HANDBOOK OF RESEARCH
ON MULTICULTURAL EDUCATION

◆

HANDBOOK OF RESEARCH ON MULTICULTURAL EDUCATION

James A. Banks
EDITOR

Cherry A. McGee Banks
ASSOCIATE EDITOR

MACMILLAN PUBLISHING USA

Simon & Schuster Macmillan

New York

Prentice Hall International

London   Mexico City   New Delhi   Singapore   Sydney   Toronto

Macmillan Publishing USA
Simon & Schuster Macmillan
1633 Broadway
New York, NY 10019-6785

Library of Congress Catalog Card Number: 94-28862

Printed in the United States of America

Printing number
        3   4   5   6   7   8   9   10

Library of Congress Cataloging-in-Publication Data

Handbook of research on multicultural education / James A. Banks,
    editor ; Cherry A. McGee Banks, associate editor.
        p.   cm.
    Includes bibliographical references and indexes.
    ISBN 0-02-895797-0 (alk. paper)
    1. Multicultural education—United States—Handbooks, manuals,
etc.   2. Multicultural education—Research—United States—
Handbooks, manuals, etc.   3. Minorities—Education—United States—
Handbooks, manuals, etc.   I. Banks, James A.   II. Banks, Cherry A.
McGee.
LC1099.3.H35   1995
370.19′6—dc20   94-28862
                                                            CIP

The paper used in this publication meets the minimum requirements of American National Standard for Information Sciences—Permanence of Paper for Printed Library Materials. ANSI Z39.48-1984. ∞™

CONTENTS

Part I
HISTORY, GOALS, STATUS, AND ISSUES

Part II
RESEARCH AND RESEARCH ISSUES

Part
III
KNOWLEDGE CONSTRUCTION

Part
IV
ETHNIC GROUPS IN HISTORICAL AND SOCIAL SCIENCE RESEARCH

Part
V
IMMIGRATION POLICY AND THE EDUCATION OF IMMIGRANTS

Part
VI
THE EDUCATION OF ETHNIC GROUPS

Part
VII
LANGUAGE ISSUES

Part
VIII
ACADEMIC ACHIEVEMENT: APPROACHES, THEORIES, AND RESEARCH

Part
IX
INTERGROUP EDUCATION APPROACHES TO SCHOOL REFORM

Part
X
HIGHER EDUCATION

Part
XI
INTERNATIONAL PERSPECTIVES ON MULTICULTURAL EDUCATION

INTRODUCTION

Multicultural education is a field of study and an emerging discipline whose major aim is to create equal educational opportunities for students from diverse racial, ethnic, social-class, and cultural groups. One of its important goals is to help all students to acquire the knowledge, attitudes, and skills needed to function effectively in a pluralistic democratic society and to interact, negotiate, and communicate with peoples from diverse groups in order to create a civic and moral community that works for the common good.

Because of its focus on equity, justice, and cultural democracy, multicultural education is consistent with the democratic ideals of the basic documents of the United States such as the Declaration of Independence, the U.S. Constitution, and the Bill of Rights. One of its major aims is to actualize for all the ideals that the founding fathers intended for only an elite few at the nation's birth.

Multicultural education has deep historical roots. It is linked directly to African American scholarship that emerged in the late 19th and early 20th centuries and indirectly to the intergroup education and research movement that was formulated in the 1940s and that had largely vanished when the civil rights movement emerged in the 1960s.

In its contemporary manifestation, multicultural education emerged out of the civil rights movement of the 1960s and 1970s. The civil rights movement emerged when African Americans, frustrated by deferred and shattered dreams, took to the streets and used the ballot box to demand symbolic and structural changes throughout U.S. society. Many of their demands focused on changes in the nation's schools, colleges, and universities. Individuals from many other ethnic and racial groups participated in and strongly supported the civil rights movement initiated by African Americans.

The first wave of responses by educational institutions resulted in the establishment of *ethnic studies* courses and programs in the nation's schools, colleges, and universities. As the ethnic studies movement grew and was becoming institutionalized, the realization arose among scholars and practitioners that although ethnic studies was a necessary component of educational reform, it was not sufficient to bring about the structural changes in schools, colleges, and universities that were needed to create educational equality for low-income students and students of color.

Consequently, *multiethnic education* was developed. It was designed to reform each of the variables in the educational environment in order to create equal educational opportunities for all students. Multiethnic education involves systemic and structural reform of these variables in schools, colleges, and universities: (a) policy and politics; (b) the attitudes, perceptions, beliefs, and actions of teachers and professors; (c) the formalized curriculum and course of study; (d) assessment and testing procedures; (e) the languages and dialects sanctioned within educational institutions; (e) teaching styles and strategies; and (f) instructional materials.

The ethnic studies and multiethnic education movements inspired other groups on the margins of society to push for change in the nation's educational institutions that would reflect their cultures, experiences, hopes, and dreams. One of the most successful political interest groups was made up of people with disabilities and their supporters. Using arguments borrowed from the 1954 *Brown v. Board of Education of Topeka* desegregation decision and from the civil rights movement, advocates for the rights of people with disabilities were able to win a number of important legal victories that resulted in substantial educational reforms. One of their most significant victories was the passage of Public Law 94-142, enacted by Congress in 1975. Known as the Education for All Handicapped Children Act, it requires free public education for all students with disabilities, nondiscriminatory evaluation, and an individualized education program (IEP) for each student with a disability. It also stipulates that each student with a disability should be educated in the least restricted environment.

Feminists were also inspired by the civil rights movement to renew their historical quest for more rights for women in U.S. society, including equity in educational institutions. One of the most significant victories of the women rights movement was Title IX of the 1972 Educational Amendments. Title IX prohibits sex discrimination in all educational programs receiving federal support. At the university level, women studies programs emerged. Today they are becoming institutionalized in colleges and universities throughout the United States, although they face important challenges.

One of the most significant developments within the last three decades has been the emergence of feminist scholarship. It seriously challenges the traditional disciplines such as philosophy, the social and behavioral sciences, and the natural and physical sciences. New paradigms, concepts, and epistemological assumptions have emerged that are forcing scholars in the traditional disciplines to rethink and to reconceptualize some of their major paradigms, concepts, and assumptions. Ethnic studies scholarship is also challenging the established disciplines and mainstream scholarship in similar ways.

As a new field of study and interdisciplinary discipline, multicultural education draws upon, reflects, and echoes concerns in ethnic studies, multiethnic education, women studies, and—to a lesser extent—research and scholarship on exceptionality. Multicultural education incorporates concepts, paradigms, theories, assumptions, and pedagogy rooted in each of these interdisciplinary fields and applies them to practical educational settings in schools, colleges, and universities. The interrelationships of variables such as race, class, and gender—and the ways they interact to influence education—are an important concern in multicultural education theory and research.

Multicultural education not only draws content, concepts, paradigms, and theories from specialized interdisciplinary fields such as ethnic studies and women studies (and from history and the social and behavioral sciences), it also interrogates, challenges, and reinterprets content, concepts, and paradigms from the established disciplines. Multicultural education applies content from these fields and disciplines to pedagogy and curriculum development in educational settings. *Consequently, we may define multicultural education as a field of study designed to increase educational equity for all students that incorporates, for this purpose, content, concepts, principles, theories, and paradigms from history, the social and behavioral sciences, and particularly from ethnic studies and women studies.* It is because of these characteristics that Edmund W. Gordon calls multicultural education a *metadiscipline*.

An important aim of this *Handbook* is to clarify the meaning and boundaries of multicultural education and to stem the tide of the multiple misconceptions of the concept that are widespread and pernicious. Multicultural education focuses on ethnic, racial, cultural, and gender groups within the boundaries of a nation-state, such as the United States, the United Kingdom, and Canada. Yet there is a widespread confusion among scholars, practitioners, publishers, and the public that multicultural education is the same as global education and international education.

Global and international education focus on the interrelationships among nations and the study of foreign nation-states respectively. Even though multicultural education and global education both try to help students to develop cross-cultural competencies and skills, each field has unique contributions to make to the education of students. Consequently, the two fields should not be confused. The integrity of each field should be recognized and respected.

THE NATURE OF THE HANDBOOK

The main purpose of this *Handbook* is to assemble in one volume the major research and scholarship related to multicultural education that has developed since the field emerged in the 1960s and 1970s. Research is defined broadly in this *Handbook* and includes studies using experimental and quasi-experimental designs, historical and philosophical inquiry, ethnographic studies, case studies, survey research, scholarship broadly defined, and insights gained from practice.

The chapters in the *Handbook* reflect the diverse disciplinary roots that constitute the foundations of the field. Consequently, contributors include researchers and scholars from a wide range of disciplines, including anthropology, history, psychology, social psychology, sociology, English and literature, and various fields within education.

THE DEVELOPMENT OF THE HANDBOOK

The idea for a handbook of research on multicultural education grew out of conversations between the editors on the state of multicultural education that occurred over several months. They concluded that the interdisciplinary nature of the field necessitated a volume in which the work of leading researchers and scholars in multicultural education and associated disciplines could be identified and discussed. They further concluded that the intended audience for the volume would be the community of researchers, scholars, and practitioners in multicultural education and associated disciplines.

The editors agreed that the sponsor for the *Handbook* should be the Center for Multicultural Education. The Center, located at the University of Washington, Seattle, was uniquely positioned to draw upon the expertise of scholars who were Faculty Associates of the Center in multicultural education, ethnic studies, women studies, and associated disciplines. With initial ideas about the mission and audience for the *Handbook* in place, the editors began conversations with leaders in the field and began a survey of the multicultural education literature.

The first working outline for the *Handbook* was developed by the editors after they surveyed the literature in multicultural education and consulted with key leaders in the field. Some of the individuals consulted later became members of the Editorial Advisory Board. The Editorial Advisory Board was then established. The draft outline was sent to the Editorial Advisory Board. The Board members made comments and suggestions that the editors incorporated into the next draft outline. After the working outline was revised, the editors solicited the advice of the Board regarding individuals who should be invited to contribute to the *Handbook*. The editors used the suggestions from Board members and their own knowledge of researchers and scholars in the field to develop the final list of individuals who were invited to contribute to the *Handbook*.

In part because multicultural education is a nascent field without an established tradition of standardized sub-areas and divisions, the outline underwent further changes as the editors communicated with individuals who agreed to participate in the project. In some cases contributors modified the topics on which they were asked to write. In at least two cases, contributors suggested new topics for themselves and recommended other individuals for the topics that had been assigned to them by the editors. During this process of discussions with contributors, members of the Editorial Advisory Board, and of sharing the outline with other scholars and practitioners in the field, the working outline grew from a projected 35 chapters to the 47 chapters that now constitute this *Handbook.*

The contributors were asked to critically review the research and scholarship within their topic areas in as comprehensive and balanced a way as possible, to conceptualize research broadly, to describe the implications of the research reviewed for further research, policy, and practice, and to use their own judgment to determine the scope and depth of their chapters. Most of the individuals invited to write chapters were established scholars with national and international reputations. However, the editors invited and encouraged contributors to work with colleagues early in their careers if they chose. A number of authors invited a colleague or several to co-author their chapters. In several cases the co-authors are scholars in the early phases of their careers. The editors viewed the *Handbook* as a project not only to present the work of established scholars, but to mentor future scholars in the field.

The reviewers played a significant role in shaping the contents of the *Handbook* chapters. Each chapter had at least two reviewers; some had more. The reviewers gave the authors comments on their chapter outlines and on the first drafts of their chapters. The contributors incorporated the comments of the editors and the reviewers into their final chapter drafts

Four chapters in the *Handbook* are reprinted—in revised form—from previous publications. This was done to provide comprehensive coverage of the field and to fill gaps created by several invited chapters that did not materialize.

THE ORGANIZATION OF THE HANDBOOK

The *Handbook* is divided into 11 parts. Part I describes the nature, history, goals, status, and key issues in the field. The major purpose of the chapters in this section is to provide readers with a description of the way in which the field has developed historically, its various components and dimensions, its status in schools, colleges, and universities, and the challenges and opportunities it faces as we enter the 21st century.

Part II focuses on research and research issues in multicultural education. The chapters in this part describe examples of research in multicultural communities and classrooms as well as guidelines for conducting sound research in the field. The ways in which knowledge is constructed is a major research topic in feminist and in ethnic studies scholarship. Part III focuses on knowledge construction and critical theories. The chapters in Part IV examine ways in which researchers have described various ethnic groups in past and contemporary research and publications.

Throughout U.S. history, immigration and issues related to the education of immigrants have been enduring and significant problems. A persistent tension has existed between pro-

viding cultural freedom for immigrants and shaping a national civic culture with shared values and democratic ideals. The tension between *pluribus* and *unum* that has existed since the nation was established still exists today. The two chapters that constitute Part V describe the historical factors and forces related to immigration to the United States and the forging of a common civic culture and the education of immigrants respectively.

The challenges and opportunities of educating specific ethnic groups is the focus of Part VI. The chapters in this part describe the research, issues, and guidelines involved in educating ethnic groups of color in the past, present, and future. Effective ways to educate language minority groups and to help all students to acquire second language competencies is becoming increasingly important as the percentage of students who speak a first language other than English increases in U.S. schools, colleges, and universities. The chapters in Part VII examine the research on second language teaching and learning and describe its policy implications.

The mean academic achievements of students such as Mexican Americans, Puerto Ricans, American Indians, and African Americans are significantly below that of Whites. The chapters in Part VIII examine, summarize, and derive policy implications from the research regarding ways to increase the academic achievement of students from diverse racial, ethnic, and social-class groups.

An important aim of multicultural education is to help all students—including White mainstream students—to acquire the knowledge, attitudes, and values needed to function effectively in a pluralistic democratic society. The chapters in Part IX focus on intergroup education and intercultural relations. They summarize research and describe guidelines for improving interracial and interethnic relations in the nation's educational institutions.

Institutions of higher education, in part because of the increasing numbers of women and students of color that have entered their doors since the 1970s, are facing tremendous challenges and opportunities in their efforts to respond effectively to these population groups and to deal with increasing racial tension on campus. The chapters in Part X summarize research in higher education that deals with students, ethnic studies, women studies, curriculum reform, and multicultural teacher education.

Many individuals in the United States think of multicultural education and interracial problems as unique to this nation. Yet multicultural education is an international discipline and field of study. It takes unique forms in each nation, yet it shares a number of overarching issues, concepts, and paradigms cross-nationally. The chapters in Part XI describe the historical development and current status of multicultural education research and developments in Australia, the United Kingdom, Canada, and Germany.

ACKNOWLEDGMENTS

In conceptualizing and developing this *Handbook* the editors have incurred enormous debts. It is with pride that we acknowledge publicly the professionals who made this project possible. First, we would like to thank the members of the Editorial Advisory Board, whose names were previously identified. Without their support, advice, wisdom, and encouragement, this *Handbook* would not have been possible. The Board members strongly supported the project from its inception, gave us wise advice and counsel, recommended contributors, agreed to read manuscripts, and—with skill and diplomacy—helped us to make several difficult and sensitive publication decisions. Nine of the 15 Board members also wrote chapters for the *Handbook*.

We would like to give special thanks to these Board members for going beyond the call of duty and serving as reviewers of specific chapters in addition to writing chapters for the *Handbook*: Geneva Gay, Evelyn Hu-DeHart, Sonia Nieto, and Christine E. Sleeter.

We are grateful to the contributing authors who wrote chapters for the *Handbook*, revised them using feedback from the editors and the reviewers, and invested an enormous amount of time in this project because they believed in it and gave us their trust. We are deeply grateful to the reviewers for preparing excellent comments on chapter outlines and on chapter drafts. The *Handbook* is a much stronger publication because of their hard work and strong commitment to the profession. We hope the *Handbook* will be a source of continuing pride for the Advisory Board, the contributors, the reviewers, and the profession.

Since its inception, this *Handbook* has been a major project of the faculty affiliated with the Center for Multicultural Education at the University of Washington, Seattle. Most members of the Center have been heavily involved in its conception and development. The Center is also initiating a project to facilitate its dissemination.

The Center staff involved in the conception and development of the *Handbook* include the Editor, who is the Center's Director, and the Associate Editor, who is a Faculty Associate of the Center. Other Faculty Associates of the Center served as either contributors or reviewers. Geneva Gay, Michael Knapp, and K. Tsianina Lomawaima are contributing authors. Ronald T. Butchart, Erasmo Gamboa, Geneva Gay, Nancy Hansen-Kren-

ing, and James K. Morishimi reviewed manuscripts for the *Handbook*.

Agnes Roche and Michael R. Hillis, former research assistants in the Center, helped to shepherd the *Handbook* from its conception to its publication. We extend a special thanks to Agnes Roche for overseeing many of the daily details of the *Handbook* project. We wish to thank Timothy C. Standal, Chair of the Area of Curriculum and Instruction in the College of Education—where the Center for Multicultural Education is housed—for his encouragement and support of the *Handbook* project. We wish to acknowledge the encouragement given to us by Allen D. Glenn, Dean of the College of Education, during the early phase of the *Handbook* project when support was especially needed.

We wish to thank Philip Friedman, our Macmillan editor, who not only believed in the *Handbook* idea from its inception but also gave us both freedom and support—in the right amounts—that greatly facilitated our work. Michael Sander, our project manager and editor, greatly strengthened the *Handbook* with his keen insight, wisdom, and perceptive attention to details. Andrew Ambraziejus and Sabrina Bowers ably coordinated the production of the *Handbook* at Macmillan. Kimberly McKaig helped the editors with proofreading. Finally, we wish to acknowledge our daughters, Angela Marie and Patricia Ann, whose presence and commitment to equity have been sources of continuing inspiration for our work.

We conceived and initiated the *Handbook* project because we believed that multicultural education had come of age and that the field needed a *Handbook* not only to help legitimize and institutionalize it, but also to help educate future scholars and provide them with a one-volume overview and summary of the theory and research in multicultural education. Our colleagues—and the future—will determine the extent to which our efforts were successful.

James A. Banks
Editor

Cherry A. McGee Banks
Associate Editor

CONTRIBUTORS

Rod Allan is coordinator of primary (elementary) teacher education at Charles Sturt University-Mitchell at Bathurst, New South Wales, Australia. Since 1976 he has variously been editor and co-editor of *Mitchell Studies,* a handbook of teaching ideas for the social studies. His research interests include multicultural education and the analysis of political processes and their impact on tertiary students, details of which have been published in national and international journals.

Cherry A. McGee Banks is Assistant Professor of Education at the University of Washington, Bothell. Her current research interests focus on race and gender in educational leadership. She has contributed to such journals as the *Phi Delta Kappan, Social Education, Educational Policy,* and *Social Studies and the Young Learner.* Professor Banks is co-editor (with James A. Banks) of *Multicultural Education: Issues and Perspectives* and co-author (with James A. Banks) of *March Toward Freedom: A History of Black Americans.* She serves on several national committees and boards including the American Bar Association's Special Advisory Committee on Youth Education for Citizenship, the National Council for the Social Studies' Carter G. Woodson Book Award Committee, and the Board of Examiners for the National Council for the Accreditation of Teacher Education. Professor Banks serves on the editorial boards of *The Social Studies, Educational Foundations,* and *New Communities.* She is active in efforts to increase parent and community participation in education and currently serves on the Board of Trustees of the Shoreline Community College (Seattle, Washington).

James A. Banks is Professor of Education and Director of the Center for Multicultural Education at the University of Washington, Seattle. He has been President of the National Council for the Social Studies and has held fellowships from the National Academy of Education, the Kellogg Foundation, and the Rockefeller Foundation. Known internationally for his work in social studies and multicultural education, he was named a Distinguished Scholar/Researcher on Minority Education by the American Educational Research Association

(AERA). He received an honorary Doctorate of Humane Letters (L.H.D.) from the Bank Street College of Education in 1993. He was the recipient of the AERA Research Review Award in 1994. Professor Banks has published more than 100 articles in such journals as *Educational Researcher, Phi Delta Kappan, Social Education,* and *Educational Leadership.* His books include *Teaching Strategies for Ethnic Studies, Teaching Strategies for the Social Studies, An Introduction to Multicultural Education,* and (with Cherry A. McGee Banks) *Multicultural Education: Issues and Perspectives.*

Christine I. Bennett is Professor of Social Studies and Multicultural Education at Indiana University in Bloomington. She is also director of the Teacher as Decision Maker Program, a graduate studies program dedicated to multicultural teacher education in a global context. Her funded research and research publications have focused on the impact of a multicultural social studies curriculum on African American, Anglo, and Latino youth; classroom climates in desegregated middle schools; causes of racial inequities in school suspensions and expulsions in desegregated high schools; explanations of minority student attrition in predominantly White universities, and the impact of multicultural teacher education. She is the author of *Comprehensive Multicultural Education: Theory and Practice.*

Josephine A. Bright is Assistant Professor of Human Development and a researcher at the Wheelock College Center on Families, Communities, Schools and Children's Learning. Her primary interests are reflected in the courses she teaches which include: "Contemporary Research and Reflections on African American Families" and "Working with Children and Families of Diverse Cultures." Her current research, supported by the U.S. Department of Education, involves an ethnographic exploration of how African American families prepare children for success in the primary grades. She received her doctorate in child and family studies from Syracuse University. Her dissertation is entitled *High-Achieving, Low-Achieving, Low-Income Black Children: What Makes the Difference?*

Johnnella E. Butler is Professor and former Chair of the American Ethnic Studies Department at the University of Washington, Seattle. She formerly taught at Smith College, where she served as Chair of the Afro-American Studies Department and developed the Smith program in African American Studies. A specialist in African American literature and women's studies, Professor Butler is particularly interested in how ethnic studies and women's studies can be interrelated. She is the author of *Black Studies: Pedagogy and Revolution* and co-editor of *Transforming the Curriculum: Ethnic Studies and Women's Studies.* Professor Butler has contributed to many different journals and several books, including *Women's Place in the Academy: Transforming the Liberal Arts Curriculum, Feminist Pedagogy,* and *Toward a Balanced Curriculum.*

Carlos E. Cortés is Professor of History at the University of California, Riverside. The recipient of two book awards, Cortés also received his university's Distinguished Teaching Award and Faculty Public Service Award, the 1980 Distinguished California Humanist Award, and the American Society for Training and Development's 1989 National Multicultural Trainer of the Year Award. Cortés has lectured widely throughout the United States, Latin America, Europe, and Asia on such topics as multicultural education, media literacy, and the implications of diversity for government and private business. The author of many publications and documentary films and former guest host on the PBS national television series, "Why in the World?" Cortés is currently working on a three-volume history of the U.S. motion picture treatment of race, ethnicity, foreign nations, and world cultures.

Linda Darling-Hammond is Professor of Education and Co-Director of the National Center for Restructuring Education, Schools, and Teaching (NCREST) at Teachers College, Columbia University. Her research focuses on policy issues related to teaching quality and educational equity. She is a member of the National Academy of Education and the National Board for Professional Teaching Standards. She has edited the *Review of Research in Education* and co-edited *The New Handbook of Teacher Evaluation.* Her books include *Professional Development Schools: Schools for Developing a Profession, A License to Teach: The Foundation for 21st Century Schools,* and *Authentic Assessment in Action: Case Studies of Schools and Students at Work.*

Joyce L. Epstein is Co-Director of the National Center on Families, Communities, Schools and Children's Learning, Principal Research Scientist, and Professor of Sociology at Johns Hopkins University. She is author of more than 100 publications on school and family partnerships; middle grades education; school, family, and peer group effects on student learning and development; and materials for educators to improve school and classroom practices. An internationally known scholar, she was the recipient of the Academy for Educational Development's 1991 Eurich Education Award for her work on school and family partnerships. Her recent book is *School and Family Partnerships: Preparing Educators and Improving Schools.*

Peter Figueroa is a Reader in the School of Education, University of Southampton, England. He has also been a Lecturer and Research Officer at Oxford University, the Australian National University, and the University of the West Indies, Jamaica. His interests lie mainly in interrelated aspects of sociology, philosophy, and education. Known internationally for his work in multicultural and anti-racist education, he has also been a Visiting Professor at the University of Frankfurt and the University of Dar-es-Salaam. His books include *Education and the Social Construction of 'Race,' Sociology of Education: A Caribbean Reader* (with G. Persaud), and *Education for Cultural Diversity* (with A. Fyfe).

Ann K. Fitzgerald is Director of Student Services for Marymount Manhattan College. She has previously worked for the Child Care Action Campaign and the Association of Junior Leagues. Dr. Fitzgerald has also served as consultant to the Carnegie Council on Adolescent Development, as a faculty member at the annual Lilly Endowment workshop on the liberal arts, and as a staff member of the women's studies summer institute at the University of Michigan. At Denison University, where she taught for twelve years, Dr. Fitzgerald was co-founder and director of the women's studies program as well as Dean for Educational Services, Affirmative Action Officer, and Assistant to the President. She was educated at Mt. Holyoke College, St. Andrews University, and the University of Wisconsin. She has written on the women's movement, adolescent development, and contemporary political issues.

Michele Foster is Professor of Education at Claremont Graduate School. Named a Distinguished Scholar on Minority Education by the American Educational Research Association, she has held post-doctoral fellowships from the National Academy of Education and the University of North Carolina, Chapel Hill. Some of her research interests include the social and cultural context of learning, urban education, and the ethnography of speaking. Known for her research on African American teachers, her articles have appeared in *Language in Society, Urban Education, Theory into Practice, NWSA Journal,* and *Educational Theory.* She is also the editor of *Readings on Equal Education, Volume 11: Qualitative Investigations into Schools and Schooling.*

Lawrence H. Fuchs is the Meyer and Walter Jaffe Professor of American Civilization and Politics at Brandeis University. He is the acting chair and permanent vice chair of the U.S. Commission on Immigration Reform. He served as the Executive Director of the U.S. Select Commission on Immigration and Refugee Policy (1979–81), whose recommendations formed the basis for the Immigration Reform and Control Act of 1986 and the Immigration Act of 1990. He has written dozens of articles on immigration, race, and ethnicity in the United States and several books on these subjects. His latest book, *The American Kaleidoscope: Race, Ethnicity, and the Civic*

Culture, won the Carey McWilliams Award for the best book on multiculturalism, the John Hope Franklin Award for the best book in American studies, and the Theodore Saloutos Award for the best book in immigrant history (1992). Professor Fuchs was a pioneer in multicultural education in the 1960s and 1970s and was the principal scholar in the creation of *Black in White America,* a four-volume curriculum for high school students, and *E Pluribus Unum: The American Experiment,* a curriculum for community colleges, both of which were developed at the Education Development Center.

Eugene E. García is Director of the Office of Bilingual Education and Minority Languages Affairs of the U.S. Department of Education in Washington, D.C. He has published extensively in the areas of language teaching and bilingual development. His most recent research is in the areas of language and education as they relate to linguistically and culturally diverse children and families. Prior to joining the U.S. Department of Education, Dr. García was Dean of the Division of Social Sciences and Professor of Education and Psychology at the University of California, Santa Cruz. He has served as a Post-Doctoral Fellow in Human Development at Harvard University and as a National Research Council Fellow. He was also a Kellogg National Fellow.

Geneva Gay is Professor of Education and Faculty Associate with the Center for Multicultural Education at the University of Washington, Seattle. She has been a fellow of the Kellogg National Leaders Fellowship Program. She was the recipient of the Distinguished Scholar Award, presented by the Committee on the Role and Status of Minorities in Educational Research and Development of the American Educational Research Association. She is known nationally and internationally for her scholarship on multicultural education, particularly as it relates to curriculum design, classroom instruction, staff development, and the culture and learning of students of color. Her writings include more than ninety articles and book chapters, as well as the co-editorship of *Expressively Black: The Cultural Basis of Ethnic Identity.* She is the author of *At the Essence of Learning: Multicultural Education.*

Donna M. Gollnick is Vice President of the National Council for Accreditation of Teacher Education (NCATE), where she oversees all accreditation activities. She has held this position since 1990. Dr. Gollnick has been writing about multicultural education for the past twenty years. She is the co-author with Philip Chinn of the textbook, *Multicultural Education in a Pluralistic Society.* She is a member of the writing team for the tenth edition of *Introduction to the Foundations of American Education.* In addition, she has written and made numerous presentations on teacher education and accreditation.

Beverly M. Gordon is Associate Professor of Curriculum in the Department of Educational Policy and Leadership at The Ohio State University. She has served as President and Program Chair of AERA's Research Focus on Black Education SIG,

and as curriculum consultant for the National Afro-American Museum and Cultural Center in Wiberforce, Ohio. She has received research funding from the National Education Association, the Ohio Historial Society, and the Howard Hughes Medical Institute. Her scholarship weaves together curriculum theory and history, knowledge production and dissemination in teacher education, and African American epistemology. She has published in journals such as *The Journal of Education, The Journal of Negro Education, Theory into Practice, Theory and Research in Social Education,* and *Urban Review.* She has authored several book chapters.

Carl A. Grant is Hoefs-Bascom Professor in the Department of Curriculum and Instruction at the University of Wisconsin, Madison. He has written or edited fifteen books in multicultural education and teacher education. These include *Research and Multicultural Education* (1993), *Making Choices for Multicultural Education* (with Christine E. Sleeter) (1988), *After the School Bell Rings* (with Christine E. Sleeter) (1986), *Bringing Teaching to Life* (1983), and *Community Participation in Education* (1979). He has also written more than ninety articles and chapters in books. Several of his writings have received awards. He is a former classroom teacher and administrator. Professor Grant was a Fulbright Scholar in England in 1982–1983. The Association of Teacher Educators named him one of the seventy leaders in teacher education in 1990. In 1993 Professor Grant became President of the National Association for Multicultural Education (NAME).

Ramón A. Gutiérrez is Professor of Ethnic Studies and History, the founding chair of the Ethnic Studies Department, and the Director of the Center for the Study of Race and Ethnicity at the University of California, San Diego. His publications include *When Jesus Came, the Corn Mothers Went Away; Marriage, Sexuality and Power in New Mexico, 1500–1846; Recovering the U.S. Hispanic Literacy Heritage; The Encyclopedia of the North American Colonies;* and *Festivals and Celebrations in American Ethnic Communities.* He received a fellowship from the MacArthur Foundation.

Beverly Guy-Sheftall is Anna Julia Cooper Professor of Women's Studies and founding director of the Women's Research and Resource Center at Spelman College. She is co-editor of *Sturdy Black Bridges: Visions of Black Women in Literature* and *Double Stitch: Black Women Write About Mothers and Daughters;* author of *Daughters of Sorrow: Attitudes Toward Black Women, 1880–1920;* and founding co-editor of *SAGE: A Scholarly Journal on Black Women.* She consults and speaks widely on issues relating to race, gender, and multiculturalism.

Kenji Hakuta is Professor of Education at Stanford University. He received his Ph.D. in experimental psychology from Harvard University, and has taught at Yale University and the University of California, Santa Cruz. His major research interests are in the psycholinguistics and sociolinguistics of bilingualism, especially as applied to schooling. He is the author of *Mirror of Language: The Debate on Bilingualism.* He chaired the Stanford Working Group on Federal Education Programs for Limited-English-Proficient Students that made recommendations for major reform of federal legislation for language minority students.

Shirley Brice Heath is Professor of English and Linguistics (and, by courtesy, of Anthropology and of Education) at Stanford University. She has held fellowships from the National Endowment for the Humanities, the Guggenheim Foundation, and the MacArthur Foundation. Known internationally for her work in literacy studies and language socialization, she has won awards from professional organizations across several fields, including English, anthropology, and education. Her books include *Telling Tongues: Language Policy in Mexico, Colony to Nation,* and *Ways with Words: Language Life and Work in Communities and Classrooms.* She is the co-author of *The Braid of Literature: Children's Worlds of Reading* and *Identity and Inner-city Youth: Beyond Ethnicity and Gender.*

Nitza M. Hidalgo is Associate Professor of Education at Westfield State College, Massachusetts. She teaches in the areas of multicultural education, teacher education, and urban school reform. Her current research involves an ethnographic investigation of Puerto Rican families' influence on their children's school achievement. She is the author of "I Saw Puerto Rico Once: A Review of the Literature of Puerto Rican Families and School Achievement in the United States." She is a past chairperson of the editorial board of the *Harvard Educational Review,* and is the co-editor of *Facing Racism in Education.*

Bob Hill teaches social education at Charles Sturt University-Mitchell, Bathurst, New South Wales, Australia. Since 1980 he has variously been editor and co-editor of *Mitchell Studies,* a handbook of teaching ideas for the social studies. His research interests include Aboriginal education, intercultural education, and the analysis of political processes and their impact on tertiary students, details of which have been published in national and international journals. He is the author of *Overcoming Inequality* and co-author of *The First of Its Kind.*

Gerd R. Hoff is Professor of Primary Education, Director of the Institute for Sociology of Education, and Joint Director of the Institute for Intercultural Education at the Free University, Berlin, Germany. As a permanent Guest Lecturer he introduced intercultural education into teacher training in the former German Democratic Republic state of Brandenburg at the University of Potsdam. He is the German coordinator of the I.A.I.E. (International Association for Intercultural Education) and is one of the General Coordinators for Europe of NESA (Network Educational Science Amsterdam). He has been a Visiting Fellow at the Centre for Multicultural Education at the Institute of Education, University of London. His recent books include *Interkulturelle Erziehung im Internationalen Vergleich* (with Michele Borrelli) and (with Hans Barkowski) *Berlin Interkulturell.*

Evelyn Hu-DeHart is Professor of History and Director of the Center for Studies of Ethnicity and Race in America at the University of Colorado, Boulder. She has degrees from Stanford University and the University of Texas, Austin, and is the recipient of numerous honors and fellowships, including two Fulbrights (to Brazil and Peru) and the Kellogg National Fellowship. Her current work focuses on researching the Asian diaspora in Latin America and the Caribbean, and on theorizing "diaspora studies" as a direction for ethnic studies. Her publications are in English, Spanish, and Chinese, and appear in scholarly journals in the United States, Great Britain, Mexico, Peru, Taiwan, and China.

Jacqueline Jordan Irvine is the Charles Howard Candler Professor of Urban Education at Emory University, Atlanta. Her research interests are multicultural education and urban teacher education. Her book, *Black Students and School Failure,* received two national book awards—The 1991 Outstanding Writing Award from The American Association of Colleges of Teacher Education and An Outstanding Academic Book of 1990 from The Association of College and University Research Librarians. She was named the 1992 Distinguished Woman Scholar by Virginia Commonwealth University, Georgia State University's College of Education's 1992 Distinguished Alumna, and the 1992 Outstanding Alumna of Howard University. She has served on the editorial boards of *The Journal of Curriculum and Supervision, The Journal of Negro Education,* and the *American Educational Research Journal.*

Joyce Elaine King is Professor of Education and Associate Vice Chancellor for Academic Affairs and Diversity Programs at the University of New Orleans. She is recognized for her expertise in the sociocultural foundations of education, emancipatory pedagogy, and culture-centered research. Professor King lectures widely in the U.S. and abroad on the education of African American people, women's leadership, and social change. She has served on the California Curriculum Commission and has held fellowships from the Kellogg Foundation and the American Council on Education. Her publications include "Dysconscious Racism: Ideology, Identity and the Miseducation of Teachers" and "In Search of African Liberation Pedagogy," a *Journal of Education* theme issue. Recent books are *Black Mothers to Sons: Juxtaposing African American Literature with Social Practice* (with C. A. Mitchell) and *Teaching Diverse Populations* (co-edited).

Michael S. Knapp is Associate Professor in the Educational Leadership and Policy Studies Area and Faculty Associate of the Center for Multicultural Education at the University of Washington, Seattle. Trained as an educational sociologist, he has specialized over the past decade in research on policies and programs aimed at "disadvantaged" populations, the nature of government policies and their implementation, and the improvement of schooling. Numerous reports and papers have emerged so far from these lines of inquiry, and with them two volumes: *Better Schooling for the Children of Poverty* (with Patrick Shields) and *Teaching Advanced Skills to At-Risk Students* (with Barbara Means and Carol Chelemer). Dr. Knapp's current research examines the integration of education and human services offered to high-risk children and families.

Gloria Ladson-Billings is Assistant Professor of Education in the Department of Curriculum and Instruction at the University of Wisconsin, Madison, where she teaches courses in social studies methods, multicultural education, and culturally relevant pedagogy. She has been a recipient of the National Academy of Education's Spencer post-doctoral fellowship for her work on effective instruction for African American students. She is a member of numerous national committees and advisory boards including the National Council for the Social Studies Standards Task Force, the Equity and Cultural Diversity Panel of the National Board for Professional Teaching Standards, the State University of New York, Buffalo, History Center, and several committees of the American Educational Research Association.

Paul Lauter is Allan K. and Gwendolyn Miles Smith Professor of Literature at Trinity College (Hartford). He is general editor of the ground-breaking *Heath Anthology of American Literature* and author or editor of a number of other books, including *Canons and Contexts, Reconstructing American Literature,* and *The Politics of Literature* (with Louis Kamp). Lauter has been a faculty member at Dartmouth, Smith, the State University of New York at Old Westbury, the John F. Kennedy Institute, San Jose State University, and the University of California, Santa Cruz, among other colleges and universities. He also taught in the Mississippi freedom schools and in Upward Bound, and directed the Adams Morgan Community School project in Washington, D.C. He is a graduate of New York, Indiana, and Yale Universities. He is the 1994–95 president of the American Studies Association.

Carol D. Lee is on the faculty of the School of Education and Social Policy at Northwestern University in Evanston, Illinois. She received her Ph.D. in Curriculum and Instruction from the University of Chicago. In addition, Professor Lee has many years of experience as a classroom teacher at the elementary, high school, and community college levels. She is a founder and former director of a twenty-year-old independent school in Chicago that integrates African American culture throughout its curriculum. Her research interests and publications focus on cultural contexts for literacy instruction. She is the author of *Signifying as a Scaffold for Literary Interpretation.*

Daniel U. Levine is Professor of Educational Administration at the University of Nebraska, Omaha. A former high school teacher in Chicago, he has conducted numerous studies dealing with urban education, compensatory education, school effectiveness, desegregation, and other topics. He has written textbooks in educational sociology and in the foundations of education. His most recent publications include the eighth edition of *Society and Education,* the fifth edition of *Foundations of Education,* and an analytic paper examining the potential of school-based management. He currently serves as an advisor to school improvement projects in several urban school districts.

Lawrence W. Lezotte is senior vice president of Effective Schools Products, Ltd., in Okemos, Michigan, an organization that provides consultation and publications for school districts that are engaged in reform. A former professor of educational administration and director of the Center for Effective Schools Research at Michigan State University, Dr. Lezotte is one of the pioneers in effective schools research. He is a co-author, with Wilbur B. Brookover and others, of *Creating Effective Schools: An Inservice Program for Enhancing School Learning Climate and Achievement.* His articles have appeared in such journals as *Educational Leadership, The American School Board Journal,* and *The Journal of Negro Education.*

Kathryn J. Lindholm is Associate Professor of Child Development at San Jose State University (SJSU), where she teaches courses on multicultural child development and serves on committees to integrate multicultural perspectives into all SJSU courses. She received her Ph.D. in developmental psychology from the University of California, Los Angeles. Professor Lindholm's research interests are currently focused on assessing the effectiveness of the increasingly popular two-way bilingual education model to promote bilingualism, academic achievement, and true integration in the school setting among native English speakers and native speakers of other languages. She serves as a consultant to many school districts, the California Department of Education, and the Center for Research on Cultural Diversity and Second Language Learning. She has authored or co-authored numerous journal articles and chapters on child bilingualism, two-way bilingual education, and multicultural themes in child development.

Angela Lintz is a doctoral student in sociology at the University of California, San Diego. She is currently writing a dissertation on African American independent schools. Her research focuses on the sociology of education, ethnic identity, and religion.

William T. Liu is Professor Emeritus of Sociology at the University of Illinois, Chicago, and Professor of Social Sciences at the Hong Kong University of Science and Technology. He received his Ph.D. in sociology from Florida State University and did his post-doctoral studies at the University of Chicago (social psychology and demography), and at Yale University (psychiatric epidemiology). He was Professor of Sociology and Director of the Center for the Study of Man at the University of Notre Dame, Director of the National Asian American Mental Health Research Center (affiliated with the University of Illinois), and served on the Board of Education of the City of Chicago. His books include *Kinship and Fertility* (with Elena Yu) and *Transition to Nowhere: Vietnamese Refugees in America.*

K. Tsianina Lomawaima is Associate Professor of American Indian Studies at the University of Arizona, Tucson. She formerly taught at the University of Washington, Seattle.

She earned her graduate degrees from Stanford University, where she was a Dorothy Danforth Compton fellow. Her research on the experiences of American Indian alumni of a federal off-reservation boarding school appears in *They Called It Prairie Light: The Story of Chilocco Indian School,* winner of the 1993 North American Indian Prose Award. She teaches history and contemporary policy issues in the areas of Indian education, economy, and law. In 1991 she received a Distinguished Teaching Award from the University of Washington.

Hugh Mehan is Professor of Sociology and Director of the Teacher Education Program at the University of California, San Diego, appointments that link his commitments to research and practice. He has studied the organization of schooling and the construction of identities such as the "competent student," the "learning disabled student," the "mentally ill patient" and the "genius." He works closely with K-12 educators so that they can make informed decisions to ensure that equitable education is available to all children. Currently President of the Council of Anthropology and Education of the American Anthropology Association, he is the author of three books (*The Reality of Ethnomethodology, Learning Lessons,* and *Handicapping the Handicapped*), and the editor of four.

Masahiko Minami is a doctoral candidate in the human development and psychology program at Harvard University, having received his Ed.M. from the same program in 1988. He received two B.A. degrees, in economics and in American literature, from Kyoto University in Japan. His research interests include developmental psychology and psycho-sociolinguistics with a particular emphasis on cross-cultural comparisons of language development and narrative/discourse structure. He has published a number of articles and reviews and presented papers on this subject. He is the co-editor of *Language Issues in Literacy and Bilingual/Multicultural Education.* Mr. Minami has also contributed chapters to books covering Asian narratives, East Asian students' experiences in U.S. classrooms, and child care quality in Japan.

Kogila A. Moodley is Associate Professor in the Department of Social and Educational Studies at the University of British Columbia (UBC) in Vancouver, Canada. She has served as Director of Multicultural Liaison in the Office of the President at UBC, and has held visiting appointments at the University of Cape Town in South Africa. She has published widely on issues of race and ethnicity as well as in policy studies. Her books include *Beyond Multicultural Education: International Perspectives* and *The Opening of the Apartheid Mind* (with Heribert Adam).

Carrol E. Moran is a Title VI Fellow at Stanford University. She has been involved in bilingual education (Spanish and Portuguese primary language students) for the past fifteen years. She has combined the roles of teacher, curriculum writer, consultant, and researcher. Her books include *Keys to the Classroom: A Teacher's Guide to the First Month of School* and *The Bridge: Spanish to English,* a guide to literacy development in a bilingual setting. She has worked with the Education for Democracy project in Nicaragua. Her doctoral work is on the development of scientific language in a bilingual setting.

Don T. Nakanishi is Director of the Asian American Studies Center at the University of California, Los Angeles. He is one of the nation's foremost authorities on American race relations and the politics of diversity. A Yale-Harvard trained political scientist, he is the author of more than fifty books and articles on topics relating to the access, representation, and influence of Asian Pacific Americans and other populations of color in major political, social, and educational institutions and sectors. Professor Nakanishi is a former national president of the Association of Asian American Studies (the principal scholarly association for the field of Asian American studies) and a recipient of numerous research awards and fellowships. He previously served on the Commission on Minorities in Higher Education of the American Council on Education, and on the Board of Governors of the Association of Yale Alumni.

Sonia Nieto is Professor of Education in the Cultural Diversity and Curriculum Reform Program at the School of Education, University of Massachusetts, Amherst. Her research interests include curriculum issues in multicultural education, the education of Latinos in the United States, and Puerto Ricans in children's books. She has written many articles and book chapters on these issues, as well as a number of books, including *Affirming Diversity: The Sociopolitical Context of Multicultural Education* and *The Education of Latino Students in Massachusetts* (co-edited with Ralph Rivera). Professor Nieto has worked extensively with teachers and schools and has served as an advisor on many boards and commissions with a focus on educational equity and social justice for all children.

John U. Ogbu is Alumni Distinguished Professor of Anthropology at the University of California, Berkeley. He is one of the world's leading educational anthropologists. He is a member of the National Academy of Education and the Social Science Research Council Committee on Research on the Urban Underclass. He has been a member of the National Research Council's Committee on Child Development and Public Policy and has served on several study panels and committees of the National Academy of Sciences, including the Committee on the Status of Black Americans. Professor Ogbu specializes in the comparative study of minority education, for which he has received grants from the Carnegie Corporation, the Ford Foundation, the W.T. Grant Foundation, the MacArthur Foundation, the National Institute of Education, the Rockefeller Foundation, and the Russell Sage Foundation. He was named a Distinguished Scholar/Researcher on minority education by the American Educational Research Association. His publications include *The Next Generation: An Ethnography of Education in an Urban Neighborhood; Minority Education and Caste: The American System in Cross-Cultural Perspective;*

and (with M. A. Gibson) *Minority Status and Schooling: A Comparative Study of Immigrant and Involuntary Minorities.*

Dina Okamoto is a graduate student in sociology at the University of Arizona. She completed her undergraduate work at the University of California, San Diego, under the direction of Professor Hugh Mehan. Ms. Okamoto is interested in the fields of social stratification, gender and labor, and multiculturalism and education.

Michael R. Olneck is Professor of Educational Policy Studies and Sociology at the University of Wisconsin, Madison, where he teaches courses in sociology of education, cultural pluralism and education, racial and ethnic inequality in education, and public policy and education. His recent analyses of the Americanization movement, intercultural education, and contemporary multiculturalism are published in a series of articles in the *American Journal of Education.* With Marvin F. Lazerson, he has published analyses of immigrants and schooling in the *History of Education Quarterly* and the *Harvard Encyclopedia of American Ethnic Groups.* He is a co-author of *Who Gets Ahead?: The Determinants of Economic Success in America,* as well as several articles in the area of education and social stratification.

Carlos J. Ovando is Professor of Education and Chair of the Department of Curriculum and Instruction at Indiana University, Bloomington. He has taught at Oregon State University, the University of Alaska, Anchorage, and the University of Southern California. Professor Ovando is a specialist in bilingual and multicultural education and has contributed to numerous publications in these fields. He has served as guest editor of two special issues of the *Educational Research Quarterly* and contributed to the *Phi Delta Kappan, Educational Leadership, WCCI Forum, Kappa Delta Pi Record, National Forum,* and the *Harvard Educational Review.* He is the co-author of *Bilingual and ESL Classrooms: Teaching in Multicultural Contexts.* Professor Ovando has made presentations in Canada, Egypt, England, Guam, Mexico, Nicaragua, the Netherlands, and the Philippines.

Amado M. Padilla is Professor of Education at Stanford University. He received his Ph.D. in experimental psychology from the University of New Mexico. Prior to his appointment at Stanford University, he was Professor of Psychology at the University of California, Los Angeles, and Director of the Spanish Speaking Mental Health Research Center. Currently, he is chairperson of the Graduate Training Program in Language, Literacy and Culture at Stanford. He has published extensively on acculturation, bilingualism, foreign language education, and the mental health of Latinos. He is the founding editor of the *Hispanic Journal of Behavioral Sciences,* which has appeared quarterly for fifteen years.

Valerie Ooka Pang is Associate Professor in the School of Teacher Education at San Diego State University. She teaches multicultural education, elementary social studies, and social foundations courses. Her research interests include multicultural curriculum development, the mental health of Asian Pacific American children, and multicultural children's literature. Her publications have appeared in various journals including *Social Education, The Social Studies, The Reading Teacher, Journal of Research and Development in Education,* and *Harvard Educational Review.* She is presently on the Asian American advisory board for Sesame Street. Pang was a principal co-investigator and the project director of the Multicultural Education Infusion Center funded by the Office of Bilingual Education and Minority Language Affairs at San Diego State University.

Clara E. Rodríguez is a Visiting Scholar at the Russell Sage Foundation and Professor of Sociology and Urban Studies at Fordham University's College at Lincoln Center. She has also been a Visiting Scholar at the Massachusetts Institute of Technology and at Yale University. She has served as Dean of Fordham University's School of General Studies. Professor Rodríguez's most recent books are *Puerto Ricans: Born in the USA* and *Hispanics in the Labor Force: Issues and Policies,* which she co-edited with Edwin Melendez and Janice Barry Figueroa. She has written numerous articles on Latinos in the United States and is currently investigating the social construction of race among Latinos and other groups.

Deborah Rosenfelt is Professor of Women's Studies and Director of the Curriculum Transformation Project at the University of Maryland, College Park. She is the former director of the Women's Studies Program at San Francisco State University, where she also directed Cross-Cultural Perspectives in the Curriculum. Her publications on curriculum development and curricular change include two volumes of the Female Studies Series; *Teaching Women's Literature from a Regional Perspective* (co-editor); *Cross-Cultural Perspectives in the Classroom: Resources for Change;* and numerous essays.

Betty Schmitz is Senior Associate, Cultural Pluralism Project, Washington Center for Undergraduate Education, Evergreen State College, and Visiting Scholar, American Ethnic Studies, University of Washington, Seattle. She also serves as Senior Fellow, Association of American Colleges. A nationally recognized leader in curriculum transformation, she has developed and directed long-term faculty development projects and institutes at several major colleges and universities. She has lectured, written, and consulted extensively on curriculum change, institutional change, classroom climate, and diversity curricula. Dr. Schmitz has also been a volunteer in numerous advocacy programs for women and served as the coordinator of the Northwest Women's Studies Association. Her books include *Integrating Women's Studies into the Curriculum* and *Core Curriculum and Cultural Pluralism.*

Janet Ward Schofield is Professor of Psychology and a Senior Scientist in the Learning Research and Development Center at the University of Pittsburgh. She has also served as a faculty member at Spelman College. She received a B.A. magna cum laude from Radcliffe College where she was elected to Phi Beta Kappa. She received her Ph.D. from Harvard University in 1972. Professor Schofield is a social psychologist whose major research interest for more than twenty years has been social processes in desegregated schools. She has published more than two dozen papers in this area as well as two books. One of these, *Black and White in School: Trust, Tension or Tolerance?* was awarded the Society for the Psychological Study of Social Issues' Gordon Allport Intergroup Relations Prize.

Sau-Fong Siu is Associate Professor of Social Work Education and Director of the Social Work Program at Wheelock College in Boston. As a researcher in the research consortium, Center on Families, Communities, Schools, and Children's Learning, she is currently conducting an ethnographic study of Chinese American families with young children. A former chairperson of the Committee on Ethnic and Racial Affairs of the Massachusetts Chapter of the National Association of Social Workers, she is also a member of the Asian-American Social Work Educators' Association and of MAAEA (Massachusetts Asian-American Educators' Association). Her publications include articles on minority children in the child welfare system and on Chinese American educational achievement.

Diana T. Slaughter-Defoe is Professor of Education and Social Policy in the Human Development and Social Policy Program, Northwestern University. She has a secondary appointment in the Department of African American Studies. Her recent research focuses on family influences on academic achievement, and on Black education and early intervention studies. She is the co-editor (with Edgar G. Epps) of a special issue of the *Journal of Negro Education* (Winter 1987) that focuses on the home environment and achievement of African American students. Professor Slaughter-Defoe is editor of *Black Children and Poverty: A Developmental Perspective* and co-editor of *Visible Now: Blacks in Private Schools.*

Robert E. Slavin is Director of the Early and Elementary School Program at the Center for Research on Effective Schooling for Disadvantaged Students at Johns Hopkins University. He received his B.A. in psychology from Reed College in 1972, and his Ph.D. in social relations in 1975 from Johns Hopkins University. Dr. Slavin has authored or co-authored more than 140 articles and fourteen books, including *Educational Psychology: Theory into Practice, School and Classroom Organization, Effective Programs for Students at Risk, Cooperative Learning: Theory, Research, and Practice,* and *Preventing Early School Failure.* He received the American Educational Research Association's Raymond B. Cattell Early Career Award for Programmatic Research in 1986, and the Palmer O. Johnson award for the best article in an American Educational Research journal in 1988.

Christine E. Sleeter is Professor of Teacher Education at the University of Wisconsin, Parkside. She teaches both graduate and undergraduate courses in multicultural education, and

consults nationally in this area. On the basis of her active record of publication, she was recently awarded the University of Wisconsin, Parkside, annual award for Excellence in Research and Creative Activity. She has published numerous articles about multicultural education in a variety of journals. Her most recent books include *Empowerment through Multicultural Education, Keepers of the American Dream,* and *Making Choices for Multicultural Education* (with Carl A. Grant). She also edits a series of books for the State University of New York Press, entitled "The Social Context of Education."

C. Matthew Snipp is Professor of Rural Sociology and Sociology, and Director of the American Indian Studies Program at the University of Wisconsin, Madison. He has been a Research Fellow at the U.S. Bureau of the Census and a Fellow at the Center for Advanced Study in the Behavioral Sciences. Professor Snipp has published numerous works on American Indian demography, economic development, poverty, and unemployment. He is the author of *American Indians: The First of This Land* and *Public Policy Impacts on American Indian Economic Development.* His current research and writing deals with poverty and unemployment on American Indian reservations, and American Indian ethnic identity.

Derald Wing Sue is Professor of Counseling Psychology at the California School of Professional Psychology, Alameda, and President of Cultural Diversity Training. He is a Fellow of the American Psychological Association, the American Association for Applied and Preventive Psychology, and the American Psychological Society. He was the first president of the Asian American Psychological Association and has been active in the practice, theory, and research of multicultural counseling. He is the author of *Counseling the Culturally Different: Theory and Practice* (with David Sue) and *Counseling American Minorities: A Cross-Cultural Perspective* (with Donald Atkinson and George Morten).

Susan M. Swap is Director of the Center on College-School Community Partnerships and the Center on Families, Communities, Schools, and Children's Learning at Wheelock College. She has had extensive experience working with families and educators in schools, offering workshops and courses, and developing parent involvement and in-service programs. She has written many books and articles, including *Building Home-School Partnerships: From Concepts to Practice.* She has taught many different courses at Wheelock in education and child development, and is former chair of the Department of Professional Studies. Her B.A. is from Radcliffe College, and her M.A. and Ph.D. (in psychology and education) are from the University of Michigan.

William F. Tate is Assistant Professor in the Department of Curriculum and Instruction at the University of Wisconsin, Madison. He teaches courses in mathematics and urban education. His research interests include educational equity and the political and cultural dimensions of mathematics and mathematics education. He is a member of several national committees including the Research Advisory Committee of the National Council of Teachers of Mathematics. He was the recipient of the University of Wisconsin's Anna J. Cooper Postdoctoral Fellowship (1991–1992) and was awarded a Ford Foundation Fellowship to study at the University of Ghana. "The Brown Decision Revisited: Mathematizing Social Problems," with Gloria Ladson-Billings and Carl A. Grant, in *Educational Policy* (September, 1993), reflects his research on the role of mathematics in society.

John S. Wills is a Postdoctoral Research Fellow in the Teacher Education Program at the University of California, San Diego, and a Visiting Assistant Professor in the School of Education at the University of California, Riverside. In 1991–1992 he was the recipient of a Spencer Postdoctoral Fellowship from the National Academy of Education. His work includes studies of classroom histories of the cold war and multicultural education in history classrooms, reflecting his interests in social studies education and citizenship.

Sara Woolverton is associated with the Educational Leadership and Policy Studies Area, College of Education, University of Washington, Seattle. She specializes in research on issues of power and disenfranchisement in schools. She has a background in anthropology and special education, and an interest in critical theory and critical research.

Darlene Eleanor York is Visiting Professor of Education at Emory University in Atlanta, Georgia. A graduate of Emory University, she specializes in cross-cultural conflict and contact research, particularly cross-cultural training for educators in culturally diverse schools. She is the recipient of the 1992 Outstanding Research Award from the Georgia Educational Research Association and the 1990 Innovation in Teacher Education Award from the Southeastern Regional Association of Teacher Educators. She is the author of several articles and one book, *Cross-Cultural Training Programs*.

Elena S. H. Yu is Professor of Public Health in the Division of Epidemiology and Biostatistics, Graduate School of Public Health, San Diego State University, San Diego. She received her doctorate degree in sociology from the University of Notre Dame, and a degree in public health from Columbia University. Born in China and raised in the Philippines in a multilingual and multicultural society, she speaks several languages and has conducted research in mainland China, Hong Kong, and the United States. Her areas of research interest are Asian American and Pacific Islander populations, minority and women's health, aging and dementias in the aged, and caregiving and caregivers' burden. Her publications span several fields, including journals in sociology, clinical epidemiology, neurology, survey methodology, and public health.

REVIEWERS

David W. Adams
Cleveland State University

Carl Allsup
University of Wisconsin, Platterville

James D. Anderson
University of Illinois, Urbana-Champaign

Jean Anyon
Rutgers University

Elliot Aronson
University of California, Santa Cruz

Arnetha F. Ball
University of Michigan, Ann Arbor

H. Prentice Baptiste
Kansas State University

Andres Barona
Arizona State University

Leonard Beckam
Duke University

Marilynne Boyle-Baise
Indiana University, Bloomington

Brian M. Bullivant
Monash University, Australia

Raymond Buriel
Claremont College

Ronald E. Butchart
University of Washington, Tacoma

J. Manuel Casas
University of California, Santa Barbara

Virgie Chattergy
University of Hawaii, Manoa

John Brown Childs
University of California, Santa Cruz

Elizabeth G. Cohen
Stanford University

Gloria Contreras
University of North Texas

James Cummins
Ontario Institute for Studies in Education, Toronto

Roger Daniels
University of Cincinnati

Boyd Davis
University of North Carolina, Charlotte

Vine Deloria, Jr.
University of Colorado, Boulder

Carlos F. Diaz
Florida Atlantic University

Mary E. Dilworth
American Association of Colleges
  for Teacher Education
Washington, DC

John Eggleston
University of Warwick, United Kingdom

Edgar G. Epps
University of Chicago

Frederick D. Erickson
University of Pennsylvania

Vivian Gadsden
University of Pennsylvania

Erasmo Gamboa
University of Washington, Seattle

Antoine M. Garibaldi
Xavier University, New Orleans

Geneva Gay
University of Washington, Seattle

Maureen D. Gillette
College of St. Rose, Albany, NY

Gerald Graff
University of Chicago

Jill Moss Greenberg
Mid-Atlantic Equity Consortium
Chevy Chase, MD

Donald Grinde
California Polytechnic State University

Robin Grinter
Manchester Polytechnic, United Kingdom

Nancy Hansen-Krening
University of Washington, Seattle

Gabriel Haslip-Viera
City College
City University of New York

Willis D. Hawley
University of Maryland, College Park

Hilda Hernandez
California State University, Chico

José Hernández
Hunter College
City University of New York

Michael R. Hillis
East Tennessee State University

Etta R. Hollins
California State University, Hayward

Evelyn Hu-DeHart
University of Colorado, Boulder

Christopher J. Hurn
University of Massachusetts, Amherst

Anthony W. Jackson
Carnegie Corporation of New York

Harvey A. Kantor
University of Utah

Peter N. Kiang
University of Massachusetts, Boston

David F. Labaree
Michigan State University

Gloria Ladson-Billings
University of Wisconsin, Madison

Kofi Lomotey
Louisiana State University, Baton Rouge

Robert E. Lowe
National-Louis University

Carol Markstrom-Adams
University of Guelph, Canada

Renée Martin
University of Toledo

Oscar J. Martinez
University of Arizona

William McDiarmid
Michigan State University

Peter L. McLaren
University of California, Los Angeles

Barry M. McLaughlin
University of California, Santa Cruz

Keith McLeod
University of Toronto, Canada

LaMar P. Miller
New York University

Janice Monk
University of Arizona

James K. Morishima
University of Washington, Seattle

Peter C. Murrell
Alverno College, Milwaukee

Caryn McTighe Musil
Association of American Colleges
Washington, DC

Joane Nagel
University of Kansas, Lawrence

Sonia Nieto
University of Massachusetts, Amherst

Michael Omi
University of California, Berkeley

Flora I. Ortiz
University of California, Riverside

Carlos J. Ovando
Indiana University, Bloomington

Young Pai
University of Missouri, Kansas City

Walter C. Parker
University of Washington, Seattle

Paul Pedersen
Syracuse University

Joel Perlmann
Harvard University

Robert S. Peterkin
Harvard University

Manuel Ramírez
University of Texas, Austin

Agnes M. Roche
University of Washington, Seattle

Robert S. Rueda
University of Southern California

Richard Ruiz
University of Arizona

Virginia Sanchez Korrol
Brooklyn College
City University of New York

Hugh J. Scott
Hunter College
City University of New York

Diane Scott-Jones
Temple University

Jack Shaheen
Southern Illinois University

Christine E. Sleeter
University of Wisconsin, Parkside

Catherine Snow
Harvard University

Gita Steiner-Khamsi
University of Zürich, Switzerland

Stanley Sue
University of California, Los Angeles

Elizabeth Blue Swadener
Kent State University

Barbara O. Taylor
National Center for Effective Schools
Madison, Wisconsin

Edward Taylor
University of Washington, Seattle

Mary Kay Thompson Tetreault
California State University, Fullerton

Roland G. Tharp
University of California, Santa Cruz

Russell Thornton
University of California, Berkeley

Maria E. Torres-Guzmàn
Teachers College, Columbia University

G. Richard Tucker
Carnegie Mellon University

Wayne J. Urban
Georgia State University

Jesse M. Vázquez
Queens College
City University of New York

Ana Maria Villegas
Educational Testing Service
Princeton, NJ

Emilie Siddle Walker
Emory University

William H. Watkins
University of Utah

Anthony R. Welch
University of Sydney, Australia

David L. Williams, Jr.
Southwest Educational Development
   Laboratory
Austin, TX

Arthur E. Wise
National Council for the Accreditation
   of Teacher Education
Washington, DC

Allen L. Woll
Rutgers University

Kenneth Wong
University of Chicago

Roberta Woolever
San Francisco State University

Jürgen Zimmer
Freie Universität
Berlin, Germany

HISTORY, GOALS, STATUS, AND ISSUES

MULTICULTURAL EDUCATION: HISTORICAL DEVELOPMENT, DIMENSIONS, AND PRACTICE

James A. Banks

UNIVERSITY OF WASHINGTON, SEATTLE

The heated discourse on multicultural education, especially in the popular press and among nonspecialists (Gray, 1991; Leo, 1990; Schlesinger, 1991), often obscures the theory, research, and developing consensus among multicultural education specialists about the nature, aims, and scope of the field. Gay (1992), as well as J. A. Banks (1993c), has noted the high level of consensus about aims and scope in the literature written by multicultural education theorists. Gay, however, points out that there is a tremendous gap between theory and practice in the field. In her view, theory development has outpaced development in practice, and a wide gap exists between the two.

Gibson (1976) reviewed the multicultural education literature and identified five approaches. She noted how the approaches differ and how they overlap and interrelate. In their review of the literature, published 11 years later, Sleeter and Grant (1987) also identified five approaches to multicultural education, four of which differ from Gibson's categories. Sleeter and Grant noted the lack of consensus in the field and concluded that a focus on the education of people of color is the only common element among the many different definitions of multicultural education. Although there are many different approaches, statements of aims, and definitions of multicultural education, an examination of the recent literature written by specialists in the field indicates that there is a high level of consensus about its aims and goals (J. A. Banks, 1993c; Bennett, 1990; Nieto, 1992; Parekh, 1986; Sleeter & Grant, 1988; Suzuki, 1984).

A major goal of multicultural education, as stated by specialists in the field, is to reform the school and other educational institutions so that students from diverse racial, ethnic, and social-class groups will experience educational equality. Another important goal of multicultural education—revealed in this literature—is to give male and female students an equal chance to experience educational success and mobility (Klein, 1985; Sadker & Sadker, 1982). Multicultural education theorists are increasingly interested in how the interaction of race, class, and gender influences education (J. A. Banks, 1993c; Grant & Sleeter, 1986; Sleeter, 1991). However, the emphasis that different theorists give to each of these variables varies considerably.

Although there is an emerging consensus about the aims and scope of multicultural education (J. A. Banks, 1992), the variety of typologies, conceptual schemes, and perspectives within the field reflects its emergent status and the fact that complete agreement about its aims and boundaries has not been attained (Baker, 1983; J. A. Banks, 1994; Bennett, 1990; Garcia, 1991; Gollnick & Chinn, 1990). Because of its forensic and polarized nature, the current acrimonious debate about the extent to which the histories and cultures of women and people of color should be incorporated into the study of Western civilization in the nation's schools, colleges, and universities has complicated the quest for sound definitions and clear disciplinary boundaries within the field (Asante, 1991; Asante & Ravitch, 1991; Ravitch, 1990; Schlesinger, 1990).

GOALS AND SCOPE

There is general agreement among most scholars and researchers that, for multicultural education to be implemented successfully, institutional changes must be made, including

Adapted with permission from *Review of Research in Education,* vol. 19 (pp. 3–49), edited by Linda Darling-Hammond, 1993. Washington, D.C.: American Educational Research Association.

changes in the curriculum; the teaching materials; teaching and learning styles; the attitudes, perceptions, and behaviors of teachers and administrators; and the goals, norms, and culture of the school (J. A. Banks, 1992; Bennett, 1990; Sleeter & Grant, 1988). However, many school and university practitioners have a limited conception of multicultural education, viewing it primarily as curriculum reform that involves only changing or restructuring the curriculum to include content about ethnic groups, women, and other cultural groups. This conception of multicultural education is widespread because curriculum reform was the main focus when the movement first emerged in the 1960s and 1970s (Blassingame, 1972; Ford, 1973), and because the multiculturalism discourse in the popular media has focused on curriculum reform and largely ignored other dimensions and components of multicultural education (Gray, 1991; Leo, 1990; Schlesinger, 1990, 1991).

If multicultural education is to become better understood and implemented in ways more consistent with theory, its various dimensions must be more clearly described, conceptualized, and researched. Multicultural education is conceptualized in this review as a field that consists of the five dimensions formulated by J. A. Banks (1991a, 1992). The dimensions are based on his research, observations, and work in the field from the late 1960s (J. A. Banks, 1970) through 1991 (J. A. Banks, 1992). Because of the limited scope of this review, no attempt is made to review the research comprehensively in each of the five dimensions. Rather, a selected group of studies in each of the dimensions is reviewed. Race, ethnicity, class, gender, and exceptionality—and their interaction—are each important factors in multicultural education. Since it is not possible within one review to examine each of the variables in sufficient depth, this review focuses on racial and ethnic groups.

THE DIMENSIONS OF MULTICULTURAL EDUCATION

The dimensions of multicultural education used to conceptualize, organize, and select the literature for review in this chapter are (a) content integration, (b) the knowledge construction process, (c) prejudice reduction, (d) an equity pedagogy, and (e) an empowering school culture and social structure. Each of the dimensions is defined and illustrated, and a brief overview of each major section of the chapter is presented. The interrelationship of the five dimensions is discussed later.

Content Integration

Content integration deals with the extent to which teachers use examples, data, and information from a variety of cultures and groups to illustrate key concepts, principles, generalizations, and theories in their subject area or discipline. In many school districts, as well as in popular writings, multicultural education is viewed only or primarily as content integration. This widespread belief that content integration constitutes the whole of multicultural education might be the factor that causes many teachers of subjects such as mathematics and science to

view multicultural education as an endeavor primarily for social studies and language arts teachers.

The historical development of content integration movements is discussed, beginning with the historical work of George Washington Williams (1882–1883), usually considered the first African American historian in the United States (Franklin, 1985). The early ethnic studies movement, which began with Williams, continued quietly until the ethnic studies movement of the 1960s and 1970s. The rise and fall of the intergroup education movement is also described in this section.

Knowledge Construction

The knowledge construction process describes the procedures by which social, behavioral, and natural scientists create knowledge, and the manner in which the implicit cultural assumptions, frames of reference, perspectives, and biases within a discipline influence the ways that knowledge is constructed within it (Berger & Luckman, 1966; Gould, 1981; Harding, 1991; Kuhn, 1970). When the knowledge construction process is implemented in the classroom, teachers help students to understand how knowledge is created and how it is influenced by the racial, ethnic, and social-class positions of individuals and groups.

This section describes how the dominant paradigms about ethnic groups that were established by mainstream social scientists were challenged by revisionist social scientists in the 1960s and 1970s; many of these revisionists were scholars of color (Acuña, 1972; Blassingame, 1972; Ladner, 1973), whereas others were not (Daniels, 1988; Genovese, 1972; Levine, 1977). Literature that illustrates how paradigm shifts are taking place and identifies models that can be used to teach students to understand the knowledge construction process is also described in this section.

Prejudice Reduction

The prejudice reduction dimension of multicultural education describes the characteristics of children's racial attitudes and suggests strategies that can be used to help students develop more democratic attitudes and values. Researchers have been investigating the characteristics of children's racial attitudes since the 1920s (Lasker, 1929). Since the intergroup education movement of the 1940s and 1950s (Miel with Kiester, 1967; Trager & Yarrow, 1952), a number of investigators have designed interventions to help students to develop more positive racial attitudes and values. This section briefly reviews selected studies on the characteristics of children's racial attitudes, and studies that describe the results of interventions designed to help students to acquire more democratic racial attitudes (J. A. Banks, 1991b).

Equity Pedagogy

An equity pedagogy exists when teachers use techniques and methods that facilitate the academic achievement of students from diverse racial, ethnic, and social-class groups. This section consists of a review of selected studies of approaches, theories, and interventions that are designed to help students who are members of low-status population groups to increase their academic achievement (Delpit, 1988; Ogbu, 1990; Shade, 1989).

The literature reviewed in this section is discussed within a historical context. The kinds of theories that have been constructed to help teachers develop more effective strategies for use with students of color and low-income students have varied throughout time. In the early 1960s the cultural deprivation paradigm was developed (Bloom, Davis, & Hess, 1965; Davis, 1948/1962; Riessman, 1962). The cultural difference theory emerged in the 1970s and challenged the cultural deprivationists (Baratz & Baratz, 1970; Ginsburg, 1972; Ramírez & Castañeda, 1974). Today the "at-risk" conception has emerged, which is akin to the cultural deprivation paradigm (Cuban, 1989; Richardson, Casanova, Placier, & Guilfoyle, 1989).

Empowering School Culture

The concept of an empowering school culture and social structure is used in this chapter to describe the process of restructuring the culture and organization of the school so that students from diverse racial, ethnic, and social-class groups will experience educational equality and cultural empowerment (Cummins, 1986). Creating an empowering school culture for students of color and low-income students involves restructuring the culture and organization of the school.

Among the variables that need to be examined in order to create a school culture that empowers students from diverse ethnic and cultural groups are grouping practices (Braddock, 1990; Oakes, 1985), labeling practices (Mercer, 1989), the social climate of the school, and staff expectations for student achievement (Brookover, Beady, Flood, Schweitzer, & Wisenbaker, 1979). This section reviews literature that focuses on institutionalized factors of the school culture and environment that need to be reformed in order to increase the academic achievement and emotional growth of students from diverse ethnic, racial, and social-class groups.

Limitations and Interrelationships of the Dimensions

The dimensions typology is an ideal-type conception in the Weberian sense. It approximates but does not describe reality in its total complexity. Like all classification schemas, it has both strengths and limitations. Typologies are helpful conceptual tools because they provide a way to organize and make sense of complex and disparate data and observations. However, their categories are interrelated and overlapping, not mutually exclusive. Typologies are rarely able to encompass the total universe of existing or future cases. Consequently, some cases can be described only by using several of the categories.

The dimensions typology provides a useful framework for categorizing and interpreting the extensive and disparate literature on diversity and education. The five dimensions are conceptually distinct but highly interrelated. Content integration, for example, describes any approach that is used to integrate content about racial and cultural groups into the curriculum. The knowledge construction process describes a method by which teachers help students to understand how knowledge is created, and how it reflects the experiences of various ethnic and cultural groups.

Content integration is a necessary but not sufficient condition for the knowledge construction process (i.e., content integration can take place without the knowledge construction process). Teachers can, for example, insert into the curriculum content about Mexican Americans without helping students to view the content from Mexican American perspectives. However, the knowledge construction process cannot be included in the curriculum without content integration first taking place.

Some of the publications examined for this review crossed several of the categories. Cooperative learning techniques, for example, can help students to increase their academic achievement, as well as to develop more positive racial attitudes. Consequently, some cooperative learning studies can be categorized as both equity pedagogy and prejudice reduction strategies (Aronson & Bridgeman, 1979; Slavin, 1985).

Criteria for selecting studies in each of the five dimensions included the extent to which the study or publication (a) is a prototype of the particular dimension being discussed; (b) has been influential in the field, as determined by the extent to which it is cited and has contributed to the theoretical and empirical growth of the field; and (c) has promise, in the author's judgment, of contributing to the future development of theory, research, and practice in multicultural education.

CONTENT INTEGRATION

The literature on content integration focuses on what information should be included in the curriculum, how it should be integrated into the existing curriculum, and where it should be located within the curriculum (i.e., whether it should be taught within separate courses or as part of the core curriculum). Another important issue discussed in this literature concerns who should be the audience for ethnic content (i.e., whether it should be for all students or primarily for students of color).

An exhaustive body of literature describes the various debates, discussions, and curricula that have focused on the integration of content about ethnic groups and women into school, college, and university curricula (J. A. Banks, 1991c; Butler & Walter, 1991; Lauter, 1991). The scope of this section is limited primarily to a description of the literature that focuses on the integration of content about racial and ethnic groups into the curriculum. The literature that describes the effects of curricular materials on students' racial and ethnic attitudes is reviewed in the section that discusses the prejudice reduction dimension.

The Need for a Historical Perspective

It is important to view the movements by ethnic groups to integrate school, college, and university curricula with ethnic content from a historical perspective (see Table 1–1). A historical perspective is necessary to provide a context for understanding the contemporary developments and discourse in multicultural education and to restructure schools, colleges, and universities to reflect multicultural issues and concerns.

TABLE 1–1. Landmark Events and Publications in the Historical Development of Ethnic Studies and Multicultural Education

Year(s)	Event/Publication
1882–1883	*History of the Negro Race in America* by George Washington Williams
1896	*The Suppression of the African Slave Trade to the United States of America 1638–1870* by W. E. B. DuBois
1899	*The Philadelphia Negro* by W. E. B. DuBois
1915	The Association for the Study of Negro Life and History is founded in Chicago
1916	*The Journal of Negro History* begins publication
1921	The Associated Publishers is established
1922	*The Negro in Our History* by Carter G. Woodson and Charles C. Wesley
1929	*Race Attitudes in Children* by Bruno Lasker
1930	*Mexican Immigration to the United States* by Manuel Gamio
1933	*The Mis-Education of the Negro* by Carter G. Woodson
1936	Eugene Horowitz's study of young children's attitudes toward the Negro
1937	*The Negro History Bulletin*, designed for schools, begins publication
1939	*Negro Education in Alabama: A Study in Cotton and Steel* by Horace Mann Bond; first reported study by Kenneth B. and Mamie P. Clark on young children's racial attitudes
1941	*Deep South: A Social Anthropological Study of Caste and Class* by Allison Davis, Burleigh B. Gardner, and Mary R. Gardner
1944	*An American Dilemma: The Negro Problem and Modern Democracy* by Gunnar Myrdal with Richard Sterner and Arnold Rose
1945	*Democratic Human Relations: Promising Practices in Intergroup and Intercultural Education in the Social Studies*, 16th yearbook of the National Council for the Social Studies, edited by Hilda Taba and William Van Til; *Black Metropolis: A Study of Negro Life in a Northern City* by St. Clair Drake and Horace R. Cayton
1947	A review of research on intergroup education is published in the *Review of Educational Research* by Lloyd A. Cook; first edition of *From Slavery to Freedom: A History of Negro Americans* by John Hope Franklin
1950	*College Programs in Intergroup Relations* by Lloyd A. Cook; *The Authoritarian Personality* by. T. W. Adorno et al.
1951	*Intergroup Relations in Teacher Education* by Lloyd A. Cook
1952	*Intergroup Education in Public Schools* by Hilda Taba, Elizabeth H. Brady, and John T. Robinson; *They Learn What They Live: Prejudice in Young Children* by Helen G. Trager and Marian R. Yarrow; *Race Awareness in Young Children* by Mary Ellen Goodman
1954	*The Nature of Prejudice* by Gordon W. Allport
1962	*Social-Class Influences Upon Learning* by Allison Davis
1965	*Compensatory Education for Cultural Deprivation* by Benjamin S. Bloom, Allison Davis, and Robert Hess
1966	*Equality of Educational Opportunity* by James Coleman et al.
1972	*Inequality: A Reassessment of the Effect of Family and Schooling in America* by Christopher Jencks et al.
1973	*No One Model American* (American Association of Colleges for Teacher Education); *Teaching Ethnic Studies: Concepts and Strategies*, National Council for the Social Studies 43rd yearbook, edited by James A. Banks
1974	*Cultural Democracy, Bicognitive Development, and Education* by Manuel Ramírez and Alfredo Castañeda: *The Next Generation: An Ethnography of Education in an Urban Neighborhood* by John U. Ogbu; *Students' Right to Their Own Language*, a position statement by the National Council of Teachers of English
1975	*Adolescent Prejudice* by Charles Y. Glock, Robert Wuthnow, Jane A. Piliavin, and Metta Spencer, sponsored by the Anti-Defamation League of B'nai B'rith
1976	*Curriculum Guidelines for Multiethnic Education*, a position statement issued by the National Council for the Social Studies; *Race, Color, and the Young Child* by John E. Williams and J. Kenneth Morland—a synthesis of research conducted in the late 1960s and 1970s on young children's racial attitudes
1977	*Multicultural Education: Commitments, Issues and Applications*, edited by Carl A. Grant, published by the Association for Supervision and Curriculum Development; *Pluralism and the American Teacher: Issues and Case Studies*, edited by Frank H. Klassen and Donna M. Gollnick, published by the American Association of Colleges for Teacher Education; *Pluralism in a Democratic Society*, edited by Melvin M. Tumin and Walter Plotch, sponsored by the Anti-Defamation League of B'nai B'rith; *Standards for the Accreditation of Teacher Education*, issued by the National Council for the Accreditation of Teacher Education, includes a requirement for multicultural education in teacher education programs
1983	*Ways with Words: Language, Life, and Work in Communities and Classrooms* by Shirley Brice Heath
1985	*Beginnings: The Social and Affective Development of Black Children*, edited by Margaret B. Spencer, Geraldine K. Brookins, and Walter R. Allen
1988	*The Education of Blacks in the South, 1860–1935* by James D. Anderson
1989	*A Common Destiny: Blacks and American Society*, edited by Gerald D. Jaynes and Robin M. Williams, Jr., National Research Council report
1991	*Shades of Black: Diversity in African-American Identity* by William E. Cross, Jr.

Contemporary reformers need to understand, for example, why the intergroup education movement of the 1940s and 1950s ultimately failed (Cook, 1947; Taba & Wilson, 1946) and why early ethnic studies leaders such as Woodson (1919/1968), DuBois (1935), Wesley (1935), and Franklin (1947), and their successors, were able to continue the early ethnic studies movement quietly with publications, research, and teaching from the turn of the century to the 1960s, when the new ethnic studies movement began.

At least a partial explanation is that the early ethnic studies movement was sustained by ethnic self-help organizations such as the Association for the Study of Negro Life and History (ASNLH; now the Association for the Study of Afro-American Life and History) and The Associated Publishers—two organizations cofounded and headed by Woodson. The Associated Publishers published many important and seminal works by and about African American scholars such as Woodson (1919/1968), Wesley (1935), and Bond (1939). African American schools and colleges were the major consumers of Black scholarship during the first decades of the 20th century. Ethnic community support might be essential for sustaining interest in ethnic studies and multicultural concerns over the long haul. Further investigations are needed to determine the different fates of the early ethnic studies and intergroup education movements.

African Americans led the movement that pushed for the integration of ethnic content into the curriculum during the 1960s and 1970s. Consequently, it is appropriate to provide a brief historical discussion of the movement to integrate the curriculum with ethnic content, using African Americans as a case study.

The Early Ethnic Studies Movement

The Black studies movement that emerged in the 1960s and 1970s has historical roots in the early national period (Brooks, 1990; White, 1973; Woodson, 1919/1968). It is more directly linked to the work in ethnic studies research and the development of teaching materials by African American scholars such as G. W. Williams (1882–1883), Woodson and Wesley (1922), and DuBois (1935, 1973). Scholars such as G. W. Williams, Wesley, Woodson, and DuBois created knowledge about African Americans that could be integrated into the school and college curriculum. Educators such as Woodson and Wesley (1922) worked during the early decades of the 20th century to integrate the school and college curriculum with content about African Americans.

Brooks (1990) discusses the early history of schools for African American children. He points out that from slavery to today, Black education has been characterized by desegregation in the colonial and early national periods, a push for segregation in the early 1800s, a movement toward desegregation during the 1950s and 1960s, and another swing toward segregation today.

The first public schools that were organized in Massachusetts and Virginia in the 1640s were desegregated (Brooks, 1990; White, 1973; Woodson, 1919/1968). However, because of the discrimination they experienced in these schools, African Americans took the leadership in establishing separate schools for their children. When the city of Boston refused to fund separate schools for African American children in 1800, the Black community set up its own schools and hired the teachers. In 1818 the city of Boston started funding separate schools for African American children. The first schools established for African Americans in the South after the Civil War were segregated by laws formulated by White legislators.

Separate schools for African Americans proved to be a mixed blessing, especially in the southern states and later in northern cities. In the South, African American schools were separate and unequal in terms of expenditures per pupil, the salaries of teachers and administrators, and the quality and

newness of textbooks and other teaching materials (Anderson, 1988; Bond, 1939).

Although separate Black public schools in the South had African American teachers and administrators, their school boards, curricula, and textbooks were White controlled and dominated. Consequently, integration of the curriculum with content about African Americans was problematic. In his influential book *The Mis-Education of the Negro,* Woodson (1933) stated that schools and colleges were miseducating African Americans because they were being taught about European civilization but not about the great African civilizations and cultures of their own people. He described what he felt were the harmful effects of neglecting Black history and civilization on the thinking and self-esteem of African American youth.

From 1920 until his death in 1950, Woodson probably did more than any other individual to promote the study and teaching of African American history in the nation's schools and colleges. He spent most of his career writing histories, editing journals, and building ASNLH. Woodson taught high school in Washington, D.C., from 1909 to 1918, and received his doctorate in history from Harvard in 1912. He was one of the founders of ASNLH and established the *Journal of Negro History* in 1916. In 1921 he established The Associated Publishers, a subsidiary of ASNLH, which published a score of histories about African Americans, many of them written by Woodson and his historian colleagues.

Woodson's books were widely used in African American high schools and colleges. He started Negro History Week (now National Afro-American History Month) in 1926 to promote the study and teaching of African American history in the elementary and secondary schools. In 1937 he started publishing the *Negro History Bulletin to* provide historial materials for use by elementary and secondary school teachers. Other early African American scholars, such as G. W. Williams (1882–1883), DuBois (1935), Wesley (1935), Quarles (1953), and Logan (1954), played key roles in constructing the knowledge needed to develop teaching materials for the schools and colleges. However, none of these scholars were as directly involved as Woodson in promoting the inclusion of content about African Americans into the curriculum of the nation's schools and colleges.

The Intergroup Education Movement

The intergroup education movement, although not a direct link to the work of early African American scholars such as Woodson, Wesley, DuBois, and Logan, is an important precedent to the ethnic studies movement that emerged in the 1960s and 1970s. The intergroup education movement is linked to the work of these scholars because content about religious, national, and racial groups was one of the variables it used to reduce prejudice and discrimination (Cook & Cook, 1954; Trager & Yarrow, 1952). It is linked to the contemporary multicultural education movement because it shared many of the goals of today's multicultural education movement and experienced many of the same problems (Taba & Wilson, 1946; J. A. Banks, 1994).

The social forces that gave rise to the intergroup education movement grew out of the consequences of World War II. The demands of the war created job opportunities in the North and the West that were not available in the South. Consequently, many African Americans, Mexican Americans, and Whites living in rural areas migrated to northern and western cities to find jobs in war-related industries. Ethnic and racial tension developed as Anglos and Mexican Americans in western cities and African Americans and Whites in northern cities competed for jobs and housing. These tensions resulted in a series of racial incidents and riots that stunned the nation.

Intergroup education emerged as an educational response to the racial and ethnic tension in the nation (Taba, Brady, & Robinson, 1952). One of its major goals was to help reduce prejudice and create interracial understanding among students from diverse national, religious, and racial groups (Cook & Cook, 1954; Taba & Wilson, 1946). Several national organizations, such as the Progressive Education Association (Locke & Stern, 1942), the National Council for the Social Studies (NCSS) (Taba & Van Til, 1945), and the American Council on Education (Cook, 1950), sponsored projects, activities, and publications in intergroup education. Projects and activities were developed for both elementary and secondary schools (Taba et al., 1952), as well as for teachers colleges (Cook, 1951).

Many of the intergroup education publications, like multicultural education publications today, were practical sources that described ways to set up an intergroup relations center (Clinchy, 1949), identified objectives and methods for schools (Vickery & Cole, 1943), described curricula and units for schools (Taba, 1950, 1951, 1952), and described intergroup education programs and projects in colleges and universities (Cook, 1951). Some of these publications were based on intergroup theories developed by social scientists such as Louis Wirth (1928) and Gordon W. Allport (1954).

Some of the nation's leading social scientists and philosophers participated in the development of theoretical ideas about the reduction of interracial tensions during the intergroup education era. Wirth, the University of Chicago sociologist, and Allport, the Harvard social psychologist, contributed chapters to a book edited by Lloyd A. Cook (1952), a leading intergroup educator. Wirth's paper was titled "Freedom, Power and Values in Our Present Crisis"; Allport's was called "Resolving Intergroup Tension: An Appraisal of Methods."

Alain Locke, the African American philosopher of Howard University, coedited a background book on intergroup education for the Progressive Education Association (Locke & Stern, 1942). This comprehensive book on race and culture consists of reprinted articles by some of the leading social scientists of the day, including Ruth Benedict, Franz Boas, John Dollard, E. Franklin Frazier, Melville J. Herskovits, Otto Klineberg, Ralph Linton, and Margaret Mead.

Allison Davis, the noted African American anthropologist at the University of Chicago and coauthor of *Deep South: A Social Anthropological Study of Caste and Class,* a classic study of an old southern city (Davis, Gardner, & Gardner, 1941), wrote a chapter for NCSS's 16th yearbook. The chapter is titled "Some Basic Concepts in the Education of Ethnic and Lower-Class Groups." Davis urged social studies teachers to teach students "a devotion to democratic values, and group disapproval of injustice, oppression, and exploitation" (Taba & Van Til, 1945, p. 278). He also believed that teachers should teach social

action: "Teach the underprivileged child to learn to help organize and improve his community" (p. 279). The fact that scholars of the stature of Davis and Locke contributed to books on intergroup education sponsored by educational organizations indicated that some of the leading social science scholars of the 1940s believed that they should become involved in a major social problem facing the nation and the schools.

Several landmark studies in race relations were published during the intergroup education era. Jewish organizations, such as the American Jewish Committee and the Anti-Defamation League of B'nai B'rith, sponsored several of these studies. One important factor that contributed to the rise of the intergroup education movement was anti-Semitism in Western nations, which reached its peak in Germany during World War II. Jewish organizations were especially interested in taking actions and sponsoring research that would ease racial tension and conflict. They were poignantly aware of the destructive power of ethnic hate (Wyman, 1984).

In 1950 *The Authoritarian Personality* (Adorno, Frenkel-Brunswik, Levinson, & Sanford, 1950) was published. In this landmark study the authors identify the personality factors that contribute to the formation of prejudice. Although they overemphasize personality-factor explanations of prejudice and give insufficient attention to structural factors, their study remains an important one.

Allport's seminal study, *The Nature of Prejudice,* was published in 1954. In this book Allport formulates his influential principles about ways to create effective intergroup interactions. He states that effective contact situations must be characterized by equal-status, cooperative rather than competitive interactions, and by shared goals. Positive interracial contact must also be sanctioned by authorities. Allport's principles are highly influential in social science research today and provide an important theoretical base for the work of researchers such as Cohen (1972), Aronson and Bridgeman (1979), and Slavin (1985).

Important theoretical and research work related to children's racial attitudes was also completed during the intergroup education period. The Anti-Defamation League of B'nai B'rith sponsored a major study by Goodman that was published in 1952. This study provided evidence that supported earlier findings by researchers such as E. L. Horowitz (1936), R. E. Horowitz (1939), and a series of studies by Kenneth B. and Mamie P. Clark (1939a, 1939b, 1940, 1947). These studies established the postulate that preschool children have racial awareness and attitudes that mirror those of adults.

Intergroup educators wanted to help students to develop more democratic racial attitudes and values (Cook, 1947; Taba & Wilson, 1946). Investigations designed to determine the effects of curricular interventions on students' racial attitudes were an important part of the intergroup education movement. Significant intervention studies conducted during this period include those by Trager and Yarrow (1952) and by Hayes and Conklin (1953). Most of these studies support the postulate that multicultural lessons, activities, and teaching materials, when used within a democratic classroom atmosphere and implemented for a sufficiently long period, help students to develop more democratic racial attitudes and values. Studies both prior to and during this period established that children internalize the adult attitudes that are institutionalized within the structures and institutions of society (Clark & Clark, 1947; Goodman, 1952; E. L. Horowitz, 1936).

Important textbooks and reports published during the intergroup education era include those by Locke and Stern (1942), Cook (1950), Taba et al. (1952), and Cook and Cook (1954), which reveal that intergroup educators emphasized democratic living and interracial cooperation within mainstream American society. The ethnic studies movements that both preceded and followed the intergroup education movement emphasized ethnic attachment, pride, and empowerment. The focus in intergroup education was on intercultural interactions within a shared, common culture (Cook, 1947; Taba & Wilson, 1946).

The Early Ethnic Studies and Intergroup Education Movements Compared

Woodson (1933) and DuBois (1973) were concerned that African Americans develop knowledge of Black history and culture, and a commitment to the empowerment and enhancement of the African American community. This was in contrast to the emphasis in intergroup education, which promoted a weak form of diversity and the notion that "we are different but the same."

The Sleeter and Grant (1987) typology consists of five categories: (a) teaching the culturally different, (b) human relations, (c) single-group studies, (d) multicultural education, and (e) education that is multicultural and social reconstructionist. Most of the literature and guides that were produced during the intergroup education era can be categorized as human relations. In this approach, according to Sleeter and Grant (1987), multicultural education is "a way to help students of different backgrounds communicate, get along better with each other, and feel good about themselves" (p. 426).

Like the human relations books and materials examined by Sleeter and Grant that were published in the 1970s and 1980s, intergroup education materials devote little attention to issues and problems such as institutionalized racism, power, and structural inequality. However, unlike most of the human relations materials examined by Sleeter and Grant, some of the materials published during the intergroup education period are based on theories developed by psychologists and social psychologists (Taba, 1950, 1951; Taba & Wilson, 1946).

The intergroup education publications and projects emphasized interracial harmony and human relations. The early ethnic studies advocates endorsed ethnic empowerment and what Sleeter and Grant call "single group studies." Thus, the aims and goals of the intergroup education and ethnic studies movements were quite different. The ethnic studies movement emphasized the histories and cultures of specific ethnic groups (single-group studies). Taba and Wilson (1946) identified the following focuses in intergroup education: concepts and understandings about groups and relations, sensitivity and goodwill, objective thinking, and experiences in democratic procedures.

The racial backgrounds and cultural experiences of the leaders of the two ethnic studies movements and those of the leaders of the intergroup education movement were factors that influenced the goals, aims, and nature of these movements. Most of the influential leaders of the early ethnic studies movement in the United States and the one that emerged in the 1960s and 1970s were people of color. Most of the leaders of the intergroup education movement were White liberal educators and social scientists who functioned and worked within mainstream colleges, universities, and other institutions and organizations. Hilda Taba (who taught at the University of Chicago and directed the Intergroup Education in Cooperating Schools Project for the American Council on Education) and Lloyd A. Cook (who taught at Wayne State University and directed the College Programs in Intergroup Relations project) were the most prolific and noted intergroup education leaders.

The different cultural experiences, perceptions, and values of the leaders of the ethnic studies and intergroup education movements significantly influenced their perceptions of the goals of citizenship education and the role of ethnic content in instruction. Ethnic studies scholars and educators probably endorsed a more pluralistic view of citizenship education than did intergroup educators because they worked and functioned primarily outside mainstream institutions and believed that parallel ethnic institutions were essential for the survival and development of ethnic groups in the United States. The experiences of most intergroup educators in mainstream institutions influenced their view that assimilation into mainstream culture and its institutions was the most appropriate way to resolve ethnic tensions.

The history of the early ethnic studies and intergroup education movements and an analysis of current curriculum reform efforts reveal that movements related to the integration of ethnic content into the curriculum move cyclically from a single-group to an intergroup focus. The fact that single-group studies movements continue to emerge within a society with a democratic ethos suggests that the United States has not dealt successfully with the American dilemma related to race that Myrdal (with Sterner & Rose, 1944) identified nearly 50 years ago.

The Ethnic Studies Movement of the 1960s and 1970s

A prominent vision within the intergroup education ideology was interracial harmony and desegregation. Another name for the movement was *intercultural education*. Intergroup education emerged when the nation was sharply segregated along racial lines and was beginning its efforts to create a desegregated society. The early goal of the civil rights movement of the 1960s was racial desegregation. However, by the late 1960s many African Americans had grown impatient with the pace of desegregation. Imbued with racial pride, they called for Black power, separatism, and Black studies in the schools and colleges that would contribute to the empowerment and advancement of African Americans (Carmichael & Hamilton, 1967).

When the civil rights movement began, the intergroup education movement had quietly died without a requiem. The separatist ideology that emerged during the 1970s was antithetical to the intergroup education vision. The America envisioned by most intergroup educators was a nation in which ethnic and racial differences were minimized and all people were treated fairly and lived in harmony.

During the late 1960s and early 1970s, sometimes in strident voices, African Americans, frustrated with deferred and shattered dreams, demanded community control of their schools, African American teachers and administrators, and the infusion of Black history into the curriculum. At the university level, frequent demands included Black studies programs and courses, heritage rooms or houses, and Black professors and administrators. During this period there was little demand for the infusion of ethnic content into the core or mainstream curriculum—that demand would not emerge until the 1980s and 1990s. Rather, the demand was primarily for separate courses and programs (Blassingame, 1971; Ford, 1973; Robinson, Foster, & Ogilvie, 1969).

As schools, colleges, and universities began to respond to the demand by African Americans for curriculum changes, other ethnic groups of color that felt victimized by institutionalized discrimination in the United States began to demand similar programs. These groups included Mexican Americans, Puerto Ricans, American Indians, and Asian Americans. A rich array of books, programs, curricula, and other materials that focused on the histories and cultures of ethnic groups of color was edited, written, or reprinted between the late 1960s and the early 1970s.

One major development during this period was the reprinting of books and research studies that had been written during the early and more silent period of ethnic studies. A few of these publications had remained in print for many years, and had been best-sellers at all-Black colleges; such books included John Hope Franklin's popular history, *From Slavery to Freedom,* first published in 1947, and *The Souls of Black Folk* by W. E. B. DuBois, first published in 1953.

However, more frequent was the reprinting of long-neglected works that had been produced during the earlier period of ethnic studies. George Washington William's *History of the Negro Race in America* (1882–1883) was reissued by Arno Press in 1968. Important earlier works on Hispanics reprinted during this period included Carey McWilliams's *North from Mexico: The Spanish-Speaking People of the United States* (1949), which provides an informative overview of Hispanic groups in the United States, and Manuel Gamio's *Mexican Immigration to the United States* (1930), a well-researched description of the first wave of Mexican immigrants to the United States. Two important earlier works on Filipino Americans were also reissued during this period: *Filipino Immigration to the Continental United States and Hawaii,* by Bruno Lasker (1931), and *Brothers Under the Skin,* by Carey McWilliams (1943).

More significant than the older books that were kept in print or reissued was the new crop of publications that focused primarily on the struggles and experiences of particular ethnic groups. The emphasis in many of these publications was on ways that ethnic groups of color had been victimized by institutionalized racism and discrimination in the United States. The quality and meticulousness of research of this rash of books varied widely. However, they all provided perspectives that gave Americans new ways to view the history and culture of the United States. Many of them became required reading in ethnic studies courses and degree programs. Among the significant books of this genre are *Japanese Americans* by Harry H. L. Kitano (1969); *The Story of the Chinese in America* by Betty Lee Sung (1967); *Occupied America: The Chicano's Struggle Toward Liberation* by Rudy Acuña (1972); *Custer Died for Your Sins: An Indian Manifesto* by Vine Deloria, Jr. (1969); and *The Rise of the Unmeltable Ethnics* by Michael Novak (1971), a highly rhetorical and ringing plea for justice for White ethnic groups such as Poles, Italians, Greeks, and Slavs.

The Evolution of Multicultural Education

The intergroup education movement is an important antecedent of the current multicultural education movement but is not an actual root of it. The current multicultural education movement is directly linked to the early ethnic studies movement initiated by scholars such as G. W. Williams (1882–1883) and continued by individuals such as DuBois (1935), Woodson (1919/1968), Bond (1939), and Wesley (1935). The major architects of the multicultural education movement were cogently influenced by African American scholarship and ethnic studies related to other ethnic minority groups in the United States.

Baker (1977), J. A. Banks (1973), Gay (1971), and Grant (1973, 1978) have each played significant roles in the formulation and development of multicultural education in the United States. Each of these scholars was heavily influenced by the early work of African American scholars and the African American ethnic studies movement. They were working in ethnic studies prior to participating in the formation of multicultural education. Other scholars who have helped to fashion multicultural eduation since its inception, and were also influenced by the African American ethnic studies movement, include James B. Boyer (1974), Asa Hilliard III (1974), and Barbara A. Sizemore (1972).

Scholars who are specialists on other ethnic groups, such as Carlos E. Cortés (1973; Mexican Americans), Jack D. Forbes (1973; American Indians), Sonia Nieto (1986; Puerto Ricans), and Derald W. Sue (1981; Asian Americans), also played early and significant roles in the evolution of multicultural education.

The first phase of multicultural education emerged when educators who had interests and specializations in the history and culture of ethnic minority groups initiated individual and institutional actions to incorporate the concepts, information, and theories from ethnic studies into the school and teacher-education curricula. Consequently, the first phase of multicultural education was ethnic studies.

A second phase of multicultural education emerged when educators interested in ethnic studies began to realize that inserting ethnic studies content into the school and teacher-education curricula was necessary but not sufficient to bring about school reform that would respond to the unique needs of ethnic minority students and help all students to develop more democratic racial and ethnic attitudes. Multiethnic education was the second phase of multicultural education. Its aim was to bring about structural and systemic changes in the total school that were designed to increase educational equality.

A third phase of multicultural education emerged when

other groups who viewed themselves as victims of the society and the schools, such as women and people with disabilities, demanded the incorporation of their histories, cultures, and voices into the curricula and structure of the schools, colleges, and universities. The current, or fourth, phase of multicultural education consists of the development of theory, research, and practice that interrelate variables connected to race, class, and gender (J. A. Banks & Banks, 1993; Grant & Sleeter, 1986). It is important to note that each of the phases of multicultural education continues to exist today. However, the later phases tend to be more prominent than the earlier ones, at least in the theoretical literature, if not in practice.

During the 1970s a number of professional organizations, such as the American Association of Colleges for Teacher Education (AACTE), the National Council of Teachers of English (NCTE), and NCSS, issued position statements and publications that encouraged schools to integrate the curriculum with content and understandings about ethnic groups. In 1973 AACTE published its brief and widely quoted statement, *No One Model American*. That same year, the NCSS 43rd yearbook was titled *Teaching Ethnic Studies: Concepts and Strategies* (J. A. Banks, 1973). The following year, NCTE (1974) issued *Students' Right to Their Own Language*. An early landmark conference on multicultural education through competency-based teacher education was sponsored by AACTE in 1974 (Hunter, 1974). In 1976 NCSS published *Curriculum Guidelines for Multiethnic Education* (J. A. Banks, Cortés, Gay, Garcia, & Ochoa, 1976). This publication was revised and reissued in 1992 with a title change to "Curriculum Guidelines for Multicultural Education" (NCSS Task Force, 1992).

Several landmark developments in the emergence of multicultural education occurred in 1977. The Association for Supervision and Curriculum Development (ASCD) published a book on multicultural education (Grant, 1977). That same year, AACTE published *Pluralism and the American Teacher; Issues and Case Studies* (Klassen & Gollnick, 1977). This book resulted from its conference series on the topic that was supported by a grant from the U.S. Office of Education. Using the grant funds, AACTE established the Ethnic Heritage Center for Teacher Education, its unit that sponsored the conferences and the book. One of the most influential developments during the early emergence of multicultural education was the issuance of *Standards for the Accreditation of Teacher Education* by the National Council for Accreditation of Teacher Education (NCATE) in 1977. These standards required all of its member teacher-education institutions, which comprised about 80% of the teacher-education programs in the United States, to implement components, courses, and programs in multicultural education. The standards were later issued in revised form (NCATE, 1987).

Many professional associations, school districts, and state departments of education published guidelines and teacher's guides to help school districts integrate content about ethnic groups into the elementary and high school curriculum. The United Federation of Teachers published *Puerto Rican History and Culture: A Study Guide and Curriculum Outline* (Aran, Arthur, Colon, & Goldenberg, 1973). This curriculum guide, like most materials produced by professional organizations,

school districts, and commercial publishers during this period, focused on a single ethnic group. Publications and materials that focused on more than one ethnic group were developed later. One of the first publications to recommend a multiethnic approach to the study of ethnic groups was the NCSS 1973 yearbook (J. A. Banks, 1973). The guides and books published during this period varied in quality. Many were produced quickly, but others provided teachers with sound and thoughtful guidelines for integrating their curricula with ethnic content.

Research Developments Since the 1960s

A rich array of research in the social sciences, humanities, and education focusing on people of color has been published since 1960. Much of this research challenges existing interpretations, paradigms, assumptions, and methodologies and provides pertinent data on long-neglected topics (Gates, 1988; King & Mitchell, 1990; Slaughter, 1988). The three decades between 1960 and 1990 were probably the most productive research period in ethnic studies in the nation's history. St. Claire Drake (1987, 1990), shortly before his death, completed a massive two-volume anthropological study, *Black Folk Here and There*. Bernal's (1987, 1991) comprehensive two-volume work, *Black Athena: The Afroasiatic Roots of Classical Civilization*, challenges existing historical interpretations about the debt that ancient Greece owes to Africa, and supports earlier works by African and African American scholars such as Diop (1974) and Van Sertima (1988). Many of the insights from this new scholarship are being incorporated into the school, college, and university curriculum.

THE KNOWLEDGE CONSTRUCTION PROCESS

The ethnic studies research and literature published during the 1960s and 1970s (Acuña, 1972), like the ethnic studies scholarship in the early decades of the century (DuBois, 1935; Woodson, 1919/1968), challenged some of the major paradigms, canons, and perspectives established within mainstream scholarship (Blea, 1988; Gordon, 1985; Gordon, Miller & Rollock, 1990; Ladner, 1973). Ethnic studies scholarship also challenges some of the key assumptions of mainstream Western empiricism (J. A. Banks, 1993b; Gordon & Meroe, 1991).

The construction of descriptions and interpretations of the settlement of the West (Turner, 1894/1989) and of slavery (Phillips, 1918) are two examples of how people of color have been described and conceptualized in mainstream U.S. history and social science. Frederick Jackson Turner (1894/1989) constructed a view of the settlement of European Americans in the West that has cogently influenced the treatment and interpretation of the West in school, college, and university textbooks (Sleeter & Grant, 1991). Turner described the land occupied by the Indians as an empty wilderness to which the Europeans brought civilization. He also argued that the wilderness in the West, which required individualism for survival, was the main source of American democracy. Although revisionist historians have described the limitations of Turner's theory, its influence on the curricula of the nation's elementary and high schools, and on textbooks, is still powerful.

The treatment and interpretation of slavery within mainstream U.S. scholarship provide another revealing example of how ethnic groups of color have been depicted in such scholarship. Ulrich B. Phillips's interpretation of slavery remained dominant from the time his book was published in 1918 to the 1950s, 1960s, and 1970s, when the established slavery paradigm was revised by a new generation of historians (Blassingame, 1972; Genovese, 1972; Stampp, 1956). Phillips's interpretation of slavery, which is essentially an apology for southern slaveholders, was one of the major sources for the conception of slaves as happy, contented, and loyal to their masters that dominated textbooks in the 1950s and 1960s (J. A. Banks, 1969).

The description of the settlement of Europeans in the western United States and the treatment of slavery in U.S. scholarship from the turn of the century to the 1950s indicate the extent to which knowledge reflects ideology, human interests, values, and perspectives (Habermas, 1971). Yet a basic assumption of Western empiricism is that knowledge is objective and neutral and that its principles are universal (Kaplan, 1964). Multicultural scholars (Acuña, 1972; Hilliard, Payton-Stewart, & Williams, 1990; King & Mitchell, 1990)—like critical theorists such as Habermas (1971) and Giroux (1983) and feminist postmodernists such as Farganis (1986), Code (1991), and Harding (1991)—reject these assumptions about the nature of knowledge.

Multicultural scholars maintain that knowledge reflects the social, cultural, and power positions of people within society, and that it is valid only when it "comes from an acknowledgment of the knower's specific position in any context, one always defined by gender, class, and other variables" (Tetreault, 1993, p. 142). Multicultural and feminist theorists maintain that knowledge is both subjective and objective and that its subjective components need to be clearly identified (Code, 1991; hooks, 1990; King & Mitchell, 1990). Multicultural theorists also contend that by claiming that their knowledge is objective and neutral, mainstream scholars are able to present their particularistic interests and ideologies as the universal concerns of the nation-state (Asante, 1991; Hilliard et al., 1990). According to Gordon and Meroe (1991):

We often wonder if the socially adapted human being, who happens to be a scholar, is truly capable of discarding her or his individual frame of reference when it comes to the study of a subject to which she or he has chosen to commit her or his life's work. This is a precarious and dangerous situation because too many times "objectivity" has served as a mask for the political agenda of the status quo, thus marginalizing and labeling the concerns of less empowered groups as "special interests." (p. 28)

A number of conceptualizations have been developed by multicultural and feminist theorists that are designed to help teachers acquire the information and skills needed to teach students how knowledge is constructed, how to identify the writer's purposes and point of view, and how to formulate their own interpretations of reality.

Four approaches used to integrate ethnic content into the elementary and high school curriculum and to teach students about ethnic groups were conceptualized by J. A. Banks (1993a): *contributions, additive, transformation,* and *social action* (see Figure 1–1). The contributions approach focuses on heroes and heroines, holidays, and discrete cultural elements. When using the additive approach, teachers append ethnic content, themes, and perspectives to the curriculum without changing its basic structure. In the transformation approach, which is designed to help students learn how knowledge is constructed, the structure of the curriculum is changed to enable students to view concepts, issues, events, and themes from the perspectives of various ethnic and cultural groups. In the social action approach, which is an extension of the transformation approach, students make decisions on important social issues and take action to help solve them.

Tetreault (1993) describes a model for teaching content about women that is also designed to help students understand the nature of knowledge and how it is constructed. In this curriculum model, the teacher moves from a male-defined curriculum to one that is gender balanced. The phases are as follows: contributions curriculum, bifocal curriculum, women's curriculum, and gender-balanced curriculum. In the contributions curriculum, a male framework is used to insert women into the curriculum; the world is viewed through the eyes of women and men in the bifocal curriculum; subjects of primary importance to women are investigated in the women's curriculum; and the gender-balanced curriculum investigates topics and concepts that are important to women but also considers how women and men relate to each other.

PREJUDICE REDUCTION

The prejudice reduction dimension of multicultural education is designed to help students develop more democratic attitudes, values, and behaviors (Gabelko & Michaelis, 1981; Lynch, 1987). Researchers and educators who are concerned about helping students develop more democratic attitudes and behaviors have devoted much of their attention to investigating how children develop racial awareness, preferences, and identification (Clark, 1963; Katz, 1976; Milner, 1983; Phinney & Rotheram, 1987). This discussion is divided into two sections: (a) the nature of children's racial attitudes and identities and (b) the modification of students' racial attitudes.

The Nature of Children's Racial Attitudes

A common belief among elementary school teachers is that young children have little awareness of racial differences and hold positive attitudes toward both African Americans and Whites. Many teachers with whom I have worked have told me that because young children are unaware of racial differences, talking about race to them will merely create racial problems that do not exist. This common observation by teachers is inconsistent with reality and research.

During a period of nearly 50 years, researchers have established that young children are aware of racial differences by the

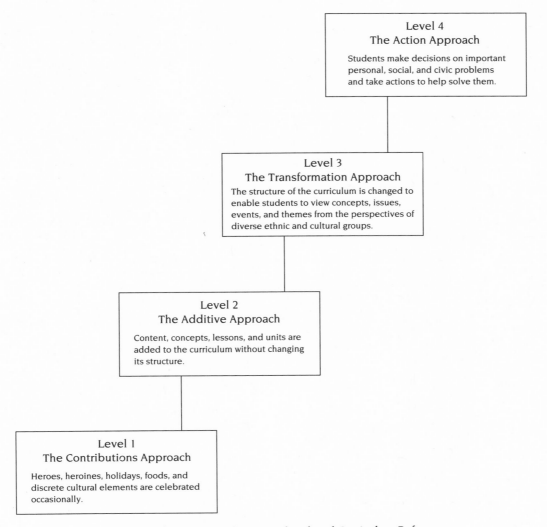

FIGURE 1–1. Approaches to Multicultural Curriculum Reform

age of three (Phinney & Rotheram, 1987; Ramsey, 1987) and have internalized attitudes toward African Americans and Whites that are established in the wider society. They tend to prefer white (pinkish-colored) stimulus objects, such as dolls and pictures, to brown dolls and pictures, and to describe white (pinkish) objects and people more positively than brown ones.

Early studies by Lasker (1929) and Minard (1931) indicate that young children are aware of racial differences and that children's racial attitudes are formed early in life. Studies by E. L. Horowitz (1936) and R. E. Horowitz (1939) indicate that both African American and White nursery school children are aware of racial differences and show a statistically significant preference for Whites. The Horowitzes interpreted their findings to mean that the African American children in their studies evidenced self-rejection when they showed a White bias in their responses to stimulus objects and pictures.

In a series of pioneering studies conducted between 1939 and 1950, Kenneth B. and Mamie P. Clark confirmed the find-

ings of the Horowitzes and gave considerable support to the self-rejection paradigm first formulated by the latter (Cross, 1991). The Clarks are usually credited with originating the self-rejection paradigm; however, Cross states that the Horowitzes, and not the Clarks, created the paradigm. Nevertheless, the famous Clark studies gave the self-rejection paradigm its widest visibility and credibility.

In the series of studies conducted by the Clarks, African American nursery school children were the subjects; the stimuli were brown and white (pinkish) dolls. The Clarks studied racial awareness, preference, and identification (Clark & Clark, 1939a, 1939b, 1940, 1947, 1950). They concluded that the children in their studies had accurate knowledge of racial differences, sometimes made incorrect racial self-identifications, and often expressed a preference for white. The Clarks concluded that many of the African American children in their studies evidenced self-rejection.

The self-rejection paradigm associated with the Clarks has

had a cogent influence on research and the interpretation of research on children's racial attitudes and self-esteem for nearly a half century. A series of significant and influential studies during the 1950s, 1960s, and 1970s confirmed the early findings by the Horowitzes and the Clarks (Morland, 1966; Porter, 1971; Radke & Trager, 1950; J. E. Williams & Morland, 1976)—that young children are aware of racial differences and that both African American and White children tend to evidence a white bias.

The self-rejection paradigm has been strongly challenged during the last decade on both methodological and interpretative grounds (W. C. Banks, 1976; Cross, 1991; Spencer, 1987). During the 1980s and 1990s, Spencer (1982, 1985, 1987) and Cross (1985, 1991) developed concepts and theories and conducted research that challenge the interpretation that the Horowitzes and the Clarks used to explain their findings. They have made a useful distinction between *personal* and *group* identity and have reinterpreted the early findings, as well as their own research findings, within this new paradigm.

An important group of studies by Spencer (1982, 1985, 1987) indicates that young African American children can distinguish their personal and group identities. They can express high self-esteem and a white bias at the same time. She formulates a cognitive theory to explain these findings: African American children often make white bias choices because they have learned from the wider society (a cognitive process) to make these choices, not because they reject themselves or have low self-concepts. In other words, the children are choosing the "right" answer when asked to select the white or colored stimulus. Research by J. A. Banks (1984) supports the postulate that African American children make choices related to race that indicate that personal and group identity are distinguished. Cross (1991) also provides strong theoretical and empirical evidence to support this conceptual distinction.

The Modification of Children's Racial Attitudes

Studies designed to modify children's racial attitudes have been conducted at least since the 1940s (Agnes, 1947; Jackson, 1944). However, the literature that describes the characteristics of children's racial attitudes is much richer than the modification literature. In two comprehensive reviews of the modification literature, J. A. Banks (1991b, 1993d) identifies four types of modification studies: (a) curricular intervention studies, (b) reinforcement studies, (c) perceptual differentiation studies, and (d) cooperative learning studies.

Curricular studies are the earliest type of intervention studies; they date back to the intergroup education period of the 1940s. In their studies, Agnes (1974) and Jackson (1944) concluded that reading materials about African Americans helped students develop more positive racial attitudes. However, most of the early studies have serious methodological problems. One of the most well-designed and significant studies of the intergroup education period was conducted by Trager and Yarrow (1952). They found that a democratic curriculum had a positive effect on the racial attitudes of both students and teachers. Hayes and Conklin (1953), with an experimental treatment that took place over a two-year period, also found that an inter-

cultural curriculum had a positive effect on the racial attitudes of students. However, the description of the intervention is imprecise.

Studies of the effects of units, courses, and curriculum materials have also been conducted by Fisher (1965), Leslie and Leslie (1972), Yawkey (1973), Lessing and Clarke (1976), Litcher and Johnson (1969), Litcher, Johnson, and Ryan (1973), and Shirley (1988). Most of these studies provide evidence for the postulate that curricular materials and interventions can have a positive effect on the racial attitudes of students. However, the studies by Lessing and Clarke and Litcher et al. had no measurable effects on the racial attitudes of students.

In an important study, Litcher and Johnson (1969) found that multiethnic readers had a positive effect on the racial attitudes of second-grade White students. However, when they replicated this study using photographs rather than readers (Litcher et al., 1973), no significant effects were attained. The investigators believe that the shorter duration of the latter study (one month compared with four) and the different ethnic compositions of the cities in which the studies were conducted may explain the conflicting findings in the two studies. In summarizing the effects of curriculum intervention studies, J. A. Banks (1991b) concludes:

The studies . . . indicate that curriculum intervention can help students to develop more positive racial attitudes but . . . the effects of such interventions are likely not to be consistent. . . . The inconsistencies may be due in part to the use of different measures to assess attitude change and because the duration of the interventions has varied widely. The duration of the intervention has rarely been varied to determine the effects. (p. 464)

J. E. Williams and his colleagues have conducted a series of reinforcement studies with young children since the 1960s (J. E. Williams & Edwards, 1969; J. E. Williams & Morland, 1976). These experiments are designed to reduce white bias in young children. In the typical design of these experiments, the children are given pictures of black and white animals or objects and are reinforced for choosing the black objects or animals and for describing them positively. When they choose the white objects or animals, they receive negative reinforcement or no reinforcement. Williams and his colleagues (J. E. Williams, Best, Wood, & Filler, 1973; J. E. Williams & Edwards, 1969) have found that these types of interventions reduce white bias in children and that the children's responses are generalized from objects and animals to people. Laboratory reinforcement studies by other researchers have generally confirmed the findings by Williams and his colleagues (Hohn, 1973; Parish & Fleetwood, 1975; Parish, Shirazi, & Lambert, 1976).

Katz and her colleagues have conducted a series of studies that have examined the perceptual components of the racial attitudes of young children. In one study she confirmed her predictions that young children can more easily differentiate the faces of in-group members than the faces of out-group members and that if young children are taught to differentiate the faces of out-groups, prejudice is reduced (Katz, 1973). She and Zalk (Katz & Zalk, 1978) examined the effects of four different interventions on the racial attitudes of second- and fifth-grade White students: (a) perceptual differentiation of minority group faces, (b) increased positive racial contact, (c) vicarious interracial contact, and (d) reinforcement of the color black. Each of the interventions reduced prejudice. However, the most powerful interventions were vicarious contact and perceptual differentiation.

Most of the research on cooperative learning has been conducted since the 1970s. Cooperative learning studies tend to support the postulate that cooperative learning situations, if based on the principles formulated by Allport (1954), can increase the academic achievement of minority students and help all students to develop more positive racial attitudes and cross-racial friendships (Aronson & Bridgeman, 1979; Cohen, 1972; Slavin, 1979, 1985). Cohen emphasizes the importance of providing students with experiences that will prepare them for equal-status interactions prior to assigning group tasks to students from different races. Her research indicates that if this is not done, both minority and White students will expect the White students to dominate the group situation. She calls this phenomenon *interracial interaction disability* and has demonstrated that pregroup treatment activities can enable African American students to experience equal status in group situations with Whites (Cohen, 1972; Cohen & Roper, 1972).

EQUITY PEDAGOGY

When the civil rights movement began in the 1960s, much attention was focused on poverty in the United States. In *The Other America,* Michael Harrington (1962) stirred the nation's conscience about the plight of poor people. Educational concepts and theories developed that reflected the national concern for low-income citizens and were designed to help teachers and other educators to develop teaching techniques and strategies that would improve the academic achievement of low-income students.

The Cultural Deprivation Paradigm

The educational theories, concepts, and research developed during the early 1960s reflected the dominant ideologies of the time, as well as the concepts and theories used in the social sciences to explain the behavior and values of low-income populations. Social scientists developed the *culture of poverty* concept to describe the experiences of low-income populations (Lewis, 1965). In education, this concept became known as *cultural deprivation* or *the disadvantaged.* Cultural deprivation became the dominant paradigm that guided the formulation of programs and pedagogies for low-income populations during the 1960s (Bereiter & Engelmann, 1966; Bloom et al., 1965; Crow, Murray, & Smythe, 1966; Riessman, 1962).

A paradigm can be defined as a system of explanations that guides policy and action (Kuhn, 1970). When a paradigm becomes established and dominates public discourse, it becomes difficult for other systems of explanations to emerge or to become institutionalized. When one paradigm replaces another, Kuhn states, a scientific revolution takes place. However, in education and the social sciences, rarely does one paradigm

replace another. More typically, new paradigms compete with established ones and they coexist. Particular paradigms have been dominant at various times in the history of the education of low-income populations since the 1960s, but the educational landscape is usually characterized by competing paradigms and explanations.

A paradigm is not only a system of explanations, it is also a perspective on reality that reflects the experiences, perceptions, and values of its creators (Code, 1991; Harding, 1991). The cultural deprivation theorists, unlike the geneticists (Herrnstein, 1971; Jensen, 1969), believe that low-income students can attain high levels of academic achievement, but that socialization experiences in their homes and communities do not enable them to attain the knowledge, skills, and attitudes that middle-class children acquire and that are essential for academic success.

Cultural deprivation theorists consequently believe that the major focus of educational reform must be to change the students by enhancing their early socialization experiences. Cultural deprivation and disadvantaged theorists believe that the school must help low-income students to overcome the deficits that result from their early family and community experiences. The focus on the deficits of low-income children often prevents cultural deprivation theorists from seeing their strengths. The emphasis on the students' deficits also does not allow the deprivationists to consider seriously structural changes that are needed in schools.

When it emerged, the cultural deprivation paradigm was the most enlightened and liberal theory of the day about educating low-income populations. Some of the nation's most eminent and committed social scientists contributed to its formulation. Allison Davis did pioneering work on the education of low-income students (Davis, 1948/1962). Davis was one of the organizers of the landmark Research Conference on Education and Cultural Deprivation, held at the University of Chicago in June 1964. Some of the nation's most eminent educators and social scientists participated in this conference, including Anne Anastasi, Basil Bernstein, Benjamin Bloom, Martin Deutsch, Erik Erikson, Edmund W. Gordon, Robert Havighurst, and Thomas Pettigrew. In the book based on the conference, Bloom et al. (1965) defined *culturally deprived* children:

We refer to this group as culturally disadvantaged or deprived because we believe the roots of their problem may in large part be traced to their experiences in homes which do not transmit the cultural patterns necessary for the types of learning characteristic of the schools and the larger society. (p. 4)

The book was highly influential among educational leaders.

Another influential book resulted from a conference held two years earlier at Teachers College, Columbia University, led by A. Harry Passow (1963), who edited *Education in Depressed Areas.* Like the Chicago conference, the Teachers College conference included papers by some of the nation's leading social scientists and educators, including David P. Ausubel, Kenneth B. Clark, and Robert J. Havighurst.

Probably the most influential book published for teachers was *The Culturally Deprived Child* by Frank Riessman (1962), which was used widely in teacher-preparation and in-service programs. He told teachers to respect low-income students and pointed out that he thought *culturally deprived* was an inappropriate term but was using it because it was popular. He wrote: "The term 'culturally deprived' refers to those aspects of middle-class culture—such as education, books, formal language—from which these groups have not benefited" (p. 3). Implicit in this statement is the assumption that a student must be middle class to have a culture.

The Cultural Difference Theorists

When the 1970s began, a new group of scholars strongly challenged the explanations and values that underlie the cultural deprivation paradigm. Some of the critics of the cultural deprivationists used powerful language in their critiques (Baratz & Baratz, 1970; Ryan, 1971). Head Start preschool programs were funded generously during the war on poverty of the 1960s. The most popular educational models used in these programs were based on the cultural deprivation paradigm. One of the most commercially successful of these programs was marketed as Distar, and was popularized by Bereiter and Engelmann (1966). In a highly influential article published in the *Harvard Educational Review,* Baratz and Baratz argued that many of these programs and models were an expression of institutional racism. Ryan stated that middle-class professionals were blaming the poor, who were victims.

The critics of the cultural deprivationists constructed a different explanation for the school failure of low-income students. They contend that these students are not having academic success because they experience serious cultural conflicts in school. The students have rich cultures and values, but the schools have a culture that conflicts seriously with the cultures of students from low-income and ethnic minority groups (Hale-Benson, 1982; Shade, 1982).

In developing their concepts and theories about the rich cultures of low-income students and students of color, the cultural difference theorists make far more use of ethnic culture than do cultural deprivationists (Ramírez & Castañeda, 1974). The cultural deprivationists focus on social class and the culture of poverty and tend to ignore ethnic culture as a variable. The cultural difference theorists emphasize ethnic culture and devote little attention to class. Ignoring the ethnic cultures of students has evoked much of the criticism of the cultural deprivationists. The lack of attention to social class is problematic in the cultural difference literature (J. A. Banks, 1988). Cultural difference theorists have developed lists of cultural characteristics designed to help teachers build on the cultural strengths of ethnic students (Hale-Benson, 1982; Ramírez & Castañeda, 1974). However, the lists become problematic when teachers interpret them as static characteristics that apply to all members of the ethnic group (Cox & Ramírez, 1981).

The most influential work related to the cultural difference paradigm deals with learning styles, teaching styles, and language (Heath, 1983). In their seminal book, Ramírez and Castañeda (1974) delineate two major types of learning styles, *field independent* and *field sensitive.* They describe theoretical and empirical evidence to support the postulate that traditional Mexican American students tend to be more field sensitive in their learning styles than Anglo students. The school, however, most often uses a field-independent teaching style. Consequently, Mexican American students tend not to achieve as well as Anglo students. Ramírez and Castañeda state that the school should help all students, including Mexican American and Anglo students, to become bicognitive in their learning styles.

Theories similar to the one described by Ramírez and Castañeda have also been formulated by Hale-Benson (1982) and Shade (1982, 1989). Hale-Benson (1987), for example, states that the African American child, more than the Anglo child, tends to be "highly affective, expresses herself or himself through considerable body language . . . [and] seeks to be people oriented" (p. 123). Shade (1982), in a comprehensive review article, summarizes an extensive body of research that supports the cultural learning style concept. In a study by Damico (1985), African American children took more photographs of people and Anglo children took more photographs of objects, thus confirming her hypothesis that African American students are more people oriented than object oriented and that Anglo children are more object oriented.

Kleinfeld (1975, 1979) has spent much of her career researching the characteristics of effective teachers of Native American students. She has become skeptical of the learning-style concept and its usefulness in instruction. After they reviewed the few studies of the educational effects of adapting instruction to Native American learning styles, Kleinfeld and Nelson (1991) concluded that "virtually no research has succeeded in demonstrating that instruction adapted to Native Americans' visual learning style results in greater learning" (p. 273). The few weak studies reviewed by Kleinfeld and Nelson do not constitute a sufficient reason to abandon the learning-style paradigm. However, the paradigm is a contentious one. Both its advocates and its critics are strongly committed to their positions.

The controversy about learning-style theory and research is difficult to resolve. J. A. Banks (1988) examined the research literature on learning style to determine the extent to which learning style is a variable related to class and ethnicity. He concluded that the issue is a complex one, and that class mobility mediates but does not eliminate the effects of ethnic culture on the learning characteristics of Mexican American and African American students.

Some researchers believe that the best way to understand the learning characteristics of students of color is to observe and describe them in ethnographic studies, rather than classifying them into several brief categories. These researchers believe that thick descriptions of the learning and cultural characteristics of ethnic minority students are needed to guide educational practice. Influential ethnographic studies of the cultural characteristics of students of color have been conducted by researchers such as Ogbu (1974), Heath (1983), and Philips (1983).

Since the 1960s, cultural difference theorists have done rich and pioneering theoretical and empirical work on the language characteristics of ethnic minority students. Prior to the 1960s, most teachers considered the version of English spoken by most low-income African Americans as an abnormal form of standard English. Within the last three decades, linguists have produced a rich body of literature that documents that Black English (Ebonics) is a legitimate communication system that has its own rules and logic (Heath, 1983; Labov, 1969; Smitherman, 1977; F. Williams, 1970). Spanish-speaking children in schools of the Southwest were prohibited from speaking their first language for many decades. However, research in recent decades has revealed that it is important for the school to recognize and make use of children's first languages (Ovando & Collier, 1985).

The Rebirth of the Cultural Deprivation Paradigm

The history of the ethnic studies and intergroup education movements indicates that ideas related to these movements reemerge cyclically. We can observe a similar phenomenon in cultural deprivation. The cultural difference paradigm dominated discourse about the education of ethnic groups throughout much of the late 1970s and the early 1980s. However, since the late 1980s the cultural deprivation/disadvantaged conception has been exhumed and given new life in the form of the novel concept "at-risk" (Richardson et al., 1989; Slavin, Karweit, & Madden, 1989). Like cultural deprivation, the definition of at-risk is imprecise. The term is used to refer to students who are different in many ways (Cuban, 1989).

One of the reasons that at-risk is becoming popular is that it has become a funding category for state and federal educational agencies. When a term becomes a funding category, it does not need to be defined precisely to attain wide usage and popularity. One reason that at-risk is politically popular is that it can be used to refer to any population of youth experiencing problems in school. Consequently, every interest group can see itself in the term. Although the term is problematic, as Cuban (1989) points out in a thoughtful article, it is increasingly used among both researchers and practitioners (Richardson et al., 1989; Slavin et al., 1989). The term *disadvantaged* has also reemerged from the 1960s. Disadvantaged children are the subject of an informative book by Natriello, McDill, and Pallas (1990).

AN EMPOWERING SCHOOL CULTURE AND SOCIAL STRUCTURE

The four dimensions of multicultural education discussed above—content integration, the knowledge construction process, prejudice reduction, and an equity pedagogy—each deal with an aspect of a cultural or social system: the school. However, the school can also be conceptualized as one social system that is larger than its interrelated parts (e.g., its formal and informal curriculum, teaching materials, counseling programs, and teaching strategies). When conceptualized as a social system, the school is viewed as an institution that "includes a social structure of interrelated statuses and roles and the functioning of that structure in terms of patterns of actions and interactions" (Theodorson & Theodorson, 1969, p. 395). The school can also be conceptualized as a cultural system (Bullivant, 1987) with a specific set of values, norms, ethos, and shared meanings.

A number of school reformers have used a systems approach to reform the school in order to increase the academic achievement of low-income students and students of color. There are a number of advantages to approaching school reform from a holistic perspective. To implement any reform successfully in a school, such as effective prejudice reduction teaching, changes are required in a number of other school variables. Teachers, for example, need more knowledge and need to examine their racial and ethnic attitudes; consequently, they need more time as well as a variety of instructional materials. Many school reform efforts fail because the roles, norms, and ethos of the school do not change in ways that will make the institutionalization of the reforms possible.

The effective school reformers constitute one group of change agents that has approached school reform from a systems perspective. This movement emerged as a reaction to the work of Coleman et al. (1966) and Jencks et al. (1972); their studies indicate that the major factor influencing student academic achievement is the social-class composition of the students and the school. Many educators interpreted the research by Coleman et al. and Jencks et al. to mean that the school can do little to increase the academic achievement of low-income students.

Brookover (Brookover & Erickson, 1975) developed a social psychological theory of learning that states that students internalize the conceptions of themselves that are institutionalized within the ethos and structures of the school. Related to Merton's (1968) self-fulfilling prophecy, Brookover's theory states that student academic achievement will increase if the adults within the school have high expectations for students, clearly identify the skills they wish them to learn, and teach those skills to them.

Research by Brookover and his colleagues (Brookover et al., 1979; Brookover & Lezotte, 1979) indicates that schools populated by low-income students within the same school district vary greatly in student achievement levels. Consequently, Brookover attributes the differences to variations in a school's social structure. He calls the schools in low-income areas that have high academic achievement *improving* schools. Other researchers, such as Edmonds (1986) and Lezotte (1993), call them *effective* schools.

Brookover and his colleagues (Brookover et al., 1979; Brookover & Lezotte, 1979) have identified the characteristics that differentiate effective from ineffective schools. Staff in effective or improving schools emphasize the importance of basic skills and believe that all students can master them. Principals are assertive instructional leaders and disciplinarians and assume responsibility for the evaluation of the achievement of basic skills objectives. Staff members accept the concept of accountability, and parents initiate more contact than in nonimproving schools.

Edmonds (1986), who was a leading advocate of effective schools as an antidote to the doom that often haunts inner-city schools, identified characteristics of effective schools similar to those formulated by Brookover and his colleagues. Rutter, Maughan, Mortimore, Ouston, and Smith (1979) studied 12 secondary schools in an urban section of London. They concluded that some schools were much better than others in promoting the academic and social success of their students. Effective schools researchers have conducted a large number of studies that provide support for their major postulates (see Chapter 29 of this *Handbook*). However, some educators have a number of concerns about the effective schools movement, including the use of standardized tests as the major device to ascertain academic achievement (Bliss, Firestone, & Richards, 1991; Cuban, 1983; Purkey & Smith, 1982).

Comer (1988) has developed a structural intervention model that involves changes in the social psychological climate of the school. The teachers, principals, and other school professionals make collaborative decisions about the school. Parents also participate in the decision-making process. Comer's data indicate that this approach has been successful in increasing the academic achievement of low-income, inner-city students. He started the program in New Haven, Connecticut, that is now being implemented in a number of other U.S. cities using private foundation support.

IMPLICATIONS FOR RESEARCH AND PRACTICE

Research

The historical development of multicultural education needs to be more fully described. Careful historical descriptions and analyses will help the field to identify its links to the past, gain deeper insights into the problems and promises of multicultural education today, and plan more effectively for the future. Studies are needed to determine the details of the teaching of African American history in the schools and colleges from the turn of the century to the 1960s. Studies are also needed to determine the extent to which the intergroup education movement intersected with the ethnic studies tradition initiated by George Washington Williams in 1882 and continued by his successors until the new ethnic studies movement began in the 1960s. The role of African American institutions, such as churches, schools, sororities, fraternities, and women's clubs (Hine, Brown, & Terborg-Penn, 1993), in promoting the study and teaching of African American history also needs to be researched (Dabney, 1934).

The broad outlines of the early ethnic studies movement related to African Americans have been described here. Studies are needed that will reveal the extent to which scholarship and teaching sources about other ethnic groups, such as American Indians and Mexican Americans, were developed from the turn of the century to the 1960s and 1970s.

A comprehensive history of the intergroup education movement is needed. We also need to determine the extent to which intergroup education practices became institutionalized within the typical school. The publications reviewed for this chapter indicate that intergroup education was often implemented as special projects within schools that were leaders in their cities or districts. Many of the nation's schools were tightly segregated when the movement arose and died, especially in the South. The geographical regions in which intergroup education project schools were located, as well as the types of schools, are important variables that need to be investigated.

Other major issues that warrant investigation are: (a) the reasons why the movement had failed by the time the new ethnic studies movement emerged in the 1960s, and (b) why its leaders, such as Hilda Taba, Lloyd A. Cook, and William Van Til, did little work in intergroup education after the mid-1950s. Seemingly, intergroup education was not a lifetime commitment for its eminent leaders. In the 1960s Taba became a leading expert and researcher in social studies education. However, in her posthumously published book, coauthored with Deborah Elkins (Taba & Elkins, 1966), *Teaching Strategies for the Culturally Diadvantaged,* Taba incorporated concepts and strategies from the intergroup education project that she directed in the 1940s, funded by the National Conference of Christians and Jews and sponsored by the American Council on Education. Intergroup education concepts and aims also had a significant influence on her famous social studies curriculum (Taba, 1967). This curriculum focuses on thinking, knowledge, attitudes, feelings, and values, as well as on academic and social skills. These components are similar to the aims that Taba stated for intergroup education in an article she coauthored with Harold W. Wilson (Taba & Wilson, 1946).

Empirical studies need to be undertaken of each of the five dimensions of multicultural education described in this chapter. Content integration studies, using both interview and ethnographic techniques, should describe the approaches that teachers use to integrate their curricula with ethnic content, the problems they face, and how they resolve them. The major barriers that teaches face when trying to make their curricula multicultural also need to be identified.

The knowledge construction process is a fruitful topic for empirical research. Most of the work related to this concept is theoretical and philosophical (J. A. Banks, 1993c; Code, 1991; Gordon, 1985; Harding, 1991). This concept can be investigated by interventions that present students with documents describing different perspectives on the same historical event, such as the Japanese American internment, the westward movement, and Indian removal. Studies could be made of teacher questions and student responses when discussing the conflicting accounts.

Studies that describe students' racial attitudes and intervention studies designed to modify them need to be conducted. A literature search using ERIC, PsychLit, and Sociofile revealed that few intervention studies related to children's racial attitudes have been conducted since 1980. Most of the studies related to children's racial attitudes reviewed here were conducted before 1980. Since 1980 there has been little support for research in race relations; consequently, there are few studies. Perhaps multicultural researchers could implement small-scale observational studies funded by civil rights organizations. Jewish civil rights organizations funded a number of important studies during the intergroup education era.

Research related to effective teaching strategies for low-income students and students of color (equity pedagogy) needs to examine the complex interaction of race, class, and gender, as well as other variables such as region and generation (Grant & Sleeter, 1986). The rising number of outspoken African American conservatives, such as Carter (1991), Sowell (1984), Steele (1990), and Wortham (1981), should help both the research and wider community understand the enormous diversity within the African American community. Conservative Mexican American writers, such as Rodriguez (1982) and Chavez (1991), reveal the ideological and cultural diversity within the Mexican American community.

Since the 1960s, diversity within U.S. ethnic minority groups has increased greatly, as a significant number of African Americans, Mexican Americans, and Puerto Ricans have joined the middle class and the exodus to the suburbs (Wilson, 1987). White flight has become middle-class flight. A sharp class schism has developed within ethnic minority communities (Wilson, 1987). Consequently, research on people of color—especially studies on learning styles and their cultural characteristics—that does not examine class as an important variable is not likely to result in findings that are helpful and generalizable.

Practice

The most important implication of this research review is that multicultural education must be conceptualized and implemented broadly if it is to bring about meaningful changes in schools, colleges, and universities. Several serious problems result when multicultural education is conceptualized only or primarily as content integration. Teachers in subjects such as mathematics and science perceive multicultural education, when it is conceptualized only as content integration, as appropriate for social studies and language arts teachers but not for them.

When multicultural education is narrowly conceptualized, it is often confined to activities for special days and occasions, such as Martin Luther King's birthday and Cinco de Mayo. It may also be viewed as a special unit, an additional book by an African American or a Mexican American writer, or a few additional lessons. The knowledge construction dimension of multicultural education is an essential one. Using this concept, content about ethnic groups is not merely added to the curriculum. Rather, the curriculum is reconceptualized to help students understand how knowledge is constructed and how it reflects human interests, ideology, and the experiences of the people who create it. Students themselves also create interpretations. They begin to understand why it is essential to look at the nation's experience from diverse ethnic and cultural perspectives to comprehend fully its past and present.

The research reviewed in this chapter indicates that children come to school with misconceptions about outside ethnic groups and with a white bias. However, it also indicates that students' racial attitudes can be modified and made more democratic and that the racial attitudes of young children are much more easily modified than the attitudes of older students and adults (Katz, 1976). Consequently, it suggests that if we are to help students acquire the attitudes needed to survive in a multicultural and diverse world, we must start early. Beginning in kindergarten, educators need to implement a well-conceptualized and sequential curriculum that is multicultural.

A school experience that is multicultural includes content, examples, and realistic images of diverse racial and ethnic groups. Cooperative learning activities in which students from diverse groups work to attain shared goals is also a feature of the school, as well as simulated images of ethnic groups that present them in positive and realistic ways. Also essential within such a school are adults who model the attitudes and behaviors they are trying to teach. Actions speak much louder than words.

Jane Elliott (as described in Peters, 1987) has attained fame for a simulated lesson she taught on discrimination that is described in the award-winning documentary *The Eye of the Storm.* One day Elliott discriminated against blue-eyed children; the next day brown-eyed children experienced the sting of bigotry. In 1984, 11 of her former third graders returned to Riceville, Iowa, for a reunion with their teacher. This event is described in another documentary, *A Class Divided,* in which the students describe the power of a classroom experience that had taken place 14 years earlier.

Elliott, who taught third grade in an all-White Iowa town, was moved to act because of the racial hate she observed in the nation. Racial incidents are on the rise throughout the United States (Altbach & Lomotey, 1941). The research reviewed in this chapter, and in two previous reviews (J.A. Banks, 1991b, 1993b), can help empower educators to act to help create a more democratic and caring society. Jane Elliott acted and made a difference; she is a cogent example for us all.

References

Acuña, R. (1972). *Occupied America: The Chicano's struggle toward liberation.* San Francisco: Canfield Press.
Adorno, T. W., Frenkel-Brunswik, E., Levinson, D. J., & Sanford, R. N. (1950). *The authoritarian personality.* New York: Norton.
Agnes, M. (1947). Influences of reading on the racial attitudes of adolescent girls. *Catholic Educational Review, 45,* 415–420.
Allport, G. W. (1954). *The nature of prejudice.* Cambridge, MA: Addison-Wesley.
Altbach, P. G., & Lomotey, K. (Eds.). (1991). *The racial crisis in American higher education.* Albany: State University of New York Press.
American Association of Colleges for Teacher Education. (1973). *No one model American.* Washington, DC: Author.
Anderson, J. D. (1988). *The education of Blacks in the South, 1860–1935.* Chapel Hill: University of North Carolina Press.

Aran, K., Arthur, H., Colon, R., & Goldenberg, H. (1973). *Puerto Rican history and culture. A study guide and curriculum outline.* New York: United Federation of Teachers.
Aronson, E., & Bridgeman, D. (1979). Jigsaw groups and the desegregated classroom: In pursuit of common goals. *Personality and Social Psychology Bulletin, 5,* 438–446.
Asante, M. K. (1991). The Afrocentric idea in education. *Journal of Negro Education, 60,* 170–180.
Asante, M. K., & Ravitch, D. (1991). Multiculturalism: An exchange. *The American Scholar, 60,* 267–276.
Baker, G. (1977). Multicultural education: Two preservice approaches. *Journal of Teacher Education, 28,* 31–33.
Baker, G. (1983). *Planning and organizing for multicultural instruction.* Menlo Park, CA: Addison-Wesley.

Banks, J. A. (1969). A content analysis of the Black American in textbooks. *Social Education, 33,* 954–957, 963.

Banks, J. A. (1970). *Teaching the Black experience: Methods and materials.* Belmont, CA: Fearon.

Banks, J. A. (Ed.). (1973). *Teaching ethnic studies: Concepts and strategies* (43rd yearbook). Washington, DC: National Council for the Social Studies.

Banks, J. A. (1984). Black youths in predominantly White suburbs: An exploratory study of their attitudes and self-concepts. *Journal of Negro Education, 53,* 3–17.

Banks, J. A. (1988). Ethnicity, class, cognitive, and motivational styles: Research and teaching implications. *Journal of Negro Education, 57,* 452–466.

Banks, J. A. (1991a). The dimensions of multicultural education. *Multicultural Leader, 4,* 5–6.

Banks, J. A. (1991b). Multicultural education: Its effects on students' ethnic and gender role attitudes. In J. P. Shaver (Ed.), *Handbook of research on social studies teaching and learning* (pp. 459–469). New York: Macmillan.

Banks, J. A. (1991c). *Teaching strategies for ethnic studies* (5th ed.). Boston: Allyn and Bacon.

Banks, J. A. (1992). Multicultural education: Approaches, developments, and dimensions. In J. Lynch, C. Modgil, & S. Modgil (Eds.), *Cultural diversity and the schools, Vol. 1, Education for cultural diversity: Convergence and divergence* (pp. 83–94). London: The Falmer Press.

Banks, J. A. (1993a). Approaches to multicultural curriculum reform. In J. A. Banks & C. A. M. Banks (Eds.), *Multicultural education: Issues and perspectives* (2nd ed., pp. 195–214). Boston: Allyn and Bacon.

Banks, J. A. (1993b). The canon debate, knowledge construction, and multicultural education. *Educational Researcher, 22*(5), 4–14.

Banks, J. A. (1993c). Multicultural education: Characteristics and goals. In J. A. Banks & C. A. M. Banks (Eds.), *Multicultural education: Issues and perspectives* (2nd ed., pp. 3–28). Boston: Allyn and Bacon.

Banks, J. A. (1993d). Multicultural education for young children: Racial and ethnic attitudes and their modification. In B. Spodek (Ed.), *Handbook of research on the education of young children* (pp. 236–250). New York: Macmillan.

Banks, J. A. (1994). *Multiethnic education: Theory and practice* (3rd ed.). Boston: Allyn and Bacon.

Banks, J. A., & Banks, C. A. M. (Eds.). (1993). *Multicultural education: Issues and perspectives* (2nd ed.). Boston: Allyn and Bacon.

Banks, J. A., Cortés, C. E., Gay, G., Garcia, R. L., & Ochoa, A. S. (1976). *Curriculum guidelines for multiethnic education.* Washington, DC: National Council for the Social Studies.

Banks, W. C. (1976). White preference in Blacks: A paradigm in search of a phenomenon. *Psychological Bulletin, 83,* 1170–1186.

Baratz, S. S., & Baratz, J. C. (1970). Early childhood intervention: The social science base of institutional racism. *Harvard Educational Review, 40,* 29–50.

Bennett, C. I. (1990). *Comprehensive multicultural education* (2nd ed.). Boston: Allyn and Bacon.

Bereiter, C., & Engelmann, S. (1966). *Teaching disadvantaged children in the preschool.* Englewood Cliffs, NJ: Prentice-Hall.

Berger, P. L., & Luckman, T. (1966). *The social construction of knowledge: A treatise in the sociology of knowledge.* Garden City, NY: Doubleday.

Bernal, M. (1987, 1991). *Black Athena: The Afroasiatic roots of classical civilization* (Vols. I & 2). New Brunswick, NJ: Rutgers University Press.

Blassingame, J. W. (Ed.). (1971). *New perspectives in Black studies.* Urbana: University of Illinois Press.

Blassingame, J. W. (1972). *The slave community: Plantation life in the antebellum South.* New York: Oxford University Press.

Blea, I. I. (1988). *Toward a Chicano social science.* New York: Praeger.

Bliss, J. R., Firestone, W. A., & Richards, C. E. (Eds.). (1991). *Rethinking effective schools: Research and practice.* Englewood Cliffs, NJ: Prentice-Hall.

Bloom, B. S., Davis, A., & Hess, R. (1965). *Compensatory education for cultural deprivation.* New York: Holt.

Bond, H. M. (1939). *Negro education in Alabama: A study in cotton and steel.* Washington, DC: The Associated Publishers.

Boyer, J. B. (1974). Needed: Curriculum diversity for the urban economically disadvantaged. *Educational Leadership, 31,* 624–626.

Braddock, J. H., II (1990). Tracking the middle grades: National patterns of grouping for instruction. *Phi Delta Kappan, 71,* 445–449.

Brookover, W. B., Beady, C., Flood, P., Schweitzer, J., & Wisenbaker, J. (1979). *School social systems and student achievement: Schools can make a difference.* New York: Praeger.

Brookover, W. B., & Erickson, E. (1975). *Sociology of education.* Homewood, IL: Dorsey.

Brookover, W. B., & Lezotte, L. W. (1979). *Changes in school characteristics coincident with changes in student achievement.* East Lansing: Institute for Research on Teaching, College of Education, Michigan State University.

Brooks, R. L. (1990). *Rethinking the American race problem.* Berkeley: University of California Press.

Bullivant, B. M. (1987). *The ethnic encounter in the secondary school.* New York: The Falmer Press.

Butler, J. E., & Walter, J. C. (Eds.). (1991). *Transforming the curriculum: Ethnic studies and women's studies.* Albany: State University of New York Press.

Carmichael, S., & Hamilton, C. V. (1967). *Black power: The politics of liberation in America.* New York: Vintage.

Carter, S. L. (1991). *Reflections of an affirmative action baby.* New York: Basic Books.

Chavez, L. (1991). *Out of the barrio: Toward a new politics of Hispanic assimilation.* New York: Basic Books.

Clark, K. B. (1963). *Prejudice and your child.* Boston: Beacon Press.

Clark, K. B., & Clark, M. P. (1939a). The development of consciousness of self and the emergence of racial identification in Negro preschool children. *Journal of Social Psychology, 10,* 591–599.

Clark, K. B., & Clark, M. P. (1939b). Segregation as a factor in the racial identification of Negro preschool children. *Journal of Experimental Education, 8,* 161–163.

Clark, K. B., & Clark, M. P. (1940). Skin color as a factor in racial identification and preference in Negro children. *Journal of Negro Education, 19,* 341–358.

Clark, K. B., & Clark, M. P. (1947). Racial identification and preference in Negro children. In T. M. Newcomb & E. L. Hartley (Eds.), *Readings in social psychology* (pp. 169–178). New York: Holt, Rinehart & Winston.

Clark, K. B., & Clark, M. P. (1950). Emotional factors in racial identification and preference of Negro Children. *Journal of Negro Education, 19,* 341–350.

Clinchy, E. R. (1949). *Intergroup relations centers.* New York: Farrar, Straus & Company.

Code, L. (1991). *What can she know? Feminist theory and the construction of knowledge.* Ithaca, NY: Cornell University Press.

Cohen, E. G. (1972). Interracial interaction disability. *Human Relations, 25,* 9–24.

Cohen, E. G., & Roper, S. S. (1972). Modification of interracial interaction disability: An application of status characteristics theory. *American Sociological Review, 37,* 643–657.

Coleman, J. S., Campbell, E. G., Hobson, C. J., McPartland, J., Mood, A. M., Weinfeld, F. D., & York, R. L. (1966). *Equality of educational opportunity.* Washington, DC: U.S. Government Printing Office.

Comer, J. P. (1988). Educating poor minority children. *Scientific American, 259,* 42–48.

Cook. L. A. (1947). Intergroup education. *Review of Educational Research, 17,* 267–278.

Cook, L. A. (1950). *College programs in intergroup relations.* Washington, DC: American Council on Education.

Cook, L. A. (1951). *Intergroup relations in teacher education: An analytical study of intergroup education in colleges and schools in the United States: Functions, current expressions, and improvements.* Washington, DC: American Council on Education.

Cook, L. A. (Ed.). (1952). *Toward better human relations.* Detroit: Wayne State University Press.

Cook, L., & Cook, E. (1954). *Intergroup education.* New York: McGraw-Hill.

Cortés, C. E. (1973). Teaching the Chicano experience. In J. A. Banks (Ed.), *Teaching ethnic studies: Concepts and strategies* (pp. 181–199). Washington, DC: National Council for the Social Studies.

Cox, B. G., & Ramírez, M., III (1981). Cognitive styles: Implications for teaching ethnic studies. In J. A. Banks (Ed.), *Education for the 80s: Multiethnic education* (pp. 61–71). Washington, DC: National Education Association.

Cross, W. E., Jr. (1985). Black identity: Rediscovering the distinction between personal identity and reference group orientation. In M. B. Spencer, G. K. Brookins, & W. R. Allen (Eds.), *Beginnings: The social and affective development of Black children* (pp. 155–171). Hillsdale, NJ: Erlbaum.

Cross. W. E., Jr., (1991). *Shades of Black: Diversity in African American identity.* Philadelphia: Temple University Press.

Crow, L. D., Murray, W. I., & Smythe, H. H. (1966). *Educating the culturally disadvantaged child: Principles and programs.* New York: David McKay.

Cuban, L. (1983). Effective schools: A friendly but cautionary note. *Phi Delta Kappan, 64,* 695–696.

Cuban, L. (1989). The "at risk" label and the problem of urban school reform. *Phi Delta Kappan, 70,* 780–801.

Cummins, J. (1986). Empowering minority students: A framework for intervention. *Harvard Educational Review, 56,* 18–36.

Dabney, T. L. (1934). The study of the Negro. *Journal of Negro History, 19,* 266–307.

Damico, S. B. (1985). The two worlds of school: Differences in the photographs of Black and White adolescents. *The Urban Review, 17,* 210–222.

Daniels, R. (1988). *Asian America: Chinese and Japanese in the United States since 1850.* Seattle: University of Washington Press.

Davis, A. (1962). *Social-class influences upon learning.* Cambridge, MA: Harvard University Press. (Original work published 1948)

Davis, A., Gardner, B. B., & Gardner, M. R. (1941). *Deep South: A social anthropological study of caste and class.* Chicago: University of Chicago Press.

Deloria, V., Jr. (1969). *Custer died for your sins: An Indian manifesto.* New York: Avon.

Delpit, L. D. (1988). The silenced dialogue: Power and pedagogy in educating other people's children. *Harvard Eductional Review, 58,* 280–298.

Diop, C. A. (1974). *The African origin of civilization: Myth or reality.* New York: Lawrence Hill.

Drake, St. C. (1987, 1990). *Black folk here and there* (Vols. I & 2). Los Angeles: University of California, Center for Afro-American Studies.

DuBois, W. E. B. (1935). *Black reconstruction.* New York: Harcourt, Brace.

DuBois, W. E. B. (1953). *The souls of Black folk.* New York: The Blue Heron Press.

DuBois, W. E. B. (1973). *The education of Black people: Ten critiques, 1906–1960.* New York: Monthly Review Press.

Edmonds, R. (1986). Characteristics of effective schools. In U. Neisser (Ed.), *The school achievement of minority children* (pp. 93–104). Hillsdale, NJ: Erlbaum.

Farganis, S. (1986). *The social construction of the feminine character.* Totowa, NJ: Rowman and Littlefield.

Fisher, F. (1965). *The influence of reading and discussion on the attitudes of fifth graders toward American Indians.* Unpublished doctoral dissertation, University of California, Berkeley.

Forbes, J. D. (1973). Teaching Native American values and cultures. In J. A. Banks (Ed.), *Teaching ethnic studies: Concepts and strategies* (pp. 201–225). Washington, DC: National Council for the Social Studies.

Ford, N. A. (1973). *Black studies: Threat -or- challenge.* Port Washington, NY: Kennikat Press.

Franklin, J. H. (1947). *From slavery to freedom: A history of Negro Americans.* New York: Knopf.

Franklin, J. H. (1985). *George Washington Williams: A biography.* Chicago: University of Chicago Press.

Gabelko, N. H., & Michaelis, J. U. (1981). *Reducing adolescent prejudice: A handbook.* New York: Teachers College Press.

Gamio, M. (1930). *Mexican immigration to the United States. A study of human migration and adjustment.* Chicago: University of Chicago Press.

Garcia, R. L. (1991). *Teaching in a pluralistic society: Concepts, models, strategies* (2nd ed.). New York: HarperCollins.

Gates, H. L., Jr. (1988). *The signifying monkey: A theory of African-American literary criticism.* New York: Oxford University Press.

Gay, G. (1971). Ethnic minority studies: How widespread? How successful? *Educational Leadership, 29,* 108–112.

Gay, G. (1992). The state of multicultural education in the United States. In K. Adam-Moodley (Ed.), *Education in plural societies: International perspectives* (pp. 47–66). Calgary, Alberta, Canada: Detselig.

Genovese, E. D. (1972). *Roll, Jordon, roll: The world the slaves made.* New York: Pantheon Books.

Gibson, M. A. (1976). Approaches to multicultural education in the United States: Some concepts and assumptions. *Anthropology and Education Quarterly, 7,* 7–18.

Ginsburg, H. (1972). *The myth of the deprived child: Poor children's intellect and education.* Englewood Cliffs, NJ: Prentice-Hall.

Giroux, H. A. (1983). *Theory and resistance in education.* South Hadley, MA: Bergin and Garvey.

Gollnick, D. M., & Chinn, P. C. (1990). *Multicultural education in a pluralistic society* (3rd ed.). Columbus, OH: Merrill.

Goodman, M. A. (1952). *Race awareness in young children.* New York: Collier.

Gordon, E. W. (1985). Social science knowledge production and the Afro-American experience. *Journal of Negro Education, 54,* 117–133.

Gordon, E. W., & Meroe, A. S. (1991). Common destinies—Continuing dilemmas. *Psychological Science, 2,* 23–30.

Gordon, E. W., Miller, M., & Rollock, D. (1990). Coping with communicentric bias in knowledge production in the social sciences. *Educational Researcher, 19,* 14–19.

Gould, S. J. (1981). *The mismeasure of man.* New York: Norton.

Grant, C. A. (1973). Black studies materials do make a difference. *Journal of Educational Research, 66,* 400–404.

Grant, C. A. (Ed.). (1977). *Multicultural education: Commitments, issues, and applications.* Washington, DC: Association for Supervision and Curriculum Development.

Grant, C. A. (1978). Education that is multicultural: Isn't that what we mean? *Journal of Teacher Education, 29,* 45–48.

Grant, C. A., & Sleeter, C. E. (1986). Race, class, and gender in education research: An argument for integrative analysis. *Review of Educational Research, 56,* 195–211.

Gray, P. (1991, July 8). Whose America? *Time,* pp. 12–17.

Habermas, J. (1971). *Knowledge and human interests.* Boston: Beacon Press.

Hale-Benson, J. (1982). *Black children: Their roots, culture and learning styles* (Rev. ed.). Baltimore: Johns Hopkins University Press.

Hale-Benson, J. (1987). Black children: Their roots, culture, and learning styles. In J. B. McCracken (Ed.), *Reducing stress in young children's lives* (pp. 122–129). Washington, DC: National Association for the Education of Young Children.

Harding, S. (1991). *Whose science? Whose knowledge? Thinking from women's lives.* Ithaca, NY: Cornell University Press.

Harrington, M. (1962). *The other America.* New York: Macmillan.

Hayes, M. L., & Conklin, M. E. (1953). Intergroup attitudes and experimental change. *Journal of Experimental Education, 22,* 19–36.

Heath, S. B. (1983). *Ways with words: Language, life, and work in communities and classrooms.* New York: Cambridge University Press.

Herrnstein, R. J. (1971). *I.Q. in the meritocracy.* Boston: Little, Brown.

Hilliard, A. G., III (1974). Restructuring teacher education for multicultural imperatives. In W. A. Hunter (Ed.), *Multicultural education through competency-based teacher education* (pp. 40–55). Washington, DC: American Association of Colleges for Teacher Education.

Hilliard, A. G., III, Payton-Stewart, L., & Williams, L. O. (Eds.). (1990). *Infusion of African and African American content in the school curriculum.* Morristown, NJ: Aaron Press.

Hine, D. C., Brown, E. B., & Terborg-Penn, R. (Eds.). (1993). *Black women in America: An historical encyclopedia.* Brooklyn, NY: Carlson.

Hohn, R. L. (1973). Perceptual training and its effect on racial preference of kindergarten children. *Psychological Reports, 32,* 435–441.

hooks, b. (1990). *Yearning: Race, gender, and cultural politics.* Boston: South End Press.

Horowitz, E. L. (1936). The development of attitude toward the Negro. In *Archives of Psychology* (No. 104). New York: Columbia University.

Horowitz, R. E. (1939). Racial aspects of self-identification in nursey school children. *Journal of Psychology, 7,* 91–99.

Hunter, W. A. (Ed.). (1974). *Multicultural education through competency-based teacher education.* Washington, DC: American Association of Colleges for Teacher Education.

Jackson, E. P. (1944). Effects of reading upon the attitudes toward the Negro race. *The Library Quarterly, 14,* 47–54.

Jencks, C., Smith, M., Acland, H., Bane, M. J., Cohen, D., Gintis, H., Heyns, B., & Michelson, S. (1972). *Inequality: A reassessment of the effect of family and schooling in America.* New York: Basic Books.

Jensen, A. R. (1969). How much can we boost IQ and scholastic achievement? *Harvard Educational Review, 39,* 1–123.

Kaplan, A. (1964). *The conduct of inquiry: Methodology for behavioral science.* San Francisco: Chandler.

Katz, P. A. (1973). Perception of racial cues in preschool children: A new look. *Developmental Psychology, 8,* 295–299.

Katz, P. A. (Ed.). (1976). *Towards the elimination of racism.* New York: Pergamon.

Katz, P. A., & Zalk, S. R. (1978). Modification of children's racial attitudes. *Developmental Psychology, 14,* 447–461.

King, J. A., & Mitchell, C. A. (1990). *Black mothers to sons: Juxtaposing African American literature with social practice.* New York: Peter Lang.

Kitano, H. H. L. (1969). *Japanese Americans: The evolution of a subculture.* Englewood Cliffs, NJ: Prentice-Hall.

Klassen, F. H., & Gollnick, D. M. (Eds.). (1977). *Pluralism and the American teacher: Issues and case studies.* Washington, DC: Ethnic Heritage Center for Teacher Education of the American Association of Colleges for Teacher Education.

Klein, S. S. (Ed.). (1985). *Handbook for achieving sex equity through education.* Baltimore: Johns Hopkins University Press.

Kleinfeld, J. (1975). Effective teachers of Eskimo and Indian students. *School Review, 83,* 301–344.

Kleinfeld, J. (1979). *Eskimo children on the Andrearsky.* New York: Praeger.

Kleinfeld, J., & Nelson, P. (1991). Adapting instruction to Native Americans' learning styles: An iconoclastic view. *Journal of Cross-Cultural Psychology, 22,* 273–282.

Kuhn, T. S. (1970). *The structure of scientific revolutions* (2nd ed., enlarged). Chicago: University of Chicago Press.

Labov, W. (1969). *The study of nonstandard English.* Urbana, IL: National Council of Teachers of English.

Ladner, J. A. (Ed.). (1973). *The death of White sociology.* New York: Vintage Books.

Lasker, B. (1929). *Race attitudes in children.* New York: Holt, Rinehart & Winston.

Lasker, B. (1931). *Filipino immigration to the continental United States and Hawaii.* Chicago: University of Chicago Press.

Lauter, P. (1991). *Canons and contexts.* New York: Oxford University Press.

Leo, L. (1990, November 12). A fringe history of the world. *U.S. News and World Report,* pp. 25–26.

Leslie, L. L., & Leslie, J. W. (1972). The effects of a student centered special curriculum upon the racial attitudes of sixth graders. *Journal of Experimental Education, 41,* 63–67.

Lessing, E. E., & Clarke, C. (1976). An attempt to reduce ethnic prejudice and assess its correlates. *Educational Research Quarterly, 1,* 3–16.

Levine, L. W. (1977). *Black culture and Black consciousness: Afro-American folk thought from slavery to freedom.* New York: Oxford University Press.

Lewis, O. (1965). *La vida: A Puerto Rican family in the culture of poverty—San Juan and New York.* New York: Random House.

Lezotte, L. W. (1993). Effective schools: A framework for increasing student achievement. In J. A. Banks & C. A. M. Banks (Eds.), *Multicultural education: Issues and perspectives* (2nd ed., pp. 303–316). Boston: Allyn and Bacon.

Litcher, J. H., & Johnson, D. W. (1969). Changes in attitudes toward Negroes of White elementary school students after use of multiethnic readers. *Journal of Educational Psychology, 60,* 148–152.

Litcher, J. H., Johnson, D. W., & Ryan, F. L. (1973). Use of pictures of multiethnic interaction to change attitudes of White elementary school students toward Blacks. *Psychological Reports, 33,* 367–372.

Locke, A., & Stern, B. J. (Eds.). (1942). *When people meet: A study in race and culture contacts.* New York: Progressive Education Association.

Logan, R. W. (1954). *The betrayal of the Negro.* New York: Collier.

Lynch, J. (1987). *Prejudice reduction and the schools.* New York: Nichols.

McWilliams, C. (1943). *Brothers under the skin.* Boston: Little, Brown.

McWilliams, C. (1949). *North from Mexico: The Spanish-speaking people of the United States.* Philadelphia: Lippincott.

Mercer, J. R. (1989). Alternative paradigms for assessment in a pluralistic society. In J. A. Banks & C. A. Banks (Eds.), *Multicultural education: Issues and perspectives* (pp. 289–304). Boston: Allyn and Bacon.

Merton, R. K. (1968). *Social theory and social structure.* New York: The Free Press.

Miel, A., with Kiester, E., Jr. (1967). *The shortchanged children of suburbia: What schools don't teach about human differences and what can be done about it.* New York: The American Jewish Committee.

Milner, D. (1983). *Children and race.* Beverly Hills, CA: Sage.

Minard, R. D. (1931). *Race attitudes of Iowa children.* Iowa City: University of Iowa.

Morland, J. K. (1966). A comparison of race awareness in northern and southern children. *American Journal of Orthopsychiatry, 36,* 22–31.

Myrdal, G., with the assistance of Sterner, R., & Rose, A. (1944). *An American dilemma: The Negro problem and modern democracy.* New York: Harper & Row.

National Council for the Accreditation of Teacher Education. (1977). *Standards for the accreditation of teacher education.* Washington, DC: Author.

National Council for the Accreditation of Teacher Education. (1987). *NCATE standards, procedures, and policies for the accreditation of professional education units.* Washington, DC: Author.

National Council for the Social Studies Task Force on Ethnic Studies. (1992). Curriculum guidelines for multicultural education. *Social Education, 56,* 274–294.

National Council of Teachers of English. (1974). *Students' right to their own langauge.* Urbana, IL: Author.

Natriello, G., McDill, E. L., & Pallas, A. M. (1990). *Schooling disadvantaged children: Racing against catastrophe.* New York: Teachers College Press.

Nieto, S. (1986). Excellence and equity. The case for bilingual education. *Bulletin of the Council on Interracial Books for Children, 17,* 3–4.

Nieto, S. (1992). *Affirming diversity. The sociopolitical context of multicultural education.* New York: Longman.

Novak, M. (1971). *The rise of the unmeltable ethnics.* New York: Macmillan.

Oakes, J. (1985). *Keeping track: How schools structure inequality.* New Haven, CT: Yale University Press.

Ogbu, J. U. (1974). *The next generation: An ethnography of education in an urban neighborhood.* New York: Academic Press.

Ogbu, J. U. (1990). Overcoming racial barriers to equal access. In J. I. Goodlad & P. Keating (Eds.), *Access to knowledge: An agenda for our nation's schools* (pp. 59–89). New York: The College Board.

Ovando, J., & Collier, V. P. (1985). *Bilingual and ESL classrooms: Teaching in multicultural contexts.* New York: McGraw-Hill.

Parekh, B. (1986). The concept of multicultural education. In S. Modgil, G. Verma, K. Mallick, & C. Modgil (Eds.), *Multicultural education: The interminable debate* (pp. 19–31). Philadelphia: The Falmer Press.

Parish, T. S., & Fleetwood, R. S. (1975). Amount of conditioning and subsequent change in racial attitudes of children. *Perceptual and Motor Skills, 43,* 907–912.

Parish, T. S., Shirazi, A., & Lambert, F. (1976). Conditioning away prejudicial attitudes in children. *Perceptual and Motor Skills, 43,* 907–912.

Passow, A. H. (Ed.). (1963). *Education in depressed areas.* New York: Teachers College Press.

Peters, W. (1987). *A class divided: Then and now* (Expanded ed.). New Haven, CT: Yale University Press.

Philips, S. U. (1983). *The invisible culture: Communication in classroom and community on the Warm Springs Indian reservation.* New York: Longman.

Phillips, U. B. (1918). *American Negro slavery.* New York: D. Appleton & Company.

Phinney, J. S., & Rotheram, M. J. (Eds.). (1987). *Children's ethnic socialization: Pluralism and development.* Beverly Hills, CA: Sage.

Porter, J. D. R. (1971). *Black child, White child: The development of racial attitudes.* Cambridge, MA: Harvard University Press.

Purkey, S. C., & Smith, M. S. (1982). Too soon to cheer? Synthesis of research on effective schools. *Educational Leadership, 40,* 64–69.

Quarles, B. (1953). *The Negro in the Civil War.* New York: Da Capo Press.

Radke, M. J., & Trager, H. G. (1950). Children's perceptions of the social roles of Negroes and Whites. *Journal of Psychology, 29,* 3–33.

Ramírez, M., & Castañeda, A. (1974). *Cultural democracy, bicognitive development, and education.* New York: Academic Press.

Ramsey, P. G. (1987). Young children's thinking about ethnic differences. In J. S. Phinney & M. J. Rotheram (Eds.), *Children's ethnic socialization: Pluralism and development* (pp. 56–72). Beverly Hills, CA: Sage.

Ravitch, D. (1990). Diversity and democracy: Multicultural education in America. *American Educator, 14,* 16–48.

Richardson, V., Casanova, U., Placier, P., & Guilfoyle, K. (1989). *School children at risk.* New York: The Falmer Press.

Riessman, F. (1962). *The culturally deprived child.* New York: Harper & Row.

Robinson, A. L., Foster, C. C., & Ogilvie, D. H. (Eds.). (1969). *Black studies in the university.* New York: Bantam.

Rodriguez, R. (1982). *Hunger of memory: The education of Richard Rodriguez: An autobiography.* Boston: David R. Godine.

Rutter, M., Maughan, B., Mortimore, P., Ouston, I., & Smith, A. (1979) *Fifteen thousand hours: Secondary schools and their effects on children.* Cambridge, MA: Harvard University Press.

Ryan, W. (1971). *Blaming the victim.* New York: Vintage.

Sadker, M. P., & Sadker, D. M. (1982). *Sex equity handbook for schools.* New York: Longman.

Schlesinger, A., Jr. (1990, Summer). When ethnic studies are un-American. *Social Studies Review: A Bulletin of the American Textbook Council,* pp. 11–13.

Schlesinger, A., Jr. (1991). *The disuniting of America: Reflections on a multicultural society.* Knoxville, TN: Whittle Direct Books.

Shade, B. J. (1982). Afro-American cognitive style: A variable in school success? *Review of Educational Research, 52,* 219–244.

Shade, B. J. (Ed.). (1989). *Culture, style and the educative process.* Springfield, IL: Charles C. Thomas.

Shirley, O. L. B. (1988). *The impact of multicultural education on self-concept, racial attitude and student achievement of Black and White fifth and sixth graders.* Unpublished doctoral dissertation, University of Mississippi, University, MS.

Sizemore, B. A. (1972). Social science and education for a Black identity. In J. A. Banks & J. D. Grambs (Eds.), *Black self-concept: Implications for education and social science* (pp. 141–170). New York: McGraw-Hill.

Slaughter, D. T. (Ed.). (1988). *Black children and poverty: A developmental perspective.* San Francisco: Jossey-Bass.

Slavin, R. E. (1979). Effects of biracial learning teams on cross-racial friendships. *Journal of Educational Psychology, 71,* 381–387.

Slavin, R. E. (1985). Cooperative learning: Applying contact theory in desegregated schools. *Journal of Social Issues, 41,* 45–62.

Slavin, R. E., Karweit, N. L., & Madden, N. A. (1989). *Effective programs for students at risk.* Boston: Allyn and Bacon.

Sleeter, C. E. (Ed.). (1991). *Empowerment through multicultural education.* Albany: State University of New York Press.

Sleeter, C. E., & Grant, C. A. (1987). An analysis of multicultural education in the United States. *Harvard Educational Review, 7,* 421–444.

Sleeter, C. E., & Grant, C. A. (1988). *Making choices for multicultural education: Five approaches to race, class and gender.* Columbus, OH: Merrill.

Sleeter, C. E., & Grant, C. A. (1991). Race, class, gender, and disability in current textbooks. In M. W. Apple & L. K. Christian-Smith (Eds.), *The politics of the textbook* (pp. 78–110). New York: Routledge.

Smitherman, G. (1977). *Talking and testifying: The language of Black America.* Boston: Houghton Mifflin.

Sowell, T. (1984). Civil *rights: Rhetoric or reality?* New York: William Morrow.

Spencer, M. B. (1982). Personal and group identity of Black children: An alternative synthesis: *Genetic Psychology Monographs, 106,* 59–84.

Spencer, M. B. (1985). Cultural cognition and social cognition as identity correlates of Black children's personal-social development. In M. B. Spencer, G. K. Brookins, & W. R. Allen (Eds.), *Beginnings: The social and affective development of Black children* (pp. 215–234). Hillsdale, NJ: Erlbaum.

Spencer, M. B. (1987). Black children's ethnic identity formation: Risk and resilience of caste-like minorities. In J. S. Phinney & M. J. Rotheram (Eds.), *Children's ethnic socialization: Pluralism and development* (pp. 103–116). Beverly Hills, CA: Sage.

Stampp, K. M. (1956). *The peculiar institution: Slavery in the antebellum South.* New York: Vintage.

Steele, S. (1990). *The content of our character: A new vision of race in America.* New York: St. Martin's Press.

Sue, D. W. (Ed.). (1981). *Counseling the culturally different: Theory and practice.* New York: Wiley.

Sung, B. L. (1967). *The story of the Chinese in America.* New York: Macmillan.

Suzuki, B. H. (1984). Curriculum transformation for multicultural education. *Education and Urban Society, 16,* 294–322.

Taba, H. (1950). *With a focus on human relations: A story of the eighth grade.* Washington, DC: American Council on Education.

Taba, H. (1951). *Diagnosing human relations needs.* Washington, DC: American Council on Education.

Taba, H. (1952). *Curriculum in intergroup relations: Case studies in instruction.* Washington, DC: American Council on Education.

Taba, H. (1967). *Teacher's handbook for elementary social studies.* Palo Alto, CA: Addison-Wesley.

Taba, H., Brady, E. H., & Robinson, J. T. (1952). *Intergroup education in public schools.* Washington, DC: American Council on Education.

Taba, H., & Elkins, D. (1966). *Teaching strategies for the culturally disadvantaged.* Chicago: Rand McNally.

Taba, H., & Van Til, W. (Eds.). (1945). *Democratic human relations* (16th yearbook). Washington, DC: National Council for the Social Studies.

Taba, H., & Wilson, H. (1946). Intergroup education through the school curriculum. *Annals of the American Academy of Political and Social Science, 244,* 19–25.

Tetreault, M. K. (1993). Classrooms for diversity: Rethinking curriculum and pedagogy. In J. A. Banks & C. A. M. Banks (Eds.), *Multicultural education: Issues and perspectives* (2nd ed., pp. 129–148). Boston: Allyn and Bacon.

Theodorson, G. A., & Theodorson, A. G. (1969). *A modern dictionary of sociology.* New York: Barnes & Noble.

Trager, H. G., & Yarrow, M. R. (1952). *They learn what they live: Prejudice in young children.* New York: Harper & Brothers.

Turner, F. J. (1989). The significance of the frontier in American history. In C. A. Milner II (Ed.), *Major problems in the history of the American West* (pp. 2–34). Lexington, MA: D. C. Heath. (Original work published 1894)

Van Sertima, I. (Ed.). (1988). *Great Black leaders: Ancient and modern.* New Brunswick, NJ: Rutgers University, Africana Studies Department.

Vickery, W. E., & Cole, S. G. (1943). *Intercultural education in American schools: Proposed objectives and methods.* New York: Harper & Brothers.

Wesley, C. H. (1935). *Richard Allen: Apostle of freedom.* Washington, DC: The Associated Publishers.

White, A. O. (1973). The Black leadership class and education in antebellum Boston. *Journal of Negro Education, 42,* 505–515.

Williams, F. (Ed.). (1970). *Language and poverty: Perspectives on a theme.* Chicago: Markham Publishing Company.

Williams, G. W. (1882–1883). *History of the Negro race in America from 1619 to 1880: Negroes as slaves, as soldiers, and as citizens* (2 vols.). New York: G. P. Putnam's Sons.

Williams, J. E., Best, D. L., Wood, F. B., & Filler, I. W. (1973). Changes in the connotations of racial concepts and color names: 1963–1970. *Psychological Reports, 33,* 983–996.

Williams, J. E., & Edwards, C. D. (1969). An exploratory study of the modification of color and racial concept attitudes in preschool children. *Child Development, 40,* 737–750.

Williams, J. E., & Morland, J. K. (1976). *Race, color, and the young child.* Chapel Hill: University of North Carolina Press.

Wilson, W. J. (1987). *The truly disadvantaged: The inner city, the underclass, and public policy.* Chicago: University of Chicago Press.

Wirth, L. (1928). *The ghetto.* Chicago: University of Chicago Press.

Woodson, C. G. (1933). *The mis-education of the Negro.* Washington, DC: The Associated Publishers.

Woodson, C. G. (1968). *The education of the Negro prior to 1861.* New York: Arno Press, (Original work published 1919)

Woodson, C. G., & Wesley, C. H. (1922). *The Negro in our history.* Washington, DC: The Associated Publishers.

Wortham, A. (1981). *The other side of racism: A philosophical study of Black race consciousness.* Columbus: Ohio State University Press.

Wyman, D. S. (1984). *The abandonment of the Jews: America and the Holocaust, 1941–1945.* New York: Pantheon.

Yawkey, T. D. (1973). Attitudes toward Black Americans held by rural and urban White early childhood subjects based upon multi-ethnic social studies materials. *Journal of Negro Education, 42,* 164–169.

CURRICULUM THEORY AND MULTICULTURAL EDUCATION

Geneva Gay
UNIVERSITY OF WASHINGTON, SEATTLE

Although general curriculum theorists and multiculturalists typically have not used the same conceptual paradigms, methodologies, and variables of analysis in developing their scholarship, they are not as discordant in principles, concepts, and intentions as initial analyses might suggest. Many logical and ideological similarities and potential connections exist between multicultural education and general curriculum theory, as well as among several specific curriculum theories that have emerged in the United States during the 20th century. This is particularly true of innovative thought and practice, which aim to make the educational enterprises more inclusive of, responsive to, and effective for diverse student populations. These connections and intersections are more implicit than explicit. However, they are becoming increasingly apparent as multicultural education theorists contextualize their arguments in broader educational ideas, issues, and movements, and as the work of general curriculum theorists responds more and more to the sociocultural realities of contemporary national and global societies.

The purpose of this chapter is to make explicit some of the conceptual connections between general curriculum theory and multicultural education. The concept model of education and curriculum theory developed by George Beauchamp (1968) guides this analysis. The major premises underlying it are that multicultural education is: (a) consistent with and a continuation of some trends of thought that have long-standing precedents in the history of education in the United States; (b) compatible with the basic egalitarian principles of democracy; and (c) of both intrinsic and instrumental value for translating some of the most fundamental ideals of American education into practice for select constituent groups of students.

GENERAL THEORETICAL PARAMETERS AND MULTICULTURAL EDUCATION

In a seminal document first published in the late 1960s, George Beauchamp (1968) attempts to define the conceptual parameters of curriculum theory. He argues that, like many other aspects of the education enterprise, curriculum theory and practice have been driven more by external sociocultural pressures and political expediencies than by systematic and thoughtful internal analysis. Furthermore, curriculum theory operates at both a macro- and a microlevel. It is a theory that encompasses several different subtheories, as well as being itself a subtheory within educational theory. Some of its subtheories are curriculum design, development, implementation, history, inquiry, and evaluation. As a subset of educational theory, curriculum theory is best understood when its functions and effects are explained in relation to other subtheories such as administration, instruction, educational psychology, policy studies, supervision, and evaluation (Beauchamp, 1968; Glatthorn, 1987; Schubert, 1986). These interactive relationships evoke an ecological perspective in which theories about curriculum are shaped by knowledge and practice within the field, as well as by developments in other educational and societal domains (Schubert, 1986).

Beauchamp (1968) defines curriculum theory as "a set of related statements that give meaning to a school's curriculum by pointing up the relationships among its elements and by directing its development, its use, and its evaluation" (p. 66). Subsequent definitions of curriculum theory include essentially the same elements as those stated by Beauchamp. For example, Zais (1976) describes it as "a generalized set of logically interrelated definitions, concepts, propositions, and other constructs that represent a systematic view of curriculum phenomena" (p. 87), which serves as a policy to guide curriculum practices. A decade later, Glatthorn (1987) proposed a similar definition: "A curriculum theory is a set of related educational concepts that afford a systematic and illuminating perspective on curricula phenomena" (p. 96). Ornstein and Hunkins (1988) suggest that any theory is "a set of related propositions that sheds light on why events occur in the manner they do" (p. 279). These and other theorists agree that the primary functions of curriculum theory are to define, describe, explain, and predict phenomena endemic to the field and to guide curriculum practice. Glatthorn adds that it also provides educators with a critical perspective about society and its schools.

The essentiality of these functions led Schubert (1986) to conclude that there are at least three, instead of one, generic types of curriculum theory: descriptive, prescriptive, and critical. Macdonald (1977) agrees with this conclusion, but uses different labels (controls and hermeneutic) for two of the three types of theorizing. *Descriptive* or *control curriculum theory* focuses on practice, and uses an empirical database to analyze existing realities. It is based on the linear-expert model of curriculum design that was first introduced by Franklin Bobbitt (1918) and popularized by Ralph Tyler (1949). *Prescriptive* or *hermeneutic theory* "provides new viewpoints, perspectives, and interpretations of the human condition" (Molnar & Zahorik, 1977, p. 6). It assumes that curriculum is a set of recommendations, seeks to establish norms for action, and attempts to clarify and defend those principles upon which these advocacies are founded. *Critical theory* deals with practice and perspective, understanding and control, and the dialectical relationship between theory and practice. Its ultimate value commitment is human emancipation. Its intentions are to expose contradictions in culture, to explain how curriculum perpetuates the socioeconomic class structures and patterns of exploitation and subjugation present in society at large, and to strive passionately and compassionately for a new social order of egalitarianism in schools and societies. These are made explicit through a combination of analytical, descriptive, and prescriptive reasoning that derives from examining schooling in the particular historical context and sociopolitical fabric that characterizes the dominant U.S. culture and society (Aronowitz & Giroux, 1990; Giroux, 1983; Giroux & McLaren, 1989; Kreisberg, 1992; McLaren, 1989; Molnar & Zaharik, 1977; Schubert, 1986).

Another schema for understanding various theoretical conceptions of the nature and functions of curriculum was developed by Miller and Seller (1985). They suggest that every conception of curriculum has embedded within it a particular worldview or set of beliefs about educational purposes, schooling processes, worthy content, instructional processes, and how students best learn. They identify three basic belief systems from which the educational enterprise is viewed. The *transmission position* emphasizes passing on to students the fund of knowledge, skills, and values that have accumulated over time. The *transaction position* views education as an interactive dia-

logue between students and the formal program of schooling, in which students are given opportunities for inquiring, problem solving, critical thinking, questioning status-quo norms, and reconstructing knowledge. The *transformation position* advocates individual responsibility and action, leading to the reconstruction of personal and social life. These positions parallel the descriptive, prescriptive, and critical theories, respectively, discussed earlier.

Generally, theory building must involve five key operations in order to fulfill its major purposes of defining, describing, explaining, and predicting major events, variables, processes, and relationships in disciplines or areas of scholarly inquiry. These are: (a) defining the key terms and constructs of the discipline; (b) classifying its known and assumed knowledge; (c) making and testing inferences and predictions; (d) creating physical, visual, and/or verbal models to represent key ideas, events, and interactions; and (e) formulating subtheories to broaden the overall scope and conceptual clarity of the theory, and to improve the explanation of the events or issues involved in the design, implementation, and evaluation of the discipline (Beauchamp, 1968; Glatthorn, 1987; Oliva, 1988; Ornstein & Hunkins, 1988; Zais, 1976).

In the late 1960s Beauchamp (1968) argued that uneven growth was taking place across these different components of curriculum theory. While developments in definitions, models, and subtheories were flourishing, little progress was being made in the classifying and inferring/predicting dimensions of curriculum theorizing. They were inhibited by the absence of a generally accepted conceptual framework for organizing curriculum knowledge. The inferences and predictions being made about curriculum phenomena were restricted to those emerging from analytical thought and descriptive research. Of necessity, then, most curriculum theorizing was primarily descriptive in nature, content, and function.

While this may have been true during the formative years of curriculum theory, developments since Beauchamp initially developed his conceptual model now contradict many of these claims. Several kinds of curriculum inquiry and research are now taking place, and a wide variety of classification schemata have emerged. Illustrative of the available classification schemes are those proposed for categorizing curriculum theories and theorists (Gay, 1980; Giroux, Penna, & Pinar, 1981; Glatthorn, 1987; Orlosky & Smith, 1978; Pinar, 1974, 1975), types of curriculum designs (Eisner & Vallance, 1974; Ornstein & Hunkins, 1988; Smith, Stanley, & Shores, 1957; Taba, 1962; Zais, 1976), and kinds and sources of knowledge and ways of knowing (Eisner, 1985; Foshay, 1975; Phenix, 1964). This also means that curriculum theory is not nearly as predominantly prescriptive as it once was. Increasing numbers of descriptive and critical theories are being generated.

As will become evident later on in this chapter, multicultural education encompasses elements of all three types of theorizing. *Descriptive* analyses of educational systems and conditions that ignore or deny the importance of cultural diversity are frequently used to establish a baseline point of referernce for changes. *Critical* explanations are then used to determine why these systems should be changed to be more representative of and responsive to cultural pluralism. *Prescriptive* recommendations suggest what the changes should embody in order for education to be maximally beneficial to an ever-increasing variety of culturally, ethnically, and socially pluralistic individuals, institutions, and communities. Multicultural education also is, simultaneously, transmissive, transactive, and transformative. It teaches content about culturally pluralistic contributions to humankind and U.S. society; engages students actively and interactively with their own cultural identity and the cultural identity of others; and develops the kind of social consciousness, civic responsibility, and political activism needed to reconstruct society for greater pluralistic equality, truth, inclusion, and justice.

When Beauchamp's conceptual model of curriculum theorizing is applied to multicultural education, several similarities are readily apparent. First, like general curricularists, multiculturalists use research findings, paradigms, principles, concepts, and perspectives from a variety of social science disciplines to construct their interrelated statements about why culturally pluralistic education is imperative, how it can and should be implemented, and the benefits to be derived from it. Invariably, these statements are interdisciplinary, and borrow heavily from sociology, cultural anthropology, political science, social psychology, cross-cultural communications, and sociolinguistics. Second, multicultural education theory includes the same theoretical subsets as general education theory, but those dealing with curriculum and instruction are more fully developed than those concerned with administration, counseling, and evaluation. Third, within multicultural curriculum theory, the operations having to do with making inferences from and predictions based on empirical research are very few in number and minimal in quality. However, some progress is being made in this area, as is evident by the multicultural research summarized in Shaver (1991), and in other chapters of this *Handbook*. The other operations endemic to theory building—defining key terms and constructs, creating models to represent conceptual relationships, classifying knowledge, formulating subtheories—are becoming increasingly more mature and crystallized. Fourth, like general curriculum, most of the theoretical developments during the formative years of multicultural education were devoted to defining the field and clarifying its fundamental goals and purposes. As a result, its theoretical scholarship tends to be more prescriptive and critical than descriptive.

DEFINITIONS IN GENERAL CURRICULUM THEORY

Within curriculum theory, the key technical concept demanding definition is *curriculum* itself, and the primary challenge is to explain the relationships among the variables embedded within it. Beauchamp (1968) suggests that there are three major ways in which curriculum is theoretically conceived. First, it is viewed as a *substantive phenomenon,* or a document of some sort. Thus it is common for theorists to talk about *a curriculum.* The major relationships that must be explained are those that exist among the internal components of the document. These include goals, objectives, activities and evaluation, intended outcomes and subject matter, and the

scope and sequence of instruction. Tyler (1949) describes these components as four fundamental questions that must be answered in developing any curriculum or plan for instruction. They are:

1. What educational purposes should the school seek to attain?
2. What educational experiences can be provided to achieve these purposes?
3. How can these educational experiences be effectively organized?
4. How can we determine whether these purposes are being accomplished?

Additionally, the sociocultural influences that impinge upon the curriculum need to be explained in order to make clear the reasons for primary decisions made about its components.

A second conception of curriculum is as a *system,* or an organized framework in which all curricular decisions are made. It implies a cluster of relationships having to do with the "human engineering required in the process of curriculum development and curriculum usage" (Beauchamp, 1968, p. 69). The major tasks inherent in a curriculum system determine the parameters for establishing these relationships. They deal with developing, implementing, and evaluating the curriculum.

The third theoretical definition of curriculum is as *an area of professional scholarship and research.* Its purpose is to advance knowledge about various curricula and curriculum development systems. To explain the relationships among curriculum variables, individuals involved in these pursuits typically evoke social, psychological, and philosophical foundations; historical precedents and experiences; social, political, and cultural influences; and research designs and procedures to explain the relationships among curriculum variables.

DEFINITIONS OF MULTICULTURAL EDUCATION

Definitional concepts of multicultural education illustrate Beauchamp's (1968) notion that multiple approaches to defining a discipline are natural, and need not impede its theoretical development. The kaleidoscope of available definitions of multicultural education reflects the scholarly perspectives of diverse disciplines (such as anthropology, sociology, and psychology); policies of state departments of education, accrediting agencies, and professional organizations; and experience-based statements developed by school practitioners (Hernandez, 1989). The definitions tend to fall into the categories of prescriptive and critical theories as described by Molnar and Zahorik (1977) and Schubert (1986), and they have primarily transactive and transformative purposes as defined by Miller and Seller (1985).

Specific definitions of multicultural education vary widely with respect to content selection, methodological focus, and referent group orientations. However, strong definitions can be grouped into several recurrent categories. Banks (1993c) identifies the major ones when he explains that "multicultural education is an idea, an educational reform movement, and a process whose major goal is to change the structure of educational institutions" (p. 7). Garcia (1982), Grant (1977a, 1978) and L. Frazier (1977) argue similarly. They agree that multicultural education is a concept, a framework, a way of thinking, a philosophical viewpoint, a value orientation, and a set of criteria for making decisions that better serve the educational needs of culturally diverse student populations.

As a *concept, idea, or philosophy,* multicultural education is a set of beliefs and explanations that recognizes and values the importance of ethnic and cultural diversity in shaping lifestyles, social experiences, personal identities, and educational opportunities of individuals, groups, and nations. Consequently, it has both descriptive and prescriptive dimensions. Descriptively, it recognizes the real social structure of the United States and its relationship to national institutions, value beliefs, and power systems. Multicultural education also prescribes what should be done to ensure equitable accessibility and treatment for diverse groups in schools and in society (Baptiste, 1986). Parekh (1986) equates multicultural education with a refined version of liberal education, education for freedom, and celebration of the inherent plurality of the world. Bennett (1990), Banks (1990, 1991/92), Gay (1988), and Garcia (1982) proclaim that it is a crucial part of the democratic imperative for U.S. schools and society.

Two influential professional organizations—the American Association of Colleges for Teacher Education (AACTE) and the Association for Supervision and Curriculum Development (ASCD)—published policy statements in the 1970s on multicultural education. They endorse the idea that multicultural education is a set of value beliefs or a philosophy about the importance of students' learning about cultural diversity. The essence of the AACTE statement (1973) is that since there is "no one model American," schools should design and implement instructional programs that value and preserve cultural pluralism. ASCD (Grant, 1977b) connects multicultural education to its own value traditions by defining it as a humanistic concept; establishes it as a condition of quality education for culturally pluralistic student populations; and suggests that it is based upon the principles of equality, human rights, social justice, and alternative life choices. The conception of multicultural education as an alternative way of thinking about how to provide quality education for diverse groups within the context of democratic ideas is further refined by Baptiste (1979), Bennett (1990), Banks (1990), Sleeter (1991), Garcia (1982), Gay (1988, 1990), and Nieto (1992).

Gay (1988) proposes that educational equality and excellence for children of color, from economically impoverished backgrounds, recent immigrants, and limited-English speakers are inextricably interwoven. Pedagogical equality that reflects culturally sensitive instructional strategies is a precondition for and a means of achieving maximal academic outcomes for culturally diverse students. Banks (1990) makes multiculturalism and citizenship reciprocal, interdependent processes. He explains that citizenship education in and for a culturally pluralistic society must help students to

develop the knowledge, attitudes, and skills needed not only to participate in, but also to transform and reconstruct society . . . to become

literate and reflective citizens who can participate productively in the workforce . . . [who] care about other people in their communities and . . . take personal, social, and civic action to create a humane and just society. (p. 211)

These conceptions satisfy Beauchamp's criterion that a fundamental element of educational theory building is explaining the relationship among the components of a phenomenon and its subtheories. Although they do not explain the specific details, these definitions do indicate that multicultural education includes curricular, instructional, administrative, and environmental efforts within schools. They also indicate that it is philosophically compatible with principles of democracy and good education (Banks, 1990, 1991/92; Gay, 1988; Nieto, 1992), thereby placing multicultural education well within the normative frameworks of the cultural and educational ideals of the United States.

Conceptions of multicultural education as a *reform movement* emphasize revising the structural, procedural, substantive, and valuative components of the educational enterprise to reflect the social, cultural, ethnic, racial, and linguistic pluralism present in the United States. They tend to be prescriptive in content and transactive and transformative in intent. These elements are implied in Baptiste's (1979) explanation of multicultural education as a "process of institutionalizing the philosophy of cultural pluralism within the educational system" (p. 172). The operative word here is "institutionalizing," which requires systematic efforts and systematic change (Banks, 1992; Gollnick & Chinn, 1990; Nieto, 1992; Sleeter, 1991).

Bennett (1990) extends this notion of systematic change by identifying some of the specific elements of a multicultural reform movement. According to her, it must be comprehensive in focus, governed by principles of equality and equity, and encompass (a) approaches to curricula that develop understanding of ethnic groups' cultures, histories, and contributions; (b) processes for students becoming multicultural in their attitudes, values, beliefs, and behaviors; and (c) action strategies for combating racism and other forms of oppressive practice. Similar prescriptions are offered by Banks (1977, 1992), who states that multicultural education involves modifications in the total school environment, including policies and politics; classroom instructional interactions, materials, and resources; extracurricular activities; formal and informal curricula; performance appraisal techniques; guidance and counseling; and institutional norms.

L. Frazier (1977), Gollnick and Chinn (1990), and Banks and Banks (1993) broaden the notion of multicultural education as comprehensive reform by extending the referent group parameters to include social class, gender, and disability, along with race and ethnicity. Sleeter and Grant (1988) did likewise, as well as including a strong argument for social reconstruction as the ultimate outcome in their definition of multicultural education. This goal is achieved by teaching political actions skills to youths so they can coalesce their efforts to work for the elimination of oppression in society and bring about a more equitable distribution of resources and opportunities for all oppressed groups. Therefore, social transformation and personal empowerment are fundamental themes within and characteristic traits of theoretical concepts of multicultural education as an emancipatory pedagogical and social reform movement.

Increasingly, multicultural education is seen as a *process* instead of a product. As a process, it is a way of thinking, a decision-making style, and a way of behaving in educational settings that is pervasive and ongoing (Banks, 1993c). It requires long-term investments of time and resources, and carefully planned and monitored actions. It evokes images similar to Beauchamp's conception of curriculum as a decision-making or "engineering" system for the creation, implementation, and evaluation of instructional plans. Grant (1978) captures the essence of this conception when he explains why he prefers to use *education that is multicultural* to identify the enterprise instead of *multicultural education*. Rather than a specific, discrete education program (such as social studies, bilingual, or science education), he sees multicultural education as a different approach to the entire educational enterprise in all its forms and functions.

The idea of a decision-making system also is embedded in Hunter's (1974) view of multicultural education as "the structuring of educational priorities, commitments, and processes to reflect the reality of cultural pluralism as a fact of life in the United States" (p. 36). The California State Department of Education's (1979) policy on multicultural education states explicitly (as do other state policies such as those of Iowa and Michigan) that it is "an interdisciplinary process rather than a single program or a series of activities" (p. 1), or a "mode of experience and learning to be infused and integrated throughout the curriculum and throughout the school program" (p. 9).

Suzuki (1979, 1984) and Sizemore (1981) add the element of a "program" or an "artifact" to the definitional parameters of multicultural education. These are analogous to Beauchamp's conception of curriculum as a substantive phenomenon. Suzuki (1984) describes multicultural education as an interdisciplinary instructional program that "provides multiple learning environments matching the academic, social, and linguistic needs of students (p. 305). This program also has multiple purposes, among which are: (a) develop basic academic skills for students from different race, sex, ethnic, and social-class backgrounds; (b) teach students to respect and appreciate their own and other cultural groups; (c) overcome ethnocentric and prejudicial attitudes; (d) understand the sociohistorical, economic, and psychological factors that have produced contemporary ethnic alienation and inequality; (e) foster ability to analyze critically and make intelligent decisions about real-life ethnic, racial, and cultural problems; and (f) help students conceptualize and aspire toward a vision of a more humane, just, free, and equal society, and acquire the knowledge and skills necessary to achieve it (Suzuki, 1979). Sizemore (1981) uses "process" somewhat analogously to "program" in her conception of multicultural education as "the process of acquiring knowledge and information about the efforts of different groups against adverse agencies and conditions for control of their destinies through the study of the artifacts and substances which emanated therefrom" (pp. 4–5).

A policy statement enacted by the Rochester, New York, School District in 1987 is representative of the way many local education agencies conceptualize multicultural education. This document mandates that "multicultural perspectives" and relevant facts, issues, values, and viewpoints of all cultural groups, especially those who have been historically omitted or misrepresented, be included in the development and dissemination of instructional materials (Swartz, 1989).

Probably the most inclusive and eclectic definition of multicultural education is one by Nieto (1992). While many other scholars use multiple elements such as content, process, ideology, and reform in their conceptions of multicultural education, Nieto's is by far the most comprehensive. She places multicultural education in a sociopolitical context, and incorporates substantive and procedural components, outcome expectations, and some interpretive comments. The result is a synergistic composite that includes some features of most of the various types of definition discussed above. Nieto states that multicultural education is

a process of comprehensive school reform and basic education for all students. It challenges and rejects racism and other forms of discrimination in schools and society and accepts and affirms the pluralism (ethnic, racial, linguistic, religious, economic, and gender, among others) that students, their communities, and teachers represent. Multicultural education permeates the curriculum and instructional strategies used in schools, as well as the interactions among teachers, students and parents, and the very way that schools conceptualize the nature of teaching and learning. Because it uses critical pedagogy as its underlying philosophy and focuses on knowledge, reflection, and action (praxis) as the basis for social change, multicultural education furthers the democratic principles of social justice. (Nieto, 1992, p. 208).

Multicultural education also meets the criterion of Beauchamp's third type of definition in theory building. It is a "field of study" because (a) there is a stable community of scholars who devote their professional time primarily, if not exclusively, to it; (b) a growing body of scholarship exists on philosophies and methodologies for incorporating ethnic diversity and cultural pluralism into the educational enterprise; (c) undergraduate and graduate programs at colleges and universities are preparing school teachers, administrators, and counselors to implement multicultural education; and (d) there is a considerable degree of continuity and longevity among the cadre of scholars who are leading voices in the field. Textbooks, monographs, journal articles, and book chapters about various multicultural education issues and dimensions are published regularly. These publications are not limited to the United States. A rich body of multicultural and antiracist pedagogical scholarship is being produced in England, Canada, Australia, and various other nations in Western Europe (Banks & Lynch, 1986; Crittenden, 1982; Lynch, 1986, 1989; Modgil, Verma, Mallick, & Modgil, 1986; Moodley, 1992; Samuda, Berry, & Laferriere, 1984; Verma, 1989), thereby giving an international dimension to the field (see part XI of this *Handbook*). Among the most prolific and consistent multicultural educational authors in the United States are James A. Banks, Carl A. Grant, Geneva Gay, Christine I. Bennett, Carlos Ovando, Philip Chinn, Christine E. Sleeter, H. Prentice Baptiste, Carlos E. Cortés, Donna Gollnick,

Ricardo Garcia, Joyce King, James Boyer, and Gloria Ladson-Billings. More recent additions to this list include Sonia Nieto, Hilda Hernandez, Cherry McGee Banks, Carlos Diaz, Valerie Ooka Pang, and Patricia Ramsey. Many of them are contributors to this *Handbook.*

Major colleges of education throughout the United States are actively engaged in educating students to become multicultural education K–12 teachers, college professors, researchers, and scholars. Some of the leading ones are the University of Wisconsin at Madison, the University of Washington in Seattle, the University of Massachusetts, Indiana University at Bloomington, the University of California at Santa Cruz, the University of Houston, and San Diego State University.

Another strong indicator of multicultural education as a field of study is its presence in the agenda of professional organizations. More and more it is becoming a central theme and determining influence in the programmatic activities of professional organizations. The National Council for the Social Studies (NCSS), ASCD, Phi Delta Kappa, the National Council for the Accreditation of Teacher Education (NCATE), and the National Education Association (NEA) were among the first to declare their commitments to multicultural education in overt and highly significant ways. More recently, the American Educational Research Association (AERA) has joined this influential group. Each has sponsored conferences, publications, and policy statements that became what Beauchamp (1968) calls "milestones" in the formative years of the field.

In 1973 NCSS published *Teaching Ethnic Studies* (edited by James A. Banks), which became a best-seller. Three years later it issued *Curriculum Guidelines for Multiethnic Education* (Banks, Cortés, Garcia, Gay, & Ochoa, 1976). This document—which was revised and reissued in 1992 with a change of title to *Curriculum Guidelines for Multicultural Education*—is the most comprehensive of its kind. It has served as a prototype for numerous groups and individuals interested in developing similar criteria. NCATE's premier contribution (1987) came in the form of standards that specified the need for colleges of education to include ethnically and culturally pluralistic content and experiences in their curricula as a condition of receiving unqualified accreditation. ASCD passed resolutions, developed media materials, published articles in *Educational Leadership,* and sponsored conferences on multicultural education and on ethnic and cultural pluralism. Phi Delta Kappa uses its journal, *Phi Delta Kappan,* and topical monographs to disseminate to its members and subscribers the thinking of leading multiculturalists on key issues in the field. NEA continues its long tradition of publishing monographs on ethnically diverse groups in the United States and persuading its members to embrace multiculturalism in their value commitments and political action. For example, in 1981 it published *Education in the 80s: Multiethnic Education* (edited by James A. Banks). Its most recent publication with a similar theme, purpose, and focus is *Multicultural Education for the 21st Century,* edited by Carlos Diaz and released in 1992. AERA's commitment to cultural pluralism in eduation was most evident in its 1991 annual conference, which was devoted to this theme. The publication of this *Handbook* is another compelling example of the emergence of multicultural education as a respected field of scholarly endeavor.

Two other significant events mark the emergence of multicultural education as a field of study. The first is a journal dedicated to developing a better understanding of ethnic, racial, and religious diversity. *Multicultural Review* was initiated in 1992 by Greenwood Publishers. It is intended to provide reviews of multicultural materials and information on multiculturalism for a readership primarily of librarians. The second event is the creation of a new professional organization to serve as a forum for educators committed to and actively engaged in the pursuit of multicultural education. During the 1990 annual conference of the Association for Teacher Education (ATE), 15 members of the Special Interest Group on Multicultural Education met and founded the National Association for Multicultural Education (NAME). Among the participants were nationally known multiculturalists: Carl A. Grant of the University of Wisconsin at Madison, H. Prentice Baptiste and James E. Anderson of the University of Houston, Pritchy Smith of the University of North Florida, and James B. Boyer of Kansas State University. Rose M. Duhon-Sells of Southern University was designated the first chair. She organized the first national convention, which took place in New Orleans in February 1991. NAME released the first issue of its journal, *Multicultural Education,* in Summer 1993.

CLASSIFYING CURRICULUM THEORIZING

In addition to defining their domain of inquiry and its component parts, another common activity among theorists is arranging information about curriculum phenomena into coherent, integrated schemata to enhance the clarity of its meaning (Beauchamp, 1968; Ornstein & Hunkins, 1988). These efforts have generated a variety of classification systems, based on different sets of analytical criteria, in both general curriculum and multicultural education. Illustrative of the schemata available for organizing general curriculum knowledge and theories are those devised by Eisner and Vallance (1974), Pinar (1974, 1975), Orlosky and Smith (1978), Gay (1980), and Glatthorn (1987). Frequently referenced classification systems in multicultural education are those developed by Banks (1993c), Gibson (1976), Gay (1983, 1990), and Sleeter and Grant (1988).

Some curriculum theories are classified according to developmental maturity and increasing complexity. For Glatthorn (1987), the existence of an empirical database to support speculative hypotheses is what distinguishes between basic and more complex curriculum theories. Gay (1983) uses increased depth of conceptual analysis: broad-based interdisciplinary reasoning informed by social science concepts; knowledge and perspectives about cultural pluralism; and growing levels of inclusivity, comprehensiveness, and systemic reform to compare the formative stages of multicultural education theory with more advanced theoretical thought. According to Glatthorn, *basic theory* sets up logically deduced but empirically untested hypotheses to explain curriculum phenomena, and employs concepts that are not systematically refined in great detail. By comparison, *complex theory* is "an exclusive conceptual scheme for explaining an entire universe of inquiry" (Glatthorn, 1987, p. 97).

The collective body of multicultural education theorizing is transitional and falls somewhere between these two polar positions. Much of it continues to be derived from logical deductions instead of an empirical database, and is therefore basic theory. However, the concepts and principles used to explain its major tenets are increasingly interdisciplinary and integrative, and include a greater depth of conceptual analysis; an empirical database verifying some of the theory's subtheories is gradually emerging (Gay, 1983, 1990). For example, explanations and justifications of what should be taught about cultural pluralism include reasoning that examines the intrinsic and instrumental value of multicultural knowledge and ways of knowing: the sociological and political needs of culturally pluralistic local, national, and global communities; the psychoemotional dispositions of culturally different students; the social construction of knowledge; skills needed for maximum personal development of individual students; and the reconstruction of society to achieve democratic equality within the context of cultural pluralism.

Another set of criteria employed to classify curriculum knowledge addresses the degree of innovation and unorthodoxy evident in the primary conceptual orientations that theorists use in framing their arguments. Pinar (1975) and Giroux et al. (1981) use these criteria to classify general curriculum theorists as either traditionalists, conceptual empiricists, or reconceptualists. *Traditionalists* are concerned primarily with the expeditious transmission of the cultural heritage of dominant society through a fixed body of knowledge and the perpetuation of the existing social order. Individuals such as Franklin Bobbitt, Ralph Tyler, E. D. Hirsch, and advocates of "back to basics" fall into this category. *Conceptual empiricists* such as Robert Gagne, James Popham, Joseph Schwab, and Jerome Bruner base their theorizing on data derived from research methodologies patterned after the physical and natural sciences. From these results they attempt to compile general principles that will enable educators to predict and control what happens in schools. *Reconceptualists* such as William Pinar, Henry Giroux, James Macdonald, and Dwayne Huebner interpret and explain social, political, and economic factors impinging upon the structures, processes, and effects of schooling. They also explain how class conflict and unequal distribution of power correlate with access to high-quality, high-status educational opportunities, and with academic achievement (Giroux et al., 1981; Pinar, 1974, 1975; McLaren, 1989).

This particular classification system does not work very well for multicultural education. Its theorists are not distributed across all three categories. Their advocacies are reconceptualist in intent and ideology, if not always in form, style, and text. Their ultimate goal is the redistribution of school resources, opportunities, and outcomes to achieve greater educational equity and excellence for culturally different groups in schools and society. Although insights gained from economic and political analyses are embedded within the tenets of multiculturalism, they often are not as direct, explicit, and prominent as they are in the arguments of the reconceptualists.

Eisner and Vallance (1974) and Orlosky and Smith (1978) devise independent but similar classification purposes of a curriculum. *Cognitive process* theories concentrate on developing intellectual operations such as critical thinking, problem solving, and conflict resolution. *Curriculum-as-technology* or *analytical* theorists are analogous to Pinar's traditionalists in that they emphasize expedience and efficiency in accomplishing predetermined outcomes. Theorists who see the curriculum as having *humanistic* or *self-actualization* purposes give priority to the personal growth and empowerment of students. By comparison, *social reconstruction-relevance* curriculum theorists place the needs of society over those of individuals. Those who give preeminence to *academic rationalism* endorse the importance of standard disciplinary knowledge in preparing students to participate in Western cultural traditions. What Orlosky and Smith call a *futuristic style* of curriculum theorizing is much like Pinar's reconceptualism in that both advocate analyzing current societal conditions as a basis for determining the focus of education designed to prepare students to live in a future of their own making.

Glatthorn (1987) feels each of these schemata is lacking in some way or another. This discontent prompted him to create another system for classifying curriculum theory. He relies upon the work of Huenecke (1982) and Schwab (1970) to construct the conceptual parameters of his categories. Curriculum theorists are then classified on the basis of their primary domain of inquiry within the curriculum field into one of four categories: structure-oriented, value-oriented, content-oriented, and process-oriented styles of curriculum theorizing.

Structure-oriented theorists analyze substantive components of the curriculum, their interrelationship, who makes decisions about them, and how these decisions are made. These theories are primarily descriptive in style and intent, and evoke Beauchamp's (1968) notation of curriculum as a decision-making or "engineering" system.

Curriculum theories that are *value oriented* are generally critical in nature and analyze the value beliefs and assumptions that undergird curriculum actions and artifacts. This emphasis led Glatthorn (1987, p. 101) to describe the work of such theorists as "educational consciousness-raising," and to identify them as reconceptualists and critical theorists. Leading advocates include William Pinar (1974, 1975), Henry Giroux (1983, 1988, 1992), Peter McLaren (1989), James Macdonald (1974, 1975, 1977), Michael Apple (1979), and George Counts (1932). Some, such as Macdonald, focus their discussions on the human condition, the search for personal transcendence, and the struggle of the individual to actualize the whole self. These person-oriented curriculum theorists gain support for their ideas from humanistic and perceptual psychologists such as the contributing authors to *Perceiving, Behaving, Becoming* (Combs, 1962) and Carl Rogers (1983). They contend that education is essentially a humanistic and moral endeavor: The learning process should engage students actively in constructing personal meaning; the journey toward self-actualization is a dialectic and dialogic interaction between self and society, explicit and implicit knowledge, change and stability; and the ultimate goal is to develop autonomous, self-actualizing individuals.

Other value-oriented theorists such as Apple (1979), Counts (1932), Giroux (1983, 1988, 1992), and McLaren (1989) ground their explanations of curriculum purposes and functions in analyses of the social milieu, the interrelationship between schools and society, cultural hegemony, uneven distribution of economic resources and political power, knowledge as cultural capital and a social construction, and the transformation of society and schools. More specific dimensions of these emphases are summarized by Giroux (1992) in his descriptions of border pedagogy, one of the operational tools of critical theory. Among its most salient features are linking education to critical social analysis and the imperative of representative democracy; advocating struggle against inequality; encouraging sociopolitical actions to expand basic human rights to oppressed and marginalized groups; and envisioning a new educational and social order that is more egalitarian, accessible, and inclusive of a wider variety of students from various gender, class, racial, and ethnic groups. Although Dewey typically is not identified as a critical theorist or reconceptualist, he did expound a moderate version of these same themes, particularly the dialectic relationship among individuals, schools, and societies. They are apparent in his writing, such as *My Pedagogic Creed* (1897), *Democracy and Education* (1916), and *The Child and the Curriculum* (1902).

The third type of curriculum theorizing in Glatthorn's classification is *content oriented*. It attributes primary significance either to students, the disciplines or formalized bodies of knowledge, or the social order in determining the selection and organization of curriculum content.

Theorists who espouse child-centered curricula (Combs, 1962; Dewey, 1987, 1902; Entwistle, 1970; Jervis & Montag, 1991) argue that the child is the beginning point, the determiner, the center, and the end of the educational process. Therefore, every phase of the child's development—the whole child—must be studied and provided for in the educational process. This is a pedagogical and a moral imperative (Entwistle, 1970; Frazier, 1976). Since children are psychological and social beings, and the welfare of individuals and society are inextricably interrelated, education must have both personal and societal development functions. Neither of these dimensions should be compromised, superimposed on, or subordinated to the other, for "if we eliminate the social factor from the child we are left only with an abstraction; if we eliminate the individual factor from society, we are left with only an inert and lifeless mass" (Dewey, 1897, p. 6). To achieve these goals, classroom teachers and curriculum designers must understand the conditions in which children live and how these conditions are continually shaping their intellectual powers, ideas, feelings, emotions, values, and behavior. During the last three or four decades, child-centered emphasis in education has taken the specific programmatic form of humanistic, affective, open, and developmental education.

With the exception of specific referent groups, these principles of child-centered education could easily be identified as basic tenets of multicultural education. Proponents consistently explain that multicultural education has both personal and social consequences. The personal effects usually include the self-affirmation, celebration, and empowerment of culturally different individuals and groups. The social consequences have to do with changing other people's knowledge and attitudes about ethnic, racial, and cultural groups, and making society more reflective on and responsive to cultural diversity. These goals are dialective and interactive. Ethnic and cultural perceptions of

self and others are influenced by societal forces, and social conditions can only be changed by individuals who know, value, and promote cultural diversity as a personal and societal strength to be cultivated. Furthermore, since cultural socialization influences every dimension of human values, beliefs, perceptions, and behavior, to demean, reject, or ignore the cultural heritage of diverse groups in curriculum and instruction constitutes an act of psychological and moral violence toward their human dignity (Novak, 1975; Pai, 1984).

Educators who concentrate their theorizing on what kinds of knowledge are most valid have tended to advocate either the structure-of-the-disciplines or different ways-of-knowing viewpoints. The former was argued eloquently and persuasively by Bruner (1960) in *The Process of Education* and by Schwab (1969) in "Education and the Structure of the Disciplines." Phenix (1964) feels that valid school knowledge could be derived from analyzing six distinctive modes of human understanding, or cluster domains of knowledge. These "realms of meaning" are symbolics, empirics, esthetics, synnoetics, ethics, and synoptics.

Proponents of the ways-of-knowing viewpoint include the contributing authors to the 1985 Yearbook of the National Society for the Study of Education (NSSE), edited by Eisner; Gardner (1983); and Barbe and Swassing (1979). The NSSE Yearbook identifies eight different modes of knowing: aesthetic, scientific, interpersonal, narrative, formal, practical, intuitive, and spiritual. Gardner makes basically the same observations, but calls the way of knowing *multiple intelligence*. His list includes linguistic, logical-mathematical, spatial, musical, bodily-kinesthetic, interpersonal, and intrapersonal intelligences. Barbe and Swassing maintain that the preferred sensory channels through which individuals receive, process, and retain information are major determinants of learning. The three primary channels of information processing, or "modalities of learning," are visual, auditory, and kinetic.

Consistent with these conceptual precedents, Banks (1993b) has developed a knowledge typology that might facilitate the process of multiculturizing school curricula. It includes five types of knowledge. *Personal/cultural knowledge* is "the concepts, explanations, and interpretations that students derive from . . . experiences in their homes, families, and community cultures" (p. 6). They act as reality screens through which school knowledge is made personally meaningful. *Popular knowledge* consists of facts, images, values, beliefs, and interpretations that are transmitted through and institutionalized in mass media. Within the context of schools, it is analogous to the *symbolic* (Gay, in press) and *lived curricula* (Glatthorn, 1987) in form and effect. *Mainstream academic knowledge* is the presumed objective truths—the disciplinary canons—generated by Western-centric research and scholarship. It constitutes the dominant fund of knowledge in the various disciplines, from which the content taught in schools is extracted. *School knowledge* is the information that appears in textbooks, curriculum guides, and other instructional materials routinely used by classroom teachers, as well as the teacher's mediation and interpretation of this information.

The fifth type of knowledge in Banks's typology is the bedrock of multicultural education. *Transformative academic knowledge* is concepts, paradigms, perspectives, and explanations that challenge mainstream assumptions about knowledge being neutral and devoid of particularistic human interests. Knowledge is seen as a social construction, and no one group has exclusive dominion over it. This type of knowledge provides alternative interpretations of ethnic, gender, and social groups' history, life, and culture, and expands disciplinary canons to encompass the cultural pluralism that is endemic to societies and the human story.

The underlying message in all of these conceptions of the nature of knowledge and ways of knowing constitutes a major principle of multicultural education. That is, because there are multiple ways of learning and because quality knowledge comes in many different forms, school curricula should reflect and facilitate a plurality of cultural learning styles, perspectives, experiences, contributions, and heritages.

Although many curriculum content theorists proclaim that social order must be the anchor point in all curriculum decision making, they differ on the role schools should take toward existing societal conditions. Some are *conformists* who advocate a life-adjustment agenda. This intention was the driving force of Franklin Bobbitt's *The Curriculum,* published in 1918, of the "back-to-basics" movement of the early 1980s, and of the economic, vocationalistic theme that permeates almost all proposals for school reform produced after the mid-1980s, from *A Nation at Risk* (National Commission on Excellence in Education, 1983) to *America 2000* (1991). It is ironic that issues of cultural pluralism and multicultural education are conspicuously absent from most of these reports. Their major concern seems to be perpetuation of the traditional status quo by socializing students to accept unquestioningly the present organization of work and technology, and preparing them to fit into a shrinking and fragile economic marketplace (Glatthorn, 1987).

Other society-centered curriculum theorists are *reformists.* They believe the basic foundations of U.S. education are valid, but their structural and programmatic features need to be revised periodically to make them more responsive to changing societal conditions and trends. One way this can be done is by helping students develop a strong sense of moral courage and civic responsibility. This is the essence of the theme in multicultural education theory, which argues that there is a natural compatibility among U.S. democratic principles, quality education, and multiculturalism (Banks, 1990, 1991/92; Bennett, 1990; Cushner, McClelland, & Safford, 1992; Gay, 1990).

Another group of society-centered curriculum theorists are *futurists.* They try to predict future consequences of current societal developments and design curricula that are preventive, corrective, and ameliorative. Shane (1981), for example, suggests that students of today must become responsible for and actively involved in shaping the kind of future they will inherit. Toffler (1974) argues similarly. He explains that since the future is "at least partially subject to our influence, our interest must therefore focus on 'preferable' futures as well as those that are 'possible' and 'probable' " (p. xxv). For this reason, future-conscious education should include developing a moral commitment to social justice, learning one's own mind, understanding one's own values, and making decisions and choices that have positive potential for creating desirable societal change. These emancipating and empowering emphases are especially significant for students who are female, poor, and of color because of

their "future-deprived" present, and because their proportions in the population are becoming increasingly more significant (Toffler, 1974). Multiculturalists (Banks, 1991/92; Banks & Banks, 1993; Baruth & Manning, 1992; *Education that Works,* 1990; Gay, in press; Henry, 1990; Hernandez, 1989) often present statistics about the rapidly shifting numerical distribution of ethnic, racial, linguistic, and social-class groups in schools and society to support their arguments about how current educational experiences need to be revised to ensure a qualitatively different society of the future.

Radical curriculum theorists contend that reactive reform strategies are not sufficient to bring about the massive changes required to make schools and society truly democratic, egalitarian, effective, and just. Instead, education must be transformed at its most fundamental core, or what Tye (1987) calls the deep structures of its underlying value assumptions. These efforts should be directed by emancipatory pedagogy and human liberation, and based upon the realization that because the education process is always a political act that occurs within a given social context, it can never be neutral, objective, or universally understood (Apple, 1979; Aronowitz & Giroux, 1990; Darder, 1991; Giroux, 1983, 1985, 1988, 1992; Goodman, 1989; McLaren, 1989; Shor & Freire, 1987). The proponents of this type of curriculum theorizing depend heavily upon the philosophical beliefs, analytical techniques, and conceptual orientations of influential social critical theorists such as Paulo Freire, Samuel Bowles and Herbert Gintis, Jurgen Habermas, and Henry Giroux.

Process-oriented theories constitute the fourth category in Glatthorn's (1987) classification system. They attempt to explain alternative approaches used to create curricula, or to activate what Beauchamp (1968) calls a "curriculum engineering system." They analyze the organizational levels at which curriculum development takes place; who participates in the process, their qualifications, roles, and functions; factors that influence decisions made about various curriculum phenomena; components of the substantive deliberations; how deliberative conflicts and problems are solved; how the scope and sequence of curriculum content are organized; plans for implementing and evaluating curriculum products; and criteria for assessing the quality and effectiveness of the curriculum processes and products.

Gay (1980) identifies four common ways in which curriculum theorists have conceptualized the curriculum development process. The *academic model* assumes that "curriculum development is a systematic process governed by academic rationality and theoretical logic" (p. 122). It also suggests that most curriculum decisions should be made by specialists, and that these decisions are guided by objective criteria, such as the Tyler rationale (Tyler, 1949), that can be applied universally. The *experiential model* is the reverse of the academic model. It concedes that the curriculum-creation process is a subjective, particularistic, and transactional endeavor in which the personal experiences and active involvement of students and teachers and the environmental contexts are primary factors. The *technical model* of curriculum development is, essentially, a "scientific production" approach to instructional planning that emphasizes "systems" and "management" principles. It was first articulated by Bobbitt (1918) in his references to instructional planning as "educational engineering" and "scientific curriculum-making." While the academic model appeals to academic rationality and theoretical logic to guide its decision making, and the experiential model emphasizes sociocultural and personal contexts, the technical model of curriculum development employs the logic of systems analysis, empiricism, scientific objectivity, and managerial efficiency.

A *pragmatic approach* to curriculum development is essentially an eclectic, political, reactive, and often fragmentary process. Decker Walker (1971) calls it a "naturalistic model" of curriculum development. Thus, a pragmatic approach to curriculum planning is

a particularistic, localized process that is specific to the sociopolitical milieu of school context in which it occurs. It concentrates on what individuals do in the daily operations of school bureaucracies to answer questions about what should be taught and how curriculum should be determined, organized, and evaluated. Of particular interest are the informal political negotiations, power allocations, and consensus building that take place among different interest groups. (Gay, 1980, p. 137)

GENERAL THEORY CLASSIFICATIONS AND MULTICULTURALISM

Most multicultural education theorizing tends to be eclectic in nature, cutting across many of the categories identified above. This is due to several factors. First, multiculturalists bring a wide variety of disciplinary training and perspectives to bear upon their understanding and interpretations of multicultural education purposes, goals, content, methodologies, and benefits. Yet there is a strong element of substantive consensus that undergirds this perspective and methodological diversity. All the individuals and groups involved are seeking basically the same ultimate goals—a more effective educational system for culturally diverse students from a wide variety of backgrounds, and a more democratic society in which there is much greater equality, freedom, and justice in all spheres of life. They also agree that the achievement of these goals is dependent upon changes in knowledge, attitudes, values, and human relationships among diverse groups, as well as fundamental structural changes in social, political, economic, and educational institutions (Banks, 1990; Darder, 1991; Nieto, 1992; Suzuki, 1979, 1984).

Second, multicultural education is essentially an affective, humanistic, and transformative enterprise that is situated within the sociocultural, political, and historical contexts of the United States. Endeavors of this kind are less amenable to single perspectives and interpretations because they are so strongly influenced by values and beliefs. Therefore, it is not surprising that multicultural education generates eclectic theoretical explanations influenced by multiple disciplinary perspectives and the experiential viewpoints of many groups and individuals.

A third factor that helps account for the diversity and eclecticism within multicultural education theory, and is often mistaken for a lack of clarity or consensus on key points, is the various referent-group orientations that exist in the field. Some multiculturalists use ethnicity as their primary point of refer-

ence, while others emphasize gender, social class, and/or language diversity. These perspectives on common themes are analogous, in principle, to the diversity evident among general curriculum theorists. Some of them concentrate on the design process, but view it from a variety of vantage points; others do likewise with curriculum implementation, content, or evaluation.

Delpit (1988) provides some additional insights into why multiculturalists routinely incorporate multiple perspectives in their theorizing. She explains that students of color and poverty need to be taught the power codes and skills needed to participate fully in mainstream U.S. life, and strategies for personal fulfillment and social reform. This bicentric agenda accepts as legitimate the expert knowledge of educators and the experiential knowledge of students in creating valid, culturally pluralistic educational programs. Thus, multicultural education attends simultaneously to the personal and the social, content and process, microcultures and the macroculture, facts and experience, cognition and affect, rationality and intuition, self and others, and the past, present, and future. This eclectic orientation permeates and shapes almost all multicultural education theory and scholarship.

The concentration of multicultural education theory on personal development, social reform, and critical analysis is a logical consequence of the fact that it is fundamentally a reconstructive and transformative endeavor. Specifically, child-centeredness, social consciousness and civic responsibility, revisionist scholarship, educational equity, and social reconstruction are the benchmark principles of multicultural education theory. These are seen as operating dialectically to explain why multicultural education, in its substantive components and its effects or outcomes, is imperative for all students. Thus, multiculturalists point out that their domain has many intrinsic and instrumental values. It can improve the academic achievement of culturally diverse students, as well as facilitate skill development in critical thinking, problem solving, decision making, and social activism needed for the creation of a more humane, egalitarian, democratic, and just society. It has potential for improving the personal competencies and empowerment of all students. Furthermore, multicultural education is a means of acquiring a more accurate knowledge base about the legacies of the cultural diversity in the United States and the world (Asante, 1991/92; Banks, 1990, 1991; Bennett, 1990; Garcia, 1982; Gay, 1988; Hilliard, 1991/92; Nieto, 1992; Sleeter, 1991).

The essence of these explanations is summarized cogently by Hilliard (1991/92), Banks (1990), and Mitchell-Powell (1992). Hilliard makes an appeal for diminishing the culturally hegemonic Eurocentric dominance in the disciplinary knowledge taught to students by including the contributions of culturally diverse groups. He explains that:

The primary goal of a pluralistic curriculum process is to present a truthful and meaningful rendition of the whole human experience. . . . Ultimately, if the curriculum is centered in truth, it will be pluralistic, for the simple fact is that human culture is the product of the struggle of all humanity, not the possession of a single racial or ethnic group. . . . We must awaken to the fact that no academic content is neutral nor is the specific cultural content of any ethnic group universal in and by itself. . . . The search for truth is our highest goal. . . . To foster it we must facilitate in students . . . a critical orientation [for] no cultural tradition can be regarded as immune to criticism . . . nothing less than the full truth of the human experience is worthy of our schools and our students. (pp. 13–14)

Nieto (1992) agrees with Hilliard that no one "canon of knowledge" that stems from a single monocultural base can ever be effective for a culturally pluralistic society such as the United States. Crichlow, Goodwin, Shakes, and Schwartz (1990) offer additional support and clarification of this philosophical position. They credit multicultural demands for making explicit a "politics of representation," which historically has been implicit in U.S. education. This politics of representation "has to do with how a specific kind of knowledge, conception, or symbolic image of and about a thing, event, place or people is constructed" (p. 101). It also involves the "struggle over accuracy versus misrepresentation, emancipatory versus hegemonic scholarship, and the constructed supremacy of Western cultural knowledge transmitted in schools versus the inherent primacy of the multiple and collective origins of knowledge" (p. 102). Therefore, "no school can consider that it is doing a proper or complete job unless its students develop multicultural literacy" (Nieto, 1992, p. 212). Or, as O'Connor (1989, p. 69) suggests, "teaching must always be engaged in multivoiced dialogues." One of these critical voices must be ethnicity (Garcia, 1982). To provide less is to ensure that some cultural voices and traditions will be silenced, and that some culturally and ethnically diverse students will be left confused, alienated, resistant, and uneducated. These observations are consistent with the AACTE (1973) policy statement that there is "no one model American," which concurs that no one individual's or group's tradition, culture, experience, or canon is universally valid.

Banks (1990) makes a similar argument in his interpretation of the knowledge reconstruction and social transformational themes embedded in multicultural education. He enables educators to recognize that the knowledge taught in schools is a form of cultural capital, and is a social construction that reflects the values, perspectives, and experiences of the dominant ethnic group. It systematically ignores or diminishes the validity and significance of the life experiences and contributions of ethnic and cultural groups that historically have been vanquished, marginalized, and silenced (Banks, 1990, 1991, 1991/92). Delpit (1988), McElroy-Johnson (1993), Darder (1991), and Crichlow et al. (1990) suggest that this kind of intellectual discrimination and oppression can be corrected by giving voice to those groups and cultural traditions long silenced in U.S. society and schools. "Voice" is the power of affirmation, derived from seeing one's cultural heritage accurately represented in school programs, as well as the ability of individual students to express ideas and direct and shape their lives toward a productive fulfillment of psychological and social needs. It is a sense of identity, self, relationships with others, purpose, and ethics (McElroy-Johnson, 1993).

Distorted and hegemonic research and scholarship practices can be corrected by revising the traditional canons of knowledge, and shifting the paradigms that govern mainstream educational values, structures, procedures, and programs. This shift should be toward the inclusion of more diverse representational frameworks in school knowledge and greater emancipatory teaching. Asante (1991/92), Bernal (1987), Drake (1987), and Van Sertima (1985) offer examples of how this works for African Americans. They provide new information and alternative interpretations about culture in ancient Africa and its influences in shaping contemporary African American cultural values and points of view. Different groups and cultures should be portrayed as producers, not just consumers of knowledge, and students should be exposed to multiple ways of knowing, thinking, and being (Crichlow et al., 1990). These transformations are imperative because all youths in the United States must understand that "the future of America is in their hands and that they can shape a new society when the torch is passed to their generation" (Banks, 1990, p. 213). A key part of the preparation for this future is the acquisition of an accurate base about the history, culture, contribution, and contemporary life of different ethnic and cultural groups. This new knowledge will help educators to design instructional programs that more accurately represent the contributions, experiences, and perspectives of all people. As a result, these students might be inspired to pursue vigorously the American ideals of freedom, equality, and justice in education, scholarship, and society (Asante, 1991/92; Banks, 1990; Hilliard, 1991/92).

Mitchell-Powell (1992)—speaking in a tone and text reminiscent of Hilliard, Nieto, Banks, O'Connor, and Crichlow and colleagues—highlights the themes of personal empowerment, knowledge reconstruction, and social reform ingrained in multicultural education. In her editor's notes to the April 1992 issue of *Multicultural Review,* she advises the readership (primarily librarians) to understand that appreciation of the U.S. common culture and values is enhanced by a recognition of the multiplicity of contributions that various groups have made. Moreover, for children to survive and prosper in a society and world destined for dramatic demographic, economic, social, and political changes, multicultural education is a necessity. Henry (1990) raises basically the same points and consequences in his assessment of the broad-based effects of "the browning of America" on schools and society. Barber (1992) makes a compelling argument that anticanonical curricular innovations and multiculturalism are fundamentally products of Western cultural ideals. Their key underlying ideas and principles include:

a conviction that individuals and groups have a right to self-determination; a belief in human equality coupled with a belief in human autonomy; the tenet which holds that domination in social relations, however grounded, is always illegitimate; and the principle that reason and the knowledge issuing from reason are themselves socially embedded in personal biography and social history, and thus in power relations. . . . (p. 147)

Virtually all multicultural educators endorse these arguments, and agree with the conclusion that when we educate our children for cultural pluralism, we enrich and empower ourselves, and come closer to achieving a truly democratic civic society (Mitchell-Powell, 1992).

Another common theme in multicultural education theory that makes it consonant with process-, society-, child-, and reformist-centered general curriculum theories is the evocation of the social milieu and how it affects educational decision making. Invariably, changing school demographics, disparities in educational opportunities, economic resources, and political power along ethnic, racial, class, and gender lines, and the school achievement of many students of color are cited in explaining why multicultural education is necessary, and how it should be implemented. These explanations include critical analyses perspectives, as well as deconstructive and transformative proposals for reforming schools and society.

Several recent suggestions are illustrative of these trends in multicultural education theory. Banks (1990), Bennett (1990), Nieto (1992), and Sleeter and Grant (1988) suggest that the goal of education is not merely to teach students to fit into the existing workforce, social order, and political structure, but to transform them. Conceding to the status quo "would be inimical to students from different cultural groups because it would force them to experience self alienation [since it fails] to incorporate their voices, experiences, and perspectives" (Banks, 1990, p. 211). Gay (1990) explains how the changing school demographic trends are creating a significant "social distance" between students and teachers, and how this may further complicate making schooling relevant to the personal lives of culturally diverse students. She predicts that these social, cultural, and experiential gaps will make "achieving educational equality even more unlikely in the existing structure of schooling" (p. 61).

This sample of a few prominent individuals, ideas, and explanations represents directional trends in multicultural education theory, and illustrates how they are compatible with some of the emphases and analyses in general curriculum theory. However, this is not the only kind of development taking place in multicultural education theory. Some classification schemata are emerging that are unique to the field, and serve better to organize and illuminate theoretical developments specific to multicultural education. These are not as inclusive, comprehensive, or crystallized as general curriculum theories—a reflection, undoubtedly, of the relative youth of multicultural education, an area of inquiry that has been in existence less than 25 years.

Many of the efforts at developing discrete classifications of multicultural education knowledge focus on distinguishing among the content emphasis, conceptual complexity, and outcome intentions of various program designs. Attempts of this kind have been made by several different educators and social scientists. Those by Gibson (1976) and Sleeter and Grant (1988) are of major and formative significance. They are prototypical because other multicultural educators have either built upon them or developed independent classification schemata that approximate their conceptual patterns, developmental directions, and descriptive features. For those reasons, the Gibson and the Sleeter and Grant models are discussed in greater detail. Elements of other classifications are juxtaposed to show the parallels that exist among multiculturalists in how they organize various approaches to teaching cultural pluralism.

The classifications tend to exemplify Gay's (1983, 1992) con-

tention that since its inception, multicultural education theory has been continually evolving and becoming more comprehensive, inclusive, integrative, transformative, and scholarly. This growth is evident in the greater depth of analysis, clarity of meaning, and power of persuasion with which proponents talk about issues central to multicultural education, and the linkages they are making between their particular concerns and more general educational priorities such as academic excellence, school reform, knowledge construction, and equity (Gay, 1992).

Gibson's (1976) classifications are especially noteworthy because she was one of the first to provide a conceptual, developmental framework for organizing various approaches to multicultural education. Five approaches emerged from her review of advocacy literature on teaching for and about cultural pluralism based in ethnicity. The first is *education of the culturally different*, or *benevolent multiculturalism*, the focus of which is helping students develop skills to assimilate into mainstream culture and society. The second approach, *education about cultural pluralism*, emphasizes teaching all students culturally diverse knowledge as a basis for promoting better cross-cultural and interethnic group understanding. *Education for cultural pluralism*, the third approach, concentrates on preserving the cultures and increasing the political power of ethnic minority groups. *Bicultural education* is the fourth approach, which prioritizes teaching ethnically diverse students skills needed to function effectively in their own microcultures and in the macroculture of the United States. This was as far as the field had advanced at the time of her analysis of the related scholarship, but Gibson saw the need for yet another approach to multicultural education.

Gibson proposed a fifth possibility, *multicultural education as the normal human experience*, wherein students would be taught to operate in a multiplicity of cultural contexts as a routine part of their regular educational experiences. Her proposal was prophetic in that multiculturalists came to embrace and advocate this idea and to define teaching strategies associated with it. They support this stance with arguments to the effect that multicultural education is inherent to good quality education for all students, and cultural pluralism is descriptive of the personal, social, and national realities of the United States and the world (Nieto, 1992; Parekh, 1986; Suzuki, 1979, 1984).

The most ambitious effort to date to organize scholarship systematically in the field of multicultural education was undertaken by Grant and Sleeter (1985; Sleeter & Grant, 1987, 1988). They compiled a list of approximately 200 articles on multicultural education, reviewed them, and classified them on the basis of their major themes, emphases, goals, content areas, and referent group orientations. The research technique is similar to that used by Schubert (1980) to catalog publications in the field of general curriculum. It builds upon the conceptual framework introduced by Gibson, but broadens the units of analysis to include gender, class, and exceptionality, as well as ethnicity.

The Sleeter and Grant (1988; Grant & Sleeter, 1993; Sleeter, 1991) analyses generated five prevalent techniques in multicultural education practice. They parallel Gibson's specific categories, as well as the underlying theme. That is, the relationship among the various approaches is historical, developmental, progressional, and cumulative with respect to conformity to existing educational and societal structures, versus their reform and transformation. The first approach, *teaching the culturally different,* is the most traditional and assimilationist, and analogous to Gibson's stage of "education *of* the culturally different." It emphasizes teaching to students who are different from the mainstream the cognitive skills, language, and values required to function in existing structures. It is guided by a "deficit philosophy" and often takes the form of compensatory programs such as Upward Bound, Headstart, Outreach, and English-language immersion. Pratte (1983) identifies a similar category in his typology of education for cultural pluralism as "restricted multicultural education."

The second category in Sleeter and Grant's classification of multicultural education approaches is *human relations.* It is similar to Gibson's "education *about* cultural differences" and Pratte's "modified restricted multicultural education" approaches, and is reminiscent of the 1950s intergroup education movement. All of these give priority to promoting intergroup harmony through a variety of instructional strategies to teach cultural awareness, prejudice and stereotype reduction, and group identity and pride. The expected outcomes are respect, tolerance, appreciation, and acceptance among diverse groups; self-respect; and understanding the interdependence of groups and individuals.

Because the third approach to multicultural education focuses on acquiring knowledge, awareness, respect, and acceptance of one group at a time, Sleeter and Grant identify it as *single-group studies.* The target group of analysis can be based on ethnicity, social class, gender, or exceptionality. Students learn about the targeted group's culture, contributions, and forms of oppression, as well as its perspectives, experiences, and current and historical struggles. The single-group approach to multicultural education also

views school knowledge as political rather than neutral and presents alternatives to the existing Eurocentric, male-dominant curriculum. It focuses on one specific group at a time so the history, perspectives, and worldview of that group can be developed coherently. It also examines the current social status of the group and actions taken . . . to further the interests of the group. . . .

The single-group studies approach views the student as an active learner, constantly seeking truth and knowledge and committed to reflecting on his or her learning. . . . The student works to develop what Freire calls a "critical consciousness." (Grant & Sleeter, 1993, p. 54)

Several other educators include parallel categories in their organizational schemata, but with some modifications. For example, Gay (1977) refers to her analogous category as "mono-minority studies," and restricts the referent groups to ethnicity. Comparable levels in Banks's (1993a) categories are described as "contributions" and "additive" approaches. Pratte (1983) uses "modified restricted multicultural education" to refer to curricular efforts to treat ethnic groups separately but equally. Level I in the Baptiste (1986, 1994) typology, which is product focused, encompasses all of Sleeter and Grant's first three approaches. Single-focus groups and events—such as ethnic celebrations, cultural contributions, and artifacts—and specific top-

ics or courses are added to the regular school curricula to teach culturally different, human relations, and single-group studies.

The fourth approach that emerged from the analysis by Grant and Sleeter of the literature on cultural pluralism in schools was *multicultural education.* Like the three preceding categories, it, too, emphasizes prejudice reduction, equal educational opportunities, social justice, and affirmation of cultural diversity. Its distinguishing procedures include dealing with multiple groups at the same time, reforming the total schooling process, and making all students benefactors of culturally sensitive education. The organizing center or core of curriculum reform shifts from separate groups to common concepts, themes, issues, and concerns across groups. The perspectives of multiple groups inform the analyses of these common concerns. Various school practices are revised to model equality and pluralism or, as Asante (1991/92) suggests, to achieve pluralism without hierarchy.

Proponents of multicultural education also include conceptual schemes, experiential backgrounds, ways of thinking, and learning styles along with cultural contributions in planning school reform for cultural diversity. Thus, curriculum and instruction, content and climate, cognition and affect, and text and context are all essential elements to be included in changing schooling to make it more reflective of and responsive to cultural pluralism. For these reasons, Baptiste (1986, 1994) refers to this analogous approach in his typology as Level II, and describes it as emphasizing a process for incorporating multicultural products within the conceptual infrastructure or matrix of curriculum and instruction. It integrates culturally pluralistic concepts, content, perspectives, and experiences into all educational components. This category encompasses Gibson's (1976) view that diversity is endemic to the human experience—what Gay (1977) describes as "multiple-minority" and "ethnic studies"; Banks's (1993a) category of "transformation"; the idea of "knowledge redefinition" proposed by Cushner et al. (1992); and Kendall's (1983) thoughts on multiculturizing instructional materials and school/classroom climates. Its philosophical orientations, content emphases, and intended outcomes also parallel those of the "Four M Curriculum" (multilingual, multicultural, multimodel, and multidimensional) envisioned by Sizemore (1979).

Education that is multicultural and social reconstructionist is the fifth category in Grant and Sleeter's classifications. It is committed to developing the critical and analytical thinking abilities of students to improve understanding of the sociopolitical stratification in U.S. life by race, class, gender, and ability groups, and to teaching them how to engage in social action to reconstruct society, and how to empower themselves so that they can control their own destinies. The "comprehensive approach to human relations education" proposed by Colangelo, Dustin, and Foxley (1985) advocates a similar agenda, with multicultural education being grounded in efforts to transform human relations and rethink morality in human conduct. It approximates Level III in the Baptiste (1986, 1994) typology, in which educational leaders internalize the multicultural values and processes. These, along with a related philosophical orientation, permeate the entire educational environment. The expected outcome is social activism and reconstruction to eliminate discrimination, oppression, and inequities of all kinds among racial, ethnic, and cultural groups. This transformation involves accepting the tremendous variation within and among groups of people as an inherent trait of all members of the human family.

This reconstructionist aspect of multicultural education is consonant with Gibson's (1976) notion that cultural diversity is the normal human experience, and with the ideas of multivoiced representations and the emancipatory pedagogy championed by Crichlow et al. (1990), King and Wilson (1990), O'Connor (1989), and Sleeter (1991). These authors make overt and direct appeals for students to learn social and action skills in order to reconstruct society. Colangelo et al. (1985) make a more indirect appeal. They believe that a transformative human relations approach to multicultural, nonsexist education is more promising for achieving fundamental social reform. They consider this kind of education

a challenge of the most radical nature to the entire historical pattern of human interaction. It envisions both a present learning environment free of indignity and harrassment [sic] and the foundations of a future society in which civil and personal equality are [sic] the norm, not merely the ideal. Such a goal is "radical" ("at the root") and awesome. (p. ix)

The critical analysis, knowledge reconstruction, social transformation, and personal empowerment emphases of these authors are common themes in virtually all forms of and approaches to multicultural education beyond the most initial and formative ones. They are specifically identified in the theoretical conceptions of Bennett (1990), Banks (1991/92, 1992, 1993a, 1993b, 1993c), Sleeter (1991), Nieto (1992), Banks and Banks (1993), Adams, Pardo and Schniedewind (1991/92), Gay (1993), Kendall (1983), and Sleeter and Grant (1988; Grant & Sleeter, 1993). Banks (1992) summarizes the functions of a curriculum of this kind:

A curriculum designed to empower students must be transformative in nature and help students to develop the knowledge, skills, and values needed to become social critics who can make reflective decisions and implement their decisions in effective personal, social, political, and economic action.
The transformative curriculum must help students to reconceptualize and rethink the experience of humans in both the United States and the world, to view the human experience from the perspective of a range of cultural, ethnic, and social-class groups, and to construct their own versions of the past, present, and future . . . multiple voices must be heard and legitimized. (p. 159)

Such curricula will be consistent with the basic mission of the multicultural education movement. That is, "to challenge oppression, and to use schooling . . . to help shape a future America that is more equal, democratic, and just, and that does not demand conformity to one cultural norm" (Sleeter, 1989, p. 63).

Gay (1992) analyzes the growth patterns of multicultural education theory that can be extrapolated from the various ways it is conceptualized, and how related implementation techniques are described. Evolvement of the theory from its

inception in the late 1960s to the present has been developmental and progressional, and grounded in some of the ideological framework of many common values, ideals, and principles of U.S. education in general. Gay concludes that multicultural discourse is characterized by increasing ideological depth, logical coherency, and pedagogical prowess. Out of these emerges a protrayal of multicultural education as an interdisciplinary, integrative, inclusive, comprehensive, transformative, liberative, and celebatory enterprise. Therefore, a "central theme of most theoretical perceptions of multicultural education is its potential for revolutionizing education and, ultimately, revitalizing society" (1992, p. 53).

MODELS OF MULTICULTURAL CURRICULUM DEVELOPMENT

Another theory-building activity closely related to developing classification systems for organizing knowledge about curriculum is the creation of models. They clarify, illustrate, and visualize key principles, concepts, components, and relationships in the area of inquiry. Beauchamp (1968) suggests that "It makes little difference whether models are 'borrowed' from other areas of knowledge or whether they are developed indigenously within the framework of curriculum constructs (p. 74). Thus, their functional utility is more important than their originality.

Since multicultural education is an eclectic field, it is not surprising that its theorists use elements from different conceptual models in other disciplines to construct their own. For example, Banks (1991) and Bennett (1990) often refer to Gordon Allport's (1958) work on the nature of prejudice and his social contact theory to develop antiracist and prejudice-reduction themes in multicultural education. Gay (1985) borrows from social and developmental psychologists such as William Cross (1991) and Erik Erikson (1968) in constructing models of ethnic identity development within the context of multiculturalism. Increasingly, educators such as Sleeter (1989, 1991), Sleeter and Grant (1988), Ladson-Billings and Henry (1990), King and Wilson (1990), Crichlow et al. (1990), and Darder (1991) are contextualizing multicultural education within critical theory traditions. Still others are using elements from representative democracy, interpersonal communications, ecological psychology, market-driven economics, cultural anthropology, the social construction of knowledge, and the sociology of organizational change to crystallize and communicate more effectively what multicultural education means, conceptually and operationally. These efforts are still rather formative and emerging. They are often restricted to segments of multicultural education rather than encompassing the entire field, and lack complete details. Therefore, it is more appropriate to think of multicultural education models as minimodels, partial models, or skeletal outlines of models.

Three types of models are included here as representative samples of the trends evident in the field. Bennett (1990) borrows from the 1948 United Nations Declaration of Human Rights, and from Native American traditional philosophy on respect for nature, to construct the core values of a "Model for Global and Multicultural Perspectives." Its four key democratic values are: (a) acceptance of cultural diversity, (b) respect for human dignity, (c) responsibility for global community, and (d) respect for planet earth. These values serve as guidelines for clarifying assumptions and as anchorpoints for grounding six main goals in conveying multicultural and global perspectives in education. The goals focus on multiple historical perspectives, cultural consciousness, intercultural competence, skills to combat racism and other forms of oppression, awareness about the state of the planet, and social actions skills. The dynamic interaction between the goals and values illustrates the close connections between multiculturalism and globalism, and their mutual concerns for human rights, understanding, justice, and equality.

Gay (1979) created an "Integrative Multicultural Basic Skills" (IMBS) model to demonstrate the interactive relationship between general education and multicultural curriculum planning. Of particular importance are principles of developmental growth, routine curriculum planning, and systemic change, and their implications for infusing multiculturalism into core learning skills and educational operations. The IMBS model comprises a set of three concentric circles that are reciprocally, interactively related.

The first set of circles represents the *core* of curriculum decision making—that is, universal basic skills routinely taught in schools, such as literacy, critical thinking, problem solving, and subject-specific techniques. The next layer of circles contains the activities that educators view as essential to curriculum creation. These include determining student needs, selecting instructional content and materials, identifying student activities and teaching behaviors, and choosing performance appraisal tools and techniques. The third circle is multicultural resources. It surrounds and encases the other two. This configuration suggests that multicultural resources (culturally pluralistic contributions, perspectives, experiences, histories, cultures) should provide the ecological settings and points of reference for all operational decisions made about curriculum planning for teaching basic skills to all students. When the IMBS model is used to design and implement instructional programs, students cannot avoid learning about cultural pluralism if they succeed in learning basic academic skills, because the former serves as the context and text for mastery of the latter.

Later, Gay (1988) further elaborates the underlying principle of *infusion* embedded in the IMBS model. She makes several suggestions intended to explicate some of the operational implications of infusing multiculturalism throughout the educative process. Among them are:

- Multicultural curriculum planning is an exercise in translating, integrating, and synthesizing knowledge about cultural pluralism.
- Using alternative culturally pluralistic pedagogical strategies to achieve common educational outcomes for diverse students is imperative for effective multicultural education.
- Distinguishing between curricular instructional input factors and expectations for achievement outcomes is essential.

- Distinctions between intrinsic (substantive) and instrumental (methodological) features of curriculum and instruction must be made, and the instrumental elements should be the first tiers of curriculum reform for cultural pluralism.

Three types of multicultural education model have been developed by Banks (1991). The first visualizes the idea that the organizing center or core of multicultural curriculum should be key concepts, topics, themes, events, and/or experiences common to all groups, but analyzed from the perspectives of multiple groups. He adds an international dimension to this basic construct by demonstrating how "ethno-national analyses" can be incorporated into the study of major issues affecting all groups. For example, a multiethnic model of the study of oppression would have students analyzing this issue from the perspectives of various ethnic groups in the United States, such as African Americans, Chinese Americans, and Jewish Americans. An ethnonational model would focus on how the oppression of similar groups has operated in other countries such as Germany, England, Argentina, and Japan. Thus, these models demonstrate the difference among mainstream centric, ethnic additive, multiethnic, and ethnonational approaches to multicultural education, relative to their central focus or organizing core.

Banks (1991) also has designed visual models to illustrate the principles of analyzing comparative ethnic and cultural perspectives on key social issues, and using interdisciplinary conceptual approaches to multicultural education. Both build upon three other ideas commonly advanced in multicultural education theory: (a) the interdependence of ethnic and cultural groups in the United States; (b) the contributions and influence of diverse ethnic, cultural, and social groups in shaping the life and culture of the United States and humankind; and (c) the need to use interdisciplinary, conceptual techniques to achieve maximum effectiveness in teaching multicultural education.

The third type of multicultural education model created by Banks (1991) demonstrates the relationships between the various microcultures and the macroculture of the United States. These relationships are depicted as being simultaneously distinct, overlapping, interactive, and reciprocal. The models indicate that members of ethnic groups have some cultural characteristics that are not shared with other groups; some traits that are shared with some but not with other ethnic groups; and some traits that are shared by all ethnic groups by virtue of their being citizens of the United States and members of humankind. These models also illustrate the idea proposed by most multicultural theorists that students need to become multicultural and develop cross-cultural social competencies so they can function comfortably in their own, others', and the national cultures.

The discussion above indicates that the major activities essential to curriculum theory building are evident in multicultural education scholarship. However, many are still emerging and are not yet competely definitive. This is not unexpected, given the relative youth of the field. It is encouraging to note that the field is developing along lines that scholars have identified as imperative for an area of inquiry to reach conceptual and scholarly maturity. Given sufficient time and continuation of the developmental directions it is currently pursuing, multicultural education will achieve the distinction of being a mature field of study with a fully developed theory of its own.

CONCLUSIONS AND IMPLICATIONS FOR FUTURE DIRECTIONS

The major premise undergirding the discussion presented in this chapter was that developments in multicultural education scholarship meet the general criteria of curriculum theorizing. The conceptual model of curriculum theorizing created by George Beauchamp (1968) was used to examine this idea. The analysis revealed that almost all of the elements Beauchamp identified as essential to curriculum theory building are present in multicultural education scholarship. These include defining the key concepts and parameters of the field; classifying knowledge in multicultural education; building models to clarify and explain the imperative of educating for cultural pluralism; and constructing subtheories to clarify issues related to the design, implementation, and evaluation of multicultural education. This examination also indicated that the field exhibits many of the same growth trends that are characteristic of other types of curriculum theorizing at comparable stages of development. It suggests further that multicultural education is well on the way to becoming a mature curriculum theory in its own right.

Another noteworthy observation emerged from the analysis. A high degree of consensus exists among multiculturalists on the major principles, concepts, concerns, and directions for changing educational systems to make them more representative of and responsive to the cultural pluralism that exists in the United States and the world. Differences are located more in semantics, points of emphasis, and constituent-group orientations than in the substantive content of what constitutes the core and essence of multicultural education. This observation defies the claims of many critics that multicultural education is chaotic, confused, lacking in conceptual clarity, and devoid of a consensual voice. A more comprehensive examination of this consensus needs to be conducted. The results will be helpful in minimizing some of the confusion about the purpose and meanings of multicultural education. They also will crystallize the fundamental elements of the field. These, in turn, can become quality-control criteria for designing multicultural education programs and determining their adequacy and effectiveness.

The analytical technique used in this chapter is a form of metacognition that allows for a productive and enriching reflective dialogue on multicultural education to take place. It provides a precedent and a methodology for future analysis on how multicultural education is related to other dimensions, trends, and priorities in U.S. educational theory and practice. The field has reached a level of conceptual maturity to warrant more analyses of this kind that explore how multicultural education illustrates universal pedagogical principles, and how it can be appropriately centered within U.S. educational and democratic ideals.

Two other lines of analytical inquiry worthy of pursuit are similar in kind and purpose to the one undertaken in this chapter. First is the premise that multicultural education is not ahistorical, nor does it exist in a theoretical void represented by other educational innovations and egalitarian initiatives. Many ideological analogues exist for the major principles and concerns of multicultural education in the United States. These are located in programs that attempt to extend the democratic principles of human dignity, equality, justice, and freedom to the educational arena. Similarities among these and other basic tenets of multicultural education need to be explicated. Some possibilities are progressive, affective, humanistic, open, alternative, developmental, and critical theory education. The analyses should demonstrate how each of these initiatives is a variation on the common consensus of (2) reforming education for the benefit of students who are underserved by schools, (b) being more inclusive and comprehensive by teaching the whole child, and (c) aligning schooling with the promises of democratic ideals.

The second set of analytical inquiries should explicate the commonly proclaimed contention that multicultural education is a methodological conduit, tool, or bridge for making the schooling process more relevant, representational, and effective for ethnically and culturally different students. Often these claims are made without sufficient explanation relative to their practical operations. The absence of these details limits the potential of multicultural education significantly, as well as making it susceptible to misinterpretations and distortions. Carefully executed analyses that explain the *operational* elements of multicultural education, which can be used to improve teaching and learning at the *functional level,* will be a significant contribution to its theory and practice. They also will generate a rich body of variables and hypotheses—capable of being tested empirically—about which operational features are most effective, and under what kinds of conditions.

Needing further analysis among these prominent bridging potentials of multiculturalism to make general education more successful for culturally different students are: matching teaching and learning styles; extending the democratic principles of equality, freedom, and justice to the operations of the educational enterprise; improving the empowerment of students through self-affirmation; developing personal competence and sociopolitical efficacy; increasing mastery of basic literary and subject-matter skills; and using culturally specific alternative materials and means to teach common learning outcomes to diverse students. Educational practitioners and researchers need help in specifying the action or behavioral dimension of these principles before they can act responsibly upon them. In fact, decisions to act on or not to act on implementation of multicultural education may be direct reflections of the extent to which educators understand it operationally. Therefore, more analytical research and scholarship in multicultural education are imperative to its future survival, integrity, and progress.

Future reflective analysis undoubtedly will reveal that multicultural education is very Western and American in spirit and intent. It grew out of a libertarian philosophy, and embodies its major principles. It falls well within the "critical and alternative voice traditions" of U.S. education. It shares with critics of this persuasion the belief that the democratic and human rights imperatives demand that existing educational programs, structures, and practices be reformed to make them more accessible and responsive to groups that historically have been oppressed, silenced, and disenfranchised educationally, economically, and politically.

Educational equity and excellence for all children in the United States are unattainable without the incorporation of cultural pluralism in all aspects of the educational process. Curriculum design is a key function in this process, and a powerful avenue through which multiculturalism can penetrate the core of the educational enterprise. Consequently, more exploration of the interconnections between specific types of curricular innovations and ideologies and particular elements of multicultural education is fundamental to conscientious efforts to maximize school success for students from diverse racial, ethnic, cultural, and social-class backgrounds.

References

Adams, B. S., Pardo, W. E., & Schniedewind, N. (1991/92). Changing "the way we do things around here." *Educational Leadership, 49,* 37–42.

Allport, G. (1958). *The nature of prejudice.* Garden City, NY: Doubleday.

America 2000: An education strategy. (1991). Washington, DC: U.S. Department of Education.

American Association of Colleges for Teacher Education. (1973). *No one model American.* Washington, DC: Author.

Apple, M. W. (1979). *Ideology and curriculum.* London: Routledge & Kegan Paul.

Aronowitz, S., & Giroux, H. A. (1990). *Education under seige: The conservative, liberal, and radical debate over schooling.* South Hadley, MA: Bergin & Garvey.

Asante, M. (1991/92). Afrocentric curriculum. *Educational Leadership, 49,* 28–31.

Banks, J. A. (Ed.). (1973). *Teaching ethnic studies: Concepts and strategies* (43rd yearbook). Washington, DC: National Council for the Social Studies.

Banks, J. A. (1977). Pluralism and educational concepts: A clarification. *Peabody Journal of Education, 54,* 73–78.

Banks, J. A. (Ed.). (1981). *Education in the 80s: Multiethnic education.* Washington, DC: National Education Association.

Banks, J. A. (1990). Citizenship education for a pluralistic democratic society. *The Social Studies, 81,* 210–214.

Banks, J. A. (1991). *Teaching strategies for ethnic studies* (5th ed.). Boston: Allyn and Bacon.

Banks, J. A. (1991/92). Multicultural education: For freedom's sake. *Educational Leadership, 49,* 32–36.

Banks, J. A. (1992). A curriculum for empowerment, action and change, In K. A. Moodley (Ed.), *Beyond multicultural education: International perspectives* (pp. 154–170). Calgary, Alberta: Detselig Enterprises.

Banks, J. A. (1993a). Approaches to multicultural curriculum reform. In J. A. Banks & C. A. M. Banks (Eds.), *Multicultural education: Issues and perspectives* (2nd ed., pp. 195–214). Boston: Allyn and Bacon.

Banks, J. A. (1993b). The canon debate, knowledge construction, and multicultural education. *Educational Researcher, 22*(5), 4–14.

Banks, J. A. (1993c). Multicultural education: Characteristics and goals. In J. A. Banks & C. A. M. Banks (Eds.), *Multicultural education: Issues and perspectives* (2nd ed., pp. 2–26). Boston: Allyn and Bacon.

Banks, J. A., & Banks, C. A. M. (Eds.). (1993). *Multicultural Education: Issues and perspectives* (2nd ed.). Boston: Allyn and Bacon.

Banks, J. A., Cortés, C. E., Garcia, R. L., Gay, G., & Ochoa, A. S. (1976). *Curriculum guidelines for multiethnic education.* Washington, DC: National Council for the Social Studies.

Banks, J. A., Cortés, C. E., Garcia, R. L., Gay, G., & Ochoa, A. S. (1992). *Curriculum guidelines for multicultural education* (rev. ed.). Washington, DC: National Council for the Social Studies.

Banks, J. A., & Lynch, J. (Eds.). (1986). *Multicultural education in Western societies.* New York: Holt, Rinehart and Winston.

Baptiste, H. P. (1979). *Multicultural education: A synopsis.* Washington, DC: University Press of America.

Baptiste, H. P. (1986). Multicultural education and urban schools from a sociohistorical perspective: Internalizing multiculturalism. *Journal of Educational Equity and Leadership, 6,* 295–312.

Baptiste, H. P. (1994). The multicultural environment of schools: Implications to leaders. In L. W. Hughes (Ed.), *The principal as leader* (pp. 89–109). New York: Merrill/Macmillan.

Barbe, W. B., & Swassing, R. H. (1979). *Teaching through modality strengths: Concepts and practices.* Columbus, OH: Zaner-Bloser.

Barber, B. R. (1992). *An aristocracy of everyone: The politics of education and the future of America.* New York: Ballantine.

Baruth, L. G., & Manning, J. L. (1992). *Multicultural education of children and adolescents.* Boston: Allyn and Bacon.

Beauchamp, G. A. (1968). *Curriculum theory* (2nd ed.). Wilmette, IL: The Kagg Press.

Bennett, C. I. (1990). *Comprehensive multicultural education: Theory and practice* (2nd ed.). Boston: Allyn and Bacon.

Bernal, M. (1987). *Black athena: The Afroasiatic roots of classical civilization* (Vol. 1). London: Free Association Books.

Bobbitt, F. (1918). *The curriculum.* Boston: Houghton Mifflin.

Bruner, J. S. (1960). *The process of education.* Cambridge, MA: Harvard University Press.

California State Department of Education. (1979). *Planning for multicultural education as a part of school improvement.* Sacramento: Office of Intergroup Relations.

Colangelo, N., Dustin, D., & Foxley, C. H. (Eds.). (1985). *Multicultural nonsexist education: A human relations approach.* Dubuque, IA: Kendall/Hunt.

Combs, A. W. (Ed.). (1962). *Perceiving, behaving, becoming: A new focus for education.* Washington, DC: Association for Supervision and Curriculum Development.

Counts, G. (1932). *Dare the schools build a new social order?* Carbondale: Southern Illinois University Press.

Crichlow, W., Goodwin, S., Shakes, G., & Swartz, E. (1990). Multicultural ways of knowing: Implications for practice. *Journal of Education, 172,* 101–117.

Crittenden, B. (1982). *Cultural pluralism and common curriculum.* Melbourne, Australia: Melbourne University Press.

Cross, W. E., Jr. (1991). *Shades of black: Diversity in African-American identity.* Philadelphia: Temple University Press.

Cushner, K., McClelland, A, & Safford, P. (1992). *Human diversity in education: An integrative approach.* New York: McGraw-Hill.

Darder, A. (1991). *Culture and power in the classroom: A critical foundation for bicultural education.* New York: Bergin & Garvey.

Delpit, L. D. (1988). The silenced dialogue: Power and pedagogy in educating other people's children. *Harvard Educational Review, 58,* 280–298.

Dewey, J. (1897). *My pedagogic creed.* New York: E. L. Kellogg.

Dewey, J. (1902). *The child and the curriculum*. Chicago: University of Chicago Press.

Dewey, J. (1916). *Democracy and education*. New York: Macmillan.

Diaz, C. (Ed.). (1992). *Multicultural education for the 21st Century*. Washington DC: National Education Association.

Drake, St. C. (1987). *Black folk here and now* (Vol. 1). Los Angeles: Center for Afro-American Studies, University of California.

Education that works: An action plan for the education of minorities. (1990). Cambridge: Massachusetts Institute of Technology, Quality Education for Minorities Project.

Eisner, E. W. (Ed.). (1985). *Learning and teaching: The ways of knowing* (84th Yearbook of the National Society for the Study of Education, Part II). Chicago: University of Chicago Press.

Eisner, E. W., & Vallance E. (Eds.). (1974). *Conflicting conceptions of curriculum*. Berkeley, CA: McCutchan.

Entwistle, H. (1970). *Child-centered education*. London: Methuen.

Erikson, E. H. (1968). *Identity, youth, and crisis*. New York: Norton.

Foshay, A. W. (1975). *Essays on curriculum*. New York: A. W. Foshay Fund, Columbia University.

Frazier, A. (1976). *Adventuring, mastering, associating: New strategies for teaching children*. Washington, DC: Association for Supervision and Curriculum Development.

Frazier, L. (1977). Multicultural facet of education. *Journal of Research and Development in Education, 11*, 10–16.

Garcia, R. L. (1982). *Teaching in a pluralistic society: Concepts, models, strategies*. New York: Harper & Row.

Gardner, H. (1983). *Frames of mind: The theory of multiple intelligences*. New York: Basic Books.

Gay, G. (1977). Changing conceptions of multicultural education. *Educational Perspectives, 16*, 4–9.

Gay, G. (1979). On behalf of children: A curriculum design for multicultural education in the elementary school. *Journal of Negro Education, 48*, 324–340.

Gay, G. (1980). Conceptual models of the curriculum-planning process. In A. W. Foshay (Ed.), *Considered action for curriculum improvement* (pp. 120–143). Alexandria, VA: Association for Supervision and Curriculum Development.

Gay, G. (1983). Multicultural education: Historical developments and future prospects. *Phi Delta Kappan, 64*, 560–563.

Gay, G. (1985). Implications of selected models of ethnic identity development for educators. *Journal of Negro Education, 54*, 43–55.

Gay, G. (1988). Designing relevant curricula for diverse learners. *Education and Urban Society, 20*, 327–340.

Gay, G. (1990). Achieving educational equality through curriculum desegregation. *Phi Delta Kappan, 70*, 56–62.

Gay, G. (1992). The state of multicultural education in the United States. In K. A. Moodley (Ed.), *Beyond multicultural education: International perspectives* (pp. 41–65). Calgary, Alberta: Detselig Enterprises.

Gay, G. (1993). Building cultural bridges: A bold proposal for teacher education. *Education and Urban Society, 25*, 287–301.

Gay, G. (in press). General school curriculum and multicultural education. In C. A. Grant & M. L. Gomez (Eds.), *Campus and classroom: Making school multicultural*. Columbus, OH: Merrill.

Gibson, M. A. (1976). Approaches to multicultural education in the United States: Some concepts and assumptions. *Anthropology and Education, 7*, 7–18.

Giroux, H. A. (1983). *Theory and resistance in education: A pedagogy for the opposition*. South Hadley, MA: Bergin & Garvey.

Giroux, H. A. (1985). Critical pedagogy, cultural politics, and the discourse of experience. *Journal of Education, 167*, 22–41.

Giroux, H. A. (1988). *Teachers as intellectuals: Toward a critical pedagogy of learning*. South Hadley, MA: Bergin & Garvey.

Giroux, H. A. (1992). *Border crossings: Cultural workers and the politics of education*. New York: Routledge.

Giroux, H. A., & McLaren, P. (Eds.). (1989). *Critical pedagogy, the state, and cultural struggle*. Albany: State University of New York Press.

Giroux, H. A., Penna, A. N., & Pinar, W. F. (Eds.). (1981). *Curriculum and instruction: Alternatives in education*. Berkeley, CA: McCutchan.

Glatthorn, A. A. (1987). *Curriculum leadership*. Glenview, IL: Scott, Foresman.

Gollnick, D. M., & Chinn, P. C. (Eds.). (1990). *Multicultural education in a pluralistic society* (3rd ed.). Columbus, OH: Merrill.

Goodman, J. (1989). Education for critical democracy. *Journal of Education, 171*, 88–115.

Grant, C. A. (1977a). Education that is multicultural and P/CBTE: Discussion and recommendations for teacher education. In F. H. Klassen & D. M. Gollnick (Eds.), *Pluralism and the American teacher: Issues and case studies* (pp. 63–80). Washington, DC: Ethnic Heritage Center for Teacher Education of the American Association of Colleges for Teacher Education.

Grant, C. A. (1977b). *Multicultural education: Commitments, issues, and applications*. Washington, DC: Association for Supervision and Curriculum Development.

Grant, C. A. (1978). Education that is multicultural—Isn't that what we mean? *Journal of Teacher Education, 29*, 45–49.

Grant, C. A., & Sleeter, C. E. (1985). The literature on multicultural education: Review and analysis. *Educational Review, 37*, 97–118.

Grant, C. A., & Sleeter, C. E. (1993). Race, class, gender and disability in the classroom. In J. A. Banks & C. A. M. Banks (Eds.), *Multicultural education: Issues and perspectives* (2nd ed., pp. 48–67). Boston: Allyn and Bacon.

Henry, W. A., III. (1990, April 9). Beyond the melting pot. *Time, 135*, 28–31.

Hernandez, H. (1989). *Multicultural education: A teacher's guide to content and process*. Columbus, OH: Merrill.

Hilliard, A. G., III. (1991/92). Why we must pluralize the curriculum. *Educational Leadership, 29*, 12–14.

Huenecke, D. (1982). What is curriculum theorizing? What are its implications for practice? *Educational Leadership, 39*, 290–294.

Hunter, W. A. (Ed.). (1974). *Multicultural education through competency-based teacher education*. Washington, DC: American Association of Colleges for Teacher Education.

Jervis, K., & Montag, C. (Eds.). (1991). *Progressive education for the 1990s: Transforming practice*. New York: Teachers College Press.

Kendall, F. E. (1983). *Diversity in the classroom: A multicultural approach to the education of young children*. New York: Teachers College Press.

King, J. E., & Wilson, T. L. (1990). Being the soul-freeing substance: A legacy of hope in Afro humanity. *Journal of Education, 172*, 9–27.

Kreisberg, S. (1992). *Transforming power: Domination, empowerments, and education*. Albany: State University of New York Press.

Ladson-Billings, G., & Henry, A. (1990). Blurring the borders: Voices of African liberatory pedagogy in the United States and Canada. *Journal of Education, 172*, 72–88.

Lynch, J. (1986). *Multicultural education: Principles and practice*. Boston: Routledge and Kegan Paul.

Lynch, J. (1989). *Multicultural education in a global society*. New York: Falmer.

Macdonald, J. B. (1974). A transcendental developmental ideology in education. In W. F. Pinar (Ed.), *Heightened conscience, cultural revolution, and curriculum theory* (pp. 85–116). Berkeley, CA: McCutchan.

Macdonald, J. B. (1975). Curriculum and human interest. In W. F. Pinar

(Ed.), *Curriculum theorizing: The reconceptualists* (pp. 283–298). Berkeley, CA: McCutchan.

Macdonald, J. B. (1977). Value bases and issues in curriculum. In A. Molnar & J. A. Zahorik (Eds.), *Curriculum theory* (pp. 10–21). Washington, DC: Association for Supervision and Curriculum Development.

McElroy-Johnson, B. (1993). Giving voice to the voiceless. *Harvard Educational Review, 63,* 85–104.

McLaren, P. (1989). *Life in schools: An introduction to critical pedagogy in the foundations of education.* New York: Longman.

Miller, J., & Seller, W. (1985). *Curriculum perspectives and practice.* New York: Longman.

Mitchell-Powell, B. (1992). From the editor. *Multicultural Review, 1,* 3.

Modgil, S., Verma, G. K., Mallick, K., & Modgil, C. (Eds.). (1986). *Multicultural education: The interminable debate.* London: Falmer Press.

Molnar, A., & Zahorik, J. A. (Eds.). (1977). *Curriculum theory.* Washington, DC: Association for Supervision and Curriculum Development.

Moodley, K. A. (Ed.). (1992). *Beyond multicultural education: International perspectives.* Calgary, Alberta: Detselig Enterprises.

National Commission on Excellence in Education. (1983). *A nation at risk: The imperative for educational reform.* Washington, DC: Author.

National Council for the Accreditation of Teacher Education. (1987). *NCATE standards, procedures, and policies for the accreditation of professional education units.* Washington, DC: Author.

Nieto, S. (1992). *Affirming diversity: The sociopolitical context of multicultural education.* New York: Longman.

Novak, M. (1975). Variety is more than a slice of life. *Momentum, 6,* 24–27.

O'Connor, T. (1989). Cultural voice and strategies for multicultural education. *Journal of Education, 171,* 57–73.

Oliva, P. F. (1988). *Developing the curriculum* (2nd ed.). Glenview, IL: Scott, Foresman.

Orlosky, D. E., & Smith, B. O. (Eds.). (1978). *Curriculum development: Issues and insights.* Chicago: Rand McNally.

Ornstein, A. C., & Hunkins, F. P. (1988). *Curriculum: Foundations, principles, and issues.* Englewood Cliffs, NJ: Prentice-Hall.

Pai, Y. (1984). Cultural diversity and multicultural education. *Lifelong Learning, 7,* 7–9, 27.

Parekh, B. (1986). The concept of multicultural education. In S. Modgil, G. K. Verma, K. Mallick, & C. Modgil (Eds.), *Multicultural education: The interminable debate* (pp. 19–31). London: Falmer Press.

Phenix, P. H. (1964). *Realms of meaning: A philosophy of the curriculum for general education.* New York: McGraw-Hill.

Pinar, W. F. (Ed.). (1974). *Heightened consciousness, cultural revolution, and curriculum theory.* Berkeley, CA: McCutchan.

Pinar, W. F. (Ed.). (1975). *Curriculum theorizing: The reconceptualists.* Berkeley, CA: McCutchan.

Pratte, R. (1983). Multicultural education: Four normative arguments. *Educational Theory, 33,* 21–32.

Rogers, C. (1983). *Freedom to learn for the 80s.* Columbus, OH: Merrill.

Samuda, R. J., Berry, J. W., & Laferriere, M. (Eds.). (1984). *Multiculturalism in Canada: Some social and educational perspectives.* Boston: Allyn and Bacon.

Schubert, W. H. (1980). *Curriculum books: The first eighty years.* Lanham, MD: University Press of America.

Schubert, W. H. (1986). *Curriculum: Perspective, paradigm, and possibility.* New York: Macmillan.

Schwab, J. J. (1969). Education and the structure of the disciplines. In I. Westbury and N. J. Wilkof (Eds.), *Science, curriculum and liberal education* (pp. 229–270). Chicago: University of Chicago Press.

Schwab, J. J. (1970). *The practical: A language for curriculum.* Washington, DC: National Education Association.

Shane, H. G. (1981). *Educating for a new millennium.* Bloomington, IN: Phi Delta Kappa.

Shaver, J. P. (Ed.). (1991). *Handbook of research on social studies teaching and learning.* New York: Macmillan.

Shor, I., & Freire, P. (1987). *A pedagogy for liberation: Dialogues on transforming education.* South Hadley, MA: Bergin & Garvey.

Sizemore, B. (1979). The four M curriculum: A way to shape the future. *Journal of Negro Education, 47,* 341–356.

Sizemore, B. A. (1981). The politics of multicultural education. *Urban Education, 5,* 4–11.

Sleeter, C. E. (1989). Multicultural education as a form of resistance to oppression. *Journal of Education, 171,* 510–571.

Sleeter, C. E. (Ed.). (1991). *Empowerment through multicultural education.* Albany: State University of New York Press.

Sleeter, C. E., & Grant, C. A. (1987). An analysis of multicultural education in the U.S.A. *Harvard Educational Review, 57,* 421–444.

Sleeter, C. E., & Grant, C. A. (1988). *Making choices for multicultural education: Five approaches to race, class, and gender.* Columbus, OH: Merrill.

Smith, B. O., Stanley, W. O., and Shores, J. H. (1957). *Fundamentals of curriculum development.* Yonkers-on-Hudson, NY: World Book.

Suzuki, B. H. (1979). Multicultural education: What's it all about. *Integrateducation, 17,* 43–50.

Suzuki, B. H. (1984). Curriculum transformation for multicultural education. *Education and Urban Society, 16,* 294–322.

Swartz, E. (1989). *Multicultural curriculum development: A practical approach to curriculum development at the school level.* Rochester, NY: Rochester City School District.

Taba, H. (1962). *Curriculum development: Theory and practice.* New York: Harcourt, Brace & World.

Toffler, A. (Ed.). (1974). *Learning for tomorrow: The role of the future in education.* New York: Vintage Books.

Tye, B. B. (1987). The deep structure of schooling. *Phi Delta Kappan, 69,* 281–284.

Tyler, R. W. (1949). *Basic principles of curriculum and instruction.* Chicago: University of Chicago Press.

Van Sertima, I. (1985). *African presence in early Europe.* New Brunswick, NJ: Transactions Books.

Verma, G. K. (Ed.). (1989). *Education for all: A landmark in pluralism.* London: Falmer Press.

Walker, D. F. (1971). A naturalistic model for curriculum development. *School Review, 80,* 51–65.

Zais, R. S. (1976). *Curriculum: Principles and foundations.* New York: Crowell.

· 3 ·

NATIONAL AND STATE INITIATIVES FOR MULTICULTURAL EDUCATION

Donna M. Gollnick

NATIONAL COUNCIL FOR ACCREDITATION OF TEACHER EDUCATION

In a study of national and state policies on multicultural education in 1977, Giles and Gollnick (1977) concluded that the

Legislative intent of both federal and state education laws appears most often to be concerned with protecting the rights of cultural and ethnic minorities in an effort to ensure equal educational opportunity rather than preparing all students to know about and function effectively in a multicultural society. (p. 156)

Have there been changes in state and national policies in the intervening years? The Elementary and Secondary Education Act has undergone a number of reauthorizations since that time. Federal policies and practices related to multicultural education have undergone some changes with each reiteration. States have passed legislation and adopted policies and guidelines related to multicultural education. In this chapter the nature of federal and state initiatives is examined. In addition, guidelines and standards for the preparation of school personnel are reviewed.

Federal initiatives have focused on preschool, elementary, and secondary education. State initiatives usually follow the lead of federal policies through state grants to implement federal policies, but in some cases move beyond federal requirements, especially in the area of curriculum. Many national associations have guidelines for the preparation of school personnel to work in their fields (e.g., elementary teaching and school psychology), to which institutions must respond if they seek accreditation from the National Council for Accreditation of Teacher Education (NCATE). Because the state approval, state licensure, and national accrediting systems require evaluations based on evidence in written documentation and interviews, institutions are forced to attend directly to multicultural components within these standards. Accountability at the precollegiate level is less likely to be required except in the implementation of court-ordered desegregation cases.

The conceptual framework developed by Sleeter and Grant (1989) was used in this chapter to analyze federal, state, and national policies and practices. These authors identified the following "five different teaching approaches that address human diversity—race, ethnicity, gender, social class, and disability" (p. 7).

1. *Teaching the Exceptional and Culturally Different* focuses on helping students of color, from low-income families, and with disabilities to succeed in schools and society.
2. *Human Relations* helps students learn to appreciate each other's similarities and differences and to improve intercultural relations.
3. *Single-Group Studies* includes the study of groups that often are not addressed in the curriculum, such as Native Americans, women, Muslims, and low-income populations.
4. *Multicultural Education* is a combination of the first three approaches. According to Sleeter and Grant (1989), "It [multicultural education] suggests changes to most existing school practices for all students so that the school and classroom may become more concerned with human diversity, choice, and equal opportunity. It is hoped that such changes will bring about greater cultural pluralism and equal opportunity in society at large as today's students become tomorrow's citizens" (p. 7.)
5. *Education That Is Multicultural and Social Reconstructionist* addresses social inequities in society. "The primary goals of this approach are to prepare students to work actively in groups and individually, to deal constructively with social problems, and to take charge of their own futures" (Sleeter and Grant, 1989, p. 7).

It was against this framework that national and state policies and programs were analyzed in this chapter.

FEDERAL INITIATIVES

Beginning in 1921, Congress directed the Bureau of Indian Affairs to expend funds "for the benefit, care, and assistance of the Indians throughout the United States for the following purposes: General support and civilization, including education" (U.S. House of Representatives, 1993, p. 411). Other than intervention into the education of Native Americans, the federal government did not acknowledge other ethnic and cultural diversity until after the 1954 *Brown v. Board of Education of Topeka* decision, which declared separate but equal education unconstitutional. It took another 10 years for the passage of the Civil Rights Act of 1964. This breakthrough was followed with the authorizing legislation in 1965 for the Elementary and Secondary Education Act (ESEA) that was part of President Lyndon Johnson's War on Poverty.

As a result of pressure by marginalized groups, federal legislation and policies have been rewritten over the past 30 years to address the needs of groups who do not automatically benefit from schooling because of their race, ethnicity, class, gender, language, or disability (Brown, 1992). Although concern about the Eurocentric content of the curriculum has received much attention by some writers (Asante, 1990; Banks, 1988; Hillard, 1976), "the original goals of the non-white minority population and white liberals with regard to reform in the public schools was equality of education opportunity, integration and social justice, i.e. equal treatment by the law" (Giles & Gollnick, 1977, p. 119). As of the early 1990s, most legislation had been designed to increase equal educational opportunity through the provision of compensatory education, transitional bilingual education, women's equity, homeless education, and assistance for the education of students with disabilities.

Federal legislation addressed the education of a few specific ethnic groups, for example, Native Americans and Native Hawaiians. The Indian Self-Determination and Education Assistance Act of 1975 (ESEA) supported self-determination by Native Americans. The Refugee Education Assistance Act of 1980 (ESEA) provided funds for the education of Cuban, Haitian, and Indochinese refugee children, supporting in particular the learning of English. The goal of these acts was to improve students' chances to compete equally in school with students from the dominant group. However, the legislation was based primarily on a deficit model in which academic expectations were low for students from these groups.

Although there were references to the cultural backgrounds of students in legislation for bilingual and Native American education, culture was not emphasized. Between 1972 and 1980, the Ethnic Heritage Studies Act (Title IX of ESEA) promoted the development of curriculum materials related to the history, geography, society, economy, literature, art, music, drama, language, and general culture of ethnic groups. The legislation was based on the assumption "that in a multiethnic society an understanding of the contributions of one's own heritage and those of fellow citizens can contribute to a more harmonious patriotic and committed populace" (U.S. House of Representatives, 1975, p. 148). The Ethnic Heritage Studies Act received little attention, had limited funding, and was short-lived. Soon after the inauguration of President Ronald Reagan in 1981, it was eliminated. Federal attention returned in 1980 to support for equal educational opportunity for targeted racial, ethnic, language, and women's groups. Legislation also existed for the education of students with disabilities, but neither it nor legislation for Head Start is within the purview of this chapter.

Race and Desegregation

Title VI of the 1964 Civil Rights Act prohibited discrimination in schools. It stated that "No person in the United States shall, on the ground of race, color, or national origin, be excluded from participation in, be denied the benefits of, or be subjected to discrimination under any program or activity receiving federal financial assistance" (U.S. House of Representatives, 1975, p. 40). The attorney general was authorized to file suit against school districts that maintained racially segregated school systems, and federal funds could be withheld from school districts found to be in noncompliance. "Desegregation policy and enforcement became the responsibility of the judicial and the executive branches of government" (Network of Regional Desegregation Assistance Centers, 1989, p. 16).

Title IV of the Civil Rights Act provided technical and financial assistance to local school districts that were attempting to desegregate. The Department of Health, Education and Welfare (HEW) established regional desegregation centers and offices in HEW regional offices and state education agencies to work with school systems to develop plans and provide staff training for school personnel. In the 1970s Desegregation Assistance Centers were expanded to include more than racial segregation. Separate centers were funded to address educational inequities based on race, sex, and national origin. The National Origin Desegregation Centers focused on the provision of equal educational opportunities for students whose native language was other than English.

Physical desegregation of Black and White schools was the goal of Title IV centers in the early years. By the end of the first 10 years, it became clear that segregation continued within schools even when they had been physically desegregated. Issues of unequal access to courses, teaching bias, and tracking of students were recognized as second-generation desegregation problems. By the end of the 1980s, the Desegregation Assistance Centers in 10 geographical regions of the United States had begun to focus on third-generation problems that were described as "persistent barriers to integration and equity or the attainment of equal education outcomes for all groups of students" (Network, 1989, p. 10). The centers began to work with school personnel toward improving the academic achievement of students of color, female students, and students who had limited proficiency in English. Nevertheless, schools were no less desegregated in 1990 than in 1973 (Bates, 1990).

A number of the Sleeter and Grant (1989) approaches have been utilized in the work of the desegregation centers. At first, school personnel in desegregated settings were provided training in human relations and teaching the exceptional and culturally different, focusing on working with African American students. In the third generation of desegregation activities, multicultural education had become the primary approach for staff training by the desegregation centers. Some of the Title IV centers provided an integrated approach toward decreasing gender, national-origin, and race discrimination in the nation's schools.

Education for Students from Low-Income Families

As part of the War on Poverty legislation in 1965, Title I of the ESEA was authorized to encourage schools with large concentrations of low-income students to improve their educational opportunities. It was based on the assumption that low-income children were educationally deprived and that special educational programs would help them achieve academic success in the regular school program. Eligible schools could use funds for the acquisition of equipment and materials, the hiring of special personnel, the training of school personnel, and program evaluations.

In 1988 the Augustus F. Hawkins-Robert T. Stafford Elementary and Secondary School Improvement Amendments of 1988 replaced Title I with Chapter 1 and added requirements for accountability of student outcomes, strengthened involvement of parents, and greater coordination with other instructional programs. Chapter 1 also provided financial aid for meeting the special needs of migrant students, students with disabilities, and neglected and delinquent children.

Although approximately "71 percent of all public elementary schools offer[ed] Chapter 1 services, more than one-third of the low-performing children in high-poverty schools [were] unserved" (U.S. Department of Education, 1993, p. 10). These inequalities were exaggerated for students in the most poverty-stricken communities of the country. Darling-Hammond (1993) found that

inequality is often most obvious in the contrasts between overcrowded, dilapidated schools with large classes lacking equipment and materials in poor neighborhoods and bright, airy facilities where students study in well-equipped small classes in affluent neighborhoods. Less visible but even more pronounced are inequalities in students' access to highly qualified teachers and high-quality curricula. (p. 4)

These inequalities were the result of inequalities in funding across states, among districts, and among schools within districts (Kozol, 1991). As of 1993, Chapter 1 funding was still doing little to overcome these inequities (U.S. Department of Education, 1993).

Because low-income families are disproportionately African American, Hispanic American, and Native American, a large proportion of the students in Chapter 1 programs are from these groups. In the 1989–90 school year, 5.3 million students were participating in these programs; 42% of the students were White, non-Hispanic; and 55% were male (Sinclair & Gutmann, 1992).

Although programs supported by Chapter 1 funds were intended to be supplemental to regular school instruction, researchers found that most participating students were actually pulled out of regular classes in which basic language and mathematics instruction was being provided (Millsap, Moss, & Gamse, 1993). Strang and Carlson (1991) found in their case

studies of Chapter 1 programs that the language of students was sometimes not a factor in instruction. Only 4 of the 14 provided English as a second language (ESL); 6 provided assistance in the native language.

Since its establishment as Title I in 1965, Chapter 1 has provided educational services for low-income students. It represented the largest federal investment in elementary and secondary education, comprising about one fifth of the Department of Education's budget. For fiscal year 1993, Congress appropriated $6.1 billion to serve 5.5 million children (U.S. Department of Education, 1993).

The laudable goal of the legislation was to improve the educational opportunities for low-income students—the educational approach that Sleeter and Grant (1989) labeled "teaching the exceptional and culturally different." The underlying assumptions of Chapter 1 legislation were that the lack of academic success was the fault of students and their families, and that appropriate remediation could bring them into the mainstream. The legislation did not encourage the reform of schools or instruction to serve a culturally diverse population more effectively. Instead, "the focus was on changing various subpopulations" (Winfield & Manning, 1992, p. 186).

The implementation of Chapter 1 in schools has done little so far to promote equity and high expectations for students. The learning gap between low-income and other students has not decreased as expected (U.S. Department of Education, 1993). A number of proposals for the reauthorization of ESEA in 1994 called for changes to support these outcomes (e.g., Darling-Hammond, 1993; U.S. Department of Education, 1993). Changes in the legislation are expected, but their content is unknown at the time of this writing.

Education for Girls and Women

Federal legislation related to females does not refer to their special needs as does Chapter 1. Instead, it highlights the inequity in schools that may limit the full participation of female students. Title IX of the 1972 Education Amendments prevented discrimination based on gender. It required that "no person shall, on the basis of sex, be excluded from participation in, be denied the benefits of, or be subjected to discrimination under any education program or activity receiving federal financial assistance" (U.S. House of Representatives, 1975, P.L. 92-318). This provision allowed federal funds to be withheld from schools if discrimination against female students or teachers could be proven. As one result, organized sports available to girls and women in schools and colleges have increased in number and quality since 1972. To help schools eliminate sex discrimination, the Desegregation Assistance Centers under Title IV of the Civil Rights Act initiated technical assistance in 1974 (Network, 1989).

The Women's Educational Equity Act provided grants for the implementation of Title IX. It also called attention to multiple discrimination, bias, and stereotyping based on gender, race, ethnicity, disability, and age. Support was provided for the development of curriculum materials, training programs, research, counseling, and expansion of opportunities in vocational education, career education, physical education, and educational administration. Although budget projections for fiscal year 1993 were nearly $2 million, actual expenditures for these projects in fiscal year 1992 were less than $500,000 (Executive Office of the President of the United States, 1993).

The focus of the federal legislation and programs for girls and women was on teaching the exceptional and culturally different approach identified by Sleeter and Grant (1989). Title IX (ESEA) and Title IV (Civil Rights Act) were authorized to provide equal educational opportunities for females and males by eliminating discrimination within schools. At the same time, the Women's Educational Equity Act supported projects for the development of materials on females—Sleeter and Grant's single-group studies approach.

Education for Students with Limited English Proficiency

In its authorization of the Bilingual Education Act in 1968 (Title VII of ESEA), Congress stated that its purpose was to establish equal educational opportunity for all children and to promote educational excellence. The introduction to the authorization included the following statements:

- many children [with limited English proficiency] have a cultural heritage which differs from that of English proficient persons;
- the instructional use and development of a child's non-English native language promotes student self-esteem, subject matter achievement, and English-language acquisition;
- a primary means by which a child learns is through the use of such child's native language and cultural heritage;
- large numbers of children of limited English proficiency have educational needs which can be met by the use of bilingual educational methods and techniques; and
- both limited English proficient children and children whose primary language is English can benefit from bilingual education programs, and . . . such programs help develop our national linguistic resources and promote our international competitiveness. (U.S. House of Representatives, 1993, pp. 187–188)

Although these statements suggested that bilingual education was the desired instructional mode for improving the educational opportunities for Limited English Proficient (LEP) students, Congress equivocated in its support over the years. In 1978 Title VII was restricted to transitional bilingual education that allowed the use of the native language only to help students become competent in English. By the 1990s, Title VII allowed for greater flexibility in the instructional strategies for LEP students. It also supported developmental bilingual programs in which instruction was offered in both English and the student's native language as well as other alternative instructional programs such as ESL.

There were approximately 3.5 million LEP students in the United States in 1990 (Council of Chief State School Officers, 1990). Approximately 19 to 28% of these students were served through Chapter 1; 7 to 11% were served through Title VII

projects (Stanford Working Group, 1993). Title VII was more like the Women's Educational Equity Act in that it supported programs in local education agencies, colleges, and universities. The Stanford Working Group identified the strengths of Title VII:

Title VII touches fewer LEP children than Chapter 1, but has been instrumental in fostering approaches that are far more appropriate. Programs are designed to overcome language barriers so that students are not held back in other subjects until they acquire English. Teachers are normally bilingual, certified in content areas, and versed in language development. Efforts are made to use materials that are sensitive, both culturally and linguistically. Moreover, Title VII, Part A has played an important role in highlighting the feasibility of effective bilingual approaches and in stimulating SEAs [State Education Agencies] and LEAs [Local Education Agencies] to focus on the needs of LEP students. Parts B and C have helped to shape a professional field that barely existed in 1968, by funding research, technical assistance, and staff development. (pp. 21–22)

Fiscal year 1993 appropriations for Title VII were $195 million—33% less than the 1981 appropriation (Stanford Working Group, 1993).

For the most part, federal policies treated language diversity as a deficit rather than a strength. In its analysis of Chapter 1 and Title VII, the Stanford Working Group (1993) found two assumptions imbedded in the legislation. One was the belief that LEP students are not capable of meeting high academic standards; second was that bilingualism and instruction in the native language "distracts these children from learning English" (p. 6). The focus of federal legislation was on the "teaching the culturally different" approach identified by Sleeter and Grant (1989). The National Origin Desegregation Centers provided training of school personnel to eliminate discrimination against LEP students in schools with the goal of providing equal educational opportunity. Since Hispanic students were more segregated than any other students in the 1990s (Network, 1989), much work remains to reverse this trend.

When the emphasis in bilingual programs was on rushing students into English-only classrooms with little or no attention to their native languages and cultures, many students developed identity problems, had low expectations, and experienced school failure (Cummins, 1989). In these cases, bilingual programs were designed to assimilate students into the dominant culture rather than to promote the appreciation and maintenance of cultural diversity. Federal legislation permitted both goals, but had favored the assimilation approach through the funding of transitional bilingual education programs in most school districts. Legislators themselves did not agree on the goals of bilingual education beyond helping LEP students learn English.

During the reauthorization of ESEA, the goals for bilingual education will be revisited. Advocates have proposed that the legislation should promote the attainment of high academic achievement by LEP students. In addition, they recommend that language be supported as a resource rather than a deficit. All students should have the opportunity to be bilingual. Students whose native language is not English should have the opportunity to use both languages for their own economic and personal advantages.

Education for Specific Ethnic Groups

After years of federal domination of the education of Native Americans, Congress in 1975 moved to a different relationship that supported self-determination, including tribally controlled schools. The Indian Education Act of 1988 (ESEA) also provided financial assistance to meet the special educational and culturally related academic needs of Native American students in public schools.

The Emergency Immigrant Education Act of 1984 provided support for supplementary educational services to students who were not born in the United States and had attended school in the United States for less than three years. The Refugee Education Assistance Act of 1980 supported supplementary services for Cuban, Haitian, and Indochinese refugees. These two acts were designed to help these students perform satisfactorily by providing English instruction and bilingual services.

Title IV of the Augustus F. Hawkins-Robert T. Stafford Elementary and Secondary School Improvement Amendments of 1988 (Education for Native Hawaiians) was passed to help improve the conditions of Native Hawaiians. This legislation supported, among other initiatives, the implementation of the Kamehameha Elementary Education Program (KEEP) model curriculum in appropriate public schools (Au & Jordon, 1981).

The focus of most of the legislation for specific ethnic groups was on Sleeter and Grant's (1989) teaching the culturally different approach. The primary goal was to provide equal educational opportunity for students that Congress believed were underserved by current state and local educational systems. The Education for Native Hawaiians Act encouraged the development of curriculum materials that reflected the students' culture—Sleeter and Grant's single-group studies approach.

Impact of Federal Legislation

As of the time of this writing, most federal legislation did not promote education that is multicultural. The primary focus was on the first approach identified by Sleeter and Grant (1989)—teaching the culturally different and students with disabilities. Cultural diversity received minimal attention in the language related to bilingual education, and no direct attention in other education legislation. The underlying purpose for the attention to females, low-income students, and non-European groups was to provide equal educational opportunity. Low-income status, languages other than English, race, ethnicity, and gender were treated as deficits to be overcome through special services rather than as potential strengths to be used in the development of curriculum and instruction.

Overall, there was a lack of coordination of programs providing educational services to culturally diverse groups. Darling-Hammond (1993) reported that

across federal categorical programs, the need to categorize children according to various eligibility criteria has often led to segregating or stigmatizing approaches to the delivery of services, as well as to fragmentation of services, which are funded by separate programs through separate offices using separate funding channels. (p. 2)

As an example, the desegregation centers sometimes addressed gender, race, and national origin separately even though each influences the other. More LEP students were served under Chapter 1 than under Title VII, but their language needs were often ignored in compensatory education services. Although desegregation activities were supported in the Civil Rights Act, students of color and males continued to be disproportionately placed in low-ability tracks. Students with limited English proficiency, from low-income families, and with disabilities were too often segregated for instructional purposes even within desegregated schools (Network, 1989). Coordination across these programs could improve services to underserved students (Darling-Hammond, 1993).

Federal education initiatives should encourage the integration of services to female students, LEP students, students of color, and students with disabilities. Federally funded projects usually do not pay attention to the interaction of race, socioeconomic status, ethnicity, disability, and gender in serving students effectively. Society is not served well if policies support the elimination of discrimination against one group (e.g., women) and continue to allow discrimination against another group (e.g., Haitians). Services could be further improved if the intent of federal legislation and programs moved beyond equal educational opportunity and promoted instead equal academic outcomes for all students.

STATE INITIATIVES

Because states, rather than the federal government, have the constitutional authority for education, they are able to address issues beyond the equal educational opportunity provisions. States can mandate curriculum content and control textbook selection for public schools. Appropriate state agencies develop and apply requirements for the approval of teacher-education programs and the licensure of teachers and other school personnel. Thus, states have the opportunity to require or encourage the inclusion of multicultural education in preschool through grade 12 schools and in teacher education programs.

The federal government does award grants directly to local school districts, colleges, and universities for bilingual education, women's equity, education of Native American and Hawaiian students, and education of students with disabilities. Most federal funds are set aside for states. In this way, the states help implement federal initiatives. For example, states have Offices for Equal Educational Opportunity that assist school districts in the desegregation efforts required by Title IV of the Civil Rights Act. State agencies have staffs to provide technical assistance for the provision of educational equity for female students, students with disabilities, and LEP students. States oversee the distribution of Chapter 1 funds and collect data on the number of eligible students.

For this section of the chapter, state legislation, policies, and guidelines were collected and reviewed from all states except three: Louisiana, New Hampshire, and Tennessee did not respond to my requests for information. Of the remaining 47 states, 45 had at least minimal requirements related to multicultural education. Neither Colorado nor North Carolina had requirements; South Carolina had very minimal requirements.

Legislation and policies related to multicultural education varied across states in part because of the ethnic diversity within each state. For example, bilingual education requirements were more likely to be found in states with large Hispanic populations. A course in Native American studies was sometimes required in states with large Native American populations. Requirements for multicultural content were often the result of the efforts of ethnic minority groups in the state. The map in Figure 3–1 shows the difference in the amount of cultural diversity across states. Only five states—Iowa, Maine, New Hampshire, Vermont, and West Virginia—had populations that were over 95% White. Fourteen additional states had populations that were over 90% White. Nine states had populations that were less than 75% White; six of these were in the South.

Some states had accreditation standards for elementary and/or secondary schools that required an on-site evaluation and/or

periodic reports to determine whether the state standards were being met. Almost all states conducted on-site reviews of teacher education programs and required teachers and other school personnel to be licensed by the appropriate state agency.

My analysis of state policies and regulations indicated that a few states addressed many aspects of multicultural education while others were doing little or nothing. The following discussion focuses on the groups targeted; curriculum, textbooks, and staff development; and the curriculum approaches to multicultural education that have evolved in states. Although the analysis focused on teacher education and licensure, examples from public school requirements are presented in the discussion when appropriate.

Targeted Groups

Gollnick and Chinn (1994) contend that the interaction of memberships in cultural groups, or microcultures, determines an individual's cultural identity. The microcultural memberships that are most critical to a student's cultural identity are

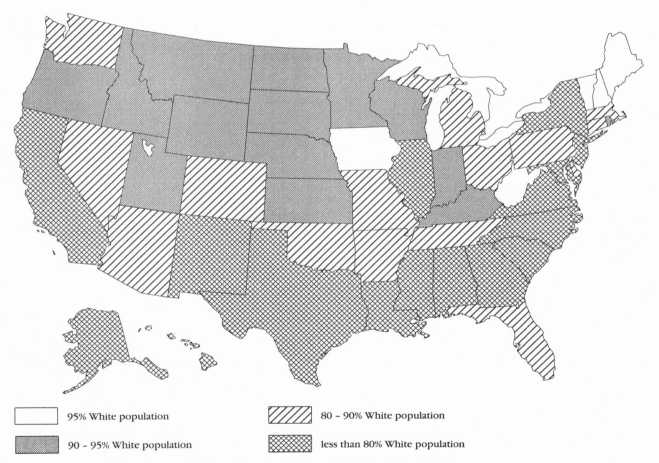

95% White population

90 - 95% White population

80 - 90% White population

less than 80% White population

FIGURE 3–1. Racial Diversity of the United States

Source: U.S. Bureau of Census, 1992, pp. 24–25.

ethnicity, race, class, gender, language, and religion. An effective multicultural curriculum includes attention to these groups (see chapter 1 of this *Handbook*).

In 1993, when this study was conducted, 35 states referred to ethnicity, race, and/or cultural groups in their regulations or policies. Generally, students and/or teacher candidates were expected to understand the cultural diversity of the nation and, in a few cases, the world. Several states referred to *minority groups;* four states required *non-Western studies.*

There were at least minimal multicultural requirements in 21 states. Most required knowledge and understanding related to the various microcultural groups. Alabama's program approval standards (1990), went somewhat beyond those expectations. They required that:

- faculty understand psychological, sociological, and cultural influences on learning;
- the general studies help candidates develop an understanding and appreciation of other cultures and the people who represent them;
- educational foundations emphasize knowledge of social, ethnic, and cultural differences among learners and their implications for school; and
- most programs expect that teacher candidates model, teach, and integrate multicultural awareness, acceptance, and appreciation throughout their teaching.

One of the 10 statements in The New York Board of Regents' "Bill of Rights for Children" stated that "all children have the right to an education which respects their culture, race, socioeconomic background, and the language of their home" (New York, 1991, p. 21). One of the goals for elementary, middle, and secondary school students was that "each student will develop the ability to understand, appreciate, and cooperate with people of different race, sex, ability, cultural heritage, national origin, religion, and political, economic, and social background, and to understand and appreciate their values, beliefs, and attitudes" (p. 20).

Twenty states included a reference to class or socioeconomic status. The reference in the general standards for a provisional teaching license in Massachusetts was similar to expectations in other states. The standards required that teachers be able to "communicate clearly, understandably, and sensitively with language appropriate to students' ages, levels of development, gender, race, ethnic, linguistic and socioeconomic backgrounds, and individual learning styles and needs" (Massachusetts, 1990, p. 9). At least one state still used the term *disadvantaged;* another state referred to *at-risk students.*

Attention to gender or sex was expected in 22 states. The reference was usually among the listing of microcultural groups that should be addressed in school and teacher-education programs. California and New York had produced several documents to assist schools and teachers in providing gender equity (e.g., California's *Sex Equity in Education: How To Tell if You're Doing Well,* n.d.; New York's *Promoting Self-Esteem in Young Women: A Manual for Teachers,* 1989, and *Women's History Month: Suggested Classroom Activities,* n.d.).

Language was sometimes among the list of concepts to receive attention in curriculum and in instruction. In a number of states the focus was on LEP students and bilingual education. New York's general school requirements included the study of a second language by all students before the 10th grade (New York, 1991). A few states required the understanding of regional dialects; 22 states included attention to language.

Students with disabilities were sometimes included with other microcultural groups to be addressed in school programs. For example, most of Indiana's program approval standards required that the professional education component include "ethnic, cultural, and disability awareness" (*Indiana Register,* 1988, p. 511). Seventeen states had similar requirements.

Eleven states included religion along with other cultural characteristics to which students and teachers should pay attention. Pennsylvania's program approval standards were typical in their requirement for the development of "appropriate teaching strategies for a diverse population of students including sex, race, religion, social economic status and national origin" (Pennsylvania, 1992, Standard IX).

States with policies and/or regulations that referenced all of these groups included Michigan, New York, and Utah. California, Kentucky, Maine, and Texas included references to all of the groups except religion. Overall, the western and midwestern states included more of these groups in their initiatives than states in the South and Northeast.

Curriculum, Textbooks, and Staff Development

Of the 47 states whose documents were reviewed for this study, 22 had policies and/or standards related to multicultural education for K–12 schools; 21 addressed multicultural education in program-approval standards for teacher education; and 14 included multicultural requirements for teacher licensure. Eighty-five percent of the states required the curriculum to reflect multicultural education. Nearly 40% of the states required staff development by schools or technical assistance from the state. Fourteen percent of the states addressed the multicultural content of textbooks. Six states (14%) referred to the elimination of cultural and linguistic biases in student and teacher assessments.

Sleeter and Grant (1989) identified five approaches for multicultural teaching: teaching the exceptional and culturally different, human relations, single-group studies, multicultural education, and education that is multicultural and reconstructionist. Each of these approaches was addressed in state initiatives except the last one. Table 3–1 indicates the states with requirements for single-group studies, human relations, and multicultural education. It also shows states with bilingual education requirements and those that require attention to cultural diversity, but do not identify the approach as multicultural.

Teaching the Exceptional and Culturally Different. All states followed federal mandates related to the education of low-income students, migrant students, and students with disabilities eligible for Chapter 1 support. The focus for these three groups was on the provision of equal educational opportunity.

When this policy was implemented in schools, members of these groups often were placed in remedial programs, tracked into low-ability or other special groups (Oakes, 1988), and not fully integrated into the regular classroom.

Students identified as LEP also fell into this category. At least 15 states required the identification of LEP students and the provision of appropriate services. Fourteen of the 15 states identified bilingual education as one of the approaches for teaching LEP students; the other state did not recommend an approach. The emphasis was to overcome a deficit (i.e., not being proficient in English). None of these states promoted the development and maintenance of at least two languages, although they did not prevent this strategy. Similar to low-income students and students with disabilities, LEP students are often segregated from the regular classroom for English and other instruction. In fact, the largest LEP group—Hispanics—are now more segregated than any other group in school settings (Valencia, 1991).

Of the 10 states with bilingual education licensure or program-approval standards, 5 also had standards for ESL. Both of these areas usually required instruction in ESL methodology, linguistics, cultural background, and the nature and grammar of English. Methodology for bilingual learners was required for a license or program in bilingual education.

In most states teacher candidates in bilingual education had to show proficiency in both English and the target language. Second-language proficiency for ESL was usually not as stringent (e.g., six hours of study in Arizona) or not required at all. Although candidates in New Jersey were required to pass a state test of English proficiency, there was no reference to proficiency in the targeted language for either bilingual education or ESL. In addition to the demonstration of language proficiency, California (1992) administered a licensure examination for (Bilingual) Cross-cultural, Language and Academic Development (CLAD/BCLAD). The examination content included:

- language structure and first- and second-language development;
- methodology of bilingual education, English-language development, and content instruction;
- culture and cultural diversity;
- methodology for primary-language instruction;
- the culture of the targeted language; and
- the language of the targeted group.

Single-Group Studies. Six states singled out the groups to be studied in K–12 or teacher-education curriculum. Montana, North Dakota, and Wisconsin required Native American studies. Teacher candidates in Alaska (1991) must have studied "the environment, indigenous and immigrant residents, and institutions of Alaska, with specific study of the social, economic, and political history of Alaska and the educational institutions and laws that affect the people of Alaska" (p. 60). The Hawaii (n.d.) state plan called for schools to provide "educational programs which enhance the understanding of Hawaii's cultural heritage" (p. A-2). New Jersey (1993) required the study of Black history and history of other minority groups. Other states were not as

specific about which ethnic groups should be included in the curriculum. Instead, they usually referred to broad descriptions like ethnic, racial, and language groups.

Human Relations. Iowa, Minnesota, and Wisconsin required teacher candidates to develop competencies in human relations. Iowa had required human relations in teacher-education programs since 1980. Its guidelines stated that "this study shall include interpersonal and intergroup relations and shall contribute to the development of sensitivity to and understanding of the values, beliefs, lifestyles, and attitudes of individuals and the diverse groups found in a pluralistic society" (Iowa, 1977, p. 6). More specifically, candidates were expected to

- recognize and deal with dehumanizing biases such as sexism, racism, prejudice, and discrimination, and become aware of the impact that such biases have on interpersonal relations;
- translate knowledge of human relations into attitudes, skills, and techniques which will result in favorable learning experiences for students;
- recognize the ways in which dehumanizing biases may be reflected in instructional materials;
- respect human diversity and the rights of each individual; and
- relate effectively to other individuals and various subgroups other than one's own. (Iowa, 1977, pp. 9–10)

In addition, the faculty for these programs were required to have appropriate background in human relations; an advisory committee had to include equal representation of various minority and majority groups; and an evaluation component had to be implemented.

Minnesota (n.d.) had similar requirements for programs preparing teachers. In addition to human relations competencies, candidates were expected to understand the contributions and lifestyles of various racial, cultural, and economic groups. The human relations components in Minnesota were also to be developed with participation by members of various racial, cultural, and economic groups. Teacher education programs were expected to have a system for assessing these competencies.

The requirements in Wisconsin had been expanded to include students with disabilities and both gender groups. They also included "study in the philosophical and psychological bases of development and change of attitudes" and the "study of constitutional and legal bases related to the status of women and various racial and cultural groups in the United States" (Wisconsin, 1992, p. 70-18). Wisconsin was the only state to have requirements for field and/or clinical experiences in this area. Teacher-education programs had to include:

- experiences to systematically evaluate the impact of the forces of discrimination, especially racism and sexism, on language, instructional materials, learning activities, learning styles, interaction between staff and pupils, tests and measurements, and school environments.
- experiences in assessing curriculum and making modifications to assure multicultural and nonsexist content.
- a minimum of 50 hours of direct involvement with adult and

TABLE 3–1. Approaches to Multicultural Education in State Policies

	Single-Group Studies	Human Relations	Cultural Diversity[a]	Multicultural Education[a]	Bilingual Education	Other
AL			P			
AK	L			L		Cross-cultural communications
AZ					P S	ESL
AR			P	S		
CA			P S	P S	P S	
CO						
CT				S[b]		
DE			S	S		
FL	S L	S		P	S	ESL; global
GA		P L	P L	P L		ESL; global
HI	S				S	
ID					S	
IL			P			
IN			P		P	
IA		P	P	S		Discrimination
KS		P S	P S	P S		Discrimination; global society
KY			P S	P S		Global society
LA						
ME			P S			Discrimination; biases
MD			P S	S		Discrimination
MA			P		P	ESL; discrimination; learning styles
MI			S	S		Encourages, but does not require
MN		P S	P S	P S		Discrimination
MS						
MO			P			Learning styles; Discrimination
MT	P	P	P	P		Prejudice
NE		P L	S	S		Discrimination
NV						
NH						
NJ				S	L	ESL
NM			L	L	L	Biased materials
NY		L S	L S		L S	ESL
NC						Recommendations only
ND	P L					
OH		S	P S	P S		
OK			P S			
OR			P			Discrimination
PA			P			

TABLE 3–1. (*continued*)

	Single-Group Studies	Human Relations	Cultural Diversity[a]	Multicultural Education[a]	Bilingual Education	Other
RI			P		P	ESL
SC	S					
SD		P				Discrimination
TN						
TX			S L	L	L	Learning styles; heterogeneous grouping
UT			P		P	Prejudice
VT						
VA						
WA		P S	P S	P S		Discrimination; prejudice; grouping
WV						
WI	P S	P S	P			Discrimination
WY			P			

P = Program Approval for Teacher Education
L = Licensure for Teachers and Other School Personnel
S = Schools, K–12 Grades

[a] Multicultural education is reported only when the state has used either that term or *multicultural perspective*. Many state documents referred to *cultural diversity, cultural pluralism*, or other concepts related to multicultural education; therefore, they are reported in the column on cultural diversity.
[b] Only under special conditions.

pupil members of groups different than the candidate, including the disabled.

• student teaching evaluation of competence in human relations skills, knowledge, and attitudes. (p. 70-18)

The human relations competencies in the program-approval standards for Nebraska and South Dakota mirrored those of Iowa. Other states required the inclusion of human or intergroup relations, but were not specific about the components.

The human relations expectations in Iowa, Minnesota, Nebraska, South Dakota, and Wisconsin went beyond Sleeter and Grant's (1989) definition of human relations in which students are helped to get along with each other. They included dealing with issues of cultural diversity and discrimination. In many ways they were stronger than the requirements for multicultural education in most other states.

Multicultural Education. The documents from 33 states included references to the inclusion of cultural diversity or cultural pluralism and sometimes discrimination and learning styles. However, only 19 states actually used the term *multicultural education* or *multicultural perspectives*.

In 1978 Iowa passed a law requiring each school board in the state to adopt a plan for multicultural, nonsexist education that addressed issues of race, ethnicity, gender, religion, and age. The plans had to include goals and objectives with timelines and specific provisions for implementation as well as staff development activities and a process for evaluating the plan.

The members of the advisory committee in each school district had to reflect cultural diversity and include persons with disabilities (Iowa, 1989). Schools were required to keep their plans on file, but did not submit them to a state agency for review. Beginning in 1985, staff from different departments of the state education agency conducted regular, on-site visits to schools as part of an equity monitoring system. These visiting teams checked adherence to federal and state laws related to equity and multicultural education (Iowa, 1993b).

In the early years of implementation, funding was available to train school personnel and publish documents on infusing multicultural education into the curriculum for specific academic areas like science and mathematics (T. Andersen, personal communication, October 22, 1993). By the 1990s, state funds were no longer available for these activities. Instead, multicultural education training and monitoring were coordinated by staff of the Office for Equal Educational Opportunity, which was supported by Title IV (Civil Rights Act) funds. Some of the state's regional education centers had equity staff who provided staff development activities for teachers and other school personnel.

Maryland, Minnesota, Nebraska, and New Jersey followed the lead of Iowa. These four states expected that K–12 curriculum be multicultural and required schools to submit plans and report regularly on their implementation. Minnesota required each school district to submit a written plan in 1990. The plan was to show how curriculum is developed and delivered so that students and staff gain understanding and appreciation of

- cultural diversity of the United States [with] special emphasis on American Indians/Alaskan Natives, Asian Americans/Pacific Islanders, Black Americans, and Hispanic Americans;
- the historical and contemporary contributions of women and men to society; and
- the historical and contemporary contributions to society by handicapped persons. (Minnesota, 1988, p. 111)

School district plans must be reviewed every six years. Although state funds could be withheld for noncompliance, the state agency had not taken that action. Instead, districts were asked for further clarification of their plans and gently encouraged to come into compliance. School district plans were reviewed and monitored under a board rule initially funded in 1977; no additional state funds were appropriated to implement the multicultural requirements (S. Jebe, personal communication, September 28, 1993).

More recently, Nebraska's legislature enacted the Multicultural Education Act of 1992 (Nebraska, 1992b), requiring each school district to make its curriculum multicultural by the 1993–94 academic year. Multicultural education was defined as "studies relative to the culture, history, and contributions of African Americans, Hispanic Americans, Native Americans, and Asian Americans. Special emphasis shall be placed on human relations and sensitivity toward all races" (Nebraska, 1992a, p. 3). It did not include gender, class, or disability studies. School districts were required to show evidence of infusing multicultural education throughout their curriculum in order to comply with state accreditation standards. Annual reports must be submitted to the state department of education. In addition, the state department was charged with developing guidelines and an assessment system to assess student cultural awareness and sensitivity every five years.

If school districts do not come into compliance with the multicultural provisions, state approval and accreditation can be withdrawn. The first assessments of students' multicultural competencies are planned for the 1997–98 academic year. The state Regional Service Centers have been asked to provide staff development for school districts; the Race Equity staff in the Department of Education has been charged with reviewing the plans. Minimal state support (i.e., approximately $75,000 in 1993–94) has been provided to help implement these requirements (J. Kubik, personal communication, September 28, 1993).

The New Jersey Administrative Code required school districts to integrate multicultural education throughout the curriculum in the provision of equal educational opportunity (New Jersey, 1993). The state's guidelines for school desegregation require school districts to "develop and implement culturally pluralistic curricula and instructional practices" (p. 7); to integrate Black history and the history of minority groups throughout the curricula and school programs; to "detect and remove or neutralize bias and stereotypes based on race, national origin, or gender in instructional materials and curriculum" (p. 8); to "teach appreciation for the value of diversity and pluralism among racial/national origin groups" (p. 8); and to "reduce the negative effects of bias among students" (p. 8). *Guidelines for Education That is Multicultural* (New Jersey, 1993) had 10

goals that encompassed Sleeter and Grant's (1989) definition of multicultural education. In addition, 1 of the goals nudged into the approach "education that is multicultural and social reconstructionist." The goal called for schools "to develop students' ability to recognize, critically analyze, and make intelligent decisions about complex social problems and issues such as discrimination and racism in contemporary society so that the students will act as agents of social change" (p. 12).

Since 1986, all New Jersey public school districts have been required to submit an annual progress report on how they are meeting the state's equity requirements. Districts must "review their curricula on a regular basis and revise, where necessary" (New Jersey, 1993, p. 9). Beginning in 1993, they must also show how they are incorporating the guidelines for multicultural education into their curriculum renewal process.

Maryland's State Board of Education (Maryland, 1993) also adopted guidelines in 1993 for education that is multicultural. Curriculum goals called for outcomes in which students would be able "to demonstrate an understanding of and an appreciation for cultural groups as an integral part of education for a culturally pluralistic society" (p. 5), and to demonstrate attitudes and actions for valuing one's own heritage and the culture of others. The guidelines for instruction promoted a school climate supportive of cultural diversity, access to "equally rigorous academic instruction" (p. 7), and the analysis of contemporary social problems. Goals for staff development activities were also outlined. Beginning in September 1994, local school systems must have established a five-year cycle of assessment and planning for the incorporation of the guidelines. Annual progress reports must be submitted to and reviewed by the State Department of Education; findings will be reported to the State Board of Education. The guidelines also required that multicultural content be infused into the state's performance assessment of pre-kindergarten through 12th-grade students.

Delaware required school districts to incorporate essential elements of a comprehensive multicultural education program. This state board policy expanded beyond curricular requirements. For example, it called for "the creation of an atmosphere which recognizes, accepts and promotes cultural, racial, and ethnic diversity and respects and values difference as a positive, integral resource of a democratic society" (Delaware, 1990, p. 22). Student counseling, assessment, discipline, and placement were expected to be culturally appropriate. The policy called for staff training and "the involvement of administrators, teachers, counselors, parents, business and community members of diverse backgrounds to serve as resources and role models" (p. 22). It also required "the establishment of a district-wide multicultural education advisory committee" (p. 22) and "the identification of an individual at the district level and in each building to coordinate the multicultural program" (p. 23). In addition, a multicultural education needs assessment was to be conducted and a plan developed to evaluate the effectiveness of the total multicultural effort in schools.

Although the Delaware plan was very comprehensive, it did not include an accountability system. School districts were required only to submit to the state agency the names of the districtwide advisory committee members and program coordinators. The State Department of Education had developed guidelines for the implementation of this policy, and staff were available for technical assistance.

Beginning in 1993, Oklahoma required school districts to submit staff development plans for helping school personnel deliver outreach programs to parents, multicultural education curriculum and instruction, and outcomes-based education. The State Board of Education required a report on these activities every four years. The regulations for staff development suggested that the training in multicultural education help teachers

1. understand their own and their students' environment and culture, including needs, abilities, attitudes, and world views;
2. recognize that different cultures exist as separate and distinct entities; acknowledge the contributions of all cultural and linguistic groups to a multicultural society; and promote a culturally sensitive curriculum representative of our diverse national population; and
3. develop strategies for the integration of cultural and linguistic teaching tools and methods in the school environment. (Oklahoma, 1993, p. 2)

West Virginia (1989) also required counties to provide staff development in multicultural education. A process for staff development was outlined, but neither the content expectations nor outcomes were described.

Florida (1991), Nevada (D. Stoker, personal communication, January 26, 1993), and West Virginia (1970) required that textbooks accurately portray racial, ethnic, and cultural diversity. Kentucky's Education Reform Act (Kentucky, 1990) required that textbooks "include the significance of the diverse ethnic contributors to society" (Kentucky, 1992, p. 4). Iowa's human relations requirements called for teacher candidates to "be able to recognize the ways in which dehumanizing biases may be reflected in instructional materials" (Iowa, 1977, p. 10). Utah (1979) required that teacher candidates be able to analyze materials for linguistic and cultural diversity.

Multicultural education was defined as

- The study of the meaning of culture, and relationship and influences between culture and education, with specific study of teaching, administration, and effectiveness of schooling as they relate to multicultural school populations (Alaska, 1991, p. 60).
- Interdisciplinary, cross-curricular education which prepares students to live, learn, and work together to achieve common goals in a culturally diverse world. It does this by (a) enabling all students to be aware of and affirmed in their own cultural roots; (b) allowing all students to understand and value diversity, fostering appreciation, respect and understanding for persons of different backgrounds; and (c) preparing students to live fruitful lives in an increasingly global society with shifting and permeable borders (Kentucky, 1992, p. 2).
- An interdisciplinary process rather than single program or series of activities. Concepts embraced by cultural pluralism, ethnic and intercultural studies and intergroup and interper-

sonal relations are included in this process. . . . The basic aim is to help students to accept themselves and other persons as having dignity and worth (Washington, 1992, p. 1).
- Education that is multicultural is a continuous, integrated multiethnic, multidisciplinary process for educating all students about diversity and commonality. Diversity factors include but are not limited to race, ethnicity, region, religion, gender, language, socioeconomic status, age, and persons with disabilities. (Maryland, 1993, p. 1)

Although labeled multicultural education, the Alaska definition focused primarily on teaching the culturally different. A strength of the Kentucky, Maryland, and Washington definitions was the attention to multicultural education as a process. These three definitions reflect Sleeter and Grant's (1989) description of multicultural education.

The definitions above captured the intent of most of the state requirements for cultural diversity and multicultural education. However, they did not measure up to the goals proposed by Gollnick and Chinn (1994):

All teaching should be multicultural and all classrooms should be models of democracy and equity. To do this requires that educators (1) place the student at the center of the teaching and learning process; (2) promote human rights and respect for cultural differences; (3) believe that all students can learn; (4) acknowledge and build on the life histories and experiences of students' microcultural memberships; (5) critically analyze oppression and power relationships to understand racism, sexism, classism, and discrimination against the disabled, young, and aged; (6) critique society in the interest of social justice and equality; and (7) participate in collective social action to ensure a democratic society.

Kentucky's (1992) learning goals and outcomes for social studies and arts and humanities reflected a number of the Gollnick and Chinn (1994) goals. The core concepts and principles for social studies included:

- the study of democratic principles (students recognize issues of justice, equality, responsibility, choice, and freedom and apply these democratic principles to real-life situations);
- cultural diversity (students interact effectively and work cooperatively with the diverse ethnic and cultural groups of our nation and world); and
- interpersonal relationships (students observe, analyze and interpret human behaviors to acquire a better understanding of self, others, and human relationships). (Kentucky, 1992, pp. 4–5)

The learning outcomes also included responsible group membership that should be demonstrated, in part, by a multicultural and world view and a mind open to alternative perspectives. Students were also expected to integrate knowledge by applying multiple perspectives based on economic, social, cultural, political, historic, physical, technical, aesthetic, environmental, and personal characteristics.

Kansas and Georgia, on the other hand, neither defined multicultural education nor described expected outcomes. The

Kansas program-approval standards (1990) required that the professional education component of teacher education "include studies in foundations of education, methods and materials of teaching, interpersonal relations, multicultural education, equal educational opportunity, human sexuality, and supervised laboratory experiences" (p. 21). Georgia (n.d.) required the incorporation of multicultural and global perspectives.

State definitions and discussions of multicultural education focused on making the curriculum more reflective of cultural diversity and improving human relations. Teacher expectations, equity in instruction, and more equal learning outcomes for all students received little attention. California was an exception in its requirements for the approval of teacher-education programs. Competencies not included by most other states were attention to equity, effective practices, and second-language acquisition (California, 1992). Teacher-education programs were expected to help candidates be able to:

• explore works of major educational theorists, review research on effective teaching practices, and examine the use of those practices among students of differing gender, ethnicity, and handicapping conditions. (p. 13)
• examine principles of educational equity and analyze the implementation of those principles in curriculum content and instructional practices. (p. 14)
• engage in multicultural study and experiences, including the study of second language acquisition and experiences with successful approaches to the education of linguistically different students. (p. 15)
• establish and sustain level of student rapport and classroom environment that promotes learning and equity. (p. 23)
• demonstrate compatibility with, and ability to teach students who are different from the candidate, including ethnic, cultural, gender, linguistic, and socioeconomic differences. (p. 31)

In 1992 the Oklahoma Legislature passed a bill to restructure teacher education as an outcome-based system. Teachers were expected to be able to "interact effectively with diverse students and overcome their own biases" and "have an understanding of different cultures" (Oklahoma, 1992, p. 4). The legislature did not stop at listing these required outcomes; it also made recommendations for how these outcomes should be achieved in a preservice teacher-education program. It suggested that programs require teacher candidates to engage in self-knowledge studies and be exposed to a variety of cultures and people; study in depth a culture other than their own; and have a community involvement experience.

Both New York (1992) and Texas (1993) included some multicultural competencies in their teacher licensure examinations. New York's *Liberal Arts and Sciences Test (LAST)* required candidates to demonstrate conceptual and analytical skills, critical thinking and communication skills, and multicultural awareness. The *Assessment of Teaching Skills—Written* was designed to assess a candidate's pedagogical knowledge. Candidates were expected to understand diverse student populations and be able to use that knowledge to address the needs of all learners. They were also to be able to foster among students a sense of community and appreciation of and respect for all individuals and groups. The communications section of the test included the analysis of how cultural and gender differences can affect communication in the classroom. The professional environment section included the application of a variety of strategies for working with parents and others to help students from diverse backgrounds reinforce in-school learning outside the school environment (New York, 1992).

Texas was in the process of developing its tests for general pedagogical knowledge. Tests based on the expected candidate competencies for early childhood education, English, industrial technology, and professional development have been developed. The Texas (1993) test expects the teachers of English/ language arts to:

• recognize factors contributing to language diversity . . . understand and use standard English while recognizing historical, social, cultural, and technical factors . . . understand social and personal conflicts that may arise from differences in language or dialect . . . use instructional approaches that help students interpret forms of written expression from different historical periods, regional perspectives, and cultural and ethnic traditions. (p. 14)
• understand written expression as [an] aspect of culture. (p. 18)

The analysis of state initiatives indicated that there was a great degree of difference in states' requirements for multicultural curriculum. At least seven states had no requirements related to curriculum. California, Iowa, Kentucky, Minnesota, and Wisconsin had comprehensive requirements for the preparation of teachers. The implementation of standards for the approval of teacher-education programs was usually checked by means of periodic on-site reviews and written reports by review teams. Texas and New York were implementing performance-based licensure tests that included the assessment of competencies related to multicultural education.

Although 14 states expected schools to make their curriculum multicultural, only Maryland, Nebraska, Minnesota, and New Jersey required accountability through regular reports of plans and implementation. Iowa conducted regular on-site reviews of schools to monitor their implementation of the state's multicultural requirements and federal equity laws. Oklahoma required regular reporting on staff development activities supporting multicultural education.

Impact of State Initiatives

A number of state initiatives have addressed making education more reflective of cultural diversity and providing equal educational opportunity for all students. It is too early to determine how effective the initiatives in most states have been in effecting changes in schools. Iowa was the first state with legislation related to multicultural education for both K–12 schools and teacher-preparation programs. Twenty-five years after the 1978 legislation, the *Educational Equity Status Report* (Iowa,

1993a) to the state board of education reported that 55% of the Iowa schools were making a good-faith effort to deliver multi-cultural education. The other 45% "had significant areas of noncompliance" (p. ii). Minnesota reported that approximately 80% of its schools were in compliance as determined by a paper, rather than on-site, review (S. Jebe, personal communication, September 28, 1993).

The accountability plans for schools in Maryland, Nebraska, and New Jersey were new, and evaluations were not planned until after 1995. In the states in which program-approval standards have required human relations or multicultural components for a number of years, the teacher-education programs may be somewhat different from those in other states. However, the author was not aware of studies to confirm this hypothesis.

There were differences in the geographic regions in which greater attention was given to multicultural education. Several midwestern states, in which Whites comprised over 90% of the population, had strong human relations requirements for teacher education. Nebraska, Minnesota, and Iowa required their schools to be accountable for the infusion of multicultural education throughout the curriculum. Three states in which Whites comprised 75% or less of the population—California, New York, and Texas—had fairly comprehensive requirements and written resources to help schools implement them. Alabama, Georgia, Kentucky, and Texas stood out among the other southern states for their attention to cultural diversity and/or multicultural education at either the K–12 level or teacher education or both. Other southern states paid little or no attention to cultural diversity at any level even though they have rather large African American populations, ranging from 3% in West Virginia to over 35% in Mississippi.

In a pattern similar to the federal government's, states did not coordinate services and support for multicultural education. The Equal Educational Opportunity office in most states dealt exclusively with desegregation issues. Many states had separate funding and departments for services to LEP students and students with disabilities. Chapter 1 funds were administered by a different office. Although the same student or teacher or school may have been eligible for services from each of the offices, efforts across departments and their staffs were seldom coordinated.

NATIONAL NONGOVERNMENTAL INITIATIVES

Some national organizations like the American Council for Education and the Anti-Defamation League began promoting the need for more effective intergroup or intercultural relations in the 1940s (Montalto, 1978; Taba, Brady, & Robinson, 1952). However, most other national education associations did not address cultural diversity and its impact on education until the 1970s. Most of the initiatives were the result of pressure and work of African, Native, Hispanic, and Asian Americans within and outside the organizations themselves. One of the first widely circulated statements was the American Association of Colleges for Teacher Education's [AACTE] *No One Model Ameri-*

can, which was written by a culturally diverse committee of teacher educators in 1973.

In the mid-1970s associations like the National Council for the Social Studies (NCSS), AACTE, the Association for Supervision and Curriculum Development (ASCD), and the National Education Association (NEA) emphasized the need for ethnic studies that included attention to ethnicity, class, and religion. In the intervening years since then, multicultural education has expanded to include other cultural differences based on gender, language, disabilities, and age. National associations call for education that is multicultural at all levels from preschool through higher education.

Another significant impetus for the continuing attention to multiculturalism has been the changing demography of the student population and the ever-increasing shortage of faculty of color at all levels. The current teaching force does not begin to match the ethnic and gender diversity in the nation. It remains primarily White and female (Dilworth, 1990). A number of associations and states have developed and implemented strategies for increasing the diversity of the teacher pool (AACTE, 1990). At the same time, it becomes even more critical that teacher candidates and practicing teachers are able to teach multiculturally. This section reviews the standards and guidelines of selected national organizations that are supportive of multicultural education.

National Accreditation Standards for Teacher Education

The inclusion of multicultural education in teacher-education programs has been a requirement of NCATE since 1978 (NCATE, 1977). Although only 500 of the 1,200 institutions that prepare teachers and other school personnel were accredited by NCATE, those institutions have probably prepared over 70% of the new teachers annually. Thus, these national standards have a major influence on the preparation of school personnel in the United States.

The NCATE standards have undergone several revisions since 1978, but making teacher education multicultural has become even more important to the national accrediting organization. Cultural diversity and/or multicultural perspectives were addressed in 4 of the 18 standards in 1992 and were expected to become even more comprehensive in the 1994 revision of the standards. The professional studies standard included the following requirements:

• The initial teacher preparation program must provide knowledge about and appropriate skills in . . . cultural influences on learning . . . instructional strategies for exceptionalities. . . . Courses and experiences ensure the development of . . . knowledge of different learning styles.

• The unit [i.e., the school, college, or department of education] provides for study and experiences that help education students understand and apply appropriate strategies for individual learning needs, especially for culturally diverse and exceptional populations.

• The curriculum for professional studies component(s) incorporates multicultural and global perspectives. (NCATE, 1992b, p. 50)

The standard on clinical and field-based experiences requires that "education students participate in field-based and/or clinical experiences with culturally diverse and exceptional populations" (NCATE, 1992b, p. 51). The standard on admission to teacher education requires that the student body be culturally diverse. A culturally diverse faculty is required in the standard on faculty qualifications, assignments, and composition.

Further changes to the NCATE standards are expected in 1994. Those revisions are likely to require that all faculty in teacher-education programs have multicultural competencies. The standard on governance will probably require that both policies and practices in teacher education be multicultural and nondiscriminatory. A new standard will require that the program help teacher candidates to integrate pedagogical and disciplinary knowledge to create culturally sensitive teaching strategies.

The NCATE standards were applied to member institutions at least twice between 1978 and 1993. However, not all institutions had yet incorporated multicultural education and cultural diversity into their programs. Table 3–2 indicates that over 80% of the institutions reviewed by NCATE between 1988 and 1993 have incorporated multicultural education into the curriculum at least at a minimal level. Institutions did not fare as well on the other standards. Only 75% provided adequate field experiences with culturally diverse and exceptional populations. Just over

60% of the institutions had student populations that were culturally diverse; only 40% had adequate diversity in their faculty.

Although teacher education has not become as multicultural as NCATE would like, these national standards have had an influence on the institutions that seek national accreditation. The curriculum is now more multicultural than in 1978, when a standard on multicultural education was first applied. However, curriculum content was the only area in which improvement was recorded. Table 3–2 indicates that there has been no improvement in the provision of culturally diverse field experiences or the degree of cultural diversity in student bodies and faculty.

State Licensure

A number of initiatives have been undertaken since 1988 to enhance the teaching profession. The most notable has been the establishment of a National Board for Professional Teaching Standards to develop standards for the advanced certification of experienced teachers, following a pattern used by accountants, architects, physicians, and other professionals (Wise and Leibbrand, 1993). The board has also been charged with developing, testing, and implementing assessment protocols to evaluate teaching proficiency. This work is now in process. Some of the assessment components will be field tested in the mid-1990s.

The National Board's advanced certification of experienced teachers has been designed as a voluntary process for individual teachers. However, all teachers and other professional school personnel such as counselors, principals, and librarians

TABLE 3–2. Attention to Multicultural Education and Cultural Diversity in the NCATE Standards

| Standard | Weakness | Dates of Visits | | | | |
		F92	S92	F91	F88–S91	All
I.E	Professional studies lack attention to cultural diversity and/or exceptionalities.	16.1% (9)	14.0% (7)	12.0% (6)	17.9% (37)	16.3% (59)
	Professional studies lack attention to global awareness.	10.7% (6)	0.4% (2)	16.0% (8)	17.9% (37)	14.6% (53)
	Professional studies lack attention to multicultural perspectives.	8.9% (5)	0% (0)	6.0% (3)	20.3% (42)	13.8% (50)
II.A	Candidates do not have adequate or systematic experiences with culturally diverse populations.	26.8% (15)	20.0% (10)	18.0% (9)	26.1% (54)	24.2% (88)
III.A	Student population is not sufficiently culturally diverse.	50.0% (28)	48.0% (24)	50.0% (25)	28.0% (58)	37.2% (135)
	The recruitment plan for a culturally diverse student population is insufficient or nonexistent.	25.0% (14)	16.0% (8)	24.0% (12)	22.7% (47)	22.3% (81)
	Alternative admission policies to encourage the admission of underrepresented groups are unclear or nonexistent.	10.7% (6)	10.0% (5)	20.0% (10)	10.6% (22)	11.8% (43)
IV.A	The faculty lacks sufficient cultural and/or gender diversity.	55.4% (31)	70.0% (35)	66.0% (33)	55.8% (120)	60.3% (219)
Total Institutions		56	50	50	207	363

These data are the Unit Accreditation Board's citations of weaknesses for all institutions reviewed under the NCATE standards between fall 1988 and fall 1993. The numbers in cells under the "Dates of Visits" are the percentage and number that were cited for not addressing the weakness statement.

must be licensed by their respective states to work in public schools. Therefore, the licensure process is not voluntary. In addition, the state licensure requirements influence the content of teacher education because institutions want to ensure that their graduates have met all of the requirements established by the profession.

Although many states required specific credit hours or courses at the time of this study, some states had begun to identify content and experiences expected, rather than specific courses. This trend is expected to continue into the next century. To assist in this effort, the Council of Chief State School Officers (CCSSO) established the Interstate New Teacher Assessment and Support Consortium (INTASC) "to enhance collaboration among states interested in rethinking teacher assessment for initial licensing as well as for preparation and induction into the profession" (INTASC, 1992, p. 1). In 1992–1993 a task force of INTASC wrote 10 performance-based principles for the initial licensure of teachers. These principles were designed to be compatible with the principles of the National Board and to serve as a base for the advanced certification of teachers after several years of experience in the classroom.

Even though the principles may be revised before publication in 1994, it is instructive to review the expectations related to education that is multicultural. Nine of the 10 principles included attention to one or more aspects of cultural diversity in the Knowledge, Dispositions, or Performances components that explicate the principle. The principle that was most directly related to teaching multiculturally required that "the teacher understands how students differ in their approaches to learning and creates instructional opportunities that are adapted to diverse learners" (INTASC, 1992, p. 14). Selected expectations that demonstrate how this principle was addressed include:

Knowledge:

- The teacher knows about the process of second language acquisition and about strategies to support the learning of students whose first language is not English.
- The teacher understands how students' learning is influenced by individual experiences, talents, and prior learning, as well as language, culture, family and community values.
- The teacher has a well-grounded framework for understanding cultural and community diversity and knows how to learn about and incorporate students' experiences, cultures, and community resources into instruction. (INTASC, 1992, p. 14)

Dispositions:

- The teacher believes that all children can learn at high levels and persists in helping all children achieve success.
- The teacher is sensitive to community and cultural norms. (INTASC, 1992, pp. 14–15)

Performances:

- The teacher seeks to understand students' families, cultures, and communities, and uses this information as a basis for connecting instruction to students' experiences.

- The teacher brings multiple perspectives to the discussion of subject matter, including attention to students' personal, family, and community experiences and cultural norms. (INTASC, 1992, p. 15)

A number of states were using these proposed standards as a model for the development of their own outcomes-based standards for licensure. Between 1993 and 1998 additional standards for teaching the content (e.g., mathematics, English, and science) will be written. These INTASC principles were also being integrated into the national accreditation system by NCATE to reinforce the need for teacher candidates to be able to work effectively in classrooms to ensure that all students learn. The collaboration among national accreditation, state licensure, and advanced certification should lead to a comprehensive system for improving teaching and learning. The resulting standards also will have a direct influence on teacher education.

Program Approval

Nearly all states have standards for the approval of programs to prepare teachers and other school personnel to work in early childhood, elementary, middle, and secondary schools. In addition, NCATE has approved curriculum guidelines for 17 specific preparation programs, such as physical education, special education, library media specialist, social studies education, and science education. Most teacher-education programs in the United States must show evidence that they are meeting either the state standards or the national guidelines that have been developed by national education organizations.

Because of their influence on teacher-education programs, I reviewed both state and national guidelines to determine how much attention they gave to cultural diversity and multicultural education. The state and national guidelines, which are approved by NCATE, that have requirements for multicultural educational are shown on Table 3–3. At least 28 states referred to one or more of the concepts supportive of multicultural education in the generic standards for professional education. However, only 16 states had references in the specific program standards. Alabama had requirements for 20 of the 27 areas included in Table 3–3. The area most likely to have state requirements was bilingual education, followed by ESL and elementary programs. The earlier section on state initiatives described some of the program-approval requirements.

Of the 17 national curriculum guidelines approved by NCATE as of 1993, all had multicultural requirements except the guidelines of the National Association of Middle Schools. Ten sets of the guidelines required attention to cultural, ethnic, socioeconomic, linguistic, and/or gender differences. Study and/or experiences with students with disabilities were required in the programs for six areas.

Multicultural education or studies was expected in six of the guidelines. Social studies and elementary education had the most references. English guidelines called for the inclusion of literature by females and authors of color. Social studies required content of non-Western and gender studies. Programs for principals and school business officials required skills in

TABLE 3–3. Multicultural Education Requirements in Teacher-Preparation Programs

	NCATE	AL	AK	AZ	AR	CA	GA	IL	IN	IA	KS	KY	ME
Generic professional studies	■	■	■		■	■	■	■		■	■	■	■
Administration	■	■					■						■
Art		■					■						
Bilingual education				■			■		■				■
Computer education	■												
Early childhood education	■								■				
Educational communications and technology	■												
Elementary education	■								■				
English/language arts	■						■						
English as a second language				■			■						
Foreign language		■				■	■						
Health education	■	■											
Home economics	■												
Library media	■												
Mathematics	■												
Middle school										■			
Music	■						■						
Physical education	■	■											
Principalship	■												■
Professional development													
Reading	■												
Counseling							■						
Psychology	■						■						
Psychometry													
Science	■	■											
Social studies	■						■						
Special education	■												
Technology education	■												

The shaded cells indicate that NCATE or the state required attention to one or more aspects of multicultural education in programs for the preparation of school personnel to teach the subject or work at the level shown in the far left column.

interpersonal relations. Study of equity issues was included in the computer education guidelines. Elementary education had the only requirements for developing skills in the selection and use of instructional materials appropriate to students' cultural and linguistic backgrounds and exceptionalities (NCATE, 1992a).

In the reviews of each program returned to NCATE by the national organizations, multicultural issues often were not being addressed adequately in the curriculum. Although courses may be offered in non-Western history and literature by females and authors of color, teacher candidates too often were not required to experience them. Instead, they were electives. However, as a result of the critique of programs using these guidelines as criteria, a number of institutions had changed their requirements and added components to ensure that at least minimal multicultural content was being included in teacher education programs.

CONCLUSIONS

Since the 1977 study of federal and state policies by Giles and Gollnick, federal legislation changed little in the way it addressed multicultural education. The focus continued to be on working with students with disabilities and culturally diverse students to provide equal educational opportunity. The

TABLE 3–3. (*continued*)

MD	MA	MN	MO	MT	NE	NJ	NM	NY	ND	OH	OK	OR	PA	RI	SD	TX	UT	WA	WI	WY
	▓	▓	▓	▓			▓	▓	▓	▓	▓	▓	▓	▓	▓		▓	▓	▓	▓
				▓												▓				
	▓					▓	▓							▓			▓			
																▓				
				▓		▓									▓	▓				
▓																				
	▓					▓		▓							▓					
	▓																			
				▓																
				▓																
																▓				
															▓					
▓				▓																
						▓										▓				
																▓				

minimal attention to ethnic diversity in the 1970s Title IX (ESEA) Ethnic Heritage Act was eliminated in the early 1980s.

Federal support for the development of curriculum materials or models received minimal funding and was addressed to specific groups (e.g., women or Hawaiians). All federal efforts were focused on the provision of equal educational opportunity for female students, students of color, LEP students, students from low-income families, and students with disabilities. Although Chapter 1 (ESEA) received about 20% of the Department of Education budget, it still did not overcome the inequities that existed across state and school districts. Federal support for desegregation efforts was inadequate to reduce the segregation of students in schools.

The number of states with requirements related to multicultural education has increased. In 1977, "at least 28 states had provisions supporting some aspects of multicultural education, including bilingual and ethnic specific aspects" (Giles & Gollnick, 1977, p. 157); that study did not include an examination of gender and exceptionalities. By 1993, 35 states had regulations or policies related to ethnicity, race, class, gender, and/ or other cultural groups. Forty states had requirements that schools and/or teacher education include the study of one or more ethnic groups, human relations, cultural diversity, multicultural education, and/or bilingual education.

Many national education associations had resolutions and/or statements that supported multicultural education, equity, and/

or equal educational opportunity at all levels of schooling (e.g., AACTE's *The Next Level,* 1990; American Federation of Teachers' *Democracy's Half-Told Story* [Gagnon, 1989]). Many had developed guidelines, which included multicultural competencies, for both school and teacher education (e.g., see the curriculum guidelines for the preparation of teachers in NCATE's *Approved Curriculum Guidelines* [1992a] from the National Association for the Education of Young Children, National Council for Teachers of English, National Council for Social Studies, et al.). Although these recommendations were commendable and were used seriously as guides for the reform of education by some educators, they were used voluntarily.

Even national accreditation by NCATE, which had requirements for cultural diversity and multicultural education, was required for all institutions in only one state—Arkansas. Nevertheless, over 500 institutions voluntarily underwent this review. In teacher education the requirements of the state program approval and licensure systems influenced the content of teacher education programs. The majority of the states expected at least minimal knowledge about cultural diversity. Alabama, California, New York, and Texas had begun the identification of expected performance for delivery in the classroom of education that is multicultural. The performance-based licensure standards being developed by INTASC delineated even further the knowledge, dispositions, and performance essential to teach all students.

States took different approaches to ensure that K–12 schools addressed elements of multicultural education. The most effective approach was legislation that required the development of plans to be monitored or assessed on a regular schedule. Laws were usually accompanied by rules for implementation that could be administered by a state department of education. Staff development activities and guidelines for multicultural education were effective short-term strategies if accompanied by sufficient funding. Without the legislative leverage, guidelines were soon ignored and staff development not supported.

There had been significant progress at the state level in the recognition of cultural diversity and the need to include it in state requirements. With few exceptions, the focus was on the first three approaches identified by Sleeter and Grant (1989)—teaching the exceptional and culturally different, human relations, and single-group studies. The requirements for multicultural education usually expected school personnel to have knowledge of cultural diversity in order to develop more effective instructional strategies for teaching culturally different students. Seldom was it expected that existing curriculum and school and classroom practices should actually be reformed to reflect cultural diversity. The application of multicultural requirements in schools and teacher education was often handled by adding a course on multicultural education or inserting units in existing courses. It is to be hoped that the next step in the realization of education that is multicultural will be the use of cultural diversity and equity as the lens through which all reform occurs.

References

Alabama Department of Education. (1990). *Alabama State Board of Education, State Department of Education administrative code.* Montgomery: Author.

Alaska Department of Education. (1991). *Alaska education regulations* (4 AAC 12.900). Juneau: Author.

American Association of Colleges for Teacher Education. (1973). *No one model American.* Washington, DC: Author.

American Association of Colleges for Teacher Education. (1990). *The next level: Minority teacher supply and demand.* Washington, DC: Author.

Asante, M. K. (1990). *Kemet, Afrocentricity and knowledge.* Trenton, NJ: Africa World Press.

Au, K. Hu-Pei, & Jordon, C. (1981). Teaching reading to Hawaiian children: Finding a culturally appropriate solution. In H. T. Trueba, G. P. Guthrie, & K. Hu Pei Au (Eds.), *Cuture and the bilingual classroom* (pp. 139–152). Rowley, MA: Newbury House.

Banks, J. A. (1988). *Multiethnic education: Theory and practice* (2nd ed.). Boston: Allyn and Bacon.

Bates, P. (1990). Desegregation: Can we get there from here? *Phi Delta Kappan, 72*(1), 8–17.

Brown, C. E. (1992). Restructing for a new America. In M. E. Dilworth (Ed.), *Diversity in teacher education: New expectations* (pp. 1–22). San Francisco: Jossey-Bass.

California Commission on Teacher Credentialing. (1992). *Standards of program quality and effectiveness, factors to consider and preconditions in the evaluation of professional teacher preparation programs for multiple and single subject credentials.* Sacramento: Author.

California Commission on Teacher Credentialing. (n.d.) *Sex equity in education: How to tell if your'e doing well.* Sacramento: Author.

Council of Chief State School Officers. (1990). *School success for limited English proficient students: The challenge and state response.* Washington, DC: Author.

Cummins, J. (1989). *Empowering minority students.* Sacramento: California Association for Bilingual Education.

Darling-Hammond, L. (1993). *Federal policy options for Chapter 1: An equity agenda for school restructuring.* New York: National Center for Restructuring Education, Schools, and Teaching.

Delaware Department of Public Instruction. Statewide Multicultural Education Committee. (1990). *Guidelines for infusing multicultural education into school curricular and co-curricular programs.* Dover: Author.

Dilworth, M. E. (1990). *Reading between the lines: Teachers and their racial/ethnic cultures* (Teacher Education Monograph No. 11). Washington, DC: ERIC Clearinghouse on Teacher Education and American Association of Colleges for Teacher Education.

Executive Office of the President of the United States. (1993). *Budget of the United States government: Fiscal year 1994.* Washington, DC: U.S. Government Printing Office.

Florida Department of Education. (1991). *Multicultural education in Florida.* Tallahassee: Author.

Gagnon, P. (1989). *Democracy's half-told story: What American history textbooks should add.* Washington, DC: American Federation of Teachers.

Georgia Professional Standards Commission. (n.d.). *Rules for the procedures of Professional Standards Commission* (Chapter 505-3, Teacher Education). Atlanta: Author.

Giles, R. H., & Gollnick, D. M. (1977). Ethnic/cultural diversity as reflected in federal and state educational legislation and policies. In F. H. Klassen & D. M. Gollnick (Eds.), *Pluralism and the American teacher: Issues and case studies* (pp. 115–160). Washington, DC: American Association of Colleges for Teacher Education.

Gollnick, D. M., & Chinn, P. C. (1994). *Multicultural education in a pluralistic society* (4th ed.). Columbus, OH: Macmillan.

Hawaii State Board of Education. (n.d.). *Hawaii state plan* [Socio-cultural advancement-Education 226-21(b)4]. Honolulu: Author.

Hillard, A. G. (1976). Introduction to the 1976 reprint. In G. G. M. James, *Stolen legacy* (pp. i–iii). San Francisco: Julian Richardson Associates.

Indiana Register. (1988, January 1). *11* (4).

Interstate New Teacher Assessment and Support Consortium. (1992). *Draft standards for teacher licensing.* Washington, DC: Council of Chief State School Officers.

Iowa Department of Education. (1977). *Guidelines for implementation of the human relations requirement for teacher education and certification and for the approval of human relations components.* Des Moines: Author.

Iowa Department of Education. (1989). *A guide to developing multicultural, nonsexist education across the curriculum.* Des Moines: Author.

Iowa Department of Education. (1993a). *Educational equity status report: 1992–93 school year.* Des Moines: Author.

Iowa Department of Education. (1993b). *Information for educational reviews: Educational equity review for civil rights issues in Iowa educational agencies.* Des Moines: Author.

Kansas State Board of Education. (1990). *General standards: Pre-service professional education* (91-1-80). Topeka: Author.

Kentucky Department of Education. (1992). *Program guidelines for multicultural education.* Frankfort: Author.

Kentucky Legislature. Session of 1990. (1990). *House bill no. 940, Kentucky Education Reform Act* (KRS 156.410). Lexington: Author.

Kozol, J. (1991). *Savage inequalities.* New York: Crown.

Maryland State Board of Education. (1993). *Annotated code of Maryland: Education article* [ss2-205(c) and 2-205(h)]. Annapolis: Author.

Massachusetts Board of Education. Massachusetts Department of Education. (1990). *Amended regulations for the certification of educational personnel.* Quincy: Author.

Millsap, M. A., Moss, M., & Gamse. B. (1993). *Chapter 1 in public schools: The Chapter 1 school implementation study.* Washington, DC: U.S. Department of Education, Office of Policy and Planning.

Minnesota Board of Education. (1988). Inclusive educational program rule (Minnesota Rules Part 3500.0550). *State Register.* Minneapolis: Author.

Minnesota Board of Teaching. (n.d.). *Components to be included in all programs leading to licensure in education* (8700.2700 Human Relations). St. Paul: Author.

Montalto, N. V. (1978). The forgotten dream: A history of the intercultural education movement, 1924–1941. *Dissertation Abstracts International, 39A,* 1061. (University Microfilms No. 78-13436).

National Council for Accreditation of Teacher Education. (1977). *Standards for the accreditation of teacher education programs.* Washington, DC: Author.

National Council for Accreditation of Teacher Education. (1992a). *Approved curriculum guidelines.* Washington, DC: Author.

National Council for Accreditation of Teacher Education. (1992b). *Standards, procedures, and policies for the accreditation of professional education units.* Washington, DC: Author.

Nebraska Department of Education. (1992a). *Chapter 16: Approval of school district multicultural education programs.* Lincoln: Author.

Nebraska Legislature. Session of 1992. (1992b). *Legislative Bill No. 922, An Act . . . to Provide for the Development and Implementation of Multicultural Education.* Lincoln: Author.

Network of Regional Desegregation Assistance Centers. (1989, June). *Resegregation of public schools: The third generation.* Portland, OR: Northwest Regional Educational Laboratory.

New Jersey Department of Education. Office of Equal Educational Opportunity. (1993). *Guidelines for education that is multicultural (GEM).* Trenton: Author.

New York State Education Department. (1989). *Promoting self-esteem in young women: A manual for teachers.* Albany: Author.

New York State Education Department. (1992). *New York state teacher certification examinations.* Albany: Author.

New York State Education Department. (n.d.). *Women's history month: Suggested classroom activities.* Albany: Author.

New York. The University of the State of New York and State Education Department. (1991). *A new compact for learning: Improving public elementary, middle, and secondary education results in the 1990s.* Albany: Author.

Oakes, J. (1988). Tracking in mathematics and science education: A structural contribution to unequal schooling. In L. Weis (Ed.), *Class, race, and gender in American education* (pp. 106–125). Albany: State University of New York Press.

Oklahoma Legislature. Session of 1992. (1992). *House Bill No. 2246, An Act Relating to Schools.* Oklahoma City: Author.

Oklahoma State Department of Education. (1993). *Regulations for local staff development programs.* Oklahoma City: Author.

Pennsylvania Bureau of Teacher Preparation and Certification. (1992). *Restructured general standards.* Harrisburg: Author.

Sinclair, B., & Gutmann, B. (1992). *A summary of state Chapter 1 participation and achievement information—1989–90.* Washington, DC: U.S. Department of Education, Office of Policy and Planning.

Sleeter, C. E., & Grant, C. A. (1989). *Turning on learning: Five approaches for multicultural teaching plans for race, class, gender, and disability.* Columbus, OH: Merrill.

Stanford Working Group on Federal Education Programs for Limited English Proficient Students. (1993). *Revising bilingual education: The second generation.* Palo Alto, CA: Author.

Strang, E. W., & Carlson, E. (1991). *Providing Chapter 1 services to limited English proficient students: Final report.* Rockville, MD: Westat, Inc.

Taba, H., Brady, E. H., & Robinson, J. T. (1952). *Intergroup education in public schools.* Washington, DC: American Council on Education.

Texas Education Agency. (1993). *Examination for the certification of educators in Texas (EXCET).* Austin: Author.

U.S. Bureau of the Census. (1992). *Statistical abstract of the United States: 1992* (112th edition). Washington, DC: U.S. Government Printing Office.

U.S. Department of Education, Office of Policy and Planning. (1993, February). *Reinventing Chapter 1: The current Chapter 1 program and new directions.* Washington, DC: Author.

U.S. House of Representatives. (1975). *A compilation of federal education laws as amended through December 31, 1974.* Washington, DC: U.S. Government Printing Office.

U.S. House of Representatives. (1993, March). *A compilation of federal education laws: Volume II—elementary and secondary education, individuals with disabilities, and related programs* (Serial No. 103-D). Washington, DC: U.S. Government Printing Office.

Utah State Board of Education. (1979). *Guidelines for cultural awareness in teacher preparation.* Salt Lake City: Author.

Valencia, R. R. (1991). The plight of Chicano students: An overview of schooling conditions and outcomes: In R. R. Valencia (Ed.), *Chicano school failure and success: Research and policy agendas for the 1990s* (pp. 3–16). New York: Falmer Press.

Washington Department of Public Instruction. (1992). *Competencies for teaching multiculturally.* Olympia: Author.

West Virginia Board of Education. (1970). Resolution: The selection of textbooks, instructional materials, and learning technologies: Inter-ethnic in content, concept, and illustration. Charleston: Author.

West Virginia Board of Education. (1989). *Legislative rule* (Chapter 18-2). Charleston: Author.

Winfield, L. F., & Manning, J. B. (1992). Changing school culture to accommodate student diversity. In M. E. Dilworth (Ed.), *Diversity in teacher education: New expectations* (pp. 181–214). San Francisco: Jossey-Bass.

Wisconsin Department of Education. Human Relations. (1992). *Wisconsin administrative code,* PI 4.11, 70-17. Madison: Author.

Wise, A. E., & Leibbrand, J. (1993). Accreditation and the creation of a profession of teaching. *Phi Delta Kappan, 75* (2), 133–136, 154–157.

• 4 •

GENDER AND RACE AS FACTORS IN EDUCATIONAL LEADERSHIP AND ADMINISTRATION

Cherry A. McGee Banks

UNIVERSITY OF WASHINGTON, BOTHELL

This chapter is a review of the status and characteristics of women and people of color in educational leadership and administration. The author's primary intention is to acquaint readers with significant studies and provide a broad overview of the characteristics and experiences of women and people of color who are superintendents and principals. The chapter reflects a dual concern for research and expert opinion. Theories and research are discussed, but the chapter also includes personal insights, interpretations, and recommendations for improving opportunities for women and people of color in educational leadership.

Available research on women and people of color in educational leadership does not support equal coverage of both groups on all of the topics covered in the chapter. Some sections of the chapter are primarily concerned with women; others focus on people of color. A major aim of the chapter is to identify gaps in the research, compare and contrast the experiences of women and people of color, and explore possible linkages between their experiences.

A major theme running throughout the chapter is the relationship of social context to the underrepresentation of women and people of color in educational leadership positions. A primary objective of this chapter is to review what we have learned and are learning about women and people of color in educational leadership and to identify ways in which a multicultural approach can help extend our knowledge by providing new insights and perspectives on leadership.

THE NATURE OF LEADERSHIP

Leadership is a relatively new field of study (Yukl, 1981). Scientific research on leadership did not begin until the late 20th century. Several of the major theories in leadership, such as social exchange theory and situational theories, were not conceptualized until the 1950s and 1960s.

Women and people of color were almost completely absent from the study of leadership until the late 1970s (Bass, 1981). The lack of research on women and people of color was not viewed as problematic because race and gender were not considered differences of consequence (Bass, 1981). Researchers seemed to assume that their findings could be applied without regard for race and gender. Theories used to frame research, such as McGregor's Theory X and Theory Y and Argyris's Model I and II, were silent on issues of race and gender (McGregor, 1960; Argyris & Schön, 1974).

Leadership theory and practice are evolving and the traditional leadership paradigm is being challenged. Scholars are working to broaden the study of leadership to include women and people of color. They are also developing preservice and continuing education programs to prepare leaders to address the changing context of educational leadership and administration (Cunningham, 1990).

Definitions

Leadership is a broad concept with many different meanings (Burns, 1979; Hemphill & Coons, 1957; Stogdill, 1974; Rost, 1991). While there is no universally accepted definition of leadership, most definitions share two assumptions. They assume that leadership is a group phenomenon and that leaders exercise intentional influence over followers (Yukl, 1981; Janda, 1960). Definitions of leadership differ in terms of who exercises influence, the reasons why influence is attempted, and the ways in which influence is exercised (Yukl, 1981; Immegart, 1988).

One widely used definition of leadership states that leadership is "the initiation and maintenance of structure in expectation and interaction" (Stogdill, 1974, p. 411). This definition incorporates two key categories of leadership behavior: *consideration* and *initiating structure* (Fleishman, 1957; Halpin & Winer, 1957; Hemphill & Coons, 1957). Consideration and initiating structure include a number of specific behaviors. Three questionnaires, the 40-item Leader Behavior Description Questionnaire (LBDQ), the Supervisory Behavior Description Questionnaire (SBDQ), and the Leader Behavior Description Questionnaire XII (LBDQ XII), were constructed by Ohio State University researchers to measure leadership behavior (Fleishman, 1953; Stogdill, 1963; Hemphill & Coons, 1957).

The LBDQ, which was normed on male samples, is still used as a research protocol. In a meta-analysis of studies that examined differences in male and female responses to the LBDQ, Shakeshaft (1979, 1985) found that there were no differences between the two sexes. Shakeshaft (1987) notes that perceptual studies using instruments like the LBDQ, as opposed to behavioral studies, may not pick up real differences in the behavior of male and female leaders. Other researchers have criticized the LBDQ for having a halo effect, reporting implicit theories and stereotypes instead of actual leader behavior, and not relating to leaders' self-descriptions of their behavior (Bass, 1981).

Current State of Leadership

There are radically different views on the status of leadership as a discipline. In a comprehensive review of research and theory on managerial leadership, Yukl (1981) concluded that the field is in a state of ferment and confusion. Yukl's concerns center on three issues: (a) the lack of agreement in the field about leadership as a concept; (b) the lack of agreement in the field as to the ability of a leader to exercise substantial influence on performance in an organization; and (c) the conceptual weaknesses of current theories of leadership and their lack of clear empirical support. Immegart (1988, p. 266), however, argues that leadership is not the "barren ground nor the frustrating arena" portrayed by critics like Yukl. In a review of research on leadership and leader behavior, Immegart notes that the knowledge base in leadership is growing, scholars are building on previous research, and the field's understanding of leadership is increasing.

Research on and conducted by women and people of color in educational leadership is growing. Women and people of color are adding an exciting element to the study of leadership. Their work raises new questions (Scott, 1983; Lomotey, 1989), challenges traditional leadership theory (Evers & Lakomski, 1991), redefines old concepts and presents new language to describe leadership (Oritz & Marshall, 1988; Shakeshaft, 1987), and is helping to create a new vision of leadership (Astin & Leland, 1991). However, there continues to be a dearth of research on both groups. Of the research that is available, there is considerably more on women than on people of color.

Major Research Approaches

Research on leadership can generally be classified into four approaches: the power-influence approach, trait approach, behavioral approach, and situational approach (Yukl, 1981). The power-influence approach regards power as a relationship that involves persuasion, coercion, indoctrination, and other forms of reciprocal influence (Bell, 1975). Leader effectiveness is measured in terms of the amount and source of power available to leaders and the ways in which power is used (French & Raven, 1960).

At the turn of the century and in the early 1900s, and then again in the 1960s and 1970s, trait theories were a topic of considerable interest in leadership. Trait theories assume that leaders can be differentiated from followers by their personality, character, and other qualities. Personal qualities such as intelligence, self-confidence, high energy, and persuasive skill are commonly identified as traits of leaders (House & Baetz, 1979; Jago, 1982; Stogdill, 1974). Trait theories are no longer in vogue. However, the idea that effective leaders have characteristics traditionally associated with men still has currency and continues to influence contemporary views of women leaders.

Behavioral approaches and situational approaches are somewhat related. Researchers use behavioral approaches to examine what leaders do (Pelz, 1952; Bales, 1950). They are particularly concerned with identifying and understanding effective behaviors and activities of leaders. Situational approaches, which are also known as contingency theories, highlight the importance of context in determining effective leadership (Fiedler, 1967; Vroom, 1976; Vroom & Yetton, 1973). For example, a specific behavior, such as praising a subordinate, is not always effective. In some cases praise may result in the desired outcome, while in other cases it may not. Situational theorists argue that effective leaders must be able to contextualize their behavior (Hersey, 1984).

It is interesting that even though situational theories were created in a society in which racism and sexism are salient, they are silent on issues of race and gender. This is especially perplexing since community factors, cultural values, and other commonly studied situational variables frequently involve issues of race and gender. Situational analysis can help increase our understanding of the behaviors of people of color and women in leadership positions as well as the behaviors of others toward them. It can also enhance our understanding of the ways in which race and gender serve as moderator variables in situations that require personal commitment, risk taking, and a quest for justice and equality.

Barbara A. Sizemore, a former superintendent of schools in Washington, D.C., argues that scholarly work on Black superintendents must be interpreted in the larger social reality of Black life and the historical context of the struggle of Blacks for education. The history of African Americans and their struggle to attend public school and gain access to jobs and positions in public schools is necessary for an informed analysis of Black educational leaders (Sizemore, 1986). Sizemore uses Black schools in Pittsburgh to illustrate her point. She states that after the Black segregated school in Pittsburgh was closed in 1867, no Black teachers were hired until 1933. The first Black principal since 1867 was hired in 1962.

SOCIAL AND ROLE THEORY

Social and role theory can help explain the status of women and people of color in leadership theory and their underrepresentation in educational leadership positions. Role theory provides a basis for examining role socialization and for explaining the behaviors of people in occupational roles such as principals and superintendents. Role theory is based on the idea that a role defines how individuals are expected to behave, how individuals occupying roles perceive what they are supposed to do, and the actual behavior of individuals (Toren, 1973; N. Gross, Mason, & McEachern, 1958).

Scholars, practitioners, and gatekeepers (those who control entry into educational leadership) are socialized and participate in a society that makes cultural assumptions about women and people of color. Those cultural assumptions grow out of societal norms and values that marginalize these two groups. Norms and values are products of socialization, and part of the process of role socialization that begins in infancy and continues through adulthood. Decisions about who is the focus of research, who is recruited and hired, and who does or does not get promoted are made within a social context in which women and people of color experience an inferior social status and are often objects of negative stereotypes.

Role socialization is commonly viewed as a two-way process in which both the socializer and the person being socialized may be changed in significant ways (Goslin, 1969). This characteristic of role socialization is particularly important when race and gender are incorporated into the study of educational leaders. On one hand, leaders learn to accept and adopt appropriate values, rules, and policies through their socialization into the profession and participation in professional organizations (E. Gross & Etzioni, 1985). Weber (1968) refers to this process as legitimation. On the other hand, women and people of color also have the potential to change the institutions in which they work and their colleagues. More research is needed to increase understanding of this dynamic interchange.

Racism and Sexism as Factors in Socialization

Women and people of color both experience prejudice and discrimination. Racism and sexism are unconscious ideologies and integral parts of the American identity (Franklin, 1993; West, 1993; Freeman, 1984). The values and norms that legitimate prejudice and discrimination are internalized and transmitted to new members of U.S. society through socialization. However, while racism and sexism are both forms of discrimination, they are not necessarily evidenced in the same way. From a sociological perspective, the prejudice and discrimination that women and people of color experience have different origins and different consequences. Developing and implementing effective strategies to reduce prejudice and discrimination require that we acknowledge and work to understand the similarities and differences in the social genesis and maintenance of gender and racial prejudice and discrimination.

Unlike people of color, women are not a numerical minority. Women are a majority in the U.S. population. They are considered a minority group because, like people of color, they lack access to power. However, even though White women lack social, political, and economic power, they enjoy a privileged status in U.S. society based on their race (McIntosh, 1988; hooks, 1990). Women of color experience discrimination based on two factors: race and sex (Butler & Walter, 1991; DuBois & Ruiz, 1990).

Women have more social contact with men and boys who are members of their ethnic or racial group than minorities have with Whites. Men and women interact with each other from birth, whereas most minorities and Whites have little voluntary social contact with each other. Children learn about sex roles directly from parents, friends, and other close associates, but most acquire information about different racial and ethnic groups from secondary sources such as books, television, and individuals who are not members of their primary groups.

Race socialization frequently privileges White characteristics and marginalizes characteristics associated with people of color (Sleeter, 1993). It is particularly pernicious because it frequently occurs in an environment where racism is a powerful though often unidentified variable in the socialization process. Racism affects individual as well as institutional responses to people of color (West, 1993; Franklin, 1993; C. McCarthy & Crichlow, 1993). Selective perception and reinforcement and other such processes are used to deny variability among people of color in areas such as intellect and accomplishment (H. J. Scott, personal communication, 1993). As a result, it is not uncommon for all members of a group to be reduced to one-dimensional representatives of their phenotype. These representations are codified in images that are presented in media, texts, and other communicative elements in society that forefront racism as an important element in race socialization.

On an institutional level, racism results in barriers that restrict people of color from access to power and privilege within the institution. Racism and its impact on race socialization make it impossible for people of color to dream their dreams free from the dire reality that color is the key that opens the door to the full range of opportunities and benefits of American citizenship (H. J. Scott, personal communication, 1993).

For the most part, race and sex socialization have been explored as independent processes. Researchers who are interested in race have basically disregarded gender and researchers who have examined issues of gender have tended to overlook race (C. McCarthy & Crichlow, 1993). This tendency ignores women of color as an integrated whole and presents them in fragments (Pinar, 1993; Dugger, 1991). Exploring race and sex as a collectivity offers exciting possibilities for future research.

Persistence of Prejudice and Discrimination

Schools reflect the race and gender stratification that exists in the wider society (Gaertner, 1980). Both women and people of color are underrepresented in educational leadership positions in schools. In 1992, 97.1% of superintendents were White and 89.5% were male (Saks, 1992). Female administrative aspirants interviewed by Edson (1987) stated that "they had to be far superior to male candidates just to be considered for an administrative position and, even then, school boards still showed a preference for hiring men" (p. 265).

Efforts to combat prejudice and discrimination, such as affirmative action, have been disappointingly ineffective for people of color and only marginally effective for women (M. McCarthy & Zent, 1981). In 1992 women held 10.5% of superintendencies while people of color held only 2.9%. African Americans constituted 1.9% of those superintendencies and Hispanics constituted .5% (Saks, 1992). Whites also held most school principalships.

Sex Roles

Over the years, researchers have used the concept of sex roles to explain why women are underrepresented in educational leadership (Schmuck, 1980). The concept of sex roles grew out of social theory and Blau's (1976) research on social exchange. Holter (1970) defines sex roles as the roles that are assigned to men because they are men and women because they are women. Sex roles are acquired through socialization in environments where there are different expectations for men and women. Each sex is socialized in ways that are consistent with specific gender expectations (Holter, 1970). Early investigations of sex roles focused on sex-role identity in terms of attitudes, values, beliefs, and behaviors (Millett, 1969/1980). These investigations were followed by studies that explored the relationship between sex and the experiences of women and men in organizations (Biklen & Brannigan, 1980).

Schmuck (1980) organized research on sex roles into three broad categories, each representing a specific perspective: the individual perspective, the social perspective, and the organizational perspective. Schmuck notes that individual perspectives on sex roles draw heavily on psychological research and focus on individual attitudes and aspirations. According to Schmuck, the individual perspective is limited by its lack of attention to societal norms, folkways, and traditions. The social perspective focuses on men's and women's work. Schmuck argues that our society maximizes the differences between men's and women's work and gives women's work less status, value, and pay. Even though most institutions in the United States have both male and female workers, Schmuck states that men generally hold the more influential positions. From an organizational perspective, competent women are often discriminated against because they are viewed as threatening and are marginalized with terms such as "girls" and "honey" (Hagen & Kahn, 1975).

The women's movement in the 1960s and 1970s increased awareness of and sensitivity to sex roles and the expectations and norms related to them (Friedan, 1963). An increased awareness of sex roles led to questions about the validity of men's investigating and interpreting research on sex roles (Schmuck, 1980). Researchers such as Huber (1973) and Rossi (1970) argue that much of the research on sex-role characteristics reflects male perspectives and is stereotyped. They question research that creates a dichotomy between males and females by suggesting, for example, that males are frank and straightforward in social relations, intellectually rational, and competent, and that females are interested in social amenities, emotional warmth, and affective matters (Huber, 1973; Rossi, 1970). Feminists have also criticized research that uses male models of organizational behavior to evaluate females. They note that even though most women are clerical or service workers, most of the research on women in organizations focuses on the roles and behavior of women in male-dominated professions (Astin, 1969; Bernard, 1964; J. White, 1967). Research on sex roles in organizations has become more diverse within the last decade. It includes studies that explore gender differences in graffiti styles, portrait posing, and assertive acts of toddlers (Loewenstine, Ponticos, & Pauldi, 1982; MIlls, 1984).

Sex-Role Stereotypes

The presence of sex-role stereotypes in our society has been extensively researched and is well documented (Fernberger, 1948; Komarovsky, 1973). Sex-role stereotypes, however, may be changing. Research on sex-role stereotypes conducted in the 1980s suggests that while sex-role stereotypes seem to remain strong, sex-biased attitudes appear to be less polarized (Ruble, 1983). Nevertheless, sex-role stereotypes continue to be pervasive.

The relationship between sex-role stereotypes and leadership is complex and has not been fully defined. However, we know that sex-role stereotypes are integrated into the self-concepts of men and women (Broverman, Vogel, Broverman, Clarkson, & Rosenkrantz, 1972). O'Leary (1974) reported that the career aspirations of women are influenced by societal sex-role stereotypes and attitudes about their competency. As late as the mid-1970s, Bem and Bem (1975) found that one third of all working women were concentrated in seven jobs: secretary, retail sales clerk, household worker, elementary school teacher, waitress, and nurse.

Many women internalize societal sex-role stereotypes and attitudes. They express these attitudes and stereotypes in role conflict, as fear of failure, and in low self-esteem (Horner, 1987; O'Leary, 1974). In investigating the relationship between sex-role stereotypes and leadership, Petty and Miles (1976) found that both males and females subscribe to sex-role stereotypes for leadership roles. Research on sex-role stereotypes suggests that there is a tendency to attribute a higher social value to behaviors that are considered masculine than to those that are considered feminine (L. T. White, 1950). Women as well as men attribute higher social value to male behaviors even when they work in female-dominated cultures, such as elementary schools. Broverman et al. (1972) found that, compared with men, women are perceived as less competent, independent, objective, and logical. Men are perceived as lacking interpersonal sensitivity, warmth, and expressiveness (Broverman et al., 1972; Williams, 1982).

Interestingly, sex-role stereotypes cause the same traits to be perceived differently in men and women (Bayes & Newton, 1978). Consequently, sex-role stereotypes can result in a no-win situation for women. Women are expected to exhibit behaviors associated with sex-role stereotypes in order to be viewed as women, and yet those very behaviors are often seen as being antithetical to effective leadership. Women who behave in ways traditionally associated with males may be passed over for promotions. L. K. Brown and Klein (1982) found that women were only allowed to advance into administrative positions when they were able to play the roles of peacemaker and nurturer as well as supervisor. Sex-role stereotypes can limit women's access to and effectiveness in leadership positions.

Since the late 1960s much of the research on sex-role stereotypes has been conducted using the Stereotype Questionnaire

(Broverman, Broverman, Clarkson, Rosenkrantz, & Vogel, 1970). Researchers using the Stereotype Questionnaire have found that sex-role stereotypes are commonly found in a variety of groups throughout the nation and are deeply ingrained in U.S. society. Research by Millham and Smith (1981), however, indicates that sex-role stereotypes may be different for African Americans than they are for Whites. In their study comparing sex-role differentiation among Black and White Americans, Millham and Smith concluded that "Blacks are generally less concerned with traditional sex-role differentiation as defined by the White majority" (p. 89).

Role Stress and Conflict

Role stress is a construct that describes a feeling of conflict that results from the inconsistent demands of a role (Goode, 1960; Merton, 1957; Parsons, 1951; Popenoe, 1971). Gross et al. (1958) found that superintendents experience conflict when they try to satisfy the conflicting desires of teachers, parents, and school board members. Conflict also results from the multiple roles minorities and women in educational administration are expected to assume. Role conflict among White males entering their first administrative positions tends to be lower than that of women and minorities entering their first administrative positions (Ortiz, 1982).

Ortiz (1982) examined the socialization processes of 350 school administrators in California. Her work is particularly important in understanding the relationship between career patterns and role conflict of women and minorities in school districts. Ortiz investigated some of the intervening processes between status and role conflict and found that organizational position can increase as well as decrease role conflict. Women and minority administrators may experience role conflict as a result of the "organization's expectations regarding their ascribed roles such as being feminine or ethnic" (p. 138). This form of role conflict is reduced when "minorities and women accentuate the positions' characteristics and when they refuse to be shattered in the face of conflicting expectations" (p. 138). Ortiz also found that role conflict is dependent on the way minorities participate in their organizations. The potential for role conflict is reduced when minorities are highly competent, limit their area of expertise to issues involving ethnicity and social bias, and do not compete with White males.

The reform role that many Black superintendents are expected to fill can also result in role stress and conflict (Sizemore, 1986). Minority administrators are challenged to maintain loyalty simultaneously to bureaucratic, personal, and community ideologies that often involve incompatible expectations, attitudes, and beliefs. Peterson (1985) makes the following comment on the role of superintendents in school reform in his book on the politics of school reform:

Reform superintendents were neither heroes nor devils, but they had an agenda that placed them at odds with a diversity of opponents that changed according to the issue at stake and the political context in which it was raised. (p. 155)

Educational administrators are frequently expected to take on the roles of educational superperson, technical manager,

and democratic leader (Cunningham & Nystrand, 1969). In his book on Black superintendents, Scott (1980) states that "the relationship Black superintendents have with other Blacks and many Whites is a manifestation of contemporary racial attitudes in America" (p. 57). Scott concludes that African American superintendents are charged with tempering Black hostility and distrust while simultaneously providing the leadership necessary to reform urban school districts.

The small number of women and people of color in educational leadership is another potential source of role stress and conflict. Kanter (1977) argues that three dynamics may result when there are small numbers of women in leadership positions: (a) women in those positions may receive more attention; (b) the additional attention may lead to more pressure to perform; and (c) the organization's cultural boundaries may be heightened due to polarization and the exaggeration of differences between males and females. Women may be channeled, through affirmative action, into special roles set aside for them. The smaller the number of individuals from other groups, the more they are seen as representatives of their group rather than as individuals. That perspective, along with the assumption that minority persons are only interested in appointments in areas such as human rights, immigration, and social assistance, limits them from being considered seriously for advancement.

GENDER AND RACE STRATIFICATION IN EDUCATIONAL LEADERSHIP

Even though both women and people of color have experienced long tenure in the field of education, there are important differences in the social contexts and experiences of the two groups. Programs designed to increase the number of people of color and women in educational leadership positions will continue to be ineffective until a better understanding is gained of the ways in which history and social context influence their underrepresentation (Ortiz & Marshall, 1988; Sizemore, 1986). This section identifies some of the key factors in the backgrounds of the two groups and provides some statistics on their past and current representation in educational leadership positions.

Effect of Gender and Race on Opportunities for Leadership

Leadership opportunities for women in school administration began to increase in the 1980s. However, women continue to be underrepresented in higher-level positions in school administration (Saks, 1992). During the 1981–1982 school year, 25% of the school administrators in the United States were women. From 1981 to 1984, the percentage of female elementary and high school principals increased from 12% to 17% (Marshall, 1984). During that same period, the percentage of female assistant superintendents increased from 9% to 15%. By 1986, 27% of principals and assistant principals were women (U.S. Bureau of the Census, 1992). In 1992 women held 12.1% of high school principalships, compared to 7.6% in 1991 (Saks, 1992). The percentage of female superintendents increased from less than

1% in 1971 to 1.8% in 1981–1982, 2.7% in 1984–1985, 7.5% in 1991, and eventually to 10.5% in 1992 (Saks, 1992).

The number of minorities in school administration did not change substantially from 1975–1976 to 1984–1985 (Snyder, 1989). During that period, the number of African American male principals declined .12% and the number of Black female principals increased 1.85%. By 1986 only 8% of all school administrators and 13% of elementary and secondary principals and assistant principals were Blacks (U.S. Bureau of the Census, 1992). A national survey of school administrators, conducted in 1985 by the American Association of School Administrators (AASA), found that African Americans held 1% of the superintendencies and 6.5% of the assistant superintendencies; Hispanics held 1.4% of the superintendencies and 1.8% of the assistant superintendencies; American Indians held .5% of the superintendencies; and Asian Pacific Islanders held .1% of the superintendencies (AASA, 1985). By 1991 the number of African American superintendents had increased only to 2.5%. The percentage of African American superintendents dropped to 1.9% in 1992 (Saks, 1992).

Historical Context of Underrepresentation

Historically, women and people of color have had limited career options. For many years education was one of the few careers open to them. Education offered an aura of respectability and professionalism, a realistic career goal, financial independence, and an opportunity to serve the community. Women constituted almost 98% of all elementary school teachers and 61.7% of elementary school principals in 1905 (Shakeshaft, 1987). By 1920 education was the seventh-ranked field of work for African American women (Shakeshaft, 1987).

Virtually all school administrators are initially recruited from the ranks of teachers (Clement, 1975). Several states require teacher certification as a prerequisite for administrative certification. For many years minorities were not hired as teachers in public schools. Even in the rural South, teaching and administrative positions in segregated schools did not open for Blacks until the first half of the 20th century (Perkins, 1989; Clifford, 1982). In a study of the early history of Black superintendents, Jones (1983) found that the first Black superintendents served in all-Black school districts between 1930 and 1958. Most of those districts were in the South. Sizemore (1986) notes that the Black superintendency did not become a reality in mixed school districts until 1954.

Teaching opportunities for African Americans began to decline during the 1960s and 1970s. Schools were integrated during those years and Black students were transferred from Black schools to White schools. African American teachers and administrators who worked in Black schools were not generally transferred to White schools. Consequently, many lost their jobs.

During the 1980s scholarships and other forms of financial aid for students entering higher education began to decrease. As a result, the number of students of color entering college and available to select education as a major decreased as well. As opportunities opened up for employment in other fields, such as business, students of color began to choose majors outside education (Perkins, 1989). In 1977 African Americans were more likely than Whites to major in education; by 1989 Whites were more likely than Blacks to elect education as their major (National Center for Educational Statistics, 1991). Between 1985 and 1990, less than 1% of American Indians, 1% of Asian Americans, 2% of Latinos, and 5% of African Americans were hired in teaching positions (Feistritzer, 1990).

The underrepresentation of women in educational leadership, like that of minorities, is embedded in a compelling historical context. After World War II the number of women administrators decreased as more men went into education. During that period, school boards tended to limit new hires to heads of households. School boards also frequently replaced retiring female principals with males (Neely & Wilson, 1978). Decision makers tended to view men as having characteristics that were more favorable in educational administration. The percentage of male elementary teachers increased from 12.8% in 1957–1958 to 14.6% during the 1967–1968 school year. During that period there was an increase of male teachers at the secondary level from 50.5% to 52.9%. In 1990 males represented approximately 15% of elementary school teachers and almost 46% of secondary teachers (U.S. Bureau of the Census, 1992).

Determining Underrepresentation

While both women and people of color are underrepresented in educational leadership positions, the determination of their underrepresentation is derived in different ways. Justification for increasing the number of women in educational administration is frequently based on the disproportionate number of women who are classroom teachers compared to the number of women who hold administrative positions. Jones and Montenegro (1990) found that even though most teachers are women, men hold 96% of superintendencies, 77% of assistant superintendencies, 88% of high school principalships, and 71% of elementary principalships.

Increasing the number of minorities in educational administration is frequently justified on the basis of the growing number of students of color in the public schools. The majority of students enrolled in public schools in California are students of color. By 2020 almost half of the students attending public school in the United States will be students of color (Spencer, 1986).

Placement of Minorities in Educational Administration

Many minorities enter administration through special projects and work on minority issues. They frequently work in schools with high minority enrollment and occupy the least powerful positions in the administrative hierarchy. In a national study of high school principals, Byrne, Hines, and McCleary (1978) found that most minority principals served in school districts with more than 20% minority enrollment. In a national survey of 210 Black school administrators, Holden (1977) found that 58% of the Black administrators worked in predominantly Black school districts with fewer than 10,000 students.

Most minority superintendents are hired in school districts that have a high proportion of students of color. The probability of African Americans being hired as superintendents increases as the number of minority students in school districts increases (Moody, 1971; Jones, 1983; Scott, 1983). By the late 1980s most Black superintendents were located in cities (Sizemore, 1986). Scott (1983) predicts that those school districts with high minority populations, critical financial conditions, and educational problems will have unwanted superintendencies, and those superintendencies will be available to Blacks.

In one of the first national studies of Black superintendents, Moody (1971) found that 72.2% of the school districts with Black superintendents were predominantly Black. Many of those districts were large urban school districts. Black superintendents have served in Chicago, Detroit, Minneapolis, Rochester, Washington, DC, Atlanta, Baltimore, Newark, and New Orleans (Scott, 1983). However, it is important to note that most school districts that have a majority of African American students do not have Black superintendents. In 1982, 66% of predominantly Black districts in the United States had White superintendents (Scott, 1983).

Role of School Boards in Underrepresentation of Women

School boards reflect the values of their communities and play an important role in the selection of administrators (Peshkin, 1978). In a 1986 survey of superintendents, personnel directors, and school board presidents, Phillips and Voorhees found that attitudes of school board presidents differed from those of superintendents and personnel directors on the ability of women to advance in educational administration. The superintendents and personnel directors believed women had the ability to advance in educational administration. The board presidents, however, believed that women could be placed in elementary administration, but should not be placed in positions such as assistant superintendent or superintendent.

In a survey of Connecticut school board members, Taylor (1971) found that board members were more likely to appoint women to positions in central office administration and as elementary principals than to positions as superintendents or secondary principals. Taylor found that female school board members, like male board members, favored males for administrative positions. However, those attitudes may be changing. In a 1978 study of California school board members, Beck found that the attitudes of male board members toward women administrators were significantly more traditional than the attitudes of female board members.

Working with women administrators seems to moderate negative attitudes toward them. Male board members who have worked with a female administrator had more favorable attitudes toward women administrators than male board members who have not worked with women administrators. Beck (1978) found that there was a positive correlation between the percentage of women hired in administrative positions and more liberal attitudes toward women.

The number of female school board members remains relatively low. In 1987, 39% of school board members were women. By 1992 that percentage had increased only to 39.9%. Minority representation on school boards is much lower than female representation. In 1987, 3.6% of school board members were Black, 1.5% were Hispanic, .1% were American Indian, and .2% were Asian American. By 1992 the percentage of African American school board members had fallen to 3.1%. It increased to .8% for American Indians. The percentage of Hispanic and Asian American board members remained the same in 1992 as it was in 1987 (Saks, 1992).

CHARACTERISTICS OF WOMEN AND MINORITIES IN EDUCATIONAL LEADERSHIP

The assumption that leadership requires male characteristics has led to a body of research in which women and people of color are compared to White men. This research results in men being held up as the ideal to which women and people of color are compared. Conceptualizing research on leadership as a mirror in which women and people of color are expected to be a reflection of White men ultimately marginalizes these two groups because they are viewed as having fewer skills and less power. In a review of empirical studies on male and female leaders, S. M. Brown (1979) concludes that "one of the popular reasons given for the differential treatment of women in management stems from stereotyping females as ineffective leaders . . . trait studies consistently supported the traditional attitude that women lack adequate leadership characteristics" (p. 595). In addition to marginalizing women and people of color, research comparing male and female leaders diverts attention away from issues like discrimination in the workplace (Fierman, 1990).

Male and Female Leaders Compared

Researchers frequently use survey instruments to gather data on the personal characteristics of male and female educational leaders. The availability of such data enables researchers to create a profile of women and men who reach high levels in school administration. In general, studies that compare male and female leaders do not demonstrate a clear pattern of difference in leadership style between the sexes (Bass, 1981; C. A. M. Banks, 1991). On occasion, however, individual studies have identified differences in leadership style. In a meta-analysis of 50 studies that compared the leadership styles of male and female principals, Eagly, Karau, and Johnson (1992) found that there is some evidence that men and women have different styles. Women tended to display a democratic and participatory style and to be more task oriented than men. However, Eagly et al. state that there are men who practice democratic leadership and women who exercise autocratic leadership. Male and female leadership styles overlap and there are considerable intragroup differences in leadership style.

Studies comparing personal characteristics and experiences of male and female leaders have had mixed results. Some studies suggest that there are differences between male and female leaders, while others suggest that there are no significant differences (Adkinson, 1981; Frasher & Frasher, 1979; Shakeshaft, 1987). Age is one variable on which differences have been consistently noted. Researchers have found that women entering school administration are older and have more school experience than men (Johnson, Yeakey, & Moore, 1980; N. Gross & Trask, 1976). Males generally have taught 5 to 7 years and females have generally taught 15 years before they enter educational administration (N. Gross & Trask, 1976).

Studies have also shown that women leaders share many commonalities. Stevens (1988) interviewed 10 women who held superintendencies in Washington State school districts. Most of the women came from homes where they were expected to achieve. Nine of the 10 female superintendents were the oldest child in their families, and 5 began their educational careers as teachers in junior high schools. All of the superintendents saw themselves as collaborative leaders.

The following studies illustrate some of the key factors found in research comparing the personal characteristics of male and female educational leaders. N. Gross and Trask (1976) conducted a major study of men and women elementary school principals. The study was part of the National Principalship Study that was carried out at Harvard University and supported by the U.S. Office of Education. Gross and Trask used a cluster sampling procedure that gave them a representative sample of 189 elementary principals in cities with a population of 50,000 or more. Secondary principals were not included in the study because the number of female junior and senior high school principals was too small. Data were gathered using a personal and school background questionnaire, a role questionnaire, and a three- to five-hour personal interview.

The average age of the women in the study was 54.3 years, with 59% of them between 50 and 59 years old. The average age of the men was 49.2 years. The largest group of men (34%) was between the ages of 40 and 49. Ninety-six percent of the women and 92% of the men were White. With one exception, the remaining individuals in the study were African American.

The N. Gross and Trask (1976) study revealed a number of important characteristics of school administrators. Over 95% of the men in the study were married, but only about one third of the women were married. Kanter (1977) notes that some high-level positions, such as superintendent of schools, seem to require two individuals: the individual hired for the position and a spouse to handle its social aspects. Traditionally, women have provided an extra hand in support of their husbands' careers. Women who are married as well as women who are not married generally have to handle both the social and professional components of their positions.

Women in the N. Gross and Trask (1976) study reported higher academic performance than the men. Twenty-three percent of women and 12% of the men indicated that their academic work was far above average; 1% of the men and none of the women reported that their academic work was below average. The women also stated that they went into teaching because they were influenced or persuaded by someone else. Men indicated that they went into teaching for financial reasons and for upward mobility. The women in the study reportedly had lower aspirations for career advancement than did the men.

Douglas and Simonson (1982) studied the life experiences and leader behaviors of 25 male and 25 female superintendents. They found that male and female superintendents did not exhibit different leader behaviors; however, they did find other differences. Four times as many male superintendents as female superintendents earned $50,000 or more. Female superintendents were less likely to be married than were male superintendents—92% of the men were married, compared to 72% of the women. All of the married male superintendents had children, but 28% of the married female superintendents had no children. The female superintendents had an average of 11.7 years of teaching experience, compared to 3.2 years for men. Fifty-four percent of the men in the study moved into superintendencies within 10 years after they started teaching. None of the women moved into superintendencies within 10 years after they started teaching. At the other extreme, 36% of the women and 4% of the men in the study became superintendents 26 or more years after their first teaching experience. Men served an average of 13.2 years in a superintendency, compared to 4.5 years for women.

In a nationwide study of 791 male and 191 female superintendents, Schuster (1987) found that males and females differ on personal and career variables, politics, and job-related costs and satisfactions. Women superintendents were more often firstborn than were male superintendents. They were more likely to be politically liberal and single, and had on average fewer children than did male superintendents. Females also read more professional books and held more doctoral degrees than did male superintendents. Increasingly, a significantly larger number of women than men sat on school boards that hired female superintendents.

In 1990 C. A. M. Banks surveyed 31 superintendents of the largest public school districts in the United States to gather data on their career patterns, personal and educational characteristics, and perceptions of managerial and leadership styles and skills (C. A. M. Banks, 1991). The respondents included 2 female superintendents and 29 male superintendents—15 European Americans, 13 African Americans, and 3 Hispanic Americans. She found that there was no significant relationship between the gender or race of the superintendents and their perceptions of their leadership styles and skills.

Hollander and Yoder (1978) reviewed research on gender and leadership and concluded that there were general areas where men and women differ in their leadership. They found that men focus more on achieving success in tasks while women seek interpersonal successes; women put more energy into creating a positive group effort; men focus on displaying recognizable leader behavior. They concluded that the differences that they noted in male and female leader behavior are related to role expectations, style, and situational characteristics.

Chapman (1975) compared the leadership styles of males and females. He concluded that differences in male and female leader behavior may result from pressures to display behaviors that are consistent with societal and cultural expectations. In a study of supervisor ratings, female supervisors received higher scores than men in the areas of being friendly, expressing appreciation for good work, and agreeing on values. In addition, female supervisors were less likely to be avoided by subordinates than were male supervisors (Munson, 1979). The Chapman and Munson studies suggest that societal expectations of appropriate female and male behavior are implicated in the ways in which leaders are evaluated. Women are expected to be warm, sympathetic, aware of others' feelings, and helpful. Men are viewed as self-assertive and dominant (Ashmore, DelBoca, & Wohlers, 1986; Williams, 1982).

Morsink (1970) measured 12 dimensions of leader behavior. There were no significant differences between male and female secondary principals on 2 of the dimensions: tolerance of uncertainty and consideration. Male principals in the study were perceived as having a greater tolerance of freedom than did women principals. While the difference was not significant, female principals were viewed as demonstrating a higher level of consideration than male principals. They generally spoke and acted as a representative of their group, maintained cordial relations with their superiors, and tried to influence them. The idea that females focus on consideration is supported by Josefowitz's (1980) finding that female managers were twice as accessible as male managers. Josefowitz noted that female managers, unlike male managers, tended to maintain an open-door rather than a closed-door policy, did not use their secretaries to screen their calls, and encouraged telephone calls to their homes in the evenings and on weekends.

Pitner (1981) observed three women superintendents for one week to determine whether male and female superintendents focus on different work activities. She found that the nature of the work that men and women superintendents performed was essentially the same. There were, however, some differences in the ways that they handled routine paper work and the ways in which they observed in schools. The female superintendents in the study interacted more frequently with their peers and female counterparts and used a more informal communication style and language than did males. They also spent more of their unscheduled time working on curriculum and instruction and tended to eat lunch alone at their desks instead of in restaurants.

Pratt (1980) used case studies of critical incidents in leaderless task-oriented small groups to examine seven leadership factors, including the leadership style of males and females. She found that there were no differences between males and females on any of the seven factors, including leadership style. Pratt concluded that, in general, there are more similarities than there are differences between male and female leaders.

In the 1980s women began to challenge openly the idea that masculine characteristics are associated with effective leadership. They argued that intuitiveness, caring, and other characteristics that are typically associated with women make for better managers and leaders (Helgesen, 1990; Loden, 1985; Rosener, 1990). While this line of research presents female characteristics in a more positive light, it maintains the dichotomy between males and females and reinforces a monolithic view of women. That limited view of women is related to their underrepresentation in educational leadership positions (Nichols, 1993). If a decision maker accepts the idea that men are self-assertive and women are caring, it is understandable why a man would be selected over a woman for a job that requires an assertive leader.

Studies of the kind reported here have several limitations. They tend not to focus on the variations within groups of males and females even though there is tremendous intragroup variation (Epstein, 1988, 1991; Fierman, 1990). Some males are more similar to females than to males and some females are more similar to males than to other females. Intragroup differences as well as similarities need further exploration. By focusing on differences between males and females we essentially deny the variation that exists within each group.

The lack of attention to variation within groups is further complicated by the methodology employed in many studies. Most use a form of survey research. Surveys rely on self-report data and are limited to the respondents' frame of reference. Research on the actual behavior of male and female managers does not always support the self-report perceptions through which male and female leaders describe themselves (Epstein, 1988, 1991).

Minorities and Educational Leadership

Research on minorities in school administration is almost exclusively on African Americans. The author was able to locate only two dissertations completed between 1964 and 1989 that were on Latino school administrators. None were located that focused primarily on Native Americans or Asians. Data on Asian Americans, Native Americans, and Latinos are limited to a small number of broad-based surveys of school administrators. In general, those studies simply indicate the number of minorities that serve in specified job categories. They do not provide information on the characteristics of Latino, Asian, or Native American administrators (Lovelady-Dawson, 1980).

Compared to women and White males, there are relatively few studies on minorities in educational leadership. Available research, however, suggests that there are significant differences in the experiences of minority, women, and White male leaders. One of the primary differences involves community relations. African American school administrators tend to be very closely tied to the minority community. Johnson, Yeakey, and Holden (1979) found that African American superintendents often reflect the needs and priorities of their client communities, and that those communities are largely Black. African American principals, to a greater extent than their White colleagues, involve parents and members of the community in school activities (Monteiro, 1977). In a study of African American principals, Lomotey (1989) found that one of the characteristics of African American principals in more successful elementary schools was "a deep compassion for, and understanding of, their students and of the communities in which they work" (p. 150).

Characteristics of Minority Female School Administrators

Edson (1987) has conducted several studies that included minority women in school administration. She argues that there may be a connection between the small number of studies on minority women in school administration and the low number of minority women actually in school administration. This intriguing hypothesis ties together two important realities: Minority females are underrepresented in leadership research and in educational administration. The lack of research on minority female school administrators makes identifying their characteristics much more problematic than identifying the characteristics of White administrators. In a national survey of school superintendents, Schuster (1987) found that no single category of minority women held more than 2% of any school administrative position. Revere (1985) found that out of 16,000 public school superintendents, only 29 were African American women. Research that highlights the nature of minority female underrepresentation in educational leadership will not only publicize this problem; it can also serve as a departure point for action to rectify it.

Research on minority women is often incorporated into larger studies of women. Edson's (1987) comprehensive study of female administrative aspirants included 36 minority females; 27 of the women were Black, 7 were Hispanic, 1 was Asian, and 1 was American Indian. Both the minority and White women in Edson's study agreed that race and gender significantly affected their career aspirations. They also acknowledged that competition exists between minority and White females. This finding raises an important question about the extent to which White women and women of color will support and cooperate with each other in what could be called a zero sum game. The reality of competition in the workplace may result in the perception that the advancement of one group of females may hinder the advancement of other groups. Edson (1988) concludes her discussion of minority female administrative aspirants by stating, "Until the field of administration welcomes all female candidates, no matter what their color, minority issues will continue to complicate the lives of minority and nonminority women alike" (p. 193).

Minority females embody two status roles—one related to gender and one related to ethnicity. Doughty (1980) argues that those status roles have negative consequences for Black women who want to enter educational administration. She states that African American female administrators have to cope with the popular myth that Black women are superhuman, capable of solving any problem and dealing with any crisis, and stronger than other women and African American men.

In 1980 Doughty surveyed Black administrators in school districts with populations of 100,000 or more. Data were collected from 1,004 Black administrators. Of those administrators, 250 were Black females. Doughty found that Black females tended to be at the bottom of the administrative hierarchy. White men held top positions such as superintendent and Black males were next, followed by White females. Black females were last. Black females in the study held positions such as supervisor, administrative assistant, and elementary principal.

Doughty (1980) also found that Black and White females who enter educational administration share a number of characteristics. Like White women, Black female administrators tend to be older than male administrators. Most of the women in the study were in their middle 40s to middle 50s before they became administrators. Also like White females, Black female ad-

ministrators, as compared to males, have more education and have spent more time teaching before moving into administration. Doughty also found that the Black females she studied had positive perceptions of themselves and their ability to do their jobs. They tended to reject descriptions of themselves as tokens and felt that they were hired and promoted because of their credentials and past performance.

In an article on Black professional women, Epstein (1972) argued that Black women were in great demand in the labor market because they satisfy two affirmative action criteria, sex and race. Doughty (1980) responded to Epstein in an article on Black female administrators. She argued that Department of Labor statistics clearly indicate that the dual status of minority and female results in lower earning power for Black women than for Black men, White women, and White men. Doughty concludes that the perception that Black women get top jobs because they are minority women is a myth. She challenges her readers to carefully look at the positions Black women hold in educational administration. She notes that they are usually assistants to superintendents, supervisors, vice principals, or elementary principals. Doughty's position that African American women may be doubly challenged by the dual barriers of gender and race is supported by Ortiz (1982) and Korah (1990). They also conclude that while women and minorities encounter barriers to leadership positions, minority women confront both gender and racial barriers.

The Effect of Race and Gender on Career Patterns

Data developed by AASA (1960, 1985) suggest that access to high-level administrative positions is limited to individuals who have followed specific career patterns (1960). While career patterns leading to superintendencies vary over time, two patterns are commonly followed. In school districts with 100,000 or more students, the typical career pattern of superintendents is teacher/principal/central office administrator/superintendent. In smaller school districts, the most common career pattern leading to a superintendency is teacher/principal/superintendent.

In a survey of 78 Black superintendents and on-site interviews with 6 of the superintendents, C. M. Banks (1988) found that Black superintendents progressed through a career path that included teacher, principal, assistant superintendent, and superintendent. Most of the Blacks in the survey were in their first superintendency and had served in that position for an average of 6.6 years. The superintendents indicated that their career development had been aided by mentors who took a personal interest in their careers.

Keim (1978) compared the career paths and expectations of 470 male and female superintendents in Pennsylvania. She found that there were significant differences between male and female career paths leading to superintendencies. Women tended to teach longer before entering administration and had more certificates and doctorates than did the men in the study.

Revere (1985) conducted one of the few studies investigating the career patterns of minority women. Based on data from her interviews, she concluded that there was no single career pattern that described the accession of minority women to the superintendency. The factors that led to their rise to the super-intendency were their self-confidence, industriousness, productivity, and ability to work well with people. Most of the women in the study were married and felt that their husbands were an important source of support.

In another study on the career paths of minority women, Bulls (1986) used ethnographic case studies to investigate the behavioral strategies used by nine Black female leaders to attain superintendencies. Attaining access to high-level administrative positions requires that African American females engage in highly purposeful behavior. For example, Bulls concluded that a doctorate was essential for African American females to become superintendents. Securing mentors, balancing feminine and masculine qualities, networking with other Black female superintendents, and obtaining a visible position in the central office were also identified as critical steps for career advancement.

Ortiz (1982) found that White males, unlike women and minorities, were socialized as teachers to enter administration. When they were assigned to vice-principalships, they were able to move away gradually from work with children and instruction and to assume more administrative responsibilities. As work demands increased, men generally had a supportive and compassionate environment in which to assimilate a new understanding of themselves and their work.

Women were more likely to move into positions where they would continue to see children as central to their work (Ortiz, 1982). Role conflict can occur when women are placed in administrative positions if they believe that children and instruction are supposed to be their primary concern. Ortiz concludes that this role conflict is often viewed as incompetency. She states that one serious consequence of this role conflict is that women may try to resolve it by accentuating male behaviors, an adaptive behavior that is often viewed as unfeminine and may result in increased role conflict.

Minorities frequently enter educational administration through special project positions (Ortiz, 1982). In general, their prior administrative work has focused on working with minorities or on minority issues. These kinds of administrative positions do not prepare them to move away from children and instruction as a primary concern and to administer and manage other adults from a wide range of ethnic groups. In similar fashion, most Whites are not given an opportunity to develop the skills and knowledge necessary to work effectively with traditional minorities and to address minority issues.

Key Factors in the Underrepresentation of Minorities and Women Educational Leaders

Educational administration is highly stratified by race and gender (Ortiz, 1982; Ortiz & Marshall, 1988). The high number of female teachers and the low number of female administrators is an example of stratification by gender (Ortiz & Marshall, 1988). A number of explanations have been offered to account for the low numbers of women and minorities in educational administration. One commonly accepted explanation is that women and minorities are not motivated to enter administration. The research, however, does not support that claim. Diaz

(1976) studied male and female teachers and found that women are more highly motivated than males to become administrators. Ortiz and Covel (1978) found that women have high career aspirations. After an extensive case study of a female principal, they concluded that "women have the same career ambitions as men, but they do not have the same opportunities" (p. 214). This conclusion is supported by Valverde (1974), who found that women and minorities held high career aspirations.

In a review of research on women in educational administration, Ortiz and Marshall (1988) concluded that women are underrepresented in educational leadership because of the way in which school administration has developed. They state that over the years school administration developed into a field that favors men over women. They identify four themes that dominated the development of educational administration: (a) teaching and administration were increasingly seen as separate but mutually dependent professions, with women in classroom teaching positions and men in administrative positions; (b) the structure of schools changed, making them more hierarchical and professional; (c) open competition decreased as sponsorship became viewed as the way to build a career in educational administration; and (d) the discussion of gender and power issues was discouraged (Ortiz & Marshall, 1988).

Research conducted by Pavan (1982) suggests that the low number of female administrators is not due to women's lack of qualifications. She found that a number of qualified females in the administrative job pool in Pennsylvania did not hold administrative positions. The women were not selected for administrative positions for several reasons, including sex-role stereotyping. Sex-role stereotyping can exist in employee selection, placement, disciplinary decisions, and preferences for supervisory behaviors (Rosen & Jerdee, 1974a, 1974b, 1974c, 1975). The extent of sex-role stereotyping is related to variables such as the percentage of women on the school board (Forlines, 1984) and the extent to which the individuals involved in the selection process have worked with a female administrator (Mack, 1981).

Woo (1985) surveyed 450 top women educational leaders. He found that many of the factors that were identified in earlier research as important variables in increasing or negating success for women were not identified as such by the women he surveyed. For example, the women in Woo's sample did not believe that affirmative action, flexible working hours, fear of success, mentors, and the "Cinderella syndrome" had any effect on their careers. They did, however, believe that factors such as assertiveness training and career guidance had a small effect on their careers. They believed the greatest obstacle to their career advancement was the lack of job opportunities.

In a 1979 nationwide survey of men and women superintendents, Richardson found that both males and females believed gender was a factor in their career development. Males believed their gender helped them attain administrative positions. Females believed their gender was of no help or was a hindrance. Even though both males and females believed that gender was a factor in access to administrative positions, affirmative action programs were not viewed positively by White males. Nasstrom and Butler (1975) found that male educators have a negative attitude toward affirmative action programs for female educators. Their attitudes were based on: (a) their belief that women were not prepared to hold a wider role, (b) perceived differences in leadership behavior between males and females, and (c) concern for their job security.

In 1979 Edson (1988) began a longitudinal study of 142 women who were seeking their first principalship. The initial data collection occurred in 1979–1980. A career update was conducted in 1984–1985. Edson's study of these 142 women provides some important information about the goals, attitudes, career progress, and concerns of women pursuing administrative careers. The subjects varied in age, race, and marital status. They lived all over the United States in cities, suburbs, and rural communities located in the South, West, Northwest, Midwest, Southeast, and Northeast. The women gave three reasons for seeking administrative careers: personal growth and challenge, concern about what was happening to children in schools, and their belief that they could do a better job than current administrators.

Edson's (1988) findings contradict earlier studies that concluded that (a) women were not interested in administration; (b) they would not move to further their careers; (c) family responsibilities were a burden and made career advancement difficult for women; and (d) female educators were uncomfortable with decision and policy making and therefore preferred support, not line, positions (Lesser, 1978; Paddock, 1981). The women Edson studied wanted careers in educational administration and the power and authority to change schools. Twenty-seven percent of the women in the study wanted to become superintendents, 13% hoped to become assistant superintendents, 14% identified secondary principalships as a career goal, and 26% named elementary school principalships as their highest career goal.

Unlike women in earlier studies, the women in the Edson (1988) study were not place-bound. Seventy-five percent of the women in the Edson study indicated that they would move out of their districts and 40% indicated that they would move out of their state for improved career opportunities. Only 26% of the 142 subjects indicated that their family responsibilities were a problem. Edson's findings on family responsibility are supported by McCamey (1976) who, in a study of African American and White female administrators, found that the women administrators did not believe that they had trouble combining family life and marriage with a career.

Epstein (1970) identified several processes by which male-dominated professions limit the participation of women. Those processes include institutionalized channels of recruitment and protégé systems that are not easily available to women. One of the pressures that women confront when they enter a male-dominated occupation is the inability to obtain information through the "good old boy" network (Harragon, 1977). Surveys of female educators often, although not always, identify the lack of mentors as an important reason why more women are not school administrators (Diaz, 1976; Jones & Montenegro, 1982; Schmuck, Charters, & Carlson, 1981). Pavan's (1987) survey of women administrators in Pennsylvania suggested that men and women have about the same number of mentoring experi-

ences. More women than men, however, reported that mentoring functions were helpful.

The importance of sponsorship and mentoring has been documented in several studies (Collins, 1983; Misserian, 1982; Valverde, 1980; Villani, 1983). While the two concepts are frequently used interchangeably, there are subtle differences between them (Villani, 1983). Sponsors help locate their protégés in positions where they receive informal career socialization experiences. These informal experiences include meeting and interacting with members of the administrator group (Valverde, 1980; Villani, 1983). Valverde (1980) interviewed six mentors to gather information on the sponsor-protégé process. He found that mentors provide 4 basic functions: exposure, advice, protection, and sanction. Misserian's (1982) survey of women managers resulted in a list of 14 mentoring behaviors. Collins (1983) surveyed 400 women and identified a similar list of 16 mentoring behaviors. Mentoring can thus be viewed as a more personal, complex process than sponsorship.

THE FUTURE STUDY OF EDUCATIONAL LEADERSHIP

A review of dissertations completed between 1964 and 1989, conducted by the author, indicates that studies of educational leaders were very limited in their scope. They tend to focus on educational leaders in a region or state. They also tend to focus on one key variable such as gender, ethnicity, leadership style, or career patterns. They do not usually examine several variables or attempt to identify intersections among them. Future research needs to have a broader scope and to reflect the dynamics of race and gender within the changing nature of our society. As a socially constructed phenomenon, leadership must also be examined within the changing meanings of race and gender.

Future research must look more deeply at the potential benefits of diverse leadership. Commenting on the state of research in educational leadership, F. I. Ortiz (personal communication, 1993) notes that research to date has not specified why it is necessary for women and people of color to assume leadership positions in educational organizations; what women and people of color contribute to educational administration, schools, and society as leaders of educational institutions; and how women and people of color are to be integrated within the leadership ranks of the educational enterprise. Ortiz's point is well taken because, while it is clear that educational administration is stratified by race and gender, relatively little is known about the employment experiences of women and people of color within the dynamics of race and gender in schools. Additional information is needed about the socialization of women and people of color in the workplace. We also need to know more about the initiation process that women and minorities experience when they enter administrative positions.

The roles of minorities and women in our society are clearly changing, and those changes may be reflected in the career patterns and in the leadership and managerial styles and skills of educational leaders. A multicultural approach to research on educational leadership invites opportunities for researchers to use a multidisciplinary approach to examine the intersections of race and gender. Important insights can be gained from comparing and contrasting the experiences of women and people of color in educational leadership. A multicultural approach adds a new dimension to the study of leadership and provides a basis for developing more comprehensive and inclusive approaches for theory and practice.

While there continues to be a significant underrepresentation of women and people of color in educational leadership, firm explanations for the underrepresentation continue to elude us. In terms of advanced training, degrees held, number of years in the profession, and total numbers in the pool from

which administrators are drawn, there is no justification for the small number of women and minority educational leaders. Research is needed to explicate the ways in which gender and race affect the recruitment, selection, and retention process for school administrators.

In conclusion, the study of women and people of color presents many challenges to researchers. It also holds out the promise that insights gained from such research will lead to more inclusive leadership that represents the diversity in our pluralistic society. As our knowledge about the experiences of women and minorities in educational leadership deepens, we may be better able to select, train, and nurture more effective leaders for schools in the 21st century.

References

Adkinson, J. A. (1981). Women in school administration: A review of the research. *Review of Educational Research, 51,* 311–343.

American Association of School Administrators. (1960). *Profile of the school superintendent.* Washington, DC: Author.

American Association of School Administrators. (1985). *Women and minorities in school administration.* Arlington, VA: Author.

Ashmore, R. D., Del Boca, F. K., & Wohlers, A. J. (1986). Gender stereotypes. In R. D. Ashmore & F. K. Del Boca (Eds.), *The social psychology of female-male relations: A critical analysis of central concepts* (pp. 69–119). Orlando, FL: Academic Press.

Argyris C., & Schön, L. A. (1974). *Theory in practice: Increasing professional effectiveness.* San Francisco: Jossey-Bass.

Astin, H. S. (1969). *The woman doctorate in America: Origins, career and family.* New York: Russell Sage Foundation.

Astin, H. S., & Leland, C. (1991). *Women of influence, women of vision.* San Francisco: Jossey-Bass.

Bales, R. F. (1950). A set of categories for the analysis of small group interaction. *American Sociological Review, 15,* 257–263.

Banks, C. A. M. (1991). *City school superintendents: Their career patterns, traits, and perceptions of leadership and managerial skill and style.* Unpublished doctoral dissertation, Seattle University.

Banks, C. M. (1988). *The Black school superintendent: A study in early childhood socialization and career development.* Unpublished doctoral dissertation, University of Pittsburgh.

Bass, B. M. (1981). *Stogdill's handbook of leadership.* New York: The Free Press.

Bayes, M., & Newton, P. M. (1978). Women in authority: Sociopsychological analysis. *Journal of Applied Behavioral Science, 14,* 7–20.

Beck, H. N. (1978). *Attitudes toward women held by California school district board members, superintendents, and personnel directors including a review of the historical, psychological, and sociological foundations.* Unpublished doctoral dissertation, University of the Pacific, Stockton, CA.

Bell, D. J. (1975). *Power, influence, and authority.* New York: Oxford University Press.

Bem, S. L., & Bem, D. J. (1975). *Training the woman to know her place: The social antecedents of women in the world of work.* (ERIC Document Reproduction Service No. ED 082 098)

Bernard, J. S. (1964). *Academic women.* University Park: Pennsylvania State University Press.

Biklen, S. K., & Brannigan, M. B. (Eds.). (1980). *Women and educational leadership.* Lexington, MA: D.C. Heath.

Blau, P. M. (1976). *Exchange and power in social life.* New York: Wiley.

Broverman, I. R., Broverman, D. M., Clarkson, F. E., Rosenkrantz, P. S., & Vogel, S. R. (1970). Sex-role stereotypes and clinical judgments of mental health professionals. *Journal of Consulting and Clinical Psychology, 34,* 1–7.

Broverman, I. R., Vogel, S. R., Broverman, D. H., Clarkson, F. E., & Rosenkrantz, P. S. (1972). Sex-role stereotypes: A current appraisal. *Journal of Social Issues, 28*(2), 59–78.

Brown, L. K., & Klein, K. H. (1982). Woman power in medical hierarchy. *Journal of American Medical Women's Association, 37,* 155–164.

Brown, S. M. (1979). Male versus female leaders: A comparison of empirical studies. *Sex Roles: A Journal of Research, 5*(5), 595–611.

Bulls, G. P. (1986). *Career development of the Black female superintendent.* Unpublished doctoral dissertation, University of Pennsylvania.

Burns, J. M. (1979). *Leadership.* New York: Harper & Row.

Butler, J. E., & Walter, J. C. (Eds.). (1991). *Transforming the curriculum: Ethnic studies and women's studies.* Albany: State University of New York Press.

Byrne, D. R., Hines, S. A., & McCleary, L. E. (1978). *The senior high school principalship.* Reston, VA: National Association of School Principals.

Chapman, J. B. (1975). Comparisons of male and female leadership style. *Academy of Management Journal, 18,* 645–650.

Clement, J. P. (1975). *Sex bias in school leadership.* Evanston, IL: Integrated Education Associates.

Clifford, G. J. (1982). Marry, stitch, die, or do worse: Educating women for work. In H. Kantor & D. B. Tyack (Eds.), *Work, youth, and schooling: Historical perspectives on vocationalism in American education* (pp. 223–268). Stanford, CA: Stanford University Press.

Collins, N. W. (1983). *Professional women and their mentors.* Englewood Cliffs, NJ: Prentice-Hall.

Cunningham, L. L. (1990). Educational leadership and administration: Retrospective and prospective views. In L. L. Cunningham & B. Mitchell. *Educational leadership and changing contexts in families, communities, and schools* (pp. 1–18). Chicago: The National Society for the Study of Education.

Cunningham, L. L., & Nystrand, R. O. (1969). Toward greater relevance in preparation programs for urban school administrators. *Educational Administration Quarterly, 5*(1), 6–23.

Diaz, S. (1976). *The aspiration levels of women for administrative careers in education: Predictive factors and implications for effecting change.* American Educational Research Association, San Francisco. (ERIC Document Reproduction Service No. ED 119 376)

Doughty, R. (1980). The Black female administrator: Women in a double bind. In S. X. Biklen & M. B. Brannigan (Eds.), *Women and educational leadership* (pp. 165–174). Washington, DC: Lexington Books.

Douglas, L. D., & Simonson, S. V. (1982). *A comparison of life experiences and leader behaviors between male and female superintendents.* Unpublished doctoral dissertation, Seattle University.

DuBois, C., & Ruiz, V. L. (Eds.). (1990). *Unequal sisters: A multicultural reader in U.S. women's history.* New York: Routledge.

Dugger, K. (1991). Social location and gender-role attitudes: A comparison of Black and White women. In J. Lorber & S. A. Farrell (Eds.), *The social construction of gender* (pp. 38–59). Newbury Park, CA: Sage.

Eagly, A. L., Karau, S. J., & Johnson, B. T. (1992). Gender and leadership style among school principals: A meta-analysis. *Educational Administration Quarterly, 28,* 76–102.

Edson, S. K. (1987). Voices from the present: Tracking the female administrative aspirant. *Journal of Educational Equity and Leadership, 7,* 261–277.

Edson, S. K. (1988). *Pushing the limits: The female administrative aspirant.* Albany: State University of New York Press.

Epstein, C. F. (1970). *Woman's place: Options and limits in professional careers.* Berkeley: University of California Press.

Epstein, C. F. (1972). Positive effects of the multiple negative: Explaining the success of Black professional women. *American Journal of Sociology, 78,* 912–915.

Epstein, C. F. (1988). *Deceptive distinctions.* New Haven, CT: Yale University Press.

Epstein, C. F. (1991). Ways men and women lead. *Harvard Business Review, 69*(1), 150–153.

Evers, C. W., & Lokomski, G. (1991). *Knowing educational administration: Contemporary methodological controversies in educational administration research.* New York: Pergamon Press.

Feistritzer, C. E. (1990). *Profile of teachers in the U.S.: 1990.* Washington, DC: National Center for Education Information.

Fernberger, S. W. (1948). Persistence of stereotypes concerning sex differences. *Journal of Abnormal and Social Psychology, 43,* 97–101.

Fiedler, F. E. (1967). *A theory of leadership effectiveness.* New York: McGraw-Hill.

Fierman, J. (1990, December). Do women manage differently? *Fortune,* pp. 115–118.

Fleishman, E. A. (1953). The description of supervisory behavior. *Journal of Applied Psychology, 37,* 1–6.

Fleishman, E. A. (1957). A leader behavior description for industry. In R. M. Stogdill & A. E. Coons (Eds.), *Leader behavior: Its description and measurement* (pp. 89–120). Columbus: Bureau of Business Research, Ohio State University.

Forlines, A. H. (1984). *Superintendents' perceptions of public opinions toward women administrators and superintendents' opinions toward women administrators.* Unpublished doctoral dissertation, George Peabody College for Teachers, Vanderbilt University.

Franklin, J. H. (1993). *The color line: Legacy for the twenty-first century.* Columbia: University of Missouri Press.

Frasher, J. M., & Frasher, R. S. (1979). Educational administration: A feminine profession. *Educational Administration Quarterly, 2,* 1–13.

Freeman, J. (Ed.). (1984). *Women: A feminist perspective* (3rd. ed.). Palo Alto, CA: Mayfield.

French, J. R. P., Jr., & Raven, B. (1960). The bases of social power. In D. Catwright & A. Zander (Eds.), *Group dynamics: Research and theory* (pp. 607–623). New York: Harper & Row.

Friedan, B. (1963). *The feminine mystique.* New York: Dell.

Gaertner, K. N. (1980). The structure of organizational careers. *Sociology of Education, 53,* 7–20.

Goode, W. J. (1960). A theory of role strain. *American Sociological Review, 25,* 483–495.

Goslin, D. A. (Ed.). (1969). *Handbook of socialization theory and research.* Chicago: Rand McNally.

Gross, E., & Etzioni, A. (1985). *Organizations in society.* Englewood Cliffs, NJ: Prentice-Hall.

Gross, N., Mason, W. S., & McEachern, A. W. (1958). *Explorations in role analysis: Studies of the school superintendency role.* New York: Wiley.

Gross, N., & Trask, A. E. (1976). *The sex factor and the management of schools.* New York: Wiley.

Hagen, R., & Kahn, A. (1975). Discrimination against competent women. *Journal of Applied Social Psychology, 41,* 362–376.

Halpin, A. W., & Winer, B. J. (1957). A factorial study of the leader behavior descriptions. In R. M. Stogdill & A. E. Coons (Ed.), *Leader behavior: Its description and measurement* (pp. 190–235). Columbus: Bureau of Business Research, Ohio State University.

Harragon, B. L. (1977). *Games mother never taught you: Corporate gamesmanship for women.* New York: Warner Books.

Helgesen, S. (1990). *The female advantage: Women's ways of leadership.* Garden City, NY: Doubleday.

Hemphill, J. K., & Coons, A. E. (1957). Development of the leader behavior description questionnaire. In R. M. Stogdill & A. E. Coons (Eds.), *Leader behavior: Its description and measurement* (pp. 147–163). Columbus: Bureau of Business Research, Ohio State University.

Hersey, P. (1984). *The situational leader.* New York: Warner Books.

Holden, R. L. (1977). *The Chicago schools: A social and political history.* Beverly Hills, CA: Sage.

Hollander, E. P., & Yoder, J. (1978). *Some issues in comparing women and men as leaders.* (ERIC Document Reproduction Service No. ED 185 883)

Holter, H. (1970). *Sex roles and social structure.* Oslo, Norway: Universitetsforlaget.

hooks, b. (1990). *Yearning: Race, gender, and cultural politics.* Boston: South End Press.

Horner, M. (1987). Toward understanding of achievement-related conflicts in women. In M. R. Walsh (Ed.), *The psychology of women* (pp. 169–184). New Haven, CT: Yale University Press.

House R. J., & Baetz, M. L. (1979). Leadership: Some empirical generalizations and new research directions. In B. M. Staw (Ed.), *Research in organizational behavior* (Vol. 1). Greenwich, CT: JAI.

Huber J. (1973). *Changing women in a changing society.* Chicago: University of Chicago Press.

Immegart, G. L. (1988). Leadership and leader behavior. In N. J. Boyan (Ed.), *Handbook of research on educational administration* (pp. 259–278). New York: Longman.

Jago, A. G. (1982). Leadership: Perspectives in theory and research. *Management Science, 28*(3), 315–336.

Janda, K. F. (1960). Towards the explication of the concept of leadership in terms of the concept of power. *Human Relations, 13,* 345–363.

Johnston, G. S., Yeakey, C. C., & Holden, R. L. (1979). An analysis of the external variables affecting the role of the Black school superintendent. *Educational Research Quarterly, 4,* 13–24.

Johnston, G. S., Yeakey, C. C., & Moore, S. E. (1980). Analysis of the employment of women in professional administrative positions in public education. *Planning and Changing, 11,* 115–132.

Jones, E. H. (1983). *Black school administrators: A review of their early history, trends, problems in recruitment.* Arlington, VA: American Association of School Administrators.

Jones, E. H., & Montenegro, X. P. (1982). *Recent trends in the representation of women and minorities in school administration and prob-*

lems in documentation. Arlington, VA: American Association of School Administrators.

Jones, E. H., & Montenegro, X. P. (1990). *Women and minorities in school administration*. (ERIC Document Reproduction Service No. ED 273 017).

Josefowitz, N. (1980, September/October). Management men and women: Closed vs. open doors. *Harvard Business Review, 58,* 56–62.

Kanter, R. M. (1977). *Men and women of the corporation*. New York: Basic Books.

Keim, A. S. (1978). *Women and the superintendency: A comparison of male and female career paths and expectations*. Unpublished doctoral dissertation, Lehigh University, Bethlehem, PA.

Komarovsky, M. (1973). Cultural contradictions and sex role: The masculine case. In J. Huber (Ed.), *Chicana women in a chicana society* (pp. 111–112). Chicago: University of Chicago Press.

Korah, S. (1990). Multiculturalism and the woman of colour: Can we bridge the gap between rhetoric and reality? *Tiger Lily: Journal by Women of Colour, 6,* 5–20.

Lesser, P. (1978). *The participation of women in public school administration*. (ERIC Document Reproduction Service No. ED 151 958).

Loden, M. (1985). *Feminine leadership or how to succeed in business without being one of the boys*. New York: Times Books.

Loewenstine, H. V., Ponticos, G. D., & Pauldi, M. A. (1982). Sex differences in graffiti as a communication style. *Journal of Social Psychology, 117,* 307–328.

Lomotey, K. (1989). *African-American principals: School leadership and success*. New York: Greenwood.

Lovelady-Dawson, F. (1980, December). Women and minorities in the principalship: Career opportunities and problems. *NASSP Bulletin, 64,* 18–28.

Mack, M. H. (1981). *A study of attitude toward women as school administrators*. Unpublished doctoral dissertation, Auburn University, AL.

Marshall, C. (1984). The crisis in excellence and equity. *Educational Horizons, 63,* 24–30.

McCamey, D. S. (1976). *The status of Black and White women in central administrative positions in Michigan public schools*. Unpublished doctoral dissertation, University of Michigan, Ann Arbor.

McCarthy, C., & Crichlow, W. (Eds.). (1993). *Race identity and representation in education*. New York: Routledge.

McCarthy, M., & Zent, A. (1981). School administrators: 1980 profile. *Planning and Changing, 12*(3), 144–161.

McGregor, D. (1960). *The human side of enterprise*. New York: McGraw-Hill.

McIntosh, P. (1988). *White privilege and male privilege: A personal account of coming to see correspondence through work in women's studies*. Wellesley, MA: Wellesley College Center for Research on Women.

Merton, R. K. (1957). *Social theory and social structure*. New York: Macmillan.

Millett, K. (1980). *Sexual politics*. New York: Ballantine. (Originally published 1969)

Millham, J., & Smith, L. (1981). Sex role differentiation among Black and White Americans: A comparative study. *Journal of Black Psychology, 7,* 77–99.

Mills, J. (1984). Self-imposed behaviors of females and males in photographs. *Sex Roles, 10*(7/8), 633–637.

Misserian, A. K., (1982). *The corporate connection: Why executive women need mentors to reach the top*. Englewood Cliffs, NJ: Prentice-Hall.

Monteiro, T. (1977). Ethnicity and the perceptions of principals. *Integrated Education, 15*(3), 15–16.

Moody, C. D. (1971). *Black superintendents in public school districts; Trends and conditions*. Unpublished doctoral dissertation, Northwestern University, Evanston, IL.

Morsink, H. M. (1970). Leadership behavior of men and women principals. *NASSP Bulletin, 54*(347), 80–87.

Munson, C. E. (1979, March). Evaluation of male and female supervisors. *Social Work, 24,* 104–110.

Nasstrom, R. R., & Butler, W. E. (1975). The professionalism of women teachers. *Kappa Delta Pi Record, 12*(1), 6–8.

National Center for Educational Statistics. (1991). *The condition of education 1991: Vol. 2. Postsecondary Education*. Washington, DC: U.S. Department of Education.

Neely, M. A., & Wilson, A. E. (1978). *A program to overcome sex bias in women's qualifications for vocational administration posts*. (ERIC Document Reproduction Service No. ED 166 391)

Nichols, N. A. (1993). Whatever happened to Rosie the riveter? *Harvard Business Review, 71*(4), 54–62.

O'Leary, V. E. (1974). Some attitudinal barriers to occupational aspirations in women. *Psychological Bulletin, 81,* 809–826.

Ortiz, F. I. (1982). *Career patterns in education: Men, women and minorities in public school administration*. New York: Praeger.

Ortiz, F. I., & Covel, J. (1978). Women in school administration: A case analysis. *Urban Education, 13,* 213–236.

Ortiz, F. I., & Marshall, C. (1988). Women in educational administration. In N. J. Boyan (Ed.), *Handbook of research on educational administration* (pp. 123–141). New York: Longman.

Paddock, S. C. (1981). Male and female career paths in school administration. In P. A. Schmuck, W. W. Charters, Jr., & R. O. Carlson (Eds.), *Educational policy and management: Sex differentials* (pp. 35–52). New York: Academic Press.

Parsons, T. (1951). *The social system*. New York: The Free Press.

Pavan, B. N. (1982). *Certified but not hired: Women administrators in Pennsylvania*. (ERIC Document Reproduction Service No. ED 263 689)

Pavan, B. N. (1987). Mentoring certified aspiring and incumbent female and male public school administrators. *Journal of Educational Equity and Leadership, 7*(4), 318–331.

Pelz, D. C. (1952). Influence: A key to effective leadership in the first-line supervisor. *Personnel, 29,* 209–217.

Perkins, L. M. (1989). The history of Blacks in teaching: Growth and decline within the profession. In D. Warren (Ed.), *American teachers: Histories of a profession at work* (pp. 344–369). New York: Macmillan.

Peshkin, A. (1978). *Growing up American*. Chicago: University of Chicago Press.

Peterson, P. (1985). *The politics of school reform 1870–1940*. Chicago: University of Chicago Press.

Petty, M. M., & Miles, R. H. (1976) Leader sex-role stereotyping in a female-dominated work culture. *Personnel Psychology, 29,* 393–404.

Phillips, D. L., & Voorhees, S. V. (1986). *Attitudes toward female school administrators in the state of Washington*. Unpublished doctoral dissertation, Seattle University.

Pinar, W. F. (1993). Notes on understanding curriculum as a racial text. In C. McCarthy & W. Crichlow (Eds.), *Race identity and representation in education* (pp. 60–70). New York: Routledge.

Pitner, N. J. (1981). *Notes on the differences in behavior of women superintendents in suburban districts*. Paper presented at the annual meeting of the American Educational Research Association, Los Angeles.

Popenoe, D. (1971). *Sociology*. New York: Meredith Corporation.

Pratt, J. M. M. (1980). *A case study analysis of male-female leadership emergence in small groups*. Unpublished doctoral dissertation, University of Minnesota, Minneapolis.

Revere, A. L. B. (1985). *A description of the Black female superintendent.* Unpublished doctoral dissertation, Miami University.

Richardson, J. A. M. (1979). *Women superintendents of public schools in the United States: Factors contributing to obtaining the position.* Unpublished doctoral dissertation, Drake University, Des Moines, IA.

Rosen, B., & Jerdee, T. H. (1974a). Influence of sex role stereotypes on personnel decisions. *Journal of Applied Psychology, 59,* 9–14.

Rosen, B., & Jerdee, T. H. (1974b). Effects of applicant's sex and difficulty of job evaluations of candidates for managerial positions. *Journal of Applied Psychology, 59,* 511–512.

Rosen, B., & Jerdee, T. H. (1974c). Sex stereotyping in the executive suite. *Harvard Business Review, 52,* 45–58.

Rosen, B., & Jerdee, T. H. (1975). Effects of employee's sex and threatening versus pleading appeals on managerial evaluations of grievances. *Journal of Applied Psychology, 60*(4), 442–445.

Rosener, J. B. (1990). Ways women lead. *Harvard Business Review, 68* (6), 119–125.

Rossi, A. S. (1970). Sex equality: The beginning of ideology. In M. L. Thompson (Ed.), *Voices of the new feminism* (pp. 113–147). New York: McGraw-Hill.

Rost, J. C. (1991). *Leadership for the twenty-first century.* Westport, CT: Praeger.

Ruble, T. L. (1983). Sex stereotypes: Issues and change in the 1970's. *Sex Roles, 9,* 397–402.

Saks, J. B. (1992, December). Education vital signs. *The American School Board Journal,* pp. 32–45.

Schmuck, P. A. (1980). Changing women's representation in school management: A systems perspective. In S. K. Biklen & M. B. Brannigan (Eds.), *Women and educational leadership* (pp. 242–263). Lexington, MA: D. C. Heath.

Schmuck, P. A., Charters, W. W., Jr., & Carlson, R. O. (Eds.). (1981). *Educational Policy and management: Sex differentials.* New York: Academic Press.

Schuster, D. J. (1987). *Male and female superintendents compared nationally: Career implications for women in educational administration.* Unpublished doctoral dissertation, Teachers College, Columbia University, New York.

Scott, H. J. (1980). *The Black school superintendent: Messiah or scapegoat?* Washington, DC: Howard University Press.

Scott, H. J. (1983). Views of Black school superintendents on school desegregation. *Journal of Negro Education, 52*(4), 378–382.

Shakeshaft, C. S. (1979). Dissertation research on women in educational administration: A synthesis of findings and paradigm for future research. (Doctoral dissertation, Texas A & M University, 1979). *Dissertation Abstracts International, 40,* 6455a.

Shakeshaft, C. S. (1985). Strategies for overcoming the barriers to women in educational administration. In S. Klein (Ed.), *Handbook for achieving sex equity through education* (pp. 124–144). Baltimore, MD: The Johns Hopkins University Press.

Shakeshaft, C. S. (1987). *Women in educational administration.* Newbury Park, CA: Sage.

Sizemore, B. A. (1986). The limits of the Black superintendency: A review of the literature. *Journal of Educational Equity and Leadership, 6*(3), 180–208.

Sleeter, C. E. (1993). How White teachers construct race. In C. McCarthy & W. Crichlow (Eds.), *Race identity and representation in education* (pp. 157–171). New York: Routledge.

Snyder, T. D. (1989). *Digest of educational statistics.* Washington, DC: National Center for Educational Statistics, Government Printing Office.

Spencer, G. (1986). *Projections of the Hispanic population: 1983–2080* (Current Population Reports, Series P-25, No. 995). Washington, DC: U.S. Bureau of the Census.

Stevens, K. M. (1988). *Profiles of Washington state women school superintendents.* Unpublished doctoral dissertation, Seattle University.

Stogdill, R. H. (1963). *Manual for the leader behavior description questionnaire—Form XII.* Columbus, OH: Bureau of Business Research, Ohio State University.

Stogdill, R. H. (1974). *Handbook of leadership: A survey of theory and research.* New York: The Free Press.

Taylor, S. S. (1971). *The attitudes of superintendents and board of education members in Connecticut toward the employment and effectiveness of women as public school administrators.* Unpublished doctoral dissertation, University of Connecticut, Storrs.

Toren, N. (1973). The bus driver: A study in role analysis. *Human Relations, 26*(1), 101–112.

U.S. Bureau of the Census. (1992). *Statistical abstract of the United States* (112th ed.). Washington, DC: Government Printing Office.

Valverde, L. A. (1974). *Succession socialization: Its influence on school administrative candidates and its implications to the exclusion of minorities from administration.* Austin, TX: University of Texas at Austin. (ERIC Document Reproduction Service No. 093 052)

Valverde, L. A. (1980). *Promotion socialization: The informal process in large urban school districts and its adverse effects on non-Whites and women.* Paper presented at the meeting of the American Education Research Association, Boston, MA.

Villani, D. (1983). *Mentoring and sponsoring as ways for women to overcome internal barriers to heightened career aspiration and achievement.* Unpublished doctoral dissertation, Northeastern University, Boston.

Vroom, V. H. (1976). Leadership. In M. Dunnette (Ed.), *Handbook of industrial and organizational psychology* (pp. 1527–1552). Chicago: Rand McNally.

Vroom, V. H., & Yetton, E. W. (1973). *Leadership and decision making.* Pittsburgh: University of Pittsburgh Press.

Weber, M. (1968). Economy and society: An outline of interpretive sociology. In G. Roth & C. Wittich (Eds.), *Wirtschaft und Gesellschaft* (E. Fischoff, Trans., pp. 28–72). New York: Bedminster Press.

West, C. (1993). *Race matters.* Boston: Beacon Press.

White, J. (1967). Women in the law. *Michigan Law Review, 65,* 1051.

White, L. T. (1950). *Educating our daughters.* New York: Harper.

Williams, J. E. (1982). An overview of findings from adult sex stereotype studies in 25 countries. In R. Rath, H. S. Asthana, D. Sinha, & J. B. Sinha (Eds.), *Diversity and unity in crosscultural psychology* (pp. 250–260). Lisse, Netherlands: Swets and Zeitlinger.

Woo, L. C. (1985). Women administrators: Profiles of success. *Phi Delta Kappan, 64*(4), 285–288.

Yukl, G. A. (1981). *Leadership in organizations* (3rd ed.). Englewood Cliffs, NJ: Prentice-Hall.

· 5 ·

AN ANALYSIS OF THE CRITIQUES OF MULTICULTURAL EDUCATION

Christine E. Sleeter

UNIVERSITY OF WISCONSIN, PARKSIDE

Until recently, when people asked me what I teach and I replied "multicultural education," I could anticipate silence, followed by a hesitant query, "What's that?" This response typifies much of the history of multicultural education, which has endured a struggle to be noticed. But a year ago, when a family friend asked the same question and I gave my usual reply, his face lit up and he exclaimed, "Oh, wow! That's really hot right now!" And so it is.

Recently there has been a voluminous amount of writing about multicultural education. In the ERIC listings of journal publications between January 1982 and June 1992, the descriptor "multicultural education" retrieved 911 entries. Most of these entries supported and advocated multicultural education in some form; for example, articles discussed the shift in demographics, curriculum strategies, teacher education, Afrocentrism, bilingual education, and teaching strategies. In other fields the volume of literature addressing multicultural education has also grown, appearing in the professional and popular literature of such fields as business, nursing, and counseling. And, as in education, most of the literature one finds under the descriptor "multicultural" advocates a perspective that is consistent with the perspective one finds in the field of multicultural education.

One might regard the number, sophistication, and visibility of critiques of any field as an indication of the field's impact. Proportionately to what has been written about multicultural education in the United States, until recently critiques of it have been few. I located 2 critiques of multicultural education in the United States that were published in the 1970s and 6 that were published in the 1980s. But I found a whopping 51 critiques that were published between 1990 and 1992. No longer does the field suffer invisibility.

In this chapter I will review the published criticisms that have been leveled against multicultural education, and discuss their implications for the field's development. In preparing this review I had to limit what I would discuss in order to keep the chapter manageable. First, I limited the discussion to critiques of multicultural education in the United States. Lively debates rage in other countries about multicultural education (e.g., debates about multicultural education versus antiracism in England), but although issues overlap, they do not cross national borders cleanly enough to include in this review in a concise and coherent manner. Second, I limited the chapter to published books, articles, and editorials that specifically discussed "multicultural education" (or "multiculturalism"). I did not seek critiques specifically of Afrocentrism, bilingual education, feminism, or ethnic studies, although many of the critiques of multicultural education mentioned these.

The great majority of the critiques take one of two opposing positions: either that multicultural education is too radical (the conservative position), or that it is too conservative (the radical leftist position). Because position on political issues defines much of the debate, before I discuss the critiques themselves I will distinguish briefly among conservative, liberal, and radical political and sociological positions on inequality (for a more developed discussion see Sleeter, 1992, pp. 9–13; also see Hoover, 1987, Jaggar, 1983).

The author is grateful to Carl Allsup, James A. Banks, Antonia Darder, Carl A. Grant, Joe Larkin, Renee Martin, Francisco Rios, and Anne Statham for their helpful comments and suggestions on earlier drafts of this chapter.

CONSERVATISM, LIBERALISM, AND RADICALISM

Conservatism champions the right of individuals to compete in the marketplace with minimal state regulation. Conservatives give priority to the individual and minimize the importance of group claims and attachments. Regulation of individuals is best performed by private institutions such as the family and the church; the moral fiber of the society at large is best protected by institutions that preserve tradition and are led by society's "natural aristocracy of talent, breeding, and, very likely, wealth" (Hoover, 1987, p. 34). Since individuals differ, inequality results naturally from differences in talent and effort; it may also be exacerbated by "dysfunctional" cultures and individual prejudices. These problems can be addressed best by encouraging the development of talent, character, and morality in "disadvantaged" children, and refusing to valorize "dysfunctional" cultures that may inhibit their successful integration into the mainstream.

Liberalism shares conservatism's focus on individual competition within a free marketplace. However, liberalism rejects conservatism's faith in private institutions and "natural aristocracy," and takes more seriously collective claims to past and present unfair treatment. Reform liberals acknowledge a history of discrimination against categories of people, and believe that the state has an obligation to remedy effects of that history in order to equalize individuals' opportunities to compete. They view programs such as Head Start and transitional bilingual education, and policies such as desegregation, as legitimate efforts to open opportunities and remedy "dysfunctional" aspects of culture. Liberals also believe that prejudice and stereotyping interfere with individuals' attempts to pursue opportunity, and that such interference can be reduced by teaching people to focus on positive rather than negative characteristics of groups.

Radical leftists reject the individual as the main unit of analysis and focus on group relations, arguing that most social behavior is structured by groups rather than individuals. Radicals also tend to reject unbridled competition for goods as the hallmark of the "good society," viewing goods as limited and rampant materialism as destructive to society at large as well as to individuals' sense of wholeness. Radicals view inequality as structured deeply into society's institutions, having been constructed by "haves" in an effort to protect and extend their power and wealth. Social inequality can be contested most effectively not by the state, which is controlled mainly by the "haves," but rather by organized collective work led primarily by oppressed groups. This requires acknowledging structural divisions among groups as well as differential vested interests in protecting those divisions. Radicals view the cultures of oppressed groups as sources of strength and insight rather than as dysfunctional, and "mainstream" culture as the ideology of the dominant groups rather than as politically neutral. Members of the radical left divide sharply, however, over the form(s) of social division they regard as most significant: social class, race, or gender.

The critiques of multicultural education consist of conservative charges that the field is too radical, and radical charges that multicultural education is too liberal and not radical enough. I should note here that the field itself is fairly diverse; one can find conservative, liberal, and radical formulations of multicultural education, ranging from very naive to quite sophisticated (Sleeter & Grant, 1988). Generally, in criticizing multicultural education, authors actually refer to specific targets rather than the field as a whole. There is also an emerging anthropological critique: Several symposia at the 1992 meeting of the American Anthropological Association were devoted to the proposition that anthropologists "must have been out of the room when the word 'cultural' acquired the prefix 'multi.'" The main concern of these symposia was that many people use the concept of "culture" in a simplistic fashion and "miss important insights that anthropologists could offer" (Coughlin, 1992, p. A8).

Since the great majority of critiques of multicultural education have come from conservatives rather than radical leftists, I will begin there.

CONSERVATIVE CRITIQUES OF MULTICULTURAL EDUCATION

While multicultural education has been the subject of occasional conservative critiques since its inception (Broudy, 1975; Glazer, 1981; Ivie, 1979; M. D. Thomas, 1981), the early 1990s saw a barrage of these critiques. They are written primarily for a popular audience. The conservative critiques first emerged in the form of conservative articulations of what children should be taught (Hirsch, 1987), then quickly escalated into a broad attack on multicultural curricula (see McLaren, 1988).

The most visible critics are Bloom (1989), D'Souza (1991a, 1991b, 1991c), Ravitch (1990a, 1990b, 1991/92), and Schlesinger (1991a, 1991b, 1991c, 1991d, 1991e, 1991f, 1992; Smoler, 1992). Their books are reviewed widely, in such highly visible publications as the *New York Times Book Review* (e.g., Kermode, 1992) and the *New Yorker* (e.g., Menand, 1991). Other essayists have published critiques in popular magazines and newspapers (Davidson, 1991; "Diversity at the Schools," 1991; "Ex Uno, Plus," 1991; Gray, 1991; Hassenger, 1992; Jackson, 1991; Krauthammer, 1990a, 1990b; Leo, 1991; "Mr. Sobol's Planet," 1991; Siegel, 1991; Sirkin, 1990; C. Thomas, 1992), in education journals and newspapers (Balch, 1992; Hogeboom, 1991; Lovin, 1992; Martel, 1991; Menand, 1992; Royal, 1992; Shanker, 1991; Stotsky, 1991a, 1991b, 1992), in other scholarly journals (Bryden, 1991; Feuer, 1991; Hardy, 1991; Howe, 1991; Wildavsky, 1991), and in monograph form (Auster, 1990). In addition, the new conservative newsletter *Heterodoxy* regularly publishes criticisms of multicultural education (see, e.g., Billingsley, 1992; Sykes & Billingsley, 1992). Some of the conservative critics such as D'Souza and Schlesinger call themselves liberals; however, I have categorized their critiques as conservative because their arguments and assumptions have more in common with conservatism as described above than with liberalism.

The target of conservative criticism is not the multicultural education literature; few critics give that literature so much as a passing nod. Rather, their targets are curricular changes and policies being instituted in schools and universities on a wide scale, particularly New York State's *A Curriculum of Inclusion* (1989) (a framework written by a task force to guide the development of new K–12 multicultural curricula), Portland, Oregon's, *African American Baseline Essays* (1989) (a series of essays that explicates six disciplines from an Afrocentric perspective, designed to help K–12 teachers reconceptualize their own curriculum), Afrocentrism in general, and revisions of core curricula on several university campuses.

Conservative critics regard education in the United States as largely politically neutral and fair to all children. For example, Balch (1992) outlines the major roles he believes schools have played quite well:

As the high road to social mobility, they sustain equality of opportunity. As sharpeners of the mind, they prepare rising generations for the responsibilities of citizenship. As purveyors of cultural understanding and technical skill, they further assimilation, national community, and the increase of the country's productive resources. As instruments for the discovery of new knowledge, they bolster expectations of material progress and ratify popular confidence in the powers of reason and science. (p. 21)

Schools may have become excessively lax in the academic rigor they expect of students, but not, in Balch's opinion, in the degree to which they serve a multicultural society fairly.

Many conservative critics acknowledge that the United States is becoming increasingly diverse. For example, Schlesinger opens a critique of multicultural education by first acknowledging, "We've always been a multiethnic country. Americans have been absorbed by diversity from the eighteenth century on" (Smoler, 1992, p. 46). D'Souza (1991c) writes that "America is becoming more diverse, ethnically and culturally, and universities are the institutions where young people of different backgrounds find themselves in close proximity"; therefore, "the objective of preparing young people for life in a multiracial society is certainly a legitimate one" (p. 34).

Their point of contention is not so much whether education should be multicultural, but what that should mean. Ravitch (1991/92) insists that the curriculum already *is* multicultural because "the common culture is multicultural" (p. 10). Stotsky (1991a) optimistically explains that reasonable citizens "should applaud the integration of non-Western cultures and the histories of various minorities—women, Hispanics, blacks, native Indian communities—into our schools' curricula" (p. 26).

Charges Against Multicultural Education

The main concern of conservative critics is that schools and universities are responding to diversity in an increasingly harmful manner, and that damaging ideas increasingly drive public education, with "myths of multiculturalism fed to *all* schoolchildren by a state monopoly" ("Ex Uno, Plus," 1991, p. 16) that is "masquerading behind the values of tolerance, diversity, and pluralism" (Stotsky, 1992, p. 65). Further, this "spread of new

multicultural perspectives throughout America's schools has taken place without much notice" (Gray, 1991, p. 13). The public needs to be aware of perilous changes in schools (Gray, 1991) and of dangerous effects of U.S. immigration policies (Auster, 1990). I will review four main concerns shared by conservatives.

Suspicious Origins of Multicultural Education. First, the conservative critics regard many of the changes taking place in education as the politically charged extremist work of a fringe of loony radicals who are succeeding in foisting new policies on a public they do not represent. For example, in *U.S. News and World Report,* Leo blasts New York State's *A Curriculum of Inclusion* (1989) as having been prepared by "prescreened worshipers at the altar of multiculturalism" who do not represent "the views of most blacks, immigrants, or New Yorkers in general" (Leo, 1991, p. 12). Krauthammer (1990a) explains that multicultural education "did not start in the New York schools. It started at the elite universities"—Stanford, in particular (p. 78). Siegel (1991) refers to multiculturalism in higher education as a "cult"—"the new orthodoxy [that] owes its most immediate inspiration to Michel Foucault" (p. 34) as well as radicals from the 1960s. Sykes and Billingsley (1992) describe multiculturalism in higher education as a movement by a small group of "multicultural mafia" who are "aware that coercion would be required to change the university," and are consequently amassing foundation money in order to buy off disciples (p. 1). D'Souza (1991a, 1991b) characterizes changes in the name of "diversity" in higher education as primarily the work of former radical student protesters of the 1960s who have returned to the university as professors to complete their conquest of it. Schlesinger (1992) complains that "ethnic ideologues" and "unscrupulous hucksters" have "imposed ethnocentric, Afrocentric, and bilingual curricula on public schools, well designed to hold minority children out of American society" (p. 130). Feuer (1991) adds the charge that multiculturalism is partly a product of Blacks who "repudiate the sciences they cannot master" during a time when scientific culture is dominant (p. 21).

To construct this origin of multicultural education, conservative critics often point to a large public of African Americans and Hispanics who presumably agree with conservative criticisms. Since "fringe radicals" do not represent the views of most people, they harass and intimidate students, professors, and citizens who question the changes they are demanding, using fear to silence their opposition. Some essayists explicitly tell readers to vote with their feet, and to transfer their children out of public schools if necessary in order to save them from state-mandated radicalism ("Ex Uno, Plus," 1991; Stotsky, 1992; C. Thomas, 1992).

Potential for Divisiveness. Second, conservatives are concerned that excessive emphasis on race and ethnicity is divisive, and will tear the United States apart in a manner similar to that experienced by the former Soviet Union, Yugoslavia, and Czechoslovakia. The curriculum is their main concern; some also address other race-conscious policies such as differential university admissions criteria, minority student organizations, and speech codes (Balch, 1992; D'Souza, 1991a, 199b).

Conservatives regard the United States as "an entirely new experiment in politics" rooted in Western political thought (Bloom, 1989, p. 27). This experiment is founded on a regard for individual rights rather than group claims:

By recognizing and accepting man's natural rights, men found a fundamental basis of unity and sameness. Class, race, religion, national origin or culture all disappear or become dim when bathed in the light of natural rights, which give men common interests and make them truly brothers. (p. 27)

The purpose of schooling is to cultivate reason so that citizens can rise above their own particular circumstances and participate rationally in a common culture based on "shared goals or vision of the public good" (p. 27). In spite of its imperfections, conservatives regard the United States as having become increasingly unified for over two centuries by a common culture and by the opportunity to shed one's past and ethnic membership in order to speak and think as an individual American.

The attention contemporary minority group members are giving to ethnic origin, they argue, subverts this trend toward inclusivity, commonality, and universalism; it also promotes White guilt and national self-hatred (Stotsky, 1991b). Schlesinger (1992), for example, notes in his discussion of the "disuniting of America":

The ethnic upsurge (it can hardly be called a revival because it was unprecedented) began as a gesture of protest against the Anglocentric culture. It became a cult, and today it threatens to become a counterrevolution against the original theory of America as "one people," a common culture, a single nation. (p. 43)

Several conservative critics contrast two different forms of multicultural education: the form they advocate—which emphasizes individual rights and cultural commonality—and the form they regard as divisive—which examines group status and cultural difference. One can find distinctions drawn between "pluralistic" and "particularistic" multicultural education (Ravitch, 1990b), multiculturalism and "militant multiculturalism" (Schlesinger, 1991f), "academic" and "ideological" multicultural education (Stotsky, 1992), and "pluralistic" and "ethnocentric" multicultural education ("More to Read," 1991).

The conservatives advocate a form of multicultural education that upholds the Western basis of U.S. institutions and thought, but incorporates diverse groups into its history and culture, with an emphasis on forging shared goals, beliefs, and allegiances. A spokesperson for what she calls "pluralistic multicultural education," Ravitch offers the California History-Social Science Framework, which she helped to draft, "as an excellent full-length multicultural curriculum" (1990a, p. 18). This framework teaches that the United States has always been multicultural, although its main institutions are rooted in Western civilization. It posits that Americans share histories of immigration to North America, but over time have become united by "the moral force of the American idea" (p. 19). As a pluralistic multicultural curriculum, it includes diverse groups in a grand narrative of America's extension of equality and freedom to all.

Particularistic (militant, ethnocentric) multicultural education and the "cult" of ethnicity in the 1980s and 1990s is a reversal of progress toward unity.

Conservatives argue that it is vital to retain the emphasis on Western thought in a multicultural society because they regard Western political thought as the source of ideas that allow individuals to rise above their origins. They argue that all civilizations have committed humanitarian crimes, but "Whatever the crimes of Europe, that continent is also the source—the *unique* source—of those liberating ideals of individual liberty, political democracy, the impartial rule of law, and cultural freedom . . . to which most of the world aspires" (Schlesinger, 1992, p. 127). In a commencement address, Mortimer Adler stated, "I would say [minority groups] should be grateful for those Western ideas they are still getting. There really is no African culture, to speak of, anyway" (Shook, 1992, p. 1). In addition, conservatives argue that America's institutions are largely British in origin, and to suggest otherwise is simply inaccurate (Bloom, 1989; Cottrol, 1991; Schlesinger, 1991f). It is important to emphasize that conservatives are underscoring not only the ideals of democracy, individual liberty, and rule of law, but also the claim that these ideals are European in origin, and that their underpinnings will be compromised if Western classics lose favor.

Some conservative critics are concerned that cultural relativism will produce not only divisiveness, but moral anarchy. Thomas (1981), for example, sees cultural pluralism as fostering disrespect for law and civility: "Pluralism leads at its worst to no ethics" (p. 592). Excessive relativism promotes self-interest rather than training people to rise above that inclination and to recognize universal principles (Bloom, 1989). Shanker (1991) speculates that multicultural education will suggest that it be taught that all cultural practices are equally good, including apartheid in South Africa, female circumcision, and Hitler's attempted genocide.

Intellectual Rigor of Multicultural Education. Third, critics argue that much multicultural curriculum is intellectually weak: it consists of a smattering of politically correct trivia and dogma that replaces sound intellectual scholarship with shoddiness, and objective fact with subjective sentiment. They criticize a variety of curricula at the K–12 levels and "diversity" courses in higher education, but their main target of criticism is Afrocentrism. The major issue that is addressed repeatedly is the Afrocentrist claim that ancient Egypt is a part of Black Africa. For example, Davidson (1991) takes issue with that claim, arguing that Afrocentrists are too "sunk . . . in a blanket rejection of Western civilization" to be swayed by evidence (p. 46). Schlesinger (1991d) refers to Afrocentric curricula as a "myth" passed off as "fact" (p. 28), and Ravitch (1990a, 1990b) regards such speculation as misdirected, ancient Egypt being removed in time so distantly from America today.

The curricula of New York and of Portland, Oregon, are criticized for both Afrocentric influence and weak scholarship. For example, Schlesinger (1991d) writes of New York's curriculum: "Its interest in history is not as an intellectual discipline but rather as social and psychological therapy whose primary function is to raise the self-esteem of children from minority groups" (p. 25); he dubs Portland's *Baseline Essays* as "bad history" (p. 27). He patronizingly describes Afrocentric thinking as having been developed as a result of Blacks' deeply wounded pride, with which "many generous-hearted people, black and white" have gone along "out of a decent sympathy for the insulted and injured of American society" (1992, p. 73). Editorials and essays in various magazines and newspapers echo Schlesinger; for example, an editorial in *The New Republic* explains: "What this [New York's] report subtly does is degrade the notion of factual truth in the American curriculum, replace factual truth with lived truth," doing so because "facts are troublesome things" that contradict what multiculturalists believe ("Mr. Sobol's Planet," 1991, p. 6). Gray (1991), writing in *Time* magazine, terms New York's report a "hatchet job on existing academic standards" (p. 13). Writing about higher education, Bryden (1991) decries the passionate orthodoxies of leftist professors, arguing that "some of its central orthodoxies are false" (p. 47) and that many of the professors are "dumb" (p. 46). Feuer (1991) regards the aim of cultural diversity in higher education as being "to entrench a place for the superficial and mediocre" (p. 21), advocating "ideological apologia for backward peoples" (p. 22). Bloom (1989), D'Souza (1991a, 1991b), and Howe (1991) offer the university curriculum of yesteryear, and particularly the Great Books curriculum, as one that may have been dominated by White men, but is intellectually sound and conveys a wide diversity of ideas, in contrast to the new multicultural curriculum.

Solutions to Minority Student Underachievement. Fourth, some conservative critics argue that multicultural education offers a poor analysis of minority student underachievement, replacing old-fashioned work with gimmicks such as self-esteem exercises. In the process, it does not give minority students the intellectual tools they need to "make it" in the real world. Ravitch (1990a), for example, explains that "particularistic" multicultural education, especially Afrocentrism, traces minority student underachievement mainly to lack of self-esteem induced by a curriculum that emphasizes Europeans. Citing the work of James Comer and Jaime Escalante, she argues that "it is dubious to assert that programs to bolster racial pride will raise children's self-esteem or their academic performance" (p. 46), because doing so locates children's identity "on another continent or in a vanished civilization" rather than in contemporary America and in doing hard work well (p. 47). She asks whether it makes more sense to teach ancient African number systems or modern mathematics, suggesting that Afrocentrism is ludicrous for emphasizing the former (1990b). Similarly, Howe (1991) and Schlesinger (1992) argue that the traditional university curriculum, particularly the classics, stretches the mind: Richard Wright, Ralph Ellison, and Chinua Achebe read Western classics, and minority students today who are assigned an incoherent multicultural curriculum are not well-served academically. Neither are Spanish-speaking students served well by bilingual education, argues Schlesinger (1992), because it retards acquisition of English and encourages segregation.

D'Souza's (1991b) main criticism of multicultural education is that it institutionalizes low expectations in higher education. He blasts universities for instituting race-based differential admissions policies, giving preference to poorly prepared minor-

ity students who find themselves set up for failure. He criticizes multicultural curricula in higher education for encouraging minority students and faculty to blame the system for their underachievement, rather than actually helping them to master academic material.

Ravitch (1990b) lists several factors that she (as well as most educators) believe will improve education for African American and Hispanic students:

They would fare better in school if they had well-educated and well-paid teachers, small classes, good materials, encouragement at home and school, summer academic programs, protection from the drugs and crime that ravage their neighborhoods, and higher expectations of satisfying careers upon graduation. (p. 349)

She acknowledges that these improvements require resources, and argues that attention to self-esteem deflects attention away from the resource problem.

Weaknesses of the Conservative Critiques

I will note three weaknesses of the conservative critiques of multicultural education, then discuss implications of these critiques for the field.

Ignore Research and Theory in Multicultural Education. First, conservative critics ignore the body of literature on multicultural education as well as a good deal of the research and theory it builds upon, produced largely by scholars of color and by feminist and critical scholars (such as the literature reviewed in this *Handbook*). None of the critics mention the work of scholars such as James A. Banks (1988), Geneva Gay (Gay & Baber, 1987), Carl Grant (1992), Sonia Nieto (1991), or Henry Trueba (1989). Instead they reduce multicultural education to New York's *A Curriculum of Inclusion* (1989), pieces of Afrocentrist work, and selected university responses to the desire of communities of color for access to higher education. Reading the critiques, one might assume that Leonard Jeffries is the main spokesperson for multicultural education, since his name appears repeatedly. Ignoring the literature on multicultural education is a serious shortcoming that undercuts these critiques. While conservatives criticize multicultural curricula as weak on scholarship, their failure to address or review literature on multicultural education reveals this very weakness in their own work.

Conservatives position themselves, rather than scholars who have developed multicultural scholarship, as spokespeople and advocates for both the broad American public in general *and* racial minority groups in particular. Most of the conservative critics are White; D'Souza, an immigrant from India, is the main (perhaps only) critic reviewed here who is not White. A few critics of other racially sensitive policies are also of color; while not directly addressing multicultural education, their positions support those of White conservative critics who do so (e.g., Chavez, 1991; Rodriguez, 1981; Sowell, 1993; Steele, 1990). Thus, White conservative critics of multicultural education find allies of color, although their numbers are small.

White conservative critics use at least two strategies to position themselves as advocates of people of color in attacking multicultural education. Arthur Schlesinger has written prolifically, so examples of both strategies will be drawn from his writing. One strategy is to call attention to their longtime advocacy of pluralism and their acquaintance with leading African American thinkers (see, e.g., Schlesinger, 1992, p. 75). Another strategy is to sprinkle their writings with the names of scholars of color such as W. E. B. DuBois, Carter Woodson, Frederick Douglass, and James Comer, who, they imply, agree with their viewpoints. Consider the following passage:

Multicultural history in its militant vein promotes fragmentation, segregation, ghettoization—all the more dangerous at a time when ethnic conflict is tearing apart one nation after another. James Baldwin once said, "To create one nation has proved to be a hideously difficult task; there is certainly no need now to create two, one black and one white." (Schlesinger, 1991f, p. 14)

Schlesinger implies that Baldwin advocated his—Schlesinger's—version of multicultural education in contrast to that of the "multicultural zealots" (p. 13) whose version he is critiquing. Note that Baldwin is not writing about Schlesinger's ideas, nor is there any indication in Baldwin's writings that he would support Schlesinger over advocates of multicultural education. This appropriation of the names of scholars and activists of color is common in the conservative critiques. The impression conveyed to readers unfamiliar with the scholarship and research that support multicultural education is that most scholars of color agree with the conservatives.

By refusing to engage with critical ideas in multicultural education literature, conservatives imply that educators of color, and particularly African American educators, cannot think rationally about schooling and disciplinary knowledge, or even about what is best for their own children. Mexican American and Puerto Rican educators tend to support bilingual education; the conservative suggestion that it is bad for Spanish-speaking students implies that Spanish-speaking educators are not using good judgment. It is one thing to recognize that educators of color disagree over many ideas. But it is quite another to tear apart Afrocentrist work wholesale as both intellectually weak and bad for African American children, and simply ignore a good deal of scholarship in other areas by educators of color. Conservatives need not agree with whatever scholars of color say, but they should at least acknowledge scholarly work and engage with it directly, rather than ignore it.

Poor Analysis of Inequality Today. A second weakness of the conservative critiques is that they offer little analysis of or reference to inequality today, framing their discussions mainly around unity versus dissension, rather than justice, and defining equality only as equal rights of individuals before the law. For example, Schlesinger (1992) writes that racism has been a "great national tragedy" in U.S. history (p. 19), relegating non-Europeans to third-class status (p. 16). However, racial inequality has been largely overcome: "The American synthesis has an inevitable Anglo-Saxon coloration, but it is no longer an exercise in Anglo-Saxon domination" (p. 118). Since contemporary American institutions and thought have the capacity to solve racism (neither he nor other conservative critics address social-

class or gender inequality), why the growing interest in ethnicity? Schlesinger traces this interest to an unsubstantiated and dangerous "decreasing confidence in the American future" (p. 41).

Absent from conservative writings is a recognition of the growing frustration that many Americans have experienced over the past 12 years as poverty rates have risen, opportunities for employment have left the country, and funding for various social programs has been cut (discussions of these trends can be found in, e.g., Barlett & Steele, 1992; Hacker, 1992; James, 1991; Kozol, 1991; Sidel, 1988). Absent, too, is a recognition that debates about the past are intimately tied to analyses of why groups continue to occupy "have not" statuses and how those statuses can be changed. Conservative critics seem to conceptualize ethnic and racial conflict as stemming from excessive group pride rather than frustration about persistent lack of access to resources. Ironically, the factors some conservatives discussed as helping the education of students of color most— well-paid teachers, small classes, good materials, summer programs, and access to satisfying careers—cost money. Rather than expending efforts criticizing multicultural education, conservatives might channel that effort into directing large amounts of resources and job opportunities into poverty areas.

The theoretical framework conservatives use to examine race relations is *ethnicity theory,* which is based on an analysis of the experience of European ethnic groups in the United States, and examines mainly the extent to which groups retain distinct cultures while becoming structurally assimilated into the dominant society. Since it is derived from the European immigrant experience, ethnicity theory focuses on cultural and ancestral distinctions within Europe, and the historic ethnic diversity among European Americans. Non-Europeans are simply added onto this list of ancestral lineages. Ethnicity theory examines how people "escape from origins" in the United States (Schlesinger, 1992, p. 15) and go about "casting off the foreign skin" (p. 112). This concept raises an interesting question, given the indelibility of skin color, and is particularly inapplicable to Native Americans, whose skin and culture are more indigenous to North America than those of European Americans.

Ethnicity theory has not conceptualized European Americans as an ethnic group in themselves, distinct visibly as well as historically from non–European Americans (see Alba, 1990). As a result, it has not formulated an analysis of race relations in the United States that examines White privilege (hooks, 1990). Yet it is the intransigence of White privilege that many advocates of multicultural education attempt to address. Conservatives do not regard alternative race- or class-based theories of racial oppression (Omi & Winant, 1986) as legitimate, nor do they give credence to questions about the social-class structure itself.

Conservatives are angered by what they regard as excessive criticism of Europe's role in the conquest and enslavement of Third World people. To argue that Europeans do not have a monopoly on cultural vice, they advocate that everyone's "warts" should be presented equally: "The sins of the West are no worse than the sins of Asia or of the Middle East or of Africa" (Schlesinger, 1992, p. 127). In that sense, we are all culturally equal. Then why are Europeans and European Americans disproportionately wealthy, and why do Americans of color and Third World nations disproportionately continue to experience poverty? The main response of conservative critics is that if we all cooperate and continue to adhere to past traditions, justice will prevail. This is a very weak response that simply does not address the current realities that many people experience. Nor does such a response acknowledge the U.S. history of oppression in which past traditions have legitimated slavery, incarceration, Jim Crow, and various forms of genocide, and in which conservative calls for gradual change have meant no change at all. (Viewed from the perspective of American Indians, the conservative response is a request that Indians accept completion of the process of cultural and national genocide.)

D'Souza's book *Illiberal Education* (1991b) merits an observation here. It can be read as an examination of the institutionalization of low expectations for academic achievement of students of color. While reading it, I was reminded of Derrick Bell's (1989) contrasting the original intent of policies advanced by African Americans (such as school desegregation) with the ultimate benefits White society derived from their implementation. Many of the higher-education policies D'Souza describes could well be subject to the same analysis Bell uses, contrasting intent of initial advocates with actual effects of White-controlled policy changes. D'Souza treats the institutionalization of low expectations for minority students as a recent event brought about by radicals; he might well ask how low expectations have been institutionalized for 300 years. Doing so might lead to an examination of institutional racism. He might also ask how scholars of color in higher education regard the policies he critiques; by failing to do so, his book portrays students of color as victims of policies desired by educators of color (among other actors in higher education). Pursuing these questions might lead him to a better appreciation than his book demonstrates of the work of scholars in multicultural education.

Politics of Conservative Viewpoint. In a third weakness of the critiques, conservatives assume that their own viewpoints are apolitical, conceptualizing them as rooted in intellectual training that enabled them to rise above their own particular circumstances in order to make an objective assessment. They frequently deride multicultural education as "political," suggesting that their own viewpoints are not, and that the way schools operate currently is not political. Some conservative rhetoric bifurcates the "political" from the "academic," such as the following passage: "Yet one of the most contentious issues in education today is what the words 'multicultural education' mean and whether the content of such programs serves academic or political ends" (Stotsky, 1991a, p. 26).

The issue here is more than rhetorical. It is embedded in a fundamental assumption of traditional Western liberal thought: that intellectual engagement with the classical ideals of Western political philosophy enables an individual to transcend personal vested interest in order to speak dispassionately for the whole society. How does one critique one's own thoughts and actions for self-interest? One does that within the framework of classical Western philosophy. If one attempts to critique ideas

from outside the framework of classical Western philosophy, or attempts to critique Western philosophy itself, one is being political, not rational (Code, 1991; Harding, 1991). Western classical thought supposedly admits a wide diversity of viewpoints, but multicultural advocates' attempts to expand intellectual inquiry beyond classical Western thought are met with charges of their being "thought police" who want everyone to think uniformly (Wildavsky, 1991). Thus, even though conservative critics argue that America is where immigrants come to "cast off their European skin" (Schlesinger, 1992, p. 25) and forge a new identity, at the same time they give primacy to Europe by arguing that this can be done only within the framework of Western thought. Further, although some conservatives regard the Afrocentrist interest in ancient Egypt as illogical, since Kemet is so far removed in time and space from the United States today, they do not apply the same standard to classical Greece.

But the conservatives uphold Western thought selectively. While several critics bemoan deconstructionism, it is certainly a school of European thought, having been born in France (Derrida, 1981; Foucault, 1979). Some argue that Afrocentrism is more Western than African (e.g., Schlesinger, 1992, pp. 81–84), yet critics attack Afrocentrism as undercutting Western ideals. Critics regard multicultural education as an attack on the West, yet "the multicultural education movement emerged out of Western democratic ideals" of equality and justice (Banks, 1991/92, p. 32). When the critics champion Western thought, it is specific strands of Western thought they actually support.

In higher education, scholars in ethnic studies and women's studies have engaged in dialogue with deconstructionists (multicultural education did not begin with deconstructionism, contrary to some critics' beliefs) largely because of a common interest in examining how one's location in the social structure, subjective identity, and vested interests shape one's beliefs and actions. Kessler-Harris (1992) observed that Black studies "raise questions not only about a common vision, but about the role of domination in constructing economic and political democracy as well" (p. 306). By questioning the very idea of political neutrality, scholars have opened many questions for analysis that earlier had not been examined (see, e.g., Code, 1991; hooks, 1990; Harding, 1991; Collins, 1991; Spivak, 1990). This leaves conservatives and advocates of multicultural education in higher education at an impasse, with one side arguing that radicals are politicizing education by refusing to adhere to standards of intellectual thought, while the other side deconstructs conservative critiques for their embodied self-interest. Both are engaging in intellectual investigation (as well as exhibiting some passionate excesses), but using different rules. An important weakness of the conservative discourse is its limited ability to examine its own vested interests in its supposed "objectivity," and the political advantage conservatives would gain if European ideas maintain primacy.

Implications of the Conservative Critiques for Multicultural Education

As I gathered documents for this review, I was surprised to note how concentrated the conservative critiques were in

1990–1992 (at the time of this writing, I do not know when they will slack off in volume). What was it about this time period that would provoke such an outpouring? And I believe it was an organized outpouring; the conservative critiques became very repetitive to read, many of them recycling the same examples and ideas over and over. Further, while those of us who have written extensively about multicultural education have labored within the normal education publication channels (textbook publishers, journals), the conservative critics gained rapid access to popular media and book publishers with wide circulation.

Afrocentricity is receiving the brunt of the anti-PC attacks; this attack is aimed specifically at people of color. The movement for multiculturalism came out of the civil rights movement. Multiculturalism can lead to action on and off campus; that's why it's considered dangerous. (Minsky, 1992, p. 19)

This statement was made by a student in a discussion about the political correctness controversy sponsored by the National Coalition for Universities in the Public Interest. I believe the student is correct. In fact, not only *can* multiculturalism lead to action, but it *is leading* to action.

The conservative critics respond not to what multicultural education scholars have said in the literature, but to actual changes in curriculum required of White students as well as students of color, and particularly changes that challenge White supremacy. Multicultural education has been around since the mid-1960s. As long as it took the form of sporadic practices in schools (largely in schools populated primarily by students of color), scholarly writings, and occasional conference themes, conservatives could ignore it. As soon as multicultural education became the foundation for required curricula at state and university levels, it could no longer be ignored because in a "tug of war over who gets to create the public culture" (Kessler-Harris, 1992, p. 310), people of color were making gains. And they were doing so during an increasingly unstable period.

The United States is experiencing many pressures that can destabilize the "New World Order." Hugh Price (1992), vice president of the Rockefeller Foundation and an outsider to the debates about multicultural education, observed:

Note the coincidence between the erosion of earnings among working-class people—white, black, and Latino—and the rise of strident multiculturalism. The social compact in America between our society and its working people—white and minority alike—is dissolving.... Those manufacturing jobs that once provided dignity and decent wages for high school graduates and dropouts alike are vanishing. All are victims of a new world industrial order that is redistributing manufacturing jobs and redefining the economic role of our communities. (p. 212)

At the same time that large numbers of Americans—disproportionately of color—have been downwardly mobile, the non-White population has been growing to the extent that Whites are no longer the majority in many cities, and are expected to lose majority status in many states during the next few decades. Auster (1990) sounds the following alarm: "The pre-1880 population from northern Europe—the original racial and cultural base of the U.S.—will have become a vanishing minority" (pp.

25–26). With whom will non-White Americans align themselves: White corporate America and its European ties, or black and brown America and its historic ties with the Third World people who increasingly constitute "cheap labor" in the American world economy?

Domestically, White middle-class America is uneasy about its own future, and can be led rather readily to pin its fears and anxieties on the threat of "diversity." Internationally, the "U.S. is now embarked on an effort to establish its supremacy as the world power, primarily through militarism.... To do this requires a sense of national unity, of a country united behind war and militarism" (Platt, 1992, p. 133). Platt argues that the conservative attacks on multicultural education represent attempts to suppress dissent, particularly that which would question U.S. military policies against Third World nations. Education, as Chomsky (1987) has argued, serves an important form of ideological control, and is increasingly under the purview of the state. He observed that the ideological spectrum of the intelligentsia in the United States has gradually narrowed, until most academic work now serves the purpose of manufacturing popular consent for U.S. military aggression and capitalist expansion. I would suggest that multicultural education threatens that ideological consensus, opening questions about both domestic and international issues that the political elite would rather not have examined publicly. By invoking racial fears as well as popular beliefs in "free speech," conservatives are attempting to shut down criticism of policy in an increasingly unstable world.

This tug-of-war over who gets to construct the public's perception of racial diversity is not new. For example, in his book *Black Athena,* Bernal (1987) points out that until around 1700 it was commonly accepted that classical European culture had important Afro-Asiatic roots. During the height of imperialism, European scholars rewrote European history to advance the Aryan theory, which holds that classical European culture arose spontaneously and was not built on the historic wisdom of any culture of color. The Aryan theory supported the cultural and political supremacy of Europe and European Americans.

Afrocentrism and multicultural education today challenge that supremacy intellectually. Politically, group relations within the United States as well as worldwide are sufficiently unstable that Europeans and European Americans, especially those of wealth, fear losing power and control. The attacks from the right are mainly about trying to maintain European and European American capitalist supremacy. Further, during 1992 the attacks were probably designed to support Bush in the 1992 election in order to allow the Reagan-Bush conservative restoration project to continue.

Conservative critiques are frequently placed in mainstream popular media because that is where the conservatives can win politically, and mainstream media are receptive to conservative "backlash" perspectives (Faludi, 1991). The average lay citizen knows very little about multicultural education (although people often draw on their own notions of culture and their understanding of the European immigrant experience to assume some understanding of it). Many people first encounter multicultural education in popular media—an encounter that is being controlled by the right. Conservatives appear to be engaged in the construction of an image of a multiculturalist that draws on racial prejudices and is designed to repel a large segment of the population.

Wolf (1991) discusses the conservative resurrection of an old image of the "ugly feminist" in order "to checkmate power at every level in individual women's lives" following successes of the women's movement (p. 19). The "ugly feminist" of the 1980s was similar to that of the 19th century: "a big masculine woman, wearing boots, smoking a cigar, swearing like a trooper" (p. 18). This image has successfully blunted the women's movement, playing on both the insecurities and the homophobia of young women who "picture a feminist as someone who is masculine and doesn't shave her legs" (pp. 208–209).

What might a caricature of the "ugly multiculturalist" look like, as portrayed in the conservative critiques? Conservatives, playing on racial stereotypes and fears, suggest that multiculturalists consist of a frenzied mob of anti-Americans trying to destroy the United States, joined by "ugly" feminists and Third World immigrants, and led by angry African American men of weak intellect. Conservatives hope to destroy public support for multicultural education and mobilize public opinion to endorse a conservative definition of how young Americans should be taught to view the United States in its diversity, and the positions of the United States and European nations within a hierarchical, capitalistic global order made up of diverse people.

The strongest implication of these conservative critiques is that a concerted effort must be made to educate the broader public about multicultural education. Most of the multicultural education literature appears in scholarly journals. As a result, the general public is receiving a distorted version of what it means. For example, conservatives portray Portland's *African American Baseline Essays* (1989) as a racist, one-sided narrative. However, writing in the *Journal of Negro Education*, one of the authors of the essays explains: "The strategy behind the *Baseline Essays* was to make the curriculum more reflective of the truly multicultural nature of American society, and to introduce co-authorship to the master narratives of this country" (Harris, 1992, pp. 306–307). In other words, the purpose of the essays is not to replace the curriculum, but to provide information and perspectives for building a multicultural curriculum. Presently many lay citizens are probably not aware of that purpose. Undoubtedly some would not support it if they were, but others would. While multicultural education scholars and activists still need to work on developing the conceptual and practical underpinnings of the field, they also need to engage in public relations.

A second implication is the need to maintain a clear sense of perspective about the main issues. Ehrenreich (1991) points out that, with many people jumping into the debates about multicultural education, relatively small issues can claim the center of attention, and relatively small academic errors or emotional excesses can become targets of public criticism. Kessler-Harris (1992) regards "political correctness" as one such red herring that should be addressed but not dwelled on. In its early days, while the field grew in relative obscurity, people could debate and disagree, experiment and make mis-

takes without much consequence. Currently, operating in the spotlight and often on the defensive, and being joined by many people who are new to multicultural education and uncertain about its main ideas, the large issues can become sidetracked.

RADICAL LEFT CRITIQUES OF MULTICULTURAL EDUCATION

Although the great majority of critiques of multicultural education have been framed by conservatives, the radical left has also produced some critiques. While conservatives may regard multicultural education as synonymous with radicalism, many radicals do not. Radical left critiques of multicultural education have been written mainly by theorists for an audience of theorists (Giroux, 1992; Mattai, 1992; McCarthy, 1988, 1990a, 1990b; Ogbu, 1992; Olneck, 1990; Popkewitz, 1988). Their purpose is not to mobilize public opinion, but rather to influence scholarly debate and, in some cases, influence multicultural education theorists.

Radical critics are committed generally to advancing a discourse that envisions structural equality. They criticize multicultural education primarily for embracing individual mobility within an economic hierarchy more than collective advancement and structural equality, and for reducing problems in the larger society to school solutions. I will first summarize their main charges against multicultural education, identify weaknesses of the radical critiques, and then discuss implications of these critiques for the field.

Charges Against Multicultural Education

Most of the radical critiques begin by distinguishing among conservative, liberal, and radical discourse for the purpose of pointing out issues in radical discourse that are not developed in multicultural education literature. These include systemic forms of racial, class, and gender oppression, and an analysis of power. For example, Olneck (1990) argues that multicultural education emphasizes the primacy of individual choice over collective solidarity, and individual mobility over collective advancement.

Radical critics then locate multicultural education within liberalism, treating it as a fairly unified body of thought and practice. While critics such as Giroux (1992) acknowledge strands of radical thought within the field, others such as Olneck (1990) regard the field as lacking a radical discourse that can be developed. In informal conversations with radical critics, I have heard exasperation with apolitical practices that White teachers term "multicultural education," such as contributions added onto Eurocentric curricula, tacit acceptance of low achievement, and cultural celebrations that deny the existence of racism. These apolitical practices resonate with liberal terminology and conceptual formulations found in much multicultural education literature.

Radical critics are particularly concerned about an absence of a critique of systems of oppression. While critics such as Olneck and Popkewitz formulate much of their work around a social-class analysis, others such as Mattai and Ogbu emphasize

White racism as the main problem, or racism and capitalism as interwoven systems of oppression. For example, Mattai (1992) argues that although multicultural education developed in response to racial debates of the 1960s, its discourse shifted from racism to culture. Culture became reified as a depoliticized expression of "otherness," and systems of oppression were ignored. JanMohamed and Lloyd (1987) suggest that the cultural pluralism of both conservatives and liberals is "the great white hope" that offers "the semblance of pluralism" while perpetuating exclusionary hierarchical systems (p. 9). It is this emphasis on culture rather than structural inequality that radicals find most problematic about multicultural education. Ogbu (1992), while discussing culture, connects it with power relations among groups historically, and criticizes multicultural education for failing to deal with culture in the context of a particular groups' historic experiences with White racism.

Radical critics fault multicultural education for putting forth psychological solutions to political and social-structural problems. Popkewitz (1988), for example, interprets discussion of learning styles as a reduction of Black culture to psychological checklists that prescribe mechanistic pedagogical solutions to Black underachievement. Critics also see multicultural education as advocating reduction of teacher prejudice as a solution to inequality, which they criticize as naive and misdirected. Radical critics regard the increasing popularity of multicultural education as a palliative White response to minority concerns that deflects attention away from structural issues, especially White racism.

Some critics see the field as misdirected but do not suggest an alternative. Others develop alternatives to multicultural education. *Border pedagogy* (Giroux, 1992) is grounded on a "recognition of those epistemological, political, cultural, and social margins that distinguish between 'us and them'" (p. 23), which Giroux regards as more politically informed and less assimilative than liberal multicultural education. Similarly, McCarthy (1988) advances *nonsynchrony*, which "recognizes the strategic importance of the historical struggles over the production of knowledge and the positioning of minorities in social theories" (p. 276), and the complexities engendered by intersections of race, class, and gender.

Weaknesses of the Radical Critiques

While radical critiques identify issues that multicultural education does not address well, they have some serious weaknesses of their own. Some of the radical critiques are oversimplified caricatures that dismiss the works by American scholars of color that span two decades (for a review of the latter, see Banks, 1992). Most of the critics write from outside the field of multicultural education. The degree to which they actually review literature in multicultural education varies; while Olneck (1990) reviewed literature in some detail, for example, Popkewitz (1988) did not review it at all. As a result, some descriptions of multicultural education, such as those by Popkewitz and McCarthy (1988), are extremely reductionistic, disregarding large bodies of scholarship. For example, Popkewitz notes the reduction of Black underachievement to psychological factors that are further simplified into learning-style checklists. While one can certainly find simplistic learning-style checklists

that do not address Black achievement in any comprehensive way, one can also find sophisticated discussions of African American cognition and worldview, developed by African American scholars such as Shade (1982) and Boykin (1982), that inform thinking in some of the multicultural education literature. Critics tend to lump together everything termed *multicultural education,* including superficialities such as food festivals, without noting that established multicultural education scholars criticize the same superficialities (Banks, 1984).

Some radical critics tacitly dismiss the work of U.S. scholars of color who draw on radical as well as liberal thinking. My own experience with multicultural education over the past 20 years has placed me in the company of many U.S. educators of color who are concerned primarily about White racism and how to confront it, and who in many cases are familiar with and contribute to intellectual scholarship in ethnic studies (see Banks, 1992). Critics of American multicultural education tend to draw on criticisms of British multicultural education that are advanced by antiracists, assuming that the issues in England and the United States are much the same. Elsewhere I have argued that they are not (Sleeter, 1989). Some radical critics use the work of White neo-Marxists and Black British antiracists to dismiss work by many American scholars of color.

McCarthy (1990b, pp. 47–48), for example, argues that multicultural education deracializes African American demands for education reform. His critique positions Baker, Banks, and Grant—three African American developers of multicultural education—against Apple and Troyna—two White neo-Marxists who are American and British, respectively. This kind of argument construction implies that the White neo-Marxists have greater insight into the nature of racial oppression than do African Americans who actively developed multicultural education. He then positions Marable (1985), an African American radical, several paragraphs after his discussion of multicultural education, suggesting that radicals of color have no association with it.

The United States as a whole tends to abhor radical discourses, treating them as "un-American." Mainstream America regards liberal discourse as "leftist" as is acceptable (and conservative Republicans during the 1992 presidential campaign touted the "L" word itself as un-American). While White racism is the primary concern of serious scholars of multicultural education, White educators are rarely receptive to appeals for change that are framed around racism. However, liberal formulations of change accept individualism and the "inevitability" of capitalism, asking mainly how to reorder individuals within a capitalistic and hierarchical social structure. The marginalization of radical thought means that many people who would find it helpful are never exposed to it in any depth. In addition, the articulation of radical discourse can itself marginalize people; groups fighting against their own marginalization tend to resist using strategies that further marginalize them if they believe such strategies—in this case, talking too radically—would do more harm than good. Neo-Marxism is the most well-developed body of radical discourse in the United States, but it is dominated by Whites, usually marginalizes race and gender, and stems from the White working-class experience that people of color have long historic reasons not to trust (see, e.g., Roediger, 1991). While White neo-Marxists can get away with radical discourse because they are protected by their race, people of color who address racism do not have that protection, and are often reluctant to discuss systemic White racism in front of Whites because of a history of negative White reactions (Barnes, 1993; Wiley, 1993).

Implications of Radical Critiques for Multicultural Education

Radical critics do point out some areas in which the field of multicultural education needs improvement. Essentially, the radical critiques suggest that multicultural education ground its theory and practice in stronger analyses of relationships among unequal groups in the United States. Multicultural education focuses on what schools can do to effect change, but in so doing, tends to decontextualize schools from broader, entrenched relations of power. While multicultural education grew out of the civil rights movements of the 1960s, much of its literature and practice have become disconnected from social movements. This decontextualization and depoliticizing weakens the potential impact of multicultural education.

Multicultural education discourse tends to conflate *race* and *ethnicity,* using racial and ethnic terminology interchangeably. The problem is that racial and ethnic theories of inequality are very different. Ethnicity theory is most often accepted by the dominant society (Omi & Winant, 1986) and is endorsed by conservative critics. Ethnicity theory suggests that groups will progress up the ladder of opportunity in a manner similar to that of European ethnic groups; attending to ethnicity means celebrating vestiges of "Old World" culture. Since ethnicity does not structure the life chances of European Americans after two or three generations, ethnicity theory does not lead to a critique of collective oppression (Alba, 1990). Basing multicultural education around assumptions of ethnicity theory leads to the superficial practices that both radicals and multicultural education theorists criticize. Terminology drawn from ethnicity theory resonates with the prior understandings of White teachers, allowing them to create multicultural teaching practices that do not acknowledge racism or White supremacy (Sleeter, 1992).

Racial theories, on the other hand, suggest that White supremacy is deeply structured into society, changing its face but not its basic nature over time. White supremacy is maintained by social institutions, and is challenged most successfully when groups of color organize to press collectively for change (Omi & Winant, 1986; Ringer & Lawless, 1989). Multicultural education should challenge racism as it is instituted in schools, as well as educating citizens about the nature of racism. The field could be strengthened by clarifying its theoretical underpinnings and its subsequent terminology.

Multicultural education does not address social class with much depth. Its theorists often criticize the persistence of poverty, but present little analysis of why poverty exists, propose no strategies to eliminate it, and fail to examine the growing concentration of national and global wealth in a small elite (Barlett & Steele, 1992; Bohmer, 1992). Multicultural education theorists should develop a critique of the social-class structure and the economic system, linking class analysis with racial and gender oppression, but not reducing economic inequality to

racism. Such critiques should also suggest actions that educators can take to address social-class inequality; with a few exceptions (Diamond & Bigelow, 1988; Shor, 1992), existing theoretical class analyses tend to develop few practical strategies.

None of the critiques develop a feminist analysis of multicultural education, although McCarthy (1988, 1990a) gives attention to gender in his critique. Multicultural education should draw more on feminist analyses of oppression, particularly the work of radical and socialist feminists (Jaggar, 1983), who have keen insights into patriarchy as well as the connections between gender inequality and capitalism (Hartsock, 1983). When sexism is mentioned at all in the multicultural education literature, it tends to be conceptualized mainly within a liberal perspective, which defines it largely as a heterosexual problem of stereotyping, subsequent differential treatment of boys and girls, and failure to include women in the curriculum (e.g., Cushner, McClelland, & Safford, 1992). In addition, sexism is often developed as a separate topic, rather than being meshed with race, ethnicity, or language (Gollnick & Chinn, 1986). Analyses of patriarchy that conceptualize gender relations as deeply institutionalized into society would broaden the treatment of sexism in the multicultural education literature, suggesting, for example, much more thorough curriculum revision, policies for shifting more power to define education toward women and girls, or policies that might challenge the entrenchment of heterosexism (hooks, 1990; Lather, 1991; Weiler, 1988). But such analyses should also be integrated with examination of racism and poverty, rather than being treated as a separate topic.

Failure to link racial oppression with runaway capitalist consumption and White patriarchy leaves advocates of multicultural education asking for limited social improvement. In a conversation with bell hooks (1990) about competition among oppressed groups, Cornel West observed:

This [competition] is true not only between male and female relations but also black and brown relations and black and Korean, and black and Asian relations. We are struggling over crumbs because we know that the bigger part of lower corporate America is already received. One half of one percent of America owns twenty-two percent of the wealth, one percent owns thirty-two percent, and the bottom forty-five percent of the population has twenty percent of the wealth. (p. 209)

Development of a comprehensive analysis of oppression would help build a "new majority for justice and peace" that can work toward "the collective path of human liberation, self-determination and sovereignty" (Marable, 1992, pp. 254–225).

When multicultural education is framed around learning about "other" cultures and displacing stereotypes, the larger structural issues are ignored. Studying "other" cultures and addressing stereotypes, or studying culture itself without examining structural inequality, gives the illusion of doing something constructive. Kozol (1991 p. 116), for example, discussed the popularity of "cultural difference" explanations used by affluent White people to justify vastly differential spending not just on schooling but also other resources such as medical care. Cultural differences *are a part* of multicultural education, but in the context of the "savage inequalities" that characterize U.S. society (Kozol, 1991), cannot receive the great bulk of attention.

Multicultural education theorists must direct attention more directly to *White racism, patriarchy,* and *capitalism,* as these intersect and are played out on various levels of society, and differentially across groups.

CONCLUSION

Gates (1991) wrote that "the challenge facing America in the next century will be the shaping, at long last, of a truly common public culture, one responsive to the long-silenced cultures of color" (p. 712). I would add additional long-silenced publics, including those who are economically poor, women, gays and lesbians, and people with disabilities. The field of multicultural education has been addressing that challenge actively for over two decades. Having experienced considerable conceptual growth and some limited gains in affecting schools, the field currently is buffeted by critiques. Those of us who work in multicultural education find ourselves walking a tightrope between naming issues accurately and antagonizing potential supporters.

The left would have the field develop a much more explicit critique of White racism, capitalism, and patriarchy, a position with which I agree. As the gap between "haves" and "have nots" in U.S. society widens and conditions among the poorest (and darkest-skinned) deteriorate, there appears to be a tendency across the general public to accept inequality as given. Many teachers, in fact, believe that the problems of racism and sexism were solved during the civil rights movement, and ascribe today's dilemmas to moral degeneration among the poor (Kozol, 1991; Sleeter, 1992).

Yet it is very difficult to work on naming social justice issues squarely in the context of the right's characterization of the field as un-American and dangerous. Multicultural education advocates have a history of trying to work with teachers and administrators in their attempt to bring about school change (Banks, 1992), and should not abandon that work. But fear of radicalism in the United States, coupled with conservative criticisms, is making it increasingly difficult to address inequality directly. Stanley (1992) notes that social reconstructionism has long experienced a tension "between pragmatism and the attempt to construct a radical program for sociocultural transformation" (p. 44). The conservative criticisms of multicultural education, advanced in a conservative climate of public opinion, aggravate that tension.

Recently Carl Grant and I received an invitation to write about the multicultural and social reconstructionist approaches to multicultural education (explicated previously in Sleeter & Grant, 1988). But the invitation, as outlined in our (unsigned) contract, contained some restrictions: The essay should be one that "respects curriculum already in place in any school, and portrays no political agenda." It should value "all cultural groups" and "not serve as a forum for attacking society," and it should be written in a "positive, nonjudgmental tone." While I have often been advised by educators in the field to tone down rhetoric, this was the most explicit restriction I had encountered on our otherwise well-received formulation of multicultural education. These were restrictions on ideas, not simply wording. They were restrictions born of a concern (I was told) that teachers will not work with multicultural education materials if they feel personally attacked.

Multicultural education means a shift in decision-making power over schooling away from dominant groups and toward oppressed groups. It should be regarded as a shift in power more than a program to be implemented. The potential of such a power shift to effect change is what has given rise to the barrage of conservative critiques. Viewing multicultural education politically suggests work for the coming decade.

At the level of theory, multicultural education should develop the structural and contextual analyses called for by the radical critics. To a large extent this conceptual work is already being done in departments of ethnic studies, women's studies, and cultural studies in universities. Some multicultural education scholars are connected with and making use of this work, but many are not. The task for education theorists is to fuse such work with schooling issues. This theoretical work will greatly enrich the field conceptually, and has the potential to focus practice.

At the level of activism, multicultural education needs to be "sold" to the public. I believe that emphasis should be placed on those publics who would be most receptive to it: multicultural education's "natural" constituencies of oppressed groups, as well as educator-activists such as those who are members of the National Coalition of Educational Activists. Various organizations exist within communities of color, such as, in the African American community, the NAACP, the National Urban League, the National Association of Black School Educators, and thousands of churches. Similarly, Latino, Asian, Native American, and low-income White communities all have various organizations to work with. Multicultural education suggests school practices, resources, and research that support agendas of such organizations. In addition, if multicultural education developed stronger linkages with bilingual education, and if language-minority publics were better informed of the field as a resource for improving schooling, such publics may constitute an additional "natural" source of political support. So would feminist organizations, especially those that have been working to bridge cultural and racial differences among women.

Yet the term *multicultural education* and much of its literature may be more familiar to White teachers (many of whom do not identify with its goals) than it is to members of community organizations who would support its goals and view the field as a helpful resource. The critiques suggest that the work to come is political in addition to being pedagogical. A great many pedagogical resources and an impressive volume of research have been developed; connecting these politically with various publics is the task ahead.

References

A curriculum of inclusion: Report of the commissioner's task force on minorities. (1989). Albany, NY: New York State Special Task Force on Equity and Excellence in Education.

African American baseline essays. (1989). Portland, OR: Portland Public Schools.

Alba, R. D. (1990). *Ethnic identity.* New Haven, CT: Yale University Press.

Auster, L. (1990). *The path to national suicide.* Monterey, VA: The American Immigration Control Foundation.

Balch, S. A. (1992). Political correctness or public choice? *Educational Record, 73*(1), 21–24.

Banks, J. A. (1984). Multicultural education and its critics. *The New Era, 65*(3), 58–65.

Banks, J. A. (1988). *Multiethnic education: Theory and practice.* Boston: Allyn and Bacon.

Banks, J. A. (1991/92). Multicultural education: For freedom's sake. *Educational Leadership, 49*(4), 32–36.

Banks, J. A. (1992). African American scholarship and the evolution of multicultural education. *Journal of Negro Education, 61*(3), 273–286.

Barlett, D. L., & Steele, J. B. (1992). *America: What went wrong?* Kansas City, MO: Andrews and McMeel.

Barnes, E. (1993). Scholars at N.Y.U. forum examine condition of Black life. *Black Issues in Higher Education, 10*(5), 16, 23.

Bell, D. (1989). *. . . And we are not saved: The elusive quest for racial justice.* New York: Basic Books.

Bernal, M. (1987). *Black Athena: The Afroasiatic roots of classical civilization* (Vol. 1). London: Free Association Books.

Billingsley, K. L. (1992). Sensitivity police brutality. *Heterodoxy, 1*(4), 4–5.

Bloom, A. C. (1989). *The closing of the American mind.* New York: Simon & Schuster.

Bohmer, P. (1992). Continuing stagnation, growing inequality. *Z. Magazine, 5*(9), 59–62.

Boykin, A. W. (1982). Task variability and the performance of Black and White school children: Vervistic explorations. *Journal of Black Studies, 12,* 469–485.

Broudy, H. S. (1975). Cultural pluralism: New wine in old bottles. *Educational Leadership, 33,* 173–175.

Bryden, D. P. (1991). It ain't what they teach, it's the way that they teach it. *Public Interest, 103,* 38–53.

Chavez, L. (1991). *Out of the barrio: Toward a new politics of Hispanic assimilation.* New York: Basic Books.

Chomsky, N. (1987). *The Chomsky reader* (James Peck, Ed.). New York: Pantheon Books.

Code, L. (1991). *What can she know? Feminist theory and the construction of knowledge.* Ithaca, NY: Cornell University Press.

Collins, P. H. (1991). *Black feminist thought: Knowledge, consciousness, and the politics of empowerment.* New York: Routledge.

Cottrol, R. (1991). *. . .* And ideas about how to do it right. *American Educator, 15*(3), 15–16.

Coughlin, E. K. (1992). Anthropologists ask how they wound up in the wings of multiculturalism debate. *Chronicle of Higher Education, 39*(17), A8.

Cushner, K., McClelland, A., & Safford, P. (1992). *Human diversity in education.* New York: McGraw-Hill.

Davidson, N. (1991). Was Socrates a plagiarist? *National Review, 43*(3), 45–46.

Derrida, J. (1981). *Positions.* Chicago: University of Chicago Press.

Diamond, N., & Bigelow, W. (1988). *The power in our hands.* New York: Monthly Review Press.

Diversity at the schools. (1991, July 8). *Christian Science Monitor,* p. 20.

D'Souza, D. (1991a). Illiberal education. *The Atlantic, 267,* 51–79.

D'Souza, D. (1991b). *Illiberal education: The politics of race and sex on campus.* New York: The Free Press.

D'Souza, D. (1991c). Investing in ignorance. *Chief Executive, 64,* 34–37.

Ex uno, plus. (1991, July 29). *National Review, 43,* 16.

Ehrenreich, B. (1991). Teach diversity—with a smile. *Time, 137*(14), 84.

Faludi, S. (1991). *Backlash: The undeclared war against American women.* New York: Doubleday.

Feuer, L. (1991). From pluralism to multiculturalism. *Society, 29*(1), 19–22.

Foucault, M. (1979). *Discipline and punish.* New York: Vintage Books.

Gates, H. L., Jr. (1991). Goodbye, Columbus? Notes on the culture of criticism. *American Literary History, 3*(4), 711–727.

Gay, G., & Baber, W. L. (Eds.). (1987). *Expressively Black: The cultural basis of ethnic identity.* New York: Praeger.

Giroux, H. A. (1992). Post-colonial ruptures and democratic possibilities: Multiculturalism as anti-racist pedagogy. *Cultural Critique, 21,* 5–40.

Glazer, N. (1981). Pluralism and the new immigrants. *Society, 19,* 31–36.

Gollnick, D. M., & Chinn, P. (1986). *Multicultural education in a pluralistic society* (2nd ed.) Columbus, OH: Macmillan.

Grant, C. A. (Ed.). (1992). *Research and multicultural education: From the margins to the mainstream.* London: The Falmer Press.

Gray, P. (1991). Whose America? *Time, 138*(1), 12–17.

Hacker, A. (1992). *Two nations: Black and White, separate, hostile, unequal.* New York: Charles Scribner's Sons.

Harding, S. (1991). *Whose science? Whose knowledge? Thinking from women's lives.* Ithaca, NY: Cornell University Press.

Hardy, J. E. (1991). Including the excluded. *Scholastic Update, 123*(8), 12.

Harris, M. D. (1992). Africentism and curriculum: concepts, issues, and prospects. *Journal of Negro Education, 61*(3), 301–316.

Hartsock, N. C. M. (1983). *Money, sex and power.* Boston: Northeastern University Press.

Hassenger, R. (1992). True multiculturalism: Setting no boundaries. *Commonweal, 119*(7), 10–11.

Hirsch, E. D., Jr. (1987). *Cultural literacy: What every American needs to know.* New York: Houghton-Mifflin.

Hogeboom, W. L. (1991). Multicultural perspectives: America has shaped us more than we have shaped it. *Education Week, 11*(14), 36, 27.

hooks, b. (1990). *Yearning.* Boston: South End Press.

Hoover, K. R. (1987). *Ideology and political life.* Monterey, CA: Brooks/Cole.

Howe, I. (1991). The content of the curriculum: Two views: The value of the canon. *Liberal Education, 77*(3), 8–9.

Ivie, S. D. (1979). Multicultural education: Boon or boondoggle? *Journal of Teacher Education, 30,* 23–25.

Jackson, K. T. (1991, October 13). Too many have let enthusiasm outrun reason. *Boston Globe,* sec. BGM, p. 27.

Jaggar, A. M. (1983). *Feminist politics and human nature.* Totowa, NJ: Rowman & Allanheld.

James, M. A. (Ed.). (1991). *The state of Native America.* Boston: South End Press.

JanMohamed, A., & Lloyd, D. (1987). Introduction: Toward a theory of minority discourse. *Cultural Critique, 6,* 5–12.

Kermode, F. (1992, February 23). Whose history is bunk? *New York Times Book Review,* sec. 7, p. 3.

Kessler-Harris, A. (1992). Cultural locations: Positioning American studies in the great debate. *American Quarterly, 44*(3), 299–312.

Kozol, J. (1991). *Savage inequalities.* New York: HarperCollins.

Krauthammer, C. (1990a). Education: Doing bad and feeling good. *Time, 135*(6), 78.

Krauthammer, C. (1990b, August 6). The tribalization of America. *Washington Post*, sec. A, p. 11.

Lather, P. (1991). *Getting smart*. New York: Routledge, Chapman & Hall.

Leo, J. (1991). Multicultural follies. *U.S. News and World Report, 111*(2), 12.

Lovin, R. W. (1992). Must we disown our past to become a multicultural society? *Liberal Education, 78*(2), 2–9.

Marable, M. (1985). *Black American politics*. London: Verso.

Marable, M. (1992). *The crisis of color and democracy*. Monroe, ME: Common Courage Press.

Martel, E. (1991). How valid are the Portland baseline essays? *Educational Leadership, 49*(4), 20–23.

Mattai, P. R. (1992). Rethinking multicultural education: Has it lost its focus or is it being misused? *Journal of Negro Education, 61*(1), 65–77.

McCarthy, C. (1988). Rethinking liberal and radical perspectives on racial inequality in schooling: Making the case for nonsynchrony. *Harvard Educational Review, 58*(3), 265–279.

McCarthy, C. (1990a). *Race and curriculum*. London: The Falmer Press.

McCarthy, C. (1990b). Race and education in the United States: The multicultural solution. *Interchange, 21*(3), 45–55.

McLaren, P. (1988). Culture or canon? Critical pedagogy and the politics of literacy. *Harvard Educational Review, 58*(2), 213–234.

Menand, L. (1991). Illiberalisms. *New Yorker, 67*(13), 101–107.

Menand, L. (1992). School daze. *Harper's Bazaar, 125*(3369), 380–381.

Minsky, L. (1992). The politics of political correctness. *Educational Record, 73*(1), 19–20.

More to read. (1991). *American Educator, 15*(3), 20.

Mr. Sobol's planet. (1991). *The New Republic, 205*(3–4), 5–6.

Nieto, S. (1991). *Affirming diversity*. New York: Longman.

Ogbu, J. U. (1992). Understanding cultural diversity and learning. *Educational Researcher, 21*(8), 5–14.

Olneck, M. (1990). The recurring dream: Symbolism and ideology in intercultural and multicultural education. *American Journal of Education, 98*(2), 147–174.

Omi, M., & Winant, H. (1986). *Racial formation in the United States*. New York: Routledge.

Platt, A. (1992). Defenders of the canon: What's behind the attack on multiculturalism. *Social Justice, 19*(2), 122–141.

Popkewitz, T. P. (1988). Culture, pedagogy, and power: Issues in the production of values and colonialization. *Journal of Education, 170*(2), 77–90.

Price, H. B. (1992). Multiculturalism: Myths and realities. *Phi Delta Kappan, 74*(3), 208–213.

Ravitch, D. (1990a). Diversity and democracy: Multicultural education in America. *American Educator, 14*(1), 16–20, 46–68.

Ravitch, D. (1990b). Multiculturalism: E pluribus plures. *The American Scholar, 59*(3), 337–354.

Ravitch, D. (1991/92). A culture in common. *Educational Leadership, 49*(4), 8–11.

Ringer, B. B., & Lawless, E. R. (1989). *Race-ethnicity and society*. New York: Routledge.

Rodriguez, R. (1981). *Hunger of memory*. Boston: D. Godine.

Roediger, D. R. (1991). *The wages of Whiteness*. New York: Verso.

Royal, R. (1992). 1492 and multiculturalism. *Intercollegiate Review, 27*(2), 3–10.

Schlesinger, A. M., Jr. (1991a). The American creed: From dilemma to decomposition. *New Perspectives Quarterly, 8*(3), 20–25.

Schlesinger, A. M., Jr. (1991b). The cult of ethnicity, good and bad. *Time, 138*(1), 21.

Schlesinger, A. M., Jr. (1991c). A dissension on multicultural education. *Partisan Review, 58*(4), 630–634.

Schlesinger, A. M., Jr. (1991d). The disuniting of America: What we all stand to lose if multicultural education takes the wrong approach. *American Educator, 15*(3), 14, 21–33.

Schlesinger, A. M., Jr. (1991e, June 25). Toward a divisive society. *Wall Street Journal*, sec. A, p. 22.

Schlesinger, A. M., Jr. (1991f). Writing, and rewriting, history. *The New Leader, 74*(14), 12–14.

Schlesinger, A. M., Jr. (1992). *The disuniting of America*. New York: Norton.

Shade, B. J. R. (1982). Afro-American cognitive style: A variable in school success? *Review of Educational Research, 52*, 219–244.

Shanker, A. (1991). The pitfalls of multicultural education. *The Education Digest, 57*(4), 5–6.

Shook, D. A. (1992, May 25). Universities losing way, Adler says. *Kenosha News*, p. 1.

Shor, I. (1992). *Empowering education*. Chicago: University of Chicago Press.

Sidel, R. (1988). *On her own: Growing up in the shadow of the American dream*. New York: Penguin.

Siegel, F. (1991). The cult of multiculturalism. *The New Republic, 204*, 34–36.

Sirkin, G. (1990, January 18). The multiculturalists strike again. *Wall Street Journal*, sec. A, p. 14.

Sleeter, C. E. (1989) Multicultural education as a form of resistance to oppression. *Journal of Education, 171*, 51–71.

Sleeter, C. E. (1992). *Keepers of the American dream*. London: The Falmer Press.

Sleeter, C. E., & Grant, C. A. (1988). *Making choices for multicultural education: Five approaches to race, class, and gender*. Columbus, OH: Macmillan.

Smoler, F. (1992). What should we teach our children about American history? An interview with Arthur Schlesinger, Jr. *American Heritage, 43*(1), 45–52.

Sowell, T. (1993). *Inside American education*. New York: The Free Press.

Spivak, G. C. (1990). *The post-colonial critic*. New York: Routledge.

Stanley, W. B. (1992). *Curriculum for utopia*. Albany: State University of New York Press.

Steele, S. (1990). *The content of our character*. New York: St. Martin's Press.

Stotsky, S. (1991a). Cultural politics. *American School Board Journal, 178*(10), 26–28.

Stotsky, S. (1991b). Is multiculturalism fostering national self-hatred? *School Administrator, 48*(4), 15–16.

Stotsky, S. (1992). Academic vs. ideological multicultural education in the classroom. *The Education Digest, 57*(7), 64–66.

Sykes, C., & Billingsley, K. L. (1992). Multicultural mafia. *Heterodoxy, 1*(5), 1, 4–6.

Thomas, C. (1992, May 3). Multiculturalism spells disaster. *Milwaukee Journal*, sec. J, p. 5.

Thomas, M., D. (1981). The limits of pluralism. *Phi Delta Kappan, 62*, 589–592.

Trueba, H. T. (1989). *Raising silent voices: Educating the linguistic minorities for the 21st century*. New York: Newbury House Publishers.

Weiler, K. (1988). *Women teaching for a change*. South Hadley, MA: Bergin & Garvey.

Wildavsky, A. (1991). Has modernity killed objectivity? *Society, 29*(1), 33–36.

Wiley, E., III. (1993). Intellectual pursuits: Examining the role of Black thinkers in a contemporary world. *Black Issues in Higher Education, 10*(5), 12–15.

Wolf, N. (1991). *The beauty myth*. New York: Morrow.

Part

$\cdot$ II $\cdot$

RESEARCH AND
RESEARCH ISSUES

·6·

QUANTITATIVE EDUCATIONAL RESEARCH WITH ETHNIC MINORITIES

Amado M. Padilla

STANFORD UNIVERSITY

Kathryn J. Lindholm

SAN JOSE STATE UNIVERSITY

Quantitative educational research with ethnic minorities has a long history. The earliest studies with educational implications focused on the intellectual assessment and school achievement of African American, immigrant, and other ethnic minority students (Brigham, 1923; Kamin, 1974; Vernon, 1982). This research legacy is well known for its failure to consider many crucial variables that we now recognize as critical in the assessment of students' abilities (Mensh & Mensh, 1991; Padilla, 1988). For example, in the assessment of intelligence the IQ test was given a special status, and it was assumed that it could be used to uncover differences in intellectual ability between individuals or racial groups (H. Gardner, 1985). With the special status ascribed to IQ tests, little attention was given to the fact that in the development of IQ tests minority children were not included in the standardization of the instrument (Kamin, 1974). Further, in actually carrying out research on differences between groups on IQ tests, little, if any, attention was given to social class, inequality in educational opportunity, language background of subjects, or cultural differences between the groups being compared. Most researchers today recognize the many problems that are inherent with the older body of IQ-related research (see especially H. Gardner, 1985; Gould, 1981).

More important here is the recognition of a set of assumptions inherent in the older IQ studies that are still operative today in educational research involving ethnic minorities. These assumptions are complex, interrelated, and conform to commonsense qualities that make them appealing. The identifiable assumptions are: (a) the White middle-class American (typically the male) is the standard against which other groups should be compared; (b) the instruments used for assessing differences are universally applicable across groups, with perhaps only minimal adjustments for culturally diverse populations; and (c) although we need to recognize the sources of potential variance such as social class, educational attainment, gender, cultural orientation, and proficiency in English, these are nuisances that can later be discarded. The overarching belief is that quantitative research is valuable because it allows the researcher to test scientific theories, which is essential to the construction of knowledge (Kuhn, 1970).

This chapter challenges these assumptions and offers numerous suggestions for improving quantitative research with ethnic minority respondents. Considerable attention is given in this chapter to methodological difficulties in conducting research with ethnic populations. In addition, problems of instrumentation and measurement of constructs are discussed. Before these issues can be investigated meaningfully, it is important to examine how the construction of knowledge has proceeded in the social sciences and what impact this has had on the study of minority populations generally, as well as in education specifically. Within this discussion questions and challenges will be directed at Eurocentric paradigms that have dominated our approach to the accumulation of scientific facts. Our critique of Eurocentric approaches to the study of ethnic minority populations in education is based on the fact that these approaches have frequently resulted in misguided interpretations because of specific biases inherent in the paradigms themselves.

97

THE SOCIAL CONSTRUCTION OF KNOWLEDGE

In a discussion of quantitative research with ethnic minority subject populations, it is important to address the topic of mainstream paradigms used by researchers to define their approach. A starting point for our discussion is the distinction between *nomothetic* and *idiographic* methods. The central tenets of these two methods were first framed by Gordon Allport (1937) with respect to their use in psychology, but the distinction is equally appropriate to educational research since historically the same paradigms have been employed by educational researchers.

The Nomothetic Approach to Educational Research

The *nomothetic* approach seeks confirmation of general laws and uses procedures that parallel the physical sciences. In contrast, the *idiographic* approach seeks to uncover a particular event in nature or society. Since its initial formulation the nomothetic-idiographic debate has been recast in terms of universalistic and relativistic principles. The universalist view rests on the assumption that concepts and methodologies are basically valid across cultures. Conversely, the relativist view maintains that concepts and methodologies do not necessarily have universal validity, and that they may be appropriate only within a restricted cultural setting.

Educational researchers have generally followed the social sciences in their adoption of acceptable paradigms that rest on a nomothetic or universal framework (Banks, 1993; Kerlinger, 1979). According to the universalistic framework, research should be guided by theory and hypothesis testing. Thus, quantitative methods are employed and statistical inferences are used to draw conclusions that support the universal principles. Since this approach eschews the importance of culture, emphasis is placed on a comparative approach that uses similar measures to compare groups of people who differ across cultures, ethnic groups, or languages. Investigators who utilize this approach argue that universal principles can be uncovered only by means of this research strategy.

The nomothetic or universal approach has come under sharp criticism from feminist and minority researchers because of its Eurocentric perspective (for a summary of this critique see Banks, 1993). The most salient feature of the Eurocentric paradigm is its focus on a monocultural, male-oriented, and comparative approach to research. The majority of instruments and research procedures used in educational research have been developed by White male researchers from a monocultural perspective using White and generally middle-class students as the normative population. These instruments and procedures are then used primarily to assess some psychological or educationally relevant construct with a White (male and female) middle-class student population. This approach lends itself to a very narrow database that results in biased conclusions of substantive educational outcomes that are even problematic for White samples who differ from the normative population. The problem is worse if use of the instruments and procedures is extended to ethnic minority populations who do not share all the demographic characteristics of the normative group. A similar point has been made by Sears (1986) who, in a provocative article, showed how research based on college students tested in academic laboratories on academic-like tasks has culminated in social psychological theories that are incompatible with the ordinary life experiences of most non–college-age majority-group adults.

There is nothing wrong with this approach to research so long as it is understood that whatever groups are being compared are equivalent in all demographic characteristics including social class, cultural background, and proficiency in English. However, there is still room for caution when, for example, men and women from the same social class and cultural background are compared on a task requiring interpersonal competition and men are found to score higher on competition (Griffen-Pierson, 1990). Is this difference due to the use of an inappropriate male-oriented task, or a real difference between the sexes resulting from a genetic disposition found in males, but not females? Obviously, an informed person would agree with the former and not the latter conclusion. Yet in comparisons of different cultural or ethnic groups, conclusions similar to the latter "genetic" interpretation can be found with no consideration for the fact that the instruments may have been biased to begin with because of a conceptual framework and set of tasks that favored one group and not the other (Griffen-Pierson, 1988, 1990).

The problem arises when "biased" instruments that favor White middle-class males are used in a comparative research framework to examine differences between racial or ethnic groups (Azibo, 1988). The comparative research framework requires a statistical test between at least two groups that have been equated on all variables known to have an influence on the behavior in question (Plutchik, 1974). However, if both the construct being assessed and the method or instrument used to assess the construct originate in the same cultural context, then a comparative approach will seriously increase the potential for bias. Thus it would be inappropriate to use the instrument developed for one cultural group to assess group differences, as necessitated by the comparative research framework. Proof that such comparisons are the mainstay of much of the empirical research in education is evident from a cursory examination of our major professional journals in education.

The situation is even more problematic because the comparative research framework assumes that there is some standard by which comparisons are made. Although not always stated explicitly, the standard is usually the White middle class (male), and any deviations therefrom are interpreted negatively as deficits or differences that possibly require intervention. An exceptionally good example would be Moynihan's (1965) report on the Black family. Because Moynihan assumed that a traditional White family model is vitally important to American life, he stated that a significant segment of the Black population was experiencing difficulty because

The family structure of lower-class Negroes is highly unstable, and in many urban centers is approaching complete breakdown. . . . [T]he emergence and increasing visibility of a Negro middle-class may beguile the nation into supposing that the circumstances of the remainder of the Negro community are equally prosperous, whereas just the opposite is true at present, and is likely to continue so. (p. 51)

To support his position, Moynihan culled data from various sources on illegitimacy rates, divorce statistics, female heads of households, and welfare dependency. These data were used to explain the "tangle of pathology" and disorganization of the African American family. Interestingly, if we studied some of the same data sources today as Moynihan employed nearly 30 years ago, but with White families in mind, we might well conclude, as have some observers (e.g., Hamburg, 1992), that the American White family is in trouble!

In sum, the central point is that when research is driven by the nomothetic approach the contention is that the really interesting theoretical questions examine ethnic group differences on some variable, without considering the potentially significant bias in the assessment instruments or procedures.

A Paradigm Shift in Ethnic Research

This nomothetic or Eurocentric approach has been challenged by African American researchers (e.g., Azibo, 1988; Khatib & Nobles, 1977) who find fault with the comparative approach that assumes a White standard reference group. This has led to an idiographic or Afrocentric approach that employs conceptual categories and worldviews adopted from traditional African cultures that serve as the standard for understanding African Americans. According to Azibo (1988), the Afrocentric approach challenges comparative studies that employ theory or methods designed to maintain African American inferiority.

In a less philosophical and more methodological challenge to the nomothetic approach, Marín and Marín (1991) argue that if researchers study Hispanics they need to understand at least some basic points about this ethnic group in order to carry out useful research with this population. Although more will be said about this later, the important point is that the Eurocentric comparative approach must be grounded in sound methodology that is fair to all the groups being compared. Yee (1992) makes a similar case when he discusses the stereotypes and misperceptions that persist when Asian Americans are studied by educational researchers.

In a paper addressed to mental-health researchers, but equally applicable to educational researchers, Rogler (1989) makes a plea for culturally sensitive research. According to Rogler:

Research is made culturally sensitive through a continuing and open-ended series of substantive and methodological insertions and adaptations designed to mesh the process of inquiry with the cultural characteristics of the group being studied. . . . The insertions and adaptations span the entire research process, from the pretesting and planning of the study, to the collection of data and translation of instruments, to the instrumentation of measures, and to the analysis and interpretation of the data. Research, therefore, is made culturally sensitive through an incessant, basic, and active preoccupation with the culture of the group being studied throughout the process of research. (p. 296)

With this definitiion of culturally sensitive research before us, we need to emphasize that we are not challenging the mer-

its of the scientific method, but are calling into question the objectivity of researchers who claim that their scientific paradigms are neutral as far as minority groups (including woman) are concerned (Code, 1987). The scientific method consists of a series of paradigms, each governed by distinct assumptions, rules, and methods of conducting research (Kuhn, 1970). But as Lakatos and Musgrave (1970) have pointed out, scientific laws, rather than being empirically discovered and valid for all time, should be examined from the perspective of the assumptions, language, and activities of the community of scientists. When the "community" does not include minority researchers, which has historically been the case until recently, then it is small wonder that culture and other salient characteristics of ethnic groups have not been considered important in mainstream research.

In sum, with Rogler's definition of culturally sensitive research in mind, as well as with our criticism of the Eurocentric paradigm, we support the new scholarship on ethnic minorities that calls for a paradigm shift, in which the study of a specific ethnic group is valued for its own sake and need not be compared to another group.

We shall now turn to a discussion of major challenges in conducting research with ethnic minority groups. Numerous important considerations that are required of the researcher intending to conduct quantitative research with ethnic groups will be identified and assessed in the following section of this chapter.

CHALLENGES IN CONDUCTING RESEARCH WITH ETHNIC GROUPS

There are numerous problems in conducting research with ethnic minority populations, many of which are frequently overlooked by investigators unfamiliar with research topics that may be particularly sensitive for these populations. Some of these issues are related to the identification and selection of a sample. In selecting a sample, one has to be careful about confounding *culture, ethnicity,* and *social class*. A related concern is the failure to recognize the heterogeneity existing within an ethnic group that can lead to variation in outcome measures and result in misinterpretation of the findings. Finally, we consider language and culture barriers confronting researchers in ethnic minority communities.

Properly Identifying, Describing, and Selecting a Sample

In the February 1989 special issue of the *American Psychologist* on "Children and Their Development: Knowledge Base, Research Agenda, and Social Policy," Horowitz and O'Brien (1989) indicate, in their essay on the "state of our knowledge and the challenges before us," that in the past 10 years there has been a "growing recognition of the influence of culture on children's development and behavior. There has also been an increasing research effort aimed at documenting the nature of those cultural influences" (p. 445). They also point out that in a previous *American Psychologist* special issue on children, published 10 years earlier, only one article on cultural influences was found, whereas in the latest *American Psychologist* special issue an entire section consisting of six articles was devoted to cultural influences.

In contrast to Horowitz and O'Brien's (1989) apparent optimism about the increasing research attention devoted to cultural influences on development, McLoyd and Randolph (1984, 1985) have shown that few publications on African American children have appeared in regular issues of *Child Development* in the period 1936–1980. The dearth of information regarding African Americans generally in American Psychological Association (APA) publications, and specifically in *Developmental Psychology* and the *Journal of Educational Psychology,* was recently documented by Graham (1992). In fact, Graham found that published articles employing African American subjects in these two journals had actually decreased over the 19-year period from 1970 to 1989, from 8.1% to 6.1% for the *Journal of Educational Psychology* and from 8% to 4.6% for *Developmental Psychology.* Moreover, 78% of the articles with African American subjects in the *Journal of Educational Psychology* had used a race comparison, whereas race comparisons were somewhat lower (65%) for articles appearing in *Developmental Psychology.*

The absence of literature of any type on children of other ethnic groups in the standard guild journals is at least as severe as it is for African Americans. Some mitigation of this situation was achieved with the April 1990 special issue of *Child Development* devoted to minority children. This collection of 24 review and research articles represents the largest single collection of information regarding minority children in any of our guild-affiliated and peer-reviewed journals.

In addition to the scarcity of information found in journals, the most recent, though dated, *Handbook of Developmental Psychology* (Wolman, 1982) contains only two references to American minority children in the chapter on cross-cultural research and theory (Adler, 1982). Otherwise, American minority children are absent entirely from this collection. The situation is no better in the fourth edition of the *Handbook of Child Psychology* (Mussen, 1983). Volume IV of the *Handbook, Socialization, Personality, and Social Development,* which might be the most likely volume to include a discussion of minority children, is totally devoid of such discussion, with the exception of a few brief passages about peer relationships and school desegregation.

The dearth of educational research involving ethnic minority students is also notable, with the exception of references to academic achievement differences among diverse groups. Even the *Handbook of Research on Teaching* (Wittrock, 1986), sponsored by the American Educational Research Association (AERA), does not make any reference to minority students in its 35 chapters and nearly 1,000 pages of text except in two chapters concerning bilingual education and mildly handicapped learners.

As indicated above, when minority students are included in quantitative research, it is usually with the intent of documenting low academic achievement of Hispanic, African American, and, to a lesser extent, Native American students in comparison to Anglo students (see California State Department of Education, 1986; Flynn, 1991; Gibson, 1988; Gibson & Ogbu, 1991; Jacob & Jordan, 1987; Neisser, 1986; Valencia, 1991) and the higher mathematics achievement of Chinese, Korean, and Japanese students relative to Caucasian students (see Flynn, 1991; Sue & Okazaki, 1990). Many educational studies involving Hispanic and African American students examine these students from the perspective of their failures in the educational system or how we can improve our understanding of factors associated with (under)achievement, such as achievement motivation (Casas, Furlong, Solberg, & Carranza, 1990; Cooper & Tom, 1984; Marchant, 1991; Schultz, in press) and parenting styles (Dornbusch, Ritter, Leiderman, Roberts, & Fraleigh, 1987; Lamborn, Mounts, Steinberg, & Dornbusch, 1991). In addition, there are a few excellent quantitative studies of the educational achievement of language-minority, usually Spanish-speaking, students in bilingual education programs (e.g., Ramirez, Yuen, & Ramey, 1991; Willig, 1985; also see chapter 25 of this *Handbook*).

Very few studies have examined ethnic minority students with respect to their successes in education. Research such as Kraft's (1991) study of what makes a Black student successful on a predominantly White campus; Alatorre Alva's (1991) examination of the academic invulnerability of Mexican American students; Duran and Weffer's (1992) study of the influential family and school factors associated with the achievement of successful Mexican American immigrant high school students; or Strom, Johnson, Strom, and Strom's (1992) investigation of programs for gifted Hispanic children and their parents is rare. Specialized topics such as desegregation and bilingual education also include ethnic minority students, but empirical research in these areas is scant.

Understanding the characteristics of the population is critical if we are to generalize the results properly and replicate the findings. However, many studies do not describe the subject population sufficiently to enable replication. Two examples of subject descriptions from recent research journals are presented below to illustrate the lack of information that would enable true replication.

1. "Subjects were 32 children from the Berkeley area. Subjects included 15 boys and 17 girls. Children came from a variety of socioeconomic and ethnic backgrounds, though most were Caucasian and middle class" (Gopnik & Meltzoff, 1992, p. 1094).
2. "In all, 423 sixth- and seventh-grade students . . . participated in the study. The school was in a predominantly working-class, [geographic location] community. The average student age was 11.87 and 13.08 for sixth and seventh graders, respectively. The sample was equally representative of males (52%) and females (48%), with 68% of the sample being Caucasian, 23% Black, 5% Hispanic, and 7% other minority status (Wentzel, 1991, p. 1068).

In each of these subject descriptions there is the basic information about number of students, gender, age, social status, and ethnicity. However, the information is too general and each variable is described for the sample as a whole. We do not know whether the social class of the Anglo non-Hispanic students was similar to that of the other ethnic groups. What does predominantly/mostly White/Causasian and middle class mean? Does that mean 51% of the sample or 89% of the sample? Does White and Caucasian include Hispanic, as it should? Does a sample of 60% White and 40% Black from diverse social backgrounds mean 50% White middle class, 35% Black working class, and the other White and Black subjects representing different social classes? Are the Hispanic students from English- or Spanish-speaking homes? Are they Mexican American, Cuban, Puerto Rican, Guatemalan, or a mixture of groups? Does diverse social background include children from homeless families or poverty conditions? What about single-parent versus two-parent families?

Contrast the previous two subject descriptions with the following subject description taken from an experimental study involving primates:

The subjects were 28 pigtailed macaque infants. Of these, 17 were classified as normal or at low risk for developmental deficits (i.e., normal birth weight, no history of clinical problems), and 11 were classified as high risk. Of the high-risk animals, 6 had experienced significant trauma at birth or during the early neonatal period (e.g., breech delivery with respiratory complications). Three high-risk subjects were part of an ongoing study examining the effects of parental reproductive history and maternal stress on growth and development. . . . The remaining 2 high-risk animals had been diagnosed as failure-to-thrive.

The infants were separated from their mothers at birth, or shortly thereafter, and were nursery-reared until they were self-feeding. . . . Then they were moved to individual cages in the main animal quarters. All animals were socialized in play groups daily . . . to prevent isolation-rearing effects. . . . (Gunderson, Fagan, & Grant-Webster, 1987, p. 672)

In this study the reader is provided with detailed information about the subjects' birth history, living conditions, and socialization experiences. One would expect such information from a controlled experimental study with animals, but the point we wish to make here is that with just some simple probing by researchers much more detailed information can be obtained about the background characteristics of ethnic-group members. With such attention to detail researchers would be on much safer ground regarding the generalizations that are made across ethnic groups. It seems ironic that so much attention is given to describing the subject population in animal research, while so little attention is given to important background characteristics in human research that employs the comparative approach.

In one of the few Subjects sections providing thorough descriptions, Knight, Tein, Shell, and Roosa (1992) provide the ethnic composition of the sample, and then go on to specify amount of education, median family income for both Anglo and Hispanic families, and acculturation information for the Hispanic families:

The original sample consisted of 303, 8–14-year-old children (M = 10.5, SD = 1.08, with only one 8-year-old and one 14-year-old participating), and either one or both of their parents. Parental participants included . . . [individuals] from English-speaking households. Ethnic composition of the current sample was 60% Anglo, 20% Hispanic, 13% Black, 4% Native American, and 2% other. The present report is based on a subset of 231 children and mothers from the original sample. The 231 children and mothers consisted of 70 Hispanic children and mothers (nearly all of whom were Mexican American) and 161 Anglo-American children and mothers. The distribution of ages was very comparable across ethnic groups.

The Anglo-American mothers reported a mean of 13.3 (SD = 2.02) years of education for themselves, 14.1 (SD = 2.18) years of education for their spouse, and a mean family income in the $20,000 to $25,000 range (with 56% of the families at or below this range). The Hispanic mothers reported a mean of 11.1 (SD = 2.58) years of education for themselves, 11.6 (SD = 3.46) years of education for their spouse, and a mean family income in the $10,000 to $15,000 range (with 60% of the families at or below this range). Among the Hispanic mothers: 14.3% were first-generation Americans (i.e., were born in Mexico and immigrated to the United States), 28.6% were second generation, and 50.0% were third generation or beyond. (p. 1395)

Clearly this level of detail cannot always be obtained, especially when the parents are not participants in the research study. However, more detail could certainly be gathered and presented in many studies involving ethnic minority subjects. How can results be generalized or studies replicated if the composition of the population is unclear? This methodological sloppiness would be unacceptable in most mainstream research journals if it applied to other subject-definition criteria. Yet it is not uncommon to find little information regarding culturally diverse children in a Method section of an article. Apparently many authors, peer reviewers, and journal editors do not question the absence of critical information when it comes to culturally diverse populations.

In identifying and selecting a sample, there are three major methodological issues:

1. What are the demographic characteristics of the population?
2. Can a random and representative sample be obtained, and how?
3. Is the sample adequately described so that a replication can be carried out?

One critical issue in identifying a population is to understand the demographic characteristics of that population. What diversity is represented in the population? Understanding the heterogeneity that exists in different communities is essential if we are to understand how best to move forward in gaining information about culturally different individuals. Further, if we are to lessen the inherent racism and biases found in research with ethnic minority individuals and in what passes as truth in the field, we need to rethink our designations of subjects. Bond (1988) cogently discusses the bias of labels and perspectives in research with culturally diverse populations. Designations such as "deprived background," "disadvantaged," "lack of stimulation," "poverty," and the more current "limited English proficient" and "at risk" have been widely associated with culturally diverse individuals. As Bond states:

Discussions of the effects of poverty on development frequently equate minority membership with the poor. Although it is important to acknowledge the disproportionate representation of certain ethnic and racial groups at the lower socioeconomic levels and the significance of such environment to these groups' development, this oversimplified equation of minority status with poverty perpetuates stereotypes and obscures the factors that contribute to this relationship. (p. 46)

When studies do incorporate culturally diverse individuals it is generally within some type of cross-cultural comparison. In many such comparisons ethnicity is confounded with class, whereby the comparison is made between a middle-class White population and a working-class African American or Hispanic (perhaps immigrant) population. Such glaring differences between groups would not be acceptable in any other area of education-related research. Imagine equating girls from upper-class backgrounds attending a private school with boys from working-class families enrolled in a public school in a study of knowledge acquisition. A reviewer of such a study would immediately recognize the problem of trying to infer gender differences from a sample that ignores differences in social class.

In addition, as mentioned previously, few Subjects sections describe the background of their research subjects sufficiently so that one knows what "Hispanic" or "Asian" means. Is the Subject a third-generation or immigrant individual from a working-class, middle-class, or upper-class background?

In order that culture, ethnicity, and social class not be confounded, it is important to understand the unique cultural features of the group. For example, issues of generation of residence, language usage, and acculturation are salient for Hispanic, African American (particularly immigrant), and Asian American families.

Few studies have actually taken these factors into account in conducting research. Over a decade ago, Laosa (1980a, 1980b, 1982) demonstrated, in a study of Anglo and Chicana mothers' teaching strategies, that any differences in teaching strategies between the two ethnic groups disappeared when the mother's level of formal education was a controlling factor. Similarly, Gutierrez and her colleagues (Gutierrez & Sameroff, 1990; Gutierrez, Sameroff, & Karrer, 1988) examined the heterogeneity of acculturation and social class in a study of Mexican American and Anglo mothers' concepts of development. Gutierrez et al. included Anglo upper- and lower-class groups and six Mexican American groups representing lower and higher socioeconomic status (SES) and low, medium, and high acculturation. Results showed significant SES effects for both Anglo and Mexican American mothers, and considerable within-group variability for the Mexican American group. In addition, comparisons between the Mexican American highly acculturated and Anglo American, both higher SES, indicated that Mexican American mothers gave more cognitively complex responses.

In another study of low-income Mexican mothers, Richman, Miller, and LeVine (1993) also demonstrated that "maternal schooling emerges from this study as an important influence on maternal responsiveness during infancy in and of itself, rather than as reflecting the social variables with which it is often associated" (p. 62). The significance of these research studies is in demonstrating the varying effects of both educational background and acculturation level in responses of Mexican American subjects, and even between similar Mexican American subgroups (e.g., grouped by acculturation level).

Several researchers have included ethnic minority individuals in their studies so that the subject sample would be representative of a particular geographic area. This representative sampling approach can be useful in understanding some component of behavior or development as reflected by the diversity of individuals in the community. An example of a representative sample is Stevenson, Chen, and Uttal's (1990) study of the achievement of 3,000 first-, third-, and fifth-grade Black, White, and Hispanic children, and a subsample of these chlidren's parents' beliefs about academic achievement. They selected "20 elementary schools covering the range of socioeconomic and ethnic groups within the area. Two classrooms each at first, third, and fifth grades within each school were randomly selected for study" (p. 509). Subsamples of students were selected for individually administered tests. Stevenson et al. provided information about the age of students by ethnic group and the percentage of students in each group born in the United States. In addition, they provided information on family structure, language spoken at home, educational level, and family income. Black, Hispanic, and White families differed significantly in both education and occupation levels, though multiple comparison analyses were not employed to examine specific differences among the groups. Stevenson et al. analyzed student achievement according to both ethnicity and SES (mother's level of education). Results indicated that ethnic differences in children's mathematics performance, but not reading performance, were no longer significant when mother's education level was controlled. There were many ethnic differences in parents' attitudes, but unfortunately, effects resulting from educational differences were not analyzed. Thus the confounding effects of education were examined in children's academic performance, but not in parental beliefs, despite the previously identified significant differences in education level among the ethnic groups.

This example illustrates one of the problems in conducting research with ethnic minority populations. The issue of confounding is substantial even in carefully conducted studies. Even when results include statistical controls, findings are not always discussed with respect to the confounding. Thus the results may be representative of the population, but the comparisons made among groups may be inappropriate because of the serious problem of confounding.

We have just seen some of the problems that may arise in representative samples. What about random samples? Culver, Wolfe, and Cross (1990) wanted to obtain a random sample from a population of 9,753 teachers who were identified as early career teachers (those with six or fewer years of full-time teaching) and who were currently teaching. However, a simple random sample would not be likely to provide enough African American teachers for the researchers' purposes because teachers from this racial group made up only 13.5% of the population. Thus they decided to "sample at random approximately equal numbers of Blacks and Whites (actually 350 Whites and 375 Blacks)" (p. 329). Since it was not possible, in this case, simply to select a random sample from the population, a different sampling procedure was used that included a random sample of White teachers and an oversample of African American teachers. In many research projects, especially of the survey type, investigators should seriously consider the advantages of oversampling of an ethnic group in order to have a large enough sample size to carry out statistical tests of significance.

In another study, Finn and Achilles (1990) conducted an experimental study of class size and used random sampling effectively in composing their classrooms:

All school systems in the State of Tennessee were invited to participate . . . . About one third of the districts, representing 180 schools, expressed an interest in participating. After negotiation, the final sample consisted of 76 elementary schools that were large enough to have at least three kindergarten classes . . . . Within each school, children entering kindergarten were assigned at random, by the project staff, to one of three class types: small, with an enrollment range of 13–17 pupils; regular, with an enrollment of 22–25 pupils; or regular with aide, with 22–25 pupils but with a teacher aide formally assigned to work with the class. Teachers were assigned at random to classes as a separate step. (pp. 559–560)

Classes were categorized by composition, as containing all White students, all minority students, or a mixture of White and minority. They were also classified by location, as inner city, urban, suburban, or rural. However, within this well-controlled experimental study was a serious confound concerning race/ ethnicity and location and social class (participation in the free lunch program was considered as designating low income). There were no inner-city classes with all White students and no urban or rural classrooms with only minority students. Only five classrooms were inner city and mixed. There was also a "strong association between minority status and participation in the free lunch program. About 70% of the student sample are either minorities receiving free lunches, or Whites not receiving free lunches; Yule's Q association measure is .78" (p. 561). Thus, in this "randomized experiment," there is certainly helpful information about class-size effects, but the effects for ethnic minority status are seriously confounded with location and social class. Fortunately, the researchers recognized this problem and conducted their analyses to take this confound into consideration.

In sum, researchers need to take seriously the problem of confounding of variables when they do research with ethnic minority populations. How a sample is selected for study can have great influence on the generalizations that can be made based on the findings. Moreover, when sufficient attention is given beforehand to possible confounding variables when selecting a subject population, misinterpretation of findings is reduced.

Understanding the Heterogeneity Within an Ethnic Group

Similar to the problem of confounding is the lack of understanding by most researchers of the heterogeneity within ethnic minority populations. Some researchers state that they include Asians without going into further detail about who these Asians are (Yee, 1992). Are they middle-class Chinese, Korean, or Japanese, are they working-class Hmong or Cambodian, or are they middle- or working-class Vietnamese? Similarly, for Hispanics, there are considerable differences among Mexican American, Cuban, Puerto Rican, Argentinean, Chilean, Colombian, Guatemalan, Central American Indian (who may be assumed to be Spanish speaking), and other subgroups. Within each of these ethnic subgroups are social-class (e.g., educational background), acculturation, language (particularly dialect and language differences among Central American Indians), and other cultural differences. For example, first-generation newly arrived immigrants differ from third- or later generation individuals in many ways (Keefe & Padilla, 1987). The older-generation Hispanics in New Mexico, who call themselves Spanish Americans, differ from the newer Mexican immigrants in the Spanish they speak, in the chile and other foods they eat, and in cultural customs. Puerto Ricans who have lived on the mainland differ from those who commute between the island and the mainland, and from those who have always lived on the mainland (Rodriguez, 1989). The earlier waves of Cubans differ in educational background and in other respects from the most recent wave of Cubans (Suarez, 1993). There are Black Cubans and Puerto Ricans who are frequently labeled as African American without any understanding of their common culture with White Cubans and Puerto Ricans. Berndt, Cheung, Lau, Hau, and Lew (1993) showed that perceptions of parenting differed among Chinese parents living in mainland China, Taiwan, and Hong Kong. In the United States, where Chinese, and Asians in general, are frequently treated as though they were homogeneous, this study demonstrates important socialization differences among Chinese families on the basis of country of origin. These studies all illustrate complex intragroup differences that must be understood in order to facilitate replicability and generalizability.

Difficulties Due to Cultural and Language Barriers

Another difficulty in conducting research with ethnic minority populations concerns language and cultural barriers. While superficial speculation on this point suggests that one can always get someone to translate instruments and mediate with the community, issues are more intricate than the simple term *language and cultural barriers* may suggest. As we asserted in the previous section, there are a number of subject-selection and -description issues that can introduce serious methodological flaws into research, though these serious flaws do not often draw the attention of journal peer reviewers. How can one interpret the results of a study involving ethnic minorities if ethnic minorities who understand that community are not included in a significant capacity on the research team? How can researchers know which members of the community are comparable to other members of the community?

Reyes and Halcón (1988) make the following assertion regarding research on Hispanics:

As Hispanic academics, our research interests often stem from . . . a compelling need to lend a dimension of authenticity to the prevailing theories about our communities. Said another way, we want to provide our own perspectives regarding prevailing negative assumptions about our values, culture, and language . . . . Our interest in these research areas is also motivated by a concern for assisting our community in improving its second-rate status in the education, economic, and political arenas. Tired of reading about ourselves in the social science literature written by non-minorities, we want to speak for ourselves, to define, label, describe, and interpret our own condition from the "inside out." We feel strongly about providing a balance to the existing literature and research on Chicanos. (p. 306)

Marín and Marín (1991) make a similar point in their book *Research with Hispanic Populations,* noting that "some [Hispanic] community members perceive social science research as a form of exploitation in which nonminority individuals reap the benefits of the data collection effort" (p. 42).

In addition, Marín and Marín (1991) delineate several other cultural barriers that make it difficult for minority and non-minority researchers alike working within an ethnic minority community. While their comments are aimed at Hispanics, many of these points are relevant for other ethnic minority groups as well:

Suspicion of government involvement in a research project is more likely when individuals or their family members and friends have lived in political climates where oppressive governments make use of informers and home visits to gather compromising information to be used in surveillance, social control, or other abuses of a person's rights. In addition, many Hispanics, regardless of their immigration status (documented, undocumented, refugee, parolee), live in fear of being stopped by agents of the Immigration and Naturalization Service and of being asked to document their citizenship or immigration status . . . . Also of relevance in determining the rate of cooperation with an investigation is the type of personal or community benefit that is to be accrued by participating in the study. (pp. 43–44)

Language barriers can also be problematic for researchers. For example, Spanish is not the same in different Hispanic communities. While Hispanics from different countries may be able to communicate with one another, there are significant dialect differences that should be reflected in letters of introduction, human subject consent forms, questionnaires, and other written and spoken forms of communication with the sample of interest. Issues in instrument translation will be discussed in the following section, "Instrumentation and Measurement."

Some cultural and language barriers can be surmounted by including members of the community on the research team. However, including a fifth-generation Mexican American raised in a middle-class suburban neighborhood who may know a little Spanish in a study of immigrant homeless parenting strategies may not be beneficial. Similarly, including a Cuban or Puerto Rican educated on the East Coast may not be particularly helpful with a Mexican American population in Texas, particularly with respect to language issues, even when the Cuban or Puerto Rican is perfectly fluent in Spanish. As another example, a highly acculturated Chinese American may not be a very effective data collector in a parenting study of traditional Chinese mothers and fathers who have not resided for very long in the United States. Unless investigators are very aware of traditional customs, they could ask questions in such a way as to promote inaccurate responses or to offend the respondents. Thus, to overcome culture and language barriers, it is necessary to understand the subject sample thoroughly.

It is equally important to know something about the language background and proficiency level of individuals who serve as translators of materials or interviewers for non–English speaking respondents. We are familiar with one instance in which an investigator working with Chinese immigrants assumed that all Chinese speakers spoke the same dialect. Consequently, when he showed up with a Mandarin-speaking interviewer to meet with parents who spoke Cantonese, he was both embarrassed by his lack of familiarity with the very community he wished to study and disappointed that his effort to identify and train an interviewer had been wasted.

In sum, the challenges in researching ethnic minority communities are considerable. We do not want to leave the impression that only minority researchers should study minority communities. But we do feel strongly that unless the researcher knows the community well, then it is a good strategy to include members of the community in the research study as true partners and not just as translators, interviewers, or computer analysts.

INSTRUMENTATION AND MEASUREMENT

Critical in any type of quantitative research are the issues of instrumentation and measurement. Regardless of whether one uses rating scales, inventories, standardized achievement tests, or any other type of performance-based outcome measure, the issues are the same. That is, the instruments must be appropriate for assessing change resulting from some experimental or educational treatment condition or for examining group differences accurately. This section will include a general discussion of these instrumentation concerns because of their relevance in identifying suitable measures when conducting research with ethnic populations.

One issue in research with ethnic minority populations concerns identifying *appropriate* outcome measures. Many instruments may be suitable for White middle-class subjects but not appropriate for culturally diverse samples. In identifying and selecting outcome measures, one has to consider the psychometric qualities of the instrument. There are at the very least three sets of related questions that should provoke serious consideration whenever we use instruments with ethnic minority respondents:

1. Are the selected instruments appropriate for use with the ethnic group in question? Is there equivalence across cultures of important concepts that are used in educational research? Have the instruments been accurately translated?
2. Is it necessary to use specially designed instruments to assess such characteristics as acculturation, ethnic identity, English-language proficiency, or culturally specific learning strategies? How are such instruments identified for use with minority populations?
3. Do minority subjects respond to questionnaires and other data-collecting instruments in the same manner as majority group members?

Are the Instruments Used Appropriate?

The first set of questions concerns the matter of appropriateness. Many studies have examined instruments to assess their suitability for particular ethnic minority populations. For example, Knight et al. (1992) evaluated the cross-ethnic equivalence of parenting and family interaction measures among Hispanic and Anglo American families. In this study they assessed four instruments: the Children's Report of Parental Behavior Inventory, the Parent-Adolescent Communication Scale, the Family Adaptability and Cohesion Evaluation Scale II, and the Family Routines Inventory. They selected these instruments because the authors believed that these inventories were the most useful in large-scale field assessments that would include ethnic minorities. They examined the interaction measures by using small panels of individuals with some training in measurement who were also members of a Hispanic culture. This examination involved having panel members evaluate each item for cultural relevance, that is, "the degree to which the behaviors and attitudes reflected in the items were applicable in the Hispanic culture" (p. 1394). Panel members also evaluated the items according to their underlying construct using two different formats. Then the panel members "identified three rejection items, three cohesion items, three adaptability items, and seven family routine items as potentially irrelevant or as questionably relevant for the Mexican American culture" (p. 1394). As Knight et al. point out,

The explanations provided by the panel members of the lack of relevance for each item fell into one of two categories: (1) the item itself, or some wording or phrasing in the item, either has an ethnically specific meaning or has unclear meaning to members of the Mexican American culture; and (2) the item was worded poorly, or vague terms were used, such that it is unlikely that subjects would understand the meaning of the item regardless of their ethnicity. (p. 1394)

The conclusions from this panel approach were that "there appears to be a small subset of items ... that are likely of limited item equivalence because the behaviors or attitudes represented in these items are of limited applicability or generalizability to the Hispanic family" (Knight et al., 1992, p. 1395). The study then went on to assess the item equivalence and functional equivalence of the latent structure and subscale intercorrelations among Hispanic and Anglo American samples. From the findings, it was clear that some scales, minus certain subscales, had sufficient cross-ethnic equivalence for English-speaking Hispanic samples, while other scales required further scale development. Many other scales have been assessed for their appropriateness for various cultural groups. Two categories of scales will be used to illustrate the psychometric work that has been conducted to address the issues of instrument appropriateness: (a) achievement scales, and (b) self-esteem scales. Numerous other types of scales could have been selected for discussion here, but achievement and self-esteem scales have a long history of use with ethnically diverse populations and serve to exemplify some points that we wish to emphasize regarding proper use of instruments with ethnic respondents.

Achievement Scales. Considerable research has examined achievement differences between ethnic minority and non-–ethnic minority students. However, it is often not clear how comparable are the various achievement measures that are used in the research. For example, Hernandez and Willson (1992) assessed the reliability of the Kaufman Assessment Battery for Mexican American children and found no significant difference in reliabilities between Mexican American and non-Hispanic Whites. Unfortunately, their samples of Mexican American children were extremely small (n = 6 to 19 per age group), which may have influenced their nonsignificant findings.

Achievement measures have been translated into other languages, but rarely are the instruments carefully assessed for their comparability. For example, the Metropolitan Achievement Test (MAT) was translated into Chinese and is used by Chinese bilingual programs because there are no alternative measures. Similarly, the Comprehensive Tests of Basic Skills (CTBS) has a Spanish version, the Spanish Assessment of Basic Education (SABE). The SABE was developed by Spanish-speaking experts and normed with a native Spanish-speaking U.S. student population. However, it is not clear that the SABE is equivalent to the CTBS. The SABE was not developed as a translation of the CTBS, but as a separate measure that was to be comparable to the CTBS; careful studies have not been conducted on the comparability of the two versions. There are also other Spanish-language achievement tests: *La Prueba Riverside de Realización en Español (La Prueba)* and *Aprenda: La Prueba de Logros en Español.* Both tests are norm-referenced with Spanish-speaking populations in the United States.

Aside from the comparability across languages is the issue of content comparability for middle-class English-speaking Anglo American students and for culturally and linguistically diverse students. In an important conceptual article, Helms (1992) has argued that cognitive ability test items are not all culturally equivalent for African Americans and Whites. As she points out, there is an "absence of clearly articulated, theoretically based models for examining the influence of race-related cultural factors on cognitive ability" (p. 1089). She concludes:

In the area of standardized cognitive ability testing, cultural equivalence per se has not been investigated empirically. Unfortunately, there seem to be no commonly accepted alternatives to the statistical approaches for instigating such investigations. Yet what is even more distressing than the lack of explicit alternatives is an apparent inability of psychologists and psychometricians to articulate the relevant issues as they affect test takers from various racial and ethnic groups within the United States. Therefore, the conclusion that whatever construct is measured by standardized CATs [Cognitive Ability Tests] constitutes universal intelligence or general cognitive ability for all racial and ethnic groups in this country is dubious at best. (p. 1090)

Achievement tests suffer from the same validity and cultural bias problems discussed above. Even criterion-referenced achievement tests based on students' classroom curriculum fall short. In Stevenson et al.'s (1990) study, discussed above, of the achievement of African American, White, and Hispanic children, the researchers carefully constructed criterion-based achievement measures of mathematics and reading. The results showed significant ethnic differences in reading, but not mathematics, even after controlling for mother's education background. Stevenson et al.'s conclusion clearly identifies the problem associated with achievement tests and even criterion-referenced tests:

Our interpretation of this finding [of significant ethnic differences in reading achievement after controlling for mother's level of education] is that the content of the material the children were asked to read was based on experiences and knowledge that were less likely to be part of the daily lives of the Black and Hispanic than of the White children. Comprehending the meaning of text is difficult when the topics lie outside the child's everyday experience. Hispanic children bore the additional burden of being asked to read a language that typically was not the native language of their parents. The content of reading classes, more than that of mathematics classes, reflects situations that exist in the dominant culture. Minority children may be penalized in reading because the materials require information to which they have had less exposure outside of school than the White children have had. However, our use of tests based on the textbooks to which the children had been exposed may have been responsible for reducing the magnitude of ethnic differences in this study compared to studies that have relied on standardized tests of achievement. Typically, standardized achievement tests are based on what children are expected to know, rather than on what they necessarily have encountered. (p. 520)

We have shown in this section that important issues regarding how achievement is conceptualized and measured across different ethnic groups are still undergoing refinement. We see this as an advancement over earlier periods, when no attempt was made to ensure that the content of a test was equivalent for all groups who took it. This point is especially important today, with increased discussion of "high-stakes" testing in schools.

Self-Esteem Scales. Another set of instruments that has been used extensively in educational research with ethnic minority students encompasses the many self-esteem scales that are available. There are some important issues exemplified by self-esteem measurement that also affect psychosocial development in children in general. One issue concerns the definition of self-esteem. Theorists have long debated how to conceptualize and measure self-esteem (Rosenberg, 1979). Two major conceptual camps are distinguished in terms of whether we view self-concept as a unidimensional construct (global view) or whether we evaluate an individual along several domains in addition to an overall global self-worth (differentiated view) (for a review, see Harter, 1983).

These theoretical perspectives have not incorporated considerations relevant to culturally diverse students. Early literature suggested that ethnic minority children showed lower levels of self-esteem than White majority group children (for reviews, see Rosenberg, 1979; Wylie, 1979), a finding contested on several methodological and conceptual grounds (Wylie, 1979). However, despite the frequency with which self-esteem measures are used, there is still little theory that is relevant to ethnic minority students. As Clark (1965) suggested almost 30 years ago, living in a racist and oppressive society that keeps people of color in poverty impinges on how a child appraises him- or herself.

Martinez and Dukes (1987) have conceptualized self-esteem according to the differentiated viewpoint, which suggests that ethnic minority students may evaluate themselves differentially along two major domains. They hypothesized that ethnic minority students would evaluate themselves lower than majority group members on *public* aspects of self-esteem (e.g., intelligence), but rate themselves high in the *private* domains (e.g., satisfaction with self). The rationale for this hypothesis was that in the public domain of self-esteem the majority group is the standard, whereas in the private domain the individual and/or the ethnic group is the standard. In their study, Martinez and Dukes found support for their thesis. The private domain self-esteem ratings of African American and Hispanic students were higher than those of Anglos, while in the public domain of intelligence, which is measured in terms of the majority culture, Hispanic and African American students rated themselves lower than White students.

Scales for measuring self-esteem among ethnic minority students also fall short. In addition to the typical psychometric problems (for a review of self-esteem scales, see Harter, 1983), they do not assess any cultural items that may affect self-esteem, and they are oriented toward middle-class norms. For example, in Harter's (1983) Perceived Competence and Social Acceptance Scale for Young Children (Grades 1–2), there is an item that asks children whether they have spent the night at a friend's house. In determining a child's social competence (which Harter views as a part of self-esteem), those first- and second-grade children who have stayed over at night at their friends' homes get higher scores than those who have not, and thus attain higher social competence scores. Clearly, this item may be culturally loaded for some ethnic children. Many ethnic minority children would not be allowed to spend the night at a friend's home as this would not be viewed as proper behavior. Many Hispanic children have never spent the night at a friend's home, even by the time they reach adulthood. These children may have stayed at their grandparents' or other family members' homes overnight, but this would not be credited on the Harter scale.

A study of Chinese children in Taiwan using the Perceived Competence Scale for Children (a translated version) reported the factorial validity of the scale for the Chinese sample (Stigler, Smith, & Mao, 1985). As with White American samples, there was a high correlation between the perceived cognitive competence and actual achievement. However, Chinese children tended to underrate their competence compared to White American children. In addition, unlike White American children, Chinese children differentiated satisfaction with self from the desire to change for the better. Stigler et al. conclude that "Whereas idealized perceptions of the self might reflect social desirability bias among American children, this same bias might produce self-effacement among Chinese children" (p. 1269). A similar finding would not be unlikely with Chinese American and other Asian American children.

In a related study, Rotenberg and Cranwell (1989) assessed the self-concept of Native American and White American children using the "20 statements" test, an open self-description measure. They found that Native American children referred more frequently in their open descriptions to kinship roles, traditional customs and beliefs, and moral worth than did White American children.

Thus different instruments yield different findings in comparisons of ethnic minority and White children. As a whole, these results clearly point out that theories of self-esteem need modification in order to accommodate the developmental and educational experiences of culturally diverse children. Only then can appropriate scales be developed to provide information about how children evaluate themselves. Very similar findings would result from an examination of other categories of scales.

Do We Need Special Instruments to Measure Ethnic Characteristics?

The second set of issues concerns the question of whether it is necessary to use specially designed instruments to assess characteristics such as acculturation, ethnic identity, and English-language proficiency. As we have seen in the above discussion, mainstream scales that assess cognitive abilities, achievement, and psychosocial development have not been generated with ethnic minority populations in mind. They have largely been produced by and for a White middle-class population. The problem becomes even more complex when we focus on culturally specific behaviors or areas of development, such as ethnic identity or acculturation, that have not been viewed as significant issues for most White middle-class individuals.

As we have discussed earlier, it is important for purposes of research to recognize the heterogeneity within certain ethnic groups. One important source of heterogeneity that has received considerable attention in recent years is acculturation (Rogler, Cortes, & Malgady, 1991; Triandis, Kashima, Shimada, & Villareal, 1986). It is well known that with contact between majority group members and immigrants, the newcomers and their offspring eventually acquire the language, values, beliefs, and behaviors of the majority group. The conceptual and methodological issues involved in the study of acculturation have been described by numerous writers (e.g., Berry, 1990; Olmedo, 1979; Padilla, 1980). Many questions have arisen regarding the process of acculturation and such considerations as gender, age, education, motivation, and degree of contact with the majority group. These questions focus primarily on the measurement of acculturation and the role of acculturation in various educational outcomes.

There is no agreed-upon universal scale for measuring acculturation; neither is there, for that matter, a single agreed-upon "best" scale for use with any particular ethnic group. However, most scales can be characterized by two general categories of items: (a) self-rated proficiency and use of the home language, and (b) preference for ethnic-related activities and friends. By way of illustration, numerous scales can be found in the literature for use with diverse ethnic groups: Koreans (Kim, 1988), Mexican Americans (e.g., Cuellar, Harris, & Jasso, 1980), Asian Americans (e.g., Suinn, Richard-Figueroa, Lew, & Vigil, 1987), and American Indians (e.g., Oetting & Beauvais, 1990–1991).

The important consideration regarding acculturation for our purposes here is that the relationship among culture change, psychosocial adjustment, and educational attainment is in need of more attention. Most of the research on acculturation involves various indexes of mental health such as depression (e.g., Moyerman & Forman, 1992), and, more recently, the relationship between acculturation and ethnic identity (Buriel & Cardoza, 1993; Marín, 1993).

There is evidence in the literature suggesting that less-acculturated immigrant students perform better academically than do their later-generation counterparts (Buriel & Cardoza, 1988; Caplan, Whitmore, & Choy, 1989; Gibson, 1988; Rumbaut, 1990; Suarez-Orozco, 1989). The consensus of these studies is that immigrant youth who identify with their ethnic group and who are more traditional in beliefs and values have better grades and are more likely to go on to college than their acculturated peers. For example, Rumbaut (1990) found that for Southeast Asian students higher grade-point average was related to how their parents answered four questions on an acculturation measure. The questions pertained to perservation of culture and identity; "sticking together" for social support and mutual assistance; living where there are people of their own ethnic group; and no interest in returning to their country of origin. Using a 0-6 point scale from "strongly disagree" to "strongly agree," Rumbaut found that high parental scores were positively related to student high school GPAs. According to Rumbaut:

This finding runs counter to assimilationist assumptions that argue that the more Americanized immigrants become, the greater will be their success in the competitive worlds of school and work. In fact, it suggests an opposite conclusion: that "Americanization" processes among the Indochinese may be dysfunctional for educational attainment. (p. 21)

A similar finding appears to hold true for Mexican immigrants (Buriel, 1984; Buriel & Cardoza, 1988), Punjabi Sikh students (Gibson, 1988), and Central American children (Suarez-Orozco, 1989). A complicating factor also has to do with whether we are describing a situation of accommodation without assimilation, or a form of biculturalism in which students acquire English-language proficiency, know the culture of their parents *and* of the school, and have friends from different ethnic groups. As a consequence, they feel more comfortable in school *and* at home and do better overall in their academic work (Alatorre Alva, 1991; Landsman et al., 1991).

In sum, the finding that immigrant students are more motivated to study and have more positive school attitudes than later-generation ethnic students is important. Further, how school achievement is influenced by ethnic and cultural maintenance via a strategy of "accommodation without assimilation" or "biculturalism" is still an open question. Much more research is required before we fully understand the relationship for immigrant students between school performance and acculturation.

Another consideration in ethnic-related research has to do with the attitude that minority group members have toward their own ethnicity. Phinney (1990) and Bernal and Knight (1993) have provided us with useful reviews of the relevant literature on ethnic identification. As Phinney states, there is much research on how majority group members perceive minority groups, but less on how minority group members perceive themselves. The issues here have to do with the evaluation of self-worth in a social context that frequently discriminates against or disparages ethnic groups.

The difficulty with ethnic identification research to date is that there are widely different approaches to the study of ethnic identity, since groups differ in their experiences as members of a minority group. This has resulted in a diversity of measurement instruments designed to assess ethnic identity. Phinney and her colleagues (Phinney & Rotheram, 1987) and Bernal and Knight and their colleagues (1993) provide a useful starting point for understanding the various avenues that have been pursued in ethnic identification research.

Assessing the Response Patterns of Ethnic Respondents

The third set of questions in this section has to do with how ethnic respondents answer questions on objective instruments such as Likert scales. This is a serious matter that merits extensive discussion. One aspect of this question in the research literature concerns what is described as *response set preferences* in answering questions on various types of objective instruments. Another has to do with *social desirability or acquiescence* in responding on instruments or during interviews.

Response Set. Bachman and O'Malley (1984) have shown that African Americans have a preference for selecting the extreme responses on instruments that use a Likert-type scale. According to Bachman and O'Malley, this is why African Americans have sometimes been found to be higher in esteem than Whites. This extreme response set means that African Americans use the extreme scores (both positive and negative) more than Whites. A positively skewed distribution of scores on a factor such as esteem may disclose inflated esteem scores that are a reflection of the response set rather than of actual differences in esteem.

Hui and Triandis (1989) have found that Hispanics are also more likely to use an extreme response set on a 5-point Likert scale than are non-Hispanic Whites. Similar findings are discussed by Marín and Marín (1991), who state that such extreme responding is particularly evident with low-acculturated Hispanic respondents. It is unknown whether other ethnic groups follow a pattern similar to African Americans and Hispanics in answering 5-point Likert-type questions.

The reason for being concerned about whether extreme response set has occurred is that such responding can seriously affect the results and interpretation of a study by giving a misleading impression of group variances. According to Bachman and O'Malley (1984), the easiest solution to the problem of extreme set responding is to collapse the extreme category on each end of the scale (e.g., collapse "Disagree" with "Strongly Disagree" on one end of the scale, and "Agree" with "Strongly Agree" on the other). Scores between ethnic and majority group subjects then become more similar. However, before collapsing the extreme categories of a 5-point scale the investigator needs to be aware that compressing a scale from 5 to 3 categories results in a scale that is no longer an interval scale, even though we may use it as such. Also, in the absence of a theory to explain why ethnic respondents prefer the extreme response categories, it may simply be sufficient to examine the pattern of responses on a Likert scale to determine whether extreme responding has occurred and to note this in reporting the results.

Social Desirability and Acquiescence. Another concern in conducting research with ethnic respondents has to do with the possible problem of social desirability and/or acquiescence in responding. Social desirability refers to the tendency to "deny socially undesirable traits and to claim socially desirable ones" (Nederhof, 1985, p. 264); responding in a socially desirable manner may occur consciously or unconsciously (Paulhus, 1984). Acquiescence refers to a type of responding wherein respondents agree (yea-saying) with statements presented to them regardless of their content. Whether or not social desirability and/or acquiescence responding is deliberate matters little, since either way it creates major concerns in assessing the validity of self-reported measures.

The question of social desirability is raised here because ethnic differences in the tendency to provide socially desirable responses have been reported in the literature. For instance, Ross and Mirowsky (1984) administered a questionnaire with a battery of measures—including social desirability, locus of control, and psychological distress—to a sample of non-Hispanic Whites and Mexican Americans in El Paso, Texas. An additional sample of Mexicans from Juarez, Mexico, was administered the same battery of instruments, but in Spanish. It was found that the greatest level of social desirability was reported by the Mexican sample, followed in turn by the Mexican Americans, and finally the non-Hispanic Whites. Ross and Mirowsky also found an inverse relationship between social class and social desirability, with individuals lower in socioeconomic status the most likely to present a pattern of socially desired responses.

Ross and Mirowsky (1984) interpreted their findings by suggesting that as we move down the socioeconomic ladder, acquiescence appears as a self-presentation strategy of those who are relatively powerless in society. According to these authors, more powerless people attempt to present "a good face" to those members of society whom they perceive to be higher in social standing in an effort to be more accepted in society.

In a reanalysis of four data sets that included responses by nearly 2,000 Hispanics and more than 14,000 non-Hispanic Whites, Marín, Gamba, and Marín (1992) reported that Hispanics showed a greater tendency to agree with items than did Whites. Two variables were found by Marín et al. to correlate with acquiescence responding. The first was educational level; those respondents, regardless of ethnicity, who possessed fewer than 12 years of formal schooling showed more response acquiescence than did the more highly educated respondents. The other variable was acculturation; it was found that more acculturated Hispanics evidenced less response acquiescence. An important cultural interpretation is offered by Marín and Marín (1991) to explain the findings. According to Marín and Marín, Hispanic culture promotes social acquiescence through the social script of "simpatia" that "mandates politeness and respect and discourages criticism, confrontation, and assertiveness. Providing socially desirable answers could be a way to promote positive, smooth relationships between researcher and participant" (p. 106).

In a study that compared foreign-born Asians, U.S.-born Asians, and White college students, Abe and Zane (1992) found that foreign-born Asian students differed significantly from Whites on the social desirability scale. However, in this case the responding was in the direction opposite that reported with Hispanics: The foreign-born Asian group was lowest in social desirability responding! The U.S.-born Asian American students fell midway between the two other groups and did not differ significantly from either group. In an interesting and related study, Smith (1990) compared Asian, White, and Hispanic women on a 40-item scale of narcissism. The results showed that Asian American women had significantly lower narcissism scores than White and Hispanic women. These two studies offer a different interpretation than that suggested for Hispanics by Marín and Marín (1991).

According to Abe and Zane (1992), the foreign-born Asian sample may have scored lower on social desirability "because the items confounded social desirability with nonself-effacing behaviors. That is, if the foreign-born Asian American group responded in a self-effacing direction, it would result in a lower social desirability score" (p. 441). Similarly, Smith (1990) suggests that narcissism is antithetical to Asian cultural values of modesty, respect for authority, and the primacy of relationships over individualism.

The review of these few studies demonstrates the importance of understanding how the cultural background that the ethnic respondent brings to the task of completing interviews, surveys, and questionnaires of various types determines the response patterns that emerge. Equipped with this understanding, the investigator might anticipate responses quite different from those obtained from the White respondents on whom most instruments are standardized. Clearly, more research is required on the question of ethnic differences in response patterns on objective measurement instruments.

Another consideration in this discussion pertains to approaching the use of an instrument with members of an ethnic group for which the scale was not normed. It is always a good practice to determine the adequacy of such a scale with the ethnic group in question. We recommend at least two methods for doing this: Cronbach alpha (internal-consistency reliability) and exploratory factor analysis. In the discussion above of a study by Knight et al. (1992), we showed how Knight and his colleagues tested their instruments for their appropriateness with ethnic samples. The discussion that follows will elaborate upon the approach taken by Knight et al. and will offer suggestions for using instruments appropriately.

Internal-Consistency Reliability. We believe that it is good practice for researchers to question the reliability of their instruments whenever they conduct a study involving ethnic samples. At the very least we recommend that an internal-consistency reliability (Cronbach alpha) be computed on whatever scales are being used in the study. This should be done for each of the ethnic groups *separately* if two or more groups are being compared. Based on the resulting alpha coefficients, the researcher needs to decide whether to proceed with the study or to search for more appropriate instruments.

What is an acceptable level of reliability to gauge the suitability of a scale for use with an ethnic sample? Our advice here is based on that given by Pedhazur and Pedhazur-Schmelkin (1991), who maintain that the acceptability of a reliability estimate depends on the "decisions made on the basis of the scores and the possible consequences of the decisions" (p. 109). Thus the reliability of an instrument should be as high as possible (minimum of r = .70) for more consequential decisions, but can be lower (r = .50) for research purposes involving few, if any, decisions to be made about the educational programming of minority students.

If the reliability estimates are low for an ethnic group, then it is always the responsibility of the investigator to point out that the estimates were low and offer caution regarding any interpretations to be drawn from the study. An item-by-item analysis may also enable the researcher to understand why the scale is more tenuous for the ethnic sample.

In conducting quantitative research with ethnic populations, it is also essential to determine, whenever possible, whether the constructs being measured by the instruments have the same meaning for each ethnic group being studied. Depending on the instrument in question and the sample size, it may be possible to examine the construct validity of instruments across groups by means of exploratory factor analysis.

Exploratory Factor Analysis. It is commonplace today for many of our educational and psychological scales to be developed using methods of factor analysis. For example, a researcher may have a theory about the underlying construct of learning anxiety, or about which attitudinal predispositions are important in learning a foreign language (e.g., R. C. Gardner, 1985). Armed with a theory, the researcher develops a set of items that appear to measure the construct in question. Then these items are administered to a large number of subjects and the data analyzed by means of an exploratory factor analysis, which is a data-analytic procedure for arriving "at a relatively small number of components that will extract most of the variance of a relatively large set of indicators (variables, items)" (Pedhazur & Pedhazur-Schmelkin, 1991, p. 598).

Those items that contribute to (or load on) a component (or a factor) are then retained and those that do not are discarded. In this way scales are developed that can be refined further to determine whether they truly measure the construct in question. Continuing our example from above, suppose that we have two instruments, one of which measures learning anxiety and the other attitudinal disposition toward foreign-language acquisition. We then hypothesize that a good second-language learner would be characterized as an individual who shows little learning anxiety and a positive attitude toward learning a new language. We can test this hypothesis by administering our two new scales to a large group of high school students studying a foreign language. As a dependent measure we could use grades in the class or, better yet, some measure of second-language proficiency. If those students who score low on anxiety and high on attitude toward foreign-language study perform better on learning of the new language than students who obtain scores that are high on anxiety and/or negative on foreign-language learning, then we can have greater confidence in the construct validity of our instruments (R. C. Gardner, 1985).

If the same or a different investigator decides to use one or both of these instruments with an ethnic population, it is important to determine whether the instrument measures the same constructs for the ethnic sample. For example, learning anxiety may be reflected very differently in a school-age population that is anxious in school because the students are not proficient in English, are aware of social-class differences between the school and home, and fear that their every action is being judged by teachers and peers who are different racially, socially, or in formal school preparation. Similarly, on the attitudes toward foreign-language study, ethnic students may already have demonstrated their positive predisposition toward language study by mastering English, which may be their second or third language.

Thus if a researcher decides to employ an instrument whose items were based on a factor analysis, we strongly recommend that the researcher include in the plan of the study a large enough sample size for an exploratory factor analysis to be computed to determine whether the items have the same factor structure as with the population on which the scale was developed. If it is a comparative study, it is particularly important that the researcher have a sample size of each ethnic group large enough to run the factor analysis (Pedhazur & Pedhazur-Schmelkin, 1991).

If the identical or a similar factor structure emerges, then the researcher can feel confident of the measures for use with the ethnic sample and can proceed with the data analysis. On the other hand, if a factor structure emerges that is different from that reported by the developers of the scale, then the researcher should rethink both the data analysis and what the difference in factor structure means from the standpoint of the ethnic group being studied.

CONCLUSION

In this chapter we have covered a number of critical issues that must be considered when doing research with ethnic minority populations. We began with a discussion of the social construction of knowledge and how two different research approaches have shaped, in different ways, how quantitative research is conducted. Central to this discussion is the Eurocentric paradigm. We showed how this paradigm has been called into question. The central problem of the Eurocentric paradigm rests on its use of the White middle-class (male) as the standard and its adherence to the comparative approach in conducting research. In recent years ethnic minority researchers and scholars have called for a shift away from the Eurocentric para-

digm and have moved toward more ethnic-sensitive paradigms (e.g., Afrocentric paradigm). These new paradigms maintain that the standard should lie with the specific ethnic group in question and that it should be based on the values and worldviews of the ethnic group alone. In addition, authors (e.g., Azibo, 1988; Marín & Marín, 1991; Rogler, 1989) have begun to call for more culturally sensitive approaches to quantitative research with ethnic communities.

In line with the culturally sensitive approaches to quantitative research, we next discussed several critical challenges to conducting quantitative research with ethnic groups. Three major challenges and solutions were presented. These challenges involved: (a) the importance of identifying, describing, and selecting a sample; (b) understanding the heterogeneity within an ethnic group; and (c) the difficulties posed by language differences. The importance of each of these challenges was discussed. It was pointed out that these challenges are not insurmountable and in fact pose no serious problem as long as there is an understanding of the ethnic group being studied.

We recommend that, whenever possible, members of the ethnic community be incorporated into the planning and implementation of the research project. This will increase the potential for more relevant research questions and approaches. Further, a more appropriate or bias-free sample may be a more likely outcome when the ethnic community is involved in the research enterprise.

The final section of this chapter was devoted to issues of instrumentation and measurement. Quantitative research is only as good as the data on which it is based, and this means that special attention must be given to the instruments used in research with ethnic populations. The importance of measurement was illustrated by a review of research involving achievement and self-esteem scales. This was followed by a discussion of acculturation and ethnic identification, which have emerged as two central constructs in ethnic-related research. It was shown that there are conceptual reasons for giving more attention to acculturation and ethnic identification in our research. This section closed with a discussion of response bias that has been found in the responses given by African American and Hispanic informants. This could be a serious concern both in the interpretation given to findings and in deciding what strategies should be followed in future development of instruments for use with ethnic populations.

Finally, the chapter closed with two analytic strategies to determine whether the ethnic informants show similar patterns of reliability and interpretation of specific items on a scale. These strategies involved internal consistency reliability and exploratory factor analysis. We are of the opinion that the research base regarding ethnic minority populations can be improved by attending to the psychometric properties of all of the instruments used in educational research.

References

Abe, J. S., & Zane, N. W. (1990). Psychological maladjustment among Asian and White American college students: Controlling for confounds. *Journal of Counseling Psychology, 37,* 437–444.

Adler, L. L. (1982). Cross-cultural research and theory. In B. Wolman (Ed.), *Handbook of developmental psychology* (pp. 76–90). Englewood Cliffs, NJ: Prentice Hall.

Alatorre Alva, S. (1991). Academic invulnerability among Mexican-American students: The importance of protective resources and appraisals. *Hispanic Journal of Behavioral Sciences, 13*, 18–34.

Allport, G. (1937). *Personality: A psychological interpretation.* New York: Holt.

Azibo, D. (1988). Understanding the proper and improper usage of the comparative research framework. *Journal of Black Psychology, 15*, 81–91.

Bachman, J. G., & O'Malley, P. M. (1984). Black-White differences in self-esteem: Are they affected by response styles? *American Journal of Sociology, 90*, 624–639.

Banks, J. A. (1993). The canon debate, knowledge construction, and multicultural education. *Educational Researcher, 22*(6), 4–14.

Bernal, M. E., & Knight, G. P. (Eds.). (1993). *Ethnic identity: Formation and transmission among Hispanics and other minorities.* Albany: State University of New York Press.

Berndt, T. J., Cheung, P. C., Lau, S., Hau, K., & Lew, W. J. F. (1993). Perceptions of parenting in mainland China, Taiwan, and Hong Kong: Sex differences and societal differences. *Developmental Psychology, 29*, 156–164.

Berry, J. (1990). Psychology of acculturation: Understanding individuals moving between cultures. In R. Brislin (Ed.), *Applied cross-cultural psychology* (pp. 232–253). Newbury Park, CA: Sage Publications.

Bond, L. A. (1988). Teaching developmental psychology. In P. A. Bronstein & K. Quina (Eds.), *Teaching a psychology of people: Resources for gender and sociocultural awareness* (pp. 45–52). Washington, DC: American Psychological Association.

Brigham, C. C. (1923). *A study of American intelligence.* Princeton, NJ: Princeton University Press.

Buriel, R. (1984). Integration with traditional Mexican American culture and sociocultural adjustment. In J. L. Martinez, Jr., & R. H. Mendoza (Eds.), *Chicano psychology* (2nd ed., pp. 95–130). Orlando, FL: Academic Press.

Buriel, R., & Cardoza, D. (1988). Sociocultural correlates of achievement among three generations of Mexican American high school seniors. *American Educational Research Journal, 25*, 177–192.

Buriel, R., & Cardoza, D. (1993). Mexican American ethnic labeling: An intrafamilial and intergenerational analysis. In M. E. Bernal & G. P. Knight (Eds.), *Ethnic identity: Formation and transmission among Hispanics and other minorities* (pp. 197–210). Albany: State University of New York Press.

California State Department of Education. (1986). *Beyond language: Social and cultural factors in schooling language minority students.* Los Angeles: Evaluation, Dissemination, and Assessment Center, California State University.

Caplan, N., Whitmore, J. K., & Choy, M. H. (1989). *The boat people and achievement in America.* Ann Arbor: University of Michigan Press.

Casas, J. M., Furlong, M., Solberg, V. S., & Carranza, O. (1990). An examination of individual factors associated with the academic success and failure of Mexican-American and Anglo students. In A. Barona & E. E. Garcia (Eds.), *Children at risk: Poverty, minority status, and other issues in educational equity* (pp. 103–118). Washington, DC: National Association of School Psychologists.

Clark, K. B. (1965). *Dark ghetto: Dilemmas of social power.* New York: Harper & Row.

Code, L. (1987). *Epistemic responsibility.* Hanover, NH: University Press of New England.

Cooper, H., & Tom, D. Y. H. (1984). Socioeconomic status and ethnic group differences in achievement motivation. In R. Ames & C. Ames (Eds.), *Research on motivation in education* (Vol. 1, pp. 209–242). San Diego, CA: Academic Press.

Cuellar, I., Harris, L. C., & Jasso, R. (1980). An acculturation scale for Mexican American normal and clinical populations. *Hispanic Journal of Behavioral Sciences, 2*, 199–217.

Culver, S. M., Wolfle, L. M., & Cross, L. H. (1990). Testing a model of teaching satisfaction for Blacks and Whites. *American Educational Research Journal, 27*, 323–349.

Dornbusch, S. M., Ritter, P. L., Leiderman, H., Roberts, D. F., & Fraleigh, M. J. (1987). The relation of parenting style to adolescent school performance. *Child Development, 58*, 1244–1257.

Duran, B. J., & Weffer, R. E. (1992). Immigrants' aspirations, high school process, and academic outcomes. *American Educational Research Journal, 29*, 163–181.

Finn, J. D., & Achilles, C. M. (1990). Answers and questions about class size: A statewide experiment. *American Educational Research Journal, 27*, 557–577.

Flynn, J. R. (1991). *Asian Americans: Achievement beyond IQ.* Hillsdale, NJ: Lawrence Erlbaum Associates.

Gardner, H. (1985). *Frames of mind: The theory of multiple intelligences.* New York: Basic Books.

Gardner, R. C. (1985). *Social psychology and second language learning: The role of attitudes and motivation.* London: Edward Arnold.

Gibson, M. A. (1988). *Accommodation without assimilation: Sikh immigrants in an American high school.* Ithaca, NY: Cornell University Press.

Gibson, M. A., & Ogbu, J. U. (Eds.). (1991). *Minority status and schooling: A comparative study of immigrant and involuntary minorities.* New York: Garland Publishing Company.

Gopnik, A., & Meltzoff, A. N. (1992). Categorization and naming: Basic-level sorting in eighteen-month-olds and its relation to language. *Child Development, 63*, 1091–1103.

Gould, S. J. (1981). *The mismeasure of man.* New York: W. W. Norton.

Graham, S. (1992). "Most of the subjects were white and middle class": Trends in published research on African Americans in selected APA journals, 1970–1989. *American Psychologist, 47*, 629–639.

Griffen-Pierson, S. (1988). *A new conceptualization of competitiveness in women.* Unpublished doctoral dissertation, University of Iowa, Iowa City.

Griffen-Pierson, S. (1990). The competitiveness questionnaire: A measure of two components of competitiveness. *Measurement and Evaluation in Counseling and Development, 23*, 108–115.

Gunderson, V. M., Fagan, J. F., & Grant-Webster, K. S. (1987). Visual recognition memory in high- and low-risk infant pigtailed macaques (Macaca Nemestrina). *Developmental Psychology, 23*, 671–675.

Gutierrez, J., & Sameroff, A. (1990). Determinants of complexity in Mexican-American and Anglo-American mothers' conceptions of child development. *Child Development, 61*, 384–394.

Gutierrez, J., Sameroff, A., & Karrer, B. M. (1988). Acculturation and SES effects on Mexican-American parents' concepts of development. *Child Development, 59*, 250–255.

Hamburg, D. A. (1992). *Today's children: Creating a future for a generation in crisis.* New York: Random House.

Harter, S. (1983). Developmental perspectives on the self-system. In P. H. Mussen (Ed.), *Handbook of child Psychology: Vol. IV. Socialization, personality, and social development* (4th ed., pp. 275–385). New York: Wiley.

Helms, J. E. (1992). Why is there no study of cultural equivalence in standardized cognitive ability testing? *American Psychologist, 47*, 1083–1101.

Hernandez, A. E., & Willson, V. (1992). A comparison of Kaufman assessment battery for children reliability for Mexican-Americans and non-Hispanic Whites. *Hispanic Journal of Behavioral Sciences, 14*, 394–397.

Horowitz, F. D., & O'Brien, M. (1989). In the interest of the nation: A reflective essay on the state of our knowledge and the challenge before us. *American Psychologist, 44*, 441–445.

Hui, C. H., & Triandis, H. (1989). Effects of culture and response format on extreme response style. *Journal of Cross-Cultural Psychology, 20*, 296–309.

Jacob, E., & Jordan, C. (Eds.). (1987). Explaining the school performance of minority students. *Anthropology and Education Quarterly, 18*, 259–392.

Kamin, L. J. (1974). *The science and politics of I.Q.* New York: Lawrence Erlbaum Associates.

Keefe, S. E., & Padilla, A. M. (1987). *Chicano ethnicity.* Albuquerque: University of New Mexico Press.

Kerlinger, F. N. (1979). *Behavioral research.* New York: Holt, Rinehart and Winston.

Khatib, S., & Nobles, W. (1977). Historical foundations of African psychology and their philosophical consequences. *Journal of Black Psychology, 4*, 91–101.

Kim, U. (1988). *Acculturation of Korean immigrants to Canada: Psychological, demographic and behavioural profiles of emigrating Koreans, non-emigrating Koreans and Korean-Canadians.* Unpublished doctoral dissertation, Queen's University, Kingston, Ontario, Canada.

Knight, G. P., Tein, J. Y., Shell, R., & Roosa, M. (1992). The cross-ethnic equivalence of parenting and family interaction measures among Hispanic and Anglo American families. *Child Development, 63*, 1392–1403.

Kraft, C. L. (1991). What makes a successful Black student on a predominantly White campus? *American Educational Research Journal, 28*, 423–444.

Kuhn, T. S. (1970). *The structure of scientific revolutions* (2nd ed.). Chicago: University of Chicago Press.

Lakatos, I., & Musgrave, A. (Eds.). (1970). *Criticism and the growth of knowledge.* Cambridge, England: Cambridge University Press.

Lamborn, S. D., Mounts, N. S., Steinberg, L., & Dornbusch, S. M. (1991). Patterns of competence and adjustment among adolescents from authoritative, authoritarian, indulgent, and neglectful families. *Child Development, 62*, 1049–1065.

Landsman, M. A., Padilla, A. M., Leiderman, P. H., Clark, C., Ritter, P., & Dornbusch, S. (1991). *Biculturalism and academic achievement among Asian and Hispanic adolescents.* Unpublished manuscript.

Laosa, L. (1980a). Maternal teaching strategies in Chicano and Anglo-American families: The influence of culture and education on maternal behavior. *Child Development, 51*, 759–765.

Laosa, L. (1980b). Maternal teaching strategies and cognitive styles in Chicano families. *Journal of Educational Psychology, 72*, 45–54.

Laosa, L. (1982). School, occupation, culture and the family: The impact of parental schooling on the parent-child relationship. *Journal of Educational Psychology, 74*, 791–827.

Marchant, G. J. (1991). A profile of motivation, self-perceptions and achievement in black urban elementary children. *Urban Review, 23*, 83–99.

Marín, G. (1993). Influence of acculturation on familialism and self-identification among Hispanics. In M. E. Bernal & G. P. Knight (Eds.), *Ethnic identity: Formation and transmission among Hispanics and other minorities* (pp. 181–196). Albany: State University of New York Press.

Marín, G., Gamba, R. J., & Marín, B. V. (1992). Extreme response style and acquiescence among Hispanics: The role of acculturation and education. *Journal of Cross-Cultural Psychology, 23*, 498–509.

Marín, G., & Marín, B. V. (1991). *Research with Hispanic populations.* Newbury Park, CA: Sage Publications.

Martinez, R., & Dukes, R. L. (1987). Race, gender, and self-esteem among youth. *Hispanic Journal of Behavioral Sciences, 9*, 427–443.

McLoyd, V. C., & Randolph, S. M. (1984). The conduct and publication of research on Afro-American children: A content analysis. *Human Development, 27*, 65–75.

McLoyd, V. C., & Randolph, S. M. (1985). Secular trends in the study of Afro-American children: A review of *Child Development*, 1936–1980. *Monographs of the Society for Research in Child Development, 50*, 78–92.

Mensh, E., & Mensh, H. (1991). *The IQ mythology: Class, race, gender, and inequality.* Carbondale: Southern Illinois University Press.

Moyerman, D. R., & Forman, B. D. (1992). Acculturation and adjustment: A meta-analytic study. *Hispanic Journal of Behavioral Sciences, 14*, 163–200.

Moynihan, D. P. (1965). *The Negro family: A case for national action.* Washington, DC: Office of Policy Planning and Research, U.S. Dept. of Labor.

Mussen, P. H. (1983). *Handbook of child psychology: Vol. IV. Socialization, personality, and social development* (4th ed.). New York: Wiley.

Nederhof, A. J. (1985). Methods of coping with social desirability: A review. *Journal of European Social Psychology, 15*, 263–280.

Neisser, U. (Ed.). (1986). *The school achievement of minority children: New Perspectives.* Hillsdale, NJ: Lawrence Erlbaum Associates.

Oetting, E. R., & Beauvais, F. (1990–1991). Orthogonal cultural identification theory: The cultural identification of minority adolescents. *International Journal of the Addictions, 25*, 655–685.

Olmedo, E. (1979). Acculturation: A psychometric perspective. *American Psychologist, 34*, 1061–1070.

Padilla, A. M. (Ed.). (1980). *Acculturation: Theory, models, and some new findings.* Boulder, CO: Westview Press.

Padilla, A. M. (1988). Early psychological assessment of Mexican-American children. *Journal of the History of the Behavioral Sciences, 24*, 111–117.

Paulhus, D. L. (1984). Two-component models of socially desirable responding. *Journal of Personality and Social Psychology, 46*, 598–609.

Pedhazur, E. J., & Pedhazur-Schmelkin, L. (1991). *Measurement, design, and analysis: An integrated approach* (2nd ed.). Hillsdale, NJ: Lawrence Erlbaum Associates.

Phinney, J. S. (1990). Ethnic identity in adolescents and adults: Review of research. *Psychological Bulletin, 108*, 499–514.

Phinney, J. S., & Rotheram, M. J. (Eds.). (1987). *Children's ethnic socialization.* Newbury Park, CA: Sage Publications.

Plutchik, R. (1974). *Foundations of experimental research.* New York: Harper & Row.

Ramirez, J. D., Yuen, S. D., & Ramey, D. R. (1991). *Longitudinal study of structured English immersion strategy, early-exit and late-exit transitional bilingual education programs for language-minority children* (Contract No. 300-87-0156). Washington, DC: U.S. Department of Education.

Reyes, M. de la Luz, & Halcón, J. J. (1988). Racism in academia: The old wolf revisited. *Harvard Educational Review, 58*, 299–314.

Richman, A. L., Miller, P. M., & LeVine, R. A. (1993). Cultural and educational variations in maternal responsiveness. *Developmental Psychology, 28*, 614–621.

Rodriguez, C. E. (1989). *Puerto Ricans born in the U.S.A.* Boston: Unwin Hyman.

Rogler, L. H. (1989). The meaning of culturally sensitive research in mental health. *American Journal of Psychiatry, 146*, 296–303.

Rogler, L. H., Cortes, D. E., & Malgady, R. G. (1991). Acculturation and mental health status among Hispanics: Convergence and new directions for research. *American Psychologist, 46*, 585–597.

Rosenberg, M. (1979). *Conceiving the self.* New York: Basic Books.

Ross, C. E., & Mirowsky, J. (1984). Socially desirable response and acquiescence in a cross-cultural survey of mental health. *Journal of Health and Social Behavior, 25*, 189–197.

Rotenberg, K. J., & Cranwell, F. R. (1989). Self-concept in American

Indian and White children. *Journal of Cross-Cultural Psychology, 20*, 39–53.

Rumbaut, R. G. (1990). *Immigrant students in California public schools: A summary of current knowledge* (Report No. 11). Baltimore, MD: The Johns Hopkins University, Center for Research on Effective Schooling for Disadvantaged Students.

Schultz, G. F. (in press). Socioeconomic advantage and achievement motivation: Important mediators of academic performance in minority children in urban schools. *Urban Review.*

Sears, D. O. (1986). College sophomores in the laboratory: Influence of a narrow data based on social psychology's view of human nature. *Journal of Personality & Social Psychology, 51*, 515–530.

Smith, B. M. (1990). The measurement of narcissism in Asian, Caucasian, and Hispanic American women. *Psychological Reports, 67*(3, pt. 1), 779–785.

Stevenson, H. W., Chen, C., & Uttal, D. H. (1990). Beliefs and achievement: A study of Black, White, and Hispanic children. *Child Development, 61*, 508–523.

Stigler, J. W., Smith, S., & Mao, L. (1985). The self-perception of competence by Chinese children. *Child Development, 56*, 1259–1270.

Strom, R., Johnson, A., Strom, S., & Strom, P. (1992). Educating gifted Hispanic children and their parents. *Hispanic Journal of Behavioral Sciences, 14*, 383–393.

Suarez, Z. E. (1993). Cuban Americans: From golden exiles to social undesirables. In H. P. McAdoo (Ed.), *Family ethnicity: Strength in diversity* (pp. 164–176). Newbury Park, CA: Sage Publications.

Suarez-Orozco, M. M. (1989). *Central American refugees and U.S. high schools: A psychosocial study of motivation and achievement.* Stanford, CA: Standford University Press.

Sue, S., & Okazaki, S. (1990). Asian American educational achievements: A phenomenon in search of an explanation. *American Psychologist, 45*, 913–920.

Suinn, R. M., Richard-Figueroa, K., Lew, S., & Vigil, P. (1987). The Suinn-Lew Asian self-identity acculturation scale: An initial report. *Educational and Psychological Measurement, 47*, 401–407.

Szapocznik, J., & Kurtines, W. (1980). Acculturation, biculturalism and adjustment among Cuban Americans. In A. M. Padilla (Ed.), *Acculturation: Theory, models and some new findings* (pp. 139–159). Boulder, CO: Westview Press.

Triandis, H. C., Kashima, Y., Shimada, E., & Villareal, M. (1986). Acculturation indices as a means of confirming cultural differences. *International Journal of Psychology, 21*, 43–70.

Valencia, R. R. (Ed.). (1991). *Chicano school failure and success: Research and policy agendas for the 1990s.* New York: Falmer Press.

Vernon, P. E. (1982). *The abilities and achievement of Orientals in North America.* New York: Academic Press.

Wentzel, K. R. (1991). Relations between social competence and academic achievement in early adolescence. *Child Development, 62*, 1066–1078.

Willig, A. (1985). A meta-analysis of selected studies on the effectiveness of bilingual education. *Review of Educational Research, 55*, 269–317.

Wittrock, M. C. (Ed.). (1986). *Handbook of research on teaching* (3rd ed.). New York: Macmillan.

Wolman, B. (Ed.). (1982). *Handbook of developmental psychology.* Englewood Cliffs, NJ: Prentice-Hall.

Wylie, R. (1979). *The self-concept: Vol. 2. Theory and research on selected topics.* Lincoln: University of Nebraska Press.

Yee, A. H. (1992). Asians as stereotypes and students: Misperceptions that persist. *Educational Psychology Review, 4*, 95–132.

7

ETHNOGRAPHY IN COMMUNITIES: LEARNING THE EVERYDAY LIFE OF AMERICA'S SUBORDINATED YOUTH

Shirley Brice Heath

STANFORD UNIVERSITY

The concept of *community* has been central to the American ethos since the settlement of the colonies, both as a fundamental ideal and an actual physical construct grounded in the interconnectedness of place, people, history, and purpose. In the widely read book of the mid-1980s, *Habits of the Heart* (Bellah, Madsen, Sullivan, Swidler, & Tipton, 1985), the authors observe that "the community of civic-minded, interlocking families rooted in two hundred fifty years of tradition—does not really exist" (p. 11) for most Americans. Instead, a wide array of organizations and regroupings serve to bond people together and include their individual voices in the "currents of communal conversation" (p. 135). Some of these communities are intentionally identified around their founders' central purpose (e.g., Mothers Against Drunk Driving). Others bear more general labels and are classified together on the basis of general perceptions about their members' shared beliefs and values (e.g., the Christian community, the gay community, the Hispanic community, or the nation as community). Still others seem shaped around a bond that unites some people and differentiates them from others at particular stages of their life (e.g., support groups, computer networks). In spite of the proliferation of what are often either temporarily or loosely aggregated communities, the quest continues for the utopia of the ideal community as a place of roots and connection, linking people to cycles of nature and grounding them in attachments to their neighbors.

Since the beginnings of social science, scholars, as well as the public at large, have quarreled over what makes and sustains *community*. (Arensberg, 1961, remains perhaps the most comprehensive discussion of this concern, particularly with respect to the community as a unit of analysis.) Of particular debate has been the question of whether or not modernity and urban industrial life within nation states force a fundamental shift away from the agricultural bases of community: shared territory, kinship, close links to nature's cycles, and consensual group solidarity. Ferdinand Toennies (1887/1963) distinguished *gemeinschaft* (community)—with emphasis on clearly defined social structure and loyalties to close personal relationships—from *gesselschaft* (society), or impersonally, even artificially, contracted associations. Emile Durkheim's (1933) analysis of organic and mechanical solidarity stressed that within modern urban society, both psychological consensus and interdependence resulting from the division of labor coexisted as two aspects of the same reality. Yet some social scientists have continued to contend that the larger society and mass communication have replaced communal associations of primary affiliations, while others argue that new "intentional communities," by their interactive nature, achieve the goals of face-to-face, homegrown, territorially based nature communities (Gusfield, 1975; Warren, 1978; Wilkinson, 1986). Pointing to the power of all-inclusive public interests and the ideology of community, B. Anderson (1983) has maintained that nations are communities because their citizens have faith in the "steady, anonymous, simultaneous activity" of fellow members moving through "homogeneous, empty time" (p. 31).

What, then, does *community* mean? This question is more difficult to answer as the 20th century closes than is the reshaped question of *who* does community mean? Rare is the contemporary individual who will claim membership in a community based on physical proximity, residence, or even face-to-face contact. Few people live close by groups with which they feel the strongest communal association. Hence, large societal institutions of all sorts—athletic, ethnic, recreational, occupational, religious, and professional—allow individuals to branch off to create their own subgroups called "communities" that provide emotional and common-interest ties as well as a sense of subjective wholeness.

This chapter considers first a brief chronology of community within American life and the influence of ideals remaining from this history. Next is a quick look through ethnographic portrayals of different kinds of contemporary communities and their ways of socializing individuals into their membership. Without the benefit of early shared learning experiences gained by playing in the same block, walking to the same school, and sharing backyards—as is the case in communities of close spatial connection—members come to association as individuals who must often undergo a self-conscious socialization to new affiliations and self-identities. All of the portrayals in this section include subtexts of members' collective views of learning through formal and nonformal education. Finally, implications of current community life for the future of research, policy, and practice in multiculturalism or pluralism in American education close the chapter.

A STEP BACK TO COMMUNITY ROOTS

In rural parts of the nation during its first 100 years, separate households at distant spots over plains and in isolated mountain hollows held their sense of connectedness by bringing residents together during particular seasons and for rites of intensification—weddings, family reunions, barn raisings, and celebrations of harvests. During the early Industrial Revolution, American villages grew up around mills, and millworker and millowner lived in sight of each other. Laborers, inventors, entrepreneurs, managers, investors, and those who hung on around the town's edges shared common spaces and came together less and less often as a group except during those occasions of sponsorship by the town's industrialists or millowners (Hall et al., 1987; Hareven & Langenbach, 1978; Wallace, 1978).

In ensuing decades, as more and more towns began to dot the countryside, weekend events, such as baseball games, parades, carnivals, and celebrations of school or church affairs, divided along gender, class, and racial lines. Competitions of male teams in local athletic events were sustained in large part by the "benevolent work" of women in local institutions, such as churches, schools, and community centers, which facilitated occasions of public congregation, celebration, and recreation. Wealthier families formed clubs, set on great expanses of land near their residential areas, to provide exclusive recreational facilities for themselves. Blacks and Whites worked, worshiped, lived, and played separately throughout not only the South but also most parts of the United States. In recently admitted states or areas preparing for statehood in the Southwest, Mexican and Anglo families often lived in separate towns despite the symbiotic nature of their economic contributions to the region's development (Camarillo, 1979; Steiner, 1969).

Despite the untenable conditions of slavery and racial division, strong coalitions of community evolved across regions and in the face of hostile opposition. These came first through the Underground Railroad and later through religious and political affiliations—often covertly and always from a sense of critical human need. In the South slavery created communities spatially based on plantations and, for freed Blacks, in the black alleys of cities such as Savannah and Richmond. As early as the 1830s more than 300,000 free Blacks lived in the United States, many forming strong middle- and upper-class communities that sustained churches, social clubs, libraries, and literary groups, primarily in northern cities. Almost entirely neglected in accounts of American history, these groups shaped key institutions, such as antislavery societies, the Black press, professional groups, and literary journals, that played significant roles in creating the cultural and social landscape during Reconstruction and into the 20th century (DuBois, 1899; Edwards, 1959; Frazier, 1947, 1957; Gatewood, 1990).

Following the Civil War and again during the period between World Wars I and II, migration to northern cities resulted in urban zones occupied exclusively by Blacks (Drake & Cayton, 1945/1962). Poverty and employment in the lowest-paying economic niches helped create ghettos of Blacks who came to compete with immigrants and refugees from Europe in the first half of the 20th century for jobs, local business development, and decent housing. Entertainment, newspapers, radio stations, occupational niches, and union memberships divided along racial, ethnic, and linguistic lines—Black, Italian, Irish, Polish, Scandinavian (Myrdal, 1944; Fishman, 1966).

Immigrant newcomers marked their identities in the architecture of homes and churches, choices of neighborhood stores and wares, and preferences for music, food, and recreational pastimes. In the late 19th century, cities such as New York, Cleveland, and San Francisco developed community schools that taught in the languages of the students until the xenophobia of World War I forced the reduction of publicly supported efforts to retain the linguistic identities of immigrant communities (Fishman, 1966). The explosion of suburbs after World War II further scattered the face-to-face commonalities of old urban neighborhoods, as the second generation of immigrants moved out to shape their lives around their chosen new American identity and to shed much of the language, traditional lore, and values of the "old country."

Social Science in the Study of Community and Society

Dynamic changes in the factors that brought people together in American life captured the attention of social scientists from the second decade of the 20th century through the 1950s. At the University of Chicago, Robert Park and his colleagues in urban sociology opened up some of the complexities of the urban community and began the tradition of the detailed case-study and ecological approach to communities that influenced social scientists such as David Riesman (1950), Oscar Lewis (1951), and Robert Redfield (1941). Sociologists described midwestern towns, documenting the increasing social stratification that created separate communities of distinct values and institutional affiliations even for those of the same ethnic and national backgrounds (Lynd & Lynd, 1929; West, 1945).

From the University of North Carolina in Chapel Hill, a team of researchers scattered across the South to document the varieties of types of communities there (Gilman, 1956; H. Lewis, 1955; Morland, 1958). Other social scientists began to study communities-in-the-making and subgroups such as gangs in urban society, purposefully formed by young and old for mutual protection of urban territory and maintenance of separate identities from other groups in poverty (Thrasher, 1927; Whyte, 1943). By the end of the 1950s the variation in what counted as *community* for social scientists ranged from occupational groupings (such as hospitals; see Becker, 1961/1976) to media-constructed entities (such as "Hollywood"; see Powdermaker, 1950).

Absence of a consensual operational definition of *community* continued to hinder social scientists from reaching any agreement on unit of analysis. Certain obvious, older, traditional requisites of community—such as territoriality, contact with the cycles of nature, and inclusion of more than one generation—were weakened considerably in favor of interactionalist perspectives that focused on attachments and common processes of formation and sustenance grounded in communication. The old issue of whether or not community disappears as society expands its influence appeared repeatedly. Throughout the 20th century in the United States, as government bureaucracies seemed to take over more and more matters previously handled informally in face-to-face encounters, social scientists periodically questioned how, and indeed if, little communities could persist with so many forces of government and mass communication at work in the society at large. Some social commentators and scholars saw this intrusion of external "problem solvers" as killing off just what communities needed for their survival: the seeking of collective solutions to their own problems. As controls of the local group over the behavior of its members weakened, communities died and larger frames of reference and temporary memberships took over former loyalties (Gallaher & Padfield, 1980).

Little Communities at the End of the 20th Century

The work of anthropologist Robert Redfield in Mexico, perhaps more than that of any other social scientist, brought together conceptual bases for distinguishing among the many types of "little communities" and the conditions of their development and persistence. In the scattered small groups of the Yucatan peninsula (1941) Redfield found what members called "communidades," and characterized these in ways that foreshadowed what would by the end of the 20th century characterize communities in North America—spatially scattered individuals brought together through communication networks and as face-to-face groups primarily in seasonal rites of intensification. He noted that habits of travel, different occupational patterns, and the mix of separate groups through intermarriage and resettlement would increasingly make of community a *sense* of bondedness rather than a *place* of mutual dwelling (Redfield, 1956/1960).

His views were echoed in work of the 1970s and 1980s that documented the diversity of Americans' responses to the need to build new shapes and formulations of group bondings from the ashes of the traditional community. Groups, seeing themselves primarily in terms of their occupations and wishing to set apart their specific abilities and interests, included in their reasons for existence not only socialization opportunities for their increased professionalization, but also advocacy and recreational goals (Salaman, 1974). Having much in common with the Underground Railroad community of the 19th century, numerous late 20th-century communities formed themselves around crises, feelings of common suffering and struggle, and the need to regroup outside "ordinary" communities to compete and survive. (Wallace's 1970 study of the rise and rebirth of the Seneca Iroquois through religion is an example of such work, as is Kreiger, 1983, a study of a lesbian community.) "Dying" communities, those attempting rebirth, and those struggling to be born all work to sustain membership and loyalties, and to overcome insecurities that spring from a lack of economic, natural, and human resources (Gallaher & Padfield, 1980, provide 10 studies of such communities beset with such problems as lack of economic and technological resources, ethnic and social class conflicts, and demographic isolation).

As the 20th century ends, membership in a community with no territorial basis or shared early socialization experience occurs at least as frequently as groupings that do bear these traditional features. Shared bonds of national origin, ethnicity, and religion are diminishing for many who find that their primary glue of community is instead a self-conscious sense of purpose and self-interest, as well as socioeconomic class ties and degree of assimilation of or resistance to mainstream values and behaviors. In earlier decades individuals were drawn together through a sense of common history; now a sense of disparate present and diverging future leads to purposeful choices of language, norms, and goals that separate many Americans from the primary-group connections of former generations.

During the civil rights era and through the 1970s, inner cities depended on the power of their subdivisions into zones of similarity in ethnicity, race, language, and religion to make self-affirming declarations (e.g., Black Is Beautiful) and to display pride in their differences. Increase in Black pride soon brought numerous efforts to revive ethnic heritages and to celebrate diversities of history, dress, music, costume, food, and art. Federal efforts, such as the Ethnic Heritage Act, encouraged artists and art institutions to take seriously the promotion of diverse art forms and traditions to widespread public attention (Kilbride, Goodale, & Ameisen, 1990). Professional and college athletics expanded efforts to recruit players from Black and Hispanic communities and to provide new opportunities for financial and educational advancement. Public consciousness about overt discrimination in public spheres, especially employment, real estate, and education, opened new possibilities of social and geographic movement to members of populations formerly subordinated in and excluded from these areas.

Within a decade these societal changes—often effected in the interest of desegregation, civil rights, and affirmative action—brought drastic shifts in allegiances to spatial communities that had previously been *all*-Black, *all*-Hispanic, *all*-Polish, *all*-Chinese (Alba, 1990; Blackwell, 1984). New economic possibilities meant chances for different patterns of residence and recreation; families began to move into new neighborhoods, many of which had only recently been the urban sites to which earlier European immigrants had come from their urban ghettos. Middle-class neighborhoods on the outskirts of cities or in towns across America were no longer predictable from household to household as to culture, race, religion, or language. Friendships came more and more to be formed through work and less through common place of residence. Telephones increasingly provided the interstices of the networks held together by communication. Soon computer networks greatly supplemented the telephone as a communication net that bound together individuals who never saw each other but coalesced around common information needs and goals. As corporations and factories steadily sought regions that would offer cheaper labor and better tax incentives, employees at executive and managerial levels were relocated frequently about the country and found safety in community formations that centered around common interests—recreational, religious, aesthetic, civic, and professional. In addition, "intentional" communities sprouted up, linking themselves together through what they termed "the technologies of cooperation and electronic communications" (see *Communities,* 1992).

In the 1960s and 1970s communities of poverty—especially those of Blacks—had been portrayed as full of pride and a centeredness in their cultural past (e.g., Stack, 1974; Hannerz, 1969). However, the late 1980s brought drastic economic changes that cut in several directions, often contradictory to one other. Numerous factors resulted in a radical decrease in the need for unskilled labor in manufacturing and construction, leaving those without formal education and specialized skills unable to find work except in the low-paying service sector (Wilson, 1987). Communities of recent migrants from Mexico struggled to establish themselves as viable economic neighborhoods with churches and businesses. Yet most were without priests from among their own group or economic entrepreneurs who could establish local businesses of sufficient strength to sustain themselves through hard times. The young turned away from their parents' older ways and tried to find themselves within a youth subculture dictated to by commercial music and entertainment (Moore & Pinderhughes, 1993). Economic migrants and political refugees entering the United States willingly stepped into low-paying jobs providing service within establishments owned by others. A few found small-business niches in the increasingly ethnically mixed and poorest inner-city areas. Many industries found that global competition meant they had to upgrade the workplace to require new technological, computational, and literacy skills of workers; displaced unskilled workers and young workers without education often could find no employment.

These changes brought rapid shifts in inner-city neighborhoods and high-rise projects that had formerly been the province of one ethnic group. By the mid-1980s urban projects often housed as many as 20 different language groups. Drug trafficking and gang violence gave "neighborhood" new meanings fraught with fear and desperation. Groups of youth claimed their own "hoods" (neighborhoods or claimed territories in various parts of the city) with automatic weapons, "beepers" as local communication resources, and fax machines and airline travel as means to stay in touch with counterparts in other

urban areas. Gang life substituted for families that had either disintegrated through alcohol and drug abuse or incarceration, or had been incomplete to start with because of single parenthood, or devolved as powerless to influence the younger generation to hope for a brighter future resulting from hard work and continued education (Hagedorn, 1988; Padilla, 1987). Young men and women found few models in their parents' lives or media representations of their ethnic heritage; instead they sought to form collective identities through gang membership (Vigil, 1993). Sexual codes centered in street norms of gender-based groups, and the value of bearing children tied more to status within these groups than to perceived role in a new generational family unit (E. Anderson, 1990). In place of the local jobs former generations of young people had held as street vendors, newspaper deliverers, and helpers in the kitchens and stockrooms of small family-owned businesses, gang members now found the entrepreneurial opportunities of gangs their only "hood" source of financial support (Padilla, 1992; Rodriguez, 1993). Male gangs shifted somewhat their earlier structures and functions of the 1940s, and they and newly organized female gangs cooperated with social scientists to document continuities and variations across as many as three generations in some neighborhoods (Moore, 1991).

WITH AN ETHNOGRAPHER'S EYE

But what is happening within these diverse groups that all go under the name of *community*? What holds these groups together, and how do they differ in the education of their members? To act responsibly, social planners have to ask both what is happening and who is calling for responses (Bellah, Madsen, Sullivan, Swidler, & Tipton, 1991, p. 283). Answers to these questions can best come from getting inside these groups and taking a comparative perspective on their historical, structural, and behavioral features. Ethnographers learn about beliefs and behaviors of groups by becoming, to the extent possible, participants and observers of these groups. But as sites of ethnographers' studies, communities and families have been the most difficult social arenas for intense study. By their very definition and rationale of existence, communities do not include outsiders such as researchers; they are not open institutions inviting general membership, and their everyday interactions are guided by unspoken (often out-of-awareness) rules of behavior and language. Writing an ethnography requires long-term immersion, continuing involvement with community members, and some degree of comparative perspective that attempts to distinguish between what is common and what is unique across such groups.

Portrayed here will be five contemporary communities of very different types, each of which has been studied by an ethnographer as insider/outsider over a long period of time. The five are: (a) a Puerto Rican barrio in New York City; (b) a pre–World War II Japanese fishing community in California and its current nonspatial community; (c) a rural-oriented African American community of the 1970s and its current nonspatially based connections; (d) a community-based youth organization in a high-crime inner-city area; (e) and a community of street youth in a university neighborhood. Taken together, these five do not give a representative picture of all possible types of communities in the final decade of the 20th century. Instead, they focus on groupings shaped in arenas that serve as the source of an increasing proportion of America's public school students. These portrayals offer insider perspectives of subordinated populations—individuals often either ignored or maligned by the public media and public policies, and badly served by the tendency toward aggregate clustering of cultural patterns in current approaches to multicultural education.

El Bloque: Then and Now

In the late 1970s in Manhattan, el bloque, home to 20 Puerto Rican families with school-age children in three five-story tenements abandoned by their landlords, buzzed on warm days with the sounds of children playing happily around open water hydrants, young men alternately washing and lounging on their cars, and women and young children sitting on the steps leading into the mailbox vestibule (see Zentella, 1981, in press). The general pattern of language was Spanish among parents and elders and often to children, and both Spanish and English among the children. Return trips to Puerto Rico, along with frequent visits from relatives, kept both the language and the sense of link to the island alive for young and old through the end of the 1970s.

Eleven of the families were related in some way to one another, but all of el bloque acted like a large family, with members alternately quarreling and caring for each other, lamenting losses together, and celebrating small victories with vigor. Stops at the local bodega, visits to nearby relatives, and occasional church celebrations punctuated the routine of daily life, which was by no means easy. Sickness, disrupted relations between husband and wife, money shortages, alcoholism, and job disappointments seemed to mark every day for someone there. Few teenagers made it through high school; the local high school had been closed down because of disrepair, violence, and failed programs. Adults worried over the educational futures of their children and the loss of blue-collar jobs for themselves; between 1950 and 1980 New York City lost 59% of its apparel and textile industry jobs. In 1985 Puerto Ricans suffered the highest unemployment rate in the city (17.5%). Of all persons below the poverty line in the city, 47.5% were Puerto Ricans, a poverty rate exceeding that of Puerto Rico, which itself fared worse than any state in the United States (Torres, 1989).

Most adults knew more Spanish than English. Those who used English most were those whose employment brought them into contact with English speakers on a daily basis, but the high unemployment rate of Puerto Ricans in the city meant that very few had this opportunity. Children became English dominant within a year of entering school, even in bilingual programs, but most were able to manage both languages, switching back and forth as needed for particular speakers, situations, or discourse strategies.

By the 1990s the close-knit community Zentella had studied a decade earlier showed the bitter effects of unemployment, drug dealing, violence, and social-service failures (Zentella, in press). Much of the sense of guardianship that families once had for each other seemed supplanted by the needs of individuals to protect themselves from the ravages of dislocation, unpredictability, and danger that ripped into their lives with regularity.

The immediate signs of loss of community for el bloque came in the displacement of its people. Most of the girls who had played sidewalk games in the 1970s under the watchful eyes of their mothers and often of fathers, relatives, and a network of older fictive kin, now were raising their own children in their parents' apartments away from the block. Their old tenements had been partially destroyed by fires in the 1980s and were slowly and haphazardly being rebuilt by city and federal authorities. The slow pace of the rebuilding, plus the appearance of unoccupied zones given the neighborhood by construction scaffolding as it cut off entrances to buildings and provided hiding places for drug activities and squatters, helped push oldtime residents to accept relocation elsewhere, usually to large city projects. As the apartments were finished, newcomers—formerly homeless—were moved in from shelters by city officials.

By the early 1990s el bloque was more African American in population than Puerto Rican, and few of the residents had been in their neighbors' apartments. The easy availability in the neighborhood of drugs and alcohol fed domestic violence and what often seemed to be open warfare on buildings and cars. Only 6 of the 20 families that had been there in the 1970s remained; 8 others lived within 12 blocks of the old block and sometimes returned to visit. The others had scattered farther afield or were no longer heard from. Several of their children now had surrogate parents or relatives or lived in foster homes. Some of el bloque's young men were headed for jail, sentenced for armed robbery, drug dealing, or domestic violence. All of the young women continued to live with their parents when they had children, because the children's fathers had unsteady jobs—if they had jobs at all—public housing had a six-year waiting list, private apartments were too expensive, and no one would rent to families on welfare.

Those left on the block or those who remembered it from their childhood lamented its passing and perhaps romanticized its former embracing role:

Una cosa que yo llamo bloque, se sentaba—era coma una familia, no como qente separada. Ahora la gente no se conocen. No se quieren ayudar. La mayoria esta en drogas. Los ninos de todo el mundo era una familia Los ninos eran de todo el mundo. [Something that I call block, it sat—it was like a family, not like separate people. Now people don't know each other. They don't want to help each other. The majority is into drugs. Everybody's children was a family. The children belonged to everybody.] (Zentella, in press)

Scattered as they now are—in domestic units that few would acknowledge to be the same as their ideal of a family and in geographic locations they do not yet acknowledge as their own communities in the ways el bloque was—the former second-generation residents of el bloque see themselves adopting and adapting aspects of other identities, both African American and Anglo.

Socialization patterns—including changes in primary agents and directions of learning—shifted in accordance with the different family living arrangements and patterns of peer friend-ships now available. Many of the young women dress, dance, and sing to the African American styles that surround them, as well as speak with African American vernacular English dialect features. For both lighter- and darker-skinned Puerto Ricans, speaking and acting Black are the natural result of intense con-tact with African Americans in schools and public housing. (See Brady, 1988, and Flores, 1988, for discussions of the doubleness of African American and Puerto Rican cultural traditions merged in Afro-Latin arts; see *Centro de Estudio Puertorri-quenos,* 1992–93, for discussion of the special problems of Puerto Rican youth and their ambivalence with regard to place and culture.) The darker-complexioned often are mistaken for African Americans, and they may identify more closely with that community, especially if they know little Spanish. But when their Spanish surname suggests to newcomers from the Carib-bean that they should speak Spanish, local non-Spanish speak-ers feel they are missing out on something.

Shifts of self-identification among the young follow the lines of both skin color and place of residence. El bloque resi-dents—both light and dark—who have moved or aspire to move to suburban areas populated by Anglos find that speaking English in ways that label them as "acting White" is a kind of self-protection and insurance for slipping into school networks. A few feel that speaking Spanish might hold them and their children back, because they have adopted the idea that only English is a ticket to a better life. They choose to think of their current interests and occupational goals for their children as providing the communal connections they need to help them in the future. This small minority tend to see themselves as Americans or Hispanic Americans.

Most individuals, even those whose behaviors and speech sometimes proclaim their affinity to things African American or Anglo, speak Puerto Rican English, a dialect that identifies them as second-generation native bilinguals. They also profess alle-giance to being Puerto Rican, and see such an identity as distinct from just being "American." In contrast to their elders, how-ever, speaking Spanish is not an indispensable part of "being Puerto Rican" for them; Puerto Rican heritage is enough. The power of English, generational change, and participation in non–Puerto Rican networks have made the pattern of retention of Spanish spotty, and the young are unwilling to exclude from the Puerto Rican family those of their sisters and brothers who do not speak Spanish.

As the mid-1990s approach, el bloque's children of the 1970s have transferred their allegiance from one block to el barrio (East Harlem) in general, and to a redefined New York Rican or Nuyorican identity in particular. Just as their parents had originally defined themselves in relation to a particular barrio in their island hometown and then became more pan–Puerto Rican in el barrio, the second generation is embracing a larger community than the one in which they were raised, but one less island-linked and more pan-Latino in the greater New York context. Both old and young share a uniform collective memory of their earlier life on el bloque "like a family," but now that it is not safe to send children to play in the syringe-filled playgrounds of the projects, they find themselves con-fined to apartments that often house three generations. This

makes the young women more dependent on their mothers than their mothers had been, because in the 1970s their grand-mothers were either in Puerto Rico or deceased. Now they rely on their mothers to care for their children while they look for jobs and schools.

In these efforts they meet other young women whose situa-tions are similar to their own. For example, job-training pro-grams become their extended network for a period of time, while they share common goals and common learning situa-tions. Once out of the program, some of these ties remain, but they tend to be more individual than communal. Ties are often bound to technology. Friends keep their networks alive by tele-phone, preferring to hold to the safety of their own households rather than risk taking the elevators or walking the streets. VCRs bring groups of people together to watch a film at home— more cheaply and safely than at movie houses. Young men were the first to keep in touch through beepers and cellular telephones; theirs is a network that circulates information re-lated to economic entrepreneurship, both legal and under-ground. Now young mothers carry beepers so they can be reached anywhere in case of a child-care emergency. Informa-tion about the latest technology is shared in the extended net-works, as is the equipment itself, along with cars, furniture, and job applications. Families respond to the similarities they see in other families struggling to survive and to make sense of the mismatch between opportunities and their hopes for the fu-ture.

Puerto Ricans in New York and other major metropolitan areas, such as Philadelphia and Chicago, have experienced many of the same expanding and contracting aspects of com-munity life as those described by Zentella (1981, in press). Latino politics, as well as community development efforts and school reform movements, have reinforced a sense of commu-nity cutting across spatial boundaries and residing in common bonds of poverty and family struggles (see, for example, Gon-zalez, 1989; Pantoja, 1989). For some, temporary communal memberships come increasingly through shared hardships and opportunities to protest these to an authority, and through newly gained opportunities to try for new housing, employ-ment, or educational opportunities. For example, neighbors in a city who formerly did not recognize each other as living in the same area create a community around a special purpose— increased safety in an elementary school where an intruder has killed several youngsters with an automatic weapon. School councils and community safety committees work to organize collections of individuals into a communal voice to pressure school boards, precinct leaders, or the mayor's office (Cabal-lero, 1989). These efforts, often led by the more upwardly mo-bile of the neighborhood, provide socialization into literacy, mathematical skills, video production, and a professional man-ner on the telephone for women and men who never found formal schooling or self-teaching sufficient motivation for pick-ing up these new skills. In another instance, the violent death of very young children in a neighborhood ballpark or nearby alley can lead to reform efforts of "community cleanup" that draw formerly reticent women into increasing public advocacy roles. In the 1990s, union groups made up almost exclusively of im-migrant women—whom outsiders formerly believed neither could nor would protest their conditions of work or lack of health benefits—learned in literacy and English as a second language classes that they could speak out about their needs and begin to reshape their unions' thinking.

Terminal Island(ers): Community Constituted, Reconstituted, and Mythologized

Located in San Pedro Bay in southern California, at the beginning of World War II Terminal Island was the residence of Japanese families who made their living primarily by fishing (see Yamashita, 1985). In the 1990s no physical traces exist of the former community, yet the Terminal Islanders Club members come together annually for celebrations and renewals of their connections to a common past. The *issei* (first generation) who immigrated from Japan at the turn of the century have disappeared, and their children, the *nisei* (second generation), are in their 70s, watching the *sansei* (third generation) gradually lose any awareness of the early life of their grandparents and parents on Terminal Island.

Between the turn of the century and World War II, Terminal Island was a microcosm of the Japanese villages left behind by the *issei* immigrants. Age and gender status relations held as they had in Japan. The social structure of families as well as that of the commercial fishing industry divided and distinguished man from woman, young from old, one type of fisherman from another. Though many of the trappings of their community seemed like that of other American communities—an elementary school, church, and several social organizations, including a Boy Scout troop—they remained very much outside or set apart, through their physical isolation on the island and through their strong retention of the habits and beliefs of the prefecture from which most of them had come. On Terminal Island, the mixture of old and new came in inexplicable social alignments: the Boy Scouts, sponsored by the Budhists, met at the Buddhist Hall. Annual Christmas festivities were held in both English and Japanese at the Baptist Mission, where the Japanese Language School also met. Judo training went on at the Shinto Shrine, and the annual Buddhist "Festival of the Dead" took place on the street in front of the Shrine. Beyond the elementary school level, students had to leave the island by the passenger ferry to San Pedro for middle or high school, but almost no friendships formed between Island *nisei* and their mainland counterparts.

By the 1940s language patterns showed some of the same kinds of mixtures. Almost all of the *issei* on Terminal Island knew standard Japanese (*kokugo*), and it was taught in the Japanese Language School. But daily contacts were carried on in *Kii-shu ben*, a dialect marked by informality and English loan words, without the honorifics of standard Japanese. Those who returned to Japan for their education (*Kibei*) and then came back to Terminal Island and used the honorific forms drew derision. Before World War II it was common for *nisei* parents to use Japanese while their children responded to them in English. The children grew up with strong receptive knowledge of Japanese, but were less than fully competent speakers of their parents' mother tongue. The mixture of Japanese and English, with the development of particular vocabulary items, came to have a distinctive form accentuated by the specialized

technical vocabulary related to the fishing industry. Those who returned to Japan as adults found that their form of Japanese learned on Terminal Island was not wholly comprehensible. These features remain in the speech of the Terminal Islanders as part of their sense of group identity. Use of any of these terms or markers of syntax and pronunciation immediately makes a Terminal Islander identifiable as such.

With the outbreak of war in December 1941, it became clear that commercial fishing for the Japanese would end. By February of 1942 all the *issei* fishermen were arrested and evicted, their homes and businesses destroyed and replaced by commercial canning facilities. Most of the Terminal Islanders lived in adjoining blocks in the internment camp at Manzanar. There was little integration with other Japanese for them, and many retained features that marked them as having *shimaguni konjo* ("an island country mentality"). They kept to themselves, excluded as a small enclave within this sea of exclusion and labeled as aggressive, rough, and uncouth.

After the war, some scattered to the East Coast but still remained in touch with those who returned to California. In a curious twist of fate for the *kibei* who had returned to Japan for education before the war, a peculiar vocational contact enabled them to obtain employment with a company in New Jersey and allowed a large number of Terminal Islander families to resettle there together. These individuals had been trained in Japan to be "chick sexers"—to differentiate between roosters and hens just shortly before birth, an important talent in the chicken-raising business. Their skills were in demand and gave them the basis for establishing a subcommunity of their former island. Others who went to New Jersey set up businesses that served those who worked in the chicken business, and still others soon became owners of food markets and other local enterprises to serve their neighbors.

Most, however, returned to California, especially the Long Beach area, where many found work in fish canneries. There they lived in either a trailer camp established as Federal Emergency Housing, in low-cost housing, or in rental units within the area of Long Beach occupied by shipyard and defense-facility workers. The mixture in the poorest sections of town of the Terminal Islanders with others in poverty—Yugoslavian-, Portuguese-, Philippine-, and Mexican-origin families—led to considerable economic competition. The few efforts of the Islanders to take up commercial fishing again were sabotaged by other immigrants who had moved into this occupation during the war. Thus returning Japanese turned to establishing small businesses that contributed goods and services desired by their Japanese neighbors. Others took up gardening and nursery services for the burgeoning Los Angeles residential areas. Many of these businesses have passed from the hands of the original owners to the next generation of Terminal Islanders.

But creating units of organization to sustain the families in their sense of togetherness, now that their physical isolation and common livelihood were gone, came with difficulty. No longer was a Fishermen's Association possible, because no central location for gathering existed; their children were minorities among minorities in the city schools, making celebrations there of New Year's *mochi-tsuki* or Girls Day or Boys Day impossible. Gradually some new units of organization were established: the Japanese church, a Buddhist temple, and the Long Beach Japanese Community Hall, all of which provided gathering places for cultural activities.

By the early 1950s the idea of a Terminal Islander reunion came about through the efforts of some *nisei* who often came together to share their memories of "the good old days." Women and men were enlisted to help locate former Terminal Islanders, and the first reunion was finally held in 1970—at a large Chinese restaurant in Los Angeles. The enthusiasm of this occasion led to the formation of the Terminal Club, which in ensuing years has sponsored the annual New Year's party (*shinnen kai*), summer picnics, and annual events such as golfing tournaments for the males. The activity building at the local California Retirement Home, constructed through funds donated from Terminal Islanders, is dedicated to the club.

Trackton: A Community Connected No More

The residents of Trackton, a working-class community of Black Americans in a rapidly growing town of the Piedmont Carolinas, were ready for the civil rights era and its accompanying proclamations of Black pride (see Heath, 1983, 1990). Textile mills had been the major employer in this region since World War I, competing with agriculture as a primary regional employer. With the lifting of legal restrictions against the employment of Blacks in the mills, and White workers moving out of the mills to what they regarded as more upwardly mobile jobs, Blacks readily took up mill jobs. In the first flush of social services and desegregated education in the 1970s, Black families looked positively on their opportunities for moving up and out of the patterns of poverty and stagnation that had encased their parents and grandparents.

In spite of the availability of public housing, many communities of working-class Blacks preferred to rent the small former mill houses scattered around small communities and in sections of larger towns that often contained several textile mills. Families shared the two-family wooden structures, whose primary identifying features were the wide open front porch and steps that led to the central dirt plaza on which residents parked their cars and children played. While some residents of these communities worked one of the shifts at the mills, others held part-time jobs as domestic laborers, and others stayed at home, "minding" the children of those who worked. Informal hierarchical social structures developed in each of these communities, often with an older male serving as unofficial "mayor," and others falling in line to help maintain social control in the community—over children as well as the adults who occasionally fell into family or neighbor disputes fueled by alcohol. Cars, tools, and household goods were shared with care and caution, each family wary of acquiring too many evident belongings and thereby becoming thought of as chief supplier for the community. Food was the exception, and young and old gave food willingly. And so long as requests did not come too often, return requests or favors were not refused and always seemed to be in balance.

Boys in the community grew up as kings of the plaza, exchanging verbal challenges with adults and older children who taunted and teased them with questions and mock attacks on their toys or games. Preschool girls rarely figured in central roles in the public roughhousing of the boys on the plaza, instead staying close to the women of the household, who spent as much time as possible on the porches. These girls played with dolls or younger siblings, talking with them and engaging in conversation with the porch sitters by the time they themselves were toddlers.

School-age children of both sexes played together often during the primary years, but as adolescence approached each group separated into specialized activities and private opportunities to talk about members of the opposite sex. Opportunities for reading and writing centered around practical matters: going to the store, reading directions for a new item to adorn a bicycle, helping parents decipher messages from school, and joining in the communal reading of letters from relatives who had moved up north. Church life, especially "meeting time" or revivals in August or homecoming weekends, drew community members together, sometimes for all-day occasions of celebration with friends from surrounding rural areas as well as different parts of town. Here men and women, young and old, separated from one another for various parts of the day. The men told stories and discussed local social and political changes in the wake of new local bureaucracies deriving from the legislation of the "Great Society." The women often worked with the choir director to create new musical performances for choir exchange with regional churches during rotating weeks of "meeting" time. Between such tasks and cleaning up the church kitchen after the midday meal, the women talked of changes in schools under desegregation, new public housing regulations and possibilities, and deaths of older community members since the last time they had held such a large church affair.

Twenty years later, the physical groupings of houses of Trackton's community no longer exist, bulldozed in the late 1980s to make room for a highway expansion. But the houses had been abandoned for several years by most of the original families, whose older members had given up their 1960s goal of independent living and gone into public housing. Many of their older children had left the area and others lived in various parts of town, subsisting on welfare and ocassional part-time jobs.

By the early 1980s it was clear that the bottom was falling out of the textile industry in the Piedmont Carolinas. Closure of the mills had been forced by a combination of factors, primary among them foreign competition and the failure of local owners to upgrade equipment to keep pace with regional divisions of textile companies now part of national and multinational conglomerates. Blacks had stayed on in many of the mills until the bitter end, unable in the recession of the time to find jobs elsewhere. When the mills finally closed, most found themselves on welfare rolls for the first time, able to secure only ocassional work in the new motels and fast-food restaurants springing up along the recently constructed interstate highways. Families that had managed to survive together in the 1970s broke apart, and public-housing units increasingly filled with mothers trying to keep their adolescents in school and out of harm's way, while taking on the additional responsibility of caring for infants born to their teenagers. Fathers had often either drifted away from the area or into heavy alcohol use.

Almost all of the Trackton youth who had entered school in the early 1970s dropped out of high school in the mid-1980s. They thereby added to their mothers' financial burdens, as they remained at home, unable to find work or to enter the Armed services or regional vocational programs because they lacked high school diplomas.

The young who moved away to major metropolitan areas generally resided in high-rise apartment units of public housing, among strangers who had also set out from rural areas and small towns of the Southeast without high school diplomas and often with infants (Heath, 1990). The communal base of church life both in the region around Trackton and in inner cities began to erode. Many country churches that had been served by circuit preachers closed for lack of support; inner-city churches were cleared for urban redevelopment or relocated to new areas of town where a rising middle class of African Americans increasingly developed and chose primarily to serve their own needs and not those of inner-city populations.

Suspicion, fear, and despair marked social relations in public-housing units, in place of the shared communal guardianship and social control hierarchy of earlier days. Dealing drugs, buying and selling handguns, stealing cars and car parts, and promoting prostitution came to be occupational choices for the young. Growing numbers of young men ended up in juvenile detention centers or jail, while the mothers of their children were left on welfare in public housing, without either the personal network or the motivational resources and modeling of older family members to inspire them to start again with their education or job seeking. As immigrants with different languages, dress, and backgrounds came to be the norm rather than the exception on the floors or in the buildings of inner-city public housing in the Southeast, ethnic differences periodically flared and subsided, as each group worked out survival strategies. For the young, membership in gangs, often ethnically based, promised affiliations and economic opportunities offered by neither families nor community-building institutions such as churches.

Community became a concept only minimally associated with affective response, and only as an appendage to the names of major public-housing units, such as "Boyd Hill Community" or "Rayland Project Community." Bonding for young people beyond the ages of 8 to 10 was increasingly not to historical traditions and a collective memory of their parents' past, but to the survival strategies and flourishes of dress, symbols, and language that marked gangs. Most of the adolescents who formed male-female bondings and tried to establish households of their own found that their educational and employment failures forced the girl to stay with her mother's household, while the male remained with his mother or stayed on a casual basis with friends. Young mothers alternated between feeling abandoned and bitter and hoping still for the ideal romance of a man who would stay with them and help take care of the children. The primary group bonding became that of "us women"—the young single mothers in high-rise projects who tried to care for their children apart from the family, church, and neighborhood supports of their own childhood.

BEST: A Safe Place in a Danger Zone

BEST is not a community that uses space in expected ways; it is not a region or a group of residences. It is only a couple of buildings located several blocks apart along the streets of an inner-city area infamous for gang-related deaths and local drug-war casualties. The same activities take place in both buildings, and a single administration looks over both. BEST is a community youth center, opened in 1963 as an outreach program of a nearby White church (see Heath & McLaughlin, 1993; Mclaughlin, Irby, & Langman, 1994). Throughout the year, in after-school and summer day programs, BEST serves as community for the youth of the nearby high-risk projects.

The neighborhood of BEST, located in a large midwestern city, provides a counterpart to the more recently built public-housing projects of the Southeast to which some of Trackton's children had gone. The housing projects of BEST's neighborhood were established back in the 1940s and renovated in the 1960s after massive urban unrest had turned their streets into battlegrounds. Here gangs of youth have been power brokers of city neighborhoods since the 1920s, though today's gangs differ considerably because of their links to drug dealing and the intense isolation of youth from older residents of the immediate neighborhood. Unlike the "tough old man" of past gang eras who lived just two apartments down the street, the bosses of "hood" gangs in the 1990s are more likely to be inmates whose communication networks spread across the state and even the nation.

Nearby schools are bullet scarred and have metal detectors at every entry; school personnel try to ban all possible signs of gang membership exhibited by students. Young people learn to walk quickly along the street, careful not to walk too close to a building held by a gang that may not regard them as "homies." Once they reach their own high-rise project buildings, they pass by the local gang members who guard the doors and sometimes use their positions of power to arrange drug deals.

For some children of this neighborhood, leaving school at the end of the day does not mean going home or heading to the streets to gangbang. It means heading for BEST, their home away from home, their surrogate family that provides help with homework, after-school activities, and friends in a safe place shut off from the streets and the projects.

Daily over 100 youngsters between the ages of 8 and 18 go to BEST. For several groups of high schoolers, BEST is their "scholarship" home, a sponsoring agency for cohorts of 20 or so member students who move as a single group through high school as BEST scholars. This special "family within a family" membership avails these young people of a sustaining primary group between ninth grade and high school graduation. The young people go to BEST daily to do homework and projects with their group leader, an adult who has committed to staying with them through their entire "scholar" cycle. Afternoon activities vary: Homework comes first, as older students team up with one or two younger peers, set out their school books, and hear about the week of work and projects ahead. On some days homework takes several hours. On other afternoons the older youngsters can join together in "club" activities in which they work on supplementary projects on African American-, Caribbean-, Puerto Rican-, and Mexican-origin heroes and heroines, with the goal of preparing a hall exhibit. On other days they plan puppet shows, story-telling, and art programs for presentation in the auditorium to their younger peers.

As the dark shadows of evening begin to fall along the streets down from the high-rise projects, the youngsters collect at the door of BEST to walk home in groups. By 6 o'clock the grade school children have left the buildings, but the junior high and high school students head down the street to a restaurant to get a quick dinner, so they can return to BEST by 7 P.M. each evening with a group of local law students and other adults who are their tutors. These sessions involve not only homework of the day or week from their schools, but also preparations for taking standardized tests, and researching scholarships, employment, and career choices. Values clarification, discussion about appropriate times for standard English, and debate over recent police crackdowns in the neighborhood also come up during these evening sessions. On weekends, tutors and BEST teens join in tennis lessons, art classes, mural projects, and an occasional movie.

BEST socializes its young along the lines of traditional family life. Manners, goals, values, speech, work, play, friendships, and current events circulate through the lives of the adults and young people within BEST's halls. BEST also provides the services often expected of communities in affluent suburbs: a safe place to congregate; library resources; reliable adults to offer advice, help, and discipline; recreational equipment, spaces, and program; and opportunities for occasional aesthetic and athletic events. In addition, BEST constantly creates and sustains a collective memory. Its "graduates"—those who have moved out of the community to jobs and higher education—return often to talk with current BEST young people. Photographs, trophies, and newspaper clippings throughout the buildings announce the achievements of those who have preceded the current generation. Many of the staff have been with BEST since its beginning in the fall of 1963, and their stories of the past bring laughter and tears on many of the informal occasions that take place in the halls of BEST.

Young people of BEST talk of their community there in romanticized terms, crediting it with "saving my life," "making me what I am now," "giving me a chance," "protecting me and being there for me," and "being there for me to trust." The institution is thus a combination of personified agent and glorified place. Friendships, sponsorships, disciplined occasions, interdependent living and learning, and motivation to grow and learn in peace mark BEST, just as they mark community in the traditional sense of something more than a building and a set of associations. The common endeavors and shared outlook, firmly but not obtrusively grounded in the Christian fellowship and ethos of the sponsoring church, ensure that daily needs (ranging from shoes to praise) can be met for youngsters. Like many communities, BEST serves as a transition or border zone between the families and households of the young and the outside world of strangers, new opportunities, and different expectations.

Homeless City: A "Kid Community" of the Streets

"Spare change?" "Excuse me, sir, can you spare a quarter for a starving kid?" "Ma'am, how about a few cents, so I don't have to sell my body?" "Could you spare some money, so I can buy milk for my kitten?" Along the streets of University Avenue, a 10-block zone near the State University located in a large Pacific Northwest city, young men and women address passersby with these greetings. Scattered strategically at different corners, in supermarket parking lots, and in doorways of video stores and "counterculture" shops, about two dozen teens are at work panhandling by noon on any given day. For six to eight hours they will shuttle back and forth between their chosen posts, collecting their change to a point where they can enter the muffin shop for a cup of coffee, a stop in the bathroom, and a quick facewash. By 8 P.M. several days of the week they are nowhere to be seen, for all of them have gathered at Teen Feed, occasions for a free hot meal at one of the local churches (see Heath, 1992a, 1992b).

Shortly before the doors of the church educational building open, the young people gather outside on the steps to have a final smoke, for rules of Teen Feed prohibit smoking, drinking, or dealing or taking drugs while in the building. Once the doors open they shuffle into a semblance of a line and move to the trays and along the cafeteria line, where they can pick up their plates of steaming hot spaghetti, garlic bread, salad, jello, and cake. Behind the cafeteria line and scattered among the tables of the auditorium are adults from the church and a few students from the university. "Hey, Mellissa, great color on those fingernails! How'd you get those sequins to stick? Did you get over to the office to see about getting your GED?" Such combinations of compliments, teasing, and nudging flow back and forth, as the young people take their seats at bare wooden tables and begin to eat. They run over their plans with each other, bringing friends up-to-date on recent trials with relationships, their latest contact with their parents, brushes with the law, and music they've heard or movies they've seen. Often they discuss plans for trips to San Francisco or perhaps the Oregon coast. They dream of these trips for months. A few save enough money to catch a bus one day and disappear for a few months. But almost always they return, striding in the door of the church sporting a new haircut or hair color and eager to share their adventures with their old friends.

By 10 P.M. on any evening of Teen Feed, they are out the door of the church building and scattering their separate ways. Some head back to their homes, trying once again for a short while to see whether they can live with their parents. Others know where they will sleep—in a now-familiar doorway of a store along Main Street or with a couple of friends who recently got enough money together to rent a room at the transient hotel. A close look at their knots of friendship illustrates the interests and circumstances that both connect and sometimes scatter them.

For a period of more than four weeks, Susie, Mel, and Jennifer were always together (Heath, 1992a). The three of them shared a "squat," the name the young people have given the abandoned buildings two streets back of Main Street. They had

plans to panhandle, save their money, and rent a room together. Once they had a room, they hoped to find jobs. Susie
and Jen had arrived in town together after meeting on the
streets of a midwestern city. Jen had left home because she
"could not stand" what she regarded as "overbearing parents
who only want to control my life." They had given her a horse
when she was 8 years old, and by the age of 16 she had ridden
her way to numerous ribbons and trophies. But at 16 she was
tired of the endless competition and was no longer sure she
even wanted to go to college. Her parents responded with
higher demands and tighter controls. She decided to run away
with Susie, whom she had met at school. Susie's life fascinated
Jen, for Susie seemed to have had everything Jen lacked in the
way of freedom, choice, and experiences. Susie had left home
at 13 because "nobody cared." Her older sister had been in a
treatment center for cocaine abuse and then in jail, and Susie's
single parent, her mother, always seemed either mentally occupied or physically absent, because she was trying "to do something with your sister." Susie took off, frustrated at "always
trying to be the good kid." She sometimes returned to her
mother's apartment for short stays, but she always left soon:
"My sister was going through a lot of shit, and I was the scapegoat. I tried so hard to take care of everyone. Mom used to say
stuff like, 'I'll be back in a couple of weeks. Call me every day,
and see if I'm back. I've got to take care of your sister.'" When
Jen joined Susie on the street, the two decided to travel. They
settled for a while in University City, a place Susie had visited a
year or so earlier and where she had thought life on the streets
was better than in other cities. The university atmosphere made
people "more giving, smarter, and not so mean."

Soon after the two arrived in University City they met Mel,
who had grown up there. Mel had left home at 14 and had been
on the streets two years when she welcomed Jen and Susie in
and agreed to teach them how to become "a part of our community here." She taught them the best places to panhandle, the
days when unfriendly policemen took their beats, the clerks at
the muffin shop who would sneak day-old muffins to the street
kids, and the restaurants whose waitresses would not yell when
you went in to use the bathroom and just have a cup of coffee.
These learning sessions came in informal talks, primarily
around the dinner table at Teen Feed and on strolls along Main
Street, where strangers would not have distinguished the girls
from their age peers who were sophomores and juniors at the
local high school. Mel introduced them to others of the "street
kid" community, giving them brief biographies of those she
knew best and dropping brief warnings about those she did not
know or had learned not to trust. The girls shared their very
different background stories. Jen and Susie listened to Mel's
stories of physical and mental abuse from her stepfather, remembering the forms abuse took in their own families—highly
restrictive outings, unpredictable support, and verbal ha-
rangues. Susie's sister had told her blood curdling tales of
events that took place when she was just an infant: Her natural
father had chased her mother around the house with a knife to
"drive the demons from her." They asked Mel about her real
father and learned that she had lived with him for three months
when she was 15, but "he kicked me out, 'cause we had differences, and he was an addict." Before she met Susie and Jen,

Mel's best friend had been a big "mutt," Jupiter, that she had
inherited from another street friend who had left the area three
months earlier. Mel coached the newcomers on the guys to stay
away from, the ones who were homosexual or bisexual, those
who had a reputation for liking "kinky sex," and how to get
condoms. For the most part the girls had little private contact
with boys of the community, who tended to hang in small
groups, as did the girls.

For several months the girls were never apart except when
they panhandled, finding it more profitable to operate on different sides of Main Street, about a block apart. They always
entered Teen Feed as a threesome, taking their places in line
with friends and sitting together to discuss their present plans,
recent incidents, and "grapevine" news about friends who had
"moved on" out of the University area. After three months the
threesome gave up their plans to rent a room together, because
"we figure we'll never find a place that would take a dog." Mel
decided to head for San Francisco as soon as she earned "some
extra money to take enough food for Jupiter." Susie found a job
through a local counseling and employment agency recommended by one of the Teen Feed adults and moved to a suburb
of town, where she was going to live in a youth center and work
with a youth coordinator. Jen decided to go back home after
her father found her and pleaded with her to come back and try
again. Susie commented: "You know it's funny about parents.
They can't stand us while we're with them, but as soon as we do
something to prove that we might be able to make something
out of life by ourselves, they just want us back."

For the short time they formed part of the transient community of the University District, the three girls shared everything
from their spare change to the ramshackle abandoned building
where they slept. They made definite plans to provide for each
other and to build a future together. The realities of disparate
needs led them to outgrow each other and to separate. Mel
knew she did not want a job, because she would find it too
confining. Susie wanted a job to prove to her mother and the
world that she could survive on her own. Jen chose to return to
her family and to put in place some lessons she had learned
from slowing her life down.

In spite of media presentations about the violence of the
streets, the "street kids" in University District have created a
"community" life. In place before the arrival and after the departure of individual community members were structures of
organization, rules of territory and exchange of goods, and
patterns of socialization. Teen Feed and the adults and students
there provided information, encouragement, conversation, and
family-like meal times when young and old came together
around "a lot of talk about nothing" (S. B. Heath, 1983). School,
church, police, physicians, and other "typical" ministering
agents of community were largely absent from the lives of these
young. Most had left school around age 14 and depended on
their mature looks and experiences to allay suspicions by
strangers that they were "school-age." They regarded the
church as "a place to eat," and, in fact, many were unaware of
any relationship between church teachings and the service that
members provided them a few nights a week at Teen Feed.
When any of them became sick enough to need a doctor, they
went to the emergency room at the hospital; those who had

families in the area went home and hoped that parents would get them help. They read papers they collected from trashcans, knew which clinics had open days for certain kinds of screenings or tests, and frequently checked the bulletin board of the local youth-counseling and employment center to see if possibilities might convince them to move on.

Each one had learned to be a "street kid," adopting and adapting as best they could certain aspects of idealized features of "family"—promises of mutual caring, some regularity of group meals, and generally regular hours of working and sleeping. They had also chosen to leave behind in their current existence features of home life they had detested: control, demands, abuse, and drugs. They had built bonds of shared exclusion and common dilemmas; they had learned how to find places of acceptance. They had spent lots of time telling stories, planning the next step in their lives, and sharing oral and written sources of information. They took advantage of the abilities of the group to get what they needed; for example, Jen could read better than Mel and Susie, so she helped Susie interpret the forms she had to fill out for her job. Among themselves, and occasionally branching out to ask for advice and help from other young people of the street, they managed access to medical services, travel information, and housing and clothing networks. Though for many their time on the street away from their damaged and damaging families was relatively short— often less than two years—they forged a sense of deep horizontal comradeship with each other and, to some extent, with "street kids" in general (as do children of the streets in cities all over the world; see Boyden, 1991; Webber, 1991). The absence of sustained time with caring adults and lack of models for their own rapid transition from child to adult throw them very much on their own resources and often into the temptation of relieving their pain through drugs. But both for those who manage to leave the streets for good and those who keep returning, there is the bond created by inclusion in being ignored by others. For years beyond their own time on the streets, they connect primarily to peers and to those who have also experienced streets as places to call home.

THE FUTURE OF COMMUNITY

As the end of the 20th century nears, the demographic profile of the United States suggests that communities such as those portrayed here may persist and even proliferate for some decades to come. Their values and realignments of dependencies and interdependencies suggest strongly that the "habits of the heart" of America have moved its citizens away from the realities of traditional spatial community and into new organizational alignments that create bondings more directly and pragmatically than did the loosely aggregated amorphous communities of the past (Bellah et al., 1985). Groups, ranging from professional affiliations to local youth recreational associations, offer protection of one sort or another and socialize their members into patterns of behavior, language use, and value systems that work for the benefit of individual members and, more vaguely, for the benefit of the group as a whole or for a particular cause or enterprise espoused by the group. Locat-

ing community in people's lives requires understanding of the nature and levels of the network of social relations that provides several different normative frameworks simultaneously (Bender, 1978; Milroy, 1992). This network approach examines sets of social relations at work at the same time and sequentially over the life course of an individual, and considers how the coincidence of normative frameworks within an individual's map of social relations amounts to one's ongoing socialization.

The togetherness of the multiple and somewhat unpredictable forms of communities in the next century will be far less spontaneous and, no doubt, considerably less enduring—in both reality and collective memory—than that of communities that dominated through most of the 20th century. Neighborhoods such as el bloque, University City, and the projects that surround BEST and take in former residents of Trackton, incorporate dysfunctional elements of society such as drugs, alcohol, and spousal and child abuse. Individuals in these situations, struggling to meet everyday subsistence needs, have few resources of reform that can bring back into place older bonds based on "little communities" occupying common spatial territory. Therefore, they will no doubt continue to turn to groupings based on needs, communication networks, and selective appeals to common histories and language ties.

Communities have historically served five central functions (Dynes, 1970, p. 84): mutual support, social control, social participation, socialization, and production. Within their provisions of mutual support and social participation, they have met key individual and group needs through interaction, generally assumed to take place on a face-to-face and regular basis. Their socialization and social control functions have ensured not only conformity to certain norms and practices, but also a process of continuation of the information, values, and behaviors of their members through enculturation processes at various points after childhood (Brim & Wheeler, 1966). Their production and distribution functions, though generally linked in the past to food and service, have also increasingly included information and technical services (often linked to further expansion of information and increased communication networks; see Gottschalk, 1975; Scherer, 1972). The array of communities noted here, with the exception of the disrupted community and current collection of individuals of Trackton, all include these key functions. Moreover, the communities described here arose out of crises or critical environmental and socioeconomic changes that thrust on their members and leaders a sense of mutual need, a feeling of loss, and a sense of connection as a way station along the path to improved conditions. In all cases, these communities have only in the past decade come to include individuals of different ethnic groups and language backgrounds. For example, whereas Trackton and el bloque were all Black and all Puerto Rican, respectively, the current neighborhoods of those who used to live in Trackton and el bloque are ethnically mixed. When BEST began, all the young people there were Black, in the 1990s some Puerto Rican children, as well as immigrant youth, became part of the community. University City's street youth include young people from several different ethnic groups; their elder counterparts, who have their special posts along the street for panhandling, also represent several different ethnic backgrounds.

What do these nontraditional and ethnically mixed communities mean for education and for the late 20th-century movement in the name of "multiculturalism"? The usual answer might be that multicultural education will bring the separate cultures that have always made up the United States population into consideration in the content of classrooms, allowing students to learn about groups other than their own and thereby grow to appreciate them. But such an answer does not adequately take into account the conditions of variety among communities today.

The ethnographic cases here reflect structural and behavioral features of communities from which an increasing percentage of American students will come in the next century. Their diversity is not that usually associated with portrayals in education of "multicultural diversity," but rather comes in diversity of access to mainstream institutions, stable predictable home lives, daily language uses and calls for particular identities, and resources on which to fall back in times of family crisis incited by poverty, illness, and random violence. Many of today's young do not see their community or their identity as that of a single ethnic group, place, or family; instead they pick and choose, change and reshape their affiliations of primary socialization. Multicultural education will be hopelessly caught in cultural lag if it tries to plead for the dignity of cultural differences and respect merely through repeated portrayals of individuals of color who have conquered their oppressive backgrounds to contribute to mainstream society, or in capsule histories of the immigration patterns of certain nationalities. Discussions of African American, Hispanic, Latino, Asian American, or Pacific cultures that present all members of each of these groups as homogeneous and securely locked within the membranes of their ethnic membership and identity as "a community" also reflect an inability to stay in touch with the out-of-school socialization networks of today's youth. Multicultural education must go considerably further than the introduction of new content into literature, social studies, and art and music classes. The history of groups taught under the rubric of "multicultural education" must not present all the struggles as those of the past, with no concurrent attention to recent and contemporary regional, economic, and social stresses and strains carrying strong influence on institutions such as families, communities, community organizations (such as gangs and other youth groups), and occupations.

The term *multicultural* is, more often than not, a collective category for "others"—those outside the perceived mainstream of ethnic background (northern European and British Isles) and Caucasian racial membership. Implicit within such a category is the notion that all those that are multicultural are non-White, defined for what they are *not* rather than for what they are. That which is White and mainstream remains very much the norm against which such projections are made. To speak of "ethnic communities" or even of "multicultural" communities is to perpetuate myths that such communities are, on the one hand, homogeneous across classes, regions, and histories of immigration, or, on the other hand, to suggest that there is homogeneity of culture, language, and socialization within local communities. Yamashita's work (1985) and that of Zentella (1981, in press) make it abundantly clear that such is not

the case, even among individuals who identify themselves as Japanese or Puerto Rican. Numerous other studies of individuals in transition and of communities responding—as those included here did—to social and economic crises and drastic shifts in conditions (Barton, 1969; Dynes, 1970; Erickson, 1976) echo the need to ensure that "multicultural education" not become a consolidating mechanism.

In such a view of education, "others" are categorized together, stripped of their variations and individual differences, and uniformly pictured as victimized and dependent on the White "majority" to come to their aid or provide their models for the future. Preferential endogamy—or choosing to marry within one's own group—as a trend toward continuity (Schermerhorn, 1978, p. xiv) cannot be assumed of all individuals or groups. More and more individuals will be of "mixed" cultures, ethnicities, and identities, and will learn to declare themselves of one or another ethnic group according to current rewards for such declarations. For example, during the 1980s the San Francisco Unified School District learned that parents and high schoolers were shifting their self-assignments of ethnic labels in order to help their argument for entry into magnet schools. The District ruled that an individual could change his or her identity only once every three years. The U.S. Bureau of the Census, national survey organizations, and local school districts present choices of ethnic identity as though they were clear-cut and permanently set along racial and group affiliations; for example, students in state colleges often have to tag themselves as "non-Hispanic White" or "non-Hispanic Black" (Brady, 1988). The offspring of families that include several ethnicities increasingly find themselves negotiating their language, dress, manners, and announcements of affiliation on a regular situational basis in job interviews, arrangements with social service agencies, and dealings with school personnel. For example, the offspring of a Jewish father from eastern Europe and a mother from Mexico may find that she can "prove" her Hispanic identity on school forms only by using her mother's maiden name as her own rather than her legal name—that of her father. Increased intermarriage and geographic mobility mean that the biological bases, cultural values, and communication patterns of ethnic groups (Barth, 1969) can no longer be counted on to create and sustain community. (For discussion of the transformation of identity among White Americans, see Alba, 1990.)

Future research must continue to integrate paradigms, bringing together census data (Farmer, Luloff, Ilvento, & Dixon, 1992), literary and historical representations, and participation observation (Bender, 1978). These must be long-term accounts that draw in every way possible from the knowledge gained by the long-term insider-outsider perspectives of anthropologists, descendants of earlier communities, and individuals who claim several communities of origin through intermarriage, acculturation, and biculturalism (E. Anderson, 1990; Driben, 1985; Yamashita, 1985). Moreover, community studies must increasingly explore the socialization powers of short-term communities, such as refugee camps (Long, 1993), drug-dealing affiliations (Adler, 1985; Agar, 1973), and communities of purposeful intent and endeavor (such as science-fiction readers and writers) linked by distance technologies (Laffler, forthcoming). Community studies can no longer take historical identities as given; researchers must attend much more to ways that groups and institutions create alternative historical identities for themselves (Dorst, 1989).

As the 20th century ends, more than one quarter of the nation's youngsters are at "serious risk" of never reaching maturity; another one quarter are at moderate risk of leading unproductive lives to the detriment of themselves and others (Dryfoos, 1990; Schorr, 1988). Many of the reasons for this state of affairs among the young of America lie within policies dominated by idealized images of community, family, school, and ethnic homogeneity. Policies and promises have tended to focus on those things the public would like to believe have gone unchanged, and to ignore those that have changed (Wilkinson,

1986). In addition, this reductionism can continue to hide the power of institutions and downplay their possibilities for both benefit and harm (Bellah et al., 1991).

The young of the projected majority of "minorities" entering the workforce at the opening of the 21st century can meet their own potential and the needs of society only if education, health, employment, and housing policies take into account contemporary diversities of communities. Myths, ideals, and dependencies on old social structures and their roles have to shift so that policy makers and contemporary institutions can provide contexts and conditions of learning that will be relevant to the present realities of American communities and facilitate their productive, positive futures.

References

Adler, P. A. (1985). *Wheeling and dealing: An ethnography of an upper-level drug dealing and smuggling community.* New York: Columbia University Press.

Agar, M. (1973). *Ripping and running: A formal ethnography of urban heroin addicts.* New York: Seminar Press.

Alba, R. D. (1990). *Ethnic identity: The transformation of white America.* New Haven, CT: Yale University Press.

Anderson, B. (1983). *Imagined communities: Reflections on the origin and spread of nationalism.* London: Verso.

Anderson, E. (1990). *Street Wise: Race, class, and change in an urban community.* Chicago: University of Chicago Press.

Arensberg, C. (1961). The community as object and as sample. *American Anthropologist, 63,* 241–264.

Barth, F. (Ed.). (1969). *Ethnic groups and boundaries.* Boston: Little, Brown.

Barton, A. H. (1969). *Communities in disaster: A sociological analysis of collective stress behavior.* Garden City, NY: Doubleday.

Becker, H. (1976). *Boys in white: Student culture in medical school.* New York: Transaction Books. (Originally published 1961)

Bellah, R. N., Madsen, R., Sullivan, W. M., Swidler, A., & Tipton, S. M. (1985). *Habits of the heart: Individualism and commitment in American Life.* Berkeley: University of California Press.

Bellah, R. N., Madsen, R., Sullivan, W. M., Swidler, A., & Tipton, S. M. (1991). *The good society.* New York: Alfred A. Knopf.

Bender, T. (1978). *Community and social change in America.* New Brunswick, NJ: Rutgers University Press.

Blackwell, J. (1984). *The black community: Diversity and unity.* New York: Harper & Row.

Boyden, J. (1991). *Children of the cities.* London: Zed Books.

Brady, V. (1988). Black Hispanics: The ties that bind. *Centro, 2*(3), 44–47.

Brim, O. G., & Wheeler, S. (1966). *Socialization after childhood: Two essays.* New York: Wiley.

Caballero, D. (1989). School board elections: Parents against the odds. *Centro, 2*(5), 86–94.

Camarillo, A. (1979). *Chicanos in a changing society: From Mexican pueblos to American barrios in Santa Barbara and Southern California, 1848–1930.* Cambridge, MA: Harvard University Press.

Centro de Estudio Puertorriquenos. (1999–93, Winter). Entire volume.

Communities, Journal of Cooperation. (1992, Fall). 79 [Entire issue].

Dorst, J. D. (1989). *The written suburb: An American site, an ethnographic dilemma.* Philadelphia: University of Pennsylvania Press.

Drake, S. C., & Cayton, H. R. (1962). *Black metropolis: A study of Negro life in a northern city.* New York: Harper Torchbooks. (Originally published 1945)

Driben, P. (1985). *We are Metis: The ethnography of a halfbreed community in Northern Alberta.* New York: AMS Press.

Dryfoos, J. G. (1990). *Adolescents at risk.* New York: Oxford University Press.

Dubois, W. E. B. (1899). *The Philadelphia Negro: A social study.* Philadelphia: University of Pennsylvania Press.

Durkheim, E. (1933). *The division of labor in society.* Glencoe, IL: The Free Press.

Dynes, R. R. (1970). *Organized behavior in disaster.* Lexington, MA: Heath Lexington Books.

Edwards, G. F. (1959). *The Negro professional class.* New York: The Free Press.

Erickson, K. T. (1976). *Everything in its path.* New York: Simon & Schuster.

Farmer, F. L., Luloff, A. E., Ilvento, T. W., & Dixon, B. L. (1992). Rural community studies and secondary data: Aggregation revisited. *Journal of the Community Development Society, 23*(1), 57–70.

Fishman, J. A. (1966). *Language loyalty in the United States.* The Hague: Mouton & Co.

Flores, J. (1988). Rappin', writin', & breakin'. *Centro, 2*(3), 34–41.

Frazier, E. F. (1947). *The Negro in the United States.* New York: Macmillan.

Frazier, E. F. (1957). *Black Bourgeoisie.* Glencoe, IL: The Free Press.

Gallaher, A., & Padfield, H. (1980). *The dying community.* Albuquerque, NM: University of New Mexico Press.

Gatewood, W. B. (1990). *Aristocrats of color: The Black elite, 1880–1920.* Bloomington: Indiana University Press.

Gilman, G. (1956). *Human relations in the industrial Southeast.* Chapel Hill: University of North Carolina Press.

Gonzalez, N. (1989). Latino politics in Chicago. *Centro, 2*(5), 46–57.

Gottschalk, S. S. (1975). *Communities and alternatives: An exploration of the limits of planning.* New York: Wiley.

Gusfield, J. R. (1975). *Community: A critical response.* Oxford, England: Basil Blackwell.

Hagedorn, J. M. (1988). *People and folks: Gangs, crime and the underclass in a rustbelt city.* Chicago: Lake View Press.

Hall, J. D., Leloudis, J., Korstad, R., Murphy, M., Jones, L. A., & Daly, C. B. (1987). *Like a family: The making of a southern cotton mill world.* Chapel Hill: University of North Carolina Press.

Hannerz, U. (1969). *Soulside: Inquiries into ghetto culture and community*. New York: Columbia University Press.

Hareven, T. K., & Langenbach, R. (1978). *Amoskeag: Life and work in an American factory-city*. New York: Pantheon Press.

Heath, S. B. (1983). *Ways with words: Language, Life, and work in communities and classrooms*. Cambridge, England: Cambridge University Press.

Heath, S. B. (1990). The children of Trackton's children: Spoken and written language in social change. In J. E. Stigler, R. A. Shweder, & G. Herdt (Eds.), *Cultural psychology: Essays on comparative human development* (pp. 496–519). Cambridge, England: Cambridge University Press.

Heath, S. B. (1992a, November 13). How can we help homeless teens in U district? *Daily of the University of Washington*, p. 9.

Heath, S. B. (1992b). *Street youth of Seattle*. Seattle, WA: University Street Ministry.

Heath, S. B., & McLaughlin, M. W. (Eds.). (1993). *Identity and inner-city youth: Beyond ethnicity and gender*. New York: Teachers College Press.

Kilbride, P. L., Goodale, J. C., & Ameisen, E. R. (1990). *Encounters with American ethnic cultures*. Tuscaloosa: University of Alabama Press.

Kreiger, S. (1983). *The mirror dance: Identity in a women's community*. Philadelphia: Temple University Press.

Laffler, J. (forthcoming). *The science fiction community of readers and writers*. Doctoral dissertation, Stanford University, Stanford, CA.

Lewis, H. (1955). *Blackways of Kent*. Chapel Hill: University of North Carolina Press.

Lewis, O. (1951). *Life in a Mexican village: Tepoztlan restudied*. Urbana: University of Illinois Press.

Long, L. D. (1993). *Ban Vinai: The refugee camp*. New York: Columbia University Press.

Lynd, R. S., & Lynd, H. M. (1929). *Middletown*. New York: Columbia University Press.

McLaughlin, M. W., Irby, M. A., & Langman, J. (1994). *Urban sanctuaries: Neighborhood organizations in the lives and futures of inner-city youth*. San Francisco: Jossey Bass.

Milroy, J. (1992). *Linguistic variation & change*. Oxford, England: Basil Blackwell.

Moore, J. W. (1991). *Going down to the barrio: Homeboys and homegirls in change*. Philadelphia: Temple University Press.

Moore, J. W., & Pinderhughes, R. (1993). *Latinos and the underclass debate: Latino communities in the United States*. New York: Russell Sage Foundation.

Morland, J. K. (1958). *Millways of Kent*. Chapel Hill: University of North Carolina Press.

Myrdal, G. (1944). *An American dilemma: The Negro problem and modern democracy*. New York: Harper.

Padilla, F. M. (1987). *Puerto Rican Chicago*. Notre Dame, IN: University of Notre Dame Press.

Padilla, F. M. (1992). *The gang as an American enterprise*. New Brunswick, NJ: Rutgers University Press.

Pantoja, A. (1989). Puerto Ricans in New York: A historical and community development perspective. *Centro, 2*(5), 20–31.

Powdermaker, H. (1950). *Hollywood: The dream factory*. New York: Columbia University Press.

Redfield, R. (1941). *The folk culture of Yucatan*. Chicago: University of Chicago Press.

Redfield, R. (1960). *The Little community*. Stanford, CA: Stanford University Press. (Originally published 1956)

Riesman, D. (1950). *The lonely crowd*. New Haven, CT: Yale University Press.

Rodriguez, L. J. (1993). *Always running: La vida loca—Gang days in L.A*. Willimantic, CT: Curbstone Press.

Salaman, G. (1974). *Community and occupation*. Cambridge, England: Cambridge University Press.

Scherer, J. (1972). *Contemporary community: Sociological illusion or reality?* London: Tavistock.

Schermerhorn, R. A. (1978). *Comparative ethnic relations*. Chicago: University of Chicago Press.

Schorr, L. B. (1988). *Within our reach*. Garden City, NY: Anchor Press/Doubleday.

Stack, C. B. (1974). *All our kin: Strategies for survival in a Black community*. New York: Harper & Row.

Steiner, S. (1969). *La Raza: The Mexican Americans*. New York: Harper & Row.

Thrasher, F. (1927). *The gang*. Chicago: University of Chicago Press.

Toennies, F. (1963). *Community and society*. New York: Praeger. (Originally published 1887)

Torres, A. (1989). New York in the year 2000: A sober assessment. *Centro, 2*(6), 48–54.

Vigil, J. D. (1993). Gangs, social control, and ethnicity: Ways to redirect. In S. B. Heath & M. W. McLaughlin (Eds.), *Identity and inner-city youth: Beyond ethnicity and gender* (pp. 94–120). New York: Teachers College Press.

Wallace, A. F. C. (1970). *The death and rebirth of the Seneca*. New York: Alfred A. Knopf.

Wallace, A. F. C. (1978). *Rockdale: The growth of an American village in the early industrial revolution*. New York: Alfred A. Knopf.

Warren, R. (1978). *The community in America*. Chicago: Rand McNally.

Webber, M. (1991). *Street kids: The tragedy of Canada's runaways*. Toronto: University of Toronto Press.

West, J. (1945). *Plainfield*. New York: Columbia University Press.

Whyte, W. F. (1943). *Street corner society*. Chicago: University of Chicago Press.

Wilkinson, K. P. (1986). In search of the community in the changing countryside. *Rural Sociology, 51*(1), 1–18.

Wilson, W. J. (1987). *The truly disadvantaged*. Chicago: University of Chicago Press.

Yamashita K. S. (1985). *Terminal Island: Ethnography of an ethnic community: Its dissolution and reorganization to a non-spatial community*. Dissertation, University of California, Irvine.

Zentella, A. C. (1981). *Hablamos los dos: Bilingualism in el bloque*. Unpublished doctoral dissertation, University of Pennsylvania, University Park.

Zentella, A. C. (in press). *Hablamos los dos: Language use and community life*. New York: Basil Blackwell.

8

ETHNOGRAPHIC STUDIES OF MULTICULTURAL EDUCATION IN CLASSROOMS AND SCHOOLS

Hugh Mehan
UNIVERSITY OF CALIFORNIA, SAN DIEGO

Dina Okamoto
UNIVERSITY OF ARIZONA

Angela Lintz
UNIVERSITY OF CALIFORNIA, SAN DIEGO

John S. Wills
UNIVERSITY OF CALIFORNIA, SAN DIEGO

This chapter reviews ethnographic studies of multicultural education in the classroom and the school. We emphasize those studies that have made self-conscious attempts to be culturally inclusive by modifying classroom organization, discourse patterns, or the curriculum. Space limitations and the focus of this chapter mean, unfortunately, that other research cannot be included. Of necessity, we have omitted studies of desegregation (e.g., Hanna, 1982; Metz, 1980, 1986; Peshkin, 1991; Rist, 1979; Schofield, 1982; Wagner, 1969) and ethnographies of urban schools (e.g., Fine, 1991; O'Conner, 1992; Ogbu, 1974; Weis, 1985, 1990).

The chapter is organized into three parts. In the first part we examine the educational and social consequences of attempts to achieve multicultural education by modifying classroom discourse patterns and participation structures. In the second part we examine what happens when the manifest content of the instructional curriculum is modified in order to (a) teach a multicultural history so that students will gain an understanding of the experiences of different groups, and (b) foster ethnoracial identity. In the third part we draw the implications of these studies for classrooms composed of students from many different linguistic and cultural backgrounds.

THE CONSEQUENCES OF MODIFYING CLASSROOM DISCOURSE

The language teachers use with students is constitutive. The way in which teachers ask questions and engage in discourse with students both constrains and enables the ways in which they can display what they know. Because of the cooccurrence relationships that operate in conversation, what students can say in lessons depends on the frames established by what teachers say, the questions they ask.

The "recitation script" (Tharp & Gallimore, 1988) is the prevailing way in which lessons are organized in U.S. classrooms. While everyday conversations are organized in two-part sequences (Sacks, Schegloff, & Jefferson, 1974), classroom lessons are organized in three-part sequences: a teacher's initiation act induces a student's reply, which in turn invokes a teacher's evaluation (Mehan, 1979). This three-part I-R-E structure exists because teachers often ask "known information questions" (Mehan, 1979; Shuy & Griffin, 1978; Sinclair & Coulthard, 1975) in which students' knowledge is tested rather than new information sought from them. Recitation lessons, therefore,

The authors wish to thank James A. Banks, Frederick Erickson, and Peter McLaren for their helpful suggestions on the first draft of this chapter.

The contribution of Hugh Mehan to this chapter was supported by the Linguistic Minority Research Institute of the University of California and OERI; the contribution of Angela Lintz and Dina Okamoto was supported by the Girard Foundation; the contribution of John Wills was supported by the Spencer Foundation.

are teacher centered and require students to respond, often individually, with student behavior evaluated quite publicly. Such lessons create a highly competitive classroom interaction situation.

Discontinuity Between the Language of the Home and the School

Students of language use in homes and schools (Cazden, 1988; Heath, 1982, 1986; Laosa, 1973; Mehan, 1979; Philips, 1982; Schultz, Florio, & Erickson, 1982) have suggested that recitation-type lessons in school may be compatible with the discourse patterns in Anglo families but may be incompatible with the discourse patterns of certain minority group families. This discontinuity, in turn, may contribute to the lower achievement and higher drop-out rate among minority students.

In the hallmark study in this tradition, Philips (1982) found that Native American children performed very poorly in classroom contexts that demanded individualized performance and emphasized competition among peers, but performed more effectively in classroom contexts that minimized the obligation of individual students to perform in public contexts. The classroom contexts in which Native American students operated best were similar in organization to local Native American community contexts, where *cooperation* and not *competition* was valued, and *sociality* and not *individuality* was emphasized. Philips attributes the generally poor performance of Native American children to differences in the "structures of participation" normatively demanded in the home and in the school. It seems that the patterns of participation normally expected in conventional classrooms create conditions that are unfamiliar and threatening to most Native American children.

Erickson and Mohatt (1982) showed that an Athabaskan Indian teacher taught Athabaskan Indian children differently than did a Canadian teacher in the same school. The Indian teacher's manner of exercising control over the classroom focused on groups; she dispensed praise in public, criticism in private, and allocated turns so that students were not obligated to participate as individuals but could choose to join in group answers to questions. More interesting than the congruence between the cultural style of this Native teacher and her Native students is the fact that the Canadian teacher began to modify his teaching practices in the direction of his students' culture. His Indian students informally socialized him to use more group-based instruction, facilitate more voluntary contributions, and keep evaluations private as they worked together through time (cf. Barnhardt, 1982).

McCullum (1989) makes a similar point about the cultural congruity of a Puerto Rican teacher's turn-allocation practices with her Puerto Rican students. While an English-speaking teacher of Puerto Rican students in Chicago allocated turns competitively and individually—in ways that conform precisely to the recitation script—a Spanish-speaking teacher of Puerto Rican students in Puerto Rico deployed turn-allocation strategies that were group oriented and permitted students to volunteer answers. McCullum suggests that the language patterns used in the Puerto Rican classroom signaled a social relationship between teacher and students that was closer to an "instructional conversation" (Tharp & Gallimore, 1988) than a rec-

itation lesson. And this instructional conversation was more consistent with the conversational patterns in everyday Puerto Rican life.

Heath (1982) compared the way White middle-income teachers talked to their Black low-income elementary school students in the classroom with the way these teachers talked to their own children at home in a community she calls "Trackton." Like Cazden (1979), she found that the teachers relied heavily on questions and language games like "Peekaboo" and "Riddles" when they talked to their children at home. The most frequent form of question was the "known information" variety so often identified with classroom discourse. Middle-income parents also talked often to preverbal children, suppling the surrounding context and hypothetical answers to questions they posed. These "quasi conversations" recapitulated the I-R-E sequence of traditional classroom lessons.

Heath (1982) reports that the children of the middle-income teachers were being taught to label and name objects and to talk about things out of context, which were just the skills demanded of students in school. These same teachers talked to the students in their classrooms in ways that were very similar to the ways in which they talked to their own children at home. They instructed students primarily through an interrogative format using "known information questions," and taught students to label objects and identify the features of things.

However, this mode of language use and language socialization was not prevalent in the homes of low-income students. Low-income adults seldom addressed questions to their school-age children at home, and even less often to preverbal children. Where Trackton teachers would use questions, Trackton parents would use statements or imperatives. And when questions were asked of Trackton children by their parents, they were much different from the types of questions asked by teachers. Questions at home called for nonspecific comparisons or analogies as answers. They were not the known information or information-seeking questions associated with the classroom. Heath (1982) concludes that the language used in Trackton homes did not prepare children to cope with the major characteristics of the language used in classrooms: utterances that were interrogative in form but directive in pragmatic function, known information questions, and questions that asked for information from books.

Modifying Classroom Discourse for Cultural Compatibility

These observations regarding home-school discontinuity spurred attempts to rearrange classroom discourse for compatibility with home-based discourse. When the discourse structure of the classroom corresponds to the discourse pattern of the low-income home, students' academic performance improves.

Piestrup (1973) documented the positive benefits of this compatible relationship in 14 predominantly African American first-grade classrooms in the Oakland Public School System. When teachers employed a style that reflected the taken-for-granted speech patterns of the African American community, instruction was the most effective. Students in classrooms where teachers implicitly incorporated the taken-for-granted features of culturally familiar speech events in classrooms, including rhythmic language, rapid intonation, repetition, alliteration, call and response, variation in pace, and creative language play, scored significantly higher on standardized reading tests than students in classrooms where teachers used other styles.

According to Foster (1989), Marva Collins, the well-known teacher from Chicago's Westside Prep School, employed strategies similar to those of the successful teachers in Piestrup's (1973) study. While Collins attributes her own success to a phonics curriculum, Foster gives more credit to the congruence between her interactional style and the children's cultural experience. Familiar language and participation structures, including rhythmic language, call and response, repetition, and deliberate body motions, comprise the interactional pattern.

Foster (1989) complemented her informal discussion of Collins's teaching with a more formal analysis of teachers in a predominantly African American community college. She found that classroom discussion increased in degree and intensity when teacher-student interaction was more symmetrical (teachers and students had equivalent numbers of turns) and cooperative learning groups were formed. This finding parallels a more general one about the value of cooperative learning for linguistic minority youth (Duran & Szymanski, 1992; Gumperz & Field, 1992; Kagan, 1986; Slavin, chapter 35 of this *Handbook*). Successful community college teachers also called for active vocal audience responses and descriptions of personal experiences, strategies that act in ways that model performance patterns in the local African American community.

In order to increase Trackton students' verbal skills in naming objects, identifying their characteristics, providing descriptions out of context, and responding to known information questions, Heath (1982) worked with the Trackton teachers on ways to adapt to the community's ways of asking questions. After reviewing tapes with researchers, teachers began social studies lessons with questions that ask for personal experiences and analogic responses, such as "What's happening there?" "Have you ever been there?" "What's this like?" These questions were similar to the questions that parents asked their children at home. Their use in early stages of instruction was productive in generating active responses from previously passive and "nonverbal" Trackton students. Once the teachers increased the students' participation in lessons using home questioning styles, they were able to move them through a zone of learning toward school-based questioning styles (cf. D. Taylor & Dorsey-Grimes, 1988).

In an analogous fashion, teachers working with the Kamehameha Early Education Program (KEEP) spontaneously introduced narratives jointly produced by the children into the beginning of reading lessons—a detail later observed by researchers associated with the project (Au, 1980; Tharp & Gallimore, 1988). In addition, they shifted the focus of instruction from decoding to comprehension, implemented small-group instruction to encourage cooperation, and included children's experiences as part of the discussion of reading materials. All of these modifications were consistent with Hawaiian cultural norms and had significant consequences. Student participation

in lessons increased and their scores on standardized tests improved. Both of these effects were notable because they contravened the notoriously low school performance of Native Hawaiians.

Moll and his colleagues (Moll, Vélez-Ibáñez, & Greenberg, 1988, 1989; see also Moll & Díaz, 1987; Díaz, Moll, & Mehan, 1986) have systematized the use of ethnographic techniques to exploit the social and cultural practices of the community for instructional purposes in the classroom. Employing a collaborative approach to research, teachers and researchers first work together to learn about the demographic and economic patterns, the social networks and the social knowledge that exist in households and neighborhoods within the local community. Then teachers mobilize the information they acquire for instructional purposes.

Moll et al. (1989) relate a provocative example in which a sixth-grade teacher incorporated information about construction gleaned from the local barrio to enliven literacy instruction. After students were sent to the library in the usual fashion to gather and read books on constructing houses and other buildings, the teacher invited members of the local community (some of whom were the parents of the students) to share their knowledge about building. A mason told the students how to mix mortar, measure straight lines, and stack bricks neatly and strongly. A carpenter told about the relative strength of brick and wood, and about sawing and nailing techniques. Students applied this knowledge to a model they built in their classroom. Analysis of the students' writing during and after the model building showed that the students incidentally acquired new vocabulary (joists, ridge hangers, waffle boards), wrote eloquently about the skills involved in the building trades, and, perhaps most important, developed an appreciation for their parents' "funds of knowledge." The students were surprised and pleased that the school would validate their parents' skills and experience, even though they did not have formal education.

This study has wider implications. It helps redefine the Latino family for educators, researchers, and the public. Educational activities such as these demonstrate that the households and neighborhoods of even the poorest families are not devoid of knowledge and are not disorganized. Economically poor conditions do not create culturally poor conditions. Rural and urban poor Latino families are connected to extensive social networks that provide different forms of economic assistance and labor cooperation that help families avoid the cost of plumbers, car mechanics, even physicians. These social networks also provide emotional and service support in the form of child care, job information, and "connections." While educators are correct when they say they are strapped for material resources in the classroom, they can learn from Moll and his colleagues that even the poorest neighborhood is rich in cultural resources that can connect the classroom to the world.

By modifying classroom discourse to emphasize inquiry and information-seeking questions, McCarty, Wallace, Lynch, and Benally (1991) help dispel the myth of the nonverbal Indian student, and in the process challenge the concept of learning styles. For decades Native American students have been portrayed in the literature as quiet, passive, nonresponsive (John,

1972). They have been said to learn by observing and doing, not through listening and saying (More, 1989; Tharp, 1989). Often in the name of cultural compatibility, educators have emphasized nonverbal means of instruction and cue-response scripted drills as a way to reach passive Indian students. McCarty et al. say that these erstwhile attempts have had an unfortunate side effect. Indian students are not taught with higher-order questioning and inquiry methods.

Working with the Navajo-staffed Native American Materials Development Center, staff members of the Rough Rock Indian reservation school implemented an inquiry-based bilingual social studies program. In the first lesson the teacher-demonstrator showed students local scenes and asked them to identify things needed in their community. After accumulating a long list, students were asked to group like items and justify their choices. Eventually they reached a consensus, identifying things needed and things they'd like to have. That consensus led to the lesson generalization: "Rough Rock is a community because people work together to meet their needs and solve mutual problems" (McCarty et al., 1991, p. 57).

The lessons in "Navajo Humanities" suggest that Navajo students will indeed respond enthusiastically to inquiry-based questioning. What made these lessons work? McCarty and his coauthors (1991) suggest that this curriculum was effective because it encouraged students to draw upon their prior knowledge to solve new problems. The materials presented familiar scenes and the teachers' questions tapped students' knowledge and experience. When the classroom environment was changed, Navajo children became verbal, assertive, and able to make innovative generalizations.

In addition to illustrating that Native American children will respond to inquiry-based instruction when it is grounded in the experiences of their everyday life, this study shows us the limitations of the cognitive styles concept. Native American and other minority children may in fact appear to be nonverbal when classroom discourse patterns limit their expression, but if the expression of students' ideas is sought, if aspects of students' life are meaningfully incorporated into curricular content, and if students are encouraged to use their cultural and linguistic knowledge to solve new problems, then Native American students will respond eagerly and verbally to questioning. This validates the observation by Cole and Scribner (1974) that cognitive differences reside more in the situations in which particular cognitive processes are applied than in the existence of a process in a cultural group and its absence in another.

Organizing classroom discourse around inquiry has produced similar results with Haitian students. Current research in the sociology of science (e.g., Knorr-Cetina & Mulkay, 1983; Latour & Woolgar, 1986) suggests that scientists do their work within a community of practice. They transform their observations into findings through interpretation and argumentation, and not simply through measurement and discovery. While scientists may claim that they discover facts passively, close observation of their practice reveals they construct findings actively. While textbooks depict the scientific *method* as orderly, logical, and rational, sociological studies show that scientific *practice* entails making sense out of contradictory observations, choosing among competing hypotheses, and convincing others about the importance of findings.

Researchers from the Technical Educational Research Center (TERC) explored this idea that scientific understanding is shaped by a community through scientific argument, rather than received from authority, with a class of seventh- and eighth-grade Haitian students in Cambridge, Massachusetts (Roseberry, Warren, & Conant, 1992). The "Water Taste Test" was designed to investigate the "truth" of a belief held by most of the junior high school students that the water from the fountain on the third floor was superior to the water from the other fountains in the school (in part because "all the little kids slobber" in the first-floor fountain). First, the students designed and then took a blind-taste test of water from several fountains. They were surprised when two thirds chose the water from the first-floor fountain even though they said they preferred the third-floor fountain. Next, they extended their study to include a wider sample of students from other classes. They discussed methodological issues of sampling, masking the identity of the water, and ways to overcome bias in voting. When the class analyzed their data they found that 88% of the junior high school students thought they preferred water from the third-floor fountain, but 55% actually chose water from the first floor. In order to interpret their findings, the students analyzed the school's water. They discovered that the water from the first-floor fountain was 20 degrees colder than that from the other fountains (and theorized that the water was cooled by underground pipes and warmed as it flowed to the third floor). Therefore, they concluded that temperature was probably a deciding factor in students' preferences.

This sense-making approach to science with language minority students is a radical departure from the textbook memorizing or even experimental demonstrations found in most classrooms. Here we see students constructing scientific understandings through an iterative process of theory building, hypothesis testing, and data collection. These students posed their own questions, generated their own hypotheses, and analyzed their own data. This activity facilitated students' appreciation of responses that were different from their own, which Vygotskians and Piagetians alike agree is essential in learning to take the perspective of the other. Like scientists in real-life laboratories, these students challenged one another's thoughts, negotiated conflicts about evidence and conclusions, and shared their knowledge in order to achieve an understanding that looks just like scientific understanding. Like scientists in real-life laboratories, these students were working in a community of practice in which the exploration of individual participants was guided and supported by the whole group (cf. Brown & Palinscar, 1989; Brown et al., in press).

The research discussed in this section reinforces a more general point made by Erickson and Schultz (1992): The engagement of students in learning activities results from a connection between social participation structure (form) and academic curriculum (content). If the social participation structure is familiar to students, then performing with new academic content is less alienating (as in the KEEP reading lessons described in Au, 1980; Tharp & Gallimore, 1988). On the other hand, if the academic content is familiar or engaging, then students may be willing to try out new ways of interacting and using language (as in the Rough Rock lessons in McCarty et al., 1991). The issue underlying both cases is safety—not having to risk looking clumsy or stupid in front of others. Lesson content and form, taken together or separately, can reduce the risk of embarrassment, which in turn triggers resistance—the withholding of assent to learn and to participate in learning activities.

THE CONSEQUENCES OF MODIFYING THE CURRICULUM

A second approach to multicultural education modifies the curriculum, especially in social studies and history, to achieve one of two goals: (a) to include the contributions of women and members of underrepresented minority groups, or (b) to build an ethnoracial identity. Since there is virtually no literature on these topics, we present our own case studies here (Lintz & Okamoto, 1993; Wills, 1993, in press).

Modifying Classroom Curriculum for Cultural Inclusion

In this section we describe the struggles of three teachers to introduce a multicultural curriculum into their classrooms using a new textbook series adopted by the state of California that was intended to provide a "multicultural history" of the United States and the world. Wills (1993, in press) examined the influence of official curricular knowledge on the representation of racial and ethnic groups in three U.S. history classrooms in one predominantly White, suburban middle school in San Diego. The approach taken by the textbook series and by the teachers Wills observed consisted mainly of injecting the contributions of African Americans, Native Americans, and other previously underrepresented groups into the existing "American Narrative of Progress" (i.e., the celebration of the expansion and progress of U.S. society).

The three teachers whose classrooms were observed—"Judy," "Ruth," and "Tom"—were chosen for their very different teaching styles and interests. Wills observed their use of different instructional materials and compared and contrasted their use of the same materials, *A More Perfect Union* (Armento, Nash, Slater, & Wixson, 1991), the textbook used in all three classrooms.

The hope of multicultural curriculum reform is that it will help teach students some degree of understanding of different racial, ethnic, and religious groups, and that this understanding will translate into improved relations in our increasingly diverse society (Banks & Banks, 1989; Sleeter & Grant, 1987). A multicultural history curriculum, by focusing on the experiences of men and women of diverse racial, ethnic, and religious groups in U.S. history, will provide students with a historical context in which to situate and understand the experiences and perspectives of these groups in American society today.

Efforts to make the curriculum multicultural have often focused on providing students of color with historical role models and on improving their self-esteem. While these goals are important, we also recognize the necessity to educate all students with a history that may ultimately improve race and ethnic relations in an increasingly diverse society. This is, after all, the goal of both proponents and opponents of the new textbook series in California, who share the belief that educa-

tion can be a positive force for social change, and that it can influence students' attitudes and beliefs regarding different racial, ethnic, and religious groups. For White students and teachers, multicultural education (what it could and should be, not necessarily what it is in practice) means challenging the assumptions and biases of mainstream White American culture (cf. Grant & Sleeter, 1986; McLaren & Estrada, 1993). The purpose of Wills's (1993, in press) ethnography was to see how well the history these three teachers taught achieved this goal, and what problems they had in realizing a truly multicultural U.S. history. In the following pages we report on his findings concerning African Americans.

African Americans in American History. The historical presence of African Americans in U.S. history was noted fairly early in the school year. While discussing early colonial history, Ruth and Tom used a population chart ("Ethnic Population, 1775") in the students' textbook, *A More Perfect Union* (Armento et al., 1991, p. 49), which shows that African Americans comprised 20% of the population of colonial America. Tom provided his students with a graphic depiction of the middle passage and the purchase of African Americans by White colonists once they had arrived in North America. Ruth also briefly discussed the conditions Africans faced on the voyage from Africa, using a model of a slave ship created by a student in a previous year—sunflower seeds representing Africans—to show students how Africans were packed into slave ships.

Most of the talk about African Americans was concerned with their enslavement—their abduction and passage from Africa to North America, their being sold at slave auctions, and the fact that the 20% mentioned in the ethnic population chart were probably all slaves. When the Constitutional Convention was discussed, the teachers noted that slavery was not abolished and that slaves were counted as three fifths of a person for purposes of representation and taxation. There were some exceptions to the equation of African Americans to slaves. For example, Tom discussed a few Black Revolutionary War heroes with his students and asked them to write a report on a Black Revolutionary War hero of their choice. While this was a sincere effort by Tom to present his students with a more inclusive history of the United States, it was not a great success. The students had great difficulty finding information on Black Revolutionary War heroes—partly due to the research skills of students, who favor the encyclopedia over other materials, but also because of a lack of good resources on this topic at the school and local public library—and most of the students ended up with very brief reports reiterating the little information they could find, and limited to the few individuals mentioned in their textbooks—Crispus Attucks, Salem Poor, and Peter Salem, the latter two being African Americans who fought on the side of the colonists in their war for independence from England (Armento et al., 1991).

While African Americans appear early in American history, the textbook focus was never specifically on them. Their presence was noted, but never examined in any depth. Students learned little or nothing about the experiences of African Americans in America during the colonial period. In fact, students learned very little about African Americans at all until the teachers began to discuss the Civil War, when their presence as slaves in the South impinges more on the story of White America. Teachers and students looked closely at the experiences of Africa Americans during their study of this period in American history.

Students in Judy's class had the opportunity to learn a lot about enslaved African Americans in the South during the Civil War. Judy spent eight weeks on the Civil War period, using the students' textbook, slides, library resources, laserdisc presentations, documentary film, literature, music from the period, and her own supplementary reference materials. She taught her students not only about the growing conflict between North and South, but also the cruelties, indignities, and injustices African Americans experienced under slavery.

Judy organized small-group Civil War projects that students presented to the class, including slide lectures, poetry recitals, reenactments of the Lincoln-Douglas debate, monologues from famous individuals of the time, point-counterpoint presentations between pro- and antislavery historical figures, reports on music from this period, skits on Civil War events, and the completion of a final essay dealing with slavery. Judy also had her students read Julius Lester's (1968) *To Be a Slave*, a collection of interviews with African Americans who experienced slavery personally, gathered by the Federal Writers' Project in the 1930s. Students kept a dialectical journal in which they recorded their personal responses to a few passages from each chapter of this book.

All the work the students did and the materials they read were focused on giving the students some sense, however imperfect, of the indignities, injustices, and brutalities that characterized the life of enslaved African Americans in the South. And the students seemed sincere, both in their writing and comments in class, in their expressions of shock and outrage at the treatment of African Americans under slavery. Slavery is on the face of it immoral, and Judy's students had difficulty understanding how White slaveholders could have been so cruel.

By the end of the school year, when Judy finished her unit on the Civil War, her students had become "virtual witnesses" (Shapin, 1984) to the experiences of African Americans under southern slavery. Wills thought that this detailed experience would provide Judy's students with a depth of historical knowledge that would prepare them to think and talk about the experiences of contemporary African Americans with some sensitivity. He thought they would be able to call upon their knowledge of the racism, brutality, and injustices experienced by African Americans under slavery when discussing the existence of these same issues and problems today. But while the unit was still in progress, he had reason to question the long-term effects of this newly gained information.

In the middle of May 1991 Judy was presented with an opportunity to connect the past to the present, to use history as a resource for discussing contemporary African American experiences in U.S. society. Judy was about halfway through her Civil War unit. Her students had read the first few chapters in *A More Perfect Union* (Armento et al., 1991) dealing with slavery and the growing conflict between North and South, and also the first few chapters of *To Be A Slave* (Lester, 1968). They'd also just finished watching the documentary "Roots of Resistance: The Underground Railroad," which discusses, among other things, the experiences of African Americans under slavery, the Underground Railroad, the Fugitive Slave Act, and the Dred Scott decision.

The uprising in Los Angeles occurred just at the time Judy had planned to discuss this documentary film with her students. After commenting briefly on the events in Los Angeles after the Rodney King verdict, and trying to stress to her students that the uprising affects all of us, Judy asked her students if things have changed very much, if the inequities they had "witnessed" in the past are still present today.

(1) Teacher: So, you know my question to you is have things changed that much? Or do we still have these same kinds of issues in our society? Do we think that our society is is um, has equality for everybody? Or not? Carl?

(2) Carl: I don't know I think, I think [inaudible] bring it upon themselves because,

(3) Teacher: Okay. How would they do that?

(4) Carl: 'Cause I don't, I mean. I mean I'm not racist against Black people or anything but if you look at like, all the minorities that we've had in our country, for the last twenty or thirty years the Japanese and the, the um Philippines and everything. They've all come to our country and they've, started businesses and, it'll have, places like the Black people do down in the hood and everything. They have their own businesses and, the Koreans have, have businesses but, I think Black people—

(5) Teacher: Let me play devil's advocate with you for a minute here, and say to you um those people were not brought here as slaves.

(6) Carl: Well ya but, I mean, there are no slaves anymore I mean. I mean, I mean there's plenty of people who are, are racist against [them], against other other minorities not just Blacks.

(7) Teacher: Uh huh.

(8) Carl: And, but they've put up with it and they've, gone and, against odds they've, started businesses but Black people, I mean—I mean I'm not saying all of them 'cause there are a lot of, successful Black people but, a lot of 'em just kind of, think that everybody's against 'em and they just stood down there and they don't, have jobs and stuff and they think that everybody's against 'em.

(9) Teacher: Okay. Patty?

(10) Patty: Well in response to what Carl said I don't know, if he thinks about this but, it's possible that a lot of Blacks feel like they're, that everyone's against them, because, through I mean, through their descendants they've been told about, through the people before them they've been told about slavery and a lot of times people, people, I guess when you start hearing things over and over again and you, when you hear that, that you're inferior, you're gonna start to believe it. It's not I mean, I understand what Carl's saying but it's not, it's not that they don't wanna try. I don't think it's just that they believe that they can't because that's what they've been told.

(11) Teacher: How many of you read *Roll of Thunder, Hear My Cry* in here? [a few hands go up] And, *Roll of Thunder* was written about a time during the Depression. And how were the Blacks treated in that book? Were they treated as if they were equals Patty?

(12) Patty: No.

(13) Teacher: And we're looking at a time that is roughly sixty years after the Civil War ended. So they weren't treated as equals then either were they?

Carl responded to Judy's question by stating that he thought African Americans "bring it upon themselves" (line 2). While assuring Judy and the other students that he's not racist (line 4), Carl wondered why other minorities like the Japanese, Koreans, and Filipinos have started businesses and succeeded economically, while African Americans have not. In response to Carl's comments Judy made an assertion (line 5) that drew upon the historical experiences of African Americans that the class was in the midst of studying: "those people [other minorities] were not brought here as slaves." Carl responded: "Well ya but, I mean, there are no slaves anymore" (line 6).

Carl is right. There are no slaves anymore. While African Americans did experience cruelty, brutality, and horrible atrocities and injustices under slavery, that is a "problem" that was corrected many years ago. Slavery is "history," a past that has no obvious connection to the present for Carl, who finally concluded that although there are some successful Blacks, a lot of African Americans simply believe that everyone is against them, and so are not motivated to get jobs.

At this point Patty (line 10) attempted to enlighten Carl about the effects the legacy of slavery has on present-day African Americans. It's not that African Americans don't want jobs, don't want to succeed economically; they believe that everyone's against them, and that they are inferior to Whites and to other minority groups, because that's what they've told themselves year after year. For Patty, the condition of Blacks today is the unfortunate consequence of remembering the history of their ancestors, a history that makes them believe in their own inferiority.

Judy rejoined the discussion (line 11), asking if any of the students had read one of the selections assigned in their literature course. Only a few of the students had read this book (M. D. Taylor, 1976, which recounts the experiences of Cassie Logan and her family, who are Black, in the South during the Great Depression, experiences that expose the racism, discrimination, and injustices African Americans have continued to endure in American society). Judy's question was meant to turn the students' attention away from the characteristics of African Americans (i.e., what's wrong with these people?) to the circumstances surrounding African Americans—how they have been treated in American society under slavery, during the Great Depression, and today. African Americans have been treated inequitably by Whites, a continuous problem in American history.

If one's goal is to provide students with a history that speaks to the present, then this brief excerpt suggests that an apparent multicultural step forward can in fact be counterproductive. A detailed study of the experiences of enslaved African Americans during the Civil War period did not help these students understand the continuing struggle of African Americans with racism and discrimination in today's society. The students' understanding of African Americans' experiences of injustice is "anchored" in slavery, with discrimination and prejudice a product of their enslavement. Outside the context of Southern slavery, the students have little historical knowledge to draw upon for thinking about African Americans' experiences of racism, discrimination, and injustice in the United States. The students think the Civil War solved these problems.

The Situation of African Americans in American History. In their analysis of the representation of race, class, gender, and disability in current textbooks for grades 1 through 8 in four different subject areas, Sleeter & Grant (1991) note the power of the narrative of U.S. history textbooks to "situate" people of color in specific time periods or events that are important to Whites. Native Americans are included as friends of the early English colonists or in their later fights with settlers, Asian Americans are noted for their work on the railroad, and African Americans are included in slavery and the civil rights struggle.

The bias of mainstream, White American culture evident in these classroom lessons and curricular materials is that the Civil War South is the only proper place to study the presence of African Americans in American history. Furthermore, it is assumed that the study of slavery is sufficient for communicating the experiences of African Americans in American history. The multicultural perspective in contemporary California classrooms emphasizes the close and careful study of slaves and slavery, so that students gain a deep understanding of the cruelties of slave life and the injustices African Americans experienced under slavery.

But as we saw in the excerpt from a discussion in Judy's class, this practice of situating African Americans in a particular time and place in American history—in the Civil War South—and focusing on their experiences as slaves during this period has some surprising consequences. Carl's comments suggest that this practice is a means of *confining* African Americans—and their experiences and concerns—to a specific time and place in U.S. history.

Examining the experiences of African Americans under southern slavery, but ignoring the experiences of African Americans outside of slavery, constructs a history that binds the racism and prejudice African Americans have experienced in United States specifically to their enslavement in the South. The history students learn from this approach denies that African Americans' experiences of injustice and discrimination are part of a continuous historical record.

In her "To Be A Slave" journal in Judy's class, Jean wrote about southern slavery as the "era of racism, prejudice, and slavery." Eric, writing in his final essay on slavery in Judy's class, noted that "less than ninety years later [after the Civil War] black people were the target of racism once again." Both students represented African American's experiences with injustice as periodic but not continuous. Finally, Diana and Sue, both writing in their overviews of U.S. history, expressed the belief that slavery was a horrible experience, but a thing of the past. Diana wrote "that was the past," while Sue wrote "in the end, as you know there is no more slavery anymore."

Students have little knowledge of the history of race relations in the United States. What they do know is the character of the relations between enslaved African Americans and their White masters. Focusing on the "evils" of slavery—cruel masters, the brutal treatment of slaves, belief in the inferiority of slaves—is important, to be sure. But it provides a history that is too narrow and limited to be of much use in discussing contemporary American society. It provides very weak links to issues of racism, discrimination, and the denial of political and civil rights, the very issues that the California State Department of Education (1988) alludes to when it talks about teaching students the history of the United States as "an unfinished struggle to realize the ideals of the Declaration of Independence and the Constitution" (p. xii). Slavery, it seems, is simply not a very useful vehicle, in an of itself, for understanding the continuous experiences of African Americans in the United States.

Realizing a Multicultural History of the United States. The approach to "multiculturalizing" the curriculum taken by this new textbook series and evident in the efforts of the teachers Wills (1993, in press) observed has been to add women and people of color to the existing narrative of American history. When done thoughtfully, as in *A More Perfect Union*'s (Armento et al., 1991) discussion of Tecumseh, The Prophet, Sequoya, and the infamous Trail of Tears, this approach can supply meaningful additions to students' history of the United States. Not only does it provide students with more diverse images of specific groups (thereby making stereotypes more difficult to sustain), but it also focuses on the experiences of racial and ethnic groups that raise such issues as injustice and racism in American history. But this additive approach to multicultural reform, while presenting a more inclusive history, is ultimately inadequate to the task at hand. While students are exposed to more women and people of color than in the past, the "American Narrative of Progress" remains unquestioned.

The problem is not simply that there are not enough African Americans, Native Americans, Asian Americans, or Hispanics in American history, but that the inclusion of these groups represents the interests and biases of mainstream, White American culture. It's not, as one history teacher complained, that multiculturalists want every group mentioned in every paragraph of American history. But the presence of these groups should do more than simply add "color" to what is still essentially a White story of America, in which the experiences, concerns, and interests of these groups are incidental and marginalized. The limited presence of diverse groups in this narrative provides students with a rather narrow range of images for representing racial and ethnic groups in U.S. history, perpetuating rather than challenging the stereotypical images of these groups that teachers and students bring with them into the classroom.

The problem with the way African Americans are included in American history is that the focus is too narrow, the goals too limited. Teachers can and should expand the focus of their studies within slavery, raising issues of injustice, liberty, and freedom. But more important is the need to begin examining the experiences of African Americans outside of slavery. For example, while *A More Perfect Union* (Armento et al., 1991) does focus extensively on southern slavery, it also discusses—albeit briefly—the existence of communities of free African Americans in both the North and the South. This is an opportunity that can be seized by teachers to provide their students with a fuller history of the experiences of African Americans in the United States, one that is likely to raise issues of injustice, discrimination, and racism.

This is easy to recommend, but more difficult to achieve in practice. Teachers and students are not just reading biased materials; they also bring their own biases to their reading of history, the "cultural baggage" of popular stereotypes of racial, ethnic, and religious groups, as well as assumptions about American history, ranging from where and when different groups should be present in American history, to notions of what form the history of the United States should take (a celebration of the expansion and progress of a shining democracy, or the story of the colonization and exploitation of a continent?). These cultural biases and assumptions are central to understanding the "politics of representation" (Holquist, 1983; Mehan & Wills, 1988; Shapiro, 1988) involved in the use of curriculum in the construction of historical knowledge in the classroom. This also suggests that the realization of a multicultural history of the United States involves not simply the remaking of educational curriculum, but also the remaking of American culture.

Modifying Classroom Curriculum to Build Racial-Ethnic Identity

Widespread dissatisfaction with the public schools has led some parents to seek alternative forms of education for their children, most notably private schools. Approximately 5.3 million students attend at least 22 different types of private schools (Key Statistics, 1989). *Religious* private schools have been created because parents and educational leaders are dissatisfied with the moral climate of the public school. Religious schools attempt to create environments where students are self-consciously exposed to deep religious values (Parsons, 1987). *African American* private schools have been created because Black children have had such limited success in public schools in the face of long-standing patterns of racism and discrimination that have not been broken down by desegregation and busing. Often affiliated with African American churches, African American independent schools offer an environment that emphasizes ethnoracial identity formation, high academic expectations, and a firm disciplinary code based on religious principles (G. E. Foster, 1991).

The life and organization of White Christian fundamentalist schools has received some attention (Parsons 1987; Peshkin, 1986; Rose, 1988). With the exception of Ratteray and Shujaa

(1987), the rise of independent schools attempting to build ethnoracial as well as religious identities is largely undocumented. The interaction of ethnoracial and religious identity politics demands academic attention, especially since more than 70% of the ethnoracial secular and religious schools Ratterjay and Shujaa surveyed have been founded *since* the landmark 1954 U.S. Supreme Court desegregation decision, *Brown v. Board of Education of Topeka.*

The Social Organization of the Church and the School. Disciple's Academic Christian Academy (DACA) is an African American independent school with an ethnoracial identity project (Lintz & Okamoto, 1993). Operating autonomously, this African American Christian fundamentalist school functions largely as a result of the political efforts of the local African American community. Most teachers, administrators, parents, and students are African American and make the decisions that define the school's character and set the school's agenda. Like most other Christian fundamentalist schools, DACA's parent organization owns the physical facilities in which its school is housed. Disciple's church is part of an African American charismatic denomination, Church of God in Christ, an association of churches (Lincoln & Maimya, 1990). In this denomination, a preacher is ordained, approved for church leadership by a local church, and then founds his own church, rather than being sent to the pulpit by a central office. A number of churches in this organization have schools, but they operate independent of any national or central church authority.

According to Bishop Ralph Jackson, founder of DACA, the school has a strong religious agenda because many of the students require direction and spiritual guidance owing to their extreme backgrounds. It is not uncommon for DACA students to be faced with one or more drug abusers in their immediate family, a family tragedy caused by gang activity, an immediate family member in jail, or to have no parents at all. Given the desperate conditions of her students' lives, the principal of the school, Sister Shiela Robinson, declared that the students' most important concern is to build self-esteem and confidence. Acknowledging that college is not for everyone, she wants to ensure that her students will mature as productive adults, and obtain jobs in the mainstream of society.

Disciple's is located in an inner city. The surrounding community is predominantly African American and Latino, and gang activity is prevalent. The school and church facilities are located in a 13,000-square-foot building. There are 114 students (K–12), nine teachers, and two teacher's aides who are supervised by the principal. While Bishop Jackson said that the teachers need not be members of his church, they must hold spiritual values derived from Christianity. The school has five classrooms, each with 23 students, which produces a teacher-student ratio much more favorable than that of public schools. Grades are combined (K–1, 2–3, 4–6, 7–8, 9–12) because there are not enough students at each grade to fill separate classrooms.

The complexion of Disciple's is striking in contrast to most U.S. public schools. Virtually all of the teachers, students, and administrators are African American, but the school is separatist in neither ideology nor practice; a small number of non-Black students and non-Black teachers participate. The very presence of so many African American staff and administrators provides a culture-affirming atmosphere. Such schools are often the only places where African American children can observe members of their own cultural group as autonomous operators and managers, as individuals in control of an important institution (G. E. Foster, 1991).

Both students and teachers wear navy and white clothing— white blouses and navy skirts for females, white shirts and navy slacks for males. This religiously motivated attention to gender, dress, and etiquette is not unique to Disciple's. It permeates Catholic and White Christian fundamentalist schools (Parsons, 1987; Peshkin, 1986; Rose, 1988).

Only one of the teachers holds a California teaching credential. Two of the teachers have credentials, one foreign and the other out-of-state, that are not accepted by the state of California. Five teachers have B.A. degrees, and of those five, two have M.A. degrees. One teacher is working toward her B.A. in secondary education at a local private university.

The physical organization of the classrooms at Disciple's, a legacy from the Accelerated Christian Education curriculum that the school once used, is different from traditional public schools. Each classroom has two larger desks for instructors, while student desks line the perimeter, with wooden slats separating them. Without compartments in the desks, books and other materials must be stacked underneath.

Disciple's classrooms are similar to public school classrooms in that teachers are constantly negotiating with the students for order. The seventh- and eighth-grade teacher frequently raises his voice to the students in a calm manner, telling them that control and discipline are the necessary determinants of success. The second- and third-grade teacher constantly gives commands and imperatives to which the students quickly respond without question. The teacher is quick to correct anyone who is out of order: "What are you doing standing up? Why were you talking? Turn around and keep working." The teachers' disciplinary style demands that students conform to externally imposed rules, a type of authority system that can produce passive, conforming students (Wilcox, 1982).

Teachers at Disciple's routinely employ the recitation script described in the first part of this chapter. Teachers structure participation by calling on individual students to perform in front of the group. The student's knowledge of almost any subject is informally tested through known information questions. Ability grouping prevails in reading and math. Because grade levels are combined, teachers often work with one grade while the other students work silently at their desks. The K–5 students are taught traditionally with textbooks and workbooks. The children learn to work quietly and must raise their hands when questions arise. Similar to many public school classrooms, the transmission of knowledge moves in only one direction, from teacher to student. Cooperative or collaborative groups, inquiry or discovery methods are virtually nonexistent.

Different participation structures are imposed in the upper grades. Students must raise their hands when a formal lesson is being taught, but otherwise may talk among themselves. The senior high class has a self-directed curriculum because so many grade levels are combined. Since lectures are not a regular part of the curriculum, students complete assignments at their desks for most of the day, but do not seem to be doing intensive work because they constantly talk to one another. There are no science labs or advanced math and literature courses. Thus the upper grades at Disciple's provide less academic content than comparable public schools, concentrating instead on building self-esteem and confidence.

The Overt Curriculum: Building Ethnoracial Identity Through Religion. The academic day at DACA begins with prayer followed by religious studies. These studies are biblical text readings with teacher-directed exegesis. Religious instruction in the primary grades comes largely from collections of biblical stories. Starting with the second- and third-grade classes, however, religious pedagogy includes reading aloud from biblical text. Tutelage in faith not being limited to morning prayer or biblical studies, students also attend chapel two days per week. Chapels may be spiritually focused (a salvation message by a visiting missionary) or instructional, but even when they are instructional—a health presentation about the dangers of smoking for example—explicit religious guidance accompanies the material. Children are not to smoke because it can cause health problems, but since their bodies are "a temple of the Holy Spirit" (I Corinthians 6:19), a habit causing physical decay of the corporal person also causes spiritual malaise.

All of the educational materials used at Disciple's are published by A Beka, a company affiliated with the ministry of Pensacola Christian College. These books present a complete Christian education program, including day-to-day lesson plans, in materials heavily infused with a religious message. For example, Bible verses are displayed at the bottom of each math workbook page; sentences that need to be written in grammatically correct form include biblical references and persons; and more than half of the fiction and poetry included in the literature books is religiously oriented. The science book for the upper grades rejects evolution and espouses creationism:

It is very important to understand that the theory of evolution is not science; it is simply an idea that certain men thought up after they rejected God's Word. To call evolution scientific is to insult science itself. (Howe, 1984, p. xx).

In the highly structured, teacher-centered classrooms, students are not encouraged to be critical thinkers or to have meaningful discourse about the different theories of origination. Students are taught to accept only one perspective, not only when studying the origins of the universe, but in other subjects as well. Even though the A Beka curriculum does give accurate representations of most facts, it ultimately limits students' understanding of the world. A paternalistic approach to gender relations and the economy is apparent throughout the curriculum and does not actively promote a sense of gender difference. The traditional family unit and traditional lifestyles are portrayed frequently. For example, sketches from the high school literature anthology reinforce traditional sex roles. Women are depicted as either wife or mother, while men are

shown in many roles (such as worker, thinker, scientist, father judge, mountain climber). Only 10 representations of women, compared with 60 of men, appeared in a 500-page textbook.

Disciple's chapel, daily prayer, and Christian curriculum constitute a spiritual exercise that is absent from the public school environment, but the religious orientation is not the only difference in its academic life. The substantial focus on African American culture and history throughout the academic year is an example of a curriculum priority that occurs uniquely in African American independent schools. The educators at Disciple's see African American culture and history as an important component of their curriculum, though somewhat less so than the spiritual. The religious and ethnoracial identity agendas are at odds with one another, however, because the fundamentalist Christian orientation of the A Beka books is so highly Eurocentric. A Beka texts portray Western societies as the most technologically advanced and attribute this developmental superiority to the belief that Christianity is the one true religion. In the fourth-grade history book, for example, the section on Native Americans discusses their heathen status and celebrates the missionaries who brought them the Christian religion. The introduction alerts the reader:

The very first Americans did not know anything about the Bible until the Europeans brought it to them. Because they did not have the Bible, which tells us about the one true God, they worshipped false gods. Their worship of false gods kept them from advancing the way the Europeans had. (Howe, 1986, p. 38)

After establishing the heathen status of the Native Americans, the text tells of how the white men "improved their way of life" with the Bible. The text states that the missionary Roger Williams was "willing to treat the Indians fairly. He offered to buy the land from them" (Howe, 1986, p. 44). This narrative of Western progressivism, which dominates public school texts described earlier in this chapter, attributes no value to any cultural perspective other than the European Christian. Other religions are simply heathen. Contact with Whites and the culture that evolved from Christianity presents the only possibility for non-White Christian cultures. The implication for African Americans is clear: Any African cultures are heathen and consequently primitive.

The commitment to ethnoracial identity at Disciple's forces teachers to use materials to supplement the Eurocentric Christian fundamentalist curriculum. To instruct students about their ethnoracial identity teachers infuse the curriculum with drama, Black history texts, and movies. They often rely on homemade learning materials and research from college-level publications. Ratteray and Shujaa (1987) found "teacher-designed materials" to be prevalent in black independent schools, because teachers insisted that "commercially produced materials inadequately represented their cultural group" (p. 6). One of the DACA teachers who said she "didn't make much of race" in fact displayed just the opposite propensity. For "Black History Month" she composed an elaborate drama for the children to perform in front of their parents. Included were the views of a variety of African American historical figures about the plight of and solution for African Americans, including Sojourner Truth:

America owes to my people some of the dividends. . . . She can afford to pay, and she must pay. I shall make them understand that there is a debt to the Negro people which they can never repay. At least, then, they must make amends.

Most of the quotations in the play, like the one above, affirm the common experience of African Americans, thereby fostering a group destiny. To enhance understanding of and pride for the students' African American heritage, teachers also include lessons from films and Black history texts. Franklin's (1969) *From Slavery to Freedom: A History of Negro Americans* and Blum's (1971) *Key Issues in the African American Experience* are examples of texts used by teachers to integrate African American history into their curriculum. The teacher who introduced these texts acquired them in a Black Studies course in college. The movie *Roots* was shown to the fourth through sixth grades. The teachers supplemented the film with commentary, explaining the historical racial-cultural context of scenes. Black identity is also expressed in prideful slogans and pictures of famous African American scientists, athletes, and educators displayed on the classroom walls.

The Covert Curriculum: A Critique of Black Linguistic and Cultural Expression. The overt instruction in ethnoracial identity during formal lessons at DACA does not proceed without tensions. Often the overt curriculum of ethnic pride is contradicted by a covert curriculum that critiques Black linguistic expression and popular culture. In addition, the collective sense of pride taught in Black history and social studies runs up against informal entreaties to the individual pursuit of success.

Much important writing has been dedicated to the subject of interaction between "Anglo" teachers and linguistic and cultural minority students. As the research we reviewed in the first part of this chapter shows, the communication challenges that result from differing linguistic patterns, beliefs, values, and experiences can interfere with the learning process. Implicit in the "cultural discontinuity" position is that closing the gap between the linguistic and cultural styles of teachers and students will facilitate the educational process. The work of Piestrup (1973), Erickson & Mohatt (1982), and M. Foster (1989) can be interpreted to suggest that employing teachers from the same ethnolinguistic background as the students can help close this gap.

African American independent schools present an opportunity for a common linguistic-cultural code between teacher and student to fortify cultural identity in classroom interaction. Our work at DACA shows that cultural-linguistic continuity between teacher and students does not necessarily result in cultural tolerance, however. Similar experiences do not essentially constitute relational fluency or support. Some communication barriers attributed to the cultural differences between "Anglo" teachers and their African American pupils also arise between African American teachers and their African American pupils, an observation made by Rist (1970) over 20 years ago about interactions between Black teachers and Black students in public schools.

Most notably, some DACA teachers denigrate the use of Black English Vernacular (BEV) by their students. They find it necessary to correct BEV whether the lesson is a discussion of a PBS educational program or a grammar exercise. One teacher referred to BEV as "ghettoese," combining a poverty term with a language suffix, thereby making this a language of destitution. This high school teacher studied African American history and Swahili as an undergraduate and feels strongly that many aspects of African American culture should be abandoned, particularly BEV.

These critiques are not limited to the students' linguistic expression; they also attack other aspects of Black popular culture. A member of the church leadership, Elder Ford, spoke to the students during a school chapel about the need to abandon such physical expressions of ethnoracial identity as hairstyle in order to achieve mobility. He advised the boys not to get "ridiculous" haircuts; otherwise, when they go to job interviews "the man" will tell them to follow one of the arrows shaved into their hair out to the next exit.

DACA students are also told that Black identity should be tempered with a positive Black heritage. The high school teacher said that there is no benefit in trying to "Africanize" because Blacks have been Americans for seven generations. Aspirations for success involve cultural change and sacrifice. Students need to aspire to "nerd" as opposed to "cool" status, finding new friends who have the same success-oriented goals, leaving old companions behind.

Another message communicated implicitly to students concerns strategies for achieving success in U.S. society. Students are encouraged to seek individual rather than collective strategies for mobility. The high school teacher also told his students: "You can't bring the whole tribe with you. You have to get there first and *then* help people." In so doing, this teacher critiques a popular effort to form an African American group identity. He discourages collective strategy as a solution for poverty in the African American community, advocating instead an individual solution. If there is to be mobility for African Americans, it will be achieved by individuals, striving personally without coalescing with others.

These critiques are not expressed out of malice. These African American teachers who unintentionally employ a culture-of-poverty perspective when encountering African American popular culture all *care* for their students, wanting them to be academically successful. In fact, critiques of student's language and culture are rendered with a motivation to encourage students to speak and behave in ways that will clear barriers on their paths to success. These critiques generated negative consequences, however, that were manifested in classroom interaction. When encountering criticism of their speech and behavior, students often acted flustered (blowing air through pursed lips, stammering) and withdrew from the lesson. That is, these *African American* students withdrew from learning situations with their *African American* teachers; but this resistance is passive, not active. Truancy, drug use, and verbal conflict with teachers are not part of the milieu at DACA. MacLeod's (1987) "hallway hangers," Willis's (1979) "lads," and Foley's (1990) "cholos" are noticeably absent from this independent school. Rather than playing the role of class clown or disrupter, which Ogbu (1974) and Hanna (1982) found in their studies of African American students in public schools, the DACA students are more likely to resist passively, conduct that has been more commonly attributed to Native Hawaiian and Native American students (Au & Jordan, 1981; Erickson & Mohatt, 1982; Philips, 1982).

Even though the overt curriculum for the entire school is religiously based, teachers do not invoke the Bible in the covert curriculum, that is, in providing explanations or guiding students' conduct. According to Peshkin (1986), teachers and administrators at Bethany Baptist Academy put Christ at the center of all subjects and concentrated on teaching proper Christian behavior. In the Bethany Baptist Academy classrooms he studied, teachers used references from the Bible as often as possible in their lessons, and students were expected to regard the Bible as the absolute truth and guide for life. By contrast, teachers and aides at Disciple's teach all subjects except devotion without reference to the tenets of Christianity or the Bible. The difference between such schools as DACA and Bethany Baptist Academy and typical public schools is found in the explicit curriculum, then, not the implicit curriculum of teacher-student discourse.

This observation does not imply that the teachers at Disciple's are not deeply religious. Brother Grant Brown, senior high school co-teacher, asserts that the most important component of Disciple's is the spiritual atmosphere. He says that students can learn to recognize their problems and use their spiritual values, knowing that God will give them strength to overcome. Brother Brown claims that if students do not learn any spiritual values, then they cannot use their knowledge correctly. Other teachers feel just as strongly about the spiritual aspect of the school, but they realize that students also need discipline, mastery of basic subjects, and confidence to succeed in the real world.

Dilemmas and Contradictions of Multicultural Education in Separate Schools. The teaching practices at DACA are not much different from those found in public schools. A major rationale for opening private schools is that they are freed from bureaucratic constraints and governmental regulations (Chubb & Moe, 1990). Even though independent schools are able to organize in any manner they choose and use any teaching techniques they wish, Disciple's has not deviated radically from the traditional approach to teaching. Supplements are used when teaching African American history, and peer tutoring is employed in one of the lower-grade classes. But these are the exceptions, not the rule. Ability grouping, rigid daily schedules, customary participant structures, and conventional teaching techniques are practiced every day. Thus there is little evidence that Disciple's exercises its freedom from bureaucratic constraints by implementing innovative instructional strategies or using time and space creatively in the classroom.

African American culture is bountifully displayed in the distinctive presence of African American educators, curriculum materials, and striking classroom wall designs. At the same time, popular Black culture is exorcised. The African American teachers at Disciple's critique their students' linguistic and cultural expressions. When communication difficulties occur with Anglo teachers, African American pupils are likely to explain the disrespect of their terminology in terms of racism. When

their linguistic and cultural patterns are censored by their African American teachers, however, they attribute the censorship to cultural treason. There are even long-lived labels for those who compromise Black cultural tradition to please Whites: "Tom," "Uncle Tom" or "oreo." Though separate independent schools are a potential solution to the cultural communication gap between teachers and students, "minority" teachers may make choices, for the same reasons as do their White counterparts, that frustrate "minority" students and thus limit classroom interaction and the learning process. Multicultural education requires more than teachers who are from the same ethnic background as their students.

The overt agenda at DACA to build a collective sense of pride, taught in the formal Black history and social studies portions of the curriculum, ran up against entreaties in the informal curriculum to pursue success individually. Students were encouraged continually to achieve success first on their own, and to worry about the African American community second. This attitude fuels Wilson's (1987) argument that the African American urban community is truly disadvantaged in part because the African American middle class has abandoned the inner city.

Because of the desperate circumstances of their student's lives, the school officials of Disciple's believe that firm discipline is required. Seeking their answer to the discipline problem in a fundamentalist Christian curriculum raises a host of other problems. This same curriculum is Eurocentric, antiscience, relies on externally imposed authority (which fosters passive students), and contradicts the thrust of the ethnic pride curriculum.

Consistent with the religious base of its supporting church, the teachers see teaching as a calling, a vocation, not a job. But these teachers have relatively little formal education and teacher training, which limits the quality of academic instruction in the upper grades, especially in math and laboratory science courses. As a result, the school's goal of building self-esteem is met better than the school's goal of developing academic sophistication.

CONCLUSIONS AND IMPLICATIONS FOR MULTICULTURAL EDUCATION

At a time when American society is grappling with the difficult issue of race and ethnic relations, and when many are looking to education as a vehicle for improving relations among diverse groups, it is important to understand the various strategies that educators have employed to incorporate diversity into the curriculum and the schools. To this end, we have reviewed ethnographic studies of multicultural education in three areas: (a) those that describe attempts to achieve equality in classroom interaction by modifying discourse patterns and participation structures; (b) those that describe attempts to implement a curriculum that stresses the contributions of previously underrepresented ethnic groups and women; and (c) those that describe attempts to build an ethnoracial identity.

If one goal of multicultural education is to construct an inclusive multiracial and multiethnic definition of American identity, then our review of the design and implementation of the multicultural textbooks being used in California public and private schools demonstrates the limitations of curricular reforms that attempt to achieve a multicultural history through the *addition* or *injection* of racially and ethnically diverse individuals into an already existing narrative of U.S. history. It seems more productive to employ totally restructured narratives of U.S. history that are both honest and respectful. Such narratives would provide students with an image of "Americans" that captures and celebrates the diversity of the United States, both today and in the past, and would acknowledge that conflict, oppression, and prejudice have been enduring features of U.S. history, not isolated incidents confined to unusual periods of time.

To be sure, we want a "critical multiculturalism" (Giroux, 1988; Grant & Sleeter, 1986; McLaren & Estrada, 1993) that encourages students to challenge inequality and to promote cultural diversity. But we feel we need to go beyond critique, to the systematic inclusion of new narratives in the curriculum. African American, Native American, and Latino narratives all have different stories, with different plots, major events, and characters. These narratives need to be juxtaposed with the mainstream "narrative of progress" so that students can recognize experiences different from their own, and learn to take the perspective of others. Exposing students to the multiplicity of narratives that comprise U.S. society and teaching them about the contested nature of our history encourages them to challenge inequality and to promote cultural diversity.

This is an important first step, but it is also problematic. Merely supplementing the prevailing narrative of American history with separate histories of different racial and ethnic groups leaves a Eurocentric narrative at the center. While the perspectives of African Americans, Native Americans, and other groups may be included, they are still confined to commenting on historical periods and events deemed important by mainstream White American culture. Ultimately, what is needed is a new narrative of U.S. history, one that focuses on the historical moments in which different groups interacted over, even fought over, issues of justice, equality, and civil and political rights.

While the studies we have reviewed are provocative, there is a problem with this line of research. The investigators have examined primarily monocultural or bicultural classrooms. Although not easy by any means, it is a relatively uncomplicated task to modify practices and reorganize classrooms when they are composed of no more than two culturally different groups. The job grows enormously in complexity when the classrooms are composed of students from many different ethnic and linguistic groups. Are there lessons to be learned from these monocultural and bicultural studies for *multi*-cultural classrooms? We glean five generalizations from these studies about ways to organize classroom practices for the benefit of many cultural groups.

1. Academic Rigor with Social Supports. Maintaining high expectations, focusing on comprehension rather than decoding, on sense making rather than decontextualized skills drills, may very well be better ways of teaching all children. When academically rigorous instruction is conducted within a community of scholarship accompanied by a system of social supports, then all students seem to benefit. But if culturally sensitive features are added to the curriculum without adding academically demanding curriculum, then minority students may not benefit and achieve.

2. Student-Centered Classroom and Discourse Organization. The use of small-group instruction instead of whole-group instruction, cooperative groups instead of individualized, competitive instruction, turn-taking rules that facilitate student-initiated participation instead of teacher-mandated participation, seem to have general appeal across cultural groups. When student-centered participation structures are employed, students are more actively engaged *and* perform at a higher cognitive level.

3. The Teacher as Ethnographer. There is a tendency for teachers, in the name of multicultural education, to want to learn details about the ethnic traditions of different cultural groups. As we have said elsewhere (Cazden & Mehan, 1989), while this strategy is attractive and has some merit, it is probably impossible and potentially dangerous—impossible because there may be too many ethnic groups in a classroom, and dangerous because limited knowledge will lead to stereotypes that impede learning. Instead of trying to learn *the generalities of ethnic groups in the abstract,* the studies we have reviewed here are recommending that teachers learn about *the details of their students' lives in the particular.* This means teachers will need to explore their students' knowledge and experiences (see 4, below) by observing their students in the classroom, on the playground, and in the community, and by talking with students, their families, and members of the community. The context-specific nature of cultural knowledge means that what the teacher learns about students one year may not apply to students in the next year. Therefore, teachers will have to engage in this ethnographic process on a regular basis.

4. Students' Knowledge as Resource. Instead of denying the coherence and personal significance of the language and culture of the home by trying to eradicate their expression within the school, this research suggests employing the knowledge and experiences that students bring to school with them as resources for instruction. When classroom discourse, curricular content, and classroom organization have been modified to incorporate students' "funds of knowledge" and everyday experiences, students are more engaged and more productive (Moll et al., 1988, 1989; Roseberry et al., 1992).

Without doubt, ethnic pride and self-esteem are essential for healthy human development. These processes develop more fully when fortified by rigorous academic instruction, which in turn is accompanied by a dynamic system of social supports. If students' language, culture, and knowledge are blocked from entering the classroom, students resist this cultural exclusion. Student resistance operates every bit as much against teachers from the same racial-ethnic background as it does against teachers from the so-called majority or dominant groups.

5. Adapt General Principles to Local Circumstances. This is itself a more general principle. No matter how impressive, no matter how provocative, general recommendations must be modified to fit local circumstances (Cazden & Mehan, 1989). Or to paraphrase Goldenberg & Gallimore (1989, p. 45): To be successful, universally valid principles must be artfully fitted to the local niches of schools and classrooms. While it is true that small-group instruction, voluntary turn-allocation procedures,

and funds of knowledge seem to be universally productive forms of instruction, each school experience, each classroom, is different. Therefore, each school will have to adopt a local version of these universal principles. As Vogt, Jordan, and Tharp's (1987) attempt to implement the Hawaiian version of the KEEP curriculum with Navajos shows, each "artful implementation" will have to be sensitive to the features of the children's experience in local circumstances.

References

Armento, B. J., Nash, G. B., Slater, C. L., & Wixson, K. K. (1991). *A more perfect union*. Boston: Houghton Mifflin.

Au, K. (1980). Participation structures in a reading lesson with Hawaiian children. *Anthropology and Education Quarterly, 11*(2), 91–115.

Au, K., & Jordan, C. (1981). Teaching reading to Hawaiian children: Finding a culturally appropriate solution. In H. Trueba, G. P. Guthrie, & K. H. Au (Eds.), *Culture and the bilingual classroom* (pp. 139–152). Rowley MA: Newberry House.

Banks, J. A., & Banks, C. A. M. (Eds.). (1989). *Multicultural education: Issues and perspectives*. Boston: Allyn and Bacon.

Barnhardt, C. (1982). "Tuning in": Athabaskan teachers and students. In R. Barnhardt (Ed.), *Cross-cultural issues in Alaskan education* (pp. 87–98). Fairbanks: University of Alaska, Center for Cross-Cultural Studies.

Blum, A. (1971). *Key issues in the African American experience*. New York: Harcourt Brace Jovanovich.

Brown, A. L., Ash, D., Rutherford, M., Nakagawa, K., Gordon, A., & Campione, J. C. (in press). In G. Salomon (Ed.), *Distributed cognitions*. New York: Cambridge University Press.

Brown, A. L., & Palinscar, A. M. (1989). Guided cooperative learning and individiual knowledge acquisition. In L. B. Resnick (Ed.), *Cognition and instruction: Issues and agendas* (pp. 393–451). Hillsdale, NJ: Lawrence Erlbaum Associates.

California State Department of Education (1988). *History-social science framework for California public schools kindergarten through grade twelve*. Sacramento: Author.

Cazden, C. B. (1979). *Peekaboo as an instructional strategy: Discourse development at home and at school* (Papers and Reports on Child Language Development #17). Stanford, CA: Stanford University, Department of Linguistics.

Cazden, C. B. (1988). *Classroom discourse*. Portsmouth, NH: Heineman.

Cazden, C. B., & Mehan, H. (1989). Principles from sociology and anthropology: Context, code, classroom and culture. In M. C. Reynolds (Ed.), *Knowledge base for the beginning teacher* (pp. 42–57). Oxford, England: Pergamon.

Chubb, J. E., & Moe, T. M. (1990). *Politics, markets and America's schools*. Washington, DC: The Brookings Institution.

Cole, M., & Scribner, S. (1974). *Culture and thought*. New York: Wiley.

Diaz, S., Moll, L. C., & Mehan, H. (1986). Sociocultural resources in instruction: A context specific approach. In *Beyond Language* (pp. 187–230). California State University, Los Angeles: Evaluation, Dissemination and Assessment Center.

Duran, R. P., & Szymanski, M. (1992, December). *Activity and learning in cooperative learning*. Paper presented at the annual meeting of the American Anthropological Association, San Francisco.

Erickson, F., & Mohatt, G. (1982). Participant structures in two communities. In G. D. Spindler (Ed.), *Doing the ethnography of schooling* (pp. 132–175). New York: Holt, Rinehart & Winston.

Erikson, F., & Schultz, J. (1992). Student experience and the curriculum. In P. W. Jackson (Ed.), *Handbook of research on curriculum* (pp. 465–485). New York: Macmillan.

Fine, M. (1991). *Framing dropouts: Notes on the politics of an urban public high school*. Albany: State University of New York Press.

Foley, D. (1990). *Learning capitalist culture: Deep in the heart of tejas*. Philadelphia: University of Pennsylvania Press.

Foster, G. E. (1991). *Independent schools owned by African Americans*. New York: Toussaint Institute Fund.

Foster, M. (1989). "It's cookin' now": A performance analysis of the speech events in an urban community college. *Language in Society, 18*, 1–29.

Franklin, J. H. (1969) *From slavery to freedom: A history of Negro Americans* (3rd ed.). New York: Vintage Books.

Giroux, H. (1988). *Schooling and the struggle for public life: Critical pedagogy in the modern age*. Minneapolis: University of Minnesota Press.

Goldenberg, C. N., & Gallimore, R. (1989). Teaching California's diverse student populations: The common ground between educational and cultural research. *California Public Schools Forum, 3*, 41–65.

Grant C. A., & Sleeter, C. E. (1986). Educational equity: Education that is multicultural and reconstructionist. *Journal of Educational Equity and Leadership, 6*(2), 105–118.

Gumperz, J. J., & Field, M. (1992, December). Paper presented at the annual meeting of the American Anthropological Association, San Francisco.

Hanna, J. L. (1982). Public policy and the children's world: Implications of ethnographic work for desegregated schooling. In G. D. Spindler (Ed.), *Doing the ethnography of schooling* (pp. 316–335). New York: Holt, Rinehart & Winston.

Heath, S. B. (1982). Questioning at home and at school: A comparative study. In G. D. Spindler (Ed.), *Doing the ethnography of schooling* (pp. 96–101). New York: Holt, Rinehart & Winston.

Heath, S. B. (1986). Sociocultural contexts of language development. In *Beyond Language* (pp. 143–186). California State University, Los Angeles: Evaluation, Dissemination and Assessment Center.

Holquist, M. (1983). The politics of representation. *The Newsletter of the Laboratory of Comparative Human Cognition, 5*(1), 2–9.

Howe, J. E. (Ed.). (1984). *Matter and motion*. Pensacola, FL: A Beka Books.

Howe, J. E. (Ed.). (1986). *The history of our United States*. Pensacola, FL: A Beka Books.

John, V. K. (1972). Styles of learning—styles of teaching: Reflections on the education of Navajo children. In C. B. Cazden, D. Hymes, & V. K. John (Eds.), *Functions of language in the classroom* (pp. 331–343). New York: Teachers College Press.

Kagan, S. (1986). Cooperative learning and sociocultural factors in school. In *Beyond Language* (pp. 231–298). California State University, Los Angeles: Evaluation, Dissemination and Assessment Center.

Key statistics for private elementary and secondary education: School year 1989–90. (1989, December) (Early Estimates, Survey Report No. NCES 90-206). Washington, DC: National Center for Educational Statistics, U.S. Department of Education.

Knorr-Cetina, K. D., & Mulkay, M. (Eds.). (1983). *Science observed: Perspectives on the social study of science.* London: Sage Publications.

Laosa, L. M. (1973). Reform in educational and psychological assessment: Cultural and linguistic issues. *Journal of the Association of Mexican-American Educators, 1,* 19–24.

Latour, B., & Woolgar, S. (1986). *Laboratory life: The social construction of scientific facts.* Princeton, NJ: Princeton University Press.

Lester, J. L. (1968). *To be a slave.* New York: Scholastic.

Lincoln, C. E., & Mamiya, L. H. (1990). *The Black church in the African American experience.* Durham, NC: Duke University Press.

Lintz, A., & Okamoto, D. (1993, May). *Dilemmas of multicultural education in African American independent schools.* Paper presented at the Conference of the Linguistic Minority Research Institute, UC Santa Barbara, CA.

MacLeod, J. (1987). *Ain't no makin' it.* Boulder, CO: Westview Press.

McCarty, T. L., Wallace S., Lynch, R. H., & Benally, A. (1991). Classroom inquiry and Navajo learning styles: A call for reassessment. *Anthropology and Education Quarterly, 22,* 42–59.

McCullum, P. (1989). Turn-allocation in lessons with North American and Puerto Rican students. *Anthropology and Education Quarterly, 20,* 133–156.

McLaren, P., & Estrada, K. (1993) A dialog on multiculturalism and democratic culture. *Educational Researcher, 22*(3), 27–33.

Mehan, H. (1979). *Learning lessons.* Cambridge, MA: Harvard University Press.

Mehan, H., & Wills, J. S. (1988). MEND: A nurturing voice in the nuclear arms debate. *Social Problems, 35*(4), 363–383.

Metz, M. H. (1980). *Classrooms and corridors: The crisis of authority in desegregated secondary schools.* Berkeley: University of California Press.

Metz, M. H. (1986). *Different by design.* London: Routledge & Kegan Paul.

Moll, L. C., & Diaz, S. (1987). Change as the goal of educational research. *Anthropology and Education Quarterly, 18,* 300–311.

Moll, L. C., Vélez-Ibáñez, C., & Greenberg, J. (1988). *Project implementation plan: Community knowledge and classroom practice: Combining resources for literacy instruction.* Tucson: University of Arizona Press.

Moll, L. C., Vélez-Ibáñez, C., & Greenberg, J. (1989). *Fieldwork summary: Community knowledge and classroom practice: Combining resources for literacy instruction.* Tucson: University of Arizona.

More, A. J. (1989) Native Indian learning styles: A review for researchers and teachers. *Journal of American Indian Education, 3,* 15–28.

O'Conner, R. P. (1992). *Black resistance in high school: Forging a separatist culture.* Albany: State University of New York Press.

Ogbu, J. U. (1974). *The next generation: An ethnogrpahy of education in an urban neighborhood.* New York: Academic Press.

Parsons, P. F. (1987). *Inside America's Christian schools.* Macon, GA: Mercer University Press.

Peshkin, A. (1986). *God's choice: The total world of a fundamentalist Christian school.* Chicago: University of Chicago Press.

Peshkin, A. (1991). *The color of strangers, the color of friends.* Chicago: University of Chicago Press.

Philips, S. U. (1982). *The invisible culture: Communication in classroom and community on the Warm Springs reservation.* New York: Longman.

Piestrup, A. (1973). *Black dialect interference and accommodation of reading instruction in the first grade* (Monographs of the Language Behavior Research Lab). Berkeley: University of California.

Ratteray, J. D., & Shujaa, M. (1987). *Dare to choose: Parental choice at independent neighborhood schools.* Washington, DC: Institute for Independent Education.

Rist, R. C. (1970). Student social class and teacher expectations: The self-fulfilling prophecy in ghetto education. *Harvard Educational Review 40*(3), 411–451.

Rist, R. C. (1979). *Desegregated schools: Appraisals of an American experience.* New York: Academic Press.

Rose, S. (1988). *Keeping them out of the hands of Satan: Evangelical schooling in America.* London: Routledge & Kegan Paul.

Roseberry, A. S., Warren, B., & Conant, F. R. (1992). *Appropriating scientific discourse: Findings from language minority classrooms* (Working Paper #1). Cambridge, MA: Technical Educational Research Center.

Sacks, H., Schegloff, E., & Jefferson, G. (1974). A simplist systematics for the organization of turn-taking in conversation. *Language, 50,* 696–735.

Schofield, J. W. (1982). *Black and White in school: Trust, tension or tolerance?* New York: Praeger.

Schultz, J., Florio, S., & Erickson, F. (1982). Where's the floor? *The Quarterly Newsletter of the Laboratory of Comparative Human Cognition, 4,* 2–9.

Shapin, S. (1984). Pump and circumstance: Robert Boyle's literary technology. *Social Studies of Science, 14,* 481–520.

Shapiro, M. J. (1988). *The politics of representation: Writing practices in biography, photography, and policy analysis.* Madison: University of Wisconsin Press.

Shuy, R., & Griffin, P. (1978). *The study of children's functional language and education in the early years.* Arlington, VA: Center for Applied Linguistics.

Sinclair, J. M., & Coulthard, R. M. (1975). *Toward an analysis of discourse.* New York: Oxford University Press.

Sleeter, C. E., & Grant, C. A. (1987). An analysis of multicultural education in the United States. *Harvard Educational Review, 57*(4), 421–444.

Sleeter, C. E., & Grant, C. A. (1991). Race, class, gender, and disability in current textbooks. In M. W. Apple & L. K. Christian-Smith (Eds.), *The politics of the textbook* (pp. 78–110). London: Routledge & Kegan Paul.

Taylor, D., & Dorsey-Grimes, C. (1988). *Growing up literate: Learning from inner city families.* Portsmouth, NH: Heinemann.

Taylor, M. D. (1976). *Roll of thunder, hear my cry.* New York: Bantam.

Tharp, R. G. (1989). Culturally compatible education: A formula for designing effective classrooms. In H. T. Trueba, G. Spindler, & L. Spindler (Eds.), *What do anthropologists have to say about dropouts?* (pp. 51–66). New York: Falmer Press.

Tharp, R., & Gallimore, R. (1988). *Rousing minds to life: Teaching, learning, and schooling in social context.* Cambridge, England: Cambridge University Press.

Vogt, L. A., Jordan C., & Tharp, R. (1987). Explaining school failure, producing school success: Two cases. *Anthropology and Education Quarterly, 18*(4), 276–288.

Wagner, J. (1969). *Misfits and missionaries.* Beverly Hills, CA: Sage.

Weis, L. (1985). *Between two worlds.* London: Routledge & Kegan Paul.

Weis, L. (1990). *Working class without work.* London: Routledge & Kegan Paul.

Wilcox, E. (1982). Differential socialization in classrooms: Implications for equal opportunity. In G. D. Spindler (Ed.), *Doing the ethnography of schooling* (pp. 268–309). New York: Holt, Rinehart & Winston.

Willis, P. (1979). *Learning to labor.* New York: Columbia Teachers College Press.

Wills, J. S. (1993, August) *The situation of African Americans in American history: Using history as a resource for understanding the experiences of contemporary African Americans.* Paper presented at the annual meeting of the American Sociological Association, Miami.

Wills, J. S. (in press). Popular culture, curriculum and historical representation: The situation of Native Americans in American history and the perpetuation of stereotypes. *Journal of Narrative and Life History, 4.*

Wilson, W. J. (1987). *The truly disadvantaged.* Chicago: University of Chicago Press.

· 9 ·

MULTICULTURAL EDUCATION THROUGH THE LENS OF THE MULTICULTURAL EDUCATION RESEARCH LITERATURE

Carl A. Grant
UNIVERSITY OF WISCONSIN, MADISON

William F. Tate
UNIVERSITY OF WISCONSIN, MADISON

Disciplined inquiry in education is a relatively new field of study. The original paradigmatic boundaries of educational research were borrowed from scholarship in psychology. Landsherre (1988) points out that educational research was first known as experimental pedagogy. Theoretical principles of experimental pedagogy were isomorphic to that of experimental psychology, a phrase credited to Wundt in around 1880 (see, e.g., Wundt, 1894). According to Landsherre (1988), experimental pedagogy was introduced around 1900 with inquiries conducted by Lay and Meumann in Germany; Binet and Simon in France; Rice, Thorndike, and Judd in the United States; Claparede in Switzerland; Mercante in Argentina; Schuyten in Belgium; Winch in England; and Sikorsky and Netschajeff in Russia. From 1900 to the present, the study of educational problems developed quickly and three major research movements evolved: (a) the child study movement, where the research was linked to applied child psychology; (b) the progressive movement, where philosophy took precedence over the tenets of science, and life experience over the scientific method; and (c) the scientific research movement, with a logical positivist approach to educational problem solving (Landsherre, 1988).

The philosophical precepts of multicultural education are most strongly connected to the progressive movement of educational research. Multicultural education as an educational philosophy and ideology was born out of the civil rights movements of the 1960s and the early 1970s. It was originally conceptualized as an educational effort to counter racism in schools (see, e.g., Baker, 1973; Banks, 1975; C.A. Grant, 1975; Sizemore, 1979; Gay, 1983; Gollnick & Chin, 1986). It soon expanded to become the umbrella term for a school reform movement that addresses issues of race, ethnicity, gender, socioeconomic class, language, and disability (C. A. Grant & Sleeter, 1986). C. A. Grant (1993) provides insight into the thinking and hopes of many multicultural education theorists (see, e.g., Baker, 1973; Hilliard, 1974; Sullivan, 1974).

Multicultural education is a philosophical concept and an educational process. It is a concept built upon the philosophical ideals of freedom, justice, equality, equity, and human dignity that are contained in American documents such as the Constitution and the Declaration of Independence. It recognizes, however, that equality and equity are not the same thing: equal access does not necessarily guarantee fairness. Multicultural education is a process that takes place in schools and other educational institutions and informs all subject areas and other aspects of the curriculum. It prepares all students to work actively toward structural equality in the organizations and institutions of the United States. It helps students to develop positive self-concepts and discover who they are, particularly in terms of their multiple group memberships. Multicultural education does this by providing knowledge about the history, culture, and contributions of the diverse groups that have shaped history, politics, and culture of the United States. Multicultural education acknowledges that the strength and riches of the United States are a result of its human diversity. It demands a college and school staff that is multiracial and multiculturally literate, including K–8 staff members who are capable of teaching in more than one language. It demands a curriculum that organizes concepts and content around the contributions, perspectives, and experiences of the myriad groups that are part of American society. It confronts social issues involving race, ethnicity, socioeconomic class, gender, homophobia, and disability. It accomplishes this by providing instruction in familiar contexts and building on students' diverse ways of thinking. It encourages student investigations of world and national events and how these events affect their lives. It teaches critical thinking skills, as well as democratic decision making, social action and empowerment skills. Finally, multicultural education is a total process: it cannot be truncated: all components of its definition must be in place in order for multicultural education to be genuine and viable. (pp. 4–5)

This chapter begins with a discussion of some of the problems associated with conducting research on race, class, and gender in education. Next, the heuristic used to analyze the literature on multicultural education is presented. We continue with an analysis of research studies on curriculum and text materials; preservice preparation of teachers; practicing teachers; and teacher-student relationships. We then delineate barriers to multicultural education research and conclude with our final discussion.

Our focus is on the philosophical tenets and the influence of multicultural education found in the research literature, rather than on research methods and procedures. We have not included research studies on bilingual and multilingual education; this research is included in chapters 24 and 25 of this *Handbook*.

We have not been able to locate all research reports that appear in special printings and volumes of limited circulation. Nevertheless, we feel that the literature reported in this chapter will provide the reader with important insight into multicultural education research.

THE TROUBLED STATE OF RESEARCH ON RACE, CLASS, AND GENDER

A substantial increase in research on race occurred after the 1954 *Brown v. Board of Education of Topeka* decision. However, this research, as Taeuber (1977) points out in the foreword to Weinberg's book, *Minority Students: A Research Appraisal* (1977), had methodological, theoretical, and conceptual problems. Weinberg frames the problems in the introduction to his book:

The present volume places research on minority students in a broader framework than is customary. Factors treated at some length include historical and legal background, the ideology of racism, a continuing reexamination and questioning of prevailing views of the role of social class and race in learning, and the impact of minority communities upon the schools. . . . Too often theoretical studies proceed in virtual ignorance of this reality. Curiously, this failing is rarely commented on in the research literature. (p. v)

Lightfoot (1980) also contends that earlier research on minority students had many shortcomings. She argues that much of this research lacked insight into the context in which students live, cope, and survive. Although she praises the historical importance of the work of Clark and Clark (1947), she argues

that their study reduced the complexities of the African American experience to "simple, understandable, dramatic data" (Lightfoot, 1980, p. 5). Lightfoot stated:

One of the obvious interpretative difficulties with using the Clarks' findings as evidence of the value of desegregation for children is that their research did not describe the natural behaviors and perceptions of children but rather their responses to a contrived experimental task. (p. 5)

Race, ethnicity, and social-class variables vital to desegregation research are also vital to multicultural education research. However, an important distinction between these two areas of research is that much of the (earlier) desegregation research was "decision oriented" (see, e.g., Tate, Ladson-Billings, & Grant, 1993). Green, Bakan, McMillan, and Lezotte (1973) made this point when they observed that most of the research funded by the federal government and foundations is decision oriented, that is, research designed to provide information to a decision maker (p. 624). Similarly, Taeuber (1977) concluded:

Despite repeated pleas for a coordinated and systematic research effort, despite establishment of sundry desegregation assistance and research centers, and despite sporadic governmental and private conferences, symposia, and reports, the flood of publications roars on, largely unharnessed by those most in need of its power. Educational administrators in search of advice on how to desegregate effectively, attorneys in search of empirical information on complex issues of feasibility and effectiveness, social scientists in search of new knowledge from a vast national experiment in social change—all find themselves inundated. (p. iii)

Besides being decision oriented, much of the desegregation research, and research in general that used race, class, and gender as variables, is narrowly conceived. Much of the desegregation research dealt with Black achievement (see, e.g., Vane, Weitzman, & Applebaum, 1966; R. Scott, 1969; Crain, 1971) and Black aspirations (see, e.g., Ausubel & Ausubel, 1963; Coleman, 1967) and did not situate race and gender in a historical context that takes into account the relationship between oppression and privilege (Weinberg, 1977).

Social class and socioeconomic status are often reduced in educational research to variables used to categorize student achievement data. This research often ignores the cultural reproduction and the transmission of knowledge related to socioeconomic status, gender, and race. For example, Apple (1979) suggests there is a relationship between the curriculum, pedagogy, and forms of evaluation in schools and the structural inequality in the larger society. He contends that researchers must get inside both the school and the workplace in order to develop a more complete analysis of the relationship between education and the state and between culture and economy in education (see also Bernstein, 1973; Bourdieu, 1973).

The following statement by Spender (1982) characterizes the troubled state of gender research in education: "Our problems had not been perceived as problems" (p. 141). Spender and other feminists point out that the perspectives of women have not appeared across the disciplines of the academy and in research conducted by the academy. The absence of women's voices in academic discourse has kept "their problems" on the margins of educational research and preserves them as the "others" in the academic community. Gender research in education has also been complicated by the failure of researchers to address different ethnic and racial group experiences within the feminist analysis (see, e.g., hooks, 1990).

In sum, for many, educational research becomes problematic when it does not include race, class, and gender, and/or when these constructs are not rigorously interrogated. For others, educational research becomes problematic when it *does* include race, class, and gender. However, not to include these social constructs, and not to provide a rigorous interrogation, means, for example, that the day-to-day life of students in their social milieu, and the interaction of the school within that milieu, are not studied. Furthermore, there is not sufficient consideration given to the idea that the school is itself reproducing racial, class, and/or gender inequities (Weinberg, 1977).

APPROACHES TO MULTICULTURAL EDUCATION

Since the conception of multicultural education and its continuous growth, there have been several approaches (e.g., C. A. Grant & Sleeter, 1985; C. A. Grant, Sleeter, & Anderson, 1986; Sleeter & Grant, 1987) or dimensions (Banks, 1992) that have been used to define or characterize research and scholarship. These approaches or dimensions have illuminated the direction taken and the epistemological boundaries of multicultural education. We will use the approaches as benchmark criteria to classify and judge the various studies that are reported in the subsequent sections of this chapter. C. A. Grant and Sleeter (1985) described the approaches as follows.

Teacher-education programs operating from the *Teaching the Exceptional and Culturally Different* approach prepare preservice students to fit K–12 students into the existing social structure and Eurocentric culture. Education methods suggest relating the subject matter taught to K–12 students to their life experiences and concentrating their learning on the basic skills. Preservice students make the curriculum relevant to the K–12 students' background and learning styles, and adapt it to their skill levels. Educational programs that prepare teachers for teaching the culturally different student raise very few, if any, questions about the dominant culture's traditional aims. Rather, the stress is on techniques for building a bridge between K–12 students and the schools they attend, and helping the students adapt to the norms of the dominant culture. The problem of cultural discontinuity remains that of the students.

The *Human Relations* approach attempts to foster positive effective relationships among members of racial and cultural groups, and/or between males and females, to strengthen student self-concept, and to increase school and social harmony. A teacher-education program stressing the human relations approach has in place curriculum that teaches preservice students how to develop lessons and activities that eliminate race, class, and gender stereotyping, and that promote individual differences and similarities. The importance of celebrating cultural holidays and highlighting heroes and heroines, and the importance of including the works of some authors of color and

women in the curriculum, are pointed out. Similarly, the importance of using cooperative grouping for teaching K–12 students how to work together, and for motivating learning, is addressed. Moreover, teacher education from a human relations perspective prepares teachers to honor diverse student backgrounds and to promote harmony among students. Real conflict among groups is often glossed over and a critical examination of race, class, and gender oppression does not take place.

The *Single-Group Studies* approach promotes social structural equality for, and immediate recognition of, an identified group. Commonly implemented in the form of ethnic studies or women's studies, these programs assume that knowledge about particular oppressed groups should be taught separately from conventional classroom knowledge, either in separate units or separate courses. Teacher-education programs advocating a single-group studies approach seek to raise consciousness concerning an identified group (e.g., Native Americans) by teaching their K–12 students about the culture and contributions of that group, as well as about how it has been oppressed by and/or has worked with the dominant groups in our society. Teacher-education programs that place the majority of their graduates in particular geographical areas or find that the majority of their graduates are employed in a particular community may stress this approach.

The *Multicultural Education* approach promotes social structural equality and cultural pluralism. The curriculum is organized around the contributions and perspectives of different cultural groups, and it examines how race, class, and gender inequities are played out in the various areas of society. Language arts methods courses as well as science methods courses see their subject matter as reflecting the concerns and culture of different ethnic groups and men as well as women. Future teachers learn how gender-biased socialization and race and social-class oppression get transmitted to their own teaching practices, and pay attention to how males and females from different ethnic backgrounds are socialized. They learn how to build on K–12 students' learning styles, adapt to their individual skill levels, and involve students actively in thinking and analyzing.

The *Education that Is Multicultural and Social Reconstructionist* (EMC-SR) approach extends the previous approaches (especially the last two) by teaching future teachers how to teach their K–12 students to analyze inequality and oppression in society critically, particularly in their own life circumstance. It also teaches K–12 students how to develop skills for social action. An EMC-SR teacher-education program would promote structural equality and cultural pluralism and prepare its graduates to work actively toward structural equality.

These approaches provide a theoretical backdrop for analyzing multicultural education research. The approaches can be applied to different research focuses (e.g., curriculum, teacher education, teacher-student relations) to determine their attention to the philosophy and ideology of multicultural education (see, e.g., C. A. Grant, 1992). The purpose of the following section is to discuss the multicultural education research on various areas of schooling in relationship to the approaches delineated above.

STUDIES IN THE MULTICULTURAL EDUCATION LITERATURE

In this section we will present a discussion and analysis of the following areas: curriculum and text materials, preservice education, practicing teachers, and teacher-student relations. These were selected in part because they represent the educational area that have received the most "multicultural" research attention and there is relatively less of a possibility that they would duplicate other research reported in this *Handbook*.

Curriculum and Text Materials

Among the practices of schooling that have received the most ongoing research attention in relation to multicultural issues are curriculum and text materials. Inspired by the outcries of parents, educators, and civic and educational organizations, along with some textbook publishers who realized that multicultural concerns have severe marketplace consequences, curriculum materials and text materials have been subjected to a good deal of research analysis to determine race, class, gender, and disability bias. We have organized our discussion of the curriculum materials in chronological order.

One of the earliest calls for attention to textbook bias was made by the National Association for the Advancement of Colored People in a 1939 pamphlet entitled *Anti-Negro Propaganda in School Textbooks*. In 1949 the American Council on Education did the first comprehensive study of text materials and reported that secondary social studies textbooks were "distressingly inadequate, inappropriate and even damaging to intergroup relations" (American Council on Education, 1949, p. 16).

In 1964 Elson's *Guardians of Tradition* was published. This book was a comprehensive analysis of 1,000 K–8 school textbooks of the 19th century. Elson was interested in discovering the ideas and beliefs of the "common man and woman," and believed that school textbooks were a solid lead to this understanding. She wrote:

Apart from the Bible, the books most widely read in nineteenth-century America were not those written by intellectuals, but schoolbooks written by printers, journalists, teachers, ministers, and future lawyers earning their way through college. The selective process by which these people decided what political, economic, social, cultural, and moral concepts should be presented to American youth undoubtedly helped to form the average American's view of the past, the present, and the possible future of man. (p. vii)

Elson offers an observation that helps to explain how xenophobia and racism became a part of our textbooks:

The American as the ideal man, is of the white race, of Northern European background, Protestant, self made. ... Although schoolbook authors consider themselves guardians of liberty, they can be more accurately described as guardians of tradition. (p. 340)

In spite of the increasing number of research studies on textbook bias that were becoming part of the educational land-

scape, the general public's first major exposure to the bias in textbooks was reported in the *Saturday Review* in 1963—"Life Is Fun in a Smiling, Fair-Skinned World," by Otto Klineberg. This report was followed by a number of research studies conducted on textbook bias.

The Michigan Department of Education (1971), Council on Interracial Books for Children (1976), Butterfield, Demos, Grant, Moy, and Perez (1979), Federbush (1973), Hirschfelder (1975), Kane (1970), Oliver (1974), Showalter (1971), Swanson (1977), Trecker (1971, 1973), and Women on Words and Images (1972) all conducted research studies of textbooks in the 1970s to determine their responsiveness to multicultural issues. These studies acknowledged that there was some improvement from the blunt racism of previous decades. However, they were in close agreement that the portrayal of Blacks, Native Americans, and other peoples of color in textbooks was still marginalized, or omitted, or presented negatively and often inaccurately (e.g., Butterfield et al., 1979; Council on Interracial Books for Children, 1976; Hirschfelder, 1975). Women and girls were for the most part stereotypes, passive, placed in secondary roles, or omitted (e.g., Council on Interracial Books for Children, 1976; Oliver, 1974). Social class and socioeconomic status were rarely discussed: at best, one or two stories would be situated in a lower socioeconomic setting (e.g., Butterfield et al., 1979) Similarly, a character with a disability, especially as a central focus, was rare (e.g., Butterfield et al., 1979). The conclusion and discussion in most of the studies on textbooks, while arguing for fairer treatment and larger representation of people of color and women, by and large situated their argument in C. A. Grant and Sleeter's (1985) Human Relations approach. Including people of color, women, and people who live at or below the poverty level in a positive manner in the American story, or in the discussion of controversial issues, were the goals suggested by the authors in their critiques of the studies. For example, the Commission on Ethnic Bias for the Association for Supervision and Curriculum Development posited, "The instructional materials of our schools are expected to reflect our national heritage, goals, and aspirations and are so accepted" (Miller, 1974, p. 11). Absent was any mention of the linkage between knowledge and power, more specifically whose knowledge is considered foremost and at whose expense the power had been acquired. These critiques lacked any discussion of the way textbooks developed on the basis of "accepted" national goals helped to perpetuate the creation of symbolic others. For example, Native American culture was usually depicted as uncivilized and savage, the opposite of the "civilized" Anglo-Saxon culture.

Studies of textbook bias, especially for sexism, have continued to receive attention in the 1980s and 1990s. Reading textbooks (Britton, Lumpkin, & Britton, 1984; Scott, 1981), social studies and economics textbooks (Hahn & Blankship, 1983; Tetreault, 1984, 1986), and science textbooks (Powell & Garcia, 1988) have been analyzed for sexism. These analyses all conclude that females appear in texts more than in the past. Males, however, still dominate, and although some women are portrayed in nontraditional roles, many are still role stereotyped. These authors assert for the most part that much more needs to be done to depict women in today's society accurately. This argument is situated in C. A. Grant and Sleeter's (1985) Single-Group Studies approach. The studies reviewed suggest that more and more textbook publishers are recognizing the prejudice inherent in past portrayals of women in "traditional" roles and are moving to represent women in a multitude of careers. Nevertheless, they point out that males remain in very "traditional" roles, thus illustrating how textbooks are still constructing female roles differently from male roles. In fact, we contend that females continue to serve as the index to frame what is considered a male role. That is, males are active, and do science, business, and athletics, whereas females are active and passive, and do art and science, language and math, and cheerleading.

Studies of racial bias in textbooks decreased in the 1980s; studies of social class and disability, while limited before, continued at a similar pace. Sleeter and Grant (1991) suggest that this might have been because many educators assumed that racial bias was being addressed by publishers. A similar argument may be applied to socioeconomic bias, class bias, and disability. In their study of grades 1–8 social studies, reading and language arts, science, and mathematics textbooks with copyright dates between 1980 and 1988, Sleeter and Grant (1991) concluded:

Treatment of diversity in textbooks has not improved much over the past fifteen years or so, generally, although a few textbooks have improved in specific, limited ways. There was a flurry of activity to "multiculturalize" textbooks during the late 1960's and early 1970's, although that activity never did address social class in textbooks. That activity may have stopped, and we may be entering an era of backsliding, a return to more White and male-dominated curricula. (p. 101)

In the 1990s studies have continued to call attention to the need for greater and more accurate inclusion of people of color, women, people with disabilities, and people living at or below poverty. The investigation of history textbooks in California is a case in point (Reinhold, 1991). This was perhaps the most extensive and publicized investigation of textbooks since the 1974 Kanawha County, West Virginia, examination of language art and English textbooks, and the 1975 *Man: A Course of Study* (Education Development Center, 1968). The California curriculum controversy came about when the history textbooks submitted for state adoption were harshly criticized for their lack of attention to diversity. Seven out of nine publishing companies submitted new history and social science textbooks that failed to meet the criteria set forth in the California's *History–Social Science Framework* (1981). Included in the criteria was that the books must represent the true multicultural nature of society and must disclose the perspective of people of color in history, not as just victims but as contributors, and not as "add-on's," but interwoven throughout the historical accounts.

These books received careful scrutiny from several educators, including Joyce King (1992) who argued that they lacked ethnic diversity and contained inaccuracies, racial stereotypes, distortions, omissions, and negative images of African American people. King and colleagues (e.g., Ladson-Billings, 1992a) were advocates of textbooks conceived on epistemological pillars more closely aligned with the multicultural education approach.

The study of text materials is perhaps among the oldest areas of multicultural education research. Several trends emerge from this research. First, this area of inquiry continues to be a very popular field of research, especially in textbook analysis of reading and social studies texts. Noticeably limited are studies involving mathematics text materials and other emerging school areas of study (e.g., computer literacy). Second, educational organizations (e.g., Council on Interracial Books for Children) and academicians are both contributing to the analysis and research of textbooks. Third, the research in this area is beginning to examine the relationship between textbooks and the economic, historical, intellectual, and social constructs of U.S. society.

Preservice Preparation

Research studies on preservice programs that focus on multicultural education are limited. At the time this chapter was written, we could locate only 47 studies. It is important that we add that research in teacher education, in general, is sparse. Houston (1990), editor of the *Handbook of Research on Teacher Education,* stated: "There has been notable recent progress, but the research basis for such important work as educating the nation's teachers is still extremely thin. Although the importance of research is being espoused, little progress is being made" (p. ix). The research studies available cluster into the following areas: university-based workshops, courses, and programs; field immersion with and without preservice courses; culturally diverse placement; and cooperating teachers and supervisors.

University Workshops. Perhaps the earliest efforts to investigate the implementation of multicultural education in preservice programs was conducted by Baker in 1973, when she sought to determine whether providing a workshop on multicultural education would benefit her preservice students (Baker, 1973, 1977). McDiarmid and Price (1990) studied the impact of a multicultural workshop on preservice students, and Henington (1981) studied the impact of short concentrated periods of multicultural instruction on preservice students. These researchers found that workshops and other short periods of multicultural instruction do not have a long-term impact on the stereotypic thinking of preservice students. McDiarmid (1990) and McDiarmid and Price (1990) report that a workshop had virtually no impact on their students. In contrast, Baker (1977) stated: Workshops and other less involved approaches to multicultural training have some benefit. . . . But when this approach is compared to more comprehensive training, it addresses that both time and intensity produce more desirable outcomes" (p. 33).

Each of the four studies focuses on race and ethnicity. However, McDiarmid's (1990) study also addressed gender and language. McDiarmid's study was assigned to the Multicultural approach because the participants examined institutional racism and the integration of multiculturalism into different subjects. Henington's (1991) study was assigned to the Teaching the Exceptionally and Culturally Different approach because it focuses mainly on preparing teachers to help K–12 students to assimilate into mainstream society. McDiarmid and Price's (1990) study was assigned to the Human Relations approach because it addresses teaching tolerance, building self-esteem, and celebrating diversity.

University Courses. Most of the research in preservice teacher education examined courses that included instruction in multi-cultural education. Most often students in foundations and methods courses were examined to see if any change in their outlook regarding race, class, and gender resulted from taking the course. Adler (1991), Ahlquist (1991), Bennett, Niggle, and Stage (1990), Dottin (1984), Gomez (1991), King and Ladson-Billings (1990), King (1991), Ladson-Billings (1991a, 1991b), Larke (1990), Mills (1984), and Sleeter (1988) report that these courses improved preservice students' understanding of multi-cultural education. For example, Bennett et al. studied a course in multicultural education that had as its goals (a) the develop-ment of historical perspectives and cultural consciousness; (b) the development of intercultural competencies; (c) the eradica-tion of racism, prejudice, and discrimination; and (d) the suc-cessful teaching of multicultural students. The authors report that "there is an overall reduction in feeling of social distance even though the course focuses primarily on race and ethnic-ity" (p. 253). These courses, for the most part, offered their students insight into race, gender, and class oppression. The students were provided an opportunity to increase their aware-ness of how certain groups are stereotyped based upon in-come, family background, skin color, gender, test scores, and language. The students were also presented with the history and background of urban students, and insights into how to implement multicultural education. All of these courses, with the exception of Larke's, were using the Multicultural approach. Larke's study focused on preservice teachers' understanding of culturally diverse families, cultural awareness, and cross-cul-tural communication (p. 29), focuses that are more in line with the Human Relations approach.

University Programs. Since the beginning of the 1990s, at-tempts to infuse multicultural education throughout the profes-sional preservice program have been reported. Diez and Mur-rell (1991), Maher (1991), Noordhoff and Kleinfeld (1991, 1993), and Stallings (1992) each report positive results from this infusion method. Noordhoff and Kleinfeld (1991) argue that simply adding multicultural courses to the teacher-prepara-tion curriculum is ineffective and potentially misleading—even damaging (pp. 6, 7).

Maher (1991) describes a teacher-education program that used a Single-Group Studies focus; it centered on gender eq-uity and equality. Diez and Murrell (1991) and Noordhoff and Kleinfeld (1991, 1993) describe programs that are consistent with the Multicultural approach. Both teacher-education pro-grams direct attention to the structural inequality related to race, class, and gender. Noordhoff and Kleinfeld (1991) argue, "It [effective teaching in a culturally diverse setting] means in-cluding in the subject matter of reflection, social, political, and ethical issues which are embedded in teachers' thinking and everyday practice, as well as reflection on teaching perfor-

mance" (p. 11). Stallings (1992) describes her preservice pro-gram goal to enhance the instruction of teachers so that urban children will improve socially, emotionally, physically, and aca-demically. Despite this stated goal, Stallings's program goals appear to have a more technical orientation toward teaching that is consistent with the Teaching the Exceptional and Cultur-ally Different approach. For example, Stallings stated:

Each week student teacher and supervising teacher panels discuss mu-tual concerns. Examples of activities that occurred through the seminars included assessing children's learning levels, conferring with parents, observing peers, preparing lessons using the children's background experiences, preparing lessons with higher order questions and higher cognitive activities, and participation in cooperative group activities. (p. 9)

University Field Experiences. The educational literature sug-gests that the field experience is the most valuable part of the preservice program (Guyton & McIntyre, 1990). Early research on the effect of student teaching or the placement of teacher-education students in urban, racially mixed, or socioeconomi-cally stratified communities is extremely thin. However, since the 1980s there have been several studies that examined the influence of the field experience in a multicultural community on the teaching attitudes and behavior of preservice students (see, e.g., Mahan, 1982a; Cooper, Beare, & Thorman, 1990; Ma-her, 1991; Noordhoff & Kleinfeld, 1991, 1993; Gomez & Tabach-nick, 1991). Results from these studies indicate that the field experience positively influences the teacher-education stu-dent's ability to work with ethnically diverse students and stu-dents whose background is different from their own. Diez and Murrell (1991) stated:

While the faculty have designed the course sequence and field experi-ence to build toward the ability to design effective learning experiences for a diverse student body, the most important context for developing this ability is in the final field seminar and student teaching. (p. 12)

The approach to multicultural education in these field expe-riences varies. The studies by Mahan (1982a), Cooper et al. (1990), Diez and Murrell (1991), and Noordhoff and Kleinfeld (1991, 1993) are consistent with the Human Relations approach because the primary focus of these programs was to prepare preservice students to become comfortable in a culture differ-ent from their own. Mahan (1982a) stated:

A major goal of a cultural immersion teacher preparation program can be to forge a few close friendships between a preservice teacher and members of a cultural group that the teacher had not previously known, understood, or been in contact with in the past. (p. 169)

As we noted earlier, Maher's (1991) course had a Single-Group Studies approach, that is, the pedagogy focused on gen-der equity and equality. Similarly, the student-teaching experi-ence in Maher's program focused on gender equity and equality. Gomez and Tabachnick (1991) used narrative and voice scholarship with preservice students to examine issues of race, class, and gender. The design of their teacher-education program was consistent with the Multicultural approach.

Field Immersion plus Course Sequence. There is growing concern among teacher educators about the need for preservice students to have both preservice courses that infuse multicultural education and field experiences (especially student teaching) in which students live full-time in a multicultural community. Research in this area suggests that students acquire greater multicultural knowledge and understanding from this combined experience. Mahan (1982a, 1984) reports that the students in the preservice program that he directs receive multicultural education in the course sequence, including working in the local community. For their student-teaching experience, these students live and do volunteer work in the Hopi or Navajo communities. Mahan (1984) states that "Young teachers, who are immersed in the local culture, do make culturally oriented adjustments in their teaching style" (p. 109). Cooper et al. (1990) conducted a study that compared two cohorts of students. One cohort of 85 was placed in culturally different classrooms in Minnesota, although they continued to live in their conventional Eurocentric neighborhoods, while the second cohort of 18 lived in a Mexican American community in Texas. Cooper et al. state that "The opportunity to student teach in Texas, with its attendant exposure to another culture, appears to generate among participants an articulated willingness to demonstrate multicultural competencies" (p. 3). Similarly, Nava (1990) reports that preservice students who participated in a cross-cultural training program, and lived with a Mexican family while student teaching in Mexico, have greater cultural sensitivity as teachers in the United States than teachers without these experiences.

All three programs fit into the Human Relations approach. Each program is concerned that student teachers develop a cultural awareness and sensitivity for teaching students who are ethnically and racially different.

Placement in Culturally Diverse Classrooms and Communities. The need is increasing for the present cohort of mostly White female teacher-education students to have a practicum experience, or to student teach in classrooms with culturally, linguistically, and socioeconomically diverse students (Diez & Murrell, 1991; Gomez & Tabachnick, 1991). However, research on the results of placement in culturally diverse classrooms or communities is very limited (Ladson-Billings, 1991b; Larke, Wiseman, & Bradley, 1990; Mahan, 1982a). The results from the available studies of students working in culturally diverse settings show mixed results. For example, Larke et al. report that having teacher-education students tutoring students of color did positively "change the attitude and perceptions of the preservice teachers towards African American or Mexican American children" (p. 7). Ladson-Billings (1991b), on the other hand, points out that these experiences are not "some kind of magic bullet" and that there were not great differences between the attitudes and beliefs of students who have taken her course and those who have not.

Larke et al. (1990) and Mahan (1982a) developed experiences that seem to be directed toward the Human Relations approach to multicultural education. These programs were mainly concerned with helping the preservice students to get to know the community residents as "people," eliminate stereo-

types, and learn about the community. Ladson-Billings (1991) had her students examine race, gender, and socioeconomic issues in the community as they related to the diverse ethnic groups living there and in the larger society. Her teaching is in keeping with the Multicultural approach.

Cooperating Teachers and Supervisors. Student teaching is considered the most salient feature in the preservice experience, so the cooperating teacher's role is extremely important. Research that examines the cooperating teacher's role from a multicultural perspective is practically nonexistent. We were able to locate only one study, and that one examined cooperating teachers' beliefs about multicultural education.

Haberman and Post (1990) conducted a survey of teachers using C. A. Grant and Sleeter's (1985) five approaches to multicultural education as a template to classify teachers' beliefs about multicultural education. The goal of multicultural education to which the teachers in the study aspired was that of Human Relations. Haberman and Post stated:

Over 80 percent of the respondents selected Items #1 (All people are individuals) and #2 (Cooperation and tolerance are vital). It is evident that respondents believed that tolerance for others and individuals should be the goals of school programs in multicultural education. (p. 33)

There is an equivalent lack of educational literature that examines the supervisors of student teachers and multicultural teaching. Gillette (1990), summarizing a review of the research literature in this area, explains:

There is a paucity of research related to the role of student teaching in facilitating the development of multicultural perspectives with student teachers.... [W]e currently know almost nothing about what techniques, methodologies or curricula facilitate or impede the development and maintenance of a multicultural perspective in student teachers. (p. 83)

Gillette (1990) studied a supervisor who was working with a student teacher attempting to implement multicultural education in a racially and socioeconomically diverse classroom. She reports that the supervisor's concerns and efforts were focused mainly on classroom routines and management. Absent was any sustained analytical inquiry regarding the student teacher's actions in general, especially those related to race, class, and gender. The supervisor efforts in Gillette's study were at best akin to the Human Relations approach to multicultural education.

Six trends emerge from the multicultural research conducted on preservice education.

1. There is a movement from research analyzing multicultural workshops to examining courses and field programs on race and gender diversity and social justice.
2. A majority of this research was undertaken by instructors examining their own courses. Further, most of these studies were conducted without external funding.
3. A majority of the courses studied used the Multicultural Edu-

cation approach or the Human Relations approach. Clearly, there is an epistemological tension between these two groups of studies. The Human Relations approach is guided by an assimilationist ideology, while the Multicultural approach examines power relationships and the perspectives of different race, class, and gender groups.

4. Many of these studies neglected the scholarship and epistemological foundations of previous research on multicultural education.

5. These studies did not provide a critique of their research design and methodology or discuss their limitations.

6. The studies failed to provide a definition of multicultural education and focused mainly on race and/or ethnicity. Consequently, the interrelationships between variables (e.g., race and gender, gender and class) were not incorporated into the analyses.

Studies on Practicing Teachers

Since the early 1970s, an increasing number of teacher educators have argued that veteran teachers need to participate in staff development in order to become more responsive to race, class, and gender concerns, especially in relationship to multicultural education (Arciniega, 1977; Banks, 1975; Gay, 1977; C. A. Grant & Melnick, 1978). These arguments have in part grown out of research that points to how the race, class, and gender of students serve as powerful influences on schooling (e.g., Apple, 1979). Protests by parents of color have also contributed to the calls for more equitable educational practices (Fantini, Gittell, & Magat, 1970; Natriello, McDill, & Pallas, 1990).

Studies of multicultural education and certified teachers not connected to the preparation of student teachers are rare. We located five. Baty (1972) conducted 10 three-hour meetings that taught teachers working with Mexican American students about Mexican American history, culture, and social heritage, and gave the teachers an opportunity to discuss issues and concerns related to teaching Mexican American students. Based upon posttest results, Baty concluded:

This increased empathy together with a greater understanding of ways in which the school system acts to remove the child from his/her culture increases the teacher's propensity to change her/his approach and to have changes introduced in the school system, in the form of greater experimentation and more deliberate attempts to harness the potential contribution of Mexican American children to the classroom. (p. 73)

Multiplying Options, Subtracting Bias is the title of a videotape used by Fennema, Wolleat, Pedro, and Becker (1981) as the intervention in a pretest-posttest study with 64 mathematics teachers (45 males and 19 females) to increase female students' selection of high school mathematics courses. Posttest results indicate very little change for the 19 female teachers, which the researchers believe was due to the near-ceiling pretest scores of the female teachers. However, the male teachers showed significant increases in their level of information on sex-related differences and on other videotape content.

Washington (1981) conducted a five-day multicultural workshop with 49 elementary school teachers. Teachers saw films, heard audiotapes, and participated in group dynamic sessions to explore racism and White consciousness. They also discussed the ideology of multicultural education, multicultural materials and methods, school desegregation, and children's racial knowledge and identities. Washington concluded on the basis of results from a self-report classroom behavior scale and an attitude-scale report that the training had a negligible effect on either attitude or behavior.

C. A. Grant and Grant (1985) conducted a two-week institute with 30 teachers and administrators from 10 Teacher Corps project schools. The purpose of the institute was to help participants develop an understanding of the necessity for EMC-SR in their teaching and school responsibilities. Based upon the results from a Curriculum Analysis and Modification pre-post assessment instrument, they reported that the participants integrated more multicultural concepts into their curriculum after having participated in the institute.

Based upon classroom observations, Ortiz and Yates (1988) reported that the attitudes of teachers were not changed after attending cultural awareness workshops and seminars. In fact, the author reasoned that the workshops strengthened the teachers' beliefs about their current practices. Similarly, Sleeter (1992) conducted an ethnographic study of 30 teachers who participated in multicultural education training for two years. Sleeter observed that although the teachers reported that the in-service training was beneficial, and that they learned a lot, the inclusion of multicultural education in their teaching was limited.

The research studies of Baty (1972) and Fennema et al. (1981) were assigned to the Single-Group Studies approach to multicultural education because they dealt with structural inequality faced by a particular group. The studies by Washington (1981), C. A. Grant and Grant (1985), and Sleeter (1992) were more closely aligned with the Multicultural Education approach. These studies dealt with the lived realities of various groups and their battles to achieve equality. For example, Sleeter's study focused on how teachers interpret social and educational issues. She used conservative, liberal, and radical structural frameworks as templates to analyze the teachers' perspectives.

The multicultural research reported in this section concerned studies examining the influence of short-term treatments on the attitude and behavior of classroom teachers. Only two of the studies (C. A. Grant & Grant, 1985; Sleeter, 1992) followed the teachers for over a year. One of the studies (Ortiz, 1988) indicated no change in the teachers' attitude, and the findings from the other studies indicate only a small change in the attitude and behavior of the classroom teachers. Three of the five studies were supported with some form of external funding. No follow-up studies by the authors were reported in the educational literature.

Teacher-Student Relationships

An increasing number of multicultural education theorists, in order to improve understanding of the context of schooling, are including the study of teacher-student relationships in their research agenda. More specifically, their agenda includes research in the following areas: teachers' prior experiences, teachers' attitude toward diversity and multicultural education, teacher-student interactions, and teachers as role models. We note that a few of the studies reviewed in this section are not thought of as "traditional" multicultural research. However, they can inform and influence the scholarship and research on multicultural education, so we believe it is important that they be included.

The research literature on teacher-student interactions has been growing steadily over the last 20 years. There are studies reporting that teachers interact with high achievers more than with low achievers (Good, 1970) and that grade level or age can influence how teachers interact with some students (Irvine, 1990). Over the years, this literature has focused on how teachers interact with students based upon their gender, socioeconomic status, and race, thereby making it useful and meaningful to multicultural education research. Studies have pointed out that teachers interact with boys more than with girls (Brophy & Good, 1970; Datta, Schaefer, & Davis, 1968; Dweck & Bush, 1976; Martin, 1972; Sadker & Sadker, 1985; American Association of University Women, 1992), especially White boys (Irvine, 1990; Sadker & Sadker, 1981). The American Association of University Women observes that although most teachers are women, they inadvertently cater classroom activities to boys and lavish more attention on them. Other pertinent observations are that the interactions with boys are more critical (Safilios-Rothschild, 1979) and in a harsher tone (Jackson & Lahadernde, 1967; Waetjen, 1962). Teacher-student interaction studies (e.g., Brophy & Everston, 1981; Sadker & Sadker, 1985; Page, 1991) have also shown that teachers interact with boys more because their behavior necessitates greater communication. According to Sadker and Sadker (1985), "boys received additional communication by asserting themselves and literally calling out for attention" (p. 361). Some of these studies have acknowledged that some teachers who were more critical of boys than of girls nevertheless praised boys more than girls (Meyer & Lindstrom, 1969; Meyer & Thompson, 1956).

Studies that describe teacher-student interactions among White females and females of color are very limited. The research that is available is mostly on the teacher interactions of White girls and African American girls. According to Irvine (1990), African American females in the lower elementary grades (K–2) receive more positive interactions from teachers than do White females in the lower elementary, and African American females in the upper elementary (3–5) receive less positive interactions than when they were in the lower grades. Irvine states:

The data from this research support the early salience of black females in the lower elementary grades, but suggest that teachers and schools have a significant influence in socializing black females to traditional female behaviors. By the time black females enter the upper elementary grades, they seem to have joined their white female counterparts in their invisibility, thereby resulting in fewer interactions with teachers. (p. 71)

Linda Grant's research includes the study of African American girls and White girls (see, e.g., L. Grant, 1983, 1984, 1985). In a study of African American and White girls in several midwest and southern elementary schools, L. Grant (1993) con-

cludes that "White girls were considerably more teacher-oriented than African-American females, spending more time interacting with teachers than with peers" (p. 94). She adds:

From the perspectives of teachers, especially white teachers, white girls are central and African-American girls peripheral. . . . Classroom experiences encouraged African-American girls to emphasize social competence over intellectual attainment. These themes appeared both in relationships with teachers, who recognized their social actions more than their academic achievement. . . . (1993, p. 108)

King (1987) and Ladson-Billings (1990, 1992b) have established lines of research that explore the "culturally relevant" interactions occurring between African American students and their teachers. King interviewed teachers of African American students to gain insight into the teachers' thinking about their own practice. She found that the teachers structured classroom social relations to help students assume responsibility for their own learning. Further, the teachers viewed the teacher-student interaction as an opportunity to prepare their students to "survive" both the educational system and society rather than "fit into it." Ladson-Billings (1990) interviewed and conducted classroom observations and found that successful teachers of African American students were not rigid or authoritarian; rather, the student-teacher interaction was equitable. These teachers shared power with the students because they viewed education as an empowering force (Ladson-Billings, 1992b). These teachers sought to establish a community of learners where students interacted collaboratively and accepted responsibility for each other's education (Ladson-Billings, 1990, 1992b).

We have noted the lack of published educational research reports about females of color, as well as the limited research data on student-teacher interaction involving students of color in general, other than a few studies on African Americans. However, our retrieval efforts did uncover two discussions of teacher interactions with Asian American students that are pertinent to our discussion. Takaki (1989) states:

Asian American "success" has emerged as the new stereotype for this ethnic minority. While this image has led many teachers and employers to view Asians as intelligent and hard-working and has opened some opportunities, it has also been harmful. Asian-Americans can find their diversity as individuals denied: many feel forced into the "model minority" mold and want more freedom to be their individual selves, to be "extravagant." (p. 477)

Yoshiwara (1983) points out that these stereotypes (e.g., "model minority") have implications for curriculum, teacher-student relations, and career aspirations. She explains:

Always being described as quiet, hard working, nonverbal, and high achieving places unfair burdens on Japanese-American students. When teachers encourage this type of behavior, they reward students for remaining stereotypic. Teachers need to encourage verbal skill and consciously select Japanese American students to engage in discussion in debates and presentation. It is very important to create an atmosphere in which Japanese American students can feel comfortable enough to pursue their own paths in society. (p. 25)

Rist (1970) and Gouldner (1978) contend that teachers marginalize low-income students. Jackson and Cosca (1974) and Sadker and Sadker (1981) report that many teachers interact with, call on with greater frequency, praise more highly, and intellectually challenge students who are middle class, male, and White. The reasons why teachers interact with students differently is not completely clear. It could be, as we noted earlier, because "boys assert themselves" (Sadker & Sadker, 1985), or because White girls are more invisible (Irvine, 1990), or perhaps because teachers have very little insight into their own interaction patterns (Sadker & Sadker, 1985). However, the teacher socialization literature, especially the socialization literature that examines teachers' biographies, may offer other critical explanations to be considered by multicultural education researchers.

Zeichner and Gore (1990), in a review of the teacher socialization literature, state:

These [life histories—autobiographies and biographies] interpretive and critical studies have begun to provide us with rich information about the ways in which teachers' perspectives are rooted in the variety of personal, familial, religious, political, and cultural experiences they bring to teaching.... (p. 334)

The influence of life histories is illuminated in teachers' interactions with students in the following narratives. Birrell (1993) documented the experiences of a beginning secondary teacher. The importance of a teacher's life history is reflected in the following comment by the beginning teacher:

I hate their ethnic attitude and their lingo. I hate to categorize it but I like Black students who act more white. They're not sitting around the classroom saying, "yo baby." Black kids hit me with their lingo and tones. I don't like it. It's a different language. Why aren't they named Mike instead of Jamal? (p. 6)

Decker (1969), a beginning teacher assigned to work in an urban school with an African American student population, claims:

I was struck ... by the blackness. Being immersed in a Negro world was new to me, and in the dim, artificial light of the corridors, faces seemed to disappear.... It was Christmas before I could understand them without watching their mouths. (p. 37)

Similarly, Parkay (1983), a neophyte White teacher, describes the culture shock and fear he experienced working with African American students. Parkay stated:

During my first year at DuSable [a high school of Chicago's southside] I was frequently very anxious and frightened. On occasion, I even had nightmares about the place. I despaired of ever understanding or accepting the students' behavior and attitudes that were so strange and threatening to me. I experienced what anthropologists and sociologists have termed "culture shock." (p. 18)

Parkay (1983) indicated other fears related to him teaching in an all-Black school: fear of being manipulated, fear of aggressiveness, fear of intrusive behavior, fear of encirclement and loss of autonomy, and fear of violent primitive behavior. She adds, "If the lower class school to which a teacher is assigned contains a significant percentage of Black students, most middle class teachers are apt to experience anxiety related to their students' race" (p. 52).

Finally, Longstreet (1978) describes how her lack of understanding of the culture of students she was teaching turned them off and annoyed her:

Many teachers at Harlem school confessed to a feeling of "strangeness" at the school.... Virtually no permanent friendships existed between Black and White teachers, and even the informal lunchroom talk fests revealed White and Black teachers were aloof from one another. Some White teachers attributed the lack of response in the children as based in anti-White feelings. And some of the Black teachers concluded that the failure of children was grounded in anti-Black feelings among White teachers. (p. 11)

Research on teacher-student interactions has been important to several social movements (e.g., racial desegregation and gender equity). As was the case with the research on text materials, teacher-student interaction research has appeared in several publication forms (e.g., biographies, journal articles, and reports). This area of research has benefited from long-term commitment by scholars (e.g., work by Brophy & Good, 1970; Brophy, 1985; L. Grant, 1983, 1984, 1985, 1993; Sadker & Sadker, 1981, 1985). The teacher-student interaction research suggests that students of color and girls are receiving treatment different from that accorded White males. This differential treatment would not be problematic if it led to greater achievement and social consciousness by all students (e.g., the Multicultural Education approach). Yet the research described above indicates differential treatment that has led to the elevation of White male students at the expense of students of color and female students. This research suggests that teachers perpetuate and reinforce the stereotypic beliefs associated with girls (e.g., reserved and quiet) and people of color (low achievers). Further, this form of indexing occurs early in the educational lives of students.

BARRIERS TO MULTICULTURAL EDUCATION RESEARCH

Several formidable barriers exist to the design and implementation of multicultural education and multicultural education research (C. A. Grant, 1992). Five of them are discussed here in hopes of informing present and future generations of scholars interested in generating a multicultural education research agenda. We have organized the barriers to multicultural education research as follows:

- Property Rights Versus Human Rights
- Researcher's Background, Knowledge, and Epistemological Bias
- Exceptionalism Within Academic Discourse
- Funding to Support Multicultural Education Research
- Conceptual Confusion over Multicultural Education

Property Rights Versus Human Rights

The civil rights roots of multicultural education position this philosophy of education in the middle of a long and seemingly endless debate over human rights (see, e.g., Allen, 1974; Williams, 1991; Marable, 1992; C. A. Grant, 1993). Many of the barriers to civil rights legislation are also connected to the ideological attacks on multicultural education. One such barrier is the tension between property rights and human rights in the United States.

Bell (1987) argues that the civil rights lawyers litigating issues involving educational equality built their cases on the belief that human rights were guaranteed by the U.S. Constitution. Bell reviews the events leading up to the Constitution's design and suggests there was a tension between property rights and human rights. This tension was heightened by the presence of African people being objectified as property (i.e., slaves). The purpose of the U.S. government, as specified by the Constitution, was to protect the main object of society—property. Thus a government constructed to protect the rights of property owners lacked the necessary incentive to secure rights for African Americans. Bell adds, "The concept of individual rights, unconnected to property rights, was totally foreign to these men of property [Constitution conventioneers]; and thus, despite two decades of civil rights gains, most blacks remain disadvantaged and deprived because of their race" (p. 239).

Like the civil rights movement, the discipline of multicultural education is built on the belief that the Constitution of the United States protects human rights (see, e.g., C. A. Grant, 1993), rather than property rights. This assumption has left proponents of multicultural education open to ideological attack from both the political right and left. For example, from the political right, Diane Ravitch (1990) wrote, "The real issue on campus and in the classroom is not whether there will be multiculturalism, but what kind of multiculturalism will there be" (p. A44). Ravitch is against "particularism," that is, approaches to multicultural education such as Afrocentricity (see, e.g., Asante, 1991). Implicit in the argument put forth by Ravitch and other conservatives (see, e.g., Hirsch, 1987) is the following question: Whose property is the school curriculum? In her historical analysis of desegregation, Ravitch (1980) stated:

In assessing the meaning of the Brown decision today, we must recognize that it deals not just with the question of access to schools, but with the question of how to define Black people, and what part Blacks should play in defining their own purposes. If Blacks are seen as a caste group that has been deprived of its culture and its history, then one set of remedies seems appropriate; if seen as a self-conscious group with a viable culture, then other remedies might be in order. But whichever perspective prevails, the role of government must be to provide Blacks with the opportunity and the means to make choices for themselves, because it was precisely this power to make decisions that was denied to Blacks in the past. (p. 44)

It appears that Ravitch, an influential writer and educational policy maker, recognized the need for African Americans to choose their own educational remedies. In fact, she delineates this argument based on the need to empower African Americans—an issue of human rights. Ten years later, Ravitch (1990) argued against one form of multiculturalism (centricity—e.g., Afrocentricity or Latino-centered education) despite her earlier endorsement of Black political empowerment. It would appear that Ravitch and others of this school of thought are trying to control the school curriculum (i.e., intellectual property) by sanctioning their "preferred" educational remedies. Estrada and McLaren (1993) point out:

What we are witnessing at this present moment in our history is an attempt by the New Right to establish its own version of multiculturalism—what I [McLaren] refer to as corporate multiculturalism—that effectively disguises its allegiance to the ideological imperatives of consumer society [property control]: that of subordinating local knowledge and interests and intercultural alliances to the promotional logic of the capitalist marketplace. Our subjectivities and identities are assaulted by and virtually saturated with a consumer ethic such that our very desires are in the process of what French philosopher Gilles Deleuze calls "reterritorialization"—an ideological process that couples our identity as citizens with neocolonist universals such that democracy and capitalism are viewed as almost synonymous. Whereas many see a deep-laid antagonism between democracy and capitalism, our society fails to challenge oppression in its many guises because oppression has become so institutionalized that we fail to recognize it. (p. 27)

Ravitch's 10-year turnaround is representative of a larger societal retreat from the civil rights era agenda of human rights to the Reagan-Bush era of protecting and securing individual property rights—both intellectual and economic (see, e.g., Crenshaw, 1988). Several scholars have suggested that multicultural education his not adequately addressed the tension between property rights and human rights. For example, Olneck (1993) claims that dominant conceptions of multicultural education are separated from sociopolitical interests (i.e., property control), and that multicultural scholars see ethnic conflict as a derivative of negative attitudes toward and ignorance about the manifestations of difference, which can be eliminated by cultivating empathy, acceptance, and understanding. Somewhat similarly, but from a different theoretical perspective, McCarthy (1990) contends: "In significant ways, too, proponents of multiculturalism fail to take into account the differential structure of opportunities that help to define minority relations to dominant white groups and social institutions in the United States" (p. 33).

Ladson-Billings and Tate (1993) raise a question that scholars interested in multicultural education research must address: "How then, in a society framed and constructed on the basis of property rights, do we seek essential human and civil rights?" (p. 7).

Researcher's Background, Knowledge, and Epistemological Bias

Researcher's Background and Knowledge. A second barrier to the development of multicultural education research is the demographic profile of higher-education faculties. In 1991, 93% of education professors were White, and of this number, 70% were male (C. A. Grant & Millar, 1992). In addition, the average age for full professors was 53, associate professors, 47, and assistant professors, 42 (C. A. Grant & Millar, 1992). Given this profile, it is reasonable to conjecture that the great majority of education professors have had little or no exposure to multicultural education during their formative years of professional development. In fact, C. A. Grant and Koskela (1986) conducted a study that included examining the publication bibliographies and course outlines of an education faculty at a large midwestern university. They found little to indicate an acceptance or a working knowledge of multicultural education.

The demographic composition of school of education faculties has also influenced the disciplinary focus of multicultural education research. Borden (1993) reports that an overwhelming number of undergraduate and graduate degrees awarded to students of color are in the humanities and social sciences. Thus it should not be surprising that a large majority of multicultural education research has focused on subjects such as history, literature, social studies, or other subtopics within the humanities and social sciences (see, e.g., Sleeter & Grant, 1988). Very little multicultural education research has addressed issues involving mathematics or science (e.g., D'Ambrosio, 1985; Anderson, 1990; Frankenstein, 1990; Yager, 1993). Although there are several possible explanations, one reason is the lack of racial and ethnic diversity within mathematics and science education faculties. The following statement represents the typical qualifications requested in classified advertising for assistant professors in mathematics education:

Earned doctorate in mathematics education or related discipline. An undergraduate degree in mathematics is required. A masters degree in mathematics or equivalent is highly desirable. At least three years of elementary or secondary mathematics teaching is required.

In 1987 only 834 African American students were awarded the undergraduate degree in mathematics (National Science Board, 1991). Two years later, the number of master's degrees in mathematics awarded to African American students was 59 (National Science Board, 1991). These figures typify the cohort of African Americans annually meeting the initial academic qualifications of an assistant professor of mathematics education. The next requirement for an academic career in mathematics education is teaching experience. How many of the students from each year's master's degree cohort have taught or will go on to teach school mathematics for three years? Current demographic trends indicate that the African American teaching force will decrease from 6.9% of all teachers to less than 5% by the year 2000 (Whitaker, 1989; Stewart, Meier, & England, 1989). Further, potential teachers from racially diverse backgrounds with science and mathematics skills will have numerous opportunities outside of education. Unless this trend is reversed, the likelihood of future multicultural education research in areas such as mathematics and science is in jeopardy.

The lack of multicultural studies for future teachers is also a product of the composition of faculties in the liberal arts. John Kenneth Galbraith, an important figure in economics, noted:

One should always be aware of a possibility of discrimination and a tendency to think of males when [academic] appointments are being considered. . . . In my lifetime, I have generally voted for the promotion of people who were most like Galbraith. (Phillip, 1993, p. 14).

Many states (e.g., Texas) have moved to or, like California, have well-established teacher-certification programs built upon a strong liberal arts background. Yet most liberal arts programs have little racial or gender diversity within their faculty ranks. For example, the American Economics Association (AEA), a society chiefly of academicians, reports that of its 12,079 members there are 1,693 (approximately 14%) women and 126 (approximately 1%) African Americans (Phillip, 1993). The rest of this academic society is composed mainly of White males.

The racial and gender composition of economics faculty (and other disciplines) has had a significant influence on how social and political problems get framed and discussed in academic discourse. Dr. Robert Solow, a 1987 Nobel Prize winner, contends there are areas in economics where discussions are seriously incomplete because they fail to consider race, class, and gender (Phillip, 1993). Solow argues that unemployment and recession periods are the most obvious topics that are often minimized or left out of the research and teaching agenda of many professors. Yet many women and people of color are the earliest and most negatively influenced by business cycles. The significantly higher jobless rate of African American teenagers versus White teens is but one of many areas that have received little treatment. Other topics include poverty, unionization, productivity growth, and free trade. The failure to apply a multicultural perspective to economic and other social problems can only allow for the perpetuation of stereotypic beliefs about people from diverse cultures and experiences. Each of these areas has a significant implication for the multicultural education of prospective teachers.

King (1991) reports that the prospective teachers described in her study—members of her educational social foundation course—suffered from an "uncritical habit of mind" when analyzing issues involving the economic and social status of culturally diverse groups and their own positions of privilege. We hypothesize that the racial, ethnic, sexual, and socioeconomic backgrounds of faculty throughout the academy have important implications for the development of courses, educational experiences, and research agendas that challenge the uncritical way many students think about inequity by accepting certain culturally sanctioned myths, stereotypes, and beliefs that justify the advantages of some groups.

Researcher's Epistemological Bias. A barrier to multicultural education research closely related to the lack of culturally diverse scholars is the resulting epistemological bias attributable to this human resources vacuum. A researcher makes conjectures about certain important features of the phenomenon of interest and how these features are related. Delgado (1990) argues that feminists and scholars of color are able to tell stories different from those heard in traditional academic discourse. Albert Einstein makes a similar argument on this point:

To the discoverer . . . the constructions of his imagination appear so necessary and so natural that he is apt to treat them not as the creations of his thoughts, but as given realities. . . . The stereotypical categories that we use are rarely without some point of tangency with reality (biological, social, medical), but their interpretation is colored by the ideology that motivates us. (Minow, 1987, pp. 173–174)

Like Einstein, Delgado (1990) recognizes that a scholar's previous experience and personal convictions will impact his or her research (see also Gould, 1981). Rather than hide behind the tenets of scientific empiricism, Delgado (1990, 1991) argues that the researcher's previous experiences are important components of disciplined inquiry (see also Banks, 1993). Delgado (1990) contends that women and people of color in our society speak with experiential knowledge that is framed by racism and sexism. This framework gives their stories a common structure warranting the term "voice." Incorporating the voice of scholars of color and women scholars challenges the manner in which political, moral, and scientific analysis is conducted in traditional educational research. Many educational scholars embrace universalism over particularity. Positivism, also referred to as scientific empiricism, will not confer the status of "real" to things not directly observable. Price (1992) remarks on the research bias of this position:

> In educational research, the most blatant expression of this view is behaviorism, which eschews mental and cognitive constructs. Although behaviorism lost its dominant position in American psychology a decide or two ago, some positivist habits linger on in educational research. Inattention to the thoughts, customs, and intentions of subjects is one such habit. This vestige of positivism in the habits of some quantitative researchers is antithetical to research on multicultural education. As argued previously, this is the vice of some quantifiers, not a vice of quantification of itself. (p. 64)

Scientific empiricism tends to minimize anything that is historical, contextual, or specific with the unscholarly labels of "literary" or "personal" (Williams, 1991). For many multicultural education scholars, social reality is constructed by the creation and the exchange of stories about individual situations (e.g., Gordon, 1992; Ladson-Billings & Henry, 1990; Soto, 1992; Tate, in press a). Delgado (1989) points out that outgroups throughout U.S. history have used stories to heal wounds caused by racism, sexism, and other forms of oppression. These stories also provide a mechanism to challenge dominant groups of society who use stock stories (e.g., stereotypes) to legitimize privilege (Crenshaw, 1988; Lawrence, 1987; Bell, 1992; Takaki, 1993). Yet these stories are in jeopardy if multicultural education researchers do not fend off arguments against research that incorporates the voices of marginalized groups (see, e.g., Delgado, 1991; Tate, in press a; Ladson-Billings & Tate, 1993; Gordon, 1992).

Exceptionalism Within Academic Discourse

Exceptionalism within academic discourse is another barrier to the implementation of multicultural programs and to sustained multicultural education research. Appleby (1992) defines exceptionalism as the United States' form of Eurocentrism. Exceptionalism is an orientation toward data that seeks to incorporate those aspects of U.S. history that help to forge a national identity and glorify the national symbols, such as open opportunity, a spirit of inquiry, freedom of speech and religion, independence, and destruction of privilege (Appleby, 1992). Exceptionalism also tries to minimize any images of the United States that may appear to challenge the national image. Appleby states:

> Most of what really happened in the colonial past was ignored because it fit so ill with the narrative of exceptionalism. The colonial settlements had to be presented as the foundations for the independent nation to come, an interpretation similar in logic to interpreting our own times in terms of the aspirations of those who will live in the twenty-second century. Embarrassing facts abounded in the colonial past. Everywhere one looked one found concerns profoundly different from those that animated citizens of the new American republic engaging the attention of women and men. The exotic cultures of Africans and native Americans could not be incorporated into American history, for those peoples' very claim to have culture would have subverted the story of progress. The self-conscious crafters of American identity took great pride in freedom of religion, but the major religious figures of the colonial era, the Puritans of New England, openly embraced orthodoxy—banishing dissidents, whipping Baptists, even executing four Quakers. And so it went with free speech. Congress composed a Bill of Rights guaranteeing free speech, but colonial legislators had been much more likely to jail their critics than to protect their speech. And then there was the elaboration of slave codes by colonial legislators. How were those laws to be integrated into the teleology of a peculiarly free people? (p. 425)

The impact of exceptionalism on the school curriculum has significant implications for the multicultural scholar and researcher. Some acts of history are slanted to paint a portrait of a fair and democratic United States. For example, social studies textbooks often describe Dr. Martin Luther King, Jr., as a preacher dreaming of democratic values and brotherhood—patriotic national symbols—while virtually ignoring the social fabric of oppression and inequitable power relations that motivated him to action (see, e.g., Swartz, 1992). Swartz states, "These separations of 'acts' from their causes and effects restrict the development of consciousness about social conditions through absorption of the 'act' into acceptable dominant ideology" (p. 35). In essence, Dr. King becomes acceptable as a preacher, while the power relations that led to his actions are "negated" in the rhetoric of opportunity to engage in civil disobedience—a symbol of American "fairness."

The danger of exceptionalism is not limited to misinterpretation of historical accounts. Exceptionalism can help shape the way a discipline is formed and, ultimately, how students come to think about a subject. School mathematics is one such example. Joseph (1987) expresses why multicultural researchers should concern themselves with how mathematics and science are embedded within an exceptionalism framework:

> Now an important area of concern for antiracists is the manner in which European scholarship has represented past and potentialities of nonwhite societies with respect to their achievement and capabilities in promoting science and technology. The progress of Europe and its cultural dependencies during the last 400 years is perceived by many as inextricably—and even causally—linked with the rapid growth of science and technology. So that in the minds of many, scientific progress becomes a uniquely European phenomenon, to be emulated only by following the European path of social and scientific development. (pp. 13–14)

Much of the literature in mathematics and mathematics education is guided by the following Eurocentric (i.e., exceptionalism doctrine) precepts (see, e.g., Cohen, 1982; Joseph, 1987; Anderson, 1990; Kamens & Benovot, 1991; Tate, in press b):

1. The tendency to separate mathematics from the economic, political, and cultural venues of society.
2. The belief that the ability to do mathematics is limited to an elite few (generally White males) who are thought to have an intellectual gift denied the rest of society.
3. The widespread agreement among mathematicians that mathematical discovery follows only from deductive axiomatic logic attributed to the Greeks; hence, empirical methods associated with indigenous people have little merit.

Space limitations prohibit discussing the implications of all three of these Eurocentric precepts as potential barriers to multicultural scholarship and research. Yet perhaps one example related to the first precept—the separation of mathematics from social, political, and cultural venues—will illustrate the impact of exceptionalism on a multicultural approach to mathematics education. Tate (in press b) describes the following situation in his secondary mathematics methods course:

A colleague presented my students with a graph of Asian Americans' graduation rates in high school and college and their incomes vis-à-vis European Americans. The students were told to use the data to develop a paragraph on what the statistical data does and does not reveal about Asian Americans as a group. As the students developed their statements they relied solely on the statistical data. Not a single student asked why Asian students who had higher achievement levels than European Americans were earning less money. None of my students' paragraphs included the possibility of racism as a potential explanation.

The power of exceptionalism is that it distorts reality by allowing unquestioning participants to hold false conceptions of a meritocratic society. The separation of mathematical analysis from social issues in school mathematics, and the resulting inability of students, including prospective teachers, to look beyond numerical solutions and toward meaningful social interpretation of data, illustrates how exceptionalism influences mathematics education. Similar arguments can be applied to science (see, e.g., Carter, 1991; Yager, 1993) and other areas of technical literacy (Apple, 1991; Pillar, 1992).

Funding to Support Multicultural Education Research

A key factor in the development of long-term and sustained multicultural education research is funding. Lack of funding is a barrier to multicultural education research for two reasons. First, formal and informal socialization of future multicultural education scholars should take place in graduate programs with the resources required for thorough scholarly preparation. Popkewitz (1984) stated:

As people are trained to participate in a research community, the learning involves more than the content or the field. Learning the examplars of a field of inquiry is also to learn how to see, think about and act towards the world. An individual is taught the appropriate expectations,

demands, and consistent attitudes and emotions that are involved in doing science. (p. 3)

In the academy, a key ingredient for providing graduate students the type of experience described above is research funding. A lack of funding can result in a void in the future leadership of multicultural education research.

A second reason lack of funding for multicultural education research is problematic is its impact on the type and length of studies that are possible. It is extremely difficult to study multiple educational systems, schools, classrooms, and/or teachers without financial backing. C. A. Grant and Secada's (1990) review of research studies on multicultural preservice and inservice programs reveals that only a few studies were supported with institutional, state, or federal funds. It is important to point out that the federal government has supported the Bureau for Equal Educational Opportunity and Multifunctional Resource Centers. However, the contractual obligations of these bureaus and centers are to provide training and technical assistance to schools and parents. The centers and bureaus are not provided a budget to conduct general research. In fact, research on the effectiveness of their training and assistance is not considered a primary focus of their mission. We consider this a lost multicultural education research opportunity.

Conceptual Confusion over Multicultural Education

The lack of an agreed-upon definition has been a barrier to multicultural education (see discussions by Banks, 1977; C. A. Grant & Sleeter, 1985; Sleeter & Grant, 1988). This lack of definition leads to competing interpretations and notions, thus allowing critics to dismiss multicultural education or to view it as an idea without theoretical underpinnings. The impact of this confusion can be found in curriculum frameworks, textbooks, teacher education, and other school artifacts that claim to be "multicultural," yet lack any coherent guiding philosophy.

GENERAL DISCUSSION

We saw as our task for this chapter to provide the reader with insights into multicultural education practices through the lens of the research literature. We soon discovered, from reviewing the many documents, that two research ideologies emerged—research on multicultural education and multicultural education research. This discovery reinforced our belief that the way words and phrases are stated provides a social construct or meaning to an idea. An example from Lewis Carroll's (1865/1934) *Alice's Adventures in Wonderland* illustrates this point:

The Hatter opened his eyes very wide . . . but all he said was, "Why is a raven like a writing-desk?"

"Come, we shall have some fun now!" thought Alice. "I'm glad they've begun asking riddles—I believe I can guess that," she added aloud.

"Do you mean that you think you can find out the answer to it?" said the March Hare.

"Exactly so," said Alice.

"Then you should say what you mean," the March Hare went on.

"I do," Alice hastily replied; "at least—at least I mean what I say—that's the same thing, you know."

"Not the same thing a bit!" said the Hatter.

"Why, you might as well say that 'I see what I eat' is the same thing as 'I eat what I see'!"

"You might just as well say," added the Dormouse, which seemed to be talking in its sleep, that 'I breathe when I sleep' is the same thing as 'I sleep when I breathe'!"

"It is the same thing with you," said the Hatter, and here the conversation dropped, and the party sat silent for a minute, while Alice thought over all she could remember about ravens and writing-desks, which wasn't much. (p. 92)

The above excerpt illustrates that the way words and phrases are stated changes meaning and purpose. There is similarity between the phrases "research on multicultural education" and "multicultural education research." Both connect in some way to the discipline of multicultural education and the discipline of educational research. Further, both often use as primary themes race, class, socioeconomic status, and gender, but there is also a distinct practical difference between "research on multicultural education" and "multicultural education research."

"Research on multicultural education" refers to the employment of the concepts and procedures of logical positivism to study the implementation of multicultural education. It includes doing research (i.e., investigation and analysis) and using, for example, quantitative and/or qualitative procedures to understand or explore the theory and practices of multicultural education. "Research on multicultural education" presently is best characterized by the following four precepts:

1. It espouses a philosophical orientation closely associated with an assimilationist policy that encourages tolerance and acceptance within the existing social structure.
2. There is an attempt to produce a rule or tenet to guide decision making.
3. There is an attempt to employ research procedures that are value-free and objective.
4. Statistical prediction techniques (i.e., correlation studies) are used to achieve the previous two characteristics.

"Multicultural education research" refers to the employment of the tenets of qualitative and/or quantitative research methodology to study social justice and power relationships that exist in educational institutions. "Multicultural education research" is best characterized by the following five precepts:

1. It is built upon the philosophical ideas of freedom, justice, equality, equity, pluralism, and human dignity.
2. It is the intent and purpose of the research to facilitate a comprehensive understanding of students in order to improve their learning experience and total education.
3. There is an attempt to understand the influence and interactions of the constructs of race, class, socioeconomic status, and gender.
4. There is an attempt to understand the relationship between knowledge and power.

5. Multiple perspectives and voices of the school community are included in the research data.

What follows in this discussion are: (a) selected observations that we believe will contribute to further understanding of the research on multicultural education and multicultural education research; and (b) suggestions to scholars interested in multicultural education research. We begin our discussion with paradigmatic frameworks.

Paradigmatic Frameworks

We contend that the character and nature of the research on multicultural education practices has taken two forms—research on multicultural education and multicultural education research. An examination of the school desegregation research literature and research conducted by multicultural theorists may help to illuminate the characteristics of both types of research. Some scholars and educators may not recognize school desegregation research as a form of research on multicultural practices. However, we argue that school desegregation as an educational practice, including much of the research conducted in this area, is consistent with the Teaching the Exceptional and Culturally Different approach and the Human Relations approach to multicultural education (see, e.g., Allport, 1954; C. W. Grant & Sleeter, 1985; Desegregation Assistance Center, 1989; Schofield, 1991). A large majority of desegregation research explored the influence of desegregation on stereotypic thinking, behavior, attitudes, achievement, and student self-concept (Schofield, 1991; Weinberg, 1977). Much of the desegregation research was guided by psychometric methodology, such as statistical analysis comparing Whites and Blacks (Weinberg, 1977). Many of these race-related educational studies were decision oriented and focused on a narrow range of outcomes rather than the social processes that might account for the outcomes (Weinberg, 1977; Desegregation Assistance Center, 1989; Schofield, 1991). That is, the research was designed to produce a rule or tenet to guide policy makers. Schofield stated:

The focus on desegregation's effects undoubtedly stemmed at least partially from the fact that researchers and funding agencies often hoped to use the results of the research in political ways to support or, less frequently, to undermine it as a national policy. Obviously, for political purposes, it is much more useful to be able to say that desegregation improves or harms intergroup relations than it is to delineate the processes that may lead to these results. (p. 344)

Reviews of the desegregation research literature report that much of this research did not explore the experiences and lived realities of students (Weinberg, 1977; Schofield, 1991). According to Schofield:

Although for many years contact theory [see Allport, 1954] was routinely invoked in reports on desegregation research, it had a remarkably small impact on the actual design and reporting of that research. For example, researchers often tip their hats to contact theory in the introductory passages of a research report and then fail entirely to give information on topics that it suggests should be vital to predicting the probable outcomes of the contact experience. (p. 360)

In contrast to research on multicultural education, multicultural education research is built upon the philosophical precepts of equity, freedom, and pluralism. These philosophical precepts represent a different worldview from the assimilationist philosophy that is often closely associated with research on multicultural education. The constructs of equity, freedom, and pluralism are subjective, thus requiring interpretive frameworks and methods. Erickson (1986) stated:

Interpretive, participant observational fieldwork research, in addition to a central concern with mind and with subjective meaning, is concerned with the relation between meaning-perspectives of actors and ecological circumstances of action in which they find themselves. This is to say the notion of the social is central in fieldwork. (p. 127)

C. A. Grant and Sleeter (1986) provide an example of multicultural education research. The philosophical orientation of this study was cultural pluralism, equity, and equality. The researchers used a theoretical framework based upon conflict theory to explore the power relations among students, teachers, and administrators in a racially mixed and mainstreamed junior high school. Grant and Sleeter employed an interpretive framework that took into account the interactions of race, social class, gender, and disabilities within the school community. They conducted classroom observations, collected field notes, and interviewed teachers, students, administrators, nonteaching school staff, and community members in order to discover the ways in which a racially mixed and mainstreamed junior high school was contributing to the reproduction of social inequality for individual students.

Sleeter (1992) provides another example of multicultural education research. She conducted a two-year ethnographic study of 30 teachers from 18 schools who participated in a staff-development program in multicultural education. Sleeter framed her study within three philosophical ideologies—conservatism, liberalism, and radical structuralism. These philosophical lenses allowed Sleeter to examine closely the relationship between the staff-development orientation and the lived realities of the teachers. She explored how the teachers' philosophical orientations were consistent across issues (e.g., social equality) involving the various combinations of race, class, and gender. Her analysis examined the relationship between knowledge and power. Sleeter argued that the knowledge acquired in staff development was more for individual growth, an issue of self-empowerment, than for institutional change.

Our analysis of the research reviewed in this chapter reveals that a good deal of it employed the precepts of multicultural education research. To illustrate this point we shall discuss the literature on curriculum and text materials, preservice preparation, and research studies on certified teachers.

The research on curriculum and text materials often was conducted to discover the relationship between knowledge and power by focusing on the extent to which texts and curriculum materials represented and portrayed people of color and women in a fair and accurate manner. These analyses examined the way that various racial, ethnic, and gender groups were included in text materials (see, e.g., Council on Interracial Books for Children, 1976; Butterfield et al., 1979; Tetreault, 1986; Powell & Garcia, 1988).

Most of the research studies on preservice programs employed the tenets associated with multicultural education research. The purpose and intent of the majority of these studies was to contribute to a literature base that informs those who prepare teachers to teach students of various racial, ethnic, and social backgrounds. Many of these studies examined knowledge/power relationships that exist in society and the teacher-education students' perspectives on these knowledge/power relationships (e.g., Baker, 1977; Dottin, 1984; Mahan, 1984; Ahlquist, 1991; King & Ladson-Billings, 1990; Gomez, 1991). Many of these studies examined the teacher-education students' perspectives on students of various race, class, and gender groups and the social issues influencing these groups (see, e.g., McDiarmid, 1990; Ahlquist, 1991; Ladson-Billings, 1991a; Bennett et al., 1990; Diez & Murrell, 1991; Noordhoff & Kleinfeld, 1993).

All of the research studies on certified teachers reviewed in our analysis were guided by the philosophical tenets of equality and equity (Baty, 1972; Fennema et al., 1981; Washington, 1981; C. A. Grant & Grant, 1985; Ortiz & Yates, 1988; Sleeter, 1992). Three of the studies examined the relationship between knowledge and power (Fennema et al., 1981; C. A. Grant & Grant, 1985; Sleeter, 1992). For example, Fennema and colleagues researched the impact of a mathematics staff-development program designed to increase females' knowledge of sex-related differences in mathematics. The staff development also sought to change the attitude and behavior of significant others within the female students' educational environment.

The movement to multicultural education research has resulted in scholarship that seeks to analyze the contextual aspects of educational resources, classrooms, and student experiences. However, much of the present multicultural education research is limited, in that it tends to examine the impact of race, class, and/or gender instead of examining the interactions of these social constructs (C. A. Grant & Sleeter, 1986b; hooks, 1990; Sleeter, 1992). For example, Sleeter stated:

It is quite possible for an individual to profess one theoretical perspective regarding one axis of inequality, such as gender, and another regarding other axes of inequality. For example, bell hooks (1990) criticizes avant-garde Whites who take a radical position on gender and/or social class, but accept implicitly more conservative believes about race; or African American men who view racism from a radical perspective but regard women, including African American women, as their inferiors. In analyzing a person's beliefs about the social structure and inequality, it is important not to assume *consistency* [emphasis added]. (pp. 13–14)

Although we see movement toward conducting multicultural education research, we have a suggestion and several issues of concern for scholars interested in pursuing this line of inquiry.

Research Suggestions and Concerns

Research questions need to be more attentive to issues of equity, power, and justice. For example, much of the earlier research and some of the present research on curriculum materials and textbooks has been concerned mainly with developing research questions that focus on fair and accurate representation of ethnically diverse students and females. This research often has provided a limited view of how textbooks present differential power relations. In illustration, mathematics textbooks usually do not provide students with real insight into the political nature of mathematics (Ernest, 1991; Frankenstein, 1990). Few mathematics textbooks offer students an opportunity to analyze the U.S. census process. Thus students do not have an opportunity to explore the role and implications of race, class, and gender categorizations in arguably the most important mathematical enterprise of this society. A majority of the textbook research has instead focused on whether or not a particular group is represented appropriately or equitably—a human relations issue—rather than on the relationship between power and race, class, and gender.

One issue of concern is the limited subject-matter focus of the research questions. Very few of the studies sought to inquire into the multicultural nature of science, mathematics, and technology education. We need scholarship that investigates how a student's cultural background and lived reality influence scientific understanding.

A second issue of concern is the lack of research that examines the implementation of multicultural education in classroom settings. There is a need to understand the possible influence of multicultural content and instructional practices on students' school experiences.

A third issue of concern is the focus and location of multicultural education research. A majority of this research has been conducted at predominately White institutions investigating the influence of multicultural education on students' attitudes and behaviors. There is a need to conduct research on the influence of multicultural education on preservice students of color.

A fourth issue of concern involves methodological practices. Our review of research on multicultural education yielded four methodological concerns:

1. Replication studies were almost totally absent. Multicultural education scholars need to conduct research on multiple sites to confirm and disconfirm findings over time and situations (Erickson, 1986). A related point is a need for multicultural education researchers to establish chains of inquiry to formulate conceptions of knowledge.

2. Many of the studies were conducted by the researcher on his or her own students or class. This raises a question of researcher bias.

3. There is a tendency for multicultural education researchers to neglect previous research related to the area of investigation, thus fragmenting and disconnecting the discipline.

4. Many of the studies do not fully describe the procedures and methods used to collect data.

These methodological concerns should be addressed in future research. Good research procedure is important to understanding the influence of multicultural education.

CONCLUDING REMARKS

We conclude with three remarks that are critical to future multicultural education research. First, we want to encourage scholars to employ the tenets of multicultural education research. From the 1960s to the early 1990s was a period when multicultural theorists devoted much, if not most, of their attention to preparing essays and writing books defining and describing multicultural education, and declaring and celebrating it as a field of scholarship. As we head into the 21st century, scholarly work in these areas must continue, but scholarship in the area of multicultural education research must take center stage. We believe that multicultural education research will increase the knowledge base of how policies and practices of schooling are influencing the learning experiences of all students.

Second, the trend toward conducting only racial or gender and sometimes socioeconomic/class analysis of schooling is very strong. Very few researchers are exploring the interrelationship among these constructs (see, e.g., Sleeter, 1992). Thus the development of scholars who conduct research on the nexus of the constructs (i.e., race, class, and gender) that make up the heart of multicultural education is paramount.

Third and finally, conducting multicultural education research must be demythicized. This scholarship is a social phenomenon that aids and illuminates. Multicultural education research involves committing your action as a scholar within the language of possibilities, a language that provides understanding and enlightenment and leads to the construction and/or reconstruction of hope and agency for all people.

References

Adler, S. (1991). Forming a critical pedagogy in the social studies methods class: The use of imaginative literature. In B. R. Tabachnick & K. M. Zeichner (Eds.), *Issues and practices in inquiry-oriented teacher education* (pp. 77–90). London: Falmer Press.

Ahlquist, R. (1991). Position and imposition: Power relations in a multicultural foundation class. *Journal of Negro Education, 60*(2), 158–169.

Allen, R. (1974). *Reluctant reformers: The impact of racism on American social reform movements.* Washington, DC: Howard University Press.

Allport, G. W. (1954). *The nature of prejudice.* Garden City, NY: Doubleday Anchor.

American Association of University Women. (1992). *How schools shortchange girls.* Washington, DC: American Association of University Women Educational Foundation.

American Council on Education (1949). *Intergroup relations in teaching materials.* Washington, DC: Author.

Anderson, S. E. (1990). Worldmath curriculum: Fighting Eurocentrism in mathematics. *Journal of Negro Education, 59*(3), 348–359.

Apple, M. W. (1979). *Ideology and curriculum*. Boston: Routledge & Kegan Paul.

Apple, M. W. (1991). The new technology: Is it part of the solution or part of the problem in education? *Computers in the Schools, 8*(1), 59–82.

Appleby, J. (1992). Recovering America's historic diversity: Beyond exceptionalism. *The Journal of American History, 79*(2), 419–431.

Arciniega, T. A. (1977). The challenge of multicultural education for teacher educators. *Journal of Research and Development in Education, 11*(1), 52–69.

Asante, M. K. (1991). The Afrocentric idea in education. *Journal of Negro Education, 60*(2), 170–180.

Ausubel, D. P., & Ausubel, P. (1963). Ego development among segregated Negro children. In H. A. Passow (Ed.), *Education in depressed areas* (pp. 109–141). New York: Teachers College Press.

Baker, G. C. (1973). Multicultural training for student teachers. *Journal of Teacher Education, 24*(4), 306–307.

Baker, G. C. (1977). Multicultural education: Two preservice training approaches. *Journal of Teacher Education, 28*(3), 31–33.

Banks, J. A. (1975). *Teaching strategies for ethnic studies*. Boston: Allyn and Bacon.

Banks, J. A. (1977). The implications of multicultural education for teacher education. In F. H. Klassen and D. M. Gollnick (Eds.), *Pluralism and the American teacher* (pp. 1–34). Washington, DC: American Association of Colleges for Teacher Education.

Banks, J. A. (1992). Multicultural education: Historical development, dimensions, and practice. In L. Darling-Hammond (Ed.), *Review of research in education* (Vol. 19, pp. 3–49). Washington, DC: American Educational Research Association.

Banks, J. A. (1993). The canon debate, knowledge construction, and multicultural education. *Educational Researcher, 22*(5), 4–14.

Baty, R. M. (1972). *Re-educating teachers for cultural awareness*. New York: Praeger.

Bell, D. (1987). *And we are not saved: The elusive quest for racial justice*. New York: Basic Books.

Bell, D. (1992). *Faces at the bottom of the well: The permanence of racism*. New York: Basic Books.

Bennett, C. T., Niggle, T., & Stage, F. (1990). Preservice multicultural teacher education: Predictors of student readiness. *Teaching and Teacher Education, 8*(1), 243–254.

Bennett, C. T. (with Okinaka, A., & Xiao-yang, W.). (1988, April). *The effects of a multicultural education course on preservice teachers' attitudes, knowledge, and behavior*. Paper presented at the annual meeting of the American Educational Research Association, New Orleans.

Bernstein, B. (1973). Social class, language and socialization. In J. Karabel & A. H. Halsey (Eds.), *Power and ideology in education* (pp. 473–486). New York: Oxford University Press.

Birrell, J. R. (1993, February). *A case study of the influence of ethnic encapsulation on a beginning secondary teacher*. Paper presented at the annual meeting of the Association of Teacher Education, Los Angeles.

Borden, V. (1993, May 20). Procedures and analysis for top 100 degree producer rankings. *Black Issues in Higher Education*, pp. 60–102.

Bourdieu, P. (1973). Cultural reproduction and social reproduction. In J. Karabel and A. H. Halsey (Eds.), *Power and ideology in education* (pp. 487–510). New York: Oxford University Press.

Britton, G., Lumpkin, M., & Britton, E. (1984). The battle to imprint citizens for the 21st century. *Reading Teacher, 37*, 724–733.

Brophy, J. (1985). Teachers' expectations, motives, and goals for working with problem students. In C. Ames & R. Ames (Eds.), *Research on motivation in education, Vol. II: The classroom milieu*. Orlando, FL: Academic Press.

Brophy, J., & Everston, C. M. (1981). *Students' characteristics and teaching*. New York: Longman.

Brophy, J., & Good, T. (1970). Teachers' communication of differential expectations for children's classroom performance: Some behavioral data. *Journal of Educational Psychology, 61*, 356–374.

Butterfield, R. A., Demos, E. S., Grant, G. W., Moy, P. S., & Perez, A. L. (1979). A multicultural analysis of a popular basal reading series in the international year of the child. *Journal of Negro Education, 48*(3), 382–389.

California State Board of Education. (1981). *History—Social Science Framework for California Public Schools*. Sacramento: Author.

Carroll, L. (1934). *Alice's adventures in Wonderland*. New York: Random House. (Original work published 1865)

Carter, C. (1991). Science-technology-society and access to scientific knowledge. *Theory into Practice, 30*(4), 273–279.

Clark, K., & Clark, M. (1947). Racial identification and preferences in Negro children. In T. M. Newcomb & E. L. Hartley (Eds.), *Reading in social psychology* (pp. 169–178). New York: Holt.

Cohen, P. C. (1982). *A calculating people: The spread of numeracy in early America*. Chicago: University of Chicago Press.

Coleman, J. S. (1967, July). *Race relations and social change*. Baltimore, MD: Center for the Study of Social Organization of Schools, Johns Hopkins University.

Cooper, A., Beare, P., & Thorman, J. (1990). Preparing teachers for diversity: A comparison of student teaching experiences in Minnesota and South Texas. *Action in Teacher Education, 12*(3), 1–4.

Council on Interracial Books for Children. (1976). *Stereotypes, distortions and omissions in U.S. history textbooks*. New York: Racism and Sexism Resource Center for Educators.

Crain, R. L. (1971). School integration and the academic achievement of Negroes. *Sociology of Education, 44*(1), 1–26.

Crenshaw, K. W. (1988). Race, reform, and retrenchment: Transformation and legitimation in anti-discrimination law. *Harvard Law Review, 101*, 1331–1387.

D'Ambrosio, U. (1985). Ethnomathematics and its place in the history and pedagogy of mathematics. *For the Learning of Mathematics, 5*, 44–48.

Datta, L., Schaefer, E., & Davis, M. (1968). Sex and scholastic aptitude as variables on teachers' rating of the adjustment and classroom behavior of Negro and other seventh-grade students. *Journal of Educational Psychology, 59*, 94–101.

Decker, S. (1969). *An empty spoon*. New York: Harper & Row.

Delgado, R. (1989). Storytelling for oppositionists and others: A plea for narrative. *Michigan Law Review, 87*, 2411–2441.

Delgado, R. (1990). When a story is just a story: Does voice really matter? *Virginia Law Review, 76*, 95–111.

Delgado, R. (1991). Brewer's plea: Critical thoughts on common cause. *Vanderbilt Law Review, 44*, 2–14.

Desegregation Assistance Center. (1989). *Resegregation of public schools: The third generation*. Portland, OR: Author.

Diez, M., & Murrell, P. (1991, April). *Assessing abilities of expert teaching practice in diverse classrooms*. Paper presented at the annual meeting of the American Educational Research Association, Chicago.

Dottin, E. S. (1984). Enhancing multicultural perspectives in teacher education through the foundations of education. *Teacher Education Quarterly, 2*(2), 46–52.

Dweck, C. S., & Bush, E. S. (1976). Sex differences in learned helplessness: Differential debilitation with peer and adult evaluators. *Developmental Psychology, 12*, 147–156.

Elson, R. M. (1964). *Guardians of tradition*. Lincoln: University of Nebraska Press.

Education Development Center. Social Studies Curriculum. (1968). *Man: A course of study*. Washington, DC: Curriculum Development Associates.

Erickson, F. (1986). Qualitative methods in research on teaching. In M. C. Wittrock (Ed.), *Handbook of research on teaching* (3rd ed., pp. 119–161). New York: Macmillan.

Ernest, P. (1991). *The philosophy of mathematics education*. London: Falmer Press.

Estrada, K., & McLaren, P. (1993). A dialogue on multiculturalism and democratic culture. *Educational Researcher, 22*, 27–33.

Fantini, M., Gittell, M., & Magat, R. (1970). *Community control and the urban school*. New York: Praeger.

Federbush, M. (1973). *Let them aspire! A plea and proposal for equality of opportunity for males and females in the Ann Arbor public schools* (4th ed.) (Research Rep. No. 143). Ann Arbor, MI: Committee to Eliminate Sex Discrimination in the Public Schools. (ERIC Document Reproduction Service No. ED 092 416)

Fennema, E., Wolleat, P. L., Pedro, J. D., & Becker, A. D. (1981). Increasing women's participation in mathematics: An intervention study. *Journal for Research in Mathematics Education, 12*(1), 3–14.

Frankenstein, M. (1990). Incorporating race, gender, and class issues into a critical mathematical literacy curriculum. *Journal of Negro Education, 59*, 336–351.

Gay, G. (1977). Changing conceptions of multicultural education. *Educational Perspectives, 16*(4), 4–9.

Gay, G. (1983). Multiethnic education: Historical developments and future prospects. *Phi Delta Kappan, 64*(8), 560–563.

Gillette, M. D. (1990). *Making them multicultural: A case study of the clinical teacher-supervisor in preservice teacher education*. Unpublished doctoral dissertation, University of Wisconsin, Madison.

Gollnick, D. M., & Chinn, P. C. (1986). *Multicultural education in a pluralistic society* (2nd ed.). Columbus, OH: Merrill.

Gomez, M. L. (1991). Teaching a language of opportunity in a language arts methods course: Teaching for David, Albert and Darlene. In B. R. Tabachnick & K. M. Zeichner (Eds.), *Issues and practices in inquiry-oriented teacher education* (pp. 91–112). London: Falmer Press.

Gomez, M. L., & Tabachnick, B. R. (1991). Telling teaching stories. *Teaching Education, 4*(2), 129–138.

Good, T. (1970). Which pupils do teachers call on? *Elementary School Journal, 70*, 190–198.

Gordon, B. M. (1992). The marginalized discourse of minority intellectual thought. In C. A. Grant (Ed.), *Research and multicultural education: From the margins to the mainstream* (pp. 19–31). Washington, DC: Falmer Press.

Gould, S. J. (1981). *The mismeasure of man*. New York: W. W. Norton.

Gouldner, H. (1978). *Teachers' pets, troublemakers, and nobodies*. Westport, CT: Greenwood Press.

Grant, C. A. (1975). Exploring the contours of multi-cultural education. In C. A. Grant (Ed.), *Sifting and winnowing: An exploration of the relationship between multi-cultural education and CBTE* (pp. 1–11). Madison, WI: Teacher Corps Associates.

Grant, C. A. (1981). Education that is multicultural and teacher preparation: An examination from the perspective of preservice students. *Journal of Educational Research, 75*(2), 95–99.

Grant, C. A. (1988). The persistent significance of race in schooling. *The Elementary School Journal, 88*, 561–569.

Grant, C. A. (1992). *Research and multicultural education: From the margins to the mainstream*. London: Falmer Press.

Grant, C. A. (1993). *Avoiding confusion and ambiguity: A definition of multicultural education*. A paper submitted for publication.

Grant, C. A., & Grant, G. W. (1985). Staff development and education that is multicultural. *British Journal of In-Service Education, 12*(1), 6–18.

Grant, C. A., & Koskela, R. (1986). Education that is multicultural and the relationship between preservice campus learning and field experiences. *Journal of Educational Research, 79*(4), 197–203.

Grant, C. A., & Melnick, S. L. (1978). Multicultural perspectives of curriculum development and their relationship to in-service education. In R. A. Edelfelt & E. B. Smith (Eds.), *Breakaway to multi-dimensional approaches: Integrating curriculum development and in-service education* (pp. 81–100). Washington, DC: Association of Teacher Educators.

Grant, C. A., & Millar, S. (1992). Research and multicultural education: Barriers, needs and boundaries. In C. A. Grant (Ed.), *Research and multicultural education: From the margins to the mainstream* (pp. 7–18). London: Falmer Press.

Grant, C. A., & Secada, W. G. (1990). Preparing teachers for diversity. In W. R. Houston (Ed.), *Handbook of research on teacher education* (pp. 403–422). New York: Macmillan.

Grant, C. A., & Sleeter, C. E. (1985). The literature on multicultural education: Review and analysis. *Educational Review, 37*(2), 97–118.

Grant. C. A., & Sleeter, C. E. (1986a). *After the school bell rings*. Philadelphia: Falmer Press.

Grant, C. A., & Sleeter, C. E. (1986b). Race, class, and gender in education research: An argument for integrative analysis. *Review of Educational Research, 56*(2), 195–211.

Grant, C. A., Sleeter, C. E., & Anderson, J. (1986). The literature on multicultural education: Review and analysis. *Educational Studies, 12*, 47–71.

Grant, L. (1983). Gender roles and statuses in elementary school children's peer relationships. *Western Sociological Review, 14*, 58–76.

Grant, L. (1984). Black females' "place" in desegregated classrooms. *Sociology of Education, 57*, 98–111.

Grant, L. (1985). Race-gender status, classroom interaction, and children's socialization in classrooms. In L. C. Wilkson and C. B. Marrett (Eds.), *Gender influences in classroom interaction* (pp. 57–77). New York: Academic Press.

Grant, L. (1993). Race and schooling of young girls. In J. Wrigley (Ed.), *Education and gender equality* (pp. 91–114). London: Falmer Press.

Green, R. L., Bakan, R. F., McMillan, J. H., & Lezotte, L. W. (1973). Research and the urban school: Implications for educational improvement. In R. M. W. Travers (Ed.), *Second handbook of research on teaching* (pp. 601–631). Chicago: Rand McNally.

Guyton, E., & McIntyre, D. J. (1990). Student teaching and school experiences. In W. R. Houston (Ed.), *Handbook of research on teacher education* (pp. 514–534). New York: Macmillan.

Haberman, M., & Post, L. (1990). Cooperating teachers' perceptions of the goals of multicultural education. *Action in Teacher Education, 12*(3), 31–35.

Hahn, C. L., & Blankenship, G. (1983). Women and economics textbooks. *Theory and Research in Education, 2*, 67–76.

Henington, M. (1981). Effect of intensive multicultural non-sexist instruction on secondary student teachers. *Educational Research Quarterly, 6*(1), 65–75.

Hilliard, A. (1974). Restructuring teacher education for multicultural imperatives. In W. A. Hunter (Ed.), *Multicultural education through competency-based teacher education* (pp. 40–55). Washington, DC: American Association of Colleges for Teacher Education.

Hirsch, E. D. (1987). *Cultural literacy*. New York: Vintage.

Hirschfelder, A. B. (1975). The treatment of Iroquois Indians in selected American history textbooks. *The Indian Historian, 8*(2), 31–39.

hooks, b. (1990). *Yearning: Race, gender and cultural politics*. Boston: South End Press.

Houston, W. R. (Ed.). (1990). *Handbook of research on teacher education*. New York: Macmillan.

Irvine, J. J. (1990). *Black students and school failure*. New York: Greenwood Press.

Jackson, G., & Cosca, C. (1974). The inequality of educational opportunity in the Southwest: An observational study of ethnically mixed classrooms. *American Educational Research Journal, 11*, 219–229.

Jackson, P., & Lahadernde, H. (1967). Inequalities of teacher-pupil contacts. *Psychology in the Schools, 4,* 204–211.

Joseph, G. C. (1987). Foundations of Eurocentrism in mathematics. *Race and Class, 27,* 13–28.

Kamens, D. H., & Benavot, A. (1991). Elite knowledge for the masses: The origin and spread of mathematics and science education in national curricula. *American Journal of Education, 99,* 137–180.

Kane, M. B. (1970). *Minorities in textbooks: A study of their treatment in social studies texts.* Chicago: Quadrangle Books.

King, J. (1987). Black student alienation and Black teachers' emancipatory pedagogy. *The Journal of Black Reading and Language Education, 3*(1), 3–13.

King, J. (1991). Dysconscious racism: Ideology, identity, and the miseducation of teachers. *The Journal of Negro Education, 60*(2), 133–146.

King, J. (1992) Diaspora literacy and consciousness in the struggle against miseducation in the black community. *The Journal of Negro Education, 61*(3), 317–340.

King, J. E., & Ladson-Billings, G. (1990). The teacher education challenge in elite university settings: Developing critical perspectives for teaching in a democratic and multicultural society. *The European Journal of Intercultural Studies, 1*(2), 15–30.

Klineberg, O. (1963, February 16). Life is fun in a smiling, fair-skinned world. *Saturday Review,* pp. 75–77.

Ladson-Billings, G. (1990). Like lightning in a bottle: Attempting to capture the pedagogical excellence of successful teachers of Black students. *The International Journal of Qualitative Studies in Education, 3,* 335–344.

Ladson-Billings, G. (1991). Beyond multicultural illiteracy. *Journal of Negro Education, 60*(2), 147–157.

Ladson-Billings, G. (1992a). *Distorting democracy: An ethnographic view of the California history-social science textbook adoption process.* Paper presented at the annual meeting of the American Educational Research Association, San Francisco.

Ladson-Billings, G. (1992b). Reading between the lines and beyond the pages: A culturally relevant approach to literacy. *Theory into Practice, 31*(4), 312–320.

Ladson-Billings, G., & Henry, A. (1990). Blurring the borders: Voices of African liberatory pedagogy in the United States and Canada. *Journal of Education, 2,* 72–88.

Ladson-Billings, G., & Tate, W. F. (1993). *Towards a critical race theory of education.* Manuscript submitted for publication.

Lambert, V., & Rohland, G. (1983). *The feasibility of teaching about sex-role stereotyping in a pre-service teacher training setting: A pilot study.* Paper presented at the Ninth Annual Midyear Conference of the AERA/SIG: Women and Education, Tempe, AZ.

Landsherre, G. D. (1988). Research perspectives. In J. P. Keeves (Ed.), *Educational research, methodology, and measurement: An international handbook* (pp. 9–16). Oxford: Pergamon Press.

Larke, P. J. (1990). Cultural diversity awareness inventory: Assessing the sensitivity of preservice teachers. *Action in Teacher Education, 12*(3), 23–30.

Larke, P. J., Wiseman, D., & Bradley, C. (1990). The minority mentorship project: Changing attitudes of preservice teachers for diverse classrooms. *Action in Teacher Education, 12*(3), 5–11.

Lawrence, C. R. (1987). The id, the ego, and equal protection: Reckoning with unconscious racism. *Stanford Law Review, 39,* 317–388.

Lightfoot, S. L. (1980). Families as educators: The forgotten people of Brown. In D. Bell (Ed.), *Shades of brown: New perspectives on school desegregation* (pp. 2–19). New York: Teachers College Press.

Longstreet, W. (1978). *Aspects of ethnicity: Understanding differences in pluralistic classrooms.* New York: Teachers College Press.

Mahan, J. M. (1982a). Community involvement components in culturally-oriented teacher preparation. *Education, 103*(2), 163–172.

Mahan, J. M. (1982b). Native Americans as teacher trainers: Anatomy and outcomes of a cultural immersion project. *Journal of Educational Equity and Leadership, 2*(2), 100–110.

Mahan, J. M. (1984). Major concerns of Anglo student teachers serving in Native American communities. *Journal of American Indian Education, 23*(3), 19–24.

Maher, F. (1991). Gender, reflexivity and teacher education: The Wheaton Program. In B. R. Tabachnick & K. M. Zeichner (Eds.), *Issues and practices in inquiry-oriented teacher education* (pp. 22–34). London: Falmer Press.

Marable, M. (1992). *The crisis of color and democracy.* Monroe, ME: Common Courage.

Martin, R. (1972). Student sex and behavior as determinants of the type and frequency of teacher-student contacts. *Journal of School Psychology, 10,* 339–347.

McCarthy, C. (1990). Multicultural approaches to racial inequality in the United States. *Curriculum and Teaching, 5,* 25–35.

McDiarmid, G. W. (1990). *What to do about differences? A study of multicultural education for teacher trainees in the Los Angeles Unified School District* (Research Rep. No. 90-11). East Lansing: Michigan State University, National Center for Research on Teacher Education.

McDiarmid, G. W., & Price, J. (1990). *Prospective teachers' views of diverse learners: A study of the participants in the ABCD project* (Research Rep. No. 90-6). East Lansing: Michigan State University, National Center for Research on Teacher Education.

Meyer, W., & Lindstrom, D. (1969). *The distribution of teacher approval and disapproval of HeadStart children.* Washington, DC: Office of Economic Opportunity.

Meyer, W., & Thompson, G. (1956). Teacher interaction with boys as contrasted with girls. *Journal of Educational Psychology, 47,* 385–397.

Michigan Department of Education. (1971). *A second report on the treatment of minorities in American history textbooks.* Lansing: Author.

Mills, J. (1984). Addressing the separate-but-equal predicament in teacher preparation: A case study. *Journal of Teacher Education, 6,* 18–23.

Miller, L. P. (1974). Evidence of ethnic bias in instructional materials. In M. Dunfee (Ed.), *Eliminating ethnic bias in instructional materials: Comment and bibliography* (pp. 11–19). Washington, DC: Association for Supervision and Curriculum Development.

Minow, M. (1987). When difference has its home: Group homes for the mentally retarded, equal protection and legal treatment of difference. *Harvard Civil Rights-Civil Liberties Law Review, 22*(1), 111–189.

National Association for the Advancement of Colored People. (1939). *Anti-Negro propaganda in school textbooks.* Washington, DC: Author.

National Science Board (1991). *Science and engineering indicators.* Washington, DC: Government Printing Office.

Natriello, G., McDill, E. L., & Pallas, A. M. (1990). *Schooling disadvantaged children: Racing against catastrophe.* New York: Teachers College Press.

Nava, A. (1990). Toward a model in applied cross-cultural education: CSUN/Ensenada teacher institute. *Social Studies Review, 29*(3), 77–79.

Noordhoff, K., & Kleinfeld, J. (1991, April). *Preparing teachers for multicultural classrooms: A case study in rural Alaska.* Paper presented at the annual meeting of the American Educational Research Association, Chicago.

Noordhoff, K., & Kleinfeld, J. (1993). Preparing teachers for multicultural classrooms. *Teaching and Teacher Education, 9*(1), 27–39.

Oliver, L. (1974, February). Women in aprons: The female stereotype in children's readers. *The Elementary School Journal*, 74(5), 253–259.

Olneck, M. (1993). Terms of inclusion: Has multiculturalism redefined equality in American education? *American Journal of Education*, 101, 234–260.

Ortiz, A. A., & Yates, J. R. (1988). *Characteristics of learning disabled, mentally retarded, and speech-language handicapped Hispanic students at initial evaluation and reevaluation*. Paper presented at the Ethnic and Multicultural Symposia, Dallas, TX. (ERIC Document Reproduction Service No. ED 298 705)

Page, R. (1991). *Lower-track class-rooms*. New York: Teachers College Press.

Parkay, F. W. (1983). *White teacher, black school: The professional growth of a ghetto teacher*. New York: Praeger.

Phillip, M. (1993, June 17). Race, gender and economics in the classroom. *Black Issues in Higher Education*, pp. 14–18.

Pillar, C. (1992, September). Separate realities. *Macworld*, pp. 218–230.

Popkewitz, T. (1984). *Paradigm and ideology in educational research*. London: Falmer Press.

Powell, R. R., & Garcia, J. (1988). What research says. . . About stereotypes. *Science and Children*, 25, 21–23.

Price, G. (1992). Using quantitative methods to explore multicultural education. In C. A. Grant (Ed.), *Research and multicultural education: From the margins to the mainstream* (pp. 58–70). London: Falmer Press.

Ravitch, D. (1980). Desegregation: Varieties of meaning. In D. A. Bell (Ed.), *Shades of brown* (pp. 30–47). New York: Teachers College Press.

Ravitch, D. (1990, October 24). Multiculturalism, yes, particularism, no. *The Chronicle of Higher Education*, p. A44.

Reinhold, R. (1991, September 29). Class struggle. *The New York Times Magazine*, p. 26.

Rist, R. C. (1970). Student social class and teacher expectations: The self-fulfilling prophecy. *Harvard Educational Review*, 40, 411–451.

Sadker, D., & Sadker, M. (1981). The development and field trial of a non-sexist teacher education curriculum. *High School Journal*, 64, 331–336.

Sadker, D., & Sadker, M. (1985). Is the o.k. classroom o.k.? *Phi Delta Kappan*, 66(5), 358–361.

Safilios-Rothschild, C. (1979). *Sex-role socialization and sex discrimination: A synthesis and critique of the literature*. Washington, DC: National Institute of Education.

Schofield, J. W. (1991). School desegregation and intergroup relations: A review of the literature. *Review of Research in Education*, 17, 335–409.

Scott, K. P. (1981). Whatever happened to Jane and Dick? Sexism in texts reexamined. *Peabody Journal of Education*, 58, 135–142.

Scott, R. (1969). Social class, race, seriating and reading readiness: A study of their relationship at the kindergarten level. *Journal of Genetic Psychology*, 115, 87–96.

Showalter, E. (1971). *Women's liberation and literature*. New York: Harcourt Brace Jovanovich.

Sizemore, B. A. (1979). The four M curriculum: A way to shape the future. *Journal of Negro Education*, 48(3), 341–356.

Sleeter, C. E. (1988). *Preservice coursework and field experience in multicultural education: Impact on teacher behavior*. Unpublished manuscript.

Sleeter, C. E. (1992). *Keepers of the American dream*. London: Falmer Press.

Sleeter, C. E., & Grant, C. A. (1987). An analysis of multicultural education in the United States. *Harvard Educational Review*, 57, 421–444.

Sleeter, C. E., & Grant, C. A. (1991). Race, class, gender and disability in current textbooks. In M. W. Apple & L. K. Christian-Smith (Eds.), *The politics of the textbook* (pp. 78–110). New York: Routledge.

Soto, L. (1992). Success stories. In C. A. Grant (Ed.), *Research and multicultural education: From the margins to the mainstream* (pp. 153–164). London: Falmer Press.

Spender, D. (1982). *Invisible women*. New York: Writers and Readers Publishing Cooperative.

Stallings, J. (1992, April) *Lessons learned from a four-year case study of preparing teachers for urban schools*. Paper presented at the Annual Meeting of the American Educational Research Association, San Francisco.

Stewart, J., Meier, K. J., & England, R. E. (1989). In quest of role models: Change in Black teacher representation in urban school districts, 1968–1986. *Journal of Negro Education*, 58, 140–152.

Sullivan, A. (1974). Cultural competence and confidence: A quest for effective teaching in a pluralistic society. In W. A. Hunter (Ed.), *Multicultural education through competency-based teacher education* (pp. 56–71). Washington, DC: American Association of Colleges for Teacher Education.

Swanson, C. (1977). The treatment of the American Indian in high school history texts. *The Indian Historian*, 10(2), 28–37.

Swartz, E. (1992). Multicultural education: From a compensatory to a scholarly foundation. In C. A. Grant (Ed.), *Research and multicultural education: From the margins to the mainstream* (pp. 32–46). London: Falmer Press.

Taeuber, K. E. (1977). Foreword. In M. Weinberg, *Minority students: A research appraisal* (p. iii). Washington, DC: Government Printing Office.

Takaki, R. (1989). *Strangers from a different shore*. Boston: Little, Brown.

Takaki, R. (1993). *A different mirror: A history of multicultural America*. Boston: Little, Brown.

Tate, W. F. (in press a). From inner city to ivory tower: Does my voice matter in the academy? *Urban Education*.

Tate, W. F. (in press b). Expanding the vision of mathematics subject matter knowledge: The need for a critical race perspective. In E. Hollins (Ed.), *A knowledge base for teaching culturally diverse learners*. Albany: State University of New York Press.

Tate, W. F., Ladson-Billings, G., & Grant, C. A. (1993). The Brown decision revisited: Mathematizing social problems. *Educational Policy*, 7(3), 255–275.

Tetreault, M. T. (1984). Notable American women: The case of United States history textbooks. *Social Education*, 48, 546–550.

Tetreault, M. T. (1986). Integrating women's history: The case of United States history high school textbooks. *History Teacher*, 19, 211–262.

Trecker, J. L. (1971). Woman's place is in the curriculum. *Saturday Review*, 54(42), 83–86, 92.

Trecker, J. L. (1973). Sex stereotyping in the secondary school curriculum. *Phi Delta Kappan*, 55(2), 110–112.

Vane, J. R., Weitzman, J., & Applebaum, A. P. (1966). Performance of Negro and White children and problem and nonproblem children on the Stanford Binet Scale. *Journal of Clinical Psychology*, 22, 431–435.

Waetjen, W. (1962). Is learning sexless? *Education Digest*, 28, 12–14.

Washington, V. (1981). Impact of antiracism/multicultural education training on elementary teachers' attitudes and classroom behavior. *Elementary School Journal*, 81(3), 186–192.

Weinberg, M. (1977). *Minority students: A research appraisal*. Washington, DC: Government Printing Office.

Whitaker, L. (1989, January). The disappearing Black teacher. *Ebony*, pp. 122–126.

Williams, P. J. (1991). *The alchemy of race and rights: Diary of a law professor*. Cambridge, MA: Harvard University Press.

Woman on Words and Images. (1972). *Dick and Jane as victims: Sex stereotyping in children's readers*. Princeton, NJ: Author.

Wundt, W. M. (1894). *Lectures on human and animal psychology* (J. E. Creighton & E. B. Titchener, Trans.) (2nd ed.). New York: Macmillan.

Yager, R. E. (1993). Science-technology-society as reform. *School Science and Mathematics*, *93*, 145–151.

Yoshiwara, F. M. (1983). Shattering myths: Japanese-American educational issues. In D. T. Nakanishi and M. Hirano-Nakanishi (Eds.), *The education of Asian and Pacific-Americans: Historical perspectives and prescriptions for the future*. Phoenix, AZ: Oryx Press.

Zeichner, K. M., & Gore, J. M. (1990). Teacher socialization. In W. R. Houston (Ed.), *Handbook of research on teacher education* (pp. 329–348). New York: Macmillan.

KNOWLEDGE CONSTRUCTION

· 10 ·

KNOWLEDGE CONSTRUCTION AND POPULAR CULTURE: THE MEDIA AS MULTICULTURAL EDUCATOR

Carlos E. Cortés
UNIVERSITY OF CALIFORNIA, RIVERSIDE

Discussions of education often, and erroneously, use "schools" and "education" as synonymous concepts. Certainly schools comprise a powerful component of the educational process. However, they do not monopolize education, nor could they even if they wished (Berger & Luckman, 1966; Cremins, 1990).

Students learn in schools. But they also learn outside of schools through the "societal curriculum"—that massive, on-going, informal curriculum of families, peer groups, neighborhoods, churches, organizations, institutions, mass media, and other socializing forces that educate all of us throughout our lives (Berry, 1980; Cortés, 1981; Leifer, Gordon, & Graves, 1974; Leiss, Kline, & Jhally, 1986; Spring, 1992). Much of that societal curriculum provides multicultural education.

Through the societal curriculum, as well as through the school curriculum, students learn language, acquire culture, obtain knowledge, develop beliefs, internalize attitudes, and establish patterns of behavior. They learn about themselves and others. They learn about the groups to which they and others belong. They learn about their nation and other nations and cultures. In short, as part of this combined process of school and societal multicultural education, students learn about diversity in various forms, including racial, ethnic, cultural, gender, religious, regional, and national.

As a major element of societal multicultural education, the mass media—through such avenues as newspapers, magazines, motion pictures, television, and radio—disseminate information, images, and ideas concerning race, ethnicity, culture, and foreignness. Media educate both for better *and* for worse. This media multicultural curriculum functions whether or not individual mediamakers actually view themselves as educators, whether or not they are aware that they are spreading ideas about diversity, and whether they operate in the realm of fact or fiction. Moreover, media-based multicultural learning may occur whether or not learners approach the media as a source of knowledge and information, whether or not they are aware that they are learning from the media, and whether or not they recognize how their previous experiences—including their media experiences—may be influencing the meanings that they consciously or unconsciously construct from their interactions with the media.

Media multicultural education plays a powerful role in the social construction of knowledge about race, ethnicity, and culture (Hall, 1977). It both fosters ethnic pride and erodes self-esteem through the repetition of themes, messages, and images (Allen & Hatchett, 1986). It sometimes contributes to intergroup understanding through sensitive examinations of ethnic experiences, cultures, and problems, but at other times exacerbates intergroup misunderstanding through repeated presentation of derogatory stereotypes and overemphasis on negative themes about selected groups or nations (MacDonald, 1992; Shaheen, 1984). It spreads fact and fiction, at times striving for truth, accuracy, sensitivity, and balance, while at other times consciously distorting for purposes of sensationalism, commercialism, and ideological message transmission. By participating in the social construction of knowledge about race and ethnicity, media multicultural education both interacts with and affects personal identity, both challenges and reinforces intergroup prejudice, contributes to both intergroup understanding and intergroup misunderstanding, and influences public norms, expectations, hopes, and fears about diversity.

Media multicultural education incorporates both the news and entertainment media. Audiences learn not only from programs and publications intended to provide information, but also from media presumably designed merely to entertain (as well as to make money). Moreover, audiences sometimes have great difficulty distinguishing nonfictional from fictional media presentations. For example, a 1989 survey revealed that 50% of U.S. television viewers considered the show *America's Most Wanted* to be a news program, while 28% considered it entertainment (Rosenstiel, 1989).

While some mediamakers state that they merely offer entertainment, in fact they simultaneously teach, whether intentionally or incidentally. Reverse the equation. Whatever the stated or unstated goals of the makers, audiences learn from and construct knowledge based on both fictional and nonfictional media, although in the case of fictional media they usually fail to realize that such media-based learning is occurring (Jowett, 1976; Singer & Kaplan, 1976; Sklar, 1975). Plato recognized the power of fictional narrative when he asserted, "Those who tell the stories also rule the society." In his book, *The Empire's Old Clothes: What The Lone Ranger, Babar, and Other Innocent Heroes Do to Our Minds,* Ariel Dorfman (1983) argued:

Industrially produced fiction has become one of the primary shapers of our emotions and our intellect in the twentieth century. Although these stories are supposed to merely entertain us, they constantly give us a secret education. We are not only taught certain styles of violence, the latest fashions, and sex roles by TV, movies, magazines, and comic strips; we are also taught how to succeed, how to love, how to buy, how to conquer, how to forget the past and suppress the future. We are taught, more than anything else, how not to rebel. (p. ix)

In a comparable manner, sociologist Herbert Gans (1967) likened television to schools and television programs to school courses:

Almost all TV programs and magazine fiction teach something about American society. For example, *Batman* is, from this vantage point, a course in criminology that describes how a superhuman aristocrat does a better job eradicating crime than do public officials. Similarly, *The Beverly Hillbillies* offers a course in social stratification and applied economics, teaching that with money, uneducated and uncultured people can do pretty well in American society, and can easily outwit more sophisticated and more powerful middle-class types. ... And even the innocuous family situation comedies such as *Ozzie and Harriet* deal occasionally with ethical problems encountered on a neighborhood level. ... Although the schools argue that they are the major transmitter of society's moral values, the mass media offer a great deal more content on this topic. (pp. 21–22)

Among this "great deal more content" the mass media have transmitted an enormous body of material on race, ethnicity, culture, and foreignness, thereby contributing to the social construction of multicultural knowledge. The *degree* to which media actually *construct* multicultural knowledge, perceptions, and stereotypes can be debated. Beyond debate, however, is the fact that they *contribute* to the construction of intercultural, interracial, and interethnic knowledge, beliefs, perceptions, and attitudes. Specifying precisely what the media have taught and identifying what different individuals, groups, or nations have learned from the media, however, pose a considerable challenge. In addressing the role of media in the social con-

struction of multicultural knowledge, scholars have explored at least four basic analytical dimensions of that process:

1. *Content Analysis*: An examination of the content of the mass media in order to assess what the media have *taught* about race, ethnicity, culture, and foreignness.
2. *Control Analysis*: An examination of the process by which mediamakers have created, repeated, modified, and disseminated this multicultural content.
3. *Impact Analysis*: An examination of the short-term and long-term influences of the media on individual and societal learning about race and ethnicity, including the roles that readers, viewers, and listeners have played in the process of the media-based social construction of multicultural knowledge.
4. *Pedagogical Analysis*: An examination of the relationship between mass media and school education in the construction of multicultural knowledge, including ways in which schools can address, contend with, and build from the media, particularly using it pedagogically as a multicultural educational tool.

CONTENT ANALYSIS: THE MEDIA CURRICULUM ON RACE AND ETHNICITY

What have the mass media taught about race and ethnicity? Three basic generalizations can be formulated about such research to date.

First, most published content analyses of race and ethnicity in the mass media deal with a single ethnic group, such as Chinese Americans, a constellation of related ethnic groups, such as Asian Americans, or a single foreign area, such as Asia. Sometimes studies link the related ethnic and foreign cultures, such as Asian Americans and Asians.

Second, most studies focus tightly on the subject group or area, with only occasional efforts to place such content analysis in the comparative context of the media treatment of other ethnic groups or foreign areas. This tight unicultural focus sometimes leads to false conclusions about the asserted or implied uniqueness of the media's treatment of the subject group. In contrast, a comparative multicultural approach may reveal that such treatment was not group specific and that, during a particular era, the media were giving similar treatment to other ethnic groups or cultures or, for that matter, to Americans in general.

Third, some of these studies reflect attempts to examine systematically and comprehensively the long-term chronological development of the treatment of the target ethnic group or culture by the media (or by one element of the media, such as television or motion pictures). However, most studies merely provide snapshots of media treatment within limited periods of time rather than longitudinal analyses of media treatment over an extended period. Such limited studies often achieve provocative and suggestive insights. However, some studies fall into the trap of asserting broad long-term generalizations about the media treatment of a group or groups or about images, messages, and stereotyping based on a relatively small number of fragmentary, overly selective, or temporally restricted pieces of media evidence. Occasionally this even leads to the stereotyping of assumed, asserted, but unproven media stereotyping.

Motion pictures have drawn the greatest degree of book-length scholarly content analysis concerning the media treatment of race and ethnicity. Numerous scholars have assessed the historical development of the U.S. motion picture treatment of specific racial and ethnic groups. African Americans in film have received the most extensive examination, ranging from Donald Bogle's (1989) engagingly iconoclastic and idiosyncratic *Toms, Coons, Mulattoes, Mammies & Bucks: An Interpretive History of Blacks in American Films*, to impressionistically provocative essays on individual films like James Snead's (1992) *White Screens/Black Images: Hollywood from the Dark Side* and the special motion picture issue (1991) of the *Black American Literature Forum*, to more archive-based studies like Thomas Cripps's (1977) *Slow Fade to Black: The Negro in American Film, 1900–1942* and (1993) *Making Movies Black: The Hollywood Message Movie from World War II to the Civil Rights Era* and Daniel Leab's (1975) *From Sambo to Superspade: The Black Experience in Motion Pictures*. Books on Jewish Americans have earned the statistical runner-up spot, with such studies as Lester Friedman's (1982) *Hollywood's Image of the Jew* and Patricia Erens's (1984) *The Jew in American Cinema*, as well as books on Yiddish cinema (discussed later).

The mainstream film treatment of U.S. Latinos has been studied in Allen Woll's (1980) *The Latin Image in American Film* and Arthur Pettit's (1980) *Images of the Mexican American in Fiction and Film*, while Gary Keller's (1985) *Chicano Cinema: Research, Reviews, and Resources* and Chon Noriega's (1992) *Chicanos and Film: Essays on Chicano Representation and Resistance* address the role of both mainstream and Chicano media in the creation of the Chicano film image. The depiction of American Indians has been discussed in Ralph and Natasha Friar's (1972) *The Only Good Indian . . . The Hollywood Gospel*, John O'Connor's (1980) *The Hollywood Indian: Stereotypes of Native Americans in Films*, and Gretchen Bataille and Charles Silet's (1980) *The Pretend Indian: Images of Native Americans in the Movies*. Other books on the film treatment of specific groups include Eugene Franklin Wong's (1978) *On Visual Media Racism: Asians in the American Motion Pictures*, Joseph Curran's (1989) *Hibernian Green on the Silver Screen*, and Les and Barbara Keyser's (1984) *Hollywood and the Catholic Church: The Image of Roman Catholicism in American Movies*. Among single-group books-in-progress are Jack Shaheen's study of the movie treatment of Arabs and Arab Americans.

For the most part, these books focus on the question of content. However, such archive-based books as Cripps's (1977) *Slow Fade to Black*, O'Connor's (1980) *Hollywood Indian*, Wong's (1978) *Visual Media Racism*, and Woll's (1980) *Latin Image* also engage the control analysis issue of the *process* by which mediamakers have created, repeated, and modified movie multicultural content, including some of the reasons and forces behind this content creation.

The treatment of ethnic groups in other media has generated far fewer comprehensive book-length content analysis efforts. The television depiction of African Americans has been examined in J. Fred MacDonald's (1992) *Blacks and White TV: African Americans in Television Since 1948,* while Jack Shaheen (1984) addressed Arab Americans as well as Arabs in *The TV Arab*. Bradley Greenberg, Michael Burgoon, Judee K. Burgoon, and Felipe Korzenny's (1983) *Mexican Americans and the Mass Media* and Janette Dates and William Barlow's (1990) *Split Image: African Americans in the Mass Media* contain essays on coverage and treatment in a variety of media.

Beyond books, there has been a cottage industry of content analysis articles on the media treatment of individual ethnic groups (Woll & Miller, 1987). These include multiple articles on certain significant television programs, such as *Roots, All in the Family,* and *The Cosby Show,* and motion pictures, such as *The Birth of a Nation, Dances with Wolves, Guess Who's Coming to Dinner,* and *The Jazz Singer* (in its various versions). Most article-length studies focus on the media depiction of individual ethnic groups (Gray, 1986; Subervi-Vélez, 1986). Yet some ethnic groups have not yet earned even a single scholarly article concerning their media treatment.

No book to date deals systematically with the larger issue of the history of the treatment of race and ethnicity by the media in general. Nor, for that matter, has there been a comprehensive history of the overall media treatment (as contrasted to treatment by an individual medium) of a specific ethnic group. Among the most comprehensive single-group studies of the popular cultural social construction of multicultural knowledge are Raymond William Stedman's (1982) *Shadows of the Indian: Stereotypes in American Culture,* Joseph Boskin's (1986) *Sambo: The Rise & Demise of an American Jester,* and Adolph Caso's (1980) *Mass Media vs. the Italian Americans.* However, the first two deal only partially with the mass media, and the latter employs a highly selective topical structure rather than a developmental historical framework.

Finally, there has been no book-length scholarly study of the comparative treatment of race and ethnicity in one segment of the media. The most comprehensive books to date are collections of essays on motion pictures. These include Randall Miller's (1978) edited volume of original essays, *The Kaleidoscopic Lens: How Hollywood Views Ethnic Groups,* Allen Woll and Randall Miller's (1987) *Ethnic and Racial Images in American Film and Television: Historical Essays and Bibliography* (most of the essays in these two books employ the traditional group-by-group approach), Lester Friedman's (1991) edited collection, *Unspeakable Images: Ethnicity and the American Cinema,* and Robert Brent Toplin's (1993) *Hollywood as Mirror: Changing Views of "Outsiders" and "Enemies" in American Movies.* Carlos Cortés's book-in-progress, *Hollywood's Multicultural Curriculum: A History of the U.S. Motion Picture Treatment of Race and Ethnicity,* addresses this topic in a chronological, cross-cultural, comparative manner.

While the themes of individual and, to a far lesser extent, comparative group treatment have dominated multicultural media content analysis, there is also the larger question of the general *categories* of multicultural knowledge that the media have disseminated. In general, the media provide three different but interrelated types of content that contribute to multicultural knowledge construction.

Media Provide Information About Race and Ethnicity

People cannot be at all places at all times, nor can they travel into the past. Therefore, they must rely on mediating forms of communication—particularly the mass media—for much of their learning about today's world as well as the past. Because individuals cannot develop in-depth knowledge about each and every racial or ethnic group or nation on the basis of personal or educational experience, they necessarily acquire much of what they know about race, ethnicity, culture, and foreignness through what historian Daniel Boorstin (1961) has termed the "pseudoenvironment," principally the mass media.

Moreover, the issue of media as multicultural information source goes well beyond the question of accuracy. In news, the constant reiteration of certain themes, even when each story is accurate in and of itself, may unjustifiably emphasize limited information about an ethnic group (Heller, 1992). Similarly, the repetition of ethnic images by the entertainment media add to viewer's pools of "knowledge," particularly if news and entertainment treatments coincide and mutually reinforce each other in theme, approach, content, perspective, and frequency.

Media Help Organize Multicultural Information and Ideas

More than simply providing information, media also influence viewer and reader structures for perceiving, receiving, thinking, and remembering—the way people process and organize information and ideas as they construct their personal multicultural knowledge (Adoni & Mane, 1984). Fictional and nonfictional narratives, for example, perform the same roles that folk stories and fairy tales have filled for years (Bettelheim, 1976). They provide a type of "ritualized glue" that helps recipients make sense out of the pseudoenvironment's increasing information overload, which assaults and often overwhelms readers, viewers, and listeners. In his book *Information Anxiety,* Richard Saul Wurman (1989) opined that the amount of information available to an individual now doubles every half decade, while a single weekday issue of the *New York Times* contains more information than the average resident of 17th-century England was likely to encounter in a lifetime.

Reporting in 1977 that there had been more than 2,300 research papers on television and human behavior, social psychologist George Comstock addressed the relationship of the entertainment media to the reification of social structures:

Several writers have argued that television is a powerful reinforcer of the status quo. The ostensible mechanisms are the effects of its portrayals on public expectations and perceptions. Television portrayals and particularly violent drama are said to assign roles of authority, power, success, failure, dependence, and vulnerability in a manner that matches the real-life social hierarchy, thereby strengthening that hierarchy by increasing its acknowledgement among the public and by failing to provide positive images for members of social categories occupying a subservient position. Content analyses of television drama support the contention that portrayals reflect normative status. (pp. 20–21)

To the degree that the media assert the normality of racial, ethnic, and social hierarchies or reiterate interethnic taboos, they serve to reinforce the legitimacy and even the naturalness of these relationships and attitudes. When news media continually reflect and disseminate selected patterns of thinking about race and ethnicity, they help to shape reader and viewer mental and attitudinal frameworks for organizing future information and ideas about certain groups (Hartmann & Husband, 1972; Hawkins & Pingree, 1981). When the entertainment media repeatedly depict interethnic or racial dominance or subservience or consistently portray members of specific ethnic groups in limited spheres of action, they contribute to the formation of viewer schema for perceiving those groups and absorbing future images into a meaningful, consistent, if distorted, conceptual framework (Wiegman, 1989). By influencing viewer, reader, and listener organizational schema, in other words, the media go well beyond spreading information (and misinformation) in contributing to the social construction of multicultural knowledge.

For example, in a study of the comparative treatment of Blacks and Whites by Chicago local television news, communications scholar Robert Entman (1990) concluded that:

In the stories analyzed, crime reporting made blacks look particularly threatening, while coverage of politics exaggerated the degree to which black politicians (as compared to white ones) practice special interest politics. These images would most feed the first two components of modern racism, anti-black affect and resistance to blacks' political demands. On the other hand, the positive dimension of the news, the presence of black anchors and other authority figures, may simultaneously engender an impression that racial discrimination is no longer a problem. . . . (p. 342)

Media Influence Multicultural Values and Attitudes

For decades, critics of the media have been asserting the value-influencing power of movies. The Payne Fund studies of motion picture impact during the 1930s, for example, included Henry James Forman's (1933) provocatively titled *Our Movie Made Children.* More recently, media historian Robert Sklar (1975) chose *Movie-Made America* as the title for his widely read cultural history of U.S. motion pictures, although he avoided the deterministic "hypodermic needle effect" leanings of some of the Payne Fund studies (Jarvis, 1991).

Hollywood's 1930 Motion Picture Production Code (the Hays Code) provides a primer on Hollywood's response to public concerns over the motion picture industry's role in teaching values (see Stanley & Steinberg, 1976, pp. 80–93). For example, one of the code's values positions, its opposition to interracial love, appeared in Section II; Rule 6, which read, "Miscegenation (sex relationship between the white and black races) is forbidden." Until that rule was deleted in 1956, Hollywood drummed home the repeated values message of the importance of avoiding miscegenation, not only between "the white and black races," but also between Whites and other people categorized as "colored." In those rare screen instances where interracial love or sex occurred or seemed about to occur, failure, punishment, and retribution predictably resulted (Cortés, 1991b).

To an extent this values element of the Hollywood movie curriculum reflected widespread American social mores. When surveys conducted for Gunnar Myrdal's (1944) classic, *An American Dilemma: The Negro Problem and Modern Democracy*, asked southern Whites what discriminatory lines must be maintained, their most common answer was "the bar against intermarriage and sexual intercourse involving white women" (p. 60). Similar Anglo opposition to intermarriage with Mexican Americans was documented through interviews for economist Paul Taylor's (1930) study of Mexican labor in the United States.

Although interracial marriage had long existed in the United States, Hollywood elevated antimiscegenation values lessons over the presentation of multiethnic reality. In adopting this pattern of portrayals, moviemakers functioned simultaneously as learners (reacting to the presence of certain social mores among many Americans), as teachers of values (creating antimiscegenation "curriculum guidelines" and consistently transmitting this "thou-shall-and-shall-not" lesson to the viewing public), and as profits-at-all-costs commercialists (fearing that movies with interracial love might not "sell" to White audiences, particularly in the South) (Cripps, 1970).

A more recent study of prime-time television drama, situation comedies, and movies suggested that these racially separatist values lessons have not disappeared, even if the separatism is less blatant or codified (Weigel, Loomis, & Soja, 1980). That study concluded that cross-racial interactions comprised only 2% of the time in which characters were on screen. Moreover, in comparison to White-White interactions, Black-White relations on fictional television were more formal, involved less intimacy, and included less shared decision making.

The media's participation in the social construction of multicultural knowledge, then, involves more than the creation and dissemination of images. Content analysis research has revealed that the media are also involved in the transmission of information (correct or incorrect, balanced or distorted, contextualized or stereotypical). Moreover, that content also involves the organization of information and ideas and the dissemination of values (Hall, 1982).

CONTROL ANALYSIS: MEDIAMAKERS AS MULTICULTURAL CURRICULUM DEVELOPERS

Content analysis of media multicultural education raises the collateral issue of control analysis—why have the media disseminated these multicultural images and messages? When it comes to reasons for the dissemination of multicultural content and ideas, media creators vary (Fisher & Lowenstein, 1967; Rubin, 1980; Wilson & Gutiérrez, 1985). Some mediamakers intentionally try to teach about race and ethnicity, while others do so only incidentally, such as by publishing news stories with multicultural dimensions or by including ethnic characters in movie or television narratives without any particular goal of ethnic image making or message sending. Yet whatever the mediamakers' intentions, their media may teach by contributing to multicultural knowledge construction (Diawara, 1992).

But what are the sources of the impetus for media creation of multicultural content? In general, control analysts have focused on three levels: the media at large; an entire media industry; or individual components of the media.

Some scholars have argued that the issue of the creation of media content must be addressed in structural terms of the media at large, including the societal context in which the media operate (Gitlin, 1979). For example, in analyzing the British media, Stuart Hall (1981) contended:

If the media function in a systematically racist manner, it is not because they are run and organized exclusively by active racists; this is a category mistake. This would be equivalent to saying that you could change the character of the capitalist state by replacing its personnel. Whereas the media, like the state, have a *structure,* a set of *practices* which are *not* reducible to the individuals who staff them. What defines how the media function is the result of a set of complex, often contradictory, social relations; not the personal inclinations of its members. (p. 46)

Other analysts have looked at specific media industries. Some critics of the media, including politicians and special-interest pressure groups, have proclaimed various types of media conspiracies to influence interethnic popular thinking. Yet, while they have discovered a few spent shells lying about, neither critics nor scholars have yet demonstrated with any evidentiary effectiveness many mediawide or even single-industry-wide smoking guns of multicultural educational intentions.

Possibly the closest they have come is through their analysis of the 1930 Motion Picture Production Code (Stanley & Steinberg, 1976, pp. 80–93), which laid out movie content rules—dos and don'ts that Hollywood filmmakers had to follow in order to earn the official industry Seal of Approval for commercial exhibition. Some of its provisions applied directly to or had serious implications for the treatment of race and ethnicity. Yet with the admittedly important miscegenation exception, even this critical document does not provide evidence of any major industry concern about the treatment of this theme.

For example, Section V of the code stated that "the Production Code Administration may take cognizance of the fact that the following words and phrases are obviously offensive to the patrons of motion pictures in the United States and *more particularly* [emphasis added] to the patrons of motion pictures in foreign countries: Chink, Dago, Frog, Greaser, Hunkie, Kike, Nigger, Spig, Wop, Yid" (Stanley & Steinberg, 1976, p. 83). The code's emphasis on the concerns of patrons in foreign countries suggests that the commercial issue of overseas ticket sales provided a stronger imperative than did the moral issues of ethnic sensitivities or interethnic bigotry.

At times, however, certain media industries and even the media at large have appeared to follow a relatively regimented approach to the treatment of specific multicultural topics. Under federal government pressure to support World War II mobilization, for example, Hollywood consciously created a prowar multicultural curriculum by cranking out movies featuring multiethnic military units, each containing at least one Grabowski, one Ginsberg, one González, one Graziano, and one O'Grady. Hollywood thereby issued a clarion call to arms by spreading the message that Americans of all backgrounds have fought for their country in the past and should be happy to do so now (Koppes & Black, 1987).

Finally, when scholars drop down from mediawide and individual media industrywide analyses, they have identified more limited collaborations around specific themes, concerns, issues, or media products. Some individual newspapers, magazines, stations, and even movie studios have had their own multicultural ideologies. Motion pictures provide a prime example of multicultural control analysis that has invited scholarly examination.

For example, in its early years Warner Brothers took a special interest in making social-problem films that often dealt with issues of racial inequality, antiethnic bigotry, and discrimination. At one time, assimilation-oriented Jewish movie studio heads took steps to reduce the screen visibility of Jewish Americans, particularly during the rise of European anti-Semitism in the 1930s (Gabler, 1988). In contrast, during the past two decades such ethnic filmmakers as Spike Lee, Edward James Olmos, Wayne Wang, Francis Ford Coppola, and Martin Scorsese have emphasized the making of movies that explore their own ethnic groups (Lourdeaux, 1990).

Alternative independent film movements, not just individual filmmakers, have occasionally arisen around selected multicultural themes and issues, such as Black "race movies" (Cripps, 1978) and Yiddish films of the 1920s and 1930s. Jewish American moviemakers in the Yiddish film movement provided a sharp contrast with mainstream Jewish studio heads by consciously emphasizing the celebration and maintenance of Jewish culture, as opposed to the assimilationist screen ideology of the Hollywood moguls. During the past decade a growing scholarly literature on Yiddish films has provided insight into the efforts of this interesting alternative effort in multicultural media curriculum development (Goldberg, 1983; Goldman, 1983; Hoberman, 1991).

Individual mediamakers have sometimes tried to influence societal attitudes toward specific ethnic groups. Over the years, selected films have consciously tried to reduce bigotry by challenging ethnic prejudice. This was a common stance in such post–World War II movie textbooks as *Home of the Brave* (African Americans), *A Medal for Benny* (Mexican Americans), *Broken Arrow* (American Indians), *Saturday's Hero* (Polish Americans), *Crossfire* (Jewish Americans), and *Knock on Any Door* (Italian Americans). Some filmmakers have tried to deliver broader multicultural messages, such as celebrating ethnic diversity as an element of American society or presenting ethnic diversity as an integral part of American national character, culture, and values. In contrast, other films have just as consciously traded on antiethnic bigotry, a process begun during the early silent era in the anti-Mexican "greaser" movies (like *The Greaser's Revenge*), the parade of Indian savage movies, and even classics like D. W. Griffith's *The Birth of a Nation,* which featured some of the most despicable depictions of African Americans ever to reach the screen.

At times moviemakers assume and take advantage of previous audience multicultural knowledge construction and the resulting audience predispositions in order to provoke media-conditioned emotional responses. Sometimes filmmakers play upon personal fears by providing an ethnic menace, iconographically generated, for example, by a band of Indians (or even just the presence of a smoke signal accompanied by the

beating of tom-toms) in movies set in the old West, or by a large group—presumably a gang—of young Latinos or African Americans in contemporary urban films. Or they may go for cheap intercultural laughs by using "odd" surnames, inserting a crowd of Japanese tourists loaded with cameras, or, in the 1978 film *The End*, presenting an asylum inmate who admits that he strangled his father because he was "too Polish" (Polish-American Guardian Society, 1982).

While trading on and manipulating this presumed constructed multicultural knowledge and these audience predispositions, moviemakers reinforce the audience's constructed knowledge and thereby make it more convenient for other mediamakers to draw upon that knowledge. However, like school textbook writers, mediamakers ultimately lose control of their multicultural creations. Once media products appear, they take on lives of their own. Media authors often find that their original conceptions become severely modified, seriously undermined, or even drastically distorted in the editing and production process. Images, depictions, and messages that ultimately appear in media creations may or may not represent the best expression of the creator's intent. Therefore, the images and messages in the media may diverge, to some degree, from the intent of the mediamakers.

The process by which makers of broadcast and print media have created ethnic content has received less attention than has the work of filmmakers. Sally Miller's (1987) seminal work, *The Ethnic Press in the United States: A Historical Analysis and Handbook*, contains a variety of histories of the manner in which ethnic newspapers and magazines have contributed to their own groups' popular knowledge construction. Other examinations of the role of the print press in ethnic knowledge dissemination and construction include Martin Dann's (1971) *The Black Press, 1827–1890: The Quest for National Identity,* Abby Arthur Johnson and Ronald Maberry Johnson's (1979) *Propaganda and Aesthetics: The Literary Politics of Afro-American Magazines of the Twentieth Century,* and Carolyn Martindale's (1986) *The White Press and Black America.* The manner in which makers of television programs have been involved in the construction of knowledge about two ethnic groups is explored in MacDonald's (1992) *Blacks and White TV* and Shaheen's (1984) *The TV Arab.* Melvin Patrick Ely's (1991) *The Adventures of Amos 'n' Andy: A Social History of an American Phenomenon* examines the rise and fall of that popular and controversial radio and later television show. The social teaching role of advertising, including teaching about ethnic groups, has also received scholarly attention (Leiss et al., 1986). Finally, recent years have witnessed the rapid growth of foreign-language television and radio in the United States, but scholars have barely begun to address the knowledge-construction aspects of this phenomenon (Cortés, 1993; Subervi-Vélez, 1986).

Ely's (1991) study, which includes an examination of the role of African American protests in affecting *Amos 'n' Andy*'s fate, also illustrates an additional aspect of control analysis: that the forces influencing the creation of media content and popular knowledge construction do not come entirely from within the media. External pressure groups—watchdog groups, ratings groups, protest groups, ethnic organizations, and multiethnic coalitions—have often tried, sometimes with success, to influence media content, including media treatment of ethnic groups (Lewels, 1974). These groups have ranged from the Catholic Legion of Decency, formed in the 1930s to assess movie content and apply content ratings, to such ethnic protest groups as the Italian-American Anti-Defamation Committee and the Polish-American Guardian Society.

Most important, both the media industry and mediamakers individually have embodied reigning or at least competing national ideologies, which are often transitory and in conflict with one another. From commitment to the idea of the melting pot to the championing of contemporary multiculturalism, from support for the U.S. government during World War II to support for (and sometimes opposition to) the civil rights movements, ideology has penetrated and provided a subtext for American mediamaking. While the media have never been the curricular monolith that critics have sometimes claimed, and while individual newspapers, magazines, networks, stations, and studios, as well as individual mediamakers, have provided varying treatments of race and ethnicity, the deeper patterns of media multicultural curricular messages often outweigh the surface variations (Hall, 1982; Gitlin, 1979).

IMPACT ANALYSIS: ASSESSING MEDIA CONSTRUCTION OF MULTICULTURAL KNOWLEDGE

As all educators know, teaching and learning are not synonymous. We teach and then, through examinations—often to our chagrin—we discover great variations in the extent, content, and quality of student learning, including learning through school multicultural education (Banks, 1991, 1993). That same teaching-learning gap applies to media teaching and reader/viewer/listener learning from media (Schwoch, White, & Reilly, 1992).

While mediamakers intentionally or unintentionally develop multicultural curriculum and while media products themselves become intended or unintended textbooks on race and ethnicity, once media output is published, broadcast, or screened, audiences become coparticipants in multicultural knowledge construction. They may react as conscious, analytical learners, pondering the media's treatment of race and ethnicity and thoughtfully integrating this pseudoenvironmental experience into their knowledge bases, ideational frameworks, attitudinal structures, and value systems. Or they may react and learn by unconsciously connecting these new ideas to their previously existent knowledge, perceptions, attitudes, values, and mental schemata. Whether or not readers, listeners, and viewers are aware of the process, a media product may well contribute to the construction of their corpus of multicultural knowledge.

Media multicultural education has been extensive, continuous, and powerful. Yet given the conscious and unconscious filtering power of media receivers, the widely varying sets of experiences, cognitive frameworks, and expectations that they bring to the media reception process, the presence of often deeply imbedded values and beliefs (including prejudices), and their differing information bases, it is clear that caution must

temper assertions concerning the *precise* content of audience learning (Korzenny, Ting-Toomey, & Schiff, 1992). Identifying the exact content of socially constructed learning—from whatever source—can be frustratingly elusive (Gilman, 1985).

Scholarly and popular analyses of the societal impact of the media have tended to become polarized. Many analysts have treated the media as virtually all-powerful forces that inculcate audiences with their beliefs (Medved, 1992; Winn, 1977). Some have taken a nearly deterministic position, drawing direct causal (sometimes unicausal) links between media and the development of individual, group, and national beliefs, attitudes, and behavior. So popular and fallacious in many early media studies, this common trap of media determinism—the assumed "hypodermic needle" media effect—remains popular in protest-group proclamations and political pontifications about media impact. While most media content analysts present only sporadic concrete evidence of media impact on the construction of audience knowledge, some content analysis scholars suggest or even categorically assert what viewers learn from the media, inappropriately using media content (teaching) to proclaim audience impact (learning). In the area of schooling, this would be analogous to substituting an analysis of textbooks and lectures for final examinations and achievement tests in assessing student learning.

In contrast to these deterministic assertions, other analysts have viewed the media as having limited power to influence audiences, treating the media as a reflector of social consensus or fulfiller of audience desires, or emphasizing the audience's activist role in constructing meaning from the media (Hall, 1982; Jenkins, 1992). Those who take these limited-influence positions comprise two basic groups. First are many mediamakers, particularly those involved in the entertainment media. Most feature filmmakers, creators of entertainment television, and makers of records and music videos generally claim that they merely entertain, reject responsibility for what their media might incidentally or unintentionally teach, and at times even deny their teaching potential. Second are those scholars, particularly proponents of certain varieties of "reception theory," who assert that the reader, viewer, and listener are the primary forces in the media-based construction of knowledge.

In the middle stand those scholars who agree that media, including movies and fictional television, do teach, but argue that research to date has generally failed to identify the precise content of audience learning. Assessing media impact on knowledge construction, therefore, poses major scholarly challenges. Yet research has provided some insights (Huston et al., 1992; Tichi, 1992). Such multicultural scholarship has generally fallen into three categories: empirical, projective, and theoretical.

Empirical Scholarship

Empirical scholarship on the impact of media on self-identity and intergroup and intragroup perceptions has been sporadic and temporally limited. Film and television impact research has focused almost entirely on the short-range effects of specific films or television shows, often in experimental settings. Even though results vary, they do coalesce convincingly around two basic conclusions. First, media, including feature films and fictional television, do influence intragroup and interethnic perceptions; viewers do learn about race and ethnicity from both nonfictional and entertainment media. Second, the nature of that influence varies with the individual reader, listener, or viewer, who provides a key variable concerning the extent, content, and tenacity of that conscious or unconscious learning. In short, scholarship confirms that old social science axiom, "*Some* people are influenced by *some* media, at *some* time."

Research has identified the influence, albeit short-range, of selected media on intergroup attitudes and perceptions, sometimes reinforcing prejudices, at others modifying them (Raths & Trager, 1948). One pioneering study of the 1930s involved the classic 1915 silent film, *The Birth of a Nation*, which included a degrading portrayal of African Americans during the Reconstruction era of U.S. history. That study concluded that when White students viewed *Birth* as part of their courses on U.S. history, an increase in student prejudice toward African Americans resulted (Peterson & Thurstone, 1933).

But media, including entertainment media, can also reduce prejudice, even if audiences do not realize it. Some scholars found that the 1947 anti-anti-Semitism film, *Gentleman's Agreement,* had such an effect (Middleton, 1960). In one study, students who saw the film reported improved attitudes toward Jews, even though most of the surveyed students also stated that the film *had not* influenced their attitudes (Rosen, 1948).

One of the most extensive examinations of the impact of the entertainment media on popular construction of knowledge was the Payne Fund motion picture impact research project carried out during the early 1930s by leading sociologists, psychologists, and educators, located principally at the University of Chicago. The Payne Fund project began in response to public expressions of concern about movie effects, and the public, particularly powerful politicians, literally demanded absolute conclusions and agendas for action, rather than traditional academic calls for more research. Fearful of being considered too cautiously academic, some of the scholars went beyond the bounds of their evidence, making claims and recommendations that ultimately brought much of their research into scholarly ill repute. While in retrospect some of their methodologies seem empirically crude, their research results—as contrasted with their often poorly grounded cries of alarm and calls for action—did provide powerfully suggestive evidence for the presence of viewer learning, including learning about race, ethnic groups, and foreign nations.

Unfortunately for those interested in the effect of films on the social construction of multicultural knowledge, such film-impact studies virtually ended in the late 1940s with the advent of television, as communications researchers turned their impact-study attention to the new kid on the media block. Moreover, by the 1960s such behaviorist pretest-posttest direct-impact studies had lost stature among communications scholars, who had become frustrated by the failure of this approach to determine more than limited and short-range media effects on attitude and overt behavior (Chaffee & Hochheimer, 1985; Hall, 1982; Rogers, Dearing, & Bregman, 1993). Instead, scholars turned their attention to other avenues for inspecting

the knowledge construction relationship between media and media recipients. They developed a variety of media impact models, such as uses and gratifications, agenda setting, and the spiral of silence (Fejes, 1984; Roberts & Bachen, 1982).

Uses-and-gratifications research emphasizes the role of viewers and readers as active seekers of specific media that serve useful functions for them or that provide certain personal gratifications (Tan & Tan, 1979). For example, some studies have concluded that Black children, more than White children, consider entertainment television to be an important source of learning about the world, including behavior with the opposite sex and other types of social adaptation (Atkin, Greenberg, & McDermott, 1978; Gerson, 1966).

Agenda-setting research began with the principle that the media may not be able to tell audiences what to think, but they can tell them what to think about (Kosicki, 1993). (The spiral-of-silence model provides the flip side to agenda setting by focusing on the power of the media to avoid certain issues and thereby limit public discussion about them.) Later agenda-setting research expanded its domain, demonstrating the ability of the media to "frame" public issues and to "prime" the public on *how* to think about those issues (Goffman, 1974; Ynegar & Kinder, 1987). As argued by agenda-setting scholars Maxwell McCombs and Donald Shaw (1993):

Agenda setting is considerably more than the classical assertion that the news tells us *what to think about.* The news also tells us *how to think about it.* Both the selection of objects for attention and the selection of frames for thinking about these objects are powerful agenda-setting roles [emphasis in original]. (p. 62)

Most agenda-setting scholars have restricted their attention to the news, ignoring the comparable role of the entertainment media. They have found evidence that racial and ethnic differences influence audience reactions to media agenda-setting efforts. For example, Oscar Gandy and Larry Coleman (1986) concluded that Black college students rejected mainstream press criticism of the Rev. Jesse Jackson during his 1984 campaign for the Democratic presidential nomination.

Other empirical research has reconfirmed the variability of learner responses to the media, particularly when audiences reflect different cultural positions (Korzenny et al., 1992) or when the subject is as emotion laden as bigotry and prejudice (Cooper & Jahoda, 1947). Scholars have taken a variety of approaches to such reception analysis in an effort to determine or posit how different audiences have or may have interpreted and drawn meaning from varieties of media (Bryant & Zillman, 1991; Jenkins, 1992). One approach to such reception research has been the intensive study of audience reactions to important media products. Two major television phenomena, *All in the Family* and *Roots*, illustrate those learning variations.

Norman Lear's weekly television series, *All in the Family,* which burst onto the American television scene in 1971, generated a series of empirical studies that revealed varying audience responses. This popular series portrayed antihero Archie Bunker as a classic bigot—racist, sexist, and just about every other kind of anti-"ist" imaginable. The show sought to critique racial and ethnic prejudice by making Bunker's expressions of bigotry appear to be comically absurd. By provoking viewers to laugh at Archie and by portraying bigotry as imbecilic, Lear consciously sought to reduce prejudice. The ploy succeeded, but only for *some* viewers. Unfortunately, others identified with the cuddly, ingratiating, laugh-provoking Archie, the lovable racist, and found his expression of bigoted beliefs to be a confirmation of the validity of their own prejudices (Leckenby & Surlin, 1976). Studies of *All in the Family* with American and Canadian audiences confirmed the operation of the "selective perception hypothesis"—that is, already highly prejudiced or dogmatic viewers tended to admire Bunker and condone his racial and ethnic slurs (Brigham & Giesbrecht, 1976; Surlin & Tate, 1976; Vidmar & Rokeach, 1974). In contrast, a comparable study concluded that the selective perception hypothesis did not seem to operate with Dutch viewers (Wilhoit & de Bock, 1976).

Roots, the January 1977, eight-night television miniseries tracing the history of the family of author Alex Haley from African origins to the post-Civil War United States, also drew a swarm of researchers. Stuart Surlin (1978) analyzed and compared the results of five studies conducted concurrently with or immediately after the showing of *Roots.* All focused on the topic of viewer "incidental learning," but results varied. The studies generally concluded that a higher percentage of Blacks than Whites viewed *Roots,* with 60–80% of the viewers believing in the accuracy of the show's treatment of history. However, while three of the studies concluded that the series seemed to have a positive impact on viewers, two of the studies tended to support the selective perception hypothesis.

Still another approach to the study of the role of media in the social construction of multicultural knowledge has involved analyses of the interaction of the media with specific ethnic audiences (Allen, 1981; Comstock & Cobbey, 1979). These include studies of the relationship of the media to: the acculturation of Asian American immigrants (Yum, 1982); American Indian communication practices (Worth & Adair, 1972); the maintenance and decline of ethnic pluralism among U.S. Latinos (Subervi-Vélez, 1986); intercultural interpretations by Inuit children (Caron, 1979); self-esteem and group identification by various sectors of the African American community (Allen & Hatchett, 1986); and White college-student perceptions of Black socioeconomic progress and decline (Armstrong, Neuendorf, & Brentar, 1992). For example, a retrospective study of Black viewers of *Roots* (Fairchild, Stockard, & Bowman, 1986) found that differences based on region, urbanicity, age, education, and income (but not gender) influenced viewers' reactions to the program in terms of their evaluation of its significance and role as evidence of Black social progress.

In contrast to the *obtrusive* empiricism of pretest-posttest and survey research, in which audiences respond to specific scholarly queries, other scholars have drawn upon already existent evidence as the basis for *unobtrusive* empiricism. For example, Chon Noriega (1988–1990) found a similar "selective perception" phenomenon among movie reviewers when he categorically examined the responses of Hispanic and non-Hispanic critics to a variety of Latino-made films about the U.S. Latino experience, like *Stand and Deliver* and *Born in East L.A.*. Noriega discovered that ethnicity served as a primary factor in separating critical reactions. Latino critics tended to focus on the cultural content and social conflict in the films, while Anglo critics tended to react negatively to the *absence* of criminality, deriding the films because they presented Latino communities as too clean and did not portray Latinos as social deviants. In short, burdened by their own media-learned expectations, Anglo critics disparaged the films because they failed to meet their own internalized stereotypes of a Latino barrio.

Other scholars have drawn upon a variety of sources as the basis for unobtrusively addressing impact within specific intergroup and international contexts. For example, in his *War Without Mercy: Race and Power in the Pacific War,* historian John Dower (1986) assessed the development of racial pride and cross-cultural stereotypes of the enemy in both Japan and the Allied nations prior to and during World War II. Casting a wide investigatory net that included media along with other forms of evidence, Dower explored multiple Japanese and Allied sources—from scholarly studies to propaganda tracts, from government reports to military training materials, and from popular periodicals to motion pictures. But Dower took an additional step, pointing to examples of both sides' political and military decisions that revealed how these stereotypes had become internalized and operationalized, even when acting on them led to military and diplomatic excesses and blunders.

Projective Scholarship

Alongside empirical scholarship stands the second category of media impact scholarship, projective studies in which scholars have attempted to assess and suggest how different audiences *may* or *are likely to* construct personal knowledge from specific media. Sam Keen's (1986) *Faces of the Enemy: Reflections of the Hostile Imagination* and Vamik Volkan's (1988) *The Need to Have Enemies and Allies: From Clinical Practice to International Relationships* argued that people *need* to hate and that "the other"—the racial other, the ethnic other, the cultural other, the foreign other—serves as a convenient outlet for that hate. Some scholars have focused on specific examples of the role of "otherness." For example, Blaine Lamb (1975) asserted that Mexican characters served that "other" role for early U.S. movie audiences, who needed an easily identifiable, easily despised foil.

Other projective studies have attempted to reconstruct historical learning. For example, some scholars have drawn upon autobiographies to suggest the impact of media learning on ethnic identity (Erben & Erben, 1991–1992). A few scholars have ventured into the challenging area of projective assessment of the ways that historical audiences may have reacted to the media treatment of racial and ethnic groups (Staiger, 1992). For example, in her article "*The Scar of Shame*: Skin Color and Caste in Black Silent Melodrama," Jane Gaines (1987) used social and cultural characteristics of African American moviegoers during the 1920s to posit how such viewers probably "read" that film, as contrasted to latter-day reinterpretations of the movie that tend to be burdened with distorting assumptions.

Some scholars have based their projections about the media-based social construction of knowledge on their own "readings" of specific media "texts." For example, such approaches have been used to address *The Cosby Show* television series, leading to nearly polaric conclusions concerning potential impact (Real, 1991). Is *Cosby* the ideal positive-role-model minority show, featuring a well-educated, sophisticated, financially successful African American family? Or, by commission and omission, whether intentionally or unintentionally, does the series provide less salutary lessons to some viewing audiences?

Although observing that racism was never mentioned in 15 episodes of the series that he analyzed, media scholar John D. H. Downing (1988) lauded the show for its dignified emphasis on Black culture, for its championing of Black familial unity, for its direct, continuous critique of sexism, and for portraying Black-White relations in a manner that challenged racist thinking by transcending racism. Yet *The Cosby Show* has drawn its share of concerned reactions from analysts who feared that the series' concentration on well-heeled African Americans and failure to deal with the Black underclass might unintentionally encourage viewers to ignore the fact that the majority of American Blacks still face tremendous social and economic problems (Dyson, 1989; Jhally & Lewis, 1992). As media scholar Paula Matabane (1988) wrote:

"The Cosby Show," for example, epitomizes the Afro-American dream of full acceptance and assimilation into U.S. society. Both the series and Bill Cosby as an individual represent successful competitors in network television and in attaining a high status. Although this achievement is certainly not inherently negative, we should consider the role television plays in the cultivation of an overall picture of growing racial equality that conceals unequal social relationships and overestimates of how well blacks are integrating into white society (if at all). The illusion of well-being among the oppressed may lead to reduced political activity and less demand for social justice and equality. (p. 30)

Finally, the media industry and the media themselves sometimes provide grudging projective recognition of their power to contribute to the social construction of multicultural knowledge. For example, prior to the 1977 U.S. national network television showing of Francis Ford Coppola's *The Godfather Saga* (a revised and expanded version of the two theatrical motion pictures, *The Godfather* and *The Godfather: Part II*), the following words appeared on screen, simultaneously intoned by a solemn voice: "*The Godfather* is a fictional account of the activities of a small group of ruthless criminals. It would be erroneous and unfair to suggest that they are representative of any ethnic group."

Forewarned that the characters were not "representative of any ethnic group," a nationwide audience watched the violent, multigenerational saga of the Corleone family. The film began in Sicily, large segments were spoken in Italian with English subtitles, and most of the characters bore such names as Clemenza, Barzini, Tattaglia, and Fanucci. Moreover, those hollow words became the model for future media disclaimers. Subsequent controversial films that exploited criminal violence in presenting other ethnic groups, such as the 1983 *Scarface* (Cuban Americans) and the 1985 *Year of the Dragon* (Chinese Americans), copied and only slightly modified the "*Godfather* disclaimer." While such words could do little to mitigate the teaching impact of these movie textbooks (in fact, howls of laughter during the disclaimers suggested that the warnings may have done more harm than good), the disclaimers did serve as a media admission that feature films do, in fact, teach and influence audience learning about ethnicity and ethnic groups.

Theoretical Scholarship

Finally, alongside scholars who conduct empirical and projective analysis are those who have addressed the process of media-based construction of knowledge by proposing and applying *theories* of audience reception (Bryant & Zillmann, 1991; Jensen, 1987; Schwartz, 1973). Some use schema theory, according to which each learner (viewer/reader/listener) develops an operational internal mental and emotional schema—referred to by such names as "ideational scaffolding," "cognitive maps," or "anticipatory schemes"—based on his or her own personal experiences, including school and societal learning. This personal schema then becomes the reception framework by which learners process, interpret, and organize new information, ideas, and images, including those disseminated by the media (Candy, 1982; Gentner & Stevens, 1983; Graber, 1984).

Related to schema theorists are media analysts who draw upon Gestalt psychology. According to this approach, viewers and readers encounter a piece of communication and alter it by omitting some of its content from their reception or memory, while supplementing or contextualizing its content based on their own beliefs and biases, thereby changing its meaning for them. In terms of ethnic groups, this Gestalt approach would suggest that if the media challenge preexistent beliefs, particularly beliefs with strong and deep emotional roots, these challenges will tend to be blunted by omission, supplementation, and contextualization (Cooper & Jahoda, 1947). In light of this theory, it can be hypothesized that media would be more likely to influence viewer beliefs about ethnic groups and intergroup relations if they dealt with topics about which viewers knew little or did not have firmly held preconceptions.

Psychologist Leon Festinger (1957) went one step further with his "theory of cognitive dissonance." According to this theory, once an individual's cognitive structure takes firm shape, it tends to repel those ideas that seem too dissonant. Application of this theory suggests that when media or school frontal assaults on firmly rooted prejudices lack subtlety, they may well be rejected by some because they create too much dissonance.

Learners are not usually aware of their reception schema, their ideational scaffolding, their cognitive structures, or for that matter many of their own prejudices, including those learned, reinforced, or shaped by the media. For example, as part of his social learning theory, psychologist Albert Bandura (1977) described the "sleeper effect," which provides insights for better understanding of how media teaching/learning works. In relation to the media, the "sleeper effect" suggests that ideas, often clothed as entertainment, can subconsciously enter and become part of a viewer's cognitive or affective storehouse, then lie dormant until provoked by some external stimulus, like a personal or mediated experience (Comstock, 1978). People may not realize that they have prejudices, including media-fostered prejudices, about a certain group until they encounter individuals from that group or are exposed to a media barrage about that group, at which point these "sleeping" beliefs and attitudes awaken and become activated.

What about media influence on behavior? Anecdotal evidence provides myriad examples of media popularizing clothing styles, verbal expressions ("Make my day"), and other forms of behavior. Aware of this penchant for imitation, protesters have railed against the release of such youth-gang films as *A Clockwork Orange* (1971), *The Warriors* (1979), *Colors* (1988), *Boyz N the Hood* (1991), and *American Me* (1992) for fear that young people would imitate the onscreen violence. Although a few fights have broken out in or near theatres, massive waves of imitative gang violence have not occurred, which came as a shock to those who have proclaimed such deterministic positions about media impact.

But more critical, more subtle, and also more delicate is the issue of "disinhibiting effects." Rather than provoking people into action, do the media, operating over a long period of time, remove certain inhibitions to previously repressed actions? Do movies that celebrate vigilantism (for example, the *Death Wish* series) reduce inhibitions to the use of violence? If films make teenage sex appear normative or "safe," do they weaken restraints against teenage promiscuity (not to mention pregnancy)? These are issues that still defy precise empirical scholarship concerning the long-range construction of media-based knowledge.

Overall, then, scholarship has demonstrated that the media do contribute to the social construction of multicultural knowledge—what people learn from the media about race, ethnicity, and culture. Content analysis has provided insight into the media multicultural curriculum—information, messages, ideas, and images that the media have disseminated. Control analysis has provided insight into the process by which mediamakers have made decisions about whether, when, and how to treat multicultural themes. Impact analysis has provided insight into the ways in which media and audiences interact in the social construction of multicultural knowledge.

Yet the *precise* assessment of the media's *long-range* historical influences on multicultural knowledge construction remains a complex scholarly challenge. Research has not dealt with the long-range impact of continuous media experience on learning about ethnic groups. For example, as Garth Jowett and James Linton (1980) noted:

Most of the research on movie influence deals with individual movies, but it is the cumulative effect of years of viewing movies which so far defies adequate measurement and which is of real interest in any assessment of the movies' impact on society and culture. (p. 10)

Among the scholarly problems has been the difficulty of controlling variables and separating media influence from the impact of other teaching forces, such as schools, families, and other societal institutions (McLeod & Reeves, 1981).

PEDAGOGICAL ANALYSIS: RELATIONSHIP OF MEDIA AND SCHOOLS IN THE SOCIAL CONSTRUCTION OF MULTICULTURAL KNOWLEDGE

The final scholarly area related to the media-based construction of multicultural knowledge is the relationship between media and school multicultural education. Two questions are most critical. First, how have the media interacted with schools in the construction of multicultural knowledge? Second, how can educational institutions build most effectively from the growing scholarship on the process of the media-based construction of multicultural knowledge?

To date, media and educational scholars have tended to operate in separate worlds as regards the social construction of multicultural knowledge. As this chapter has demonstrated, media scholars have employed a variety of approaches for looking at the roles that the media have played in the social construction of knowledge about race and ethnicity. Conversely, as reflected in this *Handbook*, scholars involved in multicultural education have explored myriad facets of multicultural teaching and learning. These parallel efforts suggest similarities and differences between educational and media scholarship.

Media scholars analyze media content, while educational scholars analyze textbooks and curricula. Media scholars examine media decision making and actions, while educational scholars dissect decision making and actions within the textbook industry, within school systems, and by teachers and administrators. Media scholars attempt to assess reader, viewer, and listener learning, while educational scholars assess student learning. Seldom have these scholarly efforts intersected (Spring, 1992; Stein, 1979).

Some communications scholars have focused on the role of the media in fostering interracial, interethnic, and intercultural learning among those of school age (Berry & Asamen, 1993; Dates, 1980; Hartmann & Husband, 1972; Rapaczynski, Singer, & Singer, 1982) and in socializing children of different racial and ethnic backgrounds (Berry & Mitchell-Kernan, 1982; Stroman, 1991). For example, Bradley Greenberg (1972) discovered that White children often considered television depictions of Blacks to be more representative than Blacks whom they knew in real life. In order to develop more effective school multicultural education, teachers and curriculum developers must become more aware of such research on media multicultural knowledge construction among young people, and integrate these findings into their pedagogical approaches. Moreover, scholars need to develop research strategies for investigating the relationship between media and school multicultural knowledge construction.

The potential for media/school multicultural educational research is raised by the article, "Harmony and Conflict of Intercultural Images: The Treatment of Mexico in U.S. Feature Films and K–12 Textbooks," by Gerald Michael Greenfield and Carlos Cortés (1991). While the article addresses the treatment of a foreign nation rather than race and ethnicity within the United

States, its methodology suggests one avenue for media education-school education intertextual research. The authors compared and contrasted the ways in which U.S. social studies textbooks and feature films have treated both Mexico in general and a series of critical themes in Mexican history, such as the immigration of undocumented Mexican workers into the United States. On the basis of their content analysis, the authors indicated the places where textbooks and feature films reinforce each others' intercultural messages, where they challenge each other, and where by omission they concede dominance to the other sector as an educational force.

While educator understanding of the role of the mass media in the social construction of knowledge about race and ethnicity is important, even more critical is the need for educators to develop more effective ways to draw upon that understanding in order to improve multicultural education. At least three areas of activity stand out. First, educators need to develop greater awareness of the different theoretical approaches to media knowledge construction, as well as the pedagogical implications of such theories (Matlin, 1991). Second, educators need to become involved in the continuous process of self-reeducation by thoughtful and critical observation of media treatment of race and ethnicity, including those media that their students tend to select. Third, and possibly most important, educators need to develop more effective pedagogical strategies for using the mass media as a multicultural teaching source (Martindale, 1993).

During the past two decades there has been a growth of interest in the areas of media literacy and critical pedagogy, including scholarship and curriculum materials aimed at helping teachers draw upon media at various grade levels (Brown, 1991; Schwoch et al., 1992). Although most of these media literacy materials deal only tangentially with race and ethnicity, a few scholars have dealt directly with the question of integrating media critically into multicultural education (Cortés, 1991a; 1992). In addition, others have dealt with the development of media for use in the effort to reduce racism and improve inter-group understanding (Hall, 1981). Yet much more needs to be done to increase the effective use of media to strengthen multicultural education.

CONCLUSION

The mass media, then, play a critical role in the social construction of knowledge concerning race and ethnicity. This involves not only knowledge about specific individual racial and ethnic groups, but also broader thinking about race and ethnicity in the United States, as well as about interracial, interethnic, and intercultural relations. Moreover, research has demonstrated that media impact varies among readers, viewers, and listeners, with the race and ethnicity of recipients often playing a significant role in this media-audience learning relationship.

The critical role of the mass media in the social construction of knowledge (as well as attitudes and perceptions) about race and ethnicity has significant implications for school multicultural education. Teachers, administrators, students, parents, and others involved in school education are exposed to the media, including intended and unintended media multicultural education. Yet most published scholarship on multicultural education and proposals for implementing multicultural education have failed to engage the existence, persistence, and power of the media as a multicultural educator, including its implications for multicultural schooling.

For the full flourishing of school multicultural education, scholars need to develop more sophisticated ways to explore and assess media-based multicultural knowledge construction. This is particularly important in terms of the analysis of the media-based multicultural knowledge, beliefs, perceptions, and attitudes that students bring to school. Educators need to develop more effective ways to draw upon this scholarship to strengthen multicultural educational pedagogy and curriculum development.

References

Adoni, H., & Mane, S. (1984). Media and the social construction of reality: Toward an integration of theory and research. *Communication Theory, 11*, 323–340.

Allen, R. L. (1981). Communication research on Black Americans. In H. A. Myrick & C. Keegan (Eds.), *In search of diversity, symposium on minority audiences and programming research: Approaches and applications* (pp. 47–63). Washington, DC: Corporation for Public Broadcasting.

Allen, R. L., & Hatchett, S. (1986). The media and social effects: Self and system orientations of Blacks. *Communication Research, 13*(1), 97–123.

Armstrong, G. B., Neuendorf, K. A., & Brentar, J. E. (1992). TV entertainment, news, and racial perceptions of college students. *Journal of Communication, 42*(3), 153–176.

Atkin, C., Greenberg, B., & McDermott, S. (1978). Race and social role learning from television. In H. S. Dordick (Ed.), *Proceedings of the sixth annual telecommunications policy research conference* (pp. 7–20). Lexington, MA: D. C. Heath.

Bandura, A. (1977). *Social learning theory*. Englewood Cliffs, NJ: Prentice-Hall.

Banks, J. A. (1991). Multicultural education: Its effects on students' racial and gender role attitudes. In J. P. Shaver (Ed.), *Handbook of research on social studies teaching and learning* (pp. 459–469). New York: Macmillan.

Banks, J. A. (1993). Multicultural education for young children: Racial and ethnic attitudes and their modification. In B. Spodek (Ed.), *Handbook of research on the education of young children* (pp. 236–250). New York: Macmillan.

Bataille, G. M., & Silet, C. L. P. (Eds.). (1980). *The pretend Indian: Images of Native Americans in the movies*. Ames: Iowa State University Press.

Berger, P. L., & Luckman, T. (1966). *The social construction of reality:*

A treatise in the sociology of knowledge. Garden City, NY: Doubleday.

Berry, G. L. (1980). Children, television and social class roles: The medium as an unplanned educational curriculum. In E. L. Palmer & A. Dorr (Eds.), *Children and the faces of television* (pp. 71–81). New York: Academic Press.

Berry, G. L., & Asamen, J. K. (Eds.). (1993). *Children and television: Images in a changing socio-cultural world*. Beverly Hills, CA: Sage.

Berry, G. L., & Mitchell-Kernan, C. (Eds.). (1982). *Television and the socialization of the minority child*. New York: Academic Press.

Bettelheim, B. (1976). *The uses of enchantment: The meaning and importance of fairy tales*. New York: Alfred A. Knopf.

Black American Literature Forum [Entire issue]. (1991). *25*(2).

Bogle, D. (1989). *Toms, coons, mulattoes, mammies & bucks: An interpretive history of Blacks in American films* (2nd ed.). New York: Continuum.

Boorstin, D. J. (1961). *The image or whatever happened to the American dream?* New York: Atheneum.

Boskin, J. (1986). *Sambo: The rise & demise of an American jester*. New York: Oxford University Press.

Brigham, J. C., & Giesbrecht, L. W. (1976). "All in the family": Racial attitudes. *Journal of Communication, 26*(4), 69–74.

Brown, J. A. (1991). *Television critical viewing skills education: Major media literacy projects in the United States and selected countries*. Hillsdale, NJ: Lawrence Erlbaum Associates.

Bryant, J., & Zillmann, D. (Eds.). (1991). *Responding to the screen: Reception and reaction processes*. Hillsdale, NJ: Lawrence Erlbaum Associates.

Candy, P. C. (1982). Personal constructs and personal paradigms: Elaboration, modification and transformation. *Interchange: A Journal of Educational Policy, 13*(4), 56–69.

Caron, A. H. (1979). First-time exposure to television: Effects on Inuit children's cultural images. *Communication Research, 6*, 135–154.

Caso, A. (1980). *Mass media vs. the Italian Americans*. Boston: Branden Press.

Chaffee, S. H., & Hochheimer, J. L. (1985). The beginnings of political communication research in the United States: Origins of the "limited effects" model. In E. M. Rogers & F. Balle (Eds.), *The media revolution in America and in Western Europe* (pp. 267–296.) Norwood, NJ: Ablex Publishing Corp.

Comstock, G. (1977). *The impact of television on American institutions and the American public*. Honolulu: East-West Communications Institute, East-West Center.

Comstock, G. A. (1978). *Trends in the study of incidental learning from television viewing*. Syracuse, NY: ERIC Clearinghouse on Information Resources.

Comstock, G., & Cobbey, R. (1979). Television and the children of ethnic minorities. *Journal of Communication, 29*(1), 104–115.

Cooper, E., & Jahoda, M. (1947). The evasion of propaganda: How prejudiced people respond to anti-prejudice propaganda. *Journal of Psychology, 23*, 15–25.

Cortés, C. E. (1981). The societal curriculum: Implications for multiethnic education. In J. A. Banks (Ed.), *Education in the 80's: Multiethnic education* (pp. 24–32). Washington, DC: National Education Association.

Cortés, C. E. (1991a). Empowerment through media literacy: A multicultural approach. In C. E. Sleeter (Ed.), *Empowerment through multicultural education* (pp. 143–157). Albany: State University of New York Press.

Cortés, C. E. (1991b). Hollywood interracial love: Social taboo as screen titillation. In P. Loukides & L. K. Fuller (Eds.), *Plot conventions in American popular film* (pp. 21–35). Bowling Green, OH: Bowling Green State University Popular Press.

Cortés, C. E. (1992). Media literacy: An educational basic for the information age. *Education and Urban Society. 24*(4), 489–497.

Cortés, C. E. (1993). Power, passivity, and pluralism: Mass media in the development of Latino culture and identity. *Latino Studies Journal, 4*, 1–22.

Cremins, L. (1990). *Popular education and its discontents*. New York: Harper & Row.

Cripps, T. (1970). The myth of the southern box office: A factor in racial stereotyping in American movies, 1920–1940. In J. C. Curtis & L. L. Gould (Eds.), *The Black experience in America: Selected essays* (pp. 116–144). Austin: University of Texas Press.

Cripps, T. (1977). *Slow fade to Black: The Negro in American film, 1990–1942*. New York: Oxford University Press.

Cripps, T. (1978). *Black film as genre*. Bloomington: Indiana University Press.

Cripps, T. (1993). *Making movies Black: The Hollywood message movie from World War II to the civil rights era*. New York: Oxford University Press.

Curran, J. M. (1989). *Hibernian green on the silver screen*. New York: Greenwood Press.

Dann, M. E. (Ed.). (1971). *The Black press, 1827–1890: The quest for national identity*. New York: Capricorn.

Dates, J. L. (1980). Race, racial attitudes and adolescent perceptions of Black television characters. *Journal of Broadcasting, 24*(4), 549–560.

Dates, J. L., & Barlow, W. (Eds.). (1990). *Split image: African Americans in the mass media*. Washington, DC: Howard University Press.

Diawara, M. (Ed.). (1992). *Black American cinema*. New York: Routledge, Chapman, and Hall.

Dorfman, A. (1983). *The empire's old clothes: What the Lone Ranger, Babar, and other innocent heroes do to our minds*. New York: Pantheon.

Dower, J. (1986). *War without mercy: Race and power in the Pacific war*. New York: Pantheon.

Downing, J. D. H. (1988). "The Cosby Show" and American racial discourse. In G. Smitherman-Donaldson & T. A. van Dijk (Eds.), *Discourse and discrimination* (pp. 46–73). Detroit: Wayne State University Press.

Dyson, M. (1989). Bill Cosby and the politics of race. *Z Magazine, 2*(9), 26–30.

Ely, M. P. (1991). *The adventures of Amos 'n' Andy: A social history of an American phenomenon*. New York: The Free Press.

Entman, R. M. (1990). Modern racism and the images of Blacks in local television news. *Critical Studies in Mass Communication, 7*, 332–345.

Erben, R., & Erben. U. (1991–1992). Popular culture, mass media, and Chicano identity in Gary Soto's "Living Up the Street" and "Small Faces." *MELUS, 17*(3), 43–52.

Erens, P. (Ed.). (1984). *The Jew in American cinema*. Bloomington: Indiana University Press.

Fairchild, H. H., Stockard, R., & Bowman, P. (1986). Impact of "Roots": Evidence from the national survey of Black Americans. *Journal of Black Studies, 16*(3), 307–318.

Fejes, F. (1984). Critical mass communications research and media effects: The problem of the disappearing audience. *Media, Culture and Society, 6*, 219–232.

Festinger, L. (1957). *A theory of cognitive dissonance*. Evanston, IL: Row, Peterson.

Fisher, P. L., & Lowenstein, R. L. (Eds.). (1967). *Race and the news media*. New York: Praeger.

Forman, H. J. (1933). *Our movie made children*. New York: Macmillan.

Friar, R. E., & Friar, N. A. (1972). *The only good Indian . . . the Hollywood gospel*. New York: Drama Book Specialists.

Friedman, L. D. (1982). *Hollywood's image of the Jew*. New York: Frederick Ungar.

Friedman, L. D. (1991). *Unspeakable images: Ethnicity and the American cinema*. Urbana: University of Illinois Press.

Gabler, N. (1988). *An empire of their own: How the Jews invented Hollywood*. New York: Crown.

Gaines, J. (1987). *The Scar of Shame*: Skin color and caste in Black silent melodrama. *Cinema Journal, 26*(4), 3–21.

Gandy, O., Jr., & Coleman, L. G. (1986). The Jackson campaign: Mass media and Black student perceptions. *Journalism Quarterly, 63*(1), 138–143, 154.

Gans, H. J. (1967). The mass media as an educational institution. *Television Quarterly, 6*(2), 20–37.

Gentner, D., & Stevens, A. L. (Eds.). (1983). *Mental models*. Hillsdale, NJ: Lawrence Erlbaum Associates.

Gerson, W. M. (1966). Mass media socialization behavior: Negro-White differences. *Social Forces, 45*(1), 40–50.

Gilman, S. L. (1985). *Difference and pathology: Stereotypes of sexuality, race, and madness*. Ithaca, NY: Cornell University Press.

Gitlin, T. (1979). Prime time ideology: The hegemonic process in television entertainment. *Social Problems, 26*(3), 251–266.

Goffman, E. (1974). *Frame analysis*. Boston: Northeastern University Press.

Goldberg, J. N. (1983). *Laughter through tears: The Yiddish cinema*. Rutherford, NJ: Fairleigh Dickinson University Press.

Goldman, E. A. (1983). *Visions, images, and dreams: Yiddish film—past and present*. Ann Arbor, MI: UMI Research Press.

Graber, D. A. (1984). *Processing the news: How people tame the information tide*. New York: Longman.

Gray, H. (1986). Television and the new Black man: Black male images in prime-time situation comedy. *Media, Culture and Society, 8*, 223–242.

Greenberg, B. S. (1972). Children's reactions to TV Blacks. *Journalism Quarterly, 49*(1), 5–14.

Greenberg, B. S. (1986). Minorities and the mass media. In J. Bryant and D. Zillman (Eds.), *Perspectives of mass media* (pp. 165–188). Hillsdale, NJ: Lawrence Erlbaum Associates.

Greenberg, B. S., Burgoon, M., Burgoon, J. K., & Korzenny, F. (1983). *Mexican Americans and the mass media*. Norwood, NJ: ABLEX.

Greenfield, G. M., & Cortés, C. E. (1991). Harmony and conflict of intercultural images: The treatment of Mexico in U.S. feature films and K–12 textbooks. *Mexican Studies/Estudios Mexicanos, 7*(2), 283–301.

Hall, S. (1977). Culture, the media and the "ideological effect." In J. Curran, M. Gurevitch, & J. Woollacott (Eds.), *Mass communication and society* (pp. 315–348). London: Edward Arnold.

Hall, S. (1981). The whites of their eyes: Racist ideologies and the media. In G. Bridges & R. Brunt (Eds.), *Silver linings: Some strategies for the eighties* (pp. 28–52). London: Lawrence & Wishart.

Hall, S. (1982). The rediscovery of "ideology": Return of the repressed in media studies. In M. Gurevitch, T. Bennet, J. Curran, & J. Woollacott (Eds.), *Culture, society and the media* (pp. 56–90). New York: Methuen.

Hartmann, P., & Husband, C. (1972). The mass media and racial conflict. In D. McQuail (Ed.), *Sociology of mass communications* (pp. 435–455). Baltimore, MD: Penguin.

Hawkins, R., & Pingree, S. (1981). Using television to construct social reality. *Journal of Broadcasting, 25*, 347–364

Heller, M. A. (1992, November). "Bad news." *Hispanic*, pp. 18–26.

Hoberman, J. (1991). *Bridge of light: Yiddish film between two worlds*. New York: Museum of Modern Art and Schocken Books.

Huston, A. C., et al. (1992). *Big world, small screen: The role of television in American society*. Lincoln: University of Nebraska Press.

Jarvis, A. R. J. (1991). The Payne Fund reports: A discussion of their content, public reaction, and effect on the motion picture industry, 1930–1940. *Journal of Popular Culture, 25*(2), 127–140.

Jenkins, H. (1992). *Textual poachers: Television fans and participatory culture*. New York: Routledge, Chapman, and Hall.

Jensen, K. B. (1987). Qualitative audience research: Toward an integrative approach to reception. *Critical Studies in Mass Communication, 4*, 21–36.

Jhally, S., & Lewis, J. (1992). *Enlightened racism: "The Cosby Show," audiences, and the myth of the American dream*. Boulder, CO: Westview Press.

Johnson, A. A., & Johnson, R. M. (1979). *Propaganda and aesthetics: The literary politics of Afro-American magazines of the twentieth century*. Amherst: University of Massachusetts Press.

Jowett, G. (1976). *Film: The democratic art*. Boston: Little, Brown.

Jowett, G., & Linton, J. M. (1980). *Movies as mass communication*. Beverly Hills, CA: Sage.

Keen, S. (1986). *Faces of the enemy: Reflections of the hostile imagination*. New York: Harper & Row.

Keller, G. D. (Ed.). (1985). *Chicano cinema: Research, reviews, and resources*. Binghamton, NY: Bilingual Review/Press.

Keyser, L., & Keyser, B. (1984). *Hollywood and the Catholic church: The image of Roman Catholicism in American movies*. Chicago: Loyola University Press.

Koppes, C. R., & Black, G. D. (1987). *Hollywood goes to war: How politics, profits and propaganda shaped World War II movies*. New York: The Free Press.

Korzenny, F., & Ting-Toomey, S., with Schiff, E. (Eds.). (1992). Mass media effects across cultures. *International and Intercultural Communication Annual, 16*. Newbury Park, CA: Sage.

Kosicki, G. M. (1993). Problems and opportunities in agenda-setting research. *Journal of Communication, 43*(2), 100–127.

Lamb, B. S. (1975). The convenient villain: The early cinema views the Mexican-American. *Journal of the West, 14*(4), 75–81.

Leab, D. J. (1975). *From sambo to superspade: The Black experience in motion pictures*. Boston: Houghton Mifflin.

Leckenby, J. D., & Surlin, S. H. (1976). Incidental social learning and viewer race: "All in the Family" and "Sanford and Son." *Journal of Broadcasting, 20*(4), 481–494.

Leifer, A. D., Gordon, N. J., & Graves, S. B. (1974). Children's television more than mere entertainment. *Harvard Educational Review, 44*(2), 213–245.

Leiss, W., Kline, S., & Jhally, S. (1986). *Social communication in advertising*. Toronto: Methuen.

Lewels, F. J., Jr. (1974). *The uses of the media by the Chicano movement: A study in minority access*. New York: Praeger.

Lourdeaux, L. (1990). *Italian and Irish filmmakers in America: Ford, Capra, Coppola, and Scorsese*. Philadelphia: Temple University Press.

MacDonald, J. F. (1992). *Blacks and White TV: African Americans in television since 1948* (2nd ed.). Chicago: Nelson-Hall.

Martindale, C. (1986). *The White press and Black America*. New York: Greenwood Press.

Martindale, C. (Ed.). (1993). *Pluralizing journalism education: A multicultural handbook*. Westport, CT: Greenwood Press.

Matabane, P. W. (1988). Television and the Black audience: Cultivating moderate perspectives on racial integration. *Journal of Communication, 38*(4), 21–31.

Matlin, M. W. (1991). The social cognition approach to stereotypes and its application to teaching. *Journal on Excellence in College Teaching, 2*, 9–24.

McCombs, M. W., & Shaw, D. L. (1993). The evolution of agenda-setting research: Twenty-five years in the marketplace of ideas. *Journal of Communication, 43*(2), 58–67.

McLeod, J. M., & Reeves, B. (1981). On the nature of mass media effects.

In S. B. Withey & R. P. Abeles (Eds.), *Television and social behavior: Beyond violence and children* (pp. 17–54). Hillsdale, NJ: Lawrence Erlbaum Associates.

Medved, M. (1992). *Hollywood v. America*. New York: HarperCollins.

Middleton, R. (1960). Ethnic prejudice and susceptibility to persuasion. *American Sociological Review, 25*(5), 679–686.

Miller, R. M. (Ed.). (1978). *The kaleidoscopic lens: How Hollywood views ethnic groups*. Englewood, NJ: Jerome S. Ozer.

Miller, S. M. (Ed.). (1987). *The ethnic press in the United States: A historical analysis and handbook*. Westport, CT: Greenwood Press.

Myrdal, G. (1944). *An American dilemma: The Negro problem and modern democracy*. New York: Harper & Brothers.

Noriega, C. (1988–1990). Chicano cinema and the horizon of expectations: A discursive analysis of recent film reviews in the mainstream, alternative and Hispanic press, 1987–1988. *Aztlan, A Journal of Chicano Studies, 19*(2), 1–31.

Noriega, C. (Ed.). (1992). *Chicanos and film: Essays on Chicano representation and resistance*. New York: Garland.

O'Connor, J. E. (1980). *The Hollywood Indian: Stereotypes of Native Americans in films*. Trenton: New Jersey State Museum.

Peterson, R. C., & Thurstone, L. L. (1933) *Motion pictures and the social attitudes of children*. New York: Macmillan.

Pettit, A. G. (1980). *Images of the Mexican American in fiction and film*. College Station: Texas A&M University Press.

Polish-American Guardian Society. (1982). Six "rounds" of court hearings "knock-out" movie "The End." *Polish-American Guardian Society Annual Newsletter*, 1–3.

Rapaczynski, W., Singer, D. G., & Singer, J. L. (1982). Teaching television: A curriculum for young children. *Journal of Communication, 32*(2), 46–55.

Raths, L. E., & Trager, F. N. (1948). Public opinion and "Crossfire." *Journal of Educational Sociology, 21*(6), 345–368.

Real, M. R. (1991). Bill Cosby and recoding ethnicity. In L. R. Vande Berg & L. A. Wenner (Eds.), *Television criticism: Approaches and applications* (pp. 58–84). New York: Longman.

Roberts, D. F., & Bachen, C. M. (1982). Mass communication effects. *Annual Review of Psychology, 32*, 307–356.

Rogers, E. M., Dearing, J. W., & Bregman, D. (1993). The anatomy of agenda-setting research. *Journal of Communication, 43*(2), 68–84.

Rosen, I. C. (1948). The effect of the motion picture "Gentleman's Agreement" on attitudes toward Jews. *Journal of Psychology, 26*, 525–536.

Rosenstiel, T. B. (1989, August 17). Viewers found to confuse TV entertainment with news. *Los Angeles Times*, sec. 1, p. 1.

Rubin, B. (Ed.). (1980). *Small voices and great trumpets: Minorities and the media*. New York: Praeger.

Schwartz, T. (1973). *The responsive chord*. Garden City, NY: Doubleday.

Schwoch, J., White, M., & Reilly, S. (1992). *Media knowledge: Readings in popular culture, pedagogy, and critical citizenship*. Albany: State University of New York Press.

Shaheen, J. G. (1984). *The TV Arab*. Bowling Green, OH: Bowling Green State University Popular Press.

Singer, R. D., & Kaplan, R. M. (Eds.). (1976). Television and social behavior [Special issue]. *Journal of Social Issues, 32*(4).

Sklar, R. (1975). *Movie-made America: A cultural history of American movies*. New York: Random House.

Snead, J. (1992). *White screens/Black images: Hollywood from the dark side*. New York: Routledge, Chapman, and Hall.

Spring, J. (1992). *Images of American life: A history of ideological management in schools, movies, radio, and television*. Albany, NY: State University of New York Press.

Staiger, J. (1992). *Interpreting films: Studies in the historical reception of American cinema*. Princeton, NJ: Princeton University Press.

Stanley, R. H., & Steinberg, C. S. (1976). *The media environment: Mass communications in American society*. New York: Hastings House.

Stedman, R. W. (1982). *Shadows of the Indian: Stereotypes in American culture*. Norman: University of Oklahoma Press.

Stein, J. W. (1979). *Mass media, education, and a better society*. Chicago: Nelson-Hall

Stroman, C. A. (1991). Television's role in the socialization of African American children and adolescents. *Journal of Negro Education, 60*(3), 314–327.

Subervi-Vélez, F. A. (1986). The mass media and ethnic assimilation and pluralism: A review and research proposal with special focus on Hispanics. *Communication Research, 13*(1), 71–96.

Surlin, S. H. (1978). "Roots" research: A summary of findings. *Journal of Broadcasting, 22*(3), 309–319.

Surlin, S. H., & Tate, E. D. (1976). "All in the Family": Is Archie funny? *Journal of Communication, 26*(4), 61–68.

Tan, A., & Tan, G. (1979). Television use and self-esteem of Blacks. *Journal of Communication, 29*(1), 123–135.

Taylor, P. S. (1930). *Mexican labor in the United States* (Vol. 1). Berkeley: University of California Press.

Tichi, C. (1992). *Electronic hearth: Creating an American television culture*. New York: Oxford University Press.

Toplin, R. B. (1993). *Hollywood as Mirror: Changing views of "outsiders" and "enemies" in American movies*. Westport, CT: Greenwood Press.

Vidmar, N., & Rokeach, M. (1974). Archie Bunker's bigotry: A study in selective perception and exposure. *Journal of Communication, 24*(1), 36–47.

Volkan, V. (1988). *The need to have enemies and allies: From clinical practice to international relationships*. Northvale, NJ: J. Aronson.

Weigel, R. H., Loomis, J., & Soja, M. (1980). Race relations on prime time television. *Journal of Personality and Social Psychology, 39*(5), 884–893.

Wiegman, R. (1989). Negotiating AMERICA: Gender, race, and the ideology of the interracial male bond. *Cultural Critique, 13*, 89–117.

Wilhoit, G. C., & de Bock, H. (1976). "All in the Family" in Holland. *Journal of Communication, 26*(4), 75–84.

Wilson, C. C., II. & Gutiérrez, F. (1985). *Minorities and media: Diversity and the end of mass communication*. Beverly Hills, CA: Sage.

Winn, M. (1977). *The plug-in drug*. New York: Viking Press.

Woll, A. L. (1980). *The Latin image in American film* (rev. ed.). Los Angeles: Latin American Center, University of California.

Woll, A. L., & Miller, R. M. (Eds.). (1987). *Ethnic and racial images in American film and television: Historical essays and bibliography*. New York: Garland.

Wong, F. E. (1978). *On visual media racism: Asians in the American motion pictures*. New York: Arno Press.

Worth, S., & Adair, J. (1972). *Through Navajo eyes: An exploration in film communication and anthropology*. Bloomington: Indiana University Press.

Wurman, R. S. (1989). *Information anxiety*. Garden City, Doubleday.

Ynegar, S., & Kinder, D. R. (1987). *News that matters: Agenda-setting and priming in a television age*. Chicago: University of Chicago Press.

Yum, J. O. (1982). Communication diversity and information acquisition among Korean immigrants in Hawaii. *Human Communication Research, 8*(2), 154–169.

· 11 ·

KNOWLEDGE CONSTRUCTION, COMPETING CRITICAL THEORIES, AND EDUCATION

Beverly M. Gordon

THE OHIO STATE UNIVERSITY

Most of the curriculum field, and indeed educational literature in both the academy and popular culture, is grounded in the Euro-American "regime of truth" (Foucault, 1970). As reflected in some of the earliest efforts to constitute American education, curriculum decisions about what knowledge and material would constitute an education, whether deliberate or not, embraced a Euro-American immigrant perspective (National Education Association [NEA], 1893, 1895). This perspective represents the canonization of "Whiteness" in the dominant narratives that are disseminated in the schools as, for example, American literature (Morrison, 1992) and American history and social studies (King, 1992a, 1992b). Even the critique of American cultural hegemony and economic capitalism in postmodern society posed within the broad purview of the reconceptualization of the educational and curriculum field—from the critical theorizing of the Frankfurt School (Aronowitz, 1981, 1992; Giroux, 1978, 1981, 1983, 1992; Grundy, 1987) and the sociology of knowledge in education (Karabel & Halsey, 1977; Young, 1975) to postmodernist theorizing and critiques (Giroux & McLaren, 1989; Gore, 1993; Giroux, 1992)—is, for the most part, situated within this regime.

Challenging the omissions and distortions of this hegemonic regime of truth is thus not merely a matter of infusing more information into a faulty premise, but of reconstituting the conceptual systems that govern models of humanness and modes of being. Yet, as humankind is infinitely capable of constructing new societies and civilizations, so is it also capable of configuring new conceptual systems, particularly new conceptualizations of humanity and hierarchy. In both form and content, the alternative realm of knowledge represented in popular culture as well as in historical and contemporary African American scholarship, institutions, and artifacts, while not monolithic, constitutes more than an extension of contemporary American society and thought; it signals the ascendance of a new world civilization.

The African American conceptual system challenges American Western ideological hegemony in two ways. First, it provides a source for critiquing the fundamental principles upon which objectivity and rationality regarding social construction of race and racism are constructed within that system. Second, by articulating the evolution and construction of an alternative realm of knowledge that can move beyond and transcend the prevailing conceptual system, this conceptual system affords non-White, non-Western peoples a foundation on which to base action for social change.

According to Taylor (1989), a society's conceptual system is based upon its realm of knowledge. This conceptual system forms or is the result of the "unique experiences" of a given society and "may take the form of scientific, metaphysical or religious knowledge" (p. 117). Moreover, Taylor adds, "the society to which each corresponds respectively regards that framework as its final premise for all thinking. From this it follows that all three types [of knowledge] are rational" (p. 118). A conceptual system thus has an internal logic, its own objectivity and rationality. In its totality, Taylor argues, it is the "rational"; however, the rational and the "sacred" are one and the same within a society because both represent ultimate truth within its confines. In Taylor's view:

Frequently, the sacred has been thought to be a "higher" order of truth. If a lower order of truth, for example, positive science, comes to be considered as the highest and only valid truth, or approach to it, then the truth of positive science has become sacred. The latter is that knowledge upon which the society conceives itself to depend; the system of concepts to which every problem in a final sense must be referred. Certainly, most societies will see fit to separate the "higher" from the "lower" [order of truth]. . . . Similarly, the social definition of sex, military prowess, age, skin color, or anything else will have sacred or profane connotations according to the place of these definitions in the system of definitions—that is, in the conceptual system. (p. 119)

184

The generation of social knowledge, science, cultural artifacts—indeed, all of our socially constructed reality—is partially influenced and informed by historical, cultural, and political contexts. This becomes particularly clear when one critically examines the paradigms traditionally used by dominant White U.S. society to understand and control subjugated groups. The Darwinist, or "evolutionary," perspective, and the way it is articulated within the Western canon, is for White Westerners (including those in the United States) the prevailing conception of what constitutes "natural law" as it relates to the conceptualization of human beings. The idea of race as a socially constructed category is but one manifestation of this ideological paradigm. Racialization, that is, the social construction of race and the hierarchical categorization of human beings within this race paradigm, continues to serve as the root cause of the racism that frames and structures the U.S. societal structure.

The African diasporic, specifically the African American, countercreation of knowledge functions as both a critique of and challenge to dominant White American society because it engenders the creation of new conceptual systems and modes of being that deserve more study and discussion. It nurtures the development of an African American epistemology generated out of the African American existential condition, that is, the knowledge and artifacts produced by African Americans based on their specific cultural, social, economic, historical, and political experience (B. Gordon, 1990).

THE AFRICAN AMERICAN AUTOCHTHONOUS CRITIQUE OF WESTERN IDEOLOGICAL HEGEMONY: EVOLUTION AND CHALLENGE

As critique, the Black challenge to Western ideological hegemony stems from a critical science that neither originated in nor is guided by European critical theory, or, for that matter, postmodern deconstructionism. This "authochthonous" or indigenous critical science sprung specifically from the American continent inhabited by its advocates. Its origins and applications reflect the unique collective experience of the reality in which Africans found themselves in the "New World."

The autochthonous critique of the dominant conceptual system in the United States exposes the ideas that rationalize the hierarchical structuring of humanity and consequent subjugation of people based on the category of race. In the American experience, Blackness, or "Africanism" (Morrison, 1992), has traditionally been the antithesis of Whiteness, or "the denotative and connotative blackness that African peoples have come to signify, as well as the entire range of views, assumptions, readings and misreading that accompany Eurocentric learning about these people" (pp. 6-7). As Morrison posits:

Africanism has become, in the Eurocentric tradition that American education favors, both a way of talking about and a way of policing matters of class, sexual license, and repression, formations and exercises of power, and meditations on ethics and accountability. Through the simple expedient of demonizing and reifying the range of color on a palette, African Americanism makes it possible to say and not say, to inscribe and erase, to escape and engage, to act out and act on, to

historicize and render timeless. It provides a way of contemplating chaos and civilization, desire and fear and a mechanism for testing the problems and blessing of freedom. (p. 7)

The Evolution of Black Studies

African Americans have long understood the importance of critiquing and countering social sciences that are intended to explain, interpret, and control individuals based on racial classifications (Carby, 1987; Hull, Bell-Scott, & Smith, 1982; Roman, 1911; Sterling, 1984; Washington, 1987). For at least the last century, African American intellectuals and artists have engaged in the creation of knowledge and institution-building efforts. Various cultural and intellectual thrusts emerged from the African American community, several of which encouraged social theorizing and the production of culture and cultural artifacts, as well as the construction of community institutions (B. Gordon, 1985, 1990). These thrusts manifested as individual campaigns, societies, movements, and institutions such as the American Negro Academy, the Association for the Study of Negro Life and History, the National Association for the Advancement of Colored People (NAACP), hundreds of historically Black educational institutions from primary school through higher education, and thousands of other efforts undertaken by multitudes of people known and unknown.

One of the early eras of great social, cultural, and intellectual movement within the African American community occurred from the 1880s to the 1920s (American Negro Academy, 1969). Although overtly hostile racist terrorism—lynchings, race riots, Jim Crow segregation—was prevalent during this era, great cultural and intellectual fervor emanated from the African American community. These were the years of the great migration of African Americans from the South to the North, as well as the age of the Harlem Renaissance, with its significant cultural flowering (Carby, 1987; Locke, 1925; Washington, 1987). The NAACP and the National Urban League, along with a number of other modern civil rights organizations, were established during this period. Other cultural and intellectual organizations came into being as "part of the Negro history and protest movement designed to promote dignity and race pride against insults and to challenge [W]hite notions of Negro inferiority and racism" (Kaiser, 1969, pp. i–ii). During its 31-year history (1897–1928), the American Negro Academy, organized by Alexander Crummell, produced and published 22 occasional papers on a variety of subjects such as race, education, industrialism, Negro suffrage, the church, peonage, and economics (American Negro Academy, 1969; B. Gordon, 1990; Moss, 1981).

During the decade from 1926 to 1936, more African American students graduated from college and attended graduate school than in the entire previous century (Fontaine, 1940). The nature of graduate work—particularly the paradigms disseminated to graduate students—was a critical factor in the shift in African American social theory from the nationalist perspective to the ecological assimilationist/integrationist perspectives that still greatly influence contemporary social science. The University of Chicago School of Sociology produced an influential second generation of highly credentialed White sociologists during this period, including Ward (1903, 1906, 1913),

Odum (1910), Park (1931; Park & Burgess, 1924; Park & Miller, 1921; see also Turner, 1967), Burgess (1928, 1961), Sumner (1966), and (Franklin) Giddings (1935). However, as Bracey, Meier, and Rudwick (1973) note, the first-generation African American sociologists, including Crummell (1897/1969), DuBois (1896/1973b, 1899/1973a, 1903; Dubois & Dill, 1911), Haynes (Bowser, 1981), Daniels (Bowser, 1981), and others, were scarcely noticed within the sociological intellectual circles dominated by Whites.

During the 1920s and 1930s, social theory in the United States was influenced, albeit indirectly, by Spencer's (1864, 1873/1961, 1885) social Darwinist theory of evolutionary determinism, which also exerted considerable influence on American educational theorizing. With its notions of superiority and inferiority, Spender's law-of-evaluation thesis, having already been used as the rationale for slavery, was employed as a sociological theoretical framework to explain problems in the urban cities caused by the massive influx of European immigrant populations and the exodus of African Americans from the South to the North (Bowser, 1981). Issues such as social conflicts between races, housing, and land-use conversion in cities had to be addressed in the early 20th century, and they, too, were explained in the context of evolutionist theory. In this view, African Americans experienced difficulties because of racial prejudice and their inability to develop complex societies like those of western Europe.

Robert E. Park was a leader in shaping the Chicago School of Sociology as well as a great influence on race relations theory and the development of urban sociology (B. Gordon, 1985). The assumptions Park held about African American people and the theoretical paradigms and concepts he employed in his research were problematic (Ellison, 1973; Jones, 1973). The ecological paradigm that permeated later Park-inspired studies of urban growth and development was a transitional notion bridging social conditionality with social Darwinism. Burgess (1928), in his study of residential segregation in American cities, postulated his thesis of "fixed conditionality," in which he contended that patterns of residential groupings followed a social Darwinist bent; that is, the most superior residents (Whites) will naturally rise to the top (secure the best homes, living conditions, and neighborhoods). Burgess, however, fails to address or include in his analytical framework the role of city planners in constructing and preserving certain sections of a city for development or underdevelopment. Although Park, Burgess, and other early White sociologists of the Chicago School were not openly racist, the rationality they employed assumed the racial inferiority and second-class status of people of African descent in the United States. However, they believed that "since Negroes theoretically could be changed, given the right environment, it was the mission of fair-minded Whites to advocate racial reform or accommodation" (Bowser, 1981, p. 189). The solution to solving the problems of African Americans, in this view and that of many African American scholars influenced by Park and others, was complete assimilation (Alkalimat, 1973).

The second generation of African American sociologists provided a countercritique of these views. Scholars such as Doyle (1937), Drake (Drake & Cayton, 1945), Johnson (1930, 1934, 1938, 1951), Frazier (1932, 1937, 1939), Reid (1936, 1939, 1940), and Woodson (1919/1968, 1933/1977) were concerned about the kind of education that African Americans were receiving, even at prestigious graduate institutions such as the University of Chicago, which instilled Black cultural self-hatred and cognitive inferiority on one hand and embraced the ecological assimilationist/integrationist perspective on the other. In a continuing effort to challenge the prevailing intellectual institutions and dominating paradigms, these scholars critiqued the prevailing paradigms and conceptual frameworks that "explained" the societal context and conditions of African Americans (Bowser, 1981; Fontaine, 1940, 1983).

Carter G. Woodson and the Association for the Study of Negro Life and History

In 1915 Carter G. Woodson (1933/1977, 1919/1968) established the Association for the Study of Negro Life and History (ASNLH) and an accompanying publication, the *Journal of Negro History* (Meier & Rudwick, 1986). Woodson believed that racism was due to ignorance and that educating Whites about the African experience in America would dispel it. Negro History Week, inaugurated by the ASNLH in 1926, was one of Woodson's ideas. Woodson was always struggling for money for the ASNLH and was not comfortable relying on foundations, philanthropic organizations and other groups for support. In the late 1920s he took the ASNLH's organizational structure to another level by getting Negro public school teachers involved with his association. In 1937 he began publishing the *Negro History Bulletin*, a periodical specifically geared toward school-aged children and their teachers in public schools. This enterprise was "sustained even though it was run at a large deficit that absorbed much of the money raised in nickels, dimes, and quarters from the black community" (Meier & Rudwick, 1986, p. 280). Woodson also became involved in the preparation of public school textbooks for border states and upper southern states.

In Woodson's view, the education, knowledge, and accompanying skills training that African Americans received in the U.S. education system crippled and greatly prohibited their development and advancement because it reinforced cultural self-hatred and cognitive inferiority. His 1933 work, *The Mis-Education of the Negro,* provides one of the most important critiques of the American school curriculum to date. In this book Woodson unmasks the conceptual systems in which the American curriculum are grounded and which have long legitimized and normalized racist hierarchical categories within biological and social science. He contends that the paradigms employed in higher education, particularly at the graduate level in the social and biological sciences, influenced as they were by social Darwinism, do little more than promote racism and rationalize the consequent colonial subordination of African Americans. This process was an insidious one, in Woodson's view, for, as he wrote: "When you control a man's thinking, you do not have to worry about his actions. . . . He will find his proper place and will stay in it" (Woodson, 1933/1977, p. xiii). To counter the imposed intellectual hegemony of White Western society and the presumed servility of persons of African descent, Woodson proposes the generation of a theoretical prescription derived from the multiple dimensions of the Black experience in America:

> After Negro students have mastered the fundamentals of English, the principles of composition, and the leading facts in the development of its literature, they should not spend all of their time in advanced work on Shakespeare, Chaucer and Anglo-Saxon. They should direct their attention also to the folklore of the African, to the philosophy in his proverbs, to the development of the Negro in the use of modern language, and to the works of Negro writers. The leading facts of the history of the world should be studied by all, but of what advantage is it to the Negro student of history to devote all of his time to courses bearing on such despots as Alexander the Great, Caesar, and Napoleon, or to the record of those nations whose outstanding achievement has been rapine, plunder, and murder for world power? Why not study the African background from the point of view of anthropology and history, and then take up sociology as it concerns the negro peasant or proletarian who is suffering from sufficient ills to supply laboratory work for the most advanced students of the social order? Why not take up economics as reflected by the Negroes of today and work out some remedy for their lack of capital, the absence of cooperative enterprise, and the short life of their establishments. Institutions like Harvard, Yale and Columbia are not going to do these things, and educators influenced by them to the extent that they become blind to the Negro will never serve the race efficiently. (pp. 150–151)

The Mis-Education of the Negro further speaks to the crisis Woodson saw in the emergence of the "New Negro," a term coined by Alain Locke (1925) to describe the literary and artistic African American intellectuals of the 1920s and 1930s. For Woodson, the most important contribution an African American could make and was obligated to make was to serve the race. He reasoned that neither the "old" nor the "new" Negro was educated in a way that would help unify the African American community and influence social change for its advancement. Classical education, as advocated by W. E. B. DuBois (1903), had not elevated a substantial number of African American thinkers and philosophers "to the height of black men farther removed from influences of slavery and segregation" such as Pushkin or Dumas (Woodson, 1933/1977, pp. 15–16). Nor had the industrial education approach of Booker T. Washington left African Americans with sufficient training and practice to compete successfully in the workforce (not surprisingly, this insufficient training also barred them from trade unions).

In Woodson's view, African Americans in U.S. schools and colleges were being indoctrinated with a Eurocentric worldview. Such an orientation, he argued, would not help impressionable young African American scholars "become a constructive force in the development of the race" (Woodson, 1933/1977, p. 3). Indeed, one of the many consequences of the miseducation of Negroes, according to Woodson, was their dissociation from the masses of their community. By rationalizing that the masses would be incapable of coalescing their economic resources, Black elites engaged in denial of their autochthonous communities and their ethnic and racial selves. Instead of joining with their community in a collective effort to advance and develop with a unified front, educated African Americans distanced themselves from the masses as a means of acquiescing to the White dominant societal (scientific) interpretations of

the ineptitude and inferiority of Black people. For instance, Woodson observed that "Negro banks, as a rule, have failed because the people, taught that their own pioneers in business cannot function in this sphere, withdrew their deposits" (p. 108). Arguing that this and other self-defeating beliefs were the manifestation of miseducation, he urged African Americans to cooperate and pull together for the good of their own communities, forgoing individual gain or conflict.

Woodson envisioned the African American community shifting from a position of dependency and assimilation to one of self-reliance and self-actualized power in which African Americans actively take charge of their circumstances and engage, on a variety of levels, in a sincere liberation struggle, the critical and emancipatory spirit of which would emanate from within the community itself. His theorizing thus offers a basis for social action. Moreover, Woodson's understanding of how social science paradigms and assumptions shape reality and influence societal policy challenges dominant theorizing and adds further substance to the evolving African American scholarly critique of these paradigms. His reconceptualization and reconstruction of higher education as a mechanism of racial upliftment predates the Afrocentric Black nationalist philosophy of African American scholars such as Asante (1980, 1987, 1990) by 60 years. Woodson's contentions that social knowledge and action had to be generated out of the context of the African American community itself, and that African Americans can neither depend on nor wait for liberal Whites to help them, were echoed over a half century later by scholars such as Childs (1981, 1991) and Aronowitz (1981). Additionally, his pedagogical model for teaching people about themselves, their own heroes, and neighbors, along with the research methodology he suggested as a preliminary step in establishing a curriculum for U.S. schools, predates Freire's (1973) notion of education for critical consciousness by about 40 years. As Woodson wrote in *The Mis-Education of the Negro*:

> To educate the Negro we must find out exactly what his back[g]round is, what he is today, what his possibilities are, how to begin with him as he is and make him a better individual of the kind that he is[.] Instead of cramming the Negro's mind with what others have shown that they can do, we should develop his la[t]ent powers that he may perform in society a part of which others are not capable. (1933/1977, p. 151)

With the increase in attendance of African Americans at institutions of higher education, African American scholars became concerned with knowledge dissemination at those institutions. Fundamental questions began to emerge about the nature of the education African American students were receiving. Some of the critical issues included: What constitutes the college curriculum? What is the impact of the curriculum on the student? What images of African Americans are being promoted in the paradigms and theories? What interests are served by the dominant ideology and the realm of knowledge being disseminated? The social critiques of these emerging African American scholars became a struggle among competing paradigms. Social theorizing became the ideological battleground for the struggle among adherents of philosophies ranging from loosely defined assimilationist to staunch nationalist positions. While social theory sympathetic to the assimilationist/integrationist perspective was, and still is, the dominant ideology, leading African American scholars continue to critique the dominant social theory and generate alternative paradigms and analyses to explain, understand, and theorize about African Americans in other than pejorative ways (B. Gordon, 1985).

W. E. B. DuBois and the *Studies of Negro Problems* Series

A most poignant example of the invisibility of African American institutional social theorizing in the U.S. conceptual system is the lack of recognition given to the work of W. E. B. DuBois. In his efforts to change the conditions and status of African American people, DuBois engaged in social critique and theorizing from an institutional viewpoint. From 1896 to 1911 DuBois, then director of publicity and research for the NAACP, edited *Studies of Negro Problems,* a 16-volume series published by Atlanta University Press. This project was conceptualized by DuBois (DuBois & Dill, 1911) as a "plan of social study of the Negro American, by means of an annual series of decennially recurring subjects covering, so far as practicable, every phase of human life" (p. 5). The series represented the thinking of a collective of scholars who met at Atlanta University's annual "Negro conferences." At these meetings, some of the leading African American thinkers of the day engaged in extensive critique of the theory and practice of racism in U.S. society and put forward agendas aimed at social reform and upliftment of the African American community. Their conference presentations, which DuBois edited, focused on various topics of concern to African Americans, including the social and physical conditions of African American life in the nation's urban areas, mortality rates in cities, social betterment, business, economic development, the church, the arts, education, health, and crime. Lack of economic resources ended the series.

The story of the *Studies of Negro Problems* series illustrates one aspect of the relationship between institutions and the scientific production and cultural fabric of society. Political control and economic autonomy within an institution can have a profound impact on the production and dissemination of knowledge and the freedom to support research and training deemed to be in the vested interests of a societal community. Unfortunately for DuBois, few philanthropists and capitalists were willing to make contributions that would sustain these activities for African Americans. DuBois's work at Atlanta University, which remains still relatively obscure in circles of critical pedagogy, began almost three decades before the formation of the Institute for Social Research, an economically independent private research institute for social science affiliated with Frankfurt University in Germany. This institute, established in 1923 by Felix Weil and with "an initial endowment providing a yearly income" (Jay, 1973, p. 8) from his father, Hermann Weil, to the University of Frankfurt, was dedicated to "the reflective critique of socially unnecessary constraints of human freedom" (Schroyer, 1975, p. 15). Like the Atlanta University collaborations that preceded it, the Institute for Social Research represented a collective of scholars working together to solve societal crises. Although both efforts were successful in their own

right, one gained significant prominence in the realm of educational history and social theorizing, while the work and influence of the other has received only scant recognition. Apparently, Weil's "gifts," as Jay (1973) describes them, "though not enormous did permit the creation and maintenance of an institution whose financial independence proved a great advantage throughout its subsequent history" (p. 8).

It is ironic that the Frankfurt School's social theory work has been criticized for failing to reconcile theory and practice, and consequently having little effect in changing the conditions and status of the working class. As Jay (1973) contends, "the Frankfurt School chose the purity of its theory over the affiliation that a concrete attempt to realize it would have required" (p. 37). As most of the young European intellectuals who were a part of the Institute were from the upper middle class, the necessity and urgency for practical application of their theorizing may have been lost to them because they had no experiential understanding of the troubles of the working class.

COMPETING DISCOURSES IN AFRICAN AMERICAN EDUCATIONAL THEORIZING

The Multicultural Premise

From the 19th century to the present postmodern, post–civil rights era, African Americans have focused on their situation and condition within the "racialized" societal structures of American society (B. Gordon, 1993). Historical examples of African American intellectual culture, educational discourse, and institution building abound in the efforts of notable figures such as W. E. B. DuBois, Carter G. Woodson, Anna Julia Cooper, Charlotte Hawkins Brown, Mary McLeod Bethune, Mary Church Terrell, and Ida B. Wells-Barnett (B. Gordon, in press). Essentially, the work of these leaders and thinkers, while not monolithic and sometimes quite oppositional within their own ranks, was dedicated to two goals: (a) winning the struggle against racism and a racialized societal order, and (b) empowering and improving the quality of life for the African American masses. Postmodern African American scholars have continued this tradition of scholar-activism in both the intellectual and popular cultural communities. The pioneering efforts of contemporary educational leaders such as Banks (1969, 1973, 1981, 1988, 1991; Banks & Banks, 1989), Grant (1977, 1984, 1992), and Gay (Gay & Baber, 1987) have resulted in scholarship and institution-building efforts supporting the reconceptualization of U.S. society as "multicultural." These scholars have attempted to transform the dominant discourse of educational theory and classroom pedagogy to make room for the realms of knowledge generated by the diverse racial, ethnic, and cultural groups within U.S. and other Western societies. Additionally, their work has addressed the inherited prejudices, biases, fears, and misconceptions about "other" people in the Americas, using school classrooms as the arenas in which to engage such issues.

The language of multicultural education has become a familiar signal and pillar in the curriculum of most classrooms, from primary through higher education. One of the main if not original tenets of multicultural education is to make students aware of difference, and of the twin truth that difference, like commonality, is normal. Still, the issue of race is central to the concept of multiculturality in U.S. society. As Carby (1992) rightly notes, the study of difference does little to change the fact that the economic, political, and social configurations of a racialized society impact directly on the economic, political, and social existence of individual members of that society. It does little to address, much less change, the real lived and living conditions of the masses of Black people in America. The dispersion of academic knowledge about the African American community does not obviate White culpability in the maintenance of what West (1992) has called the "nihilistic threat" of White domination to Black existence in the United States, nor does it exonerate society's learning institutions from their complicity in the failure rates of African American students.

Several educators have attempted to conceptualize multiculturalism as an activist liberatory mechanism, as the "emancipatory" formulation of multiculturality (Crichlow, Goodwin, Shakes, & Swartz, 1990). Their work recasts classroom pedagogical practice in part as a discourse between teacher and children engaged in critiquing the dominant narrative found within their course texts and curricula, in essence, finding the cracks—the contradictions, omissions, and myths within the materials used in schools. By this means teachers and students can unmask the "hidden" agenda of the U.S. curriculum (Anyon, 1980; Apple, 1990, 1993; Giroux, 1981, 1983; Vallance, 1977). McCarthy (1990) posits that multiculturalism offers educators a language of critique and re-creation as well as a basis for changing the school "ethos" so that students of color "have access to an academic core curriculum on par with their middle-class and white counterparts" (p. 127). As King and Wilson (1990) point out, the modern debate over multiculturalism is not an argument over ethnicity, particularism, or pluralism in the curriculum; it is a struggle over conceptual frames of reference and ideology.

Several thorny dilemmas confront those who advocate multiculturalism in the United States today. One of these is the expropriation of the term in the "real" world. As Carby (1987) maintains, "the terrain of language is a terrain of power relations" (p. 17). In that sense, terms such as "multicultural," "multiracial," "difference," "tolerance," "minority," and "majority" speak to the normative terrains of power. Carby (1992) later observes that while multicultural theory (and, to a lesser extent, feminist theory and critical pedagogy) talks about "difference," such discourse does not "unmask" the complex social, political, and economic structures in which African American people are immersed because of the racialization of U.S. society:

The theoretical paradigm of difference is obsessed with the construction of identities rather than relations of power and domination, and, in practice, concentrates on the effect of this difference on a (white) norm. ... Because the politics of difference works with concepts of individual identity, rather than structures of inequality and exploitation, processes of racialization are marginalized and given symbolic and political meaning only when the subjects are black. (p. 193)

The concept of multiculturalism currently extends far beyond its original intent. Its language, discourse, and meaning, in part born out of the civil rights movement of the 1950s and 1960s, have become gnarled in such a way that aspects of multiculturalism—hence now all of it—carry "backlash" baggage that, conveniently for some, projects an antagonistic, hierarchical, "we/them" structure. Other contemporaries offer "pluralism talk" that fails to acknowledge that Americans as a society and we as teachers particularly, have come to know our students, or "the one sharing the raft, or ... drinking next to us at the bar" (Greene, 1992, p. 256), solely by their racial affiliation because of the power of the dominant sociocultural conceptual systems of meaning that assert the primacy of race. There is also the parallel concern that the concept of multiculturalism has become a catch-basin for all the other "isms" of U.S. society, that it has become a podium of convenience for numerous persons and groups committed to issues surrounding countless diverse "others" who still enjoy skin-color privileges within American society (e.g., White women, White gays and lesbians, Whites who are differently abled). Such vulgarizations diminish and marginalize the discourse of multiculturalism and multicultural education, and trivialize actions on behalf of these efforts.

Critical and Feminist Discourses

Although postmodern emancipatory critical and feminist discourses have focused on issues of otherness and marginality and have made inroads into dominant educational discourse (either applauded or vilified), in the main these discourses have had at most a narrow and limiting engagement with the works of African American scholars who make problematic the regimes of truth operating within dominant and emancipatory narratives that constitute schools curriculum (B. Gordon, 1992). Indeed, the issue of race seems not to be part of feminist or critical pedagogical discourse; both relegate race to a liminal category. On the other side of the coin, African American scholarship on the whole seems not to be as successful in being recognized in either dominant or emancipatory discourses, particularly when it challenges Eurocentric conceptual systems of hierarchical structuring of humanity by, for example, critiquing how race functions as a historical and social construction. West (1993) implores the African American community to move beyond its current postmodern stagnation crisis, to (re)constitute concepts of leadership, coalitions, nationalism, and racial reasoning in order to develop the interests and welfare of the African American community and contribute to a genuine multiracial democracy. He also expresses concern that African Americans' racism toward Whites is obstructing the building of "meaningful coalition[s] with white progressives because of an undeniable white racist legacy of the modern Western world" (p. 66).

The blind side of critical and feminist discourses is their inability, unwillingness, or complete lack of awareness of the need to focus on the conceptual systems that construct, legitimize, and normalize the issues of race and racism. This is demonstrated through the flagrant invisibility in their works of the critical and cultural model generated by a subjugated oppressed group from its own experiences within a dominant and hostile society. Why is it that African American critiques have been overlooked? Why is it that feminist pedagogical discourse parallels strands of critical pedagogies that have been constructed within the United States (Gore, 1993), yet never mentions African American critical and liberatory pedagogy? The Black challenge to Western ideological hegemony is older than both critical and feminist discourse and was born of the need for intellectual, ideological, and spiritual liberation of people who lived under both the racist domination and sexist patriarchal subordination to which both the critical and feminist discourses react and refer. While Black autochthonous knowledge is sympathetic to fundamental issues about which both critical and feminist discourses feel passionately, its movement is in different directions, with implications that may well transcend these current discourses.

Critical Theory and the Issue of Race. Critical theory seeks to understand the origins and operation of repressive social structures (Held, 1980; Horkheimer, 1972; Jay, 1973; Marcuse, 1964; Schroyer, 1975). Critical theory is the critique of domination. It seeks to focus on a world becoming less free, to cast doubt on the claims of technological scientific rationality, and then to imply that present configurations do not have to be as they are—that it is possible to change reality, and that conditions may already exist that can make such change possible.

Over the past several decades, critical social science has entered the debates within the field of education and has produced profound critiques on the dominant narratives and discourses in the field. The critical inquiry characterized in education employs interpretive schemes grounded in European (particularly German Jewish) historical, cultural, and intellectual thought (Held, 1980; Jay, 1973; Slater, 1977). Contemporary critical discourse has put forward the argument that schools reproduce hierarchy, exclusion, and inequality among racial groups and social classes, in part by selectively disseminating differentiated knowledge—high status to low status—to children. Moreover, the linguistic and cultural capital disseminated by the school embodies the values and beliefs of the dominant society and trivializes cultural traditions that deviate from the normative structure legitimated by that dominant society (Anyon, 1980; Apple, 1993; Bourdieu, 1977; Keddie, 1975). As Bourdieu observes, the school "offers information and training which can be received and acquired only by subjects endowed with the system of predispositions that is the condition for the success of the transmission and of the inculcation of the culture" (p. 494).

Critical discourse proposes that a society is able to reproduce the relations of power and dominance that characterize its existing social and political arrangements in part through the reproduction of specific social relationships and forms of social consciousness. This mode of social control has been referred to as "ideological hegemony" (Gramsci, 1971). Ideological hegemony has become a crucial starting point for examining the negation of "others"—other cultural traditions, other intellectual theorizing, and the production of knowledge that deviates from the normative structure of reality legitimated by prevailing societal institutions. Proponents of cultural hegemony argue that society reproduces itself, in part, through the permeation of a general worldview that defines the entire system of values, attitudes, beliefs, social practices, and norms that function in various ways to universalize the ideology of the established order (Apple, 1990; Giroux, 1981, 1983). This worldview, in turn, reflects and engenders the dominant class's interests. This dominant worldview is perpetuated, to a certain extent, by institutions such as schools, families, mass media, and other agencies of socialization. While such a worldview is far from monolithic, it exerts a powerful influence in shaping social structure and societal relationships.

In the 1980s and 1990s, the critical discourse in the field of education looked to the European theater, embracing the postmodernist deconstructionist thought from France (e.g., Foucault 1970, 1977a, 1977b, 1979, 1988; Derrida, 1976, 1983; Lacan, 1988; Lyotard, 1984). The more familiar critical educational discourse focuses on theoretical work and pedagogy (e.g., Apple, 1990, 1993; Freire, 1968, 1973, 1978; Giroux, 1992; Gore, 1993; Popkewitz, 1987, 1988; Shor, 1986, 1987, 1988; Shor & Freire, 1987). Some of this discourse concentrates on the critique of issues such as the differential power relations in schooling and sites within classrooms that produce and reproduce societal power relations, the dominance of the technocratic model of educating students, and the construction and dissemination of knowledge.

Nonetheless, such a critique may not be able to account for the idiosyncratic or contradictory nature of contemporary U.S. society because of the uniqueness of racism in the Americas and the status of race as a founding societal principle used to rationalize the subjugation of an entire people. Moreover, in Western societies like the United States, both the majority and minority populations, from the working poor through the middle classes and beyond to the highest echelons of the elite, are all intertwined or embedded in an insidious "consumer capitalist" system. Countering such (socially constructed) "reality" requires a model of discourse and historical critique that encourages dialogue free from the domination and discourse within popular cultural communities and societal institutions. As Apple (1993) has noted, "being critical means something more than simply fault-finding. It involves understanding the sets of historically contingent circumstances and contradictory power relations that create the conditions in which we live" (p. 5). This belief is echoed by Giroux (1992), who contends that critical discourse must also seek to propose alternative, critical pedagogical traditions that provide for a free and open communication process that both teaches and practices the "knowledge, habits and skills of critical citizenship" in order to understand societal constraints that lead toward societal participation and transformation (p. 74). While the issue of race, as well as race in conjunction with class and gender, has been part of the history of the critical discourse as an object of study (e.g., Apple & Weiss, 1983), only recently have proponents of this discourse seriously engaged the theoretical constructs generated by African Americans (e.g., Giroux, 1992).

Feminist Theory and the Issue of Race. Feminist discourse has contributed meaningfully and substantively toward raising American consciousness of the multiple and complex issues confronting women. It has clearly made a pertinent contribution to the popular and academic literature on contemporary societal issues. However, the marginalization of the feminist deconstruction of Whiteness as race (i.e., employing "White" as a racial category), and the culpability and complicity of White women in the maintenance of systems that disadvantage people of color and other groups of outsiders, are painfully obvious (Gore, 1993; Lather, 1991). Feminist pedagogy reflects the hierarchy of issues within the dominant feminist discourse, such as the concepts of authority and empowerment, an emphasis on discourse at the expense of practical application, and sites for pedagogical practice (Gore, 1993). Little of this discourse focuses on the deconstruction of the conceptual systems that keep the concept of race and skin-color privileges in place. In light of this, statements proclaiming feminism as "the quantum physics of postmodernism" or asserting that it is "embedded in popular practice which seeks to transform the world" (Lather, 1991, p. 27) ring especially hollow.

Historically, African American women activists and scholars have sought to transform the world for themselves, their community, and finally for the dominant society at large (Blassingame & McKivigan, 1979; DuBois, 1903; P. Giddings, 1984; B. Gordon, in press). The role of African American women, many of whom were also engaged in the club movement and the struggle for women's suffrage, in establishing institutions of learning was especially notable during the early part of the 20th century (B. Gordon, in press). The work of organizations such as the National Association of Colored Women (NACW), formed in 1896, whose motto was "Lifting as We Climb," exemplify a long tradition of self-help and service to the community on the part of African American women (P. Giddings, 1984). Individual women of note include Charlotte Forten Grimke, born in 1837 in Philadelphia's free Black community, who received an upper-class education through private tutors and in the public schools of Salem, Massachusetts. Upon graduating from Salem Normal School in 1856, Grimke gave up the genteel life and volunteered her services to the War Department to help educate the thousands of freed men and women from the South Carolina Sea Islands (Lerner, 1973). Lucy Craft Laney graduated from Atlanta University in 1886 and, that same year, founded the Haines Normal Institute in Atlanta, her most famous graduate being Mary McLeod Bethune, who founded Bethune-Cookman College in 1904. Bethune was also the president of the National Association of Colored Women's Clubs (NACWC) and served as an advisor to President Franklin D. Roosevelt (Lerner, 1973; Loewenberg & Bogin, 1987).

Other significant yet generally unsung African American women whose efforts represent an autochthonous, institution-building response to the Western pedagogical hegemony include Frances (Fanny) Jackson Coppin, Anna Julia Cooper, and Charlotte Hawkins Brown. Coppin, born a slave in 1837, had her freedom purchased by an aunt, who worked for $6 a month to pay $125 for Coppin. Coppin was later sent to Bedford, Massachusetts, where she began working and attending the State Normal School. She eventually entered Oberlin College, graduating with a distinguished record in 1865. She taught at the Institute for Colored Youth in Philadelphia and served as its principal for 41 years, from 1869 to 1902, adding teacher training and industrial arts to the school's curriculum. She also established various community-based institutions to help young people acquire job skills (Lerner, 1973; Loewenberg & Bogin, 1987; Sterling, 1984). Anna Julia Cooper was born a slave in North Carolina. Cooper graduated from Augustine Normal School in 1869 and began her teaching career. She later obtained a master's degree from Oberlin College in 1884, and moved to Washington, D.C., where by 1901 she became the second woman principal at the segregated M Street High School. She secured admissions and scholarships for African American students to attend Harvard, Yale, and Brown universities (Lerner, 1973). Close to her retirement, Cooper traveled to France and earned a doctorate in Latin at the Sorbonnne. After returning to the United States, she established Frelinghuysen University in Washington, D.C., an evening college for working students, and served as its president from 1929 to 1941 (Lerner, 1973). Charlotte Hawkins Brown, born in North Carolina and raised in Boston, took classes at Wellesley, Harvard, Simmons College, and Salem State Teachers College. Her education was partially funded by Alice Freeman Palmer, president of Wellesley. In 1902 Brown founded her own school, The Palmer Memorial Institute, a finishing school for young African American women; she served as the school's president from 1904 to 1952 (Lerner, 1973).

While most women of color have been resistant to feminist theory that identifies gender relations as a primary form of oppression (Lather, 1991), some have examined the struggles being waged by African American women against sexual and class oppression as well as racism (Hull et al., 1982; James & Farmer, 1993). These issues include working in institutions of White male supremacy, patriarchal society and White skin privilege, child abuse, sexism in higher education, and multicultural feminist perspectives. Other African American women have addressed the challenge of dysfunctional families within the African American community (hooks, 1984, 1992); other voices speak of, but are not limited to, issues concerning Black lesbians (Bunch, 1975; Lorde, 1978), Black women in interracial relationships (Butler, 1992; Golden, 1992; Opitz, 1992), Black women throughout the African Diaspora (Bushby, 1992; Golden, 1992; Mirza, 1992; Sached, 1985), and Black women who constitute the working poor (Joseph, 1981).

King (1992b) has argued that African American women have been positioned in a blind spot of the dominant discourse on the African American community. As she queries: "What does this particular construction illuminate or obscure about African American life and social issues? To what extent does this construction implicitly or explicitly place African American women and men in competition against and conflict with one another?" (p. 37). Discourse and narratives based on part of a population may have problematic implications for the advancement and well-being of the community at large because discussions with such partial data may well exacerbate the problems instead of resolving them. The seductive nature of talking about gender relations as a primary form of oppression for African American women belies several issues, the least of which is that the playing field is not equal. African American men are not on the same playing field with respect to aggregate accumulation of capital, power, and control as White men; African American women are not on the same playing field with respect to aggregate accumulation of capital, power, and control as White women. Dividing a community against itself threatens the life and viability of a community that is under assault on multiple fronts.

Where does feminist discourse situate the historical and contemporary theorizing and work of African American women (and/or African American men, for that matter)? Talking about sexism may help unpack tensions between women and men, but it deflects persistent racial issues. Gore (1993) observes that during the early 1980s, when feminists were shaping their "question of pedagogy," women of color, to whom she refers as "Third Wave" and poststructuralists, had little voice and representation. Moreover, while Third-Wave feminisms "are now more widely embraced ... feminist pedagogy discourse remains strongly influenced by these earlier works" (pp. 91–92). Contemporary White feminist discourse, liberal or radical, seldom addresses or confronts the critique of the Western ideological hegemony proffered by African American women, for whom racism is the nexus around which issues of gender, politics, economics, and social class revolve.

Something unspoken may be underlying this curious silence. The issues of race and racism and the race/gender dichotomy in relation to multiple levels of discrimination are deeply rooted within the collective psyches of people in the United States and the West. While people of color and White women have historically confronted discriminatory issues, the antagonisms, albeit socially and politically constructed, center around the unspoken issue of race, specifically with regard to Whiteness and its resulting ability to influence power and control. The dominant voices within White feminism have not addressed this adequately, nor have they owned up to White middle-class, feminist ethnocentrism's share in the ideology that negates and marginalizes the experiences of women of color (Brand, 1987; Brewer, 1989; Cox, 1990; Garcia, 1989; Graham, 1991; Nain, 1991).

In asserting an Afrocentric feminism, Vivian Gordon's (1987) analysis makes the overall well-being of the whole African American community, male and female, the primary issue. She argues that coalitions between Black women and White women by their very nature negate, or at least jeopardize, Black women's ability to build stronger bonds with Black males here in the Americas as well as develop alliances and coalitions with Africans on the mother continent. She articulates a manifesto of sorts, a way of seeing the world and participating in it that confirms the writings as well as the lived experiences of African American women scholars. She further contends that, in depicting the lives of African American women, "the perspective which usually dominates [Women's Studies perspectives] is that of the radical feminist and the radial feminist lesbian who certainly present valid issues of oppression, but who do not represent the primary experiences of the pluralistic majority of Black women" (p. 15). Gordon identifies seven issues as the major concerns of African American women: education, employment, family (home and motherhood), housing (including health and crime), perceptions of self and role, leadership, and women's liberation (pp. 51–52). Her Afrocentric critique, on the other hand, "represents freedom from sexism and racism and em-

braces a Black female/male co-partnership in struggle and love" (p. 46).

Collins (1990) also has delineated aspects of the theoretical constructs and Afrocentric nature of Black feminist thought. She asserts that African American women intellectuals employ an "outsider-within" stance through which to critique the process of oppression; this allows them to look "with different eyes"— being able to see each aspect of oppression from a differing viewpoint. This outsider-within stance also reveals the contradictions between ideologies of womanhood and the devalued status of African American women. Moreover, she attests, African American women participate with but do not hold full membership in the community of the African American male, the White male, or the White feminist; to effect any change in this marginal status requires African American women to reclaim the black feminist intellectual tradition by discovering, reinterpreting, and analyzing their literary and intellectual works and societal deeds from an Afrocentric feminist standpoint. Collins's perspective employs three dimensions: concrete experience as a criterion of meaning, the use of dialogue in assessing knowledge claims, and an ethic of caring and concern for the totality of the entire African American community. In such a humanist vision of community, African American men and women alike are nurtured in order to confront oppressive social institutions.

Black feminist thought goes beyond race, gender, and class to include other social relationships of domination that revolve around religion, ethnicity, sexual orientation, and ageism. It addresses the ongoing epistemological debates in feminist theory and in the sociology of knowledge concerning ways of assessing truth. Such thought challenges the nature of proof and scientific validations of Eurocentric masculine political and epistemological requirements with which African American and other scholars are confronted within the academy. The Afrocentric feminist framework embraces social change as a change in individual consciousness coupled with the social transformation of political and economic institutions. This is especially relevant to those African American women scholars and activist leaders who are in positions to create real change in various ways.

THE BLACK STUDIES CULTURAL MODEL TOWARD A NEW WORLD CIVILIZATION

Waging the Canon War

One of the most contentious debates within U.S. contemporary higher education centers on the question of what a well-educated college graduate should know. While the nation's college campuses are the locations of the battles, at issue and at stake is the primacy of the Western or classical European tradition as represented in its sciences, metaphysics, and religion. The war is being waged to determine which canon will prevail in U.S. culture.

The canon war at the level of the university (and popular culture) could be characterized as a struggle between those identified as "liberals" who embrace "political correctness"

(Schultz, 1993) and those identified as "conservatives," traditionalists committed to preserving the Western canon. The latter count among their number individuals such as Will (1991), D'Souza (1991), Schlesinger (1992), Hirsch (1987), and Bloom (1988), and organizations such as the National Academy of Scholars (Adler, Starr, Chideya, Wingert, & Haac, 1990; Prescott, 1990). The forces behind the liberal assault on this canon have been identified by the conservatives as including postmodernist deconstructionist critics such as Lacan (1988), Derrida (1976), Foucault (1977a, 1977b, 1988), and Genovese (1991). More recently their numbers have been swelled by African Americans such as Diop (1974), Van Sertima (1976), Asante (1980, 1987, 1990), Hilliard (1976), Hale-Benson (1986), Mazrui (1986), Holloway (1990), and others who have asserted the presence of Africanisms in U.S. and world culture and the primacy of an Afrocentric (particularist) perspective. However, framing this contest in terms of a left/right dichotomy masks a more fundamental issue that both liberals and conservatives must concede: that competing realms of knowledge present alternative modes of knowing and being that challenge the conceptual system upon which the current canon is based.

As Taylor (1989) posits, when people are presented with two conceptual systems, they must reconcile the disparities between the two either by rejecting one or by seeing "each as constituting its own order of truth" (p. 118). This second alternative, "since it violates the notion of the unity of knowledge, tends to be unsatisfactory, unless some way is discovered of reconciling these orders on some more ultimate metaphysical ground" (p. 118). However, it may be that the contemporary critique of the canon of Western civilization is not a war of aggression against Western tradition, but instead a setting of the stage for a change—an attempt to call into question the current conceptual system of this society. Again, according to Taylor:

The conceptual system begins to dissolve when it questions its own foundations. The ultimate concepts of the system must remain sacred which is to say that they must remain unquestioned if they are to remain ultimate. . . . Institutional structures, whether marriage and the family, economics, educational, or state can remain sacred only so long as they are not open to question. To question is in a sense to profane, and indicates that another conceptual framework is in process of formation. (p. 123)

More interesting is the idea that the liberals may not really be desirous of straying too far from the sanctity of Western ideological hegemonic dominance; that they merely selectively accept or reject components of the canon at their convenience (Harvey, 1993). Critical academic discourses seldom reflect upon the privileging nature of Whiteness in U.S. society. It may be that both the right and the left have at the very least a vested interest in assuming that Western ascension will endure forever, and/or that there neither was a civilized world that preceded it, nor will there be such after Western domination of the global community ceases.

The fury surrounding the canon war, particularly the ferocious reaction of the conservatives to the generation of knowledge that does not use Western civilization as its ideological axis, may well speak to an effort to protect the sanctity of the currently prevailing conceptual systems rather than erode them. Yet, in a larger sense, the canon war is larger than the college and university curriculum; it is about questioning the sanctity of Western institutional structures as a whole. The nexus of relationships between the allies and opponents engaged in this conceptual discourse are complicated and provocative, and it is tempting to allow our gaze to be diverted from the issue that is the fundamental point of contention: that syllabi proceed from paradigms, collectively embraced, that describe to us who and what we are, what it is possible to know, and how we are to go about achieving such knowledge.

Framing the Cultural Question

One way of conceptualizing the perspective, criticism, and theorizing of African American intellectuals and pedagogists would be to employ what Bethel (1992) calls an African American *lieu de memoire*, a term adapted from the concept described by the French historian Pierre Nora (1984). According to Clark (1989), *lieu de memoire* refers to a setting for researching and remembering the "history of the Other." In Bethel's view, African Americans incorporate their *lieu de memoire* into "a consciously constructed history which revised and challenged the assumptions of inherent racial inferiority and the moral rightness of racial subordination implicit in the Euro-American cultural tradition" (Bethel, 1992, p. 828). Bethel's discussion is even more interesting when juxtaposed with Morrison's (1992) suggestion that the shaping of knowledge in the master narratives of traditional "canonical American literature" has been influence by Africanisms. Indeed, Morrison's critique offers several intriguing queries, such as: Are "the major and championed characteristics of our national [American] literature—individualism, masculinity, social engagement versus historical isolation . . . responses to a dark abiding, signing Africanist presence" (p. 5)? How has "the process of organizing American coherence through a distancing Africanism [become] the operative mode of a new cultural hegemony" (p. 8)? How have "agendas in criticism . . . disguised themselves and, in so doing, impoverished the literature it [*sic*] studies" (pp. 8–9)?

Using the field of literature as an example, Morrison (1992) contends that criticism, as a form of knowledge, is capable of robbing literature not only of its own implicit and explicit ideology but of its ideas as well. It can dismiss the arduous work writers perform to make an art that becomes and remains part of and significant within a human landscape. In American literature, particularly that of the United States, what becomes most obvious in this regard is the African presence and its influence in the entirety of American history and culture. Given this argument, America (the United States) would not be America as we know it today were it not for the presence and influence of Africanism. This observation becomes even more compelling in the context of the Black Studies cultural model. As described by Wynter (1990, 1992c), the Black Studies perspective is based on a cultural model, whereas the multicultural perspective is based on an infusion model. Using American literature to illustrate how these two different perspectives operate, Wynter makes the point that the original, most familiar way of thinking about American fiction is to consider it as being inclusive of the works of White American authors and, for the most part, exclusive of non-White American authors. Interestingly, this point could be surmised not only from reading Morrison (1992) but also from examining the curriculum being advocated by those critics of recent years who have given secondary school and higher education failing grades because of what they perceive as the lessening of the dominance of Western civilization (e.g., Bloom, 1988; Hirsch, 1987; Schlesinger, 1992). In an effort to preserve Western ideological and intellectual hegemony, these latter critics have proposed what has come to be called a "Great Books" response, or a curricular emphasis on the classical literature, science, arts, and humanities of Western societies. A multicultural perspective would argue for the revision of such a course to include works by non-White American authors. The Black Studies perspective, on the other hand, would raise several specific "cultural questions," such as "What are the prescriptive rules that determine [the] inclusion and exclusion [of particular forms of knowledge]?" (Wynter, 1992b, p. 6).

An example drawn from the social studies field is useful and even more compelling in showing the differences between the multicultural and Black Studies perspectives. That discussion centers around the recent textbook controversy in California, in which African American educational scholars and community leaders, along with individuals and groups representing other people of color in the state and throughout the United States, opposed the adoption of a particular series of social studies textbooks alleged to contain "egregious racial stereotyping, inaccuracies, distortions, omissions, justifications and trivialization of unethical and inhumane social practices, including racial slavery" (King, 1992a, p. 322). The controversy was categorized by those who defended the textbooks as ostensibly a multicultural argument. Resistance to the texts was framed as "a threat to national unity," to "E Pluribus Unum" itself (King, 1992a, p. 324). Multiculturalists were accused of offering "particularistic" and "racist" arguments against the texts, which claimed to depict the "pluralistic" and "true democratic" ideals of the mainstream; the ethnic studies approach was held as "un-American" (Ravitch, 1990; Schlesinger, 1990). King employs a Black Studies perspective in her critique of this controversy. She raises questions about the predominant intellectual perspectives and biases of those authoring the texts and the social interests they serve, concluding that "the clash in California is about ideology, not ethnicity; it is about how curricula and knowledge support dominating power relations through historical narratives that alienate Black students and other students of color" (p. 324).

Wynter's (1991, 1992a) perspectives on the textbook dispute reshape it as nothing less than an epistemological struggle that challenges the Anglo-Euro-American "master script" (Swartz, 1992), which conceives of America as a country of immigrants. By contrast, Wynter (1991) contends that, in the dawning of the 21st century, the United States is emerging as a unique entity in world history: the first "world" civilization, bringing with it global transformations and realignments of allegiance and power, particularly within the Third World. Her cultural question is the following: "Will America reinvest itself into a democratic egalitarian society or remain as it was originally invented,

a hierarchical society based on a structure of domination and subjugation?" For Wynter, the stakes are high: The planetary environment is at risk of being destroyed because of the logic of the collective behaviors of individuals groups and the way Western culture views science and humankind. In an earlier work, Wynter (1990) argues that, in Western culture, science is constituted by equal parts of scientific and narrative knowledge. More precisely, the narrative-knowledge side of science in Western society views humans as biogenetically evolved organisms, and it contends that there is a range or gradation within the species from the highest, most evolved, and genetically superior to the lowest, least evolved, and genetically inferior. A key component of this "scientific knowledge" is that Whiteness is situated at the highest level of genetic superiority, while Blackness is situated at the lowest level of genetic inferiority.

Wynter (1991) counters this view by proposing that humanness constitutes more than existence as a biological, genetically preprogrammed organism. That is, humans are preprogrammed to be human, but their humanness "comes into being when humans initiate a cultural system which is a moral and ethical system coded in the [founding] narrative." Her Black Studies cultural model proposes a conceptual system of a universal (world) culture in which human beings are viewed "not as genetically bonded and separated" but as symbolically kin-related. Her model fits the definition of autochthonous science in that it originates from the particular perspective of the African American reality, part of which includes the preservation of African conceptualizations and ways of thought and living—in effect, its *lieu de memoire*. These conceptualizations transform Judeo-Christianity into an Afro-Judeo-Christian popular culture that represents what Wynter considers to be the first emerging universal culture.

In articulating the contemporary challenge facing African American scholars, Wynter (1984, 1991) draws parallels with the situation facing scholars of the 13th and 15th centuries, which the lay humanist intellectuals struggled against the intellectual hegemony of the church and clergy over the people. These lay intellectuals challenged the "regimes of truth" by deconstructing intellectual knowledge, that is, the scientific and narrative knowledge, which ultimately led to the end of the church's hegemony over knowledge and to the secularization of human beings. The contemporary challenge for African American scholars is the deconstruction of the body of knowledge within the academy and the reinvention of the "unum" that reflects this vision of humanity and the emergent universal popular culture.

Implications for Praxis

Societal Institutions such as the schools, the media, and the justice system have unwittingly contributed to the political development of children in contemporary society. As increasing youth alienation and crime rates demonstrate, communities of children and youth have accurately surmised that their political position in this society is that of fringe dwellers with very little at stake in the maintenance of the societal status quo. With regard to African American communities, from the so-called middle class to the working poor, young people not only see disparity and injustice but are questioning, and even rejecting, current societal values and beliefs. Simultaneously, they are constructing their own cultural contexts. While African American (or any) popular youth culture is by no means monolithic, as demonstrated by the various controversies involving "rap" artists and the texts of their music (Baker, 1993; Lusane, 1993; Powell, 1991; Rose, 1991), it posits a political view that challenges the dominant society (Hall, 1992). The cultural artifacts to which African American youth resonate (i.e., rap, music, fashion, film, politics) challenge the current systems and institutions of American society by admonishing students not to participate in American domination and subordination of other people (Powell, 1991; Rose, 1991). These youth have developed social systems, practices, and beliefs that are drastically contrary to the traditional norms of the African American community.

Inner-city African American youth, who may not be literate in the great Western works so highly regarded by Bloom (1988) and Hirsch (1987), know the difference between the political ideologies espoused by Malcolm X and Martin Luther King, Jr., and by and large they are choosing Malcolm X's notion of obtaining justice "by any means necessary," partly because of their dawning awareness of the reality in which they live. Repeated scenarios of social injustice and inequity for people of color in the United States, coupled with these young people's growing belief that current economic social configurations will never allow them access to the realms of power enjoyed by society's elites, result in their rejection of the ideal of Whiteness as either a conceptual or an institutional system.

The danger remains that in African American youths' alienation from and rejection of Whiteness, in their equating and rejecting rigorous academic preparation as "acting White," these young people may actually contribute to their own deskilling and devaluation in society (Fordham, 1988; Fordham & Ogbu, 1986). Nonetheless, they provide an interesting barometer of what may constitute the cutting edge of the emerging "global" culture of the United States. As Troyna and Hatcher (1992) and Fuller (1991) contend, the critical theorizing and knowledge construction affecting the education of children of color, in Western societies like the United States as well as in the Third World, is a struggle over ideology rather than pedagogy.

One of the more important questions asked by the Black Studies critique is relatively straightforward: In whose interest and for what purpose will Black children and other children of color in the United States be educated? Will that education function as a mode of ideological domination, working to co-opt and adapt these groups of students to the dominant societal hierarchy, or will it function as a force of social reconstruction to help them redefine the nature of their own lives? As Wynter (1991) asks: "What must be the 'regime of truth' operating in school curriculum that manages to produce [and reproduce], regularly and precisely, the racial stratification beween and among groups we see in [American] society?" The Black Studies cultural model, as an autochthonous critique, aptly challenges this regime. However, critique alone will not change concep-

tual systems by arguing that they work in the interest of some particular groups as opposed to other groups. Theorists, working with practitioners, must expand their engagement of these conceptualizations to encompass the creation of institutions and systems that transcend the current realms of knowledge. In teacher education, this means the inclusion of African American educational theorizing and pedagogy in both preservice and inservice courses, not as an isolated multicultural course requirement but as part of the teacher-education curriculum at large. Numerous examples of African Americans' visions of praxis can guide such efforts (e.g., Crichlow et al., 1990; Gordon 1982; Henry, 1992; Hilliard, 1992; Hollins & Spencer, 1990; Jansen, 1990; King, 1992a, 1992b; Ladson-Billings, 1992; Ladson-Billings & Henry, 1990; Lee, Lomotey, & Shujaa, 1990).

In the postindustrial and postmodern American society of the 21st century, the most critical educational struggle for people of color will be for control over the academic, intellectual, and political development of their children. That this struggle will be compounded by the economics of the new world order, the downsizing and restructuring of the U.S. economy and workforce, and the emergence of the Third World makes the issue of the kind of education that African American youth receive absolutely critical. The conceptual systems that govern the production of knowledge, and that regulate educational discourse, meaning, and the resulting societal behaviors and configurations, will no doubt be marshalled to control autochthonous critiques and social action. However, the brute force of domination alone will not quell, let alone resolve, what will amount to social and, more specifically, pedagogical rebellion.

Educational pedagogists concerned with the education of African American children must address or deconstruct their own culpability in the marginalization and/or absence of the work of African American educational theorists. Outside of the academy, there are also opportunities for service in the African American community itself. African American educational scientists and theorists can work in and study community organizations, academic institutions, churches, and civic groups. As the work of Anderson (1988), Henry (1992), King (1992a, 1992b) and Lee et al. (1990) has shown, self-help efforts such as Saturday Schools, private/independent African American institutions, parent/community meetings and workshops, and church-based academic tutorial initiatives have long been part of the landscape of applied research and educational activism in the African American community.

The historical goals of the African American community's autochthonous models of knowing and being, its generation of cultural knowledge, and its efforts at institution building have been economic autonomy, political power, self-help, civic service, and nationalism (B. Gordon, 1985), or, as Crummell (1987/1969) asserted, "the generation of a civilization" (p. 4). The emergence of a "global" U.S. society from the Afro-Judeo-Christian popular culture is being born in part out of this challenge to reconfigure the dominant realms of truth and rational knowledge. Those who support as well as oppose this challenge understand well what is at stake: It is nothing less than the influence, power, and control of the future direction of this society and the global community at large.

References

Adler, J., Starr, M., Chideya, F., Wingert, P., & Haac, L. (1990, December). Taking offense: Is this the new enlightenment on campus or the new McCarthyism? *Newsweek*, pp. 48–54.

Alkalimat, A. H. I. (1973). The ideology of Black social science. In J. Ladner (Ed.), *The death of white sociology* (pp. 173–189). New York: Vintage.

American Negro Academy. (1969). *The American Negro Academy: Ocasional papers, 1–22*. New York: Arno Press and *The New York Times*.

Anderson, J. (1988). *The education of Blacks in the South, 1860–1935*. Chapel Hill: University of North Carolina Press.

Anyon, J. (1980). Social class and the hidden curriculum of work. *Journal of Education*, *162*(1), 67–92.

Apple, M. (1990). *Ideology and curriculum* (2nd ed.). New York: Routledge

Apple, M. (1993). *Official knowledge: Democratic education in a conservative age*. New York: Routledge.

Apple, M., & Weiss, L. (Eds.). (1983). *Ideology and practice in schooling*. Philadelphia: Temple University Press.

Aronowitz, S. (1981). *The crisis in historical materialism: Class, politics and culture in Marxist theory*. New York: Praeger.

Aronowitz, S. (1992). *The politics of identity: Class, culture, social movements*. New York: Routledge.

Asante, M. K. (1980). *Afrocentricity: The theory of social change*. Buffalo, NY: Amulefi.

Asante, M. K. (1987). *The Afrocentric idea*. Phildelphia: Temple University Press.

Asante, M. K. (1990). *Kemet, Afrocentricity, and knowledge*. Trenton, NJ: Africa World Press.

Baker, H. A., Jr. (1993). *Black studies, rap and the academy*. Chicago: University of Chicago Press.

Banks, J. A. (1969). A content analysis of the Black American in textbooks. *Social Education*, *33*, 954–957, 963.

Banks, J. A. (Ed.). (1973). *Teaching ethnic studies: Concepts and strategies* (43rd Yearbook). Washington, DC: National Council for the Social Studies.

Banks, J. A. (1981). *Multiethnic education: Theory and practice (1st ed.)*. Boston: Allyn and Bacon.

Banks, J. A. (1988). *Multiethnic education: Theory and practice (2nd ed.). Boston: Allyn and Bacon*.

Banks, J. A. (1991). *Teaching strategies for ethnic studies* (5th ed.). Boston: Allyn and Bacon.

Banks, J. A., & Banks, C. A. M. (Eds.). (1989). *Multicultural education: Issues and perspectives*. Boston: Allyn and Bacon.

Bethel, E. R. (1992). Images of Hayti: The construction of an Afro-American lieu de memoire. *Callaloo*, *15*(3), 827–841.

Blassingame, J. W., & McKivigan, J. R. (Eds.). (1979). *The Frederick Douglass papers, Series one: Speeches, debates and interviews, 1864–80* (Vol. 4). New Haven, CT: Yale University Press.

Bloom, A. (1988). *The closing of the American mind*. New York: Simon & Schuster.

Bourdieu, P. (1977). Cultural reproduction and social reproduction. In J. Karabel & A. H. Halsey (Eds.), *Power and ideology in education* (pp. 487–510). New York: Oxford University Press.

Bowser, B. (1981). The contribution of Blacks to sociological knowledge: A problem of theory and role to 1950. *Phylon*, *42*, 180–193.

Bracey, J., Meier, A., & Rudwick, E. (1973). The Black sociologists: The first half century. In J. Ladner (Ed.), *The death of Wite sociology* (pp. 3–22). New York: Vintage.

Brand, D. (1987). Black women and work: The impact of racially constructed gender roles on the sexual division of labour, part one. *Fireweed*, *25*, 28–37.

Brewer, R. M. (1989). Black women and feminist sociology: The emerging perspective. *American Sociologist*, *20*(1), 57–70.

Bunch, C. (1975). Not for lesbians alone. *Quest: A Feminist Quarterly*, *2*(2), 50–56.

Burgess, E. (1928). Residential segregation in American cities. *The Annals*, *140*, 105–115.

Burgess, E. (1961). Social planning and race relations. In J. Masuoka & P. Valien (Eds.), *Race relations, probelms and theory: Essays in honor of Robert E. Park* (pp. 13–25). Chapel Hill: University of North Carolina Press.

Bushby, M. (Ed.). (1992). *Daughters of Africa: An international anthology of words and writings by women of African descent from ancient Egyptian to the present*. New York: Pantheon.

Butler, D. (1992). To my father. In M Bushby (Ed.), *Daughters of Africa: An international anthology of words and writings by women of African descent from ancient Egyptian to the present* (pp. 923–924). New York: Pantheon.

Carby, H. V. (1987). *Reconstructing womanhood: The emergence of the Afro-American woman novelist*. New York: Oxford University Press.

Carby, H. (1992). The multicultural wars. In G. Dent (Ed.), *Black popular culture: A project by Michele Wallace* (pp. 187–199). Seattle, WA: Bay Press.

Childs, J. B. (1981). Concepts of culture in Afro-American political thought, 1890–1920. *Social Text: Theory/Culture/Ideology*, *2*(1), 28–43.

Childs, J. B. (1991). Notes on the Gulf War, racism and African American social thought. *Journal of Urban and Cultural Studies*, *2*(1), 81–92.

Clark, V. (1989, May 12). *Performing the memory of difference in Afro-Caribbean dance: Katherine Dunham's choreography, 1938–1987*. Paper presented at the Dunham Symposium, Stanford University, Stanford, CA.

Collins, P. H. (1990). *Black feminist thought: Knowledge, consciousness and the politics of empowerment*. New York: Routledge, Chapman & Hall.

Cox, C. (1990). Anything less is not feminism: Racial difference and the W. M. W. M. (White middle-class women's movement). *Law and Critique*, *1*(2), 237–248.

Crichlow, W., Goodwin, S., Shakes, G., & Swartz, E. (1990). Multicultural ways of knowing: Implications for practice. *Journal of Education*, *172*(2), 101–117.

Crummell, A. (1969). Civilization: The primal need for the race. In *The American Negro Academy: Occasional papers, 1–22*. New York: Arno Press and *The New York Times*. (Original work published 1897)

Derrida, J. (1976). *Of grammatology* (G. Spivak, Trans.). Baltimore, MD: Johns Hopkins University Press.

Derrida, J. (1983). The principal of reason: The universal in the eyes of its pupils. *Diacritics*, *13*(3), 3–20.

Diop, C. A. (1974). *The African origins of civilization: Myth or reality?* (M. Cook, Trans.). Westport, CT: Lawrence Hill.

Doyle, B. W. (1937). *The etiquette of race relations in the South: A study in social control*. Chicago: University of Chicago Press.

Drake, St. C., & Cayton, H. (1945). *Black metropolis: A study of Negro life in a northern city*. New York: Harcourt, Brace.

D'Souza, D. (1991). *Illiberal education: The politics of race and sex on campus*. New York: The Free Press.

DuBois, W. E. B. (1903). *The souls of Black folks*. Chicago: A. C. McClurg.

DuBois, W. E. B. (1973a). *The Philadelphia Negro: A social study*. Millwood, NY: Kraus-Thomson. (Original work published 1899)

DuBois, W. E. B. (1973b). *The Suppression of the African slave trade to the United States of America, 1638–1870.* Millwood, NY: Kraus-Thomson. (Original work published 1896)

DuBois, W. E. B., & Dill, A. G. (Eds). (1911). *The common school and the Negro American* (Atlanta University Publications No. 16). Atlanta, GA: Altanta University Press.

Ellison, R. (1973). An American dilemma: A review. In J. Ladner (Ed.), *The death of White sociology* (pp. 81–95). New York: Vintage.

Fontaine, W. (1940). An interpretation of contemporary Negro thought from the standpoint of the sociology of knowledge. *Journal of Negro History, 25*(1), 6–13.

Fontaine, W. (1983). "Social determination" in the writing of Negro scholars. In L. Harris (Ed.), *Philosophy born of struggle: An anthology of Afro-American philosophy from 1917* (pp. 89–106). Dubuque, IA: Kendall Hunt.

Fordham, S. (1988). Racelessness as a factor in Black students' school success: Pragmatic strategy or pyrrhic victory? *Harvard Educational Review, 58*(1), 54–84.

Fordham, S., & Ogbu, J. U. (1986). Black students' school success: Coping with the burden of "acting White." *The Urban Review, 18,* 176–206.

Foucault, M. (1970). *The order of things.* New York: Random House.

Foucault, M. (1977a). *Language, counter-memory, practice: Selected essays and interviews* (D. Bouchard, Ed.). Ithaca, NY: Cornell University Press.

Foucault, M. (1977b). *Power and knowledge: Selected interviews and other writings* (G. Gordon, Ed.). New York: Pantheon.

Foucault, M. (1979). *Discipline and punishment: The birth of the prison* (A. Sheridan, Trans.). New York: Vintage.

Foucault, M. (1988). *Politics, philosophy and culture: Interviews and other writings, 1977–1984* (L. D. Kritzman, Ed.). New York: Routledge.

Frazier, E. F. (1932). *The Negro in the United States.* New York: Macmillan.

Frazier, E. F. (1937). The impact of urban civilization upon Negro family life. *American Sociological Review, 2*(5), 609–618.

Frazier, E. F. (1939). *The Negro family in the United States.* Chicago: University of Chicago Press.

Freire, P. (1968). *Pedagogy of the oppressed.* New York: Seabury Press.

Freire, P. (1973). *Education for critical consciousness.* New York: Seabury Press.

Freire, P. (1978). *Pedagogy in process: Letters to Guinea-Bissau.* New York: Seabury Press.

Fuller, B. (1991). *Growing-up modern: The western state builds third world schools.* New York: Routledge, Chapman & Hall.

Garcia, A. M. (1989). The development of Chicana feminist discourse, 1970–1980. *Gender and Society, 3*(2), 217–238.

Gay, G., & Baber, W. L. (Eds.). (1987). *Expressively Black: The cultural basis of ethnic identity.* New York: Praeger.

Genovese, E. D. (1991, April). Hersey, yes—sensitivity, no. *The New Republic,* pp. 30–35.

Giddings, F. (1935). *Principles of sociology.* New York: Follett.

Giddings, P. (1984). *When and where I enter: The impact of Black women on race and sex in America.* New York: Bantam Books.

Giroux, H. (1978). Writing and critical thinking in social studies. *Curriculum Inquiry, 8*(4), 291–310.

Giroux, H. (1981). *Ideology, culture and the process of schooling.* Philadelphia: Temple University Press.

Giroux, H. (1983). *Theory and resistance in education: A pedagogy for the opposition.* South Hadley, MA: Bergin & Garvey.

Giroux, H. (1992). *Border crossings: Cultural workers and the politics of education.* New York: Routledge, Chapman & Hall.

Giroux, H., & McLaren, P. (Eds.). (1989). *Critical pedagogy, the state and cultural struggle.* Albany: State University of New York Press.

Golden, M. (1992). "Crystal," an excerpt from *A woman's place.* In M. Bushby (Ed.), *Daughters of Africa: An international anthology of words and writings by women of African descent from ancient Egyptian to the present* (pp. 819–823). New York Pantheon.

Gordon, B. (1982). Toward a theory of knowledge acquisition for Black children. *Journal of Education, 64*(1), 90–108.

Gordon, B. (1985). Toward emancipation in citizenship education: The case of African American cultural knowledge. *Theory and Research in Social Education, 12*(4), 1–23.

Gordon, B. (1990). The necessity of African American epistemology for educational theory and practice. *Journal of Education, 172*(3), 88–106.

Gordon, B. (1992). The marginalized discourse of minority intellectual thought in traditional writings on teaching. In C. Grant (Ed.), *Research and multicultural education: From the margins to the mainstream* (pp. 19–31). London: Falmer Press.

Gordon, B. (1993). African American cultural knowledge and liberatory education: Dilemmas, problems and potentials in a postmodern American society. *Urban Education, 27*(4), 448–470.

Gordon, B. (in press). The fringe dwellers: African-American women scholars in the postmodern era. In B. Kanpol & P. McLaren (Eds.), *Education, democracy and the voice of the other.* Westport, CT: Greenwood Press.

Gordon, V. (1987). *Black women, feminism and Black liberation: Which way?* Chicago: Third World Press.

Gore, J. (1993). *The struggle for pedagogies: Critical and feminist discourses and regimes of truth.* New York: Routledge.

Graham, H. (1991). The concept of caring in feminist research: The case of domestic service. *Sociology, 25*(1), 61–78.

Gramsci, A. (1971). *Selections from the prison notebooks* (Q. Hoare & G. N. Smith, Eds. & Trans.). New York: International Publishers.

Grant, C. A. (Ed.). (1977). *Multicultural education: Commitments, issues, and applications.* Washington, DC: Association for Supervision and Curriculum Development.

Grant, C. A. (Ed.). (1992). *Research and multicultural education: From the margins to the mainstream.* London: Falmer Press.

Greene, M. (1992). The passions of pluralism. *Journal of Negro Education, 61*(3), 250–261.

Grundy, S. (1987). *Curriculum: Product of praxis.* London: Falmer Press.

Hale-Benson, J. (1986). *Black children: Their roots, culture and learning styles* (rev. ed.). Baltimore, MD: Johns Hopkins University Press.

Hall, S. (1992). What is the "Black" in Black popular culture? In G. Dent (Ed.), *Black popular culture: A project by Michele Wallace* (pp. 21–33). Seattle, WA: Bay Press.

Harvey, W. B. (1993, July 29). Remembering Lani Guinier and the multiculturalist agenda. *Black Issues in Higher Education,* p. 56.

Held, D. (1980). *Introduction to critical theory: Horkheimer to Habermas.* Berkeley: University of California Press.

Henry, A. (1992). African Canadian women teachers' activism: Recreating communities of caring and resistance. *Journal of Negro Education, 61*(3), 392–404.

Hilliard, A. G., III. (1976). *Alternatives to IQ testing: An approach to the identification of gifted "minority" children* (Final report to the California State Department of Education, Special Education Support Unit). Sacramento: California State Department of Education. (ERIC Document Reproduction Service No. ED 146 009)

Hilliard, A. G., III. (1992). Behavioral style, culture, and teaching and learning. *Journal of Negro Education, 61*(3), 370–377.

Hirsch, E. D. (1987). *Cultural literacy: What every American needs to know.* Boston: Houghton Mifflin.

Hollins, E. R., & Spencer, K. (1990). Restructuring schools for cultural inclusion: Changing the schooling process for African American youngsters. *Journal of Education, 172*(2), 89–100.

Holloway, J. (Ed.). (1990). *Africanisms in American culture.* Bloomington: Indiana University Press.

hooks, b. (1984). *Feminist theory from margin to center.* Boston: South End Press.

hooks, b. (1992). Dialectically down with the critical program. In G. Dent (Ed.), *Black popular culture: A project by Michele Wallace* (pp. 48–55). Seattle, WA: Bay Press.

Horkheimer, M. (1972). *Critical theory: Selected essays* (M. J. O'Connell et al., Trans.). New York: Herder & Herder.

Hull, G., Bell-Scott, P., & Smith, B. (Eds.). (1982). *All the women are White, all the Blacks are men, but some of us are brave.* New York: Feminist Press at CUNY.

James, J., & Farmer, R. (1993). *Spirit, space and survival. African American women in (White academe.* New York: Routledge.

Jansen, J. (1990). In search of liberation pedagogy in South Africa. *Journal of Education, 172*(3), 62–71.

Jay, M. (1973). *The dialectical imagination: A history of the Frankfurt School and the Institute of Social Research, 1923–1950.* Boston: Little, Brown.

Johnson, C. S. (1930). *The Negro in American civilization: A study of Negro life and race relations in the light of social research.* New York: Henry Holt.

Johnson, C. S. (1934). *Shadow of the plantation.* Chicago: University of Chicago Press.

Johnson, C. S. (1938). *The Negro college graduate.* Chapel Hill: University of North Carolina Press.

Johnson, C. S. (1951). *Education and the cultural crisis.* New York: Macmillan.

Jones, R. (1973). Proving Black inferior: The sociology of knowledge. In J. Ladner (Ed.), *The death of White sociology* (pp. 114–135). New York: Vintage.

Joseph, G. (1981). White promotion, Black survival. In G. Joseph & J. Lewis, *Common differences: Conflicts in Black and White feminists perspectives,* Boston: South End Press.

Kaiser, E. (1969). Introduction. In *The American Negro Academy: Occasional papers, 1–22* (pp. i–xiii). New York: Arno Press and *The New York Times.*

Karabel, J., & Halsey, A. H. (Eds.). (1977). *Power and ideology in education.* New York: Oxford University Press.

Keddie, N. (1975). Classroom knowledge. In M. F. D. Young (Ed.), *Knowledge and control: New directions for the sociology of education* (pp. 133–160). London: Collier-Macmillan.

King, J. E. (1992a). Diaspora literacy and consciousness in the struggle against miseducation in the Black community. *Journal of Negro Education, 61*(3), 317–340.

King, J. E. (1992b, April). *The middle passage revisited: Diaspora literacy and consciousness in the struggle against "miseducation" in the Black community.* Paper presented at a symposium on "New Challenges to the 'Regimes of Truth': Toward a New Intellectual Order," at the annual meeting of the American Educational Research Association, San Francisco, CA.

King, J. E., & Wilson, T. L. (1990). Being the soul-freeing substance: A legacy of hope in Afro humanity. *Journal of Education, 172*(2), 9–27.

Lacan, J. (1988). *Speech and language in psychoanalysis* (A. Wilden, Trans.). Baltimore, MD: Johns Hopkins University Press.

Ladson-Billings, G. (1992). Liberatory consequences of literacy: A case of culturally relevant instruction for African American students. *Journal of Negro Education, 61*(3), 378–391.

Ladson-Billings, G., & Henry, A. (1990). Blurring the borders: Voices of African liberatory pedagogy in the United States and Canada. *Journal of Education, 721*(2), 72–88.

Lather, P. (1991). *Getting smart: Feminist research and pedagogy with/in the postmodern.* New York: Routledge, Chapman & Hall.

Lee, C., Lomotey, K., & Shujaa, M. (1990). How shall we sing our sacred song in a strange land? The dilemma of double consciousness and the complexities of an African-centered pedagogy. *Journal of Education, 172*(2), 45–62.

Lerner, G. (Ed.). (1973). *Black women in White America: A documentary history.* New York: Vintage.

Locke, A. (Ed.). (1925). *The new Negro.* New York: Albert & Charles Boni.

Loewenberg, B. J., & Bogin, R. (Eds.). (1987). *Black women in nineteenth-century American life: Their words, their thoughts, their feelings.* University Park: Pennsylvania State University Press.

Lorde, A. (1978). Scratching the surface: Some notes on barriers to women and loving. *Black Scholar, 9*(7), 31–35.

Lusane, C. (1993). Rap, race, and politics. *Race and Class, 35*(1), 41–56.

Lyotard, J. (1984). *The postmodern condition.* Minneapolis: University of Minnesota Press.

Marcuse, H. (1964). *One-dimensional man: Studies in the ideology of advanced industrial society.* Boston: Beacon Press.

Mazrui, A. (1986). *The Africans: A triple heritage.* Boston: Little, Brown.

McCarthy, C. (1990). Multicultural education, minority identities, textbooks and the challenge of curriculum reform. *Journal of Education, 172*(2), 118–129.

Meier, A., & Rudwick, E. (1986). *Black history and the historical profession, 1915–1980.* Urbana: University of Illinois Press.

Mirza, H. (1992). *Young, female and Black.* London: Routledge.

Morrison, T. (1992). *Playing in the dark: Whiteness and the literary imagination.* Cambridge, MA: Harvard University Press.

Moss, A. A., Jr. (1981). *The American Negro academy: Voice of the talented tenth.* Baton Rouge: Louisiana State University Press.

Nain, G. T. (1991). Black women, sexism and racism: Black or antiracist feminism? *Feminist Review, 37,* 1–22.

National Education Association. (1893). *Report of the committee on secondary school studies.* Washington, DC: Government Printing Office.

National Education Association. (1895). *Report of the committee of fifteen on elementary education, with the reports of the sub-committees: On the training of teachers; on the correlation of studies in elementary education; on the organization of city school systems.* New York: American Book.

Nora, P. (1984). Entre memoire et histoire, la problematique des lieux. In P. Nora (Ed.), *Les lieux de memoire* (pp. xiii–xvii). Paris: Gallimard.

Odum, H. (1910). *Social and mental traits of the Negro.* New York: Longmans, Green.

Opitz, M. (1992). Afro-German. In M. Bushby (Ed.), *Daughters of Africa: An international anthology of words and writings by women of African descent from ancient Egyptian to the present* (pp. 935–936). New York: Pantheon.

Park, R. E. (1931). The mentality of racial hybrids. *American Journal of Sociology, 36,* 534–551.

Park, R. E., & Burgess, E. (1924). *Introduction to the science of sociology.* Chicago: University of Chicago Press.

Park. R. E., & Miller, H. A. (1921). *Old world traits transplanted.* New York: Harper Brothers.

Popkewitz, T. (1987). *Critical studies in teacher education: Folklore, theory and practice.* Bristol, PA: Taylor & Frances.

Popkewitz, T. (1988). Culture, pedagogy and power: Issues in the production of values and colonialization. *Journal of Education, 170*(2), 77–90.

Powell, C. T. (1991). Rap music: An education with a beat from the street. *Journal of Negro Education, 60*(3), 245–259.

Prescott, P. S. (1990, December). Learning to love the PC canon. *Newsweek,* pp. 50–51.

Ravitch, D. (1990). Multiculturalism: E. pluribus plures? *The American Scholar, 59*, 337–354.

Reid, I. A. (1936). *Adult education among Negroes*. Washington, DC: Associates in Negro Folk Education.

Reid, I. A. (1939). *The Negro immigrant: His background, characteristics and social adjustment, 1899–1937*. New York: Columbia University Press.

Reid, I. A. (1940). *In a minor key: Negro youth in story and fact*. Washington, DC: American Council on Education.

Roman, C. W. (1911). *A knowledge of history is conducive to racial solidarity . . . and other writings*. Nashville, TN: Sunday School Union.

Rose, R. (1991). "Fear of a Black planet": Rap music and Black cultural politics in the 1990s. *Journal of Negro Education, 60*(3), 276–290.

Sached, (1985). *Working women: A portrait of South African women workers*. Braamfontein, South Africa: Raven Press.

Schlesinger, A. M., Jr. (1992). *The disuniting of America: Reflections on a multicultural society*. New York: Norton.

Schroyer, T. (1975). *The critique of domination: The origins and development of critical theory*. Boston: Beacon Press.

Schultz, D. L. (1993). *To reclaim a legacy of diversity: Analyzing the "political correctness" debates in higher education*. New York: The National Council for Research on Women.

Shor, I. (1986). *Culture wars: School and society in the conservative restoration*. Boston: Routledge & Kegan Paul.

Shor, I. (1987). *Critical teaching and everyday life*. Chicago: University of Chicago Press.

Shor, I. (Ed.). (1988). *Freire for the classroom: A sourcebook for liberatory teaching*. Portsmouth, RI: Boynton/Cook.

Shor, I., & Freire, P. (1987). *A pedagogy for liberation: Dialogues on transforming education*. South Hadley, MA: Bergin & Garvey.

Slater, P. (1977). *Origin and significance of the Frankfurt school*. London: Routledge & Kegan Paul.

Spencer, H. (1864). *First principles*. New York: D. Appleton.

Spencer, H. (1885). Education: Intellectual, moral and physical. New York: John Alden.

Spencer, H. (1961). *The study of sociology*. Ann Arbor: University of Michigan Press. (Original work published 1873)

Sterling, D. (Ed.). (1984). *We are your sisters: Black women in the nineteenth century*. New York: Norton.

Sumner, W. G. (1966). *Folkways*. Boston: Ginn.

Swartz, E. (1992). Emancipatory narratives: Rewriting the master script in the school curriculum. *Journal of Negro Education, 61*(3), 341–355.

Taylor, S. (1989). *Conceptions of institutions and the theory of knowledge* (2nd ed.). New Brunswick, NJ: Transaction.

Troyna, B., & Hatcher, R. (1992). *Racism in children's lives*. London: Routledge, Chapman & Hall.

Turner, R. (Ed.). (1967). *Robert E. Park on social control and collective behavior*. Chicago: University of Chicago Press.

Vallance, E. (1977). Hiding the hidden curriculum: An interpretation of the language of justification in nineteenth-century educational reform. In A. Bellack & H. Kliebard (Eds.), *Curriculum and evaluation* (pp. 590–607). Berkeley, CA: McCutchan.

Van Sertima, I. (1976). *They came before Columbus*. New York: Random House.

Ward, L. F. (1903). *Pure sociology: A treatise on the origin and spontaneous development of society*. New York: Macmillan.

Ward, L. F. (1906). *The psychic factors of civilization*. Boston: Ginn.

Washington, M. H. (Ed.). (1987). *Invented lives: Narratives of Black women, 1860–1960*. New York: Anchor Press.

West, C. (1992). Nihilism in Black America. In G. Dent (Ed.), *Black popular culture: A project by Michele Wallace* (pp. 37–47). Seattle, WA: Bay Press.

West, C. (1993). *Race matters*. Boston: Beacon Press.

Will, G. (1991, May 6). Curdled politics on campus. *Newsweek*, p. 72.

Woodson, C. G. (1968). *The education of the Negro prior to 1861*. New York: Arno Press and *The New York Times*. (Original work published 1919)

Woodson, C. G. (1977). *The mis-education of the Negro*. New York: AMS Press. (Original work published 1933)

Wynter, S. (1984). New Seville and the conversion experience of Bartolome de Las Casas. *Jamaica Journali, 17*(2), 25–32.

Wynter, S. (1990, September). *America as a "world": A Black studies perspective and "cultural model" framework*. Letter to the California State Board of Education.

Wynter, S. (1991, July 27). *Diaspora literacy and the Black studies perspective in curriculum change*. Lecture/Paper presented at a seminar on "Diaspora Literacy," Santa Clara University, Santa Clara, CA.

Wynter, S. (1992a, April). *The challenge to our episteme: The case of the California textbook controversy*. Paper presented at a symposium on "New Challenges to the 'Regimes of Truth': Toward a New Intellectual Order," at the annual meeting of the American Educational Research Association, San Francisco, CA.

Wynter, S. (1992b). *Do not call us Negros: How multicultural textbooks perpetuate the ideology of racism*. San Jose, CA: Aspire Books.

Wynter, S. (1992c). Re-thinking aesthetics: Notes toward a deciphering practice. In M. Cham (Ed.), *Ex-iles: Essays on Caribbean cinema* (pp. 237–279). Trenton, NJ: Africa World Press.

Young, M. F. D. (Ed.). (1975). *Knowledge and control: New direction for the sociology of education*. London: Collier-Macmillan.

ETHNIC GROUPS IN HISTORICAL AND SOCIAL SCIENCE RESEARCH

12

HISTORICAL AND SOCIAL SCIENCE RESEARCH ON MEXICAN AMERICANS

Ramón A. Gutiérrez

UNIVERSITY OF CALIFORNIA, SAN DIEGO

Historical and social science research on Mexican Americans has a long tradition in the United States that reaches back more than a century and a half. At various points in this history, Mexican Americans have been characterized as a regionally conquered people, as an immigrant group, as a minority, as a nationality, and as an emerging majority population. In this historiographical survey the extant scholarship under review has been divided thematically into five subsections: Mexicans as a Regionally Conquered People, 1821–1880; The Mexican as Immigrant, 1880–1993; The Mexican American Minority, 1920–1965; Chicanos as a Nationality, 1965–1993; and Recent Research Trends, 1985–1993. The dates following each of these subsections denote when a particular theme and specific representation of the Mexican was prominent in the scholarly literature. Sometimes the actual research was produced in the period under review, but often it was not; as any bibliophile will attest, revisionist research continues, produced every day. Bear in mind, too, that the five themes and periods elaborated here are rough approximations for the primacy of specific discourses on the Mexican population in the United States. Obviously, population movements, paradigm shifts, and the diffusion of information do not always conform to such neat temporal and thematic divides. The same can be said of ethnic Mexicans in the United States. They have moved across the U.S.-Mexico border over the course of many years, producing population nodes in which conquered residents, immigrant workers, assimilated Mexican Americans, and nationalistic Chicanos all reside side by side.

MEXICANS AS A REGIONALLY CONQUERED PEOPLE, 1821–1880

Mexicans first attracted the attention of the American reading public in 1821 when the newly independent Republic of Mexico began welcoming the world's traders and settlers. Mexico's leaders were convinced that if they did not populate the vast expanses of seemingly "vacant" national territory, it would quickly become the envy of expansionistic neighbors. To accomplish this, in 1824 Mexico promulgated a colonization law that encouraged immigrants to petition for land and settlement grants. Scouts from the United States seeking natural resources, merchants in search of markets, trappers hunting pelts, settlers desperate for land, and adventurers seeking just that, responded rapidly to Mexico's newly opened borders. They arrived in *Nuevo México* (New Mexico), which had been colonized in 1598, in *Tejas* (Texas) and the *Pimería Alta* (southern Arizona), whose settlements dated from the 1720s, and in the towns of *Alta California*, colonized in the years following 1769. These were the only population centers that had been established in Mexico's far north under Spanish colonial rule. The Kingdom of New Mexico, which in the colonial period encompassed the northern half of Arizona, was by far the most densely populated in 1820, with some 28,500 nominally "Spanish" settlers and 10,000 Christianized Indian residents. California boasted a populace of 3,400 "Spaniards" and 23,000 mission Indians; Arizona counted about 700 "Spanish" and 1,400 Indian mission residents; and Texas had roughly 4,000 "Spaniards" and 800 Christianized Indians congregated in missions (R. A. Gutiérrez, 1991, 1992).

The men and women who ventured from the United States into Mexican territory, and who were literate enough to record their observations and experiences, became important cultural mapmakers for their stay-at-home compatriots, as literary historian Martin Padget (1993) has explained. As the initial mappers of a complex cultural terrain, these early 19th-century American writers were largely responsible for creating the textual types and stereotypes of the Mexican that would be etched into the minds of militant jingoists, politicians, and patriots as they articulated the God-ordained providential mission of United States–

territorial expansion. "Manifest Destiny" became the war cry with which they impassioned their readers about the necessity to lay claim to Mexican terrain (Merk, 1963; Horsman, 1981). As the gospel of American state nationalism, Manifest Destiny was deeply steeped in anti-Spanish and anti-Catholic attitudes, anchored to a republican ideology that disparaged feudal and monarchical forms of government, and wedded to an evolutionary science that deemed it the duty of superior races to eradicate inferior mongrels.

Such sentiments are readily apparent in such best-selling narratives as James O. Pattie's *The Personal Narrative of James O. Pattie* (1831), Richard Henry Dana's *Two Years Before the Mast* (1840), and Josiah Gregg's *Commerce of the Prairies* (1844). The negative stereotypes of "Spaniard" and "Mexican" crafted by American travel writers have been extensively studied over the last 40 years by Gardiner (1952), Lacy (1959), Noggle (1959), Robinson (1963, 1977), Gunn (1974), Paredes (1977a, 1977b), Langum (1978), Meyer (1978), Weber (1979), Pettit (1980), Monsiváis (1984), and R. A. Gutiérrez (1989a).

The accumulated scholarly evidence concludes that most of the American travel narratives were but panegyrics for the territorial expansion of the United States. American travelers attested to the greatness of the United States in comparison with the moral and physical decay of Mexico, as most demonstrably embodied in Mexican men. The women were another matter. In the eyes of American men who described them, they were beautiful "Spanish" *señoritas* who suffered none of the character deficits of the "Mexican" mixed-blood men who had inherited all the degenerate traits of the Spanish and Indian races (Lacy, 1959; Meyer, 1978). Mexican men were typically portrayed as a breed of cruel and cowardly mongrels who were indolent, ignorant, and superstitious, given to cheating, thieving, gambling, drinking, cursing, and dancing. Expansionists drew on such stereotypes to build the case for territorial aggrandizement by asking: Was it not the duty of the United States to rescue such "greasers" from themselves? Dana as much as said so, speculating in his 1840 *Two Years Before the Mast*, "In the hands of an enterprising people, what a great country this could be" (Monsiváis, 1984, p. 55). So it was. First in Texas, Anglo American settlers united with a small group of elite Mexican *Tejanos* and declared their independence from Mexico as the Republic of Texas in 1835. In 1846, sparked by border conflicts between Texas and Mexico, the United States declared war—a war that ended by dispossessing Mexico of one third of its national territory.

The causes, the events, and the consequences of the United States-Mexican War have been the topic of numerous tomes from the vantage points of both the victors and the vanquished. Singletary's *The Mexican War* (1960) remains the most succinct history of the war itself, with all its various military campaigns. Mexican historian Ramón Eduardo Ruiz (1963) carefully dissected the political (the personal ambitions of President James K. Polk) and economic motives (the expansion of plantation slave economies and the desire to acquire more land) for the war in *The Mexican War: Was it Manifest Destiny?*, a theme Brack (1975) addressed largely through Mexican sources in *Mexico Views Manifest Destiny, 1821–1846*. Johannsen's *To the Halls of the Montezumas* (1985) studied the war in the Ameri-

can imagination. Horsman (1981) went one step further, teasing out the Anglo-Saxon racial ideology that justified war in Texas and Mexican territory. Finally, an interpretation best classified as "Manifest Destiny in reverse" was advanced by Weber in *The Mexican Frontier 1821–1846* (1982). He argued that American conquest was made possible, if not inevitable, by the inefficiency and decadence of Mexican civil and ecclesiastical institutions on the northern frontier. Dobyns (1991) aggressively rebutted the Weber thesis, arguing that, at least with respect to popular Catholicism in northern Mexico, no such decay was apparent.

The Texas Revolution and the Mexican War were the two events that legally transformed Mexicans into American citizens. Given the centrality of these historical events in forging the modern political identity of Chicanos, a large part of the scholarly research undertaken by Chicano scholars educated since the mid-1960s has focused on the periods right before and right after territorial annexation by the United States. The overarching themes in all of these works—themes largely of concern to the contemporary Mexican American experience—are: the nature and meaning of community and nation, the dynamics and politics of race, the sex/gender stratification of society, and the covert and overt dimensions of Mexican resistance to U.S. annexation and Anglo domination.

In rewriting and re-visioning the history of the Southwest before U.S. rule, Chicano scholars have usually focused their studies on the various regions Spain initially colonized— *Nuevo México, Tejas, Alta California*, and the *Pimería Alta*, or southern Arizona. New Mexico, the oldest and most densely populated of these territories, was the topic of R. A. Gutiérrez's *When Jesus Came, the Corn Mothers Went Away* (1991). As the title suggests, Gutiérrez investigated the nature of interactions between the Pueblo Indians and their Spanish conquerors, looking specifically at the conflictual politics that characterized marriage, religion, and patriarchal rule, as men and women, young and old, slave and free negotiated their behavior in a colonial context. Sketching the cultural concepts of *honor* (honor) and *vergüenza* (shame) that formed Spanish notions of the self, Gutiérrez shows how race and color were imagined as central components of the status hierarchy governed by honor, and how the legacy of this hierarchy persisted up to and after territorial conquest in 1848. Shorter articles on the status of Spanish women in Santa Fe (J. L. Aragón, 1976), on their property rights and wills (Veyna, 1986, 1993), and on life and labor in late 18th-century Albuquerque (Ríos-Bustamante, 1976) have also greatly enhanced our knowledge of New Mexico.

The history of Spanish, Mexican, and republican Texas has been intensely scrutinized by several generations of scholars. Herbert E. Bolton (1915) laid the foundation for Texas studies in *Texas in the Middle Eighteenth Century: Studies in Spanish Colonial History and Administration*. Chipman's *Spanish Texas, 1519–1821* (1992) covered many of the same themes over a longer historical period. Simons and Hoyt (1992), in their encyclopedic *Hispanic Texas: A Historical Guide*, cataloged the wide array of Hispanic contributions to Texas culture, including such things as architecture and cuisine. Poyo and Hinojosa (1991) have sought the origins of *Tejano* identity in the area of San Antonio in the 18th century. The arrival of Anglo American settlers, and the changes that produced, was the topic of De León's *The Tejano Community, 1836–1900* (1982), which surveyed the experiences of daily life for *Tejanos* (Texans of Mexican origin) through their religious rituals, their forms of entertainment, their work, and their politics. De León argued, sometimes without much evidence, that *Tejanos* accepted their circumstance of conquest and "developed a bicultural identity that equipped them to resist oppression" (1982, p. xii).

One such *Tejano* hero who resisted oppression was Juan Seguín, a wealthy landowner. In 1835 he allied himself with the Anglos during Texas independence, only to be removed in the 1840s as the mayor of San Antonio and driven out of Texas once the Anglos had consolidated their power. This tragic turn of events in Seguín's life has made him a resistance hero for many Mexican Americans. Seguín's story became the theme of Jesús Treviño's 1982 movie *Seguín*. De la Teja (1991) recently prepared a critical edition of Juan Seguín's diary and correspondence.

Montejano's *Anglos and Mexicans in the Making of Texas, 1836–1986* (1987) is the most comprehensive work on Anglo-Mexican race relations in Texas. Montejano examined the origin, growth, and demise of the racial order in Texas, specifically as tied to class development that evolved from a ranch, to a farm, to an urban-industrial economy. According to Montejano, unique and peculiar "racial situations" were created under each of these modes of production, resulting in years of racial quiescence (1836–1900), a period of intense "Jim Crow" segregation (1920–1940), and a period of integration (1940–1986) when Mexican-origin residents of Texas demanded their civil rights, first peacefully and then more militantly.

Studies of Spanish colonial and Mexican California produced by Chicano scholars have been few. Like R. A. Gutiérrez's work on New Mexico (1991), which explores Indian-White relations through the intimate politics of the libido, Monroy in *Thrown Among Strangers: The Making of Culture in Frontier California* (1990) and Castañeda (1990, 1993) have studied the Spanish colonization of California and the hybridization that occurred there when Spaniards, *mestizos*, and Indians mixed biologically through marriage, concubinage, and rape. Both Monroy and Castañeda tell much larger stories about how colonizers and colonized eked out a meager subsistence, how poverty and marginality precipitated sexual violence, and how constant conflicts erupted among settlers, missionaries, and Indians over labor, food, and love.

While much of the historical research on Mexicans as a conquered population has focused on New Mexico, Texas, and California, undoubtedly because of the sheer number of Mexicans who ultimately settled in these states, a few monographs have been written on Arizona and Colorado in the pre- and post-1848 periods. For Arizona, Officer's *Hispanic Arizona, 1536–1856* (1987) and Sheridan's *Los Tucsonenses: The Mexican Community in Tucson, 1854–1941* (1986) are essential baseline readings. In *Songs My Mother Sang to Me: An Oral History of Mexican American Women*, Martin (1992) interviewed 10 women regarding the role of gender and cultural resistance as Arizona's Mexican ranches were transformed into

barrios. Similar studies do not exist for Colorado. Deutsch's *No Separate Refuge: Culture, Class and Gender on an Anglo-Hispanic Frontier in the American Southwest, 1880–1940* (1987) studied the transformation of women's work and culture in northern New Mexico and southern Colorado. An anthology edited by De Onís, *The Hispanic Contribution to the State of Colorado* (1976), has contributed some groundbreaking essays on the history of Colorado's ethnic Mexicans.

During the late 19th and first half of the 20th centuries scores of works were written on the two institutions that still dominate the mythic imagination of the Southwest—the missions and the presidios. Rarely was much attention given to the third institution of colonial conquest, the independent town. Cruz (1988) filled this lacuna with *Let There Be Towns*, tracing the municipal origins of Santa Fe, New Mexico; El Paso, San Antonio, and Laredo, Texas; and Los Angeles and San José, California, focusing specifically on town plans, the institutions of town government (*cabildos*), and how they actually functioned. Though very institutional and legalistic in his approach, Cruz set down the foundation for more detailed town studies. Indeed, M. J. González (1993) used Cruz's work in his study of the municipal origins of Los Angeles, which explored the republican philosophy of the town founders, the ecclesiopolitical ideals manifested in town planning, and the role of Indians in the town's economy both before and after secularization.

What all of these studies indicate is that in New Mexico, Texas, and California, and by implication in Arizona and Colorado, the personal identities that European settlers developed were initially based on membership in a religious community as Old Christians or as New Christian converts. Residence on New Spain's northern frontier gradually transformed the Old World regional consciousness that the colonists initially proclaimed as Castilians, Catalans, Leonese, and Galicians into a single national identity as Spaniards. But the Spaniards of Mexico's north, as a contingent largely of young and single men, by necessity took American Indian and African slave women as lovers, concubines, and occasionally as legal brides. Quickly a cultural *mestizaje* developed, resulting in a syncretic culture born of biological, linguistic, and social mixing. Thus when the colonists proclaimed that they were "Spaniards" they did so to differentiate themselves culturally from those they defined as "Indians."

Despite the realities of extensive physical amalgamation, the Spaniards maintained the fiction that they were biologically pure in order to create and to perpetuate their social privileges in relationship to the Indians, whom they stigmatized through conquest, subjugation, and toil. In the 18th century, as racial mixing rapidly rendered physical color categories meaningless as visual markers of status, new strictures were established in law to regulate relations that could no longer be assessed visually. The legal color categories of the *Régimen de Castas* (The Society of Castes) defined in excruciating detail the precise racial status of every particular mix of ancestry, thus buttressing the authority of local pigmentocracies at precisely the moment when they were most contested from below. Since racial codes were largely cultural fictions used to create social boundaries and hierarchies of prestige, they, too, ultimately gave way in the 1790s to a renewed consciousness of place, a *conciencia de sí*, and an identification with the *patria chica*, or the "small fatherland." By the early 1800s *Tejanos* proclaimed their uniqueness as settlers of this zone. The *Californios* celebrated their own pastoral ways. The *Tucsonenses* (residents of Tucson, then Arizona's major settlement) explained that their character had been forged by the aridity of their desert terrain. And the *Nuevo Mexicanos* boasted of the distinct regional culture they had preserved. The highly developed sense of regional and local community that developed in each of these areas was undergirded by a common religion, a common cycle of rites of passage and calendric events, a common language, and an identity as "Spaniards" forged in opposition to and conflict with "Indians" (R. A. Gutiérrez, 1989b). This sense of community was what gave Spaniards, transformed into Mexicans with independence in 1821, the will and the strength to resist their domination by Anglos.

Sketching the parameters of Anglo American legal domination, though crucial to any history of Mexican Americans, has yet to gain much sustained attention. The legal incorporation of Mexicans into the United States transpired with the ratification of the Treaty of Guadalupe-Hidalgo in 1848, and with its extension through the 1853 Gadsden Purchase. The U.S. government assured Mexicans residing in the conquered territory that their lands would be protected, their religion honored, their language preserved, and their livelihoods left undisturbed. Mexican American and Chicano scholars since the mid-1960s have repeatedly shown how those legal protections were violated and rendered meaningless. The history of the Treaty of Guadalupe-Hidalgo, its debate, and its ultimate ratification by the United States was the topic of a monograph by Griswold del Castillo (1992). Martínez, in *Troublesome Border* (1988), also focused on the 1848 treaty within a broader history of border conflicts between Mexico and the United States, from 1795 to the present.

How Mexicans residing in the United States after 1848 lost their lands and power, despite promises by the U.S. government that these would be protected, has been the topic of extensive study. Most of the book-length monographs to date have examined this process as it unfolded in California. Pitt (1971) studied Mexican-Anglo relations in northern California from the gold rush until 1890. Griswold del Castillo (1979) focused on the morselization of land rights, the disappearance of livestock production, and the political disenfranchisement of *Californios* in the Los Angeles Basin, parallel themes splendidly explored by Hass (1994) in her book on the history of racial identities in Santa Ana, California.

But undoubtedly the best of the California studies on the disenfranchisement of Mexicans is Camarillo's *Chicanos in a Changing Society: From Mexican Pueblos to American Barrios in Santa Barbara and Southern California, 1848–1930* (1979). While other historians described a dichotomous ethnic structure that pitted Anglos against Mexicans or Chicanos, Camarillo carefully documented a much more complex social structure with internal class cleavages in every ethnic group. Here was a complex story describing how California's *Mexicano* population was deprived of its land, politically disempowered, and socially segregated into ethnic enclaves or barrios. These themes were illuminated through an examination of racial and ethnic conflicts, and an analysis of ethnic and class alliances forged either to seize power or to dominate in the struggle to keep it. That Camarillo got the story right can be seen in any contemporary newspaper story about electoral reapportionment in California. By showing Chicanos precisely how Mexicans lost their political power in the state, Camarillo outlined a political strategy for how best to regain it as ethnic Mexicans become an emerging majority population in California.

A full-length history of New Mexican land and water rights controversies has yet to be written. What does exist is a splendid anthology edited by Briggs and Van Ness, *Land, Water, and Culture: New Perspectives on Hispanic Land Grants* (1987). Herein Ebright (1987) surveyed the legal background of New Mexican land grants, while Hall (1987) explored the conflicts between Hispano and Pueblo Indians over these grants. Van Ness (1987) looked at the functions of Spanish land grants at the local level. The two best contributions in the volume are those by Briggs (1987) and Rodriguez (1987). Briggs explained how oral histories could be used in land-grant litigation. Rodriguez focused on Taos, New Mexico, to show how the "Land of Enchantment" was metaphysically constructed for touristic consumption.

The history of overt and covert resistance to Anglo domination in the Southwest has been an important and recurrent theme in Chicano-inspired scholarship over the last 20 years. Writing from a lesbian feminist perspective, and interrogating her sources for their class and racial bias, D. J. González (1993) studied the facts and fiction surrounding Doña Gertrudis Barceló, a Santa Fe woman who allegedly ran a brothel in the 1850s and 1860s. González argued that Doña Barceló really was a businesswoman of considerable skill who adopted to changing social, political, and economic dislocations and adroitly profited from the American invaders. De León's *They Called Them Greasers: Anglo Attitudes Toward Mexicans in Texas, 1821–1900* (1983) analyzed the more general topic of American stereotypes of Mexicans as they were generated in Texas.

One of the persistent myths of American Western historiography has been that *Mexicanos* happily greeted American soldiers, offered little resistance to their domination, and allowed the conquest to occur without spilling a drop of blood. Rosenbaum (1981) shattered this myth in *Mexicano Resistance in the Southwest*. He chronicled how New Mexicans assassinated the occupational governor, Charles Bent, in 1847; how *Mexicanos* fought and died during numerous campaigns of the Mexican War; and how, when overpowered militarily by 1848, they maintained a resistance to domination and the dispossession of their lands. Rosenbaum showed how resistance to displacement took various forms: so-called "bandit" activity (Tiburcio Vásquez and Joaquín Murieta in California; Gregorio Cortez, José Mosqueda, and Mariano Reséndez in Texas), secret societies (New Mexico's *La Mano Negra* and *Las Gorras Blancas*), political parties (*El Partido del Pueblo Unido*), and anarchist and syndicalist groups. Castillo and Camarillo (1973) contributed immensely to this general theme by proposing that *Mexicano* resistance fighters had to be understood as primitive rebels and not as the unruly "bandits" of the Anglo American imagination.

One of the most exciting developments in historical scholarship on Mexican Americans has been the revival of Spanish and *Mexicano* literary voices from 1598 to the early 1900s. Two recent anthologies analyzing these writings have appeared: Herrera-Sobek's *Reconstructing a Chicano/a Literary Heritage* (1993) and R. A. Gutiérrez and Padilla's *Recovering the U.S. Hispanic Literary Heritage* (1993). While the former primarily focused on Spanish colonial texts produced within what is now the United States, the latter delved into nontraditional sources such as periodical literature (Kanellos, 1993), the privately published works of 19th-century New Mexican novelists Vicente Bernal and Felipe Maximiliano Chacón (Gonzales-Berry, 1993), the *Californio* oral histories collected by Hubert H. Bancroft's assistants in the 1880s (R. Sánchez, 1993), Mexican American autobiographies (G. Padilla, 1993b), and the bibliographic sources for the study of Mexican American literary culture in the United States from 1821 to 1945 (R. A. Gutíerrez, 1993b).

At a more detailed and monographic level, G. Padilla expanded our knowledge of the 19th-century formation of Mexican American autobiographical identity in *History, Memory and the Struggles of Self-Representation* (1993a). Herein he analyzed the ways in which war and social domination shaped the contours of the Mexican American autobiographical voice from 1836 on, arguing that Mexican Americans wrote autobiographies as a response to their fear, both real and imagined, of social erasure and literary oblivion. As a literary archaeologist, Padilla recovered the autobiographical utterances of his colonized compatriots, reminding moderns that to do this we must imagine a historical moment that did not exclusively privilege the individual. The men and women Padilla studied—Juan Seguín, Rafael Chacón, Mariano Vallejo, Manuel Otero, Cleofas Jaramillo—were representatives of the larger communitarian politics in which these subjects were engaged.

Much research yet remains to be done in the conquest period. The literary voices of Mexican women are still waiting to be heard. Little has been written about the politics of conquest. No one has yet written the history of Mexicans in Colorado or in any area outside of the Southwest. And much more has yet to be said about the intimate politics of daily life in which men and women, Anglo and Mexican, young and old, rich and poor constantly interacted.

THE MEXICAN AS IMMIGRANT, 1880–1993

Once the U.S. military victory over Mexico's ceded territory was complete and the economic, political, and cultural subordination of Mexicans residing in the Southwest had been accomplished, Mexico became a close and convenient source of cheap immigrant labor. The development of Arizona, California, New Mexico, and Texas as economically productive areas necessitated cheap, tractable, unskilled labor. One sector of the American economy after another called on Mexicans, first to mine the vast mineral deposits of the West, then to construct the railroads that moved these minerals to ports and eastern manufacturing centers, and finally, when rail lines made it possible to transport agricultural products to markets quickly and cheaply, as laborers to till, tend, and harvest the fields.

Mexicans became the immigrant laborers of choice in the 1880s, primarily because the Chinese workers who had provided the bulk of California's labor during the gold rush were excluded from entry into the United States in 1882 by the Chinese Exclusion Act. In 1882 as well the Alien Contract Labor Law was repealed, prohibiting labor contractors from recruiting workers in distant lands. Experimentation with Japanese workers ended with the so-called Japanese Gentlemen's Agreement of 1907, which restricted the number of Japanese immigrant laborers allowed into the country. Mexico was thus the closest and most abundant source of workers available. By 1930 the census of the United States listed 16,668 Mexicans legally employed in "mining," 70,799 in "transportation and communication" (primarily as railroad field hands), and 189,000 in "agricultural industries" (initially sugar beets and cotton, and later citrus and table vegetables) (McWilliams, 1949; R. A. Gutiérrez, 1976; Reisler, 1976; Cardoso, 1980).

Mexican peasant laborers began entering the United States in the 1880s largely because of the rural poverty they faced at home, a situation that culminated in the 1910 Mexican Revolution. Landless and increasingly unable to produce or purchase the basic necessities of life, these men and women were forced to migrate to known work sites. In the 1880s President Porfirio Díaz began a massive modernization program in Mexico, centered on the creation of an extensive infrastructure that ultimately connected the country's productive areas with markets. Railroad construction was the cornerstone of this plan, primarily through rail links between Mexico and the United States. Many landless peasants left their ancestral homes in search of work on railroad construction in Mexico's northern states. Once there, they found it quite easy to continue their trek further north into the United States. No physical barrier other than the easily forded Rio Grande separated Mexico from the United States before 1924. The availability of jobs at wages significantly higher than those found in Mexico made the move all the more irresistible. Caught in the midst of the revolutionary violence that rocked Mexico between 1910 and 1924, many migrants found the United States a peaceful and attractive haven.

The Mexican emigration/immigration literature published in Mexico and the United States is immense and often contradictory. Some of it is based on facts. Much of it is based on fallacious assumptions that have been widely accepted as facts and compounded through dissemination as national fictions. It is impossible to summarize all of this literature here, but what follows illustrates some of the major themes.

Two very different and often contradictory representations of the "Mexican immigrant" exist in the public policy and scholarly literature. The Mexican immigrant has been viewed either as a "problem" that threatens the racial, hygienic, and economic basis of life in the United States (Jenks & Lauck, 1917; Bamford, 1923–24), or a valuable asset that contributes to American prosperity by performing tasks at wages that citizen workers will not accept, and by contributing taxes from which the immigrant rarely benefits (Borjas, 1990). Advocates of the Mexican-as-problem position have demanded severe immigration restrictions, particularly at times of economic hardship. The Mexicans-as-assets advocates have generally favored open doors or more tempered governmental regulation, particularly during times of prosperity. The average person on the street probably embodies attitudes about immigrants drawn from both viewpoints.

The tenor of these polemics and debates has been remarkably consistent, whether in 1903 or 1993. In 1908, for example, labor contractors in the Southwest explained to Victor S. Clark, a U.S. Bureau of Labor economist, that they preferred Mexican to Japanese laborers because "when you have occasion to dismiss one Japanese, all quit. If a Mexican proves poor or an undesirable workman, you can let him go without breaking up the gang" (V. S. Clark, 1908, p. 478). Clark characterized the Mexican immigrant laborer as

ambitious, listless, physically weak, irregular and indolent. On the other hand, he is docile, patient, usually orderly in camp, fairly intelligent under competent supervision, obedient, and cheap. If he were active and ambitious, he would be less tractable and would cost more. (p. 496)

From this point of view—that of California growers—the Mexican was still characterized by many of the same negative stereotypes that American travel writers had first created in the 1820s.

At the opposite end of the spectrum, in the 1920s, nativist and patriotic societies and eugenicist organizations demanded a solution to the "Mexican Problem" through immigration restriction because, explained sociologist Robert L. Garis (1930) of Vanderbilt University:

Their minds run to nothing higher than animal functions—eat, sleep, and sexual debauchery. In every huddle of Mexican shacks one meets the same idleness, hoards of hungry dogs, and filthy children with faces plastered with flies, disease, lice, human filth, stench, promiscuous fornication, bastardy, lounging, apathetic peons and lazy squaws, beans and dried chili, liquor, general squalor, and envy and hatred of the gringo . . . . Yet there are Americans clamoring for more of this human swine to be brought over from Mexico. (p. 436)

Princeton economist Robert Foerster (1925) voiced similar opposition to Mexican immigration on purely racial grounds. He asked rhetorically whether Mexican *mestizo* and African mulatto racial stocks should be welcomed in the United States. Foerster argued that they should not because "These groups merely approach but do not attain the race value of the white stocks, and therefore that the immigrants from these countries—Latin America—tend to lower the average of the white population of the United States" (p. 55). He warned that it was foolhardy to succumb to momentary profits while the racial purity of the nation was under attack (p. 57).

As various interest groups in the United States have attempted to advance their agendas, the question of appropriate policy about Mexican immigrants has been a recurrent concern. Of primary interest to these debates has been: How many Mexicans emigrate to the United States? This has not been a simple question to answer. Statistics on Mexican entries into the United States along the southern border were not kept until 1924. Before that, the only Mexicans who entered U.S. immigration records were those who arrived at official ports of entry, such as New York and San Francisco. Since few Mexicans ever saw the Statue of Liberty, those numbers rarely reached the hundreds before 1924. Estimates gathered by the U.S. Census in 1930 placed the number of Mexicans permanently residing in the United States at one million, a number Mexican scholars fiercely contested as too high. The census had been taken in July, at the peak period in the use of Mexican labor, Gamio maintained (1930a, 1930b, 1931); if one estimated the number of immigrants on the basis of monetary remittances in December, after the temporary migrants had returned home, the number of permanent residents was closer to 500,000.

The first systematic statistical count of Mexicans living in the United States came shortly after the 1929 economic depression. Restrictionist pressures mounted and eventually led to the deportation of many Mexicans. From 1930 to 1937 massive repatriation campaigns were conducted throughout the U.S. Southwest and Midwest. According to state and federal reports, the deportees were all Mexicans, but the reality was that many Americans of Mexican descent were deported or emigrated back to Mexico under duress. From official Mexican records Carreras (1974, p. 145) concluded that 311,717 Mexicans had reentered Mexico between 1930 and 1933. Working with American welfare records, newspaper accounts, and state and federal statistics, Hoffman (1974) placed the number of Mexican deportees at 458,039, a number comparable to that advanced by Gamio in 1930. Further information on the repatriation movement can be found in Kiser and Silverman (1972), Betten and Mohl (1973), and Dinwoodie (1977).

Not until 1942, as the United States entered World War II, were Mexican immigrants allowed to reenter in large numbers. To stem labor shortages in industries that were deemed essential to the war effort, Congress authorized Public Law 45, which became widely known as the Bracero Program. Though this legislation was initially deemed a temporary emergency war measure, it was repeatedly extended in various forms and under slightly different names until 1964. To stem some of the most notorious abuses suffered by Mexican immigrant laborers—unsanitary living conditions, payment failures, peonage-like contracts, overt racism—Mexico and the United States agreed that firms requiring workers would petition the U.S. Department of Labor. The Labor Department would serve as the contracting agent, guaranteeing the wage, the length of work, and the living conditions of the contracted workers. The Labor Department also made provisions to hold a portion of the workers' wages in escrow until they returned to Mexico, thereby assuring that temporary guests would not become permanent residents (Galarza, 1964, 1977; Samora, 1971; Craig, 1971; Gamboa, 1990; Calavita, 1992). Approximately 4.6 million braceros entered the United States between 1942 and 1964, a statistic considered accurate by most American and Mexican authorities.

The initiation of the Bracero Program coincided with another major trend in Mexican emigration—the movement of undocumented immigrants into the United States. According to official statistics compiled by the Immigration and Naturalization Service, 22 million undocumented Mexican immigrants have been apprehended and deported back to Mexico since 1942. The precise meaning of this number has been the topic of heated debate. Statistics often do not account for repeat offenders; the same individual may have been apprehended by American authorities as many as 50 times in a lifetime. Nevertheless, depending on the user, the number can be exaggerated to show how the nation's borders have been eroded, or conversely, the necessity of better monitoring and more accurate statistics.

Some clarity was brought to the issue with the passage of the U.S. Immigration Reform and Control Act of 1986. Undocumented immigrants who had entered the country before January 1, 1982, were given the right to legalize their status; a special amnesty was extended to those persons who had spent at least 90 days working in agriculture in the year preceding May 1, 1986. A mere 2.3 million applicants came forward (Durand & Massey, 1992), thus greatly deflating the 1980s projections of 7 to 8 million undocumented Mexican immigrants in the United States. Of course, the critics of these numbers have argued that not all Mexicans eligible for legalization took advantage of the statute.

Who migrated? The standard historical truism worldwide has been that the poorest cannot afford to move and the rich have no reason to, so the stratum in between is the one that has the wherewithal and motives to move. But the answers one finds to this question in the emigration literature on Mexicans are as varied as the scholars who framed them. Some have asserted that it was the landless and poor who migrated (Reichert, 1979; Stuart & Kearney, 1981). Other scholars have confirmed the above-stated truism, noting that the migrants were poor but not at the bottom of the social hierarchy (Cornelius, 1976; Wiest, 1973). And one scholar (E. J. Taylor, 1986) argued that no relationship between social class and migration could be established.

The most insightful analysis of who migrates has been offered by Douglas Massey and his coauthors (Massey, Alarcón, Durand, & González, 1987). Massey et al. argued that the class composition of migrants was a historically varied, dynamic, and ever-shifting process dependent on the age of the migration stream from a particular Mexican locality to the United States and the social inequality present in the community of origin. In a typical scenario, when the migrant stream from a particular Mexican area initially developed, the individuals who migrated were from the middle sectors of the social hierarchy as reckoned by wealth and/or occupation. They left Mexico without kinship or social ties in the United States to draw on, and thus were the only social group economically capable of risking a move to initiate a migrant stream from their home community. Once they were established in the United States, ties of kinship and friendship made it possible for poorer members of their home community to enter and eventually to dominate the migrant stream, because they could join an established support network when they arrived. Once the support networks became extensive, migration was less dependent on class or the resources a particular migrant could garner.

What geographic regions did Mexican migrants come from and where have they settled in the United States? Gamio (1930a, 1931) studied the geographic origin of Mexicans who migrated to the United States, as did his Mexican compatriot Loyo (1969) in the mid-1960s. Both concluded that the bulk of migrants left the central Mexican states of Guanajuato, Michoacán, México, and Jalisco; since 1965 many have also come from the state of Oaxaca. And while the revolutionary violence between 1910

and 1917 probably accounted for the majority of emigrants during those years, abundant work, higher wages, and the possibility of upward mobility have continued to attract them to the United States in the years that followed. Mexicans historically have settled overwhelmingly in the Southwest, with California and then Texas receiving the bulk. Recently, however, Washington (Gamboa, 1992), the Great Lakes region (Valdés, 1991; Vargas, 1993), and New York have developed sizable Mexican communities. Both the geographic distribution and demographic profile of these immigrants have been studied by Alvarez (1966), Bean and Tienda (1987), Boswell (1979), Martínez (1975), and Teller, Estrada, Hernández, and Alvírez (1977).

Much of the writing produced by Chicano scholars in the period after 1965 has focused on the work experiences of Mexican laborers in the United States. Undoubtedly part of the reason for this focus was the scholars' desires to trace their own immigrant roots. But one cannot dismiss the influence of one historian, Juan Gómez-Quiñones, founder of the UCLA Chicano Studies Research Center. As mentor of the first generation of Chicano scholars at UCLA, it was inevitable that the research themes of his students and disciples would bear the mark and concerns of the master. Much of the important work of Gómez-Quiñones has been on Mexican immigrants as workers (1972, 1982), focusing on their culture (1977), on their relationships with state authorities (1975), and on their political organizations on both sides of the border (1990).

His own students, and those influenced by his models, have studied the origins of labor union activism in the form of fraternal organizations and mutual aid societies (Briegel, 1974; Hernández, 1983; Vélez-Ibañez, 1983), the role of the Mexican consulates in protecting workers in the United States (Balderrama, 1982), Mexican workers in Texas (Zamora, 1993), and the roles of various labor unions and political parties, such as the Communist Party of the United States (Arroyo, 1975; Almaguer & Camarillo, 1983). The bulk of this literature focused on class and class formation in the United States and gave little attention to the dynamics of racism. For these authors race was but an ideological ploy the ruling class used to divide workers; it was a form of false consciousness that had no role in the activity of militants. The only strategy for seizing power was a class strategy, or so claimed the Socialist and Communist organizers of Mexican workers from the 1920s to the 1960s. How Chicanos reacted to this formulation of their oppression will be examined in some detail in the section on the Chicano movement.

The published story of the Mexican immigrant has largely been a heroic male tale. Women have rarely entered the historical and sociological record. But whatever the mythology, the reality has been that women have formed a major component of the migrant stream since the 1880s. Between 1930 and 1933, for example, Carreras (1974) discovered that of the 311,717 Mexicans repatriated, two thirds were women. More recent studies have estimated that since 1945, slightly more than one half of all Mexican immigrants have been women (V. L. Ruiz & Tiano, 1987; Cardenas & Flores, 1986).

Historically, Mexican women usually entered the migrant stream only after their particular community had a well-established immigrant support network in the United States. Men usually migrated first, familiarized themselves with labor markets and work demands, and, when they felt secure, sent for their wives and children (Durand & Massey, 1992). Thus those communities that have had long histories of sending emigrants to the United States usually also have had a large number of women among those migrants. If the community's history of sending workers to the United States is more recent, the number of women in that migrant stream is usually smaller.

The nature of gender relations in Mexican immigrant families has been of some concern to feminist scholars. Studying a sample of 26 families containing 44 adult women, and controlling for the length of separation between a husband and wife caused by the migration process, Hondagneu-Sotelo (1992) found that the longer a couple was separated, the greater was the erosion of domestic patriarchy. During long periods of separation women became independent and "were no longer accustomed or always willing to act subserviently before their husbands." When the separation was only a few years, "daily housework arrangements were not radically transformed once the families were reconstituted in the United States" (pp. 408–409).

The newest research trends in the Mexican immigration literature can be found in the work of D. Gutiérrez (1994) and Foley (1990). In *Walls and Mirrors: Mexican Americans, Mexican Immigrants, and the Politics of Ethnicity in the American Southwest, 1910–1986*, Gutiérrez focused on the differences that were generated over 150 years within the Mexican and Mexican American communities as their populations were transformed into Americans. Over the course of these years, as Mexicans forged a situational ethnicity, responding to forces generated both within their communities and outside of them by the discriminatory practices of American society, they constantly grappled with the "crucial distinctions between 'native' and 'foreigner,' 'citizen' and 'alien,' 'American' and 'Mexican'" (p. 12). How these statuses were mobilized for political purposes, to promote or curtail the flow of Mexican immigrants, is the story that Gutiérrez tells with considerable finesse. It is a story full of nuance and complexity; a story devoid of black or white, but quite florid in its various hues of gray. There are Mexican Americans who hate Mexicans and ally themselves with Americans to curtail Mexican immigration, just as there are working-class Mexican Americans who favor continued immigration, while cursing their middle-class ethnic brothers who want to stem the flow.

Foley also explored social complexity, linking theoretical concerns in Chicano and African American history with issues central to labor history and postemancipation studies. In *The New South in the Southwest: Anglos, Blacks, and Mexicans in Central Texas, 1880–1930* (1990), Foley examined the complex triangular relationship that developed among Anglo owners and tenants, Black and Mexican sharecroppers, and Mexican migrant workers in the fertile cotton-producing area of Central Texas from 1880 to 1930. Historically, Central Texas (roughly from Dallas in the north to San Antonio and Corpus Christi in the south) represented the boundary between the cotton-growing U.S. South, with its history of slavery and emancipation, and the semiarid region of southwestern Texas, with its history of ranching and migrant Mexican labor. At the end of the 19th century the populations from these two geographically distinct regions began to overlap. Mexicans began moving north, pushed by political and economic turmoil in Mexico and pulled by economic opportunities in the fertile fields to the north and east. By 1900 large numbers of Mexicans had settled in the cotton-producing counties north of San Antonio where, along with African Americans, they began displacing Anglo share tenants on farms and came to form the labor supply in this predominantly Anglo region.

The trend in Chicano-inspired immigration studies increasingly has been to look at conflicts within and between ethnic groups, incorporating information from diverse fields of study.

THE MEXICAN AMERICAN MINORITY, 1920–1965

The emergence of a Mexican American minority population in the United States between 1920 and 1965 is the theme that has received the least attention in the vast scholarly corpus examined here. The very appellation *Mexican American* signifies that something Mexican and something American have mixed, and from this mixture an entirely new hybrid has been produced. This hybridity historically has been studied by anthropologists and sociologists as *assimilation*, a process initiated by marriage, by acquiring a new language or religion, by obtaining a distinct job, and by entering a new culture.

The Mexican's transition from the status of conquered group to assimilated American has been long and rather confining. From the time the first Anglo American settlers arrived in the Mexican territory that eventually became the United States, extensive Anglo-Mexican intermarriage occurred. Racially mixed progeny were born. Protestants converted to Catholicism and vice versa, to make a good or advantageous match. Spanish-English bilingualism became a necessity for anyone who married exogamously or traded in the labor or products of the Southwest. Social scientists have long described this process of cultural mixing and blending, in which cultural partners both give and take from each other, as *transculturation*. Historically, transculturation has been the norm when cultures and peoples reside side by side, sharing foodways and folkways, love and life. But when a relationship of domination and subordination has developed that was coded as a racial, ethnic, or national divide, transculturation was no longer the operative process. Instead, power was exercised by the dominant group to make the subordinate become more like them. In social science writing such cultural movement in one direction only, toward the ideals of the dominant culture, has been described as *acculturation*, which can occur either at the structural or personal level. At the personal level, acquisition of the dominator's language, forms of comportment, dress and demeanor, as well as aspirations, has been defined as *assimilation*.

By the 1880s, given some 60 years of cohabitation in the Southwest, there were sizable numbers of the Mexicans who thought of themselves as Americans, as indeed they were by law, and who objectively had assimilated or were in the process of assimilating to the dominant Anglo American culture. They had accepted or passively acquiesced to the realities of the domination under which they lived. Some married Anglos, some learned the language, and a few had even mastered it (Dysart, 1976; Myres, 1982; Miller, 1982; Carver, 1982).

Then, starting in the 1880s, large numbers of dirt-poor Mexican immigrants started to arrive in the old Spanish towns and villages of the Southwest, resuscitating latent Anglo perceptions of the social types that had inspired vicious stereotypes of Mexicans in the 1820s. In the Anglo American imagination, once again the Mexican was poor, dirty, indolent, disease-ridden, superstitious, and dumb. Such caricatures fed the racist science and xenophobic ideologies of the day. Indeed, in the 1880s one did not call another a "Mexican," a "Meskin," or a "Mex" in polite company. It was considered an insult, particularly to women and men who had resided in the Southwest since the times of the Spanish doñas and dons.

As was noted in the first section of this chapter, in the 1820s a bifurcated image of Mexicans developed in American travel literature. The beautiful women were described as "Spanish," and the indolent men as "Mexican." In the 1880s this bifurcation was reanimated, with the longtime Mexican residents of the Southwest labeled "Spanish" and "Spanish Americans," and the recent immigrants "Mexicans." With this naming strategy, ethnic Mexicans resident in the United States were distanced and differentiated as a distinct nationality from Mexican immigrants. This differentiation also had racial implications, for by accepting and even proclaiming a Spanish identity, ethnic Mexicans created a genealogy rooted in Europe that lacked the degenerate racial elements present in Mexican *mestizos* (mixed-bloods) (R. A. Gutiérrez, 1989b, 1993a).

One cannot make sense of the sociological and anthropological literature on Mexican Americans as a minority group published from roughly 1920 to 1965 without understanding this "Mexicans" and "Spaniards" distinction. In this period the three major analytic paradigms of societal analysis—biological determinism, environmental/structural determinism, and cultural determinism—repeatedly invoked the "Spanish" and "Mexican" categories to explain why Mexican Americans, despite many years of residence in the United States, were not assimilating as quickly or as completely as northern Europeans had. The assimilation models of the day had been constructed largely on the basis of the experiences of the "old" northern European immigrants who had settled the Northeast between 1776 and 1880. However, with the United States seemingly flooded by the arrival of numerous "new" immigrants from southern and eastern Europe and Mexico between 1880 and 1930, new models were necessary to explain everything from the desirability of racial mixing with these immigrants, to the biological determinants of the crimes they committed, their poor health, and unemployment rates.

Strongly influenced by the racial science of the late 19th and early 20th centuries, the biological determinists in psychology sought to confirm empirically what many already suspected: that Mexicans and southern and eastern European immigrants were innately less intelligent. The IQ test was the instrument used to prove this; when administered to non–native English speakers, these tests invariably confirmed that these groups had lower IQs. The work of Young (1922) on mental difference in immigrant groups; of Garth (1923) on the intelligence of Mexican American, American Indian, and mixed-blood children; of

Garretson (1928) on the causes of retardation among Mexican children in Arizona; and of Haught (1931) on the language difficulties of "Spanish American" children, all conclusively pointed to the linguistic shortcomings of their research subjects as measured by intelligence tests—proof positive of their inferior mental abilities. These were studies and findings, coincidentally, that advocates of immigration restrictions were always quick to publicize in their testimony before congressional committees; such studies persisted as late as 1950 (Carlson & Henderson, 1950).

The riposte to these biological determinists came from anthropologists, sociologists, and educational psychologists who rejected biological explanations and instead turned their attention to the structural environment in which Mexican Americans lived, learned, and worked to explain the characteristics of Mexican workers. The very organization of the American agricultural economy, rather than the mental capacities of individual Mexicans, had to be examined to understand the "Mexican problem." Why Mexican Americans as a group were "unstable, subject to irregular employment, low earning, and more importantly the social and political disabilities of non-residents," explained Paul S. Taylor (1938, p. 226), had more than anything else to do with the fact that the demand for their labor was largely seasonal, widely dispersed regionally, and poorly compensated.

Emory Bogardus (1940) and Norman D. Humphrey (1943) echoed similar sentiments when they explained that the structure of work and levels of discrimination were the environmental factors that most affected the life outcomes of Mexican workers. Migratory labor begot "deplorable housing accommodations, and the Mexican and his family have suffered," noted Bogardus (p. 170). Mexican American boys were attracted to gangs, not because they had low IQs or were culturally deprived, but because they were "discriminated against occupationally. Some of the work opportunities open to other youth are closed to him because he is 'Mexican'" (Bogardus, 1943, p. 65). Writing about Mexican immigrants in Detroit, Humphrey concluded that "Discrimination against Mexicans in the southern and western states is neither favorable to assimilation nor to the acquisition of United States citizenship" (p. 333).

In scathing critiques of IQ testing, native New Mexican George I. Sánchez (1932, 1934, 1940) demanded that test instruments be more carefully constructed and that investigators build in environmental variables (such as diet, home environment, social class, the physical nature of schools, rural vs. urban setting) to explain school and test score performance. On the basis of his own studies Sánchez argued that Mexican American children were no less intelligent than any other American group. The racist policies of school boards and teachers were the real problem, as demonstrated "in the nature and quality of the educational facilities available to these children. . . . In the counties with the largest proportions of Spanish-speaking people," Sánchez argued, "school terms are shorter, teachers are less well prepared and their salaries are lower, and materials of instruction and school buildings are inferior to those found elsewhere in the state [of New Mexico] . . . . The unresponsiveness of the school to the environment of New Mexican children tends to force them out of school" (1940, pp. 31–32). In fact,

Sánchez demonstrated (1932) that Spanish-speaking children who had initially been judged dull and feebleminded on the basis of intelligence tests had, after only two years of English-language tutoring, shown perfectly normal IQs.

The powerful correctives offered by Sánchez in psychology were buttressed by others who were eager to understand the relationship between environment and educational success. West (1936) wanted to know whether teachers' racial prejudices influenced their assessment of a child's performance. Comparing a Southwestern sample of "Spanish-American" and "Anglo-American" teachers, he found that the Anglo teachers "were more strongly inclined than were the Spanish to claim superiority for pupils of their own race" (p. 337).

Thomas Garth and his colleagues (Garth, Elson, & Morton, 1936) used three achievement tests (one nonverbal, two verbal) to assess the role English-language competence played in the intelligence test results of Anglo and Mexican school-aged children. Controlling for age and grade, the I.Q. scores of the Mexican American children on the nonverbal test were "about equal to the American White I.Q." (p. 58), though they scored much lower than Anglo students on the verbal tests.

Keston and Jiménez (1954) extended this line of research on the relationship between language and intelligence by administering Spanish and English versions of the Stanford-Binet Intelligence Test to bilingual children in Albuquerque, New Mexico. The results were quite unexpected. The children had higher IQs when tested in English than in Spanish, explained largely by the fact that though the children were verbally competent in Spanish, they had no formal training in reading and writing the language—skills necessary to do well on the standardized tests. From this study it became clear that simply translating a test into Spanish was no solution to the larger educational problems faced by Mexican Americans.

The third major paradigm shift used extensively to analyze Mexican Americans—cultural determinism—grew out of 19th-century racial science and studies of national character precipitated by the rise of state nationalisms. In country after country historians, philosophers, and pedants intensively scrutinized the behaviors of their compatriots to sketch the collective portrait of the nation.

The national character of Mexico was largely depicted by psychologist Samuel Ramos (1938), philosopher Leopoldo Zea (1952), and poet/critic Octavio Paz (1961). These three men generally agreed that the Mexican psyche had been deeply affected by three centuries of Spanish colonial domination and repeated foreign penetration of their sovereign national space. The living legacy of this past was a profound sense of inferiority among Mexicans, compensated for and displayed by men as hypermasculinity, or *machismo*. Using observations from his own practice, psychiatrist Diaz-Guerrero (1955) delineated precisely how this inferiority/hypermasculinity manifested itself. For him, the dominant Mexican family pattern consisted of the absolute and unquestioned authority of the father and the necessary and absolute self-sacrifice of the mother. Boys were socialized to display *machismo*, while girls were taught that their femininity was tied to the home and maternity. In adolescence men simultaneously sought both homey maternal wives and eroticized sexual playmates. Their strength, courage, and viril-

ity, symbolized by the size of their penis and testicles, were displayed by the convention of protecting one's own women-folk while trying to seduce those of other men. While before marriage men placed women on pedestals as queens, after marriage they became slaves who had to submit to the unquestioned authority of their husbands. Diaz-Guerrero concluded that the inability of both sexes, particularly the females, to fulfill these expectations commonly led Mexicans to develop neuroses. Many Mexican personality disorders were due to the exaggerated *machismo* in the culture, a thesis that found validation in works by Lewis (1951) and Gilbert (1959). While Lewis's study was largely impressionistic, Gilbert reached the conclusion by administering 106 Rorschach tests to residents of a mestizo village close to Mexico City. There was a pronounced tendency, he argued,

to either severely constricted affect or to morbid-depressed-hypochon-driacal types of responses among the older males.... [T]his may be indicative of increasing impotence and "castration anxiety" as the males fail in the life-long struggle to live up to the demands of machismo.... (p. 212)

The study of Mexicans living in the United States followed similar lines of inquiry. Mexicans were deemed initially identical on both sides of the border, with assimilation fundamentally transforming generational power relations within the home. "Mexican men in Detroit generally expect their wives to behave in much the same fashion that they did in Mexico," explained Humphrey (1944). "Most Mexican women in Detroit have remained subordinate, home-centered creatures" (p. 624). Assimilation produced a role reversal that effectively emasculated the father and elevated the eldest assimilated son to the role of "protector, orderer, and forbidder; in short a foster parent, schooled in American ways" through the mastery of English and monetary earnings. The mother retained her status as the guardian of "Mexican meanings and understandings" (p. 624). Jones (1948) reached the similar conclusion that the impact of emigration to the United States was to break up the "web of culture" that previously had kept the Mexican family intact (p. 452).

Throughout the 1950s and early 1960s, little substantive research was added to these psychological profiles. Increasingly, though, Mexican American culture came to be seen as based on "values" and "value orientations" that were diametrically different from those found in Anglo culture, values that bred underachievement and educational failure (Saunders, 1954; Kluck-hohn & Strodtbeck, 1961). Mexican Americans would best enjoy the benefits of assimilation, explained educational psychologist H. T. Manuel (1965), only by embracing "Anglo-American values, both because of the weight of numbers in the dominant group and because of better adaptation ..." (p. 44). In the chapter "Failure of the Culture," Carter (1970) explained that Mexican American culture itself was responsible for orienting its children to "devalue formal education," to place interpersonal relationships over material goods, to fatalism, stasis, apathy, presentism, superstition, and devaluation of time; "the Anglo concept of wasting time is not understood" (p. 42).

In general, Spanish Americans were portrayed as "a poor,

proud, stable and cohesive group, with a value orientation strongly emphasizing interpersonal relations rather than ideas, abstractions or material possessions." They scorned upward mobility and equated it "with craft and dishonor," or so opined sociologist Robert G. Hayden (1966, p. 15). In their domestic relations,

The family is under the firm authority of the father, while the mother assumes the traditional subservient and severely proscribed role of homemaker, the model of purity, bearer and trainer of children. This is a reflection of "hombría" or "machismo," i.e., supreme male dominance, and male individualism, assertiveness, and extreme pride . . . . (p. 20)

Harking back to the work of Ramos (1938) and Paz (1961), Madsen (1964) proposed that *machismo* was a reactive response to the Mexican American male's subordination in the United States. "To a large extent the supremacy of the male within his own home compensates for subservience he may have to demonstrate on the job or in the presence of a social superior" (p. 48).

As obtuse and ethnocentric as these research results may now seem, their impact was far-reaching. Many of the conclusions of the biological determinists and value orientation theorists were diffused broadly through American culture via films. Woll (1977, 1980), Pettit (1980), Keller (1985), Greenfield and Cortés (1991), and Cortés (1992) have all shown that Hollywood films turned to such "scientific" caricatures of the Mexican and Mexican American to underscore the point that they lacked the values for upward mobility and full citizenship in the United States. Though some thematic variations were screened, Mexicans largely were portrayed in the movies as bandits and villains who rarely managed to romance the beautiful girls or to triumph in the conflicts in which they found themselves (Woll 1977, 1980). That triumph was always reserved for Anglo men. American social science and image making persistently emasculated Mexican men and rendered the women passive and erotic trophies of conquest.

Much of this scholarship and popular mythmaking that blamed the victims for their own marginalization and subordination in American life was gradually eclipsed in the early 1960s as a result of social protest. Given the passivity, docility, and apathy social scientists said characterized the culture of African Americans, American Indians, and Mexican Americans, how was it possible that these groups had mobilized themselves to demand change?

CHICANOS AS A NATIONALITY, 1965–1993

Mexican Americans fought in World War II to make the world safe for democracy (Morin, 1966). Fighting beside other assimilated immigrants, they believed the national promise that when they returned home, the American dream of social mobility and middle-class status would be theirs. The troops returned to what became a period of unprecedented economic growth in the United States. It was between 1945 and 1960 that America's global economic hegemony was truly consolidated. For

White American men the dream was indeed realized. The G.I. Bill of Rights helped educate many of them. The consumer goods, the cars, the stocked refrigerators, money to spare, and government loans to educate their children soon followed. But by 1960 it had become clear to African Americans, Mexican Americans, and Asian Americans that the benefits, the dreams, and the cash had not been distributed equitably. Indeed, the 1960 census graphically showed that minorities lagged far behind White America in terms of household income, education, and occupations.

For Mexican Americans these realizations were made potent in the mid-1960s. Though denied equality at home, Mexican Americans saw their sons drafted and killed in the escalating war in Vietnam. They read in newspapers about the worldwide crumbling of imperialism and the rise of new nationalisms, and at home they were moved by the peaceful activism of Cesar Chavez, who was trying to win better wages and work conditions for farm workers, and by Reies López Tijerina's attempts to regain lands fraudulently stolen from New Mexico's *Hispanos*. This complex conjuncture of structural forces was what sparked the Chicano movement. What differentiated the Chicano movement from the civil rights activities of such groups as the League of United Latin American Citizens (LULAC), the American G.I. Forum, or the numerous mutual aid societies that *Mexicanos* had created to better their socioeconomic situation, was the *Movimiento's* radical political stance. The civil rights movement of the 1940s and 1950s had sought slow, peaceful change through assimilation, petitions for governmental beneficence, and appeals to White liberal guilt. The Chicanos, largely a contingent of educated students in a revolution sparked by rising expectations, demanded equality with White America and an end to racism, and asserted their right to cultural autonomy and national self-determination.

Chicanos saw themselves confronted by social emasculation and cultural negation, and thus sought strength and inspiration in a heroic Aztec past that emphasized the virility of warriors and the exercise of brute force. Young Chicano men, a largely powerless group, invested themselves with images of power—a gendered symbolic inversion commonly found in the fantasies of powerless men worldwide. Aztlán, the legendary homeland of the Aztecs, was the nation Chicanos claimed, which they situated in a global community of oppressed nations and theorized through the emerging paradigm of internal colonialism.

Internal colonialism had initially emerged as a social science model in the 1950s in an attempt to understand the dynamics of racism, the isolation of racial groups from the sociopolitical and economic institutions of the dominant class society, and the use of minorities as surplus labor and cannon fodder in White America's imperial wars. The model was originally elaborated to explain the "development of underdevelopment" in Africa, Asia, and Latin America (Frank, 1967). Employed by Latin American Marxists as an explanation for the backwardness of Indian areas, internal colonialism eventually was developed as a theory of ethnic relations between indigenous groups and the larger *mestizo* (mixed blood) class societies in Mexico, Guatemala, and Peru. The theory proposed that structural constraints, very similar to those through which the metropolis systematically underdeveloped its periphery (colonies), were reproduced internally in a nation-state in relations between the dominant center and Indian communities. Thus the discrimination Indians suffered had not only a cultural manifestation, but a structural foundation as well (González-Casanova, 1969; Stavenhagen, 1965; Cotler, 1967–68).

Nationalist protest movements in the United States were deeply influenced by the colonial paradigm. Harold Cruse (1962) characterized race relations in the United States as "domestic colonialism." Three years later Kenneth Clark in *Dark Ghetto* advanced the proposition that the political, economic, and social structure of Harlem was essentially that of a colony (1965), a model Stokely Carmichael and Charles Hamilton employed as internal colonialism in *Black Power* (1967). But it was Robert Blauner (1972) who best articulated the theory in relationship to American minorities. Blauner maintained that while the United States was never a "colonizer" in the 19th-century European sense, it had nonetheless established its development through the conquest and seizure of Indian lands, the enslavement of Africans, and the usurpation of Mexican territory through war. Thus "Western colonialism brought into existence the present-day patterns of racial stratification; in the United States, as elsewhere, it was a colonial experience that generated the lineup of ethnic and racial divisions" (p. 12).

Blauner (1972) admitted that internal colonialism by itself could not be used to theorize race relations and social change in the United States because the country was a combination of colonial-racial and capitalist class realities. Internal colonialism was a modern capitalist practice of oppression and exploitation of racial and ethnic minorities within the borders of the state, characterized by relationships of domination, oppression, and exploitation. Such relationships were apparent as (a) *forced entry*—"The colonized group enters the dominant society through a forced, involuntary, process"; (b) *cultural impact*—"The colonizing power carries out a policy which constrains, transforms, or destroys indigenous values, orientations, and ways of life"; (c) *external administration*—"Colonization involves a relationship by which members of the colonized group tend to be administered by representatives of the dominant power. There is an experience of being managed and manipulated by outsiders in terms of ethnic status"; and (d) *racism*—"Racism is a principle of social domination by which a group seen as inferior or different in terms of alleged biological characteristics is exploited, controlled, and oppressed socially and psychically by a superordinate group" (p. 84).

White-skin racial privilege was at the heart of the colonial relationship, manifested as an "unfair advantage, a preferential situation or systematic 'headstart' in the pursuit of social values, whether they be money, power, position, learning, or whatever" (Blauner, 1972, p. 22). White people had historically advanced at the expense of and because of the presence of African Americans, Chicanos, and other Third World peoples, particularly in the structure of dual labor markets and occupational hierarchies. Given these realities, racism was not a form of false consciousness; it resulted in concrete benefits for Whites.

Chicano militants widely accepted the internal colonial model and by the 1960s and 1970s increasingly conceptualized themselves as a socially, culturally, and economically subordi-

nated and regionally segregated people. These ideas received extensive expression in Acuña (1972) and R. A. Gutiérrez (1976) in the discipline of history, Almaguer (1971, 1974, 1975) in the field of sociology, and Barrera (1979) and Barrera, Muñoz, and Ornelas (1972) in political science.

When internal colonialism was taken from the realm of the global and applied as a local concept, the *barrio*, or ghetto, became its focus, as evidenced in the titles of scholarly works by Camarillo, *Chicanos in a Changing Society: From Mexican Pueblos to American Barrios in Santa Barbara and Southern California, 1848–1930* (1979); Griswold del Castillo, *The Los Angeles Barrio, 1850–1890* (1979); and Romo, *East Los Angeles: A History of a Barrio* (1983).

If anything defined the ethics of the Chicano moral community, it was the belief in collectivism and an explicit rejection of individualism (Acuña, 1972, p. 230). *Chicanismo* meant identifying with *la raza* (the race or people), and collectively promoting the interests of *carnales* (brothers) with whom they shared a common language, culture, and religion.

Examining any of the Chicano scholarly or artistic productions between 1965 and 1975 clearly indicates one point. The history of Chicanos was thought to have begun in 1848, at the end of the U.S.-Mexican War. This date emphasized the legacy of Anglo racism toward Chicanos. As Armando Navarro (1974) would write, "Chicano politics [and history have] always been imbued with a spirit of resistance toward Anglo-American oppression and domination." The relationship between Anglos and Chicanos "was conceived out of a master-servant relationship between the Anglo conqueror and the Chicano conquered" (pp. 57–58).

The years 1965 to 1969 saw extensive Chicano activism in the Southwest. As Chicano students were recruited to college and university campuses, the protest from the streets was brought into the classroom. Chicanos demanded Chicano Studies Programs, cultural pride days, and diversification of the curriculum. Coming predominantly from working-class backgrounds and feeling privileged by their college draft exemptions, these Chicanos identified with workers and peasants, and indeed imagined themselves as speakers for these groups.

Few Chicano militants, however, were willing to consider women as an important component of their emancipatory project. By 1969, at the very moment Corky Gonzales was trying to weld a regionally fractured Chicano student movement into a national force, the more radical Chicanas were beginning to see themselves as triply oppressed—by their race, their gender, and their class. "Women students were expected by their male peers to involve themselves actively but in subordination," recalled Adelaida del Castillo (1980). It was not uncommon in those days for the movement's men "to request sexual cooperation as proof of commitment to the struggle, by gratifying the men who fought it" (p. 7). Although the movement persistently had advocated the self-actualization of all Chicanos, women soon discovered that Chicanos meant only men.

Within the Chicano student movement, women were denied leadership roles and were asked to perform only the most traditional stereotypic tasks—cleaning up, making coffee, executing the orders given by men, and servicing their needs.

Women who did manage to assume leadership positions were ridiculed as unfeminine, sexually perverse, promiscuous, and, at the extreme, all to often were taunted as lesbians.

Consequently, by the early 1970s articles began to appear in the movement press highlighting the contradiction between racial and sexual oppression in the Chicano movement. Irene Rodarte (1973) posed the question, "Machismo or revolution?," which Guadalupe Valdes Fallis (1974) reformulated as "tradition or liberation?" Chicano men initially regarded the feminist critique as an assault on their Mexican cultural past, their power, and, by implication, their virility, and responded with crass name calling, labeling Chicana feminists as *malinchistas*, traitors who were influenced by ideas foreign to their community—namely, bourgeois feminist ideology.

The men exhorted the women to be Chicanas first and foremost, to take pride in their cultural heritage, and to reject women's liberation (Longauex y Vásquez, 1970, 1972). Theresa Aragón (1980) was but one of the many women who responded by stating clearly and unequivocally that Chicanas, by incorporating feminist demands in their anticolonial revolution, were not dupes of White bourgeois feminists. "The white women's movement at present is not generally aware of or sensitive to the needs of the Chicana," Aragón wrote, and as such, "Chicanas would have to define their own goals and objectives in relationship to their culture, and their own feminist ideology in relation to those goals" (p. 27).

Just as Chicanos interested in interpreting the history of the Southwest as a history of racial conflict between Anglos and Mexicans explicitly chose 1848 as the beginning of Chicano history, Chicana feminists began envisioning a history ordered by a different sense of time. For women it was not the U.S.-Mexican War that was most important; instead, it was the first major act of conquest in the Americas, Spain's defeat of the Aztec empire (Sweeney, 1977; Mirandé & Enríquez, 1979). A Chicana history that began in 1519, not 1848, placed the issues of gender and power at the very center of the political debate about the future and the past. By choosing 1519, women focused attention on one of Mexico's most famous women, Doña Marina, a Maya woman of noble ancestry who befriended Hernán Cortés in 1517. Cortés availed himself of Doña Marina's considerable knowledge of the local political geography and of various indigenous languages. Acting as his mistress, translator, and confidant, Marina helped Cortés to forge local antipathies toward the Aztecs into a fighting force that Cortés successfully unleashed on Tenochtitlan.

In Mexican history Doña Marina, or la Malinche, had always been seen as a villain, as the supreme betrayer of her race. Luis Valdez, in his 1971 play *The Conquest of Mexico*, depicted Malinche as a traitor because "Not only did she turn her back on her own people, she joined the white men and became assimilated" (p. 131). For activist Chicanas, historical representations of Malinche as a treacherous whore who betrayed her own people were but profound reflections of the deep-seated misogynist beliefs in Mexican and Mexican American culture. The only public models open to Mexican women were those of the virgin and the whore (Stevens, 1973). If women were going to go beyond them, then they had to begin by rehabilitating Malinche, seeing her as the primordial source of *mexicanidad* and *mestizaje*. Malinche, noted del Castillo (1977),

is the beginning of the mestizo nation, she is the mother of its birth, she initiates it with the birth of her mestizo children .... Thus any denigration made against her indirectly defames the character of the ... chicana female. If there is shame for her, there is shame for us; we suffer the effects of those implications. (p. 126)

Whatever the facts—in the case of Malinche there are dreadfully few—the crafting of a *her*story and feminist chronology had shifted the debate away from racism to sexism, away from the male ethos of *carnalismo*, or brotherhood, and *chicanismo*, to *mexicanidad* and *mestizaje*, or pride in one's Mexican ancestry and a recognition of race mixture.

The aim of the male Chicano movement was to decolonize the mind. Chicanas wanted to decolonize the body. Male concerns over job discrimination, access to political power, entry into educational institutions, and community autonomy and self-determination gave way to female demands for birth control (Delgado, 1978; Flores, 1976; Aragón, 1980) and against forced sterilization (Velez-Ibañez, 1980), for welfare rights, prison rights for *pintas*, protection against male violence, and, most important, for sexual pleasure both in marriage and outside of it.

Even more revolutionary was that Chicanas began to write and to express a complex inner emotional life, exploring their sexuality (Alarcón, Castillo, & Moraga, 1989), particularly lesbianism (Trujillo, 1991; Anzaldúa, 1987). Given the importance of sexuality in the Chicana feminist movement, much of the writing explored the mother-daughter relationship. The confrontation between two cultures and between two ways of life was often played out as a generational struggle between mothers and daughters. For Tina Bénitez (1988), the love/hate relationship that existed between Chicanas and their mothers was the result of the mother's desire to reproduce in her daughter the values of a patriarchal culture. "The mother blocks her desires by telling her what 'good girls' should and should not do," asserted Bénitez, "thereby condemning her to emulate a role of powerlessness" (p. 24).

Mothers often came to be regarded with very mixed emotions by their Chicana daughters, in large part because of their subordination/accommodation to patriarchal power. The mothers, who often favored assimilation, urged their daughters to learn English, get educated, marry well (to wealthy Anglo men, if possible), and, if necessary, abandon their cultural past. The generational conflict took on its most confrontational and accusatory tones when daughters, be they lesbian or heterosexual, started to assert their sexuality. To an older generation, sex was not a topic for public discussion, and even in private was not a topic broached comfortably. To daughters, many as participants in the sexual revolution of the 1960s, female sexuality was something to celebrate openly, to talk about, write about, and represent in a myriad of open ways. Mothers viewed such behavior as tantamount to the abandonment of *mexicano* cultural values and acceptance of Anglo ways. Mothers thus accused their daughters of assimilationism; daughters accused their mothers of accommodationism—and here was the problem (Moraga, 1983).

Gradually some women came to realize that they could not blame their mothers for what their mothers themselves had not been able to control. The ultimate solution to this conflictual relationship, according to one Chicana feminist (Burroughs, 1988), was for mothers to give their love and approval to their daughters freely, and for daughters to relieve their mothers of all the psychic burdens they, too, had endured. "The choice is to either passively sit and watch our sisters and mother be beaten into the ground, or to help them rise above by giving them the love and support they so often seek from men" (p. 56).

As should be apparent from these writings, the impact of Chicano-inspired scholarship and activism was to challenge the status quo and to displace the century-old stereotypes and caricatures of Mexicans and Mexican Americans in the dominant imagination. The alleged passivity of the Mexican American could no longer be reconciled with the images that appeared daily on network television news and in newspapers. "Docile" Mexican Americans had demanded their rights; had affirmed the vibrancy and importance of their culture, religion, and language; and, like other nationalist movements in the United States, were demanding a reinscription into the body politic.

RECENT RESEARCH TRENDS, 1985–1993

Since 1985 there has been a great deal of research activity generated by scholars of Chicano ancestry, by individuals who were active in the movement, and by sympathetic fellow travelers. Foremost in the minds of many has been serious reexamination of the Chicano movement, focusing on the social origins of the leaders and the ideologies that inspired them and that they espoused. Ernesto Chavez (1993) studied the history of the Chicano movement in Los Angeles, largely through oral histories conducted with the actual movement activists. Mario García and Ramón Gutiérrez are also at work on histories of the movement that undoubtedly will challenge the notion that a unified movement ever really existed at the national and grassroots levels.

Studies critical of the Chicano movement's ideology have started to appear. Almaguer's recent essay, "Ideological Distortions in Recent Chicano Historiography" (1989), lays open the historiography on Chicanos, exposing the false epistemological closures and simplistic ideas that he, as well as other Chicano radicals and intellectuals, claimed as their credo in the 1960s. Almaguer argues that, motivated primarily by the desire to challenge the dominant assimilationist model of the 1950s, Chicano radicals embraced a colonial analysis that depicted the history of Chicanos as that of a colonized minority. However strongly these sentiments were felt in the 1960s, Almaguer now maintains that the analysis was largely wrong. A cursory examination of Chicano histories showed that Native Americans had been ignored; that Mexican Americans historically had occupied several classes; and that in the racial hierarchy, Mexicans occupied an intermediate position between Anglos and Indians. In short, much of what he and others had written was an ideological distortion of the past, fashioned to fit the political tenor of the day.

Writing from a Jewish, *Tejana*, lesbian, *mestiza*, working-class perspective, Gloria Anzaldúa (1987) employed a slightly different strategy to destabilize the unitary mythology of the masculine-centered Chicano movement. In her book *Borderlands/La Frontera: The New Mestiza*, Anzaldúa described her fractured identities, identities fractured not only by her gender, class, race, religion, and homosexuality, but also by the reality of life along the U.S.-Mexico border. In one chapter, "How to Tame a Wild Tongue," Anzaldúa vividly showed through the example of language just how complex Mexican American culture along the U.S.-Mexico border really was. She identified eight forms of Spanish:

> My "home" tongues are the languages I speak with my sister and brothers, with my friends. They are [*Pachuco* (called *caló*), Tex-Mex, Chicano Spanish, North Mexican Spanish dialect, and Standard Mexican Spanish, with Chicano Spanish] being the closest to my heart. From school, the media and job situations, I've picked up standard and working class English. From Mamagrande Locha and from reading Spanish and Mexican literature, I've picked up Standard Spanish and Standard Mexican Spanish. From *los recién llegados*, Mexican immigrants and *braceros*, I learned Northern Mexican dialect. . . . (pp. 55–56)

Anzaldúa then described how and when she used each form of Spanish, concluding that the relationship between language and identity was complex and that Mexican Americans and Chicanos were a complexly stratified ethnic group.

As the Chicano movement has been eclipsed politically, both nationally and on college and university campuses, scholars have once again turned their attention to older research themes that traditionally were studied under the rubric of immigration. Mexican immigrant men were primarily studied as workers, and this is a focus that has been carried over into feminist-inspired research on Mexican immigrant women, Mexican American women, and Chicanas. Women's rates of labor-force participation, their incomes in comparison to men, their occupational preferences, and their roles in secondary labor markets have been abundantly documented (Cardenas, 1982; Cooney, 1975; Kossoudji & Ranney, 1984; Sullivan, 1984). V. L. Ruiz (1987) explored the work activities of Mexican and Mexican American women in northern California food-processing plants between 1920 and 1950, particularly their labor union activism. Zavella (1985, 1987) took up the issue of conflicts between work and family, studying women cannery workers in the Santa Clara Valley of northern California. She showed how mechanization had contributed to female labor segregation and how the labor market reinformed traditional family roles within the household. In Zavella's sample, men, be they Mexican, Mexican American, or Chicano, viewed working wives as symbols of their own shortcomings as husbands and providers, and worried about the effects of an absent mother on their children. Since this initial research, Zavella has published extensively and quite brilliantly on the organization of work among Chicanas (1991a, 1991b).

Segura (1984, 1989a, 1989b, 1992, 1993) has contributed

immensely to an analysis of the intersection of race, class, and gender among Mexican American women and Chicanas through investigation of their labor market experiences. She has been keenly interested in the "effects of family relationships upon employment options . . . [labor force] points of entry and occupational advancement" (1984, p. 77).

What all of this recent research has poignantly established is that the Mexican-origin population of the United States is complexly stratified by class, color, gender, generation, and level of assimilation, and that it is no longer a minority, but an emerging majority population in the Southwest. Hayes-Bautista and Chapa (1988) explored the implication of these facts for the well-being of the American economy in *The Burden of Support: Young Latinos in an Aging Society*, wherein they generated a set of demographic projections to determine the shape and nature of California's population in the year 2030. Since the Immigration Reform Act of 1965, California's population has changed tremendously, marked by high levels of immigration from Asian and Latin American countries. As the authors noted, these immigrants were by and large relatively young and unskilled, and have demonstrated very high fertility rates (1980 = 3.14, or slightly more than 3 children per woman of childbearing age). California's Anglo population, on the other hand, had declined as a proportion of the state's total population since 1965, had shown low fertility rates (1.31, or roughly 1 child for every woman of childbearing age), and had seen a dramatic increase in life expectancy (from 58.6 years for males in 1930 to 71.3 years in 1980). What these demographic facts portended was an increasingly aged Anglo minority population dependent for social services and governmental transfer payments on a Mexican emerging majority that was largely uneducated, unskilled, and politically disenfranchised. The authors argued that if resources were not invested in the state's human capital, decades of intense racial and generational conflict and a lowered standard of living would be California's future—a model that applied to other geographic areas of the United States as well.

Another important result of the 1965 Immigration Reform Act was a profound change in demographic composition of Latin American-origin immigrants. Whereas up to 1965 the majority of these had been Mexican, after 1965 larger numbers came from the Caribbean, Central America, and Latin America. To acknowledge this change, scholars have increasingly turned their attention to a new political identity—that of Latinos. F. Padilla (1987) explored this identity in *Latino Ethnic Consciousness*, in which he described attempts in Chicago by Puerto Ricans, Cubans, Mexican Americans, Mexicans, and other Latin American immigrant groups to forge a common identity and coalition as Latinos, as speakers of a Latin-origin language—Spanish. This identity stemmed from years of community organization and action, and a clear realization that without orchestrated unified action, no one group standing alone will be able to wrestle concession from the municipal government.

The common interests, experiences, and struggles of Latinos also recently resulted in the first major study of Latino political participation in American politics. De la Garza, DeSipio, García, García, and Falcón (1992) undertook what they called the La-

tino National Political Survey, a sample of extensive interviews with 1,546 Mexicans, 589 Puerto Ricans, and 682 Cubans residing in the United States concerning their political attitudes.

IMPLICATIONS FOR RESEARCH AND PRACTICE

Looking over the course of almost 200 years, this chapter has surveyed the historical and social science literature on Mexicans, Mexican Americans, Chicanos, and, to some extent, Latinos. What becomes apparent is that in each of the periods reviewed here the ethnic Mexican population of the United States was negatively stigmatized by its culture and its occupations, and persistently and repeatedly viewed as a problem that had to be cured, if not eradicated. Scholarship written by Chicanos themselves, and by intellectuals who were sympathetic to their aspirations, did a great deal to change the topics and tenor of the research. Studies that once vilified Mexicans, that blamed the victims for their own problems, or that celebrated victimization were supplanted by scholarship that explored historical agency, subjectivity, and differentiation.

If one glances over the research corpus herein discussed, it is readily apparent that there are still numerous themes in the history of Mexican Americans desperately in need of study. The issue of transculturation has been only slightly explored, and much remains to be written on the process of assimilation and acculturation as it has affected a highly mobile population that has consistently refused to cut its ties to Mexico. Most of the theoretical work on assimilation and acculturation was based on the experiences of European immigrants who were separated by an ocean from their country of origin, who rarely visited Europe once they emigrated, and who quickly cast their lot with their new home in the United States. Mexicans have never fit this pattern, and thus perhaps it is time to rethink assimilation as an explanatory model for Americanization.

Undoubtedly because so much of the scholarship on ethnic Mexicans in the United States focused on immigration, little has been written on the upward social mobility of second- and third-generation Mexican immigrants. This oversight may soon be remedied as social scientists turn increasingly to the study of Latinos, which by necessity requires comparing the experiences of Cubans, Mexicans, Central Americans, and Puerto Ricans in the United States.

Issues of gender still animate many feminist intellectuals, a trend that will surely continue. Gay, lesbian, and bisexual Mexican American scholars and cultural workers are interrogating both the actual past and how it was represented, noting the politics of textual erasure, the epistemology of the closet, the privileges of masculinity and heterosexuality, and how all of these prejudices have been textually naturalized.

As the United States tries to imagine its future in a new world order devoid of the threat of communism, how the nation's borders are constructed both physically and metaphysically will be an issue of utmost importance. To respond to the challenges and opportunities posed by the rise of global corporations and major regional trading blocs, the hemispheric relationship among Mexico, Canada, and the United States is being renegotiated. Perhaps in the not-too-distant future physical borders will cease to exist in North America and workers will move about freely without constraint, pushed and pulled by market forces rather than the forces of state repression.

These, then, are some of the challenges and opportunities that await scholars, researchers, students, and cultural workers—reimagining the Mexican past in order to change the future before us.

References

Acuña, R. (1972). *Occupied America: The Chicano struggle toward liberation*. New York: Canfield Press.

Alarcón, N., Castillo, A., & Moraga, C. (1989). *Third woman: The sexuality of Latinas*. Berkeley, CA: Third Woman Press.

Almaguer, T. (1971). Toward the study of Chicano colonialism. *Aztlán*, 2(1), 7–21.

Almaguer, T. (1974). Historical notes on Chicano oppression: The dialectics of racial and class domination in North America. *Aztlán*, 5(1–2), 27–56.

Almaguer, T. (1975). Class, race, and Chicano oppression. *Socialist Revolution*, 25, 71–99.

Almaguer, T. (1989). Ideological distortions in recent Chicano historiography. *Aztlán*, 18(1), 7–27.

Almaguer, T., & Camarillo, A. (1983). Urban Chicano workers in historical perspective: A review of the literature. In *The State of Chicano Research on Family, Labor, and Migration: Proceedings of the First Stanford Symposium on Chicano Research and Public Policy* (pp. 3–32). Stanford, CA: Stanford University Center for Chicano Research.

Alvarez, H. (1966). A demographic profile of Mexican immigration to the United States, 1910–1950. *Journal of Inter-American Studies*, 8(1), 471–496.

Anzaldúa, G. (1987). *Borderlands/la frontera: The new mestiza*. San Francisco: Ante Lute Press.

Aragón, J. L. (1976). The people of Santa Fe in the 1790s. *Aztlán*, 7(3), 391–417.

Aragón, T. (1980). Organizing as a political tool for the Chicana. *Frontiers: A Journal of Women Studies*, 5(2), 9–34.

Arroyo, L. (1975). Notes on past, present and future directions of Chicano labor studies. *Aztlán*, 6(2), 137–150.

Balderrama, F. E. (1982). *In defense of La Raza: The Los Angeles Mexican consulate and the Mexican community, 1929–1936*. Tucson: University of Arizona Press.

Bamford, E. F. (1923–24). The Mexican casual problem in the southwest. *Journal of Applied Sociology*, 8, 364–371.

Barrera, M. (1979). *Race and class in the Southwest: A theory of racial inequality*. Notre Dame, IN: Notre Dame University Press.

Barrera, M., Muñoz, C., & Ornelas, C. (1972). The barrio as internal colony. *Urban Affairs Annual Reviews*, 6, 465–498.

Bean, F. D., & Tienda, M. (1987). *The Hispanic population of the United States*. New York: Russell Sage.

Bénitez, T. (1988). The mother daughter relationship. In L. Hernández & T. Bénitez (Eds.), *Palabras Chicanas* (pp. 23–29). Berkeley, CA: Third Woman Press.

Betten, N., & Mohl, R. A. (1973). From discrimination to repatriation: Mexican life during the great depression. *Pacific Historical Review*, 42(3), 370–388.

Blauner, R. (1972). *Racial oppression in America*. New York: Harper & Row.

Bogardus, E. (1940). Current problems of Mexican immigrants. *Sociology and Social Research*, 24, 168–173.

Bogardus, E. (1943). Gangs of Mexican-American youth. *Sociology and Social Science Research*, 27, 60–72.

Bolton, H. E. (1915). *Texas in the middle eighteenth century: Studies in Spanish colonial history and administration*. Berkeley: University of California Press.

Borjas, G. J. (1990). *Friends or strangers: The impact of immigrants on the U.S. economy*. New York: Basic Books.

Boswell, T. D. (1979). The growth and proportional distribution of the Mexican-stock population of the United States: 1910–1970. *Mississippi Geographer*, 7(1), 57–76.

Brack, G. (1975). *Mexico views manifest destiny, 1821–1846*. Norman: University of Oklahoma Press.

Briegel, K. L. (1974). *The Alianza Hispano Americana, 1894–1965: A Mexican fraternal insurance society*. Unpublished doctoral dissertation, University of Southern California, Los Angeles.

Briggs, C. (1987). Getting both sides of the story: Oral history in land grant research and litigation. In C. L. Briggs & J. R. Van Ness (Eds.), *Land, water, and culture: New perspectives on Hispanic land grants* (pp. 217–268). Albuquerque: University of New Mexico Press.

Briggs, C. L., & Van Ness, J. R. (1987). *Land, water, and culture: New perspectives on Hispanic land grants*. Albuquerque: University of New Mexico Press.

Burroughs, F. (1988). Joining the future and the past. In L. Hernández & T. Benítez (Eds.), *Palabras Chicanas* (pp. 55–57). Berkeley, CA: Third Woman Press.

Calavita, K. (1992). *Inside the state: The bracero program, immigration, and the I.N.S.* New York: Routledge.

Camarillo, A. (1979). *Chicanos in a changing society: From Mexican pueblos to American barrios in Santa Barbara and southern California, 1848–1930*. Cambridge, MA: Harvard University Press.

Cardenas, G. (1982). Undocumented immigrant women in the Houston labor force. *California Sociologist*, 5(2), 98–118.

Cardenas, G., & Flores, E. T. (1986). *The migration and settlement of undocumented women*. Austin: Mexican American Studies Center, University of Texas.

Cardoso, L. (1980). *Mexican emigration to the United States, 1897–1931*. Tucson: University of Arizona Press.

Carlson, H., & Henderson, N. (1950). The intelligence of American children of Mexican parentage. *Journal of Abnormal Psychology*, 33, 540–553.

Carmichael, S., & Hamilton, C. V. (1967). *Black power*. New York: Random House.

Carreras, M. (1974). *Los mexicanos que devolvió la crisis 1929–1932*. Mexico City: Secretaría de Relaciones Exteriores.

Carter, T. (1970). *Mexican Americans in school: A history of educational neglect*. New York: Russell Sage.

Carver, R. (1982). *The impact of intimacy: Mexican-Anglo intermarriage in New Mexico, 1821–1846*. El Paso: Texas Western Press.

Castañeda, A. (1990). *Presidarias y pobladoras: Spanish-Mexican women in frontier Monterey, California, 1770–1821*. Unpublished doctoral dissertation, Stanford University.

Castañeda, A. (1993). Sexual violence in the politics and policies of conquest: Amerindian women and the Spanish conquest of Alta California. In A. de la Torre & B. M. Pesquera (Eds.), *Building with our hands: New directions in Chicana studies* (pp. 15–33). Berkeley: University of California Press.

Castillo, P., & Camarillo, A. (1973). *Furia y muerte: Los bandidos Chicanos*. Los Angeles: Aztlán Publishers.

Chavez, E. (1993). *The Chicano movement in Los Angeles, 1966–1978*. Unpublished doctoral dissertation, University of California, Los Angeles.

Chipman, D. E. (1992). *Spanish Texas, 1519–1821*. Austin: University of Texas Press.

Clark, K. (1965). *Dark ghetto*. New York: Harper & Row.

Clark, V. S. (1908). Mexican labor in the United States. *United States Bureau of Labor Bulletin, 78*, 450–503.

Cooney, R. S. (1975). Changing labor force participation of Mexican-American wives: A comparison with Anglos and Blacks. *Social Science Quarterly, 56*, 252–261.

Cornelius, W. A. (1976). *Mexican migration to the United States: The view from rural sending communities*. Cambridge, MA: MIT Center for International Studies.

Cortés, C. E. (1992). To view a neighbor: The Hollywood textbook on Mexico, In J. Coatsworth & C. Rico (Eds.), *Images of Mexico in the United States* (pp. 91–118). San Diego: Center for U.S.-Mexican Studies, University of California, San Diego.

Cotler, J. (1967–68). The mechanics of internal domination and social change in Peru. *Studies in Comparative International Development, 3*(12), 229–246.

Craig, R. (1971). *The bracero program: Interest groups and foreign policy*. Austin: University of Texas Press.

Cruse, H. (1962). *Rebellion or revolution*. New York: Morrow.

Cruz, G. R. (1988). *Let there be towns: Spanish municipal origins in the American Southwest, 1610–1810*. College Station: Texas A&M University Press.

Dana, R. H. (1840). *Two years before the mast*. New York: Harpers.

De la Garza, R. O., DeSipio, L., García, F. C., García, J., & Falcón, A. (1992). *Latino voices: Mexican, Puerto Rican, & Cuban perspectives on American politics*. Boulder, CO: Westview Press.

De la Teja, F. J. (1991) *A revolution remembered: The memoirs and selected correspondence of Juan N. Seguín*. Austin: Texas Historical Society.

De León, A. (1982). *The Tejano community, 1836–1900*. Albuquerque: University of New Mexico Press.

De León, A. (1983). *They called them greasers: Anglo attitudes toward Mexicans in Texas, 1821–1900*. Austin: University of Texas Press.

De Onís, J. (1976). *The Hispanic contribution to the state of Colorado*. Boulder, CO: Westview Press.

del Castillo, A. R. (1977). Malintzin Tenépal: A preliminary look into a new perspective. In R. Sánchez (Ed.), *Essays on la mujer* (pp. 124–149). Los Angeles: Chicano Studies Center, UCLA.

del Castillo, A. R. (1980). Mexican women in organization. In M. Mora & A. R. del Castillo (Eds.), *Mexican women in the United States* (pp. 7–16). Los Angeles: Chicano Studies Center, UCLA.

Delgado, S. (1978). Young Chicana speaks up on problems faced by young girls. *Regeneración, 1*(1), 5–7.

Deutsch, S. (1987). *No separate refuge: Culture, class and gender on an Anglo-Hispanic frontier in the American Southwest, 1880–1940*. New York: Oxford University Press.

Diaz-Guerrero, R. (1955). Neurosis and the Mexican family structure. *American Journal of Psychiatry, 112*, 411–417.

Dinwoodie, D. H. (1977). Deportation: The immigration service and the Chicano labor movement in the 1930s. *New Mexico Historical Review, 52*(3), 193–206.

Dobyns, H. F. (1991). Do-it-yourself religion: The diffusion of folk Catholicism on Mexico's northern frontier 1821–1846. In N. R. Crumrine & A. Morinis (Eds), *Pilgrimage in Latin America* (pp. 53–70). New York: Greenwood Press.

Durand, J., & Massey, D. S. (1992). Mexican migration to the United States: A critical review. *Latin American Research Review, 27*(2), 3–42.

Dysart, J. (1976). Mexican women in San Antonio, 1830–1860: The assimilation process. *Western Historical Quarterly, 7*(4), 365–377.

Ebright, M. (1987). New Mexican land grants: The legal background. In C. L. Briggs & J. R. Van Ness (Eds.), *Land, water, and culture: New perspectives on Hispanic land grants* (pp. 15–66). Albuquerque: University of New Mexico Press.

Flores, K. (1976). Chicano attitudes toward birth control. *Imagenes de la Chicana, 1*(1), 19–21.

Foerster, R. F. (1925). *The racial problems involved in immigration from Latin America and the West Indies to the United States: A report to the Secretary of Labor*. Washington, DC: Government Printing Office.

Foley, N. (1990). *The new South in the Southwest: Anglos, Blacks, and Mexicans in Central Texas, 1880–1930*. Unpublished doctoral dissertation, University of Michigan, Ann Arbor.

Frank, A. G. (1967). *Capitalism and underdevelopment in Latin America*. New York: Monthly Review Press.

Galarza, E. (1964). *Merchants of labor: The Mexican bracero story*. Santa Barbara, CA: McNally & Loflin.

Galarza, E. (1977). *Farm workers and agribusiness in California, 1947–1960*. Notre Dame, IN: Notre Dame University Press.

Gamboa, E. (1990). *Mexican labor and World War II: Braceros in the Pacific Northwest, 1942–1947*. Austin: University of Texas Press.

Gamio, M. (1930a). *The life story of the Mexican immigrants*. Chicago: University of Chicago Press.

Gamio, M. (1930b). *Número, procedencia y distribución geográfica de los inmigrantes mexicanos en los Estados Unidos*. Mexico City: Talleres Gráficos y Diario Official.

Gamio, M. (1931). *Mexican immigration to the United States*. Chicago: University of Chicago Press.

Gardiner, H. (1952). Foreign travelers' accounts of Mexico, 1810–1910. *The Americas, 8*(3), 321–351.

Garis, R. L. (1930). Mexican immigration: A report by Roy I. Garis for the information of the members of congress. In United States House of Representatives, *Western hemisphere immigration* (pp. 420–455). Washington, DC: Government Printing Office.

Garretson, O. (1928). A study of causes of retardation among Mexican children in a small public school system in Arizona. *Journal of Educational Psychology, 19*, 31–40.

Garth, T. (1923). A comparison of the intelligence of Mexican, mixed, and full blood Indian children. *Psychological Review, 30*, 388–401.

Garth, T., Elson, T. H., & Morton, M. M. (1936). The administration of non-language intelligence tests to Mexicans. *Journal of Abnormal Psychology, 23*, 101–145.

Gilbert, G. M. (1959). Sex differences in mental health in a Mexican village. *International Journal of Psychiatry, 5*(3), 208–213.

Gómez-Quiñones, J. (1972). The first steps: Chicano labor conflict and organizing, 1900–1920. *Aztlán, 3*(1), 13–50.

Gómez-Quiñones, J. (1975). Piedras contra la luna, México en Aztlán y Aztlán en México: Chicano-Mexican relations in the Mexican consulates, 1900–1920. In *Contemporary Mexico: Papers of the 4th international congress of Mexican history* (pp. 43–97). Mexico City: El Colegio de México.

Gómez-Quiñones, J. (1977). On culture. *Revista Chicano-Riqueña, 5*(2), 35–53.

Gómez-Quiñones, J. (1982). *Development of the Mexican working class north of the Rio Bravo: Work and culture among laborers and artisans, 1600–1900*. Los Angeles: Chicano Studies Research Center Publications, UCLA.

Gómez-Quiñones, J. (1990). *Chicano politics: Reality and promise, 1940–1990*. Albuquerque: University of New Mexico Press.

Gonzales-Berry, E. (1993). Two texts for a new canon: Vicente Bernal's *Las Primicias* and Felipe Maximiliano Chacón's *Poesía y prosa*. In R. A. Gutiérrez & G. Padilla (Eds.), *Recovering the U.S. Hispanic literary heritage* (pp. 129–152). Houston, TX: Arte Público Press.

González, D. J. (1993). La Tules of image and reality: Euro-American attitudes and legend formation on a Spanish-Mexican frontier. In A. de la Torre & B. M. Pesquera (Eds.), *Building with our hands: New directions in Chicana studies* (pp. 75–90). Berkeley: University of California Press.

González, M. J. (1993). *In search of the plumed serpent: Mexican Los Angeles, 1781–1850*. Unpublished doctoral dissertation, University of California, Berkeley.

González-Casanova, P. (1969). Internal colonialism and national development. In I. L. Horowitz (Ed.), *Latin American radicalism* (pp. 118–137). New York: Random House.

Greenfield, G. M., & Cortés, C. E. (1991). Harmony and conflict of intercultural images: The treatment of Mexico in U.S. feature films and K–12 textbooks. *Mexican Studies/Estudios Mexicanos, 7*(2), 283–301.

Gregg, J. (1844). *Commerce of the prairies*. New York: H. G. Langley.

Griswold del Castillo, R. (1979). *The Los Angeles barrio, 1850–1890*. Berkeley: University of California Press.

Griswold del Castillo, R. (1992). *The treaty of Guadalupe-Hidalgo: A legacy of conflict*. Norman: University of Oklahoma Press.

Gunn, D. W. (1974). *American and British writers in Mexico, 1556–1973*. Austin: University of Texas Press.

Gutiérrez, D. (1994). *Walls and mirrors: Mexican Americans, Mexican immigrants, and the politics of ethnicity in the American Southwest, 1910–1986*. Berkeley: University of California Press.

Gutiérrez, R. A. (1976). *Mexican migration to the United States, 1880–1930: The Chicano and internal colonialism*. Unpublished master's thesis, University of Wisconsin, Madison.

Gutiérrez, R. A. (1989a). Aztlán, Montezuma, and New Mexico: The political uses of American Indian mythology. In R. A. Anaya & F. Lomelí (Eds.), *Aztlán: Essays on the Chicano homeland* (pp. 172–190). Albuquerque, NM: Academia/El Norte Publications.

Gutiérrez, R. A. (1989b). Ethnic and class boundaries in America's Hispanic past. In S. Chan (Ed.), *Intersections: Studies of ethnicity, gender, and inequality* (pp. 47–63). Lewiston, NY: Edwin Mellin Press.

Gutiérrez, R. A. (1991). *When Jesus came, the corn mothers went away: Marriage, sexuality and power in New Mexico, 1500–1846*. Stanford, CA: Stanford University Press.

Gutiérrez, R. A. (1992). The colonial worlds: The southern part of the United States. In M. Ramírez (Ed.), *Ibero-American heritage: Latinos in the making of the United States of America* (Vol. 2, pp. 719–738). Albany: New York State Education Department.

Gutiérrez, R. A. (1993a). Nationalism and literary production: The Hispanic and Chicano experiences. In R. A. Gutiérrez & G. Padilla (Eds.), *Recovering the U.S. Hispanic literary heritage* (pp. 309–314). Houston, TX: Arte Público Press.

Gutiérrez, R. A. (1993b). The UCLA bibliographic survey of Mexican American literary culture, 1821–1945: An overview. In R. A. Gutiérrez & G. Padilla (Eds.), *Recovering the U.S. Hispanic literary heritage* (pp. 309–314). Houston, TX: Arte Público Press.

Gutiérrez, R. A., & Padilla, G. (1993). *Recovering the U.S. Hispanic literary heritage*. Houston, TX: Arte Público Press.

Hall, G. E. (1987). The Pueblo grant labyrinth. In C. L. Briggs & J. R. Van Ness (Eds.), *Land, water, and culture: New perspectives on Hispanic land grants* (pp. 67–140). Albuquerque: University of New Mexico Press.

Hass, L. (1994). *Conquests and identities in California, 1769–1936*. Berkeley: University of California Press.

Haught, B. F. (1931). The language difficulty of Spanish-American children. *Journal of Applied Psychology, 15*, 92–95.

Hayden, R. G. (1966). Spanish-Americans of the Southwest: Life style patterns and their implications. *Welfare in Review, 4*(4), 14–25.

Hayes-Bautista, D., & Chapa, J. (1988). *The burden of support: Young Latinos in an aging society*. Stanford, CA: Stanford University Press.

Hernández, J. A. (1983). *Mutual aid for survival: The case of the Mexican Americans*. Malabar, FL: Krieger.

Herrera-Sobek, M. (1993). *Reconstructing a Chicano/a literary heritage: Hispanic colonial literature of the Southwest*. Tucson: University of Arizona Press.

Hoffman, A. (1974). *Unwanted Mexican Americans in the great depression: Repatriation pressures, 1929–1939*. Tucson: University of Arizona Press.

Hondagneu-Sotelo, P. (1992). Overcoming patriarchal constraints: The reconstruction of gender relations among Mexican immigrant women and men. *Gender & Society, 6*(1), 393–415.

Horsman, R. (1981). *Race and manifest destiny: The origins of American racial Anglo-Saxonism*. Cambridge, MA: Harvard University Press.

Humphrey, N. D. (1943). The Detroit Mexican immigrant and naturalization. *Social Forces, 22*, 332–335.

Humphrey, N. D. (1944). The changing structure of the Detroit Mexican family: An index of acculturation. *American Sociological Review, 9*(6), 622–626.

Jenks, J. W., & Lauck, W. J. (1917). *The immigrant problem: A study of American immigration conditions and needs*. New York: Funk and Wagnalls.

Johannsen, R. W. (1985). *To the halls of the Montezumas: The Mexican war in the American imagination*. New York: Oxford University Press.

Jones, R. C. (1948). Ethnic family patterns: The Mexican family in the United States. *American Journal of Sociology, 53*(6), 450–452.

Kanellos, N. (1993). A socio-historic study of Hispanic newspapers in the United States. In R. A. Gutiérrez & G. Padilla (Eds.), *Recovering the U.S. Hispanic literary heritage* (pp. 107–126). Houston, TX: Arte Público Press.

Keller, G. D. (1985). *Chicano cinema: Research, reviews, and resources*. Binghamton, NY: Bilingual Review Press.

Keston, M., & Jiménez, C. (1954). A study of the performance on English and Spanish editions of the Stanford-Binet intelligence test by Spanish-American children. *Journal of Genetic Psychology, 85*, 263–269.

Kiser, G. C., & Silverman, D. (1972). Mexican repatriation during the great depression. *Journal of Mexican American History, 2*(2), 122–142.

Kluckhohn, F., & Strodtbeck, F. (1961). *Variations in value orientations*. Evanston, IL: Row, Peterson & Co.

Kossoudji, S. A., & Ranney, S. I. (1984). The labor market experience of female migrants: The case of temporary Mexican migration to the United States. *International Migration Review, 18*(3), 1120–1143.

Lacy, J. H. (1959). New Mexico women in early American writings. *New Mexico Historical Review, 34*(2), 41–59.

Langum, D. J. (1978). Californios and the image of indolence. *Western Historical Quarterly, 9*(2), 181–196.

Lewis, O. (1951). *Life in a Mexican village*. Urbana: University of Illinois Press.

Longauex y Vásquez, E. (1970). The Mexican-American woman. In R. Morgan (Ed.), *Sisterhood is powerful* (pp. 379–840). New York: Random House.

Longauex y Vásquez, E. (1972). Soy Chicana primero. *El cuaderno, 1*, 17–22.

Loyo, G. (1969). Notas preliminares de Gilberto Loyo sobre la migración de Mexicanos a los Estados Unidos de 1900 a 1967. In M. Gamio (Ed.), *El inmigrante mexicano: La historia de su vida* (pp. 28–37). Mexico City: Universidad Nacional Autónoma de México.

Madsen, W. (1964). *The Mexican-Americans of south Texas*. New York: Holt, Rinehart, and Winston.

Manuel, H. T. (1965). *Spanish-speaking children of the Southwest*. Austin: University of Texas Press.

Martin, P. P. (1992). *Songs my mother sang to me: An oral history of Mexican American women*. Tucson: University of Arizona Press.

Martínez, O. J. (1975). On the size of the Chicano population: New estimates, 1850–1900. *Aztlán, 6*(1), 43–67.

Martínez, O. J. (1988). *Troublesome border*. Tucson: University of Arizona Press.

Massey, D., Alarcón, R., Durand, J., & González, H. (1987). *Return to Aztlán: The social process of international migration from western Mexico*. Berkeley: University of California Press.

McWilliams, C. (1949). *North from Mexico: The Spanish-speaking people of the United States*. Philadelphia: Lippincott.

Merk, F. (1963). *Manifest destiny and mission in American history*. New York: Random House.

Meyer, Doris L. (1978). Early Mexican-American responses to negative stereotyping. *New Mexico Historical Review, 53*(3), 75–91.

Miller, D. A. (1982). Cross-cultural marriages in the southwest: The New Mexico experience, 1846–1900. *New Mexico Historical Review, 57*(4), 335–359.

Mirandé, A., & Enríquez, E. (1979). *La Chicana: The Mexican-American woman*. Chicago: University of Chicago Press.

Monroy, D. (1990). *Thrown among strangers: The making of culture in frontier California*. Berkeley: University of California Press.

Monsiváis, C. (1984). Travelers in Mexico: A brief anthology of selected myths. *Diogenes, 125*, 48–74.

Montejano, D. (1987). *Anglos and Mexicans in the making of Texas, 1836–1986*. Austin: University of Texas Press.

Moraga, C. (1983). *Loving in the war years: Lo que nunca pasó por sus labios*. Boston: South End Press.

Morin, R. (1966). *Among the valiant: Mexican-Americans in WWII and Korea*. Alhambra, CA: Borden Publishing Company.

Myres, S. L. (1982). Mexican Americans and westering Anglos: A feminine perspective. *New Mexico Historical Review, 57*(4), 317–333.

Navarro, A. (1974). The evolution of Chicano politics. *Aztlán, 5*(1–2), 57–84.

Noggle, B. (1959). Anglo observers of the southwest borderlands, 1825–1890: The rise of a concept. *Arizona and the West, 1*(2), 105–131.

Officer, J. E. (1987). *Hispanic Arizona, 1536–1856*. Tucson: University of Arizona Press.

Padget, M. (1993). *Cultural geographies: Travel writing in the southwest, 1869–97*. Unpublished doctoral dissertation, University of California, San Diego.

Padilla, F. (1987). *Latino ethnic consciousness*. Notre Dame, IN: Notre Dame University Press.

Padilla, G. (1993a). *History, memory and the struggles of self-representation: The formation of Mexican American autobiography*. Madison: University of Wisconsin Press.

Padilla, G. (1993b). Recovering Mexican American autobiography. In R. A. Gutiérrez & G. Padilla (Eds.), *Recovering the U.S. Hispanic literary heritage* (pp. 153–178). Houston, TX: Arte Público Press.

Paredes, R. A. (1977a). The Mexican image in American travel literature, 1831–1869. *New Mexico Historical Review, 52*(1), 5–29.

Paredes, R. A. (1977b). The origins of anti-Mexican sentiment in the United States. *The New Scholar, 6*, 139–165.

Pattie, J. O. (1831). *The personal narrative of James O. Pattie*. Cincinnati, OH: John. H. Wood.

Paz, O. (1961). *The labyrinth of solitude: Life and thought in Mexico*. New York: Random House.

Pettit, A. G. (1980). *Images of the Mexican American in fiction and film*. College Station: Texas A&M University Press.

Pitt, L. (1971). *The decline of the Californios: A social history of the Spanish-speaking Californians, 1846–1890*. Berkeley: University of California Press.

Poyo, G., & Hinojosa, G. (1991). *Tejano origins in eighteenth-century San Antonio*. Austin: University of Texas Press.

Ramos, S. (1938). *El perfil del hombre y la cultura en México*. México, D.F.: Pedro Robredo.

Reichert, J. A. (1979). *The migrant syndrome: An analysis of U.S. migration and its impact on a rural Mexican town*. Unpublished doctoral dissertation, Princeton University, Princeton, NJ.

Reisler, M. (1976). *By the sweat of their brow: Mexican immigrant labor in the United States, 1900–1940*. Westport, CT: Greenwood Press.

Ríos-Bustamante, A. (1976). New Mexico in the eighteenth century: Life, labor and trade in la villa de San Felipe de Albuquerque, 1706–1790. *Aztlán, 7*(3), 357–389.

Robinson, C. (1963). *With the ears of strangers: The Mexican in American literature*. Tucson: University of Arizona Press.

Robinson, C. (1977). *Mexico and the Hispanic southwest in American literature*. Tucson: University of Arizona Press.

Rodarte, I. (1973). Machismo vs. revolution. In D. Moreno (Ed.), *La mujer en pie de lucha* (pp. 4–34). Mexico City: Espina del Norte.

Rodríguez, S. (1987). Land, water and ethnic identity in Taos. In C. L. Briggs & J. R. Van Ness (Eds.), *Land, water, and culture: New perspectives on Hispanic land grants* (pp. 313–403). Albuquerque: University of New Mexico Press.

Romo, R. (1983). *East Los Angeles: A history of a barrio*. Austin: University of Texas Press.

Rosenbaum, R. J. (1981). *Mexicano resistance in the southwest: The sacred right of self-preservation*. Austin: University of Texas Press.

Ruiz, R. E. (1963). *The Mexican war: Was it manifest destiny?* New York: Holt Rinehart.

Ruiz, V. L. (1987). *Cannery women, cannery lives: Mexican women, unionization, and the California food packing industry, 1930–1950*. Albuquerque: University of New Mexico Press.

Ruiz, V. L., & Tiano, S. (1987). *Women on the U.S.-Mexico border: Responses to change*. Boston: Allen and Unwin.

Samora, J. (1971). *Los mojados: The wetback story*. Notre Dame, IN: Notre Dame University Press.

Sánchez, G. I. (1932). Scores of Spanish-speaking children on repeated tests. *Pedagogical Seminary and Journal of Genetic Psychology, 40*(1), 223–231.

Sánchez, G. I. (1934). Bilingualism and mental measures: A word of caution. *Journal of Applied Psychology, 18*(6), 765–772.

Sánchez, G. I. (1940). *Forgotten people*. Albuquerque: University of New Mexico Press.

Sánchez, R. (1993). Nineteenth-century Californio narratives: The Hubert H. Bancroft collection. In R. A. Gutiérrez & G. Padilla (Eds.), *Recovering the U.S. Hispanic literary heritage* (pp. 279–292). Houston, TX: Arte Público Press.

Saunders, L. (1954). *Cultural difference and medical care: The case of the Spanish-speaking people of the southwest*. New York: Russell Sage Foundation.

Segura, D. (1984). Labor market stratification: The Chicana experience. *Berkeley Journal of Sociology, 29*, 57–91.

Segura, D. (1989a). Chicana and Mexican immigrant women at work: The impact of class, race, and gender on occupational mobility. *Gender & Society, 3*(1), 37–52.

Segura, D. (1989b). The interplay of familism and patriarchy on the employment of Chicana and Mexican immigrant women. In *Renato Rosaldo lecture series monographs* (Vol. 5, pp. 35–53). Tucson, AZ: Mexican American Studies and Research Center.

Segura, D. (1992). Walking on eggshells: Chicanas in the labor force. In S. Knouse, P. Rosenfeld, & A. Culbertson (Eds.), *Hispanics in the workplace* (pp. 173–193). Newbury Park, CA: Sage Publications.

Segura, D. (1993). Ambivalence or continuity?: Motherhood and employment among Chicanas and Mexican immigrant women workers. *Aztlán, 20*(1–2), 119–151.

Sheridan, T. (1986). *Los Tucsonenses: The Mexican community in Tucson, 1854–1941*. Tucson: University of Arizona Press.

Simons, H., & Hoyt, C. (1992). *Hispanic Texas: A historical guide*. Austin: University of Texas Press.

Singletary, O. (1960). *The Mexican War*. New York: Oxford University Press.

Stavenhagen, R. (1965). Classes, colonialism, and acculturation. *Studies in Comparative International Development*, *1*(6), 53–77.

Stevens, E. (1973). Marianismo: The other face of machismo in Latin America. In A. Pascetello (Ed.), *Female and male in Latin America* (pp. 89–102). Pittsburgh: University of Pittsburgh Press.

Stuart, J., & Kearney, M. (1981). *Causes and effects of agricultural labor migration from the Mixteca of Oaxaca to California*. La Jolla: Center for U.S.-Mexican Studies, University of California, San Diego.

Sullivan, T. A. (1984). The occupational prestige of women immigrants: A comparison of Cubans and Mexicans. *International Migration Review*, *18*(1), 1045–1062.

Sweeney, J. (1977). Chicana history: A review of the literature. In R. Sánchez (Ed.), *Essays on la mujer* (pp. 99–123). Los Angeles: Chicano Studies Center, UCLA.

Taylor, E. J. (1986). Differential migration, networks, information and risk. In O. Stark (Ed.), *Research in human capital and development: Migration, human capital, and development* (pp. 147–171). Greenwich, CT: JAI.

Taylor, P. S. (1938). Migratory agricultural workers on the Pacific coast. *American Sociological Review*, *35*, 220–239.

Teller, C., Estrada, L., Hernández, J., & Alvírez, D. (1977). *Cuantos somos: A demographic study of the Mexican American population*. Austin: Mexican American Studies Center, University of Texas.

Trujillo, C. (1991). *Chicana lesbians*. Berkeley, CA: Third Woman Press.

Valdés, D. (1991). *Al norte: Agricultural workers in the great lakes region, 1917–1970*. Austin: University of Texas Press.

Valdes Fallis, G. (1974). The liberated Chicana: A struggle against tradition. *Women: A Journal of Liberation*, *3*(4), 20–21.

Valdez, L. (1971). *La conquista de Méjico. Actos y el teatro campesino*. San Juan Bautista, CA: Menyan Publications.

Van Ness, J. R. (1987). Hispanic land grants: Ecology and subsistence in the uplands of northern New Mexico and southern Colorado. In C. L. Briggs & J. R. Van Ness (Eds.), *Land, water, and culture: New perspectives on Hispanic land grants* (pp. 141–216). Albuquerque: University of New Mexico Press.

Vargas, Z. (1993). *Proletarians of the north: Mexican industrial workers in Detroit and the midwest, 1917–1933*. Berkeley: University of California Press.

Vélez-Ibañez, C. G. (1980). Se me acabó la canción: An ethnography of nonconsenting sterilizations among Mexican women in Los Angeles.

In M. Mora & A. del Castillo (Eds.), *Mexican women in the United States* (pp. 71–94). Los Angeles: Chicano Studies Center, UCLA.

Vélez-Ibañez, C. G. (1983). *Bonds of mutual trust: The cultural systems of rotating credit associations among urban Mexicans and Chicanos*. New Brunswick, NJ: Rutgers University Press.

Veyna, A. F. (1986). Women in early New Mexico: A preliminary view. In T. Córdova (Ed.), *Chicana voices: Intersections of class, race, and gender* (pp. 120–135). Austin: University of Texas Press.

Veyna, A. F. (1993). "It is my last wish that . . . ": A look at colonial Nuevo Mexicanas through their testaments. In A. de la Torre & B. M. Pesquera (Eds.), *Building with our hands: New directions in Chicana studies* (pp. 91–108). Berkeley: University of California Press.

Weber, D. J. (1979). "Scarce more than apes": Historical roots of Anglo American stereotypes of Mexicans in the border region. In D. J. Weber (Ed.), *New Spain's far northern frontier: Essays on Spain in the American West, 1540–1821* (pp. 295–307). Albuquerque: University of New Mexico Press.

Weber, D. J. (1982). *The Mexican frontier 1821–1846: The American Southwest under Mexico*. Albuquerque: University of New Mexico Press.

West, G. A. (1936). Race attitudes among teachers in the Southwest. *Journal of Abnormal Psychology*, *23*, 146–159.

Wiest, R. (1973). Wage-labor migration and the household in a Mexican town. *Journal of Anthropological Research*, *29*(1), 108–209.

Woll, A. L. (1977). *The Latin image in American film*. Los Angeles: University of California Press.

Woll, A. L. (1980). Bandits and lovers: Hispanic images in American film. In R. M. Miller (Ed.), *The kaleidoscopic lens: How Hollywood views ethnic groups* (pp. 54–72). New York: Jerome S. Ozer.

Young, K. (1922). *Mental differences in certain immigrant groups*. Eugene: University of Oregon Publications.

Zamora, E. (1993). *The world of the Mexican worker in Texas*. College Station: Texas A&M University Press.

Zavella, P. (1985). "Abnormal intimacy": The varying work networks of Chicana cannery workers. *Feminist Studies*, *11*(3), 541–557.

Zavella, P. (1987). *Women's work and Chicano families*. Ithaca, NY: Cornell University Press.

Zavella, P. (1991a). Mujeres in factories: Race and class perspectives on women, work, and family. In M. di Leonardo (Ed.), *Gender at the crossroads of knowledge: Feminist anthropology in the postmodern era* (pp. 312–336). Berkeley: University of California Press.

Zavella, P. (1991b). Reflections of diversity among Chicanas. *Frontiers: A Journal of Women Studies*, *12*(2), 1–16.

Zea, L. (1952). *Conciencia y posibilidad del Mexicano*. Mexico City: Porrua y Obregón.

13

PUERTO RICANS IN HISTORICAL AND SOCIAL SCIENCE RESEARCH

Clara E. Rodríguez

FORDHAM UNIVERSITY

This review of the literature finds that colonialism has been a principal factor in, an orienting influence of, and a focus for critical writing. Because of space limitations, the review focuses on major English-language books. This omits many otherwise significant articles, monographs, and reports. The literature is divided into two periods: books published before and after 1970. In general, the majority of books published before 1970 were, implicitly or explicitly, reflective (and in some cases supportive) of Puerto Rico's colonial relationship to the United States. The bulk of works published after 1970 were critical of this relationship, and attempted to deconstruct the earlier literature and contextualize Puerto Rico and Puerto Ricans.

The review of the pre-1970s literature reveals a number of subthemes. These are: (a) an obfuscation of the colonial relationship and the neglect of political sovereignty issues; (b) an exclusive, noncomparative focus on Puerto Rico—as if Puerto Rico existed in isolation; (c) a preponderance of non-Puerto Ricans writing about Puerto Ricans; (d) the dominance of an assimilationist, immigrant paradigm; (e) a tendency to overgeneralize from small numbers or extreme cases to all Puerto Ricans; and (f) the application of paradigms, categories, and contexts developed in the United States but not necessarily relevant to Puerto Ricans. As a result, Puerto Ricans tended to be defined by others, and Puerto Rican history tended either to be excluded or presented from a Eurocentric perspective. Implicit deficit models highlighted negative as opposed to positive dimensions among Puerto Ricans, and revisionist or critical work tended to be marginalized.

In the late 1960s and early 1970s there was a surge in English-language literature that challenged these earlier perspectives. This literature came about as a result of a number of

factors. One was the development of English-language works by Puerto Ricans in Puerto Rico. Another factor was the growth of a new generation of English-dominant, activist Puerto Ricans in the United States who were influenced by (a) the political and social currents of the time, such as the Black power and the civil rights struggles, the antiwar movement, and the general challenge to social and ethical mores of the time; and by (b) the long-standing Spanish-language tradition of political radicalism on the status issue in Puerto Rico. These contributed to the development of a historically based, clearly articulated anticolonial perspective. The early literary works and autobiographical works of second-generation Puerto Ricans also served to stimulate and support more critical work (e.g., Thomas, 1967). In addition, the establishment of Puerto Rican Studies programs were a stimulus to, as well as a result of, the development of this literature.

This chapter is organized in the following way. It begins by emphasizing the political and thematic similarities in the literatures of Puerto Ricans and Native American peoples. This comparison is meant to illuminate the unique political relationship both groups have had with the U.S. government, and to emphasize how this relationship has influenced the literature written. Works on the early 1898–1910 period, subsequent governors' memoirs, and the major political, economic, and anthropological-sociological books written in the 1950s and 1960s are then examined, and their relevant characteristics denoted. An analysis of Oscar Lewis's *La Vida* follows as a detailed case study of literature sculpted by colonialism. Next, the literature in the post-1970 period is reviewed, highlighting the proclivity in these works to deconstruct colonialism and to contextualize the earlier works in a way that represents the Puerto Rican reality

The author would like to thank the following for important contributions to this chapter: S. Baver, H. Cordero-Guzmán, T. Feliciano, G. Haslip-Viera, J. Hernández, M. Hyacinth, S. Nieto, F. Ortiz, V. Sánchez-Korrol, A. Torres, and J. Vásquez. Permission to quote from the following is gratefully acknowledged: *La Vida: A Puerto Rican Family in the Culture of Poverty—San Juan and New York,* by Oscar Lewis. New York: Random House, 1966. *The Culture Facade: Art, Science, and Politics in the Work of Oscar Lewis* by S. M. Rigdon. Urbana and Chicago: University of Illinois Press, 1988.

more validly. The chapter ends with a discussion of the implications of this literature for multicultural education.

Puerto Ricans and Native American Peoples

The comparison of Puerto Ricans and Native American peoples is a departure from current and past practice. In the past Puerto Ricans were often compared with previous European immigrant groups (e.g., Fitzpatrick, 1971; Glazer & Moynihan, 1970). More recently, analogies have been found between Puerto Ricans and African Americans (e.g., F. Bean & Tienda, 1988; Torres, 1994). These comparisons are important because Puerto Ricans share many characteristics with both African Americans and previous immigrant groups. However, they have tended to obfuscate the importance (and the history) of the political relationship between Puerto Rico and the United States. Because the relationship of Native American nations to the U.S. government is one of even longer duration, it provides a distinct historical perspective within which to discuss the relationship between the United States and Puerto Rico. An analysis of the similarities between Native American nations and Puerto Ricans facilitates greater insight into the subtle distinctiveness of, and difficulties with, the literature on Puerto Ricans.

Both Puerto Ricans and Native Americans share a historical and still unresolved issue—political sovereignty in relation to the United States (Tinker, 1992). Indeed, the "Domestic Dependent Nation Policy," which was applied to Puerto Rico in 1898, was first articulated in Supreme Court decisions regarding the Cherokee nation (Hernández, 1992). In contrast with Native American peoples, who originally participated in treaty making as nations, Puerto Ricans did not participate in the 1898 Treaty of Paris negotiations and have never entered into bilateral agreements with the United States. However, because of their common political histories as wards of the U.S. Congress, both groups have experienced difficulty in bringing forward their concerns. This is because in so doing they bring attention to policies of inequity (e.g., colonial, military, legal, economic, and imperialist) that the United States would prefer either not to discuss or to define in quite different ways. For example, it has taken a long time for the American majority to understand that the "expansion of the West" also meant "the vanishing of the West" from the perspective of Native Americans. Similarly, in the case of Puerto Ricans, the U.S. victory in the war with Spain in 1898 also meant the invasion and conquest of Puerto Rico by a foreign power.

In essence, the study of the history of Puerto Rico requires us to examine the United States' foray into colonial administration in the 20th century. This is neither pleasant nor easy to do in those academic contexts that have been created to gloss over or interpret these aspects of U.S. history in seemingly positive ways. For this reason, the political situation of Puerto Rico vis-à-vis the United States is often better understood outside of the United States than within it. As a consequence, both Native Americans and Puerto Ricans often look to international law and international arenas as courts of appeal and for definitions of their status and rights.

Both also share issues involving current and past political prisoners and a history of invasion, land takeovers, and installation of authoritarian regimes by the U.S. government. Both groups were administered, for a time, by the Department of War and then by the Department of the Interior. Moreover, both groups have had decades of persistent exposure to programs of forceful cultural assimilation, language dominance, and economic exploitation. Yet both groups have also resisted attempts to be completely assimilated or to be recreated as marginal laborers "in the White man's image." Finally, socioeconomic data on both groups presents a similarly bleak picture of disadvantage.

Education and Colonialism: The Puerto Rico Case

Although quite real in its consequences, the control and influence that has been exerted by the United States on Puerto Rico is seldom noted. The history of education and language is a good example of this somewhat concealed, but quite determining, control. The first American educators who came to the island after 1898 thought that "the Spanish spoken in Puerto Rico was not an appropriate vehicle to transmit the culture the people already had and much less the culture the educators wanted to introduce" (Rodríguez Bou, 1966, p. 159). Indeed, Dr. Victor S. Clark, prior to his 1900 report on Puerto Rico, said: "There does not seem to be among the masses the same devotion to their native tongue or to any national ideal that animates the Frenchman" (quoted in Rodríguez Bou, 1966, p. 159). Subsequent events would prove this observation wrong, because—even after 95 years of U.S. rule and strenuous efforts to make them English speaking—Puerto Ricans persisted in their strong loyalty to the Spanish language. In fact, as compared with all Latino groups in New York City, they have a higher proportion who speak Spanish at home (Rodríguez, 1989).

Nonetheless, Clark's idea was shared by many others who proceeded to alter the school system and institute English as the sole language of instruction. At the time this decision was made, the people of Puerto Rico had been Spanish-speaking for close to 400 years. This was 250 years longer than the majority of the people in the United States (who were not of British origin) had been speaking English. Until 1949 the Commissioners of Education in Puerto Rico were appointed by the presidents of the United States. Although they were responsible for educational policy, many of these commissioners had no previous experience in educational administration or practice, nor had they ever been to Puerto Rico prior to their appointment. They were political appointees sent to enforce the English-only policy.

Soon after the U.S. occupation began, a strong popular resistance developed against the English-only policy (Morales-Carrión, 1983). Deprived of any political means of expressing their dissatisfaction with the new regime, Puerto Ricans demonstrated their discontent by continuing to speak their language. Spanish was spoken at home and in public when American officials were not present. The wisdom of the English-only policy was continuously questioned. It became apparent that the Spanish-speaking students did not have a clue as to what many of the English-only, U.S.-imported teachers were trying to say. This was also evident in the poor academic performance of students, who left school recalling the boredom, frustration, and humiliation of the experience (Negrón de Montilla, 1975). However, it took decades for an educational language policy to be established that took into account Puerto Ricans' native tongue and cognitive pattern of learning. It was not until 1949 that Spanish was used as the language of instruction in all grades, and English was taught as a second language.

Educational language policies fluctuated depending in large part on who had been appointed commissioner. The consequences of these changing policies for Puerto Ricans have never been fully assessed; nonetheless, their impact was clearly felt. For example, one policy that was in effect for some time during the period 1916–1934 had Spanish as the language of instruction in grades 1–4 and English as the language of instruction in grades 6–8. The fifth grade was a grade of transition. The consequences of this policy become clearer when we consider the average fourth- to fifth-grade educations of many Puerto Rican elderly. As one elderly Puerto Rican gentleman vividly related, he had been an enthusiastic, bright, and eager student in school until the fifth grade when, frustrated by his English-language books, he angrily cast them into a ditch on his way home from school, never to return.

This anecdote and dimension of Puerto Rican history emphasize, in a personalistic way, how determinant colonialism has been in the everyday lives of Puerto Ricans and in most of the policies developed in Puerto Rico. Actual implementation of the policies varied widely, being perhaps stronger in large cities, where the strength of U.S. control was greater. Although the control over educational policy is less stringent today, U.S. educational associations and educational training in the United States continue to influence education. The past history of language and education in Puerto Rico demonstrates the absolute necessity of viewing Puerto Rico and Puerto Ricans contextually.

PRE-1970 LITERATURE

Despite the significance and pervasiveness of the colonial structure in the history of Puerto Ricans, close attention to the U.S. role in this structure is generally absent from the literature written prior to 1970. The colonial relationship tends to be obfuscated or depicted as benign, as creating more opportunities than obstacles to progess, and/or as eminently "fixable." Consequently, and as in the case of Native American peoples and other groups, Puerto Ricans who read the literature on their people are confronted with unquestioned myths, sins of omission and commission, and distortions and suppression of evidence concerning their historical relationship with the United States.

These distortions, assumptions, and perceptions are often quite subtle as regards Puerto Rico. They are also typically wrapped in verbal complexity. An example of this subtlety and complexity can be seen in a seemingly innocuous statement written by one of the United States' more socially committed presidents, Franklin D. Roosevelt. In a letter appointing José M. Gallardo to be Puerto Rico's Commissioner of Education, he states:

What is necessary, however, is that the American citizens of Puerto Rico should profit from their unique geographical situation and the unique historical circumstance which has brought to them the blessings of American citizenship by becoming bilingual. (quoted in Rodríguez Bou, 1966, p. 163)

Implicit in this statement is the assumption that Puerto Ricans are fortunate to have been blessed with American citizenship. The letter contains no indication that this citizenship was thrust upon Puerto Ricans, without their consent and just prior to World War I, as a justification for their recruitment into the armed forces and U.S. military use of Puerto Rico. (A Puerto Rican request for an opportunity to vote on this issue was denied.) It is not clear that "the unique historical circumstance" alluded to in the letter was a war in which Puerto Rico was invaded by the United States—a war in which some Puerto Ricans supported the United States because they thought that the United States would assist them in their struggle for independence from Spain. But the result was that Puerto Rico enjoys less independence in its current relationship with the United States than it did in 1897 with Spain (Rodríguez, 1989).

Glossed over in Roosevelt's statement was the fact (made clear in later histories) that those who profited from the "unique geographical situation" were actually U.S. government and business (Dietz, 1986; L. Figueroa, 1974; Maldonado Denis, 1972). Indeed, soon after the 1898 war ended, Puerto Rico's military importance to the United States was made clear (Hernández, 1992). Puerto Rico still serves this role. In 1991 Puerto Rico had half of the U.S. military personnel in the Caribbean, with military installations covering 72,634 acres of Puerto Rico's land (García Muñiz, 1993).

What is also not stated in Roosevelt's letter is that historically, "becoming bilingual" has often meant assimilating monoculturally to the U.S. Anglo way of life—without regard for traditional Puerto Rican customs and language. Last, there is no indication in the letter that the citizenship referred to does not allow Puerto Rico to have political representation in the U.S. Congress. Discontent over lack of representation in the British Parliament was one of the reasons the American colonists fought a war with England and became the United States.

Earliest Literature

Immediately after the U.S. invasion in 1898, the earliest descriptions of Puerto Rico were stock-taking accounts. Although one American geographer's book about Puerto Rico prior to the conquest found the economic and social situation to be relatively stable and comfortable (Hernández, 1992), North American reports after the conquest (Carroll, 1898; Davis, 1900) found a backward society with a great number of social problems, including high illiteracy, low health standards, and inadequate sanitation facilities. Another perspective on this period is offered by Morales-Carrión (1952) and Berbusse (1966), who portray the initial period of occupation as one fraught with conflict. The "temporary" military government, which persisted for two years, proclaimed the supremacy of the military and published copies of the Constitution of the United States and its territorial laws. Other changes were put into effect: The name of the island was changed to "Porto Rico," which remained the official name until 1932, when Puerto Ricans succeeded in passing legislation to return it to its original spelling, Puerto Rico. In 1899, when rumors of revolt spread, all periodicals were placed under the direct control of the military. Berbusse concludes that the greatest failings of the military governors were their lack of understanding of a people with a different tradition and their rather blunt expression of chauvinism.

Puerto Rico's political situation changed to civilian rule after the military government ceased in 1900 as a result of the Foraker Act. However, despite Puerto Rican expectations (of liberation and greater political and economic freedoms), the change did not result in improvement. A total of 13 Anglo American governors would be appointed between 1900 and 1946—without consulting Puerto Ricans. Most of the appointments were political payoffs for men who lacked any prior experience with the island. Many could not speak the language, had little interest in the culture, felt the job carried little prestige, and "were interested in being elsewhere" (G. Lewis, 1963, p. 119). In 1947 Puerto Ricans managed to have legislation passed that would enable them to elect their own governor.

Governors' Memoirs

The memoirs of two appointed governors (Tugwell, 1946/1977; Roosevelt, 1937/1970) provide insight into official government perspectives at the time. Theodore Roosevelt, Jr., served as the Governor of Puerto Rico between 1929 and 1932. He was the son of President Theodore Roosevelt, who had a decisive role in planning and carrying out the U.S. war with Spain and had become president in 1901, soon after the invasion of Puerto Rico. It is clear from Roosevelt's memoirs that he was imbued with an imperialistic vision similar to the one his father had earlier articulated as president (p. 83). His memoirs also make clear the previous policy of the United States, which was in the main "to Americanize Puerto Rico and thereby confer on her the greatest blessing, in our opinion, within our gift" (p. 97). In accordance with this policy of Americanization, all the laws were changed to conform with U.S. laws. The civil code in Puerto Rico, which had been derived from Roman law, was "superseded in general with our adaptation of the English common law" (p. 98). Roosevelt also was quite explicit about the perceived need to change the language of the people as part of the Americanization policy: "Perhaps more significant of the line we were following was our attitude on education. . . . We set out deliberately to change this [the fact that Puerto Ricans spoke Spanish] and to make Puerto Rico English speaking" (p. 99).

Roosevelt's views on the ability of Puerto Ricans to govern themselves are more subtle. But it is apparent that he implicitly minimizes the level of political knowledge, participation, and especially resistance among the Puerto Rican people. He also viewed as natural and inevitable the dissatisfaction of Puerto Ricans. He said: "The fact remains, however, that never in any part of the world have I known a country financed by foreign capital and administered by foreigners where there was not local dissatisfaction and irritations" (Roosevelt, 1937/1970, p. 103). Mintz (1990) describes the changes during this period differently, and underscores the economic gain that accrued to the "sugar bosses":

Almost overnight, the island's placid countryside was remade by the conquerors, so that Puerto Rico could supply her colossal northern neighbor with the ever vaster quantities of sugar, molasses, and rum her fertile lands would yield. The central highlands, with their coffee lands and small farmers, declined, while the sugar coasts rapidly grew in extent and importance. . . . Between the First World War and the crash, Puerto Rico was turned into an enormous agrosocial sweatshop; during the Great Depression, its workers suffered while the sugar corporations, both Puerto Rican and North American, prospered. (p. 2)

Rexford Tugwell, a member of Franklin D. Roosevelt's brain trust, was the appointed governor of Puerto Rico between 1941 and 1946. In his memoirs he painted a more sympathetic and detailed picture of the economic and political control the United States exercised over Puerto Rico. Indeed, he remarked that Puerto Rico was just as much a colony as Massachusetts and New York had been under George III. He also discussed the president's concern over "the frightening increase of the population" (Tugwell, 1946/1977, p. 35) and the need for this to be stopped. Last, he recognized the lack of sympathy of the U.S. Congress and the generally difficult odds Puerto Rico faced there. Tugwell drew a distinction between the policy of the government and the attitude of the American people. He said: "Americans intend well for Puerto Ricans, but the United States somehow does not intend well for Puerto Rico" (p. 93). With regard to actual government practice, Tugwell said there was "no policy" and he described the prevailing governmental attitude as one that was "neither selfish nor generous; it was indifferent" (p. 7).

As Mintz (1990) has said more recently: "The propensity to view Puerto Rico as not very significant has never vanished from either the official North American psyche or the popular view" (p. 2). According to Tugwell (1946/1977), time spent on Puerto Rico was seen as "a political waste" (p. 71). What was demanded of a Puerto Rican governor "was that Puerto Rico should never be heard of" (p. 84). There was also the predominant attitude that it was "better to keep issues foggy" (p. 71). These attitudes influenced the subsequent economic and political changes Puerto Rico would undertake, as well as its literature.

Tugwell's departure was immediately followed by the appointment of the first Puerto Rican governor, Jesus Piñero, and subsequently by the election of a Puerto Rican governor, Luis Muñoz Marín, in 1948, and the development of a constitution that was approved through popular vote in 1952. The economy of the island also went through a series of transitions. First, socialist principles were used to reform Puerto Rico's economy. This was followed by a labor-intensive industrial economy called "Operation Bootstrap," which gave way after 1960 to the present "Capital-Intensive Economy" (Hernández, 1992). Both of the latter economic approaches relied heavily on the use of tax incentives, low wages, and lenient regulation to attract foreign capital and industry to the island. In this regard Puerto Rico became the U.S. model for programs established in other developing parts of the world. It also served as a well-publicized and convenient counter to socialist models inspired by the Cuban Revolution. During this period (1950s–1970s)

Puerto Rico made major advances in education, housing, electrification, water and sewage systems, roads, and transportation. There was a large increase in consumerism, as well as growth of the middle class. This was also the period during which Puerto Rico developed its tourism industry and experienced the greatest exodus of its residents to the States.

Economic and Political Studies of Puerto Rico

In the period following World War II a number of studies focused on the politics and economics of Puerto Rico. These works were limited exclusively to the island, with little critical attention paid to the colonial relationship between the United States and Puerto Rico. The economic analyses included an early study by Perloff (1950), which focused on the future of the economy, and later works that assessed the consequences of economic growth. For example, L. G. Reynolds and Gregory (1965) focused on the Puerto Rican economy, with particular attention to economic push-and-pull factors affecting migration, wages, productivity, and industrialization. Another major economic treatise was Friedlander's (1965) study of labor migration and economic growth. This study documented the relative decline of employment in the agricultural sector and the accompanying decrease in agricultural output in Puerto Rico. It noted that despite changes in the kinds of work done by the total employed, such as labor shifts into mining, manufacturing, construction, services, and government, the volume of unemployment and underemployment remained high. These studies also noted that unemployment would have been higher but for the high rate of out-migration. However, these works gave little attention to contextual or political factors affecting the economic planning, or the decisions previously made by the U.S. colonial administration.

Political analyses included works by Anderson (1965), Hanson (1960), Wells (1969), and Goodsell (1965). These works also tended to focus exclusively on Puerto Rico and on the dramatic economic and political changes occurring in Puerto Rico after World War II, while avoiding explicit discussion of the colonial relationship. Anderson, for example, says the intent of his book is to explain "the dynamics of Puerto Rican party politics in terms of the perceptions and expectations of the political actors involved, not in terms of the relations—real or desired—between Puerto Rico and the United States" (p. vii). Nonetheless, these books reflect (some more explicitly than others) the ability of Puerto Ricans to cope successfully with the limitations imposed by the colonial relationship. Hanson describes how Puerto Rico was able to challenge radically the political dominance of absentee sugar interests. Goodsell analyzes politics in Puerto Rico after 1917 and demonstrates how the political elite in Puerto Rico managed to defeat U.S. political control. He describes how appointed governors were blocked or circumvented by the Puerto Rican legislature, and how the governors' attempts to supervise their political administrations were often impeded by their own cultural unfamiliarity, the language barrier, their short tenure, and an informal system developed by Puerto Rican leaders to facilitate legislation useful to the island.

There was also in the literature a more celebratory tone.

This shift of perspective is referred to by Anderson (1965) in his preface. He declares:

In the years since the Second World War there has been a marked change in the literature on Puerto Rico. . . . During the thirties and early forties the island territory was usually described in terms of despair and hopelessness. . . . After the war Puerto Rico became an island of hope. . . . Such words as "miracle," "showcase of democracy," "the answer to Communism in Latin America" have been used to describe the transformation of this island over the past twenty years. (p. vii)

Although this review is limited to books, two very significant articles produced during this period reflected a similar orientation. They were an article by Baggs (1962) and an article by Galbraith and Shaw Soto (1953). Both emphasized the success of Puerto Rico's economic development program. Galbraith and Shaw Soto also chronicle the success of the governor, Luis Muñoz Marín, in eliciting popular support for the program and for political reforms.

Sociological, Anthropological, and Journalistic Works

Between 1938 and 1972 there were a total of 20 major social science works written on Puerto Ricans. These include, in order of publication, books that focused specifically on Puerto Rico by Vincenzo Petrullo (1947), Julian Steward et al. (1956), David Landy (1959), Sidney W. Mintz (1960), Melvin Tumin and Arnold Feldman (1961), Gordon K. Lewis (1963), and Anthony La Ruffa (1971). The following authors focused specifically on Puerto Ricans in the United States: Lawrence Chenault (1938/ 1970), C. Wright Mills, Clarence Senior, and Rose Goldsen (1950), Elena Padilla (1958), Oscar Handlin (1959), Beatrice Berle (1958), Dan Wakefield (1959/1975), Clarence Senior (1961), Patricia Cayo Sexton (1965), Nathan Glazer and Daniel P. Moynihan (1970), Eva Sandis (1970), and Rev. Joseph Fitzpatrick (1971). Only Handlin and Glazer and Moynihan focus on other groups as well as Puerto Ricans, while Oscar Lewis's *La Vida* (1966) examines three families in Puerto Rico and two in New York. Christopher Rand's (1958) work discusses both Puerto Rico and Puerto Ricans in the United States. With few exceptions, this literature was characterized by an approach that emphasized fieldwork, community studies, structured questionnaires, and personal accounts. The social scientists generally used a variety of descriptive, ethnographic, and survey research methods in their studies, while the journalists based their works on conversations and impressions.

CHARACTERISTICS OF THE LITERATURE

With a Blind Eye: Exclusive Focus and Obfuscation of the Colonial Relationship

In the literatures on both Puerto Ricans and Native American peoples can be found a number of common themes that flow from the unique political relationship between these groups and the U.S. government. One is the tendency to ignore the larger political-economic contexts affecting the groups. In the earlier literature there was often an exclusive focus on the group without (a) the standard contrast and comparison methodologies used to study and assess groups, and (b) much analysis of U.S. motives, policies, and impact on the group. Hawaiians and the South Pacific peoples in the U.S. territories often see their historical and contemporary situation as similar to that of Native Americans, and yet these groups are seldom compared or studied together. Puerto Ricans were viewed as "unique" and apparently without parallel. This tendency was particularly evident in the early literature, but in the case of Puerto Ricans there are still, for example, few comparative analyses of U.S. territories such as Guam. This "one-case" focus delimited analysis of more contextual and structural issues that may have been common to people similarly situated. For example, Puerto Rico's status issue is analyzed without reference to the experiences of such other nations as Cuba, the Dominican Republic, and the Philippines, and without reference to the United States' own resolution of its status issue.

There was a concurrent obfuscation of the colonial relationship. Although some works made reference to the "status" issue or to the all-consuming preoccupation with the status issue in Puerto Rico, few discussed the role of the United States in originating or sustaining the issue. When the colonial relationship was not overlooked, it was viewed as benign, commensurate with what Puerto Ricans wanted, or eminently fixable. Certain inequalities were acknowledged, but it was thought that, with certain reforms and more education in English, these could be improved. Thus, although the colonial relationship was a very significant influence in the everyday life of the people, it and its consequences tended to be ignored or obfuscated in many of the major English-language works.

This characteristic of the early literature reflects, to a degree, the nonreflexive view that most Americans had (and many still have) of Puerto Rico. Puerto Rico is often approached as if it didn't have a historical and current-day political and economic context. Visitors to Puerto Rico are often surprised at the all-pervasive nature of the status issue in Puerto Rico—the extent to which it permeates political and social life, as well as the extent to which it influences decisions in education, the environment, language policy, and economic planning.

The methodologies and approaches common in much of the early literature contributed to the exclusive focus on Puerto Rico and the tendency to obfuscate the colonial relationship. Reports on the island and memoirs were, by definition, exclusive focuses on the island written by representatives of the U.S. government. Many of the subsequent political analyses (Anderson, 1965; Goodsell, 1965; Hanson, 1960; Wells, 1969) also represented insular, noncontextualized views of the island. Economic studies of the island (e.g., Friedlander, 1965; Perloff, 1950; L. G. Reynolds & Gregory, 1965) gave scant attention to contextual or political factors affecting economic planning, or to comparative situations. In addition, the works written by sociologists, anthropologists, and journalists—which constituted the bulk of the pre-1970s literature on Puerto Ricans—also focused exclusively on Puerto Rico or on Puerto Ricans in the continental United States. In many cases the ethnographic approaches used in these works also reinforced these tendencies and allowed for Eurocentric biases (Rodríguez, 1994b).

Despite this tendency to obfuscate the colonial relationship, it was the colonial relationship that allowed and facilitated works on Puerto Ricans by many noted North Americans. Ironically, it is also the presumed need for "fixing" that has facilitated the production of so many works by North Americans. With regard to research, Puerto Rico has been accessible, exploitable, enjoyable, and fundable. Last, and most unfortunate, it has been this colonialist relationship that has also predisposed some authors either to view Puerto Ricans negatively and/or to misunderstand them totally. As Gordon Lewis (1963) pointed out, Puerto Ricans have the dubious distinction of being one of the most researched but least understood people in the United States, if not in the world.

Preponderance of Non-Puerto Ricans

Just as there is a preponderance of non-Native Americans who write Native American Indian literature, the English-language literature on Puerto Ricans was also dominated by non-Puerto Ricans. Of the 20 major social science works noted above, only one author was Puerto Rican. Puerto Ricans were used in some cases as fieldworkers and assistants, but they were viewed merely as helpers and their contributions were seldom acknowledged. The University of Puerto Rico Social Science Research Center was administered for a considerable period of time by Anglo Americans who consistently identified young Anglo scholars who came to do their doctoral dissertations (Lauria-Perricelli, 1990). Many of these works were published by major presses and were conducted by persons who were either prominent at the time or were to become celebrated scholars.

Consequently, autonomous indigenous perspectives tended to lack representation. Much of the literature suffered because there was little cultural, linguistic, and/or historical familiarity with the group studied. Given that language, culture, and knowledge of a people's history are basic bridges to be crossed when studying groups different from one's own, it is surprising how little attention this issue received in the early literature. For example, few works bothered to indicate how many of their research personnel were familiar with these three areas, nor did they discuss how their own lack of familiarity may have influenced their work.

As a result, much of the literature suffered from an "otherness" approach, in which Puerto Ricans were examined as "others" without histories or "convincing" cultural rationales. Although there were works written by Puerto Ricans on Puerto Ricans in the early 1970s (e.g., Seda Bonilla, 1973; Fernández Méndez, 1972; Buitrago Ortiz, 1974), they were few in number and, with scant exceptions (e.g., E. Padilla, 1958), did not receive as much attention as the works by non-Puerto Ricans.

Dominance of the Assimilationist, Immigrant Paradigm

Another characteristic of this literature was the tendency to view Puerto Ricans within an assimilationist, immigrant paradigm. There are significant differences between the Puerto Rican migration and the migration of previous immigrant groups to the United States. For example, their arrival as U.S. citizens and colonial subjects—as colonial (im)migrants—their Caribbean as opposed to European point of origin, and their multiracial composition are key differentiating factors. Nonetheless, it was the immigrant paradigm that was predominantly used in the pre-1970 literature to analyze Puerto Ricans in the United States (see, e.g., Chenault, 1938/1970; Fitzpatrick, 1971; Glazer & Moynihan, 1970; Handlin, 1959; Mills et al., 1950). In keeping with this paradigm, it was expected that, despite initial difficulties, Puerto Ricans would assimilate in due time, as had previous European immigrants. To the degree that the multiracial nature of the group was recognized, it was predicted that those who could not pass for White would assimilate into communities of African origin, called "Negro" at that time.

A number of factors combined to make this the paradigm of choice. First, it was the reigning paradigm, within which many of those who studied Puerto Ricans were educated. It was also the paradigm that coincided with the "melting pot" ethos that evolved with the large migrations at the end of the 19th and the beginning of the 20th centuries. In addition, Puerto Ricans arrived in greatest numbers in the 1950s, which was a unique historical period. The immigration laws of 1921 and 1924 had closed U.S. doors to free, unrestricted immigration, so large numbers of immigrants had not arrived for a number of years. New York, in particular, had lost much of its earlier and current ethnic immigrant flavor.

This was also a period of extreme political conservatism—the McCarthy era. The degree to which this conservative political climate influenced the reception of Puerto Ricans has not yet been fully assessed. Baver (1984) has noted that Puerto Ricans' political resistance to U.S. domination had a negative effect on the position that established political parties took vis-à-vis Puerto Ricans. But within this politically conservative context, groups that were culturally and linguistically distinct—as were migrating Puerto Ricans—were seen to be "immigrants." Citizenship status, multiracial composition, or U.S. military experience did not matter—these were minor ripples that would eventually be smoothed out. Puerto Ricans were seen as the last in the continuum of (European) immigrant groups to this country. That this was not the "best-fitting" paradigm within which to understand Puerto Ricans would become evident as the work of revisionist writers and protestors helped to usher in an era in which diversity and multiculturalism would combine with the arrival of greater numbers of immigrants from Asia and Latin America and begin the formation of a new paradigm.

Overgeneralizations: Assuming the Part to Be the Whole

Another important and cross-cutting theme that is still to be found in the literature on Puerto Ricans is the tendency to generalize from a small number of observations and extreme cases to the whole group. Such generalization presents a homogeneous but very distorted picture of the group. The rich and heterogenous reality that typifies not just Puerto Ricans but most groups is missed. There is a selectivity of observation, and the complexity of the structures affecting individuals is not understood—especially the social, economic, and political institutions within which behavior takes place. It is this tendency that has been the most problematic and unfortunately the most

recurrent in the literature on Puerto Ricans. (For a discussion, see Torres & Rodríguez, 1991).

Misapplication of Categories, Concepts, and Contexts

The use of categories and concepts developed in one context and applied uncritically to another context was another theme in the literature that continues in the present. A recurring example involves the socioeconomic categories used by researchers, which often place federal government employees in Puerto Rico in lower status positions than they are seen to occupy by the population they serve. This tendency to apply categories and concepts uncritically is often evident in studies relying on secondary data. In such studies basic issues, such as contextual analysis, the definition and measurement of variables, and the validity and relevance of constructs, seldom surface as points of discussion. While this approach is common and accepted in mainstream social science research, its primary purpose is not to generate knowledge about Puerto Rico and Puerto Ricans. Hypotheses often flow from, and build upon, the results of preceding studies that have used methodological and theoretical orientations that are similarly abstract. Consequently, the correct application and execution of the preestablished methodology becomes the basis upon which the research is evaluated. The extent to which it reveals new, useful, and accurate information about Puerto Ricans is often secondary. This tendency has been particularly evident in recent journal articles written about Puerto Ricans.

Neglect of Indigenous Voices and Histories

The cultural traditions and literatures of both Puerto Ricans and Native Americans have been severely neglected. Histories of both groups tend to begin with the official date of conquest, and are thereby constructed within the official U.S. canon. Thus, in the case of Puerto Ricans, the literature "began" after 1898. Literature written prior to that time by Puerto Ricans, or by others, tended not to be incorporated into the new English-language literature on Puerto Ricans. It was as if there had not been at least a 3500-year history in Puerto Rico prior to its conquest by the United States. An example of this continuing neglect is the work of Eugenio M. de Hostos, who was an eminent social writer, philosopher, and intellectual leader in the late 19th century. Although he is quite well known in Latin American literature, not one of his works has yet been translated into English. In addition, references to de Hostos in the literature in English are limited to his political role as an advocate for the independence movement at the time of conquest.

Definitions

The struggle over definitions and perspectives has become more evident in the literatures of both Native American peoples and Puerto Ricans (Churchill, 1992; Jaimes, 1992). "Indigenous" writers seek to find their own voice and often struggle against definitions of themselves by others as "others." This conflict is most clearly seen in discussions over the ostensibly straightforward task of counting people. The criteria, issues, and consequences of defining what constitutes a "Native American person" or "Indian" have been well detailed by Snipp (1989). Different criteria have resulted in different counts. Historically, Native American peoples have preferred criteria identifying them as members of various nations instead of the genetically based criteria of the U.S. government. Genetically based criteria (like the proportion of Indian "blood") have resulted in lower numbers of Native Americans counted, as well as in fewer persons being declared eligible for entitlement programs that grew out of treaty stipulations or tribal agreements with the U.S. government.

Similarly, for most intents and purposes, the data generally presented on Puerto Ricans is on the 2,727,754 Puerto Ricans who reside in the continental United States. Yet in 1989 there were also 3,522,037 Puerto Ricans living in Puerto Rico. This practice continues despite the fact that both mainland and island Puerto Ricans are citizens of the United States. Consequently, this practice underestimates (a) the absolute numbers of Puerto Ricans, (b) the number and proportion of Latinos in the United States, and (c) the proportion of Puerto Ricans that are Latinos. Indeed, the Puerto Rican share of the Latino population in the United States almost doubles when Puerto Ricans from Puerto Rico are included in the count—from 12.2% to 24.1% (U.S. Bureau of the Census, 1990a, 1990b). The practice also underestimates the needs of Puerto Ricans in Puerto Rico and Puerto Ricans in the States, and in some instances pits the groups against one another as they define themselves in regard to government programs and are encouraged to compete for public and private funds, such as scholarships and student financial aid.

In both the Native American and Puerto Rican cases, the key issues are "who" is to be considered a member of the group, who is to determine the criteria for group membership, and what are the political consequences of the group membership criteria? In both cases it is the official government figures that determine the "true" population. In both cases it is in the government's interest to subdivide and make these populations smaller.

In summary, many of the works produced in the pre-1970s period manifested the problems noted above. They ignored issues of political sovereignty; they obfuscated or viewed as benign the political relationship; they focused exclusively on Puerto Ricans without contrasting them with similar groups; they misrepresented, underrepresented, or totally ignored indigenous histories and voices; they utilized inappropriate contexts, categories, and concepts to examine Puerto Ricans; and they generalized from extreme cases to the whole population. Although some works were less problematic than others, as a whole the works conveyed a strong sense of "otherness" in their depictions of Puerto Ricans.

The literature that emerged after the 1970s would critique the earlier literature on a number of grounds. These included: (a) overuse of the Malthusian view that Puerto Rico's problems are the result of overpopulation (see Hernández, 1992; Hernández Cruz, 1988; and History Task Force, 1979, for criticisms of this view); (b) the tendency to apply an accusative or deficit model that views Puerto Rico and Puerto Ricans as "a problem," the source of their own problems, or an expensive liability with

few accomplishments or contributions; (c) the incorrect assumption that the history of the Puerto Rican community in the United States has been undistinguished and of fairly short duration; (d) a tendency to ignore issues and perspectives of concern to Puerto Ricans; (e) inordinate concern with racial issues and race mixture (see Rodríguez, 1994a, 1994b); and (f) disparagement of Puerto Rican language and culture.

OSCAR LEWIS AND *LA VIDA*

A Significant Study

Oscar Lewis's *La Vida* (1966) represents most dramatically some of the difficulties found, in greater and lesser degree, in the early works. It is also the book that received the greatest attention in the popular press and in the scholarly community. Lewis wrote the book for "teachers, social workers, doctors, priests, and others—who bear the major responsibility for carrying out anti-poverty programs . . . " (Rigdon, 1988, p. 151). It was written in a narrative form and is highly readable. It also appeared during the peak of the Johnson administration's War on Poverty and reflected to some degree the concerns of this period.

As a glance at the *Book Review Digest* for 1966 and 1967 will attest, in the first two years of its publication *La Vida* was reviewed in a wide variety of major journals and newspapers by some of the foremost authors of the day. It was also the subject of a special issue of the *Revista de Ciencias Sociales*, the social sciences journal of the University of Puerto Rico (Maldonado Denis, 1967b). The year after the publication of *La Vida*, *Current Anthropology* invited 55 international associates to comment on Lewis's works (O. Lewis, 1967). Prior to its publication, portions of the book had been printed in *Scientific American*, *Harper's*, and *Commentary*. In 1967 it won the National Book Award for nonfiction.

La Vida was perhaps the most controversial book ever written on Puerto Ricans. English-language assessments of the work varied widely. Theodore Caplow (1967) is typical of the negative side:

La Vida would be unreadable without its large component of pornography. It is jumbled and chaotic and conveys the impression that the author is implacably hostile to his unfortunate subjects. . . . The result is a nasty book in every sense, unfair to its readers as well as its subjects. (p. 486)

Other writers expressed gratitude for Lewis's brilliant contribution and used superlatives congratulating his extraordinary anthropological achievement. On the whole, those reviewers who favored the book far outnumbered those who opposed it. Within Puerto Rico and Puerto Rican communities in the United States, the book generally elicited outrage, as evidenced by letters to the press (von Eckardt, 1967), a review by Monserrat (1967) (then head of the Migration Division of Puerto Rico's Department of Labor), and less publicized discussions. However, the academic community in Puerto Rico presented a wider range of response in their reviews (Maldonado Denis, 1967b).

Some indication of the response to the book, and consequently the image it projected, can be garnered from its major reviews. The *New Republic* (1965) said the "impact is genuine and frightening"; *Newsweek* (1966) announced that "the language and its human context will shock the squeamish"; *Time* (1966) stated flatly, "the effect is suffocating and ugly." *The New York Times Book Review* asked Michael Harrington (1966) to do a front-page review. He said:

The middle class reader is in danger of being overwhelmed. How exactly does he assimilate to his experience the reminiscence of a crippled child who tells of having played the "game" of prostitution? . . . and one mother entertains her children by singing "dirty songs." (p. 1)

Along with the sensationalism and shock of the book, we see in the reviews a tendency to overgeneralize. For example, Harrington concludes that this family of five was "a single yet archetypical family of the poor" (pp. 1, 92).

Reviewers were divided on whether Lewis misrepresented Puerto Ricans or whether readers "misinterpreted" the work (see, e.g., von Eckardt, 1967; Fitzpatrick, 1966; Glazer, 1967). Still others felt the problems with the work went beyond misrepresentation of Puerto Ricans to the misrepresentation of people in poverty. Opler (1967), for example, argued that the concept of the culture of poverty blurred, leveled, and stereotyped the indigent of various cultures of the world, and that this was "a middle-class or ethnocentric stereotype" (p. 488). Charles Valentine (see Rigdon, 1988) argued that Lewis's work had more pragmatic, negative implications; he maintained that it was Lewis's works and his concept of the culture of poverty that deserved part of the blame for the failure of the War on Poverty program.

Regardless of the reaction, it was obvious that Lewis's book was a very significant book; it was seen as an "important part of the literature building up on the Puerto Rican community in New York City and its background in Puerto Rico" (Glazer, 1967, p. 83). It also undoubtably affected the image construction of Puerto Ricans. But to what extent was the work a reflection of the contextual reality of colonialism and of the biases inherent within this structure? Was Lewis's work methodologically sound? Was Lewis aware of the image he would project? Was he informed about the consequences of his work and, if so, did he care?

The Colonial Context Displayed

La Vida illustrates a good many of the themes discussed above. It was an ethnography written by an Anglo American with a strong assimilationist and immigrant background. Oscar Lewis was born Yehezkiel Lefkowitz, the son of Polish immigrants. He had "tried to blend in by changing his name and suppressing Yiddish-influenced syntax and a New York accent" (Rigdon, 1988, p. 24). The book had an exclusive focus, obfuscated the colonial relationship, conveyed a strong sense of "otherness," utilized a deficit model, applied inappropriate contexts for analysis, generalized from extreme cases to the whole group, and depreciated the indigenous view of political events.

These characteristics are evident in the structure and text of the book, as well as in Lewis's writings about the book.

The book focuses exclusively on one extended family living in a slum area of San Juan, Puerto Rico, and in New York City. There is an introduction followed by five chapters, each of which is devoted to one person in the family. The family consists of the mother plus her four children. Each chapter describes a day in their lives and then presents a narrative by an individual family member. The book is heavily laced with sex. Indeed, one reviewer said: "When I first dipped into this book, the language, the bald descriptions of sexual intercourse—anatomical in detail—so appalled me that I put it aside for some weeks" (Day, 1967, p. 74).

The colonial relationship is only obliquely referred to in the narrative, as when Lewis's respondents express their opinions about politics or about Americans. (His respondents are, incidentally, supporters of statehood.) However, the effect of the colonial relationship weaves its way implicitly into the narrative. It is evident in the need of the Ríos family members to move to the United States to work. Family members indicate they came to New York to live and earn money away from the island they consistently profess to love and prefer.

Lewis refers to the political relationship in his introduction. He uses it to support his decision to study the culture of poverty in Puerto Rico. His earlier book, *The Children of Sánchez* (1961), had come in for some devastating criticism in Mexico, and its continued publication was held up for a time because of charges that the book was "a complete invention" and "obscene" (Geltman, 1967, p. 427). In his introduction to *La Vida*, Lewis (1966) indicates that:

In the course of my anthropological studies . . . in Mexico, a number of my Mexican and other Latin American friends have sometimes delicately suggested that I turn to a study of poverty in my own country, the United States. (p. xi)

Lewis decided Puerto Rico would be the "first step in that direction" (p. xi). Although one might wonder, as did von Eckardt (1967), to what degree Lewis could generalize from the Puerto Rican case to the United States, Lewis argued that Puerto Rico had been under U.S. control and influence since 1898, it was an unincorporated territory, Puerto Ricans had citizenship status, and there had been a large migration of Puerto Ricans to the United States (Lewis, pp. xi ff.). (Curiously, he then noted the various indicators of economic and social affliction among Puerto Ricans in the United States.)

There were other related factors favoring the choice of Puerto Rico. Two prime ones were funding and the period's policy climate. As Rigdon (1988) states: "With the new priority given by the Kennedy administration to social welfare policy in the early 1960s, research proposals to test the culture of poverty thesis were eminently fundable" (p. 72). Lewis received grants from the Social Security Administration, the Guggenheim Foundation, the Wenner-Gren Foundation, the Institute for the Study of Man, and from his university. He did not pursue a similar plan to research Mexicans in Chicago because of problems with the accessibility of informants. Since Puerto Ricans were legally citizens, fears of repercussions or deportation, or potential problems of cooperation were not anticipated (Rigdon, 1988). Thus it appears that crucial to Lewis's study of Puerto Rico were important components of Puerto Rico's colonial context: political approval and timing, funding, and the availability of informants.

That these factors take on particular meanings when viewed within Puerto Rico's colonial context can be seen when we contrast the Puerto Rico experience with that of the other two Latino countries he studied. Having secured a visa from the State Department, an invitation from Fidel Castro, and some money from the Ford Foundation, Lewis left the Puerto Rico project to undertake a similar three-year research project in Cuba. However, his project in Cuba was closed down by the Castro regime about midway, one of his informants was arrested, and Lewis was formally accused of being a CIA spy in Cuba (Rigdon, 1988). His experience in Mexico with *The Children of Sánchez* (1961) was not dissimilar with regard to its outcome. In Mexico public and official opposition made it impossible to produce a film version of the book, the book was widely criticized and attacked, and he was accused of being an FBI spy (Rigdon, 1988). Regardless of the truth of the charges that he was an FBI or CIA spy—both Lewis and Rigdon maintained that the charges were false—one wonders if he would also have been asked to leave Puerto Rico had that been an independent country as well.

Despite his argument that Puerto Rico was part of his own country, Lewis used a Mexican framework to examine Puerto Rico. In his introduction Lewis faults Puerto Ricans for not developing "a great revolutionary tradition" (O. Lewis, 1961, p. xvi) like that of Mexico, and for not identifying as richly and as deeply with their traditions as do the Mexicans. Lewis also argues that the native culture in Puerto Rico was relatively simple and never reached the high degree of civilization achieved by Mexico in pre-Hispanic times. He states that the Spanish conquest was much more devastating for Puerto Rico than for Mexico because the Spaniards wiped out most of the Indian population. All of these differences, he argues, account for the differences he finds in his research between Puerto Ricans and Mexicans.

Muna Muñoz Lee, his principal translator, attempted to discuss with Lewis the difficulties she saw with using a Mexican context to study Puerto Rico. Muñoz Lee was the daughter of the then-governor of Puerto Rico and of a North American woman from Mississippi. She was also the granddaughter of one of the leading political figures of 20th-century Puerto Rico, Luis Muñoz Rivera. By virtue of her bicultural and political background, Muñoz Lee was uniquely positioned to provide insight and advice to Lewis. She argued that trying to fit the history of Puerto Rico into a Mexican framework could only produce distortion (letter from Muñoz Lee to Lewis, May 25, 1965, cited in Rigdon, 1988).

She objected to his "Indianista" approach (Muñoz Lee to Lewis, June 4, 1965, cited in Rigdon, 1988, p. 248) and argued that "Lewis understated the level of colonial resistance by Puerto Ricans and overstated the importance of their Indian past" (p. 82). Indeed, she wrote to him that to attribute any deficiency in Puerto Rican personalities to a lack of knowledge

of our Indian background was equivalent to interpreting the personalities of New Yorkers on the basis of their ignorance of their "indian backgrounds" (p. 247). Nor did she agree that Puerto Ricans were more "broken" by the Spanish conquest and for that reason less overtly hostile to Spain (Muñoz Lee to Lewis, May 25, 1965, cited in Rigdon, 1988).

Although she questioned the validity of utilizing a Mexican framework to examine Puerto Rico, what concerned her even more was that "she did not accept the logic that allowed Lewis to jump from historical events to personality traits" (Rigdon, 1988, p. 82). For Lewis (1966) argued:

When I compare my findings on the Ríos and the other families that I have studied in Puerto Rico with my findings on my Mexican families, a number of differences emerge, differences which are undoubtedly related to the different histories of Mexico and Puerto Rico. (p. xv)

In this regard, Lewis generalized from extreme cases to the whole population and its history.

Muñoz Lee also challenged Lewis's condescending view of Puerto Rico's Autonomous Charter of 1897. Lewis (1966) argued that the charter represented "a bit more autonomy" and "the wresting of a few more concessions" (p. xvi) from Spain. Muñoz Lee wrote that:

What P. R. finally got from Spain, one year before the American conquest, was . . . full status as a Province of Spain, with representation in the Cortes. To call this "a bit more autonomy" is like saying Hawaii and Alaska "wrested a bit more autonomy from the U.S." when they were made States of the Union. (Rigdon, 1988, p. 246)

Part of Lewis's response to Muñoz Lee's letters was curious. He responded by seeking to relocate Puerto Rico into the U.S. context. He asked:

I wish I knew what Puerto Rican Negroes were taught about their past. . . . Here in the U.S. there has been a major trend to portray the great achievements of the Negro people of Africa in pre-European conquest time. Has the same thing been happening in Puerto Rico? (Lewis to Muñoz Lee, June 1, 1965, cited in Rigdon, 1988, p. 346)

What is apparent is that he continued to view Puerto Ricans through outside contexts and to apply concepts and categories developed in another context without taking the Puerto Rican experience (or Muñoz Lee's views) into consideration.

Lewis (1966) also demonstrated an astounding lack of awareness of the consequences of a colonial policy. Contrasting Puerto Ricans with Mexicans, he said:

In Mexico even the poorest slum dwellers have a much richer sense of the past and a deeper identification with the Mexican tradition than do Puerto Ricans with their tradition. . . . In San Juan the respondents showed an abysmal ignorance of Puerto Rican historical figures. Some knew more about George Washington and Abraham Lincoln than about their own heroes. (p. xvii)

In making this statement Lewis was oblivious to the fact that, along with changes in language policy, colonialism had brought changes in the content of education. For several years after publication of the Lewis book, Puerto Ricans were still taught the history of the United States and not the history of Puerto Rico (or Spain). This was not the case in Mexico. Moreover, Lewis overlooked some idiosyncrasies common in colonial and neocolonial settings, namely that some of his Puerto Rican respondents may have wanted to make the "Americano" feel more comfortable by noting these American heroes, or may have wanted to impress this representative of the colonial center with their knowledge of U.S. history.

Obliviousness within the colonial context is a common, but complex, concept. Despite the fact that Lewis was aware that his knowledge of Puerto Rican history and culture was superficial and limited (Rigdon, 1988), he was resistant to other views; even his "continuous debate" (Rigdon, p. 81) with Muñoz Lee did not alter his views. However, the ultimate irony in the colonial process is when social scientists such as Lewis chastise Puerto Ricans for not knowing their own history. In so doing, Lewis ignored the colonial history and policies that the United States thrust upon Puerto Rico.

A number of Marxists in Puerto Rico defended Lewis's work, and it is important to understand why—for their position further highlights the colonial context of Puerto Rico. Maldonado Denis (1967), for example, argued that Lewis's respondents represented the double alienation that comes from the combination of class and colonialist oppression. In essence, the Ríos family was seen to represent the lumpenproletariat within a colonial structure. He contended that the politically conservative attitudes of the Ríoses indicated that Marx was right when he said the lumpenproletariat were a potential ally of the propertied classes. He (and von Eckardt, 1967) took issue with those who were concerned with the image of Puerto Ricans that Lewis's work projected. He argued that bourgeois Puerto Ricans preferred not to see this reality and were obsessed with maintaining a positive "public image" that had been artificially created. In essence, Marxists argued that it was important to confront this reality so as to change the structure that gave rise to it; others argued that the image was not representative.

This debate raises a number of still-unanswered questions:

1. Was Lewis accurately representing a marginalized group in the society that Puerto Ricans preferred not to see?
2. Were the Ríoses (as a marginalized unit within the society) used by Lewis and his funders because it suited capitalist-colonialist interests to depict Puerto Ricans in an inferiorization narrative?
3. Was the focus on the Ríoses an intentional, but commonplace, misrepresentation of a society that was conveniently available and fundable because of its colonial relationship to the United States?
4. Were those who supported Lewis influenced by elitist, classist views?

These questions are still being disputed in current-day discussions of the underclass. Perhaps the best that can be said is that the issue is not *whether* there is a problem, but *how* that problem is to be described and categorized—within pathological, deficit models, or within more structuralist frameworks.

Methodological Critiques

Oscar Lewis's *La Vida* (1966) received two major methodological criticisms: his use of a selective sample and of a selective site (E. Padilla, 1967). Although Lewis had originally intended to conduct his research in four distinct neighborhoods, he selected all five of the members of his family from one barrio (Rigdon, 1988). Lewis selected his informants "from a group Lewis thought was most likely to manifest subculture traits" (Rigdon, p. 109). Thus, by "relying on individuals who were the most accessible and willing to cooperate, Lewis selected out many people who were fully employed and hard working, as well as those with a strong sense of personal privacy" (p. 111).

Lewis never explains exactly how or why he selected the family (von Eckardt, 1967). The Ríos family was one of 120 multiproblem families that had been under study by the School of Social Work at the University of Puerto Rico. They had been classified—along with 19% of the sample—as being in the pseudoeffective category. These families were characterized as being characteristically flattering to professional authorities, telling them what they wanted to hear, verbally quite facile, and demanding but unstable in their demands (Marín, 1967). One reviewer suggested that Lewis's subjects might have tended to dramatize and exaggerate both language and sexual exploits in order to impress the anthropologist's fieldwork aides (Opler, 1967). Whatever the truthfulness of the respondents' stories, a serious flaw in the book is Lewis's inability to demonstrate the representativeness of his respondents. As Glazer (1967) says: "Who is he describing? exceptional people, leading exceptional lives, who resemble Puerto Ricans in only limited ways? Prof. Lewis is ambiguous on this crucial question" (p. 83).

Lewis (1966) conveys contradictory messages as to whom the Ríoses represent. On the one hand, he announces: "I should like to emphasize that this study deals with only one segment of the Puerto Rican population and that the data should not be generalized to Puerto Rican society as a whole" (pp. xii–xiii). But then he declares subsequently:

The intensive study of the life of even a single extended family by the methods used in this volume tells us something about individuals, about family life, about lower-class life as a whole, and about the history and culture of the larger society in which these people live. It may also reflect something of national character, although this would be difficult to prove. (p. xv)

As Rigdon (1988) indicates:

By the end of the introduction the reader cannot be certain if Lewis meant the Ríoses to represent the culture of poverty or if he meant to present them as just one family who happened to be poor and Puerto Rican. (p. 79)

Moreover, although Lewis provides some formal disclaimers in his introduction, the following 700 pages are "of quite a different order" (Glazer, 1967, p. 83).

Another issue raised is the typicality of the area chosen. As Elena Padilla (1967) notes in her review, "La Esmeralda, as any

San Juan resident would tell, is a center of prostitution, the unofficial red light district of the city" (p. 651). Glazer (1967) described it similarly, as being the "oldest slum in San Juan, on the beaches under the wall of the old city, near where the ships come in and the sailors land" (p. 84). Susan Rigdon (1988), an associate of Lewis's, describes the area as

a community of outcasts. It was a community for the most down-and-out of Puerto Rico's poor; alcoholics, drug addicts, and some mentally ill and emotionally disturbed people, who for lack of money or social welfare programs, had nowhere else to go. (p. 97)

There is also in Lewis's work little awareness of the role of class. This is curious, because his work is premised on the assumption that cultural differences exist because of class. In von Eckhardt's (1967) own study of middle-class Puerto Rican youth, she shows that the values that predominate in this group are opposite to those in *La Vida*. She argues that Lewis should have placed the Ríos family more clearly within the Puerto Rican societal structure. E. Padilla (1967) agrees, and adds that Lewis "has failed to use unbiased sampling procedures in the selection of his respondents and has neglected to use historical methods to place the Ríoses in their proper historical and social perspective" (p. 652). This "contextualizing" is especially important when the intended readership is English speaking and non-Puerto Rican. As Pérez de Jesús (1967) suggests, such a study can misrepresent Puerto Ricans, especially in the United States, where so little is known about them.

The representativeness of the Ríos family was also questioned because they were engaged in prostitution, while only a minority of families in the area studied were so engaged (Glazer, 1967; Pérez de Jesús, 1967). As one reviewer commented: "An account of a prostitute's family may produce a sensational best-seller, but our studies of Puerto Ricans—employed, on relief, from the highland jivaro background and from other strata—indicate it is not at all representative" (Opler, 1967, p. 488). (This reviewer had been engaged in a 10-year study of randomly drawn samples of Puerto Rican families in New York and on the island.) Fitzpatrick (1966) also questioned the representativeness of the sexual patterns depicted and cited other studies in Puerto Rico (e.g., Landy, 1959; Mintz, 1960; Steward et al., 1956) that had found results quite at variance with Lewis's presentation of "unbridled ids."

Although the emphasis in the book on sex reflects, to some degree, the fact that the family selected was involved in prostitution, one Puerto Rican reviewer (Rodríguez Bou, 1967) commented that the incessant references to sex elicited reservations about the subjects, who appear to speak almost exclusively about sex during all their conscious hours and to practice it the rest of the time. He notes that even the children's lullabies and songs are of a sexual nature, and that references to other activities—dances, baths, movies, wakes, trips—are all related to sex. He also noted that although Puerto Rican children exhibit sexual precociousness, examples of sexual crudity such as those found in *La Vida* are extremely rare.

Another question raised about the respondents' representativeness is the degree to which they may have been mentally ill. Lewis included as a member of his staff a Mexican psychologist,

Carolina Luján, with whom he had previously worked in Mexico. Her job was to administer psychological tests to the respondents. Luján "was consistently diagnosing paranoid and schizoid tendencies in his [Lewis's] Puerto Rican informants" (Rigdon, 1988, p. 91). Susan Rigdon, who also worked on the Puerto Rico study, said: "Among his Puerto Rican informants in particular were a number of people whose behavior was, in the context of their own communities, deviant and even bizarre" (p. 97). However, Lewis took issue with Luján's conclusions and said the tests had cross-cultural and class biases. He took this position despite the fact that he had originally included them in his study and also relied on them to support his list of social and psychological traits in the culture of poverty (Rigdon, 1988).

Lewis's work is also criticized because he never clarified the criteria he used to select or edit his original tapes. Lewis says that, in the process of taping, he asked informants to repeat the histories that he already knew with the goal of having them "in their own words" (Lewis, 1966, p. xx). He also says that few notes were taken during the day, when observation took place, and that memory was relied on to reproduce the dialogue and the details. According to Rigdon (1988), Lewis never kept records, logs, or diaries in the field (pp. 75–76). It is unclear what was included and what was excluded from the tapes, and what criteria were used to select themes and conversations in *La Vida* (Beattie, 1967; Rodríguez Bou, 1967). Yet, in a participant observation study, it is important to make clear the criteria used to compile the observations because we rely on the observer's interpretation of his or her observations, and because there is also a tendency to present evidence that supports one's view—to have selective perception (Rodríguez Bou, 1967).

There are other questions that could be raised about Lewis's research in Puerto Rico. Contrary to earlier studies in which he was quite actively involved, in Puerto Rico he personally administered only a small number of questionnaires (Rigdon, 1988). One assistant, Francisca Muriente, did nearly half of all the interviewing. Lewis was also in failing health. According to Rigdon (1988), "by the mid-1960s some of the people closest to him noted the impact his health problems were beginning to have on his memory and critical faculties" (p. 76). She adds that "it is not surprising that under these circumstances Lewis had difficulty grasping the meaning of the Puerto Rican materials" (p. 76). Another factor that may have influenced Lewis's thinking on the work was "his degree of dependence . . . on collaborators and assistants" (p. 83). Most of his assistants were non-Puerto Rican.

There is also a question as to the "fit" between his theory and his data. Rigdon (1988) says: "The use of culture of poverty theory to force an integration was not only artificial but led Lewis to postulate relationships he did not demonstrate, let alone prove, with his own data" (p. 81). Some of the evident contradictions in his work can be explained to some degree by Rigdon's comment that toward the end of his career he began to apply generalizations from one research study to another, sometimes adding contradictory or competing findings. "For this reason almost everything he published in the 1960s is full of contradictions" (Rigdon, p. 176). Rodríguez Bou (1967) also notes data discrepancies between Lewis's description of the area studied and data derived from other contemporaneous studies of the same area.

Did Lewis hold latent biases toward Puerto Ricans? Rigdon (1988) argues that Lewis had a "tendency to view Puerto Rico and its people as suffering from a psychology of oppression, a fatalistic outlook resulting from a prolonged period of victimization and insufficient resistance" (p. 82). She suggests that this tendency affected his interpretation of the Puerto Rico material: "I believe that this attitude colored all of Lewis's attempts to interpret the Puerto Rican material and was reinforced by his overconcentration on the poorest and most deviant of his informants" (p. 82).

In short, the book was used to generalize to many groups, most importantly Puerto Ricans, yet the representativeness of this one family can be questioned on a variety of grounds. It is clear that they are not representative of all Puerto Ricans, it seems evident that they are not representative of Puerto Ricans in poverty or of most people in poverty, and it is questionable whether they are even representative of the barrio within which they lived. Although the book is subtitled *A Puerto Rican Family in the Culture of Poverty*, it is difficult to determine whether this is a study of the culture of poverty or a study of prostitution within the culture of poverty. Some have argued that *La Vida* is a study that projected the "poverty of culture" (Geltman, 1967, p. 428) among Puerto Ricans and among those in poverty (Maldonado Denis, 1967a).

Limited Perspective, Not Limited Knowledge

La Vida has been criticized on a number of other grounds, but the questions that remain are: To what extent was Oscar Lewis aware of the image he would project? Was he informed about the consequences of his work? Did he care? Was he, as one reviewer commented, "guilty of professional and social irresponsibility" (Monserrat, 1967, p. 51)?

Lewis was clearly aware of the image *La Vida* projected. In response to criticisms about his work, Lewis (1967) declared:

Most Mexican and Puerto Rican critics have not challenged the essential truth of the data in my books. The only question that has been raised has concerned the advisability of publishing such data because of possible harm to the Mexican or Puerto Rican image. (p. 498)

(Apparently Lewis did not accept as valid the criticisms of his method; see Lewis, 1967.) We also get some indication of his awareness from letters he wrote to colleagues and collaborators. With regard to the role of prostitution, Luján, his psychologist, wrote to him and said,

I am not quite happy about including the Ríos family in "The Culture of Poverty" because prostitution is their way of life and colors every aspect of their experience. This I do not believe to be a trait of the culture of poverty. (Luján to Lewis, January 25, 1966, cited in Rigdon, 1988, p. 256)

Lewis rejected this position, saying: "Indeed, she [Luján] urges me to emphasize in my introduction that this is not a typical culture of poverty family because of the prostitution factor. My own tendency goes in the other direction" (Lewis to Elizabeth Herzog, March 29, 1966, cited in Rigdon, p. 260).

It seems that Lewis was very aware of the image the book would project and that it would be seen as shocking. In a letter to Lloyd Ohlin, a sociologist, he said: "I am afraid my new book on the Ríos family will be a shock even to social workers whose middle-class values and experiences will probably make the Ríos family seem animal-like and unreachable" (March 22, 1966, cited in Rigdon, 1988, p. 257). He had also written to Luján about this, but as noted above was not inclined to follow her advice. Luján wrote to Lewis and said:

As far as presenting a denigrating image of the Puerto Rican, I believe you can avoid this by avoiding generalizations in your introduction. ... If you can put it across that your study is a study of prostitution in a culture of poverty, and not a characteristic of the culture of poverty, this would seem convenient. (March 23, 1966, cited in Rigdon, p. 259)

Lewis ignored the advice and appeared to rationalize his approach. In a letter to anthropologist Michael Kenny he asserted:

I am afraid that my first volume on Puerto Rican families will cause a scandal here in New York among Commonwealth officialdom who are so desperately and understandably trying to build a positive image of the Puerto Rican, stimulate community organization and solidarity, etc. I am sympathetic to their goals but find that they are out of touch with a large sector of their own people. Either that, or they manage to conceal even from themselves the knowledge of the serious problems of Puerto Rican family life. (June 7, 1965, cited in Rigdon, p. 295)

Note that in this letter he generalizes from the problems of his one family to "the serious problems of Puerto Rican family life" and concludes: "I am afraid this will not make a pretty picture but I believe it is an accurate one" (Rigdon, p. 297).

In a letter to Luján, it is unclear whether Lewis is interested in lessening the possible outcry over the book or in using Puerto Rican intellectuals to legitimate it. He says: "In the case of the Puerto Rico volume, I had better ask three or four Puerto Rican intellectuals to read the manuscript and get their advice before I send it to the press" (February 28, 1965, cited in Rigdon, 1988, p. 295). One is less inclined to a sympathetic interpretation of this when one reads in the same letter:

The big mistake was my allowing publication of the Sánchez book in Spanish. You may recall that I once offered Orfila a thousand dollars to tear up our contract and he laughed at my worrisome nature, etc. Now he is charged with social dissolution for publishing it. I certainly don't want to have a Spanish edition of my work on the P. R. families. None of the family members read English. (Rigdon, p. 295)

The Irony

The greatest irony in the Lewis saga is that, after the publication of *La Vida*, Lewis began to rethink what he had so strongly defended. His study comparing three generations of Puerto Rican women in one family prompted Lewis to rethink his culture of poverty construct (Rigdon, 1988). Lewis decided that "home environment" and "socialization" (Rigdon, p. 95) were not the only factors at work reproducing the subculture life style. He could not account for how people from the same family came out differently (Rigdon, 1988). In a letter to Manuel Maldonado Denis he says:

The more I study the poor, the more impressed I am by the wide range of variation and the subtle differences from family to family. No generalizations can really encompass the richness and variety of the lives which I am attempting to portray in the words of the poor. . . . (cited in Rigdon, p. 93)

His awareness of the impact on Puerto Ricans and of his own doubts concerning his theory are revealed in a letter he wrote to Lloyd Ohlin:

The impact of my book on the Puerto Rican image would be less damaging if I could sustain the thesis that what we are dealing with is essentially a universal condition rather than a distinctively Puerto Rican one. . . . (Letter dated March 22, 1966, cited in Rigdon, p. 257)

Lewis never published the study of three generations of Puerto Rican women that aroused his doubts and his rethinking. He also rushed *La Vida* into print before he had completed the comparative studies he had originally intended to do of 100 families in four San Juan slums. When *La Vida* first came out, a number of reviewers gave him the benefit of the doubt, saying they would have to await the results of the other studies (Rodríguez Bou, 1967). However, as von Eckardt (1967) said, it would have been more prudent of Lewis not to publish *La Vida* until another study in another country (e.g., England) was done. Why, then, was *La Vida* published? Perhaps, as Rigdon (1988) notes, "Time, funding, availability of informants, and pressures to publish—not the conviction that the necessary data had been collected—were what brought these studies to a close" (p. 174).

In the meantime, the Puerto Rican communities dealt with the spillover effects generated by the book. Teachers read it in their faculty lounges, well-intentioned social workers and other service providers read it en route to work. They concluded, after a titillating, albeit somewhat repulsive, 700 pages, that they now understood Puerto Ricans. As Rodríguez Bou (1967) argued, the study would have a negative impact on the poor, because many poor people would now be rejected by the non-poor, who would assume they followed the practices depicted in *La Vida*. He also asserted that the study would have a negative impact on Puerto Ricans in general because the general readership (especially in communities filled with prejudices) could find abundant "confirmation" for their ideas and preconceived notions.

In the end, the book served important, if dispiriting, political purposes. Writes Rigdon (1988):

In the 1960s the eradication of poverty was a central political issue and the culture of poverty was a dramatic yet conveniently vague phrase that helped to call attention to the problems of the poor—or, from another perspective, to the problem of the poor. (p. 87)

Puerto Ricans became further identified with the problem of the poor. Subsequent funded research on Puerto Ricans would focus on poverty, and *La Vida* would provide a major point of departure. But what is perhaps most lamentable is that even if we were to accept Lewis's study as representative or legitimate, it would have taught us nothing new, nor could it prescribe policy that would alleviate the dramatic expression of hunger and deprivation (Rodríguez Bou, 1967).

DECONSTRUCTING AND CONTEXTUALIZING: THE POST-1970 LITERATURE

Many of the themes in the earlier literature still persist (see, e.g., Hauberg, 1974), some in slightly altered fashion; for example, the culture of poverty thesis was transformed into the underclass conception. There was also a shift from a focus on Puerto Rico and Puerto Ricans to the more generic Hispanic group, within which Puerto Ricans were subsumed. (Within this rubric, there was a tendency to lose sight of what was specific to one group and what was common to all Latino groups). There was also a shift to a more quantitative approach. Private and public funding would assist these shifts. However, there was also the development of a literature that was deconstructionist in its intent and that sought to contextualize Puerto Rico and Puerto Ricans. As was to be expected, resistance to, and misinterpretation of, the new literature would also become manifest.

The early efforts (in English and in Spanish) to combat and correct the homogeneous and distorted views of Puerto Ricans were often ignored or summarily dismissed because they challenged the prevailing notions. Often these pioneering writers and researchers were accused of reflecting bias and were perceived as lacking in competence or qualifications. At best they were seen as marginal, or not important in addressing the major research questions of the day. In addition, until very recently, publisher interest in these efforts was minimal. Unless the images coincided with stereotypical expectations, most publishers did not avail themselves of these transformative works, arguing that they would have no market. Consequently, many of these works were not published in mainstream outlets. This was the case both in the United States and in Puerto Rico, where the internalized colonialism and the divisions created by it restrained publishers from accepting materials written in English by Puerto Ricans. If critical or revisionist works were printed at all, it was often through less well-established and less prestigious avenues, with distribution networks that were typically not extensive. Thus they became in many respects phantom or fugitive works—seldom referenced, less well known, and less read.

Moreover, there was a subtle academic exclusion. Scholars who might have been considered "deconstructionists" or "postmodernists" were instead often "derogatively labeled 'ghetto' scholars" (Vázquez, 1992, p. 1043). According to Vázquez, their work was often devalued because, in large measure, their subject matter was devalued. Despite the fact that

others could and did study Puerto Rico and Puerto Ricans in great profusion during the 1940s, 1950s, and 1960s, [when] Puerto Ricans started studying other Puerto Ricans it was seen as nothing more than the scholarly contemplation of one's own navel. If American scholars [studied] American culture and society through American studies, this was considered serious scholarship. However, when a Puerto Rican researcher [studied] the Puerto Rican culture—any aspect of it—it [was] not seen as quite scholarly enough. (p. 1043)

Nonetheless, despite the protestations of more traditional (and threatened) mainstream academics, the energetic efforts of the new writers succeeded in transforming the literature on Puerto Ricans. The number of Puerto Ricans contributing to the literature increased significantly after 1970.

It was also during the late 1960s and early 1970s that many Puerto Rican Studies programs were started. These programs rejected traditional approaches to learning about Puerto Ricans and defined new sources of learning that stemmed from within the Puerto Rican experience. Puerto Rican Studies discarded apologist and colonizing ideologies and designed new theoretical constructs within which fresh analyses about the Puerto Rican condition were generated (Nieves, 1987). The Puerto Rican Studies thrust emphasized the accountability of scholars to represent the community accurately.

The literature that surfaced during this period reflected these new intentions. It also focused directly on the colonial relationship and its negative consequences. Challenging the assimilationist, immigrant paradigm, it questioned the use of deficit models and gave attention to indigenous issues and histories that had been neglected. It compared Puerto Ricans with other, similar groups and examined Puerto Ricans within national and international contexts. As was the case with the literatures of other racial-ethnic groups, there was a search for a "buried past." And the histories of the Puerto Rican communities in the States began to be constructed and, in some cases, reconstructed.

Falcón (1984) refers to the late 1960s and early 1970s as a period of "nationalist revitalization" within the Puerto Rican communities in the States. During this period a number of works appeared that were widely read and that stressed the heretofore neglected perspectives of "independentistas." Significant among these were Figueroa (1974), Maldonado Denis (1972), Silén (1971), and López (1973). Many of these works offered an interpretation of Puerto Rico's history that emphasized the inequality of the colonial relationship and the consequences of domination. López and Petras (1974) and López (1980) were similar in their criticism. They were also critical of earlier studies that focused on symptoms and did not point out that these symptoms were consequences of larger exploitative relationships that had been cultivated and institutionalized over time. A number of the articles were devoted to "the Puerto Rican diaspora" in the States. In this new literature, the political relationship was central, not obscured or seen as benevolent.

Many works began to unearth the history of the independence movement and to clarify its current-day distortions. Ribes Tovar's (1971) volume on the independence leader Albizu Campos is an example of such a work oriented to a less academic audience. All of these works were instrumental in establishing in the States a literary tradition that had already existed in Puerto Rico in Spanish. Other works that would follow in this tradition are those by G. Lewis (1974), Závala and Rodríguez (1980), Liden (1981), Blaught (1987), Fernández (1988, 1992), and Meléndez and Meléndez (1993). Meléndez and Meléndez presented critical perspectives on contemporary Puerto Rico, and focused on questions often neglected in earlier research, such as the extent of military control and ownership of land in Puerto Rico; the struggle for independence in the 21st century; and an assessment of Puerto Rico's current role in the Caribbean economy. What was evident in this ongoing tradition of

scholarship was that "Behind the complacency that sometimes seems to dominate U.S. colonial rule over Puerto Rico lurks a will of national affirmation that refuses to die" (Carrión, 1993, p. 75).

In keeping with more radical and revisionist perspectives were works examining the impact of the political relationship on Puerto Rico (Heine, 1983; Maldonado Denis, 1980; Marquez, 1976) and upon Puerto Ricans in the United States (History Task Force, 1979). This relationship was no longer viewed as benign and malleable, but rather as highly determinant. For example, the earlier literature had viewed migration as a response to push-and-pull forces, but still very much the result of individual choice. The Centro de Estudios Puertorriqueños focused upon the influence of the political-economic relationship on migration (History Task Force, 1979). Scholars at the Centro argued that one cannot separate analysis of migration from analysis of economic structure and change; that the massive migration of Puerto Ricans to the States in the post-World War II period was a labor migration that could only be understood by examining the colonial-capitalist framework of Puerto Rico; that it was, in effect, driven by U.S. capitalist forces functioning within a colonial context.

In subsequent works, the political-economic relationship and the post-World War II industrialization program in Puerto Rico received closer examination (see, e.g., Baver, 1993; Bloomfield, 1985; Bonilla & Campos, 1986; Carr, 1984; Dietz, 1986; López, 1987; Meléndez & Meléndez, 1993; Pantojas-García, 1990; Ross, 1976; Weisskoff, 1985). Similarly, an emphasis on examining larger contextual and structural issues affecting Puerto Ricans in the United States was provided by Rodríguez (1974, 1989), Morales (1986), and F. Padilla (1987). These works began with the assumption that Puerto Ricans in the States and in Puerto Rico could not be accurately understood without understanding the context from which they came, the context they had entered, and the structural contexts within which they functioned.

These perspectives were also to be found among authors who utilized larger quantitative databases. Hernández (1983), for example, found that human capital theory could not be applied to Puerto Rican youth without considering their health, family, and residential situation, migration background, and veteran status. Meléndez, Rodríguez, and Barry Figueroa's (1992) collection examined structural economic factors affecting Puerto Ricans, as well as the effect of national and international intersections of race, color, class, and colonialism. Some authors developed innovative perspectives within traditional subject areas. For example, Burgos, Rodríguez-Vecchini, and Torre (1993), building on the earlier work of Hernández (1967) and Torruellas and Vásquez (1984), developed new perspectives on return migration. These works differed from the earlier literature in that they focused more on the structures affecting Puerto Ricans as opposed to the cultural attributes considered to be characteristic of the group.

Closely allied to this approach was the growing research that went beyond exclusive focus on Puerto Ricans and examined Puerto Ricans in relation to similar groups. Examples include F. Padilla's (1985) account of the factors responsible for the development of Latino ethnic consciousness among Puerto Ricans and Mexicans in Chicago; Acosta-Belén and Sjostrom's (1988) collection of articles on Hispanics in the United States; de la Garza, Desipio, Garcia, Garcia, and Falcón's (1992) study of political attitudes; and R. Morales and Bonilla's (1993) study of Latinos in a changing U.S. economy. Another instance is Hernández's (1992) text, an interdisciplinary work, that surveys the peoples and nations made part of the United States by war and occupation, and focuses on Puerto Ricans, Filipinos, Hawaiians, Chicanos, and Native Americans. Finally, the work by Torres (1994) compares the effects of national and regional trends on Puerto Ricans and African Americans in New York City.

In addition to deconstructing and reconstructing earlier views, works began to focus on issues that had been ignored in the previous literature (e.g., Hardy-Fanta, 1992; Harwood, 1977; Morales-Dorta, 1976; F. Padilla, 1992; F. Padilla & Santiago, 1993). The collection of readings edited by Rodríguez, Sánchez Korrol, and Alers (1980/1984) is an early example of a work that focuses on previously ignored issues. Developed as a reader for Puerto Rican Studies courses, it included articles that were vital to the Puerto Rican community at the time, but were generally ignored within more mainstream contexts. Articles on Puerto Rican women, the Young Lords, Latin music, the struggle for local political control, spiritualism, the struggles within the Catholic church, the Puerto Rican Day Parade, race within ethnicity, political activism, the economy, and a beginning critique of the conceptual models and methods used to "measure" the quality of life among Puerto Ricans were included in this interdisciplinary volume. This attention to neglected issues was a first step in developing knowledge that would help to resolve community issues. The highly interdisciplinary nature of the articles, ranging from literary selections by nonacademic writers to more traditional social science commentaries, would also typify other works published during this period.

This reader also departed from traditional approaches in that it asserted that the experience of being Puerto Rican would enhance the work, if based on valid observations related to commonly accepted knowledge. It was not suggested that one had to be Puerto Rican to write accurately about the Puerto Rican community, or that being Puerto Rican was any guarantee of accuracy or insight, but that the experience of being Puerto Rican, if understood correctly, would be an asset in dealing with the issues. Thus it was no accident that nearly all involved with this collection were second-generation Puerto Ricans or had experienced life in U.S. Puerto Rican communities. The editors stated that "the authors have been intimately involved in the issues they address and this sets their work apart from many traditional social scientists" (Rodríguez et al., 1980, p. 3). The collection also endeavored to speak to "the new reality of Puerto Ricans, their future, and a more accurate past than had been depicted in the traditional literature" (p. 3). This collection and the others described here attempted to put forth a more representative view by allowing those affected to speak for themselves within a framework of personal integrity and dignity. Other works that followed (e.g., Acosta-Belén, 1986; Hidalgo & McEniry, 1985) were similar in their orientations, which was targeted to government officials and service providers interested in the Hispanic community.

The post-1970 literature contained the same search for a "buried past" undertaken by Native Americans and other groups that have been excluded from official U.S. history. Examples include the continuing work of the Centro de Estudios Puertorriqueños in assembling historical documentation on the migration and on Puerto Rico (Flores, 1987; History Task Force, 1983; Oral History Task Force, 1986; Reynolds, Rodríguez-Fraticelli, & Vásquez Erazo, 1989) and the volumes by Wagenheim and Jiménez de Wagenheim (1973) and Acosta (1987). In women's studies, the reconstruction of migrant women's lives utilizing oral history methods is another example (Benmayor, Juarbe, Alvarez, & Vásquez, 1987). Moreover, there are a number of works that present "portraits of the early migration" (Hernández Cruz, 1988), such as those by Sánchez Korrol (1983), which depicts the pre-World War II Puerto Rican community, and by Iglesias (1984), which compiles the memoirs of Bernardo Vega, an early migrant and socialist writer who gives us a glimpse of life in the late 19th- and early 20th-century Puerto Rican community. Works by Acosta-Belén and Sánchez Korrol (1993) and Colón (1982) describe the Puerto Rican community in the 1930s, 1940s, and 1950s. There is also the work of Pérez y Mena (1991) on the historical roots of spiritualism, Bloch (1973) on Puerto Rican music, and Stevens-Arroyo (1988) and Rouse (1992) on the world of the Taínos, the pre-Columbian inhabitants of Puerto Rico.

These works and others began to contest the generally accepted notion that the Puerto Rican community in the States began at about the time that *West Side Story* made its debut on Broadway in 1957. There were also numerous works documenting more recent history, both verbally (e.g., Bonilla-Santiago, 1988; Cardona, 1974; Díaz-Stevens, 1993; J. Figueroa, 1989; Estades, 1978; Haslip-Viera & Baver, 1994; Martínez, 1974; Ribes Tovar, 1968, 1970, 1972; Rogler, 1972; Sanchez & Stevens-Arroyo, 1987) and pictorially (Maldonado, 1984; Young Lords Party, 1971). Many of the works also moved the Puerto Rican perspective to a more national level (see, e.g., U.S. Commission on Civil Rights, 1976; Wagenheim, 1975).

In addition, there were works that began to reassess or take a critical view of such long-standing issues as language, religion, race, residential segregation, employment, and education. Much of this discussion is to be found not in published books, but rather outside the realm of this review in reports and monographs published by community organizations, especially ASPIRA, the Puerto Rican Forum, the National Puerto Rican Coalition, the Institute for Puerto Rican Policy, and the Latino Institute; in theses; and in articles in journals developed by Puerto Ricans, such as *The Rican, Revista, Centro Boletín, Journal of Latino Studies,* and *METAS*. It is also to be found in the monographs produced by the Hispanic Research Center (1990), and in the work on culture and language by the Centro de Estudios Puertorriqueños (Alvarez, Bennett, Greenless, Pedraza, & Pousada, 1988; Attinasi, Pedraza, Poplack, & Pousada, 1988; Benmayor, Torruellas, & Juarbe, 1992; Cultural Studies Task Force, 1987; Pedraza, 1987; Poplack & Pousada, 1981; Torruellas, Benmayor, Goris, & Juarbe, 1991).

Language, a perennial issue, has received particular attention in the Centro de Estudios Puertorriqueños's Working Papers (Language Policy Task Force, 1978, 1980, 1982). Book-length treatments are found in Fishman, Cooper, and Ma (1971) and in Zentella (1994), both of which examine the development of language and identity in the United States, while Walsh (1991) reexamines language issues in Puerto Rico.

Questions were raised in many works about earlier assimilationist assumptions, but the following authors gave particular attention to this area: Fishman et al., 1971; Flores, 1993; Morales, 1986; F. Padilla, 1985, 1987; Rodríguez, 1974, 1989; Rogler and Santana Cooney, 1984. In keeping with the new thrust and research in the post-1970 literature, the updated edition of Fitzpatrick's *Puerto Rican Americans* (1987) moderated former claims about assimilation. Although a number of works would continue to reflect the perspectives of the past (e.g., Aliotta, 1991), there was also evidence of a shift to a more sympathetic albeit sometimes patronizing and stereotypic view (e.g., Sheehan, 1976; Steiner, 1974). There were also a number of attempts to provide profiles of commonplace Puerto Ricans (e.g., C. Bean, 1974; Cooper, 1972) or of the perspectives of Puerto Rican leaders (Cordasco & Bucchioni, 1973; Mapp, 1974).

Although many of the works cited above contributed to this new perspective, Jennings and Rivera's *Puerto Rican Politics in Urban America* (1984) is a good example of the expression of many of these themes. The book addresses the generally neglected or stereotyped view of Puerto Rican politics in the States by taking a broad view. It includes articles on the history of Puerto Rican politics, from mid-19th century to current times, both in and outside of New York. The book also focuses on topics often neglected, such as labor activism and the Puerto Rican struggle for educational equality. In addition, it begins to detail the growing literature on the Puerto Rican community in the States, noting the still-assimilationist perspective of some writers and a more analytical shift in perspective with regard to Puerto Rican politics. Finally, it draws attention to the repression of Puerto Rican political activists (Falcón, 1984).

The literature on, and by, women also increased in the post-1970 period. Although many Latina women were critical of Ribes Tovar's (1972) book on Puerto Rican women because of what appeared to be unsubstantiated and subjective generalizations, it did provide a popular history of women and drew attention to famous women of the 19th and 20th centuries. Acosta-Belén's (1979, 1986) works served a number of important purposes. They provided a link between the work being done in Puerto Rico and in the United States, and they focused on areas that had generally been neglected, including images of women in literature, role expectations, discrimination, lesbianism, the Black Puerto Rican woman, and stories of success. The work of Sánchez Korrol (1983) emphasized the unacknowledged contributions of women to the household economy and to the functioning of the early Puerto Rican communities in the States. The personal essays of Levins Morales and Morales (1986) shed light on identity struggles of Puerto Rican women, while Hidalgo and McEniry (1985) gave particular emphasis to service delivery issues affecting women.

The works on women by Benmayor et al. (1987, 1992) and Torruellas et al. (1991) were interesting in that they utilized the same oral history method employed by Oscar Lewis but arrived at very different depictions. Cafferty San Juan and Rivera-Martínez (1981) examined the issues in bilingual education, while García Coll and Mattei's (1989) collection explored the psychological and social development of Puerto Rican women from a lifespan developmental perspective. These works have served to stimulate newer efforts; see, for example, Ortiz (1994) and Lamberty and García Coll (1994). They have also continued the traditions established of incorporating work from both Puerto Rico and the States, and of focusing on important areas often neglected in the earlier literature.

Work at the intersection of Women's Studies and Puerto Rican Studies expanded the boundaries of the field. According to Acosta-Belén (1992), there is emerging a literary discourse based upon cultural subjectivities that involve being a Latina and sharing experiences (both at individual and interethnic levels) that transcend national origins and speak to a spirit of solidarity and identification with the liberation movements of all women and other groups oppressed because of class position, race, ethnicity, or sexual preference.

In the literary arena, there were developments that paralleled the trends of the post-1970s. Acosta-Belén (1992) argues that the literature produced by Puerto Ricans in the States provided cultural validation and affirmation of a collective sense of identity. Analyzing this literature, she finds that these qualities served to counteract the detrimental effects of the marginalization experienced in the States. She cites a number of other characteristics of this literature, including its antiestablishment cast, its commitment to denouncing inequality and injustice, and its use as a consciousness-raising tool for promoting social change. Furthermore, she finds that the writings revealed the prevalence of a strong political activism, cultural effervescence, and communal spirit, which helped to counter the alleged cultural deficiency notions promulgated by earlier writers. The book by Rodríguez de Laguna (1987) on Puerto Rican literature reflected "the bridging tradition"; it examined images and identities in the creative literature of Puerto Ricans in two world contexts.

Acosta-Belén (1992) views the literature produced in the States as part of the larger multicultural revitalization movement that was a component of ethnoracial minorities' response to their structural and cultural marginalization and to the assimilation pressures from the dominant Anglo American society. This multicultural revitalization challenged cultural hegemony and engendered, within U.S. academic circles, an intellectual reevaluation and redefinition of "ethnocentric Western cultural theories and canons" (p. 983).

IMPLICATIONS

The implications of this literature review for teachers and students in multicultural education are many. Given the previous literature on Puerto Ricans, it would seem important to develop material that is more sensitive to Puerto Rican culture, writings, insights, and ideas. This would counter, to a degree, the earlier errors. It would also introduce students to knowledge and perspectives to which, in all likelihood, they have not been exposed. When teaching, it would seem that the following are some of the more urgent needs.

1. Clarify the role of the United States in Puerto Rico, both historically and currently. It would seem incumbent on teachers to be very specific when discussing the current situation—for example, to talk about the lack of representation in the U.S. Congress, the lack of control Puerto Rico has over immigration to Puerto Rico, commercial trade with other countries, Caribbean security issues, U.S. military bases, environmental policy, and the cultural impact of Anglo American industry and tourism. It would also seem important to discuss how these issues affect Puerto Ricans.

It would seem just as necessary to discuss how creatively and cleverly Puerto Ricans have coped with these limitations on a historical basis. Thus it is important to discuss how colonialism induces not just a colonized mentality but also an "oppositional mentality" (Rodríguez, 1989).

2. Make clear that Puerto Rico has:

(a) at least a 3,500-year history before 1898;
(b) a Native American civilization prior to 1493 that has continued influencing Puerto Rican culture;
(c) a history of enslavement and forced migration of Africans from 1510 to 1876, the contributions of which became important components of Puerto Rican culture;
(d) a Puerto Rican community in the States with a history dating back to the 19th century;
(e) a culture that is a blend of European (mainly Spanish), African, Native American, and Anglo American traditions.

3. Stress the need to view Puerto Ricans as a heterogeneous people, having various racial and ethnic backgrounds, as well as divergent cultural and political views and migrant status. Given the confusion and general lack of information about Puerto Ricans, teachers may have to be prepared to dispel students' previous homogeneous or stereotypic images.

4. Given the tendency in the literature to overgeneralize (i.e., to go from specific or extreme cases to the whole group), it would seem that special efforts would need to be made to avoid falling into this trap when utilizing personal stories or singular cases for illustrative purposes.

5. Given the earlier exclusive and limiting focus, it would

seem important to highlight the similarities and differences between Puerto Ricans and such other groups as Native Americans, other Latinos, African Americans, Asian Americans, and migrants to Europe from former European colonies. However, teachers might well have to be prepared to discuss Puerto Ricans within more conventional frameworks, for example, why and how Puerto Ricans fit into this society as U.S. citizens, and how they also fit into Latin American history and culture.

6. Given the extent to which Puerto Rican history has been omitted or obscured in the curriculum, it is important to stress the accomplishments of Puerto Ricans prior to 1898, including the work of ordinary people who contributed to the island's wealth, but were kept as slaves; the long struggle for liberation; and the establishment of a unique self-determination in 1897.

7. Similarly, it would also seem to be especially important to stress the contributions of Puerto Ricans from 1898 to the present, both in Puerto Rico and in the United States.

8. The unique political position of Puerto Rico also implies that it is important to discuss both the benefits and problems of Puerto Rico as a U.S. territory, such as the gains in standard of living after Puerto Ricans elected their own governor, along with the disruptions caused by industrialization and mass migration.

9. Last, Puerto Rico's political status lends itself to lively discussions among students regarding continued commonwealth, statehood, or independence. However, students should be reminded that this issue will ultimately be decided by the U.S. Congress and the American people as well, and that other territories may be affected, such as the District of Columbia, Guam, and the Virgin Islands. The comparison of Puerto Ricans and Native American peoples should help the students to reflect on the colonial policies of the United States and the consequences of these policies on affected groups.

A broader, multicultural approach should result in a more valid presentation of Puerto Ricans. It should also assist in the integration of Puerto Rican Studies into a broader perspective that is inclusive and representative of the commonalities and differences among all groups.

References

Acosta, U. (1987). *New voices of old: Five centuries of Puerto Rican cultural history.* Santurce, PR: Permanent Press.

Acosta-Belén, E. (Ed.). (1979). *The Puerto Rican woman.* New York: Praeger.

Acosta-Belén, E. (Ed.). (1986). *The Puerto Rican woman* (2nd ed.). New York: Praeger.

Acosta-Belén, E. (1992). Beyond island boundaries: Ethnicity, gender, and cultural revitalization in Nuyorican literature. *Callaloo, 15*(4), 979–998.

Acosta-Belén, E., & Sánchez Korrol, V. (1993). *The way it was and other writings.* Houston, TX: Arte Público Press.

Acosta-Belén, E., & Sjostrom, B. (Eds.). (1988). *The Hispanic experience in the U.S.* (2nd ed.). New York: Praeger.

Aliotta, J. J. (1991). *The Puerto Ricans.* New York: Chelsea House Publishers.

Alvarez, C., Bennett, A., Greenless, M., Pedraza, P., & Pousada, A. (1988). *Speech and ways of speaking in a bilingual Puerto Rican community.* New York: Centro de Estudios Puertorriqueños, Hunter College, City University of New York.

Anderson, R. (1965). *Party politics in Puerto Rico.* Stanford, CA: Stanford University Press.

Attinasi, J., Pedraza, P., Poplack, S., & Pousada, A. (1988). *Intergenerational perspectives on bilingualism.* New York: Centro de Estudios Puertorriqueños, Hunter College, City University of New York.

Baggs, W. C. (1962). *Puerto Rico: Showcase of development.* San Juan:

Commonwealth of Puerto Rico. (Reprinted from the *1962 Britannica Book of the Year*)

Baver, S. (1984). Puerto Rican politics in New York City: The post-World War II period. In J. Jennings & M. Rivera (Eds.), *Puerto Rican politics in urban America* (pp. 43–59). Westport, CT: Greenwood Press.

Baver, S. (1993). *The political economy of colonialism: The state and industrialization in Puerto Rico*. New York: Praeger.

Bean, C. (1974). *My name is José*. Chicago: Herald Press.

Bean, F., & Tienda, M. (1988). *The Hispanic population in the U.S.* New York: Russell Sage Foundation.

Beattie, J. H. M. (1967). Review of *The Children of Sánchez, Pedro Martínez*, and *La Vida*. *Current Anthropology, 8*(5), 484.

Benmayor, R., Juarbe, A., Alvarez, C., & Vásquez, B. (1987). *Stories to live by: Continuity and change in three generations of Puerto Rican women* (Working paper). New York: Centro de Estudios Puertorriqueños, Hunter College, City University of New York.

Benmayor, R., Torruellas, R. M., & Juarbe, A. L. (1992). *Responses to poverty among Puerto Rican women: Identity, community and cultural citizenship*. New York: Centro de Estudios Puertorriqueños, Hunter College, City University of New York.

Berbusse, E. J. (1966). *The United States in Puerto Rico, 1898–1900*. Chapel Hill: University of North Carolina Press.

Berle, B. (1958). *80 Puerto Rican families in New York City*. New York: Columbia University Press.

Blaught, J. (1987). *The national question: Decolonizing the theory of nationalism*. London: Zed Books.

Block, P. (1973). *La-le-lo-lai: Puerto Rican music and its performers*. New York: Plus Ultra.

Bloomfield, R. (1985). *Puerto Rico: The search for a national policy*. Boulder, CO: Westview Press.

Bonilla, F., & Campos, R. (1986). *Industry and idleness*. New York. Centro de Estudios Puertorriqueños, Hunter College, City University of New York.

Bonilla-Santiago, G. (1988). *Organizing Puerto Rican migrant farmworkers: The experience of Puerto Ricans in New Jersey*. New York: Lang.

Buitrago Ortiz, C. (1974). *Esperanza: An ethnographic study of a peasant community in Puerto Rico*. Tucson: University of Arizona Press.

Burgos, W., Rodríguez-Vecchini, H., & Torre, C. A. (Eds.). *The commuter nation: Perspectives on Puerto Rican migration*. San Juan: Editorial de la Universidad de Puerto Rico.

Cafferty San Juan, P., & Rivera-Martínez, C. (Eds.). (1981). *The politics of language: The dilemma of bilingual education for Puerto Ricans*. Boulder, CO: Westview Press.

Caplow, T. (1967). Review of *The Children of Sánchez, Pedro Martínez*, and *La Vida*. *Current Anthropology, 8*(5), 485–486.

Cardona, L. A. (1974). *The coming of the Puerto Ricans*. Washington, DC: Unidos.

Carr, R. (1984). *Puerto Rico: A colonial experiment*. New York: New York University Press.

Carrión, J. M. (1993). The national question in Puerto Rico. In E. Meléndez & E. Meléndez (Eds.), *Colonial dilemma: Critical perspectives on contemporary Puerto Rico* (pp. 67–75). Boston: South End Press.

Carroll, H. K. (1898). *Report on the island of Porto Rico*, Submitted by the Special Comissioner for the United States to Puerto Rico to President William McKinley, Washington, DC.

Chenault, L. (1970). *The Puerto Rican migrant in New York City*. New York: Columbia University Press. (Original work published 1938)

Churchill, W. (1992). Naming our destiny: Towards a language of Indian liberation. *Global Justice, 3*(2 & 3), 22–33.

Colón, J. (1982). *A Puerto Rican in New York and other sketches*. New York: International Publishers.

Cooper, P. (1972). *Growing up Puerto Rican*. New York: Arbor House.

Cordasco, F., & Bucchioni, E. (Eds.). (1973). *The Puerto Rican experience: A sociological sourcebook*. Totowa, NJ: Rowman & Littlefield.

Cultural Studies Task Force. (1987). *Aprender a luchar, luchar es aprender*. New York: Centro de Estudios Puertorriqueños, Hunter College, City University of New York.

Davis, General M. (1900). *Report on civil affairs to Porto Rico, 1899*. Washington, DC: Government Printing Office.

Day, D. (1967, April-May). How blessed the poor. *The Critic*, pp. 74–76.

de la Garza, R., Desipio, L., Garcia, C., Garcia, J., & Falcón, A. (1992). *Latino voices: Mexican, Puerto Rican, and Cuban perspectives on American politics*. Boulder, CO: Westview Press.

Díaz-Stevens, A. M. (1993). *Oxcart Catholicism on fifth avenue*. Notre Dame, IN: University of Notre Dame Press.

Dietz, J. L. (1986). *Economic history of Puerto Rico*. Princeton, NJ: Princeton University Press.

Estades, R. (1978). *Patterns of political participation of Puerto Ricans in New York City* (translated and printed in Spanish). Rio Piedras: Editorial Universitaria, Universidad de Puerto Rico.

Falcón, A. (1984). An introduction to the literature of Puerto Rican politics in urban America. In J. Jennings & M. Rivera (Eds.), *Puerto Rican politics in urban America* (pp. 145–154). Westport, CT: Greenwood Press.

Fernández, R. (1988). *Los Macheteros: The violent struggle for Puerto Rican independence*. Westport, CT: Greenwood.

Fernández, R. (1992). *The disenchanted island: Puerto Rico and the United States in the twentieth century*. New York: Praeger.

Fernández Méndez, E. (Ed.). (1972). *Portrait of a society: Readings in Puerto Rican sociology*. Rio Piedras: University of Puerto Rico Press.

Figueroa, J. (1989). *Survival on the margin: A documentary study of the underground economy in a Puerto Rican ghetto*. New York: Vantage Press.

Figueroa, L. (1974). *History of Puerto Rico*. New York: Anaya.

Fishman, J. A., Cooper, R. L., & Ma, R. (1971). *Bilingualism in the barrio*. Bloomington: University of Indiana Press.

Fitzpatrick, J. P. (1966, December 10). Oscar Lewis and the Puerto Rican family. *America, 115,* 778–779.

Fitzpatrick, J. P. (1971). *Puerto Rican Americans*. Englewood Cliffs, NJ: Prentice-Hall.

Fitzpatrick, J. P. (1987). *Puerto Rican Americans* (2nd ed.). Englewood Cliffs, NJ: Prentice-Hall.

Flores, J. (Ed.). (1987). *Divided arrival: Narratives of the Puerto Rican migration, 1920–50*. New York: Centro de Estudios Puertorriqueños, Hunter College, City University of New York.

Flores, J. (1993). *Divided borders: Essays on Puerto Rican identity*. Houston, TX: Arte Público Press.

Friedlander, S. L. (1965). *Labor migration and economic growth*. Boston: MIT Press.

Galbraith, J. K., & Shaw Soto, C. (1953). Puerto Rican lessons in economic development. *Annals of the American Academy of Political and Social Sciences, 1*(285), 55–59.

García Coll, C., & Mattei, M. (Eds.). (1989). *The psychosocial development of Puerto Rican women*. Westport, CT: Praeger.

García Muñiz, H. (1993). U.S. military installations in Puerto Rico controlling the Caribbean. In E. Meléndez & E. Meléndez (Eds.), *Colonial dilemma: Critical perspectives on contemporary Puerto Rico* (pp. 53–65). Boston: South End Press.

Geltman, M. (1967, April 18). Electronic anthropology. *National Review*, pp. 426–428.

Glazer, N. (1967, February). One kind of life. *Commentary*, pp. 83–85.

Glazer, N., & Moynihan, D. P. (1970). *Beyond the melting pot* (2nd ed.). Cambridge, MA: M.I.T. Press.

Goodsell, C. (1965). *Administration of a revolution*. Cambridge, MA: Harvard University Press.

Handlin, O. (1959). *The newcomers: Negroes and Puerto Ricans in a changing metropolis.* Cambridge, MA: Harvard University Press.

Hanson, E. P. (1960). *Puerto Rico: Land of wonders.* New York: Alfred A. Knopf.

Hardy-Fanta, C. (1992). *Latina politics: Latino politics.* Philadelphia: Temple University Press.

Harrington, M. (1966, November 20). Everyday hell. *New York Times Book Review*, pp. 1, 92.

Harwood, A. (1977). *Rx-spiritist as needed: A study of a Puerto Rican community mental health resource.* New York: Wiley.

Haslip-Viera, G., & Baver, S. (Eds.). (1994). *Latinos in New York: A community in transition.* Notre Dame, IN: University of Notre Dame Press.

Hauberg, C. A. (1974). *Puerto Rico and the Puerto Ricans.* New York: Twayne.

Heine, J. (1983). *Time for decision: The United States and Puerto Rico.* Lanham, MD: North-South.

Hernández, J. (1967). *Return migration to Puerto Rico.* Berkeley: University of California Press.

Hernández, J. (1983). *Puerto Rican youth employment.* Maplewood, NJ: Waterfront Press.

Hernández, J. (1992). *Conquered peoples in America* (4th ed.). Dubuque, IA: Kendall/Hunt.

Hernández Cruz, J. E. (1988). Puerto Rico in the Ibero-American heritage project. In *The Ibero-American heritage curriculum project: Latinos in the making of the United States of America: Yesterday, today, and tomorrow: Conference proceedings of the second annual meeting of the International Advisory Panel at Santillana del Mar, Spain, October 6–9, 1988* (pp. 165–176). Albany: University of the State of New York, State Education Department.

Hidalgo, H., & McEniry, J. L. (Eds.). (1985). *Hispanic temas: A contribution to the knowledge bank of the Hispanic community.* Newark, NJ: Rutgers University, Puerto Rican Studies Program.

Hispanic Research Center. (1990). *Report of activities, 1977–1990.* New York: Hispanic Research Center, Fordham University.

History Task Force. (1979). *Labor migration under capitalism.* New York: Monthly Review Press.

History Task Force. (1983). *Sources for the study of Puerto Rican migration 1879–1930.* New York: Centro de Estudios Puertorriqueños, Hunter College, City University of New York.

Iglesias, C. A. (Ed.). (1984). *Memoirs of Bernardo Vega.* New York: Monthly Review Press.

Jaimes, M. A. (1992). Federal Indian identification policy. In M. A. Jaimes (Ed.), *The state of Native America: Genocide, colonization and resistance.* Boston: South End Press.

Jennings, J., & Rivera, M. (Eds.). (1984). *Puerto Rican politics in urban America.* Westport, CT: Greenwood Press.

La Ruffa, A. (1971). *San Cipriano: Life in a Puerto Rican community.* New York: Gordon and Breach Science Publishers.

Lamberty, G., & García Coll, C. (Eds.). (1994). *Puerto Rican women and children: Issues in health, growth, and development.* New York: Plenum.

Landy, D. (1959). *Tropical childhood.* Chapel Hill: University of North Carolina Press.

Language Policy Task Force (1978). *Language policy and the Puerto Rican community.* New York: Centro de Estudios Puertorriqueños, Hunter College.

Language Policy Task Force (1980). *Social dimensions of language use in East Harlem.* New York: Centro de Estudios Puertorriqueños, Hunter College.

Language Policy Task Force (1982). *Intergenerational perspectives on bilingualism: From community to classroom.* New York: Centro de Estudios Puertorriqueños, Hunter College.

Lauria-Perricelli, A. (1990). *A study in historical and critical anthropology: The making of* The People of Puerto Rico. Ann Arbor, MI: University Microfilms.

Levins Morales, A., & Morales, R. (1986). *Getting home alive.* Ithaca, NY: Firebrand Books.

Lewis, G. K. (1963). *Puerto Rico: Freedom and power in the Caribbean.* New York: Monthly Review Press.

Lewis, G. (1974). *Notes on the Puerto Rican revolution: An essay on American dominance and Caribbean resistance.* New York: Monthly Review Press.

Lewis, O. (1961). *The children of Sánchez.* New York: Random House.

Lewis, O. (1966). *La Vida: A Puerto Rican family in the culture of poverty—San Juan and New York.* New York: Random House.

Lewis, O. (1967). Reply to reviews of *The Children of Sánchez, Pedro Martínez,* and *La Vida. Current Anthropology, 8*(5), 497–499.

Liden, H. (1981). *History of the Puerto Rican independence movement, 19th century* (Vol 1). Maplewood, NJ: Waterfront Press.

López, A. (1973). *The Puerto Rican papers.* New York: Bobbs-Merrill.

López, A. (Ed.). (1980). *The Puerto Ricans: The history, culture and society.* Cambridge, MA: Schenkman.

López, A. (1987). *Doña Licha's island: Modern colonialism in Puerto Rico.* Boston: South End Press.

López, A., & Petras, J. (Eds.). (1974). *Puerto Rico and Puerto Ricans.* Cambridge, MA: Schenkman.

Maldonado, A. A. (1984). *Portraits of the Puerto Rican experience.* Bronx, NY: IPRUS.

Maldonado Denis, M. (1967a). Oscar Lewis, *La Vida,* y la enajenacion. *Revista de Ciencias Sociales, 11*(2), 253–259.

Maldonado Denis, M. (Ed.). (1967b). *Revista de Ciencias Sociales* [Special issue], *11*(2). Rio Piedras: Universidad de Puerto Rico.

Maldonado Denis, M. (1972). *Puerto Rico: A socio-historic interpretation.* New York: Random House.

Maldonado Denis, M. (1980). *The emigration dialectic: Puerto Rico and the U.S.A.* New York: International Publishers.

Mapp, E. (Ed.). (1974). *Puerto Rican perspectives.* Metuchen, NJ: Scarecrow Press.

Marín, R. C. (1967). Ponencia sobre *La Vida,* el libro de Oscar Lewis. *Revista de Ciencias Sociales, 11*(2), 226–234.

Márquez, R. (1976). *The docile Puerto Rican.* Philadelphia: Temple University Press.

Martínez, A. (Ed.). (1974). *Rising voices.* New York: New American Library.

Meléndez, E., & Meléndez, E. (Eds.). (1993). *Colonial dilemma: Critical perspectives on contemporary Puerto Rico.* Boston: South End Press.

Meléndez, E., Rodríguez, C. E., & Barry Figueroa, J. (Eds.). (1991). *Hispanics in the labor force: Issues and policies.* New York: Plenum Press.

Mills, C. W., Senior, C., & Goldsen, R. (1950). *The Puerto Rican journey: New York's newest migrants.* New York: Harper & Bros.

Mintz, S. W. (1960). *Worker in the cane: A Puerto Rican life history.* New Haven, CT: Yale University Press.

Mintz, S. W. (1990). The island. In J. Delano (Ed.), *Puerto Rico mio: Four decades of change/photographs* (pp. 1–6). Washington, DC: Smithsonian Institution Press.

Monserrat, J. (1967). Review of Oscar Lewis' *La Vida. Natural History, 76*(70), 50–51.

Morales, J. (1986). *Puerto Rican poverty and migration: We just had to try elsewhere.* New York: Praeger.

Morales, R., & Bonilla, F. (1993). *Latinos in a changing U.S. economy.* Newburg Park, CA: Sage Publications.

Morales-Carrión, A. (1952). *Puerto Rico and the non-Hispanic Caribbean: A study in the decline of Spanish exclusivism.* San Juan: University of Puerto Rico Press.

Morales-Carrión, A. (1983). *Puerto Rico: A political and cultural history.* New York: W.W. Norton.

Morales-Dorta, J. (1976). *Puerto Rican espiritismo: Religion and psychotherapy.* New York: Vantage Press.

Negrón de Montilla, A. (1975). *Americanization in Puerto Rico and the public school system, 1900–1930.* Rio Piedras: University of Puerto Rico Press.

New Republic. (1965, December 3). [Review of *La Vida*], p. 155.

Newsweek. (1966, November 21). [Review of *La Vida*], p. 131.

Nieves, J. (1987). Puerto Rican studies: Roots and challenges. In M. Sánchez & A. Stevens-Arroyo (Eds.), *Toward a renaissance of Puerto Rican studies: Ethnic and area studies in university education* (pp. 3–12). Boulder, CO: Social Science Monographs; Highland Lakes, NJ: Atlantic Research and Publications.

Opler, M. K. (1967). Review of *The Children of Sánchez, Pedro Martínez,* and *La Vida. Current Anthropology, 8*(5), 488–489.

Oral History Task Force: (1986). *Extended roots: From Hawaii to New York.* New York: Centro de Estudios Puertorriqueños, Hunter College, City University of New York.

Ortiz, A. (Ed.). (1994). *Puerto Rican women workers in the twentieth century: New perspectives on gender, labor and migration.* Philadelphia: Temple University Press.

Padilla, E. (1958). *Up from Puerto Rico.* New York: Columbia University Press.

Padilla, E. (1967, December). Book review of *La Vida. Political Science Quarterly, 82,* 651–652.

Padilla, F. (1985). *Latino ethnic consciousness: The case of Mexican-Americans and Puerto Ricans in Chicago.* Notre Dame, IN: University of Notre Dame Press.

Padilla, F. (1987). *Puerto Rican Chicago.* Notre Dame, IN: University of Notre Dame Press.

Padilla, F. (1992). *The gang as an American enterprise.* New Brunswick, NJ: Rutgers University Press.

Padilla, F., & Santiago, L. (1993). *Outside the wall: The struggle of a Puerto Rican prisoner's wife.* New Brunswick, NJ: Rutgers University Press.

Pantojas-García, E. (1990). *Development strategies as ideology: Puerto Rico's export-led industrialization experience.* Boulder, CO: Lynne Rienner.

Pedraza, P. (1987). *An ethnographic analysis of language use in the Puerto Rican community of East Harlem.* New York: Centro de Estudios Puertorriqueños, Hunter College, City University of New York.

Pérez de Jesús, M. (1967). Comentarios en torno a *La Vida,* obra publicada por el Dr. Oscar Lewis. *Revista de Ciencias Sociales, 11*(2), 264–274.

Pérez y Mena, A. I. (1991) *Speaking with the dead: Development of Afro-Latin religion among Puerto Ricans in the United States.* New York: AMS Press.

Perloff, H. S. (1950). *Puerto Rico's economic future: A study in planned development.* Chicago: University of Chicago Press.

Petrullo, V. (1947). *Puerto Rican paradox.* Philadelphia: University of Pennsylvania Press.

Poplack, S., & Pousada, A. (1981). *A comparative study of gender assignment to borrowed nouns.* New York: Centro de Estudios Puertorriqueños, Hunter College, City University of New York.

Rand, C. (1958). *The Puerto Ricans.* New York: Oxford University Press.

Reynolds, L. G., & Gregory, P. (1965). *Wages, productivity and industrialization in Puerto Rico.* Chicago: Richard D. Irving.

Reynolds, R. M., Rodríguez-Fraticcelli, C., & Vásquez Erazo, B. (Eds.). (1989). *Campus in bondage: A 1948 microcosm of Puerto Rico in bondage.* New York: Centro de Estudios Puertorriqueños, Hunter College, City University of New York.

Ribes Tovar, F. (1968). *Handbook of the Puerto Rican community* (Vol. 1). New York: El Libro Puerto Rico.

Ribes Tovar, F. (1970). *Enciclopedia puertorriquena ilustrada: The Puerto Rican heritage encyclopedia.* New York: Plus Ultra.

Ribes Tovar, F. (1971). *Albizu Campos: Puerto Rican revolutionary.* New York: Plus Ultra.

Ribes Tovar, F. (1972). *The Puerto Rican woman.* New York: Plus Ultra.

Rigdon, S. M. (1988). *The culture facade: Art, science, and politics in the work of Oscar Lewis.* Urbana and Chicago: University of Illinois Press.

Rodríguez, C. E. (1974) *The ethnic queue: The case of Puerto Ricans.* San Francisco: R & E Research Associates.

Rodríguez, C. E. (1989). *Puerto Ricans: Born in the USA.* Boston: Unwin & Hyman. (Reissued by Westview Press, Boulder, CO, 1991)

Rodríguez, C. E. (1994a). Challenging the racial hegemony: Puerto Ricans in the U.S. In R. Sanjek & S. Gregory (Eds.), *Everyone's business: The politics of race and identity* (pp. 131–145). New Brunswick, NJ: Rutgers University Press.

Rodríguez, C. E. (1994b). Racial themes in the literature. In G. Haslip-Viera & S. Baver (Eds.), *Latinos in New York: A community in transition.* Notre Dame, IN: University of Notre Dame Press.

Rodríguez, C., Sánchez Korrol, V., & Alers, O. (Eds.). (1984). *The Puerto Rican struggle: Essays on survival in the U.S.* Maplewood, NJ: Waterfront Press. (Original work published 1980)

Rodríguez Bou, I. (1966). Significant factors in the development of education in Puerto Rico. In United States-Puerto Rico Commission on the Status of Puerto Rico, *Status of Puerto Rico: Selected Background Studies of the Status Commission Report* (pp. 147–314). Washington, DC: Government Printing Office.

Rodríguez Bou, I. (1967). Comentarios en torno a *La Vida* de Oscar Lewis. *Revista de Ciencias Sociales, 11*(2), 205–225.

Rodríguez de Laguna, A. (Ed.). (1987). *Images and identities: The Puerto Rican in two world contexts.* New Brunswick, NJ: Transaction Books.

Rogler, L. H. (1972). *Migrant in the city: The life of a Puerto Rican action group.* New York: Basic Books.

Rogler, L. H., & Santana Cooney, R. (1984). *Puerto Rican families in New York City: Intergenerational processes.* Maplewood, NJ: Waterfront Press.

Roosevelt, T. (1970). *Colonial policies of the United States: American imperialism.* New York: Arno Press & The New York Times. (Original work published 1937)

Ross, D. (1976). *The long uphill path: A historical study of Puerto Rico's program of economic development.* San Juan, PR: Editorial Edil.

Rouse, I. (1992). *The Tainos: Rise and decline of the people who greeted Columbus.* New Haven, CT: Yale University Press.

Sánchez, M. E. and Stevens-Arroyo, A. (Eds.). (1987). *Toward a renaissance of Puerto Rican Studies: Ethnic and area studies in university education.* Boulder, CO.: Social Science Monographs; Higland Lakes, NJ: Atlantic Research and Publications.

Sánchez Korrol, V. (1983). *From colonia to community: The history of Puerto Ricans in New York City, 1917–1948.* Westport, CT: Greenwood Press.

Sandis, E. (Ed.). (1970). *The Puerto Rican experience.* New York: Selected Academic Readings.

Seda Bonilla, E. (1973). *Social change and personality in a Puerto Rican agrarian reform community.* Evanston, IL: Northwestern University Press.

Senior, C. (1961). *Strangers, then neighbors: From pilgrims to Puerto Ricans.* New York: Freedom Books.

Sexton, P. C. (1965). *Spanish Harlem.* New York: Harper & Row.

Sheehan, S. (1976). *A welfare mother.* Boston: Houghton Mifflin.

Silén, J. A. (1971). *We, the Puerto Rican people: A story of oppression and resistance.* New York: Monthly Review Press.

Snipp, M. C. (1989). *Native Americans: The first of this land.* New York: Russell Sage Foundation.

Steiner, S. (1974). *The islands: The worlds of the Puerto Ricans.* New York: Harper & Row.

Stevens-Arroyo, A. M. (1988). *The cave of the Jagua: The mythological world of the Taínos.* Alburqueque: University of New Mexico Press.

Steward, J. H., Manners, R. A., Wolff, E. R., Padilla Seda, E., Mintz, S. W., & Scheele, R. L. (1956). *The people of Puerto Rico: A study in social anthropology.* Chicago-Urbana: University of Illinois Press.

Thomas, P. (1967). *Down these mean streets.* New York: Alfred A. Knopf.

Time. (1966, November 25). [Review of *La Vida*], p. 133.

Tinker, G. (1992). Indigenous autonomy and the next 500 Years. *Global Justice, 3*(2 & 3), 1–3.

Torres, A. (1994). *Between melting pot and mosaic: African Americans and Puerto Ricans in the New York political economy.* Philadelphia: Temple University Press.

Torres, A., & Rodríguez, C. E. (1991). Latino research and policy: The Puerto Rican case. In E. Meléndez, C. E. Rodríguez, & J. Barry Figueroa (Eds.), *Hispanics in the labor force: Issues and policies* (pp. 247–263). New York: Plenum Press.

Torruellas, R. M., Benmayor, R., Goris, A., & Juarbe, A. L. (1991). *Affirming cultural citizenship in the Puerto Rican community.* New York: Centro de Estudios Puertorriqueños, Hunter College, City University of New York.

Torruellas, L. M., & Vásquez, J. L. (1984). *Puertorriqueños que regresaron: Un analisis de su participación laboral.* Rio Piedras: University of Puerto Rico.

Tugwell, R. G. (1977). *Stricken Land: The story of Puerto Rico.* New York: Greenwood Press. (Original work published 1946)

Tumin, M., & Feldman, A. (1961). *Social class and social change in Puerto Rico* (2nd ed.). Princeton, NJ: Princeton University Press.

U.S. Bureau of the Census. (1990a). *1990 Census of the population,* series #1990 CP-1-1, table 253, p. 323 (General population characteristics). Washington, DC: Government Printing Office.

U.S. Bureau of the Census. (1990b). *The summary: Population and housing characteristics,* series #CPH-1-53, table 1, August 1990, pp. 1–17. Washington, DC: Government Printing Office.

U.S. Commission on Civil Rights. (1976). *Puerto Ricans in the continental United States: An uncertain future.* Washington, DC: Author.

Vázquez, J. M. (1992). Embattled scholars in the academy. *Callaloo, 15*(4), 1039–1051.

von Eckardt, U. M. (1967). *La Vida* de Oscar Lewis: Reseña y comentario. *Revista de Ciencias Sociales, 11*(2), 240–252.

Wagenheim, K. (1975). *A survey of Puerto Ricans on the U.S. mainland in the 1970s.* New York: Praeger.

Wagenheim, K., & Jiménez de Wagenheim, O. (Eds.). (1973). *The Puerto Ricans: A documentary history.* New York: Praeger.

Wakefield, D. (1975). *Island in the city: The world of Spanish Harlem.* New York: Arno Press. (Original work published 1959)

Walsh, K. (1991). *The struggle for voice: Issues of language, power, and schooling for Puerto Ricans.* New York: Bergin & Garvey.

Weisskoff, R. (1985). *Factories and food stamps.* Baltimore, MD: Johns Hopkins University Press.

Wells, H. (1969). *The modernization of Puerto Rico: A political study of changing values and institutions.* Cambridge, MA: Harvard University Press.

Young Lords Party. (1971). *Palante: Young Lords Party.* New York: McGraw-Hill.

Závala, I. M., & Rodríguez, R. (1980). *The intellectual roots of independence: An anthology of Puerto Rican political essays.* New York: Monthly Review Press.

Zentella, A. C. (1994). *Growing up bilingual: Puerto Rican children in New York.* London, Cambridge: Basil Blackwell.

·14·

AMERICAN INDIAN STUDIES

C. Matthew Snipp
UNIVERSITY OF WISCONSIN, MADISON

American Indian studies is an interdisciplinary blend of many fields in the social sciences and humanities; history and anthropology have been especially prominent, along with contributions from education, sociology, psychology, economics, and political science. In recent years American Indian writers and artists have produced a substantial body of original writings, literary criticism, and other artistic works. A casual glance at the literature in American Indian studies will reveal that it is divided about equally between historical research and studies of contemporary American Indians, no doubt reflecting the strong influence of history and anthropology. Historical studies of American Indians tend to focus on culture and tradition, precontact social structure, or episodes in relations with Euro-Americans. Contemporary research focuses on a wide range of issues, from modern culture to socioeconomic conditions to law and public policy.

American Indian studies overlaps many disciplines, and is better characterized as an "area study," like Soviet studies or Latin American studies, rather than a traditional academic discipline. American Indian studies also lacks a single coherent theoretical paradigm that structures intellectual inquiry. Instead, a plethora of intellectual perspectives from a diversity of disciplines have been used to explain a variety of subjects related to American Indians. In fact, the single unifying theme of American Indian studies is its link to the culture and experiences of American Indians, as a people separate from the mainstream of American society and Euro-American culture.

This literature can be roughly classified into several major subject areas encompassing both historical and contemporary interests; specifically they are demographic behavior, socioeconomic conditions, political and legal institutions, and culture and religion. Of course, a great deal of overlap exists among these areas. Another notable point is that this literature deals almost exclusively with North American aboriginals and their descendants. As the field has evolved, relatively little attention has been devoted to the natives of South America or the Pacific Islands. Finally, this review focuses mainly on work done in the social sciences and history. Reviews are necessarily selective, and an in-depth discussion of work in the arts and literature is far afield from the issues addressed in this chapter.

AMERICAN INDIANS

Before pursuing further the topical areas of American Indian studies, some background information about American Indians may be helpful. No one knows with certainty when populations of *Homo sapiens* first appeared in North America. It is widely believed that the first immigrants to North America migrated from what is now Siberia, perhaps in pursuit of game, across the Beringia land bridge now submerged in the Bering Sea. This land bridge has existed during several ice ages, leading to speculation that the first populations arrived as early as 40,000 years ago or as recently as 15,000 years ago—24,000 years ago is considered a particularly credible estimate (Thornton, 1987, p. 9).

Moving southward, these populations settled throughout the Americas. In North America, dense populations developed along the East and West coasts, in the Southeast and Southwest regions, and in the Mississippi River valley. The size of the 15th-century aboriginal population is currently the subject of intense debate (cf. Verano & Ubelaker, 1992). Once thought to number less than 1 million, the precontact native population is now believed to have been much larger. The most conservative estimates calculated that 3 to 5 million natives were living in North America in 1492, though other, more controversial estimates

An abbreviated version of this chapter appears in *Encyclopedia of Sociology*, edited by E. F. Borgatta and M. L. Borgatta, 1992, New York: Macmillan. Joane Nagel and Russell Thornton provided helpful comments on an earlier draft. The author, of course, bears full responsibility for any factual errors and misstatements that may remain.

range upward to 18 million (Dobyns, 1983; Thornton, 1987; Ramenofsky, 1987).

The aboriginals of North America did not prosper after the arrival of Europeans. European-borne diseases were devastating and, along with warfare, genocidal practices, forced removals, and a changing ecology, very nearly annihilated American Indians. Census records indicate that by the end of the 19th century fewer than 250,000 American Indians survived in the United States. By 1900 the culture, lifestyle, social organization, and even the languages of these survivors were vastly different from their ancestors of 400 years earlier.

Since 1900 American Indians in the United States and Canada have staged a remarkable comeback. Growing in number throughout this century, there were 1.9 million American Indians and Alaska Natives counted in the 1990 U.S. Census. About half of this population lives in rural areas, most often on specially designated tribal lands—reservations or trust properties. Though more numerous than in the past, American Indians are still not prosperous. The standard of living for most American Indians in the United States is about the same as for African Americans, and well below the standards of White Americans (Snipp, 1989).

Although less variegated than in the past, American Indians today retain a diverse representation of tribal cultures. Broad generalizations about American Indians are often difficult to make, and exceptions are usually easy to find. The American Indian Studies literature typically deals with this problem by focusing exclusively on a single tribe or a group of similar tribes, or by seeking reasonable generalizations that appear valid for many tribal cultures. The literature concerned with American Indian demography has most often been concerned with large-scale processes affecting American Indian people across the nation.

AMERICAN INDIAN DEMOGRAPHY

American Indian demography focuses on the size, distribution, and composition of the American Indian population. Improvements in the data for American Indians, especially that gathered by the U.S. Census, have facilitated studies of their contemporary demography, and this work has been especially important in planning and public policy applications. However, a great deal of attention has been given to pre-Columbian historical demography, and since the mid-1960s this literature has been filled with significant breakthroughs and controversies.

Historical Demography

Understanding the prehistoric and historic demographic behavior of American Indians is a prerequisite for gaining knowledge about the indigenous societies of North America and for assessing the impact of European contacts. For example, large populations are usually associated with economic surpluses, and complex societies with highly developed systems of religion, culture, and governance. Archaeological evidence of such societies exists in the Southwest, Pacific Northwest, and the Mississippi River valley (Thornton, 1987; Willey, 1966). And be-

cause American Indians almost disappeared in the late 19th century, large numbers of earlier generations of Indians would indicate that the arrival of Europeans had a substantial, if not devastating, impact on native mortality and, by implication, native social organization.

The first systematic estimates of the American Indian population were published in 1918 by a Smithsonian anthropologist, James Mooney (Thornton, 1987). He reckoned that 1.15 million American Indians were living around 1600. Alfred Kroeber reviewed Mooney's early estimates in 1938 and deemed them essentially correct, though he adjusted the total population estimate downward to 900,000 (Deneven, 1976). The Mooney-Kroeber estimates of around 1 million in 1600 have been the benchmark for scholars throughout this century, though other estimates were published. However, the Mooney-Kroeber estimates were flawed because they failed to take into account the effects of epidemic disease.

Noting the shortcomings in the Mooney-Kroeber figures, Dobyns (1966) published a revised estimate for the 1492 population. According to Dobyns, the 1492 North American population was perhaps as large as 12 million. This launched a debate that is still far from being resolved. Despite these disagreements, it is fairly certain that the Mooney-Kroeber figures were too low. Even very conservative estimates now number the indigenous 1492 population at approximately 3 to 5 million (Ubelaker, 1976; Thornton, 1987). At the other end of the spectrum, Dobyns's most recent estimates (1983) suggest a population numbering 18 million.

Dobyns's work in particular has started lively debates about a variety of issues in American Indian historical demography. Some of these disputes are disagreements about methodology (Driver, 1969; Thornton & Marsh-Thornton, 1981). For example, the projection methods used in this work depend heavily on estimates of the nadir population, that is, the approximate year and numeric size of the Indian population before it began to rebound in number. Some critics make a convincing case that Dobyns's 1966 estimates are flawed because he uses the wrong nadir (Driver; Thornton & Marsh-Thornton). However, there is little agreement about the nadir population, except that it happened around the turn of the 20th century and was much smaller than the precontact population. For example, Thornton (1987) suggests that the nadir was around 228,000 in 1890, but Ubelaker (1992) argues that it was later and larger than Thornton's figure, namely, 530,000 in 1900. The geographic areas about which Thornton and Ubelaker are writing are not strictly comparable, but this discrepancy exemplifies the current debate.

Despite the apparent ubiquity of disputes in this literature, there is little disagreement that the population estimates by Mooney and Kroeber are too low, and that Dobyns's revisions are probably too high. But some observers find this range, between 1 million and 18 million, troubling. Henige (1986, 1992), for instance, argues that the theory, methodology, and data for estimating precontact populations are irredeemably flawed, so defective that it is simply impossible to draw any conclusions whatsoever about the size of the populations in the Western Hemisphere before 1492. Perhaps, but precontact population estimates are so heavily laden with implications about precontact societies that it seems unlikely scholars will heed Henige's advice to abandon this effort.

In fact, there is a growing body of archaeological research that deals with this issue. Substantially larger population estimates than the Mooney-Kroeber figures are certainly consistent with the archaeological record (Ramenofsky, 1987). This work clearly indicates that relatively complex societies occupied regions of North America before the arrival of Europeans (Milner, 1992). However, the archaeological work also makes it abundantly evident that the process of depopulation was considerably more complex than it often has been portrayed. In fact, there is a growing body of evidence that the American Indian population did not precipitously collapse all at once. Instead, diseases reached some populations sooner than others, and affected populations in some areas more than in others (cf. Verano & Ubelaker, 1992). This body of literature shows that the impact of European contact was certainly greater than once believed, as the introduction of European diseases, slavery, and genocidal practices, and the intensification of conflict nearly exterminated the native population (Stannard, 1992). Recent research has noted that population recoveries normally follow epidemic mortality; the European recovery following the spread of the bubonic plague is evidence for this observation (Thornton, Warren, & Miller, 1992). This poses the vexing question of why North American native populations did not recover in the same manner as Europeans. One possible explanation is that the expansion of mercantile capitalism and the attendant depredations by Europeans (e.g., slavery and genocide), as well as the loss of traditional subsistence sources, made population recovery impossible for American Indians, at least until the late 19th century (Thornton, 1992).

Massive population losses also undoubtedly caused a large-scale amalgamation and reorganization of groups struggling to survive, and profound changes in the cultures and social structures of these populations (Merrell, 1989; Nagel & Snipp, 1993). Beyond the archaeological record, not much is known about the distribution and composition of these populations before and after the arrival of Europeans (Milner, 1992). This remains a promising subject for future studies of American Indian historical demography.

Contemporary Demography

As mentioned, the American Indian population stopped declining and began to increase sometime around 1890 to 1900. Since that time the American Indian population has grown very quickly, especially since 1950. As Figure 14–1 shows, population growth was modest in the first half of this century, and the deadly influenza epidemic of 1918–1919 (Prucha, 1984, pp. 854–855) resulted in a slight population decline in 1920. This low rate of growth is somewhat surprising considering that American Indian women had (and have) relatively high fertility rates (Thornton et al., 1991). However, high infant mortality rates and the propensity of mixed-ancestry offspring to shed their Indian identity may have kept American Indian population growth at low levels.

There was a sharp increase in the Indian population beginning in about 1950. Some (and possibly a great deal) of this

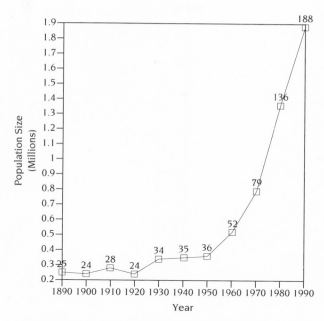

FIGURE 14–1. American Indian Population, 1890–1990

increase was due to procedural changes in the 1960 census that resulted in a more accurate enumeration, but other factors, such as improved health care, also played a role. For instance, in 1955 health-care delivery to reservations was improved when the Indian Health Service was moved from the Bureau of Indian Affairs (BIA) to the Public Health Service (Sorkin, 1988). Studies indicate that because American Indians often have better access to health care (from the Indian Health Service) than do other equally impoverished groups, infant mortality has diminished and longevity has increased (Taffel, 1987; Snipp, 1989).

While other types of deaths, such as those related to alcoholism and violence, continue to be a problem (Sorkin, 1988), American Indian fertility is exceedingly high, even higher than that of Black women (Snipp, 1989; Thornton et al., 1991). The large excess of American Indian births over deaths has contributed significantly to the population growth of this century.

A peculiar characteristic of American Indian population growth, at least since 1970, is that a large share of this increase can be attributed to changing racial identification. That is, much of the expansion in the American Indian population since 1970 has been the result of persons switching their racial identification to American Indian from some other racial category (Passell, 1976; Passell & Berman, 1986). The U.S. Census, virtually the only comprehensive source of data for American Indians, depends on the voluntary self-identification of respondents to identify and enumerate members of the American Indian population as well as all other racial groups. Declining social discrimination, growing ethnic pride, and a resurgence in tribal organization have been cited as possible reasons why so many individuals have switched their racial identity to American Indian (Passell & Berman, 1986; Quinn, 1990).

The fluid boundaries of the American Indian population underscore a particularly problematic concern for demographers and anyone else desiring to study the American Indian population—namely, defining who is a member of the American Indian population. Definitions are abundant and there is no single agreed-upon standard. Some federal agencies and a number of tribes use an arbitrary measure of descendancy, such as ¼ blood quantum. Blood quantum standards for tribal membership vary greatly from ½ to ¹⁄₆₄ Indian blood.

For many other applications the genealogical verification of blood quantum standards is too complex. This leads agencies such as the Census Bureau to rely simply on self-identification. By default, most studies of American Indians also rely on self-identification, especially if they use secondary data from federal government sources. To complicate this matter for comparative purposes, the Canadian government uses a somewhat different set of standards for defining the boundaries of its native Indian population.

Beyond the complexities of counting American Indians, studies show that American Indians, more than other minorities, are concentrated in rural areas; slightly fewer than half reside in metropolitan regions. Most American Indians live west of the Mississippi River, mainly because of 19th-century removal programs directed at eastern American Indians. A number of studies document that American Indians are one of the least educated, most unemployed, poorest, and least healthy groups in American society (cf. Snipp, 1989). Nonetheless, American Indians are more likely than other groups, especially African Americans, to live in a large husband-wife household, and about a third of the population speaks a native language—provisional evidence of the continuing influence of traditional culture in family organization and language use (Sandefur & Sakamoto, 1988; Snipp, 1989).

The recent movement of American Indians to urban areas is a demographic event of major significance. As late as 1930, when about half of American society lived in cities, only about 10% of the American Indian population could be found in urban environs. However, World War II, federal policy, and prevailing migration streams in the postwar era were responsible for urbanizing the American Indian population. World War II was significant because American Indian participation in this conflict was widespread; approximately 25,000 American Indians served in the military (Hagan, 1979, p. 158). This experience provided many American Indians with their first glimpse of life away from the reservation. It also gave many in the service an opportunity to learn job skills and, perhaps even more important, skills in dealing with the cultural practices and expectations of Euro-American society. The impact of the GI Bill following the war also should not be underestimated. This program gave many American Indians an opportunity for higher education, resulting in a generation of relatively well-educated Indian men for whom there were no job opportunities on the reservation (Fixico, 1986). Needless to say, job opportunities in expanding postwar urban America were a powerful incentive for migration away from rural reservations. Because of their limited participation in the uniformed services, Indian women benefited little from the GI Bill, and neither their education nor their labor-force participation in-

creased noticeably after the war in the same way as Indian men (Snipp, 1989).

Federal relocation policies also have had an impact on Indian urbanization. In the 1950s and 1960s federal relocation programs were established to encourage reservation Indians to move to preselected relocation centers in cities such as Los Angeles, San Francisco, Chicago, and Denver (Sorkin, 1978). Participants in these programs typically were provided job training and/or counseling, moving expenses, and a stipend until they found work. Critics faulted these programs for being ineffective as well as being a reservation "brain drain" (Fixico, 1986; O'Brien, 1989). Nonetheless, they had a significant impact on Indian urbanization insofar as more than 100,000 American Indians participated in these programs until they were sharply curtailed in the early 1970s (Margon, 1976; Sorkin, 1978).

Despite the abolition of relocation programs in the early 1980s, American Indians continue to be a highly mobile population. However, evidence from the 1980 census suggests that while American Indians have higher migration rates than either African Americans or Whites, they tend to follow the same migration streams as other Americans (Snipp, 1989). In the 1970s American Indians joined the streams moving out of the Northeast and upper Midwest in favor of destinations in the West and South (Snipp, 1989).

These developments have tended to produce "generations" of urban Indians. For example, studies in Los Angeles have found distinct generations of urban Indians, divided between those who moved there in the 1930s or 1940s and those who came later in the relocation programs. These groups have distinctive characteristics with respect to their reservation ties, tribal allegiances, and the Indian organizations in which they are active (Price, 1968; Weibel-Orlando, 1991).

Urbanization has profound implications for the American Indian population that are manifest in several ways. This development is directly related to other social and economic characteristics, as well as to measures of well-being for the Indian population. Urbanization also has influenced American Indian political ideologies, in addition to cultural events and practices. These issues are addressed below.

STUDIES OF SOCIAL AND ECONOMIC STATUS

The literature on the social and economic status of American Indians is relatively large. One area of research, development studies, includes a wide variety of perspectives concerned with the structure of economic relations between Euro-Americans and Indians. This literature is often historical, but there is also a small but growing body of work that deals with contemporary economic processes that affect the well-being of American Indians. Another research perspective concerns the human resources of American Indians, especially in terms of education, unemployment, and the prevalence of poverty.

Development Studies

From a historical perspective, most recent studies of the early social and economic status of American Indians focus on the development of so-called dependency relations between Euro-Americans and American Indians (White, 1983; Hall, 1989). Dependency theory, a variant of neo-Marxist World System theory, has been widely criticized for a number of shortcomings, but it has gained a measure of provisional acceptance among scholars of White-Indian relations (Wolf, 1982; White, 1983; Hall, 1989). In this perspective, economic dependency arises from trade relations in which Euro-Americans enjoy a disproportionate economic advantage over American Indians. The source of this advantage stems from a near monopoly over items such as manufactured goods and rum (Wolf, 1982; White, 1983). The introduction of such European business practices as the use of credit also played a role in fostering dependency.

Dependency relations between Euro-Americans and American Indians led to highly exploitive trading conditions that were often detrimental to American Indians. Trade relations were a frequent source of conflict that periodically erupted into serious violence. Unscrupulous traders and a growing commerce in Indian captives, for example, ignited the Yamassee War that marked the end of Indian slavery in the Southeast (Merrell, 1989). Early colonial officials frequently complained about the conflicts created by the unethical practices of frontier traders and sought to curb their abuses, though with little success (Bateman, 1989). Beyond the conflicts between traders and their Indian clients, the introduction of European innovations such as guns, horses, and metal implements represents a subtler and more profound impact of economic dependency that is not fully appreciated; such items altered forever the culture and lifestyles of North American Indians. In the Southwest, for example, the introduction of guns and horses restructured relations between nomadic and sedentary groups, and allowed the Spanish to exploit for their own advantage the traditional antagonisms that existed between these groups (Hall, 1989).

The onset of the Industrial Revolution, growing urbanization, and an influx of immigrants from Europe and slaves from Africa changed dramatically the relations between Euro-Americans and American Indians. The role of American Indians as trading partners decreased in favor of policies and measures designed to remove them from lands desired for development by Euro-Americans. The emergence of industrial capitalism diminished the importance of American Indian productivity in the national economy while the natural resources belonging to American Indians have become ever more valued (Jacobsen, 1984). Throughout the 19th century, American Indians were more or less forcibly induced to cede their lands for the development of agriculture, timber, and water. Efforts to develop petroleum, coal, and other minerals on tribal lands were first initiated in the late 19th century (Miner, 1976).

The exploitation of Indian lands has continued throughout the 20th century. This has prompted some scholars to argue that American Indian tribes have a quasi-colonial status within the U.S. economy. Natural resources such as timber, water, and minerals are extracted from reservations and exported to distant urban centers where they are processed. In exchange, manufactured goods are imported for reservation consumption. The value of the imported goods typically exceeds the value of the exported resources (Snipp, 1988a). The difference in value between imports and exports plays a significant role in the

persistent poverty and low levels of economic development characteristic of many reservations. And indeed, those American Indians who reside on reservations with significant energy resources do not enjoy a standard of living appreciably higher than those on other reservations (Snipp, 1988b).

Tribes have responded by organizing to prevent the wholesale expropriation of reservation resources. For example, the Council of Energy Resource Tribes (CERT) is an intertribal consortium that provides technical assistance and information to reservations seeking to lease or develop oil, gas, or other energy resources (Ambler, 1990). This organization was formed in the mid-1970s to help tribes negotiate effectively with highly sophisticated multinational energy corporations. In this period, when energy prices were rising rapidly, there were numerous cases of gross incompetence and a few cases of fraud involving federal officials responsible for managing tribal energy resources (Ambler; Richardson & Farrell, 1983). In the aftermath of these cases, the tribes became more heavily involved in the negotiations for exploration and development leases; CERT has often played a major role in these discussions as a technical adviser.

Many other reservations have struggled to achieve economic self-sufficiency. There are various explanations for the limited success that tribes have had in stimulating economic activity on reservations. Some studies of reservation economies blame the isolated locales for many of the economic woes that are experienced (Sorkin, 1971; Levitan & Johnston, 1975). These studies argue that lack of physical infrastructure, absence of raw materials, distance from markets, and a workforce with few skills severely limit development opportunities, especially in manufacturing.

Economic development in Indian country is also frequently complicated by the collision of traditional native values and the ethics of capitalism and business development (Vinje, 1982). In fact, Cornell and Kalt (1990, 1992a, 1992b) argue that for economic development to be successful, development projects must be structured in ways that are consonant with tribal culture and practices. Projects with authoritarian or highly centralized management practices will be neither welcome nor likely to succeed in reservation communities that are highly egalitarian and communalistic.

A recently published collection of papers by a group of public-choice economists takes a sharply different view of reservation economies and their problems (Anderson, 1992). At the risk of oversimplifying public-choice theory, this perspective views individual initiative and private property as the foundations for economic growth. According to this model, reservation economies are stagnant because individual initiative and private property have been stifled by institutions such as tribal and federal government agencies (McChesney, 1992). The remedy for curing the economic ills of reservations, in this view, is to encourage more private ownership and individual entrepreneurship.

Given the importance of tribalism and other communalistic values in the organization of reservation life, some of these ideas seem strangely out of context and stretched to their logical limits. They are also vaguely reminiscent of the disastrous allotment and termination policies adopted earlier in this century (Hoxie, 1984; Fixico, 1986). At least one of the contributors to Anderson (1992) was aware of the less-than-perfect theoretical fit of public-choice theory for reservation economies:

I recall that when [we] began this project on Indians and Property Rights, we had high hopes of discovering a property rights innovation that would help the Indians become richer. In many respects, we began with all the enthusiasm of the "Friends of the Indian" who initiated the disastrous Dawes Act. I am now much less hopeful that the Indians will learn anything from us. (Roback, 1992, p. 24)

Despite the many obstacles to economic development, in recent years a number of reservations have enjoyed limited and, in a few instances, spectacular success in spurring economic growth, especially in tourism, gambling, and light manufacturing (Snipp & Summers, 1991). For example, White (1990) describes the development successes of the Passamaquoddy in Maine and of the Mississippi Choctaw. The Passamaquoddy are particularly interesting because they parlayed a substantial land claims settlement into an even larger estate through investments in agriculture, manufacturing, and investment portfolios. The Passamaquoddy are not alone in their use of a legal decision to obtain economic leverage. In Washington State, tribes have used a court decision affirming their fishing rights to build a successful aquaculture industry; such processes have been called "the legal road to economic development" (Olson, 1988).

There are many paths to the legal road to economic development. Reservation tobacco outlets gain a competitive advantage because tribal sovereignty makes them immune from state taxes, and hence able to sell their products for lower prices than their off-reservation competitors. States have been known to complain bitterly about this loss of tax revenue, and merchants about unfair competition. However, the sums of money and the controversies related to reservation tobacco sales pale in comparison to the disputes surrounding gambling. Reservation gambling is a relatively recent development that started with a 1980 court decision (*Seminole Tribe of Florida v. Butterworth*) that allowed high-stakes bingo on the Florida Seminole reservation (Kersey, 1992). Within a few years reservation gambling has grown explosively. Some of these operations are small-scale, marginally profitable bingo operations, but others, such as the one owned by the Pequot tribe in western Connecticut, are large, full-service casinos that take in millions of dollars annually. Surprisingly, there are a few studies of reservation gaming (Cordeiro, 1992; Cornell & Kalt, 1992a; Midwest Hospitality Advisors [MHA], 1992), and most of what has been published is in trade publications such as the one published by the Indian Gaming Association.

Human Resources

Contemporary studies of the social and economic status of modern American Indians consistently point to the widespread poverty and economical hardships facing them. The Meriam Report, published in 1928 (Institute for Government Research), furnished the first systematic empirical assessment of the economic status of American Indians. Since the publication of this report, numerous studies have documented the disadvantaged status of American Indians (cf. Brophy & Aberle, 1966; Levitan & Hetrick, 1971; Snipp, 1989).

Although a number of studies have described in detail the economic conditions among American Indians, fewer have attempted to isolate the causes of poverty and unemployment. However, it is clear that a number of factors can be blamed for these conditions. Primary among them is that American Indians have very low levels of education, and this, of course, limits access to job opportunities, especially well-paid jobs (Trosper, 1980).

The persistent finding that American Indians lack the skills, and especially the education, to compete successfully in the job market underscores a pressing problem. In 1970 only 22% of American Indian adults had completed high school, while 55% of White adults had done so (Snipp, 1989). Ten years later, 56% of American Indians reported 12 or more years of schooling (69% for White adults), but such gains are somewhat misleading because GEDs are widespread among American Indians (Snipp, 1989). Perhaps a more telling statistic is that in 1980, 26% of Indian youths aged 16 to 19 had withdrawn from school without a diploma (U.S. Bureau of the Census, 1983).

The lack of education among American Indians should not be construed as resulting from a lack of exposure to educational institutions. American Indians have a long history of experience with Western education under the auspices of missionaries and federal authorities (Szasz, 1977, 1988; Fuchs & Havighurst, 1972). Until recently these schools have been far more concerned with "civilizing" American Indians—detribalizing and acculturating them—than with educating them (Fuchs & Havighurst; Szasz, 1977; Hoxie, 1984).

Changes in federal policy since the mid-1970s facilitated the participation of American Indians in educational systems (Gross, 1989). Indian school board members and tribally controlled school systems are considerably more common than in the past. Perhaps most significant is that 24 tribally controlled colleges have formed in the past 25 years (Carnegie Foundation, 1989). Most of these fledgling institutions are two-year community colleges, though a few offer baccalaureate and master's degrees. These institutions are especially meaningful because of the dearth of American Indians with advanced education.

The sharp rise in the number of high school graduates has not translated into an equal rise in college attendance. In fact, there is some evidence to suggest that transitions to college have diminished for American Indians since the 1960s (Snipp, 1989). American Indians who attend college are enrolled overwhelmingly in public institutions, approximately 88% (Fries, 1987). Furthermore, from 1975 to 1981 the number of American Indian baccalaureate degree recipients stayed nearly constant—about 3,500—despite an increase in the "college-age" population (Fries). There was a small increase in American Indian doctorates, but the numbers are exceedingly low, rising from 93 in 1975–1976 to 130 in 1980–1981 (Fries).

American Indian students have marked preferences for certain areas of study. Over half of these degrees were in the social sciences, education, and the humanities. Barely 20% were in the physical or biological sciences. The relative underrepresentation of American Indians in the latter fields may reflect a preference for subjects that promise to ameliorate the problems or meet the needs of their communities. For example, an education major would allow one to become a teacher and serve a pressing need on many reservations.

The role of economic discrimination in limiting opportunities for American Indians is unclear. Some research suggests that discrimination is not a significant disadvantage for American Indians (Sandefur & Scott, 1983), while other studies disagree with this conclusion (Gwartney & Long, 1978). However, unlike the case with women and African Americans, there is little research showing that American Indians are systematically segregated into lower-status, lesser-paid occupations. That is, there is little evidence to suggest that there are "Indian jobs" in the same manner as there is "women's work" such as, for instance, lower-paid clerical employment. The absence of systematic *labor market* discrimination does not mean that American Indians are immune from other types of discrimination, such as in housing or education.

Of course, American Indian women are not exempt from gender discrimination. American Indian women are systematically paid less than their male counterparts in comparable circumstances (Snipp, 1989, 1990; Snipp & Aytac, 1990). American Indian women also appear to be constrained by many of the same concerns that affect other women. For example, family obligations such as child-rearing duties limit their ability to participate in the workforce, and the so-called "feminization of poverty" has been especially burdensome for Indian women. Unfortunately, very little has been written about the special circumstances of American Indian women; this is an area in which much more work needs to be done.

The economic conditions on reservations, where many Indians reside, are particularly harsh. Reservations are typically located in remote rural areas and are often bereft of economic activity and job opportunities. Reservation unemployment rates in excess of 50% are not unusual. The impact of spatial isolation or lack of economic opportunity is underscored by data that typically show that urban American Indians enjoy a higher standard of living than their counterparts living in rural areas, usually reservations (Sorkin, 1978).

There is disagreement about the benefits of rural-urban migration for American Indians; some studies have identified tangible benefits for urban immigrants (Clinton, Chadwick, & Bahr, 1975; Sorkin 1978), while other research finds evidence to the contrary (Gundlach & Roberts, 1978; Snipp & Sandefur, 1988). One argument against programs that assist urban migration is that such efforts typically help most those who need the least help; that is, such efforts assist the brightest and most able-bodied. Conversely, these same programs take poorly educated and unemployed Indians from reservations and turn them into poorly educated and unemployed urban Indians. Federal policies that encouraged urban immigration for American Indians in the 1950s and 1960s were abandoned amid controversies over their effectiveness and overall impact (Fixico, 1986; O'Brien, 1989).

Persistently high poverty rates have led some researchers to suggest that some reservations are ripe for the development of an "underclass" (Sandefur, 1989). However, there is little or no research about reservation "underclasses," and disagreements about the meaning of this concept are certain to limit work on this subject (Sandefur). Along similar lines, informal economies are known to thrive on reservations but little has been written about them (Sherman, 1988).

The poverty and economic hardship facing rural and urban American Indians alike have been a major source of other serious distress. Alcoholism, suicide, and homicide are leading causes of death for American Indians (Office of Technology Assessment [OTA], 1986). One study found that programs sponsored by the Indian Health Service have improved some measures of public health, such as infant mortality. However, other health problems associated with poverty and social malaise, such as mental disorders and alcoholism, are likely to remain unchanged in the absence of significant improvements in economic conditions (Sorkin, 1988).

POLITICAL ORGANIZATION AND LEGAL INSTITUTIONS

Historical Background

The political and legal status of American Indians in the United States is an extremely complicated subject, tangled in a conflicting multitude of treaties, formal laws, bureaucratic regulations, and court decisions. Unlike any other racial or ethnic group in American society, American Indians have a distinctive niche in the legal system acquired through a long history of conflicts and agreements with federal authorities. As a result of this history, a separate agency within the federal government (the Bureau of Indian Affairs), a volume of the Code of Federal Regulations (25), and a multiplicity of other rules exist for dealing with American Indians.

The current legal and political status of American tribes is the product of a long and circuitous history. The relevant literature overlaps modern studies in law and political science, as well as in history (Dippie, 1982; Deloria, 1985; Deloria & Lytle, 1983; O'Brien, 1989). Initially, before the arrival of Europeans, the indigenous societies of the Western Hemisphere were self-governing entities with political systems of varying degrees of complexity. The Mississippian culture (approximately A.D. 1200–1400) may have had a highly complex political structure akin to the systems of pre-Columbian Central and South America (Champagne, 1992; Milner, 1992).

The arrival of Europeans in the Western Hemisphere certainly altered the political systems of these societies, but this did not mean that these populations were no longer self-governing. On the contrary, dwindling numbers in the aftermath of disease may have manifest simpler, devolved systems of governance. At the same time, there is some evidence that political consolidation occurred for the purpose of mobilizing military power and controlling access to European traders. For example, the Iroquois confederation may have become more tightly knit for monopolizing trade with Europeans. This allowed them to drive the Huron out of upstate New York and to gain exclusive trading rights with Europeans in this part of the country (Bradley, 1987).

The English Crown maintained a healthy respect for the sovereign rights of tribes. The Royal Proclamation of 1763 made it clear that the colonies were obligated to respect the rights of tribes (Prucha, 1984; O'Brien, 1989). Needless to say, this was an extremely unpopular position among the colonists, and this proclamation was eventually repealed. Nonetheless, this was an important document because it established doctrine for dealing with Indian tribes that was later to shape Indian policy in the new United States (O'Brien).

Early Federal–Indian Relations

Dealings with American Indian tribes by the new United States were at first highly circumscribed. The new U.S. government had neither the financial nor the military resources to wage a protracted war (Prucha, 1984). There was little choice for federal authorities except to negotiate with tribes on a "government-to-government basis." Prucha writes about a memorandum from Henry Knox, Secretary of War, to George Washington, in which

he [Knox] concluded that to crush the Indians would require men and money "far exceeding the United States' ability to advance, consistently with a due regard to other indispensible objects." To treat the Indians by a "conciliatory system" would not only cost far less but, more important, would absolve the nation from "blood and injustice which would stain the character of the nation . . . beyond all pecuniary calculation." (pp. 61–62)

The War of 1812 and conflicts with Indians after the war were a turning point in federal policy (Dippie, 1982). The War of 1812 decisively limited Britain's influence in North America, especially as an ally of the Indians against the expanding U.S. frontier. Perhaps more significant, Andrew Jackson successfully prosecuted the Creek Wars and established beyond doubt the federal government's ability to wage war successfully against a formidable Indian force. This made negotiation merely a convenient alternative to military action and considerably expanded the options available to the rapidly expanding nation.

Although the federal government initially dealt with tribes as equals, this practice was short-lived, especially after 1812, when pressure to remove Indians from the eastern United States resulted in a series of measures that culminated in the infamous removal legislation of the 1830s. This legislation also prompted a succession of legal confrontations that have made the political status of American Indian tribes difficult to characterize. In 1831 Chief Justice John Marshall described Indian tribes as "domestic, dependent nations" (*Worcester v. Georgia*). In another decision (*Cherokee v. Georgia*, 1832) Marshall affirmed the idea that tribes were sovereigns with the same rights as "foreign powers," and that treaties with them had the same standing in law. With these opinions he set forth the principle that tribes are autonomous political entities that enjoy a quasi sovereignty, subject only to the authority of the federal government (Barsh & Henderson, 1980; O'Brien, 1989).

The limits on tribal political autonomy have fluctuated as a result of court decisions and federal legislation that curtail or extend tribal powers. The Congress forbade any further treaties

to be made with Indian tribes in the Appropriations Act of 1871. This action reflected congressional impatience in dealing with Indian tribes as political entities with sovereign rights, especially when the wherewithal existed to conduct successful military campaigns. And in fact, the prohibition against treaty making left military action as the only recourse for resettling tribes reluctant to give up their homes and move to their appointed reservations. Passage of this statute was followed by outbreaks of bloodshed and violence in which the tribes of the West were forcibly settled on reservation lands, distant from tribal lands rapidly being occupied by Euro-American settlers.

Sixteen years later, in an effort to break up the reservations and liquidate the remaining tribal lands, the disastrous General Allotment (Dawes) Act was passed. The Dawes Act, which became law in 1887, and related legislation were designed to parcel out small, privately owned tracts of land to individual Indian families. It was expected that this land, along with the gift of a mule and a plow, would be enough to turn Indians into yeoman farmers (Carlson, 1981; Hoxie, 1984). But Indians who were once nomadic hunters had little knowledge of agriculture and little desire to pursue small-scale farming as a livelihood, while among Indian farmers agricultural production actually fell because allotment disrupted traditional systems (Carlson).

Twentieth-Century Federal–Indian Relations

The allotment process continued until the early 1930s and very nearly succeeded in completely dispersing Indian lands. Ultimately, this policy caused nearly 90 million acres of Indian land to pass into non-Indian hands through sales, fraud, and tax seizures. By 1934 Indian tribes controlled only a third of the land they had possessed in 1887 (O'Brien, 1989). A number of tribes are trying to cope with this problem today by repurchasing property or reclaiming land illegally seized during allotment.

The allotment programs were curtailed as policy by the passage of legislation known as "The Indian New Deal." The most significant enactment in the Indian New Deal was the Wheeler-Howard Indian Reorganization Act (IRA), passed in 1934. This act rescinded earlier federal legislation outlawing tribal governments. The IRA permitted tribes to organize their own governments to handle a limited number of issues on their reservations. However, tribal governments wishing to organize under the IRA legislation were required to adopt a system of representative democracy similar in form to the federal government (Prucha, 1984; O'Brien, 1989); other forms of government, such as traditional theocracies, were not permitted. For many years these tribal governments had little real power and very circumscribed jurisdictions, but this began to change in the early 1970s.

In the years following World War II the federal government unilaterally decided to extricate itself from Indian affairs with a three-pronged public policy known as "Termination and Relocation." The first step in this process began shortly after World War II, when the federal government established the Indian Claims Commission (ICC). This commission was created to settle outstanding claims made by Indian tribes involving such disputes as treaty violations and illegally seized land. Although it was expected that the ICC would expedite these claims, many of them were still pending when the commission was dissolved in 1978 (Fixico, 1986, p. 186). The second part of Termination and Relocation involved dissolving reservation boundaries and withdrawing federal recognition from tribal governments. Ultimately only two reservations were terminated, the Menominee in Wisconsin and the Klamath in Oregon, and the former was restored to reservation status in 1975. In theory, once the claims were settled and the reservations abolished, the third step would be to move American Indians from isolated rural areas to urban labor markets. To accomplish this objective, in the early 1950s the BIA established programs to encourage reservation Indians to move to preselected urban "relocation centers" in cities such as Seattle, Los Angeles, and San Francisco. By 1972 more than 100,000 American Indians had participated in these programs (Sorkin, 1978).

Termination and Relocation came under increasing attack from numerous quarters. Supporters complained that it was not implemented quickly or effectively enough, while opponents argued that these policies did more harm than good (Fixico, 1986). By the mid-1960s the time was ripe for a dramatic change in federal policy toward American Indians. Until the 1960s, federal actions more often curtailed than extended tribal rights. However, the past 25 years have marked a political resurgence among American Indians (Cornell, 1988). Active opposition to Termination and Relocation eventually led to the passage of a number of legislative acts affirming, among other things, Indian religious freedom and rights to self-government. The Indian Self-Determination and Educational Assistance Act of 1975 was an especially important bill. This legislation formally recognized the rights of tribes to administer their reservations with minimal interference from Congress, the courts, or the BIA. In particular, the BIA was directed to hand over control of many of its programs and activities.

Tribal sovereignty, as mentioned, is a complex legal doctrine affecting the political autonomy of tribal governments. It is distinct from a closely aligned political principle known as self-determination. The principle of self-determination, unlike tribal sovereignty, is relatively recent in origin and initially was meant as a claim for administrative control of reservation affairs. As a political ideology, self-determination developed in response to the unilateral actions of the federal government in implementing policies such as the Termination legislation of the 1950s. In the 1960s self-determination was a rallying theme for promoting greater tribal involvement in the development and implementation of federal policies affecting American Indians. This principle was formally enacted into public law with the passage of the Indian Self-Determination and Educational Assistance Act of 1975. Federal agencies have complied with the mandates of this legislation by gradually divesting control over programs and services, such as those once administered by the BIA. For example, many tribal governments now have contracts to provide social services similar to the arrangements formerly made with state and local governments.

Arguments promoting self-determination have been enlarged in recent years to the point where self-determination is indistinguishable from tribal sovereignty (Gross, 1989). The most influential statement merging these principles is a report presented to the Senate by the American Indian Policy Review Commission (AIPRC) in 1976. The AIPRC report was a comprehensive though highly controversial evaluation of federal Indian policy. The Reagan and Bush administrations acknowledged the principle of self-determination as mandated by Congress, but did not seek to expand tribal powers. At this time there is no indication that the Clinton administration plans either to restrict or expand the principle of self-determination as it has been implemented during the Reagan-Bush administrations.

Pan-Indian Political Ideology

Pan-Indianism is a supratribal ideology that places the common interests and well-being of American Indians as a collectivity above the narrower interests of individual tribes. Not surprisingly, the goals of tribalism and pan-Indianism do not always coincide. The roots of modern pan-Indian organizations can be traced to the Omaha leader Pontiac, and later to the Shawnee leader Tecumseh, and to Joseph Brant, a Mohawk. These leaders organized pan-Indian movements opposing Euro-American frontier settlement in the late 18th and early 19th centuries (e.g., Pontiac's Revolt, 1763).

In the late 19th century, pan-Indian messianic movements known as Ghost Dances swept across the West (Thornton, 1986). There were two major episodes of the Ghost Dance. The first began in the early 1870s and was confined mainly to California, Nevada, and Oregon. The second was more widespread, with adherents across the Southwest and the Plains, and started around 1890. The Ghost Dances began with the visionary dreams of Paviotso spiritual leaders. Wodziwob's visions sparked the first movement, and another Paviotso, Wovoka, was responsible for the second movement. The practice of the Ghost Dance varied, but adherents believed that the dance would resurrect dead warriors, bring back wildlife, and remove Euro-Americans from the land. Some believed that the special shirts worn for the Ghost Dance would protect them from soldiers' bullets (Thornton).

The federal government moved aggressively to repress the Ghost Dance and forbade its practice on reservations. This ultimately led one group of Sioux, led by Big Foot, to leave the reservation. The military was dispatched to force them back. The confrontation between the military and Big Foot's followers ended in the 1890 Wounded Knee massacre in which 146 men, women, and children were killed and buried in a mass grave, and another 7 died later from their wounds (Prucha, 1984, p. 729). This was the last major conflict involving American Indians and the U.S. military.

Despite the Ghost Dance tragedy, pan-Indian organizations have persisted since the late 19th century. Federal boarding schools were established in the late 1800s for "civilizing" and detribalizing Indian children. Ironically, boarding schools became seedbeds for pan-Indianism as Indian youth realized that the experiences of their tribe were not unique, and that American Indians shared many problems in common regardless of tribal affiliation (Dippie, 1982, pp. 263–269; Nagel, 1992). In the early decades of this century, especially before 1930, many of these students migrated to urban areas. They organized urban-based pan-Indian organizations to promote the well-being of American Indians across the nation (Hertzberg, 1971). These organizations were particularly active in the 1910s and 1920s, but most had disappeared before World War II.

Creation of the National Congress of American Indians in 1944 marked the renewal of pan-Indian interests, although the next major burst of pan-Indian activity did not occur until the late 1960s and early 1970s. The political resurgence of American Indians coincided with the gains of the civil rights movement. It is impossible to credit this development to civil rights activism alone, but certainly they are not unrelated. The political climate of the 1960s and early 1970s was clearly favorable to social change, especially for ensuring equal rights for ethnic minorities. American Indian leaders and their supporters moved quickly to capitalize on these sentiments.

Some observers also have suggested that Indian political activism in the 1960s was a response to the postwar Termination policies that aimed to liquidate the special status accorded to Indian tribes. For example, restoration of the Menominee reservation in Wisconsin served as a focus for Indian activists in the Midwest. Relocation programs in the Termination era accelerated the urbanization of American Indians and contributed eventually to building the "critical mass" necessary for the political mobilization of urban Indians (Fixico, 1986).

The highly diverse tribal composition of the urban Indian population has meant that it is virtually impossible to organize urban Indians around narrowly defined issues germane to only one or a few tribes. In the face of this constraint, the ideology of "pan-Indianism" is a theme peculiar to urban Indian groups (Hertzberg, 1971), a supratribal ideology committed to broad issues such as economic opportunity and social justice, and to the preservation of Indian culture through pan-Indian events such as intertribal pow-wows.

The urbanization of American Indians in the 1950s and 1960s accelerated the development of pan-Indian organizations and activities (Nagel 1992). Some of these organizations, such as the National Congress of American Indians, have moderate political agendas focused on lobbying, while others, such as the American Indian Movement, are highly militant. The latter was involved in the occupation of the Washington, DC, BIA office in 1972, and later participated in the armed conflict at Wounded Knee, South Dakota, in 1973 (Churchill & Vanderwall, 1988). Today, most cities with large Indian populations have pan-Indian organizations involved in political activities, cultural events, and social service delivery (Weibel-Orlando, 1991).

It is important to note that pan-Indian ideology and issues have somewhat less appeal in reservation communities. It is not that pan-Indian sentiments are absent among reservation Indians, but rather that tribal homogeneity is much greater on and near reservations, and issues directly affecting the reservation and the structure and function of tribal government are typically more salient than more global kinds of intertribal concern.

CULTURE AND RELIGION

The cultures of American Indians are extremely diverse and broad generalizations are difficult to make, although contemporary American Indians are probably less heterogeneous than their ancestors were before the arrival of Europeans. The same can be said about the religions of American Indians. Not much is known about the spiritual life of American Indians before the 15th century; such information is available only from archaeological evidence and, regrettably, material remains seldom capture the rich complexity of religious symbol systems. Most knowledge about American Indian religions is based on the reports of explorers, missionaries, traders, and anthropologists (Brown, 1982).

Spirituality

The spiritual practices of contemporary American Indians reflect several different types of religious observances: Christian, neotraditional, and traditional. Participation in one or another of these observances may or may not limit participation in another. For example, adherents to Christianity may feel that participation in other religious ceremonies is a violation of their beliefs. But these practices are not always mutually exclusive, and are sometimes blended into new religious practices. Besides the variation in religious beliefs, it is also important to keep in mind that there is a great deal of tribal variation in these practices.

American Indians who are practicing Christians represent the legacy of European missionaries. The Christian affiliation of many, if not most, American Indians reflects their tribal membership and the denomination of the missionaries responsible for their tribe's conversion. Numerical estimates are not available, but there are many Catholic Indians in the Southwest, while American Indians in the Midwest are often Lutheran, to mention only a few examples.

American Indians who participate in neotraditional religions often belong to a branch of the Native American Church (NAC). NAC is a pan-Indian religion that is practiced throughout the United States and Canada. The NAC combines elements of Christian religion with traditional religious beliefs and practices. A particularly controversial NAC practice is the use of peyote, a hallucinogenic drug and an otherwise illegal substance, as a sacrament paralleling the use of wine in the Christian Church.

In the early part of this century, prior to World War I, reformers seeking to "civilize" American Indians advocated the abolition of peyote. This effort, along with other endeavors such as the Prohibition movement, which led to the Harrison Act, prompted a small group of Indians in Oklahoma to organize the NAC. This was a deliberate strategy designed to preserve peyote ceremonies under the constitutional protections of religious freedom. After numerous legal challenges the NAC won the right to use peyote within narrowly defined limits prescribed by the courts (Prucha, 1984). However, the Supreme Court has recently upheld a decision (*Employment Division, Department of Human Resources v. Smith*, 110 S. Ct. 1595, 1990) involving the use of peyote that raised serious questions about its legality. This has fostered concerns about how the conservative Court will interpret freedom-of-religion cases in the future (Deloria, 1992).

Traditional American Indian religious practices often take place in the context of informally organized groups such as sweatlodge or feasting societies. Some of these groups are remnants of the older religious movements, such as the Ghost Dance discussed earlier. Not much is written about these groups because they are ordinarily not open to outsiders. An exception is the Sun Dance, and the ceremonies of this belief have attracted numerous chroniclers. The ceremony is held in a number of locations, mainly in the northern plains, and involves the participation of numerous tribes. It is perhaps best known for the ritual scarification and trances of the Sun Dancers (Jorgensen, 1972).

The secrecy in which many traditional religions are practiced may be the result of the intense repression once directed at these observances by the federal government. In 1883 the BIA established Courts of Indian Offenses that prosecuted American Indians for practicing their traditional culture. Among other things, the courts forbade the use of traditional medicines, shaman healers, and all ceremonial observances, including religious ceremonies. Despite their dubious legal foundation, the Courts of Indian Offenses were active until their mandate was rewritten in 1935 (Prucha, 1984).

In 1935 the federal government ended its official opposition to the practice of tribal culture and religion. However, this did not end the conflicts between government authorities and American Indians trying to practice a non-Christian religion. Many American Indians regard freedom of religion as an elusive promise. Besides the controversies surrounding NAC ceremonies, the preservation of sacred areas and the repatriation of religious artifacts and skeletal remains from museum collections are highly contentious issues that concern many American Indians (Loftin, 1989).

Preservation of sacred areas is an issue that places Indian groups at odds with land developers, property owners, local governments, and others who would develop sites deemed sacred by American Indian spiritual leaders. In one such case, the Navajo and Hopi went to court in 1983 to petition against the development of a ski resort that was alleged to intrude on sacred ground. In this and in several similar cases, the courts ruled against the Indians (Loftin, 1989). A more recent case (*Lyng v. Northwest Indian Cemetary Protective Association*, 108 S. Ct. 1319, 1988) challenged the U.S. Forest Service's authority to construct a logging road that would desecrate an area in northern California deemed sacred by Yurok, Karok, and Tolowa tribes. The upshot of these rulings is that the courts have little tolerance for Indian claims when they threaten economic interests (Deloria, 1992).

Similar conflicts have arisen over the repatriation of religious artifacts and skeletal remains held in museums, pitting academics such as scientists and museum curators against Indian groups. Scientists, especially archaeologists, claim that these remains are important "data" that may hold the keys to scientific discoveries in the future. Tribes and other Indian organizations counter that these are the remains of their ancestors, over whom no one has a proprietary right, and who should be left to rest undisturbed. In some instances remains and artifacts have been returned to tribes; Stanford University returned burial remains to the Ohlone tribe in California, for example. Other institutions have opposed repatriation or are studying the matter. The Smithsonian Institution has developed a complex policy for repatriation, and the University of California has appointed a committee to develop such a policy. For the foreseeable future this controversy is likely to linger in the courts, Congress, and academic institutions.

Cultural Survival

Compared with repatriation, cultural studies are a less controversial though no less important domain of American Indian Studies. While the doctrine of religious freedom and its impact on the practice of Indian religion defines one of the central forms of native culture, cultural studies emphasize the content of Indian lifestyles, values, and symbol systems. Some of these studies focus on the internal content of tribal culture, while other research deals with the impact of tribal culture on other forms of behavior.

Two other themes have been extremely important in the study of American Indian culture. One has been the study of traditional cultural knowledge for the purpose of renewing and extending it to others. For example, there has been a well-known renaissance in Pueblo pottery (Nagel, in press), but the resurrection of tribal arts and crafts also has included basketry, wood carving, and decorative arts such as beadwork and jewelry made from porcupine quills. A second theme has been manifest in the use of native materials or knowledge to express the contemporary experience of American Indians. For example, the use of native folklore in contemporary novels or poetry is a common practice among American Indian writers.

For decades, studies of American Indians were dominated by ethnologists recording for posterity details about Indian culture, especially material culture, or documenting the ways that European contact influenced the content of tribal culture. Much of this research was spurred by the belief that American Indians were destined for extinction, and thus it was necessary to chronicle tribal culture before it disappeared; one scholar describes this tradition as "salvage ethnography" (Dippie, 1982, pp. 222–242). The popularity of this type of research has declined significantly, partially because there are few "pristine" cultures left anywhere in the world, much less North America. It is also fairly clear to most observers that American Indians are not in imminent danger of extinction. Another, perhaps more damaging reason for the decline in research is the growing realization among scholars that studies purporting to document precontact Indian culture were based on secondhand accounts of periods that were themselves not truly "pristine." The influence of European diseases and trade goods often arrived far in advance of the physical presence of Europeans (Dobyns, 1983).

Although American Indian ethnologies have fallen out of favor, studies of American Indian culture have persisted. Such studies now resemble literary or artistic criticism, and a discussion of this work is somewhat far afield for this chapter. Nonetheless, it is noteworthy that writers such as Leslie Silko, Scott Momaday, Joy Harjo, Louise Erdrich, and Michael Dorris have received a great deal of public recognition, as well as artists such as R. C. Gorman and William Rabbit. This work is especially notable insofar as it blends the themes, concepts, and experiences of American Indian tribal culture with non-Indian media such as literary styles or printmaking.

Other work has focused on how European innovations have been incorporated into tribal culture in ways that are unique among American Indians; silversmithing and rug weaving are two well-known examples. Still other studies have examined how the symbolic culture of American Indians has gradually adapted to changing environmental conditions (Fowler, 1987). For example, urban Indians from Oklahoma living in Los Angeles have constructed their churches and conduct their services in ways that closely mirror the practices of Indian churches in Oklahoma (Weibel-Orlando, 1991).

A related set of studies deals with the resurgence in American Indian culture. Cultural resurgence among American Indians is manifest in a number of different ways. The spread of pan-Indianism described above is clearly one sign of cultural renewal. Another is that the use of American Indian languages and the number of native speakers have increased significantly in recent years (Leap, 1988). The resurgence of American Indian language use is particularly fascinating. The number of American Indians who do not speak English, especially among those under age 40, is very small (Snipp, 1989). Despite the widespread use of English, about a fourth of the American Indian population also regularly use a native language, and there is some evidence that this may be on the increase (Leap; Snipp).

One reason for this resurgence is that many tribes are engaged in active efforts to encourage native-language use (White, 1990). In areas where there are large concentrations of native-language speakers, such as the Navajo reservation, it seems likely that these efforts to preserve the language will be successful. However, some tribes such as the Catawba in South Carolina have all but lost their language (the last two native speakers died in the 1950s) and it remains to be seen whether it will be possible to reintroduce a native language (Taukchiray & Kasakoff, 1992). It seems likely that for some tribes the native language will remain a vital part of the culture, while for others native-language instruction will not be unlike Latin training, something to be learned and used occasionally but not in everyday life.

The influence of American Indian culture on other types of behavior is perhaps most prominent in a large literature on American Indian mental health, education, and rehabilitation (Bennett & Ames, 1985; Foster, 1988). The bulk of these studies show that education and rehabilitation efforts can be made more effective if they are sensitive to cultural nuances. In fact, many specialists take this idea as a given point of departure and focus their research on the ways in which Euro-American educational and therapeutic practices can be adapted to the cultural predisposition of American Indian clients. For example, substance-abuse programs might incorporate elements of tribal culture such as sweat lodges or talking circles as a part of their therapeutic regime, or traditional values such as respect for elders or for women may be advocated as a device for preventing domestic abuse.

CONCLUSION

It was once widely believed that the American Indian was destined for extinction, the "Vanishing American." This led to a plethora of early studies of American Indians that sought to document and catalog the culture and lifestyles of American Indians before they disappeared forever. Along with this effort, a great deal of work was done to classify disparate elements of tribal culture such as family and kinship structures, language, property relations, housing design, and artwork. This work adopted a view of American Indians as the passive objects of scientific inquiry.

Modern American Indian studies are a sharp departure from this earlier tradition of scholarship in a number of important respects. One crucial difference is that American Indians are viewed as a dynamic and vital population that shows no sign of disappearing from the ethnic mosaic of American society. Another difference is that American Indian studies focus on tribal culture as an evolving phenomenon that is continuously changing as American Indians adapt to the world around them. In fact, it is the dynamic character of American Indian culture that has made possible the survival of American Indians into the 20th century and beyond. In many respects, the raison d'etre of American Indian studies arises from a fundamental concern about American Indian culture, lifestyles, and traditions, and a basic commitment to the well-being of American Indian people.

Like the American Indian population, American Indian studies is a highly diverse and growing field of inquiry. It is interdisciplinary and extremely eclectic in the perspectives it employs. Once primarily the domain of historians and anthropologists, American Indian studies has rapidly expanded beyond the bounds of these disciplines with contributions from scholars in a wide variety of fields. Given the scope and breadth of these endeavors, the field of American Indian studies will continue to expand and develop for the foreseeable future.

References

Ambler, M. (1990). *Breaking the iron bonds.* Lawrence: University Press of Kansas.

Anderson, T. L. (Ed.). (1992). *Property rights and Indian economies.* Lanham, MD: Rowman and Littlefield Publishers.

Barsh, R. L., & Henderson, J. Y. (1980). *The road: Indian tribes and political liberty.* Berkeley: University of California Press.

Bateman, R. (1989). *The deerskin trade in the southeast.* Unpublished manuscript, Johns Hopkins University, Department of Anthropology, Baltimore, MD.

Bennett, L. A., & Ames, G. M. (Eds.). (1985). *The American experience with alcohol: contrasting cultural perspectives.* New York: Plenum.

Bradley, J. W. (1987). *Evolution of the Onondaga Iroquois.* Syracuse, NY: Syracuse University Press.

Brophy, W. A., & Aberle, S. D. (1966). *The Indian: America's unfinished business.* Norman: University of Oklahoma Press.

Brown, J. E. (1982). *The spiritual legacy of the American Indian.* New York: Crossroad.

Carlson, L. A. (1981). *Indians, land, and bureaucrats*. Westport, CT: Greenwood Press.

Carnegie Foundation for the Advancement of Teaching. (1989). *Tribal college: Shaping the future of Native Americans*. Princeton, NJ: Princeton University Press.

Champagne, D. (1992). *Social order and political change*. Stanford, CA: Stanford University Press.

Churchill, W. A., & Vanderwall, J. K. (1988). *Agents of repression: The FBI's secret wars against the Black Panther party and the American Indian movement*. Boston: South End Press.

Clinton, L., Chadwick, B. A., & Bahr, H. M. (1975). Urban relocation reconsidered: Antecedents of unemployment among Indian males. *Rural Sociology, 40,* 117–133.

Cordeiro, E. E. (1992). The economics of bingo: Factors influencing the success of bingo operations on American Indian reservations. In S. Cornell and J. P. Kalt (Eds.), *What can tribes do? Strategies and institutions in American Indian economic development* (pp. 205–238). Los Angeles: American Indian Studies Center, University of California.

Cornell, S. (1988). *The return of the native*. New York: Oxford University Press.

Cornell, S., & Kalt, J. P. (1990). Pathways from poverty: Economic development and institution-building on American Indian reservations. *American Indian Culture and Research Journal, 14,* 89–125.

Cornell, S., & Kalt, J. P. (1992a). Reloading the dice: Improving the chances for economic development on American Indian reservations. In S. Cornell and J. P. Kalt (Eds.), *What can tribes do? Strategies and institutions in American Indian economic development* (pp. 1–59). Los Angeles: American Indian Studies Center, University of California.

Cornell, S., & Kalt, J. P. (Eds.). (1992b). *What can tribes do? Strategies and institutions in American Indian economic development*. Los Angeles: American Indian Studies Center, University of California.

Deloria, V., Jr. (Ed.). (1985). *American Indian policy in the twentieth century*. Norman: University of Oklahoma Press.

Deloria, V., Jr. (1992). Trouble in high places: Erosion of American Indian rights to religious freedom in the United States. In M. A. Jaimes (Ed.), *The state of native America* (pp. 267–290). Boston: South End Press.

Deloria, V., Jr., & Lytle, C. M. (1983). *American Indians, American justice*. Austin: University of Texas Press.

Denevan, W. M. (Ed.). (1976). *The native population of the Americas in 1492*. Madison: University of Wisconsin Press.

Dippie, B. W. (1982). *The vanishing American*. Lawrence: University Press of Kansas.

Dobyns, H. F. (1966). Estimating aboriginal American population: Estimating techniques with a new hemispheric estimate. *Current Anthropology, 7,* 395–416.

Dobyns, H. F. (1983). *Their number become thinned*. Knoxville: University of Tennessee Press.

Driver, H. E. (1969). *Indians of North America* (2nd rev. ed.). Chicago: University of Chicago Press.

Fixico, D. L. (1986). *Termination and relocation*. Albuquerque: University of New Mexico Press.

Foster, D. V. (1988). Consideration of treatment issues with American Indians detained in the federal bureau of prisons. *Psychiatric Annals, 18,* 698–701.

Fowler, L. (1987). *Shared symbols, contested meanings*. Ithaca, NY: Cornell University Press.

Fries, J. E. (1987). *The American Indian in higher education 1975–1976 to 1984–1985*. Washington, DC: Center for Education Statistics, U.S. Department of Education.

Fuchs, E., & Havighurst, R. J. (1972). *To live on this earth*. Albuquerque: University of New Mexico Press.

Gross, E. R. (1989). *Contemporary federal policy toward American Indians*. Westport, CT: Greenwood Press.

Gundlach, J. A., & Roberts, A. D. (1978). Native American Indian migration and relocation: Success or failure? *Pacific Sociological Review, 12,* 117–128.

Gwartney, J. D., & Long, J. E. (1978). The relative earnings of Blacks and other minorities. *Industrial Labor Relations Review, 31,* 336–346.

Hagan, W. T. (1979). *American Indians* (Rev. ed.). Chicago: University of Chicago Press.

Hall, T. D. (1989). *Social change in the southwest, 1350–1880*. Lawrence: University Press of Kansas.

Henige, D. (1986). Primary source by primary source? On the role of epidemics in new world depopulation. *Ethnohistory, 33,* 293–312.

Henige, D. (1992). Native American population at contact: Standards of proof and styles of discourse in the debate. *Latin American Population History Bulletin, 22,* 2–23.

Hertzberg, H. W. (1971). *The search for an American Indian identity*. Syracuse, NY: Syracuse University Press.

Hoxie, F. E. (1984). *A final promise: The campaign to assimilate the Indians, 1880–1920*. Lincoln: University of Nebraska Press.

Institute for Government Research. (1928). *The Problem of Indian Administration* [The Meriam Report]. Baltimore, MD: Johns Hopkins University Press.

Jacobsen, C. K. (1984). Internal colonialism and Native Americans: Indian labor in the United States from 1871 to World War II. *Social Science Quarterly, 65,* 158–171.

Jorgensen, J. C. (1972). *The sun dance religion*. Chicago: University of Chicago Press.

Kersey, H. A. J. (1992). Seminoles and Miccosukees: A century in perspective. In J. A. Paredes (Ed.), *Indians of the southeastern United States in the late 20th century* (pp. 102–119). Tuscaloosa: University of Alabama Press.

Leap, W. L. (1988). Indian language renewal. *Human Organization, 47,* 283–291.

Levitan, S. A., & Hetrick, B. (1971). *Big brother's Indian programs: With reservations*. New York: McGraw-Hill.

Levitan, S. A., & Johnston, W. B. (1975). *Indian giving: Federal programs for Native Americans*. Baltimore, MD: Johns Hopkins University Press.

Loftin, J. D. (1989). Anglo-American jurisprudence and the Native American tribal quest for religious freedom. *American Indian Culture and Research Journal, 13,* 1–52.

Margon, A. (1976). Indians and immigrants: A comparison of groups new to the city. *Journal of Ethnic Studies, 4,* 17–28.

McChesney, F. S. (1992). Government as definer of property rights: Indian lands, ethnic externalities, and bureaucratic budgets. In T. L. Anderson (Ed.), *Property rights and Indian economies* (pp. 109–146). Lanham, MD: Rowman and Littlefield Publishers.

Merrell, J. H. (1989). *The Indian's new world: Catawbas and their neighbors from European contact through the era of removal*. Chapel Hill: University of North Carolina Press.

Midwest Hospitality Advisors (MHA). (1992). *Impact: Indian gaming in Minnesota*. Minneapolis: Marquette Partners.

Milner, G. R. (1992). Disease and sociopolitical systems in late prehistoric Illinois. In W. Verano & D. H. Ubelaker (Eds.), *Disease and demography in the Americas* (pp. 103–116). Washington, DC: Smithsonian Institution Press.

Miner, H. C. (1976). *The corporation and the Indian*. Columbia: University of Missouri Press.

Nagel, J. (in press). *The political construction of American Indian ethnic identity*. New York: Oxford University Press.

Nagel, J., & Snipp, C. M. (1993). Ethnic reorganization: American Indian social, economic, political, and cultural strategies for survival. *Racial and Ethnic Studies, 16,* 203–235.

O'Brien, S. (1989). *American Indian tribal governments*. Norman: University of Oklahoma Press.

Office of Technology Assessment (OTA). (1986). *Indian health care*. Washington, DC: Government Printing Office.

Olson, M. (1988). The legal road to economic development: Fishing rights in western Washington. In C. M. Snipp (Ed.), *Public policy impacts on American Indian economic development* (pp. 77–112). Albuquerque: Institute for Native American Development, University of New Mexico.

Passell, J. S. (1976). Provisional evaluation of the census count of American Indians. *Demography, 13*, 397–409.

Passell, J. S., & Berman, P. A. (1986). Quality of 1980 census data for American Indians. *Social Biology, 33*, 163–182.

Price, J. A. (1968). The migration and adaptation of American Indians to Los Angeles. *Human Organization, 27*, 168–175.

Prucha, F. P. (1984). *The great father*. Lincoln: University of Nebraska Press.

Quinn, W. W., Jr. (1990). The southeast syndrome: Notes on Indian descendant recruitment organizations and their perceptions of native American culture. *American Indian Quarterly, 14*, 147–154.

Ramenofsky, A. F. (1987). *Vectors of death: The archaeology of European contact*. Albuquerque: University of New Mexico Press.

Richardson, J., & Farrell, J. A. (1983, November 20–27). The New Indian wars. *Denver Post*, special reprint.

Roback, J. (1992). Exchange, sovereignty, and Indian-Anglo relations. In T. L. Anderson (Ed.), *Property rights and Indian economies* (pp. 5–26). Lanham, MD: Rowman and Littlefield Publishers.

Sandefur, G. D. (1989). American Indian reservations: The first underclass areas? *Focus, 12*, 37–41.

Sandefur, G. D., & Sakamoto, A. (1988). American Indian household structure and income. *Demography, 25*, 44–68.

Sandefur G. D., & Scott, W. J. (1983). Minority group status and the wages of Indian and Black males. *Social Science Research, 12*, 44–68.

Sherman, R. T. (1988). *A study of traditional and informal sector microenterprise activity and its impact on the Pine Ridge Indian reservation economy*. Unpublished manuscript.

Snipp, C. M. (Ed.). (1988a). *Public policy impacts on American Indian economic development*. Albuquerque: Institute for Native American Development, University of New Mexico.

Snipp, C. M. (1988b). Public policy impacts and American Indian economic development. In C. M. Snipp (Ed.), *Public policy impacts on American Indian economic development* (pp. 1–22). Albuquerque: Institute for Native American Development, University of New Mexico.

Snipp, C. M. (1989). *American Indians: The first of this land*. New York: Russell Sage Foundation.

Snipp, C. M. (1990). A portrait of American Indian women and their labor force experiences. In S. E. Rix (Ed.), *The American woman, 1990–1991: A status report* (pp. 265–272). New York: W. W. Norton.

Snipp, C. M., & Aytac, I. (1990). The labor force participation of American Indian women. *Research in Human Capital and Development, 6*, 189–211.

Snipp, C. M., & Sandefur, G. D. (1988). Earnings of American Indians and Alaska natives: The effects of residence and migration. *Social Forces, 66*, 994–1008.

Snipp, C. M., & Summers, G. F. (1991). American Indians and economic poverty. In C. M. Duncan (Ed.), *Rural poverty in America* (pp. 155–176). Westport, CT: Auburn House.

Sorkin, A. L. (1971). *American Indians and federal aid*. Washington, DC: Brookings Institution.

Sorkin, A. L. (1978). *Urban American Indians*. Lexington, MA: D. C. Heath.

Sorkin, A. L. (1988). Health and economic development on American Indian reservations. In C. M. Snipp (Ed.), *Public policy impacts on*

American Indian economic development (pp. 145–165). Albuquerque: Institute for Native American Development, University of New Mexico.

Stannard, D. E. (1992). *American holocaust*. New York: Oxford University Press.

Szasz, M. C. (1977). *Education and the American Indian*. Albuquerque: University of New Mexico Press.

Szasz, M. C. (1988). *Indian education in the American colonies, 1607–1783*. Albuquerque: University of New Mexico Press.

Taffel, S. M. (1987, June 19). *Characteristics of American Indian and Alaska native births: United States* (NCHS Monthly Vital Statistics Report, vol. 36, no. 3). Hyattsville, MD: U.S. National Center for Health Statistics.

Taukchiray, W. D., & Kasakoff, A. B. (1992). Contemporary Native Americans in South Carolina. In J. A. Paredes (Ed.), *Indians of the southeastern United States in the late 20th century* (pp. 72–101). Tuscaloosa: University of Alabama Press.

Thornton, R. (1986). *We shall live again* (Rose Monograph Series). New York: Cambridge University Press.

Thornton, R. (1987). *American Indian holocaust and survival*. Norman: University of Oklahoma Press.

Thornton, R. (1992, October). *North American Indians and the demography of colonialism: Population dynamics, the epidemic disease "myth," and adaptations following 1492*. Paper presented at the conference *Discovery: Meaning, Legitimations, Critiques*, University of Wisconsin, Madison.

Thornton, R. T., & Marsh-Thornton, J. (1981). Estimating prehistoric American Indian population size for the United States area: Implications of the nineteenth century population decline and nadir. *American Journal of Physical Anthropology, 55*, 47–53.

Thornton, R., Sandefur, G. D., & Snipp, C. M. (1991). American Indian fertility in 1910, and 1940 to 1980. *American Indian Quarterly, 15*, 359–367.

Thorton, R., Warren, J., & Miller, T. (1992). Depopulation in the southeast after 1492. In J. W. Verano and D. H. Ubelaker (Eds.), *Disease and demography in the Americas* (pp. 187–195). Washington, DC: Smithsonian Institution Press.

Trosper, R. L. (1980). *Earnings and labor supply: A microeconomic comparison of American Indians and Alaskan natives to American Whites and Blacks* (Publication no. 55). Boston: Social Welfare Research Institute, Boston College.

Ubelaker, D. H. (1976). The sources and methodology for Mooney's estimates of North American Indian populations. In W. M. Denevan (Ed.), *The native populations of the Americas in 1492* (pp. 243–288). Madison: University of Wisconsin Press.

Ubelaker, D. H. (1992). North American Indian population size: Changing perspectives. In J. W. Verano and D. H. Ubelaker (Eds.), *Disease and demography in the Americas* (pp. 169–176). Washington, DC: Smithsonian Institution Press.

U.S. Bureau of the Census. (1983). *1980 census of population, general social and economic characteristics, United States summary*. Washington, DC: Government Printing Office.

Verano, J. W., & Ubelaker, D. H. (Eds.). (1992). *Disease and demography in the Americas*. Washington, DC: Smithsonian Institution Press.

Vinje, D. C. (1982). Cultural values and economic development: U.S. Indian reservations. *Social Science Journal, 19*, 87–99.

Weibel-Orlando, J. (1991). *Indian country, L.A.* Urbana: University of Illinois Press.

White, R. (1983). *The roots of dependency*. Lincoln: University of Nebraska Press.

White, R. H. (1990). *Tribal assets*. New York: Holt.

Willey, G. R. (1966). *An introduction to American archaeology*. Englewood Cliffs, NJ: Prentice-Hall.

Wolf, E. R. (1982). *Europe and the people without history*. Berkeley: University of California Press.

·15·

ASIAN AMERICAN STUDIES

William T. Liu

HONG KONG UNIVERSITY OF SCIENCE AND TECHNOLOGY

Elena S. H. Yu

SAN DIEGO STATE UNIVERSITY, SAN DIEGO

The term *Asian American* is used in the United States by federal, state, and local governments to designate people of Asian descent, including Pacific Islanders (residents from the Pacific islands that are under U.S. jurisdiction, such as Guam, American Samoa, and the Marshall Islands). Although historically relevant and geographically appropriate, inclusion of the Pacific islands in the generic term *Asian American* stemmed from administrative convenience for the federal government rather than from racial or ethnic identifications.

Historically, in 1917 the Congress of the United States created the Asiatic Barred Zone, which stretched from Japan in the east to India in the west. People from within the zone were banned from immigration. The geographic concept was incorporated into the Immigration Act of 1924 (Oriental Exclusion Act), a law that had a profound impact on the demographic structure of Asian American communities as well as on U.S. foreign policy. Although it is generally assumed that the term *Asian American* has a racial basis, particularly from the perspective of U.S. immigration history, the racial overtone is muted by the inclusion in the 1980 census of people from India in the "Asian and Pacific Islander" category; they had been classified as "White" prior to 1980.

IMMIGRATION AND RESTRICTIONS OF ASIAN AMERICANS

Asian immigration can be divided into two periods: the old and the new. The old immigration period was marked by nonoverlapping waves of distinct Asian populations who came largely in response to the sociopolitical conditions in their homelands and to the shortage of unskilled labor experienced by special-interest groups in the United States. The new immigration was characterized by the simultaneous arrival of people from the Asia-Pacific Triangle, spurred principally by the 1965 legislative reforms in U.S. immigration policy, shortages of certain skilled and professional labor, the involvement of the United States in Asia, and sociopolitical situations in Asia.

The year 1848 marked the beginning of Asian immigration to the United States when the coastal Chinese—mostly from Guangdong—responded to failures in the rural economy of China and to the gold rush in California, seeking new opportunities on the West Coast. Within less than 35 years the Chinese became the first group in U.S. history to be legally barred from becoming citizens because of race. The 1882 Anti-Chinese Exclusion Act was followed by an influx of immigrants from the southern prefectures of Japan during the last decade of the 19th century—until that flow ended abruptly with the Gentlemen's Agreement of 1907–1908. Unlike the termination of Chinese immigration, cessation of entry by Japanese was accomplished through a diplomatic compromise between the two governments rather than through an act of Congress. Without a continuous flow of Japanese farm workers to ease the labor shortage on Hawaiian plantations, contractors turned to the Philippine Islands—which had been a U.S. possession since 1898—for cheap labor. From 1906 to the independence of the Republic of the Philippines in 1946, over 125,000 (predominantly single) Filipino males, the majority from the Ilocos region, labored on Hawaiian sugar plantations.

The exclusions of Asians enacted into the National Origins Act of 1924 essentially remained in effect until 1965. By act of

Reprinted with modifications from *Encyclopedia of Sociology*, edited by E. F. Borgatta and M. L. Borgatta, 1992, New York: Macmillan.

Congress in 1943, however, 105 Chinese were permitted to immigrate annually, and in 1952, under the McCarran-Walter Act, a token 100 persons from each Asian country were allowed entry. The symbolic opening of immigration doors to Asians was attributed to Walter Judd, a congressman from Minnesota who had spent many years in China as a medical missionary. Provision of a quota of 100 persons seemed to be an important moral victory for those who wanted elimination of the exclusion act, but it was in fact a restatement of the 1924 national origin quota basis for immigration.

The new stream of Asian immigrants to the United States is the artifact of the 1965 legislative reform that allowed an equal number of persons (20,000) from each country outside the Western Hemisphere to immigrate. Family unification and needed skills became the major admission criteria, replacing national origin. Besides China and the Philippines, Korea and the Indian subcontinent became, and continue to be, the major countries of origin of many newly arrived Asian immigrants. Refugees from Vietnam, Cambodia, and Laos began to enter the United States in 1975. By 1990 peoples from Indochina had become the third largest Asian group, following Chinese and Filipinos. In contrast, Japan's immigration to the United States practically ceased from 1945 to 1965, when it resumed at a much lower rate than those reported for other Asian countries.

SOCIAL CONSEQUENCES OF IMMIGRATION RESTRICTIONS

Several distinct demographic characteristics provide graphic illustration of past restrictions and recent reforms in the immigration laws. Earlier immigrants from China and the Philippines were predominantly single males. As a result of racial prejudice that culminated in the passage in many western and southwestern states of antimiscegenation laws directed primarily against people of color, the majority of these earlier Asian immigrants remained unmarried. The lack of family life caused unattached immigrants to depend on one another, creating an apparent great solidarity among people of the same ethnic group. Many of the earlier studies of Chinese and Filipino communities depicted themes of social isolation and loneliness, which did not apply to the Japanese community. A well-known portrayal of the extreme social isolation of Chinese laundrymen in Chicago was published by Paul Siu (1952) only as a paper entitled "The Sojourner." Although Siu's work was written under the direction of Robert E. Park and Ernest W. Burgess, it was not included in the Chicago School sociological series published by the University of Chicago Press. Thus a major piece of Asian American research, *The Chinese Laundryman: A Study in Social Isolation* (Siu, 1987), remained unpublished until after the author's death.

The existence of single-gender communities of Filipinos and Chinese is clearly demonstrated in the U.S. censuses between 1860 and 1970. In 1860 the sex ratio for Chinese was 1,858 men for every 100 women. By 1890, following the peak of Chinese immigration during the previous decade, the ratio was 2,678 males for every 100 females—the highest recorded. Sex ratios for the Chinese population later declined steadily as the result of legislative revisions in 1930 (46 U.S. Stat. 581) and 1931 (46 U.S. Stat. 1511) that enabled women from China to enter the United States.

A second factor that helped to balance the sex ratio in the Chinese community, particularly among the younger age cohorts, was the presence of an American-born generation. In 1900 U.S.-born persons constituted only 10% of the Chinese American population. By 1970 the figure was 53%. Nevertheless, in the 1980 census the sex ratio remained high for some age groups within certain Asian American subpopulations; among Filipinos, for example, the highest sex ratio was found in those 65 and older.

The demographic characteristics of Japanese Americans present yet another unusual feature. Under the Gentlemen's Agreement between Japan and the United States, Japanese women were allowed to land on the West Coast to join their men even though the immigration of male laborers was curtailed. The majority of the women came as picture brides (Glenn, 1986) within a narrow span of time. Thus the years following 1910 were the decade of family building for the first (*issei*) generation of Japanese Americans. Since almost all issei were young and their brides were chosen from a cohort of marriageable applicants of about the same age, it was not surprising that issei began their families at about the same time after marriage. Controlled migration of brides resulted in a uniform age cohort of second-generation Japanese Americans (*nisei*). The relatively homogeneous age group of the nisei generation meant that their children, the third generation (known as *sansei*), were also of about the same age. The fourth generation followed the same pattern. The amazingly nonoverlapping age and generational cohorts among Japanese Americans is not known to have had parallels in other population groups.

Third, while Asian Americans in general continue to grow in number as a result of new immigration, increases in the size of the Japanese American population are primarily dependent on the addition of new generations of U.S.-born babies. It is generally believed that offspring of Japanese women who marry Whites have lost their Japanese identity, even though there are no estimates of the impact of intermarriages upon the shrinkage of the Japanese American community. Given the fact that Japanese immigrants had lower fertility rates than women in Japan during the period prior to and shortly after World War II, and that the number of new immigrants since the war has remained small, Japanese American communities have larger percentages of older people than do other ethnic minority populations, including other Asian Americans. In short, Japanese Americans will be a much smaller ethnic minority in the future. The plurality ranking for all Asian groups placed the Japanese at the top of the list in 1970; they dropped to third place in 1980, to fourth in 1990, and are expected to be ranked last by 2000.

One more demographic fact is worthy of note. Hawaii and the West Coast states continue to draw large numbers of new immigrants from Asia. Through a process known as chain migration, relatives are likely to follow the immigrants soon after their arrival. This leads to sudden increases in population within the ethnic enclaves. The post-1965 pattern of population growth in many Chinatowns, for instance, is an example of the renewal and revitalization of ethnic communities—which were experiencing a decline prior to 1965—as is the formation and expansion of Koreantowns and Filipinotowns. Moreover, the settlement of post-1965 immigrants from Asia is more dispersed than that of the earlier groups, owing to the fact that the need for professional and skilled workers is widely distributed throughout the country. The emergence of Thai, Malaysian, and Vietnamese communities in major metropolitan areas has added a new dimension to the ethnic composition of Asian Americans.

Two separate chains of immigration resulted from the new immigration legislation of 1965. One chain, largely found in Chinese and Filipino communities, is kin-selective in that the process of settlement follows the family ties of earlier immigrants. The other process is occupation-selective, based on skills and professional qualifications. These two processes created significantly different immigrant populations, with clearly discerned bimodal distributions of status characteristics. It is therefore common to find recent immigrants from Asia among the high-income groups as well as among families living below the poverty level; some find their homes in the ethnic enclaves of central cities while others live in posh suburban communities. Any attempt to describe Asian Americans by using average measures of social status characteristics, such as income, education, and occupation, can produce a distorted profile that fits no particular group except in the abstractions of a myth that is of little use either to researchers or planners. A more useful description would involve the use of standard errors—to show the polarities or deviations of the immigrant group from the norm of the majority.

In short, the sociodemographic and socioeconomic characteristics of all Asian American communities since 1850 have been greatly influenced by federal immigration legislation. It is impossible to have a clear grasp of the structure and change of Asian American communities without an understanding of the history of immigration legislation.

ASIAN AMERICAN RESEARCH

Asian American research may be divided into five periods: (a) the early period before World War II, which was influenced by the Chicago School of thought; (b) the World War II period, which saw a preponderance of Japanese American studies; (c) the postwar era, with a strong emphasis on culture and personality studies; (d) a shift toward "ethnic studies" as a result of the civil rights movement; (e) the emergence of a new generation of Asian American studies in the 1980s.

The Early Period

The pioneer sociological studies on the assimilation of immigrants in American urban communities may be attributed to the work of Robert E. Park (1922, 1950; Park & Burgess, 1937). Although Park had done little empirical investigation, he supervised a large number of graduate students and formulated what was known as the race cycle theory, which stressed the unidirectional process of competition, accommodation, and assimila-

tion as the basis of race relations in urban America. Park led a group of researchers to study Chinese and Japanese communities on the Pacific Coast. The results failed to prove the race-cycle theory. In defending his theory, according to Lyman (1977), Park employed the Aristotelian doctrine of "obstacles," which suggests that among Chinese and Japanese the assimilation progress in the hypothesized direction was delayed.

Early published sociological research on Asian Americans included the works of Bogardus (1928, 1930), who attempted to delineate degrees of prejudice against minorities in terms of social distance. There were special topics such as "Oriental crime" in California (Beach, 1932); school achievement of Japanese American children (Bell, 1935); and anti-Asian sentiments (Ichihashi, 1932; Sandmeyer, 1939). A noted pioneer community study of Japanese Americans conducted by Frank Miyamoto (1939) in Seattle in the late 1930s paved the way for the long and significant bibliography on Japanese American studies that followed.

Perhaps the most significant and ambitious piece of work during the prewar era was the study of the social isolation of Chinese immigrants, which took more than a decade to complete. The author, Paul Siu, lived and observed, in extreme poverty, the life of Chinese laundrymen. The product of his research endeavors offers a classic text in the study of "unmeltable" immigrants, from which new sociological concepts were developed (Siu, 1952, 1987).

World War II and Japanese American Studies

Large-scale systematic studies on Asian Americans began shortly after the Japanese attack on Pearl Harbor, when the United States declared war on Japan. The U.S. government stripped Japanese Americans of their property, relocated them, and housed them in internment camps for several years. Alexander Leighton, a psychiatrist, recruited nisei social science graduates to assist in his work in the camps, monitoring the morale and loyalty of internees; this was perhaps the pioneer work in assessing their group cohesion and structure. A few of Leighton's nisei assistants completed their doctoral studies after the war, maintaining a close and affectionate relationship with him. All had made their own contributions as social scientists and as Asian American specialists. Leighton's work on the internment of these civilians (both citizens and noncitizens) resulted in the publication of a classic text on loyalty (Leighton, 1945).

Careful documentation of the internment was recorded by Thomas and Nishimoto (1946), Thomas (1952), and Broom and Kitsuse (1955). Home front conditions in the United States had sparked an area of development in social science research, and it had increased the general knowledge base on Japanese Americans, including their families, their communities, and their sacrifices and contributions during a time of trial.

Culture and Personality Studies in the Postwar Era

During World War II, the U.S. government had reason and opportunity to question the suitability of Asians as American citizens in regard to loyalty and civic responsibilities. It was also a time to test the myth that Asian immigrants could not assimilate into American society. Social scientists were intrigued by the way culture shapes the personality. Ruth Benedict's (1946) classic work on the Japanese personality and society opened a new vista for research. A cohort of young scholars at the University of Chicago, which included Japanese American graduate students, became known for their pioneer work in studying Japanese behavioral patterns. It had a profound effect on a generation of interested social scientists and resulted in the publication of many classic works in culture and personality (Babcock & Caudill, 1958; Caudill, 1952; Caudill & DeVos, 1956; Caudill & Scarr, 1961; DeVos, 1955; Jacobson & Rainwater, 1953; Kitano, 1961, 1962, 1964; Meredith, 1966; Vogel, 1961). Similar studies on other Asian American groups are conspicuously absent.

Ethnic Studies and the Civil Rights Movement

In the 1960s the civil rights movement, sparked by the death of Martin Luther King, Jr., led, perhaps indirectly, to the passage of an unprecedented immigration-legislation reform. At the time there existed among Asian Americans a collective search for identity that shared many of the goals and rhetoric of the Black movement on the Pacific Coast, principally in California. Research into ethnic (Asian) U.S. communities had added two dimensions. The first was the need to raise consciousness as a part of the social movement. Personal testimonials of experiences as members of an oppressed minority provided insight into the psychology of ethnic minorities. The cathartic as well as the cathectic quality in many of the writings of the postwar era reflected the mood of the period and was perhaps necessary in the absence of an appropriate theoretical model, with empirical data, to argue against the assimilation model in standard texts on racial and ethnic studies. The second dimension, consistent with the radical theme, was the apparent influence on race and ethnic relations of Marxian views, which posited that African Americans and other minorities are victims of oppression in a capitalist society.

Expectedly, the civil rights movement began a renewed interest in research on the experiences of the earliest Asian Americans. With time the titles ranged from well-documented academic publications to insightful popular readings for the lay public (Chen, 1980; Choy, 1979; Daniels, 1988; Ichioka, 1988; Miller, 1969; Nee & de Bary, 1973; Saxton, 1971; Sung, 1971; Takaki, 1989; Wilson & Hosokawa, 1980).

Asian American studies was established as an academic discipline at a time when there were only a few major publications as sources of information for undergraduates (see Kitano, 1961, 1962, 1964, 1976; Lyman, 1974a, 1974b; Petersen, 1971). The birth of the specialty was marked by the conspicuous absence of available materials, particularly on Filipinos, Koreans, Vietnamese, and the peoples of India. In response to this void, the Asian American Studies Center at the University of California at Los Angeles published two collections of papers (Tuchiki, Wong, Odo, with Wong, 1971; Gee et al., 1976) and starting in 1971, a quarterly, *Amerasia Journal*. On the Atlantic Coast, also beginning in 1971, a group of U.S.-born professionals published an intellectual nonacademic monthly, *Bridge: An Asian American Perspective*. For more than a decade these publications were popular reading materials for college students interested in Asian American studies.

New Generation of Asian American Studies and Research

Stanley Lyman of the University of California, Berkeley, is generally acknowledged as a pioneer in Asian American research. Through his numerous papers and books he has demonstrated a combination of theoretical relevance and historical insight into the origin and growth of Asian American communities, especially those of the Chinese and Japanese (Lyman, 1961, 1964, 1968). As a social historian he based his research, by and large, on archival documents (see Lyman, 1970a).

In the 1980s some well-trained sociologists began to emerge, many of them foreign-born and foreign-educated— the "first-generation new immigrants"—scholars who pursued advanced degrees in the United States. Arriving at a time when the United States as a whole had become sensitive to diverse cultures, the new Asian American researchers are increasingly vocal, questioning traditional sociological theories and concepts based on studies of European-based cultures. Their studies of Asian American communities have added much to a field that had been underserved by the social sciences. Similarly, they have even questioned neutral and descriptive federal statistics on Asian and Pacific Islander populations, in terms of both inadequate sample design and culturally biased instrument design.

Members of the new generation of researchers generally work on specific topical areas that previously had not been systematically scrutinized. The works of Bonacich (1972, 1975, 1978) and her associates (Bonacich, Light, & Wong, 1976; Bonacich & Modell, 1980) have concentrated on the theory of the split labor market and Asian American—particularly Korean immigrant—small business in America. Light has begun to build an impressive series of research works on Asian American small businesses (Light, 1972; Light & Wong, 1975). Korean communities have become the favorite subject for many publications that have contributed significantly to the literature on new immigrant communities and urban America (Hurh & Kim, 1984; I. Kim, 1981; K. C. Kim, Kim, & Hurh, 1981; S. D. Kim, 1975; E. Y. Yu, 1977).

A lack of statistics remains a major problem in Asian American studies. Whereas estimates of the social and economic characteristics of White, African American, and other groups may be obtained from Current Population Surveys and other sources, as well as from the U.S. Bureau of the Census, the only useful and comprehensive source materials for Asian Americans are census data. However, such information is available for only three major Asian groups from 1940 through 1970 (Chinese, Japanese, Filipino). In 1980, for the first time, the census provided separate counts for three other major Asian groups: Koreans, Asian Indians, and Vietnamese. Through special publications, the Census Bureau has provided excellent data on the socioeconomic status and social mobility of Asian Americans (Gardner, Robey, & Smith, 1985; Hirschman & Wong, 1984; Wong, 1982), but the information is rather limited, and it is not always possible to disaggregate the different Asian subgroups from the generic category "Asian Americans."

The use of averages to represent the social and economic characteristics of diverse groups of Asians in the United States, or reliance on data from a few older immigrant groups of Asians (such as Japanese, Chinese, and Filipinos) to represent all Asian Americans, masks the significantly different levels of social attainment experienced by subgroups of Asian Americans, thereby furthering the myth, popularized in the 1970s, that Asians are a "model minority."

During the 1980s a number of studies began to counter the myth of Asians as a model minority; they cover a wide spectrum of specific topics that had not been previously investigated. These include the achievement of Asian Americans in school (Hsia, 1988; Stevenson, Lee, & Stigler, 1985, 1986; Vernon, 1982); health statistics and mental-health issues (Liu, 1986a,

1986b; Liu & Yu, 1985; Liu, Yu, Chang, & Fernandez, 1990; Sue & Morishima, 1982; Yu & Liu, 1987a, 1987b, 1989); families and kinship (Glenn, 1986; Li, 1977); political participation (Jo, 1980); religion (Cho, 1979); and business and income (Chiswick, 1978, 1980; Zhou & Logan, 1989).

Though rigorous and systematic studies on Asian America are still in their infancy, a solid beginning was launched in the late 1980s. Asian America as a field of academic study and as a research topic became a new section of the American Sociological Association, with more than 300 members in 1990. Nearly all major universities on the Pacific Coast have established Asian American Studies programs, and new Pacific or Asian Centers have been set up on the East Coast. In addition, many academic programs on Asian Americans are available as part of broader and undifferentiated ethnic-studies programs throughout the United States.

References

Babcock, C. E., & Caudill, W. (1958). Personal and cultural factors in treating a nisei man. In C. Seward (Ed.), *Social studies in culture conflict*. New York: Ronald Press.

Beach, W. C. (1932). *Oriental crime in California*. Stanford, CA: Stanford University Press.

Bell, R. (1935). *Public school education of second generation Japanese in California*. Stanford, CA: Stanford University Press.

Benedict, R. (1946). *The chrysanthemum and the sword*. Boston: Houghton Mifflin.

Bogardus, E. S. (1928). *Immigration and race attitudes*. Boston: D.C. Heath.

Bogardus, E. S. (1930). A race relations cycle. *American Journal of Sociology, 35*, 612–617.

Bonacich, E. (1972). A theory of ethnic antagonism: The split labor market. *American Sociological Review, 37*, 549–559.

Bonacich, E. (1975). Small business and Japanese American ethnic solidarity. *Amerasia Journal, 3*, 96–113.

Bonacich, E. (1978, August 14–19). *U.S. capitalism and Korean immigrant small business*. Paper presented at the Ninth World Congress of Sociology, Uppsala, Sweden.

Bonacich, E., Light, I., & Wong, C. C. (1976). Korean immigrant small business in Los Angeles. In R. S. Bryce-Laporte (Ed.), *Sourcebook on new immigration* (pp. 167–184). New Brunswick, NJ: Transaction Books.

Bonacich, E., & Modell, J. (1980). *The economic base of ethnic solidarity: Small business in the Japanese American community*. Berkeley: University of California Press.

Broom, L., & Kitsuse, J. (1956). *The managed casualty*. Berkeley: University of California Press.

Caudill, W. (1952). Japanese-American personality and acculturation. *Genetic Psychology Monographs. 45*, 3–102.

Caudill, W., & DeVos, G. (1956). Achievement, culture, and personality: The case of Japanese Americans. *American Anthropologist, 58*, 1102–1126.

Caudill, W., & Scarr, H. A. (1961). Japanese value orientations and cultural change. *Ethnology, 1*, 53–91.

Chen, J. (1980). *The Chinese of America*. New York: Harper and Row.

Chiswick, B. R. (1978). The effect of Americanization on the earnings of foreign born men. *Journal of Population Economy, 86*, 891–921.

Chiswick, B. R. (1980). Immigrant earnings patterns by sex, race and ethnic groupings. *Monthly Labor Review, 103*, 22–25.

Cho, P. J. (1979, August 28). *The Korean church in America: A Dahrendorf model*. Paper presented at the Asian American Sociological Meeting, Boston.

Choy, B. Y. (1979). *Koreans in America*. Chicago: Nelson-Hall.

Daniels, R. (1988). *Asian America: Chinese and Japanese in the United States since 1850*. Seattle: University of Washington Press.

DeVos, G. (1955). A quantitative Rorschach assessment of maladjustment and rigidity in acculturating Japanese Americans. *Genetic Psychology Monographs, 52*, 51–87.

Gardner, R. W., Robey, B., & Smith, P. C. (1985). *Asian Americans: Growth, change and diversity*. Washington, DC: The Population Reference Bureau.

Gee, E. (Ed.). (1976). *Counterpoint: Perspectives on Asian America*. Los Angeles: UCLA Asian American Studies Center.

Glenn, E. N. (1986). *Issei, nisei, war bride*. Philadelphia: Temple University Press.

Hirschman, C., & Wong, M. G. (1984). Socioeconomic gains of Asian Americans, Blacks and Hispanics: 1960–1976. *American Journal of Sociology, 90*, 584–607.

Hsia, J. (1988). *Asian Americans in higher education and at work*. Hillsdale, NJ: Lawrence Erlbaum Associates.

Hurh, W. M., & Kim, K. C. (1984). *Korean immigrants in America*. Teaneck, NJ: Fairleigh Dickinson University Press.

Ichihashi, Y. (1932). *Japanese in the United States*. Stanford, CA: Stanford University Press.

Ichioka, Y. (1988). *The issei*. New York: The Free Press.

Jacabson, A., & Rainwater, L. (1953). A study of management representative evaluations of nisei workers. *Social Forces, 32*, 35–41.

Jo, Y-h. (1980). *Political participation of Asian-Americans: Problems and strategies*. Chicago: Pacific/Asian American Mental Health Research Center.

Kim, I. (1981). *New urban immigrants: The Korean community in New York*. Princeton, NJ: Princeton University Press.

Kim, K. C., Kim, H. C., & Hurh, W. M. (1981). Job information deprivation in the United States: A case study of Korean immigrants. *Ethnicity, 8*, 219–232.

Kim, S. D. (1975, March 20–21). *Findings of national inquiries on Asian wives of U.S. servicemen*. Paper presented at the Methodist Conference, Tacoma, WA.

Kitano, H. H. L. (1961). Differential child-rearing attitudes between first and second generation Japanese in the U.S. *Journal of Social Psychology, 53,* 13–19.

Kitano, H. H. L. (1962). Changing achievement patterns of the Japanese in the United States. *Journal of Social Psychology, 58,* 257–264.

Kitano, H. H. L. (1964). Inter-generational differences in maternal attitudes towards child-rearing. *Journal of Social Psychology, 63,* 215–220.

Kitano, H. H. L. (1976). *Japanese Americans: The evolution of a subculture.* Englewood Cliffs, NJ: Prentice-Hall.

Leighton, A. (1945). *The governing of men.* Princeton, NJ: Princeton University Press.

Li, P. (1977). Fictive kinship, conjugal ties, and kinship chain among Chinese immigrants in the United States. *Journal of Comparative Family Studies, 8,* 47–63.

Light, I. H. (1972). *Ethnic enterprise in America.* Berkeley: University of California Press.

Light, I. H., & Wong, C. C. (1975). Protest or work. *American Journal of Sociology, 80,* 1342–1368.

Liu, W. T. (1986a). Asian/Pacific American elderly: Mortality differentials, health status, and use of health services. *Journal of Applied Gerontology, 4,* 35–64.

Liu, W. T. (1986b). Health services for Asian elderly. *Research on Aging, 8,* 156–183.

Liu, W. T., & Yu, E. (1985). Ethnicity and mental health: An overview. In L. Maldonaldo & J. Moore (Eds.), *Urban ethnicity in the United States: New immigrants and old minorities* (Vol. 29, pp. 211–248). Beverly Hills, CA: Sage.

Liu, W. T., Yu, E., Chang, C. F., & Fernandez, M. (1990). The mental health of Asian American teenagers. In A. R. Stiffman & L. E. Davis (Eds.), *Ethnic issues in adolescent mental health* (pp. 92–114). Newbury Park, CA: Sage.

Lyman, S. (1961). *The structure of Chinese society in nineteenth century America.* Unpublished doctoral dissertation, University of California, Berkeley.

Lyman, S. (1964). The Chinese secret societies in the Occident: Notes and suggestions for research in the sociology of secrecy. *Canadian Review of Sociology and Anthropology, 1*(2), 79–102.

Lyman, S. (1968). Contrasts in the community organization of Chinese and Japanese in North America. *Canadian Review of Sociology and Anthropology, 5,* 2.

Lyman, S. (1970a). *The Asian in North America.* Santa Barbara, CA: ABC-Clio.

Lyman, S. (1970b). *Asians in the West.* Reno: University of Nevada Press.

Lyman, S. (1974a). *Chinese Americans.* New York: Random House.

Lyman, S. (1974b). Conflict and the web of group affiliation in San Francisco's Chinatown, 1850–1910. *Pacific Historical Review, 43*(4), 473–499.

Lyman, S. (1977). *The Asian in North America.* Santa Barbara, CA: ABC-Clio.

Meredith, G. M. (1966). Acculturation and personality among Japanese-American college students in Hawaii. *Journal of Social Psychology, 68,* 175–182.

Miller, S. C. (1969). *The unwelcome immigrant: The American image of the Chinese, 1775–1882.* Berkeley: University of California Press.

Miyamoto, F. (1939). Social solidarity among the Japanese in Seattle. *University of Washington Publications in the Social Sciences, 11*(2), 57–130.

Nee, V. C., & de Bary, B. (1973). *Longtime Californ': A documentary study of an American Chinatown.* New York: Pantheon.

Park, R. E. (1922). *The immigrant press and its control.* New York: Harper & Brothers.

Park, R. E. (1950). *Race and culture.* Glencoe, IL: The Free Press.

Park, R. E., & Burgess, E. W. (1937) *Introduction to the science of sociology.* Chicago: University of Chicago Press.

Petersen, W. (1971). *Japanese Americans.* New York: Random House.

Sandmeyer, E. C. (1939). *The Anti-Chinese movement in California.* Urbana: University of Illinois Press.

Saxton, A. (1971). *The indispensable enemy: Labor and the anti-Chinese movement in California.* Berkeley: University of California Press.

Siu, P. C. P. (1952). The sojourner. *American Journal of Sociology, 58,* 34–44.

Siu, P. C. P. (1987). *The Chinese laundryman: A study in social isolation.* New York: New York University Press.

Stevenson, H. W., Lee, S. Y., & Stigler, J. W. (1985). Cognitive performance and academic achievement of Japanese, Chinese, and American children. *Child Development, 56,* 718–734.

Stevenson, H. W., Lee, S. Y., & Stigler, J. W. (1986). Mathematics achievement of Chinese, Japanese and American children. *Science, 231,* 693–699.

Sue, S., & Morishima, J. (1982). *The mental health of Asian Americans.* San Francisco: Jossey-Bass.

Sung, B. L. (1971). *The story of the Chinese in America.* New York: Collier Books.

Takaki, R. (1989). *Strangers from a different shore: A history of Asian Americans.* Boston: Little, Brown.

Thomas, D. S. (1952). *The salvage.* Berkeley: University of California Press.

Thomas, D. S., & Nishimoto, R. (1946). *The spoilage.* Berkeley: University of California Press.

Tuchiki, A., Wong, E., Odo, F., with Wong, B. (Eds.). (1971). *Roots: An Asian American reader.* Los Angeles: UCLA Asian American Studies Center.

Vernon, P. E. (1982). *The abilities and achievements of Orientals in North America.* New York: Academic Press.

Vogel, E. (1961). The go-between in a developing society: The case of the Japanese marriage arranger. *Human Organization, 20,* 112–120.

Wilson, R. A., & Hosokawa, B. (1980). *East to America: A history of the Japanese in the U.S.* New York: Morrow.

Wong, M. (1982). The cost of being Chinese, Japanese and Filipino in the United States, 1960, 1970, 1976. *Pacific Sociological Review, 25,* 59–78.

Yu, E., & Liu, W. T. (1987a). Measurement of depression in a Chinatown clinic. In W. T. Liu (Ed.), *A decade review of mental health research, training, and services.* Chicago: University of Illinois Press.

Yu, E., & Liu, W. T. (1987b). The Underutilization of mental health services by Asian Americans: Implication for manpower training. In W. T. Liu (Ed.), *A decade review of mental health research, training, and services.* Chicago: University of Illinois Press.

Yu, E., & Liu, W. T. (1989). Suicide prevention and intervention among Asian youths. In ADAMHA, *Report of the secretary's task force on youth suicide* (Vol. 3) (DHHS Publication no. ADM 89–1623). Washington, DC: Government Printing Office.

Yu, E. Y. (1977). Koreans in America. *Amerasia Journal, 4,* 117–131.

Zhou, M., & Logan, J. R. (1989). Returns on human capital in ethnic enclaves: New York City's Chinatown. *American Sociological Review, 54,* 809–820.

CULTURE-CENTERED KNOWLEDGE: BLACK STUDIES, CURRICULUM TRANSFORMATION, AND SOCIAL ACTION

Joyce Elaine King

UNIVERSITY OF NEW ORLEANS

At this level of Otherness the "negro" was not even considered, since he was not imagined to have languages worth studying, nor to partake in culture, so total was his mode of Nigger Chaos.
—*Sylvia Wynter, 1984*

... it is not merely defiant; it is not merely black ... [but] a way of maintaining their dignity through collective autonomy when confronted with the school's undermining doubt about their ability.
—*Perry Gilmore, 1985*

Everybody was a nigger these days. Women, gays, always comparing their situations with blacks.
—*Ishmael Reed, 1993*

The problem here is that few Americans know who and what they really are ... most American whites are culturally part Negro American without even realizing it.
—*Ralph Ellison, 1986*

This chapter is an interpretive review of selected sources in Black studies, historical and literary scholarship, and research in the social sciences and multicultural education. One purpose of this review is to clarify the nature and production of culture-centered knowledge in African American (Diasporan/African) intellectual thought, educational research, and practice. A second purpose is to summarize and draw conclusions from this literature regarding the uses of cultural knowledge and culture-centered knowledge in curriculum transformation and social action, particularly for the educational benefit of Black people. All but the culturally conservative "Western Traditionalists" (Banks, 1993) recognize the partiality of knowledge and the importance of understanding how culture and ideology affect knowledge, its production, and its social uses. In addition, crite-

ria are needed to distinguish between dominating as compared to liberating culture-centered knowledge and curriculum transformation. For example, a central concern in Black studies (and in some variants of multicultural education) has been: How can education be used as a social weapon for human freedom (Rodney, 1990; Williams, 1991)? While this chapter does not include a comprehensive review of the discipline of Black studies, it discusses relevant scholarship and research directions that address this critical issue. The literature has been selected in accordance with these aims.

THE BLACK STUDIES CRITIQUE: EDUCATION FOR HUMAN FREEDOM

Education and knowledge are contested, non-neutral terrains. Contestation about education in the last decades of the 20th century has frequently taken the form of vituperous debate and media hyperbole about curriculum transformation at all levels. Irruptions in the academy over the curriculum (Erickson, 1992; Graff, 1993) have coincided with community struggles over racism in education, including ostensibly multicultural textbooks (Epstein & Ellis, 1992; J. E. King, 1992; Sanford, 1990; Cornbleth & Waugh, 1993; Wynter, 1992a). This academic and public discourse raises questions about the meaning and future of Black studies and multicultural education as well as the legitimacy of African-centered theorizing and curriculum development (Asante, 1991a, 1991b; Banks, 1992; Gates, 1992a, 1992b; Gay, 1983; Ogbu, 1992; Ravitch, 1990b; Sleeter, 1991). Disagreements about education and curriculum transformation among liberals, progressives, and conservatives—that appear to be about what should be included in the literary canon or taught in the school curriculum—are as much about the society's failure to resolve the problems of racial hierarchy and cultural hegemony in a purported democracy. As Giroux (1992) and others observe, attacks on multicultural education have "used the language of liberalism and pluralism to give credence to the new nativism and racism that has been resurgent in the last decade in the media, mass culture, and American schools" (p. 234). Erickson (1992) analyzes this collapse of liberalism and also concludes that the current dispute about the humanities curriculum and the literary canon in higher education is "not merely academic." Rather, this debate is so fierce because it "involves the attempt to redefine American cultural identity under new historical circumstances" (p. 97).

The United States has never been the "White" country of popular imagination and ideology, and "American cultural identity" continues to be formed not only along the boundaries of the "color line"—that enduring problem of the 20th century that DuBois predicted (DuBois, 1903/1953; Franklin, 1993)—but also within the normative cultural demarcations that denote and connote degrees of assimilation to an idealized White Euro-American middle-class cultural norm (Cruse, 1987). These social divisions along racial and cultural lines require equally trenchant analysis because, as Cruse (1967) observes:

Racial democracy is, at the same time, cultural democracy; and the question of cultural democracy in America [continues to be] posed in a way never before seen or considered in other societies. This uniqueness results historically from the manner in which American cultural developments have been influenced by the Negro presence. (p. 96)

In contrast to the current waves of newly arriving immigrants, this troublesome "Negro presence" is not a new historical circumstance. And it is in the context of persisting systemic social inequity and injustice that this chapter asks: What needs to be analyzed and understood about curriculum transformation and social action that is in the best interest of African Americans? Close consideration of the contestation over the curriculum reveals a recurring pattern of cultural negation/assimilation versus cultural affirmation/revitalization within a historical dialectic of ideological conflict and cultural hegemony (Semmes, 1992). This dialectic, which is often oversimplified as a choice between integration or separatism, has a long history in concrete struggles that African Americans have waged for liberating knowledge, intellectual autonomy, and education for human freedom (Wright, 1970). The epistemological critique of knowledge brought on by the modern Black studies movement is one legacy of this struggle.

The Black Studies Legacy and Multiculturalism

Current debates about Black studies and multicultural curriculum transformation have been argued in earlier historical periods, albeit in different vocabularies. For example, objections to Black studies arose as this movement converged with the Black Arts movement to challenge Eurocentric intellectual

and cultural hegemony in the academy and liberate African American and African culture, consciousness, and aesthetics from institutionalized White cultural supremacy. Both of these movements had historical antecedents that go back at least to David Walker's *Appeal to the Colored Citizens of the World but in Particular and very Expressly to those of the United States of America* in 1829 (D. Walker, 1829/1971), to the Garvey Movement, and to the Harlem Renaissance in the 1920s (Locke, 1925/1977). The base of contemporary African American, Caribbean, and African literary scholarship can also be located in the "New Negro, Indigenist and Negritude movements of the 1920s and 1930s" (V. Clark, 1991, p. 40). In the 1960s both Black studies and the new letters movement were correctly linked to the political and cultural values in the concept of Black Power (Gayle, 1971). Calls for "education for liberation" (Banks, 1973; Sizemore, 1973a) and "Black feminist criticism" in the 1970s emerged from the convergence of the "new Black consciousness" and the women's movement. This convergence influenced subsequent developments in ethnic and women's studies, "minority" literary theory and criticism, multicultural education, and teacher education (Banks, 1992; B. Gordon, 1985a, 1992; Guy-Sheftall, 1992; Ladson-Billings, 1991a). Christian (1989) recounts that this conjuncture of Black consciousness and the women's movement "provided a context to imagine questions" about Black women's writing that were "never imagined before" (p. 61).

From its inception as an "interdisciplinary mode of critical investigation" (Marable, 1992, p. 31), Black studies distinguished itself from Negro history and ethnic studies (Aldridge, 1992; J. H. Clarke, 1992). Black studies evolved beyond Negro history and Black history to encompass a particular epistemological and axiological mission across the disciplines. Harding (1970) explains the crucial difference between Black history and Negro history: "Black History does not seek to highlight the outstanding contributions of special black people to the life and times of America. Rather our emphasis is on exposure, disclosure, on reinterpretation of the entire American past" (p. 279). In other words, Black history raises questions that were never asked by Negro history—questions about the European heritage of the United States, for example. That is, Black history is "forced to ask about the meaning of America itself" (p. 281). Such questions are not only about "exclusively black things" and Black people, for Black history "sees with Indian eyes as well" (p. 280). Black studies is an interdisciplinary fulfillment of the task and hope of Black history: to create a newly defined world "in which the best of blackness has prevailed" and Black manhood and womanhood "will be vindicated" (p. 291). Or as Margaret Walker envisioned in her poem, "For My People," this is a world that "will hold all the people" (Harding, 1970, p. 291).

More recently, Semmes (1992) states that the interdisciplinary body of knowledge that constitutes "Black, African American, or African studies"

is tied to explicating social and historical processes that affect the status and development of people of African descent on a global scale . . . [and] this emerging discipline is able to provide universals for understanding the human experience in general. (p. ix)

The point is that Black studies links the development of African-descent people with the *transmutation* of knowledge. Rather than merely "multiculturalizing" knowledge or "opening up" the traditional disciplines (Gates, 1992a, p. 6), this intellectual perspective asks: "Where is the social philosophy, the social, political and economic theory that could *change the condition* of African Americans?" (Semmes, 1992, p. 72, emphasis added). Black studies offers the possibility of an epistemological critique of social reality and the social organization of knowledge. The object of this critique includes the societal obstacles to Black people's development as well as the knowledge that sustains and legitimates societal inequity.

Black Studies, African-Centered Thought, and Cultural Democracy

Watkins (1993) describes the "Black studies curriculum development movement of the past twenty-five years" as an evolution of the "Black nationalist orientation" that combined "Pan Africanist," "cultural nationalist," and "separatist" views on education (p. 329). According to Watkins, this nationalist outlook in curriculum development contrasts sharply with the optimism of earlier Black liberal education aims. Watkins concludes that "its focus on separateness indicates little optimism for integration" (p. 331), and that this nationalist outlook is "reflected in part in contemporary renditions of Afrocentrism" (p. 331). From the perspective of Black studies as a mode of critical investigation, however, it is the ideology *underlying* the social ethic of integration that should be analyzed (Cruse, 1967; Semmes, 1992). Semmes stresses this aspect of Afrocentrism or "Afrocentric social science" that is the "act of examining phenomena in terms of their relationship to the survival and prosperity of African peoples." Such critical examination is "crucial to developing a social science approach within the context of African American studies," or Black studies (p. 18). Semmes's description of African-centered theorizing emphasizes "the importance of an epistemological center" (p. 18) in Black studies/Afrocentric social science that also affirms the importance of the humanities (1981, p. 14) in analyzing the Black experience and Euro-American cultural hegemony.

Semmes (1992) compares the way E. Franklin Frazier (1957, 1973) and Harold Cruse (1967) systematically examined the liberal integrationist ethic. He concludes that their scholarship demonstrates that this ethic requires African American cultural or group negation, and this negation blocks the kind of group-based strategies that enabled other groups to develop (Semmes, p. 75; Cruse, p. 476). This suggests that achieving racial and cultural democracy is not a dualistic either/or choice between integration or separation but requires overcoming "blocked cultural pluralism." It is in this context that Semmes identifies group-affirming African-centered thought with the Black studies tradition of intellectual autonomy that extends legitimacy to the "study of plural impulses among African Americans" (p. 76). That is, studying group-based strategies for social action can be legitimately pluralist; such study need not be equated with "separatism" or "self-segregation." Semmes also shows that "over time dominant society elites have

changed the meaning of segregation for African Americans to fit their political needs" and interests (p. 105):

The label "segregation" is incorrectly applied to any group-focused effort by African Americans and others to meet the social and cultural needs that are not automatically provided to African Americans, as they are to European Americans, or to rectify the past and current effects of White supremacist oppression and structured inequality. (p. 105)

Thus, equating the "variegated expressions" of African-centered theorizing and "group-directed strategies" (p. 105) with separatism/segregation uncritically accepts normative liberal assumptions concerning integration and social change.

Moral and Epistemological Panics. In the 1960s the Black studies critique of liberal assumptions, "mainstream" knowledge, and ideology across the disciplines precipitated a series of stunning breakaways from Western traditional forms of knowledge, thought, and influence (V. Clark, 1991; Sizemore, 1973b; West, 1985). Both epistemological and "moral panics" ensued in reaction against the alternative perspective and social action possibilities that the Black studies critique of knowledge and society represents. The term *moral panic* refers to "the emergence of a perceived threat to the values and interests of a society in its mass media" (Carby, 1987, p. 190, n. 15). (Cohen, 1972, originated the term, and S. Hall, Critcher, Jefferson, Clarke, & Roberts, 1978, use it in the British context.) *Epistemological panic* is used here to suggest a corollary perceived threat to certain values and interests in the disciplines and curriculum knowledge (Schlesinger, 1991). These epistemological and moral panics can be seen in a book on teaching social studies published as Black history challenged Negro history over two decades ago (Banks & Joyce, 1971).

Banks (1971a), McIntosh (1971), and other contributors to Banks and Joyce (1971) make explicit social justice claims upon the social studies to make the curriculum relevant to the lives and needs of "culturally different" children. Particularly revealing are articles by Cuban (1971), which first appeared in *Saturday Review* in 1968, and an essay critique by Grambs (1971) of a 1965 children's biography of Crispus Attucks. (See Swartz, 1992, for a more recent discussion of the transformation of curriculum knowledge about Attucks.) Cuban stressed that Negro history belonged in the public schools because of its "restraint and balance," but not Black history, which, despite its merits, aimed at "instilling racial pride" through "propaganda" (pp. 317–318). Cuban preferred Negro history to both the presumed "mythology" of Black history and the "white mythology" of the existing school curriculum that Negro history could rectify. Grambs complained that the children's biography featuring Crispus Attucks as a hero distorted the historical facts by substituting "non-history" and "ethnic chauvinism" for "authentic history" (p. 327). Banks (1971b) wrote a lengthy response to these criticisms in a letter to the editors of the *Harvard Educational Review* (which had published the Grambs essay). He argued that their liberal assumptions about and interpretation of the "canons of scholarly objectivity and historical accuracy" (Cuban, 1971, p. 318), as well as their claim that these standards of historicity are lacking in Black history, were not only profoundly misguided but missed the point of teaching history in general.

The Restoration Agenda. The complaint that Black history lacks scholarly objectivity and appropriate "balance" and promotes propagandistic "ethnic chauvinism" persists in the current "culture wars" in education. As Black studies has become institutionalized, the object of moral and epistemological panics about curriculum transformation has shifted to African-centered theorizing and education practice. Critics describe African-centered education as academic "separatism" and excoriate it as "filiopietism (i.e., excessive reverence for one's ancestors)" (Ravitch, 1990a, p. 46). The current "restoration agenda" involves efforts by both conservatives and liberals to constrain the transformation of the curriculum in schools and the academy (Asante, 1991a, 1991b; Banks, 1993; Cornbleth & Waugh, 1993; J. E. King, 1992; Ladson-Billings, 1991b; Shor, 1986; Sizemore, 1990). Notwithstanding its various perspectives, multicultural education risks being appropriated and positioned as a more politically and academically acceptable alternative to African-centered curriculum reform, as Negro history was positioned in relation to the perceived threat of Black history.

Liberals, progressives, and conservatives alike condemn the political implications of African-centered scholarship and curriculum, but usually without adequately acknowledging the ideological distortion of knowledge and cultural hegemony this alternative epistemological approach seeks to rectify (Semmes, 1992, pp. 12–13). For example, Eugene Genovese, Nathan Glazer, Arthur Schlesinger, Jr., Diane Ravitch, and C. Vann Woodward, to name a few, criticize aspects of multicultural curriculum reform but unequivocally denounce the "Afrocentric idea" in education (Asante, 1987, 1991a). While these scholars may not equally support the opinion stated by George F. Will in the *Baton Rouge Morning Advocate* (December 19, 1989, p. 3, cited in McCarthy, 1990, p. 118), his position expresses the ideology of Euro-American superiority to which African-centered theorizing responds. Will states: "Our country is a branch of European civilization.... "Eurocentricity" is right, in American curricula and consciousness, because it accords with the facts of our history...."

Another exchange among historians more than 20 years ago is also relevant. In a response to C. Vann Woodward's criticism of W. E. B. DuBois, Stuckey (1971) addressed the "long history" of White historians and the media admonishing and "disrespecting" Black scholars and Black studies (pp. 280–281). (See Genovese, 1971, for another example of the tendency of White scholars in this regard.) Woodward had chided DuBois for publishing "uninhibited" expressions of "racial pride." This exchange further illustrates that the anxiety (or panics) about Black intellectual autonomy and group consciousness—be it Black history or African-centered theorizing—is a recurring theme. Stuckey's rejoinder to Woodward included this closing comment:

Of this we may be certain: white historians, save perhaps the most radical of the future, will never acknowledge what blacks have done for the country or what Americans have done to blacks. To do so would be tantamount to blotting out the America they have known and written

about and would bring to an end ways in which, as white men, they look out on the world and in at themselves. (p. 286)

Since these exchanges, scholarly debate about the epistemological legitimacy and theoretical adequacy—or truthfulness—of Black studies has become more complex as the importance of perspective as an epistemological (not biological) issue has been realized (Asante, 1992, p. 22). Internal differences exist among scholars representing divergent postmodern, progressive, Marxist, conservative, liberal pluralist, and feminist epistemological perspectives and theoretical positions. Within this shifting intellectual terrain and complex political landscape, knowledge, culture, and cultural identity intersect and are *used* for different theoretical, ideological, and educational purposes. It is with respect to this intersection of culture, ideology, and knowledge that a heuristic construct of culture-centered knowledge is used in this chapter as a conceptual tool to analyze forms of curriculum knowledge and transformation that can be identified with hegemony and autonomy. Such an analysis is needed to distinguish between dominating versus liberating forms of knowledge of, by, for, and about African-descent people and their education. This examination of culture-centered knowledge and curriculum transformation builds on the epistemological critique and axiological foundations of the modern Black studies movement.

KNOWLEDGE PRODUCTION, SOCIAL INTERESTS, AND CONCEPTUAL PARADIGMS

It is a common understanding in the social sciences that knowledge is a social construction of reality and that both reality and knowledge pertain to specific social contexts (Berger & Luckmann, 1967, p. 3). Yet according to E. Gordon (1985) and others, "mainstream" social science has inadequately and insufficiently addressed the life experiences of African Americans and other cultural groups (p. 118). African American scholars have revealed links among culture, ideology, hegemony, and methodological bias in social science knowledge production (Alkalimat, 1969; Ani, 1994; Childs, 1989; Dixon, 1971; Ladner, 1973; Semmes, 1992). In addition to exposing ethnocentric perspective bias in social science knowledge production, African American scholars are exploring a liberatory role for African American cultural knowledge as an alternative to hegemony and ideology in education and in the arts (Childs, 1989; B. Gordon, 1985b, 1990; King & Mitchell, 1990; Peeples, 1984). This includes using "culture as a weapon for liberation" (B. Gordon, 1993, p. 458).

Alternatives to Cultural Hegemony and Ideology

According to McLaren (1989), hegemony refers to processes of domination that are maintained "not by sheer force" but through "consensual social practices." It is a struggle by which the "powerful win the consent of those who are oppressed" (p. 173). Palestinian educator Fasheh (1990) describes one effect of hegemony in education:

Generally speaking, hegemonic education produces intellectuals who have lost their power base in their own culture and society and who have been provided with a foreign culture and ideology, but without a power base in the hegemonic society. (p. 25)

Semmes (1992) emphasizes this key element of hegemony with respect to African Americans: "progress for the subordinated group meant the uncritical assimilation and regurgitation of the conquering culture" (p. 3). In other words, as Semmes writes, "the perspective of the oppressed shifted to that of the imperial group. This rotation in perspective affirmed the legitimacy of the world view of the oppressor, which sought to present subordination as a normative order" (p. 3). This does not mean that dominated social groups are homogeneous and exist with no internally stratifying divisions or opposing interests. However, as Collins (1990) points out, such "contradictory elements" can "foster both compliance with and resistance to oppression" (p. 18, n. 4). Also, as Semmes explains, hegemonic domination of African Americans has been complicated because of the "self-generative character of the human spirit" that has produced "distinctive parameters for cultural reconstruction" and revitalization (pp. 2–3). Black studies and African-centered theorizing are indicative of such opposition to cultural hegemony and ideological constraints on thought.

E. Gordon, Miller & Rollock (1990) also criticize the tendency among researchers to "make one's own community the center of the universe and the conceptual frame that constrains all thought." This applies to conceptual paradigms as well as to the methodological paradigms used to study social phenomena. "The problem," as they put it, "is cultural and methodological hegemony" (p. 15). E. Gordon et al. suggest an approach to this problem of "communicentric bias" that is consistent with a holistic and critical interdisciplinary Black studies approach to knowledge. They suggest that a "marriage between the arts, humanities and the social sciences" is needed "in order to understand the lived experiences of Blacks, Latinos and Native Americans" (p. 18). Gordon et al. write: "We may need to turn to the arts and humanities ... because the meanings of our behavior are often better explicated in artistic and fiction work" (p. 18). Because literature can also function as a vehicle of hegemonic domination, however, its use in research, social theorizing, and curriculum transformation may require demystification. Churchill (1992) addresses the problematic role that literature has played for American Indians:

Literature from the very first arrival of white people on the continent has been written in the service of dominating American Indians "to provoke and sanctify systematic warfare." ... In the final stage, literature and stereotyping of culture establishes complete control "over truth and knowledge." It finally replaces troops and guns as the relevant tool of colonization. (pp. 1–2)

Writers in the Black Arts movement, theorists/critics of literature, including Black children's literature (Johnson, 1990; Sims, 1982), as well as intellectuals in formerly colonized societies in the West Indies and Africa, have written extensively on both the need to combat literature as a tool of cultural domination/colonization (Cesaire, 1960; Mudimbe, 1988; Touré, 1969; Wa Thiong'o, 1986) and its potential as a tool for liberation. The novelist John O. Killens stressed the role of "art as a weapon" that could be used to liberate all people. That is, art (literature) could also "liberate white people ... of their prejudice, their preconceived notions of what the world is about" (Peeples, 1984, p. 12; also quoted in King & Mitchell, 1990, pp. 78–79). This reviewer found it both necessary and constructive to include examples of literary theory and criticism in this chapter in order to examine oppositional discursive practices in African American and African diaspora thought that have implications for curriculum transformation.

Conceptual Intervention Is Needed

Though a problem of bias in knowledge production may be acknowledged, it can also be argued that the existing organization of knowledge sustains and legitimates the social framework through cultural hegemony and ideology in education. Rectifying the ideological and partial nature of knowledge production in the disciplines and school curricula has been one focus of the Black studies movement. Conceptual confusion continues to exist regarding what constitutes ideological bias and hegemony. This confusion, partly related to a tendency to conflate ideology, worldview or philosophical perspective, and identity, generates questions like: "Who is qualified to teach Black studies?" (Aldridge, 1992, p. 63). "Can White teachers/professors teach Black literature?" "Can't a White person write a multicultural textbook?" J. E. King (1992) explains the specious nature of such questions when ideology is conflated with identity. To the latter question, King responds: "The answer, of course, is yes; the issue, however, is the social interests of the perspective from which any scholar writes, regardless of ethnicity, gender, religion, etc." (p. 325; see also Wiggington, 1991/ 1992, p. 62). Moreover, Carruthers (1994) argues that ideology ought not to be confused with worldview (or a philosophical perspective). He writes: "The concept of an African world-view must be distinguished from any connotation of ideology ... [that] is largely associated with the rationalization of class interests...." (p. 53). W. M. King (1990) makes a similar point with respect to the scholar's "mind-set." The issue is "not so much the color of the scholar's skin," he writes, "as the mind-set that is brought to the examination of the intergroup dynamic..." (p. 170). These scholars are writing about ideology in education, but the educational research literature is not presently organized in a way that permits one to locate references such as these that address the relationship among culture, identity, ideology, hegemony, and knowledge production in education.

Nor are computerized databases like ERIC and RIES organized to access publications about cultural knowledge. A computer search of these databases using this concept was not possible: The system indicates that the word *culture* appears in the databases, but not with the word *knowledge*. Therefore, relevant studies in journals known to the author of this chapter were accessible only by using the names of authors or key words like *multicultural* and *African American*—a search strategy that generates far too many citations to be useful. This is despite the fact that several publications discussed in this chapter contain the words "cultural knowledge" in their titles and or content (Banks, 1993; B. Gordon, 1985b, 1993; Lee, 1991). Relevant book chapters were also difficult to access through a computer search using these concepts (e.g., Sleeter & Grant, 1991). One finding of the literature review undertaken for this chapter, therefore, is that the Black studies epistemological critique has not sufficiently influenced the conceptual paradigms-in-use in education research or those used to organize these computerized databases. Conceptual intervention in the educational research literature is needed to facilitate a systematic examination of scholarship that addresses ideological influence on knowledge in curriculum and education practice, particularly with regard to the education of Black people.

CULTURE-CENTERED KNOWLEDGE AND CURRICULUM TRANSFORMATION

Before examining other sources that were ultimately identified and selected for this review (by a manual search of journals and books, in many cases), it will be useful to consider some basic definitions of the key concepts that will be used to analyze culture-centered knowledge in this chapter (as compared to the cultural knowledge of a specific racial/ethnic group). These concepts include culture and cultural knowledge, culture-centered knowledge, and African American cultural knowledge.

Culture and Cultural Knowledge

The concept of *culture* can be used broadly to refer to humans in general, a nationality, or a particular group. Culture usually refers to group ways of thinking and living. At the most specific level, it is a group's "design for living" (Nobles, 1985); it includes the shared knowledge, consciousness, skills, values, expressive forms, social institutions, and behavior that enable their survival as a people. This usage is consistent with a definition Bullivant (1989) prefers: Culture is "a social group's design for surviving in and adapting to its environment" (p. 27). In other words, culture is the total product of a people's being and consciousness that "emerges from their grappling with nature and living with other humans in a collective group" (Ogundipe-Leslie, 1984, p. 81). Culture is also "both enduring and changing" as it adapts to changing societal needs and goals (Semmes, 1981, p. 4).

A people's particular ways of interpreting and perceiving reality—their social thought and folk wisdom—constitute one aspect of collectively generated autochthonous cultural knowledge. The term *cultural knowledge* refers to the learned behaviors, beliefs, and ways of relating to people and the environment that members of a cultural group acquire through normal processes of enculturation (Spradley, 1972). In a typology of knowledge that Banks (1993) constructs, this sociocultural dimension is the first of five categories of knowledge: (a) personal/cultural; (b) popular; (c) mainstream academic; (d) transformative academic; and (e) school. African American cultural knowledge will be discussed following an explanation of culture-centered knowledge.

Culture-Centered Knowledge

Culture-centered knowledge (CCK) is used in this chapter generically as an organizing concept (not a descriptive category) to denote integrating factors that aid in holding a social framework together. This concept includes forms of knowledge, that is, thought, perception, and belief structures that—by making certain ways of knowing oneself and the world possible—function in behalf of integrating the extant (or an envisioned) social framework. The centered nature of CCK denotes its role in generating the coherence a referent social framework requires to secure the loyalty, motivated participation, and relevant consciousness of its subjects (adherents). For example, individuals from different subgroups can be socially integrated (assimilated) within the referent (White, Anglo-Saxon, or European American) middle-class culture because CCK induces the perceptions and interpretations of social reality, behaviors, consciousness, and consensual (but not necessarily conscious) meanings that support the middle-class normative cultural model of the social framework. Culture-centered knowledge, as ideology, can make certain perceptions and interpretations of reality (of self and "different" others) possible or "dysconsciously" improbable. Dysconsciousness is defined as "an uncritical habit of mind (including perceptions, attitudes, assumptions, and beliefs)"; it is a form of thought that "justifies inequity and exploitation by accepting the existing order of things as given" (J. E. King, 1991a, p. 135).

This formulation of the concept of culture-centered knowledge attempts to denote objectively the manner in which certain ways of knowing and perceiving social reality function within a given social framework. It is adapted from Wynter's (1991) discussion of ideology, not in the pejorative sense of false-consciousness, but as a description of the "system function," as Ricoeur (1979) and others suggest, that "all Ideologies serve" (p. 252). This formulation of CCK also draws on Asante's (1992) explanation of how Afrocentricity differs from the ideology of Eurocentricity.

For example, Euro-American cultural knowledge that is represented and valorized in school curricula is culture-centered with respect to its referent, the existing U.S. social framework, not because it is Eurocentric, but because it serves to *legitimate* the dominant White middle-class normative cultural model (Castenell & Pinar, 1993; C. Clark, 1973). This is so even if White American culture is actually hybrid, or "culturally part Negro" (Ellison, 1986, p. 108). In contrast, an Afrocentric or African-centered worldview refers to the culture-specific social thought or perspective of African-descent people (not in terms of biology but of social and historical experience). In contrast to Eurocentric thought, this worldview does not rationalize or justify a universal or normative cultural model of being and way of knowing the world. That is, as Asante (1992) states, "Afrocentricity is not a black version of Eurocentricity" (p. 22). This would imply that White cultural authority in the curriculum or the disciplines would simply be replaced by the hegemony of Black cultural authority. There has been a failure to distinguish among differing conceptions of Black studies and African-centered thought (Weider 1992), and these differences involve more than "ongoing debate over nomenclature" in the field of Black studies (Hine, 1990, p. 15).

Hegemony and Autonomy. Analysis is required in order to determine whether the referent social framework of culture-centered knowledge (i.e., that CCK holds together) is dominating or democratic (liberating). Under conditions of domination, race and ethnic difference, for example, is negated and a single, normative "common culture" model based on individualism is emphasized. In this instance culture-centered knowledge can be identified with hegemony, if it induces the belief that the social interests of various groups are indivisible (e.g., isomorphic), whereas diverse communities of interests actually exist (Alinsky, 1971). Such socially constructed consensus is in the particular interest of a dominant group that prevails over and against the various interests of less powerful groups. On the other hand, culture-centered knowledge that enables social cohesion through democratic or "shared pluralism" (A. Walker, 1991, p. 25)—recognizing and valuing group differences and freedom in choice and thought—can be identified with autonomy. In this instance the larger interest of human freedom predominates. Under conditions of autonomy differences are not suppressed or ranked. In addition, under conditions either of hegemony or autonomy, CCK produces (and/or privileges) forms of subjectivity and thought that dislocate or locate individual and collective identity, behavior, and consciousness.

To recapitulate, culture-centered knowledge (like knowledge more generally), because it is a social product, is built up as a result of the social activity of men and women (Cornforth, 1971, p. 149), but also in particular social and cultural contexts. An important point is that under conditions of hegemony, CCK conflicts with or disparages the cultural knowledge and interests of dominated groups, and the "sameness" of individuals (e.g., "e pluribus unum") serves as a rationalizing principle for domination that is represented as societal cohesion (e.g., "our" national identity, national security interest). Curiously, sameness can be represented ideologically as pluralism: "We are all multicultural."

The Belief Structure of Race. A final point is that the culture-centered knowledge that constitutes a given society's claims about itself does not necessarily correspond to the reality of how the social framework actually works. In the Caribbean and in Brazil a socially integrating belief structure of race powerfully contradicts the appearance of pluralism in these societies (Goveia, 1970; Moore, 1964; Wynter, 1992a). Because the Caribbean Islands are peopled by diverse groups, the islands are thought to constitute "plural societies" with no "common culture or common set of values, shared by the population as a whole" (Goveia, p. 9). However, Goveia points out that the integrating factor (or CCK) that unifies the Caribbean in a way that transcends "internal divisions" of class, language, and politics is the "acceptance of the inferiority of Negroes to whites" (p. 9). The social framework in Brazil is also sustained by such a system-integrating structure of belief in Black inferiority. This culture-centered knowledge legitimates "racial democracy," the central myth of societal cohesion in Brazil, that is, one

becomes "White" with enough money. Despite the reality of racial hierarchy in Brazil, the idea of Brazil as a racial democracy was documented and promulgated for years in government-sponsored social science research (Fontaine, 1985).

In the United States people also proclaim their society to be a democracy, yet the social framework is also based on a system of racial hierarchy and a belief structure of racial superiority/inferiority (Hacker, 1992). Wynter (1984) maintains that one of the ways that social cohesion has been forged in U.S. society is through the collectively imagined threat of "Nigger Chaos" that inheres in the alter ego role of the conceptual "black" or "Negro" (p. 2). The conceptual Black embodies a totalizing belief in Black inferiority that rationalizes racial inequality in the social framework. Such beliefs, induced by culture-centered knowledge in the education system and as part of normal processes of enculturation, indicate some of the ways in which the social framework of these societies is sustained by a lack of cognitive autonomy. Such hegemonic CCK can either enable certain social illusions to be maintained or provoke the cognitive or intellectual autonomy needed to call the belief structure into question. Before analyzing and comparing different forms of culture-centered knowledge in educational discourse and curriculum transformation, a discussion of African American cultural knowledge and the tradition of autonomous Black social thought follows.

African American Cultural Knowledge and Thought

To acknowledge that individuals enculturated within a common group experience share a distinct mode of social thought and a shared body of cultural knowledge is not to imply an essentialized, romantic, biocentric ethnorationality. Although certain individuals will no doubt prove the exception, empirical evidence exists in various disciplines that African American culture differs from European American culture(s) in various ways including: perceptual and value orientations, language patterns, ethos, and worldview (Collins, 1990; Cox, Lobel, & McLeod, 1991; Dixon, 1971; Heath, 1989; Kochman, 1981; Meyers, 1988; Nobles, 1985; Shade, 1982; A. Walker, 1991; S. W. Williams, 1991). This shared cultural knowledge includes the skills, awareness, consciousness, and competence that permit African American people to participate meaningfully in their culture—in all of its changing socioeconomic and regional variations. The cultural competence involved is more than learning "a conglomeration of superficial aspects of life such as dance, dress, hairstyles" or other artifacts (Ogundipe-Leslie, 1984). This literature also suggests that, despite the rupturing effects of enslavement and dislocating miseducation, the cultural knowledge that enables African American people to maintain a collective group identity has been passed on, at least in part, through oral and literate expressive traditions (Asante, 1987; Gay & Baber, 1987; Harris, 1992; Heath, 1989; Holloway, 1990; Stuckey, 1987). Spirituality, a recognizable feature in African cultures worldwide, is a distinctive and profoundly important dimension of African American cultural knowledge and consciousness as well (Cone, 1972; Drake, 1977; Levine, 1977; Mitchell, 1991; Richards, 1980; Thompson, 1983). It is expressed in both religious music, such as spirituals, and the secularized blues. According to Cone, this spirituality, and particularly the blues, affirms the worth of Black humanity (Allen, 1991), embraces the value of universal humanism, and acknowledges but refuses to accept "the absurdity of White society" (Cone, 1972; p. 117). The literature also suggests that African American cultural knowledge includes a "distinctly African American mode of rationality" that evolved out of the shared history of "resistance against the various effects of capitalism and racism" (B. Gordon, 1985b, p. 7).

Competing Perspectives and Positions. The suggestion that African Americans share a distinct cultural perspective or worldview evokes skepticism about the cultural and "racial identity politics" that are implied. Scholars writing from within various theoretical positions—about African American social thought, Black studies, and multicultural education reforms, for example, including Black feminist scholars and literary critics and theorists—tend to stress the importance of recognizing gender and social-class differences. Emphasis is also placed on the "duality" of African American identity (Gates, 1992b; Marable, 1993). What many perceive to be problematic and to which they take exception in "narrow notions of Afro-American identity" (Giroux, 1992, p. 127) that are equated with African-centered theorizing includes: "scholarly" versus "vulgar" positivist claims to universality and cultural "authenticity" (Lemelle, 1993; Marable, 1993); "an untenable binary opposition" or (false) dichotomy between Europeans/Africans or Whites/Blacks (White, 1990, p. 84); "ethnic absolutisms" (Gilroy, 1993, p. 3); or unitary, fixed, biological conceptions of cultural identity that are reflected in conceptions of the "subject" as generically White/female or Black/male (Gates, 1992b; Giroux, 1992; S. Hall, 1991; Guy-Sheftall, 1992; hooks, 1984, 1990; hooks & West, 1991; Said, 1993; West, 1993). Black feminist scholar D. K. King (1988) criticizes the "theoretical invisibility of black women" in "mainstream" scholarship and Black studies, while Collins (1990) locates her theoretical analysis of Black women's thought and experience in the nexus of race, class, and gender *within* an Afrocentric epistemological paradigm. She defines Black women's standpoint as Afrocentric feminist consciousness:

Because Black women have access to both the Afrocentric and the feminist standpoints, an alternative epistemology used to rearticulate a black women's standpoint should reflect elements of both traditions.... While an Afrocentric feminist epistemology reflects elements of epistemologies used by African-Americans and women as groups, it also paradoxically demonstrates features that may be unique to Black women. (pp. 206–207)

White (1990), on the other hand, is critical of both Afrocentric theorizing and Collins's Afrocentric feminist standpoint. White asserts that "Black feminists do not have any essential, biologically-based claim on understanding black women's experience" because this group is "divided by class, region, and sexual orientations" (p. 82). White also argues that Afrocentric theorizing, like the Eurocentric perspective it criticizes, is essentially positivist, and therefore also makes false claims to

universal truth (p. 93). Other objections are raised based on the perception that this theoretic is counterproductive to interracial collaboration, that it represents a form of racial "essentialism," "cultural separation," or an overdetermined modernist notion of the "fixed subject" (McCarthy & Crichlow, 1993). Giroux (1992) suggests that the writing of women of color avoids such problems (pp. 113–118). In a discussion of "some meanings of blackness," Gates (1992b, pp. 131–151) disparages what he calls "the paranoid dream of cultural autarky." Gates indicates his preference for "blackness without blood," that is to say, "elective affinities, unburdened by an ideology of descent" over the "cultural ensolacements of nationalism" (p. 151).

S. A. Clarke (1991) describes some positive uses of a "soft" racial identity politics. Clarke acknowledges that "political practices and mobilizations that are based on cultural and social identities" such as race have "serious limitations," but he argues that racial identity politics "also embody possibilities for empowerment" because "the most powerful constructions of common sense about identity politics . . . are deeply influenced by racial symbols, racial meanings, and racial understandings" (p. 37). Yet this potential for empowerment must contend with "formidable hostility," because political mobilizations around race appear (to liberals and conservatives) to constitute a "danger to the body politic" (p. 37). That is, "identity politics are positioned"—in a socially constructed and media-supported "common sense" way—"to starkly reflect the need for a reassertion of 'traditional' liberal values of individualism, privatism, and authoritarian nationalism" (p. 38). Progressives argue that racial identity politics ignore divergent cultural differences within groups (e.g., immigrant Africans, Haitians) and block class-based coalition building with other groups (Marable, 1993). Clarke suggests, however, that

social representations—narratives, symbols, images—that privilege race as a sign of social disorder and civic decay can be thought of as part of a socially constructed "fear of a black planet" that has traditionally functioned to blunt progressive political possibilities. (p. 38)

"Fear of a Black Planet," an allusion to a popular politically oriented rap album, also applies to hostile reactions to African-centered theorizing and practice. One problem, of course, is who decides what is progressive (or valid), and by which criteria? Clearly, the race of the protagonists in such discussions is not a reliable indicator either of their political perspective or theoretical position.

Cultural Assimilation/Miseducation/Liberation. It is not necessary to conclude that African American social thought is homogenous to recognize that one of its predominant concerns, well-represented in the work of DuBois (H. Aptheker, 1973), Woodson (1933), and others, is the relationship between preserving African American cultural originality and liberating education. In his introduction to a collection of essays on the education of Black people, H. Aptheker, DuBois's editor and biographer (and a radical White historian in his own right), explains that:

DuBois saw education (to be truly education) as partisan and—given the realities of the social order—fundamentally subversive. Specifically, in this connection, he wrote as a Black man in the United States; in this sense he was concerned in the first place with the education of his people in the United States, and that education as part of the process of the liberation of his people. Thus, his writing on education—as on everything else—has a kind of national consciousness, a specific motivation which—while directed towards his people—at the same time and therefore was meant to serve all humanity. (p. xi)

That education ought to be for service to "all humanity" while preserving African American culture—and not just for class-based personal gain and profit making—constituted no contradiction for DuBois. This is indicative of the significant human interest in the social thought of African American intellectuals like DuBois who were at the same time committed to "saving the race" (Carruthers, 1994). One of DuBois's last commentaries on this matter was written in 1960, just three years before his death:

Any statement of our desire to develop American Negro culture, to keep up our ties with coloured people, to remember our past is being regarded as "racism." I, for instance, who have devoted my life to efforts to break down racial barriers, am being accused of desiring to emphasize differences of race. This has a certain truth about it. (quoted in H. Aptheker, 1973, p. 150)

It is interesting to note that scholars of various persuasions cite DuBois's (1903/1953) *The Souls of Black Folk* to support both pluralist and nationalist interpretations of the aims of Black studies, curriculum transformation, and social action (Gates, 1992a, p. 6; Marable, 1993, p. 121; Stuckey, 1987). However, DuBois explained that he was "not fighting to settle the question of racial equality" in America by "getting rid of black folk" (p. 150). Rather his commitment was to the "possibility of black folk and their cultural patterns existing in America without discrimination; and on terms of equality" (p. 150). This requires the "preservation of African history and culture as a valuable contribution to modern civilization as it was to medieval and ancient civilization" (pp. 150–151).

DuBois's commitment to these multiple goals was long-term and not one-dimensional. As early as 1897 he wrote that he did not believe Black folk were destined to "imitate Anglo-Saxon culture" but to maintain an "originality which shall unswervingly follow Negro ideals" (Stuckey, 1987, p. 398, n. 59). According to Stuckey, DuBois "considered originality the highest nationalist objective intellectually and spiritually" yet he also expressly admired aspects of Euro-American culture and emphasized the worth of all humanity (p. 398, n. 61). In order to take into consideration the importance of economic and psychological factors, Stuckey notes that DuBois later modified his early belief in "racial gifts as the motive force of history" (pp. 265; 398, n. 59).

This commitment to uplifting humanity by struggling to transform the United States into a "socially just society" (Semmes, 1992, p. 73) while valorizing African American culture and autonomy is an important dimension of the tradition of Black studies and African American social thought (Childs,

1989). Other Black intellectuals who have demonstrated this commitment (the list could be longer) include Ida B. Wells-Barnett (1969), John Henrik Clarke (Adams, 1992; J. H. Clarke, 1992), Anna Julia Cooper (Carby, 1987; Cooper, 1892/1988), Vincent Harding (1974, 1990), C. L. R. James (Hamilton, 1992, C. L. R. James, 1948, 1970), Arturo Schomburg (Childs, 1989), and Sylvia Wynter (1992b, 1992c). As Frazier (1973) also observed, this struggle requires "intellectual freedom" from "an implied or unconscious assimilationist philosophy, holding that Negroes should enter the mainstream of American life as rapidly as possible leaving behind their social heritage and becoming invisible as soon as possible" (p. 56). Earlier, Woodson (1933) had described how the "mis-education of the Negro" produced the abject conformity that contributed to this "failure of the Negro intellectual" that Frazier (1957, 1973) and Cruse (1967) also criticize.

HEGEMONY/AUTONOMY: CULTURE-CENTERED KNOWLEDGE AND CURRICULUM TRANSFORMATION

The remainder of this chapter will use the formulation of CCK presented earlier to compare different forms of culture-centered knowledge in educational discourse and curriculum transformation. Culture-centered knowledge that represents divergent conceptions of "difference" and social interest can be organized into four overlapping categories of curriculum transformation. The knowledge in these categories is identified as culture-centered because each category is associated with a type of curriculum transformation (or restoration) that can serve a socially integrating function in behalf of a particular social framework. The four categories are: *Marginalizing Knowledge, Invisibilizing Knowledge, Expanding Knowledge,* and *Deciphering Knowledge.* Each category corresponds to divergent ways of perceiving and knowing social reality, particularly with regard to the social constructions of "sameness" or "difference." These social constructions have implications for the way social interests are represented—as "indivisible," for example, or as "communities of interest." Table 16–1 shows the four categories of culture-centered knowledge and curriculum transformation in relation to the conception of sameness/difference and the interest with which each is associated.

As Table 16–1 shows, these categories are also identified with hegemony or autonomy. As such, each also involves domi-

TABLE 16–1. Categories of
Culture-Centered Knowledge and
Curriculum Transformation

Hegemony/Sameness Indivisible Interest	Autonomy/Difference Communities of Interest
Marginalizing Knowledge	Expanding Knowledge
Invisibilizing Knowledge	Deciphering Knowledge

nating or liberating forms of curriculum transformation and education practice as social action. The two categories identified with hegemony and indivisible social interests are Marginalizing Knowledge and Invisibilizing Knowledge. Both emphasize sameness; that is, the social construction of difference (as sameness) corresponds to a unitary conception of social interests, but to a greater (Invisibilizing Knowledge) or lesser (Marginalizing Knowledge) extent. Expanding Knowledge and Deciphering Knowledge are forms of curriculum transformation that can be identified with autonomy; that is, knowledge and curriculum transformation in these categories are autonomous or free to a greater (Deciphering Knowledge) or lesser (Expanding Knowledge) extent from socially constructed cognitive constraints (beliefs) that suppress difference. Under such conditions of autonomy, culture-centered curriculum knowledge values cultural difference and recognizes diverse communities of social interests. Democracy or "pluralism without hierarchy" (Asante, 1992, p. 22) and cultural affirmation is the "Ideological" interest (in the Wynterian sense) in the social framework this type of curriculum transformation seeks to bring about. These four categories, as presented here, are not intended to be mutually exclusive but are dynamically interrelated. Each one contains in itself the conditions of possibility of another category (C. L. R. James, 1948).

Marginalizing Knowledge

Marginalizing Knowledge is a form of curriculum transformation that can include selected "multicultural" curriculum content that simultaneously distorts both the historical and social reality that people actually experienced. Marginalization can take the form of bias and omission (McCarthy, 1990; Swartz, 1992), but it is most particularly a form of selective inclusion. The ideology of pluralism in California's *History/Social Science Framework* (California State Department of Education [CSDE], 1987) and state-adopted textbooks illustrates this kind of Marginalizing Knowledge in the transformation of a curriculum. This form of marginalizing inclusion is justified in the (indivisible) interest of "our common culture." That diverse cultures make the United States a multicultural society; that the perspectives of diverse groups should be acknowledged; and that the right to "be different" should be "respected" are clearly stated principles in this document. The *Framework* also states that it "incorporates a multicultural perspective throughout" (CSDE, p. 5). However, the ideology of pluralism in this curriculum guide marginalizes the actual experiences of African Americans, Latinos, and American Indians in the development of U.S. society. This is done through the use of conceptual terms that privilege the historical experiences of White Euro-American immigrant groups. J. E. King (1992) and Wynter (1992a) analyze the conceptual flaws in the *Framework* and the state-adopted textbooks; they demonstrate how the conceptualizations of "immigrant" and "immigration" in these curriculum materials reify the historical experiences of dominant Whites and rationalize the social construction of racial hierarchy and societal inequity in textbooks. These representations of "our common culture" mask the enduring significance of racial and cultural social divisions.

An example from the *Framework's* course guide for the fifth-grade "story of the development of the nation" is illustrative. The focus is on "one of the most remarkable stories in history: the creation of a new nation peopled by *immigrants* from all parts of the globe" (CSDE, 1987, p. 50, emphasis added). In chapter one of the state-approved fifth-grade textbook, *America Will Be* (Armento, Nash, Salter, & Wixson, 1991), ideological representations of this (mis)conceptualization are stated as incontrovertible fact (about which historians agree). This statement appears in the text: "Everyone who lives in the United States is either an immigrant or a descendant of immigrants." Alongside it, to provide reinforcement, a study question asks: "Why do you think historians call the United States 'a nation of immigrants?'" (p. 13). The contradictory interests that are suppressed by this representation of everyone in the United States in terms of the idealized Euro-American immigrant "model of being" becomes apparent when this construct is applied to the actual historical experiences of American Indians, Native Hawaiians and Alaskans, or the indigenous peoples of the Southwest and their ongoing struggles over the land, including disputed claims, resistance to the disposal of toxic wastes in their communities, their rights to natural resources, and their right not to be treated as "illegal aliens" in their ancestral homelands. This representation makes the African American experience of enslavement an anomaly of the normative cultural model (J. E. King, 1992).

Yet students are to be taught that all groups have the same indivisible social interest. Descriptions of U.S. society as a "common community" that mask the racially and economically divided social reality is another way that dominant-group interests are represented as the indivisible interest of all individuals and groups. Consider this statement:

We are strong because we are united in a pluralistic society of many races, cultures, and ethnic groups; we have built a great nation because we have learned to live in peace with each other, respecting each other's right to be different and supporting each other as members of a common community. (CSDE, 1987, p. 56)

This *Framework* passage adroitly transforms difference into a form of homogenizing pluralism or sameness in the ostensible interest of "our common public culture." According to J. E. King (1992), possible interests of dominant power groups that are at stake in the promulgation of this form of culture-centered knowledge include the official validation of "established" scholars and the reification of the White Euro-American immigrant experience as a model of success to be emulated by Latino and Asian immigrant "newcomers." This representation of social reality does not provide students with culture-centered knowledge needed to critique the basis of social cohesion in the U.S. social framework (e.g., the belief structure of race) or the motivation to participate in continued struggle against racism and injustice (J. E. King, 1992, pp. 324–326). B. Gordon (1992) suggests that this may be because "pluralism is used and defended in the United States because pluralism can assist the dominant power in maintaining their structures" (p. 28). Gates (1992b) ridicules this critical view of the "ideology of pluralism" as a kind of delusion of a "Hard Left" position.

To "caricature" this position, Gates states that this ideology is "distasteful" for the "Left" (in contrast to a "liberal pluralist" position) because it "disguises real power relations ... leaves the concept of hegemony unnamed ... fails to be adequately emancipatory [and] it leaves oppressive structures intact" (p. 177).

Invisibilizing Knowledge

Curriculum transformation and knowledge in this category also serve the ideology of the sameness and indivisibility of social interests, but not in terms of pluralism. Rather, Invisibilizing Knowledge is monocultural; it simply obliterates the historical presence, unique experience, contributions, and perspectives of diverse people in the development of the United States and Western civilization. This category can include not only forms of erasure but also defamation or denial of group achievements (LaFrance, 1992). The interest involved is the restoration or preservation of Western cultural and intellectual dominance through the curriculum. This occurs in curriculum narratives like the "We-came-to-an-empty-land" White colonial settler identity story of the development of the United States, and the "Our-Western-heritage-of-Ancient-Rome-Greece-Egypt-and-Sumer-but-not-Africa" White ethnic identity story (Bernal, 1987; Diop, 1981; Hilliard, 1992; Young, 1990).

The "we" and "our" terms induce the conceptually excluded to identify with these social constructions of the self-identity of the dominant group (LaFrance, 1992; Martinez, 1992/1993; Wynter, 1992a). Such narratives also constitute a discourse of cultural hegemony that transmutes the "real environment" (Fasheh, 1990) into an ideological one: Cultural identity is positioned hegemonically within the dominant group's social interest. This erasure does not just marginalize difference; it obliterates the self-identities and communities of interest of the dominated as well. Paradoxically, this erasure may even be achieved by means of "structured absences" and silences on certain topics (Morrison, 1989) that writers use to construct an imagined "White self" or national identity. Curriculum restoration of Western dominance through Invisibilizing Knowledge is articulated by Neusner (1989) in an example of CCK that is vigorously defended as universally valid objective scholarship in the popular media (Leo, 1989) and in academic writing such as this:

A critical question that demands our study of other cultures is why it is that the West has created what the rest of the world now wants. Why did capitalism not begin in India, for example? ... Why is there no science in Africa? Why has democracy only been grafted onto the political structures in Asia? And conversely, why are all of them to be found indigenously in the West? To answer such questions, we must begin where science, economics, politics, and technology began and from whence they were diffused. They uniquely flourished in the West, and, to begin with, in Western Europe. (Neusner, 1989, p. B1)

Sizemore (1990, p. 78) cites the above statement to make the point that such claims to the superiority, objectivity, and universality of the disciplines of Western knowledge are themselves based on "distinctly political ideologies" (p. 77). Consequently, the sociohistorical record becomes an unrelenting monocul-

tural narrative of White superiority, while denial of any influence of culture and ideology on knowledge also invisibilizes the connection between the power to define reality and ideological distortions of knowledge and curriculum transformation (restoration). Both Expanding Knowledge and Invisibilizing Knowledge are responses to the moral and epistemological panics discussed above.

Expanding Knowledge

The other two categories of curriculum transformation recognize that various perspectives on knowledge, divergent social interests, and multiple social identities exist in consequence of the diversity of people's historical and lived experiences. In the Expanding Knowledge category curriculum transformation incorporates multiple narratives and rotating standpoints from which to view and interpret social reality, such as "from the margin to the center" (hooks, 1984). This category can be likened to an "additive" model of multicultural curriculum change (Banks, 1989). Curriculum transformation that expands knowledge can replace "Whiteness" in the mode of the subject (the normative representation of the social framework's desired self) with a racially "hybrid" middle-classness (not homelessness or wagelessness). However, this rotation in the perspective of the subject can multiculturalize knowledge without changing fundamentally the norm of middle-classness in the social framework's cultural model of being (Wynter, 1992c). With the expansion and inclusion of the multiple perspectives of diverse "Others," traditional knowledge in the curriculum and the disciplines can be multiculturalized and thereby "saved" (Wynter, 1992c). Only "incremental additions to a body of knowledge" (Aldridge, 1992, p. 65) or to the disciplines are possible as curriculum expands in this way (Asante, 1992, pp. 22–23). These additions do not undo, uninvent, or uncover the social framework's prescriptive rules governing inclusion and exclusion (Wynter, 1992b, 1992c). Ishmael Reed's (1993) novel about multicultural change at a fictional college satirizes this limitation of Expanding Knowledge. As the number of oppositional (i.e., multicultural) studies programs increase and vie for centrality, Professor Puttbutt, the novel's Black protagonist, concludes sardonically that "Everybody was a nigger.... Women, gays, always comparing their situations [subject positions] with blacks" (p. 9). In other words, traditional disciplines can be transformed (e.g., "multiculturalized," "genderized," or "Africanized") by adding the perspectives of the formerly excluded, but fundamental assumptions of human existence in the social organization of knowledge can remain unquestioned and thereby leave in place faulty conceptions of being within those disciplines.

The inclusion of African American literature at all levels of education is a common form of curriculum transformation in the category of Expanding Knowledge (McElroy-Johnson, 1993; Spears-Bunton, 1990). Gates (1992a, 1992b) is widely recognized for his successful efforts to "open up" mainstream literature to include a Black literary canon. Both Gates (1988) and Baker (1984) have used "vernacular" forms of African American expressive culture like blues music and "signifyin'" (indirect, boastful, critical, or reproachful speech) to articulate complex, complementary theories of the distinctive character of African American literature and writing. Their stated aim is to "enlarge" the literary canon by institutionalizing this vernacular tradition (Gates, 1992a, 1992b). Although Gates (1988, p. 259, n. 5) credits Baker with strongly influencing his thinking, and Baker indicates that he suggested that Gates use the word *vernacular* for his theory of literary criticism (p. 111), the two scholars alternately support and publicly criticize each other's work. For instance, Baker "signifies" on Gates's (1988) theory of signifyin' with this bit of doggerel by the poet Amiri Baraka: "When I die, the consciousness I carry I will to black people. May they pick me apart and take the useful parts, the sweet meat of my feelings. And leave the bitter bullshit rotten white parts alone" (Baker, 1984, p. 111).

Baker's point is to accuse Gates of "curiously apolitical" arguments about the meaning of the vernacular tradition and to equate "the bitter ... rotten white parts" of Gates's literary theory with a "troubling" and "overly professional careerist" approach. Baker criticizes what he regards as elitism in Gates's use of vernacular forms (Baker, 1988, pp. 103–104), as well as his appropriation of this tradition for careerist ends (Baker, 1993, pp. 64–65). Christian (1989) and R. Gilmore (1993) also caution that the "system" can "reproduce itself" through the work of "individualistic" scholars who have become a "multi-culturalized professional managerial class" by virtue of opportunistically studying whatever is "politically and oppositionally 'new'" (R. Gilmore, 1993, pp. 71–72). According to Gilmore,

this individualistic "careerism in academic work" promotes one particular aspect of social change without integrating that struggle into the larger struggle ... [but] assigns primary importance to the fact—and survival—of oppositional studies within the social structure of the university.... (p. 72)

West (1990) argues against scholarly textual analysis that is disassociated from the "effects and consequences these dismantlings have in relation to the operations of military, economic and social power" (p. 588).

In Wynter's (1992c) estimation, the theory of literary criticism offered by Gates does not liberate people's knowledge and consciousness from dominating social constructs, but is instead a culturally original way of *interpreting* Black texts. Wynter is also doubtful about the establishment of what she calls Gates's "ethno-literary" or "cultural-indigenous" school of thought in the arts (pp. 263–266). In sum, individual scholars and practitioners engaged in Expanding Knowledge may exercise sufficient cognitive autonomy to increase the available perspectives, but perhaps not so "vastly" as is often asserted (Adell, 1990; Baker, 1984, p. 63; Gates, 1992a; Giroux, 1992; West, 1993). Other critical analyses of Black vernacular traditions (Childs, 1989; Cone, 1972; Stuckey, 1987), when compared to theorizing that is aimed primarily at institutionalizing a Black literary canon, reveal autonomous critiques of the social framework in African American thought that are articulated in analyses that not only expand but transcend the "mainstream" canon. As Frazier (1973) once observed:

The philosophy implicit in the folklore of the Negro folk is infinitely superior in wisdom and intellectual candor to the empty repetition of platitudes concerning brotherly love and human dignity of Negro intellectuals who are tyrants within the Negro world and never had a[n] [autonomous] thought in their lives. (p. 60)

These limitations of curriculum transformation through Expanding Knowledge are also suggested in a critical comparison of "capitalistic" and "democratic" versus "liberationist" forms of Afrocentrism (Weider, 1992).

Other forms of curriculum transformation that involve Expanding Knowledge in schools and the academy include collaborative efforts among teachers, students, and researchers to recover and use in school learning students' cultural knowledge related to their home and community experiences (Wiggington, 1989). Lee (1991, 1992) extends Gates's theory of African American vernacular oral traditions to create "culturally sensitive scaffolding," an innovative teaching strategy that uses "students' existing cultural knowledge" of traditional African American community language practices like signifyin' to enable them to interpret figurative language in Black literary texts. Moll, Amanti, Neff, and Gonzalez (1992) are training teachers to use the tools of anthropology to study the "funds of knowledge" in the households of Mexican American and African American families. A team of researchers and teachers then translates this cultural knowledge into meaningful classroom lessons. The object in both of these research projects is the improvement of student academic learning. Sleeter and Grant (1991) also provide ethnographic data that supports, as an alternative to disabling, reified school knowledge, the use of students' cultural knowledge to expand classroom lessons and teach students more productively (p. 56).

Deciphering Knowledge

Examination of the theoretical and literary analyses of Wynter (1984, 1989, 1991, 1992a, 1992c) and Morrison (1989, 1992) will show that Deciphering Knowledge that is aimed at changed consciousness and cognitive autonomy can be a foundation for curriculum transformation. This is not to imply that Deciphering Knowledge alone can change society; social action directed at fundamental social change requires the "emancipation of human cognition" (C. L. R. James, 1948; Semmes, 1992). Both Wynter and Morrison use a theoretical and methodological vocabulary like that of Foucault's (1972) "archaeology of knowledge" to expose the belief structure of race in literature, school texts (Wynter, 1992a), and other discursive practices. Foucault's method involves "deciphering," "excavating," and analyzing "discursive literary formations" in the social organization of knowledge "whose lineage can be traced and whose regularities are discoverable" (Baker, 1984, pp. 17–18). Wynter locates her theoretical project within Black studies and describes her method as a "deciphering practice." She uses Foucault's (1970) insights regarding knowledge and power to "decipher" the governing cultural rules of knowledge in the academic disciplines and in society. One such rule is the classifying duality of "conceptual" Whiteness and Blackness, which, Wynter (1984, 1989, 1992b) argues, sustains and legitimates human misery.

In two analytical essays, Morrison (1989, 1992) examines critically the socially constructed nature of Whiteness and

Blackness in the "literary imagination." Morrison deciphers the presence and use of invented "ideological Africanism" in fiction (1992, p. 80) by "excavating" the "denotative and connotative blackness that African peoples have come to signify" in literature (p. 6). She writes:

Africanism is the vehicle by which the American self knows itself as not enslaved, but free; not repulsive, but desirable; not helpless, but licensed and powerful; not history-less, but historical; not damned, but innocent; not a blind accident of evolution, but a progressive fulfillment of destiny. (p. 52)

Together these analyses demonstrate the liberating possibilities of curriculum transformation that uses autonomous culture-centered knowledge to decipher the social framework and the social organization of knowledge that legitimates it.

The Perspective Advantage of "Alterity"

Wynter's (1992a) examination of the belief structure of race suggests that the social constructions of Blackness/Whiteness embedded in literature that Morrison has uncovered reveal the "cultural mode of rationality" of the social framework. Wynter demonstrates that the founding integrative conception of the U.S. social framework is a "prescriptive value-opposition between Black and White" (p. 7), to which the society's racially based classifying system—or episteme that values and ranks people, their knowledge, and culture unequally—is a *logical* response. Within this classifying system, the conceptual Black is the alter ego (of the conceptual White) that "embodies the alternative of (Nigger) chaos" (Wynter, 1984, p. 2) to the "orthodox behaviors" that express the "normative national [White] identity" (Wynter, 1992a, p. 17). This conceptual difference between Blackness and Whiteness is the CCK upon which racialized social cohesion and inequity are founded. Wynter analyzes the epistemology of this prescriptive conception of human difference and concludes that *alterity* gives Black studies a perspective advantage. Semmes also argues that the "normative Eurocentric propensity" of cultural hegemony gives an advantage to Black studies as a social and epistemological critique (Semmes, 1992, p. 44).

This perspective advantage is not due to an inherent racial/cultural difference, Wynter (1992a) argues, but is the result of the dialectical nature of constructed otherness that prescribes the liminal status of Blacks (and, e.g., American Indians) as beyond the normative boundary of the conception of Self/Other. A. Davis (1983a) makes an analogous observation about the dialectical nature of the Black/White experience of oppression/liberation, or what Morrison describes as the "parasitical nature of white freedom" (Morrison, 1992, p. 57). This perspective advantage of alterity can be likened to the "second-sight" Negroes are "gifted with" in the "American world" (DuBois, 1903/1953, pp. 16–17). This is not a racial advantage but a function of the normative racial categories of value that are operative in the social framework.

Reasoning that curriculum transformation that simply adds on multiple perspectives (i.e., by "pivoting" the center) is inherently more inclusive (or valid) than a Black studies or Afri-

can-centered perspective, because more perspectives are included, accepts an "either/or" epistemology that elides the particularity of the "Black perspective" (Drake, 1987, p. 1). The alternative suggested herein is not a dualistic position that there are multiple (and equally partial) standpoints that are either equally valid (because equally partial) or inexorably ranked hierarchically. Recognizing the alterity perspective of Black studies (or "seeing with Indian eyes, as well") does not essentialize "Blackness" as a homogenizing reverse epistemic (West, 1990, p. 585). Nor does Wynter's analysis of the perspective of alterity reduce the social complexity to a single explanatory factor. At times other differences (e.g., gender) may assume centrality in an analysis of the social reality, but *within* the belief system of race, given the way the classifying system of race functions as a belief structure in the society. Collins (1990) also recognizes the contradictions and limitations of "either/or" epistemology with respect to the intersection of race, class, and gender (pp. 206–207, 230–235). The alternative to the prescriptive hierarchy of Otherness, insofar as curriculum transformation is concerned, is neither imposing an inverted "Black over White" hegemony nor emphasizing "multiple identities." The solution Wynter proposes is abolition of the race-based classifying belief structure itself (Wynter, 1992b, 1992c).

The next section of this chapter, which further considers the social effects of Deciphering Knowledge and its explanatory power to penetrate social myths, suggests a specific role for Black studies in curriculum transformation that abolishes this belief structure. It is also important to emphasize that the referent social framework of the deciphering culture-centered knowledge in the work of Morrison and Wynter is not a world dominated by Blackness or a world that multiculturalizes the Other and leaves conceptual Blackness intact. Rather, the social "Imaginary" (Wynter, 1989, p. 639) is the "newly defined world" (Harding, 1970, p. 290) that will "hold all the people" (p. 292) and constitute an altogether different "order of knowledge" and "changed quality of consciousness" (Blumenburg, 1983, p. 205; cited in Wynter, 1989, p. 643). According to Wynter, cognitive autonomy from the social framework's existing "cultural specific model of reality" is a necessity of human freedom (pp. 640–641). This suggests that liberating education can make more visible "the mode of production of the symbolic" (Simon, 1992, pp. 109–110) as well as the "real environment and power relations" (Fasheh, 1990, p. 28).

This section presented four types of culture-centered knowledge and curriculum transformation that can be identified with hegemony or autonomy. The next section presents a further explication of the belief structure of race in the work of Wynter and Morrison.

DECIPHERING THE SOCIAL ORGANIZATION OF KNOWLEDGE

Henry and Buhle (1992) note that Wynter's "critical works contain one of the most powerful and comprehensive recastings of the problems of colonial discourses in the light of post-structuralist theory" (p. 116). Their assessment is perhaps a reflection of the interdisciplinary breadth and scope of Wynter's theoretical project. Her analysis of the belief structure of race draws together recent theory in biology, environmental studies, the history of European thought and colonization of the "New World," and African/Diaspora theorizing and social analysis. It presents a comprehensive, interdisciplinary analysis of the epistemological and axiological foundations of a Black studies approach to curriculum transformation. Wynter's theoretical project is grounded in a commitment to scientific description and ethical concern for social justice that is shared by other Caribbean, African, and African American scholars, including Angela Davis (U.S., 1983a, 1983b), Chiekh Anta Diop (Senegal, 1981), Frantz Fanon (Martinique and Algeria, 1963), Elsa Goveia (Jamaica, 1970), Vincent Harding (U.S., 1970, 1974, 1990), C. L. R. James (Trinidad, 1948, 1963), Asmarom Legesse (Eritrea, 1973), Donna M. Richards (U.S., 1980; Ani, 1994), Walter Rodney (Guyana, 1975, 1990), Arturo Schomburg (U.S., Childs, 1989), Ida B. Wells-Barnett (U.S., 1969), and Carter G. Woodson (U.S., 1933), to name only a few. One of Wynter's major contributions is that her work brings together elements of a transnational tradition of intellectual autonomy in African/Diaspora social thought. Wynter (1989) points out, for instance, that Frantz Fanon (1963) and the Martiniquan writer Edouard Glissant (1981) had been "impelled" by their recognition of the "Abject Otherness" of African-descent people to raise the "question of the historical and, therefore, relative nature of our modes of subjectivity" *before* Foucault (1970, 1972) was awakened to this problem in the aftermath of the 1968 "cultural revolts" in France (Wynter, 1989, p. 640).

Wynter's work extends that of African American scholars like George Washington Ellis, an ethnographer whose work appears in the *Journal of Race and Development* as early as 1915, W. E. B. DuBois, and Carter G. Woodson, who raised the issue of subjectivity in racist scholarly justifications of slavery (Childs, 1989, pp. 83–87). According to Childs, "Ellis argued that scholarly activity had to be moved from the ideological position of racism to the ideological position of democracy" (p. 87). Childs notes that Ellis's "sense of the partiality of knowledge" was "intimately linked" to his "belief in the multifariousness of social reality" (p. 94). Ida B. Wells-Barnett exposed economic motives for the lynching of African Americans that were masked in racial and sexual rationalizations (B. Aptheker, 1982; Carby, 1987; A. Davis, 1983b; Wells-Barnett, 1969).

Deciphering the Belief Structure of Race

Wynter uses an interdisciplinary approach across the humanities and science to decipher the belief structure of race as a founding element of the Western model of culture, knowledge, and the "mode of the subject." This "cultural model analysis" calls for a *rewriting* of the academic disciplines from a "Black Studies Intellectual Perspective" (of alterity). This belief structure is *in* the disciplines and needs to be abolished in order to "emancipate human knowledge" from the semiolinguistic (symbolic) rules of inclusion/exclusion—the sign systems that inhere in the very "Founding Narratives of Origin" that "we tell ourselves." These rules govern all human cultures (Wynter, 1991, 1992c). Wynter argues that as humans we are neither consciously aware of them nor do we knowingly

choose these behavior-orienting rules because we are subjects within an episteme or our "order of knowledge" and, as such, we are "always already" socialized by these rules. (The term *always already,* as used by Derrida, 1976, denotes the socially determining power of language practices and is frequently found in the work of scholars writing from within "poststructuralist" and "deconstructionist" theoretical positions.) These governing rules represent the order's "desired mode of the subject" to us—what it means, for example, to be a good man or woman—and govern our behaviors and attitudes towards ourselves and others. Wynter explains how our present order of knowledge came into being.

Feudal Europe's "theocentric" order of scholastic knowledge was founded on a unifying narrative that was eventually overturned by the emergent class of lay humanists who had been "written" out of that order's story (culture-centered knowledge of what it meant to be a human). In the feudal theocracy, because only God's "Word" was knowable, only the clergy could "know." To break with this epistemic order, lay humanists like Columbus and Copernicus reinvented "Man" and the universe in relation to the established order that was dominated by God and the Church, and in the process reconceptualized what was ultimately knowable by man (Foucault, 1970; Wynter, 1991). (The belief in women's "naturally" sinful nature and lower order of being as an obstacle to knowledge was not overturned.)

As the feudal order was giving way to mercantilism and ultimately to capitalism, this rupture was paving the way for the "Age of Reason" and the "Enlightenment." Thus, new possibilities of scientific knowledge and "discovery" of new lands and peoples ensued—all of which was literally *un*thinkable within the previous scholastic order of knowledge. Our existing order of knowledge has given us symbolically constructed categories of subjective identity—categories of the desired "Self" and "Other" (Wynter, 1989)—that have "ordered human groups in terms of degrees of possession of (or lack of) reason" and justified the domination of peoples who lack these desired qualities (Henry & Buhle, 1992, p. 117). The terms of inclusion/exclusion, for example, include: head/body; civilized/primitive; order/chaos; parent/child; us/not us; and property/no property (p. 117). Europeans justified their colonial domination of others in these terms, and the colonized have been socially induced to adopt dislocating, disorienting, hegemonic self-definitions within the terms of this dominant order of knowledge that defines them as Other and "establishes the bases of [their] self-negating and imitative behavior" (p. 118).

Deciphering Invented Africanism/The White Literary Imagination

Morrison (1992) deciphers the ways that race, in the form of invented "Africanism," functions dialectically in literature and in the social imagination of White authors and readers. "Through a close look at 'literary blackness,'" she writes, "it may be possible to discover 'literary whiteness'" (p. 9). Morrison examines the "impact of racial hierarchy, racial exclusion, and racial vulnerability and availability" in fiction on non-Black readers and writers (p. 11). This examination of the "problem that race causes" in the nation's literature (p. 14) shows how writers position readers as "white" by using "serviceable" representations of "the Black." Thus Morrison's analysis also reveals how the "sycophancy of white identity" (p. 19) functions hegemonically in these relations of representation. Because hegemony legitimates the social framework's White normative cultural model of being and identity, the analyses by both Wynter and Morrison suggest that Black people's humanity can only be affirmed and valued—and everyone else freed from the conceptual incarceration of the belief structure of race—if society is reinvented and reorganized around a different cultural model of the human. As Morrison explains: "Statements to the contrary, insisting on the meaninglessness of race to the American identity are themselves full of meaning. The world does not become raceless or will not become unracialized by assertion" (p. 46).

Therefore, a condition of a radically changed social framework is autonomous knowledge, and according to Wynter, autonomous knowledge must include knowledge of the "cultural model" itself. Both Morrison and Wynter point out that the belief structure of race that sustains the existing social framework is built into the culture, in the epistemic or social organization of knowledge, including the education system, the academic disciplines, curriculum knowledge, and the national literature. The disciplines of the West's cultural heritage are deeply implicated. That is why Wynter traces the history of their development through the intellectual, economic, and political expansion that followed the Middle Ages.

A Deciphering Role for Black Studies in Curriculum Transformation

Just as the bourgeoisie had to disestablish (theocentric) scholasticism to find freedom for their own proper being, Wynter (1992c) argues that postcolonial subjects must "establish a new order" of knowledge to get beyond the present crisis of societal and self-negation. Wynter contends that the Black studies intellectual perspective can bring into being an epistemological break from the biological/racial/hierarchical narrative about humanity's origins that "we" still tell ourselves. Wynter finds support for her position in the work of Woodson (1933) and of Fanon, a psychiatrist and revolutionary theoretician who documented his empirical observations of the psychological consequences of "alienating material conditions" and "alienated consciousness" (Hansen, 1977) in his book *Black Skins, White Masks* (Fanon, 1967). As with Fanon, a primary concern of both Wynter and Morrison is to explicate the conditions of human freedom from all forms of alienation and oppression. Since people have the capacity to question and to act upon humanly instituted ideological and self-negating cultural structures, such as the belief in the "genetic defectivity of race," cognitive autonomy is a condition of freedom (Wynter, personal communication, September 15, 1993).

Wynter urges Black studies scholars to investigate the conditions under which autonomous thought and social action are possible. Citing Hartmann's (1980) observation that "literature is to the modern mind as the Bible was to medieval thought," Wynter (1992c, p. 263) points out that literary criticism must

perform a deciphering "allegorical exegesis" to provide cognitive alternatives to the social framework's governing mode of knowledge and being. Wynter's critical aesthetics project is for liberating knowledge not only in behalf of African-descent people, but also for the most inclusive interest of human freedom. Both Wynter and Morrison are contributing to an emergent body of Deciphering Knowledge that exemplifies the dynamically evolving Black studies epistemological critique.

THE PRACTICE OF FREEDOM: DECIPHERING CULTURE-CENTERED KNOWLEDGE

The remainder of this chapter presents selected examples of culture-centered knowledge in research and education practice that deciphers aspects of the social framework to prepare people for the practice of freedom, that is, to change society and themselves (Freire, 1980). It should be clear from the above discussion that culture-centered knowledge can serve different interests and purposes with different outcomes (e.g., invisibilization, marginalization, expanding the canon). The literature discussed below will demonstrate this point further and suggest criteria that can be used to distinguish between the two forms of autonomous culture-centered knowledge identified in this chapter. There are several important reasons to focus on identifying differences between curriculum transformation that expands the canon and Deciphering Knowledge in education practice and research. One is that scholars not only conceptualize Black studies, African-centered, and multicultural curriculum transformation differently, but also conceptualize and use African American cultural knowledge in very different ways in curriculum transformation. A second reason to examine closely such applications of cultural knowledge is because scholars using the same conceptual paradigm and theoretical vocabulary (e.g., Fanon, Foucault, or DuBois) can, of course, reach very different conclusions (Robinson, 1993). For example, Wynter's (1992c) critical exegesis or "re-thinking" of aesthetics identifies "signifying practices" in both popular films and Black music, as do Gates (1988) and Baker (1984, 1993), but with different theoretical aims. In another example, Asante (1992) uses "dislocation, location and relocation" as theoretical terms within the "Afrocentric position" to describe what he calls the "locational fallacy," or what occurs when a person is "de-centered, misoriented, or disoriented" from his or her own cultural reality (p. 20). When writing about theorists who "displace" dominating/colonial representations (master narratives) that relegate difference to marginalized "otherness," Giroux (1992) cites Young's (1990) notion of "dislocating" postcolonial discourse (p. 20).

The literature reviewed in this section of the chapter suggests two primary criteria that can be used to identify Deciphering Knowledge in education practice and research. The first criterion is the *social effects of knowledge,* particularly with respect to the uses of knowledge for social action in organic connection with "the larger struggle for social change" (R. Gilmore, 1993, p. 72). Deciphering Knowledge gives priority to the most urgent needs of real-life citizens as a criterion of validity—as compared to whether new scholarship is institutionalized as a discipline or expands a traditional academic canon. An important example of this criterion is Wynter's insistent plea urging intellectuals to "marry their thought" to the jobless, "the global new poor," or "les damnés (de la terre)" — Fanon's (1963) "wretched of the earth" — the "captive populations of the U.S. inner cities and the Third World shantytown archipelagoes" (Wynter, 1992c, p. 241). Stated another way, Deciphering Knowledge is necessarily holistic, explicitly accountable to and linked to the needs of real communities (J. James, 1993b; Orr, 1992). Both Expanding and Deciphering Knowledge can make useful contributions to curriculum transformation and social action, but by different means. For example, a growing body of African-centered curriculum materials that are not reviewed in this chapter is expanding the curriculum knowledge available to schools.

The ethos of Deciphering Knowledge is nonelitist and inclusive, with regard to the fluid roles of the scholar/activist/knower (intellectual, teacher, student, researcher, or community person), who is committed to rigorous truth-seeking demystification (Harding, 1974; J. James, 1993a; J. James & Farmer, 1993). A second criterion follows from this: the *effects of knowledge on consciousness or cognitive autonomy,* that is, the extent to which culture-centered knowledge penetrates social myths linked to objective and subjective problems of human existence and gives people "power over their own lives" (Boggs, 1974, p. 80). Such knowledge is necessarily nonassimilationist and embraces democratic racial and cultural pluralism. These criteria assume the dialectical mutability of the social framework and people (Giddens, 1979). Liberating, autonomous knowledge can change consciousness, and a new social "Imaginary" (Wynter, 1989) can empower and motivate people to take action, that is, to take charge of their circumstances.

Deciphering Knowledge, Consciousness, and Social Change

This next section presents several examples of research and scholarship that demonstrate these criteria in different contexts, though not necessarily to the same extent. The researchers and practitioners involved aim to make the curriculum and other education practices more liberating and inclusive, while also meeting the real and urgent needs of people by using knowledge for action and change. (Personal biographical information that is included about several researchers, such as race, accords with an "ethic of personal accountability," or a value-based criterion, that Collins, 1990, pp. 216–219, suggests is useful for assessing knowledge claims in an alternative Afrocentric epistemology.)

Education to Govern. Grace Lee Boggs, a Chinese American woman formally trained in philosophy, is a grassroots scholar-activist in the Black community of Detroit. She and her late husband, James Boggs (noted for publications like *Pages from a Negro Worker's Notebook* and *Racism and the Class Struggle*), have been at the forefront of radical social change for decades. An essay Boggs first published in 1970, and still powerfully relevant, critiques society and education from the perspective of the Black experience. As the title of a later version of this essay suggests, "Education: The Great Obsession" (Boggs, 1974), this work penetrates pervasive social myths like "making it"—that is, that education is for "achieving the *good life*" and for "fitting people into the framework of our present industrial society" (p. 72). Although Boggs explains how a new role for education would benefit all students, she demonstrates how the education system works to the particular disadvantage of the Black community. Because the education system supports the social framework, Boggs observes that "the overwhelming majority of black youth see no relationship" between education, "their daily lives in the community or the problems of today's world which affect them so intimately" (p. 69). That is, education promotes opportunist individualism over communal needs; unquestioning acceptance of textbook authority; and irrelevance in the face of changing economic conditions. Boggs proposes a new role for education to prepare students "to govern" in the best interests of their communities and the society. The key principles of this new system of education are:

1. *Education must be based on a philosophy of history* to enable students to realize their "highest potential as a human being" with the "unique capacity . . . to shape and create reality in accordance with conscious purposes and plans" (pp. 72–73).
2. *Education must include clearly defined goals* and social purposes "for changing society and changing ourselves simultaneously" (p. 72).
3. *Education must be responsive to the community,* that is, "the community itself with its needs and problems must become the curriculum of the schools. . . . [T]hrough a realistic curriculum, research becomes a means of building the community. . .rather than pacification programs against the community" (p. 74).
4–5. *Education must include a wide variety of resources and environments* (e.g., the city and countryside, books and computers) and *productive activity* as well, because "experiencing the consequences of their own activity" is the way students learn best (pp. 75–76).
6. *Education must include living struggles* to enable students "to develop the technical skills to rebuild their communities" and "transform themselves along with their communities" (p. 76).
7–8. *Education must include development in bodily self-knowledge and well-being;* and *education must include preparation to govern.* This is because "young people whose *self-concept* has undergone a fundamental change must be given concrete opportunities to change the *actual* conditions of their life" (p. 77, emphasis in original).

Since Boggs first articulated these principles, the U.S. education system has not enabled most young Black people to develop the "sense of black pride, black consciousness, and total rejection of the present social system" that Boggs envisioned (p. 77). Yet a body of scholarship has developed, here and in other parts of the world, that critiques curriculum knowledge and provides empirical and conceptual support for liberating education. This scholarship accords with many of the principles Boggs articulated and contributes in various ways to culture-centered knowledge, curriculum transformation, and pedagogy that can benefit African American students and is also in the interest of a more just and equitable world. Selected examples include:

1. *Critiques of the curriculum/alternative knowledge:* Anyon, 1981; Banks, 1991, 1993; B. Gordon, 1985b; Grant, 1989; Harding, 1970; Hilliard, 1991/1992, 1992; J. E. King, 1992; J. E. King and Wilson, 1990; Ladson-Billings, 1991b; McCarthy, 1990; Obenga, 1990; Sleeter and Grant, 1991.

2. *Teaching approaches that recuperate, valorize, and/or use African American/Diaspora/student cultural knowledge and social practice:* Asante, 1991a; Ballenger, 1992; Heath, 1989; Hollins, 1982; Hollins and Spencer, 1990; Jordan, 1988; J. E. King, 1994; Moses, Kamii, Swap, and Howard, 1989; S. W. Williams, 1991.

3. *Critical teaching of African American literature:* Lee, 1991, 1992; McElroy-Johnson, 1993; Johnson, 1990; Jordan, 1988; Sims, 1982; Spears-Bunton, 1990.

4. *Oppositional/emancipatory pedagogy:* Childs, 1991; Crichlow, Goodwin, Shakes, and Swartz, 1990; J. James and Farmer, 1993; J. E. King, 1990, 1991b; Ladson-Billings and Henry, 1990; MacLeod, 1991; Shujaa, 1994).

These examples and categories are only illustrative and not mutually exclusive. Other sources can be identified related to critical pedagogy, multicultural education, and African-centered curriculum strategies that aim to empower and influence student development positively (e.g., Bigelow, 1990; Gay, 1988; Nieto, 1992; Simon, 1990, 1992; Sleeter & Grant, 1987; Swartz, 1992; Tatum, 1992). An extensive body of research also exists on culturally responsive pedagogy for culturally different children, of which research with Native Hawaiian children is one of the best-known examples (Au & Kawakami, 1994).

Next is an important historical precedent for the kind of education that Boggs proposes. With few exceptions, the research just cited is disconnected from this historical legacy. Contemporary education theorizing and practice related to liberating knowledge, curriculum transformation, and social action for change rarely build on the philosophical foundations and living struggles that influenced scholar-activists like Boggs.

The Historical Legacy of the Mississippi Freedom Schools. Striking parallels exist between what Boggs proposes as "education to govern," the Citizenship Schools the Southern Christian Leadership Conference organized across the South to prepare disenfranchised Black people to assert their voting rights, and the Mississippi Freedom Schools organized by the Student Non-violent Coordinating Committee (SNCC) in 1964. The purpose of the Freedom Schools was to "start young Mississippians thinking about how they could change the society in which they lived" (Perlstein, 1990, p. 319). Educators and community activists organized these schools to awaken students and adults to their highest human potential. The problems in southern Black communities dominated by virulent racism be-

came the curriculum for these schools, and the "scars of the system" possessed by the people, as well their survival knowledge and "living struggles," provided creative learning resources. As Perlstein reports: In SNCC schools for Black Mississippi teenagers, "Teachers generally incorporated students' lives into lessons and worked to break down the authority of whiteness" (p. 317). Often this pedagogy was constructed with the students, whom the volunteer teachers believed had as much to teach them as the other way around. The "art, dance, song, drama" and "the emancipatory capacities of these free forms . . . helped to promote a synthesis of experience, learning and politics [that] depended on the opportunities for activism that other components" of the Freedom Schools provided (p. 318). Both the Citizenship and Freedom schools embodied what Freire (1980) later called "education as the practice of freedom." The expectation in these schools was that people would become empowered to govern themselves and their communities (S. Clark, 1986; Perlstein, 1990; Stembridge, 1971).

Cultural Knowledge and Curriculum Transformation

The struggle for education that redirects learning toward community needs and control of Black communities and schools seems to have been taken up in some independent Black educational institutions (Lee, Lomotey, & Shujaa, 1990; Shujaa, 1994). In addition, the "Algebra Project," the inspiration of former SNCC activist Bob Moses, is recognized as a legacy of the civil rights movement's popular education activities (Ayers, 1989; Moses et al., 1989). Teacher retraining and curriculum development in this project make algebra, traditionally a "gatekeeping" course, accessible to middle school students in inner city and southern schools. Some Algebra Project lessons build on African American cultural knowledge to teach math concepts (M. Moses, personal communication, August 20, 1993).

Other approaches get students directly involved in studying their culture and emphasize the need for social action through collaborative research that also enhances their academic learning. MacLeod (1991) adapted the "Foxfire" method that had been developed by Wiggington (1985, 1991/1992) to engage Black Mississippi high school students in studying the history of their own community's involvement in the civil rights movement. "The Bloodlines Project" enabled these students to use "tools of social analysis" to understand and decipher "how inequities in wealth, power, and privilege affect them" (MacLeod, 1991, p. 274). According to MacLeod, "this critical awareness of selfhood in relation to society" becomes for some a motivating force to struggle for a better world (p. 274). MacLeod's students published their study in *Minds Stayed on Freedom* (Youth of the Rural Organizing and Cultural Center, 1991). Other innovative educator-student collaborative projects with Puerto Rican/Latino and Native American students use community-mediated research and study projects to link service to academic learning and curriculum change (M. Hall, 1991; Torres-Guzmán, Mercado, Quintero, & Rivera-Viera, 1994). The skills and knowledge these students gain through these projects also accord with many of Boggs's education principles.

Lessons from the Decolonized World

Other examples of liberating knowledge, curriculum transformation, and social action-oriented practice created out of urgent necessity in the African Diaspora and the decolonized world share elements in common with the new education system Boggs proposes (Coard, 1971; Gonçalves e Silva, 1992; Jansen, 1990). Two will be discussed briefly; the first example is from Palestine, the second is from Mali (West Africa). They exemplify ways that cultural knowledge and curriculum transformation can make education more responsive to community needs. They also point to new directions in research.

Munir's Mother's Math. Just as extreme social disruption in France in 1968 enabled Foucault to rethink the nature of knowledge, Munir Fasheh, a Palestinian teacher and professional mathematician, was compelled to regard his discipline in an entirely new way and rethink the relationship between knowledge and hegemony. The urgent reality of war in his society and the Palestinian youth rebellion—the Intifadeh—brought the real needs of the Palestinian people to his attention. Fasheh (1990) compares his math with his mother's math. Her math consists of turning rectangles of fabric into "perfectly fitted clothing for people" (p. 21) and her sewing, despite her "illiteracy," "demonstrated another way of conceptualizing and doing mathematics, another kind of knowledge, and the place of that knowledge in the world" (p. 24). Even with "few measurements and no patterns," his mother's sewing involved math nonetheless in the way that "it embodied order, pattern, relations, and measurement" (p. 21). Fasheh discovered, by looking at their math in their two contexts, that his math was "biased toward the manipulation of symbols and theories linked . . . to technological advancement . . . that usually lead(s) to military, political, and economic power and control" (p. 22), whereas his mother's math was "biased toward life, action, production, and personal experience, and it was linked to immediate and concrete needs in the community" (p. 22). Yet her math and her knowledge, while not "intrinsically disempowering," were "continually discredited by the world around her" (p. 24). Although Fasheh is an experienced teacher and math professional, he realized that his mother's math was "beyond" his comprehension; it was "so deeply embedded in the culture that it was invisible to eyes trained by formal education" (p. 22).

Fasheh also realized that "the power of Western hegemony rests on claims of superiority, universality, and ethical neutrality of Western math, positivistic science, technology, and education" (1990, p. 25). He concludes that continuing to accept these Western claims of superiority, universality, and authoritativeness in math, science, and education "is detrimental to creating a healthier and more humane world" (p. 25). For education to be responsive to this challenge, according to Fasheh, it must play a new role in community transformation by enabling people to critique the "basic premises and values that govern their conceptions, practices, and production" (p. 25). The kind of math people need involves organic praxis, a combination of the practical aspects of his mother's math that is linked to community needs and the articulated theoretical constructs of his discipline. This kind of education will allow people to "reclaim

and develop what has been made invisible by hegemony" (p. 25).

The Gao, Mali, School Museum. Hassimi Maiga, another professional educator and senior researcher, developed an innovative educational approach in Mali, West Africa, that plays the kind of role in community transformation that both Fasheh and Boggs envision. From its philosophy to classroom practice and learning-by-doing-service in the community, the Gao School Museum approach exemplifies the principles of the new system of education that Boggs outlines. In each classroom the students and teachers collaboratively develop a repository of materials, resources, and teaching aids that they use to balance the theoretical knowledge in the school curriculum with students' cultural knowledge, practical skills, and know-how. Maiga (1993) explains that the Gao School Museum permits "each child to learn the curriculum content and to put what he or she is learning into practice . . . by actively participating with the teacher in the search for, creation and production of knowledge" (p. 9). In the process the teachers and students are able "to transcend the limitations of the present curriculum in so far as the future needs of the students, their community and society are concerned" (p. 11).

The Gao School Museum is also innovative in the preparation and training of teachers as researchers: It enables them to rethink their subject matter so as to meet real community needs. This innovation was partly designed to improve the implementation of Mali's national ruralization program, which created practical learning activities such as gardening, tending animals and poultry, carpentry, and sewing to enhance the academic learning of Malian students (Maiga, 1993, p. 40). In the Malian context of severe environmental and economic constraints (e.g., recurring drought), education is constantly endangered. Behind this visible and urgent economic crisis lies a deeper one: Students need to develop the kind of knowledge and skills that will enable them to be flexible, self-directed creators of solutions to their economic and social problems. The aim of the Gao School Museum is to develop students who are problem solvers for the positive transformation of their society. As Fasheh (1990) observed in the Palestinian context, this requires using the theoretical insights of the disciplines of the school curriculum, and recovering and reclaiming indigenous cultural knowledge and autonomous cognitive resources for education and social change. Consequently, the methodology of the Gao School Museum requires that teachers carefully study the curriculum first, then select and integrate learning activities that reinforce this kind of experiential learning across the curriculum. Teachers and students form research teams to study, analyze, and produce selected aspects of the curriculum together; they engage in productive community problem solving to test their knowledge and apply what they learn in situations with real, immediate consequences. The underlying philosophy serves as a "concrete bridge between learners and their social, cultural and economic environment; as a laboratory for studying and improving the presentation of school subjects; and therefore as a permanent pedagogical support for both teachers and students" (Maiga, 1993, p. 21).

Indigenous Cultural Knowledge, Professional Education, and Grassroots Development

Recent developments in the professional education of lawyers, teachers, social workers, and international development specialists, among others, demonstrate the importance of recuperating indigenous cultural knowledge, as these lessons from the decolonized world also suggest. From preparation for professional advocacy in environmental poverty law (Cole, 1992), to the use of the clients' "subjugated knowledge" in social work (Hartman, 1992), to reexaminations of the value of indigenous knowledge systems by development specialists (D. L. Williams & Muchena, 1991) and environmentalist educators (Orr, 1992), there is an interest in identifying and using (indigenous) cultural knowledge for liberating purposes. Community educators and grassroots development specialists in Africa (Hope & Timmel, 1984; National Education Crisis Committee, 1987), Latin America (Kleymeyer & Moreno, 1988), and in the United States are using participatory research "by-the-people-for-the-people" strategies (Dubell, Erasmie, & de Vries, 1980) as well as critical pedagogies of organic social action research to recuperate subjugated cultural knowledge (King & Mitchell, 1990; Borda, 1980). These strategies involve participants in the study of their own lives and community needs in ways that can enable people to recognize and value their cultural knowledge and promote cultural "revitalization" and group self-help (Kleymeyer & Moreno, 1988, p. 36).

The research discussed thus far in this chapter underscores the importance of considering the social effects of knowledge and the ways that curriculum transformation can contribute to demystification of the social framework and thereby prepare people to change themselves and society. Research that bridges "street and school" can be a form of organic praxis that links scholarly work with community needs and with the cultural knowledge of the people engaged in the research. Two examples of this type of research are summarized briefly in the next section. This section will also point to directions in research that can support these effects.

ORGANIC PRAXIS, RESEARCH, AND SOCIAL ACTION

King and Mitchell (1990) provide a model of participatory Afrocentric research that can engage participants in thinking critically about changing themselves and society. This research is a grounded (Rodney, 1975) model of organic praxis that involves professionals and community participants in analyzing, theorizing, and discussing African American literature, their own social practice as mothers of sons, and myths of the social framework and the education system. Together the researchers and participants collectively decipher and recuperate cultural knowledge they can use in family, school, and community contexts. This methodology, according to King and Mitchell, "recognizes that particular knowledge of the world contained in people's daily cultural practice and social experience is not just distorted by the dominant ideology . . . but can be liberating as well" (pp. 89–90). One criterion of validity the researchers use

in this praxis-oriented research is the impact of collaborative inquiry on the "consciousness and practice" of the participants (p. 100). This study is an organic approach to the collective production of cultural knowledge "for the sake of the communal good and individual human liberation" (J. James, 1993b, p. 133, n. 17).

Ballenger (1992), a White professional preschool teacher of young Haitian children, describes another research approach that values and uses the cultural knowledge of a community and enables the researcher to reflect critically upon her own knowledge and assumptions. Ballenger's research method parallels the engaged scholarship of King and Mitchell. By comparing her own methods and language of classroom control with those of Haitian teachers and parents, and by engaging in reflective discussion with them, Ballenger learned that the "process of gaining multicultural understanding in education must . . . be a dual one" (p. 207). What she learned from the children and their Haitian teachers enabled her to reevaluate the emphasis on (and the presumed superiority of) individualism in North American teaching practice, compared with the shared values and responsibilities of membership in a moral community that Haitian children derive within their cultural group at a very young age. Ballenger describes her attempts to use the cultural knowledge of the community by emulating the language (reciprocal dialogue) and methods of classroom control that she learned from the Haitian teachers, parents, and children. She reports that she feels "especially connected to the children" when she gets "it right" (p. 205).

A Lack of Conceptual and Pedagogical Resources

As Black students move through the education system, they face "the school's undermining doubt about their ability" (P. Gilmore, 1985, p. 124). Their dignity and positive group identity may be further undermined by hegemonic school knowledge and curricula that traumatize and humiliate many Black students, especially when dealing with topics concerning their ancestry, such as slavery (Hawkins, 1990; J. E. King, 1992). While some educators admit that they lack conceptual tools to intervene in this dynamic (Hawkins, 1990), others are oblivious, or are able to perceive ethnocentric bias and ideology only in materials that depart from and attempt to rectify a normative Eurocentric perspective bias (J. E. King, 1991a). That the problem of dislocating cultural hegemony in education persists, even as textbooks have become more multicultural, reveals a conceptual, methodological, and pedagogical lack in curriculum knowledge and research (Wynter, 1992a). In fact, there has been generalized silence about these matters in research in the disciplines and fields of pedagogical inquiry that might otherwise be of help to teachers. This is partly because educational researchers fail to draw upon the insights of research and theorizing in Black studies (B. Gordon, 1992; J. James, 1993b).

Weinburg's (1991) research provides an intriguing example of this lack in research on learning, teaching, and curriculum. Weinburg is an "educational psychologist interested in how people learn from texts," and he presents evidence that even "bright," "successful" high school students with in-depth factual knowledge of history and excellent academic and "generic" reading skills do not recognize distortion, polemic, or bias in history texts. Weinburg asks: "How could they know so much history, yet have so little sense of how to read it?" (p. 511). The Black studies epistemological critique can aid in the search for answers to such important questions.

Woodson's (1933) observations more than 50 years ago—that African Americans are miseducated as a result of the social organization of knowledge; that this bias has "invaded the teaching profession" (p. 20); and that "false education" contributes to social nefariousness—are still relevant. Woodson wrote: "There would be no lynching if it did not start in the classroom" (p. 3). Organic, praxis-oriented research is needed that enables students, teachers, and researchers to recognize ways that ideological bias and hegemony in the disciplines constrain their own thinking (Rodney, 1990). This applies not just to the humanities, but to science (Bazin, 1993) and mathematics (Fasheh, 1990), as well. As the research and experiences of Ballenger (1992), Fasheh (1990), King (1994), King and Mitchell (1990), MacLeod (1991), and Maiga (1993) indicate, rethinking the disciplines can be linked fruitfully with community praxis and inquiry related to the use of cultural knowledge. Such organic, praxis-oriented research is a first step toward rethinking the social framework and the knowledge that legitimates it. Educators at all levels need to study the intellectual and historical antecedents of Black studies and African-centered approaches to education to clear away the mystification and confusion surrounding group-based perspectives and strategies for education, curriculum transformation, and social change.

In addition, community needs should become a subject and object of study and a resource for learning as well (J. James, 1993a, 1993b). Finally, in contrast to "the pattern of thinking about racialism in terms of its consequences on the victim" (Morrison, 1992, p. 11), research is needed that examines how students, teachers, and academics (including textbook authors) are affected by and can overcome various societal myths, such as the belief system of race, that are embedded in the social organization of knowledge. Before they can decide whether to "challenge the status quo" (Farmer, 1993) in order to reinvent school knowledge and transform the curriculum (Bigelow, 1990), "teach the conflicts" (Graff, 1993), or teach "against the grain" (Simon, 1992), educators at all levels need to be able to recognize and overcome their own miseducation (J. E. King, 1991a).

These research directions have not been pursued by the general research community. For example, explorations of critical theory, ideology, and hegemony are examined without regard to the Black experience. Ewart's (1991) review of educational applications of Habermas's (1968) critical theory addresses the role of emancipatory knowledge and the critique of ideology. However, none of the topics and issues discussed relate to ideological distortions in school knowledge or the kinds of distortions or concern noted here (Anyon, 1979; Apple, 1979, 1993). Similarly, in a literature review that identifies "knowledge constructs" in research on learning and literacy,

there is no mention of the knowledge and skills Weinburg (1991) indicates are needed by students (or teachers) to critique distortions in school texts (Alexander, Schallert, & Hare, 1991). Finally, research that focuses on the education of Black students often emphasizes sociocultural deficits as an obstacle to assimilation or acculturation (Ogbu, 1992; Steele, 1992). This research paradigm misses the point of a fundamental insight of Black studies: Cultural and racial democracy require pluralism, not cultural negation or absorption.

Concluding Comments

This examination of culture-centered knowledge and curriculum transformation suggests that marginalizing and/or invisibilizing historical reality can alienate the identity and consciousness of subordinated groups or create the conditions of intellectual autonomy that are a requisite of cultural and racial democracy and human freedom. That is, a dialectical theory of social change suggests that the experience of subordination and liminality can also give such groups a perspective advantage of alterity. While expanding knowledge through the inclusion of multiple perspectives on reality is an alternative to dominating curriculum transformation and knowledge, Wynter (1984, 1989, 1992c) and Morrison (1989, 1992), from such a perspective of alterity, decipher the belief structure that legitimates the social framework and contributes to alienated and self-negating consciousness. Both these analyses suggest that the knowledge in the academic disciplines themselves needs to be changed. Such changes could create further possibilities for cognitive autonomy and human freedom. The "canon wars" over curriculum transformation are deflecting attention from the "war against the cities" where the marginalized are struggling for survival (M. Davis, 1993; R. Gilmore, 1993). Gilmore is right to criticize scholars who are benefiting from the "privatization" of intellectual work that does little to reveal the deteriorating material conditions that require "public oppositional action" (p. 78). Deciphering knowledge, like oppositional aspects of African American cultural knowledge—and the intellectual autonomy of the Black studies tradition—is a resource that can be used to link curriculum transformation with the "wider struggle" for social change in order to bring about the alternative social vision of Black studies: "a world that will hold all the people."

Coda

To have any practical relevancy to the actual conditions and problems experienced by African American people, Black Studies must conceive itself as a type of praxis, a unity of theory and practical action. It is insufficient for black scholars to scale the pristine walls of the academic tower, looking below with calculated indifference to the ongoing struggles of black people. We must always remember that we are the product and beneficiaries of those struggles, and that our scholarship is without value unless it bears a message that nourishes the hope, dignity and resistance of our people. (Marable, 1992, p. 32)

References

Adams, B. E. (1992). *John Henrik Clarke: The early years.* Hampton, VA: United Brothers and Sisters Communications.

Adell, S. (1990). A function at the junction. *Diacritics, 20*(4), 43–56.

Aldridge, D. P. (1992). The kitchen's filled—But who are the cooks? What it takes to teach Black Studies. *Phylon, 49*(1/2), 61–70

Alexander, P., Schallert, D., & Hare, V. (1991). Coming to terms: How researchers in learning and literacy talk about knowledge. *Review of Educational Research, 61*(3), 315–343.

Alinsky, S. (1971). *Rules for radicals.* New York: Random House.

Alkalimat, A. H. [Gerald McWorter]. (1969). The ideology of Black social science. *The Black Scholar, 4*(2), 28–35.

Allen, N. (Ed.). (1991). *African-American humanism: An anthology.* Buffalo, NY: Prometheus Books.

Ani, M. [D. M. Richards]. (1994). *Yurugu: An African-centered critique of European cultural thought and behavior.* Trenton, NJ: Africa World Press.

Anyon, J. (1979). Ideology and United States history textbooks. *Harvard Educational Review, 49*(3), 361–386.

Anyon, J. (1981). Social class and school knowledge. *Curriculum Inquiry, 11,* 3–42.

Apple, M. (1979). *Ideology and curriculum.* Boston: Routledge & Kegan Paul.

Apple, M. (1993). *Official knowledge: Democratic education in a conservative age.* New York: Routledge.

Aptheker, B. (1982). *Women's legacy.* Amherst: University of Massachusetts Press.

Aptheker, H. (Ed.). (1973). *The education of Black people: Ten critiques by W.E.B. DuBois, 1906–1960.* New York: Monthly Review.

Armento, B., Nash, G., Salter, K., & Wixson, K. (1991). *America will be.* Boston: Houghton Mifflin.

Asante, M. K. (1987). *The Afrocentric idea.* Philadelphia: Temple University Press.

Asante, M. K. (1991a). The Afrocentric idea in education. *Journal of Negro Education, 60*(2), 170–180.

Asante, M. K. (1991b). Multiculturalism: An exchange. *The American Scholar, 60*(2), 267–276.

Asante, M. K. (1992). African American Studies: The future of the discipline. *The Black Scholar, 22*(3), 20–29.

Au, K. H., & Kawakami, A. J. (1994). Cultural congruence in instruction. In E. R. Hollins, J. E. King, & W. C. Hayman (Eds.), *Teaching diverse populations: Formulating a knowledge base* (pp. 5–23). Albany: State University of New York Press.

Ayers, W. (1989). "We who believe in freedom cannot rest until it's done": Two dauntless women of the Civil Rights Movement and the education of a people. *Harvard Educational Review, 59*(4), 520–528.

Baker, H. A., Jr., (1984). *Blues, ideology and Afro-American literature: A vernacular theory.* Chicago: University of Chicago Press.

Baker, H. A., Jr., (1993). *Black Studies, rap and the academy.* Chicago: University of Chicago Press.

Ballenger, C. (1992). Because you like us: The language of control. *Harvard Educational Review, 62*(2), 199–208.

Banks, J. A. (1971a). Relevant social studies for Black pupils. In J. A. Banks & W. W. Joyce (Eds.). *Teaching social studies to culturally different children* (pp. 202–209). Menlo Park, CA: Addison-Wesley.

Banks, J. A. (1971b). Varieties of history: Negro, Black, White. In J. A. Banks & W. W. Joyce (Eds.), *Teaching social studies to culturally different children* (pp. 329–332). Menlo Park, CA: Addison-Wesley.

Banks, J. A. (1973). Curriculum strategies for liberation. *School Review, 81*(3), 405–414.

Banks, J. A. (1989). Integrating the curriculum with ethnic content: Approaches and guidelines. In J. A. Banks & C. A. Banks (Eds.), *Multicultural education: Issues and perspectives* (pp. 189–207). Boston: Allyn and Bacon.

Banks, J. A. (1991). Multicultural literacy and curriculum reform. *Educational Horizons, 69*(3), 135–140.

Banks, J. A. (1992). African American scholarship and the evolution of multicultural education. *Journal of Negro Education, 61*(3), 273–286.

Banks, J. A. (1993). The canon debate, knowledge construction, and multicultural education. *Educational Researcher, 22*(5), 4–13.

Banks, J. A., & Joyce, W. W. (Eds.). (1971). *Teaching social studies to culturally different children.* Menlo Park, CA: Addison-Wesley.

Bazin, M. (1993). Our sciences, their science. *Race & Class, 34*(4), 35–47.

Berger, P. L., & Luckmann, T. (1967). *The social construction of reality.* Garden City, NY: Doubleday Anchor.

Bernal, M. (1987). *Black Athena: The Afro-Asiatic roots of classical civilization* (Vol. 1). London: Free Association Books.

Bigelow, W. (1990). Inside the classroom: Social visions and critical pedagogy. *Teachers College Record, 91*(3), 437–448.

Blumenberg, H. (1983). *The legitimacy of the modern age* (R. M. Wallace, Trans.). Cambridge, MA: MIT Press.

Boggs, G. L. (1974). Education: The great obsession. In Institute of the Black World (Ed.), *Education and Black struggle: Notes from the colonized world* (pp. 61–81). *Harvard Educational Review,* Monograph No. 2.

Borda, O. F. (1980). Science and the common people. In F. Dubell, T. Erasmie, & J. de Vries (Eds.), *Research for the people—Research by the people* (pp. 13–40). Linkoping, Sweden: Linkoping University.

Bullivant, B. M. (1989). Culture: Its nature and meaning for educators. In J. A. Banks & C. A. Banks (Eds.), *Multicultural education: Issues and perspectives* (pp. 27–45). Boston: Allyn and Bacon.

California State Department of Education. (1987). *History/Social Science Framework.* Sacramento, CA: Author.

Carby, H. (1987). *Reconstructing womanhood: The emergence of the African American women novelist.* New York: Oxford University Press.

Carruthers, J. H. (1994). Black intellectualism and the crisis in Black education. In M. J. Shujaa (Ed.), *Too much schooling, too little education: A paradox of Black life in White societies.* (pp. 37–55). Trenton, NJ: Africa World Press.

Castenell, L. A., Jr., & Pinar, W. F. (Eds.). (1993). *Understanding curriculum as racial text: Representations of identity and difference in education.* Albany: State University of New York Press.

Césaire, A. (1960). *Return to my native land.* (2nd ed.; E. Snyders, Trans.). Paris: Présence Africaine.

Childs, J. B. (1989). *Leadership, conflict and cooperation in Afro-American social thought.* Philadelphia: Temple University Press.

Childs, J. B. (1991). The pedagogy of peace and war. *Journal of Urban and Cultural Studies, 2*(1), 81–92.

Christian, B. (1989). But what do we think we're doing anyway: The state of Black feminist criticism(s) or my version of a little bit of history. In C. A. Wall (Ed.), *Changing our own words: Essays on criticism, theory, and writing by Black women* (pp. 58–74). New Brunswick, NJ: Rutgers University Press.

Churchill, W. (1992). *Fantasies of the master race: Literature, cinema and the colonization of American Indians.* Monroe, ME: Common Courage Press.

Clark, C. [Sayed Malik Khatib]. (1973). The concept of legitimacy in Black psychology. In E. G. Epps (Ed.), *Race relationships: Current perspectives* (pp. 332–354). Cambridge, MA: Winthrop.

Clark, S., with C. S. Brown (Ed.). (1986). *Ready from within: Septima Clark and the civil rights movements*. Navarro, CA: Wild Trees Press.

Clark, V. (1991). Developing Diaspora literacy and *Marasa* consciousness. In H. Spillers (Ed.), *Comparative American identities* (pp. 40–61). New York: Routledge.

Clarke, J. H. (1992). The influence of Arthur A. Schomburg on my concept of Africana studies. *Phylon, 49*(1/2), 4–9.

Clarke, S. A. (1991). Fear of a Black planet: Race, identity politics and common sense. *Socialist Review, 21*(3/4), 37–56.

Coard, B. (1971). *How the West Indian child is made educationally subnormal by the British school system*. London: New Beacon Books.

Cohen, S. (1972). *Folk devils and moral panics: The creation of the Mods and Rockers*. London: MacGibbon and Kee.

Cole, L. W. (1992). Empowerment as the key to environmental protection: The need for environmental poverty law. *Ecology Law Quarterly, 19*, 619ff.

Collins, P. H. (1990). *Black feminist thought: Knowledge, consciousness, and the politics of empowerment*. London: Unwin Hyman.

Cone, J. H. (1972). *The spirituals and the blues*. New York: Seabury Press.

Cooper, A. J. (1988). *A voice from the South*. New York: Oxford University Press. (Original work published 1892)

Cornbleth, C., & Waugh, D. (1993). The great speckled bird: Education policy-in-the-making. *Educational Researcher, 22*(7), 31–37.

Cornforth, M. (1971). *The theory of knowledge*. New York: International Publishers.

Cox, T. H., Lobel, S. A., & McLeod, P. L. (1991). Effects of ethnic group cultural differences on cooperative and competitive behavior on a group task. *Academy of Management Journal, 34*(4), 827–847.

Crichlow, W., Goodwin, S., Shakes, S., & Swartz, E. (1990). Multicultural ways of knowing. *Journal of Education, 172*(2), 101–117.

Cruse, H. (1967). *The crisis of the Negro intellectual: From its origins to the present*. New York: Morrow.

Cruse, H. (1987). *Plural but equal: A critical study of Blacks and minorities and America's plural society*. New York: Morrow.

Cuban, L. (1971). Black history, Negro history, and White folk. In J. A. Banks & W. W. Joyce (Eds.), *Teaching social studies to culturally different children* (pp. 317–320). Menlo Park, CA: Addison-Wesley.

Davis, A. (1983a). Unfinished lecture on liberation—II. In L. Harris (Ed.), *Philosophy born of struggle: Anthology of Afro-American philosophy from 1917* (pp. 130–136). Dubuque, IA: Kendall/Hunt.

Davis, A. (1983b). *Women, race & class*. New York: Vintage Books.

Davis, M. (1993, June). Who killed L.A.? The war against the cities. *CrossRoads*, no. 32, pp. 2–19.

Derrida, J. (1976). *Of grammatology*. Baltimore, MD: Johns Hopkins University Press.

Diop, C. A. (1981). *Civilization or barbarism: An authentic anthropology*. Chicago: Lawrence Hill Books.

Dixon, J. (1971). African-oriented and Euro-American-oriented world views: Research methodologies and economics. *Review of Black Political Economy, 7*(2), 119–156.

Drake, S. C. (1977). *The redemption of Africa and Black religion*. Chicago: Third World Press.

Drake, S. C. (1987). *Black folk here and there* (Vol. 1). Los Angeles: Center for Afro-American Studies, UCLA.

Dubell, F., Erasmie, T., & de Vries, J. (Eds.). (1980). *Research for the people—Research by the people*. Linkoping, Sweden: Linkoping University.

DuBois, W. E. B. (1953). *The souls of Black folk*. New York: Fawcett. (Original work published 1903)

Ellison, R. (1986). What America would be like without Blacks. In R. Ellison, *Going to the territory* (pp. 104–112). New York: Random House.

Epstein, K. E., & Ellis, W. F. (1992). Oakland moves to create its own multicultural curriculum. *Phi Delta Kappan, 73*(3), 635–638.

Erickson, P. (1992). Multiculturalism and the problem of liberalism. *Reconstruction, 2*(1), 97–101.

Ewart, G. (1991). Habermas and education: A comprehensive overview of the influence of Habermas in educational literature. *Review of Educational Research, 61*(3), 345–378.

Fanon, F. (1963). *The wretched of the earth*. New York: Grove Press.

Fanon, F. (1967). *Black skins, white masks*. New York: Grove Press.

Farmer, R. (1993). Place but not importance: The race for inclusion in academe. In J. James & R. Farmer (Eds.), *Spirit, space and survival: African American women in (White) academe* (pp. 196–217). New York: Routledge.

Fasheh, M. (1990). Community education: To reclaim and transform what has been made invisible. *Harvard Educational Review, 60*(1), 19–35.

Fontaine, P. (Ed.). (1985). *Race, class and power in Brazil*. Los Angeles: Center for Afro-American Studies, UCLA.

Foucault, M. (1970). *The order of things: An archeology of the human sciences*. New York: Vintage Books.

Foucault, M. (1972). *The archeology of knowledge*. (A. M. Sheridan Smith, Trans.). New York: Harper & Row.

Franklin, J. H. (1993). *The color line*. Columbia: University of Missouri Press.

Frazier, E. F. (1957). *Black bourgeoisie: The rise of a new middle class*. New York: The Free Press.

Frazier, E. F. (1973). The failure of the Negro intellectual. In J. A. Ladner (Ed.), *The death of White sociology* (pp. 52–66). New York: Vintage Books.

Freire, P. (1980). *Education for critical consciousness*. New York: Continuum.

Gates, H. L. (1988). *The signifying monkey: A theory of African-American literary criticism*. New York: Oxford University Press.

Gates, H. L. (1992a). African American Studies in the 21st Century. *The Black Scholar, 22*(3), 3–11.

Gates, H. L. (1992b). *Loose canons: Notes on the culture wars*. New York: Oxford University Press.

Gay, G. (1983). Multiethnic education: Historical developments and future prospects. *Phi Delta Kappan, 64*, 560–563.

Gay, G. (1988). Designing relevant curricula for diverse learners. *Education and Urban Society, 20*(4), 327–340.

Gay, G., & Baber, W. L. (Eds.). (1987). *Expressively Black: The cultural basis of ethnic identity*. New York: Praeger.

Gayle, A. (Ed.). (1971). *The Black aesthetic*. Garden City, NY: Doubleday & Company.

Genovese, E. D. (1971). Black studies: Trouble ahead. In J. W. Blassingame (Ed.), *New perspectives on Black Studies* (pp. 104–115). Urbana: University of Illinois Press.

Giddens, A. (1979). *Central problems in sociological theory*. Berkeley: University of California Press.

Gilmore, P. (1985). "Gimme room": School resistance, attitude, and access to literacy. *Journal of Education, 167*(1), 111–128.

Gilmore, R. W. (1993). Public enemies and private intellectuals: Apartheid USA. *Race & Class, 35*(1), 69–78.

Gilroy, P. (1993). *The Black Atlantic: Modernity and double consciousness*. Cambridge, MA: Harvard University Press.

Giroux, H. (1992). *Border crossings: Cultural workers and the politics of education*. New York: Routledge.

Glissant, E. (1981). *Le discours antillais*. Paris: Seuil.

Gonçalves e Silva, P. B. (1992, April). *Black-women-teachers' resistance to racism in Sao Carlos (Sao Paulo, Brazil)*. Paper presented at the meeting of the American Educational Research Association, San Francisco.

Gordon, B. M. (1985a). Teaching teachers: "Nation at risk" and the issue of knowledge in teacher education. *The Urban Review, 17,* 33–46.

Gordon, B. M. (1985b). Toward emancipation in citizenship education: The case for African-American cultural knowledge. *Theory and Research in Social Education, 12*(4), 1–23.

Gordon, B. M. (1990). The necessity of African-American epistemology for educational theory and practice. *Journal of Education, 172*(3), 88–106.

Gordon, B. M. (1992). The marginalized discourse of minority intellectual thought in traditional writings on teaching. In C. A. Grant (Ed.), *Research and multicultural education: From the margins to the mainstream* (pp. 19–31). London: Falmer Press.

Gordon, B. M. (1993). African American cultural knowledge and liberatory education: Dilemmas, problems and potentials in a postmodern American society. *Urban Education, 27*(4), 448–470.

Gordon, E. W. (1985). Social science knowledge production and minority experiences. *Journal of Negro Education, 54*(2), 117–133.

Gordon, E. W., Miller, F., & Rollock, D. (1990). Coping with communicentric bias in knowledge production in the social sciences. *Educational Researcher, 19*(3), 14–19.

Goveia, E. (1970). The social framework. *Savacou, 1,* 7–15. Mona, Jamaica: University of the West Indies.

Graff, G. (1993). *Beyond the culture wars: How teaching the conflicts can revitalize American education.* New York: Norton.

Grambs, J. (1971). Crispus Attucks. In J. A. Banks & W. W. Joyce (Eds.), *Teaching social studies to culturally different children* (pp. 320–328). Menlo Park, CA: Addison-Wesley.

Grant, C. A. (1989). Urban teachers: Their new colleagues and the curriculum. *Phi Delta Kappan, 70*(10), 764–770.

Guy-Sheftall, B. (1992). Black women's studies: The interface of women's studies and Black studies. *Phylon, 49*(1/2), 33–41.

Habermas, J. (1968). *Knowledge and human interests.* Boston: Beacon Press.

Hacker, A. (1992). *Two Nations: Black, White, separate, hostile, unequal.* New York: Scribner's.

Hall, M. (1991). Gadugi: A Model of service-learning for Native American communities. *Phi Delta Kappan, 72*(10), 754–757.

Hall, S. (1991). Brave new world. *Socialist Review, 21*(1), 57–64.

Hall, S., Critcher, C., Jefferson, T., Clarke, J., & Roberts, B. (1978). *Policing the crisis: Mugging, the state and law and order.* London: Macmillan.

Hamilton, C. (1992). A way of seeing: Culture as political expression in the works of C. L. R. James. *Journal of Black Studies, 22*(3), 429–443.

Hansen, E. (1977). Freedom and revolution in the thought of Frantz Fanon. *Pan-African Journal, 10*(1), 1–22.

Harding, V. (1970). Beyond chaos: Black history and the search for the new land. In J. A. Williams & C. F. Harris (Eds.), *Amistad 1* (pp. 267–292). New York: Vintage Books.

Harding, V. (1974). The vocation of the Black scholar and the struggles of the Black community. In Institute of the Black World (Ed.), *Education and Black struggle: Notes from the colonized world* (pp. 3–29). *Harvard Educational Review.* Monograph No. 2.

Harding, V. (1990). *Hope and history: Why we must share the story of the movement.* Mary Knoll, NY: Orbis Books.

Harris, V. (1992). African-American conceptions of literacy: A historical perspective. *Theory into Practice, 31*(4), 276–286.

Hartman, A. (1992). In search of subjugated knowledge. *Social Work, 37*(6), 483–484.

Hartmann, G. (1980). *Criticism in the wilderness: A study of literature today.* New Haven, CT: Yale University Press.

Hawkins, J. A. (1990, June/July). The cries of my ancestors: The "uncomfortable" story of slavery must be told honestly. *Teacher Magazine,* pp. 8–9.

Heath, S. B. (1989). Oral and literate traditions among Black Americans living in poverty. *American Psychologist, 44*(2), 367–373.

Henry, P., & Buhle, P. (1992). Caliban as deconstructionist: C.L.R. James and postcolonial discourse. In P. Henry & P. Buhle (Eds.), *C.L.R. James's Caribbean* (pp. 111–142). Durham, NC: Duke University Press.

Hilliard, A. G. (1991/1992). Why we must pluralize the curriculum. *Educational Leadership, 49*(4), 12–14.

Hilliard, A. G. (1992). The meaning of KMT history. *Phylon, 49*(1/2), 10–22.

Hine, D. C. (1990). Black Studies: An overview. In R. L. Harris, D. C. Hine, & N. McKay, *Three essays: Black Studies in the United States* (pp. 15–25). New York: Ford Foundation.

Hollins, E. R. (1982). The Marva Collins Story revisited: Implications for regular classroom instruction. *The Journal of Teacher Education, 33*(1), 37–40.

Hollins, E. R., & Spencer, K. (1990). Restructuring schools for cultural inclusion: Changing the schooling process for African American youngsters. *Journal of Education, 172*(2), 89–100.

Holloway, J. E. (Ed.). (1990). *Africanisms in American culture.* Bloomington: University of Indiana Press.

hooks, b. (1984). *Feminist theory: From margin to center.* Boston: South End Press.

hooks, b. (1990). *Yearning: Race, gender and cultural politics.* Boston: South End Press.

hooks, b., & West, C. (1991). *Breaking bread: Insurgent Black intellectual life.* Boston: South End Press.

Hope, A., & Timmel, S. (1984). *Training for transformation: A handbook for community workers.* Gweru, Zimbabwe: Mambo Press.

James, C. L. R. (1948). *Notes on dialectics.* Westport, CT: Lawrence Hill.

James, C. L. R. (1963). *The Black Jacobins.* New York: Vintage Books.

James, C. L. R. (1970). The Atlantic slave trade and slavery: Some interpretations of their significance in the development of the United States and the Western world. In J. A. Williams & C. F. Harris (Eds.), *Amistad 1* (pp. 119–164). New York: Vintage Books.

James, J. (1993a). African philosophy, theory, and "living thinkers." In J. James & R. Farmer (Eds.), *Spirit, space and survival: African American women in (White) academe* (pp. 31–46). New York: Routledge.

James, J. (1993b). Teaching theory, talking community. In J. James & R. Farmer (Eds.), *Spirit, space and survival: African American women in (White) academe* (pp. 118–135). New York: Routledge.

James, J., & Farmer, R. (Eds.), (1993). *Spirit, space and survival: African American women in (White) academe.* New York: Routledge.

Jansen, J. (1990). In search of liberation pedagogy in South Africa. *Journal of Education, 172*(2), 62–71.

Johnson, D. (1990). *Telling tales: The pedagogy and power of African American literature for youth.* New York: Greenwood.

Jordan, J. (1988). Nobody mean more to me than you and the future life of Willie Jordan. *Harvard Educational Review, 58*(3), 363–374.

King, D. K. (1988). Multiple jeopardy, multiple consciousness: The context of a Black feminist ideology. *Signs, 14*(1), 42–72.

King, J. E. (Ed.). (1990). In search of African liberation pedagogy: Multiple contexts of education and struggle (Theme issue). *Journal of Education, 172*(2).

King, J. E. (1991a). Dysconscious racism: Ideology, identity, and the miseducation of teachers. *Journal of Negro Education, 60*(2), 133–146.

King, J. E. (1991b). Unfinished business: Black student alienation and Black teachers' emancipatory pedagogy. In M. Foster (Ed.), *Readings on equal education* (Vol. 11, pp. 245–271). New York: AMS Press.

King, J. E. (1992). Diaspora literacy and consciousness in the struggle against miseducation in the Black community. *Journal of Negro Education, 61*(3), 317–340.

King, J. E. (1994). The purpose of schooling for African American children: Including cultural knowledge. In E. R. Hollins, J. E. King, & W. C. Hayman (Eds.), *Teaching diverse populations: Formulating a knowledge base* (pp. 25–56). Albany: State University of New York Press.

King, J. E., & Mitchell, C. A. (1990). *Black mothers to sons: Juxtaposing African American literature with social practice.* New York: Peter Lang Publishers.

King, J. E., & Wilson, T. L. (1990). Being the soul-freeing substance: A legacy of hope in Afro humanity. *Journal of Education, 172*(2), 9–27.

King, W. M. (1990). Challenges across the curriculum: Broadening the base of how knowledge is produced. *American Behavioral Scientist, 34*(2), 165–180.

Kleymeyer, C., & Moreno, C. (1988). La feria educativa: A wellspring of ideas and cultural pride. *Grassroots Development, 12*(2), 32–40.

Kochman, T. (1981). *Black and white styles in conflict.* Chicago: University of Chicago Press.

Ladner, J. A. (Ed.). (1973). *The death of White sociology.* New York: Vintage Books.

Ladson-Billings, G. (1991a). Beyond multicultural illiteracy. *Journal of Negro Education, 60*(2), 147- 157.

Ladson-Billings, G. (1991b, November). *Distorting democracy: Social studies curriculum development and textbook adoption in California.* Paper presented at the meeting of the National Council for the Social Studies, Washington, D.C.

Ladson-Billings, G., & Henry, A. (1990). Blurring the borders: Voices of African liberatory pedagogy in the United States and Canada. *Journal of Education, 172*(2), 72–88.

LaFrance, J. (1992). Lessons from Maine. *Harvard Educational Review, 62*(3), 384–395.

Lee, C. D. (1991). Big picture talkers/words walking without masters: The instructional implications of ethnic voices for an expanded literacy. *Journal of Negro Education, 60*(3), 291–304.

Lee, C. D. (1992). Literacy, cultural diversity, and instruction. *Education and Urban Society, 24*(2), 279–291.

Lee, C. D., Lomotey, K., & Shujaa, M. J. (1990). How shall we sing our song in a strange land? The dilemma of double consciousness and the complexities of an African-centered pedagogy. *Journal of Education, 172*(2), 45–61.

Legesse, A. (1973). *Gada: Three approaches to the study of an African society.* New York: The Free Press.

Lemelle, S. J. (1993). The politics of cultural existence: Pan-Africanism, historical materialism and Afrocentricity. *Race & Class, 35*(1), 93–112.

Leo, J. (1989, November 27). Teaching history the way it happened. *U.S. News & World Report,* p. 73.

Levine, L. W. (1977). *Black culture and black consciousness: African American folk thought from slavery to freedom.* New York: Oxford University Press.

Locke, A. (Ed.). (1977). *The new Negro.* New York: Atheneum. (Original work published 1925)

MacLeod, J. (1991). Bridging street and school. *Journal of Negro Education, 60*(3), 260–275.

Maiga, H. O. (1993). *From whole to part: The Gao School Museum— Restoring a learning tradition.* San Francisco: Aspire Books.

Marable, M. (1992). Blueprint for Black studies and multiculturalism. *The Black Scholar, 22*(3), 30–36.

Marable, M. (1993). Beyond racial identity politics: Towards a liberation theory for multicultural democracy. *Race & Class, 35*(1), 113–130.

Martinez, E. (1992/1993). How Calif. texts portray Latinos. *Rethinking Schools, 7*(2), 10–11.

McCarthy, C. (1990). Multicultural education, minority identities, textbooks, and the challenge of curriculum reform, *Journal of Education, 172*(2), 118–129.

McCarthy, C., & Crichlow, W. (Eds.). (1993). *Race, identity, and representation in education.* New York: Routledge.

McElroy-Johnson, B. (1993). Giving voice to the voiceless. *Harvard Educational Review, 63*(1), 85–104.

McIntosh, G. A. (1971). Black liberation and the social studies curriculum. In J. A. Banks & W. W. Joyce (Eds.), *Teaching social studies to culturally different children* (pp. 366–369). Menlo Park, CA: Addison-Wesley.

McLaren, P. (1989). *Life in schools: Introduction to critical pedagogy in the foundations of education.* New York: Longman.

Meyers, L. J. (1988). *Understanding the Afrocentric world-view.* Dubuque, IA: Kendall/Hunt.

Mitchell, C. A. (1991, Autumn). "I love to tell the story": Biblical revisions in *Beloved. Religion & Literature, 23*(3) 27–42.

Moll, L., Amanti, C., Neff, D., & Gonzalez, N. (1992). Funds of knowledge for teaching: Using a qualitative approach to connect homes and classrooms. *Theory into Practice, 31*(2), 132–141.

Moore, C. (1964). Cuba: The untold story. *Présence Africaine, 52*(24), 177–229.

Morrison, T. (1989). Unspeakable things unspoken: The Afro-American presence in American literature. *Michigan Quarterly Review, 28*(1), 1–34.

Morrison, T. (1992). *Playing in the dark: Whiteness in the literary imagination.* Cambridge, MA: Harvard University Press.

Moses, R. P., Kamii, K., Swap, S. M., & Howard, J. (1989). The algebra project: Organizing in the spirit of Ella. *Harvard Educational Review, 59*(4), 423–443.

Mudimbe, V. Y. (1988). *The invention of Africa: Gnosis, philosophy and the order of knowledge.* Bloomington: University of Indiana Press.

National Education Crisis Committee (1987). *What is history? A new approach to history for students, workers and communities.* Johannesburg, South Africa: Skotaville Publishers.

Neusner, J. (1989). It is time to stop apologizing for Western civilization and start analyzing why it defines world culture. *The Chronicle of Higher Education, 35*(23), B1–B2.

Nieto, S. (1992). *Affirming diversity: The sociopolitical context of multicultural education.* White Plains, NY: Longman.

Nobles, W. W. (1985). *Africanity and the Black family.* Oakland, CA: Black Family Institute Publications.

Obenga, T. (1990). *The African origin of philosophy.* Paris: Présence Africaine.

Ogbu, J. (1992). Understanding cultural diversity and learning. *Educational Researcher, 21*(8), 5–14, 24.

Ogundipe-Leslie, M. (1984). African women, culture and another development. *Journal of African Marxists, 5,* 77–92.

Orr, D. W. (1992). *Ecological literacy: Education and the transition to a postmodern world.* Albany: State University of New York Press.

Peeples, K. (1984). The artist as liberator: An interview with John Oliver Killens. *Community Review, 5*(2), 6–14.

Perlstein, D. (1990). Teaching freedom: SNCC and the creation of the Mississippi Freedom Schools. *History of Education Quarterly, 30*(3), 287–324.

Ravitch, D. (1990a). Diversity and democracy. *American Educator, 14*(1), 16–20ff.

Ravitch, D. (1990b). Multiculturalism: E pluribus plures. *The American Scholar, 59*(3), 337–354.

Reed, I. (1993). *Japanese by spring.* New York: Atheneum.

Richards, D. M. (1980). *Let the circle be unbroken: The implications of African spirituality in the Diaspora.* Trenton, NJ: Red Sea Press.

Ricoeur, P. (1979). Ideology and utopia as cultural imagination. In D. M. Borchert & D. Stewart (Ed.), *Being human in a technological age* (pp. 107–126). Athens: Ohio University Press.

Robinson, C. (1993). The appropriation of Frantz Fanon. *Race & Class, 35*(1), 79–91.

Rodney, W. (1975). *The groundings with my brothers.* London: Bogle-L'Ouverture.

Rodney, W. (1990). *Walter Rodney speaks: The making of an African intellectual.* Trenton, NJ: Africa World Press.

Said, E. W. (1993). *Culture and imperialism.* New York: Alfred A. Knopf.

Sanford, A. (1990). An education agenda. *Essence, 21*(4), 126.

Schlesinger, A., Jr. (1991). *The disuniting of America: Reflections on a multicultural society.* Knoxville, TN: Whittle Direct Books.

Semmes, C. E. (1981). Foundations of an Afrocentric social science. *Journal of Black Studies, 12*(1), 3–17.

Semmes, C. E. (1992). *Cultural hegemony and African American development.* Westport, CT: Praeger.

Shade, B. (1982). Afro-American cognitive style: A variable in school success? *Review of Educational Research, 52*(2), 219–244.

Shor, I. (1986). *Culture wars: School and society in the conservative restoration 1969–1984.* Boston: Routledge & Kegan Paul.

Shujaa, M. J. (Ed.). (1994). *Too much schooling, too little education: A paradox of Black life in White societies.* Trenton, NJ: Africa World Press.

Simon, R. I. (1990). Jewish applause for a Yiddish Shylock: Beyond the racist text. *Journal of Urban and Cultural Studies, 1*(1), 69–86.

Simon, R. I. (1992). *Teaching against the grain: Texts for a pedagogy of possibility.* New York: Bergin & Garvey.

Sims, R. (1982). *Shadow and substance: Afro-American experience in contemporary children's fiction.* Urbana, IL: National Council of Teachers of English.

Sizemore, B. A. (1973a). Education for liberation. *School Review, 81*(3), 389–404.

Sizemore, B. A. (1973b). Shattering the melting pot myth. In J. A. Banks (Ed.), *Teaching ethnic studies: Concepts and strategies.* Forty-third Yearbook of the National Council for the Social Studies (pp. 73–101). Washington, DC: NCSS.

Sizemore, B. A. (1990). The politics of curriculum, race, and class. *Journal of Negro Education 59*(1), 77–85.

Sleeter, C. E. (1991). *Empowerment through multicultural education.* Albany: State University of New York Press.

Sleeter, C. E., & Grant, C. A. (1987). An analysis of multicultural education in the United States. *Harvard Educational Review, 57*(4), 421–444.

Sleeter, C. E., & Grant, C. A. (1991). Mapping terrains of power: Student cultural knowledge versus classroom knowledge. In C. E. Sleeter (Ed.), *Empowerment through multicultural education* (pp. 49–68). Albany: State University of New York Press.

Spears-Bunton, L. A. (1990). Welcome to my house. African American and European American students' responses to Virginia Hamilton's *House of Dies Drear. Journal of Negro Education, 59*(4), 566–576.

Spradley, J. P. (1972). Foundations of cultural knowledge. In J. P. Spradley (Ed.), *Culture and cognition: Rules, maps, and plans,* (pp. 3–38). Prospect Heights, IL: Waveland Press.

Steele, C. M. (1992). Race and the schooling of Black Americans. *The Atlantic, 269*(4), 68–78.

Stembridge, J. (1971). Notes on a class. In S. Carmichael, *Stokely speaks: Black power to Pan-Africanism* (pp. 3–4). New York: Vintage Books.

Stuckey, S. (1971). Twilight of our past: Reflections on the origins of black history. In J. A. Williams & C. F. Harrison (Eds.), *Amistad 2* (pp. 261–296). New York: Vintage Books.

Stuckey, S. (1987). *Slave culture: Nationalist theory and the foundations of Black America.* New York: Oxford University Press.

Swartz, E. (1992). Multicultural education: From a compensatory to a scholarly foundation. In C. A. Grant (Ed.), *Research and multicultural education: From the margins to the mainstream* (pp. 32–43). London: Falmer Press.

Tatum, B. D. (1992). Talking about race, learning about racism: The application of racial identity development theory in the classroom. *Harvard Educational Review, 62*(1), 1–24.

Thompson, R. F. (1983). *Flash of the spirit: African and Afro-American art and philosophy.* New York: Random House.

Torres-Guzmán, M., Mercado, C. I., Quintero, A. H., & Rivera-Viera, D. (1994). Teaching and learning in Puerto Rican/Latino collaboratives: Implications for teacher education. In E. R. Hollins, J. E. King, & W. C. Hayman (Eds.), *Teaching diverse populations: Formulating a knowledge base* (pp. 105–128). Albany: State University of New York Press.

Touré, S. (1969). A dialectical approach to culture. *The Black Scholar, 1*(1), 11–26.

Wa Thiong'o, N. (1986). *Decolonizing the mind: The politics of language in African literature.* London: James Currey.

Walker, A. (1991). *Reach wisely: The Black cultural approach to education.* San Francisco: Aspire Books.

Walker, D. (1971). Article 11. Our wretchedness in consequence of ignorance. In H. A. Baker, Jr. (Ed.), *Black literature in America* (pp. 55–65). New York: McGraw-Hill. (Original work published 1829)

Watkins, W. H. (1993). Black curriculum orientations: A preliminary inquiry. *Harvard Educational Review, 63*(3), 321–338.

Weider, A. (1992). Afrocentrism: Capitalist, democratic, and liberationist portraits. *Educational Foundations, 6*(2), 33–43.

Weinburg, S. (1991). On the reading of historical texts: Notes on the breach between school and academy. *American Educational Research Journal, 28*(3), 495–519.

Wells-Barnett, I. B. (1969). *On lynchings.* New York: Arno Press & New York Times.

West, C. (1985). The dilemma of the Black intellectual. *Cultural Critique, 3*(1), 109–124.

West, C. (1990). The new cultural politics of difference. In R. Ferguson, M. Gever, & T. Minh-ha (Eds.), *Out there: Marginalization and contemporary cultures* (pp. 577–589). Cambridge, MA: MIT Press.

West, C. (1993). *Race matters.* Boston: Beacon Press.

White, E. F. (1990). Africa on my mind: Gender, counter discourse and African-American nationalism. *Journal of Women's History, 2*(1), 73–97.

Wiggington, E. (1985). *Sometimes a shining moment: The Foxfire experience.* Garden City, NY: Doubleday.

Wiggington E. (1989). Foxfire grows up. *Harvard Educational Review, 59*(1), 24–49.

Wiggington, E. (1991/1992). Culture begins at home. *Educational Leadership, 49*(4), 60–64.

Williams, D. L., & Muchena, O. N. (1991). Utilizing indigenous knowledge systems in agricultural education to promote sustainable agriculture. *Journal of Agricultural Education, 32*(4), 52–57.

Williams, S. W. (1991). Classroom use of African American language: Educational tool or social weapon? In C. E. Sleeter (Ed.), *Empowerment through multicultural education* (pp. 199–216). Albany: State University of New York Press.

Woodson, C. G. (1933). *The mis-education of the Negro.* Washington, DC: Associated Publishers.

Wright, N. (Ed.). (1970). *What Black educators are saying.* San Francisco: Leswing Press.

Wynter, S. (1984). The ceremony must be found. *Boundary/2, 12*(3)/ *13*(1), 19–61.

Wynter, S. (1989). Beyond the word of man: Glissant and the new discourse of the Antilles. *World Literature Today, 63,* 637–648.

Wynter, S. (1991). Columbus and the poetics of the *Propter Nos.* In D. Kadir (Ed.), *Discovering Columbus. Annals of Scholarship, 8*(2), 251–286.

Wynter, S. (1992a). *Do not call us "negros": How multicultural textbooks perpetuate racism.* San Francisco: Aspire Books.

Wynter, S. (1992b). No humans involved: An open letter to my colleagues. *Voices of the African Diaspora, 8*(2), 13–16.

Wynter, S. (1992c). Rethinking "aesthetics": Notes towards a deciphering practice. In M. Cham (Ed.), *Ex-iles: Essays on Caribbean cinema* (pp. 237–279). Trenton, NJ: Africa World Press.

Young, R. (1990). *White mythologies: Writing history and the West.* London: Routledge.

Youth of the Rural Organizing and Cultural Center. (1991). *Minds stayed on freedom.* Boulder, CO: Westview Press.

Part

·V·

IMMIGRATION POLICY AND THE EDUCATION OF IMMIGRANTS

· 17 ·

THE AMERICAN CIVIC CULTURE AND AN INCLUSIVIST IMMIGRATION POLICY

Lawrence H. Fuchs
BRANDEIS UNIVERSITY

This chapter describes the evolution of an inclusivist immigration and naturalization policy implicit in the founding myth of the United States as an asylum for all persons seeking freedom, a myth that was constantly challenged by tribal and racial ideas of national membership similar to those on which most other nations were founded. Universality in immigration policy is possible in the United States only because Americans are united by the principle of individual rights—rather than group rights—embodied in the 1st and 14th Amendments to the Constitution. Principles of individual rights enable Americans from dozens of different ancestral backgrounds to participate in a system of voluntary pluralism that allows them, if they choose, to carry forward, in new and old ways, important aspects of their ancestral cultures while participating in a civic culture that defines their shared American identity.

At a visit to the Cheltenham School in Denver in February 1980 as Executive Director of the Select Commission on Immigration and Refugee Policy, I spent time with a third-grade class learning to count in three languages. After class I talked informally with the youngsters. To a towheaded, blue-eyed third grader, I pointed out George Washington's picture on the wall and asked if he knew who it was. "George Washington," came back a quick reply. "And what did he do?" I asked. The youngster looked puzzled, thought a bit, and exclaimed, "He died." His classmate, a Vietnamese refugee who had been in the country only six months, spoke up and said: "He's the father of our country."

THE FOUNDING MYTH OF THE AMERICAN REPUBLIC

The answer exemplified the inclusivist American immigration tradition. The republic, more than 200 years old, was still a country of immigration. The triumph of the inclusivist American tradition of immigration resulted in part from the founding myth of the American republic. Founding myths, accounting for the origins of a nation and explaining its destiny, usually are tribal (based on genealogy or blood), as with the Abraham story in the Old Testament (God told Abraham to create a new nation), or the tale of Theseus, the mythical Athenian king who defeated the horrible Minotaur of Crete and united the 12 small, independent states of Attica, making Athens its capital. The foundation of Rome was attributed to Romulus, son of Mars, the god of war. After having been saved from drowning and raised with his brother Remus by a she wolf, Romulus built a new city on the Tiber River on the spot where the brothers' lives had been saved. Japan, according to its traditional founding myth, was established because a favorite descendant of the Sun Goddess created the Japanese islands and became the first emperor, from whom all other emperors were descended.

Early in its history, spokesmen for the new American nation explained that the United States was created by God as an *asylum* in which *liberty, opportunity*, and *reward for achievement* would prosper. It was a powerful new myth that provided an ideological rationalization for the selfish interest Americans had in recruiting European immigrants to claim the land, fight Indians, and later to work in the mines and factories. It became the founding myth of a new political culture that united White Americans from different religious and national backgrounds. Belief in the myth constituted the American faith that motivated Americans to create new political institutions and practices that became the basis for American patriotism early in the life of the republic.

Of course, racism was also well entrenched in American life, making the myth a travesty for persons of color (Franklin, 1993; Horsman, 1991). But European immigrants in the early 19th century were quickly included in the new republic, making it easy for them to make claims upon it and to speak of Washington as "the father of our country," just as the Vietnamese Ameri-

293

can youngster did in Denver in 1980 (Jones, 1992). It was relatively easy for the Europeans to claim an American identity because the American founding myth was ideological and not tribal (Gleason, 1980). The three ideas that constituted the basis of what Americans called "republicanism" were not marked by tribal boundaries: (a) first, that ordinary men and women can be trusted to govern themselves through their elected representatives, who are accountable to the people; (b) second, that all who live in the political community (essentially, adult White males at the time) are eligible to participate in public life on the basis of equal rights; and (c) third, that individuals who comport themselves as good citizens are free to differ from each other in religion and other aspects of their private lives (Fuchs, 1990).

VOLUNTARY PLURALISM

The third idea constituted the basis for a kind of *voluntary pluralism* in which immigrant settlers from Europe and their progeny were more or less free to maintain affection for and loyalty to their ancestral religions and cultures, while being encouraged at the same time to claim an American identity by embracing the founding myths and participating in the political life of the republic (Fuchs, 1990). It was a system of pluralism that began mainly in colonial Pennsylvania, where immigrants of various nationalities and different Protestant denominations—as well as Catholics and Jews—moved with relative ease into political life. This new invention of Americans in which individuals could choose how and when or not to be ethnic (by moving easily across group boundaries) was sanctioned and protected by a unifying civic culture based on the American founding myth, its institutions, heroes, rules, and rhetoric.

THE INCLUSIVIST IMMIGRATION TRADITION

The inclusivist immigration tradition that accepted Europeans regardless of nationality and put them on a clear, fast track to citizenship was in competition with two other traditions that originated in colonial America. The first gained prominence in colonial Massachusetts, and the second mainly in the Chesapeake Bay colonies of Virginia and Maryland, called here the Virginia idea. To oversimplify the three approaches to immigration and the rights and privileges of immigrants, Pennsylvania sought immigrants who would be good citizens regardless of religious or national background; Massachusetts wanted as members only those who were religiously pure; and Virginia, with its increasing reliance on a plantation economy, wanted workers as cheaply as it could get them without necessarily welcoming them to membership in the community.

Out of the Massachusetts and Virginia ideas there emerged two powerful exclusivist American traditions regarding immigration. The first made religion, nationality, and *especially* race criteria for accepting would-be immigrants. It began with the decision by the theocratic community in the Massachusetts Bay Colony to turn back 60 English Protestant passengers on board the ship *Handmaiden* because there was insufficient testimony

as to their character and godliness (Ruthman, 1965). The second held that certain kinds of laborers admitted to work should not necessarily be admitted to the political community, especially, as it turned out, those of color. The planters in Virginia and Maryland, who wanted to maximize tobacco profits, sought workers and not visible saints, and began to import indentured servants regardless of their religious backgrounds, laborers who would serve those who paid their transportation for a period of four to seven years before becoming free. As a result, immigration to the Chesapeake for 100 years after 1607 was eight times as large as the Puritan migration to New England (Bailyn, 1986). The Virginia idea as applied to Whites was undermined partly because servants could not be kept as servants forever. When they became free they preferred to work for themselves, taking advantage of the cheap public land that was available in Virginia and elsewhere. More important, efforts to import and control White servants proved more costly than Black slavery. One way to counter the restlessness and rebelliousness of freed poor Whites was to buy Black slaves and, at the same time, link the hopes of poor Whites for a better life to a social, economic, and political system based largely on freedom and opportunity for all White newcomers on near equal terms with native-born Americans.

The Massachusetts idea was vitiated by the drive for capital expansion, which required new labor and capital. Even the Massachusetts Bay Colony succumbed to the desire for settlers, to the point of accepting Jews after rigidly excluding them throughout the 17th century. The idea that membership in the polity should be based on belonging to a particular Protestant denomination, or even on adherence to Protestantism, was overwhelmed by the general desire for immigrants in the colonies.

That was the general idea in Pennsylvania. Following the leadership of William Penn in 1681, by the early 18th century Pennsylvania had established a policy of encouraging the immigration of Europeans regardless of their religious background, and of admitting them to membership in the civic life of the colony on roughly equal terms with native-born Pennsylvanians. As a result, Pennsylvania became home to Scotch-Irish Presbyterians, Baptists and Presbyterians from Wales, and a variety of German Pietists. There were elements of exclusivism in Pennsylvania and New York, the other colony that achieved considerable cultural diversity. A Scottish-born counselor to the governor of New York, Cadwallader Colden, spoke angrily of "Dutch boors grossly ignorant and rude who could neither write nor read nor speak English" (quoted in Forbes & Limos, 1981, p. 24) In Pennsylvania, Benjamin Franklin wondered in 1753:

Why should Pennsylvania, founded by the English, become a colony of *aliens* [emphasis in original] who will shortly be so numerous as to Germanize us instead of us Anglifying them and will never adopt our Language or Customs any more than they can acquire our complexion? (Quoted in Forbes & Limos, 1981, p. 24)

Both Colden and Franklin eventually saw the advantages of a liberal, inclusivist approach to European immigration in a new nation hungry for settlers. By the time of the Revolution, some

Anglo-Europeans were still hostile toward speakers of Dutch and German and even toward the English-speaking Scotch-Irish, the newest large immigrant group, but none of the newcomers were kept from easy naturalization or from participating in politics on roughly equal terms with the native-born. That such persons could be good citizens even though they were Scotch-Irish Presbyterians, French Huguenots, German Pietists, English Quakers, or even Jews and Catholics had become a commonly accepted idea, although much more so in Pennsylvania and New York, the Middle Atlantic colonies, and even in the South, than in New England.

Neither the Massachusetts nor the Virginia ideas died. The leaders of the early Bay Colony wanted immigrants to be true believers. So did Thomas Jefferson, who cared not a fig whether the newcomers were practicing Episcopalians or Congregationalists or were unaffiliated, but who was uncertain that immigrants from monarchical nations could learn the principles of republicanism easily. He speculated that immigrants from monarchical nations would distort and warp the spirit of republicanism, and transmit their values to their children (Peterson, 1977). Although Jefferson was skeptical about taking vigorous measures to speed immigration, he did not oppose it, and later became a champion of easy naturalization, partly for partisan reasons, but also because as the United States expanded it needed more settlers. Capitalism and territorial expansion were the driving forces behind an inclusivist open immigration policy toward Europe, but Americans did not stop worrying about the potentially divisive effects of immigration. How could one tell if the strangers were fit for citizenship? How would one know if they were capable of becoming good Americans? The Constitution said nothing about immigration or naturalization policy, but stipulated that immigrants could not be eligible for the presidency and that a newcomer would have to wait seven years before being eligible for election to the House of Representatives, with an additional two years for the Senate. It left it for Congress to establish a uniform rule of naturalization, which it did in 1790 by legislating that any "free White person" could become a citizen who had resided for two years in the United States and at least one year in the state where he sought admission, simply by proving good character and taking an oath to support the Constitution. Even two years seemed a long time to one congressman from Virginia, an apostle of inclusion, when he said:

We shall be inconsistent with ourselves, if, after boasting of having opened an asylum for the oppressed of all nations . . . we make the terms of admission to the full enjoyment of that asylum so hard as is now proposed. It is nothing to us, whether Jews or Roman Catholics settle amongst us; whether subjects or kings, or citizens of free states wish to reside in the United States they will find it in their interest to be good citizens. (Quoted in Ringer, 1983, pp. 109–110).

While nothing was said in the debate about establishing religious, cultural, or linguistic tests for citizenship, making membership terms for Whites unprecedentedly inclusivist, it was assumed that dark-skinned persons would be excluded from immigration altogether. The view that there should be no religious test for immigration or naturalization was soon challenged by the enormous influx of Irish Catholic immigrants.

Anti-Catholic Prejudice and Nativism

Anti-Catholic prejudice was endemic in the United States in the 1830s and 1840s, based, from the perspective of Protestant militants, on the belief that the Roman Catholic Church was an enemy of freedom and that Catholics were subservient to the tyrannical foreign power of a pope in Rome (Bennett, 1988). The newcomers were also disliked for reasons of culture and class. Crowding into wretched tenements in the cities or shacks in the marshlands or outlying districts, frequently plagued by disease and drink, many entered almshouses, mental institutions, and prisons. Often willing to work at hauling heavy loads, cleaning stables, and sweeping streets for wages lower than those acceptable to native-born Americans, they would have provoked the antagonism of poor, unskilled native workers even if they had not practiced a "foreign" religion with its statues, crucifixes, and ornate vestments.

As hostile as the Protestant working men and women were to the newcomers—there was street fighting in several cities between poor Catholics and Protestants in the 1830s and 1840s, the burning of churches, and the stoning of homes—no major movement arose to stop immigration (Higham, 1972). Cheap labor was badly needed to work in the factories and mines, build the bridges and roads, and serve as domestics to the wives of businessmen, merchants, and professional men. Upper-middle-class Whigs wanted the Irish to do the dirty jobs; leaders of the Democratic Party wanted their votes. In opposing nativist efforts to lengthen the waiting time of newcomers for naturalization and to restrict their privileges as citizens, the Democratic platforms of 1840, 1844, 1848, and 1852, employing language based on the founding myth, praised "the liberal principles embodied by Jefferson in the Declaration of Independence and sanctioned in the Constitution, which makes ours the land of liberty, and the asylum of the oppressed of every nation" (Porter & Johnson, 1956/57, p. 2).

In some states the position of the Democratic Party on immigration was overwhelmed by the growing power of the nativists. The American Party of the 1850s, whose members were sworn to exclude all immigrants—and Roman Catholics in particular—from places of trust, profit, or honor, had phenomenal success, carrying the Massachusetts and Delaware state elections in 1854, and even won in Pennsylvania in alliance with the Whigs. In the fall congressional election about 75 members of the party were sent to Washington, and in the next year the legislative elections of Rhode Island, New Hampshire, and Connecticut were won by nativists. By 1856, 7 governors, 8 U.S. senators, and 104 members of the U.S. House of Representatives were elected after campaigning on the American Party platform, and talk of a Know-Nothing President became commonplace (Billington, 1938).

Most leaders of the Democratic Party not only resisted anti-Catholic hysteria but made a strong appeal for immigrant support. The party platform in 1856, once more faithful to the original Pennsylvania idea of American nationality, insisted that "no party can justly be deemed national, Constitutional or in accordance with American principles which bases its exclusive organization upon religious opinions and accidental birthplace." Opposing what it called a "crusade ... against Catholics and foreign born ..," the platform denounced it as not "in unison with the spirit of toleration and enlarged freedom which peculiarly distinguishes the American system of popular government" (Porter & Johnson, 1956/57, pp. 24–25).

The platform was both right and wrong. The Pennsylvania approach of "toleration and enlarged freedom" was an important feature of American life in the 1850s, but the Massachusetts approach, growing out of its Puritan origins, also was deeply embedded in the consciousness of Americans. By disbanding Irish military companies and keeping the Irish from the police force and state agencies, the new Puritans believed they were protecting republicanism. But even in Massachusetts no action was taken to restrict the voting of naturalized citizens, as had been demanded previously by many nativist leaders. The militant attacks of the Americanists had little appeal to politicians, especially in states where a growing number of newcomers voted. But the most important reason for the quick disintegration of the American Party was that the nation was seized by a wrenching debate over slavery (Franklin, 1967). As that debate intensified, religious passions and the issue of how long a residency period should be required for aliens to become citizens were overwhelmed by feelings on the race question; the American Party disappeared, and with it the issue of a religious test for membership in the American polity.

Largely forgotten after the Civil War were the opposition of the urban Irish to the cause of abolition, the July 1863 riots of the Irish against the draft law in New York City, and the alleged papal conspiracy to destroy republican government (Higham, 1972). More likely to be remembered were the heroes of General Thomas Meagher's Irish Brigade, two thirds of whom had been killed in the Battle of Fredericksburg, and the thousands of Catholic soldiers who fought in the Union Army and lived to celebrate their patriotism.

Even if there had been no Civil War, the Irish were well on their way toward becoming Irish Americans, just as the Germans were becoming German Americans, even though, unlike the Germans, the Irish were overwhelmingly poor and suffered from high rates of family separation, crime, and disease (Portes & Rumbaut, 1990). More than the Germans, who were suspected by some nativists as being bad material for American membership because of their cultural and linguistic separatism, the Irish Catholics provided a severe test of the capacity of the civic culture to permit and sanction voluntary pluralism while unifying newcomers around republican principles (Bennett, 1988). Like the Germans and the Scandinavians, they showed that it was possible for immigrant-ethnic groups to retain separate communal, cultural, and educational institutions at the same time that they participated increasingly in the wider economic and political life of the nation (Greeley, 1981).

The Inclusivist Tradition First Restricts Persons of Color

The inclusivist tradition prevailed with respect to Europeans throughout the 19th and into the early 20th centuries, but it was

never intended for newcomers of color (Franklin, 1976). Their labor was desired, but not at the price of membership. After the Civil War and passage of the 13th, 14th, and 15th Amendments, it was no longer possible to keep Black persons born in the United States from citizenship, and the naturalization law of 1870 provided for the first time that persons of African descent could be naturalized. During the debate, Republican Senator Charles Sumner of Massachusetts proposed an amendment that would permit naturalization for other groups of color. But senators from the western states, determined to exclude alien Chinese from citizenship, persuaded enough of their colleagues to defeat Sumner's motion overwhelmingly (Ringer, 1983). To most Americans, naturalization of the Chinese or other groups of color was unthinkable. They were, as the Democratic Party platform of 1884 said, "unfitted by habits, training, religion or kindred ... for the citizenship which our laws confer" (Porter & Johnson, 1956/57, p. 67). But employers wanted Asian workers, and from 1850 to 1944 those in Hawaii and on the West Coast sought laborers successively from China, Japan, Korea, and the Philippines (Daniels, 1988). Primarily they wanted single males, who would work hard, fast, and cheap at the most menial jobs and could never, under American law, be admitted to membership in the political community. It was an old story. The writers of the Democratic platform insisted that the ideals of the republic were sound, but the Chinese were seen, as nativists saw the Irish in the 1850s, as being incapable of becoming members of a self-governing republic (Chan, 1991).

Asian Immigration

The inclusivist tradition was for Europeans only because there was something else besides "habits, training, religion or kindred" that kept the Chinese as outsiders. It was race. Popular literature, political speeches, and government reports tended to stigmatize the Chinese as inherently immoral (Chan, 1991; Takaki, 1989). Called "Celestials," "Mongolians," "Coolies," and "Chinks," they were portrayed as inured to filth, disease, and immorality (Miller, 1969). The racist stigmatizing of the Chinese, repeated in time toward the Japanese, Koreans, Filipinos, and Mexicans, became a handy basis for their exclusion from political rights and for their often vicious maltreatment, especially in contrast to the reception afforded Europeans. At the same time that police authorities and immigration inspectors chased and sometimes beat the Chinese in the West, German and Scandinavian aliens in Wisconsin, Wyoming, and Nebraska were being urged to vote (seven states had laws permitting alien suffrage up to the outbreak of World War I). At the very time that the California Constitution of 1878 stipulated that "no alien ineligible to become a citizen of the U.S. shall ever be employed on any state, county, municipal or other public work in this state ..." (Ringer, 1983, p. 592), there were more than 50 Irish Catholics on the Boston police force; in five years that city would elect the immigrant Hugh O'Brien for the first of five terms as mayor.

More than 322,000 Cantonese-speaking male peasants arrived in the United States between 1850 and 1882, most of whom worked in American railroads, in mines, on plantations, at logging camps, and in vineyards, orchards, and ranches, with no expectation by them or their employers that they would ever be anything but Chinese alien sojourners who would go home to wives or prospective wives when the Americans decided that their labor was no longer needed (Fuchs, 1961). But by the late 1870s it was clear that tens of thousands of them would neither return home nor be confined to servile labor. In 1882, when nearly 40,000 Chinese nationals arrived and only 10,000 went home, Congress decided to oblige employers to look elsewhere for muscle by passing the first law to exclude Chinese laborers (in no other year in the 19th century would there be a net immigration of Chinese).

But the idea of importing sojourner laborers from Asia was very much alive. Temporary alien workers were sought first among the Japanese, but as their numbers grew, various state laws were passed to keep the Japanese in their place, including a 1907 congressional statute that provided that any American woman who married a foreigner—keeping in mind that only Asian nationals were ineligible to become Americans—would have to take the nationality of her husband. Although that law was repealed in 1922, female citizens who married aliens ineligible for citizenship continued to be deprived of their American citizenship until 1931, a rule that discouraged women from marrying Asians even in states that had no antimiscegenation ban. Since the ratio of male to female sojourners was enormous, especially for the Chinese (26 to 1 in 1890) and Filipinos (10 to 1 in 1910), such legislation kept many newcomers from marriage and from becoming parents of American-born children (Kitano & Daniels, 1988; Lai, 1980; Melandy, 1980).

As with the Chinese, it was not enough to keep the Japanese ineligible from becoming citizens; it became increasingly necessary to enforce the system of sojourner pluralism against those already in the United States. In 1913 Congress passed its Alien Land Law, prohibiting aliens ineligible for citizenship from owning land, although they were allowed to rent it (Millis, 1915). And under pressure from the United States, the government of Japan agreed in 1907 to impose limitations on Japanese emigration rather than suffer the indignity of a statute aimed at the Japanese comparable to the repeatedly enacted Chinese exclusion laws.

But the pressure mounted for Japanese exclusion specifically and Asian exclusion generally. There was still a loophole for employers seeking Asian workers. Since Filipinos lived in a territory of the United States, they could come to and go from the mainland, but as aliens ineligible for citizenship they were pushed to the bottom of the system of stratified sojourner pluralism in the West and in Hawaii. As bad as the situation was for Chinese and Japanese aliens in the 1930s, it was worse for Filipinos, who were relegated to the lowest status in that polylaminated system. But they kept coming to the United States without restriction until 1934, when, with the passage of the Philippines Independence Act by Congress, a quota of 50 immigrants per year was established.

Mexican Immigration

Employers in the West and Southwest looked to Mexico for workers, who came, as did all immigrants from other Western Hemisphere nations, without numerical limits until 1965 (McWilliams, 1968; Weber, 1973). But even though there were no numerical restrictions, many Mexicans entered illegally to avoid immigration fees and various exclusionary tests, including the requirement that they not become a public charge, and, after 1917, the literacy test. It was much easier to move back and forth two or three times a year without having to obtain a visa. How many illegal aliens came to the United States during any one period is impossible to say, but the speculations started early in the 20th century. The Commissioner General for Immigration in 1911 guessed that for the period 1900–1910 there were 10 to 20 times as many "unofficial immigrants" coming north from Mexico as those who entered lawfully. There was no way of knowing how many entered illegally and his guess was probably wildly exaggerated, but the actual number undoubtedly was substantial (Steiner, 1969).

From an employer's point of view, immigration policy with respect to Mexico was almost flawless. The large number of illegal aliens who came to work meant a steady supply of particularly vulnerable workers who would depress wages and labor standards, thereby keeping costs down and preventing the formation of an effective labor organization. The growers of perishable fruits and vegetables particularly appreciated the influx since they never knew just how many workers they would need, depending upon the vagaries of weather. Since Americans generally benefited economically from a system that made low-cost, unskilled help available for all kinds of menial tasks, such as hospital orderlies, dishwashers, and housemaids, and from the reduced cost of lettuce, strawberries, and other fruits and vegetables, opposition to the system tended to be limited to unions. So strong was the system that growers could rely not just on the flow of undocumented labor but on the cooperation of government in helping to manage that flow as their needs required.

By 1921 there were three immigration policies in the United States, shaped to a considerable extent by employer needs. The first, which applied to Europe, was inclusive with respect to nationality (Jones, 1992). The second, applied to Asia, was based on keeping Asians ineligible for citizenship until such time as they were barred by the 1924 immigration law. The third depended upon a system of formal and informal regulation that adjusted the flow of Mexican labor. The informal part depended upon the continuing flow of illegal aliens; the formal aspect began with the creation of the first *bracero* program for Mexican farm workers in World War I, which later was expanded to allow some of them to be employed in non-farm work. It was a system of sojourner pluralism that continued to a considerable extent up to the 1980s, enforced first by the local police in Texas, later by the Texas Rangers, and to some extent in subsequent periods by the Immigration and Naturalization Service (INS). When employer desires for Mexican labor waned in 1928, the U.S. authorities cooperated in keeping the Mexicans out by applying a literacy test that had been enacted by Congress in 1917 but had not been implemented for Mexicans for years. In the beginning years of the Depression, between 1929 and 1934, more than 400,000 Mexicans were sent home without formal deportation proceedings, including thousands of U.S. citizens of Mexican descent who were deported mistakenly and illegally (Weber, 1973). Sympathetic to the needs of the local economy and amenable to political pressures, the INS stepped up enforcement when laborers became difficult, such as in the crackdown following the so-called "Wetback Strikes" of 1951 and 1952 (Moore, with Pachon, 1976; Samora, 1971).

The *bracero* program that began in July 1942 epitomized the willingness of the U.S. government to subsidize southwestern and California agriculture with cheap labor. The *braceros*, who basically were limited to the agricultural sector and could not be drafted or join unions, each cost less than an average of $500 a year in wages during the war (Meier & Rivera, 1972; Samora, 1971). To help growers obtain additional Mexican workers, the INS began a practice known as "drying out," which involved giving undocumented workers employed by American farmers identification slips, deporting them, and then allowing them to reenter the United States legally.

Employers found the system not as reliable as the *bracero* program, and when the Korean War commenced in 1951 a third *bracero* program was established in which the Department of Labor became the labor contractor. But this time the creation of a *bracero* program did not stop the accelerating flow of illegal aliens, as returning *braceros* actually became recruiting agents for growers by describing to others the opportunities to earn good money in the United States. The Border Patrol could now vigorously apprehend aliens, and employers could still count on large numbers of them getting through. Actually, many illegal aliens were ex-*braceros* or relatives of *braceros*. The program turned out to be not just a replacement for illegal migration, but a stimulus to it (Samora, 1971).

For the most part, the issue of illegal migration and the question of importing temporary workers to the Southwest and West did not become a national issue until the 1960s. When the liberal Senator Paul Douglas (D-Illinois) offered an amendment to the 1952 Immigration and Nationality Act to provide for penalties against employers of illegal aliens, it was defeated overwhelmingly by a vote of 69 to 12. The Congress made it illegal to harbor an undocumented alien, but specifically provided that employment did not constitute harboring, an aspect of the law that became known as the "Texas Proviso" in recognition of the benefit that it brought to employers in Texas and the Southwest. Instead of employer sanctions, the Eisenhower administration launched "Operation Wetback" in June 1954. Special mobile forces of the INS began sweep operations in California and Texas, and eventually 1,750,000 undocumented aliens were rounded up. But the basic immigration-labor importation policy for the West and Southwest remained intact. Because of the Texas Proviso and the *bracero* program, employers could tolerate the roundups and summary deportations. Of the 3,075,000 *mojados* deported between 1950 and 1955, only 63,000 went through formal deportation proceedings. Between 1955 and 1959, when an average number of 430,000 *braceros* entered annually, they constituted about one quarter of all the farm workers hired in the states of Texas, California, Arizona, and New Mexico, and in 1960 they accounted for 26% of the nation's seasonal agricultural labor force (Cortés, 1980).

European Immigration

Congress did not focus on the anomalies and abuses of the third immigration policy until the 1970s and 1980s, but became extremely preoccupied with immigration from Europe between 1900 and 1910, when almost 9 million immigrants, the vast majority of whom were European, came to the United States, the heaviest migration in any single decade (Jones, 1992). When more than 4 million immigrants arrived during the next four years, the political demand to stop what was commonly perceived to be a tidal wave of immigration became irresistible. But the question was not just one of numbers. From the perspective of the Immigration Restriction League, founded in 1894 by four Boston-born and -bred graduates of Harvard College who inherited the old Massachusetts exclusivist tradition toward immigration, the immigrants were the wrong kind, coming as they did overwhelmingly from what they perceived to be the strange and almost exotic environments of Catholic and Jewish communities in southern and eastern Europe.

The plea for immigration restriction met strong opposition—employers wanting more muscle, ethnics wanting more brothers and sisters, and a growing band of social workers and politicians wanting more clients. The standoff between the pro- and anti-immigration forces was reflected in the schizophrenic immigration bill of 1907 which gave the secretary of commerce the power to admit immigrants in borderline cases if he deemed them needed for work, and which also required immigrants to pay a head tax of $4, twice the amount prescribed before. The most important part of the legislation was the creation of an Immigration Commission, which reported three years later, on December 5, 1910, a recommendation (with only one dissent) that a reading and writing test, which had passed the Congress in 1897 but had been successfully vetoed by President Grover Cleveland, was the most practical single method of restricting undesirable immigration (Hutchinson, 1981).

With so many conflicting pressures, the political parties straddled the issue of immigration policy toward Europe in the early 1900s. While both the Republican and Democratic Party platforms promised a continuation of the exclusion of Chinese labor, they were uncertain with respect to European immigration until 1912, when the Republicans pledged "the enactment of appropriate laws to give relief from the constantly growing evil of induced or undesirable immigration, which is inimical to the progress and welfare of the people of the United States" (Porter & Johnson, 1956/57, p. 187). Finally, growing opposition to the new immigration led in 1917 to passage of the literacy test over President Wilson's veto. But the test was insufficient in curbing the number of immigrants from eastern and southern Europe, and in 1921 and 1924 Congress applied the exclusivist tradition in American immigration policy to Europeans. The Johnson-Reed Act, commonly known as the National Origins Act of 1924, provided for an annual limit of 150,000 Europeans (plus the wives, parents, and minor children of U.S. citizens); a complete prohibition on Japanese immigration; the issuance and counting of visas against quotas abroad rather than on arrival; and the development of quotas based on the numerical contribution of each nationality to the overall U.S. population rather than on just the proportions of the foreign-born population, as had been stipulated in the 1921 legislation. The old Pennsylvania approach of accepting White Europeans as Americans regardless of their national background was repudiated. Instead, immigrants were accepted according to annual quotas of 2% of each nationality's proportion of the U.S. population in 1890, leading to absurdly low quotas for Italians of 4,000, Poles of 6,000, and Greeks of only 100. The Commissioner of Immigration reported one year after the 1924 legislation took effect that virtually all immigrants now "looked" exactly like Americans (Drachsler, 1820). The tide of darker-skinned Catholics and Jews had been stopped.

THE EXCLUSIVIST TRADITION

The exclusivist tradition applied not just to immigration policy but also to the immigrants already in the United States. Although many American institutions welcomed the immigrants, xenophobia in the post-World War I era was widespread (Bennett, 1988; Higham, 1972). Even as immigrants embraced American institutions, and especially the civic culture of the United States, the old Massachusetts idea that certain kinds of people were not fit to become Americans persisted. Consider the outrageous behavior expressed in a letter from President Herbert Hoover in 1930, responding to criticism from an Italian-born mayor, Fiorello LaGuardia of New York: "You should go back to where you belong and advise Mussolini on how to make good honest citizens in Italy . . . like a lot of other foreign spawn, you do not appreciate the country which supports and tolerates you" (quoted in Baltzell, 1965, p. 30). It was an offensive expression of bigotry against a man who, in addition to being a distinguished mayor of the largest and most important city in the United States, had flown in the U.S. Air Force in World War I and would play a major role in directing the national war effort in World War II. Did Hoover make LaGuardia feel like an outsider? Probably not. Like many other talented, imaginative immigrants from eastern and southern Europe, he found it easy to claim membership in the American civic culture because its ideals, symbols, and founding myth did not require him to stop feeling Italian, although social and cultural pressures on newcomers to conform to American mass culture were always strong.

What LaGuardia and many of his immigrant constituents had discovered was that no matter how much they were disparaged in social situations or discriminated against in employment, the American founding myth, its heroes, and its Constitution were on their side. The immigrants who understood and believed that—and especially their children—were likely to develop an even keener sense of their civic identity as Americans than those Americans who had been born in the United States

THE INCLUSIVIST TRADITION

How could foreign-speaking and -acting newcomers feel any relationship to the founding fathers, those Anglo-Americans who really were the charter members of the new republic? Abraham Lincoln knew the answer in 1860, when he observed that even though the German, Irish, French, and Scandinavian immigrants of his time could not identify personally with the Revolution and the early days of the republic, they felt "a part of us" because

when they look through that old Declaration of Independence, they find that those old men say that "we hold these truths to be self-evident,

that all men are created equal," and then they feel . . . that they have a right to claim it as though they were blood of the blood and flesh of the flesh of the men who wrote the Declaration of Independence," [and] so they are. (quoted in Eastland & Bennett, 1979, p. 53)

The inclusivists had the immigrants, the founding myth, and the Constitution on their side. The immigrants could speak easily of "our forefathers." The founding myth said that "all men are created equal," and the Constitution guaranteed immigrants and their children fundamental rights, including the right to develop an ethnic-American identity. In a series of three landmark decisions in the mid-1920s, Justice J. C. McReynolds, writing for the Supreme Court, made it clear that although he sympathized with those who would make the newcomers conform culturally, it was his and the Court's responsibility to uphold the principles of freedom that gave rise to ethnic and religious diversity. The supreme courts of Iowa, Ohio, and Nebraska had upheld legislation that forbade the teaching of modern foreign languages in the public schools, but McReynolds, acknowledging that "the foreign born population is very large, that certain communities use foreign words, follow foreign leaders, move in a foreign atmosphere . . ." (Meyer v. Nebraska, 1923), saw such legislation as inimical to basic rights in the United States. Such a law would have been fine in ancient Sparta, said McReynolds, but in the United States the parents had a right to engage teachers to instruct their children in the subject matter that they chose. "The protection of the Constitution," the Court insisted, "extends to all, to those who speak other languages as well as to those born with English on the tongue" (Meyer v. Nebraska 1923).

In a 1925 decision the Court ruled that an attempt by the state of Oregon to stamp out Catholic and other parochial schools by requiring all students to attend public schools also was inimical to the Constitution. An inclusive approach, under the Constitution, made room for such schools, dear to the hearts of many of the immigrants (Pierce, Governor of Oregon, et al., v. The Society of Sisters, 1925). A third decision in 1926 struck down a Territory of Hawaii law intended to hamstring foreign-language schools in the islands (a large proportion of Japanese American children continued to speak Japanese in their homes, and a majority went to Japanese language schools in addition to the public schools). After noting that there were 163 foreign-language schools in the territory, Justice McReynolds, while once again sympathetic to the point of view of the Americanizers, found that parents had the right to create such schools and send their children to them (Farrington, Governor of Hawaii, et al., v. Tokushige et al., 1926). The practical effect of the three decisions was to encourage American patriotism not by stamping out old cultural sensibilities and sensitivities, as many of the exclusivists wished and as many of the children of immigrants actually tried to do, but by giving legal permission to immigrants to carry on their ethnic traditions.

The power of the founding myth—the United States as an asylum for those who seek freedom and opportunity—was all but shut down in the racist 1920s and the Depression years of the 1930s. But it was given renewed strength in the 1960s by a variety of factors: the revivification of American ideals in World War II; the propaganda values attached to those ideas in the Cold War with the Soviet Union; the rise to power of second- and third-generation Italian, Jewish, Greek, and other eastern and southern European political and civic leaders who identi-fied with the inclusivist tradition; and especially the civil rights revolution against racism, with its emphasis on the universality of human rights in the United States regardless of religion, nationality, or color.

NEW IMMIGRATION POLICY

The civil rights revolution put a spotlight on the racist basis that the United States had employed for selecting immigrants from Europe and excluding those from Asia in the 1924 act, and the racism that stultified expressions of diversity of all kinds. It was a cruel system, which kept out Jewish refugees in the 1930s and Italian, Greek, and other would-be immigrants who were barred by the narrow quotas assigned to their countries imme-diately after World War II. Italian, Polish, and Jewish Americans lobbied hard for a change in the system and won after President John F. Kennedy, a strong opponent of the national origins quota method of selecting immigrants, was assassinated.

Following the landslide election of Lyndon Johnson in 1964 and passage of the Civil Rights Act in 1964 and the Voting Rights Act in 1965, Congress passed amendments to the Immigration and Nationality Act in 1965 that opened up immigration to the entire world. But because the system of allocating visas was linked so strongly to a potential immigrant's being related to someone already in the United States—out of six preference systems, four were based on family reunification, and immedi-ate relatives of U.S. citizens could immigrate without restric-tion—it was not expected that there would be much immigra-tion from Asia or other parts of the world that had not sent large numbers of immigrants in recent decades (immigration from Asia had constituted only 5% of all immigrants between 1931 and 1960).

The results were quite different from what had been antici-pated because non-Europeans, including increasing numbers of Asians, persons from the Caribbean basin, Latin Americans, and even Africans, found a variety of ways to enter the United States initially in some other manner than as close relatives of U.S. citizens or resident aliens, and eventually to adjust their status to that of immigrant (permanent resident alien). One way was to be admitted as immigrants under one of the two prefer-ences in the system that were not based on family reunification (professionals and artists or as needed skilled or unskilled workers), and in the 1980s about half of the persons admitted as immigrants actually were in the United States at the time of immigration, having entered lawfully as nonimmigrant aliens (mostly students and tourists) or as refugees or asylees, or unlawfully as illegal aliens.

Although immigration was now open to all nations, the Western Hemisphere was assigned a ceiling for the first time in U.S. history. Concern with increased immigration from Mexico was the major reason for establishing a 120,000-person ceiling for the hemisphere, at first without any limitation per country, as a companion to the 290,000 ceiling established for the East-ern Hemisphere, including refugees. (Immediate relatives of U.S. citizens in both hemispheres still could immigrate without numerical restriction, although subject to exclusions based on

individual characteristics, such as disease, as is true for all im-migrants.) In response to concern about Mexican immigration, a 20,000-per-country Western Hemisphere ceiling was enacted in 1976, in addition to application of the family-based prefer-ence system utilized in the Eastern Hemisphere. Two years later a worldwide ceiling was created, with a per-country limita-tion of 20,000 for all nations.

Immigration policy had become uniform with respect to legal immigrants (especially with the ending of the *bracero* program in 1964). In one sense the system discriminated against persons in countries where there was a high demand for immigration by applying an equal per-country ceiling. But equality in ceilings could assure the United States of diversity in immigration. By 1980 the proportion of foreign-born was not as great as it had been in 1880 and only one half of what it had been in 1920, but there were more than twice as many national-ities as there had been 100 years earlier. No longer did two or three groups dominate the immigration flow, as was true at the turn of the century, when Italians, Jews, and Poles accounted for 45% of all immigration between 1899 and 1910.

By the early 1980s the top three countries (Mexico, Vietnam, and the Philippines) were responsible for less than 30% of the total number of immigrants. In 1987 the top three (Mexico, the Philippines, and Korea) accounted for 26%, the top five coun-tries less than 36% (U.S. Bureau of the Census, 1991). Immi-grants in the 1980s came from 174 nations and colonies—34 in Europe, 26 in North America, 20 in Central and South America, 42 in Asia and the Middle East, and 52 in Africa. As late as 1976 only 4 African countries accounted for over 500 immigrants (Cape Verde, Egypt, Nigeria, and South Africa) (U.S. Bureau of the Census, 1991); by 1985 there were 9 (the new ones were Ethiopia, Ghana, Kenya, Liberia, and Morocco). By the late 1980s Asians, who not very long before had been excluded altogether, constituted almost one half of all lawfully admitted immigrants to the United States (Gardner, Robey, & Smith, 1985).

Ethnic Diversity and the American Civic Culture

The welcome given to new immigrants in the 1970s and 1980s was fundamentally different from that which had been extended to newcomers in other periods of large immigration, because Americans now generally celebrated ethnic diversity instead of disparaging it (Fuchs, 1990). Millions of Americans and foreign nationals visiting the U.S.A. Exhibition at Epcot Center in Disney World in the 1970s and 1980s saw a multime-dia show including figures from U.S. history in which one of the two narrators, Mark Twain (the other was Benjamin Franklin), exclaimed, "We built America out of different races and the process made us Americans. . . ." The Pilgrims, who came to America to enforce religious conformity on their children, were portrayed as dedicated to religious freedom. Frederick Douglass, who spoke frequently with bitter fury against slavery and caste, was shown as a man of great optimism and hope. Chief Joseph, who lamented the destruction of his people, the Nez Percé, by American intruders, was misleadingly quoted as speaking of "one government for all."

The idea behind the exhibit certainly was not to give an

authentic U.S. history lesson, but to help Americans leave it feeling uplifted and united. The search for unifying themes to unite Americans was understandable and even useful at a time when immigrants and refugees were arriving in the United States from all over the world in large numbers, and when African Americans and American Indians talked openly about the history of the oppression of their peoples (Deloria & Lytle, 1983; Harding, 1981). Designers of exhibits such as the one at Disney World, politicians and movie makers, comic strip writers, and leaders in all aspects of American public and popular culture celebrated the diverse racial, religious, and national backgrounds of Americans. As articulated by them, ethnic diversity in the United States was a unique and unifying American characteristic. Ethnic diversity itself had become a shared core value of Americans.

The idea that American identity was determined by its predominantly Anglo-Saxon origins breathed its last in the eloquent but failed efforts by Senator Sam J. Ervin, Jr. (D-North Carolina) to maintain the national origins quota system in the debate on the 1965 amendments to the Immigration and Nationality Act. Ervin thought that his argument—that preference should be given to applicants for immigration who had a closer kinship with people who had already made seminal historical contributions to the United States—sounded plausible. "Do you not believe that it is much easier to assimilate into our nation people who bear a likeness to those who are here?" he asked. "Do you not believe it is much easier to assimilate into this nation people who have, more or less, similar ideas in respect to government and in respect to philosophy?" (quoted in Morgan, 1978, p. 104).

The facts of American life had passed that argument by. The descendants of Greeks, Italians, Jews, Japanese, and others who testified against the national origins quota system were living refutations of Ervin's position. These hyphenated Americans had not made the United States into a polyglot culture or a society without a core national identity. When Anthony J. Celebrezze, the secretary of the Department of Health, Education and Welfare, testified on behalf of the 1965 amendments, he did so as the 17th immigrant to have been a member of a U.S. presidential cabinet. Ervin's argument collapsed under the weight of history. The children of the "Palatine boors," as Franklin had called the Germans, had become Americans easily, as had the children of the "Hunkies," "Dagos," "Kikes," "Frogs," "Chinks," "Greasers," and all those other immigrants whose parents were viewed suspiciously as outsiders and unfit for membership.

In the 1930s and 1940s most Americans agreed with the charter member approach to immigration policy. Not only were they against admitting immigrants and refugees altogether, but they had strong nationality preferences concerning those to be admitted (Simon, 1985). By 1965, as the civil rights revolution gained momentum, the national origins system was in increasing disfavor among Americans. When the Gallup Poll asked Americans that year if they would favor changing the immigration law "so that people would be admitted on the basis of their occupational skills rather than on the basis of the country they came from," 51% favored such a change, with only 30% against it (Simon, 1985, p. 40).

When respondents in one 1984 survey ("Public Attitudes on Refugees," 1984) were asked whether "a man from Taiwan who wants to come to the U.S. to be with his daughter, who immigrated here ten years ago," should be admitted, only 16% said no, compared to 75% who said yes. When the sample was asked if "a Jew from the Soviet Union facing persecution because he is Jewish should be admitted," only 14% said no and 79% yes. Sixty-six percent believed that "a man from El Salvador who comes from a town in which many people were killed by fighters from both sides of that country's civil war and who fears that if he is forced to return he will be in danger" should be admitted, while only 24% said no. Most surprising of all, perhaps, while 52% said that they would admit a man from England "who wants to start a new life for himself in this country," 57% said that they would admit a man from Mexico with the same intention. An immigration policy that had once been governed to a large extent by considerations of color, nationality, and religion had been transformed to one largely free of those considerations.

People in areas and institutions of the United States who had once believed in and practiced an Anglo-Saxon tribal view of insiders and outsiders changed their beliefs and practices dramatically. In Iowa, whose only president, Herbert Hoover, had attacked Italian Americans as outsiders, a higher proportion of Southeast Asian refugees was settled in relationship to the population than in any other state. Iowa's Anglo-Saxon governor pointed out what he called our formerly "homogeneous communities . . . are now the beneficiaries of contributions the refugees are making as productive members of our society" (*Refugees*, 1985).

From a world perspective, an extraordinary paradox developed in American society in the 1970s and 1980s. In dozens of nations throughout the world—such as Barundi, Ethiopia, the Soviet Union, Sri Lanka—ethnic diversity was perceived as a threat to national unity. But in the United States ethnic diversity was celebrated as a feature of national unity, not just in popular culture but in museums, textbooks, and other educational settings. It was acclaimed increasingly on such national holidays as Independence Day and Thanksgiving, and also in a series of special holidays and events—those massive cultural displays—including the centennial of the Statue of Liberty, the bicentennial of the Constitution, and the Ellis Island restoration, and periodically in mass naturalization ceremonies.

Instead of being portrayed as a threat to American unity, immigrants invariably were displayed in the news media of the 1980s as exemplars of the American dream of freedom and opportunity for all. Occasional articles would appear on Jamaican drug gangs or the Chinese mafia, but the dominant emphasis was on freedom received and freedom cherished; opportunity seized and achievements won in art, literature, and business. Immigrants and ethnicity became romanticized regularly in newspapers, television specials, and news features. A widely used advertisement for the *Wall Street Journal* in 1986 showed a picture of immigrants debarking at Ellis Island, captioned with the headline: "They Didn't Bring Riches. They Brought Something Better." In a widely distributed comic strip, "Fun Facts with Nikki, Todd and Randy," the three youngsters debated whether or not they should buy only American cars, as

Todd, the young African American boy, suggested. Randy, the Asian youngster, demurred, reminding the blonde girl, Nikki, that her great-grandfather came from Ireland, and Todd that his great-great-great-grandfather came from Africa. "And my parents came here from Cambodia . . . so in a way, aren't we all imports?" asked Randy (*Boston Sunday Globe,* 1985).

In other nations, cultural and political conservatives generally were hostile to immigrants, whereas in the United States immigrants often were portrayed by conservative columnists in the 1980s as confirming and reinvigorating American values. Columnist George F. Will (1980) wrote that he was convinced that "the newest citizens have the clearest idea of what we are celebrating when we raise a red, white and blue ruckus on the Fourth of July" (p. 76). Another conservative, Jeane Kirkpatrick (1986), Ambassador to the United Nations under President Ronald Reagan, wrote that

only those who do not understand America believe that families that have been here for ten generations are more American than the tens of thousands of new citizens naturalized last year. And only those who do not understand America think it is un-American for Cuban-Americans to have a special interest in Cuba, or Black Americans to have a special interest in Africa, or Polish-Americans in Poland, or Jews in Israel. (p. A-11)

The values of the republic, she wrote, receive "continual renewal by new citizens, who bring to us a special personal sense of the importance of freedom." She cited one Vietnamese refugee who arrived in 1979 after suffering for two years in Vietnam prisons: "Perhaps it is the immigrants' function from generation to generation to remind them [Americans] of what a treasure it is they own" (p. A-11).

One distinctly American cultural display, the mass naturalization ceremony, gave journalists and headline writers sentimental material for patriotic stories. Headlines in the newspapers about such ceremonies became opportunities for teaching about the civic culture, not just to immigrants but to native-born Americans. The celebratory headlines obscured the fact that immigrants often chose to become Americans for more selfish reasons than to affirm the values of the Constitution. They naturalized to obtain petitioning rights to be reunited with their relatives, to be able to hold a job that required government clearance, or to receive the protection that a U.S. passport gave them when traveling abroad. But the media reveled in stories about newly naturalized citizens choosing to affirm the ideals, heroes, heroines, symbols, and rituals of the civic culture, because that presumably is what their readers enjoyed hearing about (Benevenuto, 1983; Cahoun, 1985; Cummings, 1984; Freedman, 1986; Loo, 1983; Morale, 1981; Pave, 1985; Rodricks, 1983).

The mass naturalization ceremonies, the celebration of July Fourth and Thanksgiving, and especially the celebration of the centennial of the Statue of Liberty, which one reporter called "a convocation of a common secular faith," constituted a triumph of at least the rhetoric of the civic culture and civil religion. A reporter who saw subway passengers in New York spontaneously burst into patriotic song on liberty weekend concluded that "the Indian news dealer, the Haitian cabbie, the Greek cook—with their energy and their dreams, they nourish and

redeem a nation's soul" (Freedman, 1986, p. 17). There was reason to doubt that the nation's soul had been redeemed—after all, the covenant demanded by the civil religion called upon Americans to sacrifice for the ideals of freedom and equality, and such sacrifice did not characterize Ronald Reagan's America—but most reporters and politicians knew by the mid-1980s that the rewriting of history to make cultural diversity a part of the American founding myth, and the glorification of diversity to help unify the country, sold papers and was good politics, too, because Americans generally accepted that new history (McDaniel, 1984).

The Persistence of Xenophobia and Racism

Notwithstanding the new celebration of diversity, xenophobia, racism, and ethnic prejudices persisted. The welcome to the newcomers, while more accepting than that given to the southern and eastern Europeans or the Irish Catholics before them, was not always warm. Fear and dislike of newcomer immigrants erupted in many cities against Cubans, Haitians, Asian Indians, Vietnamese, Mexicans, and Puerto Ricans (who, of course, were citizens and not immigrants). The nature and extent of the hostility expressed toward newcomers depended upon the size of the target group, the suddenness with which they arrived in any particular community, and the economic conditions at the time. For example, when the federal government decided to allow 100,000 Cuban refugees to seek permanent U.S. residency in 1984, two Miami radio talk-show hosts initiated a campaign to send postcards opposing the decision to the White House, producing a jamming of its switchboards, with 95% of the callers phoning to protest the decision to allow the "Marielitos" to stay (Barbar, 1984).

In Jersey City, where a substantial number of Indians settled over a short period of time, Indian women found that wearing the traditional sari made them a target for harassment by native-born Whites and African Americans (and some Hispanic youths, too). "We will go to any extreme to get Indians to move out of Jersey City" (Marriot, 1987, p. B-1), wrote one correspondent to the *Jersey Journal* in 1987, in an atmosphere that forced the 9,000 members of the Indian community to remain indoors after dark and to avoid walking alone. One young White boy said, "It's White people against the Hindus," and an Indian woman wondered, "Why they kill us? . . . We are Americans, too" (Marriot, 1987, p. B-1).

So common and severe were episodes of harassment and violence against Asians, including those who were already citizens, that the U.S. Commission on Civil Rights undertook a study to examine the incidence of intimidation and vandalism against Asians, conducting field investigations in eight states and the District of Columbia. The rapid growth of the Asian population in the 1980s was followed by attacks on Korean merchants in Washington and New York, Kampucheans in several cities in Massachusetts, H'mong (Laotian highlanders) in Philadelphia, and Vietnamese in Florida, Texas, and California. One Justice Department official called violence against Asians "the fastest growing area of discrimination" in the country (U.S. Commission on Civil Rights, 1986).

African Americans and immigrants clashed sharply in some cities. Blacks in Los Angeles complained that Koreans treated them rudely in stores, would not hire them, and made money from the African American community without giving anything back (Ingweson, 1991). In Philadelphia, where about 5,000 H'mong refugees were resettled in a poor, mostly Black neighborhood, the local residents showed so much hostility in 1984 that hundreds of H'mong fled the city as if they were fleeing a war zone once more. Although the H'mong encountered some hostility wherever they went, even in Minneapolis, where their resettlement probably was more successful than elsewhere, the brutality in Philadelphia—muggings and pistol whippings—was greater than anywhere else (Coakley, 1984; "Immigrants: New Victims," 1986).

Hostility toward Latinos often focused on the language issue. Although it was a surrogate for many other questions, it surfaced wherever a large number of Hispanics lived, resulting in the campaign for making English an official language in more than a dozen states in the 1980s. "It isn't our town any more . . . it isn't an American city any more" (Lemann, 1988, p. 57), said one White in Monterey Park, California, a town of 60,000 that had become three fourths Asian and Hispanic in the late 1980s. Mexican Americans resented the achieving Asians and their success, and many Whites, seeing street signs in foreign languages, viewed the Mexicans, Vietnamese, and Chinese as outsiders who were taking over the city (Lemann, 1988).

With so much movement of population in the major cities, turf fights between newcomers and oldtimers were common. When the Chinese expanded into neighborhoods beyond the area deemed "Chinatown" on the Lower East Side of New York City in the early 1970s, Italians organized the Little Italy Restoration Association to resist encroachment on their territory (Kessner & Caroli, 1981). American-born Chinese labeled newcomers from Hong Kong *chook kok* (bamboo stalks closed at one end with the roots intact, presumably seen as rigid and old-fashioned), while young immigrants from Hong Kong and Taiwan retaliated by calling the native-born Americans *chook sing* (bamboo stalks empty at both ends, presumably lacking in content). Italian Americans took to calling recently arrived Italians "Guineas," an epithet that had been used in earlier decades against all Italian immigrants (Kessner & Caroli, 1981).

Despite these outbursts of hostility toward newcomers, the nativist xenophobia of earlier periods of large immigration had diminished. That was partly because the vast majority of immigrants came as members of families already in the United States, partly because they generally were better educated and more highly skilled than immigrants in earlier periods of massive immigration, and also because of the new conception Americans had of their own history and identity as a nation of immigrants. Underscoring those factors was the reality of economic growth in the 1980s, which tended to dissipate opposition to legal immigration.

EXPANDED IMMIGRATION POLICIES

The report of the Select Commission on Immigration and Refugee Policy in 1981 marked a point at which Congress began to think of legal immigration as good for the nation, even as it struggled with the problem of reducing the flow of illegal workers into the United States. When Congress passed the Immigration Reform and Control Act five years later, it was substantially in accord with the Select Commission's recommendations to open the front door wider to legal immigration in several ways (even as it tried to close the back door to illegal migration). It passed a comprehensive program to legalize illegal aliens (1.77 million applicants), all of whom would become eligible for resident alien status. It also passed a special legalization program for formerly illegal aliens who claimed successfully to have worked in agriculture for 90 days in the previous year (who also were made eligible for eventual resident alien status). Another group who could persuade the INS that they had worked for 90 days in each of three successive previous years were put on a somewhat faster track to resident alien status. These special agricultural workers (altogether 1.3 million applied) represented some concession to the old immigration tradition of the Southwest and California that supplied workers to employers with the help of the government. But it represented a fundamental departure from that tradition by specifying that the workers would not be confined to agriculture or to any section of the country and that they could become eligible for permanent residency.

In addition to these major increases in lawful immigration, Congress in 1986 also increased the immigration ceilings for colonies and dependencies from 500 to 6,000; provided for adjustment of the status of special entrants who came from Cuba and Haiti in the early 1980s to that of permanent resident alien; and added 5,000 immigrants annually for two years, to be chosen by lottery from persons who were nationals of countries with low rates of immigration attributed to the emphasis in the 1965 amendments on family reunification (36 countries, mostly European). The last provision was extended to 15,000 additional immigrants in 1989 and 1990. In 1988 Congress increased immigration once more by providing 10,000 additional visas for 1990 and 1991 for would-be immigrants from 162 countries, also to be chosen by lottery, one application per potential immigrant. (In the 5,000-a-year program, would-be immigrants could submit multiple applications.)

Another major provision of the Immigration Reform and Control Act of 1986 that stemmed from the American inclusivist tradition toward immigrants was passage of an amendment that made it illegal to discriminate against aliens in employment. The same amendment also created an Office of Special Counsel that was authorized not only to receive complaints but to make independent investigations of possible discrimination against persons on the basis of alienage, in response to the concern of many critics of the measure that the threat of employer sanctions against those who hired illegal aliens would increase discrimination against foreign-sounding and -looking legal aliens and citizens.

Congress and the courts in the 1970s and 1980s tended to make more uniform the rights of all those who lived and worked in the United States regardless of their status. An excellent illustration of how the United States narrowed differences in the law between naturalized and native-born citizens was in the field of expatriation. Less than two years after passage of the liberalized Immigration Act of 1965, the Supreme Court decided in *Afroyim v. Rusk* (1967) that Congress lacked the constitutional power to pass laws depriving a U.S. citizen of his or her nationality without consent, even when the person involved was a naturalized citizen who had voted in foreign elections. The decision, reversing earlier cases, made it clear that citizenship and allegiance were voluntary. Hugo Black, writing for the majority, concluded:

Citizenship in this nation is part of a cooperative affair ... we hold that the Fourteenth Amendment was designed to, and does, protect every citizen of this Nation against a Congressional forcible destruction of his citizenship, whatever his creed, color or race. Our holding does no more than to give to this citizen that which is his own, a Constitutional right to remain a citizen in a free country unless he voluntarily relinquishes that citizenship. (*Afroyim v. Rusk,* 1967, p. 268)

Another example of the narrowing gap between naturalized and American-born citizens came in February 1988, when a federal district court judge ruled in a suit brought by two naturalized citizens of Vietnamese birth that naturalized citizens had the same rights as other Americans to security clearances that gave them access to government secrets. The ruling affected an estimated 23,600 naturalized citizens who were employees of the Department of Defense or who were employed by contractors working for the department (Halloran, 1988).

Aliens did not have equal rights with naturalized citizens (they were subject to deportation on several grounds, for example) and nonresident aliens did not have all of the same rights as those who had been admitted as immigrants, but the clear trend of the 1970s and 1980s was to reverse the derogation of alien rights that had begun in reaction to the large immigration at the turn of the century, and had continued for several decades. Reacting in a xenophobic way to eastern and southern Europeans, many states began limiting the rights of resident aliens in the 1890s, when ordinances were passed denying them licenses to operate certain kinds of businesses (Higham, 1972). Virtually all states excluded resident aliens from dentistry, medicine, engineering, optometry, and the law, and those with the largest number of aliens tended to have the most severe restrictions (Hull, 1985; Ueda, 1992). Some states discriminated against resident aliens in ludicrous fashion, not trusting them as undertakers or barbers or pool hall operators. A Cincinnati law that prohibited aliens from owning and operating poolrooms actually was upheld by the Supreme Court, which found that the premise of the legislation—that citizen proprietors were not as likely as aliens to allow the poolrooms to become social nuisances—was reasonable. In Rhode Island in 1924, a state court upheld the law that prohibited aliens from driving motor buses because, the court reasoned, "aliens as a class are naturally less interested in the state, the safety of its citizens, and the public welfare" (Hull, 1985, p. 40).

In 1971, just as immigration from non-European countries was beginning to increase substantially, the Supreme Court ruled that most of these restrictions were invalid. The specific case involved a law that made welfare payments available only to citizens or long-term resident aliens. Such a law, the court decided, was in conflict with the 14th Amendment's equal protection clause, since there was no compelling public interest in denying welfare payments to recent immigrants. Having invited immigrants to come to the United States, it was no longer permissible to enact laws that sharply limited their ability to receive fundamental benefits or to make a living. States could no longer discriminate to keep immigrants from practicing law, working as civil engineers, or attending educational institutions, as they had in the past (*Graham v. Richardson,* 1971; Hull, 1985).

The decision did not invalidate state laws that were deemed to have a political function, such as those barring aliens from being public school teachers, police officers, probation officers, jurors, voters, and government officials involved in making public policy. Other distinctions between resident aliens and citizens were continued, even one that excluded aliens from Medicare supplemental insurance programs unless they had resided in the United States for at least five years. Constitutional scholars and advocates of alien rights argued forcefully against many of the distinctions that remained (Aleinikoff, 1987; Hull, 1985).

Citizenship clearly was the highest form of membership, and some distinctions in rights and privileges persisted among different categories of aliens into the 1990s. Resident aliens, for example, were the only group of aliens allocated an immigration preference that enabled them to petition for their immediate relatives to become permanent resident aliens as well. Those foreign nationals granted refugee or asylee status were eligible for a full range of federally funded services and, after one year for refugees and two for asylees, could adjust their status to that of permanent resident. Those permitted to stay in the country through extended voluntary departure, or who were given special entrant status, or were paroled into the United States by the attorney general, were eligible for work permits and Supplemental Security Income (SSI), and sometimes for Aid for Families with Dependent Children (AFDC) and Medicare, but asylum applicants (applications pending) normally did not have access to any of these programs and sometimes were denied authorization to work.

Asylum applicants presented a serious problem for immigration policy when they came in large numbers, as Central Americans did in late 1980 and early 1989. The Refugee Act of 1980 provided the right of asylum, but the Carter, Reagan, and Bush administrations did not want asylum claims to become a back door to immigration. There was no right to immigration comparable to the right to asylum, and the dilemma presented to governments all over the world was how to enforce asylum law fairly and efficiently without having the right to asylum abused by persons with plausible but not compelling claims to exercise that right. The issue had much less to do with the inclusivist-exclusivist debate in American immigration than with the fear of large numbers of persons coming to the United States who, by claiming asylum, would burden the INS adjudication process, make heavy demands on local services and benefits, and create serious domestic political difficulty.

The asylum issue also had to do with U.S. foreign policy, since it was obvious from the way in which the asylum law was administered—each individual had to demonstrate a well-founded fear of persecution—that those fleeing Communist regimes or other countries out of favor with the United States, such as Iran, had a better chance at winning asylum than those leaving countries whose rulers were friendly to the United States, such as El Salvador (Zucker & Zucker, 1987). Since asylum applicants were entitled to a hearing and additional appeals under American law, it was possible for many of them to remain in the United States even after their claims had been denied.

But the largest source of back-door immigration remained the border crossers and visa abusers who never bothered to claim asylum, a majority of whom came from Mexico and from other countries, such as Ireland, where it would be extremely difficult to establish a well-founded fear of persecution. The effort to curtail the flow of illegal migrants into the United States through more efficient enforcement authorized by the employer sanctions provision of the Immigration and Reform Act of 1986 was achieving modest results by 1989, although eventually it would become necessary for Congress to link sanctions to a more secure system of identifying those eligible to work, such as an upgraded, highly counterfeit-resistant Social Security card, as recommended by many members of the Select Commission.

In the meantime, the sharpest distinction with respect to rights among those working in the United States was between those who were in the country illegally and lawfully admitted aliens; but even illegal aliens, and especially their children, had some rights. In 1982 the Supreme Court ruled that the equal protection clause of the 14th Amendment prevented the state of Texas from keeping undocumented school-age children from enjoying the same free public education that it provided to children who were citizens of the United States or legally admitted aliens. In speaking for the Court, Justice William Brennan exposed the fundamental hypocrisy of a policy (changed in 1986) that deliberately exempted employers of illegal aliens from any penalty while denying the children of such alien workers the most elemental right of public education. "This situation," wrote Brennan, "raises the specter of a permanent caste of undocumented resident aliens, encouraged by some to remain here as a source of cheap labor, but nevertheless denied the benefits our society makes available to citizens and lawful residents" (*Plyler v. Doe,* 1982, p. 215), which was precisely the point of coercive sojourner pluralism as applied to many Mexican workers throughout most of the 20th century.

The 14th Amendment conferred additional rights on illegal aliens. The undocumented worker who established the necessary domicile could pursue remedies available under Workers Compensation laws in the event of injury while involved in the course of employment. In addition, the tendency in the 1980s was to expand slightly the due process rights of illegal aliens confronted with deportation. In 1987 the Supreme Court even ruled that an illegal alien reentering the country after being deported could not be prosecuted for illegal reentry if he or she could show that the original deportation order was invalid because of the basic constitutional right of due process (Taylor, 1987).

Three years earlier the Court had ruled that it was an unfair labor practice for an employer to report illegal aliens to the INS in retaliation against the aliens' effort to organize a union, since

under then-existing law it was not illegal to hire an undocumented alien; in 1987 the 11th Circuit Court of Appeals ruled that undocumented aliens were entitled to a minimum wage and overtime pay guaranteed by federal law under the Fair Labor Standards Act of 1938 (*Annual Report of the Mexican-American Legal Defense and Education Fund,* 1987/88). In another case, a federal district court ruled in 1986 that federal authorities acted improperly when they prohibited Medicaid assistance for illegal aliens, because the 1966 statute authorizing Medicaid contained "no express restriction on alien eligibility" ("Illegal Aliens Are Eligible for Medicaid," 1986, p. 6).

There were no constitutional rights to Medicaid or most other benefits for illegal aliens, and the Immigration Reform and Control Act of 1986 limited benefits sharply even for the newly legalized aliens. But the tendency to weaken strong distinctions between different categories of aliens, including illegal aliens, and citizens was manifest in a variety of state and local actions and even in decisions by the INS, as when it ruled in 1988 that undocumented alien children who are or have been in foster care were no longer disqualified from becoming legal residents of the United States under the legalization program (Howe, 1988).

Such rulings did not affect the vast majority of illegal aliens, who lived in an underclass easily exploited by employers, and were often afraid to report to doctors, hospitals, or law-enforcement officials to protect themselves. Many illegal aliens hesitated to claim benefits available to their children or themselves for fear of being caught. Most who were caught at the border were turned around without any hearing, and although the courts expanded due process remedies in some respects for illegal aliens, they narrowed them in others. The rights of illegal aliens, resident aliens, and sometimes citizens, too, were infringed on occasion by INS practices, such as raids to catch illegal aliens in neighborhoods and places of employment (Isgro, 1985).

It was partly the vulnerability of the underclass of illegal aliens who had been in the United States for a relatively long time that led Congress to enact the legalization program of the 1986 law, and illegal aliens who applied for legalization were well aware that they were moving out of underclass status into something much closer to full membership in U.S. life. "This means I won't have to live like a second class person," said a legalization applicant from El Salvador who had been in the United States for eight years. "Now I will no longer be at a lower level than other people. I can do what I want" (Narvaez, 1987, p. 44). "This is our country now," said a Nicaraguan as he applied for legalization on the very first day of the program (Jolidom, 1987, p. 1). A 35-year-old Brazilian man who had been trained as an engineer but worked as a busboy exclaimed, "I feel great that I have some rights now, to be here, to be free and to be accepted" (Wong, 1987, p. 46).

As the main legalization program unfolded, officers of the INS, hoping to avoid the mistakes of France, Canada, and other nations whose earlier amnesty programs had disappointing results, saw legalization as an opportunity not just to proselytize for the agency's image, but also to participate in a celebration of ethnic diversity. In the 13 states of its southern region the INS isolated rural pockets of illegal aliens to be reached by its employees, who stuffed bilingual flyers into 580,000 packages of tortillas. One legalization officer wrote a song, "Amnestia," to be played on Spanish language radio stations along the Rio Grande. INS floats and information booths appeared at ethnic celebrations, and the agency conducted statewide radio remote broadcasts. The INS, whose main responsibilities at a time of massive illegal migration had to do with enforcement, was anxious to show that it, too, belonged to the inclusivist tradition of American immigration. Two years later the Congress created another category of admissions for Amerasian children fathered by U.S. servicemen in Vietnam and their families (essentially meaning mothers and other children), giving 37,658 such persons immigrant status from 1989 through 1991.

In 1990, a time of economic uncertainty, with the nation about to enter a prolonged recession and a war in the Persian Gulf, Congress acted again to expand immigration, providing for additional visas for family reunification immigration and almost tripling from the earlier limit of 54,000 the number of immigrants to be admitted for work independent of family ties in the United States (including the immediate families of the principal beneficiaries). Another provision established a safe haven for those already in the United States fleeing civil war

TABLE 17–1. Immigrants, by Country of Birth: 1961–1989 (in thousands)

Country of Birth	1961–1970, total	1971–1980, total	1981–1988, total	1989	Country of Birth	1961–1970, total	1971–1980, total	1981–1988, total	1989
All countries	3.321.7	4.493.3	4,710.7	1,090.9	Thailand	5.0	44.1	46.2	9.3
Europe[a]	1.238.6	801.3	510.3	82.9	Turkey	6.8	18.6	16.4	2.0
Czechoslovakia	21.4	10.2	9.1	1.0	Vietnam	4.6	179.7	314.9	37.7
France	34.3	17.8	17.7	2.6					
Germany	200.0	66.0	55.8	6.8	North America[a]	1,351.1	1,645.0	1,560.0	607.4
Greece	90.2	93.7	23.9	2.5	Canada	286.7	114.8	90.2	12.2
Hungary	17.3	11.6	6.9	1.2	Mexico	443.3	637.2	569.0	405.2
Ireland	42.4	14.1	15.5	7.0	Caribbean[a]	519.5	759.8	688.4	88.9
Italy	206.7	130.1	26.7	2.9	Barbados	9.4	20.9	14.1	1.6
Netherlands	27.8	10.7	9.3	1.2	Cuba	256.8	276.8	138.6	10.0
					Dominican Republic	94.1	148.0	182.9	26.7
Poland	73.3	43.6	61.8	15.1	Haiti	37.5	58.7	106.2	13.7
Portugal	79.3	104.5	32.2	3.8	Jamaica	71.0	142.0	164.3	24.5
Romania	14.9	17.5	29.7	4.6	Trinidad and Tobago	24.6	61.8	27.4	5.4
Soviet Union	15.7	43.2	47.4	11.1					
Spain	30.5	30.0	12.3	1.6	Central America[a]	97.7	132.4	211.5	101.0
Sweden	16.7	6.3	7.9	1.1	Costa Rica	17.4	12.1	10.7	2.0
Switzerland	16.3	6.6	5.4	0.8	El Salvador	15.0	34.4	76.5	57.9
United Kingdom	230.5	123.5	112.1	14.1	Guatemala	15.4	25.6	36.6	19.0
Yugoslavia	46.2	42.1	13.9	2.5	Honduras	15.5	17.2	29.9	7.6
					Nicaragua	10.1	13.0	23.7	8.8
Asia[a]	445.3	1,633.8	2,166.7	312.1	Panama	18.4	22.7	22.1	3.5
Afghanistan	0.4	2.0	20.2	3.2					
Cambodia	1.2	8.4	105.3	6.1	South America[a]	228.3	284.4	311.2	58.9
China: Mainland	96.7	202.5	295.5	32.3	Argentina	42.1	25.1	17.0	3.3
Taiwan				14.0	Brazil	20.5	13.7	16.2	3.3
Hong Kong	25.6	47.5	43.9	9.7	Chile	11.5	17.6	16.4	3.0
India	31.2	176.8	200.0	31.2	Colombia	70.3	77.6	85.0	15.2
Iran	10.4	46.2	108.6	21.2	Ecuador	37.0	50.2	36.0	7.5
Iraq	6.4	23.4	16.3	1.5	Guyana	7.1	47.5	73.2	10.8
Israel	12.9	26.6	27.4	4.2	Peru	18.6	29.1	38.5	10.2
Japan	38.5	47.9	32.7	4.8	Venezuela	8.5	7.1	12.7	2.1
Jordan	14.0	29.6	24.3	3.9					
					Africa[a]	39.3	91.5	131.2	25.2
Korea	35.8	272.0	272.3	34.2	Egypt	17.2	25.5	23.6	3.7
Laos	0.1	22.6	122.7	12.5	Nigeria	1.5	8.8	21.3	5.2
Lebanon	7.5	33.8	30.3	5.7	South Africa	4.6	11.5	11.8	1.9
Pakistan	4.9	31.2	43.6	8.0					
Phillipines	101.5	360.2	374.5	57.0	Australia	9.9	14.3	10.6	1.5
Syria	4.6	13.3	14.9	2.7	Other countries[b]	9.2	23.0	20.7	2.8

[a] Includes countries not shown separately.

[b] Includes New Zealand.

Note: From U.S. Bureau of the Census, *Statistical Abstract of the United States: 1991*, 111th ed. Washington, DC: Government Printing Office, 1991.

and natural disasters; this provision was made applicable immediately to Salvadoreans for a minimum of 18 months, and was subsequently renewed. Other pro-immigration measures included an expansion of visas for persons from Hong Kong, and 40,000 visas annually for nationals of 33 nations that had low rates of immigration in recent years (16,000 Irish per year in what was called a transitional diversity program).

Under the 1990 law, the total number of persons to be awarded permanent resident status (including refugees and asylees who adjust their status) will average at least 700,000 a year through the rest of the 1990s. Most will come from Asia, Latin America, the Caribbean, Africa, and the Middle East, plus at least 100,000 refugees and asylees, probably doubling the annual average of newcomers compared with the 20 years between 1961 and 1980 (see Table 17–1).

Changes in the composition of the immigrant population have been at least as dramatic as the increase in its overall size. In 1964, the year before passage of legislation ending discrimination against immigrants from eastern Europe and Asia, there were more French nationals admitted than Koreans, more than twice as many Germans as Filipinos, and 8 times as many Italians as immigrants from India. In 1991 those three Asian countries accounted for almost 10 times as many immigrants as the three European countries (108,169 to 11,578) (U.S. Bureau of the Census, 1991).

THE TRIUMPH OF THE CIVIC CULTURE

Critics often claim that racism has gotten worse since the death of John F. Kennedy (Bell, 1992; Hatcher, 1992). That claim cannot be supported by immigration policy, where the principles of the civic culture have triumphed. Even as public sentiment in 1993 rose to restrict the total number of immigrants, no significant leader of either political party called for a return to national origins quotas or racial discrimination. The founding myth of the United States as an asylum for those seeking opportunity has been extended to large numbers of people from all parts of the world, most of whom are people of color and not Protestant or English-speaking. More immigrants were admitted in 1992 from Nigeria than from France, from Ethiopia than from Italy, from Ghana than from Greece (U.S. Bureau of the

Census, 1991). More became resident aliens (immigrants) from the Philippines than from Germany, Ireland, and the United Kingdom combined.

Indeed, more than twice as many Asians as Europeans became immigrants and were placed on a fast, clear track to citizenship, including nearly 40,000 each from China and India, and almost 78,000 from Vietnam, or nearly twice the number emigrating from the former Soviet Union (U.S. Bureau of the Census, 1991). Protection for those newcomers to express the cultures, languages, and religions of their ancestors has never been more secure and has never achieved such heights as in the United States in the 1990s. The central principle of the civic culture—that individuals should be protected in their right to express themselves as they wish so long as they abide by the laws that protect the safety and well-being of the country as a whole—has never been more secure. Voluntary pluralism has triumphed because of that principle, a principle secured by the heroic struggles of Americans whose ancestors came from all over the world, most recently in the civil rights revolution led by Martin Luther King, Jr. It should be understood that voluntary pluralism has its origins in the founding myths of the nation and the rhetoric of Anglo-Europeans like Jefferson who played such a decisive role in its formation. To understand how we came to the place where voluntary pluralism thrives, it is necessary for teachers and professors of U.S. history to teach about the heroes and heroines, the great documents, the symbols, the principles, the values, and the institutions that make the American civic culture and voluntary pluralism in the United States unique (Fuchs, 1990). Given the vast diversity of immigration to the United States, a civic-centered education is necessary now more than ever in the teaching of U.S. history. An approach to U.S. history that emphasizes the evolution of the civic culture will teach about the possibilities of multiculturalism without promoting any kind of ethnic or racial chauvinism. The danger to the civic culture and *voluntary* pluralism comes from those on the left and the right who espouse a view that one's primary identity is tribal. That view is hostile to the civic culture, whether it comes from fundamentalist Christians who insist that children in public schools should be taught their brand of morality, or from Afrocentric or any other ethnocentric approach to history that denies the common, shared civic identity that makes voluntary pluralism possible.

References

Afroyim v. Rusk. (1967). 387 U.S. 253.
Aleinikoff, T. A. (1987). *Aliens, citizens and constitutional membership.* Unpublished manuscript.
Annual report of the Mexican-American Legal Defense and Education Fund (May 1987–April 1988). p. 10.
Bailyn, B. (1986). *The people of British North America.* New York: Knopf.
Baltzell, E. D. (1965). *Aristocracy and caste in America.* New York: Vintage.
Barbar, B. (1984, December 6). Cuban influx alarms Miami Whites. *U.S.A. Today*, p. 3A.
Bell, D. (1992). *Faces at the bottom of the well: The permanence of racism.* New York: Basic Books.

Benevenuto, M. (1983, July 12). America gave me a home—A chance to be somebody. *National Enquirer*, p. 11.
Bennett, D. H. (1988). *The party of fear: From nativist movements to the new right in American histoy.* Chapel Hill: University of North Carolina Press.
Billington, R. A. (1938). *The Protestant crusade, 1800–1860: A study of the origins of American nativism.* New York: Rinehart and Company.
Boston Sunday Globe comics. (1985, March 31).
Cahoun, J. (1985, June 18). Red, white and blue rose is an all-American beauty at 83. *Cleveland Plain Dealer*, p. 10.
Chan, S. (1991). *Asian Americans: An interpretive history.* Boston: Twayne Publishers.

Coakley, M. (1984, October 21). Laotians came for refuge, they got rage. *Chicago Tribune*, p. 4

Committee on the Judiciary, U.S. Senate (1979, May). *U.S. immigration law and policy: 1952–1979*. Washington, DC: Government Printing Office.

Cortés, C. E. (1980). Mexicans. In S. Thernstrom, A. Orlov, & O. Handlin (Eds.) *Harvard encyclopedia of American ethnic groups* (pp. 697–719). Cambridge, MA: Harvard University Press.

Cummings, J. (1984, December 1). New citizens: A sense of belonging spiced with opportunity. *New York Times*, p. 8.

Daniels, R. (1988). *Asian America: Chinese and Japanese in the United States since 1850*. Seattle: University of Washington Press.

Deloria, V., Jr., & Lytle, C. M. (1983). *American Indians, American justice*. Austin: University of Texas Press.

Drachsler, J. (1820). *Democracy and assimilation*. New York: Macmillan.

Eastland, J., & Bennett, W. J. (1979). *Counting by race: Equality from the founding fathers to Bakke and Weber*. New York: Basic Books.

Farrington, Governor of Hawaii, et al., v. Tokushige et al. (1926). 284 U.S. 298.

Forbes, S. F., & Limos, P. (1981). A history of American language policy. *Papers on U.S. immigration history: U.S. immigration policy and the national interest* (Appendix A to the staff report of the Select Commission on Immigration and Refugee Policy). Washington, DC: Government Printing Office.

Franklin, J. H. (1967). *From slavery to freedom: A histoy of Negro Americans* (3rd ed.). New York: Knopf.

Franklin, J. H. (1976). *Racial equality in America*. Chicago: University of Chicago Press.

Franklin, J. H. (1993). *The color line: Legacy for the twenty-first century*. Columbia: University of Missouri Press.

Freedman, S. G. (1986, July 6). A cheerful celebration of the good-hearted American idyll. *New York Times*, p. 17.

Fuchs, L. H. (1961). *Hawaii pono*. New York: Harcourt Brace Jovanovich.

Fuchs, L. H. (1990). *The American kaleidoscope: Race, ethnicity and the civic culture*. Hanover, NH: Wesleyan University Press.

Gardner, R. W., Robey, B., & Smith, P. C. (1985). *Asian Americans: Growth, change, and diversity*. Washington, DC: Population Reference Bureau.

Gleason, P. (1980). American identity and Americanization. In S. Thernstrom, A. Orlov, & O. Handlin (Eds.), *Harvard encyclopedia of American ethnic groups* (pp. 30–58). Cambridge, MA: Harvard University Press.

Graham v. Richardson. (1971). 403 U.S. 365.

Greeley, A. M. (1981). *The Irish Americans: The rise to money and power*. New York: Harper & Row.

Halloran, R. (1988, February 15). Judge gives naturalized citizens right to U.S. security clearances. *New York Times*, p. A-10.

Harding, V. (1981). *There is a river: The Black struggle for freedom in America*. New York: Harcourt Brace.

Hatcher, A. (1992). *Two nations: Black and White: Separate, hostile, unequal*. New York: Ballantine Books.

Higham, J. (1972). *Strangers in the land: Patterns of American nativism 1860–1925*. New York: Atheneum.

Horsman, R. (1991). *Race and manifest destiny.: The origins of American racial Anglo-Saxonism*. Cambridge, MA: Harvard University Press.

Howe, M. E. (1988, March 26). I.N.S. ruling benefits illegal immigrant children. *New York Times*, p. 28.

Hull, E. (1985). *Without justice for all: The constitutional rights of aliens*. Westport, CT: Greenwood Press.

Hutchinson, E. P. (1981). *Legislative history of American immigration policy, 1798–1965*. Philadelphia: University of Pennsylvania Press.

Illegal aliens are eligible for Medicaid. (1986, July 20). *New York Times*, p. 6.

Immigrants: New victims (1986, May 12). *Newsweek*, p. 57.

Ingweson, M. (1991, June 16). Korean merchants in Watts trying to defuse resentment. *Los Angeles Times*, pp. 1, 11.

Isgro, F. (1985). Review of significant cases decided by the federal courts in 1984. *Migration Today*, 12(4/5), 35.

Jolidom, L. A. (1987, May 5). Amnesty day: "This is our country now." *U.S.A. Today*, p. 1.

Jones, M. A. (1992). *American immigration* (2nd ed.). Chicago: University of Chicago Press.

Kessner, T., & Caroli, B. B. (1981). *Today's immigrants, their stories: A new look at the newest Americans*. New York: Oxford University Press.

Kirkpatrick, J. (1986, June 30). We need the immigrants. *Washington Post*, p. A-11.

Kitano, H. H. L., & Daniels, R. (1988). *Asian-Americans: Emerging minorities*. Englewood Cliffs, NJ: Prentice-Hall.

Lai, H. M. (1980). Chinese. In S. Thernstrom, A. Orlov, & O. Handlin (Eds.), *Harvard encyclopedia of American ethnic groups* (pp. 217–234). Cambridge, MA: Harvard University Press.

Lemann, N. (1988, January). Growing pains. *Atlantic Monthly*, p. 57.

Loo, L. (1983, July 14). Smiles light up the dark: 2500 gain citizenship. *Honolulu Advertiser*, p. A3.

Marriot, M. (1987, October 12). In Jersey City, Indians face violence. *New York Times*, p. B-1.

McDaniel, M. A. (1984, December). *The Crisis*, p. 10.

McWilliams, C. (1968). *North from Mexico: The Spanish speaking people of the United States*. New York: Greenwood Press.

Meier, M. S., & Rivera, F. (1972). *The Chicanos: A history of Mexican-Americans*. New York: Hill and Wang.

Melandy, H. B. (1980). Filipinos. In S. Thernstrom, A. Orlov, & O. Handlin (Eds.), *Harvard encyclopedia of American ethnic groups* (pp. 354–362). Cambridge, MA: Harvard University Press.

Meyer v. Nebraska. (1923). 262 U.S. 390, pp. 401–403.

Miller, S. C. (1969). *The unwelcome immigrant: The American image of the Chinese, 1785–1882*. Berkeley: University of California Press.

Millis, H. A. (1915). *The Japanese problem in the United States*. New York: Macmillan.

Miss Liberty to embrace new citizens. (1984, August 30). *New Jersey Star-Ledger*, p. 1.

Moore, J. W., with Pachon, H. (1976). *Mexican Americans* (2nd ed.). Englewood Cliffs, NJ: Prentice-Hall.

Morale, L. (1981, July 12). My life is complete—And this is the land that made it all possible. *National Enquirer*, p. 11.

Morgan, T. (1978). *On becoming American*. Boston: Houghton Mifflin.

Narvaez, A. A. (1987, August 9). Illegal aliens find freedom at immigration center. *New York Times*, p. 44.

New U.S. citizen's heart beats "Because it's American." (1985, July 31). *Chicago Tribune*, p. 4.

Pave, M. (1985, April 21). They wore U.S. flag on their hearts. *Boston Globe*, p. 29.

Peterson, M. D. (Ed.). (1977). *The portable Thomas Jefferson*. New York: Penguin Books.

Pierce, Governor of Oregon, et al., v. The Society of Sisters. (1925). 262 U.S. 510.

Plyler v. Doe. (1982). 457 U.S. 202, p. 215.

Porter, K. H., & Johnson, D. B. (Eds.). (1956/57). *National party platforms, 1840–1868*. Urbana: University of Illinois Press.

Portes, A., & Rumbaut, R. G. (1990). *Immigrant America: A portrait*. Berkeley: University of California Press.

Public attitudes on refugees. (1984, June 7). *Refugee Reports,* U.S. Committee on Refugees.

Refugees. (1985, February). *Refugee Reports,* U.S. Committee on Refugees, p. 29.

Ringer, B. R. (1983). *We, the people, and others.* New York: Tavistock Publications.

Rodricks, D. (1983, June). 127 new Americans proudly step forward. *Baltimore News-American,* p. 7.

Ruthman, D. B. (1965). *Winthrop's Boston: The portrait of a Puritan town, 1630–1649.* Chapel Hill, University of North Carolina Press.

Samora, J. (1971). *Los Mojados: The wetback story.* Gary, IN: University of Notre Dame Press.

Simon, R. J. (1985). *Public opinion and the immigrant: Print media coverage, 1880–1980.* Lexington, MA: Lexington Books.

Steiner, S. (1969). *La Raza: The Mexican-American.* New York: Harper & Row.

Takaki, R. (1989). *Strangers from a different shore: A history of Asian Americans.* Boston: Little, Brown.

Taylor, S., Jr. (1987, May 27). Court backs illegal aliens in a deportation case. *New York Times,* pp. 1–2.

Ueda, R. (1992). *New citizens and the American civic tradition: Naturalization, Americanization, and Americanism in European and Asian immigration, 1870–1950.* Unpublished manuscript.

U.S. Bureau of the Census, (1991). *Statistical abstract of the United States: 1991* (111th ed.). Washington, DC: Government Printing Office.

U.S. Commission on Civil Rights. (1986). *Recent activities against citizens and residents of Asian descent.* Washington, DC: Clearinghouse Publication Number 1986.

Weber, D. (Ed.). (1973). *Foreigners in their native land: Historical roots of the Mexican American.* Albuquerque: University of New Mexico Press.

Will, G. F. (1980, July 18). *Newsweek,* p. 76.

Wong, D. S. (1987, August 27). Immigrants feeling good about amnesty. *Boston Globe,* p. 46.

Zucker, N. L., & Zucker, N. F. (1987). *The guarded gate: The reality of American refugee policy.* New York: Harcourt Brace Jovanovich.

· 18 ·

IMMIGRANTS AND EDUCATION

Michael R. Olneck

UNIVERSITY OF WISCONSIN, MADISON

The schooling of immigrants holds substantial symbolic power in American culture. Educators' responses to immigrants in the early part of this century established an ideology of social reform and provided terms of debate that endure (D. K. Cohen, 1970; Fass, 1989). What Americans believe about the schooling of immigrants in the past has significant bearing on their expectations for both recent immigrants and minorities whose origins lie outside the immigrant experience (Montero-Sieburth & La Celle-Peterson, 1991). For these reasons, research on immigrants and education illuminates important societal beliefs and aspirations, prevailing educational policies and practices, and contentious debates about multiculturalism.

This chapter examines the ways in which educators and schools have responded to the children of immigrants, the nature of the encounter between immigrants and the schools, and the patterns, causes, and consequences of educational outcomes among immigrants and their children. The literature upon which it draws is diverse, encompassing the work of both historians and social scientists. In the case of the historical work, analysis of immigrants and schooling is often embedded in analysis of larger problematics, such as the development of urban schooling. For these reasons, it is not possible to speak of "the" literature on immigrants and education in the same way as it may be possible to speak of the literature on other topics treated in this *Handbook*. The chapter, therefore, primarily synthesizes the findings and interpretations of research pertaining to particular questions and draws on exemplars rather than delineates a coherent body of research.

EDUCATIONAL RESPONSES TO THE PRESENCE OF IMMIGRANTS

The responses of schools to immigrants are shaped by a range of influences. These include social changes concomitant with immigration, broader political currents, professional educational philosophies and paradigms, and local school ethoses.

Across the variations shaped by broader forces, there has been a continuity of purpose to acculturate immigrants and to assimilate them into existing or emergent social structures, moral orders, and symbolic systems. The discussion in this section centers on the goals of and means to immigrant acculturation, immigrants' responses to these goals and means, the accommodations that schools have made to immigrants' cultural differences, and the degree of conflict attending each of these.

The Goals of and Means to Immigrant Acculturation

While the impetus to expanded schooling in the 19th century came from multiple sources (Kaestle, 1983), historical research has demonstrated close relationships between immigration and the development of common schooling. Cities such as New York and Boston experienced rapid growth in their Irish and non-English-speaking immigrant populations beginning as early as the 1830s. Inextricably related to capitalist industrialization, the growth of urban immigrant populations became associated in the minds of native-born Americans with class conflict, persistent poverty, crime, social disorganization and disorder, cultural deviance and foreign habits, and the threat of Catholicism (Kaestle, 1973, 1983; Schultz, 1973).

Anxious social reformers promoted schooling as an institution in which to inoculate immigrant children against the moral depravity of their environment, to inculcate principles of republican virtue, and to cultivate American habits and identities through association with native-born children (Kaestle, 1973; Schultz, 1973). Schools were intended to serve as "culture factories" (Schultz, 1973) in which polyglot populations were to be homogenized.

On the assumptions that the social morality of the nation depended crucially on the moral character of each individual, and that extant American institutions were both superior and fragile, antebellum schools stressed a pan-Protestant ideology of unity, assimilation, obedience, restraint, self-sacrifice, and industriousness that was directed at all, but deemed especially necessary for lower-class immigrants (Kaestle, 1983; see also Troen, 1975). To these ends, educators placed reliance on moralizing textbooks (Elson, 1964; Schultz, 1973) and on the educative effects of "nonsectarian" King James Bible reading and Protestant prayers.

The responses of 19th-century immigrants to the common schools cannot be easily summarized (Kaestle, 1983). For many the cultural and religious alienation and denigration with which the public schools confronted their children sparked political protest, and provided reasons to attend parochial schools or not to attend schools at all (Kaestle, 1973, 1983; Ravitch, 1974; Schultz, 1973). For others the opportunities provided by the schools, or the local accommodations compelled by developing political power among immigrant communities, such as permitting scriptural choice and purging textbooks of ethnic slurs, or making provisions for the use of non-English vernaculars, sufficed to make attendance attractive. Indeed, in some cities such as Boston, immigrant demand for school attendance outstripped available spaces before the enactment of compulsory attendance laws (Schultz, 1973). Whether immigrants accommodated to and cooperated with the evolving public schools, or whether they ignored them or resisted them, varied significantly among and within groups, geographically and temporally (Kaestle, 1983).

While Americans expected 19th-century schools to transform immigrants, decentralized control of schools (Kaestle, 1983; Tyack, 1974), belief in the assimilative power of everyday exposure to the American environment and American institutions, and belief in the civic efficacy of simple literacy training and moral didacticism (Lazerson, 1971) militated against, though did not entirely preclude, special practices directed specifically toward immigrant acculturation rather than toward the socialization of all.

In the contexts of rapid and large turn-of-the-century population influxes from southern and eastern Europe to crowded and disorderly urban centers (see, e.g., Lazerson, 1971), intensified and widespread anxiety over American national identity and social cohesion, and transformations in the nature of the workplace, educators both broadened the reach of the school in socializing all children through such measures as "community civics" (Olneck, 1989), and adopted distinctive curricular, extracurricular, and disciplinary innovations intended primarily, though not exclusively, to "Americanize" the children of immigrants. These included, among other measures, kindergartens; instruction in hygiene, manners, and the conduct of daily life; home visitations; and special classes for teaching English. A number of historians have detailed these efforts (see, e.g., Lazerson, 1971; Berrol, 1978; Tyack, 1974; Brumberg, 1986; R. Cohen & Mohl, 1979; Raftery, 1992).

No account of the schooling of European immigrants in the early part of this century is more meticulous than that by Steven Brumberg (1986). Reconstructing the efforts of New York's schools during the first quarter of the century to transform immigrant children from "aliens" into "Americans," Brumberg emphasizes the connections educators made between outward behavior and inner identity. In explicitly instructing youngsters in middle-class hygiene and manners, diet and food preparation, home management, dress, aesthetic and literary standards,

recreation, the rights and duties of citizenship, accentless English, and the myths and legends of U.S. history, and in providing them with role models, educators sought not merely to induce behavioral conformity, but, more fundamentally, to inculcate American values, logics, sensibilities, and identities. Similarly, regimentation of movement, patriotic assemblies, the flag salute, exhortative speeches, and other rituals were intended not merely to regulate behavior and to extract professions of loyalty, but to reorder students' dispositions, orientations, and the communities and symbols with which they identified.

Despite recognizing the denigration implied by the exclusion of immigrant culture from curricular recognition and by prohibitions on children's use of their native languages, Brumberg (1986) rejects the characterization, prevalent among revisionist scholars, of Americanization in the schools as coercive or paternalistic cultural imposition by elites intent on preserving WASP hegemony or on developing new forms of social discipline (see, e.g., Greer, 1972; Violas, 1973; Carlson, 1987). Instead, based on the facts that many of the approaches utilized by the New York Public Schools were innovated by private philanthropic institutions that were heavily and voluntarily patronized by immigrants; that immigrants faced a real need for structure and direction in a difficult new environment; and that immigrant parents, at least the eastern European Jews upon whom his study concentrates, appear to have endorsed the schools' efforts, Brumberg gives credence to the Americanizers' desires to "share" American life with the newcomers, and to provide them with the knowledge required for successful participation in a modern, urban society (see also Weinberg, 1977).

A less sympathetic interpretation of Americanization in the public schools is advanced in R. Cohen and Mohl's (1979) study of Gary, Indiana. Cohen and Mohl associate Americanization with the nativist impulse to regulate and reorder the behavior of immigrants coercively so as to ensure adherence to dominant social norms, and to ensure social stability. They also associate the schools' day-to-day regimen of Americanization with the cultivation of a compliant industrial workforce. More so than Brumberg, Cohen and Mohl highlight the ways in which schools denigrated immigrants and their cultures.

However, unlike some who interpret Americanization as an attempt to institutionalize social control (e.g., Carlson, 1987), R. Cohen and Mohl (1979) question the extent to which Americanizers imposed their requirements upon unwilling families and students. Immigrant values, Cohen and Mohl observe, were not necessarily antagonistic to those of the public schools. Immigrants might well have valued the opportunities for economic mobility that schooling offered more than they objected to assaults on their cultural integrity, which, in any case, could be nurtured outside the schools. Finally, public school attendance remained high in Gary despite the availability of parochial school alternatives.

Brumberg's (1986) sympathetic interpretation of Americanization is consistent with Timothy Smith's (1969) findings that turn-of-the-century immigrant community organizations were themselves heavily involved in Americanizing activities. It is also consistent with my own distinction between "popular

Americanizers," whose activities took on "anti-hyphen" and "100 percent Americanism" forms, and "professional Americanizers," including teachers, who sought to promote cultural conformity in order to integrate the population and to enhance immigrants' participation in national life (Olneck, 1989). David Tyack (1974) may have best summarized the dual nature of Americanization by observing that it cultivated both modern habits and Anglo-conformity, and that it promoted both equal opportunity and social control.

Despite the evidence that many immigrants welcomed the opportunities provided by public schools, there is reason to believe that what Brumberg (1986) has interpreted as congruence between the interests of the schools and those of first-generation immigrant parents might better be interpreted, at least in some respects, as acquiescence. Deborah Dash Moore (1981) has found that New York's second-generation Jewish immigrant adults, having attained the political power associated with middle-class status, pressured the schools to recognize and accommodate Jewish ethnicity, most prominently by including Hebrew as a foreign language in the high schools, and by accommodating the schools' calendars to the demands of Jewish observances. Attainment of the political capacity to press ethnic demands, albeit modest ones, rather than intergenerational change in ethos away from assimilation toward pluralism, most probably accounts for this shift.

Elsewhere, immigrant groups, such as Poles and Czechs in Chicago, pressured school authorities for inclusion of homeland languages in school curricula (Hogan, 1978), thereby signifying resistance to the exclusively English school environment upon which Americanizers insisted. Catholic immigrants rejected as well linkages between Americanization and Protestantism like those forged in the released-time plan adopted by the Gary, Indiana, public schools and the city's Protestant churches (R. Cohen & Mohl, 1979).

European immigrants during the first quarter of this century entered schools that were intent not only on Americanizing them culturally, but on sorting them and their native peers scientifically into distinct academic tracks and differentiated vocational destinations (see, e.g., Lazerson, 1971; Tyack, 1974). To this end schools adopted the use of standardized aptitude tests patterned on the classification tests developed for the army during World War I (see, e.g., Raftery, 1992).

Revisionist scholars have interpreted the testing movement in the light of the eugenics and immigration restriction movements, seeing the use of tests as racist mechanisms to put a meritocratic facade on discrimination and class exploitation (Karier, 1973). Others have offered more benign interpretations. Paula Fass (1989), for example, characterizes IQ testing as a way to codify social perceptions of heterogeneity while providing the means to solve the institutional problems generated by expanded school populations (see also D. K. Cohen & Rosenberg, 1977). The former interpretation neglects the cultural complexity of institutional practices, while the latter ignores the role of unequal power in establishing hegemonic beliefs.

While immigrants may have for the most part accepted, and even supported, the efforts of the schools to acculturate their children, they were less accepting of the efforts to differentiate and vocationalize secondary education. Immigrant communities sometimes collectively and publicly resisted plans, like the Gary Plan, that intensified curricular differentiation and appeared to limit their children's opportunities for social mobility through schooling (Brumberg, 1986).

After enactment of immigration restriction in 1924, and with abatement of anxieties over the threat to national cultural identity, the schools shifted their emphasis on Americanizing new immigrants to addressing an already long-standing "second-generation problem," a problem recognized earlier by settlement-house workers (Davis, 1967), but heretofore largely ignored by the schools. Hoping to overcome the alienation experienced by relatively acculturated children of immigrants who were cut off from their parents but not fully accepted into the American mainstream, and hoping to reduce the ongoing tensions between hyphenated Americans and Anglo-Saxons, between Jews and Gentiles, and even between White and Black Americans, educators began to develop "intercultural education" to recognize the contributions of diverse groups to American history and society, to teach appreciation of cultural differences, and to enhance the self-respect of minority children (see Goodenow, 1975; Montalto, 1982; Olneck, 1990).

Foreshadowing aspects of the debates over multicultural education in the post-1965 period, interculturalists debated the relative emphasis that should be placed on recognizing distinctive contributions and cultures of particular groups as compared with the emphasis that should be placed on commonalities among individuals of diverse origins. In the context of World War II, the latter position prevailed (Montalto, 1982).

As the preceding account suggests, the historiography of immigrant education has been overwhelmingly devoted to the schooling of European immigrants. Historians investigating the schooling of Mexican and Asian immigrants in the Southwest and West detail Americanization, IQ testing, and vocationalizing measures paralleling those applied to European immigrants, and find similar tensions between coercion and beneficence, and between immigrant acquiescence and resistance, as found by those studying the schooling of European immigrants (see, e.g., San Miguel, 1987; Gonzalez, 1990; Raftery, 1992). They detail, as well, the somewhat paradoxical ties, unique to non-White immigrants, between Americanization, on the one hand, and systematic racial segregation and economic, political, and social subordination, on the other.

After passage of the Immigration Act of 1965, revoking the 1924 national quota regulations, large-scale immigration into the United States resumed, particularly from Mexico, Latin America, and Asia, and once again the question of how to school immigrant children arose, persisting into the present. Despite contemporary rhetoric rejecting melting-pot ideology and celebrating cultural pluralism (Olneck, 1990), recent ethnographic research shows that schools continue to seek to integrate immigrant children into an assumed American mainstream (see, e.g., Goldstein, 1985; Grey, 1990). Voicing concern that immigrant children be provided equal opportunity to acquire the skills necessary for participation in U.S. labor markets and social arenas, contemporary educators insist that newcomers be encouraged and prepared to enter "regular" classrooms and to participate in the elaborate social life of U.S. schools (see, e.g., Becker, 1985; Goldstein, 1985; Gibson, 1988).

They do so, however, in a context ostensibly more accommodating of cultural diversity than the contexts of the past.

Accommodations to Cultural Diversity

The degree and manner in which schools have acknowledged and accommodated cultural differences varies over time and locale. Accommodations by the public schools have, however, been generally limited and conflictual.

Throughout much of the 19th century, the combination of decentralized control and concentrations of immigrant settlement in the agricultural upper Midwest, especially Germans in Wisconsin, permitted considerable use of vernacular mother tongues in rural schools, the hiring of native homeland language speakers as teachers, and modifications or benign neglect of Protestant-inspired observances such as Bible reading (Kuyper, 1980; Kaestle, 1983). School officials turned a blind eye to such practices, even when they were legally prohibited, both because of the political power of immigrant communities, and because of the officials' desire to entice immigrant children into the "Anglicizing" environment of the common school and away from the isolating influences of private, religiously sponsored schools in which the use of English was minimal.

Such accommodations in rural areas, while widespread, were nevertheless subject to criticism and controversy. English-language parents objected when their own children were assigned to schools in which instruction in German predominated, necessitating the redrawing of district lines and time-sharing of school buildings (Kuyper, 1980; Schlossman, 1983). At the state level, nativist-inspired legislation limiting language of instruction to English, even when it had little instrumental effect, took on great symbolic importance (Tyack, 1974; Jorgenson, 1987).

Mid- to late-19th-century urban school officials in such cities as St. Louis and Milwaukee were motivated, for reasons similar to those of their rural counterparts, to provide opportunities for the study of German as a subject in elementary schools. By 1874 almost half of St. Louis's elementary students availed themselves of this opportunity, and by 1880, 80% of the German students had been drawn into the public schools (Troen, 1975). But even as they provided for the study of German in their schools, urban school officials, with rare exception, insisted that the amount of time devoted to such study be strictly limited, that such study be a bridge into a wholly English-language curriculum, and that non-German students be encouraged to participate in German-language programs (Schlossman, 1983). School authorities did not consider similar measures for linguistic groups whose numbers were fewer than the Germans, and whose children were already within the embrace of the public schools (Troen, 1975).

Even in relatively favorable contexts, linguistic accommodation engendered ongoing debate. Opponents of German-language instruction in St. Louis, particularly the Irish, invoked arguments over cost, interference with the regular curriculum, threats to the standing and universality of English, and special privilege, and succeeded in eliminating such instruction even before the onset of anti-German hysteria in the middle 1910s (Troen, 1975; Schlossman, 1983).

Outside of the Midwest, accommodations were fewer and less durable. New York City, for example, experimented with a small number of schools for German-speaking students beginning in 1837, but refused requests for similar schools for Italians. The German schools were abolished in 1850 because students remained in the schools longer than was necessary to acquire facility with English, postponing their integration with native children, and because the teachers extended the use of instruction in German beyond stipulated subject matter (Kaestle, 1973). A request for a similar school by Germans in Boston in 1851 was denied on the grounds of not being "necessary to Americanizing foreigners" (Schultz, 1973, p. 290).

Accommodation to the religious and cultural demands of 19th-century Catholic immigrants proved inherently more difficult than accommodation to the linguistic demands of Germans. Common-school reformers sought an inclusive school system that would culturally and morally reform and homogenize the republic's children (Kaestle, 1973, 1983). To this end they demanded and won, despite opposition from Catholics and from a minority of officials sympathetic to local pluralism, a public school monopoly on tax monies for schooling, and insisted upon practices like nonsectarian moral education and Bible reading without commentary that were anathema to Catholic immigrants and their clerical leaders (Kaestle, 1973; Troen, 1975; Ravitch, 1974; Sanders, 1977; Jorgenson, 1987). They also confronted immigrant children with texts that denigrated Catholicism, Catholics, the nations from which Catholic immigrants originated, and the moral character of immigrant populations, most notably the Irish (Elson, 1964; Kaestle, 1973; Sanders, 1977; Jorgenson, 1987). The result was periodic eruption of intense conflict between Catholics and Protestants over school policy; periods of uneasy and tenuous local accommodation, such as banning Bible reading; and the growth of parochial schooling (see, e.g., Ravitch, 1974; Kaestle, 1973; Troen, 1975; Schultz, 1973; Sanders, 1977; Jorgenson, 1987).

While impelled in large measure by the hostility of the surrounding society, the 19th-century growth of parochial schooling did not depend solely on the nativism of the public schools or on overt conflict between Catholics and Protestants over school issues (Troen, 1975; Sanders, 1977). Those immigrants, such as the German-speaking Lutherans and Catholics in St. Louis, who looked to schooling to guarantee their children's membership in ongoing ethnic, linguistic, and religious communities, rather than as training for wider civic participation, relied upon parochial schooling until their linguistic demands were met. As of 1860, four years before the public schools introduced German language classes, four times as many German students in St. Louis attended "German" schools as attended public schools (Troen, 1975).

Patterns and rates of growth of urban parochial schools were determined by ongoing immigration, economic conditions, concentrations of population, and the size and attitudes of particular groups (Sanders, 1977). Schools proliferated, in particular, as ethnically and linguistically specific parishes were established (Troen, 1975; Sanders, 1977). By 1900, more than half of the parochial school students in Chicago were attending schools in national parishes—that is, parishes officially associated with an ethnic population rather than with an all-inclusive geographic district (Sanders, 1977). While the question of national parishes divided Catholics, conflict among groups and between particular groups and the episcopate over school staffing, supervisory authority, language use, and textbook selection propelled the creation of new schools into the 20th century.

The extent to which 19th-century immigrants attended parochial schools is not easily established. Sources rarely distinguish the proportion of students attending such schools at any one time from the proportion of students having ever attended such schools. What is clear is that attendance varied temporally, geographically, and ethnically. For example, while Kaestle (1983) observes that during the 1860s over 80% of Chicago's elementary school students attended public schools, Sanders (1977) finds that over the course of the 19th century, about half of the city's Catholic students attended parochial schools. In contrast to Chicago during the 19th century, during the first decade of the 20th century, only 13 to 15% of Massachusetts students were attending parochial schools (Lazerson, 1971).

Public schools during the first quarter of this century made even fewer and more grudging accommodations to cultural diversity than had 19th-century schools. While a few experts advocated and a few schools occasionally experimented with the employment of bilingual teachers and even some bilingual instruction, educational orthodoxy held that any use of home languages in the classroom detracted from English acquisition and perpetuated the use of non-English languages in immigrant homes. Moreover, educators intent upon facilitating immigrant children's rapid assimilation were exceedingly reluctant to separate them from their English-speaking classmates (Olneck, 1989). Nevertheless, teachers and administrators recognized that sink-or-swim practices and the placement of older children into primary grades could cause difficulty and be counterproductive.

To facilitate the speedy acquisition of English by immigrant children, various localities experimented with "vestibule" or "steamer" classes and "special rooms" that were intended to equip non-English-speaking students with sufficient English comprehension to enable them to join regular classrooms (Lazerson, 1971; Berrol, 1978; Montero-Sieburth & La Celle-Peterson, 1991). Such experimental classes were regarded as expedients, intended to be conducted solely in English and limited to language instruction, and were to be attended only for so long as was absolutely necessary. Nor were they universal or necessarily prevalent. In Gary, Indiana, during the mid-1920s, only one school had even one special class in which to teach immigrant children English (R. Cohen & Mohl, 1979).

For schooling that was linguistically and culturally responsive, late-19th- and early-20th-century eastern, central, and southern European immigrants relied in varying degrees upon parochial schools (Sanders, 1977; R. Cohen & Mohl, 1979). The appeal of parochial schools during this period was especially strong among Slavic groups, whose use of schooling was directed more toward ethnic solidarity than toward economic mobility (Hogan, 1978; R. Cohen & Mohl, 1979; Bodnar, 1976, 1982).

While scholars have often contrasted the culturally conservative functions of parochial schools with the Americanizing functions of public schools (see, e.g., R. Cohen & Mohl, 1979),

under the impact of immigration restriction, diminished ethnic cohesion, residential dispersal and ethnic commingling, social mobility, language attrition, and the centralizing and standardizing policies of the Church hierarchy, parochial schools from the 1920s onward played more the role of organizing an Americanized Catholic community than of preserving ethnically bounded immigrant communities (Sanders, 1977; see also Fass, 1989). While compromises continued to be required, such as permitting catechism in home languages or permitting supplementary language texts, declines were pronounced in the teaching and utilization of home languages in even ostensibly national parish schools, and in the numbers of such schools and their enrollments (Sanders, 1977).

During the 1920s and 1930s, in the absence of continuing infusions of new, non-English-speaking immigrants into the schools, the issue of accommodating linguistic diversity receded. As second-generation immigrants constructed American-based ethnic identities, the question became the extent to which the public schools were permissible arenas in which to organize and express these identities collectively.

Introduction of foreign languages like Hebrew and Italian as subjects of study in the high schools came to serve as ethnic insignias of Americanized middle-class groups, even as the proportion of ethnic students enrolling in such courses was minimal (Dash Moore, 1981).While school boards looked askance at the formation of religio-ethnic clubs and associations within the schools, or at the use of school facilities for community-based religio-ethnic activities, school principals proved more accommodating (Dash Moore, 1981; Raftery, 1992). The social distance between the schools and immigrant children diminished as second-generation Euro-Americans entered the teaching force in increasing numbers, and as school officials endeavored to place ethnic teachers with coethnic student populations (Berrol, 1978).

In the period since the 1965 Immigration Reform Act, the schooling of immigrants has been conditioned by the assumptions of policies and practices pertaining to the schooling of students of color and nonimmigrant linguistic minorities (Glazer, 1985). Official educational policy assumes that the limited recognition and incorporation of minority cultural and linguistic repertoires is an appropriate, and perhaps necessary, means to assure students that they are respected and that they belong, and to facilitate levels of linguistic and subject-matter comprehension adequate to participation in regular classrooms. This assumption is most commonly implemented through transitional bilingual education and English as a Second Language (ESL) programs, which schools provide with varying degrees of willingness and levels of support, and which are structured so as to leave undisturbed the normal school programs and prevailing local academic values (Goldstein, 1985). Similarly, when immigrants' recreational cultures are recognized, it is in a manner that highlights immigrant marginality, such as the funding of soccer clubs as a "nonestablished" sport (Grey, 1990).

School ethnographers have found that by virtue of physical and social isolation from the "regular" academic program, the very programs intended to facilitate the incorporation of immigrant students can highlight and perpetuate those students' and their teachers' marginal and peripheral status within the school (Grey, 1990; Becker, 1985; Goldstein, 1985; Gibson, 1988). Immigrant parents and students, while often appreciative of the support and guidance offered by these programs, are aware that the education that they provide is not fully recognized, and express concern that students not be assigned to them needlessly or retained in them unnecessarily (Gibson, 1988; Montero-Sieburth & La Celle-Peterson, 1991; Suarez-Orozco, 1991).

Nevertheless, it is usually only within such "special" programs or classrooms that teachers are willing to modify curriculum and pedagogy to accommodate the distinctive learning needs of immigrant children, and that immigrant children may comfortably express themselves (Goldstein, 1985; Trueba, Jacobs, & Kirton, 1990). Moreover, immigrant children who are not placed in "special" programs, or who have completed ESL, are likely to be placed in lower-level ability groups and curricular tracks in the "regular" program, further limiting their opportunities (Goldstein, 1985; Gibson, 1988).

Despite the fact that local bilingual and ESL programs are highly circumscribed and are often supported with federal and state funds, they are a source of protest by established Americans. Resistance arises because the programs do not mesh with perceptions of what the local school is and does, and how it is related to the existing community (Grey, 1990); because local parents fear that special programs will interfere with their own children's educations, and resent "their" tax dollars being used to fund instruction that uses "other people's" languages (Gibson, 1988); because some community members fear that bilingual education impedes assimilation (Gibson, 1988); and because some community members hold nativist sentiments of the sort exemplified by the English-only movement (Montero-Sieburth & La Celle-Peterson, 1991; Kiang, 1990).

The unwillingness of communities to respond more fully to and accommodate the distinctive needs of immigrant communities has, in some cases, prompted those communities to organize on the model of and sometimes in cooperation with long-term American minority communities (Montero-Sieburth & La Celle-Peterson, 1991; Kiang, 1990).

THE ENCOUNTER BETWEEN THE IMMIGRANT AND THE SCHOOLS

The encounter between immigrant children, families, and communities and the schools is conditioned by local school cultures; by perceptions relevant actors hold of one another and themselves; by the diverse meanings immigrants and educators assign to schooling; by tacit as well as explicit pedagogical, curricular, and administrative practices; by the degree of discontinuity that obtains between immigrant and school cultures; and by the structural characteristics and cultural practices of immigrant communities. The results of that encounter may be seen in status orders within schools, in the nature of mutual interactions, in the degree of acculturation immigrants experience, in the manner in which immigrants appropriate and utilize their educational experiences, and in the ways that schooling becomes a site for the construction and experience of ethnic identity.

Local School Cultures

Immigrants do not enter undifferentiated "American" schools. They enter specific schools whose immediate contexts, histories, memories, and commitments shape their organization and practices. Mediated by day-to-day routines and by the interpretations assigned to events, differences among schools may be highly consequential for the ways in which boundaries between immigrant and native students are either transcended or solidified.

Goode, Schneider, and Blanc (1992), for example, found appreciable differences in the practices and outcomes of two neighboring Philadelphia schools serving socioeconomically comparable populations. One, a public school, symbolically celebrated schooling as an avenue of individual mobility, and deemphasized cultural differences. It provided short-term rather than long-term English for Speakers of Other Languages (ESOL) or ESL programs, and established classroom and lunchroom assignment and seating rules that ensured intermingling. The school's policies and practices appeared to encourage easy interactions and strong attachments among students from diverse groups, as well as the muting of expressions of ethnic distinctiveness, including the informal use of languages other than English. The other school, a parochial school, symbolically recognized distinctive community entities, addressed recruitment appeals explicitly to particular identity groups, and recognized and supported group-based activities and associations. This school's policies and practices appeared to accentuate the salience of group boundaries.

Goode et al.'s (1992) specific findings should not be generalized. In some contexts it is institutional silence about immigrant cultural distinctiveness that seems to reinforce separation and lack of communication between immigrant and native students (Grey, 1990). What Goode et al.'s findings demonstrate more generally is the salience of immediate school contexts for social relations between immigrants and natives.

The terms on which immigrants encounter native students may be affected by school ethoses that antedate their entrance into particular schools. In her ethnographic study of two contrasting high schools, Goldstein (1985) found that in one school, institutional commitments to sustaining a public reputation for academic rigor and to upholding strict academic standards encouraged bilingual/bicultural programs markedly isolated from the remainder of the school, while in the other school a prior commitment to strong discipline and racial integration encouraged the placement of immigrant students in classes among natives, though in pedagogical regimes not conducive to constructive interactions.

Intergroup Perceptions

The views that students, parents, and teachers hold of one another significantly shape the degree, quality, and consequences of interactions between immigrants and their fellow students and teachers, and the views immigrant youth come to hold of themselves. Often the result is exacerbated social distance and marginality for immigrant students even in the absence of intentional exclusion.

In the eyes of many American students and teachers, immigrants have entered, even intruded, into "our" country, and are therefore obligated to adopt "our" ways and evaluative standards (Gibson, 1988). Native students and teachers are especially frustrated by the lack of participation by immigrants in the social and extracurricular lives of the schools and, echoing complaints of previous generations of educators and students, complain about immigrants' "clannishness." Students often do not comprehend the restrictions some immigrant parents place on their children, immigrants' apparent lack of concern with dating, or the degree to which immigrant students seem to take school seriously (Gibson 1988; Goldstein, 1985). Generally, neither American-born teachers and students nor immigrant students recognize the extent to which their assessments of one another are complicated by misinterpretations of behavior, and by mutual ignorance of differing subjective values and standards (Goldstein, 1985; Delgado-Gaitan & Trueba, 1991).

Both in earlier periods and in contemporary times, teachers have categorized immigrant groups according to their conformity to prevailing definitions of the "good student," and have held mixed views of the educational values, capabilities, and futures of immigrant students. Early 20th-century educators praised the studiousness and academic talent displayed by Jewish students, while criticizing Italians as nonacademic (Brumberg, 1986; Cowan & Cowan, 1989; Olneck & Lazerson, 1974; Ravitch, 1974). Contemporary educators frequently stereotype many Latinos, Portuguese, and Hmong as academically limited, likely to drop out, and suitable only for special, remedial programs, while praising the academic prowess and hard work of Vietnamese and other "Asian" students (Becker, 1985; Grey, 1990; Gibson, 1988; Goldstein, 1985; Caplan, Choy, & Whitmore, 1991; Delgado-Gaitan & Trueba, 1991; Trueba et al., 1990; Matute-Bianchi, 1991). Certain groups, like the Hmong, newly arrived Mexican immigrants, and Central American refugees, enjoy the approval of teachers for their efforts and comportment, despite their being perceived as academically deficient (Goldstein, 1985; Matute-Bianchi, 1991; Suarez-Orozco, 1991).

Immigrant students are well aware of the negative judgments being passed upon them, though the degree to which they are critical of teachers in return seems to vary by their length of residence or membership in a group that has a collective memory of discrimination within the United States. In Garden City, Kansas, for example, Latino students explain their high drop-out rate as a reaction, in part, to the low expectations their teachers express toward them (Grey, 1990). Recent Portuguese immigrants in New England see their teachers as being helpful, and interpret their teachers' more favorable views toward African Americans and Southeast Asians as an effect of the larger school environment, not of their teachers' volition (Becker, 1985). In contrast, earlier Portuguese arrivals perceive their teachers as neglecting them, favoring other groups, and ignoring their language.

The judgments that teachers render of immigrant students' academic competence are integrated into the students' views of themselves. When these are negative, not only are students deterred from learning, but their sense of marginality is accentuated (Trueba et al., 1990).

The hostility, disapproval, condescension, and indifference they sense from native-born students can injure immigrant students, leading to even greater hesitance and withdrawal than produced merely by newcomer status and cultural uncertainty (Becker, 1985; Goldstein, 1985). While some researchers have observed that immigrants, in contrast to indigenous minorities, may explain away and tolerate the prejudice they encounter (Gibson, 1988; Suarez-Orozco, 1991), it cannot be supposed that immigrant youth are inured to the effects of rejection.

Just as native students assess immigrant students, so, too, immigrants assess the natives with whom they come into contact. These assessments can impede mutual interaction. In particular, many immigrants judge African Americans unfavorably, significantly affecting relationships in the urban schools that both attend (Becker, 1985; Caplan et al., 1991).

Immigrant students are often disconcerted by American students' apparent disrespect toward teachers, and by the constant socializing that occurs in classes, making them likely to rebuff overtures made toward them in the classroom setting (Goldstein, 1985). On the other hand, immigrant youth, recognizing the status enjoyed by native students, often do aspire to friendships and associations with their established fellows (Goldstein, 1985).

Tacit and Explicit Pedagogical, Curricular, and Administrative Practices

Pedagogical, curricular, and administrative practices, even when ostensibly responsive to the needs of immigrant students, leave intact or minimally disturb prevailing definitions of mainstream schooling. These practices can create the boundaries and strengthen the hierarchies that define the immigrant's marginal location within the school, and that limit relationships among immigrants and natives.

For example, laissez-faire practices ceding students appreciable choice in their patterns of association inhibit cooperation and interaction between immigrant and native students. Exempting immigrant girls from gym requirements, while responsive to particular cultural prohibitions, fails to provide inclusive accommodations to immigrant needs (Becker, 1985).

Reliance on whole-class instruction and on public student participation renders immigrants whose skills in English are limited, and who are reluctant participants, problematic to teachers. They are less of a dilemma in the lower ability-level classes that rely on individual worksheets, drills, and in-class exercises than in the upper ability-level classrooms that rely on lectures and homework (Goldstein, 1985). Even in lower ability-level classes, immigrants may be seated apart, encouraged to rely upon one another, and graded for effort alone, resulting in isolation from mainstream students and ongoing classroom activities.

Teachers' perceptions and interpretations of immigrant youth guide their practices with them. Expectations of poor performance, early school departure, and resistance to assimilation, as held by New England teachers of Portuguese immigrants, result in neglect and indifference to poor academic performance, while high expectations, like those held with respect to Asian students, result in encouragement and individualized attention (Becker, 1985). Interpretation of immigrants' reticence as lack of interest, coupled with practices dependent upon student voluntarism and initiative, limit immigrant students' classroom participation.

Cultural Discontinuities

The schools have historically presented and continue to present a challenge to the valued ways and inherited meanings of immigrant groups. More than just behavioral patterns are at issue. Rather, concepts of God, personhood, family, community, and society, responsibilities and futures, right and wrong, and gender identities and roles are at stake. These challenges have had profound consequences for the experiences of immigrant youth, for rending relationships between the generations, and for transforming immigrant culture and identities.

The most obvious challenge is to the place of community languages. Among turn-of-the-century eastern European Jewish immigrant youth, Yiddish rapidly became a source of shame that was to be readily relinquished (Brumberg, 1986). At the same time, reliance on Yiddish deterred parental visits to the schools, no doubt to the relief of children who dreaded exposure of their parents' broken and accented English (Dash Moore, 1981). In similar fashion, contemporary Portuguese immigrant students abandon the use of Portuguese at school despite continuing to use it at home, while their parents eschew contact with the schools (Becker, 1985). On the other hand, students alienated by the school's rejection and exclusion of their own cultural practices may, in turn, reject the use of English, and pointedly use their own language in the school setting (Delgado-Gaitan & Trueba, 1991).

More generally, American teachers and fellow students present immigrant youth with models that put in doubt their own sense of what is normal, right, and proper, and that beckon them away from the worlds of their families and communities. Immigrant youth face the dilemma of how both to fulfill the roles and responsibilities that family and community membership require, such as assuming early employment or entering marriage at a young age, and at the same time to conform to the expectations of American culture and institutions (Goldstein, 1985).

Social scientists and historians have frequently commented upon the power of individualism in American culture and social structure. The practices and values of American schooling are premised on deeply ingrained perceptions of the "individual" as the fundamental sociological and moral unit of society. In contrast, family and community are the fundamental sociological and moral constructs for many immigrants, and the practices and values of American schools that are rooted in individualism are a source of tension, discomfort, and conflict (Goldstein, 1985; Gibson, 1988; Caplan et al., 1991; Trueba et al., 1990).

The extracurricular and social lives of American schools, for example, may not only compete with the obligations of many immigrant students to contribute to the family's economic well-being, but may, in their premise that individuals must discover and develop their unique interests during a period of adolescence, present a foreign model of personhood (Goldstein, 1985). Expectations that students must develop their skills as "decision-makers" who "make up their own minds" may conflict with models of family and community decision making that rely on collective wisdom and respect for elders (Gibson, 1988). Expectations that students will compete academically on an individualistic basis may conflict with immigrants' practices of cooperation, aversion to atomistic behavior, and reluctance to distinguish oneself publicly (Gibson, 1988; Goldstein, 1985; Delgado-Gaitan & Trueba, 1991).

Classrooms and schools are governed by linguistic, sociocultural, and social interaction codes that may well diverge from those governing the home, peer, and community lives of immigrant children (Delgado-Gaitan & Trueba, 1991). Language and literacy acquisition, in particular, may be impeded when the social organization of teaching and learning ignores these differences, and fails to provide opportunities and activities that permit students to integrate and build upon the culture, cognitive patterns, and skills they bring to the classroom.

Delgado-Gaitan and Trueba (1991) found, for example, that pedagogical practices in the California elementary schools they studied contradicted culturally sanctioned patterns of sharing, leadership, and oral storytelling among Mexican American students. Mainstream teachers, rather than modify their pedagogies to accommodate their students, attributed students' difficulties to "deficiencies," and insisted upon adherence to Anglo norms. Trueba et al. (1990) report similar findings for the elementary school attended by the Hmong students they studied. In both cases students did not necessarily or successfully adopt the American patterns insisted upon in the classrooms. Rather, they engaged in a variety of strategies to resist or to disengage from classroom learning, further reinforcing their teachers' negative assessments of the students' academic capabilities.

It is perhaps in the matter of gender relations that schooling poses the greatest challenge to immigrant communities. While the education of sons is regarded with some anxiety, it is nevertheless viewed positively as a means to furthering family economic security. But, across a number of immigrant groups, researchers have found that the education of girls has been more problematic than that of boys. Hmong, Portuguese, Sikh, and other immigrant parents worry that schools, which are typically coeducational, undermine the close supervision and protection that they seek to exercise over their daughters. They also worry that American ideas of individual fulfillment, particularly as achieved through higher education, will lead their daughters away from their responsibilities as caretakers of the home and as future mothers, and possibly into marriages with native-born Americans (Goldstein, 1985; Becker, 1985; Gibson, 1988; Matute-Bianchi, 1991). To mitigate the potential harm schooling may cause, parents (and brothers) may insist that daughters (and sisters) attend the schools attended by their brothers (Goldstein, 1985), and may limit support for higher education to community college programs destining their graduates for office work (Gibson, 1988).

Schooling has offered the girls models of less burdened and constrained lives, but has posed them with highly charged conflicts that are not easy to resolve (Goldstein, 1985). Sikh young women in Northern California respond to the conflicting messages they receive, the criticisms they endure, and the uncertainty of parental support for further education with lower grades and higher absenteeism rates than their male counter-parts (Gibson, 1988).

Cross-Group Interactions

The interactions between immigrant students and natives that arise out of the kinds of mutual perceptions, cultural discontinuities, and educational practices discussed above often range from virtually nonexistent to hostile. There is little evidence of sustained and mutually fruitful interaction across boundaries, either within or beyond the confines of the school.

Not one of the sample of Becker's (1985) Portuguese immigrant students, irrespective of time of arrival, or any members of their families, had an Anglo friend with whom they socialized outside of work or school, nor did the students participate in the social life of the school organized around dances and sports. Since Becker's study was conducted in the Portuguese section of "Old City," and does not include subjects whose families left the East End immigrant community, the generalizability of this finding to residentially mobile Portuguese is, however, uncertain.

In the midwestern city studied by Goldstein (1985), virtually no Hmong high school students met with American classmates outside of school. Within the high schools Goldstein studied, on those rare occasions when social conversations occurred between Americans and Hmong, they were filled with misunderstood responses and disparaging undertones on the part of the American students. On occasion the Hmong encountered subtle forms of discrimination, such as American students deliberately speaking fast, making plays on words, and using sarcasm at their expense. Direct discrimination also occurred in the use of racial slurs. The Northern California Sikhs studied by Gibson (1988) encountered a similarly unfriendly environment.

For many immigrant parents, American schools are remote and opaque (Trueba et al., 1990). Among the Hmong that Goldstein (1985) studied, parents believed that it was inappropriate to bother teachers with requests about their children's progress, and they felt impeded from approaching the schools by their lack of facility with English. Consequently, they did not display the kind of involvement with their children's schooling that teachers interpret as evidence of "caring about" and "supporting" education (Lareau, 1989). Similarly, among the Sikhs studied by Gibson (1988) and the Mexican Americans studied by Delgado-Gaitan and Trueba (1991), parents were reluctant to attend school meetings or to visit the schools otherwise unless their children were experiencing particular difficulties.

The Meaning of Schooling to Immigrants and Educators

While myths and symbols exaggerate and idealize reality, the identification of education with opportunity in America, and of the school with American society itself, is of crucial significance in conditioning the encounter between immigrant communities and American schools. Immigrants tend to regard schools, despite the cultural threats they pose, as welcome avenues to participation and mobility (Gibson, 1991).

For Russian Jewish immigrants in the early 20th century, for example, American public schools stood in stark contrast with the Russian state system that limited the number of Jews who could attend secondary schools and universities, and that insisted upon suppression of Jewish identity (Dash Moore, 1981; Cowan & Cowan, 1989). Moreover, American schools opened vistas for young women denied admission by both Russian schools and traditional Jewish cheders and yeshivas.

Contemporary Hmong, while largely preliterate and unschooled, already recognized in Laos the value of formal schooling for the attainment of urban, white-collar jobs, and came to realize in the refugee camps in Thailand the crucial importance of schooling to the future of their children in their anticipated destinations (Goldstein, 1985). Once in the United States, they appreciated the contrast between humane teaching styles as compared with the more harsh methods of Laotian teachers (Trueba et al., 1990).

Northern California Sikh parents and students express confidence that educational credentials will be respected and rewarded in the United States irrespective of the origins of their holders, as do Central American refugees and those Mexican American students who have retained an orientation toward Mexico (Gibson 1988; Suarez-Orozco, 1991; Matute-Bianchi, 1991). Indo-Chinese refugees press strongly upon their children the connections between educational success and occupational attainment, as do Mexican immigrants (Caplan et al., 1991; Delgado-Gaitan & Trueba, 1991).

The value that immigrants assign to schooling arises in part from the recognition that only superior educational credentials will overcome discriminatory barriers to advancement (Gibson, 1988). Heavy pragmatic reliance on schooling as an instrument of advancement impels commitments and academic trajectories that cannot be explained alone by traditional respect for education. Success in school is not, however, necessarily perceived by parents or children as an instrument of individual mobility or competitive success. Rather, in a number of immigrant or refugee communities, among them Sikhs, Vietnamese, and Central Americans, schooling is collectively supported and pursued as a strategy for enhancing family status and mobility, and for recompensing adults for their sacrifices on behalf of children (Gibson, 1988; Caplan et al., 1991; Suarez-Orozco, 1991).

Immigrant belief in and dependence on the efficacy of schooling is not an obdurate article of faith that is unresponsive to objective realities and to shifts in a group's perception of its status and opportunities. While Sikh confidence in higher education is strong in Northern California, in Britain it is on the wane as awareness of persistent discrimination becomes more acute (Gibson & Bhachu, 1991). In California, immigrant "Mexicanos" hold a far stronger faith in the efficacy of education than do nonimmigrant Mexican Americans and Chicanos (Matute-Bianchi, 1991).

School as a Site for Constructing and Evolving Ethnic Identity

Ethnic identities are not inheritances or preservations but are, rather, ongoing active constructions that emerge out of interactions among groups within sociopolitical and symbolic contexts. The nature of those identities depends upon the interpretations parties make of their interactions, which, in turn, depend both on the cultural systems they bring to the contexts of interaction, and on modifications of these arising out of sustained interaction.

Within American schools, immigrant youth become ethnic as they develop images of themselves and of their place on the "map" of American society (Goldstein, 1985), and as they cope with the confusions inherent in wanting to continue to be of their own people and to become Americans (Trueba et al., 1990). Processes of ethnic differentiation, stratification, and identification define, as much as do processes of cultural diffusion and incorporation, the manner of Americanization (Fass, 1989).

For example, from the social distance induced by school sorting mechanisms and classroom management practices, from the treatment they received from American teachers and students, from the competition of their own cultural and power orders with those of the dominant society, and from the necessity of self-consciously making cultural choices, the Hmong high school students whom Goldstein (1985) studied developed a distinctive sense of themselves as a separate category, and as a marginal and inferior group. So, too, did the younger Hmong students studied by Trueba and his colleagues (1990). A social identity as Hmong immigrants was, therefore, not simply the projection forward of premigration identities, nor was it inconsistent with the adoption of American cultural symbols and behavioral norms (Goldstein, 1985).

Not only is ethnic identity among immigrants constructed, its expression may vary situationally and may be systematically patterned by gender, suggesting that the school is itself salient in the refashioning of identity (Becker, 1985; Fass, 1989). For example, among long-term Portuguese immigrant students in New England, within the school context, boys approximate their Anglo counterparts culturally far more than do girls, yet within the home and community no gender differences obtain in the expression of Portuguese identity. Nor are there differences between long-term residents and recent arrivals in the expression of identity in the home and family, while pronounced differences obtain at school. Ethnicity, in this view, provides resources and strategies that may be maneuvered to secure favorable terms of adaptation, and to reduce stress and dissonance (Becker, 1985).

The world of extracurricular activities, as much as the classroom, may be a stage upon which ethnicity is contingently and variably enacted, and is thus a sphere in which variable patterns of association and acculturation arise. Paula Fass (1989) found pronounced ethnic differences, particularly among young men, in patterns of extracurricular participation in New York City's high schools during the 1930s and 1940s. More important, the nature of those differences varied from school to school, depending upon patterns of social class and ethnic composition. This latter variation suggests strongly that the dynamics of ethnic participation were not simple extrapolations of traditional affinities, but arose out of context-specific interaction between groups seeking a place within each school's prestige and status hierarchies. Despite the intentions of educators that extra-

curriculars serve as a homogenizing force, the actions of immigrant youth in appropriating activities for their own ends configured new patterns of association and relationship that resulted in patterns of incorporation, participation, and identification divergent from the patterns intended by those seeking to direct and control immigrant assimilation.

As immigrant students negotiate the world of schooling, they acquire competencies, make choices, and take on roles that both transform their own identities and alter their relationships with their families and communities, and, indeed, begin to reconfigure family and community. In very real ways, immigrant children take school home with them. But what they take is selected, filtered, reinterpreted, applied in novel contexts, and transformed through processes that cannot be readily comprehended as "assimilation" (Brumberg, 1986; Goldstein, 1985).

In part as a reaction to ostracism and discrimination, and in part as an expression of wanting to belong, immigrant children readily adopt the outward manifestations of American culture—including the use of English, American clothing styles, listening to American music, and eating American food—and they develop a distance from and ambivalence about their native culture (Becker, 1985; Goode et al., 1992; Gibson, 1988). Delgado-Gaitan and Trueba (1991) suggest that the deeper interactional, linguistic, and cultural codes that immigrant students appropriate at school are also transported into familiar family, peer, and community contexts.

In their adoption of American practices, immigrant children are ambivalently encouraged by parents eager that their offspring not incur the objections of natives and equally eager that they take advantage of opportunity (Trueba et al., 1990; Gibson, 1988). Such acculturation is not intended or regarded as relinquishing inherited identities, but is rather part of elaborating a dual identity (Gibson, 1988). Indeed, peer pressures to socialize solely within the group may intensify even as acculturation proceeds apace.

More significant than the acquisition of outwardly American cultural practices is the necessity for immigrant children and their parents to come to terms with new standards of evaluation and new sources of authoritative knowledge that undermine the authority and efficacy of the adult community. In the case of early 20th-century Jews, for example, the texts of "Western Civilization" replaced the Talmud; teachers, to some extent, replaced parents and rabbis; and the general community replaced the Jewish community as sources of authority (Brumberg, 1986; Cowan & Cowan, 1989). Among contemporary Hmong youth, the family is less and less a center of activity or a source of self-esteem (Trueba et al., 1990).

Schooling is not merely a site at which immigrant students work out their identities. Their relationship to schooling may become an integral component of students' collective and individual identities. This may be seen most clearly when diverse orientations toward school characterize distinctive identities within a single ethnic group. Maria Matute-Bianchi (1986, 1991) has, for example, detailed, for one high school in a California coastal community, the ways in which positive and negative orientations toward school are highly salient in defining the identities, respectively, of "Mexicanos," or recent Mexican immigrants and long-term immigrants retaining an orientation toward Mexico, and "homeboys" and "homegirls," or Chicanos, who are largely second-generation or longer U.S. residents from lower socioeconomic strata.

In the school Matute-Bianchi studied, students whose perceptions and understandings accord with the modal immigrant model, emphasizing opportunity (Ogbu, 1987, 1991; Gibson, 1991), incorporate favorable outlooks about schooling into their sense of what it means to be a "Mexicano." Students who hold to the modal involuntary minority model, stressing opposition to the culture of historical and contemporary oppressors, incorporate rejection of schooling into their sense of what being a "homeboy" or "homegirl" means.

THE CAUSES AND CONSEQUENCES OF EDUCATIONAL ACHIEVEMENT AND ATTAINMENT AMONG IMMIGRANTS

There is a long-standing fascination with educational outcomes among immigrants. During the last 25 years social scientists and historians have attempted to assess and explain the dimensions and variability of immigrant school performance, and to assess and explain the socioeconomic consequences of that performance. This section attempts to elucidate the questions they have asked, the findings they have reported, and their interpretations of their findings.

Patterns of Educational Performance Among Prerestriction Immigrant Groups

David Cohen (1970) pioneered recent historical study of immigrant school achievement by attempting to exploit studies published during the first third of the 20th century concerning school "retardation," that is, rates of grade-specific over-age enrollments, as well as studies of school retention or persistence and studies of standardized test results. Cohen hoped to establish the extent to which achievement varied among immigrant groups, the reasons for that variation, and the extent to which variation among groups diminished over time.

Cohen (1970) identified a relatively consistent rank ordering of groups' performances that persisted over the first three decades of this century. Children of parents from England, Scotland, Wales, Germany, and Scandinavia did about as well as children of native Whites. Eastern European Jews ranked at or above native White averages, while non-Jewish central and southern Europeans and, to a lesser extent, the Irish were at a serious disadvantage.

The studies that Cohen (1970) utilized were inadequate for disentangling the effects of ethnicity per se from the effects of other relevant factors on which ethnic groups might differ, such as premigration literacy rates, average length of residence in the United States, and occupational distributions or economic resources. To the small extent that Cohen could compare immigrant groups within categories of possibly confounding variables, he found that ethnic differentials were only modestly attenuated. To explain persistent and unaccounted for ethnic differentials, Cohen cautiously, and with qualifications, speculated that independent variations in ethnic-specific "motivation and culture" were at play.

Stimulated in part by Cohen's work, Olneck and Lazerson (1974) attempted a more rigorous analysis of the school achievement of immigrants during the first third of this century. Still working with published sources rather than with survey data for individuals, but drawing on a wider array of studies than Cohen had used, Olneck and Lazerson attempted to manipulate and combine cross-sectional results from a number of sources in ways that would more precisely distinguish direct "ethnic" effects from the effects of confounding and intervening influences.

Olneck and Lazerson (1974) found that, true to the myth of immigrants as eager to avail themselves of educational opportunity, immigrant children were as likely as comparably aged children of native Whites to have been in school and, while in primary school (Grades 1–4), to have been making comparable progress. However, immigrant children were more likely to have been behind in their progress in grammar school (Grades 5–8), in part because they had entered school late, and they were noticeably less likely to have entered high school. Once in high school, however, immigrants were as likely as natives to make normal progress, a finding to be expected in light of the selectivity governing high school entrance.

Olneck and Lazerson's (1974) principal findings relate not to comparisons between immigrants and native Whites, but to comparisons among specific ethnic groups. They found pronounced and fairly consistent differences among national origin groups in rates of grammar school "retardation," likelihoods of entering high school, and rates of progress in high school. As did D. Cohen (1970), Olneck and Lazerson found that the children of Italian and Polish parents fared particularly poorly, while the children of Eastern European Jews fared well.

Olneck and Lazerson (1974) devoted considerable effort to an unsuccessful attempt to account for the disparities between Russian Jews and southern Italians. Even when such factors as average age of entrance into school, length of time students' families had lived in the United States, average incomes of the two groups, and scores on standardized tests were, albeit crudely, taken into account, pronounced differences in educational progress and attainment remained between the two groups.

Having failed to explain educational disparities with the effects of differences on measured factors known to influence educational outcomes, Olneck and Lazerson (1974) advanced a cultural explanation, though they were careful to note that ethnic cultures were not free-floating and static, but were rooted in historical experiences that shape collective outlooks. They argued that cognitive and intellectual orientations, such as facility with words and abstractions, as well as attitudinal and behavioral dispositions toward schooling, such as the ability and willingness to obey and follow a prescribed institutional regimen, responsiveness to a school's reward system, and belief in the importance of continuing in school, influenced performance and persistence in school. Drawing on anthropological sources, immigrant novels, and sociological studies, they offered evidence that Russian Jewish culture prepared that group for education success, while the opposite was true for southern Italians (see also Tyack, 1974).

By far the most significant study of the determinants and consequences of immigrant school achievement and attainment in the past is that by Joel Perlmann (1988). Utilizing local and state school and census records, and the manuscript U.S. Census, Perlmann assembled and analyzed longitudinal data for individuals from Providence, Rhode Island, covering the period 1880–1930. Because it analyzes data for panels of individuals over time, Perlmann's study is able to assess rather precisely the factors associated with immigrant school performance and attainment, and to assess trends in the interrelationships among ethnicity, immigrant status, socioeconomic background, school performance, and educational attainment.

Perlmann (1988) sets as his task distinguishing the relative influence of factors associated with premigration history, levels of discrimination encountered in the United States, and groups' locations within the local political economy and social-class structure. More generally, Perlmann aims to distinguish the effects of "cultural" factors from those of "structural" factors. He assumes that ethnic differentials not otherwise explained by measures of social structural location might legitimately be attributed to unmeasured cultural factors. While the effects of so-called structural factors may arise in part out of cultural processes specific to social-class locations (Willis, 1977; Connell, Ashenden, Kessler, & Dowsett, 1982), the distinction between the effects of current social locations and demographic configurations, on the one hand, and the effects of ethnic-specific determinants, on the other, remains useful.

Perlmann's (1988) findings attest to the salience of both structural and cultural factors. Increasing political, social, and economic power and participation among the Irish appear, for example, to account for the convergence between 1880 and 1890 of Irish and Yankee high school entry and school enrollment rates among youth from similar socioeconomic and demographic backgrounds. On the other hand, cultural factors appear implicated in persistent disadvantages for Italians in school progress, grades, and high school entry that cannot be explained by differentials in socioeconomic background or nativity.

Perlmann's (1988) findings accord with those of others that Russian Jews displayed a distinctive propensity to persist in school that cannot be explained by socioeconomic factors. By 1915, and through the remainder of the period of Perlmann's study, Jews were disproportionately likely to enter and to graduate from high school, and to enroll in the college preparatory track. In contrast to the results of some of the early studies upon which Olneck and Lazerson (1974) rely, Perlmann does not find that Jewish high school students received higher grades than their classmates. This suggests a utilitarian commitment to schooling, rather than a distinctive fondness for academic learning (see also Slater, 1969).

A number of scholars have questioned the extent to which independent cultural factors are implicated in educational differentials among immigrant groups. Stephen Steinberg (1981) advances a "social class theory" that does not deny the role of cultural influences, but which maintains that cultural factors are influential only insofar as they are conditioned by and interact with class factors. Steinberg argues that only after they secured an economic foothold through small-scale entrepreneurial success or savings from arduous labor were Jews able to act upon values conducive to lengthier schooling. Colin Greer (1972) advances a similar claim.

If Steinberg and Greer are correct, certain patterns, which neither spells out, should be evident in empirical data. Differentials in educational attainment favoring the children of Jewish immigrants should occur only above certain socioeconomic thresholds, and the degree to which Jews enjoy educational advantages in comparison with others should rise, at least up to a point, with socioeconomic status. The average socioeconomic level of a group, creating a socioeconomic context or environment beyond that of the family, might be expected to influence individuals' educational attainments. No such patterns are evident in Perlmann's data, nor have such patterns been demonstrated in other data.

Furthermore, while it is true that among contemporary Chinese immigrants, a group whose distinctively high educational attainment is sometimes compared with that of earlier Jewish immigrants, the children of proprietors hold an educational advantage (Sanchirico, 1991), taking into account self-employment status explains a negligible portion of the advantage in educational attainment that Asian Americans hold over others (Hirschman & Falcon, 1985).

Without gainsaying the powerful impact of socioeconomic status and social-class location on differentiating educational outcomes among individuals and groups, both direct and inferential evidence suggests the salience of cultural factors that distinguish otherwise structurally comparable groups. But cultural factors do not operate in a vacuum, nor are they impervious to material and historical circumstances, so the durability of distinctive educational ethoses and of their consequences is an open question.

Durability of Educational Differences Among Ethnic Groups

Steinberg (1981) rightly observes that immigrant groups that started out with less favorable cultural dispositions with respect to education did experience educational mobility once they experienced economic mobility. While he is unpersuasive in inferring from this that economic mobility is a necessary perquisite for enjoying educational advantages, he is correct that ethnic differentials do not persist unchanged.

In a similar vein, Miriam Cohen (1982) argues that increasing levels of persistence in schooling among Italian Americans in New York City, beginning in the 1930s, demonstrate that socioeconomic and demographic circumstances, as well as labor-market incentives, explain what otherwise appears to be ethnically determined educational behavior. While Cohen, like Steinberg, is unpersuasive that her findings refute claims of culturally determined educational differentials, she does demonstrate that educational strategies are in some substantial measure pragmatic responses to circumstance and context.

David Hogan (1978), whose stated interest lies not in explaining ethnic educational inequalities as such, but in elucidating the salience of the class structure of social relations for culturally mediated educational behavior, has nonetheless provided evidence relevant to the convergence of levels of educational attainment among immigrant groups. Hogan explains the lengthier schooling pursued by various Chicago immigrant groups in the 1920s as an outcome of the evolution among working-class immigrants of an instrumental attitude toward schooling necessitated by the imperative of ensuring their children's economic welfare. Whereas earlier, groups differed substantially in their reliance on opening their homes to boarders, utilizing their children's labor for supplementary income, investing in home ownership, or investing in their children's lengthier schooling (see also R. Cohen & Mohl, 1979; Bodnar, 1982), over time all came to rely more uniformly on their children's remaining in school. Hogan's argument implies that diminishing educational differentials among immigrant groups can be interpreted as the result of accommodations to an increasingly narrow range of economic options, not necessarily as the convergence of cultural values occasioned by assimilation.

The convergence of educational outcomes among diverse European immigrant groups evident in local data is evident as well in national survey data. Beverly Duncan and Otis Dudley Duncan (1968), for example, analyzed nationally representative data for male, native-born, nonfarm-background Whites and non-Whites other than Blacks who were 25 to 64 years old in 1962, and found that Poles and Italians, often cited as immigrant groups with unfavorable educational outcomes, received a half-year more schooling than men of similar socioeconomic backgrounds. Conversely, men from the North and the West with native-born parents enjoyed no advantage beyond that conferred by more favorable socioeconomic origins. On the other hand, men born in the Soviet Union, presumably largely Russian Jews, received almost a year and a half more schooling than expected on the basis of their socioeconomic origins.

Duncan and Duncan's (1968) findings suggest that while Jewish educational behavior remained distinctive, that of other eastern and central European ethnic groups converged on common patterns determined in large measure by socioeconomic background rather than ethnicity. This finding has been amply confirmed in Featherman and Hauser's (1978) analysis of more broadly representative data from a 1973 replication of the survey upon which Duncan and Duncan relied; in Hirschman and Falcon's (1985) analysis of data drawn from the 1977–1983 National Opinion Research Center (NORC) General Social Surveys; in Lieberson's (1980) analysis of 1970 U.S. Census data; and in Lieberson and Waters's (1988) analysis of 1980 U.S. Census data.

Taken together, these findings reinforce the conclusion that, for the most part, whatever culturally distinctive orientations toward schooling late 19th- and early 20th-century European immigrants may have brought to the United States, their effects were exhausted in the earlier part of this century. While cross-group variations in average or median educational attainment are noticeable among men born before 1905—that is, among members of the cohorts whose progress is reflected in the results of the U.S. Immigration Commission's 1908 study—they are substantially attenuated among those born after 1915, and

are generally negligible among those born after 1935 (Lieberson, 1980). Nor do contemporary group differences in details of educational distributions that are not readily captured by the mean or the median distinguish the descendants of eastern, central, and southern European immigrants from those of northern and western European immigrants (Lieberson and Waters, 1988).

Beyond the findings pertaining to Euro-Americans, persistently distinctive patterns of educational attainment that cannot be explained by socioeconomic origins have been reported among Asian Americans and Mexican Americans. In Featherman and Hauser's (1978) sample, second-generation Chinese and Japanese acquired a year and a half or more schooling than would be predicted on the basis of their socioeconomic origins. Hirschman and Falcon (1985) report similar findings.

In Featherman and Hauser's (1978) sample, second-generation Mexicans received eight tenths of a year less schooling than expected on the basis of their socioeconomic origins. The net disadvantage evidenced by Mexican Americans was, however, considerably less than the net disadvantage evidenced by foreign-born Mexicans (and Puerto Ricans), and considerably less than the overall disadvantage of almost three years that they evidenced when socioeconomic origins were uncontrolled (see also Hirschman & Falcon, 1985). No adequate data exist with which to disentangle the effects of linguistic, cultural, political economy, and school and classroom factors on the net Mexican American disadvantage in educational attainment.

Another of Featherman and Hauser's (1978) findings warrants note. If we compare men from the same ethnic heritage groups, we find that those who were foreign-born received somewhat less schooling than would be expected on the basis of their socioeconomic origins; second-generation men received over one third of a year more schooling than otherwise expected; and third-generation men evidenced neither a net disadvantage nor advantage in schooling. On the assumption that a substantial number of foreign-born men received their schooling outside the United States, these results suggest that being born into and growing up in an immigrant household confers educational benefits. The plausibility of a distinctive immigrant ethos, commented upon by recent anthropological analysts of contemporary immigrant education behavior (e.g., Gibson, 1991; Suarez-Orozco, 1991), therefore receives support in these data.

Education and Immigrant Occupational Attainment

The mythology of the immigrant experience celebrates schooling as an avenue out of poverty into the middle class. While mythology no doubt exaggerates both the degree of immigrant mobility and the role of schooling in mobility (Berrol, 1982), the value of schooling for socioeconomic attainment is well established (Olneck, 1979). Featherman and Hauser's (1978) analyses permit us to ask about the extent to which education has been an avenue of occupational attainment for immigrant groups.

It is clear that education has been the key means by which a number of groups have attained occupational advantages. Men whose parents were from Great Britain, for example, enjoyed an advantage in 1973 of approximately one fifth of a standard deviation on a frequently employed sociological measure of occupational status (Featherman & Hauser, 1978). This advantage could be attributed almost entirely to more favorable educational attainment. In an even sharper case, men with Chinese and Japanese parents also enjoyed approximately one fifth of a standard deviation occupational advantage, but in the absence of favorable educational levels would have been expected to suffer a small occupational disadvantage (Featherman & Hauser). Examining data from the 1976 Survey of Education and Income, Hirschman and Wong (1984) found similar results, and concluded that "It is only through overachievement in education that Asian Americans reach socioeconomic parity with the majority population" (p. 600).

Some groups enjoy occupational advantages to which educational advantages have contributed substantially, but that must be explained by other influences as well. In Featherman and Hauser's (1978) 1973 sample, men presumed to be Russian Jews enjoyed an almost two thirds of a standard deviation advantage on occupational status, only about half of which is explained by their unusually high educational attainment. The occupational advantages enjoyed by men of Irish and of Latin American other than Mexican parentage are associated in the same sample in substantial measure with educational advantages. The offspring of German, Polish, and certain other miscellaneous European immigrant groups, however, enjoy modest occupational advantages that are largely, though not entirely, unrelated to educational attainment. Among Italians, educational attainment appears to have had an impact that, while absolutely small, sufficiently counteracted the lingering influences of lower socioeconomic origins to enable Italians to attain average occupational status in the second generation. Schooling has therefore been one, but by no means the sole, avenue of mobility for Euro-American immigrant groups.

Just as atypically high educational attainment has facilitated the mobility of some immigrant groups, lack of schooling has severely impeded the occupational mobility of other groups. Most notably, both foreign-born and second-generation Mexican men suffer an occupational disadvantage of roughly 60% of a standard deviation, 80% of which is associated with their unfavorable levels of educational attainment.

The Educational Performance of Recent Immigrants

The educational performance of the children of recent immigrants is a matter of both public and scholarly attention. News media routinely comment on Vietnamese valedictorians, Chinese science fair winners, and the other accomplishments of Asian "model minorities." More generally, the success of Asian immigrants in the schools is contrasted with the persistently high dropout rates and low test scores of inner-city African Americans, Native Americans, and Chicanos. Social science data largely accord with popular perceptions. While there is considerable variation among individuals within any ethnic group, the above-average success of Vietnamese, ethnic Chi-

nese from Vietnam, Chinese, Korean, and Asian Indian students seems incontrovertible.

The most systematic study of the school achievement of Asian immigrant children is reported by Caplan and associates (Caplan, Whitmore, & Choy, 1989; Caplan et al., 1991). Drawing on school records from 1984 for over 500 students in Grades 7 to 12 from four major American cities and Orange County, California, Caplan found that the "children of the Boat People," despite having been in the United States only an average of 3.5 years, and usually from households in which no one came to the United States knowing English, received grades averaging slightly over B, and scored at the 54th percentile on the California Aptitude Test (CAT). On the math section of the CAT they scored at the 72nd percentile.

Informal comments and transcripts recorded teachers' and principals' perceptions that the students in question were the schools' highest achievers and were exceptionally eager to learn. This finding is consistent both with the authors' finding of strong family pressure on Asian immigrant children to succeed in school, and the findings in a nationally representative sample that Asian high school students do considerably more homework than their White peers, hold far higher educational expectations, and are far more likely to report that their parents monitor their schoolwork (Wong, 1990).

Unfortunately, Caplan et al. (1989, 1991) had no data on the performance of the refugee children's classmates. However, Portes and Rumbaut (1990) report data that permit comparisons among students from diverse groups. The data pertain to 39,000 high school students in San Diego during 1986–1987. These data reveal a familiar pattern of lower grade-point averages (GPA) among African Americans, Pacific Islanders, and Mexican-origin students, higher GPAs among White Anglos, and highest GPAs among Chinese, Korean, and Asian Indian students. The most noteworthy finding in the Portes and Rumbaut study is that within linguistic minority groups, students who were bilingual and fully proficient in English outperformed students who were monolingual in English. In a subsample of Indochinese students for whom data on socioeconomic background was available, the advantage of bilinguals persisted even when socioeconomic background was controlled.

In this same sample, an index of cultural reaffirmation was positively associated with higher grades. Portes and Rumbaut (1990) conclude from these findings that "it is not parents most willing to assimilate—in the sense of 'subtracting' from their cultural background—who seem to motivate their children effectively, but those most inclined to reaffirm their cultural heritage within ethnic neighborhoods" (p. 214).

Portes and Rumbaut are not alone in finding that affirmative ethnic identities and commitment to ethnically rooted values among immigrants and their children, rather than assimilation, are associated with greater success in school. In her study of Mexican-descent students in a California high school, Matute-Bianchi (1991) found that more recent immigrants, those longer-term U.S. residents who maintained a strong "Mexicano" identity, and American-born students who were "Mexican-oriented" fared relatively well, while those identified as "Mexican American" had more variable success, and those identified as Chicanos and Cholos fared least well. Interestingly, teachers in Matute-Bianchi's study were unaware of the role of positive ethnic identity in their students' achievement, and tended to assume that the more successful students were those most fully acculturated to American norms (Matute-Bianchi, 1991).

In their study of Indochinese students, Caplan et al. (1991) found, on the basis of demographic, social-psychological, and attitudinal survey measures, that while neither parental facility with English nor prior socioeconomic status explained variations in the children's school performance, those having the strongest respect for the past and its relevance to the present, and those most committed to familial and communal loyalty and responsibilities, enjoyed the most success at school. Similarly, summarizing both her own study of Punjabi Sikhs in "Valleyside," California, and other case studies of immigrant students, Margaret Gibson (1991) concluded that immigrant children's school success is explained not by assimilation, but by "strong home cultures and a strong and positive sense of their ethnic identities" (p. 375).

The success of immigrant students in American schools should not be exaggerated. In Becker's (1985) study of a New England high school, the dropout rate for Portuguese students was four times higher than expected on the basis of enrollment figures. In Lowell, Massachusetts, in 1986–1987, half of the Lao high school students dropped out (Kiang, 1990). In the early 1980s, while boys rarely dropped out, 85% of Hmong young women dropped out of "Lakewood's" high schools (Goldstein, 1985). Even among the Punjabi Sikhs, whose relative success Gibson (1988, 1991) emphasizes, students who arrived in the United States after fourth grade experienced particular difficulties, numerous students graduated with their academic courses having been primarily within the ESL program, the performance of boys exceeded that of girls, and substantial disparities in standardized test scores obtained between Punjabi and Anglo students. More generally, Wong (1990) found only very modest advantages in high school grades among Filipino and Japanese students in the nationally representative 1980 High School and Beyond sample.

The apparent relative success of children of immigrants in comparison with nonimmigrant students of color and linguistic minorities has been the focus of considerable theoretical debate. John Ogbu (1987, 1991) and his students and colleagues (e.g., Matute-Bianchi, 1986, 1991; Gibson, 1987, 1988, 1991; Suarez-Orozco, 1987, 1991) have advanced a "cultural ecological" model premised on the distinction between "voluntary" or immigrant minorities and "involuntary" minorities, as well as on the associated distinction between "primary" and "secondary" cultural characteristics (see chapter 32 of this *Handbook*).

Primary cultural characteristics entail those beliefs, practices, and values that derive from immigrant groups' premigration pasts. Secondary cultural characteristics entail beliefs, practices, and values that are formed in response to the historical oppression and exploitation involved in the incorporation of involuntary minority groups into society. Secondary cultural traits are characterized by oppositional social identities, cultural inversions, and pessimistic folk theories of success, which render engagement with the demands of majority institutions a

betrayal of group allegiance and collective identity. In contrast, immigrants are said to hold a "dual frame of reference" that, in light of the homeland conditions propelling emigration, dismisses majority hostility and embraces opportunity. In this model, immigrants see their cultural differences as "barriers to be overcome," while involuntary minorities see the "cultural differences they encounter at school as markers of identity to be maintained" (Ogbu, 1987, p. 330).

Ogbu's model has been criticized on a number of grounds. One is its sparse evidentiary base. Ogbu does not present direct evidence linking the operation of secondary cultural characteristics to school behavior or performance (Trueba, 1988; Foley, 1991).

A second ground of criticism of Ogbu's model is that while it perfunctorily recognizes the role of "school and classroom forces," including classroom practices that denigrate and clash with minority culture and norms, it substantially underestimates the impact of the social organization of teaching and learning on minority school performance. Henry Trueba, in particular (e.g., Trueba 1988; Trueba et al., 1990), argues that the absence of culturally appropriate classroom "activity settings" that integrate cognitive socialization across home, community, peer, and schooling sites is implicated in minority school failure.

However valid Trueba's argument about the importance of culturally congruent learning environments, it is difficult to see how that argument refutes the claims of the cultural ecology model. That model addresses the paradox that some minorities, on average, enjoy greater success in school despite experiencing more severe cultural incongruity with classroom social organization than do certain less successful minorities. In Trueba's argument, this paradox should not even arise. Trueba's analysis is most helpful for understanding the difficulties of minority students who, from the perspective of the cultural ecology model, might be expected to enjoy greater school success than they do. The Hmong stand as the most obvious case in point (Trueba et al., 1990; Goldstein, 1985).

A further line of argument by Trueba denies Ogbu's premise that so-called involuntary minority groups necessarily remain at the bottom of the educational ladder. In particular, Trueba (1988) argues that educational progress can be documented for Mexicans in the Southwest. Rather than refuting the central claim of the cultural ecology model—that educational behavior is shaped by cultural practices and social identities that evolve in response to perceptions of social location and social structure—this evidence may simply suggest that Ogbu erred in classifying Mexicans as an involuntary minority.

Both Foley (1991) and Matute-Bianchi (1986, 1991) demonstrate the salience of a variety of emergent Mexican American identities, some of which exemplify the dispositional profile of voluntary or immigrant minorities, and others that exemplify the dispositional profile of involuntary minorities. The finding that the descendants and possibly even offspring of immigrants can evidence a dispositional profile characteristic of "involuntary" minorities is consistent with the finding that immigrants' initial perceptions of the absence of discrimination can yield to the recognition of rejection and barriers (Portes, 1984). On the other hand, the finding that heretofore oppressed and subordinated minority groups can undertake cultural revitalization movements that redefine ethnic identities in ways conducive to educational achievement and attainment (Foley, 1991) is evidence that the distinctions Ogbu draws need not be permanent, and that they are imperfectly associated with original conditions of incorporation into society.

Frederick Erickson (1987) has attempted to reconcile the cultural ecology argument with the cultural discontinuity argument. Erickson's contention that engagement in school is a form of political assent, while disengagement is a form of political resistance, is entirely consistent with the premises of cultural ecology theory. What Erickson adds is that cultural incongruities can become politicized not only by the actions of students, as the cultural ecology model would emphasize, but by the actions of teachers as well.

Teachers may, for example, denigrate and disparage students for failing to adopt mainstream cultural usages. If such denigration were more frequently directed at indigenous minorities than at immigrant minorities, or if indigenous minorities interpreted such responses in light of shared experiences of cultural oppression, relations of trust necessary to learning would be less readily forged between indigenous minority students and their teachers than between immigrant students and their teachers. On the other hand, culturally responsive instruction might not only be more comprehensible to all minority students than culturally hegemonic instructional practices, but might also allay indigenous minorities' historic distrust of dominant institutions. On this argument, it is the intersection of cultural intelligibility and sociopolitical factors that determines classroom outcomes, and may explain the success of immigrant minorities relative to that of indigenous minorities.

CONCLUSION

The results of scholarship about immigrants and schooling unsurprisingly reveal greater ambiguity and complexity than popular mythology represents. Immigrants have embraced American schools, but not as unreservedly as mythology holds. Schools have been places where immigrant children joined American society, but not necessarily on the terms educators preferred or with the ease that is sometimes imagined. American schools have, however reluctantly, always had to revise their practices and policies to accommodate immigrant languages, cultures, and identities, but their success in educating immigrant children has been uneven. Immigrants have availed themselves of schooling as an avenue of social mobility, but not with equal success, and often as a hedge against discrimination, not as an affirmation of equal opportunity.

The results of the historical research this chapter has reviewed suggest that contemporary opposition to multiculturalism is often premised on mistaken representations of the past. The charge of "Eurocentricity" that people of color raise against the contemporary curriculum is not a novel kind of charge. Nineteenth-century Catholics, especially the Irish, were acutely aware that public school textbooks, staffing patterns, and approaches to socialization were Anglo-Protestant. Conflict over

the monocultural character of the public schools persisted into the 20th century.

The demand for African American immersion schools, whatever its merits, is not the first demand of its kind. European immigrants in the 19th century sought similar accommodations on occasion. The demand that public school curricula incorporate culturally specific content has precedent in the incorporation of European immigrant languages into post-World War I course offerings. The contemporary use of schools for ethnic expression also has precedent in the use of schools during the interwar period for Euro-American religio-ethnic organizations and activities. Most notably, while there may be no "American tradition" of bilingual education (Schlossman, 1983), there is ample precedent for the incorporation of non-English vernaculars into pedagogical repertoires.

Valid representation of the past would not dictate particular resolutions to our contemporary dilemmas. It could, however, challenge the claim that the authority of history denies legitimacy to the multiculturalist critique and program.

Valid representation of the past, as well as scrutiny of recent ethnographic and survey data, could also lend support to the claim that it is culturally responsive schools, not monocultural schools, that are most integrative and least divisive. While insistence on Anglo-Protestant schools during the 19th century impelled many Catholic immigrants to foreswear the public schools, accommodation to the linguistic demands of Germans drew German immigrant children into the public schools.

Insistence on culturally discontinuous pedagogical regimes can often provoke disengagement and resistance, while culturally responsive pedagogy seems more often to prompt engagement and assent to learning. Maintenance of ethnic loyalty, not assimilation, appears associated with stronger school performance among immigrant children.

There remains theoretical and practical need to integrate historical research on the schooling of European immigrants more fully with research on the schooling of Latino and Asian immigrants, and to integrate social scientific research on the schooling of contemporary immigrants more fully with research on the schooling of involuntary minorities.

Because, as Sylvia Wynter has pointed out, the European immigrant has been represented as the "generic" American (see Olneck, 1993), it is necessary to a more inclusive symbolic representation of American identity that the connotation of the historical "immigrant" embrace Latinos and Asians. Theoretically, historical research that paid comparative attention to Latino, Asian, and European immigrants could better elucidate the dynamics of ethnicity, race, and class that are entailed in the political economy of the schooling of immigrants.

Finally, both because immigrants and involuntary minorities are compared in the popular imagination, and because recent theoretical work has turned on the distinction between the immigrant experience and that of involuntary minorities, it is important that richer empirical work be undertaken to establish how the dynamics of schooling differ and overlap between immigrants and involuntary minorities.

In particular, ethnographic research is needed at sites in which immigrants and involuntary minorities attend school together. Such research could not only bring into sharper relief the perspectives of diverse students, but could also better address whether and how teachers' ideologies, pedagogies, and social relations with students distinguish between immigrant youths and involuntary minorities. Those distinctions might prove as relevant to educational disparities as any distinctions in students' frames of reference.

References

Becker, A. (1985). *The role of the public school in the maintenance and change of ethnic group affiliation*. Unpublished doctoral dissertation, Brown University, Providence, RI.

Berrol, S. (1978). *Immigrants at school, New York City, 1898–1914*. New York: Arno Press.

Berrol, S. (1982). Public schools and immigrants: The New York City experience. In B. Weiss (Ed.), *American education and the European immigrant: 1840–1940* (pp. 31–43). Urbana: University of Illinois Press.

Bodnar, J. (1976). Materialism and morality: Slavic-American immigrants and education, 1890–1940. *Journal of Ethnic Studies, 3*(4), 1–19.

Bodnar, J. (1982). Schooling and the Slavic-American family. In B. Weiss (Ed.), *American education and the European immigrant: 1840–1940* (pp. 78–95). Urbana: University of Illinois Press.

Brumberg, S. E. (1986). *Going to America, going to school: The Jewish immigrant public school encounter in turn-of-the-century New York City*. New York: Praeger.

Caplan, N., Choy, M. H., & Whitmore, J. K. (1991). *Children of the boat people: A study of educational success*. Ann Arbor: University of Michigan Press.

Caplan, N., Whitmore, J. K., & Choy, M. H. (1989). *The boat people and achievement in America: A study of family life, hard work, and cultural values*. Ann Arbor: University of Michigan Press.

Carlson, R. (1987). *The Americanization syndrome: A quest for conformity*. New York: St. Martin's Press.

Cohen, D. K. (1970). Immigrants and the schools. *Review of Educational Research, 40*(1), 13–27.

Cohen, D. K., & Rosenberg, B. (1977). Functions and fantasies: Understanding schools in capitalist America. *History of Education Quarterly, 17*(2), 113–137.

Cohen, M. (1982). Changing education strategies among immigrant generations: New York Italians in comparative perspective. *Journal of Social History, 15*(3), 443–466.

Cohen, R., & Mohl, R. (1979). *The paradox of Progressive education: The Gary Plan and urban schooling*. Port Washington, NY: Kennileat.

Connell, R., Ashenden, D. J., Kessler, S., & Dowsett, G. W. (1982). *Making the difference: Schools, families, and social division*. Sydney, Australia: G. Allen and Unwin.

Cowan, N. M., & Cowan, R. S. (1989). *Our parents' lives: The Americanization of Eastern European Jews*. New York: Basic Books.

Dash Moore, D. (1981). *At home in America: Second generation New York Jews*. New York: Columbia University Press.

Davis, A. (1967). *Spearheads for reform: The social settlements and the Progressive movement, 1890–1914*. New York: Oxford University Press.

Delgado-Gaitan, C., & Trueba, H. (1991). *Crossing cultural borders: Education for immigrant families in America*. London: Falmer Press.

Duncan, B., & Duncan, O. D. (1968). Minorities and the process of stratification. *American Sociological Review, 33*(3), 356–364.

Elson R. (1964). *Guardians of tradition: American schoolbooks of the nineteenth century*. Lincoln: University of Nebraska Press.

Erickson, F. (1987). Transformation and school success: The politics and culture of educational achievement. *Anthropology and Education Quarterly, 18*(4), 335–356.

Fass, P. (1989). *Outside in: Minorities and the transformation of American education*. New York: Oxford University Press.

Featherman, D., & Hauser, R. (1978). *Opportunity and change*. New York: Academic Press.

Foley, D. (1991). Reconsidering anthropological explanations of ethnic school failure. *Anthropology and Education Quarterly, 22*(1), 60–86.

Gibson, M. (1987). The school performance of immigrant minorities: A comparative view. *Anthropology and Education Quarterly, 18*(4), 262–275.

Gibson, M. (1988). *Accommodation without assimilation: Sikh immigrants in an American high school*. Ithaca, NY: Cornell University Press.

Gibson, M. (1991). Minorities and schooling: Some implications. In M. A. Gibson & J. U. Ogbu (Eds.), *Minority status and schooling: A comparative study of immigrant and involuntary minorities* (pp. 357–381). New York: Garland.

Gibson, M., & Bhachu, P. K. (1991). The dynamics of educational decision making: A comparative study of Sikhs in Britain and the United States. In M. A. Gibson & J. U. Ogbu (Eds.), *Minority status and schooling: A comparative study of immigrant and involuntary minorities* (pp. 63–95). New York: Garland.

Glazer, N. (1985). Immigrants and education. In N. Glazer (Ed.), *Clamor at the gates: The new American immigration* (pp. 213–239). San Francisco: Institute for Contemporary Studies Press.

Goldstein, B. L. (1985). *Schooling for cultural transitions: Hmong girls and boys in American high schools*. Unpublished doctoral dissertation, Department of Educational Policy Studies, University of Wisconsin, Madison.

Gonzalez, G. (1990). *Chicano education in the era of segregation*. Philadelphia: Balch Institute Press.

Goode, J. G., Schneider, J. A., & Blanc, S. (1992). Transcending boundaries and closing ranks: How schools shape interrelations. In L. Lamphere (Ed.), *Structuring diversity: Ethnographic perspectives on the new immigration* (pp. 173–213). Chicago: University of Chicago Press.

Goodenow, R. (1975, Winter). The Progressive educator, race and ethnicity in the Depression years: An overview. *History of Education Quarterly, 15*, 365–394.

Greer, C. (1972). *The great school legend: A revisionist interpretation of American education*. New York: Basic Books.

Grey, M. A. (1990). Immigrant students in the heartland: Ethnic relations in a Garden City, Kansas, high school. *Urban Anthropology, 19*(4), 409–427.

Hirschman, C., & Falcon, L. M. (1985). The educational attainment of religio-ethnic groups in the United States. In A. C. Kerckhoff (Ed.), *Research in sociology of education and socialization* (Vol. 5, pp. 83–120). Greenwich, CT: JAI Press.

Hirschman, C., & Wong, M. G. (1984). Socioeconomic gains of Asian Americans, Blacks, and Hispanics: 1960–1976. *American Journal of Sociology, 90*(3), 584–607.

Jorgenson, L. (1987). *The state and the non-public school, 1825–1925*. Columbia: University of Missouri Press.

Kaestle C. (1973). *The evolution of an urban school system: New York City, 1750–1850*. Cambridge, MA: Harvard University Press.

Kaestle, C. (1983). *Pillars of the republic: Common schools and American society, 1780–1860*. New York: Hill and Wang.

Karier, C. (1973). Testing for order and control in the corporate liberal state. In C. Karier, P. Violas, & J. Spring, *Roots of crisis: American education in the twentieth century* (pp. 108–137). Chicago: Rand McNally College Publishing Company.

Kiang, P. N. (1990). *Southeast Asian parent empowerment: The challenge of changing demographics in Lowell, Massachusetts*. Jamaica Plains, MA: MABE Monographs.

Kuyper, S. J. (1980). *The Americanization of German immigrants: Language, religion and schools in nineteenth century rural Wisconsin*. Unpublished doctoral dissertation, Department of History, University of Wisconsin-Madison.

Lareau, A. (1989). *Home advantage: Social class and parental intervention in elementary education*. London, England: Falmer Press.

Lazerson, M. F. (1971). *The origins of the urban school: Public education in Massachusetts, 1870–1915*. Cambridge, MA: Harvard University Press.

Lieberson, S. (1980). *A piece of the pie: Blacks and white immigrants since 1880*. Berkeley: University of California Press.

Lieberson, S., & Waters, M. (1988). *From many strands: Ethnic and racial groups in contemporary America*. New York: Russell Sage Foundation.

Matute-Bianchi, M. E. (1986). Ethnic identities and patterns of school success and failure among Mexican-descent and Japanese American students in a California high school: An ethnographic analysis. *American Journal of Education, 95*(1), 233–255.

Matute-Bianchi, M. E. (1991). Situational ethnicity and patterns of school performance among immigrant and nonimmigrant Mexican-descent students. In M. A. Gibson & J. U. Ogbu (Eds.), *Minority status and schooling: A comparative study of immigrant and involuntary minorities* (pp. 205–247). New York: Garland.

Montalto, N. (1982). *A history of the intercultural education movement*. New York: Garland.

Montero-Sieburth, M., & La Celle-Peterson, M. (1991). Immigration and schooling: An ethnohistorical account of policy and family perspectives in an urban community. *Anthropology and Education Quarterly, 22*(4), 300–325.

Ogbu, J. U. (1987). Variability in minority school performance: A problem in search of an explanation. *Anthropology and Education Quarterly, 18*(4), 312–334.

Ogbu, J. U. (1991). Immigrant and involuntary minorities in comparative perspective. In M. A. Gibson & J. U. Ogbu (Eds.), *Minority status and schooling: A comparative study of immigrant and involuntary minorities* (pp. 3–33). New York: Garland.

Olneck, M. (1979). The effects of education. In C. Jencks, S. Bartlett, M. Corcoran, J. Crouse, D. Eaglesfield, G. Jackson, K. McClelland, P. Mueser, M. Olneck, J. Schwartz, S. Wald, & J. Williams, *Who gets ahead?: The determinants of economic success in America* (pp. 159–190). New York: Basic Books.

Olneck, M. (1989). Americanization and the education of immigrants: An analysis of symbolic action. *American Journal of Education, 97*(4), 398–423.

Olneck, M. (1990). The recurring dream: Symbolism and ideology in intercultural education and multicultural education. *American Journal of Education, 98*(2), 147–174.

Olneck, M. (1993). Terms of inclusion: Has multiculturalism redefined equality in American education? *American Journal of Education, 101*(3), 234–260.

Olneck, M. R., & Lazerson, M. F. (1974, Winter). The school achievement of immigrant children: 1900–1930. *History of Education Quarterly, 14*, 453–482.

Perlmann, J. (1988). *Ethnic differences: Schooling and social structure among the Irish, Italians, Jews and Blacks in an American city, 1880–1935*. New York: Cambridge University Press.

Portes, A. (1984). The rise of ethnicity: Determinants of ethnic perceptions among Cuban exiles in Miami. *American Sociological Review, 49*(3), 383–397.

Portes, A. & Rumbaut, R. G. (1990). *Immigrant America: A portrait*. Berkeley: University of California Press.

Raftery, J. R. (1992). *Land of fair promise: Politics and reform in Los Angeles schools, 1885–1941*. Stanford, CA: Stanford University Press.

Ravitch, D. (1974). *The great school wars: A history of the New York City Public Schools*. New York: Basic Books.

San Miguel, G., Jr. (1987). *"Let all of them take heed": Mexican Americans and the campaign for educational equality in Texas, 1910–1981*. Austin: University of Texas Press.

Sanchirico, Andrew. (1991). The importance of small-business ownership in Chinese American educational achievement. *Sociology of Education, 64*(4), 293–304.

Sanders, J. W. (1977). *The education of an urban minority: Catholics in Chicago, 1833–1965,* New York: Oxford University Press.

Schlossman, S. L. (1983). Is there an American tradition of bilingual education?: German in the public elementary schools, 1840–1919. *American Journal of Education, 91*(2), 139–186.

Schultz, S. (1973). *The culture factory: Boston public schools, 1789–1860*. New York: Oxford University Press.

Slater, M. (1969). My son the doctor: Aspects of mobility among American Jews. *American Sociological Review, 34*(3), 359–373.

Smith, T. L. (1969). Immigrant social aspirations and American education, 1880–1930. *American Quarterly, 21*(3), 523–543.

Steinberg, S. (1981). *The ethnic myth: Race, ethnicity, and class in America*. New York: Atheneum.

Suarez-Orozco, M. (1991). Immigrant adaptation to schooling: A Hispanic case. In M. A. Gibson & J. U. Ogbu (Eds.), *Minority status and schooling: A comparative study of immigrant and involuntary minorities* (pp. 37–61). New York: Garland.

Troen, S. K. (1975). *The public and the schools: Shaping the St. Louis school system, 1838–1920*. Columbia: University of Missouri Press.

Trueba, H. (1988). Culturally based explanations of minority students' academic achievement. *Anthropology and Education Quarterly, 19*(3), 270–287.

Trueba, H., Jacobs, L., & Kirton, E. (1990). *Cultural conflict and adaptation: The case of Hmong children in American society*. New York: Falmer Press.

Tyack, D. (1974). *The one best system: A history of American urban education*. Cambridge, MA: Harvard University Press.

Violas, P. (1973). Jane Addams and the new liberalism. In C. Karrier, P. Violas, & J. Spring, *Roots of crisis: American education in the twentieth century* (pp. 66–83). Chicago: Rand McNally College Publishing Company.

Weinberg, D. (1977). The ethnic technician and the foreign-born: Another look at Americanization ideology and goals. *Societas, 7*(3), 209–227.

Willis, P. (1977). *Learning to labour: How working class kids get working class jobs*. Farnborough, England: Saxon House.

Wong, M. (1990). The education of White, Chinese, Filipino, and Japanese students: A look at "High School and Beyond." *Sociological Perspectives, 33*(3), 355–374.

Part

·VI·

THE EDUCATION OF ETHNIC GROUPS

19

EDUCATING NATIVE AMERICANS

K. Tsianina Lomawaima

UNIVERSITY OF ARIZONA, TUCSON

Educating Native Americans. Those three words encapsulate a 500-year-old battle for power: first, the power to define what education is—the power to set its goals, define its policies, and enforce its practices—and second, the power to define who native people are and who they are not. European and American colonial governments, operating through denominations of the Christian Church, first defined "education" for Native Americans as the cleansing, uplifting, thoroughly aggressive and penetrating force that would Christianize, civilize, and individualize a heathen, barbaric, and tribal world (Axtell, 1981; Hoxie, 1984; Prucha, 1979, 1984; Szasz, 1988; Szasz & Ryan, 1988; Van Well, 1942).

In the last two centuries the U.S. colonial administration of Indian affairs has diligently built a bureaucracy dedicated to controlling every aspect of native lives (Biolsi, 1992; Castile & Bee, 1992; Hoxie, 1984; R. Nelson & Sheley, 1985). Rules and regulations have been promulgated to mandate schooling, control individual bank accounts, direct land use, and authorize mineral extraction—in short, to construct an edifice of federal surveillance that might astonish the average U.S. citizen secure in the image of a democratic nation. This chapter will lay bare the educational edifice designed largely by non-Indians to instruct American Indians, then elucidate the Indian response to that instruction, and Indian movements to design and control the education of their own children and communities. In this chapter I use the terms *Native American, Indian,* and *Indian education* to refer to all Indian people in the lower 48 states and to Alaska Natives. The federal government, however, maintains two separate listings of American Indian tribes and Alaska Native villages.

The chapter begins with a discussion of tribal sovereignty, federal policy, and the special government-to-government relationship that exists between tribes and the United States. A brief overview of the demographic history and characteristics of the Indian population within the United States includes statistics on

educational participation, achievement, and degrees earned. The history of federal Indian policy began with colonial efforts to Christianize and civilize indigenous people, and continued through the establishment of mission and federal boarding schools. Boarding schools shaped thousands of Native American people, and their attitudes and responses to those institutions are discussed briefly.

The review of contemporary research on Indian education covers the topical literature on dropouts, learning styles, interactional styles in classrooms, theories of cultural congruence or discontinuity and their shortcomings, self-determination in Indian education, curriculum development, and language policy. After a discussion of current trends in educational research, the chapter concludes with an assessment of the past and implications for the future of Native American education.

TRIBAL SOVEREIGNTY AND FEDERAL INDIAN POLICY

Federal powers have devised an educational system wedding content and practice in order to reshape Native American people (Adams, 1988b; Haig-Brown, 1988; Littlefield, 1989, 1993; Lomawaima, 1993). Other arms of the federal bureaucracy have manufactured definitions of Indian-ness, tribal rolls, lists of recognized (versus unrecognized) tribes, and certificates of degree of Indian blood—all to control who has American Indian or Alaska Native status and who has not (Pascal, 1991; Weatherhead, 1980; National Archives, 1988a, 1988b). Native nations have creatively resisted the extension of federal powers even as they have had to adapt to those same powers (Nabokov, 1991; Olson & Wilson, 1984). The assertion of tribal power is and has always been the assertion of sovereignty: to retain and/or reclaim rights to self-government, self-definition, and self-

The author is grateful for the assistance of Mark Hein, University of Washington, in compiling and annotating sources for this chapter.

education (Barsh & Henderson, 1980; Castile & Bee, 1992; Wilkinson, 1987). Indian education can only be understood against this historical, political, economic, and social battleground.

In the latter half of this century, the balance of power has shifted as tribes have struggled with changing definitions of self-government in an attempt to strengthen and expand tribal sovereignty (V. Deloria & Lytle, 1984; Fixico, 1986; Philp, 1986). The shift in power has not been uniform, or rapid, or uncontested; it has grown slowly from deep roots. It has significantly changed educational practice and policy but has by no means reformed schools to satisfy all the needs of Native American children, parents, and communities (Szasz, 1977).

The tug-of-war between tribal sovereignty and federal power has carved contours across the landscape of Indian education. Research into the character and quality of that education has at times illuminated those contours; at other times researchers have been so engulfed by the gullies carved by the contest they have not been able to see the horizon. It is the aim of this chapter to delineate the course of research on Indian education without losing sight of the larger political context, where Indian people patiently labor to check the erosion of their sovereign rights. We need the higher vantage point in order to imagine what Indian education should be and might become.

Since the federal government turned its attention to the "problem" of civilizing Indians, its overt goal has been to educate Indians to be non-Indians (Hoxie, 1984; Szasz, 1988; Szasz & Ryan, 1988). Since the late 1800s, most federal policy has not equated the civilizing process with simple assimilation into U.S. society. Educational policies have been designed to prepare Indians as a working class, amenable to federal control, to provide domestic and manual labor to the U.S. economy (Adams, 1988b; Hoxie, 1984; Littlefield, 1993; Lomawaima, 1993; Trennert, 1988). Native Americans have challenged that model of Indian education by seeking access to Euro-American schools, and to academic and professional training. In the last century tribes and the courts have refined a theory of political rights that posits educational opportunity as a treaty right promised in partial exchange for the cession of huge tracts of land (see Deloria & Lytle, 1984, for "traditional Indians'" view of treaty rights; see Biolsi, 1993, for a case study of Lakota interpretations of treaty rights; see Wilkinson, 1987, for changing judicial interpretations). As nations exercising limited sovereignty, tribes occupy a unique legal and political space within the United States. American Indian tribes and Alaska Native villages are federally defined as entities with a special government-to-government relationship with the United States, and that status distinguishes them from all other ethnic or racial minorities.

Most Native Americans believe their right to education should not necessitate eradication of native language, culture, religion, or identity (Jaimes, 1983; Johnson, 1968). As Native American parents and communities have challenged and changed the working definition of Indian education, and created education for and by native people, the questions and solutions proposed by educational researchers (native and nonnative) have also evolved.

One of the great challenges to research on Native Americans

is the exhilarating range of diversity among our cultures. The federal government currently recognizes 510 tribes, including more than 200 Alaska Native villages (U.S. Department of the Interior, 1991). Federal officials have estimated there are as many as 250 native groups who are not recognized, that is, groups who do not have a special government-to-government relationship with the United States (Prucha, 1984, p. 1196). Each native community is distinguished by its own language, customs, religion, economy, historical circumstances, and environment. Native people are not all the same. A fluent member of a Cherokee Baptist congregation living in Tahlequah, Oklahoma, is different from an English-speaking, powwow-dancing Lakota born and raised in Oakland, California, who is different from a Hopi fluent in Hopi, English, Navajo, and Spanish who lives on the reservation and supports her family by selling "traditional" pottery in New York, Santa Fe, and Scottsdale galleries. The idea of being generically "Indian" really was a figment of Columbus's imagination.

It is a cornerstone of tribal sovereignty today that tribal governments set the criteria for their tribal membership; the criteria vary widely across the nations. Some tribes specify a "blood quantum" (often one quarter) for membership; others do not. Some tribes specify native language fluency as a condition for service in the tribal government; others do not. Despite tribal control of tribal membership, certain federal criteria for Native American identity still carry weight. The federal government, for instance, requires one-quarter blood quantum (proved by a federal "certificate of Indian blood" based on agency records) to qualify for Bureau of Indian Affairs (BIA) college scholarships. Other federal agencies or programs—such as the census, or educational opportunity entitlement funds—rely on self-identification. An American Indian or Alaskan Native is someone who checks the right box on the right form.

POPULATION AND DEMOGRAPHIC TRENDS

The scholarly effort to piece together a demographic history of the Native American population has proved a difficult and depressing chore. There is no consensus on exactly how many native people lived on the North American continent prior to 1492 (see Ramenofsky, 1987, pp. 1–21, and Ubelaker, 1992, for an overview of the debate). We do know indigenous Americans were devastated by European expansion and newly introduced epidemic diseases, smallpox foremost among them (although pre-Columbian America was not a disease-free paradise; see Verano & Ubelaker, 1991). Although scholars do not agree on absolute native population numbers, they have slowly but surely revised Indian population numbers upward to current estimates for precontact native North America ranging from over 5 million in the present United States (Thornton, 1987, p. 2) to the highest estimate, 18 million north of Mexico (Dobyns, 1983, p. 289).

Native populations plummeted as much as 90 to 95% to their nadir of less than 250,000 at the beginning of this century. The U.S. Census Bureau first attempted a complete census of American Indians in 1890, when they counted 248,000. By 1900 that number had shrunk to 237,000. The numbers have been climbing ever since, as populations recovered and as census methods changed: 357,000 in 1950, 524,000 in 1960 (U.S. Bureau of the Census, 1988).

The numbers shot upward as the census allowed more citizens to self-identify, and altered the questions on race and ethnicity beginning in 1960: 793,000 Native Americans in 1970, 1.42 million in 1980, 2.06 million in 1990 (U.S. Bureau of the Census, 1988, 1992). Self-identification has influenced the count, as "only about 40% of the difference between the 1970 and 1980 census counts of American Indians can be accounted for by natural increase" (Thornton, Sandefur, & Snipp, 1991, p. 365). Of the 1.37 million (not including Alaska Natives) enumerated in the 1980 census, "fewer than 900,000 were enrolled as members in federally recognized" tribes (p. 365).

By 1980 approximately half of the Native American population lived in the West; approximately half of the total lived on or near reservations, and the rest lived in or near urban areas. The 1980 census counted over 270 identified reservations and tribal trust lands, and over 200 Alaska Native villages (U.S. Bureau of the Census, 1984).

In 1980 the 1.42 million Native Americans (American Indians and Alaska Natives) enumerated by the census constituted 0.6% of the total U.S. population of 226.5 million (U.S. Bureau of the Census, 1984). In 1990, 2,065,000 Native Americans constituted 0.8% of the national population (U.S. Bureau of the Census, 1992, p. 17). Since the early 1970s Native American students have constituted 0.7 to 0.9% of the enrollment in public elementary and secondary schools—the native population has been statistically younger than the U.S. norm (U.S. Bureau of the Census, 1992, p. 18). Roughly 76% of the native students in 1980 attended public or private schools, and the remaining 24% attended schools operated by the BIA or by tribes (U.S. Bureau of the Census, 1988, p. 10). In the 1990–1991 school year, the BIA funded 180 educational facilities for Indian children, including 48 day schools, 39 on-reservation boarding

schools, 5 off-reservation boarding schools, and 8 dormitories attached to public schools. In the same year, contracting tribes received BIA funds to run 62 day schools, 11 on-reservation boarding schools, 1 off-reservation boarding school, and 6 dormitories. In addition, federal funds to public schools supported about 225,870 Indian students enrolled in those schools (U.S. Department of the Interior, 1991). In 1980 Native American students made up 0.7% of the total enrollment in institutions of higher education. They have been awarded 0.4% of the bachelor's degrees, 0.3 to 0.4% of the master's degrees, and 0.3 to 0.4% of the doctoral degrees throughout the decade of the 1980s (National Center for Education Statistics [NCES], 1981, 1985–86, 1990a).

These figures reflect the fact that Indian children and young adults have not gone on to higher education at rates close to national norms. In 1980, 8% of the native population completed four years of college, half the national rate of 16% (U.S. Bureau of the Census, 1988, p. 5). Narrowing the focus to natives in Alaska reveals a sharper disparity. In 1980, 3% of Alaska natives completed four years of college, compared to the state rate of 21% (U.S. Bureau of the Census, 1988, p. 18). See Table 19–1 for a graphic representation of Native American participation in U.S schooling and degrees awarded. The higher in education and awarded degrees one looks, the more serious the underrepresentation of native people.

Closer examination of degrees awarded, especially graduate degrees, reveals that Native Americans have concentrated their studies in a few fields and disciplines, particularly education. In 1989–1990, for example, 14% (598) of the bachelor's degrees, 37% (405) of the master's degrees, and 37% (38) of the doctoral degrees earned by native people were in education. In that same academic year, Native Americans earned only 5 Ph.D.'s in the physical sciences and 4 Ph.D.'s in the life sciences (NCES, 1992, pp. 273–280). Table 19–2 shows the number of doctorates earned by Native Americans from 1975 to 1991, and the percentages of those degrees earned in education. This table

TABLE 19–1. Native American Students and Degrees, 1978–1990

(numbers rounded to nearest thousand)	1978	1980	1986	1988	1990
Number of Native Americans enrolled in public schools (K–12)	329	306	N.A.	N.A.	N.A.
Percent of totals (all races)	0.8	0.8	0.9		
Number of Native Americans enrolled in higher education	77.9	83.9	N.A.	92.5	102.6
Percent of totals (all races)	0.7	0.7		0.7	0.8

Bachelor's and Master's Degrees Earned by Native Americans

	1976–77	1984–85	1989–90
Bachelor's degrees	3,326	4,246	4,338
Percent of total (all races)	0.4	0.4	0.4
Master's degrees	967	1,256	1,108
Percent of total (all races)	0.3	0.4	0.3

Sources: Based on data from:

Digest of Education Statistics, National Center for Education Statistics, 1981, 1985–86, 1990, 1992; Washington, DC: Government Printing Office.

Doctorate Recipients from United States Universities [Summary Report], National Research Council, 1991, Washington DC: National Academy Press.

TABLE 19–2. Doctorates Earned by Native Americans: Disparate Statistics

	NRC-SR Data[a]		NRC 1991 Data[b]	DES Data[c]	MSGE Data[d]
	U.S.	A.I.	A.I.	A.I.	A.I.
1975	27,009	143	36		
		34% (% of A.I. doctorates earned in education)			
1976	27,195	148	40		148
		35%			
1977	26,007	220	65	95	
		31%			
1978	25,186	174	60		
		32%			
1979	25,369	165	81	104	
		39%		41%	
1980	25,108	106	75		
		50%			
1981	24,990	89	85	130	89
		47%			
1982	24,309	77	77		
		38%			
1983	24,292	81	81		
		54%			
1984	23,951	74	74		
		43%			
1985	23,241	93	96	119	
		42%			
1986	22,984	100	99		
		26%			
1987	22,863	116	115	104	
		35%			
1988	23,172	93	94		
		38%			
1989	23,172	93	94		
		26%			
1990	N.A.	N.A.	93	102	
				37%	
1991	24,721	130			
		41%			

U.S. = total doctorates earned by citizens in U.S.;
A.I. = American Indian doctorates

Note: Where statistics were unavailable for a source, the table was left blank.

[a] *Doctorate Recipients from United States Universities* [Summary Report], National Research Council, 1976, 1977, 1978, 1979, 1980, 1981, 1982, 1983, 1986a, 1986b, 1987, 1989a, 1989b, 1990, 1993, Washington, DC: National Academy Press.

[b] *Summary Report 1990: Doctorate Recipients from United States Universities*, by D. Thurgood, 1991, Washington, DC: National Academy Press. Despite its similarity to NRC reports cited above, this summary report has a different Library of Congress catalog number, and the numbers Thurgood cites vary drastically from statistics reported in other NRC Summary Reports.

[c] *Digest of Education Statistics*, National Center for Education Statistics, 1981, 1985–86, 1990, 1992, Washington, DC: Government Printing Office.

[d] "Minority Students in Graduate Education," by J. Vaughn, 1985. In B. Smith (Ed.), *The State of Graduate Education* (pp. 151–168), Washington, DC: The Brookings Institution.

also illuminates disturbing disparities among various statistical sources in number of degrees reported as earned. The NCES and the National Research Council (NRC) cite significantly different numbers of doctorates earned by American Indians. The NRC (1976) says there were 143 American Indian doctorates in 1975 (Vaughn, 1985, p. 152), but other sources cite only 36 (Thurgood, 1991, p. 39). The NRC (1982) cites 89 American Indian doctorates in 1981, but NCES (1990a) cites 130. Which numbers are to be believed?

It is difficult, if not impossible, to discuss trends in higher education enrollment and degrees earned by American Indians when statistics vary so widely. One can only wonder about the validity of any measures of American Indian participation in education. If the NRC is to be believed, Native Americans, out of all ethnic groups, hold the longest RTD, or time actually registered in school between the baccalaureate and doctoral degrees. Their RTD is 8.3 years, compared to 7.2 years for Whites, 7.5 years for Hispanics, 8.2 years for African Americans, and 6.8 years for Asians (NRC, 1991, p. 46).

HISTORICAL BACKGROUND: POLICIES OF EDUCATING INDIANS

If history is the bequest of meaning from the past to the present, then Indian education has had a remarkably constant inheritance until recent times. Unfortunately, school-based education has not often included the education of Indian children by their parents or by other tribal adults. Native American autobiographies (Brumble, 1981) provide an excellent source of information on tribal methods of education (Eastman, 1916/1977; Sekaquaptewa, 1969), and Eggan (1974) insightfully summarized how Hopi traditional instruction creates an enduring and emotionally profound commitment to Hopi life.

Euro-American nations and churches have consistently sought to replace those profound lessons with a new language, Christianity, patriarchal family structure, subordinate political status, and capitalist economy—all part of a conscious agenda to disenfranchise Indians from their land (Adams, 1988b). Four principal methods have been utilized to accomplish these goals.

Four Methods of Disenfranchisement

First, colonial authorities relocated Native Americans into newly created political units: well-controlled communities separate from European settlements. Spanish missions (Van Well, 1942), French Jesuit "reductions" (J. W. Grant, 1984; Moore, 1982), and Puritan Praying Towns (N. Salisbury, 1982) were Indian enclaves within foreign societies.

Second, although the degree of literacy training varied among the European states, native peoples were instructed in the language of civilized society, be it French, Spanish, English, or some other.

Third, these newly created native communities were shaped religiously by diverse European colonizers. Conversion to Christianity was a fundamental necessity, whether the conversion was to Catholicism or Protestantism.

Fourth, native economies were restructured to fit European notions of sedentary agriculture, small-scale craft industry, and gendered labor. Segregated native communities were designed to teach trades and agriculture to men and domestic skills to women (Szasz, 1988; Szasz & Ryan, 1988; Wright, 1989). These four components of colonization—relocation under political control, replacement of language, religious conversion, and gendered economic reconstruction—permeate American Indian education to the present day.

The hopes of colonial educators are epitomized by Eleazar Wheelock, who sought "to save the Indians from themselves and to save the English from the Indians" (Axtell, 1981, p. 97). Wheelock founded Moor's Charity School for Indians, as well as Dartmouth College—the two schools were separate institutions, although Dartmouth ostensibly focused on Indian education.

American Indian parents and children resisted these programs of total assimilation in a variety of ways. From armed revolts in the Southwest to epidemic-induced conversions in the Northeast, the course of proselytization was never smooth (Bowden, 1981). Reprisals for resistance could be harsh. The Spanish flogged, amputated hands and feet, or set aflame Pueblo "heretics" in the 17th century (Simmons, 1979), and in 1895 the United States sent Hopi men who resisted federal agents to Alcatraz (James, 1974). More recent assimilatory practices, such as boarding-school enrollment, may seem humane compared to earlier horrors, yet they have also provoked resistance. Indian children have devised ingenious ways to subvert or escape the disciplines of boarding-school life (Adams, 1988a; Coleman, 1993), from smuggling sandwiches to building whiskey stills disguised as Boy Scout outdoor ovens (Lomawaima, 1994).

In the late 18th and early 19th centuries, the United States left Indian education in the hands of the clergy, subsidizing the work of mission boards in agricultural, domestic, manual-labor, and academic instruction (Prucha, 1979). Diverse native nations met diverse denominations—Quakers, Moravians, Catholics, Presbyterians, Mennonites—some of whom were dedicated to high academic standards and to developing writing systems and literacy in both English and native languages (Neely, 1975). Noley (1979) has pointed out that missionaries began bilingual and bicultural education in the early 1800s for Choctaws and other Eastern tribes. Tribal governments continued this educational tradition after Eastern tribes were relocated to Indian Territory (to become the state of Oklahoma) by the middle of the 19th century. The Creek, Choctaw, and Cherokee nations, among others, established their own academies and seminaries in Indian Territory, such as the Cherokee Female Seminary, established in 1851 (Mihesuah, 1993).

By the late 1800s the federal government began to displace missions as the primary educator of Native Americans (Prucha, 1979). In 1875 Col. Richard Henry Pratt began a successful federal experiment in education among Kiowa and Cheyenne prisoners of war incarcerated at Fort Marion, St. Augustine, Florida. After three years of imprisonment, a number of the young Kiowa and Cheyenne requested further schooling. Convinced that equal educational opportunity was all that separated native people from the advantages of civilization, Pratt tried in vain to locate an agricultural college that would accept his students. Samuel Armstrong accepted them into Hampton Institute, a school for African Americans, but the Indian college at Hampton was short-lived. Armstrong, a staunch conservative committed to a racist hierarchy of humankind, and Pratt, with his progressive notions of racial equality, could not tolerate one another (Adams, 1977; Utley, 1964).

Pratt successfully lobbied Secretary of the Interior Carl Schurz and the Congress to establish the first federal off-reservation boarding school for American Indian youth at unused military barracks in Carlisle, Pennsylvania (Ryan, 1962; Utley, 1964). Carlisle Indian School opened in 1879. Within five years similar schools were established: Chilocco Indian School in Oklahoma; Genoa Indian School in Nebraska; and Haskell Institute at Lawrence, Kansas. By the turn of the century the federal government ended its subsidies of mission schools, opened 25 off-reservation boarding schools, and operated dozens of local day schools and on-reservation boarding schools.

Federal policy of total cultural assimilation of Indian people and federal educational practices of military regimentation, strict discipline, and intensive manual labor clearly reveal federal intent to train young Indians in subservience to federal authority (Adams, 1988b; Lomawaima, 1993; Littlefield, 1989, 1993). Non-native and native reformers have objected to the principles and/or the practices of assimilatory education since its inception. Religious or political groups have, at various times, fought corruption and graft in the federal administration of Indian affairs and advocated more humane treatment of Indian students. Perhaps the best-known, and most effective, exposé of federal Indian administration was the 1928 report, *The Problem of Indian Administration* (Meriam, 1928). The Meriam report's chapter on Indian education targeted boarding schools as inappropriate places to raise children, and recommended public and on-reservation day schools as alternatives.

Under the leadership of John Collier, President Franklin D. Roosevelt's Commissioner of Indian Affairs, the education division of the BIA began to shift support from boarding to day schools, from federal to public schools, from assimilatory to respectful attitudes toward native cultures (Philp, 1977; Szasz, 1977; see Barman, Hébert, & McCaskill, 1986–1987, for a historical and contemporary review of federal/mission education of Native Canadians). The assimilatory view has not disappeared from the scene, however. As recently as 1989, BIA schools were advised to provide "bonified [*sic*] vocational preparation" and to beware the "consequences" of teaching any language but English, or even English as a second language (Latham, 1989).

Research on the Boarding School Experience

Indian resistance to the federal agenda of assimilation in the boarding schools has proved a rich ground for historical and contemporary research on what federal/mission education has meant to Indian individuals and communities. Early research on boarding schools tended to focus on the social, cultural, psychological, or intellectual pathologies of Indian students or the pathologies of the environment (Birchard, 1970; Krush, Bjork, Sindell, & Nelle 1966). Alternatively, authors investigated the history of particular schools by focusing on federal policy and the documentary evidence left by school staff (Ryan, 1962; Trennert, 1988).

In 1983, McBeth introduced the voices and opinions of native alumni of federal boarding schools in Oklahoma. Her work paved the way for research and films revealing the opinions and experiences of native people in U.S. boarding schools (Loma-waima, 1994) and Canadian residential schools (Haig-Brown, 1988; Johnston, 1988; Pittman, 1989). Basil Johnston's memoir of his education at "Spanish," a Jesuit boarding school in northern Ontario in the 1930s, is the contemporary counterpoint to Francis LaFlesche's (1900/1978) moving account of Presbyterian mission education of young Omaha children in the 1880s. Boarding-school attendance has left a range of legacies, from family enrollment at an "alma mater" over successive generations (McBeth, 1983; Lomawaima, 1994; Stull & Kendall, 1986) to very negative attitudes toward all schools (Butterfield & Pepper, 1991).

Ethnographic study of contemporary boarding-school students has been carried out largely in Alaska, rather than the lower 48 states (Kleinfeld, 1973c). In 1985 the governors of the 19 Pueblos of New Mexico sponsored an oral history of the Santa Fe Indian School. The resulting museum exhibit and catalog (Hyer, 1990) eloquently convey native voices, native lives, and native self-determination in education.

RESEARCH ON INDIAN EDUCATION

Scholarly and professional discussion of Indian education began as early as 1884, when the Indian Service (later called the BIA) began an annual tradition of summer institutes for its teachers. By summer 1903 Superintendent of Indian Schools Estelle Reel had organized 10 such institutes (Reel, 1903). As part of her plan to professionalize her teacher corps, Reel successfully applied to the National Education Association (NEA) for recognition as a subgroup. In 1899 the group on Indian education met for the first time to present papers and exchange ideas at the NEA annual meeting. Teachers, principals, and administrators discussed, among other topics, the relation between literary and industrial education, teacher training, trades instruction for Indian boys, and domestic training for girls, "the uplifter[s] of the home" (NEA, 1900, p. 701).

In 1936 the education division of the Indian Service began to publish a field letter entitled *Indian Education* to present "concise and clear-cut statements of the philosophy, policy and preferred procedures of Indian education" (Beatty, 1953, p. 10). Volumes of reprinted articles from the newsletter focus on education for cultural change (Beatty, 1953) and education for cross-cultural enrichment (Thompson, 1964). Willard Walcott Beatty, a proponent of Progressive education, was the Indian Bureau's Director of Education from 1936 to 1952. "Sympathetic and understanding of the customs and heritage of other peoples," Beatty endeavored to develop an education relevant to Indian life (Szasz, 1977, p. 49).

Although Beatty was not ultimately successful, the concept of community schooling, the construction of reservation day schools, and bilingual education programs did flourish under his administration. Beatty was succeeded by Hildegard Thompson (1952–1965), who guided the education division through difficult years. Congressional legislation to terminate tribes' special government-to-government relation with the federal

government, and mandates to relocate Indians to urban areas, threatened tribal sovereignty during her tenure (Szasz, 1977).

Self-Determination: Rhetoric or Reality?

The civil rights movement of the 1950s and 1960s radically shifted the status quo on reservations. More and more Indian children had been enrolling in public schools, and Indian parents and communities exercised newfound political power to reform existing schools or establish new schools of their own (Johnson, 1968). Congressional and federal investigations of Indian education uncovered scandals and advocated reforms (Aurbach & Fuchs, 1970; Committee on Labor and Public Welfare, 1969; Fuchs & Havighurst, 1972; NAACP Legal Defense and Educational Fund, 1971). Congress responded with a landslide of legislation promoting tribal self-determination in education. This legislation included the 1965 Elementary and Secondary Education Act (P.L. 89-10, amended in 1966 to include BIA schools), the 1964 Economic Opportunity Act, the 1972 Indian Education Act (Title IV of Public Law 92-318), the 1975 Indian Self-Determination and Education Assistance Act (P.L. 93-638), and the Educational Amendments Act of 1978 (P.L. 95-561 and its technical amendments P.L. 98-511, 98-89, and 100-297).

The Indian Self-Determination and Education Assistance Act of 1975 (P.L. 93-638) exemplifies how rhetoric—what sounds good on paper—has collided with administrative reality in American Indian education. P.L. 93-638 regulated the existing practice of contracting federal monies (administered through the BIA) to Indian communities to run local programs (Senese, 1986, p. 153). The practice of "638 contracting" has been praised by some as the greatest opportunity in history for Indian people to control their own destiny (Szasz, 1977), while others damn it as yet another link in the chain of BIA bureaucratic oppression (Barsh & Trosper, 1975; Grell, 1983; Senese, 1986). Senese argued that 638 contracting offers Indian communities only an "illusion of control and competency" (p. 154), while the language of the law, its implementation, and the flawed disbursement of funds have crippled community-based education.

Senese began with Flannery's (1980) findings that "the growth in contracting operations in schools slowed *after* the passage of P.L. 93-638" (Senese, 1986, p. 155), and went on to quote tribal leaders who call 638 the "BIA self-perpetuation act" and who equate self-determination with "job insecurity" (pp. 161–162). Senese identified four major ways 638 reinforces BIA control and weakens community direction of education: the broad discretion of the secretary of the interior to decline or terminate contracts; late and unpredictable funds available only on a cost-reimbursable basis; no budgetary provisions for raises or promotions; and the "lack of bureau accountability" for technical assistance funds (p. 161). In a case study of 638 contracting at the Kickapoo Nation School, Grell (1983) repeated all of Senese's criticisms and concluded that "control of the school is not a panacea" for Indian education because "the incompatibility of externally imposed restrictions and tribally-oriented values in education remains" (p. 9). McCarty (1987, 1989) detailed identical problems of program instability, student transfers, staff turnover, and unpredictable funding as major obstacles to community school success on the Navajo reservation.

The Disadvantaged Child

Throughout the late 1960s and early 1970s, educational and social scientists began to study the school experiences of American Indian (and other minority) children and to document their achievement levels on standardized tests. Some researchers focused on the validity of testing instruments, others on the inadequacies or underpreparation of minority children. Two articles in the *Journal of Learning Disabilities* exemplify the latter focus. The authors used standardized developmental tests to "document" that Nez Percé kindergarten students had "less developed" visual perception (Lowry, 1970, p. 303) and "severe linguistic inadequacy" (Ramstad & Potter, 1947, p. 493) compared with their White classmates.

A "culture of poverty" model labeled children, their families, and communities as fundamentally "disadvantaged"—culturally, socially, and/or economically unable to melt into the great American pot (Crow, Murray, & Smythe, 1966; Webster, 1966). L. Salisbury's (1974) research in Alaska attributed to cultural disadvantage the maladjustment of native students to college life. Students had "communication problems" because of their "cultural attitude toward [not verbally] sharing problems" (pp. 194–199). Salisbury hoped to teach the students to "verbalize problems freely" in order to make the "transition toward a culture in which [they] must find a place" (p. 199). "Disadvantage" models continued the assimilationist thrust of two centuries of Indian education with assumptions that Indian children must "find their place."

Other scholars removed the onus of disadvantage from Indian students, and placed responsibility elsewhere for minority student "failure." Bryde's (1970) classic study of scholastic failure and personality conflict examined the "cross-over phenomenon" (Brown, 1979) among Sioux students. These students achieved at or above national norms in their first few school years, then crossed over and "reverse[d] their performance by underachieving for the rest of their scholastic lives" (Bryde, 1970, p. i). By the seventh or eighth grade, students sensed "themselves caught by forces beyond their command" and responded with rejection, depression, alienation, and anxiety (p. 67). Bryde and others recognized that systematic social inequities were being played out in the schools as well as in the larger society (Ogbu, 1983, 1987, 1989; Parmee, 1968).

The Drop-Out Rate: Problems of Comparability

Disproportionately high drop-out rates and low graduation or retention rates for Native American students, at all educational levels, have been a matter of statistical inquiry and policy concern for decades. The NCES sponsored three longitudinal studies of drop-out rates during the 1970s and 1980s (NCES 1988, 1989, 1990b). The studies were hampered by very small sample sizes of American Indian/Alaska Native students, making statistical analysis impossible (but see descriptive reports for some of the data sets; e.g., BIA, 1988). The 1980 survey of 30,000

sophomores and 28,000 seniors across the country found a 31.8% drop-out rate for American Indian females, 27.2% for American Indian males, 18% for Hispanics, 14.1% for Blacks, 2.7% for Asian-Americans, and 11.5% for Whites (Peng & Takai, 1983). The National Educational Longitudinal Study of 1988 tracked 24,599 eighth graders (including 307 students coded as Native American) and reported drop-out rates of American Indian/Alaska Native, 9.2%; Black, non-Hispanic, 10.2%; Hispanic, 9.6%; White, non-Hispanic, 5.2%; and Asian/Pacific Islander, 4% (NCES, 1990b).

In 1992 the *Journal of American Indian Education* (Swisher, 1992b, 1992c) devoted two special issues to drop-out research, as

> the statistics regarding these rates among Indian/Native students have been highly speculative, inaccurate, and/or embedded in the innocuous category of "other" when reported . . . there is not a clear picture of the reasons that Indian/Native students are leaving school. (Swisher, 1992a, p. 1)

Swisher and Hoisch (1992) reviewed drop-out studies from the 1960s through the 1980s, revealing disparities from study to study among measurement techniques, sample sizes and compositions, and data sets that made nationally comparable or meaningful figures very difficult to obtain.

In an effort to calculate Indian drop-out rates more accurately, Swisher, Hoisch, and Pavel (1991) drew data from 26 state and national educational agencies, BIA offices, and tribal entities in the 20 states identified by the census with the largest Indian/Native populations. While state data response was quite timely and complete, data were difficult to impossible to obtain and/or compare across BIA and tribal sources. A subsequent follow-up study focusing on BIA schools found a 25% drop-out rate in grades 9 through 12 (no data were available before grade 7) (Swisher & Hoisch, 1992, p. 9).

Swisher and Hoisch (1992) summarized the major stumbling blocks to drop-out research: widely varying statistical methods and/or incomparable data sets, frequency of student transfers, and minimal attention to the reasons why students leave school. The phenomenon of transferring is especially confounding for drop-out statistics. Swisher and Hoisch reported transfer rates from 10% in BIA elementary schools to 30% in BIA high schools to 50% at Chemawa, a BIA boarding school in Oregon (p. 20).

Researchers who have explored students' school experiences and reasons for dropping out have identified a variety of important social, cultural, economic, and academic factors. Their studies tend to focus on "school-based" reasons for dropping out, such as uncaring teachers or inappropriate curriculum (Reyhner, 1992); on "home-based" reasons, such as lack of parental support or first language other than English (Platero, Brandt, Witherspoon, & Wong, 1986); or on "student-based" reasons, such as boredom, life goals unrelated to school instruction, pregnancy, or substance abuse (Bowker, 1992). Many studies incorporate one or more of these perspectives on school stayers and school leavers.

Coladarci (1983) interviewed students who had dropped out of a Montana high school district and identified noncaring teachers, objectionable school curriculum, irrelevant school-ing, problems at home, lack of parental support, and lack of peer support as major influences on the decision to drop out. Platero et al. (1986) found Navajo and Ute students were mostly "bored." Their academic problems were minor, but social friction with other students, absenteeism due to pregnancy, and grade retention resulting from absenteeism pushed them out of school. Similarly, in an NEA-sponsored study, Swisher and Hoisch (1992) found that "apparently, in New Mexico [Native American] students are more likely than any other ethnic group to become dropouts because, for one reason or another, the district removes them from school, a fact that warrants further investigation" (p. 17).

Brandt (1992) reported the findings of the Navajo Area Student Dropout Study (NASDS) (Platero et al., 1986). Prior to NASDS, reported drop-out rates across the reservation ranged from 30 to 95% (Brandt, 1992, pp. 48–49). NASDS tracked students through their Navajo census numbers, and interviewed 889 students—670 stayers and 219 leavers. The investigators found that "over 50% of the students that the schools identified as 'dropouts' had in fact either transferred to another school or had graduated" (p. 52). NASDS estimated a transfer rate for the study area of 30%, a dropout rate of 31%, and rank-ordered the reasons students gave for dropping out, from number 1, "bored with school," through "problems with other students," to number 15, "having to work" (p. 57). Academic factors were minimally involved for school leavers; strong Navajo cultural ties were found among stayers and leavers; and bilingual proficiency in Navajo and English was positively linked to persistence in school. Brandt concluded that, whether students chose to stay or leave, schools were not "challenging or engaging Navajo students socially or intellectually" (p. 61).

Bowker (1992) reviewed the extensive literature on American Indian student dropouts as she focused on female students to determine what factors contribute to women's school success (graduation) or nonsuccess (nongraduation). Bowker's two-year study of 991 Indian females of diverse backgrounds from seven northern Plains groups (all grew up on reservations) found that many of the girls "academically . . . were confident in their abilities to do their school work, yet many of them did not choose to do so" (p. 14). Bowker found "strong evidence" that "American Indian girls drink no more than non-Indian girls," but noted that 50% of the Indian female dropouts were due to pregnancy, compared to 40% for the national norm (p. 15). The strongest indicator Bowker found for school success was "the support of their families," especially their mothers and grandmothers (p. 16). She could not find strong correlates for school "failure." "In the final analysis, this study found no formula for success or dropping out. Women who dropped out were those whom most educators would not consider at risk; others succeeded with the deck stacked against them" (p. 17).

Deyhle's (1992) seven-year ethnographic study of Navajo and Ute "school leavers" provides a rich source of evidence and data. She followed six class cohorts (1984–1989), interviewing students and leavers at a border town high school and at a Navajo reservation high school. Deyhle found that native students and non-native teachers/administrators neither trusted

nor cared for one another. Students were not blind to the institutional racism of the schools or to their limited economic and social opportunities in the surrounding community. Deyhle calls their decision to leave school "a rational response" to racism (p. 25).

Deyhle found Ogbu's (1987) concept of castes useful in understanding "failure" among the native students attending the border town high school. She accounted for school success among the students attending the on-reservation school through cultural integrity of school and community (Deyhle, 1992, pp. 26–27). Deyhle concluded that "when youth revealed the feelings they had of being 'pushed out' of schools and 'pulled into' their own Indian community, one must look beyond 'individual failure' as pivotal reasons for leaving school" (p. 43). "As many as 18% of these Indian youth were physically in school for 12 years and still did not graduate," and 55% of those who dropped out did so in the 12th grade (pp. 27–28). She established an overall dropout rate of 21.3%.

Learning and Interactional Styles

As educators have struggled to develop culturally relevant classroom materials and pedagogic methods (Lipka, 1991), researchers have addressed the issue of how children might learn and exhibit knowledge in culturally specific ways. Swisher and Deyhle (1987), in their review of this literature, define learning style as "the way in which knowledge is acquired," and interactional style as "the way in which knowledge is demonstrated" (p. 345). The cultural discontinuity/congruence hypothesis predicts that cultural discontinuities between teachers and students (King, 1967; Sindell, 1974; Vogt, Jordan, & Tharp, 1987), between Indian and non-Indian learning styles (Cazden & John, 1971; John, 1972), or between teacher-imposed and community-sanctioned interactional styles (Philips, 1972, 1983) will hinder children's achievement as measured by standardized tests. Deyhle (1983) raised a provocative issue for standardized testing in an article documenting the transition of Navajo students from eager test takers (grades one and two) to test resisters (grades six, seven, and eight). She posits that a culture that values process over product, coupled with students' gradual realization of the personal judgment entailed in passing or failing, conspire to create students who reject testing itself.

Learning-style researchers have focused on, among other critical parameters defining how children learn and how they display what they learn: (a) linguistic performance (Cazden & Leggett, 1981; Philips, 1972, 1983; Scollon & Scollon, 1981) and linguistic nonperformance, or silence, in the classroom (Dumont, 1972; Wax, Wax, & Dumont, 1964); (b) observational or "private" versus trial-by-error learning (John, 1972; Wolcott, 1967); (c) cooperative versus competitive learning strategies (Brown, 1980; Miller & Thomas, 1972); (d) field-dependent versus field-independent perceptual and personality organization (Dinges & Hollenbeck, 1978); (e) cultural congruence; and (f) brain hemispheric dominance (not discussed further here; see Chrisjohn & Peters, 1989, and Rhodes, 1990, for rebuttals to the idea of "right-brained" or "whole-brained" Indians).

Linguistic Performance. Philips's (1972, 1983) seminal study of Warm Springs (Oregon) reservation education outlined different standards of linguistic performance in the community and in the school. She called these linguistic standards "communicative competencies." Communicative competency is defined and judged through a framework of rules governing who speaks when, for how long, in what order, and in what context. Philips called the framework of rules that govern speech "participant structures." Philips concluded that Indian children at Warm Springs resisted participant structures that were school-defined and teacher-dominated, and that required students to recite publicly as a sign of mastery over content knowledge. One of the most cited studies of Indian education, her 1972 work laid the framework for two decades of research on linguistic performance and classroom interaction.

The classroom interaction model has been productively applied to studies of reading instruction. Au and Jordan (1981) described the Kamehameha Early Education Program (KEEP) developed for native Hawaiian children. KEEP successfully integrates native Hawaiian values of informal education into formal classroom reading lessons, building on the Hawaiian "talk story" or storytelling model. Van Ness (1981) analyzed a similar program for getting Alaskan Athabascan children ready for reading.

Greenbaum and Greenbaum (1983) reviewed the literature on cultural differences in classroom interaction, and the possible effects of sociolinguistic interference that result when teachers and students nonverbally regulate conversation in conflicting ways. They identify three possible kinds of interference: (a) misinterpretation of intent or content; (b) value conflicts, such as cooperative versus competitive learning; and (c) "converged accommodation," the degree to which participants in a conversation may shift speech styles to conform to another speaker as a sign of approval or disapproval. While concluding that Indian and non-Indian classroom interactions do differ in the frequency/duration of utterances, voice loudness, and degree of visual attention, they caution that "it has yet to be shown empirically that such differences obstruct the students' comprehension of what they are being taught" (p. 28).

Thielke and Shriberg (1990) suggest that Indian children's delays in language and speech development and reduced educational achievement may be related to the high incidence of otitis media (inflammation of the middle ear) among native populations. This study raises important questions that warrant further research on Native American health problems and their educational impacts (see Dorris, 1989, for the disturbing implications of fetal alcohol syndrome [FAS]).

Philips (1972, 1983) also discussed how Warm Springs adults taught children to pay attention, to observe, to practice on their own, and only then to undertake public performance or demonstration of a new skill or knowledge. This notion of "private learning" (Swisher & Deyhle, 1989, p. 4) has been attested as well for Navajo children (Longstreet, 1978), Oglala Sioux children (Brewer, 1977), and Yaqui children (Appleton, 1983).

Private Learners. In addition to characterizing Indian children as private learners, many researchers also see them as silent students. Studies have attempted to demonstrate empirically what teachers report anecdotally: that Indian children are much quieter than other children in the classroom. In their study of Oklahoma Cherokee children's behavior in classrooms, Dumont and Wax (1969) posit a "Cherokee School Society" shaped by the students in response and resistance to an imposed, alien institution. By the seventh and eighth grades the students

surrounded themselves with a wall of silence impenetrable by the outsider, while sheltering a rich emotional communion among themselves. The silence is positive, not negative or withdrawing, and it shelters them so that ... they can pursue their scholastic interests in their own style and pace. By their silence they exercise control over the teacher. (p. 222)

Guilmet (1978, 1981) examined the oral-linguistic and non-oral-visual behavioral patterns of Navajo and White children in the classroom and the playground to determine if the Navajo students were more or less quiet. Differentiating the assumptions of (a) learning-style theory—Navajo children learn non-orally and visually at home, therefore they are culturally predisposed to quieter behavior at school—and (b) interference theory—classrooms are an alien environment unsuited to expression of Navajo oral-linguistic competencies, therefore children are quieter at school than at home—Guilmet observed a small sample of 16 Navajo and 7 White children. Navajo children were strikingly less oral-linguistic and strikingly more nonoral-visual than White children. This difference was more marked on the playground than in the classroom. Based on earlier research on Navajo mothers (1979), Guilmet proposed a "culturally appropriate [Navajo] mode of attending" (1981, p. 149) that defines intense speech interactions and high levels of physical activity as discourteous, self-centered, and undisciplined (1979).

Cooperation or Competition? It is commonly asserted that Indian children are raised to be more "cooperative" than White children, and that competition is expressed by Indian children only in group contexts, such as team sports. Miller and Thomas (1972) compared 48 Blood children from a reserve school in Alberta, Canada, with 48 non-Indian children in an urban school. The children, all between the ages of 7 and 10, were tested with the Madsen Cooperation Board under two experimental reward conditions. In the first experiment, cooperative behavior was necessary to ensure a high rate of reward for each player. Both Indian and non-Indian groups cooperated effectively to achieve a group reward. Under the individual reward system, however, the "performance level of Indian children continued to increase while that of the non-Indian children deteriorated" (p. 1109). The Indian children developed verbal strategies to cooperate, and reprimanded competitive behavior. The authors note in their conclusion that "it is tempting to relate these differences to differences in the cultural background of the groups ... but the specific ways that these ... cultural factors find expression in cooperative behaviors ... are not known in detail at the present time" (p. 1110).

Field-Dependent or -Independent? Swisher and Deyhle (1989) note that the little research on Indian students' degree of field dependence/field independence contradicts the model Ramírez and Castañeda (1974) developed, based on their study of Mexican American children. Mexican American children tested higher in the direction of field dependence than Anglo children, who tested higher toward field independence. This cognitive model proposes that formally organized families who promote strong individual identity produce field-independent children, and that shared-function families (especially in groups isolated from the U.S. mainstream) who promote group identity will produce field-dependent children (Ramírez & Castañeda, 1974). The Ramírez and Castañeda model predicts that Navajo children would be more field dependent than White children. The 1978 study by Dinges and Hollenbeck demonstrates exactly the opposite. Dinges and Hollenbeck propose genetic, environmental, experiential, and linguistic factors to account for this unexpected result. Their recognition of cultural and grammatical imperatives that privilege "perceptual-cognitive abilities" is noteworthy, but their devaluation of Navajo creativity is not. Dinges and Hollenbeck claimed that Navajo women do not create rug patterns according to a cultural aesthetic, but that they merely "duplicate" them "from memory" (p. 218).

Cultural Congruence. Mohatt and Erickson (1981) used Philips's (1979) model of participant structures to analyze culturally patterned aspects of classroom behavior as they scrutinized the teaching styles of two "effective and experienced" teachers, one an Indian female, the other a non-Indian male, in a school on the Odawa reserve (Canada). They were interested in the "cultural congruence of each [teacher's] style with the pattern of interaction customary for Indian children in everyday life" (p. 117). Their observation of how the non-Indian teacher adapted his style over the course of a year helped convince the native board of directors to pledge research monies to "see whether more culturally congruent participant structures will increase achievement among native students" (p. 119).

Kleinfeld (1974) examined whether altering nonverbal cues that communicate "warmth" in teaching styles would stimulate learning, question answering, and question asking among 20 White and 20 Eskimo students. The cues were ethnographically defined according to Eskimo values. She found that "warm" college guidance sessions did increase learning for both groups, but that "ethnic group differences were few and not altogether consistent" (p. 3). Earlier research (Kleinfeld, 1973a) provided some evidence suggesting that "warmth" expressed by a test administrator could raise intelligence test scores for Athabascan Indian and Eskimo students.

Cultural Discontinuity/Congruence Theory and Criticisms

The theoretical perspective of cultural discontinuity/cultural congruence unites many of these studies across the divide of whether they see school failure as a student pathology (the student "drops out") or a school pathology (the school "pushes out") or a home/cultural pathology (native home/community "pulls out" student). Simply put, this theory predicts that cultural/linguistic difference among teacher, school, and student can result in student underachievement or failure; cultural/linguistic congruence among teacher, school, and student leads to student success.

Ledlow (1992) tackled the whole question of cultural discontinuity between home and school as an adequate explanation for dropping out. She critically reviewed earlier research and found "little or no explicit research to prove the hypothesis" that cultural discontinuity contributes to school failure or that culturally relevant curricula and pedagogy contribute to school success (p. 21). Ledlow supports the cultural discontinuity/cultural compatability hypothesis as a research question, but objects to unquestioned assumption of its validity. She proposes that macrostructural explanations of minority schooling, rooted in a Marxist perspective, might more productively focus on "economic and social issues"—pregnancy, drugs, boredom, institutional racism, poverty—"which are not culturally specific to being Indian" (p. 29) in order to address dropping out. Evidence from Deyhle (1992) and others indicates that "a strong sense of traditional cultural identity ... provides a student with an advantage in school. The idea that traditional Indian students may have an academic advantage over more 'acculturated' students is an important issue" (Ledlow, 1992, p. 34). McShane (1983) also critiqued Indian education research as "theoretically naive" (p. 34). He turns to psychological analysis for "powerful" models to interrelate cognition, affect, and behavior.

Ogbu (1989), in his differentiation of voluntary and involuntary minorities, has pointed out that some minority groups who do well in school are more culturally different from the "mainstream" school culture than groups who do poorly (pp. 182–183). A simple model of cultural congruence does not account for their school success. In Indian education, Osborne (1989) called into question the whole rationale of the cultural congruence hypothesis by pointing out that complete cultural congruence between Indian (specifically Zuni Pueblo, New Mexico) and U.S. values is not possible in the classroom. Classrooms are incongruous institutions within Zuni culture. He questioned the desirability of cultural congruence, since Zuni parents want their children prepared to survive and excel in mainstream U.S. society. Osborne proposed a conceptual framework of "fused biculturalism" to describe the juxtaposition of irreconcilable but coexisting cultural traditions.

Yet another critique of research in Native American education zeroes in on the lack of evidence to support the abundance of literature about Indian students' "visual learning styles" (Kleinfeld & Nelson, 1988, p. 2). Kleinfeld and Nelson directed an extensive computer search of the literature that suggests that Indian children have "special strengths" in spatial abilities and visual memory (p. 1). They searched the psychological, ethnographic, and educational research for studies that empirically *tested* the claim that "instruction adapted to Native American learning styles increases achievement" (p. 8). They found three. Two studies (McCartin & Schill, 1977; Shears, 1970) did not show that Native American students learn more with visually based instruction. The third (Erickson, 1972) found support for the claim in one site but not another, but also found that visually based instruction was even more effective for White than for Indian children. Kleinfeld and Nelson concluded that the lack of evidence notwithstanding, the "learning-style" construct remains popular because educators want to avoid "deficit" language and because the terminology is useful in grant proposals and in describing the plethora of adjustments teachers make when dealing with specific Native American groups.

Curriculum Development

The debatable efficacy of learning-style/teaching-style research should not lead us to forget the equally important issue of curriculum content. How we teach children, and how they learn, should not obscure the critical nature of what they are being taught. Any Native American who has suffered through a television miniseries on "How the West Was Lost," or a high school history lecture lauding the bold, adventurous spirit that led Columbus to his "discovery," or an elementary classroom reenactment of the first Thanksgiving, knows this lesson. What if teachers scrupulously develop culturally/linguistically sensitive pedagogical methods, but never alter the content of what they teach? Can we expect Indian children to "succeed" in school so long as Indian history, cultures, and people are systematically excluded from, marginalized within, or brutalized by curricular content? Research findings from the Rough Rock Demonstration School on the Navajo reservation underscore this question. When an experimental social studies curriculum based on local values and ideas was introduced, children blossomed from silent "concrete" learners into talkative, analytical students (Benally, Lynch, McCarty, & Wallace, 1991).

Projects in curriculum development have achieved positive results in some Indian-controlled schools. The Kickapoo Nation School introduced new curriculum in 1985 and reversed declining performance on test scores (Dupuis & Walker, 1989). McCarty (1987, 1989) described the fractious and difficult process of curriculum and language development at Rough Rock Demonstration School as an exercise in frustration; Okakok's (1989) more optimistic view stressed the benefits of integrating Inupiat and Western Alaskan cultural values into the administration and curriculum of the North Slope Borough School District.

What goes on within schools is only part, of course, of the influences to which children are exposed. DeMarrais, Nelson, and Baker's (1992) delightful description of the cognitive skills reinforced by "storyknifing," the storytelling activity of young Alaska Native girls along the muddy banks of the Kuskokwim River, concluded with the discouraging observation that this childhood pastime has been supplanted by hours in front of the TV.

Language Policy and Language Renewal

Native American language use, language maintenance, and language renewal are tremendously important influences on educational experiences and policies, but would require another chapter to review adequately. As many as 200 native languages are still spoken in the United States today, but patterns of fluency vary widely among communities (Leap, 1981). At one end of the continuum, groups such as the Navajo tribe try to maintain a language still spoken by a majority of members

(Rosier & Holm, 1980). Along the middle, the Tachi-Yokuts in central California struggle to revive interest in a language spoken only by an elderly few (Britsch-Devany, 1988). At the other end of the continuum, native languages have virtually disappeared, leaving their traces in a locally specific version of "Indian English" (Leap, 1977).

Long-standing federal policy to eradicate native languages has only recently been revised to provide grudging support of the idea of bilingual education (McCarty, 1992; Zepeda, 1990). Since the passage of the Bilingual Education Act in 1968 (other federal titles also supply monies to support bilingual/bicultural education) at least 70 native communities have developed language-education projects (McCarty, 1992; St. Clair & Leap, 1982). Federal language policies have intended primarily to establish "transitional" bilingual programs, to move children from a native language to fluency in English (J. H. Grant & Goldsmith, 1979; Spolsky, 1972, 1978). Most native people, however, are committed to maintaining native language as well (Palmer, 1988). Native-language use is being fostered from Makah on the northwest tip of Washington state (Renker & Arnold, 1988) to Passamoquoddy in Maine (Spolsky, 1978).

Tribes have turned to professionally and academically trained linguists to help develop educational programs in spoken and written language (Hale, 1973; Leap, 1988; Watahomigie & Yamamoto, 1987; Young, 1972). Fluent native speakers of Hopi, Navajo, Papago, and other languages have also obtained graduate degrees in linguistics and applied their training to educational development. Despite a dramatic reduction in federal funds for bilingual education initiated by President Reagan in the early 1980s, it seems unlikely that Native Americans will willingly or easily surrender their languages. Many communities are deeply troubled, however, by the challenges of language maintenance or renewal as truly fluent speakers grow fewer and older, and younger generations grow up inundated by the constant English chatter transmitted via cable, satellite dish, and videos.

Trends

Research on Indian education has tended to move away from models that propose deficiencies in the student's language abilities (Philion & Galloway, 1969; L. Salisbury, 1974), or neural organization (Ross, 1989), or cultural background, to theories of social and economic discrimination (Ogbu, 1983, 1987, 1989) that contextualize schools within the larger community. Current research trends define native cognitive skills as strengths, not weaknesses (Macias, 1989), and try to discover the characteristics of successful students (Benjamin, Chambers, & Reiterman, 1993; Grantham-Campbell, 1992; Shutiva, 1991). DeMarrais et al. (1992) focus on storytelling skills of Alaska Native girls; Kleinfeld (1973b) studies Eskimos' visual skills; Nelson and Lalami (1991) discuss Tohono O'odham children's "visual-spatial, pattern-symbol and kinesthetic" skills for the creative process.

American Indian participation in higher education promises to grow as more and more tribes establish their own community colleges. Since Navajo Community College, the first tribally controlled community college, was established in 1969, this area of educational opportunity has grown by leaps and bounds. Today 27 tribal colleges across the United States offer Native American adults an alternative in higher education that is structured upon native values and philosophies (Carnegie Foundation for the Advancement of Teaching, 1989). At Sinte Gleske college in Sioux country, native scholars map the constellations and their earthly correlates among the geographic features of the Black Hills (P. Deloria, 1984); native scholars gather at the Institute for Native Knowledge at Humboldt State University in Northern California to exchange ideas; finally, native scholarship is being shaped by native people.

ASSESSMENTS AND IMPLICATIONS FOR FUTURE RESEARCH

Native Americans face multiple challenges in the coming century as they work to maintain sovereignty, develop economically, preserve or regain language, and ensure educational access and achievement for their young people. Significant obstacles to all these goals exist within U.S. society, as the states and Donald Trump battle to restrict Indian gaming, as Congress legislates arts and crafts production, and as the Supreme Court whittles away at religious freedoms (*Lyng v. Northwest Indian Cemetery Protective Assn.,* 1988; *Employment Division v. Smith,* 1990).

It is perhaps ironic that a pan-tribal identity has become more real over time, but that pan-tribal linkage today complicates educational policy making and educational research. Too much policy has been predicated on creating viable solutions to "Indian" problems, generically defined. Too much research has been predicated on the hope that one teaching method or learning style or classroom environment or curriculum package will serve all Native Americans equally well.

One of the unfortunate consequences of too little educational research, and a high proportion of research focused on culturally/tribally specific sites or isolated reservations, is that provocative but slender evidence is generalized to all "Indian" children. Educators need to acknowledge the diversity of native cultures and experiences, and work locally to develop relevant content and methods. It may be that their achievements will never be generalizable to all "Indian" children. We need a wider range of research in the increasingly multicultural, increasingly poor urban schools where more and more children are being educated, far from "traditional" tribal homes.

Diversity in the classroom means we must attend to the skills, strengths, and needs of each child as an individual, building on native values without romanticizing them. Fiordo (1988) presents a Canadian example of education to eliminate alcohol and drug abuse, the Four Winds Development Project, that develops native cultural metaphors without stereotyping an "Indian Learning Style." The impulse is there for well-meaning teachers, curriculum developers, school administrators, and federal policy makers to discover the perfect learning style, pedagogical method, or curricular content for all Indian students, be it left-brain learning, whole-language instruction (Kasten, 1992), or generic spirituality (Locust, 1988). The search for the single teaching method or learning style that best serves or typifies a racially, linguistically, ethnically, or economically de-

fined subgroup of U.S. society is like the search for the Holy Grail. It risks becoming a sacred calling that consumes resources in the search for an illusory panacea for complex social and educational ills.

History, politics, and education have been inextricably bound up with one another in Indian America. Activism for educational change and empowerment has served as a political proving ground for Native American leadership. In the wake of the 1960s civil rights movement, the birth of the National Indian Education Association offered a forum for nationwide communication and organization. Alternative, native-run presses such as The Indian Historian Press, *Wassaja,* and *Akwesasne Notes* linked tribal communities and provided unprecedented opportunity to disseminate information and exchange ideas. The Chicago Indian Conference in 1961, the formation of the National Indian Youth Council in the early 1960s, and the first Convocation of American Indian scholars at Princeton in 1970 brought people together and developed new levels of political consciousness and cooperation (Indian Historian Press, 1970; Josephy, 1982; Lynch & Charleston 1990).

Locally controlled schools, such as Rough Rock Demonstration School, served as exemplars of community organization and educational self-determination. Rough Rock has hosted thousands of visitors and observers since it opened its doors. Schools have frequently been the flash point for political organization in Indian communities. In the South, for example, the desegregation of a tripartite school system (White, Black, and Red) focused the energies of the Poarch Band of Creeks, who eventually achieved federal recognition (Paredes, 1992). When Native Americans occupied Alcatraz Island in San Francisco Bay on November 20, 1969, they resolved to "plan our own futures and educate our own children" (blue cloud, 1972, p. 21). Their plan for Alcatraz included a Center for Native American Studies with "traveling colleges" to visit reservations, a training school, and a museum. Education was foremost in their minds, and their vision was realized in part when D-Q University was established at Davis, California (blue cloud, 1972; Lutz, 1980). The vision flourishes today on the campuses of 27 tribally run community colleges. Education, politics, and history still walk hand in hand across Indian country, while economic development too often trots at their heels like a half-grown hound.

Native American communities know their own history well, and that highly developed historical consciousness tends to make them skeptical of federal promises of change or educators' promises of improvement. The special legal and political status of tribes and the implications of sovereignty may mitigate against a wholehearted acceptance of multicultural education if "multicultural concepts seem to promote the assimilative trend by standardization at the expense of self-determination in Indian education" (Jaimes, 1983, p. 17). If self-determination means a tribal community college, or an all-Indian urban school (Butterfield & Pepper, 1991), it may appear to run counter to U.S. ideals of desegregation and cultural sharing. Native America has insisted for 500 years on the right to its own ideals. If Native American people are making educational decisions according to their own ideals—ideals of cultural survival and sovereign status—then they must be respected. Nothing less than the Constitution of the United States promises them that sovereign right.

References

Adams, D. (1977). Education in hues: Red and Black at Hampton Institute, 1878–1893. *The South Atlantic Quarterly, 76,* 159–176.

Adams, D. (1988a). Bullets to boarding schools. In P. Weeks (Ed.), *The American Indian experience* (pp. 218–239). Arlington Heights, IL: Forum Press.

Adams, D. (1988b). Fundamental considerations: The deep meaning of Native American schooling, 1880–1900. *Harvard Educational Review, 58*(1), 1–28.

Appleton, N. (1983). *Cultural pluralism in education.* New York: Longman.

Au, K., & Jordan, C. (1981). Teaching reading to Hawaiian children. In H. Trueba, G. Guthrie, & K. Au (Eds.), *Culture and the bilingual classroom* (pp. 139–152). Rowley, MA: Newbury House.

Aurbach, H., & Fuchs, E. (1970). *The status of American Indian education.* University Park: Pennsylvania State University Press.

Axtell, J. (1981). Dr. Wheelock's little red school. In J. Axtell (Ed.), *The European and the Indian: Essays in the ethnohistory of colonial North America* (pp. 87–109). Oxford, England: Oxford University Press.

Barman, J., Hébert, Y., & McCaskill, D. (Eds.). (1986–1987). *Indian education in Canada* (Vols. 1–2). Vancouver: University of British Columbia Press.

Barsh, R., & Henderson, J. (1980). *The road: Indian tribes and political liberty.* Berkeley: University of California Press.

Barsh, R., & Trosper, R. (1975). Title I of the Indian self-determination and education assistance act of 1975. *American Indian Law Review, 3,* 361–395.

Beatty, W. (1953). *Education for culture change.* Chilocco, OK: Bureau of Indian Affairs.

Benally, A., Lynch, R., McCarty, T., & Wallace, S. (1991). Classroom inquiry and Navajo learning styles: A call for reassessment. *Anthropology and Education Quarterly, 22,* 42–59.

Benjamin, D.P., Chambers, S., & Reiterman, G. (1993). A focus on American Indian college persistence. *Journal of American Indian Education, 32*(2), 24–40.

Biolsi, T. (1992). *Organizing the Lakota: The political economy of the new deal on the Pine Ridge and Rosebud Reservations.* Tucson: University of Arizona Press.

Biolsi, T. (1993). The political economy of Lakota consciousness. In J. Moore (Ed.), *The political economy of North American Indians* (pp. 20–42). Norman: University of Oklahoma Press.

Birchard, B. (1970). *Boarding schools for American Indian youth.* National Study of American Indian Education, ser. 2, no. 2. Minneapolis: University of Minnesota Center for Urban and Regional Affairs.

blue cloud, P. (Ed.). (1972). *Alcatraz is not an island.* Berkeley: Wingbow Press.

Bowden, H. (1981). *American Indians and Christian missions.* Chicago: University of Chicago Press.

Bowker, A. (1992). The American Indian female dropout. *Journal of American Indian Education, 31*(3), 3–20.

Brandt, E. (1992). The Navajo area student dropout study: Findings and implications. *Journal of American Indian Education, 31*(2), 48–63.

Brewer, A. (1977). An Indian education. *Integrateducation, 15,* 21–23.

Britsch-Devany, S. (1988). The collaborative development of a language renewal program for preschoolers. *Human Organization, 47,* 297–302.

Brown, A. D. (1979). The cross-over effect: A legitimate issue in Indian education? In *Multicultural education and the American Indian* (pp. 93–113). Los Angeles: American Indian Studies Center, University of California.

Brown, A. D. (1980). Cherokee culture and school achievement. *American Indian Culture and Research Journal, 4,* 55–74.

Brumble, H. D., III. (1981). *An annotated bibliography of American Indian and Eskimo autobiographies.* Lincoln: University of Nebraska Press.

Bryde, J. (1970). *The Indian student: A study of scholastic failure and personality conflict* (2nd ed.). Vermillion, SD: Dakota Press.

Bureau of Indian Affairs. (1988). *Report on BIA education: Excellence in Indian education through effective school process.* Washington, DC: U.S. Department of the Interior.

Butterfield, R., & Pepper, F. (1991). Improving parental participation in elementary and secondary education for American Indian and Alaska Native students. In *Indian nations at risk task force commissioned papers.* Washington, DC: Department of Education. (ERIC Document Reproduction Service No. ED 343 763)

Carnegie Foundation for the Advancement of Teaching. (1989). *Tribal colleges: Shaping the future of Native America.* Princeton, NJ: Author.

Castile, G., & Bee, R. (1992). *State and reservation: New perspectives on federal Indian policy.* Tucson: University of Arizona Press.

Cazden, C., & John, V. (1971). Learning in American Indian children. In M. L. Wax, S. Diamond, & F. Gearing (Eds.), *Anthropological perspectives on education* (pp. 253–272). New York: Basic Books.

Cazden, C., & Leggett, E. L. (1981). Culturally responsive education: Recommendations for achieving Lau remedies II. In H. Trueba, G. Guthrie, & K. Au (Eds.), *Culture and the bilingual classroom* (pp. 69–86). Rowley, MA: Newbury House.

Chrisjohn, R. D., & Peters, M. (1989, August). The right-brained Indian: Fact or fiction? *Journal of American Indian Education* [Special issue], pp. 77–83.

Coladarci, T. (1983). High school dropouts among Native Americans. *Journal of American Indian Studies, 23*(1), 15–22.

Coleman, M. C. (1993). *American Indian children at school, 1850–1930.* Jackson: University of Mississippi Press.

Committee on Labor and Public Welfare, U.S. Senate. (1969). *Indian education: A national tragedy—A national challenge.* Washington, DC: Government Printing Office.

Crow, L., Murray, W., & Smythe, H. (1966). *Educating the culturally disadvantaged child.* New York: David McKay.

Deloria, P. (Director). (1984). *Eyanopopi: Heart of the Sioux* [Film]. Boulder, CO: Centre Productions.

Deloria, V., Jr., & Lytle, C. (1984). *The nation within: The past and future of American Indian sovereignty.* New York: Pantheon Books.

DeMarrais, K., Nelson, P., & Baker, J. (1992). Meaning in mud: Yup'ik Eskimo girls at play. *Anthropology and Education Quarterly, 23,* 120–144.

Deyhle, D. (1983). Measuring success and failure in the classroom: Teacher communication about tests and the understandings of young Navajo students. *Peabody Journal of Education, 61*(1), 67–85.

Deyhle, D. (1992). Constructing failure and maintaining cultural identity: Navajo and Ute school leavers. *Journal of American Indian Education, 31*(2), 24–47.

Dinges, N. G., & Hollenbeck, A. R. (1978). Field dependence-independence in Navajo children. *International Journal of Psychology, 13,* 215–220.

Dobyns, H. F. (1983). *Their number become thinned.* Knoxville: University of Tennessee Press.

Dorris, M. (1989). *The broken cord.* New York: Harper & Row.

Dumont, R. (1972). Learning English and how to be silent: Studies in Sioux and Cherokee classrooms. In C. Cazden, V. John, & D. Hymes (Eds.), *Functions of language in the classroom* (pp. 344–369). New York: Teachers College Press.

Dumont, R., & Wax, M. (1969). Cherokee school society and the intercultural classroom. *Human Organization, 28,* 217–226.

Dupuis, V. L., & Walker, M. (1989). The circle of learning at Kickapoo. *Journal of American Indian Education, 28*(1), 27–33.

Eastman, C. (1977). *From the deep woods to civilization.* Lincoln: University of Nebraska Press. (Original work published 1916)

Eggan, D. (1974). Instruction and affect in Hopi cultural continuity. In G. Spindler (Ed.), *Education and cultural process* (pp. 311–332). New York: Holt, Rinehart, and Winston.

Employment Division v. Smith, 494 U.S. 108, L.Ed.2d 876, 110 S.Ct. 1595 (1990).

Erickson, D. (1972). *Verbal and diagram-supplemented institutional strategies and achievement for Eskimo students.* Qualifying paper submitted to Harvard Graduate School of Education.

Fiordo, R. (1988). The great learning enterprise of the four winds development project. *Journal of American Indian Education, 27*(3), 24–34.

Fixico, D. (1986). *Termination and relocation: Federal Indian policy, 1945–1960.* Albuquerque: University of New Mexico Press.

Flannery, T. (1980). *The Indian self-determination act: An analysis of federal policy.* Unpublished doctoral dissertation, Northwestern University, Evanston, IL.

Fuchs, E., & Havighurst, R. (1972). *To live on this earth.* New York: Doubleday.

Grant, J. H., & Goldsmith, R. (1979). *Bilingual education and federal law: An overview* (Project report). Austin, TX: Dissemination and Assessment Center for Bilingual Education.

Grant, J. W. (1984). *Moon of wintertime: Missionaries and the Indians of Canada in encounter since 1534.* Toronto: University of Toronto Press.

Grantham-Campbell, M. (1992, December). *Successful Alaska Native students: Implications 500 years after Columbus.* Paper presented at the meeting of the American Anthropological Association, San Francisco, CA.

Greenbaum, P. E., & Greenbaum, S. D. (1983). Cultural differences, nonverbal regulation, and classroom interaction: Sociolinguistic interference in American Indian education. *Peabody Journal of Education, 61*(1), 16–33.

Grell, L. (1983). *Indian self-determination and education: Kickapoo Nation School.* Paper presented at the meeting of the American Anthropological Association, Chicago, IL. (ERIC Document Reproduction Service No. ED 247 056)

Guilmet, G. M. (1978). Navajo and Caucasian children's verbal and nonverbal visual behavior in the urban classroom. *Anthropology and Education Quarterly, 9*, 196–215.

Guilmet, G. M. (1979). Maternal perceptions of urban Navajo and Caucasian children's classroom behaviors. *Human Organization, 38*, 87–91.

Guilmet, G. M. (1981). Oral-linguistic and nonoral-visual styles of attending: Navajo and Caucasian children compared in an urban classroom and on an urban playground. *Human Organization, 40*, 145–150.

Haig-Brown, C. (1988). *Resistance and renewal: Surviving the Indian residential school.* Vancouver, BC: Tillacum Library.

Hale, K. (1973). The role of American Indian linguistics in bilingual education. In R. Turner (Ed.), *Bilingualism in the Southwest* (pp. 203–225). Tucson: University of Arizona Press.

Hoxie, F. (1984). *A final promise: The campaign to assimilate the Indians, 1880–1920.* Lincoln: University of Neberaska Press.

Hyer, S. (1990). *One house, one voice, one heart: Native American education at Santa Fe Indian School.* Santa Fe: Museum of New Mexico Press.

Indian Historian Press. (1970). *Indian voices: The first convocation of American Indian scholars.* San Francisco: Author.

Jaimes, M. A. (1983). The myth of Indian education in the American education system. *Action in Teacher Education, 5*(3), 15–19.

James, H. (1974). *Pages from Hopi history.* Tucson: University of Arizona Press.

John, V. (1972). Styles of learning—styles of teaching: Reflections on the education of Navajo children. In C. Cazden, D. Hymes, & V. John (Eds.), *Functions of language in the classroom* (pp. 331–343). New York: Teachers College Press.

Johnson, B. (1968). *Navaho education at Rough Rock,* Rough Rock, AZ: Rough Rock Demonstration School, D.I.N.E., Inc.

Johnston, B. H. (1988). *Indian school days.* Norman and London: University of Oklahoma Press.

Josephy, A. M., Jr. (1982). *Now that the buffalo's gone.* Norman and London: University of Oklahoma Press.

Kasten, W. (1992). Bridging the horizon: American Indian beliefs and whole language learning. *Anthropology and Education Quarterly, 23*, 108–119.

King, A. R. (1967). *The school at Mopass: A problem of identity.* New York: Holt, Rinehart, & Winston.

Kleinfeld, J. S. (1973a). Effects of nonverbally communicated personal warmth on the intelligence performance of Indian and Eskimo adolescents. *The Journal of Social Psychology, 91*, 149–150.

Kleinfeld, J. S. (1973b). Intellectual strengths in culturally different groups: An Eskimo illustration. *Review of Educational Research, 43*, 341–359.

Kleinfeld, J. S. (1973c). *A long way from home: Effects of public high schools on village children away from home.* Fairbanks, AK: Center for Northern Educational Research.

Kleinfeld, J. S. (1974). Effects of nonverbal warmth on the learning of Eskimo and white students. *The Journal of Social Psychology, 92*, 3–9.

Kleinfeld, J., & Nelson, P. (1988). *Adapting instruction to Native Americans' "learning styles": An iconoclastic view.* (ERIC Document Reproduction Service No. ED 321 952)

Krush, T., Bjork, J., Sindell, P., & Nelle, J. (1966). Some thoughts on the formation of personality disorder: Study of an Indian boarding school population. *American Journal of Psychiatry, 122*, 868–876.

LaFlesche, F. (1978). *The middle five.* Lincoln: University of Nebraska Press. (Original work published 1900)

Latham, G. (1989). Thirteen most common needs of American Indian education in BIA schools. *Journal of American Indian Education, 29*(1), 1–11.

Leap, W. (1977). *Studies in southwestern Indian English.* San Antonio, TX: Trinity University Press.

Leap, W. (1981). American Indian language maintenance. In B. Siegel (Ed.), *Annual review of anthropology* (Vol. 10, pp. 209–236). Palo Alto, CA: Annual Reviews Inc.

Leap, W. (1988). Applied linguistics and American Indian language renewal: Introductory comments. *Human Organization, 47*, 283–291.

Ledlow, S. (1992). Is cultural discontinuity an adequate explanation for dropping out? *Journal of American Indian Education, 31*(3), 21–36.

Lipka, J. (1991). Toward a culturally based pedagogy: A case study of one Yup'ik Eskimo teacher. *Anthropology and Education Quarterly, 22*, 203–223.

Littlefield, A. (1989). The B.I.A. boarding school: Theories of resistance and social reproduction. *Humanity and Society, 13*, 428–441.

Littlefield, A. (1993). Learning to labor: Native American education in the United States, 1880–1930. In J. Moore (Ed.), *The political economy of North American Indians* (pp. 43–59). Norman: University of Oklahoma Press.

Locust, C. (1988). Wounding the spirit: Discrimination and traditional American Indian belief systems. *Harvard Educational Review, 58*, 315–330.

Lomawaima, K. T. (1993). Domesticity in the federal Indian schools: The power of authority over mind and body. *American Ethnologist, 20*(2), 1–14.

Lomawaima, K. T. (1994). *They called it Prairie Light: The story of Chilocco Indian School*. Lincoln: University of Nebraska Press.

Longstreet, W. S. (1978). *Aspects of ethnicity*. New York: Teachers College Press.

Lowry, L. (1970). Differences in visual perception and auditory discrimination between American Indian and White kindergarten children. *Journal of Learning Disabilities, 3*, 359–363.

Lutz, H. (1980). *D-Q University: Native American self-determination in higher education*. Davis: University of California, Native American Studies/Applied Behavioral Sciences, Tecumseh Center. (ERIC Document Reproduction Service No. ED 209 049)

Lynch, P. D., & Charleston, M. (1990). The emergence of American Indian leadership in education. *Journal of American Indian Education, 29*(2), 1–10.

Lyng v. Northwest Indian Cemetery Protective Assn., 485 U.S. 439, 108 S. Ct. 1319 (1988).

Macias, C. J. (1989, August). American Indian academic success: The role of indigenous learning strategies. *Journal of American Indian Education* [Special issue], pp. 43–52.

McBeth, S. (1983). *Ethnic identity and the boarding school experience of west-central Oklahoma American Indians*. Washington, DC: University Press of America.

McCartin, R., & Schill, W. (1977). Three modes of instruction. *Journal of American Indian Education, 17*(1), 14–20.

McCarty, T. L. (1987). The Rough Rock demonstration school: A case history with implications for educational evaluation. *Human Organization, 46*, 1103–1112.

McCarty, T. L. (1989). School as community: The Rough Rock demonstration. *Harvard Educational Review, 59*, 484–503.

McCarty, T. L. (1992). *Federal language policy and American Indian education*. (Rev.). (ERIC Document Reproduction Service No. ED 355-060)

McShane, D. (1983). Explaining achievement patterns of American Indian children: A transcultural and developmental model. *Peabody Journal of Education, 61*(1), 34–48.

Meriam, L. (1928). *The problem of Indian administration*. Baltimore, MD: Johns Hopkins Press for the Institute for Government Research.

Mihesuah, D. A. (1993). *Cultivating the rosebuds: The education of women at the Cherokee Female Seminary, 1851–1909*. Urbana: University of Illinois Press.

Miller, A. G., & Thomas, R. (1972). Cooperation and competition among Blackfoot Indian and urban Canadian children. *Child Development, 43*, 1104–1110.

Mohatt, G., & Erickson, F. (1981). Cultural differences in teaching styles in an Odawa school. In H. Trueba, G. Guthrie, & K. Au (Eds.), *Culture and the bilingual classroom* (pp. 105–119). Rowley, MA: Newbury House.

Moore, J. (1982). *Indian and Jesuit: A seventeenth century encounter*. New Orleans: Loyola University Press.

NAACP Legal Defense and Educational Fund. (1971). *An even chance: A report on federal funds for Indian children in public school districts*. Annandale, VA: Graphics 4.

Nabokov, P. (Ed.). (1991). *Native American testimony*. New York: Penguin Books.

National Archives. (1988a). Indian tribal entities within the contiguous 48 states recognized and eligible to receive services from the U.S. B.I.A. *Federal Register, 53*, 52829–52831.

National Archives. (1988b). Native entities within the state of Alaska recognized and eligible to receive services from the U.S. B.I.A. *Federal Register, 53*, 52832–52835.

National Center for Education Statistics. (1981). *Digest of education statistics*. Washington, DC: Government Printing Office.

National Center for Education Statistics. (1985–86). *Digest of education statistics*. Washington, DC: Government Printing Office.

National Center for Education Statistics. (1988). *High school and beyond—A descriptive summary of 1980 high school sophomores: Six years later* (DOE Report No. CS88-404). Washington, DC: Government Printing Office.

National Center for Education Statistics. (1989). *Analysis report: Dropout rates in the United States 1988* (NCES 89-609). Washington, DC: Office of Educational Research and Improvement, U.S. Department of Education.

National Center for Education Statistics. (1990a). *Digest of education statistics*. Washington, DC: Government Printing Office.

National Center for Education Statistics. (1990b). *National education longitudinal study of 1988: A profile of the American eighth grade* (NCES 90-458). Washington, DC: Office of Educational Research and Improvement, U.S. Department of Education.

National Center for Education Statistics. (1992). *Digest of education statistics*. Washington, DC: Government Printing Office.

National Education Association. (1900). *Journal of the proceedings and addresses of the 39th annual meeting of the NEA*. Chicago: University of Chicago.

National Research Council. (1976, 1977, 1978, 1979, 1980, 1981, 1982, 1983, 1986, 1987, 1989, 1990, 1991, 1993). *Doctorate recipients from United States universities* [Summary reports]. Washington, DC: National Academy Press.

Neely, S. (1975). The Quaker era of Cherokee Indian education, 1880–1892. *Appalachian Journal, 2*, 314–322.

Nelson, A., & Lalami, B. (1991). The role of imagery training on Tohono O'odham children's creativity scores. *Journal of American Indian Education, 30*(3), 24–32.

Nelson, R., & Sheley, J. (1985). Bureau of Indian Affairs influence on Indian self-determination. In V. Deloria, Jr. (Ed.), *American Indian policy in the twentieth century* (pp. 177–196). Norman: University of Oklahoma Press.

Noley, G. (1979). Choctaw bilingual and bicultural education in the nineteenth century. In *Multicultural education and the American Indian* (pp. 25–39). Los Angeles: American Indian Studies Center, University of California.

Ogbu, J. U. (1983). Cultural discontinuities and schooling. *Anthropology and Education Quarterly, 13*, 290–307.

Ogbu, J. U. (1987). *Minority education and caste: The American system in cross-cultural perspective*. New York: Academic Press.

Ogbu, J. U. (1989). The individual in collective adaptation: A framework for focusing on academic underperformance and dropping out among involuntary minorities. In L. Weis, E. Farrar, & H. Petrie (Eds.), *Dropouts from school: Issues, dilemmas, and solutions* (pp. 181–204). Albany, NY: State University of New York Press.

Okakok, L. (1989). Serving the purpose of education. *Harvard Educational Review, 59*, 405–422.

Olson, J., & Wilson, R. (1984). *Native Americans in the twentieth century*. Urbana: University of Illinois Press.

Osborne, B. (1989). Cultural congruence, ethnicity, and fused biculturalism: Zuni and Torres Strait. *Journal of American Indian Education, 28*(2), 7–20.

Palmer, G. (1988). The language and culture approach in the Coeur d'Alene language preservation project. *Human Organization, 47*, 307–321.

Paredes, J. A. (1992). *Indians of the southeastern United States in the late 20th century*. Tuscaloosa: University of Alabama Press.

Parmee, E. (1968). *Formal education and culture change: A modern Apache Indian community and government education programs*. Tucson: University of Arizona Press.

Pascal, R. (1991). The imprimatur of recognition: American Indian tribes and the federal acknowledgment process. *Washington Law Review, 66*, 209–226.

Peng, S. S., & Takai, R. T. (1983). *High school dropouts: Descriptive information from high school and beyond* (Bulletin, pp. 1–9). Washington, DC: National Center for Educational Statistics.

Philion, W. L., & Galloway, C. G. (1969). Indian children and the reading program. *Journal of Reading, 12,* 553–560, 598–602.

Philips, S. U. (1972). Participant structures and communicative competence: Warm Springs children in community and classroom. In C. Cazden, V. John, & D. Hymes (Eds.), *Functions of language in the classroom* (pp. 370–394). Prospect Heights, IL: Waveland.

Philips, S. U. (1983). *The invisible culture: Communication in classroom and community on the Warm Springs Indian reservation.* New York: Longman.

Philp, K. (1977). *John Collier's crusade for Indian reform, 1920–1954.* Tucson: University of Arizona Press.

Philp, K. (Ed.). (1986). *Indian self-rule: First-hand accounts of Indian-White relations from Roosevelt to Reagan.* Salt Lake City, UT: Howe Brothers.

Pittman, B. (Director). (1989). *Where the spirit lives* [Film]. Canada: Amazing Spirit Productions.

Platero, P. R., Brandt, E., Witherspoon, G., & Wong, P. (1986). *Navajo students at risk. Final report for the Navajo area student dropout study.* Window Rock, AZ: Platero Paperwork Inc.

Prucha, F. P. (1979). *The churches and the Indian schools.* Lincoln: University of Nebraska Press.

Prucha, F. P. (1984). *The Great Father* (Vols. 1–2). Lincoln: University of Nebraska Press.

Ramenofsky, A. (1987). *Vectors of death: The archaeology of European contact.* Albuquerque: University of New Mexico Press.

Ramírez, M., & Castañeda, A. (1974). *Cultural democracy, bicognitive development, and education.* New York: Academic Press.

Ramstad, V., & Potter, R. (1974). Differences in vocabulary and syntax usage between Nez Perce Indian and White kindergarten children. *Journal of Learning Disabilities, 7,* 491–497.

Reel, E. (1903). *Report of the superintendent of Indian schools.* Estelle Reel papers, Arden Sallquist collection, Cheney-Cowles Museum, Eastern Washington State Historical Society, Spokane, WA.

Renker, A., & Arnold, G. (1988). Exploring the role of education in cultural resource management: The Makah cultural and research center example. *Human Organization, 47,* 302–307.

Reyhner, J. (1992). American Indians out of school: A review of school-based causes and solutions. *Journal of American Indian Education, 31*(3), 37–56.

Rhodes, R. W. (1990). Measurements of Navajo and Hopi brain dominance and learning styles. *Journal of American Indian Education, 29*(3), 29–40.

Rosier, P., & Holm, W. (1980). *The Rock Point experience: A longitudinal study of a Navajo school program (Saad naaki bee Na'nitin).* Bilingual Education Series, no. 8. Arlington, VA: Center for Applied Linguistics.

Ross, A. C. (1989, August). Brain hemispheric functions and the Native American. *Journal of American Indian Education* [Special issue], pp. 72–76.

Ryan, C. (1962). *The Carlisle Indian industrial school.* Unpublished doctoral dissertation, Georgetown University, Washington, DC.

Salisbury, L. H. (1974). Teaching English to Alaska Natives. In R. Deever, W. Abraham, G. Gill, H. Sundwall, & P. Gianopulos (Eds.), *American Indian education* (pp. 193–203). Tempe: Arizona State University.

Salisbury, N. (1982). *Manitou and providence: Indians, Europeans, and the making of New England, 1500–1643.* Oxford, England: Oxford University Press.

Scollon, R., & Scollon, S. (1981). *Narrative, literacy, and face in interethnic communication.* Norwood, NJ: Ablex.

Sekaquaptewa, H. (1969). *Me and mine* (as told to L. Udall). Tucson: University of Arizona Press.

Senese, G. (1986). Self-determination and American Indian education: An illusion of control. *Educational Theory, 36,* 153–164.

Shears, B. (1970). Aptitude, content and method of teaching word recognition with young American Indian children. *Dissertation Abstracts International, 31,* 2221A. (University Microfilms No. 70–20, 250). University of Minnesota.

Shutiva, C. (1991). Creativity differences between reservation and urban American Indians. *Journal of American Indian Education, 31*(1), 33–52.

Simmons, M. (1979). History of Pueblo-Spanish relations to 1821. In A. Ortiz (Ed.), *Handbook of North American Indians* (Vol. 9, pp. 178–193). Washington, DC: Smithsonian Institution Press.

Sindell, P. (1974). Some discontinuities in the enculturation of Mistassini Cree children. In G. Spindler (Ed.), *Education and cultural process* (pp. 333–341). New York: Holt, Rinehart, & Winston.

Spolsky, B. (Ed.). (1972). *The language education of minority children: Selected readings.* Rowley, MA: Newbury House.

Spolsky, B. (1978). American Indian bilingual education. In B. Spolsky & R. Cooper (Eds.), *Case studies in bilingual education* (pp. 332–361). Rowley, MA: Newbury House.

St. Clair, R., & Leap, W. (1982). *Language renewal among American Indian tribes: Issues, problems, and prospects.* Rosslyn, VA: National Clearinghouse for Bilingual Education.

Stull, D., & Kendall, D. (Producers). (1986). *Another wind is moving* [Film]. Lawrence: University of Kansas and Kickapoo Nation School.

Swisher, K. (1992a). Preface. In K. Swisher (Ed.), *Journal of American Indian Education* [Special issue], *31*(2), 1.

Swisher, K. (Ed.). (1992b). *Journal of American Indian Education* [Special issue], *31*(2).

Swisher, K. (Ed.). (1992c). *Journal of American Indian Education* [Special issue], *31*(3).

Swisher, K., & Deyhle, D. (1987). Styles of learning and learning of styles: Educational conflicts for American Indian/Alaskan Native youth. *Journal of Multilingual and Multicultural Development, 8*(4), 345–360.

Swisher, K., & Deyhle, D. (1989, August). The styles of learning are different, but the teaching is just the same: Suggestions for teachers of American Indian youth. *Journal of American Indian Education* [Special issue], pp. 1–14.

Swisher, K., & Hoisch, M. (1992). Dropping out among American Indians and Alaska Natives: A review of studies. *Journal of American Indian Education, 31*(2), 3–23.

Swisher, K., Hoisch, M., & Pavel, D. (1991). *American Indian/Alaska Native dropout study, 1991.* Washington, DC: National Education Association.

Szasz, M. (1977). *Education and the American Indian: The road to self-determination, 1928–1973* (2nd ed.). Albuquerque: University of New Mexico Press.

Szasz, M. (1988). *Indian education in the American colonies, 1607–1783.* Albuquerque: University of New Mexico Press.

Szasz, M., & Ryan, C. S. (1988). American Indian education. In W. Washburn (Ed.), *Handbook of North American Indians* (Vol. 4, pp. 284–300). Washington, DC: Smithsonian Institution Press.

Thielke, H. M., & Shriberg, L. D. (1990). Effects of recurrent otitis media on language, speech, and educational achievement in Menominee Indian children. *Journal of American Indian Education, 29*(2), 25–35.

Thompson, H. (1964). *Education for cross-cultural enrichment.* Lawrence, KS: Bureau of Indian Affairs.

Thornton, R. (1987). *American Indian holocaust and survival.* Norman: University of Oklahoma Press.

Thornton, R., Sandefur, G., & Snipp, C. M. (1991). American Indian Fertility Patterns: 1910 and 1940 to 1980. A research note. *American Indian Quarterly, 15,* 359–367.

Thurgood, D. (1991). *Summary Report 1990: Doctorate recipients from United States universities*. Washington, DC: National Academy Press.

Trennert, R. (1988). *The Phoenix Indian School: Forced assimilation in Arizona*. Norman: University of Oklahoma Press.

Ubelaker, D. (1992). North American Indian population size: Changing perspectives. In J. Verano & D. Ubelaker (Eds.), *Disease and demography in the Americas* (pp. 169–176). Washington, DC: Smithsonian Institution Press.

U.S. Bureau of the Census. (1984). *American Indian areas and Alaska Native villages: 1980*. Supplementary report PC80-S1-13. Washington, DC: Government Printing Office.

U.S. Bureau of the Census. (1988). *We, the first Americans*. Washington, DC: Government Printing Office.

U.S. Bureau of the Census. (1992). *Statistical abstract of the United States* (112th ed.). Washington, DC: Government Printing Office.

U.S. Department of the Interior. (1991). *American Indians today* (3rd ed.). Washington, DC: Author.

Utley, R. (Ed.). (1964). *Battlefield and classroom: Four decades with the American Indian*. New Haven, CT: Yale University Press.

Van Ness, H. (1981). Social control and social organization in an Alaskan Athabaskan classroom: A microethnography of "getting ready" for reading. In H. Trueba, G. Guthrie, & K. Au (Eds.), *Culture and the bilingual classroom* (pp. 120–138). Rowley, MA: Newbury House.

Van Well, Sister M. (1942). *The educational aspects of the missions in the Southwest*. Milwaukee, WI: Marquette University Press.

Vaughn, J. C. (1985). Minority students in graduate education. In B. L. R. Smith (Ed.), *The state of graduate education* (pp. 151–168). Washington, DC: The Brookings Institution.

Verano, J., & Ubelaker, D. (1991). Health and disease in the pre-Columbian world. In H. Viola & C. Margolis (Eds.), *Seeds of change* (pp. 209–223). Washington, DC: Smithsonian Institution Press.

Vogt, L., Jordan, C., & Tharp, R. (1987). Explaining school failure, producing school success: Two cases. *Anthropology and Education Quarterly, 18*, 276–286.

Watahomigie, L., & Yamamoto, A. Y. (1987). Linguistics in action: The Hualapai bilingual/bicultural education program. In D. D. Stull & J. J. Schensul (Eds.), *Collaborative research and social change: Applied anthropology in action* (pp. 77–98). Boulder, CO: Westview Press.

Wax, M., Wax, R., & Dumont, R. (1964). Formal education in an American Indian community. *Social Problems, 11*[Suppl.], 95–96.

Weatherhead, L. (1980). What is an "Indian tribe"?—The question of tribal existence. *American Indian Law Review, 8*(1), 1–47.

Webster, S. (Ed.). (1966). *Understanding the educational problems of the disadvantaged learner*. San Francisco: Chandler Publishing.

Wilkinson, C. (1987). *American Indians, time, and the law*. New Haven, CT: Yale University Press.

Wolcott, H. (1967). *A Kwakiutl village and school*. New York: Holt, Rinehart, & Winston.

Wright, B. (1989, November). *The "Untameable Savage Spirit": American Indian responses to colonial college missions*. Paper presented at the meeting of the American Society for Ethnohistory, Chicago.

Young, R. (1972). *Written Navajo: A brief history* (Navajo Reading Study Progress Report 19). Albuquerque: University of New Mexico. (ERIC Document Reproduction Service No. ED 068 229)

Zepeda, O. (1990). American Indian language policy. In K. Adams & D. Brink (Eds.), *Perspectives on official English* (pp. 247–256); J. Fishman (Gen. Ed.), *Contributions to the sociology of language* 57. Berlin/New York: Mouton de Gruyter.

20

HISTORICAL AND SOCIOCULTURAL INFLUENCES ON AFRICAN AMERICAN EDUCATION

Carol D. Lee

NORTHWESTERN UNIVERSITY

Diana T. Slaughter-Defoe

NORTHWESTERN UNIVERSITY

In this chapter on African American education, we explore the influences of culture and political status on the schooling experiences and educational achievement of African Americans. We also discuss the influences of culture and political status on educational research regarding African Americans. In scope, this chapter focuses primarily on elementary through secondary school education. Using culture and political status as filters, we trace the educational status of African Americans historically. We analyze the historical foundations of critical contemporary issues in the education of African Americans and document major educational problems that can be traced to issues of culture and political status. We describe both theoretical and programmatic responses, based on culturally responsive foundations, to the educational needs of African American children and adolescents. The studies reported include theoretical research and historical studies, as well as qualitative and quantitative research. Because of space limitations, the chapter does not include issues of school administration, higher education, and early childhood education. Where possible, however, continuities between early and later schooling experiences are noted.

MAJOR EDUCATIONAL PROBLEMS IN SCHOOLS

Several studies published during the Reagan-Bush years (1980–1992) indicate that African Americans, particularly males from lower socioeconomic backgrounds, are disproportion- ately represented in the grade-retention, school-suspension, and drop-out rates of public schools (Bennett & Harris, 1981; Campbell, 1982; Hess & Lauber, 1985; Hess & Greer, 1987; Kaufman, 1991). Prior to leaving school during the adolescent years, the same students are frequently poor academic achievers in the elementary grades, and experience academic suspensions for related disciplinary problems.

Further, since the beginning of public schooling in the United States, African American children have been labeled, and even misclassified and tracked, relative to educational standing, as a combined result of inequitable resource alloca- tions; the application of inadequately developed and normed intelligence and achievement tests; disproportionately inappro- priate placements in special educational classrooms and set- tings; and insufficient attention to the learning styles evidenced by many of the children (e.g., Myrdal, 1944; Hilliard, 1976; De- signs for Change, 1982; Shade, 1982; Hale-Benson, 1986; Miller- Jones, 1988, 1989; Epps, 1992).

The studies of the Chicago Panel on Public School Policy and Finance, and others of similar persuasion, suggest that preven- tion and/or intervention begin early in the elementary schools the students attend, focusing particularly on raising the level of teacher academic expectations for African American students and improving teacher quality, in addition to revitalizing the overall school climate of the public schools attended by these youth (e.g., K. Clark, 1965; Baron, Tom, & Cooper, 1985; Hess & Greer, 1987; Comer, 1988a; Anson, Cook, & Habib, 1991;

The authors are indebted to Craig Brookins, North Carolina State University, for his assistance with the sections of this chapter that discuss the rites of passage.

Haynes & Comer, 1993). Other intervenors have emphasized the importance of preschool intervention for school readiness, including the contribution of such national programs as Project Head Start, to the early development of social and academic competence among African American children (e.g., V. Washington & Oyemade, 1987; Schorr, 1988). Today, many who stress intervention to improve the educational prospects of African American children offer strategies for effectively involving parents and family within the social context of the school (Comer, 1980, 1988b; Slaughter & Epps, 1987; Slaughter-Defoe, 1991; K. R. Wilson & Allen, 1987). It is encouraged that evaluations of the longer-term effects of Head Start, for example, apply a two-generational model in which outcomes for parents and families, as well as children, are stressed (Slaughter, Washington, Oyemade, & Lindsey, 1988; Slaughter, Lindsey, Nakagawa, & Kuehne, 1989; Grimmett & Garrett, 1989; Head Start Research and Evaluation: A Blueprint for the Future, 1990).

Perhaps the most radical effort at reform of public schools in the past 15 years was introduced by Chicago's School Reform Act, effective July 1, 1989. The Chicago School Reform Act followed the assertion of then-Secretary of Education William Bennett in November 1987 that Chicago's public schools were the worst in the United States, whether measured by drop-out rates, disciplinary incidents, or achievement scores. This act established Local School Councils at each of the 539 Chicago public schools that had the authority and power to establish a school improvement plan, allocate appropriate resources for implementation, and evaluate the performance of the principal in relation to realization of the goals of that plan at four-year intervals (Chicago Schools, 1991). The Chicago plan essentially sought to take power from school administrators and give it to the parents of attending schoolchildren.

The overall strategy is consistent with efforts to involve parents meaningfully, particularly lower-income, minority-status, and culturally different parents, in their children's education (Slaughter & Epps, 1987; Epps, 1992). However, despite best intentions, monitors of this effort suggest that African American and other parents have not yet achieved the measure of authority in their children's education and schooling toward which restructuring and decentralization efforts have aimed (Ayers, 1991; Boo, 1992). The observers note that teacher involvement and commitment to the reform effort have been minimal, and that restructuring has not directly impacted the classroom, including teacher behavior and teacher-pupil interaction. Thus the mere presence of parents may be necessary, but is not sufficient, to impact school administrative policies and practices. This was particularly true because school resources continued to be limited, the councils had limited powers to raise revenues or set curricula, and teachers and administrators were better positioned to "wait out 'reform' until public interest wanes" (Boo, 1992, p. 23).

The data on disproportionate rates indicative of educational failure on the part of African American children, as well as contemporary approaches to the educational problems presented by African American students, are familiar. However, we appreciate less often the considerable historical continuity between the failures of schools in relation to African American children and families today, and such failures throughout the

history of the African American presence in the United States. At the least, these historic and continuing experiences have influenced attitudes held by African Americans toward the educational system of the United States. Valuing education highly, African Americans typically have less positive responses toward the educational system itself. Indeed, we posit that a major aspect of the relationship between U.S. educational institutions and African Americans has been the struggle between educational ideology and related policies and practices, including access and equity of resources advanced. Traditional learning environments, including public schools, in which African Americans have participated in the greatest numbers have emphasized cultural assimilation, rather than cultural difference or competence, the latter two of which would affirm the African American cultural heritage.

HISTORICAL FOUNDATIONS OF CRITICAL CONTEMPORARY ISSUES

J. D. Anderson (1988) states that "there have been essential relationships between popular education and the politics of oppression. Both schooling for democratic citizenship and schooling for second-class citizenship have been basic traditions in American education" (p. 1). In the history of African American education, tensions surrounding the content and focus of schooling and the question of who should control the schools can be traced from Reconstruction through the present (Bullock, 1967; Butchart, 1980; Woodson, 1991). There is significant evidence that the African American community has historically recognized the political ramifications of education and how education could be used as either a tool of liberation or a tool for maintaining second-class citizenship (Woodson, 1969). Woodson (1991) documents efforts of African Americans to gain education prior to the Civil War. The intensity of the interests in education of the newly freed African Americans after the Civil War ended has been well documented by many researchers (J. D. Anderson, 1988; Franklin, 1984; Stowe, 1879; B. T. Washington, 1902). Anderson quotes from one ex-slave who said: "There is one sin that slavery committed against me which I will never forgive. It robbed me of my education" (p. 5). Harding (1981) notes the observations of White northern journalist Sidney Andrews in 1866:

Yesterday's "ignorant slaves" . . . now seemed fiercely determined to educate themselves and their people . . . the epitome of this quest could be seen in Macon, Georgia: "a young negro woman with her spelling book fastened to the fence, that she might study while at work over the wash tub." Such testimony of black determination to master the printed word came from every corner of the South. . . . (p. 308)

In response to this tremendous desire for education and the new legal rights of citizenship, the government established the Freedman's Bureau in 1865. Among the responsibilities assigned to the Freedman's Bureau was to establish and provide oversight for schooling for the newly freed African Americans. From 1867 to 1872 the Freedman's Bureau established day schools, night schools, and industrial schools. However, from the end of the Civil War and before the inroads of the Freedman's Bureau, an entire movement of independent schools had been established by African Americans themselves. According to J. D. Anderson (1988), both the Freedman's Bureau and northern missionaries discovered "that many ex-slaves had established their own educational collectives and associations, staffed schools entirely with black teachers, and were unwilling to allow their educational movement to be controlled by 'civilized' Yankees" (p. 6). John W. Alvord, the national superintendent of schools for the Freedman's Bureau, in astonishment conducted many investigations of what he called, in part because of his own incredulity, "native schools." His investigations provide one body of evidence on the quantity, distribution, and administration of these schools established by African Americans. In 1866, one year after the end of the Civil War, Alvord estimated that there were "at least 500 schools of this description . . . already in operation in the South" (p. 7). These schools were supported by the monetary and labor contributions of formerly enslaved African Americans; who were responsible as well for the supervision and administration of the schools (J. D. Anderson, 1988; Gutman, 1979). Gutman notes that this educational movement had its foundations in African American communal values. Butchart (1980) has documented not only that the formerly enslaved African Americans developed and supported their own schools in large numbers, but also that they resisted efforts to control these schools from outside their own communities. Anderson writes, "A white observer noted that 'in all respects apart from his or her competency to teach—they will keep their children out of school, and go to work, organize and [*sic*] independent school and send their children to it'" (p. 12).

An additional significant component of African American efforts in education after the Civil War was through church-operated schools called "Sabbath schools." They were conducted in the evenings and on weekends, providing basic instruction in literacy for those who could not attend regular schools during weekdays. According to reports in 1869 by Alvord's field agents, conservative estimates indicated there were "1,512 Sabbath schools with 6,146 teachers and 107,109 pupils" (J. D. Anderson, 1988, p. 13).

Out of both the missionary interests and the emerging interests of northern capitalist philanthropists issued a vision of an appropriate education for African Americans based on an industrial model of education. These interests were intricately linked to the interests of the class of traditional planters in the South. The combined efforts of African American communities, the Freedman's Bureau, and northern missionaries had laid the foundations in practical terms for universal public schooling in the South for both Blacks and Whites (DuBois, 1935/1962). According to J. D. Anderson (1988), "proponents of southern industrialization increasingly viewed mass schooling as a means to produce efficient and contented labor and as a socialization process to instill in black and white children an acceptance of the southern racial hierarchy" (p. 27). This model was exemplified in the curriculum and administration of both Hampton Normal and Agricultural Institute of Virginia, founded by White Brigadier General Samuel Chapman Armstrong, and the Tuskegee Institute developed in Alabama by Booker T.

Washington (J. D. Anderson, 1978). This model of education reflected both market interests and the interests of maintaining the existing racial hierarchy (J. D. Anderson, 1975). However, the schools developed and operated by African Americans (with the notable exception of Booker T. Washington and the Tuskegee Institute) did not accept this model as appropriate for the interests of the African American community. According to J. D. Anderson (1988), Black educators of the postwar common school movement believed that

education could help raise the freed people to an appreciation of their historic responsibility to develop a better society and that any significant reorganization of the southern political economy was indissolubly linked to their education in the principles, duties and obligations appropriate to a democratic social order. (p. 28)

Ironically, the curriculum model adopted by Black schools did not differ significantly from courses taught in northern White schools (Woodson, 1969). J. D. Anderson (1988) suggests that although this curriculum did not focus on "the historical and cultural forces that enabled Afro-Americans to survive the most dehumanized aspects of enslavement" (p. 29), it did counter the prevailing attitudes that Blacks were intellectually inferior and incapable of learning. An interesting example of how educated African Americans related their studies of European classics to the liberatory aims of education as they envisioned them is captured in the 1883 testimony of Richard Wright to the U.S. Senate Committee on Education and Labor about the education and work conditions of Georgia Blacks. Wright was the principal of the only public high school for Blacks in the state of Georgia. He stated:

I believe too, that our methods of alphabetic writing all came from the colored race, and I think the majority of the sciences in their origin have come from the colored races. . . . Now I take the testimony of those people who know, and who, I feel are capable of instructing me on this point, and I find them saying that the Egyptians were actually woolly-haired negroes. (J. D. Anderson, 1988, p. 29)

According to Anderson, although the short-range goals of schooling envisioned by Blacks were for basic literacy and citizenship training, the long-range goals were to develop "a responsible leadership class that would organize the masses and lead them to freedom and equality" (p. 31).

The tensions inherent in this brief history of the beginnings of formal education for African Americans in the United States capture conflicting themes and interests that have been maintained into the present. Four educational philosophers who wrote from the turn of the century through the 1920s capture the essence of the conflicting positions regarding what an appropriate education for African Americans should be and who should control educational institutions providing services to Black students: W. E. B. DuBois, Booker T. Washington, Horace Mann Bond, and Carter G. Woodson. The core of these tensions revolved around how a responsible leadership class would best be educated.

Between 1860 and 1935, roughly three models for educating a responsible leadership class developed. The first model was based on a combination of curriculum modeled on the New

England *liberal classical curriculum*, implemented in schools established both by northern missionary societies and by the Black education movement organized by former enslaved African Americans. The second model was based on the model of *industrial education* developed at Hampton Institute of Virginia, founded by Samuel Chapman Armstrong in 1868 and later propagated by Armstrong's tutee, Booker T. Washington. The third model *critiqued* the limitations of both models.

The industrial model, whose foundation was laid through the model of Hampton Institute, was aimed at influencing generations of leaders in the Black community who would become teachers. Armstrong himself said, "Let us make the teachers and we will make the people" (J. D. Anderson, 1988, p. 45). Armstrong argued against Black political participation. Booker T. Washington reactivated that same position when he said, "In their present condition it is a mistake for them to enter actively into general political agitation and activity" (Anderson, p. 52). At the famous Atlanta Exposition in 1895, Washington announced that Tuskegee Institute would produce Black workers who would be "the most patient, faithful, law abiding and unresentful people that the world has seen" (Anderson, p. 73). This model of Black education received widespread support from political and philanthropic leaders including Ulysses S. Grant, Rutherford B. Hayes, James A. Garfield, Theodore Roosevelt, William Howard Taft, Woodrow Wilson, Andrew Carnegie, John D. Rockefeller, and Julius Rosenwald. In contrast, there was a highly vocal opposition to the industrial model by leaders of northern missionary societies, but most importantly by the leadership of the Black intelligentsia. This debate did not begin with W. E. B. DuBois, as is commonly thought; in fact, the Hampton industrial model was initiated the year DuBois was born, 1868. However, the debate reached its pinnacle within the first two decades of the 20th century. The vocal Black leadership who opposed this industrial model of Black education included such figures as William Monroe Trotter, editor of the *Boston Guardian*, Charles Chestnutt, John S. Durham, John Hope, Bishop Henry McNeil Turner, Ida Wells-Barnett, and W. E. B. DuBois. The critical difference was that these Black leaders believed that education should provide training for direct political empowerment along with an intellectual curriculum. This was believed to be especially important for education at the secondary and college levels, from which professional leadership for the Black community developed. DuBois (1903/1968, 1908/1969) labeled these incipient leaders the "talented tenth." By 1905 DuBois and other members of the opposition organized the Niagara Movement, which advocated direct action to achieve civil rights for African Americans. By 1910 the Niagara Movement had organized the National Association for the Advancement of Colored People (NAACP).

This ideological battle continued long after the death of Booker T. Washington in 1915, primarily because of the heavy investment of capital and political pressure from northern capitalists and politicians. Much of this investment was intended to develop alternative industrial normal schools to train teachers, and county training schools in rural districts to provide secondary education where public high schools did not exist. In fact, by 1933, 66% of Black high school students in the south were being educated in county training schools based on the indus-

trial model (J. Anderson, 1988, p. 147). However, by 1935 many of these schools were phased out because of more stringent licensing requirements for those preparing to teach, and the evolution of a public, though segregated, school system in the South. DuBois and Dill (1911) accurately noted that the existence of a public education system in the South is due in large part to the efforts of African Americans to be adequately educated in order to compete both economically and politically.

DuBois's critique of Black education spanned a period from 1903 through 1960. In an address at Howard University in 1930 (DuBois, 1973a), DuBois succinctly and elegantly summarized the tensions between the New England model of education aimed at Euro-classic intellectual traditions and the industrial model aimed at training a docile workforce. Whether based on a Euro-classical model (Howard, Fisk, and Atlanta Universities) or an industrial education model (the land-grant colleges and former industrial schools like Hampton Institute or Tuskegee), by 1930 the Black college still mimicked curriculum and social organization patterns found in predominantly White colleges. DuBois acknowledged the tremendous increase in Black school enrollment (p. 65) and the Black leadership produced from the Black colleges, "trained in modern education, able to cope with the white world on its own ground and in its own thought, method, and language" (p. 66). However, DuBois criticized the Black colleges for focusing inadequately on the problems of economic development within the Black community, training graduates to cluster in white-collar jobs without building a solid foundation for businesses and independent institutions within the African American community. He also criticized a social milieu in which Black college men focused more on superficial social life (athletics and Greek-letter societies) than on rigorous intellectual study. He argued that these colleges were producing a generation of leaders who were committed to personal wealth rather than to the service and leadership of the masses of their communities. DuBois reasoned that changes in technology required a different kind of education that neither the intellectual focus of the Black colleges nor the antiquated vocational focus of the industrial schools addressed. He wrote:

The industrial school secured usually as teacher a man of affairs and technical knowledge, without culture or general knowledge. The college took too often as teacher a man of books and brains with no contact with or first-hand knowledge of real everyday life and ordinary human beings . . . . Both types of teacher failed. (p. 76)

As had been the case throughout his many years of critique, this challenge laid by DuBois in 1930 is no less relevant today. DuBois said in 1930 before his Howard University audience:

We are not going to share modern civilization just by deserving recognition. We are going to force ourselves in by organized far-seeing effort— by outthinking and outflanking the owners of the world today who are too drunk with their own arrogance and power successfully to oppose us, if we think and learn and do. (DuBois, 1973a, p. 77)

DuBois recognized throughout his illustrious intellectual career that the problem of education for African Americans was no simple matter. He articulated in 1946 and again in 1960 the delicate tensions between political and economic integration of African Americans into the fabric of American life and the maintenance of African American cultural integrity. Any analysis of the movement to integrate public education in the United States and current trends in multicultural education must acknowledge the insights of DuBois. DuBois wrote that although in 1960 some resolutions to the problems of Blacks' right to vote and equal protection under the law were in sight, "it brings not as many assume an end to the so-called Negro problems, but a beginning of even more difficult problems of race and culture" (Dubois, 1973c, p. 149). DuBois continued:

I am not fighting to settle the question of racial equality in America by the process of getting rid of the Negro race; getting rid of black folk, not producing black children, forgetting the slave trade and slavery, and the struggle for emancipation; of forgetting abolition and especially ignoring the whole cultural history of Africans in the world. What we must . . . do is to lay down a line of thought and action which will accomplish two things: The utter disappearance of color discrimination in American life and the preservation of African history and culture as a valuable contribution to modern civilization as it was to medieval and ancient civilization. (pp. 150–151)

Dubois's Harvard-educated contemporary, Carter G. Woodson, founder of the Association for the Study of Negro Life and History (later African American Life and History) and of the concept of Black History Week (later African American History Month), made similar criticisms of education offered in Black colleges based on a Euro-classical model:

No systematic effort toward change has been possible, for, taught the same economics, history, philosophy, literature and religion which have established the present code of morals, the Negro's mind has been brought under the control of his oppressor. The problem of holding the Negro down, therefore, is easily solved. When you control a man's thinking you do not have to worry about his actions. . . . You do not need to send him to the back door. He will go without being told. In fact, if there is no back door, he will cut one for his special benefit. His education makes it necessary. (Woodson, 1969, p. xxxiii)

We have articulated this history of the major conceptions of what education for African Americans should entail because they form the foundation on the basis of which current trends and issues must be understood. In fact, many of the critical contemporary issues around the education of African Americans parallel in fundamental ways these same historical tensions (Franklin & Anderson, 1978). Table 20–1 summarizes these three foundational models and their contemporary manifestations. For a full review of these historical tensions and how they have been treated by historians of African American education, see Butchart (1988).

AFRICAN AMERICAN ACHIEVEMENT IN EDUCATION

J. D. Anderson (1984) offers an extensive review of data documenting the evolution of African American achievement in education from Reconstruction through the 1980s. Anderson

TABLE 20–1. Historical Models of Education Appropriate for Blacks, 1860–1935 and Contemporary Parallels

	Euro-Classical Liberal Curriculum	Industrial Education Hampton/Tuskegee Model	Education for Black Self-Reliance
Supporters	Northern missionary societies; White liberals; Blacks who supported liberal education	Booker T. Washington; northern capitalists; national, state, and local White political leaders	W. E. B. DuBois, William Monroe Trotter, Ida B. Wells, Martin Delaney, Carter G. Woodson, Mary McLeod Bethune
Historical Sites of Operation	Black land-grant colleges; normal schools; missionary colleges	Black land-grant colleges; southern county school system; Hampton Institute; Tuskegee Institute	Schools set up by formerly enslaved Africans; Sabbath schools; Black literary societies (Porter, 1936)
Key Characteristics	1. Curriculum content drawn from Euro-classical traditions 2. Belief that understanding foundations of Western civilization is a necessary prelude to participation in democratic citizenship	1. Train workers who are dutiful, hard working, and capable of contributing to the growing labor needs of the postwar South 2. Do not focus on politics and oppression 3. Train teachers for public schools	1. Administration controlled by Blacks 2. Curriculum reflecting African and African American cultural and historical traditions 3. Explicit goals related to political empowerment 4. Education to challenge existing political and cultural norms
Contemporary Parallels	Movement to integrate public schools without an explicit focus on the content and delivery of instruction that is culturally diverse and sensitive	Tracking in vocational programs and inequitable tracking in less challenging academic courses and special education	Freedom schools of civil rights movement; Black independent school movement; Black studies in higher education; Afrocentric curriculum movement; rites-of-passage movement

proposes that an appropriate framework for analyzing data regarding the educational achievement of African Americans should "chart the ingroup achievement patterns of black school children through the twentieth century, to study those patterns on their own terms, and to see how recent developments compare with those of earlier decades" (p. 103). He also proposes that these developments can be properly understood only in the context of the political and economic conditions under which they were achieved. It is also important to note that the standards and instruments by which educational achievement have been measured since the late 1800s have changed in response to the expansion of mandatory public education, the educational requirements of the labor market, and the development of formalized instruments for measuring proficiency in basic school subject matters. Thus the data for achievement reflect the historical era during which they were collected, and any broad conclusions to be drawn from such data must be considered tentative.

Definitions of minimal literacy as measured by school attendance between Reconstruction and the first decade of the 20th century are substantively different from definitions of minimal literacy as measured by high school completion rates after 1960. From the Reconstruction era through the dawn of the 20th century, literacy rates were measured using census data on school enrollment. By 1930 high school enrollment became the benchmark. Any discrepancies between Whites and Blacks concerning high school enrollment are certainly influenced by the fact that at this period there were only a small number of high schools available for Blacks in the South, and the vast majority of African Americans lived in the South. According to the Bureau of Education in 1917, in 1915, 90% of African American schoolchildren lived in the South, with only 64 public secondary schools available for Blacks (J. D. Anderson, 1984, p. 114). After the introduction of standardized IQ testing in the U.S. Army during World War I, the formal study of standardized measures of mental ability sharply increased. From the late 1920s on, these standardized measures were used to assess the (presumed) native abilities of American students, including African Americans, and thus were initiated as a gauge of educational achievement. Following *Brown v. Board of Education of Topeka,* from 1954 on, college enrollment and, later, graduation rates were added as a measure of educational achievement. Achievement according to each of these measures must be weighed in light of the extreme political, social, and economic hardships that Blacks had to overcome in order to attend school and achieve. In addition, the motivation for schooling within the African American community should also be evaluated in relationship to the economic and political benefits achievable from schooling during different historical periods. For example, it was not unusual in the 1940s and 1950s to see Black college graduates working as mail carriers, waiters, railroad porters, and redcaps (Lincoln, 1969). In 1982 the jobless rate among African American teenagers was reported at 50%, in contrast with 16.5% in 1954 (cited in J. D. Anderson, 1984, p. 120).

In the decades immediately following Reconstruction, literacy rates were measured by percentages of school-age children enrolled in school. It should be noted that the ranges specifying

school age substantively changed over time as well. The period from 1860 to 1880 reveals the greatest rate of increase in rates of literacy within the African American community, from a 2% literacy rate in 1860 to a 34% literacy rate in 1880 (J. D. Anderson, 1984, p. 105). Following Reconstruction there was a harsh political backlash that resulted in terrorism and Jim Crowism. Thus between 1880 and 1900, although there was a 25% increase in the number of school-age children within the African American community (in itself a devastating commentary on the mortality rates under the African holocaust of enslavement), there was a decrease in the percentage of Black school-age children enrolled in school (Anderson, p. 108). Under the most dire of political, economic, and social conditions, however, illiteracy rates in the Black community decreased drastically, from 70% in 1880, to 44% in 1900, and to 19% by 1910, as defined by rates of school enrollment. By 1910 school enrollment for Blacks and Whites in the North and West were nearly the same. The biggest discrepancies in school-enrollment figures were in the South, where no mandatory school attendance laws were in effect. As noted earlier, DuBois and Dill (1911) credit the evolution of a public school system in the South to the educational demands of the African American community and to federal efforts to support those demands. Despite differences in high school enrollment figures in the South due to lack of adequate availability of facilities for Blacks, analysis of growth figures within the African American community indicates that the period between 1917 and 1931 records the greatest increase in high school enrollment (J. D. Anderson, 1984, p. 112).

In the period following the landmark 1954 Supreme Court decision, *Brown v. Board of Education of Topeka,* the benchmarks that served as measures of educational achievement began to shift. The *Brown* decision made possible greater opportunity for college enrollment among African Americans. The greatest increases in high school completion, college enrollment, and college graduation rates within the African American community occurred between 1960 and 1980. Between 1966 and 1976 there was a 275% increase in Black student college enrollment (J. D. Anderson, 1984, p. 188). During the same period, the data reveal that Blacks were more likely to enroll in two-year colleges than four-year institutions (p. 118). College enrollment and graduation rates decreased between 1980 and 1986, and thereafter increased to slightly more than the 1980 level (Carter & Wilson, 1993).

Around the 1920s, standardized test data began to be used as a measure of educational achievement in the United States. Most of the data involved the use of standardized measures of native intelligence in the form of IQ tests. There is ample evidence to support the claim that IQ testing was used from its inception in the United States to justify claims of native mental inferiority among African Americans (Gould, 1981; Hilliard, 1991b). From the beginning there were challenges to the assumptions that these measures were unbiased instruments. Foreman (1932), a White Georgian who became advisor on racial matters to President Franklin Delano Roosevelt, had as his assistant African American educator and researcher Horace Mann Bond (J. D. Anderson, 1984, p. 114; Urban, 1993). Foreman and Bond studied test scores of African American children enrolled in Black schools in Jefferson County, Alabama, operated by the Tennessee Coal, Iron and Railroad Company. The company had dedicated itself to providing the best possible resources to its schools. Foreman and Bond found that average scores for these Black children at the third grade were consistent with national norms. They concluded that better educational and social environments had a positive effect on the educational achievement of African American children, and thus challenged the assumptions of Black intellectual inferiority fostered by mainstream research on standardized testing and Blacks (J. D. Anderson, 1984, p. 114).

Similar arguments can be made today about the effects of the quality of educational environments and resources on African American student achievement on standardized measures. Dreeben and Gamoran (1986) found "that when black and nonblack first graders are exposed to similar instruction, they do comparably well" (p. 667). Mullis, Dossey, Foertsch, Jones, and Gentile (1991) have analyzed data on the trends in academic progress among American students between 1969 and 1990 on the National Assessment of Educational Progress (NAEP). This analysis focuses on trends according to subject matter, age, race, ethnicity, and gender. While there were significant gains in achievement by African Americans as measured by the NAEP tests between 1969 and 1990, Black and Latino students continue to score significantly below Whites on every measure. The improvements in Black achievement on these measures are evident in each subject. In science, gains between 1969 and 1990 have been for 9-year-olds (statistically significant) and 11-year-olds; 17-year-old African Americans maintained their level of achievement, while that for 17-year-old Whites decreased. In mathematics and reading, there were significant improvements for all three ages, 9, 13, and 17. Despite these improvements, the gaps between African Americans and Whites remain great. It can be argued that these continuing gaps in Black and White achievement may be attributable in part to the continuing distinctions in quality of educational practice and resources—as they relate to tracking, course content, classroom pedagogy, and technological facilities—between schools serving predominantly White student populations and schools serving predominantly African American and Latino students (Page, 1991; Oakes, 1985, 1990; Darling-Hammond, 1985; Darling-Hammond & Green, 1990; Mullis et al., 1991; Means & Knapp, 1991; Marshall, 1990; Scott, Cole, & Engel, 1992).

Standardized testing measures have been used to categorize and limit educational access for African American students. Such measures include both achievement tests and IQ tests. A special issue of the *Negro Educational Review* (Hilliard, 1987), republished as *Testing African American Students* (Hilliard, 1991b), provides critiques of the historical and psychological foundations of standardized psychological assessment as they relate to the educational opportunities of African American youth.

Irvine and Irvine (1983) assert that any discussion of discrepancies in educational achievement between Black and White students must address the consequences of the 1954 Supreme Court decision that called for the desegregation of public schooling. These consequences may be viewed at inter-

personal, institutional, and community levels. Epps (1992) offers a comprehensive overview of key events and issues in the evolution of the battle over segregated public schools. While the *Brown* decision did not address issues of school achievement, there was an underlying assumption that the desegregation of public schools would have a positive impact on the life chances of African American students. Irvine and Irvine challenge the research community to provide "analyses which assess the effect of desegregation on black pupil achievement and on life outcome chances for black children" (p. 410). Offering an in-depth analysis of the broader social ramifications of school desegregation, they cite Charles Johnson (1954) of Fisk University, who predicted that the *Brown* decision would result in the "demise of racially separate schools" and in "dramatic . . . changes in the institutional structures of the black community" (Irvine & Irvine, p. 412).

Irvine and Irvine (1983) argue that, at the interpersonal level, teacher-pupil interactions and relationships that they say characterized traditionally all-Black schools were changed as a result of the significant loss in number of Black teachers and principals in those historically all-Black schools, particularly in the South (M. Foster, 1993; Gadsden, 1993). Picott (1976) collected data that indicated "a 90% reduction in the number of black principals in the South between the years 1964 and 1973" (Irvine & Irvine, p. 417). It should be noted, however, that the number and percentage of African American teachers in some northern districts, such as Chicago, increased significantly after 1954 (E. G. Epps, personal communication, October 1993). Irvine and Irvine cite Beady and Hansell (1981), who found that the race of the teacher "was strongly associated with expectation for students' future success in college" (Irvine & Irvine, p. 414). They conclude that the factors influencing student achievement prior to the *Brown* decision were reflective of an interaction between pupil ability and social class. After the *Brown* decision, the influencing interaction included race.

At the institutional level, Irvine and Irvine (1983) claim that the school in the African American community prior to the *Brown* decision served, along with the Black church, as a central pillar of the community. Schools under desegregation were relatively autonomous. Sowell (1976) states:

Under the dual school system in the era of racial segregation the lack of interest in black schools by all-white boards of education allowed wide latitude to black subordinates to run the black part of the system so long as no problems became visible. (pp. 36–37)

The Black school in this context provided inspirational role models for upward mobility (the professionals associated with the school lived in the community), emphasized social values that promoted positive self-concept and identity, and was a site for communitywide events and support services. Similar observations about the centrality of the Black school prior to the widespread desegregation of public schools, particularly the Black high school in the African American community, have been made by F. C. Jones (1981) and Rodgers (1975). While a case has been made for the positive role of the model Black school, others have noted the class biases and tracking in schools such as the famous Dunbar High School of Little Rock, Arkansas (E. G. Epps, personal communication, October 1993).

The third level on which desegregation has influenced educational achievement in the Black community, according to Irvine and Irvine (1983), is that of the community. They state that "understanding the black community involves understanding its basis for solidarity, its implied sense of control, its values and its collective aspirations for its young" (p. 419). In what they call the "historic black community," members of the community functioning through the community's primary institutions, the church and the school, served as a source of achievement and socialization for youngsters. They cite Billingsley's (1968) historic study on the African American family:

In every aspect of the child's life a trusted elder, neighbor, Sunday school teacher, school teacher, or other community member might instruct, discipline, assist, or otherwise guide the young of a given family. Second, as role models, community members show an example to and interest in the young people. Third, as advocates they actively intercede with major segments of society (a responsibility assumed by professional educators) to help young members of particular families find opportunities which might otherwise be closed to them. Fourth, as supportive figures, they simply inquire about the progress of the young, take a special interest in them. Fifth, in the formal roles of teacher, leader, elder, they serve youth generally as part of the general role or occupation. (p. 99)

Irvine and Irvine conclude that desegregation has changed the concept of "the collective whole, the collective struggle, and the collective will" to a focus on individual achievement through individual effort for individual development (p. 420). They cite Kroll (1980), who found no "statistically significant research from 1955–77 which showed that desegregation influenced black student achievement positively" (Irvine & Irvine, 1983, p. 421).

Orfield and Ashkinaze (1991) take just the opposite view on the effects of school desegregation on Black student achievement. While a primary focus of their study of the Atlanta metropolitan area is on the effects of national and local political and economic policies on opportunities for Blacks, particularly low-income Blacks, to achieve upward mobility, they offer extensive data on the achievement of Black and White students on standardized achievement tests over time in segregated and desegregated schools. They conclude that the overwhelming evidence for the Atlanta region between 1975 and 1987 is that the schools with the highest achievement on the standardized measures were those schools that were integrated, regardless of economic background of students, and regardless of whether the schools were within metropolitan Atlanta or the surrounding suburbs. Crain and Mahard (1981) also found that desegregation had a positive effect on education, especially when initiated in the early grades. They also found "that desegregation enhances IQ test scores as much or more than it does achievement test scores" (p. 76). Thus, 40 years after *Brown v. Board of Education of Topeka,* race continues to be a salient issue in African American education. Lewis and Nakagawa (1994), for example, report that race played a significant role during the

late 1980s and early 1990s in the restructuring efforts of Chicago and other big city school systems throughout the nation.

BLACK STUDIES, AFROCENTRICITY, AND MULTICULTURAL EDUCATION: FOUNDATIONS

Banks (1992) and Karenga (1992) acknowledge the interrelationships among Black studies within the university, the conceptual frameworks of Afrocentricity, and multicultural education. Banks illustrates that key leaders in the current movement for multicultural education were initially grounded in the intellectual foundations of African American studies. Banks (1988) distinguishes between multiethnic studies and multicultural studies, with the latter including not only the perspectives and interests of specific ethnic groups, but also considerations related to gender, sexual orientation, and exceptionality or disability. Karenga, however, argues that the foundations of critique and corrective that characterize what he calls the Africana Studies project imply considerations of diversity to include variables such as gender.

The links among the evolution of Black studies as a discipline within the university, Afrocentricity, and multicultural education are evident in the history of Black studies. The struggle for Black studies began in the 1960s and was influenced by the radicalism of the civil rights movement, the antiwar movement, and the student movement (Karenga, 1982). Leadership of the Student Non-Violent Coordinating Committee (SNCC) trained thousands of Black students as well as White students in social and political activism. Radical White students who initiated the free speech movement at the University of California at Berkeley in 1964, as well as students leading the antiwar movement, including leadership of the Students for a Democratic Society (SDS), were initially trained as SNCC workers in the South (Carson, 1981; Karenga, 1982). In its opposition to the Vietnam war, the student movement challenged the political links of the university to the structures of power that sustained the war. SNCC opposed the war because it saw the war as another example of U.S. intervention in Third World liberation struggles and felt that the war deflected resources and energy needed to correct injustices against African Americans (Carson, 1981; Karenga, 1982).

Out of this political environment, fueled in 1966 by the Watts revolt and a more broadly defined Black power movement, Black students in 1966 at San Francisco State College demanded the establishment of the first Department of Black Studies. At that time the Black Student Union at San Francisco State initiated the Experimental College, which carried out service activities with the surrounding community. After an extensive student strike in 1968 that included formal organizational support from other Third World student groups, the first Black Studies program and department was founded under the leadership of Nathan Hare (Hare, 1972). The Third World Liberation Front that supported the Black Student Union in the strike included the Mexican American Student Confederation, the Asian-American Political Alliance, the Intercollegiate Chinese for Social Action, the Philippine American Collegiate Endeavor, and the Latin American Student Organization (Karenga, 1982). The model for Black studies established by Hare (1972, p. 33) included the call to "bring both the college to the community and the community to the college," increasing the enrollment of Black students as well as their representation in decision-making bodies, and improving their overall treatment on campus. This early model for Black studies also strove to develop a leadership of Black intellectuals who would view service to the Black community as fundamental, reflecting earlier positions stated by scholars and activists such as DuBois (1973b), Woodson (1969), and Bethune (1939). By 1969 most of the major universities and colleges had agreed to the establishment of some form of Black studies (Karenga, 1982). Initially there was resistance on the part of many historically Black colleges to organize Black studies programs and departments, but after universities such as Harvard, Yale, and Columbia had established such programs, many of the Black colleges began to follow suit (Brisbane, 1974; Karenga, 1982). R. Allen (1974) reports that by 1971 at least 500 colleges and universities had established Black studies programs; however, by 1974 that number had dropped to 200.

Black studies has faced and continues to face challenges to its rigor as an intellectual discipline, as well as a diminution of power by relegation of the discipline to program and institute status, rather than full departmental status within the university (Karenga, 1982). These challenges mirror in many ways the challenges to implementation of multicultural education at both the precollegiate and collegiate levels. The Black studies movement introduced the concept of relevance in educational curriculum, expanding curriculum to include ethnic studies, and infusing curriculum with a concern for social consciousness, commitment, and action. The movement for multicultural education at both K–12 and collegiate levels, as well as current movements toward African-centered pedagogy, clearly rests on the legacy of the history of the Black studies movement (Banks, 1992; see also Banks, chapter 1 of this *Handbook*).

The intellectual construct of Afrocentricity provides the philosophical foundation of the Black studies movement as well as the historical movement we have labeled in Table 20–1 as "Education for Black Self-Reliance." The early educational philosophy of DuBois (1973b), Bond (1935), Woodson (1969), and Bethune (1939) can be generally grouped under the umbrella of Afrocentric thought. Karenga (1992) states:

When one speaks of the Afrocentric project, one should always keep in mind that one is not talking about a monolithic position, but rather a general conceptual orientation among Africana Studies scholars whose fundamental point of departure and intellectual concerns and views are centered in the African experience. (p. 7)

The African experience is broadly defined as a shared orientation among peoples of African descent both on the continent of Africa and throughout the Diaspora, based on similar cultural, historical, and political experiences (Skinner & Nwokah, 1987; Herskovits, 1958; Asante, 1987; Stuckey, 1987; Bastide, 1979; J. R. King, 1976; Mbiti, 1970; Nobles, 1974, 1985; Pasteur & Toldson, 1982). Karenga (1992) states that this shared orientation or

African worldview minimally includes the following principles: "1) the centrality of community; 2) respect for tradition; 3) a high level spirituality and ethical concern; 4) harmony with nature; 5) the sociality of selfhood; 6) veneration of ancestors; and 7) the unity of being" (p. 12). Adaptations of these themes are also reflected in the literature on Black learning styles that will be discussed later in this chapter. As was the case with the arguments at the turn of the century among African American leaders against the industrial model of education for Blacks, contemporary articulations of Afrocentric theories have engendered an ideological battle.

Karenga (1992) emphasizes the difference between the terms *Afrocentrism* and *Afrocentricity*. He advocates use of the term *Afrocentricity* to delineate an intellectual category, a quality of thought and practice, rather than simply an ideological tool. Although the term *Afrocentricity* was introduced by Asante (1980) in the late 1970s, what Banks (1992) calls the African American ethnic studies movement has a long tradition of scholarship linking the culture, experiences, and worldview of African Americans, Africans in other parts of the Diaspora, and Africans on the continent. That tradition of scholarship does not represent a monolithic view, but rather an ongoing discussion among African scholars, bounded by a broad sense of shared cultural and historical experience (Carruthers & Karenga, 1986; Diop, 1974). Afrocentric thought has been made institutionally operational in the freedom schools of the civil rights movement (Howe, 1965), the independent school movement from the 1970s until the present (Lee, 1992), the current rites-of-passage movement in African American communities across the nation (Warfield-Coppock, 1992), and the production of history texts and readers reflecting African and African American experiences (Harris, 1990, 1992; D. Johnson, 1991). All of these manifestations of Afrocentric orientations in education highlight the importance of linking intellectual study to service in the Black community, and of grounding intellectual thought in the cultural experiences and the historical traditions of Black people (Bethune, 1939; Bond, 1935; DuBois, 1973b; Hare, 1972; Woodson, 1969). Karenga (1992) argues that Afrocentricity has both particular and universal dimensions. He writes: "For even as there are lessons for humanity in African particularity, there are lessons for Africans in human commonality" (p. 9). These lessons in human commonality include "respect and concern for truth, justice, freedom [and] the dignity of the human person" (p. 10).

CULTURAL CONTEXTS INFLUENCING AFRICAN AMERICAN EDUCATION

In this section we look at research that explores how African American culture has been used to improve teaching and learning for Black students. Spradley (1980) defines "culture as *the acquired knowledge people use to interpret experience and generate behavior* [emphasis in original]" (p. 6). This acquired knowledge is often transmitted through language and includes knowledge about social roles and relationships, structures for communicating, norms about what is appropriate to be communicated to whom and under what circumstances, and conceptions about the natural world and the individual's role in it (Hymes, 1974; Gee, 1989). Farr (1991) writes, "culture can be viewed as a (cognitive) system of knowledge that both gives rise to behavior and is used to interpret experience" (p. 365). Thus any discussion of African American education within a multicultural context must use as a primary filter the implications of African American cultural knowledge, values, and language for the learning process.

Language and Literacy

Language is an essential tool through which we not only communicate, but through which we construct knowledge or think through new problems. Thus any discussion of factors influencing the learning of African American children, adolescents, and adults must take into account the variable of language use. This variable becomes particularly problematic in a society, such as the United States, in which language varieties are valued hierarchically. The conditions under which there are low- and high-prestige language varieties in a society have been labeled *diglossia* by Saville-Troike (1989). Sociolinguists have pointed out that developing communicative competence in a language variety entails learning not only the structure, phonology, and lexicon of the language or dialect, but also learning a set of cultural values that determine what is appropriate to be said, how the communication should be articulated, and under what circumstances (Hymes, 1974; Gee, 1989; Robinson, 1988). Such communicative competence entails what Saville-Troike terms *biculturalism*. Because of the low prestige that Black English carries, especially in its vernacular variety (in contrast to standard Black English), the influences of language on learning for African Americans are both complex and problematic.

The discussion that follows, on the impact of competency in Black English (standard or vernacular) on the acquisition of literacy competencies, is influenced by two major trends in the reconceptualization of what it means to be literate in contemporary terms. Langer (1984) proposes that literacy be conceptualized as a way of thinking, as opposed to being limited to the ability to decode and comprehend printed matter, especially extended texts, at basic levels. She suggests that the ability to analyze critically, for example, a television newscast not only displays literate thinking, but is also a prerequisite to democratic citizenship. Pursuing the same concept, Cole and Keyssar (1985) discuss the idea of film literacy. This reconceptualization of literacy as a way of thinking critically may focus on knowledge communicated through both print and oral mediums. In the same vein, Denny Taylor (1989) proposes thinking about teaching reading and writing as problem-solving activities, methods through which readers think through problems and construct new knowledge.

The variety of English spoken by the majority of African Americans is referred to as Black English or African American English. Although much attention has been paid by researchers to its vernacular variety, Orlando Taylor (1992) argues that there are both standard and vernacular forms of Black English (see also Labov, 1969; Smitherman, 1977; Dillard, 1972; Kochman, 1981). The syntax of the standard variety may more closely

approximate the syntax of the standard variety of English. However, standard Black English shares with its vernacular counterpart essential defining features related to phonology, intonation, and other tonal characteristics, and formal modes of discourse. Smitherman classifies Black modes of discourse into the following general categories: call and response, signification, tonal semantics, and narrative sequencing. These genres of discourse have been studied extensively (Abrahams, 1970; Smith, 1972a, 1972b; Mitchell-Kernan, 1981; Kochman, 1972). Smitherman and others (Vass, 1979; Gates, 1988; Turner, 1949) document the influence of West African languages on the structure, phonology, lexicon, and modes of discourse of Black English. In fact, Smitherman specifically refers to Black English vernacular as "Africanized English" (p. 103). While this body of linguistic research documents the logic of the grammar (Labov, 1969, 1972), as well as its creative and imaginative qualities (Delain, Pearson, & Anderson, 1985; Gates, 1988; Mitchell-Kernan, 1981; Smitherman), research on practical implications for teaching and learning has been limited. Research that has investigated the practical implications for educational settings has fallen into three broad categories: educational programming based on deficit assumptions; analyses of the effects of mismatches between the language of the school and that of the community, based on the assumption that competence in Black English is not a deficit but a difference; and proactive research that builds upon the identified strengths of Black English.

In the late 1960s and early 1970s there were many funded educational programs to implement curriculum aimed at compensating for what was termed "cultural deprivation," largely reflected in the language uses displayed by many African American children (see Hall & Guthrie, 1980, for a full review). Attempts were made to organize what were called "dialect" readers based on the assumption that the phonology and syntax of Black English interfered with the abilities of Black children to learn to read. A review of the research shows mixed results, with no clear advantage to the use of dialect readers and no substantive support for the claim that use of Black English interfered with learning to read (Hall & Guthrie, 1980).

In contrast to these educational interventions and research based on models of cultural and linguistic deprivation, and in response to the research cited above regarding the distinctive and positive qualities of Black English, other researchers have investigated the effects of the home/school language differences on learning, without attributing fault to the child or the home. O. Taylor and Lee (1987), Michaels (1981, 1986), and Cazden, Michaels, and Tabors (1985) conducted ethnographic observations of sharing time in primary grade classrooms. They found that the African American children told stories in what Michaels called a topic-associative style, whereas the White children used a more linear narrative style that more closely approximated the linear expository style of writing and speaking into which the school was attempting to apprentice the students. In the topic-associative style, African American children told stories in which the segments of the story appeared on the surface as anecdotal, with no explicit relationship to one another. Instead, the relationships between segments of the story must be inferred, and often relate to some unarticulated internal point of view of the narrator. This stands in contrast to the sequential series of events and explicit thematic cohesion of the topic-centered storytelling style used by the White children in the studies. The teachers saw no logic to the Black children's narratives and were thus unable to coach them to make connections between episodes and to make details more explicit. Cazden (1988) reports differences in the judgments of White and Black adults about topic-centered and topic-associative children's narratives:

> White adults were much more likely to find the episodic stories hard to follow and they were much more likely to infer that the narrator was a low-achieving student. Black adults were more likely to evaluate positively both topic-centered and episodic stories, noticing differences, but appreciating both. (p. 17)

Gee (1989) extended this analysis of the topic-associative narrative style by arguing that it was more aligned with a high literary style and was, in fact, more complex and subtle than the topic-centered style that the school advocated.

This issue of narrative style is significant because children's sense of genres influences how they approach writing tasks and what story grammars they use as templates for comprehending stories (Stein & Palicastro, 1984). Ball (1992) investigated the expository structures used by a group of African American high school students in their school and personal expository writing. She found a preference for the use of structures grounded in African American linguistic traditions among these students, although they were not necessarily conscious of why they used them. Lee (1991, 1992a, 1993) and Delain et al. (1985) investigated how competencies in Black English related to procedural knowledge or heuristics in interpreting figurative language. Delain et al. showed that competency in Black English was the most significant variable influencing comprehension of figurative language for the middle school Black children in their study, whereas general language ability was the determining factor for the White children. Lee demonstrated how signifying, a genre of Black discourse, could be successfully used to teach skills in interpreting fiction. Lee argued that the language experiences of African American students at the middle school and high school levels offered rich cognitive models from which to extrapolate strategies for interpreting fiction. In addition, she claimed that the prior knowledge such students brought, particularly to texts of African American fiction, when coupled with the teaching of culturally scaffolded reading strategies, offered a rich learning environment for complex thinking about literary texts. Lee proposed that such learning environments helped apprentice students into a community of readers that would then address a diverse array of literary texts. Mahiri (1991) investigated how a group of adolescent African American boys in a youth basketball organization used specific aspects of Black English to develop skills in argumentation and as a jumping-off point for extensive reading about sports. Moss (1994) investigated how specific forms of argumentation are structured within the African American sermon and the many uses of literacy in the Black churches she studied. These studies are important because they take a proactive stance on specific ways in which education for African American children can be im-

proved by drawing on particular language strengths evident in Black English.

In addition to the research on using specific characteristics of Black English to teach and learn academic skills related to literacy, there is also a body of research that considers the socializing effects of competency in Black English and the implications of that socializing for schooling. Delpit (1986, 1988) warned that misunderstandings often occurred in classrooms when teachers used an indirect communicative and teaching style with African American children. She argued that teachers should be direct and explicit about the power relationships embedded in the use of different language varieties. DiPardo (1993) investigated the effects of interventions on a college campus to help basic writers, often from ethnically and linguistically diverse backgrounds, make successful transitions to college-level composition classes. Case studies including African American students and tutors revealed tremendous ambivalence about what it meant to adapt standard English and an academic expository essay style to their writing and personal communication. DiPardo argued that universities, although well intentioned, need to give more careful thought to the organization and goals of basic writing programs for ethnically and linguistically diverse students. Ogbu (1987) and Fordham (1988) have argued that African American students sometimes develop an oppositional attitude toward school in part because they equate success in school with "acting White." This possibility of learning to act White as a prelude to success in school is inevitably tied to learning to speak standard English and potentially divorcing oneself from appropriate uses of Black English. Marsha Taylor (1982) stresses that "in Black Language, attention is paid not only to *what* is said but *how* it is said, *where* it is said, and *who* is doing the 'saying'" (p. 68). Because the investment in developing competency in a particular language variety is so intimately linked to social competence in a given community as well as to concepts of self, Farr (1991) recommends that schools stress what she calls bidialectism or bilingualism, as well as biculturalism.

Several other studies have investigated how African American English is used in socializing children not only to attitudes about school and about evaluating social realities, but also to attitudes toward language. Williams (1991) investigated how a group of middle-class African American families socialized their children about goals for education in conjunction with developing African American cultural identities, many trying to help their young children steer their way through values that may conflict. Potts (1989) analyzed stories of personal experience told by children living in a public housing project in Chicago. The stories were individually and jointly constructed with a parent. Potts found the stories to be structurally complex, using Labov's (1972) framework for narratives. Heath (1983) conducted ethnographic investigations of two working-class Piedmont communities of the Carolinas, one White, one Black. She found the language socialization patterns and the norms for what constituted a good story very different in the two communities. She also found that expectations about language use and narrative strategies in the two communities differed greatly from those of the school. Within the African American working-class community of Trackton, the rules observed by Heath for turn taking within conversations and for getting the floor, as well as the norms for good narratives, are consistent with the characteristics of Black English usage described earlier. Although this literature on socializing through use of Black English offers great promise, little formal research has been conducted to investigate its practical implications for schooling. Two exceptions are Heath (1983) and Lee (1993).

Cultural Variables in Learning and Teaching Mathematics

While most of the research and educational practices linking culture to learning have been in humanities-related fields, focusing on relationships between language and literacy or cultural learning styles, too little attention has been paid to the implications of African American cultural knowledge and/or experiences for learning and teaching mathematics. Unfortunately, one of the most widely acknowledged works in this area posits a deficit model. Orr (1987) argues that African American English serves as a barrier impeding Black children's understanding of certain mathematical concepts that she claims are counterintuitively expressed in Black English. In a comprehensive review of issues of culture and mathematics by Stigler and Baranes (1989), the only reference to African American culture and mathematics is the questionable Orr study. Baugh (1988) critiques Orr's argument on the following grounds, among others: (a) the fact that the school in which she made these observations catered primarily to wealthy Whites, and thus the faculty was not sufficiently familiar with the language and cultural variables influencing the education of inner-city Black students; (b) weaknesses and contradictions in the pedagogy of the classes; (c) a lack of understanding of Black English vernacular on the part of the author; and (d) an impoverished research design. In addition, Baugh (p. 403) cites criticisms of the work raised by Wolf Wolfram of the Center for Applied Linguistics in Washington, D.C., who served as the primary linguistic consultant on the Orr project. J. A. Jones (1990) offers additional criticisms of the Orr study, focusing on the limitations of the mathematical pedagogy employed.

Culture and mathematical learning are joined in what Stigler and Baranes (1989) refer to as "a new sociology of mathematics [that] has arisen that takes as its premise that the foundations of mathematics are to be found through examination of the cultural practices in which the activities of mathematicians are embedded" (p. 258). Mathematicians, in this sense, are not merely those who have chosen mathematics as a professional study, but are also all of us who carry out routinized daily activities that involve problem solving related to number, space, time, volume, and probability. Stigler and Baranes argue that culture may influence mathematical understanding and practices through cultural tools, cultural practices, and cultural institutions. The conceptualization of ethnomathematics as a framework in the discipline of mathematics education is now influencing instruction (D'Ambrosio, 1985; Zaslavsky, 1979, 1993; Frankenstein, 1990; Stiff & Harvey, 1988; Ascher, 1991).

Consistent with recent National Council of Teachers of Mathematics' *Standards* (1989), others have called on schools to organize curriculum and instruction around the real-life experiences of culturally diverse students (S. Anderson, 1990; Frankenstein, 1990; Joseph, 1987). Tate (1993) argues that mathematics education should empower African American students and others to protect their rights and interests, particularly in a society where mathematics may be used to stereotype and in which mathematical models are used to represent particular political and economic interests within societal decision making. He asserts that mathematics instruction for African American students should be grounded in a critical base of racial knowledge. Both Tate and Secada (1993) encourage teachers to engage students in problem solving that is situated in the real-life struggles of the communities in which students live.

At least three major projects involving the learning of mathematics by African American students include a cultural frame of reference: The Algebra Project, founded by civil rights activist and mathematician Bob Moses (Moses, Kamii, Swap, & Howard, 1989); the work of Uri Treisman at the University of California at Berkeley, helping African American students master calculus at the collegiate level (Fullilove & Treisman, 1990); and the historic work of Abdulalim Shabazz at Clark-Atlanta University in Atlanta (Hilliard, 1991a; Kostelecky, 1992). A special issue of the *Journal of Negro Education* (Jones-Wilson, 1990), "Black Students and the Mathematics, Science and Technology Pipeline: Turning the Trickle into a Flood," highlights other projects and approaches that have proven successful for African American students learning mathematics.

Moses explicitly states that he started The Algebra Project to empower African American, Hispanic, and other "minority" youth to master the rudiments of algebra, which serves as the gatekeeper to the study of higher mathematics and sciences (Moses et al., 1989). The Algebra Project introduces an extensive study of algebra in the middle grades in order to prepare students, predominantly African American, to enter high school ready for advanced mathematics. The Algebra Project uses the structure of an urban transit system as a metaphor for the directionality of positive and negative numbers in algebra. The project draws on culturally specific norms by consciously encouraging students to express a descriptive representation of algebraic problems using African American English, Spanish, Creole, or whatever the indigenous language of the student may be (Silva, Moses, Rivers, & Johnson, 1990; Kamii, 1990). Recent extensions of the project in small southern African American communities have included drawing mathematical metaphors for key concepts from African drumming. The project emphasizes a curricular process that draws upon students' existing social knowledge and experiences and links that knowledge to the more fundamental and powerful ideas that undergird the domain of algebra. The project started at the King Elementary School in Cambridge, Massachusetts. As a result of the project, "40 percent of King's 1989 graduates passed the high school algebra exam and most of the others were placed in honors algebra as freshmen" (Klonsky, 1990, p. 8). The project has now expanded to other large and small school districts across the United States.

The Math Workshop Program at the University of California at Berkeley was established by Philip Uri Treisman. Treisman (Jackson, 1989; Fullilove & Treisman, 1990) discovered that African American students entering the university who had been high achievers in high school were not faring well in calculus. Asian American students, by contrast, were doing exceptionally well. Treisman observed that Asian American students often worked cooperatively in study groups for calculus. African American students, on the other hand, had come from high schools where individual hard work was emphasized and viewed as necessary in order to distance high-achieving students from others who did not appear to value school success. These African American students came to Berkeley thinking it was inappropriate to work together and share knowledge. Drawing in part on the work on cooperative learning that suggests that African American students achieve well in such groupings (Slavin, 1977; Slavin & Oickle, 1981; Boykin, 1983, 1994), Treisman formed the Math Workshop Program to foster cooperative learning. The program has been tremendously successful and has received national recognition. Treisman's observations support claims by Irvine and Irvine (1983) and Fordham (1988) that academic success is often interpreted by African American students as requiring cultural and social transformations that are not consistent with more traditional African American values of group cooperation and social responsibility.

Abdulalim Shabazz, Black mathematician at Atlanta University (now Clark-Atlanta University), between 1956 and 1963 trained 109 African American students who received master's degrees in mathematics. Hilliard (1991a) states:

It is estimated that nearly 50 percent of the present African-American mathematicians in the United States (about 200) resulted either directly or indirectly from Atlanta University's 109 master's degree recipients during the seven-year period from 1956 to 1963. . . . Shabazz, directly or indirectly, is linked to the production of more than half the African-American holders of the Ph.D. in mathematics. (p. 31)

Shabazz explicitly states that his approach links a sense of social activism, social responsibility, and cultural awareness, and includes a history of African and African American contributions to the history of mathematics (A. G. Hilliard, personal communication, October 1993). Shabazz attributes the tremendous success of his program to these cultural focuses.

Teachers and Cultural Contexts for Learning

According to M. Foster (1993), the literature that examines the effects of the thinking, beliefs, and values of teachers on their delivery of instruction has not investigated the effects of cultural background and racial identity on those beliefs, values, and thinking. That body of literature that specifically looks at African American teachers teaching African American students tends to fall into two broad categories. One body portrays African American teachers as uncaring and unable to relate to African American students of working-class backgrounds (Conroy, 1972; Rist, 1970; D. Spencer, 1986). The second body portrays successful teachers of African American students as professionals who draw upon community norms in order to establish close personal ties with students, emphasizing both cognitive and affective personal development (Lightfoot, 1978; Sterling, 1972; Lerner, 1972; Siddle-Walker, 1993). Studies of African American teachers from this second body of literature conclude from personal testimonies that such teachers bring their political views into play within the classroom, believing that it is their responsibility to prepare African American students with the explicit knowledge and attitudes they will need to succeed in a racist society (Baker, 1987; S. Clark, 1962; Monroe & Goldman, 1988; see M. Foster, 1993, for a full review). An emerging core of African American researchers has begun to argue that culturally conscious teachers who are effective with African American students espouse a distinct educational philosophy and pedagogy that is rooted in African American cultural norms and political history (M. Foster, 1989, 1993, chapter 31 of this *Handbook;* Henry, 1992; J. E. King, 1991; Ladson-Billings, 1991; Lomotey, 1993; Murrell, 1991). The arguments of these researchers share much in common with the educational philosophies advocated by DuBois (1973b), Woodson (1969), Bond (1935), and Bethune (1939). The concept of what makes these teachers effective aligns consistently with the expressed philosophy of education that emphasizes acquiring knowledge not only of the world, but also specifically about African American history and culture in order to empower students to succeed in an antagonistic world and society. M. Foster (1993) initiates the concept of "community nomination" wherein parents and community members nominate teachers who they determine are outstanding, and these community-nominated teachers become the subjects of research. Ladson-Billings (1990, 1992) introduces the concept of "culturally relevant teaching" and distinguishes it from "assimilationist" teaching. In the former, teachers see their "role as helping students to see the contradictions and inequities that existed in their local community and the larger world" (1992, p. 382). According to Ladson-Billings, culturally relevant teaching involves "a pedagogy that empowers students intellectually, socially, emotionally, and politically by using cultural referents to impart knowledge, skills, and attitudes" (p. 382). Ladson-Billings argues that culturally relevant teaching reflects a state of mind. She documents the teaching style of a teacher whom she labels "biologically White" and "culturally Black" (p. 383). Similar observations have been made by Gay (1993) and Cazden (1976).

The studies cited on African American teachers and teachers who have proven effective in teaching African American students have included ethnographic investigations involving interviews, surveys of community residents, and, to a limited extent, classroom observations. An elaborate study by Lightfoot (1973) investigated the relationships between the expressed political ideology of two teachers and the social and cognitive development of the African American children they taught. Lightfoot's study involved not only interviews of teachers and extensive classroom observation, but also interviews with students in the classrooms. Both teachers in the study expressed desires to prepare their students to succeed in a hostile society, but their beliefs about how best to confront the societal contradictions differed dramatically. Lightfoot concludes that in analyzing how the politics of teachers influences the delivery of instruction, one must also consider their attitudes about student assertiveness, expressiveness, and dissonant reasoning.

Some of the research on African American teachers has investigated the effects of racism on these teachers in desegregated schools (Tyack, 1974; Franklin, 1979; Curry, 1981; J. Anderson, 1988; Ethridge, 1979). M. Foster (1990) notes:

Historically, paid less than their white counterparts, rarely employed except to teach African American pupils, opposed by unions seeking to preserve seniority rights of their largely white constituencies, dismissed in large numbers following the *Brown vs. Board of Education Decision,* and denied access to teaching positions through increased testing at all levels, African American teachers' lives and careers have been seriously affected by racism. (p. 3)

MAJOR POLICIES AND STRATEGIES TO IMPROVE AFRICAN AMERICAN EDUCATION: CULTURAL PARADIGM

Educational research and practices that reflect a cultural paradigm emphasize cultural solidarity, education for self-reliance in the African American community, and specific ways in which cultural knowledge, practices, and values that characterize the historic and contemporary African American experience can be drawn upon to improve the education of African Americans. These contemporary approaches have foundations in the history of African American education (Watkins, 1993), foundations that are explored from a variety of perspectives in a special issue of *Urban Education* entitled "Social and Cultural Tensions in the Schooling and Education of African-Americans: Critical Reflections" (Shujaa, 1993b). Many of the researchers, policy makers, and practitioners operating under this framework explicitly draw upon the educational philosophies of W. E. B. DuBois (1973b), Carter G. Woodson (1969), Horace Mann Bond (1935, 1976), and Mary McLeod Bethune (1939), among others.

The manner in which preferred modes or styles for learning are influenced by culture has been an issue of interest to educational researchers as well as practitioners working with African American students. The research that informs this question draws in part from work in educational psychology (Boykin, 1982, 1983; Boykin & Allen, 1988; Nobles, 1985; Shade, 1982, 1983, 1986) and in part from work in language socialization patterns (Ward, 1971; Heath, 1983), child socialization patterns (McAdoo, 1988), and narrative traditions (Smitherman, 1977; Labov, 1972) within the African American community. Willis (1989) provides a full review of the research literature on African American learning styles, as do Irvine and York (chapter 27 in this *Handbook*).

Boykin (1979, 1983), Shade (1982), Nobles (1986), and Karenga (1992) each have outlined sets of variables that, in their opinions, characterize African American culture. Each argues that the origin of these characteristics can be traced to the continuity of African belief systems within African American culture. Herskovits (1958) and DuBois (1903/1968, 1908/1969) have made similar arguments regarding family structure; L. Jones (1963) and Southern (1971) around musical patterns; Vass (1979), Smitherman (1977), and Dillard (1972) around language patterns; and Hale-Benson (1986) and Billingsley

(1968) around family socialization. Shade (1983, 1986) found Blacks to be more "spontaneous, flexible, open-minded, and less structured in their perceptions of people, thoughts, and events" (Willis, 1989, p. 51).

The critical challenge to this line of research is in defining its implications for classroom practice. One conclusion has been that the mismatches between the styles of learning exhibited by African American students and the behavioral expectations and pedagogical styles of schools result in low levels of achievement among African American students (Irvine, 1990; B. Allen & Boykin, 1991). According to Hilliard (1989/1990), such mismatches can lead to underestimation of the intellectual potential of both individuals and groups. This problem has been particularly virulent with regard to language use (O. Taylor & Lee, 1987; Hilliard, 1983; Cazden, John, & Hymes, 1972; Cook-Gumperz, 1986) and discipline. The high levels of physical activity often attributed to young African American males have led to increased instances of negative discipline (Hale-Benson, 1986), as well as increased grade failures and placement in special education classes (Obiakor, 1992; Harry, 1992). Hilliard (1976) has suggested ways that the culture of the school can change to accommodate learning styles and needs of diverse student populations. He suggests that schools become more flexible, creative, holistic, and people-centered in their teaching strategies.

One line of research that supports the learning-styles argument and informs classroom practice is the work on cooperative learning. Slavin (1977) and Slavin and Oickle (1981) have found that African American students appear to achieve at higher levels when cooperative learning instructional strategies are used. Boykin, in a series of studies, extends Slavin's findings by positing a cultural argument to account for the success of cooperative learning strategies with African American students (Tuck & Boykin, 1989; see Boykin, 1994, for a full review of related studies). In these studies Boykin provided middle school African American and White children differing conditions under which to learn a set of materials. These conditions included cooperative groups that worked together for group competition; groups that worked together for no reward; and situations in which the format of the learning was varied, a circumstance that Boykin has labeled *verve*. Boykin found consistently that the African American students preferred to work cooperatively in groups for which there was no external reward. They preferred group work for its intrinsic value, and learning environments that were characterized by verve. They learned more new material under these conditions. Boykin argues that elements of African American cultural norms and socialization influence the success of these strategies with African American students. Ladson-Billings's (1990, 1992) work on culturally responsive pedagogy is consistent with this line of research, which is grounded in the premise of distinctive ways of learning within the African American community.

Current community organizing efforts for African-centered curriculum in both public and private schools are linked directly to educational research and educational philosophies that highlight the relationships among African American cultural norms and knowledge bases and effective learning and teaching of African American students. "In Search of African

Liberation Pedagogy: Multiple Contexts of Education and Struggle," a special issue of the *Journal of Education* (J. E. King, 1990), and "Africentrism and Multiculturalism: Conflict or Consonance?" a special issue of the *Journal of Negro Education* (S. Johnson, 1992b), offer in-depth analyses of theoretical and practical issues related to African-centered curriculum and pedagogy. A special issue of *Educational Leadership,* "Whose Culture?" (Brandt, 1991/1992), captures the controversies and disagreements of the debate about the common American culture to be emphasized in school curriculum, as opposed to curriculum that reflects the distinctive contributions of different groups. Lee, Lomotey, and Shujaa (1990) articulate the need for and offer definitions of African-centered pedagogy, while at the same time acknowledging both its limitations within and contributions to public education. Lee et al. theorize that an effective African-centered pedagogy does the following:

1. legitimizes African stores of knowledge; 2. positively exploits and scaffolds productive community and cultural practices; 3. extends and builds upon the indigenous language; 4. reinforces community ties and idealizes service to one's family, community, nation, race, and world; 5. promotes positive social relationships; 6. imparts a worldview that idealizes a positive, self-sufficient future for one's people without denying the self-worth and right to self-determination of others; 7. supports cultural continuity while promoting critical consciousness. (p. 50)

Similar arguments have been made by Gordon (1993), Shujaa (1993a), J. E. King and Wilson (1990), and Ladson-Billings (1992).

There are at least three practical contexts in which such a pedagogy can be observed: (a) independent African-centered schools, (b) African American public school academies (including all-male academies), and (c) community rites-of-passage programs. Each of these educational environments can be found in cities and towns nationwide, although clearly the majority of African American students are enrolled in traditional public school arrangements.

Slaughter and Johnson (1988) provide a comprehensive overview of African Americans in private schools. K–12 private schools attended by African American students generally fall within three broad categories: (a) Catholic schools, (b) predominantly White elite schools, and (c) Black independent schools with either a religious philosophy or an African American cultural orientation. These three categories of institutions differ widely in terms of educational philosophy and the distribution of African American students attending. Franklin and McDonald (1988) provide a historical overview of the participation of African Americans in Catholic education. Black parents who choose Catholic schools for their children tend not to be Catholic, and choose the schools for academic rather than religious reasons (Hoffer, 1988). African American students in Catholic schools perform academically better than their counterparts in public schools, although there is still a gap between Black and White achievement within Catholic schools (Coleman & Hoffer, 1987; Hoffer, Greeley, & Coleman, 1985). African American students who attend predominantly White elite schools represent a minority in terms of enrollment and face some of the same racist tensions that African Americans face in public schools and the larger society (Speede-Franklin, 1988;

Epps, 1988). However, the presence of African American faculty seems to help students to overcome these tensions (Epps, 1988). Black parents seriously consider the effects of racial isolation in such schools on the self-image and social development of their children, but make their choices based on the assumption that the academic benefits will ultimately outweigh the effects of racial isolation (Brookins, 1988).

Private schools owned and operated by African Americans with African American student populations differ in history and philosophy from Catholic and predominantly White private schools. Independent African American schools can be traced back to the late 18th century, including the school founded in Boston by Prince Hall in 1798 and a school founded in 1829 in Baltimore by the Oblate Sisters of Providence, an order of Black nuns, which is still functioning today (Ratteray & Shujaa, 1988; Bond, 1976; Franklin, 1979). Among the oldest African American schools still in existence are Piney Woods Country Life School, a residential school in Mississippi in operation since 1909, and Laurinburg Institute in North Carolina, founded in 1909 (Ratteray & Shujaa, 1988). Ratteray and Shujaa (1987), in a survey of parents whose children attend African American independent schools, analyzed a wide array of characteristics important to parents choosing this type of schooling. Their data indicate that parents choose African American independent schools for a variety of reasons: 48% for the learning environment, 29% for academic reasons, 12% for religious education (where applicable), 7% for the cultural emphasis; 4% were concerned about cost (Ratteray & Shujaa, 1987). Although the survey included 399 parents at 40 schools, in interpreting the results it is important to keep in mind that the low percentages reported for religious education and cultural emphasis may reflect the relative percentages of schools with such emphases within the sample. Those private Black schools that have the greatest emphasis on culture include those in the Council of Independent Black Institutions (CIBI) (Lomotey & Brookins, 1988), founded in 1972, although there are other schools emphasizing African American culture that are not part of the CIBI organization, such as the Marcus Garvey School in Los Angeles and the Chad School in Newark. A special issue of the *Journal of Negro Education* (S. Johnson, 1992a), "African Americans and Independent Schools: Status, Attainment, and Issues," examines successful culturally responsive independent schools (Lee, 1992b; G. Foster, 1992), as well as the school system of the Nation of Islam (Rashid & Muhammad, 1992). While there is a standing tradition of private education that centers on African American cultural foundations, there is a growing movement in public education for public schools to include curriculum content that reflects African American and African historical experiences. Since the late 1980s this movement has been manifested in two basic thrusts. The first has been to change the content of curriculum and textbooks used by all children (Banks, chapter 1 of this *Handbook*). The second has been to focus the organization of certain schools on supporting the explicit development of African American males (Leake & Leake, 1992; Holt, 1991/1992). In some instances, public schools with predominantly African American student populations are being challenged to include African-centered curriculum (Asante, 1991/1992; Hilliard, Payton-Stewart, & Williams, 1990; Shujaa, 1993a).

The critique of curriculum content centers mostly on the representation of African and African American history, particularly in textbooks (J. E. King, 1992; Swartz, 1992). The following criticisms have been summarized by Hilliard et al. (1990, pp. xx–xxi):

1. "No significant history of Africans in most academic disciplines before the slave trade."
2. "No 'People' history."
3. "No history of Africans in the African Diaspora."
4. "No presentation of the cultural unity among Africans and the descendants of Africans in the African Diaspora."
5. "Little to no history of the resistance of African people to the domination of Africans through slavery, colonization, and segregation apartheid."
6. "The history of African people that is presented fails to explain the common origin and elements in systems of oppression that African people have experienced, especially during the last 400 years."

King refers to this knowledge base as *Diaspora literacy*. She was intimately involved in the critique of the California History/Social Science Framework of 1988 and the 1990 history textbook adoption policies of the state of California. As a result of this controversy, "at least five communities . . . have refused to buy the books in California" recommended by the state (J. E. King, 1992, p. 323; Epstein & Ellis, 1992). According to King, groups of teachers, parents, and students have made similar critiques of the content of curriculum and textbooks:

The Rochester (NY) Public Schools Multicultural Office, TACT (The Association of Chinese Teachers in San Francisco), CURE (Communities United Against Racism in Education in Berkeley), TACTIC (Taxpayers Concerned About Truth in the Curriculum in Sacramento), NABRLE (National Association of Black Reading and Language Educators in Oakland), and the Rethinking Schools Collective (in Wisconsin). (p. 323)

The New York State Board of Regents (Hancock, 1990) has faced similar political battles over its curriculum project to infuse African-centered content into curriculum and textbooks. Perhaps the most widely cited example of a major urban school district infusing African-centered content into the wider curriculum is that of Portland, Oregon (O'Neil, 1991/1992). The Portland school system commissioned African American scholars in each of the major academic disciplines to write overviews, known as *Baseline Essays*. The Portland *African American Baseline Essays* (Hilliard & Leonard, 1990) have been used as references for other school districts, while at the same time resulting in significant controversy (Martel, 1991/1992).

While historians may disagree over interpretations and definitions of what counts as evidence, few multiculturalists take exception to the need to address gaps in the representation of African and African American history in traditional school curricula and textbooks. Some, in fact, argue that teaching historical controversies may provide a powerful way of apprenticing students into the formal study of history as a discipline (Lee et al., 1990; Seixas, 1993; Wineburg, 1991). Perhaps the most controversial of these initiatives in public education has been the call for African-centered all-male academies. These all-male academy initiatives are a result in part of current concern about the appalling statistics describing the low educational achievement and life chances of African American males (Madhubuti, 1990; Wright, 1991/1992). A special issue of the *Journal of Negro Education,* "Focus on Black Males and Education" (S. Johnson, 1992c), explores the political, educational, and economic variables that influence this state of affairs, as well as exploratory programs that seek to empower African American male students. The African American Immersion project in the Milwaukee Public School system received much attention in the early 1990s (Holt, 1991/1992; Leake & Leake, 1992). There have been similar efforts to establish African American all-male academies in Detroit, Washington, Baltimore, Dallas, and Brooklyn (Dent, 1989), although several of these efforts have been challenged in court for gender segregation. In these instances, as in Milwaukee, the school systems have reconfigured the proposals to include an emphasis on African American culture and male development, but have agreed to include both male and female student populations. These programs often invite members of the community to serve as mentors for male students, modeling the rites-of-passage movement outside of schools.

Insufficient attention has been given to models of academic success in predominantly African American public schools. Sizemore (1985, 1987, 1988) documents organizational features, academic routines, qualities of leadership, and staff support that resulted in sustained academic achievement as measured by standardized tests. Among the features identified by Sizemore (1988) are the following:

1. The use of staff and teacher expertise, skills, information, and knowledge to conduct problem-directed searches for the resolution of school concerns and dilemmas.
2. The involvement of parents in some participatory and meaningful way in the school's program.
3. The prompt evaluation of teacher and staff performances and the provision of assistance, help, and inservice where necessary; however, the rating of performances as unsatisfactory where warranted, including persuading such teachers to transfer in spite of central office resistance.
4. The demand for the use of materials which prove functional for elevating achievement when such are not approved by the Board of Education, especially in the areas of phonics, African American History and Culture, and mathematics problem solving.
5. The denial of student placement in Educable Mentally Retarded divisions unless all strategies for regular learning had occurred and had been exhausted.
6. The refusal to accept system programs which consumed administration and supervision time normally given to the regular program unless such programs increased the school day. (pp. 244–245)

While it may not be evident on the surface, Sizemore's analysis includes both cultural and political dimensions. She emphasizes the need for leaders at the school level who are willing to confront bureaucratic restrictions and struggle to institute curriculum, academic routines, and staff necessary to bring about academic achievement in underachieving African American public schools. She also emphasizes the need to include African American history and culture as a foundational component of the academic curriculum. Sizemore (1988) concludes:

> While there is much in the literature citing teacher leadership and parent involvement as important criteria for high achievement, our findings do not confirm these notions. It may be that the African American school needs a different mix of ingredients for a successful recipe. Since there has never been a consensus among the American polity around full citizenship for the African American, and since the institutional value of white superiority still dominates the social reality, strong leadership may continue to emerge as the most important factor in the elevation of achievement in African American schools until the education of teachers comes to include content which reflects the true history and condition of African Americans so that they are enlightened and better prepared to teach African American children. (p. 265)

Strong consideration must be given to Sizemore's analysis, as her work demonstrates evidence of sustained high academic achievement.

According to Warfield-Coppock (1992), community-based rites-of-passage programs have been growing steadily since the 1970s. These rites-of-passage programs may be sponsored by community organizations, schools, agencies, churches, or groups of families, or function as part of outpatient services in therapeutic environments. Programs in school contexts are still community driven in that the schools often depend on mentoring from members of the community. The argument is that adolescent rites-of-passage programs can develop cultural and social values and coping strategies that can help African American youth to develop positive self-concepts and self-esteem, and promote positive social relationships (Warfield-Coppock, 1992; Dunham, Kidwell, & Wilson, 1986; Hare & Hare, 1985; Oliver, 1989; Perkins, 1986). The self-concept of African American youth is endangered by negative socialization through the media, institutions, and the street culture (Hare & Hare, 1985; Ogbu, 1985; M. Spencer, 1990), economic disadvantage (Muga, 1984; M. Spencer, 1987; Oliver, 1989), and racism (M. Spencer, 1987). The theoretical underpinning of the rites-of-passage movement has been that a positive ethnic identity is essential to the development of a healthy self-concept and positive functioning in U.S. society, especially for adolescents making the transition to adulthood. There is, however, very little research-based evaluation of such programs. Since the 1960s the rites-of-passage movement has developed programmatic models that draw on traditional African models of adolescent socialization (Warfield-Coppock, 1990).

IMPLICATIONS FOR FURTHER RESEARCH, POLICY, AND PRACTICE

One of the most immediate needs in future research is to recognize the cultural diversity now present within African American families and communities throughout the United States (Slaughter-Defoe, Nakagawa, Takanishi, & Johnson, 1990). These communities presently include children descended from the entire Caribbean, South American, African,

and African American experience. While these families collectively share the consequences of the political, economic, and social oppression of U.S. Blacks, they have and are devising their own strategies for establishing and maintaining cultural competence. If, as Spencer and colleagues have posited (M. Spencer, Swanson, & Cunningham, 1991), ethnicity and ethnic identity are pivotal to competence formation, then these groups will have overlapping and unique approaches to educational environments that could be informative to those endorsing multicultural educational policies and practices (e.g., Miller-Jones, 1988; Ogbu, 1987, 1988).

Yet another important trend is the growing appreciation for the overriding importance of development and continuity to what and how children learn. When Clark published *Dark Ghetto* in 1965, he perceived compensatory programs such as Project Head Start to have mistakenly blamed African American parents and families for their children's educational difficulties. In contrast, he placed blame squarely on teachers and school administrators for not assuming proper responsibility and accountability for the education of lower-income and minority children. In 1991, the contemporary Project Head Start program endorsed a set of "multicultural principles." Further, elementary and secondary educators increasingly acknowledge the importance of family and community as *active, positive* contributors to the educative process both inside and outside the classroom (Lightfoot, 1978; Slaughter-Defoe, 1991; Strickland & Ascher, 1992). Collaborative partnerships must be established with children's families at all grade levels if the recent academic and learning challenges occasioned by the deepening crises of chronic and persistent poverty are to be ameliorated (Comer, 1988a; McLoyd, 1990; Scott-Jones, 1991; Slaughter, 1988; Slaughter-Defoe, Kuehne, & Straker, 1992; M. N. Wilson, 1989). The ideals of these elementary and secondary educators are very similar to those always held by prevailing Head Start preschool programs. Thus today, preschool, elementary, and secondary teachers increasingly acknowledge that they contribute collectively to the continuities in children's learning and development.

As we enter the 21st century, it is likely that increasing numbers of African American children will be educated with other, culturally different populations in the same school and/or classroom at both elementary and secondary levels. For example, in a study of the Comer process in Chicago, several participating lower-income elementary schools include Asian, Hispanic, and African American student populations (Cook, Slaughter-Defoe, & Payne, 1994). Given the earlier research on Black-White populations, we are aware that the early experience of desegregation is likely to enhance IQ performance test scores (e.g., see Crain & Mahard, 1981; Moore, 1987). However, we know very little about how these newer intergroup experiences will influence the children's academic and social competencies, including their intellectual and achievement performances. More research in this area is indicated, as well as into how African American parents will effect school choices in the public school arena given the newer options relative to school community composition (Yeakey, 1988; Slaughter, Johnson, & Schneider, 1988).

Finally, the challenges inherent in the education of African American students demand increased investigation by researchers and practitioners into the abiding influences of culture, not from the deficit models of prior decades, but rather as an important strand in the ongoing multicultural education project. Such research holds great promise for the emerging disciplines of cultural psychology (Stigler, Shweder, & Herdt, 1990) and everyday cognition (Rogoff & Lave, 1984). Investigations into the roles of culture in learning among African American children and adolescents offer opportunities for new understandings, not only about learning in specific school subject matters, but also in issues of socialization and character development. While the sociolinguistic research agenda of the 1970s provided significant insights into the complex structures and functions of different language varieties (Gumperz & Hymes, 1986) and their implications for teaching and learning (Cazden, John, & Hymes, 1972), that research had little impact on instruction in school and nonschool settings (Lee, 1993). The research

agenda we are proposing should include both basic and applied research, as well as action research by both university-based and school-based researchers. Bridges between theoretical and applied research are needed, for example, to investigate the effects of movements calling for authentic and dynamic assessment of African American achievement in education and opportunities for advanced schooling (Wolf, Bixby, Glenn, & Gardner, 1991; Brandt, 1992). Clearly, the problem of attracting African Americans into the field of education is another area requiring additional research (S. H. King, 1993).

Miller-Jones (1988) argued that research into the development of African American children positively influenced the formulation of new paradigms in child development. We propose that the research directions we have recommended will not only have a similar enriching effect on the quality of educational experiences for African American students, but will also impact fundamental understandings about learning and teaching that will support the development of all children.

References

Abrahams, R. (1970). *Deep down in the jungle: Negro narrative folklore from the streets of Philadelphia.* Chicago: Aldine.

Allen, B., & Boykin, A. (1991). The influence of contextual factors on Afro-American and Euro-American children's performance: Effects of movement opportunity and music. *International Journal of Psychology, 26,* 373–387.

Allen, R. (1974). Politics of the attack on Black studies. *The Black Scholar, 6*(1), 2–7.

Anderson, J. D. (1975). Education as a vehicle for the manipulation of Black workers. In W. Feinberg & H. J. Rosemont (Eds.), *Work, technology and education: Dissenting essays in the intellectual foundations of American education* (pp. 15–40). Urbana: University of Illinois Press.

Anderson, J. D. (1978, Winter). Northern foundations and southern rural Black education, 1902–1935. *History of Education Quarterly, 18,* 371–396.

Anderson, J. D. (1984). The schooling and achievement of Black children: Before and after Brown v. Topeka, 1900–1980. In M. L. Maehr & D. E. Bartz (Eds.), *The effects of school desegregation on motivation and achievement* (pp. 103–121). Greenwich, CT: JAI Press.

Anderson, J. D. (1988). *The education of Blacks in the south, 1860–1935.* Chapel Hill: University of North Carolina Press.

Anderson, S. (1990). Worldmath curriculum: Fighting Eurocentrism in mathematics. *Journal of Negro Education, 59,* 348–359.

Anson, A., Cook, T., & Habib, F. (1991). The Comer school development program: A theoretical analysis. *Urban Education, 26*(1), 56–82.

Asante, M. (1980). *Afro-centricity: The theory of social change.* Buffalo: Amulefi.

Asante, M. (1987). *The Afrocentric idea.* Philadelphia: Temple University Press.

Asante, M. (1991/1992). Afrocentric curriculum. *Educational Leadership, 49*(4), 28–31.

Ascher, M. (1991). *Ethnomathematics: A multicultural view of mathematical ideas.* Pacific Grove, CA: Brooks/Cole.

Ayers, W. (1991). Perestroika in Chicago's schools. *Educational Leadership, 48*(8), 69–71.

Baker, H. (1987). What Charles knew. In L. Rubin (Ed.), *An apple for my*

teacher: 12 authors tell about teachers who made the difference (pp. 123–131). Chapel Hill, NC: Algonquin.

Ball, A. F. (1992). Cultural preference and the expository writing of African-American adolescents. *Written Communication, 9*(4), 501–532.

Banks, J. A. (1988). *Multiethnic education: Theory and practice.* Boston: Allyn and Bacon.

Banks, J. A. (1992). African American scholarship and the evolution of multicultural education. *Journal of Negro Education, 61*(3), 273–286.

Baron, R., Tom, D., & Cooper, H. (1985). Social class, race and teacher expectations. In J. Dusek (Ed.), *Teacher expectations* (pp. 251–269). Hillsdale, NJ: Erlbaum Publishers.

Bastide, R. (1979). *African civilization in the new world.* London: C. Hurst.

Baugh, J. (1988). Twice as less, Black English and the performance of Black students in mathematics and science [Book review]. *Harvard Educational Review, 58,* 395–403.

Beady, C., & Hansell, S. (1981). Teacher race and expectations for student achievement. *American Educational Research Journal, 18,* 191–206.

Bennett, C., & Harris, J. J. (1981). *A study of the causes of disproportionality in suspensions and expulsions of male and black students. Part I: Characteristics of disruptive and non-disruptive students.* Washington, DC: U.S. Office of Education.

Bethune, M. M. (1939). The adaptation of the history of the Negro to the capacity of the child. *Journal of Negro History, 24,* 9–13.

Billingsley, A. (1968). *Black families in White America.* Englewood Cliffs, NJ: Prentice Hall.

Bond, H. M. (1935, April). The curriculum of the Negro child. *Journal of Negro Education, 4*(2), 159–168.

Bond, H. M. (1976). *Education for freedom.* Lincoln, PA: Lincoln University Press.

Boo, K. (1992, October). Reform school confidential. *Washington Monthly,* pp. 17–24.

Boykin, A. W. (1979). Psychological/behavioral verve: Some theoretical explorations and empirical manifestations. In A. W. Boykin, A. Franklin, & J. Yates (Eds.), *Research directions of Black psychologists* (pp. 351–367). New York: Russell Sage.

Boykin, A. W. (1982). Task variability and the performance of Black and White schoolchildren: Vervistic explorations. *Journal of Black Studies, 12,* 469–485.

Boykin, A. W. (1983). On academic task performance and Afro-American children. In J. Spencer (Ed.), *Achievement and achievement motives* (pp. 324–371). Boston: W. H. Freeman and Company.

Boykin, A. W. (1994). Harvesting culture and talent: African American children and educational reform. In R. Rossi (Ed.), *Educational reform and at risk students*. New York: Teachers College Press.

Boykin, A. W., & Allen, B. (1988). Rhythmic-movement facilitated learning in working-class Afro-American children. *Journal of Genetic Psychology, 149,* 335–347.

Brandt, R. (Ed.). (1991/1992). Whose culture? *Educational Leadership, 49*(4).

Brandt, R. (Ed.). (1992). Using performance assessment. *Educational Leadership, 49*(8).

Brisbane, R. (1974). *Black activism.* Valley Forge, PA: Judson Press.

Brookins, G. K. (1988). Making the honor roll: A Black parent's perspective on private education. In D. T. Slaughter & D. J. Johnson (Eds.), *Visible now: Blacks in private schools* (pp. 12–20). New York: Greenwood Press.

Bullock, H. A. (1967). *A history of Negro education in the south: From 1619 to the present.* Cambridge, MA: Harvard University Press.

Butchart, R. E. (1980). *Northern schools, southern Blacks, and reconstruction: Freedmen's education, 1862–1875.* Westport, CT: Greenwood Press.

Butchart, R. E. (1988). Outthinking and outflanking the owners of the world: A historiography of the African-American struggle for education. *History of Education Quarterly, 28*(3), 333–336.

Campbell, E. L. (1982). *School discipline: Policy, procedures, and potential discrimination—A study of disproportionate representation of minority pupils in school suspensions.* New Orleans, LA: Mid-South Educational Research Association.

Carruthers, J., & Karenga, M. (Eds). (1986). *Kemet and the African world view: Selected papers of the proceedings of the first and second conferences of the Association for the Study of Classical African Civilization.* Los Angeles: University of Sankore Press.

Carson, C. (1981). *In struggle: SNCC and the Black awakening of the 60's.* Cambridge, MA: Harvard University Press.

Carter, D., & Wilson, R. (1993). *11th annual status report on minorities in higher education.* Washington, DC: American Council on Education.

Cazden, C. (1976). How knowledge about language helps the classroom teacher—or does it: A personal account. *Urban Review, 9*(2), 74–90.

Cazden, C. (1988). *Classroom discourse.* Portsmouth, NH: Heinemann.

Cazden, C., John, V., & Hymes, D. (Eds.). (1972). *Functions of language in the classroom.* New York: Teachers College Press.

Cazden, C., Michaels, S., & Tabors, P. (1985). Spontaneous repairs in sharing time narratives: The intersection of metalinguisitic awareness, speech event and narrative style. In S. Freedman (Ed.), *The acquisition of written language: Revision and response.* Norwood, NJ: Ablex.

Chicago schools must do worse. (1991, January 19). *The Economist,* p. 26.

Clark, K. (1965). *Dark ghetto.* New York: Harper.

Clark, S. (1962). *Echo in my soul.* New York: E. P. Dutton.

Cole, M., & Keyssar, H. (1985). The concept of literacy in print and film. In D. R. Olson, N. Torrance, & A. Hildyard (Eds.), *Literacy, language and learning: The nature and consequences of reading and writing* (pp. 50–72). New York: Cambridge University Press.

Coleman, J. S., & Hoffer, T. (1987). *Public and private high schools.* New York: Basic Books.

Comer, J. (1980). *School power.* New York: The Free Press.

Comer, J. (1988a, November). Educating poor minority children. *Scientific American, 259*(5), 42–48.

Comer, J. (1988b). *Maggie's American dream.* New York: New American Library.

Conroy, P. (1972). *The water is wide.* Boston: Houghton Mifflin.

Cook, T., Slaughter-Defoe, D., & Payne, C. (1994). *Comer school development program in Chicago schools: Unpublished proposal to the MacArthur foundation.* Northwestern University, Center for Urban Affairs and Policy Research, Evanston, IL.

Cook-Gumperz, J. (Ed.). (1986). *The social construction of literacy.* New York: Cambridge University Press.

Crain, R. L., & Mahard, R. E. (1981). Minority achievement: Policy implications of research. In W. Hawley (Ed.), *Effective school desegregation: Equity, quality, and feasibility* (pp. 55–84). Newbury Park, CA: Sage.

Curry, L. (1981). *The free Black in America 1800–1850.* Chicago: University of Chicago Press.

D'Ambrosio, U. (1985). Ethnomathematics and its place in the history and pedagogy of mathematics. *For the Learning of Mathematics, 5,* 44–48.

Darling-Hammond, L. (1985). *Equality and excellence: The educational status of Black Americans.* New York: The College Board.

Darling-Hammond, L., & Green, J. (1990). Teacher quality and equality. In J. Goodlad & P. Keating (Eds.), *Access to knowledge: An agenda for our nation's schools* (pp. 237–258). New York: College Entrance Examination Board.

Delain, M., Pearson, P., & Anderson, R. (1985). Reading comprehension and creativity in Black language use: You stand to gain by playing the sounding game. *American Educational Research Journal, 22*(2), 155–173.

Delpit, L. (1986). Skills and other dilemmas of a progressive Black educator. *Harvard Educational Review, 56*(4), 379–385.

Delpit, L. (1988). The silenced dialogue: Power and pedagogy in educating other people's children. *Harvard Educational Review, 58*(3), 280–298.

Dent D. (1989). Readin', ritin' & rage: How schools are destroying Black boys. *Essence, 20*(7), 54–59.

Designs for Change. (1982). *Caught in the web: Misplaced children in Chicago's classes for the mentally retarded.* Chicago: Author.

Dillard, J. (1972). *Black English.* New York: Random House.

Diop, C. A. (1974). *The African origin of civilization: Myth or reality* (M. Cook, Trans.). New York: Lawrence Hill and Company.

DiPardo, A. (1993). *A kind of passport: A basic writing adjunct program and the challenge of student diversity.* Urbana, IL: National Council of Teachers of English.

Dreeban, R., & Gamoran, A. (1986). Race, instruction, and learning. *American Sociological Review, 51,* 660–669.

DuBois, W. E. B. (1962). *Black reconstruction in America: An essay toward a history of the part which Black folk played in the attempt to reconstruct democracy in America, 1860–1880.* Cleveland: World, Meridian Books. (Original work published 1935)

DuBois, W. E. B. (1968). *The souls of Black folk: Essays and sketches.* Greenwich, CT: Fawcett. (Original work published 1903)

DuBois, W. E. B. (1969). *The Negro American family.* New York: Afro-American Studies, New American Library. (Original work published 1908)

DuBois, W. E. B. (1973a). Education and work. In H. Aptheker (Ed.), *The education of Black people: Ten critiques, 1906–1960* (pp. 61–82). New York: Monthly Review Press.

DuBois, W. E. B. (1973b). *The education of Black people: Ten cri-*

tiques, 1906–1960 (H. Aptheker, Ed.). New York: Monthly Review Press.

DuBois, W. E. B. (1973c). Whither now and why. In H. Aptheker (Ed.), *The education of Black people: Ten critiques, 1906–1960* (pp. 149–158). New York: Monthly Review Press.

DuBois, W. E. B., & Dill, A. G. (1911). *The common school and the Negro American.* Atlanta: Atlanta University Press.

Dunham, R., Kidwell, J., & Wilson, S. (1986). Rites of passage at adolescence: A ritual process paradigm. *Journal of Adolescent Research, 1,* 139–154.

Epps, E. G. (1988). Summary and discussion. In D. T. Slaughter & D. J. Johnson (Eds.), *Visible now: Blacks in private schools* (pp. 86–90). New York: Greenwood Press.

Epps, E. G. (1992). Education of African Americans. In M. C. Alkin (Ed.), *Encyclopedia of educational research* (Vol. 1, pp. 49–60). New York: Macmillan.

Epstein, K., & Ellis, W. (1992). Oakland moves to create its own multicultural curriculum. *Phi Delta Kappan, 73*(3), 635–638.

Ethridge, S. (1979). Impact of the 1954 Brown v. Topeka board of education decision on Black educators. *Negro Educational Review, 30*(3–4), 217–232.

Farr, M. (1991). Dialects, culture and teaching the English language arts. In J. Flood, J. M. Jensen, D. Lapp, & J. R. Squire (Eds.), *Handbook of research on teaching the English language arts* (pp. 365–371). New York: Macmillan.

Fordham, S. (1988). Racelessness as a factor in Black students' school success. *Harvard Educational Review, 58,* 54–84.

Foreman, C. (1932). *Environmental factors in Negro elementary education.* New York: Norton.

Foster, G. (1992). New York city's wealth of historically Black independent schools. *Journal of Negro Education, 61*(2), 186–201.

Foster, M. (1989). It's cookin' now: An ethnographic study of a successful Black teacher in an urban community college. *Language in Society, 18*(1), 1–29.

Foster, M. (1990, April). *The politics of race: Through African-American teachers' eyes.* Paper presented at the Annual Meeting of the American Educational Research Association, Boston.

Foster, M. (1993). Educating for competence in community and culture: Exploring the views of exemplary African-American teachers. *Urban Education, 27*(4), 370–394.

Frankenstein, M. (1990). Incorporating race, gender, and class issues into a critical mathematical literacy curriculum. *Journal of Negro Education, 59,* 336–351.

Franklin, V. P. (1979). *The education of Black Philadelphia.* Philadelphia: University of Pennsylvania Press.

Franklin, V. P. (1984). *Black self-determination: A cultural history of the faith of the fathers.* Westport, CT: Lawrence Hill and Company.

Franklin, V. P., & Anderson, J. (Eds.). (1978). *New perspectives on Black educational history.* Boston: G. K. Hall.

Franklin, V. P., & McDonald, E. B. (1988). Blacks in urban Catholic schools in the United States: A historical perspective. In D. T. Slaughter & D. J. Johnson (Eds.), *Visible now: Blacks in private schools* (pp. 93–108). New York: Greenwood Press.

Fullilove, R. E., & Treisman, P. U. (1990). Mathematics achievement among African American undergraduates at the University of California, Berkeley: An evaluation of the math workshop program. *Journal of Negro Education, 59*(3), 463–478.

Gadsden, V. L. (1993). Literacy, education, and identity among African-Americans: The communal nature of learning. *Urban Education, 27*(4), 352–369.

Gates, H. L. (1988). *The signifying monkey: A theory of Afro-American literary criticism.* New York: Oxford University Press.

Gay, G. (1993). Ethnic minorities and educational equality. In J. A. Banks & C. A. M. Banks (Eds.), *Multicultural education: Issues and perspectives* (2nd ed., pp. 171–194). Boston: Allyn and Bacon.

Gee, J. P. (1989). What is literacy? *Journal of Education, 171*(1), 18–25.

Gordon, B. (1993). African-American cultural knowledge and liberatory education: Dilemmas, problems, and potentials in a postmodern American society. *Urban Education, 27*(4), 448–470.

Gould, S. J. (1981). *The mismeasure of man.* New York: W. W. Norton.

Grimmett, S., & Garrett, A. (1989). A review of evaluations of project Head Start. *Journal of Negro Education, 58*(1), 30–38.

Gumperz, J. J., & Hymes, D. (Eds). (1986). *Directions in sociolinguistics: The ethnography of communication.* New York: Basil Blackwell.

Gutman, H. G. (1979, 17–18 August). *Observations on selected trends in American working-class historiography together with some new data that might affect some of the questions asked by historians of American education interested in the relationship between education and work.* Paper presented at the Conference on the Historiography of Education and Work, Stanford University, Stanford, CA.

Hale-Benson, J. (1986). *Black children: Their roots, culture, and learning styles.* Baltimore, MD: Johns Hopkins University Press.

Hall, W. S., & Guthrie, L. F. (1980). On the dialect question and reading. In R. Spiro, B. Bruce, & W. Brewer (Eds.), *Theoretical issues in reading comprehension: Perspectives from cognitive psychology, linguistics, artificial intelligence and education* (pp. 439–452). Hillsdale, NJ: Lawrence Erlbaum Associates.

Hancock, L. (1990, April 24). Whose America is this anyway? *Village Voice,* pp. 37–39.

Harding, V. (1981). *There is a river: The Black struggle for freedom in America.* New York: Harcourt Brace Jovanovich.

Hare, N. (1972). The battle of Black studies. *The Black Scholar, 3*(9), 32–37.

Hare, N., & Hare, J. (1985). *Bringing the Black boy to manhood: The passage.* San Francisco: Black Think Tank.

Harris, V. (1990). African-American children's literature: The first one hundred years. *Journal of Negro Education, 59,* 540–555.

Harris, V. (1992). Contemporary Griots: African-American writers of children's literature. In V. Harris (Ed.), *Teaching multicultural literature in grades K–8* (pp. 55–108). Norwood, MA: Christopher-Gordon Publishers.

Harry, B. (1992). *Cultural diversity, families, and the special education system.* New York: Teachers College Press.

Haynes, N., & Comer, J. (1993). The Yale school development program: Process, outcomes, and policy implications. *Urban Education, 28*(2), 166–199.

Head start research and evaluation: A blueprint for the future. (1990). DHHS Publication No. (ACY) 91-31195). Washington, DC: U.S., DHHS, Administration for Children and Families, ACYF, Head Start Bureau.

Heath, S. B. (1983). *Ways with words: Language, life and work in communities and classrooms.* New York: Cambridge University Press.

Henry, A. (1992). African Canadian women teachers' activism: Recreating communities of caring and resistance. *Journal of Negro Education, 61*(3), 392–404.

Herskovits, M. J. (1958). *The myth of the Negro past.* Boston: Beacon Press.

Hess, G. A., & Greer, J. (1987). *Bending the twig: The elementary years and the dropout rates in the Chicago Public Schools.* Chicago: Spencer Foundation and the Chicago Panel on Public School Policy and Finance.

Hess, G. A., & Lauber, D. (1985). *Dropouts from the Chicago public schools: An analysis of the classes of 1982, 1983, 1984.* Chicago: Lloyd A. Frey Foundation and the Chicago Panel on Public School Policy and Finance.

Hilliard, A. G. (1976). *Alternatives to IQ testing: An approach to the assessment of gifted "minority" children* (Final Report to the Special Education Support Unit). Sacramento: California State Dept. of Education. (ERIC Document Reproduction Service No. ED 147 009)

Hilliard, A. G. (1983). Psychological factors associated with language in the education of the African-American child. *Journal of Negro Education, 52*(1), 24–34.

Hilliard, A. G. (Ed.). (1987). Testing African American students [Special issue]. *The Negro Educational Review, 38*(2–3).

Hilliard, A. G. (1989/1990, December/January). Teachers and cultural styles in a pluralistic society. *Rethinking Schools,* p. 3.

Hilliard, A. G. (1991a). Do we have the *will* to educate all children? *Educational Leadership, 49*(1), 31–36.

Hilliard, A. G. (Ed.). (1991b). *Testing African American students: Special re-issue of The Negro Educational Review.* Morristown, NJ: Aaron Press.

Hilliard, A. G. & Leonard, C. (Eds.). (1990). *African American baseline essays.* Portland, OR: Portland Public Schools.

Hilliard, A. G., Payton-Stewart, L., & Williams, L. O. (Eds.). (1990). *Infusion of African American content in the school curriculum: Proceedings of the first national conference, October, 1989.* Morristown, NJ: Aaron Press.

Hoffer, T. B. (1988). Catholic schools and Black children: Summary and discussion. In D. T. Slaughter & D. J. Johnson (Eds.), *Visible now: Blacks in private schools* (pp. 157–160). New York: Greenwood Press.

Hoffer, T. Greely, A. M., & Coleman, J. S. (1985). Achievement growth in public and Catholic schools. *Sociology of Education, 58*(2), 74–97.

Holt, K. C. (1991/1992). A rationale for creating African-American immersion schools. *Educational Leadership, 49*(4), 18–19.

Howe, F. (1965). Mississippi's freedom schools: The politics of education. *Harvard Educational Review, 35*(2), 144–160.

Hymes, D. (1974). *Foundations in sociolinguistics.* Philadelphia: University of Philadelphia Press.

Irvine, J. (1990). *Black students and school failure.* New York: Praeger.

Irvine, R. W., & Irvine, J. J. (1983). The impact of the desegregation process on the education of Black students: Key variables. *Journal of Negro Education, 52*(4), 410–422.

Jackson, A. (1989, Spring). Minorities in mathematics: A focus on excellence, not remediation. *American Educator,* pp. 22–27.

Johnson, C. S. (1954). Some significant social and educational implications of the U.S. Supreme Court's decision. *Journal of Negro Education, 23*(3), 364–371.

Johnson, D. (1991). *Telling tales: The pedagogy and promise of African American literature for youth.* Westport, CT: Greenwood Press.

Johnson, S. (Ed.). (1992a). African Americans and independent schools: Status, attainment, and issues [Special issue]. *Journal of Negro Education, 61*(2).

Johnson, S. (Ed.). (1992b). Africentrism and multiculturalism: Conflict or consonance? [Special issue]. *Journal of Negro Education, 61*(3).

Johnson, S. (Ed.). (1992c). Focus on Black males and education [Special issue]. *Journal of Negro Education, 61*(1).

Jones, L. (1963). *Blues people: Negro music in White America.* New York: Morrow.

Jones, F. C. (1981). *A traditional model of educational excellence: Dunbar High School of Little Rock, Arkansas.* Washington, DC: Howard University Press.

Jones, J. A. (1990). *Look at math teachers, not 'Black English'* (Policy Studies on Education series). Washington, DC: Institute for Independent Education.

Jones-Wilson, F. C. (Ed.). (1990). Black students and the mathematics, science and technology pipeline: Turning the trickle into a flood [Special issue]. *Journal of Negro Education, 59*(3).

Joseph, G. (1987). Foundations of Eurocentrism in mathematics. *Race and Class, 27,* 13–28.

Kamii, M. (1990). Opening the algebra gate: Removing obstacles to success in college prepatory mathematics courses. *Journal of Negro Education, 59*(3), 392–405.

Karenga, M. (1982). *Introduction to black studies.* Los Angeles, Kawaida Publications.

Karenga, M. (1992). *Afrocentricity and multicultural education: Concept, challenge and contribution.* Unpublished paper, Department of Black Studies, California State University, Long Beach.

Kaufman, P. (1991). *Dropout rates in the United States: 1990.* Washington, DC: National Center for Education Statistics.

King, J. E. (Ed.). (1990). In search of African liberation pedagogy: Multiple contexts of education and struggle [Special issue]. *Journal of Education, 172*(2).

King, J. E. (1991). Black student alienation and Black teachers' emancipatory pedagogy. In M. Foster (Ed.), *Readings on equal education, Vol 11: Qualitative investigations into schools and schooling* (pp. 245–271). New York: AMS.

King, J. E. (1992). Diaspora literacy and consciousness in the struggle against miseducation in the Black community. *Journal of Negro Education, 61*(3), 317–340.

King, J. E., & Wilson, T. L. (1990). Being the soul-freeing substance: A legacy of hope in Afro humanity. *Journal of Education, 172*(2), 9–27.

King, J. R. (1976). African survivals in the Black community: Key factors in stability. *Journal of Afro-American Issues, 4*(2), 153–167.

King, S. H. (1993). The limited presence of African-American teachers. *Review of Educational Research, 63*(2), 115–149.

Klonsky, M. (1990, October). Civil rights leader promoting algebra for all. *Catalyst, Voices of Chicago School Reform,* pp. 8–9.

Kochman, T. (Ed.). (1972). *Rappin' and stylin' out: Communication in urban Black America.* Urbana: University of Illinois Press.

Kochman, T. (1981). *Black and White: Styles in conflict.* Chicago: University of Chicago Press.

Kostelecky, J. (1992, Summer). The will and the way to educate. *Technos,* pp. 11–14.

Kroll, R. (1980). A meta analysis of the effects of desegregation on academic achievement. *Urban Review, 12,* 211–224.

Labov, W. (1969). *The study of nonstandard English.* Urbana, IL: National Council of Teachers of English.

Labov, W. (1972). *Language in the inner city: Studies in the Black English vernacular.* Philadelphia: University of Pennsylvania Press.

Ladson-Billings, G. (1990). Like lightning in a bottle: Attempting to capture the pedagogical excellence of successful teachers of Black students. *International Journal of Qualitative Studies in Education, 3*(4), 335–344.

Ladson-Billings, G. (1991). Returning to the source: Implications for educating teachers of Black students. In M. Foster (Ed.), *Readings on equal education, Vol. 11: Qualitative investigations into schools and schooling* (pp. 227–244). New York: AMS.

Ladson-Billings, G. (1992). Liberatory consequences of literacy: A case of culturally relevant instruction for African American students. *Journal of Negro Education, 61*(3), 378–391.

Langer, J. (1984). Literacy instruction in American schools: Problems and perspectives. In N. Stein (Ed.), *Literacy in American schools, learning to read and write* (pp. 111–136). Chicago: University of Chicago Press.

Leake, D. O., & Leake, B. L. (1992). Islands of hope: Milwaukee's African American immersion schools. *Journal of Negro Education, 61*(1), 24–29.

Lee, C. D. (1991). Big picture talkers/words walking without masters: The instructional implications of ethnic voices for an expanded literacy. *Journal of Negro Education, 60*(3), 291–304.

Lee, C. D. (1992a). Literacy, cultural diversity, and instruction. *Education and Urban Society, 24*(2), 279–291.

Lee, C. D. (1992b). Profile of an independent Black institution: African-centered education at work. *Journal of Negro Education, 61*(2), 160–177.

Lee, C. D. (1993). *Signifying as a scaffold for literary interpretation: The pedagogical implications of an African American discourse genre.* Urbana, IL: National Council of Teachers of English.

Lee, C. D., Lomotey, K., & Shujaa, M. (1990). How shall we sing our sacred song in a strange land? The dilemma of double consciousness and the complexities of an African-centered pedagogy. *Journal of Education, 172*(2), 45–61.

Lerner, G. (Ed.). (1972). *Black women in White America: A documentary history.* New York: Vintage.

Lewis, D., & Nakagawa, K. (1994). *Race and reform in the American metropolis.* Albany, NY: State University of New York Press.

Lightfoot, S. L. (1973). Politics and reasoning: Through the eyes of teachers and children. *Harvard Educational Review, 43*(2), 197–244.

Lightfoot, S. L. (1978). *Worlds apart: Relationships between families and schools.* New York: Basic Books.

Lincoln, E. (1969). The relevance of education for Black Americans. *Journal of Negro Education, 38*(3), 218–222.

Lomotey, K. (1993). African-American principals: Bureaucrat/administrators and Ethno-humanists. *Urban Education, 27*(4), 395–412.

Lomotey, K., & Brookins, C. C. (1988). Independent Black institutions: A cultural perspective. In D. T. Slaughter & D. J. Johnson (Eds.), *Visible now: Blacks in private schools* (pp. 163–183). New York: Greenwood Press.

Madhubuti, H. (1990). *Black men: Single, dangerous and obsolete.* Chicago: Third World Press.

Mahiri, J. (1991). Discourse in sports: Language and literacy features of preadolescent African American males in a youth basketball program. *Journal of Negro Education, 60*(3), 305–313.

Marshall, J. D. (1990). *Discussions of literature in lower-track classrooms* (Report Series Number 2.10). Albany, NY: Center for Learning and Teaching of Literature, State University of New York.

Martel, E. (1991/1992). How valid are the Portland baseline essays? *Educational Leadership, 49*(4), 20–23.

Mbiti, J. (1970). *African religion and philosophy.* New York: Anchor Books.

McAdoo, H. (Ed.). (1988). *Black families.* Beverly Hills, CA: Sage.

McLoyd, V. (1990). The impact of economic hardship on Black families and children: Psychological distress, parenting, and socioemotional development. *Child Development, 61,* 311–346.

Means, B., & Knapp, M. S. (1991). *Teaching advanced skills to educationally disadvantaged students: Final report.* Washington, DC: U.S. Department of Education.

Michaels, S. (1981). "Sharing time," Children's narrative styles and differential access to literacy. *Language in Society, 10,* 423–442.

Michaels, S. (1986). Narrative presentations: An oral preparation for literacy with first graders. In J. Cook-Gumperz (Ed.), *The social construction of literacy* (pp. 94–115). New York: Cambridge University Press.

Miller-Jones, D. (1988). A study of African-American children's development: Contributions to reformulating developmental paradigms. In D. T. Slaughter-Defoe (Ed.), *Black children and poverty: A developmental perspective* (pp. 75–92). San Francisco: Jossey-Bass.

Miller-Jones, D. (1989). Culture and testing. *American Psychologist, 44*(2), 360–368.

Mitchell-Kernan, C. (1981). Signifying, loud-talking and marking. In A. Dundes (Ed.), *Mother wit from the laughing barrel* (pp. 310–328). Englewood Cliffs, NJ: Prentice-Hall.

Monroe, S., & Goldman, P. (1988). *Brothers: Black and poor, a true story of courage and survival.* New York: Ballantine.

Moore, E. G. (1987). Ethnic social milieu and Black children's intelligence test achievement. *Journal of Negro Education, 56*(1), 44–52.

Moses, R. P., Kamii, M., Swap, S. M., & Howard, J. (1989). The algebra project: Organizing in the spirit of Ella. *Harvard Educational Review, 59*(4), 423–443.

Moss, B. (1994). Creating a community: Literacy events in African American churches. In B. Moss (Ed.), *Literacy across communities.* Cresskill, NJ: Hampton Press.

Muga, D. (1984). Academic sub-cultural theory and the problematic of ethnicity: A tentative critique. *The Journal of Ethnic Studies, 12,* 1–51.

Mullis, I. V., Dossey, J. A., Foertsch, M. A., Jones, L. R., & Gentile, C. A. (1991). *Trends in academic progress: Achievement of U.S. students in science, 1969–70 to 1990, mathematics, 1973 to 1990, reading, 1971 to 1990, writing, 1984 to 1990* (Prepared by Educational Testing Service). Washington, DC: Office of Educational Research and Improvement, U.S. Department of Education.

Murrell, P. (1991). Cultural politics in teacher education: What's missing in the preparation of minority teachers. In M. Foster (Ed.), *Readings on equal education, Vol 11: Qualitative investigations into schools and schooling.* New York: AMS.

Myrdal, G. (1944). *An American dilemma: The Negro problem and modern democracy* (Vols. 1 and 2). New York: Harper and Brothers.

National Council of Teachers of Mathematics. (1989). *Professional standards for teaching mathematics.* Reston, VA: Author.

Nobles, W. (1974). African roots and American fruit: The Black family. *Journal of Social and Behavioral Sciences, 20*(2), 52–64.

Nobles, W. (1985). *Africanity and the Black family: The development of a theoretical model.* Oakland, CA: The Institute for the Advanced Study of Black Family Life and Culture.

Nobles, W. (1986). *African psychology: Toward its reclamation, reascension and revitalization.* Oakland, CA: Black Family Institute.

Oakes, J. (1985). *Keeping track: How schools structure inequality.* New Haven, CT: Yale University Press.

Oakes, J. (1990). *Multiplying inequalities: The effects of race, social class and tracking on opportunities to learn mathematics and science.* Santa Monica, CA: Rand Corporation.

Obiakor, F. E. (1992). Embracing new special education strategies for African-American students. *Exceptional Children, 59*(2), 104–106.

Ogbu, J. (1985). A cultural ecology of competence among inner-city Blacks. In M. Spencer, G. Brookins, & W. Allen (Eds.), *Beginnings: The social and affective development of Black children* (pp. 45–66). Hillsdale, NJ: Lawwrence Erlbaum Associates.

Ogbu, J. (1987). Opportunity structure, cultural boundaries, and literacy. In J. Langer (Ed.), *Language, literacy and culture* (pp. 149–177). Norwood, NJ: Ablex.

Ogbu, J. (1988). Cultural diversity and human development. In D. T. Slaughter (Ed.), *Black children and poverty: A developmental perspective* (pp. 11–28). San Francisco: Jossey-Bass.

Oliver, W. (1989). Black males and social problems: Prevention through Afrocentric socialization. *Journal of Black Studies, 20,* 15–39.

O'Neil, J. (1991/1992). On the Portland plan: A conversation with Matthew Prophet. *Educational Leadership, 49*(4), 24–27.

Orfield, G., & Ashkinaze, C. (1991). *The closing door: Conservative policy and Black opportunity.* Chicago: University of Chicago Press.

Orr, E. W. (1987). *Twice as less: Black English and the performance of Black students in mathematics and science.* New York: Norton.

Page, R. (1991). *Lower track classrooms: A curricular and cultural perspective.* New York: Teachers College Press.

Pasteur, A., & Toldson, I. (1982). *Roots of soul: The psychology of Black expressiveness.* Garden City, NY: Doubleday.

Perkins, U. E. (1986). *Harvesting new generations: The positive development of Black youth.* Chicago: Third World Press.

Picott, R. (1976). *A quarter century of elementary and secondary educa-*

tion. Washington, DC: Association for the Study of Negro Life and History.

Porter, D. B. (1936). The organized educational activities of Negro literary societies, 1828–1846. *Journal of Negro Education, 5*(4), 555–576.

Potts, R. (1989, April). *West side stories: Children's conversational narratives in a Black community.* Paper presented at the biennial meeting of the Society for Research in Child Development, Kansas City, MO.

Rashid, H. M., & Muhammad, Z. (1992). The Sister Clara Muhammad schools: Pioneers in the development of Islamic education in America. *Journal of Negro Education, 61*(2), 178–185.

Ratteray, J. D., & Shujaa, M. (1987). *Dare to choose: Parental choice at independent neighborhood schools.* Washington, DC: Institute for Independent Education.

Ratteray, J. D., & Shujaa, M. (1988). Defining a tradition: Parental choice in independent neighborhood schools. In D. T. Slaughter & D. J. Johnson (Eds.), *Visible now: Blacks in private schools* (pp. 184–198). New York: Greenwood Press.

Rist, R. (1970). Student social class and teacher expectations: The self-fulfilling prophecy in ghetto education. *Harvard Educational Review, 40*(3), 411–451.

Robinson, J. L. (1988). The social context of literacy. In E. R. Kintgen, B. M. Kroll, & M. Rose (Eds.), *Perspectives on literacy* (pp. 243–253). Carbondale: Southern Illinois University Press.

Rodgers, F. A. (1975). *The Black high school and its community.* Lexington, MA: D.C. Heath.

Rogoff, B., & Lave, J. (Eds.). (1984). *Everyday cognition: Its development in social context.* Cambridge, MA: Harvard University Press.

Saville-Troike, M. (1989). *The ethnography of communication.* New York: Basil Blackwell.

Schorr, L. (1988). *Within our reach: Breaking the cycle of disadvantage.* New York: Doubleday.

Scott, T., Cole, M., & Engel, M. (1992). Computers and education: A cultural constructivist perspective. In G. Grant (Ed.), *Review of research in education* (Vol. 18, pp. 191–254). Washington, DC: American Educational Research Association.

Scott-Jones, D. (1991). Adolescent childbearing: Risks and resilience. *Education and Urban Society, 23,* 53–62.

Secada, W. G. (1993). *Towards a consciously-multicultural mathematics curriculum.* Paper presented at the Teachers College Conference on Urban Education, Teachers College, Columbia University, New York.

Seixas, P. (1993). The community of inquiry as a basis for knowledge and learning: The case of history. *American Educational Research Journal, 30*(2), 305–326.

Shade, B. J. (1982). Afro-American cognitive style: A variable in school success? *Review of Educational Research, 52,* 219–244.

Shade, B. (1983). Cognitive strategies as determinants of school achievement. *Psychology in the Schools, 20,* 488–493.

Shade, B. (1986). Is there an Afro-American cognitive style? *The Journal of Black Psychology, 13,* 13–16.

Shujaa, M. (1993a). Education and schooling: You can have one without the other. *Urban Education, 27*(4), 328–351.

Shujaa, M. (Ed.). (1993b). Social and cultural tensions in the schooling and education of African-Americans: Critical reflections [Special issue]. *Urban Education, 27*(4).

Siddle-Walker, E. V. (1993). Caswell County Training School, 1933–1969: Relationships between community and school. *Harvard Educational Review, 63*(2), 161–182.

Silva, C. M., Moses, R. P., Rivers, J., & Johnson, P. (1990). The algebra project: Making middle school mathematics count. *Journal of Negro Education, 59*(3), 375–392.

Sizemore, B. A. (1985). Pitfalls and promises of effective schools research. *Journal of Negro Education, 54,* 269–288.

Sizemore, B. A. (1987). The effective African American elementary school. In G. W. Noblit & W. T. Pink (Eds.), *Schooling in social context: Qualitative studies* (pp. 175–202). Norwood, NJ: Ablex.

Sizemore, B. A. (1988). The Madison elementary school: A turnaround case. *Journal of Negro Education, 57*(3), 243–266.

Skinner, E., & Nwokah, O. (1987). Communication and continuity in the diaspora: Some personal reflections on cultural connections. In W. Baber & G. Gay (Eds.), *Expressively Black: The cultural basis of ethnic identity* (pp. 321–344). New York: Praeger.

Slaughter, D. T. (Ed.). (1988). *Black children and poverty: A developmental perspective.* San Francisco: Jossey-Bass.

Slaughter, D. T., & Epps, E. G. (1987). The black child's home environment and student achievement. *Journal of Negro Education, 56*(1), 3–20.

Slaughter, D. T., & Johnson, D. J. (Eds.). (1988). *Visible now: Blacks in private schools.* New York: Greenwood Press.

Slaughter, D. T., Johnson, D. J., & Schneider, B. (1988). The educational goals of black private school parents. In D. T. Slaughter & D. J. Johnson (Eds.), *Visible now: Blacks in private schools* (pp. 224–250). New York: Greenwood Press.

Slaughter, D. T., Lindsey, R. W., Nakagawa, K., & Kuehne, V. (1989). Who gets involved? Head Start mothers as persons. *Journal of Negro Education, 58*(1), 16–29.

Slaughter, D. T., Washington, V., Oyemade, U. J., & Lindsey, R. (1988). *Head Start: A backward and forward look.* Social Policy Report, 3(2). Washington, DC: Society for Research in Child Development, Washington Liaison Office. (Available from SRCD Executive Office, University of Michigan, Ann Arbor, MI, John Hagen, Executive Director.

Slaughter-Defoe, D. T. (1991). Parental educational choice: African American dilemmas. *Journal of Negro Education, 60*(3), 354–360.

Slaughter-Defoe, D. T., Kuehne, V., & Straker, J. (1992). African-American, Anglo-American, and Anglo-Canadian grade 4 children's concept of old people and of extended family. *International Journal of Aging and Human Development, 35*(2), 161–178.

Slaughter-Defoe, D. T., Nakagawa, K., Takanishi, R., & Johnson, D. J. (1990). Toward cultural/ecological perspectives on schooling and achievement in African- and Asian-American children. *Child Development, 61,* 363–383.

Slavin, R. (1977). *Student team learning techniques: Narrowing the achievement gap* (Report No. 228). Baltimore, MD: Johns Hopkins University, Center for Social Organization of Schools.

Slavin, R., & Oickle, E. (1981). Effects of cooperative learning teams on student achievement and race relations: Treatment by race interactions. *Sociology of Education, 54,* 174–180.

Smith, A. (1972a). Markings of an African concept of rhetoric. In A. Smith (Ed.), *Language, communication and rhetoric in Black America* (pp. 363–374). New York: Harper & Row.

Smith, A. (1972b). Socio-historical perspectives of Black oratory. In A. Smith (Ed.), *Language, communication and rhetoric in Black America* (pp. 295–305). New York: Harper & Row.

Smitherman, G. (1977). *Talkin and testifyin: The language of Black America.* Boston: Houghton Mifflin.

Southern, E. (1971). *The music of Black Americans: A history.* New York: Norton.

Sowell, T. (1976). Patterns of Black excellence. *The Public Interest, 43,* 26–58.

Speede-Franklin, W. A. (1988). Ethnic diversity: Patterns and implications of minorities in independent schools. In D. T. Slaughter & D. J. Johnson (Eds.), *Visible now: Blacks in private schools* (pp. 21–31). New York: Greenwood Press.

Spencer, D. (1986). *Contemporary women teachers: Balancing school and home.* New York: Longman.

Spencer, M. (1987). Black children's ethnic identity formation: Risk and resilience of castelike minorities. In J. Phinney & M. Rotheram (Eds.), *Chidlren's ethnic socialization: Pluralism and development* (pp. 103–116). Newbury Park, CA: Sage.

Spencer, M. (1990). Parental values transmission: Implications for the development of African-American children. In H. Cheatham & J. Stewart (Eds.), *Black families: Interdisciplinary perspectives* (pp. 111–130). New Brunswick, NJ: Transaction Publishers.

Spencer, M., Swanson, D. P., & Cunningham, M. (1991). Ethnicity, ethnic identity, and competence formation: Adolescent transition and cultural transformation. *Journal of Negro Education, 60*(3), 366–387.

Spradley, J. (1980). *Participant observation.* New York: Holt, Rinehart and Winston.

Stein, N., & Policastro, M. (1984). The concept of a story: A comparison between children's and teachers' viewpoints. In H. Mandl, N. Stein, & T. Trabasso (Eds.), *Learning and comprehension of text.* Hillsdale, NJ: Lawrence Erlbaum Associates.

Sterling, P. (1972). *The real teachers: 30 inner-city schoolteachers talk honestly about who they are, how they teach and why.* New York: Random House.

Stiff, L., & Harvey, W. (1988). On the education of Black children in mathematics. *Journal of Black Studies, 19,* 190–203.

Stigler, J., & Baranes, R. (1989). Culture and mathematics learning. In E. Z. Rothkopf (Ed.), *Review of research in education* (Vol. 15, pp. 253–307). Washington, DC: American Educational Research Association.

Stigler, J. W., Shweder, R. A., & Herdt, G. (Eds.). (1990). *Cultural psychology: Essays on comparative human development.* New York: Cambridge University Press.

Stowe, H. B. (1879, June). The education of the freedmen. *North American Review,* pp. 605–615.

Strickland, D. S., & Ascher, C. (1992). Low income African-American children and public schooling. In P. W. Jackson (Ed.), *Handbook of research on curriculum* (pp. 609–625). New York: Macmillan.

Stuckey, S. (1987). *Slave culture.* New York: Oxford University Press.

Swartz, E. (1992). Emancipatory narratives: Rewriting the master script in the school curriculum. *Journal of Negro Education, 61*(3), 341–355.

Tate, W. F. (1993, April). *Can America have a colorblind national assessment in mathematics?* Paper presented at the annual meeting of the American Educational Research Association, Atlanta.

Taylor, D. (1989). Toward a unified theory of literacy learning and instructional practices. *Phi Delta Kappan, 71*(3), 184–193.

Taylor, M. (1982). *The use of figurative devices in aiding comprehension for speakers of Black English.* Unpublished doctoral dissertation, University of Illinois, Urbana.

Taylor, O. (1992, June). *Toward a redefinition of standard Black English.* Paper presented at the African American English in Schools and Society Conference, Stanford University, Stanford, CA.

Taylor, O., & Lee, D. (1987). Standardized tests and African-American children: Communication and language issues. *Negro Educational Review, 38*(2/3), 67–80.

Tuck, K., & Boykin, A. (1989). Verve effects: The relationship of task performance to stimulus preference and variability in low-income Black and White children. In A. Harrison (Ed.), *The eleventh conference on empirical research in Black psychology* (pp. 84–95). Washington, DC: NIMH Publications.

Turner, L. (1949). *Africanisms in the Gullah dialect.* Chicago: University of Chicago Press.

Tyack, D. (1974). *The one best system: A history of American urban education.* Cambridge, MA: Harvard University Press.

Urban, W. J. (1993). *Black scholar: Horace Mann Bond 1904–1972.* Athens: University of Georgia Press.

Vass, W. (1979). *The Bantu speaking heritage of the United States.* Los Angeles: Center for Afro-American Studies, University of California.

Ward, M. (1971). *Them children: A study in language learning.* New York: Holt, Rinehart and Winston.

Warfield-Coppock, N. (1990). *Afrocentric theory and applications, Volume 1: Adolescent rites of passage.* Washington, DC: Baobab Associates.

Warfield-Coppock, N. (1992). The rites of passage movement: A resurgence of African-centered practices for socializing African American youth. *Journal of Negro Education, 61*(4), 471–482.

Washington, B. T. (1902). *Up from slavery: An autobiography.* New York: Doubleday.

Washington, V., & Oyemade, U. J. (1987). *Project Head Start: Past, present, and future trends in context.* New York: Garland.

Watkins, W. H. (1993). Black curriculum orientations: A preliminary inquiry. *Harvard Educational Review, 63*(3), 321–338.

Williams, K. (1991). Storytelling as a bridge to literacy: An examination of personal storytelling among Black middle-class mothers and children. *Journal of Negro Education, 60*(3), 399–410.

Willis, M. G. (1989). Learning styles of African American children: A review of the literature and interventions. *The Journal of Black Psychology, 16*(1), 47–65.

Wilson, K. R., & Allen, W. (1987). Explaining the educational attainment of young Black adults: Critical familial and extra-familial influences. *Journal of Negro Education, 56*(1), 64–76.

Wilson, M. N. (1989). Child development in the context of the Black extended family. *American Psychologist, 44*(2), 380–385.

Wineburg, S. (1991). On the reading of historical texts: Notes on the breach between school and academy. *American Educational Research Journal, 28*(3), 495–520.

Wolf, D., Bixby, J., Glenn, J., & Gardner, H. (1991). To use their minds well: Investigating new forms of student assessment. In G. Grant (Ed.), *Review of Research in Education* (Vol. 17, pp. 31–74). Washington, DC: American Educational Research Association.

Woodson, C. G. (1969). *The mis-education of the Negro.* Washington, DC: The Associated Publisher. (Original work published 1933)

Woodson, C. G. (1991). *The education of the Negro prior to 1861.* Salem, NH: Ayer Company Publishers. (Original work published 1919)

Wright, W. J. (1991/1992). The endangered Black male child. *Educational Leadership, 49*(4), 14–16.

Yeakey, C. C. (1988). The public school monopoly: Confronting major national policy issues. In D. T. Slaughter & D. J. Johnson (Eds.), *Visible now: Blacks in private schools* (pp. 284–307). New York: Greenwood Press.

Zaslavsky, C. (1979). *Africa counts: Number and pattern in African culture.* Chicago: Lawrence Hill Books.

Zaslavsky, C. (1993). *Multicultural mathematics: Interdisciplinary cooperative-learning activities.* Portland, ME: J. Weston Walch.

21

EDUCATING MEXICAN AMERICAN STUDENTS: PAST TREATMENT AND RECENT DEVELOPMENTS IN THEORY, RESEARCH, POLICY, AND PRACTICE

Eugene E. García

UNITED STATES DEPARTMENT OF EDUCATION

Our understanding of population diversity as it relates to educational endeavors continues to expand in its utilization of diverse theories of language, learning, thinking, teaching, socialization, and culture (August & Garcia, 1988). What was once considered the study of values and behavior (Mead, 1937; Skinner, 1957) has become today an interlocking study of linguistic, psychological, and social domains, each independently significant, but converging in a singular attempt to reconstruct the nature of the cultural experience at the micro (smallest unit of social analysis, such as a speech event) and macro (larger unit of social analysis, such as social class) level. It is this complex set of understandings upon which an educator must depend when addressing teaching and learning in today's classrooms. For the educator of culturally and linguistically diverse students in general and Mexican American students in particular, the issue of culture—what it is and how it directly and indirectly influences academic learning—becomes particularly important (Ogbu, 1992).

This reality of global diversity and interrelatedness pertains directly to our own nation's heterogeneity and interdependence. The United States is itself a country of incredible cultural and linguistic diversity. This trend of ethnic and racial population diversification continues most rapidly among its young and school-age children. California has already been transformed into a minority/majority state, with 52% of today's students coming from "minority" categories; in fewer than 20 years, 70% of California's students will be non-White, and one half will speak a language other than English on their first day of school. Nationwide, White, non-Hispanic student enrollment has decreased since 1976 by 13%, or a total of 5 million students. As the overall total of the U.S. student population has decreased

from 43 million to 41 million students (pre-K to grade 12) since 1976, the following demographic student indicators have become educationally significant:

1. Minority enrollment as a proportion of total enrollment in elementary and secondary education rose from 24% in 1976 to 30% in 1986.
2. As a proportion of total enrollment, Hispanics increased from 6.4% in 1976 to 10% in 1986. The number of Hispanic students increased from almost 3 million in 1976 to more than 4 million in 1986, an increase of 45%.
3. During this same period, Asian/Pacific Islander students increased from 535,000 to 1,158,000, an increase of 116%. (National Center for Educational Statistics [NCES], 1991)

The new foundations related to the schooling initiatives targeted at Mexican American students in the United States will be the focus of this chapter. I will include an expanded discussion of the issues that bring together research, theory, and educational policy and practice of significance to these students. Even more specifically, the chapter will address educationally related conceptual/theoretical pursuits that attempt to "explain," and therefore lay the foundation for, educational "action."

Within the last few decades, research and practice in culture and education has shifted from a focus on "Americanization" (Gonzalez, 1990) and educational equity (Ramírez & Castañeda, 1974) to multicultural education (Banks, 1991; Sleeter & Grant, 1987), and more recently to the "culturally" relevant instruction of children from culturally and linguistically diverse groups (Garcia, 1991; Ogbu, 1992; Tharp, 1989; Trueba, 1988). The following discussion introduces the demographic contexts of schooling and the theoretical and empirical knowledge bases related to an understanding of culture and education as they relate to Mexican American students. Teaching/learning will be addressed as it relates to linguistic, cognitive, and social research and theory that has developed over the last two decades. Such contributions have reshaped in a dramatic way our view of "Americanization," equal educational opportunity, multicultural education, and the overall role of cultural "difference" in education.

THE DEMOGRAPHIC CONTEXT

The U.S. Census Bureau never fails to confuse us in its attempts to provide clarifying demographic information. With regard to documenting the racial and ethnic heterogeneity of our country's population, it has arrived at a set of highly confusing terms that place individuals in separate exclusionary categories: White, White non-Hispanic, Black, Hispanic (with some five subcategories of Hispanics). Unfortunately, outside of the census meaning of these terms, they are for the most part highly ambiguous and nonrepresentative of the true heterogeneity that the bureau diligently seeks to document. Therefore, it is important to note at the outset of this discussion that these categories are useful only as the most superficial reflection of our nation's true diversity. I do not know many census-identified "Whites," "Blacks," or "Hispanics" who believe that they are truly "White," "Black," or any other restrictive label. But given the limited responses allowed them in census questionnaires, they are constrained by these choices. Racially and culturally we are not "pure" stock, and any separation by the Census Bureau, the NCES, or other social institutions that attempt to address the complexity of our diverse population is likely to impart a highly ambiguous sketch.

Having consented to this significant restriction with regard to efforts aimed at documenting population diversity in this country, I must still conclude that an examination of the available data in this arena does provide a fuzzy but useful portrait of our society and the specific circumstances of various groups within our nation's boundaries. The demographic portrait of Mexican Americans in the United States is even more unfocused than the norm. National data are difficult to obtain in such a specific ethnic format, which is generally concerned with identifying "Hispanics." Although the term *Hispanic* is a relatively new census-related identifier, it is quite evident that populations thus identified (Mexicans, Mexican Americans, Puerto Ricans, Cubans, Chicanos, Latinos, etc.) are often presumed to be one ethnic group, with little appreciation for the diversity among them. Because of this "forced marriage" of demographic data at the national level, I will utilize the data on Hispanics whenever it is required by the nature of the information source, but whenever possible will restrict my analysis to Mexican American populations. Although this is awkward, it is reflective of the problems that exist in utilizing myriad ethnic data sources.

Table 21–1 attempts to summarize present data relevant to the Hispanic subpopulations in the United States. However, due to the difficulties inherent in reporting related data, the table combines these subgroups in focusing on general demographic indicators, as well as on the specific educational character of the population and specific social indexes that mark this population as particularly vulnerable to U.S. institutions. It is quite evident, either independently or comparatively, that the plight of Hispanics (some 60% Mexican American) in the United States is highly problematic; the table depicts consummate vulnerability for Hispanic families, children, and students. On almost every indicator, Hispanic families, children, and students are "at-risk," likely to fall into the lowest quartile on indicators of "well-being": family stability, family violence, family income, child health and development, and educational achievement. Yet this population has grown significantly in the last two decades and will grow substantially in the decades to come.

At the student level, the most comprehensive report with regard to this growth trend was published by The College Board and the Western Interstate Commission for Higher Education (1991). That report indicates that the U.S. non-White and Hispanic student population will increase from 10.4 million in 1985–1986 to 13.7 million in 1994–1995. These pupils will constitute 34% of public elementary and secondary school enrollment in 1994–1995, up from 29% in 1985–1986. White enrollment, meanwhile, will rise by just 5%, from 25.8 million to 27 million, and the White share of the student population will drop from 71% to 66%. According to this study, non-White and Hispanic student enrollment will grow from 10 million in 1976 to nearly 45 million in 2026. *In 2026, we will have the exact inverse of student representation as we knew it in 1990: Hispanic and non-White students will make up 70% of our enrolled K–12 student body, with an estimated 40% of these students of Mexican American descent.*

Of distinctive educational significance is the reality that in 1986, 30 to 35% (3 million) of non-White and Hispanic students were identified as residing in homes in which English was not the primary language (August & Garcia, 1988). By the year 2000 our schools will be serving 6 million limited-English-proficient students. By 2026 that number will conservatively approximate 15 million students, or in the vicinity of 25% of total elementary and secondary school enrollments. In the decades to come it will be virtually impossible for a professional educator to serve in a public school setting, and probably any private school context, in which his or her students are not consequentially diverse—racially, culturally, and/or linguistically.

ACADEMIC WELL-BEING

Drop-out Rate

One major indicator of public school success in our present society is completion of high school. The second national educational goal adopted by the 1990 Education Summit in Charlottesville, Virginia, aims to increase the high school completion rate to 90% by the year 2000. Unfortunately, the dynamics of school completion are not well understood and the cause-and-effect relationships are unclear (Fernandez & Shu, 1988). Much confusion stems from the variety of methods utilized to document the school completion phenomenon. The NCES has

TABLE 21-1. Hispanic Demographic Synthesis

I. General Demographic Character
A. Of the 18.8 million Hispanics in the continental U.S., the following characterizes the population's ethnic diversity:

Country/Area of Origin	Number	Percent
Mexico	11.8 million	62.8
Puerto Rico	2.3 million	12.2
Central/South America	2.1 million	11.2
Cuba	1.0 million	5.3
Other	1.6 million	8.5

B. 82% of this Hispanic population is found in 8 states: Arizona (3%), California (31%), Colorado (3%), Florida (6%), Illinois (4%), New Mexico (3%), New York (11%), and Texas (20%).
C. Average age of this population is 25.1 years, compared to 32.6 years for the general population.
D. 200,000 Hispanics immigrate legally to the U.S. yearly (40% of all legal immigrants; an estimated 200,000 Hispanics immigrate illegally).
E. The Hispanic population grew by 61% from 1970 to 1980, compared to an 11% growth in the general population.
F. 11 million Hispanics report speaking Spanish in the home.
G. 7% of Hispanics live in metropolitan areas; 50% in central cities.

II. Education
A. 40% of Hispanics leave school prior to graduation (40% of these leaving do so by grade 10).
B. 35% of Hispanics are held back at least one grade.
C. 47% of Hispanics are overaged at grade 12.
D. 85% of Hispanic students are in urban districts.
E. 70% of Hispanic students attend segregated schools (up 56% in 1956).
F. Hispanics are significantly below national norms on academic achievement tests of reading, math, science, social science, and writing at grades 3, 7, and 11, generally averaging 1–2 grade levels below the norm. At grade 11, Hispanics average a grade 8 achievement level on these tests.

III. Indexes of "Vulnerability"
A. Median family income has fluctuated for Hispanics (1972—$18,880; 1982—$16,227; 1986—$19,995), remaining below non-Hispanics (1972—$26,261; 1982—$23,907; 1986—$30,321).
B. 29% of Hispanic families live below the poverty line, up from 21% in 1979 (10.2% of White families live below the poverty line).
C. 905,000 (23%) of Hispanic families are maintained by female head-of-household (up from 17% in 1970). 53% of these households live below the poverty line.
D. 50% of Hispanic women are in the labor force.
E. Hispanics are twice as likely to be born to an unmarried, teen mother compared to Whites.
F. 56% of Hispanics are functionally illiterate, compared to 46% for Blacks and 16% for Whites.
G. 65% of Hispanics hold unskilled and semiskilled jobs, compared to 35% of non-Hispanics.

Sources:
Conditions of Hispanics in America Today, U.S. Bureau of the Census, 1984, Washington, DC: Government Printing Office.
The Hispanic Population in the United States: March 1986 and 1987, U.S. Bureau of the Census. 1987, Washington, DC: Government Printing Office.
Change, May/June 1988, Washington, DC: American Association of Higher Education.
The Nation's Report Card: NAEP, by A. N. Appleby, J. Langer, & I. J. S. Mullis, Princeton, NJ: Educational Testing Service.
Education in the United States, National Center for Educational Statistics, 1992, Washington, DC: Author.

begun to address this confusion. NCES issued two reports (Frase, 1989; Kaufman & Frase, 1990) that attempt to provide a systematic window of understanding with regard to high school completion by enumerating a set of drop-out rates:

Event rates report—within a single year—the percentage of students who left high school without finishing work toward a diploma. This is a measure of the actual event of dropping out.

Status rates report—at any given point in time—the percentage of the population of a given age range who either (a) have not finished high school, or (b) are not enrolled. This measure reflects the current status of a given group in the population at large (not just students).

Cohort rates report—over a given time period—what happens to a single group of students. This measure reflects changes in any given group over time.

Status and cohort reports provide a view of high school completion, since they take into consideration what happens to students after they leave school. Reports of this type indicate that high school completion rates for ages 16 to 24 have generally declined in the last 20 years. In this age group, the status rate went from 16% in 1968 to less than 13% in 1989 (Kaufman & Frase, 1990). In 1989 about 4 million persons in the United States aged 16–24 were high school dropouts. Roughly, then, 87% of all U.S. students receive their high school diploma or its equivalent by the age of 24. Unfortunately, this is not the case for subsets of students. Measured by either event or status measures, non-White and Hispanic students drop out at two to three times the rate of White students. Hispanic youth have the highest national drop-out rate, Blacks the second highest, and Whites the lowest. During the period of 1987–1989, about 8% of Hispanic students dropped out of school each year, an event rate almost twice as high as that for Whites. In 1989, among the population aged 16–24, only 67% of Hispanics had completed high school or its equivalency (Kaufman & Frase, 1990). These same data indicate that high school completion rates are lowest in cental city, metropolitan, and rural areas, and highest in suburban areas. Hispanics are concentrated in central city, metropolitan, and rural areas.

Academic Achievement

Having determined that high school completion is problematic for the students of concern in this *Handbook,* how do these students do while they are in school? The NCES has again generated a set of data that addresses this question (NCES, 1991). The most revealing data concern the modal grade-level achievement as measured by standardized measures of academic achievement over several years, 1983 to 1989. This measure attempts to assess the relative number of students who are not achieving at the "normal" and expected level.

Overall, these data indicate that the percentage of students one or more years below modal grade level has increased for boys and girls and for Whites, Blacks, and Hispanics at each age level. For 8-year-olds the percentage of students in this category increased from 20% to 24.5%; for 13-year-olds the increase was from 26.2% to 33.4%. However, an interesting pattern emerges for Whites as compared to Hispanics. At the age of 8 there is little difference between Whites (24.5%) and Hispanics (25.0%) with regard to academic nonachievement. But at age 13 the discrepancy is quite significant: Whites, 28.8%, and Hispanics, 40.3%. From roughly third grade to eighth grade, academic achievement drops off significantly for Hispanics as compared to Whites. Moreover, this effect is more attenuated for boys than for girls. The unfortunate result is that 40% or more of Hispanic students are one grade level or more below expected and normal achievement levels by the eighth grade. This revelation, in concert with the previously discussed high school completion and drop-out data, raises substantive educational concerns. Clearly, as this population grows in size and nothing changes to effect intervention, this underachievement will be an extreme waste of intellectual resources that we cannot in the least afford.

Financial Resources

Educational financing in the United States is not without its national, state, and local complications. On the average, 90% of any educational expenditure consists of tax dollars flowing directly from local or state sources. Less than 10% of these expenditures come from federal sources. Although funding for education increased substantially in the United States during the 1980s, education spending as a proportion of the gross national product actually declined slightly to just over 3.5%, lowest for all "developed" countries. While in real terms overall state and local spending rose 26% between 1980 and 1988, the federal share actually decreased by 2% (Committee for Economic Development, 1991).

Hispanic children reside primarily in central city, metropolitan, and rural areas in highly populated pockets of racial and ethnic segregation, immersed in neighborhoods of concentrated poverty (Kozol, 1991). These children are likely to attend troubled schools with fewer resources and larger classes than schools attended primarily by White students (National Commission on Children, 1991). Moreover, they have been more negatively affected than others by recent changes in educational funding policies. The reduction of federal assistance to education, including that for compensatory education and desegregating school districts, has reduced the fiscal resources directly available for the education of Hispanic students (Levin, 1986). Districts that cannot be integrated because they lack White students are not eligible for enhanced funding available to establish science and math magnet schools, an emerging federal funding priority (Oakes, 1991). In such troubled schools, educational personnel are not occupied with the educational buzzwords of the 1980s—"restructuring," "reform," "teacher empowerment," "site-based management," "teacher competencies," "outcome accountability," "national goals." Instead they are concerned about the bare necessities: windows, books, typewriters, heat, working bathrooms, lighting, and building renovations (Kozol, 1991; Rose, 1989).

These schools have been transformed into institutions that must spend valuable time seeking the resources for basic survival. They are much like developing countries that beg for grants, loans, and other forms of assistance from one source after another. These schools "beg" from city, state, federal, business, and charity sources, only because the basic resources are not provided by present funding structures and formulas. In fact, those structures and formulas are working to their disadvantage. Most Hispanics attend schools in cities and taxing entities in which competition for tax dollars is great. These same communities have high unemployment and underemployment, and are pressed to provide a higher level of related social services. They are competing with wealthier communities to retain businesses. These variables directly affect the resources that can be directed to education.

Most directly, students in these schools are underfunded, even in times that argue for "fairness" in school financing. Our society makes quite clear that we abhor the notion of social privilege. We strongly believe that an individual's or his or her family's wealth is not a deterrent to educational success. Yet such beliefs are not upheld in the ways in which we allocate educational resources. Fiscal disparities were identified over two decades ago. In a now-famous 1968 legal case, Demetrio Rodriguez, a parent in the Edgewood School District in San Antonio, Texas, argued that his children were underfunded relative to children in an adjacent school district, only a few miles away from his own. Residents of the Edgewood School District (96% non-White) paid a higher tax rate than residents of that nearby district, a predominantly White school district and community. Yet they were able to generate only $37 for each pupil. With resources provided by the state, Edgewood was able to spend $231 per student on a yearly basis. The neighboring school district generated $412 per student from its locally lower tax rate, and with resources from the state was able to generate a yearly per pupil expenditure of $543, a differential amounting to over 100%.

Coons, Clune, and Sugarman (1970) documented the distinct differential funding between "rich White" districts and "poor minority" districts identified in this legal action as a national phenomenon. They argued that there is something incongruous about the American ideology of fairness in such funding discrepancies, "a differential of any magnitude the sole justification for which is an imaginary school district line" (p. 137). These boundaries and funding inequalities combined to make the public schools into institutions that educated the rich and kept the poor uneducated (Coons et al.). This preferential education for the rich and denial of the poor continues today. Twenty years after the realization and documentation that educational funding was creating a "class" structure, with Hispanics at the lower end, we have achieved no substantive remedy. Court actions seeking such remedies are being revisited by the Edgewood School District as well as by school districts in California, Illinois, New Jersey, and New York.

Kozol (1991) sums up this situation best:

These are Americans. Why do we reduce them to this beggary—and why, particularly in public education? Why not spend on children here [in schools underfunded] at least what we would be investing in their education if they lived within a wealthy district like Winnetka, Illinois, or Cherry Hill, New Jersey, or Manhasset, Rye, or Great Neck in New York? Wouldn't this be a natural behavior in an affluent society that seems to value fairness in so many other areas of life? Is fairness less important to Americans today than in earlier times? Is it viewed as slightly tiresome and incompatible with hard-nosed values? What do Americans believe about equality?" (p. 41)

Professional Educational Personnel

The previous demographic information has indicated that the diversity in our schools is a recent, but an explosive and long-term, phenomenon. Teachers, administrators, and other educational professionals receiving their training over a decade ago were not encumbered by the challenges facing preservice teaching candidates today. They did not "need" to be ready to respond to the challenge presented by a highly diverse student body. Moreover, few individuals from the ranks of the emerging majority succeeded academically a decade ago, and so were not and are not in the teaching profession. In fact, for the 1987–1988 school year, of the 2.6 million public and private school teachers and the 103,000 school administrators, over 88% were White, and fewer than 12% were non-White and Hispanic—3% Hispanic. In this same academic year, Hispanic academic enrollment was at 24% (NCES, 1991).

It remains quite evident that the vast majority of schoolteachers and administrators are White and will continue to be White in the near future, while the proportion of non-White and Hispanic students continues to increase rapidly (NCES, 1991). Although it is difficult to identify the specific attributes of teachers who have served a diverse student body effectively, recent efforts have attempted to do so. Unlike earlier reports that merely identified and described effective programs, recent efforts have sought out effective programs and/or schools, then attempted to describe the specific instructional and attitudinal character of the teacher (Carter & Chatfield, 1986; Garcia, 1992; Pease-Alvarez, Garcia, & Espinosa, 1991; Tikunuff, 1983; Villegas, 1991). Dwyer (1991) identifies four domains in which "good" teachers excel: (a) content knowledge; (b) teaching for student learning; (c) creating a classroom community for student learning; (d) teacher professionalism. Villegas (1991) has added a fifth domain when the student population served by the teacher is culturally and linguistically diverse. She suggests that "good" teachers in these classroom contexts are required to incorporate culturally responsive pedagogy.

Concern for the effectiveness of teachers is not new. From the earliest days of education program evaluation, the quality of the instructional staff has been considered a significant feature (Heath, 1983). Unfortunately, for programs serving "minority" students, the evaluation of "effectiveness" has been subsumed to an empirical concern regarding the significance of the multicultural aspect of the curriculum, and, for limited-English-speaking students, the use/nonuse of the students' native language and the academic development of the English language (August & Garcia, 1988). Very little attention is given to the attributes of the professional and paraprofessional staff that implements the array of models and program types required in the service of these students in compensatory education programs. Typically, attention to the characteristics of such staff is restricted to years of service and extent of formal educational training received (Olsen, 1988). Yet most educational researchers will grant that the effect of any instructional intervention is directly related to the quality of that intervention's implementation by the instructor(s). In a recent report issued by the California Commission on Teacher Credentialing (1991), it is verified that a disproportionate number of poor and minority students are taught during their entire school career by the least-qualified teachers, because of high teacher turnover, large numbers of misassigned teachers, and classrooms staffed by teachers holding only emergency (temporary and not state-approved) credentials.

It is important to note that professional teaching organizations such as the National Education Association (NEA), the American Federation of Teachers (AFT), and the National Association for the Education of Young Children (NAEYC), to name a few of the largest professional educational organizations, have addressed the specific need for teachers to receive special training in areas that relate to teaching the increasingly diverse student body. Certification agencies, such as the California Commission on Teaching Credentialing, have included particular provisions related to "multicultural" education that institutions of higher education must implement if they are to be accredited as teacher-training institutions and their graduates considered positively as candidates for state teacher credentialing.

Unfortunately, even with this universal acceptance that addresses the specific need to train and assess teachers with regard to their competence in teaching culturally diverse students, the present modes of training and assessment are highly problematic. The data are quite clear with regard to the problems of individual assessment of teacher professional competence. Present professional assessment can be criticized on several levels (McGahie, 1991; Sternberg & Wagner, 1986; Shimberg, 1983):

1. Professional competence evaluations usually address only a narrow range of practice situations. Professionals engage in very complex planning, development, implementation, problem solving, and crisis management. These endeavors do not usually require technical skills and knowledge that are easily measured.

2. Professional competence evaluations are biased toward assessing formally acquired knowledge, probably because of the preponderance of similar assessments of student academic achievement. We assess teachers as we assess students, even though we have differing expectations regarding these populations.

3. Despite the presumed importance of "practice" skills, professional competence assessments devote little attention to the assessment of enunciated practice skills. With regard to teachers of highly diverse students, we do have some understanding of specific skills that "might" be necessary. Lack of specific research in this domain makes it difficult to articulate the exact skills that would be recommended as candidates for assessment.

4. Almost no attention is given to what has earlier been identified as the "disposition" and "affective" domains of the teacher. In recent "effective" teacher analysis, these teacher attributes were identified as being as significant as content knowledge and practice skills (Pease-Alvarez et al., 1991; Villegas, 1991).

In addition to the above concerns, professional assessment instruments are subject to severe violations of reliability and validity. Feldt and Brennan (1989) have demonstrated that components of measurement error are highly inconsistent in the arena of professional assessment. Similarly, test validity is a fundamental problem for professional assessment (Berk, 1986). Inferences about professional competence or ability to practice are actually inferences about specific constructs. This is the old and dangerous "chicken-and-egg-problem." We construct an assessment and soon we are willing to say that whoever scores at "such-and-such" on that assessment is competent. At the base of this assessment, however, is the legitimacy of the constructs that generated it. We presently lack any definitive body of research and knowledge regarding the constructs that embody good teachers in general, and good teachers specifically of culturally diverse students. That knowledge base is developing, but it is presently not substantive in nature (Garcia, 1991).

In summary, the teaching expertise of those professionals charged with meeting the challenges of diversity is highly questionable. These individuals have not been well prepared. We are beginning to react to that challenge. Many of you are reading this *Handbook* because of the interest, concern, and specific professional obligations that will be yours in teaching or in related educational professions. It is important to recognize that we are struggling together in this enterprise. We are far from achieving the instructional expertise that will effectively meet the growing challenges of diversity. Those challenges are not dissipating, and you will likely be called upon directly to assist in developing and implementing educational initiatives that will address them. You will not just be an actor in this domain, you will be strategically involved in writing the script.

Summary

Making sense of demographic data within the realm of education and related domains is like trying to make sense out of the economy only by exploring the vast array of statistics that we as Americans compile about our nation. No one can obtain a clear understanding of the "economy" merely by examining those statistics, no matter how comprehensive, strategic, or ingenious the numbers are. The same is true for the education of Mexican American and Hispanic students in this country. However, much like the economic game, education is an important part of our social fabric. Most of us have been to school. In fact, most of us have spent a majority of our lives in formal schooling activities. And we utilize demographic statistics, much as we use economic statistics, to help us understand the nature of the enterprise through the description of the status or well-being of individual and business players. In the demographic analysis presented in this chapter, specific status indicators for specific groups and individuals have been presented with the understanding that such description can add some depth, but not total understanding, to the challenge faced by today's and tomorrow's educators.

What do these descriptive data tell us about that challenge? It is unmistakable that the students who will populate our schools, who will play the "game," will be radically different with regard to race, culture, and language within a relatively short period. In less than two decades, one half of our students will be non-White and Hispanic, with one quarter of the total student body speaking a language other than English on their first day of school. A teacher receiving a teaching credential today will probably be responsible for the education of a more diverse student body than any teacher at any time in the history of formal education. This will be true at all levels of education. Mexican American students, coming from social and economic circumstances that will make them particularly vulnerable, will undertake their schooling with several "strikes" against them.

They are likely to be underequipped with school materials, not the best that money can buy, but only the least that society is willing to spend after investing in higher-priority endeavors, or willing to spend differentially on more "selective" students. They are likely to be "taught" by individuals who do not meet the highest standards or by teachers who themselves are learning teaching responsibilities. Moreover, many of these students will require instruction in a language that is not their own. They will need to acquire the knowledge of the schooling culture along with the language in which that culture is immersed.

Yet these same data unequivocally indicate that the future of our society rests with these students. As they emerge as the majority in the schools, their success is our success and their failure is our failure. They must succeed. We have no other alternative short of disbanding the "game." To think of disbanding education in this country is analogous in impossibility to thinking of disbanding the economy. Can education rise to this challenge and accommodate students it has historically under-served? There is no doubt that we have the resourcefulness to meet this challenge. The remainder of this chapter will address aspects of this country's past and more recent educational responses to the education of Mexican American students. It is important to add that type of depth to the demographic understanding of this challenge.

THE EDUCATIONAL RESPONSE

Americanization

Historically, "Americanization" has been a prime institutional education objective for culturally diverse children (Elam, 1972; Gonzalez, 1990). "Americanization" schooling practices were adopted whenever the population of these students rose to significant numbers in a community. This adoption led to the establishment of special programs that were applied to both children and adults in urban and rural schools and communities. The desired effect of "Americanizing" students was to socialize and acculturate the diverse community. In essence, if schools could teach these students English and "American" values, then educational failure could be averted. Ironically, social economists have argued that this effort was coupled with systematic efforts to maintain disparate conditions between Anglos and "minority" populations. Indeed, more than anything else, past attempts at addressing the "Black, Hispanic, Indian, and Asian educational problem" have actually preserved the political and economic subordination of these communities (Spencer, 1988).

Coming from a sociological theory of assimilation, "Americanization" has traditionally been recognized as a solution to the problem of immigrants and ethnicity in the modern industrialized United States. "Americanization" was intended to merge small ethnic and linguistically diverse communities into a single dominant national institutional structure and culture. Thomas and Park (1921) argued that the immigrants' "Old World" consciousness would eventually be overcome by "modern" American values. Rather than provide here a detailed review of the literature regarding the historical circumstances of the many immigrant populations that came to the United States, I will rely on recent analyses by Gonzalez (1990) and Spencer (1988). According to Gonzalez, there were important distinctions between European immigrants and the experiences of other immigrant groups regarding assimilation. First, the "Americanization" of the non-European community has been attempted in a highly segregated social context that shows little sign of diminishing. Mexican American and other non-White students are more segregated today than three decades ago. Second, assimilation of these groups had both rural and urban aspects, whereas the European experience was overwhelmingly urban. Third, this assimilation was heavily influenced by the regional agricultural economy, which retarded a "natural" assimilation process. Finally, immigrants from Mexico could not escape the effects of the economic and political relationship between an advanced industrialized nation, the United States, and a semi-industrialized, semifeudal nation, the latter increasingly under the political and economic sway of the United States. This relationship led to a very constrained immigration pool, with only farm and low-skilled labor immigrating continuously to the United States. None of the contributory European nations had such a relationship with the United States, and thus their national cultures tended to be judged more on an equal footing with nations/territories struggling to realize their interests against the nationalism of a rising world power. This factor alone would have made for a significant modification in the objectives and manner in which "Americanization" was applied to non-European background communities.

It can be argued that "Americanization" is still the goal of many programs aimed at Mexican American students (Weis, 1988; Rodriguez, 1989). "Americanization" for Mexican American students unfortunately still means the elimination not only of linguistic and cultural differences, but of an undesirable culture. "Americanization" programs seem to assume a single homogeneous ethnic culture in contact with a single homogeneous modern one, and the relationship between the two is not that of equals. The dominant community, enjoying greater wealth and privileges, claims its position by virtue of cultural superiority (Ogbu, 1986). In one way or another, every Mexican American child, whether born in the United States or in Mexico, is likely to be treated as a foreigner, an alien, or an intruder. The Los Angeles school superintendent voiced a common complaint in a 1923 address to district principals: "We have the [Mexican] immigrants to live with, and if we Americanize them, we can live with them. . . ." Unfortunately, even today the objective is to transform the diversity in our communities into a monolithic English-speaking and American-thinking and -acting community. This attitude was recently articulated by Ken Hill, a California superintendent who has received national and state distinction for his efforts in a district serving a large number of Mexican American students: "We've got to attend to the idea of assimilation and to make sure that we teach English and our values as quickly as we can so these kids can get in the mainstream of American life" (quoted in Walsh, 1990). Hill is echoing the "Americanization" solution articulated repeatedly over the last century. It is important to note that the drop-out rate for Mexican American students in Hill's school district was recently reported as over 40% (Matute-Bianchi, 1990).

The "Americanization" solution has not worked. Moreover, it depends on the flawed notion of group culture. The "Americanization" solution presumes that culturally different children are culturally flawed as a group. To fix them individually, the individuals must be acted on as members of a cultural group. It is assumed that changing the values, language, and culture of the group will provide the solution to the educational underachievement of students who represent that group. In essence, the groups should "melt" into one large and more beneficial "American" culture. But the challenge facing educators with regard to Mexican American students is not to "Americanize" them. Instead, it is to understand them and act responsively to the specific diversity that they bring and to the educational goal of academic success for all students. Is the adoption of this notion of education equity enough?

Educational Equity

For at least the last four decades equal access to educational opportunities has served as a basic assumption of U.S. educational activities. This was clearly brought home by the 1954 Supreme Court *Brown v. Board of Education of Topeka* decision. This landmark case concluded that separate/segregated education for Black Americans was unequal to that education provided for White Americans, and inherently unequal. In essence, the court argued that every effort must be made to address equal access to education regardless of race. This decision was reinforced for Hispanic Americans, Asian Americans, Native Americans, and women in the significant U.S. congressional activity during the War On Poverty era of the 1960s and 1970s. The major legislative act was the Civil Rights Act of 1964, Title IV of which banned discrimination on the grounds of race, color, or national origin in any program receiving federal financial assistance (Title VII of that act addressed educational equity across gender). Not coincidentally, the Elementary and Secondary Act of 1965 began to provide millions of federal dollars in assistance to state and local school systems. If these school systems were to make use of federal funds, they were held accountable to the standard of nondiscrimination.

The 1964 legislation directly banned recipients of federal resources from "restricting an individual in any way in the enjoyment of any advantage or privilege enjoyed by others receiving any service, financial aide or benefit under the (federally) funded program." Moreover, the recipient of federal funds was prohibited from utilizing criteria or methods that would have the effect of impairing accomplishment of the objectives of the federally funded program with respect to individuals of a particular race, color, or national origin. Significantly, other provisions of this legislation provided the possibility of a private cause of action (a lawsuit) against the federally funded institution to rectify issues of discrimination. Students and their parents did not have to wait for the federal government to find funded programs out of compliance; they could move to the courts independently to seek relief. And they did. A barrage of legal action aimed at addressing education inequities soon followed passage of the legislation.

In addition to legal action, further administrative and legislative activity also was a consequence of this initial legislative attention to equal educational opportunity, aimed particularly at Mexican American students. In 1970 the Department of Health, Education, and Welfare issued a memorandum, later referred to as the "May 25 Memorandum," that clarified the mandate of the 1964 Civil Rights Act with respect to non-English-speaking populations of students: "Where a liability to speak and understand the English language excludes national origin minority group children from effective participation in the educational program offered by a school district, the district must take affirmative steps to rectify the language deficiency in order to open instructional programs to these students." The Equal Educational Opportunities and Transportation Act of 1974 placed this administrative protection for language-diverse students into formal law. The act makes "the failure by an educational agency to take appropriate action to overcome lan-guage barriers that impede equal participation by its students in its educational programs" an unlawful denial of equal educational opportunities.

Taken together, these legal and legislative initiatives placed the societal values regarding the importance of education into a form of direct relevance to culturally diverse populations. In essence, any child, regardless of race, color, national origin, and language, is equally entitled to the benefits of educational endeavors. This equal educational approach to the growing number of culturally diverse students pervaded our schools for over a decade, and is still a part of what drives many educational initiatives for these students. In 1990 the *Phi Delta Kappan,* a respected publication of this country's professional education community, dedicated its entire September issue (Grant, 1990), to those concerns still presently confronted by efforts of school desegregation and equal educational opportunity. But equal access has not been the only stimulus driving our educational interest for Mexican American students.

Multicultural Education

From the educational establishment and minority groups themselves came another important educational thrust of particular consequence to culturally diverse students. Aimed mostly at curriculum reform, this initiative suggested that curriculum in the United States should reflect the diverse character of the country's cultural and linguistic groups. A *multicultural education* was recommended for several reasons. First and foremost, the curriculum should represent the actual contributions by various cultural groups to this country's society. Curriculum was criticized for its unbalanced perspectives, which emphasized Western European values, history, literature, and general worldview (Banks, 1984). The United States was not one monolithic culture, and the curriculum should reflect that cultural diversity. Second, a multicultural curriculum would inform "majority" group children of "minority" group contributions, and would at the same time reaffirm the "minority" group significance to the society. Third, multicultural education was perceived as a school reform movement aimed at changing the content and process within schools. Its goal was not only to provide equal educational opportunity, but also to enhance the schooling experience for all students (Sleeter & Grant, 1987).

The multicultural education concept took on several distinct approaches to the instruction of students in general, and culturally diverse students in particular. However, the major impact of this reform movement has been in the curriculum areas, that is, the area of schooling that addresses the content of instruction. In essence, this major reform attempted to address *what* students should be learning. The reform made it quite clear that we needed to know more about this country's diverse cultural groups, and that after we had uncovered such knowledge we needed to dispense it in our everyday schooling endeavors. This overall agreement about the importance of including curriculum that addressed diversity was quite significant, since there was some disagreement with regard to the goals of such activity.

Sleeter and Grant (1987) have provided an excellent review of these discrepant goals and the overall limited consequences of the multicultural education reform movement for American education. Within a model described as "Teaching the multiculturally different," the goal was to assist educators in assisting culturally different students to succeed in mainstream schooling. Although not directly implicating the need to "change" or "assimilate" children of different backgrounds into the mainstream, this goal seemed to serve as a foundation for that form of multicultural education. The prescription was usually subtractive in nature. That is, children with different cultures and languages were asked to leave these attributes behind through the assistance of bridgelike educational programs that promised access to and success in academic and, later, other societal domains. Within this view, multicultural education was seen as a temporary, highly directed educational endeavor that would lead to a melting pot of a successful and more homogeneous student population.

Early vestiges of Head Start reflect this multicultural approach. For preschool children ages three to four, Head Start and its extension for the early elementary student, Follow Through, were perceived as bridges to the mainstream academic environment. Other compensatory education programs like Title I and now Chapter I programs that address underachievement directly are in this same category of educational programs meant to bridge nonachieving students with achievement. They are temporary in nature, with goals of providing a transition for unsuccessful students to success through a process likened to natural cultural assimilation. In such assimilation, immigrants with very diverse cultures and languages come to embrace mainstream American values and acquire English as their main mode of communication. Schools were asked to serve, positively, as an organized vehicle to hasten this natural form of assimilation.

The bridging goal of some multicultural education efforts was combined with another goal: enhancing human relations (Perry, 1975; Colangelo, Foxley, & Dustin, 1982). Such a goal was seen as best achieved by learning about and with each other. In so doing, diverse populations would be able to understand each other, and the corollary of this better understanding would be enhanced communication and social relations. Distinct from the assimilation and bridging goals and procedures, educational programs reflecting this approach to multicultural education asked students to add knowledge about other groups not like their own and utilize it in ways that would enhance social accommodation of diversity—"let's learn to get along better." The most dramatic example of a large-scale program of this type actually occurred in Canada, where French-speaking populations (Francofones) in the province of Quebec were in constant social and economic dispute with English-speaking populations (Anglofones). The solution to this social relations problem was Bilingual-Bicultural Immersion Education. Anglofone children were placed in French only schooling programs for the first three years of their educational experience. Over time, the goal of the program was for children to acquire knowledge of both the language and the culture of Francofones, with the expected product of better human relations. Evaluation of these programs indicate that these expectations were achieved without any cost in academic achievement through children's learning academic content in a language other than their own home language.

Yet another approach to multicultural education has been much more "activist" in nature. Its goals serve to promote respect for diversity. Beyond just acquiring and disseminating information regarding cultural diversity, this approach is aimed at developing intellectual and societal acceptance of cultural diversity as a goal in and of itself (Banks, 1984, 1988; Fishman, 1989; R. Garcia, 1979; Gay, 1975; Gollnick & Chinn, 1986; Grant, 1977). This approach has been the most popular and most influential in the last decade, and has attempted to bring together issues of race, ethnicity, gender, and social class. The thrust of such initiatives has been to permeate the curriculum with issues of diversity—diversity in literature, social thought, scientific approaches, historical construction—while at the same time serving up criticism of "standardized" curriculums, particularly those that reflect Western European contributions as the standard. A corollary of this approach is the overall multicultural and social reconstructionist perspective that is also espoused (Appleton, 1983). In essence, students are asked to become social critics, particularly relative to issues of social injustice. Adoption of this multicultural educational approach would rid society of pervasive social injustices inflicted on the basis of race, ethnicity, and gender.

An example of a proactive stance with regard to multicultural education for Mexican Americans has emerged from the bilingual education community in this country. Starting in 1988, Double Immersion programs have begun to be introduced into large Mexican American school districts of California and Texas. The goal of these programs is to produce a student population that is bilingual and bicultural. For Anglo, English-speaking students, the goal is English- and Spanish-language fluency and literacy, with the program beginning in kindergarten. These students are exposed to Spanish-language instruction in classrooms with Latino Spanish-speaking students and to a curriculum that addresses bicultural concerns. The goals for Mexican American students in the programs are the same. These goals are in concert with the notion of actively promoting cultural diversity, with a healthy academic respect for the linguistic and cultural attributes of the diverse students involved. Similar programs in the public schools of San Francisco, San Diego, and Chicago are housed in "magnet" schools. The intent is to have a highly culturally diverse set of students come together around a thematically designed curriculum that is multilingual and multicultural. Such programs attempt to integrate African American, Mexican American, Asian American, and other culturally diverse student populations by recognizing diversity as a potential positive in addressing equal educational opportunity and multicultural education agendas (Grant & Sleeter, 1987).

Attention to multicultural education in this country over the last two decades has produced a series of debates and substantive accomplishments. Publishing companies have launched new curriculum efforts to address concerns of "bias" raised by proponents of multicultural education (Gollnick & Chinn, 1986). Teacher-training programs have been required to provide specific training at the preservice level (California Commission on Teacher Credentialing, 1991). School-based programs such as the "magnet" and Double Immersion bilingual education programs described above find their roots, at least partially, in the values and goals of multicultural education. The above discussion has attempted to place multicultural education into three broad categories based on the goals of distinct but not necessarily exclusive goal agendas. These goals range from those related to bridging/assimilation for Mexican American students, to enhancing human relations, to actively promoting cultural diversity as a societal goal. Such goals build upon the previous historical and ongoing initiatives dealing with equal educational opportunity—no child should be denied the benefits of education. These two educational initiatives—equal educational opportunity and multicultural education—have individually and together changed the educational response to the growing presence of cultural diversity in our schools.

Beyond Multicultural Education

Equal educational opportunity and multicultural education efforts have failed to address a number of important educational concerns. For the most part they have lacked strong theoretical foundations, addressed only curriculum (not instructional methods or pedagogy), produced many single-case studies of ethnic groups, and produced little empirical data to substantiate the positive effects of implementation. Academic achievement in many culturally diverse populations has not been enhanced significantly over the past decades. Equal educational opportunity activity has generated ongoing legislative and legal policy along with concomitant resources to address this core societal value. But such action has not dealt, in any comprehensive manner, with how educational equity should be achieved. Similarly, educational inertia in and around multicultural education has espoused important societal values and has led to advances on a number of educational fronts. But it has not produced a set of comprehensive strategies that address the educational concerns it has raised (Sleeter & Grant, 1987). Therefore, the result of these educational equity and multicultural reform initiatives has been to raise issues. In accomplishing that outcome, they have been assisted by the demographic reality of a changing, culturally diverse society.

An era of equal educational opportunity and multicultural education has left us with a legacy of some clearly identifiable results. First, educational endeavors related to culturally diverse students have been pragmatically oriented. That is, they have focused on a set of problems—discrimination, desegregation, underachievement, low self-esteem, non-English proficiency—and have forwarded programs to address these problems. However, these efforts have tended to lack any substantive theoretical underpinnings. Instead, the proposed solutions were driven by the social values associated with educational equity and pluralism. A more theoretical approach would still consider the same "problems," but would attempt first to understand why such problems exist, and then address solutions on the basis of those understandings (E. Garcia, 1991; Tharp, 1989).

Another legacy of the last three decades of educational activity centered on culturally diverse populations, particularly the result of multicultural education endeavors, has been the extended case-study approach to cultural diversity. The educational community has produced an extensive literature on the characteristics of different racial, ethnic, and ethnolinguistic groups. The goal of this work was to document the cultural and linguistic attributes of different groups in the United States so that these attributes could be understood and used to serve these populations better. It was not uncommon to learn that American Indian children were nonverbal (Appleton, 1983), Asian American children were shy (Sue & Okazaki, 1990), Mexican American children were cooperative (E. Garcia, 1983), African American children were aggressive (Boykin, 1986), and Anglo children were competitive (Kagan, 1983). Although this case-study work was meant to advance our understanding of culturally diverse students, it often had the effect of promoting stereotypes. Moreover, it did not recognize the broader, well-understood axiom of social scientists who study culture: There is as much heterogeneity within any cultural group as there is between cultural groups. Unfortunately, descriptively useful indicators took on explanatory values: If that student is Mexican American, she must be cooperative, field-sensitive, and speak Spanish. Educational programs were developed to address these cultural attributes, only to discover that many Mexican American children were not cooperative, were field-independent, and did not speak Spanish. If all Mexican Americans are not alike, if all African Americans are not alike, and if all American Indians are not alike, then what set of knowledge about those groups is educationally important? What overarching conceptualization of culture is useful in understanding the educational framework of culturally diverse groups?

Theoretical/Conceptual Frameworks

Before addressing the above questions directly, it seems appropriate to locate this discussion within a broad, educationally relevant theoretical continuum. At one end of this continuum it is argued that addressing culturally diverse populations calls for a deeper understanding of the interaction of the students' culture and the prevailing school culture (Tharp, 1989). This cultural significance position is supported by a rich contribution of research that suggests that the educational failure of "diverse" student populations is related to culture clash between home and school. Evidence for such a position comes from Boykin (1986) for African American students, Heath (1983) for poor White students, Wiesner, Gallimore, and Jordan (1988) for Hawaiian students, Vogt, Jordan, and Tharp (1987) for Navaho students, and Garcia (1988) for Mexican American students. In essence, these researchers have suggested that without attending to the distinctiveness of the contribution of culture, educational endeavors for these culturally distinct students are likely to fail. Theoretically, students do not succeed because the difference between school culture and home culture leads to an educationally harmful dissonance—*a home-to-school "mismatch."* Sue and Padilla (1986) directly enunciate the argument of this position: "The challenge for educators is to identify critical differences between and within ethnic minority groups and to incorporate this information into classroom practice" (p. 62).

At the other extreme of this theoretical continuum lies the position that instructional programs must ensure the implementation of appropriate *general principles of teaching and learning.* The academic failure of any student rests on the failure of instructional personnel to implement what we know "works." Using the now-common educational analytical tool known as meta-analysis, Walberg (1986) suggests that educational research synthesis has identified robust indicators of instructional conditions that have academically significant effects across various conditions and student groups. Other reviews (Baden & Maehr, 1986; Bloom, 1984; Slavin, 1989) have articulated this same position. A number of specific instructional strategies, including direct instruction (Rosenshine, 1986), tutoring (Bloom, 1984), frequent evaluation of academic progress (Slavin, Karweit, & Madden, 1989), and cooperative learning (Slavin, 1989), have been particular candidates for the "what works with everyone" category. Expectations play an important role in other formulations of this underachievement dilemma. I. Levin (1988) has suggested that students, teachers, and school professionals in general have low academic expectations of culturally and linguistically diverse students. The popular dramatization of high school math instructor Jaime Escalante in the film *Stand and Deliver* exemplifies this position. Raising student motivation in conjunction with enhancing academic expectations with challenging curriculum is a prescribed solution. Implied in this "general principle" position is that the educational failure of "diverse" populations can be eradicated by the systemic and effective implementation of these understood general principles of instruction that work with "all" students.

At various positions within this continuum are other significant conceptual contributions that attempt to explain the academic underachievement of culturally and linguistically diverse students. Paulo Fiere (1970) has argued that educational initiatives cannot produce academic or intellectual success under social circumstances that are oppressive. He and others (Cummins, 1986; Pearl, 1991) suggest that such oppression taints any curriculum or pedagogy, and only a pedagogy of empowerment can attain the lofty goals of educational equity and achievement. Similarly, Bernstein (1971), Laosa (1982), and Wilson (1987) point to socioeconomic factors that influence the organization of schools and instruction. Extensive exposure over generations to poverty and related disparaging socioeconomic conditions significantly influences the teaching/learning process at home, in the community, and in schools. The result is disastrous, long-term educational failure and social disruption of family and community. Ogbu and Matutue-Bianchi (1986) offer an alternative, macrosociological perspective with regard to the academic failure of culturally and linguistically diverse students. Such a conceptualization interprets this country's present social approach to several immigrant and minority populations as "caste-like." In this theoretical attempt to explain underachievement, the authors argue that these populations form a layer of our society that is not expected to excel academically or economically, and is therefore treated as a "caste-like population." These expectations are transformed into parallel self-perceptions by these populations, with academic underachievement and social withdrawal the result.

Clearly, the above conceptualizations are not presented here in any comprehensive manner. They are further articulated in other chapters of this *Handbook.* Moreover, the "cultural match/mismatch" to "general principles" continuum need not be interpreted as a set of incompatible approaches in the attempt to understand the educational circumstances of culturally diverse students. Instead, this short introduction should make evident that a wide variety of scholars have dealt seriously with this topic of attempting to understand why so many culturally and linguistically diverse students are not well served by today's educational institutions. These conceptual contributions have not espoused multicultural education principles or educational equity policies. Rather, they have attempted to address the conditions surrounding the education of a culturally diverse population by searching for explanations for those conditions.

These contributions take into consideration the work of Fiere (1970), Bernstein (1971), Cummins (1979, 1986), Heath (1986), Ogbu (1986), Trueba (1987), Levin (1988), and Tharp and Gallimore (1989), all of whom have suggested that the schooling vulnerability of culturally diverse students must be understood within the broader contexts of a society's circumstances for students in and out of schools. That is, no quick fix is likely under social and schooling conditions that mark the student for special treatment of his or her cultural difference without consideration for the psychological and social circumstances in which that student resides. This approach warns us against the isolation of any single attribute (poverty, language difference, learning potential) as the only variable of importance. This more comprehensive view of the schooling process includes an understanding of the relationship between home and school, the psycho-socio-cultural incongruities between the two, and the resulting effects on learning and achievement (Tharp & Gallimore, 1989).

Embedded in this perspective is the understanding that language, culture, and their accompanying values are acquired in the home and community environment (Cummins, 1986; Goldman & Trueba, 1987; Heath, 1981); that children come to school with some knowledge about what language is, how it works, and what it is used for (Hall, 1987; Goodman, 1980; Smith, 1971); that children learn higher-level cognitive and communicative skills as they engage in socially meaningful activities (Duran, 1987); and that children's development and learning is best understood as the interaction of linguistic, sociocultural, and cognitive knowledge and experiences (Trueba, 1988). A more appropriate perspective of learning, then, is one that recognizes that learning is enhanced when it occurs in contexts that are both socioculturally and linguistically meaningful for the learner (Diaz, Moll, & Mehan, 1986; Heath, 1986; Scribner & Cole, 1981; Wertsch, 1985).

Such meaningful circumstances are not generally accessible to culturally diverse children. Those schooling practices that contribute to the academic vulnerability of this student population, and tend to dramatize the lack of fit between student and school experience, are reflected in the monolithic culture transmitted by the schools in the forms of pedagogy, curricula, instruction, classroom configuration, and language (Walker, 1987). Such practices include systematic exclusion of the students' histories, language, experience, and values from classroom curricula and activities (Giroux & McLaren, 1986; Ogbu,

1982), "tracking" that limits access to academic courses, learning environments that do not foster academic development and socialization (Duran, 1986; Eder, 1982; Oakes, 1990) and perception of self as a competent learner and language user, and limited opportunities to engage in developmentally and culturally appropriate learning that are not limited to teacher-led instruction (E. Garcia, 1988).

This rethinking has profound implications for the teaching/learning enterprise related to culturally diverse students (E. Garcia, 1991). The new pedagogy is one that redefines the classroom as a community of learners in which speakers, readers, and writers come together to define and redefine the meaning of the academic experience. It might be described by some as a pedagogy of empowerment (Cummins, 1986), by others as cultural learning (Heath, 1986; Trueba, 1987), and by others as a cultural view of providing instructional assistance/guidance (Tharp & Gallimore, 1989). In any case, it argues for the respect and integration of the students' values, beliefs, histories, and experiences, and recognizes the active role that students must play in the learning process. This responsive pedagogy expands students' knowledge beyond their own immediate experiences while using those experiences as a sound foundation for appropriating new knowledge. For many minority students, this includes utilization of the native language and/or bilingual abilities that are a substantive part of a well-functioning social network in which knowledge is embedded.

Furthermore, a responsive pedagogy for academic learning requires a redefinition of the instructor's role. Instructors must become familiar with the cognitive, social, and cultural dimensions of learning. They need to recognize the ways in which diversity of instruction, assessment, and evaluation affect learning. They should become more aware of the classroom curriculum, its purpose, and the degree of its implementation. Of significance is the configuration of the classroom environment and the nature of interaction of students with teacher and with other students. Instructors must also recognize that the acquisition of academic content requires helping students display their knowledge in ways that suggest their competence as learners and language users. Analysis of these dimensions will underscore the potential for equipping the classroom for the particularly sensitive task of ensuring success with culturally diverse students.

Finally, teachers must destroy preconceived myths about learning processes and the potentially underprepared student and, in particular, about those who come from lower socioeconomic households and/or from homes in which English is not the primary language. For those embracing this new concept of responsive pedagogy, new educational horizons for themselves and their students are not only possible but inevitable. What follows is a more explicit analysis of educational research that attests to the appropriateness of this conceptual and abstract articulation of responsive educational practices that "work" with Mexican American students.

Effective Instructional Practices

The present synopsis and analysis rests on the foundations established by recent research that has documented educationally effective practices with Mexican American students in se-

lected sites throughout the United States (Tikunoff, 1983), in Carpenteria, California (Cummins, 1986), San Diego, California (Carter & Chatfield, 1986), Phoenix, Arizona (E. Garcia, 1988; Moll, 1988), and the San Francisco Bay Area, California (Delgado-Gaitan, 1992; E. Garcia, 1992; Lucas, Henze, & Donato, 1990; Pease-Alvarez et al., 1991). These descriptive studies identified specific students, as well as schools and classrooms that served Mexican American students and were particularly academically successful. The case-study approach adopted by these investigators included examination of preschool, elementary, and high school classrooms. Teachers, principals, parents, and students were interviewed, and specific classroom observations were conducted that assessed the dynamics of the instructional process.

The results of these studies provide important insights with regard to general instructional organization, literacy development, academic achievement, and the perspectives of students, teachers, administrators, and parents. With regard to instructional organization within classrooms, a high degree of common attributes were identified. Classrooms generally emphasized—more than might be expected in a regular classroom—the functional communication between teacher and students and among students themselves. Teachers were constantly checking with students concerning the clarity of assignments and student roles in those assignments. Classrooms were characterized by a high, sometimes noisy, volume of communication, emphasizing student collaboration on small-group projects organized around "learning centers." Such an organization minimized individualized work tasks, involved few "worksheet" exercises, and provided a very informal family-like social setting in which the teacher either worked with a small group of students, never larger than eight and sometimes as small as one, or traveled about the room assisting individuals or small groups of students as they worked on their projects. Large-group instruction was rare, usually confined to start-up activities in the morning.

Significantly, instruction of basic skills and academic content was consistently organized around thematic units such as "bears," "butterflies," and "dinosaurs" in the early grades, and "pop music," "gardens," "pesticides," and "peace/war" in the higher grades. In the majority of classrooms studied, the students actually selected the themes in consultation with the teacher, either through direct voting or some related negotiation process. The teacher's responsibility was to ensure that the instruction that focused on the chosen themes covered the content and skill-related goals and objectives for that grade level in that school district. This theme approach allowed the teacher to integrate content and skills. The major thrust in these classrooms was the appropriation of knowledge centered around these themes, with the realization that basic skills were necessarily developed as a means to appropriate this knowledge. Students became "experts" in these thematic domains while also acquiring the requisite academic skills.

Reported "micro" analysis of instructional events in literacy and math, along with analysis of actual literacy (dialogue journals, learning logs, writing workshop publications, etc.) and math (learning logs, homework, surveys, etc.) products, indicated that teachers organized instruction in a manner that required students to interact with each other utilizing cooperative learning techniques. It was during these student-student dialogues that most higher-order cognitive and linguistic discourse was observed. Students asked each other "hard" questions and challenged each other's answers more readily than in their interaction with the teacher. Moreover, students were likely to seek assistance from other students, and were successful in obtaining it. With regard to the language of instruction in these classrooms, lower-grade teachers used both Spanish and English, while upper-grade teachers used mostly English. Students were allowed to use either language, although the same trend was observed for limited-English-speaking students. With regard to the literacy development of non-English-speaking students, observations revealed:

1. Writing moved in a systematic progression from the native language in the early grades to writing in English in the later grades.
2. Writing in English emerged at or above the grade level of writing in Spanish.
3. The quality of writing in various forms was highly conventional, with few spelling or grammatical errors, along with systematic use of "invented" spelling. Limited-English-speaking students in these classrooms were making the transition from Spanish to English without any detrimental effects.

Interviews with classroom teachers, principals, and parents revealed an interesting set of perspectives regarding the education of the students in these schools. Classroom teachers (average teaching experience of 6.70 years—these "effective" teachers were all seasoned professionals) were highly committed to the educational success of their students; perceived themselves as instructional innovators utilizing "new" learning theories and instructional philosophies to guide their practice; continued to be involved in professional development activities, including participation in small-group support networks; had a strong, demonstrated commitment to student-home communication (several teachers were utilizing a weekly parent interaction format); and felt that they had the autonomy to create or change the instruction and curriculum in their classrooms, even if it did not meet with exact district guidelines. Significantly, these instructors "adopted" their students. They had high academic expectations for all their students ("everyone will learn to read in my classroom") and also served as advocates for their students. They rejected any suggestion that their students were intellectually or academically disadvantaged.

Principals (average administrative experience of 11.7 years) tended to be highly articulate regarding the curriculum and instructional strategies undertaken in their schools. They were also highly supportive of their instructional staff, taking pride in their accomplishments. They reported their support of teacher autonomy, although they were quite aware of the potential problems regarding the pressure to conform strictly to district policies concerning standardization of curriculum and the need for academic accountability (testing). Parents (average education level of 7.1 years) expressed a high level of satisfaction and appreciation with regard to their children's education experience in these schools. All indicated or implied that the academic success of these children was tied to their future economic success. Anglo and Hispanic parents were both quite involved in the formal parent support activities of the schools. However, Anglo parents' attitudes were much more in line with a "child advocacy" position, somewhat distrustful of the schools' specific interest in doing what was right for their child. Conversely, Mexican American parents expressed a high level of trust for the teaching and administrative staff.

This recent research addresses some significant practice questions regarding effective academic environments for Mexican American students:

1. *What role did native-language instruction play?* These "effective" schools considered native-language instruction key in the early grades (K–3).
2. *Was there one best curriculum?* No common curriculum was identified. However, a well-trained instructional staff implementing an integrated "student-centered" curriculum, with literacy pervasive in all aspects of instruction, was consistently observed across grade levels. Basals were utilized sparingly and usually as resource material.
3. *What instructional strategies were effective?* Consistently, teachers organized so as to ensure small collaborative academic activities requiring a high degree of heterogeneously grouped student-to-student social (and particularly linguistic) interaction. Individual instructional activity such as worksheets/workbooks was limited, as was individual competition as a classroom motivational ingredient.
4. *Who were the key players in this effective schooling drama?* School administrators and parents played important roles. However, teachers were the key players. They achieved the educational confidence of their peers and supervisors. They worked to organize instruction, create new instructional environments, assess effectiveness, and advocate for their students. They were proud of their students, academically reassuring but consistently demanding. They rejected any notion of academic, linguistic, cultural, or intellectual inferiority regarding their students (E. Garcia, 1991, p. 8).

Conclusion

The preceding discussions have attempted to highlight important data and theory that serve to provide an understanding of effective instruction for Mexican American students. These same data and theory have influenced the educational treatment of language-minority students. As indicated previously, the knowledge base of this area continues to expand, but is in no way to be considered complete or comprehensive. In addition, it would be an error to conclude that the data and theory that have emerged have been a primary factor in determining the educational treatment of language-minority students. However, it does seem appropriate to identify in the present discussion possible program, policy, and future research implications derived from research and theory, as highlighted by our own discussion and that of Hakuta and Snow (1986), August and Garcia (1988), Hakuta and Garcia (1989), and E. Garcia (1992).

A. One major goal of education in direct response to Mexican American students should be the development of the full repertoire of linguistic skills in English, in preparation for participation in mainstream classes. Future research should delineate alternative routes that will allow for effective achievement of this goal. Achieving such a goal should consider that time spent learning the native language is not time lost in developing English. Children can become fluent in a second language without losing the first language, and can maintain the first language without retarding the development of the second language. Presently, it is not clear what processes or mechanisms facilitate this positive transfer. Identifying such processes is a challenge awaiting future research.

B. Education programs for Mexican Americans should have the flexibility of adjusting to individual and cultural differences among children. Furthermore, educators should develop the expectation that it is not abnormal for some students to need instruction in two languages for relatively long periods of time. We do not yet know how much time in the native language positively influences academic outcomes in the second language. This type of research will greatly enhance our educational outcomes for language-minority students.

C. Educators should not have lower expectations of language- and ethnic-minority students. The clear distinction between specific expectations and academic achievement requires further academic-related research.

D. A major problem for Mexican American children is that young Anglo children share the negative stereotypes of their parents and the society at large. Any action that upgrades the status of all children and of their language contributes to the child's opportunities for friendship with other children. Future research with these children must link issues of ethnic identity, general self-concept, and specific academic self-concept.

In summary, theoretical (and to some extent, research) support can be identified for educational interventions that successfully serve Mexican American students. The present state of research and theory with respect to the education of these students does allow highly specific conclusions or prescriptive details. However, it is appropriate to recommend that educational professionals, in their quest to intervene for betterment of Mexican American students, carefully scrutinize relevant theory and research and utilize that analysis to design, implement, and evaluate interventions of significance to their particular educational circumstances.

References

Appleton, C. (1983). *Cultural pluralism in education: Theoretical foundations*. New York: Longman.

August, D., & Garcia, E. (1988). *Language minority education in the United States: Research, policy and practice*. Chicago: Charles C. Thomas.

Baden, B., & Maehr, M. (1986). Conforming culture with culture: A perspective for designing schools for children of diverse sociocultural backgrounds. In R. Feldman (Ed.), *The social psychology of education* (pp. 289–309). Cambridge, MA: Harvard University Press.

Banks, J. A. (1984). *Teaching strategies for ethnic studies* (3rd ed.). Boston: Allyn and Bacon.

Banks, J. A. (1988). *Multiethnic education: Theory and practice* (2nd ed.). Boston: Allyn and Bacon.

Banks, J. A. (1991). *Teaching strategies for ethnic studies* (5th ed.). Boston: Allyn and Bacon.

Berk, R. A. (Ed.). (1986). *Performance assessment: Methods and applications*. Baltimore, MD: Johns Hopkins University Press.

Bernstein, B. (1971). *Class, codes and control* (Vol. 1). London: Routledge & Kegan Paul.

Bloom, B. (1984). The search for methods of group instruction as effective as one-to-one tutoring. *Educational Leadership, 41*(8), 4–17.

Boykin, A. (1986). The triple quandary and the schooling of Afro-American children. In U. Neisser (Ed.), *The school achievement of minority children* (pp. 57–92). New York: New Perspectives.

Brown vs. Board of Education of Topeka, 347 US 483 (1954): 686.

California Commission on Teacher Credentialing. (1991). *Teacher credentialing in California: A special report*. Sacramento: Author.

Carter, T. P., & Chatfield, M. L. (1986). Effective bilingual schools: Implications for policy and practice. *American Journal of Education, 5*(1), 200–234.

Civil Rights Act of 1964. Public Law 88-352, as approved by the President on July 2, 1964. Chicago: Commerce Clearinghouse.

Colangelo, N., Foxley, C. H., & Dustin, D. (Eds.) (1982). *The human relations experience*. Monterey, CA: Brooks/Cole.

The College Board and the Western Interstate Commission for Higher Education. (1991). *The road to college: Educational progress by race and ethnicity*. New York: The College Board.

Committee for Economic Development. (1991). *The unfinished agenda: A new vision for child development and education*. New York: Author.

Coons, J. E., Clune, W., III, & Sugarman, S. D. (1970). *Private wealth and public education*. Cambridge, MA: Harvard University Press.

Cummins, J. (1979). Linguistic interdependence and the educational development of bilingual children. *Review of Educational Research, 19*, 222–251.

Cummins, J. (1986). Empowering minority students: A framework for intervention. *Harvard Educational Review, 56*(1), 18–36.

Delgado-Gaitan, C. (1992). School matters in the Mexican American home: Socializing children to education. *American Educational Research Journal, 29*(3), 495–513.

Diaz, S., Moll, L. C., & Mehan, H. (1986). Sociocultural resources in instruction: A context-specific approach. In *Beyond language: Social and cultural factors in schooling language minority students* (pp. 197–230). Sacramento: Bilingual Education Office, California State Department of Education.

Duran, R. (1986). *Improving Hispanics' educational outcomes: Learning and instruction*. Unpublished manuscript, Graduate School of Education, University of California, Santa Barbara.

Duran, R. (1987). Factors affecting development of second language literacy. In S. Goldman & H. Trueba (Eds.), *Becoming literate in English as a second language* (pp. 33–55). Norwood, NJ: Ablex.

Dwyer, C. (1991). *Language, culture and writing* (Working paper 13). Berkeley: Center for the Study of Writing, University of California.

Eder, D. (1982). Difference in communication styles across ability groups. In L. C. Wilkinson (Ed.), *Communicating in the classroom* (pp. 167–184). New York: Academic Press.

Elam, S. E. (1968). Acculturation and learning problems of Puerto Rican children. In F. Corrdasco & E. Bucchini (Eds.), *Puerto Rican children in mainland schools* (pp. 344–351). Metuchen, NJ: Scarecrow Press.

Equal Educational Opportunities and Transportation Act of 1974, 294(f).20 U.S.L.

Equal Educational Opportunity Act, 20 U.S.C. 1703(f).

Feldt, L. S., & Brennan, R. C. (1989). Reliability. In R. L. Linn (Ed.), *Educational measurement* (3rd ed., pp. 105–146). New York: Macmillan.

Fernandez, R., & Shu, G. (1988). School dropouts: New approaches to an enduring problem. *Education and Urban Society, 20,* 363–386.

Fiere, P. (1970). *Pedagogy of the oppressed.* New York: Seabury Press.

Fishman, J. (1989). *Language and ethnicity in minority sociolinguistic perspective.* Philadelphia: Multilingual Matters Ltd.

Frase, M. (1989). *Dropout rates in the United States: 1988* (Analysis report). Washington, DC: Superintendent of Documents, Government Printing Office.

Garcia, E. (1983). *Bilingualism in early childhood.* Albuquerque: University of New Mexico Press.

Garcia, E. (1988). *Effective schooling for language minority students.* Arlington, VA: National Clearinghouse for Bilingual Education.

Garcia, E. (1991). *The education of linguistically and culturally diverse students: Effective instructional practices.* Washington, DC: Center for Applied Linguistics.

Garcia, E. (1992). Effective instruction for language minority students: The teacher. *Journal of Education, 173*(2), 130–141.

Garcia, R. (1979). *Teaching in a pluralistic society.* New York: Harper & Row.

Gay, G. (1975). Organizing and designing culturally pluristic curriculum. *Educational Leadership, 33,* 176–183.

Giroux, H. A., & McLaren, P. (1986). Teacher education and the politics of engagement: The case for democratic schooling. *Harvard Educational Review, 56*(3), 213–238.

Goldman, S., & Trueba, H. (Eds.) (1987). *Becoming literate in English as a second language: Advances in research and theory.* Norwood, NJ: Ablex.

Gollnick, D. M., & Chinn, P. C. (1986). *Multicultural education in a pluristic society.* New York: Macmillan.

Gonzalez, G. (1990). *Chicano education in the segregation era: 1915–1945.* Philadelphia: The Balch Institute.

Goodman, Y. (1980). The roots of literacy. In M. P. Douglass (Ed.), *Reading: A humanizing experience* (pp. 286–301). Claremont, CA: Claremont Graduate School.

Grant, C. A. (Ed.). (1990). School desegregation [Special issue]. *Phi Delta Kappan, 72*(1).

Grant, G. W. (1977). *In praise of diversity: Multicultural classroom applications.* Omaha: University of Nebraska Press.

Hakuta, K., & Garcia, E. (1989). Bilingualism and bilingual education. *American Psychologist, 44*(2), 374–379.

Hakuta, K., & Snow, C. (1986, January). *The role of research in policy decisions about bilingual education* (Testimony). Washington, DC: U.S. House of Representatives Education and Labor Committee.

Hall, N. (1987). *The emergence of literacy.* Portsmouth, NH: Heinemann Educational Books.

Heath, S. B. (1981). Towards an ethnohistory of writing in American education. In M. Farr-Whitman (Ed.), *Writing: The nature, development and teaching of written communication: Vol. 1. Variation in writing: Functional and linguistic-cultural differences* (pp. 225–246). Hillsdale, NJ: Lawrence Erlbaum.

Heath, S. B. (1983). *Ways with words.* Cambridge, England: Cambridge University Press.

Heath, S. B. (1986). Sociocultural contexts of language development. In *Beyond language: Social and cultural factors in schooling language minority students* (pp. 143–186). Sacramento: Bilingual Education Office, California State Department of Education.

Kagan, S. (1983). Social orientation among Mexican American children: A challenge to traditional classroom structures. In E. Garcia (Ed.), *The Mexican American child* (pp. 163– 182). Tempe: Arizona State University.

Kaufman, P., & Frase, M. J. (1990). *Dropout rates in the United States: 1989.* Washington, DC: National Center for Education Statistics.

Kozol, J. (1991). *Savage inequalities: Children in America's schools.* New York: Crown.

Laosa, L. M. (1982). School, occupation, culture and family: The impact of parental schooling on the parent-child relationship. *Journal of Educational Psychology, 74*(6), 791–827.

Levin, H. M. (1986). *Educational reform for disadvantaged students: An emerging crisis.* Washington, DC: National Education Association.

Levin, I. (1988). *Accelerated schools for at-risk students* (CPRE Research Report Series RR-010). New Brunswick, NJ: Rutgers University Center for Policy Research in Education.

Lucas, T., Henze, R., & Donato, R. (1990). Promoting the success of Latino language minority students: An exploratory study of six high schools. *Harvard Educational Review, 60*(3), 315–334.

Matute-Bianchi, E. (1990). *A report to the Santa Clara County School District: Hispanics in the schools.* Santa Clara, CA: Santa Clara County School District.

McGahie, W. C. (1991). Professional competence evaluation. *Educational Researcher, 20*(1), 3–9.

Mead, M. (1937). *Cooperation and competition among primitive people.* New York: McGraw Hill.

Moll, L. (1988). Educating Latino students. *Language Arts, 64*(10), 315–324.

National Center for Educational Statistics (1991). *The condition of education, 1991: Vol. 1. Elementary and secondary education.* Washington, DC: Government Printing Office.

National Commission on Children. (1991). *Beyond rhetoric. A new American agenda for children and families: Final report of the national commission on children.* Washington, DC: Author.

Oakes, J. (1990). *Multiplying inequalities: The effects of race, social class, and tracking on opportunities to learn mathematics and science.* Santa Monica, CA: Rand Corp.

Oakes, J. (1991). *Lost talent: The underparticipation of women, minorities, and disabled persons in science.* Santa Monica, CA: Rand Corp.

Ogbu, J. (1982). Socialization: A cultural ecological approach. In K. M. Borman (Ed.), *The social life of children in a changing society* (pp. 253–267). Hillsdale, NJ: Lawrence Earlbaum Associates.

Ogbu, J. (1986). The consequences of the American caste system. In U. Neisser (Ed.), *The school achievement of minority children: New perspectives* (pp. 19–56). Hillsdale, NJ: Lawrence Erlbaum.

Ogbu, J. (1992). Understanding cultural diversity and learning. *Educational Researcher, 21*(8), 5–14.

Ogbu, J., & Matute-Bianchi, M. E. (1986). Understanding sociocultural factors: Knowledge, identity and school adjustment. In *Beyond language: Social and cultural factors in schooling language minority students* (pp. 73–142). Sacramento: Bilingual Education Office, California State Department of Education.

Olsen, L. (1988). *Crossing the schoolhouse border: Immigrant students and the California public schools.* San Francisco: California Tomorrow Policy Research.

Pearl, A. (1991). Democratic education: Myth or reality. In R. Valencia (Ed.), *Chicano school failure and success* (pp. 101–118). New York: Falmer Press.

Pease-Alvarez, L., Garcia, E., & Espinoza, P. (1991). Effective instruction for language-minority students: An early childhood case study. *Early Childhood Research Quarterly, 6,* 347–361.

Perry, J. (1975). Notes toward a multi-cultural curriculum. *English Journal, 64,* 8–9.

Ramírez, M., III, & Castañeda, A. (1974). *Cultural democracy, bi-cognitive development and education.* New York: Academic Press.

Rodriguez, C. E. (1989). *Puerto Ricans born in the U.S.A.* Winchester, MA: Unwin Hyman, Inc.

Rose, M. (1989). *Lives on the boundary.* New York: The Free Press.

Rosenshine, B. (1986). Synthesis of research on explicit teaching. *Educational Leadership, 43,* 60–69.

Scribner, S., & Cole, M. (1981). *The psychology of literacy.* Cambridge, MA: Harvard University Press.

Shimberg, B. (1983). What is competence? How can it be assessed? In M. R. Stern (Ed.), *Power and conflict in continuing professional education* (pp. 17–37). Belmont, CA: Wadsworth.

Skinner, B. F. (1957). *Verbal behavior.* Englewood Cliffs, NJ: Prentice-Hall.

Slavin, R. E. (1989). The PET and the pendulum. Fadism in education and how to stop it. *Phi Delta Kappan, 70*(10), 752–759.

Slavin, R. Karweit, N., & Madden, N. (1989). *Effective programs for students at risk.* Boston: Allyn and Bacon.

Sleeter, C. E., & Grant, C. A. (1987). An analysis of multicultural education in the United States. *Harvard Educational Review, 57*(4), 421–444.

Smith, F. (1971). *Understanding reading.* New York: Holt, Rinehart and Winston.

Spender, D. (1988). Transitional bilingual education and the socialization of immigrants. *Harvard Educational Review, 58*(2), 133–153.

Sternberg, R. J., & Wagner, R. K. (Eds.). (1986). *Practical intelligence.* New York: Cambridge University Press.

Sue, S., & Okazaki, S. (1990). Asian-American educational achievements: A phenomenon in search of an explanation. *American Psychologist, 45*(8), 913–920.

Sue, S., & Padilla, A. (1986). Ethnic minority issues in the United States: Challenges for the educational system. In *Beyond language: Social and cultural factors in schooling language minority students* (pp. 35–72). Sacramento: Bilingual Education Office, California State Department of Education.

Tharp, R. G. (1989). Psychocultural variables and k constants: Effects on teaching and learning in schools. *American Psychologist, 44,* 349–359.

Tharp, R. G., & Gallimore, R. (1989). *Challenging cultural minds.* London: Cambridge University Press.

Thomas, S. V., & Park, B. (1921). *Culture of immigrants.* Cambridge, MA: Newcome Press.

Tikunoff, W. J. (1983). *Compatibility of the SBIF features with other research on instruction of LEP students.* San Francisco: Far West Laboratory (SBIF-83-4.8/10).

Trueba, H. (1987). *Success or failure? Learning and the language minority student.* New York: Harper & Row.

Trueba, H. (1988). *Rethinking learning diabilities: Cultural knowledge in literacy acquisition.* Unpublished manuscript, Office for Research on Educational Equity, Graduate School of Education, University of California, Santa Barbara.

Villegas, A. M. (1991). *Culturally responsive pedagogy for the 1990's and beyond.* Princeton, NJ: Educational Testing Service.

Vogt, L., Jordan, C., & Tharp, R. (1987). Explaining school failure, producing school success: Two cases. *Anthropology and Education Quarterly, 18*(4), 276–286.

Walberg, H. (1986). Synthesis of research on teaching. In M. Wittrock (Ed.), *Handbook of research on teaching* (3rd ed., pp. 15–32). New York: Macmillan.

Walker, C. L. (1987). Hispanic achievements: Old views and new perspectives. In H. Trueba (Ed.), *Success or failure? Learning and the language minority student* (pp. 15–32). Cambridge, MA: Newbury House.

Walsh, R. (1990, October 12). Minority students in Santa Clara county continue to deteriorate academically. *San Francisco Examiner,* pp. B1–4.

Weis, L. (1988). *Class, race and gender in American education.* Albany: State University of New York Press.

Wertsch, J. V. (1985). *Vygotsky and the social formation of mind.* Cambridge, MA: Harvard University Press.

Wiesner, T. S., Gallimore, R., & Jordan, C. (1988). Unpackaging cultural effects on classroom learning: Native Hawaiian peer assistance and child-generated activity. *Anthropology and Education Quarterly, 19*(4), 327–353.

Wilson, W. J. (1987). *The truly disadvantaged: The inner city, the underclass, and public policy.* Chicago: University of Chicago Press.

22

A HISTORY OF THE EDUCATION OF PUERTO RICAN STUDENTS IN U.S. MAINLAND SCHOOLS: "LOSERS," "OUTSIDERS," OR "LEADERS"?

Sonia Nieto

UNIVERSITY OF MASSACHUSETTS, AMHERST

Puerto Ricans have achieved the dubious distinction of being one of the most undereducated ethnic groups in the United States. How this has come to pass is a long story, infused with controversy concerning political status, conflicts over the role of culture and language in school and society, the experience of racism and discrimination, and fierce community determination to define and defend itself. This chapter is an attempt to document that history and provide some insights into what can be learned from it.

According to the U.S. Census Bureau, Puerto Ricans living in the United States numbered 2,651,815 in 1990, about 15% of the total Latino population and the second largest Latino ethnic group in the nation (Institute for Puerto Rican Policy, 1992). This number represents approximately two fifths of the Puerto Rican people, arguably one of the most dramatic diasporas of any people in the world. Yet whether they reside in Puerto Rico or in the United States itself, Puerto Ricans have been "born in the U.S.A." since 1898, because they have been subject to U.S. policies as a result of a change of sovereignty from one colonial power to another (Rodriguez, 1991).

Because of this colonial relationship, Puerto Ricans even in Puerto Rico have been in U.S.-controlled schools since 1898, shortly after the Spanish-American War, when the island was taken over by the United States. The U.S. Congress mandated that Puerto Rican children learn English and the "American way of life" as soon as the island was ceded by Spain in 1898 (Negrón, 1971; Cafferty & Rivera-Mártinez, 1981). Additionally, U.S. ideals have been instilled through language policies and U.S. textbooks, materials, and methods, as well as through teacher preparation and the celebration of national U.S. holidays, including, ironically, U.S. independence (Walsh, 1991).

Puerto Ricans who have lived in the continental United States have been even more directly affected by U.S. educational policies than those living in Puerto Rico. Current educational data tell a tale of unfulfilled dreams and unrealized expectations not very different from the conditions of 50 or 60 years ago. In spite of the fact that the 1980s were heralded as "The Decade of the Hispanic," few educational gains were made during these years among Latinos, and fewer still among Puerto Ricans.

PURPOSE AND ORGANIZATION

The subject of numerous studies and research reports carried out since the 1930s, Puerto Ricans in U.S. schools have been portrayed as "problems," "losers," "dropouts," "culturally deprived," "disadvantaged," or "at risk," among other labels (see, e.g., Association of Assistant Superintendents, 1948; Margolis, 1968; Lewis, 1965; Gallardo, 1970). The purpose of this chapter is to document the difficult history of Puerto Rican students in U.S. schools in order to understand the impact of this experience, to analyze how and why it has occurred, and to explore some directions for a more promising future. First, three persistent dilemmas related to the topic will be addressed: the issue of appropriate ethnic labels; the inconsistency of data available about Puerto Ricans; and the drop-out crisis, the major educational dilemma facing the Puerto Rican community.

A brief history of Puerto Ricans in the United States, focusing on the migration experience as it has influenced education, will be presented. Following will be a brief discussion of a number of recurring themes in the education of Puerto Ricans in the United States. After this, through selected studies and reports beginning in the 1930s and extending into the present, the education of Puerto Ricans and the panoply of labels accompanying this experience will be reviewed. The chapter will end with a discussion of lessons to be learned from the struggle of Puerto Ricans for equal and quality education.

PERSISTENT DILEMMAS

The Meaning of Ethnic Labels

A perpetual problem facing researchers and policy makers interested in the education of Puerto Ricans has been that of definition. First, there is the question of which overarching term is most appropriate for persons of Spanish-speaking origin. Over the years, terms have included *Spanish origin*, *Hispanic*, *Latin American*, and *Latino(a)*. Recently the debate has focused on whether *Hispanic* or *Latino(a)* is the most relevant term. As Murguia suggests, "Struggles over ethnic labels are not meaningless. Fundamentally, they are ideological in nature, attempts to define a group and to direct its future" (Murguia, 1991, p. 8). He suggests that, unlike *Hispanic*, *Latino* has a connotation of cultural inclusiveness and maintenance that takes into account the African and indigenous roots of this group.

A more basic problem has been how to discern the very real differences among Latino groups. While the terms *Latino(a)* or *Hispanic* may be useful in describing the deep connections among all those in the Americas who are descendants of the indigenous inhabitants, Spanish and other European colonizers, and enslaved Africans, or any combination of these, they become less useful in recognizing historic, regional, linguistic, racial, social-class, and other important differences (Marín & Marín, 1983). The tendency in the literature to lump all groups together has thus resulted in an obfuscation of crucial differences that can help explain such issues as poverty, language dominance, political orientation, and school success or failure.

As a subgroup within the Latino population, Puerto Ricans generally fare the worst of all Latino groups in educational outcomes (Orum, 1986; Carrasquillo, 1991; Meier & Stewart, 1991; Institute for Puerto Rican Policy, 1992; Latino Commission on Educational Reform, 1992). Pertinent data are often hard to come by, however, because Puerto Ricans are usually categorized within the larger framework of *Hispanic* or *Latino(a)*, rather than by their specific national origin, as most Latinos prefer. For example, a recent report has determined that Latinos are the only ethnic group that experienced no improvement whatsoever in socioeconomic status between 1980 and 1990, and that more than a third of all Latino children compared to just one eighth of White children live in poverty (Perez, 1991). Although useful, this information fails to reveal that *Puerto Rican* children specifically have by far the greatest risk of being poor of any racial or ethnic group, with 58% living in poverty (NCLR, 1993; ASPIRA Institute for Policy Research, 1993). Thus, because data concerning specific ethnic groups within the larger Latino category are generally unavailable, the severe situation of Puerto Ricans is further obscured.

Nevertheless, general data provide a glimpse into the deplorable educational conditions faced by all Latinos, and therefore can be helpful in suggesting the particularly unsatisfactory situation confronted by Puerto Ricans. Orfield has found, for instance, that despite differences in education levels, income, and political power of students from different Latino backgrounds, all face increasing levels of school segregation in all parts of the country (Orfield, 1986). Equally troubling, less money is spent on Latino students in the United States than on other students in general. Large urban school districts, which are 27% Latino, tend to be chronically underfunded. Such districts spent an average of $5,200 per pupil in 1991, compared with $6,073 for suburban schools (ASPIRA, 1993). Although academic achievement levels among Latinos have improved since the 1970s, they continue to lag behind national averages. For instance, only 37.7% of Latinos are enrolled in algebra or accelerated math classes, while they are twice as likely as Whites to be enrolled in remedial math classes (ASPIRA, 1993). In addition, the percentage of Latino teachers and other professionals is exceptionally low: Although Latinos constituted 11.3% of all elementary school students and 10.4% of all high school students in 1990, only 3% of teachers were Latinos (ASPIRA, 1993).

There is a need to disaggregate the data on Latinos by ethnicity, but this is more easily said than done. In this chapter, data specific to Puerto Ricans will be used whenever possible. However, because Puerto Ricans are often studied only in conjunction with other Latino groups, this is not always an option. In addition, it is sometimes helpful to consider research that focuses on other Latinos in order to explore specific strategies, programs, or philosophical orientations that have been successful with them. Therefore, in cases where such research might be useful for the purposes of this chapter, it will be included.

Lack of Consistent Data

Another problem of definition has been the seeming contradiction between few data being available and enough research having been conducted to document the educational crisis faced by Puerto Ricans. These differing perceptions can be understood by looking at the kinds of data available and determining how they have been used. A 1976 national report by the U.S. Commission on Civil Rights, for instance, concluded that, in spite of the fact that Puerto Ricans "have been studied to death," the research had been performed largely by social scientists, not policy makers, and government agencies had failed to document socioeconomic data adequately. At the same time, the commission found that the study of so-called "problem groups" such as Puerto Ricans and African Americans amounted almost to "an industry within the social sciences," and concluded: "There is no need for further study to prove that Puerto Rican problems merit special attention, even though the full extent of their problems are inadequately documented. Lack of data is no longer a valid excuse for government inaction" (U.S. Commission on Civil Rights, 1976, p. 1).

The complaint that enough is already known is not new; in 1968 a study commissioned by ASPIRA stated that "The many Puerto Rican parents who complain that their children 'are not being taught to read or do their arithmetic' are usually right. No new study is required to confirm their anxieties" (Margolis, 1968, p. 1). The same study documented that by 1968, Frank Cordasco, an educator with a deep interest in the Puerto Rican community, had compiled an impressive bibliography of 450 articles and studies devoted to the issue of Puerto Rican children in U.S. schools. Because most studies have focused on deficiencies, the literature on the Puerto Rican experience in education has been characterized by a lack of a vision for building effective strategies and models for instruction. The problem, therefore, has not necessarily been lack of data, but lack of action and will to remedy the many educational problems faced by Puerto Ricans. As this chapter will document, major reports over the past 50 years have defined problems and made recommendations to solve them in remarkably similar ways, but these recommendations have been largely overlooked.

The Drop-out Crisis

Dropping out of high school has been a constant and recurring dilemma in the educational experience of Puerto Ricans documented since the 1960s, although it probably existed even before then. The data are not firm, but anecdotal and other sources suggest that the drop-out dilemma has been evident since Puerto Rican students began attending U.S. schools. For example, as early as 1920 it was suggested that a major cause of Puerto Rican students' poor academic performance was their inability to understand the language of instruction (Cafferty & Rivera-Martínez, 1981). No doubt contributing to the early drop-out crisis were practices such as placing students behind their peers or in "special" classes (such as those for the mentally retarded or slow learners) because they were Spanish speaking (Sánchez Korrol, 1983).

In one of the first reports on the educational status of Puerto Ricans commissioned by ASPIRA, the drop-out crisis was identified and, although the data were described as "murky" and accurate statistics could not be provided, the author concluded: "The public schools are like a giant sieve, sifting out all but the strongest, the smartest, or the luckiest" (Margolis, 1968, p. 3). Ironically, the identical metaphor was used almost twenty years later in a publication of the National Council of La Raza (NCLR):

The American educational system is often portrayed as a pipeline, successfully transporting individuals from childhood to college or full participation in the world of work. However, it is becoming increasingly clear that this pipeline more closely resembles a sieve where Hispanic children are concerned. (Orum, 1986, p. i)

Low high school completion has been dismally similar over the years wherever Puerto Ricans go to school, with drop-out rates of 71% reported in Chicago (U.S. Commission on Civil Rights, 1976; Kyle & Kantowicz, 1991); 70% in Philadelphia and 90% in Boston (Cafferty & Rivera-Martínez, 1981); 80% in New York City (Calitri, 1983); and 72% in Holyoke, Massachusetts (Frau-Ramos & Nieto, 1993).

Dropping out of high school remains one of the most severe problems affecting Latinos. Depending upon measures used, data differ widely concerning the drop-out crisis, but the fact remains that Latinos in general, and Puerto Ricans in particular,

are regarded as having the highest drop-out rate of any group. The NCLR has reported that one half of all Puerto Rican students in U.S. schools do not graduate (NCLR, 1989). Although the situation improved slightly during the late 1970s and mid-1980s, by the 1990s more Latinos were dropping out than ever: In 1991, 35.3% of Latinos were high school dropouts, compared to 34.3% in 1972 (ASPIRA, 1993).

Another report (Hispanic Policy Development Project, 1990) found that 40% of all Latinos aged 25 to 34 had not completed four years of high school, and an additional 25% had graduated without the skills that would help them in the workplace. The report concluded: "Being undereducated is undoubtedly the single biggest obstacle to the overall economic assimilation of Hispanics" (p. 12). As documented by the NCLR, Latinos not only have higher drop-out rates but also tend to leave school earlier than any major population group (NCLR, 1990). By the age of 17, almost 20% of Latinos leave school without a diploma and, among those aged 19 and over, 43% are out of school and without a high school diploma. National data also reveal that after American Indians, Latinos are more likely to be held back for two or more grades than any other racial/ethnic group, and this places them at a higher risk for dropping out (NCLR, 1990).

The Inadequacy of Traditional Explanations. Tackling the vexing problem of dropouts has been on the Puerto Rican agenda for decades. A number of reasons, explanations, and theories concerning the drop-out crisis have been formulated over the years. The NCLR, for example, has described a combination of factors that place many Latinos in a "high risk" category for dropping out. Single-parent family status plus low family income, and low parental education plus limited English proficiency, are reported as two significant combinations. Among Puerto Ricans, 40.8% are more likely to have two or more of these "risk factors" than are other Latinos. In addition, single-parent family status has also been identified as a major risk factor affecting Latino students, and percentages of Puerto Rican children living in single-parent households (33%) and headed by females (29%) are greater than that of any Latino group (NCLR, 1990).

Although data such as these are interesting and the resulting theories may help explain some of the drop-out phenomenon, it should be noted that many Latino students from single-parent households and with other so-called "risk factors" are nevertheless successful in school. Relying simply on family structural issues for explanations of school failure is inadequate in accounting for the complex issues involved. School policies and practices, therefore, began to be viewed more critically in much of the research carried out in the 1980s.

Traditional research on school failure had focused almost exclusively on three areas: student characteristics (social class, race and ethnicity, family structure, native language), school policies related to student behavior (discipline problems, suspension, and absenteeism), and poor academic performance (poor grades and retention). By the mid-1980s this kind of analysis was being called into question for failing to look more deeply into the role played by schools in actually promoting failure (Wehlage & Rutter, 1986; Fine, 1991).

A More Comprehensive View of High School Dropouts. Looking beyond family, personal, and socioeconomic characteristics to a more wholistic explanation of school failure, recent research has suggested that school policies and practices themselves negatively influence Latino students' academic performance, behavior, and decisions to stay in or leave school. For instance, Fernández and Shu (1988) found that Latinos had higher drop-out rates than their non-Latino peers *even* when they did not fall into the "risk" categories. That is, they had higher drop-out rates even if their grades were higher than those of other students; they were in academic rather than general tracks; they were not from poor families; they did not have parents with less schooling; or they did not have problems with their teachers. The only possible clue the researchers uncovered was that many Latinos expressed more negative feelings about their schools than did other students (thus confirming the issue of marginality, to be discussed later).

Another recent theory posits that certain conditions in schools encourage success or failure, thereby constituting a set of circumstances termed the *holding power* of schools (Wehlage & Rutter, 1986). That is, a combination of factors, including student characteristics and school conditions, is responsible for academic success or failure. Much of the research that began in the mid-to-late 1960s focused on such factors as grade retention, overage status of students, placement practices, and confrontation of students with school authorities (Hispanic Policy Development Project, 1990; NCLR, 1990; Vélez, 1989; Fernández & Vélez, 1990). This comprehensive perspective may prove to be more helpful than earlier theories in suggesting strategies to resolve the drop-out crisis among Puerto Ricans.

PUERTO RICANS IN THE UNITED STATES: A BRIEF HISTORY

It is impossible to understand the Puerto Rican experience in the United States, including the persistence of the drop-out crisis, without first understanding the reasons that brought Puerto Ricans here in the first place. As U.S. citizens since 1917 (albeit an imposed citizenship that was neither asked for nor particularly desired), Puerto Ricans can travel freely to and from the United States, and have come in large numbers since the beginning of the century to seek better economic opportunities for their families (Chenault, 1938/1970; History Task Force, 1979, 1982; Colón, 1961/1982; Sánchez Korrol, 1983; Iglesias, 1984; Fitzpatrick, 1971, 1987; Rodriguez, 1991; Acosta-Belén & Sánchez Korrol, 1993). Virtually no Puerto Rican has remained untouched by this experience; at least one third of the population has at one time or another lived in the continental United States, most for periods of fewer than 10 years (Cafferty & Rivera-Martínez, 1981).

The migration of Puerto Ricans to the United States has been a unique experience for several reasons (History Task Force, 1982). First, Puerto Ricans represent the first group of newcomers to arrive as citizens; there has been no need for them to focus inordinate attention on the process of becoming citizens or severing ties with the home country, as is customary with other immigrants. Thus the term *migration* rather than *immigration* is the one most often used to describe this movement.

Second, Puerto Rican migration was the first "jet-age" movement to the United States. Travel to and from the island became relatively easy and inexpensive with the growing accessibility of air travel beginning in the 1940s, the period that has been called "the Great Migration" (Sánchez Korrol, 1983). Third, the major Puerto Rican migration occurred at a time when a strong back was less important than technical or professional skills, and this has had a detrimental effect on the economic advancement of the entire group (Fitzpatrick, 1971, 1987). That is, the low-skill jobs generally available to earlier immigrants have been largely eliminated in the past several decades and, consequently, a high school diploma is a minimum requirement for most jobs in the current economy.

Finally, the migration has been characterized by a back-and-forth movement and thus has been dubbed "the revolving door," a "circulatory migration" (Bonilla & Campos, 1981), or "a process of Puerto Rican commuting" (Fitzpatrick, 1971). This particular kind of migration has even made its way into contemporary Puerto Rican fiction: In a short story entitled "The Flying Bus," Luis Rafael Sánchez, a Puerto Rican novelist, describes one of the passengers as "a well-poised woman ... [who] informs us that she flies over *the pond* every month and that she has forgotten on which bank of it she really lives" (Sánchez, 1987, p. 19; emphasis in original).

Result of Circulatory Migration

There have been two major results of this circulatory migration, both of which have left their mark on the educational experiences of Puerto Ricans in the United States. First, it has provided a cultural and linguistic continuity not afforded previous or even some recent immigrants, and this has been manifested by a practical need for use of the Spanish language and familiar cultural patterns. Puerto Ricans have in general continued to identify with their culture and language more than was the case with former European immigrants. In fact, Latinos in general have resisted to a great extent the pressures of the assimilationist ideology that characterized the experiences of European immigrants.

Examples of cultural maintenance among Puerto Ricans abound. For instance, the first major study of bilingualism among Puerto Ricans, based on a series of interviews with leaders in the community, revealed that they placed great importance on maintaining and speaking Spanish and identifying as Puerto Ricans (Fishman, Cooper, & Ma, 1971). Furthermore, in 1981 it was reported that over 70% of Puerto Rican migrants in New York were faithful listeners of Spanish-language radio stations (Cafferty & Rivera-Martínez, 1981). A more recent study, based on interviews with 100 families, revealed that not one person in any of the families identified as exclusively "American," but rather they all continued to identify as either "Puerto Rican" or "Puerto Rican American" (Colleran, Gurick, & Kurtz, 1984). Studies focusing on bilingualism among Puerto Ricans in New York City have generally concluded that there is tremendous allegiance to maintaining the Spanish language as a marker of identity (Durán, 1983).

The second effect of the circulatory migration for Puerto Ricans has been to redefine immigration from "a single life-transforming" experience to "a way of life" (National Puerto Rican Task Force, 1982). While for the majority of Europeans immigration was a new beginning, albeit an often painful one, for many Puerto Ricans migration has tended to be a series of periodic movements to and from the island. The situation has been disruptive, to be sure, but it has also reframed the migration experience as a normal part of life in which cultural patterns are renewed, transformed, and recreated, and it has redefined Puerto Ricans not as traditional immigrants but as "a community in movement" in "a process of commuting" (Fitzpatrick, 1971). Consequently, what Puerto Ricans as a group have expected of U.S. schools has not necessarily been assimilation, but rather accommodation to, and even protection and maintenance of, their language and culture.

To understand the disruption caused by migration, one need only look at the immensity of the exodus from the island. By 1957, 550,000, or fully a quarter of the Puerto Rican people, lived in the United States (Rand, 1958). In 1992, two fifths of all Puerto Ricans, or over 2,600,000, lived at least some portion of their lives in the United States (Institute for Puerto Rican Policy, 1992). Under any definition, this represents a dramatic unsettling of the population and cannot help but influence such issues as educational achievement, employment, and health.

Causes of Migration of Puerto Ricans to the United States

Puerto Ricans are not new migrants, but have lived in the continental United States for well over a century. By 1830 there was a Sociedad Benéfica Cubana y Puertorriqueña (translated at the time as the Spanish Benevolent Society) comprised primarily of Puerto Rican and Cuban merchants in New York City, largely the result of trade among Cuba, Puerto Rico, and the mid-Atlantic states (Sánchez Korrol, 1983). Political activists, especially those supporting independence for Cuba and Puerto Rico and dedicated to an Antillean federation, found their way to New York City by the 1860s, where they published newspapers and started political and civic organizations. By the early 1900s both skilled craftspeople and unskilled workers, particularly in the tobacco industry, had migrated to Florida and New York. In 1910 there were over a thousand Puerto Ricans living in 39 states and Hawaii, and by 1920 Puerto Ricans could be found in 45 states (Puerto Rican Forum, 1970; Sánchez Korrol, 1983).

The major reason for the migration was not simple overpopulation, as has frequently been advanced (Fitzpatrick, 1971), but the effect of dramatic structural economic changes that virtually destroyed traditional patterns of individual land ownership and consolidated the domination of large corporations from the United States (Sánchez Korrol, 1983; Rodriguez, 1991). These changes have persisted. At present a full 70% of Puerto Rican industries are owned by U.S. corporations, making Puerto Rico a dependent stepchild of the U.S. economy (Hidalgo, 1992). Structural changes such as these have resulted in an increase in unemployment and the growth of a marginal work force. Thus the possibility of job opportunities, not overpopulation, is the

single most important factor encouraging migration to the continental United States.

Puerto Rican migration to the United States has been described as a "push-pull" phenomenon, with the U.S. economy acting as both a "pull" and a "push" factor. In a 1950 study it was documented that from 1908 on, the ups and downs of the U.S. economy and the waves of migration from Puerto Rico were highly correlated (Mills, Senior, & Goldsen, 1950). While structural changes in the Puerto Rican economy represent an important "push" factor, the direct recruitment of Puerto Rican workers beginning early in the 20th century provides an example of a "pull" factor. Such early recruitment efforts took Puerto Ricans as far as Hawaii where, in 1903, 539 children were enrolled in Hawaiian schools (History Task Force, 1982).

The contract farm worker program that began in 1940 was another important source of migrants, bringing in an average of 20,000 workers every year to harvest crops in such diverse states as Michigan, Connecticut, New Jersey, and Massachusetts. These arrangements continued into the 1970s in formal contracts, and informally into the present. Many Puerto Rican communities in the United States began as a result of former agricultural workers remaining and bringing other family members to join them (Fitzpatrick, 1971, 1987).

New York City, a "Home Away From Home," and Other Destinations

At the beginning of the 20th century only 37% of Puerto Ricans living in the United States were concentrated in New York City, but by 1940 fully 85% were residing there (Sánchez Korrol, 1983), making it the preeminent "home away from home" for most Puerto Ricans. One of the earliest studies of the Puerto Rican community (Chenault, 1938/1970) found that in 1930, half of all Puerto Ricans in the United States were living in East Harlem (soon to be known as El Barrio, or Spanish Harlem), but, as the author correctly predicted, the past migration "constituted only a small beginning of the migration which will soon take place" (p. 4). In fact, he described Spanish Harlem in 1935 almost as one might describe it and many other Puerto Rican communities in the years to come:

The community has, to a large degree, taken on the color and customs of the Spanish-speaking countries. In certain sections Spanish is generally spoken. Some of the stores have no signs in English at all, and seem to depend entirely upon Spanish-speaking customers.... The entire settlement seems to take on an increased activity at night. There are many people on the streets, Spanish music can be heard from the music and radio shops, dances are in progress, and the bars and restaurants are prosperous. (pp. 129–130)

During this early period, many of the migrants were agricultural workers, domestics, or needleworkers, while others were factory workers, many of whom worked in one of the two largest employers of Puerto Ricans, a large biscuit company and a pencil factory (Chenault, 1938/1970). By 1948 some 200,000 Puerto Ricans lived in New York City.

The Puerto Rican community in New York was a vibrant and active one even in the early years, when the first wave of migrants, known as "the pioneers," made their pilgrimage to the United States. As early as 1923 the *Hermandad Puertorriqueña*, a community organization with a focus on mutual assistance, was created, and in the 1930s the Puerto Rican Merchants Association, representing over 500 small businesses, mostly *bodegas* (small, family-owned grocery stores with Caribbean products), was founded (Sánchez Korrol, 1983).

Although the Puerto Rican community was largely concentrated in New York City between 1940 and 1960, it later dispersed throughout the Northeast. Migration to New York City increased 206% between 1940 and 1950, but in other states it increased an astounding 443%. By 1955 it was estimated that there were as many as 175,000 Puerto Ricans in cities outside of New York, with another half million in New York City itself (Padilla, 1958). For example, in Philadelphia the Puerto Rican population doubled to over 14,000 between 1950 and 1960 (Koss, 1965). This pattern has held true in the past several decades. By 1970 there were about 260,000 Puerto Ricans living outside New York City and another 600,000 in the city (Puerto Rican Forum, 1970). In 1990 over 60% of all Puerto Ricans in the United States resided outside of New York State (Institute for Puerto Rican Policy, 1992).

The number of Puerto Ricans living in the United States has increased steadily throughout the century. Although the return migration has sometimes surpassed the numbers coming into the United States, a study of the migration from 1982 to 1988 found that the annual migration resulted in a net gain during each of those years (Mélendez, 1991). By 1981 there were 1.8 million Puerto Ricans living in the United States (Cafferty & Rivera-Martínez, 1981); this number had increased to 2,651,815 by 1990 (Institute for Puerto Rican Policy, 1992).

The Relationship Between Migration and Education

This brief review of migration has highlighted several issues that are relevant when considering the history of the education of Puerto Ricans in the United States. First, the migration of Puerto Ricans cannot be neatly placed within the traditional framework of the immigration of other newcomers. Second, the colonial relationship of Puerto Rico to the United States should not be overlooked in analyzing either the presence of Puerto Ricans or their history of underachievement in U.S. schools. Third, although many Puerto Ricans have dreams of returning to the island—indeed, migration and return migration are parallel processes—the truth is that Puerto Ricans as a community are in the United States to stay. The following section will describe a number of recurring themes evident in the history of the education of Puerto Ricans in the United States, which is inextricably linked to the migration.

RECURRING THEMES IN THE EDUCATION OF PUERTO RICAN STUDENTS

Interwoven throughout the history of the education of Puerto Ricans in the United States are a number of related themes that have appeared and reappeared over the past 60 years. Winding their way through this complex story, some of these themes have at times receded into the background and at other times become prominent motifs that help explain the educational experience of Puerto Rican students in U.S. schools. They have remained consistent benchmarks in signaling the centrality of education for the Puerto Rican community.

These themes should not be understood as isolated phenomena, but rather as interconnected issues that sometimes overlap while helping to place the experience in a context that makes sense. Three themes that emerge throughout the history of the education of Puerto Ricans in the United States are the legacy of colonialism; the role of racism, ethnocentrism, and linguicism; and the struggle for self-determination. Each will be briefly described below and will become evident throughout the remainder of this chapter.

The Legacy of Colonialism

The preceding discussion concerning migration makes it abundantly clear that colonialism has always played an important role in the Puerto Rican experience. Puerto Rico and the United States are connected through colonial ties, and this gives the migration a unique character. According to Rodriguez, the fact that Puerto Rico and the United States were joined as a result of "an act of conquest" is often overlooked or minimized in the literature, with Puerto Ricans too generally perceived as simply one of the latest "newcomers" in the traditional conception of the immigration experience (Rodriguez, 1991). Early writers were especially fond of focusing on the "overpopulation problem" as an overriding reason for the migration (Chenault, 1938/1970; Mills et al., 1950; Fitzpatrick, 1971), conveniently avoiding U.S. imperialism and the structural changes it brought about in the Puerto Rican economy as contributing factors. Later work by Sánchez Korrol (1983), Rodriguez (1991), Campos and Bonilla (1976), Mélendez (1991), and even Fitzpatrick's own later work (1987) challenge this analysis as overly simplistic.

The Colonial Impact in Puerto Rico. In Puerto Rico itself, policies and practices in schools and other educational institutions geared toward assimilating the population to U.S. values and ideals have had an enormous impact (Negrón, 1971). English is a required subject in all Puerto Rican public schools, beginning in the very earliest grades. More significantly, Puerto Rican youngsters are barraged with U.S. cultural images not only in schools, but also through the media and marketing. They are thus presented with cultural icons from two different contexts, leading inevitably to cultural confusion and dislocation. For example, children in Puerto Rico learn both the American national anthem and the Puerto Rican anthem; they celebrate the birthdays of U.S. heroes and Puerto Rican heroes; and they hear both salsa (Caribbean music) and rap on the radio. This also results in Puerto Rican youngsters' being more familiar and comfortable with mainstream U.S. culture than is true of other immigrant groups.

Although Puerto Rican resistance to assimilation and cultural homogeneity has been sporadic, contradictory, and uneven, challenging the role of schools has been a characteristic of the Puerto Rican educational experience throughout its history.

The Colonial Impact in the United States. Given its status as a stepchild of larger colonial powers, first Spain and later the United States, Puerto Rico has been at the mercy of policies and practices over which it has had little control. This powerlessness has left its mark on the Puerto Rican community. Ogbu's theory concerning the difference between *voluntary* and *involuntary* minorities is helpful in understanding this phenomenon (Ogbu, 1987). According to this theory, it is important to look not only at a group's cultural background but also at its situation in the host society and its perceptions of opportunities available in that society. Thus the major problem in U.S. Puerto Ricans' academic performance is not that they possess a different language, culture, or cognitive or communication style, but the nature of the history, subjugation, and exploitation they have experienced, together with their own responses to their treatment.

Research with newly arrived Puerto Ricans seems to confirm this theory. It has been found that these students tend to be more successful academically and to have higher self-esteem than those born in the United States (Prewitt-Díaz, 1983). In addition and certainly not coincidentally, Puerto Ricans are racially mixed, and the issue of race remains paramount in explaining their experiences in the U.S. context (Rodriguez, 1991).

Puerto Rican students bring this colonial heritage to the schoolhouse door. They are U.S. citizens, not immigrants, and therefore language, culture, and ethnicity, rather than nationality, are what separate them from their peers (Cafferty & Rivera-Martínez, 1981). Furthermore, the colonial condition, which makes migration a constant experience, has created what have been called "the students in between," those who spend time on both island and mainland (Quality Education for Minorities Project, 1990). For example, between 1969 and 1973, 51,000 Puerto Rican youngsters went from Puerto Rico to New York City schools, while another 63,000 traveled in the opposite direction. In addition, about 30% of all New York City Puerto Rican students reported between one and four changes in school between grades 7 and 9 (Quality Education for Minorities Project, 1990). Special programs and policies to help ease the transition from island to mainland, or vice versa, have been suggested (Morrison, 1958; Gallardo, 1970; Rivera-Medina, 1984).

Racism, Ethnocentrism, and Linguicism

As in the case of many other students of color, Puerto Ricans have faced varying degrees of racism and other forms of ethnocentrism in the schools and throughout their experiences in the United States. In this section, issues related to racial, cultural, and linguistic bias will be considered. Puerto Ricans are racially mixed and represent a challenge to the rigid White/Black categories traditionally employed in the United States. Puerto Ricans tend to identify primarily in cultural ways rather than racially (Rodriguez, 1991). This includes identification with Spanish, their native language. *Linguicism*, which refers to discrimination based on native language, is a preeminent reality in the Puerto Rican educational experience. It has surfaced

time and again and has led to demands for bilingual education and Spanish-language maintenance (Skutnabb-Kangas, 1988).

Early Examples. Conflicts in communities where Puerto Ricans live have been documented for many years. As early as the 1920s, near race riots between Puerto Ricans and Jews were reported (Chenault, 1938/1970; Sánchez-Korrol, 1983). In Brooklyn a factory was said to have put up a sign that read "No Negroes or Porto [*sic*] Ricans wanted" (Chenault, 1938/1970, p. 79). Chenault's study, one of the first of Puerto Ricans in New York City, focused on characteristics of Puerto Ricans that defined them in primarily negative ways, citing their lack of ambition and reliability and even their "sensitive dispositions." Wrote Chenault, "The opinion . . . exists that the Puerto Rican worker is inclined to be quick-tempered and sensitive. It is probably true that he is inclined to protest quickly against what he considers to be mistreatment" (p. 81). Another early study quoted Lait and Mortimer, two journalists, who described Puerto Ricans as

mostly crude farmers, subject to congenital tropical diseases . . . [who are] almost impossible to assimilate and condition . . . [and who] turn to guile and wile and the steel blade, the traditional weapon of the sugar cane cutter, mark of their blood and heritage. (Mills et al., 1950, p. 80)

Puerto Rican students were often perceived as inheriting the negative characteristics ascribed to their families, found to be evident in the attitudes and behaviors they brought to school, including impulsiveness, lack of discipline, and destructiveness, all of which led to an inability to profit from their educational experience. In the words of Chenault:

Some observers are of the opinion that the Puerto Rican, as well as members of the other Spanish-speaking groups, is less inclined to seek out educational advantages and follow them up by regular attendance than individuals of some of the other cultural groups. (1938/1970, p. 145)

Another sociologist, commenting on Puerto Ricans in New York schools, concluded:

A high percentage of Puerto Ricans in a school drags the teaching down almost inevitably, because of the language problem, and when Puerto Rican children are in a majority on a street they can, like any such majority, make life almost unbearable for other children. (Rand, 1958, p. 5)

Throughout the history of the education of Puerto Ricans in the United States, negative responses of teachers and other educators have ranged from denial of cultural differences (being "color-blind"), to insensitivity, to outright discriminatory policies, and all have left their mark on students' perceptions of whether or not they can achieve academic success (Ogbu, 1987; Hidalgo, 1992). Even children's literature has not been exempt, as research on the images of Puerto Ricans in U.S. children's books and school textbooks has documented that they are full of stereotypes that are at best misleading and incomplete, and at worst racist, sexist, and assimilationist (Nieto, 1983, 1992).

From "Color-Blindness" to Ignorance. An inability to confront cultural differences has been evident in much of the research concerning teachers of Puerto Rican youngsters. In an early paper, Margolis (1968) explains: "Because [the teacher] subscribes to the great American abstraction that 'prejudice is bad,' she abhors the more barbarous symptoms of bigotry and allows herself the luxury of feeling tolerant. The tolerance often turns to condescension" (p. 7). Prejudice denied inevitably leads to overlooking real differences among students as well.

Sometimes teachers have been puzzled by their students' behavior, and have made remarks that demonstrate an obvious lack of awareness concerning language development, cultural issues, and the importance of relating education to students' experiences. Frequently their remarks have centered on the students' inability to learn based on supposed cultural characteristics. Typical of these is the following comment made by a teacher in the 1960s:

Things just don't make an impression on these children. We haven't found the way to teach them. For some reason they don't relate to school. The reason is that their whole culture is different. The only way to teach them is to repeat things twenty-five times unless for some reason it means something to them. (Sexton, 1965, p. 58)

Attitudes such as these are not limited to the 1960s. Research undertaken as late as the 1990s echoes a continued lack of awareness. Darder and Upshur (1993), for instance, found that a significant number of the teachers they interviewed in four Boston public schools felt that their academic preparation was inadequate with respect to the educational needs of Latino children. This situation also indicates a lack of awareness on the part of teacher educators.

Marginalization. Feelings of marginalization among Latino students have been a chief consequence of the negative perceptions of teachers and others concerning them and their academic abilities. For example, Zanger (1993) found that Latino students in one high school in Boston felt excluded, invisible, and subordinate to other students. She also found that some teachers were just as contemptuous of Latinos as the most racist students, and that Puerto Rican students had encountered the worst instances of racism on the part of teachers. One student, for example, described how stunned he was when a teacher called him a "spic" in class.

Examples of discriminatory practices and racist attitudes have been apparent throughout the history of the education of Puerto Ricans in U.S. schools. It is important to highlight this theme not to focus on past grievances, but rather to understand how such attitudes and practices have influenced students' low academic achievement and high drop-out rates. Puerto Rican communities have generally reacted to racism and discrimination, even in the earliest years of migration, by insisting on their right to self-determination.

Self-Determination

The struggle to define their own reality has been a constant theme in the experience of Puerto Ricans in the United States.

This was apparent even during the 1920s and 1930s when the community, in its infancy, formed numerous community agencies and organizations (Sánchez Korrol, 1983), and became more pronounced as both professional and grassroots leaders began to emerge during the 1950s.

Examples from the 1950s. Even well-meaning non-Puerto Ricans have tended to perceive issues quite differently from Puerto Ricans. Thus, while "Americanization" and "cultural adaptation" were called for by early efforts focusing on Puerto Rican educational problems, Puerto Ricans themselves, even at this time, were pressing for some form of Spanish-language maintenance (Morrison, 1958).

Similarly, at about the same time that overwhelmingly negative perceptions of Puerto Ricans were holding sway, Elena Padilla (1958), a noted anthropologist and a Puerto Rican herself, challenged them squarely by suggesting that the problems of Puerto Ricans are neither unidimensional nor necessarily created by those on whom they are blamed. Commenting on the cultural strengths of the community and people's ability to confront inequities, she added: "Regarded as a problem in New York City, Puerto Ricans have problems of their own and solutions to them that, while not always recognized or acceptable to the larger society, make their lives tick" (p. 162).

Developing Community Organizations to Meet the Challenges. The quest for self-determination became even more apparent in the way Puerto Ricans, particularly the small but growing professional class, began organizing themselves beginning in the 1950s. The numerous self-help and advocacy organizations, the trademark of a community bent on defining itself and seeking its own solutions to problems, invariably centered on issues of education. In the mid-1950s a group of young Puerto Rican professionals established the Puerto Rican-Hispanic Leadership Forum (now the National Puerto Rican Forum), a communitywide organization to promote their interests in New York City (Fitzpatrick, 1971; ASPIRA Association, 1991). Chief among the organizers was Antonia Pantoja, called the "inspiration and guiding spirit" of these early movements (Fitzpatrick, 1971). A Puerto Rican social worker, Pantoja was born in Puerto Rico and raised and educated in New York City, working her way up as a factory worker, artist, student, and teacher (ASPIRA, 1991). Many educational and social reform efforts of the past four decades can be traced to her vision. She has remained a formidable model of strength and perseverance in the Puerto Rican community.

A primary example of the kind of organization that reflected the growing self-awareness and incipient spirit of self-determination of these years was ASPIRA. A Spanish word meaning "to aspire," ASPIRA was founded by the Puerto Rican Forum in 1961 to promote education among Puerto Rican youths. Through its long and distinguished history as the primary agency promoting the educational rights of Puerto Ricans, it has been responsible for motivating countless youths to continue their education by providing educational guidance and leadership in schools and communities. ASPIRA has been instrumental in promoting higher education for Puerto Rican youth through the establishment of clubs in high schools (where student members become Aspirantes); many Puerto Ricans who have gone on to become leaders in their communities trace their success to their involvement with ASPIRA. With national headquarters in Washington since 1985, ASPIRA now has affiliates in six states and Puerto Rico and has expanded its services to other Latinos besides Puerto Ricans, and even to non-Latinos in the neighborhoods it serves (ASPIRA, 1991).

Other grassroots, educational, and political organizations that have emerged over the past three decades echo the theme of self-determination first enunciated in the early part of the century (Sánchez Korrol, 1983; Iglesias, 1984), but most evident in the 1960s. These include the National Puerto Rican Coalition in Washington, D.C., and in what is still the location with the largest and most influential Puerto Rican community, New York City, the Institute for Puerto Rican Policy, the Puerto Rican Educators Association, the National Congress for Puerto Rican Rights, the Puerto Rican/Latino Education Roundtable, the Puerto Rican Legal Defense and Education Fund, and El Puente. The National Council of La Raza and the Hispanic Policy Development Project, both located in Washington, D.C., although not focused exclusively on Puerto Ricans, include them prominently.

A New Militancy Develops. Demands that Puerto Ricans be heard became increasingly militant after the 1960s. Political and community struggles, an outgrowth of the civil rights movement in the United States, were characterized by a growing frustration among students, parents, and other previously disenfranchised segments of the population. This new militancy was evident in numerous struggles for community control, bilingual and ethnic studies education, decentralization of the city's schools, and, in higher education, in demands for Puerto Rican studies departments and open enrollment at CUNY, the City University of New York, that eventually led to the development of several such departments and a research center, the Centro de Estudios Puertorriqueños (Fitzpatrick, 1971, 1987; M. E. Sánchez & Stevens-Arroyo, 1987).

Self-definition in the Puerto Rican community has grown in tandem with the growth of the community itself, and is a major theme evident in the many commissions, reports, studies, and grassroots efforts of the past 30 years. How the self-determination agenda has developed in the political context of this period will be evident in the nature of these efforts, to be discussed in the following section.

THE EDUCATION OF PUERTO RICANS IN U.S. MAINLAND SCHOOLS: A CHRONOLOGY OF LABELS

It is instructive to look at the many labels that have been used to characterize Puerto Rican students in U.S. schools in order to understand how labels have reflected their historical and political contexts. Generally applied from a paradigm of privilege, that is, from the perspective of the dominant White,

Anglo-Saxon middle class, the labels have ranged from considering Puerto Ricans as "problems" and "culturally deprived" to "at risk." Through the years these terms have been challenged by Puerto Ricans and other progressive educators in order to reframe the discussion. Although the characterizations used here do not always fit neatly into the time frames suggested, they provide an idea of the ways in which Puerto Rican students have generally been defined, and thus of the pedagogical and social policies and strategies developed to meet their needs.

In this section major reports, studies, and research projects from the 1930s to the present will be reviewed, along with their prevailing assumptions about Puerto Ricans in general and Puerto Rican students in particular. Recurring issues, problems, and solutions will be highlighted.

Before 1960: The Puerto Rican Student as a "Problem"

The fact that Puerto Ricans face tremendous problems in U.S. schools has been recognized for many years, but how these problems have been identified and defined over the years has varied. For example, the early literature was replete with references to the "Puerto Rican problem," thus situating the issue squarely on the experiences, culture, language, and social class with which Puerto Rican students arrive in the United States and subsequently at the schoolhouse door.

The existence of the "Puerto Rican problem" was defined as early as the 1930s, with the release of a report from the New York City Chamber of Commerce in 1935 that claimed Puerto Rican children were "slow learners," based on the results of an experiment in which 240 Puerto Rican children were given intelligence tests (Iglesias, 1984; Sánchez Korrol, 1983, in press). The release of this report was met by fierce rebuttals from the community and became, according to Sánchez Korrol, one of the primary issues addressed by Vito Marcantonio, the beloved Italian American politician who represented Spanish Harlem for many years. In what was probably the first challenge to the discriminatory effects of standardized tests for Puerto Rican youngsters, he concluded that such tests made inadequate allowances for the social, economic, linguistic, and environmental factors of Puerto Rican children's lives.

In 1948, with the publication of the first major report on Puerto Ricans in the New York City schools, the "problem" label was once again used in relation to Puerto Rican students (Association of Assistant Superintendents, 1948). As a result of this investigation, the position of Substitute Auxiliary Teacher (SAT) was created by the New York City Board of Education. To be filled by Spanish-speakers who could qualify for substitute licenses, the primary duty of SATs was to assist principals and teachers in working with Puerto Rican pupils and parents. By 1949 there were 10 such positions citywide. Other Teaching Personnel (OTPs), who were hired to teach English to Puerto Ricans, and Puerto Rican Coordinators, teachers at the junior high school level, were added to these specialists and numbered 50 citywide by 1954 (Morrison, 1958). In the first years of efforts focusing on educational problems, most Puerto Rican staff filled low-level, low-status, and substitute positions.

The Puerto Rican Study, 1953–1957. A massive project conducted by the New York City Board of Education from 1953 to 1957, *The Puerto Rican Study* was undertaken to investigate the education and adjustment of Puerto Rican students in the public schools, who already numbered over 53,000 (Morrison, 1958). Although certainly not as negative in tone as previous studies, it still reflected the tendency to focus on perceived deficits of Puerto Rican students. For instance, one of the reasons for conducting the study was that the "problem" of Puerto Ricans, which had been limited until the 1950s to "San Juan Hill" and Spanish Harlem, was now spreading to other schools in the city (Morrison, 1958). It was also guided, as were many of the early reports, by the assumption that quick "Americanization" was a primary objective of schooling (Fitzpatrick, 1971).

The major objectives of *The Puerto Rican Study* were to gather accurate data on the number and characteristics of Puerto Rican pupils in New York City schools, and to determine the most effective methods and materials for teaching English to them in order to promote their adjustment. As a result of this extensive, $1 million study, six reports and 16 resource unit volumes were generated, and 23 short- and long-range recommendations were made, many of which were to be repeated in the next 40 years. Included among these were specific recommendations on teaching English, developing closer working relationships with parents, and formulating new policies for working with "non-English-speaking" pupils. Although bilingual education was not specifically mentioned, the report flirted with the issue of how best to use the language skills that Puerto Rican students already had. One of the more forward-thinking recommendations reminded teachers and administrators that "whatever is done for the non-English-speaking child is, in the long run, done for all the children" (Morrison, 1958, p. 238).

Lack of Puerto Rican Involvement in Early Studies. Most of the early reports and studies concerning Puerto Rican students in U.S. schools were conceived, developed, and conducted by non-Puerto Ricans (Chenault, 1938/1970; Association of Assistant Superintendents, 1948; Mills et al., 1950; Morrison, 1958; Rand, 1958). It is instructive to note, for example, that *The Puerto Rican Study* had only 1 member of 17 on the Advisory Panel and 1 consultant of 9 who were Puerto Rican (Morrison, 1958). The lack of Puerto Rican perspectives no doubt colored the way problems were defined and recommendations made. Sánchez Korrol (1983), for example, has noted that few if any positive role models for young Puerto Ricans were to be found amidst the reports:

Seeking historical roots, the children of the early migration were too often surprised to find themselves as statistics on the city's welfare rolls, school dropouts, truants, health and correctional hazards, a rootless people, devoid of a history and a culture, according to published reports and sound research. (p. 208)

Nevertheless, one of the major accomplishments of *The Puerto Rican Study* was to upgrade the teaching of English as a Second Language (ESL), thus setting the stage for increasing the presence of Puerto Ricans in the schools as aides, community liaisons, teachers, and counselors. By 1961 the SAT position, a low-status role mostly filled by Puerto Ricans and other Latinos, was elevated to Regular Auxiliary Teacher (RAT), and by 1965 there were 142 such positions in the New York City public schools (Fitzpatrick, 1971). With an increase in personnel came an increase in curriculum development and adaptation of materials to meet the educational needs of Puerto Rican youngsters. This probably signaled the beginning of a real Puerto Rican imprint, particularly of Puerto Rican women educators, on the New York City educational system (Sánchez Korrol, in press).

"The Culture of Poverty," "The Losers," and Tentative Challenges to the Melting Pot: Perspectives from the 1960s

The 1960s ushered in an era characterized by a growing dichotomy between how Puerto Ricans and non-Puerto Ricans interpreted the Puerto Rican experience, a divergence that has continued in some ways to the present. Although not all Puerto Ricans speak with one voice, recommendations and demands made by the Puerto Rican community concerning education have been remarkably consistent over the past 30 years, while actual policies and practices, generally developed and carried out by non-Puerto Ricans, have lagged behind. This pattern was first established to a great extent during the 1960s.

The Social and Political Context. Social and political contexts, with their competing ideologies, must be kept in mind if we are to understand how the educational problems of Puerto Ricans were defined during the 1950s and the 1960s. At the same time that the civil rights, Black Power, and other liberation movements were sweeping the country, a conservative ideology that centered on cultural and linguistic differences as deficiencies was taking hold in academia and schools, especially those serving students of color (Reissman, 1962; Bereiter & Englemann, 1966; Jensen, 1969).

For Puerto Ricans, this paradigm of cultural deficiency was nowhere more devastatingly articulated than in *La Vida* (Lewis, 1965; see Rodriguez, Chapter 13 of this *Handbook*, for a more detailed discussion), an extensive study of 100 Puerto Rican families living in poverty in New York City and San Juan, Puerto Rico. In an in-depth study of the Ríos family, described by the author as "closer to the expression of an unbridled id than any other people I have studied" (p. xxvi), Lewis virtually defined "the culture of poverty" and all its negative ramifications for generations to come. This had grave consequences for Puerto Ricans. A particularly insidious description of his subjects reads:

The people in this book, like most of the other Puerto Rican slum dwellers I have studied, show a great zest for life, especially for sex, and a need for excitement, new experiences and adventures. . . . They value acting out more than thinking out, self-expression more than self-constraint, pleasure more than productivity, spending more than saving, personal loyalty more than impersonal justice. They are fun-loving and enjoy parties, dancing and music. They cannot be alone; they have an almost insatiable need for sociability and interaction. (p. xxvi)

Attitudes such as these were reflected by others who worked in communities and schools with large numbers of economically disadvantaged Puerto Ricans. In a sociological study published that same year concerning the Puerto Rican, African American, and Italian populations of Spanish Harlem (Sexton, 1965, p. 11), a youth worker is quoted as saying: "No wonder they can't learn anything in school.... They have sex on their minds 24 hours a day." A teacher, referring specifically to Puerto Rican and African American children, stated: "They love to dance and move their bodies. They can't sit still. The ones that do well in school usually don't like to dance or move around."

By the 1960s few of the recommendations of *The Puerto Rican Study* had been carried out, and educational opportunities for Puerto Ricans had in fact worsened. For example, by 1960 only 13% of Puerto Ricans 25 years and older had completed high school, and more than half had less than an eighth-grade education (Puerto Rican Forum, 1970). Furthermore, 1960 census data indicated that Puerto Ricans were the lowest in both education and occupational status in New York City (Fitzpatrick, 1971). A 1961 study of a Manhattan community found that fewer than 10% of Puerto Rican children in third grade were reading at grade level or above (Puerto Rican Forum, 1970). In addition, only a small number of Puerto Ricans graduated from New York City high schools with academic diplomas in 1963 (331, or 1.6% of the 21,000 academic diplomas granted), at a time when the total Puerto Rican school population was over 150,000 (Fitzpatrick. 1971). Even of these 331, only 28 went on to college (Cafferty & Rivera-Martínez, 1981).

As reported by the Puerto Rican Forum, this dire situation was reflected in other arenas as well: A 1964 study found that Puerto Ricans had the highest percentage of poverty in New York City, along with the worst housing and the lowest level of education and income. Probably not coincidentally, as of 1970 there was no Puerto Rican elected official in the city administration (Puerto Rican Forum, 1970). Outside of New York City, the situation was frequently even worse. For instance, between 1966 and 1969 only four Puerto Rican students graduated from the Boston public schools (Cafferty & Rivera-Martínez, 1981). A 1972 study in Massachusetts estimated that at least 2,500 Puerto Rican children in Boston were not attending school, and that a third of all students in one Springfield junior high school quit *before* going on to high school (Massachusetts State Advisory Committee, 1972).

Growing Puerto Rican Involvement in Research and Advocacy.

The worsening educational situation for Puerto Ricans led to a change in how these problems were addressed in the community, apparent in three major ways. First, educators and community activists led a more aggressive challenge of the "melting pot" and "cultural deprivation" models and other negative characterizations of their community. Boycotts and other protests for quality education were frequent occurrences during the 1950s and 1960s in New York City. Second, there were initial, although somewhat tentative, demands for programs such as bilingual education, ethnic studies, and cross-cultural education that later grew into major rallying cries for educational equality. Thus, a new paradigm of cultural and linguistic

inclusion was beginning to form. Third, demands began to be made for more Puerto Rican educators and policy makers.

The growing militancy was also apparent to one degree or another in the reports and studies. Given the grave situation and growing frustration in the Puerto Rican community, the slow trickle of studies that had begun in the 1930s had grown steadily by the 1960s. The next major report on the education of Puerto Ricans in the United States, this time with substantial community involvement, was based on the First Citywide Conference of the Puerto Rican Community that took place in April 1967 (Office of the Mayor, 1968). A total of 32 recommendations, many similar or identical to those made previously by *The Puerto Rican Study*, were submitted to the mayor of New York City. However, new and different recommendations reflected the changes in the political climate of the 1960s and the prominent Puerto Rican participation in the conference. Among these were bilingual programs and courses in Puerto Rican culture, literature, and history.

Hemos Trabajado Bien (1968). Bilingual and ethnic studies education were also a feature of the ASPIRA Symposium of 1968, *Hemos Trabajado Bien* (ASPIRA of New York, 1968), a conference on the education of Puerto Ricans and Mexican Americans that received widespread national attention and for which another report was commissioned (Margolis, 1968). Titled *The Losers*, the report served as a common starting point for understanding the status of the education of Puerto Rican youth. According to its author, the title "losers" referred to several different groups, including the children, the community, and society at large. Visiting 16 schools in seven cities with large Puerto Rican communities, Margolis examined major educational problems, including high drop-out and low attendance rates, poor academic achievement, and uninformed and unsympathetic teachers and administrators.

Because of its focus on teachers, students, and parents, this report signaled a new emphasis on parental involvement that was to become a hallmark of all subsequent reports on the education of Puerto Rican youth. Although it did not make any concrete recommendations, the report's findings concerning poor record keeping, biased and unimaginative teaching, and low expectations for Puerto Rican students were compelling. Margolis (1968) concluded, based on these findings, that the longer Puerto Rican children attended public school, the less they learned.

Especially noteworthy in the ASPIRA report was the fact that it was among the first to challenge the "melting pot" ideology so prevalent until then. Saying that teachers who refused to acknowledge their students' differences were practicing "a subtle form of tyranny" (Margolis, 1968, p. 7), the author continued:

They are saying, "All people should pretend to be like everyone else even when they are not." That is how the majority culture imposes its standards upon a minority—a cruel sort of assimilation forced onto children in the name of equality. (p. 7)

This was not the first critique of the "melting pot," which had come under serious scrutiny some years before. In a statement with a flavor more of the 1980s than of 1950, Mills et al., writing specifically about Puerto Ricans, roundly condemned this ideology:

With the recent decline of immigration, cultural pluralism, a new approach to the solution of problems arising from the presence of divergent cultures, has been taken seriously by small circles of people. This perspective assumes the bankruptcy of the "melting pot theory," asserting that to attack group values is likely to strengthen them. More importantly, it proposes that each cultural group may have something to contribute to American civilization as a mixed cultural whole. (p. 84)

This kind of thinking marked the turning point in the way problems facing Puerto Rican youth were defined and addressed, at least by Puerto Rican and other progressive educators.

Pressure Toward Assimilation. In spite of these challenges, schools continued to reflect the conventional "melting pot" ideology by stressing the assimilationist role of education. A 1965 ethnographic doctoral study by Bucchioni provides a glimpse into the daily and consistent pressures toward assimilation that took place in New York City schools with Puerto Rican majorities (Bucchioni, 1982). The researcher, who participated in extensive observations in a number of classrooms, used the case of "Miss Dwight" for detailed analysis and discussion. Subtle and not-so-subtle assimilationist pressures were evident in her classroom in curriculum content, teaching methods, and other messages to children about the inherent worth or value of their experiences and culture. These included admonitions about not speaking Spanish, choosing the best students to be "Mr. and Mrs. America" for the morning pledge to the flag, a discussion about what constitutes a good nutritious diet (in which no Puerto Rican foods were included), learning how to do the square dance, and a disturbing discussion about different neighborhoods in New York City. In the latter discussion, Juan, a student who is astonished that some families have their very own bathrooms, concludes that only very rich people can live in those places. He is reassured by Miss Dwight: "Not exactly rich, Juan. But they do work hard, and every day," to which Juan answers, "My papa, he say he work hard, every day—eben on Sunday" (p. 210).

The curriculum, teaching strategies, and messages chronicled in Miss Dwight's classroom do not, in and of themselves, necessarily undermine a child's self-image. It was becoming clear to many educators, however, that their cumulative effect can be disastrous for young people struggling to maintain a sense of integrity in a dominant culture hostile to them. Miss Dwight's attitudes can best be described as patronizing, while those of one of her fellow teachers were more blatantly ethnocentric and defeatist: "What's the use of worrying about these kids? Between their lousy way of living and their Spanish, we're lost before we begin," she concluded (Bucchioni, 1982, p. 213). That the attitudes of teachers and schools can affect young people directly is more than evident.

The messages in both the expressed and the hidden curriculum above emphasize that everything associated with the lives of Puerto Rican youth (their native language, foods, lifestyles, music, and even their parents) was perceived as somehow lacking and deficient. The theory of "cultural deprivation" so popular during the early 1960s thus became subject to more critical analysis by those most affected by it. Kenneth Clark, a leading African American psychologist, for instance, challenged it directly: "The concept of the culturally deprived child is a new stereotype, a new excuse, a new rationalization for inadequate education of minority group children" (quoted in Sexton, 1965, p. 60). This challenge began to be felt in the Puerto Rican community as well.

Fighting the Labels: A Growing Militancy and Other Perspectives from the 1970s

Labels are not always the result of imposition from above. In the case of Puerto Ricans in the United States, labels sometimes emerged from the very tensions that were the outcomes of colonialism and the migratory experience. In the 1970s Puerto Ricans from the island tended to address the experience of Puerto Ricans in the United States in a naive way, focusing on assimilation as a necessary goal, with the assumption that learning English would inevitably solve the educational problems of Puerto Rican youngsters. The growing conflicts between Puerto Rican perspectives from the island and those from the U.S. mainland were exemplified at a 1970 conference, held in Puerto Rico, on the education of Puerto Rican children in the United States (Gallardo, 1970). The conference organizers, largely educators from Puerto Rico, focused on the "problems" of Puerto Ricans in the United States, and also presented a viewpoint of great naivete, suggesting that within the next 25 years Puerto Ricans would know English sufficiently well so that bilingual programs would no longer be needed (Gallardo, 1970).

These educators were clearly unprepared for the more militant Puerto Rican educators from the mainland, who demanded that the format of the conference be changed to include their perspectives because educators from the island were unaware of, and in some cases unsympathetic to, the reality of Puerto Ricans in the States. These differences were becoming increasingly evident in these years and were to mark the future relationships of Puerto Ricans in a number of ways.

At this conference there was much anger reported from speakers in the audience for conference organizers' characterization of Puerto Rican youngsters as "pitiful" and "victimized." One activist U.S.-based educator, Awilda Orta, confronted this patronizing tone by asserting, "Puerto Ricans in the continental United States are not looking for affection, they are looking for their civil rights given to them as people" (Gallardo, 1970, p. 65). Another U.S. Puerto Rican activist, Joseph Monserrat, criticized the cultural content of the conference as completely off the mark:

We can talk about "compadrazco" [godparent relationships], and we can talk about extended families, and we can talk about "machismo," and we can talk about the Puerto Rican syndrome [a term used in the mental health literature referring to the behavior of women in stressful situations, characterized by screaming and fainting], and it is interesting to talk about these things. But as long as we talk about the Puerto Rican, we will never talk about the problem, because the problem is not the Puerto Rican.... The problem basically is the realities that exist in the communities into which Puerto Ricans move. (p. 67)

He suggested instead that the task at hand was to break "the monolingual, monocultural barrier" and to challenge the melting pot ideology.

The 1970s thus brought with them not only internal tensions between Puerto Ricans on the island and U.S. Puerto Rican urban communities, but also greater militancy and definition within these communities in the United States. The growing educational militancy can be understood as part of the larger civil rights movement, although civil rights were defined in a particularly Puerto Rican context. Two examples will help illustrate these developments. The next part of this section highlights the struggle for equal educational opportunity in two cases in New York City, followed by a description of the prominence of bilingual education in the Puerto Rican community.

Puerto Rican Educational Militancy: Two Cases. Although less well documented than the formal reports, or the conferences and research studies on Puerto Rican communities, there are in the literature some concrete examples of how these more militant demands were manifested in the community. Two of the most fully chronicled cases of Puerto Rican educational militancy occurred as part of the community control and decentralization movements of the mid-1960s and early 1970s and took place in Intermediate School 201 in Harlem and District 1 on the Lower East Side (Gittell, 1972; Fuentes, 1976; U.S. Commission on Civil Rights, 1976). Along with African Americans, Puerto Ricans had been involved in demanding two-way integration since the 1950s. IS 201, a huge, windowless structure built in 1966 in Harlem, was to be the setting for this integration. Because they feared a White exodus, however, neither the mayor nor the Board of Education pursued integration, thus setting the stage for parent demands to control the school in order to guarantee quality education.

Boycotts and prolonged community activism led to the establishment of three experimental school districts in the summer of 1966 in New York City: IS 201, Two Bridges, and Ocean Hill-Brownsville. Parents and other community members were to have a major voice in the educational decisions affecting their children in these districts (Gittell, 1972). Puerto Rican students were a significant population in each of the schools involved. Although the combined power of the Board of Education and the United Federation of Teachers (UFT) was able to crush these grassroots movements, they left an important legacy. For example, one of the first bilingual programs established without federal or state support was set up as a mini-school in Ocean Hill-Brownsville in 1968 (Fuentes, 1980; Wasserman, 1969; Rubinstein, 1970). It was largely due to parent demands that this program was established. Parents also helped in the selection of the staff and in determining the focus of the curriculum (Rubinstein, 1970).

Two Bridges, a community in lower Manhattan, was the setting for the other important early 1970s educational movement

in which Puerto Ricans were well represented (Fantini & Magat, 1970). This neighborhood, known as Community District 1, became the setting for one of the longest and most bitterly fought campaigns for the rights of Puerto Rican and other community students and parents during the early 1970s (Fuentes, 1976, 1980). By 1972, parents and other activists secured control of the majority of seats on the school board and made immediate changes, including hiring Luis Fuentes (principal of the Ocean Hill-Brownsville school that had begun the bilingual program a number of years before) as community superintendent, as well as hiring other Latino, African American, and Chinese American personnel, and instituting programs such as bilingual education and a systematized reading program (Fuentes, 1976).

These changes were greeted with skepticism and fear by the educational establishment, including the UFT, which claimed that because of the campaign waged by the community, the schools had become "arenas of political extremism, racism and patronage" (Shanker, 1973). Although the UFT-backed coalition called itself the "Brotherhood Slate," it ran candidates in the 1973 and 1974 elections that totaled 17 White and only 1 Black, in spite of the fact that the district's pupil population was 73% Puerto Rican and only 6% White. In addition, none of these candidates had children in the public schools.

Grassroots elements of the local Puerto Rican community organized an opposing parent slate that consisted of four Puerto Ricans, two African Americans, one Chinese, and one White citizen, all parents of children in the district's public school system. Interestingly, this slate was termed "separatist" by the opposition (Fuentes, 1976). The UFT president called for the election of "people of good will" to the community school boards, with the obvious implication that the majority of such people would be middle-class Whites (Shanker, 1973).

The UFT spent more than $100,000 to the parent slate's $4,000, and by 1974 the community school board was restored to a White majority; the controversial Luis Fuentes, who had been supported by most residents of the community, was fired. In spite of these setbacks, District 1 had struggled and in some ways even flourished as an educational experiment in which new and innovative programs were started, including the hiring of 120 bilingual Chinese- and Spanish-language teachers, the development of interviewing and hiring committees that included parents and students, and a school lunch program selected and supervised by parents (Fuentes, 1976).

Report of the U.S. Commission on Civil Rights: A New Era Begins. It was against this backdrop that the U.S. Commission on Civil Rights conducted a series of regional studies and open meetings between 1971 and 1976, and issued an influential national report on the condition of Puerto Ricans in the United States (U.S. Commission on Civil Rights, 1976). This report was noteworthy for a number of reasons. First, with the exception of surveys by the Census Bureau, it represented the first time a federal government agency had focused specifically on the entire population of mainland Puerto Ricans. Second, it was the first effort to document accurately the socioeconomic status of Puerto Ricans in the entire United States. It was found, for example, that as of 1975, more than 1.7 million Puerto Ricans were living in the United States, with an incidence of poverty and unemployment more severe than that of virtually every other ethnic group.

Third, the report comprehensively documented for the first time the educational status of Puerto Ricans in the entire continental United States. What the commission found was a population that was severely undereducated and an educational establishment that consistently failed to respond to the needs of the Puerto Rican community. For instance, while 62% of all U.S. adults had completed a high school education, only 28.7% of Puerto Ricans had done so. The report also chronicled the catastrophic drop-out problem among Puerto Ricans, including a drop-out rate of over 70% in Chicago (U.S. Commission on Civil Rights, 1976). Furthermore, the commission reported chronic underachievement among Puerto Rican youngsters.

This report was notable in its insistence that school policies and practices contributed in a significant way to the failure of Puerto Rican students, rather than the traditional explanation of "cultural deprivation" to explain such failure. It documented how tracking, IQ and achievement tests, assignment practices, little support for parent and community involvement, and insensitive teachers and counselors unfairly jeopardized Puerto Rican students, and it highlighted how Puerto Rican and other low-income students, compared to middle-class and wealthier students, had unequal access to quality education.

A focus on school policies and practices represented a fundamental shift from the paradigm of cultural deprivation and "blaming the victim" (Ryan, 1972) that had been the norm, and it signaled a new systemic way of looking at the problems that Puerto Ricans were having in school. The U.S. Commission on Civil Rights report was significant because it redefined language and cultural differences as potential assets rather than liabilities. Hernán LaFontaine, who had been the principal of the first wholly bilingual school in New York City and first director of the Board of Education's Office of Bilingual Education, was quoted as saying:

Our definition of cultural pluralism must include the concept that our language and culture will be given equal status to that of the majority population. It is not enough simply to say that we should be given the opportunity to share in the positive benefits of modern American life. Instead, we must insist that this sharing will not be accomplished at the sacrifice of all those traits which make us what we are as Puerto Ricans. (U.S. Commission on Civil Rights, 1976, p. 103)

The recommendations made by the commission included the establishment of affirmative action plans to recruit Puerto Rican faculty; the elimination of ability grouping in all but the most absolutely necessary cases; and, most important, bilingual-bicultural education in all school districts with significant enrollments of Puerto Rican and other language-minority students (U.S. Commission on Civil Rights, 1976). This last recommendation was very much in keeping with the resurgence of bilingual education since the late 1960s as the primary means to improve the education of Puerto Rican students. A brief review of bilingual education will explain how it became the preeminent issue in the community's demands for equitable education during the 1970s and beyond.

Bilingual Education in the Puerto Rican Community

Bilingual education was not a new idea in the 1960s, and in fact the history of bilingual education is closely linked to the history of the United States itself (Castellanos, 1983). That is, the cycle of policies and practices related to languages and language use in society in general, and in schools in particular, reflects the many ways in which the United States has attempted to resolve the issue of language diversity. These have ranged from "sink or swim" policies (i.e., immersing language-minority students in English-only classrooms to fend on their own), through the imposition of English as the sole medium of instruction, to encouraging the flourishing of bilingual education, such as through German-English bilingual schools in the 1800s (Castellanos, 1983; Keller & van Hooft, 1982).

In the context of the huge influx of new immigrants at the turn of the century, the accompanying xenophobic hysteria, and a policy of isolationism, bilingual education had virtually disappeared between the two world wars. During the late 1960s, as yet another consequence of the civil rights movement, renewed demands for bilingual education began to be heard.

Bilingual Education as a Remedy for Unequal Education. While integrating schools remained the primary focus in the African American community for achieving equality of education, Puerto Rican and other Latino communities did not have as much faith in this process. This was because integration was generally viewed as a Black/White issue rather than because the process of integration itself was viewed pessimistically. An in-depth study of two school systems by ASPIRA, for instance, found that school desegregation had not led to a greater understanding of Latinos by school administrators or teachers, and that racist stereotypes remained common (ASPIRA of America, 1979). ASPIRA concluded that desegregation plans needed to distinguish the needs of African Americans and Latinos, and to adhere to state and federal guidelines for bilingual education. Thus, in the Puerto Rican and other language-minority communities, bilingual education became the cornerstone of educational equality (Báez, Fernández, Navarro, & Rice, 1986). Most language-minority communities began to view bilingual education as their central civil rights issue because it represented the best guarantee that youngsters who did not speak English would be provided education in a language they understood. Without it, they might well be doomed to educational underachievement and severely limited occupational choices in the future.

Bilingual education was also seen as helping to counteract the assimilationist agenda of schooling that resulted in young people's shifting their cultural and class identification away from their own communities and toward that of the larger society. Parents, community activists, and educators began to fear that through the hidden and expressed curriculum and the educational power of the media, young Puerto Ricans were being encouraged to develop patterns of thought and behavior that more closely conformed to the middle-class White ideal. In effect, they were being taught to reject the values of their own communities, including their language and culture. Bilingual education was seen as an antidote to this pressure.

Demands for bilingual education should not be understood as outside "the American dream," but as part and parcel of it. For example, the main objectives Puerto Ricans envision for education are economic security and what one might call "the good life," objectives not really different from those of the larger society and the educational system. There are, however, some fundamental differences between the ways these objectives are defined. "The good life" for Puerto Ricans has rarely included the assimilation and cultural rejection referred to above. On the contrary, Puerto Ricans have demonstrated an almost unbridled enthusiasm for education *while at the same time* displaying a fierce tenacity with respect to maintaining their language and culture. In the Puerto Rican community, and in the larger Latino community in general, there has not been a contradiction between getting a good education and retaining their ethnic identity. Thus in 1982, in spite of the fact that Latinos have been in the United States for years, many for generations, 80% of them still lived in households in which Spanish was spoken, quite an achievement in view of the extraordinary pressure to drop it (NCLR, 1982). For Puerto Ricans the percentage is 91%, higher than for any other Latino group (Rodriguez, 1991).

Some Results of Demands for Bilingual Education. Activism for bilingual education in the Puerto Rican community resulted in programs in specific schools, such as in Ocean Hill-Brownsville and in PS 25 in the Bronx, the first totally bilingual school in the Northeast, established in 1968 (Fuentes, 1976; LaFontaine et al., 1973). At the national level, protests and demands among activists in the Mexican American, Puerto Rican, American Indian, and other language-minority communities led to passage of the Bilingual Education Act of 1967 (part of the Elementary and Secondary Education Act of 1968), which provided funding for a small number of demonstration projects throughout the country (Bilingual Education Act of 1967, 1968). This act provided for a program of instruction that would enable students to achieve equal proficiency in English and their native language, develop pride in and awareness of their cultural heritage, and aid them in increasing their academic achievement. State-level activism on the part of Puerto Ricans and others in Massachusetts led to the passage of Chapter 71A, the first law to mandate bilingual education, which became the model for virtually every other such state-mandated law in the country (Bureau of Transitional Bilingual Education, 1971).

Recourse to the Courts and Local and Federal Legislatures. Two key arenas for the political demands of the Puerto Rican and other linguistic-minority communities became the legislatures at both state and national levels, and the local and federal courts. In 1969 plaintiffs representing 1,800 Chinese-speaking students sued the San Francisco Unified School District for failing to provide non-English-speaking students with an equal chance to learn. Although the case was lost at the state level, by 1974 it had reached the Supreme Court. In the landmark *Lau v. Nichols* (1974) case, the Court, recognizing the relationship of language to equal educational opportunity, ruled unanimously that the civil rights of students who did not understand the language of instruction were indeed being violated.

Although the Court did not impose any particular remedy, the results of its decision were immediate and extensive. By 1975 the Office for Civil Rights and the Department of Health, Education, and Welfare issued a document popularly known as "The Lau Remedies," which provided guidance in identifying, assessing the language abilities of, and providing appropriate programs for students with a limited proficiency in English (Office of Civil Rights, 1975). This document has served as the basis for determining whether or not school systems are in compliance with the findings of *Lau*. Bilingual programs have been the common remedy of most school systems.

One of the Puerto Rican community's most important campaigns for educational equity through bilingual education took place in 1972, when the New York City Board of Education was sued by the Puerto Rican Legal Defense and Education Fund (PRLDEF) on behalf of 15 schoolchildren and their parents, with ASPIRA of New York, Inc., ASPIRA of American, Inc. (now the ASPIRA Association), and other organizations representing the educational interests of Puerto Rican youngsters (Santiago-Santiago, 1986; ASPIRA Association, 1991). The suit, a landmark case in the history of bilingual education because it involved the largest school system in the country and the largest class of plaintiff children (over 80,000), was based on evidence that Puerto Rican youngsters of limited English proficiency were being denied equal educational opportunity (Santiago-Santiago, 1986). After a great deal of litigation and negotiation, the suit was resolved in August 1974 and resulted in the ASPIRA consent decree mandating bilingual education in the New York City school system (ASPIRA, 1991).

According to Santiago-Santiago (1986), the ASPIRA consent decree, and bilingual education in the Puerto Rican community in general, need to be placed in the context of the sociopolitical relationship of Puerto Rico to the United States, particularly given the special citizenship status of Puerto Ricans, a fact that is often overlooked in bilingual education literature. Some Puerto Ricans have maintained that specific educational and language policies need to be developed that respond to the conditions of this citizenship status. Thus, although the reasons for bilingual education may be just as urgent in other language-minority communities, the situation of Puerto Ricans is unique in that they are not immigrants, but citizens who are as free to move within national borders as any other citizens. Says Santiago-Santiago: "When Puerto Rican parents request bilingual maintenance programs, the parents are more often viewed as 'un-American' rather than as parents who wish to foster the freedom their children should have in moving between the island and the continent" (p. 157).

It is understandable that bilingual education became inextricably linked with demands for equal educational opportunity in the Puerto Rican community, as demonstrated in numerous reports and studies released beginning in the late 1960s (Margolis, 1968; Puerto Rican Forum, 1970; Massachusetts State Advisory Committee, 1972; U.S. Commission on Civil Rights, 1976; Cafferty & Rivera-Martínez, 1981; National Puerto Rican Task Force, 1982). Although bilingual education continues to be a key element in calls for educational reform for Puerto Rican students, it became only one of many strategies recommended during the 1980s and 1990s, to which we will now turn.

Puerto Rican Students "At Risk" and as "Outsiders": Redefining Complex Issues in the 1980s and 1990s

The 1980s represented a period of retrenchment and retreat from the more liberal educational policies of the 1960s and 1970s, a trend no better defined than in the educational reform movement that officially began with the publication of *A Nation at Risk* (National Commission on Excellence in Education, 1983). While educational concerns during the previous two decades had focused on educational equality by challenging the deficit theories popularized in the 1960s and espousing strategies such as busing, integration, ethnic studies, and cross-cultural and multicultural education, the 1980s brought with them a concern that equity had been won at the expense of excellence. This led to calls for raising standards, longer school days and years, reinstatement of the classics, a return to the "basics," and the forging of a common cultural experience for all students (National Commission on Excellence in Education, 1983; Bloom, 1987; Hirsch, 1987).

As a result of this educational reform movement, the term *at risk*, referring to students whose socioeconomic, experiential, and cultural characteristics made them likely candidates for school failure, became the label in vogue in the 1980s. Although often meant to point out unequal educational access for youngsters based on their race, language, or social class, this term was a legacy of the "culturally deprived" label of the 1960s because it was frequently used to blame students for perceived shortcomings rather than to attend to the shortcomings of school systems.

This change in perspective was felt in the Puerto Rican community, but the terms associated with the reform movement were given different meanings in an attempt to advance the specific community agenda. Puerto Rican activists and professionals embarked on a process of redefining educational equity and excellence through a profusion of studies and reports centering on the education of Puerto Ricans and other Latinos (National Commission on Secondary Education for Hispanics, 1984; Orum, 1986; Valdivieso, 1986).

Although bilingual education remained a key ingredient in all calls for reform, the educational agenda of the 1980s and 1990s expanded to include a more serious look at other policies and practices leading to educational failure among Puerto Rican youths. For instance, in a review of the ASPIRA consent decree over a decade after it was implemented, Santiago-Santiago (1986) suggested that one of its shortcomings was that it would not ensure equal educational opportunity for fully 60% of Puerto Rican youngsters in New York City because they were not enrolled in bilingual programs. Some of these were youngsters who did not qualify for bilingual education under the consent decree because they were deemed to be proficient enough in the English language (youngsters who were proficient in English, even if they were also proficient in Spanish, could not qualify for such programs). Bilingual education continued to be identified as a compensatory rather than an enrichment program. Some students who were found to be "bilingual" were actually not proficient in either language and were generally placed in special education classes. Although they might have benefited from placement in bilingual classrooms, most of these students were denied such placement and were therefore largely unaffected by the decree.

In analyzing the new position of bilingual education as just one among many important educational issues for Latinos, rather than as the preeminent issue it had been for two decades, Orfield (1986) explained:

Until recently in many communities, Hispanic educational problems were often defined almost exclusively as language problems. Hispanic teachers and administrators were hired primarily for bilingual programs. The image of what was wrong was the first grader sitting helpless in a class where he could not understand anything the teacher was saying. This was, of course, a very serious problem. The great majority of Hispanic students, however, spoke English, lived in metropolitan areas, and still had serious educational problems. (pp. 6–7)

Puerto Rican and other Latino communities began to recognize that lack of English skills alone did not explain poor academic achievement or high drop-out rates. For example, Cuban American students, who have the highest educational levels of all Latinos, are also the most likely to speak Spanish at home. In their case, middle-class status, with its accompanying access to higher-level education, has been found to have more salience in terms of academic achievement (Valdivieso & Davis, 1988). In addition, educational policies and practices were being scrutinized more carefully by activists in the community, and calls for more political participation were heard (Caballero, 1986).

National Commission on Secondary Education for Hispanics. While much of the research of these years concerned Latinos in general rather than only Puerto Ricans, key features of some of these reports and studies will be reviewed because of their relevance for the Puerto Rican community. The focus of many of the reports undertaken by Latino advocacy groups during the 1980s and 1990s shifted from defining students as failures to defining the schools they attended as failures. For example, in a move that countered the prevailing ideology of reform movement reports, the National Commission on Secondary Education for Hispanics was created to explore why so many inner-city public high schools were not more successful in educating Latinos. For several months during 1983 and 1984, members of the commission traveled to cities with large Latino communities (New York City, Miami, Los Angeles, Chicago, and San Antonio), visiting schools and holding hearings with students, parents, teachers, administrators, counselors, and business people.

In a marked departure from the majority of reports and studies carried out in the previous two decades, the commission chose to stay out of what they characterized as the "acrimonious debate" over bilingual education, but rather concluded that there were two major language needs at the high school level for Latino students: to teach them English efficiently and effectively, and to foster biliteracy and bilingualism insofar as possible (National Commission on Secondary Education for Hispanics, 1984). The major focus of the report thus shifted from language to academic achievement in general.

The report chronicled the failure of schools to educate Latino students through data concerning dropouts, placement practices, test scores, and tracking. For example, the data revealed that 40% of all Latinos who drop out do so before 10th grade, information that would be useful in influencing the nature of drop-out prevention programs, since these are generally targeted for high school students and are too late to be of any help. The commission also found that 25% of all Latino students who entered high school were overage for their grade, and that, of Puerto Rican students in particular, 45% who began high school never finished. The effects of tracking, testing, and low expectations of students were found to be especially severe for Latino students, with 76% of those who took the High School and Beyond (HSAB) achievement tests scoring in the bottom half of national results and with 40% of all Latinos in a general track (National Commission on Secondary Education for Hispanics, 1984).

The commission reported that schools that were most successful with Latinos were characterized by strong links to the community, active parent involvement, dedicated principals and teachers who had high expectations for all students, and a good number of Latino teachers and other adults in guidance, mentoring, and supervisory roles. In fact, students who testified at the hearings attributed their success in these schools to a quality of "caring," or, in the words of one of them: "Teachers lean on us and get on our case but we know they care about us …"(National Commission on Secondary Education for Hispanics, 1984, Vol. 1, p. 29). Not surprisingly, the major findings of the commission centered on the importance of the quality of life in schools, suggesting that personal attention, contact with adults, and family involvement with the schools are the keys to improving the performance and retention of Latino students.

National Council of La Raza. Another national report using the momentum of *A Nation at Risk* was released by the NCLR and was designed to provide an overview of the educational status of Latinos in order to explore the implications for educational policy makers (Orum, 1986). The report took most reform initiatives to task because they were not designed to improve education for Latino and other "at-risk" youngsters. In fact, it maintained that many of the reform initiatives actually increased the proportion of Latinos who left school without diplomas.

The findings of the NCLR report echoed earlier warnings about the dire effects of tracking on Latino students, who were less likely to be placed in programs for the gifted and in honors classes and more likely to be in remedial classes than either White or African American students. The report also concluded that Latinos were the most undereducated group of Americans, according to measures of below-grade-level enrollment, number of years of school completed, and drop-out rates, with the rate of about 50% for Puerto Ricans the highest of any Latino group (Orum, 1986). The report ended with a list of recommendations emphasizing reforms in school policies and practices, including programs designed to improve early school success, courses in multicultural education and the education of language-minority students in teacher education programs, and the establishment of academic tutorial programs and drop-out prevention and recovery efforts.

Other Research Studies and Reports. Also responding to the inadequacy of reforms of the 1980s after the release of *A Nation at Risk* was a report that asked the plaintive question, *Must They Wait Another Generation?* (Valdivieso, 1986). It reported drop-out rates for Latinos as high as 70% in Chicago and 80% in New York City in the early 1980s. Among 20- to 24-year-old Puerto Ricans, 46% were not high school graduates, the worst standing of any Latino group. Claiming that current reforms were inadequate for the needs of Latinos because many of the issues important to them had been overlooked, the author suggested strategies that focused on improved and more sensitive counseling, recognition of the role of work in the lives of Latino high school students, and major changes in the organization of secondary schools, including tracking, ability grouping, and access to high-level curriculum (Valdivieso, 1986).

Because of its history, as well as its large number of Puerto Rican professionals and the size of its Puerto Rican community, New York City has remained in the forefront of many of the educational struggles of the Puerto Rican community. In 1987 ASPIRA of New York established an educational group consisting of the Puerto Rican/Latino Educational Roundtable of the Centro (Center for Puerto Rican Studies) at CUNY, the Puerto Rican Educators Association (PREA), and other organizations concerned with the education of Puerto Ricans in New York City (Reyes, 1988). Their report, another response to the national reform movement, made recommendations regarding systematic drop-out prevention efforts, bilingual/bicultural programs, parental participation, recruitment of bilingual and Latino professionals at all levels, and affirmation of cultural and linguistic diversity. A series of other reports released during the next several years came to very similar conclusions (Latino Commission, 1992, 1994).

Orum and Vincent (1984) found that 68.1% of Latino students attended schools that were predominantly "minority." Added the authors: "Hispanics now have the dubious distinction of being not only the most undereducated group of American children, but also the most highly segregated" (p. 26). Orfield and Monfort (1988) found an even more severe situation for Puerto Rican students: In the Northeast, where most Puerto Ricans live, 77.5% of all Latinos attended extremely segregated schools. In a summary of available data on the educational attainment of precollegiate Latino students, Arias (1986) suggested that their increasing segregation in central cities was contributing to the continuing limited access to English-language development, college preparatory, and advanced placement curriculum, and that it was this isolation, more than anything else, that posed a great threat to the ideal of equal educational opportunity.

An extensive quantitative, historical, and legal analysis of 142 U.S. school districts was undertaken to explore these kinds of inequities in Latino education, and to find suggestions for what can be done about them (Meier & Stewart, 1991). Although the authors agreed that Latino students were more segregated than African Americans, they argued that segregation is not the only impediment to equal educational opportunity. Other, more subtle methods are equally effective in denying access to education, including ethnic disparities in discipline (e.g., dress codes that are more rigidly enforced among Latinos) and academic grouping (through special education, curriculum tracking, ability grouping, and segregated bilingual education). Coined "second-generation educational discrimination," these kinds of strategies can induce Latino students to drop out of school, thus attaining a lower quality of education (Bullock & Stewart, 1979).

Meier & Stewart (1991) also found that second-generation discrimination exists because Latinos lack the political power to prevent such actions, and that school districts with greater Latino representation on school boards and among teaching faculty experienced significantly less of this discrimination. Calling the situation for low-income Puerto Ricans "especially grim," the authors claimed that they fared the worst of any Latino subgroup because, while their educational experiences resembled those of African Americans, they did not have the compensating political resources of this group (Meier & Stewart, 1991).

Puerto Rican Student Marginalization. During the early 1990s, more research on Puerto Rican students attempted to discern the reasons for low achievement and high drop-out rates, and therefore focused on comprehensive analyses of actual school experiences. Darder and Upshur (1993), for instance, in a study of four Boston public schools, conducted extensive meetings and interviews with teachers, principals, students, and parents, and also administered questionnaires and took part in long hours of classroom observation. They found that the overall environment in these schools, which had student bodies that were 45–55% Latino, was "deficient" both because of physical dilapidation and because the curriculum and instructional strategies were largely irrelevant to the lives of the children. In addition, in a replay of "cultural deprivation" research of the 1960s, the authors found that most principals and teachers tended to view the source of the educational problems faced by Latinos as originating either in their environment or in the children themselves. The children, on the other hand, located the problems squarely at the school door, and wanted more sports activities, better food in the cafeteria, more interesting books, more computers, cleaner bathrooms, teachers who did not yell at them, and a safe environment.

Examples of student marginalization have been found in other recent research as well. For example, an extensive review of school records in Holyoke, Massachusetts, high schools found that Puerto Rican students in nonbilingual programs were more than twice as likely (69% compared to 31%) to drop out as those in bilingual programs (Frau-Ramos & Nieto, 1993). The same study quoted one young man, in explaining his reason for dropping out, as saying that he felt like "an outsider," not really belonging to the community of the school.

Zanger (1993), through research based on a panel discussion of 20 high-achieving Latino students in a college-skills course in a Boston high school who were asked to reflect on their school experiences, found that many expressed similar feelings of marginalization. In the words of one student: "They won't accept you if you're not like them. They want to monoculture [you]" (p. 169). Students used words such as "below," "under," "low," and "down" to describe what they felt was their

position in the school. If this is the case among academically successful students, we can only speculate that low-achieving students feel even more marginalized and disempowered.

Finally, an ethnographic study of high school dropouts who had returned to attend an alternative high school program in New York City examined the reasons these young people gave for dropping out (Saravia-Shore, 1992). Criticisms of their former school experiences included teacher favoritism toward better students, and the lack of respect, care, and concern of teachers for them. These students gave specific instances of teachers' discrimination: "They would say things like, 'Do you want to be like the other Puerto Rican women who never got an education? Do you want to be like the rest of your family and never go to school?'" (p. 242).

In spite of experiences of this kind, about one half of the students who attended this alternative high school went on to higher education. This success rate was attributed to a number of factors that were in keeping with family and community values, among them teachers' caring and an emphasis on student decision-making skills (Saravia-Shore, 1992).

The Latino Commission. The most recent report in the long history chronicling the education of Puerto Ricans in New York City was released by the Latino Commission on Educational Reform, formed in October 1991 to examine issues of concern to the 334,000 Latino children in the New York City public schools, about 50% of whom are Puerto Rican (Latino Commission, 1992, 1994). This total represents 35% of the student body in the public schools. Chaired by Board of Education member Luis Reyes, the commission comprised 35 Latino leaders representing community-based organizations, colleges and universities, and government agencies, as well as students, parents, and teachers.

It is instructive to note the differences between the commission and its predecessor of almost 40 years, *The Puerto Rican Study* (Morrison, 1958). Although the issues of concern were strikingly familiar, the differences between them were dramatic. Among the similarities were the charge (to make recommendations to help the Board of Education fulfill its commitment to Latino students) and the findings of high drop-out rates, poor achievement, and lack of access to rigorous academic programs (Latino Commission, 1994). In a replay of the dismal educational conditions of the 1950s, Latino students were still likely to be attending segregated and underachieving schools and to have a drop-out rate 40% higher than all other students. Among Puerto Ricans the drop-out rate was still the highest of all, estimated at 35% (Latino Commission, 1994).

The Latino Commission was dramatically different from *The Puerto Rican Study* for a number of reasons. First, in a marked departure from such labels as "losers" and "at risk," the commission concentrated its efforts on characterizing Latino youngsters as potential "leaders." Thus its focus was on rigorous academics, high expectations, innovative pedagogy, community service, and empowerment, as well as the establishment of a "Leadership School" so that students could develop sound skills, a social conscience, a connection to other ethnic groups, and leadership abilities for a multicultural society. The circle that began with Puerto Ricans defined as "problems" in *The Puerto Rican Study* (Morrison, 1957) had been closed with Latino youths recognized as potential "leaders" of their community.

The commission, in designing a vision for the education of Latinos, recommended the following components in its interim report: developing a sense of identity based on a study of Latino history and culture; acknowledging and affirming Latino diversity and shared values; developing and maintaining bilingual literacy; and linking schools with the community and with the growing sectors of the labor market (Latino Commission, 1992). The final report focused on the status of the initial recommendations (Latino Commission, 1994).

There were other differences between the two documents as well. In dramatic contrast to *The Puerto Rican Study*, whose membership was almost entirely non-Latino, all 35 commission members were Latinos. The voices of Latino professionals, parents, and community activists were loud and strong, something that would have been unthinkable 40 years earlier. Latino student voices were also represented through a series of surveys and interviews carried out by Latino college student researchers from Fordham University, working under the supervision of sociologist Clara Rodriguez. The major findings of these surveys and interviews echoed those of similar research: Schools with low Latino drop-out rates were characterized by student perceptions of cohesive school spirit and teacher and counselor cultural sensitivity. The interim report concluded: "The respect and value in which students were held was extremely important in separating the schools with low Latino dropout rates from those with high rates" (Latino Commission, 1992, Vol. 2, p. 79).

Thus, as the 1990s approached their midpoint, the research on Puerto Rican students in the United States had increased dramatically from its beginnings in the 1930s. Furthermore, the research is expanding outside its traditional New York City borders, as is evident in projects being developed and reported in other states (Hidalgo, 1992; Rivera & Nieto, 1993). Lessons from this long and troubled history will be the focus of the next section of this chapter.

WHAT HAVE WE LEARNED? BUILDING ON THE STRUGGLES AND PREPARING FOR THE FUTURE

A number of lessons that may be helpful in developing a vision and strategies for the future education of Puerto Ricans in the United States can be gleaned from the review presented in this chapter. These lessons, described in three broad contexts, can be found throughout the extensive literature covered, and will be reviewed briefly along with examples from additional research.

Building on Family Strengths

The family has been recognized as a major force in the education of Puerto Ricans throughout their history in the United States. Whether it has been through parent involvement,

the community control movement, or inclusion of family perspectives in the curriculum, the family can have a positive impact on students' attitudes and achievements (see Hidalgo, Bright, Siu, Swap, & Epstein, chapter 28 of this *Handbook*). Yet, although the literature is replete with evidence of the high expectations of Puerto Rican parents for their children's achievement, it has also shown that they have received little direct help in providing environments for their children's success (Mills et al., 1950; Koss, 1965; Orfield, 1986; Díaz-Soto, 1988; Hidalgo, 1992).

Special strengths of the Puerto Rican community lie in close family relationships, conception of community responsibility, and resilience in the face of adversity. Given Puerto Rican parents' high aspirations and stubborn insistence on the rewards of education, it becomes imperative that these be used in any strategy to improve the education of their children (Nieto, 1988; Saravia-Shore, 1992). One example of using the family strengths of Puerto Rican and other children as the core of the curriculum has been described by a teacher working with two professors in western Massachusetts: (Keenan, Willett, & Sosken, 1993). They explain: "Unlike other approaches that focus on changes the families must make to support schools, we begin with ways that schools must change to support families" (p. 57). Through visits by families of culturally diverse backgrounds to the classroom, the researchers document the wide range of knowledge, skills, and teaching capabilities used by parents with their children at home that can enrich their education in school as well.

Research such as this documents how students' experiences, culture, and language are important sources for curriculum development, and thus for their academic achievement, and can serve as a promising practice for other schools working with a culturally diverse population, including Puerto Rican children.

Cultural and Linguistic Maintenance

Throughout much of the history of the education of Puerto Ricans in the United States, cultural and linguistic maintenance have served as both a defense against a hostile environment and as a nonnegotiable demand for educational improvement. Even during periods of "Americanization" and other assimilationist pressures, Puerto Ricans have insisted on retaining Spanish and their cultural roots, while at the same time learning English and becoming biculturally adept. Nowhere is this more evident than in the demands for bilingual education that began in the 1960s. Research over the past two decades has reaffirmed the academic and linguistic benefits of maintaining the native language and becoming bilingual (Cummins, 1981, 1989; Hakuta, 1987; Ramirez, 1991).

Other indications of how cultural and linguistic maintenance can be helpful in learning can be found in research focusing on the impact of culture and cultural behaviors on the classroom (Hernández & Santiago-Santiago, 1983; Solá & Bennett, 1985; McCollum, 1989; Hornberger, 1990; Sayers, 1991; Torres-Guzmán, 1992; Walsh, 1991). Zentella (1992), in research focusing on 19 Puerto Rican families in New York City, discovered that the most successful students in the study were also the most fluent bilinguals. Walsh's research points out how Puerto Rican youngsters maintain their culture and language, albeit in limited ways, even in schools where they are disparaged. She found that fourth-grade Puerto Rican students often maintained cultural nuances in the meanings they gave to words in Spanish in spite of the fact that they had lost the same meaning in English. For instance, "neighborhood" in English was described as a place with buildings, while its Spanish equivalent, "comunidad," was described as "a place where there's a lot of family" (p. 73). This intriguing research points out how children internalize reality from two opposing worlds and can end up either being enriched or as "cultural schizophrenics," with implications for the classroom and student learning.

An ethnographic study that tells the stories of teachers struggling to give hope and provide environments for the empowerment of Latino students is also instructive (Torres-Guzmán, 1992). Two examples of critical pedagogy in action were used: an integrated environmental science curriculum in an alternative high school in New York City, housed in a community-based organization; and a student-experience approach that organized curriculum to validate students as learners. In both cases students' experiences were used as the basis for their education and to help them become more active learners.

The environmental science curriculum described by Torres-Guzmán (1992) resulted in the formation of "The Toxic Avengers," a student group that investigated toxic wastes in their Brooklyn neighborhood and eventually led to the cleanup of a particularly polluted lot. In 1989 the Toxic Avengers received an award from the Citizens' Committee of New York for their efforts. Concludes Torres-Guzmán:

The message of the stories is not complex: incorporating student experiences as a way of giving primacy to students' voices changes the relationships of power and collaboration in the classroom. Learning can become meaningful and purposeful for the individual and can create spaces for exploring what the relationship of the individual is within the broader social context. (p. 488)

A review of the literature on the interactions of Latino students and their teachers also found that explicit or positive acknowledgment of Latinos' cultural base is valuable in the classroom experience (Rodriguez, 1991). Another review on linguistically and culturally diverse students in general found that promoting students' native as well as second languages was an effective strategy in their learning. The researcher concluded that the more linguistically and culturally diverse the children, the more closely must academic content be related to the child's own environment and experience (García, 1991). All of these examples point to the importance of linguistic and cultural maintenance, through bilingual and multicultural programs, as important cornerstones of any strategy to improve the education of Puerto Rican youngsters.

Revisiting School Policies and Practices

Much research on the education of Puerto Ricans has emphasized, either directly or indirectly, the need to reexamine the impact of school policies and practices on their academic achievement and high school completion. These policies and practices have included inequitable school funding (Meier & Stewart, 1991; ASPIRA, 1993), overcrowding (Orfield, 1986), ability grouping (National Commission, 1984; Valdivieso, 1986), retention (Margolis, 1968; Orfield, 1986; Fernández & Vélez, 1990), testing (Keller, Deneen, & Magallán, 1991; Mestre & Royer, 1991), curriculum reform (Fine, 1991; Latino Commission, 1994), disciplinary policies (Wehlage & Rutter, 1986), and the need for work-study programs (Valdivieso, 1986; Hispanic Policy Development Project, 1990).

Rather than continuing to focus on students or their families as "the problem," research instead suggests that schools need to look at their own policies and practices in order to improve the education of Puerto Rican students. While this in no way means minimizing the responsibility of Puerto Rican families and communities in the process, it simply reaffirms the traditional responsibility of U.S. schools to educate *all* students, not just those from English-speaking, middle-class, and well-educated families. Thus, rather than focus on issues about which they can do precious little, such as poverty, low parental educational levels, or single-parent family structure, schools need to focus on what they *can* change. At the same time, Puerto Rican families and communities need to feel that they have an important role to play in the education of their children, and partnerships need to be formed among families, schools, and the larger community in order to tackle the plague of underachievement and high drop-out rates.

CONCLUSION

Puerto Ricans have been attending schools in the continental United States in large numbers since the late 1930s, and numerous problems with their educational achievement have been identified throughout these years. In this chapter the troubled history of the educational experiences of Puerto Ricans has been reviewed, including a description of the migration to the United States and its impact on education. Three themes characterizing the education of Puerto Ricans in U.S. schools were briefly explored: the legacy of colonialism; the role of racism, ethnocentrism, and linguicism; and the quest for self-determination. Following this, an extensive review of research, based on a chronology of labels used to describe Puerto Rican students over the years, documented the extent of high drop-out rates and low achievement. Schools' responsibility in fueling these problems through negative and racist attitudes and low expectations, and through such practices as ability grouping, grade retention, inadequate counseling, and irrelevant curriculum, were discussed. Finally, lessons drawn from this history were reviewed, including building on family strengths, the importance of linguistic and cultural maintenance, and the need to reexamine school policies and practices in order to make schools more accommodating to the needs of Puerto Rican students.

The long history of Puerto Rican students in U.S. schools has been one of unfulfilled expectations and broken dreams. The failure of schools to educate this population has jeopardized both the students and our society at large. In the meantime, labels used to characterize Puerto Rican students have almost taken on a life of their own, leaving in their wake a legacy of neglect and hopelessness. Ironically, the labels used to describe Puerto Rican youngsters can also be used to describe our schools and our society. As Margolis (1968) so aptly stated:

"The Losers"—refers to us all. The children are losing all hopes of learning or succeeding; the schools are losing all hopes of teaching; and

the nation is losing another opportunity, perhaps its last, to put flesh on the American dream. (p. i)

Similarly, "outsiders" can refer to Puerto Rican students who feel marginalized as well as to school systems that remain on the outskirts of the Puerto Rican experience. In the same way, "leaders" refers to us all, for not only will Puerto Rican students become leaders if their educational needs are met, but schools and society will become leaders as well by providing them with the excellent and equitable education that all youngsters deserve.

References

Acosta-Belén, E., & Sánchez Korrol, V. (Eds.). (1993). *The way it was and other writings*. Houston, TX: Arte Público Press.

Arias, M. B. (1986). The context of education for Hispanic students: An overview. *American Journal of Education, 95*(1), 26–57.

ASPIRA of America. (1979). *Trends in segregation of Hispanic students in major school districts having large Hispanic enrollments. Final report*. New York: Author.

ASPIRA Association. (1991). *The ASPIRA story: 1961–1991*. Washington, DC: Author.

ASPIRA Institute for Policy Research. (1993). *Facing the facts: The state of Hispanic education, 1993*. Washington, DC: Author.

ASPIRA of New York. (1968). *Hemos trabajado bien. Proceedings of the ASPIRA National Conference of Puerto Ricans, Mexican-Americans, and Educators*. New York: Author.

Association of Assistant Superintendents. (1948). *A program of education for Puerto Ricans in New York City*. Brooklyn: New York City Board of Education.

Baez, T., Fernández, R. R., Navarro, R. A., & Rice, R. I. (1986). Litigation strategies for educational equity: Bilingual education and research. *Issues in Education, 3*(3), 198–214.

Bereiter, C., & Engleman, S. (1966). *Teaching disadvantaged children in the preschool*. Englewood Cliffs, NJ: Prentice-Hall.

Bilingual Education Act of 1967. (1968). U.S. Code 20.

Bloom, A. (1987). *The closing of the American mind: How higher education has failed democracy and impoverished the souls of today's students*. New York: Simon & Schuster.

Bonilla, F., & Campos, R. (1981). A wealth of poor: Puerto Ricans in the new economic order. *Daedalus, 110*, 133–176.

Bucchioni, E. (1982). The daily round of life in the school. In F. Cordasco & E. Bucchioni (Eds.), *The Puerto Rican community and its children on the mainland* (3rd rev. ed., pp. 201–238). Metuchen, NJ: Scarecrow Press.

Bullock, C. S., III, & Stewart, J., Jr. (1979). Incidence and correlates of second-generation discrimination. In M. L. Palley and M. B. Preston, (Eds.), *Race, sex, and policy problems* (pp. 115–129). Lexington, MA: Lexington Books.

Bureau of Transitional Bilingual Education. (1971). *Two way: Bilingual bicultural is two way education*. Boston: Department of Education.

Caballero, D. (1986). *New York school board elections: A fight for the future of our children*. Testimony presented by the Puerto Rican/Latino Education Roundtable at the New York State Assembly Public Hearing on School Board Education Reforms, June 5. New York: Puerto Rican/Latino Education Roundtable, Hunter College.

Cafferty, P. S. J., & Rivera-Martínez, C. (1981). *The politics of language: The dilemma of bilingual education for Puerto Ricans*. Boulder, CO: Westview Press.

Calitri, R. (1983). *Racial and ethnic high school dropout rates in New York City*. New York: ASPIRA.

Campos, R., & Bonilla, F. (1976). Industrialization and migration: Some effects on the Puerto Rican working class. *Latin American Perspectives, 3*(3), 66–108.

Carrasquillo, A. L. (1991). *Hispanic children and youth in the United States: A resource guide*. New York: Garland.

Castellanos, D. (1983). *The best of two worlds*. Trenton, NJ: State Department of Education.

Chenault, L. R. (1970). *The Puerto Rican migrant in New York City*. New York: Columbia University Press. (Original work published 1938)

Colleran, K., Gurick, D., & Kurtz, M. (1984). *Migration, acculturation, and family processes*. New York: Hispanic Research Center, Fordham University.

Colón, J. (1982). *A Puerto Rican in New York and other sketches*. New York: International. (Original work published 1961)

Cummins, J. (1981). The role of primary language development in promoting educational success for language minority students. In Office of Bilingual Bicultural Education, California State University (Ed.), *Schooling and language minority students: A theoretical framework* (pp. 3–49). Sacramento: Evaluation, Dissemination, and Assessment Center.

Cummins, J. (1989). *Empowering minority students*. Sacramento: California Association for Bilingual Education.

Darder, A., & Upshur, C. (1993). What do Latino children need to succeed in school? A study of four Boston public schools. In R. Rivera & S. Nieto (Eds.), *The education of Latino students in Massachusetts: Research and policy considerations* (pp. 127–146). Boston: Gastón Institute for Latino Public Policy and Development.

Díaz-Soto, L. (1988, April). *The home environment and Puerto Rican children's achievement: A researcher's diary*. Paper presented at the annual conference of the National Association for Bilingual Education, Houston, TX.

Durán, R. P. (1983). *Hispanics' education and background: Predictors of college achievement*. New York: College Entrance Examination Board.

Fantini, M., & Magat, R. (1970). *Community control and the urban school*. New York: Praeger.

Fernández, R. R., & Shu, G. (1988). School dropouts: New approaches to an enduring problem. *Education and Urban Society, 20*(4), 363–386.

Fernández, R. R., & Vélez, W. (1990). Who stays? Who leaves? Findings from the ASPIRA five cities high school dropout study. *Latino Studies Journal, 1*(3), 59–77.

Fine, M. (1991). *Framing dropouts: Notes on the politics of an urban public high school*. Albany: State University of New York Press.

Fishman, J. A., Cooper, R. L., & Ma, R., et al. (1971). *Bilingualism in the barrio*. Bloomington: Indiana University Press.

Fitzpatrick, J. P. (1971). *Puerto Rican Americans: The meaning of migration to the mainland*. Englewood Cliffs, NJ: Prentice-Hall.

Fitzpatrick, J. P. (1987). *Puerto Rican Americans: The meaning of migration to the mainland* (2nd ed.). Englewood Cliffs, NJ: Prentice-Hall.

Frau-Ramos, M., & Nieto, S. (1993). "I was an outsider": Dropping out among Puerto Rican youths in Holyoke, Massachusetts. In R. Rivera and S. Nieto, (Eds.), *The education of Latino students in Massachusetts: Research and policy considerations* (pp. 147–169). Boston: Gastón Institute for Latino Public Policy and Development.

Fuentes, L. (1976). Community control did not fail in New York: It wasn't tried. *Phi Delta Kappan, 57*(10), 692–695.

Fuentes, L. (1980). The struggle for local political control. In C. E. Rodriguez, V. Sánchez Korrol, & J. O. Alers (Eds.), *The Puerto Rican struggle: Essays on survival in the U.S.* (pp. 111–120). New York: Puerto Rican Migration Research Consortium, Inc.

Gallardo, J. M. (Ed.). (1970). *Proceedings of conference on education of Puerto Rican children on the mainland*. Santurce, PR: Department of Education.

García, E. (1991). *Education of linguistically and culturally diverse students: Effective instructional practices*. Santa Cruz, CA: National Center for Research on Cultural Diversity and Second Language Learning.

Gittell, M. (1972). Decentralization and citizen participation in education. *Public Administration Review, 32*, 670–686.

Hakuta, K. (1987). Degree of bilingualism and cognitive ability in mainland Puerto Rican children. *Child Development, 58*(5), 1372–1388.

Hernández, S. M., & Santiago-Santiago, I. (1983). Toward a qualitative analysis of teacher disapproval behavior. In R. V. Padilla (Ed.), *Theory, technology, and public policy on bilingual education* (pp. 99–111). Rosslyn, VA: National Clearinghouse for Bilingual Education.

Hidalgo, N. M. (1992). *"i saw puerto rico once": A review of the literature on Puerto Rican families and school achievement in the United States* (Report #12). Boston: Center on Families, Communities, Schools and Children's Learning.

Hirsch, E. D. (1987). *Cultural literacy: What every American needs to know*. Boston: Houghton Mifflin.

Hispanic Policy Development Project. (1990). *A more perfect union: Achieving Hispanic parity by the year 2000*. New York: Author.

History Task Force, Centro de estudios puertorriqueños. (1979). *Labor migration under capitalism: The Puerto Rican experience*. New York: Monthly Review Press.

History Task Force. (1982). *Sources for the study of Puerto Rican migration: 1879–1930*. New York: Centro de Estudios Puertorriqueños, Research Foundation of the City University of New York.

Hornberger, N. (1990). Creating successful learning context for bilingual literacy. *Teachers College Record, 92*(2), 212–229.

Iglesias, C. A. (1984). *Memoirs of Bernardo Vega*. New York: Monthly Review Press.

Institute for Puerto Rican Policy. (1992, June). The distribution of Puerto Ricans and other selected Latinos in the U.S.: 1990. *Datanote on the Puerto Rican Community, 11*. New York: Author.

Jensen, A. R. (1969). How much can we boost I.Q. and scholastic achievement? *Harvard Educational Review, 39*(1), 1–123.

Keenan, J. W., Willett, J., & Solsken, J. (1993). Constructing an urban village: School/home collaboration in a multicultural classroom. *Language Arts, 70*, 56–66.

Keller, G. S., Deneen, J. R., & Magallán, R. J. (Eds.). (1991). *Assessment and access: Hispanics in higher education*. Albany: State University of New York Press.

Keller, G. S., & van Hooft, K. S. (1982). A chronology of bilingualism and bilingual education in the United States. In J. Fishman & G. Keller (Eds.), *Bilingual education for Hispanic students in the United States* (3–19). New York: Teachers College Press, Columbia University.

Koss, J. D. (1965). *Puerto Ricans in Philadelphia: Migration and accommodation*. Unpublished doctoral dissertation, University of Pennsylvania, Department of Anthropology.

Kyle, C., & Kantowicz, E. (1991). Bogus statistics: Chicago's Latino community exposes the dropout problem. *Latino Studies Journal, 2*(2), 34–52.

LaFontaine, H., Colon, E., Hernandez, M., Melendez, G., Orta, A., Pagan, M., Perez, C., Quiñones, N., & Rivera, S. (1973). Teaching Spanish to the native Spanish speaker. In J. W. Dodge (Ed.), *Sensitivity in the foreign-language classroom: Reports of the working committees* (pp. 63–86). Northeast Conference on the Teaching of Foreign Languages.

Latino Commission on Educational Reform. (1992). *Toward a vision for the education of Latino students: Community voices, student voices. Interim report of the Latino Commission on Educational Reform* (2 Vols.). Brooklyn: New York City Board of Education.

Latino Commission on Educational Reform (1994). *Making the vision a reality: A Latino action agenda for educational reform. Final report of the Latino Commission on Educational Reform* (2 vols.) Brooklyn: New York City Board of Education.

Lau v. Nichols, 414 U.S. 563 (1974).

Lewis, O. (1965). *La Vida: A Puerto Rican family in the culture of poverty, San Juan and New York*. New York: Vintage.

Margolis, R. J. (1968). *The losers: A report on Puerto Ricans and the public schools*. New York: ASPIRA, Inc.

Marín, G., & Marín, B. V. (1983). Methodological fallacies when studying Hispanics. *Applied Social Psychology, 3*, 99–117.

Massachusetts State Advisory Committee to the U.S. Commission on Civil Rights. (1972). *Issues of concern to Puerto Ricans in Boston and Springfield*. Boston: U.S. Commission on Civil Rights.

McCollum, P. (1989). Turn-allocation in lessons with North American and Puerto Rican students: A comparative study. *Anthropology & Education Quarterly, 20*(2), 133–156.

Meier, K. J., & Stewart, J., Jr. (1991). *The politics of Hispanic education: Un paso pa'lante y dos pa'tras*. Albany: State University of New York Press.

Meléndez, E. (1991). *Los que se van, los que regresan: Puerto Rican migration to and from the United States, 1982–1988*. New York: Commonwealth of Puerto Rico, Department of Puerto Rican Community Affairs.

Mestre, J. P., & Royer, J. M. (1991). Cultural and linguistic influences on Latino testing. In G. S. Keller, J. R. Deneen, & R. J. Magallán (Eds.), *Assessment and access: Hispanics in higher education* (pp. 39–66). Albany: State University of New York Press.

Mills, C. W., Sr., & Goldsen, R. K. (1950). *The Puerto Rican journey: New York's newest migrants*. New York: Harper & Row.

Morrison, J. C. (1958). *The Puerto Rican study, 1953–1957*. Brooklyn: New York City Board of Education.

Murguia, E. (1991). On Latino/Hispanic ethnic identity. *Latino Studies Journal, 2*(3), 8–18.

National Commission on Excellence in Education. (1983). *A nation at risk: The imperative for educational reform*. Washington, DC: Government Printing Office.

National Commission on Secondary Education for Hispanics. (1984). *"Make something happen": Hispanics and urban school reform* (2 Vols.). Washington, DC: Hispanic Policy Development Project.

National Council of La Raza. (1982). *The educational status of Hispanic-American children*. Washington, DC: Author.

National Council of La Raza. (1989). *Multiple choice: Hispanics and education*. Washington, DC: Author.

National Council of La Raza. (1990). *Hispanic education: A statistical portrait, 1990*. Washington, DC: Author.

National Council of La Raza. (1993). *Moving from the margins: Puerto Rican young men and family poverty.* Washington, DC: Author.

National Puerto Rican Task Force. (1982). *Toward a language policy for Puerto Ricans in the U.S.: An agenda for a community in movement.* New York: City University of New York Research Foundation.

Negrón, A. (1971). *Americanization in Puerto Rico and the public school system, 1900–1930.* Río Piedras, PR: Editorial Edil.

Nieto, S. (Ed.). (1983). Puerto Ricans in children's literature and history texts: A ten-year update [Special issue]. *Bulletin of the Council on Interracial Books for Children, 14,* 1 & 2.

Nieto, S. (1988). Challenges and opportunities: Four sides of the same coin. In *The Ibero-American heritage curriculum project: Latinos in the making of the United States of America: Yesterday, today, and tomorrow* (Conference proceedings, pp. 117–126). Albany: State University of New York Press.

Nieto, S. (1992). We have stories to tell: A case study of Puerto Ricans in children's books. In V. A. Harris (Ed.), *Teaching multicultural literature in grades k–8* (pp. 171–201). Norwood, MA: Christopher-Gordon Publishers.

Office of Civil Rights. (1975). *Task force findings specifying remedies for eliminating past educational practices ruled unlawful under Lau v. Nichols.* Washington, DC: Department of Education.

Office of the Mayor. (1968). *Puerto Ricans confront problems of the complex urban society: A design for change* (Community conference proceedings). New York: Author.

Ogbu, J. U. (1987). Variability in minority school performance: A problem in search of an explanation. *Anthropology and Education Quarterly, 18*(4), 312–334.

Orfield, G. (1986). Hispanic education: Challenges, research, and policies. *American Journal of Education, 95*(1), 1–25.

Orfield, G., & Monfort, F. (1988). Are American schools resegregating in the Reagan era? In H. W. Stanley & R. G. Niemi (Eds.), *Vital statistics on American politics* (pp. 326–327). Washington, DC: Congressional Quarterly Press.

Orum, L. S. (1986). *The education of Hispanics: Status and implications.* Washington, DC: National Council of La Raza.

Orum, L. S., & Vincent, A. (1984). *Selected statistics in the education of Hispanics.* Washington, DC: National Council of La Raza.

Padilla, E. (1958). *Up from Puerto Rico.* New York: Columbia University Press.

Perez, S. (1991). Hispanic child poverty: Signs of distress, signs of hope. *Agenda, 10*(2), 15–17.

Prewitt-Díaz, J. O. (1983). A study of self-esteem and school sentiment in two groups of Puerto Rican students. *Educational and Psychological Research, 3,* 161–167.

Puerto Rican Forum, Inc. (1970). *A study of poverty conditions in the New York Puerto Rican community.* New York: Author.

Quality Education for Minorities Project. (1990). *Education that works: An action plan for the education of minorities.* Cambridge, MA: Author.

Ramirez, J. D. (1991). *Final report: Longitudinal study of structured English immersion strategy, early-exit and late-exit transitional bilingual education programs for language minority children.* Washington, DC: Office of Bilingual Education.

Rand, C. (1958). *The Puerto Ricans.* New York: Oxford University Press.

Reissman, F. (1962). *The culturally deprived child.* New York: Harper & Row.

Reyes, L. (1988). *Su nombre es hoy.* New York: ASPIRA of New York.

Rivera, R., & Nieto, S. (Eds.). (1993). *The education of Latino students in Massachusetts: Research and policy considerations.* Boston: Gastón Institute for Latino Public Policy and Development.

Rivera-Medina, E. J. (1984). The Puerto Rican return migrant student: A challenge to educators. *Educational Research Quarterly, 8*(4), 82–91.

Rodriguez, C. (1991). *Puerto Ricans: Born in the U.S.A.* Boulder, CO: Westview Press.

Rubinstein, A. T. (1970). *Schools against children: The case for community control.* New York: Monthly Review Press.

Ryan, W. (1972). *Blaming the victim.* New York: Vintage Books.

Sánchez, L. R. (1987). The flying bus. In A. Rodrigeuz de Laguna (Ed.), *Images and identities: The Puerto Rican in two world contexts* (pp. 17–25). New Brunswick, NJ: Transaction Books.

Sánchez, M. E., & Stevens-Arroyo, A. M. (Eds.). (1987). *Toward a renaissance of Puerto Rican studies: Ethnic and area studies in university education.* Highland Lakes, NJ: Atlantic Research and Publications.

Sánchez Korrol, V. E. (1983). *From colonia to community: The history of Puerto Ricans in New York, 1917–1948.* Wesport, CT: Greenwood Press.

Sánchez Korrol, V. (in press). Beyond bilingual education: Puerto Rican women educators in New York City, 1947–1967. In A. Ortiz (Ed.), *New perspectives on gender, labor and migration.* Philadelphia: Temple University Press.

Santiago-Santiago, I. (1986). *ASPIRA v. Board of Education* revisited. *American Journal of Education, 95*(1), 149–199.

Saravia-Shore, M. (1992). An ethnographic study of home/school role conflicts of second generation Puerto Rican adolescents. In M. Saravia-Shore & S. F. Arviza (Eds.), *Cross-cultural literacy: Ethnographies of communication in multiethnic classrooms* (pp. 227–251). New York: Garland.

Sayers, D. (1991). Cross-cultural exchanges between students from the same culture: A portrait of an emerging relationship mediated by technology. *The Canadian Modern Language Review, 47*(4), 678–696.

Sexton, P. C. (1965). *Spanish Harlem.* New York: Harper & Row.

Shanker, A. (1973, April 29). Where we stand. *New York Times,* p. E11.

Skutnabb-Kangas, T. (1988). Multilingualism and the education of minority children. In T. Skutnabb-Kangas & J. Cummins (Eds.), *Minority education: From shame to struggle* (pp. 9–44). Clevedon, England: Multilingual Matters.

Solá, M., & Bennett, A. T. (1985). The struggle for voice: Narrative, literacy, and consciousness in an East Harlem school. *Journal of Education, 167,* 88–110.

Torres-Guzmán, M. E. (1992). Stories of hope in the midst of despair: Culturally responsive education for Latino students in an alternative high school in New York City. In M. Saravia-Shore & S. F. Arvizu (Eds.), *Cross-cultural literacy: Ethnographies of communication in multiethnic classrooms* (pp. 477–490). New York: Garland.

U.S. Commission on Civil Rights. (1976). *Puerto Ricans in the continental United States: An uncertain future.* Washington, DC: Author.

Valdivieso, R. (1986). *Must they wait another generation? Hispanics and secondary school reform.* New York: Clearinghouse on Urban Education, Institute for Urban and Minority Education, Teachers College, Columbia University.

Valdivieso, R., & Davis, C. (1988). *U.S. Hispanics: Challenging issues for the 1990s.* Washington, DC: Population Trends and Public Policy.

Vélez, W. (1989). High school attrition among Hispanic and non-Hispanic White youths. *Sociology of Education, 62*(2), 119–133.

Walsh, C. E. (1991). *Pedagogy and the struggle for voice: Issues of language, power, and schooling for Puerto Ricans.* New York: Bergin and Garvey.

Wasserman, M. (1969, June). The I.S. 201 story: One observer's version. *Urban Review, 2,* 3–15.

Wehlage, G., & Rutter, R. (1986). Dropping out: How much do schools contribute to the problem? *Teachers College Record, 87*(3), 374–392.

Zanger, V. V. (1993). Academic costs of social marginalization: An analysis of Latino students' perceptions at a Boston high school. In R. Rivera & S. Nieto (Eds.), *The education of Latino students in Massa-* *chusetts: Research and policy considerations* (pp. 170–190). Boston: Gastón Institute for Latino Public Policy and Development.

Zentella, A. C. (1992). Individual differences in growing up bilingual. In M. Saravia-Shore & S. F. Arvizu (Eds.), *Cross-cultural literacy: Ethnographies of communication in multiethnic classrooms* (pp. 211–225). New York: Garland.

• 23 •

ASIAN PACIFIC AMERICAN STUDENTS: A DIVERSE AND COMPLEX POPULATION

Valerie Ooka Pang

SAN DIEGO STATE UNIVERSITY

To many educators, Asian Pacific American students seem to look and to be alike; they are perceived as model minority students. Like many other stereotypes, this perception is more easily believed than subjected to careful examination. In fact, most Asian Pacific American students are neither "superbrains" nor gang members. They do represent many cognitive strengths and weaknesses, have diverse ethnic roots, live in many parts of the United States, and range from being newly immigrated to having roots over 200 years old in the United States (Cordova, 1983). Educators and researchers need to become aware of the diversity and complexities within the Asian Pacific American student population.

Asian Pacific Americans encompass a number of highly diverse groups, including those of Cambodian, Chinese, East Indian, Filipino, Guamanian, Hawaiian, Hmong, Indonesian, Japanese, Korean, Laotian, Samoan, and Vietnamese cultural heritages (Takaki, 1989). The U.S. Bureau of the Census included smaller Asian Pacific American groups within the category of all other Asians in the 1980 Census (U.S. Bureau of the Census, 1983). These were Bangladeshi, Bhutanese, Bornean, Burmese, Celbesian, Cernan, Indochinese, Iwo-Jiman, Javanese, Malayan, Maldivian, Nepali, Okinawan, Sikkimese, Singaporean, and Sri Lankan (Gardner, Robey, & Smith, 1985). In total, Asian Pacific Americans make up the fastest-growing minority group in the United States. From 1970 to 1980 the Asian population increased by approximately 143% (Suzuki, 1988). And from 1980 to 1990 the Asian Pacific American population continued to grow, numbering 7.3 million people and representing almost 3% of the U.S. population in 1990 (Ong & Hee, 1993). Ong and Hee project that by the year 2020, the Asian Pacific

American population will number from 17.9 million to 20.2 million, representing an increase of 145 to 177 percent.

The Asian Pacific American student population has also seen dramatic growth. During the 1980s the number of Asian Pacific American children increased from a little over 900,000 to 1.7 million (Kiang & Lee, 1993). In states like California, New York, New Jersey, and Pennsylvania, the number of Asian Pacific school-age students grew during this decade at a rate of over 100%. A force that has contributed to the increasing number of Korean immigrants is the adoption of children by U.S. families (Chan, 1991). In one district in Massachusetts, Kiang and Lee reported that over 35 to 50 new Cambodian and Laotian students registered for school each week in 1987. Taking into consideration birthrate and continued immigration, it may be safely surmised that the Asian Pacific American student population will continue to increase at an impressive rate.

Though the number of students who are of mixed parentage is not known, it is important to note that Asian Pacific American youth include a number of Eurasian Pacific Americans, Asian Latino Americans, Asian Black Americans, Asian Native Americans, and other racially mixed children. Interracial marriages have been occurring since the first Filipino immigrants made Louisiana their home in 1763 and wed outside their ethnic community (Cordova, 1983). An increase in mixed-parentage children also resulted from the military involvement of U.S. soldiers in Korea from the beginning of the Korean War in 1950 until 1990. Many Korean women became wives of soldiers, and their children added to the increase of interracial children (Chan, 1991). More recently, of course, there have been many mixed children conceived during the Vietnam War who were rejected both in Vietnam, because of their White American roots, and in the United States, because of their Vietnamese background (Carlin & Sokoloff, 1985). Many Amerasian children from Vietnam entered the United States under the Amerasian Homecoming Act of 1987, which allowed those born from 1962 through 1975 to be admitted to the country (Chan, 1991). In addition, many Japanese Americans, Korean Americans, and Filipino Americans marry outside of their ethnic group (Lee & Yamanaka, 1990), which adds to the number of children with multiple ethnic roots.

Before a general discussion of the Asian Pacific American population, a word must be said about the label *Oriental*. Though this term is often used in education to identify students with Asian roots, its use in reference to U.S. citizens and residents ignores the negative connotations of an outgroup status of foreigners, and perhaps even of "yellow peril." The term *Oriental* may also generate Western imperialistic images of rugs and spices, rather than people. Asian Pacific Americans have resided in the United States for over 200 years, some being able to trace their roots back over 10 generations. Soldiers from the Filipino American community fought in the War of 1812 (Cordova, 1983). "Asian Pacific American" or, more inclusively, "Asian and Pacific Islander American" is the most appropriate term to describe groups with roots in Asia and the Pacific Islands.

FACTORS CONTRIBUTING TO DIVERSITY

Asian Pacific American Students, Native or Immigrant

An important variable to consider when teaching or doing research with Asian Pacific American students is place of birth—U.S.-born or immigrant. The experiences of the two groups may differ greatly, as do the manners in which they identify themselves. Though it is dangerous to overgeneralize across individuals within a group, U.S.-born students are likely to be more highly assimilated into mainstream society than immigrant students (Cabezas, 1981). Individuals who do not reside in ethnic communities are also more likely to be assimilated (D. Sue, Sue, & Sue, 1983). For example, many Japanese American students who live in middle-class suburban neighborhoods may not choose to identify themselves along ethnic lines (Kitano, 1976). Matute-Bianchi (1986) found that such high school students from central California often identify themselves by their school activities, such as student government and social clubs, rather than by ancestry. Most did not want to engage in school activities that were ethnically tied. For example, though attempts had been made at one school to establish a club focusing on Japanese history, no students of Japanese descent joined the group.

However, many American-born English learners may readily identify themselves through ethnic lines, and even boast, "I can be President of the United States." These students may come to school unable to speak English because they have spoken their home languages all their lives. Kindergarten could be the very first setting requiring them to use English. On the other hand, many American-born students speak only English (Cabezas,

1981). They can be categorized as bicultural, and may look positively at ethnic membership and life in an environment that mixes both mainstream and traditional Asian values (D. Sue & Sue, 1971). These children may be family oriented, respect elders, and value education, while at the same time they participate in mainstream afterschool activities like football or ballet. They may not choose to take part in Asian Pacific American activities at school, but can be members of, for example, a local Buddhist temple, participating in ethnically specific activities in that context (Matute-Bianchi, 1986).

Like their American-born counterparts, immigrant students clearly relate to their cultural background in various ways. Some may be highly assimilated young people who feel compelled to blend into U.S. society, and so relinquish ancestral cultural values, behaviors, and traditions. They may, for example, refuse to speak their first language, and view their ethnic ties as obstacles to being accepted into the mainstream. In contrast, there are those who are extremely proud of their background. The parents of these children speak their native language, and children may attend a special Saturday or afterschool language school built to ensure that the values, beliefs, and language of the originating culture remain in the community (Guthrie, 1985; Kim, 1980; Cheng, 1991).

Many people from Asian countries have migrated to the United States in search of economic stability. Prior to 1965, Chinese American, Filipino American, Japanese American, and Korean American communities consisted of families who had long U.S. roots, since immigration had been prohibited for the Chinese after 1882, the Asian Indians in 1917, the Japanese in 1924, and the Filipinos after 1934 (Kim, 1978; Takaki, 1989). With passage of the Immigration Act of 1965 (which became effective in 1968), the number of Chinese, Korean, Asian Indian, and Filipino immigrants rose dramatically (Chan, 1991; Hing, 1993). Immigration was no longer based upon "national origins"; rather, 20,000 people per year could migrate to the United States from each country in the Eastern Hemisphere (Takaki, 1989). In addition, special emphasis was placed upon reuniting families, and a large majority of the immigration from Asian nations is based upon this provision (Hing, 1993).

More recently, Asian immigration increased after the governments of South Vietnam, Cambodia, and Laos fell in 1975. Thousands of Vietnamese, Chinese, Cambodian, and other Asian refugees fled Southeast Asia because of political strife (Hune, 1979). The Indochinese Resettlement Assistance Act of 1971 and reauthorization of the Refugee Act of 1980 provided federal assistance for refugees. The largest proportion of the refugee population was Vietnamese, with smaller numbers of Laotians, Chinese-Vietnamese, and Hmong refugees. They represented a large diversity in socioeconomic and educational levels (Rumbaut, 1985). Some were fluent English speakers, while others had no English-language skills at all. Many of the first refugees who left Indochina in 1975 were Vietnamese who were forced from Vietnam because they had worked for the U.S. government (Chan, 1991). Many of these individuals fled in airplanes and helicopters without their families, knowing they would be unable to return (Takaki, 1989). In the first wave, many of the refugees were highly educated. Takaki reported that "37 percent of heads of households had completed high school and 16 percent had been to college. Almost two thirds could speak English well or with some fluency" (p. 451). In addition, many were familiar with U.S. culture (Cheng, 1991).

The second wave of refugees, from 1979 until 1982, consisted of Vietnamese, Cambodians, Laotians, and Hmong. Many of these refugees escaped by boat or foot and sought safety in refugee camps in Thailand (Cheng, 1991). Whole families attempted to escape in leaky boats, only to encounter storms, pirates, and Vietnamese soldiers. The second wave included fewer professionals than the first wave, and more people who had lived in rural areas, like fishermen, farmers, and owners of small shops (Takaki, 1989). Many had no formal schooling.

As the Asian Pacific population has changed, difficulties have sometimes developed between immigrant and U.S.-born Asian Pacific American students. Differences between the two categories of students, their values and feelings, can affect their interactions at school (Lau, 1988). U.S.-born students often have little knowledge of the factors that forced new immigrants to the United States. They may not understand that refugees from Vietnam, Cambodia, and Laos had few choices; these individuals sought protection from the tyranny of Communist-backed governments (Takaki, 1989). New Asian Pacific American students may find themselves living in a hostile environment in which their cultural beliefs and behaviors are in conflict with their U.S.-born peers (Caplan, Choy, & Whitmore, 1991; Trueba, Cheng, & Ima, 1993).

Possible Intragroup Conflicts

Many Asian Pacific Americans have found themselves with increasing feelings of marginality (D. Sue & Sue, 1971); the pressure of cultural assimilation can produce ambivalent feelings about ethnic group membership (Gordon, 1964). Marginality refers to conflicting attitudes that may develop when a member of a minority group finds himself or herself at cultural odds with the dominant society. A marginal person can develop personality traits of insecurity, hypersensitivity, and excessive self-consciousness. Even within the Asian Pacific American population, those students whose families are several generations American may not feel comfortable with new immigrant students. They may fear being identified with the immigrants who, they feel, are old fashioned, "nerds," or "weird" in dress and behavior. When new immigrants are being harassed by other students, the established Asian Pacific Americans may feel the pressure to "join in" the mainstream so as not to be perceived as associated with the newcomers. Or they may ignore the harassment without trying to discourage the taunting. Educators should be aware of this possible area of conflict and not routinely choose other Asian Pacific Americans as buddies for immigrant students, assuming incorrectly that U.S.-born students of the same ethnic background can be of the most help to newly arrived pupils. Asking students to volunteer for this responsibility may reduce the potential for such conflict.

The second source of intragroup conflict may lie in the past, in the form of "old country" animosities. Many new immigrant students may find themselves placed in classes with others from groups that, historically, have been fierce enemies. Antagonism has cropped up in some school incidents involving Asian Pacific

American students battling each other. In one instance, a teacher who had Vietnamese American and Cambodian American students learned about these animosities in a peer teaching situation. The Vietnamese American student had lived in the United States for about seven years and spoke English well; the Cambodian American student had been in the United States for only three years and was having some difficulties understanding the material. The teacher mistakenly assumed that they would be happy to work with each other, since they had similar refugee experiences. He asked the Vietnamese youth to help the Cambodian. Since such students generally have a high regard for teachers, they were reluctant to speak out, but the Vietnamese student explained diplomatically that he did not think the other student would accept his help. This greatly surprised the teacher, but the prediction of the student was confirmed when the Cambodian student said, "I do not want to accept help from a Vietnamese." These feelings were worked through, but even then it was difficult for students who had been in adversary roles to view situations in a new light. Historical sentiments may come with new immigrants, and educators need to be aware of such long-standing animosities.

Of course, immigrant and U.S.-born youth may not generally form close friendships with each other. There can exist a mutual feeling of mistrust, reflecting a lack of understanding of each other's values and beliefs. Sometimes language barriers contribute to the distance. Those born in the United States who do not speak an Asian language may feel unable to communicate with immigrants who are speaking a first language other than English. And immigrant youngsters may not understand English sufficiently well to feel comfortable participating in peer-group conversations. School staff should be sensitive to these possible sources of conflict in encouraging cooperative activities. Students with varied roots can be placed in small mixed groupings where personal experiences can help reduce prejudicial attitudes. Here, again, the danger of overgeneralizing is ever present, as the dynamics within groups are not always apparent. Educators need to react to their Asian Pacific American students as individuals, and to understand how the differing experiences of these students can influence their behaviors in school.

Socialization of Children

Parental attitudes and child-rearing practices definitely influence the development of students. Though quite a few studies have examined general tendencies of Asian Pacific Americans as one group, only two large projects could be located that compared varying practices within that large group. One study, conducted by Cabezas (1981), examined the early childhood development of 233 Asian Pacific American families (Chinese, Japanese, Korean, and Vietnamese) from the San Francisco-Oakland metropolitan area, focusing upon parental values, child rearing, and interactional styles. The author found, in Asian Pacific American mothers born both here and overseas, a predominance of question-asking behavior over modeling, cueing, or direct commands, with American-born mothers showing a higher incidence of the behavior than those born elsewhere. Chinese and Filipino mothers born overseas used more direct commands and were more authoritarian in their beliefs than the other mothers. In those families where mothers asked more questions, the children (preschool and primary grades) also responded with more questions and sought more verbal approval from their mothers. The results of this study seem to be in conflict with the belief that Asian Pacific American students do not have the verbal skills to involve themselves in an interactive school setting. An Asian Pacific American child's failure to participate may reflect a lack of encouragement to engage in interaction, rather than lack of ability. If Asian American students are not being consistently included in class discussions, they may feel reticent about participating because of strong respect for authority (Trueba, Cheng, & Ima, 1993). If they go into the school with strong verbal interaction skills, but these skills are not being developed in classrooms, they could become less apt to participate as they progress through the educational system.

The second study was by Rumbaut and Ima (1988), who examined parent-child relationships of the Southeast Asian Pacific American refugee community in the San Diego city schools. Extensive data were collected on 579 youth, while general comparative information was collected on 1,485 junior and senior high school students. Lao and Khmer parents were found to stress academic discipline and to pressure youth to achieve less than Vietnamese, Chinese Vietnamese, and Hmong parents. In addition, there was less of a sense of obligation toward elders and parents in Lao and Khmer communities. Vietnamese, Chinese Vietnamese, and Hmong parents had stronger parental controls and domination over their children, and they emphasized the importance of collective survival. In contrast, the Lao and Khmer, rural in origin and less educated, seemed to value a more individualistic adjustment to U.S. life (e.g., in moving out as quickly as possible from shared living arrangements). Yet their communities also had a fatalistic point of view toward life, which seemed to manifest itself in the lack of an aggressively competitive attitude toward academic success. The Lao of upper-class background are more likely to have migrated to France, and many of the Khmer elite were killed in Kampuchea. Therefore, many of the refugees who settled in the United States have had fewer resources and hold values that do not advance a strong desire for "success."

Parents in the Vietnamese American community, in particular, seemed to have much more strict control over their children than Khmer and Lao parents, regardless of social class. Vietnamese American students are more likely to feel familial obligation and to be competitive in school. In elite Vietnamese families, a complex bicultural manner of resolving conflicts with children was found—though the word of parents was highly respected, children were permitted in some instances to explain, in a polite tone, their perspective in the conflict situation. Parents wanted children to feel that they had some control over their own existence. Meanwhile, the discipline Hmong parents have instilled in their children, coupled with strong respect for authority, seemed to result in high levels of motivation in some students. These students demonstrated great tenacity and discipline in their school work. Unfortunately, though many Hmong students do well in high school, very few continue studies on the college level. There is a great deal of

pressure to have a family, and many Hmong youth marry young (Trueba et al., 1993). Of course, they then find it difficult to support a family with only a high school diploma.

The socialization of children is a dynamic process. The longer Asian Pacific Americans live in the United States, the stronger is a shift toward a bicultural existence, especially in young people. Demographers project the continual influx of Asian immigrants (Hing, 1993). Consequently, many Asians will experience a transition into a bicultural existence. Some Asian Pacific parents, though somewhat unsure about the effect of cultural adaptation, seem to be pragmatic about the changes they see in their children. Caplan, et al. (1991) cite the responses of various parents:

I want my children to know Laotian culture. But it is very hard to teach it to them. We don't have any temple to show them our religion and culture. They go to school; they are going to learn more and more about American culture (Lao) (p. 83)

I am used to Americans, learn about their ways of working, and try my best to socialize. In the meantime I still maintain the moral values inside my small family and plan to teach my children that they have to get Americanized while still being Vietnamese. It's hard, but I have no choice. (Vietnamese) (pp. 83–84)

Other Asian Pacific American parents may not feel that assimilation into the American mainstream is desirable or inevitable. Gibson (1988) found in the Punjabi Sikhs (Asian Indian) community in California that parents were strongly opposed to cultural assimilation into the mainstream. Though parents advocated academic achievement, they did so without loss of cultural values because they were able to maintain a strong community separate from the school.

Language Differences

Asian Pacific American students bring a wide range of languages to schools. More than half of all Asian Pacific children come to school with a home language other than English (Trueba, et al., 1993). In 1970 a class action suit, brought by Kinney Lau and 11 other Chinese American students against Alan Nichols and the San Francisco Board of Education, demonstrated the language needs of Asian students in public schools (Kiang & Lee, 1993). This suit led to the historic 1974 *Lau v. Nichols* Supreme Court decision that ruled that all students are entitled to an equal education. The San Francisco School Board argued that the district was providing equal education because the instruction, materials, and teachers were the same for all students. The Chinese American community argued that equal education was not possible in a classroom where children were Cantonese-speaking and instruction was in English. The Supreme Court ruled that the civil rights of the Chinese American students were violated because they did not understand instruction in English (Nieto, 1992).

The first language of Asian Pacific American children may be one of the following: Burmese, Chamorro, Cantonese, English, Japanese, Farsi, Fijian, Hawaiian, Hindi, Hmong, Indonesian, Khmer, Korean, Laotian, Mandarin, Polynesian, Samoan, Tagalog, Thai, Urdu, and/or Vietnamese. These languages are extremely diverse and come from five broad language roots:

Sino-Tibetan, Altaic, Malayo-Polynesian, Austro-Asiatic, and Indo-European (Cheng, 1991). The languages differ from each other in phonetics, writing systems, grammar, and sentence structure. Even those Asian Pacific students who are immigrants from the same country may not understand each other's dialects. For example, some Chinese American students come to school speaking Mandarin or Cantonese. Though both are Han dialects, they have different phonetic and tonal characteristics (Cheng, 1991). The written symbols called ideographs are the same for the two dialects, but the spoken words are different.

The written forms of Asian languages may use Chinese characters or ideographs; for example, the written forms of Japanese and Korean were created from the Chinese writing system. Yet languages like Vietnamese have developed a Romanized alphabet system to replace the Chinese character system (Cheng, 1991). Some languages, like Laotian, are primarily made up of monosyllabic words, whereas Japanese is a polysyllabic language.

Some languages also have a complex set of rules that govern word usage depending upon the person's social status. In Laotian and Japanese, the social hierarchy dictates the proper use of words in addressing distinguished speakers. The structure of language can also differ greatly from English. In Korean there are no articles or relative pronouns (Cheng, 1991). Language errors may be the result of code switching, and may not mean that children lack cognitive ability and should be placed in learning-disability classrooms. Students may be applying language rules from their first language to learning English.

Many Asian Pacific children come to school knowing tones that are not part of the English language, and not knowing phonemes included in English. Students must often learn to master new sounds. Japanese speakers do not use the sounds of *v* and *l*, and so often substitute the English sounds for *b* or *r*. Some languages, like Laotian, are monotonous (Cheng, 1991), so students may not understand the importance of using inflection in speaking a polysyllabic language like English. In tonal languages like Cantonese, the syllable *ma* may represent many different meanings depending upon the tone it is given (Cheng, 1991). The high-level tone of *ma* may mean mother, while the falling tone of *ma* may mean to scold. A child who is familiar with a tonal language may be expecting words to have various definitions and be listening for tonal differences. Trueba et al. (1993) provided other examples explaining why some students may say *sree* instead of *tree* or *te'lvsion* instead of *television*. Additionally, students may have trouble with understanding grammatical differences and say "You no like it" or "I first go, you later come." These incidents demonstrate the need for teachers to understand the structure and language patterns of Asian Pacific American students who may come to school with a home language other than English.

SOCIOCULTURAL AND ACADEMIC NEEDS

Self-Concept and Psychological Needs

To many U.S. educators, Asian Pacific American students appear to have fewer and less severe personal problems than other students. Though teachers are often aware of the academic problems of those from Southeast Asia, the needs of other students may not be readily apparent. It is easy for educators to spot problems of language proficiency, but it is much more difficult to identify internal conflicts in students.

Needless to say, Asian Pacific American students must deal with the stresses of racism and the existence of conflicting cultural messages communicated by the images frequently portrayed of Asian Pacific Americans ("Whiz Kids," 1987; Pang, Colvin, Tran, & Barba, 1992). One of those images is the "model minority," which is often accompanied by the belief that Asian Pacific Americans are the students who raise the grading curve. They are usually not the football stars or cheerleaders, and they may be perceived as "nerds." Students who do well must cope with the social image, and it is not always an asset to stand out academically, to be considered "eggheads." Yet they often come from families in which education is highly valued. Many Asian Pacific parents will sacrifice material comfort in order to provide the best educational experience for their children (Mordkowitz & Ginsburg, 1986). Some parents expect not only "good" grades, but "exceptionally high" grades from their offspring (Pang, 1991). Thus students who feel pressure from their families must deal with possible rejection from their peers.

On the other hand, there are Asian Pacific American students who are not intellectually gifted and cannot reach the high academic standards that parents or teachers have set for them. These students have a difficult time dealing with negative feelings of being a "loser." One *sansei* (third-generation Japanese American) high school student said about himself, "My folks just gave up on me because I didn't get into college." Unfortunately, this message was reiterated by his teacher, who told the student, "Your sister was an A student—how come you only get C's? You're not trying." The model minority image can be a terrible liability for students who are not academically inclined, especially when teachers assume that students from certain Asian Pacific American groups will be top achievers. These students are trying to deal with the powerful process of assimilation, and mixed messages regarding their acceptance into mainstream society can be a heavy burden for them to carry.

The impact of being a member of a visibly different minority group can also have a forceful effect on the fragile and developing self-image of children. The findings of a study examining the self-concept of Asian Pacific American youth show a disturbing pattern of generally lower levels of self-esteem than Caucasian and African American youngsters (Tidwell, 1980). Another study reported Vietnamese American students as scoring lowest on overall self-concept in comparison to non-Vietnamese Asian, Caucasian, African American, and Mexican American students (Oanh & Michael, 1977). Similarly, Korean American and Chinese American students may not feel as positive about their physical self-image as African American or White American students (Chang, 1975; Fox & Jordan, 1973). In another study of the general self-concept of Japanese American students in the fourth through sixth grades, lower physical self-concept scores were offset by high academic self-image scores, to make the general scores less than revealing (Pang, Mizokawa, Morishima, & Olstad, 1985). These findings may be surprising to many educators who believe that Asian Pacific Americans are well-adjusted, competent students. Such studies point to the need for schools, colleges, and universities to take steps to help Asian Pacific American students develop more positive perceptions of themselves.

Since Asian Pacific American students are often perceived as well adjusted and achieving, eductors may not realize that many young people are losing their ability to speak their home language. The resultant impact of this "language shift" (Kiang & Lee, 1993) is not only a lack of home language proficiency in a native language, but also a disturbance of family relationships and personal self-image. When children lose the ability to speak a home language and parents are unable to speak English, communication between different generations of a family are hampered. This cultural dissonance can also result in a weakened sense of self. There is a great need for language programs for Asian Pacific American students that will help to maintain cultural ties and keep ethnic identities strong.

Parental Factor in Test Anxiety and Achievement

The importance of parental support in Asian Pacific American families cannot be overestimated. For example, Pang (1991) found that the parental support felt by middle school students of Chinese, Filipino, Korean, and East Indian heritages was predictive of mathematics grades. However, these students were also more test anxious than their White American counterparts because of their desire to please their parents. The side effect of high parental expectations and need for approval may be test anxiety. In comparison with their White American peers, Asian Pacific American students report more support and encouragement from their parents. Asian Pacific American parents, more than their White American counterparts, believe that their children try to please them. The socialization of Asian Pacific American students follows a complex interpersonal process that transforms into an intrapersonal one (Cole, John-Steiner, Scribner, & Souberman, 1978). The quest for approval through doing well becomes internalized, though children are typically unaware of the process. Besides, it may be the support felt by Asian Pacific American children that helps them to diffuse, to an extent, the pressure of high parental academic expectations.

The role of parents in academic achievement was also perceived as extremely important by Hess and his associates (Hess, McDevitt, & Chih-Mei, 1987). In contrast with Caucasian Americans, Chinese American mothers of sixth-grade students placed more responsibility for their children's poor performance in mathematics upon the training received at home. While acknowledging the training their children received at school to be critical, these mothers explained that it was the duty of parents to instill in their children the value of education. In addition, they lacked confidence in the school and felt it necessary to take an active part in remedying its shortcomings. They revealed high academic expectations, stressing the importance of the child's effort. These studies display not only the prominence of parental attitudes and values in the academic process, but also the influence of child-rearing practices. Many Asian Pacific American students come from family environments that emphasize schooling. In some cases, families take an active part in monitoring the progress of students.

Academic Achievement of Students

Research on the academic achievement of Asian American students has typically indicated high levels of scholarship, and, in fact, the popular press often labels them "whiz kids" ("Whiz Kids," 1987). Unfortunately, this portrayal does not accurately reflect the actual achievement levels found across the group. The Admissions Testing Program of the College Board collected data for five years (1980–1985) on college-bound seniors (Ramist & Arbeiter, 1986). The 1985 sample included the responses of 1,052,351 high school seniors. Among them were 42,637 Asian Pacific American students, or 4% of all candidates, which was almost a 50 percent increase from the beginning of the study in 1980. The sample represented a broad spectrum of Asian communities. On the Scholastic Aptitude Test in 1985, the Asian Pacific American verbal mean scores of 404 was below the national average of 431, but the mathematics mean of 518 was above the national average of 475. Table 23–1 shows the mean verbal and mathematics scores for White American and Asian Pacific American high school seniors from 1975–1991 on the Scholastic Aptitude Test (Snyder, 1992). There is a significant decrease in the average verbal scores of Asian Pacific American students during the years 1976 through 1984. The most dramatic drop in mean scores of Asian Pacific students came in 1978, 1979, and 1982 school years, when their average scores were 396, 396, and 395, respectively. These scores may reflect the lower scores obtained by the large number of refugee students who entered U.S. schools speaking languages other than English during the first and second waves of immigration from Southeast Asia.

The observed trend of Asian Pacific American students doing better in mathematics than in verbal areas had been reported earlier (Stodolsky & Lesser, 1967), but the literature does not, unfortunately, indicate specific realms of strengths or weaknesses within these broad subject areas. However, the Admissions Testing Program did provide information regarding the SAT reading comprehension and vocabulary subscores (Ramist & Arbeiter, 1986). On the reading comprehension subscale, Asian Pacific Americans scored 40.7, in contrast with the White American mean of 44.9. On the vocabulary subscale, the scores were 40.4 for Asian Pacific Americans and 45.0 for White Americans. In the questionnaire administered by the Admissions Testing Program, seniors were asked how many years they had studied mathematics. The Asian Pacific American mean was 3.89 years, in contrast with the White American mean of 3.72. The additional two months of instruction may be reflected in the difference in mathematics performance. Another reason may be the strong interest Asian Pacific American seniors show in mathematics and science. While 58.6% of these students indicated that their intended area of study in college was the biological or physical sciences, only 38.8% of the White American seniors intended to study the sciences. This may mean that more Asian Pacific American than White American college-bound students had become interested in science at an earlier age, and had participated in extracurricular activities that fos-

TABLE 23–1. Scholastic Aptitude Test Score Averages of
White American and Asian Pacific American
High School Seniors, 1975–1991

Test	Racial/Ethnic Background	1975–76	1976–77	1977–78	1978–79	1979–80	1980–81	1981–82	1982–83	1983–84	1984–85	1986–87	1987–88	1988–89	1989–90	1990–91
SAT-Verbal																
	White	415	448	446	444	442	442	444	443	445	449	447	445	446	442	441
	Asian American	414	405	401	396	396	397	398	395	398	404	405	408	409	410	411
SAT-Mathematical																
	White	493	489	485	483	482	483	483	484	487	490	489	490	491	491	489
	Asian American	518	514	510	511	509	513	513	514	519	518	521	522	525	528	530

Source: Digest of Education Statistics 1992 (p. 125) by T. Snyder, 1992. Washington, DC: National Center for Educational Statistics.

tered the development of knowledge and skills in science. In addition, if their parents indicated a preference for careers in mathematics and sciences, the children would be more likely to have pursued that route.

In English instruction, on the other hand, the College Board study found almost the same amount of time of study (Ramist & Arbeiter, 1986). The mean years of instruction were 3.97 for Asian Pacific Americans and 4.00 for White Americans. In spite of the equivalence in the length of instruction, a lack of strong English-language skills plagues many Asian Pacific American students. Of the 1985 Asian Pacific American high school seniors who indicated that English was not their best language, the SAT verbal median score was a low 272; the median for others who reported English as being their best language was 434, still lower than the mean of 449 for White Americans. The large number of Asian Pacific American immigrants who have migrated to the United States since the 1970s, many of whose families have home languages other than English, may account for such findings. Program development in both oral and written communication skills for Asian Pacific American students is an area that educators, policy makers, and researchers need to address. This need is perceived by Asian Pacific American seniors themselves. Even though 73% rated themselves high on mathematics abilities, only 56% so rated themselves for oral expression (in comparison with 64% for all students) (Ramist & Arbeiter, 1986). Asian Pacific American students seem to have "communication anxiety"—they not only feel the inability to do well, but reveal a fear of writing and speaking. Such apprehension in itself may attract them into more technical and scientific fields of study.

Relevant information is currently gathered by a few large school districts according to specific Asian ethnic groups. Their data clearly show that there are both successful and failing Asian Pacific American students. For example, the Seattle School District's 1986–1987 student population contained 19.5% Asian Pacific Americans, a total of 8,532 (Seattle Public Schools, 1987). These students represented nine ethnic groups: Chinese, East Indian, Filipino, Japanese, Korean, Other Asian, Samoan, Other Southeast Asian, and Vietnamese. The district defined students to be "at risk" if they scored below the 50th

percentile on the California Achievement Test (1977 norms). Over 39% of the Asian Pacific American high school students who took the California Achievement Test in the Seattle School District during the 1986–1987 academic year scored below the 50th percentile in reading. A similar pattern was found in 40.9% of Chicano/Latino students, but only 18.3% of White American students were found "at risk." Table 23–2 provides a more complete description of the data, including the results in language and mathematics. Just as there were many students who were "at risk," many others were dropouts; Table 23–3 presents details for Asian Pacific American youth. The wide difference among group drop-out rates is seen in the 1985–1986 Seattle School District figures. Though only 5.1% of the Japanese American students dropped out of school, 34.6% of the Samoan American students left school before graduation. Over one third of all Samoan students in Seattle schools

TABLE 23–2. Proportions of High School Students
Scoring below the 50th Percentile on the
California Achievement Test, 1986–1987

Ethnic Group	Subject		
	Reading	Language	Mathematics
Asian Pacific American	39.8%	34.4%	20.5%
Japanese	12.8	12.1	11.3
East Indian	28.1	37.5	31.3
Korean	28.4	22.2	12.3
Chinese	29.2	23.9	8.1
Other Asian	34.2	42.5	37.5
Filipino	40.7	35.6	28.6
Vietnamese	55.7	46.4	15.8
Samoan	76.9	69.8	65.4
Other Southeast Asian	79.1	65.1	36.7
American Indian	50.0	57.1	57.8
Black American	54.9	59.8	58.6
Chicano/Latino American	40.9	41.9	41.8
White American	18.3	23.4	25.4

Source: Adapted from *Data Profile District Summary* (pp. 85, 87, 89) by Seattle Public Schools, 1987. Seattle, WA: Author.

TABLE 23–3. Proportions of Asian Pacific American High School Dropouts, 1985–1986

Ethnic Group	Proportion
Asian Pacific American	11.0%
Japanese	5.1
Chinese	5.3
Korean	8.6
Other Asian	10.4
Filipino	11.0
Vietnamese	11.8
East Indian	12.7
Other Southeast Asian	17.9
Samoan	34.6
White American	16.1

Source: Adapted from *Data Profile District Summary* (p. 135) by Seattle Public Schools, 1987. Seattle, WA : Author.

TABLE 23–4. Mean Percentile Ranks of the CTBS Reading Scores, May 1987

Ethnic Group	Grade											
	K	1	2	3	4	5	6	7	8	9	10	11
Asian Pacific American												
Japanese[a]	58[b]	69	67	60	65	70	74	72	82	71	67	71
Korean[a]	53	64	60	52	59	60	49	62	47	47	36	50
Chinese	40	53	51	43	47	48	46	45	39	41	33	39
Filipino	50	57	49	42	49	45	37	39	37	32	35	34
White American	67	56	68	57	69	69	70	73	77	68	71	73
American Indian[a]	52	40	36	46	59	63	68	64	50	41	50	35
Black American	33	31	27	27	27	34	31	32	28	26	24	33
Hispanic American	31	30	29	28	32	32	27	32	26	25	19	22

[a] Fewer than 60 students were tested at each grade level.

[b] The percentile rank of 50 represents the national average.

Source: Adapted from *Districtwide (CTBS/U) Test Results* (p. 28) by San Francisco Unified School District, 1987. San Francisco, CA: Author.

dropped out of school, which puts the community "at risk" of losing the potential of its youth.

Samoan Americans are one group of Asian Pacific Americans who are struggling to keep their culture and community intact (Jung, 1993). The following quote describes the difficulty that faces Asian Pacific Islanders: "A certain seabird has a long feather in its tail, and whenever he loses it, he loses his balance. So is tradition to the Samoan" (p. 3). The strength of the Samoan community comes from the maintenance of the family, which may include a large extended network of members. As with many other ethnic communities, parents may not understand the policies and culture of schools. For example, since Samoan culture is highly verbal, parents may not respond to written notes from teachers, which can be a source of miscommunication (Jung, 1993).

It is obvious that educators, policy makers, and researchers should not facilely generalize when dealing with such a diverse population as Asian Pacific American youth. They are like any other group in that some students do well, while others may be struggling in school. Each child should be treated as an individual. The general descriptions of various Asian Pacific groups in this chapter should not be used to stereotype any of the subgroups.

Patterns of academic achievement similar to those of the Seattle School District have been found in the San Francisco School District. In the analysis of the May 1987 reading scores on the Comprehensive Tests of Basic Skills (CTBS) by youngsters in kindergarten through the 11th grade, Japanese American students had the highest mean percentile rank among Asian Pacific Americans, followed by Korean Americans, Chinese Americans, and finally, Filipino Americans (San Francisco Unified School District, 1987). The details are presented in Table 23–4. Because there were many limited-English-proficient students in the district, the scores were recalculated for those who were proficient in English, based on oral and written assignments, class progress, and achievement at or above the 36th percentile on standardized tests. As seen in Table 23–5, the patterns for such subgroups were similar to those for the Asian Pacific American students in general. Japanese American students again scored well, followed by Chinese Americans, and

then Korean Americans. Filipino students were demonstrating mean ranks close to the national average.

It is as difficult to identify all the variables that affect achievement among Asian Pacific American students as it is among White American students. There are, at least, some definite differences in relation to the varied background and experiential factors reviewed here. The literature on academic achievement does point to the need for the continuance of bilingual education for Asian Pacific American students. It also points to a lack of research that carefully examines the needs of diverse Asian Pacific American groups in the area of language and reading skills.

Impact of Prejudice and Ethnic Bias

The impact of ethnic prejudice as an influential factor on the sociopsychological development of Asian Pacific American stu-

TABLE 23–5. Mean Percentile Ranks of the CTBS Reading Scores of English-Proficient Students, May 1987

Ethnic Group	Grade											
	K	1	2	3	4	5	6	7	8	9	10	11
Asian Pacific American												
Japanese[a]	71[b]	73	85	65	76	72	81	78	85	72	68	73
Korean[b]	55	68	69	63	70	68	63	73	67	65	59	59
Chinese	68	71	70	62	64	63	66	65	63	62	60	62
Filipino	56	62	55	52	56	53	46	50	48	44	50	47
White American	68	57	70	59	70	70	71	74	78	70	71	76
American Indian[a]	52	42	35	48	59	63	69	67	50	41	50	35
Black American	33	31	27	27	27	34	31	32	28	26	24	33
Hispanic American	51	47	49	43	45	46	41	43	40	36	36	39

[a] The number (and proportion) of "English-proficient" students varied from one group to another, as well as from one grade to another. Consult the cited source for details.

[b] The percentile rank of 50 represents the national average.

Source: Adapted from *Districtwide (CTBS/U) Test Results* (p. 36) by San Francisco Unified School District, 1987. San Francisco, CA: Author.

dents must also be addressed by teachers, researchers, and policy makers. There are many reports of the frustrations Asian Pacific American students experience in dealing with prejudicial attitudes and remarks. For instance, Kim (1978) found 30% of the Korean American students she studied reporting discrimination at school in the form of harassment or name calling. Such incidents involved not only other students but also some school personnel. She recounted an incident in which a five-year-old boy said, "They [his classmates] call me Chinese!" Apparently this child was hurt because he was singled out for his difference in physical appearance. In addition, many Asian Pacific American students who are not Chinese resent being automatically identified as a member of this group. Often people use the category of Chinese as a generic Asian label because they do not know how many different groups exist in the Asian Pacific American community. This plays into the stereotype that all Asians look the same. These feelings can lead to frustrations and anger in children about their bicultural or multicultural identities. Similar concerns were expressed by Japanese American high school students in central California. They were upset because of the perceived image their peers had of Japanese Americans.

As one ninth grader said: "They [the school community] think we're all smart and quiet. We're not, but they think we are." Another student indicated that Japanese-American "students have a reputation for being really good in science and math." And another student said he was not particularly "good" in math but "the teacher expected me to do good in it." (Matute-Bianchi, 1986, p. 247)

To understand the experiences of Southeast Asian Pacific American students in the San Diego city schools in California, the district surveyed 521 junior high students and found strong resentment against Southeast Asian Pacific Americans (Rumbaut & Ima, 1988). Approximately 30% of the nonrefugee students made disturbing remarks such as: "Get rid of the Cambodians"; "I think the Blacks and Whites get along great but it's the Vietnamese we can't stand"; "Move some Nips to other schools" (Rumbaut & Ima, 1988, p. 59). The bigotry against Asian Pacific Americans has resulted in the death of students. In 1987 in Lowell, Massachusetts, during a period of community unrest surrounding busing and anti-immigration sentiment, an 11-year-old White male beat up Vandy Phorng, a 13-year-old Cambodian student. Phorng was pushed into a canal, where he drowned (Kiang, 1990). In January 1989 in Stockton, California, a White male shot and killed five Southeast Asian American children at Cleveland School (Kiang, 1990). The violence against Asian Pacific American students is a shocking expression of the prejudice that exists in American society.

Southeast Asian American students provided recommendations on how to improve intercultural relationships (Rumbaut & Ima, 1988). They wanted school staff to do something about, among other things, the name calling, as it often escalated into physical violence between Vietnamese and nonrefugee students. Cambodian American students were greatly offended by derogatory remarks that abusers considered to be casual statements. In addition, some Southeast Asian American youth felt that some teachers were biased against them, making negative

statements about Vietnam or giving them unfair punishment. These biases found in school experiences can greatly affect the emerging bicultural identity of Asian Pacific American youth. Educators need to understand the choices and dilemmas such students face in the cultural assimilation process, and to help them in developing the personal confidence and coping skills to deal with the ethnic discrimination they will most likely encounter. Students may withdraw from the school community or fight back, verbally or physically, if they feel powerless to deal with prejudicial situations.

Implications for Research

A complex issue that researchers must consider is the nature of their beliefs about Asian Pacific Americans and Asians. For many educators, both terms refer to the same communities. Though Asian Pacific Americans may have strong connections with their Asian relatives, there are also many Asian Pacific American students who are fifth-generation or beyond U.S. citizens, speak English only, and have become highly assimilated into U.S. society. Though there is research that focuses upon the achievements and characteristics of Japanese, Chinese, and other Asian student populations (Stevenson, Lee, & Stigler, 1986; Stevenson, 1991), researchers must be cautious in their use of research on Asians in explaining the behavior and beliefs of Asian Pacific American students.

Another issue that continues to dominate the literature is the overemphasis placed upon Confucian values in explaining the academic achievement of Asian Pacific American students. The process of achievement is an extremely complex one in which numerous variables contribute to the success of students in school. Many researchers may think mistakenly that Confucian values are similar to American mainstream values. Confucian and American mainstream values are quite different, yet they both encourage academic achievement (Cheng, 1991; Caplan et al., 1991). In addition, since Asian Pacific American communities are located within the larger American society, the Confucian values of some individuals are changing. Trueba et al. (1993) found that some Asian Pacific American students are finding that the values of humility, obedience, moderation, and harmony may not be functional in a technological society. Hirschman and Wong (1986) believe the success of groups like the Japanese and Chinese was encouraged by the closure of immigration from Asian countries at the end of the 1800s and early 1900s. These communities were not asked to use their few resources to support an increasing population; instead, the few funds available were concentrated, in some instances, on supporting small businesses, developing agricultural methods, and sending their children to college.

Much of the research on racial and cultural differences has compared African American and White American samples. For many years the United States government did not attempt to collect information on the demographics of Asian Pacific Americans, and merely classified the population with various groups into an "other" category. This explains the invisibility of Asian Pacific American students in many research projects. Research by Mizokawa and Rychman (1990) demonstrates how the aggregation of data can hide critical differences among cultural groups. Mizokawa and Rychman found in their research on six Asian Pacific American student groups that distinguishing patterns arose on four attributional choices of ability, effort, luck, and task ease in success and failure situations. Their sample of 2,511 students included 836 Chinese, 562 Filipino, 232 Japanese, 166 Korean, 344 Vietnamese, and 371 Southeast Asian youth. In this study the authors found that Asian Pacific American students believed that effort was more important than ability in explaining success or failure. Of the six groups studied, Korean Americans had the highest attribution scores, followed by Filipino Americans, Chinese Americans, Japanese Americans and Southeast Asian Americans, with the lowest effort scores in the Vietnamese American sample. It is recommended that more attention be placed on providing information on ethnic-group membership. When using gross categories like ethnicity, it is also important for researchers to examine such other characteristics as generation in the United States, home language, English-language proficiency, socioeconomic status, gender, gender-role expectations, family values, neighborhood/geographical location, and occupation of parents. In addition, some research on Asian Pacific American students has limited generalizability because of small sample sizes and the grouping of diverse Asian groups into one gross category.

Though there seems to be a growing body of knowledge about the historical experience of Asian Pacific Americans, there is much less quantitative and qualitative research on educational issues such as learning styles, motivational styles, sociocultural communication styles, effective language strategies, and metacognitive processing. Not only is there a need for data on the patterns of various Asian Pacific American groups as they relate to these areas, but it is also important for researchers to examine the impact of individual differences (Slaughter-Defoe, Nakagawa, Takanishi, & Johnson, 1990). In addition, the research that exists has customarily utilized college students rather than younger children; research that centers upon Asian Pacific American children is rare. Longitudinal studies of Asian Pacific American students are also scarce.

The most promising type of research involving Asian Pacific American students is exemplified by the ethnographic work of Ima (1992), who utilized a cultural ecological approach (Ogbu, 1981). In his exploratory study of newcomer students to a large district in southern California, Ima extended his original study of Asian Pacific American students (Rumbaut & Ima, 1988), investigating the effectiveness of schooling for newcomers. Ima reviewed the court proceedings that mandated integration, interviewed personnel, learned about community cultural values, reviewed district policies, examined data from bilingual and English as a Second Language (ESL) programs, gathered student grade-point averages, made observations in classrooms, and gathered information on the political and social context of school neighborhoods. Ima interviewed students, parents, aides, counselors, resource faculty, teachers, counselors, vice principals, principals, and central office administrators. The focus of his study was five secondary schools, with an average population of 2,000 students per school, and their surrounding neighborhoods. These schools included many Cambodian, Filipino, Hmong, Lao, and Vietnamese American students. Ima found that Asian Pacific American students were being served by different kinds of schools whose efficacy depended upon the goals of the school. One was a college preparatory school in which immersion into English was the norm and the curriculum was basically Eurocentric. At this school few teachers addressed the cultural and linguistic needs of students. Another school was so beset with social problems that it could only provide minimal time for instruction; most time was spent "keeping order." None of the schools provided a culturally affirming environment. The "American Dream" for many of the Asian Pacific American newcomer students Ima interviewed was only a fantasy. Many newcomers fell behind in their classes because the district did not provide adequate bilingual and ESL programs. There was a lack of teaching materials written in the home language of students. Finally, the district was not effective in monitoring the success of students and assessing student progress. The impact of schooling that does not provide a culturally affirming learning environment in which student values and languages are respected can be devastating. Students will not have an "equal chance" to develop, learn, and mature, and this will limit their ability to realize their dreams.

Implications for Practice

Educators need to begin to examine their attitudes toward and knowledge of Asian Pacific American students. Asian Pacific students constitute an extremely diverse population that has complex needs. The inaccurate "model minority" myth and belief in the homogeneity of the Asian Pacific American student population have limited the development of educational programs that address their varied needs. New perspectives on these students should be adopted by educators. Educational institutions should develop comprehensive multicultural education programs that address the need for curriculum reform and transformation (Banks, 1991).

One area of concern is the self-concept of Asian Pacific students. Utilizing a general self-concept score for Asian Pacific students does not provide information regarding specific needs. Students may also suffer from test anxiety and pressures for high academic achievement. Some appear to be highly influenced by a desire to please their parents, an impetus potentially stronger than direct parental pressure. Additionally, educators may be unconsciously contributing to students' heightened anxiety by assuming that most Asian Pacific American students are high achievers. Another important concern is the inability of many educators to recognize feelings of depression, frustration, and desperation in Asian Pacific American students. Educational institutions should consider instituting programs to help students and parents to understand the pressures for high academic achievement and to assist highly anxious students in developing effective coping skills.

Positive role models can serve as examples of how others have been able to strike a balance among the diverse expectations young people face from their ethnic, religious, peer, family, neighborhood, and school communities. The increased use of positive role models can benefit Asian Pacific American and other students by presenting diverse perspectives and an expanded view of successful individuals within a culturally diverse society. Employment of Asian Pacific administrators, teachers, and community resources can help Asian Pacific students expand their own beliefs about their potentialities, while also providing other students with a heightened awareness of the contributions of Asian Pacific Americans in U.S. society. Positive role models can also be integrated into the curriculum through the careful selection and use of literature (Pang, et al., 1992).

As the number of Asian Pacific American students steadily increases, it is important that educators use teaching materials and resources that promote sensitive, positive, and accurate portrayals of Asian Pacific Americans. As this chapter has indicated, Asian Pacific students are often confronted with biases from peers, teachers, and friends. Literary resources can present protagonists who are empowered people. These role models should not be generalized depictions of politeness, martial arts, and stilted speech. The characters should represent real people whose cultural background enriches and guides their lives and who illustrate the struggles of individuals with their bicultural identity (Pang et al., 1992). When instructors use literature with Asian role models, students may feel validated to express their beliefs because the instructor's use of Asian perspectives gives legitimacy to those viewpoints. Asian Pacific American literature can expand all students' viewpoints of complicated social issues by providing new perspectives and demonstrating the value of diverse cultural worldviews (Pang & Park,1992). Asian Pacific literary selections and books can stimulate students to discuss the complexities of life that all students face, and thereby help them understand their own lives.

Many excellent books and materials with Asian Pacific American protagonists focus upon human and civil rights (Pang et al., 1992). These resources can be used to generate discussion in issues-centered lessons focusing upon citizenship in a culturally diverse democracy (Shaver, 1992; Evans & Pang, 1992). Instructors can use novels, films, books, and other print media to begin in-depth discussions in the classroom on issues with which Asian Pacific American students may be dealing on a personal level, such as bicultural identity, ethnic discrimination, employment, cultural pluralism, immigration, and nationalism. For example, instructors may discuss various events of World War II, but few discuss the impact of the internment of Japanese Americans from the viewpoint of Japanese Americans, and fewer teachers may discuss the internment from a Chinese American, African American, or West Coast viewpoint (Pang & Park, 1992). Resources for older students, like Frank Chuman's *The Bamboo People* (1976) and Peter Irons's *Justice at War* (1983), read along with novels like Yoshiko Uchida's *Desert Exile* (1982) and Frank Okada's *No-No Boy* (1976), can provide a comprehensive view of the impact of the internment of Japanese Americans by examining historical, emotional, and psychological perspectives. To give younger readers information, instructors can have available materials like Sheila Hamanaka's *The Journey: Japanese-Americans, Racism, and Renewal* (1990) and Yoshiko Uchida's *Journey to Topaz* (1971). Films like "Color of Honor" (Ding, 1988) and "Unfinished Business" (Mouchette Films & Okazaki, 1986) are also excellent resources for educators. Materials that provide an Asian Pacific American perspective not only give Asian Pacific students the opportunity to hear viewpoints from the Asian Pacific communities, but can also help them to develop their own "voice."

A subscription to *Amerasia* is an important contribution to any institutional or personal library. This landmark journal is published by the Asian American Studies Department at the University of California, Los Angeles. *Amerasia* is an especially valuable resource because it provides information on crucial historical, literary, and psychological issues that affect the diverse Asian Pacific American community.

The increase in anti-Asian crimes points to the need for educators to include discussion of current social issues, such as the devastation of Koreatown after the Rodney King verdict. When Korean American students returned to school in Koreatown, many asked to go home early because of headaches and stomach pains resulting from their uneasiness over events in society (Kiang & Lee, 1993). There has also been a sharp rise of "Japan-bashing" violence, which is unsettling for Asian Pacific students (Kiang & Lee) who are seen as foreigners and threats to the economic well-being of the United States. Bringing into the classroom issues that affect many Asian Pacific students will help to make formal education more relevant, bridging the gap between home and school (Trueba et al., 1993).

In order for Asian Pacific American students to experience equal educational opportunity and develop their "voice," educational institutions must provide students with effective bilingual and second-language education. The right of students to receive instruction in their home language was officially mandated by the *Lau v. Nichols* Supreme Court decision. There is controversy as to what remedies should be implemented. Even those Asian Pacific American students who speak and write English well point to the need for schools to institute educational programs to help them become confident in communication skills, both oral and written. Research does support the concern that Asian Pacific American students feel about their verbal abilities. Researchers have found Asian Pacific students to score lower than their White American peers on the verbal portion of standardized instruments like the Scholastic Aptitude Test (Ramist & Arbeiter, 1988; S. Sue & Abe, 1988; Reglin & Adams, 1990). Because these students often exhibit competencies in technical and scientific fields, educators may overlook their lower grades in English, creative writing, or composition. There are some Asian groups whose children are dropping out of school at a rate of 50%, and the effects can be devastating on the economic and political survival of their communities. In addition, there are sufficiently high numbers of "at risk" students in certain groups to call for a balanced view of Asian Pacific American students and their families.

One of the most promising programs that has involved Asian Pacific American students is the Kamehameha Elementary Education Program (KEEP) for at-risk Hawaiian American students (Tharp & Gallimore, 1988). A 10-year study of the program involving 3,345 students demonstrated significant achievement in reading. Using Vgotsky's sociocultural context of learning, the KEEP program focused upon the interaction of teacher and student and of student and student where literacy developed along with cognition. Much emphasis was placed upon the experiences of children and the sharing of their experiences in discussion and within the context of learning centers. In these learning centers, children worked collaboratively with each other rather than in highly structured teacher-directed instruction. One of the culturally based approaches used in the KEEP program was "talk story" (Au, 1980). In utilizing "talk story," students were allowed to discuss in a group in which there was "overlapping speech, joint performance (cooperative production of responses) by a group, and informal turn-taking" (Tharp & Gallimore, p. 151). Utilizing this culturally familiar method of communication, children were allowed to develop language skills in a natural context.

Like any other group, Asian Pacific American students have strengths and needs. U.S. society is still saddled with an educational system that has difficulty dealing with students who come to school with varying values, languages, and motivational backgrounds. Understanding the great diversity among Asian Pacific American students is crucial; otherwise, their needs may continue to be overlooked. Creation of alternatives in curriculum, policies, materials, counseling, and instructional strategies demands a change in the educators' attitudes toward, and knowledge of, Asian Pacific American students. Educators can provide an equal educational opportunity when schooling is guided by accurate information and in-depth understanding of the cultural needs of Asian Pacific American students.

References

Au, K. (1980). Participation structures in a reading lesson with Hawaiian children: Analysis of a culturally appropriate instructional event. *Anthropology and Education Quarterly, 11*(2), 91–115.

Banks, J. A. (1991). *Teaching strategies for ethnic studies* (5th ed.). Boston: Allyn and Bacon.

Cabezas, A. (1981). *Early childhood development in Asian and Pacific American families: Families in transition.* San Francisco: Asian Inc.

Caplan, N., Choy, M. & Whitmore, J. (1991). *Children of the boat people: A study of educational success.* Ann Arbor: University of Michigan Press.

Carlin, J., & Sokoloff, B. (1985). Mental health treatment issues for Southeast Asian refugee children. In T. Owen (Ed.), *Southeast Asian mental health: Treatment, prevention, services, training and research* (DHHS Publication No. ADM 85-1399, pp. 91–112). Washington, DC: U.S. Department of Health and Human Services.

Chan, S. (1991). *Asian Americans: An interpretive history.* Boston: Twayne.

Chang, T. (1975). The self-concept of children in ethnic groups: Black American and Korean American. *Elementary School Journal, 76,* 52–58.

Cheng, L. (1991). *Assessing Asian language performance: Guidelines for evaluating limited-English-proficient students.* Oceanside, CA: Academic Communications Associates.

Chuman, F. (1976). *The bamboo people: The law and Japanese-Americans.* Del Mar, CA: Publisher's Inc.

Cole, M., John-Steiner, V., Scribner, S., & Souberman, E. (Eds.). (1978). *Mind in society.* Cambridge, MA: Harvard University Press.

Cordova, F. (1983). *Filipinos: Forgotten Asian Americans.* Dubuque, IA: Kendall/Hunt.

Ding, L. (Producer & Director). (1988). *Color of honor* [Film]. San Francisco: Crosscurrent Media.

Evans, R., & Pang, V. (1992). Resources and materials for issues-centered social studies education. *The Social Studies, 83*(3), 118–119.

Fox, D., & Jordan, V. (1973). Racial preference and identification of American Chinese, Black and White children. *Genetic Psychology Monographs, 88,* 220–286.

Gardner, R. W., Robey, B., & Smith, P. C. (1985) *Asian Americans: Growth, change, and diversity.* Washington, DC: Population Reference Bureau.

Gibson, M. (1988) *Accommodation without assimilation: Sikh immigrants in an American high school.* Ithaca, NY: Cornell University Press.

Gordon, M. (1964). *Assimilation in American life.* New York: Oxford University Press.

Guthrie, G. P. (1985). *A school divided.* Hillsdale, NJ: Lawrence Erlbaum Associates.

Hamanaka, S. (1990). *The journey: Japanese-Americans, racism, and renewal.* New York: Orchard Books.

Hess, R., McDevitt, T., & Chih-Mei, C. (1987). Cultural variations in family beliefs about children's performance in mathematics: Comparison among People's Republic of China, Chinese-American, and Caucasian American families. *Journal of Educational Psychology, 79,* 179–188.

Hing, B. O. (1993). Making and remaking Asian Pacific America: Immigration policy. In *The state of Asian Pacific America: A public policy report: Policy issues to the year 2020* (pp. 127–140). Los Angeles: LEAP Asian Pacific American Public Policy Institute and UCLA Asian American Studies Center.

Hirschman, C., & Wong, M. (1986). The extraordinary educational attainment of Asian-Americans: A search for historical evidence and explanations. *Social Forces, 65*(1), 1–27.

Hune, S. (1979) U.S. immigration policy and Asian and Pacific Americans: Aspects and consequences. In S. Hune (Ed.), *Civil rights issues of Asian and Pacific Americans: Myths and realities* (pp. 283–291). Washington, DC: U.S. Commission on Civil Rights.

Ima, K. (1992). *Testing the American dream: A case study of educating secondary newcomer students.* Unpublished manuscript, San Diego State University.

Irons, P. (1983). *Justice at war.* New York: Oxford University Press.

Jung, S. (1993, May 19–June 1). Samoans: Struggling to keep traditions alive. *International Examiner,* pp. 3, 7, 10.

Kiang, P. (1990). *Southeast Asian parent empowerment: The challenge of changing demographics in Lowell, Massachusetts,* (Monograph No. 1). Jamaica Plain, MA: Massachusetts Association for Bilingual Education.

Kiang, P., & Lee, V. W. (1993). Exclusion or contribution? Education K–12 policy. In *The state of Asian Pacific America: A public policy report: Policy issues to the year 2020* (pp. 25–48). Los Angeles: LEAP Asian Pacific American Public Policy Institute and UCLA Asian American Studies Center.

Kim, B. (1978). *The Asian Americans: Changing patterns, changing needs.* Montclair, NJ: Association of Korean Christian Scholars in North America.

Kim, B. (1980) *The Korean-American child at school and at home.* Washington, DC: U.S. Department of Health, Education, and Welfare.

Kitano, H. (1976). *Japanese Americans: The evolution of a subculture* (2nd ed). Englewood Cliffs, NJ: Prentice-Hall.

Lau, G. (1988). *Chinese American early childhood socialization in com-*

munication. Unpublished doctoral dissertation, Stanford University, Palo Alto, CA.

Lee, S., & Yamanaka, K. (1990). Patterns of Asian American intermarriage and marital assimilation. *Journal of Comparative Family Studies, 21*(2), 287–305.

Matute-Bianchi, M. (1986). Ethnic identities and patterns of school success and failure among Mexican-descent and Japanese-American students in a California high school: An ethnographic analysis. *American Journal of Education, 94,* 233–255.

Mizokawa, D., & Rychman, D. (1990). Attributions of academic success and failure: A comparison of six Asian-American ethnic groups. *Journal of Cross-Cultural Psychology, 21*(4), 434–451.

Mordkowitz, E., & Ginsburg, H. (1986, April). *The academic socialization of successful Asian Pacific American college students.* Paper presented at the annual meeting of the American Educational Research Association, San Francisco.

Mouchette Films (Producer) & Okazaki, S. (Director). (1986). *Unfinished business: The Japanese American internment cases* [Film]. San Francisco: Crosscurrent Media.

Nieto, S. (1992). *Affirming diversity: The sociopolitical context of multicultural education.* New York: Longman.

Oanh, N. T., & Michael, W. B. (1977). The predictive validity of each of ten measures of self-concept relative to teacher's ratings of achievement in mathematics and reading of Vietnamese children and of those from five other ethnic groups. *Educational and Psychological Measurement, 37,* 1005–1016.

Ogbu, J. (1981). Origins of human competence: A cultural ecological perspective. *Child Development, 52,* 413–429.

Okada, F. (1976). *No-No Boy.* Seattle: University of Washington Press.

Ong, P., & Hee, S. (1993). The growth of the Asian Pacific American population: Twenty million in 2020. In *The state of Asian Pacific America: A public policy report: Policy issues to the year 2020.* Los Angeles: LEAP Asian Pacific American Public Policy Institute and UCLA Asian American Studies Center.

Pang, V. (1991). The relationship of test anxiety and math achievement to parental values in Asian-American and European-American middle school students. *Journal of Research and Development in Education, 24*(4), 1–10.

Pang, V., Colvin, C., Tran, M., & Barba, R. (1992). Beyond chopsticks and dragons: Selecting Asian-American literature for children. *The Reading Teacher, 46*(3), 216–224.

Pang, V. O., Mizokawa, D., Morishima, J., & Ostad, R. (1985). Self concepts of Japanese-American children. *Journal of Cross-Cultural Psychology, 16,* 99–109.

Pang, V., & Park, C. (1992). Issues-centered approaches to multicultural education in the middle grades. *The Social Studies, 83*(3), 108–112.

Ramist, L., & Arbeiter, S. (1986). *Profiles: College-bound seniors 1985.* New York: College Entrance Examination Board.

Reglin, G., & Adams, D. (1990). Why Asian-American high school students have higher grade point averages and SAT scores than other high school students. *The High School Journal, 73*(3), 143–149.

Rumbaut, R. (1985). Mental health and the refugee experience: A comparative study of Southeast Asian refugees. In T. Owen (Ed.), *Southeast Asian mental health: Treatment, prevention, services, training and research* (DHHS Publication No. ADM 85-1399, pp. 433–486.). Washington, DC: U.S. Department of Health and Human Services.

Rumbaut, R., & Ima, K. (1988). *The adaptation of Southeast Asian refugee youth: A comparative study.* Washington, DC: US Department of Health and Human Services, Family Support Administration, Office of Refugee Resettlement.

San Francisco Unified School District. (1987). *Districtwide (CTBS/U) test results.* San Francisco: Author.

Seattle Public Schools. (1987). *Data profile district summary.* Seattle, WA: Author.

Shaver, J. (1992). Rationales for issues-centered social studies education. *The Social Studies, 83*(3), 95–99.

Slaughter-Defoe, D., Nakagawa, K., Takanishi, R., & Johnson, D. (1990). Toward cultural/ecological perspectives on schooling and achievement in African- and Asian-American children. *Child Development, 61,* 363–383.

Snyder, T. (1992). *Digest of Education Statistics 1992.* Washington, DC: National Center for Education Statistics.

Stevenson, H. (1991). Japanese elementary school education. *Elementary School Journal, 92*(1), 109–120.

Stevenson, H., Lee, S. Y., & Stigler, J. W. (1986). Mathematics achievement of Chinese, Japanese, and American children. *Science, 231,* 693–699.

Stodolsky, S., & Lesser, G. (1967). Learning patterns in the disadvantaged. *Harvard Educational Review, 37,* 546–593.

Sue, D., & Sue, D. (1971). Chinese American personality and mental health. *Amerasia Journal, 1,* 95–98.

Sue, D., Sue, D., & Sue, D. (1983). Psychological development of Chinese-American children. In G. Powell (Ed.), *The psychological development of minority group children* (pp. 159–166). New York: Brunner/Mazel Publishers.

Sue, S., & Abe, J. (1988). *Predictors of academic achievement among Asian-American and White students* (Report No. 88-11). New York: College Entrance Examination Board.

Suzuki, B. (1988, April). *Asian Americans in higher education: Impact of changing demographics and other social forces.* Paper presented at the National Symposium on the Changing Demographics of Higher Education, Ford Foundation, New York.

Takaki, R. (1989). *Strangers from a different shore.* Boston: Little, Brown.

Tharp, R., & Gallimore, R. (1988). *Rousing minds to life.* New York: Cambridge University Press.

Tidwell, R. (1980). Gifted students' self-images as a function of identification process, race and sex. *Journal of Pediatric Psychology, 5,* 57–69.

Trueba, H., Cheng, L., & Ima, K. (1993). *Myth or reality: Adaptive strategies of Asian Americans in California.* Washington, DC: Falmer Press.

U.S. Bureau of the Census. (1983). *1980 census population: Characteristics of the population.* Washington, DC: Government Printing Office.

Uchida, Y. (1971). *Journey to Topaz.* New York: Scribner's.

Uchida, Y. (1982). *Desert exile.* Seattle: University of Washington Press.

Whiz kids. (1987, August 31). *Time.* pp. 42–51.

LANGUAGE ISSUES

· 24 ·

LANGUAGE ISSUES IN MULTICULTURAL CONTEXTS

Masahiko Minami
HARVARD UNIVERSITY

Carlos J. Ovando
INDIANA UNIVERSITY, BLOOMINGTON

Over the past 30 years, a rich, exciting, and complex body of literature addressing language, literacy, and multicultural/bilingual education has emerged. The major goal of this chapter is to serve as a resource for those who are interested in language issues in multicultural contexts. We shall find that while the scholarship of the 1960s and 1970s tended to be generally theoretical, the major trend in the 1980s and 1990s has been for scholars to shift from a linguistically oriented, theoretical focus to one in which language, literacy, and multicultural/bilingual education are viewed as the products of socioculturally mediated processes among individuals and groups in school and nonschool settings.

The theoretical-linguistic nature of language studies in the 1960s and 1970s reflected the influence of Noam Chomsky's (1957) revolution, which brought with it the importance of conceptualizing links between the role of language and the human mind. Since the latter half of the 1970s, however, language studies have addressed more social and pragmatic linguistic concerns, focusing on literacy and multiculturalism/bilingualism within a sociocultural framework. The shift in language studies is, perhaps, a reflection of the demographic changes that have occurred in the United States in the second half of the century. During the 10 years between 1970 and 1980 in particular, U.S. society became increasingly multicultural as well as multilingual (Ovando, 1993). Crawford (1992) states:

Immigration to the United States has increased noticeably in recent years and, more important, its source countries have changed. In 1965, Congress abolished the national-origins quota system, a racially restrictive policy that long favored northwestern Europeans and virtually excluded Asians. As late as the 1950s Europe was still supplying more than half of all immigrants to the United States. By the 1980s the Third World was providing 85 percent of them, not counting the undocumented. These newcomers were far less familiar, racially and culturally, and so was their speech. After half a century of decline, minority tongues were suddenly more audible and, to many Americans, more dissonant as well. (p. 3)

The 1980s indeed witnessed a rapid influx of immigrants from Asia and Latin America into the United States. The upswing in immigration has resulted in large numbers of school entrants whose first language is not English. Summarizing the most recent census data concerning demographic changes from 1980 to 1990, the *New York Times* of April 28, 1993 (Barringer, 1993), reports that the number of U.S. residents for whom English is a foreign/second language increased nearly 40% to 32 million. In 1992 the U.S. Department of Education (USDE, 1992) estimated that in 1990–1991 approximately 2.3 million children lived in language-minority households, made substantial use of minority languages, and were Limited-English-Proficient (LEP) students. According to the Stanford Working Group (1993), the number of LEP children is much greater, perhaps as many as 3.3 million children between the ages of 5 and 17. Furthermore, the 1990 Census (cited in Stanford Working Group) counted more than 6 million school-aged children who used languages other than English at home. Language-minority children are now the fastest-growing group in schools in the United States (McKeon, 1992). Among language-minority groups, Spanish-speaking households are the fastest-growing sector and are expected to become this country's largest minority in the not-so-distant future.

Most educational discourse and learning environments to date have tended primarily to reflect the discourse practices of mainstream society, with often unfortunate results for non-

This chapter evolved from the conceptual framework that the first author formulated when he edited "Language Issues in Literacy and Bilingual/Multicultural Education," which was published by the *Harvard Educational Review* in 1991.

We are grateful to James A. Banks, Norma González, Kristina J. Lindborg, Michael Sander, G. Richard Tucker, and Roland Tharp for their helpful comments on an earlier draft of the chapter. We also thank Catherine Snow for her comments on an outline of the chapter.

mainstream students, including many language-minority students (Cazden, 1988; Cazden, Michaels, & Tabors, 1985; Gee, 1990, 1991; Michaels, 1981, 1991; Michaels & Collins, 1984). Using the term *match-mismatch*, some linguists (e.g., Cook-Gumperz & Gumperz, 1982; Erickson & Mohatt, 1982; Heath, 1982a; Mehan, 1991; Philips, 1982) have postulated that language-minority students do not prosper academically in such contexts because the discursive practices of their homes do not match the discursive practices of the school environment. In turn, such a mismatch between the discursive practices of the home and those of the school tends to limit language-minority students' access to and participation in higher educational and occupational opportunities (Spener, 1988). In other words, while children from middle- and upper-class cultural and speech communities are sociolinguistically advantaged in the school environment, children from poor, non-English, and nonstandard English speech communities are more likely to be disadvantaged and even at risk of being marginalized in school environments. Through language studies in multicultural contexts, researchers have addressed in a variety of ways the language issues that have emerged since the 1960s regarding such students. These studies have the potential to help educators working with those who are from distinct cultural and speech communities. Reviewing the research on language diversity, ethnic minorities, and learning is, therefore, important in many respects.

The relevant studies can be organized into the following three interrelated sections: classic theoretical approaches to language, language as a socioculturally mediated product, and multicultural and bilingual issues in relation to language. Despite the apparent differences in focus, these three approaches can be integrated into a continuum. Specifically, the first section presents an overview of the classic theoretical approaches to language studies, connecting two different disciplines of linguistics—generative grammar represented by Noam Chomsky, and sociolinguistic studies represented by Dell Hymes, William Labov, and Basil Bernstein. The second section, which emphasizes sociocultural aspects, discusses language-related issues in different societies. The third section further extends the issues discussed in the preceding section to multicultural and bilingual educational settings within a culturally diverse society such as the United States.

Through these three interrelated sections, we will be examining the following key questions:

1. What does past research tell us about cross-cultural differences in the process of language acquisition and literacy skills development?
2. Does the linguistic match-mismatch conception adequately capture the relationships between the primary speech community where an individual was raised and the secondary speech community represented by the school?
3. If languages are conceptualized as social possessions, with literacy thus being perceived from a sociocultural standpoint, what significance does this realization have for education in multicultural/bilingual contexts?

CLASSIC THEORETICAL APPROACHES TO LANGUAGE

The Chomskyan Revolution and Its Influence on Language Studies

In the 1950s most explanations of child development were dominated by behaviorist interpretations. This was especially true in Western societies, and the United States in particular. Noam Chomsky (1959), however, criticized the behaviorist approach represented by B. F. Skinner (1957), who suggested that language development is largely determined by training based on trial and error, and not by maturation. Instead, Chomsky (1965) emphasized that humans have a biological endowment, which he called a language acquisition device (LAD), that enables them to discover the framework of principles and elements common to attainable human languages. The LAD includes basic knowledge about the nature and structure of human language, which is termed "universal grammar" (UG). Although grammatical rules of sentence structure are limited, no one could exhaust all the possible sentences of language; thus, triggered by input, this internalized system of rules can generate an infinite number of grammatical sentences. Believing in a self-charged "bioprogram" whereby language acquisition is autonomous, Chomsky (1985) writes:

UG consists of various subsystems of principles; it has the modular structure that we regularly discover in investigation of cognitive systems. Many of these principles are associated with parameters that must be fixed by experience. The parameters must have the property that they can be fixed by quite simple evidence, because this is what is available to the child; the value of the head parameter, for example, can be determined from such sentences as *John saw Bill* (versus *John Bill saw*). Once the values of the parameters are set, the whole system is operative. (p. 146)

Chomsky thus hypothesizes that, in their language acquisition process, children move from the initial state to the steady state, as if by simply flipping a series of switches.

The linguistic revolution originated by Chomsky has exerted an enormous influence on contemporary studies (e.g., Slobin, 1985; Wanner & Gleitman, 1982). Brown and Bellugi (1964), for example, stress the rule-governed nature of language acquisition. If the behaviorist theory were applied to language acquisition, it would be assumed that the child's behavior is reinforced by the caretaker's approval and self-satisfaction only when the child follows the caretaker's lead. Brown and Bellugi, while acknowledging the significant influence of environmental or parental interactions (e.g., mothers modify their speech to their child by simplifying, repeating, and paraphrasing), emphasize that the process of language acquisition cannot be explained by the behaviorist stimulus-response-reinforcement system alone. They pay particular attention to three processes that characterize the child's acquisition of syntactic structures. Analyzing toddlers' language acquisition, Brown and Bellugi conclude that mother-child interaction, which is a cycle of imitations, reductions, and expansions, helps the inductive processing of the latent structure of the target language.

Similarly, Carol Chomsky (1969, 1972), examining elementary schoolchildren's language development (between the ages of 6 and 10), finds a relationship to reading. With a particular emphasis on the innate mechanism for language learning, she suggests that this natural process of children's language development continues actively into their elementary school years. (Her finding that schoolchildren are still in the process of their first-language acquisition serves as a strong logical foundation for supporting "late-exit" bilingual programs, discussed in this chapter under "Multicultural and Bilingual Issues.") According to her, the degree of sophistication in language acquisition is reflected in the ability to understand grammatically complex sentences, such as "John told Bill to leave" versus "John promised Bill to leave." Further, despite diverse individual differences (Nelson, 1981), particularly in terms of the rate of development, all children construct implicit grammatical rules and pass through a developmental sequence of linguistic stages.

Carol Chomsky's study, which was conducted in elementary schools in the Boston area, neither pays attention to sociocultural differences nor emphasizes conversational or social interactions, and thus it is illustrative of the theoretical-linguistic focus of this period. Influenced by Noam Chomsky's (1965) conception of an innate LAD, her study focuses only on inborn linguistic competence and analyzes the underlying rule-governed nature of the target language. However, sociocultural differences and social interactions play a major role in the school environment in relation to a realignment of the function of language, from oral language used in everyday life to written language with fewer nonlinguistic and situational cues. Because of the need to address such issues, studies of a more sociolinguistic nature emerged in the 1970s.

Sociolinguistic Studies of the 1970s

The corrective emphasis on biology was an oversimplification just as extreme as the Skinnerian one, though on the opposite end of the nature-nurture continuum. Generative grammar, represented by Noam Chomsky, was challenged by sociolinguists because of the necessity of reconceptualizing childhood environments in other societies and cultures. Chomsky (1965), using the *language-parole* distinction originally proposed by the Swiss linguist Ferdinand de Saussure (1915/1959), presented the dichotomy of competence (a person's internalized grammar of a language) and performance (the actual use of language in concrete situations). Challenging this dichotomy of competence and performance, Dell Hymes (1974a), an advocate of the ethnography of communication, introduced the concept of "communicative competence," the ability not only to apply the grammatical rules of a language in order to construct a grammatically correct sentence, but also to know when, where, and with whom to use these correct sentences in a given sociocultural situation. Criticizing Chomsky's definition of "competence," Hymes writes:

Chomsky's redefinition of linguistic goals appears, then, a half-way house. The term "competence" promises more than it in fact contains.

It is restricted to knowledge, and, within knowledge, to knowledge of grammar. Thus, it leaves other aspects of speakers' tacit knowledge and ability in confusion, thrown together under a largely unexamined concept of "performance." (pp. 92–93)

Claiming that Chomsky's dichotomy of competence and performance is misleading, Hymes suggests that, unlike the nativist (or innatist) position that tends to disregard sociocultural differences, these differences affect the process of language acquisition and later language skills development at a variety of levels. In other words, while Chomsky focuses on the universal nature of language acquisition, Hymes stresses characteristic features of the outcome of language acquisition in a specific sociocultural context. Hymes's work is an example of how researchers in the 1960s and 1970s—whether they agreed with Chomsky or not—were greatly influenced by the Chomskyan revolution.

While, as Hymes suggests, language development is considered the ability to participate fully in a set of social practices, those who support generative grammar still explain the process of language acquisition very differently. For example, when applying the theory of generative grammar to Standard English and to nonmainstream varieties of American English such as Black English Vernacular (BEV), it is possible to claim that, despite different surface features/expressions, they share the same underlying (deep) structure. The double negative (e.g., "I didn't see nothing") is sometimes considered one of the stigmatized features of BEV, particularly in school settings (Orr, 1987). To show that there are no logical foundations for such stigmatization, according to the nativist position, multiple negation can be explained as a result of the acquisition of a different rule-governed system; that is, exposure to a distinct set of examples in early childhood leads to different types of unconscious rules for sentence production. In this way, those who support generative grammar conclude that "Standard English is better because we assume it to be better" (Robinson, 1990, p. 63).

Like Hymes, William Labov (1972), in studying performance, has shifted a paradigm from isolated linguistic form (i.e., the grammatical sentences of a language) to linguistic form in human context, and analyzed the sequential use of language. While studying the structure of BEV in order to show that nonstandard dialects are also highly structured systems, Labov has taken a very different route from that of the nativist. Labov's particular solution to the problem was to examine how people use BEV in a natural context. In interviewing inner-city youth he used so-called "danger-of-death" prompts, such as "Were you ever in a situation where you were in serious danger of being killed?" (1972, p. 363), to elicit narratives. Labov's method is called "high point analysis" (Peterson & McCabe, 1983) because of the central importance of ascertaining the emotional climax—the high point—of the narrative. Labov and his colleagues define narrative technically as "one method of recapitulating past experience by matching a verbal sequence of clauses to the sequence of events which (it is inferred) actually occurred" (Labov, 1972, pp. 359–360; Labov, Cohen, Robins, & Lewis, 1968, p. 287; Labov & Waletzky, 1967, p. 20). By using this high point analysis, Labov and his followers present the linguistic techniques employed to evaluate experience within the speaker's particular cultural set, such as BEV, and study the basic structure of narrative within a particular culture. In other words, these researchers stress that some linguistic variables, such as structural components in story/narrative, are under the great influence of sociocultural variation (which, as later sections will reveal, is a significant factor in multicultural educational settings).

The British sociologist Basil Bernstein (1971) interprets competence-performance in a more sociocultural way. According to him, "competence refers to the child's tacit understanding of the rule system," but "performance relates to the essentially social use to which the rule system is put" (p. 173). Bernstein thus reframes performance by combining Chomsky's notion of "performance" and Hymes's conception of "communicative competence."

Bernstein (1971) further claims that there is substantial evidence suggesting effects of sociocultural variables; for example, working-class and middle-class people use different linguistic codes. According to Bernstein, middle-class speakers in England employ an *elaborated code* that facilitates the verbal elaboration of subjective intent, while working-class speakers, to greater or lesser degree, employ a *restricted code,* a speech mode in which it is unnecessary for the speaker verbally to elaborate subjective intent. However, Bernstein's notion of codes has been criticized because they fail to acknowledge an overriding concern with collaborative message construction by working-class speakers (Hemphill, 1989). Furthermore, since his conception has often been regarded as a "verbal-deficit" theory and additionally confused with social class, it has tended to be misused, especially in the United States (Brandt, 1990), where it was employed as a mechanism to explain the academic failure of children of linguistically nonmainstream backgrounds (including children from working-class homes). Despite these criticisms, as later sections will reveal, his theory greatly influenced those studies in the 1980s that examined how children deal with tasks in school settings.

In summary, tracing the pros and cons of the nativist explanations for language development is important because such debate influenced the direction of later language studies. For instance, while criticizing Chomsky, who tends to ignore the significance of language performance, Brown (1973) still tries to measure competence through children's performance data. At the same time, Hymes's (1974a) notion of "communicative competence" lays the groundwork for the 1980s, especially in the educational arena. Cook-Gumperz and Gumperz (1982) summarize:

The task of exploring the cultural transmission of knowledge as communicative competence requires us to see the interactional face-to-face relationship of teacher to student as embedded interactively within a context of the procedures of classroom practices within schools, which themselves are part of an institutional system of education policies and ideology. (pp. 19–20)

As this statement illustrates, those theories that were developed in the 1960s and 1970s have been incorporated into studies in the 1980s and 1990s. As regards communicative competence in particular, the next section will focus on socialization, the process whereby children acquire the ability to recognize and interpret the types of social activities that are taking place in their culture-specific environment.

LANGUAGE AS A SOCIOCULTURALLY MEDIATED PRODUCT

Starting in the latter half of the 1970s, and increasingly in the 1980s and 1990s, the shift toward more social and pragmatic concerns deepened the sociocultural nature of many language studies. Specifically, studies of language acquisition and socialization in a variety of settings flourished during this period and explored issues related to language within a sociocultural framework. The core assumption of these studies is the social interaction paradigm advocated by the Russian psychologist Lev Vygotsky (1978) and by Jerome Bruner (1977).

According to this social interaction theory, children's communicative competence, reflecting a certain cultural identity, develops in accordance with socially accepted rules. This communicative style will be important when considering children's entry into school, which may require a realignment of language use. This realignment is often necessary because there is a difference between the language use of the primary speech community (generally the oral language style used at home) and the language use of the secondary speech community (school literacy, in addition to a certain type of oral language used at school).

Looking more specifically at literacy, it can be defined in more than one way. Some researchers (e.g., Garton & Pratt, 1989) define literacy as both spoken and written language because of their belief that a strong connection exists between learning to talk and learning to read and write. This theory assumes that early oral language development is directly related to the later development of written language. In this hypothesis, literacy can be defined as "the mastery of spoken language *and* reading and writing" (p. 1). While accepting this position, to avoid unnecessary confusion (and to make a clear distinction between the terms) we basically adopt Catherine Snow's (1983) definition of oral language and literacy, in which oral language simply means "all oral forms of communication, speaking and listening," and literacy includes "the activities and skills associated with the use of print—primarily reading and writing" (p. 166).

To represent the idea that "the contextual clues to interpretation are in the text itself" (Scollon & Scollon, 1981, p. 48), the term *decontextualization* is used. Since "decontextualized" means "self-contained" or "self-sufficient," some researchers prefer *self-contextualization* (Dickinson & Smith, 1990); others prefer *recontextualization* because a "decontextualized text is impossible . . . every text has a context" (Shuman, 1986, p. 118). Following the convention, however, we use the term *decontextualization* throughout.

The Social Interaction Approach:
A *Theoretical Background*

Studies of language development and language skills acquisition have increasingly focused on communicative social interactions in the earliest stages of children's speech patterns. Since there are remarkably wide individual differences (Nelson, 1981) as well as cultural differences (Schieffelin & Ochs, 1986), researchers have come to conceptualize that children are not passive beneficiaries of their environments but active agents in their own socialization throughout life. The progress in this viewpoint is predicated on the theory that individuals and society construct one another through social interaction (Ochs, 1986).

Vygotsky's (1978) ideas form a basis for the view of language as a socioculturally mediated product. For instance, Vygotsky hypothesized that children's cognitive skills first develop through social interactions with more mature members of society and then become internalized after long practice. Specifically, he interpreted children's cognitive skills in terms of the "zone of proximal development," which he defined as the relationship between the following two types of children's problem-solving behaviors: (a) the behaviors when children solve a problem by interacting with adults who can provide them with some guidance, such as structuring the problem, solving parts of the problem, or providing suggestions (i.e., interpsychological behavior corresponding to the potential level of development); and (b) the behaviors when children can solve the problem by themselves (i.e., intrapsychological behavior in accordance with the actual level of development). As the child matures, the relationship between interpsychological and intrapsychological behaviors changes for a given task, so that children gradually come to solve on their own problems that previously they could solve only partially, or not at all, except through interpersonal supports provided by adults.

The zone of proximal development is thus the process of social interaction between adults and children, providing children with a tool to establish a complex series of actions in problem-solving situations. Since this process takes place before children have the mental capacities to take appropriate actions to solve the problem on their own, adults need to regulate children's actions. Through the process of interaction, these regulatory behaviors taken by adults gradually become part of the children's own behavior. The relationship between cognitive development and social interaction, particularly early social interactions between children and more mature members of society, can be summarized by Vygotsky's claim that all higher mental functions appear twice in development: (a) first as social or interpsychological functions during interactions with other social agents, and (b) only later, through the internalization of social-interactive processes, as individualized or intrapsychological functions.

Inspired by Vygotsky's zone of proximal development, Bruner (1977) maintains that, for learning to take place, children must have opportunities for cooperative verbal and nonverbal interactions with adults. He uses the term *scaffolding* to describe these adult-child interactions, which are initially scripted and played by adults, but then allow children to take an increasingly major role in creating and performing the joint script. Bruner (1990) further emphasizes that understanding the properties of the narrative is important because they illustrate how the narrator constructs his or her logic in the process of interaction with others. Bruner specifically proposes that: (a)

at an early stage of development the child, interacting with the caregiver, enters into the world of meaning construction; and (b) the meaning creation process in narrative discourse is closely related to a specific style of cultural representation. Bruner argues that "four-year-olds may not know much about the culture, but they know what's canonical and are eager to provide a tale to account for what is not" (pp. 82–83).

Jean Lave (1991), on the other hand, emphasizes learning within several "apprenticeship" situations, such as Mayan midwives in the Yucatan, supermarket butchers in an on-site training program, and Alcoholics Anonymous groups. Since she claims that learning occurs within what she calls "communities of practice," she situates learning in a particular pattern of social participation; that is, a person moves from being a peripheral participant to a full participant in sociocultural practices of the community in which he or she lives. Lave's emphasis on "apprenticeship" is thus synonymous with social interaction. In this regard, Lave and Wenger (1991) write:

Children are, after all, quintessentially legitimate peripheral participants in adult social worlds. But various forms of apprenticeship seemed to capture very well our interest in learning in situated ways—in the transformative possibilities of being and becoming complex, full cultural-historical participants in the world—and it would be difficult to think of a more apt range of social practices for this purpose. (p. 32)

When applied to the use of language, the social interaction paradigm suggests a culturally ideal adult-child relationship. In terms of first-language acquisition, for example, children acquire their language through interactions with more competent members, usually mothers (see, e.g., Snow, 1977, 1983, 1986). When applying the social interaction approach to the classroom context, an ideal situation can be conceptualized as one in which, through the constructive dialogue between teacher and student, the teacher fully understands the student's needs and assists his or her internalization of subject matter (Tharp & Gallimore, 1991a, 1991b). In multicultural contexts, an ideal situation would be one in which, through interactive processes of teaching and learning, the teacher's questions scaffold the child's constructing process of knowledge based on his or her own cultural identity.

Children and their environments have thus come to be conceptualized as a dynamic system in which they actively interact with and influence each other. Even infants and small children are influential in socializing other members of their family as well as their peers. For instance, later-born children are said to tend toward slower language development than firstborn children, perhaps because the existence of siblings causes parental attitudinal changes, such as shortening of conversation directed at later-born children, and because siblings are not good language models for later-born children (Ochs, 1986). Similarly, it is easy to imagine that children socialize their peers into gender-specific modes of action and communication that they have acquired through social interactions such as game situations (Cook-Gumperz, 1992). It is further possible to assume that the links between gender and linguistic practices are culturally constructed (Borker, 1980) and, more important, developed through early social interactions (Gal, 1992). The social interactionist paradigm has thus greatly influenced language studies in the 1980s and 1990s.

Language Socialization in Diverse Cultural Contexts: *Becoming a Member of a Speech Community*

As discussed earlier in this chapter, Hymes (1974a) stresses that, from early childhood on, children in different cultural settings learn the appropriate use of their language, as well as its grammar and vocabulary. The acquisition of a culture-specific communicative competence thus plays a significant role in the process of language acquisition and the development of language skills. Peggy Miller (1982) describes a variety of culture-specific routinized interactions between mothers and their children in South Baltimore. She calls such interaction "direct instruction," which includes: (a) directing the children to speak appropriately (e.g., "please," "excuse me," and "thank you"); (b) conversing with dolls appropriately; (c) rhyming, singing, and playing verbal games; (d) using correct grammar, pronunciation, and intonation; and (e) counting, reciting the alphabet, and identifying the colors.

Different cultures have different priorities with respect to caring for, socializing, and educating young children. The primary intent of Miller's (1982) study is to suggest that while children from lower-class families in South Baltimore are being taught distinct styles of language, they are not linguistically deprived. In different cultural settings people can observe dissimilarities in parental expectations and their resultant different communicative styles. Sarah Michaels (1981, 1991) observed "sharing time" classes (an oral language activity in early elementary classrooms), and distinguished the ways that African American and White (or European American) children describe past events in their narratives during sharing time. Similarly, Shirley Brice Heath (1982b, 1983, 1986) states that children growing up in White middle-class, White working-class, and African American working-class families in Appalachia have different experiences with literacy, and thus develop different expectations concerning behavior and attitudes surrounding reading and writing events. Each of their communicative styles reflects a unique culture-specific perspective toward socialization.

According to Hymes (1982), among the Chinook and some other North American Indian tribes, newborn babies were believed not to be babbling but to be speaking a special language that they shared with the spirits. Ochs and Schieffelin (1984) claim that "what a child says and how she or he says it will be influenced by local cultural processes, in addition to biological and social processes that have universal scope" (p. 277). While admitting Noam Chomsky's (1965) notion of a highly abstract core of structures that is applicable to any language, these researchers put particular emphasis on the influence of environmental/sociocultural factors. The following claims proposed by Ochs and Schieffelin (1984) clearly support Hymes's notion of "communicative competence":

1. The process of acquiring language is deeply affected by the process of becoming a competent member of society.

2. The process of becoming a competent member of society is realized to a large extent through language, by acquiring knowledge of its functions, social distribution, and interpretations in and across socially defined situations, i.e., through exchanges of language in particular social situations. (p. 277)

Through different processes, from a very early age children are socialized into culturally specific modes of organizing knowledge, thought, and communicative style. Language acquisition and socialization are, therefore, two sides of the same coin.

Through investigation of the language acquisition and socialization process of the Kaluli of Papua New Guinea, Ochs and Schieffelin (1984), Schieffelin and Eisenberg (1984), and Schieffelin (1986) find another example of how language is strongly dependent on social patterns. According to these researchers, Kaluli mothers do not believe that baby-babbling is language, and instead claim that language begins at the time when the child uses two critical words, "mother" and "breast." More important, Kaluli mothers do not recast their children's utterances, nor do they modify their own language to fit the linguistic ability of the young child. During the first 18 months or so, very little sustained dyadic verbal exchange takes place between adult and infant. The infant is only minimally treated as an addressee, and not treated as a communicative partner in dyadic exchanges.

The Kaluli mother's attitude toward her child's language development shows a remarkable contrast to that of the Anglo-American middle-class mother who accommodates situations to the child from birth on. Kaluli mothers consider finely tuned child-directed speech (sometimes called "motherese") inappropriate. Instead, they train their children to imitate adult forms of speech, believing that complex adult speech will be tuned into the child's comprehension. The Anglo-American middle-class mother treats her young child as an addressee in social interaction; she simplifies her speech to match more closely what she considers to be the communicative competence of the young child (Snow, 1977, 1983, 1986, 1989a, 1989b; Snow & Ninio, 1986). Note, however, that since communicative competence is culturally shaped, it represents culture-specific norms and aspirations. In other words, because differing environmental and sociocultural factors are operating in the Anglo-American middle-class and Kaluli speech communities, the communicative competence required for each community is consequently different. Therefore, arguing whether finely tuned child-directed speech and recasts contribute universally to an optimal course of language development is obviously irrelevant.

In summary, cross-cultural studies have suggested that different patterns of social interaction are being used in different environments. This is especially true as regards language socialization, which is the critical area of socialization for the propagation of culture-specific communicative competence. Language studies in the 1980s thus emphasize that children from different cultures are driven in divergent directions by models endorsed by the adults around them, and that, following culturally specific norms, different language goals and plans are implemented in a wide variety of forms.

The Relationship Between Oral Language and Literacy: *Consequences of Literacy*

This section has thus far examined from a linguistic point of view how socialization serves to generate members of a society who are competent in socioculturally specific ways. An individual is socialized from babyhood on, with the primary agent of socialization being the family. However, once a child has started schooling, which is widespread in modern societies, the main agent of socialization changes from the primary speech community—the family and local community where the child was raised—to the secondary speech community, the school, in which the child's narrative discourse style and subsequent literacy practices are often reshaped.

Regarding this point, David Olson (1977) has stated that the acquisition of literacy proceeds from context-dependent (i.e., contextualized), oral ways of thinking to the acquisition of context-free (i.e., decontextualized), logical, message-focused skills, such as reasoning and problem solving. Olson equates the acquisition of literacy with that of higher-level critical-thinking skills, claiming that the function of schooling is to make children's language skills increasingly explicit and decontextualized.

Snow (1983) suggests many similarities between learning to talk (i.e., language acquisition) and learning to read and write (i.e., literacy) in the early stages of the child's development. According to Snow, the specific oral discourse style employed by middle-class families at home, which has the characteristic features of being decontextualized and detached, closely matches school language use, a factor that accounts for the later literacy success of children from these homes. In other words, since Snow regards early oral language development as having direct influence on the development of later language skills, her emphasis will naturally be placed on the importance of the continuity between oral language and literacy.

The above hypothesis suggests that oral language skills at home are necessary precursors to later literacy skills in an educational context. Conversely, it can be seen that if the nature of conversational interactions in children's homes and in school do not parallel each other, those children's academic success may be jeopardized. This is the earlier mentioned match-mismatch formulation of literacy. The conflict between contextualized home language use and decontextualized school language use has been a recurrent issue throughout the 1980s and 1990s, and will be discussed from a slightly different angle in relation to bilingual education in the next section of this chapter.

Some researchers have opposed the literacy-as-development view and its resulting match-mismatch formulation of literacy. Based on their research, Scribner and Cole (1978, 1981) have challenged Olson's (1977) view, in which literacy, in combination with schooling, is supposed to equip children with the skills necessary for the transition from context-dependent thought (characteristic of oral language used in everyday life) to decontextualized abstract thinking (characteristic of literacy). Scribner and Cole studied the unschooled but literate Vai people of Liberia, who invented a syllabic writing system to represent their language. They suggest that in the case of the Vai,

literacy is not associated with decontextualized thought. Scribner and Cole's argument is supported by other studies, such as research on the Cree-speaking people's syllabic script in northern Canada (Bennett & Berry, 1991). These research findings conclude that the relationship between higher-order intellectual skills and literacy practices is very complex, as is the relationship between literacy and schooling. Research conducted in other cultures thus warns that various modes of learning usually considered to be related to one another in Western societies may function differently in different cultures and societies.

There is another criticism of a depiction of language use as developing from context-bound orality to context-free literacy (Robinson, 1990). According to Deborah Brandt (1989, 1990), Olson's "strong-text" view of literacy, which is based on the oral-literate dichotomy (an "explicit," elaborated literate style versus an "ambiguous," restricted oral style), in fact originates in Bernstein's (1971) theory of codes, which has been used to explain why some children do better than others in school (Torrance & Olson, 1985). The oral-literate dichotomy is considered dangerous because it is likely to be connected with the "deficit hypothesis" that assumes that the parents in some sociocultural groups fall short of the skills necessary to promote their children's success at school. For example, examining literacy programs to support low-income, minority, and immigrant families, Elsa Auerbach (1989) warns that the so-called transmission of school practices model, which promotes parents' efforts toward school-like literacy practices in the home, functions under the deficit hypothesis. Since this hypothesis either implicitly or explicitly condemns children's environmental, sociocultural, and/or linguistic background for their failure in the classroom context, it implies that the family, not the teacher, is responsible for providing adequate educational support. The oral-literate dichotomy has thus served as a basis for the match-mismatch formulation of literacy and its resulting deficit hypothesis. As Brandt (1990) puts it, "in match-mismatch formulations, students are deemed at risk in school literacy performance to the extent to which their home language is at odds with the so-called explicit, decontextualized language of the school" (p. 106).

To overcome criticism that the match-mismatch formulation of literacy has tended to be confounded with social class, Snow, Barnes, Chandler, Goodman, and Hemphill (1991) examined the home and classroom environments and family-school relationships "within social class." Believing it is "necessary to look elsewhere to understand the differences between the children who did well and those who did poorly" (p. 3), they restricted their study to children from low-income families and found that frequent parent-teacher contact was one of the most important factors contributing to children's academic growth (discussed at the end of the next section under "Parental Participation"). Overall, the match-mismatch formulation of literacy has been dominant, although it has remained controversial because of its close association with the oral-literate dichotomy, which is easily confounded with social class and, above all, with the deficit hypothesis.

Yet it is still true that the match-mismatch formulation sheds light on the role of socialization and reflects the relationships between the primary speech community in which an individual was raised and the secondary speech community represented by the school. In order to capture the mutual relationships, narrative study, which Labov (1972) has stressed, plays an important role because a specific narrative discourse style not only reflects the language socialization process, but also represents a fundamental structure that has been socioculturally cultivated.

Michaels (1981, 1991) distinguishes the ways that African American and White (or European American) children describe past events in their narratives, such as those used during sharing time at school. According to Michaels, White middle-class teachers who have been accustomed to a discourse with a clearly identifiable topic (i.e., topic-centered) tend to misunderstand African American children, whose culture encourages them to use a discourse consisting of a series of implicitly associated personal anecdotes (i.e., topic-associating). Susan Philips (1972) describes how, because of differences in unconscious interactional norms, the verbal as well as nonverbal communicative style of Native American students causes conflicts and misunderstandings in interactions with Anglo teachers. An extension of such contrast may be described as follows: Through socialization, children from some cultures may be more accustomed to an analytic or deductive style, while children from other cultures may feel more comfortable with an inductive style of talking, in which the main theme of the talk must be inferred from a series of concrete examples. Thus, by describing how children's habitual ways of communicating at home may not necessarily work in the school setting, Michaels and Philips suggest that educators who are sensitive to and supportive of children's linguistic and communicative styles will be better able to understand children from different cultures.

To understand culture-specific patterns of narrative, James Gee (1985) has used stanza analysis, which has been applied successfully to narratives from various cultures (Minami & McCabe, 1991a, 1991b, 1993, in press). Introducing the concept of stanza, Hymes (1982) cites a short story from the Zuni, a Native American tribe in New Mexico, and develops his argument about a culture-specific pattern of narrative structure. Extending Hymes's (1981, 1990) verse analysis, Gee (1985, 1989) specifies the notion of stanza as an ideal structure containing "lines," each of which is generally a simple clause; overall, a stanza consists of a group of lines about a single topic.

Applying this stanza analysis to the sharing time data (Cazden, 1988; Cazden et al., 1985; Michaels, 1981), Gee (1985, 1986b, 1989) illustrates differences in narrative between an African American girl and a White (or European American) girl. He categorizes the former as an oral-strategy (or poetic) narrative and the latter as a literate-strategy (or prosaic) narrative. Gee (1986b) then attributes this difference to whether a society is founded on an orality-oriented culture or a literacy-oriented culture, and concludes that a so-called residually oral community, less influenced by written-language styles than the White middle-class community, still retains ties to an oral tradition with a particular narrative pattern.

Gee (1990) has made another contribution to language studies by rejecting the traditional view of literacy, which has been construed as each individual's ability to read and write in order to achieve an autonomous, higher-level cognitive skill. Gee claims that this traditional view of literacy is too naive to capture the sociocultural role of literacy. Rather, following Brazilian educator Paulo Freire's (1970a, 1970b) conceptualization of literacy as emancipatory process, Gee argues that languages are always social possessions, and the notion of "literacy" has been used to oppress nonliterate individuals and underrepresented groups, and thus to consolidate the preestablished social hierarchy, especially in Western societies. Culture-related domains for the mastery of communicative competence include discourse, appropriateness, paralinguistics, pragmatics, and cognitive-academic language proficiency (Ovando, 1993). Gee's (1990) notion of "Discourse" with a capital "D," including more than sequential speech or writing, represents a sociocultural aggregate model that consists of "words, acts, values, beliefs, attitudes, social identities, as well as gestures, glances, body positions and clothes" (p. 142). Rather than simply using the linguistic match-mismatch conception, Gee argues that diverse sociocultural variables are irrationally affecting children's school success and failure.

In summary, an examination of studies of social interaction, socialization, and the resulting acquisition of communicative competence in diverse cultural contexts, suggests the many complex relationships between oral language and literacy. Above all, the issue of ambiguous oral discourse contrasted with explicit literate discourse has received a lot of attention, particularly in the United States. As Gee (1986a) argues, however, "the oral/literate contrast makes little sense because many social groups, even in high-technology societies, fall into such mixed categories as residual orality" (p. 737). This argument by Gee corresponds to Heath's (1983) statement that "the traditional oral-literate dichotomy does not capture the ways other cultural patterns in each community affect the uses of oral and written language" (p. 344), as well as to Hymes's (1974b) view that "it is impossible to generalize validly about 'oral' vs. 'literate' cultures as uniform types" (p. 54).

As Kieran Egan (1987) suggests, since the child's language development should be understood as developing from orality to a composite of orality and literacy, effective use of children's orality during the early school years should then lead to their subsequent development of literacy. By emphasizing this composite model of orality and literacy, the Kamehameha Early Education Program (KEEP) in Hawaii has been successful. KEEP has acted on the premise that teachers from mainstream culture should appreciate minority children's early socialization patterns and home discourse practices without molding those children into the patterns of Anglo-American middle-class children (Au & Jordan, 1981; Jordan, 1984; Jordan, Vogt, & Tharp, 1993). As in the example of KEEP, educators can facilitate students' academic success by combining new areas of linguistic knowledge with the communicative skills the students already have acquired at home. Therefore, with the establishment of culturally compatible classroom practices, home language can further facilitate children's effective participation in school activities.

This section has also emphasized that narrative discourse styles, which represent communicative competence, mirror the society in which they are employed. Studies on different cultural settings within and outside U.S. society have identified different communicative styles. As Gee (1985) puts it, "Just as the common core of human language is expressed differently in different languages, so the common core of communicative style is expressed differently in different cultures" (p. 11). Cazden (1988) states, "Narratives are a universal meaning-making strategy, but there is no one way of transforming experience into a story" (p. 24). This line of thinking is further advanced by Bruner (1990), who suggests that the meaning-creation process in narrative discourse is closely related to a specific style of cultural representation.

What is problematic is that, based on the oral-literate dichotomy and its resulting match-mismatch formulation of literacy, the essayist style of literacy, which is assumed to be the cultural norm of mainstream schooling, is performing a gatekeeper's role in Western societies. Scollon and Scollon (1981) observed that their 2-year-old daughter Rachel, a product of a mainstream U.S. environment, was already on her way to Western literacy even though she could not yet read and write. On the other hand, the way in which a 10-year-old Athapaskan girl in Alaska talked or wrote, despite its being grammatical, was regarded by her teachers as oral and nonliterate. The Athapaskan girl's style, which was ambiguous, was considered inappropriate according to the Western norm of literacy.

Along similar lines, African American children who are accustomed to disambiguating pronouns in oral narrative discourse by means of prosody (largely depending on intonation contours such as vowel elongation) are predicted by teachers to produce ambiguous, poorly written narratives (Michaels & Collins, 1984). In U.S. society, unfortunately, such ambiguity tends to be confounded with preliteracy skills and further connected with social class, with little consideration of cultural differences. Therefore, it is not the match-mismatch formulation per se that is responsible for the controversy. Rather, the real issue is that, coupled with biases against minorities, there seems to be a general assumption in mainstream U.S. society that an oral style is ambiguous and valued negatively, whereas a literate style is explicit and characterized positively.

MULTICULTURAL AND BILINGUAL ISSUES IN RELATION TO LANGUAGE

Because of rapid social diversification, multicultural and bilingual education is playing an increasingly important role in U.S. schools. But while educational settings are becoming increasingly multicultural, particularly in urban areas in the United States, educators are often ill-prepared to work effectively in such culturally and linguistically diverse contexts. In this section we will look more specifically at bilingual and multicultural education, and discuss further the socioculturally embedded nature of language acquisition and mastery of language skills.

Although this section includes bilingual education, we do not intend to lump first-language proficiency and bilingualism together. It is certainly true that, unlike first-language acquisition, second-language acquisition (or bilingualism) is influenced by knowledge of the first language. At the same time,

however, second-language acquisition (or bilingualism) is, like first-language acquisition, influenced by active hypothesis testing under the control of a rule-governed system (N. Chomsky, 1965). What is emphasized here is that this and the preceding section of this chapter constitute a continuum in the sense that even if the same language is spoken, if the manner of presentation and interaction style are different, communication may be difficult, and that if different languages are spoken, communication problems may become even more serious. The potential problems that are raised in these sections, therefore, are the same: (a) When a child who has acquired a certain paradigm for communication in one culture enters into another cultural setting, what happens? (b) Since the habitual way of communication in one cultural setting does not necessarily work in a new setting, what should educators keep in mind and, moreover, do for these children?

Misconceptions Regarding Bilingualism

More than half a million immigrants from nearly 100 different countries and cultures enter the United States every year, most speaking languages other than English (Crawford, 1989). To help them master the new language, immigrant children who speak little or no English are placed in a variety of programs, such as Maintenance Bilingual Education (MBE) (or additive/late-exit), Transitional Bilingual Education (TBE) (or early-exit), or English as a Second Language (ESL). Researchers, policy makers, administrators, the public, and those actively involved in bilingual and ESL programs have been engaged for the past 25 years in heated debates for and against bilingual education. For example, Baker and de Kanter's (1981, 1983) evaluation studies generally conclude that bilingual programs are no more effective in promoting language and academic skills than alternative programs, such as structured immersion programs in which content-area instruction is provided through a monolingual English approach with modified use of ESL techniques. In contrast to Baker and de Kanter, Willig (1985), Ramírez, Yuen, and Ramey (1991), and Rosier and Holm (1980) found evidence supporting the efficacy of bilingual programs; that is, bilingual education promotes the learning processes of bilingual children and, moreover, programs with substantial native-language components seem effective in promoting education achievement by minority students (see chapter 25 of this *Handbook* for a review of the literature).

Differences exist even among those who support bilingual programs, with some advocating an MBE program, claiming that in these programs children have an opportunity to become proficient in English while maintaining their home language, while others support a TBE program. TBE is the approach used in most bilingual education programs in the United States (Crawford, 1989), the purpose of these TBE programs being to help LEP children become familiar with subject matter temporarily through their native language while also developing English proficiency. However, since many TBE programs provide only a very limited period of native-language instruction and do not guarantee the mastery of English, these programs may prevent LEP children from attaining proficiency in either their native language or English (Spener, 1988).

Reflective of the large number of early-exit TBE, as opposed to MBE, programs, there seems to be widespread sentiment throughout the United States that language-minority children should use as little of the home language as possible, under the assumption that this will lead to quicker proficiency in English (Hakuta, 1986; Huddy & Sears, 1990). In the early literature, in the 1920s and 1930s in particular, a generally pessimistic view of bilingualism can be found (see chapter 25 of this *Handbook* for a view of the literature). Madorah Smith (cited in Hakuta, 1986), for example, studied a group of Hawaiian children; she concluded that bilingualism caused retardation and that second-language learning in childhood is arduous, handicapping, and fraught with problems. Barry McLaughlin (1992) notes the following myths about bilingualism, which cause people to support programs that use as little of the home language as possible: (a) "Children learn second languages quickly and easily"; (b) "The younger the child, the more skilled in acquiring a second language"; (c) "The more time students spend in a second language context, the quicker they learn the language"; (d) "Children have acquired a second language once they can speak it"; and (e) "All children learn a second language in the same way" (pp. 1–7). These misunderstandings, based on simplistic and erroneous assumptions, have been used as arguments against the use of children's home language in school settings.

In sharp contrast, research by Peal and Lambert (1962) refuted the pessimistic view of bilingualism and instead showed bilinguals to be intellectually normal and, especially in the domain of "cognitive flexibility," superior to monolinguals. A variety of research findings in the late 1970s, the 1980s, and the 1990s further refute the arguments against bilingual education. Contextualized language mainly used for conversational purposes is quite different from decontextualized language used for school learning. Furthermore, the former develops earlier than the latter (Cook-Gumperz & Gumperz, 1982). In the context of bilingual education in the United States, this means that children become conversantly fluent in English before they develop the ability to use English in academic situations.

Jim Cummins (1979), for example, suggests that while children may pick up oral proficiency in as little as two years, as measured on standardized tests, it may take five to seven years to acquire the decontextualized language skills necessary to function successfully in an all-English classroom. To represent these two separate skills—contextualized/context-embedded communication and decontextualized/context-reduced language—Cummins (1980) originally proposed Basic Interpersonal Communicative Skills (BICS) and Cognitive/Academic Language Proficiency (CALP). According to him, BICS is the communicative capacity to function well in everyday interpersonal/social (thus contextualized/context-embedded) contexts, whereas CALP is related to the higher-level language skills required for cognitively demanding content such as literacy (thus decontextualized/context-reduced). BICS and CALP, therefore, correspond respectively to what Olson (1977) terms *utterance* and *text*. Emphasizing that conversational skills are significantly less important in achievement than are academic skills, Cummins used this BICS-CALP distinction as evidence in favor of MBE programs. (Note, however, that since social-language de-

velopment is closely related to the later development of academic language skills, BICS and CALP constitute a continuum rather than separate categories; see Ovando & Collier, 1995, for more on this topic. Because of this continuity argument, Cummins, 1984, 1991b, later dropped this BICS-CALP distinction and now uses the term Common Underlying Proficiency [CUP] to discuss transfer of academic knowledge from the first language to a second language in an educational context. See our discussion below.)

Cummins (1991a, 1991b), Cummins et al. (1984), and Williams and Snipper (1990) suggest that first-language and second-language proficiency are interdependent, and that a strong native-language foundation therefore acts as a support in the learning of English, making the process easier and faster. Moreover, using the concept of CUP, Cummins (1991b) argues that since most of the learning that goes on in the native language transfers readily to a second language, transfer of academic knowledge from the first language to a second language in an educational context is highly probable. For example, once decontextualization skills have been acquired in one's first language, they are available for use in a second language (Snow, 1990; Snow, Cancino, De Temple, & Schley, 1991).

Similarly, once the basic principles of reading are mastered in the home language, such reading skills transfer quickly to a second language (Cummins, 1991b). Collier (1987) has found that five-, six-, and seven-year-old arrivals to the United States, because of limited literacy skills in their first language, tend not to acquire English academic skills adequately compared to older arrivals, who can transfer knowledge of reading in their native language to reading in English. Studies examining language-minority students' long-term academic achievement in the United States generally confirm that students who have been in late-exit programs perform better than those who exited bilingual programs early (Collier, 1992; Ramírez et al., 1991). The premise of interdependence between the two languages thus supports additive bilingual programs that develop proficiency in English while maintaining minority children's first language.

As stated above, becoming fluent in a second language does not have to mean losing the first language; conversely, maintaining the first language does not retard the development of a second language. However, as one of the myths cited previously indicates, many people still believe that if children have not mastered the second language by early school years, they never will. Wallace Lambert (1975, 1977, 1981) has classified bilingual education into two types: "additive bilingualism," in which, as in MBE programs, children's first language is maintained and supported, and "subtractive bilingualism," in which the language of instruction is likely to replace children's first language with a so-called "prestigious" national or international language. The erroneous belief that children are fast and effortless second-language learners constitutes the logical foundation of such subtractive bilingualism, as seen in many TBE programs that promote replacing the first language with a second language as soon as possible. When second-language acquisition is understood as a composite of cognitive development and proficiency in the first language (Collier, 1989), the dangers of subtractive bilingualism become apparent. Research in Canada, for example, suggests that while students immersed in a second language at an older age (secondary school) showed less nativelike communicative competence than students immersed in the second language at a younger age (Hart, Lapkin, & Swain, 1991), the second-language skills shown by late-immersion students are far ahead of the skills of early-immersion students in some academic discourse domains (Harley, 1991). Similarly, Genesee (1983) reports that only one year of immersion in a second-language classroom in the seventh grade provides as much development in second language as three years of immersion starting in the first grade; that is, late-immersion students show high levels of communicative competence, particularly in academic settings. Therefore, the commonsense notion that it is beneficial to immerse children in their second language as soon as possible is not a well-founded idea.

While it may be difficult to make any conclusive statements concerning the long-term comparison between transitional and maintenance programs because of such variables as district differences (Cazden, 1992), the research of the 1980s and 1990s tends to suggest the effectiveness of maintenance programs for the child's first- as well as second-language development. Furthermore, research findings from Canada in particular refute the linguistic match-mismatch hypothesis discussed in the preceding section; comparison of late-immersion and early-immersion students does not support the theory that the conflict between home language use and school language use results in academic difficulties (Cummins, 1991b). Research into the late-immersion programs in Canada demonstrates that ideal bilingual education programs increase fluency in both languages by treating a nonmainstream first language as an asset rather than a handicap. Therefore, maintenance bilingual programs hold the edge in helping to educate children to be confident and capable in the academic environment.

Empowerment of Minority Students, Parents, and Communities

Facing diverse approaches to the education of LEP children, many researchers have recently begun to support maintenance programs. Two-way (or interlocking) bilingual/immersion education programs in particular have attracted attention. In these programs, non-English-background students and English monolingual students are placed in the same classroom and study the content areas in each other's language (Lindholm, 1992; Ovando, 1990a, 1990b). There is no isolation of language-minority students in this educational setting, and children have the opportunity to play and talk together in each other's language (Morison, 1990). Thus, two-way bilingual education plays a crucial role in helping language-minority children to maintain their ethnic identity and, at the same time, in exposing majority children to a minority language and culture.

However, the story is not such a simple matter. In some bilingual programs majority children learn virtually no second language, even when minority students outnumber the majority children in the program. For example, it has been reported in the evaluations of the bilingual program in Culver City, California, that the immersion students who had the program as English monolinguals had not attained mastery of Spanish even

after six years of immersion in the language (Genesee, 1985; Wong Fillmore & Valadez, 1986). Similarly, the bilingual component of the Brookline Early Education Project (BEEP) in Massachusetts, in which language-majority (English) and language-minority (Spanish) children were brought together, reports that while all Spanish-speaking children eventually learned English while maintaining Spanish, the effects of the program on English-speaking children's proficiency were not as evident (Hauser-Cram, Pierson, Walker, & Tivnan, 1991). Although the Culver City program and BEEP may have played an important role in sensitizing language-majority children to different cultures, the findings in terms of second-language proficiency are educationally disappointing.

The clue to understanding this problem may be found in studies on language and literacy on the Navajo Reservation, where about two thirds of school-age Navajo children are currently attending public schools (Holm & Holm, 1990) but a diglossic situation still exists. Two different languages coexist, each encompassing a different range of social functions (D. McLaughlin, 1990, 1992). English is generally used in schools and churches and is thus regarded as a language with greater social prestige. Navajo, basically used in informal situations such as family conversation, has been relegated to a vernacular status and consequently considered less prestigious. Though accepting the use of vernacular Navajo in formal situations, schools and churches limit its use; the message they are conveying to Navajo children is nothing but the stigmatized image of their indigenous language. The case on the Navajo Reservation may explain why language-majority children in some bilingual programs do not attain mastery of a minority language. It might be that adults, administrators, and teachers in those programs send children a conscious or unconscious negative message about minority languages and cultures.

As the above examples indicate, while the home environment and family-school relationships are important (Snow, Barnes, Chandler, Goodman, & Hemphill, 1991), many researchers have tended to discuss students' school success and failure simply in the match-mismatch formulation of literacy and discourse patterns. Children's academic success should be studied and emphasized in a different way.

Cummins (1986) has long examined the pattern of minority students' academic success and failure, and stressed ways in which educators can promote the empowerment of minority students and their parents and communities so that those children can become confident and capable in academic environments. Carole Edelsky (1991), however, strongly criticizes Cummins for his heavy reliance on test scores in his analysis of the social and cognitive nature of children's language skills. According to Edelsky, while advocating the empowerment of minority students, Cummins is in reality using culturally biased conventional test scores in order to measure their academic progress. Edelsky claims that what Cummins is measuring has nothing to do with how minority children have become truly confident and capable in academic environments; Edelsky concludes that Cummins's ideal and practice are contradictory and antinomic.

It is certainly true that standardized tests do not necessarily serve as an accurate or fair measure of language-minority students' diverse strengths (Edelsky, 1991; McCloskey & Enright, 1992). Yet, as Cummins emphasizes, the function of educators and policy makers should be to empower minority students. Moreover, as Collier (1992) argues, ignoring minority students' performance on standardized tests means nothing but denying those students "access to a meaningful education and equal opportunity to benefit in life from their education" (p. 194).

The importance of minority students' empowerment is further clarified in the writing of Freire (1970a, 1970b), who suggests that the literacy process should be conceptualized as playing a central role in empowering those who are, in many ways, oppressed in a given social system, so that those people can participate fully in the system. Similarly, Williams and Snipper (1990) have broken literacy down into three levels: (a) *functional literacy* indicates the minimum skills, such as the ability to read signs on the street or at the railroad station, necessary for an individual to function in everyday life in a given society; (b) *cultural literacy* emphasizes cultural ties and traditions in a given society; (c) *critical literacy* identifies political elements intrinsic to reading and writing events, thus involving the ability to use print for empowerment in society. Thus the ultimate goal of literacy education is to achieve a practice based on authentic dialogue between equally well-informed individuals. While these three levels differ from one another, they are similar in their conceptualization of literacy as reflecting the relationship between an individual and the society in which he or she lives, and in their implication that literacies should equip an individual to function well and, above all, to fight against inequity prevalent in society. It has been observed that many students may need at least four years of second-language study to reach functional literacy in the second language (Collier, 1992; Williams & Snipper, 1990). Having arrived at this level, students can then proceed toward cultural and critical literacy. (Note that this evidence supports Cummins's 1979 threshold hypothesis, in which he claims that in order to learn a second language, a certain minimum "threshold" level of proficiency must be attained in the first language.)

In considering the empowerment of language-minority students, the circumstances of their presence in the majority society have to be taken into account. As John Ogbu (1992) puts it, "To understand what it is about minority groups, their cultures and languages that makes crossing cultural boundaries and school learning difficult for some but not for others, we must recognize that there are different types of minorities" (p. 8). According to Ogbu, minority groups consist of different types, such as (a) immigrant or voluntary minorities, and (b) castelike or involuntary minorities. He claims that voluntary immigrant minorities are more likely to achieve academic success because they appraise their situation very differently from involuntary minorities; they believe that the life in the United States will be better than the life in their countries of origin. Involuntary minorities are less likely to succeed in school because they tend to try to preserve linguistic and cultural differences as symbolic of their ethnic identity and their separation from the oppressive mainstream culture; their appraisal of the situation is not likely to have a positive influence on their academic performance.

Lisa Delpit (1988) provides some suggestions for overcom-

ing such social injustice. According to Delpit, children from middle-class communities are advantaged because they know what she calls the codes/culture of power; children from lower-class communities or African American communities are disadvantaged because they lack this knowledge. Delpit claims that social injustice is embedded in the social norms of communicative interaction of the dominant group; her argument parallels Bernstein's (1971) codes and the match-mismatch formulation of literacy. In order to empower minority students, Delpit argues that teachers should make the rules of the "culture of power" explicit and teach those rules to all students as a first step toward a more fair education and society. This concept corresponds to the idea proposed by Jay Robinson (1990), who advocates that equal opportunities should be provided to all students to practice and develop language competencies in response to concrete situations, especially in the classroom.

Those who advocate minority students' empowerment do not necessarily agree as to what exactly, in the domains of language and literacy, offers such empowerment. For example, recall that Freire (1970a, 1970b) argues for educational practice based on an authentic dialogue between teachers and learners as equally knowing subjects. He sharply criticizes the use of social norms held by the dominant culture to legitimate only a few modes of communication, because this restrictive approach leads to the devaluation and thus subtle oppression of minority-language speakers and speakers of nonmainstream varieties. Instead, Freire strongly advocates that literacy process should play the role in empowering those who are oppressed within the system, and thus function as a means of cultural action for freedom.

In contrast to Freire, in her discussion of the debate over the process-oriented/whole-language versus the skills-oriented approach to education, Delpit (1988) stresses that educators, particularly those who support whole language, do not adequately provide minority students with knowledge of the rules needed to function in the culture of power. Whole-language classrooms are usually characterized as valuing students' home cultures and thus accepting a plurality of literacies (Edelsky, 1991). Under this pedagogical ideal the teacher's roles are different than they would be in a traditional teacher-centered/skills-oriented classroom; in whole-language classrooms teachers are guides, participants, and, above all, learners in their own domains. Delpit has been criticized for her lack of sensitivity to the diversity within the whole-language and process-writing movements (Reyes, 1992). What she emphasizes, however, is that it is the educators, and not minority children's homes, that should provide a beneficial environment for those children and facilitate their academic performance. Thus, while Freire and Delpit do not necessarily agree on politically acceptable multiculturalism, they share the same ultimate goals for the empowerment of minority students.

In summary, language researchers have shown in a variety of ways how children's home environment and language community affect their academic development. The way in which a teacher perceives this background can be crucial to the child's academic success or failure. For example, Snow, Barnes, Chandler, Goodman, and Hemphill (1991) report parent-teacher miscommunications and misunderstandings as well as teachers' biases against low-income families and their children as factors hindering those children's academic growth. It may be true that some children, minority children in particular, arrive in school with distinct external disadvantages when compared with peers whose home environments have afforded them ample opportunities to learn the language used in school. No one can deny that children need good environmental support for learning. Moreover, Ogbu (1992) criticizes multicultural education for tending to emphasize change of teacher attitudes and practices instead of focusing on the minority students' own responsibility for their academic performance. However, when one looks at the language research that shows the great variation in linguistic styles and functions, it becomes apparent that educators do need a good understanding of the potential difficulties that language differences can produce, but without lowering their expectations for children who come from linguistically nonmainstream backgrounds.

Lessons from Successful Cases

Our discussion on minority students' empowerment has stressed that sociocultural and linguistic differences alone cannot account for their academic success and failure. There are many elements that should be taken into consideration, such as teacher-student or peer collaborative learning, positive self-image, and the level of teachers' expectations for students. As Eugene García (1991) aptly states, lessons from successful cases will "provide important insights with regard to general instructional organization, literacy development, academic achievement, and the perspectives of students, teachers, administrators, and parents" (p. 2). This subsection will discuss factors in minority students' success.

Parental Participation. Between 1976 and 1989, college participation rates among White high school graduates increased from 33.0% to 38.8%; in contrast, rates for African American and Hispanic high school graduates declined from 33.5% to 30.8% and from 35.8% to 28.7%, respectively (Carter & Wilson, 1990). In addition to smaller numbers going on to college, high dropout rates, low test scores, and poor attendance records indicate that most high schools have failed to meet the needs of Hispanic language-minority students.

Not all schools have failed in their response to these needs. Reporting on language-minority students' success in secondary schools, Lucas, Henze, and Donato (1990) identify the following factors that are related to successful outcomes with language-minority students: (a) "Value is placed on the students' languages and cultures"; (b) "High expectations of language-minority students are made concrete"; (c) "School leaders make the education of language-minority students a priority"; (d) "Staff development is explicitly designed to help teachers and other staff serve language-minority students more effectively"; (e) "A variety of courses and programs for language-minority students is offered"; (f) "A counseling program gives special attention to language-minority students through counselors" who understand those students linguistically as well as culturally; (g) "Parents of language-minority students are encouraged

to become involved in their children's education"; and (h) "School staff members share a strong commitment to empower language-minority students through education" (pp. 324–325).

As can be seen above, one of the factors in language-minority students' success is parental involvement, which is also exemplified in successful late-exit programs (Cazden, 1992). Similarly, Snow, Barnes, Chandler, Goodman, and Hemphill (1991) report positive correlation between parental expectations and low-income children's academic achievement. At the same time, however, these researchers warn of a dangerous situation in which parents are not as involved with teachers at the high school level as they were with teachers at the elementary school level, because of increased parent-teacher miscommunications and misunderstandings, as well as teachers' biases against children with certain backgrounds.

Community Participation. The second factor in minority students' academic success is a community's active participation in school curriculum design in order to cater to the needs of a particular student population. Carlos Ovando (1984) reports such efforts in Nulato, a remote indigenous Athapaskan village in Alaska. According to Ovando, Nulato students and their parents believe that one of the important reasons for getting an education is to learn about Athapaskan traditions. Thus, they have worked actively with administrators to see that the curriculum includes native culture and that an effort is made to hire native teachers. The community's efforts have achieved a positive school environment in which there is little conflict in socialization patterns between the primary speech community (home) and the secondary speech community (school).

Another positive outcome of the community's participation in school curriculum takes the form of preserving that community's traditions. While various traditional customs are still alive, language loss is a serious issue in Nulato in the 1990s. Since parents in the current generation of better-schooled, English-speaking Athapaskans have experienced an intergenerational language communication gap with their own parents, they are trying to find ways to preserve their ancestral language and culture (Ovando, 1994). In order to solve or lessen this critical issue, the community and the school are currently exploring the creation of ecological niches in the school environment in which grandparents can promote the use of the Athapaskan language with schoolchildren. The lessons from Nulato indicate that the school and the community can work together to explore ways of encouraging preservation of the language and culture of children's primary speech community without sacrificing their academic prosperity. In the past, local community movements have played a major role in the development of national language policies, such as the formulation and passage of the Native American Languages Act (Hale, 1992). In this sense, language-maintenance programs that involve the community and the school provide a good lesson for those who seek empowerment of minority students, parents, and communities.

In summary, educators need to promote the empowerment of minority students, their parents, and communities. We should also not forget that the quality of multicultural/bilingual education programs vary with the teachers. Teachers also need to experience the elements necessary to empower language-minority students (Ada, 1986). In this sense, not only minority students, their parents, and communities, but teachers themselves should be empowered.

CONCLUSION AND IMPLICATIONS

In this chapter we have extended the traditional discussion of language issues to multicultural educational settings by looking at how language shapes and is shaped by diverse cultural experiences. This section answers the questions posed at the outset of this chapter:

1. What does past research tell us about cross-cultural differences in the process of language acquisition and literacy skills development?
2. Does the linguistic match-mismatch conception adequately capture the relationships between the primary speech community where an individual was raised and the secondary speech community represented by the school?
3. If languages are conceptualized as social possessions, with literacy thus being perceived from a sociocultural standpoint, what significance does this realization have for education in multicultural/bilingual contexts?

With regard to the first question, this review of existing studies shows that the acquisition of culture-specific communicative competence and socialization patterns plays a significant role in the process of language acquisition and the development of language skills. Because of the differences in social structure and practices, direct comparison among differing speech communities may not be possible. The findings and implications presented in this chapter, however, suggest that U.S. educators should reconsider their cultural approaches and assumptions.

With regard to the second question, the linguistic match-mismatch conception does not adequately capture the primary and secondary speech community relationships. The second section has discussed biases that are often operating behind the match-mismatch hypothesis. The third section has further identified rebutting evidence from the Canadian immersion bilingual program. Thus, what has been emphasized throughout this chapter is that regardless of home environments, children can learn to internalize new expectations of classroom life.

Obviously, our answers to questions 1 and 2 are intricately related to question 3. As reviewed in the third section, empowerment of language-minority students and their parents and communities is an issue that cannot be ignored in the discussion of successful language development for language-minority students. To achieve this end, the importance of teacher-student interaction (and peer interaction in the case of two-way bilingual education programs) should be conceptualized and put into practice by using the framework presented by Vygotsky (1978) and Bruner (1977). The nature of the teacher-student interaction is particularly relevant to the promotion of minority children's academic success. Teachers who understand the linguistic issues, so that they can develop communicative compe-

tence in response to meaningful situations in the classroom, will be better prepared to provide equal opportunities to all students. As we have seen through the research, there are many potential obstacles to smooth teacher-student interactions. For example, even if interlocutors exchange their ideas about a particular topic and acknowledge each other's comments, they may define the same discourse/narrative topic somewhat differently if they have different cultural backgrounds, and communication may eventually break down. Thus, cultural components play a crucial role in keeping a collaborative activity on track.

Biases against socioculturally disadvantaged groups should not be ignored. Take mathematics and science classrooms, for example. Following the Sapir-Whorf hypothesis (Whorf, 1956) that the language one speaks profoundly affects the manner in which one thinks about the world, Orr (1987) erroneously concludes that BEV serves as a barrier to African American students' success in mathematics and science; the deficit hypothesis condemning African American children's home environment is operating behind her argument. Similarly, it has been reported that teachers tend to miss many opportunities to include female students in the conversation. Through choice of language, the teacher may not provide clear or explicit instructions to female students, or may tend to call on White middle-class male students much more frequently than minority working-class female students (Lemke, 1990). Unequal time allocation between males and females in classrooms may be attributed not only to differences in gender-specific language socialization (Maltz & Borker, 1982; Tannen, 1990), but also to the fact that women tend to be kept unfairly silent and powerless in society (Lakoff, 1973, 1990, 1992).

Considering all of the above mentioned obstacles, the result is that classroom teachers do tend to interact differently with children from different sociocultural backgrounds (Cazden, 1988; Cazden et al., 1985; Michaels, 1981, 1991; Michaels & Collins, 1984), and that some do lower their expectations for those minority students' academic achievement (e.g., Cummins, 1986). As anthropological sociolinguists (e.g., Schieffelin & Ochs, 1986) claim, there are behavioral similarities for children of a given age in each cultural setting. Rather than accepting species-specific characteristics, such as the language acquisition process claimed by Noam Chomsky (1965), finding such population-specific characteristics is necessary for understanding what language socialization is all about.

Some classroom teachers tend to view minority students as a group, simply ignoring their individual differences. To make matters worse, in such classrooms the "we" (mostly White middle-class teachers) and "they" (minority students as a bundle) notion of multiculturalism may also exist. Not only is it true that even if they speak the same first language (e.g., Spanish), children from one community (e.g., Mexico) and those from another (e.g., Puerto Rico) are different; it is also necessary that each minority student from each community be perceived as a distinct individual. If classroom teachers attribute Hispanic children's discipline problems to their parents and home environments, in statements such as "The Hispanic students come from restrictive environments; when they arrive in school they go wild" (Penfield, 1987, p. 31), these teachers' view delineates, based on the deficit hypothesis, nothing but a bias against minority students. A "one size fits all" approach never applies in any sense (Reyes, 1992). As Floden, Buchmann, and Schwille (1987) stress, today's schools are responsible for presenting students with a series of options for living and thinking, and providing them with diverse experiences and disciplinary concepts. Thus, contrary to the deficit hypothesis, it is the teacher, not the family, who takes the main responsibility for providing adequate educational support.

The classroom teacher's major responsibility is, then, as Carol Winkelman (1990) puts it, to perform the role of an "experienced participant in the community rather than sole authority" and to facilitate classroom discourse, so that all "students feel more comfortable about being innovative and taking risks with their language" (p. 117). To create such an interactive classroom, the teacher needs to understand the interwoven relationship among language-minority students' linguistic, sociocultural, and cognitive processes (Ovando & Collier, 1995). Based on this understanding, a classroom, a school, and above all, education can then become a forum in which, regardless of race, ethnicity, social background, and gender, everyone is treated equally, so that children from different sociocultural backgrounds can fully nurture their identities and self-esteem.

References

Ada, A. F. (1986). Creative education for bilingual teachers. *Harvard Educational Review, 56*(4), 386–394.

Au, K. H., & Jordan, C. (1981). Teaching reading to Hawaiian children: Finding a culturally appropriate solution. In H. Trueba, G. P. Guthrie, & K. H. Au (Eds.), *Culture in the bilingual classroom: Studies in classroom ethnography* (pp. 139–152). Rowley, MA: Newbury House.

Auerbach, E. R. (1989). Toward a social-contextual approach to family literacy. *Harvard Educational Review, 59*(2), 165–181.

Baker, K. A., & de Kanter, A. A. (1981). *Effectiveness of bilingual education: A review of the literature.* Washington, DC: Office of Planning, Budget and Evaluation, U.S. Department of Education.

Baker, K. A., & de Kanter, A. A. (1983). Federal policy and the effectiveness of bilingual education. In K. A. Baker & A. A. de Kanter (Eds.), *Bilingual education* (pp. 33–86). Lexington, MA: Lexington Books.

Barringer, F. (1993, April 28). Immigration in 80's made English a foreign language for millions. *The New York Times,* pp. A1, A10.

Bennett, J. A., & Berry, J. W. (1991). Cree literacy in the syllabic script. In D. R. Olson & N. Torrance (Eds.), *Literacy and orality* (pp. 90–104). New York: Cambridge University Press.

Bernstein, B. (1971). *Class, codes and control: Vol. 1. Theoretical studies towards a sociology of language.* London: Routledge & Kegan Paul.

Borker, R. (1980). Anthropology. In S. McConnell-Ginet, R. Borker, & N. Furman (Eds.), *Women and language in literature and society* (pp. 26–44). New York: Praeger.

Brandt, D. (1989). The medium is the message: Orality and literacy once more. *Written Communication, 61,* 31–44.

Brandt, D. (1990) *Literacy as involvement: The acts of writer, reader, and texts.* Carbondale: Southern Illinois University Press.

Brown, R. (1973). *A first language.* Cambridge, MA: Harvard University Press.

Brown, R., & Bellugi, U. (1964). Three processes in the child's acquisition of syntax. *Harvard Educational Review, 34*(2), 133–151.

Bruner, J. (1977). Early social interaction and language development. In H. R. Schaffer (Ed.), *Studies in mother-child interaction* (pp. 271–289). London: Academic Press.

Bruner, J. (1990). *Acts of meaning.* Cambridge, MA: Harvard University Press.

Carter, D., & Wilson, R. (1990). *Ninth annual status report: Minorities in higher education.* Washington, DC: American Council on Education.

Cazden, C. B. (1988). *Classroom discourse: The language of teaching and learning.* Portsmouth, NH: Heinemann.

Cazden, C. B. (1992). *Language minority education in the United States: Implication of the Ramírez report* (Educational Practice Report 3). Santa Cruz, CA: National Center for Research on Cultural Diversity and Second Language Learning.

Cazden, C. B., Michaels, S., & Tabors, P. (1985). Spontaneous repair in sharing time narratives: The interaction of metalinguistic awareness, speech event, and narrative style. In S. W. Freedman (Ed.), *The acquisition of written language* (pp. 51–64). Norwood, NJ: Ablex.

Chomsky, C. (1969). *The acquisition of syntax in children from 5 to 10.* Cambridge, MA: MIT Press.

Chomsky, C. (1972). Stages in language development and reading exposure. *Harvard Educational Review, 42*(1), 1–33.

Chomsky, N. (1957). *Syntactic structure.* The Hague: Mouton & Co.

Chomsky, N. (1959). Review of *Verbal behavior* by B. F. Skinner. *Language, 35*(1), 26–58.

Chomsky, N. (1965). *Aspects of the theory of syntax.* Cambridge, MA: MIT Press.

Chomsky, N. (1985). *Knowledge of language: Its nature, origin, and use.* New York: Praeger.

Collier, V. P. (1987). Age and rate of acquisition of second language for academic purposes. *TESOL Quarterly, 21*(4), 617–641.

Collier, V. P. (1989). How long? A synthesis of research on academic achievement in a second language. *TESOL Quarterly, 23*(3), 509–531.

Collier, V. P. (1992). A synthesis of studies examining long-term language-minority student data on academic achievement. *Bilingual Research Journal, 16*(1 & 2), 187–212.

Cook-Gumperz, J. (1992). Gendered talk and gendered lives: Little girls being women before becoming (big) girls. In K. Hall, M. Bucholtz, & B. Moonwomon (Eds.), *Locating power: Proceedings of the 1992 Berkeley Women and Language Conference* (Vol. 1, pp. 68–79). Berkeley: Berkeley Women and Language Group, University of California.

Cook-Gumperz, J., & Gumperz, J. J. (1982). Communicative competence in educational perspective. In L. C. Wilkinson (Ed.), *Communicating in the classroom* (pp. 13–24). New York: Academic Press.

Crawford, J. (1989). *Bilingual education: History, politics, theory, and practice.* Trenton, NJ: Crane Publishing.

Crawford, J. (1992). *Hold your tongue: Bilingualism and the politics of "English only."* Reading, MA: Addison-Wesley.

Cummins, J. (1979). Linguistic interdependence and the educational development of bilingual children. *Review of Educational Research, 49,* 222–251.

Cummings, J. (1980). The cross-lingual dimensions of language proficiency: Implications for bilingual education and optimal age issue. *TESOL Quarterly, 14*(2), 175–187.

Cummins, J. (1984). Wanted: A theoretical framework for relating language proficiency to academic achievement among bilingual students. In C. R. Rivera (Ed.), *Communicative competence approaches to language proficiency assessment* (pp. 2–19). Clevedon, England: Multilingual Matters.

Cummins, J. (1986). Empowering minority students: A framework for intervention. *Harvard Educational Review, 56*(1), 18–36.

Cummins, J. (1991a). Interdependence of first- and second-language proficiency in bilingual children. In E. Bialystok (Ed.), *Language processing in bilingual children* (pp. 70–89). New York: Cambridge University Press.

Cummins, J. (1991b). Language development and academic learning. In L. M. Malavé & G. Duquette (Eds.), *Language, culture and cognition* (pp. 161–175). Clevedon, England: Multilingual Matters.

Cummins, J., Swain, M., Nakajima, K., Handscombe, J., Green, D., & Tran, C. (1984). Linguistic interdependence among Japanese and Vietnamese immigrant students. In C. Rivera (Ed.), *Language proficiency and academic achievement* (pp. 60–81). Clevedon, England: Multilingual Matters.

Delpit, L. D. (1988). The silenced dialogue: Power and pedagogy in educating other people's children. *Harvard Educational Review, 58*(3), 280–298.

Dickinson, K. D., & Smith, M. W. (1990, April). *Bookreading as a setting for the use of self-contextualizing language with low-income preschoolers.* Paper presented at the annual meeting of the American Educational Research Association, Boston.

Edelsky, C. (1991). *With literacy and justice for all.* Bristol, PA: Falmer Press.

Egan, K. (1987). Literacy and the oral foundation of education. *Harvard Educational Review, 57*(4), 445–472.

Erickson, F. D., & Mohatt, G. (1982). Cultural organization of participation structures in two classrooms of Indian students. In G. D. Spindler (Ed.), *Doing the ethnography of schooling: Educational anthropology in action* (pp. 132–175). New York: Holt, Rinehart, & Winston.

Floden, R. E., Buchmann, M., & Schwille, J. R. (1987). Breaking with everyday experience. *Teachers College Record, 88*(4), 485–506.

Freire, P. (1970a). The adult literacy process as cultural action for freedom. *Harvard Educational Review, 40*(2), 205–225.

Freire, P. (1970b). *Pedagogy of the oppressed.* New York: Seabury Press.

Gal, S. (1992). Language, gender, and power: An anthropological view. In K. Hall, M. Bucholtz, & B. Moonwomon (Eds.), *Locating power: Proceedings of the 1992 Berkeley Women and Language Conference* (Vol. 1, pp. 153–161). Berkeley: Berkeley Women and Language Group, University of California.

García, E. (1991). *Education of linguistically and culturally diverse students: Effective instructional practices* (Educational Practice Report 1). Santa Cruz, CA: National Center for Research on Cultural Diversity and Second Language Learning.

Garton, A., & Pratt, C. (1989). *Learning to be literate: The development of spoken and written language.* New York: Basil Blackwell.

Gee, J. P. (1985). The narrativisation of experience in oral style. *Journal of Education, 167,* 9–35.

Gee, J. P. (1986a). Orality and literacy: From the savage mind to ways with words. *TESOL Quarterly, 20*(4), 719–746.

Gee, J. P. (1986b). Units in the production of narrative discourse. *Discourse Processes, 9,* 391–422.

Gee, J. P. (1989). Two styles of narrative construction and their linguistic and educational implications. *Discourse Processes, 12,* 287–307.

Gee, J. P. (1990). *Social linguistics and literacies: Ideologies in discourse.* Bristol, PA: Falmer Press.

Gee, J. P. (1991). Memory and myth: A perspective on narrative. In A. McCabe & C. Peterson (Eds.), *Developing narrative structure* (pp. 1–25). Hillsdale, NJ: Lawrence Erlbaum Associates.

Genesee, F. (1983). Bilingual education of majority-language children: The immersion experiments in review. *Applied Psycholinguistics, 4,* 1–46.

Genesee, F. (1985). Second language learning through immersion: A review of U.S. programs. *Review of Educational Research, 55*(4), 541–561.

Hakuta, K. (1986). *Mirror of language: The debate on bilingualism.* New York: Basic Books.

Hale, K. (1992). On endangered languages and the safeguarding of diversity. *Language, 68*(1), 1–3.

Harley, B. (1991). The acquisition of some oral second language skills in early and late immersion. In L. M. Malavé & G. Duquette (Eds.), *Language, culture and cognition* (pp. 232–249). Clevedon, England: Multilingual Matters.

Hart, D., Lapkin, S., & Swain, M. (1991). Secondary level immersion French skills: A possible plateau effect. In L. M. Malavé & G. Duquette (Eds.), *Language, culture and cognition* (pp. 250–265). Clevedon, England: Multilingual Matters.

Hauser-Cram, P., Pierson, D. E., Walker, D. K., & Tivnan, T. (1991). *Early education in the public schools: Lessons from a comprehensive birth-to-kindergarten program.* San Francisco: Jossey-Bass.

Heath, S. B. (1982a). Questioning at home and at school: A comparative study. In G. Spindler (Ed.), *Doing the ethnography of schooling* (pp. 102–131). New York: Holt, Rinehart, & Winston.

Heath, S. B. (1982b). What no bedtime story means: Narrative skills at home and school. *Language in Society, 11,* 49–76.

Heath, S. B. (1983). *Ways with words: Language, life and work in communities and classrooms.* New York: Cambridge University Press.

Heath, S. B. (1986). Taking a cross-cultural look at narratives. *Topics in Language Disorders, 7*(1), 84–94.

Hemphill, L. (1989). Topic development, syntax, and social class. *Discourse Processes, 12,* 267–286.

Holm, A., & Holm, W. (1990). Rock Point, A Navajo way to go to school: A valediction. In C. B. Cazden & C. E. Snow (Eds.), *English plus: Issues in bilingual education* (pp. 170–184). Newbury Park, CA: Sage.

Huddy, L., & Sears, D. O. (1990). Qualified public support for bilingual education: Some policy implications. In C. B. Cazden & C. E. Snow (Eds.), *English plus: Issues in bilingual education* (pp. 119–134). Newbury Park, CA: Sage.

Hymes, D. (1974a). *Foundations in sociolinguistics: An ethnographic approach.* Philadelphia: University of Pennsylvania Press.

Hymes, D. (1974b). Speech and language: On the origins and foundations of inequity among speakers. In E. Haugen & M. Bloomfield (Eds.), *Language as a human problem* (pp. 45–71). New York: Norton.

Hymes, D. (1981). *"In vain I tried to tell you": Studies in Native American ethnopoetics.* Philadelphia: University of Pennsylvania Press.

Hymes, D. (1982). Narrative as a "grammar" of experience: Native Americans and a glimpse of English. *Journal of Education, 2,* 121–142.

Hymes, D. (1990). Thomas Paul's Sametl: Verse analysis of a (Saanich) Chinook jargon text. *Journal of Pidgin and Creole Languages, 5*(1), 71–106.

Jordan, C. (1984). Cultural compatibility and the education of Hawaiian children: Implications for mainland educators. *Education Research Quarterly, 8*(4), 59–71.

Jordan, C., Vogt, L., & Tharp, R. G. (1993). Explaining school failure, producing school success: Two cases. In E. Jacob & C. Jordan (Eds.), *Minority education: Anthropological perspectives.* (pp. 53–65). Norwood, NJ: Ablex.

Labov, W. (1972). *Language in the inner city.* Philadelphia: University of Pennsylvania Press.

Labov, W., Cohen, P., Robins, C., & Lewis, J. (1968). *A study of the nonstandard English of Negro and Puerto Rican speakers in New York City* (Vol. 2) (Cooperative Research Project No. 3288). Washington, DC: U.S. Office of Education.

Labov, W., & Waletzky, J. (1967). Narrative analysis: Oral versions of personal experience. In J. Helm (Ed.), *Essays on the verbal and visual arts* (pp. 12–44). Seattle: University of Washington Press.

Lakoff, R. (1973). Language and woman's place. *Language in Society, 2,* 45–80.

Lakoff, R. T. (1990). *Talking power.* New York: Basic Books.

Lakoff, R. T. (1992). The silencing of women. In K. Hall, M. Bucholtz, & B. Moonwomon (Eds.), *Locating power: Proceedings of the 1992 Berkeley Women and Language Conference* (Vol. 2, pp. 344–355). Berkeley: Berkeley Women and Language Group, University of California.

Lambert, W. E. (1975). Culture and language as factors in learning and education. In A. Wolfgang (Ed.), *Education of immigrant students: Issues and answers* (pp. 55–83). Toronto: The Ontario Institute for Studies in Education.

Lambert, W. E. (1977). The effects of bilingualism on the individual: Cognitive and sociocultural consequences. In P. A. Hornby (Ed.), *Bilingualism: Psychological, social, and educational implications* (pp. 15–27). New York: Academic Press.

Lambert, W. E. (1981). Bilingualism and language acquisition. In H. Winitz (Ed.), *Native language and foreign language acquisition* (pp. 9–22). New York: New York Academy of Science.

Lave, J. (1991). Situating learning in communities of practice. In L. B. Resnick, J. M. Levine, & S. D. Teasley (Eds.), *Perspectives on socially shared cognition* (pp. 63–82). Washington, DC: American Psychological Association.

Lave, J., & Wenger, E. (1991). *Situated learning: Legitimate peripheral participation.* New York: Cambridge University Press.

Lemke, J. (1990). *Talking science: Language, learning, and values.* Norwood, NJ: Ablex.

Lindholm, K. J. (1992). Two-way bilingual/immersion education: Theory, conceptual issues, and pedagogical implications. In R. V. Padilla & A. H. Benavides (Eds.), *Critical perspectives on bilingual education research* (pp. 195–220). Tempe, AZ: Bilingual Press/Editorial Bilingüe.

Lucas, T., Henze, R., & Donato, R. (1990). Promoting the success of Latino language-minority students: An exploratory study of six high schools. *Harvard Educational Review, 60*(3), 315–340.

Maltz, D., & Borker, R. (1982). A cultural approach to male-female miscommunication. In J. Gumperz (Ed.), *Language and social identity* (pp. 195–216). New York: Cambridge University Press.

McCloskey, M. L., & Enright, D. S. (1992). America 2000: A TESOL response. In *TESOL resource packet* (pp. 1–9). Alexandria, VA: TESOL.

McKeon, D. (1992). Introduction. In *TESOL resource packet* (p. i). Alexandria, VA: TESOL.

McLaughlin, B. (1992). *Myths and misconceptions about second language learning: What every teacher needs to learn* (Educational Practice Report 5). Santa Cruz, CA: National Center for Research on Cultural Diversity and Second Language Learning.

McLaughlin, D. (1990). The sociolinguistics of Navajo literacy. *Journal of Navajo Education, 7*(2), 28–36.

McLaughlin, D. (1992). *When literacy empowers: Navajo language in print.* Albuquerque: University of New Mexico Press.

Mehan, H. (1991). *Sociological foundations supporting the study of cultural diversity* (Research Report 1). Santa Cruz, CA: National Center for Research on Cultural Diversity and Second Language Learning.

Michaels, S. (1981). "Sharing time": Children's narrative styles and differential access to literacy. *Language in Society, 10,* 423–442.

Michaels, S. (1991). The dismantling of narrative. In A. McCabe & C. Peterson (Eds.), *Developing narrative structure* (pp. 303–351). Hillsdale, NJ: Lawrence Erlbaum Associates.

Michaels, S., & Collins, J. (1984). Oral discourse styles: Classroom interaction and the acquisition of literacy. In D. Tannen (Ed.), *Coherence in spoken and written discourse* (pp. 219–244). Norwood, NJ: Ablex.

Miller, P. (1982). *Amy, Wendy, and Beth: Language acquisition in South Baltimore.* Austin: University of Texas Press.

Minami, M., & McCabe, A. (1991a). Haiku as a discourse regulation device: A stanza analysis of Japanese children's personal narratives. *Language in Society, 20,* 577–600.

Minami, M., & McCabe, A. (1991b, October). *Rice balls versus bear hunts: Japanese and Caucasian family narrative patterns.* Paper presented at the 16th Annual Boston University Conference on Language Development.

Minami, M., & McCabe, A. (1993, July). *Social interaction and discourse style: Culture-specific parental styles of interviewing and children's narrative structure.* Paper presented at the 4th International Pragmatics Conference, Kobe, Japan.

Minami, M., & McCabe, A. (in press). Rice balls and bear hunts: Japanese and North American family narrative patterns. *Journal of Child Language.*

Morison, S. H. (1990). A Spanish-English dual-language program in New York City. In C. B. Cazden & C. E. Snow (Eds.), *English plus: Issues in bilingual education* (pp. 160–169). Newbury Park, CA: Sage.

Nelson, K. (1981). Individual differences in a language development: Implications for development and language. *Psychological Bulletin, 17,* 170–187.

Ochs, E. (1986). Introduction. In B. B. Schieffelin & E. Ochs (Eds.), *Language socialization across cultures* (pp. 1–13). New York: Cambridge University Press.

Ochs, E., & Schieffelin, B. B. (1984). Language acquisition and socialization: Three developmental stories. In R. Schweder & R. LeVine (Eds.), *Culture theory: Essays on mind, self and emotion* (pp. 276–320). New York: Cambridge University Press.

Ogbu, J. U. (1992). Understanding cultural diversity and learning. *Educational Researcher, 21*(8), 5–14.

Olson, D. R. (1977). From utterance to text: The bias of language in speech and writing. *Harvard Educational Review, 47*(3), 257–281.

Orr, E. W. (1987). *Twice as less: Black English and the performance of Black students in mathematics and science.* New York: Norton.

Ovando, C. J. (1984). School and community attitudes in an Athapaskan bush village. *Educational Research Quarterly, 8*(4), 12–29.

Ovando, C. J. (1990a). Intermediate and secondary school curricula: A multicultural and multilingual framework. *The Clearing House, 63*(7), 294–298.

Ovando, C. J. (1990b). Politics and pedagogy: The case of bilingual education. *Harvard Educational Review, 60*(3), 341–356.

Ovando, C. J. (1993). Language diversity and education. In J. A. Banks and C. A. M. Banks (Eds.), *Multicultural education: Issues and perspectives* (2nd ed., pp. 215–235). Boston: Allyn and Bacon.

Ovando, C. J. (1994). Change in school and community attitudes in an Athapaskan village. *Peabody Journal of Education, 69*(2), 43–59.

Ovando, C. J., & Collier, V. P. (1995). *Bilingual and ESL classrooms: Teaching in multicultural contexts* (2nd ed.). New York: McGraw-Hill.

Peal, E., & Lambert, W. E. (1962). The relation of bilingualism to intelligence. *Psychological Monographs, 76*(27, Whole No. 546).

Penfield, J. (1987). ESL: The regular classroom teacher's perspective. *TESOL Quarterly, 21*(1), 21–39.

Peterson, C., & McCabe, A. (1983). *Developmental psycholinguistics: Three ways of looking at a child's narrative.* New York: Plenum.

Philips, S. U. (1972). Participant structures and communicative competence: Warm Springs children in community and classroom. In C. B. Cazden, V. P. John, & D. Hymes (Eds.), *Functions of language in the classroom* (pp. 370–394). Prospect Heights, IL: Waveland Press.

Philips, S. U. (1982). *The invisible culture: Communication in classroom and community on the Warm Springs Indian reservation.* New York: Longman.

Ramírez, J. D., Yuen, S. D., & Ramey, D. R. (1991). *Longitudinal study of structured English immersion strategy, early-exit and late-exit tran-*

sitional bilingual education programs for language-minority children. Final report to the U.S. Department of Education. (Executive Summary and Vols. 1 & 2). San Mateo, CA: Aguirre International.

Reyes, M. L. (1992). Challenging venerable assumptions: Literacy instruction for linguistically different students. *Harvard Educational Review, 62*(4), 427–446.

Robinson, J. L. (1990). *Conversations on the written word: Essays on language and literacy.* Portsmouth, NJ: Heinemann.

Rosier, P., & Holm, W. (1980). *The Rock Point experience: A longitudinal study of a Navajo school program.* Washington, DC: Center for Applied Linguistics.

Saussure, F. de. (1959). *Course in general linguistics* (W. Baskin, trans.). New York: McGraw-Hill. (Original work published 1915).

Schieffelin, B. B. (1986). Teasing and shaming in Kaluli children's interactions. In B. B. Schieffelin & E. Ochs (Eds.), *Language socialization across cultures* (pp. 165–181). New York: Cambridge University Press.

Schieffelin, B. B., & Eisenberg, A. R. (1984). Cultural variation in children's conversations. In B. B. Schieffelin & J. Picker (Eds.), *The acquisition of communicative competence* (pp. 378–420). Baltimore, MD: University Park Press.

Schieffelin, B. B., & Ochs, E. (Eds). (1986). *Language socialization across cultures.* New York: Cambridge University Press.

Scollon, R., & Scollon, S. (1981). *Narrative, literacy and face in interethnic communications.* Norwood, NJ: Ablex.

Scribner, S., & Cole, M. (1978). Literacy without schooling: Testing for intellectual effects. *Harvard Educational Review, 48*(4), 448–461.

Scribner, S., & Cole, M. (1981). *The psychology of literacy.* Cambridge, MA: Harvard University Press.

Shuman, A. (1986). *Storytelling rights: The uses of oral and written texts by urban adolescents.* New York: Cambridge University Press.

Skinner, B. F. (1957). *Verbal behavior.* Englewood Cliffs, NJ: Prentice-Hall.

Slobin, D. I. (1985). Introduction: Why study acquisition crosslinguistically? In D. I. Slobin (Ed.), *The crosslinguistic study of language acquisition: Vol. 1. The data* (pp. 3–24). Hillsdale, NJ: Lawrence Erlbaum Associates.

Snow, C. E. (1977). Mother's speech research: From input to interaction. In C. E. Snow & C. A. Ferguson (Eds.), *Talking to children: Language input and acquisition* (pp. 31–49). New York: Cambridge University Press.

Snow, C. E. (1983). Literacy and language: Relationships during the preschool years. *Harvard Educational Review, 53*(2), 165–189.

Snow, C. E. (1986). Conversation with children. In P. Fletcher & M. Garman (Eds.), *Language acquisition* (pp. 69–89). New York: Cambridge University Press.

Snow, C. E. (1980a). Imitativeness: A trait or a skill? In G. Spiedel & K. Nelson (Eds.), *The many faces of imitation in language learning* (pp. 73–90). New York: Springer-Verlag.

Snow, C. E. (1989b). Understanding social interaction and language acquisition: Sentences are not enough. In M. H. Bornstein & J. S. Bruner (Eds.), *Interaction in human development* (pp. 83–103). Hillsdale, NJ: Lawrence Erlbaum Associates.

Snow, C. E. (1990). The development of definitional skill. *Journal of Child Language, 17,* 697–710.

Snow, C. E., Barnes, W. S., Chandler, J., Goodman, I. F., & Hemphill, L. (1991). *Unfulfilled expectations: Home and school influences on literacy.* Cambridge, MA: Harvard University Press.

Snow, C. E., Cancino, H., De Temple, J., & Schley, S. (1991). Giving formal definitions: A linguistic or metalinguistic skill? In E. Bialystok (Ed.), *Language processing in bilingual children* (pp. 90–112). New York: Cambridge University Press.

Snow, C. E., & Ninio, A. (1986). The contracts of literacy: What children learn from learning to read books. In W. Teale & E. Sultzby (Eds.), *Emergent literacy; Written and reading* (pp. 116–138). Norwood, NJ: Ablex.

Spener, D. (1988). Transitional bilingual education and the socialization of immigrants. *Harvard Educational Review, 58*(2), 133–153.

Stanford Working Group. (1993). *Federal education programs for limited-English-proficient students: A blueprint for the second generation.* Palo Alto, CA: Stanford University.

Tannen, D. (1990). *You just don't understand: Women and men in conversation.* New York: Morrow.

Tharp, R. G., & Gallimore, R. (1991a). *The instructional conversation: Teaching and learning in social activity* (Research Report 2). Santa Cruz, CA: National Center for Research on Cultural Diversity and Second Language Learning.

Tharp, R. G., & Gallimore, R. (1991b). *Rousing minds to life: Teaching, learning, and schooling in social context.* Cambridge, England: Cambridge University Press.

Torrance, N., & Olson, D. R. (1985). Oral and literate competencies in the early school years. In D. R. Olson, N. Torrance, & A. Hildyard (Eds.), *Literacy, language, and learning: The nature of consequences of reading and writing* (pp. 256–284). New York: Cambridge University Press.

U.S. Department of Education. (1992). *The condition of bilingual education: A report to the Congress and the president.* Washington, DC: Government Printing Office.

Vygotsky, L. S. (1978). *Mind in society: The development of higher psychological processes.* Cambridge, MA: Harvard University Press.

Wanner, E., & Gleitman, L. R. (Eds.). (1982). *Language acquisition: The state of the art.* New York: Cambridge University Press.

Whorf, B. L. (1956). *Language, thought, and reality: Selected writings* (J. B. Carroll, Ed.). Cambridge, MA: MIT Press.

Williams, J. D., & Snipper, G. C. (1990). *Literacy and bilingualism.* New York: Longman.

Willig, A. C. (1985). A meta-analysis of selected studies on the effectiveness of bilingual education. *Review of Educational Research, 55,* 269–317.

Winkelman, C. L. (1990). Talk as text: Student on the margins. In J. L. Robinson (Ed.), *Conversations on the written word: Essays on language and literacy* (pp. 115–128). Portsmouth, NJ: Heinemann.

Wong, Fillmore, L., & Valadez, C. (1986). Teaching bilingual teachers. In M. C. Wittrock (Ed.), *Handbook of research on teaching* (3rd ed., pp. 648–684). New York: Macmillan.

· 25 ·

BILINGUAL EDUCATION: BROADENING
RESEARCH PERSPECTIVES

Carrol E. Moran   *Kenji Hakuta*

STANFORD UNIVERSITY   STANFORD UNIVERSITY

The United States was founded as a multilingual society. Bilingual education has existed in various forms for a variety of linguistic groups since that founding over 200 years ago (Fishman & Hofman, 1966; Kloss, 1977). While early U.S. efforts in bilingual education, as well as present-day bilingual programs in Canada, cited the development of bilingualism as their goal, the majority of bilingual programs in the United States today promote bilingual education only as a means to achieving the goal of literacy in English.

The focus of this chapter is on research in bilingual education in the United States, its history, practices, and potential. The introductory section of this chapter will describe a variety of models of bilingual education and lay a foundation of terminology for those new to the field. The second section looks historically at research in the field of bilingual education, both in the development of evaluation research agendas and in basic research on bilingualism, to examine some of the forces that have influenced that research and have helped to shape the present state of the field. The third section contrasts two very different approaches to studying bilingual education, examining the design and methodology as well as the results and implications of these studies. The final section suggests a new approach to looking at research in the field that aims to broaden the goals of bilingual education toward promoting a language-rich society (Ruiz, 1988; Padilla, 1990), and proposes an inclusive approach to research that brings the bilingual education community into full participation in the research process and suggests a new role for the bilingual education researcher.

The modern era of bilingual education in the United States may be dated back to 1963, to Coral Way Elementary School in Dade County, Miami, Florida (Mackey & Beebee, 1977). This original bilingual program served an equal ratio of English to Spanish native speakers. The goal was to promote bilingualism among both groups of students. Each group received native-language instruction in the morning and second-language instruction in the afternoon, with mixing encouraged through art, physical education, and music in the middle of the day. The program was deemed a success both in the development of language and content and in the affective domain. It improved attitudes across ethnic groups and enhanced the self-esteem of students. Teachers and administrators observed that students were broadening their perspectives and preparing to contribute to their bilingual community (Mackey and Beebe). Despite the initial promise of the Coral Way experiment, the past 30 years have been fraught with controversy, resulting in a scattered variety of programs designed to serve the growing number of Limited-English-Proficient (L.E.P.) students. (The term LEP is controversial for both its deficiency orientation and the unfortunate auditory association with leper. It is, however, the official legal designation and most commonly used term for students who have not achieved a locally specified degree of proficiency in English. For this reason it will be used in this chapter of the *Handbook* with periods between the letters, encouraging the reader to read the letters independently.)

The authors would like to acknowledge the contributions of James A. Banks, Elizabeth Burris, Carlos Diaz, Barry McLaughlin, Jean Mahoney, Carlos Ovando, Richard Ruiz, Judy Stobbe, and Alison Woolpert, who read early outlines and drafts of this chapter and made useful suggestions for improvements. We would also like to thank the many people in the field who allowed themselves to be interviewed so a diversity of voices might be presented.

MODELS OF BILINGUAL EDUCATION

From their auspicious beginnings in Coral Way, bilingual programs in the United States have grown, but do not come close to serving the approximately 5.2 million children between the ages of 5 and 17 whose home language is other than English (National Center for Education Statistics, 1993). Nor do programs exist to accommodate the roughly 2.3 to 3.5 million L.E.P. school-age children (Aleman, 1993). Title VII (federally funded bilingual programs) services reached just 290,000 students in 1993.

The term *bilingual program* has come to represent many different approaches to educating children who are acquiring a second language. (See C. Baker, 1993, for a comprehensive explanation of models used throughout the world.) These approaches may be characterized by the amount of native languages utilized or the number of years the native language or mother tongue is supported. Native language may not be used at all by teachers but allowed by students (immersion or submersion), or it may be used sparingly as a vehicle to help students into the second language (Transitional Bilingual Education [TBE]). TBE programs vary greatly in the amount of native language used and the length of time that language is maintained. Early-exit programs generally place students in English-only classrooms as early as first or second grade without fully developing literacy in the native language. Late-exit programs move children into English-only classrooms after the fourth grade, usually no later than the sixth grade. Native language may be encouraged and supported beyond the time when a student functions in English (maintenance). The distinction between late-exit and maintenance programs is not always clear, since local politics and policy may play a role in the choice of naming a program TBE, late-exit, or maintenance. Dual-language immersion programs—also called two-way immersion programs or biliteracy immersion programs—have the goal of maintaining the native language of language-minority students and promoting the minority language among majority-language students.

Programs may be further characterized by the second-language usage patterns. Languages may be alternated every other day or week. The native language may be developed in the language arts block and the second language developed in the content areas, as in the California case studies approach (Samaniego & Eubank, 1991; Crawford, 1989). Second language is often taught through the content areas by using strategies designed to increase students' ability to acquire the language (sheltered language approaches).

Programs may also be differentiated by their approach to staffing. Staffing patterns often vary with the linguistic proficiencies of the teacher and, more specifically, with the availability of bilingual teachers. Staffing patterns resulting from accommodations to the dearth of bilingual teachers include: (a) a waivered bilingual program in which the teachers do not meet the qualifications to be considered fully proficient in language, culture, or curriculum to teach language-minority students but are granted a waiver due to shortages of such teachers; (b) a team-teaching model that may team bilingual and monolingual teachers to meet the language needs of students; and (c) a bilingual strand/track that provides a segment of bilingual classes within a monolingual school site, with one or more bilingual teachers at each grade level or in multigraded classes.

Alternatively, a program may be characterized by its goals. Both TBE programs and structured English immersion programs have the eventual goal of enabling students to function in English-only classrooms. TBE programs have been the most prevalent approach in the United States. A maintenance bilingual program continues to support the primary language of language-minority students even after proficiency in English has been reached, striving for a goal of producing fully proficient bilinguals. A biliteracy program has the goal of developing students who are bilingual and biliterate, as in a maintenance program; English is added to the curriculum rather than replacing the student's native language for instruction. A dual language immersion program has the goal of bilingualism for students of both the dominant and minority cultures (Lindholm & Aclan, 1991). The minority language is the medium of instruction initially for the dual purpose of developing native language for language-minority students and developing second language for language-majority students, moving toward full bilingualism for both language groups. In this model English is used approximately 10% of the time in kindergarten, with the percentage increased each year until a level of 50% of instruction is being offered in each language.

The variety of approaches to bilingual programs is a response to varied populations as well as to the political, social, and educational objectives of different school sites. Communities differ not only in terms of the number and mix of students of various language groups and the language capacity of the school system staff, but also in terms of the goals of the community for those students. These goals are determined, if not always articulated, by the community, the parents, and the administrators, as well as by local, state, and federal policy makers and the educational staff.

The role of bilingual education research in this context has been predominantly evaluative, confined to a narrow emphasis on determining the effectiveness of the schools to meet their goals, usually defined as English proficiency.

Most of the evaluation research to date has been an attempt to determine the best way to "do" bilingual education (Ramirez, Pasta, Yuen, Ramey, & Billings, 1991; Baker & De Kanter, 1983). These studies have looked at which model works best or which curriculum is more successful. Other research with more basic orientations has looked at specific aspects of the realm of bilingual education related to various theories, such as second-language acquisition (C. Snow, 1992), native-language shift (Veltman, 1983; Hakuta & D'Andrea, 1992), bilingualism and cognition (Ben-Zeev, 1977; Bialystok, 1987a, 1987b; Diaz, 1983; Ianco Worral, 1972; Peal & Lambert, 1962), and cooperative learning (Johnson, Johnson, & Maruyama, 1983; Kagan, 1986).

With the goal of improving the relationship of research to the policy and practice of bilingual education, it is important to reflect on what has influenced the field of research to date. Rather than provide an overview of the literature, the next section will cover the historical development of research, and the following section will compare two types of evaluation research studies in depth. For broader reviews of research on bilingual education see Baker (1993), Cziko (1992), Crawford (1989), Trueba (1989), Wong Fillmore and Valadez (1986), Ramírez et al. (1991), and Ramírez, Yuen, Ramey, and Pasta (1990). (For further discussion on language issues see chapter 24 of this *Handbook*.)

THE HISTORICAL DEVELOPMENT OF RESEARCH IN BILINGUAL EDUCATION

Historical reflection is an effective instructional approach (Arons, 1983) because it allows the student to see the development of knowledge as a fallible process rather than a fact to be accepted without question. Understanding the historical context can help us make informed decisions about what knowledge to accept as truth and what to reject. The history of research in bilingual education is a tale of many different social and political climatic forces and changes at work.

Research, whether basic or applied, is never independent from political influence. Most researchers need the backing of a funding institution. Such institutions fund research according to their own intellectual, social, or political agendas. One important difference between basic and evaluative research lies in the constraints that shape research projects. Whereas evaluative research tends to be commissioned by government agencies and so shaped by prevailing policies, basic research, which is initiated by individuals within the research community, is primarily influenced by the intellectual climate of the times.

The Historical Development of Bilingualism and Cognition

This section will examine the history of basic research in the area of bilingualism and cognition with an eye to its development, its impact on bilingual education, and possible areas for improvement in the relationship among basic research, policy, and practice.

A look at the general context of research on intelligence that prevailed in the first half of the 20th century provides a basis for understanding the research on bilingualism and intelligence conducted at that time (Gould, 1981). Alfred Binet, professor of psychology at the Sorbonne, was hired in 1904 to identify children who would not be successful in regular classes and who should be separated for special instruction. Binet developed a variety of tasks for children to perform that afforded the assignment of a "mental age" of the child. He was opposed to the notion of a fixed entity of intelligence and was vehement that his test not be used as a general intelligence measure (Hakuta, 1986).

In America, however, through the efforts of Goddard (1917) and Terman (1916), Binet's work was turned into a general intelligence test that was administered to immigrants and in the military in the early part of the century (with no regard for language proficiency, socioeconomic status, or literacy background), thus adding to the general belief of the time in the

inferior intelligence of immigrant and non-White populations (Hakuta, 1986).

This intellectual and social climate—one of belief in innate intelligence (nature over nurture) and a lack of awareness of the impact of socioeconomic status and language proficiency as confounding factors in testing—had a great effect on the research findings. In addition, the anti-immigrant attitudes of the society, particularly against southern European stock, encouraged an environment that supported such biased research (Higham, 1965). This was the social milieu surrounding research on bilingualism and intelligence in the first half of this century. It is not surprising that the extensive and rigorous (by standards of the time) quantitative research found negative consequences of bilingualism as related to intelligence. Baker (1993), who refers to this as the "period of detrimental effects," extends the list of methodological flaws beyond linguistic factors into bias in sampling procedures and analysis of data using simple averages.

Inferior performance by bilinguals on IQ tests allowed the researcher to determine either that the bilinguals were genetically inferior, as such hereditarians as Terman, Young, and Goodenough concluded (Hakuta, 1986), or that bilingualism caused retardation in the development of verbal skills, as the language handicap notion suggested (Hakuta, 1986). In this context Saer (1924) studied English-Welsh bilinguals, Yoshioka (1929) tested Japanese American bilinguals, and Smith (1939) studied bilinguals in Hawaii. The studies compared bilinguals to monolinguals, with the bilinguals being found inferior. When the question of a language handicap was considered by researchers, it was perceived as a result either of inferior intelligence (the hereditarian viewpoint) or of negative experiential influence (being raised bilingually). Neither school of researchers considered the inadequacy of the instrument used to measure intelligence. It is important to note that this deficit theory of bilingualism lingers in the present approach to bilingual education in this country. The very term *Limited English Proficient* and the notion of compensatory education and transitional models of bilingual education are founded on this construct, the idea that entering school with a different language background is a negative factor in school success. Early-exit programs and English-immersion programs are based on the deficit notion that the native language is a handicap, that learning occurs best in English, and the sooner the better.

Research, as the next body of literature will show, has gone beyond the deficit notion, but that deficit has been institutionalized in our school culture, language (L.E.P.), and practices, and in the transitional model of bilingual education.

The research on bilingualism and cognition since the early 1960s has reported positive consequences of bilingualism (Ben-Zeev, 1977; Bialystok, 1987a; Diaz, 1983; Ianco Worral, 1972; Peal & Lambert, 1962). This research grew out of a very different sociological climate. In Canada, where bilingualism in French and English became a necessity, a new phenomenon took place. The citizens of the dominant language group, English, were choosing to become bilingual and putting their children into French-immersion schools. This created a very different climate for research and a very different group of bilinguals to be studied. These were not lower socioeconomic status students, but rather the middle class. They were not newly arrived immigrants, but the established dominant class. The research that was spawned in this context yielded very different information on the relationship between bilingualism and intelligence.

Elizabeth Peal and Wallace Lambert (1962) set new methodological standards in the research on bilinguals that required measuring language proficiency in both first and second language. They noted the importance of controls for both socioeconomic status and for language proficiency of bilinguals in research. Their method required sampling only among "balanced bilinguals" with proficiency in both first and second language (bias inherent in using "balanced bilinguals" will be discussed later in this chapter) and contrasting them with monolingual students from the same school. Both groups were middle-class students. In the Peal and Lambert study the bilinguals outperformed the monolinguals on verbal and nonverbal measures, particularly in tasks that required mental or symbolic flexibility. This was the first study to demonstrate the advantage of bilinguals in terms of "cognitive flexibility" (Hakuta, 1986). In the tradition of basic research, many studies followed, building on the methodological standards and the theory of cognitive advantages to bilingualism developed by Peal and Lambert.

Diaz (1983) provides a comprehensive review of the literature on the studies following in the footsteps of the Peal and Lambert (1962) study that suggest the cognitive advantages of bilingualism. Diaz divides these advantages into cognitive flexibility, linguistic and metalinguistic skills, concept formation, and divergent and creative thinking. To move out of the deficit notion of bilingualism, it is important to build on the body of literature that suggests the cognitive strengths that bilinguals bring to the classroom.

Cognitive flexibility was a term coined by Peal and Lambert (1962) to describe the superior performance of bilinguals on a range of cognitive tasks, including verbal and nonverbal measures of general intelligence. Peal and Lambert noted that the nonverbal advantages of balanced bilinguals were more apparent on tests requiring manipulation and reorganization of symbols than on tasks requiring perceptual or spatial abilities (Diaz, 1983). In a study with Hebrew-English bilingual children, Ben-Zeev (1977) found that bilinguals showed superiority in symbol substitution and verbal transformation tasks. One such task had children substituting the word "spaghetti" for "I," necessitating sentences like "Spaghetti am cold," which violates the normal grammar rules. Ben-Zeev (1977) noted that bilingual children seemed more attentive to structure and detail as well as to feedback from the experimenter. This notion of cognitive flexibility has potential for enticing dominant-language students to become bilingual. What parents wouldn't want their children to increase their cognitive flexibility? More research in this area might define the term more clearly and provide more specific evidence of how cognitive flexibility works.

A more widely researched aspect of bilinguals and cognition is the metalinguistic advantage of bilingualism. Case studies (Leopold, 1939; Ronjat, 1913) suggest that early bilingualism fosters advantages for both cognitive and linguistic development. Leopold suggests that bilingualism aids children in developing an early separation of sound and meaning, leading to an understanding of the arbitrariness of language. Vygotsky (1935/1973) suggests that bilingualism frees the mind "from the prison of concrete language and phenomena" (as cited in Cummins, 1976, p. 34). In a study of English-Afrikaans bilingual children, Ianco-Worral (1972) administered a semantic-phonetic preferences test. When asked to choose among such words as cap, can, and hat, children choosing cap and can would demonstrate a phonetic preference, while those choosing cap and hat would demonstrate a semantic preference. Ianco-Worral found that semantic preference increased with age, and that bilingual children showed semantic preferences at an earlier age than monolingual children.

A number of other studies conducted with various groups of bilingual children support the metalinguistic advantages of bilinguals (Cummins, 1977; Lambert & Tucker, 1972; Hakuta & Diaz, 1985; Galambos & Hakuta, 1988; Bialystok, 1987a, 1987b). Despite a significant body of literature on the role of metalinguistic awareness in literacy development (Tunmer & Herriman, 1984), little work beyond that of Bialystok has attempted to bring this research together with that on bilingualism and metalinguistic awareness. Such intersections of research agendas might yield information on issues raised by teachers concerning appropriate strategies for second-language literacy.

Numerical concept formation is another cognitive area in which bilinguals seem to outperform monolinguals. Vygotsky (1935/1973) contends that language influences the development of new cognitive structures. Liedtke and Nelson (1968) and Bain and Yu (1974) tested bilinguals versus monolinguals regarding formation of linear measurement concepts and additive rules in number strings, respectively, and found support for the notion that bilinguals were superior to monolinguals in these areas of concept development. Further research on the relationships between bilingualism and numerical concept formation might yield new pedagogical approaches to working with bilinguals. Future research might pursue ways to capitalize on these possible advantages of bilingualism.

Just as negative associations between bilingualism and cognition were based on faulty methodological practice, the research on cognitive advantages has been criticized for its methodological shortcomings (Reynolds, 1991). The use of "balanced" bilingualism may be confounded with innate cognitive ability. The lack of randomness of the sample is another methodological flaw that is hard to overcome (Reynolds). The cognitive advantages shown by balanced bilinguals may indicate a bias caused by such factors as parental attitudes, experiences, and motivation (C. Baker, 1993). The cause-and-effect relationship is difficult to determine. Are the cognitive advantages the result of bilingualism, or is the balanced bilingualism a result of cognitive advantages? Hakuta (1986) also questions how much the researcher's motivations may determine the results of the research. Despite these flaws, the positive consequences show what is "possible" with balanced bilinguals under positive circumstances, and this line of research merits further attention.

This brief look at the development of basic research in the area of cognition and bilingualism reveals the limitations as well as the potential role of basic research in bilingual education. Theories are shaped by the historical and social context of the time as well as the intellectual pursuits of the researcher. As theories develop, the underlying biases as well as the methodological rigor with which the theories are tested in different settings must be examined. Many minority-language parents still fear that time spent in native-language instruction will retard their child's progress in English. Majority-language parents might be more interested in placing their children in bilingual programs if the findings of advantages noted above were common knowledge. The studies that followed Peal and Lambert (1962) in the area of cognition and bilingualism are little known beyond the bilingual research community, and most educators are not aware of the historical evolution of the deficit theories that have been institutionalized in the school system. Even teachers who are aware, for example, of a possible metalinguistic advantage of bilingualism generally do not see its relevance to pedagogy. As theories such as those regarding bilingualism and cognition develop, they should be brought to the educational community for discussion of what implications such theories might have and how those implications might be studied in the context of the classroom. This approach to research will be discussed further in the final section of this chapter.

A History of Bilingual Education Program Evaluation Research

The historical perspective on bilingualism and cognition has provided some insights into what might be considered "macro-level" encroachment of the prevalent social and political views into the conduct of basic research. That relationship between politics and research will appear quite indirect and distal when compared with the more direct influence of politics in the area of program evaluation in bilingual education in the United States.

From its relatively early stages as a federal program, as Title VII of the Elementary and Secondary Education Act [ESEA] of 1968, bilingual education has been host to ideological drama. A major cluster of sentiments about bilingual education was expressed in a monograph by journalist Noel Epstein (1977), who labeled the bilingual education movement as one of "affirmative ethnicity." Evaluation research on the question of the effectiveness of bilingual education programs reached an early crescendo in January 1978 with the release of a study funded by the Department of Health, Education, and Welfare (DHEW), conducted by the American Institutes of Research (AIR, 1978). With reauthorization of ESEA scheduled for that year, the main question underlying the AIR study was whether bilingual education programs were, on average, more effective than English as a Second Language (ESL) programs. The results indicated that there were few differences between the programs. Bilingual education advocates were quick to point out, among other things, that the study did not come to grips with the quality of the bilingual programs (Gray, Convery, & Fox, 1981). Despite its many shortcomings, the study succeeded in stirring up doubts about the effectiveness of bilingual programs, and contributed to a broad perception of bilingual education as being a jobs program for Hispanic American educators rather than a serious pedagogical innovation (see Epstein, 1977).

The 1978 amendment to the Bilingual Education Act, in large part reacting to the AIR study, included a new section on research instructing the assistant secretary of education to "coordinate research activities of the National Institute of Education with the Office of Statistics and other appropriate agencies in order to develop a national research program for bilingual education" (Sec. 742). Thus, in spring 1978 an Education Division Coordinating Committee was established to implement the broad mandate, and came to be called the "Part C Committee" after the section of the legislation requiring its establishment. The committee was chaired by the deputy assistant secretary for education policy development, and included representatives from the National Institute of Education (NIE), the National Center for Education Statistics (NCES), the Office of Education (both the Office of Bilingual Education and the Office of Evaluation and Dissemination), and ad hoc representatives of the assistant secretary for planning and evaluation of DHEW.

The memo establishing the committee (U.S. DHEW, 1979) identified three areas where research might be directed: investigation of various national needs for bilingual education; research to improve the effectiveness of services for students; and research and evaluation to improve the management and operation of the Title VII program (Education Division, U.S. DHEW). In the area of service improvement, the following research studies were specified:

(b) (1) studies to determine and evaluate effective models of bilingual-bicultural programs;
    (2) studies to determine
        (A) language acquisition characteristics and
        (B) the most effective method of teaching English (in a bilingual-bicultural program);
    (3) 5-year longitudinal study [On the effectiveness of this title];
    (4) studies [on] . . . methods of [identifying children needing services];
    (6) studies [on] . . . teaching reading to L.E.P. children and adults;
    (8) studies of . . . teaching about culture.

The Part C Committee ended up embodying the tensions underlying the debate over what type of research would ultimately prove most useful for policy purposes. NIE's emphasis was on basic learning and instructional processes, whereas the Office of Evaluation and Dissemination emphasized effectiveness of ongoing programs.

A major backdrop to these tensions was the status of the Lau remedies that had been proposed by the Office for Civil Rights (U.S. DHEW, 1975) in response to the 1974 Supreme Court decision (Lau v. Nichols, 1974) supporting the rights of L.E.P. children to special assistance to enable them to participate equally in the school program. Although the remedies had never been proposed as regulations, they were used as such and served as the basis for negotiation with hundreds of school districts (Crawford, 1989). Bilingual education was the method of choice in the Lau remedies. The main questions facing the Part C Committee involved what evidence it could gather to shed light on whether it was wise to prescribe bilingual education, and whether this policy could be reinforced through the types of programs that could be awarded under Title VII.

It would probably be accurate to say the NIE approach enjoyed the initial advantage. The program started in 1979, in the middle of the Carter administration, when NIE was still a strong agency within DHEW. Thus, soon after its inception, in 1979, the Part C Committee commissioned a major four-year study of the characteristics of effective bilingual practices. Considering the hailstorm of criticism that followed the AIR study, it was probably wise for even the critics of bilingual education to enable data collection on the basics of program functioning.

Issuance of the proposed Lau regulations was delayed by the Carter administration until August 5, 1980, as Carter struggled for reelection. The proposal would mandate bilingual education in schools with at least 25 L.E.P. students from same-language groups in K–8. This controversial proposal was popular with the Hispanic constituencies that Carter desperately needed, although their support was not sufficient to stem the tide of politics. The proposed regulations were withdrawn by the Reagan administration on February 2, 1981. Secretary of Education Bell (now at the helm of the recently formed, separate Department of Education, which Reagan promised to dismantle) called them "harsh, inflexible, burdensome, unworkable, and incredibly costly," and criticized native-language instruction as "an intrusion on state and local responsibility." He went on, "We will protect the rights of children who do not speak English well, but we will do so by permitting school districts to use any way that has proven to be successful" (quoted in Crawford, 1989, p. 42).

As early as September 1981, Bell's statement was bolstered by departmental analysis. An internal document circulated by Office of Planning, Budget, and Evaluation (OPBE) staff members Keith Baker and Adriana de Kanter, titled "Effectiveness of Bilingual Education: A Review of the Literature" (K. Baker & de Kanter, 1983c), called into question the wisdom of a single approach. Baker and de Kanter collected studies that compared bilingual education approaches with nonbilingual procedures, and concluded that there was no evidence to support the department's policy of requiring Title VII grant programs to be reserved for bilingual purposes.

The K. Baker and de Kanter document was criticized on a number of grounds (1983a), including the underhanded way in which it was leaked to the press and congressional staff without benefit of external review. Indeed, the paper never became an official department document, and was rendered into a document suitable for citation only through nonofficial channels

when Baker and de Kanter included it, along with other Department of Education analyses, in a book on bilingual education (K. Baker and de Kanter, 1983b). In addition, flaws in the paper's method of summarizing across studies have been questioned; a subsequent reanalysis by Willig (1985) of the same studies summarized by Baker and de Kanter, this time using meta-analysis, showed positive effects of bilingual programs. Nevertheless, through its timeliness the document served to strengthen the position that there should be no federal prescription of bilingual education.

By 1982 the Department of Education, in particular the OPBE, was fully engaged in formulating research to reinforce this position. Two major Requests for Proposals (RFPs) were issued that year and funded the following year. The first, titled "Longitudinal Study of Immersion and Dual Language Instructional Programs for Language Minority Children," was funded for a five-year period from December 1983, on a budget of $1.4 million in its first year. The justification section of the RFP (U.S. Department of Education, 1982a) for this study borrowed text heavily from the K. Baker and de Kanter (1983c) document, and sought to compare traditional forms of bilingual education with English immersion, using a traditional treatment-comparison design. This study is reviewed in greater detail later in this chapter.

The second RFP was for a "National Longitudinal Evaluation of the Effectiveness of Services to Language Minority Limited English Proficient Students" (U.S. Department of Education, 1982b), funded for a five-year period starting in September 1983, on a budget of $1.5 million in its first year. This RFP (U.S. Department of Education, 1982b) noted the AIR (1978) study as well as the K. Baker and de Kanter (1983c) analysis, referring to the study as

an attempt to synthesize results from diverse research studies [that] demonstrated again the importance of complete documentation of service, school, child, and home characteristics for drawing conclusions about service effectiveness. . . . [Al]though in the past such evaluations may have been appropriate for the Department, this is not the case now. For the Department to formulate federal education policy regarding services provided to language minority limited English proficient students in a time of decreasing federal monies and regulation, a comprehensive information base is required—a base containing information about the broad range of services being provided to such students. (U.S. Department of Education, 1982b, p. 1)

The purpose of the study would be to provide a comprehensive, nationally representative picture of the types of services provided to L.E.P. students, and to conduct a longitudinal study

TABLE 25–1. Projects in Bilingual Education Research Funded by Federal Government (by fiscal year)

Agency	1979	1980	1981	1982	1983	Total
National Institute of Education	4	9	28	1	4	46
Office of Bilingual Education and Minority Languages Affairs	2	1	5	0	4	12
Office of Planning and Evaluation	3	5	6	1	8	23
National Center for Education Statistics	2	0	1	0	0	3
Total	11	15	40	2	16	84

TABLE 25–2. Total Budget for Projects Funded by Federal Government (by fiscal year)

Agency	1979	1980	1981	1982	1983	Total
National Institute of Education	$ 325,034	$1,021,225	$3,608,523	$ 225,000	$ 268,896	$ 544,867
Office of Bilingual Education and Minority Languages Affairs	63,276	443,610	381,006	0	903,232	$ 1,791,124
Office of Planning and Evaluation	1,288,457	1,536,392	1,242,058	2,273,650	3,880,505	10,221,062
National Center for Education Statistics	289,283	0	225,000	0	0	514,283
Total	1,966,050	3,001,227	5,456,587	2,498,650	5,052,633	17,975,147

that might enable extraction of factors that contribute to successful outcomes of such programs.

These two evaluation studies constituted the department's major effort at understanding program effectiveness. The value of this ambitious approach and the technical merits of these studies were analyzed by a National Academy of Sciences panel (Meyer & Fienberg, 1992), and will be described in our review. These studies were controlled by OPBE rather than NIE or the Office of Bilingual Education and Minority Languages Affairs (OBEMLA), and represented a fundamental shift in bureaucratic power as well as in research paradigm, from a basic to an evaluation orientation. The shift was true across the department during this time period, as can be seen in Tables 25–1 and 25–2, based on the department office controlling studies related to bilingual education (Part C funds), as reported in official department publications (National Clearinghouse for Bilingual Education, 1982, 1984). As seen most clearly in Table 25–1, NIE's control of studies peaked in 1981, paralleling the demise of the agency, and by 1983 OPE, with its program evaluation orientation, controlled the bulk of the department's activities.

These brief passages through the history of bilingual education research in the areas of both basic research and program evaluation supply the context for looking at two very different approaches to evaluation research in the field of bilingual education.

ANALYSIS OF TWO APPROACHES TO BILINGUAL EDUCATION RESEARCH

In this section the complex nature of design issues and methodological difficulties will be looked at more carefully in a comparison of two federally funded studies that represent very different approaches to research. The Significant Bilingual Instructional Features (SBIF) study is a three-year analysis of five different ethnic community bilingual programs (Tikunoff, 1983). The Longitudinal Immersion study is a five-year longitudinal evaluation of three Spanish-language bilingual programs.

The Significant Bilingual Instructional Feature Study

The SBIF study (1980–1983) was designed to examine the successful instruction of L.E.P. students. This study attempted to determine the requirements for L.E.P. students to function proficiently in accomplishing instructional tasks. The study took place in diverse cultural settings, yet because of a strong theoretical framework and clear operational definitions, the findings from these unique contexts are both credible and generalizable.

The SBIF study was in two parts. The first part studied 58 bilingual teachers and 232 L.E.P. students during 10 full days of instruction. Instructional features were described and some were identified as being "significant." As defined in the parameters of the study, to be "significant" means: (a) the feature had to have been identified in the research literature as positively impacting instruction for L.E.P. and other students; (b) the feature had to occur frequently and with high quality in each of the 58 classes; (c) teachers had to identify the feature during analysis of their instructional protocols; and (d) the feature or a cluster of features had to be associated with positive outcomes for L.E.P. students.

Despite great diversity in districts, programs, and classrooms, five instructional features were found to be significant, appearing frequently, consistently, and with high quality. These are the five significant features found:

1. Successful teachers utilized active teaching strategies, including: (a) emphasizing clear communications during instruction, clear descriptions of tasks, and appropriate strategies for explaining, clarifying, and organizing information; (b) maintaining students' engagement in instructional tasks, keeping students focused, pacing instruction appropriately, and communicating expectations clearly; and (c) monitoring students' progress and providing immediate feedback to students.

2. Successful teachers used both primary and second language to mediate instruction, alternating between the languages to increase student understanding of the instruction.

3. Successful teachers integrated English-language development with academic skills even when students' primary language was used for some of the instruction.

4. Successful teachers incorporated the home culture into the classroom, including references to the culture, building on cultural discourse modes, and observing the values and norms of the L.E.P. students' home culture while the majority culture norms were being taught.

5. Successful teachers had congruency among their instructional goals, organization and delivery of lessons, and student outcomes. They communicated high expectations for L.E.P. students and had confidence in their ability to teach all students (see Tikunoff, 1985).

These five instructional features resulted in L.E.P. students' being able to understand and acquire the skills and concepts that their teachers expected. They knew what was expected during instructional tasks, and were able to achieve a high rate of accuracy and to obtain appropriate feedback when necessary. While the findings of this study are not earth-shattering in terms of revealing new information, they are credible because of the rigorous design of the study with respect to its objectives. An essential feature of the SBIF study was the operationalization of terms. By creating succinct definitions of classroom experiences, researchers were able to make sense of the behaviors they were observing. After dividing instructional tasks into distinct types, they were able to measure success of L.E.P. students based on competence at these tasks.

According to the researchers' definition, Student Functional Proficiency (SFP) was determined by demonstrated participative, interactional, and academic competence in a classroom conducted primarily in English. This, by the way, reflects the prevailing deficit perspective of bilingual programs, as a student was considered deficient (not functionally proficient) unless that student functioned in the absence of the primary language.

Concise definitions of terms can serve research. However, the definitions themselves are susceptible to the same biases that limit all theoretical constructs. For example, one way the SBIF study measures student participation is in terms of Academic Learning Time (ALT). A student's academic learning time consists of: (a) the amount of time the teacher allocated to a subject area; (b) the proportion of this time a student is engaged in completing tasks in the subject area; and (c) the proportion of time a student achieves high accuracy in task completion. Such a definition reflects the time-on-task preoccupation of its day (time-on-task theory will be discussed further in regard to the implications of the Longitudinal Immersion study) and a value of high accuracy on defined tasks. As the focus of educational research has shifted from product to process, the usefulness of these constructs has been questioned. The definition of ALT is no longer informative.

A number of effective strategies pointed out by the SBIF study have found their way into common use. One such strategy was the integration of English-language development with content instruction. Writes Tikunoff (1983), "Students learn the language of instruction while engaged in completing class tasks while using that language. . . . Proficiency is best developed with relation to learning the language of instruction while learning to participate competently in completing class tasks" (p. 35).

Another important mediation of effective instruction found in the SBIF study is the use of students' home cultural information to enhance instruction. One example cited was the use of the term *mijito* (my son) by a Hispanic American teacher to soften a reprimand of a young male student. This use of home cultural information included the home-versus-school discourse patterns of students from differing cultures. Teachers of Chinese American L.E.P. students, for example, noted the importance of teaching students to proceed independently and not wait for instructions from an adult. Native American teachers were careful not to assign boys and girls from the same Navajo tribal clan to the same reading groups. Hispanic American students were encouraged to work cooperatively, in keeping with the values of the home. This is an example of a feature that is unique to each cultural context, but the use of such a feature is generalizable across contexts.

The SBIF study was able to look at a variety of bilingual programs in highly diverse settings. It had specific criteria for identifying features that cut across the diversity of contexts. It also had a clearly developed theory of what constituted success of L.E.P. students in any bilingual setting. This clarity of criteria and underlying theory are necessary to create precise standards of measurement that allow generalizability across what would otherwise be viewed as unique, context-embedded programs.

One of the methodological concerns of the study was the identification of effective classrooms by nomination rather than by student outcomes. The study proposed that if teachers were nominated as effective by their administrators and peers, and if they met the ALT standards, then their classrooms should be deemed effective. Tying effectiveness to student outcomes would have created a stronger base from which to derive effective practices. However, lack of availability of dependable outcome measures, particularly those that could be applied in diverse contexts, is one of the problems that continues to plague the field. Available measures generally focus on low-level skills and are out of synch with current instructional practice. There are also no reliable measures available in the native language for most language-minority groups.

The SBIF study validates the methods regularly employed by effective teachers, that they can articulate and on which they generally agree, and that have already been discussed in the literature. It also provides frames for looking at the classroom and at instruments for measuring success. It does not allow us to go beyond the fairly obvious successful classroom practice, however, to the complexities of why teachers use these strategies and why they are successful. In fact, the initial constructs served to limit the findings greatly. Any classroom innovations that had not been previously discussed in the literature would not appear significant even though they might be related to positive outcomes. Such strict constructs for significance did not allow the study to report much beyond what was generally known and accepted in the field. Such research often receives the response, "So tell us something we don't already know." This study validated bilingual educators, saying, in effect, "You're going in the right direction. Using native language, bringing students' culture into the classroom, and teaching language through content is what effective bilingual education looks like." The study also contributed a useful lexicon for observing classroom behaviors. Clarity of theory and operational definitions allowed for information from diverse classroom contexts and cultures to generate data that could be brought together to create basic constructs significant in effective bilingual classrooms. This approach stands in great contrast to many of the evaluative studies that operate on a more traditional program comparison design.

The Longitudinal Immersion Study

A more recent study (1986–1990) compares the effects of three types of bilingual programs (Ramírez et al., 1990). The Longitudinal Immersion study was commissioned as a direct result of the findings of a federally funded 1981 study on TBE programs (K. Baker & de Kanter, 1983c). After reviewing more than 300 studies of TBE programs, Baker and de Kanter found only 28 that met their research standards. Based on these studies, Baker and de Kanter found:

> Although TBE has been found to work in some settings, it also has been found ineffective and even harmful in other places. Furthermore, both major alternatives to TBE—structured Immersion and ESL—have been found to work in some settings. (p. 51)

This five-year Longitudinal Immersion study was originally set up to compare the relative effectiveness of English immersion with the more traditional TBE model, the early-exit bilingual program. The comparison of late-exit bilingual programs was later added by the researchers for the purpose of greater contrasts in the comparison. The study set criteria for each of the program types in terms of the use and amount of primary language. In immersion programs English is used exclusively for instruction, though teachers are bilingual and occasionally use the primary language to help students. Early-exit programs use the primary language as well as English for instruction, and children are mainstreamed into English-only programs within two or three years after entry into the program. Late-exit programs use both primary language and English for instruction, but use may be differentiated by the teaching staff (teacher A used one language and teacher B used another) and primary language is used at least 50% of instructional time. Children are not mainstreamed into English-only classes until after fifth or sixth grade.

The schools were located through a telephone network that called state departments of education and other educational agencies to recommend programs of the three different types. Immersion and early-exit programs were chosen only if they occurred together in the same school or district. It was found that districts with late-exit programs offered no alternative program, so examples were chosen independent of a comparison program. The four sites that were chosen after on-site visits and agreement to participate in the immersion and early-exit studies were located in New York, Texas, and California. A fourth state, which had originally agreed to participate, did not, thus creating a design problem. There was not adequate representation of all three models in any one state.

In the immersion and early-exit programs cohorts of kindergarteners and first graders were chosen to be followed for five years. In the late-exit program kindergarten and third-grade cohorts were selected. This particular design was chosen to test the facilitative effects theory, which suggests that instruction in the L.E.P. child's primary language becomes apparent after grade four (Ramírez et al., 1991). The rationale for the difference in cohorts between programs was that in the immersion and early-exit programs children would be mainstreamed rapidly, and this design would allow the study to follow students for a year or two in the mainstream classroom. The late-exit programs did not mainstream their students until after fifth or sixth grade. New kindergarten and third-grade cohorts were begun in the second year of the study, and a new site was added

during the second year. Participation in the immersion program included all schools (except those in one district) and all kindergarten and first-grade teachers within those schools implementing the immersion strategy program. The early-exit and late-exit sites were chosen arbitrarily by program administrators. The potential for bias in such selection is clear, and points the way toward more design problems.

Scores on standardized tests in English (California Test of Basic Skills) given in the fall and in the spring were the primary measures of student growth. A statistical method called Trajectory Analysis of Matched Percentiles (TAMP) was utilized to compare the changes in test scores of groups of students. This method for creating growth curves was used to compare student growth across cohorts even though students in the cohorts were not necessarily in the same grades. TAMP is a graphical tool for comparing change from cross-sectional data. It allows scores of two populations to be compared as a whole rather than pairing individual student scores, and provides a useful explanatory method of comparing growth curves when two groups are comparable. Unfortunately, comparability did not exist in the Longitudinal Immersion study (Meyer & Fienberg, 1992). In the late-exit programs student cohorts may have been in third through sixth grade, while immersion and early-exit cohorts were available only in kindergarten through third grade. This statistical growth curve was used for the comparison of projected growth curves across groups in different grade levels. A fancy statistical device cannot save a poor design.

Which program was more effective? Effectiveness was measured by student scores on tests in English language arts, reading, and mathematics, all administered in English. Students in the immersion and early-exit programs were compared directly within the schools and districts. All three groups were compared to the norming population (normed on a national sample of predominantly native English speakers, 1972–1973). The conclusion reached was: "There appears to be no difference in the academic growth relative to the norming population between immersion strategy and early-exit students. Moreover, the form of this growth is similar to that found for late-exit students" (Ramírez et al., 1991, p. 641).

A number of methodological problems give cause for some concern about the generalizability of these findings. The late-exit programs could not be compared with the early-exit and immersion programs because they did not occur in the same districts or states as the other programs (Cazden, 1992; Meyer & Fienberg, 1992). Therefore, the effects of school or district cannot be considered. In addition, the late-exit programs had great differences in the amount of English used after the fourth grade (60%, 75%, and 94%). This brings into question the validity of grouping the late-exit programs together after fourth grade.

As a study of this magnitude (eight years and $4.3 million) warrants, analysis and critiques abound. In 1990 the U.S. Department of Education requested the National Academy of Sciences to review evaluation studies in bilingual education. The resulting publication (Meyer & Fienberg, 1992) performs a thorough analysis of the Ramírez et al. (1990, 1991) study. Three of the conclusions of this report merit particular attention:

- The formal design of the study was ill-suited to answer the important policy questions that appear to have motivated it.
- The absence of clear findings in the Immersion study that distinguish among the effects of treatments and programs relating to bilingual education does not warrant conclusions regarding differences in program effects, in any direction.
- Taking fully into account the limitations of the study, the panel still sees the elements of positive relationships that are consistent with empirical results from other studies and that support the theory underlying native language instruction in bilingual education (Meyer & Fienberg, 1992, p. 104).

These points represent concerns over both design and implications of the study. The design of this study was doomed from the beginning. The addition of late-exit programs for purposes of greater contrast, though well intentioned, left the study wide open for criticism. The late-exit programs were not found in districts with immersion and early-exit programs, thereby prohibiting within-district and within-school comparisons and allowing for confounding district or school variables. In addition, one late-exit program was a six-year program and the other two were only three- to four-year programs. Comparisons of students in the cohorts could not be made except through the TAMP comparison of growth curves, which was not an appropriate use of TAMP.

Dolson and Mayer (1992) also question the particular early-exit bilingual programs that were chosen, since they utilized such a small amount of native-language instruction in comparison with early-exit programs that utilized native language to a much greater extent and would have provided a greater contrast to structured immersion. Allowing programs to be compared according to their names rather than according to strict criteria that distinguish between them produces muddied results. The lack of theory as the basis for the design was also criticized: "Explicit theory of bilingual education, including explicit objectives, is required to both motivate and structure the sensible statistical design of a study to evaluate alternative forms of bilingual education" (Meyer & Fienberg, 1992, p. 90).

K. Baker (1992) suggests it is "bad theory" rather than no theory that guided the study. The assumptions of the facilitative theory (first-language learning facilitates second-language learning) and the threshold hypothesis (a certain "threshold level of L1 is needed to have facilitative effects in L2," Cummins, 1977), he argues, were the theoretical assumptions that lead to the findings that late-exit programs had a greater effect. He concludes that the data suggest the opposite—that the greater effect in the early grades should be recognized.

Had the study set out to disprove the time-on-task theory with regard to second-language acquisition, the study design could have been much cleaner. The time-on-task theory, promoted by forces opposed to bilingual education, would suggest that the more time a student spends in English, the greater the success in English. Programs would have been differentiated by the amount of time students spent in instruction in English, and the results would have been hard to dispute. In fact, despite the design problems created by the absence of theory, findings from the Ramírez et al. (1990, 1991) study should put this time-on-task theory to rest (K. Baker, 1992; Cazden, 1992). Students

in immersion programs and early-exit programs did not do any better on English tests—and in some regards did worse—than students in late-exit programs that utilized considerably less English. In an attempt to counter this argument, K. Baker (1992) offers a "spaced practice" theory, which suggests that giving students pauses in learning a second language by providing them with "rest breaks" in their native language would provide a better explanation of the data in the Ramírez study.

Another design criticism was the limitation of immersion programs to those that taught Spanish-language speakers only (Rossell, 1992) and those whose teachers were bilingual in Spanish and English (Dolson & Mayer, 1992). Rossell suggests that the majority of immersion programs contain a variety of language groups and, in fact, are most appropriate in those situations; Dolson and Mayer point out the impracticality and inappropriateness of utilizing bilingual teachers (whose language abilities are in great demand) in immersion programs that place little demand on use of the students' primary language. Those realities notwithstanding, Ramírez et al. (1990, 1991) limited the bias in the study by choosing programs that differed only in the amount and extent to which the native language was utilized, rather than confounding the study with other language groups or with teachers incapable of understanding student responses or communicating with parents.

Despite the need for longitudinal information, such studies are by nature fraught with design problems (Collier, 1992). The attrition of students, as occurred in this study, is the greatest problem in longitudinal studies, particularly with L.E.P. students, who move frequently. In addition, the lack of fidelity of treatment in a program in which students progress through different teachers over the years dilutes the findings. In the Ramírez et al. (1990, 1991) study one of the early-exit programs more closely resembled an immersion program in terms of amount of native-language instruction used, and one of the late-exit programs abruptly transitioned students into English at the fourth grade. Again, a governing theory, such as time-on-task, or strict adherence to criteria and definition, such as amount of native language spoken, would have averted this problem. In addition, the inescapable problem of lack of random assignment of students or teachers to bilingual programs will plague any experimental design of bilingual programs.

Concerns regarding the implications of the study have come from a variety of directions. The concern voiced by the panel to review evaluation studies of bilingual education programs (Meyer & Fienberg, 1992) suggests we should not interpret the results as supporting or denying the benefits of any of the treatment groups. Yet such interpretations will be made. Some will interpret the findings as supportive of late-exit programs. Dolson and Mayer (1992) write: "Of the three program models investigated in the Longitudinal Study, the late-exit design appears to be the most effective in reversing the negative educational outcomes experienced by many language-minority students in the United States" (p. 145).

Others will find support for negative interpretations of current theories. Notes K. Baker (1992):

Ramírez et al.'s arguments favoring late-exit programs are grossly speculative and contradicted by their own data. They are interesting only because they provide a degree of fit with the facilitation hypothesis. If the facilitation hypothesis were a decent theory, we might be able to overlook the weaknesses of Ramírez et al.'s analysis, but the facilitation hypothesis is so lacking empirical support in the literature that it merits no further consideration. (p. 84)

Rossell (1992) comments:

It could also be inferred from this study that we ought to get rid of *all* special language acquisition programs, since they are expensive and they appear to be no better for LEP students than regular classroom enrollment with ESL pull-out. I infer this from the fact that the most common finding of the studies comparing ESL pull-out to transitional bilingual education is that there is no difference between the two [Rossell & Ross, 1986; Rossell, 1990]. If there is no difference between immersion and bilingual education and no difference between bilingual education and ESL pull-out, it is not unreasonable to assume that there is no difference between immersion and ESL pull-out, although they were not compared directly in this study. (p. 183)

It is clear from the varied responses that the Ramírez et al. (1990, 1991) findings will be interpreted within the context of the theoretical framework of the reader of those findings. The panel to review evaluation studies of bilingual education (Meyer & Fienberg, 1992) provides a more reasoned perspective. These findings, though not necessarily statistically significant, should be reviewed in the context of their trends in supporting other findings in the literature. Despite the problematic relationship of the research design to the questions being researched, we can still learn some things from this study. McLaughlin (1985) made this point regarding studies in second-language acquisition that apply to the Ramírez et al. study:

It can be argued that a great deal can be learned from less than perfect research and less than fully generalizable findings. If one accepts the notion that knowledge in social science grows by accretion, every bit of information contributes to the process. What one must avoid is misinformation, and the more rigorous the research and the more careful the researcher is to deal with the problems that have been discussed here, the greater the contribution to knowledge about the effects of bilingual education. (p. 245)

The Ramírez et al. study, because of its problematic design, could not answer the policy questions regarding which bilingual education treatment is most effective among the three models described, nor does it answer pedagogical questions such as how and when second language should be introduced. It does, however, present some findings that are worth pursuing in future research for their pedagogical implications.

In looking at the characteristic differences among programs, the amount of relative use of English and Spanish by teachers and students was the most salient. In the immersion strategy program teachers used English at least 97% of the time at all grade levels. In the early-exit program English was used approximately 66% of the time in kindergarten and first grade, 75% in grade two, 80% in grade three, and 97% in grade four. In contrast, the late-exit program used English less than 10% of the time in kindergarten, increasing to 33% for grade two, 50% for grades three and four, 64% for grade five, and 80% in grade six. In all grades of the late-exit programs student patterns of

language use were similar to that of the teacher. The authors summarized this information to suggest that, across grade levels and within programs, students tend to mirror the patterns of language use of their teachers (Ramírez et al., 1991). As suggested earlier, time-on-task theory of learning English would predict, according to these usage patterns, that immersion program students should excel on tests of English. Such was not the case. Results on tests of English at the upper grades were very similar, and there was actually surprisingly little difference in the lower grades, although late-exit students had not yet received literacy instruction in English.

Teachers across programs tend to say the same things to students regardless of language proficiency, yet the discourse patterns may vary depending on the group being addressed: Teachers speaking to heterogeneous groups (L.E.P. and Fluent English Speaker [FEP]/English Only [EO] mixed) consistently explained and modeled more than when they spoke to single-language groups. Single-language groups (L.E.P.-only and FEP/EO-only) were questioned almost twice as often and received more feedback. The implications of these behaviors for student learning invite more research.

All programs presented a teacher-dominated, passive-language learning environment. From the standpoint of minimizing the variability among programs in the study, this was positive. However, from a pedagogical standpoint, this was dismal (Cazden, 1992). Although this pattern of teacher-dominated talk and low-level questioning strategies is prevalent in many classrooms (Cazden, 1984; Lemke, 1990), it is particularly inappropriate for classrooms in which a major objective is second-language development. Further research into the quality of the language-learning environment, coupled with greater dissemination of findings, would help to advance pedagogy in this area.

Teacher qualifications were a variable that distinguished late-exit programs from immersion and early-exit programs. Late-exit teachers were more proficient in Spanish and had greater education and training for working with language-minority children. Qualitative data on why late-exit teachers were more highly qualified would be useful. Is it the presence of proficient and trained teachers that encourages the existence of late-exit programs? Do late-exit programs encourage teachers to become more proficient and better qualified? Do communities that foster late-exit programs also encourage the development of bilingual professionals? What motivates teachers to receive greater levels of training? This is an area of research that warrants further study.

Parent involvement was greatest in the late-exit bilingual programs, and there was more homework assigned in the late-exit program. Such variables could be considered a bias of the study (Rossell, 1992) or a discovery of features that distinguish between programs. A reasonable theory might suggest the following: When teachers are more proficient in the language of the parents, parents feel more comfortable and involved in the program. Involved parents would then be more apt to understand assignments in their native language and to participate in homework, making homework a more valuable and effective strategy. Recent studies on parent involvement (Snow, Barnes, Chandler, Goodman, & Hemphill, 1991; Moll, 1992) suggest that it is a benefit for language-minority students. Exactly what kinds of parent involvement and what parental behaviors bene-fit minority-language student learning is another area for fur-ther study.

These provocative findings were discovered within the pro-grams through classroom observations, and were not the result of the longitudinal study. The major criticisms of the study are of the comparison design and the longitudinal statistical analy-sis of the standardized tests.

Many of the criticisms mentioned go beyond this particular study to include most program comparison evaluation studies in bilingual education, and support the need for change in the current paradigm of program evaluation. Communities have differing populations, differing school personnel, and differing access to research and training. It is therefore understandable that differing programs would evolve to meet student needs. If it is required that districts encompass a variety of programs in order to participate in evaluation studies, it will seriously limit the evaluation that can take place as well as hamper districts in their pursuit of programs that seem best suited to their commu-nity needs. In addition, teachers are not robots; they make choices, regardless of program design, that create variation in the student's educational program. Any attempt to assign teach-ers randomly to varying programs would disregard the prerog-ative of teachers to instruct in ways they believe best suit their situation. Comparison of nominal programs from one site or another will never adequately capture the factors involved in the success or failure of an approach. Samaniego and Eubank (1991) noted that

the effect of a given bilingual education initiative will vary with the environment in which it is implemented. In particular, a treatment which works well in one setting may fail in another, or may require nontrivial modifications if it is to be effective elsewhere. (p. 13)

It seems clear from the criticism of the Ramírez et al. (1990, 1991) study that the traditional design of comparison of treat-ment groups based on random assignment and blind evaluation is not possible to attain or perhaps even desirable in studying bilingual education. The panel reviewing evaluation studies on bilingual education (Meyer & Fienberg, 1992) makes the case clearly in stating the criteria required for an effective evaluation in this experimental model:

1. the intervention is acute and *a priori,* is expected to yield an acute outcome (produce a large effect);
2. the intervention acts rapidly, and the evaluation can be carried out over a short period of time;
3. the imposition of controls for the trial does not create an envi-ronment for the study that is substantially different from the environ-ment in which the proposed therapy would be used on a routine basis. . . .
It is the panel's judgment that virtually all bilingual education inter-ventions violate, at least to some extent, all three conditions. (p. 95)

Concerned parents are not likely to allow their children to be randomly assigned to a treatment group, nor would philo-sophically grounded educators participate in randomly as-signed educational treatments that do not suit their theoretical frameworks or successful practical experiences. Administrators

will not be willing to set up programs that do not respond to the needs and goals of their communities. Researchers must take into account the complexity of the variables, and imple-ment studies based on theory and sound design that capture the reality of the classroom and take into account the needs of the research audience.

The Ramírez et al. (1990) study has compiled massive amounts of data that, despite design problems, may be re-garded as a source for adding to the pool of knowledge sur-rounding bilingual education. In addition, the design and meth-odological problems might serve as an impetus to rethink the current paradigm in bilingual education research.

This next section will advocate the need for a broadened yet cohesive view of the field of research in bilingual education. Such a view must expand the goal of bilingual education and address the needs of all those involved in the field, including policy makers, administrators, teachers, teacher educators, par-ents, and students. This broadened view may require a rede-fined role for the researcher.

TOWARD A NEW PERSPECTIVE ON RESEARCH IN BILINGUAL EDUCATION

Educational research in general suffers from what Kaestle (1993) calls an "awful" reputation. He quotes many education officials and researchers as to why this negative image exists. Emerson Elliot suggests, "At the policy level, you have to think about supporting research primarily on the grounds that ulti-mately it is expected to have some impact on the performance of American education" (quoted in Kaestle, p. 23). One of the most common criticisms of educational research is "the lack of connection between their [the researchers'] research and teach-er's practice" (p. 27). Some suggest it is because the wrong questions are being asked, others that the findings are not effec-tively disseminated. Research in bilingual education suffers from the same disparity between research and practice. In addi-tion, policy makers have been disappointed that bilingual edu-cation research has not proven definitively that bilingual educa-tion works, or that one type of program works better than another. Teachers have been disappointed that specific peda-gogical questions have not been settled, such as when is the right time to introduce reading in a second language and what are the most effective strategies for teaching content to a mixed group. Parents want to know what kind of program will offer their child the best chance of achieving success in U.S. society.

Just as bilingual educators have to meet the needs of a di-verse group of students, researchers in bilingual education must consider the expectations of a heterogeneous audience consisting of administrators, teachers, and parents. Bilingual teachers, confronted with students of varying proficiencies in different languages as well as varied degrees of readiness for the academic tasks of school, have developed some effective strategies to communicate with this diverse group. Perhaps drawing on the strategies of effective bilingual teaching and using the language of the bilingual class can help researchers reframe their role in the field of bilingual education. To reinforce this notion, research on effective bilingual instruction will be woven into our discussion.

One of the effective practices that has been adopted widely in bilingual classrooms is interactive group work or cooperative learning (Kagan, 1986; Cohen, 1984; Johnson, Johnson, & Maruyama, 1983; Slavin, 1981). In cooperative or collaborative group work students learn language and content by working together and talking with one another (see chapter 35 of this *Handbook*). The proficient bilingual students in the group play a key role in translating between students of different language backgrounds. They are the "brokers" for the group. Extending this concept broadly to the audience of bilingual education research, such an approach brings people who speak the language of policy, practice, and parenting to the table with researchers who speak and write "researchese." Though policy makers have at times attempted to translate research for practitioners, the researcher, from a greater position of objectivity, seems the more likely candidate to take on the role of "broker" to facilitate cooperation and collaboration among those involved in the field of bilingual education. Reflecting on education and informing policy and practice are the charges educational researchers are expected to accomplish. The perceived ineffectiveness of educational research to attain these goals may be a result of an inability to communicate in the language of the intended audience. Speaking the language of the various participants in this research audience and translating between participants would facilitate such communication.

Imagine the researcher in the role of translator/facilitator, bringing together this heterogeneous group of policy makers, practitioners, and parents to discuss the research agenda. Drawing again on effective practices from the classroom in which learners are involved in the choosing of topics and themes (Garcia, 1991), the researcher would look to the group to generate the questions to be researched. As the practitioners, policy makers, and parents negotiate and prioritize the concerns of their community, they also begin to share each other's perspectives. The effective teacher asks, "What do we know? What do we want to know about this topic/problem?" The researcher would draw upon the literature and discuss implications of research for the problem at hand. A good example of this translation of basic research into practitioner language is offered by Catherine Snow (1992) on questions of second-language acquisition. She cites the common questions generated by teachers. Then she draws from the research on second-language acquisition to point out the implications that address those concerns. In this role as "broker" the researcher can also help to formulate the larger contexts and problems of the field of bilingual education based on theoretical frameworks. A broadened vision or perspective based on research findings, historical patterns, and sound theoretical reasoning would benefit the participants in the community of bilingual education.

The present frame within which bilingual education operates is based on the notion of compensating for the deficiencies of language-minority children, as was discussed earlier. The questions that have hung from this frame have revolved around whether native-language instruction works and how much native language instruction is enough to get L.E.P. students into English-only programs.

Many researchers feel the need to change the questions in the research away from whether bilingual education works, or whether one program works better than another, to whether bilingual programs can be improved in their response to the diverse communities they serve (Cziko, 1992; Hakuta, 1986; Lindholm & Fairchild, 1990; Padilla, 1990; Willig, 1985). Cziko suggests moving from what is "probable" in all bilingual programs to what is "possible," suggesting that we look at what can be done under the best of circumstances.

One group that has been left out of the discussion until recently has been parents of English speakers who place their students in bilingual programs to learn the language and culture of the minority group in their community. Their concerns with "What does bilingual education offer my child?" have been largely ignored in the compensatory model of bilingual education that sees its role as "fixing" L.E.P. students so they fit into the existing English-only classrooms. Despite the extensive literature from Canada on the benefits of bilingual programs for children of the dominant culture (Lambert & Tucker, 1972; Swain & Lapkin, 1991), and the recent literature on two-way immersion programs (Lindholm & Aclan, 1991), little has been written about how bilingual education in the United States benefits the majority-culture student or the majority-cultural community. Taking the concern of majority parents to heart suggests increasing the breadth of the goal of bilingual education programs from compensation to enrichment, making foreign-language teaching an important component. Padilla (1990) suggests the goal of a "language competent society" may serve to unify researchers to pursue a more coherent path in bilingual education research:

Research and development in science have historically been connected to a "mission" that is supported by a majority of the general population and by policy makers. Missions are characterized by a joining together of people, organizations and institutions that mobilize to seek a solution to common problems.

If the mission of bilingual education became one of creating a language-rich society, by logical extension native languages would be viewed as a natural resource (Ruiz, 1988) and bilingualism would be considered a gift (Hakuta, in press). Foreign-language program planners would merge their efforts with bilingual program planners to capitalize on the linguistic resources of the immigrant communities.

A broader pool of resources would be employed in both the teaching and researching of language in schooling. The audience for the research would become greater and more diverse, increasing the significance of the role of researcher as "a broker of knowledge" in a diverse community of interests. This revised vision of bilingual education could have important sociological and political implications for the field.

This section of the chapter will suggest that breaking down the isolation that exists in present research will improve the effectiveness of research, policy, and practice. In an attempt to sample the variety of perspectives, a number of people were interviewed from our perceived research audience across the United States. Their voices will speak for the diversity of the field. Names are used only when more extensive comments are given. Some survey participants chose to remain anonymous.

The Heterogeneous Audience of the Bilingual Education Researcher

Interviews with a variety of parents, practitioners, and policy makers in the bilingual research audience brought to life Moll's (1992) notion of "funds of knowledge": Each member of a community brings a wealth of knowledge to the learning environment. Research needs to reflect these diverse voices.

This was not a scientific survey but rather an informal sampling from people around the country. The interviews opened with the question, "What are the issues that you feel should be addressed in the field of bilingual education?" As one might imagine, the responses reflected the diversity of the audience. Quan Cao, Director of Bilingual Education in Florida, elaborated on a policy perspective regarding what research issues need to be addressed:

- How do appropriate legislation and levels of funding affect bilingual education in such particulars as teacher training and system building?
- How does the larger restructuring movement tie into bilingual education?
- What influence will the setting of the national goals and standards have on L.E.P. kids?

In general, teachers have more classroom-oriented concerns. A bilingual fourth-grade teacher in California suggests that research address "The appropriate role of decoding in a whole-language program for L.E.P. kids." A bilingual kindergarten teacher from Texas is interested in how literacy acquisition and second-language research intersect. A language specialist in Florida is concerned about how to test L.E.P. students so they are not discriminated against and kept out of special services programs. A bilingual sixth-grade teacher from a small rural town asks, "How do we teach science to best develop language? What strategies really work? Which strategies give status to Spanish language?" A language consultant from a large city asks, "What do we do about mixed dominant children [those who mix languages or have neither language fully developed]?" Those involved in teacher professional development ask, "How do we change what really happens in school? What influences teachers to change so that teachers reflect on what they are doing and why they are doing it?"

In contrast to both administrators and teachers, parents shared a different set of concerns. One English-speaking parent wonders, "How do we bring middle-class Anglo students and poor Mexican kids together and not develop negative stereotypes?" A Mexican parent asks, "Is my child going to learn enough English?"

In an attempt to understand how research is reaching its intended audience, another interview question asked, "What sources do you draw on for your information regarding research on bilingual education?" Policy makers utilized government publications and information from agencies such as the National Clearinghouse for Bilingual Education and the Multifunctional Resource Centers. Teachers answered, "workshops, journals such as *Language Arts, Educational Leadership, Phi Delta Kappan.*" Parents read newspapers.

The importance of a good "road show" should not be overlooked in the dissemination of research and the inclusion of teachers and parents in the research community. Researchers need to get their findings into the educational community in a way that will catch the attention of members of that community. When policy makers were asked, "How could dissemination of research be improved?" Maria Trejo, Director of Categorical Programs, California State Department of Education, suggested that teachers be approached to rewrite the research findings in a language fellow teachers could understand. Teachers, on the other hand, felt that administrative support for attendance at workshops would be beneficial. Teachers also mentioned the need to condense research findings:

I want someone to synthesize the research and tell me how those understandings translate into classroom practice. There should be a journal of effective practices with L.E.P. students which synthesizes the literature around themes or issues. I want something that is a little predigested. If we're going to focus on the classroom, people have to facilitate that [reading of the research] for us. (Susana Dutro, bilingual mentor teacher, California)

Teri Marchese, a sixth-grade teacher, suggests that research be available on audiotapes so teachers can listen to it. State documents and important findings could be made available in staff lounges. Teachers agreed that bringing researchers out to the schools to talk with teachers was important. Judy Stobbe, bilingual kindergarten teacher, suggests that both a bottom-up approach, "piquing teachers' interest on issues that are important to them," and a top-down approach, "pushing through the hierarchy and having administrators expect informed teaching," were needed to close the gap between research and practice.

The final question asked of practitioners was in regard to researchers' practice: "What sensitivities should researchers be aware of on coming into the classroom?" One central theme emerged: Research should be done in the classroom, not in laboratories. This sentiment was reiterated by Kaestle (1993), who cites the transformation of Anne Brown's research from laboratory to classroom. Brown states, "I'm not telling the teacher what I want done. . . . I watch her implement it, and I watch her change it. Actually, I'm totally dependent on a gifted teacher" (quoted in Kaestle, p. 16). Jim Greeno adds that work done in a laboratory rather than a classroom creates an insurmountable "translation problem" (Kaestle, p. 16) between the controlled environment and the real world. Teachers interviewed, sensitive to the discomfort of being scrutinized like a germ under a microscope, have a lot to say to researchers entering the classroom:

- Build a relationship with the teacher and strategize together about the research.
- Don't judge a 10-minute observation outside of the greater context; managing a classroom is a complex task.
- Engage teachers in reflective practice by asking questions that not only give information to the researcher but also stimulate teachers to reflect on why they engage in a particular activity.
- Don't just take from the classroom; give something back to the teacher and the class.

Judy Stobbe suggests, "Researchers need to empower teachers by saying, 'You have taught 30 children per year for 10 or 20 years. What has worked? You, as the kindergarten teacher, have something to say that I want to listen to.' " The voices of teachers ought to be reflected in the research.

The responses from these informal interviews do not pretend to be scientific or to reveal any surprises to the research community. They do, however, validate the diversity of the perspectives and the need to acknowledge these diverse perspectives when formulating research agendas. They also suggest new directions for the role of the researcher: the researcher as listener, collaborator, and disseminator of knowledge.

An Inclusive Approach to Research in Bilingual Education

This chapter has looked broadly at the historical, political, and sociological influences on the practice and research of bilingual education. It has also looked in depth at two distinct approaches taken by federally funded studies in bilingual education. With knowledge of the diversity of the research audience and a redefined role for the researcher, what, then, should research look like? Borrowing from effective bilingual classroom practice to improve the research process, it's time to synthesize and look for applications to the real world (Moran, 1992). What do we now know about bilingual education research? How can what we know help us improve the relationship between research and practice?

By now, the complexity of the issues surrounding bilingual education research should be clear. Researchers are influenced by ever-changing political, social, and intellectual forces. Their work is expected to satisfy the diverse needs of a heterogeneous audience of administrators, teachers, and parents. In addition, there is a need to strengthen the theoretical underpinnings of research in the field by drawing on basic research studies. The contrasting approaches of the SBIF study and the Longitudinal Immersion study demonstrate the important role of theory in the validity and generalizability of research findings. The SBIF study illustrated the strengths and limitations of strong a priori theory. The Longitudinal Immersion study demonstrated the impracticality of applying the traditional model of experimental research to such a complex dynamic social situation as bilingual education. Given the complexity and constraints of the project, what might be an alternative way to improve research in bilingual education?

A more inclusive approach to research needs to be attempted that would bring in all the groups of stake holders in the field: practitioners, policy makers, parents, and students. This community should be involved in creating the research questions. This necessitates studies that are localized in specific cultural contexts and address questions of specific concern to those involved in the learning community. Nationwide studies could be created around theories that integrate findings from the smaller localized studies. The panel reviewing evaluation research in bilingual education supports this notion: "For the evaluation of bilingual education treatments, the panel believes that multiple highly focused studies are likely to be much more

informative than a single large study" (Meyer & Fienberg, 1992, p. 96).

Multiple studies built around clear theoretical constructs such as how language is acquired, and around clearly defined terms such as language proficiency and amount of language use, would allow greater generalizability across the contexts. In addition, clear descriptive information depicting the factors that characterize each setting, such as teacher and student discourse patterns, numbers of language-minority students, and attitudes of the community toward primary language, would allow researchers to look at constellations of factors in school settings that might influence the success or failure of a given treatment.

In addition to strong theory, the design of the study is a crucial issue. It is important to consider a design that allows the various members of the research audience to define and participate in the evaluation of the program. The panel to review the evaluation of bilingual education research studies (Meyer & Fienberg, 1992) suggests a possible model to be adapted: The "evolutionary operation" study design developed by Box and Draper (1969, 1987) utilizes the results of subexperiments to inform the next level of research. Tharpe and Gallimore (1979) adapted this approach in studying Hawaiian children in the Kamehameha project. The approach suggests that researchers enter the classroom to collect qualitative data that will inform the theoretical questions. These theoretical questions then suggest a treatment variable that will lend itself to quasi experimentation. After determining whether the treatment effect is great enough, the researcher returns to a qualitative personal approach to evaluate the data and translate them into possible elements of a program. These elements are then established and tested in an experimental approach to determine if they work in the setting in which they are employed.

A hypothetical description of how this process might work follows: The researcher is invited in because policy makers are concerned that language-minority students aren't doing well in English. The teacher notes that language-minority students rarely speak in class. During consultation with the parents, the parents contend that their children understand English very well but are reticent about speaking it. The researcher, after observing the class, notes that recitation mode is the most common form of student-teacher dialogue, and that whole-class discussions are the common grouping. In discussions with language-minority students the researcher learns that they feel shy about making mistakes with their English in front of the class. The researcher may then suggest an intervention that consists of one or more options drawn from basic research theory: (a) moving from whole-group to small-group discussions; (b) encouraging majority-language students to use the minority language (which would allow minority-language students both to be experts and to see mistakes being made by their peers); (c) reversing student-teacher roles; or (d) putting students in charge of teaching certain aspects of the curriculum to their peers.

Any of these treatments would then be tried in the particular setting and evaluated as to their results in terms of increased participation of minority-language students. When one or a combination of treatments is found to be effective, the researcher might then discuss with students and teachers why that particular treatment seemed to increase participation. This discussion may lead to a new understanding and a variation on the treatment. The new treatment, such as encouraging minority-language students to have small-group discussions in their native language before participating in whole-class discussions in English, could then be tried out in other situations. Again, going back and forth between an experimental approach and a qualitative collection of data would improve the treatment and increase understanding of why and under what conditions it works.

The researcher shares information with policy makers, parents, and practitioners, both to inform them of research progress and to discuss further research steps.

If it is theory-based, operationalized in its definitions, and explicit in the descriptions of context, this approach to research in bilingual education could add to the general pool of knowledge regarding bilingual education. It could also serve as an evaluation tool to assess various theories and aspects of bilin-

gual education within different naturally occurring settings. At the same time, it could serve the purpose of improving instructional practices within local settings.

If research in bilingual education is going to serve its diverse audience, it must follow a dynamic design that allows for the interplay of political and social forces within the context of the communities served. It must be inclusive in its involvement of the educational community in every step of the research. To accomplish this, the researcher must play a role that includes being listener and broker at the research table, bringing together the entire educational community and facilitating the creation of innovative approaches to researching the significant issues in bilingual education. Those significant issues should be influenced by a broadened perspective that includes foreign-language teaching as a goal of bilingual education; a view of minority languages as a natural resource; and bilingualism as a gift to be cherished.

References

Aleman, S. R. (1993). *CRS report for Congress: Bilingual education act: Background and reauthorization issues.* Washington, DC: Congressional Research Service, The Library of Congress.

American Institutes for Research. (1978). *Evaluation of the impact of ESEA Title VII Spanish/English bilingual program.* Washington, DC: Author.

Arons, A. B. (1983). Achieving wider scientific literacy. *Daedalus, Journal of The American Academy of Arts & Sciences, 112*(2), 91–122.

Bain, B. & Yu, A. (1974). Bilingualism and cognition: Toward a general theory. In S. T. Carey (Ed.), *Bilingualism, biculturalism, and education: Proceedings from the conference at College Universitaire Saint Jean* (pp. 119–128). Edmonton: University of Alberta.

Baker, C. (1993). *Foundations of bilingual education and bilingualism.* Cleveland, OH: Multingual Matters Ltd.

Baker, K. (1992). Ramírez et al. Misled by bad theory. *Bilingual Research Journal, 16*(1&2), 63–90.

Baker, K., & de Kanter, A. (1983a). An answer from research on bilingual education. *American Education, 56*(4), 157–169.

Baker, K., & de Kanter, A. (1983b). (Eds.) *Bilingual education: A reappraisal of federal policy.* Lexington, MA: Lexington Books.

Baker, K., & de Kanter, A. (1983c). Federal policy and the effectiveness of bilingual education: A review of the literature. In K. Baker & A. de Kanter (Eds.), *Bilingual education: A reappraisal of federal policy* (pp. 33–86). Lexington, MA: Lexington Books.

Ben-Zeev, S. (1977). The influence of bilingualism on cognitive strategy and cognitive development. *Child Development, 48*, 1009–1018.

Bialystok, E. (1987a). Influences of bilingualism on metalinguistic development. *Second Language Research, 3*(2), 154–166.

Bialystok, E. (1987b). Words as things: Development of word concept by bilingual children. *Studies in Second Language Learning, 9*, 133–140.

Bilingual Education Act of 1978. P. L. 95-561 (1978).

Box, G. E. P., & Draper, N. R. (1969). *Evolutionary operation: A statistical method for process improvement.* New York: Wiley.

Box, G. E. P., & Draper, N. R. (1987). *Empirical model-building and response surfaces.* New York: Wiley.

Cazden, C. B. (1984). *Effective instructional practices in bilingual education.* Washington, DC: National Institute of Education. (ERIC Document Reproduction Service No. ED 249 768)

Cazden, C. B. (1992). *Language minority education in the United States:*

Implications of the Ramirez report. Santa Cruz: National Center for Research on Cultural Diversity and Second Language Learning, University of California.

Cohen, E. (1984). Talking and working together: Status, interaction and learning. In P. Peterson, L. C. Wilkinson, & M. Hallinan (Eds.), *The social context of instruction* (pp. 171–186). New York: Academic Press.

Collier, V. (1992). A synthesis of studies examining long-term language-minority student data on academic achievement. *Bilingual Research Journal, 16*(1&2), 87–212.

Crawford, J. (1989). *Bilingual education: History, politics, theory, and practice.* Trenton, NJ: Crane Publishing Company.

Cummins, J. (1976). The influence of bilingualism on cognitive growth: A synthesis of research findings and explanatory hypothesis. *Working Papers on Bilingualism, 9*, 1–43.

Cummins, J. (1977). Metalinguistic development of children in bilingual education programs: Data from Irish and Canadian Ukranian-English programs. In M. Paradis (Ed.), *The Fourth Locus Forum* (pp. 127–138). Columbia, SC: Hornbeam.

Cummins, J. (1978). Educational implications of mother tongue maintenance in minority language group. *Canadian Modern Language Review, 34*, 395–416.

Cziko, G. A. (1992). The evaluation of bilingual education. *Educational Researcher, 21*(2), 10–15.

Diaz, R. (1983). Thought and two languages: The impact of bilingualism on cognitive development. In E. W. Gordon (Ed.), *Review of research in education* (10th ed., pp. 23–54). Washington, DC: American Educational Research Association.

Dolson, D. P., & Mayer, J. M. (1992). Longitudinal study of three program models for language minority students: A critical examination of reported findings. *Bilingual Research Journal, 16*(1&2), 105–158.

Elementary and Secondary Education Act of 1968. P.L. 90-247 (1968).

Epstein, N. (1977). *Language, ethnicity, and the schools: Policy alternatives for bilingual-bicultural education.* Washington, DC: Institute for Educational Leadership.

Fisher, C. W., Guthrie, L. T., & Mandinach, E. B. (1983). *Verification of bilingual instructional features* (Doc. SPIF 83-R. 12). San Francisco: Far West Laboratory for Educational Research and Development.

Fishman, J. A., & Hofman, J. E. (1966). Mother tongue and nativity in the

American population. In J. A. Fishman (Ed.), *Language loyalty in the United States* (pp. 34–50). The Hague: Mouton.

Galambos, S., & Hakuta, K. (1988). Subject-specific and task-specific characteristics of metalinguistic awareness in bilingual children. *Applied Psycholinguistics, 9*, 141–162.

Garcia. E. (1991). *Education of linguistically and culturally diverse students: Effective instructional practices.* Santa Cruz: National Center for Research on Cultural Diversity and Second Language Learning, University of California.

Goddard, H. H. (1917). Mental tests and the immigrant. *Journal of Delinquency, 2*, 243–277.

Gould, S. J. (1981). *The mismeasure of man.* New York: Norton.

Gray, T. C., Convery, H. S., & Fox, K. M. (1981). *The current status of bilingual education legislation* (Bilingual Education Series, 9). Washington, DC: Center for Applied Linguistics.

Hakuta, K. (1986). *Mirror of language: The debate on bilingualism.* New York: Basic Books.

Hakuta, K. (in press). Bilingualism as a gift. In *Proceedings of the Esther Katz Rosen Symposium in the Psychological Development of Gifted Children.* Washington, DC: American Psychological Foundation.

Hakuta, K., & D'Andrea, D. (1992). Some properties of bilingual maintenance and loss in Mexican background high school students. *Applied Linguistics, 13*, 72–99.

Hakuta, K., & Diaz, R. M. (1985). The relationship between degree of bilingualism and cognitive ability: A critical discussion and some new longitudinal data. In K. Nelson (Ed.), *Children's language* (5th ed., pp. 319–345). Glendale, NJ: Lawrence Erlbaum.

Higham, J. (1965). *Strangers in the land: Patterns of American nativism 1860–1925.* New York: Atheneum.

Ianco-Worral, A. (1972). Bilingualism and cognitive development. *Child Development, 43*, 1390–1400.

Johnson, D. W., Johnson, R. T., & Maruyama, G. (1983). Interdependence and interpersonal attraction among heterogeneous and homogeneous individuals: A theoretical formulation and a meta-analysis of research. *Review of Educational Research, 53*, 5–54.

Kaestle, C. (1993). The awful reputation of education research. *Educational Researcher, 22*(1), 23–31.

Kagan, S. (1986). Cooperative learning and sociocultural factors in schooling. In Bilingual Education Office, California State Department of Education, *Beyond language: Social and cultural factors in schooling language minority students* (pp. 231–298). Los Angeles: Evaluation, Dissemination and Assessment Center, California State University.

Kloss, H. (1977). *The American bilingual tradition.* Rowley, MA: Newbury House.

Lambert, W. E., & Tucker, G. R. (1972). *Bilingual education of children: The St. Lambert experiment.* Rowley, MA: Newbury House.

Lau v. Nichols, 414 U.S. 563 (1974).

Lemke, J. L. (1990). *Talking science: Language, learning and values.* Norwood, NJ: Ablex.

Leopold, W. F. (1939). *Speech development of a bilingual child: A linguist's record: Vol. 1. Vocabulary growth in the first two years.* Evanston, IL: Northwestern University Press.

Liedtke, W. W., & Nelson, L. D. (1968). Concept formation and bilingualism. *Alberta Journal of Educational Research, 14*, 225–232.

Lindholm, K., & Aclan, Z. (1991). Bilingual proficiency as a bridge to academic achievement: Results from bilingual/immersion programs. *Journal of Education, 173*(3), 99–113.

Lindholm, K., & Fairchild, H. H. (1990). Evaluation of an elementary school bilingual immersion program. In A. M. Padilla, H. H. Fairchild, & C. M. Valadez (Eds.), *Bilingual education issues and strategies* (pp. 126–136). Newbury Park, CA: Sage Publications.

Mackey, W. F., & Beebe, V. N. (1977). *Bilingual school for a bicultural community: Miami's adaptation to the Cuban refugees.* Rowley, MA: Newbury House.

McLaughlin, L. B. (1985). *Second-language acquisition* (Vol. 2). Hillsdale, NJ: Lawrence Erlbaum.

Meyer, M., & Fienberg, S. (1992). *Assessing evaluation studies: The case of bilingual education strategies.* Washington, DC: National Academy Press.

Moll, L. C. (1992). Bilingual class studies and community analysis. *Educational Researcher, 21*(2), 2–24.

Moran, C. (1992). Content area instruction for students acquiring English. In J. Tinajero and A. Flor Ada (Eds.), *The power of two languages: Literacy and biliteracy* (pp. 264–275). New York: Macmillan/McGraw Hill.

National Center for Education Statistics (1993). *Language characteristics and schooling in the United States, a changing picture: 1979 and 1989* (NCES 93-699). Washington, DC: U.S. Department of Education, Office of Educational Research and Improvement.

National Clearinghouse for Bilingual Education. (1982). Update: Part C Bilingual education research. *FORUM, 5*(3), 1–8.

National Clearinghouse for Bilingual Education. (1984, March). Update: Part C Bilingual education research agenda. *FOCUS, 14*, 1–5.

Padilla, A. M. (1990). Bilingual education issues and perspectives. In A. M. Padilla, H. H. Fairchild, & C. M. Valadez (Eds.), *Bilingual education issues and strategies* (pp. 11–26). Newbury Park, CA: Sage Publications.

Peal, E., & Lambert, W. E. (1962). The relation of bilingualism to intelligence. *Psychological Monographs: General and Applied, 76* (546), 1–23.

Ramírez, J. D., Pasta, D., Yuen, S. D., Ramey, D. R., & Billings, D. (1991) *Final report: Longitudinal study of structured English immersion strategy, early-exit and late-exit bilingual education programs for language-minority children* (Vol. 2) (Prepared for U.S. Department of Education). San Mateo, CA: Aguirre International (No. 300-87-0156).

Ramírez, J. D., Yuen, S. D., Ramey, D. R., & Pasta, D. J. (1990). *Final report: Longitudinal study of immersion strategies, early-exit and late-exit transitional bilingual education programs for language-minority children* (Submitted to U.S. Dept. of Education). San Mateo, CA: Aguirre International.

Reynolds, A. G. (Ed.). (1991) *Bilingualism, multiculturalism, and second language learning: The McGill Conference in Honor of Wallace E. Lambert.* Hillsdale, NJ: Lawrence Erlbaum.

Ronjat, J. (1913). *Le développement du langage observé chez un enfant bilingue.* Paris: Champion.

Rossell, C. H. (1990). The effectiveness of educational alternatives for limited-English–proficient children. In G. Imhoff (Ed.), *The social and cultural context of instruction in two languages: From conflict and controversy to cooperative reorganization of schools* (pp. 71–121). New Brunswick, NJ: Transaction.

Rossell, C. H. (1992). Nothing matters? A critique of the Ramírez et al. longitudinal study of instructional programs for language minority children. *Bilingual Research Journal, 16*(1 & 2), 159–186.

Rossell, C., & Ross, J. (1986). The social science evidence on bilingual education. *Journal of Law and Education, 15*(4), 385-419.

Ruiz, R. (1988). Orientations in language planning. In S. L. McKay & S. Wong (Eds.), *Language diversity: Problem or resource?* (pp. 3–25). Rowley, MA: Newbury House.

Saer, D. J. (1924). The effect of bilingualism on intelligence. *British Journal of Psychology, 14*, 25–38.

Samaniego, F. J., & Eubank, L. A. (1991). *A statistical analysis of California's case study project in bilingual education* (Technical Report 208). Davis: Division of Statistics, University of California, Davis.

Slavin, R. (1981). Effects of cooperative learning teams on student achievement and race relations: Treatment by race interactions. *Sociology of Education, 54*, 174–180.

Smith, M. E. (1939). Some light on the problem of bilingualism as found from a study of the progress in mastery of English among pre-school children of non-American ancestry in Hawaii. *Genetic Psychology Monographs*, *21*, 119–284.

Snow, C. (1992). Perspectives on second-language development: Implications for bilingual education. *Educational Researcher*, *21*(2), 16–19.

Snow, C. E., Barnes, W. S., Chandler, J., Goodman, F., & Hemphill, L. (1991). *Unfulfilled expectations: Home and school influences on literacy*. Cambridge, MA: Harvard University Press.

Swain, M., & Lapkin, S. (1991). Additive bilingualism and French immersion education: The roles of language proficiency and literacy. In A. G. Reynolds (Ed.), *Bilingualism, multiculturalism, and second language learning: The McGill Conference in honor of Wallace E. Lambert* (pp. 203–216). Hillsdale, NJ: Lawrence Erlbaum.

Terman, L. M. (1916). *The measurement of intelligence*. Boston: Houghton Mifflin.

Tharpe, R., & Gallimore, R. (1979). The ecology of program research and evaluation: A model of evaluation succession. In L. Sechrest, S. West, M. A. Philips, R. Redner, & W. Yeaton (Eds.), *Evaluation studies review annual* (Vol. 4, pp. 39–60). Beverly Hills, CA: Sage Publications.

Tikunoff, W. J. (1983). *Utility of the SBIF features for the instruction of LEP students*. San Francisco, CA: Far West Laboratory for Educational Research and Development.

Tikunoff, W. J. (1985). *Applying significant bilingual instructional features in the classroom* (Part C Bilingual Education Research Services). Rosselyn, VA: National Clearinghouse for Bilingual Education.

Trueba, H. T. (1989). *Raising silent voices: Educating linguistic minorities for the 21st century*. Boston: Heinle & Heinle.

Tunmer, M. & Herriman, L. (1984). The development of metalinguistic awareness: A conceptual overview. In W. E. Tunmer, C. Pratt and M. L. Herriman (eds.) *Metalinguistic awareness in children*. Berlin: Springer-Verlag.

U.S. Department of Education (1982a). *Description and longitudinal study of immersion programs for language minority children*. Request for Proposal, Office of Planning, Budget, and Evaluation.

U.S. Department of Education (1982b). *National longitudinal evaluation of the effectiveness of services for language minority limited English proficient students*. Request for Proposal (RFP 82-057), Office of Planning, Budget, and Evaluation.

U.S. Department of Health, Education, and Welfare (1975). *Task force findings specifying remedies available for eliminating past educational practices ruled unlawful under Lau v. Nichols*. Office for Civil Rights.

U.S. Department of Health, Education, and Welfare (1979, July). *Proposed research plan for bilingual education*. Education Division.

Veltman, C. (1983). *Language shift in the United States*. Berlin: Morton Publishers.

Vygotsky, L. (1973). *Mind in society: The development of higher psychological processes* (M. Cole, V. John-Steiner, S. Scribner, & E. Souberman, Eds.). Cambridge, MA: Harvard University Press. (Original work published 1935)

Willig, A. C. (1985). A meta-analysis of selected studies on the effectiveness of bilingual education. *Review of Educational Research*, *55*, 269–317.

Wong Fillmore, L., & Valadez, C. (1986). Teaching bilingual learners. In M. C. Wittrock (Ed.), *Handbook of research on teaching* (3rd ed., pp. 648–658). New York: Macmillan.

Yoshioka, J. G. (1929). A study of bilingualism. *Journal of Genetic Psychology*, *26*, 473–479.

· VIII ·

ACADEMIC ACHIEVEMENT: APPROACHES, THEORIES, AND RESEARCH

· 26 ·

INEQUALITY AND ACCESS TO KNOWLEDGE

Linda Darling-Hammond

TEACHERS COLLEGE, COLUMBIA UNIVERSITY

As a consequence of structural inequalities in access to knowledge and resources, students from racial and ethnic "minority" groups in the United States face persistent and profound barriers to educational opportunity. In this chapter we document the extent of these inequalities, identify some of their sources, describe certain of their consequences for the nature and quality of education provided to different groups of students in the United States, and suggest policy changes needed to correct continuing inequities. We believe that documentation of and serious policy attention to these ongoing, systematic inequalities are critical for improving the quality and outcomes of education for all students. Without acknowledgment that students experience very different educational realities, policies will continue to be based on the presumption that it is students, not their schools or classroom circumstances, that are the sources of unequal educational attainment.

We begin with a brief discussion of the history and current state of segregation and exclusion confronting historically designated "minority" groups within the U.S. public education system. It is this isolation that creates the conditions for systematically unequal access to learning opportunities. In the second section we describe the role played by funding inequities in perpetuating unequal access to resources and knowledge. In the third section we explore questions of access to educational resources, including qualified teachers, courses, curriculum materials, and equipment. The fourth section addresses the ways in which tracking serves to exacerbate existing discrepancies by further rationing curricular opportunities. In the final section we put forward a number of proposals concerning school finance equalization, professional teaching policies, curriculum and testing reforms, and governmental roles in improving access to knowledge and educational resources for all students in the United States.

THE STRUCTURE OF INEQUALITY IN U.S. EDUCATION

Institutionally sanctioned discrimination in access to educational resources is older than the American nation itself. In his history of 18th-century colonial education, Lawrence Cremin (1970) writes:

> For all of its openness, provincial America, like all societies, distributed its educational resources unevenly, and to some groups, particularly those Indians and Afro-Americans who were enslaved and even those who were not, it was for all intents and purposes closed.... For the slaves, there were few books, few libraries, [and] few schools ... the doors of wisdom were not only not open, they were shut tight and designed to remain that way.... [B]y the end of the colonial period, there was a well-developed ideology of race inferiority to justify that situation and ensure that it would stand firm against all the heady rhetoric of the Revolution. (pp. 411–412)

Indeed, the legacy of discrimination did persist: "While [19th-century] publicists glorified the unifying influence of common learning under the common roof of the common school, black Americans were rarely part of that design" (Tyack, 1974, p. 110). From the time southern states made it illegal to teach an enslaved person to read, throughout the 19th century

---

This chapter draws in part on another chapter by Linda Darling-Hammond entitled "Teacher Quality and Equality" in *Access to Knowledge: An Agenda for Our Nation's Schools*, edited by J. Goodlad and P. Keating, 1990. NY: College Entrance Examination Board.

This chapter was prepared with the research assistance of Tamar Gendler and Elaine Joseph.

and into the 20th, African Americans faced de facto and de jure exclusion from public schools throughout the nation, as did Native Americans and, frequently, Mexican Americans (Tyack, pp. 109–125; Kluger, 1976; Meier, Stewart, & England, 1989; Schofield, 1991).

Twentieth-century statistics reveal the long-term effects of this pattern. African Americans and Hispanic Americans have, on the whole, completed significantly fewer years of school than Whites. In 1940 only 7% of African Americans over 25 had graduated from high school, as compared to 24% of Americans generally (U.S. Bureau of the Census, 1992). By 1985, 78% of White American adults had completed 12 or more years of school, compared to fewer than half of Mexican American and Puerto Rican American adults, and 60% of African Americans (U.S. Bureau of the Census, 1989). Similar patterns are true for Native Americans, although comparable data are less frequently available.

Educational experiences for "minority" students continue to be substantially separate and unequal. In 1964, fully a decade after *Brown v. Board of Education of Topeka*, 98% of African American students in the South were still enrolled in all-Black schools, and over 70% of northern Black students were still enrolled in predominantly minority schools (Schofield, 1991, p. 336). Though progress was made after passage of the 1964 Civil Rights Act, it was steady for only about a decade. The percentage of "minority" students in predominantly minority schools remained virtually unchanged between 1972 and 1986 (at 63.6% and 63.3%, respectively). Meanwhile, the percentage of Black students in intensely segregated schools (90% or more minority enrollment) dropped only slightly, from 38.7% to 32.5%, during the same period (Orfield, Monfort, & Aaron, 1989, cited in Schofield, 1992, p. 336). Hispanic students have been increasingly segregated over the years, with the proportion located in predominantly minority schools increasing from 55% in 1968 to 71% by 1986 (Orfield et al., 1989).

African American and Hispanic American students continue to be concentrated in central city public schools, many of which have become majority "minority" over the past decade. As of 1989, 52% of students in central city schools were Black or Hispanic (National Center for Education Statistics [NCES], 1992, p. 104). As we describe below, these schools are typically funded at levels substantially below those of neighboring suburban districts. The continuing segregation of neighborhoods and communities intersects with funding formulas and school administration practices that create substantial differences in the educational resources made available in different communities. Together, these conditions produce ongoing inequalities in educational opportunity by race and ethnicity.

Not only do funding systems and other policies create a situation in which urban districts receive fewer resources than their suburban neighbors, but schools with high concentrations of "minority" students receive fewer resources than other schools within these districts. And tracking systems exacerbate these inequalities by segregating many "minority" students within schools, allocating still fewer educational opportunities to them at the classroom level. How these layers of inequality are constructed is described below.

The Legacy of Funding Inequality

In 1857 a group of African American leaders testified before a state investigating committee about the striking discrepancies between the finances allocated to White and to Black students. While the New York Board of Education spent $16 per White child for sites and school buildings, the comparable figure per Black child was one cent; while Black students occupied school buildings described as "dark and cheerless" in neighborhoods "full of vice and filth," White students had access to schools that were "splendid, almost palatial edifices, with manifold comforts, conveniences, and elegancies" (Tyack, 1974, p. 119).

Over a century later, after the Supreme Court had already declared "separate but equal" education to be a violation of the 14th Amendment, James Bryant Conant's *Slums and Suburbs* (1961) and Francis Keppel's *The Necessary Revolution in American Education* (1966) documented continuing disparities in educational opportunity. According to Conant, "the expenditure per student in the wealthy suburban schools is as high as $1000 per year. The expenditure in a big city school is half that amount" (quoted in Wise, 1972, p. 6). Kluger (1976) documents large disparities in funding of segregated Black and White schools at the elementary, secondary, and postsecondary levels through the 1960s.

These disparities existed—and continue to exist—between predominantly White and minority schools even within the same district. In 1967 the Washington, D.C., District Court found that Black and poor children were denied equal educational opportunity not only because of de facto segregation in Washington's schools, but because of unequal spending as well. The court held that:

> If Whites and Negroes, rich or poor, are to be consigned to separate schools, pursuant to whatever policy, the minimum the Constitution will require and guarantee is that for their objectively measurable aspects these schools be run on the basis of real equality, at least unless any inequalities are adequately justified. (*Hobson v. Hansen,* 1967)

The court subsequently ordered a program of massive reallocation of school resources, ranging from textbooks to teachers and facilities construction. Similar circumstances have continued to obtain in large cities like Philadelphia, Chicago, and New York throughout the intervening years. In 1990 the Los Angeles City School District was sued on similar grounds (*Rodriguez et al. v. Los Angeles Unified School District,* 1992). Students there in predominantly minority schools, which are overcrowded and less well funded than other schools, were found to be disproportionately assigned to inexperienced and unprepared teachers hired on emergency credentials. This unequal assignment of teachers creates ongoing differentials in expenditures and access to educational resources, including the knowledge well-prepared teachers rely on in offering high-quality instruction.

Though some progress has been made since the 1960s, dramatic disparities persist. Jonathan Kozol's 1991 *Savage Inequalities* describes the striking differences between public schools in urban settings—schools whose population is between 95 and 99% non-White (p. 3)—and their suburban counterparts. While Chicago public schools spent just over $5,000 per student in 1989, nearby Niles Township High School spent $9,371 per student. While central city Camden, New Jersey, schools spent $3,500 that year, affluent suburban Princeton spent $7,725 per student. Schools in New York City spent $7,300 in 1990, while those in nearby suburbs like Manhasset and Great Neck spent over $15,000 per student for a population with many fewer special needs (pp. 236–237).

Savage Inequalities is replete with familiar yet poignant stories: MacKenzie High School in Detroit, where word-processing courses are taught without word processors because the school cannot afford them (Kozol, 1991, p. 198); Public School 261 in New York City, which has no windows in many classrooms and where recess is not possible because there is no playground (pp. 85–87); or East St. Louis Senior High School, whose biology lab has no laboratory tables or usable dissecting kits (p. 28). Meanwhile, children in neighboring suburban schools enjoy features like a 27-acre campus (p. 65), an athletic program featuring golf, fencing, ice hockey, and lacrosse (p. 157), and a computer hookup to Dow Jones to study stock transactions (p. 158).

The students notice. As one New York City 16-year-old notes of his school, where holes in ceilings expose rusty pipes and water pours in on rainy days, in comparison with others:

You can understand things better when you go among the wealthy. You look around you at their school, although it's impolite to do that, and you take a deep breath at the sight of all those beautiful surroundings. Then you come back home and see that these are things you do not have. You think of the difference. (Kozol, 1991, p. 104)

His classmate adds:

If you . . . put white children in this building in our place, this school would start to shine. No question. The parents would say: "This building sucks. It's ugly. Fix it up." They'd fix it fast—no question. . . . People on the outside may think that we don't know what it is like for other students, but we visit other schools and we have eyes and we have brains. You cannot hide the differences. You see it and compare. . . . (Kozol, 1991, p. 104)

The disparities in physical facilities are just the tip of the iceberg. Shortages of funds make it difficult for urban and poor rural schools to compete in the marketplace for qualified teachers or to provide the equipment and learning materials students need. As we describe later in this chapter, measurable and compounded inequalities leave most "minority" children with fewer and lower-quality books, materials, computers, labs, and other accoutrements of education, as well as less-qualified and -experienced teachers, fewer counselors, and social service providers working under greater stress with larger loads. It all adds up.

Such discrepancies in resource allocation are a function of how public education in the United States is funded. In most cases, education costs are supported by a system of general taxes—primarily local property taxes, along with state grants-in-aid (Guthrie, Garms, & Pierce, 1988). Because these funds

are typically raised and spent locally, districts with higher property values have greater resources with which to fund their schools, even when poorer districts tax themselves at proportionally higher rates. In Texas, for instance, the 100 wealthiest districts taxed their local property at an average rate of $.47 per $100 of assessed worth in 1989; at that level of effort, they were able to spend over $7,000 per student. Meanwhile, the 100 poorest districts, taxing themselves at a rate of over $.70 per $100, were able to raise only enough to spend some $3,000 per student (Kozol, 1991, p. 225).

Differences of the same kind exist among states, with per-pupil expenditures ranging from over $8,000 in New Jersey in 1989–1990 to under $3,000 in Utah (Educational Testing Service [ETS], 1991, p. 4). And while states generally make some effort to provide fiscal aid that has some equalizing effect on spending among districts, the federal government thus far plays no such role with respect to differentials among states in wealth and ability to pay for education.

These disparities translate into real differences in the services provided in schools: Higher-spending districts have smaller classes, higher-paid and more experienced teachers, and greater instructional resources (Hartman, 1988), as well as better facilities, more up-to-date equipment, and a wider range of course offerings (ETS, 1991). Districts serving large proportions of poor children have fewer resources. Thus, those students least likely to encounter a wide array of educational resources at home are also least likely to encounter them at school (ETS, 1991).

In their review of resource allocation studies, MacPhail-Wilcox & King (1986) summarize the resulting situation as follows:

School expenditure levels correlate positively with student socioeconomic status and negatively with educational need when school size and grade level are controlled statistically. . . . Teachers with higher salaries are concentrated in high income and low minority schools. Furthermore, pupil-teacher ratios are higher in schools with larger minority and low-income student populations. . . . Educational units with higher proportions of low-income and minority students are allocated fewer fiscal and educational resources than are more affluent educational units, despite the probability that these students have substantially greater need for both. (p. 425)

Studies of resource disparities in New York State bear this out. By virtually any resource measure—state and local dollars per pupil, student-teacher and student-staff ratios, class sizes, teacher experience, and teacher qualifications—districts with greater proportions of poor and minority students have access to fewer resources than others (Berne, 1992; New York Study Group, 1993).

The Legality of Unequal School Funding

Although concern about unequal school funding was expressed as early as the turn of the century (Cubberly, 1906; Updegraff & King, 1922), it was not until the mid-1960s that the legality of traditional inequities of school finance was subjected to judicial review. In 1965 Arthur Wise published an article challenging the constitutionality of school finance schemes that produce radically disparate per-pupil expenditures within states (Wise, 1965; see also Benson, 1961). Arguing that such unequal spending leads to unequal educational opportunities, he suggested that this might constitute a denial by the state of equal protection under the law (Wise, 1965, 1972; also Guthrie et al., 1988).

A number of lawsuits were filed on these grounds, and in 1973, in *Robinson v. Cahill,* the New Jersey Supreme Court declared the state's school financing system to be in violation of the New Jersey Constitution's education clause, which called for a "thorough and efficient system of free public schools" for all children between the ages of 5 and 18 (Wise & Gendler, 1989, p. 14). That same year, in *San Antonio Independent School District v. Rodriguez* (1973), however, the U.S. Supreme Court rejected the argument that education constitutes a fundamental right under the federal Constitution, thus stemming further federal court challenges of educational funding inequities.

Although hopes for a sweeping indictment of school funding traditions on federal grounds were dashed by the *San Antonio* decision, state-level challenges continued in several dozen state courts during the 1970s (Taylor & Piche, 1991). In 1976, in *Serrano v. Priest,* California's Supreme Court ended nearly a decade of debate by ruling that the state's system of school finance violated both the federal Constitution's 14th Amendment and California's own equal protection clause (Wise & Gendler, 1989; Guthrie et al., 1988). Other victories were achieved in West Virginia and Connecticut. However, most of the challenges were unsuccessful. Taylor and Piche note the differences in how state courts have approached similar problems:

In each case, the state court was confronted with significant fiscal disparities, but the opinions reflect that they each engaged in their own unique legal reasoning, applying different standards, and ultimately drawing different conclusions. The indisputable impact then of the "Federalist" approach, forged by the Supreme Court in *Rodriguez,* is that children in the poor districts of states like Connecticut and West Virginia are guaranteed some measure of equity, while those who live in the property-poor and urban districts of states like New York and Maryland are condemned to inferior educations. (p. 67)

Disparities in funding ratios of 3 to 1 between high- and low-spending districts were and are common within states in which challenges have been both successful and, more commonly, unsuccessful. These disparities create differences among students' educational opportunities as a function of race and socioeconomic status as well as geography. As Taylor and Piche (1991) demonstrate:

Inequitable systems of school finance inflict disproportionate harm on minority and economically disadvantaged students. On an inter-state basis, such students are concentrated in states, primarily in the South, that have the lowest capacities to finance public education. On an intrastate basis, many of the states with the widest disparities in educational expenditures are large industrial states. In these states, many minorities and economically disadvantaged students are located in property-poor urban districts which fare the worst in educational expenditures. In

addition, in several states economically disadvantaged students, white and black, are concentrated in rural districts which suffer from fiscal inequity. (pp. xi–xii)

Furthermore, this connection between inadequate funding and the race and social status of students exacerbates the difficulties of creating either integrated or adequately funded schools. The vicious cycle was described early on in the fight for school funding reform:

School inequality between suburbia and central city crucially reinforces racial isolation in housing; and the resulting racial segregation of the schools constantly inhibits progress toward funding a therapeutic answer for the elimination of school inequality. If we are to exorcise the evils of separateness and inequality, we must view them together, for each dimension of the problem renders the other more difficult to solve—racially separate schools inhibit elimination of school inequality, and unequal schools retard eradication of school segregation. (Silard & Goldstein, 1974, p. 324)

In total, courts in 10 of the 31 states in which suits have been filed have found their state's school finance scheme to be unconstitutional on one of three grounds: the federal Constitution's 14th Amendment, the state constitution's equal opportunity clause, or the state constitution's education article (McUsic, 1991, p. 307). A series of state challenges in the 1970s was followed by a decade of little activity, during which time there remained substantial variation in the share of school funding provided by different states, with less activism aimed at equalization in states in which judicial pressure had been absent (Wong, 1989). The issue was rejoined in the late 1980s, when successful finance suits were brought in New Jersey, Texas, Montana, Kentucky, and Tennessee (ETS, 1991).

Although the legal intricacies by which the courts have made their decisions are beyond the scope of this chapter, some of the conceptual grounds on which opponents of such decisions rest their arguments are not. In particular, opponents of school finance reform often argue (a) that concerns about local control outweigh concerns about equalizing funding across districts, and (b) that differences in per-pupil expenditures are irrelevant to issues of equity, since financial input does not affect the quality of education a district offers.

In response to the local control argument, defenders of school finance reform have pointed out that local control of schools has already been subjected to such erosion that, as the Texas Supreme Court wrote in its 1988 *Edgewood v. Kirby* decision,

the only element of local control that remains undiminished is the power of wealthy districts to fund education at virtually any level they choose, as contrasted with property-poor districts who enjoy no such local control.... Most of the incidents in the education process are determined and controlled by state statute and/or State Board of Education rule, including such matters as curriculum, course content, textbooks, hours of instruction, pupil-teacher ratios, training of teachers, administrators and board members, teacher testing, and review of personnel decisions and policies. (quoted in Wise & Gendler, 1989, p. 16)

Although local control in the form of parental and community involvement in the public schools remains an important factor in successful education, it does not provide justification for radically inequitable allocation of financial resources. Indeed, a more equitable distribution of resources might be a precondition for genuine local control (Yudof, 1991).

Proponents of the argument that "money doesn't make a difference" suggest that low-cost attitudinal and administrative changes contribute more than financial resources to educational quality within districts, and that no definitive correlation has been shown between money spent and educational quality. Defenders of finance reform argue that although money *can* be misspent, and although significant changes can be made without maximum resources, the question must be considered within the larger framework of the possibilities that are created and constrained at differing levels of resources. Within that framework, money makes a substantial difference (Minow, 1991; Murnane, 1991).

HOW MONEY MAKES A DIFFERENCE

The relationship between educational funding and educational achievement was placed in question in 1966, when James Coleman and a team of researchers issued *Equality of Educational Opportunity* (Coleman et al., 1966), which later came to be known as the Coleman report. Although the report argued that sources of inequality that it identified should be remedied, its statement that "schools bring little influence to bear on a child's achievement that is independent of his background and general social context" (quoted in Ferguson, 1991, p. 468) became widely viewed as a claim that school funding does not affect school achievement. As later analyses pointed out, it is in part the high correlation between students' backgrounds and their schools' resources that makes it difficult in macroanalytic studies to identify an independent effect of schooling on achievement (see, e.g., MacPhail-Wilcox & King, 1986). The "no effects" finding in the Coleman report was also a predictable result of the use of gross measures of inputs and outcomes aggregated to the school level, a shortcoming of the data also noted by the report's authors.

Nonetheless, while the Coleman report did not say so, the received view became the belief that additional resources play no role in producing better-educated students. Other studies have sought to confirm this view (e.g., Hanushek, 1990; Jencks et al., 1972), while newspapers have reveled in reporting the counterintuitive conclusion that "money doesn't buy better education.... The evidence can scarcely be clearer" (*Wall Street Journal,* June 27, 1989, cited in Kozol, 1991, p. 133).

Recent studies, however, have begun to provide statistical justification for the view that money *does* make a difference. Analyzing a set of data on Texas school districts even larger than that available to Coleman and his team of researchers, Ronald Ferguson (1991) found that the single most important measurable cause of increased student learning was teacher expertise, measured by teacher performance on a statewide recertification exam, teacher experience, and master's degrees. He also found that class size, at the critical point of a teacher:student ratio of 1:18, is also a statistically significant determinant of student outcomes.

Both of these findings have been confirmed elsewhere. As described in the next section, a large number of studies have found positive effects of teacher expertise on student achievement. In addition, smaller class sizes (below a threshold that is often in the low 20s or below) can make a substantial difference in achievement, especially in the early grades and for low-income students (Glass, Cahen, Smith, & Filby, 1982; Walberg, 1982; Centra & Potter, 1980; Educational Research Service, 1980). Ferguson (1991) concludes: "What the evidence here suggests most strongly is that teacher quality matters and should be a major focus of efforts to upgrade the quality of schooling. Skilled teachers are the most critical of all schooling inputs" (p. 490).

Ferguson (1991) further demonstrated that expenditure levels make a difference in increasing student performance as they influence district capacity both to buy higher-quality teachers and to provide other instructional services, such as extracurricular programs. When regional cost differentials are accounted for by controlling for local salaries in competing occupations and competing school districts, school district operating expenditures exert a significant positive effect on student achievement.

The strength of effects on achievement increases as funding moves closest to direct instruction of students: While all are significant, proportionally equivalent investments in teachers' salaries produce higher marginal gains in student performance than investments in general instructional expenditures, and investments in instructional expenditures produce higher marginal gains in achievement than proportional increases in general operating expenditures. Money makes a difference, and the difference increases as it is spent on instructionally crucial resources. Ferguson (1991) notes that this finding "strongly supports the conventional wisdom that higher-quality schooling produces better reading skills among public school students, and that when targeted and managed wisely, increased funding can improve the quality of public education" (p. 488).

Ferguson's (1991) conclusion—that more qualified teachers produce an increase in test scores, which is strengthened with smaller class sizes as well—led him to recommend a radical reallocation of resources:

Equal salaries will not attract equally qualified teachers to dissimilar school districts: for any given salary, teachers prefer school districts with higher socioeconomic status and judge the attractiveness of teaching in a given district against the allure of other opportunities. This suggests that a state policy of salary differentials ... will be necessary if each district is to get its proportionate share of the best teachers. (p. 489)

His recommendation reprises a theme struck in early school finance research during the 1970s: that teacher salaries and working conditions are both important in creating incentives for teacher recruitment (see, e.g., Hall & Carroll, 1973). Lacking strength in both arenas, poor districts generally lose out in the competition for highly qualified teachers (Darling-Hammond, 1988).

ACCESS TO GOOD TEACHING

In "Closing the Divide," Robert Dreeben (1987) describes the results of his study of reading instruction and outcomes for 300 Black and White first graders across seven schools in the Chicago area. He found that differences in reading outcomes among students were almost entirely explained, not by socioeconomic status or race, but by the quality of instruction the students received:

Our evidence shows that the level of learning responds strongly to the quality of instruction: having and using enough time, covering a substantial amount of rich curricular material, and matching instruction appropriately to the ability levels of groups.... When black and white children of comparable ability experience the same instruction, they do about equally well, and this is true when the instruction is excellent in quality and when it is inadequate. (p. 34)

However, the study also found that the quality of instruction received by African American students was, on average, much lower than that received by White students, thus creating a racial gap in aggregate achievement by the end of first grade. In fact, the highest ability group in Dreeben's sample was in a school in a low-income African American neighborhood. However, these students learned less during first grade than their lower-aptitude White counterparts. Why? Because their teacher was unable to provide the kind of appropriate and challenging instruction this highly talented group deserved.

Another study of African American high school youth randomly placed in public housing in the Chicago suburbs rather than in the city found similar results (Kaufman & Rosenbaum, 1992). Compared with their comparable city-placed peers, who were of equivalent income and initial academic attainment, the students who were enabled to attend largely White and better-funded suburban schools had better educational outcomes across many dimensions: They were substantially more likely to have the opportunity to take challenging courses, receive additional academic help, graduate on time, attend college, and secure good jobs.

These examples are drawn from carefully controlled studies that confirm what many other studies have suggested: Much of the difference in school achievement found between African American students and others is due to the effects of substantially different school opportunities, in particular greatly disparate access to high-quality teachers and teaching (see, e.g., Barr & Dreeben, 1983; Dreeben & Gamoran, 1986; Dreeben & Barr, 1987; College Board, 1985; Oakes, 1990a; Darling-Hammond & Snyder, 1992).

The Unequal Distribution of Teachers

Minority and low-income students in urban settings are most likely to find themselves in classrooms staffed by inadequately prepared, inexperienced, and ill-qualified teachers be-

cause funding inequities, distributions of local power, and labor market conditions conspire to produce teacher shortages of which they bear the brunt. The data confirm that these difficulties continue to be structural conditions of urban schooling:

- In 1983, the most recent year for which national information is available, shortages of teachers—as measured by unfilled vacancies—were three times greater in central cities than in rural areas or suburbs (NCES, 1985).
- More than 14% of all newly hired teachers in central city school districts in 1983 were uncertified in their principal field of assignment, nearly twice the proportion in other types of districts (NCES, 1985).
- A survey of high school teachers in 1984 found that the schools in which uncertified teachers were located were disproportionately central city schools with higher than average percentages of low-income and minority students (Pascal, 1987, p. 24).
- In 1985, 5,000 untrained teachers were hired on emergency certificates in New York, Los Angeles, and Houston alone. Many of these districts' vacancies were not filled when schools opened that fall (Darling-Hammond, 1987).
- In 1986, shortages stimulated the issuance of over 30,000 emergency and temporary teaching certificates in just the fewer than a dozen states that keep records on such matters. The national totals are probably several times this number. The vast majority of these teachers were hired in central city and poor rural school districts and placed in the most disadvantaged schools. The same is true of teachers recruited through alternative certification routes, who have often had only minimal preparation (Darling-Hammond, 1990c).
- In 1992, 2,600 of New York City's new hires were uncertified, bringing the total number of such teachers in the city at that time to 9,600. Cancellation of the state and city mentoring programs because of budget cuts meant that most of these teachers were also unsupervised.

All of this means that districts with the greatest concentrations of poor children, minority children, and children of immigrants are also those in which incoming teachers are least likely to have learned about up-to-date teaching methods or about how children grow, learn, and develop—and what to do if they are having difficulties (Darling-Hammond, 1988).

Teacher shortages subvert the quality of education in a number of ways. They make it hard for districts to be selective about the quality of teachers they hire, and they often result in the hiring of teachers who have not completed (or sometimes even begun) their pedagogical training. In addition, when faced with shortages, districts must often hire substitutes, assign teachers outside their fields of qualification, expand class sizes, or cancel course offerings. No matter what strategies are adopted, the quality of instruction suffers.

In recent years, shortages of qualified teachers in subject areas such as early childhood education, bilingual education, special education, mathematics, science, and foreign languages have forced cities to hire thousands of teachers who are not fully prepared. The vast majority of these are assigned to the most disadvantaged central city schools, where working conditions are least attractive and turnover rates are highest (Darling-Hammond, 1990c; 1992). Since many of the more expert and experienced teachers transfer to more desirable schools and districts when they are able, new teachers are typically given the most difficult teaching assignments in schools that offer the fewest supports (Wise, Darling-Hammond, & Berry, 1987; Murnane, Singer, Willett, Kemple, & Olsen, 1991). Because of these challenges, attrition rates for new teachers, especially in cities, average between 40 and 50% over the first five years of teaching (Wise et al., 1987; Grissmer & Kirby, 1987).

This high attrition rate adds problems of staff instability to the already difficult circumstances in which central city youth attend school. Where shortages are acute and enduring, many children in central city schools are taught by a parade of short-term substitute teachers, inexperienced teachers without support, and underqualified teachers who know neither their subject matter nor effective teaching methods. This sets up the school failure that society predicts for low-income and minority children—a failure that it helps to create for them by its failure to deal effectively with the issues of teacher supply and quality.

Emergency hiring, assignment of teachers out of their fields of preparation, and high turnover in underfunded schools conspire to produce the finding of the California Commission on the Teaching Profession: that disproportionate numbers of minority and poor students are taught throughout their entire school career by the least qualified teachers (California Commission, 1985). This finding is confirmed by many other studies over several decades (Darling-Hammond, 1990c, 1992).

Oakes's (1990a) nationwide study of the distribution of mathematics and science opportunities across hundreds of schools found patterns that are pervasive across communities and across school subjects. Based on teacher experience, certification status, preparation in the discipline they are teaching, higher degrees, self-confidence, and other teacher and principal perceptions of competence, it is clear that low-income and minority students have less contact with the best-qualified science and mathematics teachers. Principals of high-minority and low-income schools report that they have high levels of teaching vacancies and great difficulty filling them with qualified teachers. Students in such schools have only a 50% chance of being taught by math or science teachers who are certified at all, and an even lower chance of being taught by those who are fully qualified for their teaching assignments by virtue of the subject area(s) they have prepared to teach. Oakes concludes:

Our evidence lends considerable support to the argument that low-income, minority, and inner-city students have fewer opportunities. . . . They have considerably less access to science and mathematics knowledge at school, fewer material resources, less-engaging learning activities in their classrooms, and less-qualified teachers. . . . The differences we have observed are likely to reflect more general patterns of educational inequality. (pp. x–xi)

Just as Dreeben (1987) found in his study of early reading teaching, Oakes (1990a) also discovered that "High-ability students at low-socioeconomic status, high-minority schools may actually have fewer opportunities than low-ability students who

attend more advantaged schools" (p. vii). The pattern of systematic underexposure to good teaching tends to put all children in high-minority schools at risk.

What Matters in Teaching?

Over the last 20 years, educational research has exploded the myths that any teaching is as effective as any other, and that unequally trained and experienced teachers are equally advantageous to students. In a study documenting the positive influence of teaching experience on teaching effectiveness, Murnane and Phillips (1981) note:

The question of whether teachers become more productive as they gain teaching experience has been of interest to policymakers for many years. One reason is that schools serving children from low-income families have typically been staffed with less experienced teachers than schools serving middle-class children. This has led to court tests of whether the uneven distribution of teaching experience constitutes discrimination against low-income children. (pp. 453–454)

Although the correlation between teacher experience and effectiveness is not unvarying over the course of a career, studies consistently find that new teachers—those with fewer than three years of experience—tend to be much less effective than more experienced teachers (Murnane & Phillips, 1981; Moskowitz & Hayman, 1974; Rottenberg & Berliner, 1990). Especially in the unsupported environment most encounter, beginning teachers experience a wide range of problems in learning to teach; problems with classroom management, motivating students, being aware of and dealing appropriately with individual learning needs and differences, and developing a diverse repertoire of instructional strategies are among the most commonly noted (Veenman, 1984; Johnston & Ryan, 1983; Rottenberg & Berliner, 1990).

Having confirmed that teacher experience does make a difference, researchers are now identifying what expert veterans do in the classroom that distinguishes their teaching from that of novices (see, e.g., Berliner, 1986; Shulman, 1987; Grossman, 1990). Among other things, expert teachers are much more sensitive to students' needs and individual differences; they are more skilled at engaging and motivating students; and they can call upon a wider repertoire of instructional strategies for addressing student needs. Much of this research also demonstrates the importance of teacher education for the acquisition of knowledge and skills that, when used in the classroom, improve the caliber of instruction and the success of students' learning (Berliner, 1984; Darling-Hammond, 1992).

This is particularly important in light of the fact that policy makers have nearly always answered the problem of teacher shortages by lowering standards, so that people who have had little or no preparation for teaching can be hired. These teachers are disproportionately assigned to teach minority and low-income students in central cities and poor rural districts. Although this practice is often excused by the assumption that virtually anyone can figure out how to teach, a number of reviews of research summarizing the results of more than 100 studies have concluded that fully prepared and certified teachers are more highly rated and more successful with students than teachers without full preparation (Darling-Hammond, 1992; Evertson, Hawley, & Zlotnik, 1985; Ashton & Crocker, 1986, 1987; Greenberg, 1983; Druva & Anderson, 1983). Thus, policies that resolve shortages in poor districts by supporting the hiring of unprepared teachers serve only to exacerbate the inequalities experienced by low-income and minority children.

The extent and kind of teacher preparation are especially important in determining the effectiveness of teachers in "school-based" subjects (those subjects students tend to learn primarily in school rather than through informal learning outside of school), such as mathematics, science, and early reading (Hice, 1970; LuPone, 1961; McNeil, 1974). Teacher education is also a critical determinant of the use of teaching strategies that encourage higher-order learning and are responsive to students' needs and learning styles.

A number of studies have found that teachers who enter without full preparation are less able to plan and redirect instruction to meet students' needs (and less aware of the necessity to do so), less skilled in implementing instruction, less able to anticipate students' knowledge and potential difficulties, and less likely to see it as their job to do so, often blaming students if their teaching is not successful (Bledsoe, Cox, & Burnham, 1967; Copley, 1974; Rottenberg & Berliner, 1990; Bents & Bents, 1990; Grossman, 1989, 1990).

These findings are reflected in Gomez & Grobe's (1990) study of the performance of alternate-route candidates hired in Dallas with only a few weeks of prior training. The performance of these candidates was much more uneven than that of trained beginners, with markedly lower ratings on their knowledge of instructional techniques and instructional models, and with a much greater proportion (from 2 to 16 times as many) likely to be rated "poor" on each of the teaching factors evaluated. The proportions rated "poor" ranged from 8% on reading instruction to 17% on classroom management. The effects of this unevenness showed up most strongly in students' achievement in language arts, where students of the alternate-route teachers scored significantly lower than students of fully prepared beginning teachers, after adjusting for initial achievement levels.

The reasons for this are no mystery. Strickland (1985) stresses that, for early literacy development, teachers must be able to develop programs that accommodate a variety of cognitive styles and learning rates, with activities that broaden rather than reduce the range of possibilities for learning. Teachers must receive preparation that prepares them to understand the nature of language and language development as well as the nature of child growth and development. These understandings undergird knowledge of appropriate procedures for fostering language growth at various stages of development.

Comer (1988) also emphasizes the importance of preparing teachers with a strong background in child development as a key to the kind of teaching that has been so successful in his School Development Program. The evidence clearly indicates that such preparation makes a difference in what children learn. Yet very few teachers have received serious preparation regarding child and adolescent development, and even fewer of them are teaching in high-poverty schools.

It seems that appropriate preparation in planning and classroom management is one of the factors that allow teachers to focus on the kind of complex teaching that is needed to develop higher-order skills. Since the novel tasks required for complex problem solving are more difficult to manage than the routine tasks associated with learning simple skills, lack of classroom management ability can lead teachers to "dumb down" the curriculum in order to control student work more easily (Carter & Doyle, 1987; Doyle, 1986).

When school staffing patterns create substantial imbalances in teacher expertise across schools, the effects are profound. When Armour-Thomas, Clay, Domanico, Bruno, and Allen (1989) compared a group of exceptionally effective elementary schools with a group of low-achieving schools with similar demographic characteristics in New York City, they found that differences in teacher qualifications and experience accounted for roughly 90% of the variance in student reading and mathematics scores at grades three, six, and eight. Far more than any other factor, teacher expertise made the difference in what children learned.

Access to Courses, Curriculum Materials, and Equipment

In addition to being taught by less qualified teachers than their suburban counterparts, urban students face dramatic differences in courses, curriculum materials, and equipment. While Goudy Elementary School, which serves a predominantly African American student population in Chicago, uses "15-year-old textbooks in which Richard Nixon is still president" and has "no science labs, no art or music teachers . . . [and] two working bathrooms for some 700 children," the neighboring town of New Trier (more than 98% White) provides its high school students with "superior labs . . . up-to-date technology . . . seven gyms [and] an Olympic pool" (Kozol, 1991, pp. 63–65).

From a more cross-cutting statistical vantage point, Oakes (1990a) found in a study of access to mathematics and science-related educational resources across hundreds of schools that:

Students in low-income, high-minority schools have less access than students in other schools to computers and to the staff who coordinate their use in instruction, to science laboratories, and to other common science-related facilities and equipment. (p. ix)

As just one easily measured resource important to preparation for work in the modern world, a number of studies of computer availability demonstrate that access to and use of computers differs significantly for minority and White students, both at home and at school. Only about 7% of African American and Hispanic students, as compared to 23% of White students, had access to computers at home in 1989, and schools did not equalize access. About one third of African American and Hispanic students used computers at school, as compared to 46% of White students (U.S. Bureau of the Census, 1989).

Among schools, students in low socioeconomic status (SES) and high-minority schools have much less access—in terms of number of computers per student and amount of time they are available to individual students—than students in other schools, and their schools have far fewer teachers trained in the uses of computers (Becker, 1983, 1986; Oakes, 1990a; Sutton, 1991). Furthermore, in predominantly minority schools and classrooms, microcomputers are used much more frequently for drill and practice and much less frequently to teach students to program, access data, and solve problems using the computer as a tool, rather than as a master (Becker, 1983; Winkler, Shavelson, Stasz, Robyn, & Feibel, 1984; Sutton, 1991).

Even more important are deep-seated inequalities in access to curriculum. High-minority schools are much less likely to offer advanced and college preparatory courses in mathematics and science than are schools that serve affluent and largely White populations of students (Matthews, 1984; Oakes, 1990a, 1990b). Schools serving predominantly minority and poor populations offer fewer advanced and more remedial courses in academic subjects, and they have smaller academic tracks and larger vocational programs (NCES, 1985; Rock, Hilton, Pollack, Ekstrom, & Goertz, 1985).

California is not unique in finding that both the size and rigor of college preparatory programs within its schools vary with the race and socioeconomic status of school populations (California State Department of Education, 1984). As plaintiffs noted in the New Jersey school finance case, wealthy and predominantly White Montclair offers foreign languages at the preschool level, while poor and predominantly Black Paterson does not offer any until high school—and then relatively few. And while 20% of 11th and 12th graders in wealthy Moorestown participate in Advanced Placement courses, none are even offered in any school in poor and predominantly Black Camden and East Orange (ETS, 1991, p. 9).

When high-minority, low-income schools offer any advanced or college preparatory courses, they offer them to only a very tiny fraction of students. Thus, at the high school level, African Americans, Hispanics, and American Indians have traditionally been underrepresented in academic programs and overrepresented in vocational education programs, where they receive fewer courses in areas such as English, mathematics, and science (College Board, 1985). Furthermore, minority students in vocational education programs are enrolled earlier and more extensively than are White students in programs training specifically for low-status occupations (Oakes, 1983). Even among the college bound, non-Asian minority students take fewer and less demanding mathematics, science, and foreign-language courses (Pelavin & Kane, 1990).

The National Education Longitudinal Survey of 1988 shows that African American, Latino, Native American, and low-income students continue to be much more likely than White or upper-income students to be placed in remedial and low-level courses (NCES, 1991). As Oakes (1992) explains:

The extraordinarily complex connections between tracking and social stratification play out in two ways. First, schools with predominantly low-income and minority student populations tend to be "bottom heavy." That is, they offer smaller academic tracks and larger remedial and vocational programs than do schools serving whiter, more affluent student bodies. . . . The second link between tracking and students' race and social class is forged in racially mixed schools through the dispro-

portionate assignment of African-American and Latino students to low-track classes. (p. 13)

Unequal access to high-level courses and challenging curriculum explains much of the difference in achievement between minority students and White students. For example, analyses of data from the High School and Beyond surveys demonstrate dramatic course-taking differences among students of various racial and ethnic groups in such areas as mathematics, science, and foreign language (Pelavin & Kane, 1990). These data also demonstrate that, for students of all racial and ethnic groups, course taking is strongly related to achievement; among students with similar course-taking records, achievement test score differences by race or ethnicity narrow substantially (College Board, 1985, p. 38; Jones, 1984; Jones, Burton, & Davenport, 1984; Moore & Smith, 1985).

TRACKING AND THE RATIONING OF CURRICULUM

The same forces that produce the flow of good teachers and rich educational resources to advantaged schools, and the ebb of opportunities from disadvantaged schools and students, are at work within schools wherever tracking persists. Tracking endures in the face of growing evidence that it does not substantially benefit high achievers and tends to put low achievers at a serious disadvantage (Oakes, 1985, 1986; Hoffer, 1992; Kulik & Kulik, 1982; Slavin, 1990), in part because good teaching is a scarce resource, and thus must be allocated. Scarce resources tend to get allocated to the students whose parents, advocates, or representatives have the most political clout. This results—not entirely but disproportionately—in the most highly qualified teachers teaching the most enriched curricula to the most advantaged students.

Evidence suggests that teachers themselves are tracked, with those judged to be the most competent, experienced, or with the highest status assigned to the top tracks (Oakes, 1986; Davis, 1986; Finley, 1984; Rosenbaum, 1976; Talbert, 1990). In one study of secondary school curriculum, for example, 42% of teachers of remedial, vocational, and general mathematics had been teaching for five years or less, compared with 19% of those in the pre-algebra and algebra sections (McDonnell, Burstein, Ormseth, Catterall, & Moody, 1990, cited in Wheelock, 1992).

Expert, experienced teachers who are in great demand are rewarded with opportunities to teach the students who already know a lot. New teachers, unprepared teachers, and those teaching outside their field of preparation are often assigned to the students and the classes that others do not care to teach, which leaves them practicing on the students who would benefit most from the skills of the expert, experienced teachers.

Another major reason for the persistence of this practice is the kind of preparation teachers receive generally. Managing a heterogeneous classroom requires preparation that relatively few teachers receive and skills that relatively few of them acquire (Darling-Hammond, 1990b; Wheelock, 1992). It requires refined diagnostic ability, a broad repertoire of teaching strategies, and the ability to match strategies to varied learning styles and prior levels of knowledge. It requires skill in using inquiry and cooperative learning strategies, as well as skills in classroom management even more considerable than those required in a homogeneous classroom. Because relatively few teachers are prepared to manage heterogeneous classrooms effectively, tracking persists.

Tracking is much more extensive in U.S. schools than in most other countries. Starting in elementary school, with the designation of instructional groups and programs based on test scores and recommendations, it becomes highly formalized by junior high school. The result of this practice is that challenging curricula are rationed to a very small proportion of students, and far fewer U.S. students ever encounter the kinds of curriculum typically experienced by students in other countries (McKnight et al., 1987; Usiskin, 1987; Useem, 1990; Wheelock, 1992).

Students placed in lower tracks are exposed to a limited, rote-oriented curriculum, and ultimately achieve less than students of similar aptitude who are placed in academic programs or untracked classes (Gamoran, 1990; Gamoran & Mare, 1989; Oakes, 1985, 1992). Teacher interaction with students in lower-track classes is less motivating and less supportive, as well as less demanding of higher-order reasoning and responses (Good & Brophy, 1987). These interactions are also less academically oriented and more likely to focus on behavioral criticisms, especially for minority students (Eckstrom & Villegas, 1991; Oakes, 1985). Presentations are less clear and less focused on higher-order cognitive goals (Oakes, 1985).

These curricular differences are widespread, and they explain much of the disparity between the achievement of White and minority students and between those of higher and lower income levels (Oakes, 1985; Lee & Bryk, 1988). When students of similar background and initial achievement level are exposed differentially to either more or less challenging curriculum material, those given the richer curriculum opportunities outperform those placed in less challenging classes (Alexander & McDill, 1976; Oakes, 1985; Gamoran & Berends, 1987).

Most studies have estimated effects statistically based on naturalistic occurrences of different tracking policies. However, one study that randomly assigned seventh-grade "at-risk" students to remedial, average, and honors mathematics classes found that, at the end of the year, the at-risk students who took the honors class offering a pre-algebra curriculum outperformed all other students of similar background (Peterson, 1989, cited in Levin, 1992).

Tracking exacerbates differential access to knowledge. As Oakes (1986) notes, assignments of poor and minority students to lower tracks are predictable:

One finding about placements is undisputed.... Disproportionate percentages of poor and minority youngsters (principally black and Hispanic) are placed in tracks for low-ability or non-college-bound students (NCES, 1985; Rosenbaum, 1980); further, minority students are consistently underrepresented in programs for the gifted and talented (College Board, 1985).

Though test scores and prior educational opportunities may provide one reason for these differential placements, race and socioeconomic status play a distinct role. As Gamoran (1992) found, race and socioeconomic status determined assignments to high school honors courses even after test scores were controlled. This is true in part because of prior placement of students in upper tracks in earlier grades, in part because of counselors' views that they should advise students in ways that are "realistic" about their futures, and in part because of the greater effectiveness of parent interventions in tracking decisions for higher-SES students.

For similar reasons, race and socioeconomic status also affect students' placements in vocational and academic programs and in more or less challenging courses within them (Oakes, Selvin, Karoly, & Guiton, 1992; Useem, 1990). The seeds of this tracking are planted in "ability grouping" in elementary school, and students' placements are well established long before high school begins (Moore & Davenport, 1988).

From "gifted and talented" programs at the elementary level through advanced courses in secondary schools, teachers who are generally the most skilled offer rich, challenging curricula to select groups of students, on the theory that only a few students can benefit from such curricula. Yet the distinguishing feature of such programs, particularly at the elementary level, is not their difficulty, but their quality. Students in these programs are given opportunities to integrate ideas across fields of study. They have opportunities to think, write, create, and develop projects. They are challenged to explore. Though virtually all students would benefit from being similarly challenged, the opportunity for this sort of schooling remains acutely restricted.

In many instances, the reason for the restriction is the scarcity of teachers who can teach in the fashion such curricula demand. In addition, schools continue to believe that few students need or will profit from such demanding instruction. Those beliefs are especially strong with respect to students of color. The disproportionately small enrollment of non-Asian minority students in "gifted and talented" programs is widespread. In most districts, though there are exceptions, African American and Hispanic students are represented in such courses at well under half their representation in the total student population (College Board, 1985, pp. 31–33). Statistical patterns are brought alive by descriptions of sorting such as this one offered by Kozol (1991) of a school in New York City:

The school is integrated in the strict sense that the middle- and upper-middle class white children here do occupy a building that contains some Asian and Hispanic and black children; but there is little integration in the classrooms.... (p. 93)

He describes how minority children are disproportionately assigned to special education classes that occupy small, cramped corners and split classrooms, while classes of the "gifted and talented," almost exclusively White with a few Asian students, occupy the most splendid spaces, filled with books and computers, where they learn, in the children's words, "logical thinking," "problem-solving," "respect for someone else's logic," and "reasoning." Students are recommended for these classes by their teachers and parents as well as by their test scores. Kozol wrote in his notes: "Six girls, four boys. Nine white, one Chinese. I am glad they have this class. But what about the others? Aren't there ten black children in the school who could enjoy this also?" (p. 97).

Testing and Tracking

These differential allocations of resources are maintained and justified in substantial measure by the continued use of standardized testing for allocating curriculum opportunities. Over many decades, standardized tests have been used to define both teaching goals and students' opportunities to learn. As a tool for tracking students into different courses, levels, and kinds of instructional programs, testing has been a primary means for limiting or expanding students' life choices and their avenues for demonstrating competence. Increasingly, these uses of tests are recognized as having the unintended consequence of limiting students' access to further learning opportunities (Darling-Hammond, 1991; Oakes, 1985; Glaser, 1990).

For over 100 years, standardized testing has been a tool used to exert control over the schooling process and to make decisions about educational entitlements for students. Testing proved a convenient instrument of social control for those late 19th-century superintendents who sought to create the "one best system" of education (Tyack, 1974). It also proved enormously useful as a means of determining how to slot students for either more or less rigorous (and costly) curricula when public funding of education and compulsory attendance vastly increased access to schools in the early 20th century.

Given the massive increase in students, the limits of public budgets, and the relatively meager training of teachers, strategies were sought to codify curriculum and to group students for differential instruction. IQ tests were widely employed as a measure of educational input (with intelligence viewed as the "raw material" for schooling) to sort pupils so they could be efficiently educated according to their future roles in society (Cubberly, 1919; Cremin, 1961; Watson, in press). The tests were frequently used to exclude students from schooling opportunities altogether (Glaser, 1981).

Though many proponents argued that the use of these tests as a tool for tracking students would enhance social justice, the rationales for tracking—like those for using scores to set immigration quotas into the United States—were often frankly motivated by racial and ethnic politics. Just as Goddard "proved" with his testing experiments in 1912 that 83% of Jews, 80% of Hungarians, 79% of Italians, and 87% of Russians were feeble-minded (Kamin, 1974), so did Terman "prove" in the early 1900s that "Indians, Mexicans, and negroes . . . should be segregated in special classes. . . . They cannot master abstractions, but they can often be made efficient workers" (Terman, quoted in Oakes, 1985, p. 36).

Terman found many performance inequalities among groups on his IQ test, adapted from Binet's work in France. Most, but not all, seemed to confirm what he, and presumably every "intelligent" person, already knew: that various groups were inherently unequal in their mental capacities. However, when girls scored higher than boys on his 1916 version of the Stanford-Binet, he revised the test to correct for this apparent flaw by selecting items to create parity among genders in the scores (Mercer, 1989). Other inequalities—between urban and rural students, higher- and lower-SES students, native English speakers and immigrants, Whites and Blacks—did not occasion such revisions, since their validity seemed patently obvious to the test makers (cited in Einbender, 1992).

The role of testing in reinforcing and extending social inequalities in educational opportunities has by now been extensively researched (Gould, 1981; Mercer, 1989; Oakes, 1985; Kamin, 1974; Watson, in press) and widely acknowledged. Use of tests for placements and promotions ultimately reduces the amount of learning achieved by students placed in lower tracks or held back in grade (Darling-Hammond, 1991). Minority students are disproportionately subject to both of these outcomes of testing.

Neither outcome ultimately improves achievement. Students who are retained in grade fall consistently behind on both achievement and social-emotional measures when compared with students of equivalent achievement levels who are promoted (Holmes & Matthews, 1984; Shephard & Smith, 1986). Furthermore, the practice of retaining students is a major contributor to increased drop-out rates (Mann, 1987; Carnegie Council on Adolescent Development, 1989; Wehlage, Rutter, Smith, Lesko, & Fernandez, 1990; Massachusetts Advocacy Center, 1988).

In addition, many studies have found that students placed in the lowest tracks or in remedial programs—disproportionately low-income and minority students—are most apt to experience instruction geared only to multiple-choice tests, working at a low cognitive level on test-oriented tasks that are profoundly disconnected from the skills they need to learn. Rarely are they given the opportunity to talk about what they know, to read real books, to write, or to construct and solve problems in mathematics, science, or other subjects (Oakes, 1985; Cooper & Sherk, 1989; Davis, 1986; Trimble & Sinclair, 1986). In short, they have been denied the opportunity to develop the capacities they will need for the future, in large part because commonly used tests are so firmly pointed at educational goals of the past.

Enriching an Impoverished Curriculum

Cooper & Sherk (1989) describe how worksheet-based instruction focused on the discrete "skill" bits featured on multiple-choice tests impedes students' progress toward literacy:

When hundreds of these worksheets, each of which presents a small, low-level skill related to reading, have been completed, children are said to have completed the "mastery" skills program. Often, these children still cannot read very well, if one defines reading as the ability to discern connected prose for comprehension. . . .

[Furthermore], worksheets are devised in such a way, teachers are told, that the material teaches itself. As a result, the amount of oral communication between pupil and teacher and between pupil and pupil is drastically reduced. . . . [Yet] if children are to learn language, a part of which is reading, they must interact and communicate. They must have some opportunity to hear words being spoken, to pose questions, to conjecture, and to hypothesize. . . . (p. 318)

Their discussion of what teachers should be able to do to support children's literacy development maps onto more general principles of effective instruction. Teachers must be able to construct active learning opportunities involving student collaboration and many modes of oral and written language use; help students access prior knowledge that will frame for them the material to be learned; structure learning tasks so that students have a basis for interpreting the novel experiences they encounter; and stimulate and engage students' higher-order thought processes, including their capacities to hypothesize, predict, evaluate, integrate, and synthesize ideas (Cooper & Sherk, 1989; see also Resnick, 1987; Bowman, 1993; Braddock & McPartland, 1993; Garcia, 1993).

In recent years the school reform movement has engendered widespread efforts to transform the ways in which students' work and learning are organized and assessed in schools. These alternatives are frequently called performance-based or "authentic" assessments because they engage students in "real world" tasks rather than multiple-choice tests, and evaluate them according to criteria that are important for actual performance in that field (Wiggins, 1989). Such assessments include oral presentations or exhibitions, along with collections of students' written products and their solutions to problems, experiments, debates, constructions and models, videotapes of performances and other learning occasions, and results of scientific and other inquiries (Archbald & Newman, 1988).

Much of the rationale for these initiatives is based on growing evidence that traditional norm-referenced, multiple-choice tests fail to measure complex cognitive and performance abilities. Furthermore, when used for decision making, such tests encourage instruction that tends to emphasize decontextualized, rote-oriented tasks imposing low cognitive demands rather than meaningful learning. Thus efforts to raise standards of learning and performance must rest in part on efforts to transform assessment practices.

If performance-based assessments that are currently being developed point at more challenging learning goals for all students, they may ameliorate some of the current test-induced sources of inequality (Darling-Hammond, 1994; Glaser, 1990). However, this will be true only to the extent that teachers are able to teach in the ways demanded by these assessments—that is, in ways that support the development of higher-order thinking and performance skills and in ways that diagnose and build upon individual learners' strengths and needs. Equalization of educational opportunities must rest as much on improving the caliber of teaching encountered by low-income and minority students as it does on changing the testing instruments or other technologies of schooling to which they are subject.

POLICY FOR EQUALITY: TOWARD EQUALIZATION OF EDUCATIONAL OPPORTUNITY

The common assumption about educational inequality is that it resides primarily in those students who come to school with inadequate capacities to benefit from what education the school has to offer. In line with the sorting philosophy described above, students must prove themselves "worthy" to receive a rich, challenging, and thoughtful curriculum. If they do not, the fault is thought to be in their own capacities as learners, not in the schools' capacities to teach them. Too few policy makers, educators, and members of the public at large presume that students are entitled to such a curriculum as a matter of course. In fact, some state defendants have countered school finance cases arguing for equalization of school expenditures with assertions that equalization is not required unless it can be proven that equal expenditures will produce equal outcomes.

The fact that U.S. schools are structured such that students routinely receive dramatically unequal learning opportunities based on their race and social status is simply not widely recognized. If the academic outcomes for minority and low-income children are to change, aggressive action must be taken to change the caliber and quantity of learning opportunities they encounter. These efforts must include equalization of financial resources; changes in curriculum and testing policies and practices; and improvements in the supply of highly qualified teachers to all students.

Resource Equalization

Progress in equalizing resources to students will require attention to inequalities at all levels—among states, districts, schools within districts, and students differentially placed in classrooms, courses, and tracks that offer substantially disparate opportunities to learn. As a consequence of systematic inequalities at each of these levels, minority and low-income students are not only frequently "at risk" from poverty or community factors, they are placed further at risk by the schools they attend.

Special programs such as compensatory or bilingual education will never be effective at remedying underachievement so long as these services are layered on a system that educates minority and low-income children so poorly to begin with. The presumption that "the schools are fine, it's the children who need help" is flawed. The schools serving large concentrations of low-income and minority students are generally not fine, and many of their problems originate with district and state policies and practices that place the schools at risk as well.

The inherently unequal effect of current policies should be considered as attention focuses on the special circumstances of the students put at greatest disadvantage by those policies. Current initiatives to create special labels and programs for "at-risk" children and youth are unlikely to succeed if they do not attend to the structural conditions of schools that place children at risk, not only from their home or community circumstances but from their school experiences as well. Pressures are great to respond to special circumstances with special categorical programs, and the tradition of succumbing to those pressures in an add-on fashion is well established, in education as in other areas of national life. But special programs, with all their accoutrements of new rules and procedures, separate budgets, and fragmented, pull-out programs, will be insufficient so long as the status quo remains unchanged in more significant ways.

As the 1992 interim report of an independent commission on Chapter 1 observes: "Given the inequitable distribution of state and local resources, the current notion that Chapter 1 provides supplemental aid to disadvantaged children added to a level playing field is a fiction" (Commission on Chapter 1, 1992, p. 4). The commission proposes that each state be held accountable for assuring comparability in "vital services" among all its districts as well as in all schools within each district. Among these vital services, perhaps the most important is highly qualified teachers, not just for specific Chapter 1 services but for all classrooms.

The new wave of school finance lawsuits that are challenging both within-state and within-district resource allocation disparities is promising. These suits are increasingly able to demonstrate how access to concrete learning opportunities is impaired by differential access to money, and how these learning opportunities translate into academic achievement for students. Intradistrict suits challenging the unequal distribution of qualified teachers and other curriculum opportunities are also being considered in many cities, following an initial success in Los Angeles (*Rodriguez et al. v. Los Angeles,* 1992). These strategies should continue to be pursued.

The goal of these activities should be to ensure that, at least at the state level where constitutional responsibility for education resides, all students have access—both across and within districts—to equal financial resources, adjusted for student poverty and cost-of-living differentials. Ferguson's (1991) recommendation that equalization focus on district capacity to hire high-quality teachers is an important one with empirical support. In addition to the weight of evidence indicating the central importance of qualified teachers to student learning, there is real-world experience with the positive effects of such policies on teacher quality and distribution. When Connecticut raised and equalized beginning teacher salaries under its 1986 Education Enhancement Act, shortages of teachers (including those that had plagued urban areas) evaporated. By 1989 many teaching fields showed surpluses, leading the state to consider ending its alternative certification program, since it appeared an expedient no longer necessary to staff schools (Darling-Hammond, 1992; Bliss, 1992). This is a useful beginning point for other policies aimed at equalizing access to good teaching.

Curriculum and Assessment Reform

Many studies have pointed out that the curriculum offered to most students in most U.S. schools is geared toward lower-order "rote" skills (National Assessment for Educational Progress [NAEP], 1981; Boyer, 1983; Goodlad, 1984; Sizer, 1984), and that it is far less challenging than that encountered by the

majority of students in many other countries (McKnight et al., 1987). As in times of past national concern—for example, the post-Sputnik years—major curriculum reform projects have been launched by the federal government as well as by many states.

These efforts to create a "thinking curriculum" for all students are important to individual futures and to our national welfare. They are unlikely to pay off, however, unless other critical changes are made as well. Among these are changes in the ways U.S. schools track students in order to differentiate curriculum, and the ways in which teachers are prepared and supported. Although mounting evidence indicates that low-tracked students are disadvantaged by current practice and that high-ability students do not benefit more from homogeneous classrooms than from heterogeneous grouping, the long-established American tracking system will be difficult to reform until there is an adequate supply of well-trained teachers. Such teachers must be prepared both to teach the more advanced curriculum that U.S. schools now fail to offer most students and to assume the challenging task of teaching many kinds of students with diverse needs, interests, aptitudes, and learning styles in integrated classroom settings.

Other important changes concern the types and uses of achievement tests in U.S. schools. As a 1990 study of the implementation of California's new mathematics curriculum framework points out, when a curriculum reform aimed at problem solving and the development of higher-order thinking skills encounters an already-mandated rote-oriented basic skills testing program, the tests win out (Darling-Hammond, 1990a). As one teacher put it:

Teaching for understanding is what we are supposed to be doing ... [but] the bottom line here is that all they really want to know is how are these kids doing on the tests.... They want me to teach in a way that they can't test, except that I'm held accountable to the test. It's a Catch 22.... (S. Wilson, 1990, p. 318)

Initiatives to develop more complex and authentic modes of assessment may begin to offset this problem. But the bigger issue for enhancing learning opportunities is how tests are used. Many current proposals for performance-based assessment view these new kinds of tests as serving the same screening and tracking purposes as more traditional tests, assuming that more "authentic" assessments would both motivate and sort students more effectively. Others see a primary goal of assessment reform as transforming the purposes and uses of testing as well as its form and content. They argue for shifting the use of assessment from a sorting device to a tool for identifying student strengths and needs so that teachers can adapt instruction more successfully (Glaser, 1981, 1990).

Assessment initiatives that hope to embed authentic assessment in the ongoing processes of teaching and curriculum development share the view offered by Glaser (1990) that schools must move from a selective mode to an adaptive mode. They must shift from an approach "characterized by minimal variation in the conditions for learning" in which "a narrow range of instructional options and a limited number of paths to success are available" (p. 16), to one in which "conceptions of learning and modes of teaching are adjusted to individuals—their backgrounds, talents, interests, and the nature of their past performances and experiences" (p. 17). Fundamental agreement with this view leads to a rejection of the traditional use of testing, even performance-based testing, as an externally controlled tool for the allocation of educational opportunities. If teachers are to engage in the pursuit of "individually configured excellence" (Gardner, 1991) for all students, they must be able to tap multiple intelligences and employ multiple pathways to learning. As students are offered wider opportunities for learning and the assessment of their achievement becomes an integral part of learning and teaching, assessments must provide multidimensional views of performance that inform ever more effective instruction.

The outcomes of the current wave of curriculum and assessment reforms will depend in large measure on the extent to which assessment developers and users use assessments in ways that serve teaching and learning rather than sorting and selecting; pursue broader reforms to improve and equalize access to educational resources and opportunities; and support the professional development of teachers along with the organizational development of schools, so that assessment is embedded in teaching and learning, and is used to inform more skillful and adaptive teaching that enables more successful learning for all students (Darling-Hammond, 1994).

Investing in Good Teaching for All Students

A key corollary to this analysis of inequality is that improved opportunities for minority students will rest in part on policies that professionalize teaching by increasing the knowledge base for teaching, and on the mastery of this knowledge by all teachers permitted to practice. This means providing *all* teachers with a stronger understanding of how children learn and develop, how a variety of curricular and instructional strategies can address their needs, and how changes in school and classroom organization can support their growth and achievement.

There are two reasons for this assertion. First, the professionalization of an occupation raises the floor below which no entrants will be admitted to practice. It eliminates practices of substandard or irregular licensure that allow untrained entrants to practice disproportionately on underserved and poorly protected clients. Second, professionalization increases the overall knowledge base for the occupation, thus improving the quality of services for all clients, especially those most in need of high-quality teaching (Darling-Hammond, 1990c; Wise & Darling-Hammond, 1987).

The students who have, in general, the poorest opportunities to learn—those attending the inner-city schools that are compelled by the current incentive structure to hire disproportionate numbers of substitute teachers, uncertified teachers, and inexperienced teachers, and that lack resources for mitigating the uneven distribution of good teaching—are the students who will benefit most from measures that raise the standards of practice for all teachers. They will also benefit from targeted policies that provide quality preparation programs and financial aid for highly qualified prospective teachers who will teach in central cities and poor rural areas.

Investments in better-prepared teachers are also needed to support current education reforms that envision greater teacher responsibility in educational decisions at all levels. Restructured schools require changes in the nature of teaching work and knowledge, including a more active, integrated, and intellectually challenging curriculum, and a broader range of roles for teachers in developing curriculum and assessments of student performance; coaching and mentoring other teachers; and working more closely with families and community agencies. Because restructured schools are also redesigning classroom organization so that "push-in" rather than "pull-out" methods are more likely to be used for children with special needs, and interdisciplinary approaches to a "thinking curriculum" are more common, teachers will need to know more about both subjects and students than they have in the past. Finally, school-based management and shared decision-making initiatives rely for their success on the capacity of education practitioners to make knowledgeable judgments about curriculum and assessment, school organization, and program evaluation. Teachers will need to be prepared to make such decisions responsibly. Teacher preparation and licensing should reflect the demands of teachers' evolving roles. In addition, providing equity in the distribution of teacher quality requires changing policies and long-standing incentive structures in education so that shortages of trained teachers are overcome, and schools serving low-income and minority students are not disadvantaged by lower salaries and poorer working conditions in the bidding war for good teachers.

Building and sustaining a well-prepared teaching force will require local, state, and federal initiatives. To recruit an adequate supply of teachers, states and localities will need to upgrade teachers' salaries to levels competitive with those of college graduates in other occupations, who currently earn 25–50% more, depending on the field. This should occur as part of a general restructuring effort that places more resources as well as decision-making authority at the school level, and allocates a greater share of education dollars to classrooms than to the large bureaucracies that oversee them (see, e.g., Darling-Hammond, 1990b).

Incentive structures must be reshaped to encourage the provision of highly qualified teachers to low-income and minority students. Some models are emerging. In Charlotte–Mecklenberg, North Carolina, and in Rochester, New York, for example, master teachers who have been recognized for their demonstrated expertise can be called upon, as part of their privilege and their obligation, to teach children and create new programs in the schools that currently most lack expert teaching. In such experiments, and in the policy changes they incorporate, lies one part of the hope for equalizing opportunities to learn.

States must also strengthen teacher education and certification. In almost all colleges and universities, teacher education is more poorly funded than other schools or departments (Ebmeier, Twombly, & Teeter, 1990; Sykes, 1985). It has long been used as a revenue producer for programs that train engineers, accountants, lawyers, and future doctors. Rather than bemoaning the quality of teacher training, policy makers must invest in its improvement.

Accreditation and licensing are two major quality-control mechanisms for any profession. In the field of teaching, these mechanisms have historically been weak. Although all of the other established professions require graduation from an accredited school as one condition of the license to practice, most states do not require departments or schools of education to be accredited, nor do they require candidates for licensure to have graduated from such schools. The National Council for Accreditation of Teacher Education (NCATE) accredits only approximately 500 of more than 1,200 institutions that prepare teachers. Meanwhile, "the generally minimal state-prescribed criteria remain subject to local and state political influences, economic conditions within the state, and historical conditions which make change difficult" (Dennison, 1992).

The historic lack of rigorous standard setting in teaching is changing, however. Autonomous professional standards boards for teaching now exist in 12 states, a threefold increase over the number only a few years ago. In these 12 states educators set standards for teacher preparation and licensing and ask legislators for a mandate to enforce them, rather than legislators' setting standards themselves, as has traditionally been the case. A growing number of states are improving teacher education programs by encouraging their accreditation under the new, more rigorous standards that are being implemented by NCATE. The foundation of the new accreditation system is the body of growing knowledge about teaching and learning, including understandings about how to teach diverse learners well.

Improvement of teacher education depends as well on major changes in the content and governance of teacher licensing. Virtually no one believes that most current state licensing requirements provide meaningful standards of teacher knowledge and competence: not the public, not the profession, not even the policy makers who are themselves responsible for setting the requirements. Their willingness to avoid their own regulations by creating emergency, temporary, and alternative routes to certification is the most obvious indictment of the system they have established. Meaningful standards must be established and then met by all entrants to the profession. Shortages must be met by offering enhanced incentives to teach rather than by lowering standards, especially for those who teach children in central cities and poor rural schools. While accreditation will improve the quality of teacher education, professional licensing, coupled with targeted financial supports

for recruitment, is needed to ensure that every child will have access to a well-prepared teacher.

The federal government must play a leadership role in providing an adequate supply of well-qualified teachers just as it has in providing an adequate supply of well-qualified physicians. When shortages of physicians were a major national problem more than 30 years ago, Congress passed the 1963 Health Professions Education Assistance Act to support and improve the caliber of medical training, create and strengthen teaching hospitals, provide scholarships and loans to medical students, and create incentives for physicians to train in shortage specialties and to locate in underserved areas.

Similarly, federal initiatives in education should seek to:

1. *Recruit new teachers,* especially in shortage fields and in shortage locations, through scholarships and forgivable loans for high-quality teacher education.
2. *Strengthen and improve teachers' preparation* through improvement incentive grants to schools of education and supports for certification reform.
3. *Improve teacher retention and effectiveness* by improving clinical training and support during the beginning teaching stage, when 30–50% of new teachers drop out. This would include funding internship programs for new teachers in which they receive structured coaching and mentoring, preferably in urban schools supported to provide state-of-the-art practice.

If the interaction between teachers and students is the most important aspect of effective schooling, then reducing inequality in learning has to rely on policies that provide equal access to competent, well-supported teachers. The public education system ought to be able to guarantee that every child who is required by public law to go to school is taught by someone who is prepared, knowledgeable, competent, and caring. That is real accountability. As Grant (1989) puts it: "Teachers who perform high-quality work in urban schools know that, despite reform efforts and endless debates, it is meaningful curricula and dedicated and knowledgeable teachers that make the difference in the education of urban students" (p. 770). When it comes to equalizing opportunities for students to learn, that is the bottom line.

References

Alexander, K. L., & McDill, E. L. (1976). Selection and allocation within schools: Some causes and consequences of curriculum placement. *American Sociological Review, 41,* 963–980.

Archbald, D. A., & Newman, F. M. (1988). *Beyond standardized testing: Assessing authentic academic achievement in the secondary school.* Reston, VA: National Association of Secondary School Principals.

Armour-Thomas, E., Clay, C., Domanico, R., Bruno, K., & Allen, B. (1989). *An outlier study of elementary and middle schools in New York City: Final report.* New York: New York City Board of Education.

Ashton, P., & Crocker, L. (1986). Does teacher certification make a difference? *Florida Journal of Teacher Education, 38*(3), 73–83.

Ashton, P., & Crocker, L. (1987). Systematic study of planned variations: The essential focus of teacher education reform. *Journal of Teacher Education, 38*(3), 2–8.

Barr, R., & Dreeben, R. (1983). *How schools work.* Chicago: University of Chicago Press.

Becker, H. J. (1983). *School uses of microcomputers: Reports from a national survey.* Baltimore, MD: Johns Hopkins Center for Social Organization of Schools.

Becker, H. J. (1986). *Computer survey newsletter.* Baltimore, MD: Johns Hopkins Center for Social Organization of Schools.

Benson, C. S. (1961). *The economics of public education.* Boston: Houghton Mifflin.

Bents, M., & Bents, R. B. (1990, April). *Perceptions of good teaching among novice, advanced beginner and expert teachers.* Paper presented at the annual meeting of the American Educational Research Association, Boston.

Berliner, D. C. (1984). Making the right changes in preservice teacher education. *Phi Delta Kappan, 66*(2), 94–96.

Berliner, D. C. (1986). In pursuit of the expert pedagogue. *Educational Researcher, 15*(7), 5–13.

Berne, R. (1992). Educational input and outcome inequities in New York State. In *The road to outcome equity. Report of the New York study group on outcome equity.* Albany: New York State Education Department.

Bledsoe, J. C., Cox., J. V., & Burnham, R. (1967). *Comparison between selected characteristics and performance of provisionally and professionally certified beginning teachers in Georgia.* Washington, DC: U.S. Department of Health, Education, and Welfare.

Bliss, T. (1992). Alternate certification in Connecticut: Reshaping the profession. *Peabody Journal of Education, 69*(3), 35–54.

Bowman, B. (1993). Early childhood education. In L. Darling-Hammond (Ed.), *Review of research in education* (Vol. 19, pp. 101–134). Washington, DC: American Educational Research Association.

Boyer, E. (1983). *High School.* New York: Harper & Row.

Braddock, J., & McPartland, J. M. (1993). Education of early adolescents. In L. Darling-Hammond (Ed.), *Review of research in education* (Vol. 19, pp. 135–170). Washington, DC: American Educational Research Association.

California Commission on the Teaching Profession. (1985). *Who will teach our children?* Sacramento: Author.

California Sate Department of Education. (1984). *California high school curriculum study: Path through high school.* Sacramento: Author.

Carnegie Council on Adolescent Development. (1989). *Turning points: Preparing youth for the 21st century.* New York: Carnegie Corporation of New York.

Carter, K., & Doyle, W. (1987). Teachers' knowledge structures and comprehension processes. In J. Calderhead (Ed.), *Exploring teacher thinking* (pp. 147–160). London: Cassell.

Centra, J. A., & Potter, D. A. (1980). School and teacher effects: An interrelational model. *Review of Educational Research, 50*(2), 273–291.

Coleman, J. S., Campbell, E. Q., Hobson, C. J., McPartland, J., Mood, A. M., Weinfeld, F. D., & York, R. L. (1966). *Equality of educational opportunity.* Washington, DC: Government Printing Office.

College Board. (1985). *Equality and excellence: The educational status of Black Americans.* New York: College Entrance Examination Board.

Comer, J. P. (1988). Educating poor minority children. *Scientific American, 259*(5), 24–48.

Commission on Chapter 1. (1992). *High performance schools: No exceptions, no excuses.* Washington, DC: Author.

Conant, J. B. (1961). *Slums and suburbs.* New York: McGraw-Hill.

Cooper, E., & Sherk, J. (1989). Addressing urban school reform: Issues and alliances. *The Journal of Negro Education, 58*(3), 315–331.

Copley, P. O. (1974). *A study of the effect of professional education courses on beginning teachers.* Springfield: Southwest Missouri State University. (ERIC Document Reproduction Service No. ED 098 147)

Cremin, L. (1961). *The transformation of the school: Progressivism in American education, 1876–1957.* New York: Vintage Books.

Cremin, L. (1970). *American education: The colonial experience 1607–1783.* New York: Harper & Row.

Cubberly, E. P. (1906). *School funds and their apportionment.* New York: Teachers College Press.

Cubberly, E. P. (1919). *Public education in the United States: A study and interpretation of American educational history.* Boston: Houghton Mifflin.

Darling-Hammond, L. (1987). What constitutes a "real" shortage of teachers? Commentary. *Education Week, 6*(16), 29.

Darling-Hammond, L. (1988, Summer). Teacher quality and educational equality, *The College Board Review,* no. 148, pp. 16–23, 39–41.

Darling-Hammond, L. (1990a). Instructional policy into practice: "The

power of the bottom over the top." *Educational Evaluation and Policy Analysis, 12*(3), 233–242.

Darling-Hammond, L. (1990b). Teacher professionalism: Why and how. In A. Lieberman (Ed.), *Schools as collaborative cultures: Creating the future now.* (pp. 25–50). Philadelphia: Falmer Press.

Darling-Hammond, L. (1990c). Teacher quality and equality. In J. Goodlad & P. Keating (Eds.), *Access to knowledge: An agenda for our nation's schools* (pp. 237–258). New York: College Entrance Examination Board.

Darling-Hammond, L. (1991). The implications of testing policy for quality and equality. *Phi Delta Kappan, 73*(3), 220–225.

Darling-Hammond, L. (1992). Teaching and knowledge: Policy issues posed by alternate certification for teachers. *Peabody Journal of Education, 67*(3), 123–154.

Darling-Hammond, L. (1994). Performance-based assessment and educational equity. *Harvard Educational Review, 66*(1), 5–30.

Darling-Hammond, L., & Snyder, J. (1992). Traditions of curriculum inquiry: The scientific tradition. In P. W. Jackson (Ed.), *Handbook of Research on Curriculum.* New York: Macmillan.

Davis, D. G. (1986, April). *A pilot study to assess equity in selected curricular offerings across three diverse schools in a large urban school district.* Paper presented at the annual meeting of the American Educational Research Association, San Francisco.

Dennison, G. M. (1992). National standards in teacher preparation: A commitment to quality. In *The Chronicle of Higher Education, 39*(15), A40.

Doyle, W. (1986). Content representation in teachers' definitions of academic work. *Journal of Curriculum Studies, 18,* 365–379.

Dreeben, R. (1987). Closing the divide: What teachers and administrators can do to help Black students reach their reading potential. *American Educator, 11*(4), 28–35.

Dreeben, R., & Barr, R. (1987, April). *Class composition and the design of instruction.* Paper presented at the annual meeting of the American Education Research Association, Washington, DC.

Dreeben, R., & Gamoran, A. (1986). Race, instruction, and learning. *American Sociological Review, 51*(5), 660–669.

Druva, C. A., & Anderson, R. D. (1983). Science teacher characteristics by teacher behavior and by student outcome: A meta-analysis of research. *Journal of Research in Science Teaching, 20*(5), 467–479.

Ebmeier, H., Twombly, S., & Teeter, D. (1990). The comparability and adequacy of financial support for schools of education. *Journal of Teacher Education, 42*(3), 226–235.

Eckstrom, R., & Villegas, A. M. (1991). Ability grouping in middle grade mathematics: Process and consequences. *Research in Middle Level Education,15*(1), 1–20.

Edgewood Independent School District v. Kirby, 777 S.W. 2d 391 (Texas 1989).

Educational Research Service. (1980). *Class size: A summary of research.* Reston, VA: Author.

Educational Testing Service. (1991). *The state of inequality.* Princeton, NJ: Author.

Einbender, L. (1992). *Coming to terms with standards and standardization in student assessment.* Unpublished manuscript.

Evertson, C., Hawley, W., & Zlotnick, M. (1985). Making a difference in educational quality through teacher education. *Journal of Teacher Education, 36*(3), 2–12.

Ferguson, R. F. (1991). Paying for public education: New evidence on how and why money matters. *Harvard Journal on Legislation, 28*(2), 465–498.

Finley, M. K. (1984). Teachers and tracking in a comprehensive high school. *Sociology of Education, 57,* 233–243.

Gamoran, A. (1990, April). *The consequences of track-related instructional differences for student achievement.* Paper presented at the annual meeting of the American Educational Research Association, Boston.

Gamoran, A. (1992). Access to excellence: Assignment to honors English classes in the transition from middle to high school. *Educational Evaluation and Policy Analysis, 14*(3), 185–204.

Gamoran, A., & Berends, M. (1987). The effects of stratification in secondary schools: Synthesis of survey and ethnographic research. *Review of Educational Research, 57,* 415–436.

Gamoran, A., & Mare, R. (1989). Secondary school tracking and educational inequality: Compensation, reinforcement or neutrality? *American Journal of Sociology, 94,* 1146–1183.

Garcia, E. (1993). Language, culture, and education. In L. Darling-Hammond (Ed.), *Review of research in education* (Vol. 19, pp. 51–98). Washington, DC: American Educational Research Association.

Gardner, H. (1991). *The unschooled mind.* New York: Basic Books.

Glaser, R. (1981) The future of testing: A research agenda for cognitive psychology and psychometrics. *American Psychologist, 39*(9), 923–936.

Glaser, R. (1990). *Testing and assessment: O tempora! O mores!* Pittsburgh: University of Pittsburgh, Learning Research and Development Center.

Glass, G. V., Cahen, L. S., Smith, M. L., & Filby, N. N. (1982). *School class size: Research and policy.* Beverly Hills, CA: Sage.

Gomez, D. L., & Grobe, R. P. (1990, April). *Three years of alternative certification in Dallas: Where are we?* Paper presented at the annual meeting of the American Educational Research Association, Boston.

Good, T. L., & Brophy, J. (1987). *Looking in classrooms.* New York: Harper & Row.

Goodlad, J. (1984). *A place called school: Prospects for the future.* New York: McGraw-Hill.

Gould, S. J. (1981). *The mismeasure of man.* New York: Norton.

Grant, C. A. (1989). Urban teachers: Their new colleagues and curriculum. *Phi Delta Kappan, 70*(10), 764–770.

Greenberg, J. D. (1983). The case for teacher education: Open and shut. *Journal of Teacher Education, 34*(4), 2–5.

Grissmer, D. W., & Kirby, S. N. (1987). *Teacher attrition: The uphill climb to staff the nation's schools.* Santa Monica, CA: Rand Corporation.

Grossman, P. L. (1989). Learning to teach without teacher education. *Teachers College Record, 91*(2), 191–208.

Grossman, P. L. (1990). *The making of a teacher: Teacher knowledge and teacher education.* New York: Teachers College Press.

Guthrie, J. W., Garms, W. I., & Pierce, L. C. (1988). *School finance and education policy: Enhancing educational efficiency, equality and choice* (2nd ed.). Englewood Cliffs, NJ: Prentice Hall.

Hall, W. C., & Carroll, N. E. (1973, January). The effect of teachers' organizations on salaries and class size. *Industrial and Labor Relations Review, 26,* 834–841.

Hanushek, E. A. (1990, March). *The impact of differential expenditures on school performance.* Issue analyses, American Legislative Exchange Council, Washington, DC.

Hanushek, E. A. (1991). When school finance "reform" may not be good policy. *Harvard Journal on Legislation, 28*(2), 423–456.

Hartman, W. T. (1988). District spending disparities: What do the dollars buy? *Journal of Education Finance, 13*(4), 436–459.

Hice, J. E. L. (1970). The relationship between teacher characteristics and first-grade achievement. *Dissertation Abstracts International, 25*(1), 190.

Hobson v. Hanson, 269 F. Supp. 401, 496 (D.D.C. 1967).

Hoffer, T. B. (1992). Middle school ability grouping and student achievement in science and mathematics. *Educational Evaluation and Policy Analysis, 14*(3), 205–227.

Holmes, C. T., & Matthews, K. M. (1984). The effects of nonpromotion on elementary and junior high school pupils: A meta-analysis. *Review of Educational Research, 54,* 225–236.

Jencks, C., Smith, M., Acland, H., Bane, M. J., Cohen, D., Gintis, H., Heyns, B., & Michelson, S. (1972). *Inequality: A reassessment of the effect of family and schooling in America.* New York: Basic Books.

Johnston, J. M., & Ryan, K. (1983). Research on the beginning teacher. In K. R. Howie & W. E. Gardner (Eds.), *The education of teachers: A look ahead* (pp. 136–162). New York: Longman.

Jones, L. V. (1984). White-black achievement differences: The narrowing gap. *American Psychologist, 39,* 1207–1213.

Jones, L. V., Burton, N. W., & Davenport, E. C. (1984). Monitoring the achievement of black students. *Journal for Research in Mathematics Education, 15,* 154–164.

Kamin, L. (1974). *The science and politics of IQ.* New York: Wiley.

Kaufman, J. E., & Rosenbaum, J. E. (1992). Education and employment of low-income Black youth in White suburbs. *Educational Evaluation and Policy Analysis, 14*(3), 229–240.

Keppel, F. (1966). *The necessary revolution in American education.* New York: Harper & Row.

Kozol, J. (1991). *Savage inequalities.* New York: Crown.

Kluger, R. (1976). *Simple justice.* New York: Alfred A. Knopf.

Kulik, C. C., & Kulik, J. A. (1982). Effects of ability grouping on secondary school students: A meta-analysis of evaluation findings. *American Education Research Journal, 19,* 415–428.

Lee, V., & Bryk, A. (1988). Curriculum tracking as mediating the social distribution of high school achievement. *Sociology of Education, 61,* 78–94.

Levin, H. M. (1992). The necessary and sufficient conditions for achieving educational equity. In R. Berne (Ed.), *New York equity study.* Unpublished Report of the Equity Study Group, New York State Education Department, Albany.

LuPone, L. J. (1961). A comparison of provisionally certified and permanently certified elementary school teachers in selected school districts in New York State. *Journal of Educational Research, 55,* 53–63.

MacPhail-Wilcox, B., & King, R. A. (1986). Resource allocation studies: Implications for school improvement and school finance research. *Journal of Education Finance, 11,* 416–432.

Mann, D. (1987). Can we help dropouts? Thinking about the undoable. In G. Natriello (Ed.), *School dropouts: Patterns and policies* (pp. 3–19). New York: Teachers College Press.

Massachusetts Advocacy Center and the Center for Early Adolescence. (1988). *Before it's too late: Dropout prevention in the middle grades.* Boston: Author.

Matthews, W. (1984). Influences on the learning and participation of minorities in mathematics. *Journal for Research in Mathematics Education, 15,* 84–95.

McDonnell, L. M., Burstein, L., Ormseth, T., Catterall, J., & Moody, D. (1990). *Discovering what schools really teach: Designing improved coursework indicators.* Washington, DC: U.S. Department of Education.

McKnight, C. C., Crosswhite, J. A., Dossey, J. A., Kifer, E., Swafford, S. O., Travers, K. J., & Cooney, T. J. (1987). *The underachieving curriculum: Assessing U.S. school mathematics from an international perspective.* Champaign, IL: Stipes Publishing.

McNeil, J. D. (1974). Who gets better results with young children— Experienced teachers or novices? *Elementary School Journal, 74,* 447–451.

McUsic, M. (1991). The use of education clauses in school finance reform litigation. *Harvard Journal on Legislation, 28*(2), 307–340.

Meier, K. J., Stewart, J., Jr., & England, R. E. (1989). *Race, class, and education: The politics of second-generation discrimination.* Madison: University of Wisconsin Press.

Mercer, J. R. (1989). Alternative paradigms for assessment in a pluralistic society. In J. A. Banks & C. A. M. Banks (Eds.), *Multicultural education* (pp. 289–303). Boston: Allyn and Bacon.

Minow, M. (1991). School finance: Does money matter? *Harvard Journal on Legislation, 28*(2), 395–400.

Moore, D., & Davenport, S. (1988). *The new improved sorting machine.* Madison, WI: National Center on Effective Secondary Schools.

Moore, E. G., & Smith, A. W. (1985). Mathematics aptitude: Effects of coursework, household language, and ethnic differences. *Urban Education, 20,* 273–294.

Moskowitz, G., & Hayman, J. L. (1974). Interaction patterns of first year typical and best teachers in inner-city schools. *Journal of Educational Research, 67,* 224–230.

Murnane, R. J. (1991). Interpreting the evidence on "Does money matter?" *Harvard Journal on Legislation, 28*(2), 457–464.

Murnane, R. J., & Phillips, B. R. (1981). Learning by doing, vintage, and selection: Three pieces of the puzzle relating teaching experience and teaching performance. *Economics of Education Review, 1*(4), 453–465.

Murnane, R. J., Singer, J. D., Willett, J. B., Kemple, J. J., & Olsen, R. J. (1991). *Who will teach? Policies that matter.* Cambridge, MA: Harvard University Press.

National Assessment of Educational Progress. (1981). *Reading, thinking, and writing: Results from the 1979–80 national assessment of reading and literature.* Denver, CO: Author.

National Center for Education Statistics. (1985). *The condition of education.* Washington, DC: U.S. Department of Education.

National Center for Education Statistics. (1991). *National education longitudinal survey* (88, NCES No. 91-460). Washington, DC: Office of Educational Research and Improvement.

National Center for Education Statistics. (1992). *The condition of education.* Washington, DC: U.S. Department of Education.

New York Study Group on Outcome Equity. (1993). *The road to outcome equity: Final report of the study group on outcome equity.* (R. Berne, Ed.). Albany: New York State Education Department.

Oakes, J. (1983). Limiting opportunity: Student race and curricular differences in secondary vocational education. *American Journal of Education, 91*(3), 328–355.

Oakes, J. (1985). *Keeping track.* New Haven: Yale University Press.

Oakes, J. (1986, June). Tracking in secondary schools: A contextual perspective. *Educational Psychologist, 22,* 129–154.

Oakes, J. (1990a). *Multiplying inequalities: The effects of race, social class, and tracking on opportunities to learn mathematics and science.* Santa Monica, CA: The RAND Corporation.

Oakes, J. (1990b). Opportunities, achievement, and choice: Women and minority students in science and mathematics. In C. C. Cazden (Ed.), *Review of research in education* (Vol. 16, pp. 153–222). Washington, DC: American Educational Research Association.

Oakes, J. (1992). Can tracking research inform practice? Technical, normative, and political considerations. *Educational Researcher, 21*(4), 12–21.

Oakes, J., & Lipton, M. (1990). Tracking and ability grouping: A structural barrier to access and achievement. In J. I. Goodlad & P. Keating (Eds.), *Access to knowledge: An agenda for our nation's schools* (pp. 187–204) New York: College Entrance Examination Board.

Oakes, J., Selvin, M., Karoly, L., & Guiton, G. (1992). *Educational matchmaking: Academic and vocational tracking in comprehensive high schools.* Santa Monica, CA: The RAND Corporation.

Orfield, G. F., Monfort, F., & Aaron, M. (1989). *Status of school desegregation: 1968–1986.* Alexandria, VA: National School Boards Association.

Pascal, A. (1987). *The qualifications of teachers in American high schools.* Santa Monica, CA: The RAND Corporation.

Pelavin, S. H., & Kane, M. (1990). *Changing the odds: Factors increasing access to college.* New York: College Entrance Examination Board.

Resnick, L. B. (1987). *Education and learning to think.* Washington, DC: National Academy Press.

Robinson v. Cahill, 303 A. 2d 273, 294 (1971).

Rock, D. A., Hilton, T. L., Pollack, J., Ekstrom, R. B., & Goertz, M. E. (1985). *A study of excellence in high school education: Educational policies, school quality, and student outcomes.* Washington, DC: National Center for Education Statistics.

Rodriguez et al. v. Los Angeles Unified School District, Superior Court of the County of Los Angeles #C611358 (Consent decree filed Aug. 12, 1992).

Rosenbaum, J. (1976). *Making inequality: The hidden curriculum of high school tracking.* New York: Wiley.

Rosenbaum, J. E. (1980). Social implications of educational grouping. In D. C. Berliner (Ed.), *Review of research in education* (Vol. 8, pp. 361–401). Washington, DC: American Educational Research Association.

Rottenberg, C. J., & Berliner, D. C. (1990, April). *Expert and novice teachers' conceptions of common classroom activities.* Paper presented at the annual meeting of the American Educational Research Association, Boston.

Schofield, J. W. (1991). School desegregation and intergroup relations. In G. Grant (Ed.), *Review of research in education* (Vol. 17, pp. 335–409). Washington, DC: American Educational Research Association.

Serrano v. Priest, 487 P. 2d 1241 (1971).

Shepard, L., & Smith, M. L. (1986). Synthesis of research on school readiness and kindergarten retention. *Educational Leadership, 44*(3), 78–86.

Shulman, L. S. (1987). Knowledge and teaching: Foundations of the new reform. *Harvard Educational Review, 57*(1), 1–22.

Silard, J., & Goldstein, B. (1974, July). Toward abolition of local funding in public education. *Journal of Law and Education, 3,* 324.

Sizer, T. (1984). *Horace's compromise: The dilemma of the American high school.* Boston: Houghton Mifflin.

Slavin, R. E. (1990). Achievement effects of ability grouping in secondary schools: A best evidence synthesis. *Review of Educational Research, 60*(3), 471–500.

Strickland, D. (1985). Early childhood development and reading instruction. In C. Brooks (Ed.), *Tapping potential: English and language arts for the Black learner* (pp. 88–101). Washington, DC: National Council of Teachers of English.

Sutton, R. E. (1991). Equity and computers in the schools: A decade of research. *Review of Educational Research, 61*(4), 475–503.

Sykes, G. (1985). Teacher education in the United States. In B. R. Clark (Ed.), *The school and the university* (pp. 264–289). Los Angeles: University of California Press.

Talbert, J. E. (1990). *Teacher tracking: Exacerbating inequalities in the high school.* Stanford, CA: Center for Research on the Context of Secondary Teaching, Stanford University.

Taylor, W. L., & Piche, D. M. (1991). *A report on shortchanging children: The impact of fiscal inequity on the education of students at risk.* Prepared for the Committee on Education and Labor, U.S. House of Representatives. Washington, DC: Government Printing Office.

Trimble, K., & Sinclair, R. L. (1986, April). *Ability grouping and differing conditions for learning: An analysis of content and instruction in ability-grouped classes.* Paper presented at the annual meeting of the American Educational Research Association, San Francisco.

Tyack, D. B. (1974) *The one best system.* Cambridge, MA: Harvard University Press.

U.S. Bureau of the Census. (1989). *Current population survey, October, 1989.* Washington, DC: U.S. Department of Commerce.

U.S. Bureau of the Census. (1992). *Statistical abstract of the United States: 1992* (112th ed.). Washington, DC: U.S. Department of Commerce.

Updegraff, H., & King, L. A. (1922). *Survey of the fiscal policies of the state of Pennsylvania in the field of education*. Philadelphia: University of Pennsylvania.

Useem, E. L. (1990). You're good, but you're not good enough: Tracking students out of advanced mathematics. *American Educator, 14*(3), 24–27, 43–46.

Usiskin, Z. (1987). Why elementary algebra can, should, and must be an eighth grade course for average students. *Mathematics Teacher, 80,* 428–438.

Veenman, S. (1984). Perceived problems of beginning teachers. *Review of Educational Research, 54*(2), 143–178.

Walberg, H. (1982). What makes schooling effective. *Contemporary Education: A Journal of Review, 1,* 22–34.

Watson, B. (in press). *Essays from the underside*. Philadelphia: Temple University Press.

Wehlage, G. G., Rutter, R. A., Smith, G. A., Lesko, N., & Fernandez, R. R. (1990). *Reducing the risk: Schools as communities of support.* New York: The Falmer Press.

Wheelock, A. (1992). *Crossing the tracks.* New York: The New Press.

Wiggins, G. (1989). Teaching to the (authentic) test. *Educational Leadership, 46*(7), 41–47.

Wilson, S. (1990). A conflict of interests: Constraints that affect teaching and change. *Educational Evaluation and Policy Analysis, 12*(3), 309–326.

Winkler, J. D., Shavelson, R. J., Stasz, C., Robyn, A., & Feibel, W. (1984). *How effective teachers use microcomputers for instruction.* Santa Monica, CA: The RAND Corporaiton.

Wise, A. E. (1965). Is denial of equal educational opportunity constitutional? *Administrator's Notebook, 13,* 1–4.

Wise, A. E. (1972). *Rich schools, poor schools: The promise of equal educational opportunity.* Chicago: University of Chicago Press.

Wise, A. E., & Darling-Hammond, L. (1987). *Licensing teachers: Design for a teaching profession.* Santa Monica, CA: The RAND Corporation.

Wise, A. E., Darling-Hammond, L., & Berry, B. (1987). *Effective teacher selection: From recruitment to retention.* Santa Monica, CA: The RAND Corporation.

Wise, A. E., & Gendler, T. (1989). Rich schools, poor schools: The persistence of unequal education. *College Board Review, 151,* 12–17, 36–37.

Wong, K. K. (1989). Fiscal support for education in American states: The "parity-to-dominance" view examined. *American Journal of Education, 97*(4), 329–357.

Yudof, M. G. (1991). School finance reform in Texas: The Edgewood saga. *Harvard Journal on Legislation, 28*(2), 499–505.

LEARNING STYLES AND CULTURALLY DIVERSE STUDENTS: A LITERATURE REVIEW

Jacqueline Jordan Irvine
EMORY UNIVERSITY

Darlene Eleanor York
EMORY UNIVERSITY

The research on the learning styles of culturally diverse students is neither a panacea nor a Pandora's box. The complexity of the construct, the psychometric problems related to its measurement, and the enigmatic relationship between culture and the teaching and learning process suggest that this body of research must be interpreted and applied carefully in classrooms of culturally diverse students. The analyses presented in this chapter suggest that the widespread conclusions in the literature that African American, Hispanic, and Indian students are field-dependent learners who prosper academically when taught with comparable field-dependent teaching strategies are premature and conjectural. However, the learning-styles research has significant possibilities for enhancing the achievement of culturally diverse students. This body of research reminds teachers to be attentive not only to individual students' learning styles but to their own actions, instructional goals, methods, and materials in reference to their students' cultural experiences and preferred learning environments.

Consequently, the purpose of this chapter on the learning styles of culturally diverse students is to review critically: (a) the definitions of the construct and the instruments used to measure it; (b) assumptions regarding the cultural influences on teaching and learning; (c) conclusions about the field-dependent learning styles of African American, Hispanic, and Indian students; (d) suggested field-dependent teaching strategies; (e) problems of the learning-styles research; and (f) potential promises of the learning-styles research.

DEFINITIONS AND INSTRUMENTATION

The concept of learning styles is based on the theory that an individual responds to educational experiences with consistent behavior and performance patterns. These patterns are composed of a constellation of cognitive, affective, and physiological behaviors that are created and maintained by the interaction of culture, personality, and brain chemistry (American Association of School Administrators, 1991; Bennett, 1990). Technically, *learning styles* is an umbrella term encompassing three distinct styles or substyles: cognitive, affective, and physiological.

The division of learning styles into cognitive styles, affective styles, and physiological styles serves both to differentiate and to specify related research. Cognitive-styles research, for example, focuses on how learners prefer to receive and process information and experiences, how they create concepts, and how they retain and retrieve information. Affective-styles research, in contrast, emphasizes differences in interpersonal skills and self-perception, curiosity, attention, motivation, arousal, and persistence. Finally, physiological-styles research measures how gender, circadian rhythms, nutrition, and general health impact learning processes. In education, the central focus of research is on cognitive styles, defined by Messick (1984) as "characteristic self-consistencies in information processing that develop in congenial ways around underlying personality trends" (p. 61). Thus, although cognitive styles can be distinguished theoretically from affective and physiological styles, in research and in practice the terms *learning style* and *cognitive style* are often used interchangeably.

When learning-styles measures began to appear, the diagnosis of a specific student-learning preference seemed so simple and accessible, its applicability so apparent, and its potential so vast that learning-style identification was believed to be a fundamental key in reconceptualizing what educators meant by thinking and learning. Contributing theorists such as Benjamin Bloom (1976) proposed that learning occurred as a result of the interactions of an individual's prior knowledge, attitudes toward learning, self-perception, and his or her immediate environment. Others suggested that "thinking" could be subdivided into several distinct, measurable processes (McKenney & Keen, 1974). Kolb's (1984) theory that learning is a cycle based on the learner's preferences for some combination of concrete-abstract and reflective-active experiential learning dimensions further enhanced the idea that learning is a negotiated activity, not the display of an ascriptive ability. These theories have called into question both the appropriateness and efficacy of the traditional search for "pure" intelligence.

Maintaining a theoretical distinction between learning style and ability has proven difficult. For example, Anthony Gregorc (1979) explored "mindstyles," suggesting that learners filter, order, process, and evaluate information congruent with their perceptions of reality. These filtering, ordering, processing, and evaluative functions seem related both to ability and style. Gregorc suggests that learning ability is mediated by deep psychological constructs, sociocultural variables, and socialization patterns—a consortium influencing learning style. More recently, Howard Gardner (1983) suggested that the interaction of culture, affect, and cognition allows the learner to develop "multiple intelligences," including spatial sensitivity, musical ability, kinesthetic/body intelligence, interpersonal intuition, and deep knowledge of oneself. Hence the theoretical distinction between style and ability is unclear.

In a recent review of cognitive styles research, Tiedemann (1989) used Messick's (1984) contrasting properties of cognitive styles and intellectual abilities as a means of differentiating style from ability. First, intellective abilities concern the learner's scope of information, the level of complexity of the information, and the quality and speed of information processing. Cognitive styles concern how the information is processed, the modes or patterns of information processing.

Second, ability implies a "measurement of competencies in terms of maximal performance, with the emphasis on accuracy and correctness of response" (Tiedemann, 1989, p. 263). In contrast, style is a measure of preference or habit. It measures not potentials, but propensities.

Third, ability is unidimensional. That is, it is a higher measure of some ability, such as abstract reasoning, and implies that more of that particular competency is present in the learner with a higher score than in the learner with a lower score. Cognitive style, however, is presumed to be multidimensional. Ranges of style indicate a variety of cognitive responses; each direction is a type of zero-sum equation. For example, a learner whose style is less concrete is therefore more abstract.

Fourth, the multidimensionality of styles implies that all styles are appropriate within given learning contexts, and when the context is congruent with style, learners with that style may enjoy an advantage. The measure of ability is presumed to be more universal: Higher-ability learners are believed to have an advantage over those with lower abilities in every learning context.

Fifth, ability indicates the presence of domain-specific competencies such as verbal or mathematical ability. Cognitive styles, however, represent learning preferences across domains and thus may signal the pattern of underlying personality constructs.

Finally, ability is viewed as a variable that helps or enables the learner to achieve a given competency. Style, in contrast, is presumed to be a variable that "contribute[s] to the selection, combination, and sequence of both substance and process" as well as regulating "the direction, duration, intensity, range, and speed of functioning" (Tiedemann, 1989, p. 263). In other words, ability aids behavioral competency; style organizes and controls the processing of information.

Since the development of learning-style theory, a search has been underway to capture and observe distinct cognitive, affective, and physiological behaviors. Testing instruments have been developed in recent years in an attempt to measure different styles and to categorize them along a meaningful and reliable continuum. More than 30 learning-styles instruments have been constructed, and the tests have been administered to a broad cross-section of populations. Table 27–1 is a representative, though not exhaustive, list of some of the major learning-styles instruments presently in use.

Despite the continuing popularity of the instruments, the surrounding research has not fully supported the underlying theory of learning styles. As early as 1963, Zigler suggested that cognitive-style instruments were confounded with measures of cognitive ability, a distinction that continues to be problematic. Other researchers have addressed other problems. Paulsen (1978), for example, suggests that cognitive style may be partially a function of physiological maturity. O'Leary, Calsyn, and Fauria (1980), in a comparison test of brain-impaired and non-impaired subjects, found that learning-styles instruments may measure cognitive impairment more accurately than they do underlying personality constructs. Many have suggested that learning-styles measures are gender related (Zeitoun & Fowler, 1981) or age related (Gjerde, Block, & Block, 1985). Furthermore, several learning-style tests, such as the Rod-and-Frame Test (RFT) and the Group Embedded Figures Test (GEFT), which are designed to measure the same construct, have produced low correlations when administered to the same subjects (Witkin, Dyk, Faterson, Goodenough, & Karp, 1962). Hence, the theory and measurement of learning styles are the focus of ongoing debate. In broad terms, the concept of learning style continues to face three central challenges: (a) the persistence of weak links between instruments and theory; (b) the persistence of internal weaknesses in the learning-style instruments themselves, particularly the difficulties with validity and reliability; and (c) the importance of these weaknesses in light of the growing popularity of the instruments and calls for the creation

TABLE 27–1. Selected Learning-Styles Identification Instruments

Title and Reference	Assessment Type	Categories of Learners	Format Style and Length
ELSIE (Edmonds Learning Style Identification Exercise) (Reinert, 1976)	Cognitive style	Visualization Reading Listening Kinesthetic	50 common English words are analyzed according to learner's patterns of response.
GEFT (Group Embedded Figures Test) (Witkin, 1971)	Cognitive style	Analytical Global	Subjects are asked to identify simple shapes hidden in complex figures. The test takes 15 minutes.
Transaction Ability Inventory (Gregorc, 1982)	Cognitive style	Concrete Abstract Random Sequential	Subjects rank their responses to learning using 40 words in 10 sets of 4 words each.
Cognitive Profiles (Letteri, 1980)	Cognitive style	Field independence/ dependence Scan/focus Breadth of categorization Cognitive complexity/ simplicity Reflectiveness/ impulsiveness Leveling/sharpening Tolerant/intolerant	7 separate tests used in combination to predict standardized achievement-test scores.
Group Embedded Figures Test (Witkin, 1971)	Cognitive style	Field-dependence Field-independence	15-minute test in which subjects must find geometric figures within larger patterns, differentiated by task.
MFFT (Matching Familiar Figures Test) (Kagan, 1965)	Cognitive style	Impulsivity-reflectivity	12 pictures are shown with, in each case, 6 alternatives, only one of which is correct. Impulsives tend to choose more quickly and inaccurately than reflectives.
Student Motivation Information Form (Wlodkowski, 1978)	Affective style	Intrinsic motivation Extrinsic motivation	35 incomplete sentences are used to elicit information about motivation.
I/E Scale (Rotter, 1959)	Affective style	Internal/external locus of control	29 paired alternatives that describe beliefs about life events. Subjects choose one alternative they believe to be true.
LSI (Learning Style Inventory) (Dunn, Dunn, & Price, 1978)	Learning style	Environmental Emotional Sociological Physical	Comprehensive style indicator containing 36 computer-scored subscales.
MBTI (Myers-Briggs Type Indicator) (Myers & Briggs, 1976)	Learning style	Judgment Perception Introversion Extraversion Feeling Thinking Sensing Intuition	550 questions assessing multilevel personality indicators. Requires training to administer and score.
CSII (Cognitive Style Interest Inventory) (Hill, 1971)	Learning style	Abstract Visual Tactile Auditory Coordination Social interaction	Self-reported ranking of learning preferences and beliefs. Test takes 50 minutes.
Swassing-Barbe Modality Index (Barbe & Swassing, 1979)	Learning style	Visual Auditory Tactile/kinesthetic	Subject must process the order of geometric shapes in each of the three modalities. Scores from each tell the preferred modality.

Note: No measures exist to isolate physiological style preferences. The learning-styles measures include both cognitive and affective; those listed also contain items that address physiological aspects of learning.

of style-sensitive educational environments based on the results of learning-style measures.

Recent reviews of learning style have been critical of both the theory and instrumentation used to explain and identify style. For example, in a longitudinal study of children at ages 3, 4, 5, and 11, Gjerde et al. (1985) found that the consistency of error scores over time using the Matching Familiar Figures Test (MFFT) was related to IQ measures. They conclude that this learning-style instrument may measure cognitive competence rather than the underlying theoretical construct of conceptual tempo it is designed to measure. Similarly, in a thorough review of the research on the 1976 Learning Style Inventory (LSI), Atkinson (1991) found that the design strategy, reliability, and validity of the inventory were largely unsupported by the research evidence. Furthermore, Atkinson suggests that the revised LSI, the LSI 1985, may be vulnerable to similar weaknesses. The "feeling," "watching," "thinking," and "doing" differences in preferred learning modalities remain unsubstantiated. Tiedemann (1989), in a review of the research on five theoretical characteristics believed to qualify as style indicators, concludes that the research fails to support the theory or to legitimize the continued use of style measures: "The gap between the conceptual and empirical level is enormous. It cannot be reduced by revising the theory" (p. 272). Tiedemann's criticisms rest in what he views as an irreconcilable conflict. If the theory were modified to "fit" research results, Tiedemann argues that the current concept of learning style would have to be abandoned. If, however, current definitions of the concept are retained, some new method of measuring the concept is needed. Researchers have as yet had little success in devising an instrument that operationally distinguishes "behavior correlates of different performance dimensions," or competence, from style (p. 273).

There has been rapid growth, not only in the use of learning-style measures within education, but also in the research surrounding learning styles. Even a cursory examination of the educational and psychological research literature reveals several thousand studies conducted within the last decade. One area of interest has been the link between measures of learning style and academic achievement. This is an important field of examination, particularly since learning-style theory suggests that educational experiences designed to be more congruent with student learning style may enhance academic achievement.

The prediction (not simply the correlation) of academic achievement plays a critical role in both research and application. In research, the presence of predictive validity enables one to forecast individual performance or estimate current performance on variables that are different from a learning-styles inventory (American Psychological Association, 1966). This form of validity is an important tool in educational test design and construction. In practice, the prediction of performance based on the results of a test can exert a powerful influence over thousands of transactions between teacher and student. When children's scores on a learning-style measure are used as a predictor of future achievement, and when teaching and learning environments are correspondingly mediated to enhance future achievement, the strength of the predictive validity of learning-styles measures becomes apparent.

Since 1966, only 29 studies have been conducted measuring the predictive validity of learning-styles instruments. Of those published since 1978, several address predictive validity in areas other than academic achievement, such as studies that try to predict emotional or psychological maturity, levels of skill, or coordination in sports. Other studies examine whether learning-styles instruments can be used to predict career choices. Several others draw from a preschool or postsecondary population. However, there are limited studies published since 1978 that test the predictive validity of learning-styles instruments relative to academic achievement among K–12 populations; this research can be analyzed using the categories of field dependence/independence, locus of control, impulsivity-reflectivity, and other learning-styles measures.

Field Dependence/Independence

Field dependence/independence refers to psychological constructs that define the ways individuals respond cognitively to confusing information or unfamiliar situations. These responses produce observable behaviors. Field-dependent behaviors include high levels of impulsivity, low reflectivity, and reliance on the social environment and on authority figures. Field-dependent persons prefer to work with people rather than in isolation and tend to conform to the prevailing social context. Field-independent behaviors are more conceptual and analytical in nature. Field-independent persons tend to be autonomous, detached, goal oriented, and self-aware. Neither of these styles is mutually exclusive. All individuals may exhibit, at different times, elements of both field-dependent and field-independent behaviors (Ramirez & Castaneda, 1974; Saracho & Spodek, 1984).

In a 1978 study, Buriel tested a mixture of Mexican American and Anglo American first and second graders and compared them with a mixture of Mexican American and Anglo American third and fourth graders to see if three separate measures of field dependence/field independence could predict achievement on reading and math sections of the Metropolitan Achievement Test. Only one instrument, the Children's Embedded Figures Test (CEFT), revealed a relationship strong enough to predict mathematics scores, and only for Mexican American children. Given achievement domains, culture, gender, and age, Buriel found that none of the instruments used to measure field dependence/independence could predict academic achievement.

In a later study of the predictive strength of field dependence/independence, Swanson (1980) tested learning-disabled third-grade females. The CEFT, the Nowicki-Strickland Locus of Control test for children, and an intelligence test were given, and the results compared with scores on the Peabody Achievement Test in reading and mathematics. Swanson, like Buriel (1978), found that the CEFT contained some predictive power, but related more to intelligence than to style. Swanson concludes that learning-style measures are no better than IQ tests for predicting academic achievement.

Blaha (1982) measured fifth-grade African American and White children in three domains: attitude toward reading, locus of control measure, and field dependency/independency. The measures were used to predict scores on the Iowa Test of Basic

Skills (ITBS) in reading, mathematical concepts, and mathematical computation. Blaha found that attitude toward reading was strongly related to reading achievement. Field independence related more strongly to reading achievement than to achievement in mathematics. The locus of control measure proved to be an important predictor for reading and mathematical computation but not for mathematical concepts. These results call into question the generalizability of learning styles and the validity of learning-styles measures. Interestingly, Blaha found no predictions that could be made based on gender or race.

Taken together, these three studies challenge the ability of current field-dependence/independence measures to predict academic achievement. Three problems exist. First, there seems to be no configuration of school-aged subjects that has yet established a predictive relationship. For example, although testing has involved different-aged male and female children from different cultures, from different backgrounds, and with different abilities, no "group style" has been found that can predict academic achievement. Second, although there are some indications that some tests seem related to the achievement of some children, the relationship does not establish one of the fundamental tenets of learning-style theory: that "style" supersedes content-based knowledge. For example, tests of field independence that show the presence of a dominant learning style in reading should show evidence of the same preferred style in mathematics as well. They do not. Finally, these learning-styles measures fail to produce as strong a predictive relationship as intelligence tests. In theory, learning style may be distinct from learning ability, but the instruments used to measure style have made little distinction between them.

Locus of Control

The distinction between internal and external locus of control was first measured by Julian Rotter (1959). His I/E Scale measures the degree to which respondents feel some sense of control over their lives. For example, a student who believes that high test scores occur because of a "lucky pencil" is more externally controlled than one who believes that high test scores are attributable to drive and effort.

As pointed out earlier, Blaha (1982) found that locus of control was a predictor of reading and mathematical computation but not of mathematical concepts. Other researchers have examined the strength of locus of control measures as predictors of academic achievement. For example, in a study of third, fourth, and fifth graders, Creek, McDonald, and Ganley (1991) divided the children into gifted (average IQ of 140) and nongifted (average IQ of 120). They then subdivided the groups, using the Nowicki-Strickland Locus of Control Scale, into those internally motivated and externally motivated. All the children were given the California Achievement Test. The test results showed that the nongifted internals scored as high as the gifted externals. As noted earlier, the relationships among intelligence, style, and achievement are unclear. If learning styles supersede intelligence in the determination of school achievement, then Creek, McDonald, and Ganley's work should have produced different results. Instead, their results suggest that the

construct of learning styles and the instruments used to measure it are receiving more attention than they deserve.

Impulsivity-Reflectivity

Impulsivity and reflectivity refer to the speed and accuracy of a student's response to questions. An impulsive learner is one who is likely to answer quickly and inaccurately; a reflective learner is likely to take more time pondering a question (Becker, Bender, & Morrison, 1978).

In a longitudinal study of kindergarten children, Wood (1979) investigated the predictive power of four measures of cognitive style. She tested the kindergarten children using the MFFT, an instrument designed to measure potential learning problems, the Metropolitan Readiness Test (MRT), and the teacher's assessment of student self-concept. At the end of their first-grade year, these measures were compared with their scores on the ITBS. Wood found that none of the measures predicted achievement scores. The single exception was the MFFT, which predicted achievement for boys only, and only when the MRT was removed from the equation.

In another study of impulsivity-reflectivity, Margolis and Brannigan (1978) found that impulsivity predicts achievement in reading. They also used a kindergarten sample of average-ability children, administering the MRT, the MFFT, and several other cognitive-style measures. These results were compared with scores on a reading inventory. Although Margolis and Brannigan found that impulsivity is related to achievement, it is perhaps significant that separate equations for achievement were calculated based on outcomes from the MFFT. This reliance on a single measure of impulsivity-reflectivity, coupled with their small sample size ($n = 22$ for each group), suggests the need for replication of the study.

Butter, Kennedy, and Shoemaker-Kelly (1982) used a similar design to measure third-grade children whose IQ scores were unknown. The MFFT was administered, as was the Auditory Impulsivity Test (AIT)—a test of how well students can select a series of sounds that mimics a previously heard series of beeps and pauses. These results were compared with the California Achievement Test of reading comprehension and vocabulary. Butter et al. found that both cognitive-styles measures predicted reading achievement; however, the combined scores accounted for only 22% of the variance in achievement. In this study, both reflectives and impulsives were considered in a single regression equation. Furthermore, because no IQ scores were taken, it is unclear how well the instruments predict compared to intelligence tests.

Other Learning-Styles Measures

Raile (1980) compared outcomes on the Structure of Intellect–Learning Abilities Test (SOILAT) with a test that predicts foreign-language achievement. The tests were administered to secondary students enrolled in Spanish classes and in French classes, and to students not enrolled in foreign-language classes. Raile found that, although there was a significant relationship between the measures, the relationship was not consistent across the two foreign languages. Furthermore, the correlations between bilingual Mexican American students and English-speaking students studying a foreign language were insignificant. Although some of the six SOILAT subtests showed a greater predictive ability than others, the test was an inconclusive predictor of achievement.

Asbury, Stokes, Adderley-Kelly, and Knuckle (1989) tested 100 right-handed African American sixth graders. In all, 16 predictor variables were tested, including intelligence, dexterity, ethnic identity, and brain function. These were used to categorize the students into a modified scoring scheme of the Wechsler Intelligence Scale for Children-Revised (WISC-R) and to compare with students' grades in academic subjects. Asbury et al. found no predictive ability from ethnic identity, but they did find that the Symbol Digit Modalities Test (SDMT)—a test that asks respondents to substitute numbers for geometric designs in written and oral responses—was significant and was also related to IQ scores. Along with the SDMT, gender was also a significant predictor, leading the authors to conclude that "sex, an organismic variable, and SDMT-O, a neuropsychological measure . . . may suggest an intimate connection between physiological function . . . and test performance" (p. 188).

In another interesting study of the relationship of learning styles to achievement, Kampwirth and MacKenzie (1989) tested first graders using the Swassing-Barbe Modalities Index (SBMI) and the visual and auditory subtests of the Illinois Test of Psycholinguistic Abilities (ITPA). These were compared with the children's scores on a lesson in which they were to learn nonsense words. The children were assigned to two groups based on their learning style preferences. In one group a lesson in the words was presented using primarily auditory teaching methods; in the other group primarily visual teaching methods were presented. Kampwirth and MacKenzie found that the strongest correlations were between the scores of the children taught by auditory means and those taught by visual means. No significant difference between groups or methods was noted. Children whose learning-style tests indicated a preferred modality were taught in accordance with that modality, but even under those circumstances the learning-style measures could not predict the achievement of the children.

Although all learning-style measures have produced equivocal findings on many different scales of reliability and prediction, these results across the field-dependence/independence, locus of control, reflectivity-impulsivity, and other dimensions suggest that learning-style instruments perform more of a dialogic than a diagnostic function. Results from learning-styles measures may alert both teachers and students to individual learning preferences, but to use the results as an indicator of potential achievement is clearly unwarranted from research findings. Furthermore, while teachers who utilize a variety of teaching styles undoubtedly encourage learning in their students, a repertoire of teaching styles tailored to the learning styles of students will not assure student achievement because there is evidence that matching teaching styles with learning style will not predict achievement (Kampwirth & Mackenzie, 1989). This research suggests that a wider, more inclusive understanding of children is necessary in order to encourage achievement.

THE RELATIONSHIP BETWEEN LEARNING STYLES AND CULTURE

Culture is the sum total of ways of living (Hoopes & Pusch, 1979), a way of life that is shared by members of a population (Ogbu, 1988) and includes rites and rituals, legends and myths, artifacts and symbols, and language and history, as well as "sense-making devices that guide and shape behavior" (Davis, 1984, p. 10). Culture is what one thinks is important (values); what one thinks is true (beliefs); and how one perceives things are done (norms) (Owens, 1987).

The cultures of students of color or their "way of life" (Ogbu, 1988) are often incongruous with expected middle-class cultural values, beliefs, and norms of schools. These cultural differences often result in cultural discontinuity or lack of cultural synchronization between the student and the school (Irvine, 1990), and has led researchers to conclude that cultural differences, particularly differences among mainstream and diverse students' approaches to learning, are major contributors to the school failure of students of color.

Bennett (1990) identifies five cultural factors that appear to influence learning: (a) childhood socialization, (b) sociocultural tightness, (c) ecological adaptation, (d) biological effects, and (e) language. *Childhood socialization* refers specifically to the child-rearing practices of a particular culture. For example, authoritative socialization practices are associated with field dependence, laissez-faire practices with field independence. Serpell (1976) claims that mothers of field dependents hamper independence in their children because they tend to be overly protective, restrictive of their children's exploration and originality, impulsive and arbitrary disciplinarians, and overly indulgent. Chimezie (1988) attributes African American children's more developed motor proficiency skills to the observed fact that African American mothers have more physical contact with their babies than do Euro-American mothers. Since African American homes generally have more people in them, African American children receive more frequent and intense verbal and physical stimulation than White children. Bermudez's (1986) research on Hispanics concludes that Hispanic parenting styles are significantly different from the parenting styles of Anglos. She found that Hispanic parents were less likely than Anglo parents to encourage self-dependent and analytic skills.

The concept of *sociocultural tightness* (Hall, 1989) distinguishes between high- and low-context cultures. High- and low-context cultures differ along several dimensions: time orientation, social roles, interpersonal relations, reasoning, verbal messages, and social organization. Field-dependent learning styles are typical for individuals in high-context cultures. For example, high-context cultures operate on polychronic time, with loose schedules and multiple and simultaneous activities. Knowledge is gained through intuition and spiral logic. Low-context cultures are thought to operate on tight schedules with linear events, with knowledge gained through analytical reasoning.

Ecological adaptation affects learning styles. For example, some cultures depend on highly developed perceptual skills for survival in their environment. Navajo children are taught to recognize their families' herd at great distances and are cognizant of danger signs of changing weather and approaching predators (Swisher & Deyhle, 1989).

The *biological effects* refer to such factors as nutrition, physical development, and brain development. McShane and Plas (1982) conclude that the psychoneurological literature suggests that Indians may have a neurologically based cognitive style that "may interfere in some cases with left hemisphere processing of its own specialized function, resulting in deficit linguistic processing and overuse of the spatial mode" (p. 14). They also suggest that otitis media, or middle-ear infection, a condition that plagues half of the Indian population, may be related to Indian students' preference for certain learning styles. Pasteur and Toldson (1982) hypothesize that African Americans and Whites are governed by different hemispheres of the brain. These authors note that African Americans are thought to be right-brain dominated—intuitive, nonverbal, creative, spontaneous, and expressive—while Whites are likely to be left-brain dominated—logical, mathematical, and sequential. Perhaps the most extreme example of the biological basis of learning style is the assertion by Dunn, Gemake, and Jalali (1990) that boys are less able to sit for long periods of time because they are "less well padded exactly where they need to be" (p. 71). These authors conclude that there appears to be a biological basis for learning style.

Finally, *language* is an important variable in learning style. For African American students, there are obvious differences from mainstream language usages not only in students' pronunciation, vocabulary, rhythm, pacing, and inflection, but also in assumptions regarding what is spoken and left unspoken, whether one interrupts, defers to others, or asks direct or indirect questions (Erickson, 1986). Many Asian and Hispanic students who are not native speakers encounter barriers in school because their language is not valued and is perceived as a cultural deficit rather than an asset. Some researchers believe that the Navajo language has influenced Indian students' mastery of mathematics; the absence from the language of agreed-upon meanings for concepts such as multiply, divide, if, cosine, and sine is thought to be a contributory factor to some Indian students' difficulty with certain mathematical functions and syllogistic reasoning (Bradley, 1984; Moore, 1982).

THE LEARNING STYLES OF AFRICAN AMERICAN, HISPANIC, AND INDIAN STUDENTS

In spite of methodological, conceptual, and pedagogical problems in the learning-styles research (discussed later in this chapter), researchers persist in identifying certain learning-styles characteristics of various ethnic groups. The following represents a summary of some of these works.

African American Learning Styles

A summary of the research (Baruth & Manning, 1992; Boykin & Toms, 1985; Cushner, McClelland, & Safford, 1992; Hale-Benson, 1986; Shade, 1982, 1989a, 1989b) suggests that African Americans are field-dependent learners as contrasted to field-

independent (some writers prefer to use the terms *relational, field sensitive,* or *global* learners) and tend to:

- respond to things in terms of the whole instead of isolated parts;
- prefer inferential reasoning as opposed to deductive or inductive;
- approximate space and numbers rather than adhere to exactness or accuracy;
- focus on people rather than things;
- be more proficient in nonverbal than verbal communications;
- prefer learning characterized by variation and freedom of movement;
- prefer kinesthetic/active instructional activities;
- prefer evening rather than morning learning;
- choose social over nonsocial cues;
- proceed from a top-down processing approach rather than a bottom-up approach;
- prefer "vervistic" (Boykin & Toms, 1985) learning experiences.

Hispanic Learning Styles

The research (Baruth & Manning, 1992; Casteñeda & Gray, 1974; Grossman, 1984; Ramírez & Castañeda, 1974), like that on African American students, characterizes Hispanic students as field-dependent and relational learners, indicating that these students tend to:

- prefer group learning situations;
- be sensitive to the opinions of others;
- remember faces and social words;
- be extrinsically motivated;
- learn by doing;
- prefer concrete representations to abstract ones;
- prefer people to ideas.

Indian Learning Styles

Many researchers (Baruth & Manning, 1992; Bradley, 1984; McShane & Plas, 1982; Sawyer, 1991; Swisher & Deyhle, 1989; Tharp, 1989) have noted that Indian students also tend to be field dependent, although Shade (1989b) identifies most Indians, regardless of tribe, as field independent. However, a summary of the findings reveals that Indians tend to be field dependent, like their African American and Hispanic counterparts, and:

- prefer visual, spatial, and perceptual information rather than verbal;
- learn privately rather than in public;
- use mental images to remember and understand words and concepts rather than word associations;
- watch and then do rather than employ trial and error;

- have well-formed spatial ability;
- learn best from nonverbal mechanisms rather than verbal;
- learn experientially and in natural settings;
- have a generalist orientation, interested in people and things;
- value conciseness of speech, slightly varied intonation, and limited vocal range;
- prefer small-group work;
- favor wholistic presentations and visual representations.

SUGGESTED FIELD-DEPENDENT TEACHING STRATEGIES

Advocates believe that the closer the match between a student's learning style and the teacher's instructional methods, the more likely the student will experience academic success (Cushner et al., 1992; Gregorc, 1979; Dunn & Dunn, 1979, cited in Bennett, 1990). Shade (1982) speculates that the differences in performance between African American students and mainstream students can be related to "Afro-American cognitive or perceptual style preference which emphasizes a person rather than an object orientation" (p. 236).

Several researchers have translated these findings into recommendations for teaching and organizing instruction. Clarkson (1983) describes field-dependent instructional techniques for an "urban" learning style, although he notes that minorities and women also are likely to be field-dependent learners. He recommends that teachers develop a strong personal relationship with their students, deliver clear and direct verbal instructions, and use advance organizers in a highly structured presentation of instructional materials. He advises teachers to arrange classroom seating so that field-dependent learners are physically close to the teacher and physically distant from other students in order to minimize distractions and discourage interaction. He recommends "that nondirect teaching strategies, such as independent project work, independent seatwork, and 'do-your-own thing-times,' in the classroom *not* [emphasis in original] be used with this type of student" (p. 124).

Clarkson's work is contradictory to recommendations by Gilbert and Gay (1989), who state that field-dependent African American students function better in loosely structured, cooperative environments in which teachers and students work together. These researchers state that "multimodal, multidimensional" (p. 278) classrooms are not distracting to African American students, and "the orderly environment that the teacher considers most desirable for learning seems dull, stagnant, and unstimulating to black students" (p. 279). Hale-Benson's (1986) observations are similar, indicating that physical and motoric activities like dancing and hand clapping contribute to the achievement of African American students.

In reference to Hispanics, Ramírez and Casteñeda (1974) advise instructional methods such as cooperative learning, a curriculum humanized through use of humor, fantasy, or drama, personalized rewards, modeling, informal class discussions, global emphasis on concepts rather than attention to details, and explicit rules regarding classroom behavior. Grossman (1984) extends these researchers' work and advocates that teachers who work with Hispanic students include community group projects, use personal rewards such as hugs and pats, avoid debating as an instructional technique, avoid long-term projects in favor of daily assignments, include religion, saints, and the supernatural in the curriculum, de-emphasize the question-answer format, and stand close to the students when teaching.

A list of teaching behaviors for Indian students is presented by Sawyer (1991). She suggests that teachers avoid highlighting individual students' success, accept silence, reduce lecturing, de-emphasize competition, use personal teaching styles, allow longer pauses after questions, use whole-language approaches to language instruction, and use minimal teacher directions. Bradley (1984) cautions teachers to avoid discovery learning when planning instruction for Indian students; peer learning and learning stations with visual, motor, tactile, or auditory games or tasks are advised.

Cooperative teaching is one of the techniques most often recommended for all culturally diverse students. Slavin (1987) found that African American students' achievement is enhanced when cooperative learning groups incorporate group rewards based on group members' individual learning. He speculates that African American students excel in cooperative learning because it captures "the social and motivational dynamics of team sports" (p. 66).

PROBLEMS OF THE LEARNING-STYLES RESEARCH

The research on learning styles and culturally diverse populations should be interpreted cautiously. Several aspects of this emerging body of knowledge warrant careful consideration and further deliberation. The critical questions for consideration are:

1. Is culture the primary variable that influences learning styles of students of color? Are there other significant variables?
2. Do characteristics of the cultural group apply uniformly to individual members of the group?
3. What is the relationship between teachers' instructional methods and students' learning style?
4. Should students of color always be taught using their preferred learning style?

Critical Variables that Influence Learning Styles

The research on learning styles of culturally diverse students is based preponderantly on the cultural anthropological literature. Relevant examples can be found in the works on African Americans' African cultural retentions and are summarized by Boykin (1986), who proposes that African American culture contains at least nine interrelated dimensions: (a) spirituality—an approach in which life is viewed as vitalistic rather than mechanistic; (b) harmony—the idea that humans and nature live interdependently; (c) movement—an emphasis on rhythm, music, and dance; (d) verve—a propensity for high levels of stimulation; (e) affect—an emphasis on emotions and feelings; (f) communalism—a commitment to social connectedness; (g) expressive individualism—a value on genuine personal expression; (h) oral tradition—a preference for oral/aural communication; and (i) social time perspective—an orientation to time as social rather than material space. These observations are directly related to consequent instructional recommendations, summarized in this chapter, that suggest that African American students learn best through physical movements, personal teacher-student relationships, cooperative groups, and oral/aural communication.

Similarly, Slonim (1991) posits that Hispanic culture is founded on core values of: (a) mutualism that stresses sharing and cooperation; (b) interpersonal relationships based on trust and respect; (c) modesty in regard to personal or sexual matters; (d) a relaxed perception of time; (e) a fatalistic attitude toward life; (f) a preference for physical proximity; and (g) a value on machismo in which men embrace traditional sex-role behavior. The recommended instructional strategies for Hispanic students are synchronous with the values of cooperation and a focus on interpersonal relationships.

Although it is clear that culture, particularly ethnicity, is a powerful force that influences students' predispositions toward learning, it must be emphasized that cultural practices are learned behavior that can be unlearned and modified. Culture is neither static nor deterministic; people of color are not solely products of their culture. Consequently, culture affects individuals in different ways. Hanson (1992) states that culture is not a strict set of prescribed behaviors, but is a "framework through which actions are filtered or checked as individuals go about daily life" (p. 3). She adds that culture is constantly evolving and that although some students may share the same cultural background and predispositions, not all members of the same cultural group behave in identical ways.

Individuals who belong to a particular cultural group vary in the degree to which they identify with their culture. Banks (1987) identifies a six-stage typology of ethnic identity that traces development from ethnic psychological captivity, through ethnic encapsulation, ethnic identity clarification, biethnicity, and multiethnicity, to global competency. Banks emphasizes that his schema is not a hierarchy in the sense that individuals begin at stage one and move progressively to stage six; rather, individuals can move among the stages depending on their experiences.

The cultural influence on learning styles is mediated by such additional factors as social class and gender. Banks (1988) writes that although people in the same social class do exhibit some similar learning-styles characteristics, there is evidence that the effects of ethnicity persist across social-class segments within an ethnic group (p. 462). Women tend to be more field dependent than men (Cushner et al., 1992). Although Shade's (1989a) review of studies does not identify social class or gender differences in African American cognition, she speculates that her findings are probably related to previous researchers' omission of these variables in their work. Child-rearing practices and the home environment are also significant factors,

although Nieto (1992) notes that children raised in the same home can have different learning styles. Using the LSI, Jacobs (1990) found differences between the learning approaches of high- and low-achieving African American students. African American high achievers were teacher motivated and preferred less structure than low achievers. Bell and McGraw-Burrell (1988) found that African American high achievers shared similar learning styles with White students, a finding consistent with Kreuze and Payne's (1989) conclusion that Hispanic and White students' learning styles did not differ significantly from each other.

Not to be underestimated is the growing number of various ethnic subcultures. Valentine (1971) observes that there are at least 14 African American subcultures "with more or less distinct cultures" (p. 140). Hispanics also are represented by many subcultures. They do not all share a common language, religion, or racial identification. Hispanics in the United States come from 19 different countries and have disparate socioeconomic and migrational characteristics (Marin & Marin, 1991). These subcultural differences have surfaced in learning-styles differences. Ramírez and Castañeda (1974) found that the variability of learning styles within Hispanic populations is related to degree of assimilation, distance from the Mexican border, length of residence in the United States, degree of urbanization, and degree of prejudice experienced.

In summary, it appears that culture and ethnicity are frameworks for the development of learning-styles preferences. However, other factors can play a significant role in changing and modifying initial cultural predilections.

The Dangers of Generalizations

Stereotyping exists when exaggerated and inaccurate characteristics of a group are ascribed to an individual. This phenomenon is different from sociotyping, which involves accurate generalizations about groups (Bennett, 1990). For example, we know that the majority of students of color score lower on standardized tests than their White counterparts. This is an accurate generalization or sociotype, but it is a stereotype when extrapolated to a particular individual Indian or Hispanic student. The learning-styles research, if not carefully interpreted and implemented, poses some danger in this regard, particularly when style assumptions limit students' experiences or infer negative characteristics about ability. For example, students thought to be field dependent may be discouraged from participating in solo performances or from taking leadership roles. Negative teacher expectations can be fueled if teachers incorporate generalized and decontextualized observations about children of color without knowledge of the limitations of learning-styles labels. Research in which conclusions are unsupported or insufficiently supported by the data may be not only misleading but harmful. For example, Cureton (1978), in describing African American students' auditory skills, states: "They are not accustomed to listening for long periods" (p. 752). Dunn et al. (1990) revealed that Whites, in comparison to African Americans, prefer bright lights while learning, a trait correlated with a successive-analytic-left processing style. On the other hand, they add, low-light preference is associated with a simultaneous-global-right processing style. Based on such limited evidence, the authors conclude: "Thus Euro-Americans may be more analytical than Afro-Americans" (p. 73).

Teachers' Instructional Methods and Students' Learning Style

As indicated earlier in this chapter, numerous writers (Clarkson, 1983; Cureton, 1978; Gilbert & Gay, 1989; Ramírez & Castañeda, 1974; Sawyer, 1991) have presented recommendations that associated learning-styles research with specific instructional strategies for culturally diverse students. Other researchers (Boykin, 1986; Foster, 1989) have extended this application from teaching methods to teaching style, and inferred that there are teacher personality types that are more effective with particular groups. Boykin (1986; Boykin & Toms, 1985) describes African American students' preference for verve or high stimulation and their low tolerance for routine and monotonous tasks, and implies (Chimezie, 1988) that teachers of African American students must also be vervistic, a personality style characterized by high energy and performance. Other researchers suggest that effective teachers of African American students use a "style filled with rhythmic language, rapid intonation, and many encouraging gestures" (Foster, 1989, p. 5), with many instances of repetition, call and response, variation in pace, high emotional involvement, creative analogies, figurative language, vowel elongation, catchy phrases, gestures, body movements, symbolism, aphorisms, and lively discussions with frequent and spontaneous student participation. Foster, quoting Piestrup (1972), calls this the Black Artful Style reminiscent of the admired Black preaching style.

Irvine (1990) suggests that all children, regardless of race, would benefit from more active and stimulating teaching approaches. In his seminal work, *A Place Called School,* Goodlad (1984) observed over 1,000 classes and found that 60% of class time in elementary school was spent doing the following: preparing for and cleaning up after assignments, listening to teachers explain or lecture, and carrying out written assignments. What Goodlad discovered was a lack of variability for most children. Seldom (except in art, music, and physical education) were children being taught with methods involving physical movement, varied techniques, or high affect. There was minimal student movement, minimal student-to-student interaction, minimal teacher-to-student interaction, and minimal intimate affect. Irvine notes, "Given these conditions, all children, particularly black children, would welcome 'verve inducement' in these classrooms" (p. 91).

Kleinfeld (1992) and Shade (1989a) agree that, given the limitations of the learning-styles research, it is premature to conclude that any one method of teaching is effective with a particular cultural group. Shade, who appears to have modified her earlier position (Shade, 1982), refers to the learning-styles research as propositions that have strong intuitive elements, yet are "insufficient to produce the types of changes necessary in the teaching-learning process and in the assessment of skills" (1989a, p. 110). Hilliard (1989/90) makes a more definitive statement by warning educators that "it is premature to draw conclusions for classroom strategy based on style; or to prescribe pedagogical practice in a general way" (p. 3).

Teaching to Preferred Learning Style

Inherent in the learning-styles literature is the assumption that diverse students can learn only if they use their preferred style. One avenue for examining this assumption critically is to pose a historical question: Prior to the emergence of a defined learning style for African American students, is there any evidence that African American teachers in segregated schools employed teaching techniques that attended to learning style? In an impressive ethnographic study of a pre-*Brown* (*Brown v. Board of Education of Topeka,* 1954) segregated school in North Carolina, Siddle Walker (1993) documents that African American teachers' success was related to their interpersonal caring rather than to a particular method or teaching style. She states: "Students spoke much more vehemently about the degree to which they felt cared about than they did about the particular teaching methods used by the teachers" (p. 75). The works of Sowell (1976), Jones (1981), and Baker (1982) support Siddle Walker's observations.

The assumption that diverse students can learn only if they use their preferred style also ignores what developmental psychologists call the malleability (Gallagher & Ramey, 1987) and plasticity (Lerner, 1987) of children. These researchers note that people do not develop in a standardized or normative fashion; researchers have too often ignored the active role that individuals play in shaping their own development. Culturally diverse students have demonstrated their resilience and adaptability and can, if provided the psychological and instructional support, master various learning styles. Hilliard (1992) adds: "All students have an incredible capacity for developing the ability to use multiple learning styles, in much the same way that multiple language competency can be accomplished" (p. 373). Gilbert and Gay (1989) and Chimezie (1988) recommend, in fact, that African American students shift their preferred verbal and kinesthetic style to more school-compatible written and sedentary performance.

Saracho and Spodek (1984) acknowledge the work of several learning-styles theorists who advocate this kind of bicognitive flexibility for culturally diverse students. Although the authors support the theoretical concept, they raise concerns about the teachability of cognitive flexibility. Some research (Kogan, 1971) indicates that field-independent learners are better able to switch learning strategies than field-dependent learners, and that field dependents may resist style modification. Furthermore, a culturally diverse student who is achieving with his or her preferred style has no obvious or compelling reason to switch learning styles. Teaching cognitive flexibility to certain students is not only an unwise use of valuable instructional time, but may also be frustrating to students and lead to less, not more, learning. More important, there is no empirical evidence that these strategies enhance student achievement.

PROMISING ASPECTS OF THE LEARNING-STYLES RESEARCH

Although the research on learning styles is plagued by methodological, conceptual, and pedagogical problems, and is "thin and fragmented" (Banks, 1988, p. 465), there are many aspects of the literature that have significant potential for enhancing the achievement of culturally diverse students.

First, learning-styles research emphasizes the cultural context of teaching and learning (Irvine, 1992). Cultural variables are powerful, yet often overlooked, explanatory factors in the school failure of children of color. African American, Hispanic, and Indian students bring to the school setting a distinctive set of cultural forms and behaviors, including their group's history, language, values, norms, rituals, and symbols.

It must be emphasized that effective teachers of these students must contextualize the teaching act, giving attention to their students' cultural forms, behaviors, and experiences. Teachers also must negotiate and construct their understanding of teaching by examining the intersection of contexts and culture as well as their own behaviors, talents, and preferences. The cultural context of teaching and learning reminds teachers to be attentive not only to individual students' learning styles but to their own actions, instructional goals, methods, and materials as they relate to their students' cultural experiences and preferred learning environment. The teacher should probe the school, community, and home environments in a search for insights into diverse students' abilities, preferences, motivations, and learning approaches. Villegas (1991) calls this process "mutual accommodation in which both teachers and students adapt their actions to the common goal of academic success with cultural respect" (p. 12).

The learning-styles research reminds teachers to (a) understand and appreciate students' personal cultural knowledge, and (b) use their students' prior knowledge and culture in teaching. This process calls for the construction and design of relevant cultural metaphors and images in an effort to bridge the gap between what the students know and appreciate and the new knowledge or concepts to be taught. This process requires finding pertinent cultural examples, applying, comparing, and contrasting them, and creating authentic discourse and authentic teacher questions that relate what is being taught to what the student knows. Giroux (1992) adds:

This is not meant to suggest that the experiences that students bring to school be merely affirmed. On the contrary, one begins with such experiences but does not treat them as undisputed nor allow them to limit what is taught. Knowledge needs to be made meaningful in order to be made critical and transformative. (p. 9)

Second, the learning-styles research documents the importance of affect in teaching culturally diverse students. Teaching is an act of social interaction, and the resultant classroom climate is related directly to the interpersonal relationship between student and teacher. Learning-styles theories accentuate the significance of teacher-student interactions that include eye contact, facial expressions, body posture, physical space, use of

silence, and interpersonal touching (Longstreet, 1978). The foundation for success for students of color appears not to be teacher knowledge of specific learning styles, but committed, caring, dedicated teachers who are not afraid, resentful, or hostile, and who genuinely want to teach at schools with culturally diverse populations.

Third, learning-styles research is extremely helpful in that it rightly places the responsibility for student learning with teachers, instead of ascribing blame to students and their parents. It holds teachers responsible and accountable for designing instruction to meet students' individual learning needs by making them aware that all students are capable of learning, provided the learning environment attends to a variety of learning styles. In addition, learning-styles research alerts teachers to ways in which their unique teaching styles and pedagogical preferences may contribute to lack of achievement by certain students. It stresses the importance of increasing the number of instructional methods and amount of materials in the classroom and abandoning more traditional teacher-dominated methods of teaching. Kleinfeld (1992) states that learning styles "reminds teachers to create rich and interesting classrooms where children learn in different ways" (p. 2).

CONCLUSION

Learning-styles research is based on the theory that individuals respond to learning situations with consistent patterns of behavior. When applied to culturally diverse students, learning-styles research proposes to explain why children of the same culture and ethnicity often employ similar strategies for learning.

Learning-styles instruments, which attempt to operationalize the theoretical variables, have been moderately successful in distinguishing many of these styles. However, the applicability of the learning-styles research is limited. Understanding this limitation is particularly important in the education of children of color. One core assumption inherent in the learning-styles research is that children outside of mainstream culture learn better when teaching matches their preferred style. However, research on learning styles using culturally diverse students fails to support the premise that members of a given cultural group exhibit a distinctive style. Hence, the issue is not the identification of a style for a particular ethnic or gender group, but rather how instruction should be arranged to meet the instructional needs of culturally diverse students. Teachers who understand the preferred style of a student can use that knowledge to design and plan instruction and to encourage students to experiment with a wider repertoire of learning approaches. Clearly, learning-styles research is a useful beginning point in designing appropriate instruction for culturally diverse students, and not an end in itself.

References

American Association of School Administrators. (1991). *Learning styles: Putting research and common sense into practice.* Arlington, VA: Author.

American Psychological Association. (1966). *Standards for educational and psychological tests and manuals.* Washington, DC: Author.

Asbury, C. A., Stokes, A., Adderly-Kelly, B., & Knuckle, E. P. (1989). Effectiveness of selected neuropsychological, academic, and socio-cultural measures for predicting Bannatyne pattern categories in black adolescents. *Journal of Negro Education, 58*(2), 177–188.

Atkinson, G. (1991). Kolb's Learning Style Inventory: A practitioner's perspective. *Measurement and Evaluation In Counseling and Development, 23*(4), 149–161.

Baker, S. (1982, December). *Characteristics of effective urban language arts teachers: An ethnographic study of retired educators.* Paper presented at the meeting of the American Reading Forum, Sarasota, FL.

Banks, J. A. (1987). *Teaching strategies for ethnic studies* (4th ed.). Boston: Allyn and Bacon.

Banks, J. A. (1988). Ethnicity, class, cognitive, and motivational styles: Research and teaching implications. *Journal of Negro Education, 57*(4), 452–466.

Barbe, W., & Swassing, R. (1979). *Swassing-Barbe modality index.* Columbus, OH: Zaner-Bloser.

Baruth, L. G., & Manning, M. L. (1992). *Multicultural education of children and adolescents.* Boston: Allyn and Bacon.

Becker, L. D., Bender, N. N., & Morrison, G. (1978). Measuring impulsivity-reflection: A critical review. *Journal of Learning Disabilities, 11*(10), 626–632.

Bell, Y. R., & McGraw-Burrell, R. (1988). Culturally-sensitive and traditional methods of task presentation and learning performance in black children. *The Western Journal of Black Studies, 12*(4), 187–193.

Bennett, C. I. (1990). *Comprehensive multicultural education* (2nd ed.). Boston: Allyn and Bacon.

Bermudez, A. (1986, March). *Examining the effects of home training on problem-solving styles.* Paper presented at the meeting of the Teachers of English to Speakers of Other Languages, Anaheim, CA.

Blaha, J. (1982). Predicting reading and arithmetic achievement with measures of reading attitudes and cognitive styles. *Perceptual and Motor Skills, 55,* 107–114.

Bloom, B. S. (1976). *Human characteristics and school learning.* New York: McGraw-Hill.

Boykin, A. W. (1986). The triple quandary and the schooling of Afro-American children. In U. Neisser (Ed.), *The school achievement of minority children* (pp. 57–92). Hillsdale, NJ: Lawrence Erlbaum Associates.

Boykin, A. W., & Toms, F. D. (1985). Black child socialization. In H. P. McAdoo & J. L. McAdoo (Eds.), *Black children: Social, educational, and parental environments* (pp. 33–51). Beverly Hills, CA: Sage Publications.

Bradley, C. (1984). Issues in mathematics education for Native Americans and directions for research. *Journal for Research in Mathematics Education, 15*(2), 96–106.

Brown v. Board of Education of Topeka, 347 U.S. 483 (1954).

Buriel, R. (1978). Relationship of three field-dependence measures to the reading and math achievement of Anglo American and Mexican American children. *Journal of Educational Psychology, 70*(2), 167–174.

Butter, E. J., Kenned, C. B., & Shoemaker-Kelly, K. E. (1982). Prediction of third grade reading ability as a function of performance on visual, auditory and visual-auditory cognitive style tasks. *The Alberta Journal of Educational Research, 28*(4), 347–359.

Casteñeda, A., & Gray, T. (1974). Bicognitive processes in multicultural education. *Educational Leadership, 32,* 203–207.

Chimezie, A. (1988). Black children's characteristics and the schools: A selective adaptation approach. *The Western Journal of Black Studies, 12*(2), 77–85.

Clarkson, J. (1983). Urban learning styles. In J. M. Lakebrink (Ed.), *Children's success in school* (pp. 115–139). Springfield, IL: Charles C. Thomas.

Creek, R. J., McDonald, W. C., & Ganley, M. A. (1991). *Internality and achievement in the intermediate grades* (Report No. SP-032-968). Office of Educational Research and Improvement. (ERIC Document Reproduction Service ED No. 330 656)

Cureton, G. O. (1978). Using a black learning style. *The Reading Teacher, 31*(7), 751–756.

Cushner, K., McClelland, A., & Safford, P. (1992). *Human diversity in education.* New York: McGraw-Hill.

Davis, S. M. (1984). *Managing corporate culture.* Cambridge, MA: Ballinger Press.

Dunn, R. S. , & Dunn, K. J. (1979). Learning styles/teaching styles: Should they . . . Can they be matched? *Educational Leadership, 36,* 238–244.

Dunn, R., Dunn, K., & Price, G. E. (1978). *Learning style inventory.* Lawrence, KS: Price Systems.

Dunn, R., Gemake, J. G., & Jalali, F. (1990). Cross-cultural differences in learning styles of elementary-age students from four ethnic backgrounds. *Journal of Multicultural Counseling and Development, 18*(2), 68–93.

Erickson, F. (1986). Culture difference and science education. *The Urban Review, 18*(2), 117–124.

Foster, M. (1989). "It's cooking now": A performance analysis of the speech event of a Black teacher in an urban community college. *Language in Society, 18,* 1–29.

Gallagher, J. J., & Ramey, C. T. (1987). *The malleability of children.* Baltimore, MD: Paul H. Brookes Publishing Co.

Gardner, H. (1983). *Frames of mind: The theory of multiple intelligences.* New York: Basic Books.

Gilbert, S. E., & Gay, G. (1989). Improving the success in school of poor black children. In B. J. R. Shade (Ed.), *Culture, style, and the educative process* (pp. 275–283). Springfield, IL: Charles C. Thompson.

Giroux, H. A. (1992). Educational leadership and the crisis of democratic government. *Educational Researcher, 21*(4), 4–11.

Gjerde, P. F., Block, J., & Block, J. H. (1985). Longitudinal consistency of Matching Familiar Figures Test performance from early childhood to preadolescence. *Developmental Psychology, 21*(2), 262–271.

Goodlad, J. (1984). *A place called school.* New York: McGraw-Hill.

Gregorc, A. F. (1979). Learning/teaching styles: Potent forces behind them. *Educational Leadership, 36,* 234–236.

Gregorc, A. F. (1982). *Transaction ability inventory.* Department of Secondary Education, University of Connecticut, Storrs.

Grossman, H. (1984). *Educating Hispanic students.* Springfield, IL: Charles C. Thomas.

Hale-Benson, J. E. (1986). *Black children: Their roots, culture, and learning styles.* Baltimore, MD: Johns Hopkins University Press.

Hall, E. T. (1989). Unstated features of the cultural context of learning. *The Educational Forum, 54,* 21–34.

Hanson, M. J. (1992). Ethnic, cultural, and language diversity in intervention settings. In E. W. Lynch & M. J. Hanson (Eds.), *Developing cross-cultural competence* (pp. 3–18). Baltimore, MD: Paul H. Brookes Publishing Co.

Hill, J. (1971). *Personalized education programs utilizing cognitive style mapping*. Bloomfield Hills, MI: Oakland Community College Press.

Hilliard, A. G. (1989/90). Teachers and cultural styles in a pluralistic society. *Rethinking Schools, 14*(2), 3.

Hilliard, A. G. (1992). Behavioral style, culture, and teaching and learning. *Journal of Negro Education, 61*(3), 370–377.

Hoopes, D. S., & Pusch, M. D. (1979). Definitions of terms. In M. D. Pusch (Ed.), *Multicultural education: A cross-cultural training approach* (pp. 2–8). Yarmouth, ME: Intercultural Press.

Irvine, J. J. (1990). *Black students and school failure: Policies, practices, and prescriptions*. Westport, CT: Greenwood Publishing Group.

Irvine, J. J. (1992). Making teacher education culturally responsive. In M. E. Dilworth (Ed.), *Diversity in teacher education* (pp. 79–92). San Francisco: Jossey-Bass.

Jacobs, R. L. (1990). Learning styles of black high, average, and low achievers. *The Clearing House, 63*, 253–254.

Jones, F. C. (1981). *A traditional model of educational excellence*. Washington, DC: Howard University Press.

Kagan, J. (1965). *Learning and the educational process*. Chicago: Rand McNally.

Kampwirth, T. J., & MacKenzie, K. (1989). Modality preference and word learning: The predictive ability of the Swassing-Barbe Modality Index and the Illinois Test of Psycholinguistic Abilities. *Educational Research Quarterly, 13*(2), 18–25.

Kleinfeld, J. (1992). *Learning styles and culture*. Fairbanks: University of Alaska Press.

Kogan, N. (1971). Educational implications of cognitive styles. In G. S. Lesser (Ed.), *Psychology and educational practice* (pp. 242–292). Glenview, IL: Scott, Foresman.

Kolb, D. A. (1984). *Experiential learning: Experience as the source of learning and development*. Englewood Cliffs, NJ: Prentice-Hall.

Kreuze, J. G., & Payne, D. D. (1989). The learning styles preferences of Hispanic and Anglo college students: A comparison. *Reading Improvement, 26*(2), 166–169.

Lerner, R. M. (1987). The concept of plasticity in development. In J. J. Gallagher & C. T. Ramey (Eds.), *The malleability of children* (pp. 3–14). Baltimore, MD: Paul H. Brookes Publishing Co.

Letteri, C. A. (1980). *Cognitive profile: Basic determinant of academic achievement*. Burlington, VT: Center for Cognitive Studies.

Longstreet, W. C. (1978). *Aspects of ethnicity*. New York: Teachers College Press.

Margolis, H., & Brannigan, G. G. (1978). Conceptual tempo as a parameter for predicting reading achievement. *Journal of Educational Research, 71*(6), 342–345.

Marin, G., & Marin, B. V. (1991). *Research with Hispanic population*. Newbury Park, CA: Sage Publishers.

McKenney, J. L., & Keen, P. G. W. (1974). How managers' minds work. *Harvard Business Review, 53*, 79–90.

McShane, D. A., & Plas, J. M. (1982). Wechsler scale performance patterns of American Indian children. *Psychology in the Schools, 19*(1), 8–17.

Messick, S. (1984). The nature of cognitive styles: Problems and promise in educational practice. *Educational Psychologist, 19*, 59–74.

Moore, C. G. (1982). *The Navajo culture and the learning of mathematics*. Washington, DC: The National Institute of Education. (ERIC Document Reproduction Service No. ED 214 708)

Myers, I. B., & Briggs, K. C. (1976). *Myers-Briggs type indicator*. Palo Alto, CA: Consulting Psychologists Press.

Nieto, S. (1992). *Affirming diversity: The sociopolitical context of multicultural education*. New York: Longman.

Ogbu, J. (1988). Cultural diversity and human development. In D. T. Slaughter (Ed.), *Black children and poverty: A developmental perspective* (pp. 11–28). San Francisco: Jossey-Bass.

O'Leary, M., Calsyn, D. A., & Fauria, T. (1980). The Group Embedded Figures Test: A measure of cognitive style or cognitive impairment. *Journal of Personality Assessment, 44*(5), 532–537.

Owens, R. G. (1987). *Organizational behavior in education*. Englewood Cliffs, NJ: Prentice-Hall.

Pasteur, A. B., & Toldson, I. L. (1982). *The roots of soul: The psychology of black expressiveness*. New York: Anchor Press.

Paulsen, K. (1978). Reflection-impulsivity and level of maturity. *Journal of Psychology, 99*(1), 109–112.

Piestrup, A. M. (1972). *Black dialect interference and accommodation of reading instruction in first grade* (Monograph of the Language Behavior Research Laboratory). Berkeley: University of California.

Raile, F. N. (1980). *Structure of intellect factors and foreign language learning* (Structure of intellect studies Report No. FL-016-807). (ERIC Document Reproduction Service No. ED 288 346)

Ramírez, M., & Casteñeda, A. (1974). *Cultural democracy, bicognitive development, and education*. New York: Academic Press.

Reinert, H. (1976). One picture is worth a thousand words? Not necessarily! *The Modern Language Journal, 60*, 160–168.

Rotter, J. B. (1959). Generalized expectations for internal versus external control of reinforcements. *Psychological Issues, 1*(4), 11–12.

Saracho, O. N., & Spodek, B. (1984). *Cognitive style and children's learning: Individual variation in cognitive processes*. Urbana, IL: ERIC Clearinghouse on Elementary and Early Childhood Education. (ERIC Document Reproduction Service No. 247 034)

Sawyer, D. (1991). Native learning styles: Shorthand for instructional adaptations? *Canadian Journal of Native Education, 18*(1), 99–104.

Serpell, R. (1976). *Culture's influence on behaviour*. London: Methuen & Co.

Shade, B. J. (1982). Afro-American cognitive styles: A variable in school success? *Review of Educational Research, 52*(2), 219–244.

Shade, B. J. (1989a). Afro-American cognitive patterns: A review of the research. In B. J. Shade (Ed.), *Culture, style, and the educative process* (pp. 94–115). Springfield, IL: Charles C. Thomas.

Shade, B. J. (1989b). The influence of perceptual development on cognitive style: Cross ethnic comparisons. *Early Child Development and Care, 51*, 137–155.

Siddle Walker, E. V. (1993). Interpersonal caring in the "good" segregated schooling of African American children: Evidence from the case of Caswell County Training School. *Urban Review, 25*, 63–77.

Slavin, R. E. (1987). Cooperative learning and the education of black students. In D. S. Strickland & E. J. Cooper (Eds.), *Educating black children: America's challenge* (pp. 63–68). Washington, DC: Howard University Press.

Slonim, M. B. (1991). *Children, culture, and ethnicity*. New York: Garland.

Sowell, T. (1976). Patterns of black experience. *The Public Interest, 43*, 26–58.

Swanson, L. (1980). Cognitive style, locus of control, and school achievement in learning disabled females. *Journal of Clinical Psychology, 36*(4), 964–967.

Swisher, K., & Deyhle, D. (1989). The styles of learning are different, but the teaching is just the same. *Journal of American Indian Education* [Special Issue], 1–13.

Tharp, R. G. (1989). Psychocultural variables and constants: Efects on teaching and learning in schools. *American Psychologist, 44*(2), 349–359.

Tiedemann, J. (1989). Measures of cognitive style: A critical review. *Educational Psychologist, 24*(3), 261–275.

Valentine, C. A. (1971. Deficit, difference, and bicultural models of Afro-American behavior. *Harvard Educational Review, 41*(2), 137–157.

Villegas, A. M. (1991). *Culturally responsive pedagogy for the 1990s and beyond*. Washington, DC: American Association of Colleges of Teacher Education.

Witkin, H. A. (1971). *Group embedded figures test*. Palo Alto, CA: Consulting Psychologists Press.

Witkin, H. A., Dyk, R. B., Faterson, H. F., Goodenough, D. R., & Karp, S. A. (1962). *Psychological differentiation*. New York: Wiley.

Wlodkowski, R. J. (1978). *Student motivation information form*. Washington, DC: National Education Association.

Wood, C. M. (1979, April). *Cognitive style, school readiness and behavior as predictors of first-grade achievement*. (Report No. PS-011-098). Paper presented at the annual meeting of the American Educational Research Association, San Francisco. (ERIC Document Reproduction Service ED No. 182 014)

Zeitoun, H. H., & Fowler, H. S. (1981, April). *Predicting Piagetian cognitive levels of teacher education students at the Pennsylvania State University*. (Report No. SP-016-378). Paper presented at the annual meeting of the National Association for Research in Science Teaching, Ellenville, NY. (ERIC Document Reproduction Service No. ED 204 136)

Zigler, E. A. (1963). A measure in search of a theory. *Contemporary Psychology, 8,* 133–135.

· 28 ·

RESEARCH ON FAMILIES, SCHOOLS, AND COMMUNITIES: A MULTICULTURAL PERSPECTIVE

Nitza M. Hidalgo
WESTFIELD STATE COLLEGE

Sau-Fong Siu
WHEELOCK COLLEGE

Josephine A. Bright
WHEELOCK COLLEGE

Susan M. Swap
WHEELOCK COLLEGE

Joyce L. Epstein
JOHNS HOPKINS UNIVERSITY

Studies of families and studies of schools have grown to include research on the simultaneous influences of these two important contexts on children's learning and development. Researchers are examining not only what families do to influence their children's development, or what schools do to educate young-sters, but also what schools and families do together and with their communities to support and motivate children to do their best as students.

Research in this field is still in its infancy. Although based on a long tradition of research on families and on schools studied separately, attention to issues of "partnership" is relatively new. Since the early 1980s, however, the field has begun to attract researchers from many disciplines studying many facets of school, family, and, more recently, community partnerships across the ages from infancy to adolescence, and across grade levels from preschool through high school. Questions have broadened and measures have deepened each year to improve the focus and increase the importance of the field. Local or regional studies have helped to identify key topics of interest to researchers and to educators. National data are now available (such as the National Education Longitudinal Survey [NELS] and the National Household Education Survey [NHES]) to check patterns that were identified in smaller studies, or to raise ques-tions for new small- or large-scale studies.

The early research not only defined a broad agenda, but also has helped to redirect and improve policy and practice. Ad-vances in theory, research, and program development over the past decade have made it possible for schools, districts, and states to go beyond rhetoric to develop programs of school, family, and community partnerships ("Paths to Partnership," 1991).

Although progress has been steady, results of research, changes in policies, and improvements in practice have been fragmented through reporting in a wide variety of journals, books, and documents. It should help, then, to review briefly some of the progress that has been made in the ways research-ers and educators think about and work to improve school, family, and community partnerships.

This research was supported by the U.S. Department of Education's Office of Educational Research and Improvement (R117Q00031). The opinions expressed are the authors' and do not represent OERI positions or policies.

498

PROGRESS IN RESEARCH ON SCHOOL, FAMILY, AND COMMUNITY PARTNERSHIPS

The Importance of Family Environments and Involvement

For over a quarter century, studies have shown that children benefit when their parents support and encourage their education. On average, more educated families are more involved in schools and with their children's formal education. As important, however, some families from all situations—regardless of the formal education or income level of the parents, and regardless of the grade level or ability of the student—use strategies to encourage and influence their children's education and development. Studies are accumulating that show that family practices concerning children's education are more important for helping students succeed in school and in general than are family structure, economic status, or characteristics such as race, parent education, family size, and age of child (e.g., Becker & Epstein, 1982; R. M. Clark, 1983; Comer, 1980, 1988; Davies, 1991; Epstein, 1986b, 1990; Scott-Jones, 1986, 1987). Families can compensate for lack of material or economic resources when they draw on their strengths to develop supportive relationships with their children and monitor and guide their children's education. The more schools do to involve families, the less parent behavior or student success can be explained by status variables.

The Importance of Schools Helping All Families Become Involved

Early studies that documented the importance of family environments for student success opened a new research question: *If* family involvement and encouragement is important, *how* can schools and communities help more families at all grade levels become involved in ways that help their children succeed in school? Research is accumulating that shows that schools must take leadership in developing and implementing practices that enable more parents to become and remain involved in their children's education. Evidence is also growing that when schools develop their programs of partnership, families appreciate the assistance, more families become involved, and more students improve their achievements, attitudes, and behaviors (Davies, 1990; Dornbusch & Ritter, 1988; Epstein, 1991; Epstein & Dauber, 1991; see also Epstein, 1992, and Swap, 1993, for two more complete reviews of the growing field of research and practice of school, family, and community partnerships and their effects).

A New Theory to Explain School and Family Influence on Children's Learning

The data that accumulated during the 1980s challenged prevailing theories of social organization that assumed that organizations were most effective when they operated independently and separately (Waller, 1932; Weber, 1947). As a result of a series of studies, Epstein (1987) offered a different theory for student learning and success in school, the model of "overlapping spheres of influence" of family and school, and extended it (Epstein, 1988) to family, school, community, and peer group to account for the major contexts that influence children's learning and development. Her social-organizational perspective integrates and extends the ecological model of Bronfenbrenner (1979, 1986), the educational insights of families as educators of Leichter (1974), the sociological perspectives on connections of professional and nonprofessional institutions and individuals of Litwak and Meyer (1974), the emphasis on shared responsibility of Seeley (1981), and a long tradition of sociological and psychological research on school and family environments and their effects.

The model of overlapping spheres of influence includes both external and internal structures. The external structure represents the multiple contexts and dynamic options for more or less overlap based on the philosophies and practices of families and schools. It also accounts for the age or grade level of the student and period of time or history that may affect the contexts, practices, and participants. The internal model represents the patterns of interactions of the participants within contexts at the institutional and individual levels. Because it is assumed that the child is the reason for the connections between home and school, the model focuses on the key role of the "child as student" in interactions between families and schools, parents and teachers, or other influential participants. The students are key to successful school and family partnerships. They are the main actors in their own education, and the main conductors of the two-way communications between school and home.

Overall, the external and internal structures of overlapping spheres of influence recognize the interlocking histories of institutions that motivate, socialize, and educate children, and the changing and accumulating skills and interactions of the individuals in those contexts as the basis for studying the connections that affect children's learning and development. The general model allows for different practices and relationships that may be needed at various age and grade levels and with families of differing educational and cultural backgrounds.

Continuing Questions

The traditional and new lines of research are needed to continue to increase knowledge and improve practice. These include studies of family environments and influence; studies of school effectiveness and effects; studies of community contexts and their influence on families, schools, and students; and studies of the *partnerships, connections,* or *collaborations* between and among these contexts and the individuals in them.

One of the topics that still needs research attention is the nature of school, family, and community partnerships for families and children with diverse cultural backgrounds. Researchers have begun to study how parents of all educational and cultural backgrounds teach their children and work with their children's schools (Chavkin, 1993). This includes studies of African American families (Clark, 1983; Comer, 1980, 1988; Dauber & Epstein, 1993; Epstein & Dauber, 1991; Epstein, Herrick, & Coates, in press; McAdoo, 1981; Scott-Jones, 1987), Chinese American families (Sung, 1987; Wong, 1990), Indochinese families (Caplan, Choy, & Whitmore, 1992), and Hispanic families (Canino, Earley, & Rogler, 1989; Delgado & Humm-Delgado, 1982; Delgado-Gaitan, 1990; Delgado-Gaitan & Trueba, 1991; Moll & Greenberg, 1990). These studies form an important base of knowledge about the approaches and possibilities of partnership by all families in their children's education. Many questions remain, however, about patterns of family influence as children progress through school, and about the strategies schools need to implement in order to reach, inform, and involve all families in their children's education.

About This Chapter

This chapter summarizes information that emerged from the first phase of a study of family influence and family-school-community connections of four ethnic groups in the Boston area. The research (one of the projects in the Center on Families, Communities, Schools, and Children's Learning, sponsored by the U.S. Department of Education's Office of Educational Research and Improvement) is a collegial effort of four researchers: Nitza Hidalgo, studying Puerto Rican families; Josephine Bright, studying African American families; Sau-Fong Siu, studying Chinese American families; and Susan McAllister Swap, studying Irish American families. Joyce L. Epstein introduces and discusses the chapter, new directions, and conclusions, drawing from her research on school and family partnerships with diverse groups of families.

The researchers are exploring how families from the four ethnic groups support their children's school success in the early primary grades (kindergarten through second grade), how definitions of success change from year to year as children proceed through the grades with new teachers, and how families respond to their children's development and new school demands and expectations. The results of this study will be important because schools in the United States need to know how to improve programs in which large numbers of children fail, particularly those from ethnic minority groups. Better partnerships among schools, families, and communities will be part of the solutions for increasing the motivation of minority and immigrant children to learn and succeed in school.

The first four sections that follow contain literature reviews of the history of the immigration of each ethnic group to the United States, including the treatment of the early immigrants and experiences of each group with education. Each of the four sections discusses family influence on children's education, and the involvement in education at home, at school, and in the community of families in each cultural group.

PUERTO RICAN FAMILY INVOLVEMENT IN EDUCATION

The literature on Puerto Rican family involvement in children's schooling is limited for a number of reasons. First, many studies tend not to distinguish Puerto Ricans from Latinos, making information on Puerto Rican families difficult to discern.

Second, Puerto Rican students' lack of school achievement has been the traditional focus of investigations, resulting in explanations that attribute failure to cultural deficits and to home/school discontinuities without focusing on family influences. Third, studies of large or social populations such as students, families, or schools operationalize the units of analysis using definitions of family and parental involvement that lack sensitivity to cultural variations within particular groups. The subtleties of cultural socialization patterns, ethnicity (often confused with race), and the group's sociohistorical experiences are rarely analyzed.

In studies of ethnic families, researchers have problematically combined culture with socioeconomic lifestyle (Staples & Mirandé, 1980). A conceptual model that investigates Puerto Rican family involvement in children's schooling would emphasize types of families, including the meaning and function of extended families, and the values and practices of families within particular contexts: home, school, and community. Inquiry into the relationship of these factors to Puerto Rican family socialization of children and involvement in childrens' schooling would result in informative and culturally sensitive profiles of Puerto Rican family involvement in schooling.

One such model constructed by Auerbach (1989) in the area of family literacy, called the social-contextual approach, may have applications in investigations of ethnic family involvement in children's schooling. As applied to parental involvement, the social-contextual approach uses parental knowledge, values, beliefs, and at-home practices to construct a definition of involvement (Volk, 1992). The approach reevaluates the parental activities considered beneficial for children's academic success. Auerbach notes that researchers have used the model of school as the framework for defining the activities parents should conduct at home, deeming school-like practices as most beneficial for academic success. The author suggests that researchers look at the socially (and culturally) meaningful activities in daily family life that may promote school achievement. Shifting the lens of analysis, Auerbach suggests we change the questions we are asking, from whether the home activities match the expectations of schools (see Goldenberg, 1987), to how specific cultural parent/child activities (like storytelling and relating traditional sayings and expressions) may influence children's academic development.

This section analyzes literature on Puerto Rican parental involvement in schools from a framework that is inclusive of cultural definitions and practices. After a brief review of background information on Puerto Rican families in the United States, the definition of family is looked at more closely using the Puerto Rican model. Current research on Puerto Rican involvement in the home, school, and community is reviewed. A twofold criterion was used for inclusion of research and other literature. Studies on Puerto Ricans were chosen if their focus on parental involvement embraced cultural considerations, or if they incorporated cultural beliefs and practices into their investigative paradigms.

Background Information

The Latino population in the United States is growing at a significantly higher rate than non-Latino populations. Latinos will add more people to the U.S. population than any other racial or ethnic group in the coming decade (U.S. Department of Commerce, 1993). By 2010 the Latino population will be the second largest ethnic group, with 13.2% of the total U.S. population (U.S. Department of Commerce, 1993; Rivera, 1991); by 2020 the Latino population will be 15.2% of the total U.S. population (U.S. Department of Commerce, 1993).

As of 1990, Puerto Ricans constituted 12.1% of the total national Latino population (Institute for Puerto Rican Policy, 1992). In 1990 Puerto Ricans, whose median age was 26.9, numbered 2,382,00 in the continental United States. Only 58% of Puerto Ricans aged 25 and older had graduated from high school in 1990, while only 10.1% aged 25 and older had completed four years of college. The median household income for Puerto Rican families in 1990 was $16,169. Thirty-seven percent of Puerto Rican families had incomes below the 1990 poverty rate, while 56.7% of those in poverty were children under 18 (Institute for Puerto Rican Policy).

While small numbers of Puerto Ricans have lived in the United States since the 19th century, the mass migration began in the 1940s. During the 1960s and 1970s, although many Puerto Ricans continued to arrive in the United States, a reverse migration to the Island exceeded the number of arrivals (Hidalgo, 1992). The back-and-forth movement of families continues to date. One can say that there are three distinct categories of Puerto Ricans in the United States: (a) the recently arrived migrants in search of employment; (b) the migrant workers moving back and forth as work demands; (c) the U.S.-born second-, third-, and fourth-generation Puerto Ricans (Santiestevan & Santiestevan, 1984).

Intragroup differences within ethnic groups result from various factors: educational experiences, socioeconomic status, length of time living in the country, area of residence, whether one lives in an ethnic enclave, the generational position of individuals (age), and the amount of intermarriage with other ethnic groups. For Puerto Ricans in the United States the additional factors that influence intragroup differences are Spanish or English dominance, place of educational experiences (Puerto Rico or the United States), where the formative years were spent, migration patterns, and intensity of personal connection to the Island.

Redefinition of Family

Variations in Puerto Rican family composition are evident in the United States. Mizio (1974) writes: "The Puerto Rican family system must be viewed on a continuum. At one end is an extended family system with traditional Puerto Rican values, and at the other end the nuclear family system with an American value system" (p. 78). Salgado (1985) presents five family types that exemplify Puerto Rican families:

1) the nuclear family similar to the U.S. model
2) the traditional extended family with its network of kin and kin-like relations
3) the modified extended family in which the nuclear family has close relationships and extended family support
4) the female-dominant family in which the maternal relatives have an important role in the socialization of children and in which the father's role is reduced [the single-parent family is subsumed under this category]
5) the sub-extended family in which the family unit has a nuclear composition, but in which the extended family has a major psychological and social role. (p. 40)

The nuclear family may include the mother, father, their children, the children of other unions, and the children of friends. Extended families might include parents, children, and grandparents, with frequent visits from aunts and uncles. According to Harry (1992b), extended families may be seen as an "integral part of the family's identity and authority structure" (p. 388).

The extended family serves various functions: It is a source of ethnic identification and language maintenance for children, a source of caring and affection for children (Hidalgo, 1994), a provider of child care (Bird & Canino, 1982), a provider of transportation, and a fountain of emotional support for family members in times of crisis. An economic analysis of extended family households (Angel & Tienda, 1982) provided evidence of the importance of extension as a financial coping strategy, which may not be solely related to cultural preferences.

Thus, when inquiring into family structures of Puerto Ricans, parental-involvement models should be inclusive of the extended family (see Epstein, 1992, for an expanded formulation of parental involvement). While a single parent may not be informed of her child's day-to-day school progress, the grandmother may be so informed. The grandparent is a valid representative of the family. Active involvement of the grandparent may change the nature of the decision-making process of single-parent households to resemble more closely the style found in two-parent households, the model that—according to Dornbusch and Strober (1988)—supports the higher school achievement of children. Insight into ethnic/racial differences in the definition of family should lead investigators necessarily to study the active and multiple roles played by extended family members.

Parental Involvement in the Home

Discerning the influence of Puerto Rican families on school achievement requires an understanding of the particular mechanisms of socialization that exist within the culture. Given the various types of family composition and the fluid migration patterns, there are as many variations and differences in socialization patterns as there are similarities.

The literature on Puerto Rican culture reveals a number of values and child-rearing practices that have been preserved and maintained in some form despite the transition to the United States. Close communication, connections to the Island, the existence of the extended family, and the back-and-forth movement of people are the mechanisms facilitating the maintenance of cultural values and practices.

Family obligation is deeply ingrained in Puerto Rican culture, in which the fundamental obligations are to family and friends. Puerto Rican individuals present themselves within the framework of the family to which they belong. Fitzpatrick

(1987) writes that "individual confidence, sense of security and identity are perceived in the relationship to others who constitute the family" (p. 70). Inner self-worth and sense of integrity come from doing what is expected, especially with regard to family obligations.

Harry (1992a) found that Puerto Rican "parents spoke of their children's strengths and weaknesses in terms of family characteristics" (p. 32). She found that Puerto Ricans share a collective identity in which the achievements or conditions ascribed to one member, such as a child, reflect back to the family as a whole. The parents trace the child's characteristics to particular family members, as traits inherited from adults in the family. A sense of family identification is holistic in nature and not individualized.

Family unity and interdependency are highly valued; close and frequent contact among family members is expected. Mizio (1974) writes that "family unity refers to the desirability of close and intimate kin ties" (p. 187). The genuine expression of generosity toward others and a concern about closeness and caring are part of interpersonal relationships in which one is expected to reciprocate kindness. Reciprocity is taught by the example of parents and by oral expressions that are repeated during the childhood years, such as the saying *Hoy por tí, mañana por mí* (Today for you, tomorrow for me). Reciprocity is most significant and expected among family members and neighbors.

Interdependence among family members is expected and viewed positively. No one is expected to do everything alone (Mizio, 1974). Sánchez-Ayéndez (1988) states that "the interdependency framework conceptualizes the individual as unable to do everything or to do everything well and therefore in need of others for assistance" (p. 177). The interdependence framework provides a support system for individuals.

Vázquez-Nutall and Romero-García (1989) looked at differences between how Puerto Rican girls are taught in the home and the expectations of U.S. teachers for student behavior. They found that the U.S. model promotes individual achievement, while the Puerto Rican approach is geared to family satisfaction. Puerto Rican parents value interdependence and nurture cooperation in children.

Child-rearing behavior reflects the value of respect. Lauria (1972) differentiates between the two varieties of respect (*respeto*) in Puerto Rican culture. The first definition refers to respect for human dignity in a general sense, "generalized deference" (p. 38). Respect of this kind is a precondition for all social relations. The second form of respect, according to Lauria, is respect for another's authority and stature, "particularized forms of *respeto*" (p. 38), which stem from certain types of social relations. Respect of the second kind encompasses particular kinds of regard for others according to status.

The concept of *respeto* may be expressed in parental deference toward teachers' authority in educational matters, but, as Harry (1992a) notes, deference should not be interpreted as trust, because trust has to be earned and is a quality of good interpersonal relations between teachers and parents.

Children are expected to be obedient and dedicated to the family. Parents are the authorities who require respect, and their decisions should not be questioned. The Puerto Rican family is "one with close emotional and psychological ties in which the child becomes well-acquainted with the hierarchy of power and the role expectations of each family member" (Nieves Falcón, quoted in Salgado, 1985, p. 40). Although mothers control decisions on child rearing, children are taught to have unquestioned respect for both parents, especially for the father's authority.

Lourdes Díaz-Soto (1988, 1989, 1990), in her study of 57 Puerto Rican families of high- and low-achieving students, found that "parents acted as facilitators within an organized framework of expectations" (1990, p. 19). Díaz-Soto found a number of recurrent themes in the homes of high achievers: *language* (parents used both Spanish and English in communicating with their children), *aspirations* (parents held high expectations for their children's future careers), *discipline* (parents employed consistent controlling strategies), and *protectiveness* ("parents always knew where their children were") (p. 12).

The Díaz-Soto study is significant because it dispels the myth that all Puerto Rican children are low achievers, and because she finds that Puerto Rican parents do support their children's school achievement.

Dinah Volk (1992), in one of the few studies that directly addresses Puerto Rican parental involvement (Goldenberg, 1987, included 1 Puerto Rican family in his sample of 10 families), investigated the parent/child home interactions of three kindergarten children. Employing the social-contextual model (Auerbach, 1989), Volk found both formal and informal learning activities in the home. She concluded that even those parents who did not employ teacher-like talk with their children provided various learning activities (such as natural conversation strategies) that stimulated children's development.

There are many subtle ways that parents positively influence their children that are often overlooked in studies of ethnic family involvement in education. Díaz-Soto (1992) delineates some of these subtle activities:

> the caring attitude of parents, the high educational expectations both parents and children relate, the value placed on family life and immediate responses to human needs . . ., the value placed on childhood, the giving attitudes, the neat, orderly, colorful environments in the midst of chaotic neighborhoods, the higher order values placed on religious life, hospitality, [and] respect for educational personnel. . . . (p. 159)

Studies that provide culturally sensitive insight into ethnic families expand the model of home practices that influence student achievement. Using an approach inclusive of the multiple ways of interpreting behavior allows Puerto Rican family beliefs and practices to be understood within their social context.

Parental Involvement in the School

Much of the research on the influence of the home on Puerto Rican student achievement focuses on the differences between child-rearing practices in the home and in the school. Differences in verbal and nonverbal behavior in particular are seen as resulting in miscommunication between teachers and students and misinterpretation by teachers of student behavior.

Salgado (1985) presents an example of the misunderstanding of cultural differences between the school and the Puerto Rican home. Teachers may believe the Puerto Rican child is too passive

because she does not talk too much, remains by herself during play period and when the teacher talks to her about the observed behavior, the child does not look at her or respond. While the teacher anticipates that the child's behavior is peculiar, the mother finds it very proper. The child is behaving in a manner that pleases the mother and fulfills the expectations of what "a good child is." (p. 47)

Lack of information about the high value Puerto Ricans place on respect and obedience within the family unit obscures insight into culturally based child behavior in the classroom.

Reinaldo Ortíz-Colón (1985), in a study of Head Start children that explores subtle cultural factors, found that the Anglo teachers and Puerto Rican mothers of Head Start children agreed on the behaviors and skills or outcomes of children's learning. Ortíz-Colón found differences in the importance teachers and mothers placed on particular behaviors. While teachers ranked behaviors based on independence and verbal assertiveness as more important, mothers placed more value on obedience and mindfulness of rules. The goal desired by both mothers and teachers was that the children, regardless of their sex, learn effectively and be successful in school.

Results also showed differences among the Puerto Rican mothers themselves. The behavior and skill rankings of the more acculturated mothers was similar to the Anglo teachers' ranking. Ortíz-Colón (1985) concludes: "Cultural and socioeconomic differences in ideologies about how best to socialize the child, then, are factors that influence the discontinuities between mothers and teachers" (p. 111). The acculturated mothers were aware of the Anglo teachers' expectations and were able to communicate similar expectations to their children within a Puerto Rican family orientation (see Hidalgo, 1993, for a discussion of teachers' expectations of Puerto Rican home support). The less acculturated mothers were also supportive of their children's school achievement, but in uniquely Puerto Rican ways.

In a study of low-income Puerto Rican families' interactions with the special education system, Harry (1992a, 1992b) examined how ethnicity influenced parents' understanding of their children's placement in special education. She found that Puerto Rican parents used broader definitions of normal child development than the definitions used by educators. Harry also found ethnic differences operating in the definition of family, in parenting styles and discipline strategies, and in parent/child interactions.

Two additional studies explore the importance of family influence on Puerto Rican and Latino school achievement. Durán (1983) summarizes a 1975 study by Alicea and Mathis (1975) of factors influencing Puerto Rican students' decisions to remain in high school. The study found that the factors affecting school achievement were language proficiency and

[students'] communication with parents, parental guidance and support in education, presence of significant adults at school providing help and encouragement, knowledge of and pride in Puerto Rican cultural heritage, students' perceptions of broader societal opportunities, and students' professional and higher education goals. (p. 29).

While the quality of the school environment and its effects on school retention should not be underestimated, this study illustrates the importance of Puerto Rican family involvement in the education of their children. Conversely, when Puerto Rican high school students do not perceive family support, they are more likely to drop out of school (Colón-Tarrats, 1988). This study found that the subtle means of family support for academic achievement seemed to be missing for Puerto Rican student dropouts who have a high reliance on familial support systems.

Research on home/school discontinuities that judge differences by nonethnic paradigms may miss insights on the ways cultural beliefs shape home practices. The different activities found in the home can be interpreted and understood on their own terms. Differences between home and school, when understood within a sociocontextual model, are seen as cultural boundaries (Erickson, 1987), which are neutral differences that have not been negatively charged by the imposition of dominant cultural definitions.

Parental Involvement in the Community

Within Latino communities parents have joined together to form coalitions to advance community educational and social interests. Community-based organizations have been created to meet educational and political needs. According to Uriarte (1988), who studied the historical development of a Puerto Rican community agency, the purpose of the agencies is the "continuous struggle to develop vehicles that will advance the groups' needs through direct confrontation of state and private institutions as well as the demand for autonomy and community control of these organizations" (p. 36). The role of the Latino community-based agencies is essential in offering alternative educational opportunities for Latino students (Weiser Ramírez, 1990). The community-based agencies, by employing Latino staff, designing programs that build on students' cultural strengths, and the validity they derive from having the community's trust (Weiser Ramírez), may provide the effective education that schools have not traditionally presented. Projects to promote Latino parental involvement in schools have been created by many Latino agencies, including the Aspira Association (Weiser Ramírez), the Hispanic Policy Development Project (Nicolau & Ramos, 1990), and the Intercultural Development Research Association (Robledo Montecel, 1993).

Latino parent groups have organized locally and statewide to promote equal educational opportunity and appropriate bilingual educational programs. In 1975 Puerto Rican parents and the Aspira Association pressed the New York City Board of Education to establish bilingual programs. A *consent decree* was reached that dictated mandatory bilingual education for all eligible children (Fitzpatrick, 1987). The implementation of bilingual education programs, mandated by federal and state laws, has opened access to Latino parental involvement in schools (Nieto, 1992).

In "Home-School Linkages," Arvizu (1992) describes the formation of the United Bronx Parents in New York City as the result of an awareness by parents that the public schools were not serving the best interests of their children. The United Bronx Parents developed decentralization plans (Fitzpatrick, 1987) and organized a series of parent-training strategies to provide information on how to make the school system more responsive to their children's needs.

On a statewide level in Massachusetts, *Padres Unidos en Educación y el Desarrollo de Otros* (PUEDO) (1989) (Parents United in Education and the Development of Others) have organized in cities with substantial Latino populations to push for language services and quality education for Spanish-speaking students.

As Latino parents collaborate to fight for equal educational opportunities for their children, school systems will have to respond to these pressures.

Patterns of Parental Involvement: Implications for Educators, Administrators, and Researchers

To encourage the active participation of Puerto Rican families in schools, educators should note some unique Puerto Rican interrelational considerations. The Puerto Rican interpersonal style of communication views directness as rude. Diplomacy in communicating with parents is advised. Educators should consider providing personal attention and outreach to parents, especially by the use of the Spanish language, with such actions as employing bilingual front office staff. Educators are encouraged to employ community liaisons who have established their validity as community members. Furthermore, members of the extended family should be treated with the same respect and authority as parents (Robledo Montecel, 1993); members of the extended family are legitimate representatives of family interests.

This section has reviewed research on the influences of Puerto Rican families on their children in the home, in the school, and in the community. The conceptualization of family was expanded to include both nuclear and extended families, as these are appropriate definitions for Puerto Rican families. The review defined a framework for reviewing literature that included the influence of ethnicity in defining and studying family involvement. Puerto Rican cultural values and child-rearing practices were delineated to gain a more complete picture of how Puerto Rican families structure the learning environment for their children. Research studies that examined the subtle variations of Puerto Rican families' expectations and strategies to ensure school achievement were highlighted.

Examination of Puerto Rican family involvement in education that does not include in the investigational framework the meaning of parental practices and values within the culture will neglect the ethnically derived contributions made by families. Puerto Rican families could be viewed as part of a multidimensional support system (within the home, within the school, and between home and school) (Delgado-Gaitán, 1990). Such an approach may allow families and communities to create strategies that contribute to their children's advancement.

Researchers should build upon and enhance the strong support system found in Puerto Rican families by investigating Puerto Rican families in culturally sensitive ways, by promoting parent learning about the requirements of school, and by promoting the training of teachers on the socialization and strengths of Puerto Rican families.

FAMILY-HOME CONTRIBUTIONS TO AFRICAN AMERICAN STUDENT ACHIEVEMENT

I'm a very pushy mother, and I show my child that I'm interested and I care. And when he lays his books down and says "I'll do it later," I say "No. Go back and do it now. I'll check it. Then if you want to go play Nintendo or whatever, you [can] go do that." It brings smiles of joy when they have plays at school and different types of activities. I get off of work at 3:30, and if it's after school hours, I'll be there. They have no doubt I will be there. I say that to them. They see me walk in and their smiles grow bigger. Why? Because Mom is there. (Excerpt from interview with African American mother; Bright, 1992)

In 1990 African Americans numbered 29,986,000 and were the largest ethnic minority group in the United States, about 12% of the total population (U.S. Bureau of the Census, 1990). Without a doubt, African Americans have achieved remarkable gains in education, income, and occupation over the last three decades (Eshleman, 1988; Staples, 1988). However, education still pays better dividends for Whites than for African Americans. Between 1970 and 1985 the median years of schooling completed by Whites increased from 10.9 to 12.5 years. During this same period the median years of schooling completed by African Americans soared from 8.0 to 12.0 years, virtually eliminating the Black/White education gap (Gay, 1989). Yet, as census data show, this increase in education has produced few economic benefits for African Americans. In fact, the economic gulf that separates African Americans from White Americans has widened. In 1985 median income for White families ($29,152) was $12,366 more than that for Black families ($16,786) (Eshleman, 1988). By 1987 median income for White families had climbed to $32,274, but was only $18,098 for African American families, a difference of $14,176 (Ploski & Williams, 1989).

Equally significant is the finding that the Black/White income gap *increases* with education. Staples (1988) has noted that barriers to employment are encountered by less-educated Whites as well as African Americans. However, college-educated African Americans also experience employment barriers. Not only is the unemployment rate for African American male college graduates four times that of their White counterparts (Staples, 1986), but African American male college graduates earn less income and are unemployed as frequently as White male high school dropouts (Staples, 1985).

The economic oppression of significant numbers of African American men to the extent that they cannot secure steady employment at decent wages has profoundly affected Black families. In 1960 almost 75% of Black men were in the labor force. Among all African American families in the same year, 21% were headed by women. By 1982 only 54% of Black men were working, and 42% of all Black families were headed by women (Staples, 1985). A consequence of these trends has been a tremendous increase in the percentage of African American children living in one-parent households with incomes below the poverty level.

African American children are among the poorest children in the United States. For the population as a whole, the rate of child poverty in the United States has increased 50% since 1969, and affects nearly one out of every three children under the age of six (Kozol, 1988). Among African American children, the incidence is even higher. In 1983, 41% of all Black children lived in families with incomes below $7,510 per year (Staples, 1988). By 1986 almost half of all African American children were being reared in poverty (Eshleman, 1988).

Living in poverty places many African American children at risk for school drop-out and educational failure. Factors within schools also conspire against achievement in African American children (see, e.g., Calabrese, 1990; Grant, 1984; Hare, 1987). At the same time, some African American children do well in the very same schools and classrooms distinguished by the failure of their peers. This disparity may occur among children who live in the same inner-city communities, come from similar family structures, and share similar experiences of poverty and discrimination.

The presence of these exceptions is strong evidence for the feasibility of overcoming a wide range of adverse conditions (see, e.g., Pollard, 1989; Shields, 1989). How do these children achieve academic excellence despite their being categorized as "socially disadvantaged," "educationally at risk," and "likely to fail"? How do lower-income African American parents promote and support their children's educational achievements? What can we learn from these successful children and their families that will bring us closer to the goal of success for *all* of our children? These are the questions that will be addressed in this section.

A perusal of the school achievement research literature suggests that the experiences of African American children and families have not been represented adequately. In a pattern that continues to the present, this literature has been characterized by an overwhelming emphasis on achievement failures rather than on the successes of African American children (for a review see Slaughter-DeFoe, Nakagawa, Takanishi, & Johnson, 1990). Deficit-oriented models have typically explained academic failure in African American children by reference to presumed problems in "disorganized" and "pathological" Black family life (e.g., Moynihan, 1965).

This "tangle of pathology" conception does not represent African American families or the complexities related to school success or failure. Such labels not only overlook the richness of African American culture (Hill, 1971) and the diversity within Black family lifestyles (Willie, 1981), they also fail to consider variability in family forms, family processes, and family outcomes as they are encountered in low-income African American communities (Swan & Stavros, 1973).

When applied to the experiences of low-income African American families, deficit models fail to consider that these families make resourceful and creative adaptations as they cope with the stresses associated with trying to survive on very little money (Stack, 1991), and develop supportive child-rearing strategies that empower African American children in the midst of conditions beyond their control (Hale, 1991). Also seldom

acknowledged is the role of social and economic discrimination in perpetuating the disadvantaged status of African Americans (Davis, 1981).

While it is known that children of poverty face increased risk and vulnerability, newer perspectives emphasize that a low income does not uniformly predict family functioning, especially achievement socialization (Slaughter-DeFoe et al., 1990). Family processes are more predictive of student achievement than family income or structure (see, e.g., R. M. Clark, 1983; Scott-Jones, 1987).

A growing literature dispels the myth that African American families lack values, attitudes, and skills that are useful to their children in school. Stevenson, Chen, and Uttal (1990) found that low-income African American mothers have positive attitudes about education and are eager to help their children succeed in school. Additional research shows that African American parents contribute substantially to their children's intellectual and cognitive development, a finding that holds true across socioeconomic groups (see Slaughter & Epps, 1987). In the next few sections, issues that are salient to academic success in African American children are discussed.

Family and Community Influences on School Achievement

It is generally agreed that teacher and school variables, especially quality teaching and expectations among teachers that all children can achieve, positively affect young African American children's school performance (e.g., Comer, Haynes, & Hamilton-Lee, 1990). But some social scientists have argued that parents may be the primary factors in contributing to school success (see, e.g., Bloom, 1982). Parents are the child's first teachers, and experiences within the home may set the stage for independence and achievement later in childhood (Slaughter-DeFoe, 1991). School-related skills learned within the parent-child system were found to enhance young African American children's potential for performing well in school (Scott-Jones, 1987).

The literature review provided by Slaughter and Epps (1987) cites specific parental influences on children's intellectual and cognitive development. African American children's advancement in language development, for example, is stimulated by maternal verbal responsiveness to the child's speech behaviors, and by verbal and nonverbal signals that communicate active interest in the child's play behaviors. Other work reviewed emphasizes the key role of positive parent-child relationships in influencing competence and good adjustment in children. Low-income African American preschool children identified as successful achievers through the first kindergarten year had mothers who set clear and consistent standards for behavior, but who also were warm, accepting, and willing to consider the child's point of view.

Almost identical themes have been identified in other studies. Swan and Stavros (1973) found a positive association between the cognitive styles of low-income African American preschoolers identified as effective learners and their parents' child-rearing practices. While specific techniques and individual child-rearing methods varied considerably among these families, several similar themes emerged, notably the positive influences present in the home. Parents of children with effective learning styles interacted verbally with them in situations that were not conflictual or punishing. Parents valued their children the most when they were happy, independent, and helpful. When asked what strategies they might recommend to other parents to help them raise their children, these parents identified encouragement, trust, respect for autonomy, didactic interaction, and love as key ingredients in child rearing.

Research with grade-school children has also delineated the importance of parenting variables. Focusing on maternal teaching styles in the homes of high- and low-achieving, low-income African American first graders, Scott-Jones (1987) found that in high-readiness homes, teaching and school-related activities were integrated into the flow of pleasant play activities, and seemed incidental rather than formal and intentional. High-readiness children took the lead in their own activities. Mothers acted as "supportive others," responding to their children's requests for help and attention rather than directing their activities. Related comparisons point to greater emphasis on "good behavior" and fewer books in the homes of low-readiness children. By contrast, being "smart," being a good student, and getting good grades were stressed in the homes of high-readiness children.

The importance of supportive parental figures becomes even more pronounced when research on African American adolescents is considered. When asked to name persons who influenced them to strive in school, high achievers included one or both parents without exception (Edwards, 1976). Similarly, the family profiles of academically successful African American high school students presented by R. M. Clark (1983) indicate a home atmosphere that is strongly supportive of academic achievement. Students recalled the prominent place of literacy-enhancing activities (e.g., reading, writing, word games, and hobbies) in their early childhood experiences. Further, high-achieving students' parents saw themselves as persons who were capable of coping successfully with life's problems.

The beneficial role of extended family networks in African American parents' overall well-being and ability to carry out parenting responsibilities effectively has been well documented in the research literature. Extended family members can be sources of support for both single- and two-parent families in caring for school-age children (H. P. McAdoo, 1982). African American mothers who feel supported by extended family members are more effective teachers of their children in the home (Slaughter & Epps, 1987); assistance from extended family members in general, and from their own mothers in particular, has a positive effect on African American adolescent mothers' educational and economic achievements, on their parenting skills, and on their children's development (see Taylor, Chatters, Tucker, & Lewis, 1990).

The role of the church in the informal support network of African American families has also been investigated. Church involvement can have positive effects on African American families (Taylor et al., 1990). In a study of low-income African American fifth-grade children and their parents, Bright (1992) found that family church attendance correlated strongly with children's academic achievement. Families of high achievers were

significantly more likely to attend church than families of low achievers. When questioned about the importance of church in their own lives, parents' responses indicated that religious involvement and participation in church-related activities reduced psychological distress, enhanced self-esteem and feelings of personal well-being, and gave them a sense of control. One mother stated simply, "There is strength in church" (Bright, p. 112).

In previous discussions of the socialization process in African American families, it has been noted that the Black child-rearing task has an added layer of complexity (Hale, 1991; London & Devore, 1988; H. P. McAdoo, 1985; Peters, 1985). Peters, for example, points out that African American parents must teach their children the skills needed for potential success in both an African American cultural context and a mainstream American culture that insidiously devalues the qualities attributed to Blackness.

LeVine (1988) has suggested that all cultures evolve a set of customs for responding to environmental hazards that might jeopardize the attainment of child-rearing goals. Consistent with this view, Holliday, Henning, and Johnson's (1983) research on African American maternal beliefs indicates that mothers' concerns with the social contexts of child rearing include awareness that Black children need to be prepared for social realities that might complicate, confound, or obstruct their development, and for the social competence necessitated by these realities. Mothers were particularly concerned that their children be well informed about Black history, feel good about being Black, and actively engage any obstacles encountered.

Racial identity and its relation to achievement has also been explored. The research suggests that parents of academically successful African American students may place more emphasis on pride in racial heritage, positive attitude toward ethnicity, and racial-social awareness than do parents of less successful students. Bowman and Howard (1985) found that school grades correlated significantly with African American adolescents' reports of parental support for positive Black identity development. Youths whose parents had given them no information about race relations in the United States scored the lowest grades.

Another issue that has received attention is the alarming rate of academic failure among African American males as compared with African American females; the latter generally perform better in school (see, e.g., Slaughter-DeFoe et al., 1990). This situation, which has sparked much debate (see, e.g., Dent, 1991; Hare, 1985; Hare & Castanell, 1985; Kunjufu, 1983), has prompted the development of comprehensive educational programs or "immersion" schools, designed exclusively for African American children, primarily for males (see Murrell, 1993, for a discussion of issues in this area). As described by Dent, the primary goal of such efforts is to bolster the self-esteem, self-confidence, and self-worth of African American children and youth in order to prepare them to deal with racism and other issues of concern to Black males. To achieve these objectives, curricula emphasize Black history and culture in addition to academic work. While it is not clear whether these programs have yet been evaluated with any rigor, preliminary reports suggest they have been successful in increasing student motivation and in improving school retention rates and standardized test scores among economically disadvantaged Black children and youth (see Dent).

Some researchers have attempted to identify protective factors that might promote healthy development of African American children in spite of chronic poverty and discrimination (see, e.g., R. M. Clark, 1983; Edwards, 1976; Pollard, 1989; Shields, 1989). Pollard, for example, has discussed successful school achievement of inner-city African American children in terms of resiliency or childhood coping behavior. She suggests that resilient children encounter the same stresses as their peers, but are buffered against the adverse effects of these stresses by mediating factors within themselves, their families, and the school/community environments. These sources of support are associated with social-psychological factors such as self-perceptions, attitudes, aspects of intrinsic motivation, and interpersonal relationships (see Werner, 1984).

There is no denying that living in blighted urban areas can impose powerful limitations on the support networks children can construct for themselves; deteriorating housing and inadequate health care and social services also affect children profoundly. Yet inner-city children and youth can and do differ in their personal social networks in ways that then affect their life chances. Ogbu (1981), for example, has noted that attitudes of hopefulness or of despair are acquired through social networks in which members share and reinforce these attitudes. Ogbu has also emphasized that neighborhood networks can orient young people toward or away from behaviors that promote school success. Supportive home and neighborhood/community environments can impart positive influences on low-income African American urban children's life goals and school attendance and achievement (R. M. Clark, 1983).

Parental Involvement in the School

Educators are recognizing to an increasing degree the importance of engaging low-income families and communities as partners in the educational process (see Heleen, 1990). Partnerships between families/communities and schools provide continuity between the child's home/community and school environments (J. L. McAdoo, 1979), a factor that is crucial in the case of economically and socially disadvantaged African American children who may lack a secure home-school link (Comer, 1985; Spencer, 1985). Collaborative efforts among families, communities, and schools can extend the resources available to the school and broaden opportunities for children's learning (Swap, 1993). Even more compelling, higher levels of parental involvement in the school have been found to be associated with higher levels of academic achievement in African American children (Slaughter-DeFoe, 1991).

Although these arguments make rational and factual sense, there are still many obstacles to parental involvement in schools. Historically, public schools serving impoverished families and communities have not concerned themselves with the need for massive societal change. Indeed, some have argued that public schools have served as agents to perpetuate the status quo (see, e.g., Kozol, 1975, 1991). In accounting for widespread school failure among African American children and youth, schools have frequently shifted the blame to the victims themselves (see, e.g., Murrell, 1993). Because of these and other factors, schools have been a source of alienation for many minority parents (see, e.g., Calabrese, 1990; Comer, 1985; Hare, 1987).

What can be done to improve relationships between minority parents and schools and, in so doing, create conditions that are more beneficial for children? Steven Leonard, an African American inner-city public school principal (quoted in Thompson, 1991), has noted that many parents are "misinformed or intimidated or feel unwelcomed, at best, when they walk into a school" (p. 34). While also stressing the importance of helping teachers become "master teachers," in the sense that they can all teach *every* student in the classroom, Leonard describes himself as "somebody [whose] mission it is to serve the needs of parents," because "if you are supporting parents, then you're supporting children in the best way that anyone can support them" (p. 34). Some programs are having measurable success in helping public schools build their partnerships with low-income African American families (see Epstein & Dauber, 1991; Epstein, Herrick, & Coates, in press).

In spite of the many challenges they face, there is evidence that low-income African American parents can feel empowered in their relationships with schools. In interviews with 58 mothers and fathers of low-income African American fifth-grade students, Bright (1992) found that many of these parents were intimately involved in their children's educational experiences and felt they had good relationships with their children's schools. When asked, "Does the school play an important role in the way you raise your child?," one mother said:

> Yes, myself and the school, play a very important part together because we're working on the same thing, and that is to see a child get an education, to show the child that we care, and to let them know also what they're doing wrong. We both play very, very important roles in their lives. (Bright, 1992)

The importance of family involvement is also evident during the middle grades (Dauber & Epstein, 1993) and at the secondary school level (e.g., R. M. Clark, 1983; Edwards, 1976; Shields, 1989; Swap, 1993). Clark's findings indicate that parents of academically successful African American high school students were more likely to be assertive in their attempts to keep informed about their children's progress in school.

The research reviewed on African American family involvement in education indicates that social supports to families, parental involvement in the home and in the school, and parental support for positive racial/cultural identity development are central to our understanding of school achievement in low-income African American children. Highlighting forces within families that contribute to school success should encourage a movement beyond stereotypical and limited perspectives of all low-income African American families and children. By focusing on the positive outcomes that can be achieved, we will be better able to formulate strategies and policies that are supportive of the successful progress of low-income African American children and their families.

As shown in this review, low-income African American parents believe strongly in the value of an education and contribute substantially to their children's achievement development. However, it is not enough to focus upon family beliefs and modes of functioning. The review included literature suggesting that successful implementation of the factors necessary to construct a positive educational experience requires addressing issues of inequality within the school, the workplace, and society itself.

CHINESE AMERICAN FAMILY INVOLVEMENT IN EDUCATION

"My biggest headache as a teacher is the non-involvement of Chinese parents. They only care about their work and how much money they make. They have no idea how their children are doing in school.... Phone calls to discuss the child's progress are not returned. Invitations to come to school for parent-child conferences are ignored. It seems that no matter what the school does, Chinese parents simply don't want to be involved. Why are they so busy?" So complained a White teacher who has taught in New York City's Chinatown for over ten years. (Interview reported in Ming Sum, 1990)

To what extent is this description of Chinese parental involvement with the schools an accurate one? Are there other pieces that must be considered to make the picture complete? What do we mean by parental involvement with education? Does it make any difference in the school performance of Chinese American children?

What Does the Literature Reveal about the Relationship between Chinese American Parents and Schools?

A comprehensive review of literature on family processes and educational achievement (Dornbusch & Wood, 1989) finds that better school performance is associated with frequent parental participation in school functions, but this finding is not generalizable to Asian American student populations. As we will show in this literature review, Asian American parents generally care deeply about their children's education and contribute substantially to the child's learning environment, but parental support may take forms different from those of other cultures. To acknowledge the tremendous diversity among Asian Americans and to avoid overgeneralization, this section of the chapter will focus on Chinese Americans, the largest Asian American ethnic group and the one with the longest history in the United States.

According to the 1990 census (*Asians in America*, 1991), the nation's 1.5 million Chinese Americans constitute 0.7% of the U.S. population. If trends in the last three decades are any indication, and barring any drastic change in immigration policy, the number of Chinese Americans is expected to increase.

They are concentrated in urban areas of six states, in descending order by size of Chinese American population: California, New York, Hawaii, Texas, New Jersey, and Massachusetts. Immigrants outnumber American-born Chinese by roughly two to one. Despite more than a century of severe discrimination in immigration, employment, housing, education, citizenship, marriage, and social life, Chinese Americans as a group have taken advantage of educational and career opportunities that opened up after World War II. With changes in the immigration law in 1965 favoring the professionally trained, the educational profile of Chinese Americans has been transformed. Since the 1970s, Chinese American students have been perceived by the American public as superachievers or math whiz kids. On a number of commonly accepted indicators of educational achievement—such as drop-out rates, college enrollment rates, and college graduation rates—Chinese Americans as a group have indeed fared well, even outperforming Whites (Hsia, 1988).

However, aggregate data do not tell the whole story. The diversity in country of origin, language, socioeconomic status, educational background, and degree of acculturation makes it extremely difficult to make generalizations about the contemporary Chinese American community. As pointed out by Kwong (1987), the Chinese American community has become a bimodal community of "uptown Chinese" and "downtown Chinese." Roughly 30% of Chinese Americans are professionals and entrepreneurs, well educated, some American-born and some immigrants, enjoying high incomes, and living outside of Chinatowns. Another 30% are manual and service workers, more recent immigrants, speaking no English, having little education, and residing in Chinatowns. This bimodal distribution must be kept in mind when discussing educational achievement and parent involvement, or any other characteristic of Chinese Americans.

The literature examining the educational achievement of Chinese Americans is vast. (See Siu, 1992, for a recent literature review and bibliography on this subject.) Although the "model minority" myth about Asian Americans has been debunked (e.g., Hu, 1989; Kim & Chun, 1992; Suzuki, 1977), and the adequacy of the cultural thesis to explain school success has been challenged (Ogbu, 1990; Siu, 1992; Sue & Okazaki, 1990), the public as well as the professional community continues to be deeply interested in the role of Chinese culture in children's academic achievement.

Given the amount of attention to the ways Chinese family structure, practices, and values influence children's educational achievement, the dearth of research studies on Chinese American parental involvement in education is surprising. There is no book or article in research journals that deals exclusively with the frequency and nature of Chinese American (not generic Asian American) parental contacts with the schools and/or their participation in the community around educational issues. The possible relationship between extent and nature of parental involvement and outcome (school achievement of the children) remains an unexplored field. Available information about Chinese American parental involvement tends to be limited and anecdotal. To give a complete picture of Chinese American parental involvement in education, this review has drawn on oral histories, unpublished works such as doctoral dissertations, and sources in the Chinese language.

Parental Involvement in the Home

The literature is replete with references to the value Chinese American parents place on education. While valuing education is by no means a claim unique to Chinese Americans, what is distinctive is the tendency of Chinese Americans to define their cultural identity in terms of academic achievement (e.g., Lau, 1988; P. S. Lee, 1983); to be a scholar and do well in school is to be Chinese. Education is also seen as an important, perhaps the only, avenue for upward social mobility.

Findings from studies of family socialization patterns conducted in China, Taiwan, and Hong Kong, as well as those conducted in the United States (e.g., Chen & Uttal, 1988; Hess, Chang, & McDevitt, 1987; D. Y. F. Ho, 1986; Lin, 1988; Schneider & Lee, 1990; Sue & Sue, 1971; Yao, 1985), are surprisingly consistent. When compared with their American Caucasian counterparts, Chinese parents tend to exercise more control over family members, emphasize a greater sense of family obligation, value grades more than general cognitive achievement in children, evaluate more realistically a child's academic and personality characteristics, be less easily satisfied with a child's accomplishments, and believe more in effort and less in innate ability as a factor in school success. These descriptions reflect a traditional Chinese perspective, but there is some evidence (e.g., Lau, 1988) to suggest that even American-born Chinese parents retain some traditional Chinese parenting values and practices.

According to Epstein (1992), one type of school and family partnership consists of "basic parental obligations to make children ready for school" (p. 1145). Another type is involvement in home-based learning activities. These are the types of child-centered involvement with which Chinese American parents feel most comfortable and in which they probably excel. As Epstein notes, the term "parental involvement" needs to be conceptualized broadly as "school and family partnerships" to include members of the extended family, which assumes great significance in Chinese culture. One should never assume that parents are the only ones who involve themselves with the children's education. Grandparents, aunts, uncles, cousins, and even older siblings are sometimes key players in a child's schooling, whether or not they live under the same roof (e.g., Siu, 1994; Wong, 1990). A review of the literature (e.g., Schneider & Lee, 1990; Slaughter-Defoe et al., 1990; Wong, 1990; Yao, 1985) reveals many ways in which Chinese American families attempt to support children's school performance: reducing the number of household chores for children; using Chinese proverbs and folk stories to motivate children to study; purchasing workbooks; establishing study times; scheduling children's free time; taking children to the library; teaching the three R's before children enter kindergarten; enrolling children in language schools and music classes on weekends or after school; and assisting them with homework. These practices are not limited to families that are educated and affluent. Wong's (1990) ethnography of family literacy activities pursued by low-income, non-English-proficient parents documents the considerable amount of money, time, and energy committed to helping children get good grades. Creating homework, for example, seems to be a common strategy. The practice is motivated by a firm belief that practice makes perfect, a desire to keep children occupied, and a need to compensate for the perceived lax practice of the American public schools.

The above positive picture of active family involvement in the Chinese American child's education must be counterbalanced by the one portrayed in a comprehensive study of new immigrant children in New York City's Chinatown (Sung, 1987). Sung concluded that "parental absence is a pervasive phenomenon" (p. 224). The poorer new immigrant Chinese American family has in fact delegated many of its functions (e.g., feeding, medical attention, providing supervision, monitoring homework) to the school or to an after-school program. Older children take jobs to supplement the family income; in many instances, education takes a back seat to the economic survival of the family.

Parental Involvement in the School

Whereas parents are actively engaged in the home with their children's education, there is not a matching interaction between school personnel and parents. "A cool response to school activities; a hiding of dissatisfaction deep in the heart" is the title of the lead article of a Chinese newspaper's special issue on Chinese American parental involvement in the schools (K. Ho & Fong, 1990, p. 1). These two phrases perhaps best capture the general state of the Chinese American parent-school relationship. A recent survey (Ho & Fong) in New York City of a broad spectrum of parents with regard to educational level, children's age, and length of residency in the United States yields some disturbing findings. The child's report card was for many the only means of school-home communication, but only 42% of all respondents could read and understand everything without the help of a dictionary or translator, and 1% of the parents surveyed did not read the report card. While most claimed that parental involvement was necessary to improve education for children, only 27% regularly attended parent-teacher conferences and other school functions; only 11% voted in parents' council elections or on school issues.

Although school participation was minimal across the board, parents who had only an elementary school level of education (22.5%) had the least parental involvement, presumably because of the long working hours necessary for their survival. These respondents did not believe their involvement could have an impact on the quality of their children's education.

Lack of English proficiency and long working hours are often cited by school personnel and parents as barriers to more active involvement in the schools (e.g., First & Carrera, 1988; E. Lee, 1988; New York City Board of Education, 1980). While those obstacles can be formidable, attitudinal factors cannot be discounted, since available data suggest that parental involvement remains low even when Chinese-speaking teachers and counselors are available and all notices are written in both Chinese and English (Ming Sum, 1990). In Yao's study (1985) comparing Chinese American parents with Caucasian parents, the former, though college educated and of a middle- or upper-middle-class background, still visited the school and attended activities less frequently than did their Caucasian counterparts. A number of explanations have been offered for the minimal Chinese American parental presence in the schools as volunteer assistants, advocates for their own children, or participants in policy making. These include unwillingness to appear to challenge school authority (Davino, 1993; Hsu, 1993; Yao, 1985); an unfamiliarity with established protocols for scheduling appointments with the teacher (Chou, 1991); and skepticism about the efficacy of speaking out (K. Ho & Fong, 1990; Hsu, 1993). Of course, these explanations may be more applicable to Chinese immigrants than to American-born Chinese parents. In the 1992 election, several American-born Chinese in California won seats on school committees. Unfortunately, no study has yet compared the parental involvement of Chinese immigrants with that of American-born Chinese.

Could the low level of participation indicate trust in the school? The educated, suburban parents in Yao's study (1985) seemed satisfied with the quality of education. These findings, however, contradicted those of two other surveys (Hirata, 1975; K. Ho & Fong, 1990). While it is true that Chinese American parents tend to accord legitimacy to the school and the teacher, it does not automatically follow that they are satisfied with them. Ogbu's assertion (1983) that Chinese immigrants tend to think of this country's education as superior to that in the home country refers to access to educational opportunities, not necessarily the quality of education. While many Chinese Americans see higher education as more accessible in the United States, and this sometimes provides the motivation for immigration, they have grave concerns about the lax discipline in the schools, lack of moral education, poor mathematics training, and insufficient homework (Chan, 1991; Hirata, 1975; K. Ho & Fong, 1990; Kenny Lai, quoted in J. F. J. Lee, 1991, p. 74). Instead of complaining to school authorities, the prevailing Chinese American parental strategy is to take compensatory measures—inventing homework, sending children to church or to Chinese-language school to learn discipline and moral values, hiring a tutor, and enrolling children in after-school programs such as Kumon Math Workshops.

Some strategies to involve Chinese American parents further have been tried by schools and found somewhat useful, such as setting up telephone networks (New York City Board of Education, 1980), offering ESL classes in the schools (New York City Board of Education, 1990), and cosponsoring with local colleges a guest speaker program featuring prominent Chinese Americans from different fields (Young, Scorza, & Sica, 1984).

Parental Involvement in the Community

This is an area in which there is practically no research. The famous *Lau v. Nichols* case (1974), which went all the way to the Supreme Court, is perhaps the best-known illustration of how Chinese American parents mobilized themselves to demand appropriate education for non-English-proficient students. When the San Francisco Unified School District delayed implementation of this court ruling, parents formed a citizens' task force to develop a master plan for bilingual education (Wang, 1976).

One of the most successful information and referral services set up by and for Chinese American parents is the Chinese American Parents' Association of New York City, which has a membership of over 800 in seven districts. Its hotline handles over 1,500 calls per year from parents. In addition, the organization offers newsletters and workshops to familiarize recent immigrants with the American educational system, and mediates disputes between school systems and Chinese American parents. Other local and national community groups support Chinese American family involvement in the schools or advocate for Chinese American students. (See Appendix at the end of this chapter for a sample of resource organizations.)

Chinese American parental involvement in education is largely uncharted territory, ripe for exploration. First, more is known about parental involvement in the home than about school governance and advocacy. Second, little data exists on the effects on achievement of different degrees and types of involvement. Finally, more is known about the involvement of overseas-born Chinese parents than about American-born Chinese parents, primarily because research access is made easier by the concentration of Chinese immigrants in Chinatowns. We know little about parental involvement patterns of Chinese Americans who are scattered in suburban communities and whose children are not enrolled in bilingual programs. Shoho's 1992 study of three generations of parental involvement among Japanese Americans in Hawaii is instructive. First-generation Japanese American parents show a different pattern of family-school partnership from third-generation parents, with the latter being more directly and actively involved in the schools. Is such a pattern true of Chinese Americans?

Three lines of inquiry could prove fruitful and close the gaps in the literature: (a) a comparison of immigrant and native-born parental involvement; (b) a study of the effects of differential involvement on achievement; and (c) a comparison of family-school relationships of several generations of Chinese Americans.

IRISH AMERICAN PARENTAL INVOLVEMENT IN EDUCATION

Why Study Irish Americans?

The inclusion of a White European ethnic group in this chapter may seem odd. It is. First, there is almost no information about current achievement levels of Irish youngsters or the practices and values of Irish families related to their children's success in school. Research studies that explore the link between family practices and school achievement in White families rarely distinguish among different ethnicities. Second, the patterns of discrimination and minimal school achievement that affected the Irish as a group from 1840 to about 1920 have all but disappeared. Thus there is no current "problem" with the achievement of Irish youth that would justify research, except perhaps differential achievement by class (e.g., Lightfoot, 1983), which affects all ethnicities. Third, there is a question of whether contemporary Irish Americans even have a distinct identity, or whether the long process of assimilation has re-

RESEARCH ON FAMILIES, SCHOOLS, AND COMMUNITIES: A MULTICULTURAL PERSPECTIVE • 511

sulted in an undifferentiated "American" identity or, as Alba (1900) suggests, a slightly less amalgamated identification as "European Americans." Is there perhaps no culture left to study?

There are cogent reasons to investigate the current and past meanings of a White ethnic identity. First, multicultural education embraces all ethnicities, and many contend that the development of cultural sensitivity and the ability to take another's perspective begin with an exploration of one's own roots and family values. Since only about 11% of our teachers are people of color (Hawley, 1989), and the Irish have been well represented in the ranks of teachers for generations (e.g., Perlmann, 1988), an exploration of Irish American values and their origins could be a useful entry point into multicultural studies for many current teachers and the children they teach.

Second, there is evidence that Irish American identity still has meaning for many Americans. D. Clark (1991), drawing on his research in contemporary Philadelphia, argues that Irish ethnicity is neither disappearing nor transforming, but continues to be deeply influential in contributing to a recognizable Irish American identity composed of character traits, behaviors, and beliefs. Alba (1990), in lengthy interviews with 524 randomly chosen residents of the Albany-Troy-Schenectady area in 1984–1985, discovered that about two thirds of those with Irish ancestry identified with their heritage, and of these, half considered their Irish background to be of at least moderate importance. With as much as one sixth of the nation now reporting Irish ancestry, there are thus a good number of families for whom an in-depth exploration of their heritage and its meaning for children's success in school could be illuminating.

Finally, although the Irish no longer experience overt discrimination, what has been learned from their history of seeking access is instructive, so long as that information is understood in context, and caution is exercised in generalizing to the struggles of other groups. For example, in exploring the historical differences in the political experiences of American Blacks and White ethnics, Cornacchia and Nelson (1992) point out that "of great significance was the fact that Blacks were forced to participate in a continuous politics of seeking basic citizenship rights, while white ethnic groups could take their citizenship rights for granted after early years of immigration to America" (p. 102).

Background

Early Immigration Patterns. Small numbers of Irish immigrated to the United States during the 17th and 18th centuries. They were quite skilled and economically successful—merchants and artisans with confidence and resources. Many were Protestants and Ulstermen of Scottish ancestry, and some became prosperous and prominent citizens (see Griffin, 1990). As the economy of Ireland declined and failures multiplied in the subsistence crop of potatoes, the number of immigrants increased, but the skills and resources they brought with them were minimal. From 1841 to 1850 about 781,000 of the "famine Irish" came to America's shores. From 1851 to 1860 the number climbed to about 914,000. Between 1820 and 1850 the Irish

constituted 42.3% of all American immigrants and were the single largest immigrant group in Boston, New York, Baltimore, and Cincinnati (see Fallows, 1979; Handlin, 1941; Swap & Krasnow, 1992).

These 19th-century Irish were generally hired as unskilled laborers at the bottom of the economic ladder. Many of the jobs available to men were dangerous; the Irish experienced an extremely high rate of accident and death in their work on the nation's canals, bridges, railroads, and mines. The predominant occupation of Irish women was as servants (Diner, 1983). Employers and want ads during this period often stated explicitly that "No Irish need apply."

Extensive stereotyping of Irish Americans occurred during the period from 1820 to 1865. Perhaps most surprising to us now is that some people believed that there was "scientific" evidence to support the widespread belief that the Irish were inherently inferior. Evidence was provided through the pseudoscience of phrenology, a method of reading character from the shape and protuberances of the skull. Roediger (1991) noted: "Some suggested that the Irish were part of a separate caste or a 'dark' race, possibly originally African. Racial comparisons of Irish and Blacks were not infrequently flattering to the latter group" (p. 133). The negative stereotypes, fed by nativism and the emergence of the Know-Nothing Party, characterized the Irish as rough, uncivilized, and brutal. As Fraser (1979) summarized the process: "As has so often happened in American history, the poor were blamed for all of the problems they faced. The Irish were seen as drunks; they were the ones arrested; they were the ones on the poor rolls" (p. 38).

The schools reflected the social stereotyping of the larger society, and education provided a persistent, fundamental, and emotional focal point in the many conflicts between nativists and Irish Catholics. The public schools welcomed Irish children with ambivalence. On the one hand, it was the mission of the common school to serve as the primary agent of civilization and assimilation and to "make every Irish Catholic a good Yankee" (Fraser, 1979, p. 32). On the other hand, in many communities, especially in the Northeast, Irish children were not treated with respect, as Ravitch (1974) explains in her history of the New York City schools: "The public schools were reproachful, disapproving of their habits and morality, disparaging their family, their religion, and their culture" (p. 33).

Transition from "Famine Irish" to Respectability. The Irish made a transition from poverty to respectability in the period from 1865 to 1930 (see Fallows, 1979; Miller, 1985; Perlmann, 1988; Shannon, 1963). In a more extensive review of the literature, Swap and Krasnow (1992) argue that there were several factors that supported this transition. One important factor was the locations in which Irish families chose to settle: Irish Americans assimilated relatively quickly into communities such as Philadelphia and San Francisco that were expanding, had accessible housing, offered options for skilled and unskilled work, and had social and community organizations open to the Irish.

The Irish used their numbers to advantage in gaining control of local politics in most major cities of the Midwest and Northeast during this period. Their success was based on "gifts of organization and eloquence, a sense of cohesion, and the beginnings of a political tradition in the nationalist agitation of Ireland" (Shannon, 1963, p. 60). Political control of the cities spurred access to jobs and economic security, and the daughters of the Irish became heavily represented among the teachers and administrators of the schools (Perlmann, 1988).

The Irish have had a long tradition of relying on the community to support its members, and Funchion's (1983) *Irish American Voluntary Organizations* is a weighty tome. Irish American voluntary organizations served many purposes. Among the most important were support for new immigrants (giving advice and information, helping them find jobs and housing) and socialization of newcomers into the social, literary, and economic traditions of mainstream culture (see Light, 1985). The Catholic Church also provided an important sense of community and continuity for Irish immigrants. Church members founded many social institutions such as orphanages and hospitals, "fashioning an almost self-sufficient Catholic urban ethnic America" (McCaffrey, 1992, p. 13).

A key factor in the achievement and upward mobility of the peasant Irish was the establishment of Catholic schools as alternatives to the public schools. Different cities enrolled varying numbers of their Catholic children in parochial schools. In 1908, for example, sample percentages were: Boston, 26%; Cleveland, 71%; Newark, 76%; New York, 47%; and Philadelphia, 69% (Perlmann, 1988). States Fass (1989):

[Catholic schools] became an alternative and complex school system which, by the middle of the twentieth century, enrolled around 14 percent of all children of school age and included in 1962 almost five and one-half million children. . . . Of all Catholic children, the number of those who attended Catholic schools has rarely exceeded 50 percent throughout the twentieth century. (p. 191)

According to Perlmann's analysis of the contribution of Catholic schools to upward mobility for Irish youngsters in Providence, Rhode Island, Irish children in these schools were more likely than their cohorts in the public schools to enroll in college preparatory programs and to graduate from high school. Moreover, the Catholic Church itself was a place where paths to success were open for Irish youngsters.

Current Status. The levels of educational achievement and occupational status of Irish Americans have been above the national average for several decades (Fallows, 1979). Drawing upon data published by the National Opinion Research Center from 1972 to 1984, Vosburgh and Juliana (1990) calculated that the Irish had higher occupational prestige and educational levels than either Italians or "Other Whites." Access to college as a result of the G.I. Bill after World War II was an important stimulus.

A lingering negative stereotype, sometimes presented as fact, is that Catholics in general and Irish Americans in particular have not distinguished themselves as scholars, scientists, and academicians. Steinberg (1981) tackles the myth of Catholic anti-intellectualism by presenting data documenting that, in terms of their numbers in the general population, by 1974 Catholics had achieved parity with Protestants in their representation among college faculty in this country and almost achieved parity in their representation among the faculty of our most prestigious academic institutions. In a comparison of Catholics with Protestants and Jews, he argues that the slower entry of Irish into the ranks of academia was not due to ethnic differences but to initial social-class disadvantages in the form of literacy and occupational skills.

Family Support for Educational Achievement

Celtic Heritage. The long scholarly tradition of the Irish and its importance as an enduring value even during eras of oppression is fundamental to the understanding of current Irish American values about achievement. Irish intellectual and artistic achievement has a proud history dating back to about 400 B.C. Celtic influence forged cultural unity: a common language and a rich oral tradition of poetry and song; laws that reflected customs and values of the entire island population; and a distinctive artistic style used in stone carvings, sculpture, and metalwork that continued to influence artists throughout the Middle Ages. Early Catholic missionaries who came to Ireland around 500–400 B.C. acknowledged and incorporated aspects of the Celtic tradition into the rituals of the Catholic Church. They also established monasteries that both preserved the learning of antiquity and became centers of scholarship. From the fifth to the eighth centuries A.D., while chaos reigned in most of Europe, Celtic Ireland was experiencing its golden age (Fitzgibbon, 1983).

Celts in Ireland had an important scholarly tradition whose emissaries were Druids, poets, and bards. As Fitzgibbon (1983) explained, Druids were the spiritual and temporal advisors to the tribal leaders as well as the custodians of the tribe's beliefs and education. He contends that "in Ireland, some if not all of these men could write and some knew Latin and probably Greek" (p. 49). To become a Druid required long and arduous training, as the tribe's sagas and genealogies were committed to memory rather than written. Poets were powerful courtiers, responsible for creating verses to glorify the chief and curse his enemies. However, they were also scholars; the 10th and highest grade of poet had to memorize at least 350 stories. Bards carried the poets' words through the countryside, often with musical accompaniment. The legacy of history and language conveyed by the bards was so important to the Irish that they maintained bardic schools to carry on these traditions until the beginning of the 18th century. It can be argued (e.g., Greeley, 1972) that the Irish veneration of scholarship, appreciation of polished gifts in poetry and language, emphasis on the hero and the heroic, and use of Gaelic are all legacies from the Celtic past that continue to shape today's Irish and Irish Americans.

Denial of Access to Formal Education by the English. The continuous flowering of an Irish intellectual tradition was suppressed by the English conquest and persecution of the Irish Catholics. The English began the tradition of seeing the Irish as savages as early as the 12th-century Norman invasion (Deane, 1991). The history of English incursions and failed rebellions extended over many centuries. Cromwell's supporters sold thousands of Irish into servitude in the West Indies, and by the end of the 17th century the English owned 95% of the property of Ireland and enjoyed a complete monopoly over political power (Greeley, 1972). The Penal Codes of 1691 prohibited Irish Catholics from voting, serving on a jury, teaching school, entering the university, becoming a lawyer, maintaining schools, speaking in Gaelic, or sending their children abroad to be educated.

Maintaining the Heritage. Nonetheless, Gaelic language and history was transmitted orally within communities; itinerant schoolmasters (often friars or priests) taught the classics and Gaelic culture in "hedge schools" (behind a hedge to avoid detection), though their work was limited and illegal. As Fitzgibbon (1983) insists: "A respect, even a reverence for learning was part of the Irish tradition" (p. 251). Some of those with means fled to Europe for an education, and European theological colleges provided opportunities for the training of priests, many of whom returned. The Catholic Church, though suppressed, provided continuity with an honored past, connection with the community, some access to education, and justification for suffering. But especially in the 19th century, immigration to America, "the land of opportunity," embodied the best hope of poor Irish Catholics for owning land, becoming financially successful, and obtaining formal education—if not for oneself, then for one's children.

Maintaining Irish Values Related to Achievement in America

Parental Support. How did Irish American parents support the achievement of their children in school? Information is available from oral histories, letters, autobiographies, novels, and plays; very limited information is available from psychological or educational research (see Swap & Krasnow, 1992). At least through 1920, many Irish immigrants and their children were unable to take advantage of much formal education, as earning enough to keep the family together was the priority. In Curran's (1948/1986) autobiographical novel *The Parish and the Hill,* for example, a major theme is the need for a brilliant son to give up his dreams for a college education in order to support the family, though the veneration for books, history, literature, and poetry is a shaping force in the family. Becoming educated to be economically successful is one important component of the Irish reverence for education; appreciating scholarship for its own sake is another (see Fanning, 1990); becoming educated so as to have a voice at the table and participate in the ritual of conversation and debate is a third (see Fanning; Swap & Krasnow).

In a sociological analysis, Biddle (1981) asserts that the Irish Catholic family of the parish she was investigating (1920–1950) emphasized being respectable (doing the right thing and being polite), encouraged achievement, and valued family cohesion and stability more than individual achievement, especially for girls. Differences between enclaved and middle-class families were found in the former's "lesser amount of overt affection, the favoritism toward sons, the preference for action, the use of alcohol to increase sociability, the obligations of families to one

another, and the gathering of family members for rituals and holidays" (p. 106). Although Biddle found considerable differences within her subset of middle-class families, children's achievement in school was consistently an important value, especially encouraged by mothers. Sociologists Vosburgh and Juliana (1990) analyzed the responses of Irish and Italian respondents to National Opinion Research data. Members of both groups valued highly the trait "trying hard to succeed."

Genova (1981) conducted ethnographic and questionnaire studies to explore the interaction effects of school and home environments on students of varying race, class, ethnicity, and gender. As one of the five groups studied, the ethnographic portion employed a sample of eight Irish American middle school children from a working-class community, each of whom was visited by the researchers 10 times. Household routines were not formally structured to encourage achievement, but a parental emphasis on children doing well in school was mentioned. Children were aware that they were Irish, but did not know what that entailed or how they knew it. Most parents in this sample attended sports activities, but did not facilitate their children's participation in other organized programs.

The questionnaire study tapped 1,290 seventh- and eighth-grade students from several communities. Of the five groups studied, the Irish American children ($n = 162$) gave the highest ratings to home climate variables that emphasized school learning and out-of-school learning. In terms of outcome variables, the Irish were second only to the French in terms of reading achievement and about in the middle of the distribution in terms of grades and teachers' ratings. Methodological limitations made it difficult to ascertain whether the differences that were found among ethnic groups were due to class, recency of immigration, mixed or particular ethnicity, or some combination of these and other variables. However, it was a fruitful study in setting directions for future research.

Unlike the considerable research devoted to the study of child-family interactions among, for example, African American families, no studies were found that explored communication patterns, family processes, family structures, or family practices specifically of Irish American families that may be related to school achievement. Although there have been several important studies that explore differential achievement of students by class or race, patterns of parental involvement in their children's schooling, and the significance of school practices that involve families regardless of race or class (e.g., Epstein, 1986b; Lareau, 1989; Snow, Barnes, Chandler, Goodman, & Hemphill, 1991), White families in these studies are not differentiated by ethnicity.

Parental Involvement in School and Community Activities. In general, parental involvement studies do not identify White families and their patterns of involvement by ethnicity or explore the particular kinds of activities at home and/or school that Irish American families develop to support children's achievement. No studies were found that explore similarities and differences in Irish American family involvement in parochial versus public school settings. Although one could speculate (and observation confirms) that Irish Americans are part of the legions who make up the cadre of school volunteers and who participate in parent-teacher organizations (PTOs), there are no data available about involvement by ethnicity.

Community activities (e.g., athletic competitions, church groups, and particularly Irish activities such as step-dancing classes) are available for families, although the relative involvement of Irish families in community activities as compared with other ethnic groups is not known. Irish societies and community organizations still flourish, particularly in larger cities, and provide opportunities for fellowship, charitable enterprises, support for new immigrants, educational pursuits, and connections to Ireland. Advocacy for Irish American students as a defined ethnic group does not appear to be a focus of these activities or organizations.

Exploration of the discrimination and negative stereotyping experienced historically by the Irish and Irish Americans provides interesting analogues to current patterns of discrimination. Particularly notable are the ways in which Irish Catholics held on to their beliefs about the value of education and the importance of scholarly traditions throughout the 19th century, despite lack of access to formal schooling in Ireland and minimal expectations for the achievement of the sons and daughters of the famine Irish in America.

The question of whether there are traceable Irish patterns of interest and emphasis (such as the importance of the oral tradition) remains to be resolved. Whether such "traits" could be drawn upon to support the success of Irish children in school is an open question, as is the question of whether there are patterns of support for schooling and achievement that are more characteristic of Irish families than of other groups. Clearly these are not questions that must be resolved to support the overall success of Irish American children in school; the hope of this work is that such questions might intrigue teachers and provide another window into multicultural education.

SUMMARY AND DISCUSSION

Crosscutting Themes

Several themes that crosscut the four summaries provide guiding principles for understanding school partnerships with families of diverse backgrounds. Families in all four cultural groups:

love and care for their children;
have, historically, valued and supported their children's education;
have, traditionally, drawn from the strengths of their extended families and communities for support, guidance, and motivation in raising and educating their children;
have made (and continue to make) personal sacrifices and investments so that their children will have the education they need to succeed in mainstream U.S. society.

All four groups experienced prejudice and discrimination in the United States because of their race, culture, and language. Yet, through their support for education, many families in all four groups have guided their children away from poverty to-ward greater prosperity, away from disdain toward greater respect. The Puerto Rican saying *Hoy por tí, mañana por mí* sounds very much like the commitments of other early immigrant groups, in which parents and older siblings worked overtime or on many jobs so that children (first mainly males) could graduate from high school and attend college. The first generation of college-goers in every racial or ethnic group always has been celebrated by their families and communities.

Most important:

• Differences within racial or ethnic groups may be greater than differences between them on all of these family factors, including support for their children's education, use of extended families and community networks, and involvement in schools.

This chapter describes the intragroup differences that show how wrong it is to generalize about a particular group. All Asian American families are not "model minorities" and, indeed, no group could fulfill such expectations. Of course, negative labels are no more correct or useful than positive stereotypes, as the chapter attests.

Members of every group did, do, and will vary widely in social class, recency of immigration, English- and native-language competencies, family educational background, area of residence, ethnicity of neighborhood, age of parents, intermarriage, and other measures of assimilation or acculturation. These variables are likely to be as or more important influences on family attitudes toward and behaviors about their children's education than country of origin, race, or ethnicity.

Puerto Rican family attitudes and practices in children's education also may be affected by the locale of parents' and/or students' early years and education, migration patterns, and the intensity of family connections with the Island or home country. African American families vary in levels of poverty and prosperity, family structure of one- or two-parent homes, and employed or unemployed (or underemployed) parents. Students in all ethnic groups respond differently to these variations in family situations, making some students more "resilient" than others to stressors (Winfield, 1991). Equally interesting, some children are nonresponsive to *advantages* that are offered by their families.

Thus, other variables that are likely to be more important than race or ethnicity concern the direct connections of families with children's learning:

• Research and practice have focused on children's and families' *failures*, but more will be learned from their *successes*.

Much of the literature on African American and on Latino children and their families focuses on their failures instead of their successes. Similarly, many negative stereotypes have guided educators to hold the lowest expectations for children of color and their families, and for most immigrant groups. At one time this was true for Chinese American and for Irish American children and families. When the focus is on student *success*, however, research suggests that there are some common factors and influences in families from all groups that override other factors: the presence of reading matter at home, family praise and guidance for being a good student and getting good grades, and family support for many literacy activities such as reading, writing, word games, poetry, and stories.

This chapter highlights another similarity across groups that remains a variable for focused study:

• Families teach their children about their multiple memberships.

For example, African American, Latino, and Chinese American families help their children to develop bicultural identities and competencies about their own ethnicity and about mainstream America. Perry (1993) describes this as encouraging students to learn to exercise their multiple memberships. She recognizes that African American youngsters may hold several racial, ethnic, and mainstream memberships. This perspective has even broader importance. Irish American children (and all White children) may need to become more aware of their own multiple memberships. This often is portrayed as a burden of minority or immigrant groups, but actually is everyone's burden or opportunity.

Research that accounts for the ways families within and across cultural groups vary on the numerous characteristics and behaviors described above will illuminate the real influences on family involvement in children's education and the dynamics by which school and family connections affect children's learning. The variables of importance go beyond the characteristics of students and their families.

For all four cultural groups:

• The school plays an important role in whether and how all families become involved in their children's education.

Although parents value education, they have traditionally been given little information about exactly how to support their children as students each year in school. Until recently, parents have mainly been left on their own to learn about their children's development, and to figure out whether and how to become involved at school. The new research on partnerships is showing, however, that in addition to the personal characteristics and experiences of families, the *school's leadership* to develop a program of partnership determines whether all families (including those of various educational and cultural backgrounds) are "enabled" to become and remain effective partners in their children's education (Epstein, 1992; Swap, 1993). The four summaries of groups in this chapter make important distinctions between family experiences with and readiness for involvement *at home* and *at school.* As our own studies have found, parents mostly want to know *how to help their own child at home each year.* Yet schools tend to focus heavily on parental visits to the school building. As schools build their programs, a better balance will be needed between practices to involve parents at home and at school.

Finally, for all four cultural groups:

• The concept of "partnership" acknowledges that neither families nor schools alone can educate and socialize children for their work in society.

Emerging from research and new practices is the understanding that neither family nor school alone can help children solve learning and development problems. Partnerships make it more likely that ideas, energy, and resources will be targeted to improve schools, strengthen families, and increase students' chances for success. School practices should help parents understand the school and their children's opportunities and programs. Two-way communication should help schools understand families' cultures, strengths, and goals. Both school and family need to exchange information about the children they share. And children need to know that their families and their teachers have similar expectations for them to work hard in the role of "student" in order to succeed in school and in society.

Following the Crosscutting Themes

The reviews of the four ethnic groups in this chapter suggest that differences in the nature and extent of family involvement and influence on children's education and on children's learning are not simply the result of fixed, unchangeable, culturally determined values and practices, but are likely to be explained by variations in family factors, community contexts, and school programs that systematize or organize practices of partnership. These variables must be examined and explained in comparative studies across cultural groups to address the questions:

• How much is *similar* and how much is *different* between and among families of different cultural groups? How should these features guide school programs to inform and involve families in their children's education?

For example:

• Do Puerto Rican parents value interdependence and cooperation more than other parents? Or is this a quality that varies within groups as much as or more than between them? Researchers have reported that Hispanic Americans, African Americans, Native Americans, Native Hawaiians, and other groups emphasize cooperation, interdependence, and exchange in their cultures. Others report that cooperation and interaction are general teaching tools that help all children learn.

• Do Chinese American families work more or better as managers of their children's education, or does this skill vary across families? Are these approaches determined by parents' education and experiences with schools, as some studies report (Baker & Stevenson, 1986; Useem, 1992), or by the schools' practices of informing parents about how to monitor and discuss schoolwork and homework with their youngsters, as other studies document (Epstein, 1986b; Dauber & Epstien, 1993)?

• Do Chinese American families make more explicit than other groups their desire that their children become fully competent in mainstream U.S. society, or do otherwise similar families make that goal equally explicit? How do families help their children attain the goal of competence in mainstream America? How do schools help families conduct the activities that will help their children reach this goal? How is this goal affected or balanced by family goals to help children retain and benefit from their cultural identities?

- Do Puerto Rican families value home life more than other families, or do these values and behaviors vary among families in all groups? Religiosity and ties to their churches are key factors in Irish American, Latino, and African American family life. All four groups' emphasis on the importance of extended families, relatives, and connections with their communities suggest similarities and variations among the families in all groups in terms of warmth, hospitality, and other qualities of home life.

- Do African American families emphasize standards for behavior, respect for the child's point of view, and frequent interaction at home more than other families, or are these variables distributed about equally among similar families in all groups? If these factors are important for student learning and success in school, which school practices of partnership will help more families adopt these approaches with their children?

- Is the Puerto Rican concept of "respect" similar to or different from the African American emphasis on "reciprocity" or the Chinese concept of "harmony" in relationships, and the Irish American emphasis on respect and respectability? Do all of these family teachings help children prepare for interactions with teachers and children in school and others in their communities? How do these factors help schools and families develop and maintain the mutual respect that is needed for their partnerships in children's education?

Studies of families with different cultural backgrounds, such as the research that is being conducted by the authors and the emerging questions discussed here, will help to determine both *how families are alike* and *how they are different* in their hopes for their children, their approaches to learning, and their needs for information and assistance from schools. This point is important to elaborate:

Effective school programs of partnership need to include both common and unique practices in order to respond to the similar and different needs of families. Common practices help to construct a sense of a school community for all families, children, and educators without regard to cultural or other differences. All families need to feel welcome at the schools their children attend. All families need and want good and useful information to maintain their involvement and influence in their children's lives, even when that information must be provided in different forms and languages.

Some schools find families with different cultural, racial, and language backgrounds "hard to reach." They set up barriers to communication based on differences (real or assumed) of one group from another. Other schools have implemented policies and practices that enable them to reach and include all families (Davies, Burch, & Johnson, 1992; Epstein et al., in press). As knowledge about partnerships grows, all schools will have access to a wider repertory of practices for involving all families.

Some practices that schools initiate must be common for all families (such as invitations to join the PTA); other practices may be tailored for different groups in order to attain common goals (such as translations needed to communicate with families who do not speak English, or meetings or conferences that must be scheduled at night to reach parents who work during the day); still other practices must be unique in order to respond to family situations and needs (such as special meetings with new immigrant families to welcome them and orient them to the school, or family literacy programs that are conducted by community adult literacy agencies for parents who want to learn or improve English or reading skills).

NEW DIRECTIONS

Linking School and Family Partnerships and Multicultural Education

The similarities and differences among families within and between cultural groups and the common and unique practices that schools must implement to involve families identify new directions for research and practice that link the fields of school and family partnership and multicultural education. Two new directions are needed.

Multicultural education must incorporate school and family partnerships to assure student success in school, and to assure the success of multicultural programs. The term *multicultural education* seems to create controversy whenever it is discussed. Opponents of multicultural education believe that attention to differences among people undermines the idea of America as a "melting pot" in which all immigrants develop an American identity. They fear that multicultural education will cause divisions among groups and reduce the extent to which individuals from different groups treat each other with respect. In schools, they worry that celebrations of differences emphasize student attitudes and self-esteem instead of academics, and thereby lower standards for excellence in education.

Proponents of multicultural education see America as a "stew" or "tossed salad" in which groups maintain their racial and cultural identities even as they develop their American identity. They believe that attention to differences reduces divisions among groups by increasing understanding and respect for each other. In schools, they expect that additions to curricula that recognize the contributions and perspectives of various cultures will increase all students' interest and achievement in those subjects. They anticipate improvements in standards and increased success of students.

Behind the widely different attitudes toward the label *multicultural education,* the proponents and opponents have similar goals. They seek to reduce racism, improve attitudes toward those who differ from oneself, report accurate histories and perspectives, and create a sense of community and commitment to America. Even Schlesinger (1991), who believes that multiculturalism pays too much attention to the *pluribus* and not enough to the *unum* among Americans, acknowledges the basic goals of education to be the promotion of equity, respect, recognition of contributions, and a sense of community. These goals were not met in the past when different cultures and language uses were ignored, denied, or punished by schools, or when immigrant or poor families were excluded from their children's education. Indeed, some point to the fact that this nation is and always has been divided by race, class, gender, and ethnicity, and that a different direction is needed to set a positive course for pluralism (J. A. Banks, 1993a, 1993b).

The four sections of this chapter help to redirect the debate by showing why *schools* must take leadership to develop programs that are clear, inclusive, and excellent in three areas: curriculum and instruction, interpersonal and race relations, and school and family partnerships. The first two have been traditional components of multicultural education. The third topic—school and family partnerships—must be added in order for schools to succeed in the other aspects of multicultural education.

Well-designed programs of partnership mobilize all families to help their children at home (and other children in school) develop pride in their history and culture, bolster self-esteem, and contribute to a sense of community. Parents of different cultural groups who work together at schools and in the community send powerful images and messages to children about the importance of families in education and about cooperation among adults.

By contrast, weak or poorly designed programs exclude families who are from various cultures, label them "hard to reach," find them unresponsive, ignore their strengths, avoid their cultures and customs, deny their aspirations for their children or their knowledge of their children's talents, and treat them as part of (or as a cause of) their children's problems in school. Research suggests that when this happens, children suffer, schools and communities lose skills and investments, and families become isolated from each other.

Strong programs of school and family partnerships will increase the chances of reaching three of the goals for multicultural education—knowledge construction, prejudice reduction, and an empowering school culture and social structure (J. A. Banks, 1993b). For example, family reflections and experiences can be incorporated into school activities and in homework assignments to contribute to students' construction of personal cultural knowledge. It is hard to imagine a deep sense of "empowerment" for students *unless* they know that their families are accepted and valued in the school culture and social structure.

C. A. M. Banks (1993) notes that students from various groups must "cross barriers of language, values, cognitions and culture" (p. 43) in school. This is another way of recognizing the multiple memberships that individuals must exercise to succeed in mainstream society. These barriers will be crossed with the restructuring of schools to make their programs more "congruent" with students' families (C. A. M. Banks, 1993; Nieto, 1992; Torres-Guzman, 1990). Epstein (1987) calls these congruent constructions "school-like families" and "family-like schools," within the theory of overlapping spheres of influence. The restructuring of both environments—school and home—is necessary to make each more aware of, responsive to, appreciative of, and in partnership with the other to support children as students.

Students' self-acceptance and self-confidence as learners within the school setting are affected by how the school accepts, respects, and appreciates them and their families. By participating in their children's construction of knowledge about their heritage and culture, by participating at their chil-

dren's schools and contributing with other families to the school culture and structure, families can help students develop pride without prejudice. By sharing celebrations about knowledge, families can help children realize that gaining skills is a way of gaining strength for the student, the family, and the community. Although including families complicates multicultural education by requiring attention to another context (home) and another set of actors (parents and other family members), this hard work will be needed to attain the main goals of multicultural education—to improve learning and to help all youngsters function effectively in a culturally and ethnically diverse nation and world (J. A. Banks, 1993b).

School and family partnerships must incorporate multicultural education in order to assure student success in school, and to involve all families successfully. Topics and approaches of multicultural education must be added to the design and implementation of school and family partnership programs. This includes synthesizing and applying the results of research on families from different cultural groups, and selecting the common and different practices that will involve all families in their children's education. These program designs are complicated by the need to give attention to bilingual education and other programs for children with limited English proficiency.

In an earlier discussion, Epstein (1986a) tailored her framework of major types of involvement to the needs of families in which the children and parents have limited English skills. Six types of involvement guide schools in their development of comprehensive programs of partnership. Practices to operationalize each type of partnership may be selected or revised to accommodate families of students with diverse cultural backgrounds, accounting for the parents' language of proficiency or English reading skills, as the following discussion suggests.

In the framework for partnerships, Type 1 practices to involve families refer to workshops or other activities that help families create *home conditions that support student learning.* These activities should be offered to all families, not just those with proficiency in English. Providing translators for non-English-speaking families is a way of demonstrating the schools' belief in the value of all families to their children's education and to the schools.

For example, at a workshop for parents in St. Paul, Minnesota, translators worked simultaneously with the main speakers in three languages and sign-language sections of an audience, clearly conveying the message that all parents were wanted and welcome at the event. Most schools have low attendance at workshops and other meetings at school. It is not surprising that participation is low in places where parents are not understood or made welcome through communications in their own language. When tapes, videos, summaries of workshops, and other information on child development and child rearing are shared, they, too, must be dubbed or translated for accessibility in the languages of all families.

As another Type 1 activity, students and families share their cultures and customs with their children's schools. For example, in Boston, an elementary school used numerous bulletin boards to celebrate diversity with pictures and stories by children about their families' favorite foods, games, holidays, and other family experiences. The displays revealed the similarities and differences among children and families, and the school's awareness and appreciation of these aspects of family life.

Type 2 activities to *communicate information about school programs and children's progress* also require English translations for language-minority families, as well as better English writing for parents who are not advanced readers. Letters, memos, notices, report cards, and other materials that are sent home must be translated if families do not read English or do not read English well. This can be accomplished without losing information and without patronizing families. Conferences at school or telephone calls to and from school may require translators to assure that parents and teachers are equally effective in communicating with each other about the children they share. California was a state leader in requiring communications in three languages to reach students' families, and other states and districts have been adding similar responsive policies.

Type 3 activities refer to parents or other *volunteers* or *audiences* for student presentations and events at school. Although many parents cannot come to the school because of their own work schedules, many others—particularly those from diverse cultural and language groups—do not come because they do not feel welcome or have not been invited. Parents who live far from the school, or those whose own school experiences were negative and who feel insecure in school, will stay away from the school building.

In well-designed programs of partnership, all families—regardless of their languages—are asked to volunteer their time and talents to assist teachers, administrators, and students at home or at school, and to come to school as audiences for student events. Schools may conduct surveys or phone calls in the parents' languages to obtain volunteers. When the parents come to school to volunteer, there must be a bilingual parent, other volunteer, or school staff member who can welcome, direct, and instruct them about how to help without creating feelings of discomfort or inadequacy. Some schools are establishing "parent rooms" or "parent centers" where families and others can complete volunteer work and communicate with other families and teachers in a setting other than the classroom (Johnson, 1993). Similarly, when parents come as audiences for student performances or assemblies, other parents or students with bilingual skills may be needed to welcome and assist parents who may not be familiar with or comfortable at school.

Type 4 refers to parents' involvement with their own children's *learning activities at home.* This may include homework or other learning activities designed by the school to boost students' progress, or learning activities that parents design and supervise. As the four reviews in this chapter suggest, parents from all backgrounds feel comfortable monitoring their children's education at home, but just about all parents need information about how to do this from year to year as their children progress through the grades. In Type 4 activities, information is shared with parents using language that is clear about what their children are learning; the skills needed to pass the grade; how to encourage and assist their children in reading, math, science, or other skills at home; how to interact about homework; and other connections to curriculum and learning. Families need to know that the school wants them to supervise,

support, monitor, encourage, and interact with their children about homework, and that they can do so in the language used at home, even as the student completes homework in English.

Type 5 refers to memberships in *decision-making, governance, and advocacy* groups to bring parents' voices to the table in decisions about school and classroom programs. It is not enough to involve token representatives of bilingual or economically disadvantaged families in limited decision-making roles, or only on committees about bilingual or Chapter 1 programs. Parent representatives must be helped to make contact with all of the families they represent, so that all parents have some input into school decisions that affect them and their children. Parent representatives must also be helped to give information back to all families, in the language they speak and understand, about decisions that are made.

Type 6 refers to *collaborations with community groups* that the school arranges, including information for families about community services that may help them and their children. Some community agencies and community advocacy groups include bilingual staff or volunteers to help families understand the services in the community that may assist them and their children.

Schools use other Type 6 activities, such as enabling children, families, and the schools to learn about their community's strengths and resources. One New York elementary school used field-trip activities to compile a neighborhood "portrait" (Goode, 1990) that identified the many resources in the neighborhood of the school.

The types of involvement can be used to link school and family partnership to multicultural education. The general framework of six types of partnership can be tailored as described above to help build stronger multicultural education programs that explicitly involve families. This approach has been used to guide program development at the state level (as in California, Utah, and Wisconsin) where policy leaders are working to involve all families from diverse cultural groups—African American, Hispanic American, Asian American, and Native American—in their children's education.

The framework has been similarly helpful in many districts with the same agenda. For example, in Arlington, Virginia, the framework of six types was adopted, expanded, and implemented in schools with large numbers of Latino families. (Voiland-Sanchez, Sutton, & Ware, 1991). The framework also has proven useful in schools with African American families, including inner-city schools in economically depressed neighborhoods (Davies, Palanki, & Burch, 1993; Epstein & Dauber, 1991; Epstein et al., in press; Warner, 1991).

The connections of school and family partnership with multicultural education suggest a rewording of the historic *Lau v. Nichols* (1974) decision that altered education for children with limited English proficiency. Epstein (1986a) made a "modest proposal" to change the words of the *Lau* decision to reflect the results of research on school and family partnerships:

Where the inability of *parents* of school children to speak and understand the English language *excludes the children* from effective participation in the education program, *the school district* must take affirmative steps *to open its instructional program to these parents* and their children [emphasis added]. (pp. 14–15)

This revision recognizes that language barriers between parents and school, just as between child and school, impede the equal participation of the children because parents cannot effectively monitor student work and progress, raise questions or concerns with teachers, assist their children as knowledgeable partners with the school, or act as advocates. School districts and individual schools have not typically taken this affirmative action with bilingual parents, nor have most schools responded appropriately to Chapter 1 regulations to involve in their children's education poor, language-minority, and other parents who may have difficulty reading English (D'Angelo & Adler, 1991).

Preparing Educators to Connect Partnerships with Families and Multicultural Education

The perspective on partnerships, information on families from four cultural groups, and framework for school programs to involve all families discussed in this chapter reveal a major flaw in the present educational system that must be corrected:

• The new perspectives and directions linking school and family partnership and multicultural education must be added to preservice and in-service teacher and administrator education programs.

The nation is becoming more diverse as immigration continues and as families grow. Through the 1980s, African American and Latino students constituted a majority of public school students in central cities (U.S. Department of Education, 1993). It is estimated that by 2000 about 40% of all school-aged children in the United States will come from racial and ethnic minority families. Most of the students and their families will be in central cities, and most of them will be poor. About 90% of their teachers will be White.

These facts and projections raise many questions: How will all teachers be prepared to work with the families of their students? How, when, and where will educators learn about the various cultures, values, and histories of the families of students they may teach during their careers? How, when, and where will educators learn about the particular families in their present school? How will educators learn to communicate with all families so that parents will understand their schools and their children's programs each year?

The reviews on the four ethnic groups testify loudly to the need for educators to have better information about the diversity among families, including family backgrounds, cultures, histories, languages, strengths, values, and goals for their children. They must understand the similarity of family needs for information; the connections of multicultural education with school and family partnerships; and the common, tailored, and unique practices in all six types of involvement that can be used to create comprehensive programs to include all families in

their children's education. Because these goals have neither been set nor met for educators in the past, most teachers and administrators today are confused by and less successful with children and families who differ in background from themselves.

CONCLUSION

Families are an inevitable, continuous, and important part of children's school life. All families—whatever their background, culture, or language—want and need assistance from schools in helping their children succeed each year. Based on emerging knowledge of the influence of families from all cultural groups on their children through the years of school, and new knowledge of the importance of school and family partnerships, two connections must be made and strengthened. The field of multicultural education needs to be more explicitly aware of the part families play in student learning and in supporting the goals of multicultural programs. The field of school and family partnerships needs to be more explicitly aware of the goals and approaches of multicultural education in order to design responsive programs to involve all families. In U.S. schools in the next century, this combination of educational restructuring will help all students succeed.

APPENDIX: SELECTED RESOURCE ORGANIZATIONS

1. Art, Research, and Curriculum (ARC) Associates (Contact person: Sau-Lim Tsang), 310 Eighth Street, Suite 220, Oakland, CA 94607. (510)834-9455. Aim is to forge vital links between school and other institutions, such as family and community programs. Offers parent institutes in different languages to teach parents the skills necessary for involvement in their children's education. Bilingual Ombudsman Program intervenes on behalf of non-English-proficient parents and students.
2. Chinese American Parents' Association (Contact person: Pauline Chu), 36-09 Main Street, Suite 7-C, Flushing, NY 11354. (718)359-6810. Helps Chinese American parents, especially new immigrants, deal with education-related matters. Publishes *The Next Generation,* a bilingual magazine for parents.
3. National Association for Asian and Pacific American Education (Contact person: Annie Ching), c/o ARC Associates, 310 Eighth Street, Suite 220, Oakland, CA 94607. (510)834-9455. Encourages research on education topics, operates bilingual education workshops and service projects, and promotes inclusion of Asian and Pacific American culture and history and social curricula. Publishes quarterly newsletters.

References

* Indicates sources in the Chinese language.

Alba, R. (1990). *Ethnic identity: The transformation of White America.* New Haven, CT: Yale University Press.

Alicea, V. G., & Mathis, J. (1975). *Determinants of educational attainment among Puerto Rican youth in the U.S.* Washington, DC: Universidad Boricua.

Angel, R., & Tienda, M. (1982). Determinants of extended household structure: Cultural pattern or economic need? *American Journal of Sociology, 87,* 1360–1383.

Arvizu, S. (1992). Home-school linkages: A cross-cultural approach to parent participation. In M. Saravia-Shore & S. Arvizu (Eds.), *Cross-cultural literacy* (pp. 37–56). New York: Garland.

Asians in America: 1990 Census classification by states. (1991). San Francisco: *Asian Week.*

Auerbach, E. (1989). Toward a social-contextual approach in family literacy. *Harvard Educational Review, 59*(2), 165–181.

Baker, D. P., & Stevenson, D. L. (1986). Mothers' strategies for children's school achievement: Managing the transition to high school. *Sociology of Education, 59,* 156–166.

Banks, C. A. M. (1993). Restructuring schools for equity: What have we learned in two decades? *Phi Delta Kappan, 75*(1), 42–48.

Banks, J. A. (1993a). The canon debate, knowledge construction and multicultural education. *Educational Researcher, 22*(5), 4–14.

Banks, J. A. (1993b). Multicultural education: Historical development, dimensions and practice. In L. Darling-Hammond (Ed.), *Review of research in education* (pp. 3–50). Washington, DC: American Educational Research Association.

Becker, H. J., & Epstein, J. L. (1982). Parent involvement: A study of teacher practices. *Elementary School Journal, 83,* 85–102.

Biddle, E. (1981). The American Catholic Irish family. In C. Mindel & R. Habenstein (Eds.), *Ethnic families in America: Patterns and variations* (2nd ed., pp. 86–114). New York: Elsevier.

Bird, H., & Canino, G. (1982). The Puerto Rican family: Cultural factors and family intervention strategies. *Journal of the American Academy of Psychoanalysis, 10,* 257–268.

Bloom, B. S. (1982). *All our children learning: A primer for parents, teachers and other educators.* New York: McGraw-Hill.

Bowman, P., & Howard, C. (1985). Race-related socialization, motivation, and academic achievement: A study of Black youth in three-generation families. *Journal of the American Academy of Child Psychiatry, 24,* 134–141.

Bright, J. A. (1992). *High-achieving, low-achieving, low-income Black children: What makes the difference?* Unpublished doctoral dissertation, Syracuse University, Syracuse, NY.

Bronfenbrenner, U. (1979). *The ecology of human development: Experiment by nature and design.* Cambridge, MA: Harvard University Press.

Bronfenbrenner, U. (1986). Ecology of the family as a context for human development: Research perspectives. *Developmental Psychology, 22,* 723–742.

Calabrese, R. L. (1990). The public school: A source of alienation for minority parents. *Journal of Negro Education, 59*(2), 148–154.

Canino, I., Earley, B., & Rogler, L. (1989). *The Puerto Rican child in New York City: Stress and mental health* (Monograph No. 4). Bronx, NY: Hispanic Research Center.

Caplan, N., Choy, M. H., & Whitmore, J. K. (1992). Indochinese refugee families and academic achievement. *Scientific American, 263*(5), 36–42.

Chan, C. K. (1991, September).* Is American education suitable for your children? *Sing Tao Daily,* p. 13 (New York City).

Chavkin, N. (Ed.). (1993). *Families and schools in a pluralistic society.* Albany: State University of New York Press.

Chen, C., & Uttal, D. H. (1988). Cultural values, parents' beliefs, and children's achievement in the United States and China. *Human Development, 31,* 351–358.

Chou, B. J. (1991, May 14, 15, 16).* What is a child supposed to learn in preschool education? A Chinese-American parent's perspective. *World Journal* (Taipei, Taiwan).

Clark, D. (1991). *Erin's heirs: Irish bonds of community.* Lexington: University Press of Kentucky.

Clark, R. M. (1983). *Family life and school achievement: Why poor Black children succeed or fail.* Chicago: University of Chicago Press.

Colón-Tarrats, N. (1988). *Cimarrones: A life history analysis of Puerto Rican dropouts in Boston.* Unpublished doctoral dissertation, Harvard University, Cambridge, MA.

Comer, J. P. (1980). *School power: Implications of an intervention project.* New York: The Free Press.

Comer, J. P. (1985). Empowering Black children's educational environments. In H. P. McAdoo & J. L. McAdoo (Eds.), *Black children: Social, educational, and parental environments* (pp. 123–138). Beverly Hills, CA: Sage.

Comer, J. P. (1988). Educating poor minority children. *Scientific American, 259*(5), 42–48.

Comer, J. P., Haynes, N. M., & Hamilton-Lee, M. (1990). School power: A model for improving Black student achievement. In J. Dewart (Ed.), *The state of Black America (1990)* (pp. 225–238). New York: National Urban League.

Cornacchia, E., & Nelson, D. (1992). Historical differences in the political experiences of American Blacks and White ethnics: Revisiting an unresolved controversy. *Ethnic and Racial Studies, 15*(1), 102–124.

Curran, M. D. (1986). *The parish and the hill.* (Afterword by A. Halley) New York: The Feminist Press. (Original work published 1948)

D'Angelo, D., & Adler, C. R. (1991). Chapter 1: A catalyst for improving parent involvement. *Phi Delta Kappan, 72*(3), 350–354.

Dauber, S. L., & Epstein, J. L. (1993). Parents' attitudes and practices of involvement in inner-city elementary and middle schools. In N. Chavkin (Ed.), *Families and schools in a pluralistic society* (pp. 53–71). Albany: State University of New York Press.

Davies, D. (1990). Shall we wait for revolution? A few lessons from the Schools Reaching Out Project. *Equity and Choice, 6*(3), 68–73.

Davies, D. (1991). Schools reaching out: Family, school and community partnerships for students' success. *Phi Delta Kappan, 72*(3), 376–382.

Davies, D., Burch, P., & Johnson, V. (1992). *A portrait of schools reaching out: Report of a survey on practices and policies of family-community-school collaboration* (Center Report No. 1). Baltimore, MD: Center on Families, Communities, Schools and Children's Learning.

Davies, D., Palanki, A., & Burch, P. (1993). *Getting started: Action research in family-school-community partnerships* (Center Report No. 17). Baltimore, MD: Center on Families, Communities, Schools and Children's Learning.

Davino, C. F. (1993, January 29). Op-Ed: Who will be the voice for our children? *Asian Week,* p. 16.

Davis, A. (1981). *Women, race & class.* New York: Vintage Books.

Deane, S. (Ed.). (1991). *The field day anthology of Irish writing* (Vols. 1, 2, & 3). Derry, Northern Ireland: Field Day Publications, distributed by W. W. Norton & Company.

Delgado, M., & Humm-Delgado, D. (1982). Natural support systems:

Source of strength in Hispanic communities. *Social Work, 27*, 81–90.

Delgado-Gaitán, C. (1990). *Literacy for empowerment: The role of parents in children's education.* New York: The Falmer Press.

Delgado-Gaitán, C., & Trueba, H. (1991). *Crossing cultural borders.* New York: The Falmer Press.

Dent, D. J. (1991, April). Survival lessons. *Essence,* pp. 88–93.

Díaz-Soto, L. (1988). The home environment of higher and lower achieving Puerto Rican children. *Hispanic Journal of Behavioral Sciences, 10*(2), 161–167.

Díaz-Soto, L. (1989). Relationship between home environment and intrinsic versus extrinsic orientation of higher achieving and lower achieving Puerto Rican children. *Educational Research Quarterly, 13*(1), 22–36.

Díaz-Soto, L. (1990). *Families as learning environments: Reflections on critical factors affecting differential achievement.* (ERIC Document Reproduction Service No. ED 315 498)

Díaz-Soto, L. (1992). Success stories. In C. Grant (Ed.), *Research and multicultural education* (pp. 153–164). London: The Falmer Press.

Diner, H. (1983). *Erin's daughters in America: Irish immigrant women in the nineteenth century.* Baltimore, MD: Johns Hopkins University Press.

Dornbusch, S. M., & Ritter, P. L. (1988). Parents of high school students: A neglected resource. *Educational Horizons, 66,* 75–77.

Dornbusch, S. M., & Strober, M. (1988). Feminism, children, and the new families. New York: The Guilford Press.

Dornbusch, S. M., & Wood, K. D. (1989). Family processes and educational achievement. In W. Weston (Ed.), *Education and the American family: A research synthesis* (pp. 66–95). New York: New York University Press.

Durán, R. (1983). *Hispanics' education and background.* New York: College Entrance Examination Board.

Edwards, O. L. (1976). Components of academic success: A profile of achieving Black adolescents. *Journal of Negro Education, 45,* 408–422.

Epstein, J. L. (1986a). Parent-involvement: Implications for limited-English proficient parents. In C. Smith-Dudgeon (Ed.), *Proceedings of the Symposium on Issues of Parent Involvement and Literacy* (pp. 6–15). Washington, DC: Trinity College, Department of Education and Counseling.

Epstein, J. L. (1986b). Parents' reactions to teacher practices of parent involvement. *Elementary School Journal, 86,* 277–294.

Epstein, J. L. (1987). Toward a theory of family-school connections: Teacher practices and parent involvement. In K. Hurrelman, F. Kaufman, & F. Losel (Eds.), *Social intervention: Potential and constraints* (pp. 121–136). New York: DeGruyter.

Epstein, J. L. (1988). *Schools in the center: School, family, peer, and community connections for more effective middle grades schools and students.* Baltimore, MD: Johns Hopkins University Center for Research on Elementary and Middle Schools.

Epstein, J. L. (1990). Single parents and the schools: Effects of marital status on parent and teacher interactions. In M. Hallinan (Ed.), *Change in societal institutions* (pp. 91–121). New York: Plenum.

Epstein, J. L. (1991). Effects on student achievement of teacher practices of parent involvement. In S. Silvern (Ed.), *Literacy through family, community, and school interaction* (pp. 261–276). Greenwich, CT: JAI Press.

Epstein, J. L. (1992). School and family partnerships. In M. Alkin (Ed.), *Encyclopedia of educational research* (6th ed., pp. 1139–1151). New York: Macmillan.

Epstein, J. L., & Dauber, S. L. (1991). School programs and teacher practices of parent involvement in inner-city elementary and middle schools. *Elementary School Journal, 91*(3), 289–303.

Epstein, J. L., Herrick, S. C., & Coates, L. (in press). Effects of summer home learning packets on student achievement in language arts in the middle grades. *School Effectiveness and School Improvement.*

Erickson, F. (1987). Transformation and school success: The politics and culture of educational achievement. *Anthropology & Education Quarterly, 18*(4), 335–356.

Eshleman, J. R. (1988). *The family: An introduction* (5th ed.). Boston: Allyn and Bacon.

Fallows, M. (1979). *Irish Americans: Identity and assimilation.* Englewood Cliffs, NJ: Prentice-Hall.

Fanning, C. (1990). *The Irish voice in America.* Lexington: University Press of Kentucky.

Fass, P. (1989). *Outside in: Minorities and the transformation of American education.* Oxford, England: Oxford University Press.

First, J. M., & Carerra, J. W. (1988). *New voices: Immigrant students in U.S. public schools.* Boston: National Coalition of Advocates for Students.

Fitzgibbon, C. (1983). *The Irish in Ireland.* New York: W. W. Norton.

Fitzpatrick, J. (1987). *Puerto Rican Americans: The meaning of migration to the mainland* (2nd ed.). Englewood Cliffs, NJ: Prentice-Hall.

Fraser, J. (1979). Reform, immigration, and bureaucracy, 1820–1870. In J. Fraser, H. Allen, & S. Barnes (Eds.), *From common school to magnet school* (pp. 28–42). Boston: Trustees of the Public Library of the City of Boston.

Funchion, M. (Ed.). (1983). *Irish American voluntary organizations.* Westport, CT: Greenwood Press.

Gay, G. (1989). Ethnic minorities and educational equality. In J. A. Banks, and C. A. M. Banks (Eds.), *Multicultural education: Issues and perspectives* (pp. 167–188). Boston: Allyn and Bacon.

Genova, W. (1981). *A study of interaction effects of school and home environments on students of varying race/ethnicity, class, and gender: Vol. 1. Summary and conclusions; Vol. 2. Ethnographies of five racial/ethnic groups; Vol. 3. A practitioner's guide for achieving equity in multicultural schools.* Newton, MA: TDR Associates. (ERIC Document Reproduction Service Nos. UD 022 515–518)

Goldenberg, C. N. (1987). Low-income Hispanic parents' contribution to their first-grade children's word-recognition skills. *Anthropology & Education Quarterly, 18*(3), 149–179.

Goode, D. A. (1990). The community portrait process: School community collaboration. *Equity and Choice, 6*(3), 32–37.

Grant, L. (1984). Black females' "place" in desegregated classrooms. *Sociology of Education, 57,* 98–111.

Greeley, A. (1972). *That most distressful nation: The taming of the American Irish.* Chicago: Quadrangle Books.

Griffin, D. W. (1990). *The book of Irish Americans.* New York: Random House.

Hale, J. (1991). The transmission of cultural values to young African-American children. *Young Children, 46*(6), 7–15.

Handlin, O. (1941). *Boston's immigrants.* Cambridge, MA: Harvard University Press.

Hare, B. R. (1985). Reexamining the achievement central tendency: Sex differences within race and race differences within sex. In H. P. McAdoo & J. L. McAdoo (Eds.), *Black children: Social, educational, and parental environments* (pp. 139–155). Beverly Hills, CA: Sage.

Hare, B. R. (1987). Structural inequality and the endangered status of black youth. *Journal of Negro Education, 56,* 100–110.

Hare, B. R., & Castanell, L. (1985). No place to run, no place to hide: Comparative status and future prospects of Black boys. In M. B. Spencer, G. K. Brookins, & W. R. Allen (Eds.), *Beginnings: The social and affective development of Black children* (pp. 201–214). Hillsdale, NJ: Lawrence Erlbaum Associates.

Harry, B. (1992a). Making sense of disability: Low-income Puerto Rican parents' theories of the problem. *Exceptional Children, 59*(1), 27–40.

Harry, B. (1992b). Developing cultural self-awareness: The first steps in values clarification for early interventionist. *Topics in Early Childhood Special Education, 12*(3), 333–350.

Hawley, W. D. (1989). The importance of minority teachers to the racial and ethnic integration of American society. *Equity and Choice, 5*(2), 31–36.

Heleen, O. (Ed.). (1990). Schools reaching out: Families and schools build new partnerships [Special issue]. *Equity and Choice, 6*(3).

Hess, R. D., Chang, C.-M., & McDevitt, T. M. (1987). Cultural variations in family beliefs about children's performance in mathematics: Comparisons among Peoples' Republic of China, Chinese American, and Caucasian-American families. *Journal of Educational Psychology, 79*(2), 179–188.

Hidalgo, N. (1992). *"I saw Puerto Rico once": A review of the literature on Puerto Rican families and school achievement in the United States* (Center Report No. 12). Baltimore, MD: Center on Families, Communities, Schools and Children's Learning.

Hidalgo, N. (1993). *Teachers' perceptions of home support.* Manuscript submitted for publication.

Hidalgo, N. (1994). Profile of a Puerto Rican family's support for school achievement. *Equity and Choice, 10*(2), 14–22.

Hill, R. (1971). *The strengths of Black families.* New York: Emerson Hall Publishers.

Hirata, L. C. (1975). Youth, parents, and teachers in Chinatown: A triadic framework of minority socialization. *Urban Education, 10*(3), 279–296.

Ho, D. Y. F. (1986). Chinese patterns of socialization: A critical review. In M. H. Bond (Ed.), *The psychology of the Chinese people* (pp. 1–36). Hong Kong: Oxford University Press.

Ho, K., & Fong, M. (1990).* A cool response to school activities; a hiding of dissatisfaction deep in the heart. *Herald* [Special issue on Chinese-American parent involvement], *3*(9), 1 (New York City).

Holliday, B. G., Henning, R. C., & Johnson, D. J. (1983, May–June). *Black maternal beliefs.* Paper prepared at the Groves Conference on Marriage and the Family, Freeport, Grand Bahama Island.

Hsia, J. (1988). *Asian Americans in higher education and at work.* Hillsdale, NJ: Lawrence Erlbaum Associates.

Hsu, C. W. (1993, January 15). Bringing China into the American classroom. *Sampan,* p. A-19 (Boston).

Hu, A. (1989). Asian-Americans: Model minority or double minority? *Amerasia Journal, 15,* 243–257.

Institute for Puerto Rican Policy. (1992). *Datanote on the Puerto Rican community.* New York: Institute for Puerto Rican Policy.

Johnson, V. R. (1993). *Parent/family centers in schools: Expanding outreach and promoting collaboration* (Center Report 20). Baltimore, MD: Center on Families, Communities, Schools and Children's Learning.

Kim, U., & Chun, M. B. J. (1992, April). *Educational "success" of Asian Americans: An indigenous perspective.* Paper presented at the annual meeting of the American Educational Research Association, San Francisco.

Kozol, J. (1975). *The night is dark and ...m far from home.* New York: Bantam Books.

Kozol, J. (1988). *Rachel and her children.* New York: Crown Publishers.

Kozol, J. (1991). *Savage inequalities: Children in America's schools.* New York: Harper Perennial.

Kunjufu, J. (1983). *Countering the conspiracy to destroy Black boys.* Chicago: African American Press.

Kwong, P. (1987). *The new Chinatown.* New York: Hill & Wang.

Lareau, A. (1989). *Home advantage: Social class and parental intervention in elementary education.* Philadelphia: Falmer Press.

Lau v. Nichols, 414 U.S. 563 (1974).

Lau, G. M. H. (1988). *Chinese American early childhood socialization in*

communication. Unpublished doctoral dissertation, Stanford University.

Lauria, A. (1972). Respeto, relajo and interpersonal relations in Puerto Rico. In F. Cordasco & E. Buccioni (Eds.), *The Puerto Rican community and its children on the mainland* (pp. 36–48). Metuchen, NJ: Scarecrow Press.

Lee, E. (1988). *Ten principles on raising Chinese-American teens.* San Francisco: Chinatown Youth Center.

Lee, J. F. J. (1991). *Asian American experiences in the United States.* Jefferson, NC: MacFarland.

Lee, P. S. (1983). *Intraethnic diversity: An exploratory study of ethnic identity of Chinese-American adolescents.* Unpublished doctoral dissertation, Oregon State University, Corvallis.

Leichter, H. J. (1974). *The family as educator.* New York: Teachers College Press.

LeVine, R. A. (1988). Human parental care: Universal goals, cultural strategies, individual behavior. *New Directions for Child Development, 40,* 3–11.

Light, D. (1985). The role of Irish-American organizations in assimilation and community formation. In P. Drudy (Ed.), *The Irish in America: Emigration, assimilation, and impact* (pp. 113–141). Cambridge, England: Cambridge University Press.

Lightfoot, S. L. (1983). *The good high school: Portraits of character and culture.* New York: Basic Books.

Lin, C.-Y. C. (1988). *A comparison of childrearing practices among Chinese, Chinese-American, and non-Asian American parents.* Unpublished doctoral dissertation, Virginia Polytechnic Institute and State University, Blacksburg.

Litwak, E., & Meyer, H. J. (1974). *School, family, and neighborhood: The theory and practice of school-community relations.* New York: Columbia University Press.

London, H., & Devore, W. (1988). Layers of understanding: Counseling ethnic minority families. *Family Relations, 37,* 310–314.

McAdoo, H. (1981). *Black families.* Newbury Park, CA: Sage.

McAdoo, H. P. (Ed.). (1982). Stress absorbing systems in Black families. *Family Relations, 31,* 479–488.

McAdoo, H. P. (1985). Racial attitude and self-concept of young black children over time. In H. P. McAdoo, and J. L. McAdoo (Eds.), *Black children: Social, educational, and parental environments* (pp. 213–241). Beverly Hills, CA: Sage.

McAdoo, J. L. (1979). Father-child interaction patterns and self-esteem in black preschool children. *Young Children, 34*(2), 46–53.

McCaffrey, L. (1992). Irish textures in American Catholicism. *Catholic Historical Review, 78*(1), 1–18.

Miller, K. (1985). Assimilation and alienation: Irish emigrants' responses to industrial America, 1871–1921. In P. Drudy (Ed.), *The Irish in America: Emigration, assimilation, and impact* (pp. 87–112). Cambridge, England: Cambridge University Press.

Ming Sum. (1990).* Why does the school emphasize parent participation? *Herald* [Special issue on Chinese-American parent involvement], *3*(9), 12 (New York City).

Mizio, E. (1974). Impact of external systems on the Puerto Rican family. *Social Casework, 55*(2), 76–85.

Moll, L. C., & Greenberg, J. B. (1990). Creating zones of possibilities: Combining social contexts for instruction. In L. C. Moll (Ed.), *Vygotsky and education* (pp. 319–348). Cambridge, England: Cambridge University Press.

Moynihan, D. (1965). *The Negro family: The case for national action.* Washington, DC: U.S. Department of Labor.

Murrell, P. (1993). Afrocentric immersion: Academic and personal development of African-American males in public schools. In T. Perry and J. W. Fraser (Eds.), *Freedom's plow: Teaching in the multicultural classroom* (pp. 231–259). New York: Routledge.

New York City Board of Education. (1980). *Comprehensive high school bilingual program, 1979–80, Final evaluation report.* Brooklyn: New York City Board of Education Office of Educational Evaluation. (ERIC Document Reproduction Service No. ED 206 749)

New York City Board of Education. (1990). *Chinese opportunities in career education (Project Choice), 1989–90, Final Evaluation Report.* Brooklyn: New York City Board of Education Office of Research, Evaluation, and Assessment. (ERIC Document Reproduction Service No. ED 331 926)

Nicolau, S., & Ramos, C. (1990). *Together is better: Building strong relationships between schools and Hispanic parents.* Washington, DC: Hispanic Policy Development Project.

Nieto, S. (1992). *Affirming diversity.* New York: Longman.

Ogbu, J. (1981). Origins of human competence: A cultural ecological perspective. *Child Development, 52,* 413–429.

Ogbu, J. (1983). Minority status and schooling in plural societies. *Comparative Education Review, 27*(2), 168–190.

Ogbu, J. U. (1990). Overcoming racial barriers to equal access. In J. Goodlad (Ed.), *Access to knowledge: An agenda for our nation's schools* (pp. 59–89). Princeton, NJ: College Entrance Examination Board.

Ortíz-Colón, R. (1985). *Acculturation, ethnicity and education: A comparison of Anglo teachers' and Puerto Rican mothers' values regarding behaviors and skills for urban HEADSTART children.* Unpublished doctoral dissertation, Harvard University, Cambridge, MA.

Padres Unidos en Educación y el Desarrollo de Otros. (1989). *Boletín Informativo.* Boston: Author.

Paths to partnership [Special section on parent involvement, ed. J. L. Epstein]. (1991). *Phi Delta Kappan, 72*(3), 344–388.

Perlmann, J. (1988). *Ethnic differences: Schooling and social structure among the Irish, Italians, Jews, and Blacks in an American city, 1800–1935.* Cambridge, England: Cambridge University Press.

Perry, T. (1993). *Toward a theory of African American school achievement* (Center Report 16). Baltimore, MD: Center on Families, Communities, Schools and Children's Learning.

Peters, M. F. (1985). Racial socialization of young Black children. In H. P. McAdoo & J. L. McAdoo (Eds.), *Black children: Social, educational, and parental environments* (pp. 159–173). Beverly Hills, CA: Sage.

Ploski, H. A., & Williams, J. (Eds.) (1989). *The Negro almanac: A reference work on the African American* (5th ed.). Detroit, MI: Gale Research.

Pollard, D. S. (1989). Against the odds: A profile of academic achievers from the urban underclass. *Journal of Negro Education, 58,* 297–308.

Ravitch, D. (1974). *The great school wars.* New York: Basic Books.

Rivera, R. (1991). *Latinos in Massachusetts and the 1990 U.S. Census: Growth and geographical distribution.* Boston: Mauricio Gaston Institute for Latino Community Development and Public Policy.

Robledo Montecel, M. (1993). *Hispanic families as valued partners: An educator's guide.* San Antonio, TX: Intercultural Development Research Association.

Roediger, D. (1990). *The wages of whiteness: Race and the making of the American working class.* London: Verso.

Salgado, R. (1985). The Puerto Rican family. In L. Nuñez (Ed.), *Puerto Ricans in the mid '80s: An American challenge* (pp. 29–44). Alexandria, VA: National Puerto Rican Coalition.

Sánchez-Ayéndez, M. (1988). The Puerto Rican American family. In C. Mindel, R. Habenstein, & R. Wright (Eds.), *Ethnic families in America* (pp. 173–195). New York: Elsevier.

Santiestevan, H., & Santiestevan, S. (Eds.). (1984). *The Hispanic Almanac.* Washington, DC: Hispanic Policy Development Project.

Schlesinger, A. M., Jr. (1991). *The disuniting of America: Reflections on a multicultural society.* Knoxville, TN: Whittel Direct Books.

Schneider, B., & Lee, Y. (1990). A model for academic success: The school and home environment of East Asian students. *Anthropology and Education Quarterly, 21*(4), 358–377.

Scott-Jones, D. (1986). The family. In J. Hannaway & M. E. Lockheed (Eds.), *The contributions of the social sciences to educational policy and to practice, 1965–1985* (pp. 11–31). Berkeley, CA: McCutchan.

Scott-Jones, D. (1987). Mother-as-teacher in the families of high- and low-achieving low-income Black first graders. *Journal of Negro Education, 56,* 21–34.

Seeley, D. S. (1981). *Education through partnership: Mediating structures and education.* Cambridge, MA: Ballinger.

Shannon, W. (1963). *The American Irish: A political and social portrait.* Amherst: University of Massachusetts Press.

Shields, P. H. (1989). Holy angels: Pocket of excellence. *Journal of Negro Education, 58,* 203–211.

Shoho, A. R. (1992, April). *An historical comparison of parental involvement in three generations of Japanese Americans (isseis, niseis, sanseis) in the education of their children.* Paper presented at the annual meeting of the American Educational Research Association, San Francisco.

Siu, S.-F. (1992). *Toward an understanding of Chinese-American educational achievement: A literature review* (Center Report No. 2). Baltimore, MD: Center on Families, Communities, Schools and Children's Learning.

Siu, S.-F. (1994). Taking no chances: A profile of a Chinese-American family's support for school success. *Equity and Choice, 10*(2), 23–32.

Slaughter, D. T., & Epps, E. (1987). The home environment and academic achievement of Black American children and youth: An overview. *Journal of Negro Education, 56,* 3–20.

Slaughter-DeFoe, D. T. (1991). Parental educational choice: Some African American dilemmas. *Journal of Negro Education, 60,* 354–360.

Slaughter-Defoe, D. T., Nakagawa, K., Takanishi, R., & Johnson, D. J. (1990). Toward cultural/ecological perspectives on schooling and achievement in African- and Asian-American children. *Child Development, 61,* 363–383.

Snow, C., Barnes, W., Chandler, J., Goodman, I., & Hemphill, L. (1991). *Unfulfilled expectations: Home and school influences on literacy.* Cambridge, MA: Harvard University Press.

Spencer, M. B. (1985). Racial variations in achievement prediction: The school as a conduit for macrostructural tension. In H. P. McAdoo & J. L. McAdoo (Eds.), *Black children: Social, educational, and parental environments* (pp. 85–111). Beverly Hills, CA: Sage.

Stack, C. B. (1991). Sex roles and strategies for survival in an urban Black community. In R. Staples (Ed.), *The Black family: Essays and studies* (4th ed., pp. 106–116). Belmont, CA: Wadsworth Publishing Company. (Original work published 1974)

Staples, R. (1985). Changes in Black family structure: The conflict between family ideology and structural conditions. *Journal of Marriage and the Family, 47,* 1005–1015.

Staples, R. (1986). The political economy of Black family life. *Black Scholar, 17,* 2–11.

Staples, R. (1988). The Black American family. In C. H. Mindel, R. W. Habenstein, & R. W. Wright (Eds.), *Family lifestyles of America's ethnic minorities: An introduction.* New York: Elsevier.

Staples, R., & Mirandé, A. (1980). Racial and cultural variations among American families: A decennial review of the literature on minority families. *Journal of Marriage and the Family, 42,* 887–903.

Steinberg, S. (1981). *The ethnic myth: Race, ethnicity, and class in America.* New York: Atheneum.

Stevenson, H. W., Chen, C., & Uttal, D. H. (1990). Beliefs and achievement: A study of black, white and Hispanic children. *Child Development, 61,* 508–523.

Sue, S., & Okazaki, S. (1990). Asian-American educational achievement:

A phenomenon in search of an explanation. *American Psychologist, 45*(8), 913–920.

Sue, S., & Sue, D. W. (1971). Chinese American personality and mental health. *Amerasia Journal, 1*(2), 36–49.

Sung, B. L. (1987). *The adjustment experience of Chinese immigrant children in New York City.* New York: Center for Migration Studies.

Suzuki, B. H. (1977). Education and the socialization of Asian Americans: A revisionist analysis of the "model minority" thesis. *Amerasia Journal, 4*(2), 23–51.

Swan, R. W., & Stavros, H. (1973). Child-rearing practices associated with the development of cognitive skills of children in low-socio-economic areas. *Early Child Development and Care, 2,* 23–38.

Swap, S. M. (1993). *Developing home-school partnerships: From concepts to practice.* New York: Teachers College Press.

Swap, S. M., & Krasnow, J. (1992). *A saga of Irish-American achievement: Constructing a positive identity.* Baltimore, MD: Center on Families, Communities, Schools and Children's Learning.

Taylor, R. J., Chatters, L. M., Tucker, M. B., & Lewis, E. (1990). Developments in research on Black families: A decade review. *Journal of Marriage and the Family, 52,* 993–1004.

Torres-Guzman, M. E. (1990) Recasting frames: Latino parent involvement. In C. Faltis & M. McGroary (Eds.), *In the interest of language: Contexts for learning and using language* (pp. 529–552). The Hague, Netherlands: Mouton.

Thompson, S. (1991). Moving in a current of new possibilities: Boston's Martin Luther King, Jr. Middle School. *Equity and Choice, 7*(2–3), 25–34.

U.S. Bureau of the Census. (1990). *Statistical abstract of the United States 1992* (112th ed.). Washington, DC: Government Printing Office.

U.S. Department of Commerce, Bureau of the Census. (1993). *Hispanic Americans today. Current population report, population characteristics* (pp. 23–183). Washington, DC: Government Printing Office.

U.S. Department of Education, National Center for Education Statistics. (1993). *The condition of education—1993.* Washington, DC: Government Printing Office.

Uriarte, M. (1988). *Organizing for survival: The emergence of a Puerto Rican community.* Unpublished doctoral dissertation, Boston University.

Useem, E. L. (1992). Middle schools and math groups: Parents' involvement in children's placement. *Sociology of Education, 65,* 263–279.

Vázquez-Nutall, E., & Romero-García, I. (1989). From home to school: Puerto Rican girls learn to be students in the United States. In C.

García Coll & M. de Lourdes Mattei (Eds.), *The psychosocial development of Puerto Rican women* (pp. 60–83). New York: Praeger.

Voiland-Sanchez, E., Sutton, C. P., & Ware, H. W. (1991). *Fostering home-school cooperation: Involving language minority families as partners in education.* Washington, DC: National Clearinghouse for Bilingual Education.

Volk, D. (1992, April). *A case study of parental involvement in the homes of three Puerto Rican kindergartners.* Paper presented at the annual meeting of the American Educational Research Association, San Francisco.

Vosburgh, M., & Juliana, R. (1990). Contrasts in ethnic family patterns: The Irish and the Italians. *Journal of Comparative Family Studies, 21*(2), 270–286.

Waller, W. (1932). *The sociology of teaching.* New York: Russell and Russell.

Wang, L. L.-C. (1976). Lau v. Nichols: History of a struggle for equal and quality education. In E. Gee (Ed.), *Counterpoint: Perspectives on Asian America* (pp. 240–263). Los Angeles: Asian American Studies Center, University of California, Los Angeles.

Warner, I. (1991). Parents in touch: Indianapolis public schools' investment in family involvement. *Phi Delta Kappan, 72*(3), 372–375.

Weber, M. (1947). *The theory of social and economic organization.* New York: Oxford University Press.

Weiser Ramírez, E. (1990). *Hispanic community organizations: Partners in parental involvement.* Washington, DC: Aspira Association.

Werner, E. E. (1984). Resilient children: The search for protective factors. *Young Children, 40*(1), 68–72.

Willie, C. V. (1981). *A new look at Black families* (3rd ed.). Dix Hills, NY: General Hall.

Winfield, L. F. (Ed.). (1991). Resilience, schooling and development in African-American youth [Special issue]. *Education and Urban Society, 24*(1).

Wong, L. C. (1990). *An ethnographic study of literacy behaviors in Chinese families in an urban school community.* Unpublished doctoral dissertation, University of Michigan, Ann Arbor.

Yao, E. L. (1985). A comparison of family characteristics of Asian-American and Anglo-American high achievers. *International Journal of Comparative Sociology, 26*(3–4), 198–207.

Young, J., Scorza, M. H., & Sica, M. (1984, April). *Evaluation report of Newtown High School project capable, 1982–83.* Brooklyn: New York City Board of Education Office of Educational Evaluation. (ERIC Document Reproduction Service No. ED 250 432)

· 29 ·

EFFECTIVE SCHOOLS RESEARCH

Daniel U. Levine

UNIVERSITY OF NEBRASKA, OMAHA

Lawrence W. Lezotte

EFFECTIVE SCHOOLS PRODUCTS, LTD.

Reviews of research dealing with school effectiveness can be broadly conceived to incorporate studies assessing effective classroom teaching practices, change processes that result in enhanced effectiveness, varying concepts and methods used to define and measure effectiveness, and other general themes concerned with portraying or promoting student learning. Since it is not feasible to analyze so many large research topics adequately in one chapter or even an entire book, this chapter will delimit the field by focusing on studies that have tried to identify the characteristics (or "correlates") of elementary and secondary schools that are unusually effective, in the sense that their students have higher academic achievement than those in most other schools in which students are similar in socioeconomic status. Thus it will concentrate on the so-called "effective schools" movement associated with the work of Wilbur Brookover (1985), Janet Chrispeels (1992a), Ronald Edmonds (1982), Lawrence Lezotte (1982, 1993), Peter Mortimore (Mortimore, Sammons, Stoll, Lewis, & Ecob, 1988), David Reynolds (1992), Barbara Taylor (1984), and other researchers and practitioners who have contributed to our understanding of unusually effective schools.

However, because many studies dealing with the school improvement process in general, administrative leadership, student motivation, and other topics bearing on effectiveness have direct implications for and sometimes are conceptually almost inseparable from research on unusually effective schools, results of selected studies involving these related topics will be considered or referred to as appropriate in this chapter. It also should be noted that parts of this chapter are modified versions of sections in a monograph published by the National Center for Effective Schools Research and Development (Levine & Lezotte, 1990). The chapter will begin with a review and analysis of correlates that frequently have been cited as generators of

unusual effectiveness, and then will consider some of the research dealing with creation of unusually effective schools and with several "contextual" variables (grade level, social class of the student body, urban/rural location) that should be taken into account in assessing effectiveness.

ANALYSIS AND DISCUSSION OF CORRELATES

Research on unusually effective schools supports the conclusion that they generally rank high on certain characteristics frequently referred to as "effective schools correlates." The purpose of this section is to clarify the meaning of some of the major correlates as indicated by research associated with the effective schools movement as well as other related areas of analysis and inquiry. Most of the research cited in this section has been concerned with elementary and intermediate schools. Although such research generally is applicable to secondary schools, implications may be somewhat different because of their greater complexity and size. Issues dealing with effective secondary schools are discussed in a subsequent section of this chapter.

Productive School Climate and Culture Reflecting Shared Values

Some of the characteristics of schools with unusually high achievement involve various aspects of school climate and culture. Among the most frequently cited of these aspects are *safe and orderly environment,* a *shared faculty commitment to improve achievement, orientation focused on identifying and solving problems, high faculty cohesion, collaboration, and col-*

legiality, high faculty input in decision making, and *schoolwide emphasis on recognizing positive performance.*

Safe and Orderly Environment. An "orderly, safe environment conducive to teaching and learning" (Edmonds, 1982, p. 4) and similar aspects of school climate frequently have been identified as constituting a characteristic of unusually effective schools. Citations of this correlate are found most often in descriptions and case studies of individual schools (e.g., Sizemore, Brossard, & Harrigan, 1983; Taylor, 1984), whereas several studies distinguishing between groups of more and less effective schools did not find it to be a discriminating factor (e.g., Brousseau, 1988).

It is not surprising that orderly environment appears to be a characteristic of unusually effective schools, but does not necessarily differentiate between more effective and less effective schools. For one thing, there are many schools—particularly those low in socioeconomic status (SES)—in which great gains and/or acceptable conditions have been registered on this correlate, but little has been accomplished in improving instructional arrangements. In addition, research indicates that orderliness seldom is a major problem in schools that are relatively high in SES, so in these circumstances it should not be expected to differentiate between more and less effective schools (Hallinger & Murphy, 1985, 1986).

Support for the importance of orderly environment as a prerequisite for effectiveness also can be found in many case studies of "out-of-control" schools in which poor or ineffective discipline obviously hampers learning (e.g., Payne, 1984), descriptions of schools in which systematic efforts to improve discipline clearly constitute a critical precondition in moving toward instructional effectiveness (e.g., Comer, 1980, 1987, 1988; Kozberg & Winegar, 1981), and descriptions of the sequence of events in schools that have become much more effective (e.g., Bullard & Taylor, 1993; Rossmiller, Holcomb, & McIsaac, 1993; Stringfield & Teddlie, 1987, 1988; Taylor, 1984). Actions taken at unusually effective schools to provide an orderly and productive climate typically include a broad array of activities such as the following:

- establishment of a "Mental Health Team" or other family-support agencies to bolster services for disruptive or maladjusted students and coordinate internal and external resources designed to help improve students' social skills (Comer, 1980, 1987, 1988; Dolan & Haxby, 1992);
- development and implementation of rigorous discipline policies (Chrispeels, 1992a; McCormack-Larkin & Kritek, 1982).

Faculty Commitment to a Shared and Articulated Mission Focused on Improving Achievement. Research on unusually effective schools indicates that faculty commitment to the task of helping all students master important learning objectives is a key consideration differentiating between more and less effective schools. For example, case studies conducted by Brookover and his colleagues (1979) found that schools achieving above prediction were differentially characterized by "teachers' acceptance of responsibility for student achievement" (p. 118), and that this attitude was manifested in a variety of actions

involving unusual commitment of their time and energy to help students succeed. Similar conclusions, though usually using slightly different terminology, have been reached by Bullard and Taylor (1993), Clancy (1982), Lezotte (1991), Rossmiller et al. (1993), Sizemore et al. (1983), and Taylor (1984).

High commitment to improved achievement among all faculty in an unusually effective school seems to constitute a central part of their organizational culture, to the extent that in effect it not only defines their core mission but helps them cope with and overcome the many frustrations and obstacles encountered in striving to improve learning for all students. Thus Taylor's (1984) study of unusually effective elementary schools found that their principals had articulated and successfully communicated a central "criterion of effectiveness" emphasizing in one way or another that "All kids can learn" (pp. 37–38).

Examples of ways in which unusually effective schools have acted to operationalize a clear mission focused on improving academic achievement include the following:

- At elementary schools in Milwaukee's RISE project, faculty have checked each student leaving the building to make sure that he or she takes materials home, have cancelled recess during inclement weather that interferes with expeditious movement in and out of the classroom, and have refused to take time to teach extraneous subject matter (McCormack-Larkin & Kritek, 1982).
- At an unusually effective school in Los Angeles, students who failed any subject were retained in grade if they did not attend summer school, and parents were notified of their children's progress or lack of progress every week during the academic year (Levine, Levine, & Eubanks, 1984).

Problem-Solving Orientation. Closely related to cultural norms emphasizing improved learning for all students, faculty and administrators at schools identified in case-study research as unusually effective have exemplified an attitude summarized in the dictum, "If what we are doing is not working for students, particularly low achievers, we will identify the obstacles we face and try something else that may overcome them." Thus observers at these schools have been struck by the problem-solving orientation and capabilities of their faculties and by administrators' and teachers' willingness to modify current practices and other approaches (e.g., Doll, 1969; Levine & Stark, 1981, 1982; Sizemore et al., 1983).

Faculty Cohesion, Collaboration, Communications, and Collegiality. Faculty members committed to a schoolwide mission focusing on academic improvement for all students tend to exemplify greater cohesiveness and consensus regarding central organizational goals than do faculty at less effective schools. High cohesiveness also implies that such faculties may exemplify more and/or better communications that may both stimulate and reflect consensus and cooperation. As pointed out in extensive analysis by Purkey and Smith (1983), Rosenholtz (1985), and others, cohesion and consensus are particularly important in organizations, such as schools, in which staff are challenged to accomplish a number of difficult and sometimes conflicting goals, means to accomplish them are not clear, and external as well as internal considerations tend to reduce goal clarity and to fragment improvement efforts. Many analysts also have concluded that "collegiality" is important in improving cohesion and communications, identifying and solving problems, and bolstering other aspects of effectiveness (Armor, et al., 1976; McCormack-Larkin & Kritek, 1982; Rossmiller et al., 1993; Taylor, 1984).

Faculty Input in Decision Making. Given the evidence cited above that unusually effective schools exemplify high levels of communication and an orientation focused on solution of priority problems, it is no surprise that numerous researchers have found that such schools rank high on faculty input into decision making. For example: Pollack, Watson, and Chrispeels (1987) reported that unusually effective schools in San Diego County scored high on collaboration in problem solving; Mortimore et al. (1988) found that students in inner-city London registered greatest progress in schools in which "the deputy and/or teaching staff were involved in decisions about the allocation of pupils and of teachers to classes" (p. 225); principals of unusually effective urban schools examined in journal articles (e.g., Fliegel, 1971; Lonoff, 1971; Levine & Stark, 1982) and in systematic case studies (e.g., Duckett, 1980; Taylor, 1990) have been described as having established mechanisms to provide for staff input; Newark elementary schools that gained most in achievement while participating in an effective schools project had higher scores on "participative" decision making than did lower-achieving schools (Azumi, 1989); and Levine and Eubanks (1983) described a successful inner-city school in which teachers made decisions about assigning students to classes and about whether grouping would be homogeneous or heterogeneous.

Schoolwide Emphasis on Recognizing Positive Performance. Obviously related to expectations, leadership, focus on learning, and other correlates, schoolwide emphasis on recognition of academic success has been identified as a characteristic of some unusually effective schools in studies reported by Chrispeels (1992a), Hallinger and Murphy (1985), Levine et al. (1984), and Teddlie, Kirby, and Stringfield (1989). In addition, some studies have extended this characteristic beyond the academic realm in describing unusually effective schools that systematically recognize and reward pupils for citizenship, attendance, and other aspects of positive behavior (Hallinger & Murphy, 1985, 1986; Levine et al., 1984).

Focus on Student Acquisition of Central Learning Skills

Closely related to aspects of school climate and culture described above, unusually effective faculties focus on making good use of time for learning and on ensuring student mastery of central learning skills.

Maximum Availability and Use of Time for Learning. As noted above, research on unusually effective schools indicates that they are characterized by a climate in which committed faculty work together to emphasize mastery for all students. One of the clearest indications that a school functions in accordance with this characteristic is the determination of faculty in unusually effective schools that time needed for learning is "squeezed" from the available schedule. Thus various authors have described unusually effective schools in which relatively little time is expended in passing between classes or recess (Love, 1988; McCormack-Larkin & Kritek, 1982; Sizemore, 1985, 1987; Stringfield, Teddlie, & Suarez, 1986; Teddlie et al., 1989; Teddlie & Stringfield, 1985, 1993).

Emphasis on Mastery of Central Learning Skills. Numerous studies and descriptions of unusually effective elementary schools have identified emphasis on mastery of academic content as an important aspect of their instructional programs. For example, Clancy's (1982) study of 19 such schools in Michigan found that "Mastery Learning Put Into Practice" and "Insisting on Concept Mastery" tied for 5th in a list of 48 "factors" that knowledgeable observers used to rank the reasons for their success. In some cases, unusually effective elementary schools have implemented a formal mastery-learning approach utilizing a well-defined sequence of teach/test/reteach/retest (e.g., Mamary & Rowe, 1985; Menahem & Weisman, 1985; Nagel, 1986); in other cases; a less formal approach has been used to ensure that nonmasters are identified and given opportunities to receive help and assistance (e.g., Levine & Stark, 1982).

It should be noted that many schools nationally have been implementing Bloom-type mastery learning or other mastery-type approaches with little or no noticeable impact on achievement (Levine & Jones, 1988). Schools attempting to implement mastery learning encounter many serious obstacles, and as often as not mastery learning has been misimplemented or implemented largely on paper (Levine & Cooper, 1991; Levine & Jones, 1988). Thus emphasis on mastery approaches is not likely to be successful in the absence of other effectiveness correlates, and emphasis on mastery should be viewed as a building-block antecedent to rather than a "guarantee" of effectiveness.

Appropriate Monitoring of Student Progress

Research support for monitoring of student progress as an effective school correlate probably provides weaker specific guidance for practice than is true with respect to any other frequently cited correlate. Although some studies have identified such monitoring as a major characteristic of unusually effective schools (e.g., Ferguson, 1984; McCormack-Larkin & Kritek, 1982), there has been little agreement among researchers and analysts on how to define it in practice. For example, McCormack-Larkin and Kritek refer to the correlate simply as "Evaluation" and then mention "Frequent assessment of student progress on a routine basis" (p. 17); Mackenzie (1983) cites "continuous diagnosis, evaluation, and feedback" (p. 8); Brookover (1985) refers to "ongoing" [rather than frequent] monitoring of student progress . . . including diagnosis and regular feedback to pupils" (p. 266); Sizemore (1985) makes reference to "consistent monitoring of students' reading and mathematics progress" (p. 271); and Mortimore et al. (1988) find support for administrators' insistence on keeping and using records to analyze students' progress.

Practice-Oriented Staff Development at the School Site

Descriptions of unusually effective schools indicate that in-service training and other forms of staff development generally are ongoing activities carried out in large measure at the school site and focused on practical considerations in improving implementation of the instructional program and other school and district priorities (e.g., Fliegel, 1971; Glenn, 1981; Hallinger & Murphy, 1985; Lonoff, 1971; Menaham & Weisman, 1985; Mortimore et al., 1988). Much of the staff development at unusually effective elementary schools has taken the form of both intragrade and cross-grade-level meetings and planning sessions at which teachers work together to improve coordination of instruction, select key learning objectives for a mastery-oriented approach to instruction, and otherwise work to attain schoolwide objectives identified elsewhere in this chapter (Ferguson, 1984; Levine & Stark, 1981).

Ongoing, practice-oriented staff development at the school site is the antithesis of traditional in-service training, which remains the most common approach to staff development in elementary and secondary schools. Traditional in-service training is characterized by "one-shot" sessions that fill all or part of a day devoted to presentations by outside "experts." Occasionally the participants in this activity are designated "trainers of trainers" who are expected to go back and teach their colleagues effective use of new methods and techniques, even though they have not developed adequate skills for doing so and little if any time or other resources are subsequently devoted to follow-up and adaptation at the building or classroom levels. Traditional training of this kind is not just unproductive but counterproductive, because it frequently manifests an "informal covenant" in which teachers agree to listen to speakers for a few hours in return for administrators' agreement to leave them fundamentally undisturbed in their classrooms (Parish, 1981).

Outstanding Leadership

Although a few analysts have described isolated examples wherein the major leadership at unusually effective schools has been provided by someone other than the principal, the large majority of studies and examples identify the building principal as the most critical leadership determinant of effectiveness (e.g., Clancy, 1982; Doll, 1969; Duckett, 1980; Glenn, 1981; Sizemore et al., 1983; Taylor, 1984; Teddlie et al., 1989; Weiss, 1984). In addition, there appears to be considerable agreement regarding some of the leadership activities and emphases that are characteristic of unusually effective principals.

Vigorous Selection and Replacement of Teachers. Research describing principals of unusually effective schools makes it clear that they are much more likely than the average principal to assume and/or seize a major role in selecting teachers who will serve on their faculty and in transferring out those per-

ceived as detracting from the effectiveness of the school (Doll, 1969; Levine & Eubanks, 1983; Sizemore et al., 1983: Stringfield & Teddlie, 1987, 1988; Teddlie, Wimpelberg, & Kirby, 1987). In many cases this function of leadership has required large expenditures of time and energy on the part of the principal, as well as willingness to test the limits of contractual agreements with teacher organizations and to challenge central office procedures and practices regarding assignment and removal of teachers.

"Maverick" Orientation and Buffering. Principals of unusually effective schools frequently have been identified as "mavericks" who are willing to "bend" rules and challenge or even disregard pressures or directives from the central office or other external forces perceived as interfering with the effective operation of their schools (e.g., Doll, 1969; Glenn, 1981; Sizemore, 1985, 1987; Sizemore et al., 1983; Stringfield & Teddlie, 1987). Actions of this type include refusal to utilize instructional materials required by the central office; unwillingness to participate in mandated procedures dealing with teacher evaluation; "buffering" the school and its faculty from influential external agents, even though this may generate criticism of the principal and/or the faculty; practicing "creative insubordination" when external regulations are dysfunctional; and violating central office guidelines on class size or other matters in order to provide resources for staff development, improve coordination of instruction, or accomplish other central school goals (e.g., Doll, 1969; Glenn, 1981; Sizemore et al., 1983).

Frequent, Personal Monitoring of School Activities, and Sense Making. Nested within the general observation that the principal usually is a key factor in accounting for leadership behaviors associated with school effectiveness is the well-supported finding that one aspect of these behaviors involves frequent visits to classrooms combined with constant personal surveillance of activities taking place in the school (Lezotte, 1982). This particular aspect of the principal's leadership has emerged as a correlate of unusual effectiveness in virtually every study in which it has been included as a variable (e.g., Armor et al., 1976; Jackson, 1982; Mortimore et al., 1988; Sizemore et al., 1983; Taylor, 1984; Teddlie et al., 1989). Thus research on unusually effective schools indicates that their principals are frequently in and out of classrooms (usually at least once a day in elementary schools), the lunchroom, and other facilities, and often engage staff in short conversations in hallways, lounges, and elsewhere. Deal and Peterson (1991) have pointed out that frequent movement through the school is one of the ways in which the principal can shape its organizational culture.

Taylor (1984) has pointed out that the effective principal's propensity to appear frequently for short periods of time on an unscheduled basis in classrooms and elsewhere helps enable him or her to effectuate the "sense-making" function of leadership, that is, to figure out what is taking place in an uncertain and complex situation and determine what short- and long-range actions may contribute to attainment of the school's priority goals—particularly its "criteria of effectiveness," focusing on improvement in learning for all students. Principals skilled in this endeavor exemplify a "knowledge-in-action" that enables them to recognize and overcome complicated obstacles to effectiveness, even though they may not be able to articulate a clear theoretical explanation of what they are doing. Equally important, the effective principal's frequent "strategic dialogue" with faculty enables him or her continually to focus and refocus staff efforts on strategic enterprises central to attainment of the school's mission.

High Expenditure of Time and Energy on School Improvement Actions. Several case studies of unusually effective schools have remarked on the tendency of their principals to work very long hours on demanding activities that deplete their physical and mental energy (Bullard & Taylor, 1993; Doll, 1969; Venezky & Winfield, 1979). High expenditure of time and energy by principals and other leaders of unusually effective schools exemplifies an effectiveness correlate that is not limited to education but has been described as a key leadership characteristic in many types of organizations.

Some comments are relevant regarding the high expenditure of time and energy characteristic of principals of unusually effective schools. First, hard work by itself is insufficient; many principals of less effective schools work equally long and difficult hours. Other actions and organizational characteristics, as discussed elsewhere in this chapter, also must be present. Second, it is not now and perhaps never will be very clear whether high expenditure of time and energy is more important as a prerequisite for handling the difficult tasks inherent in improving schools or as a means to communicate and spread commitment in the organization, or whether it is equally important for both purposes.

Support for Teachers. Several portrayals of leadership at unusually effective schools have described their principals as providing abundant support for their teachers (e.g., Bullard & Taylor, 1993; Doll, 1969; Glenn, 1981; Levine & Stark, 1981; Rosenholtz, 1985; Sizemore, 1985). Supportive behaviors of these unusually effective principals include both emotional encouragement and practical assistance in acquiring materials, handling difficult teaching assignments, and otherwise working to function successfully as a member of a motivated faculty. Levine and Stark interpreted this orientation as representing "a pervasive concern for problems teachers face every day . . . and an attempt to perceive problems and respond with understanding of the teacher's point of view" (p. 45).

Acquisition of Resources. Perhaps related to their orientation of providing emotional and practical support for teachers, principals of unusually effective schools also have sometimes been described or have described themselves as going to great lengths to obtain additional resources for their schools (Glenn, 1981; Venezky & Winfield, 1979). Strenuous efforts to obtain resources involve a wide range of activities, such as writing grant proposals, soliciting funds or other resources in the community, stretching and bending rules along with skillful politics aimed at acquiring all possible district resources, and in-school fund raising.

Superior Instructional Leadership. Instructional leadership is a wide-ranging topic that cannot be treated comprehensively in a single chapter. Fortunately, Joseph Murphy (1989) has analyzed and summarized much of the literature on instructional leadership. After reviewing the literature in eight "related areas" of research bearing on instructional effectiveness, Murphy concluded that instructionally effective leaders tend to be outstanding with respect to four major dimensions subdivided into specific administrative "functions," as follows:

1. *Developing Mission and Goals,* including *framing* a limited number of well-defined goals that apply to all children in the school and actually are used for planning and decision making; *communicating* schoolwide goals effectively to all school constituencies.
2. *Managing the Educational Production Function,* including *promoting quality instruction* through attention to considerations that promote high achievement; *supervising and evaluating* instruction in a manner that affects classroom practice; *allocating and protecting instructional time* through scheduling of activities in classes, ensuring coordination of time usage among teachers, allocating relatively large amounts of time for instruction, and reducing interruptions and other threats to instructional time; *coordinating the curriculum* effectively through attainment of continuity across grade levels and provision of consistency within and between various regular and special support services; *promoting content coverage,* including development and enforcement of policies that require regular homework assignments; and *monitoring student progress* using a wide variety of techniques and instruments.
3. *Promoting an Academic Learning Climate,* including *establishing positive expectations and standards,* particularly for previously low-achieving students; *maintaining high visibility* on the campus and in classrooms; *providing incentives for teachers and students* through rewarding and otherwise recognizing teachers for their efforts, delegating appropriate responsibilities, and making sure that high percentages of students receive recognition and rewards, particularly for academic performance; and *promoting professional development* of teachers, particularly through schoolwide staff development.
4. *Developing a Supportive Work Environment,* including *creating a safe and orderly environment* that reflects a consistent and well-coordinated discipline program; *providing opportunities for meaningful student involvement* in school activities; *developing staff collaboration and cohesion* through collaborative processes; *securing outside resources in support of school goals* and related assertive action; and *forging links between the home and the school,* particularly with respect to the school's primary mission of educating students.

Availability and Effective Utilization of Instructional Support Personnel. With the possible exception of a handful of nearly superhuman individuals assigned to very small elementary schools, principals require assistance from one or more instructional support persons if they are to function successfully as instructional leaders. Given the wide range of concerns that require attention in working to enhance student performance, it is virtually impossible for a principal to orchestrate a successful improvement campaign without substantial on-site assistance. Evidence for the importance of instructional support personnel at unusually effective schools has been provided by a Los Angeles study in which schools that gained most in achievement used some of their discretionary budget to provide "resource staff to assist teachers" (Armor et al., 1976, p. 28); a London study (Mortimore et al., 1988) in which deputy headmasters (i.e., assistant principals) played a "key role" in accounting for unusual effectiveness; Menahem and Weisman's (1985) description of the contributions of six central-office reading specialists and a full-time staff developer at each school in bringing about large achievement gains at 27 inner-city schools in Brooklyn; and Glenn's (1981) study of effective elementary schools at which substantial contributions were made by grade-level leaders, on-site curriculum specialists, and other specialized instructional support personnel. In some of these schools, principals had persuaded or coerced teachers to accept larger classes in order to create a position equivalent to assistant principal for instruction or full-time staff developer. In several cases principals were mavericks who violated school-board policies in creating such a position without official approval from central decision makers.

Salient Parental Involvement

For several reasons, parental involvement has been a difficult variable to assess or identify as an effectiveness correlate. First, involvement is so highly correlated with SES that controlling for SES in regression studies frequently eliminates its relationships with achievement. Even if a relationship remains, it may be questionable whether the researcher controlled adequately for SES and related variables. Second, there are many forms and varieties of involvement, thus making it difficult to define or measure. Third, involvement seems to have received little attention in some studies, perhaps in part because many early leaders of the effective schools movement worried that emphasis on parental involvement might become a form of blaming the victim through minimizing educators' responsibility for introducing effective reforms (O'Neill & Shoemaker, 1989).

Research generally supports the conclusion that it is desirable to enhance parents' involvement in education and to have high levels of school-home cooperation (Ascher & Flaxman, 1987; Chrispeels, 1992b; Henderson, 1987). However, some research studies specifically related to parental involvement and school effectiveness either have failed to find support for a relationship between involvement and unusual effectiveness or have concluded that less effective schools may have more involvement of some kinds than more effective schools (Brookover & Lezotte, 1979; Hallinger & Murphy, 1985, 1986). In addition, some researchers who have portrayed unusually effective schools have not perceived (or at least have not recorded) particularly high levels of involvement.

On the other hand, several studies comparing more and less effective schools have reported that effectiveness is positively associated with involvement. For example, Armor et al. (1976) found that among predominantly African American (but not Hispanic) elementary schools, gains in achievement after controlling for SES were greatest at schools with high "school/community integration," as indicated by data showing that parents were "in and around the building fairly continuously," were included on "planning and monitoring committees for all school events and activities," and were active participants in school advisory councils (pp. 54–55). Similarly, Mortimore et al. (1988) reported that elementary students in inner-city London made greatest progress at schools in which "parents helped in the classrooms . . . [and with] outings and . . . other kinds of assistance," "regular progress meetings [were held] for parents to discuss their children's work," rooms or other facilities were provided for parents' use, and parents were allowed to "call in at any time to see the head" (p. 226).

Numerous authors have described high levels of parental involvement in portrayals of unusually effective schools. Stedman (1987) summarized general parent participation activities in some of these schools as involving "good communications between the school and the home," facilitation of parents' involvement "in their children's learning," "getting parents politically involved on behalf of the school," garnering "vital parental support for the school's daily academic efforts," and, in some cases, sharing in school governance (p. 219). Specific ways in which parents have been described as having been part of improvement efforts at unusually effective schools include the following:

- "exerting pressure on public officials" in order to help obtain and retain resources (Fliegel, 1971, p. 342);
- participating in school meetings designed to promote use of "games and other instructional materials at home" and to "improve their youngsters' attitudes toward school and learning" (Ferguson, 1984, p. 630);
- helping maintain an orderly climate in the lunchroom and the schoolyard (Lonoff, 1971, p. 339);
- participating in signing of annual contracts specifying rigorous discipline policies for their children and of weekly progress reports describing their son or daughter's mastery or nonmastery of skills taught that week (Levine et al., 1984);
- sitting in classrooms (as encouraged by the principal) in order to "observe and monitor teacher performance and student learning" (Sizemore et al., 1983, p. 16);
- participating in a parental group that helped buffer the school from other parents attempting to change school policies (Sizemore et al., 1983, p. 16);
- informing the administration when homework is "makework" rather than productive assignments coordinated with classroom instruction (Levine & Stark, 1981, 1982);
- helping their children use local library resources identified by teachers as useful for schoolwork (Levine & Stark, 1981, 1982);
- participating in a "building-level governance and management group" particularly involved in planning "programs sensitive to child development and behavior principles" (Comer, 1987, p. 15).

It is hard to find any common denominator in the foregoing examples of parental involvement at unusually effective schools, no doubt because there are many diverse ways in which schools can and do promote positive parental involvement. However, examining case studies of unusually effective schools with high parental involvement and/or visiting such schools in person suggests that these schools have identified and emphasized parental involvement activities that are somehow particularly salient in terms of the most serious problems they face at a given point in time (Chrispeels, 1992b; Lezotte, 1991). Stated differently, these schools are doing more than merely engaging in some general effort to increase parental communications or build more positive school-home relationships.

Effective Instructional and Organizational Arrangements

Research on unusually successful schools indicates that, in one way or another, they have devised and implemented arrangements to group students effectively for instruction and to utilize staff and other organizational resources in a manner that helps students—particularly low-achieving students—engage in active learning and succeed academically.

Grouping and Related Organizational Arrangements. Grouping of students is an extremely complex issue both theoretically and practically (Burns, 1987; Oakes, 1992). Practitioners and researchers must deal with a host of complicated and interrelated considerations involving such questions as the following:

How much spread in prior achievement should there be within and across classes?
On what criteria should students be grouped?
Should students be grouped homogeneously in some subjects, such as reading, but not others?
Which teachers function best with which students?
How can disadvantages of homogeneous or heterogeneous grouping be overcome if a school goes in one direction or another?
How do class size, availability of material, sequencing of learning objectives, and other considerations affect teachers' capacity to implement homogeneous or heterogeneous grouping successfully?

Descriptions of unusually effective schools indicate that, among other arrangements, some use mostly homogeneous grouping; some group students almost entirely on a heterogeneous basis; some use homogeneous grouping within classes while others group across classes or use a combination of both approaches; some individualize instruction substantially or teach students in small groups and regroup frequently; others emphasize whole-class instruction in groups that are either relatively homogeneous or heterogeneous; some use grouping arrangements that differ from grade to grade or teacher to teacher; and some utilize practices different from any of those alluded to above. A sense of this wide variation has been pro-

vided in the following description by Brookover and Lezotte (1979) in their study of Michigan elementary schools that had improved substantially in achievement over a three-year period:

Although . . . there are some relatively common characteristics . . . [very little] can be said about the common organizational characteristics. They vary from very traditional self-contained classrooms to somewhat open pod organization with team teaching. Various types of both homogeneous and heterogeneous grouping of students are used and various degrees of emphasis are placed on individualized instruction. (p. 62)

Several studies have concluded that one of the characteristics of an unusually effective school is the introduction and implementation of workable arrangements for helping low achievers (Levine & Stark, 1981, 1982; Levine et al., 1984, 1985; Sizemore et al., 1983). Grouping arrangements at schools described in these studies have been diverse, but in general they have been particularly focused on helping low achievers and have been thoughtfully designed and implemented to attain this overriding goal. Among unusually effective arrangements that have been described in case studies or in related analysis dealing with instructional interventions for low achievers are the following:

- "parallel classes" of the lowest readers who receive special help in small classes (Glickman & Pajak, 1986; Levine & Stark, 1981, 1982);
- "parallel scheduling" of reading so as to offer instruction in small groups for students grouped by previous achievement (Canady, 1988, 1989; Canady & Hotchkiss, 1985; Canady & Reina, 1993);
- individualized and small-group instruction in schools that have sufficient resources, commitment, and leadership to make this approach workable (Fliegel, 1971; Mamary & Rowe, 1985);
- assignment of two teachers to classes of Chapter 1 students with low reading achievement (Levine, Hollingsworth, & Aquila, 1987);
- extensive use of certified teachers to help provide tutoring in reading and small-group reading instruction in the primary grades (Madden, Slavin, Karweit, & Livermon, 1989; Slavin, Karweit, & Wasik, 1992);
- a variety of developmental and remedial learning opportunities during or outside the regular school day (e.g., Sizemore et al., 1983);
- reduction of primary-grade class size to 20–22 or fewer at inner-city schools (Groom, 1989);
- placement of nonpromoted students in transitional classes or units taught by teachers specially selected, qualified, and trained to help them improve and return to their previous cohort (Carter, Madison, Hall, & Lockamy, 1990; Sudlow, 1990);
- provision of special help in algebra during time formerly devoted to study halls and physical education in order to make sure that initial low achievers perform adequately in

this critically important "gate-keeping" course (Sudlow, 1990);

- provision of tutoring and after-school and/or summer school developmental learning opportunities to introduce learning skills and materials before their introduction in regular classrooms, in order to plug gaps in students' prior knowledge and thereby reduce demotivating failure experiences and the necessity for remediation for nonmastery students (Smith, 1985);

- utilization of paraprofessionals to provide additional help for low achievers (Glenn, 1981; Venezky & Winfield, 1979);

- "walking reading" or related approaches through which elementary students are grouped across or within grades by current performance level during a common reading period (Levine & Stark, 1981; Sizemore et al., 1983).

This chapter cannot provide a comprehensive analysis and discussion of all the important issues and research involving grouping of students and related aspects of organizational arrangements, but a number of considerations and conclusions that are essential for educators involved in efforts to improve school effectiveness are discussed briefly below.

1. *Improvement of grouping and related organizational arrangements at unusually effective Chapter 1 schools frequently has involved reduction or elimination of pullout approaches that take students out of their regular classes for compensatory instruction.* Potential and actual detrimental effects of pullout in Chapter 1 and other remedial or special-needs programs have been widely recognized during the past decade. Among these detrimental effects are confusion in school scheduling and functioning, unclear accountability for student progress, multiplication of record-keeping chores, and lack of coordination between regular and compensatory instruction (Allington, 1991). Although some unusually effective Chapter 1 schools have found ways to overcome these problems and implement pullout successfully, it appears that many or most have reduced or eliminated pullout in favor of other Chapter 1 approaches that generally are easier to implement effectively.

2. *Class size and, particularly, the number of low achievers per class are important considerations in working to provide effective grouping and related organizational arrangements.* Research on class size constitutes a sizable literature that cannot be reviewed comprehensively in this chapter, but several studies and conclusions that seem most salient for the effective schools process can be summarized as follows:

- Class size may be particularly important with respect to effective schools goals involving improvement of low achievers' performance on higher-order skills such as comprehension, critical thinking, and problem solving, because research indicates that such improvement requires careful *mediation* by a teacher or other instructional agent (Presseisen, Smey-Richman, & Beyer, 1992). This conclusion is compatible with those of several studies indicating that unusually effective schools have worked out arrangements for providing students with some assistance in learning individually (but usually not through comprehensive individualization) and in small groups (e.g., Duckett, 1980; Sizemore et al., 1983).

- The number of low achievers in a class may be even more important than overall class size, particularly as it affects teachers' decisions regarding pacing of instruction, their ability to respond appropriately and provide effective assistance to students, and overall behavioral dynamics in a classroom (Barr & Dreeben, 1983; Dreeben & Barr, 1988a, 1988b; Leinhardt & Pallay, 1982; Levine, 1985a).

- Class size, along with the number of low achievers and heterogeneity/homogeneity in grouping arrangements, interacts with other variables (e.g., teachers' skills, methodology, and experience; students' levels of performance) in affecting process outcomes such as whether and to what extent teacher-centered direct instruction for the whole class will be effective, whether small-group and investigative learning methods will be productive, and whether many or most students will waste time in seatwork (Madden et al., 1989). For example, some unusually effective schools appear to have improved reading achievement in part through limiting the number of reading groups per class to two or three (Block, 1983; Sizemore et al., 1983), but the feasibility of this approach clearly depends on such considerations as overall class size, number of low achievers, and size and composition of the subgroups.

3. *In schools with significant numbers of low achievers, some degree of leveling probably will be required in attempting to provide effective instruction.* The term *leveling* refers to the practice of classifying students into a few broad groupings or levels based on current reading performance. For example, Sizemore and her colleagues concluded that unusually effective inner-city schools in their study had been able to improve achievement partly through "differentiation of treatment for advanced, average, and slow learners with the provision of intense concept development instruction to increase growth rates" (Sizemore, 1985, p. 272); South Boston High School registered large gains in reading after classifying ninth- and tenth-grade students as (a) average or above average or (b) below average or nonreaders, and providing comprehensive and intensive instruction in reading and writing for the latter grouping (Kozberg & Winegar, 1981; Levine & Eubanks, 1989); and an unusually effective intermediate school in inner-city Los Angeles provided differential instruction after distinguishing among nonreaders, low readers, and average or above readers (Levine et al., 1984). *Leveling* may be a more useful term than *homogeneous grouping* because it implies an effort to avoid overuse of homogeneous grouping and tracking, along with an insistence on helping low achievers master skills needed to function successfully in more heterogeneous learning environments.

4. *To the extent that some degree of leveling is used within classes or across a grade level, strong efforts must be made to avoid the potentially negative consequences of homogeneous arrangements.* Frequently encountered in analysis of school functioning as well as formal research reviews, these negative consequences include low expectations for students in low-performing groups, slow pacing of instruction, reinforcement of low achievers' negative self-concept, and magnification of negative classroom dynamics. In this regard, Leinhardt and Pallay (1982) reviewed research on "restrictive" settings for low

achievers, and concluded that potentially negative consequences can be minimized or avoided through: (a) small class size; (b) high overlap between teaching/learning activities and criterion tasks; (c) mastery learning systems emphasizing monitoring of progress; (d) increased time in cognitive activities; (e) reasonably rapid pacing; (f) a formal classroom management system; (g) positive teacher affect; (h) increased instructional time; and (i) an emphasis on positive student self-concept.

Appropriate Pacing and Alignment. Closely related to issues involving mastery of central skills and to grouping concerns discussed in preceding sections, appropriate pacing of instruction has been identified as an important effective schools correlate in several studies of unusually successful schools. For example, analysis by McCormack-Larkin and Kritek (1982) of inner-city schools in an effective schools project in Milwaukee indicated that the fastest-improving schools exemplified "planning and monitoring for full content coverage" while also emphasizing "use of the accelerated learning approach . . . [to attain] more than one year's growth" for low achievers who otherwise would have little opportunity to achieve at the national average (pp. 17–18).

Support for the importance of pacing as a key variable in improving student achievement also has been provided in much classroom-level research, such as the series of intensive first-grade studies conducted by Barr and Dreeben (1983; Dreeben & Barr, 1988a, 1988b). After analyzing reading gains in 50 reading subgroups within 13 classes in seven schools, Barr and Dreeben reported that achievement in word learning and reading strongly reflected amount of coverage of content combined with allocation of sufficient time and other indicators of opportunity to learn (Dreeben & Barr, 1988b). The authors point out that these considerations interact with numerous other important variables, such as aptitude level and size of classes and reading subgroups, district and school policies regarding selection and use of instructional materials, and teachers' choice of instructional methods. Ways in which instructional pacing has been accelerated at low-achieving schools participating in effective schools projects include the following:

- "spiraling up" approaches in which whole-class direct instruction is used to introduce materials at students' current instructional level, but teachers quickly move beyond that level after providing appropriate help to pupils;
- "spiraling down" approaches in which whole-class direct instruction is used to introduce grade-level material, but action is taken to help nonmasters acquire key entry skills required to function at this level;
- faculty identification of skills that do and do not deserve reduced emphasis (or additional emphasis) at each grade level (Niedermeyer & Yelon, 1981; Wick & Turnbaugh, 1983);
- emphasis on materials and objectives at grade level for whole-class instruction, but at students' performance level in subsequent small-group instruction (McCormack-Larkin & Kritek, 1982);
- prohibition of ditto sheets and workbooks that mire students in unproductive small-skills assignments;

- drastic alignment of curriculum and instruction such that teachers receive only carefully selected portions of basal readers and therefore cannot proceed slowly through every page to make sure that every student has fully mastered every small skill (Levine, Levine, & Eubanks, 1985);
- limitation of district and/or school scope-and-sequence guidelines and testing practices to a small number of essential skills that emphasize higher-order learning rather than low-level, mechanical learning (Levine & Stark, 1981).

Active/Enriched Learning. Several authors have reported that unusually effective schools tend to emphasize instructional approaches that encourage and support active and enriched learning by students in a context that involves considerable interaction with teachers and other students. For example, one of the schools described in a Phi Delta Kappa volume portraying successful urban schools used Teaching Reading Through Drama, Outdoor Education, and other active learning approaches (Gregory & Mueller, 1980); teachers at effective schools in Louisiana were observed using "interactive" instruction more frequently than teachers in less effective schools (Stringfield & Teddlie, 1988; Teddlie et al., 1989); one of the unusually effective inner-city schools described by Levine and Stark (1982) spent much of its Chapter 1 funding to operate a TV production studio that facilitated development of students' language and communications skills; several of the schools in this same study implemented comprehensive arrangements to link classroom learning to use of library and media resource centers; a successful inner-city school described by Levine et al. (1984) systematically emphasized "language bees" and other active learning techniques; Mortimore et al. (1988) found that teachers at more effective elementary schools in London placed greater stress on "stimulating" higher-order learning than did teachers in less effective schools; an unusually effective school described by Comer (1980, 1987, 1988) integrated language arts and social studies learning in various ways, including student operation of a school store; several of the unusually effective schools described by Brookover et al. (1979) emphasized spelling bees and math competitions; and numerous schools that have registered substantial improvement gains have made extensive use of cooperative student-learning techniques (Brookover, 1985; Slavin & Madden, 1989).

That unusually effective schools apparently emphasize active, enriched learning is no surprise inasmuch as a great deal of research identifies overemphasis on small, mechanical skills associated with passive seatwork as a central consideration in generating and perpetuating low achievement (Allington, 1991; Cooper & Levine, 1993; Cooper & Sherk, 1989). Many studies have not cited active and enriched learning as an effective schools correlate, but this, too, is not surprising, because many or most studies have not included it as a variable; because emphasis on active learning cannot be expected to result in large achievement gains unless other effective schools correlates also are present; and because criteria for success often center on or at least include scores in language mechanics, math computation, or other low-level skills that can be bolstered somewhat through worksheets and other passive learning assignments.

Active and enriched learning approaches are difficult to implement effectively, particularly in schools with large proportions of low achievers who are not well prepared to learn independently. Successful implementation often requires substantial increases in supplies and equipment, provision of much technical assistance, reduction of teachers' loads, and willingness of staff to tolerate and be able to function in a relatively "messy" and complex working environment. It is easy to see why successful utilization of active, enriched learning in turn depends on other effective schools correlates such as skilled leadership, strong commitment on the part of teachers, unusually effective instructional arrangements for low achievers, and a problem-solving orientation throughout the entire faculty (Presseisen et al., 1992; Rossmiller et al., 1993).

Emphasis on Higher-Order Learning in Assessing Instructional Outcomes. Closely related to imperatives cited above regarding pacing and alignment of instruction, provision of active/enriched learning, and grouping arrangements to counteract emphasis on low-level learning, assessment in unusually effective schools has utilized tests and other measures that focus on comprehension and other nonmechanical skills. Despite the fact that most widely used and available standardized and criterion-referenced tests provide educators with very little help in assessing students' performance with respect to higher-order skills (Porter, 1989), faculties in many of these schools have found ways to collect and utilize data focusing on comprehension and other higher-order learning. Examples of assessment approaches and practices that appear to have played an important part in improving achievement at such schools include the following:

- New Orleans elementary schools that have registered achievement gains using the Degrees of Reading Power Test (which emphasizes students' ability to read with understanding) as part of an effective schools project stressing instructional leadership, parent involvement, and other correlates (Southern Coalition for Educational Equity, 1986);
- Glendale, Arizona, high schools at which testing and reporting policies give greater weight to skills classified as high on Bloom's taxonomy (Becker & Barry, 1990);
- Spencerport, New York, schools that emphasize the taxonomy in developing local criterion-referenced tests (Sudlow, 1990);
- primarily middle-class elementary schools at which functional reading performance is assessed by classroom teachers who then concentrate on providing materials at suitable levels of difficulty rather than on teaching reading subskills (Wick & Turnbaugh, 1983);
- inner-city schools in New York City District #19, in which large gains in reading comprehension have been registered utilizing Degrees of Reading Power scores as one part of a much larger, comprehensive effort to address many of the instructional issues discussed in this chapter (Menahem & Weisman, 1985).

Coordination in Curriculum and Instruction. Identified in several studies as a variable distinguishing between more and less effective elementary schools, coordination in curriculum and instruction has been defined in terms of: sharing of "information pertaining to reading materials and student progress . . . between grades, within grades, between the school and community, [and] with specialists and aides" (Stoll, 1978–79, p. 3); "consistency" in the "continual development of competencies" across grades and in "the approaches used to teach these skills" (Venezky & Winfield, 1979, p. 31); implementation of "grade level expectations . . . [defined in terms of] prerequisites for success at the next grade" together with "coordination of supportive services" (McCormack-Larkin & Kritek, 1982, pp. 17–18); and "consistency among teachers" in using district or school guidelines for subject matter (Mortimore et al., 1988, pp. 224, 250). Such considerations frequently have been addressed as part of the curriculum alignment process.

Easy Availability of Abundant, Appropriate Instructional Materials. Levine and Stark (1981) were struck by the strenuous efforts of administrators and teachers at several unusually effective inner-city schools to ensure that an abundance of suitable materials was easily available for use in delivering instruction. Somewhat similarly, Venezkey and Winfield (1979) remarked on the great lengths to which administrators at such schools went to provide a surfeit of appropriate instructional materials. Stoll (1978–79) found that teachers in more effective schools in Florida were more satisfied with the amount and variety of materials than were teachers at less effective schools, and Glickman and Pajak's (1986) study of Georgia districts and schools that had improved in achievement cited provision of abundant teaching resources keyed to central learning objectives as an important consideration in bringing about gains.

Classroom Adaptation. Several studies of unusually effective elementary schools have concluded that teachers in these schools tend to adapt curriculum materials and instructional methods for use in their respective classrooms, as contrasted with mechanical implementation following highly prescribed steps and sequences. Thus Sizemore et al.'s (1983) in-depth study of two such schools in Pittsburgh concluded that teachers were active in adapting basal readers and sequencing tests; Armor et al. (1976) found that encouragement for teachers to "adapt or modify the reading program on an individual classroom basis . . . [rather than conforming] closely to . . . program guidelines" (p. 28) strongly differentiated between more and less effective schools; and Jackson (1982) concluded that teachers in less effective schools in her study seemed "to be controlled by the mechanics in the management aspects" of their instructional system, as contrasted with more effective schools in which the "driving force" involved student needs (p. 151).

Stealing Time for Reading, Language, and Math. Schools with a high proportion of low achievers face an extremely difficult task in striving to ensure that students can function with sufficient understanding and independence to handle curriculum content on or near grade level, and to perform productively in seatwork and other independent learning activities. Accordingly, faculties at such schools have had to find ways to upgrade student performance in reading, language, and math. In some cases such gains have been registered largely through increasing time allocated to reading and to application in language (e.g., greater use of libraries) and mathematics. Movement in this direction is not so easy as it sounds, because parents of students at low-achieving schools may view such an approach as inequitable or discriminatory, state or district tests may include components in social studies, science, or other subjects in which student performance may well decline, and teachers may be reluctant or unwilling to "give up" favorite topics dealing with U.S. history, art, or other subjects. In the face of these and other criticisms and obstacles, success in improving reading and math through increased time allocations will depend on considerations such as a unified faculty mission, good communications with the community and/or willingness to withstand parental criticism, leadership of the principal in motivating or replacing recalcitrant teachers, acquisition of additional, appropriate reading and math materials, improved efficiency in scheduling and conducting classes, and disregard of state or district pressures to raise or maintain average scores in all testing categories—in other words, other correlates of effectiveness.

Time on Task/Opportunity to Learn. Teachers' efforts in emphasizing higher-order skills, coordinating instruction, obtaining appropriate materials, stealing time for central learning activities, and otherwise attending to instructional improvement, are to no avail unless students have realistic opportunities to learn required subject matter and actually expend time and energy doing so. Thus, it is no surprise that unusually effective schools have impressed analysts with their emphasis on ensuring that students work meaningfully and diligently in mastering the content of instruction. Unusually effective schools at which the teachers modify instruction to take account of students' learning styles, utilize class time as fully and expeditiously as possible, scrutinize and revise grouping arrangements, implement classroom and school-level climate improvement plans, and otherwise act to ensure high time on task and opportunity to learn have been described by Bullard and Taylor (1993), Glenn (1981), Jackson (1982), Levine and Sherk (1990), Levine and Stark (1982), Love (1988), Stringfield and Teddlie (1988), and other researchers.

High Operationalized Expectations and Requirements for All Students

The presence of high expectations for acceptable student performance and behaviors, along with requirements and other policies that help communicate and effectuate such expectations, has been cited as a crucial characteristic of virtually all unusually effective schools described in case studies (e.g., Armor et al. 1976; Brookover & Lezotte, 1979; Levine & Stark, 1981; Sizemore et al., 1983; Stringfield et al., 1986; Taylor, 1984; Teddlie & Stringfield, 1993; Venezky & Winfield, 1979; Weber, 1971). In addition, high expectations sometimes have been identified as a correlate of effectiveness in multiple regression studies (e.g., Weiss, 1984), even though multivariate analyses usually use questionnaires on which respondents generally are reluctant to describe themselves or their school as less than highly expectant.

Several additional points should be stressed regarding the operationalization of high expectations and rigorous requirements for students. First, setting high instructional expectations and requirements generally involves difficult work on the part of teachers. For example, teachers who minimize workbooks and ditto sheets in effect give up a relatively easy way to keep students occupied and out of trouble, and frequently encounter some opposition from those students who prefer mechanical assignments that require little thought or effort and may enhance their feelings of success (Doyle, 1983). Similarly, maintaining strong discipline and rigorous behavioral requirements requires constant vigilance and extra effort by the entire faculty in many schools, particularly inner-city secondary schools (Payne, 1984). Second, the specific methods used to operationalize high expectations and requirements may be less important than the fact that *something* is being done systematically and vigorously to communicate and ensure a strong academic press and a climate conducive to learning. For example, strong homework policies that have been utilized at many unusually effective schools (e.g., Levine & Stark, 1981; McCormack-Larkin & Kritek, 1982), and the departures from social promotion also found frequently at such schools (e.g., Eubanks & Levine, 1983; Glickman & Pajak, 1986; McCormack-Larkin & Kritek, 1982), may sometimes be less valuable for their direct impact on student behavior and performance than for their indirect transmittal of high expectations and their positive effect on school climate.

Multicultural Instruction and Sensitivity

Stedman (1987) reviewed information on unusually effective schools with high proportions of low achievers and concluded that most of these schools exemplified "ethnic and cultural pluralism" in the sense that their faculties were committed to "breaking down institutional and community barriers to equality," emphasized the use of multiethnic materials, and/or "displayed a great deal of sensitivity to linguistic minorities" (p. 219). Other unusually effective schools that appeared to emphasize these or other aspects of multicultural instruction are described in Comer (1980) and Sizemore et al. (1983), while Bamburg and Andrews (1987) found that teachers in more effective schools ranked the goal of developing "strong multicultural understanding among students and staff" higher than did faculty at less effective schools. For a variety of reasons, multicultural aspects of curriculum and instruction constitute an important consideration in striving to improve the achievement of disadvantaged minority students (Gilbert & Gay, 1985). Operating schools according to the principle that all children can learn is a central component in respecting and recognizing differences in their cultures and environments. Both researchers and practitioners connected with effective schools projects should give more explicit attention in the future to issues and possibilities involving multicultural sensitivity and instruction.

CREATING EFFECTIVE SCHOOLS

Prior to the 1980s, most of the unusually effective schools described in the literature had been isolated institutions that attained this status basically on their own, with little or no external assistance or participation in a school-improvement "project." Many schools that have participated in effective schools projects or similar school-improvement efforts have failed to register substantial and lasting gains in student achievement or other major indicators reflecting student performance. On the other hand, many other schools have improved substantially while participating in such efforts (Bullard & Taylor, 1993; Chrispeels, 1992a; Eubanks & Levine, 1983; Gauthier, Pecheone, & Shoemaker, 1985; Groom, 1989; McCormack-Larkin & Kritek, 1982; Nagel, 1986; Reynolds & Cuttance, 1992; Taylor, 1990). The remainder of this section will review some of the most important guidelines that have emerged and several key issues that are still unresolved in formulating and carrying out systematic efforts to enhance the effectiveness of groups of schools participating in significant improvement projects.

1. *Substantial staff development time must be provided for participating faculties, preferably at least in part during the regular teacher workday.* In agreement with research indicating that teachers' acquisition and successful utilization of new or improved instructional approaches requires considerable time and practice extending to coaching and practice at the classroom level, staff development must be an integral and ongoing activity in projects to make schools more effective. The magnitude of time required to provide teachers with more effective methods for improving students' comprehension skills has been underlined by Kurth and Stromberg (1984), who worked with a small group of teachers to promote more independent reading in a suburban elementary school and found that success depended on "continuous, almost Herculean" staff development efforts (p. 2). School districts that have made progress in improving student achievement through effective schools projects have utilized such approaches for delivering staff development as the following:

- stipend budgets for in-service training after school, on Saturdays, and/or during the summer (Eubanks & Levine, 1983);
- reduction of teachers' duty periods to provide time for staff development and collaboration during the regular school day (Glickman & Pajak, 1986);
- creation of "early closing" days when the student day is shortened in order to provide staff development;
- "early dismissal" of students during the last week of school to provide more time for staff and organizational development (Carter et al., 1990);
- provision of a full-time staff-development specialist to work with faculty members released from planning and/or duty periods through assignment of substitute teachers (Levine & Sherk, 1989, 1990).

2. *Faculties engaged in effective schools projects must not wait very long before beginning to address issues involving improvement of instruction.* Unfortunately, some faculties participating in effective schools projects tend to become fixated on climate, parental involvement, or other correlates that do not directly involve instruction (Azumi, 1989; Taylor, 1990), perhaps in part because instructional issues are more difficult to address, involve fundamental intrafaculty differences in philosophy and values, and/or tend to require more resources than do climate improvements (Pecheone & Shoemaker, 1984). Such an approach is unproductive because school effectiveness also depends on a mixture of key characteristics that involve organizational arrangements, active learning, and other instruction-related variables. In particular, school improvement plans should pay particular attention to grouping, higher-order skills, compensatory services, pacing, and other key aspects of instruction (Levine & Leibert, 1987).

3. *Improvement goals must be sharply focused to avoid teacher and school overload.* One of the most common reasons why effective schools projects fail is because they try to do too much in too short a time (Henderson & Lezotte, 1988). This is particularly the case when staff-development and other resources are limited (as they almost always are), but the overload problem is present even when resources are substantial, and in some cases resources contribute to the problem by encouraging school officials to try too much at one time. Similarly, there is reason to believe that many inner-city schools are hampered by the presence of too many concurrent compensatory programs.

One common example of counterproductive overload involves school-improvement projects in which faculties of inner-city elementary schools are expected to improve instruction in reading, language arts, math, science, and social studies, all in one year (Levine, 1985b). Overload of faculties participating in effective schools projects is but one small subset of a widespread national and perhaps international tendency to expect teachers to improve all aspects of instruction within a very short period of time. Thus success in an effective schools project sometimes may depend on bringing about an "organized abandonment" of numerous existing activities that are fragmented and incoherent. Observing the organizational tenet that you cannot succeed if you change just one small part of a system does not require that you introduce a multiplicity of large changes all at once. Instead, priorities should be determined and resources allocated as part of a realistic plan that takes account of constraints and overload.

4. *Significant technical assistance must be made available to faculties participating in effective schools projects.* Primarily in the form of specialized personnel, technical assistance is critically important in helping faculties assess their current levels of effectiveness and problems, develop the capacity to work together productively, and initiate and carry out significant changes in educational programming and delivery. Depending on the nature, scope, history, stage, and origins of a given effective schools project, technical assistance may involve state department of education or central office specialists, other external consultants, and/or in-school staff or organizational development personnel. For example, Pecheone and Shoemaker (1984) have described substantial specialized assistance made available by the New York State Department of Education;

Clark and McCarthy (1983) and Eubanks and Levine (1983) described arrangements for technical assistance in New York City projects that sometimes required a facilitator in each school for the equivalent of one day a week or more; and Groom (1989) portrayed a successful big-city project in which three full-time effective-schools staff and other external resources, as well as full-time instructional specialists at each school, were available to 18 elementary schools.

Part of the reason why technical assistance and large amounts of staff development time are so essential is because true school effectiveness is increasingly defined in terms of improvement in students' comprehension and other higher-order skills (Cooper & Sherk, 1989; Cooper & Levine, 1993). Recently developed instructional methods for improving comprehension have been sufficiently widespread and impressive to constitute a virtual revolution in educators' capacity for attaining this goal (Pearson, 1985). But until very recently there has been "essentially nothing in instructional materials or in teacher training that helps the teacher learn what to do when the child does not understand" (MacGinitie & MacGinitie, 1986, p. 258). One result of this discrepancy is that teachers at most schools will require large-scale assistance of various kinds in order to enhance the effectiveness of their instruction.

5. *Effective schools projects should be "data-guided" in the sense that appropriate information should be collected and interpreted to help participants prepare and carry out plans for improvement.* Faculty attention in effective schools projects should include a focus on discrepancies between advantaged and disadvantaged students in acquiring key learning skills, particularly those involving higher-order learning. School-level analysis of such data not only provides a basis for designing pertinent improvement efforts, but, equally important, calls attention to the educational outcomes to which school and district personnel assign highest priority (Rossmiller et al., 1993). Examples of effective schools projects in which appropriate data played a central part in shaping effective implementation have been provided in portrayals by the Southern Coalition for Educational Equity (1986) and by Groom (1989) of big-city projects; Everson, Scollary, Fabert, and Garcia's (1986) description of a small suburban project; Azumi's (1989) description of an elementary school project in Newark; Chrispeel's (1992a) analysis of an effective schools project in San Diego County; and Bullard and Taylor's (1993) description of districts that have substantially improved student performance.

6. *Effective schools projects should seek out and consider using materials, methods, and approaches that have been successful in schools and projects elsewhere.* Improving school effectiveness is a difficult undertaking that faculties of a participating school or project cannot be expected to reinvent successfully entirely on their own initiative (Lezotte & Bancroft, 1985; Rossmiller et al., 1993; Taylor, 1990). As noted above, approaches developed elsewhere seldom can be transported successfully without considerable adaptation, and "packaged" approaches for initiating change or improving instruction can be dangerous when they are introduced as a substitute for the hard work and often considerable resources required to bring about significant improvement. Nevertheless, prospects for success in effective schools projects are greatly enhanced when

participants judiciously consider and adapt approaches developed and successfully implemented in other locations. In the terminology used by Peters (1988), "creative swiping" should replace the "not invented here" syndrome.

Examples of approaches that should be considered for many or most projects include the following: use of Teacher Expectations and Student Achievement (TESA) training early in a project to sensitize teachers and help develop their skills in reaching low achievers (Sudlow, 1990); curriculum materials designed specifically to develop students' comprehension skills (Levine & Stark, 1982); approaches for involving parents and other community representatives (Chrispeels, 1992b; Comer, 1980, 1988; O'Neill & Shoemaker, 1989); instruments, such as the Degrees of Reading Power Test, designed to help in planning and delivering instruction focused on improvement in students' comprehension (Levine & Sherk, 1990; Cooper & Levine, 1993); assertive discipline or similar approaches (Sudlow, 1990); and student-team learning arrangements that help engage students more actively in learning (Brookover, 1985; Slavin & Madden, 1989). Additional approaches that have shown considerable utility when adapted to local projects are described in various chapters of a 1990 book edited by Barbara Taylor.

7. *The success of an effective schools project depends on a judicious mixture of autonomy among participating faculties and a measure of direction from the central office, a kind of "directed autonomy."* Flexibility and independence in making decisions about the implementation of instruction and other aspects of education have been identified as correlates of effectiveness at both the school and classroom levels. On the other hand, except in the case of isolated maverick schools that have become effective largely on their own, success also requires considerable direction and support from central office administrators. This conclusion is compatible with those of researchers who have studied innovation and planned change in general and found that it is most likely to be successful when it combines elements of "bottom-up" planning and decision making with "top-down" stimuli and support in setting directions and guiding the change process (Fullan, 1991; Corbett, Dawson, & Firestone, 1984; Huberman & Miles, 1982; Pajak & Glickman, 1989).

8. *Some form of site-based management is an important and perhaps even indispensable component of plans to improve school effectiveness, but it must not be viewed or treated as a substitute for the larger instructional improvement process.* As mentioned earlier, staff input and faculty participation in decision making frequently have been identified as correlates of unusual effectiveness, but outstanding schools in these studies have attended assiduously to the full range of correlates and improvement guidelines identified in this chapter and other reviews. Tendencies to equate or confuse site-based management or other recent teacher empowerment approaches with the comprehensive process and agenda involved in improving the performance of low-achieving students are particularly unfortunate when they result in neglect or ignorance of knowledge and strategies that have been identified by school-effectiveness researchers in the past two decades (Taylor & Levine, 1991).

Assumptions of internally initiated school improvement. Experience in working to create unusually effective schools suggests that successful projects typically embody a set of key assumptions that can be useful in helping to shape the thinking and analysis of teachers and administrators. Among these assumptions (Lezotte, 1991) are the following:

- Every school can improve, regardless of current levels of success.
- The potential for improvement already resides in every school.
- In improving instruction, no adults in the school are unimportant.
- School improvement is a process, not an event.
- The people now working in the school are in the best position to manage the change process.

District leadership and responsibilities. Specialists who have conducted effective schools projects and analysts who have examined their implementation have been virtually unanimous in observing that leadership and support from central office decision makers are vital considerations in determining whether such projects will succeed or fail (e.g., Bullard & Taylor, 1993; Menahem & Weisman, 1985; Pecheone & Shoemaker, 1984). This same conclusion frequently has been emphasized in research on change in general (e.g., Fullan, 1982, 1991).

Shoemaker (1982, 1986) has pointed out that district leadership is particularly important in ensuring continuity of committed leadership and effort at the building level; several researchers have identified lack of such leadership as a key consideration in the demise of promising efforts at schools that received a new principal unwilling or unable to maintain initial momentum. Some effective schools projects have been either severely compromised or virtually destroyed in districts where central administrators maintained the facade and terminology associated with a project, but diverted participants' attention to other topics temporarily spotlighted in the latest educational journals and magazines (Bullard & Taylor, 1993).

Research on district responsibilities in implementing effective schools projects or otherwise contributing to school effectiveness has been limited, but here, too, results confirm the central importance of district leadership and support. For example, Murphy and Hallinger (1986) studied superintendents of 12 unusually effective school districts in California and concluded that they were "actively involved" and "influential" in developing both district and school goals, originating procedures for actually selecting staff (particularly new administrators), supervising and evaluating principals, establishing and regularly monitoring a "district wide instructional and curricular focus," and ensuring consistency in "technical core" operations such as functioning of categorically funded programs, use of standardized and timely teacher-evaluation procedures, and monitoring of curriculum and instruction.

Acknowledging that successful school improvement projects generally require some "top-down" initiative (see above), and that central office decision makers also are responsible for providing many kinds of assistance at each step in the improvement process, one can view the central office role as typically involving some mixture of *decisive mandating of general directions combined with sufficient technical and financial assistance* (cf. Brickell, 1980) to allow for successful implementation of the mandate. Examples of productive action combining central mandates and provision of adequate assistance to schools participating in effective school projects have included the following:

- specification of an instructional management system incorporating an aligned curriculum emphasizing higher-order skills, combined with technical assistance regarding relevant testing and instructional strategies and with clerical assistance and computers to make record keeping manageable for teachers;
- requirements that English teachers assign and grade written papers, combined with funding to limit their daily and weekly student load;
- setting of reading comprehension minimal scores to identify students requiring remedial help, combined with funding and technical assistance to provide appropriate compensatory services (both Connecticut and New York State use the Degrees of Reading Power Test to implement this type of approach);
- preparation of district-level discipline codes emphasizing attainment of an orderly and safe environment, combined with provision of resources for in-school suspension rooms, "time-out" rooms, security guards, or other implementation components that may be required to ensure that the code is consistent, effective, and equitable;
- introduction of a firm and specific promotions/retention policy (as has been evident at some unusually effective schools), combined with monetary resources and supervision to ensure that retained students are placed with outstanding teachers who provide responsive instruction and that additional after-school, summer, and other special learning opportunities are provided for retainees;
- guidelines to encourage heterogeneous grouping, combined with resources to provide relatively small classes so that teachers can deal effectively with heterogeneity.

When central decision makers abdicate their responsibilities for providing meaningful assistance to implement their mandates, the result is likely to be an outcome variously described by informed observers as "nonimplementation" (Brieschke, 1987), "illusory" implementation (Popkewitz, Tabachnick, & Wehlage, 1982), "chaotic" displacement of priorities (Taylor, 1984), "cosmetic" reform (Orlich, 1989), "symbolic" implementation (Mann, 1989), and "phantom" implementation (Pogrow, 1983). Our own favorite term is "hallucinatory" implementation.

Promising Intervention Practices

Practitioners and specialists who direct effective schools projects have explored and developed a variety of approaches for helping to ensure a successful outcome at participating schools. Approaches that have been successful or appear to have significant potential in this regard include the following:

- establishment and facilitation of an informal group of participating principals who meet regularly and work together to provide overall guidance for the project (McCormack-Larkin & Kritek, 1982);
- district development and sponsorship of individual school audits focusing on effective schools correlates and implementation (Groom, 1989);
- redesign and utilization of personnel evaluation instruments to emphasize effective schools correlates (Adams, Allen, & Fortenberry, 1990);
- assignment of new or weak principals for several weeks of observation and shadowing of more effective principals (O'Neill & Shoemaker, 1989).

The Staff Development and School Improvement Process

Guidelines for initiating and carrying on staff development to increase school effectiveness are identical to those that have been identified as desirable or necessary for any significant school improvement effort. As summarized by Fleming and Buckles (1987), some of the considerations that must be attended to include the following: "identification of consultants and trainers; provision of substitutes or teachers' stipends; purchase of materials; availability of meeting space and planning time; [and] availability of travel/meeting expenses" (p. 4).

Effective schools projects typically involve the establishment of building-level planning committees and subcommittees that prepare annual or longer-range improvement plans that deal, in one way or another, with various correlates of effectiveness. Many of the correlates discussed in the preceding pages, such as site-level staff development, provision of substantial technical assistance, and orientation toward practical problem solving, have clear implications concerning the preparation and implementation of effectiveness improvement plans. Beyond such obvious implications, little is known about how to shape and carry out the planning process. However, a few comments may be helpful regarding experiences reported by persons who have participated in successful school-improvement projects.

1. As pointed out by Fraatz (1988), much of the evaluation activity that takes place in schools can be viewed more as bureaucratic "politics of efficiency" designed to enhance organizational maintenance than as a "warrant for intervention" to bring about fundamental improvements in effectiveness and equity (pp. 45–46). Similarly, Shujaa and Richards (1989) have made a distinction between "organizational learning cultures" (OLCs) at schools that view test data as "symbolic" opportunities to alleviate or prevent public criticism, and OLCs at schools that treat testing as a "strategic" opportunity to identify and address real problems. Examples of data that have been helpful in modifying attitudes and behavior in order to focus on strategic equity and effectiveness goals include: curriculum-alignment activities in which faculties analyze a variety of data in collaborating to select specific skills to emphasize and de-emphasize at and across grade levels (Levine & Stark, 1981, 1982; Niedermeyer & Yelon, 1981; Wick & Turnbaugh, 1983); analysis of Degrees of Reading Power data that in effect forces teachers to consider possibilities for change when their text and other materials are mismatched with their students' current comprehension levels (Harris & Cooper, 1985; Levine & Sherk, 1989; Cooper & Levine, 1993); and information on student and faculty "time-on-task" that school-improvement specialists help faculty collect and analyze as part of their participation in effective schools projects (Everson et al., 1986). Many of the schools and districts that have become substantially more effective have attained their goals in part through collecting and attending to disaggregated achievement data that show the extent to which economically disadvantaged students are or are not obtaining scores on important learning outcomes comparable to those of middle-class students (Bullard & Taylor, 1993; Chrispeels, 1992a; Rossmiller et al., 1993).

2. A clear signal indicating that a school is concerned largely with "organizational maintenance" and the "politics of efficiency" (Fraatz, 1988) rather than fundamental improvement is when its plan specifies that most or all teachers or grades will participate to the same extent in the same intervention and/or will receive exactly the same resources. Since imperatives for improvement and needs for increased resources almost always vary from teacher to teacher and grade to grade, equivalence in interventions or parity in resources throughout a school usually mean that faculty have seized on simplistic solutions that require minimal change in instruction. Examples of plan components that probably represent an "easy way out" with little or no modification of ineffective practice include the following:

- components specifying that every teacher receive exactly the same funding for supplementary materials;
- computer lab arrangements providing that all classes in a large school attend the same number of periods per week, resulting in a pattern wherein students virtually are whisked in and out of the lab;
- "schoolwide" plans that redirect Chapter 1 resources to bring about a slight reduction in the size of every elementary class, with no fundamental intervention in arrangements for delivering instruction;
- provision of the same fraction of a (fragmented) paraprofessional's time for every classroom teacher;
- purchase of a computer lab without a teacher or aide to maintain it, or with too few computers to allow for effective utilization;
- purchase of truckloads of consumable workbooks and ditto sheets that keep students occupied in seatwork.

3. If they are to make much difference, school improvement plans generally will involve changes that some or many faculty will find distasteful, frequently because the modifications will upset customary arrangements or interfere with faculty "rights" and privileges. A few examples that occur with some frequency include the following:

- regrouping arrangements that reduce senior faculty privileges in deciding who they will teach;
- agreement within a department, grade, or entire school to follow common testing practices, homework policies, and/or discipline rules, in a school where some or many faculty are satisfied with current idiosyncratic practices;
- reassignment of rooms, which may require senior teachers to forgo space they have worked to customize and improve.

Willingness of faculty in an effective schools project to join together in planning and implementing changes that involve discomfort or loss of privileges is precisely the core manifestation of the effective schools correlate involving faculty commitment to a common, clear school mission. In the absence of such willingness, expressed support for other correlates such as high expectations for all students and focus on mastery of central learning objectives should not be expected to translate into achievement gains among students.

Potentially Successful Multischool Approaches

School reformers have developed a number of approaches that have improved student achievement substantially across groups or subgroups of participating schools when they have been well implemented. Several such approaches have become widely known to educators and/or are described elsewhere in this *Handbook,* and thus will not be discussed in this section. Among these approaches are the Higher Order Thinking Skills (HOTS) program developed by Stanley Pogrow (1983, 1990, 1992) and his colleagues at the University of Arizona; the Accelerated Schools approach developed by Henry Levin (1987) and his colleagues at Stanford University; the Success for All approach developed by Robert Slavin (Slavin, Karweit, & Wasik, 1992) and his colleagues at The Johns Hopkins University; and the School Development Program developed by James Comer (1980, 1988) and his colleagues at Yale University.

Since most multischool projects and approaches have dealt exclusively or largely with elementary schools attended primarily by students from low-income families, it is important to note that systematic interventions also are being developed and implemented to enhance school effectiveness across elementary and secondary grade levels and at differing types of schools. For example, both the Comprehension and Cognition approach, sponsored by the National Urban Alliance for Effective Education, and the School-Based Instructional Leadership Program, sponsored by the National Center for Effective Schools Research and Development, appear to have produced impressive gains in student achievement at both elementary and secondary schools that have implemented them within a framework focused on key effective schools correlates such as stress on active/engaged learning and higher-order thinking skills, provision of outstanding leadership at both the school site and central office, maintenance of high expectations for all students, and modification of organizational and instructional arrangements to provide adequate assistance for low achievers. Each of these approaches combines substantial change in instructional content with recognition of principles drawn from the literature on organizational development and change in schools.

The Comprehension and Cognition approach, where fully implemented, is organized initially around administration of the Degrees of Reading Power test originally developed by the College Board. The test provides reading comprehension scores that, unlike those derived from other standardized tests, indicate how well a student actually can understand prose he or she encounters inside and outside the classroom. The second step is to align instructional materials with the comprehension level of one's students, in order to provide materials that do not frustrate students in completing independent learning activities. At the same time, materials slightly beyond students' current functional level are used during instruction designed to improve their comprehension. The third and most extensive step is to help faculty introduce teaching and learning strategies that can improve students' cognitive processes and thinking skills, within a larger framework that addresses the correlates of unusually effective schools and the processes involved in improving effectiveness. Successful results have been reported at schools in Kansas City, New York, Orlando, Prince George's County, and other locations (Ivens, 1988; Levine & Sherk, 1989; Cooper & Levine, 1993; Office of Research & Evaluation, 1993).

The School-Based Instructional Leadership Program codifies achievement-enhancement approaches originally developed by Ronald Edmonds (1982), Lawrence Lezotte (1982), Joan Shoemaker (1982), Barbara Taylor (1990), and other leaders of the so-called "effective schools" movement. As described by Holcomb (1991) and Rossmiller et al. (1993), the program explicitly addresses correlates (e.g., clear and focused mission, "opportunity to learn and time on task," high expectations for student success, positive home-school relations, "frequent monitoring of student progress," "positive environment for teaching and learning") that historically have constituted central tenets identified by effective schools researchers and practitioners. Particular attention in implementing the program is given to provision of systematic staff development, the management of change, disaggregation of data to portray the relative performance of differing groups of students, the critical importance of vigorous leadership at the school and district-office levels, and building teamwork at participating schools. Schools that have become substantially more effective utilizing central concepts and components delineated in the School-Based Instructional Leadership Program are described in Bullard and Taylor (1993), Chrispeels (1992a), and Taylor (1990).

CONTEXT DIFFERENCES: GRADE LEVEL, SOCIOECONOMIC STATUS, AND URBAN/RURAL LOCATION

Because much of the research on unusually effective schools has dealt primarily with elementary schools—particularly inner-city elementary schools enrolling mostly working-class students—many analysts have cautioned against automatically assuming that results and conclusions apply equally well to secondary schools and schools with mixed- or middle-class enrollment (e.g., Reynolds & Cuttance, 1992). In addition to these two major aspects of school context (grade level and SES), many other contextual variables, such as urban/rural location, public/private sponsorship and control, lack of experience/experience of staff, complex/simple instructional technology, strong/weak external pressures to improve, and voluntary/involuntary participation in an improvement project, may well generate differentials in the characteristics that are associated with effectiveness at differing schools and in the kinds of changes that are likely to improve effectiveness (Hallinger & Murphy, 1985). Thus Wimpelberg, Teddlie, and Stringfield (1989) have argued convincingly that effective schools research in the future should pay increasing attention to considerations such as grade level, availability of additional resources from parents and community, size of school and district, and other contextual factors that may have a decisive impact on school effectiveness and on the success of improvement projects.

Secondary Schools

For various reasons, observers have expressed doubt that characteristics associated with unusual effectiveness in research conducted mostly on elementary schools also differentiate between effective and ineffective schools at the secondary level. For one thing, upper intermediate schools (i.e., junior highs and middle schools) and senior high schools usually are much larger and more complex than elementary schools. In addition, secondary schools generally have more diffuse goals (e.g., career preparation and drop-out prevention) that frequently become more salient as students proceed through school, thereby complicating attempts to attain or identify unusual effectiveness. Third, measurement of performance is even more difficult than at the elementary level because of ceiling and floor effects in achievement testing, potentially confounding effects on achievement scores of success in reducing dropouts, and other causes. Finally, it frequently is considerably more difficult to convince secondary teachers than it is elementary teachers to try promising approaches such as cooperative learning or mastery learning.

Consideration of specific correlates of effectiveness also raises questions concerning their functioning and applicability in large secondary schools. For example, successful instructional leadership involving the supervision of numerous subject-area specialists may be very different from the situation with elementary-school generalists. High expectations may have little discernible impact if many students lack prerequisite learning skills, vigorous selection of teachers may fail to affect a critical mass of a large faculty, and administrators may be unable to monitor developments frequently and personally unless they make an impractical attempt to spend all their time "wandering around" large secondary schools. In addition, some correlates such as students' "time on task" may have a vastly different meaning at the secondary than at the elementary level.

Nevertheless, some empirical studies as well as related analyses do support the conclusion that correlates associated with effectiveness among elementary schools also help in accounting for, or at least in describing, unusually effective secondary schools. Although systematic studies of effectiveness at the secondary level are much more difficult to carry out and are more susceptible to varying interpretations and criticisms, several analysts have reported that unusually effective secondary schools tend to exhibit correlates frequently identified in research on elementary schools. Researchers in California studied 18 high schools that had been nominated as unusually effective and reported that they appeared to exemplify a "clear sense of purpose," "high expectations," "commitment to educate each student as completely as possible," and a "safe, orderly learning environment" (Murphy & Hallinger, 1985, p. 18). Somewhat similarly, Garibaldi (1987) and Firestone and Corbett (1988) independently examined information on two differing sets of high schools nominated as unusually effective and concluded that they ranked high on orderly climate, administrative leadership and support, and high expectations.

Since secondary schools generally are more complex and difficult to improve than are elementary schools, unusual success at the secondary level almost certainly involves action that goes "beyond" the usual correlates, as well as differing manifestations of the correlates in practice. In this regard, several authors have identified characteristics of unusual effectiveness that they believe have particular salience for secondary schools. Thus Hallinger and Murphy's (1985) analysis of successful high schools in California cites a "core set of standards within a rich curriculum," a "special reason for each student to go to school," a "sense of community," and "resiliency" in "bounding back" from loss of funds and other crises as correlates of unusual effectiveness (p. 18).

In a related formulation, Levine and Eubanks (1989) described several urban high schools they had reason to believe were unusually effective, and summarized some of their "commonalities" as follows: concentration on "improving comprehension" and other fundamental learning skills, "provision for alternative types of learning arrangements and experiences," and "substantial staff turnover and/or selection" (p. 49). Regarding intermediate schools, Levine et al. (1984) described a group of unusually effective inner-city schools and characterized them in terms of their common emphasis on higher-order cognitive development, students' personal development, and high expectations implemented on a schoolwide basis. It is easy to understand how and why a "rich" and "relevant" curriculum with alternative learning opportunities and career programs, substantial staff turnover, a sense of community, emphasis on both cognitive and personal development, and resilience in the face of massive obstacles may be more difficult to attain—and perhaps for this reason more crucial to success—at the secondary than at the elementary level.

As mentioned above, some of the correlates usually identified for elementary schools may have little applicability or may function quite differently in secondary schools. An excellent example is provided by time-on-task variables, which numerous studies have associated with gain in student achievement at the classroom level and several authors have identified as a characteristic of unusually effective elementary schools (e.g., Stringfield et al., 1986). A study by Teddlie and Virgillo (1988), however, reported that student time on task at "more effective" junior high schools was clearly below the level registered at "typical" junior highs. If replicated by other research, this type of differential pattern may mean that high time on task at the junior high level frequently is attained through expending class time on seatwork that keeps students occupied with low-level chores.

This brief review of the scant literature dealing explicitly with unusually effective secondary schools has not included examination of a useful and growing strand of research that focuses on the establishment and functioning of small "alternative" units inside or separate from "regular" junior and senior high schools. Generally aimed at improving educational opportunities for disaffected and/or low-achieving students, alternative units can overcome many of the problems that hamper effective instruction for a significant proportion of so-called "marginal" students (Levine, 1975, 1992; Wehlage, 1983; Wehlage, Rutter, & Turnbaugh, 1987).

In the case of secondary classes, schools, or programs designed to help initially low-achieving students, instructional coordination appears to be particularly crucial. Among other possibilities, instructional coordination can involve efforts to plan and deliver instruction across subject areas (e.g., by introducing vocabulary terms in several subjects during the same day or week) to ensure that management techniques are consistent from one class to another, and to emphasize reading and math skills that are immediately applicable in content studies such as history, science, and literature. It is easier to obtain this type of coordination to support the learning of initial low achievers in small alternative units that facilitate teacher collaboration in planning and delivering instruction—a consideration that helps account for the impressive achievement gains sometimes registered among low-achieving secondary students in school-within-a-school units at inner-city intermediate and high schools (Levine, 1992).

Socioeconomic Status

The most comprehensive and important studies explicitly seeking to determine whether or how unusually effective low-status schools differ from their more affluent counterparts have been conducted by Hallinger and Murphy (1985, 1986) and their colleagues in California, and by Teddlie and Stringfield (1985) and their colleagues in Louisiana. The California study involved extensive analysis of eight elementary schools, selected from among more than 3,100 statewide, that registered third- and sixth-grade reading and math scores above predictions based on SES for three consecutive years beginning in 1978–1979. Two of these schools were low in SES, two were classified as lower-middle, two were in middle-income communities, and two were upper-middle (Hallinger & Murphy, 1986).

The researchers found that the unusually effective schools in their study were generally similar in the sense that both those that were relatively low and high in SES exemplified several of the commonly cited correlates, namely a safe and orderly environment, a clear mission, capable instructional leadership, high expectations, a "well-coordinated curriculum," "monitoring of student progress," and "structured staff development" (Hallinger & Murphy, 1986, p. 351). However, the data also indicated that the effective low-SES schools differed from the effective high-SES schools in the following ways:

- Curriculum and instruction in the low-SES schools were more narrowly focused on fundamental learning skills, and alignment of curriculum with instruction was "moderate" rather than "tight."
- Instructional leadership emphasized both "technological and climate" goals, whereas administrators in the high-SES schools primarily stressed technological goals. In addition, though principals in both types of schools "played an active role in coordinating curriculum and instruction," those in unusually effective low-SES schools were "more forceful in asserting themselves in making instructional decisions and in intervening in classrooms where teachers were not meeting their expectations" (Hallinger & Murphy, 1985, p. 3).
- Control of instruction by the administration was "high" rather than "low to moderate."
- Administrative task orientation was "high" and relationship orientation was "low to moderate," rather than "moderate" and "moderate to high," respectively.
- "Home-school cooperation" was weak and parent involvement was "limited," rather than "strong" and "pervasive," respectively.
- "Rewards and recognition" were relatively frequent and visible rather than less frequent and intrinsic.
- High expectations for students originated largely from the school rather than the "home and school," and "future expectations" for students were "moderate" rather than "high" (Hallinger & Murphy, 1986, p. 337).

In close agreement with the findings reported by Hallinger and Murphy, Teddlie and Stringfield (1985, 1993) and their colleagues studied 76 elementary schools in Louisiana and found that the clearest difference between unusually effective and less effective middle-SES schools involved a tendency for teachers in the former group to push students harder academically and to take greater responsibility for students' achievement than did teachers in "typical" middle-SES schools. As regards low-SES schools, expectations and aspects of academic climate also were higher in the unusually effective subset, and teachers in the unusually effective low-SES schools placed a greater emphasis on reading, math, and homework than did teachers in the less effective low-SES schools. In addition, principals in the more effective low-SES schools apparently visited classrooms more frequently and played a larger role in hiring teachers than did principals in the less effective low-SES schools.

Urban/Rural Location

One of the few studies that has specifically examined possible differences between rural and urban schools bearing on the definition and enhancement of effectiveness is an investigation at a rural school of short-term awareness sessions, graduate-level courses, and "actual conduct" of a "school assessment and improvement process" involving the literature on effective schools (Buttram & Carlson, 1983, p. 73). The authors concluded that it was difficult to focus faculty attention on the

EFFECTIVE SCHOOLS RESEARCH • 543

achievement of disadvantaged students; climate concerns tended to "revolve" around the adequacy of instructional space and building maintenance; assessment of leadership at small schools lacking principals centered on head teachers or other leaders; lack of resources for staff development time and travel and for development and implementation of an improvement plan was a particular problem; traditional indicators of student SES did not appear to be reliable; and the awareness stage seemed to last for an inordinately long time. More research is needed to determine whether these kinds of problems are particularly or unusually widespread among rural schools participating in an effective schools project.

Among observers who have attempted to analyze rural schools from the viewpoint of the literature associated with the effective schools movement, Conklin and Olson (1988) and Stringfield and Teddlie (1988) concluded that, although the small size and isolation of rural schools frequently inhibit attention to unique needs of disadvantaged students, rural schools may be in a relatively advantageous position to develop faculty consensus, work productively with parents and the community, and involve students in school activities.

In general, there currently is little or no reason to believe that correlates identified as characterizing unusually effective schools are less important or relevant in rural than in urban settings, even though most of the research has been conducted in urban schools and, in many cases, in poverty areas in big cities. Although analysis cited above suggests that resource limitations typical of many rural schools may constrain implementation of effective school projects, this disadvantage may be counterbalanced by considerations facilitating communication and student involvement at small schools in rural areas.

CONCLUDING OBSERVATIONS

Rather than providing a comprehensive summary of conclusions delineated in the preceding pages, this section will briefly review and elaborate on several that have particularly important implications for the design and implementation of effective schools projects.

First, correlates of unusual effectiveness should be viewed more as prerequisites for attaining high and equitable levels of student achievement than as any kind of "guarantee" that a school will be successful. This is partly because success in dealing with one or a few correlates will not bring about effective and equitable outcomes in the absence of action dealing with other correlates.

Second, the correlates represent issues and challenges that faculty must grapple with to make their school effective, not detailed prescriptions or recipes for attaining that status. There are innumerable steps that can be taken to make a school's climate and culture productive, improve leadership, enhance expectations and requirements for satisfactory student performance, strengthen instructional arrangements for low achievers, or bring about schoolwide improvement with respect to other correlates. No specific action or set of actions is "right" for every school. From this point of view, we know both

more and less about making schools effective than we sometimes acknowledge. Research has identified the kinds of actions that faculties should consider to make their schools more effective, but it cannot tell them exactly how to proceed in their inevitably unique situation.

Third, much of what happens at unusually effective schools involves teachers' and administrators' awareness and insight in explicitly identifying and addressing obstacles to success inherent in whatever approaches are being used to deliver instruction or otherwise improve educational opportunities. For example, if some form of leveling is being used to provide special assistance for low achievers, care must be taken to overcome potentially negative effects of homogeneous arrangements. Alternately, faculties emphasizing individualized and small-group instruction in a heterogeneous setting must make sure that sufficient material, technical, and human resources are available to ensure the success of this approach to instruction.

Similarly, if day-to-day instructional leadership is to be provided primarily by the principal, other persons must be available and designated to help carry out responsibilities involving matters such as financial management, community relations, and student discipline. Alternately, the principal may concentrate largely on a range of noninstructional functions, but specialists must then be available to work with teachers on a daily basis.

Comparable requirements are present with respect to other correlates. For example, if a rigorous retention policy is initiated to help improve climate and raise expectations, comprehensive policies and actions are required to make sure that retention is not punitive. Alternately, eliminating or forgoing retention will not be productive in many schools unless a workable system exists to make sure that students achieving far below grade level receive the special assistance required to help them function successfully in classrooms with meaningful standards.

Fourth, faculties struggling to improve their effectiveness necessarily face many profound dilemmas built into the underlying school reform process. Whatever choices are made with respect to climate, expectations, parental involvement, instructional arrangements, or other correlates present a variety of difficult challenges. To keep challenges manageable, faculty probably will need to undertake an "organized abandonment" of abstractly desirable functions and activities in order to enhance their capacity to deal with their most central goals.

Fifth, effective schools research in the future must devote much more systematic attention to considerations involving emphasis on or neglect of active/engaged learning and higher-order skills in implementing and assessing instruction. Unfortunately, the importance of these correlates frequently has been masked by deficiencies in defining and measuring effectiveness.

Finally, it is difficult to overestimate the importance of several key dispositions that characterize the faculties of unusually effective schools. Among these dispositions are *insistence* that teachers, students, support personnel, and others in the school adhere to high standards in the face of difficult circumstances (Lonoff, 1971). To attain these standards, faculty at unusually effective schools must be very *persistent* in overcoming numerous obstacles and roadblocks, and they also must be *resilient* in the sense that they cannot allow occasional setbacks to thwart their plans for continuing improvement. As noted at several points in this chapter, unusually effective faculties also are *consistent* in devising and implementing coordinated curricula and instructional arrangements that result in high achievement levels among all groups of students. Insistence that faculty, students, and other parties take responsibility for improvement, persistence in doing what must be done to attain high standards, resiliency in moving forward despite discouraging obstacles and developments, and consistency in implementing coordinated and coherent programs to improve instruction—these are some of the key characteristics that will continue to be associated with unusual effectiveness for the foreseeable future.

References

Adams, C. R., Allen, H. L., & Fortenberry, R. N. (1990). Effective schools do make a difference in Jackson, Mississippi. In B. O. Taylor (Ed.), *Case studies in effective schools research* (pp. 143–154). Dubuque, IA: Kendall/Hunt.

Allington, R. L. (1991). How policy and regulation influence instruction for at-risk learners, in L. Idol and B. F. Jones (Eds.), *Educational values and cognitive instruction: Implications for reform* (pp. 273–296). Hilldale, NJ: Lawrence Erlbaum Associates.

Armor, D., Conry-Oseguera, P., Cox, M., King, N., McDonnell, L., Pascal, A., Pauly, E., & Zellman, G. (1976). *Analysis of the school preferred reading program in selected Los Angeles minority schools*. Santa Monica, CA: Rand.

Ascher, C., & Flaxman, E. (1987). Parent participation and the achievement of disadvantaged students. In D. S. Strickland & E. J. Cooper (Eds.), *Educating Black children: America's challenge* (pp. 70–76). Washington, DC: Howard University Press.

Azumi, J. E. (1989, April). *Effective schools characteristics, school improvement, and school outcomes*. Paper presented at the annual meeting of the American Educational Research Association, Washington, DC.

Bamburg, J., & Andrews, R. L. (1987, April). *Goal consensus in schools and student academic gains*. Paper presented at the annual meeting of the American Educational Research Association, Washington, DC.

Barr, R., & Dreeben, R. (1983). *How schools work*. Chicago: University of Chicago Press.

Becker, M. S., & Barry, J. N. (1990). Schools effectiveness at the secondary level: The Glendale Union model. In B. O. Taylor (Ed.), *Case studies in effective schools research* (pp. 39–49). Dubuque, IA: Kendall/Hunt.

Block, A. B. (1983). *Effective schools: A summary of research*. Arlington, VA: Educational Research Service.

Brickell, H. N. (1980). How to change what matters. *Educational Leadership, 38*(3), 202–207.

Brieschke, P. A. (1987). A study of the implementation of regulatory policy in the urban elementary school. In G. W. Noblit & W. T. Pink (Eds.), *Schooling in social context: Qualitative studies* (pp. 119–144). Norwood, NJ: Ablex.

Brookover, W. B. (1985). Can we make schools effective for minority students? *The Journal of Negro Education, 54*(3), 257–268.

Brookover, W. B., Beamer, L., Efthin, H., Hathaway, D., Lezotte, L., Miller, S., Passalacqua, J., & Tornatzky, L. (1979). *School social systems and student achievement*. New York: Praeger.

Brookover, W. B., & Lezotte, L. W. (1979). *Changes in school characteristics coincident with changes in school achievement*. East Lansing: Michigan State University Institute for Research on Teaching.

Brousseau, B. A. (1988). *A test of five correlates from effective schools research using hierarchical linear modeling*. Unpublished doctoral dissertation, Michigan State University, East Lansing.

Bullard, P., & Taylor, B. O. (1993). *Making school reform happen*. Boston: Allyn and Bacon.

Burns, R. B. (1987). Steering groups, leveling effects, and instructional pace. *American Journal of Education, 96*(1), 24–56.

Buttram, J. L., & Carlson, R. V. (1983). Effective schools research: Will it play in the country? *Research in Rural Education, 2*(2), 73–78.

Canady, R. L. (1988). A cure for fragmented block schedules in elementary schools. *Educational Leadership, 46*(2), 65–67.

Canady, R. L. (1989). Design scheduling structures to increase student learning. *Focus on Change, 1*(2), 1–2, 7–8.

Canady, R. L., & Hotchkiss, P. R. (1985). Scheduling practices and policies associated with increased achievement for low achieving students. *The Journal of Negro Education, 54*(3), 344–355.

Canady, R. L., & Reina, J. M. (1993). Parallel block scheduling: An alternative structure. *Educational Leadership, 72*(3), 26–29.

Carter, G. R., Madison, A. B., Hall, E. D., & Lockamy, T. B. (1990). A case for equity and quality: How one team is making it happen. In B. O. Taylor (Ed.), *Case studies in effective schools research* (pp. 39–50). Dubuque, IA: Kendall/Hunt.

Chrispeels, J. H. (1992a). *Purposeful restructuring*. Bristol, PA: Falmer.

Chrispeels, J. H. (1992b). *Using an effective schools framework to build home-school partnerships for school success*. Madison, WI: National Center for Effective Schools Research and Development.

Clancy, P. L. (1982). *19 improving schools and why*. Ypsilanti: Eastern Michigan University Press.

Clark, T. A., & McCarthy, D. P. (1983). School improvement in New York: The evolution of a project. *Educational Research, 12*(4), 17–24.

Comer, J. P. (1980). *School power*. New York: Free Press.

Comer, J. P. (1987). New Haven's school-community connection. *Educational Leadership, 44*(6), 13–16.

Comer, J. P. (1988). Educating poor minority children. *Scientific American, 259*(5), 42–48.

Conklin, N. F., & Olson, T. A. (1988). *Toward more effective education for poor, minority students in rural areas: What the research suggests*. Portland, OR: Northwest Regional Educational Laboratory.

Cooper, E. J., & Levine, D. U. (1993). A comprehension and cognitive development approach to school reform. *The Journal of Negro Education, 62*(1), 91–99.

Cooper, E. J., & Sherk, J. (1989). Addressing urban school reform: Politics, issues, and alliances. *The Journal of Negro Education, 58*(3), 315–331.

Corbett, H. D., Dawson, J. A., & Firestone, W. A. (1984). *School content and school change*. New York: Teachers College Press.

Deal, T. E., & Peterson, K. D. (1991). *The principal's role in shaping school culture*. Washington, DC: U.S. Department of Education.

Dolan, L. J., & Haxby, B. (1992). *The role of family support and integrated human services in achieving success for all in the elementary school* (Report No. 31). Baltimore, MD: The Johns Hopkins University Center for Research on Effective Schooling for Disadvantaged Students.

Doll, R. C. (1969). *Variations among inner city elementary schools*. Kansas City: University of Missouri School of Education.

Doyle, W. A. (1983). Academic work. *Review of Educational Research,* *63,* 169–199.

Dreeben, R., & Barr, R. (1988a). Classroom composition and the design of instruction. *Sociology of Education, 61,* 129–142.

Dreeben, R., & Barr, R. (1988b). The formation and instruction of ability groups. *American Journal of Education, 97*(1), 34–64.

Duckett, W. R. (Ed.). (1980). *Why do some urban schools succeed?* Bloomington, IN: Phi Delta Kappa.

Edmonds, R. E. (1982). Programs of school improvement: An overview. *Educational Leadership, 40*(3), 4–12.

Eubanks, E. E., & Levine, D. U. (1983). A first look at effective schools projects in New York City and Milwaukee. *Phi Delta Kappan, 64*(10), 697–702.

Everson, S. T., Scollary, S. J., Fabert, B., and Garcia, M. (1986). An effective schools program and its results: Initial district, school, teacher, and student outcomes in a participating district. *Journal of Research and Development in Education, 19*(3), 35–49.

Ferguson, B. (1984). Overcoming the failure of an inner-city school. *Phi Delta Kappan, 65*(9), 629–630.

Firestone, W. A., & Corbett, H. D. (1988). Planned organizational change. In N. J. Bogan (Ed.), *Handbook of research on educational administration* (pp. 321–338). New York: Longman.

Fleming, D. S., & Buckles, C. (1987). *Implementing school improvement plans.* Andover, MA: Regional Laboratory for Educational Improvement of the Northeast and Islands.

Fliegel, S. (1971). Practices that improved academic performance at an inner-city school. *Phi Delta Kappan, 52*(6), 341–342.

Fraatz, J. B. (1988, April). *Managed equality.* Paper presented at the annual meeting of the American Educational Research Association, New Orleans.

Fullan, M. (1982). *The meaning of educational change.* New York: Teachers College Press.

Fullan, M. (1991) *The new meaning of educational change* (2nd ed.). New York: Teachers College Press.

Garibaldi, A. M. (1987). Effective high schools. In G. W. Noblit and W. T. Pink (Eds.), *Schooling in context: Qualitative studies* (pp. 250–261). Norwood, NJ: Ablex.

Gauthier, W. J., Jr., Pecheone, R. L., & Shoemaker, J. (1985). Schools can become more effective. *The Journal of Negro Education, 54*(3), 388–408.

Gilbert, S. E., II, & Gay, G. (1985). Improving the success in school of poor Black children. *Phi Delta Kappan, 67*(2), 122–138.

Glenn, B. (1981). *What works? An examination of effective schools for poor black children.* Cambridge, MA: Harvard University Center for Law and Education.

Glickman, C. D., & Pajak, E. F. (1986). *A study of school systems in Georgia which have improved criterion referenced test scores in reading and mathematics from 1982 to 1985.* Athens, GA: University of Georgia, Department of Curriculum and Supervision. (ERIC Document Reproduction Service No. ED 282 317)

Gregory, K., & Mueller, S. G. (1980). Leif Ericson Elementary School Chicago, IL. In W. R. Duckett (Ed.), *Why do some urban schools succeed?* (pp. 60–74). Bloomington, IN: Phi Delta Kappa.

Groom, B. (1989). Striving towards excellence in the performance of students: An effective schools project. *Effective School Report, 7*(2), 8, 7.

Hallinger, P., & Murphy, J. (1985). Instructional leadership and school socioeconomic status: A preliminary investigation. *Administrator's Notebook, 31*(5), 1–4.

Hallinger, P., & Murphy, J. (1986). The social context of effective schools. *American Journal of Education, 94*(3), 328–354.

Harris, T. L., & Cooper, E. J. (1985). *Reading, thinking, and concept development.* New York: College Entrance Examination Board.

Henderson, A. T. (1987). *The evidence continues to grow.* Columbia, MD: National Committee for Citizens in Education.

Henderson, A., & Lezotte, L. W. (1988). SBI and effective schools: A perfect match. *NETWORK for Public Schools, 13*(5), 1, 3–5.

Holcomb, E. L. (1991). *School-based instructional leadership.* Madison, WI: National Center for Effective Schools Research and Development.

Huberman, A., & Miles, B. (1982). *Innovation up close: A field study in 12 school settings.* Andover, MA: The Network.

Ivens, S. H. (1988). High stakes tests and the assessment of comprehension. *Teaching, Thinking, and Problem Solving, 10*(5), 7–11.

Jackson, S. C. (1982). *Instructional leadership behaviors that characterize schools that are effective for low socioeconomic urban Black students.* Unpublished doctoral dissertation, Catholic University of America, Washington, DC.

Kozberg, G., & Winegar, J. (1981). The South Boston story: Implications for secondary schools. *Phi Delta Kappan, 62*(8), 565–567.

Kurth, R. J., & Stromberg, L. J. (1984, April). *Improving the teaching of reading in elementary schools.* Paper presented at the annual meeting of the American Educational Research Association, New Orleans.

Leinhardt, G., & Pallay, A. (1982). Restrictive educational settings: Exile or haven? *Review of Educational Research, 52*(4), 557–578.

Levin, H. M. (1987, June). *New schools for the disadvantaged.* Paper prepared for the mid-continent Regional Educational Laboratory, Denver.

Levine, D. U. (1975). Educating alienated inner-city youth: Lessons from the street academies. *The Journal of Negro Education, 44*(2), 138–148.

Levine, D. U. (Ed.). (1985a). *Improving student achievement through mastery learning programs.* San Francisco: Jossey-Bass.

Levine, D. U. (1985b). A mini-description of initially-unsuccessful attempts to introduce outcomes-based instruction. *Outcomes, 4*(2), 15–19.

Levine, D. U. (1992). Implementation of an urban school-within-a-school approach. In C. Hersholt, H. C. Waxman, J. W. de Felix, J. E. Anderson, & H. P. Baptiste, Jr. (Eds.), *Students at risk in at-risk schools* (pp. 233–249). Newbury Park, CA: Sage/Corwin.

Levine, D. U., & Cooper, E. J. (1991). The change process and its implications in teaching thinking. In L. Idol & B. F. Jones (Eds.), *Educational values and cognitive instruction: Implications for reform.* (pp. 387–410). Hillside, NJ: Lawrence Erlbaum Associates.

Levine, D. U., & Eubanks, E. (1983, April). *Instructional and organizational arrangements at an unusually effective inner-city elementary school in Chicago.* Paper presented at the annual meeting of the American Educational Research Association, Montreal.

Levine, D. U., & Eubanks, E. (1989). Organizational arrangements at effective secondary schools. In H. J. Walberg & J. J. Lane (Eds.), *Organizing for learning* (pp. 41–49). Reston, VA: National Association of Secondary School Principals.

Levine, D. U., Hollingsworth, S., & Aquila, F. (1987). Achievement gains in self-contained Chapter 1 classes in Kansas City. *Educational Leadership, 44*(6), 22–23.

Levine, D. U., & Jones, B. F. (1988). Mastery learning. In R. A. Gorton, G. T. Schneider, & J. C. Fisher (Eds.), *Encyclopedia of school administration and supervision* (pp. 166–167). Phoenix, AZ: Oryx.

Levine, D. U., & Leibert, R. E. (1987). Improving school improvement plans. *Elementary School Journal, 87*(4), 397–412.

Levine, D. U., Levine, R. F., & Eubanks, E. E. (1984). Characteristics of effective inner-city intermediate schools. *Phi Delta Kappan, 65*(10), 707–711.

Levine, D. U., Levine, R. F., & Eubanks, E. E. (1985). Successful implementation of instruction at inner-city schools. *The Journal of Negro Education, 54*(3), 313–332.

Levine, D. U., & Lezotte, L. W. (1990). *Unusually effective schools.* Madison, WI: National Center for Effective Schools Research and Development.

Levine, D. U., & Sherk, J. K. (1989). Implementation of reforms to improve comprehension skills at an unusually effective inner-city intermediate school. *Peabody Journal of Education, 66*(4), 87–106.

Levine, D. U., & Sherk, J. K. (1990). *Effective implementation of a comprehension development approach in secondary schools.* Unpublished manuscript, University of Missouri, Kansas City.

Levine, D. U., & Stark, J. C. (1981). *Instructional and organizational arrangements and processes for improving academic achievement at inner-city elementary schools.* Kansas City: University of Missouri, Kansas City.

Levine, D. U., & Stark, J. C. (1982). Instructional and organizational arrangements that improve achievement in inner-city schools. *Educational Leadership, 40*(3), 41–46.

Lezotte, L. W. (1982). A response to D'Amico: Not a recipe but a framework. *Educational Leadership, 40*(3), 63.

Lezotte, L. W. (1991). *Correlates of effective schools.* Okemos, MI: Effective School Publications.

Lezotte, L. W. (1993). Effective schools: A framework for assuring increased achievement for all students. In J. A. Banks & C. A. M. Banks (Eds.), *Multicultural education: Issues and perspectives* (2nd ed., pp. 303–316). Boston: Allyn and Bacon.

Lezotte, L. W., & Bancroft, B. A. (1985). Growing use of the effective schools model for school improvement. *Educational Leadership, 42*(6), 23–27.

Lonoff, R. (1971). Supervisory practices that promote academic achievement in a New York City school. *Phi Delta Kappan, 52*(6), 338–340.

Love, I. (1988). Getting the most out of the school day. *Educational Leadership, 45*(7), 81–82.

MacGinitie, W. H., & MacGinitie, R. K. (1986). Teaching students not to read. In S. de Castell, R. A. Luke, & K. Egan (Eds.), *Literacy, society, and schooling* (pp. 256–269). Cambridge, England: Cambridge University Press.

Mackenzie, D. H. (1983). Research for school improvement: An appraisal of some recent trends. *Educational Researcher, 12*(3), 5–16.

Madden, N. A., Slavin, R. E., Karweit, N. L., & Livermon, B. J. (1989). Restructuring the urban elementary school. *Educational Leadership, 46*(5), 14–18.

Mamary, A. & Rowe, L. A. (1985). Flexible and heterogeneous instructional arrangements to facilitate mastery learning. In D. U. Levine (Ed.), *Improving student achievement through mastery learning programs* (pp. 203–222). San Francisco: Jossey-Bass.

Mann, D. (1989). *Conditional deregulation.* Unpublished paper, Teachers College, Columbia University, New York.

McCormack-Larkin, M., & Kritek, W. J. (1982). Milwaukee's project RISE. *Educational Leadership, 40*(3), 16–21.

Menahem, M., & Weisman, L. (1985). Improving reading ability through a mastery learning program: A case study. In D. U. Levine (Ed.), *Improving student achievement through mastery learning programs* (pp. 223–240). San Francisco: Jossey-Bass.

Mortimore, P., Sammons, P., Stoll, L., Lewis, D., & Ecob, R. (1988). *School matters.* Berkeley: University of California Press.

Murphy, J. (1989). Principal instructional leadership. In P. W. Thurston & L. S. Lotto (Eds.), *Advances in educational leadership* (pp. 163–200). Greenwich, CT: JAI Press.

Murphy, J., & Hallinger, P. (1985). Effective high schools—What are the common characteristics? *NASSP Bulletin, 69*(477), 18–22.

Murphy, J., & Hallinger, P. (1986). The superintendent as instructional leader: Findings from effective school districts. *Journal of Educational Administration, 22*(2), 213–236.

Nagel, T. (1986, April). *A longitudinal study of systematic efforts to raise standardized achievement test scores using factors from school effectiveness research.* Paper presented at the annual meeting of the American Educational Research Association, San Francisco.

Niedermeyer, F., & Yelon, S. (1981). Los Angeles aligns instruction with basic skills. *Educational Leadership, 38,* 618–620.

Oakes, J. (1992). Can tracking research inform practice? *Educational Researcher, 21*(4), 12–21.

Office of Research & Evaluation. (1993). *Sustained effects of Chapter 1 student performance.* Bowie, MD: Prince George's County Public Schools Chapter 1 Office.

O'Neill, K., & Shoemaker, J. (Eds.) (1989). *A conversation between James Comer and Ronald Edmonds.* Madison, WI: National Center for Effective Schools Research and Development.

Orlich, D. C. (1989). Educational reforms: Mistakes, misconceptions, miscues. *Phi Delta Kappan, 70*(7), 512–517.

Pajak, E. F., & Glickman, C. D. (1989). Dimensions of school district improvement. *Educational Leadership, 46*(8), 61–64.

Parish, R. (1981). *Discontinuation of innovative programs in Missouri schools.* Unpublished doctoral dissertation, University of Oregon, Eugene.

Payne, C. (1984). *Getting what we ask for: The ambiguity of success and failure in urban education.* Westport, CT: Greenwood.

Pearson, P. D. (1985). *The comprehension revolution.* (Report No. 57). Urbana: University of Illinois at Urbana-Champaign, Center for the Study of Reading.

Pecheone, R., & Shoemaker, J. (1984). *An evaluation of the school effectiveness program in Connecticut.* Hartford: Connecticut State Department of Education.

Peters, T. J. (1988). *Thriving on chaos.* New York: Knopf.

Pogrow, S. (1983). *Education in the computer age.* Beverly Hills, CA: Sage.

Pogrow, S. (1990). A Socratic approach to using computers with at-risk students. *Educational Leadership, 47*(5), 61–66.

Pogrow, S. (1992). What to do about Chapter 1: An alternative view from the streets. *Phi Delta Kappan, 73*(8), 624–630.

Pollack, S., Watson, D., & Chrispeels, J. (1987, April). *A description of factors and implementation strategies used by schools in becoming effective for all students.* Paper presented at the annual meeting of the American Educational Research Association, Washington, DC.

Popkewitz, T. S., Tabachnik, R. R., & Wehlage, G. (1982). *The myth of educational reform.* Madison: University of Wisconsin Press.

Porter, A. (1989). A curriculum out of balance. *Educational Researcher, 18*(5), 9–15.

Presseisen, B. Z., Smey-Richman, B., & Beyer, F. S. (1992). *Cognitive development through radical change: Restructuring classroom environments for students at risk.* Unpublished manuscript, Research for Better Schools, Philadelphia.

Purkey, S. C., & Smith, M. W. (1983). Effective schools—A review. *Elementary School Journal, 83,* 427–452.

Reynolds, D. (1992). School effectiveness and school improvement. In D. Reynolds and P. Cuttance (Eds.), *School effectiveness* (pp. 1–24). London: Cassell.

Reynolds, D., & Cuttance, P. (Eds.) (1992). *School effectiveness.* London: Cassell.

Rosenholtz, S. J. (1985). Effective schools: Interpreting the evidence. *American Journal of Education, 93*(3), 352–388.

Rossmiller, R. A., Holcomb, E. L., & McIsaac, D. N. (1993). *The effective schools process.* Madison, WI: National Center for Effective Schools Research and Development.

Shoemaker, J. (1982). Effective schools: Putting the research to the ultimate test. *Pre-Post-Press, 7*(2), 1.

Shoemaker, J. (1986, Winter). Developing effectiveness in the district, school and classroom. *Equity and Choice, 2,* 1–8.

Shujaa, M. J., & Richards, C. E. (1989). Designing state accountability systems to improve school-based organizational learning. *Administrator's Notebook, 33*(2), 1–4.

Sizemore, B. A. (1985). Pitfalls and promises of effective schools research. *The Journal of Negro Education, 54*(3), 269–288.

Sizemore, B. A. (1987). The effective African American elementary school. In G. W. Noblit & W. T. Pink (Eds.), *Schooling in social context: Qualitative studies* (pp. 175–202). Norwood, NJ: Ablex.

Sizemore, B. A., Brossard, C. A., & Harrigan, B. (1983). *An abashing anomaly: The high achieving predominantly black elementary school* (Abstract NIE-G-80-0006). Pittsburgh: University of Pittsburgh.

Slavin, R. E., Karweit, N., & Wasik, B. A. (1992). Preventing early school failure: What works? *Educational Leadership, 50*(4), 10–18.

Slavin, R. E., & Madden, N. A. (1989). What works for students at risk: A research synthesis. *Educational Leadership, 46*(5), 4–13.

Smith, W. J. (1985). Incorporating testing and retesting into the teaching plan. In D. U. Levine (Ed.), *Improving student achievement through mastery learning programs* (pp. 241–254). San Francisco: Jossey-Bass.

Southern Coalition for Educational Equity. (1986). *Annual Report 1986.* Jackson, MS: Author.

Stedman, L. C. (1987). It's time we changed the effective schools formula. *Phi Delta Kappan, 69*(3), 215–224.

Stringfield, S., & Teddlie, C. (1987, April). *A time to summarize: Six years and three phases of the Louisiana school effectiveness study.* Paper presented at the annual meeting of the American Educational Research Association, Washington, DC.

Stringfield, S., & Teddlie, C. (1988). A time to summarize: The Louisiana school effectiveness study. *Educational Leadership, 46*(2), 43–49.

Stringfield, S., Teddlie, C., & Suarez, S. (1986). Classroom interaction in effective and ineffective schools: Preliminary results from phase III of the Louisiana school effectiveness study. *Journal of Classroom Interaction, 20*(2), 31–37.

Sudlow, R. E. (1990). Implementing effective research in a K–12 suburban district: The Spencerport model. In B. O. Taylor (Ed.), *Case studies in effective schools research* (pp. 155–182). Dubuque, IA: Kendall/Hunt.

Taylor, B. O. (1984). *Implementing what works: Elementary principals and school improvement programs.* Unpublished doctoral dissertation, Northwestern University, Evanston, IL.

Taylor, B. O. (Ed.) (1990). *Case studies in effective schools research.* Dubuque, IA: Kendall/Hunt.

Taylor, B. O., & Levine, D. U. (1991). Effective schools projects and school-based management. *Phi Delta Kappan, 72*(5), 394–397.

Teddlie, C., Kirby, P. C., & Stringfield, S. (1989). Effective versus ineffective schools: Observable differences in the classroom. *American Journal of Education, 97*(3), 221–236.

Teddlie, C., & Stringfield, S. (1985). A differential analysis of effectiveness in middle and low socioeconomic status schools. *Journal of Classroom Interaction, 20*(2), 38–44.

Teddlie, C., & Stringfield, S. (1993). *Schools make a difference: Lessons learned from a 10-year study of school efforts.* New York: Teachers College Press.

Teddlie, C., & Virgillo, I. R. (1988, April). *School context differences across grades: A study of teacher behaviors.* Paper presented at the annual meeting of the American Educational Research Association, New Orleans.

Teddlie, C., Wimpelberg, R., & Kirby, P. (1987, April). *Contextual differences in effective schools in Louisiana.* Paper presented at the annual meeting of the American Educational Research Association, Washington, DC.

Venezky, R. L., & Winfield, L. F. (1979). *Schools that succeed beyond expectations in teaching reading.* Newark: University of Delaware. (ERIC Document Reproduction Service No. Ed 177 484)

Weber, G. (1971). *Inner-city children can be taught to read: Four successful schools.* Washington, DC: Council for Basic Education.

Wehlage, G. G. (1983). *Effective programs for the marginal high school student.* Bloomington, IN: Phi Delta Kappa.

Wehlage, G. G., Rutter, R. A., & Turnbaugh, A. (1987). A program model for at-risk high school students. *Educational Leadership, 44*(6), 70–73.

Weiss, A. S. (1984). *The effectiveness of Project RISE in raising achievement levels of pupils in Milwaukee public schools inner-city schools.* Unpublished doctoral dissertation, Marquette University, Milwaukee. WI.

Wick, J. W., & Turnbaugh, R. C. (1983). *A successful program to improve student performance.* Evanston, IL: Northwestern University School of Education Division of Field Studies.

Wimpelberg, R., Teddlie, C., & Stringfield, S. (1989). Sensitivity to context: The past and future of effective schools research. *Educational Administration Quarterly, 25*(1), 82–107.

·30·

SOCIAL CLASS AND SCHOOLING

Michael S. Knapp
UNIVERSITY OF WASHINGTON, SEATTLE

Sara Woolverton
UNIVERSITY OF WASHINGTON, SEATTLE

"Teachers do it with class."
—*popular bumper sticker*

The familiar slogan above, a variant on a decades-old risqué theme, could be edited slightly to express, or at least hint at, the theme of this chapter: "Teachers do it with social class." But the amended phrasing would never make it in contemporary American society, either as humor or as a statement about the role of educators in society. We prefer not to see social class permeating institutions so long associated with social mobility. If anything, Americans would rather cling to the notion of schools as the great social equalizer, offering a set of experiences that permit individuals to transcend the boundaries of social class. But our ideologies are not our realities, and no amount of wishing will eliminate the pervasiveness of social-class dynamics in the lives of teachers and learners. Educators and the educated alike need clarity and insight regarding the presence, interplay, and power of social class in their encounters with one another.

The purpose of this chapter is to illuminate these social-class dynamics within educational institutions. We address this topic with the system of schooling from preschool through high school primarily in mind, but with attention to postsecondary institutions as well. To shed light on the roles played by social class in these institutions, we draw together diverse threads of theory and scholarship over the last half century. In essence, we are answering the question: "What is known—and thought—about the relationship of social class and schooling by scholars who have studied that relationship?" Our review is thus both a conceptual and an empirical effort to synthesize concepts, frameworks, and evidence that shed light on the question at hand. As will quickly become evident, our review does not assume a unified "body of knowledge" about the topic, but rather a set of claims and conceptions that are often at odds with one another. Somewhere in the diversity of views lies the great, gray truth, as best we know it to date, and the ground for future discoveries.

Although we have attempted to approach the topic in a comprehensive fashion, we make no claim to exhaustiveness. Rather than think of the review task as a meta-analyst might, we have conceived of our role as builders of useful conceptual frameworks. To accomplish that goal, we have drawn on various bodies of work. Most are, in some respect if not in name, sociological—the social science field most directly and continuously concerned with social class—though we have also borrowed heavily from work in anthropology and psychology or social psychology. More specifically, we have concentrated on classical and modern branches of the sociology of education drawing on writing in the functionalist tradition, neo-Marxist and non-Marxist conflict theory, interpretivist tradition, and various critical perspectives (e.g., Apple, 1978; LeCompte & Dworkin, 1988). We have focused on seminal work, both conceptual and empirical, and recent syntheses of work in the field. In addition, we have relied on educational research aimed at understanding inequality and educational opportunity, disadvantagement, the nature of curriculum, the phenomenon of learner differences, the profession of teaching, and the nature of teachers' work. (Our "watershed" includes other tributaries, among them a review of key journals such as *Sociology of Education* and a search of the ERIC database for work that bears descriptors related to both social class and schooling.)

We embark on this review in full recognition of the fact that social class is hard—perhaps impossible in some respects—to disentangle from other categorical social descriptors such as race, ethnicity, and gender; from culture (viewed as the set of shared meanings held by social groups); and from ideology (the system of values and beliefs to which societies subscribe and that serve as a justification for actions). The interactions between race and class, for example, are an ongoing topic of research (see Banks, 1993) and the subject of various discussions elsewhere in this *Handbook*. A growing number of researchers, primarily in the critical theory tradition, are beginning to attend to gender as a social-class issue (e.g., Weiler,

548

1988). The interactions between culture and class are the topic of various lines of research, most recently in a critical tradition (e.g., Bourdieu & Passeron, 1977), less recently in work on the "culture of poverty" (e.g., Lewis, 1966). The relationship between ideology and class permeates (and often clouds) the work of scholars, as it does the vision of many individuals in society. Nonetheless, we will proceed on the assumption that conceptual distinctions are at least possible and probably helpful, if never entirely clear. Empirical distinctions are less easily made, but are instructive, and so we bring them into discussion wherever relevant.

Given that it is entwined with other social conditions, why does social class as a force in educational institutions deserve the scrutiny we will give it? We believe the scrutiny is essential for at least the following reasons. First, decades of sociological work and the intuitions of thoughtful people suggest that social class is fundamental to understanding the workings and consequences of educational institutions. Second, social class is hidden, in schooling and elsewhere. American mythologies obscure the fact of social class, hide its potential or actual influence on other aspects of educational or social life, and limit our capacity to see and understand social conflicts related to class. Third, social class is central to social inequality. Whether or not one accepts inequalities as inevitable or necessary (and most Americans would not), they are deeply rooted in the social order. In order to imagine greater equality, and the roles that education might play in bringing that about, one must come to terms with the meanings and dynamics of social class. The matter takes on some urgency at the present time, when social inequalities in America are apparently increasing and, along with them, the shape of the social-class structure is changing.

Finally, education is implicated in both the conception and the measurement of social class. Put another way, it is hard to talk about one without the other, whether one is simply referring to indexes of social-class position (which often use educational level as one component), describing the process by which individuals attain a position within the social order (which almost always involves their path through a succession of educational institutions), or identifying the educational institutions' overt or covert roles in guiding the individuals' development (which typically imply "opportunities" for "advancement" and "preparation" for a place in the occupational structure).

We have organized our review in five parts that reflect a thematic rather than chronological review of work. First, to clarify key terms and paradigms within which ideas are located, we discuss the concept of social class and alternative perspectives adopted by scholars in considering the relationships between society and schools. We then examine the enduring correlation between measures of social class and most measures of educational outcomes.

The succeeding three sections attempt to "unpack" the correlation by considering, in turn, how social class is related to: (a) the community context of schools, the social organization of the student population, and the teaching force; (b) the learner; and (c) the nature of curriculum and instruction. We conclude the chapter with a review of the principal explanations for the pattern of differentiated schooling that emerges in these discussions, followed by an examination of promising directions for new research.

CONCEPTIONS OF SOCIAL CLASS AND THE PURPOSES OF SCHOOLING

To understand the relationship of social class and schooling, one must first recognize that reasonable scholars have differing views of social class, the purposes of schooling, and the relationship between the two. We review below the range of conceptions for each, and sketch a working definition that enables us to think productively about the topic at hand.

Thinking About Social Class

All societies are *stratified* in some degree; members of these societies view themselves and each other as occupying differing social positions that are hierarchically ordered from those that have more of some socially desired goods to those with less. The geological metaphor of *strata,* or layers, of people suggests a more concrete, fixed, and visible phenomenon than is typically the case (though there are instances of fixed and visible stratification), but nonetheless the fact of stratification is evident to all members of the society. They may disagree with one another about where (or whether) to draw boundaries between the strata, where to place themselves or others, and what meaning to attach to their social positioning, but all accept the existence of some social ranking.

To begin with, the different social classes in a stratification system are distinguished in economic terms, with those individuals having greatest wealth or access to resources typically occupying the "highest" classes. There are other, less tangible grounds for distinguishing class, including political power, status, prestige, and what might be referred to as "cultural power." These social "goods" can be thought of as both determinants and consequences of one's social-class position. The distribution of these social goods and hence social position is rarely fixed, except in the most rigid "caste" systems, as most social stratification systems permit mobility across class boundaries. Thus, except for members of a caste, one's social position at birth need not determine one's social position later in life.

Intellectual traditions in the social sciences approach the conceptual definition of *social class* differently. While all recognize the economic roots of class, they give it different meaning and, in varying degrees, attach to the concept other social, political, and cultural baggage. Following the ideas of Weber (1946), many social theorists and scholars see social class as deriving from relative economic power, resulting in a *positional* ranking of occupations in terms of their presumed social value and corresponding rewards. Marxist and neo-Marxist scholars assert an alternative, "objective" basis for class rooted in the *relationship* of people to the means of production (Dahrendorf, 1970), though more recent formulations in this tradition (e.g., McLaren, 1989) speak of class more broadly, including within the concept economic, social, and political relationships affecting how people in a social order live their lives. Contemporary elaborations of this theme address "production" as a multilevel concept that includes the relationship of the individual to systems of ownership, the structure of authority, and the process of one's own work activity (e.g., Anyon, 1981). Non-Marxist conflict theorists (e.g., Collins, 1979) are more apt to emphasize the cultural basis of social class, whereby members of society distinguish one another on the basis of tastes, preferences, and manners as much as anything else. Scholars approaching the matter from one or another critical perspective (e.g., Apple, 1978) are also likely to assert that social class has a cultural as well as economic basis and is intimately connected to the individual's construction of a social identity.

Reflecting the differences in intellectual tradition, the precise number, boundaries, and character of social classes remain in dispute. Sociologists operating from a positional view of social class tend to identify three to six classes (e.g., Bensman & Vidich, 1971), while Marxists distinguish three to four (e.g., Wright & Perrone, 1977). The great majority of empirical work is done with a positional breakdown of classes—working class, lower-middle class, middle class, and so on, or, more simply, high, middle, and low positions on some scale such as socioeconomic status (SES).

These distinctions among classes, and the analytic work based on them, may objectify social class more than is warranted. We prefer to think of social classes and one's own position within them as socially constructed, and reconstructed, to reflect changing conditions within society and changing views of the way society works. In this sense social class is a fiction, albeit a useful one. Such fictions change slowly when held by many people, and though one may exert influence over one's own "class consciousness," one has little control over others' views.

In ways that will become apparent as the discussion unfolds, education is inextricably part of the layering of society into distinct classes. At the least, social class is an attribute of all individuals engaged in the enterprise of schooling, of educators as well as learners. In addition, the communities served by schools can be characterized in terms of their aggregate social-class position (and also in terms of variability within them). But these characterizations are static and do not reveal the heart of the processes by which the social positions of participants in education influence schooling and, in turn, are influenced by it. To describe these processes we must first acknowledge that different assumptions may be made about society and the role(s) that formal schooling may play within it.

Thinking About the Purposes of Schooling

To consider the relationships between social class and schooling, one must make assumptions about the purposes of schooling and, along with them, the nature of society and the role of schools in preparing individuals for lives in the larger social context. These assumptions set the stage for interpretation of class-related phenomena in the context of schools.

In a pluralistic, democratic society such as that of the United States, it is a commonplace to recognize that there are multiple and competing purposes for education. There are as well competing assumptions made by analysts who wish to make sense of the behavior and results of schooling. We distinguish three sets of assumptions, or perspectives, that have been especially prominent in the scholarship of the last half century related to schooling in a social context: functionalist, conflict, and interpretive/critical perspectives.

Functionalist Perspectives. Functionalist thinking visualizes societies as analogous to organisms, containing institutions that carry out vital functions. The vital function of schools is the transmission of mainstream culture and the preparation of citizens for technical demands of modern society (Bennett & LeCompte, 1990).

Within functionalism, however, transmission of culture is not conceived of in narrow terms solely as the teaching of mainstream cultural skills, values, and behavioral norms. Functionalists also see schooling as an arena for sorting and selecting individuals for various future roles. Modern-day society is conceived of as an *expert society,* relying on highly trained individuals for economic and social growth, as well as a *meritocracy* in which ability and effort count for more than privilege and inherited social position (Hurn, 1993). Schools are viewed as instruments of this meritocratic expert society, in that they allow "the best and the brightest" to rise to the top. Theoretically, those who demonstrate the most ability and expend the most effort receive expert training in order to take high-status positions in the social and economic structure—regardless of race, gender, or social-class origins. Tracking and other forms of institutionalized differential treatment are justified by this notion of specific educational needs for individuals of different (greater or lesser) abilities to perform different types of occupations. Schools are thus perceived to be the link between an individual's cognitive abilities and his or her later occupation or social class.

In simplistic form, functionalism's view of social class is tied to the notion of meritocracy. If social and occupational status are dependent primarily on merit, then social class must, in some sense, be a reflection of effort and ability. Upper classes are comprised of the exceptionally capable and motivated, lower classes of the least capable and industrious. Social-class boundaries are seen as permeable; highly capable and motivated lower-class individuals may move upward through the class structure by diligence and intelligence, while individuals of upper-class origins may experience downward socioeconomic mobility in the absence of ability and effort. Schooling is thus viewed as the sorter and selector of human talent, and in that role is conceived of as mainstream culture's instrument of upward social and economic mobility for the lower classes.

Conflict Perspectives. Arising initially from Marxist thought, conflict perspectives offer an alternative view of society and education that focuses on the unequal property and power distribution in modern society (Bennett & LeCompte, 1990). Like functionalism, conflict perspectives presume a transmission theory of schooling. Unlike functionalism, however, conflict theorists believe that schools transmit unequal power relationships and the value systems of the elite rather than shared popular culture, values, and skills. Building on the work of

Bowles and Gintis (1976) in the Marxist tradition and others in non-Marxist traditions (e.g., Collins, 1979), conflict theorists have argued that, through use of the language and behavioral expectations of the dominant elite, differential treatment systems such as tracking, and the reinforcing of the social and political status quo, schools serve the interests of the elite (Bennett & LeCompte). Rather than transmitting intellectual and academic skills that prepare one for the workplace, schools inculcate the attitudes and values sought by future employers, including loyalty, compliance, promptness, submission to authority, and docility, and the credentials and "status culture" that are the "tickets of admission" to positions in the societal hierarchy (Bennett & LeCompte; Hurn, 1993). Schools are thus viewed by conflict theorists as institutions that reinforce class inequality in modern society.

From this perspective social-class position arises inescapably by virtue of one's current economic, political, and cultural relationship to those who control the means of production in the society and, along with it, the status culture of elite groups. Because elites control production and organize society to foster their own interests, members of other social classes are likely to stay where they are, unless the inevitable "struggle among the classes" effects a new hierarchy (or in the original Marxist ideal view, which has yet to appear, a "classless" society).

Interpretive and Critical Perspectives. Functionalism and conflict theory are both theories of cultural transmission, though they differ in notions of what schools transmit. Interpretive and critical theories, on the other hand, focus on cultural transformation by viewing "actors within social settings as active, rather than passive, participants in the social construction of their own reality" (Bennett & LeCompte, 1990, p. 21).

Growing out of the phenomenological tradition, interpretive theory focuses on the construction of meanings in social interaction. Unlike functionalism and conflict theories, which typically rely on quantitative research and concentrate on macro issues of culture and society, interpretivists use qualitative methods and center on the actual interactions of teachers, students, and peers in the construction of the school experience at the micro level. The concern of interpretivists is the meaning brought to social interactions by all parties, the behavior of individuals based on those meanings, and the resultant relationships formed and new meanings constructed in student interactions in schools.

Critical theory combines elements of the works of neo-Marxist conflict theorists and interpretivists, and was developed to explain both macro- and micro-level phenomena of education. Like interpretive theory, critical perspectives emphasize the social construction of meaning; like conflict perspectives, critical theory attends to questions of power in the larger social structure, particularly around social, economic, and political inequality. Thus one of the primary concerns of critical theory is injustice and oppression in modern society. Gramsci's (1971) work on the imposition of the worldview of the elite, a phenomenon he named "hegemony," and Freire's (1970) emphasis on the ways in which state hegemony structured the lives of Brazilian peasants reflect critical theory's attention to the role of

elite ideology in shaping meanings that support the domination and oppression of the lower social classes. The institution of formal schooling, according to critical theorists, is a societal force that contributes to domination and oppression by mirroring the worldview of the elite, and by instruction that results in differential outcomes that support the elite worldview.

Although this sounds much like conflict theory, critical perspectives go a step further by visualizing individuals and schools in a more "transformative" way (Apple, 1980). Central to critical perspectives is the assumption that individuals and social groups construct their own reality regardless of the oppressive elite-dominated social hierarchy in which they exist, and thereby have the capacity to resist and reconstrue their relationship to it. Learners are not passive recipients of curriculum, whether overt or covert. Meanings created in schools, which typically reflect the elite worldview, grow out of actions, reactions, and interactions among students, teachers, and others involved in the educational process. These meanings are open to change and reinterpretation by any of the parties to the meaning-construction process.

Social class, from this point of view, is more a "subjective" construction than "objective" reality. The "class consciousness" that may develop provides a stimulus to, and basis for, class-based resistance to oppressive conditions.

Analysts approaching the question of social class and schooling bring to their quest fundamentally different assumptions about the phenomenon. Nonetheless, virtually all agree on a few central facts regarding the strong and enduring association between social class, however measured, and the outcomes of education. As in much of the debate among researchers from the various perspectives, we take these facts, described in the next section, as the starting point for our examination.

SOCIAL CLASS AND THE OUTCOMES OF SCHOOLING

There is an enduring correlation between social class and educational outcomes. It is almost universally true that averages of educational attainment, measured by years in school or rates of dropping out, and educational achievement, measured by grades and test scores, vary by social class (e.g., Coleman et al., 1966; Jencks, 1972; Natriello, McDill, & Pallas, 1990). In general, higher class status correlates with high levels of educational attainment and achievement, low social class correlates with low levels of educational attainment and achievement, and the middle classes fall somewhere in between (Coleman et al., 1966; Goldstein, 1967; Mayeske et al., 1972; Persell, 1977, 1993). The possession of educational credentials also follows this pattern, with upper-class individuals on average holding more credentials than members of the middle class, who in turn possess more than lower-class individuals (Coleman et al.; Goldstein; Mayeske et al.; Persell).

These correlations hold over time and across cultures (Persell, 1977; Hurn, 1993). There has been ample research documenting the fact that despite increases in the availability of schooling, the rate of change in the correlation between social class and educational outcomes has been inconsequential (Thurow, 1972; Boudon, 1974; Hurn). Hurn reviews literature on a number of European studies demonstrating the enduring link between educational attainment and measures of social class, primarily fathers' income, occupation, and educational attainment (e.g., Halsey, Heath, & Ridge, 1980, regarding Great Britain; Garnier & Raffalovich, 1984, regarding France; Boudon, for a review of European data). Students in Europe and the United States from higher social-class backgrounds are most likely, for example, to pursue postsecondary education, to do so in four-year institutions, and to go to private colleges and universities. Students from lower social-class backgrounds are not only less likely than their middle- and upper-class peers to graduate from high school, they are less likely to go on to college (Sewell & Shaw, 1967). If they seek postsecondary education, they are more likely to attend two-year or vocational institutions rather than four-year colleges and universities (Karabel, 1972) and are less likely to pursue graduate degrees (Sewell & Hauser, 1976). One recent review of literature pertinent to the link between educational attainment and social class concludes: "The most powerful predictor of how much education individuals obtained was the social class background of their parents, as measured by their income level, occupation, and education" (Bennett & LeCompte, 1990, p. 170).

The correlational research base has some limitations. It only tells us about a certain set of outcomes—those valued enough by the mainstream social scientific community to be well studied. The research also depends heavily on quantifiable measures. Further, like most social scientific research it has focused primarily on White males, and may not be generalizable to interclass differences between females or non-Whites (Ayella & Williamson, 1976; Rosenfeld, 1980). Finally, most correlational data has focused on paternal status as a measure of social class and may not adequately reflect the impact on social class of mothers' education and occupation (Bennett & LeCompte, 1990).

Educational attainment, achievement, and credentialing are the most commonly studied direct outcomes of schooling. Other outcomes of schooling, which have been overlooked by the research community when considering the link between social class and educational outcomes, may be equally important in the long run. Many of these, such as self-esteem, expectancy for success, and aspirations, fall into what might be termed the *affective* domain. Persell (1993), for instance, in reviewing literature pertinent to the link between students' social status and self-esteem, concluded that the length of time in school is negatively correlated with lower-class student self-esteem. Aspirations for educational success and occupational roles also vary by social class, with lower-class students reporting lower aspirations, on average, than those of their peers in the middle and upper classes (Kahl, 1953; Cicourel & Kitsuse, 1963; Sewell & Hauser, 1976; Hurn, 1993). Students' expectations for their own success correlate with both teacher feedback and the students' histories of success or failure in school settings (Weiner, 1985), both of which correlate with social class. Because the affective dimension of schooling appears to be more extensively studied with reference to female students, and in light of Weiler's

(1988) suggestion that gender is a class issue, the research base offered by studies of gender might offer great opportunities for studying the links between social class and affective outcomes.

The centrality of the enduring correlation between social class and the direct outcomes of the educational process is of clear relevance in a discussion of social class and schooling. Also relevant to the discussion—though a detailed examination of these correlations is beyond the scope of this chapter—are the relationships between social class and occupational outcomes, which are always mediated by the outcomes of schooling.

Occupational and economic outcomes of schooling are often considered the most salient of the correlates of social class. Though the relative impact of social class and education on occupational outcomes has not been definitively established (and may never be), it cannot be denied that both education (e.g., Sewell & Shaw, 1967) and social class (e.g., Wright & Perrone, 1977) play some role in occupational attainment and earnings. Education is most clearly linked to occupational outcomes in situations in which credentials are required for job acquisition. Collins (1979) maintains that education constitutes a kind of "cultural capital" that allows the holder to "purchase" certain roles in society; the currency that allows the acquisition of higher-status jobs is the credential. Meyer (1977) asserts that it is not necessarily education that gives individuals advantages in the job market, but the wider societal belief that educated people are better able to perform jobs. Regardless of the relationship between education and the tasks of the job, education is used as a criterion in the allocation of individuals to different occupations.

It is difficult to sort the contributions of social class from those of education in their influence on occupation because social class, as will be argued in this chapter, is itself a contributor to educational outcomes such as achievement, attainment, and credentials. Wright and Perrone (1977), in seeking to determine the relative influence of education and social class, looked at occupational stratification in Marxist terms, and concluded that social class is better than educational attainment as a predictor of future occupational status. Bennett and LeCompte (1990) summarize the findings of this study as follows:

> Class matters more than education, and even overrides the effects of education. Thus, even with high levels of education, working class children will not achieve as much prestige as children from the upper classes. This is because working class children are handicapped by their background; they cannot translate their education into as much occupational prestige and economic success as can upper and middle class children with the same or inferior levels of education. (p. 171)

The research reviewed above establishes the correlation between social class and occupational outcomes, but does little to explain *how* the two are linked. If one envisions schooling as a "black box" into which students of a given social class enter, and from which emerge individuals of varying educational attributes, one must examine this "black box" to understand the subtle role social class may play in shaping educational and occupational outcomes.

SOCIAL CLASS IN THE COMMUNITY CONTEXT, STUDENT POPULATION, AND TEACHING FORCE OF SCHOOLS

We investigate the relationship between social class and the outcomes of schooling from the outside in—that is, we start in this section with the community context of schools, then examine the social organization of the student population, and finally discuss the teaching force. In subsequent sections we will proceed to the nature of the learner and to instruction itself (including both formal and "hidden" curriculum).

Our understanding of community context, social organization, and the teaching force comes from various sources. Along with large-scale studies of community demography, ethnographic and observational studies of schools and school-community relations provide the most useful insights into the ways that the social class of the community conditions what school people do. Research on tracking is especially helpful in revealing the sorting processes at the heart of the school's "macro"-social organization. Studies of the demography of the teaching force and the teacher in workplace contexts help illuminate the social-class nature of the educator.

Drawing on these sources, we describe three sets of linkages between social class and educational outcomes. First, the character of the community served by the school is shaped to a large extent by social class, and this in turn defines the social makeup of the student population, the community's expectations of that population, and the resources available to schools. Second, in part reflecting the social topography of communities, schools serve populations—and within schools, particular programs serve subpopulations—that are surprisingly homogeneous in social-class composition. This homogeneity comes about over time as schools, in effect, "sort" young people by social class. Third, the teaching force brings to the school certain class-based sensibilities rooted in their own social origins and life trajectory, as well as in the class-related positioning of "teaching" within the occupational structure.

Social Class and the Community Context of Schooling

The starting point for understanding the role of social class in schooling is to recognize that schools serve communities, and that communities are more than a defined geographical place. Rather, they reflect "patterned social interaction" and exhibit a "collective identity" (Hunter, 1975, as cited in Louis, 1990). From the perspective of both community members and outsiders, community interaction and identity are suffused with the social class of community members. More often than not, one broad social-class identity predominates; we routinely refer to a particular community as a "working-class town," an "upper-middle-class suburb," and so on.

While this labeling of communities usually masks a more complex social structure, it hints at a basic fact of U.S. social topography: Residential arrangements are profoundly segregated by social class. And there is historical evidence that, in the wake of World War II, social-class segregation has increased (Kantor & Brenzel, 1992) with the relocation of middle- and upper-middle-class groups from diverse central-city areas to the patchwork of suburbs that constitute the nation's metropolitan areas. Segregation by social class is especially noticeable when one considers the immediate "community" served by a given school, defined by its attendance area. Thus a given high school serves a "poor area of town" or an elementary school draws its students primarily from a "wealthy professional neighborhood." Alternatively, where people of different social classes live in close proximity to one another, as in some urban areas, segregation results from parental choice when, for example, large proportions of the affluent send their children to private schools (Persell, 1993).

Besides the obvious effects on the nature of the student population, the social-class makeup of the community influences what it expects of the schools and what it expects of its young people. The community embodies a value system (Louis, 1990) and a "social class culture" (McLaughlin, Talbert, & Bascia, 1990) to which educators must respond. Communities "develop a common consciousness" that constitutes a class-based context in which teachers and administrators do their work, and these contexts can differ considerably one from another depending on the social composition of the community (Anyon, 1980, 1981; Connell, Ashenden, Kessler, & Dawsett, 1982; Metz, 1990). A rich account of these influences emerges from recent ethnographic research on high schools in communities of varying SES levels:

It is clear that class issues get into the schools primarily through community pressures and through the students. The three communities [in this study] had different priorities for their schools' goals and daily practice. All the schools' staffs, especially principals, took community priorities seriously. These priorities were visibly a part of each school's life, particularly in the overall policies of each school, but also to a significant degree in classroom teaching. (Metz, 1990, p. 92)

According to this and other studies (e.g., Hemmings & Metz, 1990; Anyon, 1981; Wilcox, 1982), communities varying by social class want different things for their children. For example, the predominantly working-class communities in the Metz study placed a high priority on acquiring credentials and following rules, whereas the higher-SES communities, in which wealthier business and professional families were the dominant social group, placed emphasis on students' gaining particular kinds of knowledge and skills.

Observational research makes clear, however, that broad class characterizations of communities and what they expect of schools or students are oversimplified and not particularly useful if the subtle variations within social-class groupings are not considered (Metz, 1990). Among communities of the same social class, for example, there is considerable diversity in priorities and expectations, reflecting various factors including generational differences (e.g., how recently community members arrived at their current class position), the basis of high or low status (e.g., education, occupation, or wealth), and a community's cohesiveness or "functional integration" (Coleman, 1990). In addition, within broad social-class groupings (and to an extent cutting across class lines), other social markers shape the character of the community and its relationship to its schools. As studies of desegregation demonstrate, race and ethnicity play an especially prominent role in this regard, as do other factors (e.g., religious beliefs and political interests) that define the culture of a community. Social class is only one condition among many that give communities their flavor, their distinctive character, and their propensity to pressure the schools in particular ways.

The social class of the community translates into other important influences on schools. The first is simply a matter of resources. Higher social-class communities generally have the wherewithal to provide teachers with ample resources to do their work, whereas chronic shortages of resources and less adequate facilities are common in schools serving communities lower in the social-class hierarchy (e.g., Persell, 1993; Metz, 1990; Kozol, 1991). While not a simple linear contributor to the quality of teaching or ultimately to educational outcomes (as Coleman et al., 1966, and subsequent related research have demonstrated), resource levels are clearly an important element in the conditions of teachers' work (Louis, 1990). Second is a matter of expressed power. Higher-status communities are not passive in their relationships with schools, but rather take active steps to advocate their interests, either as a group or on behalf of individual children, and have the political clout to make themselves heard. Lower-status groups lack such a political voice (though there are notable exceptions); generally they are easily ignored, or simply not heard at all. Social-class position is thus intimately linked to the distribution and exercise of power.

The Social Organization of the Student Population

The student populations of schools and school programs are not consciously or intentionally organized along social-class lines. If anything, quite the opposite is the case—educators intend to organize schools, and programs within schools, to address particular kinds of learning needs, to convey certain kinds of knowledge to those who can make best use of them, and to prepare students for further educational experiences of various kinds. On the face of it, entry into a school or a program within a school is based on geography, parental preferences, students' interests, or some measure of the students' aptitude or ability.

But beneath the surface, social class plays several potentially major roles in the social organization of the school population, both across and within schools, with the net result that students are progressively sorted into groupings that are relatively homogeneous by social class (Persell, 1977, 1993).

Much of this sorting across schools can be said to happen by default, as a result of parental choice (in the case of private and parochial schools) or the residential segregation described above. Especially at the elementary level, public schools (and, to a lesser extent, many private schools) serve a residential area with a particular social-class composition. In the simplest case, the "neighborhood school" serves a residential area that is largely homogeneous in social-class terms. In more complex cases the attendance area of the school embraces different neighborhoods, thus diversifying the aggregate class character of the student population, but usually a particular social class

will predominate. Thus students are likely to go to school with people like themselves, that is, who share a common social-class identity (Persell, 1993).

Such characterizations gloss over diversity, and do not describe well the socially heterogeneous nature of some magnet schools, certain private schools, and large schools serving complex, transitional attendance areas. As students progress up the ladder from elementary to senior grade levels through schools that serve ever-wider attendance areas, the overall social-class diversity of the student population is likely to increase. The social heterogeneity of such instances can be compounded by parental choice, but in all probability when parents opt for private schools they are selecting a social group for their children that more closely resembles their own than the public school options available to them.

Within schools, especially those with larger, socially heterogeneous student populations, further sorting by social class takes place (Persell, 1977). Here the role of social class is both subtle and profound, and is part of a complex story describing the assignment of students to declared or de facto tracks, classrooms, groupings within classrooms, or supplemental services for individuals with a specialized learning need. The story changes somewhat at different levels of schooling.

In the elementary grades some social-class sorting takes place whenever students are assigned by "ability" (either among or within classrooms). In the younger years, when ability (or achievement) is harder to assess, the teacher's *perceptions* of ability predict placement more accurately than do standardized scores (Bennett & LeCompte, 1990). The most telling forms of social-class grouping probably occur *within* the classroom in the form of ability grouping. Classic ethnographic studies (e.g., Rist, 1970) have demonstrated that class-related characteristics of kindergarten children—their appearance, behavior, and parents' welfare status—are important determinants of teachers' expectations for the children's performance and, hence, of their placement in high- or low-ability groups for reading instruction in first grade. Other research suggests that similar factors, such as degree of politeness and willingness to follow the teachers' directions—which are related to class-based upbringing—play an important role in early ability-group assignment (Mackler, 1969, as cited in Hurn, 1993). However, in research relying on cruder quantitative measures, which so far has failed to find a direct effect of social class on ability-group assignment at the elementary level (e.g., Haller & Davis, 1981), these observational results have not yet been substantiated.

The research reviewed so far establishes only that, in the absence of concrete information about performance, *initial* assignment to groups draws heavily on traits that are closely linked to children's social class. As the years go on, teachers rely increasingly on measures of achievement (though some degree of teacher judgment is always part of the grouping decisions). But because grouping assignments have considerable permanence (see, e.g., Rist, 1970), and because of the differentiated nature of instruction in ability groups (described later in this chapter), initial group assignments can exert an enduring influence on students' progress through school.

The pattern in the secondary grades, described in research on tracking (e.g., Findley & Bryan, 1975; Heyns, 1978; Oakes, 1985), continues the sorting processes begun in elementary school. At the secondary level, the explicit bases for track assignment are three (Oakes, 1985): (a) student test-score performance, (b) teacher and counselor recommendations, and (c) student and parental choice. Social class and ethnicity are likely to be a further consideration, though not conscious or deliberate (Persell, 1993), especially in the perceptions and actions of teachers and counselors. For example, in research at the junior high school level, even when ability and teacher recommendations are similar, social class has been found to be directly related to track assignments (e.g., Kariger, 1962, as cited in Persell, 1993). Observational research has documented that markers of social-class identity—among them speech patterns, clothing, and behaviors—are important considerations in counselors' grouping decisions at the high school level (Cicourel & Kitsuse, 1963). Drawing on this and other studies, a recent review concludes: "Secondary students from different backgrounds are given different types of information, advice, and counselor attention and . . . social, class-based placements are produced in the advising process" (Oakes, Gamoran, & Page, 1992, p. 577). It is plausible that high school teachers make judgments about students that draw subliminally on the same kinds of factors (Oakes, 1985). In addition, for reasons that are deeply embedded in their nature as cultural beings, students tend to choose (or parents choose for them) to be with students who are most like themselves. Though not the only factor, the ability to be among peers with a similar social background is likely to rank high in the choice of courses or program placements.

There are forms of grouping within schools other than assignment to ability groups in the elementary grades or tracks at the secondary level. Assignment to specialized educational services such as compensatory or special education reflects class-related characteristics, and hence can be considered a subsidiary sorting mechanism that isolates students for part or all of the school day in groupings with similar social-class backgrounds. Federal and state compensatory education programs, for example, are explicitly targeted to low-performing students in schools that serve concentrations of low-income children (Birman et al., 1987). Poverty level, which is for obvious reasons closely related to social class, is considered a major indicator of educational disadvantagement or "at-riskness," and hence a focus of many specialized services (Natriello et al., 1990). Special education labeling and program assignments reflect class-based differences both in the disproportionate number of lower social-class students served and in the differential labeling of students with perceived learning and behavioral handicaps. For example, learning disabilities, the largest category of educational handicap, originated as a less stigmatizing response to demands by middle-class parents to meet the educational needs of their underachieving children, though over the years this category has become a repository for children from lower-status groups (Sleeter, 1991). In addition, social class and class-based resistance are implicated in the debate over the inclusion of "socially maladjusted" students in programs serving the be-

haviorally disordered (Nelson, Rutherford, Center, & Walker, 1991).

Social Class and Educators

Having considered the community and the social organization of the student population in and among schools, we have one other category of participant in the social drama of education: the educators themselves. Rarely considered in research on schooling, the social-class background and identity of teachers, administrators, and specialists within the school building is a potentially influential element in the interactive story of teaching, learning, and credentialing. To the extent that the encounter between students and educators is a central part of that story (as we will argue in subsequent sections of this chapter), it is important to know where *both* parties to the encounter "are coming from."

Educators hold dual class identities, one deriving from their "class of origin" and the other from their current occupational position as teacher, administrator, counselor, or other role. In many cases the two are one and the same—in crude positional terms, teachers are considered "middle class," occupying a rung in the middle of the occupational status hierarchy, and large numbers of them come from middle-class families (Bennett & LeCompte, 1990). The same is not true of all teachers; for many, teaching is a means to improve social status. This was especially so in the past; as recently as 1960, more than half of all teachers were from farm or blue-collar families (Betz & Garland, 1974, cited in Bennett & LeCompte, 1990). Thus, though teachers occupy a relatively common station in the stratification of society, they arrive from very different places.

No discussion of the class-based nature of the teaching force can ignore the fact that teaching is a segmented labor market that has been largely feminized at the lower levels, and increasingly so at the secondary levels, a pattern that has long historical roots in U.S. schools. In this respect the class-based dynamics of the teaching profession differ markedly for men and women (Weiler, 1988). Teaching offers men, for example, a better avenue of continuing upward mobility than it does women (Bennett & LeCompte, 1990). More recent formulations of the issues from a feminist perspective treat the feminization of teaching as another instance of a dual "class" system in which women tend to end up with lower-status occupations, and higher-status occupations tend to be reserved for men (Weiler). A prominent critical perspective argues that all teachers, male and female, are placed in subordinate positions in the labor structure; increasingly, these positions have been deprived of professional discretion ("deskilled") by a patriarchal power structure (Apple, 1986).

Educators bring class-based sensibilities to their work—a curious omission of the teacher socialization literature (Zeichner & Gere, 1990), which focuses on the influence of formally designated agents of socialization such as teacher-preparation institutions. These sensibilities derive in part from the teachers' class of origin, in part from their professional and life trajectory, and in part from their current patterns of association outside of school. Ethnographic research on the workplace context of high school teachers highlights the phenomenon as follows:

Teachers participate in communities and in kinship and friendship networks that also are part of the social class system. While teachers have formally similar educational credentials and participate in a single, undifferentiated occupation, they not only come from a range of social class backgrounds but participate as adults in networks that vary significantly in their social class. We were struck with the differences in attitude, lifestyle, and associates, among [the teachers we studied] . . . .

Teachers' own class affected their definitions of their work. Teachers who associated with managers and professionals defined their responsibilities more in terms of being sure to do a good job, whatever that required, while those with working class associates defined their responsibilities more in terms of conscientiously putting in required hours . . . . (Metz, 1990, pp. 94–95)

Seen from this perspective, teachers' past and current social-class affiliations are part of what equips them to cope with the varied demands of educating young people. It certainly shapes their views of their role as educators, but it also may predispose them to perceive, and interact with, students in certain ways (Weiler, 1988). And in many instances teachers' social-class identities equip them poorly to deal with youngsters whose social-class origins differ from their own (Bennett & LeCompte, 1990). That is not to say that teachers deal more effectively with students who match them in social-class background, though this is often the case; rather, teachers who have become "multicultural" are more likely to do well with student populations that represent a variety of backgrounds. At present, the institutions that prepare people for teaching do little to instill multicultural perspectives, knowledge, and skills. And the bulk of today's teacher workforce was trained in times when issues of diversity and multicultural teaching skills were not comprehensively addressed (Gay, 1986).

One further dynamic reinforces the influence of educators' social class on schooling: Some evidence suggests that teachers, like students, are subtly sorted by class background among schools and, within schools, among programs (e.g., Anyon, 1980, 1981; Metz, 1990). Social class is not the only variable controlling where educators are assigned, nor is it the most powerful. Teachers are not passive participants in their assignment to one school or another, as the "sorting" metaphor may imply; depending on the individual and the school system, a great deal of active choice enters into the process. But whether or not they are active agents, the net effect is the same: Teachers are likely to gravitate to teaching situations in which their colleagues' social-class sensibilities resemble their own. (Over time, faculties will construct shared sensibilities as well.) Thus the cadre of teachers at a typical "working-class" school and those serving predominantly upper-middle-class students are likely to look very different.

Implications for Educational Outcomes

The preceding discussion explores the connections between social class and the community context, social organization of students, and staffing of schools, and argues that, in each

realm, social class contributes to stratification within and across schools. We have argued that social class is an important influence on these realms, and that, in turn, each of these conditions the work of the school. We have not yet established that these influences change the outcomes of education, nor does most of the research we have reviewed so far purport to do so. At best, the class-based expectations of the community, the social sorting of students into relatively homogeneous groupings by class, and the class-based sensibilities of educators are indirect influences that can affect outcomes only by a chain of events. In the next two sections we will carry the argument forward, tracing that chain of events as learners enter the school building, interact with educators, and engage in—or resist—instruction.

SOCIAL CLASS AND THE LEARNER

As individuals and in peer groups, learners enter the school building with a worldview, language, values, and apparent intellectual capacities. Various lines of research help us to see how social class may shape the learners' approaches to the intellectual and social work of school. The research base for this discussion draws on sociological and anthropological studies focusing on cultural differences and cultural discontinuities. In addition, literature on peer groups and student resistance is also helpful, as is psychological work on testing and student responses to adverse conditions in schooling.

It must be remembered in any discussion of social class and children that children do not, themselves, have social class. Children and youth are assigned social-class membership on the basis of their parents' or guardians' occupation, educational attainment, earnings, lifestyle, or other markers. Consequently, discussions of social class and schooling must consider the ways in which parents', families', and communities' interactions with schools may vary due to factors associated with social class.

This section begins with the relationship between social class and the learner's "intelligence," which is often assumed to explain class-based differences in schooling outcomes. The inadequacies of intelligence concepts and measures lead us to examine the role of social class in the learner's approach to intellectual work. Following that, we consider the way the learner confronts the gap between the social and linguistic codes of home and those of school. Next, we examine the role of social class in adult and peer perceptions of learners and their capabilities, followed by a consideration of social class in the peer culture.

Social Class and the Learner's "Intelligence"

Attuned as they are to cognitive functioning, educators are soon aware that students appear to display different capacities for intellectual work. Generations of educators and scholars have assumed that this meant differences in the learners' intelligence, and have settled for intelligence quotient (IQ) measures as a reasonable proxy for the expression of these differences. These measures have a long history in efforts to understand the relationship between social class and schooling because (a) indicators of social class (such as SES) are highly correlated with IQ, and (b) IQ is highly predictive of most schooling outcomes (see, for example, Coleman et al., 1966; Jencks, 1972).

A long-standing assertion in educational sociology is that IQ is the principal means by which social class influences schooling outcomes (Hurn, personal communication, 1993). Put in the simplest and baldest terms, this argument holds that, on average, individuals born into higher social classes either grow up with more optimal conditions for cognitive development (e.g., better nutrition, more cognitive stimulation), inherit greater cognitive potential (e.g., because over time smart people are assumed to gravitate to high-status positions in society), or both. These conditions are assumed to produce young people who score higher on IQ tests. Because IQ tests capture how well students do on tasks related to the cognitive work of schooling, these individuals are more likely to succeed in school. Their success in school is likely to be rewarded with higher-status jobs and social circumstances, and the cycle then repeats itself.

Many scholars (ourselves included) view this assertion and the premises on which it rests as problematic (e.g., Davis, 1951; Reissman, 1962; Ballantine, 1993). First, it is unclear exactly what IQ tests measure, and there is considerable doubt that these tests measure "intelligence" in any absolute sense. To compound matters, the scholarly community has yet to agree on a definition of "intelligence," or even to establish that a single mental ability is involved—multiple abilities are included in many definitions of intelligence (e.g., Gardner, 1987). More than three decades ago, an analysis of IQ testing put the matter this way:

Intelligence tests measure how quickly people can solve relatively unimportant problems making as few errors as possible, rather than measuring how people grapple with relatively important problems, making as many productive errors as necessary with no time factor. (Murray, 1960, quoted in Reissman, 1962, p. 49)

Second, there is reason to doubt the stability of the tests. They are supposed to produce a constant score, and most often this is the case, but there have been numerous demonstrations in which the scores of individuals, particularly those from lower-status backgrounds, have risen dramatically following some coaching in test-taking strategies (e.g., Haggard, 1954; Heber, 1979, cited in Ballantine, 1993). Third, the content and format of IQ tests reflect particular culturally based experiences, thereby favoring certain social and ethnic groups over others (Ballantine). Fourth, it is not clearly established that higher-status positions are awarded on the basis of talent (Hurn, 1993), as noted earlier in this chapter in the discussion of conflict and critical perspectives on schooling and its relationship to society.

We find it more productive to look at IQ testing in the same way that we examine everything else involved in the relationship between social class and schooling. IQ testing—the activity that produces IQ scores—is a *social* act governed by the same norms and cultural rules that guide most of what goes on in schools (Reissman, 1962). From the student's perspective, it is intellectual work that results in a performance, like many things done in school or school-like contexts. Students come to these contexts with different social and linguistic codes, cultural understandings, presentations of self, and peer affiliations. As the ensuing discussion demonstrates, these factors all influence how students engage in intellectual tasks, what they produce as a result of this engagement, and how they are viewed by others.

Put another way, rather than social class being a natural correlate and consequence of intelligence, it is just as likely that apparent intelligence levels are "assigned," in part on the basis of social-class position. No doubt there are still *individual* variations in intelligence (by a more satisfactory definition of the concept) within social groups and across the population as a whole, but there is little compelling evidence that clear *group* differences in intelligence (by the same definition) exist or are passed on from one generation to the next (Hurn, 1993). In sum, trying to explain the relationship between social class and schooling in terms of how smart people are is a fruitless task; more satisfactory explanations emerge from a closer examination of the characteristics of the learner that are clearly class based.

Social Class and the Learner's Approach to Intellectual Work

Students are born into a social environment formed, in varying degrees, by families and communities, and comprised of a complex web of social and linguistic patterns (Heath, 1983; McDermott, 1987; Delpit, 1988; Haviland, 1990). From these patterns grow expectations that inform the behaviors and interactions of members of each family and community. These social and linguistic "codes" are determined by numerous factors, including elements of culture grown up around ethnicity, gender, religious beliefs, and position in the social-class hierarchy (Haviland). Secondary factors arise out of interactions between families and communities and the larger sociopolitical milieu, and include the types and levels of education attained and available, familial and community history, and the perceived employment opportunities available to family and community members (Ogbu, 1979; Delpit).

The defining elements of social class—relationship to economic resources, work roles, access to power, and the cultural resources (including education) that govern entry to status positions—are thus all present in the learner's experience outside of school. Regardless of formal schooling, a child in a given community will learn language and behaviors that suit her or him to take up adult roles specific to females or males in that family or community.

In the broadest sense, children are taught by the culture of family and community how to think, behave, and communicate. Research and theory have yet to develop a full account of the roles of social class in defining this culture—class and culture are, after all, distinct and should not be equated with one another. But three themes emerge from work to date, each of which contributes to our understanding of the learners' approach to the intellectual work of schooling. First, the social class of home and community shapes the learners' approach to authority, especially as manifested in work roles. Second, social class contributes to a particular kind of meaning system embedded in linguistic codes. Third, class-based conditions offer varying degrees of material security, which influences children's physical reality and attendant anxiety or contentment.

With regard to authority and work roles, the social class of family and community members can offer children an initial definition of their future places in the larger occupational structure. This definition both helps to shape students' aspirations and expectations and results in behaviors and interactive patterns that optimize chances for success in occupations common to their parents' social class. There is some evidence that middle- and upper-class parents, as a group, exhibit parenting styles that foster independence, creativity, and problem-solving and reasoning skills, while lower-class parenting methods are said to emphasize docility and obedience in the face of authority and a passive learning style (Ogbu, 1979; Bernstein, 1970, 1977; Bennett & LeCompte, 1990). These class-related parenting styles do not indicate success or failure in socializing children adequately. Rather, parenting styles reflect adaptations that maximize the chances that children will grow up to find employment in a job typical of their social class of origin (Ogbu, 1979). By this argument, working-class parents socialize their children to be responsive to authority and receptive to subservience because those are competencies required in many working-class jobs. Middle-class parents socialize their children in the competencies of reasoning, questioning, and independence because those are skills thought to be required for middle-class jobs.

With regard to class-based linguistic meaning systems, a number of researchers have focused on the nature of linguistic patterns that vary by social class. Bernstein (1977), for example, found that working-class life—organized around authority based on age, class, and gender—generates communicative codes characterized by a "particularistic" meaning system. The resulting verbal shorthand reflects the assumption that listeners are familiar with intents and meanings. Meanings are usually not made explicit by the speaker and directives are grounded in authority rather than rational explanation. In contrast, middle-class families tend to use a "universalistic" language code in which meaning and context are more elaborately spelled out. While working-class linguistic codes may be entirely satisfactory in homes and communities, students who do not know the nuances of universalistic communication are at a disadvantage in school systems in which universalistic patterns predominate and middle-class teachers may be unfamiliar with lower-class students' intents and meanings.

Research focused on the linguistic teaching of nonmainstream cultural groups—which occupy lower levels of the social-class hierarchy—arrive at similar conclusions. Consider, for example, work on interrogative patterns (Heath, 1983) and the learning of "the culture of power" (Delpit, 1988). While such research does not single out social class as the primary source of linguistic meaning systems, there is good reason to understand it as an important contributing condition.

Other factors related to the economic and social concomitants of social class can also affect students' ability to learn. Many lower-class students live in poverty and are faced with somatic concerns revolving around unmet physical needs. Hunger, inadequate clothing, inadequate medical care, transient status, and overcrowded or inadequate housing are part of daily life for a growing percentage of children (Bennett & LeCompte, 1990; Natriello et al., 1990; Children's Defense Fund, 1991). Psychological distress arising from uncertainty about daily needs, cultural incongruence with the schools, the social stigma of poverty, and high levels of familial stress is commonplace for impoverished children (Schorr, 1988; National Commission on Children, 1991; Kozol, 1991; Rafferty & Shinn, 1991). Anxieties generated by uncertainties in physical, emotional, and social survival detract from capacity to learn, in that anxious students must devote a portion of their energy and intellectual capacity to coping with physical and emotional concerns unrelated to the academic tasks of school (Tobias, 1979). While there are many social, emotional, and physical stressors that affect learners of all social classes, lower-class students are far more likely to experience anxiety due to the economic realities of social class than are their middle- and upper-class peers. On the other hand, some learners from the upper classes may face a greater degree of pressure than their middle- and lower-class peers to succeed in intellectual tasks, and this pressure may result in personal anxiety that impacts ability to learn.

The Match or Mismatch Between Social Class of Learners and of School

As the earlier discussion of educators' social class suggests, schools display a way of thinking, behaving, and communicating that is shaped by social class. Students walking through a classroom door are entering a well-established culture complete with linguistic codes, behavioral expectations, and assumptions about the nature of teaching and learning. Most of these communicative and behavioral codes reflect the values, power dynamics, and knowledge base of mainstream middle- or upper-class cultures (Delpit, 1988; Hurn, 1993; Persell, 1977; Bourdieu & Passeron, 1977; Nelson-Barber & Meier, 1990). To the degree to which learners have been raised in family and community environments with similar middle-class assumptions and expectations, students have a good chance of experiencing cultural congruence between family and school; that is, mainstream students in mainstream schools are more likely to understand overt communications and expectations, as well as the unspoken rules of middle-class behavior. To the degree that learners' linguistic and behavioral codes and expectations differ from those of the mainstream, students may experience cultural incongruity.

Researchers have begun to identify "communicative code differences" that arise in situations of cultural incongruence. Students and teachers

produce communicative breakdowns by simply performing routine and practical everyday activities in ways their subcultures define as normal and appropriate. Because behavioral competence is differently defined by different social groups, many children and teachers fail in their attempts to establish rational, trusting and rewarding relationships across ethnic, racial or class boundaries in the classroom. (McDermott, 1987, p. 173)

According to McDermott's (1987) theory of cultural incongruence, school failure for lower-class children is built of the culturally incongruent actions, reactions, and interactions between middle-class teachers and lower-class "pariah" students. Because many researchers studying cultural incongruence (e.g., scholars such as McDermott, Ogbu, Delpit) have studied populations in which race and class differences intersect, it is not always possible to disentangle the effects of one or the other of these characteristics. However, it is possible to make a good argument about the class-based nature of much racially generated cultural incongruence by demonstrating that middle-class members of racial minorities experience a greater degree of cultural harmony with mainstream schools than do lower-class racial minorities.

Another way of looking at the match between the class-based cultures of students and schools is suggested by the work of Bourdieu (e.g., Bourdieu & Passeron, 1977), who observed, primarily in French schools, the teaching of the superiority of elite culture, especially as reflected in familiarity with the arts and use of elegant language forms. Hurn (1993) summarizes the essential argument:

Students who lack familiarity with this style, who lack what Bourdieu calls "cultural capital," will appear dull, plodding, and (at best) merely earnest, and they will be consistently typed as worthy members of the middle or lower class but as unsuitable for elite positions.... Schools work to conceal the real character of domination by teaching that there is only one legitimate culture and one form of approved consciousness—that of the highly educated elite. (p. 197)

Lower-class children frequently lack the "cultural capital" that is valued in schools, in that they use different language forms and bring to school familiarity with different (not necessarily classical) art forms. The cultural capital that working-class children bring to school constitutes a sort of "foreign currency" that is undervalued in the mainstream school context (Bourdieu & Passeron, 1977).

Social Class as a Basis for Perceptions of the Learner's Capabilities

The match between what the learner brings to school—class-based modes of thinking, behaving, and communicating—and the prevailing class-based culture of the school conditions other people's perceptions of the child. In particular, adults in the school, other learners, and the students' own parents ascribe capabilities and characteristics to the student when there is no direct or "objective" evidence on which to base these perceptions. Here, once again, social class is closely entwined with matters of race, ethnicity, and culture. But the underlying pattern is clear: Learners who are identifiably from lower-class backgrounds (regardless of race) tend to be perceived negatively, as less capable than they probably are, while those from families and communities located higher in the social-class hierarchy tend to be perceived positively (Persell, 1977, 1993; McDermott,1987; Rosenholtz & Rosenholtz, 1981).

Adults' Perceptions of the Learners' Capabilities. Historically, educators, researchers, and educational policy makers have tended to attach notions of deficit and asset to differences in cultures, languages, behavioral norms, and educational preparedness (e.g., Baratz & Baratz, 1970; also see review discussions in Bennett & LeCompte, 1990; Hurn, 1993). Not surprisingly, mainstream cultural values, Standard English, compliant but inquisitive behaviors, and a functional knowledge of mainstream school norms and academic skills have been considered assets for students. When educators speak about educational preparedness, socialization, or enculturation, they are often referring to this or a similar set of skills and standards (Nelson-Barber & Meier, 1990). To the extent that students possess *different* qualities, languages or dialects, behaviors, and knowledge, they have been considered deficient. This deficit model has worked to the disadvantage of lower-class learners in that they often have been viewed as "culturally deprived" or "culturally disadvantaged," and the learning environment from which they originate (their families and communities) has been considered "culturally impoverished":

By characterizing the environment of lower-class children as deprived, disorganized, or pathological, the cultural deprivation argument shifted attention away from the failings of the schools and of biased testing instruments to the supposed failure of poor people to bring up their children correctly. (Hurn, 1993, p. 152)

This assumption of deficit in the lives and academic readiness of lower-class students has been reified in the form of policies and programs that objectify "economic disadvantage" or "cultural deprivation." The Head Start program, for example, was created in order to overcome the deprivation of disadvantage perceived to be symptomatic of low-income families (Hurn, 1993; Baratz & Baratz, 1970). Through repeated use of terms like "economic disadvantage" and "cultural deprivation," educators and policy makers have objectified the conception of learner deficit due to low social class as something real and all but inevitable (Bloom, Davis, Hess, & Silverman, 1965; Reissman, 1962). This objectification of learner deficit slipped into the unconscious assumptions of educators; most teachers automatically assume deficiencies in the skills and abilities of lower-class students (Persell, 1977, 1993). These assumptions are compounded by the influence on teachers of "information" about students gleaned from academic records, test scores, and narrative accounts, all influenced by social class. This is significant because "much of the information teachers gain about low income children seems to be negative" (Persell, 1993, p. 80). As discussed elsewhere in this chapter, unconscious and conscious assumptions of deficit on the part of school personnel can have a profound impact on the treatment of learners through such mechanisms as differential classroom treatment (Brophy & Good, 1970; Rosenholtz & Rosenholtz, 1981; Chaikin, Sigler, & Derlega, 1974), labeling (Rist, 1977), tracking (Oakes, 1985), and career counseling. Furthermore, teacher modeling of low expectations for students is a factor in students' evaluations of their peers' skills and abilities, as discussed below (Cohen, 1986b).

Peers' Perceptions of the Learners' Capabilities. The influence of social status on perceptions of learner skills, abilities, and characteristics in the school environment is not limited to adults. Students are actively engaged in rank-ordering each other and forming social hierarchies. Although the process of peer stratification and establishing dominance is more characteristically a male than a female phenomenon (Daniels-Bierness, 1989), most students do form opinions about each other's characteristics and abilities, and frequently these opinions are initially fashioned on the basis of "diffuse status characteristics" such as race, gender, and perceived social class (Cohen, 1982, 1986b). Cohen has demonstrated that peer perceptions of learners' abilities influence social dynamics in the classroom in such a way that low-status peers are given fewer opportunities to participate meaningfully in group activities, while high-status peers tend to participate more, be listened to, and be allowed to take authority roles. Lack of low-status student participation in group activities not only reduces learning opportunities for these students, but reduces social opportunities as well by eliminating chances for them to demonstrate skills and abilities. When students do or do not demonstrate skills and abilities, peers evaluate them differently on the basis of student social status in order to avoid what Hymel (1986) terms "affective incongruence." High-status peers are given the benefit of the doubt when not behaving as expected, while low-status student behavior tends to be negatively valued regardless of its actual content. While it must be emphasized that *social status* and *social class* are conceptually distinct, these findings are important because, as mentioned above, perceived social class is one of the diffuse status characteristics used by students in assessments and assignments of social status.

Given the predictable way in which the perceptions of adults and peers in the school building are shaped by social class and other factors that bear little relationship to capabilities, it is no wonder that efforts to reform the schooling available to lower-status children have targeted the deficit model just described. "Accelerated schools" (Levin, 1988) and "complex instruction" (Cohen, 1986a), to mention only two reform proposals, have created approaches to schooling and curriculum that assume a multidimensional "asset model" of the learner. Other efforts to promote academically challenging instruction in schools serving high concentrations of low-status children are also explicit about the need to reconceive the learner (e.g., Means, Chelemer, & Knapp, 1991; Knapp & Shields, 1990).

Parents' Perceptions of the Learners' Capabilities. Parents' perceptions of student capabilities and opportunities must also be considered in a discussion of social class. While parents of any social class may have faith in their children's intellectual capabilities, lower-class parents frequently do not trust the schools' ability to elicit the cognitive capacities of their children. That is, many lower-class parents are cognizant that the abilities of their children may not be the ones valued by middle-class teachers and anticipated by school curricula, and many understand that their children do not possess some of the skills valued by mainstream culture. The ensuing cultural mismatch can result in mutual distrust between parents and teachers and the loss of hope on the part of lower-class parents that schools will educate their children adequately (Comer, 1988).

Social Class in the Peer Culture

Students in schools group themselves into peer groups of like individuals, and one of the dimensions of familiarity influencing peer-group formation is social class. Research and theory points to important effects of class-based peer culture on educational outcomes.

Because students form peer groups with others who are like themselves, speak in familiar languages (and vernaculars), behave in predictable ways, and are perceived to be academically similar, social-class sensibilities are a large, though certainly not the only, determinant of peer-group membership. It is not inconceivable that the shared experiences of peer-group members along social-class lines in a school context may be the primary factor in setting the tone for the peer-group response to the institution of schooling. Even peer groups explicitly formed along lines of race and gender inevitably invoke class issues, through the inextricable relationships between these two characteristics and social class. It is known, for example, that disaffection with and resistance to schooling is far more common among individuals and groups of lower-class origin than among those from upper- and middle-class families and communities (Solomon, 1992; Fordham, 1988). Of course, there are exceptions to this pattern among individuals and groups; that lower-class students are the most likely to be disaffected does not mean that most lower-class children *are* disaffected. Contented and discontented students exist at all levels of the social-class hierarchy.

The peer culture provides a sense of community and belonging to students (Fordham & Ogbu, 1986). In essence, one's peer culture is analogous to one's family within the school; it plays a similar role in providing models, shaping aspirations, establishing expectations, and forming identity. As students get older and less dependent on adult approval, peer-group influence strengthens. Indeed, any casual observer of youth is likely to note that the opinions of peers are a great deal more salient to adolescents than those of school staff.

One of the common tasks of a peer culture within a school is to define its members' response to the social and academic learning environment. If the school provides a safe, stimulating, validating, and reinforcing environment for members of the peer group, the spoken or unspoken standards of the group may well emphasize success within the social and academic parameters of the school. For instance, some middle- and upper-class peer groups may consist of successful students who are active in the formal extracurricular culture of school, including participation in athletics, cheerleading, debate clubs, chess clubs, student government, or other sanctioned school activities. Conversely, peer groups consisting of students who find school an unfamiliar, unfair, unstimulating, or hostile environment may develop a culture that is centered around or includes elements of resistance to the formal culture of the school (Anyon, 1980; McDermott, 1987; Neufeld, 1991). This resistance may take many forms, including noncompliance or nonparticipation in the classroom, outright defiance of school staff and school regulations, "cutting" class, dropping out, or engaging in illegal activities on or off school grounds (Solomon, 1992).

How the Learner's Social Class Relates to Educational Outcomes

When one brings the learner into focus, the web of potential influences on educational outcomes becomes more interconnected and richly textured. Differing social-class backgrounds condition learners' approaches to the intellectual work of schooling. The gap between the class-based world from which the learner comes and the essentially middle-class culture of the school compounds the matter: Teachers and learners may misunderstand each other in their daily interactions, and both adults and other students will form impressions of the learner's capabilities based on visible class-related characteristics, among other traits. Finally, peer groups form, in part influenced by the learners' social class, and may provide a united response to schooling, whether supportive or resistant.

Taken together, these class-based dynamics predispose learners from higher social-class backgrounds to perform more effectively in the typical school setting, and those from lower-class backgrounds to perform less so, regardless of their innate abilities. However, student performance also reflects the nature of instruction itself, to which we now turn.

SOCIAL CLASS AND THE NATURE OF INSTRUCTION

We have considered the role of social class in setting the community and school context for instruction and in shaping what the principal participants—teachers and learners—bring to instructional interactions. In this section we turn to instruction itself by examining, first, what is taught (content) and, second, how it is taught (pedagogy) in the different "class contexts" that result from the sorting processes described earlier in the chapter. In our analysis of instruction we include both the formal and the "hidden" curricula of schooling. In organizing our discussion by what is taught and how it is taught, we acknowledge the difficulty of separating content from pedagogy. Nonetheless, the distinction is analytically useful in ways that will become apparent as we proceed.

What we know about the relationship of social class and instruction comes from various sources, especially from the growing literature on "curriculum differentiation" (see Oakes et al., 1992, for a recent comprehensive review) and from interpretive research on the sociology of the curriculum (see Bennett & LeCompte, 1990, for a review of this work). Even within these traditions, relatively few studies have attempted to trace the links between social class and instruction in any detail and with any attention to the complexities inherent in the concept of "class." More often, one encounters "SES" or "parents' income level" as one among many variables predicting, or correlated with, some feature of content and pedagogy. While such

quantitative research offers the statistical power of larger samples and provides clues to the puzzle, it does not produce a compelling account of the mechanisms by which social class connects with instruction. To trace such links, we must rely more extensively on observational and ethnographic research (e.g., Anyon, 1980, 1981; Wilcox, 1982; Metz, 1990).

Research on the relationship between social class and instruction reveals a consistent pattern: Both content and pedagogy vary systematically with the class context of schooling. Put simply, the instruction available to students lower down on (any) social-class scale is, on average, academically less challenging, more repetitive, and more dominated by a concern for social control than that offered to students of higher social-class background. Thus, in the aggregate, learners from different social-class backgrounds are typically taught different content and are taught it in a distinctive manner.

What Is Taught (Content)

When considering what is taught, one must examine the content both of the formal curriculum and of the hidden curriculum embedded in instructional materials and the design of learning tasks. We include within the content of the formal curriculum the kinds of information and knowledge—and also the implied conception of knowledge and its sources—conveyed by materials, learning tasks, direct instruction, articulation of content across grades, and the array of informational resources to which learners have predictable access. These sources offer explicit statements of values, beliefs, and ideologies that are also part of the formal curriculum content. The content of the hidden curriculum includes values, norms, and beliefs regarding the organization of society, authority, work, the economy, achievement, success or failure, the purpose of learning, and the place of the individual in relation to these concerns. This content is implied rather than stated and is conveyed in a myriad of ways, most subconscious.

Social class enters the examination of curricular content in two ways. First, the curriculum teaches *about* class—what it is, how social classes relate to one another. Second, the curriculum *reflects* (some would argue, is tailored to) the social-class context of instruction. Put another way, systematic differences in the curriculum *are associated with* the social-class composition of the student population.

Social Class as Part of the Content of Instruction. Regarding social class as a focus or topic of study, the formal curriculum says relatively little. Systematic reviews of leading textbooks, for example, reveal remarkably little about social class in any subject area (Sleeter & Grant, 1991; Anyon, 1979). Rather, instructional materials in common use are "class-blind," conveying the message that social class is not a significant feature of life. In examining the kinds and conceptions of knowledge taught in differing class contexts, Anyon's classic research (1980, 1981) found that upper elementary children were taught little about the history, prevalence, or operation of class-related phenomena in the United States. Thus the curriculum teaches about social life as much by what it excludes as what it includes. The same phenomenon has been noted in studies of the treatment of gender (see Sadker, Sadker, & Long, 1993).

If anything, the formal curriculum systematically under-represents the experience of individuals living at either extreme of the social-class hierarchy, as well as the variety of perspectives that can be brought to bear on these experiences or the hierarchy as a whole. Conversely, the curriculum typically overrepresents the experience and worldview of middle-class America, in line with prevailing ideologies of the nation as an egalitarian society in which individual effort counts most. The "class-blind" character of the curriculum thus mirrors what has long been a fact of life in U.S. society—namely, that the lives of the poor and rich are relatively invisible to the great majority of Americans (Bennett & LeCompte, 1990).

Differentiation of Content by Social Class. Regarding the correspondence between curricular content and the social-class composition of the student population, most of what has been learned derives from careful comparative inquiry into what is taught in different social-class contexts. Such research (e.g., at the elementary level, Anyon, 1980, and 1981; Wilcox, 1982; at the secondary level, Oakes, 1985) reveals a pattern of formal content differentiated on at least the following dimensions: focus on "advanced" versus "basic" skills, focus on conceptual understanding, range and variety of academic tasks, degree of repetition, extent of topical coverage, and attention to "practical" knowledge (i.e., with immediate vocational applications). In broad strokes, the content taught to learners in higher-status class contexts is typically more conceptual, varied, challenging, wide ranging, and more focused on "advanced" skills than the content taught in lower-status class contexts, and at the same time less repetitive and less focused on knowledge with immediate practical application.

Underlying these differences are divergent conceptions of knowledge itself. Consider, for example, how Anyon (1981) contrasts the prevailing conception of knowledge in the two working-class elementary schools she studied with the conception that predominated in an affluent professional elementary school:

What counts as knowledge in these two working class schools is not knowledge as concepts, cognitions, information or ideas about society, language, math, or history, connected to conceptual principles or understandings of some sort. Rather, it seems that what constitutes school knowledge here is (1) fragmented facts, isolated from context and connection to each other or wider bodies of meaning, or to activity or biography of the students; and (2) knowledge of "practical" rule-governed behaviors—procedures by which the students carry out tasks that are largely mechanical. Sustained conceptual or "academic" knowledge has only occasional, symbolic presence here. (p. 12)

Knowledge in the affluent professional school is not only conceptual, but is open to discovery, construction, and meaning making; it is not always given. Knowledge is often concepts and ideas that are used to make sense, and that thus have personal value. Although knowledge may result from personal creativity and independent thinking, there are constraints and directives on what counts as answers. Knowledge has individualistic goals, but it also may be a resource for social good. It is analytical and more realistic about society than knowledge in the middle class and working class schools. The children are also getting a good

dose of two dominant ideologies: that the system itself will be made more humane by expressions of concern for the less fortunate, and that individuals, not groups, make history. (p. 23)

These differences in formal content are accompanied and reinforced by a hidden curriculum of values, norms, and beliefs related to society, work roles, and the students' relationship to these roles. One comparative ethnographic study of first-grade classrooms in both a lower-middle-class and an upper-middle-class elementary school identifies clear differences in lessons about the child's self-presentation skills, relationship to authority, and images of self at present and in the future (Wilcox, 1982). In the lower-status school, children were taught to see themselves as part of an externally controlled hierarchical system, given limited opportunities to develop self-presentation skills, and focused on the present with little reference to their futures. Their counterparts in the upper-middle-class school were taught to internalize control over their actions, given daily practice in self-presentation skills, and helped to develop images of their prospects for the future (in second grade, for example, but also in the distant future, at college and beyond).

A parallel pattern pertains at the secondary level, though with differences that relate to the organization of schooling at this level. Unlike the elementary level, where the official scope and sequence of subject matter to be taught in the respective schools were relatively similar, the formal and hidden content of what is taught in secondary schools is, in varying degrees, formally differentiated by tracks (or their equivalent) that are designed for learners with presumably different educational and occupational futures (Oakes, 1985; Page, 1991; Oakes et al., 1992). The differentiated pattern occurs both across tracks (e.g., college prep, general, vocational) and, within track, by ability (e.g., the top, middle, and lower English classes within a given grade). The variable array of elective courses is itself deployed informally along a continuum from more to less demanding.

There are various ways for the differences in content to be associated with class context at the secondary level. First, as in the case of elementary schools, high schools serve attendance areas that reflect some residential segregation by class, which gives the schools as a whole a distinctive class-related character (Metz, 1990). Second, within high schools, learners from different social classes are unequally distributed among tracks (and even within tracks), and these disparities grow with time (Oakes et al., 1992). Predictably and consistently, learners from lower-status social backgrounds are concentrated in lower-track classrooms. In general terms, such placement means a pronounced departure from what is taught in "more advanced" courses: Less material is covered overall, the knowledge is more fragmented, and less is asked of the learner. While nominally addressing the same subject matter as more advanced classrooms (and generating the same credit toward graduation), low-track classrooms may offer "less detail" (i.e., less demanding content), "practical skill building" (i.e., reading skills rather than substance), "relevance" (i.e., topics chosen for their appeal to disaffected adolescents), or some combination of these components (Page, 1991, p. 181).

The ostensible basis for the selection of course content (and for track placement, as discussed earlier in the chapter) is the learner's presumed or demonstrated level of ability and achievement. It is thus easy to assume, as many educators do, that social background plays no real part in these differences. By this argument, the unequal social distribution of learners is simply an unfortunate side effect.

While there is no clear empirical evidence to resolve the matter, there are grounds for a counterposition. First, the contrasts in curriculum across schools of differing social-class contexts are striking. Unless one assumes that whole populations of learners are simply less capable overall—a dubious assumption in the light of Advanced Placement calculus results from "turnaround" inner-city high schools (e.g., Matthews, 1988)—then there is likely to be less matching of curriculum with actual ability than educators claim. Second, because differential grouping by ability appears to compound the measured differences in achievement over time, any intrusion of social background factors in the process will be carried forward over time (Goodlad & Oakes, 1988). Third, the correspondence between what is taught and the knowledge requirements of the work roles of learners' parents is remarkably close. If one makes the assumptions that (a) society needs an array of skilled and unskilled workers in roughly similar proportions to the present, and (b) in the absence of good information teachers will assume that learners' capabilities and occupational futures will resemble those of their parents, then the correspondence between what is taught and social-class background is not accidental but, instead, highly functional (Wilcox, 1982). Without necessarily intending to do so, teachers and schools thus "tailor" curriculum to social-class background (this linkage is still an association more than a clear causal claim).

To put this argument in some perspective, there are many similarities in curriculum across class contexts, perhaps more than the ethnographic research base suggests. Analysts find, for example, a great deal of repetition in the curriculum at all levels, an emphasis on coverage of factual material, and relatively little intellectual challenge (Gehrke, Knapp, & Sirotnik, 1992). Interpretive research on high school lower-track classrooms finds them "paradoxically different *and* similar . . . as versions of a particular school's regular classes, rather than as readily distinguishable phenomena" (Page, 1991, p. 237).

We should point out that differences in the formal and hidden curricula across class contexts often reflect more than social class. Race, ethnicity, and gender, among other social factors, also appear to be implicated in the differentiation of content, in ways that are analytically distinct from, though often intertwined with, social class. Nonmainstream ethnic backgrounds and experiences, for example, are systematically underrepresented in curriculum materials or the selection of content and, by implication, are undervalued. In many instances in which minority-group members are concentrated in lower-status groupings, instructional content is differentiated concurrently by ethnicity and social class.

How the Content Is Taught (Pedagogy)

The manner in which curricular content is taught also differs systematically by class context and reinforces the messages embedded in instructional materials, learning tasks, and the scope and sequence of content. Pedagogy conveys overt and covert lessons about learners' intrinsic worth, prospects for success in school, and relationships with authority and control. For our purposes, *pedagogy* includes the teacher's approach to teaching subject matter, classroom management (to the extent this can be distinguished from content-specific pedagogy), personal style of interacting with learners, and control over learning tasks. We assume that pedagogy, as we have defined it, is interactive and thus jointly constructed by teachers and learners.

The prevailing pattern of instruction in lower- and working-class contexts emphasizes "transmission" teaching (e.g., Hargreaves, 1988; Knapp & Shields, 1991; Oakes, 1990), tight control of classroom interactions, heavy-handed discipline, teacher control of learning tasks, reliance on seat work and worksheet activities, and an impersonal, authoritarian style that is often disrespectful of learners. This instructional style responds to, and in reciprocal fashion aggravates, the often-identified pattern of resistance to schooling by students in such contexts (Anyon, 1981; Erickson, 1987; Bennett & LeCompte, 1990). This approach to pedagogy teaches students that little is expected of them (except perhaps minimal compliance); they are not highly valued; they cannot be trusted to guide their own learning or conduct themselves responsibly in the classroom; and they must accept low-level positions in a rigidly controlled hierarchy.

The prevailing pattern in higher-status social-class contexts contrasts in predictable ways. Teachers in such schools tend to rely less on transmission modes of teaching (though there is still plenty of it), employ a wider range of approaches to classroom control and discipline, and offer more opportunities for learner control of learning tasks (see Oakes et al., 1992, for a review of studies related to this point). Teachers tend to interact with learners in more personalized and respectful ways. On their part, learners are more outwardly cooperative (Metz, 1990) and accepting of the school's implicit premise (LeCompte & Dworkin, 1988). In ways that are both obvious and subtle, this pedagogical pattern encourages students to develop a greater sense of self-worth, higher expectations for school success, and a wider range of possibilities for fitting into hierarchies of control at different levels.

Though it probably describes much of what teachers and learners experience in schools at all levels, this stark contrast in pedagogy by class contexts masks some complexities and ambiguities. First, though most closely matched with the culture of the school and most likely to be accepting of schooling, learners from middle-class and affluent families are not the only ones who "buy into" the teaching and learning patterns they encounter in the school building. For example, the children of recent immigrant families and refugees, while often positioned in a lower social class, are typically highly responsive to schooling, transmission teaching and all (Bennett & LeCompte, 1990). Second, the learners' experience of lower-track and upper-track pedagogy is more varied than the preceding scenario suggests. In some instances learners do not find the former pedagogy oppressive and may even feel that it facilitates academic learning, while the latter can be highly routinized and skill based (Oakes et al., 1992). The distinctive culture of the school may provide remarkably different meanings to lower-track participation, as in the following summary by Oakes et al. of findings from Metz's (1978) study of two desegregated junior high schools:

In one school, lower-track placement was stigmatizing, exacerbated racial divisions, and provoked uneasy truces or classroom mayhem. At the other school, lessons proceeded and there were more positive relations between and among teachers and students. Worksheets predominated in both schools' lower-track curriculum, but in one context they signified the teachers' distance from and control of students, whereas in the second, they signified the provision of manageable assignments, shelter from public failure, and reassuring routine. (Oakes et al., 1992, p. 588)

Consequences for Learning and Credentialing

Differentiated instruction entails various consequences for learning, and because the different curricula are received by learners with divergent social-class profiles, the net effect is for students of different social classes to absorb, on average, different kinds and amounts of knowledge, or to differ otherwise in learning outcomes. At least the following kinds of effects have been considered in research to date: normative and attitudinal learning, cognitive learning, and credentialing.

Regarding the learning of specific norms and attitudes, the discussion of differentiated instruction has already summarized the principal evidence available. Because normative learning is subtle, subliminal, and pervasive, no large-scale database presents satisfactory evidence for assessing claims in this regard. We must rely on the more closely examined small-scale studies, which suggest, in effect, that divergent norms—ranging from obedience and respect for external authority at the lower end of the social-class hierarchy to independence and individual initiative at the upper end—are communicated and learned by students in their respective class contexts. The evidence also suggests that learners are by no means passive and compliant in this regard; for example, students in lower-track contexts may internalize norms of resistance as much as they come to accept external control. Similarly, most researchers agree that learners form distinctive attitudes about schooling that vary with social-class context, with those in higher-status contexts forming generally more positive attitudes. However, the sources of these attitudes are much in dispute. In all probability, differentiated instruction is only one of a complex of forces both inside and outside the school that contribute to their formation.

Regarding cognitive learning, the predominant bodies of research rely on large-scale quantitative databases in which achievement-test scores are the principal dependent variable (see Hurn, 1993, and Oakes et al., 1992, for reviews of this evidence base). The evidence base is mixed, but on the whole appears to demonstrate that learners in higher-ability groups or track placements gain more than those lower in the school stratification system. Furthermore, considerable evidence indicates that the disparities in cognitive achievement increase with time, suggesting that there are cumulative effects of differentiated instruction.

Regarding persistence in school and the acquisition of credentials, the evidence is relatively consistent and strong: Participation in higher-track programs and experiences increases the likelihood that learners will persist in school and attain higher-status educational credentials (Hurn, 1993; Oakes et al., 1992). It is a reasonable inference, then, that the differentiated instruction available to the learners of different social-class backgrounds contributes in no small measure to these outcomes.

PUTTING THE STORY TOGETHER

This chapter suggests a broad general argument about the nature of the relationship between social class and schooling. In brief, we have argued that social class contributes to an increasingly differentiated pattern of schooling over time, and that this differentiation is one determinant of educational outcomes. Drawing on the alternative perspectives noted at the beginning of the chapter, we review the principal explanations offered to date for this pattern and its consequences. These explanations and the research base on which they rest leave a number of issues for future research to explore, which we suggest at the close of the chapter.

Explanations for the Differentiation of Schooling and Its Consequences

Each of the realms we have examined—the community context, social organization of the student population, the teaching force and the conditions under which it works, the learners as individuals and peer groups, and instruction—appears to contribute to class-related differentiation in the learners' schooling experience. Associated with these experiences are systematic differences in educational outcomes. To what extent can the differentiated pattern and its consequences be attributed to social class? Put another way, is it plausible, theoretically and empirically, that social class exerts an influence on outcomes, and, if so, how does it do so?

Explaining the differentiation of schooling and its consequences is not an easy matter and depends heavily on the analyst's framework. The explanations typically offered combine one or more of the following: (a) the composition and expectations of the communities served by schools; (b) the capabilities and background of the teaching force; (c) the conditions under which teachers work; (d) the nature of the students and their response to schooling; and (e) the explicit intentions of powerful interests inside and outside the school system.

The Nature of Communities Served by the Schools. Communities that differ in social-class profile demand different things of the schools and of their children. Reflecting differences in power and the ability to advocate their interests both individually and collectively, community members express and press their demands more or less effectively. Furthermore, whatever community members actually feel about the school, school personnel tend to perceive the communities' wants differently depending on social-class context. Finally, communities that are higher in social class typically have greater collective resources to offer educational institutions, as well as greater individual resources to enable (private) school choice. As detailed earlier in the chapter, lower- and working-class contexts are less likely to make active and sustained demands for academically challenging instruction; are more likely to expect tight control of instruction and student behavior; are less likely, on average, to encourage high academic achievement, or at least to model the meaning of high academic achievement; are more likely to be perceived as preferring tight control and caring less about academic challenges; and are more likely to perceive the school as a hostile institution (the role of social class in this pattern of hostility is complicated in mixed-race situations).

Social class thus plays a major role in shaping parents' aspirations for their children, parental access to school personnel, ability to bring pressure to bear on the schools, expectations for instructional behavior, perceptions of community demands, and resources for school support or school choice. The more homogeneous in terms of social class one assumes that communities are, the stronger this argument becomes. The more diverse the school community, the more it is likely to send mixed signals and raise for school people the question of which signals to attend.

The Nature and Capabilities of the Teaching Force. A second set of explanations holds that schooling differs by class context and produces different outcomes because different kinds of teachers work in each context. Seen with a functionalist lens, teachers in lower- and working-class contexts are less capable, on average, than those in a higher social-class context. Teachers of talent are drawn to schools serving a higher social-class population by greater rewards, improved working conditions (discussed below), and enhanced prestige that come with higher-status students. Viewed from a critical perspective, the matter is less one of teaching ability and more the match between the teachers' own social-class sensibilities and the individuals they teach. Teachers gravitate (by choice, assignment, or both) to a social-class context in which they feel most at home, or at least are more closely matched with the student population they are teaching. Thus teachers in lower-status schools are more likely to originate from lower- and working-class backgrounds and hence are more likely to be guided by the aspirations and styles typical of individuals from these backgrounds.

Here, social class serves either as a source of prestige to which people of talent are attracted, or as a primary consideration, conscious or unconscious, in the sorting of teachers by social-class context.

Conditions Under Which Teachers Work. From this perspective, differentiated schooling and unequal outcomes reflect variations in the conditions of work (e.g., defined by the resource environment, rewards and incentives, degree of professional autonomy, and collegial culture), which are in part shaped by the social class of communities, students, and teachers. Teachers in lower- and working-class contexts are more likely to experience severe resource constraints, receive fewer rewards for good work, see fewer incentives to work hard, have less autonomy, and work within a professional culture that discourages complex forms of teaching. Hence it is understandable that teachers gravitate to the least demanding forms of teaching (e.g., transmission teaching), and plausible that these forms of teaching should produce lower educational outcomes, on average.

Social class enters into this set of explanations in complex ways, for example, by shaping the availability of resources (for rewards, facilities, or materials), influencing the teachers' assessment of the quality of their work lives, or influencing the formation of a collegial culture within the school.

The Nature of the Students and Their Response to Schooling. This explanation holds that students are increasingly segregated by social class as they move through schools. The social composition of the students in a given ability group, classroom, track, or school shapes perceptions of ability, expectations for success, the education offered to them, and their way of responding to it. In comparison with higher-status contexts, lower- and working-class contexts present teachers with a student population that uses communicative codes different from the teachers', appears to be less capable in a mainstream context, and is arguably more difficult to teach. Such populations include a higher proportion of students with specialized learning needs. Students in such contexts are more likely to manifest active or passive forms of resistance, as discussed earlier in the chapter. Given the typical mismatch in cultural and social-class terms between these students and the school, they are likely to appear deficient and be judged less capable. As a consequence, instruction that demands less and controls more is a natural (default) approach to the teaching task. It is natural, even inevitable, that students who are asked for less will achieve less on conventional measures of educational outcomes.

Here, social class affects instructional outcomes by influencing the way students are perceived, distributing specialized learning needs unequally, encouraging class-based grouping, and encouraging resistance to schooling. This explanation is complicated by the tendency for lower- and working-class contexts to present the teacher with greater ethnic and cultural diversity.

The Intentions of Powerful Interests Inside and Outside the School System. The fifth set of explanations posits a driving force that is external to teachers, students, and the interaction among them. In this view, the mandates, requirements, and other decisions of educational leaders respond to key constituencies for education (e.g., corporate interests) and, in so doing, encourage different curricula to be taught to children with different class origins. From this perspective, lower- and working-class contexts tend to be targeted by corporate interests as a source of unskilled and semiskilled labor; viewed as deficient in basic skills by the educational establishment, hence needing a less challenging curriculum; or viewed as too numerous for, or less deserving of, exposure to the "status culture," which would lose its meaning if too many people acquired it.

Here, social class acts as a marker of appropriateness for particular niches in the social and occupational hierarchy, where appropriateness is judged by those with greater power in society. The argument rests on the demonstration of intentionality on the part of the various powerful interests and the degree of confluence between their interests or desires and educational practices.

Using Different Perspectives to Weigh These Explanations.
The three frameworks presented at the beginning of the chapter combine elements of these five explanations in differing ways, and are more or less convincing in the following respects.

Critical perspectives leave the most room for individual and group construction of the meaning of social-class position; acknowledge power differentials explicitly; explain resistance patterns well; and demonstrate clearly how "class consciousness" might be passed on from parents to children, among peers in school, and to a limited extent by teachers who come from similar social origins. Critical perspectives assert the greatest role for social class in the "subjective" experience of the individual.

Conflict accounts offer the most satisfactory explanations of the unequal power distribution among social groups and the consequences of these power disparities for the kinds of schooling available to members of these groups. Conflict accounts also identify pervasive influences of social class in the schooling process, particularly with regard to sorting, tracking, and streaming. These accounts, however, tend to assume tighter coupling of schooling to societal outcomes and greater, more direct control of schooling by power elites than is warranted by the evidence to date. In addition, conflict accounts do a better job of describing social prospects in the aggregate than at the individual level.

Functional accounts are the weakest of the three in explaining the prevailing patterns of peer interaction, sorting, and instructional differentiation when these are viewed as group phenomena. Functional explanations do a better job of explaining individual mobility across social-class lines at the margins, and incremental shifts in social-group prospects over time. Functional accounts assert that social-class-related forces have the least to do with the processes of schooling itself. Like conflict accounts, functional arguments insist on greater coupling between schooling and society than the existing evidence suggests.

Challenges for Future Research

There are many puzzles left by the existing base of research and theory that should be addressed. The following seem especially important:

1. *The actual mechanisms of social-class influence suggested by the five explanations above have not been adequately documented to date and deserve closer scrutiny.* Such mechanisms are subtle and often unconscious, and are therefore difficult to apprehend. For example, research that closely observes transactions between teacher and student or parent and school personnel has much to offer in this regard, as do studies that probe the beliefs, assumptions, and operating theories of educators and students. Think-aloud research, now popular in cognitive research, might have interesting applications here, as do many forms of ethnographic inquiry. Relying as they must on relatively crude measures of a small number of variables, large-scale quantitative studies are unlikely to be helpful with this kind of investigation.

2. *Questions about the ultimate causal influence of social class are unresolved, and should be investigated further.* The great majority of evidence to date, both qualitative and quantitative, demonstrates an association between social class and nearly every feature of the schooling process. Plausible arguments can be made, and have been suggested in this chapter, that there is some causal direction to these associations, and that they indicate a complex, cumulative pattern of influences on educational outcomes. Nonetheless, plausible alternative arguments can be fashioned that imply little causality, suggesting instead that social-class differentiation is merely a by-product of other causal processes. Though "causation" is a slippery slope in the social sciences, we encourage further attempts to traverse it by, for example, attempts to look longitudinally at relationships between social class and schooling. One might undertake historical research of schools or school districts that have undergone substantial change in the social-class composition of the student population over periods of time that exceeded a single generation of teachers (e.g., 40–50 years). If social class plays a causative role in such instances, one would expect to see changes in instructional and institutional practices designed to "fit" the class-based nature of changes. Other kinds of research, at a more micro level, might investigate the careers of individual teachers to establish that they changed their approach to teaching when confronted with students of differing social-class backgrounds, in ways predicted by the preceding arguments.

3. *Attention should be paid to the deeper meanings of social class and the variability within any particular social class.* Our understandings of the role of social class in educational processes are still too dependent on empirical work relying on crude categorical markers of class identity, which assumes a high degree of constancy of composition or meaning within any particular class category. We know from ethnographic studies that there is more to class than meets the eye, and this needs to be explored. Further research could productively explore the differences among working-class communities or affluent professional communities, as Metz (1990) and her colleagues have done with regard to teachers' relationship to their workplace, to identify and describe the development of distinctive class-based relationships with schooling. Students' class sensibilities probably vary within broad social-class groupings in important ways that are as yet unexplored, reflecting the subtle variations in the meaning of social class in the communities from which they come. Interpretive research aimed at uncovering these meanings could make a significant contribution to current understandings.

4. *Attempts to reconcile the findings of case-based research with larger-sample studies should be continued.* There are significant disjunctures between the findings of small-sample qualitative studies and large-sample quantitative research, with regard to particular aspects of the argument presented in this chapter (for example, research related to the role of social-class background in ability-grouping decisions at the elementary school level). The lack of confirmation may reflect a number of things, from epistemology and measurement to simple rejection of one or another hypothesis. While these matters are not easily resolved (and in a paradigmatic sense, some can never be resolved), we urge that further attempts be made to explore the intersection of case-based studies with large-sample research. Special attention needs to be paid to alternative ways of mea-

suring quantitatively the key variables implied by qualitative studies.

5. *Research and theory should move aggressively to explore the intersections between the existing research base and both feminist views of class and views rooted in race and ethnicity.* The connections among class, race, and gender are numerous and deserve to be more fully explored than they have been to date (an exploration of these connections has not been attempted in this chapter). But the task is greater than merely disentangling highly correlated variables or demonstrating instances in which two or more of these variables form a reinforcing social pattern. The task involves a reconsideration of the meaning of "class," for example, in light of feminist thinking, which approaches class in a way that departs markedly from conventional positional conceptions of stratification systems.

In closing, we urge a touch of humility in the aspirations and claims of those who study social class and schooling. The goal is not to identify simple, powerful relationships between discrete variables, but rather to understand the subtle yet profound roles of a pervasive social condition in the lives of educators and those they educate. In this vein, we find ourselves subscribing to the view argued by Metz (1990) and others that

class positions are not simply determinative of either attitude or action. Every school will have students, teachers, and administrators who bring a somewhat distinctive mix of class (and racial and gender) perspectives to the social life inside a school building. While class is a crucial element in constituting the life of every school, it never determines that life in any simple or complete sense. (p. 99)

References

Anyon, J. (1979). Ideology and United States history textbooks. *Harvard Educational Review, 49*(3), 361–386.

Anyon, J. (1980). Social class and the hidden curriculum of work. *Journal of Education, 162,* 67–92.

Anyon, J. (1981). Social class and school knowledge. *Curriculum Inquiry, 11*(1), 3–42.

Apple, M. (1978). The new sociology of education: Analyzing cultural and economic reproduction. *Harvard Educational Review, 48,* 495–503.

Apple, M. (1980). The other side of the hidden curriculum: Correspondence theories and the labor process. *Journal of Education, 162,* 47–66.

Apple, M. (1986). *Teachers and texts: A political economy of class and gender relations in education.* New York: Methuen.

Ayella, M. E., & Williamson, J. B. (1976) The social mobility of women: A causal model of socioeconomic success. *Sociological Quarterly, 17,* 334–354.

Ballantine, J. H. (1993). *The sociology of education: A systemic analysis* (3rd ed.). Englewood Cliffs, NJ: Prentice-Hall.

Banks, J. A. (1993, April). *What does it mean to integrate race, ethnicity, class, and gender in theory and research?* Paper presented at the annual meeting of the American Education Research Association, Atlanta.

Baratz, S. S., & Baratz, J. C. (1970). Early childhood intervention: The social science base of institutional racism. *Harvard Educational Review, 40,* 29–50.

Bennett, K. P., & LeCompte, M. D. (1990). *The way schools work.* New York: Longman.

Bensman, J., & Vidich, A. J. (1971). *The new American society: The revolution of the middle class.* Chicago: Quadrangle Books.

Bernstein, B. (1970). *Class, codes and control: Vol. I. Theoretical studies towards a sociology of language.* London: Routledge & Kegan Paul.

Bernstein, B. (1977). *Class, codes and control: Vol. III. Towards a theory of educational transmission.* London: Routledge & Kegan Paul.

Betz, M., & Garland, J. (1974). Intergenerational mobility rates of urban school teachers. *Sociology of Education, 47,* 511–522.

Birman, B. F., Orland, M. E., Jung, R., Anson, R. J., Garcia, G. N., Moore, M. T., Funkhauser, J. E., Morrisen, D. R., Turnbull, B. J., & Reisner, E. R. (1987). *The current operation of the Chapter 1 program.* Washington, DC: U.S. Department of Education.

Bloom, B. S., Davis, A., Hess, R. D., & Silverman, S. B. (1965). *Compensatory education for cultural deprivation.* New York: Holt, Rinehart, & Winston.

Boudon, R. (1974). *Education, opportunity and social inequality.* New York: Wiley.

Bourdieu, P., & Passeron, J. (1977). *Reproduction in education, society and culture.* London: Sage.

Bowles, S., & Gintis, H. (1976). *Schooling in capitalist America: Educational reform and the contradictions of economic life.* New York: Basic Books.

Brophy, J. E., & Good, T. L. (1970). Teachers' communication of differential expectations for children's classroom performance: Some behavioral data. *Journal of Educational Psychology, 61,* 365–374.

Chaikin, A. L., Sigler, E., & Derlega, V. J. (1974). Nonverbal mediators of teacher expectancy effects. *Journal of Personality and Social Psychology, 30,* 144–149.

Children's Defense Fund. (1992). *The state of America's children, 1992.* Washington, DC: Author.

Cicourel, A. V., & Kitsuse, J. (1963). *The educational decision makers.* Indianapolis: Bobbs-Merrill.

Cohen, E. G. (1982). Expectation states and interracial interaction in school settings. *Annual Review of Sociology, 8,* 209–235.

Cohen, E. (1986a). *Designing groupwork: Teaching strategies for heterogeneous classrooms.* New York: Teachers College Press.

Cohen, E. (1986b). On the sociology of the classroom. In J. H. Hannaway & M. E. Lockheed (Eds.), *The contributions of the social sciences to educational policy and practice: 1965–1985* (pp. 127–162). Berkeley, CA: McCutchan.

Coleman, J. S. (1990). *Equality and achievement in education.* Denver: Westview Press.

Coleman, J. S., Campbell, E. Q., Hobson, C. J., McPartland, J., Mood, A. M., Weinfeld, F. C., & York, R. L. (1966). *Equality of educational opportunity.* Washington, DC: Government Printing Office.

Collins, R. (1979). *The credential society.* New York: Academic Press.

Comer, J. P. (1988). Educating poor minority children. *Scientific American, 259*(5), 42–48.

Connell, R. W., Ashenden, D. J., Kessler, S., & Dawsett, G. W. (1982). *Making the difference.* Sydney: George Allen & Unwin.

Dahrendorf, R. (1970). Marx's theory of class. In M. Tumin (Ed.), *Readings on social stratification* (pp. 3–16). Englewood Cliffs, NJ: Prentice-Hall.

Daniels-Bierness, T. (1989). Measuring peer status in boys and girls: A problem of apples and oranges? In B. Schneider, G. Attili, J. Nadel, & R. Weissber (Eds.), *Social competence in developmental perspective* (pp. 107–120). The Netherlands: Kluwer Academic Press.

Davis, A. (1951). Socio-economic influences on learning. *Phi Delta Kappan, 32,* 253–256.

Delpit, L. D. (1988). The silenced dialogue: Power and pedagogy in educating other people's children. *Harvard Educational Review, 58,* 280–298.

Erickson, F. (1987). Transformation and school success: The politics and culture of educational achievement. *Anthropology and Education Quarterly, 18,* 335–356.

Findley, W., & Bryan, M. (1975). *The pros and cons of ability grouping.* Washington, DC: National Education Association.

Fordham, S. (1988). Racelessness as a factor in Black students' school success: Pragmatic strategy or phyrric victory? *Harvard Educational Review, 58,* 54–84.

Fordham, S., & Ogbu, J. (1986). Black students' school success: Coping with the burden of acting White. *Urban Review, 18,* 176–206.

Freire, P. (1970). *Pedagogy of the oppressed.* New York: Continuum.

Gardner, H. (1987). The theory of multiple intelligences. *Annual Dyslexia, 37,* 19–35.

Garnier, M., & Raffalovich, L. (1984). The evolution of equality of educational opportunities in France. *Sociology of Education, 57,* 1–10.

Gay, G. (1986). Multi-cultural teacher education. In J. A. Banks & J. Lynch (Eds.), *Multicultural education in Western societies* (pp. 154–177). London: Holt, Rinehart, & Winston.

Gehrke, N., Knapp, M. S., & Sirotnik, K. (1992). In search of the school curriculum. In G. Grant (Ed.), *Review of Research in Education,* (Vol. 18, pp. 51–110). Washington, DC: American Educational Research Association.

Goldstein, B. (1967). *Low-income youth in urban areas: A critical review of the literature.* New York: Holt, Rinehart, & Winston.

Goodlad, J., & Oakes, J. (1988). We must offer equal access to knowledge. *Educational Leadership, 45,* 16–22.

Gramsci, A. (1971). *Selections from the prison notebooks.* New York: International.

Haggard, E. A. (1954). Social status and intelligence. *Genetic Psychology Monographs, 49,* 141–186.

Haller, E. J., & Davis, S. A. (1981). Teacher perceptions, parental social status, and grouping for reading instruction. *Sociology of Education, 54,* 162–173.

Halsey, A. H., Heath, A. F., & Ridge, J. M. (1980). *Origins and destinations: Family, class, and education in modern Britain.* Oxford: Clarendon Press.

Hargreaves, A. (1988). Teaching quality: A sociological analysis. *Journal of Curriculum Studies, 20*(3), 211–231.

Haviland, W. A. (1990). *Cultural anthropology.* Fort Worth, TX: Holt, Rinehart, & Winston.

Heath, S. B. (1983). *Ways with words: Language, life, and work in communities and classrooms.* Cambridge, England: Cambridge University Press.

Heber, R. (1979). Sociocultural mental retardation—A longitudinal study. Paper cited in T. F. Hoult (1979), *Sociology for a new day* (2nd ed.). New York: Random House.

Hemmings, A. E., & Metz, M. H. (1990). Real teaching: How high school teachers negotiate societal, local community, and student pressures when they define their work. In R. Page & L. Valli (Eds.), *Curriculum differentiation: Interpretive studies in U.S. secondary schools* (pp. 91–112). Albany: State University of New York Press.

Heyns, B. (1978). Social selection and stratification within schools. *American Journal of Sociology, 79,* 1434–1451.

Hunter, A. (1975). The loss of community: An empirical test through replication. *American Sociological Review, 40,* 537–552.

Hurn, C. (1993). *The limits and possibilities of schooling* (3rd ed.). Boston: Allyn and Bacon.

Hymel, S. (1986). Interpretations of peer behavior: Affective bias in childhood and adolescence. *Child Development, 57,* 431–445.

Jencks, C. (1972). *Inequality: A reassessment of the effect of family and schooling in America.* New York: Basic Books.

Kahl, J. H. (1953). Educational and occupational aspirations of "common man" boys. *Harvard Educational Review, 53,* 186–203.

Kantor, H., & Brenzel, B. (1992). Urban education and the "truly disadvantaged": The historical roots of the contemporary crisis, 1945–1990. *Teachers' College Record, 42,* 521–562.

Karabel, J. (1972). Community colleges and social stratification: Submerged class conflict in American higher education. *Harvard Educational Review, 42,* 521–562.

Kariger, R. B. (1962). The relationship of lane grouping to the socioeconomic status of parents of seventh-grade pupils in three junior high schools (Doctoral dissertation, Michigan State University). *Dissertation Abstracts, 23,* 4586.

Knapp, M. S., & Shields, P. (1990). Reconceiving academic instruction for the children of poverty. *Phi Delta Kappan, 71*(10), 752–758.

Knapp, M. S., & Shields, P. (1991). *Better schooling for the children of poverty.* Berkeley, CA: McCutchan.

Kozol, J. (1991). *Savage inequalities: Children in America's schools.* New Haven, CT: Yale University Press.

LeCompte, M. D., & Dworkin, A. G. (1988). Educational programs: Indirect linkages and unfulfilled expectations. In H. R. Rodgers, Jr. (Ed.), *Beyond welfare: New approaches to the problem of poverty in America* (pp. 135–167). Armonk, NY: M. E. Sharpe.

Levin, H. M. (1988). Accelerating elementary education for disadvantaged students. In Council of Chief State School Officers (Ed.), *School success for students at risk* (pp. 209–226). Orlando, FL: Harcourt Brace Jovanovich.

Lewis, O. (1966). The culture of poverty. *Scientific American, 215,* 19–25.

Louis, K. S. (1990). Social and community values and the quality of teacher work life. In M. W. McLaughlin, J. E. Talbert, & N. Bascia (Eds.), *The context of teaching in secondary schools: Teachers' realities* (pp. 17–39). New York: Teachers College Press.

Mackler, B. (1969). Grouping in the ghetto. *Education and Urban Society, 2,* 80–96.

Matthews, J. (1988). *Jaime Escalante: The best teacher in America.* New York: Holt.

Mayeske, G. W., Wisler, D. E., Beaton, A. E., Weinfeld, F. D., Cohen, W. M., Okada, T., Proshed, J. M., & Tabler, K. A. (1972). *A study of our nation's schools.* Washington, DC: Government Printing Office.

McDermott, R. (1987). Achieving school failure: An anthropological approach to illiteracy and social stratification. In G. Spindler (Ed.), *Education and cultural process* (2nd ed., pp. 173–209). Prospect Heights, IL: Waveland Press.

McLaren, P. (1989). *Life in schools.* New York: Longman.

McLaughlin, M. W., Talbert, J. E., & Bascia, N. (Eds.). (1990). *The context of teaching in secondary schools: Teachers' realities.* New York: Teachers College Press.

Means, B., Chelemer, C., & Knapp, M. S. (1991). *Teaching advanced skills to at-risk students.* San Francisco: Jossey-Bass.

Metz, M. H. (1978). *Classrooms and corridors: The crisis of authority in desegregated secondary schools.* Berkeley: University of California Press.

Metz, M. H. (1990). How social class differences shape teachers' work. In M. W. McLaughlin, J. E. Talbert, & N. Bascia (Eds.), *The context of teaching in secondary schools: Teachers' realities* (pp. 40–107). New York: Teachers College Press.

Meyer, J. W. (1977). The effects of education as an institution. *American Journal of Sociology, 83,* 55–77.

Murray, W. (1960). Some major assumptions underlying the development of intelligence tests. Unpublished paper cited in F. Reissman (1962), *The culturally deprived child.* New York: Harper & Brothers.

National Commission on Children. (1991). *Speaking of kids: A national survey of children and parents.* Washington, DC: Author.

Natriello, G., McDill, E. L., & Pallas, A. M. (1990). *Schooling disadvantaged children: Racing against catastrophe.* New York: Teachers College Press.

Nelson, C. M., Rutherford, R. B., Center, D., & Walker, H. (1991). Do public schools have an obligation to serve troubled children and youth? *Exceptional Children, 57*(5), 406–415.

Nelson-Barber, S., & Meier, T. (1990, Spring). Multicultural context: A key factor in teaching. *Academic Connections,* 1–9. Princeton, NJ: College Entrance Examination Board.

Neufeld, B. (1991). Classroom management and instructional strategies for the disadvantaged learner: Some thoughts about the nature of the problem. In M. S. Knapp & P. M. Shields (Eds.), *Better schooling for the children of poverty: Alternatives to conventional wisdom* (pp. 257–272). Berkeley, CA: McCutchan.

Oakes, J. (1985). *Keeping track: How schools structure inequality.* New Haven, CT: Yale University Press.

Oakes, J. (1990). *Multiplying inequalities: The effects of race, social class and teaching.* Santa Monica, CA: Rand.

Oakes, J., Gamoran, A., & Page, R. N. (1992). Curriculum differences: Opportunities, outcomes, and meanings. In P. Jackson (Ed.), *Handbook of research on curriculum* (pp. 570–608). New York: Macmillan.

Ogbu, J. (1979). Social stratification and the socialization of competence. *Anthropology & Education Quarterly, 10*(1), 3–20.

Page, R. N. (1991). *Lower-track classrooms: A curricular and cultural perspective.* New York: Teachers College Press.

Persell, C. H. (1977). *Education and inequality: The roots and results of stratification in America's schools.* New York: Free Press.

Persell, C. H. (1993). Social class and educational equality. In J. Banks and C. A. McGee Banks (Eds.), *Multicultural education: Issues and perspectives* (2nd ed., pp. 71–89). Boston: Allyn and Bacon.

Rafferty, Y., & Shinn, M. (1991). The impact of homelessness on children. *American Psychologist, 46,* 1170–1179.

Reissman, F. (1962). *The culturally deprived child.* New York: Harper & Brothers.

Rist, R. C. (1970). Student social class and teacher expectations: The self-fulfilling prophecy in ghetto education. *Harvard Educational Review, 40,* 411–451.

Rist, R. C. (1977). On understanding the processes of schooling: The contributions of labeling theory. In J. Karabel & A. H. Halsey (Eds.), *Power and ideology in education* (pp. 292–305). New York: Oxford University Press.

Rosenfeld, R. A. (1980). Race and sex differences in career dynamics. *American Sociological Review, 45,* 583–609.

Rosenholtz, S., & Rosenholtz, S. (1981). Classroom organization and the perception of ability. *Sociology of Education, 54,* 134–140.

Sadker, M., Sadker, D., & Long, L. (1993). Gender and educational equality. In J. A. Banks & C. A. McGee Banks (Eds.), *Multicultural education: Issues and perspectives* (2nd ed., pp. 71–89). Boston: Allyn and Bacon.

Schorr, L. B. (1988). *Within our reach: Breaking the cycle of disadvantage.* New York: Doubleday.

Sewell, W. H., & Hauser, R. M. (1976). Causes and consequences of higher education: Modes of the attainment process. In W. H. Sewell, R. M. Hauser, & D. L. Featherman (Eds.), *Schooling and achievement in American society* (pp. 9–28). New York: Academic Press.

Sewell, W. H., & Shaw, V. P. (1967). Socioeconomic status, intelligence, and the attainment of higher education. *Sociology of Education, 40,* 1–23.

Sleeter, C. (1991). Learning disabilities: The social construction of a category. In S. Sigmon (Ed.), *Critical voices on special education: Problems and progress concerning the mildly handicapped* (pp. 21–34). Albany: State University of New York Press.

Sleeter, C., & Grant, C. (1991). Race, class, gender, and disability in current textbooks. In M. Apple & L. K. Christian-Smith (Eds.), *The politics of the textbook* (pp. 78–110). London: Routledge & Kegan Paul.

Solomon, R. P. (1992). *Black resistance in high school.* Albany: State University of New York Press.

Thurow, L. C. (1972, Summer). Education and economic equality. *Public Interest, 72,* 66–81.

Tobias, S. (1979). Anxiety research in educational psychology. *Journal of Educational Psychology, 71,* 573–582.

Weber, M. (1946). *From Max Weber: Essays in sociology.* New York: Oxford University Press.

Weiler, K. (1988). *Women teaching for change: Gender, class, and power.* New York: Bergin & Garvey.

Weiner, B. (1985). An attributional theory of achievement motivation and emotion. *Psychological Review, 92,* 548–573.

Wilcox, K. (1982). Differential socialization in the classroom: Implications for equal opportunity. In G. Spindler (Ed.), *Doing the ethnography of schooling: Educational anthropology in action* (pp. 268–309). New York: Holt, Rinehart, & Winston.

Wright, E. O., & Perrone, L. (1977). Marxist class categories and income inequality. *American Sociological Review, 42,* 32–55.

Zeichner, K. M., & Gere, J. M. (1990). Teacher socialization. In W. R. Houston (Ed.), *Handbook of research on teacher education* (pp. 329–348). New York: Macmillan.

31

AFRICAN AMERICAN TEACHERS AND CULTURALLY RELEVANT PEDAGOGY

Michele Foster

CLAREMONT GRADUATE SCHOOL

In the 1950 Inglis Lecture delivered at Harvard University, Margaret Mead noted:

Teachers who are members of any group who are in a minority in their particular community will have to add . . . in their own words that they are Negro teachers . . . as the case may be, redefining themselves against an image of a woman who for most of the country is white, middle-class, middle-aged and of Protestant background. (Mead, 1950, p. 6)

This lecture delivered more than 40 years ago succintly captures the situation of African American teachers in the research literature, where for the most part they are not well represented despite the fact that, for the first six decades of this century, teaching was one of the few occupations open to college-educated African Americans.

Although there is little information about African American teachers in the early centuries of the United States, according to the Philadelphia directory of 1795, which listed the occupations of 104 free African Americans, 4 among the 83 men and 22 women listed were teachers. Among these teachers was an African-born schoolmistress named Eleanor Harris, who was hired by the Society of Friends in 1793 to teach African American children in a school on Cherry Street in Philadelphia, where she taught until her death four years later (Nash, 1988). By 1799 at least two other African American teachers were conducting schools for African American children under the auspices of the Philadelphia Society for the Abolition of Slavery, but they were dismissed when an inspecting committee decided they were too indulgent with the children. After deciding that "it is not practical at present that black children be properly taught by a black person," the Philadelphia Society for the Abolition of Slavery withdrew its support from three schools staffed by African American teachers and opened another conducted by White teachers (Nash, 1988, p. 204).

Throughout the 19th century, largely as the result of activism in the African American community, the number of African American teachers increased steadily. Several factors—heightened self-esteem, racial pride and solidarity, an increase in the number of trained African American teachers, and an increasing dissatisfaction with the qualifications of White teachers assigned to Black schools—coalesced, encouraging Blacks to press for Black teachers. As early as 1827, dissatisfied with the White teachers placed in their children's school, New York Blacks complained:

We are skeptical, that we cannot believe that almost anyone is qualified to keep a school for our children. Enemies may declaim upon their dullness and stupidity; but we would respectfully inquire, have they not had dull and stupid instructors; who if placed in any other than a colored school, would hardly be considered as earning their salt. (Curry, 1981, p. 169)

In some cities, such as Boston, African Americans were split over whether to pursue desegregated schools or to opt for segregated schools with all African American teachers ("Segregated Education," 1951/1990; Horton & Horton, 1979; Tyack, 1974). Faced with intransigent school boards, African Americans frequently chose to fight for African American teachers. In 1877, 50 years after the African American residents of New York complained about the White teachers assigned to their schools, members of the St. Louis African American community, decrying the quality of Whites teaching in Black schools and protesting the fact that Whites frequently were hired over more qualified African American candidates, lobbied the school board, demanding that only African American teachers be employed in African American schools. In some cases securing African American teachers became a political cause taken up by national organizations. In 1879, only two years after Blacks in St. Louis won their battle for African American teachers, Frederick Barnett addressed the issue at the National Convention of Colored Men in Nashville:

White teachers in colored schools are nearly always mentally, morally, or financially bankrupt, and no colored community should tolerate the imposition. High schools and colleges are sending learned colored teachers in the field constantly, and it is manifestly unjust to make them stand idle and see their people taught by those whose only interest lies in securing their monthly compensation in dollars and cents. Again, colored schools thrive better under colored teachers. The St. Louis schools furnish an excellent example. (Painter, 1976, p. 49)

Other communities, having fought for and been refused access to desegregated schools, and encouraged by the success in St. Louis, decided to change their tactics. Instead of seeking desegregated schools, they petitioned that only Black teachers be assigned to Black schools. African Americans in San Antonio, New Orleans, Lexington, and Nashville met little resistance and succeeded in having such resolutions adopted (Painter, 1976).

As the number of Black teachers increased through the 19th and 20th centuries, so did the percentage of African American women teachers. In 1890 African American females comprised slightly more than half of all African American teachers in the United States. Twenty years later more than two thirds of all African American teachers were females (Lerner, 1972; Collier-Thomas, 1982). According to the 1920 census, 22,528 African American women were working as teachers (Bowles, 1923). Forty years later, six years after the Supreme Court's 1954 *Brown v. Board of Education of Topeka* decision, 84% of all Black elementary school teachers and 84% of all African American secondary teachers were female.

The results of the movement to secure African American teachers were mixed. Although the number of African American teachers grew dramatically through the 19th century, in most instances African Americans became the victims of their success. Indeed, by the end of the 19th century a number of school boards were arguing that providing jobs for African American teachers was the principal reason for maintaining and expanding schools for African American children (Franklin, 1979; Tyack, 1974).

African American teachers, especially women, have not only distinguished themselves professionally, but through their participation in the self-help efforts of African American religious denominations, social clubs, civic associations, and other organizations have contributed to the development of the African American community as well (Collier-Thomas, 1982). Some of these African American educators are historically significant. The names of educators such as Mary McLeod Bethune, founder of the Daytona Educational and Industrial Training School, later Bethune-Cookman College; Fanny Coppin Jackson, principal of the Philadelphia Institute for Colored Youth, subsequently Cheney College; Charlotte Hawkins Brown, founder of the Palmer Memorial Institute; and Lucy Laney, founder of the Haines Normal and Industrial School in Augusta, Georgia, are more familiar than those of other educators who also made substantial contributions to African American education. Also historically significant though less well known are Maria Baldwin, Maria

Becraft, Mattie Booth, Cornelia Bowen, Jennie Deane, Sarah Dicket, Mary Peake, and Georgia Washington, all of whom played major roles in creating the educational infrastructure of the African American community (Collier-Thomas, 1982). Countless other African American teachers are not to be found in history texts. Fortunately, some of them, like Kathleen Redding Adams, Alice Allison Dunnigan, Frances Olivia Grant, Julia Hamilton Smith, Bazoline Estelle Usher, and Addie Luck Williams, have had their experiences recorded in oral history collections (Hill, 1991).

In 1950 half of the African American professionals employed in the United States were teachers; by 1977, of the 58,515 bachelor's degrees earned by African Americans, only 22%, or 12,922, were in education (Cole, 1986). Wider career opportunities that emerged in the late 1960s and early 1970s, the most commonly cited reason for the decline in number of teachers of color, have taken their toll on the number of minorities who choose to enter the teaching profession. By 1983 only 9%, or 5,456, of the bachelor's degrees earned by African Americans were in education (Stern, 1988).

This chapter presents an overview of the research on African American teachers. Three categories of research are addressed in this review. First is the large body of literature written by policy analysts. A second body of literature reviewed consists of first-person narratives. A final body of literature is sociological and anthropological.

POLICY RESEARCH

In response to the declining numbers of African American teachers that characterized the 1980s and were predicted into the 21st century, many policy analysts focused solely on the declining numbers, while others examined the reasons for the current and projected shortages (Graham, 1987; Irvine, 1988; Murnane & Schwinder, 1988; Perkins, 1989).

Even historically Black colleges located in the southern and border states, which over the years had prepared the majority of African American teachers, experienced a marked decrease in the number of students studying education. Nationwide in 1974, historically Black institutions graduated 9,051 teachers, compared with only 4,027 seven years later (Cole & Horton, 1984). Although comprehensive data are not available for all historically Black colleges, the literature demonstrates the severity of the decline. In 1963 Florida A&M graduated 300 education majors; in 1985 it enrolled fewer than 100. Two historically Black institutions in Louisiana awarded 33% and 41% of their degrees in education in 1976 and 1977, respectively, whereas in 1982 and 1983, respectively, only 11% and 14% of the degrees awarded were in education (Irvine, 1988). Norfolk State University graduated 69 special education teachers, 42 early childhood education teachers, and 18 English education majors in 1975; in 1983 Norfolk awarded only 22, 18, and 2 degrees, respectively, in each of these fields (Witty, 1984).

Other literature from the policy arena examined the effect of increased teacher testing—at both entry and exit stages—on the number of candidates who qualified to enter the teaching ranks. Although 85% of all candidates who took the Florida

Teacher Exam in 1980 passed, the pass rate for African American candidates was only 35–40% (Dupre, 1986). The 1980 failure rate for African American teacher candidates in North Carolina was even greater; 87% of African Americans who sat for the test failed, compared with only 17% for Whites. Results such as these prompted one researcher to predict that, given these statistics, North Carolina would soon have a teaching force that is 96% White (Hilliard, 1980).

According to this literature, these statistics were exacerbated because qualifying tests were required not only for certification, but in many states were required of candidates seeking admission into teacher-training programs. A required score of 835 on the Scholastic Aptitude Test (SAT) reduced Florida's entire candidate pool by 25%; this cutoff score reduced by 90% the number of African American candidates who were eligible to matriculate into teacher-training programs (Bray, 1984). Of 6,644 minority candidates who sat for exams given to prospective teacher candidates in California in 1983, 58% failed. Angios passed at a rate of 76%, with 18,856 of 24,540 candidates qualifying for admission into teacher-education programs. African Americans had the highest failure rate, with only 530, or 26% of 2,040 candidates, passing (Gifford, 1986). The literature revealed comparable statistics for a number of other states, including Alabama, Texas, Pennsylvania, Georgia, Oklahoma, and Louisiana (Collins, 1989; Irvine, 1988; Gifford, 1986; Bray, 1984).

A second fact directly influencing the number of African American teachers, but addressed with far less frequency in the research literature, is the smaller number of African American students enrolling in and completing college. For instance, although African Americans comprise 13% of all 18- to 24-year-olds, they represent only 9.6% of those enrolled in college. Half of all African American high school graduates enrolled in college in 1977, but by 1982 that figure had fallen to 36%. Of African Americans who do go to college, 42% attend two-year colleges; of these, only 25% matriculate and graduate from four-year colleges (Irvine, 1988).

Given the complex and interactive nature of causes of this dropoff, it is impossible to try to account for the extent to which each of these factors is individually responsible for the declining numbers of African American teachers. While instructive, few of these analyses adequately considered the negative effect that school desegregation had on African-American teachers, who were disproportionately affected by court-ordered desegregation. An immediate consequence of desegregation was that between the 1954 *Brown v. Board of Education* decision and the early 1970s, approximately 31,584 African American teachers lost their jobs in 17 southern and border states (Ethridge, 1979). African American teachers in Kentucky declined by 41 during the 10 years between 1955 and 1965, even though an additional 401 would have needed to be hired merely to keep pace with the increasing number of pupils. Moreover, a study of 467 southern school districts revealed that 127 of them had dismissed 462 African American teachers, so that by 1970 the African American teacher-to-student ratio in the South was over twice that of the White teacher-to-student ratio (Stewart, Meier, & England, 1989). Negative evaluations resulted in dismissal for many. In some cases African American teachers were demoted

or stripped of their responsibilities. In other situations, the most competent African American teachers were reassigned to White schools ("Blacks Losing Teaching Jobs," 1970). Historically, because of dual school systems, African American teachers were less severely underrepresented in southern than in northern states. The permanence of the aftereffect is not surprising, for African American teachers have been in greater demand in dual school systems than they have been in unitary school systems (Tyack, 1974).

The policy literature of the 1980s was not the first to note the absence of African American teachers. Analyses similar to those written in the 1980s can be found in the policy writings of the 1930s, which was a period when the number of African American teachers was insufficient compared to the number of African American students enrolled in school (Bond, 1934).

In a 1987 policy statement entitled *Minority Teacher Recruitment and Retention: A Call to Action,* the American Association of Colleges for Teacher Education (AACTE) drafted a set of policy initiatives designed to reverse the declining numbers of teachers of color. While not specifying programmatic details, the AACTE did broadly sketch several approaches to ameliorating the problem. Some of the recommendations included the creation of national as well as state scholarship programs; high school and college work-study programs; two-year/four-year college articulation programs; assistantship and grant programs; early incentive programs; support programs for reentry and career change; teacher induction programs; and assessment demonstration grant programs (AACTE, 1987).

The literature reveals that a number of programs have been developed to recruit African American candidates into teacher education. Programs are of two types—precollege and postsecondary—depending on the educational level of the population they serve. Future Teachers of America clubs, reminiscent of clubs of the same name of the 1940s, 1950s, and 1960s, and magnet and theme high schools that focus on teaching careers are examples of precollege programs (Foster, 1990). Loan-forgiveness programs, college courses that deal with schooling issues and/or require students to tutor individual or small groups of students, test-preparation programs, and articulated transfer agreements between community colleges and universities are examples of postsecondary programs. Because the programs are relatively new, little data are available by which to evaluate them. Thus it is too early to determine whether these programs will stay and perhaps eventually reverse the declining numbers of African American teachers. While adaptation to local needs and contexts leads to program differentiation, the interventions undertaken share two common elements. Each has at least one person who is directly responsible for implementing and overseeing the program, and each program depends on collaborative efforts within and between institutions (Foster, 1990).

FIRST-PERSON NARRATIVES

Despite countless examples of first-person teacher narratives, many of which were written by socially conscious teacher-activists during the 1960s, the experiences of African American teachers are not well represented in this genre (Decker, 1969; Haskins, 1971; Herndon, 1968; Kozol, 1968; Kohl, 1967). One author who reviewed 65 first-person narratives written in this century found only 5 written by African American teachers (Foster, 1990). In part this void exists because many of the autobiographies by African American women published from the turn of the century through the late 1950s and early 1960s are no longer in print. An examination of these out-of-print autobiographies reveals that many were written by African American women born in the early part of the 20th century who were employed as schoolteachers (Adams, 1956; Anderson, 1956; Barlow, 1959; Broughton, 1907; Browne, 1969; Clark, 1962; Coppin, 1913; Dunningham, 1974; Fields with Fields, 1985; Guadet, 1913; Hedgeman, 1964; Hicks, 1959; Morton, 1965; Robinson, 1978; Terrell, 1940; Williams, 1961; Young, 1929).

While part of the autobiographies deal with their lives as schoolteachers, these experiences are embedded in a larger account of their lives. These autobiographies provide a revealing glimpse of African American teachers. Two descriptions are offered by Mamie Fields and Septima Clark, two Charleston schoolteachers. In *Lemon Swamp: A Carolina Memoir,* Fields (with Fields, 1985) portrays Aunt Eliza, affectionately called "Lala," a teacher who had been trained at Avery Institute, a Charleston normal school founded after the Civil War by the American Missionary Association, that trained many African American teachers who taught in the South Carolina low country:

She [Lala] gave us a very good basis in spelling, arithmetic, and especially geography, which she loved. Her geography lessons made us feel we were going all around the world. We knew what rivers we would cross, where and when we would have to go over the mountains, what cities we would find. Sometimes we would find the places on the maps or on the globe and then look at the pictures in the *National Geographic.* Geography wasn't boring with her, as it is with some teachers. Lala made it easy for us to learn even the difficult foreign names by using songs and rhythm. The same in arithmetic. We learned the times-tables with songs. And I can remember her teaching us the Roman numerals by a song and hand-claps: "One-i-*one*, two-i-*two*, three-i-*three*, four i-*vee*-four," right on up to "M one thous*and*!" (p. 42)

Later in her memoirs Fields describes how Lala circumvented the Charleston custom that placed the Battery, the peninsula overlooking the harbor, off limits to African Americans.

But just the same, my teacher found a way to let the children enjoy it.... Of course, we couldn't go in. But Lala knew how to tell a story. We learned about pirates sailing in and out of the tidal creeks with "contraband" (a word Lala taught us), the one-eyed captain with the bandanna who shot cannon from his ship, the squint-eyed captain who took out of Wadmalaw Creek with his sails on fire. Oh, Lala could make it very realistic, but she would be teaching at the same time: "'Contraband,' c-o-n-t-r-a, now who can spell 'band'?" Lala would keep on walking and talking and teaching; "Many pirates smuggled contraband, but some would kidnap you." It turned out that the red-eyed pirate snatched a certain rich young man and kept him until his father paid for him in solid gold. (p. 53)

In her autobiography *Echo in My Soul,* Septima Clark (1962) characterizes the pedagogical approach of her unnamed primary school teacher, also an Averyite:

Although she was a strict disciplinarian, I greatly admired the woman who operated our school. I suspect that my admiration for her influenced in some way at least my early ambition to be a teacher.... She had great pride and demanded that her children, her school pupils, have pride too...she had a rather unusual but very effective way for teaching spelling. If you missed a word, she would bring you up to the front of the room and whip each letter into the palm of your hand. Pity the poor youngster who missed *Constantinople.* But I remember her as a great deal more effective than some modern ones extolled by highly trained educators. (pp. 18–19)

These positive portraits of African American teachers contrast sharply with other characterizations of African American teachers (Conroy, 1972; Rist, 1970, 1973) that were written at a time when segregated Black urban and rural schools with all of the liabilities, including African American teachers, came under sharp attack from the White community. Thus, given the era during which these texts were written, the negative portrayals of African American teachers are perhaps understandable. But this excessively negative depiction does not correspond to the delineation of African American teachers embedded in essays, narratives, and sociological studies written by and from the point of view of African Americans. Though largely anecdotal, these accounts portray African American teachers as individuals who not only forged productive relationships with their African American students but, by encouraging many of them to succeed, challenged the status quo (Cohen, 1991; Reed, 1990; Blauner, 1989; Monroe & Goldman, 1988; Anson, 1987; Baker, 1987; Fields with Fields, 1985; Kluger, 1975; Murray, 1970; Clark, 1962).

Consider the characterization of Mamie Williams in *Simple Justice* (Kluger, 1975), a salient work on *Brown v. Board of Education.* In describing the teachers who worked in the all-Black school of Topeka, Kansas, the author provides the following description:

Mamie Williams became a master teacher. A forceful taskmaster and disciplinarian, she was no ogre. Her classroom was never a place for rote learning, and she readily acknowledged that "children with their sincerity and candor can teach adults something new every day." She was a great one for mottos. One of her favorites: "Life is infinitely rich in fine and adequate compensations. Never a door is shut but several windows are opened." Mamie Williams was a window-opener. She designed special projects of the kind she had heard about at Columbia. One of the most popular was a communal lesson in self-government: the whole school was organized like a state, with a constitution, by-laws, officers, and a legislative council. There were campaign speeches and elections, rousing inauguration ceremonies, and regular legislative reports to be filed and posted on the bulletin board in every classroom. And she organized a "Little Theatre" project for which her pupils dramatized stories they had read together in class. One time, she turned her classroom into an art gallery; those who liked to draw contributed their works, the others brought in what they liked from magazines or other sources, and everyone was excited and stimulated and learned how widely human notions of beauty can vary. (p. 378)

SOCIOLOGICAL AND ANTHROPOLOGICAL LITERATURE

The third section of this chapter draws on several bodies of literature, but concentrates primarily on the work of a small number of scholars, many but not all African American, whose work employs the qualitative methodology of sociology, anthropology, sociolinguistics, and the ethnography of speaking, and takes the cultural and social aspects of the Black community and its integrity as a starting point. For the most part, this research rejects the dominant psychological paradigm in educational research because of its overreliance on normative characteristics—individually valued personality, behavioral and cognitive traits—and its failure to consider the collective meaning systems that characterize different cultural groups. In so doing, it seeks to counter the excessively negative portrayal of Black teachers by researchers who, with few exceptions (Lerner, 1972; Sterling, 1972; Lightfoot, 1973, 1978), have characterized African American teachers in decidedly unfavorable ways, a point discussed earlier.

The majority of the literature reviewed in this section was written after the mid-1960s. My choice of this particular period has been influenced by two factors. First, prior to the mid-1960s, the majority of African-American teachers were concentrated in schools that were, de facto or de jure, segregated. Therefore, as noted above, most of the literature about African Americans prior to this time concerns desegregation, with a particular focus on African American students rather than teachers. The second condition influencing my decision to focus on the period is that 1966 is the first year that the Educational Resources Information Center (ERIC) database became available.

We must consider a number of limitations and problems evident in the database itself that limit the review that follows. When one examines the database on African American teachers, it becomes clear that most of the research concerns their relationship to the larger social order. Indeed, while the research literature prior to the 1960s concerns the need to desegregate the schools, the research literature of the 1980s deals almost entirely with the declining numbers of African American teachers and offers various analyses of the causes of this decline. Some of the literature of this more recent period stresses the need to increase the number of African American teachers. The justification advanced most often is a role-model argument, rather than an analysis of any unique characteristics, pedagogy, or philosophy of education believed to be possessed by African American teachers who work primarily with African American students (Foster, 1994).

Another limitation of the research base on teachers has been that, except for issues of access, its analyses do not adequately consider the influence of ethnic background. Research on teachers, though extensive, has generally failed to highlight the practice of African American teachers (Foster, 1994). This is true for the various bodies of literature, including the research on effective teachers, as well as the anthropological, sociological, and first-person literature on teaching (Foster).

Research on Effective Teaching. A substantial body of literature on effective and successful teachers exists in the ERIC database. Nonetheless, despite more than 4,500 and 7,018 entries on effective teachers in 1983 and 1991, respectively, as well as 5,887 on African American teachers in 1991, there are no records in the database that include both the descriptors effective or successful and African American. Neither does the literature on effective teaching contained in the ERIC database link the descriptors effective teachers with teacher characteristics. Thus, though the literature on effective teachers is quite large, it does not differentiate between Anglo teachers and teachers of color, particularly African American teachers. The literature reviewed in this section concentrates on those studies that explicitly link teachers' racial and ethnic identity and background with effective practice.

Research on Teacher Thinking. Most of the studies of teacher thinking, including the more recent "wisdom of practice" studies (Shulman, 1987), do not consider the influence of the racial identity of teachers on their belief systems. This is so despite the fact that the previous life experience of teachers—their backgrounds, identities, cultures, and the critical incidents in their lives—help shape their view of teaching as well as essential elements of their practice (Goodson, 1988). Though limited, research comparing the views of African American teachers with those of majority-group teachers has concluded that these groups differ in their job satisfaction patterns; their perception of the status of the profession and of the school environment; and the changes each group believes are required in order to educate African American students effectively (Provenzo, 1988; Metropolitan Life Insurance Company, 1988). Some of the literature on teacher thinking has also found differences between the beliefs of preservice Anglo teachers and those held by candidates of color (Murrell, 1991).

Sociological and Anthropological Literature. The sociological and anthropological literature on teaching is substantial. In large measure, however, this literature—like that on teacher thinking and the wisdom of practice studies—has failed to include African American teachers, or to view African American teachers in a favorable light. As mentioned earlier, except for the few balanced portrayals of Black teachers (Casey, 1993; Lightfoot, 1973, 1978; Sterling, 1972; Lerner, 1972), this literature has characterized African American teachers as insensitive, authoritarian individuals, upholders of the status quo who are ill suited to teaching African American students effectively (Rist, 1970, 1973; Conroy, 1972; Spencer, 1986). Positive portrayals of African American teachers are infrequent, especially when compared with those of White teachers. As a result researchers have, perhaps unwittingly through omission, distortion, and excessively negative portrayals, conveyed the idea that African American teachers are indifferent, uncaring, and unsympathetic.

A few of the studies analyzed in this section specifically target African American teachers whose students have shown significant gains in achievement as measured by test scores. However, the scholarship of other researchers on effective African American teachers is included because they argue rather convincingly that such narrow criteria obscure the search for effective African American teachers, especially since their practice is often concerned with aspects of education broader than achievement. Most of these researchers have used some version of "community nomination" (Foster, 1987, 1989a, 1990, 1991a, 1991b, 1992, 1993). Community nomination, a method of selection and a term coined by Foster (1990), is specifically designed to capture what anthropologists call an "emic," an insider's perspective. In this case, the emic is the Black community's perspective on an effective teacher. Informants are secured through direct contact with African American communities. African American periodicals, churches, organizations, and individuals—parents, students, principals—provide the names of the teachers.

These limitations notwithstanding, there is a small body of literature on African American teachers that will be discussed in detail and then used as a conceptual framework from which key factors will be derived. The critical and overriding factor that characterizes effective African American teachers is their reliance on the cultural and social underpinnings of the Black community.

Cultural Solidarity

Similar background does not guarantee productive, fluid, or uncomplicated relationships between teacher and student. Teachers of similar background will sometimes judge students more harshly because they remind them of their former selves. Cazden (1976, 1988) has argued conversely that some of the most effective schooling occurs in settings—Amish schools, Black Muslim schools, Catholic schools, Jewish shtetels—where cultural solidarity and power are combined.

When students and teachers share a common cultural background and are able to engage in productive interactions, it is possible that they might develop attachments to education that they otherwise might not. This sense of cultural solidarity can be implicit and unspoken, accepted as given because teachers are recognized members of the particular reference group. Or the cultural solidarity may be explicit and continuously reinforced in classroom interactions, a point discussed later in this chapter.

Researchers who have examined the beliefs and practices of effective African American teachers have found that such teachers have strong attachments to the Black community and consider themselves a part of it (Foster, 1990, 1991a, 1991b; Ladson-Billings, 1991a, 1991b; Ladson-Billings & Henry, 1990). Often, but not always, these attachments are expressed in the teachers' use of kin terms as well as in their use of metaphors to express a particular kind of alliance between themselves and their students (Foster, 1991a, 1993; Casey, 1990, 1993). From her study of 20 effective African American teachers, Foster (1991b) has noted that, unprompted, irrespective of gender and grade level, over half of them used kin terms or metaphors to describe their relationship with students. The following quotes taken from Foster (1991b) illustrate the metaphorical references to this conception of solidarity and connectedness:

I couldn't begin to tell you some of the problems I've encountered. I'm the kind of teacher who kids come and tell me their problems. I have brought kids, well one child I eventually brought home for two weeks until I could find a foster home for her because her mother put her out. I have had to take a child who tried to do an abortion on her own to take her back to the doctor and get her straightened out. Other little situations where the father was beating the child. I mean this is what my teaching job consists of, not just the physical education program, but an *extended family* program because I feel as though this is a part of what I'm about [emphasis added]. (p. 273)

Black people have to convince Blacks of how important it [education] is. And how they are all part of that Black *umbilical* cord because a lot of [Black] teachers, they don't do it consciously, but we are forgetting about our roots, about how we're *connected to this cord,* and about everyone we've left behind. We have it now, and we don't have time for the so-called underclass. But we have to educate ourselves as a group because otherwise what's going to happen to us all? You see what I mean. If I can't see that kid out there in the biggest project, if I can't see how he and I or she and I are of the same *umbilical cord* and do not strive to make us more *connected to that cord,* with a common destiny, then we're lost [emphasis added]. (p. 274)

In an ethnographic history of Caswell County Training School, a segregated Black school in North Carolina, Siddle-Walker (1993a, 1993b) emphasizes the salience and pervasiveness of caring relationships within the educational environment. Specifically, she shows how caring was expressed in the daily interactions between teachers and students and how students responded to an atmosphere of interpersonal caring. She also analyzes the implications of these findings for current school reforms.

In many cases these attachments were further strengthened by intergenerational employment and long-term community residence patterns of African American teachers. The evidence suggests further that often these interactions extend beyond school into the larger community (Foster, 1990, 1991a, 1991b; Casey, 1990; Ladson-Billings, 1991a, 1991b).

Connectedness is a prominent theme in the work of scholars who have examined historic and contemporary African American family life (Guttman, 1976; Jones, 1985). These studies describe the strong kinship bonds and sense of mutual obligation that have existed in African American communities and are reflected in fictive kin relationships and the use of kin terms, as well as the tendency of nonkin to take on parental social roles. These extensive kin networks have made significant contributions historically to both the material and nonmaterial well-being of children. Contemporary anthropological studies of both urban and rural Black communities demonstrate the continuing significance of these extended kin networks to the well-being of African American children (Hill, 1972; Stack, 1974). Only recently have scholars of African American life extended this analysis to relationships among nonintimates, in particular to those occupying institutional roles, such as teachers. Nonetheless, almost without exception, connectedness to Black communities seems to be a recurring theme characterizing the practice of excellent African American teachers (Foster, 1990, 1991a, 1991b; Casey, 1993; Ladson-Billings, 1991a, 1991b; Siddle-Walker, 1993a, 1993b).

Scholars who have applied the concepts of connectedness and care to schooling argue that the ability to relate to others is a critical component of responsible teachers (Noddings, 1984; Lyons, 1983). Other researchers have noted that increased motivation and engagement exist in schools where students, especially those labeled "at risk," are able to develop personal bonds with adults (McLaughlin & Talbert, 1990). Finally, a personalized style and a close and caring relationship between Hispanic teachers and pupils, characterized as *cariño*, has been noted as one of several influential factors in classrooms that exhibit high degrees of comembership (Cazden, 1988). Complementing these findings are those of Gallo (1969), Meltzer and Levy (1970), cited in Massey, Scott, and Dornbusch (1975), Woods (1979), and Payne (1984), who found, in separate studies, that students differentiate among teachers, form their perceptions of them, and respond to their behaviors based on their ability to interact with them on a personal level.

This is not to suggest that African American teachers are overly permissive, nor does it suggest—as some scholars have contended—that African American teachers, like African American mothers, are unnecessarily authoritarian and controlling (Conroy, 1972; Rist, 1970, 1973; Spencer, 1986). Neither do African American teachers display excessive warmth without communicating correspondingly high expectations for effort and achievement, as has been noted in some school settings (Massey, Scott, & Dornbusch, 1975). On the contrary, the modal description of excellent African American teachers, found in the scholarly as well as the more popular literature, is of concerned adults who command respect, are respectful of pupils, and who, though caring, require all students to meet high academic and behavioral standards (Cohen, 1991; Foster, 1989a, 1990; Ladson-Billings, 1991a, 1991b; Casey, 1990; Reed, 1990; Blauner, 1989; Monroe & Goldman, 1988; Wyatt, cited in Cazden, 1988; Anson, 1987; Baker, 1987; Fields, 1985; Kluger, 1975; Murray, 1970; Clark, 1962).

This style of teaching closely resembles the authoritative parenting style, which integrates acceptance and involvement, firm control, and psychological autonomy (Baumarind, 1971, 1972, 1978; Dornbusch, Ritter, Liederman, Roberts, & Fraleigh 1987; Lanborn & Mounts 1990; Steinberg, Mounts, Lanborn, & Dornbusch, 1990). Quoting an African American female, Casey's (1990) research provides an example of what she calls a teacher's "sensitive and benevolent assertion of her authority" (p. 317), which illustrates how an authoritative style that integrates acceptance and involvement, firm control, and psychological autonomy is enacted in a teacher-pupil relationship:

There were times when I said, "If you skip my class, I'm coming down to the mall to get you. So sometimes, I would go down to the mall, and it would be a big scene because the class would be waiting there, anticipating my coming back with these six feet, you know, men. And I would go down to the mall, and I would say, "Hi John!" "Uh, Hi!" You know. They were always really surprised. I said, "Well, we come to get you." And they looked, "We?"

Those kind of confrontations could really get to be sticky, because you had to measure how you were going to approach that, and you had to know who you were talking to and what kind of child this was, and how they gonna react to you. The students, of course, thought I was just walking into it, and not thinking each step of the way as to how I was going to do it, because some of these students were very, very belligerent about coming to class, and some of the classes they didn't go to. And it was just kind of, they'd like pass the word, "Don't skip _____'s class, I mean, she'll come and get you and that's embarrassing you know."

. . . We would start up the stairs together, and then I would notice that they were walking ahead of me. And that was my signal, to not go in the door at the same time with them, because that would be really embarrassing, and the objective was not to embarrass somebody once you get them to class. (p. 317)

Research on mother-daughter relationships has also concluded that African American mothers are admired, respected, and feared precisely because of their ability to balance the toughness required for discipline with the tenderness required for emotional support (Joseph & Lewis, 1981). When excellent African American teachers take on the role of kin, they embrace a complex set of behaviors that demand appropriate doses of firmness and nurturance.

Linking Classroom Content to Students' Experiences

Linking classroom content to student experiences characterizes the practice of effective African American teachers. Students are encouraged to bring community experiences into the classroom (Foster, 1987, 1989a; Ladson-Billings, 1991a, 1991b; Henry, 1990; Ladson-Billings & Henry, 1991). Teachers deliberately structure classroom activities to make this possible. The literature provides evidence that some classroom speech events reflect these community-classroom linkages (Hollins, 1982; Foster, 1987, 1989). Finally, these teachers do not silence student voices (Fine, 1987) by avoiding controversial topics (Foster, 1987; Ladson-Billings, 1990; Henry, 1990; Ladson-Billings & Henry, 1991).

Focus on the Whole Child

Excellent African American teachers concern themselves with the complete development of children, not just with their cognitive growth. The African American teachers described in the literature conceive of their role more broadly than that assigned them by the narrow, utilitarian purposes of schooling. Thus, while they accept the institutional goal of promoting cognitive growth, their personal definition of the teachers' role is not confined to developing academic skills but includes as well the social and emotional growth of students.

Their practice reflects this belief. Excellent African American teachers accept responsibility for nurturing in their students prerequisite skills and knowledges needed for success in school. They explicitly teach and model personal values—patience, persistence, responsibility to self and others—that can serve as a foundation to current as well as future learning; they foster the development of student attitudes and interests, motivation, aspiration, self-confidence, and leadership skills; they are also aware of the structural inequalities in society, and their practice evidences a "hidden curriculum" of self-determination designed to help students cope with the exigencies of living in a society that perpetuates institutional racism while professing a rhetoric of equal opportunity (Foster, 1987; King, 1991; Ladson-Billings & Henry, 1991; Hollins, 1982; Casey, 1990).

Interviews with several of the teachers in Foster's (1990) study provide evidence of a "hidden curriculum" that encourages students to understand the personal value, the collective power, and the political consequences of choosing academic achievement. Observing that African American students no longer "hunger and thirst" after education, one Black male teacher with 43 years of experience in both segregated and desegregated southern schools described some of the means he used to convey the importance of academic achievement to African American students. In the following excerpt, he reconstructs his critical dialogue with his African American students, a dialogue he believes is necessary to engage students in their own learning, but one that has been compromised in desegregated settings:

The big difference was that I can see we were able to do more with the Black students. In other words, if I wanted to come in this morning, have my kids put their books under the desk or on top of the desk and I'd get up on top of my desk and sit down and just talk to them. "Why are you here? Are you here just to make out another day? Or are you here because the law says you must go to school? Are you here to try to better yourself?" This kind of thing I could talk to them about. "Well, now I'm here to better myself. Well what must you do? What are the requirements? Do you know where your competition is?" And I could talk to them about things like that. "Your competition is not your little cousin that's sittin' over there. Your competition is that White person over there in that other school. He's your competition. He's the one you've got to compete with for a job. And the only way that you're going to be able to get that job is that you can't be as good as he is, you got to be better." And I could drill that into their heads. But once you integrated, I mean you didn't feel, I didn't—I don't feel comfortable really in a mixed setting to really get into the things that the Whites did to us as Black people. I don't really feel too comfortable doing that in a mixed group because I think I know how I felt when they talked about me. And surely they have feelings even though sometimes I didn't think they had any, but that kind of thing we, I mean I, couldn't do. I didn't want to pull them aside because then they would feel that they had been moved out of the mainstream because then you were just talking to just Blacks. But, this is the big difference that I saw, that you couldn't do. Well, I guess another thing, I got disillusioned with integration because of that type thing, because I could not get to my people and tell them all the things that they needed to know. I could not beat into their minds that they had to be better—that to compete with that White kid on an equal basis was not enough. I couldn't tell them that. I couldn't stop my class and tell him that so that he would understand. I think this is one of the things that they miss, Black kids, in general. (pp. 133–134)

Siddle-Walker (1993a, 1993b) confirms these findings. She found that one of the manifestations of interpersonal caring in the day-to-day life of Caswell County Training School was faculty commitment to counseling students, which they readily assumed for students both in and outside the classroom.

Use of Familiar Cultural Patterns

Anthropological research indicates that the African American community has maintained the cultural values of equality and collective responsibility in the domain of work as well as in many other tasks, including literacy activities, that are generally performed within a group context rather than by individuals alone (Stack, 1974; Szwed & Abrahams, 1979; Heath, 1983). Most of what occurs in traditional classrooms encouraged competitive behavior and individual achievement. Yet some research has shown that tremendous gains have been achieved in schools and classrooms for Black students in which learning is organized as a social event, not as a competitive or individual endeavor (Triesman, 1985; Bishop, 1985).

Excellent African American teachers embrace cultural patterns of collectivity, incorporating them into classroom activities. Students are encouraged to support each other, work together, and study collaboratively (Foster, 1987, 1989a; Ladson-Billings, 1991a, 1991b). Ladson-Billings reports that the teachers she interviewed continually stressed the need to build "a community or family," and that both they and their students were more at ease working in cooperative, collaborative classrooms. Rituals and routines reinforce this sense of collectivity, and there are also negative sanctions for belittling, humiliating, and embarrassing others (Foster, 1987; Dempsey & Noblit, 1993; Noblit, 1993).

Incorporation of Culturally Compatible Communication Patterns

Several researchers have noted the significance of interactional style between teachers and their students (e.g., Cazden & Leggett, 1981). Philips's (1972, 1983) study of the Warm Springs Indian Reservation addresses the cultural discontinuities in instructional style between Anglo teachers and Native American students. Less well known, but equally compelling, is Dumont's (1972) study of two Cherokee classrooms in which students would participate actively or remain silent depending on whether the teachers' interactional strategies were compatible with their own. A more recent study illustrating the significance of interactional style in improving the education of "caste group minority students" can be found in the work of the Kamehameha Early Education Project (KEEP), a research program aimed at improving the reading achievement of Hawaiian children. By successfully incorporating into its classrooms aspects of talk story, a familiar Hawaiian speech event, KEEP dramatically improved students' reading achievement (Au, 1980; Au & Jordan, 1981). With reference to this research literature, it should be noted that studies documenting congruent interactional style between African American teachers and African American students are rare. In fact, as noted earlier, most studies that examine the interaction between African American teachers and their students document the failures rather than the successes (e.g., Rist, 1970, 1973).

The Piestrup (1973) study is a notable exception. Trying to determine whether certain teaching styles were more successful than others in teaching Black-dialect-speaking students to read, Piestrup studied 14 first-grade classrooms in the Oakland, California, area. She identified four distinct teaching styles, but determined that one, which she labeled the Black Artful Style, was the most successful. She found that students taught with this style not only demonstrated greater achievement on standardized reading tests than children taught using another style, but that pupils of Black Artful teachers used dialect more appropriately in context. Piestrup concluded that this style may have been the most effective because it resembled many of the expressive art forms of African American culture.

Heath's (1983) decade-long research in North Carolina, which examined language learning and use in Trackton, an African American community, and then incorporated some of its interactional features into the classroom, is another study that demonstrates that reducing the sociolinguistic discontinuity between home and school positively influences African American students' participation in school lessons. Each of these studies, as well as the more theoretically oriented literature, highlights the fact that individual growth always occurs within particular social and cultural groups, which suggests that learning is facilitated and enhanced when it occurs in settings that are socioculturally familiar and linguistically meaningful to students (Vygotsky, 1962, 1978; Scribner & Cole, 1981).

Excellent African American teachers incorporate aspects of African American communicative patterns into classroom events (Hollins, 1982; Ladson-Billings & Henry, 1990; Foster, 1987, 1989a). In one of the few analyses of the teaching methods of Marva Collins, founder of Westside Prep, a school well known for its students' high rate of achievement on standardized tests, Hollins found evidence of cultural congruence between aspects of African American communicative behavior and Collins's teaching style. According to Hollins, familiar participation patterns—call and response, use of analogies, and rhythm—were all important characteristics of Collins's teaching style.

In their studies of effective Black teachers, both African American and African Canadian researchers have alluded to the incorporation of familiar communicative patterns into classroom activities. Henry (1990) and Ladson-Billings and Henry (1990) suggest that the rhythms, call and response, and use of proverbs extant in the expressive vocal communication patterns of the African diaspora characterize the pedagogy of the effective Black teachers they studied. Finally, in a systematic sociolinguistic analysis of a successful African American teacher, Foster (1987, 1989a) found evidence of code switching between the teacher's more standard English, used for regulatory purposes, and the African American expressive speech found in raps and sermons, which she labeled *performances*, used during academic tasks (cf. Cazden, 1988). This study also documents a highly systematic use of metaphors around which this teacher structured classroom activities (cf. Heath, 1983). In many cases the use of African American expressive language, manipulation of metaphors, and code switching into familiar African American English patterns are conscious and deliberate choices made by teachers (Foster, 1987, 1989a; Ladson-Billings & Henry, 1990).

CONCLUSION

To summarize, though based on a limited empirical research base, this review suggests that several factors character-

ize the pedagogy of effective African American teachers. These teachers express cultural solidarity, affiliation, and connectedness with the African American community. Often reinforced by long-term residence and employment patterns, this solidarity is manifest in the way teachers characterize their relationship to students; the responsibility they take for educating the whole child by teaching values, skills, and knowledge that enable school success and participation in the larger society; and their demonstrated competence in the norms of the African American community. Excellent African American teachers draw on community patterns and norms in structuring their classrooms. They link classroom activities to students' out-of-school experiences and incorporate familiar cultural and communicative patterns into their classroom practices, routines, and activities.

The main thesis of this chapter has been twofold: first, that despite large numbers of African Americans who have been employed as teachers, they are not commensurately represented in the research literature; and second, when they are portrayed it has typically been negatively. This is so despite recent policy documents that decry the shrinking numbers of African American teachers and call for actions that will augment the profession. The scholarly literature on African American teachers is meager, and there are very few scholars who are engaged in research on African American teachers.

Consequently, there are many questions concerning research, policy, and practice that remain unaddressed. For example, although there is considerable evidence that African American teachers were discriminated against both before and following the *Brown v. Board of Education of Topeka* decision, we know very little about the philosophy and practice of contemporary African American teachers. Do African American teachers have a distinct educational philosophy? If so, how does this affect their practice? To what extent do social class, age, gender, geographic region, and type of teacher-training institution attended shape the attitudes, behavior, philosophy, and practice of African American teachers? How do these and other factors shape African American teachers' attitudes toward African American pupils of varying social classes? Does the "wisdom of practice" (Shulman, 1987) of African American teachers differ from that of other groups of teachers? If so, in what ways? What can be learned from excellent African American teachers about educating African American pupils effectively? What attitudes do African American teachers hold toward recent school reform efforts and to what extent are African American teachers involved in them? Besides opening up other professions, how has desegregation shaped African Americans' attitudes toward the teaching profession? How do African American teachers in predominantly White school systems differ from those in systems in which African American students make up the majority?

While this list is not intended to be exhaustive, it presents a few of the questions that need to be explored in order to develop a comprehensive scholarly base on African American teachers. This chapter is intended to encourage additional research on the topic. If this chapter were to be revised in 10 years, at which time this situation has been ameliorated, then it will have met its goal.

References

Adams, E. F. (1956). *Experiences of a Fulbright teacher.* Boston: Christopher Publishers.

American Association of Colleges for Teacher Education. (1987). *Minority teacher recruitment and retention: A call to action.* Washington, DC: Author.

Anderson, R. C. (1956). *River, face homeward.* New York: Random House.

Anson, R. S. (1987). *Best intentions: The education and killing of Edmund Perry.* New York: Random House.

Au, K. (1980). Participation structures in a reading lesson with Hawaiian children: An analysis of a culturally appropriate instructional event. *Anthropology and Education Quarterly, 11*(2), 91–115.

Au, K., & Jordan, C. (1981). Teaching reading to Hawaiian children: Finding a culturally appropriate solution. In H. Trueba, G. P. Guthrie, & K. H. Au (Eds.), *Culture and the bilingual classroom: Studies in classroom ethnography* (pp. 139–152). Rowley, MA: Newbury House.

Baker, H. (1987). What Charles knew. In L. D. Rubin, Jr. (Ed.), *An apple for my teacher: 12 authors tell about teachers who made the difference* (pp. 123–131). Chapel Hill, NC: Algonquin Books.

Barlow, L. M. (1959). *Across the years: Memoirs.* Montgomery, AL: Paragon.

Baumarind, D. (1971). Current patterns of parental authority. *Developmental Psychology Monographs, 4*(1, Pt. 2).

Baumarind, D. (1972). An exploratory study of socialization effects on Black children: Some Black-White comparisons. *Child Development, 43,* 261–267.

Baumarind, D. (1978). Parental disciplinary patterns and social competence in children. *Youth and Society, 9,* 239–276.

Bishop, M. (1986, February 10). Update. *Sports Illustrated,* pp. 43–44.

Blacks losing teaching jobs. (1970, December 9). *Race Relations Reporter,* pp. 5–7.

Blauner, B. (1989). *Black lives, White lives: Three decades of race relations in America.* Berkeley: University of California Press.

Bond, H. M. (1934). *The education of the Negro in the American social order.* New York: Prentice-Hall.

Bowles, E. D. (1923, March 1). Opportunities for the educated Colored woman. *Opportunity, 1,* 8–10.

Bray, C. (1984). *The Black public school teacher: Alabama's endangered species.* Berkeley: University of California. (ERIC Document Reproduction Service No. ED 255 476)

Broughton, V. (1907). *Twenty years experience of a missionary.* Chicago: Pony Press.

Browne, R. B. (1969). *Love my children: An autobiography.* New York: Meredith Press.

Casey, K. (1990). Teachers as mother: Curriculum theorizing in the life histories of contemporary women teachers. *Cambridge Journal of Education, 20*(3), 301–320.

Casey, K. (1993). *I answer with my life: Life histories of women teachers working for social change.* New York: Routledge

Cazden, C. (1976). How knowledge about language helps the classroom teacher—or does it: A personal account. *Urban Review, 9*(2), 74–90.

Cazden, C. (1988). *Classroom discourse: The language of teaching and learning.* Portsmouth, NH: Heinemann

Cazden, C., & Leggett, E. (1981). Culturally responsive education: Recommendations for achieving Lau remedies. In H. Trueba, G. P. Guthrie, & K. H. Au (Eds.), *Culture and the bilingual classroom: Studies in classroom ethnography* (pp. 69–86). Rowley, MA: Newbury House.

Clark, S. (1962). *Echo in my soul.* New York: Dutton.

Cohen, M. (1991, February 24). Growing up segregated. *Chapel Hill Newspaper,* pp. C1–2.

Cole, B. (1986). The Black educator: An endangered species. *Journal of Negro Education, 55*(3), 326–334.

Cole, E., & Horton, F. (1984, March). *Trends in recruitment, retention and placement of prospective Black teachers.* Paper presented at the fifth National Invitational Conference on Teacher Preparation and Survival, Norfolk, VA. (ERIC Reproduction Service No. ED 263 046)

Collier-Thomas, B. (1982). The impact of Black women in education: An historical overview. *Journal of Negro Education, 51*(3), 173–179.

Collins, H. (1989, May 17). Most pass teaching exam, but Blacks don't fare as well. *Philadelphia Inquirer,* pp. B1–B6.

Conroy, P. (1972). *The water is wide.* Boston: Houghton Mifflin.

Coppin, F. J. (1913). *Reminiscences of school life and hints on teaching.* Philadelphia: AME Book Concern.

Curry, L. P. (1981). *The free Black in America, 1800–1850: The shadow of the dream.* Chicago: University of Chicago Press.

Decker, S. (1969). *An empty spoon.* New York: Harper & Row.

Dempsey, V., & Noblit, G. (1993). The demise of caring in an African-American community: One consequence of school desegregation. *Urban Review, 25*(1), 47–61.

Dornbusch, S., Ritter, P., Liederman, P., Roberts, D., & Fraleigh, M. (1987). The relation of parenting style to adolescent school performance. *Child Development, 58,* 1244–1257.

Dumont, R. V. (1972). Learning English and how to be silent: Studies in Sioux and Cherokee classrooms. In C. B. Cazden, V. John, & D. Hymes (Eds.), *Functions of language in the classroom* (pp. 344–369). New York: Teachers College Press.

Dunningham, A. A. (1974). *A Black woman's experience: From school-house to White House.* Philadelphia: Dorrance.

Dupre, B. (1986). Problems regarding the survival of future Black teachers. *Journal of Negro Education, 55*(2), 55–66.

Ethridge, S. (1979). Impact of the 1954 Brown v. Topeka Board of Education decision on Black educators. *Negro Educational Review, 30*(3–4), 217–232.

Fields, M., with K. Fields (1985). *Lemon swamp: A Carolina memoir.* New York: The Free Press

Fine, M. (1987). Silencing in public schools. *Language Arts, 64*(2), 57–74.

Foster, M. (1987). *"It's cookin' now": An ethnographic study of a successful Black teacher in an urban community college.* Unpublished doctoral dissertation, Harvard University.

Foster, M. (1989a). "It's cookin' now": A performance analysis of the speech events of a Black teacher in an urban community college. *Language in Society, 18*(1), 1–29.

Foster, M. (1989b). *Recruiting teachers of color: Problems, programs and possibilities* (Monograph of the Far West Holmes Group). Tempe: Arizona State University.

Foster, M. (1990). The politics of race: Through African-American teachers' eyes. *Journal of Education, 172*(3), 123–141.

Foster, M. (1991a). Constancy, change and constraints in the lives of Black women teachers: Some things change, most stay the same. *NWSA Journal, 3*(2), 233–261.

Foster, M. (1991b). "Just got to find a way": Case studies of the lives and practice of exemplary Black high school teachers. In M. Foster (Ed.), *Readings on equal education: Qualitative investigations into schools and schooling* (Vol. 11, pp. 273–309). New York: AMS Press.

Foster, M. (1992) African-American teachers and the politics of race. In K. Weiler (Ed.), *What schools can do: Critical pedagogy and practice* (pp. 177–202) Albany: State University of New York Press.

Foster, M. (1993). Education for competence in community and culture:

Exploring the views of exemplary African-American teachers. *Urban Education, 27*(4), 370–394.

Foster, M. (1994). Effective Black teachers: A literature review. In E. R. Hollins, J. E. King, & W. C. Hayman (Eds.), *Teaching diverse populations: Formulating a knowledge base* (pp. 225–241). Albany: State University of New York Press.

Franklin, V. P. (1979). *The education of Black Philadelphia: The social and educational history of a minority community, 1900–1950.* Philadelphia: University of Pennsylvania Press.

Gallo, D. (1969). *Student voices: A study of student preferences in a de facto segregated junior high school* (Working Paper No. 1, Pathways Project). Cambridge, MA: Harvard Graduate School of Education.

Gaudet, F. J. (1913). *He leadeth me.* New Orleans: Author.

Gifford, B. (1986). Excellence and equity in teacher competency testing: A policy perspective. *Journal of Negro Education, 55*(3), 251–271.

Goodson, I. (1988). Teachers, life histories and studies of curriculum and school. In *The making of the curriculum: Collected essays.* Philadelphia: Falmer Press.

Graham, P. A. (1987). Black teachers: A drastically scarce resource. *Phi Delta Kappan, 68*(8), 598–605.

Guttman, H. (1976). *Black family life in slavery and freedom.* New York: Pantheon Books.

Haskins, J. (1971). *Diary of a Harlem schoolteacher.* New York: Grove Press.

Heath, S. (1983). *Ways with words: Language, life and work in communities and classrooms.* New York: Cambridge University Press.

Hedgeman, A. A. (1964). *The trumpet sounds: A memoir of Negro leadership.* New York: Holt, Rinehart, & Winston.

Henry, A. (1990, April) *Black women, Black pedagogies: An African-Canadian context.* Paper presented at the annual meeting of the American Educational Research Association, Boston.

Herndon, J. (1968). *The way it spozed to be.* New York: Simon & Schuster.

Hicks, E. B. (1959). The golden apples: Memoir of a retired teacher. New York: Exposition.

Hill, R. (1972). *The strengths of Black families.* New York: Emerson Hall.

Hill, R. E. (Ed.). (1991). *The Black woman oral history project.* Cambridge, MA: Radcliffe College, Arthur and Elizabeth Schlesinger Library on the History of Women in America.

Hilliard, A. (1980, June). *The changing Black teacher and diminishing opportunities for Black teachers.* Paper presented at the First National Invitational Conference on Problems, Issues, Plans and Strategies Related to the Preparation and Survival of Black Public School Teachers, Norfolk State University, VA. (ERIC Document Reproduction Service No. ED 212 565)

Hollins, E. (1982). The Marva Collins story revisited: Implications for regular classroom instruction. *Journal of Teacher Education, 33*(1), 37–40.

Horton, J. O., & Horton, L. E. (1979). *Black Bostonians: Family life and community struggle in the antebellum north.* New York: Holmes & Meier.

Irvine, J. (1988). An analysis of the problem of the disappearing Black educator. *Elementary School Journal, 88*(5), 503–513.

Jones, J. (1985). *Labor of love, labor of sorrow: Black women, work and the family from slavery to the present.* New York: Basic Books.

Joseph, G., & Lewis, J. (1981). *Common differences: Conflicts in Black and White feminist perspectives.* Boston: South End Press.

King, J. (1991). Black student alienation and Black teachers' emancipatory pedagogy. In M. Foster (Ed.), *Readings on equal education: Qualitative investigations into schools and schooling* (Vol. 11, pp. 245–271). New York: AMS Press.

Kluger, R. (1975). *Simple justice.* New York: Vintage.

Kohl, H. (1967). *36 Children.* New York: Signet.

Kozol, J. (1968). *Death at an early age: The destruction of the hearts and minds of Negro children in the Boston public schools.* Boston: Houghton Mifflin.

Ladson-Billings, G. (1990). Culturally relevant teaching: Effective instruction for Black students. *College Board Review, 155,* 20–25.

Ladson-Billings, G. (1991a). Like lightning in a bottle: Attempting to capture the pedagogical excellence of successful teachers of Black students. *International Journal of Qualitative Studies in Education, 3*(4), 335–344.

Ladson-Billings, G. (1991b). Returning to the source: Implications for educating teachers of Black students. In M. Foster (Ed.), *Readings on equal education: Qualitative investigations into schools and schooling* (Vol. 11, pp. 227–244). New York: AMS Press.

Ladson-Billings, G., & Henry, A. (1990). Blurring the borders: Voices of African liberatory pedagogy in the United States and Canada. *Boston Journal of Education, 172*(2), 72–88.

Lanborn, S., & Mounts, N. (1990). *Patterns of competence and adjustment among adolescents from authoritative, authoritarian, indulgent and neglectful families.* Unpublished manuscript, University of Wisconsin, National Center on Effective Secondary Schools, Madison.

Lerner, G. (1972). *Black women in White America: A documentary history.* New York: Vintage.

Lightfoot, S. (1973). Politics and reasoning: Through the eyes of teachers and children. *Harvard Educational Review, 43*(2), 197–244.

Lightfoot, S. (1978). *Worlds apart: Relationships between families and schools.* New York: Basic Books.

Lyons, N. (1983). Two perspectives: On self, relationships and morality. *Harvard Educational Review, 53*(2), 125–145.

Massey, G. C., Scott, M. V., & Dornbusch, S. M. (1975). Racism without racists: Institutional racism in urban schools. *Black Scholar, 7*(3), 10–19.

McLaughlin, M., & Talbert, J. (1990). Constructing a personalized school environment. *Phi Delta Kappan, 72*(3), 230–235.

Mead, M. (1950). *The school in American culture.* Cambridge, MA: Harvard University Press.

Meltzer, M., & Levy, B. (1970). Self-esteem in a public school. *Psychology in the Schools, 7*(1), 15.

Metropolitan Life Insurance Company. (1988). *The American teacher 1988: Strengthening the relationship between teachers and students.* New York: Author.

Monroe, S., & Goldman, P. (1988). *Brothers: Black and poor, a true story of courage and survival.* New York: Ballantine Books.

Morton, L. B. (1965). *My first sixty years: Passion for wisdom.* New York: Philosophical Library.

Murnane, R., & Schwinden, M. (1988). *Who became certified to teach and who has entered teaching between 1979 and 1985: Evidence from North Carolina.* (ERIC Document Reproduction Service No. ED 301 559)

Murray, A. (1970). *Black experience and American culture.* New York: Vintage.

Murrell, P. (1991). Cultural politics in teacher education: What's missing in the preparation of minority teachers. In M. Foster (Ed.), *Readings in equal education: Qualitative investigations into schools and schooling* (Vol. 11, pp. 205–225). New York: AMS Press.

Nash, G. (1988). *Forging freedom: The formation of Philadelphia's Black community, 1720–1840.* Cambridge, MA: Harvard University Press.

Noblit, G. W. (1993). Power and caring. *American Educational Research Journal, 30*(1), 23–38.

Noddings, N. (1984). *Caring.* Berkeley: University of California Press.

Painter, N. I. (1976). *Exodusters: Black migration to Kansas after reconstruction.* New York: W. W. Norton.

Payne, C. M. (1984). *Getting what we ask for: The ambiguity of success and failure in urban education.* Westport, CT: Greenwood Press.

Perkins, L. (1989). The history of Blacks in teaching: Growth and decline within the profession. In D. Warren (Ed.), *American teachers: Histories of a profession at work* (pp. 344–369). New York: Macmillan.

Piestrup, A. (1973). *Black dialect interference and accommodation of reading instruction in first grade* (Monograph of the Language Behavior Research Laboratory). Berkeley: University of California.

Philips, S. (1972). Participant structures and communicative competence. In C. B. Cazden, V. John, & D. Hymes (Eds.), *Functions of language in the classroom* (pp. 370–394). New York: Teachers College Press.

Philips, S. (1983). *The invisible culture: Communication in the classroom and community on the Warm Springs Indian Reservation.* White Plains, NY: Longman Press.

Provenzo, E. (1988, April). *Black and White teachers: Patterns of similarity and difference over twenty years.* Paper presented at the meeting of the American Educational Research Association, New Orleans.

Reed, I. (1990, August 19). Reading, writing and racism. *San Francisco Examiner Image Magazine,* pp. 27–28.

Rist, R. (1970). Student social class and teacher expectations: The self-fulfilling prophecy in ghetto education. *Harvard Educational Review, 40*(3), 411–451.

Rist, R. (1973). *The urban school: A factory for failure.* Cambridge, MA: MIT Press.

Robinson, D. R. (1978). *The bell rings at four: A Black teacher's chronicle of change.* Austin, TX: Madrona Press.

Scribner, S., & Cole, M. (1981). Unpacking literacy. In M. Farr-Whiteman (Ed.), *Variation in writing: Functional and linguistic-cultural differences* (pp. 71–88). Hillsdale, NJ: Lawrence Erlbaum Associates.

Segregated education: Two views, 1850. (1990) In H. Aptheker (Ed.), *A documentary history of the Negro people in the United States* (Vol. 1, pp. 297–299). New York: Carol Publishing Group. (Original work published 1951)

Shulman, L. S. (1987). Knowledge and teaching: Foundations of the new reform. *Harvard Educational Review, 57*(1), 1–22.

Siddle-Walker, E. V. (1993a). Caswell County Training School, 1933–1969: Relationships between community and school. *Harvard Educational Review, 63*(2), 161–182.

Siddle-Walker, E. V. (1993b). Interpersonal caring in the "good" segregated schooling of African-American children: Evidence from the case of Caswell County Training School. *Urban Review, 25*(1), 63–77.

Spencer, D. (1986). *Contemporary women teachers: Balancing school and home.* New York: Longman.

Stack, C. (1974). *All our kin: Strategies for survival in a Black community.* New York: Harper & Row.

Steinberg, L., Mounts, N., Lanborn, S., & Dornbusch, S. (1990). *Authoritative parenting and adolescent adjustment across varied ecological niches.* Unpublished manuscript, University of Wisconsin, National Center on Effective Secondary Schools, Madison.

Sterling, P. (1972). *The real teachers: 30 inner-city schoolteachers talk honestly about who they are, how they teach and why.* New York: Random House.

Stern, J. (1988). *The condition of postsecondary education.* Washington, DC: U.S. Department of Education, Office of Educational Research and Improvement.

Stewart, J., Meier, K., & England, R. (1989). In quest of role models: Change in Black teacher representation in urban school districts 1968–86. *Journal of Negro Education, 58*(2), 140–152.

Szwed, J., & Abrahams, R. (1979). After the myth: Studying Afro-American cultural patterns in the plantation literature. In D. Crowley (Ed.), *African folklore in the new world* (pp. 65–86). Austin: University of Texas Press.

Terrell, M. E. C. (1940). *A colored woman in a white world.* Washington: Randsdell.

Triesman, U. (1985). *A study of the mathematics performance of Black students at the University of California at Berkeley.* Unpublished doctoral dissertation, University of California, Berkeley.

Tyack, D. (1974). *The one best system: A history of American urban education.* Cambridge, MA: Harvard University Press.

Vygotsky, L. (1962). *Thought and language.* Cambridge, MA: MIT Press.

Vygotsky, L. (1978). *Mind in society.* Cambridge, MA: Harvard University Press.

Williams, R. B. C. (1961). *Black and white orange: An autobiography.* New York: Vintage.

Witty, E. (1984, March). *Introduction: Attracting gifted and talented Blacks to the teaching profession.* In Fifth National Invitational Conference on Problems, Issues, Plans and Strategies Related to the Preparation and Survival of Black Public School Teachers, Norfolk State University, VA. (ERIC Reproduction Document Service No. ED 263 046)

Woods, P. (1979). *The divided school.* London: Routledge and Kegan Paul.

Young, R. (1929). *Light in the dark belt: The story of Rosa Young as told by herself.* St. Louis, MO: Concordia.

32

UNDERSTANDING CULTURAL DIVERSITY
AND LEARNING

John U. Ogbu
UNIVERSITY OF CALIFORNIA, BERKELEY

Cultural diversity has become a household phrase in education, especially minority education. I suspect, however, that there is some misunderstanding about what it means and its relevance to minority education. As an anthropologist, I am sensitive to the use of the phrase cultural diversity; as a student of minority education, I am concerned about its application or misapplication with respect to the school adjustment and performance of minority children.

This chapter addresses two contrasting educational responses to cultural diversity: (a) a core curriculum education movement and (b) a multicultural education movement. I argue that neither of the two responses will have an appreciable impact on the school-learning problems of those minorities who have not traditionally done well in school. The reason is that they are not based on a good understanding of the nature of the cultural diversity or cultural differences of minority groups.

I first summarize the two responses and their shortcomings. Second, I attempt to explain the nature of the cultural diversity and its implications for minority schooling. I do so by first distinguishing and describing different types of minorities and the difference in the relationship between their cultures and the mainstream American culture. Third, I examine their differing educational implications. I will conclude with some recommendations.

RESPONSES TO CULTURAL DIVERSITY

Core Curriculum Education

Explicit advocates of a core curriculum for the U.S. public schools come largely from the humanities (Bennett, 1984; Bloom, 1987; Finn, 1989; Hirsch, 1987, 1988). Their critics call them "assimilationists" (Carroll & Schensul, 1990). I believe, however, that core curriculum advocates are more concerned about U.S economic and technological status in international competition than about assimilating culturally diverse groups into the mainstream culture. They think that U.S. schools should teach a core curriculum like schools in Germany, Japan, South Korea, and Taiwan, countries that have made remarkable economic and technological advances. Americans attribute the technological advances to their superior education as evidenced by the fact that their students outperform American students by every academic measure.

Will this movement improve the school performance of those minorities who have not traditionally done well in school? One assumption in the core curriculum movement (and in related school reform movements) is that the academic performance of both the majority and the minority students depends on what goes on inside the schools and that what

Reprinted with permission of the American Educational Research Association from *Educational Researcher, 21*(8), pp. 5–14. An earlier version of this chapter was presented as an invited address to Division D, annual meeting of the American Educational Research Association, Chicago, March 1991.

needs to be done is to "fix" the schools (Ogbu, 1988; Weis, 1985). Fixing the school will certainly have some positive effects, seen in increasing numbers of minorities graduating from high school and college as well as entering the fields of math and science as a result of intervention programs.

However, the ability of a core curriculum to increase the school performance of some minority groups will be limited because it does not address the nature of minority cultural diversity. Past experience with compensatory education and other remedial programs suggests that it is not enough simply to announce higher academic standards and expectations (Passow, 1984). What goes on inside the schools, including the kind of curriculum taught, is very important for minority students (Edmonds, 1986; Ogbu, 1974), but more is involved. What the children bring to school—their communities' cultural models or understandings of "social realities" and the educational strategies that they, their families, and their communities use or do not use in seeking education—is as important as within-school factors (Ogbu, 1988).

Multicultural Education

The other response is multicultural education. The current movement, led largely by minorities, emerged primarily in the 1960s, initially in response to cultural deprivation theory. Before then, minorities, such as Black Americans, protested against a differential and inferior curriculum; they wanted the same curriculum that was available to Whites (Bullock, 1970; Ogbu, 1978). Today, however, multicultural education is linked to cultural diversity (Yee, 1991). Moreover, the current demand for multicultural education is for both minorities who are doing relatively well in school and those who are not.

There is, however, no clear definition of multicultural education (see Appleton, 1983; Banks, 1989a, 1989b; Bullivant, 1981; G. Gay, 1979; Gibson, 1976; Grant & Sleeter, 1986; Suzuki, 1984). Furthermore, many writers propose diverse "models" of multicultural education that are rarely based on ethnographic or empirical studies of minorities' cultures. Gibson's (1976) survey found five models in the mid-1970s: (a) multicultural education for cross-cultural understanding, which, among other things, stresses teaching strategies affirming the right to be different and the need for members of different cultures to respect one another; (b) "culturally responsive education" at the elementary and secondary schools to enhance minority school learning by including minority cultures in the content of the curriculum and as a medium of instruction; (c) bicultural education, often associated with bilingual education programs, designed to reinforce minority students' cultures, languages, and identities while teaching the language and other skills functional in mainstream culture; (d) cultural pluralism in education, designed to preserve and strengthen ethnic-group identity and to increase minority groups' social, political, and economic participation in society; and (e) multicultural education as the normal human experience, enabling individuals to participate competently in a multicultural society.

James A. Banks, probably the most prolific theorist, has also reviewed various models of multicultural education (Banks, 1981). He criticizes them for emphasizing cultural differences

and deficiencies. He proposes a "multiple acculturation" model that would promote "cross-cultural competency" (Banks, 1981). Sleeter and Grant (1987) classify multicultural education into four types and add a fifth: (a) teaching the "culturally different," an assimilationist approach; (b) a human relations approach to improve interpersonal relations; (c) single-group studies to promote cultural pluralism by raising consciousness; (d) multicultural education within the regular curriculum to reflect diversity and thereby enhance pluralism and equality; (e) education that is multicultural and social reconstructionist (p. 423), proposed by the authors to encourage students to challenge social inequality and to promote cultural diversity. Baker (1978), Baptiste (1979), G. Gay (1979, 1988, 1990), and Suzuki (1984) have proposed other models.

Taken together, multicultural education fosters pride in minority cultures, helps minority students develop new insights into their culture, reduces prejudice and stereotyping, and promotes intercultural understandings (Rubalcava, 1991). But the crucial question is to what extent will multicultural education improve the academic performance of those minorities who have not traditionally done well in school? Rarely do multicultural education models address this question explicitly. Two exceptions are bicultural education and culturally responsive education (Gibson, 1976).

Multicultural education may indeed improve school learning for some minority children. However, for several reasons it is not an adequate strategy to enhance the academic performance of those minorities who have traditionally not done well in school. One reason is that multicultural education generally ignores the minority students' own responsibility for their academic performance. Multicultural education models and actual programs convey the impression that educating minority students is a process whereby teachers and schools must change for the benefit of the students. They should acquire knowledge of minority cultures and languages for teaching minority children, promoting cross-cultural understanding, reinforcing ethnic identity, and so on. Multicultural education generally emphasizes changing teacher attitudes and practices. Yet a comparative study of the situation will show that school success depends not only on what schools and teachers do but also on what students do (Ogbu & Matute-Bianchi, 1986).

Second, we suspect that multicultural education theories and programs are rarely based on actual study of minority cultures and languages. To our knowledge, many proponents of multicultural education models have not studied minority cultures in minority communities, although some have studied minority children at school and some are minority-group members. However, membership in a minority group is not a sufficient basis for theorizing about cultural influences on learning. For example, I have found that some members of my research team studying their own local communities initially did not recognize some relevant cultural data, including cultural assumptions underlying their own behaviors. Research with minority children at school provides a very limited access to the cultural assumptions underlying the children's distinctive attitudes and behaviors. Furthermore, a good study of a minority group's culture or language may turn up some cultural/language differences that actually cause learning problems that cannot be remedied through cultural infusion into the curriculum or teaching and learning styles (Closs, 1986; Orr, 1987). What is also instructive is that there are minority groups whose language expressions, mathematical or number systems, and overt cultural behaviors might be different enough from those of White Americans to be considered barriers to learning math and science but whose members, nevertheless, learn more or less successfully. That is, they are able, eventually, to cross cultural and language boundaries and succeed academically. Thus a third reason for the inadequacy of the multicultural education solution is that it fails to separate minority groups that are able to cross cultural and language boundaries and learn successfully, in spite of initial cultural barriers, from those that are not able to do so (Gibson & Ogbu, 1991; Ogbu, 1987, 1990).

The question of who needs multicultural education to enhance academic success and who does not becomes more important when one looks at the increasing diversity in U.S. schools and classrooms (Yee, 1991). For example, we found only 5 or 6 ethnic groups represented in our initial study of Stockton, California, schools in 1968–1970. However, by 1986 the ethnic representation increased to 12 at the elementary, 11 at the junior high, and 16 at the senior high schools. As in earlier years, in 1986 some of the minority groups were doing very well in school in spite of their language and cultural differences, and some were not.

In summary, neither the core curriculum response nor the multicultural education response in its various forms is likely to enhance appreciably the academic achievement of those minority groups who have not traditionally done well in school. Like the core curriculum movement, the multicultural education movement is based on the erroneous assumption that academic achievement is primarily the result of the transaction between the specific skills and abilities of the students and the teaching of the curriculum and the process of the classroom environment, including teacher attitudes. These movements fail to recognize that the meaning and value students associate with school learning and achievement play a very significant role in determining their efforts toward learning and performance. Furthermore, the meaning and value that students from different cultural groups associate with the process of formal education vary and are socially transmitted by their ethnic communities. The important point here is that neither the core curriculum approach nor the multicultural education approach will appreciably improve the school performance of some minority groups until they and other school interventions, innovations, and reforms are informed by an understanding of why children from specific minority groups are experiencing learning and performance difficulty.

The problem is not merely one of cultural and language differences, although these differences are important. What is even more significant, but thus far unrecognized, is the nature of the relationship between minority cultures/languages and the culture and language of the dominant White Americans and the public schools they control. The relationship between the minority cultures/languages and the mainstream culture and language is different for different minorities. And it is this difference in the relationship that is problematic in the ability of the minorities to cross cultural and language boundaries and that calls for understanding in order to enhance the success of

intervention and other efforts. What is the nature of this intercultural relationship and what are its implications for minority education?

CULTURAL DIVERSITY AND DIFFERENTIAL SCHOOL SUCCESS

Societal and School Influences on Minority Education

The school learning and performance of minority children are influenced by complex social, economic, historical, and cultural factors. Therefore, before describing the cultural forces, I want to make it categorically clear that I am focusing on only one group of forces. I have described elsewhere other forces at work, namely, how American society at large, the local communities, and the schools all contribute to minority problems in school learning and performance. Societal contributions include denying the minorities equal access to good education through societal and community educational policies and practices and denying them adequate and/or equal rewards with Whites for their educational accomplishments through a job ceiling and other mechanisms. Schools contribute to the educational problems through subtle and not so subtle policies and practices. The latter include tracking, "biased" testing and curriculum, and misclassification (see Ogbu, 1974, 1977, 1978, 1991). Here we are focusing on cultural forces, specifically on the relationship between minority cultures and mainstream culture and the implications of that relationship for minority schooling.

Differential Influence of Cultural Forces

There is evidence from comparative research suggesting that differences in school learning and performance among minorities are not due merely to cultural and language differences. Some minority groups do well in school even though they do not share the language and cultural backgrounds of the dominant group that are reflected in the curriculum, instructional style, and other practices of the schools. Such minorities may initially experience problems due to the cultural and language difference, but the problems do not persist.

The reason some minorities do well in school is not necessarily because their cultures are similar to the mainstream culture. For example, Gibson (1988) reports that in Valleyside, California, the Punjabis do well even though judged by mainstream culture they would be regarded as being academically at risk.

One cultural feature, namely, differential interpretation of eye contacts by White teachers and minority-group members, has been offered as an explanation for the learning difficulties among Puerto Rican children in New York (Byers & Byers, 1972), but has not had similar adverse effects on the Punjabis. Other examples of differential academic influence of minority cultural differences have been found in studies of minority education in Stockton (Ogbu, 1974), Watsonville (Matute-Bianchi, 1986; see also Woolard, 1981), and San Francisco (Suarez-Orozco, 1987).

Studies outside the United States have also found that minority children do not fail in school because of mere cultural/language differences or succeed in school because they share the culture and language of the dominant group. In Britain, students of East Asian origins, for whom the British language and culture are different, do considerably better in school than West Indian students, who have much longer been privy to the British language and culture (Ogbu, 1978; Taylor & Hegarty, 1985). In Japan (DeVos & Lee, 1981) and New Zealand (Penfold, personal communication, 1981), minority groups—even if they have similar cultures and languages but different histories—differ in school learning and academic success.

There are cases where a minority group does better in school when it is away from its country of origin, residing in a host society where its language and culture differ greatly from the language and culture of the dominant group. Take the case of the Japanese Buraku outcaste. In Japan itself, Buraku students continue to do poorly in school when compared with the dominant Ippan students (Hirasawa, 1989; Shimahara, 1991). But the Buraku immigrants in the United States are doing just as well as other Japanese immigrants (DeVos, 1973; Ito, 1967). The Koreans in Japan are another example. In Japan, where they went originally as colonial forced labor, they do very poorly in school. But in Hawaii and the continental United States, Korean students do as well as other Asians; yet Korean culture is more similar to Japanese culture than to American mainstream culture (DeVos, 1984; DeVos & Lee, 1981; Lee, 1991; Rohlen, 1981). The Koreans' case is further instructive because of their differential school success as a minority group in the United States, Japan, and China (see Kristoff, 1992, regarding Koreans in China). Korean peasants were relocated to these three countries about the same time as emigrants, except the group that went to Japan. The Koreans are academically successful in China and Hawaii, but not in Japan. West Indians are a similar example. They are academically successful in the continental United States and in the U.S. Virgin Islands, where they regard themselves as "immigrants" (Fordham, 1984; Gibson, 1991); less successful in Canada, where they regard themselves as members of "the Commonwealth" (Solomon, 1992); and least successful in Britain, which they regard as their "motherland" (Ogbu, 1978; Tomlinson, 1982).

As these studies suggest, mere cultural and language differences cannot account for the relative school failure of some minorities and the school success of others. Minority status involves complex realities that affect the relationship between the culture and language of the minority and those of the dominant groups and thereby influence the school adjustment and learning of the minority.

TYPES OF MINORITY STATUS: A PREREQUISITE FOR UNDERSTANDING CULTURAL DIVERSITY AND LEARNING

To understand what it is about minority groups, their cultures and languages that makes crossing cultural boundaries and school learning difficult for some but not for others, we must recognize that there are different types of minority groups or minority status. Our comparative study has led us to classify minority groups into (a) autonomous, (b) immigrant or voluntary, and (c) castelike or involuntary minorities.

1. Autonomous minorities are people who are minorities primarily in a numerical sense. American examples are Jews, Mormons, and the Amish. There are no non-White autonomous minorities in the United States, so we will not discuss this type further (see Ogbu, 1978).

2. Immigrant or voluntary minorities are people who have moved more or less voluntarily to the United States—or any other society—because they desire more economic well-being, better overall opportunities, and/or greater political freedom. Their expectations continue to influence the way they perceive and respond to events, including schooling, in the host society. Voluntary minorities usually experience initial problems in school due to cultural and language differences as well as lack of understanding of how the education system works. But they do not experience lingering, disproportionate school failure. The Chinese and Punjabi Indians are representative U.S. examples. Refugees are not voluntary minorities; they are not a part of this classification or the subject of this chapter (see Ogbu, 1993, for a full discussion of the distinction).

3. Castelike or involuntary minorities are people who were originally brought into the United States or any other society against their will; for example, through slavery, conquest, colonization, or forced labor. Thereafter, these minorities were often relegated to menial positions and denied true assimilation into the mainstream society. American Indians, Black Americans, early Mexican Americans in the Southwest, and native Hawaiians are U.S. examples. Puerto Ricans may qualify for membership in this category if they consider themselves "a colonized people." The Burakumin and Koreans in Japan and the Maoris in New Zealand are examples outside the United States. It is involuntary minorities that usually experience greater and more persistent difficulties with school learning.

MINORITY STATUS, CULTURE, AND IDENTITY

The different types of minorities are characterized by different types of cultural differences as well as social or collective identities. Voluntary minorities are characterized by primary cultural differences and involuntary minorities by secondary cultural differences.

Primary cultural differences are differences that existed before two groups came in contact, such as before immigrant minorities came to the United States. For example, Punjabi Indians in Valleyside, California, spoke Punjabi; practiced the Sikh, Hindu, or Muslim religion; had arranged marriages; and wore turbans, if they were male, before they came to the United States. In Valleyside they continue these beliefs and practices to some extent (Gibson, 1988). The Punjabis also brought with them their distinctive way of raising children, including teaching children how to make decisions and how to manage money.

We gain a better understanding of primary cultural differences when we examine non-Western children who attend Western-type schools in their own countries. The Kpelle of Liberia are a good example. John Gay and Michael Cole (1967) found that the arithmetic concepts in Kpelle culture were similar in some respects to those used in the American-type school but differed in other ways. The Kpelle had few geometrical concepts, and although they measured time, volume, and money, their culture lacked measurements of weight, area, speed, and temperature. These differences in mathematical concepts and use existed before the Kpelle were introduced to Western-type schools.

Secondary cultural differences are differences that arose after two populations came into contact or after members of a given population began to participate in an institution controlled by members of another population, such as the schools controlled by the dominant group. Thus, secondary cultural differences develop as a response to a contact situation, especially one involving the domination of one group by another.

At the beginning of the culture contact the two groups are characterized by primary cultural differences; later, the minorities develop secondary cultural differences to cope with their subordination. The secondary culture develops in several ways: from a reinterpretation of previous primary cultural differences or through the emergence of new types of cultural norms and behaviors.

Several features of secondary cultural differences are worth noting for their effects on schooling. First, it is the differences in style rather than in content that involuntary minorities emphasize: cognitive style (Ramírez & Castañeda, 1974; Shade, 1982), communication style (Gumperz, 1981; Kochman, 1982; Philips, 1972, 1983), interaction style (Erickson & Mohatt, 1982), and learning style (Au, 1981; Boykin, 1980; Philips, 1976).

Another feature is cultural inversion. Cultural inversion is the tendency for involuntary minorities to regard certain forms of behavior, events, symbols, and meanings as inappropriate for them because these are characteristic of White Americans. At the same time the minorities value other forms of behavior, events, symbols, and meanings, often the opposite, as more appropriate for themselves. Thus, what is appropriate or even legitimate behavior for in-group members may be defined in opposition to White out-group members' practices and preferences.

Cultural inversion may take several forms. It may be in-group meanings of words and statements (A. Bontemps, personal communication, July 1969), different notions and use of time (Weis, 1985), different emphasis on dialects and communication style (Baugh, 1984; Holt, 1972; Luster, 1992), or an outright rejection of White American preferences or what Whites consider appropriate behavior in a given setting (Fordham & Ogbu, 1986; Petroni, 1970). Cultural inversion, along with other oppositional elements, results in the coexistence of two opposing cultural frames of reference or ideals-orienting behavior, from the perspectives of involuntary minorities.

Involuntary minorities sometimes use cultural inversion to repudiate negative White stereotypes or derogatory images. Sometimes they use it as a strategy to manipulate Whites, to get even with Whites, or, as Holt (1972) puts it for Black Americans, "to turn the table against whites" (p. 154).

Secondary cultural differences seem to be associated with ambivalent or oppositional social or collective identities vis-à-vis the White American social identity. Voluntary minorities seem to bring to the United States a sense of who they are from their homeland and seem to retain this different but nonoppositional social identity at least during the first generation. Involuntary minorities, in contrast, develop a new sense of social or collective identity that is in opposition to the social identity of the dominant group after they have become subordinated. They do so in response to their treatment by White Americans in economic, political, social, psychological, cultural, and language domains. Whites' treatment included deliberate exclusion from true assimilation or the reverse, namely forced superficial assimilation (Castile & Kushner, 1981; DeVos, 1967, 1984; Spicer, 1966, 1971). Involuntary minorities, such as Black Americans, developed oppositional identity because for many generations they realized and believed that the White treatment was both collective and enduring. They were (and still are) not treated like White Americans regardless of their individual differences in ability, training, education, place of origin or residence, economic status, or physical appearance. They could not (and still cannot) easily escape from their birth-ascribed membership in a subordinate and disparaged group by "passing" for White or by returning to a "homeland" (Green, 1981). Native Americans and native Hawaiians have no other "homeland" to return to. In the past some Black Americans sought an escape by returning to Africa (Hall, 1978) and, more recently, by converting to the Muslim religion (Essien-Udom, 1964).

CULTURAL DIFFERENCES, IDENTITY, AND SCHOOL LEARNING

I have identified different types of cultural differences characteristic of the voluntary and involuntary minorities and have described the relationship between these cultural differences and mainstream (White) American culture. I turn now to the way the relationship between the minority cultures and mainstream culture affects minority schooling.

The primary cultural differences of voluntary minorities and the secondary cultural differences of involuntary minorities affect minority school learning differently. My comparative research suggests that involuntary minorities experience more difficulties in school learning and performance partly because of the relationship between their cultures and the mainstream culture. As I have come to understand it, they have greater difficulty with school learning and performance partly because they have greater difficulty crossing cultural/language boundaries in school than voluntary minorities with primary cultural differences.

Primary Cultural Differences and Schooling

What kinds of school problems are associated with primary cultural differences and why do the bearers of these differences overcome these problems and learn more or less successfully? Why do voluntary minorities successfully cross cultural boundaries?

In school, primary cultural differences may initially cause problems in interpersonal and intergroup relations as well as difficulties in academic work for several reasons. One is that children from different cultural backgrounds may begin school with different cultural assumptions about the world and human relations. Another is that the minorities may come to school lacking certain concepts necessary to learn math and science, for instance, because their own cultures do not have or use such concepts. Still another problem is that the children may be non-English-speaking. Finally, there may be differences in teaching and learning styles.

However, the relationship between the primary cultural differences and White American mainstream culture helps voluntary minority children eventually to overcome the initial problems, adjust socially, and learn and perform academically more or less successfully. First, the cultural differences existed before the minorities came to the United States or entered the public schools; the differences did not arise to maintain boundaries between them and White Americans. They are different from, but not necessarily oppositional to, equivalent features in mainstream culture in the schools.

Furthermore, because primary cultural differences did not develop in opposition or to protect their collective identity and sense of security and self-worth, voluntary minorities do not perceive learning the attitudes and behaviors required for school success as threatening their own culture, language, and identities. Instead, they interpret such learning (e.g., English) instrumentally and as additive, as adding to what they already have (their own language), for use in the appropriate context (Chung, 1992). They also believe that the learning will help them succeed in school and later in the labor market. Voluntary minorities, therefore, tend to adopt the strategy of "accommodation without assimilation" (Gibson, 1988) or "alternation strategy" (Ogbu, 1987). That is, while they do not give up their own cultural beliefs and practices, voluntary minorities are willing, and may even strive, to play the classroom game by the rules and try to overcome all kinds of schooling difficulties because they believe so strongly that there will be a payoff later (Gibson, 1987). With this kind of attitude, they are able to cross cultural boundaries and do relatively well in school.

Still another factor in favor of voluntary minorities is that they interpret the cultural and language differences they encounter as barriers to be overcome in order for them to achieve their long-range goals of obtaining good school credentials for future employment. They did not come to the United States expecting the schools to teach them in their own culture and language, although they are grateful if the schools do. Usually, they go to the school expecting and willing to learn the culture and language of the schools, and they also expect at least some initial difficulty in doing so.

Finally, primary cultural differences and the problems they cause are often specific enough to be identified through careful ethnographic research. This specificity and identifiability facilitate developing educational policies, programs, and practices to eliminate their negative impact.

Secondary Cultural Differences and Schooling

Many of the "cultural problems" caused by secondary cultural differences are similar on the surface to those caused by primary cultural differences: conflicts in interpersonal/intergroup relations due to cultural misunderstandings, conceptual problems due to absence of certain concepts in the ethnic-group cultures, lack of fluency in standard English, and conflicts in teaching and learning style.

However, the underlying factor that distinguishes these problems from those of primary cultural differences is the style, not the content. Sociolinguists stress differences in communication style; cognitive researchers emphasize cognitive styles, styles of thought, or a mismatch between teacher and minority students in cognitive maps; interactionists and transactionists locate the problem in differences in interactional style. Researchers working among native Hawaiians traced their reading problems to differences in learning style (Au, 1981).

What needs to be stressed is that secondary cultural differences do not merely cause initial problems in the social adjustment and academic performance of involuntary minorities, but that the problems appear to be extensive and persistent. One reason for this is that these minorities find it harder to cross cultural and language boundaries.

This difficulty occurs because of the nature of the relationship between the minority culture and the dominant White American culture. The cultural differences arose initially to serve boundary-maintaining and coping functions under subordination. As boundary-maintaining mechanisms, they do not necessarily disappear or change when involuntary minorities and Whites are brought together, as in desegregated schools. Secondary cultural differences evolved as coping mechanisms under "oppressive conditions," and the minorities have no strong incentives to give up these differences as long as they believe that they are still oppressed; some of the cultural differences have taken on a life of their own, and the minorities are not necessarily aware of their boundary-maintaining functions or oppositional quality.

Involuntary minorities interpret the cultural and language differences as markers of their collective identity to be maintained, not as barriers to be overcome. This results partly from coexistence of opposing cultural frames of reference discussed earlier. There is, again, no incentive to learn or behave in a manner considered consciously and unconsciously as inappropriate for the minorities.

Among involuntary minorities, school learning tends to be equated with the learning of the culture and language of White Americans, that is, the learning of the cultural and language frames of reference of their "enemy" or "oppressors." Consider the current argument by some that school curriculum and textbooks are reflective of White culture. (Note that for their part, White Americans also define minority school learning in terms of learning White culture and language as reflected in the school curriculum and practices.) Thus, involuntary minorities may consciously or unconsciously interpret school learning as a displacement process detrimental to their social identity, sense of security, and self-worth. They fear that by learning the White cultural frame of reference, they will cease to act like minorities and lose their identity as minorities and their sense of community and self-worth. Furthermore, reality has demonstrated that those who successfully learn to act White or who succeed in school are not fully accepted by the Whites; nor do such people receive rewards or opportunity for advancement equal to those open to Whites with similar education.

The important point here is that unlike voluntary minorities, involuntary minorities do not seem to be able or willing to separate attitudes and behaviors that result in academic success from those that may result in linear acculturation or replacement of their cultural identity with White American cultural identity.

There are social pressures discouraging involuntary minority students from adopting the standard attitudes and behavior practices that enhance school learning because such attitudes and behaviors are considered "White." In the case of Black students, for example, the social pressures against "acting White" include accusations of Uncle Tomism or disloyalty to the Black cause and to the Black community, and fear of losing one's friends and one's sense of community (Fordham & Ogbu, 1986; Luster, 1992; Ogbu, 1974; Petroni, 1970).

The same phenomenon has been described for American Indian students—the tendency to "resist" adopting and following school rules of behavior and standard practices (Dumont, 1972; Kramer, 1991; Philips, 1972, 1983). According to some studies, Indian students enter the classroom with a cultural convention that dictates that they should not adopt the expected classroom rules of behavior and standard practices. A good illustration is Philips's study of Indian children on the Warm Springs Reservation in Oregon, referred to earlier. She found that the Indian students and their White teachers in an elementary school held different views about how students should interact with teachers and among themselves; they also held different views about how students should participate in classroom activities. Although the teachers' views apparently prevailed, the teachers were not particularly effective in classroom management and in getting the children to learn and perform.

There are also psychological pressures against "acting White" that are just as effective in discouraging involuntary minority students from striving for academic success. An involuntary minority individual who desires to do well in school may also define the behavior enhancing school success or the success itself as "acting White." Thinking that attitudes and behaviors associated with academic success and the success itself may result in loss of peer affiliation and support, and at the same time uncertain of White acceptance and support if he or she succeeds in learning to act White, a student may feel a personal conflict. Put differently, an involuntary minority student desiring and striving to do well in school is faced with the conflict between loyalty to the minority peer group, which provides a sense of community and security, and the desire to behave in ways that may improve school performance but that the peer group defines as "White."

The dilemma of involuntary minority students, then, is that they may have to choose between "acting White" (i.e., adopting "appropriate" attitudes and behaviors or school rules and standard practices that enhance academic success but that are perceived and interpreted by the minorities as typical of White Americans and therefore negatively sanctioned by them) and "acting Black," "acting Indian," "acting Chicano," and so on (i.e., adopting attitudes and behaviors that the minority students consider appropriate for their group but that are not necessarily conducive to school success).

We noted earlier that researchers among involuntary minorities repeatedly emphasize conflicts and discontinuities in teaching and learning due to differences in style rather than content. Stylistic differences are more diffuse and less specific than the content differences of primary cultural differences. The differences in manifest contents are not the overriding problem, because they also exist within the primary cultural differences of voluntary minorities. Rather, the differences that are more problematic among involuntary minorities are differences in style and are oppositional in relation to White or mainstream culture. Moreover, it is difficult for interventionists and teachers without special training to detect the problems and help the students.

Involuntary minorities lack some instrumental factors that motivate voluntary minorities to cross cultural boundaries. The latter try to overcome cultural, language, and other barriers because they strongly believe that there will be a material payoff later. Involuntary minorities—who did not choose to come to the United States motivated by hope of economic success or political freedom—believe less strongly. Furthermore, they lack the positive dual frame of reference of the immigrants, who compare their progress in the United States with that of their peers "back home." Involuntary minorities compare their progress—if at all—with that of White Americans, and they usually conclude that they are worse off than they should be and blame Whites, the schools, and other societal institutions controlled by Whites. Thus these minorities do not have strong incentives merely to play the classroom game by the rules (Gibson, 1988).

THE INDIVIDUAL IN COLLECTIVE ADAPTATION

We have described what appears to be the dominant pattern for each type of minority. But when we enter a minority community, whether of voluntary or involuntary minorities, we usually find some students who are doing well in school and other students who are not. We also find that the members of each community know that some strategies enhance school success and other strategies do not. We may even learn about the kinds of individuals and subgroups who use the different strategies. However, the strategies of a voluntary minority community are not necessarily the same as those of the involuntary minorities (Ogbu, 1989).

Among the voluntary minorities there appears to be a collective orientation toward making good grades in school and there also appear to be social pressures, including peer pressures, that encourage making good grades. In addition, community gossips promote striving for school success. Partly to avoid ridicule (which may extend to one's family), criticism, and isolation, voluntary minority youths tend to utilize those strategies that enhance their chances to succeed in school. The community also appears to use both tangible and symbolic means to encourage school striving. While successful members of the group may live outside the ethnic neighborhood, they tend to maintain social membership there and participate in activities in which they mix informally with the residents. They thus provide concrete evidence to the youth both that they can succeed through education and that they can be bona fide members of the community in spite of their success. Finally, voluntary minority students are eager to utilize information and resources available in school.

For involuntary minorities the situation is somewhat different. Although making good grades is strongly verbalized by students, parents, and the community as a desirable goal, there is less community and family pressure to achieve it. For example, there is rarely any stigma attached to being a poor student, and there are no community gossips criticizing a poor student or his or her family. As for peer groups, their collective orientation is probably against academic striving. Therefore, peer pressures discourage making good grades. Students who adopt attitudes and behaviors enhancing school success or who make good grades may be subjected to negative peer pressures, including criticism and isolation.

Under this circumstance, involuntary minority youths who want to succeed academically often consciously choose from a variety of secondary strategies to shield them from the peer pressures and other detracting forces of the community. The secondary strategies are over and above the conventional strategy of adopting proper academic attitudes, hard work, and perseverance. These strategies provide the context in which the student can practice the conventional strategy.

I will use Black students as an example of involuntary minorities employing secondary strategies. I have identified among them the following strategies, some promoting school success, some not.

1. Emulation of Whites or cultural passing (i.e., adopting "White" academic attitudes and behaviors or trying to behave like middle-class White students). Some students say, "If it takes acting like White people to do well in school, I'll do that." Such students get good grades. The problem is, however, that they usually experience isolation from other Black students, resulting in high psychological costs.

2. Accommodation without assimilation—an alternation model—a characteristic strategy among voluntary minorities. A student adopting this strategy behaves according to school norms while at school, but at home in the community behaves according to Black norms. One school counselor in Stockton described this strategy this way: "Their motto seems to be 'Do your Black thing [in the community] but know the White man thing [at school].'" Black students who adopt this strategy do not pay the psychological costs that attend White emulators.

3. Camouflage (i.e., disguising true academic attitudes and behaviors), using a variety of techniques. One technique is to become a jester or class clown. Since peer group members are not particularly interested in how well a student is doing academically, the student claims to lack interest in school, that schoolwork/homework or getting good grades is not important. The camouflaging student studies in secret. The good grades of camouflaging students are attributed to their "natural smartness." Another way of camouflaging is to become involved in "Black activities." If a Black athlete gets As, there's no harm done.

4. Involvement in church activities. This also promotes school success.

5. Attending private schools. For some, this is a successful way to get away from peer groups.

6. Mentors. Having a mentor is another success-enhancing strategy.

7. Protection. A few students secure the protection of bullies from peer pressures in return for helping the bullies with their homework.

8. Remedial and intervention programs. Some students succeed because they participate in such a program.

9. Encapsulation. Many Black youths, unfortunately, become encapsulated in peer group logic and activities. These students don't want to do the White man's thing or don't consider schooling important for a variety of reasons. They don't do their schoolwork. Many fail.

WHAT CAN BE DONE

Prerequisites

Recognize that there are different kinds of cultural/language differences and that the different types arise for different reasons or circumstances.

Recognize that there are different types of minority groups and that the minority types are associated with the different types of cultural/language differences.

Recognize that all minority children face problems of social adjustment and academic performance in school because of cultural/language differences. However, while problems faced by bearers of primary cultural differences are superficially similar to those of bearers of secondary cultural differences, they are fundamentally different. The reason lies in the difference in the relationship between the two types of cultural differences and White American mainstream culture.

Helping Children With Primary Cultural/Language Differences

Most problems caused by primary cultural differences are due to differences in cultural content and practice. One solution is for teachers and interventionists to learn about the students' cultural backgrounds and use this knowledge to organize their classrooms and programs, to help students learn what they teach, to help students get along with one another, to communicate with parents, and the like. Teachers and interventionists can learn about the students' cultures through: (a) observation of children's behavior in the classroom and on playgrounds, (b) asking children questions about their cultural practices and preferences, (c) talking with parents about their cultural practices and preferences, (d) doing research on various ethnic groups with children in school, and (e) studying published works on children's ethnic groups.

Some problems caused by primary cultural differences can also be solved through well-designed and implemented multicultural education. Such multicultural education must be based on actual knowledge of the cultures and languages of the children's ethnic groups, how they differ from mainstream culture and language, and the kinds of problems they generate.

Helping Children With Secondary Cultural/Language Differences

First, teachers and interventionists must recognize that involuntary minority children come to school with cultural and language frames of reference that are not only different from but probably oppositional to those of the mainstream and school. Second, teachers and interventionists should study the histories and cultural adaptations of involuntary minorities in order to understand the bases and nature of the groups' cultural and language frames of reference as well as the children's sense of social identity. This knowledge will help them understand why these factors affect the process of minority schooling, particularly their school orientations and behaviors.

Third, special counseling and related programs should be used (a) to help involuntary minority students learn to separate attitudes and behaviors enhancing school success from those that lead to linear acculturation or "acting White" and (b) to help the students to avoid interpreting the former as a threat to their social identity and sense of security.

Fourth, programs are needed to increase students' adoption of the strategy of "accommodation without assimilation," "alternation model," or "playing the classroom game." The essence of this strategy is that students should recognize and accept the fact that they can participate in two cultural or language frames of reference for different purposes without losing their own cultural and language identity or undermining their loyalty to the minority community. They should learn to practice "when in Rome, do as the Romans do," without becoming Romans.

We have found from ethnographic studies (Ogbu & Hickerson, 1980) that whereas voluntary minority students try to learn to act according to school norms and expectations, involuntary minority students do not necessarily do so. Instead, they emphasize learning how to manipulate "the system," how to deal with or respond to White people and schools controlled by White people or their minority representatives. This problem should be addressed. A related approach that can be built into multicultural education programs is teaching the students their own responsibility for their academic performance and school adjustment.

Finally, society can help reorient minority youths toward more academic striving for school credentials for future employment by (a) creating more jobs in general, (b) eliminating the job ceiling against minorities, and (c) providing better employment opportunities for minorities.

The Role of the Involuntary Minority Community

The involuntary minority community can and should play an important part in changing the situation for three reasons. First, some of the needed changes can be most effectively brought about through community effort. Second, minority children do not succeed or fail only because of what schools do or do not do, but also because of what the community does. Third, our comparative research suggests that the social structure and relationship within the minority communities could be a significant influence on students' educational orientations and behaviors.

At this point in my research I suggest four ways in which the involuntary minority community can encourage academic striving and success among its children. One is to teach the children to separate attitudes and behaviors that lead to academic success from attitudes and behaviors that lead to a loss of ethnic identity and culture or language. This can be achieved partly by successful members of the group retaining their social membership in the community and not dissociating themselves from the neighborhood, labeling the less successful invidiously as "underclass," and so on. Second, the involuntary minority community should provide the children with concrete evidence that its members appreciate and value academic success as much as they appreciate and value achievements in sports, athletics, and entertainment.

Third, the involuntary minority community must teach the children to recognize and accept the responsibility for their school adjustment and academic performance. One difference between voluntary and involuntary minorities is that the former place a good deal of responsibility on the children for their school behavior and academic performance (Gibson, 1988).

Finally, the involuntary minority middle class needs to reevaluate and change its role vis-à-vis the community. We have discovered in our comparative research two contrasting models of middle-class relationship with minority community that we suspect have differential effects on minority school success. The first model is, apparently, characteristic of voluntary minorities. Here successful, educated, and professional individuals, such as business people, doctors, engineers, lawyers, social workers, and university professors, appear to retain their social membership in the community, although they generally reside outside predominantly minority neighborhoods. Such people regard their accomplishments as a positive contribution to their community, a community, not just individual, achievement. The community, in turn, interprets their accomplishments in a similar manner. The successful members participate in community events where they interact with the youth and less successful adults informally and outside their official roles as representatives of the welfare, police, school district, or White-controlled companies. In this community, the middle class provides concrete evidence to young people that school success pays and that school success and economic and professional success in the wider society are compatible with collective identity and bona fide membership in the minority community.

In contrast, involuntary minorities seem to have a model that probably does not have much positive influence on schooling. Members of involuntary minorities seem to view professional success as "a ticket" to leave their community both physically and socially, to get away from those who have not "made it." People seek education and professional success, as it were, in order to leave their minority community. White Americans and their media reinforce this by praising those who have made their way out of the ghetto, barrio, or reservation. The middle-class minorities do not generally interpret their achievements as an indication that "their community is making it"; neither does the community interpret their achievements as an evidence of the "development" or "progress" of its members. The middle class may later return to or visit the community with "programs," or as "advocates" for those left behind, or as representatives of White institutions. They rarely participate in community events where they interact outside these roles with the youth and the less successful community members. Thus, the involuntary minority middle class does not provide adequate concrete evidence to the youth and the less successful that

school success leads to social and economic success in later adult life. The involuntary minority middle class must rethink its role vis-à-vis the minority youth. What is needed is for the middle class to go beyond programs, advocacy, and institutional representation to reaffiliate with the community socially.

References

Appleton, N. (1983). *Cultural pluralism in education: Theoretical foundation.* New York: Longman.

Au, K. H. (1981). Participant structure in a reading lesson with Hawaiian children: Analysis of a culturally appropriate instructional event. *Anthropology and Education Quarterly, 10*(2), 91–115.

Baker, G. C. (1978). The role of the school in transmitting the culture of all learners in a free and democratic society. *Educational Leadership, 36*(2), 134–138.

Banks, J. A. (1981). *Multiethnic education: Theory and practice.* Boston: Allyn and Bacon.

Banks, J. A. (1989a). Integrating the curriculum with ethnic content: Approaches and guidelines. In J. A. Banks & C. A. M. Banks (Eds.), *Multicultural education: Issues and perspectives* (pp. 189–207). Boston: Allyn and Bacon.

Banks, J. A. (1989b). Multicultural education: Characteristics and goals. In J. A. Banks & C. A. M. Banks (Eds.), *Multicultural education: Issues and perspectives* (pp. 2–26). Boston: Allyn and Bacon.

Banks, J. A. (1981). The nature of multiethnic education. In J. A. Banks (Ed.), *Education in the 80's: Multiethnic education* (pp. 15–23). Washington, DC: National Education Association.

Baptiste, H. P., Jr. (1979). The rekindling of cultural pluralism. In H. P. Baptiste & M. L. Baptiste (Eds.), *Developing multicultural education process in classroom instruction: Competencies for teachers* (pp. 9–17). Washington, DC: University Press of America.

Baugh, J. (1984). *Black street speech: Its history, structure, and survival.* Austin: University of Texas Press.

Bennett, W. J. (1984). *To reclaim a legacy: A report on the humanities in higher education.* Washington, DC: National Endowment for the Humanities.

Bloom, A. (1987). *The closing of the American mind: How higher education has failed democracy and impoverished the souls of today's students.* New York: Simon & Schuster.

Boykin, A. W. (1980, November). *Reading achievement and the sociocultural frame of reference of Afro-American children.* Paper presented at NIE Roundtable Discussion on Issues in Urban Reading. Washington, DC: The National Institute of Education.

Bullivant, B. M. (1981). *The pluralist dilemma in education.* Sydney, Australia: George Allen & Unwin.

Bullock, H. A. (1970). *A history of Negro education in the South from 1619 to the present.* New York: Praeger.

Byers, P., & Byers, H. (1972). Non-verbal communication and the education of children. In C. B. Cazden, D. Hymes, & V. John-Steiner (Eds.), *Functions of language in the classroom* (pp. 3–31). New York: Teachers College Press.

Carroll, T. G., & Schensul, J. J. (Eds.). (1990). Cultural diversity and American education: Visions of the future [Special issue]. *Education and Urban Society, 22*(4).

Castile, G. P., & Kushner, G. (Eds.). (1981). *Persistent peoples: Cultural enclaves in perspective.* Tucson: University of Arizona Press.

Chung, J. P.-L. (1992). *The out-of-class language and social experience of a clique of Chinese immigrant students: An ethnography of a process of social identity formation.* Unpublished doctoral dissertation, State University of New York at Buffalo.

Closs, M. P. (Ed.). (1986). *Native American mathematics.* Austin: University of Texas Press.

DeVos, G. A. (1967). Essential elements of caste: Psychological determinants in structural theory. In G. A. DeVos & H. Wagatsuma (Eds.), *Japan's invisible race: Caste in culture and personality* (pp. 332–384). Berkeley: University of California Press.

DeVos, G. A. (1973). Japan's outcasts: The problem of the Burakumin. In B. Whitaker (Ed.), *The fourth world: Victims of group oppression* (pp. 307–327). New York: Schocken.

DeVos, G. A. (1984, April). *Ethnic persistence and role degradation: An illustration from Japan.* Paper presented at the American-Soviet Symposium on Contemporary Ethnic Processes in the USA and the USSR, New Orleans, LA.

DeVos, G. A., & Lee, C. (1981). *Koreans in Japan.* Berkeley: University of California Press.

Dumont, R. V., Jr. (1972). Learning English and how to be silent: Studies in Sioux and Cherokee classrooms. In C. B. Cazden, D. Hymes, & V. John-Steiner (Eds.), *Functions of language in the classroom* (pp. 344–369). New York: Teachers College Press.

Edmonds, R. (1986). Characteristics of effective schools. In U. Neisser (Ed.), *The school achievement of minority children: New perspectives* (pp. 93–104). Hillsdale, NJ: Lawrence Erlbaum Associates.

Essien-Udom, E. U. (1964). *Black nationalism: A search for identity in America.* New York: Dell.

Erickson, F., & Mohatt, G. (1982). Cultural organization of participant structure in two classrooms of Indian students. In G. D. Spindler (Ed.), *Doing the ethnography of schooling: Educational anthropology in action* (pp. 132–175). New York: Holt.

Finn, C. E. (1989, July 16). Norms for the nation's schools. *Washington Post,* p. B7.

Fordham, S. (1984, November). *Ethnography in a Black high school: Learning not to be a native.* Paper presented at the annual Meeting of the American Anthropological Association, Denver.

Fordham, S., & Ogbu, J. U. (1986). Black students' school success: Coping with the "burden of 'acting white.'" *Urban Review, 18*(3), 176–206.

Gay, G. (1979). Changing conceptions of multicultural education. In H. P. Baptiste & M. L. Baptiste (Eds.), *Developing the multicultural process in classroom instruction: Competencies for teachers* (Vol. 1, pp. 18–27). Washington, DC: University Press of America.

Gay, G. (1988). Designing relevant curricula for diverse learners. *Education and Urban Society, 20*(4), 327–340.

Gay, G. (1990). Achieving education equality through curriculum design. *Phi Delta Kappan, 70,* 56–62.

Gay, J., & Cole, M. (1967). *The new mathematics and an old culture: A study of learning among the Kpelle of Liberia.* New York: Holt.

Gibson, M. A. (1976). Approaches to multicultural education in the United States: Some concepts and assumptions. *Anthropology and Education Quarterly, 7*(4), 7–18.

Gibson, M. A. (1987). Playing by the rules. In G. D. Spindler (Ed.), *Education and cultural process* (2nd ed., pp. 274–281). Prospect Heights, IL: Waveland Press.

Gibson, M. A. (1988). *Accommodation without assimilation: Sikh immigrants in an American high school.* Ithaca, NY: Cornell University Press.

Gibson, M. A. (1991). Ethnicity, gender and social class: The social adaptation patterns of West Indian youths. In M. A. Gibson & J. U. Ogbu (Eds.), *Minority status and schooling: A comparative study of immigrants and involuntary minorities* (pp. 169–203). New York: Garland.

Gibson, M. A., & Ogbu, J. U. (Eds.). (1991). *Minority status and schooling: A comparative study of immigrants and involuntary minorities.* New York: Garland.

Grant, C. A., & Sleeter, C. E. (1986). Educational equity: Education that is multicultural and social reconstructionist. *Journal of Educational Equity and Leadership, 6*(2), 105–118.

Green, V. (1981). Blacks in the United States: The creation of an enduring people? In G. P. Castile & G. Kushner (Eds.), *Persistent peoples: Cultural enclaves in perspective* (pp. 69–77). Tucson: University of Arizona Press.

Gumperz, J. J. (1981). Conversational inference and classroom learning. In J. Green & C. Wallat (Eds.), *Ethnographic approaches to face-to-face interaction* (pp. 3–23). Norwood, NJ: Ablex.

Hall, R. A. (1978). *Black separatism in the United States.* Hanover, NH: New England University Press.

Hirasawa, Y. (1989). *A policy study of the evolution of Dowa education in Japan.* Unpublished doctoral dissertation, Harvard University.

Hirsch, E. D. (1987). *Cultural literacy: What every American needs to know.* Boston: Houghton Mifflin.

Hirsch, E. D. (1988, July/August). Cultural literacy: What every American needs to know, E. D. Hirsch, Jr.: A postscript by E. D. Hirsch, Jr. *Change,* pp. 22–26.

Holt, G. S. (1972). "Inversion" in Black communication. In T. Kochman (Ed.), *Rappin' and stylin' out: Communication in urban Black America* (pp. 152–159). Chicago: University of Illinois Press.

Ito, H. (1967). Japan's outcastes in the United States. In G. A. DeVos & H. Wagatasuma (Eds.), *Japan's invisible race: Caste in culture and personality* (pp. 200–221). Berkeley: University of California Press.

Kochman, T. (1982). *Black and White styles in conflict.* Chicago: University of Chicago Press.

Kramer, B. L. (1991). Education and American Indians: The experience of the Ute Indian tribe. In M. A. Gibson & J. U. Ogbu (Eds.), *Minority status and schooling: A comparative study of immigrants and involuntary minorities* (pp. 287–307). New York: Garland.

Kristoff, N. D. (1992, February 7). In China, the Koreans shine ("It's Our Custom"). *New York Times,* p. A7.

Lee, Y. (1991). Koreans in Japan and United States. In M. A. Gibson & J. U. Ogbu (Eds.), *Minority status and schooling: A comparative study of immigrants and involuntary minorities* (pp. 131–167). New York: Garland.

Luster, L. (1992). *Schooling, survival, and struggle: Black women and the GED.* Unpublished doctoral dissertation, Stanford University.

Matute-Bianchi, M. E. (1986). Ethnic identities and patterns of school success and failure among Mexican-descent and Japanese-American students in a California high school: An ethnographic analysis. *American Journal of Education, 95*(1), 233–255.

Ogbu, J. U. (1974). *The next generation: An ethnography of education in an urban neighborhood.* New York: Academic Press.

Ogbu, J. U. (1977). Racial stratification and education: The case of Stockton, California. *ICRD Bulletin, 12*(3), 1–26.

Ogbu, J. U. (1978). *Minority education and caste: The American system in cross-cultural perspective.* New York: Academic Press.

Ogbu, J. U. (1987). Variability in minority school performance: A problem in search of an explanation. *Anthropology and Education Quarterly, 18*(4), 312–334.

Ogbu, J. U. (1988). Diversity and equity in public education: Community forces and minority school adjustment and performance. In R. Haskins & D. Macrae (Eds.), *Policies for America's public schools: Teachers, equity, and indicators* (pp. 127–170). Norwood, NJ: Ablex.

Ogbu, J. U. (1989). The individual in collective adaptation: A framework for focusing on academic underperformance and dropping out among involuntary minorities. In L. Weis, E. Farrar, & H. G. Petrie (Eds.), *Dropouts from school: Issues, dilemmas and solutions* (pp. 181–204). Albany: State University of New York Press.

Ogbu, J. U. (1990). Minority status and literacy in comparative perspective. *Daedalus, 119*(2), 141–168.

Ogbu, J. U. (1991). Low school performance as an adaptation: The case of Blacks in Stockton, California. In M. A. Gibson & J. U. Ogbu (Eds.), *Minority status and schooling: A comparative study of immigrants and involuntary minorities* (pp. 249–285). New York: Garland.

Ogbu, J. U. (1993). Differences in cultural frame of reference. *International Journal of Behavioral Development, 6*(3), 483–506.

Ogbu, J. U., & Hickerson, R. (1980). *Survival strategies and role models in the ghetto.* Special Project, University of California, Berkeley, Department of Anthropology.

Ogbu, J. U., & Matute-Bianchi, M. E. (1986). Understanding sociocultural factors in education: Knowledge, identity, and adjustment in schooling. In California State Department of education, Bilingual Education Office, *Beyond language: Social and cultural factors in schooling language minority students* (pp. 73–142). Sacramento: California State University, Los Angeles, Evaluation, Dissemination, and Assessment Center.

Orr, E. W. (1987). *Twice as less: Black English and the performance of Black students in mathematics and science.* New York: Norton.

Passow, A. H. (1984). *Equity and excellence: Confronting the dilemma.* Paper presented at the First International Conference on Education in the 1990s, Tel Aviv, Israel.

Petroni, F. A. (1970). Uncle Toms: White stereotypes in the Black movement. *Human Organization, 29,* 260–266.

Philips, S. U. (1972). Participant structure and communicative competence: Warm Springs children in community and classroom. In C. B. Cazden, D. Hymes, & V. John-Steiner (Eds.), *Functions of language in the classroom* (pp. 370–394). New York: Teachers College Press.

Philips, S. U. (1976). Commentary: Access to power and maintenance of ethnic identity as goals of multi-cultural education. *Anthropology and Education Quarterly, 7*(4), 30–32.

Philips, S. U. (1983). *The invisible culture: Communication in classroom and community on the Warm Springs Indian Reservation.* New York: Longman.

Ramírez, M., & Castañeda, A. (1974). *Cultural democracy, bicognitive development and education.* New York: Academic Press.

Rohlen, T. (1981). Education: Policies and prospects. In C. Lee & G. A. DeVos (Ed.), *Koreans in Japan: Ethnic conflicts and accommodation* (pp. 182–222). Berkeley: University of California Press.

Rubalcava, M. (1991). *Locating transformative teaching in multicultural education.* Unpublished manuscript, Special Project, University of California, Berkeley, Department of Anthropology.

Shade, B. J. (1982). *Afro-American patterns of cognition.* Unpublished manuscript, Wisconsin Center for Educational Research, Madison.

Shimahara, N. K. (1991). *Social mobility and education: Buraku in Japan.* In M. A. Gibson & J. U. Ogbu (Eds.), *Minority status and schooling: A comparative study of immigrants and involuntary minorities* (pp. 249–285). New York: Garland.

Sleeter, C. E., & Grant, C. A. (1987). An analysis of multicultural education in the United States. *Harvard Educational Review, 57*(4), 421–444.

Solomon, R. P. (1992). *The creation of separation: Black culture and struggle in an American high school*. Albany: State University of New York Press.

Spicer, E. H. (1966). The process of cultural enslavement in Middle America. *36th Congress of international de Americanistas, Seville, 3,* 267–279.

Spicer, E. H. (1971). Persistent cultural systems: A comparative study of identity systems that can adapt to contrasting environments. *Science, 174,* 795–800.

Suarez-Orozco, M. M. (1987). Become somebody: Central American immigrants in U.S. inner-city schools. *Anthropology & Education Quarterly, 18*(4), 287–299.

Suzuki, B. H. (1984). Curriculum transformation for multicultural education. *Education and Urban Society, 16*(3), 294–322.

Taylor, M. J., & Hegarty, S. (1985). *The best of both worlds: A review of research into the education of pupils of South Asian origin*. Windsor, UK: National Foundation for Education Research-Nelson.

Tomlinson, S. (1982). *A sociology of special education*. London: Routledge & Kegan Paul.

Weis, L. (1985). *Between two worlds: Black students in an urban community college*. Boston: Routledge & Kegan Paul.

Woolard, K. A. (1981). *Ethnicity in education: Some problems of language and identity in Spain and the United States*. Unpublished manuscript, University of California, Berkeley, Department of Anthropology.

Yee, G. (1991). *The melting pot revisited: A literature review of current literature in multicultural education*. Unpublished manuscript, Special Project, University of California, Berkeley, Department of Anthropology.

Part

· IX ·

INTERGROUP EDUCATION APPROACHES TO SCHOOL REFORM

· 33 ·

REVIEW OF RESEARCH ON SCHOOL DESEGREGATION'S IMPACT ON ELEMENTARY AND SECONDARY SCHOOL STUDENTS

Janet Ward Schofield

UNIVERSITY OF PITTSBURGH

The *Brown v. Board of Education of Topeka* decision was based on the constitutional principle of equal protection (Read, 1975; Wisdom, 1975). Yet for most majority and minority group members alike, the most immediate and pressing concern has been how desegregation is likely to affect children—especially their own children. This widespread concern about the impact of desegregation and the controversy over what its effects might be have led to a substantial amount of research. Some research explores desegregation's impact on a wide array of outcomes, such as residential integration, community protest movements, and employment patterns for teachers and administrators from various ethnic groups. However, there is much more research on the impact of desegregation on students themselves—most notably on their academic achievement and on relations between students from different ethnic and racial groups. It is this kind of work that is the focus of this review.

Before turning to a discussion of the conclusions that have emerged from research on the social and academic outcomes of desegregation, this chapter will deal with another important issue—the methodological and other problems that typify work in this area. Some readers may find the amount of space devoted to this topic excessive. However, concern with methodology and related issues is much more than pedantic nit-picking, since poor methodology can either mask real effects or suggest false ones. Those readers who desire an even more extended treatment of these issues are referred to Schofield (1991).

PROBLEMS IN ASSESSING THE EFFECTS OF SCHOOL DESEGREGATION

Deciding on the Relevant Studies

An attempt to assess the impact of school desegregation on students is limited by several factors. First, most of the actual implementation of school desegregation plans occurred in the late 1960s and early 1970s, and studies of these plans tended to be conducted in their early years. Thus a review that limits itself to studies of court-ordered plans will of necessity deal with dated research that may not generalize well to the current situation. Furthermore, it will concentrate on desegregation's short-term rather than its long-term impact. The economic and social position of African Americans in U.S society has changed substantially since the era in which most desegregation plans were implemented (Jaynes & Williams, 1989). So have the attitudes and behavior of a significant number of White Americans (Schuman, Steeh, & Bobo, 1985). In addition, striking demographic shifts, including the surburbanization of Whites and a sharp increase in the number of Hispanics living in the United States, have markedly changed the composition of the public school population in many areas of the country. Thus this review will not restrict itself to studies of desegregation as it is most strictly construed; it will also utilize, when they are pertinent, studies comparing students in segregated and racially mixed schools

This chapter is based on a paper originally commissioned by the Department of Education of the State of Connecticut. It has been printed here with their permission.

that are not functioning under formal desegregation plans. This literature is, generally speaking, somewhat more recent than most studies of court-ordered plans. However, it, too, tends to be a decade or more old because of numerous factors, including the difficulty researchers have experienced in recent years in getting funding for this sort of work (Schofield, 1991).

A second major obstacle to assessing the impact of desegregation on students is that resegregation within formally desegregated schools is common (Desegregation Studies Unit, 1977). Resegregation can stem from many factors as varied as traditional school practices with regard to ability grouping and tracking; federally mandated programs such as special education, compensatory education, or bilingual education; and students' own fears or prejudices (Desegregation Studies Unit, 1977; Epstein, 1985; Eyler, Cook, & Ward, 1983; Oakes, 1992; Schofield, 1982, 1989; Schofield & Sagar, 1979; Sullivan, 1979). Resegregation is not only a problem in situations involving African Americans and Whites. It often occurs in desegregation involving Hispanics as well. In fact, the need to provide appropriate education for children who are not proficient in English poses a special challenge that can lead to the resegregation of many Hispanic students if it is not handled with extreme care (Aspira of America, 1979; Cardenas, 1975; Carter, 1979; Carter & Segura, 1979; Donato, Menchaca, & Valencia, 1991; Hyland, 1992; Meier & Stewart, 1991; Orfield, 1978; Parson, 1965).

Sometimes resegregation is quite extreme, but researchers often take little cognizance of this fact. For example, Cohen's (1975) review of the literature on desegregation and intergroup relations points out that only one fifth of the studies done between 1968 and 1974 indicated whether there was actual interracial contact in the school studied. Thus it is often impossible to assess the extent to which students experienced desegregation at the classroom level. Yet this is the very sort of desegregation that research and theory suggest is most likely to have positive consequences.

Recognizing the Implications of Diversity

Desegregation is a political and legal concept. But situations that may appear identical in the sense that they are all legally desegregated may vary tremendously (Hare, 1991). For example, in addition to varying in the degree to which resegregation occurs, they may differ dramatically in the relative proportions of White, African American, Hispanic, and Asian students, the social class of the students, and the extent to which there are initial social-class and academic differences among the diverse racial and ethnic groups. There is reason to believe that differences such as these will have an impact on the outcomes of desegregation. For example, research suggests that the ratio of African Americans to Whites in a desegregated situation is related to intergroup attitudes (Crain, Mahard, & Narot, 1982; Dentler & Elkins, 1967; Longshore, 1982a, 1982b; Longshore & Prager, 1985; McPartland, 1968; Rosenfield, Sheehan, Marcus, & Stephan, 1981; St. John & Lewis, 1975; U.S. Commission on Civil Rights, 1967). Hence, it seems likely that the wide variation in the racial mix of the schools studied and in the schools' community settings contributes substantially to the difficulty in drawing any overall conclusions about the impact of desegregation.

Work in the field of evaluation research suggests that even desegregated situations that may appear similar in terms of the criteria mentioned above may vary markedly in the extent and manner of their implementation (Cook & Campbell, 1976; Cook, Levitan, & Shadish, 1985; Cronbach, 1982; Guttentag & Struening, 1975). Thus, even if one program looks superficially like another, one cannot safely assume that they actually take similar shape. This has important implications for the interpretation of large-scale studies that analyze outcome variables in a number of segregated and desegregated schools and conclude that desegregation has no impact. Indeed, it could be that desegregation has an impact that is masked because of variations in outcome due to uncontrolled differences in implementation. Alternatively, the positive impact of desegregation in some schools' classrooms might be counterbalanced by the negative impact in others. Sometimes investigators recognize these kinds of problems. More often, however, the problem is completely ignored.

Facing the Reality of Methodological Problems in Desegregation Research

Yet another issue that impedes assessing the impact of desegregation is the myriad of design and measurement problems that researchers face. As Crain (1976) has pointed out, there are strong pressures on researchers involved with studies on desegregation to complete their work rapidly. Hence, for a variety of reasons, including the fact that cross-sectional studies are generally less expensive and can be completed more quickly than longitudinal studies, the majority of the research dealing with the impact of desegregation is cross-sectional (i.e., comparing *different* groups of students with varying degrees of exposure to desegregation) rather than longitudinal (i.e., measuring the *same* group or groups of students at various points in time, usually before and after desegregation). It is ironic that cross-sectional data that are attractive to policy makers because of their relatively low cost and quick payoff do not allow one to make the causal inferences with which policy makers are frequently concerned.

Although longitudinal studies have some distinct advantages compared to cross-sectional studies, they frequently embody their own serious problems. First, they demand substantial financial resources and long-term cooperation from a school district. The pressures and difficulties of doing long-term work are so great that very few desegregation studies span more than one year. Although occasional studies do span two to five or more years (e.g., Bowman, 1973; Gerard & Miller, 1975; Laird & Weeks, 1966; Savage, 1971; Schofield, 1979, 1982, 1989; L. R. Smith, 1971), almost inevitably they tend to encounter potentially serious problems. For example, Gerard and Miller lost approximately one third of their original sample during three years of data collection. Furthermore, the tendency of longitudinal studies to cover short periods at the beginning of students' desegregated schooling severely limits the extent to which generalization from their findings is appropriate.

Many longitudinal studies of desegregation employ no control group, but simply measure a group of students before and after desegregation. This is a serious problem. The importance of control groups in longitudinal studies is heightened by the fact that there are both age trends and historical trends in many of the variables studied as outcomes of desegregation. For example, studies suggest that African American and White children generally interact less with those of the other race as they grow older (S. Aronson & Noble, 1966; Deutschberger, 1946; Dwyer, 1958; Shrum, Cheek, & Hunter, 1988; Trager & Yarrow, 1952). Hence, changes in interracial attitudes owing to age may be confused with changes resulting from desegregation unless a control group is available.

Desegregation studies are also often plagued by self-selection problems at the institutional and the individual levels that limit the researcher's ability to draw accurate conclusions. As Pettigrew (1969a) points out, schools that agree to make themselves available to researchers are probably not representative of all desegregated schools. For example, a number of districts, including Cleveland, Chicago, and Los Angeles, that are often regarded as having serious problems refused to permit their students to participate in a major federal survey of desegregated schools, even though such participation was ordered by Congress in the Civil Rights Act of 1964 (Pettigrew, 1969b). Similarly, children whose parents refuse to let them participate in research on desegregation may well be different in relevant ways from those who do participate.

In sum, any review of the literature on the effect of desegregation on outcomes such as academic achievement or intergroup attitudes must face the reality that much of the research is flawed in one way or another. However, it does appear possible to draw some conclusions, and that is the task to which this chapter will now turn. Because the amount, quality, and typical problems of research on different outcomes of desegregation differ markedly, no single set of standards has been adopted that will be applied across the board to determine whether a study is sound enough to be utilized in this review. Rather, in each section the reader will be provided with information on the database on which the conclusions in that section rest.

THE EFFECT OF SCHOOL DESEGREGATION ON ACADEMIC ACHIEVEMENT

There has been a great deal of research on the academic impact of school desegregation, in large part because of the expectation that school desegregation would enhance the achievement of minority pupils, which has clearly lagged behind that of Whites (Arias, 1986; Carrasquillo, 1991; Howard & Hammond, 1985; Pearl, 1991; Valencia, 1991). The reasons for this expectation have been many and varied. Some are relatively straightforward, such as the belief that the relatively superior facilities and better-educated staffs available in many previously all-White schools should enhance achievement. Others are more complex and psychologically oriented. For example, a number of social scientists have put forward variations on a theory that Miller (1980) has called the "lateral transmission of

values hypothesis"—the idea that minority groups coming into contact with Whites, who are often from more middle-class backgrounds, would be influenced by their middle-class peers' stronger orientation toward achievement (Coleman et al. 1966; Crain & Weisman, 1972; Pettigrew, 1969a). Research has not lent credence to this notion (Maruyama & Miller 1979; Maruyama, Miller, & Holtz, 1986; McGarvey, 1977; Miller, 1980; Patchen, 1982). However, there are enough plausible conjectures about why and how desegregation might influence minority-group achievement to make the issue worthy of investigation.

Although research on desegregation's impact on achievement has focused primarily on African American students, a number of studies have also addressed its impact on White students. Very little information is available about the impact of desegregation on Hispanic students' achievement, although this topic has begun to receive some attention.

School Desegregation and Black Math and Reading Achievement

A large number of reviews of the literature on desegregation and the achievement of African American students have been published since the mid-1970s (Armor, 1984; Bradley & Bradley, 1977; Cook, 1984; Crain, 1984b; Krol, 1978; Mahard & Crain, 1983; Miller & Carlson, 1984; Stephan, 1978, 1984; St. John, 1975; Walberg, 1984; Weinberg, 1977; Wortman, 1984). Since only a handful of studies on this topic have been conducted since the most recent of the reviews (Bennett & Easton, 1988; Carsrud, 1984; Gable & Iwanicki, 1986; Pride & Woodward, 1985), and their results are generally consistent with earlier research, these reviews will constitute the basis for the discussion presented here. However, it is important to note that there has been considerable debate over whether standardized tests, which are used to assess achievement in virtually all of the studies included in this review, are a valid indication of African American students' achievement (Fleming, 1990; Hilliard, 1990).

The earliest of the reviews just cited was conducted by St. John (1975), who examined over 60 studies of desegregation and African American achievement. She included at least four different kinds of desegregation in her review—desegregation occurring through demographic changes in neighborhoods, through school-board rezoning of districts or school closings, through voluntary transfer of pupils, and through total district desegregation. Although she classified studies by their design features, she did little or no selection of studies on methodological criteria. St. John concluded that "adequate data has not yet been gathered to determine a causal relation between school racial composition and academic achievement" (p. 36). The data did make clear, however, that neither Black nor White children suffer academically as a result of desegregation. Finally, St. John found some indication that younger African American children, especially those of kindergarten age, tend to gain greater academic benefit from desegregation than do older ones.

Weinberg (1977) reviewed 23 studies of African American achievement in interracial schools and another 48 studies of desegregated schools—those in which the interracial nature of the student body was a consequence of a conscious policy designed to end segregation. Like St. John (1975), he did not select studies on strict methodological criteria. He concluded that the majority of studies of both kinds indicated minority achievement in the racially mixed school settings superior to that in the segregated ones, although a substantial proportion reported no effect. Again there was no evidence of academic harm. Stephan's (1978) review came to a similar but not identical conclusion. He reported that the majority of studies suggested no impact, but that a substantial minority suggested positive outcomes.

Bradley and Bradley (1977) concur with Weinberg (1977) that a majority of the studies conclude that desegregation has positive effects on the achievement of African American students. However, they note that each of the studies showing positive effects suffers from methodological problems. (They also criticize most of the studies that show no effect.) Thus they conclude that the evidence suggests no effect or a positive one. One other feature of this review should be noted. All of the studies of open enrollment plans and "central schools," desegregated schools in small cities that house all of a system's students in given grades, show positive effects. In contrast, relatively few of those in which desegregation was achieved by school closing or busing show gains. However, Bradley and Bradley do not interpret these patterns as having any real significance because the number and quality of studies varies so much from one type of desegregation to another.

Krol's (1978) study was the first to apply meta-analytic techniques to the literature in this area. Meta-analysis provides a statistical method for combining results from different studies (Glass, McGaw, & Smith, 1981; Hunter, Schmidt, & Jackson, 1982; Rosenthal, 1978; Schmidt, 1992). Thus Krol's review differs from the other reviews in that it yields statistical estimates of desegregation's impact. Krol concluded overall that the average effect of desegregation on African American achievement is .16 standard deviations, which can be understood more meaningfully as from 1½ to 3 months gain per academic year. (The amount of gain depends on the kind of test.) The subset of studies with good control groups yielded a more modest estimate of .10 of a standard deviation in gain. Although these estimates are both positive, they are not statistically significant—that is, typical canons of quantitative analysis would not allow one to conclude from these data that there is an unambiguous positive impact of desegregation on achievement.

The last of the pre-1984 reviews was a meta-analysis authored by Mahard and Crain (1983). These reviewers examined a group of 93 studies including, atypically, some in which *ability* measures, rather than measures designed to tap achievement, were the dependent variable. The mean effect size in this review was .08, very similar to that produced by Krol (1978) for the "better studies." However, these reviewers argue that this underestimates desegregation's real potential, since this estimate is based on studies that included students who transferred from segregated to desegregated systems as well as studies of students who experienced only desegregated education. Examining 23 studies that compared the achievement of desegregated African American students in kindergarten and first grade

with that of their segregated peers, Mahard and Crain found a much larger effect, .25 of a standard deviation, roughly one third of a grade level. They also note that studies using measures of ability, such as IQ, found improvement similar to those that utilized achievement measures.

In 1984 the National Institute of Education (NIE) commissioned seven meta-analytic review papers examining the impact of school desegregation on African American academic achievement. The scholars responsible for these reviews agreed on a set of methodological criteria to be used in selecting a core group of studies for their analyses. Then each proceeded to conduct a meta-analysis and to write a paper detailing his conclusions. Three of the reviews are precisely what one would expect from the foregoing description, although individual authors tended to add or delete a few studies from the core group of 19 (Armor, 1984; Miller & Carlson, 1984; Stephan, 1984). Although Walberg (1984) presents the results of a meta-analysis of the core studies, his emphasis is on comparing the impact of desegregation with other educational policies or practices. Wortman (1984) reports a meta-analysis on a group of 31 studies that he felt were worthy of inclusion, as well as one performed on the basic 19. Crain's (1984b) review challenges on a number of cogent grounds the wisdom of selecting only 19 studies for review. Cook's (1984) paper examines the six others and asks what overall conclusions flow from the project as a whole. Thus this discussion will focus on Cook's paper, referring to the others where necessary. However, first an important issue raised by Crain's paper will be addressed.

Crain's (1984b) major point is that the panel's procedures led them inadvertently but systematically to underestimate desegregation's effect. Specifically, the panel selected only longitudinal studies, rejecting cross-sectional survey studies as methodologically inferior. They also rejected all longitudinal studies that used different pre- and posttests. However, use of these inclusion criteria almost automatically results in exclusion of virtually all of the studies of desegregation conducted with kindergartners and first-graders, since pretests for these age groups measure "readiness" as opposed to achievement, which is measured by the posttests. Crain demonstrates that studies of children of these grade levels, no matter what their design, yield both larger estimates of desegregation's impact and more consistently positive results than studies with other age groups. Furthermore, he argues that these studies are representative of the kind of desegregation most children experience, pointing out that most desegregation plans desegregate children from kindergarten or grade one on up. This means that in the early years of a desegregation program, when research is most likely to be carried out, older children enter desegregated schools having prior experience with segregated education. Their experience is thus quite different from that of the children who follow them, who will start in desegregated rather than in segregated schools, like the kindergarten and first-grade students in the rejected studies.

Cook (1984) concedes that Crain (1984b) has raised a pertinent issue, but fails to concur that the panel has made a fundamental error. He points out that a number of the studies Crain discusses stem from one voluntary desegregation program, and thus questions the generality of Crain's conclusions. In addition, he notes some possible technical problems in Crain's analysis. I am inclined to give more credence to Crain's concerns than Cook does for two reasons. First, it seems eminently plausible that transferring from a segregated to a desegregated school might cause adjustment problems that would not occur if one started school in a desegregated environment. If one wants to know the effect of desegregated schooling in general, it seems unwise to focus on students who have had to make a transition, especially if the study measuring desegregation's impact is carried out very close to the time of transition. Second, the technical criticisms that Cook raises with regard to Crain's work do not seem to me to challenge Crain's basic conclusion. In sum, Crain's paper raises the real possibility that the panel underestimated the academic impact of desegregation. This caveat should be kept in mind as the results of the panel's work are summarized.

Cook (1984) ends his paper with several conclusions based on his own analyses and his examination of the other commissioned papers. Since these conclusions seem to be a fair summary of the project's overall outcome, I will structure the following discussion around them. First, consistent with every other review of which I am aware, Cook concludes that desegregation does not undermine African American achievement. None of the individual 1984 papers even suggest a negative impact of desegregation on African American achievement.

Second, Cook concludes that, on the average, desegregation does not lead to an increase in the mathematics achievement of African American students, a conclusion consistent with that of Armor (1984), Miller and Carlson (1984), and Stephan (1984). Wortman reported a small positive effect on math in the core studies and a larger one in his set of 31 studies. Crain (1984b) and Walberg (1984) do not deal with the distinction between reading and mathematics gains in any detailed way.

In contrast to the situation with mathematics, Cook concludes that desegregation does increase the mean reading level of African American students. All of the panelists who dealt with the issue agreed that reading gains occurred. Their estimates ranged from .06 to .26 of a standard deviation, which translates into roughly a two- to six-week gain. These gains were generally computed *per study* rather than per year. Interpreting this gain is complex. First, one can think of it as a rough estimate of what is gained in a year of desegregation, since most of the studies included in the core group spanned just one year. On the other hand, there is no evidence to justify multiplying this effect by 12 to estimate gain over a student's entire elementary and secondary career. In fact, there is some counterevidence (Mahard & Crain, 1983). While the small number of studies spanning two years tended to find larger effects than those covering just one, the reverse was the case for the three studies that lasted three years. Further, the majority of the studies in the core covered the first year of desegregation, which may differ from later years in important ways, including its impact on achievement.

Cook also urges caution in interpreting these results because, although some mean or average gain seems clearly present, other methods of looking at the data do not lead to such an optimistic conclusion. Specifically, the median scores in these reviews, the scores that have an equal number of

scores above and below them, were almost always greater than zero but lower than the means. Also, the modal gain scores, the most frequently found scores, were near zero. The explanation for these apparently somewhat contradictory findings is that all of the analyses included some studies with unusually large gains. Such gains contributed substantially to raising the overall means, but had a much less potent effect on the medians and modes.

These technical distinctions are worth making because of their implications for the interpretation of the data. Specifically, the gain in mean reading scores suggests that desegregation, on the average, will bring academic benefits. However, the less impressive results for the medians and modes suggest that not all instances of desegregation will lead to academic gains.

The fact that some schools show atypically large gains supports the point made earlier that desegregation is a varied process and that different instances of this process can be expected to have very different outcomes. It also suggests the potential utility of exploring the achievement research systematically to see if certain types of desegregation experiences tend to be associated with particularly large or small achievement gains. This task is difficult to achieve with the NIE-sponsored reviews for several reasons. First, the core group included only 19 studies of quite similar situations. Specifically, almost all of them involved just one or two years of desegregation, making comparison between initial and later gains difficult. Similarly, 15 of the 19 core studies were of voluntary desegregation, making comparison between voluntary and mandatory programs problematic. Nonetheless, these reviews and others, especially Mahard and Crain (1983), do give some tentative indications of which characteristics of desegregation programs may have a positive impact on academic achievement.

One suggestion that emerges repeatedly in the reviews is that desegregation may be most effective when carried out in elementary school, especially in the early elementary years (St. John, 1975; Cook, 1984; Crain, 1984b; Stephan, 1984). Crain and Mahard and Crain (1983) present the most detailed discussion of this issue and make the strongest case for this point of view. Mahard and Crain point out that all 11 samples of students they examined that began desegregation in kindergarten, and over three fourths of the 44 groups of students who were desegregated as first-graders, showed achievement gains. In sharp contrast, roughly 50% of the samples of students in the more advanced grades did so. In addition, the estimated effect size of the changes for the kindergartners and first-graders is greater than those previously discussed, being .25 of a standard deviation or roughly equivalent to one third of a year in school. Thus Mahard and Crain conclude that the academic "effects of desegregation are almost completely restricted to the early primary grades" (p. 125). As discussed previously, Cook raises several technical issues that somewhat weaken the apparent strength of Mahard and Crain's data. Yet Cook's own analysis of the NIE core studies supports the idea that early desegregation is the most beneficial by demonstrating gains that are largest in the second grade and tend to decrease markedly thereafter.

There is also some indication that the type of desegregation program may make a difference in achievement effects. Mahard and Crain (1983) present data suggesting that metropolitan desegregation plans may have stronger achievement effects than others. This finding is consistent with the suggestion made by Cook (1984) and Stephan (1984) that voluntary plans may have a greater impact than mandatory ones, since virtually all of the metropolitan plans in Mahard and Crain's sample involved the voluntary transfer of African American students from inner-city to suburban schools. Their findings are also consistent with Bradley and Bradley's (1977) finding that all the studies of open enrollment programs, another kind of voluntary program, reported positive effects.

The search for other variables that influence the impact of desegregation on African American students' academic achievement is greatly impeded by lack of information about the characteristics of the schools studied, as well as the methodological problems discussed earlier. Thus, rather than speculate on the basis of single studies or inadequate groups of studies, this chapter will now turn to examining the impact of desegregation on Hispanic students' academic achievement.

School Desegregation and Hispanic Achievement

There is little empirical evidence about the impact of school desegregation on the academic achievement of Hispanic students (Orfield, 1986). During the heyday of empirical work on the effect of desegregation on student outcomes, roughly 1968 to 1975, Hispanic students were virtually ignored. The extent of the phenomenon is illustrated by the fact that several discussions on the impact of desegregation on Hispanic students published during that period cite no more than two or three studies (Carter, 1979; Weinberg, 1970, 1977). This lack of attention to how desegregation affects Hispanic students undoubtedly had a number of causes, including the fact that the courts were still in the process of deciding whether Hispanic students would be treated as an identifiable ethnic minority group eligible for the same legal protections as Blacks under the *Brown* decision. In more recent years, as the number of Hispanics living in the United States has burgeoned, considerable attention has been turned to issues related to the education of Hispanic children (Alvarez, 1992; Arias, 1986; Carrasquillo, 1991; Duran, 1983; G. G. Gonzalez, 1990; Meier & Stewart, 1991; Valencia, 1991). However, with some exceptions that will be discussed below, this work has not focused on the impact of desegregation.

Another factor that makes it difficult to assess the impact of desegregation on the achievement of Hispanic students generally is that the relatively few studies of this issue that are available deal almost exclusively with Mexican Americans. Although Mexican Americans and other Hispanic groups certainly share certain aspects of language and culture, there is tremendous diversity among the groups that fall under the label *Hispanic* (Arias, 1986; Carrasquillo, 1991; Meier & Stewart, 1991; Orfield, 1986). Thus it is a mistake to assume that research results from the study of one of these groups can be applied automatically to others.

The major published source of information on the impact of desegregation on Hispanic students is a study conducted in Riverside, California (Gerard & Miller, 1975). This massive lon-

gitudinal study included over 1,700 students, 650 of whom were Mexican American. (The district was approximately 10% Mexican American, 6% African American, and 84% White.) The analyses presented in this study are numerous and somewhat complicated, but the ultimate conclusion is that desegregation did not significantly influence the achievement level of any of the groups, including the Mexican American children.

Several other studies report more positive findings. In a study of over 1,500 Mexican American junior high school students, Kimball (cited in Weinberg, 1977) found that the higher the proportion of Anglo students in the schools he studied, the greater the minority-group achievement. Feshbach and Adelman (1969) studied African American and Mexican American junior high school boys bused to a university-based private school. Not surprisingly, both groups gained markedly in achievement compared with a control group. Mahard and Crain (1980) used data from the National Longitudinal Study of the high school graduating class of 1972 to explore the impact of desegregation on Hispanics. They found a positive correlation between attendance at predominantly White schools and the achievement scores of Cuban, Puerto Rican, and Mexican American students. Arias (1989) concluded that desegregation increased the achievement of Hispanic and African American students when it raised the average socioeconomic background of the students' peers, but not otherwise. Finally, Morrison's (1972) study found that a group of desegregated Hispanic children gained significantly more in achievement during their elementary school years than did a control group of Hispanic peers in segregated schools. It is not clear why these studies suggest positive academic outcomes for Hispanic students, whereas Gerard and Miller's (1975) study does not. However, it should be noted that, to my knowledge, there is no social evidence suggesting negative academic outcomes of desegregation for Hispanic students.

Two kinds of more recent studies lend indirect support to the idea that segregation is implicated in the poor academic performance of many Hispanic students. First, a number of studies document the adverse educational conditions under which Hispanic students in segregated schools have often labored (G. G. Gonzalez, 1990; Menchaca & Valencia, 1990; Orfield, 1988). Second, there are studies that demonstrate a strong inverse relationship between the proportion of the school's student body that is Hispanic and the overall level of student achievement (Espinosa & Ochoa, 1986; Jaeger, 1987; Valencia, 1984). The existence of such a relationship does not lead inevitably to the conclusion that segregation is harmful academically or that desegregation would help. It could merely reflect the fact that Hispanic students on the average, like students from most other minority groups, come from homes that are lower in social class than White students, and that social class plays a major role in influencing students' achievement (Jencks et al., 1972). Nonetheless, these studies do document the fact that Hispanic students, like African American students, tend to be concentrated in schools in which achievement is relatively low, an environmental condition that seems likely to inhibit rather than bolster their achievement (Rumberger & Willms, 1992; Summers & Wolfe, 1977).

In summary, the data on the impact of desegregation on the academic achievement of Hispanics, while extremely fragmentary, are consistent with the more extensive data regarding African American achievement. Results appear to be either neutral or positive. However, whereas the preponderance of evidence suggests a positive outcome for African Americans, the most recent, extended, and sophisticated study of Hispanics does not. Clearly more research is needed before any firm conclusions can be drawn.

One further issue needs to be dealt with before leaving this topic. It is not uncommon for those discussing desegregation's impact on Hispanics to detail its impact on African Americans and then either to assume or to assert explicitly that "there is no reason to believe the outcomes [of desegregation for Hispanics] differ" (Carter & Segura, 1979, p. 325). This assumption ignores two potentially major differences. First, a substantial number of Hispanic children may know little if any English when they first enter school. Thus many Hispanic students face a language barrier that is less common for African Americans (Arias, 1986). Second, to the extent that culture influences students' preparation for and reaction to schooling, Hispanic children may be different from African Americans, as indeed different segments of the population labeled *Hispanic* differ from each other (Carrasquillo, 1991).

It is clearly beyond the scope of this chapter to evaluate thoroughly how the linguistic and cultural differences between African Americans and Hispanic Americans may affect the impact of desegregation. However, it is important to note that constructive thought has been given to the issue of handling the needs of children who are not proficient in English while at the same time avoiding or minimizing racial and ethnic isolation (California State Department of Education, 1983; Carter, 1979; Carter & Chatfield, 1986; Fernandez, 1978; Fernandez & Guskin, 1978; Garcia, 1976; J. M. Gonzalez, 1979; Haro, 1977; Heleen, 1987; Milan, 1978; National Institute of Education, 1977; Roos, 1978).

School Desegregation and White Achievement

There are a substantial number of studies on the impact of desegregation on White students' achievement, although nowhere near the number that have looked at African American students' achievement. This is hardly surprising, since desegregation is often seen as a strategy for improving the achievement of minority-group students and there is little reason to expect that desegregation in and of itself will improve the academic achievement of White students as measured by standardized tests. However, the issue of the impact of desegregation on White achievement demands attention since one of the major concerns expressed by Whites opposing desegregation is that it will undermine their children's academic progress. Whether this concern is based on knowledge about the link between school social class and student achievement level (Coleman et al., 1966) or on racial prejudice, it is sufficiently widespread that the issue merits consideration in this chapter.

The major review available on desegregation and White achievement is St. John's (1975). There is also an earlier review

of the literature by Weinberg (1970). Considering the age of both of these reviews, it is reasonable to question their usefulness today, since relations between Whites and African Americans have changed significantly since their publication. However, since extremely little research has been produced on this topic since the mid-1970s, I will present a summary of Weinberg's and St. John's conclusions and then briefly discuss the most important studies relevant to this topic that have been published since their reviews.

After examining dozens of studies, many of which had serious methodological flaws, Weinberg (1970) concluded that "White children fail to suffer any learning disadvantage from desegregation" (p. 88). This finding is consistent with every other summary statement on this issue of which I am aware. For example, Orfield (1978) wrote:

> What is remarkable, however, is the consistency of the finding that the desegregation process itself has little if any effect on the educational success of White students, as measured by achievement test scores. . . . Researchers operating from very different scholarly and ideological starting points support this general finding. (p. 124)

St. John's (1975) review cites 24 studies of the impact of school desegregation on White achievement. Although many of these do not meet strict standards of methodological rigor, the pattern of results is clear. The overwhelming majority suggest no impact in either direction. When statistically significant effects do appear, they are more often positive than negative. The overall pattern is such that St. John concluded, "Desegregation has rarely lowered academic achievement for either Black or White children" (p. 36). This is true not only for studies of situations in which African Americans have been bused to previously White schools but also for the few available studies of situations in which White children were bused to previously Black schools.

The only two major studies of desegregation and White achievement of which I am aware that are not covered in Weinberg (1970) and St. John (1975) do little to change the overall conclusions. The first of these, Singer, Gerard, and Redfearn (1975), concludes on the basis of the massive study in Riverside, California, described earlier that desegregation has no effect on White students' achievement. For example, they found that the standardized reading achievement scores of White elementary school students stayed consistent from the predesegregation time period to postmeasures taken from one to five years after desegregation. The second study, Patchen (1982), also concludes there is little relation between the racial composition of the schools students attend and White academic achievement. Patchen did find some indication that White students who had attended majority Black elementary schools had lower achievement scores in high school than their peers who had attended majority White schools, but the effect was *very slight* (1% of the variance in such scores). He concluded with regard to high school racial composition that "there were no substantial associations between the average grades or the average achievement scores of Whites and the racial composition of their schools" (p. 303), although he did find some decrement in the academic effort of Whites in majority Black schools.

THE EFFECT OF SCHOOL DESEGREGATION ON DROPOUTS AND SUSPENSIONS

Both suspensions and dropouts seem bound to influence the academic achievement of students, since a student not in school for either reason misses the opportunity to learn material presented to those in school. Furthermore, dropping out means, of course, that a student must face the job market without a high school diploma, a situation that virtually guarantees difficulty in attaining a stable job with any prospect of economic security. Thus, in addition to examining the impact of school desegregation on academic achievement, this review will also consider its impact on suspension and drop-out rates.

It is clear that African American children are suspended from school much more frequently than Whites and Hispanics. In fact, Black children are from two to five times more likely than Whites to be suspended (Arnez, 1978; Children's Defense Fund, 1974; Kaeser, 1979; Yudof, 1975). In contrast, the suspension rate for Hispanic children is generally not disproportionately high. While occasional studies suggest that the suspension rate for Hispanics may be somewhat lower or higher than the rate for Whites (Aspira of America, 1979; Meier & Stewart, 1991), others find it roughly proportional to the number of Hispanic students in given schools or districts (Arnez, 1978; Eyler et al., 1983). However, both African American and Hispanic students are clearly more likely than Whites to drop out of school (Fernandez & Velez, 1985). National statistics indicate a drop-out rate during high school of 12% for Whites, 15% for African Americans, and 25% for Hispanics (Rumberger, 1991). Other sources suggest drop-out rates of up to 45% for Hispanic students (National Commission on Secondary Education for Hispanics, 1984), although such overall estimates are raised by the extremely high drop-out rate for students of Mexican heritage compared to that for other Hispanic students.

The disparity in White and minority rates of suspension and dropping out is a serious issue in and of itself, but the real issue for this review is whether desegregation influences these phenomena. There is not nearly as much material available on this question as on how desegregation influences academic achievement. However, the studies that exist suggest, perhaps surprisingly, that desegregation has somewhat opposite effects on suspension and drop-out rates.

Desegregation is frequently accompanied by a marked increase in the student suspension rate (Arnez, 1978; Eyler et al., 1983). In extreme cases suspensions may double (Foster, 1977; Project Student Concerns, 1977). Trent (1981) has suggested that such increases may be limited to the first year, when concern about desegregation is apt to be very high. However, it is not clear whether the decline in suspensions frequently averred to occur after the first year of desegregation returns the situation to the predesegregation status quo. A study performed by Aspira of America (1979) concluded that suspension rates for both Hispanics and non-Hispanics are lowest in highly segregated districts and that Hispanic suspension rates are highest in moderately segregated districts. Since important control variables were omitted from this analysis, extreme caution must be utilized in interpreting these data.

There is very little evidence about whether desegregation disproportionately increases the suspension rates for minority students, but there are indications that this may be the case. For example, Larkin (1979) reports that schools in Milwaukee that were desegregated after a court order and went from being virtually all White to being 15 to 34% African American showed both a marked increase in overall suspensions and an unusually high disparity in Black/White suspension rates compared with previously integrated schools in the same city. Kaeser (1979) shows that, in spite of similar suspension rates for African American and White students in highly segregated schools in Cleveland, African Americans are disproportionately suspended in virtually all the racially mixed schools in that city. It appears that the degree to which desegregation influences the suspension rate for African American students may be linked to the racial composition of the desegregated school. Eyler et al. (1983) discuss several studies that, taken together, suggest that recently desegregated schools with a racially balanced student body are especially likely to have disproportionately high suspension rates for African American students. Analyses conducted by Meier and Stewart (1991) demonstrate even more complicated dynamics. These researchers found that the suspension rate and other measures of disciplinary action taken with regard to Hispanic students are negatively related to the rates of such disciplinary action directed toward African American students, suggesting what Meier and Stewart call "the trade-off hypothesis," the disturbing possibility that administrators select one minority group for relatively strong disciplinary action and then compensate by being relatively lenient toward the other.

There appear to be even fewer studies of desegregation and dropping out than of desegregation and suspension. In fact, a recent extensive review of the literature on Mexican American dropouts (Rumberger, 1991) does not even mention desegregation as one of the "school factors" whose effect has been studied. However, a few studies are available. Bachman (1971) found that African American students attending desegregated high schools in the North were less likely to drop out than those in segregated schools. However, the meaning of this finding is clouded by the fact that the students in the desegregated schools also came from homes of higher socioeconomic status. Crain and Weisman (1972) report a strong relation between school integration and high school graduation for northern African Americans after controlling for factors such as parents' education, stating flatly, "Integration seems to reduce the drop-out rate by one-fourth" (p. 156). The only study of which I am aware that suggests that desegregation increases the drop-out rate for minority students in the North is the Aspira of America (1979) study that found lower drop-out rates in highly segregated schools than in moderately segregated schools. This finding contrasts sharply with a study by Hess and Lauber (1985), which concluded that the drop-out rate for Hispanic students in Chicago was highest in very segregated minority schools. A study by Felice and Richardson (1977) explored the relative drop-out rate of minority students in different kinds of segregated schools. It concluded that minority students were least likely to drop out of school when their peers were of relatively high socioeconomic status and teachers had relatively positive attitudes about the minority students' capabilities. Perhaps not surprisingly, Aspira of America reports that where major bilingual programs are offered, drop-out rates for Hispanic students appear to be reduced.

In summary, although the data are sparse, there is reason for concern about the possible increase in the suspension of African American (and possibly Hispanic) students, especially in the early years of desegregation. On the other hand, desegregation, especially to schools of higher socioeconomic status, may curb the disproportionately high drop-out rate of African American and Hispanic students, perhaps an issue of ultimately greater importance.

POSTSECONDARY EDUCATIONAL AND OCCUPATIONAL OUTCOMES OF SCHOOL DESEGREGATION

As indicated earlier, there has been a great deal of research on the impact of desegregation on achievement-test scores. However, achievement scores should not be overemphasized as an end in and of themselves. They are, at best, fairly weak indicators of college grades or occupational success (Jencks et al., 1972; Martson, 1971; McClelland, 1973). In addition, there is evidence that they predict academic success less well for African American students than for White students, although this phenomenon may be limited to Blacks enrolled in predominantly White institutions (Fleming, 1990). Such scores have received disproportionate attention because they are widely administered and hence convenient rather than because they are an outcome of premier importance.

Work by a small group of researchers, most notably Braddock, McPartland, and Crain, has opened up a new and potentially rewarding line of inquiry—the impact of desegregation on later life outcomes for minority students, such as college choice and occupational attainment. Braddock and Dawkins (1984) make the case for this line of inquiry by pointing out that desegregation may have long-term social and economic consequences for minorities by providing:

(1) access to useful social networks of job information, contacts and sponsorship; (2) socialization for aspirations and entrance into "nontraditional" career lines with higher income returns; (3) development of interpersonal skills that are useful in interracial contexts; (4) reduced social inertia—increased tolerance of and willingness to participate in desegregated environments; and (5) avoidance of negative attributions which are often associated with "Black" institutions (Braddock, 1980; Braddock & McPartland, 1982; Coleman et al., 1966; Crain, 1970; Crain & Weisman, 1972; McPartland & Crain, 1980). (p. 367)

The evidence concerning desegregation's impact on such outcomes is sparse, and virtually all of it concerns African Americans to the exclusion of members of other racial or ethnic groups. Furthermore, almost all of these studies explicitly or tacitly use the word *desegregated* as a synonym for *racially mixed*. Thus they are generally not studies of the outcomes of specific desegregation programs. Yet I believe these studies are worth discussing because of the fundamental importance of such outcomes to minority-group members in particular and to American society in general. Braddock and Dawkins (1984) point out that school desegregation can influence the amount and the type of postsecondary education African Americans receive, their academic success in the postsecondary years, and their chances of attaining a well-paying job. None of the evidence of these outcomes is so clear-cut that the issue of desegregation's impact can be definitively settled. Yet some data suggestive of positive effects are available.

The data on the impact of desegregation on the amount of postsecondary education African Americans complete has been explored in a number of studies. Crain and Weisman (1972) utilized retrospective data to explore college attendance and completion patterns in a relatively small sample of northern African American adults. They found that roughly one third of the Black males from desegregated schools went to college, compared with 24% from segregated schools. Segregated and desegregated African American females evidenced much smaller differences in the same direction. College *completion* rates were also higher for African American males and females with desegregated schooling at the elementary or secondary level than for their segregated peers. Crain and Weisman's analysis suggests that these patterns were not due to initial differences in the family background of individuals attending segregated and desegregated schools. Armor (1972) reported positive effects of two small voluntary desegregation programs on college enrollment rates as well as on the quality of the institution of higher education in which African American students enrolled, although in one case in which the data allowed exploration of the issue a higher drop-out rate for the formerly desegregated students dissipated this enrollment advantage by the end of the sophomore year. Another study with a somewhat limited sample concluded that African American students who had participated in a voluntary desegregation program had higher high school and college graduation rates than a control group of peers who attended segregated schools (Crain, Hawes, Miller, & Peichert, 1986, cited in Jaynes & Williams, 1989).

In another study, Crain and Mahard (1978) explored similar issues with a database more adequate to the job. Using data on 3,000 African American high school graduates, they replicated the earlier suggestion of benefits of desegregation for those living in the North, finding that desegregation was positively associated with college enrollment and persistence for these individuals. However, this relationship was not statistically significant for African American students living in the South. Another analysis of this same data set using different control variables and exclusion criteria found no statistically significant relationship between desegregation and college attendance in either region (Eckland, 1979).

Braddock and McPartland (1982) utilized this same database merged with later follow-up surveys to explore the same issue. Their results are moderately consistent with Crain and Mahard's (1978). Controlling for family background and the students' academic qualifications, they found a weak trend suggesting a positive impact of early desegregation on enrollment in four-year colleges for African Americans living in the North. However, such a relationship was not apparent in the data for their southern peers. Since the studies just mentioned constitute, to my knowledge, most of those that deal with the impact of desegregation on the amount of postsecondary education Blacks complete, it seems reasonable to conclude that, although desegregation has no measurable impact on college attainment for southern Blacks, it appears to have a positive, though weak, effect for those living in the North.

I know of only one study relating to the impact of desegregation on the educational attainment of Hispanic students. A follow-up study of Mexican American children who had participated in the mid-1960s in the desegregation of the elementary schools in Riverside, California, was conducted 20 years later, when the students were in their late 20s and early 30s (Mercer & Phillips, 1987). Path models developed using the respondents' retrospective reports of their home and school experiences suggested that having had friends from other ethnic backgrounds in elementary school had a weak but measurable link to adult educational attainment. The study's authors conclude:

Developing interethnic friendships in grade school and high school places a student in a network of peers who encourage staying in school and who themselves will go on for higher education. This network leads to higher grades and higher adult educational achievement. (p. 19)

Of course, this study does not assess the impact of desegregation per se. Rather it compares outcomes for students in desegregated schools who take advantage of the opportunity for developing interracial friendships provided by the heterogeneous nature of the student body with those who do not. A study by Heller (1969), which found higher occupational aspirations among Mexican American males in predominantly Anglo schools than among their peers in predominantly Mexican American schools, suggests one factor that might contribute to this phenomenon.

Another issue these researchers have explored is whether desegregation makes Blacks somewhat more likely to attend predominantly White colleges rather than predominantly Black colleges. There is, of course, some controversy over whether this is a desirable outcome, since it is clear that attendance at predominantly White institutions poses certain problems for Black students that they are not as likely to confront at historically Black institutions of higher education (Allen, 1988; Allen, Epps, & Haniff, 1991; Nievers, 1977; D. H. Smith, 1981). Furthermore, historically Black institutions of higher education have played an important role in the education of professionals serving the African American community (Jaynes & Williams, 1989). However, researchers working in this area generally argue that such an outcome is valuable, since attendance at predominantly White institutions tends to have positive job-market consequences. For example, research has documented the importance of desegregated social networks for job attainment (Braddock & McPartland, 1987). In addition, some employers tend to derogate degrees received from Black institutions and prefer Black graduates from White institutions (Braddock & McPartland, 1983; McPartland & Crain, 1980; Crain, 1984b). Such factors may be at least partly responsible for indications that Black graduates of White institutions, especially African Ameri-

can male graduates, earn more than roughly equivalent graduates from African American institutions (Braddock, 1985).

There are three studies that suggest that desegregation at the precollege level encourages African American students to enroll in predominantly White colleges (Braddock, 1980; Braddock & McPartland, 1982; Dawkins, 1991). Braddock showed a fairly strong positive relation between attending a desegregated high school and enrolling in a predominantly White college. However, the number of students and colleges involved in this study, which was carried out in one southern state, was relatively small. More convincing evidence comes from the Braddock and McPartland study, based on data from 3,000 African American high school graduates. Utilizing controls for variables such as the student's social-class background and high school grades, this study found that attendance at predominantly White institutions was more likely for students who had had prior experience with desegregation than for others who had none. Braddock and McPartland interpret this as evidence that prior desegregation experience frees African American students to risk attendance at a predominantly White institution, the only kind of four-year college readily available in the North. Finally, Dawkins uses data from the National Survey of Black Americans to show a positive relation between the racial composition of the high schools respondents attended and the racial composition of the colleges in which they enrolled.

One of the major reasons there is interest in whether school desegregation influences the kind and amount of college education obtained by minority students is that this has a bearing on occupational outcomes. The first evidence of which I am aware on this topic appeared in studies by Crain (1970) and Crain and Weisman (1972). These reports, based on the same set of survey data, concluded that "Alumni of integrated schools are more likely to move into occupations traditionally closed to Blacks; they also earn slightly more money, even after education is controlled" (Crain & Weisman, 1972, p. 161). More recent evidence has been mixed. A study by Trent (1991) failed to replicate this finding. However, a study by Dawkins (1991) based on the National Survey of Black Americans did find a modest positive link between attending a desegregated high school and later occupational attainment. Although regional and age-cohort differences were apparent in this effect, with the southern sample least likely to show this link, the link was found consistently for the three youngest non-southern samples. One factor that might be conducive to creating this relationship is that employers show relatively favorable attitudes toward hiring minority-group graduates of suburban high schools (Braddock, Crain, McPartland, & Dawkins, 1986). Thus desegregation efforts that transfer students from urban to suburban settings would presumably have positive job-market consequences for the minority students involved. More recently, several studies have focused on the impact on occupational attainment of the racial composition of the *college* African American students attend. Although the results vary somewhat from study to study, a recent review of this work concludes: "On balance, Black graduates (especially males) of predominantly White institutions seem to receive labor-market advantages over those from predominantly Black institutions" (Braddock, 1985, p. 18).

As is generally the case, the data on the impact of desegregation on occupational outcomes for Hispanics is much sparser than data exploring the parallel question with respect to outcomes for African Americans. The one study of this topic of which I am aware is the study by Mercer and Phillips (1987) of Mexican American students who participated in the desegregation of the schools in Riverside, California. Mercer and Phillips conclude that reported interethnic friendship was one of only three variables in their path model that appeared to have a direct effect on occupational attainment in early adulthood. Their model suggests that the impact of interethnic friendship in grade school on occupational attainment is mediated through its impact on interethnic friendship in high school. The latter appears to have both a direct effect on occupational attainment and an indirect effect through influencing factors such as the "achievement press" from friends, which these researchers measured through questions about whether friends actively encouraged the respondents to finish high school and enroll in college. Although these findings bear more on how students in desegregated settings may be differentially affected than on the bold question of whether desegregation in and of itself has a positive impact on occupational attainment among Mexican Americans, the one study more directly related to that issue of which I am aware suggests the possibility of positive outcomes. Heller (1969) found higher occupational aspirations among Mexican American males in predominantly Anglo schools than among their peers in predominantly Mexican American schools. Although Heller measured aspirations rather than actual attainment, the enhancement of occupational aspirations by desegregation is certainly consistent with the data on African Americans, suggesting a positive effect on attainment itself.

In summary, attendance at desegregated schools appears to have some positive impact on the kind of jobs African Americans get as well as on the amount and type of college education they undertake. Although the evidence to date is sparse and suggests that these effects are moderated by both region and gender, these outcomes are so crucial for an individual's social position and economic well-being that any reliable indication that they are influenced by desegregation is of consequence.

THE EFFECT OF SCHOOL DESEGREGATION ON AFRICAN AMERICAN SELF-ESTEEM

A considerable body of research has explored the impact of school desegregation on the self-esteem of African American children, while only a few sources supply comparable data on its impact on the self-esteem of other groups (e.g., Green, Miller, & Gerard, 1975; Sheehan, 1980). Research since the mid-1970s has suggested that the belief that African American children in segregated environments have low self-esteem, which sparked much of this research, is not well founded. Although this belief was widespread for a substantial period of time (Cross, 1980), the evidence supporting it appears flawed. First, many of the studies upon which this conclusion was based had severe methodological problems (Banks, 1976; Spencer, 1976). Second, Cross and others have pointed out that the interpreta-

tion of the finding from these studies has not been entirely consistent with the data. Finally, the social conditions in which African Americans live have changed substantially in the last several decades, which may well have implications for levels of self-esteem. Reviews of the literature have generally concluded that African Americans show the same or possibly higher levels of self-esteem than Whites (Cross, 1980; Epps, 1978; Gordon, 1980; St. John, 1975; R. Taylor, 1976).

Thus the attention directed toward the issue of desegregation and self-esteem may have been out of proportion to the problem. It does seem likely that a state-enforced system of segregation might undermine the personal and group self-regard of those subject to such a system. However, studies suggest that lack of self-esteem is not a major problem for African American children. Neither does it appear to be a major problem for Hispanic children (Carter & Segura, 1979), although some researchers have suggested that the self-esteem of Mexican American students may be lower than that of Anglos (Malry, 1968; Parsons, 1965). Furthermore, there is no strong reason to believe that desegregation under the conditions experienced by many minority children would automatically increase self-esteem or regard for their own group. For example, Hare (1977) argues that one might expect to find a short-term increase in personal and academic anxiety associated with desegregation, since many minority children enter somewhat hostile environments and/or environments that provide increased academic competition.

The major reviews of school desegregation and African American self-concept or self-esteem generally conclude that desegregation has no clear-cut consistent impact (Epps, 1975, 1978; Stephan, 1978; St. John, 1975; Weinberg, 1977). Stephan reviewed a total of 20 studies, 5 of which found that self-esteem was higher in African Americans in segregated schools, with the remaining 15 suggesting no statistically significant impact of desegregation. Although some of the other reviews, most notably Weinberg, present a somewhat more positive view, none claim a consistent positive effect of desegregation on Black self-esteem. Although there are almost no data available to test this proposition directly, Epps's (1975) suggestion that desegregation is likely to have a varied effect on self-esteem, depending on students' specific experiences, seems eminently sensible. The conclusion that low self-esteem is not a problem for African American students, combined with the evidence that desegregation does not have any strong consistent impact on self-esteem, understandably led to a sharp diminution in the amount of research on these topics after the mid-1970s.

SCHOOL DESEGREGATION AND INTERGROUP RELATIONS

Rationale for Research on This Topic

As previously indicated, the lion's share of research on the effect of school desegregation has focused on its impact on academic achievement. However, a substantial body of research has also addressed its impact on intergroup relations, especially interracial attitudes. Although many of the parties concerned with desegregated schools tend to be relatively uninterested in how interracial schooling affects intergroup relations, there are some compelling arguments in favor of giving more thought to the matter. Much social learning occurs whether or not it is planned. Hence an interracial school cannot choose to have no effect on intergroup relations; it can only choose whether the effect will be planned or unplanned. Even a laissez-faire policy concerning intergroup relations conveys the message either that school authorities see no serious problem with relations as they have developed, or that they do not feel that the nature of intergroup relations is a legitimate concern for an educational institution. So those who argue that schools should not attempt to influence intergroup relations miss the fundamental fact that, whether or not they consciously try to effect such an influence, schools are extremely likely to do so in one way or another (Schofield, 1982, 1989).

Because of the pervasive residential segregation in our society, students frequently have their first relatively extended interracial experiences in schools. The growth or decrease of hostility and stereotyping may be critically influenced by circumstances there. While there is still considerable disagreement about whether the development of close interracial ties should be a high priority in the United States, there is a growing awareness of the societal costs of intergroup hostility. Unless interracial schools are carefully planned, there is the possibility that they will exacerbate the very social tensions that many initially hoped they would diminish.

A number of considerations suggest the value of turning from an almost exclusive concentration on the academic outcomes of schooling and focusing at least some attention on nonacademic outcomes such as intergroup relations. First, the ability to work effectively with out-group members is an important skill for both majority and minority groups in a pluralistic society that is striving to overcome a long history of discrimination in education and employment. In fact, a report commissioned by the U.S. Department of Labor concluded that the ability to work effectively in a context of cultural diversity is one of the basic competencies required to perform effectively in the U.S. labor force (SCANS, 1991). Many individuals lack this ability (Pettigrew & Martin, 1987). Current population trends make acquisition of this skill an increasingly important aspect of children's education. Second, Jencks et al. (1972), as well as others, have suggested that more attention should be paid to structuring schools so that they are reasonably pleasurable environments, since schools not only prepare students for future roles but are also the setting in which they spend nearly one third of their waking hours for a significant portion of their lives. This line of argument suggests that positive relationships within the school setting may be of some value in and of themselves.

Finally, there is the possibility that social relations between students in interracial schools may affect their academic achievement and their occupational success (Braddock & McPartland, 1987; Crain, 1970; Katz, 1964; McPartland & Crain, 1980; Pettigrew, 1967; Rosenberg & Simmons, 1971; U.S. Commission on Civil Rights, 1967). For example, Katz's work suggests that the academic performance of African Americans may be markedly impaired in biracial situations that pose a social

threat. A retrospective study of the Hispanic students involved in the Riverside desegregation study found that those who reported having been friends with students of another racial or ethnic background completed more years of schooling and scored higher on a measure of occupational attainment than those who did not (Mercer & Phillips, 1987). The potentially constructive effect of positive intergroup relations on minority-group outcomes is highlighted by Braddock and McPartland's (1987) finding that African American high school graduates who use desegregated social networks in their job searches are likely to attain positions with a substantially higher salary than those who use segregated social networks. Perhaps not surprisingly, they also work in environments that have, on the average, a higher percentage of White workers.

The Effect of School Desegregation on Intergroup Relations

The research on the impact of desegregation on intergroup relations can be grouped into three basic categories. First, numerous studies (a) compare the attitudes of students in a segregated school with those of students in a similar desegregated school, or (b) look at changes in student attitudes and behavior associated with the length of time children have been desegregated. Such studies generally give relatively little information about the nature of the schools studied, assuming implicitly that desegregation is an independent variable that has been operationalized similarly in a wide variety of circumstances. Such studies often contain analyses that examine the impact of such student background variables as race or sex on reactions to desegregation. However, they generally do not address directly the impact of specific policies or programs on students.

The second basic type of research in this area consists of large correlational studies that attempt to relate a wide range of school characteristics, policies, and practices to particular outcomes. Well-known studies of this kind are Patchen (1982), Forehand, Ragosta, and Rock (1976), and a substantial body of work by Hallinan and her colleagues concerning the impact of a variety of classroom characteristics, such as classroom racial composition and size, on intergroup friendship (Hallinan, 1982, 1986; Hallinan & Smith, 1985; Hallinan & Teixeira, 1987a, 1987b).

A third type of research in this area experimentally investigates the impact of particular narrowly defined innovations on intergroup relations within desegregated schools, thus allowing fairly clear conclusions about the causal linkage between these innovations and student outcomes. The majority of this work concerns various techniques for inducing cooperation between African American and White students on various kinds of academic tasks. (For reviews see Bossert, 1988–1989; D. W. Johnson & Johnson, 1982, 1992; D. W. Johnson, Johnson, & Maruyama, 1983; Slavin, 1983a, 1983b; Slavin, Sharan, Katan, & Hertz-Lazarowitz, 1985). Another body of research both demonstrates how the gap in status associated with such social categories as Black and White in U.S. society influences children's interaction patterns, and explores ways of mitigating the impact of this status differential (Aronson & Gonzalez, 1988; Cohen,

1980; Cohen, Lockheed, & Lohman 1976; Cohen & Roper, 1972).

There have been several reviews of the first type of research—work studying the link between desegregation and intergroup attitudes (Amir, 1976; Cohen, 1975; McConahay, 1978; St. John, 1975; Schofield, 1978; Schofield & Sagar, 1983). Such reviews tend to look at studies both of specific desegregation plans and of interracial schools, often without differentiating between them. Several themes reappear frequently in these reviews. The first is dissatisfaction with technical aspects of much of the work. Since many of the specific problems were discussed in an earlier section of this chapter, I will not reiterate them here. However, it is important to recognize the extent of these problems. For example, McConahay (1979) writes:

In my own review of over 50 published and unpublished studies [on desegregation and intergroup relations] done between 1960 and 1978, I did not find even one true experiment and only four of the quasi-experimental studies had enough methodological rigor to make them worth reporting in any detail (Gerard & Miller, 1975; Schofield & Sagar, 1977; Shaw, 1973; Silverman & Shaw, 1973). (p. 1)

The situation has not changed markedly since McConahay wrote these words.

A second theme common to most of the reviews is that the extant research does not allow confident statements that *consistent* effects exist. St. John's (1975) review captures the tone of many of the others in suggesting that the most striking feature of the research is the inconsistency of the findings. Many studies suggest that desegregation tends to lead to more positive intergroup attitudes (Gardner, Wright, & Dee, 1970; Jansen & Gallagher, 1966; Kingsley, 1989; Levi, 1988; Mann, 1959; Sheehan, 1980; D. Singer, 1966; U.S. Commission on Civil Rights, 1967). Others suggest precisely the opposite (Barber, 1968; Dentler & Elkins, 1967; C. P. Taylor, 1967). Still others suggest that desegregation has a positive effect on the attitudes of Whites and negative effect on the attitudes of Blacks (McWhirt, 1967) or vice versa (Crooks, 1970; Kurokawa, 1971; Webster, 1961). Finally, some, like Lombardi (1962), Trubowitz (1969), and Schwarzwald, Amir, and Crain (1992), suggest no overall effect.

Third, virtually all of the reviews emphasize the wide variety of situations covered by the existing literature. They often point out that not only do the student bodies in the schools studied vary sharply in age and social class, but that the proportion of students from different racial and ethnic backgrounds has also varied dramatically. They go on to point out that, given the variation in particular circumstances, it is reasonable, perhaps inevitable, that different instances of desegregation will have varying effects on intergroup relations. This point is well illustrated in the recent study by Schwarzwald et al. (1992). This study found no overall impact of school desegregation at the junior high and high school level on the intergroup attitudes and beliefs of Israeli soldiers from different ethnic backgrounds (Western or Middle Eastern). However, it did find that aspects of students' school experience, such as the gap in educational attainment between students of Western and Middle Eastern background, influenced affective and behavioral reactions to out-group members.

Fourth, the reviews tend to concern themselves exclusively with Black-White relations, since so few studies in this area include Hispanic or other minority students. The one major study of desegregation and intergroup relations in a situation involving Hispanics is the previously mentioned study of the Riverside, California, desegregation experience. Gerard, Jackson, and Conolley (1975) demonstrated substantial ethnic cleavage among African American, Mexican American, and Anglo students even after several years of desegregated schooling. However, the study did not address the question of whether, even with such cleavage, attitudes toward out-group members were more positive than they would have been if the children had remained in racially isolated schools.

The reviews in this area are also similar to each other in being literary reviews rather than formal meta-analyses. The most recent of them (Schofield & Sagar, 1983) explored the possibility of advancing the state of our knowledge through formal meta-analytic procedures. For a variety of reasons discussed in that paper, a formal meta-analysis did not seem appropriate. Since very few methodologically acceptable studies of desegregation and intergroup behavior have been published since 1983, the situation remains much the same today. Thus, the evidence taken as a whole suggests that desegregation has no clearly predictable impact on student intergroup attitudes.

There are at least three considerations that work against documenting positive social outcomes of desegregation when they exist. First, the dependent variables utilized in many of these studies are often seriously flawed. For example, the dependent measures used in almost two thirds of the studies considered for meta-analysis in Schofield and Sagar (1983) are structured so that improvement in minority/majority relations can occur only if students begin to choose out-group members *rather than* in-group members. They embody a hidden and questionable assumption that intergroup relations cannot improve except at the expense of intragroup relations. To some extent, this assumption reflects the nature of social reality. For example, generally a student can sit next to only a few others at lunch. If African American students begin to sit next to Whites more frequently than before, they are also likely to sit next to African Americans less frequently. However, there is no reason to think that, in general, attitudes toward out-group members can improve only if in-group members are less valued than previously. It seems perfectly reasonable to argue that students might become more accepting of out-group members and at the same time not change their attitudes toward in-group members. Yet the "zero-sum" measures used in the majority of studies pick up only the changes in out-group acceptance that occur at the expense of the in-group. Another serious measurement problem is the fact that a great many studies have used sociometric techniques that capture information on children's best friends, rather than focusing on less stringent but perhaps more appropriate outcomes such as willingness to associate with out-group members (Asher, 1993; Asher, Singleton, & Taylor, 1982; Schofield & Whitley, 1983).

Second, quantitative research on the impact of desegregation on actual in-school intergroup *behavior* is almost nonexistent, although there are quite a few qualitative studies of peer behavior in racially and ethnically mixed schools (Hanna, 1982;

Metz, 1978, 1986; Peshkin, 1991; Rist, 1979; Schofield, 1982/89). There is an obvious reason for this. As St. John (1975) has pointed out, "Interracial behavior cannot be compared in segregated and integrated settings or before and after desegregation; it can only be examined if the races are in contact" (p. 65). Although one might expect a reasonably strong relationship between attitudes and behavior, a plethora of research in social psychology suggests that behavior by no means follows automatically from attitudes (Liska, 1974; Schuman & Johnson, 1976; Wicker, 1969). In fact, one study of a newly desegregated school concluded that although abstract racial stereotypes were intensified—a negative attitudinal outcome—African American and White students came to behave toward each other much more positively (Schofield, 1982, 1989). Although it is difficult to substantiate this conclusion on anything other than a logical basis, it seems obvious in some ways that interracial behavior is more likely than intergroup attitudes to be changed by desegregation. Unless a school is completely resegregated internally, the amount of interracial contact has to increase in a newly desegregated environment. In contrast, attitudes do not have to change.

There is no guarantee that desegregation will promote positive intergroup behavior. However, the few studies that exist of actual behavior in desegregated schools suggest that although cross-racial avoidance is common (Silverman & Shaw, 1973; Schofield, 1982, 1989; Schofield & Sagar, 1977), cross-racial interaction is usually positive or neutral in tone (Peshkin, 1991; Schofield & Francis, 1982; Singleton & Asher, 1977). Thus it is important to keep in mind in interpreting the mixed findings of research on desegregation and intergroup attitudes that researchers have generally ignored intergroup behavior, which may be more malleable.

Third, there is reason to believe that desegregation may have positive long-term attitudinal and behavioral consequences that are not captured in the kind of research discussed here, which focuses on short-term in-school changes. Although just a few studies bear on this point, they suggest that in the long run desegregation may help break a cycle of racial isolation in which both minority- and majority-group members avoid each other even though this limits their educational, occupational, social, and residential choices. For example, two studies suggest that increasing levels of school desegregation are related to decreasing amounts of residential segregation (Pearce, 1980; Pearce, Crain, & Farley, 1984). At the individual rather than the community level, there is evidence that African Americans who attended desegregated schools are more likely to report living in integrated neighborhoods and having White social contacts later in life (Crain, 1984a; Crain & Weisman, 1972). A more recent study (D. A. Johnson, 1990) found a positive relation between years of desegregated schooling and acceptance of residential integration for White high school seniors; this same relationship was not found for their minority-group peers.

In the area of employment, there is also evidence that school desegregation breaks down intergroup barriers. For example, K. Green (1981, 1982) collected follow-up data in 1980 on a 1971 national sample of African American college freshmen. Individuals who had gone to a desegregated high school or college were more likely to have White work associates and White friends as adults. In a more recent paper, Braddock, Crain, and McPartland (1984) summarize the results of several national surveys (including K. Green's) and conclude that African American graduates of desegregated schools are more likely to work in desegregated environments than their peers who attended segregated schools. Additional support for this conclusion comes from Trent's (1991) examination of data from the 1979 cohort of the National Longitudinal Survey of Labor Force Behavior Youth Survey. Desegregated schooling may not only affect one's propensity to work in racially mixed settings, but also one's reactions to this experience. Specifically, Trent has concluded that

black, Latin, and white graduates of segregated schools perceive racially-mixed work groups as less friendly than racially-homogeneous ones.... Respondents from desegregated schools make ... much less of a distinction.... This suggests that desegregated school experiences can reduce negative feelings toward co-workers of other ethnic groups. (p. 35)

There is little comparable research on the long-term impact of desegregation on Whites. However, it seems reasonable to expect a parallel effect. Indeed, two studies have demonstrated that the racial composition of White students' high schools or colleges influences the likelihood that they will work in a desegregated setting later in life (Braddock, McPartland, & Trent, 1984; Trent, 1991). Perhaps this finding stems at least partially from the fact that Whites in desegregated schools frequently show a decrease in their often initially high levels of fear and avoidance of African Americans, and an increasing willingness and ability to work with them (Collins & Noblit, 1977; Noblit & Collins, 1981; Schofield, 1981). This is consistent with Stephan and Rosenfield's (1978) work suggesting that White students who have increased contact with African American and Mexican American peers in desegregated schools develop more positive attitudes toward members of these groups. It is also consistent with the finding of a National Opinion Research Center (NORC) survey (cited in Aspira of America, 1979) that desegregated White students were more likely to report both having a close Black friend and having had Black friends visit their homes.

CONCLUSIONS

What have been the outcomes flowing from the desegregation that has been achieved since the mid-1950s? First, research suggests that desegregation has had some positive effect on the reading skills of African American youngsters. The effect is not large, nor does it occur in all situations, but a modest measurable effect does seem apparent. Such is not the case with mathematics skills, which seem generally unaffected by desegregation. Second, there is some evidence that desegregation may help to break what can be thought of as a generational cycle of segregation and racial isolation. Although research on this topic is scant and often marred by unavoidable flaws, evidence has begun to accumulate that desegregation may favorably influence such adult outcomes as college graduation, income, and employment patterns. The measured effects are often weak, yet they are worth consideration because of the vital importance of these outcomes both for minority-group members individually and for U.S. society as a whole.

The evidence regarding the impact of desegregation on intergroup relations is generally held to be inconclusive and inconsistent. However, three points that are not adequately addressed by the research literature need to be considered here. First, abolishing dual systems and requiring changes in systems found to have engaged in other sorts of de jure segregation have changed certain major aspects of minority/majority relations in this country. The existence and legal sanctioning of governmental policies and practices intended to segregate African Americans or Hispanics were statements about intergroup relations. Even if no other specific benefits were to flow from the *Brown* decision, in my view, abolishing this sort of governmentally sanctioned "badge of inferiority" was an important advance in intergroup relations. Second, as discussed earlier, most studies of desegregation and intergroup relations have not addressed the question of how intergroup *behavior* has changed. They have focused almost exclusively on attitudes, because "pre" measures of attitudes are available, whereas there is no feasible way to measure intergroup behavior in segregated schools. Yet there are indications that desegregated

schooling can provide students with valuable behavioral experience that prepares them to function in a pluralistic society. In fact, some studies suggest that this occurs even when racial attitudes become more negative. In addition, there is some evidence that school desegregation may help to break down longstanding patterns of racial isolation in adult social relationships, housing, and other areas.

Finally, it is clear that desegregation can be implemented in very different ways, and that these differences have marked effects. The literature reviewed here assesses the impact of desegregation as it has been implemented in the past, often in schools that have actively resisted this change. Thus the preceding discussion of research on the effects of desegregation should not be read as an assessment of the potential of carefully structured desegregation to effect positive change. Rather, it is a summary of what has occurred, often under circumstances in which little if any serious attention was paid to creating a situation likely to improve either academic achievement or intergroup relations. Seeing racially and ethnically heterogeneous schools as having the *potential* to improve student outcomes, and focusing more attention on the actual *nature* of the students' experiences to assure that they are as constructive as possible, should enhance the likelihood of improving present outcomes.

References

Allen, W. R. (1988). The education of Black students on White college campuses: What quality the experience? In M. T. Nettles (Ed.), *Toward Black undergraduate student equality in American higher education* (pp. 57–85). New York: Greenwood Press.

Allen, W. R., Epps, E. G., & Haniff, N. Z. (Eds.). (1991). *College in Black and White*. Albany: State University of New York Press.

Alvarez, M. D. (1992). Puerto Rican children on the mainland: Current perspectives. In A. N. Ambert & M. D. Alvarez (Eds.), *Puerto Rican children on the mainland: Interdisciplinary perspectives* (pp. 3–16). New York: Garland.

Amir, Y. (1976). The role of intergroup contact in change of prejudice and ethnic relations. In P. A. Katz (Ed.), *Towards the elimination of racism* (pp. 245–308). New York: Pergamon.

Arias, M. B. (1986). The context of education for Hispanic students: An overview. *American Journal of Education, 95*(1), 26–57.

Arias, M. B. (1989). *Compliance Monitor's Fifth Semi-Annual Report: Vasques v. San Jose (CA) Unified School District*. Submitted to Honorable Robert F. Peckham, Chief United States District Judge, San Francisco.

Armor, D. J. (1972). The evidence on busing. *Public Interest, 28,* 90–124.

Armor, D. J. (1984). The evidence on desegregation and Black achievement. In T. Cook, D. Armor, R. Crain, N. Miller, W. Stephan, H. Walberg, & P. Wortman (Eds.), *School desegregation and Black achievement* (pp. 43–67). Washington, DC: National Institute of Education.

Arnez, N. L. (1978). Desegregation of public schools: A discriminatory process. *Journal of Negro Education, 47,* 274–282.

Aronson, E., & Gonzalez, A. (1988). Desegregation, jigsaw, and the Mexican American experience. In P. A. Katz & D. A. Taylor (Eds.), *Eliminating racism: Profiles in controversy* (pp. 301–314). New York: Plenum.

Aronson, S., & Noble, J. (1966). *Urban-suburban school mixing: A feasibility study.* Unpublished manuscript, West Hartford Board of Education, West Hartford, CT.

Asher, S. R. (1993, May). *Assessing peer relationship processes and outcomes in interracial and inter-ethnic contexts.* Paper presented at the Carnegie Corporation Consultation on Racial and Ethnic Relations in American Schools, New York.

Asher, S. R., Singleton, L. C., & Taylor, A. R. (1982, April). *Acceptance versus friendship: A longitudinal study of racial integration.* Paper presented at the annual meeting of the American Educational Research Association, New York.

Aspira of America, Inc. (1979). *Desegregation and the Hispano in America* (5 Vols.). New York: Author. (ERIC Document Reproduction Service No. ED 190 270-190 272)

Bachman, J. G. (1971). *Youth in transition* (Vol. 3). Ann Arbor: University of Michigan Press.

Banks, W. C. (1976). White preference in Blacks: A paradigm in search of a phenomenon. *Psychological Bulletin, 83*(6), 1179–1186.

Barber, R. W. (1968). *The effects of open enrollment on anti-Negro and anti-White prejudices among junior high students in Rochester, New York.* Unpublished doctoral dissertation, University of Rochester.

Bennett, A., & Easton, J. Q. (1988, April). *Voluntary transfer and student achievement: Does it help or hurt?* Paper presented at the annual meeting of the American Educational Research Association, New Orleans.

Bossert, S. T. (1988–1989). Cooperative activities in the classroom. In E. Z. Rothkopf (Ed.), *Review of research in education* (Vol. 15, pp.

225–250). Washington, DC: American Educational Research Association.

Bowman, O. H. (1973). *Scholastic development of disadvantaged Negro pupils: A study of pupils in selected segregated and desegregated elementary classrooms.* Unpublished doctoral dissertation, State University of New York, Buffalo. (University Microfilms No. 73-19,176)

Braddock, J. H., II. (1980). The perpetuation of segregation across levels of education: A behavioral assessment of the contact hypothesis. *Sociology of Education, 53,* 178–186.

Braddock, J. H., II. (1985). School desegregation and Black assimilation. *Journal of Social Issues, 41*(3), 9–22.

Braddock, J. H., II, Crain, R. L., & McPartland, J. M. (1984). A long-term view of school desegregation: Some recent studies of graduates as adults. *Phi Delta Kappan, 66*(4), 259–264.

Braddock, J. H., II, Crain, R. L., McPartland, J. M., & Dawkins, M. P. (1986). Applicant race and job placement decisions: A national survey experiment. *Journal of Sociology and Social Policy, 6,* 3–24.

Braddock, J. H., II, & Dawkins, M. P. (1984). Long-term effects of school desegregation on southern Blacks. *Sociological Spectrum, 4,* 365–381.

Braddock, J. H., II, & McPartland, J. M. (1982). Assessing school desegregation effects: New directions in research. In R. Corwin (Ed.), *Research in sociology of education and socialization* (Vol. 3, pp. 259–282). Greenwich, CT: JAI Press.

Braddock, J. H., II, & McPartland, J. M. (1983). *More evidence on social-psychological processes that perpetuate minority segregation: The relationship of school desegregation and employment segregation* (Report No. 338). Baltimore, MD: Johns Hopkins University, Center for Social Organization of Schools.

Braddock, J. H., II, & McPartland, J. M. (1987). How minorities continue to be excluded from equal employment opportunities: Research on labor market and institutional barriers. *Journal of Social Issues, 43,* 5–39.

Braddock, J. H., II, McPartland, J., & Trent, W. (1984, April). *Desegregated schools and desegregated work environments.* Paper presented at the annual meeting of the American Educational Research Association, New Orleans.

Bradley, L. A., & Bradley, G. W. (1977). The academic achievement of Black students in desegregated schools: A critical review. *Review of Educational Research, 47,* 399–449.

Broh, C. A., & Trent, W. T. (1981). A review of qualitative literature and expert opinion on school desegregation. In W. D. Hawley (Ed.), *Assessment of current knowledge about the effectiveness of school desegregation strategies* (Vol. 6). Nashville, TN: Vanderbilt University Press.

California State Department of Education. (1983). *Desegregation and bilingual education—Partners in quality education.* Sacramento: Author.

Cardenas, J. (1975). Bilingual education, desegregation and a third alternative. *Inequality in Education, 14,* 19–22.

Carrasquillo, A. L. (1991). *Hispanic children and youth in the United States.* New York: Garland.

Carsrud, K. B. (1984). *Does pairing hurt Chapter 1 students?* Austin, TX: Austin Independent School District, Office of Research and Evaluation.

Carter, T. (1979). *Interface between bilingual education and desegregation: A study of Arizona and California.* Washington, DC: National Institute of Education. (ERIC Document Reproduction Service No. ED 184 743)

Carter, T., & Chatfield, M. L. (1986). Effective bilingual schools: Implications for policy and practice. *American Journal of Education, 95,* 200–232.

Carter, T., & Segura, R. (1979). *Mexican Americans in school: A decade of change.* New York: College Entrance Examination Board.

Children's Defense Fund. (1974). *Children out of school in America.* Washington, DC: Author.

Cohen, E. G. (1975). The effects of desegregation on race relations. *Law and Contemporary Problems, 39*(2), 271–299.

Cohen, E. G. (1980). Design and redesign of the desegregated school: Problems of status, power, and conflict. In W. G. Stephan & J. R. Feagin (Eds.), *School desegregation: Past, present, and future* (pp. 251–278). New York: Plenum.

Cohen, E. G., Lockheed, M., & Lohman, M. (1976). The center for interracial cooperation: A field experiment. *Sociology of Education, 49,* 47–58.

Cohen, E., & Roper, S. (1972). Modification of interracial interaction disability: An application of status characteristics theory. *American Sociological Review, 36,* 643–657.

Coleman, J. S., Campbell, E. Q., Hobson, C. J., McPartland, J., Mood, A. M., Weinfeld, F. D., & York, R. L. (1966). *Equality of educational opportunity.* Washington, DC: Government Printing Office.

Collins, T. W., & Noblit, G. W. (1977). *Crossover High.* Unpublished manuscript, Memphis State University, Department of Anthropology, Memphis, TN.

Cook, T. D. (1984). What have Black children gained academically from school integration?: Examination of the meta-analytic evidence. In T. Cook, D. Armor, R. Crain, N. Miller, W. Stephan, H. Walberg, & P. Wortman (Eds.), *School desegregation and Black achievement* (pp. 6–42). Washington, DC: National Institute of Education.

Cook, T. D., & Campbell, D. T. (1976). The design and conduct of quasi-experiments and true experiments in field settings. In M. D. Dunnette (Ed.), *Handbook of industrial and organizational psychology* (pp. 223–326). Chicago: Rand McNally.

Cook, T. D., Levitan, L. C., & Shadish, W. R., Jr. (1985). Program evaluation. In G. Lindzey & E. Aronson (Eds.), *Handbook of social psychology* (Vol. 1, pp. 699–777). New York: Random House.

Crain, R. L. (1970). School integration and occupational achievement of Negroes. *American Journal of Sociology, 75,* 593–606.

Crain, R. L. (1976). Why academic research fails to be useful. *School Review, 84,* 337–351.

Crain, R. L. (1984a, April). *Desegregated schools and the non-academic side of college survival.* Paper presented at the annual meeting of the American Educational Research Association, New Orleans.

Crain, R. L. (1984b). *Is nineteen really better than ninety-three?* Washington, DC: National Institute of Education.

Crain, R. L., Hawes, J. A., Miller, R. L., & Peichert, J. R. (1986). *Finding niches: The long-term effects of a voluntary interdistrict school desegregation plan.* New York: Teachers College Press.

Crain, R. L., & Mahard, R. E. (1978). Social racial composition and Black college attendance and achievement test performance. *Sociology of Education, 51,* 81–101.

Crain, R. L., Mahard, R., & Narot, R. (1982). *Making desegregation work.* Cambridge, MA: Ballinger.

Crain, R. L., & Weisman, C. S. (1972). *Discrimination, personality, and achievement: A survey of northern Blacks.* New York: Seminar Press.

Cronbach, L. J. (1982). *Designing evaluations of educational and social programs.* San Francisco: Jossey-Bass.

Crooks, R. C. (1970). The effects of an interracial preschool program upon racial preferences, knowledge of racial differences and racial identification. *Journal of Social Issues, 26*(4), 137–144.

Cross, W. E., Jr. (1980, December). *Black identity: Rediscovering the distinction between personal identity and reference group identification.* Paper presented at the meeting of the Society of Research and Child Development, Atlanta.

Dawkins, M. P. (1991). *Long-term effects of school desegregation on*

African Americans: Evidence from the National Survey of Black Americans. Unpublished manuscript, University of Miami.

Dentler, R. A., & Elkins, E. (1967). Intergroup attitudes, academic performance, and racial composition. In R. A. Dentler, D. Mackler, & M. E. Washauer (Eds.), *The urban R's* (pp. 61–77). New York: Praeger.

Desegregation Studies Unit. (1977). *Resegregation: A second generation school desegregation issue.* Washington, DC: National Institute of Education.

Deutschberger, P. (1946). Interaction patterns in changing neighborhoods: New York and Pittsburgh. *Sociometry, 9,* 303–315.

Donato, R., Menchaca, M., & Valencia, R. R. (1991). Segregation, desegregation, and integration of Chicano students: Problems and prospects. In R. R. Valencia (Ed.), *Chicano school failure and success: Research and policy agendas for the 1990s* (pp. 27–63). London: Falmer Press.

Duran, R. P. (1983). *Hispanics' education and background: Predictors of college achievement.* New York: College Entrance Examination Board.

Dwyer, R. J. (1958). A report on patterns of interaction in desegregated schools. *Journal of Educational Sociology, 31,* 253–356.

Eckland, B. K. (1979). School racial composition and college attendance revisited. *Sociology of Education, 22,* 122–128.

Epps, E. G. (1975). Impact of school desegregation on aspirations, self-concepts and other aspects of personality. *Law and Contemporary Problems, 39*(1), 300–313.

Epps, E. G. (1978). The impact of school desegregation on the self-evaluation and achievement orientation of minority children. *Law and Contemporary Problems, 42*(3), 57–76.

Epstein, J. L. (1985). After the bus arrives: Resegregation in desegregated schools. *Journal of Social Issues, 41*(3), 23–44.

Espinosa, R., & Ochoa, A. (1986). Concentration of California Hispanic students in schools with low achievement: A research note. *American Journal of Education, 95*(1), 77–95.

Eyler, J., Cook, V. J., & Ward, L. E. (1983). Resegregation: Segregation within desegregated schools. In C. H. Rossell & W. D. Hawley (Eds.), *The consequences of school desegregation* (pp. 126–162). Philadelphia: Temple University Press.

Felice, L. G., & Richardson, R. L. (1977). The effects of desegregation on minority student dropout rates. *Integrated Education, 15*(6), 47–50.

Fernandez, R. R. (1978). *The political dimensions of bilingual education in the context of school desegregation in Milwaukee: A case study.* Unpublished manuscript.

Fernandez, R. R., & Guskin, J. T. (1978). Bilingual education and desegregation: A new dimension in legal and educational decision-making. In H. LaFontaine, B. Persky, & L. H. Glubshick (Eds.), *Bilingual education* (pp. 58–66). Wayne, NJ: Avery Publishing.

Fernandez, R. R., & Velez, W. (1985). Race, color, and language in the changing public schools. In L. Maldonado & J. Moore (Eds.), *Urban ethnicity in the United States* (pp. 123–144). Beverly Hills, CA: Sage.

Feshbach, S., & Adelman, H. (1969). *A training demonstration and research program for the remediation of learning disorders in culturally disadvantaged youth.* Unpublished manuscript, University of California, Los Angeles.

Fleming, J. (1990). Standardized test scores and the Black college environment. In K. Lomotey (Ed.), *Going to school: The African American experience* (pp. 143–162). Albany: State University of New York Press.

Forehand, G., Ragosta, M., & Rock, D. (1976). *Conditions and processes of effective school desegregation* (Report No. PR-76-23). Princeton, NJ: Educational Testing Service.

Foster, G. (1977). *Discipline practices in the Hillsborough County public schools.* Unpublished manuscript, University of Miami, Florida School Desegregation Consulting Center.

Gable, R., & Iwanicki, E. (1986). The longitudinal effects of a voluntary school desegregation program on the basic skill progress of participants. *Metropolitan Education, 1,* 76–77.

Garcia, G. F. (1976). The Latino and desegregation. *Integrated Education, 14,* 21–22.

Gardner, B. B., Wright, B. D., & Dee, R. (1970). *The effects of bussing Black ghetto children into White suburban schools.* (ERIC Document Reproduction Service No. ED 048 389)

Gerard, H., Jackson, D., & Conolley, E. (1975). Social context in the desegregated classroom. In H. Gerard & N. Miller (Eds.), *School desegregation: A long-range study* (pp. 211–241). New York: Plenum.

Gerard, H., & Miller, N. (1975). *School desegregation.* New York: Plenum.

Glass, G. V., McGaw, B., & Smith, M. L. (1981). *Meta-analysis in social research.* Beverly Hills, CA: Sage.

Gonzalez, G. G. (1990). *Chicano education in the era of segregation.* Philadelphia: Balch Institute Press.

Gonzalez, J. M. (1979). *Bilingual education in the integrated school.* Arlington, VA: National Clearinghouse for Bilingual Education.

Gordon, V. V. (1980). *The self-concept of Black Americans.* Washington, DC: University Press of America.

Green, D., Miller, N., & Gerard, D. S. (1975). Personality traits and adjustment. In H. B. Gerard & N. Miller (Eds.), *School desegregation: A long-range study* (pp. 167–192). New York: Plenum.

Green, K. (1981, April). *Integration and attainment: Preliminary results from a national longitudinal study of the impact of school desegregation.* Paper presented at the annual meeting of the American Educational Research Association, Los Angeles.

Green, K. (1982). *The impact of neighborhood and secondary school integration on educational achievement and occupational attainment of college bound Blacks.* Unpublished doctoral dissertation, University of California, Los Angeles.

Guttentag, M., & Struening, E. (1975). The handbook: Its purpose and organization. In M. Guttentag & E. Struening (eds.), *Handbook of evaluation research* (Vol. 2, pp. 3–7). Beverly Hills, CA: Sage.

Hallinan, M. T. (1982). Classroom racial composition and children's friendships. *Social Forces, 61*(1), 56–72.

Hallinan, M. T. (1986). School organization and interracial friendships. In V. Derlega & B. Winstead (Eds.), *Friendship and social interaction* (pp. 167–184). New York: Springer-Verlag.

Hallinan, M. T., & Smith, S. S. (1985). The effects of classroom racial composition on students' interracial friendliness. *Social Psychology Quarterly, 48*(1), 3–16.

Hallinan, M. T., & Teixeira, R. A. (1987a). Opportunities and constraints: Black-White differences in the formation of interracial friendships. *Child Development, 58*(5), 1358–1371.

Hallinan, M. T., & Teixeira, R. A. (1987b). Students' interracial friendships: Individual characteristics, structural effects and racial differences. *American Journal of Education, 95,* 563–583.

Hanna, J. L. (1982). Public social policy and the children's world: Implications of ethnographic research for desegregated schooling. In G. Spindler (Ed.), *Doing the ethnography of schooling* (pp. 316–355). New York: Holt, Rinehart, and Winston.

Hare, B. R. (1977). Black and White child self-esteem in social science: An overview. *The Journal of Negro Education, 46*(2), 141–156.

Haro, C. M. (1977). *Mexican/Chicano concerns and school desegregation in Los Angeles.* Los Angeles: University of California, Chicano Studies Center Publications.

Heleen, O. (Ed.). (1987, Spring). Two-way bilingual education: A strategy for equity [Special issue]. *Equity and Choice, 3.*

Heller, C. S. (1969). *Ambitions of Mexican American youth: Goals and means of mobility of high school seniors.* Unpublished doctoral dissertation, Columbia University, New York. (University Microfilms No. 64-11,296)

Hess, G. A., Jr., & Lauber, D. (1985). *Dropouts from the Chicago Public Schools*. Chicago: Chicago Panel on Public School Finances.

Hilliard, A. G., III. (1990). Limitations of current academic achievement measures. In K. Lomotey (Ed.), *Going to school: The African American experience* (pp. 135–142). Albany: State University of New York Press.

Howard, J., & Hammond, R. (1985). *Rumors of inferiority: Black America and the psychology of performance*. Unpublished manuscript.

Hunter, J. E., Schmidt, F. L., & Jackson, G. B. (1982). *Meta-analysis: Cumulating research findings across studies*. Beverly Hills, CA: Sage.

Hyland, C. R. (1992). On the growing isolation of Hispanic students in urban schools. In J. G. Ward & P. Anthony (Eds.), *Who pays for student diversity?: Population changes and educational policy*. Newbury Park, CA: Corwin Press.

Jaeger, C. (1987). *Minority and low income high schools: Evidence of educational inequality in metro Los Angeles* (Report No. 8). Chicago: University of Chicago Metropolitan Opportunity Project.

Jansen, V. G., & Gallagher, J. J. (1966). The social choices of students in racially integrated classes for the culturally disadvantaged talented. *Exceptional Children, 33,* 222–226.

Jaynes, G. D., & Williams, R. M., Jr. (1989). *A common destiny: Blacks and American society*. Washington, DC: National Academy Press.

Jencks, C., Smith, M., Acland, H., Bane, M. J., Cohen, D., Gintis, H., Heyns, B., & Michelson, S. (1972). *Inequality*. New York: Basic Books.

Johnson, D. A. (1990). The relationship between school integration and student attitude toward residential racial integration (Doctoral dissertation, Pennsylvania State University, University Park, PA). *Dissertation Abstracts International, 51,* 2527.

Johnson, D. W., & Johnson, R. T. (1982). The study of cooperative, competitive, and individualistic situations: State of the area and two recent contributions. *Contemporary Education, 1*(1), 7–13.

Johnson, D. W., & Johnson, R. T. (1992). Positive interdependence: Key to effective cooperation. In R. Hertz-Lazarowitz & N. Miller (Eds.), *Interaction in cooperative groups* (pp. 174–199). Cambridge, England: Cambridge University Press.

Johnson, D. W., Johnson, R. T., & Maruyama, G. (1983). Interdependence and interpersonal attraction among heterogeneous and homogeneous individuals: A theoretical formulation and a meta-analysis of the research. *Review of Educational Research, 53,* 5–54.

Kaeser, S. C. (1979). Suspensions in school discipline. *Education and Urban Society, 11,* 465–486.

Katz, I. (1964). Review of evidence relating to effects of desegregation on the performance of Negroes. *American Psychologist, 19,* 381–399.

Kingsley, D. E. (1989). Racial attitudes in Liberty, Missouri: Implications for school desegregation (Doctoral dissertation, Kansas State University, Manhattan, KS). *Dissertation Abstracts International, 50,* 2811.

Krol, R. A. (1978). *A meta-analysis of comparative research on the effects of desegregation on academic achievement*. Unpublished doctoral dissertation, Western Michigan University, Kalamazoo. (University Microfilms No. 79-07962)

Kurokawa, M. (1971). Mutual perceptions of racial images: White, Black, and Japanese-Americans. *Journal of Social Issues, 27,* 213–235.

Laird, M. A., & Weeks, G. (1966). *The effect of bussing on achievement in reading and arithmetic in three Philadelphia schools*. Unpublished manuscript, The School District of Philadelphia, Division of Research, Philadelphia.

Larkin, J. (1979). School desegregation and student suspension: A look at one school system. *Education and Urban Society, 11,* 485–495.

Levi, A. (1988). Attitudes and stereotypes of Eastern and Western students in integrated and nonintegrated classes in high schools in

Israel (Doctoral dissertation, Fordham University, New York). *Dissertation Abstracts International, 49,* 2171.

Liska, A. E. (1974). The impact of attitude on behavior: Attitude-social support interaction. *Pacific Sociological Review, 17,* 83–97.

Lombardi, D. N. (1962). *Factors affecting changes in attitudes toward Negroes among high school students*. Unpublished doctoral dissertation, Fordham University, New York.

Longshore, D. (1982a). Race composition and white hostility. *Social Forces, 61,* 73–78.

Longshore, D. (1982b). School racial composition and Blacks' attitudes toward desegregation: The problem of control in desegregated schools. *Social Science Quarterly, 63,* 674–687.

Longshore, D., & Prager, J. (1985). The impact of school desegregation: A situational analysis. *Annual Review of Sociology, 11,* 75–91.

Mahard, R. E., & Crain, R. L. (1980). *The influence of high school racial composition on the academic achievement and college attendance of Hispanics*. Paper presented at the meeting of the American Sociological Association, New York.

Mahard, R. E., & Crain, R. L. (1983). Research on minority achievement in desegregated schools. In C. H. Rossell & W. D. Hawley (Eds.), *The consequences of school desegregation* (pp. 103–125). Philadelphia: Temple University Press.

Malry, L. (1968). *The educational and occupational aspirations of Anglo, Spanish, and Negro high school students*. Unpublished doctoral dissertation, University of New Mexico, Albuquerque. (University Microfilms No. 66-8284)

Mann, J. H. (1959). The effects of inter-racial contact on sociometric choices and perceptions. *Journal of Social Psychology, 50,* 143–152.

Marston, A. R. (1971). It is time to reconsider the Graduate Record Examination. *American Psychologist, 26,* 653–655.

Maruyama, G., & Miller, N. (1979). Reexamination of normative influence processes in desegregated classrooms. *American Educational Research Journal, 16*(3), 273–283.

Maruyama, G., Miller, N., & Holtz, R. (1986). The relation between popularity and longitudinal test of the lateral transmission of values hypothesis. *Journal of Personality and Social Psychology, 51,* 730–741.

McClelland, D. C. (1973). Testing for competence rather than for intelligence. *American Psychologist, 28*(1), 1–14.

McConahay, J. (1978). The effects of school desegregation upon students' racial attitudes and behavior: A critical review of the literature and a prolegomenon to future research. *Law and Contemporary Problems, 42*(3), 77–107.

McConahay, J. (1979, October). *Reducing prejudice in desegregated schools*. Paper presented at the meeting of the National Panel on School Desegregation Research, Key West.

McGarvey, W. E. (1977). *Longitudinal factors in school desegregation*. Unpublished doctoral dissertation, University of Southern California, Los Angeles.

McPartland, J. M. (1968). *The segregated student in desegregated schools: Sources of influence on Negro secondary students* (Report No. 21). Baltimore, MD: Johns Hopkins University, Center for the Study of Social Organization of Schools.

McPartland, J. M., & Crain, R. L. (1980). Racial discrimination, segregation, and processes of social mobility. In V. T. Covello (Ed.), *Poverty and public policy* (pp. 97–125). Boston: G. K. Hall.

McWhirt, R. A. (1967). *The effects of desegregation on prejudice, academic aspiration and the self-concept of tenth grade students*. Unpublished doctoral dissertation, University of South Carolina, Columbia.

Meier, K. J., & Stewart, J., Jr. (1991). *The politics of Hispanic education*. Albany: State University of New York Press.

Menchaca, M., & Valencia, R. R. (1990). Anglo-Saxon ideologies in the 1920s–1930s: Their impact on the segregation of Mexican students in California. *Anthropology and Education Quarterly, 21,* 222–246.

Mercer, J. R., & Phillips, D. (1987). *Factors predicting adult status attainment of Chicano students: 20 year follow-up*. Unpublished manuscript, University of California, Riverside.

Metz, M. H. (1978). *Classrooms and corridors*. Berkeley: University of California Press.

Metz, M. H. (1986). *Different by design*. New York: Routledge & Kegan Paul.

Milan, W. G. (1978). *Toward a comprehensive language policy for a desegregated school system: Resassessing the future of bilingual education*. New York: Arawak Consulting Company.

Miller, N. (1980). Making school desegregation work. In W. G. Stephan & J. R. Feagin (Eds.), *School desegregation: Past, present, and future* (pp. 309–349). New York: Plenum.

Miller, N., & Carlson, M. (1984). School desegregation as a social reform: A meta-analysis of its effects on Black academic achievement. In T. Cook, D. Armor, R. Crain, N. Miller, W. Stephan, H. Walberg, & P. Wortman (Eds.), *School desegregation and black achievement* (pp. 89–130). Washington, DC: National Institute of Education.

Morrison, G. A., Jr. (1972). An analysis of academic achievement trends for Anglo-American, Mexican-American, and Negro-American students in a desegregated school environment (Doctoral dissertation, University of Houston, 1972). *Dissertation Abstracts International, 33,* 6024.

National Commission on Secondary Education for Hispanics. (1984). *Make something happen*. Washington, DC: Hispanic Policy Development Project.

National Institute of Education. (1977). *Desegregation and education concerns of the Hispanic community*. Washington, DC: Government Printing Office.

Nieves, L. (1977). *The minority college experience: A review of the literature*. Princeton, NJ: Educational Testing Service.

Noblit, G. W., & Collins, T. W. (1981). Gui bono? White students in a desegregated high school. *Urban Review, 13,* 205–216.

Oakes, J. (1992). Can tracking research inform practice? Technical, normative, and political considerations. *Educational Researcher, 21*(4), 12–21.

Orfield, G. (1978). *Must we bus? Segregated schools and national policy*. Washington, DC: The Brookings Institute.

Orfield, G. (1986). Hispanic education: Challenges, research, and policies. *American Journal of Education, 95*(1), 1–25.

Orfield, G. (1988, July). *The growth and concentration of Hispanic enrollment and the future of American education*. Paper presented at the National Council of La Raza Conference, Albuquerque, NM.

Parsons, T. W., Jr. (1965). *Ethnic cleavage in a California school*. Unpublished doctoral dissertation, Stanford University. (University Microfilms No. 66-2606)

Patchen, M. (1982). *Black-White contact in schools: Its social and academic effects*. West Lafayette, IN: Purdue University Press.

Pearce, D. (1980). *Breaking down the barriers: New evidence on the impact of metropolitan school desegregation on housing patterns*. Washington, DC: National Institute of Education.

Pearce, D., Crain, R. L., & Farley, R. (1984, April). *Lessons not lost: The effect of school desegregation on the rate of residential desegregation in large center cities*. Paper presented at the annual meeting of the American Educational Research Association, New Orleans.

Pearl, A. (1991). Systemic and institutional factors in Chicano school failure. In R. R. Valencia (Ed.), *Chicano school failure and success: Research and policy agendas for the 1990s* (pp. 273–320). London: Falmer Press.

Peshkin, A. (1991). *The color of strangers, the color of friends*. Chicago: University of Chicago Press.

Pettigrew, T. (1967). Social evaluation theory: Convergences and applications. In D. Levine (Ed.), *Nebraska symposium on motivation* (Vol. 15, pp. 241–315). Lincoln: University of Nebraska Press.

Pettigrew, T. (1969a). The Negro and education: Problems and proposals. In I. Katz & P. Gurin (Eds.), *Race and the social sciences* (pp. 49–113). New York: Basic Books.

Pettigrew, T. (1969b). Racially separate or together. *Journal of Social Issues, 25*(1), 43–69.

Pettigrew, T. F., & Martin, J. (1987). Shaping the organizational context for Black American inclusion. *Journal of Social Issues, 43,* 41–78.

Pride, R., & Woodward, D. (1985). *The burden of busing: The politics of desegregation in Nashville, Tennessee*. Knoxville: University of Tennessee Press.

Project Student Concerns. (1977). *Interim report*. Louisville, KY: Jefferson County Education Consortium. (ERIC Document Reproduction Service No. ED 145 066)

Read, F. (1975). Judicial evolution of the law of school integration since *Brown v. Board of Education. Law and Contemporary Problems, 39*(1), 7–49.

Rist, R. C. (Ed.). (1979). *Desegregated schools: Appraisals of an American experiment*. New York: Academic Press.

Roos, P. D. (1978). Bilingual education: The Hispanic response to unequal educational opportunity. *Law and Contemporary Problems, 42*(3), 111–140.

Rosenberg, M., & Simmons, R. (1971). *Black and White self-esteem: The urban school child*. Washington, DC: American Sociological Association.

Rosenfield, D., Sheehan, D. S., Marcus, M. M., & Stephan, W. G. (1981). Classroom structure and prejudice in desegregated schools. *Journal of Educational Psychology, 73,* 17–26.

Rosenthal, R. (1978). Combining results of independent studies. *Psychological Bulletin, 85,* 185–193.

Rumberger, R. W. (1991). Chicano dropouts: A review of research and policy issues. In R. R. Valencia (Ed.), *Chicano school failure and success: Research and policy agendas for the 1990s* (pp. 64–89). London: Falmer Press.

Rumberger, R. W., & Willms, J. D. (1992). The impact of racial and ethnic segregation on the achievement gap in California high schools. *Educational Evaluation and Policy Analysis, 14*(4), 377–396.

Savage, L. W. (1971). *Academic achievement of Black students transferring from a segregated junior high school to an integrated high school*. Unpublished master's thesis, Virginia State College, Petersburg, VA.

SCANS (Secretary of Labor's Commission on Achieving Necessary Skills). (1991). *Skills and tasks for jobs: A SCANS report for America 2000*. Washington, DC: Government Printing Office.

Schmidt, F. L. (1992). What do data really mean? Research findings, meta-analysis, and cumulative knowledge in psychology. *American Psychologist, 47*(10), 1173–1181.

Schofield, J. W. (1978). School desegregation and intergroup attitudes. In D. Bar-Tal & L. Saxe (Eds.), *Social psychology of education: Theory and research* (pp. 329–363). Washington, DC: Halsted Press.

Schofield, J. W. (1979). The impact of positively structured contact on intergroup behavior: Does it last under adverse conditions? *Social Psychology Quarterly, 42,* 280–284.

Schofield, J. W. (1981). Uncharted territory: Desegregation and organizational innovation. *Urban Review, 13,* 227–242.

Schofield, J. W. (1982). *Black and White in school: Trust, tension, or tolerance?* New York: Praeger.

Schofield, J. W. (1989). *Black and White in school: Trust, tension, or tolerance?* New York: Teachers College Press.

Schofield, J. W. (1991). School desegregation and intergroup relations: A review of the literature. In G. Grant (Eds.), *Review of research in education* (Vol. 19, pp. 335–409). Washington, DC: American Educational Research Association.

Schofield, J. W., & Francis, W. D. (1982). An observational study of peer interaction in racially-mixed "accelerated" classrooms. *Journal of Educational Psychology, 74*(5), 722–732.

Schofield, J. W., & Sagar, H. A. (1977). Peer interaction patterns in an integrated middle school. *Sociometry, 40*(2), 130–138.

Schofield, J. W., & Sagar, H. A. (1979). The social context of learning in an interracial school. In R. C. Rist (Ed.), *Desegregated schools: Appraisals of an American experiment* (pp. 155–199). New York: Academic Press.

Schofield, J. W., & Sagar, H. A. (1983). Desegregation, school practices and student race relations. In C. Rossell & W. Hawley (Eds.), *The consequences of school desegregation* (pp. 58–102). Philadelphia: Temple University Press.

Schofield, J. W., & Whitley, B. E. (1983). Peer nomination vs. rating scale measurement of children's peer preference. *Social Psychology Quarterly, 46*, 242–251.

Schuman, H., & Johnson, M. (1976). Attitudes and behavior. *Annual Review of Sociology, 2*, 161–207.

Schuman, H., Steeh, C., & Bobo, L. (1985). *Racial attitudes in America: Trends and interpretations*. Cambridge, MA: Harvard University Press.

Schwarzwald, J., Amir, Y., & Crain, R. L. (1992). Long-term effects of school desegregation experiences on interpersonal relations in the Israeli defense forces. *Personality and Social Psychology Bulletin, 18*(3), 357–368.

Shaw, M. E. (1973). Changes in sociometric choices following forced integration of an elementary school. *Journal of Social Issues, 29*(4), 143–157.

Sheehan, D. S. (1980). A study of attitude change in desegregated intermediate schools. *Sociology of Education, 53*, 51–59.

Shrum, W., Cheek, N. H., Jr., & Hunter, S. M. (1988). Friendship in school: Gender and racial homophily. *Sociology of Education, 61*, 227–239.

Silverman, T., & Shaw, M. (1973). Effects of sudden mass school desegregation on interracial interaction and attitudes in one Southern city. *Journal of Social Issues, 29*(4), 133–142.

Singer, H., Gerard, H. B., & Redfearn, D. (1975). Achievement. In H. B. Gerard & N. Miller (Eds.), *School desegregation: A long-range study* (pp. 69–87). New York: Plenum.

Singleton, L. C., & Asher, S. R. (1977). Peer preferences and social interaction among third-grade children in an integrated school district. *Journal of Educational Psychology, 69*(4), 330–336.

Slavin, R. E. (1983a). *Cooperative learning*. New York: Longman.

Slavin, R. E. (1983b). When does cooperative learning increase student achievement? *Psychological Bulletin, 94*, 429–445.

Slavin, R. E., Sharan, S., Katan, S., & Hertz-Lazarowitz, R. (Eds.). (1985). *Learning to cooperate: Cooperating to learn*. New York: Plenum.

Smith, D. H. (1981). Social and academic environments of Black students on White campuses. *The Journal of Negro Education, 50*(3), 299–306.

Smith, L. R. (1971). *A comparative study of the achievement of Negro students attending segregated junior high schools and Negro students attending desegregated junior high schools in the City of Tulsa*. Unpublished doctoral dissertation, University of Tulsa.

Spencer, M. E. B. (1976). *The social-cognitive and personality development of the Black preschool child: An exploratory study of developmental process*. Unpublished doctoral dissertation, University of Chicago.

Stephan, W. G. (1978). School desegregation: An evaluation of predictions made in *Brown v. Board of Education. Psychological Bulletin, 85*(2), 217–238.

Stephan, W. G. (1984). Blacks and Brown: The effects of school desegregation on Black students. In T. Cook, D. Armor, R. Crain, N. Miller, W. Stephan, H. Walberg, & P. Wortman (Eds.), *School desegregation and black achievement* (pp. 131–159). Washington, DC: National Institute of Education.

Stephan, W. G., & Rosenfield, D. (1987). Effects of desegregation on race relations and self-esteem. *Journal of Educational Psychology, 70*, 670–679.

St. John, N. H. (1975). *School desegregation: Outcomes for children*. New York: Wiley.

St. John, N. H., & Lewis, R. (1975). Race and the social structure of the elementary classroom. *Sociology of Education, 48*, 346–368.

Sullivan, M. L. (1979). Contacts among cultures: School desegregation in a polyethnic New York City high school. In R. Rist (Ed.), *Desegregated schools: Appraisals of an American experiment* (pp. 201–240). New York: Academic Press.

Summers, A. A., & Wolfe, B. L. (1977). Do schools make a difference? *American Economic Review, 67*, 639–652.

Taylor, C. P. (1967). *Some change in self-concept in the first year of desegregated schooling*. Unpublished doctoral dissertation, University of Delaware, Newark.

Taylor, R., (1976). Psychosocial development among Black children and youth: A re-examination. *American Journal of Orthopsychiatry, 46*(1), 4–19.

Trager, H. G., & Yarrow, M. R. (1952). *They learn what they live*. New York: Harper.

Trent, W. (1991). *Desegregation analysis report*. New York: Legal Defense and Educational Fund.

Trubowitz, J. (1969). *Changing the racial attitudes of children*. New York: Praeger.

U.S. Commission on Civil Rights. (1967). *Racial isolation in the public schools*. Washington, DC: Government Printing Office.

Valencia, R. R. (1984). *Understanding school closures: Discriminatory impact on Chicano and Black students* (Policy Monographs Series No. 1). Stanford, CA: Stanford University, Stanford Center for Chicano Research.

Valencia, R. R. (1991). The plight of Chicano students: An overview of schooling conditions and outcomes. In R. R. Valencia (Ed.), *Chicano school failure and success: Research and policy agendas for the 1990s* (pp. 3–26). London: Falmer Press.

Walberg, H. J. (1984). Desegregation and education productivity. In T. Cook, D. Armor, R. Crain, N. Miller, W. Stephan, H. Walberg, & P. Wortman (Eds.), *School desegregation and black achievement* (pp. 160–193). Washington, DC: National Institute of Education.

Webster, S. W. (1961). The influence of interracial contact on social acceptance in a newly integrated school. *Journal of Educational Psychology, 32*, 292–296.

Weinberg, M. (1970). (Ed.). *Desegregation research: An appraisal* (2nd ed.). Bloomington, IN: Phi Delta Kappa.

Weinberg, M. (1977). *Minority students: A research appraisal*. Washington, DC: National Institute of Education.

Wicker, A. W. (1969). Attitude versus actions: The relationship of verbal and overt behavioral responses to attitude objects. *Journal of Social Issues, 25*(4), 41–78.

Wisdom, J. (1975). Random remarks on the role of social sciences in the judicial decision-making process in school desegregation cases. *Law and Contemporary Problems, 39*(1), 135–149.

Wortman, P. M. (1984). School desegregation and Black achievement: An integrative view. In T. Cook, D. Armor, R. Crain, N. Miller, W. Stephan, H. Walberg, & P. Wortman (Eds.), *School desegregation and black achievement* (pp. 194–224). Washington, DC: National Institute of Education.

Yudof, M. G. (1975). Suspension and expulsion of Black students from public schools: Academic capital punishment and the Constitution. *Law and Contemporary Problems, 39*(1), 374–411.

MULTICULTURAL EDUCATION: ITS EFFECTS ON STUDENTS' RACIAL AND GENDER ROLE ATTITUDES

James A. Banks

UNIVERSITY OF WASHINGTON, SEATTLE

Consensus does not exist about the scope and boundaries of multicultural education (Sleeter & Grant, 1987). Some writers use the term to refer only to education related to ethnic groups (Baker, 1983; Bennett, 1986), a common usage in the schools. Other writers define the term to include educational issues that focus on race/ethnicity, social class, gender, and exceptionality (Gollnick & Chinn, 1986; Grant & Sleeter, 1986a). In this chapter, multicultural education is used in this more inclusive way (Banks & Banks, 1993), with multiethnic education used to denote education related to race and ethnicity (Banks, 1994). The scope of this chapter is limited to only two of the major variables of multicultural education, race and gender, so that the factors discussed in it can be treated with sufficient depth and comprehensiveness.

The major goal of this chapter is to describe the research on the effects of materials and other curricular experiences related to race and gender (i.e., knowledge and structured educational experiences such as courses and units) on the perceptions, attitudes, and beliefs of students in grades kindergarten through 12.

THE ROLE OF MULTICULTURAL CONTENT IN THE CURRICULUM

This chapter is on the effects of multicultural content on students' perceptions, beliefs, and attitudes toward racial and ethnic groups and toward females and males. However, it is important for readers to realize that the justification for the inclusion of multicultural content in the school curriculum is not grounded in the empirical demonstration of the effects of such materials on student behavior and attitudes, but rather on two other important grounds: (a) the need for historical accuracy and (b) the national commitment to a democratic society (Myrdal, with Sterner & Rose, 1944).

A study of the American Revolution is included in the social studies curriculum primarily because educators believe that it is necessary to give students an accurate depiction of the development of U.S. society and culture. Content about people of color, women, and persons with disabilities should be included in the curriculum for the same reason: to give students an accurate view of U.S. society and culture. Multicultural content should also be included in the school curriculum because of the nation's commitment to fostering a democratic society (Myrdal, with Sterner & Rose, 1944). A pluralistic democratic society functions best when its diverse groups believe they are an integral part of its institutions and social structure. When groups within a democratic society feel excluded and experience anomie and alienation, ethnic polarization develops (Patterson, 1977). Thus schools in a pluralistic democratic society, in order to promote the structural inclusion of diverse groups and help them to develop a commitment to the national ethos and ideology, should structure a curriculum that reflects the perspectives and experiences of the diverse groups that constitute the nation-state.

Even though there are important historical and philosophi-

This chapter is reprinted with permission from James P. Shaver (Ed.), *Handbook of Research on Social Studies Teaching and Learning*. New York: Macmillan, 1991, pp. 459–469.

cal reasons for including multicultural content in the school curriculum, it is also important to determine the effects of such content on students' attitudes, perceptions, and beliefs. This knowledge can help us to design curricular interventions that will help students to develop attitudes and beliefs consistent with a democratic ideology (Clark, 1955; Gabelko & Michaelis, 1981; Katz, 1976). It can also contribute to the developing theory in multicultural education and intergroup relations (Allport, 1954; Banks, 1994; Sleeter & Grant, 1987).

MODIFICATION OF STUDENTS' RACIAL ATTITUDES

Social scientists have been interested since at least the 1920s in the racial and ethnic attitudes expressed by children. Lasker's (1929) pioneering research on children's racial attitudes indicated that young children are aware of racial differences. Lasker also described some of the emotional components that accompany racial prejudice. An early study by Minard (1931) also indicated that children's racial attitudes are formed during the earliest years of life. Since the seminal research by Lasker and Minard, a number of other researchers have studied race awareness and self-identifications of young children. This research has generally confirmed Lasker's early findings (e.g., Clark, 1955; Goodman, 1952; Milner, 1983; Porter, 1971; Williams & Morland, 1976; Wilson, 1987). Most of the research on children's racial attitudes has focused on children in preschool and kindergarten. Comparatively little research has been done on the racial attitudes of adolescent youths. An exception is the important study by Glock, Wuthnow, Piliavin, and Spencer (1975).

While there is a rich literature describing the racial attitudes and racial self-identifications of children, there is a paucity of studies that describe the results of interventions designed to change students' racial attitudes. Reviews of prior research have been undertaken by Cook (1947), Proshansky (1966), Katz (1976), and Stephan (1985). The reviews by Proshansky and Stephan were focused on studies dealing with adults rather than with children; the reviews by Cook and Katz concentrated on studies dealing with children. Those studies on the modification of children's racial attitudes shared several problems. In most, the effects of short-term interventions were examined, while researchers failed to determine their long-range effects. The interventions were usually not defined in sufficient detail for other researchers to replicate the studies or for readers to determine the precise nature of the interventions. Different measures were used in most of the various studies and intercorrelations of racial attitude measures tend to be low, making comparisons of results from different studies problematic. Scores on racial attitudes measures are often influenced by the students' knowledge of the socially acceptable responses; this makes it difficult to assess their attitudes and beliefs accurately.

Measures of behavior were not included in most of the studies. Determining the relationship between attitudes and behavior is a major problem in race relations research. Another problem is that the intervention studies were usually not grounded in a theoretical or conceptual framework. Theories developed by social scientists such as Adorno, Frenkel-Brunswik, Levinson, and Sanford (1950) and Allport (1954) have been used frequently in studies of adult prejudice, but rarely in studies dealing with curriculum interventions with students. Reinforcement studies, perceptual differentiation studies, and contact studies of attempts to modify children's racial attitudes are more theoretically grounded than studies that examine the effects of courses and curriculum. Stephan (1985) pointed out that few of the intervention studies in educational settings involve comparisons of alternative approaches, and thus provide little information about which approaches are the most effective. He also noted that in most of the studies White prejudice toward African Americans is examined, limiting the generalization of the findings to other racial and ethnic groups.

Since at least the 1940s, a number of researchers have investigated the effects of educational and curricular experiences on students' racial and ethnic attitudes and beliefs. These studies have had encouraging but mixed results. They reveal that students' racial attitudes can be affected by curriculum interventions, but that the results of such interventions are inconsistent, complex, and probably influenced by many different factors, including the nature and structure of the intervention, its duration, student characteristics, characteristics of the school environment (e.g., whether cooperative or competitive), and characteristics of the community in which the school is located. Logic and wisdom of practice suggest that teacher characteristics are also an important mediating variable in curriculum intervention studies. It is surprising that only a few of the studies reviewed in this chapter examine the teacher in any detail or treat the teacher as a variable.

TYPES OF RACIAL ATTITUDE MODIFICATION STUDIES

Several major types of racial attitude modification studies exist: (a) studies in which the effects of courses, curriculum content, and units are examined (e.g., Litcher & Johnson, 1969; Trager & Yarrow, 1952); (b) studies of the effects of reinforcement techniques (e.g., McAdoo, 1985; Parish, Shirazi, & Lambert, 1976; Williams & Edwards, 1969); (c) perceptual differentiation studies (e.g., Katz, 1973; Katz, Sohn, & Zalk, 1975; Katz & Zalk 1978); and (d) studies of the effects of cooperative classroom and school environments (e.g., Slavin, 1985; Slavin & Madden, 1979).

The richest and most productive work has been done on reinforcement techniques, perceptual approaches, and the effects of cooperative-learning environments. The research using these approaches has also resulted in rather consistent positive findings. In one such study, Katz and Zalk (1978) compared the effects of four different short-term intervention techniques on the racial attitudes of high-prejudice White students in the second and fifth grades. They assessed attitudes after two weeks and again four to six months later. The four techniques were: (a) increased positive racial contact, (b) vicarious interracial contact, (c) reinforcement of the color black, and (d) perceptual differentiation of minority-group faces. All of the experimental groups experienced a short-term reduction in mean prejudice scores on combined measures. However, the reductions were greater for the vicarious contact and perceptual groups than for the racial contact and reinforcement groups. The treatment effects were less pronounced in the long-term assessment, although some experimental gains were maintained by the vicarious contact and perceptual differentiation groups. Each experimental treatment in the Katz and Zalk study lasted only 15 minutes. It is remarkable that the treatments resulted in a reduction in prejudice and even more remarkable that some effects were still in evidence four to six months later.

The results from cooperative-learning studies have indicated rather consistently that students from different ethnic groups develop more positive racial attitudes when they participate in cooperative-learning activities (Aronson & Gonzalez, 1988; Slavin, 1985; Slavin & Madden, 1979). These studies have involved African American and White students as well as White students and Mexican American students. Students not only develop more positive racial attitudes in cooperative-learning situations, but ethnic-minority students tend to experience academic achievement gains. The achievement of White students tends to be about the same in cooperative and competitive learning environments.

INTERGROUP EDUCATION IN THE 1940s AND 1950s

Race relations research, like all research, has reflected the dominant ideologies, trends, and concerns of the times. It has ebbed and flowed with dominant social concerns. The intergroup education movement emerged during the World War II period when African Americans began their exodus to northern cities and racial conflict erupted in major U.S. cities (Cook, 1947; Taba, Brady, & Robinson, 1952). Studies such as those by Trager and Yarrow (1952) and Hayes and Conklin (1953) were part of the intergroup education movement of the 1940s and 1950s. Intergroup education had become a low national priority by the late 1950s. New initiatives in race relations would not command national attention again until the civil rights movement of the 1960s and 1970s.

A number of researchers examined the effects of curriculum materials on students' racial attitudes during the 1940s and 1950s. In studies by Jackson (1944) and Agnes (1947), students who read materials about African Americans expressed more positive racial attitudes than students who did not read such materials. However, in the Jackson study, the experimental gains disappeared after two weeks. The serious limitations of the Agnes study make it impossible to generalize its findings.

Trager and Yarrow (1952) studied the effects of a democratic and a nondemocratic curriculum on the racial attitudes of first- and second-grade students. The curriculum interventions in this study consisted of reading materials, activities, and teachers who role-played democratic and nondemocratic teaching styles. After the interventions, the students who participated in the democratic intervention expressed more positive racial attitudes and behaviors than the students who participated in the intervention that taught the prevailing views and attitudes of U.S. society. The teachers also expressed more positive racial attitudes after the interventions.

The effects of a variety of curriculum interventions were examined by Hayes and Conklin (1953) in a two-year project implemented in nine schools. Each teacher selected a different technique to use with an experimental class. The use of biographies of ethnic scientists, lectures on "The Growth of Democracy," direct contact with another ethnic group, and vicarious experience with another ethnic group were some of the techniques used by teachers in the two-year project. The researchers concluded that the students in the experimental groups developed more positive racial attitudes than did the students in the control groups in each of the two years, and that vicarious experiences were more effective than direct experiences in helping students to develop more positive racial attitudes. The findings of this study, however, should be interpreted with caution. The curricular interventions were diverse and unique from school to school; consequently, it is difficult to determine exactly what experiences were compared and almost impossible to replicate the study. However, the strengths of the study are that each intervention continued for three weeks and a multiple-intervention strategy was used.

RACIAL MODIFICATION STUDIES SINCE THE 1960s

The civil rights movement of the 1960s focused the nation's attention on serious problems in race and ethnic relations. Such deepened national concern about racial and ethnic problems had not been witnessed since the intergroup education movement of the 1940s. During the 1960s and 1970s, renewed attention was given to race relations research and children's racial attitudes. These studies can be grouped into four categories: (a) curriculum units and courses, (b) curriculum materials, (c) reinforcement studies, and (d) teaching methods.

Curriculum Units and Courses

A number of researchers have studied the effects of units and courses on students' racial attitudes, including Johnson (1966), Roth (1969), and Leslie and Leslie (1972). Johnson found that an African and African American history course in a freedom school had a positive effect on African American students' attitudes and beliefs. The students became more convinced that African Americans and Whites were equal. The course was only marginally effective with girls. African American fifth-grade students who studied African American history integrated into the regular social studies curriculum developed more positive attitudes toward African Americans in the Roth study. The self-concept of the students in the experimental groups did not change as a result of the intervention.

The effects of an experimental three-month unit about Africa and African Americans on the racial attitudes of White sixth-grade students and their peers were examined by Leslie and Leslie (1972). Each student in the experimental groups also tutored and interacted with a second-grade minority child from a central-city school. The experimental students also attempted to influence the racial attitudes of control-group students with monthly class presentations. The mean racial attitude score of the students in both the experimental and control groups became more positive after the unit. Peer influence was as effective in changing attitudes as were the curricular-tutorial interventions.

The effects of selected multiethnic social studies readings with historical, cultural, and social content about African Americans on White children's attitudes toward African Americans in rural and urban settings were investigated by Yawkey (1973). The experimental treatment consisted of the teacher's reading and leading a discussion of six books that dealt with African American history and culture. The intervention had a positive effect on the students' attitudes toward African Americans in both the rural and urban settings.

Intermediate-grade students experienced statistically significant growth in their academic achievement but not in self-concept scores in a study by Yee and Fruth (1973) in which social studies units that integrated the African American experience were studied. Yawkey and Blackwell (1974) found that two interventions had a statistically positive effect on the racial attitudes of four-year-old African-American students: (a) listening to and discussing multiethnic social studies materials; and (b) listening to and discussing multiethnic social studies materials combined with taking field trips related to the readings.

An eight-week intergroup relations unit examined by Lessing and Clarke (1976) included multiethnic readings, guest speakers, and the preparation of reports. There was not a measurable effect on the racial attitudes of a sample of junior high school students in a nearly all-White suburban school. One problem with this study is that students were allowed to select the books they read about each of five ethnic groups. The investigators hypothesized that the intervention did not help the students to develop more positive racial attitudes because of unfavorable race relations in the community in which the school was located, and because the books the students read about ethnic groups may have reinforced negative feelings about ethnic minorities.

Shirley (1988) investigated the effects of integrating multicultural activities into the English, social studies, and reading curricula on the self-concept, racial attitudes, and achievement of students in racially integrated fifth- and sixth-grade classes. The teachers who taught the students in the experimental groups attended weekly training sessions. There were no statistically significant changes in the self-concept and achievement means of African American students in the experimental groups. However, the racial attitudes of the White students in the experimental groups became more positive than the racial attitudes of the White students in the control groups.

Curriculum Materials

The effects of reading six stories about American Indians on the racial attitudes of fifth-grade students were examined by Fisher (1965). The groups in the study were: a reading-only group, a group that read and discussed the stories, and a control group that had no exposure to the stories. Both reading the stories only and reading and discussing them resulted in more positive attitudes toward American Indians. However, reading and discussing the stories resulted in more attitude change than merely reading them. In a related study, Tauran (1967) found that positive and negative literary materials influenced the attitudes of third-grade students toward Eskimos in the expected directions. The ethics of this intervention are questionable because the students in one of the treatment groups were taught unfavorable information about Eskimos.

The effects of multiethnic readers on the attitudes toward African Americans of second-grade White students in a midwestern city were examined by Litcher and Johnson (1969). For four months the children in the experimental groups used a multiethnic reader that included characters from several different racial and ethnic groups. The students in the control groups used a reader that included only White characters. The students who used the multiethnic readers had more positive posttest racial attitude mean scores than did the control groups. The Litcher and Johnson study is one of the most carefully designed and implemented and, consequently, one of the most frequently cited studies of the effects of curriculum materials on students' racial attitudes.

In a study related to the earlier Litcher and Johnson (1969) study, Litcher, Johnson, and Ryan (1973) examined the effects of pictures of multiethnic interactions on the racial attitudes of White second-grade students. This intervention had no measurable effects on the students' racial attitudes. The authors posited reasons for findings that differed from Litcher and Johnson. The duration of the later study was shorter (one month compared to four). The students in the later study lived in the suburb of a metropolitan area that had a considerably higher African American population than the city in which the earlier study was conducted. Consequently, their attitudes may have been more firmly rooted or extreme and thus harder to change.

The effects of reading stories about Mexican Americans on students' racial attitudes was examined by Howell (1973). The investigator varied the length of the intervention in the two experimental groups: one group read 10 stories over a period of 10 weeks; the other group read 5 stories over a 9-week period. A control group received no treatment. The 10-week group showed statistically significant differences on three of the four measures used in the study; the 9-week group showed statistically significant differences on only one of the measures. A strength of this study is that the length of the treatment varied and four different indexes were used to measure attitude change. Racial attitude scales are not highly correlated (Katz, 1976). Katz interpreted this to mean that prejudice is a highly complex variable, involving perceptual, attitudinal, and cognitive components. Consequently, carefully designed studies of curriculum interventions to modify racial attitudes will include several scales.

The effects on social distance scores of a minority literature program integrated into the social studies, reading, and language arts curricula were examined by Kimoto (1974). Fifth- and sixth-grade students were involved in this three-month intervention. At the end of the intervention, the experimental and the control groups had means on two of the social distance scales that were statistically different; that is, the students in the experimental group had more empathy and understanding of minority groups as measured by these two scales. However, experimental- and control-group means did not differ on one of the social distance scales and on the total scale.

Koeller (1977) studied the effects of reading excerpts from stories about Mexican Americans on the racial attitudes and self-concepts of sixth-grade students attending racially integrated schools. The experimental-group students listened to excerpts from six stories with ethnic themes over a six-week period. Control-group students heard excerpts from stories with nonethnic themes. There was not a statistically significant difference in the racial attitudes mean scores of the students. However, the investigator concluded that the treatment had a positive effect on the attitudes of the boys and a reverse effect on the girls' attitudes.

Reinforcement Studies

Reinforcement techniques to help students develop more positive associations with the color black, and consequently more positive attitudes toward African Americans, were developed by Williams and his colleagues (Williams & Robertson, 1967). In a series of studies with preschool and kindergarten children, the use of these reinforcement techniques resulted in more positive associations with the color black and with African American people (Williams & Morland, 1976). However, Shanahan (1972) and Collins (1972) failed to obtain statistically significant attitude changes using the techniques.

Most of the attitude-modification studies in which reinforcement has been investigated have been conducted in the laboratory rather than the classroom. An exception was Yancey's (1972) study. He developed a curriculum based on the Williams reinforcement techniques to help White first-graders develop less bias toward the color white and toward Whites. The curriculum intervention lasted 30 minutes each day and was conducted for 30 consecutive school days. The curriculum included stories and filmstrips that depicted African Americans positively and a game designed to develop positive associations with a black box. The investigator was also the teacher. After the curriculum intervention, the students expressed more positive racial attitudes.

In an investigation by McAdoo (1970), an 18-session "Black consciousness" curriculum had no measurable effects on the racial attitudes of African American preschool children. The effects of a six-week curriculum in which African American and White kindergarten children listened to stories that depicted African Americans favorably or described African Americans and Whites interacting positively were examined by Walker (1971). The students did not develop more positive racial attitudes during the intervention.

Teaching Methods

Few researchers have examined teaching method or approach as a variable or the relative effects of different instruc-

tional techniques in modifying students' racial attitudes. Greenberg, Pierson, and Sherman (1957) found that none of three methods—a debate, a lecture, and a discussion related to prejudice and racial integration—had any statistically significant effects on the racial attitudes of students enrolled in four different sections of an introductory college psychology class. The fourth group was a control. The changes that did occur in the means were in the direction of improved attitudes for the discussion group. This study is limited because each treatment was given in only one class session.

The effects of two different ways of teaching a semester unit on Africa on students' attitudes toward African Americans and Africa were examined by Gezi and Johnson (1970). The students who participated in the study ranged in age from 8 to 11. The control-group students studied the unit in a traditional way, with lectures stressing factual information and book assignments. The students in the experimental group studied the unit by participating in firsthand experiences and learning about Africa vicariously through such activities as viewing slides, movies, and pictures, and writing letters. The experimental-group students developed more positive attitudes toward African Americans and Africans. Gray and Ashmore (1975) examined the effects of informational, role-playing, and value-discrepancy treatments on the racial attitudes of college students. The three treatments were equally effective in developing more positive racial attitudes, as compared with the control-group results. When the students were tested eight weeks after the intervention, the experimental-group students were still lower in prejudice, although the difference was not statistically significant.

Jane Elliott's use of arbitrary discrimination to help third-grade students in Riceville, Iowa, to understand discrimination has been widely publicized in two films about her teaching and consultant work, *The Eye of the Storm* and *A Class Divided* (Peters, 1987). During the first day of intervention, brown-eyed children were declared "superior" and treated as such. The next day the roles were reversed and the blue-eyed children were declared and treated as "superior." Weiner and Wright (1973), in an intervention similar to the one implemented by Elliott, divided a third-grade class randomly into Orange and Green people. On the first day the Orange children were "superior"; the Green children were "superior" on the second day. The experimental class was significantly more likely to want to picnic with a group of African American children and held less prejudiced beliefs when compared with the control group on day three as well as two weeks later.

The effects of a teaching method called principle testing on the attitudes of high school students were investigated by Kehoe and Rogers (1978) in a city in British Columbia, Canada. In this teaching method, students are given the facts of a discrimination case and are asked to state what should be done. They are then asked a series of questions to determine the consistency with which they apply the principles implicit in their decision. The investigators examined the effects of principle testing on the students' attitudes toward women, the physically handicapped, and an ethnic-minority group, East Indians. The students who participated in the principle-testing discussions developed more positive attitudes toward the physically handicapped. However, the intervention had no measurable effects on the students' attitudes toward women and East Indians.

Summary

The studies reviewed above indicate that curriculum interventions can help students to develop more positive racial attitudes, but that the effects of such interventions are likely not to be consistent. The conflicting findings from the careful studies by Litcher and Johnson (1969) and Litcher et al. (1973) attest to the difficulties of curriculum-intervention studies. The inconsistencies may be due in part to the use of different measures to assess attitude change, and to the widely varied duration of the interventions. Studies have been rare in which the duration of the intervention has been varied in order to determine the effects.

The inconsistent results from curriculum-intervention studies may also be partly due to the variety in the social settings and contexts in which the studies took place. The racial, ethnic, and social-class characteristics of the students participating in the studies also vary considerably. Lessing and Clarke (1976) believed that the racial climate of the community influenced the results of their study. The community context may have also affected the results of the Litcher et al. (1973) study. These variables must be systematically varied and examined in curriculum-intervention studies before we can understand what factors are essential for such interventions to help students acquire democratic racial attitudes and values. Although the results of curriculum-intervention studies are not always consistent, they do indicate that teaching materials and curriculum interventions can have a positive influence on students' racial attitudes and beliefs (Katz & Zalk, 1978; Litcher & Johnson, 1969; Trager & Yarrow, 1952).

GENDER AND TEACHING MATERIALS

Research indicates that sex-role attitudes and gender associations develop early, and that teaching materials, the mass media, and society at large often reinforce sex-role stereotyping (Guttentag & Bray, 1976; Katz, 1986; Klein, 1985; McGhee & Frueh; 1980; Weitzman, 1972). A number of researchers have investigated the ways in which small-scale curriculum interventions, such as stories, vocational information, and television, influence sex-role attitudes. However, there is a paucity of studies that examine the effects of curriculum units and courses on children's sex-role attitudes and gender associations.

The research on the effects of curricular interventions on students' sex-role attitudes and gender associations shares many of the problems with the research on racial attitudes and curricular interventions described above. The studies tend to be short-term interventions, to have measurement problems, and rarely to be examinations of the relationships between expressed attitudes and behavior. In hardly any of the studies was the role of the teacher examined, the teacher treated as a variable, or the effects of teacher training on the teacher's ability to help students to develop less stereotyped gender-role conceptions investigated.

In-Service Education and Materials

One of the few studies that examined the effects of both teacher training and curriculum materials on students' gender attitudes was conducted by Tetreault (1979). She compared the gender attitudes of students following participation in three experimental conditions: (a) having a teacher who had completed a 26-hour course on the inclusion of women in U.S. history and who used a classroom set of materials on women's history; (b) having a teacher who only had the in-service training; and (c) having a teacher who only used the materials on women's history. The teachers of control-group classes neither participated in the in-service training nor used the curriculum materials on women's history.

Students in the experimental classes taught by teachers who participated in the in-service course and used the curriculum materials developed less stereotyped attitudes about males and females. However, the sex-role attitudes of the teachers who participated in the in-service program and used the curriculum materials were no different from the attitudes of the teachers in the other two experimental groups and in the control group. Most of the teachers who participated in the in-service training program, however, used three times more women's history materials than did teachers who received the materials but were not trained.

This study is important for several reasons. It is one of the few studies on gender attitudes in which an intervention that lasted for an entire academic year was examined. The study also had a large sample: 1,074 students in 55 classrooms. By defining in-service training and materials as separate variables, the investigator was able to determine their separate and combined effects. The two variables were effective when combined and less effective when used alone. The results of this study underscore the need to undergird curriculum interventions designed to change sex-role attitudes with teacher in-service education.

No data were reported on the attitudes of students who were members of different racial and ethnic groups. Similarly, few of the studies of racial attitudes reviewed above analyzed data by gender. Future studies will contribute more to knowledge development if data are analyzed for the main effects of both race and gender (Grant & Sleeter, 1986b) as well as for interactions of race and gender with the treatment. The results of the Tetreault (1979) intervention, for example, may have been different for African American and White students.

Teachers who participated in several workshops that gave them access to curriculum materials designed to promote gender equity made little use of these materials in an intervention by Woolever (1976). However, there was a statistically significant positive correlation between the amount of teacher intervention and pupil-attitude changes for grades kindergarten through two. This finding, however, did not hold for grades three through six.

The Effects of Reading Materials

A number of researchers have examined the effects of fiction and factual readings on the gender-role attitudes and perceptions of students in various grades. These interventions are usually short term and their long-term effects are rarely determined.

The effects of egalitarian books and stories on the sex-type attitudes of three-, four-, and five-year-old White students enrolled in kindergarten were examined by Flerx, Fidler, and Rogers (1976). Two experiments were reported. In the first experiment the students in the experimental group were read egalitarian stories and shown pictures illustrating the stories in which males and females pursued careers and shared household duties. Another group heard stories that described men and women in traditional stereotyped roles and occupations. In the second experiment a third treatment was added, a film in which egalitarian acts were modeled by males and females. The students who participated in the egalitarian book and film groups developed more egalitarian and less stereotyped sex-role attitudes.

There was some evidence that the boys were not as strongly affected by the treatment as were the girls, and that the film had a more enduring influence than the picture books. The results of this study are encouraging because of the short duration of the treatment—2.5 hours for experiment one, and 2 hours for experiment two.

Other researchers have also found that stories can influence gender-role attitudes and sex-role choices. Three hundred preschool boys and girls participated in a study by Lutes-Dunckley (1978). One group heard a story that depicted traditional sex-role behavior; another group heard a story in which all sex roles were reversed. A control group heard no story at all. The children who heard the story in which all sex roles were reversed made more nontraditional choices when asked to indicate which of two things they would rather do or which they liked better. There were no differences in the choices made by students who heard the traditional story or those who heard no story. Berg-Cross and Berg-Cross (1978) found that listening to four books had a positive effect on students' social attitudes, including their attitudes toward boys who play with dolls, as assessed by responses to open-ended questions. Evidence of the reliability and validity of the assessment was not presented; consequently, its results should be interpreted with caution. However, the results of this study are consistent with the findings of other studies reviewed in this chapter.

The effects on children's sex-role perceptions and story evaluations of stories that portrayed a female main character in a traditionally male role were examined by Scott and Feldman-Summers (1979). Male characters were replaced with female main characters in several stories. The third- and fourth-grade students read two stories a week for four weeks. The three experimental conditions were the combination of male and female main characters in the stories: (a) female-majority, (b) male-majority, and (c) equal proportions. Students who read stories with females in nontraditional roles increased their perceptions of the number of girls who can engage in these same activities. However, their perceptions of sex-role activities not presented in the stories were not affected.

In a study with 4th-, 7th-, and 11th-grade students, Scott (1986) confirmed the results of the Scott and Feldman-Summers (1979) investigation. She found that students who read narratives that showed females and males in nontraditional roles were more likely to think that both males and females should and could do the activity of the main character than were students who read traditional narratives. Scott also found that neither comprehension nor interest was diminished by the use of sex-fair materials. However, Kropp and Halverson (1983) found that preschool children tended to prefer stories whose main characters were of the same sex as themselves and who engaged in stereotypic activities. Jennings (1975) had obtained similar results with preschool students, but they did recall better stories in which the character's sex role was atypical.

The reading of a picture book to preschool children can influence the kinds of toys they choose (Ashton, 1983). The children were observed playing with toys for two minutes. They were then read a picture book that presented a character of the same sex playing with a stereotypic or nonstereotypic toy. Next, the children were given an opportunity to play with experimental toys for two more minutes. The children who heard a nonstereotypic story more often chose a nonstereotypic toy after the intervention. The reverse was the case for the children who heard a stereotypic story.

Vocational Choices and Expectations

A number of investigators have examined the effects of curriculum interventions on male and female students' vocational choices and expectations. In general, these interventions have had statistically significant effects. Barclay (1974) examined the effects on the gender-role attitudes of suburban and inner-city kindergarten children of reading books about women working and of general career information without reference to sex. The three treatments were: (a) reading and discussing three books dealing with working women, (b) reading and discussing a career information pamplet, and (c) viewing a flannelboard demonstration of the story of the Gingerbread Man, with later discussion (a nonrelated control treatment). The treatment in each group lasted 15 minutes during each of three days. The boys and girls exposed to the books dealing with working women increased the number of jobs they considered appropriate for females. The general career information enabled girls, but not boys, to see women in a greater number of vocational roles.

The choices made by high school juniors on the basis of sex stereotypes or lack of knowledge of probability of success in a given occupation can be influenced by vocational information that describes new opportunities for women (Hurwitz & White, 1977). The attitudes of ninth-graders toward sex-typed careers can also be changed by career information that describes nontraditional role models. After reading such materials, the students in a study by Greene, Sullivan, and Beyard-Tyler (1982) thought that more of the jobs they had read about were appropriate for both females and males. The females in the study had less sex-typed attitudes about the sex appropriateness of careers than did the males. Both males and females thought that it was more appropriate for females than males to enter nontraditional sex-typed occupations. These latter two findings are consistent with those of most other investigators who have investigated the gender-role attitudes of females and males; females tend to have more flexible gender-role attitudes and perceptions than males.

The effects of an innovative economics curriculum project, Mini-Society, on students' perceptions of entrepreneurship and occupational sex stereotyping were investigated by Kourilsky and Campbell (1984). Among the strengths of the study were its large sample (938 children in grades three through six), its geographic scope (students from three cities in different states), and its ethnic mix. The duration of the intervention is also noteworthy; it lasted 10 weeks, longer than most of the interventions reviewed in this chapter. Like the Tetreault (1979) study, this intervention had a teacher in-service education component, a 24-hour workshop that took place over a four-week period. Another strength of the study is that it was an investigation of an actual school curriculum, rather than of merely reading a story or viewing a film, as was the case in most of the studies of gender attitudes reported in this chapter.

The most serious limitation of the study was the lack of a control group; a preexperimental, single-group, pretest-posttest design (Campbell & Stanley, 1963) was used. Consequently, causal inferences about the intervention are difficult. On the pretest, the students viewed entrepreneurial roles as primarily a male domain. After participation in the Mini-Society curriculum, both boys and girls placed more females in entrepreneurial positions on the posttest. However, the change for boys was not statistically significant; the boys still saw entrepreneurship as predominantly a male domain. The interaction effects of race and gender were also examined. Most of the girls, except the African American girls, did not initially attempt entrepreneurship in the early phase of the Mini-Society curriculum.

The Effects of TV and Films

Some investigators have studied the effects of television and films on children's gender-role attitudes and perceptions. Di-Leo, Moely, and Sulzer (1970) investigated the effects on the sex-typed behavior of toy choices and game preferences of nursery-school, kindergarten, and first-grade children of a film showing a model choosing non-sex-typed toys. Before the intervention the children evidenced high levels of sex-typing in their choice of toys. After viewing the film, the students in the experimental groups made fewer sex-typed toy choices. On both the pre- and posttests, males and older children made more highly sex-typed choices than did females and younger children.

The effects of television cartoons on the sex-role stereotypes of kindergarten girls were investigated by Davidson, Yasuna, and Tower (1979). The girls viewed one of three television network cartoons: high stereotype, low stereotype, or neutral. After the intervention they were tested for sex-role stereotyping. The children who viewed the low-stereotyped television cartoon scored significantly lower on the sex-role stereotype measure than did the girls who viewed the high-stereotyped or neutral cartoons. The scores of the girls who reviewed the high-stereotyped and neutral cartoons did not differ.

The findings by DiLeo, Moely, and Sulzer (1979) and by Davidson, Yasuna, and Tower (1979) were not confirmed by Drabman et al. (1981). They found that preschool, first-, and

fourth-grade students maintained their sex-role stereotypes after viewing a videotape that depicted a male nurse working with a female physician. After viewing the videotape, the students were asked to identify photographs or names of the physician and the nurse. The students in preschool, first, and fourth grade selected male names or pictures for the physician and female names or pictures for the nurse. Seventh-grade students in the study correctly identified the names of the nurse and the physician.

The investigators conducted three different experiments in order to strengthen various aspects of the study. The findings were essentially the same in the first experiment and in the two replications. The investigators concluded that the responses of the students in preschool, first, and fourth grades were influenced more strongly by their stereotypes than by the film they viewed. The nature of the experiment, the visual presentation, the social setting, and the region might be among the reasons that the findings of this study failed to confirm the two previous ones.

Summary

Although the findings are not totally consistent, the studies reviewed above indicate that different kinds of curriculum interventions can help students to develop less stereotypic gender-role attitudes. The inconsistent results may have resulted from varied interventions, pupil ages, duration of interventions, social settings, and teacher attitudes and behavior. The research reviewed also indicates that students' conceptions of gender-appropriate occupations can be modified with curriculum interventions. While the studies are, on the whole, encouraging to educators, they do share several problems. Only a few have examined the relationship between attitudes and behavior or the duration of treatment as a variable, or have been designed to modify the attitudes and behavior of teachers.

IMPLICATIONS FOR RESEARCH AND PRACTICE

Research Implications

More studies on the effects of curriculum interventions on racial and gender-role attitudes are needed. Both ERIC and Psychological Abstracts were searched for studies in these areas. None of the studies on the effects of curriculum intervention on racial attitudes was published in the 1980s; most were published in the 1960s and 1970s. Most of the studies on gender-role attitudes examined in this chapter were also conducted in the 1970s. It appears that intervention research on racial and gender-role attitudes nearly halted at the end of the 1970s. This probably indicates that the United States has entered another phase in its history in which racial and social concerns have taken a back seat in a neoconservative national atmosphere (Schlesinger, 1986). If future projections can be based on past trends (which is always risky), national attention will again focus on racial and gender issues when the nation faces a social crisis, as in the World War II period, when intergroup education emerged, and in the 1960s, when the Black studies and women's studies movements arose as a part of the civil rights movement.

Because funding for race relations and gender-related studies is likely to be scarce for the foreseeable future, there is not likely to be a rash of such studies soon. Thus any implications for research stated here should be tempered by reality.

University teacher educators face many demands, not all of which are consistent. They are expected to interpret research for practitioners, teach methods courses, become involved with schools, and write student materials. They are also expected to do research. Research, however, often becomes the lowest priority in their day-to-day involvement with practice and practitioners. Educators should be encouraged to conduct research on race and gender curriculum interventions. They can conduct small-scale descriptive studies while doing their daily chores, such as supervising student teachers, working with doctoral candidates, and consulting with school districts.

One of the major problems with existing studies is that they are not characterized by what Geertz (1973) calls "thick description." They do not contain sufficient detail about the nature of interventions, the behavior of the students and the teachers, and the interactions that took place between students and materials. By working with student teachers and the schools in which they do their practice teaching, teacher educators could conduct ethnographic and case studies of the use of units and courses designed to modify the racial and gender attitudes of students. The ethnographic studies of social studies teachers conducted at Stanford by Shulman (1987) and his students exemplify the kind of research needed.

Teacher educators could make several important contributions to the research on racial and gender-role attitude modification. They could examine ways in which such variables as race, gender, and social class interact to influence students' behavior and attitudes. Very few of the studies reviewed in this chapter included the examination of the interaction effects of race and gender. Grant and Sleeter (1986b) have pointed out why it is important to describe interaction effects. Research by teacher educators and their graduate students should also be focused on in-depth examinations of teacher characteristics and their role in multicultural education, as well as on documentation of the relationships between attitudes and behavior.

Implications for Practice

That a 15-minute intervention influenced the racial attitudes of second- and fifth-grade children from four to six months later (Katz & Zalk, 1978) is the most striking finding of this research review. Most of the studies reviewed in this chapter consist of interventions of rather short duration. If a 15-minute intervention can influence students' racial attitudes, we can only surmise that the impact of a teacher and a curriculum with which a student interacts for over 180 days must be tremendous. This is cause for both hope and concern. This situation is hopeful if the teacher and the curriculum are democratic, but a cause for deep concern if the teacher or the curriculum is status-quo oriented, biased, or nondemocratic.

An important implication of this research review for practice is that teachers must be provided with training and opportunities that will enable them to examine their feelings, attitudes, and values, and helped to develop attitudes consistent with a democratic society (Tetreault, 1979; Trager & Yarrow, 1952). Another important implication is that students must be helped to acquire more democratic attitudes and behavior. Research findings substantiate media reports of racial discrimination and violence; many students have negative racial and gender attitudes (Glock et al., 1975; Klein, 1985; Milner, 1983). Research findings also indicate that student attitudes can be changed by curricular interventions. The precise conditions that will lead consistently to attitude change are, however, not yet clear. Interventions appear to be most successful with young children, particularly preschoolers and kindergartners (Williams & Morland, 1976; Williams & Roberson, 1967). These findings suggest that if the twig is going to be straightened (Katz, 1976), we must start as early as possible. In general, girls are more influenced than boys in intervention studies related to gender issues. Studies should be undertaken to help explain this difference and to develop more effective intervention methods for boys. Efforts must also be made to ensure that teaching materials are multicultural and gender-fair. Materials apparently influence students' racial and gender-role attitudes even when they are never discussed.

The changing demographics of U.S. society and the world—one out of three people in the United States will be a member of an ethnic minority by 2000 (Commission on Minority Participation in Education and American Life, 1988)—require that educators act now and act decisively to create a more humane and caring world. Multicultural education is a road rarely taken. If taken properly, it might make a major difference. More carefully designed research is needed to help provide the direction. In the meantime, we should use the guidelines derived from the research reviewed in this chapter to help create a more caring and humane nation.

References

Adorno, T. W., Frenkel-Brunswik, E., Levinson, D. J., & Sanford, R. N. (1950). *The authoritarian personality.* New York: W. W. Norton.

Agnes, M. (1947). Influences of reading on the racial attitudes of adolescent girls. *Catholic Educational Review, 45,* 415–420.

Allport, G. (1954). *The nature of prejudice.* Reading, MA: Addison-Wesley.

Aronson, E., & Gonzalez, A. (1988). Desegregation, jigsaw, and the Mexican-American experience. In P. A. Katz & D. A. Taylor (Ed.), *Eliminating racism: Profiles in control.* New York: Plenum.

Ashton, E. (1983). Measures of play behavior: The influence of sex-role stereotyped children's books. *Sex Roles, 9,* 43–47.

Baker, G. (1983). *Planning and organizing for multicultural instruction.* Reading, MA: Addison-Wesley.

Banks, J. A. (1994). *Multiethnic education: Theory and practice* (3rd ed.). Boston: Allyn and Bacon.

Banks, J. A., & Banks, C. A. M. (Eds.). (1993). *Multicultural education: Issues and perspectives* (2nd ed.). Boston: Allyn and Bacon.

Barclay, L. K. (1974). The emergence of vocational expectations in preschool children. *Journal of Vocational Behavior, 4,* 1–14.

Bennett, C. I. (1986). *Comprehensive multicultural education: Theory and practice.* Boston: Allyn and Bacon.

Berg-Cross, L., & Berg-Cross, G. (1978). Listening to stories may change children's social attitudes. *Reading Teacher, 31,* 659–663.

Campbell, D. T., & Stanley, J. C. (1963). *Experimental and quasi-experimental designs for research.* Chicago: Rand McNally.

Clark, K. B. (1955). *Prejudice and your child.* Boston: Beacon Press.

Collins, J. (1972). *The effect of differential frequency of color adjective pairings on the subsequent rating of color meaning and racial attitude in preschool children.* Unpublished master's thesis, East Tennessee State University, Johnson City.

Commission on Minority Participation in Education and American Life. (1988). *One-third of a nation.* Washington, DC: American Council on Education.

Cook, L. A. (1947). Intergroup education. *Review of Educational Research, 17,* 266–278.

Davidson, E. S., Yasuna, A., & Tower, A. (1979). The effects of television cartoons on sex-role stereotyping in young girls. *Child Development, 50,* 597–600.

DiLeo, J. C., Moely, B. E., & Sulzer, J. L. (1979). Frequency and modifiability of children's preferences for sex-typed toys, games, and occupations. *Child Study Journal, 9,* 141–159.

Drabman, R. S., Robenson, S. J., Patterson, J. N., Jarvie, G. J., Hammer, D., & Cordua, G. (1981). Children's perception of media-portrayed sex roles. *Sex Roles, 7,* 379–389.

Fisher, F. (1965). *The influence of reading and discussion on the attitudes of fifth graders toward American Indians.* Unpublished doctoral dissertation, University of California, Berkeley.

Flerx, V. C., Fidler, D. S., & Rogers, R. W. (1976). Sex role stereotypes: Developmental aspects and early intervention. *Child Development, 47,* 998–1007.

Gabelko, N. H., & Michaelis, U. (1981). *Reducing adolescent prejudice.* New York: Teachers College Press.

Geertz, C. (1973). *The interpretation of cultures.* New York: Basic Books.

Gezi, K. I., & Johnson, B. (1970). Enhancing racial attitudes through the study of Black heritage. *Childhood Education, 46,* 397–399.

Glock, C. Y., Wuthnow, R., Piliavin, J. A., & Spencer, M. (1975). *Adolescent prejudice.* New York: Harper & Row.

Gollnick, D. M., & Chinn, P. C. (1986). *Multicultural education in a pluralistic society* (2nd ed.). Columbus, OH: Merrill.

Goodman, M. E. (1952). *Race awareness in young children.* New York: Macmillan.

Grant, C. A., & Sleeter, C. E. (1986a). *After the school bell rings.* Philadelphia: Falmer Press.

Grant, C. A., & Sleeter, C. E. (1986b). Race, class, and gender in education research: An argument for integrative analysis. *Review of Educational Research, 56,* 195–211.

Gray, D. E., & Ashmore, R. D. (1975). Comparing the effects of informational, role-playing, and value-discrepancy treatments on racial attitudes. *Journal of Applied Social Psychology, 5,* 262–281.

Greene, L. A., Sullivan, H. J., & Beyard-Tyler, K. (1982). Attitudinal effects of the use of role models in information about sex-typed careers. *Journal of Educational Psychology, 74,* 393–398.

Greenberg, H., Pierson, J., & Sherman, S. (1957). The effects of single session education techniques on prejudice attitudes. *Journal of Educational Sociology, 31,* 82–86.

Guttentag, M., & Bray, H. (1976). *Undoing sex stereotypes: Research and resources for educators.* New York: McGraw-Hill.

Hayes, M. L., & Conklin, M. E. (1953). Intergroup attitudes and experimental change. *Journal of Experimental Education, 22,* 19–36.

Howell, M. (1973). *A study of the effects of reading upon the attitudes of fifth graders toward Mexican Americans.* Unpublished doctoral dissertation, Southern Illinois University, Carbondale.

Hurwitz, R. E., & White, M. A. (1977). Effect of sex-linked vocational information on reported occupational choices of high school juniors. *Psychology of Women Quarterly, 2,* 149–154.

Jackson, E. P. (1944). Effects of reading upon attitudes toward the Negro race. *Library Quarterly, 14,* 47–54.

Jennings, S. A. (1975). Effects of sex typing in children's stories on preference and recall. *Child Development, 46,* 220–223.

Johnson, D. W. (1966). Freedom school effectiveness: Changes in attitudes of Negro children. *Journal of Applied Behavioral Science, 2,* 325–330.

Katz, P. A. (1963). Perception of racial cues in preschool children: A new look. *Developmental Psychology, 8,* 295–299.

Katz, P. A. (Ed.). (1976). *Towards the elimination of racism.* New York: Pergamon.

Katz, P. A. (1986). Modification of children's gender-stereotyped behavior: General issues and research considerations. *Sex Roles, 14,* 591–602.

Katz, P. A., Sohn, M., & Zalk, S. R. (1975). Perceptual concomitants of racial attitudes in urban grade-school children. *Developmental Psychology, 11,* 135–144.

Katz, P. A., & Zalk, S. R. (1978). Modification of children's racial attitudes. *Developmental Psychology, 14,* 447–461.

Kehoe, J. W., & Rogers, W. T. (1978). The effects of principle-testing discussions on student attitudes towards selected groups subjected to discrimination. *Canadian Journal of Education, 3,* 73–80.

Kimoto, C. K. (1974). *The effects of a juvenile literature based program on minority group attitudes toward Black Americans.* Unpublished doctoral dissertation, Washington State University, Pullman.

Klein, S. S. (Ed.). (1985). *Handbook of achieving sex equity through education.* Baltimore, MD: Johns Hopkins University Press.

Koeller, S. (1977). The effect of listening to excerpts from children's stories about Mexican-Americans on the attitudes of sixth graders. *Journal of Educational Research, 70,* 329–334.

Kourilsky, M., & Campbell, M. (1984). Sex differences in a simulated classroom economy: Children's beliefs about entrepreneurship. *Sex Roles, 10,* 53–65.

Kropp, J. J., & Halverson, C. F. (1983). Preschool children's preferences and recall for stereotyped versus nonstereotyped stories. *Sex Roles, 8,* 261–272.

Lasker, G. (1929). *Race attitudes in children.* New York: Henry Holt.

Leslie, L. L., & Leslie, J. W. (1972). The effects of a student centered special curriculum upon the racial attitudes of sixth graders. *Journal of Experimental Education, 41,* 63–67.

Lessing, E. E., & Clarke, C. (1976). An attempt to reduce ethnic prejudice and assess its correlates. *Educational Research Quarterly, 1,* 3–16.

Litcher, J. H., & Johnson, D. W. (1969). Changes in attitudes toward Negroes of White elementary school students after use of multiethnic readers. *Journal of Educational Psychology, 60,* 148–152.

Litcher, J. H., Johnson, D. W., & Ryan, F. L. (1973). Use of pictures of multiethnic interaction to change attitudes of White elementary school students toward Blacks. *Psychological Reports, 33,* 367–372.

Lutes-Dunckley, C. J. (1978). Sex-role stereotypes as a function of sex of storyteller and story content. *Journal of Psychology, 100,* 151–158.

McAdoo, J. L. (1970) *An exploratory study of racial attitude change in Black preschool children using differential treatments.* Unpublished doctoral dissertation, University of Michigan, Ann Arbor.

McAdoo, J. L. (1985). Modification of racial attitudes and preferences in young Black children. In H. P. McAdoo & J. L. McAdoo (Eds.), *Black children: Social, educational, and parental environments* (pp. 243–256). Beverly Hills, CA: Sage.

McGhee, P. E., & Frueh, T. (1980). Television viewing and the learning of sex-role stereotypes. *Sex Roles, 6*, 179–188.

Milner, D. (1983). *Children and race.* Beverly Hills, CA: Sage.

Minard, R. D. (1931). Race attitudes of Iowa children. *University of Iowa, Studies in Character, 4*(2).

Myrdal, G., with Sterner, R., & Rose, A. (1944). *An American dilemma: The Negro problem and modern democracy* (Vols. 1 & 2). New York: Harper & Brothers.

Parish, T. S., Shirazi, A., & Lambert, F. (1976). Conditioning away prejudicial attitudes in children. *Perceptual and Motor Skills, 43*, 907–912.

Patterson, O. (1977). *Ethnic chauvinism: The reactionary impulse.* New York: Stein & Day.

Peters, W. (1987). *A class divided: Then and now* (expanded ed.). New Haven, CT: Yale University Press.

Porter, J. D. R. (1971). *Black child, White child: The development of racial attitudes.* Cambridge, MA: Harvard University Press.

Proshansky, H. (1966). The development of intergroup attitudes. In I. W. Hoffman & M. L. Hoffman (Eds.), *Review of child development research* (Vol. 2, pp. 311–371). New York: Russell Sage Foundation.

Roth, R. W. (1969). The effects of "Black Studies" on Negro fifth grade students. *The Journal of Negro Education, 38*, 435–439.

Schlesinger, A. M., Jr. (1986). *The cycles of American history.* Boston: Houghton Mifflin.

Scott, K. P. (1986). Effects of sex-fair reading materials on pupils' attitudes, comprehension, and interest. *American Educational Research Journal, 28*, 105–116.

Scott, K. P., & Feldman-Summers, S. (1979). Children's reactions to textbook stories in which females are portrayed in traditionally male roles. *Journal of Educational Psychology, 71*, 396–402.

Shanahan, J. K. (1972). *The effects of modifying Black-White attitudes of Black and White first grade subjects upon two measures of racial attitudes.* Unpublished doctoral dissertation, University of Washington, Seattle.

Shirley, O. L. B. (1988). *The impact of multicultural education on self-concept, racial attitude, and student achievement of Black and White fifth and sixth graders.* Unpublished doctoral dissertation, University of Mississippi, Oxford.

Shulman, L. (1987). Knowledge and teaching: Foundations of the new reform. *Harvard Educational Review, 57*, 1–22.

Slavin, R. E. (1985). Cooperative learning: Applying contact theory in desegregated schools. *Journal of Social Issues, 41*, 45–62.

Slavin, R. E., & Madden, N. A. (1979). School practices that improve race relations. *American Educational Research Journal, 16*, 169–180.

Sleeter, C. E., & Grant, C. A. (1987). An analysis of multicultural education in the United States. *Harvard Educational Review, 57*, 421–444.

Stephan, W. G. (1985). Intergroup relations. In G. Lindzey & E. Aronson (Eds.), *The handbook of social psychology* (pp. 599–658). New York: Random House.

Taba, H., Brady, E. H., & Robinson, J. T. (1952). *Intergroup education in public schools.* Washington, DC: American Council on Education.

Tauran, R. H. (1967). *The influences of reading on the attitudes of third graders toward Eskimos.* Unpublished doctoral dissertation, University of Maryland, College Park.

Tetreault, M. K. T. (1979). *The inclusion of women in the United States history curriculum and adolescent attitudes toward sex-appropriate behavior.* Unpublished doctoral dissertation, Boston University School of Education.

Trager, H. G., & Yarrow, M. R. (1952). *They learn what they live.* New York: Harper.

Walker, P. A. (1971). *The effects of hearing selected children's stories that portray Blacks in a favorable manner on the racial attitudes of groups of Black and White kindergarten children.* Unpublished doctoral dissertation, University of Michigan, Ann Arbor.

Weiner, M. J., & Wright, F. E. (1973). Effects of undergoing arbitrary discrimination upon subsequent attitudes toward a minority group. *Journal of Applied Social Psychology, 3*, 94–102.

Weitzman, L. J. (1972). Sex-role socialization in picture books for preschool children. *American Journal of Sociology, 77*, 1125–1150.

Williams, J. E., & Edwards, C. D. (1969). An exploratory study of the modification of color and racial concept attitudes in preschool children. *Child Development, 40*, 737–750.

Williams, J. E., & Morland, J. K. (1976). *Race, color and the young child.* Chapel Hill: University of North Carolina Press.

Williams, J. E., & Robertson, J. K. (1967). A method of assessing racial attitudes in preschool children. *Educational and Psychological Measurement, 27*, 671–689.

Wilson, A. (1987). *Mixed race children: A study of identity.* Boston: Allen & Unwin.

Woolever, R. (1976). *Expanding elementary pupils' occupational and social role perceptions: An examination of teacher attitudes and behavior and pupil attitude change.* Unpublished doctoral dissertation, University of Washington, Seattle.

Yancey, A. V. (1972). *A study of attitudes in White first grade children.* Unpublished paper, Pennsylvania State University, University Park.

Yawkey, T. D. (1973). Attitudes towards black Americans held by rural and urban white early childhood subjects based upon multiethnic social studies materials. *The Journal of Negro Education, 42*, 164–169.

Yawkey, T. D., & Blackwell, J. (1974). Attitudes of 4-year-old urban Black children toward themselves and Whites based upon multiethnic social studies materials and experiences. *Journal of Educational Research, 67*, 373–377.

Yee, A. H., & Fruth, M. J. (1973). Do Black studies make a difference in ghetto children's achievement and attitudes? *The Journal of Negro Education, 42*, 33–38.

· 35 ·

COOPERATIVE LEARNING AND INTERGROUP RELATIONS

Robert E. Slavin
JOHNS HOPKINS UNIVERSITY

The year 1994 marked the 40th anniversary of *Brown v. Board of Education of Topeka* (1954) and the 30th anniversary of the 1964 Civil Rights Act, the two most important events in the dismantling of legal barriers to racial integration in the United States. The same year also saw the 40th anniversary of one of the most important events in the study of dismantling *interpersonal* barriers to racial integration: the publication of Gordon Allport's *The Nature of Prejudice* (1954). As the *Brown* decision set the tone for later judicial action against school segregation and as the Civil Rights Act set the tone for later legislative action against segregation and discrimination in society as a whole, *The Nature of Prejudice* has served as the basis for the study of intergroup relations.

At the time Allport was writing, social scientists were debating the potential impact of desegregation in general, particularly of *school* desegregation, on intergroup relations. Allport's work was central to the social science statement (Allport & 34 co-signers, 1953), which played an important role in the deliberations of the Supreme Court in the *Brown* case (see Cook, 1984).

In *The Nature of Prejudice* (1954), Gordon Allport evaluated the experience of desegregation in industrial, military, and other nonschool settings to anticipate the effects of school desegregation on intergroup relations and other outcomes. In the early 1950s integrated schools were illegal in the 17 states (plus the District of Columbia) in which most African Americans lived, and they were rare elsewhere, so direct study of integrated schools was difficult. However, Allport did have available

enough experience and research on various integrated settings to derive a set of principles to predict when interracial contact would lead to improved relationships and when it would not. He cited research that indicated that superficial contact could be detrimental to race relations, as could competitive contact and contact between individuals of markedly different status. However, he also cited evidence to the effect that when individuals of different racial or ethnic groups worked to achieve common goals, when they had opportunities to get to know one another as individuals, and when they worked with one another on an equal footing, they became friends and did not continue to hold prejudices against one another. Allport's contact theory of intergroup relations was based on these findings. While contact theory has been updated by Amir (1969), Hewstone and Brown (1986), Pettigrew (1986), and others, it has dominated social science inquiry on race relations for four decades. Allport's own summary of the essentials of contact theory is as follows:

Prejudice . . . may be reduced by equal status contact between majority and minority groups in the pursuit of common goals. The effect is greatly enhanced if this contact is sanctioned by institutional supports . . . and if it is of a sort that leads to the perception of common interests and common humanity between members of the two groups. (p. 281)

Ever since *Brown v. Board of Education,* it has been assumed that desegregation would improve relations between students of different ethnic backgrounds. Yet all too often, de-

This chapter was adapted from "Cooperative Learning: Applying Contact Theory in Desegregated Schools" by Robert E. Slavin, 1985, *Journal of Social Issues, 41*(3), pp. 45–60, by permission of the Society for the Psychological Study of Social Issues. It was written under funding from the Office of Educational Research and Improvement, U.S. Department of Education (No. OERI-R-117-R90002). However, any opinions expressed are the author's and do not necessarily represent OERI positions or policies.

The author would like to thank James A. Banks, Elizabeth Cohen, Anthony Jackson, and Elliot Aronson for comments on an earlier draft.

segregated schools are not really integrated schools. In most schools, African American, White, and Latino students remain much more likely to have friends of their own ethnic background than to make many cross-ethnic choices (Gerard & Miller, 1975; Schofield, 1991; Stephan, 1978). Although school desegregation does have a positive effect on racial toleration (Scott & McPartland, 1982), ethnicity is still a major barrier to friendship and respect in many desegregated schools.

Desegregation must be seen as an opportunity for improvement of intergroup relations, not as a solution in itself. Stuart Cook (1979) participated in the deliberations that led to the famous social science statement (F. H. Allport et al., 1953) that played a part in the *Brown v. Board of Education* decision. He has pointed out that in the early 1950s social scientists knew that school desegregation must be accompanied by changes in school practices if it were to have positive effects on relations between African American and White students.

In traditionally organized schools, desegregation rarely fulfills the conditions outlined by Allport. Interaction between students of different ethnicities is typically superficial and often competitive. African American, Anglo, Latino, and other groups compete for grades, for teacher approval, and for places on the student council or on the cheerleading squad. In the classroom, the one setting in which students of different races or ethnicities are at least likely to be sitting side by side, traditional instructional methods permit little contact between students that is not superficial. Otherwise, African American, Anglo, and Latino students usually ride different buses to different neighborhoods, participate in different kinds of activities, and go to different social functions. Opportunities for positive intergroup interaction are limited. One major exception is sports; sports teams create conditions of cooperation and nonsuperficial contact among team members.

Correlational research by Slavin and Madden (1979) has shown that students who participate in sports in desegregated high schools are much more likely to have friends outside of their own racial group and to have positive racial attitudes than are students who do not participate in integrated sports teams. Hallinan and Teixeira (1987) and Patchen (1982) found a similar effect of participation in extracurricular activities in general. Sports teams fulfill the requirements of contact theory in that interaction among teammates tends to be nonsuperficial, cooperative, and of equal status. However, there are only so many positions on teams, and schools below the high school level may not have sports teams at all.

Is there a way to change classroom organization to allow meaningful, cooperative contact to take place between students of different ethnicities? This chapter, adapted from an earlier review (Slavin, 1985), describes the results of several research programs designed to answer this question by systematically applying interventions based on Allport's contact theory to academic classrooms. The methods evaluated in this research are referred to collectively as *cooperative learning* (Slavin, 1990). This chapter reviews the research on cooperative learning methods, with an emphasis on understanding the complex changes that occur in both classroom organization and student friendship patterns when cooperative, integrated learning groups are used in the desegregated classroom.

COOPERATIVE LEARNING

Cooperative learning methods explicitly use the strength of the desegregated school—the presence of students of different races or ethnicities—to enhance intergroup relations and other outcomes. The groups in which students work are made up of four to five students of different races, sexes, and levels of achievement, with each group reflecting the composition of the class as a whole on these attributes. In most cooperative learning methods, the groups receive rewards, recognition, and/or evaluation based on the degree to which they can increase the academic performance of each member of the group. This is in sharp contrast to the student competition for grades and teacher approval characteristic of the traditional classroom. Cooperation between students is emphasized both by the classroom rewards and tasks and by the teacher, who tries to communicate an "all for one, one for all" attitude. The various methods are structured to give each student a chance to make a substantial contribution to the team, so that teammates will be equal—at least in the sense of role equality specified by Allport (1954). The cooperative-learning methods are designed to be true changes in classroom organization, not time-limited "treatments." They provide daily opportunities for intense interpersonal contact among students of different races. When the teacher assigns students of different races or ethnicities to work together, this communicates unequivocal support on the teacher's part for the idea that interracial or interethnic interaction is officially sanctioned. Even though race or race relations per se need not be mentioned (and rarely are) in the course of cooperative-learning experiences, it is difficult for a student to believe the teacher supports racial separation when the teacher has assigned the class to multiethnic teams.

Thus, at least in theory, cooperative-learning methods satisfy the conditions outlined by Allport (1954) for positive effects of desegregation on race relations: cooperation across racial lines, equal-status roles for students of different races, contact across racial lines that permits students to learn about one another as individuals, and communication of unequivocal teacher support for interracial contact.

The conditions of contact theory are not difficult to achieve in the laboratory, and a long tradition of laboratory studies has investigated and generally supported the main tenets of contact theory (e.g., Cook, 1978; Miller, Brewer, & Edwards, 1985; Miller & Harrington, 1992). However, as Harrison (1976) points out, "200 million Americans cannot be run through the laboratory one by one [to reduce prejudice]" (p. 563). If a program designed to implement contact theory in classrooms is to be anything but an academic exercise, it must not only improve intergroup relations, but must also accomplish other educational goals. For example, research on cooperative learning would be of little relevance to schools if the methods did not also improve (or at least not hinder) student achievement, or if they were too expensive, too difficult, too narrowly focused, or too disruptive of school routines to be practical as primary alternatives to traditional instruction. As a consequence, features of cooperative-learning methods other than the degree to which they are designed to improve race relations are of great importance.

Seven principal cooperative learning methods embody the principles of contact theory, have been compared with traditional methods over periods of at least four weeks in desegregated schools, and have the practical characteristics outlined above: They are cheap, relatively easy to implement, widely applicable in terms of subject matter and grade levels, easily integrated into an existing school without additional resources, and most have been shown to improve achievement more than traditional instruction (see Slavin, 1990). Three of these methods were developed and evaluated at the Center for Social Organization of Schools at Johns Hopkins University. These are Student Teams-Achievement Divisions, Teams-Games-Tournament (Slavin, 1986), and Team-Assisted Individualization (Slavin, Leavey, & Madden, 1984). A fourth technique, Jigsaw teaching (Aronson, Blaney, Stephan, Sikes, & Snapp, 1978), has been evaluated in several desegregated schools and is widely used both in its original form and as modified by Slavin (1986) and by Kagan (1991). Methods developed and assessed at the University of Minnesota (Johnson & Johnson, 1987) have been studied in desegregated schools, and Group Investigation (Sharan & Sharan, 1992) has been studied in Israeli schools that include European and Middle Eastern Jews. In addition, Weigel, Wiser, and Cook (1975) evaluated a cooperative-learning method in triethnic (African American, Latino, Anglo) classes. These techniques are described below (see Slavin, 1986, 1990, for more detailed descriptions).

1. *Student Teams-Achievement Divisions (STAD)*. In STAD the teacher presents a lesson, and then students study worksheets in four-member teams that are heterogeneous in student ability, sex, and ethnicity. Following this, students take individual quizzes, and team scores are computed based on the degree to which each student improved over his or her own past record. The team scores are recognized in class newsletters.
2. *Teams-Games-Tournament (TGT)*. TGT is essentially the same as STAD in rationale and method. However, it replaces the quizzes and improvement-score system used in STAD with a system of academic game tournaments in which students from each team compete with students from other teams of the same level of past performance to try to contribute to their team scores.
3. *Team-Assisted Individualization (TAI)*. TAI combines the use of cooperative teams (such as those used in STAD and TGT) with individualized instruction in elementary mathematics. Students work in four- to five-member heterogeneous teams on self-instructional materials at their own levels and rates. The students themselves take responsibility for all checking, management, and routing, and help one another with problems, freeing the teacher to spend most of her or his time instructing small groups of students (drawn from the various teams) working on similar concepts. Teams are rewarded with certificates if they attain preset standards in terms of the number of units mastered by all team members each week.
4. *Jigsaw and Jigsaw II*. In the original Jigsaw method (Aronson et al., 1978) students are assigned to heterogeneous six-member teams, and each team member is given a unique set of information on an overall unit. For example, in a unit on Spain, one student might be appointed as an "expert" on Spain's history, another on its culture, another on its economy, and so on. The students read their information and then discuss it in "expert groups" made up of students from different teams who have studied the same information. The "experts" then return to their teams to teach the information to their teammates. Finally, all students are quizzed, and students receive individual grades.

   Jigsaw II modifies Jigsaw to correspond more closely with the Student Team Learning format (Slavin, 1986). Students work in four- to five-member teams (as in STAD, TGT, and TAI). All students read the same chapter or story, but each team member is given an individual topic on which to become an expert. Students discuss their topics in expert groups and teach them to their teammates, as in original Jigsaw. However, quiz scores in Jigsaw II are summed to form team scores, and teams are recognized in a class newsletter, as in STAD. Kagan (1991) has described many additional variations of Jigsaw.
5. *Johnson methods*. In cooperative-learning methods developed by David Johnson and Roger Johnson (1987), students work in small, heterogeneous groups to complete a common worksheet, and are praised and rewarded as a group. These methods are the least complex of the cooperative-learning methods and the closest to a pure cooperative model, as the other methods contain individualistic and/or competitive elements.
6. *Group Investigation*. Group Investigation (Sharan & Sharan, 1992), developed by Shlomo and Yael Sharan and their colleagues in Israel, is a general classroom organization plan in which students work in small groups using cooperative inquiry, group discussion, and cooperative planning and projects. In this method, students form their own two- to six-member groups. The groups choose subtopics from a unit being studied by the entire class, further break their subtopics into individual tasks, and carry out the activities necessary to prepare a group report. The group then makes a representation or display to communicate its findings to the entire class, and is evaluated based on the quality of this report.
7. *Weigel et al. methods*. In one study in junior and senior high schools containing African American, Mexican American, and Anglo students, Weigel et al. (1975) used a combination of cooperative-learning methods, including information gathering, discussion, and interpretation of materials in heterogeneous groups. Prizes were given to groups on the basis of the quality of the group product.

RESEARCH ON COOPERATIVE LEARNING AND INTERGROUP RELATIONS

The remainder of this chapter reviews field experiments evaluating the effects of cooperative-learning methods on intergroup relations. This review emphasizes studies in which the methods were used in elementary or secondary schools for at least 4 weeks (median duration = 10 weeks), and in which appropriate research methods and analyses were used to rule out obvious bias. Study Ns ranged from 51 to 424 (median = 164), grade levels from 4 to 12, and percent minority from 10% to 61%. Most of the studies used sociometric indexes (e.g., "Who are your friends in this class?"), peer ratings, or behavioral observation to measure intergroup relations as pairwise positive relations between individuals of different ethnic backgrounds. A few studies defined intergroup relations in terms of attitudes toward various ethnic groups. Several studies used such sociometric questions as "Whom have you helped in this class?" Because only students in the cooperative-learning classes are likely to have helped their classmates, such measures are biased toward the cooperative-learning treatments; thus the results of these measures will not be discussed. Also, observations of cross-racial interaction during the treatment classes, another measure of implementation rather than outcome, are not considered as intergroup relations measures.

Main Effects on Intergroup Relations

The experimental evidence on cooperative learning has generally supported the main tenets of contact theory (G. Allport, 1954). With only a few exceptions, this research has demonstrated that when the conditions outlined by Allport are met in the classroom, students are more likely to have friends outside their own racial groups than they would in traditional classrooms, as measured by responses to such sociometric items as "Who are your best friends in this class?"

STAD. The evidence linking STAD to gains in cross-racial friendships is strong. In two studies, Slavin (1977, 1979) found that students who had experienced STAD over periods of 10 to 12 weeks gained more in cross-racial friendships than did control students. Slavin and Oickle (1981) found significant gains in White friendships toward Blacks as a consequence of STAD, but found no differences in Black friendships toward Whites. Kagan, Zahn, Widaman, Schwarzwald, and Tyrell (1985) found that STAD (and TGT) reversed a trend toward ethnic polarization of friendship choices among Anglo, Latino, and Black students. Sharan et al. (1984) found positive effects of STAD on ethnic attitudes of both Middle Eastern and European Jews in Israeli schools.

Slavin's (1979) study included a follow-up into the next academic year, in which students who had been in the experimental and control classes were asked to list their friends. Students in the control group listed an average of fewer than one friend of another race, or 9.8% of all of their friendship choices; those in the experimental group named an average of 2.4 friends outside their own race, 37.9% of their friendship choices. The STAD research covered grades two to eight, and took place in schools ranging from 13% to 61% minority.

TGT. DeVries, Edwards, and Slavin (1978) summarized data analyses from four studies of TGT in desegregated schools. In three of these, students in classes that used TGT gained significantly more friends outside their own racial groups than did

control students. In one, no differences were found. The samples involved in these studies varied in grade level from 7 to 12 and in percentage of minority students from 10% to 51%. In addition, Kagan et al. (1985) found positive effects of TGT on friendship choices among African American, Mexican American, and Anglo students.

TAI. Two studies have assessed the effects of TAI on intergroup relations. Oishi, Slavin, and Madden (1983) found positive effects of TAI on cross-racial nominations on two sociometric scales, "Who are your friends in this class?" and "Whom would you rather *not* sit at a table with?" No effects were found on cross-racial ratings of classmates as "nice" or "smart," but TAI students made significantly fewer cross-racial ratings as "not nice" and "not smart" than did control students. In a similar study, Oishi (1983) found significantly positive effects of TAI on cross-racial ratings as "smart" and on reductions in ratings as "not nice." The effect on "smart" ratings was due primarily to increases in Whites' ratings of African American classmates.

Jigsaw. The effects of the original Jigsaw method on intergroup relations are less clear than those for STAD, TGT, or TAI. Blaney, Stephan, Rosenfield, Aronson, and Sikes (1977) did find that students in desegregated classes using Jigsaw preferred their Jigsaw groupmates to their classmates in general. However, since students' groupmates and their other classmates were about the same in ethnic composition, this cannot be seen as a measure of intergroup relations. No differences between the experimental and control groups in interethnic friendship choices were reported.

Gonzales (1979), using a method similar to Jigsaw, found that Anglo and Asian American students in the Jigsaw groups had better attitudes toward Mexican American classmates than those in control groups, but he found no differences in attitudes toward Anglo or Asian American students. In a subsequent study, Gonzales (1981) found no differences in attitudes toward Mexican American, African American, or Anglo students in Jigsaw and control bilingual classes.

The most positive effects of a Jigsaw-related intervention were found in a study of Jigsaw II by Ziegler (1981) in classes composed of recent European and West Indian immigrants and Anglo Canadians in Toronto. She found substantially more cross-ethnic friendships in the Jigsaw II classes than in control classes, both on an immediate posttest and on a 10-week follow-up. These effects were for both "casual friendships" ("Who in this class have you called on the telephone in the last two weeks?") and "close friendships" ("Who in this class have you spent time with after school in the last two weeks?")

Johnson Methods. Two studies of the Johnson methods have examined intergroup relations outcomes. Cooper, Johnson, and Wilderson (1980) found greater friendship across race lines in a cooperative treatment than in an individualized method in which students were not permitted to interact. However, there were no differences in cross-racial friendships between the cooperative condition and a competitive condition in which students competed with equals (similar to the TGT tournaments). Johnson and Johnson (1981) found more cross-racial interaction in cooperative than in individualized classes during free time.

Group Investigation. In a study in Israeli junior high schools, Sharan et al. (1984) compared Group Investigation, STAD, and traditional instruction in terms of effects on relationships between Jews of Middle Eastern and European backgrounds. They found that students who experienced Group Investigation and STAD had much more positive ethnic attitudes than students in traditional classes. There were no differences between Group Investigation and STAD on this variable.

Weigel et al. Method. One of the largest and longest studies of cooperative learning was conducted by Weigel et al. (1975) in triethnic (Mexican American, Anglo, Black) classrooms. They evaluated a method in which students in multiethnic teams engaged in a variety of cooperative activities in several subjects, winning prizes based on their team performance. They reported that their cooperative methods had positive effects on White students' attitudes toward Mexican Americans, but not on White-Black, Black-White, Black-Latino, Latino-Black, or Latino-White attitudes. They also found that cooperative learning reduced teachers' reports of interethnic conflict.

The effects of cooperative-learning methods are not entirely consistent, but 16 of the 19 studies reviewed here demonstrated that when the conditions of contact theory are fulfilled, some aspect of relationships between students of different ethnicities improves. Most studies operationalized intergroup relations as friendships between students of different ethnicities, but some found positive effects on general intergroup attitudes as well (e.g., Sharan et al., 1984; Gonzales, 1979). There are a few studies in which cooperative learning resulted in improvements in majority-minority friendships but no minority-majority friendships (e.g., Slavin & Oickle, 1981; Gonzales, 1979; Weigel et al., 1975), but in most studies improvements in intergroup relations were equally strong toward majority and minority students.

Effects on Academic Achievement

It is important to note that, in addition to positive effects on intergroup relations, cooperative-learning methods have had positive effects on student achievement in a wide variety of subjects and for students of different ethnicities and backgrounds. In particular, positive effects have been seen for methods that emphasize group goals and individual accountability, where cooperating groups are recognized based on the individual learning performances of all group members (see Slavin, 1990). In studies in desegregated schools effects have often been particularly impressive for minority students. For example, in two studies of STAD (Slavin, 1977; Slavin & Oickle, 1981), African American students gained significantly more than White students in achievement (in comparison to control groups). A study of Jigsaw by Lucker, Rosenfield, Sikes, and Aronson (1976) found positive achievement effects for African American and Latino but not for White students. However, in other studies of STAD (e.g., Slavin & Karweit, 1984), of TGT

(e.g., Edwards, DeVries, & Snyder, 1972), and of TAI (Slavin, Leavey, & Madden, 1984), African American and White students gained from cooperative learning to the same degree. Sharan and Shachar (1988) similarly found that Israeli Jewish students of European and Middle Eastern backgrounds gained equally from Group Investigation.

How Close Are the New Cross-Ethnic Friendships?

It is not surprising that friendships across racial or ethnic boundaries are rare, compared with friendships within these groups. Black, Hispanic, and Anglo students typically live in different neighborhoods, ride different buses, and prefer different activities. Secondary school students of different ethnicities often come from different elementary schools. Socioeconomic and achievement differences further separate students. These factors work against friendship formation even when race is not a factor (see Lott & Lott, 1965). Racial differences accentuate students' tendencies to form homogeneous peer groups, and sometimes result in overt prejudice and interracial hostility.

Given the many forces operating against the formation of cross-racial friendships, it would seem that if cooperative learning influences these friendships, it would create relatively weak relationships rather than strong ones (see, for example, Schofield, 1991). It seems unlikely that a few weeks of cooperative learning would build strong interracial relationships among students in the classroom at the possible expense of prior same-race relationships.

A secondary analysis of the Slavin (1979) STAD study by Hansell and Slavin (1981) investigated this hypothesis. Their sample included 424 seventh- and eight-grade students in 12 inner-city language arts classrooms. Classes were randomly assigned to cooperative learning (STAD) or control treatments for a 10-week program. Students were asked on both pre- and posttests, "Who are your best friends in this class? Name as many as you wish," in a free-choice format. Choices were defined as "close" if they were among the first six made by students, and "distant" if they ranked seventh or later. The reciprocity and order of choices made and received were analyzed by multiple regression.

The results showed that the positive effects of STAD on cross-racial choices were primarily due to increases in strong friendship choices. Reciprocated and close choices, both made and received, increased more in STAD than in control classes. Thus, contrary to what might have been expected, this study showed positive effects of cooperative learning on close, reciprocated friendship choices, the kind of friendships that should be most difficult to change.

Effects on Social Networks

One limitation of existing research on cooperative learning and on contact theory in general is the concentration on dyadic relationships across racial lines or (to a lesser extent) attitudes toward entire racial groups. However, the impact of cooperative learning almost certainly involves networks of friendships rather than simple dyadic friendships. Secondary analyses of the data from Slavin's (1979) STAD study have revealed that many of the new cross-racial friendships made over the course of the STAD intervention were formed between students who had never been in the same cooperative group (Hansell & Slavin, 1981). A moment's reflection would support the inevitability of this result; in a four-member team that has two Blacks and two Whites, each student could make only two new friends from a different race if he or she made new friends only within the team. At least one of those teammates from a different race would also likely be of a different sex; norms against Black-White dating aside, cross-sex friendships are even less frequent than are cross-race friendships (Cooper et al., 1980; DeVries & Edwards, 1974). It is also possible that two or more teammates of different races were already friends, further restricting the possible number of new cross-race, within-team choices, and any deviation from a 50-50 racial split reduces the possibilities still further.

There are at least two ways in which cooperative learning might increase cross-race friendships outside particular cooperative groups. First, a cooperative-learning experience often offers students their first (or best) opportunity for cross-race friendships. Racial groups in classrooms are characterized by many friendship ties within each race group but few outside of it. However, once a cross-race friendship is formed, the new friend's friends (of her or his own race) also become likely friendship candidates. For example, if a White student makes his or her first Black friend, this relationship bridges between formerly isolated African American and White peer groups. It opens a new pool of potential African American friends, possibly reaching even beyond the confines of the classroom.

Second, even a small number of cross-race friendships may create less well-defined peer-group boundaries, formerly based on racial (and sexual) criteria, thereby allowing new, smaller cliques to form based more on mutual liking than on race and sex. This pattern was found in an analysis of sociometric data conducted by Hansell, Tackaberry, and Slavin (1981);

clique size tended to diminish as a result of a cooperative intervention similar to STAD.

CONCLUSIONS

The results of the studies relating cooperative learning to intergroup relations clearly indicate that when students work in ethnically mixed cooperative-learning groups, they gain in cross-ethnic friendships. This research indicates that the effects of cooperative learning on intergroup relations are strong and long-lasting, and are more likely on close, reciprocated friendship choices than on distant or unreciprocated choices. There are no clear patterns indicating more consistent results for some methods than for others. All methods have had some positive effects on intergroup relations.

Additional research is needed to discover the effects of cooperative learning on actual intergroup behavior, particularly behavior outside school. A few studies (e.g., Oishi, 1983; Ziegler, 1981) have found positive effects of cooperative learning on self-reported cross-racial friendships outside class, but behavioral observation in nonclassroom settings is still needed. Also, additional long-term follow-up data are needed to establish the duration of the effects of cooperative learning.

The practical implications of the research reported in this chapter are unambiguous. There is a strong positive effect of cooperative learning on intergroup relations. More than forty years after Allport laid out the basic principles, we finally have practical, proven methods for implementing contact theory in the desegregated classroom. These methods are effective for increasing student achievement as well as improving intergroup relations. However, much more work is needed to discover the critical components of cooperative learning and to inform a model of how these methods affect intergroup relations.

References

Allport, F. H., & 34 co-signers. (1953). The effects of segregation and the consequences of desegregation: A social science statement. *Minnesota Law Review, 37,* 429–440.

Allport, G. (1954). *The nature of prejudice.* Cambridge, MA: Addison-Wesley.

Amir, Y. (1969). Contact hypothesis in ethnic relations. *Psychological Bulletin, 71,* 319–342.

Aronson, E., Blaney, N., Stephan, C., Sikes, J., & Snapp, M. (1978). *The Jigsaw classroom.* Beverly Hills. CA: Sage.

Blaney, N. T., Stephan, S., Rosenfield, D., Aronson, E., & Sikes, J. (1977). Interdependence in the classroom: A field study. *Journal of Educational Psychology, 69*(2), 121–128.

Brown v. Board of Education of Topeka, 347 U.S. 483 (1954).

Cook, S. W. (1978). Interpersonal and attitudinal outcomes of cooperating interracial groups. *Journal of Research and Development in Education, 12,* 97–113.

Cook, S. W. (1979). Social science and school desegregation: Did we mislead the Supreme Court? *Personality and Social Psychology Bulletin, 5,* 420–437.

Cook, S. W. (1984). The 1954 social science statement and school desegregation: A reply to Gerard. *American Psychologist, 39,* 819–832.

Cooper, L., Johnson, D. W., Johnson, R., & Wilderson, F. (1980). Effects of cooperative, competitive, and individualistic experiences on interpersonal attraction among heterogeneous peers. *Journal of Social Psychology, 111,* 243–252.

DeVries, D. L., & Edwards, K. J. (1974). Student teams and learning games: Their effects on cross-race and cross-sex interaction. *Journal of Educational Psychology, 66,* 741–749.

DeVries, D. L., Edwards, K. J., & Slavin, R. E. (1978). Biracial learning teams and race relations in the classroom: Four field experiments on Teams-Games-Tournament. *Journal of Educational Psychology, 70,* 356–362.

Edwards, K. J., DeVries, D. L., & Snyder, J. P. (1972). Games and teams: A winning combination. *Simulation and Games, 3,* 247–269.

Gerard, H. B., & Miller, N. (1975). *School desegregation: A long-range study.* New York: Plenum.

Gonzales, A. (1979, August). *Classroom cooperation and ethnic balance.* Paper presented at the annual meeting of the American Psychological Association, New York.

Gonzales, A. (1981). *An approach to independent-cooperative bilingual education and measures related to social motives.* Unpublished manuscript, California State University at Fresno.

Hallinan, M. T., & Teixeira, R. A. (1987). Students' interracial friendships: Individual characteristics, structural effects, and racial differences. *American Journal of Education, 95,* 563–583.

Hansell, S., & Slavin, R. E. (1981). Cooperative learning and the structure of interracial friendships. *Sociology of Education, 54,* 98–106.

Hansell, S., Tackaberry, S. N., & Slavin, R. E. (1981). Cooperation, competition, and the structure of student peer groups. *Representative Research in Social Psychology, 12,* 46–61.

Harrison, A. A. (1976). *Individuals and groups: Understanding social behavior.* Monterey, CA: Brooks/Cole.

Hewstone, M., & Brown, R. (Eds.). (1986). *Contact and conflict in intergroup encounters.* Oxford, England: Basil Blackwell.

Johnson, D. W., & Johnson, R. T. (1981). Effects of cooperative and individualistic learning experiences on interethnic interaction. *Journal of Educational Psychology, 73,* 444–449.

Johnson, D. W., & Johnson, R. T. (1987). *Learning together and alone* (2nd ed.). Englewood Cliffs, NJ: Prentice-Hall.

Kagan, S. (1991). *Cooperative learning resources for teachers* (4th ed.). San Juan Capistrano, CA: Resources for Teachers.

Kagan, S., Zahn, G. L., Widaman, K. F., Schwarzwald, J., & Tyrell, G. (1985). Classroom structural bias: Impact of cooperative and competitive classroom structures on individuals and groups. In R. E. Slavin, S. Sharan, S. Kagan, R. Hertz-Lazarowitz, C. Webb, & R. Schmuck (Eds.), *Learning to cooperate, cooperating to learn* (pp. 277–312). New York: Plenum.

Lott, A. F., & Lott, B. E. (1965). Group cohesiveness as interpersonal attraction: A review of relationships with antecedent and consequent variables. *Psychological Bulletin, 64,* 259–309.

Lucker, G. W., Rosenfield, D., Sikes, J., & Aronson, E. (1976). Performance in the interdependent classroom: A field study. *American Educational Research Journal, 13,* 115–123.

Miller, N., Brewer, M. B., & Edwards, K. (1985). Cooperative interaction in desegregated settings: A laboratory analogue. *Journal of Social Issues, 41*(3), 63–79.

Miller, N., & Harrington, H. J. (1992). Social categorization and intergroup acceptance: Principles for the design and development of cooperative learning teams. In R. Hertz-Lazarowitz & N. Miller (Eds.), *Interaction in cooperative groups* (pp. 203–227). New York: Cambridge University Press.

Oishi, S. (1993). *Effects of team assisted individualization in mathematics on cross-race interactions of elementary school children.* Unpublished doctoral dissertation, University of Maryland, College Park.

Oishi, S., Slavin, R., & Madden, N. (1983, April). *Effects of student teams and individualized instruction on cross-race and cross-sex friendships.* Paper presented at the annual meeting of the American Educational Research Association, Montreal, Canada.

Patchen, M. (1982). *Black-white contact in schools: Its social and academic effects.* West Lafayette, IN: Purdue University Press.

Pettigrew, T. F. (1986). The intergroup contact hypothesis reconsidered. In M. Hewstone & R. Brown (Eds.), *Contact and conflict in intergroup encounters* (pp. 169–195). Oxford, England: Basil Blackwell.

Schofield, J. W. (1991). School desegration and intergroup relations: A review of the literature. In G. Grant (Ed.), *Review of research in education* (Vol. 17, pp. 335–409). Washington, DC: American Educational Research Association.

Scott, R., & McPartland, J. (1982). Desegregation as national policy: Correlates of racial attitudes. *American Educational Research Journal, 19,* 397–414.

Sharan, S., Kussell, P., Hertz-Lazarowitz, R., Bejarano, Y., Raviv, S., & Sharan, Y. (1984). *Cooperative learning in the classroom: Research in desegregated schools.* Hillsdale, NJ: Lawrence Erlbaum Associates.

Sharan, S., & Shachar, H. (1988). *Language and learning in the cooperative classroom.* New York: Springer.

Sharan, Y., & Sharan, S. (1992). *Expanding cooperative learning through group investigation.* New York: Teachers College Press.

Slavin, R. E. (1977). *Student learning team techniques: Narrowing the achievement gap between the races* (Report No. 228). Baltimore, MD: Johns Hopkins University, Center for Social Organization of Schools.

Slavin, R. E. (1979). Effects of biracial learning teams on cross-racial friendships. *Journal of Educational Psychology, 71,* 381–387.

Slavin, R. E. (1985). Cooperative learning: Applying contact theory in desegregated schools. *Journal of Social Issues, 41,* 45–62.

Slavin, R. E. (1986). *Using student team learning* (3rd ed.). Baltimore, MD: Johns Hopkins University, Center for Social Organization of Schools.

Slavin, R. E. (1990). *Cooperative learning: Theory, research, and practice.* Englewood Cliffs, NJ: Prentice-Hall.

Slavin, R. E., & Karweit, N. (1984). Mastery learning and student teams: A factorial experiment in urban general mathematics classes. *American Educational Research Journal, 21,* 725–736.

Slavin, R. E., Leavey, M., & Madden, N. A. (1984). Combining cooperative learning and individualized instruction: Effects on student mathematics achievement, attitudes, and behaviors. *Elementary School Journal, 84,* 409–422.

Slavin, R. E., & Madden, N. A. (1979). School practices that improve race relations. *American Educational Research Journal, 16*(2), 169–180.

Slavin, R. E., & Oickle, E. (1981). Effects of cooperative learning teams on student achievement and race relations: Treatment by race interactions. *Sociology of Education, 54,* 174–180.

Stephan, W. G. (1978). School desegregation: An evaluation of predictions made in *Brown vs. Board of Education. Psychological Bulletin, 85,* 217–238.

Weigel, R. H., Wiser, P. L., & Cook, S. W. (1975). Impact of cooperative learning experiences on cross-ethnic relations and attitudes. *Journal of Social Issues, 31*(1), 219–245.

Ziegler, S. (1981). The effectiveness of cooperative learning teams for increasing cross-ethnic friendship: Additional evidence. *Human Organization, 40,* 264–268.

IMPROVING INTERGROUP RELATIONS AMONG STUDENTS

Janet Ward Schofield

UNIVERSITY OF PITTSBURGH

Two facts make attention to the issue of how to improve intergroup relations among children and youth from different racial and ethnic backgrounds vital. First, there is clear evidence from a wide variety of situations, ranging from conflict between youth gangs of different backgrounds to racial incidents on college campuses across the United States, that, despite the marked improvement in many aspects of intergroup relations in this country since the 1950s, serious problems still exist (Hurtado, 1992; Jaynes & Williams, 1989; Levin & McDevitt, 1993; Magner, 1989). Second, demographic trends make it clear that minority-group members are becoming an increasingly large proportion of the U.S. population (De Witt, 1991; O'Hara, 1993). Thus, patterns of prejudice or discrimination that persist will exact a larger and larger social and economic toll, both in terms of the number of minority-group members affected and in terms of the loss of their potential contribution to the broader society. Furthermore, the potential for increased political power inherent in growing numbers makes it likely that minority-group members will be able to pursue their interests more effectively than has been the case in the past. While this may have many benefits, it may well also exacerbate tensions as majority-group members have to adjust to new realities. Thus, the question of how to build and maintain positive relations among the increasingly diverse racial and ethnic groups in the United States is an issue of major importance and will remain so in the foreseeable future.

Because of the pervasive residential segregation in our society (Farley & Allen, 1987; Jaynes & Williams, 1989), children frequently have their first relatively close and extended opportunity for contact with those from different racial or ethnic backgrounds in school. Hence, whether hostility and stereotyping grow or diminish may be critically influenced by the particular experiences children have there. For this reason, this chapter will focus on exploring policies and practices that are conducive to improving intergroup relations in school settings.

Much of what we know about intergroup relations in school settings stems from research in the late 1970s and early 1980s (Gerard & Miller, 1975; Hawley et al., 1983; Hewstone & Brown, 1986; Patchen, 1982; Prager, Longshore, & Seeman, 1986; Rist, 1979; Schofield, 1982, 1989). Although there is much to be learned from this body of work, three important limitations must be acknowledged. First, much of this research has the disadvantage of being correlational in nature and thus leaving open the question of the causal direction of any empirical links found between school policies and student outcomes (Schofield, 1991). Second, this work is a decade or more old. Thus it tends to focus exclusively on improving relations between Whites and African Americans rather than on the more multifaceted situations common today. In addition, this work also fails to reflect whatever generational changes in intergroup attitudes and behavior have occurred since it appeared (for a discussion of this see Jaynes & Williams, 1989). Nonetheless, because rela-

This chapter is also being published in Willis D. Hawley & Anthony Jackson (Eds.), *Realizing Our Common Destiny: Improving Race and Ethnic Relations in America* (San Francisco: Jossey-Bass, 1995). A section of this chapter originally appeared in J. W. Schofield, "Promoting Positive Peer Relations in Desegregated Schools," *Educational Policy,* 7(3), 297–317, copyright 1993 by Corwin Press. It is reprinted here with permission from Corwin Press.

tively little work focusing directly on the policies and practices that are likely to improve intergroup relations among children has been done since this time period, with the notable exception of work relating to cooperative team learning (which is discussed in chapter 35 of this *Handbook*), the following discussion will depend heavily on this early body of work.

MATCHING THE APPROACH TO IMPROVING INTERGROUP RELATIONS TO THE CURRENT STATE OF SUCH RELATIONS

Before discussing what we know about improving intergroup relations in school contexts, it is important to make some conceptual distinctions because the strategies that are likely to be effective in meeting this goal vary substantially depending on a number of factors. The first of these factors is the current state of relations among the groups in question. It seems clear that strategies that might work well in situations where there is some tension and hostility, but no major ongoing overt conflict, are quite different from those that would be needed if two or more groups are engaged in or are on the verge of intense conflict. Second, it is important to distinguish between approaches that emphasize ongoing structural features of the school situation and those that emphasize specially developed programs or other kinds of potentially valuable but circumscribed "human relations" interventions such as special assembly programs or the like. Third, it is worth noting that the goal of reducing negative intergroup attitudes or behaviors and the goal of increasing positive intergroup attitudes and behaviors are far from identical. Work by both Patchen (1982) and Schofield (1982, 1989) suggests that quite different factors may be related to change in the amount of positive and negative intergroup behavior that occurs. To take a simple example, one can stop a fight by physically separating the combatants, at least temporarily eliminating this negative behavior. However, such an action in and of itself does not foster positive attitudes or behaviors between members of the two groups involved.

The goal of this chapter is to review strategies aimed at fostering positive relations and inhibiting negative relations among members of different racial and ethnic groups in situations in which intergroup isolation and/or tensions exist, even if they have not precipitated major conflict. This state of affairs characterizes many of our racially and ethnically mixed schools. This chapter focuses primarily on ongoing structural factors and policies rather than on the design of specific "human relations" modules for insertion into the curriculum because attention to pervasive everyday policies and practices is likely to have a greater impact on intergroup relations than a focus on more limited special-purpose interventions. However, it should be noted that recent work in social psychology and other fields provides a rich basis for thinking about how the latter might best be structured (Brewer & Kramer, 1985; Deutsch, 1993; Devine, Monteith, Zuwerink, & Elliot, 1991; Dovidio & Gaertner, 1991; Eurich-Fulcer & Schofield, in press; Linville, Salovey, & Fisher, 1986; Park, Judd, & Ryan, 1991; Pruitt & Carnevale, 1993).

RESEGREGATION: A COMMON BARRIER TO IMPROVED INTERGROUP RELATIONS

The first question to ask about intergroup relations in any racially or ethnically mixed setting is the extent to which there is any kind of meaningful intergroup contact. This is especially a challenge in situations involving groups of youth whose native tongues are different from each other. It is perfectly possible for a school or other setting that has a rather diverse ethnic and racial makeup to be one in which individuals from the various groups have little or no contact with each other. Such resegregation can be extreme. For example, in one racially mixed school a student remarked to a researcher, "All the segregation in this city was put in this school," reflecting the fact that, although students from different backgrounds all attended that school, they had little contact with each other (Collins & Noblit, 1978, p. 195). So it is important to be aware of the possibility of resegregation and to plan actively to avoid or minimize it.

How does this resegregation occur? It is clear from research conducted in schools that a number of common educational practices lead, often inadvertently, to resegregation within desegregated schools. The most obvious and widespread of these are practices designed to reduce academic heterogeneity within classrooms. A whole host of social and economic factors contribute to the fact that minority-group students in desegregated schools tend to perform less well in academic subjects than their White peers. Thus, schools that categorize students on the basis of standardized tests, grades, or related criteria tend to have resegregated classrooms (Epstein, 1985).

Although much resegregation in schools stems from policies such as streaming or ability grouping, it is undeniable that children often voluntarily resegregate themselves in a variety of situations, from eating lunch in the school cafeteria to choosing playmates in their neighborhood. The extent of such voluntary resegregation is sometimes remarkable. For example, one set of studies of seating patterns in the cafeteria of a school whose student body was almost precisely half African American and half White reported that on a typical day only about 5% of the students sat next to someone of the other race (Schofield, 1979; Schofield & Sagar, 1977). This was so in spite of the fact that there was little overt racial friction. Other studies have reported similarly marked cleavage by race (Cusick & Ayling, 1973; Gerard, Jackson, & Conolley, 1975; Rogers, Hennigan, Bowman, & Miller, 1984).

On the one hand, there is nothing inherently deleterious to intergroup relations about children who share particular interests, values, or backgrounds associating with each other to achieve valued ends. However, to the extent that grouping by race or ethnic groups stems from fear, hostility, and discomfort, it is incompatible with the goal of breaking down barriers between groups and improving intergroup relations. Stephan and Stephan's (1985) work suggests that anxiety about dealing with out-group members is prevalent and can direct behavior in unconstructive ways. Other studies (Scherer & Slawski, 1979; Schofield, 1982, 1989) suggest numerous ways in which such anxiety can cause problems, including resegregation, in desegregated schools.

The importance of avoiding a pattern of resegregation, whether it stems from formal institutional policies or informal behavior patterns, is made clear by the theoretical and empirical work of many social psychologists (Pettigrew, 1969; Schofield, 1983, 1982/1989). To take just one example, a whole body of work by Tajfel and his associates (Doise, 1978; Tajfel, 1978; Tajfel & Turner, 1979) suggests that when individuals are divided into groups they tend to favor the in-group and discriminate against the out-group, even though these groups have no previous history of antipathy. Thus, if one creates racially or ethnically homogeneous groups through school policies that resegregate students, already existing tendencies toward stereotyping and discrimination are likely to be magnified.

This suggests that great care should be taken to avoid institutional policies that lead to resegregation and to adopt policies that may undercut children's tendency to cluster in racially homogeneous groups because of fear or uncertainty. The particular policies employed to discourage such resegregation would have to depend on the particular situation with which one is dealing. However, some policies and practices that undercut resegregation can be easily implemented. For example, teachers can assign seats in a way that creates substantial potential for interracial contact rather than letting students resegregate themselves. Specifically, teachers can assign students' seats alphabetically rather than letting students select their own seats and then institutionalizing this often segregated pattern with a seating chart (Schofield, 1982, 1989). Furthermore, research shows that something as simple as occasionally changing assigned seats increases the number of friends students likely to make during the school year (Byrne, 1961).

Another policy that can help to avoid resegregation is conscious planning to encourage both minority and majority students to participate in extracurricular activities. Sometimes after-school activities become the province of either minority or majority students so that one group participates in all or most activities and the other hardly participates at all. Another perhaps more common pattern is for particular activities to become associated with students from a particular background so that, although all groups of students participate in some activities, there are few activities in which students from different backgrounds participate jointly (Collins, 1979; Gottlieb & TenHouten, 1965; Scherer & Slawski, 1979; Sullivan, 1979).

Again, the way to prevent these outcomes clearly depends on the specific situation. But helpful policies can be adopted. For example, if one group of students does not participate because they live far away and transportation poses a problem, arrangements for transportation can be considered. Similarly, if adult sponsors of school- or neighborhood-based clubs take clear steps to encourage both minority and majority students to participate before these activities get a definite reputation as "belonging" to one group, they are much more likely to succeed than if they wait until the resegregation is complete and well known among the students before trying to encourage diversity of membership.

A certain amount of resegregation may be an inevitable consequence of policies designed to advance important goals. For example, it is often hard to provide an education for children for whom English is not a first language without a certain amount of resegregation, although constructive ways to deal with this complex situation have been suggested (California State Department of Education, 1983; Carter, 1979; Carter & Chatfield, 1986; Cazabon, Lambert, & Hall, 1993; Fernandez & Guskin, 1978; Garcia, 1976; Gonzalez, 1979; Haro, 1977; Heleen, 1987; Milan, 1978; National Institute of Education, 1977; Roos, 1978). Similarly, although there has recently been some movement away from the traditional ready acceptance of tracking policies on the part of policy makers and educators (Carnegie Council on Adolescent Development, 1989; National Governors' Association, 1990), many difficult and complex pedagogical and political issues remain to be resolved about how best to serve students in classrooms in which skill levels vary widely (Oakes, 1992). In addition, there may be certain extracurricular activities, such as gospel choirs or golf teams, that are likely to be both highly valued by some parts of the community and more attractive to students from certain ethnic backgrounds than others. In spite of such difficulties, any examination of the functioning of a social environment containing children of diverse racial or ethnic backgrounds needs to address the issue of resegregation, whether it be the consequence of formal policies or of children's choices, and to devote serious attention to seeing how resegregation, if found, can be eliminated or at least reduced.

CONDITIONS CONDUCIVE TO IMPROVING INTERGROUP RELATIONS

It is important to recognize that the mere absence of resegregation is not enough to create a set of experiences that foster constructive rather than neutral or destructive relations among children from different backgrounds. The quality of those relations is the crucial factor, as Pettigrew (1969) pointed out in making his classic distinction between mere *desegregation*, which refers to the existence of a racially mixed environment, and true *integration*, which refers to the creation of a setting conducive to the development of positive relations among members of different groups.

If there is one thing that social-psychological theory and research have taught us about racially and ethnically diverse environments, it is that simply putting children from different backgrounds together is not enough to ensure positive social outcomes (Allport, 1954; Cohen, 1972; Eddy, 1975; Orfield, 1975; Rist, 1979; Schofield, 1983). There are a great many things that schools and other institutions serving diverse clienteles can do to promote positive intergroup relations and minimize intergroup conflict (Chesler, Bryant, & Crowfoot, 1981; Cohen, 1980; Crowfoot & Chesler, 1981; Epstein, 1985; Forehand & Ragosta, 1976; Forehand, Ragosta, & Rock, 1976; Hallinan, 1982; Hallinan & Smith, 1985; Hallinan & Teixeira, 1987; Hawley et al., 1983; McConahay, 1981; Mercer, Iadicola, & Moore, 1980; Miller, 1980; Patchen, 1982; Sagar & Schofield, 1984; Slavin & Madden, 1979; Wellisch, Carriere, MacQueen, & Duck, 1977; Wellisch, Marcus, MacQueen, & Duck, 1976). Precisely which practices are suitable depend on factors such as the children's ages, the institution's racial and ethnic mix, the degree to which minority and majority status are related to socioeconomic background, and the like. Because space limitations make it impractical to discuss each of the myriad of possibilities separately, this chapter will discuss what theory and research suggest about the general underlying conditions that are conducive to building and maintaining positive intergroup relations.

The most influential social-psychological perspective on the conditions that are necessary to lead to positive outcomes is often called the contact hypothesis. Since 1954, when Allport first proposed it, this approach has stimulated a great deal of research that, generally speaking, supports its basic elements. (A volume reviewing, extending, and revising this theory is Hewstone & Brown, 1986.) Basically, Allport argued that three aspects of the contact situation are particularly important in determining whether positive intergroup relations develop. These are (a) the existence of equal status within the situation for members of all groups, (b) an emphasis on cooperative rather than competitive activities; and (c) the explicit support of relevant authority figures for positive relations. In discussing these three factors, this chapter will illustrate briefly the types of policies and procedures that flow from them.

Equal Status

First, Allport argues that the contact situation must be structured in a way that gives equal status to both groups. He argues that if one does not do this, existing stereotypes and beliefs about the superiority or inferiority of the groups involved and the hostility engendered by these stereotypes will be likely to persist. Although other theorists have argued that equal status is not absolutely essential for improving intergroup relations, they generally see it as quite helpful (Amir, 1969; Riordan, 1978). In a school, as in most organizations, the various positions that need to be filled are ordered in a status hierarchy. Those on top, like the superintendent at the system level or the principal at the school level, have more power and prestige than those who serve under them. Allport's argument suggests that in filling the various positions in the organization it is important that individuals from all groups be distributed throughout the status hierarchy rather than being concentrated at a particular level. For example, one could hardly claim that majority- and minority-group members have equal status in a school if the administrators and the faculty are almost all majority-group members and the teachers' aids are all minority-group members.

Even if a school or other institutional setting in which students from varied backgrounds participate does its best to see that the formal status of minority- and majority-group members is equal, it is undeniably true that members of the two groups are likely to have very different statuses outside that setting. This can create real difficulties for achieving equal status within the setting. For example, given the sizable and stubborn link between social class and academic achievement, it is likely that unequal status outside of the school will translate into unequal distribution of students into the more and less advanced tracks in schools that have academic tracks. Even if the school recognizes this and decides to avoid formalizing such group differ-

ences by eschewing tracking, students' performance levels may well still differ in ways that affect their informal statuses within the school and their peer groups.

Finding effective ways to keep the unequal status of majority- and minority-group members in the larger society from creating unequal status within the school is not easy. However, there is evidence that concerted efforts to achieve equal status within the contact situation do appear to make a difference. For example, much has been written about the way in which textbooks and other curriculum components have either ignored or demeaned the experiences and contributions of minority-group members (McAdoo & McAdoo, 1985; National Alliance of Black School Educators, 1984; Oakes, 1985). This hardly creates an equal-status environment. Although there are many barriers to remedying this situation (Boateng, 1990), change is possible and it can have constructive effects. For example, Stephan and Stephan's (1984) review of the research conducted on multiethnic curriculum components concludes that a substantial, if methodologically flawed, set of studies generally suggests that multiethnic curricula have a positive effect on intergroup relations, at least when the program elements are of some reasonable complexity and duration.

A controversial issue relating to both equal status and resegregation is the issue of the grouping of students based on their academic performance. As mentioned previously, when desegregated schools group students on the basis of test scores, they often end up with heavily White high-status accelerated groups and heavily minority lower-status regular groups. This means that students are not only resegregated but resegregated in a way that can reinforce traditional stereotypes and engender hostility. Tracking is often instituted or emphasized in schools with heterogeneous student bodies as a mechanism for coping with the diversity. However, studies comparing tracked versus untracked schools have not yielded any consistent support for the idea that tracking generally benefits students academically (Oakes, 1992). Furthermore, there is reason to believe that it may sometimes undermine the achievement and motivation of students in the lower tracks and have a negative effect on intergroup relations (Collins & Noblit, 1978; Epstein, 1985; National Opinion Research Center, 1973; Oakes, 1992; Schofield, 1979; Schofield & Sagar, 1977). Epstein's (1985) study of grouping practices in desegregated elementary schools concludes that there is a clear positive link between equal-status programs (e.g., programs that emphasize the equality and importance of both Black and White students and that avoid inflexible, academically based grouping) and higher achievement for African American students. Furthermore, equal-status programs positively influenced both White and Black students' attitudes toward desegregated schooling.

Although tracking is one of the most visible ways in which status differentials from outside the school get reinforced and formalized inside the school, there are also many other ways in which this happens. Sensitivity to this issue can suggest seemingly minor, but nonetheless worthwhile, changes in practice to minimize this. For example, schools can add the practice of honoring students who have shown unusually large amounts of improvement in their academic performance to the traditional practice of honoring students whose absolute level of achievement is outstanding. This reinforces academic values while being more inclusive than traditional practice.

Such practices are trivial in some respects. Yet students often are very sensitive to such matters. For example, Schofield (1982, 1989) reports an incident in which a racially mixed classroom of sixth graders was shown a televised quiz show in which a team of students from their school competed against a team from another school. A usually well-behaved African American child refused to watch. Later, he explained that he did not want to see the program because the team from his school, which had a student body that was just over half Black, consisted entirely of White children. He said bitterly, "They shouldn't call this school Wexler [a pseudonym]; they should call it White School" (p. 220).

Cooperative Interdependence

Allport (1954) argues that in addition to creating a situation that gives members of all groups equal status, it is also extremely important that the activities required in the situation be cooperative rather than competitive. This is important for two reasons. First, given that discrimination is both a historical fact and a present reality in many spheres of life, it is probable that the results of competition will frequently support traditional stereotypes. In addition, considerable research suggests that competition between groups can lead to stereotyping, to unwarranted devaluation of the other group's accomplishments, and to marked hostility, even when the groups initially have no history that might predispose them to negative reactions to each other (Sherif, Harvey, White, Hood, & Sherif, 1961; Worchel, 1979). It is reasonable to expect that this tendency for intergroup competition to lead to hostility and negative beliefs would be reinforced when the groups involved have a history that makes initial hostility or at least suspicion likely.

Both theory and research suggest that the type of cooperation most likely to lead to the reduction of intergroup tensions or hostility is cooperation toward achieving a shared goal that cannot be accomplished without the contribution of members of both groups (Bossert, 1988/89; Johnson & Johnson, 1992; Sherif et al., 1961). This suggests that a rich variety of activities might be appropriate in settings such as the Girl Scouts and Boy Scouts or other youth-oriented social, athletic, or service clubs. In the school setting examples of activities likely to foster this type of cooperation would be the production of a school play, team sports, and the like. The important feature of these situations is that each student is able to make a contribution to a whole that individuals could not possibly achieve alone. Even though different people may contribute different skills, each person is necessary to and interested in the final product.

Schools in the United States have historically stressed competition, so in many ways they are not milieus particularly conducive to promoting cooperation. However, this is not inevitable or completely unchangeable. First, with the advent of self-paced instructional approaches and the increasing awareness of work on mastery learning, there has been an increasing acceptance of the idea that children may benefit from working at their own pace. Second, in recent years there have been more and more voices speaking in favor of increasingly empha-

sizing the importance of teaching children how to work cooperatively with others to achieve a joint end product (Aronson & Osherow, 1980; Bossert, 1988/89; Cohen, 1984; Hertz-Lazarowitz & Miller, 1992; Johnson & Johnson, 1987; Johnson, Johnson, & Maruyama, 1984; Kagan, 1991; Sharan & Sharan, 1992; Slavin, chapter 35 of this *Handbook*). Certainly this trend is sensible given the increasing bureaucratization and complexity of our society, which means that, as adults, individuals are increasingly likely to work with others as part of an organization rather than as individual craftspeople or entrepreneurs.

The use of class committees and teams to create joint projects comes very close to being the type of cooperation toward shared goals that appears to be so important for improving intergroup relations. A large number of experiments using a variety of cooperative structures suggest that this does indeed have a positive effect. For example, DeVries and Edwards (1974) found that students who participated in racially mixed work groups that were rewarded for their performance as groups were more likely to help and to be helped by members of the other race than students who received rewards for their individual efforts. They were also somewhat more likely to name a person of the other race as a friend after one month of teamwork even though the teams met for less than an hour a day. A host of other researchers have found similar results in more recent experiments on the impact of cooperative work in the classroom (Aronson, Blaney, Sikes, Stephan, & Snapp, 1978; Aronson & Gonzales, 1988; Bossert, 1988/89; Cook, 1985; Johnson & Johnson, 1982; Johnson et al., 1984; Sharan, 1980; Slavin, 1983a, 1983b, 1985). One important feature of such cooperative groups is that they not only appear to foster improved intergroup relations but also have positive academic consequences (Johnson, Maruyama, Johnson, Nelson, & Skon, 1981).

Although cooperative activities in the classroom or in other settings such as youth clubs hold great potential for improving intergroup relations, such cooperation must be carefully structured (Hertz-Lazarowitz, Kirkus, & Miller, 1992; Miller & Harrington, 1992; Slavin, 1992). It is important that the young people involved contribute to the group efforts in effective ways that do not reinforce traditional modes of interaction between majority- and minority-group members. For example, Cohen (1972) has found that when White and African American children who are equally capable interact with each other in certain kinds of situations, the White students tend to be more active and influential even though there is no rational basis for their dominance. Only after a carefully planned program of activities that include having the Black children teach their White peers new skills does this tendency diminish or disappear (Cohen, Lockheed, & Lohman, 1976). Hence, it is vital to be constantly aware of the need to find ways to ensure that all children contribute to the group's final products rather than assuming that the existence of a cooperative group in and of itself will motivate all children to contribute and to allow others to contribute to the group's work.

The precise dynamics that lead cooperation to have a positive effect on intergroup relations are far from fully understood (Bossert, 1988/89), although considerable attention has been devoted to the issue recently (see Hertz-Lazarowitz & Miller, 1992). However, there appear to be a number of factors that are worth individual consideration because, although they are likely to be found in cooperative situations, they are neither inevitable aspects of all cooperative situations nor strictly limited to situations in which cooperation is a salient element.

Crosscutting Social Identities. One suggestion that is frequently made in the literature on intergroup relations is that one can undermine the tendency of individuals to show bias toward out-group members by creating what are called crosscutting social categories (Brewer & Miller, 1984; Deschamp & Doise, 1978; Levine & Campbell, 1972; Schofield & McGivern, 1979; Vanbeselaere, 1987). The idea is that the importance of any one basis of social categorization, such as race or ethnicity, can be mitigated by creating or making salient other orthogonal bases of social categorization. Thus, for example, having African American and White students on each of two different cooperative learning teams means that racial background and team membership are crosscut. That is, students from different racial backgrounds now share something (i.e., team membership) with some members of the racial out-group and simultaneously differ on that dimension from some members of their racial in-group. To the extent that the social category that crosscuts racial or ethnic background is valued and salient, it may well undermine the tendency to discriminate based on the former.

Although this phenomenon may help to account for some of the positive effects of cooperative learning groups, it also suggests other avenues for improving intergroup relations. For example, it suggests that strategies that create and emphasize meaningful and valued shared social-category memberships for youths of different racial and ethnic backgrounds (as members of a particular school or community) should be constructive. In fact, laboratory work by Gaertner and his colleagues (Gaertner & Dovidio, 1986; Gaertner, Mann, Murrell, & Dovidio, 1989) suggests that bias between two initially separate groups can be mitigated when they later function in a new situation that gives them a unified identity. Thus, it seems reasonable to expect that the creation of signs and symbols of *shared* identity (ranging from school T-shirts and traditions to special songs or the like) should be helpful in improving intergroup relations.

Personalization of Out-group Members. Cooperative activities by their very nature require individuals to work together, thus providing the opportunity for them to come to know each other in ways they might not otherwise. This potential for cooperative work to lead to the development of relatively close personal relationships with members of out-groups is frequently cited as one of its advantages (Miller & Harrington, 1992). The development of such personal relations and the accompanying tendency to increasingly see the out-group members as individuals with their own particular set of personality traits, skills, and experiences is potentially important for several reasons. First, it can lead to the discovery of unexpected similarities between oneself and out-group members, and there is strong evidence that perceptions of similarity play a strong role in attraction to others (Byrne, 1971; Byrne & Nelson, 1965). Second, to the extent the out-group members behave in ways that are contrary to stereotypes of that group's behavior, such stereotypes may be weakened. This is, however, far from a simple process.

Behaviors tend to be perceived in ways that are consistent with the stereotypes (Sagar & Schofield, 1980). This appears to be due to the fact that stereotypes lead to the biased processing of social information (Bodenhausen, 1988; Greenberg & Pyszczynski, 1985; Hamilton & Trolier, 1986). Individuals may perceive those who act in ways unexpected for their group as "exceptions" whose existence does not challenge the validity of the basic stereotype (Brewer, 1988; Hewstone, Hopkins, & Routh, 1992; Johnston & Hewstone, 1992; Taylor, 1981). Third, and perhaps even more important, ongoing experience with several members of the out-group may help to undermine the strong tendency to see out-group members as relatively similar to each other compared to in-group members, who are typically perceived to be much more varied (Judd & Park, 1988; Linville, Fischer, & Salvoney, 1989). Recent work by Ryan, Judd, and Park (1993) demonstrates that a tendency to perceive out-group members as quite homogeneous affects judgments of the characteristics of specific individuals belonging to that group in ways consistent with one's initial expectations. Thus, experiences that lead individuals to think of out-group members as individuals who vary in many respects should be helpful in weakening stereotypes and lessening their impact on interactions with members of the out-group.

The importance of increasing perceptions of similarity between in-group and out-group members, of exposing in-group members to out-group behavior that cannot be construed in a stereotypic fashion, and of increasing awareness of the individual variability of out-group members suggests a number of potentially usable strategies in addition to cooperative groups. Many of these ideas are frequently embodied in aspects of human-relations training programs or in attempts to produce multicultural curricula. To date there is little definitive evidence about the effectiveness of such approaches, although there is some fragmentary evidence suggesting they sometimes have weak positive effects on intergroup relations (Hawley et al., 1983; Longshore & Wellisch, 1982; Stephan & Stephan, 1984). The limited nature of many of these efforts, including the fact that they are often one-shot attempts to create change, may help to account for this weak impact. However, it is also possible that more specific attention to lessons drawn from the social-psychological literature about the complexities of the process of stereotype change would be fruitful.

Creating Affectively Positive Environments. One consequence of cooperation in achieving a valued goal that would not otherwise be obtainable is the creation of a positive atmosphere. The importance of this factor is highlighted by the experimental work of Worchel, Andreoli, and Folger (1977), which demonstrated that for groups with a history of competition and conflict, successful cooperation increased intergroup attraction, whereas unsuccessful cooperation decreased liking for out-group members. Positive emotions caused by a wide variety of events have been demonstrated to lead to increased liking for others (Gouaux, 1971; Griffitt, 1970; Veitch & Griffitt, 1976) as well as to increased self-disclosure and interaction with previously unknown others (Clark & Watson, 1988; Cunningham, 1988). In a parallel fashion, negative emotions have been shown to lead to liking others less, to perceiving them as more different, and evaluating them negatively (May & Hamilton, 1980; Shapiro 1988; Swallow & Kuiper, 1987). Patchen's finding that African American students who were generally satisfied with their life circumstances reported more positive change in intergroup attitudes in racially mixed high schools than others suggests such processes may indeed operate in desegregated settings. Thus, finding ways to make enjoyable the situation in which members of different groups encounter each other may in fact contribute to improving intergroup relations.

Support of Authorities for Positive Relations

Finally, Allport (1954) suggests that the support of authority, law, and custom for positive equal-status relationships among members of all groups is vital to producing constructive change in intergroup attitudes and behavior as a result of intergroup contact. Certainly, a court ruling that requires desegregation (or a decision on the part of a school system to desegregate) is a very important sign of government authorities' support for this policy. However, in and of themselves, such events are not nearly enough. For schoolchildren the most relevant authorities are probably their school's principal, their teachers, and their parents. Religious leaders can also be important authorities for some children. In addition, as children move from their early years into adolescence their peers become increasingly important arbiters of opinion and exert a more and more potent influence on their behavior. Thus, although Allport clearly did not mean to include peers in his definition of "authorities," it seems sensible at least to point out that finding ways to mobilize the peer group to support positive intergroup relations could be a rather powerful approach, as demonstrated by Blanchard, Lilly, and Vaughn (1991), whose work shows that peers influence each other's expression of racist opinions. Similarly, Patchen (1982) found that individuals' avoidance of out-group members was clearly related to negative racial attitudes among their same-race peers, which suggests that concerns about peer disapproval of intergroup contact can contribute to resegregation.

In school settings the importance of the principal as an authority who can facilitate improved intergroup relations can hardly be overemphasized. The principal can play a crucial role both in helping teachers adjust to the desegregated situation and in fostering a social climate that is conducive to the development of positive relations between minority and majority students (Orfield, 1975). Principals can influence the course that desegregation takes through their actions toward teachers, students, and parents.

Principals play at least four important roles in influencing desegregation's outcomes. First, they play an enabling function; that is, they make choices that facilitate or impede practices that promote positive intergroup relations. For example, the principal can play an important role by encouraging teachers to adopt cooperative learning techniques or by creating multiethnic committees designed to identify and solve problems before they turn into polarizing crises. Second, the principal can serve a modeling function. It is clear that many people tend to emulate authority. The principal sets a model of behavior for teachers and students. There is no guarantee others will follow the

principal's example, but it is certainly helpful. Third, the principal can play a sensitizing function. The principal is in a good position to argue for the importance of paying attention to the quality of intergroup relations and to put it in an important place on the school's list of priorities. Finally, of course, the principal can serve a sanctioning function by actively rewarding positive practices and behaviors and discouraging negative ones. The prevention of negative intergroup behaviors is an issue of utmost importance because negative incidents can stimulate other negative behaviors in an escalating spiral. Research that demonstrates that one of the strongest predictors of unfriendly intergroup contact for both White and African American students is the student's general aggressiveness (Patchen, 1982) suggests the importance of the principal's role in creating a well-ordered environment in which aggressive behavior of any sort is minimized.

Teachers are also vital authority figures in the school. They too can facilitate or impede the development of positive relations at the classroom level through the processes of enabling, modeling, sensitizing, and sanctioning. For example, with regard to enabling, teachers often have it within their power to create conditions that are likely to improve intergroup relations between students. Epstein (1985) demonstrates that teachers with positive attitudes toward desegregation tend to use equal-status instructional programs more than others and that students in such classrooms have more positive attitudes toward desegregation than peers in classrooms not using such approaches. Similarly, teachers with negative attitudes are more likely to use within-class ability grouping. Teachers, like principals, can also model respect for and equitable treatment of both in-group and out-group members. The importance of teachers' attitudes and behaviors is made clear in Patchen (1982), which found a clear relation between negative teacher intergroup attitudes and White students' tendency to avoid their African American classmates.

With regard to sanctioning, teachers and others in authority can make an important contribution to fostering positive intergroup relations by clearly articulating their expectation that children will respect each other's rights and by backing up their stated expectations with disciplinary measures. It is especially important that the expectation that individuals will get along with each other be made clear from the very beginning so that children know that they cannot violate others' rights with impunity. If the expectation of harmony and respect is not made clear at the beginning, children are more likely to try to test the limits of the system and to feel they are being treated unfairly when they are held accountable for their behavior in this realm.

One important way in which authorities such as principals and teachers can foster the development of positive relations through sensitizing is for them to be aware that individuals in a desegregated school may misunderstand each others' motives or intentions, either because of cultural differences or because of fears and uncertainties about out-group members (Sagar & Schofield, 1980; Schofield, 1982/89). Using this awareness constructively can help to deal with problems that arise. Parents, too, are vital authority figures for most children, especially in their younger years. This is made clear by Patchen (1982), who found that negative parental attitudes are likely to be associated with intergroup avoidance and unfriendly intergroup encounters, whereas positive parental attitudes are associated with friendly intergroup contact. Thus, finding ways to encourage parents to involve their children in racially or ethnically diverse settings and to play a constructive role in encouraging positive intergroup contact is very important. In the context of desegregated schools, practices such as involving parents early in the planning process, creating school and communitywide multiethnic committees involving parents, teachers, and students, and providing information and opportunities for contact with the school all seem helpful (Hawley et al., 1983). In fact, a study by Doherty, Cadwell, Russo, Mandel, and Longshore (1981) suggests that parent involvement in school activities can create more positive attitudes toward majority-group members on the part of minority-group students. In both school and nonschool activities it seems reasonable to expect that issues relating to their children's safety will be salient to parents, especially in communities in which tensions are high. Thus, practices that promote safety and information about these practices might be useful in encouraging positive attitudes.

It is common for principals, teachers, and other authority figures involved with racially or ethnically diverse settings to feel that the best and fairest thing they can do is to adopt a point of view sometimes called the colorblind perspective (Rist, 1974). This perspective sees racial and ethnic group membership as irrelevant to the way individuals are treated. Taking cognizance of such group membership in decision making is perceived as illegitimate and likely to lead to discrimination against minority-group members or to reverse discrimination. Two factors make serious consideration of the colorblind perspective worthwhile. First, it is widely endorsed as a desirable perspective in institutions as diverse as the schools and the judicial system. Second, although in many ways the colorblind perspective is appealing—and consistent with a long-standing American emphasis on the importance of the individual—it easily leads to misrepresentation of reality in ways that encourage discrimination against minority-group members.

It must be acknowledged that the colorblind perspective may have some positive effects. It can reduce, at least in the short term, the potential for overt racial or ethnic conflict by generally deemphasizing the salience of race and encouraging the evenhanded application of rules to all students (Miller & Harrington, 1992). It may also reduce the potential for discomfort or embarrassment in racially or ethnically mixed schools by vigorously asserting that race does not matter.

However, this perspective also has a number of potentially negative effects. Most important, the decision to try to ignore group membership, to act as if no one notices or should notice race or ethnicity, means that policies that are disadvantageous to minority groups are often accepted without examination or thought (Schofield, 1986). For example, disproportionate suspension rates for minority students may not be seen as a sign of the need to examine discipline policies if school faculty and staff think of students only as individuals rather than facing the difficult issue of whether the school may be treating certain categories of students differently than others. Similarly, a colorblind perspective can easily lead to ready adoption or tolerance of policies that lead to resegregation. Furthermore, this perspective makes it easy for a school to use textbooks and curricular materials that inadequately reflect the perspectives and contributions of minority as well as majority group members.

The fact that the colorblind perspective has some clear disadvantages does not imply that it is desirable to remind students constantly of their group membership and to emphasize group differences continually. Both theory and experimental work suggest that practices that enhance the salience of such category memberships are bound to harm rather than help intergroup relations (Brewer & Miller, 1984; Miller & Harrington, 1992). To take just one example, a study by Miller, Brewer, and Edwards (1985) found that when participants in cooperative groups believed that social-category membership was the basis for assignment, they were less likely to respond with favorable evaluations of the out-group members than when they believed assignment to the groups was on the basis of each individual's attitudes. Thus, the best course of action may be to do what one can to encourage students to deal with each other as individuals while recognizing in setting policies and making decisions that attention to how various groups are faring is not only appropriate but likely to be constructive. The apparent contradiction here is mitigated by the fact that one of the things that is likely to make group identities salient to students is the perception that their group is not being treated fairly in comparison to others. To the extent that group outcomes are equitable because attention is paid to this issue in setting policies and making decision, one important source of polarization between members of different groups is lessened.

SUMMARY

This chapter has discussed factors that theory and research in social psychology suggest are important in structuring racially and ethnically mixed environments in ways that will foster positive relations and minimize negative relations among different groups. First, it is important to avoid resegregation, which can occur either as a result of common school policies or as a result of students' negative attitudes toward members of other groups. However, avoiding resegregation is not enough. Policies and practices need to be closely examined to ensure that insofar as possible they promote equal status and cooperative interdependence between minority- and majority-group members. Efforts to create crosscutting group memberships and to heighten a sense of connection to superordinate group identities that include members of the various groups represented in a situation are likely to be beneficial, as are practices that encourage individuals to participate with out-group members in enjoyable experiences that help participants to come to know each other as individuals. Those in positions of authority can support the development of positive intergroup relations by enabling others, as well as through modeling, sensitizing, and sanctioning. Recognizing that improving intergroup relations is likely to require some attention to how groups as well as individuals are faring in a given setting should help those in authority to perform these functions in an effective manner. However, in general, practices that heighten the salience of group membership should be avoided, unless they are the only way to make sure that other vital goals are obtained.

References

Allport, G. W. (1954). *The nature of prejudice*. Cambridge, MA: Addison-Wesley.

Amir, Y. (1969). Contact hypothesis in ethnic relations. *Psychological Bulletin, 71,* 319–342.

Aronson, E., Blaney, N., Sikes, J., Stephan, G., & Snapp, M. (1978). *The jigsaw classroom*. Beverly Hills, CA: Sage.

Aronson, E., & Gonzalez, A. (1988). Desegregation, jigsaw, and the Mexican-American experience. In P. A. Katz & D. A. Taylor (Eds.), *Eliminating racism: Profiles in controversy* (pp. 301–314). New York: Plenum Press.

Aronson, E., & Osherow, N. (1980). Cooperation, prosocial behavior, and academic performance: Experiments in the desegregated classroom. In L. Bickman (Ed.), *Applied social psychology annual* (Vol. 1, pp. 163–196). Beverly Hills, CA: Sage.

Blanchard, F. A., Lilly, T., & Vaughn, L. A. (1991). Reducing the expression of racial prejudice. *Psychological Science, 2,* 101–105.

Boateng, F. (1990). Combatting deculturalization of the African American child in the public school system: A multi-cultural approach. In K. Lomotey (Ed.), *Going to school: The African American experience* (pp. 73–84). Albany: State University of New York Press.

Bodenhausen, G. V. (1988). Stereotypic biases in social decision making and memory: Testing process models of stereotype use. *Journal of Personality and Social Psychology, 55,* 726–737.

Bossert, S. T. (1988/89). Cooperative activities in the classroom. In E. Z. Rothkopf (Ed.), *Review of research in education* (Vol. 15, pp. 225–250). Washington, DC: American Educational Research Association.

Brewer, M. B. (1988). A dual process model of impression formation. In T. Srull & R. Wyer (Eds.), *Advances in social cognition* (Vol. 1, pp. 1–36). Hillsdale, NJ: Erlbaum.

Brewer, M. B., & Kramer, R. M. (1985). The psychology of intergroup attitudes and behavior. In M. R. Rosenzweig & L. W. Porter (Eds.), *Annual review of psychology* (Vol. 36, pp. 219–243). Palo Alto, CA: Annual Reviews, Inc.

Brewer, M. B., & Miller, N. (1984). Beyond the contact hypothesis: Theoretical perspectives on desegregation. In N. Miller & M. B. Brewer (Eds.), *Groups in contact: The psychology of desegregation* (pp. 281–302). Orlando, FL: Academic Press.

Byrne, D. (1961). The influences of propinquity and opportunities for interaction on classroom relationships. *Human Relations, 14,* 63–69.

Byrne, D. (1971). *The attraction paradigm*. New York: Academic Press.

Byrne, D., & Nelson, D. (1965). Attraction as a linear function of proportion of positive reinforcements. *Journal of Personality and Social Psychology, 1,* 659–663.

California State Department of Education. (1983). *Desegregation and bilingual education—partners in quality education*. Sacramento: California State Department of Education.

Carnegie Council on Adolescent Development. (1989). *Turning points: Preparing American youth for the 21st century*. Washington, DC: The Carnegie Corporation of New York.

Carter, T. P. (1979). *Interface between bilingual education and desegregation: A study of Arizona and California*. Washington, DC: National Institute of Education. (ERIC Document Reproduction Service No. ED 184 743)

Carter, T., & Chatfield, M. L. (1986). Effective bilingual schools: Implications for policy and practice. *American Journal of Education, 95,* 200–232.

Cazabon, M., Lambert, W. E., & Hall, G., (1993). *Two-way bilingual education: A progress report on the Amigos Program*. Santa Cruz, CA: National Center for Research on Cultural Diversity.

Chesler, M., Bryant, B., & Crowfoot, J. (1981). *Making desegregation work: A professional guide to effecting change*. Beverly Hills, CA: Sage.

Clark, L. A., & Watson, D. (1988). Mood and the mundane: Relations between daily life events and self-reported mood. *Journal of Personality and Social Psychology, 54,* 296–308.

Cohen, E. (1972). Interracial interaction disability. *Human Relations. 25,* 9–24.

Cohen, E. (1980). Design and redesign of the desegregated school: Problems of status, power, and conflict. In W. G. Stephan & J. R. Feagin (Eds.), *School desegregation: Past, present, and future* (pp. 251–278). New York: Plenum Press.

Cohen E. (1984). The desegregated school: Problems in status power and inter-ethnic climate. In N. Miller & M. B. Brewer (Eds.), *Groups in contact: The psychology of desegregation* (pp. 77–96). Orlando, FL: Academic Press.

Cohen, E., Lockheed, M., & Lohman, M. (1976). The center for interracial cooperation: A field experiment. *Sociology of Education, 49,* 47–58.

Collins, T. W. (1979). From courtrooms to classrooms: Managing school desegregation in a Deep South high school. In R. C. Rist (Ed.), *Desegregated schools: Appraisals of an American experiment* (pp. 89–114). New York: Academic Press.

Collins, T. W., & Noblit, G. W. (1978). *Stratification and resegregation: The case of Crossover High School, Memphis, Tennessee* (Final report). Washington, DC: National Institute of Education.

Cook, S. W. (1985). Experimenting on social issues: The case of school desegregation. *American Psychologist, 40,* 452–460.

Crowfoot, J. E., & Chesler, M. A. (1981). Implementing "attractive ideas": Problems and prospects. In W. D. Hawley (Ed.), *Effective school desegregation* (pp. 265–295). Beverly Hills, CA: Sage.

Cunningham, M. R. (1988). Does happiness mean friendliness? Induced mood and heterosexual self-disclosure. *Personality and Social Psychology Bulletin, 14,* 283–297.

Cusick, P., & Ayling, R. (1973, February). *Racial interaction in an urban secondary school*. Paper presented at the meeting of the American Educational Research Association, New Orleans, LA.

Deschamps, J. C., & Doise, W. (1978). Crossed category membership in intergroup relations. In H. Tajfel (Ed.), *Differentiation between social groups* (pp. 141–158). New York: Academic Press.

Deutsch, M. (1993). Educating for a peaceful world. *American Psychologist, 48,* 510–517.

Devine, P. G., Monteith, M. J., Zuwerink, J. R., & Elliot, A. J. (1991). Prejudice with and without compunction. *Journal of Personality and Social Psychology, 60,* 817–830.

DeVries, D. L., & Edwards, K. (1974). Student teams and learning games: Their effects on cross-race and cross-sex interaction. *Journal of Educational Psychology, 66,* 741–749.

De Witt, K. (1991, September 13). Large increase is predicted in minorities in U.S. schools. *New York Times,* p. 14.

Doherty, W. J., Cadwell, J., Russo, N. A., Mandel, V., & Longshore, D. (1981). *Human relations study: Investigations of effective human relations strategies* (Vol. 2). Santa Monica, CA: System Development Corporation.

Doise, W. (1978). *Groups and individuals: Explanations in social psychology*. Cambridge: Cambridge University Press.

Dovidio, J. F., & Gaertner, S. L. (1991). Changes in the expression of racial prejudice. In H. Knopke, J. Norrell, & R. Rogers (Eds.), *Opening doors: An appraisal of race relations in contemporary America* (pp. 119–148). Tuscaloosa: University of Alabama Press.

Eddy, E. (1975). Educational innovation and desegregation: A case study of symbolic realignment. *Human Organization, 34*(2), 163–172.

Epstein, J. L. (1985). After the bus arrives: Resegregation in desegregated schools. *Journal of Social Issues, 41*(3), 23–43.

Eurich-Fulcer, R., & Schofield, J. W. (in press). Correlated versus uncorrelated social categorizations: The effect on intergroup bias. *Personality and Social Psychology Bulletin.*

Farley, R., & Allen, W. (1987). *The color line and the quality of American life.* New York: Russell Sage Foundation.

Fernandez, R. R., & Guskin, J. T. (1978). Bilingual education and desegregation: A new dimension in legal and educational decision-making. In H. LaFontaine, B. Persky, & L. H. Glubshick (Eds.), *Bilingual education* (pp. 58–66). Wayne, NJ: Avery Publishing.

Forehand, G. A., & Ragosta, M. (1976). *A handbook for integrated schooling.* Washington, DC: U.S. Department of Health, Education, and Welfare.

Forehand, G. A., Ragosta, M., & Rock, D. (1976). *Conditions and processes of effective school desegregation* (Final report). Princeton, NJ: Educational Testing Service.

Gaertner, S. L., & Dovidio, J. F. (1986). The aversive form of racism. In J. F. Dovidio & S. L. Gaertner (Eds.), *Prejudice, discrimination, and racism* (pp. 61–89). New York: Academic Press.

Gaertner, S. L., Mann, J., Murrell, A., & Dovidio, J. F. (1989). Reducing intergroup bias: The benefits of recategorization. *Journal of Personality and Social Psychology, 57,* 239–249.

Garcia, G. F. (1976). The Latino and desegregation. *Integrated Education, 14,* 21–22.

Gerard, H. B., Jackson, D., & Conolley, E. (1975). Social context in the desegregated classroom. In H. B. Gerard & N. Miller (Eds.), *School desegregation: A long-range study* (pp. 211–241). New York: Plenum Press.

Gerard, H. B., & Miller, N. (Eds.). (1975). *School desegregation: A long-term study.* New York: Plenum Press.

Gonzalez, J. M. (1979). *Bilingual education in the integrated school.* Arlington, VA: National Clearinghouse for Bilingual Education.

Gottlieb, D., & TenHouten, W. D. (1965). Racial composition and the social systems of three high schools. *Journal of Marriage and the Family, 27,* 204–212.

Gouaux, C. (1971). Induced affective states and interpersonal attraction. *Journal of Personality and Social Psychology, 20,* 37–43.

Greenberg, J., & Pyszczynski, T. (1985). The self-serving attributional bias: Beyond self-presentation. *Journal of Experimental Social Psychology, 21,* 61–72.

Griffitt, W. (1970). Environmental effects on interpersonal affective behavior: Ambient effective temperature and attraction. *Journal of Personality and Social Psychology, 15,* 240–244.

Hallinan, M. T. (1982). Classroom racial composition and children's friendships. *Social Forces, 61*(1), 56–72.

Hallinan, M. T., & Smith, S. S. (1985). The effects of classroom racial composition on students' interracial friendliness. *Social Psychology Quarterly, 48*(1), 3–16.

Hallinan, M. T., & Teixeira, R. A. (1987). Students' interracial friendships: Individual characteristics, structural effects and racial differences. *American Journal of Education, 95,* 563–583.

Hamilton, D. L., & Trolier, T. K. (1986). Stereotypes and stereotyping: An overview of the cognitive approach. In J. F. Dovidio & S. L. Gaertner (Eds.), *Prejudice, discrimination, and racism* (pp. 127–163). Orlando, FL: Academic Press.

Haro, C. M. (1977). *Mexican/Chicano concerns and school desegregation in Los Angeles.* Unpublished manuscript, University of California, Chicano Studies Center, Los Angeles.

Hawley, W., Crain, R. L., Rossell, C. H., Schofield, J. W., Fernandez, R., & Trent, W. P. (1983). *Strategies for effective desegregation: Lessons from research.* Lexington, MA: Lexington Books, D. C. Heath.

Heleen, O. (Ed.). (1987). Two-way bilingual education: A strategy for equity [Special issue]. *Equity and Choice, 3*(3).

Hertz-Lazarowitz, R., Kirkus, V. B., & Miller, N. (1992). Implications of current research on cooperative interaction for classroom application. In R. Hertz-Lazarowitz & N. Miller (Eds.), *Interaction in cooperative groups* (pp. 253–280). Cambridge: Cambridge University Press.

Hertz-Lazarowitz, R., & Miller, N. (Eds.). (1992). *Interaction in cooperative groups.* Cambridge: Cambridge University Press.

Hewstone, M., & Brown, R. (Eds.). (1986). *Contact and conflict in encounters.* Oxford: Basil Blackwell.

Hewstone, M., Hopkins, N., & Routh, D. A. (1992). Cognitive models of stereotype change: (1) Generalization and subtyping in young people's views of the police. *European Journal of Social Psychology, 22,* 219–234.

Hurtado, S. (1992). The campus racial climate: Contexts of conflict. *Journal of Higher Education, 63*(5), 539–569.

Jaynes, G. D., & Williams, R. M., Jr. (1989). *A common destiny: Blacks and American society.* Washington, DC: National Academy Press.

Johnson, D. W., & Johnson, R. T. (1982). The study of cooperative, competitive, and individualistic situations: State of the area and two recent contributions. *Contemporary Education, 1*(1), 7–13.

Johnson, D. W., & Johnson, R. T. (1987). *Learning together and alone* (2nd ed.). Englewood Cliffs, NJ: Prentice-Hall.

Johnson, D. W., & Johnson, R. T. (1992). Positive interdependence: Key to effective cooperation. In R. Hertz-Lazarowitz & N. Miller (Eds.), *Interaction in cooperative groups* (pp. 174–199). Cambridge: Cambridge University Press.

Johnson, D. W., Johnson, R. T., & Maruyama, G. (1984). Goal interdependence and interpersonal attraction in heterogeneous classrooms: A meta-analysis. In N. Miller & M. B. Brewer (Eds.), *Groups in contact: The psychology of desegregation* (pp. 187–212). Orlando, FL: Academic Press.

Johnson, D. W., Maruyama, G., Johnson, R., Nelson, D., & Skon, L. (1981). Effects of cooperative, competitive, and individualistic goal structures on achievement: A meta-analysis. *Psychological Bulletin, 89,* 47–62.

Johnston, L., & Hewstone, M. (1992). Cognitive models of stereotype change: Subtyping and the perceived typicality of disconfirming group members. *Journal of Experimental Social Psychology, 28*(4), 360–386.

Judd, C. M., & Park, B. (1988). Outgroup homogeneity: Judgments of variability at the individual and group levels. *Journal of Personality and Social Psychology, 54,* 778–788.

Kagan, S. (1991). *Cooperative learning resources for teachers* (4th ed.). San Juan Capistrano, CA: Resources for Teachers.

Levin, J., & McDevitt, J. (1993). *Hate crimes: The rising tide of bigotry and bloodshed.* New York: Plenum Press.

Levine, R. A., & Campbell, D. T. (1972). *Ethnocentrism: Theories in conflict, ethnic attitudes, and group behavior.* New York: John Wiley & Sons.

Linville, P. W., Fischer, G. W., & Salovey, P. (1989). Perceived distributions of characteristics of ingroup and outgroup members: Empirical evidence and a computer simulation. *Journal of Personality and Social Psychology, 57,* 165–188.

Linville, P. W., Salovey, P., & Fischer, G. W. (1986). Stereotyping and perceived distributions of social characteristics: An application to ingroup-outgroup perception. In J. Dovidio & S. L. Gaertner (Eds.), *Prejudice, discrimination, and racism* (pp. 165–208). New York: Academic Press.

Longshore, D., & Wellisch, J. B. (1982). Human relations programs in desegregated elementary schools. *Evaluation Review, 6,* 789–799.

Magner, D. K. (1989, April 26). Blacks and Whites on the campuses: Behind ugly racist incidents, student isolation and insensitivity. *Chronicle of Higher Education,* pp. 1, 28–31.

May, J. L., & Hamilton, P. A. (1980). Effects of musically evoked affect on women's interpersonal attraction and perceptual judgments of physical attractiveness of men. *Motivation and Emotion, 4,* 217–228.

McAdoo, H. P., & McAdoo, J. W. (Eds.). (1985). *Black children: Social, educational and parental environments.* Beverly Hills, CA: Sage.

McConahay, J. (1981). Reducing racial prejudice in desegregated schools. In W. D. Hawley (Ed.), *Effective school desegregation* (pp. 35–53). Beverly Hills, CA: Sage.

Mercer, J. R., Iadicola, P., & Moore, H. (1980). Building effective multiethnic schools: Evolving models and paradigms. In W. G. Stephan & J. R. Feagin (Eds.), *School desegregation: Past, present, and future* (pp. 281–307). New York: Plenum Press.

Milan, W. G. (1978). *Toward a comprehensive language policy for a desegregated school system: Resassessing the future of bilingual education.* New York: Arawak Consulting Company.

Miller, N. (1980). Making school desegregation work. In W. G. Stephan & J. R. Feagin (Eds.), *School desegregation: Past, present, and future* (pp. 309–348). New York: Plenum Press.

Miller, N., Brewer, M. B., & Edwards, K. (1985). Cooperative interaction in desegregated settings: A laboratory analogue. *Journal of Social Issues, 41*(3), 63–79.

Miller, N., & Harrington, H. J. (1992). Social categorization and intergroup acceptance: Principles for the design and development of cooperative learning teams. In R. Hertz-Lazarowitz & N. Miller (Eds.), *Interaction in cooperative groups* (pp. 203–227). Cambridge: Cambridge University Press.

National Alliance of Black School Educators. (1984). *Saving the African American child.* Washington, DC: Author.

National Governors' Association. (1990). *Educating America: State strategies for achieving the national educational goals.* Washington, DC: Author.

National Institute of Education. (1977). *Desegregation and education concerns of the Hispanic community.* Washington, DC: U.S. Government Printing Office.

National Opinion Research Center. (1973). *Southern schools: An evaluation of the effects of the Emergency School Assistance Program and of school desegregation* (Vols. 1 & 2). Chicago: Author.

Oakes, J. (1985). *Keeping track: How schools structure inequality.* New Haven: Yale University Press.

Oakes, J. (1992). Can tracking research inform practice? Technical, normative, and political considerations. *Educational Researcher, 21*(4), 12–21.

O'Hara, W. T. (1993). America's minorities: The demographics of diversity. *Population Bulletin, 47*(4), 1–48.

Orfield, G. (1975). How to make desegregation work: The adaptation of schools to their newly-integrated student bodies. *Law and Contemporary Problems, 39,* 314–340.

Park, B., Judd, C. M., & Ryan, C. S. (1991). Social categorization and the representation of variability information. In W. Stroebe & M. Hewstone (Eds.), *European review of social psychology* (Vol. 2, pp. 211–245). Chichester, England: John Wiley.

Patchen, M. (1982). *Black-White contact in schools: Its social and academic effects.* West Lafayette, IN: Purdue University Press.

Pettigrew, T. (1969). The Negro and education: Problems and proposals. In I. Katz & P. Gurin (Eds.), *Race and the social sciences* (pp. 49–112). New York: Basic Books.

Prager, J., Longshore, D., & Seeman, M. (Eds.). (1986). *School desegregation research: New directions in situational analysis.* New York: Plenum Press.

Pruitt, D. G., & Carnevale, P. J. (1993). *Negotiation in social conflict.* Pacific Grove, CA: Brooks/Cole Publishing Company.

Riordan, C. (1978). Equal-status interracial contact: A review and revision of the concept. *International Journal of Intercultural Relations, 2*(2), 161–185.

Rist, R. C. (1974). Race, policy, and schooling. *Society, 12*(1), 59–63.

Rist, R. C. (Ed.). (1979). *Desegregated schools: Appraisals of an American experiment.* New York: Academic Press.

Rogers, M., Henningan, K., Bowman, C., & Miller, N. (1984). Intergroup acceptance in classrooms and playground settings. In N. Miller & M. B. Brewer (Eds.), *Groups in contact: The psychology of desegregation* (pp. 213–227). New York: Academic Press.

Roos, P. D. (1978). Bilingual education: The Hispanic response to unequal educational opportunity. *Law and Contemporary Problems, 42,* 111–140.

Ryan, C. S., Judd, C. M., & Park, B. (1993). *Effects of racial stereotypes on judgments of individuals: The moderating role of perceived group variability.* Unpublished manuscript, University of Colorado, Boulder.

Sagar, H. A., & Schofield, J. W. (1980). Racial and behavioral cues in Black and White children's perceptions of ambiguously aggressive acts. *Journals of Personality and Social Psychology, 39,* 590–598.

Sagar, H. A., & Schofield, J. W. (1984). Integrating the desegregated school: Problems and possibilities. In M. Maehr & D. Bartz (Eds.), *Advances in motivation and achievement: A research manual* (pp. 203–242). Greenwich, CT: JAI Press.

Scherer, J., & Slawski, E. (1979). Color, class, and social control in an urban school. In R. C. Rist (Ed.), *Desegregated schools: Appraisals of an American experiment* (pp. 117–153). New York: Academic Press.

Schofield, J. W. (1979). The impact of positively structured contact on intergroup behavior: Does it last under adverse conditions? *Social Psychology Quarterly, 42,* 280–284.

Schofield, J. W. (1982). *Black and White in school: Trust, tension, or tolerance?* New York: Praeger.

Schofield, J. W. (1983). Black-White conflict in the schools: Its social and academic effects. *American Journal of Education, 92,* 104–107.

Schofield, J. W. (1986). Causes and consequences of the colorblind perspective. In S. Gaertner & J. Dovidio (Eds.), *Prejudice, discrimination and racism: Theory and practice* (pp. 231–253). New York: Academic Press.

Schofield, J. W. (1989). *Black and White in school: Trust, tension, or tolerance?* New York: Teachers College Press.

Schofield, J. W. (1991). School desegregation and intergroup relations: A review of the research. In G. Grant (Ed.), *Review of research in education* (Vol. 17, pp. 335–409). Washington, DC: American Educational Research Association.

Schofield, J. W., & McGivern, E. P. (1979). Creating interracial bonds in a desegregated school. In R. G. Blumberg & W. J. Roye (Eds.), *Interracial bonds* (pp. 106–119). Bayside, NY: General Hall.

Schofield, J. W., & Sagar, H. A. (1977). Peer interaction patterns in an integrated middle school. *Sociometry, 40,* 130–138.

Schofield, J. W., & Sagar, H. A. (1979). The social context of learning in an interracial school. In R. C. Rist (Ed.), *Desegregated schools: Appraisals of an American experiment* (pp. 155–199). New York: Academic Press.

Sharan, S. (1980). Cooperative learning in teams: Recent methods and effects on achievement, attitudes, and ethnic relations. *Review of Educational Research, 50,* 241–272.

Sharan, Y., & Sharan, S. (1992). *Expanding cooperative learning through group investigation.* New York: Teachers College Press.

Shapiro, J. P. (1988). Relationships between dimensions of depressive experience and evaluative beliefs about people in general. *Personality and Social Psychology Bulletin, 14,* 388–400.

Sherif, M., Harvey, O. J., White, B. J., Hood, W. R., & Sherif, C. (1961). *Intergroup cooperation and competition: The Robbers Cave experiment.* Norman, OK: University Book Exchange.

Slavin, R. E. (1983a). *Cooperative learning.* New York: Longman.

Slavin, R. E. (1983b). When does cooperative learning increase student achievement? *Psychological Bulletin, 94,* 429–445.

Slavin, R. E. (1985). Cooperative learning: Applying contact theory in desegregated schools. *Journal of Social Issues, 41*(3), 45–62.

Slavin, R. E. (1992). When and why does cooperative learning increase achievement? Theoretical and empirical perspectives. In R. Hertz-Lazarowitz & N. Miller (Eds.), *Interaction in cooperative groups* (pp. 145–173). Cambridge: Cambridge University Press.

Slavin, R. E., & Madden, N. A. (1979). School practices that improve race relations. *American Educational Research Journal, 16,* 169–180.

Stephan, W. G., & Stephan, C. W. (1984). The role of ignorance in intergroup relations. In N. Miller & M. B. Brewer (Eds.), *Groups in contact: The psychology of desegregation* (pp. 229–255). Orlando, FL: Academic Press.

Stephan, W. G., & Stephan, C. W. (1985). Intergroup anxiety. *Journal of Social Issues, 41*(3), 157–175.

Sullivan, M. L. (1979). Contacts among cultures: School desegregation in a polyethnic New York City high school. In R. C. Rist (Ed.), *Desegregated schools: Appraisals of an American experiment* (pp. 201–240). New York: Academic Press.

Swallow, S. R., & Kuiper, N. A. (1987). The effects of depression and cognitive vulnerability to depression on judgments of similarity between self and other. *Motivation and Emotion, 11,* 157–167.

Tajfel, H. (Ed.). (1978). *Differentiation between social groups.* London: Academic Press.

Tajfel, H., & Turner, J. C. (1979). An integrative theory of intergroup conflict. In W. Austin & S. Worchel (Eds.), *The social psychology of intergroup relations* (pp. 33–47). Monterey, CA: Brooks/Cole.

Taylor, S. E. (1981). A categorization approach to stereotyping. In D. L. Hamilton (Ed.), *Cognitive processes in stereotyping and intergroup behavior* (pp. 83–114). Hillsdale, NJ: Erlbaum.

Vanbeselaere, N. (1987). The effects of dichotomous and crossed social categorization upon intergroup discrimination. *European Journal of Social Psychology, 18,* 143–156.

Veitch, R., & Griffitt, W. (1976). Good news, bad news: Affective and interpersonal effects. *Journal of Applied Social Psychology, 6,* 69–75.

Wellisch, J. B., Carriere, R. A., MacQueen, A. H., & Duck, G. A. (1977). *An in-depth study of Emergency School Aid Act (ESAA) schools: 1975–1976.* Santa Monica, CA: System Development Corporation.

Wellisch, J. B., Marcus, A. C., MacQueen, A. H., & Duck, G. A. (1976). *An in-depth study of Emergency School Aid Act (ESAA) schools: 1974–1975.* Santa Monica, CA: System Development Corporation.

Worchel, S. (1979). Cooperation and the reduction of intergroup conflict: Some determining factors. In W. G. Austin & S. Worchel (Eds.), *The social psychology of intergroup relations* (pp. 262–273). Monterey, CA: Brooks/Cole.

Worchel, S., Andreoli, V. A., & Folger, R. (1977). Intergroup cooperation and intergroup attraction: The effect of previous interaction and outcome of combined effort. *Journal of Experimental Social Psychology, 13,* 131–140.

· 37 ·

TOWARD A THEORY OF MULTICULTURAL COUNSELING AND THERAPY

Derald Wing Sue

CALIFORNIA SCHOOL OF PROFESSIONAL PSYCHOLOGY, ALAMEDA

Counselors, therapists, and other mental health professionals are increasingly coming into contact with clients who differ from themselves in race, culture, and ethnicity (Sue, Arrendondo, & McDavis, 1992). What they are experiencing is also being reenacted in our classrooms (Atkinson, Morten, & Sue, 1993) and in the workplace (Johnston & Packer, 1987; D. W. Sue, 1991a), where both teachers and employers must learn to relate to a multicultural and multiracial population.

The changing demographics in the United States have been referred to as "the diversification of America" or, literally, "the changing complexion of society" (Atkinson, Morten, & Sue, 1993). This diversification is fueled primarily by changes in immigration laws that have allowed large numbers of racial minorities (approximately 34% from Asian and another 34% from Latin American countries) to enter the United States during the 1980s (U.S. Census Bureau, 1990). Couple this trend with the fact that birthrates of White Americans have declined to 1.7 per mother while those of racial/ethnic minorities remain higher (African Americans = 2.4, Mexican Americans = 2.9, Vietnamese = 3.4, Laotians = 4.6, Cambodians = 7.4, and Hmongs = 11.9 per mother) and it becomes clear that within several short decades racial/ethnic minorities will soon become the numerical majority (U.S. Census Bureau, 1990).

Yet it appears that counselors are ill prepared to deal with the changing characteristics of the U.S. population (Pedersen, 1988). Developing culturally effective helping strategies have met with much resistance. Several major obstacles seem to stand in the way of such a movement. First, the monocultural nature of education and training has taught mental health professionals an ethnocentric perspective of the helping process, an approach that is often antagonistic to the life experiences and values of their culturally different clients (Pedersen, 1987; Ivey, Ivey, & Simek-Morgan, 1993). Second, the counseling profession has failed to realize that the traditional theories of counseling and psychotherapy are culture bound. The assumption of

universal application to all populations and problems is highly questionable (D. W. Sue & Sue, 1990; D. W. Sue, 1992). Third, the profession has been slow in developing a conceptual framework that incorporates culture as a central core concept of the counseling process (Ivey et al., 1993; D. W. Sue, 1990). This has seriously hindered the development of culturally relevant strategies, programs, and practices in working with racial/ethnic minority clients. Multicultural counseling and therapy (MCT) can be briefly defined as any helping relationship in which two or more of the participants are culturally different. As a result, the helping process and goals of counseling may be both culture specific and/or universal. The counselor's ability to recognize and provide balance among these two dimensions is crucial to the delivery of appropriate mental health services to minority constituents.

The purpose of this chapter is to begin the process of proposing a theory of MCT. Such an attempt is filled with hazards and may be a culturally biased attempt in itself. Such a criticism is inescapable, however, as all theories are necessarily culture specific. Thus, an attempt will be made to minimize such a danger by (a) analyzing the weaknesses and culture-bound biases of traditional mental health practices; (b) reviewing the literature associated with factors identified as important in MCT and "minority" mental health; and (c) identifying guidelines or characteristics of a truly multicultural theory of counseling and psychotherapy.

CHARACTERISTICS OF COUNSELING AND PSYCHOTHERAPY

Beyond general agreement that counseling is an internal approach to treating psychological problems involving interaction between one or more clients and a therapist, there is little consensus on exactly what else it is. Counseling and psycho-

647

therapy have been called "a conversation with a therapeutic purpose" (Korchin, 1976); it has also been called "the talking cure" or the "purchase of friendship" (Schofield, 1964). One observer suggests that counseling can be variously defined by goals, procedures and methods, practitioners, or the relationship formed (Reisman, 1971).

For the purposes of this chapter, traditional counseling may be defined as the systematic application of techniques derived from predominantly Eurocentric psychological principles by a trained and experienced professional counselor or therapist for the purpose of helping psychologically troubled people. It is difficult to be more succinct or precise without getting involved in specific types of counseling. Depending on their perspectives and theoretical orientations, counselors may seek to modify attitudes, thoughts, feelings, or behaviors; to facilitate the patient's self-insight and rational control of his or her own life; to cure mental disorders; to enhance mental health and self-actualization; to make clients "feel better"; to remove a cause of a psychological problem; to change a self-concept; or to encourage adaptation. Counseling is practiced by many different kinds of people in many different ways—a fact that seems to preclude establishing a single set of standard therapeutic procedures (D. Sue, Sue, & Sue, 1994). And—despite the Euro-American emphasis on the scientific basis of counseling—in practice it is often more art than science.

Diverse Eurocentric counseling approaches seem to share some common therapeutic factors. In a study of 50 publications on psychotherapy and counseling, investigators found the most common attributes to be (a) development of a therapeutic alliance; (b) opportunity for catharsis; (c) acquisition and practice of new behaviors; and (d) the clients' positive expectancies (Grencavage & Norcross, 1990). These characteristics are consistent with those proposed by Korchin (1976). First, counseling offers the client a chance to relearn—more specifically, a chance to unlearn, relearn, develop, or change—certain behaviors or levels of functioning.

Second, counseling helps generate the development of new, emotionally important experiences. It involves the experiencing of emotions that clients may have avoided along with the painful and helpless feelings fostered by these emotions. This experiencing allows relearning as well as emotional and intellectual insight into problems and conflicts.

Third, there is a therapeutic relationship. Counselors have been trained to listen, show sympathetic concern, be objective, value the client's integrity, communicate understanding, and use professional knowledge and skills. Counselors may provide reassurance, interpretations, self-disclosures, reflections of the client's feelings, or information, each at appropriate times. As a team, counselors and clients are better prepared to venture into frightening areas that clients would not have faced alone.

Finally, counseling clients have certain motivations and expectations. Most people enter counseling with both anxiety and hope. They are frightened by their emotional difficulties and by the prospect of treatment, but they expect or hope that counseling will be helpful.

The goals and general characteristics of counseling as de-

scribed seem admirable, and most people consider them so. However, counseling itself has been criticized as being biased and inappropriate to the lifestyles of many clients such as members of minority groups (Locke, 1992; Ponterotto & Casas, 1991; D. W. Sue & Sue, 1990). Indeed, the process and goals of counseling and psychotherapy have often been likened to forms of cultural oppression (Katz, 1985; D. W. Sue, 1978).

Counseling Theories and Worldviews

Elsewhere, a worldview has been broadly defined "as how a person perceives his or her relationship to the world (nature, institutions, other people, things, etc.). Worldviews are highly correlated with a person's cultural upbringing and life experiences" (D. W. Sue, 1978, p. 419). While worldviews have traditionally been applied to individuals (microunit of analysis) in how they construe meaning in the world, the concept has been increasingly applied to larger units such as gender, race, and culture (macroanalysis). Ivey has referred to the different theories of counseling and psychotherapy as "temporary cultures" with their own assumptions about the nature of people, how problems arise, and what methods must be employed to be effective (Ivey, 1981, 1986). These temporary cultures are, indeed, different worldviews (Ivey et al., 1993), associated with different theoretical orientations. A number of multicultural scholars (Ivey et al., 1993; Locke, 1992; Pedersen, 1985, 1988; Ponterotto & Casas, 1991; D. W. Sue, 1990; White & Parham, 1990) have already made a strong case that the worldviews implicit in the psychodynamic, cognitive-behavioral, existential-humanistic, and other schools of thought might conflict with the worldviews of racial/ethnic minority clients.

To be fair, most practicing clinicians consider themselves eclectics. They contend that relying on a single theory and a few techniques is correlated with inexperience; the more experienced the clinician, the greater the diversity and resourcefulness used in a session (Norcross & Prochaska, 1988). Therapeutic eclecticism has been defined as the "process of selecting concepts, methods, and strategies from a variety of current theories which work" (Brammer & Shostrom, 1984, p. 35). An example is the early "technical eclecticism" of Lazarus (1967). This approach has now been refined into a theoretical model called multimodal behavior therapy (Lazarus 1976, 1984). Although behavioral in basis, it embraces many cognitive and affective concepts as well. Yet it is important to note that for counselors to draw from the available current theories (most of which are Eurocentric) still leaves a great void. While the behavioral schools of thought see us as *behaving beings*, the cognitive schools as *thinking beings*, the humanistic schools as *feeling beings*, and the psychoanalytic as *historic and unconsciously motivated beings*, it is important to note that we are all of these and more. D. W. Sue (1992) has stated:

The problem with traditional theories is that they are culture-bound and often recognize and treat only one aspect of the human condition: the thinking self, the feeling self, the behaving self, or the social self. Few include the totality of the human experience, and few include the cultural and political self. (p. 32)

Counseling and Cultural Bias

Racial and ethnic minorities have frequently criticized counseling as being a "handmaiden of the status quo," a "transmitter of society's values," and an "instrument of oppression." Rather than helping people reach their full potential, critics say, it has often been used to subjugate the very people it was meant to free. The meaning of such statements is clear: The process and goals of counseling are culture bound and thus culturally biased against people whose values differ from those of Western societies. The following "generic characteristics of counseling," which seem to be common to most schools of thought, often conflict with clients' cultural values (Ponterotto & Casas, 1991; D. W. Sue & Sue, 1990).

One: Focus on the Individual. Most forms of counseling and psychotherapy stress the importance and uniqueness of the individual, an attitude reflected in the concept of the I-thou relationship, the one-to-one encounter, and the belief that the client must take responsibility for him- or herself. In many cultural groups, however, the basic psychosocial unit of operation is not the individual but the family, the group, or the collective society. For example, many Asians and Hispanics define their identities within the family constellation. Whatever a person does reflects not only on that person but on the entire family as well. Important decisions are thus made by the entire family rather than by the individual (Szapocznik & Kurtines, 1993).

Counselors who work with people from such cultures may see their clients as "dependent," "lacking in maturity," or "avoiding responsibility." These negative labels do much harm to the self-esteem of minority group members, especially when they become part of a diagnosis.

Two: Verbal Expression of Emotions. The psychotherapeutic process works best for clients who are verbal, articulate, and able to express their feelings and be assertive. The major medium of communication is the spoken word (in standard English). Those who tend to be less verbal, who speak with an accent, or who do not use standard English are placed at a disadvantage. In addition, many cultural groups (including Asians and Native Americans) are brought up to conceal rather than verbalize their feelings; counselors often perceive them as "inhibited," "lacking in spontaneity," or "repressed." Thus the counseling process, by valuing expressiveness, may not only force minority clients to violate their cultural norms but also label them as having negative personality traits. Counseling and psychotherapy also fail to realize major differences in communication styles and the use of nonverbal forms of communication. Asian Americans, African Americans, Hispanic/Latino Americans, and American Indians seem to rely much more on nonverbal communication or to use contextual cues more than their White counterparts.

Three: Openness and Intimacy. Self-disclosure and discussion of the most intimate and personal aspects of one's life are hallmarks of counseling. However, cultural and sociopolitical factors may make some clients unwilling or unable to engage in such self-disclosure (Ridley, 1984; D. W. Sue & Sue, 1990). For example, the "cultural paranoia" that many African Americans have developed as a defense against discrimination and oppression may be a healthy distrust that would make them reluctant to disclose their innermost thoughts and feelings to a White counselor (Grier & Cobbs, 1968, 1971). Unfortunately, counselors who encounter this reluctance might perceive their clients as suspicious, guarded, and paranoid. Likewise, many counselors do not understand the cultural implications of disclosure among Asians, who discuss intimate matters only with close acquaintances and not with strangers, which counselors may well be (D. W. Sue & Sue, 1990).

Four: Insight. Most closely associated with the psychodynamic approach but valued in many theoretical orientations, insight is the ability to understand the basis of one's motivations, perceptions, and behavior. But many cultural groups do not value insight. In China, for example, a depressed or anxious person may be advised to avoid the thoughts that are causing the distress. This contrasts sharply with the Western belief that insight is always helpful in counseling (Leong, 1986; Lum, 1982). Interestingly, the rise in popularity of cognitive-counseling approaches such as those advocated by Ellis (1962, 1989), Beck (1976a, 1985), and Meichenbaum (1985) now reveal that "healthy denial" or avoidance of "morbid thinking" is a useful counseling strategy; this is a method that has traditionally run counter to the belief in insight.

Five: Competition Versus Cooperation. In Western society, competitiveness is a highly valued trait. This is clearly reflected in our educational system, where competition among persons is created by having children sit in neatly arranged rows of individual desks; where asking and answering questions occur via raising one's hand to seek individual recognition; where a bell-shaped curve is used to grade students (for someone to get an A, others have to obtain Bs, Cs, Ds, etc.). Some groups such as American Indians and Hispanics value and prefer more cooperative efforts in the classroom (Comas-Diaz, 1990; LaFromboise, 1988). Counselors may perceive such cultural differences as indicative of passivity, noncompetitiveness, or lack of assertiveness. One of the reasons why American Indians have the highest dropout rates in our educational system may be that to achieve they must violate basic values of their cultures (Banks, 1993).

Six: Linear-Static Time Emphasis. The United States operates by "clock time," which tends to view time as static and linear. Statements such as "Time is money" and "Don't be late" indicate the importance of time consciousness. In counseling and psychotherapy, appointments are traditionally once a week, 50 minutes out of the hour. Yet many cultural groups possess a much more dynamic, flowing, and harmonious perception of time (circular vs. linear and flowing vs. rigid), or they tend to mark time by events rather than by the clock (Ho, 1987; Inclan, 1985; Kluckhohn & Strodtbeck, 1961; Spiegel & Papajohn, 1983). Such differences in temporal perspectives can lead to major misunderstandings and difficulties. A client whose cultural background differs from that of the counselor and who shows up late for an appointment may be perceived by the counselor as passive-aggressive or irresponsible (D. W. Sue, 1990; D. W. Sue & Sue, 1990).

Seven: Nuclear Versus Extended Family. Even though it is no longer the norm in the United States, the "nuclear family" is still held to be the ideal from which we conceptualize and practice family counseling. The unit of the family usually includes the husband, wife, and immediate offspring. The definition of the family in many cultural groups may be quite different from that of their White counterparts. For example, extended family systems that include aunts, uncles, godparents, and even deceased members (ancestor worship of certain Asian groups) appear to be the norm for Mexican Americans and Asian Americans (Ho, 1987; McGoldrick, Pearce, & Giordano, 1982); among African Americans and American Indians the concept *family* may extend not only to aunts and uncles but to neighbors and tribal members (Franklin, 1988; Ho, 1987; McGoldrick et al., 1982; Red Horse, 1983; Thomas & Dansby, 1985). Thus, the counselor or therapist may need to redefine family counseling in an extended manner.

Eight: Locus of Responsibility Traditional counseling stresses that responsibility for change resides with the individual and that the locus of the problem is generally internal. Thus, much of counseling is aimed at having clients explore their own conflicts, achieve insight, and become healthy in some manner. Racial and ethnic minorities, however, often view the problem as residing outside of the person and believe that change must occur in the system rather than solely in the individual (Berman, 1979; Katz, 1985; D. W. Sue, 1978; White & Parham, 1990). Racism, discrimination, and prejudice are seen as system stressors that call for new roles for counselors (e.g., change agent, advocate, or facilitator of indigenous healing; Atkinson et al., 1993).

Nine: Scientific Empiricism. The field of counseling and the broader field of psychology attempt to mimic the physical sciences. The process of asking and answering questions about the human condition is based upon the value placed on symbolic logic (D. W. Sue & Sue, 1990), and the valued approach is an atomistic, quantitative, and reductionistic analysis of phenomena that are believed to be related by cause and effect (Ponterotto & Casas, 1991). Many cultural groups believe in a more nonlinear, wholistic, and harmonious approach to the world. The counselor is often trained to engage in linear, rational, and objective thinking in helping clients to resolve problems and difficulties (Katz, 1985; Pedersen, 1988). As a result, a counselor's desire to help may unwittingly be at odds with that of the culturally different client.

The solution to this cultural gap is obvious: Counselors need to do three things. First, they should begin the process of becoming more aware of their own cultural values, biases, stereotypes, and assumptions about human behavior (D. W. Sue, Arredondo, & McDavis, 1992; D. W. Sue et al., 1982). They need to ask: What are the worldviews they bring to the counseling

encounter? What value system is inherent in our theory of helping? What values underlie the strategies and techniques used in counseling? Without such an awareness and understanding, counselors may inadvertently assume that everyone shares their worldview. When this happens, they may become guilty of cultural oppression, imposing values on their culturally different client (D. W. Sue, 1978).

Second, counselors should begin the process of acquiring knowledge and understanding of the worldviews of minority or culturally different clients (D. W. Sue et al., 1992). Counselors need to reflect on these questions about ethnic groups of color: What are their values, biases, and assumptions about human behavior? How similar or dissimilar are they to those of the helping professional's value system? Are there such things as African American, Asian American, Latino/Hispanic American, and Native American worldviews?

Third, counselors should begin the process of developing culturally appropriate intervention strategies in the counseling process (D. W. Sue, 1990). This involves developing not only individual counseling and communication skills but system intervention skills as well. Although not discussed in this chapter, indigenous healing practices and help-giving networks of different cultures and minority communities are crucial to the provision of relevant mental health services (Das, 1987; Harner, 1990; Lee, Oh, & Mountcastle, 1992).

RACIAL/ETHNIC MINORITY COUNSELING RESEARCH: IMPORTANT THEMES

In building a theory of MCT, knowledge of the limitations and weaknesses of current models is essential, which is one of the reasons this chapter has devoted a considerable amount of space to analyzing the culture-bound limitations of current theories. Another useful path is to review the current racial/ethnic minority counseling research to identify important themes, concepts, and findings of relevance to multicultural counseling. Fortunately, several excellent surveys or reviews of the field exist (Atkinson, 1983; Casas, 1984, 1985; Heath, Neimeyer, & Pedersen, 1988; Ponterotto & Casas, 1991; Ponterotto & Sabnani, 1989). This chapter will extract some of these key concepts and findings and attempt to draw out their implications for MCT.

Centrality of Culture to Theories of Counseling

All counseling theories arise from a cultural context and as such are highly culture bound (Ivey et al., 1993; Pedersen, 1986, 1987; D. W. Sue & Sue, 1990; White & Parham, 1990). Yet the counseling profession continues to ignore this fact and act as if counseling theories are equally applicable to all people regardless of differences in race, culture, and ethnicity. The multicultural counseling literature suggests that failure to understand and take into consideration the cultural assumptions of counseling may result in ineffectiveness or cultural oppression. For example, minorities are often the victims of psychological helping models that view them as inferior, deprived, or deficient in desirable characteristics (Ponterotto & Casas, 1991;

D. W. Sue & Sue, 1990; White & Parham, 1990). This generally occurs because the counseling professional is unaware of the cultural values, biases, and assumptions of the theories.

Szapocznik and Kurtines (1993) reconceptualize family psychology and counseling to include the concept of *embeddedness*. This paradigm studies the individual within the context of family, which is in turn embedded in a cultural context. There are two important things to note in this new formulation. First, an effective counseling approach does not view the individual in the context of family and culture as though they were separate, isolated dimensions. Rather, contexts are embedded and act on one another. Szapocznik and Kurtines (p. 401) state, "We have found it useful to extend our concern for culture to include the concept of the nesting of the individual within the family and the family within the culture." Second, the cultural context in which nesting occurs is not a monocultural one. The model does not apply solely, for example, to a Cuban cultural context (a very monocultural view in itself). Rather, in the United States, contexts are embedded *within a culturally pluralist milieu*, a recognition of multiculturalism. While Cuban American children may be raised in a Cuban community in Florida, they are eventually and ultimately exposed to the Eurocentric culture of the United States as well as others.

Minority Identity Development

Multicultural specialists are increasingly recognizing the importance of racial/cultural identity development of clients in the counseling process. Researchers disagree on whether we are talking about a stage model (Atkinson, Morten, & Sue, 1993; Cross, 1971, 1978, 1989; Hardiman, 1982; Helms, 1984, 1986, 1990; Jackson, 1975; Parham, 1989; Parham & Helms, 1981) or a social-learning one (Rowe, Bennett, & Atkinson, 1994). Nevertheless, these models strongly imply that the stage or level of identity attained by the minority individual may dictate different counseling strategies and approaches. They also give strong emphasis to sociopolitical factors in the formation of racial/cultural identity.

Perhaps the most influential of the Black identity development models was the one proposed by Cross (Cross, 1971, 1987, 1991). He proposed a four-stage process (originally five) in which Blacks in the United States moved from a White frame of reference: *preencounter, encounter, immersion-emersion,* and *internalization*. The preencounter stage is characterized by Blacks who devalue their own Blackness in favor of White values and ways. Adopting White Eurocentric values and ways via assimilation in and acculturation to White society is the overriding goal. In the encounter stage, a two-step process begins to occur. The person may encounter an event (for example, the slaying of Martin Luther King, Jr.) or a series of events that produce a profound challenge to the individual's previous way of thinking and behaving; this is followed by a reinterpretation of the world and a personal shift in worldviews. Anger and guilt may move the Black person to the third stage of development, immersion-emersion. Here Blacks may withdraw from the dominant culture and immerse themselves in Black culture and tradition. There may be a rise in Black pride. The final

stage, internalization, is characterized by inner security as conflicts between the old and new identities are resolved.

Because many other minority groups seem to move through similar identity processes, several multicultural psychologists (Atkinson, Morten, & Sue, 1993; D. W. Sue & Sue, 1990) have attempted to analyze the many similarities that seem to exist among them. They identify five stages through which racial/ethnic minorities may move: *conformity, dissonance, resistance and immersion, introspection,* and *synergetic articulation and awareness*. Each stage has its corresponding attitudes and behaviors. For example, the conformity stage is characterized by the minority individual's unequivocal preference for dominant cultural values over those of the minority culture. Dominant cultural ways are viewed favorably, while those of one's own cultural heritage are viewed with disdain. To make sense of this stage and others requires an understanding of the dominant-subordinate relationship between two different cultures and the concept of "cultural racism" (D. W. Sue & Sue, 1990). Each stage represents a part of the development that oppressed people experience as they struggle to understand themselves in terms of their own culture, the dominant culture, and the oppressive relationship between the two. In counseling, a minority client at the conformity stage may prefer a White counselor, while one at the resistance and immersion stage (characterized by a focus on White racism as the problem) might prefer a counselor of his or her own race. Minority-identity-development models hold much promise for improving the delivery of culturally appropriate mental health services to racial/ethnic minorities.

White Identity Development

Within the last few years, an increasing number of multicultural counseling scholars have turned their attention to studying what has become known as "White identity development" (Hardiman, 1982; Helms, 1984; 1990; Rowe et al., 1994; Sabnani, Ponterotto, & Borodovsky, 1991). Most of these models seem to share some common assumptions. D. W. Sue and Sue (1990) state:

First, racism is a basic and integral part of U.S. life and permeates all aspects of our culture and institutions. Second, Whites are socialized into U.S. society and, therefore, inherit the biases, stereotypes, and racist attitudes, beliefs, and behaviors of the society. In other words, all Whites are racist whether knowingly or unknowingly. Third, how Whites perceive themselves as racial beings seems to follow an identifiable sequence that can be called stages. Fourth, the stage of White racial identity development in a cross-cultural encounter (counseling minorities, counselor training, etc.) affects the process and outcome of an interracial relationship. Last, the most desirable stage is the one where the White person not only accepts his/her Whiteness, but defines it in a nondefensive and nonracist manner. (p. 113)

Like their minority counterparts, a White counselor at the conformity stage (belief in the superiority of White culture over all others) may do great damage to culturally different clients. Part of effective counselor training would consist of an attempt to move the White counselor from an ethnocentric-oppressive bias to a nonracist self-affirming White identity. The conclusion we can draw is fairly straightforward. It is important to understand not only minority identity development but the racial and cultural identity of the White counselor as well.

Culturally Appropriate Intervention Strategies

In the field of counseling, increasing importance is being placed upon how culture, race, ethnicity, and gender affect communication styles (Ivey, 1981, 1986; Ivey et al., 1993; D. W. Sue, 1977, 1981, 1991; D. W. Sue & Sue, 1990). A body of literature suggests that counseling style is influenced by communication style, which in turn is affected by worldviews. Different theories of counseling represent different worldviews and may greatly influence the counseling styles and strategies used by the helping professional. Process and content analysis of counseling sessions employing strategies such as Rogerian, rational emotive, and gestalt reveal major counseling style differences generally consistent with their theoretical orientations (Dolliver, Williams & Gold, 1980; Edwards, Boulet, Mahrer, Chagnon, & Mook, 1982; Lee & Uhlemann, 1984; Meara, Pepinsky, Shannon & Murray, 1981; Weinrach, 1986).

Ivey (1981, 1986) has repeatedly emphasized the fact that different theories of counseling are concerned with generating different constructs, sentences, and helping responses. Because counseling and psychotherapy are predominantly White middle-class activities, clients who differ in race, culture, ethnicity, and class may be placed at a disadvantage in the helping relationship. The process of counseling may be antagonistic to the cultural styles of helping deemed appropriate for that particular group. For example, some studies suggest that certain groups of Asian Americans, African Americans, American Indians, and Hispanic Americans may prefer more active counseling approaches than nonactive ones (Atkinson, Maruyama, & Matsui, 1978; Berman, 1979; Dauphinais, Dauphinais, & Rowe, 1981; Nwachuku & Ivey, 1991; Ruiz & Ruiz, 1983). Traditional approaches that utilize a much more nondirective and egalitarian relationship may be experienced negatively by the culturally different client. As a result, minority clients may perceive the session as unhelpful and may prematurely terminate (S. Sue, Allen, & Conaway, 1975; S. Sue & McKinney, 1975; S. Sue, McKinney, Allen, & Hall, 1974). Multicultural specialists are beginning to realize the need for developing culturally appropriate intervention strategies in working with racial/ethnic minority clients and groups.

Systems Intervention Roles

One of the strongest criticisms of counseling approaches has been aimed at the traditional role of the counselor itself (Atkinson, Morten, & Sue, 1993; Atkinson, Thompson, & Grant, 1993). While some have argued that conventional counseling can be effective across cultural groups (Pedersen, 1985), others are critical for a number of reasons (Katz, 1985; Parham & McDavis, 1987; Smith, 1985; D. W. Sue & Sue, 1990). First, conventional counseling focuses upon the individual and may perceive the problem as residing in the person rather than in the oppressive environment. Attempting to change the person to

adjust to the sick environment is to blame the victim. Second, conventional counseling roles concentrate on the development of one-to-one interpersonal skills (Grencavage & Norcross, 1990; Korchin, 1976). It is characterized by a helping professional sitting in an office engaging in verbal self-exploration of the client. Clients are asked to take responsibility for their own actions, and all treatment is confined to an office setting. Few counselors have been trained to change systems. Thus, if the problem resides in oppressive environmental conditions, counselors are ill-prepared to act as social or environmental change agents. Third, the use of helping approaches indigenous to the client's ancestral culture receives minimal study in counselor education or counseling psychology programs. Even the study of multiculturalism in the United States is predominantly Eurocentric; Afrocentric and Asian-centric perspectives are all but missing (D. W. Sue & Sue, 1990).

BASIC ASSUMPTIONS IN A THEORY OF MCT

The literature on MCT makes clear that the field is on the verge of what Kuhn (1970) has referred to as a major paradigm shift. Such a shift occurs when (a) ideas, concepts, and data cannot be adequately accounted for by the science and theory of the day and (b) when a new and competing perspective better accommodates the existing data. This chapter's review of cultural biases inherent in the theories, processes, and goals of counseling and psychotherapy points out the inadequacy of current models; and the competing multicultural perspective seems better positioned to accommodate the existing data. Pederson (1991) has coined the phrase "multiculturalism as a fourth force in counseling," which recognizes that a major change is in the works for the profession. It is probably accurate to say that this change will be one of the most important ones to occur in this century and is likely to be quite revolutionary. It will alter how we think about the nature of reality and how we define counseling, force us to reconceptualize our theories, and broaden our definition of what constitutes helping strategies. Multiculturalism will have a major impact upon the education, training, and practice of mental health professionals. It also points to a new direction toward which research will be steered, and it may require different research strategies.

While no one has developed a generally accepted or overarching theory of MCT, there are numerous perspectives that seem to possess some common assumptions and propositions. Many of these perspectives have already been reviewed, and it appears that a developed theory of MCT is not far off. The development of a new perspective (paradigm shift) from which to view the field of counseling will occur only when MCT establishes itself as a viable theoretical perspective. A review of the existing literature on MCT suggests some propositions most likely to be incorporated into such a theory. The remaining portion of this chapter will outline propositions based more upon assumptions than axioms (truths).

Proposition 1

MCT is a metatheory of counseling and psychotherapy. It is a theory about theories and offers an organizational framework for understanding the numerous helping approaches that humankind has developed. It recognizes that theories of counseling and psychotherapy developed in the Western world and those indigenous helping models intrinsic to other non-Western cultures are neither inherently right or wrong or good or bad. Each theory represents a different worldview.

As mentioned earlier, the centrality of culture in all theories of counseling and psychotherapy needs to be acknowledged and made explicit. Criticisms about counseling and psychotherapy being culture bound would become less compelling and problematic once the cultural assumptions were stated. For example, a counselor with a rational-emotive counseling orientation would realize that the emphasis on "individual" rational decision making might be inappropriate with a Chinese client who may have a collectivist approach to solving life problems.

MCT uses the theoretical approach most consistent with the experiences and cultural perspectives of the client. In some cases it may be best to incorporate a psychoanalytic perspective. With one client it may mean a cognitive-behavioral perspective. And with yet another it may mean an organic-biological one. In most cases, however, it means a systematic integration of numerous theoretical concepts, in recognition of the complexity of the human condition. Part of the complexity is the realization that we are products of our environments (familial, social, cultural, and political). In situations where integration is not possible (concepts of the models are epistemologically conflicting), a synergetic formation of a new theory or model may be called for.

Proposition 2

MCT recognizes that both counselor and client identities are formed and embedded in multiple levels of experiences (individual, group, and universal) and contexts (individual, family, and cultural milieu). The totality and interrelationship of experiences and contexts must be the focus of treatment.

In simple terms, human beings possess three levels of identity. At the individual level, we are all unique. Because no two individuals share the same biology (even if they are identical twins) or experiences, no two individuals are ever the same. At the group level of identity, we share commonalities with others by virtue of membership in some reference group (race, culture, ethnicity, gender, religion, etc.). The universal level of identity suggests that we all belong to the species *Homo sapiens*. Like the Shakespearean character who asks, "When I cut myself, do I not bleed?" we all share many characteristics. Unfortunately, most forms of counseling and psychotherapy appear to focus on either the individual or universal level of identity to the exclusion of the group level. Two reasons seem to account for this fact: (a) counseling bias in theories that value the uniqueness or universal qualities of the human condition and (b) sociopolitical discomfort in recognizing group characteristics and differences (D. W. Sue, 1992; D. W. Sue & Sue, 1990). MCT recognizes the totality of the person's multiple identities and does not prefer one over the other.

Psychology has traditionally studied the individual as an iso-

lated entity, separate and apart from external influences (Ivey et al., 1993; D. W. Sue & Sue, 1990; Szapocznik & Kurtines, 1993). This orientation is being challenged because it fails to recognize the interaction between the person and the environment. One of these challenges is the contextualist movement, which simply states that behavior cannot be understood outside the context in which it occurs (Bronfenbrenner, 1986; Steenbarger, 1991; D. W. Sue, 1991b). The context includes not only the individual but the family and culture. The new contextualist paradigm being proposed is that working with the individual requires understanding of how the person is embedded in the family, which in turn requires understanding of how the family is affected by being embedded in a pluralistic (not a singular) culture (Szapocznik & Kurtines, 1993).

Proposition 3

Cultural identity development is a major determinant of both counselor and client attitudes toward the self, others of the same group, others of a different group, and others of the dominant group. These attitudes, which may be manifested in affective and behavioral dimensions, are strongly influenced not only by cultural variables but by the dynamics of a dominant-subordinate relationship among culturally different groups. The level or stage of racial/cultural identity will influence how clients and counselors define the problem and will dictate what they believe to be appropriate counseling goals and processes.

An understanding of the level of identity consciousness displayed by the culturally different client is crucial to the provision of appropriate mental health services. Models of cultural identity development make a strong case that not all members of a minority group are the same and that within-group differences may be moderated by many variables (Atkinson, Morten, & Sue, 1993). Among the more important ones is *minority status* in a society. Here we refer to the dominant-subordinate relationship between two different cultures, one of which is oppressed. As a result, counseling needs to acknowledge the importance of sociopolitical dynamics upon the experiences of culturally different groups in a society. The manifestation of so-called psychological problems may actually be a manifestation of oppression.

Likewise, the majority-group counselor is also embedded in his or her own culture and equally affected by the sociopolitical climate (Katz, 1985; D. W. Sue, 1977, 1978). White identity development theories stress, for example, that White counselors (members of the majority culture) need to deal with their concepts of Whiteness and examine their own biases and prejudices, as well as the roles they play in oppression. These roles include not only individual acts of bias and discrimination but also the overprivileged roles that are seemingly granted to Whites in our society (McIntosh, 1989). McIntosh states, "As a white person, I realized I had been taught about racism as something which puts others at a disadvantage, but had been taught not to see one of its corollary aspects, white privilege, which puts me at an advantage" (p. 8).

Several multicultural specialists have proposed either a stage model (Helms, 1984; Ponterotto, 1988; Sabnani, Ponterotto, & Borodovsky, 1991) or a social-learning model (Rowe et al., 1994) to explain how Whites define themselves as racial beings. They point out that the stage or level of White identity developed by the counselor will affect the process and outcome of the counseling encounter with a culturally different client. Helms (1990) presents a model of how the identity stages of a minority client and majority counselor may facilitate or hinder the growth of clients.

Proposition 4

MCT effectiveness is most likely enhanced when the counselor uses modalities and defines goals consistent with the life experiences/cultural values of the client. No one helping approach or intervention strategy is equally effective across all populations and life situations. The ultimate goal of multicultural counselor/therapist training is to expand the repertoire of helping responses available to the professional, regardless of theoretical orientation.

Helping is administered differently in different cultural groups and societies (Das, 1987; Lee et al., 1992). Eurocentric methods such as self-disclosure, nondirectiveness, and verbal participation for clients have been found to be antagonistic to many culturally different groups (LaFromboise, 1988; Ponterotto & Casas, 1991; D. W. Sue, 1977). It is not that these techniques or strategies are wrong or bad; rather, they are simply inappropriate and, when applied indiscriminately, can be constricting and oppressive. If counseling is intended to liberate individuals to the possibilities of life consistent with their culture, then helping styles need to be compatible with the experiences and values of the client.

It appears that the wider the repertoire of responses the counselor possesses, the better the helper is likely to be (Nwachuku & Ivey, 1991; D. W. Sue, 1990; D. W. Sue et al., 1992). Relying on a very narrow and limited number of skills in counseling restricts the effectiveness of counseling. Theories of counseling and psychotherapy have been shown to be differentially associated with characteristic responses. The work of Ivey and colleagues (Ivey, 1986, 1988; Ivey & Authier, 1978; Ivey et al., 1993) on the relationship of microskills and theoretical orientation of the counselor is compelling and convincing in this regard. Rogerians, for example, are likely to use predominantly attending skills, while those with a behavioral orientation will use many more influencing skills. While these skills may be inherently consistent with the worldview of the theory, what happens if the culturally different client does not share that view? A traditional Chinese American client who expects advice or suggestions from the counselor (perceived as a knowledgeable and "wise" expert) might find a more nondirective approach (withholding advice and suggestions) confusing and unhelpful. Termination of the relationship is highly probable, although the need for help is still present.

MCT advocates cultural flexibility in the helping process. It recognizes that we are all thinking, feeling, behaving, social, cultural, and political beings. Those counselors who are most

able to shift their counseling styles to meet the needs of their clients are in the best position to provide needed help. This concept has been labeled cultural intentionality by Ivey et al. (1993). They state:

> The person who acts with intentionality has a sense of capability. She or he can generate alternative behaviors in a given situation and "approach" a problem from different vantage points. The intentional, fully functioning individual is not bound to one course of action but can respond in the moment to changing life situations and look forward to longer-term goals. (p. 8)

Proposition 5

MCT stresses the importance of multiple helping roles developed by many culturally different groups and societies. These roles often involve not simply a one-to-one encounter aimed at remediation in the individual but involve larger social units, systems intervention, and prevention. The conventional roles of counseling and psychotherapy are seen as only one of many others available to the helping professional.

As indicated previously, increasing emphasis is being placed upon the need for counselors to adapt themselves to work within the client's culture rather than demanding that the culturally different adjust to the counselor's culture (Pedersen, 1986, 1988). With respect to racial/ethnic minorities in the United States, for example, counselors may be more effective if they leave their offices and meet a client in the client's environment (Atkinson, Morten, & Sue, 1993; Atkinson, Thompson, & Grant, 1993). Several important reasons dictate such an orientation.

First, conventional counseling roles may unintentionally reinforce the belief that the problem resides within the individual. When in reality the problem resides outside of the person (in the environment), we may become guilty of blaming the victim. A Latino client who may be unemployed and having difficulty finding a job may be blamed for his or her life circumstance when it may be due to discrimination or prejudice on the part of employers. An African American student who frequently gets into fights in school may be the victim of racist comments and attitudes from White peers. The fighting behavior may actually be a product of a pathological situation in the school system.

Second, if the basis of the client's troubles is located in the social structure or system, the most appropriate form of intervention may call for the counselor to change the environment, a role that calls for the counselor to become active in community and social programs. The counselor may be required to act as a change agent, consultant, teacher, or community worker.

Third, the traditional counseling role is one of remediation (Atkinson, Morten, & Sue, 1993; Katz, 1985). It tends to be reactive rather than proactive. Counselors who view the social system as a major contributor to problems of their clients would direct their energies toward prevention. As such the orientation is to change the social environment that oppresses.

Egan (1985) advocates that a counselor assume the role of a change agent, which he defines as someone "who plays an important part in designing, redesigning, running, renewing, or improving any system, subsystem, or program" (p. 12).

Fourth, movement into the client's environment has the additional advantage of allowing the counselor to observe directly the environmental factors that contribute to the client's dilemmas; direct observation promotes better understanding of the client and of what he or she believes is helpful, and it enhances the counselor-client relationship. The counselor comes to understand that helping roles have evolved within cultural contexts and that they are helpful because members of the culture believe in their efficacy. For example, it appears that the *curranderismo* (Mexican or Mexican American folk healer), practitioner of Santeria, acupuncturist or Tai Chi Chuan teacher, Sufis of Islamic countries, Alfas of Nigeria, and the Hakeem and Motwaas of Saudi Arabia are viewed by their respective cultures as legitimate healers dispensing potent forms of treatment (Das, 1987; Harner, 1990; Kakar, 1982; Lee et al., 1992).

Atkinson, Thompson, and Grant (1993) have proposed a three-dimensional model of counselor roles. The selection of an appropriate counseling role depends on three major variables: (a) locus of the problem (internal vs. external); (b) level of acculturation; and (c) counseling goals or objectives (remediation vs. prevention). From this conceptual framework they identify the following roles of importance to counseling: adviser, advocate, facilitator of indigenous support systems, facilitator of indigenous healing systems, consultant, change agent, counselor, and psychotherapist. No one role is considered more important than the others.

Proposition 6

Multicultural counselor competence involves the continual development of attitudes/beliefs, knowledges, and skills related to (a) awareness of own assumptions, values, and biases; (b) understanding of the worldview of the culturally different client; and (c) culturally appropriate intervention strategies and techniques.

The development of multicultural counseling competencies has been discussed and outlined in three major works (American Psychological Association, 1993; D. W. Sue et al., 1992; D. W. Sue et al., 1982). These competencies are highly linked to propositions 1–5. The following are characteristics associated with a culturally skilled counselor:

1. Culturally skilled counselors are actively in the process of becoming aware of their own biases, preconceived notions, and assumptions about human behavior, values, and personal limitations. They understand their own worldviews, how they are the products of their cultural conditioning, and how their cultural conditioning may be reflected in their counseling and work with racial/ethnic minorities.
2. Culturally skilled counselors actively attempt to understand

the worldviews of their culturally different clients without negative judgments.
3. Culturally skilled counselors are in the process of actively developing and practicing appropriate, relevant, and sensitive intervention strategies/skills in working with their culturally different clients.

In addition to these three characteristics, the Association of Multicultural Counseling and Development Professional Standards Committee identified three dimensions of cultural competency: (a) beliefs/attitudes; (b) knowledges; and (c) skills. The first involves attitudes and beliefs of counselors with respect to racial/ethnic minorities, the need to check stereotypes and biases and to develop a positive orientation toward multiculturalism. The second recognizes that counselors need thorough understanding of their own worldviews and specific knowledge of the cultural groups with which they work. The last dimension involves the acquisition of specific skills (intervention techniques and strategies) needed to work effectively with minority groups.

Thus far, 31 competencies have been identified by the Association of Multicultural Counseling and Development (D. W. Sue et al., 1992). Because space does not allow for an elaboration of them, only a brief description will be given here.

Using their description of the culturally skilled counselor and the dimensions of cultural competency, D. W. Sue et al. (1993) developed a 3 (characteristics) × 3 (dimensions) matrix in which to organize and develop the competencies. For example, the characteristics (a) counselor awareness, (b) understanding of culturally different clients' worldviews, and (c) developing culturally appropriate intervention strategies would each be described in three dimensions: (a) belief/attitudes; (b) knowledges; and (c) skills. A total of 9 competency areas were identified. The areas were further analyzed and specific competencies were developed for each of the 9 divisions. Some examples of the 31 competency statements that were finalized are given below.

1. "Culturally skilled counselors have moved from being culturally unaware to being aware and sensitive to his/her own cultural heritage and to valuing and respecting differences" (p. 84).
2. "Culturally skilled counselors understand and have knowledge about sociopolitical influences that impinge upon the life of racial/ethnic minorities. Immigration issues, poverty, racism, stereotyping, and powerlessness all leave major scars which may influence the counseling process" (pp. 85–86).
3. "Culturally skilled counselors are able to exercise institutional intervention skills on behalf of their clients. They can help clients determine whether a 'problem' stems from racism or bias in others (the concept of healthy paranoia) so that clients do not inappropriately personalize problems" (p. 87).

It is important to note that these competencies and their earlier derivatives have been incorporated into instruments attempting to measure cross-cultural counseling competencies: the Cross-Cultural Counseling Inventory—Revised (LaFromboise, Coleman, & Hernandez, 1991), Multicultural Counseling Awareness Scale—Form B: Revised Self Assessment (Ponterotto, Sanchez, & Magids, 1991), Multicultural Counseling Inventory (Sodowsky, Taffe, Gutkin, & Wise, 1994), and the Multicultural Awareness-Knowledge-and-Skills Survey (D'Andrea, Daniels, & Heck, 1991). Several recent studies (Ottavi, Pope-Davis, & Dings, 1994; Sodowsky et al., 1994) are impressive in documenting the existence of these competency factors.

RESEARCH IMPLICATIONS

Any theory of counseling, including MCT theory, is ultimately linked to research findings that either confirm or disconfirm its assumptions and basic tenets. This review of counseling research casts doubts upon the adequacy of current models developed by primarily Eurocentic-trained psychologists either to explain, predict, or treat the mental health problems of the diversity of peoples in this world. Thus, it speaks strongly to the development of a more inclusive model of helping. A theory of MCT has clear implications for research strategies (methodology and techniques) and focus. The development of MCT theory points to promising but previously neglected areas for future research.

First, research has traditionally emphasized a cause-effect orientation based upon symbolic logic and empiricism (Goldman, 1976; Ponterotto & Casas, 1991; D. W. Sue & Sue, 1990). The reductionistic and quantitative approach to asking and answering questions so valued by the counseling profession is often not amenable to the complex study of the human condition. Furthermore, many cultures value a more holistic and experiential approach in studying human interactions. Increasingly, multicultural researchers are recognizing the importance of such matters and advocating the use of qualitative methodology or "alternative research paradigms" to investigate counseling theory and practice (Goldman, 1989; Ponterotto & Casas, 1991). They have described qualitative research as (a) descriptive in nature; (b) inductive; (c) holistic; (d) flexible; and (e) clinically significant (see detailed discussion in Ponterotto & Casas, 1991). It appears that the counseling profession would benefit greatly from using the following qualitative research strategies borrowed from anthropology and sociology: participant observation, in-depth interviewing, and life histories and case studies. The point to keep in mind is that both quantitative and qualitative research have their own strengths and limitations. One is not better than the other, but they should complement one another.

Second, MCT theory suggests that traditional Eurocentric theories of counseling and psychotherapy are culture bound and represent worldviews that are different from those of non-European cultures. Adopting a theory of helping inevitably ties the observers to the values and assumptions implicit in the model. When raised and socialized in the particular culture as well, the researcher may possess a biased perspective of cultural differences.

This matter was considered of sufficient importance that *The Counseling Psychologist,* the official publication of the Division of Counseling Psychology, ran a special issue entitled "White American Researchers and Multicultural Counseling" (Mio & Iwamasa, 1993). In a series of persuasive articles, multicultural specialists argued that:

1. The contributions of minority professionals doing cross-cultural counseling research are often ignored and given less importance than those of their White counterparts (Ivey, 1993; Parham, 1993; Ponterotto, 1993).
2. Research has presented a picture of racial/ethnic minorities as deviant and pathological (Casas & San Miguel, 1993; D. W. Sue, 1993). This has led to the development of genetic inferiority models, cultural deficit models, or cultural deficiency models applied to racial minorities.
3. By far the most powerful statement was the need for White researchers to begin considering how their own unresolved issues of race/ethnicity color their cross-cultural perceptions (Helms, 1993; Ponterotto, 1993).

Helms (1993) believes that much of the cross-cultural research now in existence is culturally biased. She states, "To the extent that White researchers have been the primary gatekeepers of cross-cultural research (e.g. journal editors, dissertation advisers), then it is possible that those with restricted worldviews encourage constricted study of cultural diversity issues" (p. 242).

It is important to note that Helms believes many minority researchers are also victims of primarily Western European training. They can also be culturally encapsulated and can inherit the biases of the larger society. It appears that individuals (majority and minority) conducting research on multicultural areas need to understand themselves as racial/cultural beings, and the possible biases, stereotypes, and assumptions about human behavior they possess (D. W. Sue, 1993).

Last, it is important to echo again the call for greater consideration and, indeed, research into indigenous models of counseling and mental health. Non-Western models of helping are unfamiliar to most Western-trained counselors and researchers. There is, therefore, a huge void in our knowledge base. Ironically, a theory of multicultural counseling and psychotherapy that recognizes culture specificity (emic) has the greatest chance of being universal (etic).

CONCLUSIONS

We are experiencing a revolution the counseling and educational fields. It is clear that multiculturalism can no longer be treated as an ancillary; rather, it is an integral part of counseling. The challenge before us is not an easy one, for it means revising our theories and expanding our definitions of the helping process. Many mental health scholars continue to hold Eurocentric theories of counseling and psychotherapy as "sacred cows" that can be universally applied. Many of them continue to be ethnocentric and culture bound. Many may resist change because it threatens the very foundations of their belief systems and may mean a redistribution of power in our society. Yet, to ignore the social reality of multiculturalism is to deny reality itself. If we are to provide equal access and opportunities for all, then the recognition of cultural diversity is essential to our survival.

Likewise, the survival of the counseling profession depends on its ability to respond to the challenge of providing appropriate mental health services to a culturally diverse population.

The MCT movement offers hope in that direction. The next step is for us to begin constructing a theory of MCT. This chapter has outlined six propositions that seem to form the foundations of such an endeavor. Future work needs to delineate basic tenets from each proposition and to translate them into a working theory of MCT.

References

American Psychological Association. (1993). Guidelines for providers of psychological services to ethnic, linguistic, and culturally diverse populations. *American Psychologist, 48,* 45–48.

Atkinson, D. R. (1983). Ethnic similarity in counseling psychology: A review of research. *Counseling Psychologist, 22,* 79–92.

Atkinson, D. R., Maruyama, M., & Matsui, S. (1978). The effects of counselor race and counseling approach on Asian American's perceptions of counselor credibility and utility. *Journal of Counseling Psychology, 25,* 76–83.

Atkinson, D. R., Morten, G., & Sue, D. W. (1993). *Counseling American minorities.* Dubuque, IA: Brown & Benchmark.

Atkinson, D. R., Thompson, C. E., & Grant, S. K. (1993). A three-dimensional model for counseling racial/ethnic minorities. *Counseling Psychologist, 21,* 257–277.

Banks, J. A. (1993). Multicultural education: Characteristics and goals. In J. A. Banks & C. A. McGee Banks (Eds.), *Multicultural education* (2nd ed., pp. 3–28). Boston: Allyn and Bacon.

Beck, A. (1976). *Cognitive therapy and the emotional disorders.* New York: International Universities Press.

Beck, A. (1985). Cognitive therapy, behavior therapy, psychoanalysis, and pharmacology: A cognitive continuum. In M. Mahoney & A. Freeman (Eds.), *Cognition and psychotherapy* (pp. 325–347). New York: Plenum.

Berman, J. (1979). Counseling skills used by Black and White male and female counselors. *Journal of Counseling Psychology, 26,* 81–84.

Brammer, L. M., & Shostrom, E. (1984). *Therapeutic psychology.* Englewood Cliffs, NJ: Prentice-Hall.

Bronfenbrenner, U. (1986). The ecology of the family as a context for human development. *Developmental Psychology, 22,* 723–742.

Casas, J. M. (1984). Policy, training and research in counseling psychology: The racial/ethnic minority perspective. In S. D. Brown & R. Lent (Eds.), *Handbook of counseling psychology* (pp. 785–831). New York: Wiley.

Casas, J. M. (1985). A reflection on the status of racial/ethnic minority research. *Counseling Psychologist, 13,* 581–598.

Casas, J. M., & San Miguel, S. (1993). Beyond questions and discussions, there is a need for action: A response to Mio and Iwamasa. *Counseling Psychologist, 21,* 233–239.

Comas-Diaz, L. (1990). Hispanic Latino communities: Psychological implications. *Journal of Training and Practice in Professional Psychology, 1,* 14–35.

Cross, W. E. (1971). The Negro-to-Black conversion experience: Toward a psychology of Black liberation. *Black World, 20,* 13–27.

Cross, W. E. (1978). The Cross and Thomas models of psychological nigrescence. *Journal of Black Psychology, 5,* 13–19.

Cross, W. E. (1987). A two-factor theory of Black identity: Implications for the study of identity development in minority children. In J. S. Phinney & M. J. Rotheram (Eds.), *Children's ethnic socialization: Pluralism and development* (pp. 117–133). Newbury Park, CA: Sage.

Cross, W. E. (1989). Nigrescence: A nondiaphanous phenomena. *Counseling Psychologist, 17,* 273–276.

Cross, W. E. (1991). *Shades of Black: Diversity in African American identity.* Philadelphia: Temple University Press.

D'Andrea, M., Daniels, J., & Heck, R. (1991). Evaluating the impact of multicultural training. *Journal of Counseling and Development, 70,* 143–150.

Das, A. K. (1987). Indigenous models of therapy in traditional Asian societies. *Journal of Multicultural Counseling and Development, 15,* 25–37.

Dauphinais, R., Dauphinais, L., & Rowe, W. (1981). Effects of race and communication style on Indian perceptions of counselor effectiveness. *Counselor Education and Supervision, 21,* 72–80.

Dolliver, R. H., Williams, E. L., & Gold, D. C. (1980). The art of gestalt therapy or: What are you doing with your feet now? *Psychotherapy: Theory, Research and Practice, 17,* 136–142.

Edwards, H. P., Boulet, D. B., Mahrer, A. R., Chagnon, G. J., Mook, B. (1982). Carl Rogers during initial interviews: A moderate and consistent therapist. *Journal of Counseling Psychology, 29,* 14–18.

Egan, G. (1985). *Change agent skills in helping and human service settings.* Monterey, CA: Brooks/Cole.

Ellis, A. (1962). *Reason and emotion in psychotherapy.* New York: Stuart.

Ellis, A. (1989). Rational-emotive therapy. In R. J. Corsini & D. Weddings (Eds.), *Current psychotherapies* (pp. 197–238). Itasca, IL: F. E. Peacock.

Franklin, J. H. (1988). A historical note on Black families. In H. P. McAdoo (Ed.), *Black families* (pp. 23–26). Newbury Park, CA: Sage.

Goldman, L. (1976). A revolution in counseling research. *Journal of Counseling Psychology, 23,* 543–552.

Goldman, L. (1989). Moving counseling research into the 21st century. *Counseling Psychologist, 17,* 81–85.

Grencavage, L. M., & Norcross, J. C. (1990). Where are the commonalities among the therapeutic common factors? *Professional Psychology: Research and Practice, 21,* 372–378.

Grier, W., & Cobbs, P. (1968). *Black rage.* New York: Basic Books.

Grier, W., & Cobbs, P. (1971). *The Jesus bag.* San Francisco: McGraw-Hill.

Hardiman, R. (1982). White identity development: A process-oriented model for describing the racial consciousness of White Americans. *Dissertation Abstracts International, 43,* 104A. (University Microfilms No. 82-10330)

Harner, M. (1990). *The way of the shaman.* San Francisco: Harper and Row.

Heath, A. E., Neimever, G. J., & Pedersen, P. B. (1988). The future of cross-cultural counseling: A Delphi poll. *Journal of Counseling and Development, 67,* 27–30.

Helms, J. E. (1984). Toward a theoretical model of the effects of race on counseling: A Black and White model. *Counseling Psychologist, 12,* 153–165.

Helms, J. E. (1986). Expanding racial identity theory to cover counseling process. *Journal of Counseling Psychology, 33,* 62–64.

Helms, J. E. (1990). *Black and White racial identity: Theory, research, and practice.* New York: Greenwood Press.

Helms, J. E. (1993). I also said, "White racial identity influences White researchers." *Counseling Psychologist, 21,* 240–243.

Ho, H. K. (1987). *Family therapy with ethnic minorities.* Newbury Park, CA: Sage.

Inclan, J. (1985). Variations in value orientations in mental health work with Puerto Ricans. *Psychotherapy, 22,* 324–334.

Ivey, A. E. (1981). Counseling and psychotherapy. *Counseling Psychologist, 9*(2), 81–98.

Ivey, A. E. (1986). *Developmental therapy.* San Francisco: Jossey-Bass.

Ivey, A. E. (1988). *Intentional interviewing and counseling.* Pacific Grove, CA: Brooks/Cole.

Ivey, A. E. (1993). On the need for reconstruction of our present practice of counseling and psychotherapy. *Counseling Psychologist, 21,* 225–228.

Ivey, A. E., & Authier, J. (1978). *Microcounseling: Innovations in interviewing training.* Springfield, IL: Charles C. Thomas.

Ivey, A. E., Ivey, M. B. & Simek-Morgan, L. (1993). *Counseling and psychotherapy: A multicultural perspective.* Boston: Allyn and Bacon.

Jackson, B. (1975). Black identity development. *Journal of Educational Diversity, 2,* 19–25.

Johnston, W. B., & Packer, A. H. (1987). *Workforce 2000: Work and workers for the twenty-first century.* Indianapolis, IN: Hudson Institute.

Kakar, S. (1982). *Shamans, mystics, and doctors: A psychological inquiry into India and its healing traditions.* New York: Knopf.

Katz, J. (1985). The sociopolitical nature of counseling. *The Counseling Psychologist, 13,* 615–624.

Kluckhohn, F. R., & Strodtbeck, F. L. (1961). *Variations in value orientations.* Evanston, IL: Row, Peterson, & Co.

Korchin, S. J. (1976). *Modern clinical psychology.* New York: Basic Books.

Kuhn, T. S. (1970). *The structure of scientific revolutions* (2nd ed.). Chicago: University of Chicago Press.

LaFromboise, T. D. (1988). American Indian mental health policy. *American Psychologist, 43,* 388–397.

LaFromboise, T. D., Coleman, H., & Hernandez, A. (1991). Development and factor structure of the cross-cultural counseling inventory—revised. *Professional Psychology: Research and Practice, 22,* 380–388.

Lazarus, A. A. (1967). In support of technical eclecticism. *Psychological Reports, 21,* 415–416.

Lazarus, A. A. (Ed.). (1976). *Multimodal behavior therapy.* New York: Springer.

Lazarus, A. A. (1984). Multimodal therapy. In R. J. Corsini (Ed.), *Current psychotherapies* (pp. 508–544). Itasca, IL: F. E. Peacock.

Lee, C. C., Oh, M. Y., & Mountcastle, A. R. (1992). Indigenous models of helping in nonwestern countries: Implications for multicultural counseling. *Journal of Multicultural Counseling and Development, 20,* 1–10.

Lee, D. Y., & Uhlemann, M. R. (1984). Comparison of verbal responses of Rogers, Shostrom, and Lazarus. *Journal of Counseling Psychology, 32,* 91–94.

Leong, F. T. (1986). Counseling and psychotherapy with Asian-Americans: Review of literature. *Journal of Counseling Psychology, 33,* 196–206.

Locke, D. C. (1992). *Increasing multicultural understanding.* Newbury Park, CA: Sage.

Lum, R. G. (1982). Mental health attitudes and opinions of Chinese. In E. E. Jones & S. J. Korchin (Eds.), *Minority mental health* (pp. 165–189). New York: Praeger.

McGoldrick, M., Pearce, J., & Giordano, J. (Eds.). (1982). *Ethnicity and family therapy.* New York: Guilford Press.

McIntosh, P. (1989, July/August). White privilege: Unpacking the invisible knapsack. *Peace and Freedom,* pp. 8–10.

Meara, N. M., Pepinsky, H. B., Shannon, J. W., & Murray, W. A. (1981). Semantic communication and expectations for counseling across three theoretical orientations. *Journal of Counseling Psychology, 28,* 110–118.

Meichenbaum, D. (1985). *Stress inoculation training.* New York: Pergamon.

Mio, J. S., & Iwamasa, G. (1993). To do, or not to do: That is the question for White cross-cultural researchers. *Counseling Psychologist, 21,* 197–212.

Norcross, J. C., & Prochaska, J. O. (1988). A study of eclectic (and integrative) views revisited. *Professional Psychology, 19,* 170–174.

Nwachuku, U., & Ivey, A. (1991). Culture specific counseling: An alternative approach. *Journal of Counseling and Development, 70,* 106–111.

Ottavi, T. M., Pope-Davis, D. B., & Dings, J. G. (1994). Relationship between White racial identity attitudes and self-reported multicultural counseling competencies. *Journal of Counseling Psychology, 41,* 149–154.

Parham, T. A. (1989). Cycles of psychological nigrescence. *Counseling Psychologist, 17,* 187–226.

Parham, T. A. (1993). White researchers conducting multicultural counseling research: Can their efforts be "mo betta"? *Counseling Psychologist, 21,* 250–256.

Parham, T. A., & Helms, J. E. (1981). The influence of Black students' racial attitudes on preferences for counselor's race. *Journal of Counseling Psychology, 28,* 250–257.

Parham, T. A., & McDavis, R. J. (1987). Black men and endangered species: Who's really pulling the trigger? *Journal of Counseling and Development, 66,* 24–27.

Pedersen, P. B. (1985). *Handbook of cross-cultural counseling and therapy.* Westport, CT: Greenwood Press.

Pedersen, P. B. (1986). The cultural role of conceptual and contextual support systems in counseling. *Journal of the American Mental Health Counselor's Association, 8,* 35–42.

Pedersen, P. B. (1987). Ten frequent assumptions of cultural bias in counseling. *Journal of Multicultural Counseling and Development, 15,* 16–24.

Pederson, P. B. (1988). *A handbook for developing multicultural awareness.* Alexandria, VA: American Association for Counseling and Development.

Pedersen, P. B. (Ed.). (1991). Multiculturalism as a fourth force in counseling [Special issue]. *Journal of Counseling and Development, 70.*

Ponterotto, J. G. (1988). Racial/ethnic minority research in the *Journal of Counseling Psychology:* A content analysis and methodological critique. *Journal of Counseling Psychology, 53,* 410–418.

Ponterotto, J. G. (1993). White racial identity and the counseling professional. *Counseling Psychologist, 21,* 213–217.

Ponterotto, J. G., & Casas, J. M. (1991). *Handbook of racial/ethnic minority counseling research.* Springfield, IL: Charles C. Thomas.

Ponterotto, J. G., & Sabnani, H. B. (1989). "Classics" in multicultural counseling: A systematic five-year content analysis. *Journal of Multicultural Counseling and Development, 17,* 23–37.

Ponterotto, J. G., Sanchez, C. M., & Magids, D. M. (1991, August). *Initial development and validation of the Multicultural Counseling Awareness Scale (MCAS).* Paper presented at the annual meeting of the American Psychological Association, San Francisco.

Red Horse, J. (1983). Indian family values and experiences. In G. J. Powell, J. Yamamoto, A. Romero, & K. A. Morales (Eds.), *The psychosocial development of minority group children* (pp. 258–272). New York: Bruner/Mazel.

Reisman, J. (1971). *Toward the integration of psychotherapy.* New York: Wiley.

Ridley, C. R. (1984). Clinical treatment of the nondisclosing Black client. *American Psychologist, 39,* 1234–1244.

Rowe, W., Bennett, S., & Atkinson, D. R. (1994). White racial identity consciousness: A social learning analysis. *Counseling Psychologist, 22*(1), 129–146.

Ruiz, P., & Ruiz, P. P. (1983). Treatment compliance among Hispanics. *Journal of Operational Psychiatry, 14,* 112–114.

Sabnani, H. B., Ponterotto, J. G., & Borodovsky, L. G. (1991). White racial identity development and cross-cultural counselor training. *Counseling Psychologist, 19,* 76–102.

Schofield, W. (1964). *Psychotherapy: The purchase of friendship.* Englewood Cliffs, NJ: Prentice-Hall.

Smith, E. M. J. (1985). Ethnic minorities: Life stress, social support, and mental health issues. *Counseling Psychologist, 13,* 537–579.

Sodowsky, G. R., Taffe, R. C., Gutkin, T. B., & Wise, S. L. (1994). Development of the multicultural counseling inventory: A self-report measure of multicultural competencies. *Journal of Counseling Psychology, 41,* 137–148.

Spiegel, J., & Papajohn, J. (1983). *Final report: Training program on ethnicity and mental health.* Waltham, MA: The Florence Heller School, Brandeis University.

Steenbarger, B. (1991). Contextualism in counseling. *Journal for Counseling and Development, 70,* 288–299.

Sue, D., Sue, D. W., & Sue, S. (1994). *Understanding abnormal behavior* (4th ed.). Boston: Houghton-Mifflin.

Sue, D. W. (1977). Barriers to effective cross-cultural counseling. *Journal of Counseling Psychology, 24,* 420–429.

Sue, D. W. (1978). Eliminating cultural oppression in counseling: Toward a general theory. *Journal of Counseling Psychology, 25,* 419–428.

Sue, D. W. (1990). Culture specific techniques in counseling: A conceptual framework. *Professional Psychology, 21,* 424–433.

Sue, D. W. (1991a). A conceptual model for cultural diversity training. *Journal of Counseling and Development, 70,* 99–105.

Sue, D. W. (1991b). A diversity perspective on contextualism. *Journalism of Counseling and Development, 70,* 300–301.

Sue, D. W. (1992). The challenge of multiculturalism: The road less traveled. *American Counselor, 1,* 7–14.

Sue, D. W. (1993). Confronting ourselves: The White and racial/ethnic minority researcher. *Counseling Psychologist, 21,* 244–249.

Sue, D. W., Arrendondo, P., McDavis, R. J. (1992). Multicultural competencies/standards: A pressing need. *Journal of Counseling and Development, 70,* 477–486.

Sue, D. W., Bernier, J. B., Durran, M., Feinberg, L., Pedersen, P., Smith, E., & Vasquez-Nuttall, E. (1982). Position paper: Cross-cultural counseling competencies. *Counseling Psychologist, 10,* 45–52.

Sue, D. W. & Sue, D. (1990). *Counseling the culturally different: Theory and practice.* New York: Wiley.

Sue, S., Allen, D., & Conaway, L. (1975). The responsiveness and equality of mental health care to Chicanos and Native Americans. *American Journal of Community Psychology, 45,* 111–118.

Sue, S., & McKinney, H. (1975). Asian Americans in the community mental health care system. *American Journal of Orthopsychiatry, 45,* 11–118.

Sue, S., McKinney, H., Allen, D., & Hall, J. (1974). Delivery of community health services to Black and White clients. *Journal of Consulting Psychology, 42,* 794–801.

Szapocznik, J., & Kurtines, W. M. (1993). Family psychology and cultural diversity. *American Psychologist, 48,* 400–407.

Thomas, M. B., & Dansby, P. G. (1985). Black clients: Family structures, therapeutic issues, and strengths. *Psychotherapy, 22,* 398–407.

U.S. Census Bureau (1990). *Statistical abstract of the United States: 1990.* Washington, DC: U.S. Government Printing Office.

Weinrach, S. G. (1986). Ellis and Gloria: Positive or negative model? *Psychotherapy, 23,* 642–647.

White, J. L., & Parham, T. A. (1990). *The psychology of Blacks.* Englewood Cliffs, NJ: Prentice-Hall.

Part
·X·

HIGHER EDUCATION

• 38 •

RESEARCH ON RACIAL ISSUES IN AMERICAN HIGHER EDUCATION

Christine I. Bennett

INDIANA UNIVERSITY

This review of racial issues in American higher education identifies the quest for community amid diversity as the major challenge facing colleges and universities today. This quest is evident in the heated controversy over multiculturalism in the curriculum, in the rise of racial incidents on campuses across the country, and in the declining percentages of minority high school graduates who enter college, even as our population becomes more ethnically diverse.

The literature reviewed for this chapter is organized into three parts: (a) the demographics of access and equity in higher education; (b) the legacy of racism in higher education; and (c) the movement toward democratic or integrated pluralism in higher education. Each segment provides evidence from research and scholarly writing that illustrates complexities and crises that must be considered in efforts to create communities amid diversity on college campuses. The chapter concludes with a possible agenda for future research.

THE DEMOGRAPHICS OF ACCESS AND EQUITY IN HIGHER EDUCATION

A review of reports on educational attainment among African Americans, American Indians, Asian Americans, and Hispanics is limited by several factors. Researchers lack a national database that is representative of American Indians, Asian Americans, and Hispanics; reports ignore diversity such as various socioeconomic backgrounds and regions within the various ethnic groups; and findings lead to contradictory conclusions when trends are reported in terms of college enrollments, the actual head counts provided by colleges and universities each fall, rather than college participation rates, the percentage of a given age group that is currently enrolled in

college or has attended for one or more years (Carter & Wilson, 1991). Despite these limitations, clear trends can be identified.

Projections based on U.S. census data estimate that, by the turn of the century, 33% of the school-age population will come from ethnic minority backgrounds—the African Americans, Hispanics, Native Americans, and Asian Americans who are emerging as "one-third of the nation" (Commission on Minority Participation in Education and American Life, 1988). These changing demographics have enhanced the racial and cultural diversity of the nation's pool of potential college and university students. Despite this potential, and after dramatic progress in the 1970s, the college participation rates of ethnic minorities are now declining, despite increases in college enrollments.

Enrollment trends are revealed in Table 38–1, showing undergraduate enrollments in 1976, 1980, 1984, and 1991. Actual enrollments grew for all ethnic groups between 1976 and 1991. The increases were most dramatic for Asians and Hispanics. However, as shown in Table 38–2, the trends look quite different when expressed in proportion rather than actual numbers. Based upon the 18- to 24-year-old age cohorts in 1976, 1984, and 1989, Table 38–2 reports the number and percentage of high school graduates, the number and participation rate of high school graduates in college, and the ever-enrolled-in-college rates for high school graduates between the ages of 18 and 24. The figures are shown by race/ethnicity and sex for African Americans, Hispanics, and Whites.

High School Graduation and Drop-out Rates

The traditional college-going cohort of 18- to 24-year-olds decreased by nearly 4 million students between 1984 and 1992. The number of high school graduates declined by about 3 million, although the high school completion rate remained steady with 84.0% of females and 80.0% of males graduating in

TABLE 38–1. Undergraduate Enrollment in Higher Education by Race and Ethnicity: 1976, 1980, 1984, and 1991

	All Students	White	Total Minority	Asian[a]	Black	Hispanic	Native[b] American
Fall 1976	8,432,240	6,899,743	1,402,487	152,533	865,147	323,540	61,267
Fall 1980	9,262,820	7,465,722	1,606,192	214,989	932,055	390,440	68,708
Fall 1984	9,063,178	7,293,747	1,579,267	284,897	830,986	399,333	64,051
Fall 1991	12,439,000	9,508,000	NA	559,000	1,220,000	804,000	106,000
Percent Change							
1976–1980	9.9	8.2	14.5	40.9	7.7	20.7	12.1
1980–1984	−2.2	−2.3	−1.7	32.5	−10.8	2.3	−6.8
1990–1991	3.9	2.4	NA	11.2	−7.1	10.7	10.7

Note: All data for 1976–1984 are from "Fall Enrollment in Colleges and Universities" (Surveys 1976, 1980, and 1984) by U.S. Department of Education (reported in Fields, 1988); all data for 1990–1991 are from "Trends in Enrollment in Higher Education by Racial/Ethnic Category: Fall 1982 through Fall 1991," by U.S. Department of Education, National Center for Education Statistics, E.D. TABS, March 1993.

[a] Includes Pacific Islanders
[b] Includes Alaskan Natives and American Indians

1992. Between 1976 and 1992 the high school completion rate for African Americans increased from 71.8% to 76.8% among females and from 62.3% to 72.2% among males. The opposite trend emerged among Hispanics; completion rates among females rose from 56.8% in 1976 to 62.3% in 1984 and remained at 62.8% in 1992, and among males the rates rose from 53.9% in 1976 to 57.4% in 1984 but dropped to 52.0% in 1992. The high school completion rates for Whites remained stable during this time period, with 85.3% of females and 81.2% of males graduating in 1992, compared to 83.3% and 81.4% respectively in 1976.

The increases in high school graduation rates among African American students are supported by trends based on the percentage of high school dropouts among 16- to 14-year-olds, by race/ethnicity (National Center for Education Statistics, 1993). The overall drop-out rate fell between 1972 and 1992, especially for Blacks. In 1972, 14.6% of all 16- to 14-year-olds were not enrolled in school, and had neither graduated from high school nor received GED credentials. This was the case for 12.3% of Whites in this age range, 21.3% of Blacks, and 34.3% of Hispanics. By 1992 the overall drop-out rate had fallen to 11.0%, with rates at 7.7% for Whites, 13.7 for Blacks, and 29.4 for Hispanics. While the drop-out difference between Blacks and Whites has narrowed, the drop-out rate for Hispanics remained high at nearly 30% in 1992, although the rate has fallen from 35.3% in 1991 (National Center for Educational Statistics, 1993, p. 37).

College Participation Rates. Although African Americans have dramatically improved their high school completion rates, their college participation rates have declined, particularly among males. The rates among females dropped from 32% in 1976 to 26% in 1984 and then moved up to 33.8% in 1992. Among males there has been a steady decline from 35.4% in 1976 to 29.7% in 1992. Hispanics echo this decline in college participation. Among Latinas the rate dropped from 33.1% in 1976 to 29.6% in 1989; the drop was even more significant among males, who fell from 39.7% in 1976 to 27.9% in 1989. This decline cannot be attributed to increased numbers of Hispanic immigrants because educational attainment among Latinos in

the United States has traditionally improved with each generation. Furthermore, the proportion of Latino immigrants in the school-age population did not increase during this period (Chapa, 1991). For White students college participation rates among 18- to 24-year-olds have increased for females from 30.7% in 1976 to 42.8% in 1992. White male students increased their college participation rates from 35.4% in 1976 to 39.4% in 1992. Given the continued growth in the college-age populations among African Americans and Latinos, and given their higher rates of high school completion (with the exception of Latinos), a major question for higher education is why their presence on our college campuses has declined.

Explanations of Low College Enrollments for Minorities. Poverty and poor academic preparation are two crucial reasons for the low college enrollment of students of color (Irvine, 1991; Solmon & Wingard, 1991). Although over half of the nation's poverty children are low-income Whites, non-Whites are vastly overrepresented. In 1991, 32.7% of all African Americans, 28.7% of Hispanics, and 13.8% of Asians and Pacific Islanders lived below the poverty level, compared to 11.3% of all Whites (U.S. Bureau of the Census, 1991a). For children under 18 the poverty rates are 38% for Mexican American children, 49% for Puerto Rican children, 46% for African American children, and 17% for White children (Carter & Wilson, 1991; U.S. Bureau of the Census, 1991a). The relationship between socioeconomic level and educational achievement is well documented (Children's Defense Fund, 1985), and financial concerns explain why some minorities and poor Whites drop out of high school or enter the workforce rather than college after completing high school. The poor academic preparation provided many Alaskan Natives, American Indians, African Americans, Mexican Americans, and Puerto Ricans in our nation's schools is also well documented (College Board, 1985; Kozol, 1991; National Coalition of Advocates for Students, 1985; National Council of La Raza, 1990; Oakes, 1985). They are overrepresented in general and in vocational tracks, in classes for the mentally retarded, and in schools that have outdated books and inadequate facilities. Inadequate precollegiate education, cou-

TABLE 38–2. High School Completion Rates and College Participation Rates by Race/Ethnicity and Sex, 1976, 1984, 1989, and 1992 (in thousands)

	Total		African American		Hispanic		White	
1976 pop. 18–24 yrs.	26,919		3,315		1,551		23,119	
Female	13,907		1,813		850		11,840	
Male	13,012		1,503		701		11,279	
High school graduates	21,677	(80.5%)	2,239	(67.5%)	862	(55.6%)	19,045	(82.4%)
Female	11,365	(81.7%)	1,302	(71.8%)	483	(56.8%)	9,860	(83.3%)
Male	10,312	(79.2%)	936	(62.3%)	378	(53.9%)	9,186	(81.4%)
Enrolled in college	7,181	(33.1%)	749	(33.5%)	309	(35.8%)	6,276	(33.0%)
Female	3,508	(30.9%)	417	(32.0%)	160	(33.1%)	3,026	(30.7%)
Male	3,673	(35.6%)	331	(35.4%)	150	(39.7%)	3,250	(35.4%)
% ever college enrolled		53.4%		50.4%		48.9%		53.5%
Female		51.4%		50.3%		46.5%		51.3%
Male		55.7%		50.3%		51.8%		55.9%
1984 pop. 18–24 yrs.	28,031		3,862		2,018		23,347	
Female	14,287		2,052		1,061		11,826	
Male	13,744		1,811		956		11,521	
High school graduates	22,870	(81.6%)	2,885	(74.7%)	1,212	(60.1%)	19,373	(83.0%)
Female	11,956	(83.7%)	1,613	(78.6%)	661	(62.3%)	10,026	(84.8%)
Male	10,914	(79.4%)	1,272	(70.2%)	549	(57.4%)	9,348	(81.1%)
Enrolled in college	7,591	(33.2%)	786	(27.2%)	362	(29.9%)	6,256	(33.7%)
Female	3,662	(30.6%)	419	(26.0%)	207	(31.3%)	3,120	(31.1%)
Male	3,929	(36.0%)	367	(28.9%)	154	(28.1%)	3,406	(36.4%)
% ever college enrolled		53.0%		45.2%		46.0%		53.8%
Female		52.4%		45.1%		46.6%		53.4%
Male		53.6%		45.2%		45.7%		54.2%
1989 pop. 18–24 yrs.	25,261		3,559		2,818		20,825	
Female	12,936		1,905		1,377		10,586	
Male	12,325		1,654		1,439		10,240	
High school graduates	20,461	(81.0%)	2,708	(76.1%)	1,576	(55.9%)	17,089	(82.1%)
Female	10,758	(83.2%)	1,511	(79.3%)	823	(59.8%)	8,913	(84.2%)
Male	9,700	(78.7%)	1,195	(72.2%)	756	(52.5%)	8,177	(79.9%)
Enrolled in college	7,804	(38.1%)	835	(30.8%)	453	(28.7%)	6,631	(38.8%)
Female	4,085	(38.0%)	511	(33.8%)	244	(29.6%)	3,409	(38.2%)
Male	3,717	(38.3%)	324	(27.1%)	211	(27.9%)	3,223	(39.4%)
% ever college enrolled		57.9%		49.1%		43.6%		58.9%
Female		58.6%		51.8%		44.5%		59.2%
Male		57.2%		45.8%		42.7%		58.5%
1992 pop. 18–24 yrs.	24,278		3,521		2,754		19,671	
Female	12,313		1,845		1,369		9,928	
Male	11,965		1,676		1,384		9,744	
High school graduates	19,921	(82.1%)	2,625	(74.6%)	1,578	(57.3%)	16,379	(83.3%)
Female	10,344	(84.0%)	1,417	(76.8%)	860	(62.8%)	8,468	(85.3%)
Male	9,576	(80.0%)	1,211	(72.3%)	720	(52.0%)	7,911	(81.2%)
Enrolled in college	8,343	(41.9%)	886	(33.8%)	586	(37.1%)	6,916	(42.2%)
Female	4,429	(42.8%)	531	(37.5%)	339	(39.4%)	3,625	(42.8%)
Male	3,912	(40.9%)	356	(29.7%)	247	(34.3%)	3,291	(41.6%)
% ever college enrolled		65.6%		53.3%		55.8%		67.0%
Female		66.9%		56.6%		57.4%		68.1%
Male		64.1%		49.4%		52.2%		65.8%

Note: All data are from *Minorities in Higher Education: Twelfth Annual Status Report* (adapted from Tables 1 and 2, pp. 44–49) by D. J. Carter and R. Wilson, 1994, Washington DC: American Council on Education.

pled with rising standards in college entrance exams and a lack of counseling and remedial support, contributes to the declines in college access and/or academic success (Wright, 1987). Traditional criteria for college admission such as standardized test scores and high school grades are not good predictors of college potential for many minorities, especially Hispanic students (Durán, 1986), yet alternatives have not been developed.

In an exemplary study of minority and nonminority access to higher education, Orfield (1988) developed a case study of declining college access and public policy in Los Angeles since the early 1970s. He points out that nearly a fifth of the nation's Hispanics live in the greater Los Angeles area, as do many African Americans and Asians. His data on dropouts, high school achievement levels, college access and retention, and job-training programs are part of the Metropolitan Opportunity Project, which has been collecting large quantities of education data in five areas: Chicago, Houston, Philadelphia, Atlanta, and Los Angeles. Orfield found that African American and Hispanic students attend schools that are inferior to those serving Whites and Asians and that the college-going pool is shrinking for African American and Hispanic youth due to: (a) high school dropouts (43% for African Americans and Hispanics compared to 25% for Whites and 15% for Asians; p. 153); and (b) failure to obtain admission into four-year colleges because only the top 7% of high school graduates are eligible for the University of California system. Most African Americans or Hispanics "are entitled to nothing but a community college system from which few earn degrees or certificates and few transfer successfully and eventually win a B.A. degree" (p. 152). Orfield (1988) writes:

The educational policies needing close examination include those that increase high school dropouts, that increase the burdens on low-income families desiring a college education, that increase standards for admission to public four-year colleges and universities, that increase reliance on community colleges to prepare successful transfer students, that reduce and de-emphasize minority recruitment and retention programs, and that curtail civil rights enforcement. (p. 157)

He is particularly critical of California's 1960 Master Plan, which established "a huge system of public higher education on the basis of a highly selective system of access to the four-year college" (p. 157) and relies on two-year community colleges for everyone else. Orfield argues that because "high school education is unequal, and [because] there are tremendous racial differences in eligibility for public education . . . low-income minority families are paying state taxes that very heavily subsidize the universities which few of their children may attend" (p. 157), especially because the state funding of community colleges is declining.

Persistence in College. Most of the research on minorities in higher education has focused on African Americans. This growing body of research suggests that African American students do not fare well at predominantly White colleges and universities. Compared to White students on the same campuses, African American students are less likely to complete their baccalaure-

ate degree, experience poorer psychological adjustment, are less likely to pursue advanced degrees, and achieve less occupational success after graduation (Allen, 1988a, 1988b; Blackwell, 1987). The research on Asian American, Latino, and Native American college students is sparse but suggests that their experiences are in some ways similar to those of many African Americans on predominantly White campuses (Bagasao, 1989; Fields, 1988; O'Brien, 1992a).

A recent study by the National Institute of Independent Colleges and Universities described college student persistence in the nation's four-year colleges and universities (Porter, 1990). The researchers identified "four categories of persistence: . . . completers (those who completed a bachelor's degree), persisters (those who were continuously enrolled), and dropouts (those who left and did not return)" (p. vii). The High School and Beyond database was selected, providing longitudinal information on approximately 28,000 high school seniors in 1980 as well as data from follow-up surveys of close to 12,000 students in 1982, 1984, and 1986. Despite its limitations (Olivas, 1992), this is considered to be the most complete national database available on college students, and it includes large samples of African American and Hispanic students as well as small samples of Asian American and American Indian students. The data track a traditional cohort of students age 17 or 18 through age 23 or 24, an age group that still represents more than 80% of students enrolled full-time on our college and university campuses (Porter, 1990).

The study's major findings are the following: (a) Only 41% of all students completed a bachelor's degree within six years, although another 14% were still enrolled for a persistence rate of 55%; (b) completion rates were higher and more timely in independent colleges and universities than in public schools, except for Latinos, for whom type of four-year college made no difference; (c) completion rates for African American and Hispanic students were between 25% and 30% compared to over 50% for Whites and Asian Americans; (d) enrollment losses were greatest during the first year, especially among African Americans (more than a quarter had dropped out by the third semester), and after the eighth semester; (e) higher levels of socioeconomic status (SES) and academic ability were linked with higher rates of persistence, a pattern found across ethnic groups, with the exception of Hispanic students and high-ability African American students; (f) the combined effect of SES and academic ability was stronger than either factor alone (because minorities are overrepresented in the low-SES category, it is important to note that college completion rates were substantially higher for high-ability/low-SES students in all the groups than they were for all students in each ethnic group as a whole; however, the completion rates of high-ability/low-SES students were lower than those of high-ability students as a whole, except for African American students); (g) financial aid grants received during the first year of college were linked to persistence into the second semester; 90% of those who received a grant persisted compared to 75% of those who did not receive a grant. (Among African American students, 40% of the freshmen who did not receive a grant dropped out by the second semester.)

TABLE 38–3. Graduate Enrollment in Higher Education by Race/Ethnicity: Biennially, Fall 1978 to Fall 1988, and 1991

	1978	1980	1982	1984	1986	1988	1991
Total	1,219,000	1,250,000	1,235,000	1,344,000	1,435,000	1,472,000	1,639,000
White, non-Hispanic	1,019,000	1,030,000	1,002,000	1,087,000	1,133,000	1,153,000	1,258,000
Total minority	120,000	125,000	123,000	141,000	167,000	167,000	205,000
African American, non-Hispanic	68,000	66,000	61,000	67,000	72,000	76,000	89,000
Hispanic	24,000	27,000	27,000	32,000	46,000	39,000	51,000
Asian American[a]	24,000	28,000	30,000	37,000	43,000	46,000	58,000
American Indian	4,000	4,000	5,000	5,000	5,000	6,000	7,000
Nonresident Alien	80,000	94,000	108,000	115,000	136,000	151,000	177,000

Note: Data for 1978–1988 are from *Minorities in Higher Education: Ninth Annual Status Report* (p. 28) by D. J. Carter and R. Wilson, 1991, Washington, DC: American Council on Education. Data for 1991 are from *Trends in Enrollment in Higher Education by Racial/Ethnic Category: Fall 1982 through Fall 1991* (p. 6) by National Center for Education Statistics, 1993, Washington, DC: U.S. Office of Education.

[a] Includes Pacific Islanders.

Trends in Graduate and Professional School Enrollment

Graduate school enrollment, both for Whites and minorities, has slowly increased since 1978 (see Table 38–3). Enrollments fell for Hispanics by about 15% between 1986 and 1988 but increased to 51,000 students in 1991, up from 46,000 in 1986 and 39,000 in 1988. Enrollments in professional schools between 1978 and 1988 declined slightly for Whites and increased slightly for minorities; in 1991 there was a larger increase for African Americans, Hispanics, and Asian Americans, while American Indian enrollments remained the same. (See Table 38–4.) Professional school enrollments for Asian Americans have grown at a rapid rate, having more than quadrupled since 1978.

The proportion of minority and White students enrolled in undergraduate, graduate, and professional schools since 1976 is shown in Table 38–5. The proportion of minorities in the overall population of college students has increased at all levels of higher education, most dramatically in professional schools. In contrast, the proportion of Whites has steadily declined at all levels. Enrollments grew at the highest rates for Asian American

students. The proportion of Hispanics has also increased in the undergraduate, graduate, and professional student populations. American Indians have gained slightly in undergraduate education and have maintained the same proportion of graduate and professional school enrollments since 1976. The proportions of African Americans in the undergraduate and graduate student population have declined since 1976, although there has been a slight increase in the professional school population.

In contrast to this trend of increasing proportions of minority students in the higher education student population, a very different trend is also evident in the school populations shown in Table 38–5. For each year shown, the proportion of Whites in the undergraduate student population is usually exceeded by the proportion of White students in the graduate and professional levels. In contrast, minority representation usually decreases. Minorities contributed 16.6% of the undergraduate population in 1976 but only 10% of the graduate school student population and 8.6% of the professional school student population. By 1991, minorities accounted for 21.8% of all undergraduates but only 12.4% of graduate students; however, their proportion of the professional school student population increased to 18.1%. Asian American students are an exception to the

TABLE 38–4. Professional School Enrollment in Higher Education by Race/Ethnicity: Biennially, Fall 1978 to Fall 1988, and 1991

	1978	1980	1982	1984	1986	1988	1991
Total	255,000	277,000	278,000	278,000	270,000	267,000	281,000
White, non-Hispanic	229,000	248,000	246,000	243,000	231,000	223,000	224,000
Total minority	22,000	26,000	29,000	32,000	36,000	39,000	50,000
African American, non-Hispanic	11,000	13,000	13,000	13,000	14,000	14,000	17,000
Hispanic	5,000	7,000	7,000	8,000	9,000	9,000	11,000
Asian American[a]	5,000	6,000	8,000	9,000	11,000	14,000	21,000
American Indian	1,000	1,000	1,000	1,000	1,000	1,000	1,000
Nonresident alien	3,000	3,000	3,000	3,000	4,000	5,000	6,000

Note: Data for 1978–1988 are from *Minorities in Higher Education: Ninth Annual Status Report* (p. 28) by D. J. Carter and R. Wilson, 1991, Washington, DC: American Council on Education. Data for 1991 are from *Trends in Enrollment in Higher Education by Racial/Ethnic Category: Fall 1982 through Fall 1991* (p. 6) by National Center for Education Statistics, 1993, Washington, DC: U.S. Office of Education.

[a] Includes Pacific Islanders.

TABLE 38–5. Enrollment by Race and Ethnicity as a Percentage of Total Undergraduate, Graduate, and Professional Enrollments: 1976, 1980, 1984, 1988, and 1991

	1976	1980	1984	1988	1991
White					
Undergraduate	81.8	80.6	80.5	78.8	76.4
Graduate	83.9	81.9	80.5	78.4	76.7
Professional	90.1	89.3	87.1	83.6	79.8
Minorities					
Undergraduate	16.6	17.3	17.4	19.2	21.8
Graduate	10.0	10.2	9.8	11.4	12.4
Professional	8.6	9.6	11.6	14.7	18.1
Asian[a]					
Undergraduate	1.8	2.3	3.1	3.6	4.5
Graduate	1.7	2.1	2.6	3.1	3.5
Professional	1.7	2.2	3.4	5.4	7.4
African American					
Undergraduate	10.3	10.1	9.2	9.2	9.9
Graduate	6.1	5.5	4.8	5.2	5.4
Professional	4.5	4.6	4.9	5.4	6.1
Hispanic					
Undergraduate	3.8	4.2	4.4	5.6	6.5
Graduate	1.9	2.2	2.2	2.7	3.1
Professional	1.9	2.4	2.9	3.5	4.1
Native American[b]					
Undergraduate	0.7	0.7	0.7	0.8	0.9
Graduate	0.4	0.4	0.3	0.4	0.4
Professional	0.5	0.4	0.4	0.4	0.5

Note: Data for 1988 and 1991 are from *Trends in Enrollment in Higher Education by Racial/Ethnic Category: Fall 1982 through Fall 1991*. (p. 6) by National Center for Education Statistics, 1993, Washington, DC: U.S. Office of Education. Data for 1976–1984 are from *Fall Enrollment in Colleges and Universities Surveys, 1976, 1980, and 1984* (reported in Change Trendlines, 1987).

[a] Includes Pacific Islanders

[b] Includes Alaskan Natives and American Indians

trend; percentages in graduate and professional school populations are close to or exceed undergraduate percentages.

With the exception of Asian Americans, the proportion of minorities in higher education is lower than what would be expected if access to college were equitable. According to the 1990 census, African Americans account for over 12% of the total population, Hispanics 9%, Asian Americans 2.4%, and American Indians about 1% (U.S. Bureau of the Census, 1991b). These disparities between the proportion of minorities in the general and higher-education populations are likely to grow unless there is greater concern for equity and excellence at all levels of education. We must address the racial and ethnic differences in quality of precollege education, high school completion rates, progression into college, college choice, college graduation rates, and enrollment in graduate and professional schools. Some of the special issues, trends, and concerns that focus specifically on African Americans, Asian Americans, Latinos, and American Indians in higher education are highlighted in the ethnic group descriptions that follow.

African Americans. African Americans have made significant gains in the pursuit of higher education since the end of World War II, when 1.2% of Blacks had completed baccalaureate de-

grees, compared to 5.4% of native Whites (Garibaldi, 1991a). While the actual numbers of Blacks enrolled in college has steadily increased since the early 1980s, the percentage of Blacks in college has actually decreased each year, particularly among males. Ironically, these declines in African American student college enrollments are occurring at a time when their college-age population is increasing and their high school graduation rate is at its highest point ever (Arbieter, 1987; Carter & Wilson, 1991).

What are the reasons? Garibaldi (1991a) attributes the decline to inadequate precollegiate education and high rates of dropping out of high school, insufficient financial aid, higher attrition rates in the first years of college, inflation of costs of a college education, inadequate counseling, and "the inability of many black students to view a college degree as a worth-while investment" (p. 95). According to Arbieter (1987), many African American high school graduates are choosing to enter the armed forces, to enter the labor force, or to continue their education in proprietary schools. Over 90% of Navy and Air Force recruits are now high school graduates and more than ever are from ethnic minorities. The number of African Americans recruited between 1980 and 1986 increased by 20,000 in the Navy and by 12,000 in the Air Force. In data reviewed for the

College Board, Arbieter refutes the argument that the decline in college attendance by African Americans is due to recent changes in the family structure, such as increases in the teenage death rate, arrest rate, and teenage pregnancy. He argues that the Black teenage cohort has not shown a decline of stability and emphasizes the significant increase in African American high school graduates. Arbieter concludes that although Black teenagers are still at a disadvantage by most social indicators when compared to Whites, those African American graduates who enter the labor force after high school are finding jobs at an increasing rate.

Oliver and Etchevery (1987) conducted a longitudinal study of factors that influence academically talented Black students to attend college. They surveyed 82% of the African American students with a cumulative grade point average of B or above who graduated from a midwestern high school during a five-year period, for a total of 184 respondents. Five influence variables that discriminated between college attendees and nonattendees were identified as significant and accounted for 42.7% of the variance. These were, in descending order of importance: career objectives, availability of financial aid, job availability, contact with professionals working in the field of interest, and peers. The researchers recommended that college recruitment efforts should be focused on jobs and careers, should include concrete information on financial aid, should use prospective students' local networks, and should strengthen connections with professionals in students' fields of interest.

Since 1981 a National Study of Black College Students (NSBCS), directed by Walter Allen at the University of Michigan, has tracked the achievements, experiences, attitudes, and backgrounds of African American undergraduates at a variety of historically Black and predominantly White colleges and universities. The research conducted by Allen and his associates reveals that attrition rates of Black students on predominantly White college campuses are 5 to 8 times higher than the attrition rates of White students on the same campuses. African American students also report more dissatisfaction and alienation than White students. Black students at historically Black colleges and universities (HBCUs) experience more academic success and are portrayed as more "satisfied, engaged in campus life, and well-adjusted" (Allen, 1987, p. 28).

In a major study of Black college students, Fleming (1984) compared their experience in historically Black and predominantly White colleges. Her cross-sectional research was designed to "be large-scale enough to approximate a survey but intensive enough to approximate a case study" and explored general issues of student development while addressing "the importance of sex, race, and individual differences in the college experience" (p. 27). Her sample included 1,455 Black students at historically Black schools and 1,062 Black students and 388 White students at predominantly White schools, for a total of 1,752 freshmen and 971 seniors. Among African American students in her sample, 58.4% were female and 41.6% were male. Among White students in her sample, 57% were male and 43% were female. The survey research was conducted in several phases on 14 different campuses, administered in personalized group settings, and followed up with personalized

interviews where feasible. Analyses of the massive amounts of data gathered in the study were organized into four factors displayed according to campus and race: academic adjustment, adjustment to college, career development, and psychosocial adjustment. Fleming concluded that African American students may be better served on Black campuses in terms of their personal, social, and cognitive development. Despite the generally superior resources and facilities on White campuses, and despite the fact that Black students attending White schools tend to have stronger college-entry-level skills, Black students attending Black schools achieve greater academic success and personal development. Fleming attributes this to a more friendly, supportive atmosphere for Blacks on Black campuses.

These findings are especially significant because since the 1960s there has been a dramatic increase in the numbers of Black students attending predominantly White colleges and universities. Prior to 1950, over 75% of Black college students attended historically Black colleges due to segregation laws and the absence of open-admission policies. By 1973 that proportion was down to 25% and declined to less than 20% in the mid-1980s (Anderson, 1988; Garibaldi, 1991b). Nevertheless, an average of 37% of the bachelor's degrees and about 30% of master's degrees earned by African Americans are awarded by HBCUs (Wilson & Carter, 1989). Garibaldi (1991a) writes, "HBCU's still play a major role in the college and graduate education of Blacks in this country, although they represent less than 5% of the more than 3,300 colleges and universities in America" (p. 96). Despite this record, HBCUs are threatened by financial cutbacks, a lack of support from the higher education community, and efforts to desegregate higher education in the South.

Another area of concern is the declining presence of African American males throughout most of the education pipeline (Garibaldi, 1992). Black women outnumber Black men in both undergraduate and graduate school enrollment by nearly two to one. African American men have suffered the worst decline at all levels of educational attainment with one exception—the doctoral level. The number of African American men awarded "first professional" degrees, such as law, medicine, and dental degrees, increased 13% from 1985 to 1987 (Conciatore, 1990, p. 7). However, this promising trend was reversed between 1987 and 1989, when African Americans fell 9.3% in the number of first professional degrees awarded. The drop was 12.4% for males and 5.8% for females (Carter & Wilson, 1991).

Asian Americans. Asian Americans represent the lone exception to the pattern of declining college enrollments among the nation's ethnic minorities. The number of Asian American undergraduates nearly tripled between 1976 and 1986 (Hsia & Hirano-Nakanishi, 1989). In 1986 national statistics reported that 3.6% of all college students and over 3% of all college faculty were Asian, even though Asians composed only 2.1% of the total U.S. population (Suzuki, 1989). According to Hsia and Hirano-Nakanishi:

In every age range, from kindergarten to young adult, higher proportions of Asian Americans enroll in school than their white, black and Hispanic peers. Asian American high school sophomores and seniors, followed for six years by the 1980 High School and Beyond (HS&B) survey, recorded the lowest high school dropout rates and the highest cumulative grade point averages among all groups. A higher proportion of Asian high school graduates went right on to college than graduating peers. Among Asian American seniors who enrolled in four-year colleges, 86 percent persisted, and 12 percent transferred to a different institution. . . . The persistence and transfer figure for Asian Americans attending two-year colleges was 91 percent compared with 75 percent among all community college students. (pp. 24–25)

It must be noted, however, that reports on Asian Americans in the U.S. education pipeline are based on samples that under-represent Southeast Asian refugees and immigrants, many of whom are experiencing academic problems and are dropping out (Bagasao, 1989; Carter & Wilson, 1991).

The dramatic academic success of many Asian Americans, coupled with the U.S. Bureau of the Census data showing that Asians' average family income also surpasses all other ethnic minorities, contributes to the model minority myth that masks the tremendous diversity among Asian Americans, some of whom are still underrepresented on college campuses (Suzuki, 1983, 1989). The portrayal of Asian Americans as a model minority refers to "a non-white group whose members have managed to 'make it' in America despite a long history of being subjected to myriad forms of discrimination" (Chan & Wang, 1991, p. 44). Recent studies show that although many Asian Americans have achieved middle-class status, this was due to a larger proportion of families in which both spouses worked, families were larger, and children contributed more to the family income (Suzuki, 1989). Jiobu's study in 1988 of Chinese, Filipinos, Japanese, Koreans, Mexicans, Vietnamese, African Americans, and European Americans in California found that, except for Japanese Americans, none of these groups had attained real economic parity with Whites. Furthermore, he noted that Japanese Americans may be experiencing intensified prejudice (cited in Suzuki, 1989).

The myth of the model minority contributes to stereotypes that create special problems for Asian Americans on college campuses. For example, Suzuki (1989) writes that "Large numbers [of Asian Americans] are encountering personal or academic difficulties; many, especially those who have recently immigrated, are struggling to learn English . . . [and] many Asian students are undergoing extreme psychological stress and alienation" (p. 18). Furthermore, there is a widespread concern in the Asian American community that the nation's prestigious universities are using unofficial quotas that will limit the number of Asian Americans admitted (Chan & Wang, 1991; Nakanishi, 1989; Wang, 1988). While Asian Americans are overrepresented in the areas of science and technology, they are nearly absent in the arts and humanities (Bagasao, 1989; Rosca, 1989). Stereotypes of the "successful student" mislead teachers and counselors who overlook language problems and pressures to achieve that are experienced by many Asian students. Asian studies programs have tended to be marginalized, and their faculties share a history of difficulty in attaining tenure and promotion (Chan, 1989; Hune, 1989). Despite a growing number of Asian American students who are not able to pass the language competency test required for graduation, Asian Amer-

icans are typically not eligible for affirmative action support programs. In sum, there appears to be a dichotomy developing within the broad category of Asian Americans: those who are highly successful in academia versus those who are in trouble.

Hispanics. A special report on Hispanics in higher education stresses the complex interaction between social, economic, and demographic factors as well as influences from elementary and secondary education (Chapa, 1991). Hispanics have a high proportion of younger age cohorts, and, as one of the largest and fastest-growing minority groups in the United States, they will have an important role in the nation's workforce. Yet their high school completion rates are among the nation's lowest and "their participation in higher education is much lower than their proportion of the college age population. . . . In fact, the rapid growth of the population masks increased attrition from the educational system" (Chapa, 1991, p. 13).

A major problem in research on Hispanic students is a failure to distinguish among groups of differing national origin within the Hispanic population. For example, Estrada (1988) points out that five regions of the United States are most affected by increased Hispanic populations due to high birth rates or immigration. In the Southwest, where the majority live, schools are most affected by changing demographics, levels of poverty are highest, and levels of literacy and school achievement are lowest. In the Northeast, where the Puerto Rican population has received an influx of Dominicans, Central Americans, and South Americans, there exists a large professional class of Hispanics coupled with some of the highest rates of poverty. South Florida, composed mainly of Cubans, is characterized by high levels of educational attainment. The Chicago Metropolitan Area is a cross-section of the Hispanic population, and although socioeconomic levels are low, educational attainment has been above average. Finally, in the Pacific Northwest, the Hispanic population is numerically small but growing rapidly, and due to the high proportion of agricultural workers the levels of education are low (Estrada, 1988).

U.S. census data reported by Fields (1988) show varying educational attainment among groups of Hispanics. (See Table 38–6.) Efforts to address educational inequities among Hispanics are hindered by a lack of knowledge about Hispanic students (Olivas, 1986b). Much of the research on Hispanic college students has lumped them into a "minority population"

TABLE 38–6. Educational Attainment Among Hispanic Groups

Population	Percent of Hispanic population	Percent with four years of high school or more	Percent with four years of college or more
Cubans	5.0	61.6	17.1
Central and South Americans	11.0	59.3	12.2
Puerto Ricans	12.0	53.8	8.0
Mexican Americans	63.0	44.8	5.8
Non-Hispanics		77.3	20.6

with African Americans and has overlooked substantive linguistic differences and cultural experiences. Educational researchers and program evaluators measure Hispanic children with instruments and methodologies evolved from studies of majority students (Olivas, 1986b) and tend to blame Hispanics for their own school failure.

Inadequate precollegiate education for Hispanics is a major barrier to college access. Explains Olivas (1986b), "In 1982 Hispanic children attended schools that were more segregated than in 1970 . . . [and] are less likely than majority or even most minority students to complete high school or graduate with their age groups" (p. 1). Bilingual education programs remain inadequate in most states; schools lack appropriate means of diagnosing students' linguistic competence and cognitive abilities, and they lack bilingual curricula and personnel. Olivas writes that these early failures of education are "mirrored in post secondary institutions. Here, issues of limited access, discriminatory employment practices, and high attrition disproportionately affect Hispanic students" (p. 3).

According to Genevieve M. Ramirez (quoted in Fields, 1988), professor of Mexican American studies at California State University at Long Beach:

The research conducted on large cross-sections of college students nationwide offers us the following facts as significant enhancements of academic success: good high school preparation, good study habits, high self-esteem, relatively well-educated and somewhat affluent family background, entry from high school directly to a four-year institution, residence on campus, receipt of financial aid grants or scholarships and no need to work, and enrollment at a selective institution. (p. 25)

She added, "Hispanic-origin students nationwide, except the limited numbers of immigrants coming from affluent refugee families, are almost item-for-item the exact opposite" (quoted in Fields, 1988, p. 25). When asked to identify the two main reasons why they or their peers must withdraw from the university, Ramirez said that Hispanic "students most highly rated the following factors, in order: need to support self or family financially, lack of interest/motivation/goals, time conflicts with job or family obligations, emotional inability to cope with college demands, academic under-preparedness, and poor academic performance" (p. 25).

Two studies have identified stress encountered in college as an important factor for understanding Hispanic undergraduates (Muñoz, 1986; Muñoz & García-Bahne, 1977). Both studies consisted of three phases: a one-hour structured interview (one-to-one), a paper-and-pencil demographic questionnaire, and administration of the College Environmental Stress Index. The second study (Muñoz, 1986) was conducted with samples of 342 Chicano students and 120 Anglo students enrolled in four California universities. The results showed that Latino college students experienced more stress than did Anglo students; Chicanas reported greater stress than did Chicanos, while Anglo men and women were similar in the stress they encountered. Despite their higher stress scores, however, Chicanas were more academically successful than Chicano students. Chicana students received less family support than Chicanos and experienced greater sex role conflicts. Furthermore, the primary support systems for Chicanas appeared to be Chicana discussion groups and campus organizations. A third study (Chacón, Cohen, & Strover, 1986) found that time spent on domestic tasks became barriers to higher education among Chicanas, a trait not encountered to the same degree among Chicanos or the Anglo women studied.

Despite the limited amount of research on Latino college students, several trends are clear (Olivas, 1986b). First, it is evident that Hispanics experience inequities in the transition from high school to college due to socioeconomic disadvantages, inadequate precollegiate education, high drop-out rates, and enrollment in two-year colleges. Second, the underlying assumptions and approaches associated with college admissions testing, counseling, and academic achievement measures are inadequate for Hispanic students. And third, financial aid packaging limits college access. All of these factors contribute to the high stress levels experienced by many Latino college students.

There is an urgent need for researchers to develop knowledge of college achievement predictors for Hispanic students (Durán, 1986). Although he realizes that high school grades and college admission test scores will continue to be used in the foreseeable future, Durán proposes that the following factors also be reviewed for Hispanic college applicants: (a) language background and proficiency in English; (b) exposure to schooling in Spanish and academic achievement in Spanish contexts; (c) high aspirations and motivation to achieve combined with lower-than-expected high school grades and admissions test scores; (d) high school grades and test scores that are higher than would be expected based on family socioeconomics (i.e., severe financial and/or family obligations during high school coupled with higher-than-expected grades and test scores); (f) involvement in significant school, home, or community activities that require academic skills; and (g) the development of significant literary skills in Spanish and the ability to use these skills at advanced levels.

Native Americans. Demographic data on the participation and achievements of Native Americans in the education pipeline are inadequate because "Statistically Indians have either been ignored or placed in the 'other' category for most national education data" (O'Brien, 1992a, p. 16). Based upon the data that are available, a disturbing portrait emerges. In 1980, American Indians had the highest school drop-out rate of all minorities: 35.8% compared to 22.2% for African Americans and 27.9% for Latinos. Indeed, Indians represented 3.1% of all school dropouts even though they accounted for only 0.9% of the nation's schoolchildren (p. 16).

American Indians are also disproportionately placed in special education and programs for the learning disabled. The authors of a 1988 report found that only 53% of Indian grade school students were termed *not handicapped* (O'Brien, 1992a, p. 16). Poverty and unemployment are chronic problems on reservations. The median income in 1980 was $13,680, while the national median was $19,920. The male unemployment rate was 58%, reaching as high as 80% on some reservations (p. 16). Estimates show that of the less than 60% of Native Americans who do complete high school, fewer than 40% will enter college. Over 50% of American Indian college students enter two-year colleges and attend part-time. Women outnumber men by about 20%. In 1988 there were 93,000 Native Americans in higher education (Carter & Wilson, 1991, p. 28), and it is estimated that about 3% will attain a four-year degree (Wright & Tierney, 1991).

Deborah La Fountaine, director of development for the American Indian Science and Engineering Society (AISES), is appalled at the college retention figures for American Indian students. She accuses colleges and universities of recruiting students for funding purposes and then ignoring the problem of high attrition rates. As a result, she says, "all of our AISES programs deal with retention.... In Indian communities the community comes first. We teach them to reconcile the two worlds" (quoted in Rodriguez, 1992, p. 25). AISES stresses leadership training, curriculum development for grades 8–12, and teacher training because many teachers are non-Indians teaching on Indian reservations and do not relate well to their students.

A growing body of qualitative research describes cultural conflict in American Indian education. In a two-year ethnographic study for the Ford Foundation, for example, Tierney (1991) found that Native American college students experienced problems that are also faced by non-Indians, such as lack of academic preparation and feelings of loneliness. He identified other problems unique to Indian students, such as

native beliefs about science that might conflict with what is taught in a biology class, or the feeling that one must return home for specific ceremonies even if it means a class must be missed or an exam skipped. Family obligations are paramount for most Indian students. (p. 36)

In their history of American Indians in higher education, Wright and Tierney (1991) describe the centuries of efforts to Christianize and "civilize" the Indians. Throughout this history of miseducation, Indians have resisted pressures to give up their cultural identity. The tribal colleges that developed in the 1970s are for the most part a "response to the unsuccessful experience of Indian students on mainstream campuses" (p. 17). Today, 24 tribal colleges (22 community colleges, and 2 four-year colleges) "serve about 10,000 American Indians and have a full-time equivalent enrollment of about 4,500 students" (p. 17). According to Paul Boyer, author of a Carnegie Foundation study on tribal colleges, "Tribal colleges are doing so well because they recognize these differences [between tribal and mainstream values] and stress tribal values and history in the curriculum" (quoted in O'Brien, 1992c, p. 28).

Some educators hypothesize that Indian students who attend public schools rather than Bureau of Indian Affairs (BIA) schools do better in mainstream colleges, but there is no research to support this theory. According to Boyer, Indians who do best in college are those who have the "strongest sense of self-identity and connections to Indianness." Students who live on reservations are more likely to develop these connections, although they also experience culture shock on White campuses. Indians who live in urban areas aren't necessarily assimilated into White culture, and many suffer from "cultural homelessness" (quoted in O'Brien, 1992c, p. 30). Because American Indians are a "minority among minorities" there is a danger that most colleges and universities will continue to be unresponsive to their needs (p. 15).

THE LEGACY OF RACISM IN HIGHER EDUCATION

Distinctions between individual, institutional, and cultural racism provide a useful framework for an analysis of the changing demographics in American higher education today. It explains why there is still the quest for community amid diversity; there has been a facade, a fantasy of community without diversity.

Racism refers to attitudes, actions, or institutional structures that subordinate a person or group because of their color (U.S. Commission on Civil Rights, 1970). Carmichael and Hamilton (1967) were among the first to distinguish between individual and institutional racism. Individual racism consists of overt acts that are committed by White individuals, directed at people of color, and cause death, injury, or violent destruction of property. Institutional racism is less overt, often hidden in established policies and practices. The authors cite the tragic act of White terrorists who bombed a Black church in Birmingham, Alabama, and killed five Black children as an illustration of individual racism. The facts that 500 African American babies in this same city die each year due to lack of proper food, shelter, clothing, and health care, and thousands more are harmed due to conditions of poverty and discrimination, are the result of institutional racism.

In another pioneering book that distinguishes between individual and institutional racism, Knowles and Prewitt (1969) state that individual acts of racism as well as racist institutional policies can sometimes occur unintentionally, without conscious prejudice, and can be based on ignorance. The authors explain the hidden power of institutions to reward and penalize people in such areas as career opportunities, health care, educational development, political participation, treatment under the law, housing, and employment opportunities.

Feagin and Feagin (1978) extend these early works in their writings about institutionalized racism and sexism in terms of direct discrimination and indirect discrimination. Examples of direct institutional racism in education include the "legally required or informally prescribed practices" that result in ethnic minority children being segregated into inferior public schools (p. 30). Direct institutional discrimination leads to indirect institutional discrimination when poorly educated minorities cannot compete with Whites and do not qualify for advanced education and/or employment even though school officials and employers may be eager to recruit ethnic minorities.

Bullock and Rogers (1976) explain how both direct and indirect institutional racism operate in higher education, particularly in admissions policies that base acceptance for undergraduate, graduate, and professional education on standardized tests that are geared to the curricula of White, middle-class schools. Many colleges now use affirmative action procedures in an attempt to redress past discrimination.

Affirmative action procedures have, however, alienated many White students and faculty who regard such programs as "reverse discrimination," even though the programs may also target low-income Whites. Perceptions of reverse discrimination, particularly among White males, may be contributing to a rise in racial incidents on college campuses in the 1980s and 1990s, and many minorities are themselves becoming disenchanted with campus affirmative action programs because they often stigmatize students and faculty who are erroneously perceived as less qualified than nonminorities on campus (Feagin & Feagin, 1993; Jones, 1981). Clearly, addressing legacies of institutional racism on campus is a major challenge.

Cultural racism refers to the "elevation of the White Anglo-Saxon Protestant cultural heritage to a position of superiority over the cultural experiences of ethnic minority groups" (Gay, 1973, p. 33). Cultural racism combines ethnocentrism, the view that other cultures are inferior to the Anglo-European, and the power to suppress or eradicate manifestations of non-Anglo-European cultures. The legacy of cultural racism can be found in the formal curriculum, in tests, media, and course offerings. It can also be detected in the hidden, informal curriculum, as in low expectations for minority student achievement held by White faculty, ethnic/racial myths and stereotypes held by students and faculty in the university community, and an unfamiliar, nonsupportive, unfriendly, or hostile campus environment.

Individual, institutional, and cultural racism are interactive on college campuses. In a sense, because colleges and universities are institutions, racism in higher education can be viewed simply as institutional racism. However, distinctions between types of racism, particularly individual versus cultural and institutional, help pinpoint the sources of racism and clarify approaches to reform.

Individual Racism

Since the early 1980s there has been a sharp increase in social tension and conflict on predominantly White college campuses (Colón, 1991; Farrell and Jones, 1988). According to Howard Ehrlich, executive director of the National Institute Against Prejudice and Violence, there was at least one incident of ethnoviolence reported at 250 colleges and universities between the fall of 1986 and December 1988 (Colón, 1991, p. 60). Colón writes:

These acts, which are part of a widening pattern of racial animosity demonstrated across the country, have occurred on the campuses of such schools as the University of Massachusetts at Amherst, The Citadel, Michigan, Dartmouth, California at Berkeley, Texas and Columbia. These incidents and the attention paid to their causes, character and consequences have forced a general recognition that there is a racial crisis in American higher education. (p. 69)

In a study of racial incidents on predominantly White college campuses, Farrell and Jones (1988) conducted a content analysis of the *New York Times* and selected local mainstream and Black-oriented newspapers and other selected publications for the period, October 1, 1986, through December 15, 1988. Thirty-eight predominantly White universities reported inci-

dents perpetrated by White students against minority students. Seven types of racial incidents emerged from their analysis: acts of racial discrimination (25%), racist remarks (18%), racist behavior (18%), and physical attacks (13%). The remaining types were cross burnings, racist literature, and "other" (30% combined). The researchers identified three underlying causes of the conflicts: White insensitivity, environmental racism, and minority and majority student characteristics. White student and faculty insensitivity to the social, economic, and cultural backgrounds of minority students was revealed in "numerous examples of the indiscriminate use of racial slurs, racial jokes, and racist paraphernalia" (p. 217) and in subtle interracial exchanges that undermine the academic and social confidence of minority students. Environmental racism occurs in restaurants, bars, and other social outlets for students in the larger university communities where business and civic leaders "appear to be taking their cues from the majority students with respect to the negative racial behaviors they will accommodate" (p. 219). Reported examples include not playing minority-oriented music, not hiring minority students as workers, permitting racial slurs and jokes, slow service or hostile treatment, and police harassment. The third factor Farrell and Jones identify is the

substantially changed social and cultural characteristics of competing racial and ethnic social groups.... Today's minority college students, largely from low-income, working-class communities, represent the most assertive minority generation ever to enter higher education... [and] more working-class, poor white students are also entering higher education, a group [that] is one of the more racially intolerant groups in society. (p. 219)

Although most of the reported incidents of racial tension on college campuses involve African Americans as victims, other students of color and Jewish Americans also experience racism and anti-Semitism (Bagasao, 1989; Feagin & Feagin, 1993; Fiske, 1988; Suzuki, 1989). Furthermore, the social dynamics are similar to those involving African Americans (Chan & Wang, 1991).

The worsening of race relations on college campuses has been explained as a part of the legacy of Reaganism (Altbach, 1991). This legacy includes a lack of concern about racial issues through a "lack of vigorous enforcement of civil rights laws, the taming of the U.S. Civil Rights Commission and official opposition to new anti-bias initiatives" (p. 7), and a lack of concern about social problems in general. Student financial aid programs were cut back, enforcement of affirmative action and anti-bias policies was weakened, and

for the first time in a number of years, subtle racism was "in." The mean spiritedness expressed in Washington was, in part, transferred to the campus. While it would be exaggeration to blame the rise in campus racial incidents entirely on the legacy [of Reaganism], there is little doubt that white students were affected by the changing national atmosphere regarding race relations. (p. 8)

One of the most difficult and complex issues facing the campus community is how to respond to racial harassment without violating free speech. In her analysis of several racial incidents at Stanford, Sally Cole (1991) writes, "Some acts of bigotry fall within the protection of the First Amendment and it is a delicate task to define the point at which free expression ends and harassment begins" (p. 230). There appears to be an assumption that even restricted limitations on free speech, as in the case of "racial slurs," are a dangerous precedent that will lead to further encroachments on the First Amendment. A *New York Times* editorial reflected the caution:

Aside from the inherent problem of defining [verbal] harassment, vilification and intolerance—is the racial hatred preached by [Black] Louis Farrakhan and Angela Davis any worse than that of skin-head neo-Nazis?—the proposed limits on freedom of expression, no matter how well meaning, should raise caution flags. (quoted in Gordon, 1991, p. 243)

On the other hand, it can be argued that verbal and emotional abuse deserve no more protection under the First Amendment than do slander or "fighting words." When university officials and faculty do not take a stand against racial harassment, ethnic minority and White students get a clear message that racism will be tolerated.

Institutional and Cultural Racism

In their research on newly desegregated public schools, Sagar and Schofield (1984) identified four ways in which the "host school" responds to minorities and that have implications for postsecondary schools: business as usual, assimilation, pluralistic coexistence (voluntary separation), and integrated pluralism. Write Sagar and Schofield:

Insofar as possible, these [business-as-usual] interracial schools tried to maintain the same basic curriculum, the same academic standards, and the same teaching methods that prevailed under segregation.... Furthermore, they strove to enforce the same behavioral standards, to espouse the same values, and to apply the same sanctions to student offenses. In short, the schools did not perceive themselves as having to adjust their traditional practices in order to handle the new student body. Rather, the students were expected to adjust to the school....

The assimilationist ideology holds that integration will have been achieved when the minority group can no longer be differentiated from the white majority in terms of economic status, education or access to social institutions and their benefits. This will be accomplished by fostering a "color-blind" attitude where prejudice once reigned.... No significant change is anticipated since the newly assimilated minority individuals will be attitudinally and behaviorally indistinguishable from the majority. Stated in its baldest form, the assimilationist charge to the schools is to make minority children more like white children. (pp. 208, 212)

When predominantly White campuses serving culturally diverse populations take a business-as-usual or assimilationist approach, they allow institutional and cultural racism to persist. Although every campus has its own unique culture (Kuh et al., 1991), there is also a common culture across predominantly White schools. Longstreet (1978) describes this common school culture as "scholastic ethnicity" composed of five aspects: verbal communication, nonverbal communication, orientation modes (uses of time and space), social values, and intellectual modes (the curriculum content and preferred pedagogy).

Academic success in college requires proficiency in Standard American English, the institution's official language. Although international students whose native language is not English are sometimes given special consideration, linguistic diversity is often overlooked and can lead to cultural conflict related to different dialects and discussion modes. Students who speak "country," or Black vernacular, or any nonstandard dialect are often perceived as less intelligent. The emphasis on monolingual standardized tests in college admissions continues despite evidence that the tests are not good predictors of college success for Latinos (Olivas, 1986b) or for African Americans in White postsecondary schools (Bennett & Bean, 1984; Fleming, 1990; Hilliard, 1990).

Nonverbal communications, the messages sent through unconscious body movements, expressions, and gestures (kinesics), conceptions of personal space (proxemics), and styles of physical touch (haptics) are other sources of potential cultural conflict on White campuses. Eye aversion (looking down or away) is a common example. In most classrooms, "good" direct eye contact signifies that students are being attentive, or (in private conversations) truthful. Latino and Asian students, for whom eye aversion is a sign of deference and respect, often experience cultural conflict on campus (Fiske, 1988).

A prevalent theme in the research on minority students attending predominantly White colleges and universities is the feeling of "culture shock" (Fiske, 1988) and alienation due to conflicts between the students' home cultures and university expectations (Chew & Ogi, 1987; O'Brien, 1992b; Pounds, 1987; Quevedo-Garcia, 1987). Boateng (1990) refers to the deculturalization process many minority children experience in public school. The process continues at the postsecondary level. Farrell and Jones (1988) write that

the behaviors, lifestyles, and values of minority students are likely to be substantially different from those of whites, [making it difficult for those students] to successfully negotiate the university environment.... Universities, on the other hand, have made limited adjustments in their organizational and administrative structures and practices to accommodate the diverse and complex needs of their minority students populations, especially Blacks, Hispanics and American Indians. (p. 212)

As a result, many minority students have dropped out of school or found needed peer support in voluntary segregation, a phenomenon that is often resented and feared by White students, adding to racial tensions and misunderstandings.

There is overwhelming evidence that college students of color on White campuses feel more alienated than their White peers and less satisfied with many aspects of academic and social life (Allen, 1987; Fleming, 1984). In a case study that compared the attitudes and characteristics of minority and White persisters with attitudes and characteristics of nonpersisters at one predominantly White university, Bennett and Okinaka (1990) found that Asian and African American persisters felt less satisfied with the university, felt more trauma, and experienced less positive interracial contact on campus than did the nonpersisters. Among Anglos and Latinos on this campus, those who felt most negative had dropped out.

It appeared that the longer African American and Asian students remained on campus, the more dissatisfied and socially alienated they felt. This study did not provide answers as to why this was the case. But possibly it is because these groups are most easily identified as racially distinct from the White majority. Neither entry-level skills nor academic performance on campus explained the high levels of dissatisfaction and social alienation because Asians were at the higher end of the GPA, SAT/ACT score continuum and African Americans were at the lower end, although the highest-achieving African American students also dropped out at a high rate. Yet Asian and African American persisters on that campus felt more alienated and dissatisfied than did their Hispanic or White classmates.

Because Whites are in control of campus life, institutional and cultural racism, even though it may be unintentional, is likely in the absence of campus-based self-scrutiny and conscious antiracist policy making. In the forward to *Latino College Students,* Madrid (1986) writes:

Racism can enter the school curriculum through written texts which depict minorities negatively or ignore them altogether. Intelligence tests may be considered a form of racism, since they measure one's knowledge of middle class culture.... The result of racism, in the educational system is continual segregation of Hispanics, ... as demonstrated [also] by the concentration of Hispanics in two-year colleges as opposed to four-year colleges. (p. xvii)

Even financial aid programs intended to improve minority student access often reflect institutional racism (Olivas, 1986a; Orfield, 1992). In a study of financial aid access, ideology, and packaging policies, Olivas obtained data from the federally funded counseling program Hispanic Talent Search, which counsels 16,000 Hispanic students each year. He obtained a sample of 521 completed files for Mexican American and Puerto Rican full-time, first-time students in 1979–80. Seventy percent of the families reported annual incomes of less than $15,000; and over 60% had incomes under $10,500 (p. 283). He discovered that over 60% of the Hispanic students received only one type of aid, Pell grants, and predicted problems should federal aid be scaled back.

This is precisely what occurred in the 1980s and reduced low-income minority students' access to college. Low-income students were expected to shift from grants to loans, but this did not occur (Orfield, 1992). Research shows that some Americans—among them women, laborers, the less educated, the poor, and Hispanics—are less willing to borrow than others. Writes Orfield (1992):

States need a system of financial aid that is simple and predictable enough for low-income families to understand, use, and build plans around. There should be early, unambiguous notification to low-income families by the beginning of high school that their children will be able to afford college, and a simple financial aid application procedure for families who receive food stamps or any other sort of poverty-based financial aid.... States should not adopt fundamental policy changes, such as much higher admissions requirements, large tuition increases, shifting funds from undergraduate to graduate student aid or from need-based to merit-based assistance, enrollment limitations in four-year institutions, or screening tests, without carefully considering possible damage to opportunities for minority students and examination of less harmful alternatives. (p. 367)

The monocultural curriculum in place in most of the nation's colleges and universities is another example of persistent racism. Gordon (1992) writes that even as Americans become

increasingly less European and more global in origin, ... there has been a subtle but systematic insistence on the examination and celebration of a "single American heritage" and its assumed "universal perspective," both of which are the result of northern European cultural traditions having gained hegemony in North America. The dominance of these cultural traditions has proceeded simultaneously with a reduction in opportunities for the examination and celebration of other heritages as the rigid boundaries of ethnic communities and ghettos have weakened. (p. 235)

Indeed, conflict over the curriculum has emerged as a major multicultural issue in higher education. In a crisp description of the polemics, Levine and Cureton (1992) write:

The competing claims about multiculturalism boom loudly today. Some say the college curriculum has been largely impermeable to multiculturalism: that it remains unalterably "Eurocentric," ignoring—or, at best, marginalizing—diversity concerns. Others counter that higher education has sold its soul in the name of multiculturalism, that the academy currently is purging the curriculum of its historic Western canon and replacing it willy-nilly with non-Western, ethnic, and gender studies (p. 25)

Media coverage of the controversy has been compared to the coverage of civil unrest in Yugoslavia. Writes Thelin (1992): "The polarities of issues seem clear, but a distant reader seldom understands the passions and details that sustain the adversaries" (p. 17). Indeed, the mass media have misinformed the public through poorly informed reporting based on superficial research (Collins, 1992).

In a study by Levine and Cureton (1992), a survey was sent to a random sample of 270 colleges and universities stratified by Carnegie type to be representative of American higher education. The survey focused on whether, and to what extent, these institutions engaged in specific multicultural activities. The researchers concluded that a third of all colleges and universities have a multicultural general education requirement and offer coursework in ethnic and gender studies, over half (54%) have introduced multiculturalism into some of their departmental course offerings (particularly English, history, and the social sciences), and a majority are seeking to increase the ethnic diversity of their faculty (36% are actively recruiting and another 22% report passive efforts). Efforts to put multiculturalism into the curriculum are uneven; they are evident in "public institutions more than private, four-year schools more than two-year schools, research universities more than other types of colleges, and middle Atlantic and western schools more than southern and northwestern institutions" (p. 29). The researchers conclude that neither the view that the curriculum is unalterably "Eurocentric" nor the view that multiculturalism has replaced the historic Western canon is correct. "Multiculturalism is widespread in higher education today," but it lacks cohesion and "so far is only a beginning of what is likely to be a very long process" (p. 29). Although the writers do not make the point, it seems noteworthy that approximately two thirds of the schools surveyed did not report any multicultural general education requirements, nearly half did not report any departments that are including multicultural content, and over half are not actively recruiting ethnic minority faculty.

In another study of multicultural education in higher education, Gaff (1992) surveyed the academic deans in 226 diverse institutions that were working to strengthen their general education curricula. Global affairs and the influence of cultural diversity emerged as the top two trends or issues being considered. Gaff asserts that the question is no longer whether students should learn about diverse cultures, but how, and provides suggestions for the design and implementation of programs that are educationally valuable. Philosophical, curricular, faculty, pedagogical, and process issues must all be addressed during the developmental process.

Critics of multiculturalism in the curriculum identify a set of problems: the narrow set of issues, tendentious definitions and heightened politicization, a focus on "special problems" of minorities and women, and an emphasis on differences (at the expense of sameness) that brings divisiveness into the academy (Butler & Schmitz, 1992). An advertisement placed in the November 8, 1989, *Chronicle of Higher Education* entitled "Is the Curriculum Biased?" illustrates the position:

The National Association of Scholars is in favor of ethnic studies, the study of non-Western cultures, and the study of special problems of women and minorities in our society, but it opposes subordination of entire humanities and social science curricula to such studies and it views with alarm their growing politicization. Efforts purportedly made to introduce "other points of view" and "pluralism" often seem in fact designed to restrict attention to a narrow set of issues, tendentiously defined. An examination of many women's studies and minority studies courses and programs discloses little study of other cultures and much excoriation of our society for its alleged oppression of women, blacks, and others. The banner of "cultural diversity" is apparently being raised by some whose paramount interest actually lies in attacking the West and its institutions. (quoted in Butler & Schmitz, 1992, pp. 38–39)

Botstein (1991) points out that protection of academic freedom and the traditions of faculty governance complicate the issue of multicultural curriculum reform in higher education. He argues that the research for multicultural perspectives is based upon "active reconstruction" of knowledge, the search for and communication of truth, which is totally compatible with the nature of higher education at its best. He writes:

Higher education as it exists today still depends on the assumption that the rhetoric of social contact theory has value; that ideas of human nature, reason and freedom can be developed in ways that hold beyond diversity; that universality in ethical terms [notions of individuality, dignity, tolerance, and respect] is desirable. (p. 97)

THE MOVEMENT TOWARD DEMOCRATIC OR INTEGRATED PLURALISM IN HIGHER EDUCATION

Advocates of educational equity seek to create campus communities where students and faculty of every cultural and racial background feel welcome and are encouraged to reach their highest potential. School desegregation research shows that good race relations, high standards of academic achievement, and personal development among all students are most likely when school policies are based upon the model of integrated pluralism rather than on that of assimilation or business as usual (Forehand & Ragosta, 1976). Most of the desegregation research has been conducted in public schools (K–12), but there is every reason to assume that these findings would apply in desegregated colleges and universities as well.

Integrated pluralism refers to a school setting characterized by equity and mutual respect among the diverse racial and cultural groups on campus. As Sagar and Schofield (1984) write, in contrast to assimilation or business as usual, in which all students are expected to conform to White middle-class culture,

Integrated pluralism affirms the equal value of the school's various ethnic groups, encouraging their participation, not on majority defined terms, but in an evolving system which reflects the contributions of all groups. However, integrated pluralism goes beyond mere support for the side-by-side coexistence of different group values and styles. It is integrationist in the sense that it affirms the educational value inherent in exposing all students to a diversity of perspectives and behavioral repertoires and the social value of structuring the school so that students from previously isolated and even hostile groups can come to know each other under conditions conducive to the development of intergroup relations. . . .

Integrated pluralism takes an activist stance in trying to foster interaction between different groups of students rather than accepting resegregation as either desirable or inevitable. (pp. 231–232)

The concept of integrated pluralism has developed out of social contact theory and interracial contact situations such as desegregated schools, housing, and workplaces that bring ethnically encapsulated groups together for the first time. According to social contact theorists, positive racial attitudes develop out of positive interracial contacts if certain conditions in the contact situations exist (Allport, 1954; Byrne, 1961; Cohen, 1976; DeVries & Edwards, 1974; Sagar & Schofield, 1984; Wiser & Cook, 1971). Based on the original work of Gordon Allport, four conditions are necessary if these contacts are to be positive: (a) an equal-status environment for minorities and nonminorities, especially in classrooms and in cocurricular activities; (b) a social climate that supports interracial association, especially as modeled by authority figures such as teachers, principals, superintendents, and college administrators; (c) contacts among minorities and nonminorities that lead to in-depth knowledge and understandings of each other's similarities and differences; and (d) opportunities for minorities and nonminorities to work together cooperatively to achieve common goals.

A policy of integrated pluralism should be reflected in curriculum and pedagogy as well as in the campus environment. Most of the higher education research to date has focused on campus climates and the characteristics of positive environments. Although much is written about the curriculum and pedagogy, there is very little research. What does exist has been conducted mainly by school of education faculty who are concerned with preparing White teachers for ethnic diversity in the classroom.

Most colleges and universities in the United States represent a classic interracial contact situation in that many undergraduates have grown up in ethnically encapsulated environments (Banks, 1991). Whether they are from rural areas, small towns, inner cities, or the suburbs, most students have been isolated from some of the other ethnic groups on campus and often hold fears, myths, and stereotypes about them. This contributes to racial unrest when neither the curriculum nor campus life provides opportunities to unlearn these negative prejudices and misunderstandings. Casual observation shows that, for most students, ethnic encapsulation continues on campus, often through unconscious or voluntary separation. A lack of integration may contribute to the high rate of attrition among African Americans, Latinos, and American Indians attending predominantly White colleges and universities.

School desegregation research has shown that minority students achieve greater academic success in integrated schools and classrooms that encourage positive intergroup contact (St. John, 1971, 1975; Weinberg, 1977). And at least one study has shown that positive interracial contact experiences on the college campus are related to minority student feelings of satisfaction and persistence (Bennett, 1984).

It must also be emphasized that ethnic isolation is a necessary component of integrated pluralism, especially on predominantly White campuses where less than 10% of the students and 3% of the faculty are minorities. A number of studies point out the necessity of intragroup organizations and supports for minority students on White campuses (Allen, 1988a; Muñoz & García-Bahne, 1977). A growing number of colleges and universities are attempting to move away from assimilationist policies that expect minorities to "fit in" and toward practices based on the idea of integrated pluralism. This movement is accompanied by a struggle to develop a sense of community out of diversity. Write Kuh, Schuh, and Whitt (1991):

Racial incidents on campuses are one manifestation of the significant challenges presented by student diversity, and the difficulties institutions face in helping students acknowledge, accept, and appreciate diversity. Balancing the need to reestablish a sense of community on campus with a commitment to appreciating differences is a major challenge for administrators, faculty members, students, and others. (p. 25)

It would be helpful to remember that many forms of isolation have existed throughout the history of higher education without destroying the sense of campus community (Cortés, 1991). Social isolation is based on the same gender, as in sororities and fraternities; shared religious beliefs, as in a Hillel or a Newman Center; common social goals, as in volunteer tutoring programs and ethnic-based student organizations where "people gather periodically in ethnic comfort zones of shared experiences, identities, and concerns" (Cortés, 1991, p. 11). It is when students, faculty, or staff of "visibly similar ethnic appearance" gather that critics proclaim this as evidence of "Balkanization" or "tribalism" (p. 11).

In a year-long investigation of 14 four-year colleges and universities, Kuh et al. (1991) describe the characteristics of colleges that are highly successful in creating positive campus climates. In selecting the institutions, a panel of 58 experts was asked to nominate colleges that were noted for the high-quality out-of-class experiences they provided for undergraduates. The panel was to nominate five colleges in each of five categories: (a) residential colleges with fewer than 5,000 students; (b) residential colleges and universities with more than 5,000 students; (c) urban institutions with large numbers of commuting and part-time students; (d) single-sex colleges; and (e) historically Black colleges. In the final selection process the researchers selected schools that had not been widely studied previously; did not have special programs or supports that would encourage student involvement, such as unusually plentiful resources; and represented a range of geographic areas as well as a balance between public and private schools. The researchers used qualitative research methodology, including 1,295 in-depth interviews of students, faculty, and administrators, on-site observations, and document analysis.

Conditions of integrated pluralism are strongly evident in the 14 *Involving Colleges* they studied. Involving Colleges engage their students in rich learning opportunities outside the classroom. They have become "one house with many rooms" (Kuh et al., 1991, p. 61) and openly value both diversity and community.

Although Involving Colleges do not refer directly to social contact theory, the 14 schools exemplify the translation of contact theory into practice. In their discussion of "The Multicultural Imperative" (Kuh et al., 1991), the researchers argue that colleges must strive

to advance knowledge and intellectual understanding of differences among groups of people; to encourage interaction among members of different subcommunities (ethnic, cultural, gender-based, academic living groups); to promote the appreciation and valuing of commonalities across all students; and to build on commonalities while acknowledging the important and unique contributions that members of different groups can make to the academic community. (p. 294)

The Involving Colleges' programs create "a sense of belonging, a feeling on the part of students that the institution acknowledges the human needs of social and psychological comfort, and that they are full and valued members in the campus community" (Kuh, et al., 1991, p. 321). Large universities can create this environment via multiple subcommunities based on race, ethnicity, or lifestyle preferences. These campus subcommunities "can encourage their student members to take risks and be more actively involved [in campus life]" (p. 313). The researchers provide guidelines for strengthening campus pluralism, avoiding assimilation, avoiding separatism/segregation, and strengthening understanding among minorities and nonminorities. They also provide guidelines for conducting a campus audit and an institutional self-study process to help create campus climates conducive to learning and development among the diverse student populations that characterize American higher education.

In another study, this one federally funded and aimed at identifying factors that help minority students succeed in college, six lessons emerged from the case studies of 10 public universities (Richardson, Simmons, & de los Santos, 1987). The universities were selected because of their strong records for awarding baccalaureate degrees to one or more of three underrepresented minority groups in higher education: African

Americans, Latinos, and Native Americans. Other criteria for selection included a commitment to providing opportunities to minorities and willingness to share their experiences (the case studies are not disguised), diverse missions and geographic locations, and a predominantly White or multicultural student population. The authors write: "While all of the universities offered some form of intervention strategies such as summer bridge programs, early outreach, remediation, tutoring, and counseling support, none believed that these special programs captured the essence of their efforts to graduate minorities" (p. 20). In their attempt to understand the perspectives of these "very diverse" institutions, the researchers identified six common themes that help explain their successes in minority student achievement. First, "minority achievement is viewed as a preparation problem rather than a racial problem" (p. 21). For the short run, these schools waive regular admission standards to achieve "acceptable levels of representation," but they are also working to expand the admissions pool of regularly qualified high school graduates through early outreach programs in the elementary and junior high schools. Second, the importance of a positive campus climate is recognized. Like the Involving Colleges studied by Kuh et al. (1991), these universities recognize the connection between student involvement in campus life and their academic success. In multicultural settings, such as Memphis State University or Florida International University, a positive environment seems to emerge on its own. One faculty member succinctly described the shift that had taken place as minority enrollments grew from tolerance ("they're here") to acceptance ("let's work with them"; Richardson et al., 1987, p. 23). On the other hand, at predominantly White schools, where minority student enrollments are closer to 10 percent, considerable attention is given to building a hospitable environment.

The four remaining lessons reflect a strong commitment from campus authority figures to strengthening diversity: (a) concerns about small numbers of minorities on the faculty and the underinvolvement of all faculty in equal opportunity strategies; (b) strong, visible leadership and commitment from the administration; (c) comprehensive and systematic (rather than fragmented and sporadic) strategies for promoting the academic success of minorities, with an emphasis on achievement rather than retention; and (d) a favorable state policy environment (though this was not present in 2 of the 10 schools). The researchers conclude with some intriguing questions that also emerged from the study. Is there a minimum presence a minority group must attain to become a vital part of the campus community? Do individuals from marginally represented groups or multicultural campuses experience the same problems as they would in predominantly White schools? Which early intervention strategies are most effective in expanding the pool of qualified minority students? What kinds of contributions from minority communities can be reasonably expected?

In a later phase of the study (Skinner & Richardson, 1988), 107 spring 1986 minority graduates from the 10 schools were interviewed by phone. "Rich portraits of minority student achievement" (p. 37) emerged through open-ended interviews that focused on precollegiate preparation, family backgrounds, and university experiences. Although every story is unique, four student types emerged:

1) well-prepared, second generation college-goers with a lifelong commitment to higher education; 2) first generation students who also grew up with a strong belief in education, but whose preparation was inadequate; 3) first and second generation students who questioned the value of education in their lives, despite adequate preparation; and 4) first generation college students with little preparation who had grown up never intending to go to college. (p. 38)

In their discussion of implications from their research, Skinner and Richardson (1988) indirectly make a case for integrated pluralism as opposed to assimilation or business as usual. When there is a mismatch between a student's background and university expectations, the authors state:

To the extent that institutions expect students to do all or most of the adjusting, they limit the range of minority students they can serve responsibly to those who resemble traditional college-goers in preparation and opportunity orientation.... Given the current socioeconomic status of blacks, Hispanics, and American Indians—the disparities in parental education and income, the deficiencies in schooling, and so on—relatively few minority students will fit the profile of the well-prepared students in category one. (p. 42)

The 10 case-study universities in their research recognize this fact and take steps to prevent discrimination and to create a positive campus climate. Overall, Skinner and Richardson (1988) show that "minorities can succeed in a variety of settings—when the *institution* accepts responsibilities for improving its environment as well as working to improve the preparation and opportunity orientations of its students" (p. 42).

"Recruitment and Retention" (1992), a special report published in *Black Issues in Higher Education,* points out the need for colleges and universities to: (a) incorporate the new Black scholarship into the curriculum; (b) appreciate the major role played by minority faculty and staff in recruiting and supporting minority students; (c) house recruitment and retention programs in academic departments with strong faculty involvement; and (d) recognize the importance of professional groups in developing an education pipeline for minority students. The report argues that efforts to recruit and graduate college minority students can be enhanced by professional organizations such as the AISES, the Society of Hispanic Professional Engineers (SHPE), the National Society of Black Engineers (NSBE), and the National Society of Hispanic MBAs (Rodriguez, 1992). Members of these organizations feel they must play a crucial role in creating educational pipelines from the primary grades through professional school by providing role models, mentors, scholarships, and networks.

The goal of integrated pluralism, an environment where all students of every ethnic and racial background feel welcome and are encouraged to reach their highest potential, cannot be attained in predominantly White colleges and universities without strong connections with African American, Asian, Latino, and Native American communities. On many if not most campuses, the connections are weak or nonexistent. One way of strengthening these connections would be through collaborative development of the cultural-brokering approach developed by Stage and Manning (1992). This cultural-broker model provides an excellent approach for enhancing integrated pluralism on college and university campuses. Each of the four components of the model—learning to think contextually, spanning boundaries, ensuring optimal performance, and taking action—has specific implications for administrators, student affairs professionals, faculty, and all students on campus. The model could be expanded to include parents, teachers, and counselors from the students' home communities. Ideally all members of the college community would become involved in the cultural-brokering process.

TOWARD AN AGENDA FOR FUTURE RESEARCH

In the quest for community amid diversity, researchers in higher education must chart a course through turbulent seas. They can take bearings from previous research that signals policies and practices evident in Involving Colleges, schools with the highest minority student graduation rates, tribal colleges, and HBCUs. They can also take bearings from the large body of scholarly literature that exists on multicultural curricula, pedagogy, and teacher education designed for the precollegiate levels.

The urgency of the quest must continue to be supported by demographic research and national surveys despite the inadequacies inherent in the attainable data. These studies must be supplemented by longitudinal case studies and qualitative research in single institutions.

Additions to the past research agenda in higher education must include language diversity, curriculum expansion (or even transformation), pedagogy, and faculty development. A linguistically and culturally diverse population requires linguistically and culturally diverse approaches to understanding cognitive processes, measuring knowledge and skills, predicting college potential, and being in tune with students' developmental needs and concerns. While some progress is being made in the area of cultural diversity (Hilliard, 1992; Ladson-Billings,

1992; Shade, 1982), there has been little interest in strengthening bilingualism at most colleges and universities. Despite dramatic increases in the numbers of nonnative speakers, proficiency in English remains a major barrier to access to a college education.

Many writers on the crisis in higher education regard curriculum reform as the best way to address the problem. A systematic and cohesive expansion of the curriculum to include multicultural perspectives will require the participation and renewal of most of the faculty on predominantly White campuses. This renewal can become part of the university's overall research mission as shown in the state of Minnesota (Beaulieu, 1991). The quest for community amid diversity involves the entire community; the curriculum becomes a map or blueprint to guide the quest. Students are deeply involved in the quest and must learn from the curriculum where we have been and where we are going because it is hoped that they will continue the quest after graduation. There is a need for research in curriculum and pedagogy that addresses college students' differing degrees of openness and readiness for multicultural education (e.g., Artiles & Trent, 1992; Bennett, Niggle, & Stage, 1989). There is a need for research that examines how cultural styles can be incorporated to strengthen the academic achievement of college students (Slavin, 1983; Treisman, 1985). Faculty readiness is also an issue that needs to be addressed and researched (Katz, 1991).

Finally, there is a need for research focusing on the diversity within the nation's ethnic minority groups. If higher education is to strengthen community outreach programs, access, and graduation rates among Asian Americans, African Americans, Latinos, and Native Americans, more must be known about cultural, gender, and socioeconomic differences within each group. An understanding of these factors is necessary if college environments are to welcome and deal effectively with diversity.

References

Allen, W. R. (1987). Black colleges vs. White colleges: The fork in the road for Black students. *Change, 19*(3), 28–34.

Allen, W. R. (1988a). Black students in U.S. higher education: Toward improved access, adjustment, and achievement. *Urban Review, 20,* 165–188.

Allen, W. R. (1988b). Improving Black student access and achievement in higher education. *Review of Higher Education, 11*(4), 403–416.

Allport, G. (1954). *The nature of prejudice.* Reading, MA: Addison-Wesley.

Altbach, P. G. (1991). The racial dilemma in American higher education. In P. G. Altbach & K. Lomotey (Eds.), *The racial crisis in American higher education* (pp. 3–17). Albany: State University of New York Press.

Anderson, J. D. (1988). *The education of Blacks in the South, 1860–1935.* Chapel Hill: University of North Carolina Press.

Arbieter, S. (1987). Black enrollments: The case of missing students. *Change, 19*(3), 14–27.

Artiles, A. J., & Trent, S. C. (1992). *Perceived changes in college students who participated in a seminar addressing multiculturalism.* Paper presented at the annual meeting of the American Educational Research Association, San Francisco.

Bagasao, P. Y. (1989). Student voices breaking the silence: The Asian and Pacific American experience. *Change, 21*(6), 28–37.

Banks, J. A. (1991). *Teaching strategies for ethnic studies* (5th ed.). Boston: Allyn and Bacon.

Beaulieu, D. (1991). The state of the art: Indian education in Minnesota. *Change, 23*(2), 31–35.

Bennett, C. I. (1984). Interracial contact experience and attrition among Black undergraduates at a predominantly White university. *Theory and Research in Social Education, 12*(2), 19–47.

Bennett, C. I., & Bean, J. (1984). A conceptual model of Black student attrition at a predominantly White university. *Journal of Educational Equity and Leadership, 4*(3), 173–178.

Bennett, C. I., Niggle, T., & Stage, F. (1990). Preservice multicultural teacher education: Predictors of student readiness. *Teaching and Teacher Education, 6,* 243–254.

Bennett, C. I., & Okinaka, A. (1990). Factors related to persistence among Asian, Black, Hispanic, and White undergraduates at a predominantly White university: Comparison between first and fourth year cohorts. *Urban Review, 22*(1), 33–60.

Blackwell, J. (1987). *Mainstreaming outsiders: The production of Black professionals* (2nd ed.). Dix Hills, NY: General Hall.

Boateng, F. (1990). Combatting deculturalization of the African-American child in the public school system: A multicultural approach. In K. Lomotey (Ed.), *Going to school: The African American experience* (pp. 73–84). Albany: State University of New York Press.

Botstein, L. (1991). The undergraduate curriculum and the issue of race: Opportunities and obligations. In P. G. Altbach & K. Lomotey (Eds.), *The racial crisis in American higher education* (pp. 89–105). Albany: State University of New York Press.

Bullock, C. S., III, & Rodgers, H. R. (1976). Institutional racism: Prerequisites, freezing, and mapping. *Phylon, 37*(3), 212–223.

Butler, J., & Schmitz, B. (1992). Ethnic studies, women's studies, and multiculturalism. *Change, 24*(1), 37–41.

Byrne, D. (1961). The influence of propinquity and opportunities for interaction on classroom relationships. *Human Relations, 14,* 63–69.

Carmichael, S., & Hamilton, C. V. (1967). *Black power: The politics of liberation in America.* New York: Vintage Books.

Carter, D. J., & Wilson R. (Eds.). (1991). *Ninth annual status report: Minorities in higher education.* Washington, DC: American Council on Education.

Carter, D. J., & Wilson R. (Eds.). (1994). *Twelfth annual status report: Minorities in higher education.* Washington, DC: American Council on Education.

Chacón, M. A., Cohen, E. G., & Strover, S. (1986). Chicanas and Chicanos: Barriers to progress in higher education. In M. S. Olivas (Ed.), *Latino college students* (pp. 296–324). New York: Teachers College Press.

Chan, S. (1989). Beyond affirmative action: Empowering Asian American faculty. *Change, 21*(6), 48–51.

Chan, S., & Wang, L. (1991). Racism and the model minority. In P. G. Altbach & K. Lomotey (Eds.), *The racial crisis in American higher education* (pp. 43–67). Albany: State University of New York Press.

Chapa, J. (1991). Special focus: Hispanic demographic and educational trends. In D. J. Carter & R. Wilson (Eds.), *Ninth annual status report: Minorities in higher education* (pp. 11–17). Washington, DC: American Council on Education.

Chew, C. A., & Ogi, A. Y. (1987). Asian American college student perspectives. In D. J. Wright (Ed.), *Responding to the needs of today's minority students.* San Francisco: Jossey-Bass.

Children's Defense Fund. (1985). *Black and White children in America: Key facts.* Washington, DC: Author.

Cohen, E. (1976, April). *Status equalization in the desegregated school.* Paper presented at the annual meeting of the American Educational Research Association, San Francisco, CA.

Cole, S. (1991). Beyond recruitment and retention: The Stanford experience. In P. G. Altbach & K. Lomotey (Eds.), *The racial crisis in American higher education* (pp. 213–232). Albany: State University of New York Press.

College Board. (1985). *Equality and excellence: The educational status of Black Americans.* New York: Author.

Collins, H. (1992). PC and the press. *Change, 24*(1), 12–20.

Colón, A. (1991). Race relations on campus: An administrative perspective. In P. G. Altbach & K. Lomotey (Eds.), *The racial crisis in American higher education* (pp. 69–88). Albany: State University of New York Press.

Commission on Minority Participation in Education and American Life. (1988). *One-third of a nation.* Washington, DC: American Council on Education.

Conciatore, J. (1990). Military option may explain college enrollment declines among mid-income Blacks. *Black Issues in Higher Education, 7*(10), 8–9.

Cortés, C. E. (1991). Pluribus and unum: The quest for community amid diversity. *Change, 23*(5), 8–13.

DeVries, D., & Edwards, K. (1974). Student teams and learning games: Their effects on cross-race and cross-sex interaction. *Journal of Educational Psychology, 66,* 741–749.

Durán, R. P. (1986). Prediction of Hispanics' college achievement. In M. S. Olivas (Ed.), *Latino college students* (pp. 221–245). New York: Teachers College Press.

Estrada, L. F. (1988). Anticipating the demographic future. *Change, 20*(3), 14–19.

Farrell, W. C., & Jones, C. K. (1988). Recent racial incidents in higher education: A preliminary perspective. *Urban Review, 20*(3), 211–225.

Feagin, J. R., & Feagin C. B. (1978). *Discrimination American style: Institutional racism and sexism.* Englewood Cliffs, NJ: Prentice-Hall.

Feagin, J. R., & Feagin, C. B. (1993). *Racial and ethnic relations* (4th ed.). Englewood Cliffs, NJ: Prentice-Hall.

Fields, C. M. (1988). The Hispanic pipeline: Narrow, leaking, and needing repair. *Change, 20*(3), 20–27.

Fiske, E. B. (1988). The undergraduate Hispanic experience: A case of juggling two cultures. *Change, 20*(3), 29–33.

Fleming, J. (1984). *Blacks in college.* San Francisco: Jossey-Bass.

Fleming, J. (1990). Standardized test scores and the Black college environment. In K. Lomotey (Ed.), *Going to school: The African American experience* (pp. 143–154). Albany: State University of New York Press.

Forehand, G. A., & Ragosta, M. (1976). *A handbook for integrated schooling.* Princeton, NJ: Educational Testing Service.

Gaff, J. G. (1992). Beyond politics: The educational issues inherent in multicultural education. *Change, 24*(1), 31–35.

Garibaldi, A. M. (1991a). Blacks in college. In C. V. Willie, A. M. Garibaldi, & W. L. Reed (Eds.), *The education of African-Americans* (pp. 93–99). New York: Auburn House.

Garibaldi, A. M. (1991b). The role of historically Black colleges in facilitating resilience among African-American students. *Education and Urban Society, 24*(1), 103–112.

Garibaldi, A. M. (1992). Educating and motivating African American males to succeed. *Journal of Negro Education, 61*(1), 4–11.

Gay, G. (1973). Racism in America: Imperatives for teaching ethnic studies. In J. A. Banks (Ed.), *Teaching ethnic studies: Concepts and strategies* (pp. 27–49). Washington, DC: National Council for the Social Studies.

Gordon, E. W. (1992). Conceptions of Africentrism and multiculturalism in education: A general overview. *Journal of Negro Education, 61,* 235–236.

Gordon, E. W., & Bhattacharyya, M. (1992). Human diversity, cultural hegemony, and the integrity of the academic cannon. *Journal of Negro Education, 61,* 405–418.

Gordon, L. (1991). Race relations and attitudes at Arizona State University. In P. G. Altbach and K. Lomotey (Eds.), *The racial crisis in American higher education* (pp. 233–248). Albany: State University of New York Press.

Hamilton, C., & Carmichael, S. (1967). *Black power: The politics of liberation in America.* New York: Random House.

Hilliard, A. G. (1990). Limitations of current academic achievement measures. In K. Lomotey (Ed.), *Going to school: The African American experience* (pp. 135–14 2). Albany: State University of New York Press.

Hilliard, A. G. (1992). Behavioral style, culture, and teaching and learning. *Journal of Negro Education, 61,* 370–377.

Hsia, J., & Hirano-Nakanishi, M. (1989). The demographics of diversity. *Change, 21*(6), 20–27.

Hune, S. (1989). Opening the American mind and body: The role of Asian American studies. *Change, 21*(6), 56–63.

Irvine, J. J. (1991). *Black students and school failure.* New York: Praeger.

Jones, J. M. (1981). The concept of racism and its changing reality. In

B. P. Bowser & R. G. Hunt (Eds.), *Impacts of racism on White Americans* (pp. 27–49). Beverly Hills: Sage.

Katz, J. (1991). White faculty struggling with the effects of racism. In P. G. Altbach & K. Lomotey (Eds.), *The racial crisis in American higher education* (pp. 187–196). Albany: State University of New York Press.

Knowles, L. L., & Prewitt, K. (1969). *Institutional racism in America.* Englewood Cliffs, NJ: Prentice-Hall.

Kozol, J. (1991). *Savage inequalities: Children in America's schools.* New York: Crown Publishers.

Kuh, G. D., Schuh, J. H., Whitt, E. J., & Associates. (1991). *Involving colleges: Successful approaches to fostering student learning and development outside the classroom.* San Francisco: Jossey-Bass.

Ladson-Billings, G. (1992). Liberatory consequences of literacy: A case of culturally relevant instruction for African American students. *Journal of Negro Education, 61,* 378–391.

Levine, A., & Cureton, J. (1992). The quest revolution: Eleven facts about multiculturalism and the curriculum. *Change, 24*(1), 25–29.

Longstreet, W. S. (1978). *Aspects of ethnicity: Understanding differences in pluralistic classrooms.* New York: Teachers College Press.

Madrid, A. (1986). Foreword. In M. S. Olivas (Ed.), *Latino college students* (pp. ix–xvii). New York: Teachers College Press.

Muñoz, D. G. (1986). Identifying areas of stress for Chicano undergraduates. In M. S. Olivas (Ed.), *Latino college students* (pp. 131–156). New York: Teachers College Press.

Muñoz, D. G., & García-Bahne, B. (1977). *A study of the Chicano experience in higher education.* Washington, DC: National Institute of Mental Health.

Nakanishi, D. T. (1989). A quota on excellence? The Asian American admissions debate. *Change, 21*(6), 39–48.

National Center for Education Statistics. (1993). *Trends in enrollment in higher education by racial/ethnic category: Fall 1982 through Fall 1991.* Washington, DC: U.S. Office of Education.

National Center for Education Statistics. (1994). *Mini-digest of education statistics 1993.* Washington, DC: U.S. Office of Education.

National Coalition of Advocates for Students. (1985). *Barriers to excellence: Our children at risk.* Boston: Author.

National Council of La Raza. (1990). *Hispanic education: A statistical portrait 1990.* Washington, DC: Author.

Oakes, J. (1985). *Keeping track: How schools structure inequality.* New Haven: Yale University Press.

O'Brien, E. M. (1992a). The demise of Native American education. *Black Issues in Higher Education, 7*(1), 15–22.

O'Brien, E. M. (1992b). A foot in each world: Striving to succeed in higher education. *Black Issues in Higher Education, 7*(1), 27–31.

O'Brien, E. M. (1992c). Tribal colleges thrive amid hardship: Building nations and preserving cultural heritage. *Black Issues in Higher Education, 7*(1), 37–39.

Olivas, M. S. (1986a). Financial aid for Hispanics: Access, ideology, and packaging policies. In M. S. Olivas (Ed.), *Latino college students* (pp. 281–295). New York: Teachers College Press.

Olivas, M. S. (Ed.). (1986b). *Latino college students.* New York: Teachers College Press.

Olivas, M. S. (1992). Trout fishing in catfish ponds. In J. M. Jones, M. E. Goertz, & C. V. Kuh (Eds.), *Minorities in graduate education: Pipeline, policy and practice* (pp. 46–54). Princeton, NJ: Educational Testing Service.

Oliver, J., & Etchevery, R. (1987). Factors influencing the decisions of academically talented Black students who attend college. *Journal of Negro Education, 56,* 152–161.

Orfield, G. (1988). Exclusion of the majority: Shrinking college access and public policy in metropolitan Los Angeles. *Urban Review, 20*(3), 147–163.

Orfield, G. (1992). Money, equity, and college access. *Harvard Educational Review, 62*(3), 337–372.

Porter, O. F. (1990). *Undergraduate completion and persistence at four-year colleges and universities: Detailed findings.* Washington, DC: National Institute of Independent Colleges and Universities.

Pounds, A. W. (1987). Black students' needs on predominantly White campuses. In D. J. Wright (Ed.), *Responding to the needs of today's minority students* (pp. 23–38). San Francisco: Jossey-Bass.

Quevedo-Garcia, E. L. (1987). Facilitating the development of Hispanic students. In D. J. Wright (Ed.), *Responding to the needs of today's minority students* (pp. 49–63). San Francisco: Jossey-Bass.

Recruitment and retention: A Black issues special report. (1992). *Black Issues in Higher Education, 8*(24), 17–40.

Richardson, R. C., Simmons, H., & de los Santos, A. (1987). Graduating minority students. *Change, 19*(3), 20–27.

Rodriguez, R. (1992). Professional groups create an educational continuum. *Black Issues in Higher Education, 8*(24), 26–27.

Rosca, N. (1989). The arts and the Asian American community: A case of the missing audience. *Change, 21*(6), 53–55.

Sagar, H. A., & Schofield, J. W. (1984). Integrating the desegregated school: Problems and possibilities. In D. E. Bartz & M. L. Maehr (Eds.), *Advances in motivation and achievement* (pp. 204–242). Greenwich, CT: JAI Press.

Shade, B. J. (1982). African-American cognitive style: A variable in school success? *Review of Educational Research, 52*(2), 219–244.

Skinner, E. F., & Richardson, R. C., Jr. (1988). Making it in a majority university: The minority graduate perspective. *Change, 20*(3), 37–42.

Slavin, R. (1983). *Cooperative learning.* New York: Longman.

Solmon, L. C., & Wingard, T. L. (1991). The changing demographics: Problems and opportunities. In P. G. Altbach & K. Lomotey (Eds.), *The racial crisis in American higher education* (pp. 19–42). Albany: State University of New York Press.

St. John, N. H. (1971, January). *School integration, classroom climate, and achievement.* (ERIC Document Reproduction Service No. ED 052 269)

St. John, N. H. (1975). *School desegregation: Outcomes for children.* New York: John Wiley & Sons.

Stage, F. K., & Manning, K. (1992). *Enhancing the multicultural campus environment: A cultural brokering approach.* San Francisco: Jossey-Bass.

Suzuki, R. H. (1983). The education of Asian and Pacific Americans: An introductory overview. In D. T. Nakanishi & M. Hirano-Nakanishi (Eds.), *The education of Asian and Pacific Americans: Historical perspectives and prescriptions for the future* (pp. 1–13). Phoenix, AZ: Oryx Press.

Suzuki, R. H. (1989). Asian Americans as the "model minority." *Change, 21*(6), 13–19.

Thelin, J. (1992). The curriculum crusades and the conservative backlash. *Change, 24*(1), 17–23.

Tierney, W. G. (1991). Native voices in academe: Strategies for empowerment. *Change, 23*(2), 36–39.

Treisman, P. U. (1985). *A study of mathematics performance of Black students at the University of California, Berkeley.* Unpublished manuscript.

U.S. Bureau of the Census. (1991a). *Poverty in the United States* (Current Population Reports, Series P-60, No. 181). Washington, DC: U.S. Government Printing Office.

U.S. Bureau of the Census. (1991b). *Statistical abstract of the United States: 1991.* Washington, DC: U.S. Government Printing Office.

U.S. Commission on Civil Rights. (1970). *Racism in American and how to combat it* (Urban Series #1). Washington, DC: U.S. Government Printing Office.

Wang, L. L. (1988). Meritocracy and diversity in higher education: Discrimination against Asian Americans in the post-Bakke era. *Urban Review, 20*(3), 189–209.

Weinberg, M. (1977). *Minority students: A research appraisal.* Washington, DC: National Institute of Education.

Wilson, R., & Carter, D. J. (Eds.). (1989). *Eighth annual status report: Minorities in higher education.* Washington, DC: American Council on Education.

Wiser, P., & Cook, S. (1971). The impact of cooperative learning experiences on cross-ethnic relationships and attitudes. *Journal of Social Issues, 31,* 219–244.

Wright, B., & Tierney, W. G. (1991). American Indians in higher education: A history of cultural conflict. *Change, 23*(2), 11–18.

Wright, D. J. (1987). Minority students: Developmental beginnings. In D. J. Wright (Ed.), *Responding to the needs of today's minority students* (pp. 5–21). San Francisco: Jossey-Bass.

39

ASIAN PACIFIC AMERICANS AND
COLLEGES AND UNIVERSITIES

Don T. Nakanishi
UNIVERSITY OF CALIFORNIA, LOS ANGELES

Research on topics dealing with Asian Pacific Americans in higher education is beginning to emerge. Until recently, relatively little media, policy, and scholarly attention focused on the experiences, characteristics, and issues of Asian Pacific Americans in colleges and universities in the United States, in part because of their relatively small numbers nationally as well as their seemingly strong academic performance levels. Indeed, in many of the more highly regarded comparative studies of minority students (Astin, 1982; Ogbu, 1978), Asian Pacific Americans were not included in the data collection and analysis because they were not considered to be "educationally disadvantaged" like other groups of color. The lack of a sustained and rigorous body of empirical and theoretical literature has had many unfortunate, albeit often unintended, consequences for Asian Pacific Americans in higher educational institutions. Policy and programmatic decisions related to significant issues of undergraduate and graduate admissions, faculty hiring and promotion, the curriculum, and other topics were often based on empirically untested assertions and monolithic interpretations about Asian Pacific Americans. Many higher educational policy debates and disputes involving Asian Pacific Americans might not have escalated and become explosive if the points of contention could have been informed by a body of scholarly literature.

In this chapter, research on several major interrelated dimensions of the Asian Pacific American higher educational experience will be presented. Interrelated dimensions are (a) the impact of major demographic trends among the Asian Pacific American population on its college-going sector; (b) the issues of Asian Pacific American faculty and administrative representation in higher educational institutions; and (c) the Asian Pacific American admissions quotas controversy, which was the most contentious and significant higher educational issue involving Asian Pacific Americans during the 1980s and early 1990s.

In this chapter, the admissions controversy will receive special attention because, on the one hand, it was the first-ever higher educational issue to occupy one of the top rungs on the leadership agendas of Asian Pacific American civil rights and community groups. It was played out in the context of the dramatic demographic transformations and growing political involvement of the Asian Pacific American population during the 1980s and 1990s. Because these trends are likely to continue to influence future Asian Pacific American higher educational issues, the admissions controversy can serve as a revealing case study. On the other hand, the admissions debate played a highly instrumental role for higher educational research. It had an unexpected, but beneficial, effect in spurring the development of a sizable body of scholarly and policy-oriented studies on many previously unexamined topics relating to the access and representation of Asian Pacific Americans in U.S. colleges and universities. It also generated a number of large-scale, empirically based investigatory reports by government agencies and individual campus committees as well as countless journalistic stories and commentaries by both the Asian Pacific American press and the mainstream media in the United States (Hsia, 1988b; Nakanishi, 1989; Sue & Abe, 1988; Takagi, 1992).

Although the field of Asian Pacific American higher educational research has been enhanced by the focus on the admissions controversy, it has also inadvertently become imbalanced by such studies. Empirical and theoretical research on many other important and compelling aspects of the higher educational experiences of Asian Pacific Americans have not received the same concerted, rigorous, and multidisciplinary examination. For example, research focusing on the increasing reports of anti-Asian sentiments and acts of violence on many college campuses during the 1980s and early 1990s have not been the focus of scholarly inquiry, although journalistic accounts in student newspapers and the mainstream media have been extensive (Asian Pacific American Education Advisory Committee, Office of the Chancellor, the California State University [APAEAC], 1990; Farrell & Jones, 1988; Morse, 1989). Similarly, systematic studies on the vast majority of Asian Pacific American college-going students who did not aspire for nor attend the highly competitive private and public colleges and universities that were at the center of the admissions controversy have been disturbingly rare (Castillo & Minamishin, 1991; Dao, 1991; Fernandez, 1988; Kraska, 1991). The brief conclusion at the end of this chapter critiques the limitations of the current body of literature on Asian Pacific Americans and higher education and attempts to anticipate salient future areas of research.

In this chapter, the term *Asian Pacific Americans* is defined in a manner similar to that of a fact-finding report issued by APAEAC (1990): "Asian Pacific Americans are defined as immigrants, refugees, and the U.S.-born descendants of immigrants from Asia, including Pakistan and the countries lying east of it in South Asia, Southeast Asia, East Asia, and the Pacific Islands" (p. 1).

THE IMPACT OF THE GROWTH AND DIVERSITY OF THE ASIAN PACIFIC AMERICAN POPULATION ON HIGHER EDUCATIONAL INSTITUTIONS

Asian Pacific Americans are the United States's fastest-growing group, having doubled during each of two decades from 1.5 million nationally in 1970 to 3.5 million in 1980 and finally to 7.2 million in 1990. Recent projections estimate that Asian Pacific Americans will continue to increase to 11 million by 2000 and to nearly 20 million by 2020 (Bouvier & Martin, 1985; California Department of Finance, 1985; Fawcett & Carino, 1987; LEAP and UCLA Asian American Studies Center, 1993; Mueller, 1984). This substantial increase can be attributed in large measure to the Immigration Act of 1965 (which eliminated the discriminatory quota provisions of the Immigration Act of 1924), the Indochinese Refugee Resettlement Program Act of 1975, and the Refugee Act of 1980. These three legislative measures, having reversed a four-decade longitudinal trend, permitted the migration and entry of close to 1 million refugees from Southeast Asia. Asian Pacifics now represent the largest group of legal immigrants to the United States. For example, between 1931 and 1960, when the provisions of the 1924 National Origins Act were in effect, 58% of the legal immigrants were from Europe, 21% from North America, 15% from Latin America, and the smallest portion, 5%, were from Asia. However, this situation involving legal immigration was nearly the opposite by the reporting period 1980–1984. Legal immigration from Europe had decreased to 12% of the overall total, that from North America to 2%, while immigration from Latin America had increased to 35% and Asian immigration had substantially increased to 48% of the country's total legal immigrants (United Way, Asian Pacific Research and Development Council, 1985).

By extension, Asian Pacific Americans also are the fastest-growing ethnic group in the U.S. college population. In fall 1976, there were 150,000 Asian Pacific American undergraduate and graduate students in higher educational institutions across the nation (Carnegie Foundation for the Advancement of Teaching, 1987). In fall 1986 there were almost three times as many, or 448,000 Asian Pacific American enrollees (Carnegie Foundation for the Advancement of Teaching, 1987). By 1992, there were 637,000 Asian Pacific American undergraduate and graduate students, who constituted 5% of all students in U.S. colleges and universities ("College Enrollment by Racial and Ethnic Group, Selected Years," 1993). Recent population projections estimate that the Asian Pacific American college-going age sector will continue to increase from now until 2020 (LEAP & UCLA Asian American Studies Center, 1993).

During the decade from 1970 to 1980, and continuing into the 1990s, the Asian Pacific American population also dramatically shifted from being largely American born to predominantly foreign born—a result of this upsurge in international migration. For example, according to the 1980 census, 63.1% of all Asian Pacific Americans in Los Angeles County were foreign born, with 92.9% of the Vietnamese, 85.9% of the Koreans, 72.8% of the Filipinos, and 70.3% of the Chinese having been born outside the United States (UCLA Ethnic Studies Centers, 1987). In marked contrast, 10.4% of the county's White residents, 2.4% of the African Americans, and 45.5% of the "Spanish-origin" population were foreign born (UCLA Ethnic Studies Centers, 1987). In 1980, 62% of the nation's Asian Pacific Americans were born abroad (Hsia & Hirano-Nakanishi, 1989). This significant demographic shift in the Asian Pacific American population from a largely American-born community to a largely foreign-born one was also reflected among Asian Pacific American college students. The majority of these students were born abroad, although most had a substantial portion of their elementary and secondary schooling in the United States. Issues of social, cultural, and linguistic adjustment and maintenance for both students and their parents remained compelling at the elementary and secondary school levels and had numerous implications for higher educational institutions (see chapter 23 of this *Handbook*). For example, in 1985, 27% of all Asian Pacific American students who took the Scholastic Aptitude Test (SAT) throughout the United States reported that English was not their best language. In contrast, 4% of all other test-takers said that English was not their best language (Rambist & Arbeiter, 1986).

California, with a population of over 3 million Asian Pacific Americans in 1990, is the state with the largest population of Asian Pacific Americans. Forty percent of the Asian Pacific Americans in the United States live in California. By extension, over 40% of all Asian Pacific Americans who are enrolled in American higher educational institutions attend a college or university in California. Large numbers of Asian Pacific American college students can also be found in New York (which now has the second-largest community of Asian Pacific Americans), Hawaii, Illinois, and Texas (Gardner, Robey, & Smith, 1985). In 1984, these five states—California (166,837), Hawaii (31,574), New York (28,779), Illinois (18,918), and Texas (16,812)—enrolled 68.9% (262,920) of the nation's Asian Pacific American college-going population (381,746). And although nearly two thirds of the Asian Pacific American population in the United States is still concentrated in the Pacific region, the recent growth of this population is nationwide. For example, whereas in 1970 there were 1.5 million Asian Pacific Americans in the United States, by 1990 there were over 2 million who lived in states bordering the Atlantic Ocean (LEAP & UCLA Asian American Studies Center, 1993). For at least two decades beginning in the early 1970s, there has been a substantial increase in the numbers of Asian Pacific American students at both private and public institutions located on the East Coast, particularly in the city and state university of New York systems and in the Ivy League colleges.

The Asian Pacific American population, as many previous studies have demonstrated, and as Pang points out in chapter 23 of this *Handbook*, should not be conceptualized as a single, monolithic group (Chun, 1980; Endo, 1980; Endo, Sue, & Wagner, 1980; Fawcett and Carino, 1987; Gardner et al., 1985; Kim, 1978; United States Commission on Civil Rights, 1979; United Way, 1985). It has become an extremely heterogeneous population with respect to ethnic and national origins, cultural values, generations in the United States, social class, religion, and other socially differentiating characteristics. In 1970, for instance, Japanese Americans were the largest Asian Pacific American ethnic group. By 1980, however, both Chinese Americans (812,178) and Filipino Americans (781,894) surpassed Japanese Americans (716,331). Other Asian Pacific groups such as Asian Indians (387,223), Koreans (357,393), and Vietnamese (245,025) grew rapidly as well through immigration. By 1990, both Chinese (1,645,472) and Filipino (1,406,770) American populations had grown to be nearly twice as large as that of Japanese Americans (847,562), who experienced relatively little immigration from Japan and a gradually declining birth rate. It is projected that by 2000 Japanese Americans will fall further down the population rankings, with practically all other major Asian Pacific American groups outnumbering them and Filipino Americans replacing Chinese Americans as the largest Asian Pacific American ethnic group (LEAP & UCLA Asian American Studies Center, 1993). This ethnic diversity is often quite visible at many U.S. colleges and universities in the form of a wide range of student organizations and activities. At the University of California, Los Angeles (UCLA), for example, there were over 60 different Asian Pacific American student organizations in 1993.

Diversity among Asian Pacific Americans is also evident from other characteristics. Perhaps the most obvious source of differentiation results from the large numbers who came as immigrants versus those who came as refugees (Le, 1993). The diversity among Asian Pacific Americans is striking in other ways as well. Much is made of the academic achievement of Asian Pacific Americans—they are frequently labeled by the U.S. mass media as "whiz kids" (Bell, 1985; Butterfield, 1986; Chun, 1980; "The Drive to Excel: Strong Families and Hard Work Propel Asian-Americans to the Top of the Class," 1984). However, census data show that nearly 25% of all Asian Pacific Americans age 25 years and over have less than a high school diploma, and some groups have large numbers who have very little formal schooling (UCLA Ethnic Studies Centers, 1987). Nearly a quarter of all Vietnamese and Guamanian women, in the working-

age group of 25 to 44 years, have fewer than eight years of schooling. At the same time, nearly 40% of the Chinese and Asian Indian women of the same age category are college graduates, but 1 out of 10 Chinese and 1 out of 10 Asian Indian women, 25 to 44 years of age, have eight or fewer years of formal education (UCLA Ethnic Studies Centers, 1987). Even though Asian Pacific Americans have a deceptively high median household income, they also have a greater percentage of individuals living below the federal poverty level than the non-Hispanic White population. In 1990, the poverty rate for Asian Pacifics was 12.2% compared to 8.8% for non-Hispanic Whites (LEAP & the UCLA Asian American Studies Center, 1993). The poverty rates for groups such as the Hmongs, Laotians, and Cambodians were over 60% (LEAP & the UCLA Asian American Studies Center, 1993). The ramifications for higher educational institutions of these wide disparities in income and educational levels are particularly critical in relation to admissions and student support services. Asian Pacific Americans are often excluded from being considered for equal opportunity admissions programs, as well as special retention, tutoring, and counseling activities, because of the sizable number of Asian Pacific American applicants who possess competitive academic credentials (APAEAC, 1990; Bagasao & Suzuki, 1989; Escueta & O'Brien, 1991). At UCLA, for example, Asian Pacific American applicants who are first-time college-goers in their families—or who come from low-income households—are given the same form of consideration in the admissions process as other applicants who come from similar backgrounds. In 1993 Asian Pacific Americans composed nearly a third of all students who were part of the academic advancement program. This program seeks to enhance the retention and graduation rates of students from historically excluded groups.

At the same time, within any particular Asian Pacific American group such as Chinese Americans, the within-group differences can be quite pronounced, reflecting different historical waves of immigration and different segments of a class hierarchical structure. In their classic ethnographic study of San Francisco's Chinatown, *Longtime Californ'*, Nee and Nee (1974) provide a revealing sociohistorical analysis of such within-group diversity among Chinese Americans. Hirschman and Wong (1981) use census data to rigorously examine within-group differences in socioeconomic achievement among immigrant and U.S.-born Chinese, Japanese, and Filipinos. In recognition of this internal diversity, a number of colleges and universities (led by Yale University in the Ivy League and the University of California and California State University systems on the West Coast) launched recruitment and outreach activities in the late 1960s to attract Asian Pacific American applicants from low-income, inner-city high schools in longstanding port-of-entry neighborhoods such as San Francisco's Chinatown and Manilatown to develop a cross-sectional diversity of Asian Pacific American applicants (Nakanishi, 1986).

In contrast to the study of other, larger minority populations, a common technical, methodological problem facing educational researchers and policy makers is that empirical data are not routinely collected or reported on Asian Pacific Americans in toto or, more important, with respect to the different ethnic subgroups of the population (Escueta & O'Brien, 1991; Hsia,

TABLE 39–1. SAT Scores and High School GPAs of University of California Freshmen, 1984

Students' Ethnicity	High School GPA	SAT Verbal	SAT Mathematics
White	3.59	512	577
All Asian Americans	3.69	456	584
Chinese	3.73	473	612
Filipino	3.56	448	520
Indian/Pakistani	3.80	520	606
Japanese	3.75	510	604
Korean	3.64	418	594
Other Asian Americans	3.72	373	556

Note: Data are from *Predictors of Academic Achievement Scores Among Asian American and White Students* (p. 4) by S. Sue and J. Abe, 1988, New York: College Entrance Examination Board. Reprinted with permission.

1988b). Census data tapes, for example, represent one of the few quantitative data sources that provide such ethnic breakdowns with respect to nine different Asian Pacific American groups: Asian Indians, Chinese, Guamanians, Hawaiians, Japanese, Koreans, Filipinos, Samoans, and Vietnamese. Census data, however, have assorted technical and substantive limitations, especially in terms of the restricted set of individual-level characteristics that are surveyed, the long periods of delay between the collection and public dissemination of data, and the special sampling problems that have persistently hampered the gathering of data from Asian Pacific Americans and other minority populations and have resulted in substantial undercounting (United States Commission on Civil Rights, 1992; Yu, 1982). However, examining some of the available higher education data that capture the internal diversity among Asian Pacific Americans reveals significant differences among groups in terms of academic preparation, access, and representation and underscores the importance of seeking and analyzing such data. For example, the University of California requests that its applicants for admissions specify, voluntarily, their ethnic backgrounds and does so in terms of 14 different racial and ethnic groups, of which 7 are Asian Pacific American designations (Chinese, Filipino, Japanese, Korean, Thai/Other Asian, East Indian/Pakistani, and Pacific Islander). Table 39–1 illustrates the variations in SAT scores and high school grade point averages for a sample of 1984 University of California freshmen (Sue & Abe, 1988). Although all Asian Pacific American groups have median high school grade point averages that are the same or higher than White freshmen, there is substantial variation in average SAT verbal and SAT mathematics scores. The freshmen who are classified as "Other Asian Americans"—who are primarily Southeast Asian Americans—have SAT verbal scores that are substantially lower than those of Whites and all other Asian Pacific American groups.

ASIAN PACIFIC AMERICAN FACULTY AND ADMINISTRATIVE REPRESENTATION

A popular notion that Asian Pacific Americans are well represented in college faculties and administrative positions probably represents an extension of the view that Asian Pacific Americans are a successful or model minority (APAEAC, 1990; Bagasao & Suzuki, 1989). The reality, however, is quite different. As in other groups of color and women, there is a substantial decline in the representation of Asian Pacific Americans as one moves up the academic pyramid from high school graduation to freshman admissions, to graduate admissions, and then to the ranks of faculty and administrators. At UCLA, for example, the representation of Asian Pacific Americans in 1992 followed a pattern of decline (common at practically all major colleges and universities): 39.1% of the entering freshman class, 16% of all entering graduate students, 14% of the nontenured faculty, and 8% of the tenured faculty. On the other hand, at most major universities in the United States, Whites reflect the opposite, upward pattern of increasing representation in the academic pyramid. For example, in 1992 at UCLA, Whites were 33% of the entering freshman class, 52% of all entering graduate students, 73% of all nontenured faculty, and 86% of all tenured faculty. Likewise, at Stanford University in 1987, Asian Pacific Americans were 16% of all freshmen, 9% of all entering graduate students, 7% of nontenured faculty, and 3% of all tenured professors. In contrast, Whites were 68% of the freshmen class, 80% of all new graduate students, 86% of nontenured professors, and 94% of tenured professors (Stanford University, 1989). At the same time, the number of Asian Pacific Americans in top administrative posts at most major universities is practically nonexistent (Chan, 1989). In 1992, only 2 of the top 75 administrators at UCLA were Asian Pacific Americans. Similar patterns have been found at other institutions (APAEAC, 1990). A 1989 survey by the Equal Employment Opportunity Commission (EEOC) found that only 1 out of 100 executive or managerial positions in American higher education were filled by Asian Pacific Americans (Escueta & O'Brien, 1991).

To be sure, at most major universities it does not appear that Asian Pacific Americans are as grossly underrepresented in the faculty ranks as African Americans, Chicanos and other Latinos, and American Indians. In contrast to the situation of other faculty of color, there are usually some Asian professors on most college faculties (and usually more than the numbers of other faculty of color), and they usually are concentrated in specific fields like the sciences, engineering, medicine, or the teaching of Asian languages. At Stanford University in 1987, according to federal government guidelines for defining minority groups, there were 46 tenure-line Asian faculty, 24 Black faculty, 24 Hispanic, and 1 Native American (Stanford University, 1989). However, this may be misleading as well, because often the professors who are classified as being Asian are Asian foreign nationals who received a substantial portion of their higher educational training in Asian countries and remain citizens of these other countries as opposed to being Asian Pacific Americans. For example, Stanford University found that in 1987, 39 (75%) of the 52 tenure- and nontenure-line faculty members who were counted as Asian at its institution were born outside the United States, and 31 (60%) of these 52 Asian faculty members received their bachelor's degrees abroad. This situation, as the Stanford report pointed out, resulted from the fact that "federal [government] guidelines are broad . . . [and] many who are counted as minorities according to these definitions—in particular faculty born and educated abroad—are not those minorities targeted by the [Stanford University] Provost's affirmative action guidelines" (Stanford University, 1989, p. 19). The Stanford report notes that "foreign-born and foreign-educated faculty members may not be as effective as role models for minority undergraduates, who are for the most part American born. Students have described gaps in communication, especially in advising and counseling, arising from what they feel are the very different life experiences of minority faculty born and raised abroad. In such instances, mentoring—so important for the successful academic experience of minority students—can be strained" (p. 19). A 1989 EEOC survey found that 40% of Asian faculty in U.S. colleges and universities were foreign nationals, not U.S. citizens (Escueta & O'Brien, 1991).

As several studies have found, Asian Pacific faculty also do not reflect the diversity of the Asian Pacific American population across the nation or of the Asian Pacific American student population on most college campuses because most are male and represent Chinese and Japanese ethnic backgrounds (APAEAC, 1990; Escueta & O'Brien, 1991). At the campuses of the California State University system in 1990, for example, only 33 of the 999 Asian Pacific American faculty were Filipino Americans, who constitute a sizable share of the student population and are projected to become the largest Asian Pacific American group by the end of the 1990s (APAEAC, 1990). Studies have also found that Asian Pacific American faculty are concentrated in a small number of academic disciplines and are underrepresented in a large number of other disciplines (APAEAC, 1990; Escueta & O'Brien, 1991). For all of the campuses of the California State University system in 1990, almost one third (304 of 999) of Asian Pacific American faculty were in the departments of business and engineering. In contrast, many of the departments in the humanities and social sciences have very few Asian Pacific American faculty members (APAEAC, 1990).

Asian American and African American full-time faculty have the lowest tenure rates of all groups. In 1989 only 41% of the full-time faculty members of both groups at institutions across the nation were tenured, in contrast to 52% of all faculty and 53% of White faculty (Escueta & O'Brien, 1991). This situation may explain in part why, beginning in the 1980s, there has been a substantial rise in the number and visibility of Asian American professors from a variety of academic fields who asserted their rights and argued that they had faced unusual and unfair treatment in their evaluations for tenure and promotions (Carmody, 1989; Minami, 1990, Nakanishi, 1993). Indeed, one of the most far-reaching U.S. Supreme Court cases dealing with the rights of professors and academic personnel during tenure and promotional review processes, *EEOC v. University of Pennsylvania*, involved a Chinese American woman professor of management, Rosalie Tung, at the Wharton School of Business at the University of Pennsylvania (Carmody, 1989; Minami, 1990). This landmark decision has led many U.S. colleges and universities to make major changes in their policies and procedures regarding the rights of faculty to gain access to academic personnel review documents and other materials during formal promotional reviews.

In higher educational institutions, Asian Pacific Americans have encountered at least two major forms of unfair and potentially discriminatory treatment. First, like other minority and women scholars who pursue research in ethnic and gender studies, Asian Pacific American professors whose scholarship focuses on topics and issues of the historical and contemporary experiences of the Asian Pacific American population encounter the same misinformed, culturally disparaging, and often hostile reactions and evaluations of their work (Hune, 1989; Minami, 1990). Ethnic and gender research, which often confronts and challenges prevailing analytical perspectives and explores sensitive issues of racism and intergroup relations, have yet to be fully accepted and embraced as important, relevant, or exciting by large majorities of faculty members (Hune, 1989; Minami, 1990, Nakanishi, 1993; Njeri, 1989).

At the same time, Asian Pacific American professors also have encountered both subtle and overt forms of racial discrimination. In Professor Rosalie Tung's lawsuit, the Supreme Court agreed with her attorneys and the EEOC that colleges and universities have no special privileges that should shield or protect them from fully disclosing relevant personnel review documents in a formal investigation of discrimination in employment. In Tung's case, she alleged that the chairman of her department made sexual advances to her, which she turned down. She alleged that he then did everything in his power as chair to orchestrate a negative evaluation of her application for tenure, especially in putting together an all-White-male committee of five senior professors—none of whom had any expertise in her area of research on U.S.-China relations—who judged that her scholarly work was not up to their standards. What she, her attorneys, and the EEOC requested were the reports written by this five-member committee as well as all reports by the chair of her department about her. She also requested copies of the tenure review files for five White males who had received tenure just before her, in order to test her claim that she had a scholarly record that was equal to or better than theirs. The university rejected each of these requests and argued that it enjoyed a special privilege of academic freedom and confidentiality. All of this eventually led to Professor Tung's lawsuit, which the Supreme Court decided unanimously in her favor in 1990.

The issue of Asian American representation and promotions in faculty and administrative positions in U.S higher educational institutions has become a significant focus of collective mobilization by Asian American civil rights leaders and organizations (Minami, 1990) and a major topic of inquiry by several government and educational fact-finding commissions (APAEAC, 1990; Attorney General's Asian and Pacific Islander Advisory Committee, 1988; U.S. Commission on Civil Rights, 1992). These inquiries have served to highlight a number of previously overlooked, but potentially unwarranted, educational and policy consequences stemming from the underrepresentation of Asian Pacific American in faculty and administrative positions. These investigative groups have made policy recommendations for immediate and long-range resolution. A special Asian Pacific American task force to California's state attorney general recommended in a report on Asian Pacific American civil rights issues:

Asian Pacific Islander Americans cannot continue to be represented predominantly as students within California's educational institutions. The poor representation of Asian Pacific Americans among the faculty and staff in those institutions can only perpetuate institutional biases that result in unfair admissions policies, financial aid decisions, academic curriculum planning and employment policies that are oblivious to the needs of Asian Pacific Islanders. (Attorney General's Asian and Pacific Islander Advisory Committee, 1988, p. 99)

THE ASIAN PACIFIC AMERICAN ADMISSIONS CONTROVERSY: A CASE STUDY OF THE POLITICS OF ASIAN AMERICAN EDUCATIONAL CONCERNS

The Political and Demographic Dimensions of the Controversy

Perhaps no educational issue has been of greater concern and attention to such a broad national cross-section of the Asian Pacific American population than the so-called Asian Pacific American admissions controversy of the 1980s and 1990s. Those concerned include civil rights leaders of high school students and their parents, from those in New York Chinatown to the suburbs of San Francisco and from those of first-generation background to others whose families have been in the United States for many decades. Perhaps no other educational concern of the Asian Pacific American population, since at least the landmark 1974 Supreme Court bilingual education case of *Lau v. Nichols,* has attracted as much national media attention and political interest (Wang, 1976). A review of this controversy as well as the substantial amount of scholarly and educational policy research that has been produced about it provides a number of insightful theoretical and empirical vantage points from which to understand many of the most significant issues of access, representation, and influence facing Asian Pacific Americans at U.S. colleges and universities.

The Asian Pacific American admissions controversy has its origins in the early 1980s, when the national press first became interested in the increased visibility of Asian Pacific Americans in the U.S. college-going population. The media initially wrote stories that touted the individual academic achievements of some of the most gifted Asian Pacific American students such as those who were Westinghouse Talent Search winners, and what appeared to be their dramatic rise in enrollment at many of the United States's most selective institutions. *U.S. News and World Report* ("Asian Americans: Are They Making the Grade?" 1984) wrote that "Asians are, in fact, flocking to top colleges. They make up about 10 percent of Harvard's freshman class and 20 percent of all students at the Juilliard School. In California, where Asians are 5.5 percent of the population, they total 23.5 percent of all Berkeley undergraduates" (p. 42). And *Newsweek* ("The Drive to Excel," 1984) asked rhetorically: "Is it true what they say about Asian American students, or is it mythology? They say that Asian Americans are brilliant. They say that Asian-Americans behave as a model minority, that they dominate mathematics, engineering, and science courses—that they are grinds who are so dedicated to getting ahead that they never have any fun" (p. 1).

Beginning in 1985, however, journalists and syndicated columnists began to portray Asian Pacific American undergraduates not only as "whiz kids," as *Time* magazine ("The New Whiz

Kids," 1985) boldly proclaimed in a major cover story, but also as possible victims of racially discriminatory admissions practices. In a highly influential story for the *Chronicle of Higher Education,* Biemiller (1985) wrote:

Charges that some elite colleges and universities may be purposefully limiting the admission of persons of Asian descent continue to worry students and parents. . . . The allegations come at a time when reports of racially motivated violence against Asians are increasing and talk of 'trade wars' with Asian countries continues, prompting concern about a possible resurgence of anti-Asian sentiment. (p. 1)

Historical analogies were often drawn with the situation that faced American Jewish students before World War II, when invidious, discriminatory policies and procedures were officially adopted to limit their access to many of the same selective institutions about which Asian Pacific Americans were now concerned. As *Los Angeles Times* reported Linda Mathews (1987) wrote:

There may be a parallel between what is happening to Asian-Americans now and what happened to Jews in the 1920s and 1930s at some Ivy League schools. . . . To keep a lid on the number of Jewish students— denounced as "damned curve raisers" by less-talented classmates—the universities imposed quotas, sometimes overt, sometimes covert. . . . Today's "damned curve raisers" are Asian-Americans, who are winning academic prizes and qualifying for prestigious universities in numbers out of proportion to their percentage of the population. And like Jews before them, the members of the new model minority contend that they have begun to bump up against artificial barriers to their advancement. (p. 23)

Conservative and liberal commentators alike also joined the fray and linked the Asian Pacific American admissions issue to their ongoing ideological donnybrooks on a range of unsettled policy topics, be it affirmative action programs, the nation's competitiveness with foreign economic powers, or recent educational reform measures. *The Retreat From Race* by Takagi (1992) provides an engaging, in-depth analysis of the ideological dimensions and consequences of this admissions debate. George F. Will, writing in April 1989, shortly after Berkeley Chancellor Ira Michael Heyman apologized to the Asian Pacific American community for his administration's past admissions policies that "indisputably had a disproportionate impact on Asian Americans" ("UC Berkeley Apologizes for Policy that Limited Asians," 1989, p. 3), declared that liberalism was to blame for the admissions controversy (Will, 1989). In echoing the highly controversial views expressed a few months earlier by former U.S. Assistant Attorney General William Bradford Reynolds, columnist Will argued that the discrimination that Asian American students encountered was due to affirmative action policies, one of the major cornerstones of the liberal social agenda. Will wrote:

Affirmative action discriminated against Asian Americans by restricting the social rewards open to competition on the basis of merit. We may want a modified meritocracy, but it should not be modified by racism and the resentment of excellence. . . . At a time of high anxiety about declining educational standards and rising competition from abroad, and especially from the Pacific Rim, it is lunacy to punish Asian Americans, the nation's model minority, for their passion to excel. (p. B7)

Clarence Page was one of many liberal commentators, along with major Asian Pacific American community leaders, who denounced the conservatives' attack on affirmative action and their attempt to connect it with the situation facing Asian Pacific American students at Berkeley. As Page (1989) wrote:

Since this announcement offers ammunition in their relentless fight against affirmative action programs, some political conservatives applaud it. Conservatives often offer the success of Asian Americans as evidence that the American system is so fair to all that blacks and other minorities jolly well better look to themselves, not to the government or "reverse discrimination" for solutions to their problems. But the Berkeley problem was not "reverse discrimination." It was plain old fashioned discrimination of a sort affirmative action programs were intended to remedy, not create. The big difference this time is that it penalizes a people who have a reputation for overachievement. (p. A15)

The media's changing portrayal of Asian Pacific American college students from the mid-1980s to the mid-1990s may have appeared to reflect a zealous search for good and provocative news stories rather than being of significance to higher educational policy making. However, beyond the catchy headlines and one-line history lessons, a new, and potentially far-reaching, controversy about undergraduate admissions was gradually, and unexpectedly, unfolding. In many respects, the points of contention appeared to be quite familiar and somehow *seemed* to be settled, especially in the aftermath of the Supreme Court decision of *Allan Bakke v. Regents of the University of California* (which dealt with affirmative action programs in higher education). Like other recent conflicts dealing with issues of access and representation of women or historically underrepresented racial minorities in U.S. higher educational institutions, the Asian American admissions debate eventually focused on the potential bias and arbitrariness of selection criteria, procedures, and policies that might limit equal educational opportunities. Broad philosophical concepts such as meritocracy and seemingly widely shared, longstanding institutional goals such as the deliberate social engineering of a "diverse" or "balanced" undergraduate student body were again debated, and their procedural implementation in the admissions process was both questioned and justified (Tsuang, 1989; Wang, 1988).

And yet, what was not anticipated was that this new admissions controversy would involve Asian Pacific Americans, a group that had not figured prominently in the earlier policy and legal disputes over admissions, and a group that did not have a reputation for being particularly assertive, visible, or efficacious in the political or other decision-making arenas. However, during the 1980s, a new and different Asian Pacific American population emerged as a result of unprecedented demographic, economic, and political trends (Nakanishi, 1991). Higher education officials, like others who were not population specialists, probably could not have foreseen the dramatic changes that were occurring among Asian Pacific Americans, nor could they have fully realized how these trends would come to seriously challenge their seemingly well-established institutional practices and policies (Nakanishi, 1989).

Contrary to the news media's interpretation at the time, the seemingly dramatic rise in Asian Pacific American enrollment in many of the nation's most competitive institutions at the start of the 1980s probably had far less to do with Asian Pacific American students suddenly becoming more academically motivated and qualified than it did with their phenomenal demographic growth. Coinciding with this demographic upsurge was the growing political maturity and influence of the Asian Pacific American population at both the national and local levels. Perhaps at no other period in the history of Asian Pacific Americans in the United States have so many individuals and organizations participated in such a wide array of political and civil rights activities, especially in relation to the U.S. political system but also related to the affairs of their ancestral homelands in Asia.

In traditional electoral politics, what had come to be taken as a common occurrence in Hawaii, namely the election of Asian Pacific Americans to public office, suddenly became a less-than-surprising novelty in the so-called mainland states with the election and appointment of Asian Pacific Americans to federal, state, and local positions in California, Washington, New York, and elsewhere (Nakanishi, 1991). And perhaps most significant, the Asian Pacific American population came to demonstrate that it, too, had resources and talents—organizational, financial, or otherwise—to advance its specific concerns in a variety of political arenas and to confront political issues that potentially were damaging to its group interests. Two widely reported grassroots campaigns of the 1980s and 1990s were illustrative of this new collective determination: (a) the successful drive in 1988 by Japanese Americans to gain redress and reparations for their World War II incarceration and (b) the national movement to appeal and overturn the light sentences that were given to two unemployed Detroit auto workers who, in 1982, used a baseball bat to kill a Chinese American named Vincent Chin. The two men mistook Chin for a Japanese and, therefore, someone who was viewed as having taken away their jobs (Nakanishi, 1991).

The enhanced political participation of the Asian Pacific American population during the 1980s had several idiosyncratic features that would have peculiar consequences for the Asian Pacific American admissions controversy. Unlike other ethnic groups that register and vote in overwhelming proportions for one or the other of the two major political parties—as African Americans and American Jews vote overwhelmingly for the Democratic party—and therefore are largely beholden to the electoral success of that one party, Asian Pacific Americans began to exhibit a very different pattern of political affiliations at both the mass and elite levels during the decade. In numerous studies conducted as part of the UCLA Asian Pacific American Voter Registration Project, Asian Pacific Americans were found to be almost evenly divided between Democrats and Republicans with respect to their registration and voting behavior (Nakanishi, 1991).

Both political parties, especially the Republicans, have attempted to register the hundreds of thousands of recent Asian Pacific immigrants and refugees who have become naturalized citizens annually, most notably in key electoral states such as

California. At the same time, Asian Pacific Americans have cultivated a strong reputation in recent years as major financial contributors to Republican and Democratic candidates alike. The estimated $10 million they gave for the 1988 presidential election was divided almost equally between George Bush and Michael Dukakis (Nakanishi, 1991). Therefore, at the mass and elite levels of voting and campaign fund-raising, Asian Pacific Americans channeled their support to both political parties during the 1980s, a pattern that will likely continue in the future. In turn, Democratic and Republican leaders attempted to appeal to their growing and valued Asian Pacific American constituents by addressing issues of special concern to them (Nakanishi, 1991).

This unusual pattern of bipartisan affiliations among Asian Pacific Americans might well explain why the Asian Pacific American admissions issue gained the support of top leaders from both political parties. In California, for example, the foremost liberal Democratic leaders in the state legislature—Tom Hayden, Art Torres, David Roberti, and Willie Brown—actively monitored the admissions controversy at the public, taxpayer-supported University of California campuses for over 5 years. They held numerous fact-finding hearings; intervened to bring together university officials and Asian Pacific American community leaders; passed special resolutions on admissions; and instructed the state auditor general to undertake an unprecedented audit of admissions procedures at Berkeley (Takagi, 1992; Wang, 1988). They, along with other key municipal leaders such as Mayor Tom Bradley of Los Angeles, frequently spoke out against potentially discriminatory admissions practices in their appearances before local Asian Pacific American communities.

At the national level, in Washington, DC, the issue was championed by liberals such as Senator Paul Simon and conservatives such as Congressman Dana Rohrabacher as well as Presidents Ronald Reagan and George Bush. Simon and Rohrabacher both took a strong interest in the Title VI compliance investigations at UCLA and Harvard by the Office of Civil Rights of the Department of Education and requested that other institutions be formally reviewed in the future. Therefore, the admissions controversy went beyond differences in political party affiliations and ideologies for Asian Pacific Americans and came to rest at the top of the leadership agendas for Asian Pacific Americans of all political persuasions. It is highly likely that Republican and Democratic Asian Pacific American leaders, working together or independently, will continue to vigorously push officials from both parties to resolve and to continue to monitor this issue for many years to come (Nakanishi, 1989).

The Points of Contention in the Admissions Controversy

All parties to the so-called Asian American admissions debate—the critics as well as admissions officers—agreed that Asian Pacific American applicants to many of the nation's most selective undergraduate institutions of the Ivy League, Stanford, and the flagship Berkeley and Los Angeles campuses of the University of California system had lower rates of admissions, or admit rates, than other groups of applicants including Whites

(Asian American Task Force on University Admissions, 1985; Brown Asian American American Students Association, 1984; Bunzel & Au, 1987; Nakanishi, 1989; Princeton University, 1985; Stanford University, 1986; Takagi, 1992; Wang, 1988; Winerip, 1985). Although disparities have existed and been acknowledged officially for several years, statistics for the entering classes of fall 1985 are illustrative. At Princeton, for example, 17% of all applicants and 14% of the Asian American applicants were admitted in that year. At Harvard, 15.9% of all applicants and 12.5% of the Asian Americans were accepted. And at Yale, 18% of all applicants and 16.7% of Asian Americans were admitted (Winerip, 1985). Put another way, Asian American applicants to Princeton were admitted at a rate that was only 82.4% of that for others applicants; to Harvard at 78.6%; and to Yale at 92.6%.

Similarly, in perhaps the most in-depth empirical investigation of this admissions controversy, the California State Office of the Auditor General (1987), at the legislative request of the California State Senate, conducted an unprecedented audit of White and Asian Pacific American freshman applicants to the Berkeley campus of the University of California. Academic records for applicants to Berkeley's seven different undergraduate colleges and programs during the seven-year period from 1981 through 1987 were examined, producing an overall total of 49 different categories of comparison between Asian Pacifics and Whites. In 37 of the 49 categories, Whites had higher admit rates than Asian Pacifics, even though Asian Pacific applicants had higher academic qualifications in practically all comparison categories.

Every fact-finding inquiry that was undertaken to examine and resolve this debate at specific institutions of higher education (Asian American Task Force on University Admissions, 1985; Brown Asian American Students Association, 1984; Princeton University, 1985; Stanford University, 1986) found that Asian Pacific applicants had stronger group-level academic profiles as measured by high school grades and standardized test scores and that those who were admitted usually had far stronger academic qualifications than other identifiable groups of admittees. Bunzel and Au (1987), for example, found that of the students who were admitted to Harvard College in 1982, "Asian Americans had average verbal and math scores of 742 and 725, respectively, for an average combined score of 1467, while the scores for Caucasians were 666 and 689, for a total of 1355, or 112 points lower" (p. 50).

These campus-specific investigative findings were consistent with other studies, such as those by the California Postsecondary Education Commission (1987) regarding student eligibility rates for the University of California system, that consistently showed that Asian Pacific Americans had the largest proportion of "academically eligible" students of any group and, thus, should have had the highest admit rate if grades and test scores were the *only* selection criteria. In the most recent study, based on the state's 1986 high school graduating class, the California Postsecondary Education Commission found that 32.8% of the Asian American graduates were eligible for the University of California, in contrast to 15.8% for Whites, 5% for Hispanics, and 4.5% for African Americans (California Postsecondary Education Commission, 1987).

Several major explanations were offered to account for these differences in admit rates (Nakanishi, 1989). Critics contended that admissions officers at highly selective institutions, both public and private, were engaged in intentionally discriminatory practices to limit the representation of Asian Pacific American students, who tended to be the fastest-growing group of applicants at these campuses (Asian American Task Force on University Admissions, 1985; Biemiller, 1985; Brown Asian American Studies, 1984; Fanucchi, 1985). The fall 1986 entering class at Harvard College, for example, was 12.5% Asian Pacific American, which far exceeded the approximately 2% of the nation's population that was Asian Pacific and would provide credence to the view that they were overrepresented. However, the total applicant pool of 13,657 from which the staff of the Harvard admissions office sought to mold and socially engineer its diverse student body was 19.8% Asian Pacific (Harvard University, 1986). Critics also contended that public institutions like the campuses of the University of California secretly, and without adequate public and legislative discussion, deviated from their longstanding academic, merit-based admissions policies by giving weight in the selection process to a variety of subjective criteria in order to "curb the decline in white enrollment" (Fanucchi, 1985, p. 1). They also argued that Asian Pacific American faculty and administrators were systematically excluded from participating in Academic Senate and other significant campus decision-making bodies and activities dealing with undergraduate selection policies and procedures at these institutions (Asian American Task Force on University Admissions, 1985; Biemiller, 1985; Fanucchi, 1985).

Admissions officers, on the other hand, denied that quotas, informal or formal, existed for Asian Pacific Americans or any other group, especially in the post-*Bakke* era (Mathews, 1987; Takagi, 1992). They contended that critics were making simplistic assertions from the disparities in admit rates between Asian Pacific American and other groups of applicants and that these critics did not fully understand the highly professional, multilevel process of admissions review that all applicants received at these institutions (Carnegie Council on Policy Studies in Higher Education, 1977; Fischer, 1976; Klitgard, 1985; Thompson, 1982; Thresher, 1966). They further argued that privacy laws like the so-called Buckley amendment of 1974 prevented access to all the relevant materials that are reviewed in an applicant's file, especially personal essays and letters of recommendation, which can play a far more decisive role in highly selective admissions situations than is generally recognized (American Association of Collegiate Registrars and Admissions Officers & the College Board, 1980).

Admissions officers at private elite institutions, and to a lesser extent their colleagues at public colleges, also acknowledged that their admissions policies were not entirely meritocratic and encompassed other significant institutional goals and traditions. A common explanation that was offered to account for lower admit rates among Asian Pacific American applicants was that they were less likely to be proportionately represented among a range of criteria that underlie a broad and flexible interpretation of the goal of seeking undergraduate student diversity. Ironically, current officials of many of the nation's most prestigious research universities, like their predecessors

at an earlier period of controversy focusing on quotas against American Jewish applicants, found themselves defending their institutional need to enroll athletes and loyal and wealthy alumni children rather than a meritocratic ideal of choosing students on the basis of their academic promise and accomplishments (Oren, 1985; Synnott, 1979; Wechsler, 1977). Indeed, the Office of Civil Rights concluded that Harvard College did not discriminate against Asian Pacific American applicants because the disparities in rates of admission and academic qualifications between Asian Pacific American and White applicants could be explained by the special preferences that Harvard gave to athletes and alumni children. The Office of Civil Rights agreed with the university that such special preferences served compelling institutional goals, particularly in alumni affairs and fund-raising activities (Jaschik, 1990).

In response to various points of contention for which empirical data and analytical interpretations had been severely lacking, the admissions controversy spurred much needed scholarly and policy-oriented research on Asian Pacific Americans in U.S. colleges and universities. One major point of disagreement, for example, focused on the value of admissions criteria such as high school GPA, SAT verbal and math scores, and achievement tests in predicting the future college performance of Asian Pacific American and other groups of students. Contrary to conventional wisdom within admissions circles, a comparative study by Sue and Abe (1988) of University of California students found that the SAT math score was a better predictor of first-year college grades than the SAT verbal score for Asian Pacific Americans. For Whites, the SAT verbal score remained the stronger predictor, as it has been demonstrated in many previous studies. Similarly, the math achievement test score was a better predictor than the English composition score for Asian Pacific Americans, while the opposite was true for Whites. The study served to challenge the common admissions practice of placing greater weight on verbal rather than math scores. Other studies that explored related aspects of the Asian American admissions controversy contributed to the field of inquiry on admissions and selection processes (Hanson & Litten, 1982). In an article in the *Yale Law Journal,* Tsuang (1989) provided a pioneering analysis of the contemporary legal issues at stake in defending and challenging upper-limit admissions quotas. Tsuang's study was the first to explore these issues since the earlier controversies dealing with upper-limit quotas against American Jewish applicants.

The prolonged and widespread attention that was paid to the admissions controversy at highly competitive colleges had an impact, albeit far from adequate, in stimulating inquiries on the vast majority of Asian Pacific American students and professors who were not at these institutions but who have major issues and concerns that deserve serious examination (Bagasao & Suzuki, 1989). This occurred in relation to the California State University system, which had not been the focus of allegations of admissions quotas or biases. In February 1989, Chancellor W. Ann Reynolds formed the Asian Pacific American Education Advisory Committee, composed of faculty, students, staff, and administrators, to hold hearings, collect and analyze data, and make recommendations on issues and concerns ranging from student retention to faculty and staff affirmative action. In its comprehensive final report, the committee noted that, while "the committee was formed in response to the burgeoning enrollment of APA [Asian Pacific American] students on the CSU [California State University] campuses, an underlying concern was the heated controversy over whether some of the most prestigious institutions of higher learning, including UC Berkeley, Stanford, Harvard, Princeton, and Brown, had imposed discriminatory 'quotas' on the numbers of Asian students admitted" (APAEAC, 1990, p. 1).

CONCLUSION

In fall 1991, a year after the Office of Civil Rights of the Department of Education had issued its findings on potential biases against Asian Pacific American applicants to Harvard University and UCLA (Jaschik, 1990), a new admissions controversy appeared to be emerging. Three campuses of the University of California system—Berkeley, with 34% Asian Pacific Americans; UCLA, with 40%; and Irvine, with 51%—had entering freshman classes in which Asian Pacific Americans outnumbered Whites. This situation continued for these three campuses in 1992 and 1993 and is projected to continue unless significant changes are made in admissions policies or there are unexpected and dramatic shifts in the ethnic composition of the applicant pools. Similar to the early stages of the admissions controversy in the 1980s, concerns have been expressed about the declining representation of White students in the freshman class, despite the fact that the decline is largely tied to decreasing numbers of White students who apply to these colleges. The UCLA Academic Senate committee that is responsible for establishing and monitoring undergraduate admissions policies and practices wrote in its annual report for 1992–93 that, "because of its admission policy, strong recruitment programs and demand for entrance, UCLA is more ethnically diverse than many universities; further, the mixture seems fairly stable. There is some concern that the number of Caucasian students entering UCLA is dropping at a time when their numbers graduating from California high schools is stable or slightly increasing" (Committee on Undergraduate Admissions and Relations With Schools, 1993, p. 37).

Other highly competitive institutions that were embroiled in the admissions controversy, such as Harvard, Yale, Stanford, and Brown, have yet to matriculate a freshman class in which Asian Pacific Americans outnumber Whites. However, these institutions have had record numbers of Asian Pacific American freshmen in their entering classes. Nearly 25% of the freshman classes in fall 1993 at these colleges and universities were composed of Asian Pacific American students, who were the largest group of entering students of color on their campuses. In contrast, when the admissions controversy began at these and other private selective institutions in the early 1980s, there were allegations that admissions officers were socially engineering freshman classes that had upper-limit quotas, in which no more than 10% of the entering classes would be Asian Pacific American students (Hsia, 1988a; Nakanishi, 1989; Takagi, 1992; Tsuang, 1989). At the same time, at many other colleges

and universities across the nation—private and public, selective as well as noncompetitive, four-year and two-year institutions alike—where the representation of Asian Pacific American students may have been minimal in the past, there are now highly visible numbers of Asian Pacific Americans in many of their student bodies.

Although the admissions controversy of the 1980s and early 1990s had a positive impact on the further development of scholarship on Asian Pacific Americans in higher education, it is evident that there are a number of new as well as persistent concerns, issues, and experiences that require empirical and theoretical attention. Among them are the following major areas for potential future inquiries.

First, research is needed on an array of topics that recognize the diversity of Asian Pacific Americans and the differences among them with respect to their participation at different levels of American higher education. Academic pipeline issues will probably continue to be very important for the representation of all Asian Pacific Americans in certain fields, particularly the humanities, and for certain groups such as Southeast Asians, Pacific Islanders, and Filipino Americans in practically all academic fields and all junctures of the pipeline from freshman admissions to tenured professorships. Special data collection efforts should be initiated to ensure that the participation rates of these latter three groups at the student, faculty, and administrative levels are accurately monitored and serious policy-related and analytical studies are undertaken to enhance their participation. At the same time, future educational research also must go beyond merely debunking the monolithic interpretation of Asian Pacific American academic achievement and provide rigorous, empirically based explanations to account for significant differences among groups in their access, representation, and performance in higher education. In contrast to the paucity of such studies at the higher education level, there are a substantial number of works on the diverse needs of different groups of Asian Pacific American children and their parents at the elementary and secondary school levels. In chapter 23 of this *Handbook,* Pang summarizes much of this recent scholarship.

Second, a full-scale research agenda needs to be developed to understand the experiences and concerns of the vast majority of Asian Pacific American students who are far from being the stellar, award-winning "whiz kids" who were the focus of the admissions controversy. Up to now, there have been very few studies that have included Asian Pacific Americans in their collection and analysis of data on issues of student affirmative action, problems in retention and graduation, transfer rates from two-year to four-year colleges, financial aid, and other topics related to various forms of academic and financial disadvantages (Escueta & O'Brien, 1991). The final report by APAEAC of the California State University system (1990) is highly instructive in this regard. It contains one of the most extensive discussions on the "unmet English as a Second Language (ESL) needs of APA (Asian Pacific American) and other immigrant and refugee students," which it says "looms as a major issue confronting the state's educational systems" (p. 26). The report noted that "sixty-two out of 92 testimonies at the statewide hearing [of the committee] confirmed that English proficiency poses a major 'obstacle' for Asian and other immigrant students from university entrance through completion of degree programs" (p. 27).

Third, research must be launched on a range of issues dealing with the status and participation of Asian Pacific Americans as colleges and universities in the United States continue to grapple with the challenges and opportunities of diversity on their campuses and in the society. Lines of inquiry on admissions that were initiated in recent years should continue to be pursued, particularly at campuses where Asian Pacific American students now constitute a sizable proportion, if not the plurality, of the student population. Will there be a backlash to the increased presence of Asian Pacific American students, and if so how will it be manifest? What lessons, if any, have college officials and Asian Pacific American leaders learned from the admissions controversy of the 1980s and early 1990s that should be applied in resolving potential conflicts? And how, if at all, will the projected demographic growth and continued political maturation of the Asian Pacific American population have an impact on future admissions controversies?

At the same time, the increasing representation of Asian Pacific Americans on many college campuses suggests that renewed research on the quality of individual and collective experiences should be rigorously pursued. Much of the pioneering research on topics such as ethnic identity crises among college students (Sue & Sue, 1971) and demands for ethnic studies (Nakanishi & Leong, 1978) were undertaken during an earlier period when Asian Pacific American students, like other students of color, were a distinct numerical minority on most college campuses. Many explanations that were offered to account for their experiences were based on their minority status. However, there is some evidence to suggest that the recent growth of the Asian Pacific American student population has not necessarily led to dramatic shifts in the quality of their college experiences. In 1981, 1984, and 1989, the California State University system administered the Student Needs and Priorities Survey (SNAP), whose samples were broadly representative of the 350,000 students that were enrolled at its campuses. Although the numbers of Asian Pacific American students on these campuses had increased during the 1980s, the surveys consistently found that Asian Pacific American students were the "least satisfied group" (APAEAC, 1990, p. 12). The 1989 SNAP survey found a

pervasive sense of dissatisfaction displayed by Asian students . . . [that] cut across all issue areas—faculty, instruction, advising, student services, and campus life. Such perceptions and attitudes appear to be unrelated to whether the student is a recent immigrant from Southeast Asia or a native citizen of Japanese or Chinese ancestry. The cultural as well as institutional factors which lie behind these findings deserve further study. (p. 12)

These findings clearly beg further systematic research. Is the potential "pervasive sense of dissatisfaction" related to the fact that other aspects of higher educational institutions—the composition of their faculties, the vision of their academic leaders, or the philosophy of their curriculum—have not changed as rapidly and dramatically as many of their student bodies?

The Asian Pacific American population is in the midst of one of its most dramatic and significant periods of transformation. There is no question that the admissions controversy placed Asian Pacific Americans on an unexpected collision course with perhaps their most prized and reliable vehicle for social mobility. Indeed, despite the extraordinary growth and diversification of the Asian Pacific American population in recent decades, there was unmistakable unanimity in the belief that higher education remained the sine qua non for individual and group survival and advancement in the United States. Consequently, it was not surprising that the admissions debate elicited powerful emotional responses from Asian Pacific American students, parents, and community leaders alike and was an ongoing front-page news story in the Asian Pacific American ethnic press for many years. And yet, as significant as higher education has been for Asian Pacific Americans, there has been a curious paucity of rigorous and systematic scholarship on topics relating to this central aspect of the Asian Pacific American experience. It is to be hoped that this situation will change and result in an increased understanding about Asian Pacific Americans as well as about higher education in the United States.

References

American Association of Collegiate Registrars and Admissions Officers & the College Board. (1980). *Undergraduate admissions: The realities of institutional policies, practices, and procedures.* New York: College Entrance Examination Board.

Asian Americans: Are they making the grade? (1984, April 2). *U.S. News and World Report,* pp. 41–47.

Asian American Task Force on University Admissions. (1985). *Task force report.* San Francisco: Author.

Asian Pacific American Education Advisory Committee, Office of the Chancellor, the California State University. (1990). *Enriching California's future: Asian Pacific Americans in the CSU.* Long Beach, CA: Author.

Astin, A. (1982). *Minorities in American higher education.* San Francisco: Jossey-Bass.

Attorney General's Asian and Pacific Islander Advisory Committee. (1988). *Final report.* Sacramento, CA: Author.

Bagasao, P., & Suzuki, B. H. (Eds.). (1989, November/December). Asian and Pacific Americans: Behind the myths [Special issue]. *Change.*

Bell, D. A. (1985, July 15, 22). The triumph of Asian-Americans. *The New Republic,* pp. 24–31.

Biemiller, L. (1985, November 19). Asian students fear top colleges use quota systems. *Chronicle of Higher Education,* pp. 1, 34–36.

Bouvier, L., & Martin, P. (1985). *Population change and California's future.* Washington, DC: Population Reference Bureau.

Brown Asian American Students Association. (1984). Asian American admission at Brown University. *Integrateducation, 22,* 31–41.

Bunzel, J., & Au, J. K. D. (1987). Diversity or discrimination? Asian Americans in college. *Public Interest, 87,* 49–62.

Butterfield, F. (1986, August 3). Why Asians are going to the head of the class. *New York Times Magazine,* pp. 18–23.

California Department of Finance. (1985). *Projected total population of California counties.* Sacramento: Author.

California Postsecondary Education Commission. (1987). *California college going rates.* Sacramento: Author.

California State Office of the Auditor General (1987, October). *Report of first-year admissions of Asians and Caucasians at the University of California at Berkeley* (Publication P-722). Sacramento: Author.

Carmody, D. (1989, December 6). Secrecy and tenure: An issue for high court. *New York Times,* p. B8.

Carnegie Council on Policy Studies in Higher Education. (1977). *Selective admissions in higher education.* San Francisco: Jossey-Bass.

Carnegie Foundation for the Advancement of Teaching. (1987, May/June). Minority access: A question of equity. *Change,* p. 36.

Castillo, C. A., & Minamishin, S. B. (1991). Filipino recruitment and retention at the University of Hawaii at Manoa. *Social Process in Hawaii, 33,* 130–141.

Chan, S. (1989, November/December). Beyond affirmative action: Empowering Asian American faculty. *Change,* pp. 48–51.

Chun, K. T. (1980). The myth of Asian American success and its educational ramifications. *IRCD Bulletin, 15,* 1–12.

College enrollment by racial and ethnic group, selected years. (1993, August 25). *Chronicle of Higher Education,* p. 13.

Committee on Undergraduate Admissions and Relations With Schools. (1993, November 9). 1992–93 annual report. In *Legislative assembly, notice of meeting, University of California academic senate, Los Angeles division* (pp. 37–38).

Dao, M. (1991). Designing assessment procedures for educationally at-risk Southeast Asian-American students. *Learning Disabilities, 24,* 594–601

The drive to excel: Strong families and hard work propel Asian-Americans to the top of the class. (1984, April 5). *Newsweek,* pp. 4–13.

Endo, R. (1980). Social science and historical materials on the Asian American experience. In R. Endo, S. Sue, & N. Wagner (Eds.), *Asian Americans: Social and psychological perspectives* (Vol. 2, pp. 304–331). Palo Alto: Science and Behavior.

Endo, R., Sue, S., & Wagner, N. (Eds.). (1980). *Asian Americans: Social and psychological perspectives* (Vol. 2). Palo Alto: Science and Behavior.

Escueta, E., & O'Brien, E. (1991). Asian Americans in higher education: Trends and issues. *Research Briefs, American Council on Education, 2*(4), 1–11.

Fanucchi, K. (1985, July 14). Reasons sought for drop in UCLA Asian enrollment. *Los Angeles Times,* pp. 1, 3.

Farrell, W. C., Jr., & Jones, C. K. (1988). Recent racial incidents in higher education: A preliminary perspective. *Urban Review, 20*(2), 211–226.

Fawcett, J. T., & Carino, B. V. (Eds.). (1987). *Pacific bridges.* Staten Island, NY: Center for Migration Studies.

Fernandez, M. A. (1988). Issues in counseling Southeast Asian students. *Journal of Multicultural Counseling and Development, 16,* 157–166.

Fischer, F. D. (1976). Day and a half in Harvard admissions office. *Journal of the National Association of College Admissions Counselors, 21,* 14–16.

Gardner, R. W., Robey, B., & Smith, P. (1985). Asian Americans: Growth, change, diversity [Special issue]. *Population Bulletin, 4*(4).

Hanson, K. H., & Litten, L. H. (1982). Mapping the road to academe: A review of research on women, men, and the college-selection process. In P. J. Perun (Ed.), *The undergraduate woman: Issues in educational equity* (pp. 73–98). Lexington, MA: Lexington Books.

Harvard University. (1986). *The official register of Harvard University.* Cambridge, MA: Office of the University Publisher, Author.

Hirschman, C., & Wong, M. G. (1981). Trends in socioeconomic achievement among immigrant and native-born Asian-Americans, 1960–1976. *Sociological Quarterly, 22,* 495–514.

Hsia, J. (1988a). Limits of affirmative action: Asian American access to higher education. *Educational Policy, 2,* 117–136.

Hsia, J. (1988b). *Asian Americans in higher education and work.* Hillsdale, NJ: Lawrence Erlbaum.

Hsia, J., & Hirano-Nakanishi, M. (1989, November/December). The demographics of diversity: Asian Americans and higher education. *Change,* pp. 20–27.

Hune, S. (1989, November/December). Opening the American mind and body: The role of Asian American studies. *Change,* pp. 56–63.

Jaschik, S. (1990, October 17). U.S. finds Harvard did not exclude Asian Americans. *Chronicle of Higher Education,* pp. A1, A6.

Kim, B. L. C. (1978). Problems and service needs of Asian Americans in Chicago: An empirical study. *Amerasia Journal, 5,* 23–44.

Klitgaard, R. (1985). *Choosing elites.* New York: Basic Books.

Kraska, M. F. (1991). Vocational education and bilingual education addressing the needs of Indochinese students in vocational classrooms. *Journal of Vocational Special Needs Education, 13,* 27–31.

Len, N. (1993). The case of the Southeast Asian refugees: Policy for a community "at-risk." In LEAP & UCLA Asian American Studies Center, *The state of Asian Pacific America: Policy issues to the year 2020* (pp. 167–188). Los Angeles: LEAP and UCLA Asian American Studies Center.

LEAP & UCLA Asian American Studies Center. (1993). *The state of Asian Pacific America: Policy issues to the year 2020.* Los Angeles: Authors.

Mathews, L. (1987, July 19). When being best isn't good enough. *Los Angeles Times Magazine,* pp. 22–28.

Minami, D. (1990). Guerrilla war at UCLA: Political and legal dimensions of the tenure battle. *Amerasia Journal, 16*(1), 81–107.

Morse, D. (1989, November 26). Prejudicial studies: One astounding lesson for the University of Connecticut. *Hartford Courant,* pp. 10–15.

Mueller, T. (1984). *The fourth wave: California's newest immigrants.* Washington, DC: Urban Institute.

Nakanishi, D. (1986). The untapped recruiters: Minority alumni and undergraduate admissions. *Journal of College Admissions, 112,* 15–19.

Nakanishi, D. (1989, November/December). A quota on excellence? The Asian American admissions debate. *Change,* pp. 38–47.

Nakanishi, D. (1991). The next swing vote? Asian Pacific Americans and California politics. In B. Jackson & M. Preston (Eds.), *Racial and ethnic politics in California* (pp. 25–54). Berkeley: Institute for Governmental Studies.

Nakanishi, D. (1993). Asian Pacific Americans in higher education: Faculty and administrative representation and tenure. *New Directions for Teaching and Learning, 53,* 51–59.

Nakanishi, D., & Leong, R. (1978). Toward the second decade: a national survey of Asian American studies programs in 1978. *Amerasia Journal, 5,* 1–19.

Nee, B., & Nee, V. (1974). *Longtime Californ': A documentary study of an American Chinatown.* Boston: Houghton Mifflin.

The new whiz kids. (1985, August 31). *Time,* pp. 42–51.

Njeri, I. (1989, September 20). Academic acrimony: Minority professors claim racism plays role in obtaining tenure. *Los Angeles Times,* p. 1.

Ogbu, J. (1978). *Minority education and caste.* New York: Academic Press.

Okamura, J. Y. (1991). Filipino educational status and achievement at the University of Hawaii. *Social Process in Hawaii, 33,* 107–129.

Oren, D. A. (1985). *Joining the club: A history of Jews and Yale.* New Haven: Yale University Press.

Page, C. (1989, April 21). Bias against excellence haunts Asians. *Oakland Tribune,* p. A15.

Princeton University. (1985). *Faculty and student committee on undergraduate admission and financial aid: Report on admission of Asian-American applicants to Princeton.* Unpublished report.

Rambist, L., & Arbeiter, S. (1986). *Profiles, college-bound seniors.* New York: College Entrance Examination Board.

Stanford University. (1986). *CUAFA subcommittee report on Asian American admissions.* Unpublished report.

Stanford University. (1989). *Building a multiracial, multicultural university community: Final report of the university committee on minority issues.* Palo Alto: Author.

Sue, S., & Abe, J. (1988). *Predictors of academic achievement among Asian American and White students.* New York: College Entrance Examination Board.

Sue, S., & Sue, D. (1971). Chinese-American personality and mental health. *Amerasia Journal, 1,* 36–49.

Synnott, M. G. (1979). *The half-opened door: Discrimination and admissions at Harvard, Yale, and Princeton, 1900–1970.* Westport, CT: Greenwood Press.

Takagi, D. Y. (1992). *The retreat from race: Asian-American admissions and racial politics.* New Brunswick, NJ: Rutgers University Press.

Thompson, D. (1982). Understanding admissions procedures at highly selective colleges. In W. R. Lowery (Ed.), *College admissions counseling* (pp. 491–508). San Francisco: Jossey-Bass.

Thresher, A. (1966). *College admissions and the public interest.* New York: College Board.

Tsuang, G. (1989). Assuring equal access of Asian Americans to highly selective universities. *Yale Law Journal, 98,* 659–678.

UC Berkeley apologizes for policy that limited Asians. (1989, April 7). *Los Angeles Times,* p. 3.

UCLA Ethnic Studies Centers. (1987). *Ethnic groups in Los Angeles: Quality of life indicators.* Los Angeles: Author.

United States Commission on Civil Rights. (1979). *Toward an understanding of Bakke.* Washington, DC: Author.

United States Commission on Civil Rights. (1992). *Civil rights issues facing Asian and Pacific Americans in the 1990s.* Washington, DC: Author.

United Way, Asian Pacific Research and Development Council. (1985). *Pacific Rim profiles: A demographic study of the Asian Pacific profile in Los Angeles County.* Los Angeles: United Way.

Wang, L.-C. (1976). *Lau v. Nichols:* History of a struggle for equal and quality education. In E. Gee et al. (Eds.), *Counterpoint* (pp. 240–263). Los Angeles: Regents of the University of California and the UCLA Asian American Studies Center.

Wang, L.-C. (1988). Meritocracy and diversity in higher education: Discrimination against Asian Americans in the post-Bakke era. *Urban Review, 20,* 189–209.

Wechsler, H. S. (1977). *The qualified student: A history of selective college admissions in America.* New York: John Wiley and Sons.

Will, G. (1989, April 16). Prejudice against excellence. *Washington Post,* p. B7.

Winerip, M. (1985, May 30). Asian-Americans question the admissions policies at Ivy League colleges. *New York Times,* p. 19.

Yu, E.-Y. (1982). Koreans in Los Angeles: Size, distribution, and composition. In E.-Y. Yu, E. H. Phillips, & E. S. Yang (Eds.), *Koreans in Los Angeles* (pp. 23–48). Los Angeles: Korean and Korean American Studies Program, California State University, Los Angeles.

40

ETHNIC STUDIES IN U.S. HIGHER EDUCATION: HISTORY, DEVELOPMENT, AND GOALS

Evelyn Hu-DeHart

UNIVERSITY OF COLORADO, BOULDER

Fire insurance, meaning political settlement or appeasement, is a term sometimes used to describe the decision by U.S. colleges and universities to create Black studies and other ethnic studies programs on their campuses (Hayes, 1992). The reasons hark back to the history of militant student activism in the last quarter century, and to the rise of Black Power, Brown Power, and Yellow Power.

BRIEF HISTORY AND CURRENT STATUS OF ETHNIC STUDIES

In the late 1960s, inspired by the civil rights movement and further buoyed by the energies of the antiwar movement, a generation of college students throughout the United States invaded and occupied administration offices on their campuses and startled and no doubt terrified a few presidents, deans, and professors.

The demonstrations occurred mainly on large, predominantly White campuses, private and public. Led by students of color—then called "Third World" students in solidarity with the imperialized Third World and from whence so many of their forebears came as slaves, coolies, or immigrants—the activists demanded some fundamental changes in higher education. The faculty and administration then were still almost exclusively White and slightly less so male. While more women and minorities were admitted to colleges in the 1960s, student bodies were only somewhat less monolithic than were the faculties and administrations. The curriculum had been fairly static

since the first decades of the century, and the idea of multiculturalism had not yet emerged.

Beginning in 1968 at San Francisco State and University of California campuses such as Berkeley and Santa Barbara—then spreading to many campuses across the nation during the course of the next quarter century to the present day—students of color have been demanding greater access to higher education, recruitment of more faculty of color, and the creation of programs that have come to be collectively known as ethnic studies, and separately by a variety of names: Black studies (also Afro-American studies, African American studies, Africana studies), Chicana/o, Mexican American, and Puerto Rican studies (also Latina/o studies), American Indian (or Native American) studies, and Asian American studies. These programs formed the beginning of multicultural curricular reform in higher education.

For 25 years, despite fits and starts, peaks and valleys, ethnic studies programs and departments have survived and proliferated hundredsfold from their origins in California to all parts of the nation. After some serious cutbacks in the budgetary crisis of the mid-1970s to the mid-1980s, they are now back bigger and stronger than ever, revitalized, reorganized, and in some cases reconceptualized, increasingly institutionalized, and definitely here to stay. They have produced a prodigious amount of new scholarship, which, as in all disciplines and fields of learning, contain some bad, some mediocre, and much work that is good and innovative. The new perspectives are intended not only to increase our knowledge base, but in time to transform all scholarship. Their deep and widespread influence is definitely being felt and debated, as discussed below.

This chapter is an expanded version of an article published in *Phi Delta Kappan* (September 1993), 75(1), pp. 50–54.

Today, there are over 700 programs and departments throughout the United States (Butler, 1991). They come in various forms, shapes, and sizes. The largest and most powerful are the departments, followed by centers or institutes that focus on research but may also have a curricular component. The smallest, weakest, and most problematic programs tend to be those described as "interdisciplinary"—in the sense that they draw their faculty from traditional disciplinary departments; yet this is also by far the most common model, for reasons that are discussed later in this chapter.

The various components of ethnic studies are in turn represented by four major professional associations: the National Council of Black Studies, the National Association of Chicano Studies, the Asian American Studies Association, and the National Association of Ethnic Studies. The American Indian Studies Association, organized around 1980, is currently inactive. A number of smaller and more specifically focused professional associations have also been formed over the years, such as the Puerto Rican Studies Association in 1992. Women's studies was born during the same time and out of similar dynamics generated by the women's movement. (See chapter 41 of this *Handbook*.) However, it was in origin and remains to this day dominated by White and middle-class feminist academics and students.

Given their history, it is not surprising that a disproportionate number of ethnic studies programs are located in public institutions, which are more susceptible to public pressure. Most are also in the western region of the United States, which has a faster growing and more diverse population. The biggest and most powerful programs are found in four public universities in the West. They incorporate more than one ethnic-specific focus, adopt a comparative approach, and have a research emphasis in addition to teaching (undergraduate and graduate). They have full or near department status, with graduate programs in place or anticipated. They also offer variations in organizational structures and approaches.

One of the oldest, largest, and probably the best-known ethnic studies programs is at the University of California, Berkeley. It was founded in 1969, in the crucible of protracted student demonstrations, as an autonomous department reporting directly to the chancellor. Originally, it had four programs: Black Studies, Chicano Studies, Asian American Studies, and Native American Studies, each offering its own undergraduate degree. In the mid-1970s, however, the Black Studies faculty (since renamed African-American Studies) voted to move out of the Ethnic Studies department and into arts and sciences as a separate department in its own right. It continues to cooperate with other Ethnic Studies programs on programmatic issues such as the creation of comparative ethnic studies B.A., M.A., and Ph.D. programs (Wang, n.d.).

In the 1990s, the four Ethnic Studies programs together offer over 150 different courses, and enroll over 8,000 students a year, turning away another 1,000 students each semester. In 1983, Berkeley became the first and in 1992 remained the only university to offer a Ph.D. in ethnic studies. Ten years later, it had over 80 doctoral candidates enrolled, and all seven graduates had been placed in academic positions (Wang, n.d., 2–3).

The University of Washington's Department of American Ethnic Studies, the next largest multiethnic program, is relatively new. It was created in 1985 by bringing together existing or new programs in Black Studies, Chicano Studies (which had been shunted off to the social work school) and Asian American Studies. The small Native American Studies faculty chose to remain within the department of anthropology. An undergraduate degree-granting department, it expects to offer an M.A. degree by the mid-1990s.

The University of California, San Diego's Department of Ethnic Studies, created in 1990, is also relatively new. It emphasizes the comparative approach and has no ethnic-specific foci or separate degrees (University of California, San Diego, 1990).

The University of Colorado, Boulder's Center for Studies of Ethnicity and Race in America was created in 1987 by consolidating existing programs in Black Studies (renamed Afro-American Studies) and Chicano Studies, with new programs in Asian American and American Indian Studies. The center retains the four ethnic-specific foci and actively promotes comparative race studies but in 1993 offered only an undergraduate degree in Afroamerican Studies. Although it has its own faculty lines, it does not yet enjoy full autonomy or department status.

In addition to these four research universities in the West, the University of California, Los Angeles (UCLA), established yet another model in the 1960s. On this campus, there are four separate and distinct research centers devoted to the study of African Americans, Asian Americans, Chicanas/os, and Native Americans.

Outside the West, Bowling Green State University in Ohio has one of the oldest ethnic studies departments, which was founded in 1979. Like the University of California, San Diego, it also does not have ethnic-specific foci. Among four-year or nonresearch institutions, San Francisco State has one of the oldest and still largest ethnic studies departments, with four distinct foci and degrees. The largest of the programs on this campus is Asian American Studies, which was founded in 1969, making it also the oldest (Hirabayashi & Alquizola, 1992). San Francisco State has also retained the original, still unique, and politically charged name of La Raza Studies, for what elsewhere is called Chicana/o or Mexican American Studies.

Other than these big, multifoci, or comparative programs, almost all ethnic studies programs are ethnic specific. Foremost among them, for historical reasons, are Black studies (Hine, 1992), now increasingly renamed Afro American or African American. More than 60 of them (Adams, 1993) have department status, some in conjunction with a research center. Notable among them are long-standing programs at flagship state institutions such as Ohio State University, the University of Wisconsin, Madison, the University of Michigan, Ann Arbor, and the University of California, Berkeley. Temple University, a public research institution in Philadelphia, has one of the oldest, largest, and most distinctive Black studies departments. Under the guidance of its founder, Molefi Asante, it is also the foremost Afrocentric or African-centered program and the only one to offer a Ph.D. degree (Asante, 1992).

Among elite private universities, Cornell, Brown, and the University of Pennsylvania have well-established centers and departments, with Harvard and Princeton relative latecomers. Yale had one of the preeminent Black studies programs until the late 1970s, when it largely disintegrated with the departure (due in part to denial of tenure) of some of its most distinguished faculty members and the subsequent decrease of institutional support.

On a few West Coast research university campuses, such as the University of California, Davis, and UC Santa Barbara—where Chicana/o Studies was formally launched in 1968 with the militant student document entitled "El Plan de Santa Bárbara"—Chicana/o studies has also achieved department status (Keller, Magallan, & Garcia, 1989). The biggest and one of the oldest Chicana/o studies departments is located on the California State University Northridge campus. Founded in 1969 by Rudolfo Acuña, it is primarily teaching and community oriented.

Leading the development of Puerto Rican studies on the East Coast is the Centro de Estudios Puertorriqueños at Hunter College of the City University of New York (CUNY), which is research and community oriented. A number of other CUNY campuses, such as Lehman College, Brooklyn College, and John Jay College, have Puerto Rican Studies departments. Both Chicana/o and Puerto Rican Studies are linked with other educational equity programs, such as bilingual education, that address the needs of largely Spanish-speaking immigrant groups. The rise of Puerto Rican studies cannot be divorced from Puerto Rico's neocolonial relationship with the United States. The rise of La Raza and Chicana/o studies is inextricably linked to the emergence of various Chicano social movements, notably César Chávez's Farm Workers Movement (Acuña, 1988).

Asian American studies has had an interesting trajectory. Although two major programs that rapidly became departments were founded in the late 1960s in California, at UC, Berkeley, and San Francisco State, the rest of the country was slow to follow suit. It was not until the 1980s, with the dramatic rise of immigration from Asia, that Asian American studies gained renewed impetus. The new immigrants not only swelled the total numbers of peoples of Asian descent in the United States, from under 1 million in 1965 to over 7 million by 1990 (Ong & Hee, 1993), it also diversified the Asian American population well beyond the dominant groups of Chinese and Japanese, to include Filipinos, Koreans, Asian Indians, Vietnamese, and other Southeast Asian ethnicities (Endo & Wei, 1987; Omatsu, 1989). UC, Santa Barbara, the University of Colorado at Boulder, and Queens College on the East Coast, all have relatively new Asian American studies programs, research centers, or departments.

The least developed of the ethnic studies programs is American Indian, or Native American, studies (Ortiz, 1980). This is no doubt related to the continuous isolation of Native peoples of this country from mainstream society and institutions, including higher education, resulting in the absolute paucity of Native Americans with much postsecondary academic training. In the 1990s, more than any other ethnic studies foci, Native American studies is still closely tied to student services. UCLA has one of the few centers devoted to research; it also edits and publishes the *American Indian Culture and Research Journal,* one of the few academic journals devoted to Native American issues. In the east, Cornell University has perhaps the most significant Native American studies programs, which combines student support service with curriculum.

Historically, there are several models or routes for introducing and implementing ethnic studies into the curriculum. In the beginning, the first ethnic studies courses were often offered not by academic departments or by regular faculty members. Rather, community activists and minority student counselors in student service units, such as Educational Opportunity Programs (EOP), began teaching courses on various and distinct minority experiences, with or without academic credit. These courses gradually gave way to more formally constituted programs located on the academic side of campus. However, some of the early instructional staff, including many community activists, were retained on the faculty.

On campuses where ethnic studies was originally established as strictly research units, such as the four ethnic-specific research centers at UCLA, these centers have been compelled to start offering courses, undergraduate and graduate, although not necessarily degree programs. At UCLA, the Asian American Studies Center appears to have responded most actively and comprehensively to student needs. It offers not only a range of undergraduate courses, but since the 1980s a well-received M.A. degree as well (although still no B.A. degree). By contrast, the lack of attention paid on this campus to the development of an undergraduate curriculum and degree in Chicana/o studies prompted a large number of mostly Chicana/o students and a few faculty members to mount a hunger strike at the beginning of summer 1993.

On most other campuses, American studies (or its variants, such as American cultures) seems to be the most common vehicle to integrate some aspect of ethnic studies into the curriculum. This model is frequently used on campuses where there is already an established African American studies program and mounting pressure—primarily from non-Black minority students, whose numbers are swelling on our campuses and in many cases exceeding Black students—to offer additional ethnic-specific or comparative ethnic courses. If forcing these new ethnic foci into the existing African American studies department or program is not feasible (for political and structural reasons), then American studies generally emerges as the most amenable unit to incorporate the new courses. Such has been the case even at large research universities such as Yale and the University of Michigan, Ann Arbor (Garcia, 1992). American studies is also attractive for small colleges that cannot afford to create new academic units.

Yet another model is the merging of ethnic studies with existing or new area studies programs. This arrangement is particularly common for African studies and African American studies, which, by using the African diaspora paradigm, has found it politically and structurally feasible to work as one academic unit. These units are often named African and African American studies or, more simply, Africana studies. It should be noted that such units, staffed as is the case with other Black studies programs predominantly by African and African American scholars, are quite distinct from traditional African area studies programs, which draw their faculty from traditional disciplines and are mostly White (Okihiro, 1991).

Latino and Latin American studies is another model, although not a common arrangement, because the merger seems to arise partially out of administrative expediency. One recent example is the City College of New York's (CCNY) Puerto Rican Studies department, which changed its name in the late 1980s to the Department of Latin American and Hispanic Caribbean Studies. Besides offering courses on and a major in Latin America, it retains the major in Puerto Rican Studies while adding a sequence in Dominican Studies, in view of upper Manhattan's swelling Dominican immigrant population. Recently, Rutgers University decided to bring together Puerto Rico (a U.S. dependency) and the independent Spanish-speaking countries of the Caribbean into a new department of Puerto Rican and Spanish Caribbean Studies. This formulation appears to make historical, political, and cultural sense, sharing as they do a historical colonial relationship to Spain and a contemporary neocolonial relationship with the United States.

There is no known instance of Asian American studies merging with Asian studies, although on some campuses the first Asian American studies courses could well have been offered through the Asian studies program. Some changes are afoot, as scholars such as Arif Dirlik and Sucheta Mazumdar of Duke University attempt to formulate an Asian-Pacific paradigm (Dirlik, 1993; Mazumdar, 1991). During the past decade, a growing number of scholars have worked with the more global concept of the "Asian diaspora" (Hu-DeHart, 1991).

WHY ETHNIC STUDIES?

Although the study of the Black experience in America has been an old, community-based practice, led by the work of African American scholars such as Carter G. Woodson and his Association for the Study of Afro-American Life and History (Adams, 1993), the rationale for establishing formal Black studies programs almost 30 years ago was, first and foremost, to recognize the growing presence of African American students on historically White U.S. campuses.

These students wanted what most students want out of an education: to study the experiences and contributions of their community to U.S. society and culture and to use the resources of the university to help solve community problems. The guiding principle was that "knowledge was to be socially relevant." In other words, the ideals of "academic excellence" and "social responsibility" were conceived as compatible and complementary (Adams, 1993, p. 27). The other side of this argument was an explicit challenge to the Eurocentric curriculum and the prevailing, but unwritten, assumption that Western civilization was superior and universal and that its values and norms are applicable to all peoples at all times.

Since the founding and subsequent proliferation of Black studies programs, the call for the establishment of Chicana/o, Puerto Rican, Asian American, and Native American studies have increased in intensity, while subscribing to the same guiding principles. The reasons have much to do with the changing nature of American society since the mid-1960s. The civil rights movement might have removed the last vestiges of legal apartheid in this country, but the rich and powerful and their political surrogates have merely invented other means to continue to segregate, divide, exclude, and in many other ways deny equal

opportunity to the historically marginalized communities of color.

Two and a half decades after the issuance of the Kerner Commission report in 1968, which spoke of two Americas, one rich, one poor, one White, one Black, the gulf between these two Americas has grown wider than ever, especially during the Reagan-Bush years. To be more specific, by 1992, 1% of the U.S. population had gained control of more wealth than 90% of this society, a situation that parallels the intolerable inequality of much of the Third World (Muwakkil, 1992; Nasar, 1992).

Dramatic and significant demographic changes have also overtaken the United States during this same quarter century. Since 1965, when U.S. immigration laws eliminated the "national origins" quotas, which had clearly favored Europeans, many new immigrants from Asia, Latin America, and the Caribbean have greatly outnumbered the traditional White European immigrants for the first time in history (Barringer, 1991; Usdansky, 1992). Additional impetus for accelerated immigration from Asia and Central America/the Caribbean have come as consequences of U.S. economic, political, and military interventions during the post–World War II era. From 1965 into the 1990s, non-Europeans have composed over 80% of all new immigrants (Usdansky, 1992). Almost 9 million came in a great surge in the 1980s. This new wave of immigration accounts for the doubling of Asian Americans and the increase of Latinos by 60% between 1980 and 1990 (Ong & Hee, 1993; Usdansky, 1992).

The upshot of these new immigration patterns is that the U.S. population is fast becoming "colored" and ever more diverse—by race, ethnicity, religion, language, food, music, art, literature, and many other cultural expressions. In fact, with over half of its population already highly diverse in 1992, California gives us a glimpse of the national future, which is projected to become by 2050, using an oxymoronic phrase, "majority minority." The relatively high reproductive rates of minority Americans as well as their lower age distribution mean that peoples of color will increasingly characterize the nation's classrooms and workforce.

In order to bring about a truly pluralistic democracy, our educational system at all levels must not only reflect this diversity of Americans in its student body, faculty, and curriculum but must seek to achieve comparable educational outcomes for all groups in American society. To reach this end, the variety of educational reforms that are gathered under the broad rubric of "multiculturalism" include the integration of ethnic studies into the college and university curriculum. It also means that *all students,* not just those of color, should be exposed to the histories and cultures of Americans of non-European descent. In other words, in the 1990s, ethnic studies is not for minorities only.

ETHNIC STUDIES DEFINED

With the exceptions discussed above regarding the merging of some ethnic studies with certain area studies, a common mistake is to confuse or conflate ethnic studies in general with global or international studies, on the basis that they are both "non-Western" and are usually organized as nondepartmental interdisciplinary programs.

Area studies arose out of the context of U.S. imperialism in the Third World and bear names such as African studies, Asian studies, and Latin American/Caribbean studies. Their original, founding purpose was to focus on U.S.-Third World relations and to train specialists to uphold U.S. hegemony in those regions of the world in which the United States had heavy economic and political investments. Although area studies scholars have become far more critical of U.S.-Third World relations since the antiwar movement of the 1960s, and many have adopted Third World perspectives in their work, they are still predominantly White male scholars entrenched in established departments, using conventional disciplinary methodologies, subscribing to disciplinary epistemologies, and benefiting from traditional patterns of distributing power and rewards in the academy, including those underwritten by private foundations and the U.S. government (Hu-DeHart, 1991; Hune, 1991; Mazumdar, 1991; Okihiro, 1991). Rather than truly interdisciplinary, these programs can better be described as multidisciplinary.

Ethnic studies, on the other hand—having grown out of student and grass-roots community challenges to the prevailing academic power structure and Eurocentric curriculum of U.S. colleges and universities—were insurgent programs with a subversive agenda from the outset. Hence, they were suspect and illegitimate even as they were grudgingly allowed into the academy. The founders of ethnic studies—students, faculty, and community supporters alike—did not mask their objective of systematically examining and dismantling institutional racism.

Within the academy, ethnic studies scholars attempt to define a distinct epistemology, struggle consciously to break or transcend the bounds of traditional disciplines in their search for new methodologies, and wrestle more deliberately to articulate a genuinely interdisciplinary approach to the discovery of new knowledge. They argue for a holistic or organic approach to the understanding of minority experiences in America and for an emic, or insider, approach. In American Indian studies, for example, the faculty speak of an "indigenous model" (Jaimes, 1987).

Program definitions vary from campus to campus and change over time. The curriculum or course offerings are not uniform and do not conform to a prescribed pattern, although they generally fall within the broad categories of historical, sociological, and cultural. What they have in common is a specific or comparative focus on groups socially constructed as "minorities" in U.S. society, a status that results from these groups' shared history of having been racially constructed as distinct from European immigrants and their descendents. The latter have dominated the United States and defined its identity as White, Western, and superior; they see differences among themselves as strictly "cultural," or ethnic. The racially defined, non-European descended groups in the United States have a "social trajectory and outcome quite diverse from that of people categorized only by cultural standards" (Liu, 1989, 275), that is, Irish Americans, Jewish Americans, Italian Americans, and Polish Americans.

By recognizing this distinction between race and ethnicity, ethnic studies scholars confront the irony that the very name of their intellectual and political project is problematic. "The term Ethnic Studies is a misleading one, confusing our students, and lending itself to much mischievous hostility by those academics who would rather not have studies of people of color in the university at all," so notes Rhett Jones of Brown University, who concludes the field should be renamed "race studies" (Jones, 1993).

John Liu (1989), in presenting his case for the consideration of ethnic studies as a separate and distinct discipline, begins with this crucial difference: "Race and ethnicity represented divergent experiences, with never the twain to meet because of institutionalized racism" (p. 276). He argues that race, ethnicity, and institutionalized racism form the central core disciplinary concepts of ethnic studies (p. 274). This assertion is sharply at odds with the views of certain influential social scientists—such as Nathan Glazer and Daniel Moynihan (1975), Alejandro Portes and Robert Bach (1985), and Thomas Sowell (1981)—who maintain that race is merely one type of ethnicity and that, in due time, all groups plunge into the "melting pot" and become Americans (Liu, 1989).

In advancing its own coherent methodological orientation, the ethnic studies approach to knowledge, described as interdisciplinary, must be more than "simply separate applications of discipline-based methodology" (Butler, 1991). Furthermore, unlike traditional disciplines, which are long divorced from any community base or origins, ethnic studies scholars must ask the question: "Why do research and for whom?"—since its *raison d'être* is to correct the omissions and distortions in mainstream academia. Ethnic studies must "give voice to the excluded" and "involve racial groups in the articulation of their own existences through various means" (Liu, 1989, p. 279). Therefore, oral history and participatory research are important tools in ethnic studies research. Furthermore, "the enunciation of a people's voice has led many ethnic scholars to organize their research around communities" (p. 280).

Ethnic studies scholars also dispute the assertion that good scholarship is necessarily "objective" and nonpolitical, again in contrast to values in traditional disciplines. On the contrary, they openly acknowledge a moral and political purpose in their work because they are simultaneously committed to scholarship and social change, to a "more equitable social order," and to "creating new social realities" (Liu, 1989, pp. 281–282).

A good definition of comparative race and ethnic studies can be found in the UC, San Diego, Ethnic Studies department's founding document. The purpose is to focus "on immigration, slavery, and confinement, those three processes that combined to create in the United States a nation of nations. Ethnic Studies intensively examines the histories, languages and cultures of America's racial and ethnic groups in and of themselves, their relationships to each other, and particularly, in structural contexts of power" (University of California, San Diego, 1990, p. 2). The attention here is on the recovery of knowledge denied or submerged and on the construction of new knowledge from the perspectives of historically marginalized and powerless groups.

To many in ethnic studies, its purpose also has to include a fundamental and explicit challenge to the dominant paradigms of academic practices. While he was specifically addressing the goals of Puerto Rican studies, Frank Bonilla, founder and director of Hunter College's Centro de Estudios Puertorriqueños, expressed guiding principles applicable to all ethnic studies:

We have set out to contest effectively those visions of the world that assume or take for granted the inevitability and indefinite duration of the class and colonial oppression that has marked Puerto Rico's history. All the disciplines that we are most directly drawing upon—history, economics, sociology, anthropology, literature, psychology, pedagogy—as they are practiced in the United States are deeply implicated in the construction of that vision of Puerto Ricans as an inferior, submissive people, trapped on the underside of relations from which there is no forseeable exit. (quoted in Vázquez, 1988, p. 25)

In the words of another scholar, ethnic studies is a "liberating educational process" (Vázquez, 1988, p. 26) that challenges the triumph of Western civilization on U.S. soil—Eurocentrism—and its claims to objectivity and universalism. In ethnic studies, peoples of color are constructed not as mere objects to study but as "creators of events" and agents of change.

Ethnic studies scholars recognize the importance of perspective and that "perspectives . . . are always partial and situated in relationship to power" (University of California, San Diego, 1990, pp. 5–6). Putting it concretely, "it is both practically and theoretically incorrect to use the experience of white ethnics as a guide to comprehend those of nonwhite, or so-called 'racial' minorities" (Chaufauros, 1991, p. 25).

Another expression of the distinctive nature of ethnic studies scholarship is provided by Johnnella Butler, former chair of the department of American Ethnic Studies at the University of Washington, Seattle. She proposes a "matrix model"—that is, "looking at the matrix of race, class, ethnicity and gender . . . within the context of cultural, political, social, and economic expression" (Butler, 1991, p. 29). The purpose of this new academic field is to recover and reconstruct the lived historical experiences and memories of those Americans whom history has neglected, to identify and credit the contributions of these Americans to the making of U.S. society and culture, to chronicle protest and resistance, and, finally, to establish alternative values and visions, institutions, and cultures.

CURRENT DEBATES AND ISSUES WITHIN ETHNIC STUDIES

The above discussion should not convey the idea that ethnic studies is totally stabilized, institutionalized, harmonious, or monolithic. In fact, it is in a state of flux and transition, structurally, organizationally, intellectually, and ideologically. There is no automatic uniformity between and among any of the 700 or so mostly ethnic-specific programs and departments across the nation. In part, the conversations and discussions within ethnic studies is no different from ongoing debates among biologists, anthropologists, and historians as their fields grow and change. At the same time, while the discussions among ethnic studies practitioners have not become vituperative and destructive,

they can become heated and reflect the state of development of a still young field and discipline. The following comments by no means exhaust the list of issues but should convey some sense of the concerns and stakes. This discussion should also suggest the likely directions that ethnic studies will take as the field and discipline move into the 21st century.

Twenty-five years after its inception, ethnic studies finds its key issue to be a structural and organizational one on the surface, which in turn fundamentally impinges on the larger issues of governance, academic or curricular legitimacy, professional certification, and educational mission: in short, the heart and soul of any academic enterprise (Hirabayashi and Alquizola, 1992). Should ethnic studies continue largely to be an interdisciplinary program along the model of area studies, drawing faculty from established departments and disciplines? Or should it push for autonomy and department status, given its self-identity as a distinctive new academic field, complete with disciplinary definition and methodology? Should it now concentrate on establishing intellectual credentials and credibility while loosening or severing ties forged in its early days with minority student services? Should the professional associations impose some clear definition of the field, clarify the necessary qualifications or credentials for the faculty, and in general impose some sort of "quality control" over the curriculum and educational mission?

Of all these issues, the most crucial one to understand is the difference between programs and departments. As programs relying on other departments for faculty and courses, ethnic studies has no control over faculty hiring or resources and minimal influence on course offerings, thus very little power to define itself intellectually and academically. It becomes nearly impossible to build a sound, coherent, and intellectually challenging program through a rather haphazard and random sampling of whatever courses may be made available through established departments. The unfortunate result of such efforts, well intentioned though they may be, is that they fuel the argument of skeptics and critics of ethnic studies that it lacks intellectual rigor and legitimacy.

Hence, in practice, such programs at best function as a mere coordinating body of a loosely related set of courses around an ethnic-specific or comparative ethnic theme, entirely reliant on the goodwill, positive attitude, and depth of understanding and appreciation of the mission of ethnic studies by traditional departments. Most often, the relationship between ethnic studies programs and academic departments is tenuous and uneasy, if not outright hostile. Built on attitudes of turf protection, competition for scarce resources, and, frankly, outright racism on the part of some traditional scholars who cannot shake off perceptions of illegitimacy and inferiority about ethnic studies as a field (and by extension ethnic studies scholars), this relationship becomes largely unmanageable. Being the weaker of the partnership, the ethnic studies program suffers disproportionately. During periods of financial constraints, such programs can be easily—both in the structural and political sense—cut back or disbanded, which is what happened to many of them during the budgetary crisis of the 1970s.

Departments, on the other hand, control budgets, do their own faculty hiring, and, most important, determine the course of study and hence define the field, including issues of pedagogy, research, and publication (both the type and place). In short, they have status and, at least structurally, enjoy equality with other disciplines and fields of study. Departments can also readily create and sponsor graduate programs. This is why there is really little dispute within ethnic studies about the desirability in theory of department over program.

However, political expediency as well as practical and financial matters often dictate the less ideal course of action. In public institutions, a program can be created by administrative fiat, whereas the creation of new departments requires extensive review and discussion by the general faculty and layers of higher education oversight bodies, a long, drawn-out process that can become contentious.

Also, in view of the limited resources of most colleges and universities, a situation that is likely to get worse in the late 1990s, a program is still the most common model, being the easiest and least costly way to start ethnic studies. Furthermore, on those campuses where administrators have yielded to the department model, these ethnic studies departments usually have very small, and often mostly untenured, faculty. Thus, they are still reduced to a weak and marginal status within the specific college or university.

Despite these dilemmas, in the 1980s and into the 1990s, administrators were often eager to establish some kind of ethnic studies presence on their campuses, for the simple reason that it is an easy way to make a positive statement of commitment to diversity and multiculturalism. If they can go the extra mile and create an ethnic studies department with its own faculty lines, they also know it is the fastest route to diversifying the faculty. Ethnic studies scholars and supporters, having been stranded on the margins for so long, see any movement toward the center as acceptable, hence their tendency sometimes to settle for less.

Whether as program or department, the undeniable fact of ethnic studies proliferation, along with the general push toward multiculturalism and diversity, however these concepts are understood, means that ethnic studies has been acknowledged and is becoming institutionalized. A further step toward its institutionalization is linked to efforts within curriculum reform movements to "integrate" ethnic studies perspectives and scholarships into the mainstream curriculum and into mainstream scholarship. This entails not only hiring ethnic studies scholars within traditional departments, such as history, sociology, psychology, political science, and literature, but also to encourage non-ethnic studies scholars to integrate the scholarship and perspectives from ethnic studies into their courses. Finally, a current debate among students and faculty on many campuses concerns the desirability of requiring an ethnic studies course as part of the core or general undergraduate education program.

Thus, beginning in the mid-1980s with faculty in-service workshops typically described as "curriculum integration projects," campuses have embarked on the voluntary reeducation of willing and self-selected existing faculty. With institutional and foundation support such as that from the Ford Foundation, the workshops have become more ambitious and recently redesignated as "curriculum transformation" (Butler & Walter,

1991). This should be, and by and large is, good news for ethnic studies. With institutionalization and widespread influence come respect and legitimacy.

Nevertheless, uneasiness has set in around these recent developments. Does the campus push for multiculturalism threaten to swallow up or co-opt ethnic studies? Would the fading argument (very audible at the inception of ethnic studies and women's studies) more than 20 years ago, that these are stopgap or transitory measures that would eventually and automatically go out of existence once the campus is integrated, be revived, in order to justify reduction or withdrawal of resources from ethnic studies?

Even as some applaud the inevitable spillover of ethnic studies into the rest of the curriculum, they also note the tension between ethnic studies and traditional fields "as people try to locate the boundaries between the two" (Magner, 1991, p. A11). In short, as summarized by the headline of a major discussion of this issue in the May 1, 1991, *Chronicle of Higher Education:* "Push for Diversity in Traditional Departments Raises Questions About the Future of Ethnic Studies" (Magner, 1991, p. A11). This explains the wariness and opposition on the part of the Black Studies faculty of San Francisco State University's School of Ethnic Studies to the hiring by the department of political science of an African American faculty to teach Black politics—a clear struggle over boundary lines.

The dispute over boundaries raises a larger issue, which will be even more hotly debated in the 1990s. When Jesse Vázquez (1988), director of Queens College's Puerto Rican Studies program, noted that "even traditional academic departments, formerly resolute in their refusal to include ethnic studies courses in their curriculum, now cross-list, and in many instances generate their own version of ethnic studies courses in direct competition with existing ethnic studies programs" (p. 23), he also sounded a warning that these multicultural curricular reforms may have "effectively managed to co-opt some of the more socially and politically palatable aspects of the ethnic studies movement of the late 1960s and early 1970s" (p. 24). At the same time, Vázquez continues,

these latest curricular trends seem to be moving us away from the political and social urgency intended by the founders of ethnic studies and toward the kind of program design which conforms to and is consistent with the traditional academic structures.... Certainly, the struggle to legitimize these programs academically has taken the edge and toughness out of the heart of some of our ethnic studies curriculum.

The question is: Does the drive for legitimacy and institutionalization entail trade-offs for ethnic studies that may, ironically, weaken it in the long run? Should ethnic studies be "seduced and lulled" into believing that institutionalization translates into authentic acceptance and full acknowledgment and signals a change in traditional faculty attitudes, behavior, and values? Vázquez thinks not.

Neither does E. San Juan, Jr., educated at Harvard in Western literature. An incisive and vociferous critic of U.S. racial politics as manifested through issues of multiculturalism and ethnic studies (San Juan, 1992), he is concerned that (n.d., n.p.) "gradual academization" of ethnic studies would force it into the dominant European orthodoxy, which emphasizes ethnicity to the exclusion of race, and therefore "systematically [erases] from the historical frame of reference any perception of race and racism as causal factors in the making of the political and economic structure of the United States."

If race and racism should remain the analytical core of the ethnic studies project, then would not total retreat into the academy be a contradiction, for how could it separate itself from the ongoing, real-life struggles of peoples of color in the United States today? That is precisely the dilemma that eminent ethnic studies scholars such as Henry Louis Gates, Jr., chair of Harvard's African American Studies department, pointed out. His solution then, in describing a Black studies agenda for the 21st century, is "an emphasis upon cultural studies and public policy, as two broad and fruitful rubrics under which to organize our discipline" (Gates, 1992, p. 7).

San Juan also seeks to recapture the "activist impulse" that had propelled the creation of ethnic studies in the first place. He and other scholars characterize this challenge as the integration of theory (or critique) and praxis. Others put it even more simply and directly: how to reconcile the academic project of ethnic studies (i.e., the production of knowledge) with the original commitment to liberating and empowering the communities of color. Asks San Juan (n.d., n.p.): "Will it try to recuperate its inaugural vision as part of wide-ranging popular movements for justice and equality, for thoroughgoing social transformation?" Or will it settle for being just another respected academic unit?

"BARBARIANS AT THE GATE": THE BACKLASH AGAINST ETHNIC STUDIES AND MULTICULTURALISM

Any discussion of ethnic studies, however brief, would be remiss without some reference to the current controversy over "PC" (for "political correctness"), in which neoconservative and liberal critics of multiculturalism accuse ethnic studies scholars, students, and supporters, among other multicultural educational reformers, of committing heinous crimes against truth (Stimpson, 1991). Multiculturalists are charged with promoting "ethnic particularism" at the expense of national unity and a "common culture." (In chapter 5 of this *Handbook*, Christine E. Sleeter offers a more thorough discussion of the critiques of multicultural education.)

Those who mounted the PC campaign can be described as "triumphalists" (term borrowed from Bell-Villada, 1990), a close-knit group of academics and scholars, writers, journalists and editors, political pundits and commentators, and highly placed members of the Reagan-Bush administrations (Aufderheide, 1992; Berman, 1992). Most of them are conservatives and neoconservatives but can increasingly count on old liberals joining their ranks. Binding them together is the fear that multiculturalism is changing—too fast, too profoundly, and in negative directions—U.S. history, society, and culture as they know and cherish and in some cases have helped to construct them.

The writings and public pronouncements of triumphalists—

polemicists such as William Bennett (Beyers, 1991; Gordon, 1992), Dinesh D'Souza (1991), Lynne Cheney (1992), Irving Kristol (1991), George Will (1991), Roger Kimball (1990), and academics such as Allan Bloom (1987), even liberal ones such as Arthur Schlesinger (1992), Eugene Genovese (1991), and C. Vann Woodward (1991)—suggest their motives. It seems quite clear that their problem really boils down to a refusal to consider and meet the challenge mounted by multiculturalists against the claim that they, the triumphalists, make for Western universalism, objectivity, and timeless truths. The triumphalists can get hostile too, as exemplified by the words chosen by Alan Kors, historian at the University of Pennsylvania and a founder of the National Association of Scholars (NAS), to describe multiculturalists as "barbarians at the gate." The mission of the NAS, then, is to "reclaim the academy" for Western civilization (Weisberg, 1991).

The threat to the multicultural movement does not lie solely in the inflammatory rhetoric and often irresponsible research and use of evidence found in the work of some polemicists, such as D'Souza's depiction of Stephen Thernstrom's troubles with several African American women students at Harvard (D'Souza, 1991; critique by Wiener, 1991). The danger is enhanced by the financial, communications, and publications network that triumphalists have created to facilitate their campaign (Wiener, 1990).

In a real sense, with the emergence of NAS on U.S. campuses and their allies outside the walls of academe—allies such as Bennett, Bloom, and Kristol's Madison Center for Educational Affairs (Washington, D.C.)—the battle between the divergent world views represented by triumphalists and multiculturalists has been joined. After all, ethnic studies faculty in U.S. colleges and universities have made no bones about their concomitant and equal commitment to producing new scholarship, dismantling institutional racism, and creating a more equitable social order. If successful, Western civilization would no longer enjoy hegemony in the curriculum, Euro-Americans would no longer have a monopoly of power and privilege. Because they refuse to give up Western hegemony in the academy and White male privilege in society, the triumphalists have every reason to fear the coming of the multiculturalists.

Actually, it is not even ethnic studies scholars that the triumphalists are most enraged at, for these have been written off as hopelessly partisan. Rather, triumphalists rail loudest at the betrayal of White administrators and colleagues who have seemingly jumped on the multicultural bandwagon: administrators because they have supported the creation and sustained the development of ethnic studies; colleagues in such fields as history, English, comparative literature, and cultural studies because they have not only integrated minority scholarship and literature into their courses and research perspectives but, most unforgiving of all, began openly questioning the sanctity of the literary and historical canon. While William Bennett, as secretary of education, failed to derail Stanford University's effort in 1988 to broaden the reading list of its Western Civilization freshman course to include works by women, American minority, and Third World authors (Beyers, 1991; Gordon, 1992), or Berkeley's effort to include a "comparative American cultures" graduation requirement, triumphalists have become far more successful in sabotaging other campus curriculum reforms.

When they do focus on ethnic studies and other forms of multicultural education, a common tactic of the critics is to draw attention to the more extreme practices, such as Afrocentrism in Black studies or the creation of Afrocentric schools in certain low-income and large minority urban districts, and portray them to an uninformed public as the norm. Thus, an Afrocentrist such as Molefi K. Asante of Temple University appears more frequently in the media than perhaps any other ethnic studies scholar as the spokesperson for ethnic studies and multiculturalism. The woes of CCNY's Black Studies professor Leonard Jeffries (also a leading Afrocentrist), removed as chair of the department for alleged racist and anti-Semitic remarks in an off-campus speech, have been more publicized in the *New York Times* and other press accounts than perhaps any other recent story related to an ethnic studies program.

Concurrent with these attacks on multiculturalism, some well-known neoconservatives, such as Jeffrey Hart of Dartmouth, Irving Kristol of the American Enterprise Institute, and former treasury secretary and current president of the affluent Olin Foundation, William Simon, unabashedly promote and finance the establishment of right-wing, often racist, student newspapers. Modeled after the notorious prototype *Dartmouth Review*—whose first editor in 1980 was Dinesh D'Souza, even then an accomplished polemicist—almost 60 such "reviews" have been founded (Butterfield, 1990; Dodge, 1991; Henson, 1991). The presence and inflammatory rhetoric of such papers sometimes encourages the formation of "white student unions" (*Chronicle of Higher Education,* 1991), which join the vociferous chorus against affirmative action, minority student organizations (charging them with "segregation"), ethnic studies, women's studies, gay and lesbian studies, cultural studies, canon revisions, ethnic- and gender-diversity core requirements, and other educational and curricular reforms that destabilize the status quo.

In addition to these right-wing campus papers, a plethora of other antimulticultural journals and magazines have appeared. Some examples are: *Campus: America's Student Newspapers; The Intercollegiate Review;* and *Diversity and Culture: A Critical Review of Race and Culture.* NAS publishes its own quasi-scholarly journal, *Academic Questions.* The latest journalistic assault on multiculturalism, edited by 1960s radicals turned passionate neoconservatives David Horowitz and Peter Collier, is *Heterodoxy: Articles and Animadversions on Political Correctness and Other Follies.* The lead article of the October 1992 issue was a savage attack on the Ford Foundation's longtime commitment to women's studies and ethnic studies (Sykes & Billingsley, 1992).

Unfortunately, after a protracted civil rights struggle in the United States, and as we approach the beginning of the third millenium, just when peoples of color are rising up to reclaim their rightful place in U.S. history, culture, and institutions, instead of shedding their defensiveness and arrogance, powerful triumphalist forces choose instead to succumb to their fears and cling to the old social and ideological order. Contrary to the triumphalists' shrill and false charges of "thought police" and "new McCarthyism," multiculturalists understand that diversity and assertion of differences need not lead at all to divisiveness if there are no social inequalities based on constructed and imposed racial and gender categories. Unless the United States eliminates these basic barriers to equal opportunity, what does a "common culture" mean, and how does the American people forge unity and a genuine democratic American future?

FUTURE CHALLENGES FOR ETHNIC STUDIES

If the United States has ever had a "pedagogy of the oppressed," following Paulo Freire (1970), it would be ethnic studies. Today, in the 1990s, it appears to have gained sufficient acceptance and respectability that some of its practitioners no longer feel subversive. Yet the challenge remains for ethnic studies to remain socially relevant, responsive, and accountable to community needs while attaining higher and higher academic status and credibility. While the future of ethnic studies is not in immediate jeopardy, its long-term survival is certainly not assured.

Perhaps the single most unstable aspect of the field is the fact that so few of the programs have departmental status. Only when ethnic studies has departmental status will it be able to control its faculty, determine its curriculum, be in charge of its teaching and research, and advance the discipline.

Furthermore, even if most ethnic studies programs achieve autonomy, there remains the question of whether sufficient ethnic studies scholars have come through the graduation pipeline to be hired by these departments. At present, the demand for Ph.D.'s in ethnic studies is greater than the supply. So an additional priority for ethnic studies, particularly those in research universities, is to develop doctoral programs, secure fellowships from their own institutions as well as from foundations, and produce more well-trained young scholars.

A continuing struggle will be over maintaining and enhancing institutional support to secure at least a fair share of resources at a time of severe budget cuts and possible restructuring. Ethnic studies programs have every reason to fear a reprise of what happened in the budget crisis of the mid-1970s, when many universities nearly decimated, directly eliminated, or consolidated existing ethnic studies programs (at that time, affecting mostly Black and Chicano studies) with each other and, worse, with other, often scarcely related programs (such as vague entities known as "interdisciplinary studies").

Again, in a budgetary crisis, those ethnic studies programs that have secured departmental status and a strong, tenured faculty are in a much better position to defend themselves, compete with other departments, and fight back. Working in favor of ethnic studies are the changes in America's general social and educational climate, which appears to have reached some kind of consensus about the need for, and value of, "multiculturalism," although there is still no clear agreement on the precise meaning and application of that concept.

The internal dialogue within and among different kinds of ethnic studies will continue, as will the debate on the intellectual desirability and political pitfalls of integrating ethnic studies content and perspectives across the curriculum. What position should ethnic studies take when traditional departments hire faculty and offer ethnic studies courses under their patronage? How, and to what extent, should ethnic studies participate in growing campus movements to mandate certain units of "cultural pluralism" as graduation requirements? And should the ethnic studies faculty be solely or even primarily responsible for creating and offering courses that fulfill such requirements?

The relationship, both institutional and political, between ethnic studies and women's studies, ethnic studies and cultural studies (or intercultural studies), ethnic studies and gay and lesbian studies, between racism and sexism, patriarchy and Eurocentrism, have yet to be fully and systematically addressed. Also nagging is the question: Can White scholars teach ethnic studies? (Some already do, but not many.)

With a quarter century of history behind the development of ethnic studies, generational differences have appeared among scholars. Some among the older generation, even as they participated in offering the first courses on Black or other minority culture and history, continue to hold skeptical views about the field. As late as 1981, Duke University English professor Kenny Williams, who is African American, "contended that the image of Black studies had come to be confused, willingly or otherwise, with the relaxation of academic and professional standards" (quoted in Hayes, 1992, p. xxxiii). She further charged that "students, faculty, and administrators perceived Black studies as a collection of easy courses that was intellectually empty and simply gratified political and emotional demands." On the other side are younger scholars, such as Lane Hirabayashi and Marilyn Alquizola, who emphatically identify ethnic studies as their primary field and reaffirm its founding purpose, which they fear may have been lost at some campuses in their rush for institutionalization. They argue that "dialogue" with "the theories and methodologies of mainstream academic disciplines" should continue to refine "counter-hegemonic discourses," the primary goal of ethnic studies (Hirabayashi & Alquizola, 1992, pp. 8–9).

The split between "cultural nationalists" and those ethnic studies scholars who work by the race, class, and gender matrix proposed by Butler and discussed above continues to divide colleagues. This dichotomy is especially sharp in Black or African American studies, exemplified by the Afrocentrists on one end (of whom Asante and Jeffries are only two variants on a broad spectrum) and, on the other end, the "liberals" (such as Henry Louis Gates of Harvard), feminists (such as bell hooks of CUNY), Marxists (such as Manning Marable of Columbia University), and other critical theorists (such as Cornel West of Harvard).

In 1992 the National Council of Black Studies appeared to have weighed in on this issue by naming its new journal the *Afrocentric Scholar*. However, in his introduction to the first issue, the editor, William A. Little, adopts a very broad approach to Afrocentrism, defining it in opposition to the "Eurocentric perspective," and as "an effort to illuminate the contributions of African people to world culture and to provide an alternative intellectual framework to the study of African people" (Little, 1992, p. i).

Some scholars in other ethnic studies fields decry the lingering "provincialism" present in some older programs, finding that this mindset precludes the faculty from pursuing "cooperative and comparative ventures and projects" (Hirabayashi & Alquizola, 1992, p. 9).

The ideological struggle between ethnic studies and their critics—those who uphold the supremacy of Western civilization against the challenge of pluralism and therefore charge ethnic studies scholars and other multicultural heretics of committing the sin of PC—will also accelerate, further polarizing U.S. society.

As this nation approaches a new millenium, it has the unique opportunity to reinvent and thus to redefine itself. Its options are clear. On the one hand, it can retain its traditional self-image as a model of triumphant Western civilization, an identity largely unchanged since the days of the Founding Fathers and reinforced by a social structure that historian Alexander Saxton bluntly describes as a "white supremacist social structure" that is "intolerant of racial diversity" (Saxton, 1990, p. 10). The alternative is for this nation to move seriously toward racial and cultural democracy.

To do so, education in the United States must begin by rectifying an official history that has been exclusive, therefore incomplete and distorted. As long as ethnic studies and multicultural education in general remain within the confines of "sensitivity training" and "celebrating diversity," it is safe and uncontested. But the minute some ethnic studies and multicultural educators take seriously the edict that education's highest purpose is to liberate and empower (as opposed to socialize), then it becomes controversial and, frankly, threatening to the status quo. However, this is precisely what makes ethnic studies so exciting and powerful, given its location at the crux of this monumental but necessary project to rethink and re-imagine America.

REFERENCES

Acuña, R. (1988). *Occupied America: A history of Chicanos* (3rd ed). New York: Harper and Row.

Adams, R. L. (1993). African-American studies and the state of the art. In M. Azevedo (Ed.), *Africana studies: A survey of Africa and the African diaspora*. Durham, NC: Carolina Academic Press.

Asante, M. K. (1992). The Afrocentric metatheory and disciplinary implications. *Afrocentric Scholar 1*(1), 98–117.

Aufderheide, P. (Ed.). (1992). *Beyond PC: Toward a politics of understanding*. Saint Paul: Graywolf Press.

Barringer, F. (1991, March 11). Census shows profound change in racial makeup of the nation. *New York Times*, p. A1.

Bell-Villada, G. (1990). Critical appraisals of American education: Dilemmas and contradictions in the work of Hirsch and Bloom. *International Journal of Politics, Culture, and Society, 3*(4), 485–511.

Berman, P. (Ed.). (1992). *Debating PC: The controversy over political correctness on college campuses*. New York: Dell.

Beyers, B. (1991, June 19). Machiavelli loses ground at Stanford; Bible holds its own. *Chronicle of Higher Education*, p. B2.

Bloom, A. (1987). *Closing of the American mind.* New York: Simon & Schuster.

Butler, J. (1991). Ethnic studies: A matrix model for the major. *Liberal Education, 77*(2), 26–32.

Butler, J., & Walter, J. (Eds.). (1991). *Transforming the curriculum: Ethnic studies and women's studies.* Albany: State University of New York Press.

Butterfield, F. (1990, October 24). The right breeds a college press network. *New York Times,* p. A1.

Chaufauros, E. A. (1991). *New ethnic studies in two American universities: A preliminary discussion.* Unpublished manuscript, Yale University, Program on Non-Profit Organizations, New Haven.

Cheney, L. (1992). *Telling the truth: A report on the state of the humanities in higher education.* Washington, DC: National Endowment for the Humanities.

Chronicle of Higher Education (1991, September 11), "Notebook," p. A37.

Dirlik, A. (1993). The Asia-Pacific in Asian-American perspective. In A. Dirlik (Ed.), *What is in a rim? Critical perspectives on the Pacific region idea* (pp. 305–329). Boulder, CO: Westview Press.

Dodge, S. (1990, May 9). A national network helps conservative students set up 58 newspapers on college campuses. *Chronicle of Higher Education,* p. A35.

D'Souza, D. (1991). *Illiberal education: The politics of race and sex on campus.* New York: Free Press.

Endo, R., & Wei, W. (1987). On the development of Asian American studies programs. In G. Okihiro, S. Hune, A. Hansen, & J. Liu (Eds.), *Reflections on shattered windows: Promises and prospects for Asian American studies* (pp. 5–15). Pullman: Washington State University Press.

Freire, P. (1970). *Pedagogy of the oppressed* (Myra Bergman Ramos, Trans.). New York: Seabury Press.

Garcia, M. T. (1992, Fall). Multiculturalism and American studies. *Radical History Review, 54,* 49–58.

Gates, H. L., Jr. (1992). African American studies in the 21st century. *Black Scholar, 22*(1), 3–10.

Genovese, E. D. (1991, April 15). An argument for counterterrorism in the academy: Heresy, yes—sensitivity, no. *New Republic,* pp. 30–35.

Glazer, N., & Moynihan, D. P. (Eds.). (1975). *Ethnicity: Theory and experience.* Cambridge: Harvard University Press.

Gordon, D. (1992). Inside the Stanford mind. *Perspectives* (American Historical Association Newsletter), *30*(4), 1–8.

Hayes, F. W., III (Ed.). (1992). *A turbulent voyage: Readings in African American studies.* San Diego: Collegiate Press.

Henson, S. (1991). The education of Dinesh D'Souza. How an angry young man parlayed right wing money into national attention. *Texas Observer, 83*(17), 6–9.

Hine, D. C. (1992). The Black studies movement: Afrocentric-traditionalist-feminist paradigms for the next stage. *Black Scholar, 22*(3), 11–19.

Hirabayashi, L., & Alquizola, M. (in press). Asian American studies and the politics of association. *New Studies on the Left.*

Hu-DeHart, E. (1991). From area studies to ethnic studies: The study of the Chinese diaspora in Latin America. In S. Hune, H. Kim, S. Fugita, & A. Ling (Eds.), *Asian Americans: Comparative and global perspectives* (pp. 5–16). Pullman: Washington State University Press.

Hune, S. (1991). Area studies and Asian American studies: Comparing origins, missions, and frameworks. In S. Hune, H. Kim, S. Fugita, & A. Ling (Eds.), *Asian Americans: Comparative and global perspectives* (pp. 1–4). Pullman: Washington State University Press.

Jaimes, M. A. (1987). American Indian studies: Toward an indigenous model. *American Indian Culture and Research Journal, 11*(3), 1–16.

Jones, R. (1993). *Ethnic studies—beyond myths and into some realities: A working paper.* Unpublished manuscript, Brown University, Center for the Study of Race and Ethnicity in America, Providence.

Keller, G., Magallan, R. J., & Garcia, A. M. (Eds.). (1989). *Curriculum resources in Chicano studies.* Tempe, AZ: Bilingual Review/Press.

Kimball, R. (1990). *Tenured radicals: How politics has corrupted our higher education.* New York: Harper and Row.

Kristol, I. (1991, July 31). The tragedy of multiculturalism. *Wall Street Journal,* p. A12.

Little, W. (1992). Introduction. *Afrocentric Scholar, 1*(1), i.

Liu, J. (1989). Asian American studies and the disciplining of ethnic studies. In G. Nomura, S. Sumida, & R. Long (Eds.), *Frontiers of Asian American studies* (pp. 273–283). Pullman: Washington State University Press.

Magner, D. (1991, May 1). Push for diversity in traditional disciplines raises questions about the future of ethnic studies. *Chronicle of Higher Education,* p. A11.

Mazumdar, S. (1991). Asian American studies and Asian studies: Rethinking roots. In S. Hune, H. Kim, S. Fujita, & A. Ling (Eds.), *Asian Americans: Comparative and global perspectives* (pp. 29–44). Pullman: Washington State University Press.

Muwakkil, S. (1992, May 27–June 9). L.A. lessons go unlearned. *In These Times,* p. 1.

Nasar, S. (1992, March 5). The 1980s: A very good time for the very rich. *New York Times,* p. A1.

Okihiro, G. (1991). African and Asian American studies: A comparative analysis and commentary. In S. Hune, H. Kim, S. Fugita, & A. Ling (Eds.), *Asian Americans: Comparative and global perspectives* (pp. 17–28). Pullman: Washington State University Press.

Omatsu, G. (Ed.). (1989). Commemorative issue—Salute to the 60s and 70s: Legacy of the San Francisco State strike. *Amerasia Journal, 15*(1).

Ong, P., & Hee, S. J. (1993). The growth of the Asian Pacific American population: Twenty million in 2020. In *The state of Asian Pacific America—a public policy report: Policy issues to the Year 2020* (pp. 11–23). Los Angeles: LEAP Asian American Public Policy Institute and UCLA Asian American Studies Center.

Ortiz, R. D. (1980). *Final report from the round table of Native American studies directors in forming the Native American Studies Association.* Albuquerque: University of New Mexico, Institute for Native American Development.

Portes, A., & Bach, R. (1985). *Latin journal: Cuban and Mexican immigrants in the United States.* Berkeley: University of California Press.

San Juan, E., Jr. (1992). *Racial formations/critical transformations: Articulations of power in ethnic and racial studies in the United States.* Atlantic Highlands, NJ: Humanities Press International.

San Juan, E., Jr. (no date). *Multiculturalism versus hegemony: Ethnic studies, Asian Americans, and U.S. racial politics.* Unpublished manuscript, no pagination, University of Connecticut, Storrs.

Saxton, A. (1990). *The rise and fall of the White republic.* London: Verso.

Schlesinger, A. M., Jr. (1991, July 8). The cult of ethnicity, good and bad. *Time,* p. 12.

Schlesinger, A. M., Jr. (1992). *The disuniting of America. Reflections on a multicultural society.* New York: Norton.

Sowell, T. (1981). *Ethnic America: A history.* New York: Basic Books.

Stimpson, C. R. (1991, May 29). New "politically correct" metaphors insult history and our campuses. *Chronicle of Higher Education,* p. A40.

Sykes, C., & Billingsley, K. L. (1992). Multicultural mafia. *Heterodoxy, 1*(5), 1–6.

University of California, San Diego (1990, January 25). *Proposal for the creation of a department of ethnic studies at the University of Cali-

fornia, San Diego. Unpublished manuscript, University of California, San Diego.

Usdansky, M. (1992, May 29–31). "Diverse" fits nation better than "normal." *USA Today,* p. 1A.

Vázquez, J. (1988). The co-opting of ethnic studies in the American university: A critical view. *Explorations in Ethnic Studies, 11*(1), 23–34.

Wang, L. L. (no date). *Ethnic studies and curriculum transformation at UC Berkeley: Our past, present and future.* Unpublished manuscript, University of California, Berkeley, Department of Ethnic Studies, Berkeley.

Weisberg, J. (1991). NAS: Who are these guys anyway? *Lingua Franca, 1*(4), 34–39.

Wiener, J. (1990, January 1). The Olin money tree: Dollars for neocon scholars. *Nation,* pp. 12–14.

Wiener, J. (1991, September 30). What happened at Harvard? *Nation,* pp. 384–388.

Will, G. (1991, April 22). Literary politics. *Newsweek,* p. 72.

Woodward, C. V. (1991). Freedom and the universities. In P. Aufderheide (Ed.), *Beyond PC: Toward a politics of understanding* (pp. 27–49). St. Paul, MN: Graywolf Press.

·41·

WOMEN'S STUDIES AND
CURRICULUM TRANSFORMATION

Betty Schmitz
UNIVERSITY OF WASHINGTON, SEATTLE

Deborah Rosenfelt
UNIVERSITY OF MARYLAND, COLLEGE PARK

Johnnella E. Butler
UNIVERSITY OF WASHINGTON, SEATTLE

Beverly Guy-Sheftall
SPELMAN COLLEGE

Women's studies has created theories about gender and the intersections of gender, race, ethnicity, and sexuality that offer important analytical frameworks for developing multicultural curricula. Similarly, in its own internal efforts to combat institutionalized racism and ethnocentrism, and its experience with curriculum transformation, women's studies has contributed significantly to the understanding of intellectual, philosophical, and pedagogical imperatives of multiculturalism. In this chapter, we review the progress of women's studies as a catalyst for transformation of U.S. higher education curricula. We focus our discussion of feminist scholarship and pedagogy on their multicultural aspects and analyze the effects of the development of women's studies and curriculum transformation on bringing more inclusive frameworks to higher education curricula.

THE EVOLUTION OF WOMEN'S STUDIES: CREATING A NEW FIELD

The catalyst for the formation of women's studies programs and departments, like African American studies and other ethnic studies, can be traced to the social protest and political dissent of the 1950s and 1960s and to the ensuing educational and demographic changes in higher education. During the civil rights, Black Power, Chicano, American Indian, and women's movements, students and supportive faculty members pushed for greater access to education and courses on groups that had been historically invisible in the curriculum. Feminists in the academy critiqued the content of the academic disciplines, the patriarchal structure of educational institutions, and the relationship of education to dominant cultural, political, economic, and social systems.

The far-reaching objectives of women's studies are well stated in the 1977 founding preamble to the National Women's Studies Association (NWSA): "to promote and sustain 'the educational strategy of break-through in consciousness and knowledge' that would 'transform' individuals, institutions, relationships, and ultimately the whole of society" (Boxer, 1982, p. 661). NWSA articulated a transformative vision of "a world free not only from sexism, but also from racism, classism, ageism, heterosexism—from all the ideologies and institutions that have consciously or unconsciously oppressed and exploited some for the advantage of others" (p. 662).

Women's studies is the most common term for the field, although some programs have chosen terms such as *feminist studies* to suggest the importance of a perspective that could be extended to subjects other than women. Other programs have defined their focus as *gender studies*, focusing on the relational nature of the social construction of femininity and masculinity and the ways in which men and women locate themselves

We gratefully acknowledge the research assistance of Andrew Bartlett and Karen Silas, Department of American Ethnic Studies, University of Washington. We wish to thank our editors, James A. and Cherry A. McGee Banks; and colleagues Suzanne Benally, Angela Ginorio, Janice Monk, and Mary Kay Tetreault, who read earlier drafts and made helpful comments. Permission to quote from the following is gratefully acknowledged: "Women's Studies at Twenty: Setting Agendas, Defining Challenges." *Women's Review of Books* 6, no. 5 (1989): p. 14.

within gender systems. The interdisciplinary field of men's studies focuses on the social and cultural construction of men and masculinity (Brod, 1987; Clatterbaugh, 1990; Gilmore, 1990; Schilb, 1982).

Development and Institutionalization of Women's Studies

Women's studies as a distinct programmatic unit within higher education began in 1969 at San Diego State University (Chamberlain, 1988). By 1977, there were 276 programs nationwide, and sections representing scholarship on women and women's caucuses had begun to appear within the traditional, disciplinary-based professional associations. Other scholarly supports—journals, research centers (many of which began with seed funding from the Ford Foundation), libraries, archives, and textbooks—developed to serve scholars and teachers (Loeb, Searing, & Stineman, 1987; Pope, 1989; Searing, 1985; Stineman, 1979). Stimpson refers to this early period of women's studies as the "take-off phase," where "submerged and marginalized traditions" emerged "explosively" (1992, p. 1967).

Women's studies built on the presence in traditional departments of a significant number of women interested in feminist issues and gender analysis. Women's studies tended to emerge as programs rather than departments, building curricula around departmentally based courses. A 1987 study indicated that 83% of women studies faculty members earn tenure in other departments (NWSA, 1990, p. 216).

Since its inception, women's studies has continued to grow. The 1990 NWSA Directory lists 621 women's studies programs, 425 of which offer the minor, certificate, or area of concentration and 187 of which offer the major. The number of institutions offering graduate work in women's studies nearly doubled between 1988 and 1990 from 55 to 102, with at least 8 institutions offering master's degrees in women's studies as opposed to master's in other fields with a concentration in women's studies. There were six doctoral programs: Clark University; Emory University; SUNY, Binghamton; SUNY, Buffalo; the Union Institute; and the University of Wisconsin, Madison.

Women's studies is a global phenomenon as well. In the 1970s and 1980s, numerous research projects, conferences, and seminars on women and development focused attention on women's issues around the world (Benería & Sen, 1981; Boserup, 1977; Kelly, 1981, 1986; Sen & Grown, 1987). The United Nations Decade for Women conferences in Mexico City (1975), Copenhagen (1980), and Nairobi (1985) and the international interdisciplinary congresses on women have also been instrumental in the international development of women's studies. At the Fifth International Interdisciplinary Women's Congress, held at the University of Costa Rica, San Jose (1993), five panels focused specifically on the status of women's studies in 30 different countries. By the end of the 1980s, at least 163 women's research centers existed worldwide: 66 in the United States and Canada; 29 in Asia; 24 in Europe; 23 in Mexico, Central America, and Latin America; 8 in northern and sub-Saharan Africa; 5 in Australia and New Zealand; 4 in the Middle East; and 4 in the Caribbean (Chamberlain, 1989).

As women's studies has become more central to the undergraduate liberal arts curriculum, there has been rising resistance. A national professional association, the National Association of Scholars (NAS), was formed to counter the advances made by feminism and multiculturalism in the academy, and a major national debate about this topic was waged in the media (Aufderheide, 1992; Carby, 1992; Graff, 1992; J. W. Scott, 1992). Serious attacks on feminism, multiculturalism, ethnic studies, cultural studies, and gay and lesbian studies have been generously underwritten by some foundations (Messer-Davidow, 1992).

Currently in the United States, many women's studies units are pursuing departmental status, despite political difficulties. While the network structures of most programs have proven effective in sustaining and disseminating women's studies, it is difficult to mount coherent curricula for certificates, minors, and majors and engage in long-term planning when faculty members owe allegiance to more powerful departments that make tenure and promotion decisions, and when program directors must negotiate with department heads to develop and schedule courses. Faculty members often feel divided between different sets of service obligations and different scholarly imperatives. Women's studies values scholarship linked to social change, invites disclosure of one's own social location, and requires familiarity with a range of texts and ideas that transcend disciplinary boundaries and sometimes question disciplinary assumptions, features not valued in many traditional disciplines (Butler & Schmitz, 1992; Coyner, 1983; Rosenfelt, 1984).

The dependence of women's studies on disciplinary-based scholarship as well as interdisciplinary work is reflected in the structure of the major as reported by Butler, Coyner, Homans, Longenecker, and Musil (1991). A typical women's studies major takes 35 semester hours including an introductory course, usually thematically arranged around topics such as identity formation, cultural representation of women, work, family, sexuality, and cultural diversity; a series of electives in the humanities and social sciences; and a final capstone course in the form of a senior seminar, field study/internship, or independent study. One third of all programs surveyed required some kind of course or courses on race, ethnicity, or cross-cultural perspectives for their majors.

Feminist Scholarship

Feminist scholarship has emerged both within specific academic disciplines, such as English, history, sociology, biology, religion, philosophy, and political science, and through the interdisciplinary work encouraged by women's studies programs, centers for research on women, and activist women outside the academy. Feminist scholars in disciplinary fields, privileged with an insider/outsider standpoint (Andersen, 1987), began to document and critique male bias embedded in their fields. DuBois, Kelly, Kennedy, Korsmeyer, and Robinson (1985) examined how "feminist scholarship from a multiplicity of disciplines is beginning to converge" (p. 6) by examining the dialectic of oppression and liberation, victimization and agency as a central axis of inquiry. An extensive literature of critique of the concepts, methods, and perspectives in traditional disciplines has emerged (e.g., Bleier, 1986; Harding, 1986; Hartman & Messer-Davidow, 1991; Hubbard, 1982; MacKinnon, 1987; Minnich, 1990; Sherman & Beck, 1979; Spender, 1981; Strathern, 1987; Thorne & Henley, 1975; Westcott, 1979). The literature of critique is complemented by an enormous new body of research that illuminates women's experiences on their own terms (e.g., works cited under "New Fields of Study" below).

Stimpson (1989) summarized the challenges of feminist scholarship by raising nine "theoretically nasty and socially grave" questions:

Why do we seek to dominate each other? ... What are the structures, psychologies, and languages of domination? How do we maintain them?
How have women mobilized on their behalf? How have they named their own interests? How have the discourses of motherhood empowered women? Imprisoned them? Both?
How do we end the sexual division of labor and the pauperization of women?
What are the new reproductive technologies? Who controls them? In what terms?
How diverse and varied are family forms?
What are the relationships among education, literacy, and gender equity?
How have gender identities and sexual identities been produced and reproduced?
What have been the connections between general historical ... and gender changes?
How do we imagine a different and better future? (p. 14)

It is important to make note of a continuing tension in feminist scholarship, the tension between an emphasis on equality—the parity of women and men before the law—and an emphasis on difference, the recognition that different social constituencies have differing histories, experiences, and consciousness and different needs, interests, and perhaps social claims (Cott, 1987; Rhode, 1990; J. W. Scott, 1988).

In its earlier manifestations, from the late 1960s to the mid-1970s, women's studies tended to focus on the unity of women's experience as women. Much of the influential theoretical work in this period sought universal explanations, structural and/or psychological, for the origins and persistence of patriarchal patterns—for example, Millett's *Sexual Politics* (1970), which identified a relatively undifferentiated pattern of sexist imagery in male-authored literature, explained with references to male domination in virtually all societies; Rubin's "The Traffic in Women" (1975), which drew on structural anthropology and Lacanian psychoanalysis to originate the term *sex-gender system*; Rosaldo's "Women, Culture, and Society: A Theoretical Overview" (1974), which proposed a structural model that related aspects of psychology and social organization to what she posited as a "public/private" split in male/female orientations; Ortner's "Is Female to Male as Nature Is to Culture?" (1974), which proposed a universal structure of perception; Chodorow's *The Reproduction of Mothering: Psychoanalysis and the Sociology of Gender* (1978), which drew on object-relations theory to posit crucial developmental differences between women and men; and Gilligan's *In a Different Voice* (1982),

which implied universal differences between women and men in their cognitive and moral development.

The emphasis on sexual difference in U.S. feminism heightened in the 1980s through the influence of French feminist theory. Special issues of *Yale French Studies* (1981, no. 62) and *Signs* (Autumn 1981), translations of texts (e.g., Cixous, 1976), and the publication of *New French Feminisms* (Marks & de Courtivron, 1980) brought French feminists' rereading of psychoanalytic and poststructuralist theory and critique of male/female binary oppositions to a wider range of scholars.

Also during the 1980s, a tendency already present in the late 1970s gained primacy, an emphasis on difference and diversity among women. Two conflicting theoretical and pedagogical concepts of "difference" emerged: (a) as primarily gender difference that united women as distinct from men and (b) as an index of incommensurability among women of different races, classes, ethnicities, and sexualities. Thus, while Jardine in her prelude to *The Future of Difference* heard among feminists "a common voice, which crosses cultural, political, and linguistic boundaries" in its inquiry into fundamental gender dichotomy (1988, pp. xxv–xxvii), and Morgan, in *Sisterhood Is Global* (1984), reiterates the universality of violence against women, poverty among women, women's limited access to social and economic power, and women's resistance in a global feminist movement as signs of women's underlying unity; simultaneously hooks's *Ain't I a Woman: Black Women and Feminism* (1981) and writers in *This Bridge Called My Back: Writings by Radical Women of Color* (Moraga & Anzaldúa, 1981) and *All the Women Are White, All the Blacks Are Men, But Some of Us Are Brave* (Hull, Scott, & Smith, 1982) offered critiques of White feminism and demonstrated that in both theory and pedagogical practice, gender alone could not define women.

Smith called attention to the few pages focused on African American women in the "thousands and thousands of books, magazines, and articles which have been devoted, by this time, to the subject of women's writing" (1977, p. 158). Sánchez called for an end to tokenism of Native American women in women's studies, given the "hundreds of resource lists or Indian-run agencies, hundreds of Indian women in organizations all over the country" (1983, p. 153). Zinn, Cannon, Higginbotham, and Dill (1986) noted that those holding the "gatekeeping positions" at major feminist scholarly journals were as White as those at any mainstream social science or humanities publication: Only nine women of color, in comparison to 116 White women, were represented on the editorial boards of the major women's studies journals. And, in "An Open Letter to Mary Daly," Lorde (1981) questioned whether White women ever read the work of Black women (given their dismissal in White women's work as anything other than victims) and called for engagement of difference: "The oppression of women knows no ethnic or racial boundaries, true, but that does not mean it is identical within those boundaries. ... To deal with one without even alluding to the other is to distort our commonality as well as our difference" (p. 97).

This critique emerged from the development of autonomous movements of women of color in the United States (often self-identified as Third World women for both ancestral heritage and related concerns of colonization) and throughout the world, spurred by new perspectives on the global political economy of women arising within the context of the United Nations Decade for Women (Albrecht & Brewer, 1990). The term *womanist* became current in the early 1980s in the writings of some African American women who wished to define their perspective as different from feminism in its incorporation of racial, cultural, national, economic, and political considerations, but similar in its critical perception of and reaction against patriarchy and sexism (Ogunyemi, 1985; A. Walker, 1983). The work of several White feminists that critiqued hegemonic feminist theory also helped to transform the field (e.g., Aptheker, 1981; Bunch, 1983; Culley, 1985; Frye, 1983; McIntosh, 1983; Palmer, 1983; Spelman, 1982, 1988), as did the availability of Fisher's anthology *The Third Woman* (1980).

Women from working-class backgrounds as well felt marginalized and disempowered within women's studies, and writers such as Helmbold (1987) and hooks (1984, 1989) wrote of the chasm between academic environments and the backgrounds of working-class women like themselves. Others critiqued the bias of feminist discourses that ignored class differences or that spoke abstractly of class while objectifying the experiences of working-class women of all races and ethnicities, and simultaneously offered new paradigms for changing attitudes and personal politics (Fisher-Mannick, 1981; McKenney, 1981; Moraga & Anzaldúa, 1981).

Likewise, lesbian feminists critiqued institutionalized heterosexism and the relative invisibility of lesbian experience within women's studies (Brown, 1980; Bulkin, 1980; Cruikshank, 1982); Muslim women spoke about their invisibility (Ahmed, 1980; al-Hibri, 1983); Jewish women criticized anti-Semitism within the women's movement and women's studies scholarship (Beck, 1988; Pogrebin, 1982); women with disabilities raised issues of access, bias, and the intersection of women's studies and disability studies (Hillyer, 1992); and a critique of ageism in women's studies (Copper, 1988; Macdonald & Rich, 1983) and a new area of emphasis—women and aging—have emerged (Bell, 1986; Porter, 1989).

Another source of challenge to the idea of unity among women, postmodernism also interrogated the idea of unity in subjectivity and textuality, emphasizing the partiality, provisionality, and situational nature of all knowledge. It "deconstructed" binary oppositions, including those between male and female, positing a plurality of subject positions in their stead. It also maintained a steady hostility to "biologism" and "essentialism" as ontological errors misreading the symbolic, culturally constructed nature of identity, including gender, race, and national identity (e.g., Flax, 1987; Haraway, 1991; Nicholson, 1990).

Early writings by women of color explored through the multiple perspectives of the authors the simultaneity of oppressions in women's lives; the intersections between and among gender, class, race, ethnicity, religion, and sexual orientation; and the biases and prejudices of each self-identified group. Coalition politics (Dill, 1983; Reagon, 1983; Smith, 1983) seemed possible because women challenged each other to learn about one another and to build connections by confronting difference. This focus has continued in more recent work (e.g., Albrecht & Brewer, 1990; Andersen & Collins, 1992; Bulkin, Pratt, & Smith, 1984; DuBois & Ruíz, 1990; Frankenberg, 1993; Joseph & Lewis, 1986; Multi-Cultural Women Writers of Orange County, 1990; Rothenberg, 1992; Shult, Searing, & Lester-Massman, 1991; Zinn & Dill, 1994).

New Fields of Study

From the politics of exclusion and inclusion in both women's studies and ethnic studies have emerged new fields of study, fields essential to the further development of women's studies and to transformation of the curriculum. The works cited below illustrate the enormous amount of scholarship, some produced as early as the 1970s, and all of it reflecting diversity among women. Much of the writing is available only because of the creation of presses and journals devoted primarily to making this work visible (e.g., Kitchen Table/Women of Color Press, Naiad Press, Spinsters/Aunt Lute, Firebrand Books, and Crossing Press).

Black Women's Studies. A new field of study, Black women's studies, emerged in part because of the failure of both Black studies and women's studies to address adequately the experiences of women of African descent in the United States and throughout the world. This field provided the conceptual frameworks for moving women of color from the margins of women's studies to the center and provided the catalyst to incorporate "minority women's studies" into courses and curricula. Cade edited a collection of works about African American women in 1970; *The Black Woman* was as important in the development of feminist theory as Millett's *Sexual Politics*, though rarely cited in this context by White feminists. Cade's work preceded Lerner's *Black Women in White America* (1973), which is often cited as having ushered in Black women's studies.

Equally important was *The Afro-American Woman: Struggles and Images* (Terborg-Penn & Harley, 1978), which provided important feminist historical perspectives. Many other critical works followed in the formative years of African American women's studies (Davis, 1981; Dill, 1979; Giddings, 1984; Jones, 1985; Lorde, 1984; Stack, 1984; Steady, 1981; Sterling, 1984; White, 1985). Giddings's history of Black women, *When and Where I Enter* (1984), underscored the significance of the argument that Black women's history and experiences are inextricably related to that of the entire community. The first interdisciplinary anthology, *All the Women Are White, All the Blacks Are Men, But Some of Us Are Brave* (Hull et al., 1982), defined the field, traced its development, provided a rationale for it; and *Women in Africa and the African Diaspora* (Terborg-Penn, Harley & Rushing, 1987) presented theoretical frameworks that united women of African descent around the world. The founding of *SAGE: A Scholarly Journal on Black Women* by Bell-Scott and Guy-Sheftall in 1983 was a major milestone in promoting research on Black women throughout the world. It signaled the "coming of age" of African American women's studies and illustrated the importance of paradigm shifts within women's studies.

A critical component in the development of Black women's studies was the emergence of Black feminist literary criticism, a response to Black women's exclusion from both African Americanist and feminist critical canons. Smith's "Toward a Black Feminist Criticism" (1977) was the first theoretical essay attempting to define a Black feminist aesthetic, followed by work by McDowell (1980) and Christian (1980). Bell, Parker, and Guy-Sheftall (1979) and Washington (1975, 1980) edited anthologies of African American women writers, providing texts for classroom use.

The field of Black women's studies continues to expand with recent works such as Washington's *Invented Lives* (1987), Carby's *Reconstructing Womanhood* (1987), P. B. Scott et al.'s *Double Stitch* (1991), Collins's *Black Feminist Thought* (1990), Grant's *White Women's Christ and Black Women's Jesus: Feminist Christology and Womanist Response* (1989), J. James and Farmer's *Spirit, Space & Survival* (1993), S. James and Busia's *Theorizing Black Feminisms* (1993), Morrison's *Race-ing Justice, En-gendering Power* (1992), and Hine's *Black Women in United States History* (1990).

American Indian Women's Studies. In the late 1970s, funding from the Women's Educational Equity Act Program provided resources for projects to achieve educational and economic equity for Native American and Alaskan Native women, including the development of the Ohoyo ("woman" in Choctaw) Resource Center, which published a bulletin for Native women in the United States and Canada (Anderson & Verble, 1980). In 1977, 12 American Indian women held a special meeting at the NWSA to formalize a network of academic Indian women; they identified the need for work on Indian women than represented their own perspectives, for increased attention to Indian women's survival networks and relationships between them and White women, and to focus on modern life rather than the past (Green, 1979). Green's *Native American Women: A Contextual Bibliography* (1983a) and *That's What She Said: Contemporary Fiction and Poetry by Native American Women* (1983b), along with such works as *American Indian Women: Telling Their Lives* (Bataille & Sands, 1984) and *A Gathering of Spirit: Writing and Art by Native North American Women* (Brant, 1983), documented the scope and cultural diversity of writings by and about Native women for whom women's issues are inextricably linked to issues of tribal sovereignty and Indian self-determination. These texts make clear that "feminist" issues such as reproductive rights, health care, and employment remain rooted in concerns for the survival of Indian peoples and their cultures and issues of land, natural resources, and treaty rights; American Indian women's activism has arisen primarily out of tribal activism rather than out of the feminist movement.

For her bibliography, Green (1983a) reviewed more than 700 bibliographic items and 200 years of writing on Native North American women, two thirds of which were written between 1960 and 1980. Although she finds some of the earlier "as told to" narratives useful today (e.g., Lurie, 1961), she faults researchers and scholars in anthropology and history for preferring to study those tribes and topics that remain visibly traditional and fit existing models. Thus, more literature may exist on American Indian women than other groups of U.S. women of color, but it is overwhelmingly selective (heavily concentrated on the Navajo, Inuit, Pueblo, Iroquois peoples), stereotypical, and romanticized.

The historical, ethnographic, and literary studies by scholars such as Albers and Medicine (1983), Allen (1986, 1989), Hogan (1982), Jacobs (1976), Kidwell (1979a, 1979b), Medicine (1981, 1987), and Witt (1976) illustrate the changing roles of women and their struggles with tradition and change as well as Indian women's leadership and power in defining contemporary familial and societal structures, in the day-to-day struggles for survival of their communities, and in the cultural production of their people. Native American women's written works challenge both aesthetic colonization and boundaries of traditional literary categories. Central themes in the work include the importance of community, loss and continuance, resistance to assimilation, an emphasis on event, attention to the sacredness of language, concern for the land and unity of all creatures, and affirmation of tribal sovereignty and cultural traditions. Contemporary women writers tell of Spider Woman, Yellow Woman, and Changing Woman stories that intertwine contemporary and past oral traditions.

Asian Pacific American Women's Studies. Asian Pacific American women's studies emerged within activist women's movements and within the struggles of Asian American communities, providing complex analyses of the intersections of race, class, and gender. Asian American women's activism grew out of the desire to overcome oppressive roles and was energized by the civil rights movement and particularly the antiwar movement, which fueled anti-Asian hostility. As early as 1974, faculty members teaching Asian American women's studies classes in eight California universities convened to discuss the connections between theoretical orientations and activism in a field in which there was a paucity of scholarship (Chu, 1986). Writings of Asian Pacific American women in the 1970s and 1980s emphasize the stereotyping of Asians as the "model minority" and of Asian Pacific American women as passive and submissive; the enormous diversity of immigration experiences among Chinese, Japanese, Filipino, Korean, Pacific Islander, and the newer South and Southeast Asian populations and their impact on women; the relationship of Asian feminist movements to Asian Pacific American movements; intergenerational conflicts and issues of assimilation and language; ways to address intolerance of women's issues within the Asian communities; and ways to maintain courses within academic curricula without a scholarly precedent (Chai, 1988; Chow, 1987; Chu, 1986; H., 1989; Kim & Otani, 1983; Lai, 1992; Lim, 1991; Uyehara, 1979; Yamada, 1979, 1981, 1990). The historical, literary critical work of Kim (1982), Glenn (1986), Matsumoto (1984), Matthei and Amott (1990), Hune, Kim, Fugita, and Ling (1991), and Chan (1991) has strengthened the scholarly underpinnings of Asian Pacific American women's studies.

Yamada's call for Asian Pacific American women to "raise our voices a little more" (1979, p. 13) has been answered beginning with less well-known efforts such as Tsuchida's *Asian and Pacific American Experiences: Women's Perspectives* (1982) and continuing through the publication of such anthologies as *Making Waves* (Asian Women United of California,

1989); *Forbidden Stitch* (Lim & Tsutakawa, 1989); *Home to Stay* (Watanabe & Bruchac, 1990); and *Unbroken Thread* (Uno, 1993). The postmodern analyses of Minh-ha (1989) and Mohanty (1991) contribute directly to connecting Asian Pacific American women's lives to those of Asian women and other Third World women.

Chicana/Latina Studies. Likewise, Chicana/Latina feminists critiqued women's studies for its exclusionary practices and lack of attention to diversity among women (González, 1977; Rebolledo, 1985; Zinn et al., 1986). While the U.S. and Central American presence of Cubanas, the fastest-growing population of Latinas in the United States, has brought new lenses to the study of Latinas, the groups that have the largest numbers and longest history are Chicanas and Puerto Ricans. Chicana studies, Puerto Rican women's studies, and other Latina studies emerged from autonomous women of color movements and from the context of community struggles and the creation of Chicano studies, Latino studies, and Puerto Rican studies.

Knowledge and sources about Chicanas became available by the mid-1970s with the publication of three major Chicana bibliographies: *La Mujer Chicana: An Annotated Bibliography* (Chapa & Andrade, 1976); *Bibliography of Writings: La Mujer* (Portillo, Ríos, & Rodríguez, 1976); and *The Chicana: A Preliminary Bibliographic Study* (Argandona, Gómez-Quiñones, & Duran, 1976). Bibliographic studies continue to emerge (Alarcón, 1989; Carr, 1988–89; Loeb, 1980, Orozco, 1990). Literary, historical, and theoretical writings by Alarcón (1985), Anzaldúa (1990), Córdova, Cantú, Cárdenas, García, and Sierra (1986), García (1989), Herrera-Sobek (1985), Ramos (1987), Rebolledo and Rivero (1993), Ruíz (1987), M. E. Sánchez (1985), R. Sánchez and Cruz (1977), Segura (1989), Segura and Pierce (1993), Trujillo (1991), Zavella (1987), and Zinn (1980, 1982) have contributed extensively to the field and to classroom study of the Chicana experience. Chicanas continue to examine their relationship to both feminism (Segura & Pesquera, 1992; Zavella, 1987) and Chicano studies and to seek self-determination through the formation of associations such as Mujeres Activas en Letras y Cambio Social and the Chicana caucus of the National Association of Chicano Studies.

Acosta-Bélén's edited collection, *The Puerto Rican Woman: Perspectives on Culture, History, and Society* (1986), first published in 1979, is a critical source for the study and understanding of Puerto Rican women's reality both on the island and in the United States. Several of the chapters originated at a 1976 symposium on the Hispanic American woman at SUNY, Albany, including an article on the Black Puerto Rican woman in the United States, which deals with racism in both worlds (Jorge, 1986). Other scholars who have contributed substantially to our knowledge about Puerto Rican women include Azize (1979), Bose (1986), García-Coll and Mattei (1989), King (1974), Picó (1986), and the Proyecto de Estudios de la Mujer (1992).

Latina feminists bring themes and paradigms to women's studies, illustrating how issues of race, class, cultural identity, and gender subordination intersect and coexist. A central task is to name their subject in the face of linguistic and geographical boundaries and classification systems ("Hispanic," "Spanish-speaking") that do not define their reality. Through their analyses of silence and voice within the context of bilingualism, they challenge monolingual English-speaking feminists to experience their own limitations and create new definitions of self through the creative use of both languages (e.g., Anzaldúa, 1987; Gómez, Moraga, & Romo-Carmona, 1983; Horno-Delgado, Ortega, Scott, & Sternbach, 1989). Like African American and Asian Pacific American women's studies, Chicana/Latina women's studies calls attention to the international roots and connections of cultures. Acosta-Belén (1993) points out how this discourse of both denunciation and revindication "has extended beyond the U.S. frontiers and transnationalized itself by its identification and solidarity with the liberation struggles of other women and oppressed groups worldwide" (p. 182).

Jewish Women's Studies. The field of Jewish women's studies has included both a critique of anti-Semitism and an exploration of the history, literature, experience, perceptions, and religious dilemmas of Jewish women. Though Jewish women have been influential participants in and shapers of women's studies since its inception, Jewish invisibility in feminist discourses of difference remains a problem. Beck (1988) suggests that this invisibility reflects less a deliberate anti-Semitism than a facile reliance on a set of variables—race, class, and gender—that obscures Jewish women's identity. Being Jewish may entail shared religious beliefs and practices, a shared history and cultural legacy, and, in the United States and other countries of the Jewish diaspora, shared status as a minority ethnicity.

Until recently, Jewish women's studies has flourished more vigorously in the contexts of Jewish studies and Jewish community life than in women's studies in the university, as Jewish women have struggled with a central dilemma: Can one be simultaneously a feminist and a Jew? Jewish women's efforts to resolve this contradiction have generated a burgeoning scholarship (Beck, 1989; Elwell, 1992; Greenberg, 1983; Heschel, 1983; Kaye/Kantrowitz & Klepfisz, 1989; Schneider, 1984). The contradiction between religious-ethnic identity and feminist consciousness is shared by feminists in other religious traditions (Ahmed, 1992; al-Hibiri, 1982; Azari, 1983; Daly, 1973; Johnson, 1989).

Jewish women have struggled to evolve new ritual and to rewrite traditional ritual and prayer in a more egalitarian language within the undeniably patriarchal context of Judaism (Plaskow, 1990; Umansky & Ashton, 1992). Jewish women's studies also includes biblical analysis and reinterpretation of biblical texts (Ostriker, 1993; Pardes, 1992; Trible, 1978); historical work on Jewish women in specific historical periods, including the Holocaust (Baum, Hyman, & Michel, 1977; Kuzmack, 1990; Schwerteger, 1989); studies of Israeli women (Hazleton, 1977; Rein, 1980; Spiro, 1980); and work, often with Palestinian women, on peace in the Middle East (Rosenwasser, 1992). An important bibliographic resource is Cantor's bibliography, *The Jewish Woman, 1900–1985* (1987).

Lesbian Studies. While many lesbians have been central theorists of women's studies, the publication of *Lesbian Nation* (Johnston, 1973); *This Bridge Called My Back* (Moraga & Anzaldúa, 1981); *Conditions, Volume 5* (Bethel & Smith, 1979); *Nice Jewish Girls: A Lesbian Anthology* (Beck, 1982/1989); *Lesbian Studies: Present and Future* (Cruikshank, 1982); *Home Girls: A Black Feminist Anthology* (Smith, 1983); and *Lesbian Nuns: Breaking Silence* (Curb & Manahan, 1985) made visible to wider audiences a tremendous amount of literary, historical, sociological, and critical work by lesbians that had been largely ignored by women's studies in the academy. Works like these began to recover the history of lesbians, gave voice to the variety of lesbian experiences, defined heterosexism as a structural form of oppression and homophobia as a form of prejudice, and provided curricular and pedagogical approaches for creating lesbian studies as a legitimate field within women's studies and for integrating lesbian studies into other fields. New journals, such as *Conditions* and *Sinister Wisdom*, deliberately locating the making of knowledge outside of academia as well as within, contributed substantially to this evolution. Research and writing on lesbians within certain cultures continues to appear and to present the complexity of women's lives as defined by sexuality, race, class, and ethnicity (Aguilar-San Juan, 1993; Brant, 1993; Gomez, 1993; Kennedy & Davis, 1993; McNaron, Anzaldúa, Argüelles, & Kennedy, 1993; Smith, 1991; Trujillo, 1991).

Postcolonialism, Feminism, and Third World Women's Studies. The critique of feminism's ethnocentrism by U.S. women of color and women of the Third World as well as the postmodernist encounter with feminism have converged in work on feminism and anticolonial discourse. Mohanty (1991) argues that representations in Western feminist discourse of the Third World woman as the powerless object of economic, religious, legal, and sexual oppression "perpetuate and sustain the hegemony of the idea of superiority of the West, setting in motion a colonialist discourse which exercises a very specific power in defining, coding, and maintaining existing first/third world connections" (p. 78). Behar (1990) suggests that some feminist anthropologists, in their efforts to invert their representations of Third World women as passive victims, have "lately stressed the existence of female cultures of resistance, thereby extending the Western feminist self-representation to their subjects" (p. 231). Mani (1990), writing about the discursive struggle over *sati* in 19th- and 20th-century India, suggests that Indian feminism may need to revert to analytic emphases on women's subjugation to interpret accurately and reorder postcolonial relations of power.

Scholars and writers in intellectual history, anthropology, literature, and cultural studies have simultaneously expanded and particularized in specific Third World contexts feminism's critique of patriarchal institutions and ideologies. Davies (1990), for example, insists on the paramount importance for Caribbean women writers of a "common cultural heritage" of "familial and historical links to the Caribbean world," so that "a shared exploration of gender and heritage is an inseparable aspect of a singular articulation of cultural identity" (p. 59). At the same time, she and Fido argue (1990, p. 11) that the three basic, interdependent ideological formulations that have guided Caribbean thought, anticolonial and postcolonial nationalism, Black power and negritude, and Marxism-Leninism, must be supplemented by a fourth formulation—feminism.

Women in nationalist movements often find themselves confronting both nationalist ideologies, which can become socially conservative in their representations of "Western" feminism as enemy, and feminist ideologies of progress, which fail to understand the symbolic, cultural, and religious dimensions of nationalist identity and commitment (Enloe, 1990; Jayawardena, 1986; Lazreg, 1990). The expansion of the women's movement in the Third World is bringing fresh perspectives on such issues as structural adjustment, the debt crisis, violence against women, reproductive rights, militarism, reproductive technologies, racism, refugees, and work and family (Fenton & Heffron, 1987). Third World feminists have enlarged the scope of feminist theory through their continuous search for theory that remains connected to the everyday struggles of women, for new strategies, and for more immediate solutions to the multiplicity of basic survival issues (Acosta-Belén & Bose, 1990).

Contemporary Theoretical Challenges. Feminist scholarship focusing on the particularity of different women's experiences continues to grow. Unfortunately, exclusion remains an issue. In her review of 12 books of American feminist criticism focusing on contemporary women's fiction published between 1985 and 1991, Rose (1993) sees a continuing selectivity in "canon" formation and the persistence of the view that women of color and lesbians are "marginal":

Of the contemporary African-American women writers discussed by Melissa Walker [1991] and other black feminist critics, only Morrison and Alice Walker are represented with any regularity in books and articles by White feminists. Of the 167 lesbian writers Zimmermann lists in *The Safe Sea of Women* [1990], only Russ is discussed in any other books reviewed in this essay.... Except for Kingston, ... where are the Asian-American women? Hispanic women? Native American women? (pp. 370–373)

The challenges facing feminist theory in the 1990s are to transform itself through the inclusion of the voices and interpretations of women of many cultures, backgrounds, and identities as they speak for themselves in a variety of forms, media, and genres; and to produce scholarship and theory reflective of an exchange between postmodernist articulators of theories of difference and the women whose daily lives and experiences, and whose written and spoken voices, most frequently seem to disappear in the critical discourses that ostensibly valorize them (Behar, 1990; Christian, 1988; Meese, 1990; Ong, 1987; Patai, 1988). Lugones (1992) proposes a new feminist model of "friendship" rather than "sisterhood" as a more appropriate and functional base for feminist solidarity within pluralistic and multicultural contexts. Friendship does not evoke familial loyalty, hence is not unconditional. It is based in respect, sustains itself through the recognition of power relations, and holds the possibility of reconstituting relationships among women divided along sociocultural differences.

Feminist Pedagogy

The 1970s produced serious interest in developing theory about the dynamics of feminist classrooms. The challenge of teaching and learning about women paralleled discussions, arising out of student activism of the period, about the impact of opening up classrooms to previously excluded groups of students and about learner-centered and social change-oriented pedagogies developed by Freire (1970), who continues to influence feminist pedagogy in the 1990s (Luke & Gore, 1992).

Howe (1984) contributed significantly to the publication of works emphasizing both the structure of course content and classroom dynamics, bringing her experiences in the Mississippi freedom classroom to an analysis of women's experiences in the college classroom. She founded (with Lauter) the Feminist Press, which published syllabi and other resources from women's studies courses in *Female Studies VI* (Hoffman, Secor, & Tinsley, 1973) and *Female Studies VII* (Rosenfelt, 1973); *But Some of Us Are Brave* (Hull et al., 1982); and *Lesbian Studies* (Cruikshank, 1982). Howe also founded the *Women's Studies Newsletter* (now the *Women's Studies Quarterly*), which along with other teaching-centered journals such as the *Radical Teacher* provided early vehicles for the exchange of information about pedagogical issues, including diversity among women students and teachers.

Gendered Subjects, edited by Culley and Portuges (1985), collected in one volume influential work from the 1970s and early 1980s and remains unusual in its attention to the dynamics of race, class, sexuality, age, and ethnicity as they intersect with gender in the classroom. The authors critique radical pedagogy for its inattention to gender and race (especially Culley, 1985, and Friedman, 1985); analyze the paradox of "female authority" in the classroom and redefine the uses of authority to empower students (especially Culley, 1985; Culley, Diamond, Edwards, Lennox, & Portuges, 1985; See also Rich, 1979); draw connections between feminist scholarship and interactive learning and nonhierarchical classrooms (Maher, 1985); validate personal experiences of students; analyze dynamics of interaction among women situated differently in relation to power; and connect knowledge to social action. Additional contributions to issues of diversity as they intersect with pedagogy include Berry and McDaniels (1980), Butler (1991b), Cannon (1990), Frankenberg (1991), González (1980), Liu (1991), and Omolade (1987).

Yet prominent and influential studies by Gilligan (*In a Different Voice*, 1982) and Belenky, Clinchy, Goldberger, and Tarule (*Women's Ways of Knowing*, 1986), which focus on male/female differences in voice and identity and based in a White, mostly middle-class context, have inadvertently served to narrow the early theoretical conceptualizations about difference in feminist pedagogy. The emphasis in these works on "voice" ignores entirely the contemporaneous writings about struggles to find voice by women of color, lesbians, and others as well as the issue of multiple sources of identity and oppression (cf. Mohanty, 1994). The theme of "women's ways of knowing," which appears ubiquitously in various formulations for papers, conferences, and training workshops, has unfortunately

played into essentialist notes of gender that once again erase difference. Thus, for example, bibliographies on feminist pedagogy appearing in mainstream women's studies journals lack significant attention to diversity among women (Goetsch, 1991; Shrewsbury, 1987).

The Classroom Climate: A Chilly One for Women? (Hall & Sandler, 1982) addressed the classroom experience outside women's studies. Describing in detail behaviors and situations contributing to the disempowerment of women in the classroom, it offers specific recommendations for administrators, faculty, and students to bring about change and provides resource materials and suggestions for further research. While one section addresses minority women, recommendations specific to their classroom experience came in two later Association of American Colleges (AAC) publications (Moses, 1989; Nieves-Squires, 1991), addressing respectively the climate for Black and Hispanic women undergraduates, graduates, faculty, and administrators.

In recent years, pedagogical researchers and theorists influenced by postmodernism have interrogated the initial emphasis on feminist pedagogy as a set of practices emphasizing collaborative and experiential learning, a nonhierarchical classroom, and an exploration of the personal in its relationship to the political. Gore, for example, worries that feminist pedagogies, like other radical pedagogies, manifest totalizing tendencies that approximate what Foucault (1980) called "regimes of truth" (Gore, 1993, pp. 64, 51–55). Lather (1991) shares her concern, arguing for a model of critical teaching that does not assume an inevitable assent to feminist values and visions. She identifies a fundamental contradiction that she sees feminist teachers inevitably confronting: on the one hand, a desire to encourage genuine independence of inquiry, on the other hand, an assumption that such inquiry will, or should, lead students to an analysis of oppression akin to their own.

A number of critics observe that, as Gore (1993) states it, "'micro' level analyses of classrooms, more characteristic of traditional conceptions of pedagogy, have tended to ignore the constitutive role of power in pedagogy. Radical pedagogies, on the other hand, have tended to focus on the 'macro' level of ideologies and institutions while down playing the instructional act" (p. xiv).

Contemporary feminists' preoccupation with poststructuralism and with the intersection of feminism and critical pedagogy has also served to narrow attention to difference. An emphasis on empowerment of an undifferentiated "woman student" or of the "female subject"—still an important theme (e.g., Finke's Lacanian analysis, 1993)—ignores crucial race and class differences among women and men. Thus, in 1992, Kenway and Modra wrote about *Gendered Subjects* in the context of gender and schooling in Australia without references to the intersections of gender, race, class, and sexuality and without citations of the (many) authors of color in the 1984 text. Likewise, the collection in which Kenway and Modra (1992) appears, *Feminisms and Critical Pedagogy* (Luke & Gore, 1992), includes only rare citations to the work of women of color and on occasion cites them as if they were concerned solely with gender (Lewis's 1992 reference to hooks, pp. 183–184).

Developing a multicultural feminist pedagogy remains a necessary goal for women's studies. A recent book by Maher and Tetreault, *The Feminist Classroom* (1994), addresses the issue of feminist pedagogy from the perspectives of classrooms with diverse students and diverse faculty members.

Evaluation of the Impact of Women's Studies

Impact on Students. The focus of most experimental research in the 1970s and 1980s centered on assessing changes in students' attitudes toward sex roles and sex stereotyping and on the impact of women's studies courses on student self-esteem, career aspirations, and feminist identity development (Bargad & Hyde, 1991). Porter and Eileenchild (1980) noted a need for a more cognitive approach to measuring the effectiveness of women's studies teaching.

A comprehensive study on student learning in women's studies published in 1992 responds to this need and demonstrates that women's studies contributes to central goals of both liberal and multicultural education. Musil's *The Courage to Question* (1992a) explores the intellectual and personal changes that occur when students take course work in women's studies and attempts to relate outcomes of student learning with the claims the field has traditionally made about its impact. Based on multiple methods of data collection and analysis at seven different colleges and universities over a 3-year period, this report suggests that women's studies, far from imposing a monolithic ideology based on "oppression studies," as critics have charged, provides students with many of the intellectual and personal skills central to calls for reform in undergraduate education. For example, this research indicates that women's studies helps students create personalized learning by linking the intellectual and the experiential and that students find women's studies to be more intellectually rigorous because it challenges them to incorporate new knowledge into their lives (Musil, 1992b, p. 2). It helps students develop a critical perspective: students in women's studies classes debate issues far more frequently both in and out of classes, and women's studies professors encourage divergent points of view that challenge students to form their own opinions (p. 3). Regarding social change, a central goal of women's studies, this research shows that women's studies students move from voice to self-empowerment to social responsibility, that they want to improve things for others as well as themselves, and that they translate these desires into citizen action (p. 4).

This report also suggests that women's studies aids in the furthering of central goals of multicultural education. Women's studies courses heighten students' awareness of diversity and difference, and students report significant change in the way they think about people who are different from themselves. In addition, "many students developed an analysis of larger systems in which differences were embedded, reinforced, and defined and from which unequal power was allocated and perpetuated" (Musil, 1992b, p. 5). Men students, while often resisting the content of women's studies, increase their number of female friends when they take women's studies courses and develop awareness of gendered power relations (p. 9). While

these results are based on a selected group of institutions, they suggest important areas for future research.

Impact on the Disciplines and Undergraduate Curricula. There can be no question about the amount of women's studies scholarship available in the disciplines: Since its inception, *Signs: Journal of Women in Culture and Society* has published extensive review essays, about half in the traditional disciplines and half in new or interdisciplinary areas. Howe and Lauter (1980) noted as one measure of impact the formation of new divisions or sections on women or women's studies in over 50 professional associations that produced bibliographies and reports of the status of women in the profession.

In an attempt to determine the degree to which feminist scholarship had transformed academic disciplines, DuBois et al. (1985) reviewed 10 leading journals in five fields between 1966 and 1980 and found a rise in the amount of feminist research incorporated. In the baseline period (1966–70), 2% of articles were devoted to women; in the period 1971–75, the percentage rose to 3.7%; and, in 1976–80, to 5.3%. The overall percentage rose from 1.9% to 7.4%. They also looked for evidence of transformation of research in these "gatekeeper" journals and found only a handful of articles that took gender into account. No similar study has been conducted for the 1980s, during which curriculum transformation projects became widespread.

Women's studies and feminist scholarship continue to gain in importance to undergraduate curricula. Graff (1992) cites feminism as one of several major advances in humanistic scholarship over the past three decades. Astin (1993) included in *What Matters in College?* the existence of a women's or gender studies program as one of the environmental variables that have the potential to influence student outcomes. This study suggests that offering women's studies courses has positive effects on self-reported improvements in general knowledge, on student retention, and on affective outcomes, while the presence of a women's or gender studies requirement had a negative effect on student satisfaction with general education requirements. Musil (1992b) demonstrates how feminist pedagogy, with its student-centered focus, has had an impact on the assessment movement in higher education.

CURRICULUM TRANSFORMATION: CHALLENGING AND CHANGING THE "MAIN" CURRICULUM

Curriculum transformation brings new scholarship, conceptual frameworks, and pedagogies from fields of women's studies, American ethnic studies, and other comparative cultural studies to faculty members who teach in other disciplines in order to help reshape them in ways that reflect the diversity and complexity of human experiences. Its goal, according to Butler, is "the closest approximation of the truth" (1991a, p. 4). The history of curriculum transformation projects in the 1980s illustrates how this goal is being achieved.

Early Projects

In 1980 Howe called for women's studies to turn to its transformative goal: to use the knowledge and the development of new courses to change the education of all students. This "call to action" became feasible through the support of many private foundations and federal funding agencies. In the mid-1970s to the early 1980s, major curricular change efforts were begun on many campuses with support from the Mellon Foundation, the newly created Women's Educational Equity Act Program (WEEAP), the National Endowment for the Humanities, the Fund for the Improvement of Postsecondary Education (FIPSE), the Lilly Foundation, and others (Schmitz, 1985). State monies were also available: the Women's Studies Program at San Francisco State University received funding from the California State University chancellor to initiate a project, Cross-Cultural Perspectives in the Curriculum, focusing on both race and gender and eventually replicated at two thirds of California's state universities (Rosenfelt, n.d.).

The impetus for creation of a national curriculum change movement based in women's studies was provided by two national invitational conferences in 1981. The Workshop on Integrating Women's Studies into the Curriculum, organized and sponsored by the Southwest Institute for Research on Women (SIROW) with support from the Rockefeller Family Fund and the National Endowment for the Humanities (August 27–30, 1981, Princeton, New Jersey), brought together directors from 17 projects around the country to exchange information and assess current theory and practice in feminist curriculum change. These projects varied greatly in scope and purpose, those with large external grants attempting more widespread change.

Project leaders discussed critical issues about change at both the individual faculty and the institutional and disciplinary levels. They recognized two complementary efforts: one aimed at course revision on individual campuses and one aimed at broader, disciplinary change (Schmitz, 1985). The project at Wheaton College, for example, targeted introductory courses, hypothesizing that since these courses contained the fundamental concepts of the disciplines, changing them would lead to change throughout the curriculum and the disciplines themselves (Spanier, Bloom, & Boroviak, 1984). The project at California State University, Hayward, focused on courses fulfilling general education and core curriculum requirements (Pointer & Auletta, 1990). Projects at the University of Arizona (Aiken, Anderson, Dinnerstein, Lensink, & MacCorquodale, 1987, 1988; Andersen, 1987) and Montana State University (Schmitz, 1985) concentrated on faculty development. Still others began by creating a women's studies presence on campus by introducing interested faculty members to the new scholarship; Lewis and Clark College, for example, conducted a 4-week summer institute on incorporating feminist scholarship into the core curriculum with support from the National Endowment for the Humanities in 1981 (Arch & Kirschner, 1984). Smith College brought together interested faculty members in seminars to explore the dimensions of feminist scholarship and its implications for teaching (Schuster & Van Dyne, 1985).

Projects aimed at reevaluating and transforming the traditional knowledge bases of the disciplines included the Reconstructing American Literature Project of the Feminist Press (Lauter, 1983, 1991); the Wellesley Center for Research on Women's Faculty Development Program, which generated working papers in different disciplines; and the Black Studies/Women's Studies Faculty Development Project (Butler, 1985). Disciplinary-based professional associations such as the Association of American Geographers (Loyd & Rengert, 1978), the Organization of American Historians (1983; Fox-Genovese & Stuard, 1983), the American Political Science Association (1983–84), the American Psychological Association (Gappa & Pearce, 1982), and the American Sociological Association (Gappa & Pearce, 1983) sponsored or cosponsored the development of teaching materials.

The second major national conference in 1981—the Wingspread Conference on "Liberal Education and the New Scholarship on Women: Issues and Constraints in Institutional Change," supported by the Ford, Lilly, and Johnson foundations (Association of American Colleges, 1982)—brought together senior academic administrators and women's studies scholars and teachers to discuss the implications of the new scholarship for the traditional goals and assumptions of liberal learning. They generated a series of recommendations to challenge the larger educational community into serious consideration of the imperatives for institutional and curricular change.

Expansion and Evaluation

The dissemination of information about early curriculum integration projects through national educational media and national professional associations resulted in the proliferation of projects. As the fiscal restraints of the 1980s began to result in retrenchment, campuses explored more cost-effective strategies such as concentrating on more limited areas of the curriculum, piggybacking on institutional processes, and working with faculty already interested in change. Consortial models emerged in which several campuses shared resources from a major grant (Schmitz & Dinnerstein, 1991). Project leaders often chose departments where support already existed and where the involvement of a new faculty member would make a difference for future efforts at the departmental level. This focus on the department as the locus of change is increasingly important in the 1990s, as national curriculum change efforts have emphasized assessment of learning and sequencing of knowledge in the major (Association of American Colleges, 1991) and as the numbers of faculty members in departments who have participated in curriculum transformation projects increase.

Problematics of Curriculum "Integration." Another response to shrinking resources for women's studies and curriculum transformation was serious debate about the best focus for women's studies work in the academy. Women's studies faculty raised questions about the impact of curriculum change projects: What happens to feminist perspectives when taught by nonfeminists? Will the radical potential of feminist scholarship be diluted? Will women again become invisible within mainstream scholarship? Can the interdisciplinary knowledge explored in women's studies ever "fit" in traditional disciplines, and what resonances among texts and voices are lost in this process? How will mainstreaming efforts influence the already fragile alliances among women separated by race, class, sexual orientation, and ethnicity (Bowles & Klein, 1983; Coyner, 1983; Rosenfelt, 1984)?

The language and funding of curriculum transformation projects were causes for concern. The earliest term used for these projects was *mainstreaming women's studies*, a term quickly abandoned for its connotations of absorption. Other project leaders used terms such as *integration, balancing the curriculum,* or *gender-balancing the curriculum,* which also implied something less than significant change. Large grants, in the range of $50,000 to $250,000, from private foundations and federal funding programs dwarfed budgets of women's studies programs and were often awarded to units outside of women's studies programs.

Concerns were further fueled by Stimpson's 1986 report, *Women's Studies in the United States,* which expressed some pessimism about the "nation-wide instability" of women's studies, given a hostile environment and the stigma still associated with it. She predicted a somewhat gloomy future for women's studies in the academy because of attacks from neoconservatives; decreased federal funding; dwindling institutional resources; too many part-time and/or junior, untenured women's studies faculty; the absence of dedicated women's studies positions; and questions about student interest, given their concern with career preparation.

In this climate, the development of truly inclusive theory and practice for women's studies became a more compelling agenda for many women's studies scholars and teachers than curriculum transformation efforts aimed elsewhere (Butler, 1984). Without such inclusiveness, transformation of the academy risked replicating the conceptual and political errors of "White" women's studies, which Butler characterized as having to divest itself of White skin privilege, racism, and the insistence on gender as a primary category of analysis, and of "male" ethnic studies, which needs to divest itself of sexism and homophobia.

Butler (1991a), arguing that ethnic studies and women's studies can provide the transformative content and pedagogy for the liberal arts, calls for paradigm shifts in women's studies and in American ethnic studies by developing what she called generative or transformative scholarship. This scholarship would include: (a) the identification of the connections between and interactions among the disciplines—the confluence and convergence of disciplinary approaches; (b) the study and definition of the experience and aesthetics of those large groups of people who are neglected, studied not in comparison to the dominant group and not as problems to the dominant group, but in and of themselves and in relation to one another; (c) the correction of distortions of the majority and the minority that have occurred due to the insistence of exclusion; and (d) the defining and structuring of a curriculum that through its content and pedagogy affirms the interconnectedness of human life, experience, and creativity and its constant evolutionary nature.

Collaborative projects between American ethnic studies and women's studies, such as the Black Studies/Women's Studies Project at the University of Massachusetts/Smith College (Butler, 1985), the Department of Ethnic and Women's Studies at California Polytechnic University, Pomona, and the project Integrating Black Women's Studies into the Curriculum, at Spelman College, attempted to make such interconnections among race, class, gender, and ethnicity. Curriculum transformation projects emerged with the goal of transforming women's studies research, courses, and curricula as well as the liberal arts curriculum (Hoffman, 1986). The Memphis State University Center for Research on Women contributed significantly to the transformation of curricula in women's studies and other fields with the working paper series "Southern Women: Intersections of Race, Class and Gender," bibliographies (e.g., Timberlake, Cannon, Guy, & Higginbotham, 1988), a database on women of color, papers on curriculum integration, and faculty development workshops aimed at curriculum integration. In 1983, Spelman College, the oldest historically Black college for women, began a two-year project to integrate African American women's studies materials into general education courses at Spelman and to carry out faculty development activities at four other institutions: Clark, Morehouse, Agnes Scott, and Kennesaw Community College. The project ended with a two-week workshop in the summer of 1985 that brought together a racially diverse group of faculty from all five institutions (Guy-Sheftall, 1986).

Likewise, attention turned to integrating scholarship on women from other countries and to collaborative projects between women's studies and international studies. In 1987, SIROW organized a national conference to promote a dialogue between leaders in women's studies and international studies programs. Participants at this conference identified the need for faculty development projects aimed at both creating new courses and revising existing ones—in all undergraduate curricula, including women's studies and international studies—to reflect international feminist perspectives. SIROW followed up this conference with a three-year project to assist women's studies faculty in Arizona, Colorado, New Mexico, and Utah to develop international perspectives in their teaching (Betteridge & Monk, 1990; Dickstein, 1991; Monk, Newhall, & Betteridge, 1991). The Organization of American Historians (1988) sponsored a project that developed teaching packets for integrating women's history into courses on Africa, Asia, Latin America, the Caribbean, and the Middle East.

Assessment of the First Decade of Curriculum Transformation. The decade between 1975 and 1985 generated important research on the theory and practice of curriculum transformation and on faculty, curricular, and institutional change. By the mid-1980s, many books and special issues of journals had appeared that analyzed project successes and failures and reproduced bibliographies and revised syllabi (Aiken et al., 1988; Coulter, 1986; Fritsche, 1984; Lauter, 1983; Schuster & Van Dyne, 1985; Spanier et al., 1984). Project leaders identified factors that contributed to the success of projects (Aiken et al.,

1987; Finn, 1985; Butler, 1985; Butler and Schmitz, 1990; Schmitz, 1985). This research showed that curriculum transformation projects have relied almost entirely on faculty interest rather than institutional mandate. Normally, project leaders secure funds and solicit applications from which they choose a group of participants and provide incentives for them to do the work. Financial support is needed to fund speakers and to provide stipends or release time for faculty to study the new material and revise their courses. Where grants were not available, program administrators sought resources for an initial speaker or workshop to introduce faculty to key concepts and worked with specific departments or disciplines through a multiyear project with funding from local faculty development sources.

Other essential project components include: (a) administrative support; (b) a project director assigned to the effort and compensated for this work; (c) women's studies expertise and resources on campus; (d) a team of faculty leaders skilled at facilitating faculty learning and versed in interdisciplinary approaches, to work with the project director to achieve change; and (e) inclusive perspectives in the seminar readings (Schmitz, 1985). Project leaders have also recommended a balance of participants—by rank, discipline, gender, and race—to ensure that various perspectives are brought into play in curriculum and course design. Emphasis on pedagogy as well as content in the choice of readings and in course design is also essential. In the science and technical areas, in particular, much of the work has concentrated on pedagogical changes.

Feminist Phase Theory. During this period, feminist teachers and scholars working on curriculum change developed feminist phase theory to describe ways faculty members approached course design and the challenges of integrating women into the curriculum (McIntosh, 1983; Schuster & Van Dyne, 1985; Tetreault, 1980, 1985). The earliest formulation came from Mary Kay Tetreault (1980, 1985), who drew upon Gerda Lerner's (1975) formulation of questions about women's history. Tetreault described five stages that she found useful in measuring the development of feminist thinking about changing courses and disciplines: (a) male scholarship, in which there is no consciousness that knowledge is partial and exclusionary; (b) compensatory scholarship, in which the absence of women is noted, but additions are merely tokens—women are added but the traditional structures do not change; (c) bifocal scholarship, in which human experience is conceptualized in dualities (men and women as complementary), but in which women are still seen in relation to and less than men; (d) feminist scholarship, which puts women at the center and asks new questions that will elucidate their multiple and varied experiences; and (e) multifocal, relational scholarship, a holistic view of human experience that begins to define what binds together and what separates the various segments of humanity.

Project leaders used phase theory primarily to help faculty members recognize patterns and progress in curricular and disciplinary change. Andersen (1987) cautions practitioners that the phases have fluid boundaries and that their development does not necessarily follow a linear progression. Albrecht and Brewer (1990) challenge feminist phase theory for ignoring race and suggest that the theory emerging out of women's studies be linked with stages formulated by Banks (1988) for multicultural education. Collins (1991) critiques phase theory for both naive interpretations of the political aspects of change and for the exclusion of race, class, heterosexism, and other primary structures of domination. She suggests an alternative approach to curriculum transformation beginning with the description and interpretation of self-defined standpoints of women of color, racial/ethnic groups, and other subordinated groups within interlocking structures of domination.

Tetreault's analysis is useful because her conception of work that is "multifocal" and "relational" correlates with much of the contemporary work on theories of multiculturalism. Maher (1985) translated the insights of feminist phase theory into a schema for analyzing classroom pedagogy, recognizing that in order to make visible the diversity of human experience an interactive pedagogy is needed in which the active participation of all students provides multiple perspectives.

Current Shape and Priorities of Curriculum Transformation Projects

There have been nearly 200 curriculum transformation projects based primarily in women's studies between the years of 1975 and 1992, according to information collected by the National Institute for Curriculum Transformation Resources at Towson State University. In the late 1980s, in spite of conservative trends in federal funding and shifts in interests of many foundations, large-scale projects have continued to emerge. FIPSE awarded grants to Towson State University for a project for Baltimore-Washington area community colleges, and to the the American Anthropological Association to develop teaching resources for introductory courses in the discipline. In 1988, the Ford Foundation, a supporter of such projects since the 1980s, initiated a grant program for university-based women's research centers to incorporate American women of color into the curriculum (Hill, 1990) and, in 1992, a similar project for community colleges.

State monies and funds internal to campuses also became a major source of support. By 1990, the state of New Jersey, which initiated a statewide project to support curriculum transformation in 1986, had placed $1.5 million into gender integration projects. This project involves all two- and four-year public and private colleges and universities in the state, supports them in integrating gender, race, class, ethnicity, and sexual orientation into the curriculum, and publishes a journal, *Transformations*. In 1990, both the Tennessee Board of Regents and the Pennsylvania State System of Higher Education, among comparable institutions in other states, issued priorities for curriculum transformation and held workshops for teams from all institutions in these systems to plan projects. More and more institutions are beginning projects with internal funding, using existing faculty development programs or funds. These new programs have benefited from more than a decade of work and have developed intellectually and pedagogically sound curricula for faculty development that take into account the diversity of women's experiences.

Curriculum and Pedagogy of Projects. Curriculum transformation requires change in faculty members' knowledge, perspectives, and teaching behaviors. Recent projects have attempted to refine pedagogical approaches (Schmitz, 1991). They bring together multiple perspectives and elucidate interconnections among gender, race, class, culture, sexual orientation, and religion. More curriculum transformation projects based in both women's studies and ethnic studies have begun, as well as those focusing more broadly on cultural diversity in the United States. Rosenfelt and Williams (1992) describe how a curriculum transformation project funded at the University of Maryland at College Park to focus on women and gender has evolved to focus on race and gender. They describe how they explicitly use dynamics that occur in the seminar to discuss the gendered, interracial, and intercultural nature of communication patterns. The faculty development program at City University of New York created a program of readings that chose themes explicitly to elucidate the multiplicity of women's experiences (Buncombe and Helly, 1990). The Different Voices Institute at the University of Washington, funded by the Ford Foundation and begun in 1988, brought together in teaching teams scholars from both women's studies and ethnic studies to elaborate theory and pedagogy for exploring the lives of women of color through narrative, poetry, sociological, legal, and historical studies (Butler and Schmitz, 1990).

The Mainstreaming Minority Women's Studies Project (Hill, 1990) fostered collaborative work between women's studies and ethnic studies. This initiative supported 13 women's research centers to conduct faculty development activities aimed at transformation of the undergraduate curriculum. The projects emphasized different groups of women of color in the United States, depending on the expertise of the sponsoring institution and the demographic composition of its location. Most notably, the program funded at the State University of New York, Albany, focused on Puerto Rican women and established collaborative working relationships with both ProMujer at the Colegio Universitario de Cayey and the Centro de Recursos y Servicios a la Mujer at the University of Puerto Rico to develop "transnational approaches that link the study of cultural and socioeconomic systems on both ends of the continuum of the migratory process" (Acosta-Belén, 1993, p. 181). Through the collaborative work between White women and women of color working within women's studies and women and men working within both ethnic studies and multicultural initiatives, curriculum transformation projects focused primarily on race and ethnicity are developing inclusive perspectives as well.

The Effects of Curriculum Transformation

Very little research on the effects of curriculum transformation projects has been published. Most of the available literature is in the form of internal campus documents or reports to foundations or federal agencies that supported the projects.

Course and Curriculum Change. Studies of the effects of curriculum transformation projects on course change has relied on pre- and post-program analyses of the changes in courses, either through analysis of syllabi or interviews with faculty members. A syllabi analysis of the Montana State University project showed that prior to the project 45% of the courses had no content on women; 50% had less than 25%; and 5% had more than 25% (these courses were primarily in the humanities or taught by feminist teachers). After the project, 45% had 25% or more; no courses were devoid of content; yet 27% still had less than 10%, as reflected in the syllabus (Schmitz & Williams, 1983). This study did not describe the presentation of material. Tetreault (1985) used her feminist phase theory model to analyze syllabi and found that prior to the project at Lewis and Clark College, 60% of the faculty conceptualized teaching about women in ways that do not fundamentally challenge the disciplines (phase 2), and 40% in phase 3 (bifocal scholarship); after the project 15% fell into phase 2, while 54% were categorized as phase 3, 8% as phase 4 (feminist scholarship), and 23% phase 5 (multifocal, relational scholarship). Evaluation of syllabi change in the Mainstreaming Minority Women's Studies Project (Ginorio & Butler, 1992) showed that of the 102 syllabi analyzed, 52% had less than 10% of their content focusing on women of color compared to 87% before the project. Seven syllabi had 30% or more content before the project, compared to 23% after the project. African American women received the most attention (included in 48% of the post-project syllabi), compared to 32% for American Indian women, 31% for Asian American women, and 20% for Latinas. The research indicates that it is rare that a faculty member participates in one of these projects without making changes: Some add one or more new texts or concepts; some integrate material throughout the course; some completely change the structure and topics of the course to make the study of gender and cultural diversity central.

Another indicator of curriculum change is the degree to which general education requirements have changed. While women's studies degrees and course offerings have grown steadily, more progress is being made in passing requirements for cultural diversity, or for gender and cultural diversity, than for gender studies alone. The Carnegie Foundation for the Advancement of Teaching (1992) reports that between 1970 and 1985 the percentage of four-year colleges and universities with general education requirements for at least one course in international/global education increased from 4.5% to 14.6%; in Third World studies from 2.9% to 7.9%; and in women's studies from zero to 1.6%.

Finally, women's studies faculty have provided crucial sources of knowledge, enthusiasm, and pedagogical expertise for initiatives in writing across the curriculum, collaborative and cooperative learning, and interdisciplinary teaching (Schmitz, 1992).

Faculty Members. Research on the impact of the faculty development carried out in curriculum transformation projects has relied on interviews or questionnaires. In the Montana State University Project, almost all of the faculty who completed both years of the project reported important changes in classroom behavior, including avoidance of biased language, greater attention to difference in student learning styles, concerted efforts to involve all students in classroom discussion, and new teaching techniques aimed at eliciting students' experiences and opinions (Schmitz & Williams, 1983). Tetreault's (1985) interview data revealed that course changes were accompanied by a re-conceptualization of what is worth learning. She also noted an increase in the number of faculty who talked about women's studies scholarship in a multidisciplinary way. Rosenfelt (1990) reports that faculty participants in an eight-week summer institute at the University of Maryland felt that it had contributed to their greater sensitivity to issues of difference as they affect human interactions and that half of the participants indicated that they expected their work in the institute to have an impact on their future research.

Students. Since most of these projects have focused on large, introductory courses central to the liberal arts curriculum and have favored required courses over electives, large numbers of students on these campuses are engaged in the study of material on women and gender. Lewis and Clark College, which has both a Gender Studies Program and an institutional priority and commitment to "balanced exploration of the perspectives, traditions, and contributions of women and men," provides a source of comparison for the relative impact on students of these complementary educational strategies. Finke, Maveety, Shaw, and Ward (1992) report that there is a crucial difference between the integration of gender across the curriculum and the kind of systematic investigation of gender that the Gender Studies minor allows; and that even the most gender-balanced courses do not provide the intensity of study or the same level of skill development as the gender-focused courses (pp. 57–58, 63). They conclude also that the strength of gender integration is in reaching students who do not choose to take a course in the Gender Studies Program. As one sophomore commented, "My time commitments to my major and minor don't allow for elective gender classes, so I'm truly glad and appreciative of the focus that gender receives in my other classes" (p. 64).

Future Directions for Women's Studies and Curriculum Transformation

Given the activity within women's studies to transform itself to reflect the different realities and experiences of women due to race, class, ethnicity, and sexuality, women's studies in the 1990s and beyond will undoubtedly continue to seek support for curricular and institutional changes toward cultural pluralism. In so doing, it faces the challenge of continued transformation through research about differences among women; exploration of the plurality of feminist approaches and paradigms

worldwide; and diversifying the teaching faculty. While women's studies has sometimes had links to programs in American ethnic studies, African American studies, Asian American and Pacific Islander studies, Chicano/Latino studies, and American Indian studies, the relationship of women's studies to multiculturalism has yet to be thoroughly addressed.

Women's studies needs expanded institutional support. The report of the National Women's Association Task Force on the women's studies major (Butler et al., 1991) makes several recommendations addressing this issue, including freeing women's studies from institutional constraints that weaken curricular offerings and providing adequate resources; increasing the overall budget in women's studies programs; removing administrative obstacles that lock both students and faculty too narrowly within one academic unit; and strengthening the women's studies major, graduate programs, internships, and feminist teaching.

In addition to strengthening programs where they already exist, women's studies must be extended to other kinds and levels of education, where it is rare—to community colleges, historically Black institutions, tribally controlled colleges; to high schools and secondary education; and to graduate and professional education. Women's studies also faces the challenge of broadening its impact to disciplines that have changed very little, such as the sciences and technical fields.

Curriculum transformation, which has reached about 10% of the institutions of higher education in the country, faces similar challenges. The overwhelming majority of faculty in these projects have come from the social sciences and humanities. Few projects have been conducted in community colleges, which enroll large percentages of women and minority students. Graduate and professional education has been virtually untouched by women's studies in any of its forms.

Expanded efforts will take place in a climate of decreased resources. Imaginative and far-reaching collaborations at many levels, across various institutional structures and touching a variety of fields, are now both possible and essential. Collaboration between women's studies and ethnic studies programs, schools of education, state boards of education, and K–12 teachers and administrators could substantially expand the impact of curriculum change efforts. More projects to explore and integrate global perspectives on women's studies, as well as the study of women in countries around the globe, relational and comparative in substance and method, are equally essential and will provide a productive base from which to engage cultural pluralism in U.S. higher education.

References

Acosta-Belén, E. (Ed.). (1986). *The Puerto Rican woman: Perspectives on culture, history, and society* (2nd ed.). New York: Praeger.

Acosta-Belén, E. (1993). Defining common ground: The theoretical meeting of women's, ethnic, and area studies. In E. Acosta-Belén & C. E. Bose (Eds.), *Researching women in Latin America and the Caribbean* (pp. 175–186). Boulder, CO: Westview Press.

Acosta-Belén, E., & Bose, C. E. (1990). From structural subordination to

empowerment: Women in development in Third World contexts. *Gender and Society, 4*(3), 299–320.

Aguilar-San Juan, K. (1993). Landmarks in literature by Asian American lesbians. *Signs, 18*(4), 936–943.

Ahmed, L. (1980). Encounter with American feminism: A Muslim woman's view of two conferences. *Women's Studies Quarterly, 8*(3), 7–9.

Ahmed, L. (1992). *Women and gender in Islam: Historical roots of a modern debate.* New Haven: Yale University Press.

Aiken, S. H., Anderson, K., Dinnerstein, M., Lensink, J. N., & MacCorquodale, P. (1987). Trying transformations: Curriculum integration and the problem of resistance. *Signs, 12*(2), 255–275.

Aiken, S. H., Anderson, K., Dinnerstein, M., Lensink, J. N., & MacCorquodale, P. (1988). *Changing our minds: Feminist transformations of knowledge.* Albany: State University of New York Press.

Alarcón, N. (1985). What kind of lover have you made me, mother? Toward a theory of Chicanas' feminism and cultural identity through poetry. In A. T. McClusky (Ed.), *Women of color: Perspectives on feminism and identity* (Occasional Papers Series 1). Bloomington: University of Indiana Women's Studies Program.

Alarcón, N. (1989). Chicana writers and critics in a social context: Toward a contemporary bibliography. *Third Woman, 4,* 169–178.

Albers, P., & Medicine, B. (Eds.). (1983). *The hidden half: Studies of Plains Indian women.* Washington, DC: University Press of America.

Albrecht, L., & Brewer, R. M. (Eds.). (1990). *Bridges of power: Women's multicultural alliances.* Philadelphia: New Society Publishers and the National Women's Studies Association.

al-Hibri, A. (Ed.). (1982). *Women and Islam.* Oxford: Pergamon Press.

al-Hibri, A. (1983). Unveiling the hidden face of racism: The plight of Arab American women. *Women's Studies Quarterly, 9*(3), 10–11.

Allen, P. G. (1986). *The sacred hoop: Recovering the feminine in American Indian traditions.* Boston: Beacon Press.

Allen, P. G. (1989). *Spider woman's granddaughters.* New York: Fawcett Columbine.

American Political Science Association. (1983–84). *Citizenship and change: Women and American politics* (Vols. 1–9). Washington, DC: Author.

Andersen, M. L. (1987). Changing the curriculum in higher education. *Signs, 12*(2), 222–254.

Andersen, M. L., & Collins, P. H. (Eds.). (1992). *Race, class, and gender: An anthology.* Belmont, CA: Wadsworth Publishing Company.

Anderson, O., & Verble, S. D. (Eds.). (1980). *Resource guide of American Indian and Native Alaskan women.* Newton, MA: Women's Educational Equity Act Publishing Center/EDC.

Anzaldúa, G. (1987). *Borderlands/La frontera: The new mestiza.* San Francisco: Spinsters/Aunt Lute.

Anzaldúa, G. (1990). *Making face, making soul, haciendo caras: Creative and critical perspectives by feminists of color.* San Francisco: Aunt Lute Books.

Aptheker, B. (1981). "Strong is what we make each other": Unlearning racism in women's studies. *Women's Studies Quarterly, 9*(4), 13–16.

Arch, E. C., & Kirschner, S. (1984). Gender balancing as a catalyst for institutional change. *Educational Record, 66*(2), 48–52.

Argandona, R. C., Gómez-Quiñones, J., & Duran, P. H. (1976). *The Chicana: A preliminary bibliographic study.* Los Angeles: Chicano Research Center.

Asian Women United of California. (1989). *Making waves: An anthology of writings by and about Asian American Women.* Boston: Beacon Press.

Association of American Colleges. (1982). Recommendations from "Liberal education and the new scholarship on women." Washington, DC: Author.

Association of American Colleges. (1991). *Liberal learning and the arts and sciences major: Vol. 2. Reports from the fields.* Washington, DC: Author.

Astin, A. W. (1993). *What matters in college? Four critical years revisited.* San Francisco: Jossey-Bass.

Aufderheide, P. (Ed.). (1992). *Beyond PC: Toward a politics of understanding.* St. Paul, MN: Graywolf Press.

Azari, F. (Ed.). (1983). *Women of Iran: The conflict with fundamentalist Islam.* London: Ithaca Press.

Azize, Y. (1979). *Luchas de la mujer en Puerto Rico: 1898–1919.* San Juan, PR: Graficor.

Banks, J. A. (1988). *Multiethnic education: Theory and practice* (2nd ed.). Boston: Allyn and Bacon.

Bargad, A., & Hyde, J. S. (1991). Women's studies: A study of feminist identity development in women. *Psychology of Women, 15*(2), 181–201.

Bataille, G. M., & Sands, K. M. (1984). *American Indian women: Telling their lives.* Lincoln: University of Nebraska Press.

Baum, C., Hyman, P., & Michel, S. (1977). *The Jewish woman in America.* New York: New American Library.

Beck, E. T. (1988). The politics of Jewish invisibility. *NWSA Journal, 1*(1), 93–102.

Beck, E. T. (1989). *Nice Jewish girls: A lesbian anthology* (rev. ed.). Boston: Beacon Press. (First published 1982)

Behar, R. (1990). Rage and redemption: Reading the life story of a Mexican marketing woman. *Feminist Studies, 16*(2), 223–258.

Belenky, M. F., Clinchy, B. M., Goldberger, N. R., & Tarule, J. M. (1986). *Women's ways of knowing: The development of self, voice and mind.* New York: Basic Books.

Bell, M. J. (Ed.). (1986). *Women as elders: Images, visions, and issues.* New York: Haworth Press.

Bell, R. P., Parker, B. J., & Guy-Sheftall, B. G. (1979). *Sturdy Black bridges: Visions of Black women in literature.* Garden City, NY: Anchor Press/Doubleday.

Bell-Scott, P. B., Guy-Sheftall, B. G., Royster, J. J., Sims-Wood, J., DeCosta-Willis, M., & Fultz, L. (Eds.). (1991). *Double stitch: Black women write about mothers and daughters.* Boston: Beacon Press.

Benería, L., & Sen, G. (1981). Accumulation, reproduction, and women's role in economic development: Boserup revisited. *Signs, 7*(2), 279–298.

Berry, L., & McDaniels, I. (1980, November). Teaching contemporary Black women writers. *Radical Teacher*, no. 17, 7–10.

Bethel, L., & Smith, B. (Eds.). (1979). The Black women's issue [Special issue]. *Conditions, 5.*

Betteridge, A., & Monk, J. (1990). Teaching women's studies from an international perspective. *Women's Studies Quarterly, 18*(1 & 2), 78–85.

Bleier, R. (1986). *Feminist approaches to science.* New York: Pergamon Press.

Bose, C. E. (1986). Puerto Rican women in the United States: An overview. In E. Acosta-Belén (Ed.), *The Puerto Rican woman: Perspectives on culture, history and society* (2nd ed.) (pp. 147–169). New York: Praeger.

Boserup, E. (1977). Preface. *Signs, 3*(1), xi–xiv.

Bowles, G., & Klein, R. D. (Eds.). (1983). *Theories of women's studies.* Boston: Routledge and Kegan Paul.

Boxer, M. J. (1982). For and about women: The theory and practice of women's studies in the United States. *Signs, 7*(3), 661–695.

Brant, B. (Ed.). (1983). A gathering of spirit: A collection by North American Indian women [Special issue]. *Sinister Wisdom, 22–23.*

Brant, B. (1993). Giveaway: Native lesbian writers. *Signs, 18*(4), 944–947.

Brod, H. (Ed.). (1987). *The making of masculinities: The new men's studies.* Boston: Allen and Unwin.

Brown, L. (1980, Spring). Dark horse: A view of writing and publishing by dark lesbians. *Sinister Wisdom*, no. 13, 45–50.

Bulkin, E. (1980, November). Heterosexism and women's studies. *Radical Teacher*, no. 17, 25–31.

Bulkin, E., Pratt, M. B., & Smith, B. (1984). *Yours in struggle: Three feminist perspectives on anti-Semitism and racism.* Ithaca, NY: Firebrand Books.

Bunch, C. (1983). Not by degrees: Feminist theory and education. In C. Bunch & S. Pollack (Eds.), *Learning our way: Essays in feminist education* (pp. 248–260). Trumansburg, NY: Crossing Press.

Buncombe, M., & Helly, D. O. (1990). The City University of New York: 1988–89 faculty development seminar on balancing the curriculum for gender, race, ethnicity, and class. *Radical Teacher,* no. 37, 14–26.

Butler, J. E. (1984). Minority studies and women's studies: Do we want to kill a dream? *Women's Studies International Quarterly, 7*(3), 135–138.

Butler, J. E. (1985). Complicating the question: Black studies and women's studies. In M. R. Schuster & S. R. Van Dyne (Eds.), *Women's place in the academy: Transforming the liberal arts curriculum.* Totowa, NJ: Rowman and Allanheld.

Butler, J. E. (1991a). Difficult dialogues. In J. E. Butler & J. C. Walter (Eds.), *Transforming the curriculum: Ethnic studies and women's studies* (pp. 1–19). Albany: State University of New York Press.

Butler, J. E. (1991b). Transforming the curriculum: Teaching about women of color. In J. E. Butler & J. C. Walter (Eds.), *Transforming the curriculum: Ethnic studies and women's studies* (pp. 69–88). Albany: State University of New York Press.

Butler, J. E., Coyner, S., Homans, M., Longenecker, M., & Musil, C. M. (1991). *Liberal learning and the women's studies major.* College Park, MD: National Women's Studies Association.

Butler, J. E., & Schmitz, B. (1992). Ethnic studies, women's studies, and multiculturalism. *Change, 24*(1), 36–41.

Butler, J. E., & Schmitz, B. (1990). Different voices: A model institute for integrating women of color into undergraduate American literature and history courses. *Radical Teacher,* no. 37, 4–9.

Butler, J. E., & Walter, J. C. (Eds.). (1991). *Transforming the curriculum: Ethnic studies and women's studies.* Albany: State University of New York Press.

Cade, T. (Ed.). (1970). *The Black woman.* New York: Signet Books.

Cannon, L. W. (1990). Fostering positive race, class and gender dynamics in the classroom. *Women's Studies Quarterly, 18*(1 & 2), 126–134.

Cantor, A. (1987). *The Jewish woman, 1900–1985: A bibliography* (2nd ed.). Fresh Meadows, NY: Biblio Press.

Carby, H. V. (1987). *Reconstructing womanhood: The emergence of the Afro-American woman novelist.* New York: Oxford University Press.

Carby, H. V. (1992). The multicultural wars. *Radical History Review, 54*(2), 7–20.

Carnegie Foundation for the Advancement of Teaching. (1992). Signs of a changing curriculum. *Change, 24*(1), 49–54.

Carr, I. C. (1988–89). A survey of selected literature on La Chicana. *NWSA Journal, 1*(2), 253–273.

Chai, A. Y. (1988). Women's history in public: "Picture brides" of Hawaii. *Women's Studies Quarterly, 16*(1 & 2), 51– 62.

Chamberlain, M. K. (Ed.). (1988). *Women in academe: Progress and prospects.* New York: Russell Sage Foundation.

Chamberlain, M. K. (1989). *International centers for research on women.* New York: National Council for Research on Women.

Chan, S. (1991). *Asian Americans: An interpretive history.* Boston: Twayne Publishers.

Chapa, O. E., & Andrade, S. (1976). *La mujer Chicana: An annotated bibliography.* Austin, TX: Chicana Research and Learning Center.

Chodorow, N. (1978). *The reproduction of mothering: Psychoanalysis and the sociology of gender.* Berkeley: University of California Press.

Chow, E. N. (1987). The development of feminist consciousness among Asian American women. *Gender and Society, 1*(3), 284–299.

Christian, B. (1980). *Black women novelists: The development of a tradition, 1892–1976.* Westport, CT: Greenwood Press.

Christian, B. (1988). The race for theory. *Feminist Studies, 14*(1), 67–79.

Chu, J. (1986). Asian American women's studies courses: A look back at our beginnings. *Frontiers, 8*(3), 96–101.

Cixous, H. (1976). The laugh of the Medusa. (K. Cohen & P. Cohen, Trans.) *Signs, 1*(4), 875–894.

Clatterbaugh, K. (1990). *Contemporary perspectives on masculinity: Men, women and politics in modern society.* Boulder, CO: Westview Press.

Collins, P. H. (1990). *Black feminist thought: Knowledge, consciousness, and the politics of empowerment.* Boston: Unwin and Hyman.

Collins, P. H. (1991). On our own terms: Self-defined standpoints and curriculum transformation. *NWSA Journal, 3*(3), 367–381.

Copper, B. (1988). *Over the hill: Reflections on ageism between women.* Freedom, CA: Crossing Press.

Cordova, T., Cantu, N., Cardenas, G., García, D., & Sierra, C. M. (Eds.). (1986). *Chicana voices: Intersections of race, class and gender.* Austin: University of Texas, Center for Mexican American Studies.

Cott, N. F. (1987). *The grounding of modern feminism.* New Haven: Yale University Press.

Coulter, S. (1986). *Resources for curriculum change.* Towson, MD: Towson State University.

Coyner, S. (1983). Women's studies as an academic discipline. In G. Bowles & R. D. Klein (Eds.), *Theories of women's studies* (pp. 46–71). London: Routledge and Kegan Paul.

Cruikshank, M. (1980, November). Lesbian studies: Some preliminary notes. *Radical Teacher,* no. 17, 18–19.

Cruikshank, M. (Ed.). (1982). *Lesbian studies: Present and future.* Old Westbury, NY: Feminist Press.

Culley, M. (1985). Anger and authority in the introductory women's studies classroom. In M. Culley & C. Portuges (Eds.), *Gendered subjects: The dynamics of feminist teaching* (pp. 209–218). Boston: Routledge and Kegan Paul.

Culley, M., Diamond, A., Edwards, L., Lennox, S., & Portuges, C. (1985). The politics of nurturance. In M. Culley & C. Portuges (Eds.), *Gendered subjects: The dynamics of feminist teaching* (pp. 11–20). Boston: Routledge and Kegan Paul.

Culley, M., Portuges, C. (Eds.). (1985). *Gendered subjects: The dynamics of feminist teaching.* Boston: Routledge and Kegan Paul.

Curb, R., & Manahan, N. (Eds.). (1985). *Lesbian nuns: Breaking silence.* Tallahassee, FL: Naiad Press.

Daly, M. (1973). *Beyond God the father.* Boston: Beacon Press.

Davies, C. B. (1990). Writing home: Gender and heritage in the works of Afro-Caribbean/American women writers. In C. B. Davies & E. S. Fido (Eds.), *Out of the Kumbla: Caribbean women and literature* (pp. 59–74). Trenton, NJ: Africa World Press.

Davies, C. B., & Fido, E. S. (Eds.). (1990). *Out of the Kumbla: Caribbean women and literature.* Trenton, NJ: Africa World Press.

Davis, A. Y. (1981). *Women, race, and class.* New York: Vintage.

Dickstein, R. (1991). Women in international studies: A bibliographic guide. *Women's Studies International Quarterly, 14*(4), 357–373.

Dill, B. T. (1979). The dialectics of Black womanhood. *Signs, 4*(3), 543–555.

Dill, B. T. (1983). Race, class, and gender: Prospects for an all-inclusive sisterhood. *Feminist Studies, 9*(1), 131–150.

DuBois, E. C., Kelly, G. P., Kennedy, E. L., Korsmeyer, C. W., & Robinson, L. S. (1985). *Feminist scholarship: Kindling in the groves of academe.* Urbana: University of Illinois Press.

DuBois, E. C., & Ruiz, V. L. (Eds.). (1990). *Unequal sisters: A multicultural reader in U.S. women's history*. New York: Routledge.

Elwell, S. L. (1992). Jewish women's studies. In B. Holtz (Ed.), *The Schocken guide to Jewish books*. New York: Schocken.

Enloe, C. H. (1990). *Bananas, beaches, and bases: Making feminist sense of international politics*. Berkeley: University of California Press.

Fenton, T. P., & Heffron, M. J. (Eds.). (1987). *Women in the Third World: A directory of resources*. Maryknoll, NY: Orbis Books.

Finke, L. (1993). Knowledge as bait: Feminism, voice, and the pedagogical unconscious. *College English, 55*(1), 7–27.

Finke, L., Maveety, E., Shaw, C., & Ward, J. (1992). Lewis and Clark College: A single curriculum. In C. M. Musil (Ed.), *The courage to question: Women's studies and student learning* (pp. 43–81). Washington, DC: Association of American Colleges and National Women's Studies Association.

Finn, M. C. (1985). The curriculum integration movement: Taking a closer look. *Women's Studies Quarterly, 13*(2), 15–22.

Fisher, D. (1980). *The third woman: Minority women writers in the United States*. Boston: Houghton Mifflin.

Fisher-Mannick, B. (1981). Race and class: Beyond personal politics. In *Building feminist theory: Essays from Quest* (pp. 149–160). New York: Longman.

Flax, J. (1987). Postmodernism and gender relations in feminist theory. *Signs, 12*(4), 621–643.

Foucault, M. (1980). Truth and power. In C. Gordon (Ed.), *Power and knowledge: Selected interviews and other writings 1972–1977* (pp. 109–133). New York: Pantheon Books.

Fox-Genovese, E., & Stuard, S. M. (Eds.). (1983). *Restoring women to history: Materials for Western civilization* (Vols. 1–2). Bloomington, IN: Organization of American Historians.

Frankenberg, R. (1991). Teaching White women, racism, and antiracism in a women's studies program. In J. E. Butler & J. C. Walter (Eds.), *Transforming the curriculum: Ethnic studies and women's studies* (pp. 89–110). Albany: State University of New York Press.

Frankenberg, R. (1993). *White women, race matters: The social construction of whiteness*. Minneapolis: University of Minnesota Press.

Freire, P. (1970). *Pedagogy of the oppressed*. (M. B. Ramos, Trans.). New York: Seabury Press.

Friedman, S. S. (1985). Authority in the feminist classroom: A contradiction in terms? In M. Culley & C. Portuges (Eds.), *Gendered subjects: The dynamics of feminist teaching* (pp. 203–208). Boston: Routledge and Kegan Paul.

Fritsche, J. M. (1984). *Toward excellence and equity: The scholarship on women as a catalyst for change in the university*. Orono: University of Maine.

Frye, M. (1983). On being White. In *The politics of reality*. Trumensburg, NY: Crossing Press.

Gappa, J. M., & Pearce, J. (1982). *Sex and gender in the social sciences: Reassessing the introductory course*. Washington, DC: American Psychological Association.

Gappa, J. M., & Pearce, J. (1983). *Sex and gender in the social sciences: Reassessing the introductory course, introductory sociology*. Washington, DC: American Sociological Association.

García, A. M. (1989). The development of Chicana feminist discourse, 1970–1980. *Gender and Society, 3*(2), 217–238.

García-Coll, C. T., & Mattei, M. D. (Eds.). (1989). *The psychosocial development of Puerto Rican women*. New York: Praeger.

Giddings, P. (1984). *When and where I enter: The impact of Black women on race and sex in America*. New York: William Morrow.

Gilligan, C. (1982). *In a different voice: Psychological theory and women's development*. Cambridge: Harvard University Press.

Gilmore, D. (1990). *Manhood in the making: Cultural concepts of masculinity*. New Haven: Yale University Press.

Ginorio, A. B., & Butler, J. E. (1992). *Incorporating American ethnic minority women into the curriculum: An evaluation of curriculum change projects* (Final report to the Ford Foundation). Seattle: University of Washington, Northwest Center for Research on Women.

Glenn, E. K. (1986). *Issei, nisei, war bride: Three generations of Japanese American women in domestic service*. Philadelphia: Temple University Press.

Goetsch, L. A. (1991). Feminist pedagogy: A selected annotated bibliography. *NWSA Journal, 3*(3), 422–429.

Gómez, A., Moraga, C., & Romo-Carmona, M. (Eds.). (1983). *Cuentos: Stories by Latinas*. Brooklyn: Kitchen Table/Women of Color Press.

Gómez, J. (1993). Speculative fiction and Black lesbians. *Signs, 18*(4), 948–955.

González, S. (1977). The White feminist movement: The Chicana perspective. *Social Science Journal, 14*(2), 67–76.

González, S. (1980). Toward a feminist pedagogy for Chicana self-actualization. *Frontiers, 5*(2), 48–51.

Gore, J. (1993). *Struggles for pedagogies: Critical and feminist discourses as regimes of truth*. New York: Routledge.

Graff, G. (1992). *Beyond the culture wars: How teaching the conflicts can revitalize American education*. New York: W. W. Norton.

Grant, J. (1989). *White women's Christ and Black women's Jesus: Feminist christology and womanist response*. Atlanta: Scholars Press.

Green, R. (1979). American Indian women meet in Lawrence. *Women's Studies Newsletter, 7*(3), 6–7.

Green, R. (1983a). *Native American women: A contextual bibliography*. Bloomington: Indiana University Press.

Green, R. (Ed.). (1983b). *That's what she said: Contemporary fiction and poetry by Native American women*. Bloomington: Indiana University Press.

Greenberg, B. (1983). *On women and Judaism: A view from tradition*. Philadelphia: Jewish Publication Society of America.

Guy-Sheftall, B. G. (1986). Women's studies at Spelman College: Reminiscences from the director. *Women's Studies International Quarterly, 9*(2), 151–156.

H., Pamela. (1989). Asian American lesbians: An emerging voice in the Asian American community. In Asian Women United of California (Ed.), *Making waves: An anthology of writings by and about Asian American Women* (pp. 282–290). Boston: Beacon Press.

Hall, R. M., & Sandler, B. R. (1982). *The classroom climate: A chilly one for women?* Washington, DC: Association of American Colleges.

Haraway, D. J. (1991). *Simians, cyborgs, and women: The reinvention of nature*. New York: Routledge.

Harding, S. (1986). *The science question in feminism*. Ithaca: Cornell University Press.

Hartman, J. E., & Messer-Davidow, E. (1991). *(En)gendering knowledge: Feminists in academe*. Knoxville: University of Tennessee Press.

Hazleton, L. (1977). *Israeli women: The reality behind the myths*. New York: Simon & Schuster.

Helmbold, L. R. (1987). Feminists pretend to deal with class. *Sojourner, 13*(1), 33–34.

Herrera-Sobek, M. (Ed.). (1985). *Beyond stereotypes: A critical analysis of Chicana literature*. Binghamton, NY: Bilingual Press.

Heschel, S. (Ed.). (1983). *On being a Jewish feminist: A reader*. New York: Schocken Books.

Hill, L. I. (1990). The Ford Foundation program on mainstreaming minority women's studies. *Women's Studies Quarterly, 18*(1 & 2), 24–38.

Hillyer, B. (1992). Women and disabilities. *NWSA Journal, 4*(1), 106–114.

Hine, D. C. (Ed.). (1990). *Black Women in United States history* (Vols. 1–16). Brooklyn: Carlson Publishing.

Hoffman, N. (1986). Black studies, ethnic studies, and women's studies:

Some reflections on collaborative projects. *Women's Studies Quarterly*, 14(1 & 2), 49–53.

Hoffman, N., Secor, C., & Tinsley, A. (Eds.). (1973). *Female studies VI: Closer to the ground, women's classes, criticism, programs—1972* (2nd ed.). Old Westbury, NY: Feminist Press.

Hogan, L. (1982). (Ed.). *Frontiers* [Special issue]. 6(3).

hooks, b. (1981). *Ain't I a woman: Black women and feminism*. Boston: South End Press.

hooks, b. (1984). *Feminist theory: From margin to center*. Boston: South End Press.

hooks, b. (1989). *Talking back: Thinking feminist, thinking Black*. Boston: South End Press.

Horno-Delgado, A., Ortega, E., Scott, N. M., & Sternbach, N. S. (Eds.). (1989). *Breaking boundaries: Latina writing and critical readings*. Amherst: University of Massachusetts Press.

Howe, F. (1980). Editorial. *Women's Studies Quarterly*, 8(4), 2.

Howe, F. (1984). *Myths of coeducation: Selected essays, 1964–83*. Bloomington: Indiana University Press.

Howe, F., & Lauter, P. (1980). *The impact of women's studies on the campus and the disciplines*. Washington, DC: National Institute on Education.

Hubbard, R. (1982). *Women look at biology looking at women*. Boston: G. K. Hall.

Hull, G. T., Scott, P. B., & Smith, B. (Eds.). (1982). *All the women are White, all the Blacks are men, but some of us are brave*. New York: Feminist Press.

Hune, S., Kim, H., Fugita, S. S., & Ling, A. (Eds.). (1991). *Asian Americans: Comparative and global perspectives*. Pullman: Washington State University Press.

Jacobs, S. E. (1976). *Women in perspective: A guide for cross-cultural studies*. Urbana: University of Illinois Press.

James, J., & Farmer, R. (Eds.). (1993). *Spirit, space & survival: African American women in (White) academe*. New York: Routledge.

James, S., & Busia, A. (Eds.). (1993). *Theorizing Black feminisms*. New York: Routledge.

Jardine, A. (1988). Prelude: The future of difference. In H. Eisenstein & A. Jardine (Eds.), *The future of difference* (pp. xxv–xxvii). New Brunswick, NJ: Rutgers University Press.

Jayawardena, K. (1986). *Feminism and nationalism in the Third World*. London: Zed Books.

Johnson, S. (1989). *From housewife to heretic*. Albuquerque: Wildfire Books.

Johnston, J. (1973). *Lesbian nation: The feminist solution*. New York: Simon & Schuster.

Jones, J. (1985). *Labor of love, labor of sorrow: Black women, work, and the family from slavery to the present*. New York: Basic Books.

Jorge, A. (1986). The Black Puerto Rican woman in contemporary American society. In E. Acosta-Belén (Ed.), *The Puerto Rican woman: Perspectives on culture, history and society* (2nd ed.) (pp. 180–188). New York: Praeger.

Joseph, G. I., & Lewis, J. (1986). *Common differences: Conflicts in Black and White feminist perspectives*. Boston: South End Press.

Kaye/Kantrowitz, M. & Klepfisz, I. (1989). *The tribe of Dina: A Jewish women's anthology*. Boston: Beacon Press.

Kelly, M. P. F. (1981). Development and the sexual division of labor: An introduction. *Signs*, 7(2), 268–278.

Kelly, M. P. F. (1986). International development and women's employment: Issues for a feminist agenda. *Women's Studies Quarterly*, 14(3 & 4), 2–6.

Kennedy, E. L., & Davis, M. D. (1993). *Boots of leather, slippers of gold: A history of a lesbian community*. New York: Routledge.

Kenway, J., & Modra, H. (1992). Women in the academy: Strategy, struggle and survival. In C. Luke & J. Gore, *Feminisms and Critical Pedagogy* (pp. 192–210). New York: Routledge.

Kidwell, C. S. (1979a). American Indian women: Problems of communicating a cultural/sexual identity. *The Creative Woman*, 2(3), 33–38.

Kidwell, C. S. (1979b). The power of women in three American Indian societies. *Journal of Ethnic Studies*, 6(3), 113–121.

Kim, E. H. (1982). *Asian American literature: An introduction to the writings and their social context*. Philadelphia: Temple University Press.

Kim, E. H., & Otani, J. (1983). *With silk wings: Asian American women at work*. [Videotapes]. Berkeley: Asian Women United.

King, L. M. (1974). Puertorriquenas in the U.S.: The impact of double discrimination. *Civil Rights Digest*, 6(3), 20–27.

Klein, R. D. (1987). The dynamics of the women's studies classroom: A review essay of the teaching practice of women's studies in higher education. *Women's Studies International Quarterly*, 10(2), 187–206.

Kuzmack, L. G. (1990). *Women's cause: The Jewish women's movement in England and the United States, 1881–1933*. Columbus: Ohio State University Press.

Lai, T. (1992). Asian American women: Not for sale. In M. L. Andersen & P. H. Collins (Eds.), *Race, class, and gender: An anthology* (pp. 163–171). Belmont, CA: Wadsworth Publishing Company.

Lather, P. (1991). *Getting smart: Feminist research and pedagogy with/in the postmodern*. New York: Routledge.

Lauter, P. (Ed.). (1983). *Reconstructing American literature: Courses, syllabi, issues*. Old Westbury, NY: Feminist Press.

Lauter, P. (1991). *Canons and contexts*. New York: Oxford University Press.

Lazreg, M. (1990). Feminism and difference: The perils of writing as a woman on women in Algeria. In M. Hirsch & E. F. Keller (Eds.), *Conflicts in Feminism* (pp. 326–348). New York: Routledge.

Lerner, G. (Ed.). (1973). *Black women in White America: A documentary history*. New York: Pantheon.

Lerner, G. (1975). Placing women in history: A 1975 perspective. *Feminist Studies*, 3(1 & 2), 5–15.

Lewis, M. (1992). Interrupting patriarchy: Politics, resistance and transformation in the feminist classroom. In C. Luke & J. Gore (Eds.), *Feminisms and critical pedagogy* (pp. 167–191). New York: Routledge.

Lim, S. G. (1991). Asian American daughters rewriting Asian maternal texts. In S. Hune, H. Kim, S. S. Fugita, & A. Ling (Eds.), *Asian Americans: Comparative and global perspectives* (pp. 239–248). Pullman: Washington State University Press.

Lim, S. G., & Tsutakawa, M. (Eds.). (1989). *The forbidden stitch: An Asian American women's anthology*. Corvallis, OR: Calyx Books.

Liu, T. (1991). Teaching the difference among women from a historical perspective: Rethinking race and gender as social categories. *Women's Studies International Forum*, 14(4), 265–276.

Loeb, C. R. (1980). La Chicana: A bibliographic survey. *Frontiers*, 5(2), 59–74.

Loeb, C. R., Searing, S. E., & Stineman, G. F. (1987). *Women's studies: A recommended core bibliography, 1980–1985*. Littleton, CO: Libraries Unlimited.

Lorde, A. (1981). An open letter to Mary Daly. In C. Moraga & G. Anzaldua (Eds.), *This bridge called my back: A collection of writings by radical women of color* (pp. 94–97). Watertown, MA: Persephone Press.

Lorde, A. (1984). *Sister outsider: Essays and speeches*. Trumansburg, NY: Crossing Press.

Loyd, B., & Rengert, A. (1978). Women in geographic curricula [Special issue]. *Journal of Geography*, 77(5).

Lugones, M. C. (1992). Sisterhood and friendship as feminist models. In

C. Kramarae, & D. Spender (Eds.), *The knowledge explosion* (pp. 406–412). New York: Teachers College Press.

Luke, C., & Gore, J. (Eds.). (1992). *Feminisms and critical pedagogy*. New York: Routledge.

Lurie, N. O. (1961). *Mountain Wolf Woman, sister of Crashing Thunder, a Winnebago Indian*. Ann Arbor: University of Michigan Press.

Macdonald, B., & Rich, C. (1983). *Look me in the eye: Old women, aging and ageism*. San Francisco: Spinsters, Ink.

MacKinnon, C. A. (1987). *Feminism unmodified: Discourses on life and law*. Cambridge: Harvard University Press.

Maher, F. (1985). Classroom pedagogy and the new scholarship on women. In M. Culley & C. Portuges (Eds.), *Gendered subjects: The dynamics of feminist teaching* (pp. 29–48). Boston: Routledge and Kegan Paul.

Maher, F., & Tetreault, M. K. T. (1994). *The feminist classroom*. New York: Basic Books.

Mani, L. (1990, Summer). Multiple mediations: Feminist scholarship in the age of multinational reception. *Feminist Review*, no. 35, 24–41.

Marks, E., & de Courtivron, I. (Eds.). (1980). *New French feminisms*. Amherst: University of Massachusetts Press.

Matsumoto, V. (1984). Japanese American women during World War II. *Frontiers, 8*(1), 6–14.

Matthei, J., & Amott, T. (1990). *Race, gender and work: A multicultural economic history of women in the United States*. Boston: South End Press.

McDowell, D. (1980). New directions for Black feminist criticism. *Black American literature forum, 14*(3), 153.

McIntosh, P. (1983). *Interactive phases of curricular revision: A feminist perspective* (Working paper No. 124). Wellesley, MA: Wellesley College Center for Research on Women.

McKenney, M. (1981). Class attitudes and professionalism. In *Building feminist theory: Essays from Quest* (pp. 139–148). New York: Longman.

McNaron, T. A. H., Anzaldúa, G., Argüelles, L., & Kennedy, E. L. (Eds.). (1993). Theorizing lesbian experience [Special issue]. *Signs, 18*(4).

Medicine, B. (1981). Contemporary literature on Indian women: A review essay. *Frontiers, 6*(3), 122–125.

Medicine, B. (1987). Indian women and the renaissance of traditional religion. In R. J. DeMallie & D. R. Parks (Eds.), *Sioux Indian religion: Tradition and innovation*. Norman: University of Oklahoma Press.

Meese, E. A. (1990). *(Ex)tensions: Re-figuring feminist criticism*. Urbana: University of Illinois Press.

Messer-Davidow, E. (1992). Doing the right thing. *Women's Review of Books, 9*(5), 19–20.

Millett, K. (1970). *Sexual politics*. Garden City, NY: Doubleday.

Minh-ha, T. T. (1989). *Women, native, other: Writing postcoloniality and feminism*. Bloomington: Indiana University Press.

Minnich, E. K. (1990). *Transforming knowledge*. Philadelphia: Temple University Press.

Mohanty, C. T. (1991). Under Western eyes: Feminist scholarship and colonial discourses. In C. T. Mohanty, A. Russo, & L. Torres (Eds.), *Third World women and the politics of feminism* (pp. 50–80). Bloomington: Indiana University Press.

Mohanty, C. T. (1994). On race and voice: Challenges for liberal education in the 1990s. In H. A. Giroux & P. McLaren, *Between borders: Pedagogy and the politics of cultural studies* (pp. 145–166). New York: Routledge.

Monk, J., Newhall, A., & Betteridge, A. (Eds.). (1991). Reaching for global feminism: Approaches to curriculum change in the Southwestern United States. [Special issue]. *Women's Studies International Forum, 14*(4).

Moraga, C., & Anzaldúa, G. (Eds.). (1981). *This bridge called my back: A collection of writings by radical women of color*. Watertown, MA: Persephone Press.

Morgan, R. (Ed.). (1984). *Sisterhood is global: The international women's movement anthology*. Garden City, NY: Anchor Press/Doubleday.

Morrison, T. (Ed.). (1992). *Race-ing justice, en-gendering power: Essays on Anita Hill, Clarence Thomas, and the construction of social reality*. New York: Pantheon Books.

Moses, Y. T. (1989). *Black women in academe: Issues and strategies*. Washington, DC: Association of American Colleges.

Multi-Cultural Women Writers of Orange County. (1990). *Sowing ti leaves: Writings by multi-cultural women*. Irvine, CA: Multi-Cultural Women Writers of Orange County.

Musil, C. M. (Ed.). (1992a). *The courage to question: Women's studies and student learning*. Washington, DC: Association of American Colleges and National Women's Studies Association.

Musil, C. M. (1992b). *The courage to question: Executive summary*. Washington, DC: Association of American Colleges.

National Women's Studies Association. (1990). *The NWSA directory of women's studies programs, women's centers, and women's research centers*. College Park, MD: Author.

Nicholson, L. (Ed.). (1990). *Feminism/postmodernism*. New York: Routledge.

Nieves-Squires, S. (1991). *Hispanic women: Making their presence on campus less tenuous*. Washington, DC: Association of American Colleges.

Ogunyemi, C. O. (1985). Womanism: The dynamics of the contemporary Black female novel in English. *Signs, 11*(1), 63–80.

Omolade, B. (1987). A Black feminist pedagogy. *Women's Studies Quarterly, 15*(3 & 4), 32–39.

Ong, A. (1987). *Spirits of resistance and capitalist discipline: Factory women in Malaysia*. Albany: State University of New York Press.

Organization of American Historians. (1983). *Restoring women to history: Materials for U.S. I and II*. (Vols. 1–2). Bloomington, IN: Author.

Organization of American Historians. (1988). *Restoring women to history: Teaching packets for integrating women's history into courses on Africa, Asia, Latin America, the Caribbean, and the Middle East*. Bloomington, IN: Author.

Orozco, C. E. (1990). Getting started in Chicana studies. *Women's Studies Quarterly, 18*(1 & 2), 46–69.

Ortner, S. (1974). Is female to male as nature is to culture? In L. Lamphere & M. Z. Rosaldo (Eds.), *Women, culture and society* (pp. 67–87). Stanford: Stanford University Press.

Ostriker, A. S. (1993). *Feminist revision and the Bible*. Cambridge, MA: Blackwell.

Palmer, P. M. (1983). White women/Black women: The dualism of female identity and experience in the United States. *Feminist Studies, 9*(1), 151–170.

Pardes, I. (1992). *Countertraditions in the Bible: A feminist approach*. Cambridge: Harvard University Press.

Patai, D. (1988). *Brazilian women speak: Contemporary life stories*. New Brunswick, NJ: Rutgers University Press.

Picó, I. (1986). The history of women's struggle for equality in Puerto Rico. In E. Acosta-Belén (Ed.), *The Puerto Rican woman: Perspectives on culture, history and society* (2nd ed., pp. 46–58). New York: Praeger.

Plaskow, J. (1990). *Standing again at Sinai: Judaism from a feminist perspective*. New York: Harper and Row.

Pogrebin, L. C. (1982). Anti-Semitism in the women's movement. *Ms, 10*(12), 45–49.

Pointer, B. P., & Auletta, G. S. (1990). Restructuring the curriculum: Barriers and bridges. *Women's Studies Quarterly, 18*(1 & 2), 86–94.

Pope, B. C. (1989). The evolution of texts for women's studies students. *NWSA Journal, 1*(3), 497–505.

Porter, N. (1989). The art of aging: A review essay. *Women's Studies Quarterly, 17*(1 & 2), 97–108.

Porter, N. M., & Eileenchild [aka O'Hara], M. T. (1980). *The effectiveness of women's studies teaching.* Washington, DC: National Institute of Education.

Portillo, C., Riós, G., & Rodríguez, M. (1976). *Bibliography of writings: La mujer.* Berkeley: Chicano Studies Library Publication.

Proyecto de Estudios de la Mujer. (1992). *Hacia un currículo no sexista.* Cayey: University of Puerto Rico, Colegio Universitario.

Ramos, J. (Ed.). (1987). *Compañeras: Latina lesbians.* New York: Latina Lesbian History Project.

Reagon, B. J. (1983). Coalition politics: Turning the century. In B. Smith (Ed.), *Home girls: A Black feminist anthology* (pp. 356–369). New York: Kitchen Table/Women of Color Press.

Rebolledo, T. D. (1985). Chicana studies: The missing text. In *Curriculum integration: Revising the literary canon* (Working Paper No. 20). Tucson: University of Arizona, Southwest Institute for Research on Women.

Rebolledo, T. D., & Rivero, E. S. (Eds.) (1993). *Infinite divisions: An anthology of Chicana literature.* Tucson: University of Arizona Press.

Rein, N. (1980). *Daughters of Rachel: Women in Israel.* New York: Penguin.

Rhode, D. (Ed.). (1990). *Theoretical perspectives on sexual difference.* New Haven: Yale University Press.

Rich, A. (1979). Taking women's studies seriously. In *On lies, secrets, and silences: Selected prose 1966–1978* (pp. 237–245). New York: W. W. Norton.

Rosaldo, M. Z. (1974). Women, culture, and society: A theoretical overview. In M. Z. Rosaldo & L. Lamphere, *Women, culture, and society* (pp. 17–42). Stanford: Stanford University Press.

Rose, E. C. (1993). American feminist criticism of contemporary women's fiction. *Signs, 18*(2), 346–375.

Rosenfelt, D. S. (Ed.). (1973). *Female studies VII: Going strong, new courses/new programs.* Old Westbury, NY: Feminist Press.

Rosenfelt, D. S. (1984). What women's studies programs do that mainstreaming can't. *Women's Studies International Forum, 7*(3), 167–75.

Rosenfelt, D. S. (1990). *Curriculum transformation project at UMCP: Report on the 1989 summer faculty institute.* Unpublished manuscript. College Park: University of Maryland, Curriculum Transformation Project.

Rosenfelt, D. S. (1990). Integrating cross-cultural perspectives in the curriculum: Working for change in the California State Universities. *Radical Teacher,* no. 37, 10–13.

Rosenfelt, D. S., & Williams, R. (1992). Learning experience: The curriculum transformation project at the University of Maryland at College Park. *Women's Review of Books, 9*(5), 33–35.

Rosenwasser, P. (Ed.). (1992). *Voices from the promised land: Palestinian women and Israeli peace activists speak their hearts.* Willimantic, CT: Curbstone Press.

Rothenberg, P. S. (Ed.). (1992). *Race, class, and gender in the United States: An integrated study* (2nd ed.). New York: St. Martin's Press.

Rubin, G. (1975). The traffic in women: Notes on the "political economy of sex." In R. Reiter (Ed.), *Toward an anthropology of women* (pp. 157–210). New York: Monthly Review Press.

Ruíz, V. (1987). *Cannery women, cannery lives: Mexican women, unionization, and the California food processing industry, 1930–1950.* Albuquerque: University of New Mexico Press.

Sánchez, C. L. (1983). Sex, class and race intersections: Visions of women of color. In B. Brant (Ed.), A gathering of spirit: A collection by North American Indian women [Special issue]. *Sinister Wisdom, 22–23,* 150–154.

Sánchez, M. E. (1985). *Contemporary Chicana poetry: A critical approach to an emerging literature.* Berkeley: University of California Press.

Sánchez, R., & Cruz, R. M. (Eds.). (1977). *Essays on La Mujer.* Los Angeles: University of California, Chicano Studies Center.

Schilb, J. (1982). Men's studies and women's studies. *Change, 14*(2), 38–41.

Schmitz, B. (1985). *Integrating women's studies into the curriculum: A guide and bibliography.* Old Westbury, NY: Feminist Press.

Schmitz, B. (1991). Diversity and collegiality in the academy. *Liberal Education, 77*(4), 19–22.

Schmitz, B. (1992). *Core curriculum and cultural pluralism.* Washington, DC: Association of American Colleges.

Schmitz, B., & Dinnerstein, M. (1991). Incorporating scholarship on women into the community college curriculum. *AAWCJC Journal,* 5–11.

Schmitz, B., & Williams, A. S. (1983). Seeking women's equity through curriculum reform: Faculty perceptions of an experimental project. *Journal of Higher Education, 54*(5), 556–565.

Schneider, S. W. (1984). *Jewish and female: Choices and changes in our lives today.* New York: Simon & Schuster.

Schuster, M. R., & Van Dyne, S. R. (Eds.). (1985). *Women's place in the academy: Transforming the liberal arts curriculum.* Totowa, NJ: Rowman and Allanheld.

Schwerteger, R. (1989). *Women of Theresianstadt: Voices from a concentration camp.* New York: St. Martin's Press.

Scott, J. W. (1988). *Gender and the politics of history.* New York: Columbia University Press.

Scott, J. W. (1992). The campaign against political correctness: What's really at stake. *Radical History Review, 54,* 59–80.

Searing, S. E. (1985). *Introduction to library research in women's studies.* Boulder, CO: Westview Press.

Segura, D. A. (1989). Chicana and Mexican immigrant women at work. *Gender and Society, 3*(1), 37–52.

Segura, D. A., & Pesquera, B. M. (1993). Beyond indifference and antipathy: The Chicana feminist movement and Chicana feminist discourse. *Aztlán, 19*(2), 69–88.

Segura, D. A., & Pierce, J. L. (1992). Chicano/a family structure and gender personality: Chodorow, feminism, and psychoanalytic sociology revisited. *Signs, 19*(1), 62–91.

Sen, G., & Grown, C. (1987). *Development, crisis, and alternative visions: Third World women's perspective.* New York: Monthly Review Press.

Sherman, J. A., & Beck, E. T. (Eds.). (1979). *The prism of sex: Essays in the sociology of knowledge.* Madison: University of Wisconsin Press.

Shrewsbury, C. M. (1987). Feminist pedagogy: A bibliography. *Women's Studies Quarterly, 15*(3 & 4), 116–124.

Shult, L., Searing, S., Lester-Massman, E. (1991). *Women, race, and ethnicity: A bibliography.* Madison: University of Wisconsin System Women's Studies Librarian.

Smith, B. (Ed.). (1977). Towards a black feminist criticism [Special issue]. *Conditions, 2.*

Smith, B. (Ed.). (1983). *Home girls: A Black feminist anthology.* New York: Kitchen Table/Women of Color Press.

Smith, B. (1991). The truth that never hurts: Black lesbians in fiction in the 1980s. In C. T. Mohanty, A. Russo, & L. Torres (Eds.), *Third World women and the politics of feminism* (pp. 101–132). Bloomington: Indiana University Press.

Spanier, B., Bloom, A., & Boroviak, D. (1984). *Toward a balanced curriculum: A sourcebook for initiating gender integration projects.* Cambridge, MA: Schenkman.

Spelman, E. V. (1982). Combatting the marginalization of Black women in the classroom. *Women's Studies Quarterly, 10*(2), 15–16.

Spelman, E. V. (1988). *Inessential woman: Problems of exclusion in feminist thought.* Boston: Beacon Press.

Spender, D. (Ed.). (1981). *Men's studies modified: The impact of feminism on the academic disciplines.* New York: Pergamon Press.

Spiro, M. E. (1980). *Gender and culture: Kibbutz women revisited.* New York: Schocken Press.

Stack, C. (1984). *All our kin: Strategies for survival in a Black community.* New York: Harper and Row.

Steady, F. C. (Ed.). (1981). *The Black woman cross-culturally.* Cambridge, MA: Schenkman.

Sterling, D. (Ed.). (1984). *We are your sisters: Black women in the nineteenth century.* New York: W. W. Norton.

Stimpson, C. R. (1986). *Women's studies in the United States. A report to the Ford Foundation.* New York: The Ford Foundation.

Stimpson, C. R. (1989). Women's studies at twenty: Setting agendas, defining challenges. *Women's Review of Books, 6*(5), 14.

Stimpson, C. R. (1992). Women's studies. In B. R. Clark & G. R. Neave, *Encyclopedia of Higher Education* (pp. 1,965–1,976). New York: Pergamon Press.

Stineman, E. (1979). *Women's studies: A recommended core bibliography.* Littleton, CO: Libraries Unlimited.

Strathern, M. (1987). An awkward relationship: The case of feminism and anthropology. *Signs, 12*(2), 276–292.

Terborg-Penn, R., & Harley, S. (Eds.). (1978). *The Afro-American woman: Struggles and images.* Port Washington: National University Publications.

Terborg-Penn, R., Harley, S., & Rushing, A. B. (1987). *Women in Africa and the African diaspora.* Washington, DC: Howard University Press.

Tetreault, M. K. (1980). Women in U.S. history: Beyond a patriarchal perspective. *Interracial Books for Children, 11,* 7–10.

Tetreault, M. K. (1985). Feminist phase theory: An experience-derived evaluation model. *Journal of Higher Education, 56,* 363–84.

Thorne, B., & Henley, N. (1975). *Language and sex: Difference and dominance.* Rowley, MA: Newbury House.

Timberlake, A., Cannon, L. W., Guy, R. F., & Higginbotham, E. (1988) *Women of color and Southern women: A bibliography of social science research, 1975–1988.* Memphis: Memphis State University, Center for Research on Women.

Trible, P. (1978). *God and the rhetoric of sexuality.* Philadelphia: Fortress Press.

Trujillo, C. (Ed.). (1991). *Chicana lesbians.* Berkeley: Third Woman Press.

Tsuchida, N. (Ed.). (1982). *Asian and Pacific American women's perspectives.* Minneapolis: University of Minnesota, Asian/Pacific American Learning Resource Center and General College.

Umansky, E., & Ashton, D. (Eds.). (1992). *Four centuries of Jewish women's spirituality.* Boston: Beacon Press.

Uno, R. (Ed.). (1993). *Unbroken thread: An anthology of plays by Asian American women.* Amherst: University of Massachusetts Press.

Uyehara, G. K. (1979). Our responsibility for outreach in sisterhood. *Bridge: An Asian American Perspective, 7*(1), 36–38.

Walker, A. (1983). *In search of my mothers' gardens: Womanist prose.* San Diego: Harcourt.

Walker, M. (1991). *Down from the mountaintop: Black women's novels in the wake of the civil rights movement, 1966–1989.* New Haven: Yale University Press.

Washington, M. H. (Ed.). (1975). *Black-eyed Susans: Classic stories by and about Black women.* Garden City, NY: Anchor Press/Doubleday.

Washington, M. H. (Ed.). (1980). *Midnight birds: Stories by contemporary Black women writers.* Garden City, NY: Anchor Press/Doubleday.

Washington, M. H. (1987). *Invented lives: Narratives of Black women, 1860–1960.* Garden City, N.Y.: Doubleday.

Watanabe, S., & Bruchac, C. (Eds.). (1990). *Home to stay: Asian American women's fiction.* Greenfield Center, NY: Greenfield Review Press.

Westcott, M. (1979). Feminist criticism of the social sciences. *Harvard Educational Review, 49*(4), 422–430.

White, D. G. (1985). *Ar'n't I a woman? Female slaves in the plantation South.* New York: Norton.

Witt, S. H. (1976). The brave-hearted women: The struggle at Wounded Knee. *Akwesasne Notes, 8*(2), 16–17.

Yamada, M. (1979). Invisibility is an unnatural disaster: Reflections of an Asian American woman. *Bridge: An Asian American Perspective, 7*(1), 11–13.

Yamada, M. (1981). Asian Pacific American women and feminism. In C. Moraga & G. Anzaldúa (Eds.), *This bridge called my back: A collection of writings by radical women of color* (pp. 71–75). Watertown, MA: Persephone Press.

Yamada, M. (1990). The cult of the "perfect" language: Censorship by class, gender, and race. In Multi-Cultural Women Writers of Orange County, *Sowing ti leaves: Writings by multi-cultural women.* Irvine, CA: Multi-Cultural Women Writers of Orange County.

Zavella, P. J. (1987). *Women's work and Chicano families: Cannery workers of the Santa Clara Valley.* Ithaca: Cornell University Press.

Zimmermann, B. (1990). *The safe sea of women: Lesbian fiction, 1969–1989.* Boston: Beacon Press.

Zinn, M. B. (1980). Employment and education of Mexican-American women: The interplay of modernity and ethnicity in eight families. *Harvard Educational Review, 50,* 47–62.

Zinn, M. B. (1982). Mexican American women in the social sciences. *Signs, 8*(2), 259–272.

Zinn, M. B., Cannon, L. W., Higginbotham, E., & Dill, B. T. (1986). The costs of exclusionary practices in women's studies. *Signs, 11*(2), 290–303.

Zinn, M. B., & Dill, B. T. (Eds.). (1994). *Women of color in U.S. society.* Philadelphia: Temple University Press.

· 42 ·

MULTICULTURALISM AND CORE CURRICULA

Ann K. Fitzgerald
MARYMOUNT MANHATTAN COLLEGE

Paul Lauter
TRINITY COLLEGE

Both of the terms of our title—*multiculturalism* and *core curricula*—represent highly contested grounds in education today (see, for example, Carnochan, 1993; Geyer, 1993). Indeed, as we shall suggest, their very definitions are matters of conflict. Core curricula are often taken to represent a single course or sequence of courses taken by all undergraduates or all those enrolled toward a particular degree such as a bachelor of arts. For an older generation of faculty, and for many in the nonacademic public, the model is that proposed by Harvard's 1945 report, *General Education in a Free Society,* also known as the "Redbook," and implemented in many colleges around the nation (though not at Harvard) during the 1950s (Bell, 1966). The model evokes the picture of a large auditorium in which an entire freshman class would attend two or three lectures a week, as well as discussion sections focused on common texts—the Bible, or works from Greek and Roman civilization. The underlying idea, much touted during the 1980s, especially by the chairpersons of the National Endowment for the Humanities (Boyer & Levine, 1981; Cheney, 1989), was to provide undergraduate students with what a generation earlier was presented as a "common experience," a "core of unity" (President's Commission on Higher Education, 1947), exposure to a set of shared texts taken to represent the shared heritage of Western culture.

On closer examination, however, few if any programs actually conform to this idealized stereotype. As the authors of one of the few studies of contemporary general education practice comment,

"core" is not used with the consistency the advocates expect. Often it is a very loose collection of electives set out in very general categories. In the public arena the idea of a common core of general studies reaching across all institutions is proposed as a solution to all sorts of societal shortcomings. At the campus level such "one-size-fits-all" encounters realities of schedules, professional preparation requirements, and local traditions. (Toombs, Amey, & Chen, 1991, p. 112)

We will consequently use a relatively broad definition of core curriculum, including within this rubric a range of curricular formats. At one pole, rarely put into practice, are core programs that require that all students take one mandated course or a series of them. The most thoroughgoing implementation of this pattern has been at St. John's College, in Annapolis, Maryland, which has mandated the entire four-year curriculum, organized around some 120 "great books" (Rudolph, 1977). Such course sequences account "for less than 5 percent of all undergraduate general education programs" (Astin, 1993, p. 425); others estimate that of the 34% of colleges and universities that have a *multicultural* general education requirement, only 13% can be called core curricula (Levine & Cureton, 1992). At the other pole, conceptions of "core" slide off into generalized distribution requirements, courses of study in which students are expected to take a number of "general education" offerings from outside their majors; these are likely to include at least introductory-level courses in the various disciplines, courses such as American literature or psychology. Between these poles are a variety of "tight" and "loose" models of core curricular organization. Some institutions require students to choose from among a relatively restricted number of courses focused on issues (such as racial or sexual discrimination) or skills (such as computer or mathematical literacy), or from among a limited number of thematic "tracks" (Levine & Cureton, 1992, estimate that 68% of general education requirements including multicultural materials follow this model). Others offer opportunities for much broader student selection among courses gathered into loosely drawn categories such as "cultural diversity" or "scientific ways of knowing." Mount Saint Mary's College—to use one concrete example of an institution that recently created a core—requires 61 hours, about half the curriculum, of general education:

The first two years are devoted to study in the humanities and sciences of Western civilization. The third year explores the American and Christian heritages, with emphasis on the Catholic tradition. The fourth year includes an examination of one non-Western culture and reflection about contemporary moral problems, with the aid of ethical theories. (Campbell & Flynn, 1990, p. 10)

We choose a somewhat eclectic strategy for discussing core curricula, not only because it better reflects the variety of collegiate practices than any narrow definition might, but also because the traditional definition of core curriculum as unitary course of study—"today is October 5 and we are all working on Thucydides"—generally contains within itself a conclusion about the virtues of this particular form of curricular organization (Brann, 1993). Part of our intent in this chapter, however, is to interrogate various methods of providing students with a core *educational* experience in relation to our second conflicted term, *multiculturalism*.

That term, as this *Handbook* and the sheer variety of recent books and articles indicate (*e.g.,* Banks & Banks, 1993; Ch'maj, 1993; Nordquist, 1992), embraces an increasing range of curricular, pedagogical, and organizational practices at every level of education. In its weaker manifestations it can represent little more than a celebration of cultural differences as these are displayed in dress, foodways, art, and language. These are not inconsequential matters, to be sure; they constituted the central elements of the popular 1930s folk festivals promoted by leaders of the intercultural educational movement of that time (Montalto, 1982). But they seem to us of less educational weight in this historical moment than forms of study that raise issues of differences in power and questions of hybridization and change in the study of cultural and social heterogeneity.

A second set of tensions concerns the different ways in which the term *multiculturalism* is used: To what groups does it refer? Should the term properly be restricted to diversity rooted in race and ethnicity? Does it also encompass differences based upon national origin, gender, class, sexual orientation, and other terms of analysis and identity formation, including "exceptionality"? Can multiculturalism be equated with non-Western or other international studies? A growing consensus among multicultural theorists distinguishes multicultural education, which is primarily focused on issues of race, class, and gender, from global education (Banks & Banks, 1993; Gaff, 1992). While we focus primarily on race and ethnicity, our analysis deals as well with certain other categories, particularly gender and class, because, implicitly or explicitly, these are seldom absent from curricula or academic discussions concerned with multiculturalism. It might be theoretically helpful to be able to draw a line between considerations, say, of race and of gender, but in practice such categories turn out to be mutually constitutive (Spelman, 1988), as can be seen by the very fragility of generalizations about "all Black people" or all women. Furthermore, in practice, among colleges and universities that have multicultural general education requirements, 12% "focus on domestic diversity," 29% "emphasize global multiculturalism," and 57% include both (Levine & Cureton, 1992).

HISTORICAL DETERMINANTS: SPECIALIZED AND GENERAL EDUCATION

In the 20th century, American collegiate curricula have responded to alternating pulls from advocates of "specialized" and of "general" education. The elective system, developed primarily at Harvard toward the end of the 19th century under the leadership of President Charles W. Eliot, enabled students to pursue virtually any course of study they chose; of equal significance, perhaps, it allowed faculty to teach whatever was of primary interest to them (Kerr, 1964; Spurr, 1970). Increasingly influenced by the German model of the research institution—introduced at Johns Hopkins University in 1876—faculty found specialization in teaching and research to be in both their intellectual and material self-interest (Bisesi, 1982). Not surprisingly, therefore, reformers from the general education movement of the 1920s (Gruber, 1975; Rudolph, 1962) to those of the 1940s (*General Education in a Free Society,* 1945) and the 1970s and 1980s (Association of American Colleges, 1985; Rosovsky, 1978) have decried faculty specialization as a main bar to sustaining viable forms of general education. Periodically, reformers have mounted campaigns to provide "coherence" and "direction" to the curriculum by exposing undergraduates to "a body of common knowledge," or—as an originator of Columbia's Contemporary Civilization program put it—to "introduce into our education a liberalizing force which will give to the generations to come a common background of ideas and commonly understood standards of judgment" (Gruber, 1975, p. 238). Just as regularly, student preoccupation with job preparation and faculty recognition that teaching outside their disciplines offered few direct professional rewards—and could present significant professional encumbrances (Lauter, 1991)—have led to the reemphasis of departmental and thus of specialized concerns.

Such an account is accurate, so far as it goes, but it tends, like many histories focused chiefly on educational institutions, to portray developments at colleges and universities in isolation from forces at work in the wider society (a problem illustrated by Allardyce, 1982). In fact, educational reforms generally, and efforts to foster core curricula most particularly, always reflect broader social forces (Hall & Kevles, 1982). Skeptics answer the "Jeopardy"-style question "what is the problem for which core curriculum is an answer?" by citing "political, moral, ethical, and social" rather than strictly educational issues (Kaplan, 1982). And they point to the need to deconstruct ideological terms such as *coherence* and *direction,* which often mask the political mandates that energize educational reforms.

Indeed, the alternating calls for general and specialized education have embedded within them certain common social imperatives. General education during and after World War I, for example, was supported in significant measure as a countervailing cultural force to the disintegrating tendencies some commentators saw in the influence of immigrants, Bolsheviks, women's suffrage, and other expressions of change in ethnic, class, and gender norms. Core courses such as Columbia's "War Issues"—the predecessor to Contemporary Civilization—mandated by the War Department, served to gather up fragments of European history against the ruin of the war-wracked culture bemoaned by modernist writers and critics; not incidentally, such programs buttressed the cultural authority of the traditionally educated classes by valorizing what was assumed to be their heritage (Bell, 1966, offers a rather more benign view of these origins).

Similarly, in our own time, core curricula focused particularly on "the Western tradition" have been posed as an antidote to the "disuniting" tendencies critics locate in multiculturalism, feminism, and Black studies (Bloom, 1987; Schlesinger, 1991). Their opponents have, by contrast, proposed that efforts to reconstruct narrowed general education cores correspond to the broader retreat in the 1980s from the commitments of earlier decades to educational experimentation dedicated "to equal opportunity, to openness, to multivalent validations," that core curricula represent, in practice, "a genteel way to retract the social commitment of the 1960s" (Kaplan, 1982, pp. 8–9). In short, a history of general education and its discontents in 20th-century America can too easily become a social history of 20th-century America. That is not our intent. It remains important, nevertheless, not to take at face value the terms, objectives, and claims to disinterestedness deployed by each cadre of educational reformers in behalf of their plans. Curricular "coherence," for example, may be a significant virtue—or it may not, depending upon the basis on which coherence is obtained (fundamentalism? Aryanism? Stalinism?) and what is sacrificed to obtain it. Similarly, "the lack of a common intellectual experience is problematic only to the extent that it is held as an institutional value" (Jones & Ratcliff, 1991, p. 100). Our aim in the narratives that follow is not to promote any one model for relating core curricula and multiculturalism—though we do conclude that certain strategies can be seen to produce particular effects—but to portray the play of social, cultural, and political forces that have marked that uneasy relationship in our time.

CHANGING PATTERNS OF THE LAST 25 YEARS

We have suggested a regular pattern of alternating tacks in 20th-century America toward general and specialized education. But history does *not* repeat itself. A measure of the distance between the general education reforms of the 1920s and those of the 1980s—and an observation to which we will return—is the extent to which most new or revised core programs, however much they might initially focus on traditional ideas of "Western civilization," soon take on additional but significant multicultural or "non-Western" elements (Schmitz, 1992a). The reasons for this new development can be seen through a close reading of social and consequent educational changes usually attributed to "the Sixties." And these may, in turn, usefully be seen in relation to core curricula widely developed, in response to the Harvard "Redbook," during the previous decade.

One such core course, which can be taken to stand for many, was the Western Civilization program implemented during the 1950s at Hobart and William Smith colleges, mainly by faculty trained at Harvard. The first year of the course was required of all students, the second year required of those pursuing bachelor of arts degrees. Year one was divided into four units: the Hebrew Bible; Greek epic, history, and drama; Roman literature and history; and the New Testament. Elaborate "briefings" had been prepared for faculty teaching the course on each of the texts—and much of the context—to be taught, and the staff gathered every Friday afternoon over sherry to discuss the following week's work, the upcoming lectures, the briefings, and strategies for conducting the discussion sections.

From one point of view, such meetings, the lectures themselves—delivered in the main by senior colleagues—and the briefing books not only furnished a wonderful education for younger, new faculty, but they provided a commonality of experience for the students. As a recent dean at Hobart put it about another college's new (and different) core courses: "To separate ourselves into twelve separate courses would end the intellectual community that we, the faculty, are becoming within the program. While commonality can become a straightjacket that crushes creativity and spontaneity, we must continue to risk that our collective common sense will prevent the strangulation of intellectual growth among the program faculty" (Schmitz, 1992a, p. 50). From another point of view, however, all the efforts at coordination—in addition to the usual academic pressures toward conformity—operated to acculturate teachers, and through them students, to the course's ideological "line." That was expressed with disarming, if stunning, clarity in the 1950s course subtitle: "The Origins of Christian Civilization." In significant ways, the course pursued that central path: it certainly never deviated into Boasian comparative cultural study by considering, for example, originary stories or epics from outside the Western framework, nor did it for a moment ponder the implications, or even the facts, of Greek and Roman, much less American, slavery. Indeed, the course did not focus on what William H. McNeill has claimed to be the original "great idea" of such programs: Western history as the evolution of human freedom (McNeill et al., 1977). In fact, it was so constructed that Christianity seemed to spring *ex nihilo* as a climax less to history than to theology.

In about 1961, Lauter—then a young professor assigned to teach the course—mildly raised the great historical gap yawning between the Old and New testaments: Wasn't that worth discussing, even if the books were, in traditional Protestant fashion, considered "Apocrypha"? Weren't there Jewish influences on early Christianity, on its theology as well as its culture, that might be of particular interest, among others, to the increasing number of Jewish students making their way through "Christian Civilization"? The older colleagues were considerate, judicious; perhaps there ought to be a lecture on Intertestamental literature; perhaps Lauter ought "to deliver it, as the one, ah, most concerned in it." Thus was expressed one fundamental dynamic of academic multiculturalism: if you are "it," you are *it*. That is, what you are supposed to know and be concerned about is, for many well-meaning people, derived from "what you are" in terms of race, gender, or ethnicity. From such assumptions arise the notions that women scholars are necessarily resident experts on women and ethnics on ethnicity.

More fundamentally, perhaps, this episode illustrates an early instance of the critique of general education curricula and core courses in particular that became widespread later in the 1960s. The problem, this critique maintained, was that existing curricula were "incomplete," narrow, perhaps even biased; in the effort to construct a coherent, progressive narrative, they omitted too much, left out rather more of society, history, and culture than they put in. Earlier advocates of general education were rather more frank about this process of selection than some of its current champions. James Harvey Robinson (1926), in many respects the intellectual father of the 1920s Western civilization programs, wrote of his own development:

He then saw that if history was to fulfill its chief function and become an essential explanation of how our own civilization came to take the form it has, and present the problems that it does, a fresh selection from the records of the past would have to be made. Much that had been included in historical manuals would of necessity be left out as irrelevant or unimportant. Only those considerations would properly find a place which clearly served to forward the main purpose of seeing more and more distinctly how this, our present Western civilization, in which we have been born and are now immersed, has come about. (p. 4)

In the 1960s the early civil rights movement raised the demand to be let in—in to the front of the bus, to public accommodations, to the ballot box. Just so, the demand began to be raised for admission, open admission to decent schools, to all colleges, even to the curriculum. "Where," civil rights activists and students asked of courses of study, especially at mostly White institutions, "where are the Blacks?" And later, "Where are the women?" "Where are *we* in your texts, your bookshelves, your syllabi, your classrooms and faculties?"

These questions, raised with increasing intensity by the movements for social change, confronted the dominantly White and male academic establishment with dilemmas, exacerbated, of course, by the widening ruptures in the society over the war on Vietnam, the transition from "civil rights" to "Black Power," and the advent of a new wave of feminist militancy. The intellectual basis for general education programs of any sort had been eroding since the response to Sputnik in 1957 accelerated a return to specialization. It became harder and harder to achieve consensus about what students ought to know—or at least to study. "When there is no longer *a* history, when history ceases to have a central narrative, there is no longer a logical necessity for students to know either the same facts or the same history" (Allardyce, 1982, p. 720). At the same time, partly in response to the perceived threat of Soviet technology, partly for other reasons, colleges and universities were rapidly expanding, thus providing unprecedented advancement opportunities to faculty (and administrators). Most faculty perceived that such opportunities were more likely to be available to those who pursued disciplinary specialties, who established professional reputations by publishing and speaking, than to those who devoted long hours to the variety of subjects with which one needed to work to teach in serious core programs (Bell, 1966). Many faculty were only too happy to see general education require-

ments dissolve and thus free them, guiltless, to pursue disciplinary self-advancement. In addition, the student movement of the 1960s demanded not only "free speech" but much freer choices in living arrangements and academic study. With the call for "relevance," students raised questions about the relation between the classroom and their lives; they decried the arbitrary powers of administrations and faculty, including those over curriculum, pointing to the (often) direct links between academic institutions and a government seemingly committed to war (Flacks, 1971; Long, 1969—one often-cited example was the Army Mathematics Research Center at the University of Wisconsin). Student questioning of the sources of this academic "illegitimate authority" accelerated the movement away from requirements altogether.

Furthermore, it would have been no easy task to reconstruct established core courses of study to be more inclusive, polycentric, responsive to a world of increasing diversity: What needed to be added and what, therefore, omitted? On what educational or political bases could such judgments be grounded? For many faculty members, answering such questions felt rather like relearning the disciplinary alphabet. And, to be truthful, what we shall call the "new scholarship" on women and minority men was not very well developed by the late 1960s: important texts were not yet widely available, commentaries on them were few, historical narratives that linked "new" and "traditional" texts were just being disseminated or formulated. Educators had barely begun to consider the more fundamental changes in the underlying paradigms of disciplinary knowledge and therefore of curricula, of the existing structures of courses of study, that the new scholarship increasingly seemed to imply. And while the movements for social change systematically linked curricular change to opening the educational system to minority and female students *and* faculty, those links were not widely accepted within academe, nor were their implications systematically considered. All of these centrifugal forces contributed to the processes that, by the mid-1970s, had eliminated much of general education, and almost all core courses, from the academic landscape.

Meanwhile, a strategy of deepening and institutionalizing the new scholarship was pursued by advocates of Black studies, women's studies, and the other forms of ethnic minority programs that began to appear in the academy. This is not the place to examine these developments in detail (see chapter 41 of this *Handbook*). Broadly speaking, in its first stage, the new scholarship tried to answer with increasing detail the questions "where are the Blacks?" and "where are the women?" It focused on a process of rediscovering history and culture that had largely been buried or forgotten, reexamining social, political, and economic structures that had marginalized women and minority men. And it concentrated on making the fruits of its searches available to scholars, students, and the wider public through new journals and presses—many of which were founded in the late 1960s or early 1970s—and in new courses such as those on women's history, African American literature, or the psychology of sex and gender difference. Syllabi of such new courses were shared in conferences as well as through publications such as the Female Studies series published alternatively by KNOW, Inc., and The Feminist Press. And academic structures such as Chicano studies, women's studies, and Black studies programs were created, or at least proposed, to accommodate such courses.

Right from these beginnings, advocates of the new scholarship had *two* curricular goals. One, of course, concerned establishing new courses, of the sort just mentioned, devoted to the primary concerns of feminist and multicultural scholarship. But the other curricular goal had to do with transforming existing "mainstream" courses, like those in American history or introductory psychology, to include materials on minorities and White women (Howe & Lauter, 1980). The objective was simple: Creating a course on women writers or on African American history might satisfy the goal of beginning to institutionalize the study of these subjects, but it also ran the risk of ghettoizing them, along with the faculty and students interested in them. How, then, could one offer the fruits of the new scholarship to the wider academic community *except* by transforming in some measure the whole curriculum? This long-term effort, begun in the late 1970s, has continued unabated. It has taken at least three forms that are of concern to us here. First, it has been directed at transforming baseline disciplinary courses—which often do double duty satisfying general education requirements—and the textbooks on which such courses generally depend; we will use as our example the Reconstructing American Literature project and the revisionist *Heath Anthology of American Literature,* which was developed from that project. Second, efforts to broaden the impact of the new scholarship have taken the form of developing new required core courses that deal with matters of central concern to multicultural study, such as racial and sexual discrimination; we will use as our initial example Denison University's first-in-the-nation requirement, established in 1979. Third, attempts to transform curricula have been directed at existing as well as at new core requirements; we will use as our initial example the struggle over Stanford University's Western Culture program.

Before we turn to these specific examples, however, it will be useful to note that the events we will be chronicling took place during the second wave of the new scholarship (cf. chapter 41 of this *Handbook*). In this phase, the fundamental issue shifted from inclusion in existing curricular and intellectual paradigms to altering the paradigms and curricular structures themselves (Spanier, Bloom, & Boroviak, 1984). Literary, historical, economic, even religious canons came to be seen not as permanent fixtures of some transcendent culture, but as social constructions, mutable, historically contingent, subject to reformulation and reconstruction *by* people *in* time. Needless to say, such challenges to the long-standing norms of disciplinary study have been met with serious—at times hysterical—resistance. Moreover, as the postmodernism of commentators such as Fredric Jameson and Jean-François Lyotard challenged *all* overarching narratives—Christian, communist, "Western"—reaction outside the academy against prophets of disbelief also heightened. It is within such an increasingly skeptical outlook and the enraged responses to it, on the one hand, and an intensifying narcissistic and venal political economy of the 1980s, on the other—in short, within a deeply conflicted society—that this stage of the encounter of multiculturalism with core curricula took place.

PARADIGM 1: TEXTBOOKS AND DISCIPLINARY-BASED CHANGE

The strategy one adopts to provide a core educational experience depends, of course, very much upon how one defines that experience. For many reformers whose work was rooted in the new scholarship, one curricular goal has been wide student exposure to texts and materials on minorities and on White women, particularly in introductory courses, both formative for study in the major and available for general education credit. Such exposure, it has been expected, would help bring minority and female concerns into collegiate culture generally and into more advanced courses in the major in particular. This may, on the face of it, seem a modest goal indeed, especially compared with the name, "curriculum transformation," given it. But narrative evidence suggests that in cultural study, including at least literature and writing, some students feel, as Victor Doyno of the State University of New York (SUNY), Buffalo, has put it, "authorized" by discovering "authors" like themselves who provide them with a sense of the "authority" necessary to write or to speak with conviction and power (Kennedy, 1991). It may be that for some students, perhaps for a majority in any given classroom, such processes of identification are relatively unimportant. Nevertheless, for some and perhaps many students, especially those from previously marginalized cultures, the effects of role-model identification can be very significant (see, for example, McQuillen, 1992). Moreover, as Cary Nelson (1993) has put it, a "priority placed on multicultural representation in the classroom helps persuade students about the priority of multicultural representation on the faculty and in the student body" (p. 47) and, implicitly, within the body politic.

Moreover, the goal of exposing most, or all, students to a particular set of ideas or texts does not altogether differ in intent—though certainly in content—from the objectives of those who have promoted Western civilization courses in this century. They, too, assimilated general education to introductory disciplinary courses, especially in history, which they wished to fill with the varied content they named "Western Civilization" (Allardyce, 1982).

The empirical evidence developed by Alexander Astin establishes significant correlations between certain collegiate environmental factors and desirable outcomes in student attitudes and behaviors. Astin (1993) writes:

As far as institutional policies and practices are concerned, this study has included two major indicators: Institutional Diversity Emphasis (having to do primarily with affirmative action and promotion of multiculturalism on campus), and Faculty Diversity Orientation (having to do mainly with the content both of the research that faculty members do and of the courses that they teach). The study also included several indicators of the individual student's direct experience with diversity activities: taking women's or ethnic or third world courses, participating in racial or cultural awareness workshops, discussing racial or ethnic issues, and socializing with someone from another racial or ethnic group. Generally speaking all these institutional and individual environmental experiences were associated with greater self-reported gains in cognitive and affective development (especially increased cultural awareness), with increased satisfaction in most areas of the college experience, and with increased commitment to promoting racial under-standing. The same variables are also negatively associated with the development of materialistic values and with the belief that the individ-ual can do little to change society. (pp. 430–431; cf. Musil, 1992)

To be sure, "associated with" does not necessarily imply causal-ity, and Astin does point out that the direct effects of curricula that emphasize minority, Third World, or women's studies ma-terials, while not inconsequential, are not strong, especially as compared with peer relationships and student involvement with course content. But curricular choices do not take place in an institutional vacuum. Those active in developing multi-cultural and gender-fair courses recognized from the outset that efforts to translate the new scholarship into course work would influence and be affected by other institutional pro-cesses, including affirmative action hiring, departmental prac-tices of course and personnel review (Dinnerstein, O'Donnell, & MacCorquodale, 1981; Spanier, Bloom, & Boroviak, 1984), recruitment of more diverse student bodies, and—perhaps most important—forms of pedagogy (Culley & Portuges, 1985; Maher, 1987). Indeed, campus discussions of altering curricula would, over time, help engage more fundamental issues of institutional purposes and priorities. Thus the modest goal of inclusion, as its conservative critics came to recognize, implied more, say, than adding to the American literature survey a Black and a woman and stirring lightly.

Two main bars to such curricular change appeared early in the process: the limits of knowledge even among faculty sympa-thetic to change, and the lack of appropriate, available text-books and other curriculum materials. The first problem, which continues to be addressed in a variety of faculty development formats, lies beyond the scope of this chapter (see Schmitz, 1992a). The second issue—that of texts—has been engaged in most humanities and social science disciplines. For example, the Curriculum Analysis Project in the Social Sciences, funded by the Women's Educational Equity Act from 1979 to 1981, developed content modules on sex and gender for use in intro-ductory sociology, psychology, and microeconomics courses (Gappa & Pearce, n.d.). The American Anthropological Associa-tion brought scholars together with textbook authors to pro-duce an "Introduction to Cultural Anthropology." The Organi-zation of American Historians produced a series of packets, directed to college faculty, for integrating material on women into a variety of history survey courses and into courses on Western civilization (see Organization of American Historians, 1988; Fox-Genovese & Stuard, 1983). Led by Johnnella Butler and Margo Culley, a project at Amherst, Hampshire, Mount Ho-lyoke, and Smith colleges and the University of Massachusetts published a collection of syllabi and other materials titled *Black Studies/Women's Studies: An Overdue Partnership* (Spanier, Bloom, & Boroviak, 1984). We know of no systematic evalua-tion of the impact of these and other such projects to dissemi-nate curriculum materials, though our experience indicates that, particularly in earlier stages of course change and before commercial publishers are willing to issue significantly altered textbooks, these projects have provided both helpful models and otherwise unavailable materials.

Historical precedent also suggests something about the im-portance of such textbooks: "From the start," Gilbert Allardyce (1982) writes, "Western Civ traveled by textbook, and it was the success of particular works that helped standardize the course across the country" (p. 714). A similar conclusion may hold about the spread of multiculturalism, especially in certain disci-plines such as literary study. The availability of a particular textbook may, in fact, underlie the construction of an entire course, as is the case in the Special Sections on Cultural Lega-cies of Tennessee State University's freshman composition course (Schmitz, 1992a; the text is Barbara Roche Rico and Sandra Mano, eds., *American Mosaic: Multicultural Readings in Context*). Moreover, as Cary Nelson (1993) has written:

The admissions policy embodied in the anthology makes an implicit comment on the admissions policy appropriate to the institution as a whole. Nor is it much of a leap to make a connection with the nation's admission policy—its immigration statutes and their mixed history of openness and racism. The problems of ethnic, racial, and gender repre-sentation in an anthology devoted to a national literature . . . speak quite directly to questions about representation in public debate and in legis-lative bodies. Anthologies empower students to make these connec-tions whether or not teachers choose to make them explicit. (pp. 47–48)

Inversely, as Margaret Wilkerson (1992) has written, "When students who are members of those groups left out of our intellectual life are present on our campuses, their invisibility calls into question their right to be there, their intellectual capacities, and their very existence" (p. 59).

The Reconstructing American Literature (RAL) project, from which *The Heath Anthology of American Literature* developed, offers an instance in which such a disciplinary-based effort of curriculum transformation can be linked both to commercial development of the product and to specific alteration of a vari-ety of courses in American literature and American studies. The project, initiated at The Feminist Press in 1978, was initially supported by the federal Fund for the Improvement of Post-Secondary Education (FIPSE), and later by the Lilly Endowment and the Rockefeller Foundation, as well as by a number of colleges and universities. The project's objectives, more modest than its title, were summarized by its slogan: "So that the work of Frederick Douglass, Mary Wilkins Freeman, Agnes Smedly, Zora Neale Hurston and others is read with the work of Na-thaniel Hawthorne, Henry James, William Faulkner, Ernest Hemingway and others."

In practice, RAL carried out a number of tasks. In June 1982 it held a two-week institute at Yale involving over 50 scholars focused on the theoretical and practical issues of transforming American literature courses. The institute helped establish a network of scholars working in the field, a process accelerated in subsequent years when, under the project's auspices, a num-ber of workshops on the issues were held in different parts of the country. In addition, The Feminist Press published the project's collection of syllabi, essays, and other helpful mate-rials titled *Reconstructing American Literature* (Lauter, 1983).

The ultimate task of the project was to produce a seriously altered anthology of American literature that would include significant numbers of African American, Latino and Spanish, Native American, Asian American, and White women writers as well as the canonical figures. To carry out that task, the editors adopted a number of innovations. Until this project, no person who was not White and only two who were not male had ever served on editorial boards of American literature anthologies. The editorial board for the RAL anthology was uniquely diverse: half its members were White, half people of color, half were male, half female; they came from every part of the country and from most kinds of collegiate institutions. But they were chosen not so much for their representational characteristics but because of their expertise: By 1982, the field called American literature had grown so quickly and in so many new directions that no small group, certainly no one individual, could possibly have kept abreast of the new scholarship, much less the accelerating changes in disciplinary paradigms. A second innovation involved asking the literary profession at large, through mailings and meetings, which writers teachers wished to see included in such an anthology. The editors were thus able to draw on the expertise of literally hundreds of American literature scholars instead of being limited to what other anthologies had traditionally included or to their own graduate school training. Furthermore, this inclusive strategy helped widen the network of faculty interested in the project, develop their sympathies with the process of change in which it was implicated, and—not so incidentally—organize a constituency for the anthology once it was actually marketed.

Eight years elapsed between the beginning of the effort to edit an anthology and its actual publication as *The Heath Anthology of American Literature* (Lauter et al., 1990). During that period, the field of American literature continued to change in terms of both the texts that were seen to constitute it and the structures of history and culture used to frame and interpret them. It is probably fair to say that the *Heath Anthology* mainly confirmed the reality of these changes by embodying them in printed form and by gaining wide acceptance within the literary profession. On the other hand, the ongoing work of the project and then the very existence of the anthology and the differences in teaching it made possible accelerated change. It is, of course, hard to measure influence or to confirm casuality in movements of culture. What is easy to demonstrate, however, are the differences in curricula before and after the *Heath Anthology* became available. *Reconstructing American Literature* contained American literature course syllabi that, for their time (1982–1983), were markedly "advanced" in terms of their inclusion of works by White women and, at least, African American writers. Compared with many of the syllabi now regularly published in the *Heath Anthology Newsletter* (probably the most widely circulated journal in the field of American literature), they appear extraordinarily limited, if not downright backward—at least with respect to multicultural content. A dramatic example of curricular change is provided by syllabi for two courses offered by Sherry Sullivan at the University of Alabama, Birmingham, in 1980 and then in 1990 using the *Heath Anthology* (Ch'maj, 1993).

To be sure, it is impossible to estimate the role of a single textbook in a much larger movement to alter one corner of the educational landscape, any more than one can trace out specifically curricular impacts on student thinking or values isolated from a variety of collegewide influences such as peer pressures,

exposure to a diverse student body, or public commitments to creating an equitable environment. And it is logically fallacious to assume that what came after the publication of the *Heath Anthology* was caused by it. For all that, the instance offered by Sullivan's two syllabi is suggestive of the role a teaching tool can play in altering what actually is studied, and thus validated, in widely enrolled and culturally influential courses that help define campus climate as well as emphases in major study. Furthermore, the visibility of the anthology—it was, for example, the subject of a front-page story in the *Los Angeles Times,* a full-page story in the *Chronicle of Higher Education,* and reviews in *TLS,* the *Nation,* and other nonacademic journals—its marketplace success in a market-driven culture, and now its imitation by other textbooks have helped to validate multicultural approaches to literary study and make them easier to carry out in practice.

PARADIGM 2: A "DIVERSITY" REQUIREMENT

In 1979, 11 years before the *Heath Anthology* was published, Denison University adopted a requirement in its core, general education curriculum that focused on themes, topics, and texts central to multiculturalism: namely, the results of racial and sexual discrimination. This requirement—stated in the University Senate minutes of May 15, 1978, as one in "Minority Studies/Women's Studies"—was the first of its kind in the nation.

The requirement was described (in institutional documents like the catalog) in these terms:

Every Denison student enrolled in BA or BS programs shall complete a course dealing primarily with some or all of the following:
  The nature and effects of discrimination against women and minority groups in America; the roles and significant contributions of women and minority groups in American society; the ways in which historical factors have shaped women's and minorities' participation in American life; the unique experiences, identity and art that these important groups have contributed to American culture; an examination of the moral values central to these issues.

The character of this requirement and the processes of its adoption provide a number of significant insights to understanding the relation of multiculturalism and core curricula.

Denison University seems, at first, an unlikely site for the emergence of so controversial a requirement. The student movements for change enacted at Berkeley, Columbia, and elsewhere had by the mid-1970s not really produced analogous action at small, primarily conservative institutions like Denison. Yet, a series of student actions informed by those political movements emerged on the Denison campus. And while no curricular models for multicultural and feminist changes in core curricula then existed, the experimental spirit of the times had filtered down even to small-town Ohio. Most important, perhaps, an unusual conjunction of factors at the university in the mid- and late-1970s proved enabling of the changes. These factors included the following.

First—in terms of its influence on the development of the requirement—a strong, popular (highly enrolled) interdisciplinary Women's Studies course had been established by Ann

Fitzgerald and Joan Straumanis in 1972 and taught in every year. From the onset, this course had undergraduate teaching assistants who led weekly discussion groups; the TAs took a seminar (for credit) that dealt with the readings for the course, pedagogy, and campus politics. Modeled as a graduate-level women's studies course, the seminar included the unusual element of self-consciously recognizing and discussing the fact that the students were employees of the university and therefore, in some sense, responsible for its shaping. The director of Women's Studies purposefully chose students for these roles who were campus leaders (often presidents of sororities or fraternities), thus creating a certain cachet for the course among students. The seminar, and in many respects the course itself, became an intriguing blend of controversy and trendiness, as by extension did the Women's Studies program. The "visible" student TAs, moreover, attracted other students in large numbers to the course, well over 100 in any given semester, on a campus that generally had 25 in a class. Given the residential nature of the campus, course topics spilled into dorm discussions and programs; the director of Women's Studies worked closely with the Dean of Students Office and residence hall assistants to ensure continuity between the curricular and residence life programs. A Women's Resource Center provided an additional hub of feminist activity. Feminist ideas were thus widely disseminated on an otherwise conservative campus.

Second, a Black Studies program had been established in 1969 with a director and a number of departmental offerings. Thus there existed a locus for the examination of curricular ideas focused on race, especially in its American manifestations. Together with the establishment of Black Studies, a number of influential White and tenured faculty had instituted courses on these issues within their own departments. Once again, therefore, educational ideas about race and racism had been widely disseminated across the campus, at least among the faculty.

Closely related to the Black Studies program, though independent from it, was the Black Student Union, a student organization provided with both a lounge/meeting space and a budget by the Denison administration. The Black Student Union had the ability, demonstrated during the final stages of the debate over the requirement, to mobilize its members to respond to incidents of campus racism. Within the student community, in fact, a cadre of Black and feminist students organized through the Black Student Union, the Women's Resource Center, and the teaching assistants program in Women's Studies played a significant leadership role. The large majority of students at the university were White, upper middle class, and unused to thinking about power; nevertheless, as the process of pushing for a requirement went on, they became increasingly intrigued by the power they began to find they could wield.

Third, ongoing administrative leadership was provided by the provost, Louis Brakeman, and the president, Robert Good, both political scientists with substantial academic and political backgrounds in global education and policy and well informed about and committed to the importance of multiculturalism and affirmative action. They helped to encourage a campus climate of self-reflection and self-criticism. They also fostered a widely felt need to grapple with the problem of creating a sense of community, a need forced by the reality of Denison's being a

small, residential college in a small Ohio town. And they provided material support to the development both of curricular innovations such as Black and Women's Studies and departures in student activities such as the Black Student Union.

Fourth, Denison's faculty was, in keeping with its commitment to undergraduate teaching, involved in the problem of student development both inside and outside the classroom and alert to the connections. The faculty were, not surprisingly, inclined to be more progressive than the students. Moreover, many shared an educational philosophy fostering interdisciplinary study and some experience in its implementation.

Last, but by no means least, Denison retained a well-established and rather unquestioned system of general education, core requirements. Unlike most colleges of its kind, Denison had maintained traditional requirements throughout the turbulent 1960s and 1970s—so there was, rather ironically, an existing educational core and mission statement, which the proponents of multiculturalism could invoke.

The factors we have listed influenced the debates leading to adoption of the requirement and to the particular character of its final shape. Yet many or most of these factors have, we think, been critical in the development of virtually all multicultural core requirements.

The idea for proposing what became the "Minority Studies/Women's Studies" requirement grew out of a series of meetings convened by members of the Women's Studies, Black Studies, and Latin American Studies staffs to discuss their differences and disagreements and to express common concerns about the racism and sexism on the Denison campus, primarily among students. The original core requirement proposed by that coalition of groups was a course focused "on the nature and effects of discrimination in the United States." Local reality, the sense of urgency forced by the prejudices evident in everyday campus life, thus shaped the design. For example, the "American multiculturalists" saw the "internationalists" as diverting attention away from the conditions of campus and community life and thus pushed for the explicit focus on the United States. The result was, in the long run, a requirement that emphasized "America"—a word repeated no less than four times in four (out of the five) final criteria for the course.

The proposal also specified that "this requirement shall be added to the existing General Education requirements," at that time all departmental, disciplinary courses designed to provide "breadth" for students. This provision signaled the special nature of this requirement: Women and minorities were to be included, *added* to the existing core curriculum in the form of distinct courses, much the way that Women's Studies and Black Studies had been *added* as separate programs, alongside the traditional departments. At the same time, this provision took advantage of the fundamental tendency in American higher education to innovate by addition. The new did not displace the existing core requirements but extended them into realms increasingly seen as important to the educational program.

Once an initial proposal to establish a requirement was submitted to the growing Academic Affairs committee in December 1977, a combination of normal academic procedures and unusual political activities influenced its shaping and final passage. This link was hardly distinctive in its time—nor, indeed, as the example of Stanford suggests, in ours. Discussion centered on the criteria to be used to determine which courses might count toward satisfying the requirement and on what body would administer the criteria and thus effectively oversee implementation of the requirement. The issues have become familiar: Should courses dealing with societies and events outside the United States count? Should courses whose content is primarily "cultural" or "artistic" rather than social or political be included? Similarly, should the requirement be administered by those most deeply "involved"—the faculty of Black Studies and Women's Studies—by a presumptively "objective" group, or by some combination thereof? Even within the best-intentioned faculty, such discussions can slow movement to a flypaper crawl. However, a series of particularly vivid and campus-shattering racial incidents in the spring of 1978 precipitated final action.

One of these incidents—hardly unique to fraternity practice—occurred the day prior to the first student hearing on the proposal, sponsored by the Academic Affairs committee. Five days after that hearing, Women's Studies students attended the annual meeting of the Great Lakes Colleges Association Women's Studies Conference, where the events on the Denison campus were a major focus. After this conference, the Women's Studies students initiated meetings with the Black Student Union, and, together in teams, they met with each member of the Academic Affairs committee. A second hearing for student response to the proposed requirement was held later in April, followed by the first demonstration held on the Denison campus in 10 years. Students argued with recalcitrant faculty that they, the students, needed the requirement, that more needed to be done to eradicate the pervasive racism and sexism from the campus, that the curriculum was a logical place for addressing this educational need, and that it was all right with them to add another requirement. Though there was sufficient administrative and faculty support to pass the requirement, it was finally student pressure that brought it out of the contentious slough of institutional haggling into an unusually popular reality.

This part of the process was, to be sure, deeply inflected by quite local events. At the same time, these events serve to dramatize the general importance of student involvement in creating curricular—in this case multicultural—change. Indeed, they raise a question about the viability of recent dominantly administrative efforts to impose such requirements or related codes of campus speech. At Denison, top-level administrative support was critical to inaugurating the requirement, but the decisive word here is *support,* not initiation. Senior administrators helped foster respect for the work being done in Women's Studies and Black Studies, they provided funds not only to set up a Women's Resource Center and a Black Student Union, but for faculty research on women and minorities and for teaching about them. But the major initiatives arose from coalitions of concerned faculty and students.

The Denison process also calls attention to the deep connection between race and sex discrimination and the development of such "Minority Studies/Women's Studies" general education requirements. As the student arguments put it: "What do you do about racism and sexism in an educational community? You teach about them." While few, if any, argued that the require-

ment did not have a strong basis in scholarly information and ideas, the engine behind the students' self-expressed desire for the course was not academic knowledge but social issues. Thus the central criterion determining whether a course might count toward this requirement was whether its major focus was the "nature and effect of discrimination against women and/or minorities."

One may draw a number of other conclusions from this brief narrative. A central one involves change within departments. Certain courses already in place, administered and staffed by the existing Women's Studies and Black Studies programs, had a multicultural and/or feminist focus; they offered a base and perspective, a locus of momentum and expertise for developing the requirement. But these programs were small and interdisciplinary—for example, they depended on individual departments to "house" separate courses—and thus they could provide only a few of the 15 or so courses that came to count toward satisfying the requirement. Thus, the traditional departments themselves had to assume primary responsibility for developing and staffing the courses. Departmental involvement was entirely optional; no department was ever mandated to change courses, develop new ones, or contribute staff for the requirement. However, there was considerable encouragement, and at times pressure, to do so from the segments of the community that had helped initiate the requirement. Furthermore, the dynamics of academic cost accounting encouraged departments to participate: Required courses meant student enrollments, and increased enrollments meant increased budgets.

In order to fulfill the requirement, departmental courses had to meet the specified criteria existing "outside" departmental structures under the umbrella of general education. Therefore, if they wanted to participate in this component of the core curriculum, departments had to develop a bipolar vision, working both "inside" and "outside" their own educational and political paradigms. In order to accomplish this, departments could "transform" existing offerings or, alternatively, develop new courses. As the requirement was being put into practice, the latter strategy—designing new departmental courses to fulfill the requirement and hiring faculty to teach them—became the dominant one. It was initially more expedient than facing the resistance of some traditional faculty and the inertia of courses entrenched in the catalog; it did, however, mean that departments were forced to rethink their hiring priorities (Talburtt et al., 1988) since additional lines of funding were not made available to them. That process, it would appear, had effects that could not initially have been anticipated. For—with certain other internal and external factors—it fostered the institutionalization of knowledge about the teaching of materials on women and minorities *within* the traditional departments that constitute the basic framework of the academy. The graduation requirement thus became a major factor in producing a striking degree of curricular and research change at Denison (Talburtt et al., 1988).

What has been less subject to research analysis is the impact of the requirement on student and faculty culture. As we indicated above, a number of factors, including the campus leadership roles played by Women's Studies teaching assistants, helped bring the academic concerns of Women's Studies courses in particular into the residential life of the student population at large. For a significant number of students, that linkage helped foster what Alexander Astin has pointed to as critical to changing student attitudes and ideas: peer-group engagement (Astin, 1993). It is unclear, however, whether this phenomenon has persisted over the years, although anecdotal evidence related at a 10th-anniversary celebration of the "Minority Studies/Women's Studies" requirement at Denison suggested that it had. Still, further study of the long-term impacts of such requirements on faculty and student culture and performance seem to us important to understanding their value as a major interface of multiculturalism with core curricula.

PARADIGM 3: RECONSTRUCTING "WESTERN CIVILIZATION"

Our third model of a core curriculum involves students taking a mandated sequence of courses, the content of which, in this century, has generally focused on Western civilization. Such courses, it has usually been said, provide students with a "common intellectual experience" by exposing them to a unified narrative of America's inherited Western culture, a narrative conveyed usually by a set of core texts, often referred to as "great books" (Brann, 1993), and by a series of lectures traditionally delivered by members of history departments. Debates about Western civilization and the curricula devised to represent it to undergraduates have, as we have noted, waxed and waned throughout this century, subject to changing social and intellectual imperatives and to the economic and ideological needs of the nation—and the university. Thus, the curriculum of such courses is always potentially in a state of flux, subject to the normal academic process of review, revision, and change (Bell, 1966). The logic internal to the curricular process mandates that widely taken courses—core courses absorbing vast amounts of institutional resources—be routinely reevaluated and that questions concerning "common intellectual experiences" be openly debated. This is the work expected of faculty, administrators, and, increasingly, of students.

Adam Yarmolinksy (1992) has noted the importance of the process by which faculty in particular determine curricula:

The faculty cannot always, or even usually, be expected to agree on what should go into the syllabus. But they must be free to reach their own decisions by their own processes, without interference from outsiders of whatever political persuasion.... Whatever their political differences, faculty members are forced by the nature of the academy to argue them out in what purports to be rational terms. And they are further required to reach at least a second-order agreement—to agree on the nature and extent of their disagreements so that the institution can function. (p. 74)

What happened at Stanford University, then, between 1986 and 1988 during its revision of the Western Culture program was not in itself remarkable as an instance of the process of curricular change; nor was the questioning of the existing core along multicultural lines—that had been a hallmark of curricular de-

bate for at least two decades, at Stanford as well as at numerous colleges and universities across the nation (Bell, 1966).

Rather, what was remarkable about these somewhat routine academic processes was that they reached the front pages of *Time* and *Newsweek,* the *New York Times* and the *Wall Street Journal* (Hitchens, 1988). In a prolonged and well-orchestrated media campaign generated primarily by William Bennett, then secretary of education and later President Bush's general in the war on drugs, and supported by neoconservative politicians and commentators, the "Stanford Controversy" came to be less an educational debate about core curricula than one of national political identity. The very questioning of the existing core list of readings and the suggestion that it be altered to reflect minority, female, and non-Western cultures and voices, texts and paradigms, was deemed to augur the fall of Western civilization, the destruction of all that was best and brightest ("The Changing Curriculum: Then and Now," 1991; Hook, 1989). What occasioned this alarm at the national level and what fueled the media coverage was the recognition that general education (e.g., a core curriculum) was to be taken seriously as a form of public policy. Bennett used Stanford to indicate that the government had needs to fulfill in educating and shaping its citizens; his actions, speeches, and writings (and those of other neoconservative commentators such as Allan Bloom, Sidney Hook, and George Will) all served to underscore the fact that a core curriculum—especially at one of the nation's elite universities—has far-reaching political implications (Bossman, 1991; McNew, 1992). The national media reflected the real politics of diversity the nation faced (encoded in the proposed multicultural curricular components for the Stanford core curriculum)—at this near end-of-the-century—by mourning in 20th-century words and pictures the death, yet again, of Socrates, this time under the sunny skies of California, amidst the palms of Stanford's campus. Stanford's story was used as synecdoche: the part taken for the whole of what was going awry with the nation at large, beset with a plurality of groups with competing identities and claims for inclusion, and even demands for a fundamental shift in America's national story (Ravitch, 1990). As the politicians, commentators, and media all pointed out in alarm, the center of the core was not holding.

In light of this national controversy spawned by the pedestrian academic processes at Stanford, it is important to see what really happened on the campus that occasioned such attention. The center of attention was a year-long, three-quarter course entitled "Western Culture," required of all freshmen and transfer students. As was the case with many other similar programs across the country, this one had historical antecedents in an earlier core course on Western civilization, established in 1935 and taught (in large lectures) primarily by the history department until the course, along with most other requirements, was eliminated in the late 1960s. Efforts to restore a similar requirement were begun in 1975 by members of the faculty in the humanities, a two-year pilot was launched in 1978, and the program was fully implemented in 1980. The shape of the program was the result of much debate, compromise, and political trading on the part of all of the parties and departments involved; there were, in fact, seven other competing proposals for a cultural requirement. The ground, then, on which the program was developed was already heavily contested (Carnochan, 1993).

Unlike its Western civilization predecessor, Western Culture offered students a choice among eight different tracks or sequences, each housed and staffed in different departments within the humanities (many of the details of this history are drawn from Thomas, 1991; she was administrator of the program during this period). Unlike Western Civilization, the course would generally have over half of its five weekly meetings in seminar discussion groups (a pedagogical factor allowing for even more variation among the groups within a given track than, say, a series of common lectures for all students in that track). Lectures were generally given by specialists in the departments housing the track, and the seminar discussions were led by younger Ph.D.'s, hired in national searches to teach exclusively in the Western Culture program. Because these seminar leaders were employed on nontenure track contracts, the resulting turnover in staff undoubtedly led to a diversity in viewpoints and intellectual priorities within the program. It is important to recognize that one of the ostensible goals of the course—the creation of a "common intellectual experience"— was thus vitiated from the start.

What gave these different tracks their common bond was a core list of readings, 15 required and 18 strongly recommended. Each track would weave around these works other materials related to the particular theme devised by the department offering the track. The list itself then became the true core, rather than the particular uses to which that list might be put, pedagogically, educationally, or politically. Ironically (especially in the light of the way the program changes were described by Bennett and others), the very list was not even conceived of as a canon; initially, the program's designers envisioned the core list as changing and evolving on some regular basis under the direction of an academic oversight committee. This did not in fact happen because participants who developed the list reported that "the difficulty of negotiating the list was one source of its permanence: the process had been so painful and so lacking in intellectual integrity that no one expressed the slightest desire to repeat it" (Pratt, 1990, p. 12).

The 15 required works that rose quietly to canonized stature in the Western Culture program were the following:

Ancient World
Hebrew Bible, *Genesis*
Plato, *Republic,* major portions of books 1–7
Homer, major selections from *Illiad, Odyssey,* or both
At least one Greek tragedy
New Testament, selections including a Gospel

Medieval and Renaissance
Augustine, *Confessions,* 1–9
Dante, *Inferno*
More, *Utopia*
Machiavelli, *The Prince*
Luther, *Christian Liberty*
Galileo, *The Starry Messenger, The Assayer*

Modern
Voltaire, *Candide*
Marx and Engels, *Communist Manifesto*
Freud, *Outline of Psychoanalysis, Civilization and Its Discontents*
Darwin, selections

This is the list that, together with its companion group of 18 "strongly recommended" works, was so enthusiastically defended and whose demise was so heatedly contested in the national arena (*e.g.,* Phillips, 1988). The list reveals a lack of specificity (*a* "Greek tragedy" on the required list and *a* "Shakespearean tragedy" and *a* "nineteenth-century novel" on the recommended) juxtaposed with a highly specific Eurocentric focus.

When this list was constituted in 1980 and the Western Culture program begun, the program had already built into it the opportunity for significant variation. For example, in 1986 the seven tracks of the program were: History; Humanities; Conflict and Change in Western Culture; Philosophy; Great Books; Structured Liberal Education; and Technology, Science, and Society (Thomas, 1991). Given this range of focuses, there was considerable difference among the sequences and quite different intellectual and pedagogical contexts in which the core list could be read and interpreted. Nevertheless, the core list served as the locus for the ideological definition of the program both for those who supported retaining it and for those arguing for change (McNew, 1992). In the case of the former, the list offered a universally agreed-upon narrative of "our" American heritage, based on the works of Western civilization tested by time and conveying truths that transcended a particular ethnic heritage or historical moment (Hook, 1989). For the latter, the list displayed a narrow canonical "Eurocentric paradigm" (Pratt, 1990), and an equally narrow sense of Europe, along with a "monumentalist attitude" to the texts themselves.

The process of change, then, took place against a backdrop of continuing debate and centered on something allegedly concrete: "The List." And, as we have noted, there were from the beginning a series of factors opening the Western Culture program to modification and rational disagreement: the variation among the tracks; the potential for the list to be changed; the different faculty members and different pedagogical formats used within a given track; and the oversight committee's disregard of the increasing reluctance of some faculty to teach all of the required works.

The local academic and institutional context also played an enabling role in the process of reform. Stanford had an established series of minority and women's studies courses and faculty members who themselves were leading scholars in the educational movements to transform intellectual paradigms along multicultural lines; some of these scholars were the new Ph.D.'s teaching in the Western Culture program. Students, 40% of whom were minorities, were also quite active on campus, coming together in relatively strong organizations with a willingness to form coalitions. The initial, formal, public move to openly question the Western Culture program and its "canon" came from the students in the form of a statement from the Black Student Union. The statement issued to the faculty and administration called for the inclusion of issues of race, sex, and ethnicity in the core list of readings: The "current program is a disservice to the Stanford community because of its failure to acknowledge the contributions [to] and impact of women and people of color on American and European culture" (Thomas, 1991, p. 10). This call resonated in a world of existing student activism (e.g., Rainbow Coalition organizing, anti-apartheid protests) and increasing faculty discontent with the narrowness of the core list (a discontent made manifest by the fact that not all were using the readings). There was thus a union of unmet needs.

In response to these concerns, in October 1986, a university task force was formed to review the entire program. The committee released an interim report in the autumn of 1987 specifying that the course be renamed "Cultures, Ideas, and Values" (CIV) and that it focus on issues relating to class, ethnicity, race, religion, gender, and sexual orientation; courses were to examine at least one European and one non-European culture. A final draft of the report then passed to the faculty senate, where it was debated during the spring of 1988. Throughout this period the faculty/staff newspaper, *Campus Report,* printed all letters and recorded speeches related to the controversy, and the senate carried on its debate in open forums, allowing all visitors with prepared statements to speak. Thus the members of the Stanford community were engaged in an open, if heated, exchange about a core syllabus and course objectives—surely "a faculty prerogative as well as an obligation" (Yarmolinsky, 1992, p. 74). Indeed, the senate, composed of 55 senior faculty and former administrators (for the most part White male faculty from science and professional schools), would pass the final verdict. Before it could do so, however, what had been an academic process exploded into the national press when William Bennett (1984) described the process as "curriculum by intimidation."

The entry into this academic process of Bennett, Hook, conservative commentators, and the national print and television media cast the debate as itself something unnatural, undesirable, and dangerous. The introduction of multicultural components in the core course became synonymous with what Bennett called the "dropping of the West" and others deplored as "leaving students ignorant of the works of genius that lie at the heart of their own civilization." In this respect, political outsiders to the ongoing discussion succeeded in interfering with the university's processes and shaping its politics. In another, perhaps more significant sense, the revisions of Stanford's core curriculum became an arena in which differing political visions of America's cultural heritage were contested.

It was finally the faculty in the program itself that crafted a compromise, a "second order agreement," that enabled the senate to break an increasingly conflicted deadlock and vote in favor of the new CIV. The course would provide a "common intellectual experience" by focusing on certain common elements (issues, authors, texts, or themes) that would be decided upon each spring by those teaching the course. Each year the "core" would change, the canon, thereby, ceasing to exist. The process of compromise underlines the importance to the harmonious functioning of core curricula of the faculty actually involved in its implementation.

But one might draw other lessons as well. One is that core curricula are never free of political agendas; while the prominence of Stanford undoubtedly occasioned the amount of national attention drawn to its revisions, any such discussion will contain, covertly or openly, conflicting political agendas. These can, of course, be minimized; on the other hand, there may be significant educational value in opening to reasoned discussion the connections between political and curricular objectives.

Moreover—a point to which we will return below—in practice the final shape of the CIV program deviated remarkably little from its Western Culture ancestor. From this fact, one might draw a number of different conclusions: Conservatives succeeded in minimizing what were to them objectionable changes; inertial forces within a university are remarkably strong; Western civilization contains within itself enormous gravitational forces that may, in practice, conflict with the development of significant multicultural study. Whatever the balance of truth in these hypotheses, the Stanford experience adumbrates many of the issues with which advocates of core curricula on the Western Civilization model must contend.

In large measure, the many recent intersections of core curricula with multiculturalism can be framed within one or another of the paradigmatic cases we have discussed—or by some combination of them. That is, in institutions that define core learning experiences loosely as those provided by a range of introductory courses—some combination of which is mandated by a "breadth requirement"—the issue for those concerned with multiculturalism is the extent to which the content of such courses has been significantly affected by the new scholarship (see Butler & Walter, 1991). Other institutions have defined the core educational experience as classroom exposure to issues directly affecting women, minority men, or "non-Westerners"; estimates are that as of 1990 46% of four-year colleges and universities (fewer among two-year institutions—Levine & Cureton, 1992) require a course on world civilizations and 20% a course with racial and/or ethnic content (Elaine El-Khawas, "Campus Trends, 1990," American Council on Education, July 1991, cited by Carnegie Foundation for the Advancement of Teaching, 1992). These figures represent a marked increase from earlier trends noted by the Carnegie Foundation for the Advancement of Teaching. In 1985 its report indicated that "International/Global Education" requirements had increased to 14.6% of institutions, up from 4.5% in 1970; that in the same time period "Third World Studies" requirements were up from 2.9% to 7.9%, and "Women's Studies" requirements up from zero to 1.6% of institutions reporting (Carnegie Foundation for the Advancement of Teaching, 1992). For institutions planning or examining such requirements, the Denison experience may be helpful. Finally, an increasing number of institutions have devised, or are trying to develop, mandated core sequences, usually with a significant emphasis on aspects of "Western civilization." The studies we have just cited show an increase from 43.1% of institutions reporting in 1970, to 48.5% in 1985, to 53% in 1990 (Carnegie Foundation for the Advancement of Teaching, 1992; cf. Gaff & Wasescha, 1991). For the many colleges and universities moving in this direction, the debates at Stanford may prove relevant. In the remainder of this chapter, we will examine what seem to us some of the central tensions, perhaps even contradictions, that emerge in efforts to sustain or develop forms of core educational experience significantly inflected by multiculturalism.

MULTICULTURALISM AND CORE CURRICULA—TENSIONS AND POSSIBILITIES

An instructor from the Western civilization courses of 50 years ago coming to most of today's crop would be surprised, perhaps even shocked, to discover how little role history now plays. Where once "European history [was] the integrating discipline of general education programs" (Allardyce, 1982, p. 709), today's courses are organized mainly along thematic or conceptual lines, rather like those at the University of Chicago in the 1930s. There, "artistic works were studied not within the flux of historical change, where everything was relative to time and to place, but within genres, forms, or topics that were deemed to be timeless or recurring in human creative production" (p. 711). For example, an administrator at Fairleigh Dickinson University describes the rationale for Core II, "The American Experience: The Quest for Freedom," in the following terms:

In Core II, we begin with an analysis of the sacred texts of the American "Western Tradition": the Bill of Rights, the Declaration of Independence, the Gettysburg address, the Battle Hymn of the Republic, and King's "I Have a Dream" speech. As we read these works, we ask our students, who are "all men"? What is the basis of individual rights? Are we a religious people? What is the American dream and who is included in it? (cited in Schmitz, 1992a, p. 16).

Similarly, the University of Richmond's interdisciplinary core course is organized around themes such as "Moral Order," "Social Order," and "Familiar Order." The unit on "Social Order" brings together quite diverse texts—*Sundiata,* Mencius, Rousseau's *Discourse on the Origins of Inequality,* and Freud's *Civilization and Its Discontents* (Schmitz, 1992a)—necessarily removed from any deeply informative historical context (other similar strategies are illustrated in "Exploring the Complexities of Culture," 1991). It is not that history has disappeared, but as Betty Schmitz has put it, "nearly all the new courses [associated with the "Cultural Legacies" project of the Association of American Colleges] are interdisciplinary, based on primary texts, and thematically organized" (p. 41).

The contraction of the role of history in most Western civilization and similar mandated core courses has itself to be seen historically. Many of these programs have been supported and significantly encouraged by the National Endowment for the Humanities, the two most recent chairpersons of which have been strong partisans of a "great books" approach to core humanities study. That strategy poses the value of such texts precisely in their "universal" qualities, their ability to "transcend" the vagaries of time and place. They are best studied, therefore, "in their own terms" or, perhaps, in relation to other isolated texts; implied herein is a formalist methodology linked to a "great ideas" focus of the sort popularized by William Bennett (1984). The revival of historicized study in literature and the

arts, on the other hand, has not only been associated with Marxist and poststructuralist ideologies but has insisted on examining the "cultural work" that texts perform in specific historical moments. Indeed, "new historicists" argue that the very meaning of a text will *change* in changing circumstances; thus texts need to be "read" within the particular contexts they inhabit (Kennedy, 1991). The tension we are outlining is by no means new; Daniel Bell poses a similar conflict between history and analysis as one of three antinomies—the others are between past and present and between east and west—central to the future of liberal arts education (Bell, 1966). Both historicized and thematic study have their virtues and limitations: both can engage students, both can be superficial, though differently. But the choice between them is *not* ideologically neutral; on the contrary, it is a choice that may well have important ramifications for multicultural study.

Betty Schmitz (1992a) is concerned that

fewer institutions in the Cultural Legacies project—about 25 percent of the total—include or propose a required course on pluralism within the United States as part of the core. It may be easier and less threatening to engage difference at a distance—where it is expected and anticipated and where one has no permanent responsibility as a citizen—than at home. (p. 29)

She may well be right and may also be correct in seeing this phenomenon partly as a legacy of the history of general education programs. It is also true that programs grounded in the humanities, where the study of "monuments of unaging intellect" has been traditional, are less likely to focus on "social" issues such as difference than programs based in the social sciences, including history. Indeed, if one wishes to emphasize issues and problems of difference—multiculturalism, gender, sexual definition—in the core educational experience presented to students, as at the University of California, Berkeley, one is more likely to build courses around specific historical and social problems, as is illustrated by Ronald Takaki's (1991) course "Racial Inequality in America: A Comparative Historical Perspective" (cf. Wilkerson, 1992). Similarly, SUNY, Buffalo's sophomore-level course "American Pluralism and the Search for Equality," which deals with race, ethnicity, gender, class, and religion, uses readings such as speeches by Sojourner Truth and essays by Simone de Beauvoir and Studs Terkel ("Exploring the Complexities of Culture," 1991).

Along similar lines, Rockland (New York) Community College has adopted as a new graduation requirement for all A.A. degree students an approved three-credit "course on pluralism and diversity in America." The basic course designed to satisfy this requirement, "Pluralism and Diversity in America," is described in the catalog as follows:

Course designed to engage the student in the increasingly important issues of cultural, ethnic and racial diversity in America. The student will explore: acculturation; class; communication and the interrelationships between culture and language; cultural customs; family, gender and sexuality; heritage; race and ethnicity; religion and ideology; and stereotypes.

Most, though not all, of the readings are drawn from social science disciplines, and the frequently used videos focus on subjects such as "American Tongues," "Customs," "Gender," and "Racism 101." Whatever else is true about such a course, it represents an institutional commitment to a core of study significantly different from most of those gathered in the AAC's "Cultural Legacies" project. But this approach is not necessarily neutral either. The "Western heritage" can be universalized by devoting major institutional resources (and student time) to it in the form of studying presumably cosmic texts, existing in the grand isolation of an aesthetic empyrean; by contrast, the cultural heritage of "others" may be approached via social scientific analyses, which, by embedding them in particular societies and histories, implicitly deny their "universality" (cf. Schmitz, 1992b).

A historically organized "Survey of Western Civilization Since 1648" at William Patterson College presents something of a middle ground but also underlines the tensions we have been exploring. The instructor faced two problems in revising the course: how to "engage our students in a relationship with their collective past" (a telling variation from the traditional objectives of "Western Civilization") and how to integrate material on women and minorities into the course (Tirado, 1987). She noted that certain topics elicited high levels of participation among her often resentful (because the course is required), busy (because a large majority work 20 and more hours per week), heterogeneous, and poorly prepared students. These included "economic and social changes of European society," "the relationship between slavery and the Western economics," and "changes in women's roles and the character of the family" (p. 36). Retaining a familiar organization for the survey course, the instructor shifted significantly the questions she asked students to pursue. For example,

Traditionally, we ask what factors explain the Industrial Revolution's birth in England? Further, we ask what the relationship was between industrialization and the Agricultural Revolution, with its higher yields, enclosures, and the freeing of agricultural labor for incorporation into other sectors of the economy. But we may also ask what the links were between the slave trade and the English textile industry, the heart of the English Industrial Revolution. What were the implications of this first industrial revolution for the non-Western world? Nonwestern nations became providers of raw materials and labor and consumers of European manufactured goods. The textile industry benefitted from a seemingly ever-expanding market, which gave the impetus for further industrial growth. How were non-European countries, such as India, once a major producer of textiles, de-industrialized? Students were assigned essays on women's roles in the Industrial Revolution. Specifically, they were to analyze the separation between the public and private spheres and how that separation affected women's position in society. (p. 40)

In the course, students read a number of texts they might also have found in more traditional "great books" formats—Hobbes's *Leviathan,* Locke's "Treatise of Civil Government," Montesquieu's "Spirit of the Laws," Wollstonecraft's "Vindication of the Rights of Woman," *The Communist Manifesto,* excerpts from Ruskin's *Sesame and Lillies.* But these were encountered in a changed intellectual framework that reflected the desire of state education authorities to encourage a "gender perspective" in traditional courses (Braun, 1987).

Coming from a traditionally defined discipline, this course evokes questions similar to those raised above about the tension between thematic and historicized organizational principles, and the relationship of this problem to including multicultural and gender concerns. It suggests that the issue can be less—or, at any rate, not only—the texts themselves than the structures within which they are framed. Mount Holyoke's "Pasts and Presences in the West" explores classical texts and "Western heritages as a series of problems and values to be analyzed and reinterpreted, not as a sequence of ideas and institutions," nor as a set of sacred documents. Thus it used Adrienne Rich's "Toward a Woman-Centered University" and David Tracy's *Plurality and Ambiguity* to introduce a unit on the ancient Greeks that presents Herodotus, Thucydides, and *Antigone* as performing significant cultural work in 5th-century Athens—and today ("Exploring the Complexities of Culture," 1991, p. 47).

A related set of concerns arises in the tensions between focusing on the "West" and on the world ("Exploring the Complexities of Culture," 1991). Betty Schmitz (1992b) has cogently analyzed the problematics of many of even the best-intentioned strategies for relating Western cultural and political traditions to those of "others." Rigidly distinguishing "West" and "non-West" will very likely establish the kind of hierarchy generally implicit in such binaries (and falsify continuing cultural interactions) as well as the separation between "we" and "they" inimical to serious study of non-Western or minority cultures. Similarly, viewing other cultures only, or primarily, within the frameworks established for the study of the West can seriously misrepresent "others" or reduce them to points of contrast for illuminating—and implicitly validating—Western norms. Stating the problems and sensitizing planners to them do not, however, guarantee solutions, for as the Stanford example suggests, deeply held political and personal systems of value are involved. More to the point, perhaps, few educational tasks are finally more difficult—or more vital—than learning to see one's own culture from another; these are, one might argue, the end points rather than the beginnings of curriculum.

The issue may be rooted in where one begins core experiences, institutionally and personally. The approach of one of the colleges in the Engaging Cultural Legacies project, LeMoyne-Owen, illustrates this point. There "students begin by examining the African and African American heritage in a yearlong interdisciplinary course, historical in approach; the course explores African roots, diaspora, and the varied experiences of Africans in the western hemisphere." Starting in the sophomore year, students then look at other major civilizations, "beginning with Egypt and Mesopotomia" (Schmitz, 1992a, p. 26). An analogous strategy seems to be implicit in Fisk's humanities sequence, which begins with "The African American Heritage" and later uses that, in part, to compare "classic texts from the Greek and Roman empire and from various religious traditions . . . with works by African Americans"—for example, Plato's *Apology, Crito,* and *Phaedo* with Martin Luther King, Jr.'s "Letters from the Birmingham Jail" ("Exploring the Complexities of Culture," 1991). These programs may be taken to engage the debate over Afrocentric curricular approaches (Asante & Ravitch, 1991; Petrie, 1991). These have often been criticized as ahistorical and exaggerated, and no doubt some are. On the other hand, Orlando Patterson (1991) has proposed that African American history vitally recapitulates the core experiences of Western civilization. Rooted in slavery—as in Athens and Rome central to economic and political development—African American culture has been energized, as in the classical period among slaves and their descendants, by the struggle for freedom. According to Patterson, the result—again in ways deeply similar to what occurred in the classical and Renaissance Italian states—has been a transformation of both the slaves' and the masters' cultures (Patterson, 1991). Like the LeMoyne-Owen course, Patterson's paradigm is suggestive of what may be perceived by placing multicultural experiences at the center rather than at the margins of study.

Still, given the emphasis recent core curriculum planners have placed on local circumstances and particular bodies of students, programs such as those at LeMoyne-Owen and Fisk may be confronted with the question of whether they are appropriate only to a traditionally Black college. One might ask in response whether they could, in fact, be even more important to schools whose predominantly White student bodies are apt to be largely ignorant of African and African American cultures and histories. More generally, should core sequences be designed differently for different student bodies, or should students, however diverse, be expected to adapt themselves to core curricula designed, like the Hobart and William Smith course described earlier or Columbia's Contemporary Civilization (Bell, 1966), to communicate an institution's vision of a collective legacy? That "there is no one right answer to such questions" is a truism that does not mitigate the tensions the questions produce in any effort to design a core sequence that honestly grapples with cultural multiplicity and difference.

These questions, in fact, evoke a critical antinomy: whether one formulates a core experience from "what we wish students to learn" or from "who the students are," a version of "Do we teach bodies of knowledge or people?" To be sure, these are hardly independent variables, but they lead in somewhat different directions, especially if a main concern—as it needs to be—is classroom dynamics. The work of Frances Maher and Mary Kay Tetreault (e.g., Maher, 1987; Maher & Tetreault, 1994) strongly suggests that the single most dominant factor in shaping patterns of classroom discussion is the mix (or relative uniformity) of people *in* the classroom. Thus "who the students are" emerges with the texts and structures of curriculum as critical to learning. For example, it is certainly desirable for an institution to consider its location and its constituency in planning the kinds of core experiences it wishes to provide. As two successful core planners correctly put it, "the search for a universal core curriculum, we believe, is a quixotic quest. Today's core curriculum must be rooted in each college's own academic focus, its special approach to the world, and the kind of students it enrolls" (Campbell & Flynn, 1990, p. 10). But at some point, what seems locally engaging and happily familiar to students can become what is parochial. Indeed, the Denison example suggests the importance of challenging a local institutional culture precisely for the sake of gender and racial equity.

These are not abstract issues, especially at institutions in which students have increasingly come to be aware of the "subject positions" through which they encounter readings and dis-

cussions. For here the issue is often not multiculturalism as distanced by texts, but racial, ethnic, and gender tensions in the real space called a classroom. In certain respects, as a number of core participants have noted, the departure of faculty members from their home disciplines into the less-known territory of core curricula turns them from expert instructors into co-learners with their students. In this new position, faculty *can* become more open to collaborative learning endeavors with their students (Wilkerson, 1992), and these, the research suggests, can be particularly fruitful (Goodsell, Maher, & Tinto, 1992). Likewise, when instructors move from positions of expertise into collaboration, they may be more inclined to replace traditional classroom hierarchies with more "open-ended" pedagogies (Wilkerson, 1992). Indeed, Astin's (1993) findings suggest that "how the students *approach* general education (and how the faculty actually *deliver* the curriculum) is far more important than the formal curricular content and structure" (p. 425).

At the same time, a classroom significantly engaged with multicultural and gender issues *can* be a tense, even a repressed location, especially when unexamined racial, ethnic, gender, and *class* differences exist between teacher and students or among the students themselves. In such a context, as Teresa McKenna suggested at the 1993 seminar on multicultural literature at Pennsylvania State University, difference itself needs to become the source of commonality among classroom participants and the differences in subject position the subject matter, in some degree, of classroom as well as out-of-class discussion. Then, however—particularly in heavily structured core courses mandating set curricula—one encounters the ongoing imperatives of syllabi: If exposure to a set of common texts lies at the heart of the syllabus, one cannot but be caught up in the tension between covering what is laid out *there* as distinct from focusing on what is going on *here* in the classroom.

One needs, in addition, to account for Astin's finding that what he calls a "true-core" curriculum (in which all students take exactly the same courses) is the only one among general education programs that appears to have any significant effects on student cognitive or affective behavior (Astin, 1993). Astin suggests that the "beneficial effects of true-core curriculum may be mediated by the peer group" (p. 425), an impact he attributes to how common experiences can spark student discussions *out* of class and provide intellectual bases for peer bonding. Ironically, a major source of student discussion out of class appears to be comparison of how instructors present the same material, which, if so, may tend to push faculty back toward more presentational modes, in the tradition of the Harvard general education approach (Bell, 1966). More important, perhaps, common *multicultural* experiences in core programs provide distinctively valuable sources of bonding, animated discussion, and shared work in an institution committed to equity, as the early years of the Denison experience suggest.

One final set of tensions, also related to this finding, concerns the relative value of diffuse as distinct from highly focused models of core curricula. The virtues of the tight, "true-core" model is apparent in Astin's findings. The value of more and less diffuse models may be harder to establish. We have pointed to a number of these in connection with the Denison case: for example, diffusion of concern for equity issues among departments. The Pennsylvania State University "cultural diversity" requirement offers certain other values. In the first place, its statement of purpose, widely disseminated in a booklet listing courses that fulfill the requirement and distributed to all students statewide, declares as an institutional goal that

Every United States citizen should understand both the progress made in eliminating discrimination and prejudice from our society and the gaps between national ideas and national performance. Diversity courses consider: (1) the concerns and contributions of women and minorities (defined by race, ethnicity, religion, and sexual orientation), and (2) a national need for more tolerant cooperation within a complex and increasingly global community.

A participant in the Faculty Senate debate over the requirement framed other of its uses this way: "A requirement underscores the value of a category of learning. It directs students to a wide range of clearly important areas of study. It promotes course development. It feeds information and ideas into the intellectual life of the campus."

To be sure, the category of "diversity focused" courses is rather loosely drawn: The courses listed in Penn State's 1991–92 brochure include, for example, "Rape and Sexual Violence," "Arts of Africa, Oceania, and Indian America," "Gender and Geography," and "Cultural Aspects of Food." Such courses, to be sure, satisfy quite different student needs and intellectual purposes; drawn together under a single rubric—"diversity"—they may suggest a lack of definition, a politics of low-level inclusion. These courses can be taken to illustrate how widely some degree of interest in diversity issues has spread through the university; but they can also be seen as confirming Astin's finding that the existence of such courses seems to breed "mistrust in the administration." He asks, do students think "that the faculty and administrators in these institutions have attempted to mollify student dissent by authorizing the inclusion of many such courses?" (Astin, 1993, p. 333). More tightly drawn requirements and curricula, especially those that engage the volatile category of "diversity," encounter resistance based on faculty autonomy and departmental authority; loosely defined categories are able to win majorities but may sacrifice real impact on student intellectual and emotional development.

NEW DIRECTIONS

That lack of impact seems to us a critical problem, for colleges and universities have, we believe, lost substantial cultural authority in the recent decade. Increasingly, students gain a sense of the world from the entertainment industry, the mass media, and other commercial institutions. They see reflected in these what they infrequently find examined in the university—even in relatively innovative global cultures programs ("Exploring the Complexities of Culture," 1991): "the experience of profound unsettlement," the violence attendant on the vast migrations of people, the breaking down of existing borders and categories, the increasing creolization of global mass culture.

"Such experience," Michael Geyer (1993) has written, "requires the study of unsettlement, rather than settlement" (p. 553). A multicultural general education able to engage what students now experience and to enable them to function as rational and cooperative human beings in the next century will, he argues,

need to overcome the limits of civilization—and settlement-bound approaches, whether they argue for civilization writ large or for plural civilizations as autonomous units of identity. Rather than concentrating on the achievements of settlement, we should keep our eyes open for regions, times, and peoples of unsettlement, for the ceaseless struggle to think and create orders and to provide meanings. (p. 533)

Geyer's proposal may be seen as a challenge to virtually all current core curricula, and especially those on Western cultures, which do tend to focus on the moments in which settled societies flower in "classic" written texts. His idea of concentrating on "unsettlement" adds a further set of conflicting priorities to efforts to design any core curriculum, particularly one that takes multiculturalism seriously.

In pointing to such conflicts, our purpose is not to cast a pall over the effort to link core curricular experiences and multiculturalism. Rather, we wish to aid practitioners in approaching this conflicted task with open eyes. In fact, from our perspective, few missions in higher education are more vital to regaining vitality in and some of the lost authority of higher education. Our reading of the literature suggests a number of conclusions about the most useful ways of bringing multiculturalism and core curricula together.

First, institutionwide core requirements, like that at Denison, focused on domestic multicultural issues can produce changes in campus culture and departmental priorities. To be sure, students tend to resist additional requirements, but it is not clear how deeply that resistance runs, especially if students are directly involved in the formulation of such new programs. Similarly, the professional basis of faculty resistance to general education needs to be respected. At the same time, material aid to faculty in changing what they teach and concrete rewards for such change can turn resistance into its opposite (Wilkerson, 1992). In this connection, it is vital to recognize—as the wide adoption of *The Heath Anthology of American Literature* suggests and as the enthusiasm for its use confirms—that multicultural teaching and scholarship can be enormously rewarding for faculty, providing they have time for study, opportunities in conferences, seminars, and institutes to interact with colleagues, and access to new books and journals. Moreover, the pedagogical implications of multicultural syllabi need to be taken seriously and the study of collaborative learning, flexible classroom arrangements, and other departures fostered *within* academic communities often indifferent to such "educational" issues; in fact, there is increasing evidence from conference programs in the humanities that such pedagogical study is increasingly popular.

Second, the Stanford experience suggests the need for honest debate about the political issues underlying educational departures such as multiculturalism. While some differences are not likely to be resolved, at least a level of civil discourse, important to establishing community on campus, can be modeled. Moreover, multiculturalism, as we have suggested, cannot be divorced from issues of difference, not just in appearance or food or customs, but of power.

Finally, it might be asked, aren't these prescriptions, however seemingly modest, altogether Utopian at a time in which higher education is under the severest fiscal constraints yet and has, not coincidentally, lost much of its cultural and civil authority? The Denison experience shows that meaningful multicultural departures can be accomplished without significant outside funding. That does not mean that changing patterns of curricula and scholarship come free. Institutions do need, in one or another form, to *invest* their resources if they wish to respond to changing intellectual priorities and help shape a multicultural future. It may well be the case that such a path is the only one, in a radically changed world, that might lead to reestablishing the cultural authority that universities should ideally wield and that democratic education seems to us to require.

REFERENCES

Allardyce, G. (1982). The rise and fall of the Western civilization course. *American Historical Review, 87,* 695–725.

Asante, M. K., & Ravitch, D. (1991). Multiculturalism: An exchange. *American Scholar, 60,* 267–277.

Association of American Colleges (1985). *Integrity in the college curriculum: A report to the academic community.* Washington, DC: Author.

Astin, A. W. (1993). *What matters in college? Four critical years revisited.* San Francisco: Jossey-Bass.

Banks, J. A., & Banks, C. A. M. (Eds.). (1993). *Multicultural education: Issues and perspectives* (2nd ed.). Boston: Allyn and Bacon.

Bell, D. (1966). *The reforming of general education: The Columbia College experience in its national setting.* New York: Columbia University Press.

Bennett, W. (1984). *To reclaim a legacy: A report on the humanities in higher education.* Washington, DC: National Endowment for the Humanities.

Bisesi, M. (1982). Historical developments in American undergraduate education: General education and the core curriculum. *British Journal of Educational Studies, 30,* 199–212.

Bloom, A. (1987). *The closing of the American mind.* New York: Simon & Schuster.

Bossman, D. M. (1991). Cross-cultural values for a pluralistic core curriculum. *Journal of Higher Education, 62,* 661–681.

Boyer, E. L., & Levine, A. (1981). *A quest for common learning.* Washington, DC: Carnegie Foundation for the Advancement of Teaching.

Brann, E. T. H. (1993). The canon defended. *Philosophy and Literature, 17,* 193–218.

Braun, R. J. (1987, February 15). State aims at "gender perspective" in public, private college courses. *Newark Star-Ledger.*

Butler, J. E., & Walter, J. C. (Eds.). (1991). *Transforming the curriculum: Ethnic studies and women's studies.* Albany: State University of New York Press.

Campbell, J., & Flynn, T. (1990). Can colleges go back to a core curriculum? *Planning for Higher Education, 19,* 9–15.

Carnegie Foundation for the Advancement of Teaching. (1992). Signs of a changing curriculum. *Change, 24,* 50–52.

Carnochan, W. B. (1993). *The battleground of the curriculum: Liberal education and American experience.* Stanford: Stanford University Press.

The changing curriculum: Then and now. (1991). *Partisan Review, 58,* 249–281.

Ch'maj, B. E. M. (Ed.). (1993). *Multicultural America: A resource book for teachers of humanities and American studies—Syllabi, essays, projects, bibliography.* Lanham, MD: University Press of America.

Cheny, L. V. (1989). *50 hours: A core curriculum for college students.* Washington, DC: National Endowment for the Humanities.

Culley, M., & Portuges, C. (Eds.). (1985). *Gendered subjects: The dynamics of feminist teaching.* Boston: Routledge and Kegan Paul.

Dinnerstein, M., O'Donnell, S. R., & MacCorquodale, P. (1981). *Integrating women's studies in to the curriculum: A report to the Association of American Colleges on the SIROW conference "Integrating women's studies into the liberal arts curriculum" (Princeton, NJ, August 27–30).* Tuscon: Southwest Institute for Research on Women.

Exploring the complexities of culture. (1991). *Liberal Education, 77,* 40–60.

Flacks, R. (1971). *Youth and social change.* Chicago: Markham.

Fox-Genovese, E., & Stuard, S. M. (1983). *Restoring women to history: Materials for Western civilization I and II* (2 vols.). Bloomington, IN: Organization of American Historians.

Gaff, J. G. (1992). Beyond politics: The educational issues inherent in multicultural education. *Change, 24,* 31–35.

Gaff, J. G., & Wasescha, A. (1991). Assessing the reform of general education. *JGE: The Journal of General Education, 40,* 51–68.

Gappa, J. M., & Pearce, J. (no date). *Sex and gender in the social sciences: Reassessing the introductory course* (3 vols.) (Sociology, Psychology, Microeconomics). Washington, DC: American Sociological Association/American Psychological Association. San Francisco: Judith Gappa.

General Education in a Free Society. (1945). Cambridge: Harvard University Press.

Geyer, M. (1993). Multiculturalism and the politics of general education. *Critical Inquiry, 19,* 499–533.

Goodsell, A., Mahes, M., Tinto, V., with Smith, B. L., & MacGregor, J. (1992). *Collaborative learning: A sourcebook for higher education.* Syracuse: National Center on Postsecondary Teaching, Learning and Assessment.

Gruber, C. S. (1975). *Mars and Minerva: World War I and the uses of higher learning in America.* Baton Rouge: Louisiana State University Press.

Hall, J. W., & Kevles, B. L. (1982). The social imperatives for curricular change in higher education. In J. W. Hall & B. L. Kevles (Eds.), *Opposition to core curriculum: Alternative models for undergraduate education* (pp. 13–38). Westport, CT: Greenwood Press.

Hitchens, C. (1988, March 4–10). Whose culture, what civilization? *Times Literary Supplement, 4431,* p. 246.

Hook, S. (1989). Curricular politics. *Partisan Review, 56,* 201–213.

Howe, F., & Lauter, P. (1980). *The impact of women's studies on the campus and the disciplines.* Washington, DC: National Institute of Education.

Jones, E. A., & Ratcliff, J. L. (1991). Which general education curriculum is better: Core curriculum or the distributional requirement? *JGE: The Journal of General Education, 40,* 70–101.

Kaplan, M. (1982). The wrong solution to the right problem. In J. W. Hall

& B. L. Kevles (Eds.), *Opposition to core curriculum: Alternative models for undergraduate education* (pp. 3–12). Westport, CT: Greenwood Press.

Kennedy, A. (1991). Memory and values: Disengaging cultural legacies. *Liberal Education, 77,* 34–39.

Kerr, C. (1964). *The uses of the university.* Cambridge: Harvard University Press.

Lauter, P. (Ed.). (1983). *Reconstructing American literature: Courses, syllabi, issues.* Old Westbury, NY: Feminist Press.

Lauter, P. (1991). *Canons and contexts.* New York: Oxford University Press.

Lauter, P., Bruce-Novoa, J., Bryer, J., Hedges, E., Ling, A., Littlefield, D. F., Jr., Martin, W., Molesworth, C., Mulford, C., Paredes, R., Spillers, H., Wagner-Martin, L., Wiget, A., & Yarborough, R. (Eds.). (1990). *The Heath anthology of American literature* (2 vols.). Lexington, MA: D. C. Heath.

Levine, A., & Cureton, J. (1992). The quiet revolution: Eleven facts about multiculturalism and the curriculum. *Change, 24,* 25–29.

Long, P. (Ed.). (1969). *The new left: A collection of essays.* Boston: Porter Sargent.

Maher, F. (1987). Toward a richer theory of feminist pedagogy. *Journal of Education, 169,* 91–99.

Maher, F., & Tetreault, M. K. T. (1994). *The feminist classroom.* New York: Basic Books.

McNeill, W. H. (1977). Beyond Western civilization: Rebuilding the survey. *History Teacher, 10,* 509–515.

McNew, J. (1992). Whose politics? Media distortions of academic controversies. *Virginia Quarterly Review, 68,* 1–23.

McQuillen, J. S. (1992). Role models in education: Their relation to students' perceived competence, stress and satisfaction. *Education, 112,* 403–407.

Montalto, N. V. (1982). *A history of the intercultural educational movement, 1924–1941.* New York: Garland.

Musil, C. M. (Ed.). (1992). *The courage to question: Women's studies and student learning.* Washington, DC: Association of American Colleges and National Women's Studies Association.

National Institute of Education. (1984). *Involvement in learning: Realizing the potential of American higher education.* Washington, DC: Author.

Nelson, C. (1993). Multiculturalism without guarantees: From anthologies to the social text. *Journal of the Midwest Modern Language Association, 26,* 47–57.

Nordquist, J. (1992). *The multicultural education debate in the university: A bibliography.* Santa Cruz, CA: Reference and Research Service.

Organization of American Historians. (1984). *Restoring women to history: Teaching packets for integrating women into United States history* (2 vols.). Bloomington, IN: Author.

Organization of American Historians. (1988). *Restoring women to history: Packets for integrating women's history into courses on Africa, Asia, Latin America, the Caribbean, and the Middle East,* Bloomington, IN: Author.

Patterson, O. (1991). *Freedom in the making of Western culture.* New York: Basic Books.

Petrie, P. (1991, August). Afrocentrism in a multicultural democracy. *American Visions,* pp. 20–26.

Phillips, W. (Ed.). (1988). Stanford documents. *Partisan Review, 55,* 653–674.

Pratt, M. L. (1990). Humanities for the future: Reflections on the Western culture debate at Stanford. *South Atlantic Quarterly, 89,* 7–25.

President's Commission on Higher Education. (1947). *Higher education for American democracy.* Washington, DC: U.S. Government Printing Office.

Ravitch, D. (1990). Multiculturalism: E pluribus plures. *American Scholar, 59,* 337–354.

Robinson, J. H. (1926). *The ordeal of civilization.* New York: Harper and Brothers.

Rosovsky, H. (1978, February 15). Report on the core curriculum. Memorandum to Harvard Faculty of Arts and Sciences.

Rudolph, F. (1962). *The American college and university.* New York: Vintage.

Rudolph, F. (1977). *Curriculum: A history of the American undergraduate course of study since 1636.* San Francisco: Jossey-Bass.

Schlesinger, A. M., Jr. (1991). *The disuniting of America.* Knoxville: Whittle Direct Books.

Schmitz, B. (1992a). *Core curriculum and cultural pluralism: A guide for campus planners.* Washington, DC: Association of American Colleges.

Schmitz, B. (1992b). Cultural pluralism and core curricula. In M. Adams (Ed.), *Promoting diversity in college classrooms: Innovative responses for the curriculum, faculty, and institutions* (pp. 61–69). San Francisco: Jossey-Bass.

Spanier, B., Bloom, A., & Boroviak, D. (eds.). (1984). *Toward a balanced curriculum: A sourcebook for initiating gender integration projects.* Cambridge: Schenkman.

Spelman, E. V. (1988). *Inessential woman: Problems of exclusion in feminist thought.* Boston: Beacon Press.

Spurr, S. (1970). *Academic degree structures: Innovative approaches.* New York: McGraw-Hill.

Takaki, R. (1991). The value of multiculturalism. *Liberal Education, 77,* 8–10.

Talburtt, M. A., et al. (1988). *Including women in the curriculum: A study of strategies that make it happen.* Ann Arbor: Formative Evaluation Research Associates.

Thomas (Rosenstock), M. (1991). *Gender, race, and the curriculum: The Western culture controversy at Stanford.* Unpublished manuscript.

Tirado, I. A. (1987). Integrating issues of gender in the survey of Western civilization since 1648. In *Initiating curriculum transformation in the humanities: Integrating women and issues of race and gender.* Wayne, NJ: William Patterson College.

Toombs, W., Amey, M. J., & Chen, A. (1991). General education: An analysis of contemporary practice. *JGE: Journal of General Education, 40,* 102–118.

Wilkerson, M. (1992). Beyond the graveyard: Engaging faculty involvement. *Change, 24,* 59–63.

Yarmolinsky, A. (1992). Loose canons: Multiculturalism and humanities 101. *Change, 24,* 6–9, 74–75.

43

MULTICULTURAL TEACHER EDUCATION:
RESEARCH, PRACTICE, AND POLICY

Gloria Ladson-Billings

UNIVERSITY OF WISCONSIN, MADISON

Even if we are successful in increasing the percentage of teachers of color from the projected 5% in [the year] 2000 to 15%, 85% of the nation's teachers will still be white, mainstream and largely female working with students who differ from them racially, culturally, and in social class status. Thus an effective teacher education policy for the 21st century must include as a major focus the education of all teachers, including teachers of color, in ways that will help them receive the knowledge, skills, and attitudes needed to work effectively with students from diverse racial, ethnic, and social class groups. (Banks, 1991, pp. 135–136)

REAL REFORM OR RHETORIC?

The 1980s ushered in an era of educational reform. The often-cited Commission on Excellence in Education report, *A Nation at Risk* (1983), alerted the world to the failings of education in the United States. Within three years there appeared a second wave of reform documents, aimed at addressing the shortcomings of the nation's teachers.

At the same time these reform reports were proliferating, the demographic landscape of the nation was undergoing dramatic shifts. Students of color would come to represent 30% of our public schools (Banks, 1991). The nation's 20 largest school districts would report that students of color were 70% of their total school enrollment (Center for Education Statistics, 1987).

However, in the two most prominent reports addressing the crises in teaching, *Teachers for Tomorrow's Schools* (Holmes Group, 1986) and *A Nation Prepared: Teachers for the 21st Century* (Carnegie Forum on Education and the Economy, 1986), these demographic changes and the need to address issues of equity and diversity received only cursory attention (Gordon, 1988; Grant & Gillette, 1987). More interested in increasing the number of minorities entering the profession, the reform movement seems to have ignored the need for teachers,

regardless of their racial, ethnic, or cultural background, to address the needs of *all* students (regardless of racial, ethnic, or cultural background).

The failure of the major reform efforts to acknowledge the multicultural needs of tomorrow's teachers is illustrative of the marginal status that issues of multicultural education and multicultural teacher education typically receive (Gordon, 1991). More specifically, Gordon asserts:

Teachers and the teacher education field are in need of a fundamental critique of how they look at, interpret, and assist people of color in the educational process. Such a critique will require fundamental shifts in the frameworks through which teachers view themselves and others in the world, not only in the paradigms they employ and validate in their teachings, but also in a willingness to acknowledge the credibility of other perspectives, particularly those that challenge comfortable, long held assumptions. (p. 20)

It is with Gordon's notion of fundamental paradigmatic shifts in mind that this chapter attempts to reexamine the literature of multicultural teacher education. The sections of this chapter discuss four areas: (a) the state of teacher education; (b) issues of quantity versus quality in the multicultural teacher education literature; (c) issues and trends in the most recent literature; and (d) assessments about the current "wisdom of practice" (Shulman, 1987).

In addressing the first issue, the chapter suggests that teacher education is problematic and that it is impossible to decontextualize multicultural teacher education (i.e., problems of multicultural education are related to problems in teacher education).

In examining the second issue the chapter revisits the seminal work of previous multicultural teacher educators to raise questions about the growth of the field and the quality of that growth. The third issue provides an opportunity to examine the most recent literature in multicultural teacher education and identify the emerging trends and patterns this literature suggests.

In examining the current literature the chapter attempts to situate the multicultural teacher education literature in the dimensions of the multicultural education paradigm outlined by Banks (1993). Thus, the chapter categorizes the multicultural teacher education literature as it addresses content integration, knowledge construction, prejudice reduction, equity pedagogy, an empowering school community, and combinations of these dimensions.

Gollnick (1991) used the typologies of Lynch (1986) and Sleeter and Grant (1987) to examine multicultural teacher education programs. Lynch's typology addresses ideological positions that influence aspects of multicultural education. These ideological positions are "economic," "democratic," and "interdependent." They affect the values, knowledge, structures, and social controls of community, state, and national policies. Sleeter and Grant's (1987) review of the multicultural education literature identifies five approaches—teaching the exceptional and culturally different, human relations, single group studies, multicultural education, and education that is multicultural and social reconstructionist.

The decision to use Banks's typology is not a rejection of the scholarship of Lynch or Sleeter and Grant. Lynch's work helps us to see the broad underlying ideological notions that drive particular multicultural education approaches. Sleeter and Grant's important derivative categories help us to make assessments about the state of much of the mainstream multicultural education literature. However, Banks's work is a significant rethinking of ideology and practice.

Thus, this chapter is an attempt to reconceptualize multicultural teacher education to address the linkages between theory and practice and to suggest that by using this frame we have the opportunity to include literature outside the mainstream multicultural paradigm. Also, the chapter uses Banks's typology because it represents multicultural (teacher) education not as a compensatory but as a scholarly field of inquiry (Swartz, 1991).

Given the storm of attacks on multiculturalism and multicultural education (see, for example, Bloom, 1987; D'Souza, 1991; Ravitch, 1990; Schlesinger, 1992), it is important to place this discussion on firm intellectual ground. Too much of the discourse about multicultural education has been situated in the language of deficit and lack of academic achievement. Thus, both practitioners and scholars who are unfamiliar with the multicultural theoretical and conceptual literature discuss terms such as *at-risk* and *low achieving* interchangeably with *multicultural education*.

The Banks typology provides a scholarly and critical lens through which to evaluate the most recent literature on multicultural teacher education. It also provides a way to make some predictive statements about the progress of multicultural teacher education vis-à-vis multicultural theory and conceptualization.

Finally, the fourth issue argues for a "wisdom of practice" that is being created and defined by individual programs and teacher educators and may form the basis for widespread replication and experimentation in multicultural teacher education.

This chapter reviews some of the research on alternative program strategies for multicultural teacher education.

Zeichner's (1992) review of the literature on educating teachers for diversity examined programs that employ either biography, attitudinal change, diverse field experiences, or increased cultural knowledge as key features of teacher education. In reexamining this literature this chapter attempts to honor the "credibility of other perspectives" (Gordon, 1991, p. 20) and broaden the range of scholarly possibilities that may contribute to an intellectually viable and reinvigorated field of multicultural teacher education.

By examining the wisdom of practice this chapter will address the social-action and critical-consciousness aspects of multicultural education that typically have been neglected in multicultural teacher education programs. Thus, this chapter takes a position about the *kind* of multicultural teacher education that represents "best practices" (Grant, 1992a).

MAKING TEACHER EDUCATION PROBLEMATIC

The space allotted this chapter does not allow for a comprehensive discussion of teacher education. However, it is important to understand multicultural teacher education vis-à-vis teacher education; that is, it makes little sense to talk about multicultural teacher education without situating it in understandings about teacher education.

Critiques of teacher education are not new (see, for example, Conant, 1963; Sarason, Davidson, & Blatt, 1962). However, more recent critiques (Goodlad, 1990; Herbst, 1989; Sarason, Davidson, & Blatt, 1986) suggest that we continue to grapple with the same issues rather than achieve solutions to some problems and move on to new ones.

Goodlad's (1990) study of teacher education revealed that teacher education suffered from low prestige and low status, an unclear mission and identity, faculty disquietude, an ill-defined body of study, and program incoherence. While each of these has some relation to multicultural teacher education, clearly the last—program incoherence—has direct bearing on the state (and status) of multicultural teacher education.

Goodlad suggests that "the constraints of misguided regulatory intrusions and lack of educational control of or influence over bureaucratically established traditional school practices" (1990, p. 189) add additional limitations to a field that is demoralized by its low prestige, lack of rewards, heavy teaching loads, and weak professional socialization processes. These "misguided regulatory intrusions" mean that schools, colleges, and departments of education are increasingly at the whim of state legislatures and state departments of education when it comes to deciding what should make up the teacher education curriculum. Thus, schools struggling with how to develop a more multicultural teacher education program become frustrated with the myriad of new (and constantly changing) state requirements.

What results from this program incoherence is a desertion of committed scholars from teacher preparation to graduate studies. This means that the intellectual base for multicultural teacher education is eroded and left to an occasional course on "human relations" or ethnic studies.

Thus, if teacher education is fraught with these issues and challenges, we cannot disentangle them from *multicultural* teacher education. Indeed, we must add to these the unique challenges of multicultural education, which include a lack of definitional clarity (Sleeter & Grant, 1987), student resistance to multicultural knowledge and issues (Ahlquist, 1991; King & Ladson-Billings, 1990), and political attacks on and distortion of multicultural education (Bloom, 1987; D'Souza, 1991; Schlesinger, 1992).

The responsibility of multicultural teacher education, then, is to ensure that it is placed squarely within the debate about teacher education in general. Consequently, reforms and changes in teacher education must by definition include reforms and changes in multicultural teacher education and vice versa.

While Goodlad's work reflects the results of an empirical study, it does not address the philosophical or theoretical platform on which various teacher education programs rest. Zeichner and Liston (1990) suggest that four traditions of practice dominate teacher education in the 20th century. Careful not to presume that actual teacher education programs operate within neat and discrete traditions, Zeichner (1991) suggests that the traditions are useful paradigms for understanding the guiding principles of particular programs:

The four traditions of practice in twentieth century U.S. teacher education that we think are represented in all teacher education programs are: (1) an *academic* tradition that emphasizes teachers' knowledge of subject matter and their ability to transform that subject matter to promote student understanding; (2) a *social efficiency* tradition that emphasizes teachers' abilities to thoughtfully apply a "knowledge base" about teaching that has been generated through research on teaching; (3) a *developmentalist* tradition that stresses teachers' abilities to base their instruction on their direct knowledge of their students—their current understandings of the content under study and their developmental readiness for particular activities; and (4) a *social reconstructionist* tradition that emphasizes teachers' abilities to see the social and political implication of their actions and to assess their actions and the social contexts in which they are carried out, for their contribution to greater equality, justice, and humane conditions in schooling and society. (p. 4)

Each of these traditions could be said to have multicultural implications: the academic tradition on the basis of the academic content that is included (and excluded); the social efficiency tradition because of our understandings of culturally specific pedagogies (see, for example, Au & Jordan, 1981; Ladson-Billings, 1992b; Mohatt & Erickson, 1981); the developmentalist tradition because of our concern for *when* and whether to address issues of prejudice, discrimination, and racism in classroom learning (see Ladson-Billings, 1992a; Paley, 1979). However, the *social reconstructionist* tradition is explicit in its multicultural (and social justice) relevance. Thus, how we understand the philosophy and purposes of a multicultural teacher education program requires the understanding of teacher education in general at specific institutions. For example, a program may require prospective teachers to take a number of courses in the history and culture of various groups. These may be high-quality courses that bring new perspectives to students' knowledge and understanding of people of color. Nevertheless, the inclusion of these courses may represent the overall academic tradition of the teacher education program. Or, these same courses might be required in a program that generally subscribes to a developmentalist tradition.

The connection between the "multicultural knowledge" that students experience and how it is applied and used in the classroom may not be strong or made clear. What becomes important in these instances is whether multicultural aspects of the certification drive or are driven by the program.

The social reconstructionist tradition attempts to promote in teachers a disposition toward opposing inequity, not just celebrating diversity. This means that the teacher education experiences must develop prospective teachers' critical abilities, their abilities to critique education—their own and their students'. The social reconstructionist position also means that teacher preparation must equip prospective teachers to "challenge established practices, institutions, and ways of thinking and conceive new and alternative possibilities" (Pai, 1990, p. 145). These challenges include confronting forms of oppression and domination, broadly construed—for example, racism, sexism, classism, and ableism.

However, if we believe Goodlad and his associates (see Edmundson, 1990; Sirotnik, 1990; Su, 1990), most prospective U.S. teachers are not participating in a social reconstructionist teacher education program (also see Gay, 1986). Thus, the "multicultural" aspect of their teacher preparation is likely to be in the form of an individual course or other add-on component. This approach of providing single, isolated courses is more likely to make the courses seem to be additional institutional hoops through which the students must jump in order to receive teacher certification. The students and the institution are tacitly, but not so subtly, saying that multicultural concerns are not *real* concerns of teaching and learning (see, for example, Rothenberg, 1988).

In addition to challenges and problems related to the structure of teacher education, the nature and background of who goes into teaching is important also. Grant (1989) suggests that the typical teacher candidate is most likely to be "a white female whose first choice for a teaching assignment [is] a suburban school" (p. 765). Haberman (1989) documents the lack of minority teacher candidates in the educational pipeline, and suggests the training of "adults" as teachers:

Whereas now the emphasis is on teacher training for college-age youth, with approximately 20 percent of the students being "older" adults (usually called special certification students or denigrated as "retreads"), I propose that the emphasis be reversed so that the majority of trainees would be adults and the exceptions (up to 20 percent) might be those young people who really have achieved the personal identity and level of experience needed to prepare for teaching. (Haberman, 1991, p. 277)

Unfortunately, other research indicates that age and maturity may not be adequate for preparing teachers for the multicultural classroom. Winfield (1986) documented that, despite their years of service and experience, many teachers hold negative beliefs toward academically at-risk youngsters in urban classrooms. More recently, Lipman (1993) found that school-level efforts at "restructuring" may have little or no impact on teacher beliefs and ideology regarding African American student achievement. Sleeter (1992) demonstrated that, over time, work with teachers explicitly designed to address and examine their ideology so they might be more receptive to multicultural thinking and ways of teaching yields small, incremental gains that will have positive multicultural results.

This chapter has hinted at some of the existing problems in teacher education and suggested that multicultural teacher education, by design, inherits these same problems. Just as there may be no connections among foundations courses, methods courses, and practicum experiences, there also may be no connections among the multicultural knowledge, skills, and dispositions that may be present in the program.

QUANTITY VERSUS QUALITY

Although the term *multicultural education* began to appear in the literature in the early 1970s, at least three widespread reviews or assessments have looked at multicultural teacher education (Baptiste & Baptiste, 1980; Commission on Multicultural Education, 1978; Grant & Secada, 1990). The Commission on Multicultural Education, working under the auspices of the American Association of Colleges for Teacher Education (AACTE), surveyed 786 member institutions in 1977. Four hundred and forty institutions responded to the survey, which attempted to see whether the institutions had courses, a major, a minor, or departments in multicultural or bilingual education, or whether some component of multicultural or bilingual education was included in the foundations or methodology courses. According to the directory (Commission on Multicultural Education, 1978), 48 of the 50 states and the District of Columbia had at least one institution that had either a multicultural education course, major, or minor or had a multicultural component within the foundations or methods courses.

More specifically, the directory indicated that 121 institutions offered a multicultural education course in the foundations sequence; 98 offered a multicultural education course in the methods sequence; 85 offered a multicultural course independent of the foundations or methods sequences; 40 offered a major in multicultural education; 42 offered a minor in multicultural education; and 24 had a department or division of multicultural education. Fifty-two institutions offered a bilingual education course in the foundations sequence; 65 offered a bilingual education course in the methods sequence; 50 offered a distinct bilingual education course (or courses); 59 offered a major in bilingual education; 55 offered a minor in bilingual education; and 29 had a department or division of bilingual education. Eighty-six of the programs had offerings in both multicultural education and bilingual education.

Of the 109 institutions that indicated they had components of multicultural education or bilingual education in the foundations or methods courses, 74 indicated that those components were multicultural education; 4 indicated that the components were bilingual education; and 31 indicated that they had both multicultural education and bilingual education components.

Some of the unique characteristics of the survey data include a learning packet in the human relations component, special field experiences in diverse communities, required cultural awareness workshops, minicourses, programs targeting specific ethnic minorities (e.g., American Indians, Spanish-speaking migrants), and a major emphasis course on women.

This AACTE directory was useful in demonstrating the broad sweep of multicultural teacher education, but it failed to provide readers with any sense of the quality of these programs. However, in defense of the AACTE effort, the directory did represent a first step. In their own words, AACTE saw the directory as an initial document to be followed by a three-volume collection on multicultural teacher education.

Actually, four volumes followed the survey. The subsequent volumes were *Multicultural Teacher Education: Preparing Educators to Provide Educational Equity* (Baptiste, Baptiste, & Gollnick, 1980), *Multicultural Teacher Education: Case Studies of Thirteen Programs* (Gollnick, Osayande, & Levy, 1980), *Multicultural Teacher Education: An Annotated Bibliography of Selected Resources* (Lee, 1980), and *Multicultural Teacher Education: Guidelines for Implementation* (AACTE, 1980). This attempt to document the existence of multicultural teacher education (and bilingual teacher education) programs and practices was consistent with the development of standards for national accreditation of multicultural teacher education programs.

The National Council for Accreditation of Teacher Education (NCATE), influenced by the Commission on Multicultural Education's work, began to draft standards to examine more systematically how teacher preparation programs addressed the multicultural education of its prospective teachers (Gollnick, 1991). In 1979 NCATE began requiring those institutions applying for accreditation to "show evidence of planning for multicultural education in their curricula" (p. 226). By 1981 NCATE expected these institutions to provide this planned-for multicultural education. More specifically, the first NCATE "multicultural education standard" stated in part:

Provision should be made for instruction in multicultural education in teacher education programs. Multicultural education should receive attention in courses, seminars, directed readings, laboratory and clinical experiences, practicum, and other types of field experiences.

Multicultural education could include but not be limited to experiences which: (i) promote analytical and evaluative abilities to confront issues such as participatory democracy, racism and sexism, and the parity of power; (ii) develop skills for values clarification, including the study of the manifest and latent transmission of values; (iii) examine the dynamics of diverse cultures and the implications for developing teaching strategies; and (iv) examine linguistic variations and diverse learning styles as a basis for the development of appropriate teaching strategies. (NCATE, 1982, p. 14)

In its 1990 revision of the accreditation standards, NCATE dropped the separate multicultural standard and integrated multicultural components into four different standards—the standard on professional studies, the standard on field-based and clinical experiences, the standard on student admission into professional education, and the standard on faculty qualifications and assignments.

Gollnick (1991) reported that "in its review of the first 59 institutions seeking accreditation under the current NCATE standards, NCATE found only 8 (13.6 percent) of the institutions in full compliance with [the] multicultural education requirements" (p. 234). Two of the most intractable areas of weakness seem to be institutions' inability to attract and retain a culturally diverse student body and the absence of culturally diverse faculty. Indeed, "60 percent of the institutions reviewed simply do not have culturally diverse faculties" (p. 235).

In Baptiste and Baptiste's (1980) "Competencies Toward Multiculturalism," the authors examined a number of the current practices in multicultural teacher education. They pointed out that in the late 1960s several projects and institutes emerged to meet the multicultural professional development needs of preservice and in-service teachers and counselors. These projects (and institutes) typically involved workshops centered on human relations training and "T" groups (Jackson & Kirkpatrick, 1967). No empirical data about the effectiveness of these projects is reported. The project and institute approach was followed by the use of teaching modules, conflict management strategies, and the merging of the competency-based teacher education movement with multicultural goals.

Baptiste and Baptiste (1980) argued that the emergence of competency-based models facilitated the development of more in-depth in-service approaches since participants would be required to demonstrate mastery of particular skills. They argued further that the federal program, Teacher Corps, took advantage of the competency-based teacher education movement by requiring preservice teachers to demonstrate mastery of competencies in multicultural field-based practicums.

Further, Baptiste and Baptiste describe multicultural teacher education efforts in Kansas City, at Clark College (in Atlanta), Jackson, Mississippi, Indiana University, University of Southern California, Boston University, and a California rural-migrant program. Unfortunately, the review does not report evaluative data about the success or failure of these programs.

Gollnick, Osayande, and Levy (1980) published a volume of 13 case studies of multicultural teacher education programs. This volume was intended to provide examples of alternative models for meeting the 1979 NCATE multicultural standard. Rather than being presented as a protocol of identical questions or key elements, the information about the quality of the programs was provided in a descriptive format.

A more recent comprehensive review of multicultural teacher education by Grant and Secada (1990) was not encouraging. Despite uncovering over 500 journal and 700 ERIC citations from 1964 to June 1988, they were left with a mere 23 books, articles, and papers that could be legitimately called empirical. They further asserted that

no empirical studies focused on the recruitment of a diverse teaching force; 16 studies addressed pre-service teacher education; and 7 dealt with inservice teacher education.... Seventeen of the studies were concerned with multicultural education; 7 with gender equity; and one, with second language issues. Three studies overlapped on multicultural and gender issues. (p. 404)

Frustrated by the paucity of empirical research in multicultural teacher education, Grant and Secada (1990) lamented:

Though we looked for research to answer our basic question, we found ourselves having to struggle with gaps in the field, with the lack of cumulative findings in programs of inquiry, and with the failure of studies to develop conceptual distinctions that would seem to be critical in the development of such chains of inquiry. (p. 404)

One of the important aspects of the Grant and Secada review is the typology they used for classifying the empirical studies. By employing the previously mentioned Sleeter and Grant (1987) categories developed for analyzing multicultural education, the authors provided a useful rubric for understanding the quality (and perhaps depth) of the multicultural teacher education studies.

Three of the empirical studies on multicultural teacher education were classified as using the "teaching the different child" approach; 2 were classified as using the "human relations" approach; 4 were classified as using the "single group studies" approach; 10 were classified as using a "multicultural" approach; 1 was classified as using the "education that is multicultural" approach; and 3 failed to fit any of the categories.

Grant and Secada (1990) concluded their review by urging more (and different) research in multicultural teacher education that (a) moves "beyond behaviorist conceptions of knowledge" (p. 419); (b) is empirically validated; (c) tracks the dissemination of knowledge about teaching diverse students within schools; (d) helps us understand how and when teacher multicultural content knowledge is transmitted in the classroom; and (e) deals with teacher expectations, particularly as they are shaped by difficult initial teaching situations with diverse student populations.

THE VIEW SINCE 1988

Since the Grant and Secada (1990) review (their database search concludes in 1988), multicultural teacher education literature continues to be generated. In an ERIC search that overlapped the Grant and Secada review (1980–1992), using the descriptors *multicultural education* and *teacher education*, 169 entries were generated. Thirty-nine entries appear between 1989 and 1992. Twenty of those entries were journal articles, 7 were papers presented at conferences and/or professional meetings, 5 were reports, and 4 were books (3 of which were edited volumes). There was 1 each of curriculum guides, monographs, and directories. Of these 39 entries 4 were empirical studies, 11 were descriptive studies, 2 were evaluative, and 18 were position or opinion papers. Four of the 39 did not fall into any of the aforementioned categories. Some of the trends that seem to be emerging are an increase in international literature published in English (e.g., Bossort, 1990; Devlin, 1991; Geach & Broadbent, 1989; Liegois, 1990), the inclusion of global studies (Merryfield, 1990; Wegner, 1991), and early childhood literature (Lee, 1989; Williams, 1991).

Beyond the description of these studies this chapter attempts to examine these studies in terms of Banks's (1993) typology of multicultural education. According to Banks:

Content integration deals with the extent to which teachers use examples, data, and information from a variety of cultures and groups to illustrate key concepts, principles, generalizations, and theories in their subject area or discipline.... The *knowledge construction* process describes the procedures by which social, behavioral, and natural scientists create knowledge and how the implicit cultural assumptions, frames of references, perspectives, and biases within a discipline influence the ways that knowledge is constructed within it.... The *prejudice reduction* dimension of multicultural education describes the characteristics of children's racial attitudes and strategies that can be used to help students develop more democratic attitudes and values.... An *equity pedagogy* exists when teachers use techniques and methods that facilitate the academic achievement of students from diverse racial, ethnic, and social-class groups.... An *empowering school culture* and social structure... describe[s] the process of restructuring the culture and organization of the school so that students from diverse ethnic groups will experience educational equality and cultural empowerment. (pp. 5–7)

This chapter uses these dimensions as a tool for examining how multicultural teacher education has been constructed in recent years. Have we moved beyond the designation of separate courses (e.g., "the ethnic studies requirement," "the human relations workshop," "the multicultural course") to symbolize our commitment to multicultural ideals? Have we begun to think of multicultural teacher education in scholarly ways that challenge the intellect of prospective and in-service teachers? How close are we to having multicultural ideals shape and drive the professional education of teachers, no matter who they are or where that professional preparation takes place?

There is an awareness in this chapter of the inherent limitations or constraints of any typology or categorical rubric to explain complex social phenomena. As Banks (1993) himself suggests:

The dimensions typology is an ideal-type conception in the Weberian sense. It approximates but does not describe reality in its total complexity. Like all classification schema, it has both strengths and limitations. Typologies are helpful conceptual tools because they provide a way to organize and make sense of complex and disparate data and observations. However, their categories are interrelated and overlapping, not mutually exclusive. Typologies are rarely able to encompass the total universe of existing or future cases. (p. 7)

With these limitations in mind, assignments of more recent multicultural teacher education literature to these dimensions are made as indicated in Table 43–1.

The number of studies totals 43, but there is some overlap. Some entries reflect a combination of dimensions—for example, content integration and knowledge construction or prejudice reduction and knowledge construction.

As Table 43–1 suggests, the one dimension that has received the most attention in the current literature is content integration. Almost one third of the recent ERIC database entries on multicultural teacher education dealt with reasons for and studies of content integration as well as with ways of attaining content integration. Clearly, this is the dimension that has brought about the most controversy in the popular literature (e.g., weekly newsmagazines, newspapers, television news coverage). However, a number of scholars point to the limitations of

ethnic content in effecting substantive change in diverse classrooms (see, for example, Diez & Murrell, 1992; McDiarmid & Price, 1990).

Less than a quarter (20%) of the entries dealt with knowledge construction; only 10% dealt with prejudice reduction; and entries dealing with equity pedagogy and an empowering school culture constituted a mere 5% each.

More disturbing than these percentages is the fact that more than one third of the entries (36%) failed to relate to any of the dimensions. This disengagement of the multicultural teacher education literature from the multicultural education theoretical and conceptual literature is reminiscent of Gay's (1992) assertion that a gap exists between multicultural education theory and practice. She contends that theory development has widely outdistanced practice, yet theorists are blamed for poor practice.

In this instance, I am suggesting that multicultural teacher education—the intermediary step between theory and classroom practice—exhibits a similar lag. However, it is important to underscore the point that theory development and practice do not happen in a vacuum or in a linear fashion. More precisely, there is a synergistic and dynamic relationship that exists between the two. Practitioners are not merely waiting for scholars to develop theory before they begin to try new ap-

TABLE 43–1. Categorization of Multicultural Teacher Education Literature (1988–1992)

1. Content Integration n = 12 (Barrera, 1992; Bina, 1991; Cockrell, 1991; Davidman, 1990; Ladson-Billings, 1991; Merryfield, 1990; Santo, 1990; Saunders, 1991; Shah, 1989; Thompson & Meeks, 1990; Williams, 1991; Yepes-Baraya, 1991)	4. Equity Pedagogy n = 2 (Howard, 1988; Poplin, 1992)
2. Knowledge Construction n = 9 (Ahlquist, 1991; Barger, 1991; Bishop, 1991; Garcia, 1990; Kennedy, 1991; King, 1991; Kissen, 1989; Shah, 1989; Shor, 1990)	5. Empowering School Culture n = 2 (Brown, 1991; Cuellar & Huling-Austin, 1991)
3. Prejudice Reduction n = 4 (Demetrulias, 1990; Haberman & Post, 1992; Martin & Koppleman, 1991; Poplin, 1992)	6. not applicable n = 14 (Boyer-White, 1988; Clayton, 1990; Curtis, 1988; Demedjian, 1992; Easterly, 1990; Flores & Merino, 1991; Krajewski, 1988; Lee, 1989; Mangano, 1988; Orieux, 1988; "Redefining Multicultural Education," 1988; Shehan, 1988; Watson, 1988; Watson & Roberts, 1988)

proaches to pedagogy. True, theory informs practice, but practice also informs theory.

It should be noted that one of the limitations of the ERIC database is that its primary resources are mainstream venues such as scholarly journals, books, and professional conferences. To be fair, the marginalization of multicultural education (and diverse perspectives) warrants the search of less traditional sources (i.e., fugitive literature, nonmainstream journals and publications, new professional conferences).

Examples of this literature are the conference proceedings of the first annual meeting of the National Association for Multicultural Education (NAME), *Toward Education That Is Multicultural,* edited by Carl A. Grant (1992b), which includes a section on multicultural teacher education consisting of 10 papers. These papers are primarily position or opinion papers and program descriptions.

By including both mainstream and fugitive literature, Zeichner (1992) has produced a comprehensive review of the literature on preparing teachers for diversity that succinctly delineates the elements that are hallmarks of effective multicultural teacher education. Briefly, these elements include:

- admission procedures that screen students on the basis of cultural sensitivity and a commitment to the education of all students
- development of a clearer sense of prospective teachers' sense of their ethnic and cultural identities
- examination of prospective teachers' attitudes toward other ethnocultural groups
- teaching about the dynamics of prejudice and racism and how to deal with them in the classroom
- curriculum that addresses the histories and contributions of various ethnocultural groups
- teaching that includes information about the characteristics and learning styles of various groups *and* individuals (and the limitations of such information)
- curriculum that gives much attention to sociocultural research knowledge about the relationships among language, culture, and learning
- teaching about various procedures by which prospective teachers can gain information about the communities represented in the classroom
- teaching about how to assess the relationship between the methods teachers use in the classroom and the preferred learning and interaction styles in their students' homes and communities
- teaching about how to use various instructional strategies and assessment procedures sensitive to cultural and linguistic variations and how to adapt classroom instruction and assessment to accommodate the cultural resources that students bring to school
- exposure to examples of successful teaching of ethnic- and language-minority students
- opportunities for complete community field experiences with adults and/or children of other ethnocultural groups with guided reflections

- opportunities for practicum and/or student teaching experiences in schools serving ethnic- and language-minority students
- opportunities to live and teach in a minority community (immersion)
- instruction that is embedded in a group setting that provides both intellectual challenge and social support

It should be noted that while these key elements (singularly and in various combinations) are mentioned in numerous studies, very little empirical evidence is provided to support their validity (see Zeichner, 1992).

The next section of this chapter discusses multicultural teacher education literature from both mainstream and nonmainstream sources.

ATTENDING TO THE WISDOM OF PRACTICE

Shulman (1987) has reminded us that one source for the knowledge base of teaching is the wisdom of practice. He defines this wisdom of practice as "the maxims that guide (or provide reflective rationalization for) the practices of able teachers" (p. 11). To the casual observer this notion might suggest that teaching lacks the rigorous, codified knowledge base of the more prestigious professions such as law or medicine. However, it is important to note that both law and medicine depend heavily on their own wisdom of practice. The development of case knowledge—that knowledge that is created from the careful documentation of practice—is essential in constructing the knowledge base of law and medicine (also business).

Thus, new scholarship in teacher education is beginning to balance the experimental and quasi-experimental research that has been prominent in much of the research literature with a more qualitative case literature that uncovers the wisdom of practice. Several trends are beginning to emerge as a result of this scholarship. We are seeing the increased use of autobiography, restructuring of field experiences, examination of "situated" and "culturally specific" pedagogies, and the return of the researcher to the classrooms of "experts."

Autobiography

Jackson (1992) suggests that autobiography provides an opportunity for the "critical examination and experience of difference" (p. 4). More specifically, she contends:

By its very nature, autobiography is a medium through which individuals speak as subjects, in their own voices, represent themselves, and their stories from their own perspectives. The study of autobiography from a multicultural approach which legitimizes the voices and experiences of diverse people, provides occasions to bring these experiences to the center—foregrounded in bold relief. Through studying autobiography in this manner, preservice teachers experience an approach to teaching which they themselves can practice and model. (p. 3)

Gomez and Tabachnick (1992) emphasized "telling teaching stories" as a way to get preservice students to reflect on their practicum experiences in diverse classrooms. This autobiographical sharing gave their students an opportunity to understand the complexity of teaching, particularly when their students were from backgrounds different from their own. Hollins (1990) refers to "resocializing preservice teachers in ways that help them view themselves within a culturally diverse society" (p. 202). A strategy she employs for this resocialization is the construction of personal/cultural autobiographies.

Similarly, King and Ladson-Billings (1990) link critical education theory and multicultural teacher education to help their students understand their own and existing ideologies and to help "students consciously re-experience their own subjectivity when they recognize similar or different outlooks and experiences" (p. 26), both in the college classroom and in their field experiences.

It is interesting to note that teaching and teacher education in general are looking increasingly to autobiographical storytelling for deeper understandings of the complexities of teaching (Carter, 1993; Gudmundsdottir, 1991; Noddings, 1991).

Restructured Field Experiences

Student teaching, the practicum, practice teaching, and *teaching internship* are all terms for the phase of teacher education that places the pre-service teacher in the classroom, more or less, under the supervision of an experienced teacher and a university professional. Increasingly, state regulations governing teacher preparation are requiring teacher candidates to have field experiences in diverse classroom settings. For example, the California Commission on Teacher Credentialing (CCTC) includes in its program evaluation two standards that read:

Prior to or during the program each candidate engages in cross-cultural study and experience, including study of language and experience with successful approaches to the education of linguistically different students.

Each candidate demonstrates compatibility with, and ability to teach, students who are different from the candidate. The difference should include ethnic, cultural, gender, linguistic, and socioeconomic differences. (CCTC, 1988, Standards 15, 30)

Gomez and Tabachnick's (1992) work with a cohort of preservice students who selected a program that placed all students in culturally diverse settings is an example of restructuring the field experience to ensure that students are aware of the institutional (or programmatic) commitment to diversity.

In some instances, university programs are changing their entire teacher education focus toward diversity (Haberman & Post, 1992). Unfortunately, Haberman and Post's data from 23 White female sophomores who participated in a remedial summer session for low-income minority children suggest that the direct experience did little more than provide a "laboratory" for students to selectively perceive and reinforce their initial (negative) preconceptions.

Perhaps more powerful than diverse student teaching experiences are teacher education programs that stress "immersion" experiences in diverse communities (Mahan, 1982; Noordhoff & Kleinfeld, 1991). For example, in an attempt to combat the "dysconscious" racism (see King, 1991) of many prospective teachers, the Santa Clara University Teacher Education Program began to require a community immersion experience for its students.

The growing disparity between teachers' and students' backgrounds means that teachers often have little or no (or distorted) knowledge about the communities and families from which their students come. By "immersing" teacher candidates in the communities they are about to serve, without the pressure of requiring them to apply newly acquired pedagogical skills, the students have the opportunity to observe and learn from the people they will eventually serve. Important in these immersion experiences is the opportunity to participate in planned debriefings and guided reflections lest the immersion experiences serve to reinforce students' initial prejudices.

Situated Pedagogies

Scholars in anthropology have produced literature that addresses culturally specific pedagogy. A variety of terms falls under the rubric of culturally specific pedagogy, including *culturally responsive* (Cazden & Legett, 1981; Mohatt & Erickson, 1981), *culturally appropriate* (Au & Jordan, 1981), *culturally compatible* (Jordan, 1985; Vogt, Jordan, & Tharp, 1987), *cultural synchronization* (Irvine, 1990), and *culturally relevant* (Ladson-Billings, 1992b).

This literature describes teachers' attempts to make the school and home cultures of diverse students more congruent. However, the preponderance of this literature has dealt with small-scale, isolated communities. Irvine (1990) and Ladson-Billings (1992b) are exceptions in this tradition because their work has examined African American children in complex urban communities.

More recently, scholars have posited theoretical, conceptual, and research possibilities for situated pedagogies that consider race, class, and gender (see, for example, Ellsworth, 1989; hooks, 1989; King, 1990; McLaren, 1989). By addressing the specificities of particular multicultural communities, this literature avoids the platitudes and unsubstantiated generalities of generic pedagogy.

Thus, teacher education programs are called upon to think more carefully about their relationships with the communities in which they are located and the school populations that their graduates are likely to serve. Unfortunately, the literature is particularly sparse in the description and assessment of pedagogy in the growing number of "culturally centered" schools (e.g., Africentric and Native American reservation schools).

Returning to the Classrooms of "Experts"

One of the "cutting edge" trends in multicultural teacher education (and teacher education) is the examination of classroom practice of successful teachers in diverse classrooms (see Foster, 1989; Henry, 1992; Ladson-Billings, 1992b; Lipka, 1991;

Sims, 1992). Most of this literature has focused on effective practice with African American students. However, a parallel literature exists in uncovering the effective practice of teachers of linguistically diverse students (for example, see Hornberger, 1990; Moll, 1988) and among anthropologists such as Lipka (1991). These classroom teachers form the budding knowledge base and case literature for effective teaching practice in multicultural settings.

J. Shulman and Mesa-Baines (1993) have begun using teacher cases in multicultural classrooms as a part of in-service/professional development experiences. By acknowledging the expertise of practitioners, researchers are attempting to forge the important bond between theory and practice that allows for a critical (and perhaps emancipatory) literature and practice to develop.

Increasingly, this willingness to listen and learn from practitioners is providing researchers and teacher educators with opportunities to build a knowledge base in conjunction and collaboration with teachers. This dialectic relationship between theory and practice may lend more credibility to teacher preparation as professional training grounded in and informed by best practices.

What remains to be researched is the practice of "expert" teacher educators who are designing and implementing multicultural teacher education program models with little or no attention. Zeichner (personal communication, March 1993) insists that his observations of innovative teacher educators working to develop teacher educator models for diversity and equity convince him that "good work" is being done by teacher educators who have little or no time (or inclination) to write and report about their work. Similarly, the experiences of practitioners in the Black Independent School movement affirms his assertion (Lee, Lomotey, & Shujaa, 1990).

Several recent efforts have looked at innovative ways to conceptualize the issues of preparing teachers for diverse classrooms. Kennedy's (1991) volume deals with the nature of the content and how it can be taught to diverse learners. Among the chapters directly confronting the preparatory needs of teachers in multicultural settings are those by Grant (1991) and McDiarmid (1991). While Grant argues that teachers can best prepare for teaching in multicultural environments by understanding their own (diverse) histories/biographies, McDiarmid suggests that teachers are best prepared to be effective in multicultural settings when they are able to make the subject matter meaningful for diverse learners.

Dilworth's (1992) edited volume, *Diversity in Teacher Education,* examines the challenges, contexts, and directives for multicultural teacher education. While the volume is not based on empirical research, it does provide several conceptual notions and program descriptions that may constitute the basis for future studies. Among the conceptual and descriptive issues contained in the volume are a look at historical antecedents of multicultural teacher education (Brown, 1992), parochialism among teacher candidates (Zimpher & Ashburn, 1992), problems in minority teacher recruitment (Chinn & Wong, 1992; Schuhmann, 1992), diversity on historically African American college campuses (Mills & Buckley, 1992), school reform (Beckum, 1992; Winfield & Manning, 1992), and restructured

and innovative teacher preparation programs (Arends, Clemson, & Henkelman, 1992; Nelson-Barber & Mitchell, 1992).

Finally, Perry and Fraser (1993) have edited a volume on teaching in the multicultural classroom. While not specifically aimed at teacher preparation, the chapters in their section entitled "The Practice of Multicultural Education: Doing the Work" are important for their theoretical and conceptual sophistication (Hidalgo, 1993; hooks, 1993) and their explication of teacher knowledge and understanding (from the teachers' perspectives) about teaching in multicultural schools and classrooms (Dickerson, 1993; Mizell, Bennett, Bowman, & Morin, 1993; Richards, 1993).

The growth of literature in multicultural teacher education signals the willingness of scholars in both multicultural education and teacher education to engage in both theoretical/conceptual and practical ideas about the ways that teachers must be educated to address not only changing demographics, but also the demand for equity in both the classroom and the society.

CONCLUSION

Each of these new trends in multicultural teacher education is instrumental in the development of a critical multicultural teacher education. Given the growing economic, political, and social disparity between dominant group members and minority group members, multicultural teacher education cannot afford the luxury of "neutrality."

Critics from the left (McCarthy, 1990; Olneck, 1990) express serious doubts about the ability of multicultural education to address the structural inequality of the society and suggest that multicultural education is an accommodationist strategy that fails to effect any real change. Too many teacher educators (and teachers) believe that they can implement an effective multicultural education program without effecting fundamental change in the classrooms and schools in which they teach. This belief contributes to the superficial and trivial treatment of issues of race, class, and gender in elementary and secondary school classrooms.

Exposure to this weak form of multicultural education is perhaps responsible for the resistance that prospective teachers exhibit when they are faced with serious engagement of issues such as racism, sexism, and other forms of oppression (Rothenberg, 1988; Tatum, 1992). Thus, to be meaningful and powerful in the lives of diverse students, multicultural teacher education must confront the limitations and problems of traditional teacher education and "business as usual." It cannot shrink from the responsibility of real change and reform.

Additionally, multicultural education scholars and teacher educators must reclaim the discourse that has suddenly become the "hot topic" for scholars from a variety of fields who have failed to read carefully the theoretical and conceptual literature of multicultural education. A key element of this reclamation is a clear articulation of the definition of multicultural education that embodies both meaning and intent. Sleeter (1989) discusses the confusion over the meanings and purposes of multicultural education extant in the literature both in the United States and in other countries.

To this end, multicultural educators must participate in rigorous intellectual debate with scholars and policy makers from a variety of fields (most notably, anthropology, history, and sociology) to challenge and eliminate the miscommunication, misperceptions, and misinformation about multicultural education. For example, Ogbu's (1992) assertion that multicultural theories and programs are rarely based on actual studies of minority cultures and languages is unsubstantiated. Further, his rigid categories of minority status (e.g., autonomous, voluntary, and castelike) lack explanatory power for those "castelike" minority members who excel and those "voluntary" minority members who fail.

Multicultural education scholars cannot allow their message to be obscured by the rhetoric of the political and ideological left or by misinterpretation of the political and ideological right. They must challenge the appropriation of the very term *multicultural,* which has, in recent years, been constructed as the watchword for apologists of the status quo (see Ravitch, 1990) and the bane of national unity (see Schlesinger, 1992).

Multicultural teacher education occupies a critical position between multicultural theory and multicultural practice. As the logical translator of theoretical and conceptual notions about diversity into real-world practice in the nation's classrooms, it may well be the determiner of the fate of multicultural education. Given what we have seen in the literature over the past 25 or more years, and the potential for creative rethinking about teacher education and multicultural teacher education, it is time for multicultural teacher education to assume a proactive leadership role or else risk a marginalization that will have dire consequences for the fate of our teachers, our schools, and our nation.

REFERENCES

Ahlquist, R. (1991). Position and imposition: Power relations in a multicultural foundations class. *The Journal of Negro Education, 60,* 158–169.

American Association of Colleges of Teacher Education. (1980). *Multicultural teacher education: Guidelines for implementation.* Washington, DC: Author.

Arends, R., Clemson, S., & Henkelman, J. (1992). Tapping nontraditional sources of minority teaching talent. In M. Dilworth (Ed.), *Diversity in teacher education* (pp. 160–180). San Francisco: Jossey Bass.

Au, K., & Jordan, C. (1981). Teaching reading to Hawaiian children: Finding a culturally appropriate solution. In H. Trueba, G. Guthrie, & K. Au (Eds.), *Culture and the bilingual classroom: Studies in classroom ethnography* (pp. 139–152). Rowley, MA: Newbury House.

Banks, J. A. (1991). Teaching multicultural literacy to teachers. *Teaching Education, 4,* 135–144.

Banks, J. A. (1993). Multicultural education: Historical development, dimensions, and practice. In L. Darling-Hammond (Ed.), *Review of Research in Education,* (Vol. 19, pp. 3–49). Washington, DC: American Educational Research Association.

Baptiste, H. P., & Baptiste, M. (1980). Competencies toward multiculturalism. In H. P. Baptiste, M. Baptiste, & D. Gollnick (Eds.), *Multicultural teacher education: Preparing educators to provide educational equity* (Vol. 1, pp. 44–72). Washington, DC: American Association of Colleges for Teacher Education.

Baptiste, H. P., Baptiste, M. L., & Gollnick, D. M. (Eds.). (1980). *Multicultural teacher education: Preparing educators to provide educational equity* (Vol. 1). Washington, DC: American Association of Colleges of Teacher Education.

Barger, R. (1991). *Evaluating multicultural education.* Charleston: Eastern Illinois University.

Barrera, R. (1992). The cultural gap in literature-based literacy instruction. *Education and Urban Society, 24,* 227–243.

Beckum, L. (1992). Diversifying assessment. In M. Dilworth (Ed.), *Diversity in teacher education* (pp. 215–228). San Francisco: Jossey-Bass.

Bina, C. (1991, October 5–7). *The bonfire of the Buffalo Commons: A multicultural view from the mid-continent.* Paper presented at the Regional Equity Consultation Meeting of the Midcontinental Regional Educational Laboratory, Aurora, CO.

Bishop, A. (1991). *Mathematical enculturation: A cultural perspective on mathematics education.* Norwell, MA: Kluwer Academic Publishers.

Bloom, A. (1987). *The closing of the American mind: How higher education has failed democracy and impoverished the souls of today's students.* New York: Simon & Schuster.

Bossort, P. (Ed.). (1990, October). Literacy 2000: Make the next ten years matter [Conference Summary]. New Westminster, British Columbia, Canada.

Boyer-White, R. (1988). Reflecting cultural diversity in the music classroom. *Music Educators Journal, 75*(4), 50–54.

Brown, B. (1991). *Supporting teachers in a multicultural school environment: An analysis of the role of a staff developer.* Paper presented at the annual meeting of the American Educational Research Association, Chicago.

Brown, C. (1992). Restructuring for a new America. In M. Dilworth (Ed.), *Diversity in teacher education* (pp. 1–22). San Francisco: Jossey-Bass.

California Commission on Teacher Credentialing. (1988). *Adopted standards of program quality and effectiveness.* Sacramento: California State Department of Education.

Carnegie Forum on Education and the Economy. (1986). *A nation prepared: Teachers for the 21st century.* New York: Carnegie Corporation.

Carter, K. (1993). The place of story in the study of teaching and teacher education. *Educational Researcher, 22*(1), 5–12, 18.

Cazden, C., & Leggett, E. (1981). Culturally responsive education: Recommendations for achieving Lau remedies II. In H. Trueba, G. Guthrie, & K. Au (Eds.), *Culture and the bilingual classroom: Studies in classroom ethnography* (pp. 69–86). Rowley, MA: Newbury House.

Center for Education Statistics. (1987). *The condition of education.* Washington, DC: U.S. Government Printing Office.

Chinn, P., & Wong, G. (1992). Recruiting and retaining Asian/Pacific American teachers. In M. Dilworth (Ed.), *Diversity in teacher education* (pp. 112–133). San Francisco: Jossey-Bass.

Clayton, T. (Ed.). (1990). The globalization of higher education [Special issue]. *Cross Currents, 17*(2).

Cockrell, K. (1991, October 10–14). *A rural professional development school: University-school collaboration in a multicultural setting.* Paper presented at the Annual Convention of the National Rural Education Association, Jackson, MS.

Commission on Excellence in Education. (1983). *A nation at risk*. Washington, DC: Government Printing Office.

Commission on Multicultural Education. (1978). *Directory: Multicultural education programs in teacher education institutions in the United States*. Washington, DC: American Association of Colleges for Teacher Education.

Conant, J. (1963). *The education of American teachers*. New York: McGraw-Hill.

Cuellar, E., & Huling-Austin, L. (Eds.). (1991). *Achieving an ethnically diverse teaching force*. Austin: Texas Education Agency.

Curtis, M. (1988). Understanding the black aesthetic experience. *Music Educators Journal, 75*(2), 23–26.

Davidman, P. (1990). Multicultural teacher education and supervision: A new approach to professional development. *Teacher Education Quarterly, 17*, 37–52.

Demedjian, V. (Ed.) (1992). *Play's place in public education for young children*. Washington, DC: National Education Association.

Demetrulias, D. (1990). Ethnic surnames. *Educational Research Quarterly, 14*(3), 2–6.

Devlin, B. (ed.) (1991, October). *Education for all*. South East Asia and South Pacific Sub-Regional Conference Report. Darwin, Northern Territory, Australia.

Dickerson, S. (1993). The blind men (women) and the elephant: A case for a comprehensive multicultural education program at the Cambridge Rindge and Latin School. In T. Perry & J. W. Fraser (Eds.), *Freedom's plow: Teaching in the multicultural classroom* (pp. 65–89). New York: Routledge.

Diez, M., & Murrell, P. (1992). *Assessing abilities of expert teaching practices in diverse classrooms*. Unpublished manuscript, Alverno College, Milwaukee.

Dilworth, M. (Ed.). (1992). *Diversity in teacher education*. San Francisco: Jossey-Bass.

D'Souza, D. (1991). *Illiberal education: The politics of race and sex on campus*. New York: Free Press.

Easterly, J. (1990). Teaching in a culturally diverse nation state. *Social Studies Review, 29*(3), 65–67.

Edmundson, P. (1990). A normative look at the curriculum in teacher education. *Phi Delta Kappan, 71*, 717–722.

Ellsworth, E. (1989). Why doesn't this feel empowering? Working through the repressive myths of critical pedagogy. *Harvard Educational Review, 59*, 297–324.

Flores, J., & Merino, R. (Eds.) (1991). Educational research and the Mexican American child [Special issue]. *Journal of the Association of Mexican American Education, 4*.

Foster, M. (1989). "It's cookin' now": A performance analysis of the speech events of a Black teacher in an urban community college. *Language in Society, 18*, 1–29.

Garcia, J. (1990). Does "Charting a Course" include a multiethnic perspective? *Social Education, 54*, 444–446.

Gay, G. (1986). Multicultural teacher education. In J. A. Banks & J. Lynch (Eds.), *Multicultural education in Western societies* (pp. 154–177). New York: Praeger.

Gay, G. (1992). The state of multicultural education in the United States. In K. A. Moodley (Ed.), *Education in plural societies: International perspectives* (pp. 47–66). Calgary: Detselig.

Geach, J., & Broadbent, J. (1989). *Coherence in diversity: Britain's multilingual classroom*. Regent's Park, London: Center for Information on Language Teaching and Research.

Gollnick, D. (1991). Multicultural education: Policies and practices in teacher education. In C. Grant (Ed.), *Research and multicultural education: From the margins to the mainstream* (pp. 218–239). London: Falmer Press.

Gollnick, D. M., Osayande, K. I. M., & Levy, J. (1980). *Multicultural teacher education: Case studies of thirteen programs* (Vol 2). Washington, DC: American Association of Colleges of Teacher Education.

Gomez, M. L., & Tabachnick, B. R. (1992). Telling teaching stories. *Teaching Education, 4*, 129–138.

Goodlad, J. I. (1990). Better teachers for our nation's schools. *Phi Delta Kappan, 72*, 185–194.

Gordon, B. (1988). Implicit assumptions of the Holmes and Carnegie reports: A view from an African-American perspective. *The Journal of Negro Education, 57*, 141–158.

Gordon, B. (1991). The marginalized discourse of minority intellectual thought. In C. Grant (Ed.), *Research and multicultural education: From the margins to the mainstream* (pp. 19–31). London: Falmer Press.

Grant, C. (1989). Urban teachers: Their new colleagues and curriculum. *Phi Delta Kappan, 70*, 764–770.

Grant, C. (1991). Culture and teaching: What do teachers need to know? In M. Kennedy (Ed.), *Teaching academic subjects to diverse learners* (pp. 237–256). New York: Teachers College Press.

Grant, C. (1992a, April). *Preparing teachers for urban schools: Who does it? Or does it best?* Paper presented at the annual meeting of the American Educational Research Association, San Francisco.

Grant, C. (Ed.). (1992b). *Toward education that is multicultural: Proceedings of the first annual meeting of the National Association for Multicultural Education, February 15–17, 1991*. New York: Silver Burdett Ginn.

Grant, C., & Gillette, M. (1987). The Holmes report and minorities in education. *Social Education, 51*, 517–521.

Grant, C., & Secada, W. (1990). Preparing teachers for diversity. In W. R. Houston, M. Haberman, & J. Sikula (Eds.), *Handbook of research on teacher education* (pp. 403–422). New York: Macmillan.

Gudmundsdottir, S. (1991). Story-maker, story-teller: Narrative structures in curriculum. *Journal of Curriculum Studies, 23*, 207–218.

Haberman, M. (1989). More minority teachers. *Phi Delta Kappan, 70*, 771–776.

Haberman, M. (1991). The rationale for training adults as teachers. In C. E. Sleeter (Ed.), *Empowerment through multicultural education* (pp. 275–286). Albany: State University of New York Press.

Haberman, M., & Post, L. (1992). Does direct experience change education students' perceptions of low-income minority children? *Midwestern Educational Researcher, 5*, 29–31.

Henry, A. (1992). African Canadian women teachers' activism: Recreating communities of caring and resistance. *The Journal of Negro Education, 61*, 392–404.

Herbst, J. (1989). *And sadly teach: Teacher education and professionalization in American culture*. Madison: University of Wisconsin Press.

Hidalgo, N. (1993). Multicultural teacher introspection. In T. Perry & J. W. Fraser (Eds.), *Freedom's plow: Teaching in the multicultural classroom* (pp. 99–106). New York: Routledge.

Hollins, E. R. (1990). Debunking the myth of a monolithic White American culture; or moving toward cultural inclusion. *American Behavioral Scientist, 34*, 201–209.

Holmes Group. (1986). *Teachers for tomorrow's schools*. East Lansing, MI: Author.

Hornberger, N. (1990). Creating successful learning contexts for bilingual literacy. *Teachers College Record, 92*, 212–229.

hooks, b. (1989). *Talking back: Thinking feminist, thinking Black*. Boston: South End Press.

hooks, b. (1993). Transformative pedagogy and multiculturalism. In T. Perry & J. W. Fraser (Eds.), *Freedom's plow: Teaching in the multicultural classroom* (pp. 91–97). New York: Routledge.

Howard, R. (1988). Broadening the teacher's perspective about language and culture. *Journal of Educational Issues of Language Minority Students, 3*, 21–26.

Irvine, J. (1990). *Black students and school failure.* Westport, CT: Greenwood Press.

Jackson, J., & Kirkpatrick, D. (1967). *Institutes for preparation of counselors and teacher leadership in desegregated schools.* Washington, DC: U.S. Office of Education.

Jackson, S. (1992). *Autobiography: Pivot points for the study and practice of multiculturalism in teacher education.* Paper presented at the annual meeting of the American Educational Research Association, San Francisco.

Jordan, C. (1985). Translating culture: From ethnographic information to educational program. *Anthropology and Education Quarterly, 16,* 105–123.

Kennedy, M. (Ed.). (1991). *Teaching academic subjects to diverse learners.* New York: Teachers College Press.

King, J. (Ed.). (1990). In search of African liberatory pedagogy [Special issue]. *Journal of Education, 172.*

King, J. (1991). Dysconscious racism: Ideology, identity, and the miseducation of teachers. *The Journal of Negro Education, 60,* 133–146.

King, J., & Ladson-Billings, G. (1990). The teacher education challenge in elite university settings: Developing critical perspectives for teaching in a democratic and multicultural society. *European Journal of Intercultural Studies, 1,* 15–30.

Kissen, R. (1989). Multicultural education: The opening of the American mind. *English Education, 21,* 211–218.

Krajewski, R. (1988). University school relationships: Building bridges for minorities. *Teacher Education and Practice, 4*(1), 65–74.

Ladson-Billings, G. (1991). Beyond multicultural illiteracy. *The Journal of Negro Education, 60,* 147–157.

Ladson-Billings, G. (1992a, November/December). I don't see color, I just see children: Dealing with prejudice and stereotyping among young children. *Social Studies and the Young Learner, 5,* 9–12.

Ladson-Billings, G. (1992b). Reading between the lines and beyond the pages: A culturally relevant approach to literacy teaching. *Theory into Practice, 31,* 312–320.

Lee, C., Lomotey, K., & Shujaa, M. (1990). How shall we sing our sacred song in a strange land? The dilemma of double consciousness and the complexities of an African-centered pedagogy. *The Journal of Education, 172,* 45–61.

Lee, M. (1980). *Multicultural teacher education: An annotated bibliography of selected resources* (Vol 3). Washington, DC: American Association of Colleges of Teacher Education.

Lee, M. (1989). Making child development relevant for all children: Implications for teacher education. *Early Child Development and Care, 47,* 63–73.

Liegois, J. (1990, June). The CDCC teacher bursaries scheme. In *Towards intercultural education: Training for teachers of Gypsy pupils.* European Teachers' Seminar, Strasbourg, France.

Lipka, J. (1991). Toward a culturally based pedagogy: A case study of one Yup'ik Eskimo teacher. *Anthropology and Education Quarterly, 22,* 203–223.

Lipman, P. (1993). *The influence of school restructuring on teachers' beliefs about and practices with African American students.* Unpublished doctoral dissertation, University of Wisconsin.

Lynch, J. (1986). *Multicultural education: Principles and practices.* London: Routledge and Kegan Paul.

Mahan, J. (1982). Native Americans as teacher trainers: Anatomy and outcomes of a cultural immersion project. *Journal of Educational Equity and Leadership, 2,* 100–110.

Mangano, N. (1988). Guidelines for integrating non-sexist, multicultural education in the university methods course. *Educational Considerations, 15*(1), 2–5.

Martin, R. J., & Koppelman, K. (1991). The impact of a human relations/

multicultural education course on the attitudes of prospective teachers. *Journal of Intergroup Relations, 18,* 16–27.

McCarthy, C. (1990). *Race and curriculum.* Bristol, PA: Falmer Press.

McDiarmid, G. W. (1991). What teachers need to know about cultural diversity: Restoring subject matter to the picture. In M. Kennedy (Ed.), *Teaching academic subjects to diverse learners* (pp. 257–269). New York: Teachers College Press.

McDiarmid, G. W., & Price, J. (1990). *What to do about differences? A study of multicultural education for trainees in the Los Angeles Unified School District* (Research Report 90-11). East Lansing: Michigan State University, National Center for Research on Teacher Education.

McLaren, P. (1989). *Life in classrooms: An introduction to critical pedagogy in the classroom.* White Plains, NY: Longman.

Merryfield, M. (1990). *Teaching about the world: Teacher education programs with a global perspective.* Columbus: Ohio State University.

Mills, J. R., & Buckley, C. (1992). Accommodating the minority teacher candidate: Non-Black students in predominantly Black colleges. In M. Dilworth (Ed.), *Diversity in teacher education* (pp. 134–159). San Francisco: Jossey-Bass.

Mizell, L., Benett, S., Bowman, B., & Morin, L. (1993). Different ways of seeing: Teaching in an anti-racist school. In T. Perry & J. W. Fraser (Eds.), *Freedom's plow: Teaching in the multicultural classroom* (pp. 27–46). New York: Routledge.

Mohatt, G., & Erickson, F. (1981). Cultural differences in teaching styles in an Odawa school: A sociolinguistic approach. In H. Trueba, G. Guthrie, & K. Au (Eds.), *Culture and the bilingual classroom: Studies in classroom ethnography* (pp. 105–119). Rowley, MA: Newbury House.

Moll, L. (1988). Some key issues in teaching Latino students. *Language Arts, 65,* 465–472.

National Council for the Accreditation of Teacher Education. (1982). *NCATE standards for the accreditation of teacher education.* Washington, DC: Author.

Nelson-Barber, S., & Mitchell, J. (1992). Restructuring for diversity: Five regional portraits. In M. Dilworth (Ed.), *Diversity in teacher education* (pp. 229–262). San Francisco: Jossey-Bass.

Noddings, N. (1991). Stories in dialogue: Caring and interpersonal reasoning. In C. Witherell & N. Noddings (Eds.), *Stories lives tell: Narrative and dialogue in education* (pp. 157–170). New York: Teachers College Press.

Noordhoff, K., & Kleinfeld, J. (1991). *Preparing teachers for multicultural classrooms: A case study in rural Alaska.* Paper presented at the annual meeting of the American Educational Research Association, Chicago.

Ogbu, J. (1992). Understanding cultural diversity and learning. *Educational Researcher, 21*(8), 5–14.

Olneck, M. (1990). The recurring dream: Symbolism and ideology in intercultural and multicultural education. *American Journal of Education, 98,* 147–174.

Orieux, C. (1988). Teacher training for multicultural classrooms. *Canadian Journal of Native Education, 15*(2), 66–69.

Pai, Y. (1990). *Cultural foundations of education.* Columbus, OH: Merrill Publishing Co.

Paley, V. (1979). *White teacher.* Cambridge: Harvard University Press.

Perry, T., & Fraser, J. W. (Eds.). (1993). *Freedom's plow: Teaching in the multicultural classroom.* New York: Routledge.

Poplin, M. (1992). Educating in diversity. *Executive Educator, 14,* A18–24.

Ravitch, D. (1990). Multiculturalism: E pluribus plures. *American Scholar, 59,* 337–354.

Redefining multicultural education: A roundtable discussion. (1988). *Equity and Choice, 4*(3), 19–23.

Richards, J. (1993). Classroom tapestry: A practitioner's perspective. In T. Perry & J. W. Fraser (Eds.), *Freedom's plow: Teaching in the multicultural classroom* (pp. 47–63). New York: Routledge.

Rothenberg, P. (1988). Integrating the study of race, gender, and class: Some preliminary observations. *Feminist Teacher, 3,* 37–42.

Santo, B. (1990, November 9–11). Bicultural education among Indian Americans. In M. Diez (Ed.), *Proceedings of the National Forum of Independent Liberal Arts Colleges for Teacher Education* (Vol 4, pp. 94–101). Milwaukee.

Sarason, S., Davidson, K., & Blatt, B. (1962). *The preparation of teachers: An unstudied problem in education.* New York: Wiley.

Sarason, S., Davidson, K., & Blatt, B. (1986). *The preparation of teachers: An unstudied problem in education* (rev. ed.). Cambridge, MA: Brookline Books.

Saunders, S. (1991). Reflections on my educational experiences as an African American. *Teaching Education, 4,* 41–48.

Schlesinger, A. (1992). *The disuniting of America: Reflections on a multicultural society.* Knoxville, TN: Whittle Direct Books.

Schuhmann, A. (1992). Learning to teach Hispanic students. In M. Dilworth (Ed.), *Diversity in teacher education* (pp. 93–111). San Francisco: Jossey-Bass.

Shah, S. (1989). Effective permeation of race and gender issues in teacher education courses. *Gender and Education, 1,* 221–236.

Shehan, P. (1988). World musics: Windows to cross-cultural understanding. *Music Educators Journal, 75*(3), 22–26.

Shor, I. (1990). [Interview]. *Language Arts, 67,* 342–352.

Shulman J., & Mesa-Baines, A. (Eds.). (1993). *Diversity in the classroom: A casebook for teachers and teacher education learners.* Philadelphia: Research for Better Schools & Lawrence Erlbaum Associates.

Shulman, L. (1987). Knowledge and teaching: Foundations of the new reform. *Harvard Educational Review, 57,* 1–22.

Sims, M. J. (1992). Inquiry and urban classrooms: A female African-American teacher in search of truth. *Theory into Practice, 31,* 342–349.

Sirotnik, K. (1990). On the eroding foundations of teacher education. *Phi Delta Kappan, 71,* 710–716.

Sleeter, C. (1989). Multicultural education as a form of resistance to oppression. *Journal of Education, 171,* 51–71.

Sleeter, C. (1992). *Keepers of the American dream: A study of staff development and multicultural education.* London: Falmer Press.

Sleeter, C., & Grant, C. (1987). An analysis of multicultural education in the U.S. *Harvard Educational Review, 57,* 421–444.

Su, Z. (1990). The function of the peer group in teacher socialization. *Phi Delta Kappan, 71,* 723–727.

Swartz, E. (1991). Multicultural education: From a compensatory to a scholarly foundation. In C. Grant (Ed.), *Research and multicultural education: From the margins to the mainstream* (pp. 32–43). London: Falmer Press.

Tatum, B. (1992). Talking about race, learning about racism: The application of racial identity development theory in the classroom. *Harvard Educational Review, 62,* 1–24.

Thompson, D., & Meeks, J. (1990, December). *Assessing teachers' knowledge of multiethnic literature.* Paper presented at the annual meeting of the American Reading Forum, Sarasota, FL.

Vogt, L., Jordan, C., & Tharp, R. (1987). Explaining school failure, producing school success: Two cases. *Anthropology and Education Quarterly, 18,* 276–286.

Watson, J. K. (1988). From assimilation to anti-racism: Changing educational policies in England and Wales. *Journal of Multilingual and Multicultural Development, 9*(6), 531–552.

Watson, J. K., & Roberts, R. (1988). Multicultural education and teacher training: The picture after Swann. *Journal of Multilingual and Multicultural Development, 9*(4), 339–352.

Wegner, G. (1991, June). *Teaching about the new Europe and the new Germany in American teacher education programs.* Paper presented at the New Europe and the New Germany in the U.S. Classrooms Conference, Indianapolis.

Williams, L. (1991). Curriculum making in two voices: Dilemmas of inclusion in early childhood education. *Early Childhood Research Quarterly, 6,* 303–313.

Winfield, L. (1986). Teacher beliefs toward academically at-risk students in inner-urban schools. *Urban Review, 18,* 253–267.

Winfield, L., & Manning, J. (1992). Changing school culture to accommodate student diversity. In M. Dilworth (Ed.), *Diversity in teacher education* (pp. 181–214). San Francisco: Jossey-Bass.

Yepes-Baraya, M. (1991, April 1–3). *Developing multicultural curricula for teacher education: A case study from SUNY College at Fredonia.* Paper presented at the conference on Multicultural Education: Programs and Strategies for Action, Springfield, IL.

Zeichner, K. (1991, April). *Teacher education for social responsibility: The conception of teaching expertise underlying elementary teacher education at the University of Wisconsin, Madison.* Paper presented at the annual meeting of the American Educational Research Association, Chicago.

Zeichner, K. (1992). *Educating teachers for cultural diversity* (Special Report). East Lansing, MI: National Center for Research on Teacher Learning.

Zeichner, K., & Liston, D. (1990). Traditions of reform in U.S. teacher education. *Journal of Teacher Education, 41,* 3–20.

Zimpher, N. L., & Ashburn, E. (1992). Countering parochialism in teacher candidates. In M. Dilworth (Ed.), *Diversity in teacher education* (pp. 40–62). San Francisco: Jossey-Bass.

INTERNATIONAL PERSPECTIVES ON MULTICULTURAL EDUCATION

44

MULTICULTURAL EDUCATION IN AUSTRALIA: HISTORICAL DEVELOPMENT AND CURRENT STATUS

Rod Allan and Bob Hill

CHARLES STURT UNIVERSITY, MITCHELL AT BATHURST

Australia's first inhabitants were the Aborigines, hunters and gatherers who arrived, according to non-Aboriginal prehistorians (Mulvaney, 1958; Rowley, 1972) some 50,000 years ago by way of the land bridge that linked Australia to Asia. They were attracted to the fertile and well-watered country of the coastal fringe, especially in the south and east of the continent. At the time of the European invasion the Aboriginal population is estimated to have been between 300,000 (Reynolds, 1982) and 750,000 (Butlin, 1983), and by this stage they had developed distinctive cultures that were finely tuned to the environment.

During the 17th century a number of European explorers, principally Portuguese and Dutch, journeyed to the northwestern and southern sections of the continent. It was not until 1770 that a British navigator, Captain James Cook, sighted the east coast of Australia. Although his account of the voyage aroused considerable interest in Britain, no attempt was made to colonize the land until the American colonies were lost in the Revolutionary War. One hundred and sixty-seven years after the Pilgrims arrived in America, a fleet of 11 ships under the command of Captain Arthur Phillip sailed from Britain on 13 May 1787 with 1,030 people on board, 736 of them convicts (Ward, 1976). The initial settlement of Botany Bay was abandoned after one week, and on 26 January 1788 the fleet sailed into Port Jackson, the site today of the country's largest city, Sydney.

Historically, the colonization of Australia has been downplayed by non-Aboriginal historians who have preferred the term *settlement* to *invasion,* despite the dramatic impact the

arrival had through war and disease upon the indigenous inhabitants. While the dominant ethos of White Australia at the opening of the postwar immigration boom was one of assimilation, the ancestors of contemporary Anglo Australians were too ethnocentric to have ever considered assimilating into Aboriginal culture. Few Whites bothered to learn local languages and then usually with the motivation of conversion.

By the end of the 19th century the Aborigines, like many indigenous peoples in the Americas, had been all but decimated. The prevailing policy of "soothe the dying pillow" was designed to make their demise comparatively humane. However, the Aboriginal people declined to fulfill the objectives of this policy, and, partly as a result of legal attempts to end the genocide and partly as a result of their development of resistance to European diseases, the Aboriginal population increased from about 70,000 in the early 1930s to around 160,000 in 1981, 1% of the population. Their current demographic profile inclines toward youth, and Aborigines now compose 2% of the elementary school population, though their numbers are unevenly distributed throughout the country's schools (Department of Aboriginal Affairs, 1984).

While recent policies of education authorities share a number of similarities in their attitudes toward Aboriginal education and multicultural education, and a common interest in antiracism, cultural studies, and strategies designed to create greater equality of educational opportunity, most Aboriginal educators are adamant about distinguishing Aboriginal education from

The authors wish to express their appreciation for the constructive criticisms provided by Dr. Anthony Welch of Sydney University, Dr. Brian Bullivant of Monash University (Melbourne), and the Multicultural Education Unit of the New South Wales Department of School Education, Sydney.

multicultural education. They argue that to conceptually incorporate indigenous Australians with immigrant Australians and their descendants is to deny Aboriginal people their unique identity and unique claim to a place in Australian education. Partly as a result of this preference, the term *multicultural education* in Australia is normally understood to exclude Aborigines. Government departments and institutions responsible for multiculturalism have rarely solicited Aboriginal participation. Institutions responsible for Aboriginal education, now increasingly Aboriginal controlled, have pursued a different, although often parallel, agenda (National Aboriginal Education Committee [NAEC], 1982). This chapter continues that tradition and, in deferring to the arguments of Aboriginal educators such as Miller (1985), will not attempt to incorporate a discussion of Aboriginal education or Aboriginal studies.

Although this chapter will concentrate on the educational response to the massive post–World War II immigration program, a wide range of ethnic groups contributed to Australian demographics and culture throughout the 19th and early 20th centuries. While the earliest immigrants to Australia in the first 40 years of European settlement were convicts and Irish political dissidents, the availability of land led to an influx of "free" settlers, not all of them British. German Lutherans, victims of political persecution in their homeland, came to South Australia under a privately financed scheme as refugees. A small number of Indians, Chinese, and Malays were imported by some pastoralists in New South Wales as "coolie" workers. In 1851 gold was discovered in New South Wales and Victoria, and before long the goldfields had a multinational flavor. Gold seekers came in numbers from southern China, provoking much resentment, which was to have a considerable and long-term impact on the attitudes of Australians. Some 20 years after the gold rush, sugar growers in northern Queensland began conscripting labor to their fledgling industry with the often forcible recruitment of people from the Pacific Islands. As pressure against this practice increased, Italians came as a new source of labor, thus beginning a process of chain migration. This process also brought Greek and Spanish immigrants. By the turn of the century there was a range of ethnic groups in Australia, but the overwhelming majority were of British origin. This is not to imply that the British were ethnically homogeneous. As Sherington (1991) points out, Britons identified themselves as Irish, Scots, English, Welsh, and Cornish, maintained their religious differences, and entrenched them in the nascent school system.

For the first half of the 20th century immigrants, albeit in small numbers, continued to arrive, mainly from Britain. Partly because of two world wars there developed a more distinctive Australian identity, although one that was embedded in British institutions and social mores to the extent that cultural differences, particularly languages, were regarded as "un-Australian."

POSTWAR MIGRATION

Despite the image of a homogeneous country and its people, an image often promoted by the Australian mass media, Australia is one of the most ethnically diverse nations in the world, with a higher proportion of its population born overseas than any other country except Israel (Kalantzis, Cope, Noble, Poynting, 1990). Australia's population is 17 million (Bureau of Immigration Research [BIR], 1992), more than double the number at the end of World War II. This increase reflects the influx of new settlers from an extensive immigration program. One person in five has been born overseas and a further one in five has at least one parent born overseas. Four million migrants from over 100 countries have settled in Australia (BIR, 1992). Over 25% of Australia's population is of non-English-speaking background, and of these 2 million reported in the 1986 census that they spoke a language other than English at home, the five most common being Italian, Greek, a Chinese language, German, and Arabic (Kalantzis et al., 1990). In both absolute terms and in relation to population, Australia is one of the leading resettlement countries for refugees. Some 450,000 displaced persons have settled in Australia since World War II. They include 170,000 from Europe as a result of the war and its aftermath; 14,000 Hungarians who fled during the uprising of 1956; 5,700 Czechoslovakians after Dubček's removal in 1968; 70,000 Indochinese since the end of the Vietnam War in 1975; and 13,000 eastern European political dissidents who have sought asylum (BIR, 1992).

In 1945 Australia's population was 7 million, 97% of whom had ancestors from the British Isles. Australia had been through the traumatic experience of having, for the first and so far only time of European settlement, its shores attacked by hostile forces: the Japanese bombed Darwin, and its midget submarines sank a ferry in Sydney harbor. The nation's psyche was shattered: Australians were made suddenly aware that the protective umbrella of Britain no longer extended to the Pacific. The capitulation of Singapore destroyed the cherished belief that membership in the British Empire was sufficient to ensure security from external menace. The prime minister, Mr. J. B. Chifley, articulated a widely held belief that the most effective means of survival was to increase the nation's population, for otherwise: "We will not be able to justify before the world our retention of such a great country" (Crisp, 1961, p. 319). However, such a natural increase was unlikely, given the limitations of population size despite the enticing cry of Australia's first minister for immigration, Mr. Arthur Calwell, who decreed that Australia must "ennoble motherhood" for we must either "populate the country or sooner or later be overrun by Asiatic peoples" (Wilton & Bosworth, 1984, p. 7). Realistic assessments showed that the need for an immigration policy based on pragmatism and humanitarianism was long overdue. Not that in developing such a policy was a multicultural nation ever envisaged. The cornerstone was to be the immigrant from Britain: "It is my hope that for every foreign migrant there will be ten from the United Kingdom," proclaimed Calwell (p. 11). Seven years later his successor to the portfolio of immigration, Harold Holt, saw no reason to disagree: "Australia, in accepting a balanced intake of other European people, can still build a truly British nation on this side of the world" (p. 17).

While there was strong community support for such principles, the reality was that Australia's immigration policies proved to be far more flexible than envisaged, as evidenced by the ethnic pluralism of today. However, community opinion about

TABLE 44–1. Top 10 Countries of Birth for Australian Immigrants

1966–1967			1976–1977			1991–1992		
Country of Birth	No.	%	Country of Birth	No.	%	Country of Birth	No.	%
UK & Ireland	75,510	54.4	UK & Ireland	19,220	27.1	UK	14,465	13.5
Italy	12,890	9.3	Lebanon	12,190	17.2	Hong Kong	12,913	12.0
Greece	9,830	7.1	New Zealand	4,840	6.8	Vietnam	9,592	8.9
Yugoslavia	7,550	5.4	Cyprus	2,770	3.9	New Zealand	7,242	6.7
Germany	3,410	2.5	Malaysia	1,770	2.5	Philippines	5,917	5.5
New Zealand	2,750	2.0	Philippines	1,680	2.4	India	5,608	5.2
USA	2,340	1.7	Yugoslavia	1,650	2.3	China	3,388	3.2
Netherlands	1,870	1.3	Greece	1,530	2.2	Taiwan	3,172	3.0
Lebanon	1,720	1.2	Italy	1,320	1.9	Malaysia	3,123	2.9
India	1,650	1.2	USA	1,220	1.7	Sri Lanka	2,777	2.6
Subtotal	119,520	86.2	Subtotal	48,190	67.9	Subtotal	68,197	63.5
Other	19,160	13.8	Other	22,730	32.1	Other	39,194	36.5
TOTAL	138,680	100.0	TOTAL	70,920	100.0	TOTAL	107,391	100.0

Source: *Immigration Update*, Bureau of Immigration Research, 1992, Canberra: Australian Government Publishing Service.

desirable sources of immigration has consistently lagged behind government policy. The United Kingdom and Ireland traditionally have been the largest source, but the numbers of immigrants from other countries has fluctuated over time. From the mid-1950s and 1960s, southern Europeans were predominant, particularly those from Italy and Greece, followed soon after by Lebanese and Turkish immigrants. From the mid-1970s, refugees and migrants have come from Southeast Asia and other Asian countries, and more recently from South America and the Pacific rim. In 1991 and 1992 the major sources were the United Kingdom, Hong Kong, and Vietnam. These trends are illustrated in Table 44–1.

Foster (1988) notes that Australian immigration was characterized by the offering of inducements to preferred immigrants. However, the definition of "preferred" widened from British to northern European, then to southern European as economic conditions in those source countries altered. The Australian economy also dictated the flow of immigration, with additional quotas in good economic years and substantial reductions in times of increased unemployment. Similar economic push-pull factors operated in western Europe during the same period. The critical difference, however, was that in western Europe immigrants generally arrived as guest workers to fulfill labor contracts with a view of returning to their country of origin. It was always assumed with Australian postwar immigration that arrivals came not as guest workers but as permanent settlers: as "New Australians."

RESPONSES TO IMMIGRATION

Popular Reaction to Postwar Immigration, 1945–1972

The reaction of Australians to this change in demographic patterns has been complex. Many historians and social commentators assert that Australia suffers an identity crisis. Its traditional roots are British, its modern popular cultural orientation is toward the United States of America, and its major export market is Japan. The country is a geographic extension of Southeast Asia, and that is where its probable economic future lies. Many Australians are uncomfortable with this new development, which contrasts with the racist ideology of previous generations (Blainey, 1984).

Russel Ward (1958) argued that the beliefs held by the dominant force in 19th-century Australia, the White Anglo Saxon male, still permeated society at the time when the country was accepting a large proportion of new settlers. Ward identified twin ideals of "mateship" and "egalitarianism" as unifying and pervasive factors. These ideals had been challenged during the gold rush era of the 19th century by the arrival of Chinese indentured labor. The Chinese people were regarded as an affront: They worked for a pittance, "invaded" claims after White diggers had vacated them, spoke a different language, and, importantly, were of a different color. Violence does not figure prominently in Australian history, except in the treatment of Aborigines, yet the goldfields were witness to scenes of vicious racial clashes. One result of the gold rush era was that various state legislatures passed restrictive laws aimed at curtailing immigration of Asian labor. The Immigration Restriction Act, passed after the federation of Australian states came into being in 1901, soon became known as the "White Australia policy." Based substantially on the U.S. Chinese Exclusion Act (1884), it prohibited the immigration of colored peoples and institutionalized the nation's xenophobia (Ward, 1958).

If we are to accept Ward's proposition, then it is reasonable to suggest that the logical outcome of institutionalized resentment to colored immigration would be extended to other immigration as well. Elements of egalitarianism and xenophobia have persisted in the reactions of Australians to the substantial immigration of the 1950s and 1960s. Such attitudes were perceptively analyzed by Jean Martin (1972), who identified a fundamental set of beliefs held by Australians about the ways in which immigrants could and should be incorporated into Australian society. She termed these beliefs the "ideology of settlement." It is an assimilationist ideology underpinned by six essential elements that are not necessarily exclusive to Australia and are still articulated in some quarters today.

The ideology is:

1. Australians are democratic and individualistic, free of class prejudice, and essentially generous hearted and open-minded to anyone who shares these central values.
2. Australia is the "lucky country," and the one salient characteristic that all immigrants share is that they are lucky to be here.
3. With a little education of public opinion and additional support from voluntary organizations, the existing social structure can and will incorporate newcomers without undergoing radical change itself.
4. National groupings are unnecessary and a potential threat to the smooth incorporation of immigrants into Australian society.
5. The process of incorporation involves the individual immigrant assimilating into the Australian way of life, and the success of this assimilation depends, fundamentally, not on structures or on government policies but on the goodwill of individual immigrants and individual Australians.
6. It would be contrary to the prevailing egalitarian values and detrimental to the assimilation of immigrants for them to be given any unique privileges or consideration of any kind.

Throughout the 1960s these attitudes were mirrored in government policy, which was one of assimilation and attendant ethnocentrism. Immigrants were expected to submit to a dominant culture and in so doing divest themselves of their cultural distinctiveness and, in particular, their languages. While such a policy had public and political support, in practice it simply did not work.

The Advent of Multiculturalism, 1972–1986

By the end of the 1960s the non-English speaking ethnic communities had become more vocal and better organized. A groundswell of opinion in the broader community was reacting against the policies developed during two decades of conservative rule. Nonetheless, toward the end of this period was enacted the federal Immigration (Education) Act of 1971, which tied grants to specific purposes within states and gave the federal government a powerful lever to influence in a direct manner state (provincial) education policies. Arguably, this was the crucial constitutional turning point for education in Australia.

The election of the reformist Whitlam Labor government in 1972 hastened the demise of assimilation and introduced the nation to a decade of sweeping multicultural initiatives. The catalyst for change was the minister for immigration, Al Grassby, a flamboyant and publicity-conscious personality, whose view was that the cultural resources of immigrants should be seen as an integral part of Australian society. Grassby constantly spoke about "the family of the nation" and in so doing placed immigration firmly in the public arena. Labor's focus was welfare-oriented, and immigrants were acknowledged as suffering both socioeconomic disadvantage and discrimination. The dismantling of the Department of Immigration and the siting of its functions within the departments of labor, social security, and education was indicative of this approach (Kalantzis et al., 1990). During his brief tenure of 18 months, Grassby began oversight of the transition to multiculturalism. Labor dismantled the White Australia policy and introduced a nondiscriminatory immigration program, thus emulating the Canadian initiative of a decade earlier (Samuda, 1986). A commitment to refugee settlement was maintained as well.

Although the Labor government was short-lived, Whitlam's successor, the leader of the conservative coalition Malcolm Fraser, maintained the momentum and commissioned the *Report of the Review of Post-Arrival Programs and Services for Migrants* (Galbally, 1978), which became widely known as the Galbally report after its chairperson, Frank Galbally. Galbally identified four basic principles to be applied in the selection of immigrants and in program development and services for them. They were:

1. All members of Australian society must have equal opportunity to realize their full potential and must have equal access to programs and services.
2. Every person should be able to maintain his or her culture without prejudice or disadvantage and should be encouraged to understand and embrace other cultures.
3. Needs of immigrants should, in general, be met by programs and services available to the whole community, but special services and programs are necessary at present to ensure equality of access and provision.
4. Services and programs should be designed and operated in full consultation with clients, and self-help should be encouraged as much as possible with a view to helping immigrants become self-reliant quickly.

The acceptance of these principles by Fraser and subsequent governments led to the establishment of adult and child migrant education programs, interpreter services within government departments and statutory authorities, and Disadvantaged Schools Programs (DSP) and the development of the Special Broadcasting Service (SBS) with its multilingual media outlets, the Multicultural Education Program (MEP), and the Australian Institute of Multicultural Affairs (AIMA).

While the Galbally report is often credited with providing the major impetus for multiculturalism, there were two other influential reports. The Australian Ethnic Affairs Council was established in 1977 to advise the Ministry for Immigration and Ethnic Affairs on immigrant issues. The council's *Australia as a Multicultural Society* (Australian Ethnic Affairs Council [AEAC], 1977), an ideological blueprint for a future multicultural society (Bullivant, 1986, p. 110), was based on three social issues: cohesion, equality, and cultural identity. The report from the Schools Commission Committee on Multicultural Education, *Education for a Multicultural Society* (1979), became the basis of MEP.

The Economic Imperative, 1986–1993

The return to power of the Australian Labor Party in 1983 under Bob Hawke saw support for these initiatives maintained until an economic downturn 3 years later necessitated severe budget cuts. AIMA was closed, although it was later replaced by the Office of Multicultural Affairs within the Department of the Prime Minister. Funds were withdrawn from MEP, and ESL teaching programs suffered substantial decreases in funding. Coinciding with these fiscal measures was the release of a national inquiry, *The Review of Migrant and Multicultural Programs and Services: Don't Settle for Less* (Jupp, 1986). This report enunciated basic rights of equity and access in the economic, social, cultural, and political life of the nation and advocated the inalienable right for all to enjoy their own culture, practice their own religion, and use their own language.

These themes were taken up by the Office of Multicultural Affairs when in 1989 it launched the *National Agenda for a Multicultural Australia* (Office of Multicultural Affairs, 1989). While the agenda had three dimensions—cultural rights, social justice, and economic efficiency—it was the last of these that acknowledged that immigration policies must address economic issues, otherwise there would be the potential for social division and perhaps conflict.

In political terms the most interesting aspect about the immigration program has been the bipartisanship it has attracted from the major political parties. Even during the "Blainey debate" in 1984, when the eminent historian Geoffrey Blainey warned of the "Asianization" of Australia, little political capital was made by the opposition. During the 1987 federal election campaign the opposition leader, John Howard, sought to exploit immigration as an issue, though he did not pursue it for long. The issue, however, was rekindled with the release of the Fitzgerald report, *Immigration: A Commitment to Australia* (Fitzgerald, 1988). The report, although supporting an increased immigrant intake, was critical of the current immigration program, claiming that there was a decline of community confidence in immigration because the program was perceived to be no longer in the public interest. Fitzgerald argued for a sharper economic focus in selection and stressed that immigration must serve national economic needs with greater emphasis on skills, English-language proficiency, and youth and less on family reunion. The report was particularly critical of multiculturalism, which was seen as divisive and threatening; what the community required was a strong sense of Australian identity. John Howard joined the debate, claiming that Asian immigration was too high and in so doing reviving some of the concerns raised by Blainey four years earlier. It served to undermine Howard's standing within his own party and contributed to his loss of the leadership in 1990 (Kelly, 1992).

In summary, this period was characterized by tighter budgetary constraints, which affected multicultural initiatives. For example, there was a marked change from cultural to economic justification, as seen by a shift in emphasis from community languages to Asian ones, justified by potential expansion of trade and tourism. Further impetus was given by Hawke's successor, Paul Keating, at a meeting of state premiers in December 1992 when additional funds were pledged for the teaching of Asian languages.

In the last decade of the 20th century, like most of the industrial world, Australia faces harsh economic conditions. With high levels of unemployment (11% in 1993), there is strong public and political support for reduced immigration and a resentment of government resources being channeled to special interest groups. In a climate of fiscal restraint, multicultural programs are likely to be funded only if universal economic benefits can be demonstrated. The *National Agenda*, with its assumption that multiculturalism is a means of maintaining cultural and economic stability, will be tested.

THE EDUCATIONAL RESPONSE

This section identifies three discernible periods relating to multicultural education in Australia. The first canvasses the postwar years through the end of a long period of conservative government (23 years) in 1972. It was during this time that Australia received its greatest number of immigrants and the educational response was clearly an assimilationist one. The years from 1972 to 1986 saw successive governments of different political persuasion involved in the transition from "migrant education" to an era of multiculturalism in which the ethnic diversity of the nation was celebrated. This was an interventionist time when the federal government encouraged and financed educational initiatives by way of grants to states for specified purposes. The current period is one characterized by fiscal restraint as Australia struggles to combat the harsh economic conditions that have beset much of the industrialized world.

From Passive to Active Assimilation, 1945–1972

The initial postwar period was characterized by passive assimilation in education. Policies consistent with Martin's ideology of settlement were implemented. These policies required immigrant children to adapt to existing school and curriculum organization. There was a minimum of structural change in the bureaucracy and schools. A statement by a school principal in 1951 typified official thinking. He described his staff as "teachers who have no special training for this work, nor do they use any foreign language, but they have met their peculiar problems with commendable initiative, patience and skill" (Martin, 1978, p. 85). Immigrant children were defined as "problems" that would be solved over time with goodwill rather than by special programs. The little educational research conducted in this early period focused on immigrant children's deficits (Roper, 1971).

The late 1960s saw a change in perspective driven by the concerns of teachers who were having difficulty in coping with non-English-speaking background (NESB) children at a time when student numbers were growing beyond the capacity of staffing and building programs. While the implicit objective of educational commitment remained assimilation, programs were introduced to pursue that aim more actively. To comprehend the dynamic behind this change to active assimilation, it is important to understand the nature of Australian federalism. Like the United States of America and Canada, Australia has a federal constitution. While the national government controls immigration, the states (provinces) have responsibility for education. From the early 1970s the federal government's advantaged fiscal base enabled it increasingly to set the educational agenda by allocating grants to the states for specified programs. A crucial example of this was the Child Migrant Education Program (CMEP), launched initially as an interim measure in 1970. This program subsidized the provision of special ESL withdrawal classes in those primary and secondary schools with high immigrant density and provided funding for teachers, short training courses, and language laboratories. This paradigm of active assimilation was accompanied by a growing body of literature designed to provide teachers with information about the cultural background and learning difficulties of immigrant children (Bullivant, 1973; Kovacs & Cropley, 1975). However, by far the major thrust of child immigrant education was teaching English as a second language.

From Immigrant to Multicultural Education, 1972–1986

The election in 1972 of a Labor government after 23 years of conservative rule ushered in an era of great expectation for change. This accelerated the trend to greater federal involvement in ethnic affairs and also resulted in a spectacular increase in resources to education. Most important, it signaled a rejection of the old paradigm of assimilation with its focus on "migrant education" for a celebration of Australia's ethnic diversity. Grassby (1979), the former minister for immigration, summed up the new ethos:

We are not talking about "migrant" children. We are talking about Australian children of many different backgrounds. Certainly it is irrelevant to talk about migrant education. What we are really talking about is education of all children to fit them for a life in a multicultural and polyethnic society.

The change was not instant and was often honored by rhetoric rather than reality. However, by the early 1980s all Australian states had adopted multicultural education policies, typified by that of the numerically largest state, New South Wales, which enunciated its objectives in 1978 in this philosophical position:

In a multicultural society each person has a right to cultural integrity, to a positive self-image, and to an understanding and respect for differences. Not only should each person be exposed to positive feelings about his or her own heritage, but must experience like feelings about the heritage of others. (New South Wales Department of Education, 1978, p. 3)

A ministerial policy statement (New South Wales Ministry of Education, 1979) was released the following year that formed the basis for the *Multicultural Education Policy Statement* (New South Wales Department of Education, 1983) and support documents:

The aims of Multicultural education encompass the provision of educational experiences which will develop in all children:

a) an understanding and appreciation that Australia has been multicultural in nature throughout its history both before and after European colonization.
b) an awareness of the contribution which people of many different cultural backgrounds have made and are making to Australia.
c) intercultural understanding through the consideration of attitudes, beliefs and values related to multiculturalism.
d) behaviour that fosters interethnic harmony.
e) an enhanced sense of personal worth through an acceptance and appreciation not only of their Australian national identity but also of their specific Australian ethnic identity in the context of a multicultural society. (New South Wales Department of Education, 1983, p. 4)

Support documents were produced in the specific areas of:

English-as-a-second-language education;
community-languages education;
ethnic studies;
intercultural education; and
multicultural perspectives to the curriculum.

The last two were to be mandatory components for all schools.

In December 1992 the New South Wales Department of School Education released its *Multicultural Education Plan 1993–1997*. This plan provides schools with a significant range of multicultural initiatives in order to "safeguard equality of access to educational opportunity for students from non-English-speaking backgrounds within the wider brief of providing all students with an understanding of the relevance of multiculturalism to their personal lives and in their future as responsible adults" (New South Wales Department of School Education, 1992b, p. 3).

This conceptualization of multiculturalism as a component of every child's education had radical curriculum implications. A wealth of teaching resources dealing with the lifestyles and cultures of Australian ethnic groups was produced (National Advisory and Co-ordinating Committee on Multicultural Education [NACCME], 1987). A plethora of literature demonstrating the potential for incorporating a multicultural perspective in a variety of subject areas including English (Kable, 1987), religion (Goosen, 1985), social studies (Mannix, 1985), and history (Cigler, 1987; Kalantzis, 1987) appeared.

Multicultural perspectives across the curriculum were explicitly designed to foster interethnic harmony. This was a belated response to the changing ethnic composition of Australian immigrants; a change accelerated by the introduction of a non-discriminatory entry policy in 1973 and the admission of relatively large numbers of Indochinese refugees.

Another characteristic of this period was a changed focus on language. Whereas CMEP had seen ESL as a major strategy to assist the assimilation of immigrant children, the focus now was on community languages and bilingual programs as a means of overcoming educational disadvantage, strengthening ethnic identity, and preserving community languages as a national asset. Community languages became emblematic of ethnic group identity (LoBianco, 1988). There was an expansion in most states of community-language electives for final-year secondary students (DEET, 1991).

Most state education departments developed language policies either separately or as a component of their multicultural education policy. There was a growing convergence in the terminology used and a concern about lack of resources, and complaints about the destabilizing effects of short-term tied federal funding were common. Policies of different states reflected their demography and educational traditions and were often seen to be written for different audiences. In Queensland, for example, the policy documents seemed designed to reduce the threat of languages other than English (LOTE) in the minds of decision makers. In Victoria, the policy reflected the strength of the ethnic lobby and pressure for language maintenance (Andreoni & Ozolins, 1985).

Administrative difficulties in staffing such subjects, caused by the geographical distribution of students and the fact that only a small minority of Australian teachers could speak a community language, resulted in the contentious solution of increasing government funding to ethnic community-controlled schools operating outside normal school hours. Encouraged by the Galbally report, the number of ethnic schools increased, and Noorst (1982) reported the existence of 1,045 separate schools involving more than 85,000 students. Government support of these schools was criticized for being potentially divisive and allowing mainstream schools to avoid responsibility for the provision of community languages. Noorst (1982) strongly supported these schools, arguing that they were crucial in the maintenance and development of language and in the preservation and promotion of cultural heritage. Bullivant (1982) was critical of the way the schools selected and transmitted culture. He argued for dual ethnic schools that might produce a "hyphenated ethnic" (Greek-Australian, Italian-Australian), although he acknowledged the difficulty in achieving this, especially as far as smaller ethnic groups were concerned. Lewins (1982) claimed that the funding of ethnic schools could not be justified on the grounds of affirmative action. Moreover, Smolicz (1984) saw such schools as contributing to ethnic separatism. Yet by 1991 the federal government had funded 196,000 enrollments through more than 500 ethnic organizations at a cost of A$6.9 million (DEET, 1991).

Three major criticisms have been raised concerning the emphasis upon culture during this multicultural phase. Although state policies exhorted teachers to incorporate multicultural perspectives, implementation, particularly in those schools with few immigrant students, was commonly tokenistic. This reflected Cahill's finding that, nationally, Australian teachers' knowledge about Australia's ethnic groups was "seriously deficient" (Cahill, 1984, p. xiii). Typical activities such as "national" days stressed traditional cultures' externalities such as food, dress, music, and dance. Bullivant (1981b) argued that to equate culture with heritage was a dangerous oversimplification that ignored the adaptive and evolutionary nature of a group's culture and the extent to which cultural convergence had taken place.

Second, curriculum implementation across the country was uncoordinated and unsystematic, a problem that was recog-

nized by the establishment of the NACCME in 1984 in an attempt to counter the duplication of resource development in different states and the ad-hoc distribution of teaching materials (Foster, 1988). There was a lack of professionalism in the production values of many of the resources produced with government funding, and rarely did resource development budgets provide funds for training teachers to use the resources (Cahill, 1984). Earlier, the *Report of the National Inquiry into Teacher Education* (Auchmuty, 1980) had criticized teacher training institutions for their inability to prepare students adequately to understand and implement programs that catered to the diverse nature of Australian society.

Finally, there was a developing criticism that the emphasis on culture promoted by Grassby and Galbally had ignored the structural underpinnings of racism in Australian society. A growing body of critics called for a greater emphasis on affirmative action and a curriculum for working-class immigrant children aimed at achieving equal outcomes and empowering them for participation in the workforce rather than singing in their community language while they danced in the dole queue (Kalantzis, 1987).

The Economic Imperative, 1986–1993

In 1986 MEP was abolished. The 1984 *Review of the Commonwealth Multicultural Education Program* had been critical of MEP's failure to achieve substantial and lasting change in Australian schooling. The review described a lack of national coordination, an unimpressive project completion rate, and widespread lack of awareness about the scheme (Cahill, 1984). Economic constraints were to dominate educational decision making in the ensuing period. Resources for multicultural education were less plentiful and more carefully targeted to meet goals of access and equity. With a half million Australian adults identified as having major literacy problems (LoBianco, 1988), ESL teaching was seen as crucial to the demands of a more sophisticated workforce. Whereas a generation before, non-English-speaking immigrants would have been consigned as "factory fodder," there developed a greater willingness to upgrade and recognize immigrant qualifications with ESL programs complementing this process. A National Office of Overseas Skills Recognition (NOOSR) was established in 1989, and an access-and-equity strategy for Commonwealth government instrumentalities was adopted (Cope, Castles, & Kalantzis, 1991). A lucrative market in Asia was tapped for the export of education based on language proficiency as the economic potential of that region was recognized.

A national policy on languages was announced in April 1987, partly in response to figures suggesting that three years earlier only 10.5% of final-year secondary students matriculated with a second language, a decrease from 44% in 1967 (LoBianco,1987). Programs funded by the language policy included the Australian Second Language Learning Program, which allocated funds to state education systems for language instruction; the Asian Studies Program, which developed curricula in Asian languages and culture; and the Cross-Cultural Supplementation Program, for training professionals and paraprofessionals in cross-cultural communication (Clyne, 1991). Under this policy the desirability of using mainstream schools to encourage language maintenance took less prominence than arguments for learning the languages of Asian trading partners.

The production of classroom resources concerning cultural difference, which peaked in the early 1980s, reflected the change in national priorities. The bicentenary of European colonization in 1988 resulted in an avalanche of teaching materials (NACCME, 1987) and a renewed commitment to Australian studies. However, by the end of the decade the emphasis had rapidly moved to the promotion of Asian studies, seen by some as reflecting the ascendancy of economic rationalism in educational decision making.

This brief summary of the educational response to ethnic diversity since the end of World War II has attempted to identify the major components of educational change. It should be stressed, however, that in a conservative institution such as education, national or state policies have not always been implemented in the classroom.

RESEARCH

The changing educational paradigms and government policies identified previously had direct and indirect impact on the amount and nature of educational research related to cultural diversity in Australia. Many of the major studies have been government funded, and the amount of research since 1986 has been considerably reduced. This section examines significant research relating to the educational outcomes of immigrant children, the incorporation of multicultural perspectives into the curriculum, the creation of harmonious interethnic relations, and language teaching in Australian schools.

Educational Performance of Immigrant Children

A major focus of research in Australian multicultural education has been on the outcomes experienced by immigrant students. The most commonly used measures have been performance on standardized educational tests, retention rates, admission to tertiary education, and indicative vocations. Comparing the findings of these studies is fraught with difficulty for a number of reasons. Definitions of immigrants vary: In some studies the criterion used is the country of birth of the child, in other cases it is the country of birth of one or both parents. In others, the term is restricted to those immigrants from non-English-speaking countries. Some studies clearly identify the specific ethnic group membership, while others combine subjects from quite different ethnic groups and categorize them as immigrants. Generalizations are difficult because of complex interactions between gender, class, and ethnicity. Nor do official statistics, which categorize immigrants according to their country of origin, accurately identify ethnicity. For example, among immigrants from Indonesia are Dutch colonials, political refugees from East Timor, ethnic Chinese business persons, as well as ethnic Indonesians who arrived in the country originally as Australian government-sponsored students (Da Costa, 1992). With these qualifications we turn to the studies.

In a major Sydney study of immigrant in-school retention rates, Meade (1983) compared the rate of secondary school completion of children whose parents were born in a non-English-speaking (NES) country with those whose parents were born in an English-speaking country (including Australia). Forty-one percent of NESB students completed secondary schooling, a significantly higher proportion than that of Anglo students who completed secondary schooling (30%). This result still held when the IQs and socioeconomic status of both groups of students were controlled. Williams (1980, cited in Marsh, 1988) had arrived at a similar conclusion in an earlier study, conducted in Melbourne, that found that children whose fathers were born in an NES country were more likely to complete secondary school than were those whose fathers were born either in Australia or in an English-speaking country. Burke and Davis (cited in Marsh, 1988) demonstrated that the proportion of second-generation immigrant children entering tertiary institutions is higher than that of Anglo Australians. However, despite common difficulties confronted by NESB children, the results for different ethnic groups were uneven. Martin and Meade (cited in Sturman, 1985) showed that Lebanese, Maltese, Italian, and Yugoslav students tended to remain at school for shorter periods than children from other ethnic groups. Further, the Australian Schools Commission pointed out that there is frequently a strong interaction between ethnicity and gender; in many ethnic groups, educational aspirations do not extend as strongly to girls. There was no evidence that the daughters of immigrant parents perform any less well than the sons, but at both 16- and 18-year-old levels in 1971, girls born in Greece, Italy, and Yugoslavia were markedly more likely to have left the educational system than were Australian girls or boys of similar background (Sturman, 1985).

With qualifications about ethnic and gender differences, these findings suggest that at least among a significant number of ethnic groups there is high pressure for academic success and a willingness to make the financial sacrifice that might be required to ensure educational retention. The higher valuation placed upon education by families from some ethnic groups may receive a positive response from teachers. Bullivant (1988a) suggested that teachers actually prefer NESB students because their attitude to work and behavior in the classroom is more supportive of teachers and contrasts favorably with Anglo Australian students. There is some evidence that teacher support for immigrant students has affected career choices. Abraham (1992) reports that the number of female teachers of Greek descent is higher than that of any other ethnic group in Sydney. He saw the impetus being the introduction in 1973 of modern Greek to the secondary syllabus, which may have encouraged Greek students to pursue a career, coupled with the imprimatur of Greek parents who saw teaching as an acceptable profession for their daughters.

In summarizing a number of research investigations into parental attitudes, Marsh (1988) uncovered clear evidence of strong preferences for a traditional academic curriculum. Connell, Connell, Sinclair, and Stroobant (1975) recorded that their immigrant respondents wished their children to be taught more science and have fewer confusing subject choices. DiFerranti (cited in Marsh, 1988) reported that immigrant parents expressed criticism about too little homework and the absence of languages in the curriculum of Australian schools. Jakubo-wicz and Wolf (cited in Marsh, 1988) noted among immigrant parents a desire for stricter schooling. Spearritt and Colman (cited in Marsh, 1988) interviewed refugee parents who were appreciative of their children's opportunities to attend school and learn English but who felt too much time was wasted by playing games and sport. Both Burke and Davis (cited in Marsh, 1988) and Sturman (1985) suggested that Catholic schools seem to be more closely aligned with the educational values of many immigrant parents than are schools in the state system. Taft and Cahill (1978), in a study of Maltese, British, and South American immigrant children, ascertained that the British and Maltese children found their Australian schooling less difficult than in their own country of origin, and majorities from all three groups found Australian schools less difficult than they had expected. Solman (1987), in a survey of an urban state high school community with a high ethnic population, found a strong correlation between parental and student views about what should be taught (literacy, numeracy, and precise informa-tion about sex and drugs). However, there were differences between teachers and immigrant parents and children concern-ing the school's role. Although the overwhelming majority of parents and students believed that it was the responsibility of the school to encourage students to complete their full six years of secondary schooling, only 20% of teachers agreed.

It is dangerous to overgeneralize about the educational per-formance of immigrant children because the pattern varies among ethnic groups. In a major study, Marjoribanks (1979) surveyed 850 Adelaide families from five different ethnic or social-class groups (Greek, Italian, Yugoslav, Anglo middle, and Anglo working class) who had children in primary school. Us-ing multiple regression analysis, he demonstrated the complex nature of the correlates of children's achievement with a range of variables including parental aspirations, parental instrumen-tal and expressive orientations, and ethnicity and class. He found that students from Italian, Greek, and Yugoslav families scored less well, particularly in the literacy components of the study, than Australian students of similar social-class back-ground.

Taft and Cahill (1978) found quite different patterns of aca-demic progress among their South American, Maltese, and Brit-ish subjects. In their longitudinal study of students' academic progress, they found that there was a slight reduction in the proportion of South American children rated as "slow learners" by their teachers over the 2-year period. By contrast, the pro-portion of Maltese children who were rated as "slow learners" at the end of their second year was 3 times as high as the proportion rated as such in their first year at the school.

Hewitt (cited in Sturman, 1985) compared the performance of 10- and 14-year-old immigrant and Australian children on a number of reading and mathematics work tests. While there was no significant ethnic difference on the mathematics tests, 59% of 10-year-old and 43% of 14-year-old immigrant children failed to achieve 80% mastery on the reading test as compared to 47% and 28% respectively of the Australian children. Wil-liams, Batten, Girling-Butcher, and Clancy (cited in Sturman, 1985) concluded that NESB immigrants were disadvantaged in

TABLE 44-2. Basic Skills Test, New South Wales, 1991

	Literacy			Numeracy		
	Number	Mean	SD	Number	Mean	SD
Year 3 students						
Total	57,410	50.4	8.1	57,410	52.7	9.0
NESB	11,454	48.8	7.7	11,454	51.2	8.9
Year 6 students						
Total	55,101	48.9	6.8	55,153	48.9	7.9
NESB	11,207	46.7	6.8	11,215	47.6	8.0

their scores on word knowledge, literacy, and numeracy, and these unsurprising findings are supported by others that sug-gest, however, that immigrant students' deficit in language tests are reduced as the students progress through secondary school (Marsh, 1988).

Since 1989 in New South Wales, all year 3 and year 6 stu-dents in state schools have undertaken a basic skills test in literacy and numeracy. As Table 44-2 shows, the NESB chil-dren's mean scores were slightly lower than the state average; the deficit in literacy was small though slightly greater. On every measure NESB children out-performed Aboriginal and Torres Strait Islander children (New South Wales Department of School Education, 1992c).

The category of immigration may also be a predictor of educational performance. Following the war in Indochina, many of the Asian immigrants were refugees who came gener-ally without resources and without qualifications recognized in Australia. Spearritt and Colman (1983, cited in Marsh, 1988) assessed the performance of a group of Indochinese refugee students in language and numeration before they undertook an educational reception program. They retested the students 3 and 8 months later and found that the Laotian and Cambodian children (but not the Vietnamese) were significantly below norms on all aspects of the test. The posttests revealed that the educational deficit was maintained in all groups in literacy and numeracy despite some increase in oral proficiency and essay writing. Bullivant (cited in Marsh, 1988) has cited evidence that longer-term Chinese immigrants are less academically moti-vated than are short-stay immigrants. According to this perspec-tive the longer immigrant children are in Australia the more they are "contaminated" by values less supportive of education (Marsh, 1988).

With restrictions on numbers of immigrants during the eco-nomic recession of the late 1980s and early 1990s, an increasing proportion of immigrants were in the category of business/professional immigration. Most of these people spoke English, had qualifications in demand, and arrived with some financial security. Increasing numbers have come from Hong Kong as the British mandate over that colony approaches its end. The children of these immigrants appear to have met with consider-able academic success. The Australian media have recently pro-jected the stereotype of Asian students as particularly conscien-tious and successful. For example, in New South Wales, articles highlighting the fact that the top two students in the Higher School Certificate (matriculation) exam were Chinese Australians featured prominently. So too was evidence of the large proportion of Asian scholars among the top 200 students (Diaz, 1992). Asians who have come as refugees without the same favorable economic circumstances appear not to have fared as well in the educational system.

While there is substantial consensus about the research findings concerning the high educational retention rates of certain ethnic groups in the 1980s and high levels of motivation among specific groups, there has been a heated debate about the implications of the findings for multicultural education. On the one hand a number of writers, including Bullivant (1988a) and Birrell and Birrell (1981), have argued that, in many ways, Anglo Australian working-class students are the new disadvantaged, and attempts to provide assistance through multicultural programs with an equity focus have bypassed them because of their low educational motivation. Defenders of multicultural education, such as Kalantzis and Cope (1988), caution against projecting 1980s retention rates into the 1990s when rising unemployment has increased school retention rates generally while simultaneously reducing the market value of secondary education. They argue that it is possible to be blinded by the high retention rates of groups such as Greeks and Asians and ignore the high levels of attrition and unemployment among others such as Turks and Lebanese. They also point to the gap between educational aspirations and outcomes for children of many immigrant groups and argue for a curriculum that combines multiculturalism and social equity. Without a focus on multiculturalism and antiracism, they argue, those NESB students who succeed academically do so at great cost.

Multicultural Perspectives in Curriculum

In most states of Australia, curriculum was centralized and highly prescriptive until the mid-1970s. Subsequently, a trend emerged empowering schools to develop curricula targeted to the specific needs of the children in relation to their location and circumstance. This made it difficult to ascertain the extent to which multicultural perspectives had been incorporated into the curriculum and to evaluate the influence of such programs on student knowledge and attitudes. The 1990s saw a collaborative move toward greater consistency in curriculum between states. In the future, generalizations about the multicultural nature of Australian curricula should be easier.

It would seem that few schools in Australia have been untouched by multicultural perspectives. The production of classroom resources reflected education department policies. NACCME (1987) produced a directory of multicultural classroom resources that listed some 300 materials in English and 200 written in community languages. Cope (1987) analyzed 650 history and social studies texts published since 1945 and discovered a fundamental paradigm shift from homogeneous Australian identity oriented toward Britain to an identity that celebrated ethnic diversity. He describes a trend from 1945 texts, which provide a narrative of progress and development in which cultural differences are described in terms of superiority and inferiority, dominance and suppression, to a new pattern in the late 1980s, in which cultures are depicted as relative, cultural difference is celebrated, and senses of superiority are

challenged as ignorant and insensitive. The risk Cope warns of is that the materials, in their patronizing niceness, may exaggerate and construct stereotypes of cultural differences, thereby providing grist for the racist mill and ignoring the potential for cultural change and convergence. Garbutcheon Singh (1987) shares Cope's concern that even some of the best multicultural material has focused on the externalities of cultural difference (food, dress, songs, and dances) and ignored the broader sociopolitical context that constrains the way in which individuals from different ethnic groups construct their lives. By omission, these materials deny issues of justice, rights, power, and participation.

Cahill (1984), in a study of teacher attitudes in the state of Victoria, found that there was widespread endorsement of multicultural education. Only 14% of teachers considered it to be a "passing fad." In a later study of Queensland primary teachers, Sachs (1989) found their concept of culture to be remarkably consistent with that of the Queensland Department of Education multicultural policy document. Alcorso and Cope (1986), in an analysis of state curricula, found a consistent advocacy that multiculturalism not be taught as a separate subject but that it should infuse the entire school curriculum. Despite finding widespread acceptance of multiculturalism among teachers, the rapid expansion of classroom resources, and the changing image of Australia in history and social science texts, Cahill (1984) also uncovered a general lack of understanding by teachers concerning ethnicity. Teachers' knowledge about ethnic groups was deficient, and they tended to exclude students of non-Anglo background from the concept "Australian."

While teachers were favorably disposed toward multiculturalism (McInerney, 1987), there is little research evidence to show that this attitude had been successfully transmitted to their students. Maddock and Ramsland (1985) administered an attitude scale measuring support for multicultural values to secondary students in the Hunter Valley of New South Wales. Results varied among classes in the school, and there was no clear pattern of interaction of attitudes with gender, religion, or parental occupation. While attitudes toward multiculturalism were generally favorable, they were considerably less supportive than those of secondary students in Florida and Hawaii, the subjects of a previous comparable study. This led the authors to conclude that multicultural values were more deeply embedded in the curricula of American high schools and that American teachers were more consistently active in promoting these values. Walker (1987), in an ethnographic study of a secondary school with high immigrant density, demonstrated the persistence of assimilationist values in a peer-group culture despite a manifest commitment to multiculturalism within the school.

Antiracism

Sachs and Poole (1989) claim that the term *antiracism* has been less frequently used in Australia than in Great Britain. They approvingly quote Humphrey McQueen: "Silence has been a source of sustenance to racism and it has not gone away just because we have not had to articulate it" (quoted in Sachs and Poole, 1989, p. 14). Most research described in this section has focused on describing the extent of racism; there is a lamentable absence of studies evaluating school-based programs to combat racism.

Rosenthal and Morrison (1979) looked at the effect of ethnic mix within the classroom on a range of attitudes and abilities using year 6 (12-year-old) children in three categories of elementary schools in Melbourne with a high, medium, and low proportion of NESB children. The results showed no significant difference between the groups in attitudes to immigrants, with one exception. In the high-immigrant school, immigrant children recorded more positive attitudes than did the nonimmigrant children. Another study investigating interethnic attitudes was conducted by Jones and de Lacey (1979) in Wollongong, an industrial city within commuting distance from Sydney. The subjects, 50 immigrant and 100 Australian-born students, completed an instrument containing multiple-choice and open-ended items relating to attitudes held toward immigrants. The authors concluded that, while negative attitudes among Australian-born students were lessening, the students were not making strong efforts to incorporate immigrants. By contrast, the immigrant students were initiating most of the intergroup interaction. Cahill and Ewen (Cahill, 1984), in a major study of 1,346 year 8 students in 50 secondary schools, found friction scores tended to be higher in schools with high immigrant density in low socioeconomic locations.

These studies represent research designed to do empirical investigation of interethnic attitudes among school students. The findings were not widely distributed, nor did they appear to have much impact on policy. For example, the impetus for antiracism programs—the Combating Prejudice in Schools Project (Skelton, 1986) and *Human Rights in Education* (Human Rights and Equal Opportunity Commission and the NSW Department of Education, 1988)—came more from media reports of racist incidents in the community and pressure from ethnic organizations responding to the concerns of their members. These concerns were elaborated in the *Report of the National Inquiry into Racist Violence in Australia* (Human Rights and Equal Opportunity Commission, 1991), which concluded that the main victims of racist violence were Aborigines, Asians, and members of the Islamic community. This report found comparatively little physical violence in schools but gave detailed accounts of verbal abuse and harassment, often inadequately dealt with by teachers. While recommending various measures that school authorities could take to prevent racism, the commissioners accurately summarized the state of research into Australian schools: "At present there appears to be little information available to school management and staff about who experiences racism, in what forms, and from whom; or how schools can successfully accommodate students from different cultural backgrounds" (p. 349).

During 1991–92 the New South Wales Department of School Education conducted two whole-school antiracism pilot projects, one in a rural area with a high proportion of Aboriginal students, the other in an urban area of high NESB density. Regrettably, the results of these projects have not been widely disseminated, but resource materials for use by other schools have been developed, and the state has released an antiracism policy statement together with antiracism grievance procedures (New South Wales Department of School Education, 1992a).

English as a Second Language

ESL has been the least controversial and most generously and consistently funded component of multicultural education programs in Australia. Overseas debates about whether ESL programs are inherently assimilationist or whether they need to be broadened to include cultural components if they are to be empowering have not had a major impact here (Polesel, 1990).

A number of studies have attempted to evaluate the success of federal ESL programs since the inception of CMEP. The Schools Commission Committee on Multicultural Education, (1979) reported that only one third of students classified as "migrant and in need of special language assistance" were being helped under the program. Many such students were reluctant to participate because of the social stigma attached to ESL withdrawal classes. Campbell and McMeniman (1985, cited in Collins, 1990) found that ESL tuition was often withdrawn before children had attained the necessary language skills. Ninety percent of ESL staff were only generalist teachers, most with inadequate in-service education. Moreover, nearly half the children who needed ESL teaching were not receiving it (Collins, 1990).

Intensive Language Centres (ILC) for newly arrived immigrants were established to remedy the inefficiencies of decentralized reception. In New South Wales in 1977 the first center was opened, and by 1992 there were 17 centers attached to secondary schools operating in the Sydney metropolitan area. These varied in size but by 1988 were servicing 3,500 students whose average stay was 6 months before transferring to mainstream schools (Wren and Johnson, 1992). The function of each center was to assess children's English-language level and maximize their chances of successful transition to secondary-school study. Yet there was no central New South Wales education policy on their status and role, no standard curriculum, and no recognized credentials for students on completion of the program.

Wren and Johnson (1992) summarized the limited research on the effectiveness of these programs: Campbell and McMeniman (cited in Wren and Johnson, 1992) found that those students who attended for longer periods were initially more successful in senior high school studies and initially better able to understand lessons and textbooks than those who had attended two terms or less. Not surprisingly, those students who had experienced greatest difficulty in transition had previously been illiterate, slow learners, refugees, or older. Gaffey (cited in Wren and Johnson, 1992) found that students who began ILC courses at a younger age and with some formal school background were more successful in the transition to mainstream classes. Kassim (cited in Wren and Johnson, 1992) found that ILC graduates were performing well in mathematics but experienced difficulty with language-embedded subjects such as geography, art, and science. Ferguson (cited in Wren and Johnson, 1992) confirmed that ILC graduates had difficulty in mainstream classrooms because they did not receive enough opportunity to write or interact with fluent English speakers and were not given texts to assist private study. In their own research, Wren and Johnson (1992) uncovered common concerns among stakeholders in the ILC program. There was a strong desire for a uniform national instrument to assess English-language proficiency and a need for recognized credentialing of graduates from these centers. There was a demand for more proactive and less ad hoc policy making for ILCs. The administrative relationship between ILCs and the secondary schools they serviced required clarification. Teachers in mainstream schools needed to be better prepared to adjust to the different learning styles and expectations of students who were coming from ILCs.

In a national evaluation of ESL provision, the authors in Herriman (1992) noted that resources tended to be allocated in favor of recent arrivals and fewer resources were directed to the transition of students from reception centers to mainstream schools. They discovered a great variation in the qualifications of ESL teachers and found that ESL teachers were occupationally marginalized with few promotion prospects. Like Wren and Johnson (1992), they noted a need for assessment instruments that could assist in evaluating the effectiveness of ESL programs in order to enhance diagnosis and educational planning.

Languages Other Than English

Smolicz and Secombe (1977) conducted an analysis of submissions to a federal government inquiry into the teaching of immigrant languages in schools. The majority of the submissions were from ethnic organizations, and the remainder could not be seen as representative of Australian public opinion. However, with this reservation, the findings suggest that a number of influential Anglo Australians were coming to value the existence of ethnic cultures and to advocate strategies that facilitated their maintenance. Ethnic languages were seen to play a major role not only in maintaining cultural heritage but in providing the benefits of cultural interaction. Submissions from the smaller ethnic groups saw support for ethnic schools as the most realistic means of language maintenance. Over half the submissions from ethnic organizations preferred the introduction of ethnic languages and cultures as separate subjects in Australian schools. While these two strategies were concerned with ethnic structural maintenance, half of those submissions that advocated bilingualism saw it as a transitional rather than maintenance strategy.

A more recent study by Kalantzis, Cope, and Slade (1986) in the Wollongong area compared attitudes toward language maintenance and language competence of students and parents from two ethnic groups: German and Macedonian. The research methodology included group interviews with parents, attitudinal questionnaires with primary and secondary students from seven Wollongong schools, and tests of their first-language competence. The German community was deemed to represent more established immigrant groups who had achieved a generally higher socioeconomic status and English-language proficiency. The Macedonians by contrast tended to be more recently arrived immigrants, less proficient in English, and more likely to use Macedonian in the home. Both groups of parents gave a high priority to their children obtaining a high degree of competence in English. There were, however, differences in the parental groups' attitudes to language maintenance

in schools. German respondents generally believed that they had little personal need for German-language instruction as they felt quite competent in English. They believed in principle that German, as an important international and scientific language, merited being taught in schools. The Macedonian parents were keen to have more resources devoted to their language but were divided as to whether those resources should be allocated to mainstream or after-hours ethnic schools. In common with other ethnic groups, their reasons for advocating language maintenance were not cognitive or pedagogical but related to the prestige of their community. At the primary school level, German students tended to be indifferent to language maintenance, though most took the opportunity to study it when offered. Those Macedonians who studied their language in school increased their proficiency and developed a more positive attitude toward Macedonian. By secondary school the majority felt that while Macedonian should be offered, and while it might provide employment opportunities, they themselves would prefer to study languages of greater prestige such as French and German. Favorable attitudes toward Macedonian were positively correlated with the number of Macedonian students in the school. The findings on language proficiency were quite disturbing. Unsurprisingly, both NESB groups gained lower scores in English than the English-speaking control group. However, their first-language proficiency was also low, and the students felt that their experiences of mother-tongue learning at community or Department of Education Saturday language schools were unsatisfactory.

The most comprehensive research into the teaching of languages other than English in schools was conducted by the Commonwealth Department of Education in 1986. The main findings are summarized below.

Almost half of Australian students had never studied a language other than English. Only 11.7% of students from homes where a LOTE was spoken were studying that language at school. At any one time, only 17.3% of all students studied one or more non-English languages. Fewer than one third of Australian schools teach one or more languages. Only 10% of elementary schools teach a second language. Fifteen percent of secondary schools do not teach any languages other than English. Those schools that do not teach other languages are more likely to be small and rural. Students who elect to study languages are more likely to be girls (20%) than boys (14.6%), and students with at least one parent from a non-English-speaking country are more likely to study a language than students from an English-speaking background. The median hours per week allocated to study a language in schools ranged from 1.0 in primary, to 2.7 in lower secondary, to 3.9 in upper secondary. Only a minute number of students (0.1%) study the language of Australia's major trading partner, Japan (LoBianco, 1987). By 1990 almost 21,000 students were studying a LOTE in their final year of secondary education (11.7% of year 12 students), the five most popular of which were French, German, Japanese, Italian, and Mandarin (DEET, 1991).

Since this study, different state education departments have attempted to promote further the teaching of LOTE. In New South Wales, under the Community Languages Program in Primary Schools, there were over 20,000 primary children in 73 government schools studying 1 of 11 community languages. An Ethnic Schools Board was established by the state government in 1992 to assist with the efficient operation of ethnic ("Saturday") schools.

In Canada and the United States there are considerable geographic concentrations of speakers of community languages (French and Spanish respectively), whereas in Australia speakers of languages other than English are relatively dispersed. Meeting the demands from ethnic communities for the teaching of community languages in schools has been logistically difficult. In New South Wales, a controversial solution has been the establishment of the Saturday School of Community Languages. Operating in 16 centers in Sydney, Newcastle, and Wollongong, it enrolled students from government and nongovernment schools and provided tuition in a range of community languages for which there was insufficient demand in mainstream schools. In 1993, over 8,000 students were enrolled in classes for 22 languages (New South Wales Department of School Education personal communication, 1993).

CONCLUSION

In Australia in recent years immigration and ethnic affairs have generally been characterized by bipartisan consensus. Multiculturalism has not represented a threat to the dominant social institutions but has been confined to the private and the cultural sphere of Australian life. Indeed, as Bullivant (1981a) argues, Australia has been polyethnic rather than multicultural where Anglo Australians could appreciate the "color" that ethnic diversity provided—as long as diversity did not involve radical redistribution of life chances and did not require Anglo Australians to change their lifestyle significantly. Meanwhile, 50 years since the beginning of the immigration program, control of the country is still largely invested in Anglo Australian hands. English is the uncontested national language, and, despite the unstoppable momentum toward republicanism, the dominant social structures of the country remain unchallenged.

Following the overview of multicultural education presented in this chapter, it is appropriate to comment briefly on future developments. We believe that four discernible trends may affect this area in Australia. These are increased government financial restraint coupled with economic pragmatism, a growing involvement of the national government in the centralization of curriculum design, a devolution to local communities of school management, and, finally, an oversupply of teachers.

Research into multicultural education has seldom been the driving force of educational policy. Policy changes have rarely used the language or findings of the research literature. Most Australian educational research is government funded, and, in the short term, resources for research into multicultural education will be significantly reduced. Economic pragmatism seems likely to determine the research agenda, and we anticipate that the two areas where funding will be concentrated are the relationship between education and workforce participation of immigrant children and the effectiveness of language teaching, particularly Asian, in Australian schools.

A number of wider changes in Australian education will affect multicultural education. In some states there has been a trend toward greater participation of local communities in the governance of their schools, the primary intentions of this involvement being to access community resources and reduce administration costs. While this may provide opportunities for more established ethnic groups to influence the direction of schools, it might tend to further marginalize newer arrivals.

The last decade has seen a national government increasingly involved in coordination of education. This increased role may lead to efficiencies, especially in nationally accredited instruments for ESL teaching, distance education curriculum materials for languages, and ethnic studies materials targeted to national curriculums.

The oversupply of teachers and increasing competition for appointments will provide an increased incentive for teachers in training to study languages other than English. The emphasis on language in primary and secondary schools could give bilingual graduates a comparative advantage when seeking employment.

References

Abraham, D. (1992, December 10). Platonic love: The Greek passion for teaching. *Sydney Morning Herald*, p. 16.

Alcorso, C., & Cope, B. (1986). *A review of Australian multicultural education policy 1979–1986* (National Advisory Co-ordinating Committee on Multicultural Education Commissioned Research Paper No. 6). Canberra: Australian Government Publishing Service.

Andreoni, H., & Ozolins, U. (1985). *Three language policy statements: Two evaluations*. Canberra: Australian Government Publishing Service.

Auchmuty, J. J. (1980). *Report of the national inquiry into teacher education*. Canberra: Australian Government Publishing Service.

Australian Ethnic Affairs Council. (1977). *Australia as a multicultural society*. Canberra: Australian Government Publishing Service.

Birrell, R., & Birrell, T. (1981). *An issue of people: Population and Australian society*. Melbourne: Longman Cheshire.

Blainey, G. (1984). *All for Australia*. North Ryde: Methuen Haynes.

Bullivant, B. M. (1973). *Educating the immigrant child: Concepts and cases*. Sydney: Angus and Robertson.

Bullivant, B. M. (1981a). *The pluralist dilemma in education: Six case studies*. North Sydney: George Allen and Unwin.

Bullivant, B. M. (1981b). *Race, ethnicity and curriculum*. South Melbourne: Macmillan.

Bullivant, B. M. (1982). Are ethnic schools the solution to ethnic children's accommodation to Australian society? *Journal of Intercultural Studies, 3*(2), 17–35.

Bullivant, B. M. (1986). Multicultural education in Australia: An unresolved debate. In J. A. Banks & J. Lynch (Eds.), *Multicultural education in Western societies* (pp. 98–124). New York: Holt, Rinehart, & Winston.

Bullivant, B. M. (1988a). Missing the empirical forest for the ideological trees: A commentary on Kalantzis and Cope. *Journal of Intercultural Studies, 9*(1), 58–69.

Bullivant, B. M. (1988b). Social engineers hoist with their own petard: A rejoinder to Kalantzis and Cope. *Journal of Intercultural Studies, 9*(2), 84–87.

Bureau of Immigration Research. (1992). *Immigration update.* Canberra: Australian Government Printing Service.

Butlin, N. G. (1983). *Our original aggression: Aboriginal populations in south eastern Australia. 1788–1850.* Sydney: George Allen and Unwin.

Cahill, D. B. (1984). *Review of the commonwealth multicultural education program.* Melbourne: Phillip Institute of Technology.

Cahill, D. B., & Ewen, J. (1987). *Ethnic youth: Their assets and aspirations.* Canberra: Australian Government Publishing Service.

Cigler, M. (1987). Community history for young Australians. *Australian History Teacher,14,* 9–12.

Clyne, M. (1991). Australia's language policies: Are we going backwards? *Current Affairs Bulletin, 68*(6), 13–20.

Collins, J. (1990). *Migrant hands in a distant land.* Sydney: Pluto Press.

Connell, W. F., Connell, R. W., Sinclair, K., & Stroobant, R. (1975). *12 to 20: Studies of city youth.* Sydney: H. Smith.

Cope, B. (1987). *Racism, popular culture and Australian identity in transition: A case study of change in school textbooks since 1945* (Occasional Paper No. 14). Wollongong: University of Wollongong, Centre for Multicultural Studies.

Cope, B., Castles, S., & Kalantzis, M. (1991). *Immigration, ethnic conflicts and social cohesion.* Canberra: Bureau of Immigration Research.

Crisp, L. F. (1961). *Ben Chifley.* Sydney: Angus and Robertson.

Da Costa, H. (1992, September). Indonesians in Australia. *Inside Indonesia, 32,* 19–20.

DEET. 1991. *Australia's language, the Australian language and literacy policy.* Canberra: Australian Government Publishing Service.

Department of Aboriginal Affairs. (1984). *Aboriginal social indicators.* Canberra: Australian Government Publishing Service.

Diaz, T. (1992, January 14). Coincidentally, they are also very clever. *Sydney Morning Herald,* p. 3.

Fitzgerald, S. (1988). *Immigration: A commitment to Australia.* Australian Government Publishing Service.

Foster, L. E. (1988). *Diversity and multicultural education: A sociological perspective.* North Sydney: Allen and Unwin.

Foster, L. E., & Stockley, D. (1988). *Australian multiculturalism: A documentary history and critique.* Clevedon: Multilingual Matters.

Galbally, F. (1978). *Report of the review of post-arrival programs and services for migrants.* Canberra: Australian Government Publishing Service.

Garbutcheon Singh, M. (1987). Towards a strategic redefinition of intercultural studies. *Discourse, 7*(2), 69–85.

Goosen, G. (1985). How multicultural is your R. E. curriculum? *Journal of Christian Education, 83,* 13–19.

Grassby, A. J. (1979). It's time for migrant education to go. In P. R. de Lacey and M. E. Poole (Eds.), *Mosaic or melting pot: Cultural evolution in Australia* (pp. 278–282). Sydney: Harcourt Brace Jovanovich.

Herriman, M. L. (Ed.). (1992). *An evaluative study of the commonwealth ESL program.* Perth: University of Western Australia.

Human Rights and Equal Opportunity Commission. (1991). *Report of the national inquiry into racist violence in Australia.* Canberra: Australian Government Publishing Service.

Human Rights and Equal Opportunity Commission and the NSW Department of Education. (1988). *Human rights in education.* Sydney: NSW Department of Education.

Jones, J. M. & de Lacey, P. R. (1979). Natives and newcomers: Mutual attitudes. In P. R. de Lacey & M. E. Poole (Eds.), *Mosaic or melting pot: Cultural evolution in Australia.* (pp. 163–172). Sydney: Harcourt Brace Jovanovich.

Jupp, J. (1986). *The review of migrant and multicultural programs and services: Don't settle for less.* Canberra: Australian Government Publishing Service.

Kable, J. (1987). Connecting literature and life. *Idiom, 22*(1), 12–18.

Kalantzis, M. (1987). Racism and pedagogy. *Teaching History, 20*(4), 45–48.

Kalantzis, M., & Cope, B. (1988). Why we need multicultural education: A review of the "ethnic disadvantage" debate. *Journal of Intercultural Studies, 9*(1), 39–57.

Kalantzis, M., Cope, B., Noble, G., & Poynting, S. (1990). *Cultures of schooling: Pedagogies for cultural difference and social access.* Basingstoke: The Falmer Press.

Kalantzis, M., Cope, B., & Slade, D. (1986). *The language question: The maintenance of languages other than English* (Vols. 1–2). Canberra: Department of Immigration and Ethnic Affairs.

Kelly, P. (1992). *The end of certainty: The story of the 1980s.* Sydney: Allen and Unwin.

Kovacs, M. L., & Cropley, A. J. (1975). *Immigrants and society: Alienation and assimilation.* Sydney: McGraw-Hill.

Lewins, F. (1982). The political implications of ethnic schools. *Journal of Intercultural Studies, 3*(2), 36–47.

LoBianco, J. (1987). *National policy on languages.* Canberra: Australian Government Publishing Service.

LoBianco, J. (1988). Multiculturalism and the national policy on languages. *Journal of Intercultural Studies, 9*(1), 25–38.

Maddock, M., & Ramsland, J. (1985). Attitudes towards multiculturalism in schools in an industrial area: A study in the Hunter Valley, New South Wales. *Journal of Intercultural Studies, 6*(3), 16–42.

Mannix, C. (1985, May). Teaching about different cultures to students in a multicultural setting. *Newsletter (Victorian Association for Multicultural Education), 103,* pp. 14–17.

Marjoribanks, K. (1979). *Ethnic families and children's achievements.* North Sydney: Allen and Unwin.

Marsh, C. J. (1988). *Policy options paper on access and success of school children from non-English speaking backgrounds.* Canberra: Office of Multicultural Affairs.

Martin, J. (1972). *Migrants: Equality and ideology.* Melbourne: LaTrobe University.

Martin, J. (1978). *The migrant presence.* Sydney: Allen and Unwin.

McInerney, D. M. (1987). Teacher attitudes to multicultural curriculum development. *Australian Journal of Education, 31*(2), 129–144.

Meade, P. (1983). *The educational experience of Sydney high school students: Comparative study of migrant students of non-English speaking origin and students whose parents were born in a non-English speaking country.* Canberra: AGPS.

Miller, J. (1985). *Koori: A will to win.* Sydney: Angus and Robertson.

Mulvaney, D. J. (1958). The Australian aborigines 1606–1929: Opinion and fieldwork—Part 1, 1606–1859. *Historical Studies, Australia and New Zealand, 8*(30), 131–151.

National Aboriginal Education Committee. (1982). Rationale, aims and objectives in Aboriginal education. In J. Sherwood (Ed.), *Aboriginal education: Issues and innovations* (pp. 61–66). Perth: Creative Research.

National Advisory and Co-ordinating Committee on Multicultural Education. (1987). *Resource materials directory.* Canberra: Australian Government Publishing Service.

New South Wales Department of Education. (1978). *Multicultural education: A consultative document.* Sydney: Government Printer.

New South Wales Department of Education. (1983). *Multicultural education policy statement.* Sydney: Government Printer.

New South Wales Department of School Education. (1992a). *Antiracism policy statement.* Sydney: Government Printer.

New South Wales Department of School Education (1992b). *Multicultural education plan 1993–1997.* Sydney: Government Printer.

New South Wales Department of School Education. (1992c). *Public report: Basic skills testing.* Sydney: Government Printer.

New South Wales Ministry of Education. (1979). *Multicultural education policy statement.* Sydney: Government Printer.

Noorst, M. (1982). Ethnic schools: What are they and what would they like to be? *Journal of Intercultural Studies, 3*(2), 6–16.

Office of Multicultural Affairs. (1989). *National agenda for a multicultural Australia.* Canberra: Australian Government Publishing Service.

Polesel, J. (1990). ESL, ideology and multiculturalism. *Journal of Intercultural Studies, 11*(1), 64–72.

Reynolds, H. (1982). *The other side of the frontier: Aboriginal resistance to the European invasion of Australia.* Melbourne: Penguin.

Roper, T. (1971). *The myth of equality.* Melbourne: Heinemann.

Rosenthal, D., & Morrison, S. (1979). On being a minority in the classroom: A study of the influence of ethnic mix on cognitive functioning and attitudes in working-class children. In P. R. de Lacey & M. E. Poole (Eds.), *Mosaic or melting pot: Cultural evolution in Australia* (pp. 140–154). Sydney: Harcourt Brace Jovanovich.

Rowley, C. D. (1972). *The destruction of Aboriginal society.* Melbourne: Pelican.

Sachs, J. (1989). Match or mismatch: Teachers' conceptions of culture and multicultural education policy. *Australian Journal of Education. 33*(1), 19–33.

Sachs, J., & Poole, M. (1989). Multicultural education policies in Australia and Britain: Social transformation or status quo? *Education and Society, 7*(1), 9–19.

Samuda, R. J. (1986). Social and educational implications of multiculturalism. *Education and Society, 4*(2), 63–68.

Schools Commission, Committee on Multicultural Education. (1979). *Education for a multicultural society.* Canberra: Schools Commission.

Sherington, G. (1991). Australian immigration, ethnicity and education. *History of Education Review, 20*(1), 61–72.

Skelton, K. (1986). Educating for cultural understanding: The work of the Combating Prejudice in Schools project. *Youth Studies, 5*(3), 36–39.

Smolicz, J. J. (1984). Who's afraid of bi-lingualism? *Education News, 18*(5), 36–39.

Smolicz, J. J., & Secombe, M. J. (1977). Mosaic or melting pot: Cultural evolution in Australia. *Australian Journal of Education, 21*(1), 1–24.

Solman, R. T. (1987). A survey of the needs of an urban high school's community. *Australian Journal of Education, 31*(2), 145–160.

Sturman, A. (1985). *Immigrant Australians, education and the transition to work.* Canberra: NACCME.

Taft, R., & Cahill, D. (1978). *Initial adjustment to schooling of immigrant families.* Canberra: Australian Government Publishing Service.

Walker, J. C. (1987). School sport, ethnicity and nationality: Dimensions of male youth culture in an inner-city school. *Australian Journal of Education, 31*(3), 303–316.

Ward, R. B. (1958). *The Australian legend.* Melbourne: Oxford University Press.

Ward, R. B. (1976). *Australia: A short history.* Sydney: Ure Smith.

Wilton, J., & Bosworth, R. (1984). *Old worlds and new Australia.* Melbourne: Penguin.

Wren, H., & Johnson, N. (1992). The role of intensive English language centres. *Journal of Intercultural Studies, 13*(1), 33–54.

· 45 ·

MULTICULTURAL EDUCATION IN THE UNITED KINGDOM: HISTORICAL DEVELOPMENT AND CURRENT STATUS

Peter Figueroa

UNIVERSITY OF SOUTHAMPTON

This chapter provides a historical review of the development of education for a multicultural society in postwar Britain, and particularly in England. It is based on existing literature but, in view of the large body of publications, makes no claim to be comprehensive in coverage, although it seeks to give a balanced picture.

THE HISTORICAL CONTEXT

Immense social change, including decolonization and extensive labor migration, has taken place worldwide since World War II. People from Europe sought new lives in other parts of the world. Black people (that is, people especially of African, African Caribbean, and Indian subcontinent origin), over-whelmingly colonials and excolonials—and many others—sought new lives in Europe.

However, the links of such Black people with Europe extend back to ancient trading links between Europe and the East and to long-standing trans-Mediterranean commerce and conflict. Bernal's (1987) thesis of African influences on Greek culture are now well known. In Britain an African division of Roman soldiers defended Hadrian's Wall in the third century A.D. (Greater London Council, Ethnic Minorities Unit, 1986).

However, it has been mainly during the last 500 years that Britain developed close relations with Africa, the Caribbean, and the Indian subcontinent and that a significant Black population grew up in Britain. The European transatlantic slave trade, the American colonies, and the Raj were the key factors, with Black people being brought to England through the slave trade by the late 1500s (see Fryer, 1984; Little, 1948). By the 19th century a substantial Black population "permeated most ranks of society, through the length and breadth" of Britain (Walvin, 1973, p. 72).

The Industrial Revolution in Britain was funded largely through the slave trade and the exploitation of the colonies (Williams, 1944). The British Empire, with White supremacy over Black "natives," was at its height in the 19th century. The dogma of racism offered a justification.

This long history of British domination of Black people substantially accounts for the postwar migrations into Britain and for present-day British attitudes toward Black people and toward multicultural Britain. In addition, structural relations today are still similar to those of the earlier era.

The author would like to express his greatest thanks to Professor James A. Banks, Professor John Eggleston, and Dr. Robin Grinter for kindly reading an earlier draft of this chapter and for making many very helpful comments.

MAJOR CHARACTERISTICS OF MULTICULTURAL POSTWAR BRITAIN

Britain has long been culturally diverse. But in the postwar era this has gained a new political importance with substantial labor in-migration due to labor shortages in a period of reconstruction. Black groups originating especially from the Caribbean and the Indian subcontinent have been seen as problematic. The main focus in this chapter is thus on multicultural education and related issues concerning the presence of, and the orientation toward, Black people in the United Kingdom. However, Britain has to be seen, too, within the wider European kaleidoscope, including the growth in European neofascism (see European Parliament Committee of Inquiry into Racism and Xenophobia, 1990).

The Black population of Britain is relatively small. The 1991 census put it at only about 5.5% of Great Britain's total population of some 54,860,000 (Owen, 1992). However, although Black people live in all parts of Britain, there are substantial concentrations in the conurbations, and, compared with White people, a larger proportion of the Black population is of school age.

Despite the great diversity, the various minority ethnic groups do share some interests and even similarities (see Eggleston, 1986), such as an aspiration to be "fully accepted as equal members" of British society (Department of Education and Science [DES], 1985, p. 760). Each group also has a strong sense of a distinctive ethnic identity (DES, 1985).

Undoubtedly, the most fundamental shared interest of the minority ethnic groups is their unequal structural position, especially as victims of racism and discrimination. The unequal social location of Black groups within the society can be seen on social indices such as housing, employment, and education (Brown, 1984; Coard, 1971; Figueroa, 1991; Jones, 1993; Tomlinson, 1982; Townsend & Brittan, 1972).

The assertion that Britain is a racist society (e.g., Brandt, 1986) is often misunderstood. Many White authors (with notable exceptions, such as Dummett, 1973), even when they present data that could be accounted for by racism, often reject such an interpretation. For instance, in their classic study Rose et al. (1969) minimized the extent of the prejudice they found (see Bagley, 1970; Figueroa, 1974; Lawrence, 1969). Racism is not just a matter of individual attitudes and beliefs and does not necessarily imply virulent hostility. It comprises individual, interpersonal, institutional, cultural, and structural aspects or dimensions (see Brandt, 1986; Figueroa, 1991).

There is a great deal of evidence of racism in postwar Britain (see, for example, Bagley, 1970; Brittan, 1976; Brown, 1984; Brown & Gay, 1985; Daniel, 1968; Smith, 1977). There has been a substantial increase in reported racially motivated attacks in recent years ("Racist Attacks and Harassment," 1993; and "Racial Violence," 1993). A Home Office report (1981b) showed that "Asians" were 50 times more likely than White people to suffer "racial" victimization, and African Caribbeans 36 times more likely. Several recent small-scale studies (e.g., Kelly & Cohn, 1988; Mac an Ghaill, 1988; Tattum & Lane, 1989; Troyna & Hatcher, 1992; Wright, 1992) have documented racism in British schools (see also Macdonald, Bhavnani, Khan, & John, 1989).

However, British society is not monolithic. Alongside racism the society is characterized by antiracist forces and democratic traditions, institutions, and ideals.

HISTORICAL DEVELOPMENT OF MULTICULTURAL EDUCATION

Several different policy approaches relating to the presence of Black people in the United Kingdom in the postwar era can be identified (see, for instance: Brandt, 1986; Craft, 1986; DES, 1985; Little & Willey, 1981; Lynch, 1986; Massey, 1991; Mullard, 1982; Rose et al., 1969; Troyna & Williams, 1986; Willey, 1984a, 1984b). Some of these approaches became salient in the education sphere at a later date than in other spheres (see Troyna & Williams, 1986).

However, although each of these approaches might have been more salient at one time than another, they do not fall neatly along some continuum, and they have not followed each other in some neat historical order of development. Contradictory forces have been characteristic of every period.

These approaches make different assumptions about what the important issues are, about their conceptualization, about social and educational values, and about the action required. Built into them are also assumptions about self and other, about Britain and who the British are, about "immigrants," and in particular about "Black" and "White" people—in short, about "identity" and nation.

It is therefore perhaps not surprising that, as with social issues of any significance, there is hardly an issue of any importance in the field of education for a multicultural society that is not contested. Similarly, one of the characteristics of this field has been the diversity of terminology, and the diversity of meaning attached to some of the terms used (see also Banks, 1981). The very expression "education for a multicultural society" is problematic.

In the education sphere some six main overlapping and interrelating approaches can be identified historically. They are:

laissez-faire;
assimilationist;
integrationist;
multicultural/pluralist;
antiracist; and
multiculturalist and antiracist.

Other approaches that relate to one or another of the above are: immigrant education; "color-blind" education; compensatory education; education for the disadvantaged; ethnic minority education; Black studies; multiracial education; multiethnic education; intercultural education; and "education for all." "Immigrant education" corresponded mainly to the assimilationist and integrationist "phases."

Laissez-faire

The approach during the early postwar period is often seen as largely laissez-faire. This approach considered that everyone was equal before a color-blind law, so that the presence of "immigrants" and the treatment they experienced called for no special provisions. The British Nationality Act of 1948 had conferred equal citizenship rights in the UK on all citizens of the Commonwealth and colonies (see Table 45–1 for a list of major

acts, events, and developments). All that was needed was the proclamation of this equality (Rose et al., 1969).

Kirp (1979) typified the education policy approach corresponding to this period as "racial inexplicitness." There was a common belief that everything would sort itself out in time and that it was best to keep quiet about "race." Kirp argued that this was the preferred approach in education even until the late 1970s. He thought that this "inexplicitness" helped the Black population: "racial inexplicitness . . . represents doing good by

TABLE 45–1. The Historical Development of Multicultural Education in the United Kingdom

1948	British Nationality Act was enacted by Parliament.	1974	*Teacher Education for a Multi-Cultural Society* was published.
1952	The Institute of Race Relations was established.	1975	Sex Discrimination Act. This established the Equal Opportunities Commission.
1958	Notting Hill and Nottingham riots, in which White people attacked Black people and their property.	1976	Third (current) Race Relations Act. This established the Commission for Racial Equality.
1962	The first Commonwealth Immigrants Act was enacted. It set up the Commonwealth Immigrants Advisory Council.	1977	*The West Indian Community*, report of the Select Committee on Race Relations and Immigration.
	Association of Teachers of English to Pupils from Overseas (ATEPO) founded. It later became the National Association for Multiracial Education (NAME), and then the National Antiracist Movement in Education.		Inner London Education Authority policy statement on multiethnic education.
1963	The Ministry of Education published *English for Immigrants.*	1980	Manchester Education Authority policy statement, *Education for a Multicultural Society.*
	Second Report of Commonwealth Immigrants Advisory Council, presented to Parliament in 1963, published in 1964. It took an assimilationist stance.		Riots in Bristol, in which mainly Black people attacked the police and property.
1964	The government sets up a National Committee for Commonwealth Immigrants.	1981	British Nationality Act, a major act defining three classes of British citizenship and removing rights previously held by "Commonwealth" citizens.
1965	First Race Relations Act enacted by a Labour government. This established the Race Relations Board.		*West Indian Children in Our Schools*, the Rampton report, was published.
	The Department of Education and Science officially stated the policy of dispersal in Circular 7/65.		Riots in Brixton, London, and across England, in which mainly Black people attacked the police and property.
	The government issued a white paper, *Immigration from the Commonwealth*, incorporating Circular 7/65.		*The Brixton Disorders 10–12 April 1981*, the Scarman report, was published.
	Campaign Against Racial Discrimination (CARD) set up.		*Racial Disadvantage*, Home Affairs Committee report.
1966	Local Government Act, providing support for education in areas with an "immigrant" population.		BBC series, *Case Studies in Multi-Cultural Education.*
	The National Committee for Commonwealth Immigrants held a conference for educators, Towards a Multi-Racial Society.	1985	Riots in Handsworth, Birmingham, in which mainly Black people attacked the police and property.
1967	*Racial Discrimination*, the Political and Economic Planning (PEP) & Research Services report, appeared.		*Education for All*, the Swann report, was published.
	The Universal Coloured People's Association founded.		*Education for Some*, the Eggleston report, was published.
	Educational Priority Areas set up, providing funds for education in deprived areas, including those with "immigrants."	1986	Public Order Act sought to remedy some defects of previous laws against incitement to racial hatred.
1968	Second Commonwealth Immigrants Act was passed, incorporating the principle of "patriality."	1988	Immigration Act replaced some sections of the 1971 act with even tougher regulations.
	Runnymede Trust set up with focus on "racial" equality and justice.		Education Reform Act was enacted by Parliament.
	Second Race Relations Act was passed. This established the Community Relations Commission.	1989	Children Act included provisions for care services to take due account of young children's religion, "race," culture, and language.
	Urban Aid Programme, providing help to deprived areas.	1991	Football (Offences) Act included sections addressing racism in connection with football.
1969	The Institute of Race Relations published the report of the Survey of Race Relations, *Colour and Citizenship.*	1992	Education (Schools) Act. Under section 10 the Framework for the Inspection of Schools includes criteria relating to equality of opportunity.
	The Problems of Coloured School-Leavers, report of the Select Committee on Race Relations and Immigration.	1994	Education (Initial Teacher Education and Student Unions) Act further increases central control.
1971	Immigration Act, to control immigration, and, via the "patriality" principle, removing rights previously held by "Commonwealth" immigrants.		

doing little" (p. 5 3). Actually, because of unstated assumptions of cultural superiority, it permitted discriminatory practices to operate unchallenged (see Troyna & Williams, 1986).

"Racial inexplicitness" seems to cover two different stances. One is that the "immigrants" shared problems such as urban deprivation, "restricted code" language, and educational disadvantage with others and should simply be treated like them. The other is that "immigrants" did have specific "problems" that needed specific attention, but these problems were social, cultural, and linguistic rather than "racial."

Troyna and Williams (1986) argue that "nonracialized discourse" is a better typification than "racial inexplicitness" of the policy approach in education at the time. In fact, neither "nonracialized discourse," "racial inexplicitness," nor "laissez-faire" is entirely satisfactory as a typification. The vocabulary, even in educational connections, did include "racial" category words such as *colored*. Besides, the term *immigrant* was commonly used as a "racial" category to mean "colored resident," whether immigrant or not. Racist and assimilationist assumptions were widespread. The policy option of controlling specifically Black immigration was addressed on several occasions (see Rose et al., 1969). The Royal Commission on Population (1949) regarded the prospect of increased immigration as undesirable because "the sources . . . of suitable immigrants are meagre and the capacity of a fully established society like ours to absorb immigrants of alien race and religion is limited" (p. 225). Benevolent paternalism—rather than an attitude of equality—was a feature during the war years and immediately afterwards. The first "teacher for immigrants" had already been appointed by the Borough of Southall in 1957 (Power, 1967), and by the early 1960s various local education authorities (LEAs) had already instituted centers, itinerant teachers, or reception schools to teach English to "immigrant" children (see House of Commons, 1963–64).

The option of immigration controls was not taken up until the beginning of the 1960s. Rose et al. (1969) consider that the Commonwealth Immigrants Act of 1962 and the 1965 white paper, *Immigration from the Commonwealth,* marked the end of the general "laissez-faire" period. Only about then, too, did explicit education policies in the field begin to emerge from central government. The end of the first education phase could be identified with the proposal during a parliamentary debate in 1963 of a dispersal policy by the minister of education, Sir Edward Boyle, who rejected a "*laissez faire* acceptance of . . . *de facto* segregation between immigrant . . . and native schools" (House of Commons, 1963–64, col. 439).

Immigrant Education and Assimilationism

Rose et al. (1969) define assimilation as the merging of an immigrant group into the "host" society, the immigrant group having completely lost its separate identity, having adapted totally, and having been completely accepted by the "host" society (see also Patterson, 1963). Assimilation, however is often seen as a one-way process in which only the immigrants adapt. British assimilationist thinking tends to assume that there is a unitary "British way of life," that, in the imperial tradition, it is superior to anything the "immigrants" bring with them, and

that they should adapt totally to it—although they may still not be accepted for "racial" reasons.

Notting Hill Anti-Black Riot, 1958. In the years after World War I there had been "a series of serious race riots" in which White people attacked Black people and their property (Fryer, 1984; Little, 1948; Walvin, 1973). Again, after World War II there were many similar incidents starting in 1948 (Fryer, 1984; Walvin, 1973). The worst such riots took place in Notting Hill, London, in 1958. Slogans used included "Down with Niggers," and "We'll kill the Blacks" (Fryer, 1984; Glass & Pollins, 1960; Hiro, 1971; Walvin, 1973). The following year Kelso Cochrane, a West Indian carpenter, was stabbed to death in Notting Hill. Hit-and-run attacks spread outside of London (Fryer, 1984).

These events had a great impact. There was a strong reaction from those who wanted Black immigration stopped and Black people "repatriated." But those who stood for fairness, equality, an end to discrimination, and greater "harmony" also reacted strongly. Self-organization among Black people increased (see Sivanandan, 1982). Lord Justice Salmon, a Jew, told the nine White youths found guilty of assault during the Notting Hill riots: "Everyone, irrespective of the colour of their skin, is entitled to walk through our streets with their heads erect and free from fear" (Rose et al., 1969, p. 214).

Control of Black Immigration Is Introduced. Yet, immigration controls seemed to be the first consequence of these events and of the burgeoning pressure groups opposed to Black immigration (Rose et al., 1969). Thus, the first postwar law to control Black immigration, the Commonwealth Immigrants Act of 1962, was passed by a Conservative government. The Aliens Act of 1905 had been directed largely against Jews.

The 1962 act was only the first of several acts that, along with various administrative arrangements including changes to immigration rules in 1969, 1974, 1977, and 1980, progressively stopped Black immigration and removed existing rights from Black groups (Macdonald & Blake, 1991; see also below). The passing of the 1962 act had the immediate countereffect of increasing immigration as many, especially from the Indian subcontinent, sought "to beat the ban" and as "temporary," single immigrants decided to settle and bring in their families.

Despite the great public concern about immigration from the 1950s on, the immigrant population remained a minute proportion of the total population. In particular the Black population in schools was very small. The first national figures available for all state schools in England and Wales were for 1972. By then, only about 3.3% of all school children were "immigrants" (Taylor, 1974). However, the "immigrant" children were concentrated in the industrial conurbations.

Dispersal of "Immigrant" Children Is Introduced. In such an area, Southall in West London, White parents of children at two primary schools, one of which was 60% "immigrants" (mainly Indians and Pakistanis), organized a protest in 1963 against the presence of these children (Rose et al., 1969). The minister of education, Sir Edward Boyle, met the parents and later stated in Parliament that, "in the interests of the general policy for racial integration," "immigrant"-only schools must be opposed. Furthermore, "on educational grounds ... no one school should have more than about 30 per cent of immigrants." He "regretfully" told the House that "one school ... must be regarded now as irretrievably an immigrant school." He offered his "strongest support" for authorities adopting a dispersal policy that did not involve compulsion (House of Commons, 1963–64, cols. 439–442). Southall in fact adopted a policy of "dispersal" for new admissions, so as to keep the proportion of "immigrants" in any one school down to about 30% in the future.

The First Report, English for Immigrants. Immediately after this parliamentary debate the first official education publication relating to the presence of "immigrants" in Britain, *English for Immigrants,* was published (Ministry of Education, 1963). An idea of the context in which this appeared can be seen from an earlier Ministry of Education (1954) publication. This saw English literature and language as "the central expression of English life and culture and as the central subject in the education of every English child" (Ministry of Education, 1954, p. 49).

English for Immigrants took an immigrant and assimilationist approach but cautioned against too quick a demand for conformity, recognizing that many immigrant parents did not want their children to abandon their culture (Ministry of Education, 1963). Stressing above all the importance of the acquisition of English, this pamphlet suggested withdrawal classes, or reception classes or centers, to provide special English courses (Ministry of Education, 1963). Such "temporary segregation" would facilitate eventual "integration."

This pamphlet highlighted "immigrants" as "problems" and the "problems" of "immigrants," saying that the greater the proportion of "immigrant" children, the greater the "problem," and raising the issue of British parents wanting reassurance "that the progress of their own children is not being impeded" (Ministry of Education, 1963, p. 10). It dismissed the notion that "color" prejudice is much more likely to occur in schools and suggested (quite wrongly—see, for instance, Davey, 1983; Milner, 1975, 1983) that younger children are "unconscious of colour differences." However, it called for "positive steps" to help young people "not succumb ... to ... irrational prejudices" after leaving school (Ministry of Education, 1963, p. 11).

The Commonwealth Immigrants Advisory Council. The Commonwealth Immigrants Act of 1962, apart from limiting immigration, had set up the Commonwealth Immigrants Advisory Council (CIAC) to advise the home secretary on matters "affecting the welfare of Commonwealth immigrants ... and their integration into the community" and "to examine the arrangements made by local authorities ... to assist immigrants to adapt ... to British habits and customs" (CIAC, 1963, p. 2).

In December 1963, shortly after the appearance of *English for Immigrants,* CIAC (1964) presented its second report, on education, to the home secretary. This took an even more assimilationist approach. It asserted that a national system of education "cannot be expected to perpetuate the different values of immigrant groups" (p. 5). The main emphasis was on the "problem" of the "large number of immigrant children" and on their assimilation through the learning of English, the "first and vital need" (pp. 10–11, 5).

The report also highlighted the visible and cultural distinctiveness of the "Commonwealth immigrants": Britain was "increasingly becoming a multi-racial society" consisting of "individuals with equal rights" but increasingly from different "races" (CIAC, 1964, p. 3). Yet it rejected the idea of mother-tongue teaching in schools.

The report supported withdrawal groups, reception classes, and reception centers for the teaching of English, seeing no problem with that form of segregation. Yet it supported dispersal, even if that meant overriding (Black) parental choice, since "*de facto* segregation ... is something to be avoided at all costs" (CIAC, 1964, p. 11). It gave ominous warnings of "very grave" social and educational consequences of "the creation of predominantly immigrant schools" (p. 10). The report also hinted at a linguistic and cultural deficit theory to account for "educational backwardness" (p. 10).

Twin Policies of "Integration" and "Immigration" Control. In 1965 the new Labour government passed the first Race Relations Act against "racial" discrimination in public places and against "incitement to racial hatred." This act also established a Race Relations Board, which, however, like the act, was weak. Simultaneously the government pursued policies very similar to those of its predecessor: dispersal, English for "immigrants," and limitation of Black immigration.

The policy of "dispersal" was set out officially in Circular 7/65 by the DES, the successor to the Ministry of Education (DES, 1965), and in a white paper shortly afterwards (Prime Minister, 1965). Circular 7/65 again stressed the "problems" supposedly created by the presence of "immigrants." It emphasized the importance of *assimilation* into a presumed monolithic society and the adjustments that "immigrant" children had to make, anticipating "serious strains" if a school or class was more than about one third "immigrant." The teaching of English was "the major educational task" (DES, 1965, p. 2).

The emphasis was on "immigrant" education. However, the only italicized sentence in the document stressed that "*the parents of non-immigrant children*" should see that "*the progress of their own children is not being restricted*"—although there was no evidence that it was (DES, 1965, p. 5). No mention was made of "race," "color," racism, discrimination, or prejudice, but everyone knew what was meant by "immigrant."

The white paper spoke of the United Kingdom as a "multiracial society" and of the "most valuable contribution" to the economy made by "Commonwealth immigrants," but it insisted that their presence, with their "different social and cultural backgrounds, raises ... problems and creates ... social tensions" (Prime Minister, 1965, p. 10). About half of the white paper dealt with "immigration" and more stringent "immigration" controls. The rest, headed "Integration," was preoccupied with an assimilationist approach to "problems" in "housing, education, employment and health" (Prime Minister, 1965, p. 10). The goal was the absorption of the "immigrants" with "mutual understanding and tolerance," avoiding the "evil of racial strife" (pp. 18, 10). Circular 7/65 was incorporated in the white paper, thus reiterating "dispersal" and the need for English.

The dispersal policy had a "very mixed reception," with only six local education authorities (LEAs) setting up dispersal schemes (Power, 1967, p. 7). Setting up special English-language classes was the commonest response of LEAs with "immigrant" children (see Rose et al., 1969). However, according to Power, Circular 7/65 opened "the way for less inhibited discussion and more constructive local policies than ... hitherto" (p. 7). On the other hand, Rose et al. stated that "the official dispersal proposals ... tended to reinforce popular views about the danger of English children being held back" (p. 270).

National Committee for Commonwealth Immigrants. As a result of a recommendation of the second report of the CIAC, the government had set up the National Committee for Commonwealth Immigrants (NCCI) in 1964. The government now decided that a new National Committee for Commonwealth Immigrants should replace it as well as CIAC itself (Prime Minister, 1965). This NCCI supported voluntary organizations, organized conferences and seminars (including some for teachers), backed a stronger Race Relations Act, and sponsored a national survey with the Race Relations Board. The survey, carried out by Political and Economic Planning (PEP) and Research Services, demonstrated the widespread existence of "color" discrimination and boosted the case for a stronger Race Relations Act (NCCI, undated, ca. 1967; PEP & Research Services, 1967; Taylor, 1974).

Local Government Act of 1966: Section 11. In 1966 there was another general election, and Labour, having, according to Dilip Hiro (1971, p. 221), "established its restrictionist *bona fides* with the voters" through the white paper of 1965, won a landslide victory. The Local Government Act of 1966 was passed. Section 11 provided a 50% rate support grant (later increased to 75%) for staffing relating to the presence of Commonwealth "immigrants" with a different language or different customs. This gave assistance with the teaching of English and later with mother-tongue teaching, especially for Asian children, and more generally with multicultural education.

Immigrant Education and Integrationsim

It was in 1966 that the new home secretary, Roy Jenkins, in a speech explaining government policy, gave his famous definition of integration "not as a flattening process of assimilation but as equal opportunity, accompanied by cultural diversity, in an atmosphere of mutual tolerance"—a goal endorsed by the NCCI (undated, ca. 1967, p. 8). Many commentators have seen this as marking a shift from assimilationism to integrationism, in which the assimilationists' assumptions favoring their own culture and social system are at least modulated so that other cultures are given some recognition and respect.

Technically, "integration" meant a form of "absorption" not as complete as "assimilation," in which the "incoming" group adapts in important ways but is allowed to retain some distinctiveness (see Patterson, 1963). As Mullard (1982) has argued, however, the ideological and practical differences between the assimilationist and the integrationist (and indeed the pluralist) approaches were not very great (see also Brandt, 1986). Both approaches tended to put the onus of adaptation onto the "im-

migrant" groups and to assume the existing power structure and the superiority of "British" culture and society. Essentially both sought consensus on the terms of the (White) majority, either totally (assimilationism) or overwhelmingly (integrationism).

Conferences and Courses for Educators. Around the early 1960s, courses, workshops, and seminars for teachers of "immigrant" children were beginning to appear (see Power, 1967; Rose et al., 1969). Many of these dealt with the teaching of English as a second language, some with prejudice, and others with the cultures and countries of origin of "colored immigrants." Such activities were organized or promoted by, for example, the Schools Council (set up in 1964), some LEAs, a few institutions of initial teacher education, and voluntary organizations, in particular the Association of Teachers of English to Pupils from Overseas (ATEPO), which was founded in 1962, becoming the National Association for Multiracial Education (NAME) in 1973 and then the National Antiracist Movement in Education in 1985.

In July 1966 the NCCI organized a conference for educators entitled Towards a Multi-racial Society. The stress was on integration, the aim being to "encourage ... awareness within the educational system of the role of ... schools and training colleges in promoting an integrated multi-racial community"; and also to help expose the "mythology of race" so as to promote equality (NCCI, undated, ca. 1966, p. 5).

The conference report (NCCI, undated, ca. 1966, pp. 6, 7) showed that aspects of multiculturalism and even of antiracism were already beginning to be explored and that assimilationism was not universally accepted. However, the view of "immigrant" children as a "problem" and the emphasis on the learning of English were in evidence. Philip Mason, director of the Institute of Race Relations (set up in 1952 with a mainly international rather than a British focus) endorsed Jenkins's goal of integration.

He also stated that everyone "must belong to some race" (NCCI, undated, ca. 1966, p. 7). Yet, in any scientific or biological sense, the concept of "race" is highly problematic (Banton, 1983; Miles, 1982; Rex, 1983). "Race" is a social construction, in a double sense, within a racist system. First, "race" is an ideological construct—that is, a product of racist thinking. Second, it is a social reality produced, maintained, and reproduced by social forces and defined by racist social relations, especially by differential relations of power (see Figueroa, 1991; see also Miles, 1982).

Professor Kenneth Little, the doyen of studies in "race" relations in Britain, stated that there was not much difference "in the treatment of coloured people in Britain today and some 200 years ago" (NCCI, undated, ca. 1966, p. 26). He called for the presentation of the total culture of other peoples, and not just of the bizarre. Lewis Waddilove, director of the Joseph Rowntree Memorial Trust, and Dipak Nandy, executive member of the Campaign Against Racial Discrimination (CARD), without using the concept, actually pointed toward institutional racism. Nandy spoke of "systematic, impersonal patterns of discrimination," arguing that the "problem" may not be one "which would disappear if only people were kinder to each other"

(NCCI, updated, ca. 1966, pp. 32–33). He also said that "race relations" was not an "immigrant problem" and that "the native community" needed educating at least as much as "the immigrant community."

Some of the academic thinking of the time can also be seen in Bowker (1968, p. 74), who clearly assumed equality of opportunity as a basic social value but saw this as being realized through acculturation "to facilitate social integration." He seemed to assume that learning a new culture must entail losing the culture of origin (Bowker, 1968). Around the same time the Schools Council was taking a strong assimilationist approach, rejecting bilingualism, at least in practice, and stressing the teaching of English since English provided "the key to cultural and social assimilation" (1967, p. 4).

Views of Local Education Authorities. A variety of views, even contradictory ones, were being expressed by some education officers in various "immigrant" areas at the time (Power, 1967). The dominant underlying model, however, seemed to favor assimilation (even though the term *integration* was sometimes used). The need to acquire English was stressed. Some education officers used stereotypes and racialized language. The "immigrant" was frequently seen as having "problems" or giving rise to them, and their linguistic, social, or even cultural situation was sometimes referred to in deficit terms (Power, 1967).

However, the chief education officer for Warley, while also referring to "problems" and the need for English, perhaps began to bring consensus into question. He wrote:

Only too often do we in our intolerance feel that we must integrate or assimilate them . . . . What right have we to deny those whose parents pay rates an education and an upbringing on the basis of their own language and traditions? (Power, 1967, pp. 53–54).

Multicultural Education

The developments in multicultural education came more from the bottom than the top, from the efforts of both White liberals and Black people. They were partly stimulated by the shift in status among Black people from that of immigrants to settlers, which the Commonwealth Immigrants Act of 1962 led to, and by the negative messages that control of immigration gave to the Black communities. They also need to be seen against the background of other developments, especially in the late 1960s and in the 1970s. There were contradictory forces at work: some were still oriented to assimilation and the "problems" of "immigrants"; others moved increasingly toward multiculturalism and even antiracism.

Significant Events. Several events stimulated the Black community and White liberals. American civil rights campaigners visited Britain in the 1960s and made an impact: Martin Luther King in 1964, Malcolm X (especially important) in 1965, and Stokely Carmichael in 1967. The findings of extensive discrimination against "colored immigrants" (PEP & Research Services, 1967) sparked Black Power supporters, who formed the Universal Coloured People's Association (UCPA) in summer 1967. About then the Inner London Education Authority (ILEA,

1967) produced a report showing that African Caribbean children were overrepresented in schools for the educationally subnormal (ESN). In 1968 it published a very influential study (ILEA, 1968) that, despite methodological problems, concluded that "minority" groups, especially those of Caribbean background, were "underachieving" (see Figueroa, 1991).

Coard (1971) argued that West Indian children were being *made* educationally subnormal by the workings of the British educational system. Subsequently, Tomlinson (1982) provided evidence supporting this view. Rose et al. (1969, p. 285) stated that at first it was "not uncommon" for all immigrant pupils to be placed with the remedial teacher. As Craft (1986) says, the assimilationist thinking of the 1950s and early 1960s meant that there was a tendency to disregard linguistic and "cultural differences in the ability testing of immigrant pupils" (p. 80). Misplacement of these pupils thus took place. The Black community responded, not only by campaigning on the broader political and social front, but also by setting up supplementary schools (Brandt, 1986; Tomlinson, 1983) and calling for action in state schools, such as the teaching of Black studies (see Taylor, 1974).

A development that "severely" shook the "immigrant" communities and organizations (Rose et al., 1969, p. 619) and led to more protests by Black people was the passing in record time of the racist Commonwealth Immigrants Act of 1968 to keep out Kenyan Asians who were British citizens with British passports. Jo Grimond, leader of the Liberal Party, condemned this measure in Parliament as being directed purely against the entry into Britain of "colored people" (cited by Rose et al., 1969, p. 614).

Also about this time Sandys and Powell, senior Conservative Members of Parliament, were making racist comments or speeches, but the attorney general refused to use against them the provisions of the Race Relations Act of 1965 proscribing "incitement to racial hatred." Apart from Colin Jordan, a leader of the fascist British National Socialists, the only convictions under these provisions between 1965 and 1976 were of Black people, including Michael X, an African Caribbean, the founder in 1965 of the Racial Adjustment Action Society (RAAS, a Jamaican swear word) (Macdonald, 1977).

Yet in 1969 the influential report of the Survey of Race Relations (sponsored by the Institute of Race Relations and funded by the Nuffield Foundation) was still giving a good deal of attention in its many recommendations to disadvantage and deprivation; the cultural background of "immigrant" communities; immigrant education; the teaching of English; compensatory education; and "adjustment to . . . an alien culture" (Rose et al., 1969, p. 698). The report also recommended instruction for student teachers "in what has been established about inheritance, cultural variation, and the sources of prejudice" (Rose et al., 1969, p. 702).

At the time, "immigrant" children often tended to be seen as deprived inner-city children, sharing the social and educational disadvantages of deprived children generally. It thus tended to be assumed that comprehensive reorganization in the 1960s and early 1970s, the implementation of the compensatory education notion of Educational Priority Areas put forward by the Plowden report (DES, Central Advisory Council for Education,

1967), the Urban Aid Programme initiated in 1968, and the raising of the school-leaving age in 1972 would benefit "immigrants" by benefiting the disadvantaged generally.

Select Committee on Race Relations and Immigration, 1969.

The latter part of the 1960s also saw another far-reaching development. Partly through the influence of CARD (1965–67), the NCCI and the PEP and Research Services report (1967), a much wider, though still weak, Race Relations Act was passed in 1968. This act set up the Community Relations Commission (CRC) to replace the NCCI. While the implementation of the law was still the concern of the Race Relations Board, the CRC was to coordinate the policy on "race" relations and to promote "harmonious community relations between Commonwealth immigrants and the host population" (Taylor, 1974, p. 19).

Furthermore, a Select Committee on Race Relations and Immigration (SCRRI) was established in November 1968 to review policies on immigration and the expanded Race Relations Act. It took evidence from the end of 1968 until the middle of 1969, publishing its report later that year. The West Indian and Asian communities took this opportunity to make representations.

For instance, Mr. J. Crawford, secretary of the West Indian Standing Conference and chair of the North London West Indian Association, told the committee that, although non-English-speaking children born abroad did present a language problem, basically there was "no immigrant problem in schools as such"; the problem was a "white problem": "hostility and . . . overt racialism" against Black people, in school, and later in life (SCRRI, 1969c, p. 1,017).

By contrast, the written evidence of the DES to the select committee (SCRRI, 1969a, pp. 150–152) focused on "problems" or strains "caused" by the "concentration" of "immigrants" in certain areas, and on the lack of English or its "limited or defective" nature. The DES evidence included circulars 7/65 and 8/67. The latter emphasized the aim of "integration," counterposed to "segregation." In speaking of the work of colleges of education, the DES referred to the provision of "courses related to the teaching of immigrant children or to the problem of a multi-cultural society" (SCRRI, 1969a, p. 169). This was perhaps one of the earliest usages of the term *multi-cultural* by the DES, and it focused on the education of "immigrants" and had the negative connotation of a "problem," cultural traditions "foreign to our own" being seen as possible handicaps at school and beyond (p. 166). The DES stated that the aim was not to assimilate the "immigrant" children, "obliterating their cultural backgrounds, but to further their integration in an alien society by assisting them to take full advantage of our system of education" (p. 152). There was no hint that any adjustment on the part of the system might be desirable.

Sir Herbert Andrew, permanent under-secretary of state, DES, accepted under later questioning that the teaching of different cultures, religious faiths, and backgrounds should figure "somewhere" in the curriculum, but not in primary schools. He made it clear that he did not consider prejudice reduction, let alone antiracism, part of the job of education in schools. He was opposed to "the inclusion of a subject known as 'race relations'" (SCRRI, 1969c, p. 1180). Instead, every subject, in partic-

ular "religious education, history, current affairs, geography," could make "a contribution" (p. 1180).

Although Sir Herbert accepted that any "color discrimination" by a LEA would constitute a contravention of the 1968 Race Relations Act, he clearly did not think that the DES needed to have any specific policy or strategy to identify or deal with such discrimination (SCRRI, 1969c). He asserted that "problems of discrimination and of social tension . . . do not arise" within schools or colleges, and the educational system could do nothing about such problems in the wider society (p. 1194). Regarding tensions that arose "between people because of the colour of their skins," educating people so that such tensions "would disappear" was not something that one could "reasonably expect" of the educational system: it was a "moral" problem (p. 1195).

He seemed to place all of the education problems at the door of the "immigrants," not of the system. The "difficulties" had to do with English-language competence, the level of "familiarity with English [*sic*] culture, social customs and so on," and living in "run-down areas" (SCRRI, 1969c, pp. 1193–1194). "Color" was not a problem, the educational problem was temporary, and, once the children received all of their education in Britain, there would be "no problem at all" (p. 1194).

In its report, SCRRI focused on the "problems" of "immigrants" but also underlined issues relating to "race" relations and cultural understanding (SCRRI, 1969d). In addition to the usual points about general deprivation, "culture shock," the need for English, and the need for immigrants to learn about "our" customs, the committee also acknowledged the bias of "normal" IQ tests and stated that schools "should prepare all their children for adult life in a multi-racial society" (p. 41). All school leavers should be taught "the main features of race relations," and, through subjects such as religion and history, all children could be given a "better understanding of the national and cultural background of immigrants" (p. 41). The report stated that a fundamental need was for "recognition of the . . . bitterness of coloured [*sic*] prejudice" and that "the main obligation for improving race relations rests with the indigenous [*sic*] people" of Britain (p. 20).

Here then is a shift from a perspective focusing only on "immigrant education" to a broader one incorporating something of multicultural education, and perhaps even the beginnings of a form of antiracism. Unfortunately, however, in seeking bridges "between cultures and communities," the committee could only mention "West Indian songs, or . . . Indian art, jewelry and costumes" (SCRRI, 1969d, pp. 40–42). Also, any focus on racism was in the limited sense of "color prejudice."

Follow-up to the SCRRI Report of 1969.

As a follow-up to the SCRRI inquiry, the DES commissioned the National Foundation for Educational Research (NFER) to investigate the "educational arrangements for schools with immigrant pupils" (Townsend, 1971, p. 15). It was found that almost half of the LEAs in England had made some special arrangements, mainly for the teaching of English. Townsend highlighted the notions of "linguistic, cultural and social deprivation" and of a compensatory approach (p. 10). It was also found that "about seven per cent of the primary ... and ... 50 per cent of the secondary schools" studied included some treatment of "race relations" in the curriculum, though not usually as a separate subject (Townsend & Brittan, 1972, p. 112). Headteachers made various comments about teaching "race relations," including: "We have no difficulty here" and "let ... sleeping dogs lie" (p. 111). Townsend and Brittan also reported the use of inappropriate, culture-bound measures of ability and attainment.

Also in the wake of SCRRI, Her Majesty's Inspectorate (HMI) carried out a "pilot survey ... into current practice and opinion concerning the educational assessment of pupils from overseas" (DES, 1971b, p. 1), and the DES produced a survey of the "education of immigrants" (DES, 1971a). This was followed by another "pilot study" of "ethnical" secondary school "immigrant pupils" (DES, 1972). In all of these, the issues continued to be conceptualized in terms of the education of "immigrants," of their "disabilities," and of "problems." The first survey concluded that high priority should be given to the assessment of English but no priority "to the development of standardized 'culture-fair' group tests of intelligence," there being "little justification for developing any means of assessing immigrants in isolation from other projects for children with social, cultural and linguistic disabilities" (DES, 1971b, p. 19).

The second and third surveys reiterated that "teaching English to immigrant children" was the "most urgent single challenge facing the schools concerned" (DES, 1971a, p. 9). However, the report on the second survey acknowledged that teachers were "no less prone than anyone else to feelings of prejudice or even acts of discrimination" but put this down largely to "a lack of knowledge of the pupils' cultural and social background and ... the sense of bewilderment ... at not knowing how to set about ... teaching these pupils" (p. 11).

This report also rather superficially saw "immigrant pupils" as giving "fresh colour and vigour to the life ... of many schools" through "the new ... art forms which they have introduced" (DES, 1971a, p. 119). It provided a rather rosy view of children of "different ethnic groups and cultural backgrounds" living "together happily" and an image of "immigrants" integrated as equals into a "cohesive, multi-cultural society," where they were permitted "the expression of differences of attitudes, beliefs and customs, language and culture ... which may eventually enrich the main stream of our cultural and social tradition" (pp. 119–120).

In discussing the substantial overrepresentation of "immigrant pupils," mainly African Caribbeans, in ESN schools, this report continued to insist—without providing any evidence—that there are "some immigrant children who are too disadvantaged educationally to prosper in ... ordinary classes. They need special arrangements ... where they do not displace native born children" (DES, 1971a, pp. 68–69). Not surprisingly, the 1973 SCRRI report was critical of the DES (see below).

The notion of multicultural education did, nevertheless, gain prominence in the 1970s. In 1970 an international conference, Education for Cultural Pluralism, was held in London (Eppel, 1972). In January 1970 the Community Relations Commission (CRC) published the first book in its series, Education for a Multi-Cultural Society. In January 1971 it jointly organized with the National Union of Students (NUS) a conference entitled Education for a Multicultural Society, held at Edge Hill College of Education.

In 1972 a Schools Council pamphlet distinguished between what was needed in "multi-racial" classrooms and for all children in all schools to help them understand that Britain had become a multiracial and multicultural society. Pupils should be given an understanding of the clash between cultures and of beliefs about physical differences (Schools Council, 1972). A notable Schools Council project at the time was the Humanities Curriculum Project (1967–72) under Lawrence Stenhouse, which proposed a "neutral chair" procedure for the teacher in dealing with controversial issues such as "race" (see Stenhouse, 1975).

About that time many uncoordinated developments were taking place, especially at the "grass-roots" level, with a greater focus on cultural diversity and on "race" relations, including prejudice reduction and the promotion of tolerance (see Taylor, 1974). In these respects, including issues to do with Black identity, two influential books in the mid-1970s were Children and Race by Milner (1975) and Race and Education Across Cultures edited by Verma and Bagley (1975).

At the Institute of Race Relations in the early 1970s, there were struggles going on between the radicals and Black staff, on the one hand, and the liberals and conservatives on the other. By the end of 1972 the "palace revolution" had taken place, and the radical Black long-serving librarian of the institute, A. Sivanandan (1974), had become its director. The new Institute of Race Relations was committed from a deeply held socialist position to the Black struggle against racism.

The SCRRI Report of 1973. The SCRRI report of 1973 made an important contribution. The main focus was again on the education of "immigrants," English as a second language, and other "handicaps." The underlying theme was that "Special problems need special remedies" (SCRRI, 1973, p. 4). But the select committee acknowledged that the term *immigrant* was unsatisfactory; recommended the phasing out of dispersal; and focused on the issue of a "multi-racial society" and the appropriate education for it. It quoted the National Union of Teachers (NUT) as calling for "an education directed towards the needs of a multi-racial society, and not to the ... isolated question of educating children from immigrant families with often the unacknowledged aim of converting them into good Europeans" (p. 21).

The select committee also reported the NFER as stating that the terms *integration, assimilation,* and *pluralism* were treated by many as interchangeable (SCRRI, 1973, p. 24). Agreeing that there was "no consensus about the future nature of the multi-racial society," the committee saw "the first task for schools as equipping their pupils with awareness of an increasingly diverse society" so that they could "develop their own attitudes" to it (p. 25). It rejected the notion of "black studies in the narrow sense" but accepted that "the history, geography and cultures of the ... minorities ... are worthy of study ... not least by indigenous children" (p. 28). Rejecting "unity through uniformity," it accepted "unity through diversity" (p. 28).

Despite the widening of the debate by the select committee, and their calls for a response from central government, the DES continued to think within the perspective of the "problems of immigrants" and to see these as part of the general problem of "educational disadvantage" (DES, 1974, p. 5). Thus, the DES set up an internal Educational Disadvantage Unit and a (short-lived) Centre of Information and Advice on Educational Disadvantage, subsuming the "needs of immigrants" within these.

Immigration Control. At the same time, central government policy on "immigration" was still, and indeed increasingly, control oriented. A wide-ranging Immigration Act of 1971 was passed by a Conservative government to "rationalize" the laws governing immigrants from the Commonwealth, and aliens, and to meet the requirements of the European Economic Community (EEC), which the UK joined about that time. This law put on a permanent basis and expanded the provisions of the Commonwealth Immigrants Act of 1962, which had required annual renewal. It incorporated and refined the principle of patriality. "Patriality" refers to an "ancestral connection," originally through the father or father's father, to the UK. This principle had been introduced into the Commonwealth Immigrants Act of 1968 with the specific purpose of excluding East African "Asians" who held British passports. The device of "ancestral connection" was used to avoid any formal or direct racism. However, Macdonald and Blake (1991) consider this patriality clause racially discriminatory. It was also in the implementation of this act that the inexcusable practice of so-called vaginal examination of "Asian" women was introduced as part of immigration controls.

The reaction of the Black communities and of those who sympathized with them to the introduction of this legislation was one of horror and increased militancy. As Fryer (1984, p. 385) states, even before this bill was introduced, "Asians and West Indians . . . went in daily fear of their lives" in many areas. The Black community had always found that, far from facilitating "integration," stricter and stricter "immigration" controls encouraged the racists. Sivanandan (1982) shows how Black people moved over the years from resistance to rebellion. On the introduction of the 1971 bill, the chairperson of the CRC stated that it would "adversely affect the establishment of harmonious community relations" and "acutely increase the insecurity which coloured people living here already feel" (CRC, 1971, p. 43).

However, the policy of strict "immigration" controls continued, and 10 years later the British Nationality Act of 1981 was passed by a Conservative government. The principle of "patriality" was essentially retained, and indeed further refined, in this major act, which divides British nationality into three categories: British citizens; British Dependent Territories citizens; and British Overseas citizens. Of these only the first have freedom of entry to and the right of abode in the UK. Previously, people covered by the other two categories had similar rights. Over the years, in particular since the 1962 act, the rights of such people, mainly Black in the wide sense, have been progressively removed. Yet such rights have not been taken away from that major source of immigrants, the (White) citizens of the Irish Republic, and have actually been extended to (mainly White)

citizens of independent Commonwealth countries who had a parent born in the UK, although birth in the UK no longer guarantees a right to British citizenship. Furthermore, people in the category British Overseas citizens, largely Black people in the wide sense, could find themselves in effect stateless. Macdonald and Blake (1991) point out that this new nationality law merely seems to enshrine "the existing racially discriminatory provisions of immigration law under the new clothing of British citizenship" (p. 117). The Conservative government's Immigration Act of 1988 introduced even tougher regulations.

Equal Opportunities Legislation. A Labour government was returned (with a very small majority) in 1974, and equal opportunities became prominent on the agenda. The Sex Discrimination Act of 1975 was passed, and the Equal Opportunities Commission (gender) was set up. In the following year a much-strengthened Race Relations Act was passed, outlawing both direct and indirect discrimination on grounds of "race," color, nationality—including citizenship—or ethnic or national origins in a very wide range of spheres, including education. This act also set up the Commission for Racial Equality (CRE) to take over the functions of the Race Relations Board and the CRC. Despite its remaining limitations, especially the weaknesses of the implementation arrangements, this act is unique in Europe. Part III of the Conservative government's Public Order Act of 1986 remedied some of the defects of previous laws against incitement to racial hatred, while section 3 of their Football (Offences) Act of 1991 gave further attention to racism, specifically in connection with football.

SCRRI Report of 1977 Recommends a Committee of Inquiry. Finally, SCRRI (1977) in its report *The West Indian Community* recommended "as a matter of urgency" that the government set up an inquiry "into the causes of the underachievement of children of West Indian origin." The Labour government (Home Office, 1978) welcomed this report and spoke, not of "immigrants," but of "ethnic minorities"—a change worth noting, whatever the drawbacks of this latter term. Committing itself to "the concept of racial equality" and to ensuring "equal opportunities" in education, the government set up an inquiry but widened its brief to encompass "the needs of all pupils for education for life in a multi-racial society" (Home Office, 1978, p. 7).

Although the government still stressed the need for English, and the need to "compensate" for "difficulties" facing "immigrants," it also stated that for the curriculum to have meaning for all pupils its content, values, and assumptions "must reflect the wide range of cultures, histories and lifestyles in our multiracial society" (Home Office, 1978, p. 6). It saw "racial disadvantage" as caused partly by "cultural difference" but largely by "the complex and pervasive nature of racial discrimination" (p. 4). About the same time a government consultative paper (DES, 1977) was asserting that the curriculum should be multicultural.

The government's decision to set up the committee of inquiry was a momentous one. It was established in 1979, with Anthony Rampton as the chairperson. Although the Conservatives under Margaret Thatcher won a landslide victory later that year, the committee proceeded, producing an interim report in 1981 (see below). Rampton resigned amid controversy, and Lord Swann was appointed as the new chairperson, the final report eventually appearing in 1985 (see below). However, before considering the Rampton and Swann reports, it is necessary to say more about the national and local developments and debates that were taking place.

National and Local Developments and Debates. In 1968 a survey found that attention was being given to the education of children from "immigrant" communities but much less to teaching in a "multi-cultural society" generally (Millins, 1970). Following this up, a joint working party of the CRC and the Association of Teachers in Colleges and Departments of Education (ATCDE) produced in 1974 a report entitled *Teacher Education for a Multi-cultural Society.* Describing Britain as a "multi-cultural" and "pluralistic" society with "black and brown Britons," it asserted that cultural diversity offered community enrichment, the ethnocentric curriculum being "dangerously inappropriate" (CRC & ATCDE, 1974, pp. 9–10, 44). Student teachers, besides needing to be prepared for teaching English as a second language and for dealing with low performance, needed to confront the issue of "prejudice" and "institutional discrimination" (pp. 10–14). Unfortunately, even by the 1990s teacher education had still not adequately addressed such issues (see Giles & Cherrington, 1981; and Siraj-Blatchford, 1990).

The Bullock report on teaching the use of English considered that the "disturbingly low pattern of attainment" of "immigrant" children related to many issues including language, "cultural identity and cultural knowledge" (DES, 1975, pp. 285, 286). It asserted that "No child should be expected to cast off the language and culture of the home as he [*sic*] crosses the school threshold . . . . The curriculum should reflect many elements of . . . his life . . . outside school" (p. 286). Bilingualism should be seen "as an asset," teachers should be aware of the "problems" relating to dialect, and a "positive attitude" to West Indian dialect and culture would help both teachers and children (pp. 294, 287).

The Schools Council funded a project, Education for a Multiracial Society, carried out between 1973 and 1976 in primary and secondary schools and published a report in 1981. The first publication resulting from this study (Townsend & Brittan, 1973) reported that a majority of headteachers, whether or not in "multiracial" areas of schools, agreed that schools should prepare pupils for life in a "multiracial" society. Nevertheless, a large proportion of schools either did not regard this as part of their job or, if so, did little about it. An earlier Schools Council paper (1970) had found that teachers often did not believe the evidence on the development of racist attitudes in children or thought that to focus on such matters might be counterproductive or seen as "political."

The Schools Council (1981) report remarked that it had become "customary" to present the range of possibilities for Britain as a continuum from assimilationism to pluralism. In the pluralist model of society, "minority cultures retain their essential identities and stand in a relationship of equality and mutual respect to the cultural mainstream" (Schools Council, 1981,

p. 15). Rejecting assimilationism, and using phrases such as "racial minorities" or "minority ethnic groups" instead of "immigrant," this report took a pluralist stance. But a limited understanding of pluralism was implied in which the "mainstream," despite "potential enrichment" by the cultures of the "minority races," remains essentially unchanged. The report addressed racism in a cautious and indirect way, conceptualizing it in terms of prejudice and stereotypes. A more direct and vivid section of five chapters on racism submitted by the project team had been vetoed.

The report stated that a "multiracial curriculum" comprised two elements: a "recognition, visually and verbally, of the multiracial complexion of British society"; and the inclusion of "minority cultures . . . in Britain and . . . other cultures in the Third World" (Schools Council, 1981, p. 10). The objectives of "multiracial education" included knowledge of "the main cultures . . . in Britain"; acceptance of "the principles of equal rights and justice"; acceptance "that prejudice and discrimination are widespread in Britain" and are damaging to "the rejected group"; acceptance of "the possibility of developing multiple loyalties"; English language skills; mother-tongue skills; and the development of "a positive self-image" (pp. 16–17). Despite advances in thinking in this report, there was a negative subtext: Minority self-image and "minority" and "Third World" cultures are problematic and need addressing.

In 1975 the CRC carried out a study of LEAs, teachers, and parents in eight urban areas with "multi-racial" population (Wallis, 1977). Not one of these LEAs, it seemed, had made a comprehensive review of its services with reference "to the needs of a multi-racial area" (Wallis, 1977, p. 43). In fact, by the mid-1970s fewer than one third of the 49 LEAs with more than 2% of "immigrant pupils" had an adviser on "immigrant education" (Little, 1978a, p. 23).

The policy makers in the eight LEAs studied stressed English as a second language, "integration," and "equality of opportunity" (Wallis, 1977). Mother-tongue and minority cultures tended to be seen as not being school matters (Wallis, 1977). Compared with policy makers, teachers "saw a far wider range of issues as relevant," although they too saw language as "the major priority" (p. 42). Although generally "satisfied with the work done in schools to create a . . . multi-cultural . . . environment," they worried about minority "under-achievement," "identity difficulties," and difficulties faced on leaving school, including "racial discrimination" (pp. 5, 16). They gave more importance than policy makers to "the preservation of minority cultures" but tended to see this as a matter for the communities rather than the schools (p. 43). Several teachers thought that "prejudice" and "discrimination" were rare in school and often seemed to think it best not to draw attention to such (difficult) issues. A "minority of teachers showed themselves to be hostile to ethnic minorities" (p. 45).

For their part, a "minority of parents considered the teachers to be racially biased or unsympathetic to their children" (Wallis, 1977, p. 45). There was quite a strong demand for "ethnic minority" teachers and, by some Asian parents, for instruction in their own religions and languages. The majority of parents, however, were generally satisfied.

The first LEA policy statement on "multi-ethnic education"

was produced by the ILEA (1977) shortly after the passing of the 1976 Race Relations Act. It was largely in response to the concerns, especially of the African Caribbean community, about the situation of Black children in the educational system. Until then the practice in the ILEA had been mainly along assimilationist lines, stressing the acquisition of English by "immigrants" and otherwise tending to adopt a universalistic approach to the immigrants' situation, which was seen simply as one of "disadvantage" (see Troyna & Williams, 1986). The new policy statement indicated the need "to take advantage of the vitality and richness" of the "multicultural society" (ILEA, 1977, p. 1). Troyna and Williams (1986) consider that this approach was very much of the "benevolent multiculturalist" type, seeking to improve the educational performance of the "underachieving" groups by becoming sensitive to their *particular* cultural backgrounds. By contrast, a 1980 multicultural education policy statement from Manchester, also one of the earliest, tended to reflect instead the universalistic "cultural understanding" approach, which is concerned with promoting understanding and acceptance of cultural differences among *all* students (see Troyna & Williams, 1986). Neither the ILEA nor the Manchester document referred explicitly to racism, but by 1979 the ILEA had added a section on "teaching against racism," and after 1981 Manchester started developing an antiracist policy (Troyna & Williams, 1986). Teaching unions were also producing policy statements and guidance. For instance, in 1978 NUT published a pamphlet that began to address racism, and in 1981 the Assistant Masters and Mistresses Association published a multicultural education statement.

In 1978 the BBC televised extracts from five talks on "race" and racism in "multi-racial" Britain (Twitchin, 1978). One of these talks was by Professor Alan Little on "School and Race." He identified two sets of issues, one concerning the "majority" vis-à-vis the "minorities," and the other concerning the "special educational needs" of the "racial or ethnic minorities"—although he said he would like to "eradicate" the notions of "minorities," and especially of "immigrants," from the "race" relations vocabulary (Little, 1978b, pp. 56, 57). The issues he underlined included disadvantage; underachievement; the "Asian" sense of "an alternative culture"; the "West Indian" "variant on the dominant culture," which, being "rejecting," brought the danger of "self-rejection"; and the facts of discrimination, "racial hostility . . . and . . . prejudice," both within the school and outside (pp. 58–64).

Many, however, still failed to see the need to address racism in schools. In 1981, in the middle of a summer of race riots (see below), the DES (1981a) was blandly stating that schools must "reflect" the "multicultural" nature of "our society," and the House of Commons Home Affairs Committee (which had replaced the SCRRI) was failing to give adequate attention to racism. This committee was sharply critical of the DES for inaction and for not separating out "multi-racial education" concerns from "the whole range of educational disadvantage arising from social deprivation" (Home Affairs Committee, 1981, p. xx). It also stated that "the fraught relationship between the police and young blacks had its deeper origins in a complex fabric of social and economic disadvantage," disadvantage "in education and employment" being "most crucial" (pp. vii, liv).

However, it stressed that, although very important, discrimination was "possibly not the prime factor" in "racial disadvantage" in the society, and racism was not "a sufficient explanation" of the continuing "educational problems confronting ethnic minority children" (pp. xiv, lv, liv). None of this committee's recommendations for education addressed racism specifically. The committee essentially called for a targeting of the "problems" and needs of "ethnic minorities," especially "racial" disadvantage, and for a promotion of "multicultural education," although mother-tongue teaching was not seen as a matter for LEAs (Home Affairs Committee, 1981). The committee reiterated the importance of (English) "language training" and made the usual error of stating that "West Indian" children "have no ready-made culture of their own"—presumably because Caribbean cultures are so much closer to British ones than are Asian cultures (pp. xvi, lv).

Thatcher's government showed itself unwilling to accept the essentially multiculturalist recommendations of this committee. Protesting that it was "wholly committed to a multiracial society in which there is full equality of opportunity irrespective of colour, race or religion," the government simply asserted the general case that "the creation of a stronger and more prosperous economy where new real jobs are created . . . and unemployment falls . . . is the most potent means of combatting . . . racial disadvantage" (Home Office, 1982, pp. 3, 6).

However, Lynch (1983, p. 15), one of the most prolific writers in the field, argued that since Britain is a multicultural society, schools needed to provide a specifically multicultural education. This should be an "initiation of children into critical-rational acceptance of cultural diversity . . . within a common humanity." The basic principle was "respect for persons," or "mutuality" (Lynch, 1983, p. 19; 1986, p. 184). Included was a challenge to bias, stereotyping, and discrimination, "prejudice reduction" being subsequently assigned a central place (Lynch, 1987). Lynch emphasized a whole school approach, including a stated policy, multiethnic staffing, and an explicit statement that "racist, sexist and credist behaviour is totally unacceptable" (Lynch, 1987, p. 72; see Lynch, 1986). However, he saw racism primarily as an individual phenomenon. He also tended to highlight the supposed "dilemma" of cohesion versus diversity.

Similarly, Craft (1984) asked, "How far can diversity be pursued before social cohesion is put at risk?" (p. 8). Seeing cultural pluralism as posing the greatest educational challenge, he stated that educators have to decide the balance between "acculturation" and "the celebration of diversity," between assimilation and divisiveness (p. 23). But Craft failed to address the questions of power and racism. Is conformity simply to be conformity to the dominant culture? Besides, it is too simple to see diversity as such as the cause of fragmentation and conflict, or to see conflict as necessarily negative, or to pose such a stark dichotomy between social cohesion and cultural diversity.

1981. As Craft (1984) has observed, the year 1981 was significant for the development of multicultural (and antiracist) education. Several important publications appeared, some of which have already been referred to. The British Nationality Act of 1981 was passed. In April 1981 Brixton ablaze was flashed across the nation's televisions screens, as "a few hundred young people—most . . . black—attacked the police on the streets" of South London (Home Office, 1981a, p. 1). Another "race riot" had taken place one year earlier in Bristol. One year before that Blair Peach had been killed, apparently "from a blow to the head . . . by a police officer with an unauthorized . . . weapon," during a confrontation between the police and protesters against a National Front meeting in Southall, West London (Unofficial Committee of Enquiry, 1980, p. 86). There have been many other "disorders" subsequently, including "disturbances" throughout the country in summer 1981, notably in Toxteth, Liverpool, and "riots" in 1985 in Handsworth, Birmingham.

From October 1981 television screens also carried a BBC series on multicultural education (see Twitchin & Demuth, 1985). Twitchin and Demuth, adopting an "electic approach," stated that teachers understood multicultural education in a range of different ways: meeting "special needs," especially for English as a second language; bringing minority cultures into the classroom and supporting self-esteem; providing a "global perspective" for *all* children; or contributing "to good race relations" (pp. 6, 7).

However, up to the early 1980s at least, there was still a wide gap between rhetoric and educational practice (Willey, 1984b). The Schools Council had established another study of the "multi-ethnic" curriculum in all LEAs, which was carried out during 1978–80 and reported on in 1981 (Little & Willey, 1981). It was found that "official assertions about a 'multicultural' society having relevance to all schools had made minimal impact" (Willey, 1984b, p. 28). Most authorities at schools with few Black students did not see "multicultural education" as a concern of theirs. Although most of the other authorities made "some arrangements to meet the 'special' needs of minority ethnic . . . pupils," these tended to be primarily for English as a second language, with very little being done across the curriculum for all pupils (Little & Willey, 1981, p. 30). Another study, also published in 1981, found that the impact had also been minimal in in-service teacher education (Eggleston, Dunn, & Purewal, 1981).

Of all the many reports and publications in 1981, however, probably the two most significant were the Rampton (DES, 1981b) and the Scarman (Home Office, 1981a) reports. The Scarman report on the Brixton riot identified "racialism and discrimination against black people—often hidden, sometimes unconscious" as "a major source of social tension and conflict" (Home Office, 1981a, p. 110). This contributed to "racial disadvantage," which along with oppressive policing was a significant cause of the "Brixton disorders." Scarman specifically highlighted housing shortages and unemployment. Yet, he also asserted that "institutional racism" did "not exist in Britain" (Home Office, 1981a, p. 135). Moreover, almost all of his recommendations on education focused on "ethnic minority education," including the usual stress on English language. In any case, action on his recommendations was disappointing (see Solomos, 1986).

The Rampton and Swann Reports. The Rampton report (DES, 1981b), concentrated on the "academic underachievement" of West Indian children but stated that their education "must be considered as part of the education of *all* children" and that the issues in the report were "relevant to *every school* and *every teacher*" in Britain (pp. 4, 5).

The report concluded that "West Indian children as a group are failing in our education system" (DES, 1981b, p. 70), the causes being complex. It recommended a "multi-cultural approach throughout education" and that all LEAs should designate a multicultural education adviser (p. 79). It called on "teachers to play a leading role . . . to bring about a change in attitudes on the part of society . . . towards ethnic minority groups" (pp. 14, 78). It paid particular attention to language, "special education," and disruptive units, but also clearly stated that "racism, both intentional and unintentional" was *one* of the important factors contributing to "underachievement" (p. 12). Yet not one of its many recommendations referred specifically to racism.

The report was critical of the "lack of leadership" of the DES and of its tendency to see "the needs of ethnic minority children . . . only as an aspect of educational disadvantage" (DES, 1981b, p. 73). In fact, four years later, the Swann report (DES, 1985, p. 218) could lament that the only recommendation of the Rampton committee to which the DES had made a formal response related to "the collection of educational statistics on an ethnic basis."

The Swann report (DES, 1985) itself traced developments through the phases of assimilation, integration, and multicultural education and noted demands for antiracist education made by some critics of multicultural education. Swann remarked that multicultural education had not been clearly defined and ranged from concerns with "the particular educational needs of ethnic minority children," and so with Black studies and mother tongue, to the preparation of "*all* pupils for life in a multi-racial society," including the combating of racism (pp. 198, 199). Moreover, multicultural education in practice had made an impact only in multiethnic schools, targeting ethnic minorities primarily.

Swann argued that a pluralist approach, with the basic principle of "diversity within unity," was the most appropriate one in a plural, "multi-racial" Britain (DES, 1985, pp. 5–8). Swann stressed the "relevance of multicultural education to all children," including the development of the full potential of *all* children—hence Swann's notion of "education for all" (p. 226). This meant "educating all children, from whatever ethnic group," to understand "the shared values" of the society; to appreciate and respect the diversity of cultural identities, lifestyles, and backgrounds in Britain and the world; to develop "positive attitudes towards the multi-racial nature of society, free from . . . inaccurate myths and stereotypes"; to be committed to "the principles of equality and justice"; and to have "confidence in their own cultural identities" (pp. 316, 320, 321, 323).

Swann even stated that "the major obstacle" to the realization of the "pluralist society" was racism—as seen in "individual attitudes and behavior" as well as in the "more pervasive 'climate' of racism," including "institutional policies and practices" (DES, 1985, pp. 8, 36). Hence, a good education must combat racism and identify and remove "those practices and procedures" in the educational system that "work, directly or indirectly, and intentionally or unintentionally, against pupils from any ethnic group" (p. 320). It must provide "true equality of opportunity" for all (p. 325). Hence it must cater to all individual educational needs, including "any particular educational needs" of ethnic minority pupils (p. 317). Swann also advocated political education to help lay "the foundations of a genuinely pluralist society," overcome "racism at both institutional and individual levels," and "equip youngsters . . . for . . . responsible participation in adult life" (pp. 334, 336, 337).

The Swann committee inquiry was a major event that stimulated a great deal of evidence and discussion before and after the publication of the report. Whereas only a handful of LEAs had multicultural or antiracist policies in the early part of the 1980s, by the end of the decade 80 out of 115 had adopted such policies, including many LEAs without a large Black population.

However, the Conservative government accepted few of the many recommendations of the Swann report. Some funds were made available for a few years for various projects and for the in-service training of teachers. The Commission for the Accreditation of Teacher Education laid down criteria on multicultural education and equal opportunities for courses in institutions of teacher education, criteria that, with subsequent changes, have virtually disappeared.

The Swann report itself is obviously a compromise document: The politics of the whole undertaking were extremely complex, reflecting social realities. Not surprisingly, then, there is a deep ambiguity within the text: Rhetorically it is pluralist, but with a deep undercurrent of conformity. Also, despite the references to "institutional racism," its conception of racism is primarily the limited one of individual attitudes, stereotypes, and ignorance.

There are, however, many rich appendixes to individual chapters in the Swann report. Furthermore, several major publications appeared in conjunction with it. There were four substantial reviews of research into the education of Black pupils (Taylor, 1981, 1987, 1988; Taylor & Hegarty, 1985). Unfortunately, no comparable attention was paid to research into the education of White pupils for a multicultural and racially just society.

Another publication linked to the work of the Swann committee, and based on research funded by the DES, was *Education for Some* by Eggleston, Dunn, Anjali, and Wright (1986). It had been assumed that this report would be published in tandem with the Swann report (Klein, 1993). Yet, although it was ready months in advance, the DES only released it months after that event, "and then only after much pressure from the research team and . . . the communities" (Klein, p. 71). Klein states that this study revealed evidence of "pervasive racism at both institutional and personal levels" (p. 71). Wright (1986) offered some evidence within the Eggleston report to suggest that in the classroom, in allocation "to sets, streams or bands and in examination entries, complex processes may be involved which can disadvantage black young people and . . . particularly those of Afro-Caribbean origin" (p. 178).

Antiracist Education

There were many critics, from the left and the right, of multiculturalism, variously understood (Banks, 1984), but many of the antiracists were among its most vigorous critics.

Jeffcoate (1984) states that antiracism "as a self-conscious educational ideology first emerged in the 1970s," and made "major political advances" in the early 1980s (pp. 143, 144). This perspective grew out of the Black experience, according to Sivanandan (1982). Mullard (1984) holds with some justification that antiracist education had always been present but emerged formally in the early 1960s in reaction to the racism of immigrant education and "within the framework of the Black Consciousness Movement" (p. 24). It had its efflorescence in the early 1980s as a "largely 'Black' response to the ethnicism of multi-cultural education," ethnicism being a culturalist, and perhaps covert, form of racism (p. 12). The antiracist education perspective gained legitimacy partly through the SCRRI, Scarman, Rampton, and Swann inquiries and reports—all of which were influenced by the evidence of the Black community. The Institute of Race Relations (IRR, 1980), in its submission on "anti-racist not multicultural education" to the Swann committee, put the case sharply that "an ethnic or cultural approach to the educational needs . . . of racial minorities evades the fundamental reasons for their disabilities . . . the racialist attitudes and the racist practices in the larger society and in the educational system itself" (p. 82).

Antiracist Thinking and Local Policy Statements. Quintin Kynaston Comprehensive School in London provides an early example of an antiracist school policy. In 1977 the ILEA had issued a document on multiethnic education to all its schools. About that time "organised overt racist activities" were on the increase, and so protest movements such as All London Teachers against Racism & Fascism (ALTARF) had become active (Lindsay, 1984, p. 195). This was the context in which Quintin Kynaston formed a multicultural antiracist working party in 1978. The policy resulting from their work was adopted by the school in 1980. Holloway Secondary School in North London provides another early example. In 1978 a National Front leaflet was found in the school, and so the Head drafted a policy statement, which was discussed and adopted at a staff meeting (Twitchin & Demuth, 1985).

In 1980 Bradford became the first LEA to run a Racism Awareness workshop "as part of its in-service training" (Twitchin & Demuth, 1985, p. 161). The chapter that Twitchin and Demuth devoted to this workshop discussed individual, cultural, and institutional racism and strategies for change, providing many ideas for exercises to help teachers raise their awareness of racism in society, in the education system, and in themselves. Twitchin and Demuth also stressed that "racism is not just a matter of overt colour prejudice and discriminatory attitudes," but also of "racial disadvantage . . . unwitting racist attitudes . . . embedded in our language and culture; and . . . institutionalised racism" (p. 7).

In 1982 a Berkshire policy document called for "a perspective emphasising equality and justice, and combating racism" rather than one emphasizing "diversity and pluralism" (Advisory Committee for Multicultural Education, 1982, pp. 5, 8). The Berkshire Adviser for Multicultural Education at the time was R. Richardson, and the committee producing the document had the advice of two Black academic external consultants, T. Mukherjee and C. Mullard (see below). This document identi-

fied three main perspectives in "race relations and education."
The first emphasized mainly *integration*, cohesion, and stability
and saw the Black community as the "problem"; the second
emphasized cultural *diversity*, conceiving of "racism as merely a
set of mental prejudices" and obscuring economic and power
differentials and discrimination; the third, which the document
endorsed, emphasized *equality* and the *"pervasive influence of
racism"* in the sense of a "combination of discriminatory practices, unequal relations and structures of power, and negative
beliefs and attitudes" (pp. 7, 9). However, this third perspective
was "not indifferent to cultural differences and diversity" but
saw them "in the wider context of promoting equality and
justice" (p. 8). In the following year the Berkshire Education
Committee formally adopted a policy statement on education
for "racial equality and justice," which included a statement of
opposition to "racism in all its forms" (Royal County of Berkshire LEA, 1983, reproduced in DES, 1985, pp. 366–370).

Another notable example of an LEA statement was the *Anti-
Racist Statement and Guidelines* published by the ILEA in 1983.
Among other local authorities that published statements including an antiracist stance were the City of Bradford (1983) and the
London Borough of Brent (1983). In 1982 a pack for teachers
published by Birmingham LEA stated that a "subtle but endemic
racism . . . permeates our society and . . . culture" and that
"white racism is a white problem" (Rudell & Simpson, 1982,
quoted by Hatcher & Shallice, 1983, p. 3). NUT has also published antiracist guidelines (e.g., NUT, 1983, 1992).

Mullard's Analysis of Antiracist Education. One of the most
influential statements on antiracist education was made by Mullard in 1984 at the NAME annual conference. Mullard identified
four main dominant "racial" forms of education—immigrant
(1950s and 1960s), multiracial (1960s and early 1970s), multiethnic (late 1970s), and multicultural (late 1970s and 1980s)—
and one dominated "racial" form: antiracist education (Mullard,
1984). The four dominant forms had all been racist, the first two
focusing on "race" as a structural phenomenon, and the last two
focusing on "race" as a cultural phenomenon. These five forms
seem to stand in a dialectical relationship with each other,
although Mullard does not use that term. Immigrant education
was assimilationist; multiracial education, integrationist; and
multiethnic and multicultural education, pluralist. The object of
antiracist education is justice, a restructured structural-cultural
order, focusing as it does on both structure and culture. Antiracist education is thus "a struggle against racism [and ethnicism]
in education in which the specific-educational relations of social liberation and change as opposed to . . . control are . . .
developed" (p. 38). Antiracist and multicultural education were
"currently oppositional and antagonistic forms" (p. 12).

Many other antiracists besides Mullard, such as Brandt
(1986), also argue the incompatibility of multicultural and antiracist education. They tend to see "multicultural education" as
an attempt by White society and the White educational system
to react to and contain the Black struggle against racism and
inequality. It is a "cooling-out" process (Stone, 1981). Grinter
(1990, 1992), abandoning an earlier position, maintains that
multicultural and antiracist education are "incompatible philosophies" (1992, p. 95). Multicultural education believes in the

assimilation of the various cultures into a "social consensus
with shared values" (p. 101). Far from being, as the right wing
considers, "the thin edge of an antiracist wedge," it is a "racist
philosophy" that "attempts to divert and minimize the black
struggle" (Grinter, 1990, p. 212). It sees racism as resting on
"misunderstanding and ignorance," overemphasizing the personal aspects, and neglecting the "political dimension and
power structures" (Grinter, 1992, p. 95; 1990, p. 212). Antiracist
education, by contrast, sees conflict as central "in a social system that concentrates power in White, middle-class and male
hands," dominant values being imposed on disempowered, un-
valued groups (Grinter, 1992, p. 101). It understands racism as
"an ideology . . . based on learnt attitudes of White superiority
to . . . groups that Europe . . . exploited" so that "an unequal
distribution of power . . . is accepted as natural" (p. 94).

Mullard's argument is complex, sophisticated and seminal: It
has sharply analyzed multiculturalism and antiracism; understood that racism is as "serious and pervasive" as sexism and
classism in "White Western history" (Mullard, 1984, p. 58); and
grasped the need to face reality critically, deconstructing institutionalized racism and racist practice and reconstructing relationships. However, the argument is stated ascetically and
leaves much insufficiently defined and undeveloped. Also, despite the dialectical character of the analysis, there is perhaps a
tendency to reify sharp dichotomies. First, despite the oppositional relationships, and therefore the oppositional interests,
between the White dominant "group" and the Black dominated
"group," the Black and White "groups" nevertheless share
some interests. This is one of the inescapable contradictions of
social reality, and Mullard's rejection of "'mutual interests' (à la
Brandt)" is perhaps too hasty (p. 15). Second, multiculturalism
tends to become for Mullard, in sharp opposition to antiracism,
not just in some forms or usages but inherently and irretrievably, an instrument of control. Yet the social reality that must be
faced is multicultural as well as racist, and culture and structure
interpenetrate, so antiracism must encompass antiracist multiculturalism.

Attack on Antiracism. In 1984 Jeffcoate launched an attack on
antiracism (Jeffcoate, 1984). He criticized the antiracists' use of
the term *racism* as being too wide, including beliefs, hostile
prejudices, discrimination, violence, and institutional racism—
which he found particularly "obscure" (p. 145). But his main
criticism was that antiracism was "illiberal" and "authoritarian,"
and tended to "indoctrination."

He stated that pupils should be "free to express their opinions in the classroom, no matter what their . . . ideological content . . . , learning . . . to test them out against publicly accredited
criteria of truth and rationality and to observe the rules of
democratic procedure (Jeffcoate, 1984, p. 154). He argued that,
apart from the question of "separating truth from falsehood,
myth from reality, rationality from irrationality," there was "a
vast area of opinion and belief, represented by the ideology of
racism in the original sense and the politics of immigration
control and race relations," and that students were entitled to
hold such opinions and beliefs (p. 161). Jeffcoate apparently
considered it inherently indoctrinatory for the teacher to question such "opinions" and to offer an alternative view—or to

question the underlying assumptions. To seek to change "opinions and attitudes" (such as National Front opinions) as distinct from "misinformation and faulty logic," apparently even by *persuasion,* was considered by Jeffcoate to "infringe" the pupil's "autonomy" (pp. 159, 160). He contended that if, despite having

> the relevant facts, some children argue that white people are as a group intellectually superior to black people, or ... favour ... [so-called] repatriation [i.e., of Black people] ... we have to accept that as their privilege. As concerned adults we may abhor these opinions. But, as teachers, our job is not to combat opinions we do not like but to uphold democratic principles and procedures. (p. 161)

The question one could ask here, however, is: Why? Does not this last sentence itself simply represent an "opinion," and, if some young people do not share our opinions about upholding democratic principles and procedures, is that not their "privilege"? Jeffcoate has not addressed basic issues about values. Education is not only about truth and falsity and how to "test" them. (Besides, "opinions" may also raise questions of truth and falsity.) Education is about the growth of the whole person as an individual who is a social being. It is also about the valued and the disvalued and whether there is any way of "testing" these. It must be, too, about exercising one's rights and privileges without infringing on, and with sensitivity to, the rights and privileges of others. If democracy is to be upheld, so must antiracism as well as multiculturalism.

Multicultural *and* Antiracist Education

There is no inherent opposition between the multicultural and antiracist concepts. Both are needed. Fundamental as racism is, it is not the only relevant cause of social conflict, nor the only significant feature of society that needs addressing. Cultural difference can also cause conflict, and cross-cultural communication also needs addressing. Besides, it is not the case that both multicultural education can only be descriptive, that it must be racist, or that it cannot be informed by a structural understanding of racism. Furthermore, antiracist education can be multicultural, as even Grinter (1990) and the IRR (1980) in fact seem to imply. Even Mullard (1984) states that "anti-racist education ... attempts to absorb certain aspects of multiracial and multicultural education" (p. 18). Francis (1984), who points out that multiculturalism often ignores the inequality in power between different cultures, the possibility that knowing more about other cultures can actually reinforce racism, and the benefits that racism gives to White people, also argues that "anti-racist teaching can co-exist with a more politicised form of multi-cultural education" (p. 87).

In fact, in the 1980s and 1990s there have been attempts to effect a "synthesis" between multicultural and antiracist education. Grinter (1985), perhaps taking his lead from Banks (1981) in the United States, sought in this earlier paper to build a "bridge" between multiculturalism and antiracism. He argued for an antiracist multicultural education, maintaining that both multicultural and antiracist education aimed to promote "a more just society" (Grinter, 1985, p. 7). Leicester (1986, 1989) also argues that a "synthesis" of multicultural and antiracist

education can, and ought, to be developed. She speaks of "antiracist multicultural education," maintaining that "it is not anti-racist ... and multicultural education that are alternative forms ..., but that there are alternative forms of multicultural education—racist ... and anti-racist," the latter being part of antiracist education (Leicester, 1989, pp. 25, 26).

Leicester (1989) states that Mullard identifies antiracist education with the structure of the educational system and multicultural education with the cultural content of the curriculum, and she argues convincingly that this content can be both multicultural and antiracist. The implication of this position seems to be that whereas both antiracist and multicultural concerns apply to the curriculum, only the antiracist ones apply to the organization and administration. On the contrary, both perspectives impinge on both the structure *and* content of education. Educational structures are informed by cultural assumptions and practices, and justice will have been achieved only when Black cultural groups take full part at the decision-making levels of the educational and schooling system.

Fyfe (1993), as the general adviser for multicultural education in Hampshire, one of the largest LEAs and an area where the proportion of the population that is Black is below the national average, considered the polarization between multicultural and antiracist education as an "irrelevant debate." Hampshire therefore decided to adopt instead the continental European concept of "intercultural education" as being "more inclusive" (p. 47). In fact, however, this concept was poorly defined and seemed little more than a consensual form of multiculturalism. Nevertheless, Hampshire did in fact move some way toward an antiracist multi- or interculturalism, providing all its schools with guidelines, not only on multicultural education, but also on how to combat "racial" harassment (Hampshire County Council Education Department, 1987, 1991).

Figueroa (1991) has argued that "education in Britain needs to be both multicultural and antiracist," but in a "thoroughgoing" way, since "Britain is both culturally diverse *and* racist ... while nevertheless being liberal and containing important antiracist forces" (p. 50; see also Parekh, 1986). The social (as also the educational) situation is complex. The society (as too the school) is structured by class, gender, "race," culture, and other factors. The society is riven and yet held together by contradictions, not only in the sense that any one "sector" might have to embrace opposing strategies (see Hatcher & Shallice, 1983), but also in the sense that there are many different, and *unequal,* "interest groups" with conflicting *and also* common interests. Different tendencies and imperatives operate within the dominant group itself (see, e.g., Hatcher & Shallice, 1983; Whitty, 1990). Structural racism is endemic, but there are also traditions and ideals of democracy.

On the assumption of at least de facto interdependence for the achievement of social and individual aims, and granted certain basic social values, such as justice—which could be seen as a social imperative for the ultimate viability of any society—education that is antiracist *and* multicultural, among other things, would seem essential for this complex social situation. Key challenges facing such education include diversity, inequality, and racism in all its forms (see Figueroa, 1993a).

Many difficult issues for social analysis, social philosophy, and epistemology, including questions about cultural relativism, are implicated here. Although some of these issues have been addressed by authors such as Mullard (1984), Brandt (1986), Leicester (1989), Zec (1980), Haydon (1987), and White (1987), they deserve much more attention, specifically with reference to multicultural and antiracist education, than they have so far received. Furthermore, as Banks (1992) rightly states, "a clearly articulated concept" of "multicultural education that can be easily understood by teachers, that promotes justice and equality for all" (that is, in fact, also antiracist), is needed at least as much as a "debate over multicultural versus antiracist education" (p. 113).

FUTURE OUTLOOK

What, then, is the outlook for the future? In 1988 the most far-reaching education legislation in England and Wales since 1944 was passed: the Education Reform Act of 1988 (ERA). Many subsequent developments have followed, including further major legislation and the reorganization of the DES, which became the Department for Education (DFE) in July 1992. The 1988 act endowed the secretary of state for education and science with numerous and wide-ranging new powers, simultaneously taking a great deal of power and status away from LEAs. It abolished the influential, and generally Labour-controlled, ILEA, where a very large proportion of Britain's Black population lives, and which, despite possible criticisms, had done more in the sphere of multicultural and antiracist education than most other LEAs.

Whitty (1990) suggests that the two main strands within the New Right thinking, the neoliberal and the neoconservative, have strongly influenced this act. This accounts for the commitment to free-market forces of much of the act, combined with much greater central control. The neoliberal stress on consumer power can be seen, for instance, in the act's budgetary devolution to individual schools and in its encouragement of schools to opt out of local government control and to receive their funding, on the basis of a formula, directly from central government. The neoconservative concerns with traditional moral values and with "traditional British heritage" can be seen in the introduction of a centrally determined national curriculum, and in the requirements for a daily act of worship, "wholly or mainly of a broadly Christian character," and for religious education (RE), which must reflect the religious traditions of Britain as "in the main Christian" (ERA, 1988, part 1, chap. 1, sections 7[1], 8[3]).

How does this act affect multicultural and antiracist education, and how does it affect Black students? On the one hand it might seem that many of its general provisions would be of benefit to Black students. In the first place the ERA requires that the curriculum should be "balanced and broadly based"; promote the "cultural . . . development of pupils . . . and of society"; and prepare "pupils for the opportunities, responsibilities and experiences of adult life" (ERA, 1988, part 1, chap. 1, section 1(2)(a), (b)). It also requires that, while RE is to give priority to the Christian tradition, it should take account, too, of the "other

principal religions" in Britain (section 8[3]). Furthermore, the introduction of greater accountability into the working of schools, and the establishment of a national curriculum, with the implication of an educational entitlement for all students, could perhaps benefit Black students, who in the past have often received an inferior education. Moreover, the early guidance to schools by the DES (1989) stressed that the ten "foundation" subjects and RE did not constitute the whole curriculum by themselves, and that coverage of multicultural and gender issues needed to be included across the curriculum.

On the other hand, the stress on market forces and on competition between schools could lead schools to avoid wherever possible accepting students from certain Black groups, since these tend to be seen as behavioral problems or as low academic achievers. Furthermore, the national curriculum as it has been developed tends to be monocultural and ethnocentric (see, for instance, Pumfrey & Verma, 1993a, 1993b; Verma & Pumfrey, 1993a, 1993b). This tendency, moreover, has been accentuated by changes that have been made, under pressure especially from teachers, to "slim down" the national curriculum.

In many ways, national curriculum developments represent a step backward from earlier trends in the field of multicultural and antiracist education. The recommendations of the Swann report have been largely ignored (see Swann, 1993). The concepts of racism and antiracism are almost completely absent from the vast official documentation relating to the national curriculum. Various proposed multicultural or "multiracial" amendments to the bill as it went through Parliament were either defeated or had to be withdrawn (Tomlinson, 1990). All of the working groups that were established to develop curricular recommendations in each of the ten national-curriculum subjects were, indeed, required to take account of ethnic and cultural diversity and of the promotion of equal opportunities regardless of ethnic origin and gender. However, such concerns were not reflected in any of the subsequent statutory orders. Relevant issues feature mainly in five National Curriculum Council (NCC) documents: circular numbers 6 and 11, curriculum guidance numbers 3 and 8, and NCC News number 5 (NCC, 1989, 1990a, 1990b, 1991a, 1991b), none of which is mandatory, and all of which are either very brief or do not focus mainly on multicultural and antiracist education. Multicultural issues—with some very sparse references to "prejudice," "discrimination," "ethnic origin," and "race"—are treated as cross-curricular matters (NCC, 1990a, 1990b), and in practice this probably means that since the national curriculum is strongly organized by subject, these issues tend to receive only marginal attention.

Furthermore, there have been some very negative signals from the NCC. In 1989 the NCC set up a Multicultural Task Group, which was to prepare "guidance on multicultural education in the National Curriculum," to be published, the task group thought, "as non-statutory guidance" (Tomlinson, 1993, pp. 29, 23). However, when the fifth draft of the task group's work was to go forward for approval in 1990, the NCC decided not to publish any specific curricular guidance on multicultural education, other than a one-page article in the NCC newsletter and a brief circular on linguistic diversity (NCC, 1991a, 1991b;

see Tomlinson, 1993). Yet the document developed by the task group was by no means a radical one. It aimed at ensuring that "the particular needs of pupils from ethnic minority backgrounds" were served and at broadening "the horizons of *all* pupils . . . so that they can understand and respect, learn from and contribute to . . . contemporary British society" (NCC Multicultural Task Group, undated, p. 6).

On the whole this document tended to use words such as *racist* and *antiracist* very sparingly, its most radical questions for schools being "Are the school's aims congruent with the development of a non-racist society and good race relations?"; "Has the school an anti-racist policy?"; "Does the school have a clear procedure following an incident of racial harrassment [*sic*]?" (NCC Multicultural Task Group, undated, pp. 56–58). Tomlinson (1993) says there were "hints of political interference but no actual information" (p. 25). However, Graham and Tytler (1993), Graham having been NCC chief executive at the time, contains evidence of political interference in, and the influence of right-wing thinkers on, the work of the NCC.

Pascall, the new chairperson of the NCC at the time, made it clear in a major speech on "the cultural dimension in education" that he had essentially a consensual and monocultural view of education. The only concession he made to multiculturalism was a general acknowledgment that the society had been enriched throughout the ages by different cultures and a vague one-line statement about providing opportunities for the young "to experience the rich cultural diversity of Britain today" (Pascall, 1992, p. 6). Nothing was said about "minority" children being taught about their own cultural traditions. Instead, Pascall spoke of "*a cultural heritage*"—defined by Christian, Greco-Roman, Liberal Enlightenment, romanticist, and modern humanist strands—that the curriculum should transmit to every child, "irrespective of their religion or . . . community" (p. 6). This was the "dominant culture," a shared culture, "a set of values and traditions . . . developed over the centuries, which incorporates the changing face of society today" (p. 5).

Taylor (1992a, 1992b) carried out a study in 1991 and early 1992 into LEA policy and practice in multicultural and antiracist education in England, Wales, and the Isles since ERA. Although a majority of advisers or inspectors reported at least some "progress" in practice, over one third said that things had either stayed "much the same" or even "slipped backwards" (Taylor, 1992a, p. 4). Taylor also found that, whereas in 1989 LEA policies had focused on multicultural education, there had since been a "notable reorientation . . . under a broader equal opportunities (EO) rubric" (pp. 3–4). This raised the question of whether there would be parity of standing between the various areas of EO, "especially in those LEAs where it has been politic to subsume racial and cultural discrimination within this general framework" (p. 4). In particular, would gender be given greater importance at the expense of "ethnicity"?

More significant, advisers and inspectors shared some serious concerns about the situation of multicultural and antiracist education (MC/ARE) in their LEAs since ERA, generally perceiving the ideological climate as unpropitious (Taylor, 1992a, 1992b). At least one fifth of the education officers were "deeply concerned about the absence of national policy and support for MC/ARE in ERA, failure of a lead from the DES, and particularly

lack of explicit curricular guidance from the NCC" (Taylor, 1992a, p. 5). Related to this were anxieties about "*maintaining the antiracist impetus*" with the perceived marginalization of racism," more attention being given to cultural diversity (p. 5). There was also a good deal of evidence of a "low level of understanding" of multicultural and antiracist education; a perception of it simply as an "extra"; and the attitude that the issues were not relevant in areas with few Black students. Multicultural and antiracist education seemed to have a "low priority in implementation in current LEA and school practice" (p. 6). Her Majesty's Inspectorate report for 1990–91 similarly found a wide gap between policy and practice in respect of equality of opportunity (DES, 1992).

At present, therefore, the outlook for multicultural and antiracist education does not seem very bright. There is the continuing ascendancy of right-wing political ideology, promoted by right-wing pressure groups (Graham & Tytler, 1993; Judd & Crequer, 1993; Tomlinson, 1990; 1993). In such circles antiracist education is universally opposed, while multicultural education is opposed by some and accepted by others, but only within a consensual, integrationist perspective. Furthermore, as Tomlinson (1990, p. 21) has indicated, there is still at the grassroots level "a range of negative views about the implementation of a more appropriate education for a multi-ethnic society." This undoubtedly relates at least in part to the issue of a British national identity in a neo-Victorian tradition, which involves "beliefs in white racial and cultural superiority" (Tomlinson, 1990, p. 43; see also Hall, Critcher, Jefferson, Clarke, & Roberts, 1978).

Besides, there have also been such developments as the reduction of the scope of funding based on section 11 of the Local Government Act of 1966, so that the support of mother-tongue teaching and multicultural and antiracist education are now excluded, although the teaching of English as a second language is still included. As Bagley (1992, p. 9) has indicated, this amounts to a reaffirmation in the 1990s of the assimilationism of the 1960s.

Nevertheless, despite the lack of a strong lead and little support from the center, there is scope in the national curriculum, and through various provisions of the ERA, for multicultural and antiracist education structures, procedures, and practices to be realized (see, for instance, Fyfe & Figueroa, 1993; Klein, 1993; Pumfrey & Verma, 1993a, 1993b; Verma & Pumfrey, 1993a, 1993b). There is clear scope in the cross-curricular "theme" of citizenship education (NCC, 1990a) but also within each of the national curriculum subjects and religious education.

Take, for example, the national history curriculum. It is true that "themes such as black British history, immigration, the Caribbean, the Indian subcontinent . . . receive . . . little attention" in the detailed programs of studies and that "multiculturalism and especially antiracism tend to be marginal and inadequately conceptualized" (Figueroa, 1993b, p. 129). However, the history statutory order calls for "stories from different periods and cultures" in years 1 and 2 and states that throughout the rest of the course pupils should be taught about "the social, cultural, religious and ethnic diversity of the societies studied" (DES, 1991, pp. 13, 16, 34, 49). Also, the British Empire features as an optional unit and as part of core study units at various stages, thus presenting the informed and committed teacher with opportunities to approach issues from the point of view of the dominated peoples, to address racism, and to offer "a critical and rich study of history with a world-wide orientation" (Figueroa, 1993b, p. 131). The local history provisions also offer scope for focusing on migration, multiculturalism, inequality, racism, and international interdependence even in "all-White" areas (see Hix, 1991).

Moreover, although recent legislation, such as the massive Education Act of 1994, has continued the move toward greater central control, there are also other legal developments relating to education that support egalitarianism, multiculturalism, and antiracism, notably some provisions of the Children Act of 1989 and the Education (Schools) Act of 1992. The United Kingdom is also a signatory to international conventions and decla-rations on human rights, such as the European Convention on Human Rights (Council of Europe, 1950), which enshrines equal rights to education and nondiscrimination; the United Nations Convention on the Rights of the Child of 1989; and the Council of Europe Summit Vienna Declaration of 1993 against racism and for human rights, openness, and cooperation. Even more crucial is the existence of active individuals, groups, and organizations and the educational materials and ideas they generate. A notable organization since its inception in 1968 has been the Runnymede Trust (1993).

Hope for the future lies in the nonmonolithic nature of the society and especially in the existence of liberal and radical forces in the society and in the educational system. There is plenty of scope for radical or liberal groups, *working together,* to bring about and maintain change, but it requires a constant effort.

References

Advisory Committee for Multicultural Education, Royal County of Berkshire. (1982). *Education for equality: A paper for discussion in Berkshire.* Reading: Author.

Aliens Act. (1905). London: His Majesty's Stationery Office.

Assistant Masters and Mistresses Association. (1981). *Education for a multi-cultural society.* London: Author.

Bagley, C. (1970). *Social structure and prejudice in five English boroughs.* London: Institute of Race Relations.

Bagley, C. A. (1992). *Back to the future—Section 11 of the Local Government Act 1966: LEAs and multicultural/antiracist education.* Slough, Berkshire: National Foundation for Educational Research in England and Wales.

Banks, J. A. (1981). *Multi-ethnic education: Theory and practice.* Boston: Allyn and Bacon.

Banks, J. A. (1984). Multicultural education and its critics: Britain and the United States. *New Era, 65*(3), 58–65.

Banks, J. A. (1992). Interchange: Banks replies to Grinter. In J. Lynch, S. Modgil, & C. Modgil (Eds.), *Education for cultural diversity: Convergence and divergence* (pp. 112–117). London: Falmer.

Banton, M. (1983). *Racial and ethnic competition.* Cambridge: Cambridge University Press.

Bernal, M. (1987). *Black Athena: The Afro-Asiatic roots of classical civilization.* New Brunswick, NJ: Rutgers University Press.

Bowker, G. (1968). *Education of coloured immigrants.* London: Longmans.

Brandt, G. L. (1986). *The realization of anti-racist teaching.* London: Falmer.

British Nationality Act. (1948). London: His Majesty's Stationery Office.

British Nationality Act. (1981). London: Her Majesty's Stationery Office.

Brittan, E. (1976). Multicultural education 2—teacher opinion on aspects of school life, part 2: Pupils and teachers. *Educational Research, 18*(3), 182–191.

Brown, C. (1984). *Black and White Britain: The third PSI survey.* London: Heinemann Educational Books.

Brown, C., & Gay, P. (1985). *Racial discrimination: Seventeen years after the act.* London: Policy Studies Institute.

Children Act. (1989). London: Her Majesty's Stationery Office.

City of Bradford Metropolitan Council, Directorate of Educational Services. (1983). *Racialist behaviour in schools* (Local Administrative Memorandum 6/83). Bradford: Author.

Coard, B. (1971). *How the West Indian child is made educationally subnormal in the British school system.* London: New Beacon Books.

Commonwealth Immigrants Act. (1962). London: Her Majesty's Stationery Office.

Commonwealth Immigrants Act. (1968). London: Her Majesty's Stationery Office.

Commonwealth Immigrants Advisory Council. (1963). *Report* (Cmnd. 2119). London: Her Majesty's Stationery Office.

Commonwealth Immigrants Advisory Council. (1964). *Second Report* (Cmnd. 2266). London: Her Majesty's Stationery Office.

Community Relations Commission. (1971). *Report of the Community Relations Commission for 1970–71.* London: Her Majesty's Stationery Office.

Community Relations Commission & Association of Teachers in Colleges and Departments of Education. (1974). *Teacher education for a multi-cultural society.* London: Authors.

Council of Europe. (1950). *European Convention for the Protection of Human Rights and Freedoms.* Strasbourg: Author.

Council of Europe Summit. (1993). *Vienna Declaration.* Vienna: Author.

Council for National Academic Awards. (1984). *Notes on multicultural education and the professional preparation and in-service development of teachers.* London: Author.

Craft, M. (1984). Education for diversity. In M. Craft (Ed.), *Education and cultural pluralism* (pp. 5–25). Lewes, Sussex: Falmer Press.

Craft, M. (1986). Multicultural education in the United Kingdom. In J. A. Banks & J. Lynch (Eds.), *Multicultural education in Western societies* (pp. 76–97). London: Holt, Rinehart and Winston.

Daniel, W. W. (1968). *Racial discrimination in England.* Harmondsworth: Penguin.

Davey, A. (1983). *Learning to be prejudiced: Growing up in multiethnic Britain.* London: Arnold.

Department of Education and Science. (1965). *The education of immigrants* (Circular 7/65). London: Author.

Department of Education and Science, Central Advisory Council for Education. (1967). *Children and their primary schools.* London: Her Majesty's Stationery Office.

Department of Education and Science. (1971a). *The education of immigrants* (Education Survey No. 13). London: Her Majesty's Stationery Office.

Department of Education and Science. (1971b). *Potential and progress in a second culture* (Education Survey No. 10). London: Her Majesty's Stationery Office.

Department of Education and Science. (1972). *The continuing need of immigrants* (Education Survey No. 14). London: Her Majesty's Stationery Office.

Department of Education and Science. (1974). *Educational disadvantage and the needs of immigrants* (Cmnd. 5720). London: Her Majesty's Stationery Office.

Department of Education and Science. (1975). *A language for life*. London: Her Majesty's Stationery Office.

Department of Education and Science. (1977). *Education in schools: A consultative document*. London: Her Majesty's Stationery Office.

Department of Education and Science. (1981a). *The school curriculum*. London: Her Majesty's Stationery Office.

Department of Education and Science. (1981b). *West Indian children in our schools* (Cmnd. 8273). London: Her Majesty's Stationery Office.

Department of Education and Science. (1985). *Education for all* (Cmnd. 9453). London: Her Majesty's Stationery Office.

Department of Education and Science. (1989). *National curriculum: From policy to practice*. London: Her Majesty's Stationery Office.

Department of Education and Science. (1991). *History in the national curriculum (England)*. London: Her Majesty's Stationery Office.

Department of Education and Science. (1992). *Education in England 1990–1991*. London: Her Majesty's Stationery Office.

Dummett, A. (1993). *A portrait of English racism*. Harmondsworth: Penguin.

Education Act. (1994). London: Her Majesty's Stationery Office.

Education Reform Act. (1988). London: Her Majesty's Stationery Office.

Education (Schools) Act. (1992). London: Her Majesty's Stationery Office.

Eggleston, J. (1986). Multicultural society: The qualitative aspects. *Research Papers in Education, 1*(3), 217–236.

Eggleston, J., Dunn, D., Anjali, M., & Wright, C. (1986). *Education for some: The educational and vocational experiences of fifteen- to eighteen-year-old members of minority ethnic groups*. Stoke-on-Trent: Trentham Books.

Eggleston, S. J., Dunn, D., & Purewal, A. (1981). *In-service teacher education in a multiracial society*. Keele: University of Keele.

Eppel, E. (Ed.). (1972). *Education for cultural pluralism*. London: World Jewish Congress, Cultural Department.

European Parliament Committee of Inquiry into Racism and Xenophobia. (1990). *Report* (Document A3-195/90; Glyn Ford, Rapporteur). Strasbourg: European Parliament.

Figueroa, P. (1974). *West Indian school-leavers in London: A sociological study in ten schools in a London borough, 1966–1976*. Unpublished doctoral dissertation, University of London, London School of Economics & Political Science.

Figueroa, P. (1991). *Education and the social construction of "race."* London: Routledge.

Figueroa, P. (1993a). Europa: Vielfalt, Ungleicheit, Rassismus und die Folgen für die Erziehung. In N. Boteram (Eds.), *Interkulturelles Verstehen und Handeln: Beiträge aus Erziehungs-, Sozial- und Sprachwissenschaften* (pp. 115–135). Pfaffenweiler: Centaurus.

Figueroa, P. (1993b). History: Policy issues. In P. D. Pumfrey & G. K. Verma (Eds.), *Cultural diversity and the curriculum: The foundation subjects and religious education in secondary schools* (pp. 122–134). London: Falmer.

Football (Offences) Act. (1991). London: Her Majesty's Stationery Office.

Francis, M. (1984). Anti-racist teaching: General principles. In All London Teachers Against Racism and Fascism (Eds.), *Challenging racism* (pp. 85–93). London: ALTARF.

Fryer, P. (1984). *Staying power: The history of Black people in Britain*. London: Pluto Press.

Fyfe, A. (1993). The role of local education authorities: Shire authorities and Hampshire's policy. In A. Fyfe & P. Figueroa (Eds.), *Education for cultural diversity: The challenge for a new era* (pp. 281–284). London: Routledge.

Fyfe, A., & Figueroa, P. (1993). *Education for cultural diversity: The challenge for a new era*. London: Routledge.

Giles, R., & Cherrington, D. (1981). *Multicultural teacher education in the United Kingdom: A survey of courses and other provisions in British institutions of higher education*. London: Commission for Racial Equality.

Glass, R., & Pollins, H. (1960). *Newcomers: The West Indians in London*. London: Allen and Unwin.

Graham, D. & Tytler, D. (1993). *A lesson for us all: The making of the national curriculum*. London: Routledge.

Greater London Council, Ethnic Minorities Unit. (1986). *A history of the Black presence in London*. London: GLC.

Grinter, R. (1985). Bridging the gulf: The need for anti-racist multicultural education. *Multicultural Teaching, 3*(2), 7–100.

Grinter, R. (1990). Developing an antiracist national curriculum: Constraints and new directions. In P. Pumfrey & G. K. Verma (Eds.), *Race relations and urban education: Contexts and promising practices* (pp. 199–213). London: Falmer.

Grinter, R. (1992). Multicultural or antiracist education: The need to choose. In J. Lynch, S. Modgil, & C. Modgil (Eds.), *Education for cultural diversity: Convergence and divergence* (pp. 95–111). London: Falmer.

Hall, S., Critcher, C., Jefferson, T., Clarke, J., & Roberts, B. (1978). *Policing the crisis*. London: Macmillan.

Hampshire County Council Education Department. (1987). *Education for a multicultural society*. Winchester: Author.

Hampshire County Council Education Department. (1991). *Combating racial harassment: County guidelines for schools, colleges and other educational establishments*. Winchester: Author.

Hatcher, R., & Shallice, J. (1983). The politics of anti-racist education. *Multiracial Education, 12*(1), 3–21.

Haydon, G. (1987). Towards "a framework of commonly accepted values." In G. Haydon (Ed.), *Education for a pluralist society: Philosophical perspectives on the Swann report* (Bedford Way Papers, No. 30, pp. 25–37). London: University of London, Institute of Education.

Hiro, D. (1971). *Black British, White British*. London: Eyre and Spottiswoole.

Hix, P. (1991). *Local history in all-White areas: Multicultural and anti-racist history teaching and learning*. Unpublished Master's thesis, University of Southampton, Southampton.

Home Affairs Committee. (1981). *Racial disadvantage* (fifth report of the committee, session 1980–81, HC 424, 1–4, Vol. 37). London: Her Majesty's Stationery Office.

Home Office. (1978). *The West Indian community: Observations on the report of the Select Committee on Race Relations and Immigration* (session 1977–78, Cmnd. 7186, Vol. 50). London: Her Majesty's Stationery Office.

Home Office. (1981a). *The Brixton disorders, April 10–12, 1981: Report of an inquiry* (Cmnd. 8427). London: Her Majesty's Stationery Office.

Home Office. (1981b). *Racial attacks*. London: Her Majesty's Stationery Office.

Home Office. (1982). *Racial disadvantage: The government reply to the fifth report from the Home Affairs Committee, session 1980–1981 HC 424* (session 1981–82, Cmnd. 8476, Vol. 51). London: Her Majesty's Stationery Office.

House of Commons. (1963–64). *Parliamentary debates* (Hansard, 1963, November 27, fifth series, Vol. 685, cols. 433–444). London: Her Majesty's Stationery Office.

Immigration Act. (1971). London: Her Majesty's Stationery Office.

Immigration Act. (1988). London: Her Majesty's Stationery Office.

Inner London Education Authority. (1967). *Immigrant children in ESN schools: Survey report*. London: Author.

Inner London Education Authority. (1968). *The education of immigrant pupils in primary schools* (February, report 959). London: Author.

Inner London Education Authority. (1977). *Multi-ethnic education*. London: Author.

Inner London Education Authority. (1983). *Race, sex and class: Antiracist statement and guidelines*. London: Author.

Institute of Race Relations. (1980). Anti-racist not multiracial education: IRR statement to the Rampton Committee on Education. *Race and Class, 22*(1), 81–83.

Jeffcoate, R. (1984). *Ethnic minorities and education*. London: Harper and Row.

Jones, T. (1993). *Britain's ethnic minorities: An analysis of the Labour Force Survey,* London: Policy Studies Institute.

Judd, J., & Crequer, N. (1993). The right tightens its grip on education. In C. Chitty & B. Simon (Eds.), *Education answers back: Critical responses to government policy* (pp. 120–125). London: Lawrence and Wishart.

Kelly, E., & Cohn, T. (1988). *Racism in schools: New research evidence*. Stoke-on-Trent: Trentham Books.

Kirp, D. (1979). *Doing good by doing little*. London: University of California Press.

Klein, G. (1993). *Education towards race equality*. London: Cassell.

Lawrence, D. (1969). How prejudiced are we? *Race Today, 1*(6), 174–176.

Leicester, M. (1986). Multicultural curriculum or antiracist education: Denying the gulf. *Multicultural Teaching, 4*(2), 4–7.

Leicester, M. (1989). *Multicultural education: From theory to practice*. Windsor, Berkshire: NFER-Nelson.

Lindsay, L. (1984). Quintin Kynaston School. In All London Teachers Against Racism and Fascism (Eds.), *Challenging Racism* (pp. 195–204). London: ALTARF.

Little, A. (1978a). *Educational policies for multi-racial areas* (Goldsmiths' College Inaugural Lecture 1978). London: University of London.

Little, A. (1978b). Schools and race. In J. Twitchin (Ed.). *Five views of multi-racial Britain: Talks on race relations broadcast by BBC TV* (pp. 56–65). London: Commission for Racial Equality.

Little, A., & Willey, R. (1981). *Multi-ethnic education: The way forward* (Schools Council Pamphlet 18). London: Schools Council.

Little, K. (1948). *Negroes in Britain: A study of racial relations in English society*. London: Routledge & Kegan Paul.

Local Government Act. (1966). London: Her Majesty's Stationery Office.

London Borough of Brent, Education Committee. (1983). *Education for a multicultural democracy*. London: Author.

Lynch, J. (1983). *The multicultural curriculum*. London: Batsford Academic and Educational.

Lynch, J. (1986). *Multicultural education: Principles and practice*. London: Routledge & Kegan Paul.

Lynch, J. (1987). *Prejudice reduction and the schools*. London: Cassell.

Mac an Ghaill, M. (1988). *Young, gifted and Black: Student-teacher relations in the schooling of Black youth*. Milton Keynes: Open University Press.

Macdonald, I. (1977). *Race relations: The new law*. London: Butterworths.

Macdonald, I., Bhavnani, R., Khan, L., & John, G. (1989). *Murder in the playground: The Burnage report* (The report of the Macdonald Inquiry into Racism and Racial Violence in Manchester Schools). London: Longsight Press.

Macdonald, I., and Blake, N. J. (1991). *Immigration law and practice in the United Kingdom* (3rd ed.). London: Butterworths.

Manchester Education Authority. (1980). *Education for a multicultural society*. Manchester: Author.

Massey, I. (1991). *More than skin deep: Developing anti-racist multicultural education in schools*. London: Hodder and Stoughton.

Miles, R. (1982). *Racism and migrant labour*. London: Routledge & Kegan Paul.

Millins, P. K. C. (1970). *Education for a multi-cultural society: Syllabuses*. London: Community Relations Commission.

Milner, D. (1975). *Children and race*. Harmondsworth: Penguin.

Milner, D. (1983). *Children and race ten years on*. London: Ward Lock.

Ministry of Education. (1954). *Langauge* (Pamphlet No. 26). London: Her Majesty's Stationery Office.

Ministry of Education. (1963). *English for immigrants* (Pamphlet No. 43). London: Her Majesty's Stationery Office.

Mullard, C. (1982). Multiracial education in Britain: From assimilation to cultural pluralism. In J. Tierney, P. Dickinson, M. Syer, C. Mullard, J. Gundara, C. Jones, & K. Kimberley, *Race, migration and schooling* (pp. 120–133). London: Holt, Rinehart and Winston.

Mullard, C. (1984). *Antiracist education: The three O's*. Cardiff: National Association for Multi-Racial Education.

National Committee for Commonwealth Immigrants. (undated, ca. 1966). *Towards a multi-racial society*. London: Author.

National Committee for Commonwealth Immigrants. (undated, ca. 1967). *Report for 1966*. London: Author.

National Curriculum Council. (1989). *The national curriculum and whole curriculum planning: Preliminary guidance* (Circular No. 6). York: Author.

National Curriculum Council. (1990a). *Curriculum guidance eight: Education for citizenship*. York: Author.

National Curriculum Council. (1990b). *Curriculum guidance three: The whole curriculum*. York: Author.

National Curriculum Council. (1991a). *Linguistic diversity and the national curriculum* (Circular No. 11). York: Author.

National Curriculum Council. (1991b). A pluralist society in the classroom and beyond. *NCC News,* 5, p. 3.

National Curriculum Council, Multicultural Task Group. (undated). *Multicultural education* (written 1990). Unpublished manuscript, National Curriculum Council, York.

National Union of Teachers. (1978). *All our children*. London: Author.

National Union of Teachers. (1983). *Combating racism in schools: A union policy statement—Guidance for members*. London: Author.

National Union of Teachers. (1992). *Anti-racist curriculum guidelines*. London: Author.

Owen, D. (1992). *Ethnic minorities in Great Britain: Settlement patterns* (1991 Census Statistical Paper No. 1). Coventry: University of Warwick, Centre for Research in Ethnic Relations, National Ethnic Minority Data Archive.

Parekh, B. (1986). The concept of multicultural education. In S. Modgil, G. K. Verma, K. Mallick, & C. Modgil (Eds.), *Multicultural education: The interminable debate* (pp. 19–31). London: Falmer.

Pascall, D. (1992, November). *The cultural dimension in education*. Speech given at a meeting organized by the National Foundation for Arts Education at the Royal Society of Arts, London.

Patterson. S. (1963). *Dark strangers: A sociological study of the absorption of a recent West Indian migrant group in Brixton, South London*. London: Tavistock.

Political and Economic Planning & Research Services. (1967). *Racial discrimination*. London: Political and Economic Planning.

Power, J. (1967). *Immigrants in school: A survey of administrative policies*. London: Councils and Education Press Ltd.

Prime Minister. (1965). *Immigration from the Commonwealth* (Cmnd. 2739). London: Her Majesty's Stationery Office.

Public Order Act. (1986). London: Her Majesty's Stationery Office.

Pumfrey, P., & Verma, G. K. (Eds.). (1993a). *Cultural diversity and the curriculum: The foundation subjects and religious education in primary schools.* London: Falmer.

Pumfrey, P., & Verma, G. K. (Eds.). (1993b). *Cultural diversity and the curriculum: The foundation subjects and religious education in secondary schools.* London: Falmer.

Race Relations Act. (1965). London: Her Majesty's Stationery Office.

Race Relations Act. (1968). London: Her Majesty's Stationery Office.

Race Relations Act. (1976). London: Her Majesty's Stationery Office.

Racial violence. (1993, September). *The Runnymede Bulletin,* No. 268, p. 4.

Racist attacks and harassment: The epidemic of the 90's? (1993, July). *Black to Black,* p. 1.

Rex, J. (1983). *Race relations in sociological theory* (2nd ed.). London: Routledge & Kegan Paul. (1st ed. published 1970).

Rose, E. J. B., Deakin, N., Abrams, M., Jackson, V., Peston, M., Vanags, A. H., Cohen, B., Gaitskell, J., & Ward, P. (1969). *Colour and citizenship: A report on British race relations.* London: Oxford University Press.

Royal Commission on Population. (1949). *Report* (session 1948–49, Cmnd. 7695, Vol. 19). London: Her Majesty's Stationery Office.

Royal County of Berkshire Local Education Authority. (1983). *Education for racial equality: Policy paper 1.* Reading: Author.

Rudell, D., & Simpson, M. (1982). *Recognising racism.* Birmingham: City of Birmingham Education Department.

The Runnymede Trust. (1993). *Equality assurance in schools: Quality, identity, society—A handbook for action planning and school effectiveness.* London: Trentham Books for The Runnymede Trust.

Schools Council. (1967). *English for the children of immigrants* (Working Paper No. 13). London: Her Majesty's Stationery Office.

Schools Council. (1970). *Immigrant children in infant schools.* London: Evans and Methuen.

Schools Council. (1972). *Race relations and the curriculum.* London: Author.

Schools Council. (1981). *Education for a multiracial society: Curriculum and context 5–13.* London: Author.

Select Committee on Race Relations and Immigration. (1969a). *The problems of coloured school-leavers: Minutes of evidence, Thursday, 13th February, 1969* (session 1968–69, 13 Feb., 58, 6, Vol. 17). London: Her Majesty's Stationery Office.

Select Committee on Race Relations and Immigration. (1969b). *The problems of coloured school-leavers: Minutes of evidence, Wednesday, 19th February, 1969* (session 1968–69, 19 Feb., 58, 7, Vol. 17). London: Her Majesty's Stationery Office.

Select Committee on Race Relations and Immigration. (1969c). *The problems of coloured school-leavers: Minutes of evidence* (session 1968–69, 413, 3, Vol. 20). London: Her Majesty's Stationery Office.

Select Committee on Race Relations and Immigration. (1969c). *The problems of coloured school-leavers: Report and proceedings of the committee* (session 1968–69, 413, 1, Vol. 19). London: Her Majesty's Stationery Office.

Select Committee on Race Relations and Immigration. (1973). *Education* (session 1972–73, 405, 1–3, Vols. 30 & 31). London: Her Majesty's Stationery Office.

Select Committee on Race Relations and Immigration. (1977). *The West Indian community* (session 1976–77, H.C. 180, 1–3, Vol. 43). London: Her Majesty's Stationery Office.

Sex Discrimination Act. (1975). London: Her Majesty's Stationery Office.

Siraj-Blatchford, I. (1990). Positive discrimination: The underachievement of initial teacher education. *Multicultural Teaching, 8*(2), 14–19.

Sivanandan, A. (1974). *Race and resistance: The IRR story.* London: Race Today Publications.

Sivanandan, A. (1982). *A different hunger: Writings on black resistance.* London: Pluto Press.

Smith, D. J. (1977). *Racial disadvantage in Britain.* Harmondsworth: Penguin.

Solomos, J. (1986). *Riots, urban protest and social policy: The interplay of reform and social control* (Policy Papers in Ethnic Relations, No. 7). Coventry: University of Warwick, Centre for Research in Ethnic Relations.

Stenhouse, L. A. (1975). Problems of research in teaching about race relations. In G. K. Verma & C. Bagley (Eds.), *Race and education across cultures* (pp. 305–321). London: Heinemann.

Stone, M. (1981). *The education of the Black child in Britain: The myth of multiracial education.* Glasgow: Fontana.

Swann, Lord. (1993). *Education for all:* A personal view. In A. Fyfe & P. Figueroa (Eds.), *Education for cultural diversity: The challenge for a new era* (pp. 1–8). London: Routledge.

Tattum, D. P., & Lane, D. A. (1989). *Bullying in school.* Stoke-on-Trent: Trentham Books.

Taylor, F. (1974). *Race, school and community: A survey of research and literature on education in multi-racial Britain.* Windsor: NFER Publishing Company.

Taylor, M. J. (1981). *Caught between: A review of research into the education of pupils of West Indian origin.* Windsor: NFER-Nelson.

Taylor, M. J. (1987). *Chinese pupils in Britain: A review of research into the education of pupils of Chinese origin.* Windsor: NFER-Nelson.

Taylor, M. J. (1988). *Worlds apart?: A review of research into the education of pupils of Cypriot, Italian, Ukranian and Vietnamese origin, Liverpool Blacks and Gypsies.* Windsor: NFER-Nelson.

Taylor, M. J. (1992a). *Equality after ERA?: Concerns and challenges for multicultural antiracist education.* Slough: NFER.

Taylor, M. J. (1992b). *Multicultural antiracist education after ERA: Concerns, constraints and challenges.* Slough: NFER.

Taylor, M. J., & Hegarty, S. (1985). *The best of both worlds . . . ? A review of research into the education of pupils of South Asian origin.* Windsor: NFER-Nelson.

Tomlinson, S. (1982). *A sociology of special education.* London: Routledge & Kegan Paul.

Tomlinson, S. (1983). *Ethnic minorities in British schools: A review of the literature, 1960–82.* London: Heinemann Educational Books.

Tomlinson, S. (1990). *Multicultural education in White schools.* London: Batsford.

Tomlinson, S. (1993). The multicultural task group: The group that never was. In A. S. King & M. J. Reiss (Eds.), *The multicultural dimension of the national curriculum* (pp. 21–29). London: Falmer.

Townsend, H. E. R. (1971). *Immigrant pupils in England: The LEA response.* Slough: National Foundation for Educational Research in England and Wales.

Townsend, H. E. R., & Brittan, E. M. (1972). *Organization in multiracial schools.* Slough: National Foundation for Educational Research in England and Wales.

Townsend, H. E. R. & Brittan, E. M. (1973). *Multiracial education: Need and innovation* (Schools Council Working Paper 50). London: Evans and Methuen.

Troyna, B. & Hatcher, R. (1992). *Racism in children's lives: A study of mainly-white primary schools.* London: Routledge.

Troyna, B. & Williams, J. (1986). *Racism, education and the state: The racialisation of education policy.* London: Croom Helm.

Twitchin, J. (Ed.). (1978). *Five views of multi-racial Britain: Talks on race relations broadcast by BBC TV.* London: Commission for Racial Equality.

Twitchin, J., & Demuth, C. (Comp.). (1985). *Multi-cultural education: Views from the classroom* (2nd ed.). London: BBC. (1st ed. published 1981)

United Nations. (1989). *Convention on the Rights of the Child.* Geneva: United Nations Children's Fund.

Unofficial Committee of Enquiry. (1980). *Southall 23 April 1979: The report of the Unofficial Committee of Enquiry* (Chair: M. Dummett). London: National Council for Civil Liberties.

Verma, G. K., & Bagley, C. (Eds.). (1975). *Race and education across cultures.* London: Heinemann.

Verma, G. K., & Pumfrey, P. (Eds.). (1993a). *Cultural diversity and the curriculum: Cross curricular contexts, themes and dimensions in primary schools.* London: Falmer.

Verma, G. K., & Pumfrey, P. (Eds.). (1993b). *Cultural diversity and the curriculum: Cross curricular contexts, themes and dimensions in secondary schools.* London: Falmer.

Wallis, S. (1977). *The education of ethnic minority children: From the perspectives of parents, teachers and education authorities.* London: Community Relations Commission.

Walvin, J. (1973). *Black and White: The Negro in English society, 1555–1945.* London: Allen Lane.

White, J. (1987). The quest for common values. In G. Haydon (Ed.), *Education for a pluralist society: Philosophical perspectives on the Swann report* (Bedford Way Papers, No. 30, pp. 13–24). London: Institute of Education, University of London.

Whitty, G. (1990). The new right and the national curriculum: State control or market forces? In B. Moon (Ed.). *New curriculum—national curriculum* (pp. 15–22). London: Hodder and Stoughton.

Willey, R. (1984a). Policy responses in education. In M. Craft (Ed.), *Education and cultural pluralism* (pp. 27–40). Lewes, Sussex: Falmer Press.

Willey, R. (1984b). *Race, equality and schools.* London: Methuen.

Williams, E. (1944). *Capitalism and slavery.* Chapel Hill: University of North Carolina Press.

Wright, C. (1986). School processes: An ethnographic study. In J. Eggleston, D. Dunn, M. Anjali, & C. Wright, *Education for some: The educational and vocational experiences of fifteen- to eighteen-year-old members of minority ethnic groups* (pp. 127–179). Stoke-on-Trent: Trentham Books.

Wright, C. (1992). *Race relations in the primary school.* London: David Fulton.

Zec, P. (1980). Multicultural education: What kind of relativism is possible? *Journal of Philosophy of Education, 14*(1), 77–86.

46

MULTICULTURAL EDUCATION IN CANADA:
HISTORICAL DEVELOPMENT
AND CURRENT STATUS

Kogila A. Moodley
UNIVERSITY OF BRITISH COLUMBIA

Canada is one of the few democratic societies that has addressed the issue of cultural and linguistic pluralism, incorporated it into its definition of national identity, and formulated it as a formal state policy of multiculturalism. In this respect, it differs from the United States, where national policy is assimilationist and transformationist initiatives that promote cultural pluralism have come primarily from minority groups and scholars advocating alternative forms of educational reform to valorize neglected groups (Banks, 1993). It was not until the civil rights, Black power, antiwar, and women's movements added their voices of protest, against a background of Supreme Court decisions, that ideas about valuing heritage cultures were given significant national attention (Friessen, 1993).

Canada has always been an ethnically heterogeneous society (Palmer, 1975). The roots of this diversity lie in four major phases of settlement:

1. Prior to European contact, indigenous native people constituted some 50 distinct segments and spoke over a dozen languages, each with numerous dialects within them. They ranged from nomadic hunting-and-gathering groups to cultivators of the soil (Jenness, 1963).
2. From the 16th and 17th centuries up until 1760, spurred by the fur trade, there was an influx of French traders and colonizers. Most accounts estimate the Native population to have been over 200,000 at this time. By the latter half of the 1800s these numbers had dwindled to 100,000 due to conquest and genocide (Palmer, 1975). French-Aboriginal contact gave rise to the distinctive Métis population (Schwartz, 1977).
3. Along with the French came the British, in the 18th century, after Canada was ceded to Britain in the Treaty of Paris in 1763. Subsequent phases of immigration, at first by the United Empire loyalists after the American Declaration of Independence in 1776, and then by other immigrants from Britain, marked the beginnings of a firm British presence (Palmer, 1975). By the mid-19th century, they outnumbered the French.
4. The need to settle the prairie provinces led to a call for "other" immigrants, who were recruited from Europe and parts of Asia. Northern European immigrants, especially of Dutch and German origin, predominated. By 1871, German immigrants constituted the largest group, numbering some 200,000 (Hawkins, 1972). In 1896 they were joined by East Europeans, in particular Ukrainians. Despite their lack of the prized Anglo-mainstream ancestry, they were nevertheless recruited because of their agricultural backgrounds, which "fitted" them for the development of the prairies. For the same reasons, nonconformist sects such as the Hutterites and Mennonites were given tracts of land to farm as communities. Asians, most of whom came as contract laborers to work on the Canadian Pacific Railway, numbered 23,700 in 1901. Among these were some 4,700 Japanese and 1,700 East Indians. Clifford Sifton's disapproval of Asian immigration led to the imposition of a "head tax" for Chinese immigrants in 1900 and 1903, but this did not deter them from coming. By 1921, the Chinese population in Canada had increased to 40,000, the Japanese to 16,000, and the East Indians of Sikh origin to 5,000. Over half the Chinese, and the majority of Japanese and Sikhs, settled in British Columbia (Palmer, 1975).

TABLE 46–1. Population by Selected Ethnic Origins,
Canada, 1991

Total population	26,994,045
Single origins	19,199,790
African	26,430
Arab	172,320
Armenian	26,005
Austrian	27,130
Balkans	131,435
Baltic	39,610
Belgian and Luxembourgian	32,091
British	5,611,050
Caribbean	94,395
Chinese	586,645
Czech and Slovak	59,125
Dutch	358,180
Finnish	39,230
French	6,146,600
German	911,560
Greek	151,150
Indochinese	116,535
Italian	750,055
Japanese	48,595
Jewish	245,840
Latin American	85,535
Magyar (Hungarian)	100,725
Native people	470,615
Pacific Islands	7,215
Polish	272,810
Portuguese	246,890
Romanian	28,650
Russian	38,220
Scandinavian	174,370
South Asian	420,295
Spanish	82,675
Swiss	23,610
Ukrainian	406,645
West Asian	81,660
Other origins	780,035
Multiple origins	7,794,250

Source: *Immigration Statistics*, Statistics Canada, 1982, Ottawa: Queen's Printer.

The period after World War II marked a resumption in immigration. In addition to the continuing influx of British settlers, there came Europeans, notably of Italian, German, Dutch, and Polish origin, from different social and occupational backgrounds. In the mid-1960s, with a booming Canadian economy, the future was optimistic. Canada needed immigrants to meet the needs of a complex industrialized, urbanized society. Previous sponsored-immigration requirements gave way in 1966 to a more selective policy known as the point system. It was based on level of education, occupational skills, local demand, and personal adaptability. The new admission procedure replaced the racial and ethnic discriminatory practices of the past with universalistic admission criteria. After 1967, Canada's ethnic mosaic began to permit, for the first time, a significant number of non-White people. By 1971, noncharter-group im-

migrants, namely those of other than French or English origin, constituted 25.3% of the overall population and have been referred to as a "third force" (Hawkins, 1972; Porter, 1972).

Unlike earlier waves of immigration aimed at opening up the interior of the country, with involvement in agricultural pursuits, recent immigrants, particularly Asians, have preferred to settle in the major metropolitan centers. Toronto, for instance, has become home to over a third of all new immigrants (Fleras and Elliott, 1992), changing its character radically from a provincial British-dominated city to a lively, culturally heterogeneous metropolis. The range of ethnic origins and the differing group strengths in Canada are reflected in the 1991 census (See Table 46–1). Increasingly more immigrants in the 1970s originated in Third World countries, so that in 1980 exactly 50% of all new arrivals came from Asian countries. This diversity is reflected in the populations of most major cities and, consequently, in the composition of schools. In Vancouver in 1992, of 54,036 students, 46% were identified as children for whom English was a second language. Toronto has a slightly larger population of those for whom English is a second language—47%. Added to the range of home languages other than English is the presence of dialects of English. This Babylonic situation clearly gave new impetus to the practical aspects of the policy of multiculturalism.

MULTICULTURAL POLICY

In the endless quest for the ever-elusive Canadian identity, the view that Canada values the cultural mosaic, unlike the assimilationist United States, has always held prominence. This difference was formalized in the 1971 Liberal government's policy of multiculturalism. It was initiated in response to the report of the Royal Commission on Bilingualism and Biculturalism in the mid-1960s and the Official Languages Act of 1969, which conferred equal status to both French and English as the official languages of the Parliament and government of Canada (Innis, 1973). The core of the government's policy presented by Prime Minister Trudeau stressed government assistance for culture maintenance:

First, resources permitting, the government will seek to assist all Canadian cultural groups that have demonstrated a desire and effort to continue to develop a capacity to grow and contribute to Canada, and a clear need for assistance, the small and weak groups no less than the strong and highly organized.

Second, the government will assist members of all cultural groups to overcome cultural barriers to full participation in Canadian society.

Third, the government will promote creative encounters and interchange among all Canadian cultural groups in the interest of national unity.

Fourth, the government will continue to assist immigrants to acquire at least one of Canada's official languages in order to become full participants in Canadian society. (House of Commons, 1971, p. 8546)

The policy was greeted in some quarters with great enthusiasm. On the whole, however, it has been received with mixed reactions. Both the French Canadians and Native people, who now claim status as First Nations, saw it as neutralizing their special claims. As founding peoples their charter rights, which entitled French Canadians to special language rights and legal codes and Native people to Aboriginal rights, were being equalized with those of many others. Multiculturalism, Native people point out, achieves nothing for the recognition of land claims and forgotten treaty rights (Kallen, 1987; Sanders, 1987; Frideres, 1990). Although the French language is recognized as one of the two official languages, the French complained about a loss of cultural hegemony by being treated like other immigrants (Bourassa, 1975; Ryan, 1975). Some European ethnics, especially Ukrainians, viewed cultural preservation without linguistic preservation as being certain to fail.

Ambiguities and contradictions in the policy have been argued ad nauseam (Burnet, 1975). As Peter maintains, there has been a tendency to view Canadian society and ethnic groups as though they existed independently, yet with the latter adding interest to the whole through diverse customs and practices (Peter, 1981). Fear is expressed that ethnic groups, in sustaining their respective cultures, will undermine national unity, and this is mitigated by a meek plea to share these cultures with the rest of Canadian society, thereby enriching it. Cultural differences are at once extolled and considered a hindrance to be removed in the interests of access to equal opportunity (Moodley, 1983). Such conceptualization is said to raise legitimate concerns about the real integration of ethnic groups into the national identity. Finally, multicultural policy has been viewed generally as a mere election ploy to garner the ethnic vote for the Liberal Party. It is indicative, though, that the Conservative Party, after its landslide victory in 1984, continued with the identical policy that now has virtually the unanimous support of all major political forces in Canada.

In 1972 a multicultural directorate was established within the Department of the Secretary of State to promote the ideals of multiculturalism, social integration, and positive race relations. Increasingly, racism has emerged as an issue of concern to community groups and superseded the goals of cultural maintenance. Several government initiatives have ensued, with the objective of eliminating racial discrimination. In July 1988, the Canadian Multiculturalism Act was passed unanimously by both houses of Parliament. Modest funds were earmarked to promote harmonious race relations, enhance cross-cultural understanding, preserve heritage languages and cultures, ensure full and equal participation of ethnic minorities, and foster cross-government commitment for all federal institutions (Secretary of State, 1988). Thereby, the Canadian government pledged its support for an active, multicultural policy as an integral part of the nation-state. In 1991–92, $25.5 million constituted the budget allocated under the Ministry of Multiculturalism (Economic Council of Canada, 1991). This is less than the cost of one missile. Regardless, Canada became the first nation to give multiculturalism full legal authority.

PROVINCIAL RESPONSES TO CULTURAL DIVERSITY

Recognition of the potential divisiveness of the issues of culture and schooling led to the shift in control of education at confederation from the national to the provincial arena, to allow the greatest freedom of expression of differences (Mallea &

Young, 1984; Stevenson & Wilson, 1977; Titley, 1990). Consequently, religious and linguistic diversity have been dealt with differently in each province. The educational autonomy of each province, resulting in different organizational provisions for linguistic and religious instruction, makes for a rather complex and confusing picture. A broad overview reveals great contrasts among the provinces.

A denominational system has operated in Newfoundland since the 19th century, providing Anglican, Pentecostal, United Church, and Roman Catholic schools with government support (Jaenen, 1977). No such legal provisions exist for sectarian schools in New Brunswick, Nova Scotia, or Prince Edward Island, but informal arrangements have been worked out in each. Special provisions exist for Acadian education in Prince Edward Island and Nova Scotia. New Brunswick has both English and French school boards. In response to the grievances of those seeking independent religious education, Ontario developed a public educational system guaranteed under the British North America Act. It comprised both common schools, which were provincially funded, nonsectarian public schools open to all, and separate public schools funded partially by the state.

Also guaranteed under the BNA Act was a dual confessional arrangement in Quebec. To this end, French and English instruction were made available. In Manitoba, separate-language schools were available for French and English, as were bilingual schools for other ethnocultural groups. A major shift took place when English was made the sole language of instruction in 1916, effectively shattering the hopes of Franco-Manitobans for French-language education, not to speak of cultural retention. Alberta, Saskatchewan, and Northwest Territories offer both public and partially public-funded separate school systems (Mallea, 1984). British Columbia has never made any provision for public funding of separate schools, except for the supply of textbooks. There has been rising political pressure for government support of private or independent schools. Where numbers warrant it, French-medium education is made available for the Francophone minority.

Although provincial autonomy in education has afforded flexibility to meet local needs, it has raised controversy. The absence of a federal guarantee of minority rights is especially notable when the language rights of different Francophone minorities are viewed (Mallea, 1984). This state of affairs made for an initially very lukewarm reception of the policy of multiculturalism in the French-speaking provinces. If language education for a sizable charter group such as French Canadians could not be guaranteed, how could linguistic and cultural preservation for a spectrum of ethnocultural groups be encouraged? Despite this contradiction, most provincial governments have officially accepted multiculturalism for implementation in educational programs.

School boards throughout Canada have expressed various forms of commitment to multicultural education and, in some cases, to race relations programs as well. No single model of multicultural education exists in Canada. What is common is acknowledgment of a changing population with different needs. Multicultural concerns have been unevenly incorporated into school programs and into in-service teacher education programs. A few faculties of education across the country have established alternative programs in multicultural education for preservice teachers. Otherwise, multicultural education has been offered either as a separate course or as a component in sociology of education courses, where it may be discussed as part of the hidden curriculum of schools. Indeed, as Henley and Young point out, teacher preparation for a multicultural society tends to be "contested, fragmented and in large measure theoretical" (Henley & Young, 1991, p. 18). Their research into teacher preparation shows that it is "not afforded a high priority in many Canadian universities and that where multicultural education is addressed it is often done through isolated course offerings which cannot possibly provide to students the kind of exposure necessary to address adequately the complexity of the culture-society dynamic" (p. 27).

Overt responses of schools to multiculturalism indicate a shift from the earlier benign assimilation to a greater acceptance of multiculturalism. A survey by Day and Shapson (1981) involving 237 central office personnel in 70 school districts in British Columbia found that most respondents favored the inclusion of multicultural activities and programs in the school curriculum. However, this acceptance has not been evenly integrated into practice. This is not surprising in view of the tremendous ambiguity about what multicultural education means (Moodley, 1984). The survey showed that in the same sample only 20% supported the inclusion of second languages as the medium of instruction for part of the curriculum. Even in provinces where the provincial government has adopted the policy, Francophones have difficulty finding education in their own language.

In 1991, the pendulum seems to have swung as the Spicer commission report on national unity documented the outcomes of a citizens' forum on Canada's future. Among the recurring themes were calls for national unity and fundamental Canadian values and a perception that funding multicultural programs is both financially wasteful and a threat to national unity. The commission was repeatedly told that reminders of different origins were less useful in building a united country than emphasizing the things we have in common. Respondents questioned the focus on citizens' origins and celebrating heritage cultures rather than embracing a uniquely Canadian national character and celebrating Canadian heritage.

On the other hand, a number of participants, including new Canadians, have told the forum that they would prefer to see available public funds spent on language training and other forms of integration assistance for newcomers to Canada rather than on heritage-culture preservation. Interesting too were the views of Canadian youth participating in the students' forum; they were much more opposed to special recognition for Aboriginal people than were adult participants. While they adopted an egalitarian approach to questions of cultural diversity, the majority of students felt Aboriginal people should integrate into a diverse Canadian society. At the same time they were more likely to mention racism and racial discrimination in Canada as a serious problem to be addressed (Spicer Commission, 1991).

In a similar vein, the 1993 Canadian elections revealed substantial support, especially in western Canada, for a populist Reform Party, which played up the values of Canadian identity and national unity and maintained a considered distance from multiculturalism and immigration.

The main difference in multicultural politics is between an ethnocultural support-service orientation, as pursued by Ontario and Nova Scotia, and a language-based view of multicultural education, as practiced in Saskatchewan, Alberta, and Manitoba.

Ontario

The Ontario Ministry of Education (1989) has actively initiated considerable curriculum reform. There has been a marked shift in approach from the 1950s and 1960s, when it was assumed that, once immigrants acquired English-language competence, there would cease to be an "immigrant problem" (Masemann, 1984). Beginning in 1968, legislation that guaranteed French-medium education passed in Ontario. Present policy guidelines also include information about the advantages of intercultural awareness in educational planning. Courses in multiculturalism are offered to in-service teachers and administrative staff. Curriculum materials are scrutinized for bias and stereotyping, and guidelines are offered to publishers and authors to promote bias-free, appropriate curriculum materials (McLeod, 1984).

Despite the controversy about offering nonofficial languages at public expense during regular school hours and criticisms about the costs, social divisiveness, and educational retrogressiveness (Cummins & Danesi, 1990), the Ontario Heritage Language Programme established in 1977 has found increasing support. In 1980–81, 44 different languages were taught after school hours to 76,017 students (Ontario Ministry of Education, 1988). The instruction time permitted was up to 2½ hours a week. Since then, responding to community pressure as well as sound educational justification (Cummins & Danesi, 1990), both federal and provincial governments have been actively engaged in implementing heritage-language programs within the school system. This has been explicitly stated in the preamble to the Official Languages Act of 1988. In that year there were "129,000 students enrolled in 1,557 supplementary heritage language programs studying sixty different languages" (Fleras & Elliott, 1992, p. 157). Immersion programs in French are offered to English speakers who want greater fluency. Their success has stimulated international interest in the Canadian approach. Among other language programs offered are the use of the minority language as a transitional language in instruction, gradually leading to mastery of the official language (Shapson & Purbhoo, 1977). Also increasingly popular are trilingual-education programs, established with community initiative. Most children in these programs are third-generation immigrants whose home language is English (Cummins, 1984).

In 1986, as a result of a provincial conference initiated by the Ontario Ministry of Education, an advisory committee was set up comprising representatives of the ministry, teachers' federations, boards of education, and the community. Through collaborative efforts the committee drafted policy and guidelines to assist boards in developing, implementing, and monitoring initiatives aimed at achieving racial and ethnocultural equity. In addition to calling for leadership from key educational office holders and community participation, the committee's report highlighted the need for research in race relations and antiracist education as a basis for the development of equity policies

(Tator & Henry, 1991). On the issue of curriculum, the committee called for procedures to critically review existing material for racial and ethnocultural bias, to educate students to understand the forces in Canadian history that contribute to racism, to ensure the incorporation into the curriculum of the local and global experiences of the many groups that make up Canada, and to offer heritage-language programs as an integral part of the educational experience. Specific policies to examine and monitor student services, assessment, placement, and streaming procedures were considered important areas, as was the need for cross-cultural counseling, and guidance boards were urged to put in place policies enabling decisive action on matters related to racial and cultural harassment (Tator & Henry, 1991).

In 1988, through elaborate consultative processes, the Ontario ministry produced a document, *Changing Perspectives: A Resource Guide for Race and Ethnocultural Equity, K–13,* to help educators toward the goal of equity in a multicultural, multiracial society. These developments must be understood in the context of deteriorating race relations in Ontario. In 1993, the ministry reiterated its commitment to these equity goals by announcing its intention to hire more minority teachers and, if they were not available locally, to broaden the search internationally. In the same year, Ontarios's New Democratic Party government mandated all school boards to develop a racial and ethnocultural equity policy and programs to implement anti-racism initiatives.

Nova Scotia

Like Ontario, Nova Scotia's policy emphasizes intercultural understanding and the broader focus on equality of opportunity and access. Attempts have also been made to update in-service teacher education and to disseminate bias-free resources (McLeod, 1984), though this does not seem to have reached official curriculum guides and handbooks (Wilson, 1984).

These initiatives remain totally inadequate for dealing in particular with the disadvantaged position of the Black population, which has a history of 300 years in this region. Blacks' struggles for social, economic, and educational advancement continue through increasing pressure from their own communal organizations (Mock, 1988; Tator & Henry, 1991).

Manitoba, Alberta, and Saskatchewan

In contrast to the intercultural awareness and after-school language programs of Ontario and Nova Scotia, Manitoba, Alberta, and Saskatchewan have implemented more integrated language programs. English and French were until 1978 the official languages of instruction in Manitoba schools. In 1978, under the amended Public Schools Act, instruction in other languages was permitted, with school board authorization. With ministerial permission, other languages could be the language of instruction for up to 50% of regular school hours (Handford, 1993; Manitoba Ministry of Education, 1980). This policy was very well received by the Ukrainian and German communities. Several pilot projects were established, and enrollment has increased notably (Mallea, 1989).

Stimulated by the energetic efforts of the Ukrainian community of Alberta to include their cultural heritage as part of the educational process, the Alberta Schools Act was amended in 1971. School boards were empowered to introduce nonofficial-language instruction where and when they deemed it appropriate. Wide-ranging curriculum reform was initiated. Pilot programs using heritage languages for instruction for up to 50% of the school day were established. In 1974 Ukrainian-English bilingual programs were offered in both private and separate public schools. Currently, several variations of bilingual education are available. Of the 10 bilingual schools in Alberta, 5 are Ukrainian, 3 Jewish, and 2 German. In addition to these are the private schools that offer instruction in different languages. Saturday schools have also increased in scope and demand, and some 20 languages are taught. These schools are privately administered by the Alberta Cultural Heritage Branch (Wilson, 1984). These directions were formalized in the new Language Education Policy in Alberta in 1988. Among the languages in use under the Bilingual Language Program are Cree, Blackfoot, Arabic, Polish, Mandarin, Hungarian, Hebrew, and Ukrainian. This programming is not unproblematic in that the learning resources and trained personnel are not always easily available, and developmental work is in progress.

At another level, Alberta responded to the landmark legal action against alleged hate propagandist James Keegstra, who engaged in systematic anti-Semitic teaching, by establishing the Ghitter Commission on Intolerance. A number of processes were initiated to ensure fair teaching practices. All curriculum resources developed by the ministry, as well as those from external sources, were expected to pass independent audits. The guidelines established include a range of criteria such as determining whether the materials include implicit or explicit statements promoting tolerance, understanding, and respect and whether the materials build positive self-images and promote critical thinking skills. All Albertan high school students are required to take a compulsory course on career and life management, which includes an optional 25-hour module entitled Cultural Bridges, to help students explore issues in multiculturalism.

Yet another area in which Alberta has made a distinctive contribution in response to its demographics is in its Native Education Project, well known for promoting meaningful partnerships between Native parents and the school board and for producing improved learning resources about Native people that were to be evaluated for use by all students (Tator & Henry, 1991).

It is noteworthy, however, that Ron Ghitter, chairperson of the Alberta government's 1984 Committee on Tolerance and Understanding, viewed multicultural policies as divisive, and in need of transformation, since they did not promote national unity (Bunner & Ingram, 1990). The government's multicultural policy itself is considered to be a source of conflict in Alberta. Ethnic minorities compete with one another for limited funds to support their activities for cultural promotion. Inevitably, the larger, better-organized groups gain more financial support and power.

The integration of heritage languages as part of a sound multicultural program is also clear in the Manitoba Teacher Society's background paper "Multiculturalism and Education in

Manitoba" (McLeod, 1984). Three essential components are highlighted: "mainstream, multicultural education, immigrant orientation and New Canadian awareness [as well as] ancestral languages of established ethnocultural groups" (quoted in McLeod, 1984, p. 41).

Saskatchewan's commitment to multiculturalism was formalized in 1974 when the Saskatchewan Multicultural Act was passed. As a step toward implementing the goals of disseminating knowledge about and pride in all cultural heritages, the legislature amended section 209 of the School Act to permit the use of languages other than English for instruction. Financial incentives were offered for the development of such instruction. In 1978 Saskatchewan's heritage-language program came into effect, followed by Manitoba in 1979. Three types of heritage-language instruction are in progress. First, bilingual programs are taught as part of the regular school offerings. Also available are heritage languages as languages of instruction for up to 50% of the school day. Second, heritage languages are taught as core subjects within regular school hours. Third, heritage-language programs may be conducted after school and on weekends, at the initiative of communities themselves, with federal and provincial support (Cummins & Danesi, 1990).

British Columbia

In British Columbia, the 1988 Sullivan Royal Commission on Education identified the need for the school system to enshrine language rights, to preserve diverse cultural heritages, and to promote social equality and justice through recognition of individual difference (Sullivan, 1988). The government of British Columbia adopted a multicultural policy in October 1990. In July 1993 Bill 39 received final approval and the Multiculturalism Act of British Columbia was passed. There is, however, still no multicultural education policy in the province. Yet British Columbia's controversial educational reform program, *Year 2000: A Framework for Learning* (Ministry of Education [British Columbia], 1992), identified the goals of human and social development and the need to understand cultural heritage and develop tolerance and respect for the ideas and beliefs of others. The document also valued global education and critical learning skills. These emphases injected a new legitimacy for multicultural education, which promised to serve these goals.

In contrast to the debilitated provincial role in advancing the aims of multiculturalism, the record of organizations such as the British Columbia Multicultural and Intercultural Education Council (BCMIEC), which is an affiliate of the Canadian Council for Multicultural and Intercultural Education (CCMIE), and the British Columbia Teachers' Federation have been consistently active in conference organization and promotion of multicultural and antiracism education. The BCTF's Program against Racism (PAR) provides support and resources to teachers throughout the province to promote positive classroom practices and deal with incidents of racism.

Since 1993, some school boards, notably the Vancouver School Board, have made progress in providing in-service teacher education in multicultural education, establishing a regular race relations advisory committee, and institutionalizing a firm race relations policy in the school district. All schools

were requested to submit proposed plans for implementing multicultural education. A detailed evaluation of the process of implementation revealed considerable reluctance in participation, unevenness in practice, and discrepancies between the curriculum-in-theory and curriculum-in-practice (Fisher & Echols, 1992).

Similarly, the Victoria School Board, with assistance from the ministry, acted upon community members' suggestions to pilot an elementary school project entitled Alternatives to Racism. The outcome is John Kehoe's *A Handbook of Selected Activities for Enhancing the Multicultural Climate of the School* (Kehoe, 1984). No significant developments in the area of bilingual education exist, other than those privately established by some ethnocultural communities. Under the climate of budgetary restraint in British Columbia that existed in 1993, multicultural and minority-language education were quickly defined as frills. They were readily targeted and shed as priorities.

Quebec

Like the Heritage Language Programme of Ontario, Quebec's Programme de l'enseignement des langues d'origine, which was established in 1978, offers children of linguistic minorities the opportunity to retain the language of the family. The program was developed in close collaboration with fluent Native speakers from the various communities who also had a sound grasp of the French language. The model used initially was half a school-day's instruction in native language and culture. The program caters mainly to new immigrants and children whose parents define themselves as belonging to a particular ethnic group.

APPROACHES TO MULTICULTURAL EDUCATION

The education of minorities in Canada has been viewed from two basic and contrasting perspectives. The social-pathological perspective focuses on the cultural background or lifestyle of the minority as the source of "the problem." Usually with benign intentions, well-meaning educators have often interpreted the causes of the failure of some minorities as being culturally rooted (Batelaan, 1987; Burtonwood, 1986). Canadian education is replete with instances of the forcible removal of Indian children from their homes and families in order to exorcise them of their "malignant" cultures (Barman, Herbert, & McCaskill, 1989; Kirkness, 1987). Similarly, Glazer and Moynihan (1963), in their much-cited study of U.S. ethnic groups, described what they saw as the deficiencies of the urban Black family, its disorganization, instability, and lack of a distinctive culture. The source of the problem was said to emanate from their home experiences, which failed to transmit the appropriate cultural patterns necessary for the types of learning required by schools and society. Characteristic of approaches that blame the victim, such a perspective overlooked the complex interrelationship between the economic, social, and political factors involved, an interrelationship that transcends the cultural basis. This view gave rise to numerous compensatory programs that sought to make good the "cultural deficits" through enrichment programs certain to lead to integration.

In stark contrast to the deficit model of culture is the more seemingly egalitarian, anthropologically based, relativistic model. Unlike the former, it stresses that all cultures warrant equal respect and value. Neither is better or worse. Cultural content can be assessed only from the perspective of the "insider." It has its roots in the works of anthropologists such as Malinowski (1944), Radcliffe-Brown (1952), and Herskovits (1948). Whereas the goal of the deficit model is to integrate the outsider, the relativist model is analogous to the pluralist view, stressing the legitimacy of living within meaningful cultural collectivities outside the mainstream.

The two perspectives outlined are interwoven in the responses of the provinces to the federal government's policy of multiculturalism. These include:

1. programs for the newcomer to acquire fluency in one of the official languages;
2. cultural maintenance programs—interested ethnocultural groups are offered support to retain their cultures of origin through nonofficial-language instruction and/or the cultivation of aspects of folk culture;
3. multicultural education as an antidote to the conventional portrayal of ethnic groups—Canadian social studies curricula have depicted them for the most part as "marginal" Canadians, as "contributors to the dominant society," as "beneficiaries" of the dominant society, and as "problems" (Werner, Conners, Aoki, & Dahlie, 1980, pp. 7–35); the acknowledgment of the valued diversity is sought;
4. antiracism education, which recognizes that prejudice and discrimination are potent forces that need to be addressed in a multicultural society.

It is worthwhile to examine each of these approaches in more detail, citing specific Canadian initiatives to concretize their practice.

Official-Language Education

Official-language education, for a second language, has aimed at enabling the minority child to function effectively both in the school and in the world outside. At least 13 identifiable programs are now being implemented in Canada. These have been categorized as self-contained programs, withdrawal programs, transitional programs, and mainstreaming (Ashworth, 1992, p. 126).

Since the late 1980s, major Canadian language education journals have portrayed a shift away from the more technical aspects of language learning alone to wider issues of language and culture (Byram, 1986; Hebert, 1992). There has been a heightened awareness on the part of language educators of the assimilationist hidden agenda of most nonofficial language teaching.

Languages of origin have also been used for "transitional" purposes in acquiring the official language. A language of origin is used as a temporary bridge to facilitate learning the new language. This procedure aims at greater security without re-

tarding academic progress in the process. While two languages may be used in the classroom, as is the case with the Italian program in Toronto, the established language facilitates the learning of the new (Shapson & D'Oyley, 1984).

In Canada a considerable amount of evaluative research has been conducted to assess the impact of bilingual programs. Immersion programs in particular have enjoyed enormous success. This has led to an influx of parental demand, nationwide, to have children placed in schools offering French immersion (Cummins, 1987a).

Although Canada and the United States share similar immigrant populations, for whom English is a second or third language, Canadian responses to minority-language education are markedly different from their U.S. counterparts. Where English-speaking Canadians are accommodating about other-language education (Bibby, 1987), Americans move toward linguistic parochialism by enshrining English as the sole language of the state (Fishman, 1989). Glazer (1987) offers the following rationale for English monolingualism in the United States:

> In the middle 1970's national policy favored the use of native languages and of distinctive approaches making use of the distinctive culture of each group. But the results of our efforts to overcome differences in educational achievement using such approaches are not encouraging. Majority and minority alike, in part for different reasons, in part for the same reasons, now come together in agreement on traditional approaches to education as the most effective means of raising the educational achievement of minority groups and groups of different language backgrounds. (quoted in Cummins, 1987a, p. 303)

This view attributes students' academic difficulties to a mismatch between home and school languages. According to this line of reasoning, more English is the answer to the problem. In contrast, Cummins (1987a) argues from a Canadian perspective in favor of bilingual minority education:

> Virtually every bilingual programme that has been evaluated (including French immersion programmes) shows that students instructed through a minority language for all or part of the school day perform, over time, at least as well in the majority language (e.g. English in North America) as students instructed exclusively through the majority language." (p. 306)

All too often, educational interventions to improve minority academic performance in the United States have given short shrift to crucial theoretical bases, and sociopolitical considerations have predominated in their influence (Cummins, 1987a). In this regard Canada's language policies are also influenced by social, historical, and legal considerations. Canada's French and English dualism made it imperative to reconcile linguistic duality within a binational and multicultural state. Whereas Canadians embrace a pluralistic perspective, Americans have moved in the direction of the melting pot. Language planning is not unaffected by these considerations.

Cultural Maintenance Programs

Cultural maintenance programs have taken different forms. In some Vancouver schools with a sizable minority of native Indian children, cultural enrichment programs are offered.

One approach has been to withdraw native Indian children from regular classes to expose them to aspects of Indian cultural heritage, from stories to folk arts, for an assigned time every day. Since this was found by some teachers to set them back even further from other children in the classroom, an alternative has been arranged. The whole class is exposed to native Indian cultural materials for a given amount of time each week. Similar programs have been established in Black studies elsewhere. The aim of these programs is to raise the self-esteem of the minority child. The assumption here is that if the group would feel more positive about itself, its members' life chances would be different. However, high self-concept does not come only from knowledge of a cultural heritage. What is ignored is the daily relegation of the group to a castelike lower status from which there is little chance of escape.

Instead of an uncritical celebration of cultural heritage in a vacuum, what is needed, as Banks illustrates, is the development of a sense of political efficacy and the knowledge and skills to influence public policy toward greater equality (Banks & Clegg, 1990). Only if teachers' awareness of cultural backgrounds were to be harnessed toward effective teaching styles, reflecting sensitive understanding as well as actively demanding standards through high expectations, could cultural content serve such groups well.

On the other hand, some immigrant parents from nonofficial-language backgrounds have expressed a desire for the education of their children in their home languages to prevent increasing alienation from their heritage cultures. In the early 1970s, for instance, members of a Chinese community in Toronto appealed to the board of education for greater compatibility between home and school cultures for their children by asking that schools offer instruction in Chinese language and culture during the school day. This led to the establishment of a Chinese Canadian bilingual bicultural program. Children were withdrawn for 30 minutes each day for instruction. Subsequent evaluation showed that academic achievement was unaffected, that children's information about their backgrounds increased, and above all that their self-esteem had improved considerably (Bhatnagar, 1982). When the program began in 1977, there were 30 Chinese classes in 13 schools. In 1988 there were 125 classes in 35 schools (Mock, 1988).

Similarly, Greeks in eastern Canada have initiated and implemented a separate program for trilingual education in English, French, and Greek using styles of teaching valued by the community. The schools operate within the Catholic or Protestant systems in Montreal, and more recently in Toronto as well. The president of the Greek community speaks in glowing terms of its success: "In 1971, only 4 per cent of our high school graduates went to university. Today, our special schools send 84 per cent of graduates into post-secondary education" (House of Commons, 1984, p. 114).

There is, however, a danger of generalizing from the above successes. Clearly, sound pedagogic arguments have been advanced in favor of home language and cultural retention for effective school performance, as Verma and Bagley (1982) and others have pointed out. A few prerequisites for their success need to be mentioned. It goes without saying that an ongoing heritage culture with a language in use in the community is one of them. Another is a concerted, organized initiative from the community itself; this ensures cooperation through increased motivation of the children. Where enrichment programs have been offered by school boards as a corrective for poor performance, they are clearly imposed programs, lacking some of the components for success.

In this respect the call of the Native Indian Brotherhood for control of their own education and the increasing number of qualified First Nations teachers have given rise to more successful outcomes in alternative programs run by First Nations people. Likewise, at the post-secondary and university levels, a number of innovative alternative programs for First Nations students have given rise to marked increases in students' completion of programs (Kirkness, 1992). The true test will lie in the acceptability of their graduates in the marketplace.

Multicultural Education

What is understood by the term *multicultural education* is indeed varied, both in terms of theory and practice. Since its inception, it has evolved through a range of interpretations as to what it is and what it should be. Multicultural education has been said to have the potential for reinforcing or challenging hegemony (Sleeter, 1989). It has been extolled as a practicable alternative to current educational practices or dismissed as a palliative for the cultural and social inequalities in Canadian society.

In the United States, multicultural education has been described "as a new curricular form, [which] dis-articulated elements of black radical demands for a restructuring of school knowledge and rearticulated these elements into more reformist professional discourses around issues of minority failure, cultural characteristics and language proficiency" (McCarthy, 1990, p. 41).

It is difficult to speak of multicultural education in Canada as an indigenous model. Indeed it is ironic that, despite the early multicultural history of Canada and a range of measures supportive of a pluralistic society, discussions of multicultural education reveal a conglomerate of perspectives cross-fertilized by American and British variants. If there is anything uniquely Canadian it is those perspectives that emerge from Quebec, even though residents there do not prefer to call their intergroup education multicultural but intercultural. As Young expresses it, "different images of Canadian society demand different responses from the school system" (Young, 1979, p. 5).

Among the many prevailing conceptions of multicultural education (Banks, 1993; McLeod, 1981; Gibson, 1976; Young, 1984; Fleras & Elliott, 1992; Magsino, 1985; Grant & Sleeter, 1985; Kehoe, 1984; Coombs, 1986; and Ouellet, 1992), the most commonly cited cross-cutting themes are education for cultural pluralism, education about cultural difference, education of the culturally different, education for cultural preservation, and education for multicultural adaptation. Many of these themes are not mutually exclusive and are often found in combination.

Three characteristic approaches may serve to demonstrate the spectrum of portrayals.

1. McLeod (1992) has categorized approaches to multi-

cultural education in Canada into three main models: *ethnic specific, problem oriented,* and *cultural/intercultural.* As defined by McLeod, however, the ethnic-specific category is clearest, while the latter two categories reveal too much overlap to be meaningful. This is probably due more to the nature of the territory rather than the conceptualization.

A distinctive dimension of the ethnic-specific model of multicultural education is the preservation and development of specific group cultures. Their aims are to counteract assimilation and to increase knowledge and understanding of the individual's ethnocultural heritage. Ethnic-specific programs aim at promoting positive self-definition. Extreme cases of ethnic-specific socialization are those of the Hutterites and, to a lesser extent, the Mennonites, both of whom maintain fairly strict boundaries to protect them from outside influences. Many other ethnocultural groups throughout Canada have also established separate school programs. Among these are Ukrainian and Mennonite schools in Alberta, Chinese, Hebrew, and Greek schools in Ontario and Quebec, and Punjabi and Hebrew schools in British Columbia.

Two types of programs are included in the problem-oriented model by McLeod (1992). These are: (a) proactive programs that help immigrants to adapt to Canadian society through, for example, English as a second language programs or that promote positive race relations, such as multicultural leadership programs offered by boards of education (Samson, Yellin, & Mercer, 1987); (b) reactive programs, which respond to issues of racism and other forms of inequality, taking individual or collective forms to challenge grievances; and (c) the cultural/intercultural model, which promotes an ethos of multiculturalism throughout the educational system. The goal of the cultural/intercultural model is to help individuals enhance self-esteem, transcend cultural barriers, and develop appropriate bicultural skills to function in a culturally plural context. Its overarching values are equality of access and shared ownership.

2. Magsino (1985) typologizes six models of multicultural education that serve to organize existing conceptions. The first model is education for an emergent society, which entails the reconstitution of cultural diversity into a new single national culture. It is in some ways analogous to the melting pot. The second model is education of the culturally different, which refers to special education of the culturally atypical child. The aim is to equalize educational opportunities by reducing the differences between home and school cultures, not by changing the school culture, but by assisting students to master an official language and, indirectly, mainstream norms. Third is education for cultural understanding, which aims at cultivating acceptance, understanding, and appreciation of different groups. This is a liberal pluralist view that sees cultural diversity as intrinsically valuable and beneficial to society. To the extent that multicultural education promotes social justice by counteracting discrimination and ethnocentrism, it is considered valuable for the education of all children. Fourth, education for cultural accommodation aims at ensuring the equality of all groups. This is accomplished by the public school's accommodation of the ethnic particularities in some form, though a regular mainstream curriculum is maintained. These inclusions may

take the form of special-language instruction or cultural enrichment programs to bolster self-esteem. Although the ultimate aim of such programs is the accommodation and maintenance of diversity, they can be exclusionary in their group-specific nature. Fifth, education for cultural preservation aims at transmitting the cultures of groups whose identities are at risk. Group-specific education is not new; it predates the institution of multicultural education and was often initiated by communities to valorize waning identities and counter the assimilationist power of schools (McLeod, 1981, p. 15).

What distinguishes cultural accommodation from cultural preservation lies in the relative openness or impermeability of the very boundaries necessary to nurture identity. At one end of the spectrum it may be seen as a loosely organized cultural pluralism, while at the other it may constitute segregation. The sixth model categorized by Magsino, education for multicultural adaptation, seeks to educate for bicultural competency. Transcending group-specific identification, this approach values the ability to develop the necessary skills in cross-cultural communicative competency by acquiring another language and/or cultural literacy.

This typology, like many others, contains many contradictions, and the categories are seldom mutually exclusive and as distinct as their labels suggest.

3. A slightly different emphasis distinguishes the approach of Fernand Ouellet's Quebec-based yet internationalist perspective. He refers to (a) the monocultural option, through which "the State has the responsibility to socialize all citizens to the 'national culture,' in which members of all ethnic groups must melt, abandoning their ethnic specificity" (1992, p. 287); (b) the multicultural option, which requires the state to assist ethnic groups in the preservation of language and culture; (c) the intercultural option, which emphasizes the state's role in enhancing relations between the various groups through increased opportunities for exchange and collaboration; and (d) the transcultural option, which proposes the state's role in encouraging groups to transcend their own boundaries and reach out to meet new challenges offered within the global arena (Ouellet, 1992).

As with both the other typologies, there is some overlap between these categories, yet there is greater distinctiveness. Culture is the central category, while inequality, power, and racism are not mentioned. Overall, multicultural education as an educational orientation is firmly located within a consensus paradigm. For most educators it is an end in itself. At best it is used as a means to create a congenial environment. Differences are to be gently reaffirmed along a guiding thread of similarities. Cultural differences must therefore be selectively laundered of controversial spots and assessed for their compatibility with mainstream values as determined from the perspective of the dominant group.

Two notions of culture coexist with one another. On the one hand there is a reified notion of culture with its essentialist elements, which allows it to be fragmented for use, out of the private sphere, into the public sphere of schools. On the other hand there is a dynamic notion of a constantly changing culture, one that describes the ordering and ongoing transformation of all people's lives.

Seldom is the term *culture* used to describe the mainstream way of life. It is always used to signify the ways in which the lives of "others" are organized. If culture were conceived as a dynamic process by educators, it might lead to greater introspection about the nature of school and classroom organization, teachers' own modes of expression, their teaching and communication styles, their expectations, their biases, and the representation of learners' experiences in curriculum materials. All of these constitute crucial features of the hidden curriculum of ethnocentrism in classroom discourse and the lived realities of learners.

Learning to understand the "other" through cultural knowledge is often undertaken in the interests of fostering intercultural understandings. Such understanding, it has been argued, entails "a process of appropriation through which the foreign is reduced to one's own concepts and values so that understanding is necessarily ethnocentric" (Bredella, 1993, p. 559).

Embedded in these definitions of multicultural education are the goals of "equivalency in achievement," "more positive intergroup attitudes," and "pride in heritage" (Kehoe, 1993, p. 1). Appropriate-language education, fair assessment and placement procedures, unbiased curriculum, culturally compatible teaching styles, accepting learning environments, sound relations between home and school, and appropriate teacher expectations would serve the goal of equalizing achievement. More positive intergroup attitudes could be built by teaching the ability to recognize differences within groups, transcending external attributes, learning about cultural similarities, teaching critical thinking and reasoning skills, as well as promoting positive contact. Finally, developing pride in heritage can be maintained through processes that valorize the student's culture by incorporating appropriate learning materials within the curriculum and by offering instruction in heritage languages (Kehoe, 1993).

In the public's awareness, however, multicultural education continues to evoke the celebration of difference, often the exotic. In this view of multicultural education, "the curriculum" is left intact and the celebration continues to persist largely as "add-on" activities. In the British Columbia survey by Shapson and Day, there was a suggestion that "after school programmes are probably most appropriate for some of the goals and objectives of multiculturalism" (quoted in Wilson, 1984, p. 69). The inclusion of multicultural content is more prevalent at elementary levels and concentrated mostly within social studies programs. Its nonintegration in the curriculum is reflected in McLeod's (1984) comment about the status of multicultural education in secondary schools: "[They] have been slower than elementary schools in adopting multicultural education because they are more discipline and subject-oriented, and their teachers have been less innovative" (McLeod, 1984, p. 41). These findings continue to be reiterated in subsequent studies (Fisher & Echols, 1989; Tator & Henry, 1991).

A broad distinction still exists between programs focusing on culture and lifestyles and those focusing on race relations, power, and life chances. There is more consensus about the former, which is viewed as noncontroversial and "positive," and it is the preferred, safer route for most teachers. The latter, being controversial and dealing with conflict, has been defined as "negative" and avoided in the past. However, judging from the focus of papers presented at the 1993 annual conference of the CCMIE held in Vancouver, antiracism education is now used almost routinely in characterizing what would in the past have been described simply as multicultural education. Closer examination of the content of papers presented in this manner did not always convey a major theoretical shift implicit in antiracism education.

In the 1989 evaluation of the Vancouver school board's race relations policy, Fisher and Echols (1989) report that among the most frequently mentioned activity categories are "curriculum," "special events days," "games, music, arts," and, for secondary schools, "multicultural clubs" and "race relations/multicultural camps" (p. 54). In commenting on these, however, students conveyed "the sense that the curriculum emphasis tended to be superficial" (p. 54).

It is highly dubious whether the common trend to increase information *about* the different groups will lead to greater tolerance. Sufficient historical evidence as well as contemporary empirical studies show that this is not the only possible outcome (Katz, 1976; Moodley, 1981). Yet Buchignani (1982) notes that, in Calgary, leaders of community groups whose members felt most discriminated against saw the dissemination of information about visible minority groups as the most efficacious approach for overcoming intolerance.

Accentuating similarities is the guiding thread of work done by Kehoe in *A Handbook of Selected Activities for Enhancing the Multicultural Climate of the School* (Kehoe, 1984). It integrates a concern with the broader issues of equality of opportunity and a concern with the hidden curriculum and links these with the way in which cultural diversity has been treated. The similarities between the attributes of minority groups and others are emphasized. Like the program discussed above, this is a popular approach. It advises against the use of "historical bad news" such as Canadian treatment of minorities and connecting "poverty" with immigrants. Based on sound short-term evaluations, the concern with victimization is seen as not necessarily ensuring that the learner will empathize with the victim. Several studies cited by Kehoe confirmed his earlier findings (Kehoe & Mansfield, 1993). This approach is not without argument about the value of in-depth education as a long-term antidote against discriminatory behavior.

Also emphasizing children's better understanding of themselves and a respect for the differences of others is a program from Alberta known as the Society for the Prevention and Elimination of Discrimination and Stereotyping (SPEDS). This program highlights the uniqueness of individuals—their needs, abilities, values, ideas, beliefs, emotions, feelings, and forms of expression. Students are taught the complementary nature of differences. Dislike and prejudice are differentiated, as well as the costs of the latter to all human beings. These themes are raised in 36 suggested lessons using an activity-oriented, experiential approach. The SPEDS course was offered as one of two approaches. The other was an ethnic studies course. Careful evaluation using pre- and posttests showed the SPEDS approach to have more positive effects on attitudes than the ethnic studies course.

Most programs in multicultural education focus on accepting and respecting differences and recognizing similarities. Diverging from this is the concern of the Association for Values Education and Research at the University of British Columbia, which looks at issues of moral education. It sees multiculturalism as a moral concern, since it is concerned with how cultural minorities are treated and conflicts resolved. The distinction between cultural and ethical relativism is considered necessary in order to understand the moral principles basic to multiculturalism. Knowledge of the concepts of person, society, culture, prejudice, and stereotyping, and the ability to distinguish factual and value claims, are considered essential in the formulation of valid arguments and the testing of moral principles. From this perspective, what multicultural education lacks is a clearly defined moral stance. "Multicultural education must develop the modes of reasoning for arriving at rational judgement concerning how people of different backgrounds should be treated. The aim has to be one of developing beliefs and modes of reasoning by which we can make intelligent decisions concerning how the needs, interests, and feelings of people should be construed, and how conflicts of interest should be resolved" (Wright and La Bar, 1984, p. 118). This can be accomplished, it is maintained, through educational efforts that promote sound reasoning and develop in learners a concept of person, a sense of self-worth, a sense of society, and an understanding of such concepts as prejudice and stereotyping. This approach has the advantage of being applicable to all children. It makes neither saints nor villains of either majority or minority group. In a similar vein, Coombs argues: "Students must be helped to understand and appreciate that cultural differences are irrelevant to the determination of moral worth and fundamental rights, and that the principle of justice, or equal consideration of interests applies to all persons regardless of cultural background. Moreover, they must acquire a considered, defensible view of the nature of justice and know how to reason responsibly about justice of individual actions towards others as well as the justice of social institutions and practices" (Coombs, 1986, p. 12).

While values-education programs would seem basic to any sound educational initiatives, they lack the flair and visibility demanded of other overtly multicultural programs. They resemble the way in which true multicultural programs ought to be inconspicuously incorporated as part of the normal human experience in a culturally diverse society.

Despite the potential of multicultural education to transform mainstream society symbolically, it has thus far served as a melting pot on a slow burner. In this respect, its capacity to absorb, assimilate, and depoliticize minority students is considerable. It is therefore highly unlikely that Canadian schools promoting multicultural education will develop the "oppositional cultures which might provide the basis for a viable political force" promoted by Giroux (1983, p. 101). Nor is it likely that multicultural education can become a "form of resistance to oppressive social relationships," as Sleeter argues (1989, p. 59).

The preoccupation, albeit at the ideological level, with multiculturalism has given short shrift to the concerns of Native people as the original inhabitants of Canada. Including Inuit and those of mixed ancestry, the Métis, they constitute 2% of the population. No longer definable in physical and cultural terms alone, two legal categories ("status" and "nonstatus") serve to distinguish their claims to various rights. Natives of both categories number 300,000 and an estimated half a million respectively (Frideres, 1983). Subject to educational colonization, they have come to occupy a castelike position in Canadian society. In an attempt to modernize Native people and rid them of "undesirable cultural practices," most were converted to Christianity, their children were forcibly removed to residential or day schools away from the community, and they were forbidden the use of their home languages. Indian education, unlike that of other minorities, has been under federal control, reflecting the paternalistic notions of Natives as wards of the state. Under these circumstances, Native people's lack of identification with mainstream education, and the extraordinarily high dropout rate of Indian children, seem a logical consequence of educational colonization. Suffice it to say that the history of Native education runs counter to all that multiculturalism purports to value.

In the literature on multicultural education, however, native Indian education has largely been ignored. This may have happened for several reasons. Indians are construed as an integrated part of what constitutes indigenous Canadian culture. Like the flora and fauna, Natives are portrayed as natural fixtures, frequent objects in biased social studies curricula (Werner et al., 1980). For most immigrants, a country of origin still exists as a manifestation of a viable culture. For Natives, on the other hand, the material basis of a cultural tradition has been drastically altered, so that Indian culture is seen as putative rather than real, relegated to the museum rather than being an everyday world. While early Indian folklore and mythology have been glorified, contemporary Indian life is widely stereotyped in pathological terms. Loss of fluency in their language of origin, which mainstream educational institutions have both directly and implicitly aided, is then cited as evidence for the absence of an enduring culture worthy of preservation, like those of other groups. The fact that Indian education is federally controlled and financed has served to act as a legitimate reason to ignore to some extent the need for concern about the group at the crucial regional level. Added to this is the suspicion with which First Nations people have viewed multiculturalism: as a mechanism that undermines their substantial rights by including them as one among "other" groups.

Antiracism Education

Neo–Marxist-inspired antiracism as the supposed radical alternative to multiculturalism must nonetheless be questioned for its implications and contradictions. Antiracism as an approach, though a British import, has permeated the Canadian discourse and is often coupled with multicultural education. So much has it become part of establishment parlance that almost every institution has had some form of multicultural education/antiracism program, whatever that may mean in practice. Furthermore, the Ministry of Multiculturalism in its allocation of funding takes those grant applications that promote an antiracism thrust far more seriously than those that uncritically embrace multiculturalism. So sanitized has the term *antiracism* become that most senior administrations of universities have initiated the establishment of some variant of race relations policies.

Antiracism education, in contrast to a consensus-based multicultural education, seeks to understand individual and group experiences within institutional and power structures. It attempts to comprehend the social and political relations embedded in internal logic (which is itself taken for granted) of educational institutions. Diversity itself is not seen as a problem. It is the significance or lack of significance attached to "difference" that poses questions about the locus of power.

Antiracism education aims to raise levels of individual and group consciousness through the development of critical thinking to grasp and question the rationality of domination and inequality. As Ungerleider (1986) has argued:

While there is little doubt that some discrimination in educational contexts is the result of stereotyping and prejudice, there is another equally plausible explanation for discrimination . . . in that discriminatory treatment accorded people who belong to particular categories is a rational response to an environment in which social and economic resources are scarce. (p. 11)

Through a knowledge and understanding of the history of racism, the process of conquest, and the different forms of domination, antiracism education promotes political education. The ultimate aim is transformation and a restructuring of the relations of dominance. Consequently, involved activism of major actors in education—teachers, staff, and students—is considered crucial. For Sefa-Dei, the challenge for the antiracism educator is to increase student awareness about "the contrast between the promise of equality offered by the school system and the actual production of inequality through the structures of schooling and of how all should work together for social transformation" (Sefa-Dei, 1993, p. 41).

The shift from multicultural education to antiracism education is from a preoccupation with cultural difference to an emphasis on the way in which such differences are used to entrench inequality. Antiracism education draws attention to the difference between the rhetoric of multiculturalism and its practice. The prime concern of antiracism initiatives is with systemic discrimination in all its manifestations, ranging from the treatment of minorities in history to the hidden curriculum of schools. A dynamic rather than static view of culture characterizes this approach. Instead of a preoccupation with the "customs of the past," antiracism education looks at the ways in which people transform their lives and respond to injustice, especially through various forms of collective action. In the school curriculum, antiracism has sometimes been implemented by incorporating representative selections of appropriate literature, oral histories, biographies, music, poetry, and art. In so doing, the lived experiences of all children are maximized and made part of "school knowledge" (Thomas, 1984). Ann Manicom analyzes how knowledge is filtered and the ways in which written materials enter into students' constructions of particular ways of understanding the world. By examining curriculum in use, she elucidates curriculum as ideology to explore the relationship among ethnic inequality, culture, and class, and whether structural functionalism or Marxism provide

more meaningful explanatory frameworks. Multicultural curriculum is contrasted with working-class curriculum materials, each of which provides students with different ways to name the world and different image repertoires by which they understand (or misunderstand) sets of social relations within which they live their lives. Manicom raises the question, "Which materials are accorded authoritative status in the schools?" (Manicom, 1984, p. 101). The shared interests of people along class lines are emphasized in contrast to their "primordial" ethnic ties. In light of its political, controversial nature, however, teachers have been somewhat reluctant to venture in this direction, unless mandated and supported by school boards. This is most evident in Ontario, where school boards in turn are being mandated by the provincial government to follow through on antiracism programs to promote sound race relations.

Of the few school boards that have included antiracism as part of their goal of multicultural education, Toronto and North York have led the way since the late 1970s, and Vancouver followed suit in 1982. Toronto and North York addressed manifestations of racism within the school system by establishing race relations subcommittees and by consulting school personnel, students, and the community.

A "total community approach" was advocated. The 1982 Vancouver School Board race relations policy brochure stated:

1. That the Board opposes and condemns any expression of racial/ethnic prejudice by its personnel, students and trustees.
2. That the Board [will] direct the Superintendent, in cooperation with all employee, parent and student organizations and trustees, to devise guidelines for the implementation of the race relations policy.
3. That the Superintendent [will] communicate . . . the Board's race relations policy and guidelines to all personnel and students . . . [and] the entire school community . . . [and] methods will be devised at the school level whereby school personnel make employee, parent and student organizations aware of the policy . . . and . . . steps taken to implement it. . . .
13. That the Board [will] direct the Superintendent to encourage Vancouver schools to develop programs within and among schools to increase multicultural understanding. Such programs should involve all school personnel as well as students and parents. (Vancouver School Board, 1984, p. 1)

Schools were requested again in 1983 to submit detailed plans on how they might implement the district's race relations policy. Along with this request was included a reminder that "each school's action plan be a cooperative endeavor of the school staff, school consultative committee, racial/ethnic groups represented in the student population, and the student councils of secondary schools" (Vancouver School Board, 1984, p. 2). The responses of 83 schools indicated that most made a verbal commitment to an integrated, community-inclusive approach.

In the Fisher and Echols (1989) *Evaluation Report on the Vancouver School Board's Race Relations Policy*, many teachers were reported to be dissatisfied with the way in which the policy was communicated to them. Both parents and teachers requested more information about the policy. The action plans submitted were for the most part words without thoughts. Concerns were expressed about the racial and ethnic imbalance in the teaching force. Whereas most administrators and teachers denied the existence of prejudice and racism, some were concerned about "Canadian culture not being valued sufficiently" and that a "culture relations" policy might be more appropriate (p. 182). Overall, this case study indicates that the mere existence of policies should hardly give cause for complacence. The reality clearly lies in implementation and careful evaluation of the outcomes.

Advocates of multicultural education of both reformist and radical persuasions continue, with great commitment, to engage themselves in institutional transformation. They have argued for increasing numbers of visible minority teachers in the teaching force. Justifications range from the value of visible minority teachers as role models, to their greater sensitivity to the needs of minority children, to their ability to engage White teachers to confront their own prejudices (Elliston, 1977).

Several schools in Ontario refer to themselves as antiracist schools. One of these is Flemington School in North York, Ontario. Of its 400 students, approximately 70% are Black. Most students in the school come from lower-income families. In this instance, antiracism was used by the North York board as a way to meet the challenge faced by making school experience an effective one. Proactive measures were introduced to increase representation of staffing from other ethnic groups, to translate report cards into twelve languages, to use interpreters for important parent-teacher communication, to establish a successful home reading program for students for whom English is either a second language or a dialect, and to increase contacts with community agencies who run school support programs. Innovative curriculum programs to increase self-images of all students and improve their skills and competencies are also being implemented.

A few other schools under the Toronto Board of Education have also begun to establish themselves as antiracist schools. Among the steps taken have been comprehensive staff development, identification of bias in curriculum materials, research into approaches to build self-esteem in students, and the development of measures to deal with racism (Tator & Henry, 1991).

The strengths of antiracism education over multicultural education lie in its incorporation of historical analysis, its differentiated discussion of how different groups experience racism, and the interconnections it draws among different kinds of oppression such as gender and racial oppression. Analysis from this perspective engages with structural racism and identifies how it affects people of color differently.

On the other hand, more sophisticated versions of multicultural education assume an antiracist focus as well. They recognize that schooling cannot be viewed as independent of the social context in which schools are located. Consequently, they too analyze racism within economic, political, and ideological contexts and deconstruct the ways in which marginalization of some groups takes place and is perpetuated.

Although antiracism education is a supposedly radical critique of liberal multiculturalism, it is increasingly suspected of being reductive in five areas.

1. It reduces racism to color discrimination and thereby tends to overlook racism based on other ethnic markers. However, color-related racism is in a special category insofar as it does not allow individual or second-generation escape from discrimination as normally occurs with the stigmatization of European immigrants with a different language or religion.

2. Antiracism portrays racism as exclusively perpetrated by Whites against Blacks. Moreover, as Sarup points out, "it treats all Whites as racists" (Sarup, 1991, p. 40). Supremacist attitudes and ethnocentricism are not confined to Whites but constitute a universal phenomenon. Asian cultures such as the Japanese display ethnochauvinism against the Burukumin, Koreans, and Europeans; similarly, in Burundi and Liberia, Africans discriminate against other Africans, and Hutus decimate Tutsis in Rwanda. The argument that the supremacist attitudes of minorities do not constitute racism, because their powerlessness does not cause any harm, must also be questioned. Therefore, the implied assumption of antiracism—as Palmer (1986) states, "that all white people and only white people are, and cannot but be racists" (p. 149)—is inaccurate. This is not to deny that there is a place for antiracism programs, but they should address a much more pervasive ethnocentrism and all that entails.

3. Since "race" represents a nonscientific, imagined construction, the essentialist focus on race, as Peter Li states, "is reified, or treated as though it were a concrete form, which it is not" (Li, 1990, p. 7). In this respect, a polarizing color consciousness may exacerbate the very stigmatization that antiracism aims to destigmatize.

4. In exclusively blaming "institutional racism" for minority disadvantage in education, dogmatic antiracism blinds itself to other causes of inequity, such as group-specific histories and traditions. The incongruence of what such traditions motivate in everyday private life and what is required and regarded in public institutions lies often at the heart of minority failure. To discredit such reasoning as "deficit" or "deprivation" models merely ignores the predicament but does not disprove it. It is also possible that minority students are actually discouraged by the antiracist emphasis on an all-pervasive institutional racism and the usual gap between reality and the opposite claims of progressive institutions. If the curriculum, the teachers, and the whole capitalist system is by definition racist, why should a minority student identify with such a hostile environment? Why should a minority student aim at high achievement in a system that is set up to serve other interests and permanently marginalize minorities? The antiracist institutional reductionism matches that of the orthodox Marxist explanation of racialism as a necessary and expedient condition of capitalism, as if ethnochauvinism was absent in the societies of "really existing socialism." This cautionary note, however, does not counsel against confronting institutional racism wherever it can be clearly identified (Mansfield & Kehoe, 1993).

5. Finally, by lumping together various immigrant groups under the label *Black* in Britain (and *visible minorities* in Canada), antiracism falsely assumes that all designated minorities identify with the label and see themselves in terms of color. Paul Gilroy (1992) criticized this practice in education for trivi-

alizing "the rich complexity of Black life by reducing it to nothing more than a response to racism" (p. 60). At least as important as the variations within each group are the obscured differences between the visible minority components.

POLICY TRENDS IN RACE RELATIONS

The debate about race relations climaxed in the 1984 report on visible minorities entitled *Equality Now* (House of Commons, 1984). The report has significantly influenced the national debate on multiculturalism, particularly on issues related to affirmative action. It is a landmark in the ongoing controversy about immigration policy and race relations in Canada. The extensive cross-country hearings by an all-party committee of the House of Commons chaired by Liberal MP Bob Daudlin resulted in 80 recommendations on new policies, from social integration, to employment, to changes in the legal and justice system, to media representations, and to educational issues. The report received the almost unanimous endorsement of ethnic organizations and is difficult to ignore.

Despite the widespread support for this imaginative and well-intentioned blueprint, many reservations have been forthcoming from voices that dislike a multiracial immigration policy in the first place, not to speak of special considerations for disadvantaged visible minorities. However, the report also raised fundamental questions to be asked even by those who will benefit from this progressive state intervention.

From a sociological perspective the most startling shortcoming of the report lies in its treatment of visible minorities as more or less monolithic. Aboriginal people, Blacks in Nova Scotia, and Chinese and Indo Canadians in British Columbia are subsumed under the concept "visible minority communities." While a common bond may lie in their exclusion, the histories of these four major visible groups in Canada are so different, their expectations and claims so varied, and their experience of and reaction to discrimination so distinct that the common denominator of "visible minorities" makes the formulation of a common policy problematic. In addition to these intergroup distinctions, there are significant intragroup differences that make the racial label meaningless, except to those who have invented it. The crucial distinction between ethnic and racial groups is not adequately dealt with by the report. Ethnic characteristics based on cultural heritage or common territory are usually considered worthy of preservation by group members as long as their individual identity is bound to this origin. In this sense, Aboriginal people form an ethnic group or a "First Nation" whose visibility merely overlaps with ethnicity. The same applies to religious or language groups.

Unlike ethnicity, however, racial characteristics have no intrinsic social significance of their own. Racial characteristics acquire salience because of discrimination. Exclusion serves as a bond only as long as discrimination lasts. In and of themselves, racial classifications have no more meaning than eye or hair color. The conceptual confusion in advocating multiracialism as a component of multiculturalism (House of Commons, 1984) is evident. Nonracialism, but not multiracialism, can be a worthy ideal. Color blindness, however, remains the logical outcome of "eradicating racism." To aim at both—multiracialism and the eradicating of racism—is surely an unrecognized contradiction. If one wishes to combat racism and achieve color blindness as much as possible, one cannot simultaneously "activate positive racial attitudes" (House of Commons, 1984, p. 124). All racial attitudes, whether positive or negative, represent stereotypes. Positive multiracialism is a dangerous supplement to a praiseworthy multiculturalism because it heightens invidious racial perceptions, whereas multiculturalism is rightly silent on the question of race.

The report failed to distinguish between immigrants and conquered or colonized groups. Visible minorities in Canada belong to both categories. The far greater portion of the estimated 1.9 million "visibles" (7% of the population) can be found in the immigrant category, while the Aboriginal people or Blacks in Nova Scotia (who migrated as slaves or escapees from U.S. slavery) would be examples of colonized or conquered segments.

There are two important differences between the two categories:

1. Conquered people can lay legitimate claims to restitution for past injustices. Native people in particular can evoke ownership rights to land and other symbolic resources. Visible immigrants do not possess such entitlement. The state does not owe immigrants anything more than equal rights.
2. Colonized people often form what anthropologist John Ogbu (1978) refers to as "caste-like minorities." They have, until recently, internalized their stigmatization. Given insurmountable societal barriers, a self-fulfilling prophecy reinforces low expectations, which lock many members of these groups into a vicious circle of poverty, underachievement, low status, and general anomie. Voluntary immigrants in search of economic improvement may face barriers, but not to quite the same extent as castelike minorities. With the backing of an extended family, insulation through another language (which enables messages of self-worth to resist societal low-status definitions), and a culturally transmitted work ethic of high motivation, many Asian immigrants to Canada soon outperform the average member of the dominant group.

On both grounds (entitlement to restitution and need) a good argument can therefore be made that colonized minorities in Canada and, above all, Native people both deserve and need affirmative action programs, while this is not so for visible immigrants. It is simply not self-evident that the statistics about "missed opportunities to education and job skills" characterizing Aboriginal people are "applicable to other visible minorities as well" (House of Commons, 1984, p. 133). The report recommended, for example, that "post-secondary institutions need to identify recruitment procedures which encourage more visible minorities to take advantage of their programs" (House of Commons, 1984, p. 133). If this advice were to apply to Canadian students of South and East Asian origin, and if the U.S. situation (where detailed racial statistics are kept) is any guide, Canadian universities would most likely find that students from the two largest visible groups (Chinese and Indo

Canadians) would be proportionally overrepresented, at least in certain disciplines. If an ill-advised racial quota system were to apply, it could in fact be used to restrict such upward mobility, since the racist backlash would want to claim its proper quota. In 1994 this was indeed the case.

Affirmative action for Asian Canadians and other visible immigrants can hardly solve continuous racism. On the contrary, a good case can be made against affirmative racial action in that it perpetuates invidious distinctions by attaching advantage to them. Affirmative action institutionalizes race. Visible minority groups will perceive a strategic value in classifying themselves as racially distinct as long as a quota favors them in the market over competitors. The proposed changes require a racial categorization of the population. This was stated in a matter-of-fact manner in the report, as some items to be included in the census. Nowhere is the morality of requesting information about racial descent questioned. Once census data on invidious distinctions are collected, both the racists and their victims find more justifications for fortifying the barriers. How liberal philosophy, which traditionally espouses universalism and the unity of humankind, can lend itself to the official racialization of Canadian society remains problematic. Where are the lines to be drawn for children of "mixed" marriages? Will the immigrants from the Middle East qualify for visibility, or will they have to undergo a test for skin fairness? When the entire civilized world abhorred the now-abandoned compulsory race classification laws of South Africa, an official report in Canada, published in 1984, was interpreted by some to have institutionalized voluntary apartheid.

The shortsightedness of such a policy is evident in the counterproductive implications for those members of visible minorities who succeed in the absence of affirmative action. They will have to cope with the suspicion that they owe their position more to the color of their skin than to their merit, whereas when the report was published those who had made it were accepted as having reached their position on their own, despite racial obstacles. Once this certainty is removed, all members of visible minorities will labor under the suspicion of incompetence and psychological insecurity. They will be restigmatized through the very efforts meant to destigmatize visibility.

TRANSLATING POLICY INTO PRACTICE

How have the conceptual frameworks for promoting racial and cultural equity discussed earlier been translated into programs and practices within the educational process? In many major Canadian cities such as Toronto and Vancouver during the past 15 years, the numbers of students who learned English as a second language have increased dramatically. Over 50% of students now fall into this category. Many of these children are subject to assessments of one form or another to establish their appropriate placement within the school system. These demographic changes pose important questions for educational institutions. Cummins (1987b) asks appropriately:

To what extent are typical IQ tests culturally and linguistically biased against minority children? How can a psychologist tell if a student's

learning difficulties are due to a genuine learning disorder as opposed to a lack of proficiency in English? How long should educators delay psychoeducational assessment for such students and what are the implications of delaying the assessment for students who have genuine learning problems? (p. 115)

In Canada, the answers to these questions are not reassuring. Surveys reveal that few boards of education have policies regarding assessment and placement of culturally and linguistically atypical students (Samuda & Crawford, 1980). Cummins's analysis of 400 psychological assessments of non-English-speaking children in a western Canadian city is revealing. Despite the fact that in a large number of these assessments "no diagnostic conclusions were logically possible ... this fact was seldom admitted by psychologists" (Cummins, 1987b, p. 115). Bias in testing continues to prevail and is said to account for the fact that minority children perform very much below norms on the commonly used Wechsler Intelligence Scale for Children-Revised (WISC-R). Decades of discussion about cultural and class bias seem to have barely touched practice. In this respect Canadian schools hardly fare better than schools in the United States. Furthermore, unlike in the United States, in Canada public discussion of these issues seldom appears in either academic journals or popular publications (Cummins, 1987b).

In a comprehensive survey sponsored by the Ministry of Multiculturalism, Tator and Henry (1991) examined effective initiatives in curriculum, pedagogy, professional development, personnel practices, and school and community relations. The survey aimed at monitoring and evaluating the "state of the art" relating to multiculturalism, race relations, and antiracist education in Canada to serve as a resource to those committed to multicultural change and racial and ethnic equity. Respondents from ministries, boards, schools, professional associations, and parent and community groups were interviewed in four provinces. The authors argue that resistance to moving beyond the concept of multicultural education as celebration of culture and ethnicity hampers progress in addressing critical issues. Over the past decade,

multicultural education ... provides only a veneer of change rather than a transformation of educational processes and institutional structures. The most pressing challenge is a recognition and response to the racial barriers which permeate the educational process, impacting upon curriculum, assessment and placement, pedagogy, hiring and promotion practices and the "ethos" of the school environment. (p. iii)

What is evident is that the existence of multicultural policies does not ensure sound practice. Many activities of institutions dealing with equity issues took place without a race relations or multicultural policy. This confirms Anderson and Fullan's (1984) findings that the relationship between policy and implementation of programs is not linear or hierarchical; it can be interactive and incremental. Action can inform policy and either point to or provoke institutional change.

Quite valuable too are the lessons that can be drawn from the Toronto Board of Education's evaluation of its race relations program, which revealed ways in which "the 'system' and the institutional arrangements within the board served to hinder the implementation of the race relations program" (Tator &

Henry, 1991, p. 139). In this instance, the major barriers to effective policy implementation were (ironically) located in the existing collegial culture—which relied on the professional integrity of colleagues, making accountability and monitoring difficult, giving short shrift to planned, focused direction in favor of discretionary interpretation—and reliance on overbureaucratized reporting lines and ineffectual program communication.

CONCLUSIONS

Much of the ambiguity surrounding the policy of multiculturalism also applies to multicultural education. It incorporates notions of cultural pluralism, special needs, and, more recently, antiracism as a change of attitudes. Underlying these, a sense of cultural harmony is pervasive but overlooks the prime goals of equality of opportunity and equality of condition.

Rosen's 1977 conceptualization of "culture" is still implicit in most views underlying multicultural education as practiced in 1994. Though the rhetoric has changed, practice has hardly been radically transformed. Culture is seen as a set of more or less immutable characteristics attributable to different groups of people. These are used to identify people and often produce stereotypes, contrary to intention (Rosen, 1977; Fisher & Echols, 1989). The notion of culture that the Royal Commission on Bilingualism and Biculturalism (1969) espouses as an afterthought under the heading "The cultural contributions of other ethnic groups" reveals a lyrical fiction that bears little resemblance to minority reality. "Culture," the commission waxes, "is a way of being, thinking and feeling. It is a driving force animating a significant group of individuals united by common tongue and sharing the same customs, habits and experiences" (p. 11). If one takes the public definition of the two most stigmatized ethnic minorities in Canada, Native people and "East Indians," neither of the cultural attributes fits their experience. Native people are united neither by indigenous languages nor by customs and habits. So-called Indo Canadians, who arrived in Canada from four continents and as members of three world religions (Hinduism, Christianity, and Islam) and various subjects (e.g., Ismailis, Sikhs, Protestants), are even more divided in the ideological lenses they use to interpret different experiences. What unites all groups, regardless of origin, is not an alleged common culture but common exposure to manifold discrimination and common experience as "outsiders." It is this experience of conflict with and uneasy accommodation to mainstream culture that unites the minorities.

Past ideological formulas for making sense of a different social environment in precolonial America or postcolonial India do not always offer a useful guide for coping with Canadian challenges, apart from giving minorities a sense of dignity to contrast with their low status in their country of adoption. Maintaining cultural heritage uncritically can be a hindrance rather than an aid to meaningful survival. The cultural baggage of immigrants is continually examined for what is useful and meaningful in the new society, and some aspects are discarded

as being culture-specific to another place and time. The outcome of this process leads to a new ethnicity that has little in common with the reified notion that official multiculturalism intends to preserve; nor is it identical with melting into a dominant mainstream.

The extension of welfare state provisions, together with the much more diverse ethnic and occupational composition of immigrants since the late 1960s, has created a new ethnicity in Canada. This is reflected in a much greater variety of adaptation and accommodation on the part of newcomers and hosts alike, which in turn amounts to a new Canadian cultural configuration for educational policy.

It is this dynamic aspect of culture that is everywhere visible and yet ignored. Seemingly homogeneous groups are in fact disparate, are at different stages of acculturation, are geographically dispersed, hail from different parts of the world, and represent a tremendous array of regional, linguistic, and religious varieties. Above all they seem unified only by their goal of success in mainstream society. There are few societies that better illustrate Malinowski's view that culture contact produces a third cultural reality for immigrants, one that is neither the immigrant's original culture nor the new host culture (Malinowski, 1945).

The complex problem of perpetuating different cultural traditions within the school in a pluralistic configuration is evident. Foremost is the challenge to teachers as inauthentic agents of cultural transmission. Expecting teachers to communicate cultural content from highly complex cultures without reifying, fragmenting, and trivializing them to the ridiculous is problematic. This is not to deny the need for teachers to come to terms with their own ethnocentrism and to have knowledge of the cultural backgrounds of their students. However, as Kirp (1979) points out, the paths to be avoided are a descent into mindless multiculturalism and a determined effort to preserve the past for the sake of preservation.

Education about different cultures need not imply a challenge to the hegemony of mainstream education. In South Africa, for example, ethnically based education has been used to limit the aspirations of subordinated groups. As Dhondy and others in Britain have argued about the history of the Raj in India, "Two hundred years of rule may have bred a complete understanding of Indian civilization, culture and habits, but this understanding did not alter the structure of Empire" (quoted in Stenhouse, Verma, Wild, & Nixon, 1982, p. 18). Similarly, Jones and Kimberly suggest that uncritical use of multiculturalism has been seen as a way of defusing conflict and pacifying vocal members of affected minorities (cited in Tierney, 1982).

While knowledge of other cultures is important for teachers, on balance it is clearly less important than the concern about race issues—how racism permeates society and the school through teacher attitudes, negative racial images, and racial bias in schools and society (AFFOR, 1983). Teacher attitudes stand out as a crucial concern. Indeed, an unbiased teacher working with biased materials within an ethnocentric curriculum may well be preferable to a biased teacher working with multiethnic learning materials and teaching ethnic history (AFFOR, 1983). Insensitive, naive use of aspects of non-Western cultures that are nonfunctional in Canada can just as easily undervalue and ridicule heritages out of context, thereby entrenching their second-class status. As Kirp (1979) maintains, it is in fusing what deserves to endure with the contribution of the present that the educational system will most effectively respond to the issues of race.

On the whole, competence, not culture, is the major concern of minority-group parents. While the two are not mutually exclusive, it is foremost the mastery of modern knowledge, as well as the retention of functional aspects of their own traditional knowledge, to which the parents most aspire (Musgrove, 1982). The former serves their instrumental, survival needs, which are the priority in the country of adoption, and the latter their expressive needs, for which they themselves assume responsibility. Whereas diverse cultural inclusion in the school curriculum is an important device for raising the self-concept of minority children, most minority parents see their children as educationally deprived rather than culturally deprived. In this respect there has been a tendency to overstate low self-concept as a cause of minority children's failure (Stone, 1981; Musgrove, 1982). On the other hand, we overlook the fact that self-concept emerges not only from cultural recognition but also from being able to have greater mastery over one's life.

What most minority parents want for their children is not condescending teaching of fragmented, diluted versions of their culture, taught secondhand by an inauthentic group member. They expect committed, demanding teaching aimed at the mastery of basic skills and the success in English, math, and science required to survive in the new home country. In many instances these expectations were the prime reasons for leaving the country of origin. Musgrove (1982) articulates a similar view for minorities in Britain:

What "other cultures" want from us many would see as most worthy, distinguished, and indeed central in our educational tradition (though perhaps a little old-fashioned)—high moral teaching and good learning: a sense of values and a strenuous disciplined pursuit of knowledge. . . . The arguments are educational, the imperialism pedagogic. (p. 180)

Along the same lines, Maureen Stone (1981) pointed to progressive multicultural teaching as contributing to West Indian children's failure in adapting to child-centered teaching and learning approaches. Quoting Gramsci, she stressed the need for minority children to acquire dominant forms of knowledge in order better to challenge it.

In these instances, despite the cultural differences of the minorities studied, immigrants' conflicts with dominant society and the system of education are about pedagogies. This overrides cultural differences. It is clear, then, that cultural content in the school curriculum takes second place to other forces that stand in the way of academic achievement. The most successful communities are those that have taken cultural and religious education into their own hands while entrusting public schools with training for the marketplace. Asian communities in Canada are examples of such groups.

What does this leave for schools to do with the multicultural curriculum? It does not prevent teachers from having information and awareness of the cultural backgrounds of pupils in order better to diagnose strengths, weaknesses, and differences in cognitive styles. It assumes that students who choose to learn their language of heritage should be given a chance to do so. It still calls for active antiracism awareness—for examining teacher expectations and detecting stereotyping and bias in school materials. It calls for appreciation of diversity in curricula material, but integrated thematically in a global perspective and not as an end in itself. These basic achievement aspirations are the substance that all minority groups share, transcending the specific differences of country of origin, language, religious affiliation, or race.

The promises of multiculturalism in Canada will depend on the ways in which an informed multiethnic education is located in the broader economic, political, and social structures.

References

AFFOR (All Faiths for One Race). (1983). *Issues and resources: Handbook for teachers in a multicultural society.* Birmingham: Russell.

Anderson, J., & Fullan, M. (1984). *Policy implementation issues from multicultural education at the school and board level.* Toronto: Ontario Institute for Studies in Education.

Ashworth, M. (1992). Projecting the past into the future: A look at ESL for children in Canada. In K. A. Moodley (Ed.), *Beyond Multicultural Education: International Perspectives* (pp. 114–131). Calgary: Detselig.

Banks, J. A. (1993). Multicultural education: Historical development, dimensions, and practice. In L. Darling-Hammond (Ed.), *Review of research in education* (Vol. 19, pp. 3–49). Washington, DC: American Educational Research Association.

Banks, J. A., & Clegg, A., Jr. (1990). *Teaching strategies for the social studies: Inquiry, valuing and decision-making* (4th ed.). New York: Longman.

Barman, J., Herbert, Y., & McCaskill, D. (1989). *Indian education in Canada: Vol. 1, The legacy; Vol. 2, The challenge.* Vancouver: University of British Columbia Press.

Batelaan, P. (1987). Intercultural education in Europe: Policy development dilemmas. In K. McLeod (Ed.), *Multicultural education: A partnership* (pp. 231–236). Toronto: Canadian Council for Multicultural and Intercultural Education.

Bhatnagar, J. (1982). Language and cultural maintenance programmes in Canada. In C. Bagley & G. Verma (Eds.), *Self-concept and multicultural education* (pp. 165–175). London: Macmillan.

Bibby, R. (1987). Bilingualism and multiculturalism: A national reading. In L. Driedger (Ed.), *Ethnic Canada: Identities and inequalities* (pp. 158–169). Toronto: Copp Clark Pitman.

Bourassa, R. (1975). Objections to multiculturalism [letter to Le Devoir, 17 November 1971]. In H. Palmer (Ed.), *Immigration and the rise of multiculturalism* (pp. 25–26). Toronto: Copp Clark Publications.

Bredella, L. (1993). Towards a pedagogy of intercultural understanding. *American Studies, 37,* 559–594.

Buchignani, N. (1982). Practical strategies to foster inter-racial harmony through the educational system. In V. D'Oyley (Ed.), *Perspectives on race, education and social development: Emphasis on Canada.* Vancouver: University of British Columbia, Center for the Study of Curriculum and Instruction.

Bunner, P., & Ingram, M. (1990, April 9). Reconsidering the mosaic. *Alberta Report,* pp. 8–10.

Burnet, J. (1975). *The definition of multiculturalism in a bilingual framework.* Paper presented at Conference on Multiculturalism and Third World Immigrants, Edmonton.

Burtonwood, N. (1986). *The culture concept in educational studies.* Windsor, England: The Nfer-Nelson Publishing Co.

Byram, M. (1986). Cultural studies in foreign-language teaching. *Language Teaching, 19*(4), 322–336.

Coombs, J. (1986). Multicultural education and social justice. In J. H. Knoll (Ed.), *International year book of adult education* (pp. 1–13). (Sonderuck). Köln: Bohlau Verlag.

Cummins, J. (1984). Heritage languages and Canadian school programmes. In J. R. Mallea & J. C. Young (Eds), *Cultural diversity and Canadian education* (pp. 477–500). Ottawa: Carleton University Press.

Cummins, J. (1987a). In Center for Research Education and Innovation (Ed.), *Multicultural Education* (pp. 303–330). Paris: OECD.

Cummins, J. (1987b). Psychoeducational assessment in multicultural school systems. *Canadian Journal for Exceptional Children, 3*(4), 115–117.

Cummins, J., & Danesi, M. (1990). *Heritage languages: The development and denial of Canada's linguistic resources.* Toronto: Garamond Press, Our Schools-Ourselves Education Foundation

Day, E., & Shapson, S. (1981). *Multiculturalism: A survey of school districts in British Columbia.* Burnaby, B.C.: Simon Fraser University.

Economic Council of Canada. (1991). *Faces in the crowd.* Ottawa: Author.

Elliston, I. (1977). *Racial attitudes and racial violence in school and community in metropolitan Toronto.* Toronto: Metropolitan Task Force on Human Relations.

Fisher, D., & Echols, F. (1989). *Evaluation report on the Vancouver School Board's race relations policy.* Vancouver: Vancouver School Board.

Fisher, D., & Echols, F. (1992). School action plans and implementation of a district race relations policy. *Canadian Ethnic Studies, 24*(1), 58–78.

Fishman, J. (1989). *Language and ethnicity in minority sociolinguistic matters.* Clevedon: Multilingual Matters.

Fleras, A., & Elliott, J. (1992). *Multiculturalism in Canada.* Scarborough, Ontario: Nelson Canada.

Frideres, J. S. (1983). *Native peoples in Canada* (2nd ed.). Scarborough, Ontario: Prentice-Hall, Canada.

Frideres, J. S. (1990). Policies on Indian people in Canada. In P. S. Li (Ed.), *Race and ethnic relations in Canada* (pp. 98–119). Toronto: Oxford University Press.

Friessen, J. W. (1993). The politics of multiculturalism in the United States and Canada. *Multicultural Education Journal, 11*(1), 2–8.

Gibson, M. A. (1976). Approaches to multicultural education in the United States: Some concepts and assumptions. *Anthropology and Education Quarterly, 7,* 7–18.

Gibson, M. (1988). *Accommodation without assimilation: Sikh immigrants in an American high school.* Ithaca, NY: Cornell University Press.

Gilroy, P. (1992). The end of racism. In J. Donald & A. Rattansi (Eds.), *Race, culture and difference* (pp. 49–68). London: Sage.

Giroux, H. (1983). *Theory and resistance in education: A pedagogy for the opposition.* South Hadley, MA: Bergin & Garvey.

Glazer, N., & Moynihan, D. P. (1963). *Beyond the melting pot.* Cambridge, MA: MIT Press.

Handford, E. (1993). Heritage languages in Manitoba public schools: 1870–1993. In K. McLeod (Ed.), *Multicultural education: The state of the art national study* (Report #1, pp. 40–43). Toronto: University of Toronto, Faculty of Education.

Grant, C., & Sleeter, C. (1985). The literature on multicultural education: Review and analysis. *Educational Review, 37*(2), 97–118.

Hawkins, F. (1972). *Canada and immigration: Public policy and public concern.* Montreal: McGill, Queens University Press.

Hebert, Y. (1992). Multicultural education and the minority language child. *Canadian Ethnic Studies, 24*(3), 56–63.

Henley, R., & Young, J. (1992). Multicultural teacher education, part 1: Faculties of education and state policies of multiculturalism. *Multiculturalism, 2*(1), 17–19.

Herskovits, M. J. (1948). *Man and his works.* New York: Knopf.

House of Commons. (1971). *Debates.* Ottawa: Government Printer.

House of Commons. (1984). *Equality now.* Ottawa: Queen's Printer.

Innis, H. R. (1973). *Bilingualism and biculturalism.* Toronto: McLelland and Stewart and Information Canada.

Jaenen, C. (1977). Multiculturalism and public education. In J. D. Wilson (Ed.), *Policy and process: Perspectives on contemporary Canadian education* (pp. 77–96). London: Alexander Blake.

Jenness, D. (1963). *The Indians of Canada* (Anthropological Series, No. 15). Ottawa: Queen's Printer.

Kallen, E. (1987). Multiculturalism, minorities and motherhood: A social scientific critique of section 27. In Human Rights Foundation (Ed.), *Multiculturalism and the charter: A legal perspective* (pp. 123–138). Toronto: Carswell.

Katz, P. (Ed.). (1976). *Toward the elimination of racism.* New York: Pergamon Press.

Kehoe, J. (1984). *A handbook of selected activities for enhancing the multicultural climate of the school.* Vancouver: University of British Columbia, Western Education Development Group.

Kehoe, J., and Mansfield, E. (1993). The limitations of multicultural education and anti-racist education. In K. McLeod (Ed.), *Multicultural education: The state of the art national study* (Report #1, pp. 3–9). Toronto: University of Toronto, Faculty of Education.

Kirkness, V. J. (1987). Indian education: Past, present, and future. *AURORA: The Professional Journal of the Northwest Territories Teachers, 5*(1), 7–10.

Kirkness, V. J. (1992). First Nations house of learning: A case of successful transformation. In K. A. Moodley (Ed.), *Beyond multicultural education: International perspectives* (pp. 264–280). Calgary: Detselig.

Kirp, D. (1979). *Doing good by doing little: Race and schooling in Britain.* Berkeley: University of California Press.

Li, P. S. (1990). Race and ethnicity. In P. S. Li (Ed.), *Race and ethnic relations in Canada* (pp. 3–17). Toronto: Oxford University Press.

Magsino, R. (1985). The right to multicultural education: A descriptive and normative analysis. *Multiculturalism, Multiculturalisme, 9*(1), 4–9.

Malinowski, B. (1944). *A scientific theory of culture and other essays.* Chapel Hill: University of North Carolina Press.

Malinowski, B. (1945). *The dynamics of culture change.* New Haven: Yale University Press.

Mallea, J. R. (1984). Cultural diversity in Canadian education. In R. J. Samuda, J. W. Berry, & M. Laferriere (Eds.), *Multiculturalism in Canada: Social and educational perspectives* (pp. 78–100). Toronto: Allyn and Bacon.

Mallea, J. R. (1989). *Schooling in a plural Canada.* London: Multilingual Matters.

Mallea, J. R., & Young, J. (Eds.). (1984). *Cultural diversity and Canadian education.* Ottawa: Carleton University Press.

Manicom, A. (1984). Ideology and multicultural curriculum: Deconstructing elementary school texts. In J. Young (Ed.), *Breaking the mosaic: Ethnic identities in Canadian schooling* (pp. 75–103). Toronto: Garamond Press.

Manitoba Ministry of Education. (1980). *Language education.* Winnipeg: Ministry of Education.

Mansfield, E., & Kehoe, J. (1993). *A critical examination of anti-racist education.* Unpublished paper, University of British Columbia, Vancouver.

Masemann, V. (1984). Multicultural programs in Toronto schools. In J. R. Mallea & J. Young (Eds.), *Cultural diversity and Canadian education* (pp. 349–369). Ottawa: Carleton University Press.

McCarthy, C. (1990). *Race and curriculum.* London: Falmer Press.

McLeod, K. A. (1981). *Multiculturalism and multicultural education: Policy and practice* (Canadian Society for the Study of Education, eighth yearbook; pp. 12–16). Saskatoon: University of Saskatchewan.

McLeod, K. A. (1984). Multiculturalism and multicultural education: policy and practice. In R. J. Samuda, J. W. Berry, & M. Laferriere (Eds.), *Multiculturalism in Canada: Social and educational perspectives* (pp. 30–49). Toronto: Allyn and Bacon.

McLeod, K. A. (1992). Multiculturalism and multicultural education in Canada: Human rights and human rights in education. In K. A. Moodley (Ed.), *Beyond multicultural education: International perspectives* (pp. 281–302). Calgary: Detselig.

Ministry of Education [British Columbia]. (1992). *Year 2000: A framework for learning.* Victoria: Ministry of Education.

Mock, K. (1988). Toronto Chinese Canadian bilingual bi-cultural program. In Multiculturalism & Citizenship Canada (Ed.), *Access to education in a multicultural society* (pp. 29–31). Ottawa: Minister of Supply and Services Canada.

Moodley, K. A. (1981). Canadian ethnicity in comparative perspective. In J. Dahlie & T. Fernando (Eds.), *Ethnicity, power and politics in Canada* (pp. 6–21). Toronto: Methuen.

Moodley, K. A. (1983). Canadian multiculturalism as ideology. *Ethnic and Racial Studies, 6*(3), 320–331.

Moodley, K. A. (1984). The ambiguities of multicultural education. *Currents: Readings in Race Relations. 2*(3), 4–7.

Musgrove, F. (1982). *Education and anthropology: Other cultures and the teacher.* Toronto: John Wiley.

Ogbu, J. (1978). *Minority education and caste.* New York: Academic Press.

Ontario Ministry of Education. (1988). *Changing perspectives: A resource guide for race and ethnocultural equity, K-13.* Toronto: Ministry of Education.

Ontario Ministry of education. (1989). *Ontario schools intermediate and senior divisions.* Toronto: Ministry of Education.

Ouellet, F. (1992). Education in a pluralistic society: Proposal for an enrichment of teacher education. In K. A. Moodley (Ed.), *Beyond multicultural education: International perspectives* (pp. 281–302). Calgary: Detselig.

Palmer, F. (1986). Moral understanding and the ethics of indignation. In F. Palmer (Ed.), *Anti-racism: An assault on education and value* (pp. 32–42). London: Sherwood Press.

Palmer, H. (Ed.). (1975). *Immigration and the rise of multiculturalism.* Toronto: Copp Clark Publications.

Peter, K. (1981). The myth of multiculturalism and other political fables. In J. Dahlie & T. Fernando (Eds.), *Ethnicity, power and politics in Canada* (pp. 22–29). Toronto: Methuen.

Porter, J. (1972). Dilemmas and contradictions of a multicultural society. *Transactions of the Royal Society of Canada, Series 4, Vol. 10,* 193–205.

Radcliffe-Brown, A. R. (1952). *Structure and function in primitive society.* London: Routledge and Kegan Paul.

Rosen, D. (1977). Multicultural education: An anthropological perspective. *Anthropology and Education Quarterly, 8*(3), 25–32.

Royal Commission on Bilingualism and Biculturalism. (1969). *Bilingualism and Biculturalism,* Book 4. Ottawa: Queen's Printer.

Ryan C. (1975). Biculturalism or multiculturalism? In H. Palmer (Ed.), *Immigration and the rise of multiculturalism* (pp. 26–27). Toronto: Copp Clark Publications.

Samson, A., Yellin, C., & Mercer, J. (1987). Peer helping human relations. In I. Brown & S. Samson (Eds.), *Graduate race relations awareness and community experience* (pp. 11–15). Scarborough, Ontario: Scarborough Board of Education.

Samuda, R., & Crawford, D. (1980). *Testing, assessment, counselling and placement of ethnic minority students.* Toronto: Ministry of Education.

Sanders, D. (1987). Article 27 and the aboriginal peoples of Canada. In Human Rights Foundation (Ed.), *Multiculturalism and the charter: A legal perspective* (pp. 155–166). Toronto: Carswell.

Sarup, M. (1991). *Education and the ideologies of racism.* Stoke-on-Trent, U.K.: Trentham Books.

Schwartz, G. (1977). *Survey of Métis and non-status Indians: National demographic and labour force report.* Ottawa: Native Council of Canada and Canada Employment and Immigration Commission.

Secretary of State. (1988, May 30). *Multiculturalism* [News release]. Ottawa: Ministry of Multiculturalism.

Sefa Dei, G. J. (1993). The challenges of anti-racist education in Canada. *Canadian Ethnic Studies, 25*(2), 36–51.

Shapson, S., & D'Oyley, V. (Eds.). (1984). *Bilingual and multicultural education: Canadian perspectives.* Clevedon: Multilingual Matters.

Shapson, S., & Purbhoo, M. (1977). A transition program for Italian children. *Canadian Modern Language Review, 33,* 486–496.

Sleeter, C. (1989). Multicultural education as a form of resistance to oppression. *Journal of Education, 171*(3), 51–71.

Spicer Commission. (1991). *The citizen's forum on Canada's future: Report to the people and government of Canada.* Ottawa: Canadian Government Publication Center.

Statistics Canada. (1982). *Immigration statistics.* Ottawa: Queen's Printer.

Stenhouse, L., Verma, G., Wild, R., & Nixon, J. (1982). *Teaching about race relations: Problems and effects.* London: Routledge and Kegan Paul.

Stevenson, H., & Wilson, J. D. (1977). *Precepts, policy and process. Perspectives on contemporary Canadian education.* London, Ontario: Blake.

Stone, M. (1981). *The education of the Black child in Britain: The myth of multiracial education.* Glasgow: Fontana.

Sullivan, H. (1988). *A legacy for learners: The report of the Sullivan Royal Commission on education.* Victoria: Queen's Printer.

Tator, C., & Henry, F. (1991). *Multicultural education: Translating policy into practice.* Ottawa: Ministry of Multiculturalism.

Thomas, B. (1984). Principles of anti-racist education. *Currents, 2*(3), 20–24.

Tierney, J. (Ed.). (1982). *Race, migration and schooling.* London: Holt, Rinehart and Winston.

Titley, B. (Ed.). (1990). *Canadian education: Historical themes and contemporary issues.* Calgary: Detselig.

Ungerleider, C. (1986). Problematic aspects of multicultural education. Unpublished manuscript.

Vancouver School Board. (1984). *Report on school multicultural action plans 1983–84.* Vancouver: Program Services.

Verma, G., & Bagley, C. (Eds.). (1982). *Self-concept, achievement and multicultural education.* London: Macmillan.

Werner, W., Connors, B., Aoki, T., & Dahlie, J. (1980). *Whose culture? Whose heritage? Ethnicity within Canadian social studies curricula.* Vancouver: University of British Columbia.

Wilson, J. D. (1984). Multicultural programmes in Canadian education. In R. J. Samuda, J. W. Berry, & M. Laferriere (Eds.), *Multiculturalism in Canada: Social and educational perspectives* (pp. 62–77). Toronto: Allyn and Bacon.

Wright, I., & La Bar, C. (1984). Multiculturalism and morality. In S. Shapson & V. D'Oyley (Eds.), *Bilingual and multicultural education: Canadian perspectives* (pp. 112–129). Clevedon: Multilingual Matters.

Young, J. (1979). Education in a multicultural society: What sort of education? What sort of society? *Canadian Journal of Multicultural Education, 4*(3), 5–21.

Young, J. (Ed.), (1984). *Breaking the mosaic: Ethnic identities in Canadian schooling.* Toronto: Garamond Press.

47

MULTICULTURAL EDUCATION IN GERMANY:
HISTORICAL DEVELOPMENT AND
CURRENT STATUS

Gerd R. Hoff
FREIE UNIVERSITÄT BERLIN

History haunts Germany. This is particularly crucial to consider when examining its recent national heritage. Of course, there are victory columns and national monuments from imperial times all over the country like anywhere else in Europe; some of them have even been carefully restored after the damages of World War II. But they tell of victories washed out by the defeat of the 1914–18 war. This war was begun out of exuberant nationalistic feelings strongly experienced in all major European nations. Only war could show who was the most eminent and predominant of all. The result was millions of young lives from all sides butchered and gassed on the battlefields, and the economies of all nations involved on the brink of collapse. Victory was for the Entente. On each side one ally broke away beforehand, with some encouragement by the respective foes: Italy to develop the first fascist empire in the modern understanding and Russia to become the Soviet Union, the model state for the dreams of socialist revolutionaries all over the world for the next 70 years.

Austria-Hungary and Germany were the losers. The emperors resigned. New nation-states were founded or regained independence after centuries of Prussian, Austro-Hungarian, or Russian imperialism. Poland was re-created by cutting off East Prussian territory from mainland Germany, a reason for endless quarrels in the future. Large German minorities in Bohemia became subjects of the newly constructed double state Czechoslovakia, later providing an excuse for the "legitimacy" of Hitler's territorial claims against this country in 1938. In 1993, free to express their own wishes for the first time in history, the Czech Republic and Slovakia decided to separate peacefully into two independent states, a decision that neglects the existence of Moravia and the large Hungarian minority in Slovakia.

The Versailles treaty did not only punish the losers of the war. By neglecting ethnic and cultural structures among the many minorities in eastern and southeastern Europe and by enforcing new states and borders without regard to languages, religious traditions, and cultural heritage, it laid the foundation for the violent ethnic conflicts Europe experiences today in the countries of the former Yugoslavia. Austria itself was diminished to a few tiny provinces in the Alps and along the river Danube. No longer a threat as an empire, Germany had to bear the entire blame for this war. Losing it was evidence that the whole war was Germany's fault in the first place and the Germans had to take all the responsibility.

What was still left to German national pride, after having to fulfill the harsh conditions of the Versailles treaty, were outstanding cultural achievements in all fields of the arts and sciences. For half a decade Berlin was not only the largest metropolis in Europe but the world center of theater, fine arts, music, and film, equaled only by New York City. This can be attributed to the multicultural structure of this urban society, which, due to the political instability of the time, was given the opportunity to flourish. For the first time there was a chance to break down class structures and religious barriers. Unfortunately, no one recognized this, and these opportunities were lost for the future. Everybody pitied their own miseries instead: The barons were stripped of their nobility, the industrial tycoons of their war profits and markets, the military ranks lost their armies, the middle-class landlords, craftsmen, and shop owners lost their property due to inflation, the workers their jobs due to recession. The political parties blamed each other, but there was also a desperate need for scapegoats. In foreign policies the victorious nations could be blamed, especially France, which kept vast former German territories occupied, and the newly founded states in the east, Czechoslovakia and Poland, which had been part of the old Habsburg or Prussian empires. Inside the country the lucky few seemed to be the most mobile people who were flourishing under the given conditions in a world of changes, immigrants such as Czechs, Poles, and German Jews. Here the root of the fascist conspiracy theory can also be found, making all Jews members of a well-organized "international merchant class," the first principle of the later denial of German citizenship to Jews according to the Nuremberg Laws in 1935.

Hitler and his Nazi party detected their chance and took over. Driven by hatred, racism, and megalomania, they forced scientists and artists into emigration or put them into concentration camps to be tortured and finally extinguished in the gas chambers, together with Jews, communists, socialists, Gypsies, and homosexuals, being of "inferior race," or *entartet* (degenerated). Their work was banned from publication, burned, or otherwise destroyed. The majority of the German people voted in favor of racial superiority, brutal power, war, and conquest of Europe.

The "1,000-years-empire" of the Nazis lasted 12 years and gained defeat, embarrassment, and humiliation. More than 55 million people died during this war, more than 6 million as victims of Nazi race politics. About 11 million lost their regional homes and became refugees inside the considerably reduced territory of their own country. Not only 4.2 million soldiers but more than 8.5 million German civilians died (Michaelis, 1965), as the survivors were made responsible for the world's crudest atrocities. They and their children had to cope with Germany's moral and economic burden of reparation for having disregarded elementary human rights.

GERMANY SINCE 1945

The generation growing up in Germany after 1945 could do nothing but hope that their own parents, loved ones, and neighbors might not have been involved, knowing very well that this could hardly be the case but trying to suppress this knowledge. They had to build or rebuild identities after the model of the victors.

The people living in the zone occupied by the Soviet Union, which became the German Democratic Republic (GDR) in 1949, were urged to copy the "big brother": "To learn from the Soviet Union means to learn to be victorious" was one of the most popular slogans flying on red banners in the streets of every East German town for four decades to come. The German Democratic Republic, the "worker's and farmer's" state, had been according to the Communist Party the state of those oppressed by Nazi terror. The few remaining fascists in East Germany who were not killed in the war or didn't flee to join the "people's enemy," West Germany, were now safely locked away in the very same prisons and camps they had been running before. Interaction with people of different cultural backgrounds meant meeting the "masters," the Soviet army and counterintelligence, who were above the law, and meeting delegations of socialistic brother-nations in peace or work camps or exchange schemes, because the planned economy could not cope with spontaneous visits.

As the economy of East Germany became more prosperous, the Communist party (SED) began to finance "international solidarity" programs, which brought over students and workers from countries such as Cuba, Vietnam, and Angola. However, these migrants were kept isolated in secluded quarters; they came as single men and women and were forbidden to marry. While citizens of the German Democratic Republic were given the official slogan "workers of the world unite," and they had to pay contributions to international solidarity programs, in everyday life they were discouraged from mixing with "foreigners."

In the western zones, which would develop later into the Federal Republic of Germany (FRG), the catchwords were *Entnazifizierung* and *Demokratisierung,* which basically meant an enormous reeducation program, controlled by U.S. and, to a much lesser extent, British and French military personnel and civil servants. Those who were allowed to participate in West Germany's political affairs were restricted to "OdF.s" (victims of fascism) and "Unbelastete" (those who were not politically involved in the Nazi regime), which meant rather old or very young, "unimportant" or perhaps some clerical people. It was wise for the public to concentrate on rebuilding houses, factories, and farms, ignore the past, pay lip service to the idea of reunification in freedom, and fight communism, as this meant relevant economic support by the U.S. government.

The consequences were, of course, not only to be found in the differing political systems of the two German states, but the official cultural systems also differed. For example, in schooling, East Germany invented a new centralized comprehensive system based on the ideas of socialistic Weimar reform pedagogues. West Germany stuck with the old imperial system of class-related threefold streaming in secondary schools. They started school reforms much later, influenced by the results of educational and social science research from the United States. East Germany kept more of the national cultural traditions, while West Germany identified the idea of a German nation with the Third Reich and was officially eager to develop a European identity. As a result, the people in the West identified with their "Land," their federal state, and understood themselves as, for example, Bavarians or Lower Saxonians. East German citizens finally learned to be proud to be German again, as their economic and technical development became one of the most advanced among the Communist countries.

In literature, East Germany cultivated the heritage of the work of socialist writers persecuted by the Hitler government—Becher, Bloch, Brecht, Heinrich Mann, Seghers—while West Germany primarily adopted modern American, French, and British authors and reestablished dubious personalities such as Benn, Bergengruen, and Hesse. Equal developments could be named in other branches of the arts, until both states developed their own genuine artists. In the aftermath of an unsuccessful workers rebellion in the GDR in 1953, West Germany attracted successful artists from the East who fled or were expelled. But it never happened the other way around, although some people moved to the East for ideological reasons, particularly after large international World Youth festivals in the 1950s.

MINORITIES, REFUGEES, AND IMMIGRANTS IN GERMANY

There are small indigenous minorities (Danes, Frisians, and Sorbes) living in Germany. They are well protected by special legislation and have been settled in their native regions for many centuries. They face few problems, are fully bilingual, get much support in mother-tongue education at school—if they are interested at all—and are well accepted in their federal states of origin. But there are smaller groups of people who have been victims of xenophobia or even racism in Germany. Most prominent among them are the Native Travellers (Sinti or Roma). In contrast to the few Jewish survivors, German gypsies never received compensation for their suffering in Hitler's concentration camps, and are likely to be considered "foreigners" even if their families have carried German passports for generations.

The immigrant population in Germany is either German or "foreign" and is specified according to official government papers and prominent sociological studies (Bade, 1992; Griese, 1984; Heckmann, 1981). Each group consists of two major subgroups. To understand the term *foreign* in this connotation requires a brief excursion into German semantics: Non-German immigrants are referred to as being "Ausländer," meaning someone who came from abroad. It does not matter when the person actually arrived. He or she might have been born in Germany and might speak no other language than German, but so long as at least one parent is not German, a person is considered a "foreigner" by law. This is particularly the case in the common understanding of people if there are any visible differences. That is why, for example, Black Germans, who in the 1980s founded their own association, report that even when they do not face open hostility or aggression they are always asked about their country of origin, because in the common understanding no Black person can be German. That is the reason why some of them, mostly descendants of German mothers and American or French fathers who served in the army in Germany, seriously consider emigration to Paris, London, New York, or other metropolitan areas outside Germany. They want to protect their children from the same experiences that they had to endure.

The term *immigrant* is not frequently used in everyday language, as neither the German constitution nor government policies define Germany as an immigration country, although it would be the only correct term according to sociological terminology.

Germans

The two major German subgroups are refugees and resettlers.

Refugees (Flüchtlinge). This term refers to an estimated 12 million people who, as a consequence of World War II, were expelled from former German territories in Czechoslovakia, Poland, and Russia between 1945 and 1989 (the fall of the Berlin Wall), and 4.4 million people who went from former East to West Germany (Hessler, 1993). Although there have always been difficulties in integrating these minorities, which include an additional 650,000 who moved to the West until unification (October 3, 1990), this group is not relevant for this study (figures: Dann, 1993, p. 337).

Resettlers (Aussiedler, literally, ex-settlers). These are people of German origin mainly from the former Eastern block countries of the Soviet Union, Romania, and Poland, meaning descendants of families who immigrated to Eastern Europe and Inner Asia to settle in sparsely populated areas centuries ago. Their identification as German was reinforced by the Nazi government in the early 1940s. Suppressed and sometimes deported by communist authorities after the war, they were encouraged to claim exit visas by the German refugee organizations. Welcome as strictly anticommunist, conservative voters, they received permission to leave their countries by only about 10,000 a year (Otto, 1990). In 1990, after the collapse of the Warsaw Pact system, the number arriving in Germany reached a high of nearly 400,000. During the economic recession of the early 1990s, they were no longer welcome in their "fatherland." The German government was eager to organize arrangements that would allow resettlement of these groups inside Russia and prevent them from returning to the main country (Blaschke, 1985). However, this only reduced the rate to an estimated 230,000 in 1991 and 1992 (figures: "Ein einig Volk," 1993). These people, arriving in large families, have very little command of German, but they are eager to integrate and to learn. They understand themselves to be German, although they are often discriminated against as aliens, due to their recognizable Slavic accents. But they fit quite well into the system, which attempts to support their assimilation in German state schools. As a result, their children are achieving well in secondary education.

"Foreigners"

The groups listed below are the most important subgroups of the *Ausländer* population.

Guest Workers (Gastarbeiter). Between 1961 and 1973 West Germany was eager to recruit workers from abroad, particularly for unskilled and physical labor, and found them in the poor Mediterranean countries in southern Europe and in Turkey. From the mid-1950s the already booming West German economy recruited the growing workforce mainly from refugees from East Germany and native Germans from Poland and Czechoslovakia. This came to an abrupt halt in 1961 when the Iron Curtain was closed and the Berlin Wall was built. In 1960 there were some 300,000 "foreigners" working in the Federal Republic (1.5% of the total workforce). In 1973 the number increased to 2.6 million (about 12% of the workforce), a cause for the German government—the world economy being shaken by the "oil crisis"—to impose a virtual ban on new recruitment from outside the EEC. But this had a paradoxical effect. Knowing that they would lose their work permits if they left Germany for more than 3 months, many hitherto itinerant "guest workers" simply decided to settle there and have their wives and children join them. Single female workers, having earned a dowry, returned to their home countries only to get married, in this way offering an opportunity for their husbands to follow. As the ban succeeded in reducing the numbers of active foreign workers to 1.6 million in 1987, the overall Turkish population rose from approximately 1 million in 1974 to more than 1.6 million in 1989, at the time of the fall of the Berlin Wall. Family dependents in the early 1990s accounted for 60% of the total "immigrant" population, whereas in the 1960s some 90% of the workers were single (all data according to Ardagh, 1991; Herrmann, 1992a; Statistisches Landesamt Berlin, 1992).

One third of today's non-German population in Germany is Turkish; one third is made up of the other guest-worker minorities from Yugoslavia, Greece, Italy, Spain, and Portugal; and all other nations make up the rest. About 68% of the Turks and more than 86% of the Spaniards in Germany have lived there for more than 10 years. But Germany has one of the lowest levels of naturalization of any Western country: Only about 0.5% of resident foreigners a year become German citizens, compared with 2% in Britain, 1.2% in France, and 5.2% in Sweden (Ardagh, 1991, p. 288).

Here lie the roots of the very problem German schools are facing in trying to provide educational programs for the children of immigrants and guest workers. Given the large numbers of people who are unsure of how long they will remain in Germany, it is extremely difficult to define the core subjects and major goals of education. Politicians, teachers, parents, and children are undecided as to whether pupils in school should be prepared to succeed in the German society or in their country of origin (Hoff, 1992).

Asylum Seekers (Asylbewerber, Asylanten). The Bochum sociolinguist Link points out that the specially created word *Asylanten* has a completely negative connotation in the German language. Subconsciously the user thinks of someone superfluous, troublesome, and annoying (Link, 1986). The law demands that the duration of the stay for asylum seekers must be terminated. For school authorities in more or less all federal states this was a welcome excuse to provide no schooling at all or only on a voluntary basis for children whose parents were insisting. In the beginning of the 1990s, due to the pressure of immigrant organizations and teacher unions, schools were forced at least to accept children of asylum seekers. Until then the excuses of shortage of staff and packed classrooms were frequently used by reluctant principals.

As a consequence of the remorse and shame felt by the generation who survived the atrocities and barbarism of the racist Nazi government, the fathers of the West German "Basic Law" provided a basic right of political asylum to anyone who enters German soil and asks for it. It is then a matter of a legal procedure in a lengthy court case, including the right of appeal, until it is finally decided whether the individual applicant is a political refugee or an "economic" one. The latter would have to leave the country again but would not be expelled forcefully

if humanitarian reasons—for example, a (civil) war taking place in his or her home country—would prevent it. While the case is being heard, which can easily take up to 3 years or more, the asylum seeker is put in a camp or hostel at public expense. The money is provided, neither by the federation nor the state, but by the local authorities. That is the reason why all asylum seekers are allocated according to a quota system and very often end up in remote rural areas. People in these areas, especially in the former East German states, might not have seen a non-German person for generations except for military personnel or foreign forced laborers during the Nazi government. To protect the German labor market, the asylum seeker was not allowed to work for the first 5 years. This law, which was changed in 1991, caused tensions to grow as Germans, quite often on low incomes themselves or in danger of losing their jobs, saw the asylum seekers as a group of "strangers" on camp sites without any links with the local community, living on "our" money.

In the late 1970s the number of asylum seekers was already in the tens of thousands. After the fall of the Warsaw Pact system, the numbers increased drastically to 256,000 in 1991. This means that Germany accepted 309 asylum seekers for every 10,000 inhabitants (many of them coming from the war-ridden former Yugoslavian countries) compared to only 70 in the United States, 58 in the United Kingdom, or 5 in Denmark or Norway (Herrmann, 1992b).

As it can be taken for granted that conflicts between established citizens and newcomers are intensified when there is chronic unemployment and increasing inflation, there is a particular problem posed by the facts that Germany is a welfare state and state support of refugees adds to the national debt. Enzensberger (1992, p. 41) points out that "in contrast to America, where no newcomer can count on a social net to catch him, the inhabitants of Germany can claim minimal safeguards of . . . social security. But the welfare state puts ever-increasing pressure on the economy and . . . its long-term financing is uncertain."

THE GERMAN SCHOOL SYSTEM

Like the United States, Germany is a federation. The old Federal Republic consisted of 11 states; after unification 16 states were created, ranging from the small city-state of Bremen with just over half a million inhabitants to Northrhine-Westfalia with over 17 million. All states are independent as far as cultural affairs, in particular schooling, are concerned. There is a federal body, the conference of the 16 state ministers, for schooling, but, as all their resolutions have to be decided upon unanimously, very little is agreed upon for matters that concern the whole of Germany. Full-time schooling is compulsory for ages 6 to 16, followed by (minimum compulsory) 2 to 4 years of vocational part-time schooling and job apprenticeship. The latter can be replaced by three years of academic second-level secondary schooling, which leads to the only German schools' final examination, the "Abitur," a state examination, which is the necessary entrance certificate for all university or other third-level higher education studies.

More than 90% of all German schools are run by the state. The teachers, in life-long contracts working as civil servants, are fairly well paid but without any right to industrial action. The private schools, most of them owned by the two major Christian confessions, are controlled by the state inspectorate and are allowed to hire only those teachers who have passed the obligatory two state examinations.

There are two lower final certificates students can receive at the end of schooling depending on the school they are sent to for secondary education: Hauptschul- or RealschulabschluB (general school or technical middle school). This qualifies them to enter the training-qualification procedure for different jobs (e.g., shop assistants, hairdressers, masons, auto mechanics, or, on the other hand, bank clerks, legal assistants, nurses, technical staff, etc.).

The obligatory subjects in all states are German language and literature, mathematics, history and social sciences, sports, one foreign language for 5 years (mostly English), music or arts, and at least one natural science. Everything else varies: there is a certain range of preschool/infant education; primary school lasts for 4 or 6 years; some states offer the fifth and sixth grade in special schools as intermediate advancement training (*Förderstufe*).

There is a streaming system consisting of three types of secondary schools.

- The Gymnasium (high school and college), leading to the Abitur and considered of the highest status, operates for 7 to 9 years.
- The Realschule (technical middle school) is run for either 4 or 6 years but is not offered in all states.
- The Hauptschule (general secondary school) is run for either 4 or 6 years and has to take in all pupils who have been rejected by the first two school types because of underachievement. It offers two leaving certificates, an ordinary and a more advanced one, in natural sciences, languages, and mathematics. It ' possible, however, to leave this school without any certificate. As pupils are not necessarily promoted to the next grade every year, it is sometimes necessary to repeat a grade. Some may even leave, after 10 years' schooling, from a lower grade without any certificate.

In competition with this system there are the following schools.

- The Gesamtschulen (comprehensive schools) follow the "setting" principle. They offer all or at least two of the possible final certificates. Some schools start at primary level. Therefore they run for either 4, 7, 9, 12, or 13 years. But they are offered only in states that are or have been under the control of Social Democratic governments.
- Day and evening classes in adult education offer courses to gain final certificates in a later stage of life. Without these documents one is not entitled to any type of apprenticeship and can only take on unskilled labor or work freelance.

There is little doubt that a "setting" system of school organization, like the one on offer in comprehensive schools, is more favorable to pupils who have to adjust themselves to a different country. It is much easier to arrange supportive and introductory courses in this sort of system. That is why immigrant children do significantly better in states and communities where comprehensive schools are available (H. Thomas, 1987, p. 41). However, it is the streaming system in secondary education that has given schooling in Germany international recognition, and teachers, parents, and government ministers are largely in favor of schools that don't introduce setting.

Immigrant parents, who in many cases have little command of German and no personal experience of German schooling, very often assume that there is always time to decide later about the schooling career of their sons or daughters. To the contrary, the system asks them to make a final decision when their children are only 10 (or in some states 12) years old. Although parent counseling has improved during recent years, there are still too many parents who are left unprepared to make these early decisions about their children's schooling.

Another common problem affecting immigrant children is that it is possible to leave school earlier in many of the countries of origin of those who have come as "guest workers." For example, in Turkey, by far the largest contributor to Germany's ethnic pupil population, students can leave school when they are as young as 12 or 13 years old. As it is unlawful in Germany to keep children below the age of 16 away from school, and parents are forced to pay fines and face possible deportation if they disregard the law, adolescents between 12 and 15 are often forced back into the schooling system without any possibility of gaining qualifications. As a result, boys who may have been working for up to three years in Turkey are constrained to return to full-time schooling in Germany with, understandably, very little motivation.

POLICIES RELATED TO MULTICULTURAL EDUCATION

As Germany has always understood itself to be a monocultural country, there was initially little room for unpopular multicultural approaches to school organization and/or curriculum. Depending on whether the states are more likely to be exclusively governed by the Conservative Party (CDU) or the Social Democratic Party (SPD), there have been considerably diversified attempts to cope with the task of schooling a permanently increasing number of immigrant students.

Although there are some differences in interpretation of goals to be achieved, it is possible to outline four main approaches to providing education for children speaking a first language other than German. Not necessarily all of them can be defined under the heading of multicultural education.

Separation policy—providing national schools, classes, or lessons for larger homogeneous groups of pupils, mainly offered to children of the main groups of the "guest-worker" population (Turks, Yugoslavs, Greeks, Italians).
Assimilation policy—compensatory approaches providing single or group tuition to help children with language "prob-

lems" (i.e., not speaking and understanding German) to acquire quickly the necessary skills to follow the teaching provided for German children in schools. This was and still is summed up under the concept of *Ausländerpädagogik* (education for foreigners).

Cooperative policy—emancipatory approaches trying to establish cultural identity, guarantee mother-tongue alphabetization, modify general curriculum toward a multicultural representation of values, offer introduction into all major and the locally represented religions, very often focusing on bicultural comparison. The term used in Germany and most (non-English-speaking) Western European states is *intercultural education*.

United Europe policy—with the beginning of the 1990s, a new variation developed in some states that are controlled by Conservatives but influenced by other coalition partners: *Kulturübergreifende Erziehung* (literally, education overarching cultures). The focus of this approach is Europe, replacing old nationalism with new Eurochauvinism. There are already two factions quarreling, those who will focus only on member states of the EEC and those who want to integrate others, basically Eastern European countries. There are intrinsically racist elements within this latter group who are intending to exclude all non-Europeans, meaning non-Caucasian, non-White, and non-Christian people.

HISTORY OF MULTICULTURAL EDUCATION IN GERMANY

Migrant workers were encouraged to come into Germany by the hundreds of thousands between 1961 and 1973 (1960: 280,000 foreign workers in the Federal Republic; 1973: 2.6 million; figures: Herrmann, 1992a). In the beginning they were working on short-term contracts and were determined to go back to their home countries as soon as they earned a substantial amount of money. But after 1973, when the ban was imposed on new recruitment and it was no longer possible to move back and forth easily, they asked their families to come to Germany.

For school authorities and teacher education in Germany there consequently developed a massive problem: What should be done with all these children who speak languages other than German and who are asking for schooling? The demand created by having "foreign" students compose between 50 and 80% of the student population in a local elementary or main secondary school (Hauptschule) met a completely unprepared educational community (Nieke, 1984).

There was not even a major tradition of teaching German as a second language (GSL). Unlike the United States, Germany does not understand herself as an immigration country; there was no obligation deriving from colonial traditions either, in contrast to the United Kingdom, France, and the Netherlands. As a result there was only a limited demand for learning and

teaching German as a foreign language (GFL). The latter could be left easily to the specialists of promoting German culture abroad, the semiofficial German Institutes (Goethe-Institute) or the Deutscher Akademischer Austausch Dienst (DAAD: German International Academic Exchange Organization).

The percentage of immigrant children in German schools has developed as follows: 1960, 0.4%; 1965, 0.5%; 1970, no data available; 1973, 3.0%; 1975, 3.6%; 1990, 8.8% (Statistisches Bundesamt, 1992). To meet this sudden demand, activities had to be started on all levels: "Foreign" students were cushioned into preparation classes (*Vorbereitungsklassen*) and/or taken to special German-language courses (*Deutsch-Förderkurse*) to develop a basic understanding of German so students could follow the ordinary lessons at schools.

Teachers received no support or only brief training in the form of short in-service courses, very often given by those without any experience in education in schools or without sufficient knowledge about second-language acquisition. The self-made first generation of "multiculturalists," trainers as well as trainees, had nothing to rely on but the existing GFL educational programs. Not until the late 1970s did universities and teacher-training colleges try to generate projects in this field and implement GSL elements into basic teacher-training curricula. This was not only complicated because of the lack of instructors and qualified personnel, but it was difficult to establish funding at this time, above all because Germany did not accept the needs of multicultural education, still claiming not to be an immigration country. Gradually, specific textbooks and materials were developed for immigrants learning German as a second language.

In spite of these drawbacks, a few major projects developed in some universities, initiated by socio- or psycholinguists such as Johannes Meyer-Ingwersen in Essen (Meyer-Ingwersen, Neumann, & Kummer, 1977), Wilfried Stölting in Oldenburg (Molony, Zobl, & Stölting, 1978), and Norbert Dittmar (1979), Ulrich Steinmüller (1981), and Hans Barkowski (1982) in Berlin. But these focused largely on linguistic issues for immigrants (i.e., the "newcomers"), thus neglecting minority issues as well as antiracist perspectives. There was little teaching of special cultural needs for groups such as Turkish German pupils or intercultural learning for the mainstream German girls and boys. Multicultural education in the first stage dealt almost exclusively with GSL and with community language tuition.

At the same time, grass-roots neighborhood organizations, churches, unions, and sometimes communal authorities started a number of projects. Most common is the popular *Laden*, the small corner shop given up by the former owner for economic reasons. This exists in the poorer parts of the inner cities where the migrant-worker families have grouped themselves. It is obtained easily for cheap rent and is turned into an ethnic neighborhood center or as centers for special interests such as reading, for girls and women, or for children.

Comparative psycho- and sociolinguistic studies and research in language education have genuinely flourished due to a growing demand in Germany. For example, the Institute for Migration Research, Education for Foreigners, and Second Language Didactics at the University and Polytechnic Essen, an initiative of Boos-Nünning and Hohmann, was one of the first institutions to focus on research related to migrant workers and is currently the most influential research center in multicultural education in Germany. It distributes a yearly register of the publications of its members, dating back as early as 1975. The most recent edition (IMAZ, 1993) includes 523 entries, of which 149 are related to GSL, linguistics, and didactics of second-language acquisition. Another 41 publications focus on the minority languages of the "guest workers."

The many projects related to foreign- and second-language acquisition have attracted research and scholars from all countries and continents. The results are widely published among the English-speaking scientific community. However, the intentions of all these efforts have been compensatory. In the beginning, multicultural education in Germany was limited to technical support by official institutions to help newcomers function within the German community, to get along with German employers, bureaucracy, landlords, and shopkeepers. The very moment educational initiatives entered the ordinary classroom, a new educational term was born: *Ausländerpädagogik* (education for foreigners). It was closely related to special-needs education for mentally or physically disabled children. The "handicap" of the Turkish, Greek, or Yugoslav child was not to be German, and not to speak German. This meant that the child was not able to follow the German educational system.

On the other hand, there was the argument that enabling students to follow the German school curricula might make them unfit to adjust inside the societies of their origin, into which they were supposed to return one day. Consequently, the more conservatively governed German states encouraged separate schooling and/or afternoon classes in the mother tongue and the "home" culture of the "guest worker" children. The more liberal and social democratic governments favored the laissez-faire attitude corresponding to their understanding that a fundamental schooling according to the much more advanced German educational system would be useful everywhere in the world (DECS/EGT, 1986).

REVIEW OF CONCEPTUAL APPROACHES

It is questionable whether there is a German-only approach to multicultural education. While many publications reflect German views, the more relevant research is very often done in a European context (Gundara, 1991), sometimes by non-German scientists residing inside the country or in other European states (Castles, 1987). At the same time, it is very difficult to describe the academic work done in multicultural education in Germany because of the general confusion about terminology (Klemm, 1985). *Interkulturell* as well as *multikulturell* were at first used to distinguish methods different from *Ausländerpädagogik*, an assimilative approach, which was translated into English as "multicultural education." The term *interkulturelle Erziehung* (intercultural education) was strongly influenced by European authorities, especially the Council of Europe Education Project No. 7 group (DECS/EGT, 1986), as it

was used in many European countries as a term denoting an integrationist approach to the schooling of immigrant children. The Paris-based scholar L. Porcher used it as early as 1976. The term was also conceptually linked with the cultural enrichment doctrine of the Council of Europe group, which helped to mastermind the founding of the International Association of Intercultural Education (IAIE) in the Netherlands.

The term *multicultural* was adopted from British, North American, and Australian publications and originally used in Germany by authors who rejected the culturalist perspective of intercultural education and intended to stress structural inequalities between immigrants and Germans. As educational research in Germany generally relies on publications in other European countries and in North America, *multicultural* and *intercultural* became synonymous in the mid-1980s after the multicultural society became a major topic of the general political debate in West Germany.

The Berlin-based interculturalists defined their position in relation to those who favored "antiracist education" in Great Britain or the Netherlands but struggled for many years to retain the term *intercultural education*. This was because *racism* and *racist,* in the German language of West Germany, were reserved exclusively to describe anti-Semitic behavior and discrimination, especially during the era of Nazism. Only in the late 1980s, even more so after the unification, did it become possible to suggest that racist thinking and behavior exist in modern Germany. To challenge this development, some scholars such as Helmut Essinger (1991) prefer to describe themselves as "antiracist" educators; others remaining in the field of multicultural or intercultural education reflect antiracist goals in their work without explicitly changing their terminology—for example, Georg Auernheimer (1992) and Gita Steiner-Khamsi (1992).

The following review of research and projects in multicultural education will reflect schools of thought, trends, and controversial debate that have taken place over the last two decades in Germany. The work of the Marburg professor Georg Auernheimer has been particularly useful here, as he provided undergraduates and teachers with the first anthology in this field (1984) and published an extremely effective reader (1990), giving insight into the schools of intercultural education and offering the specialized scholar basic information about the neighboring disciplines in the field.

Main Positions in German Research

In December 1981 the first International Conference on Intercultural Education took place in Western Europe. Teacher educators, researchers, and senior civil servants in the educational sector gathered in Breukelen in the Netherlands and agreed that their highly industrialized countries had all become immigration countries, although not always with the consent of their respective governments and "indigenous" populations. The great challenge for education was here perceived as finding a means to provide for the needs of these growing multicultural societies. The conferees developed the idea of intercultural education, which was seen as a new pedagogical principle to be implemented in school curricula as well as in basic in-service training of teachers (Batelaan, 1983).

In West Germany at this time most scholars in the field of multicultural education were still determined to work within the framework of *Ausländerpädagogik*. However, in 1980 at the Department of Education at the Free University of West Berlin, the first Institute of Intercultural Education was founded by Ünal Akpinar, Helmut Essinger, Gerd Hoff, and Jürgen Zimmer. Here the emphasis was on creating new theoretical perspectives as well as practical projects that would develop materials for schools and promote exchanges with institutions in other countries. The universities in Bremen, Frankfurt, Giessen, Hamburg, and Oldenburg responded quickly and developed similar projects.

The universities in Germany's western industrial regions had an earlier start in responding to the lack of educational programs for children of immigrant workers. In Essen, at the university that is still today the most important center of research in this field in Germany (IMAZ—Institut für Migrationsforschung, Ausländerpädagogik und Zweitsprachdidaktik), and in cooperation with the teacher-training institutes in Heidelberg and Landau, major research projects started in the early 1970s in the field of *Ausländerpädagogik*. Ursula Boos-Nünning, Manfred Hohmann, Hans Reich, Hans-Peter Schmidtke, and Frank Wittek (founding members of the Essen-based ALFA group, a research and teacher-training center with a special emphasis on multicultural education) are among those who were first associated with this concept and were certainly the promoters of the first multicultural education programs (Hohmann, 1976), but in retrospect one can see that their early emphasis on assimilation created particular problems in the progress of research and development in the field.

It is difficult to allocate individual researchers of multicultural education to any of the particular approaches defined earlier if they have been working in the field since the early 1970s. Views have changed and developed over this long period of time. Also, as there is little funding available outside government resources in the field of education in Germany, much of the work largely reflects the state's position on immigration policy as it has gone through different stages.

For this reason the concept of *Ausländerpädagogik* is no longer represented among multiculturalists at the university level. Nevertheless, the old publications are still available and attractive to many teachers and educators as they reinforce the understanding of German society as homogeneous, monoracial, and monocultural.

MULTICULTURAL EDUCATION IN GERMANY TODAY

A group of researchers (Auernheimer, 1990; Friesenhahn, 1988; Marburger, 1991; Sayler, 1991) tried to identify the different multicultural educational concepts in Germany and cluster them into groups and historical phases. In doing this, it became clear that the very same people were associated with quite different categories because they might have developed one idea and changed their opinions according to the results of

their later research. However, Diehm and Kodron (1990) see four main positions that can define practitioners of language education and that can be usefully applied throughout the field: assimilative, integrationist, pluralistic, and antiracist.

Traditional Approaches

As discussed above, *Ausländerpädagogik* was subsequently shunned in research as compensatory and deficit oriented. That is why this assimilative approach to multicultural education is rarely used today.

However, there is a large group of "mainstream multiculturalists" following integrationist intentions. This is based on an understanding of Germany as an immigrant country, but one in which those who come to live from outside aim to develop the mores and customs of the host country in return for citizenship. This approach is promoted by politicians and political scientists from the Green Party (environmentalists) to the progressive faction of the Conservatives with their understanding of Germany as a multicultural society. There has been a flood of publications relating multicultural education to teacher training (Frey, Piroth, & Renner, 1982; Sandfuchs, 1981), to social learning in schools (Gondolf, Hegele, Pommerin, Röber-Siekmeyer, Schellong, & Steffen, 1983), to individual school subjects (Aissen-Crewett, 1989/90), to school records of immigrant children (Cummins, 1984), and to student exchange programs (A. Thomas, 1988).

The pluralistic approach in current research has been on the one hand attractive to scholars who were involved in the original *Ausländerpädagogik*. This was based on a new acceptance of immigrants' languages and cultures, which now became part of the schooling process. Leaders in this field included Boos-Nünning (Boos-Nünning, Hohmann, Reich, 1977), who specialized in vocational training of immigrants; Dickopp (1982), who masterminded the "Krefelder Modell" (cf. "Putting Multicultural Education into Practice" in this chapter); and Krüger-Potratz, who like many others, changed her perspective from her early studies of *Ausländerpädagogik* (1983) to that of intercultural studies (1987). On the other hand, this group also includes scientists who began their work from an intercultural perspective as well. They began new research to describe the problems of the paradigm "intercultural/multicultural" (Klemm, 1985), to implement results of the work done in other countries, and to focus on comparative studies (Flechsig, 1985; Hoff, 1991, 1992; Kodron, 1984).

Finally, there is a group of scientists who understand their work to be explicitly antiracist. They come most often from a background of political science, sociology, and philosophy, where, as already explained, the topics of race and racism have been restricted. Here for the first time we see a different perspective; the burden is taken away from the immigrant as the person who must "integrate"; instead, education for all must include an awareness and understanding of the "racist" structures of German society itself, its laws, its institutions, and its hierarchy. This all reflects a way of thinking derived from a belief that to be German you must have German parents, speak the language without a "foreign" accent, be White, and, in general orientation, Christian.

There are, of course, other categories that fall outside the above positions. Serious advocates of separation in education can be divided into different opposing groups. One group advocates national and/or religious schooling in order to preserve the values of the inherited culture of the immigrant population. Ironically, they meet the intentions of German nationalists and clerical conservatives who want to retain "German conceptions" and old values unspoiled by divergent cultures in their own schools.

On the other hand there are the representatives of bicultural education who often come from a background of linguistic research and are working to create an identity in the immigrant population that is bilingual and bicultural (Fthenakis, Sonner, Thrul, & Walbiner, 1985). In this process, children have to be separated from the mainstream society for parts of the day during school time, or for the early years of their upbringing, to communicate in their mother tongue and learn about the cultural heritage of the country of their families' origins (Auernheimer, 1990, p. 215).

Throughout the 1980s *intercultural* and *multicultural* became catchwords for a progressive approach to education (Hohmann, 1987), to German studies (Thum, 1986), to regional studies in foreign-language teaching (Schmidt, 1980), and to cultural studies (Maas, 1984), but it meant many different things to the people who advocated it. The formerly Germany-based Italian scholar Michele Borrelli, later professor in Wuppertal, published an article entitled "Intercultural Education: Exotic Education?" (1984). Ingrid Haller, another German scholar, titled her contribution to a major journal "Multicultural Is In!" (1991). Many German school practitioners began to fear the term (Fromeyer, 1993) and, based on a speech by the Berlin minister for school affairs, Laurin, given in 1983, began to compare multicultural education with "multifruit jam," which "only tastes sweet but doesn't allow any distinction according to taste" (H. R. Laurin, personal communication, September 18, 1983). Others coined the disparaging phase *multi-kulti* (Leggewie, 1990).

In examining the research done in this field, it becomes clear that there is very little representation from academic scholars from the immigrant communities themselves. Reasons for this include the fact that Germany sees itself as a nonimmigration country and has no race equality laws; discrimination against minorities, with the exception of Jews, is therefore not illegal. Also, professors at German universities are all civil servants, appointed by a state's minister for a lifetime. To qualify to become a civil servant you have to be a German citizen. There are very few exceptions, and these are totally at the will of the authorities involved.

Among the exceptions, the Berlin-based Turkish sociologist and political scientist Ünal Akpinar is the most senior scholar. Codirector of a research project in Bonn on the situation of "guest workers" in the 1970s, he was awarded a professorship in Berlin following his publication on aspects of Turkish socialization in relation to families and schools (Akpinar, 1976). Later he published social studies comparing the German and the Turkish situations for Turkish guest-worker families. As early as 1980, he discussed the approach of intercultural education in minority education (Akpinar, 1980). Other senior representa-

tives of this group are Wassilios Fthenakis in Munich, Hakki Keskin in Hamburg, and Faruk Sen in Essen. Keskin, a political scientist, and Sen, an economist, have a special focus on the integration of the Turkish guest-worker community, very often of rural background, into the highly specialized economy of German society. Simultaneously, they observed and counseled young people in vocational training and adult education. Likewise the Greek German linguist Fthenakis belongs to this group of established immigrant scholars. Others such as the Italian political scientist Borrelli (1988), the Greek educationalist and linguist Athanassios Gotowos (1991), or the Turkish linguist Onur B. Kula (Essinger & Kula, 1987) could not find a permanent post in Germany and are now holding lectureships in their countries of origin. All three published widely in Germany throughout the 1980s and contributed substantially to the general understanding of multicultural perspectives.

Community Education and "Third World Studies"

In the interdisciplinary field of multicultural education, the work of some researchers has taken them beyond the boundaries of Germany. Renate Nestvogel did not follow the common interest in Turkish or Greek German comparative studies but did research in African countries. Her results raised questions about what we could learn from "Third World" countries (Nestvogel, 1983). Zimmer, from the Berlin Institute for Intercultural Education, endorsed this outlook even earlier (1982). He began by implementing the "situation approach," in accordance with the methods developed by Paulo Freire for the alphabetization campaign in Brazil and other Latin American countries. Zimmer applied this to the conditions given in Western Europe for semi- or illiterate immigrants and their children. He then codirected two model projects in Berlin (partly funded by the federal government) on development of learning materials for children in preschools and in primary education. Always focusing on the intercultural approach to learning, Zimmer sees this as "the thorn in the flesh of an ethnocentric educational concept" (Zimmer, 1986, p. 144).

To put these approaches into practice, the Berlin Institute organized excursions and work camps for student teachers to countries such as Turkey, Nicaragua, Brazil, and the Philippines. This led to further initiatives in the field of "community education" (Klement, 1990). This movement shared a belief in schooling and school organization that is strictly oriented according to the needs of a given multiethnic community. It follows that intercultural education would necessarily be one of the guiding principles of the curriculum and the schools' resources.

The British-based international pedagogical society International Community Education Association (ICEA) has a significant stronghold in northwest Germany, where it is known as COMED, and has influenced school development in the former East German states. Zimmer, a cofounder of the society, as well as Angelika Krüger, the European secretary, and Ursula Neumann, professor in Hamburg, have published widely in Germany on the needs of the community in multicultural education.

Integrative Education

To complete the review of research in the field of multicultural education in Germany, it is necessary to include integrative education (*integrative Pädagogik*), introduced by Wilhelmine Sayler, a scholar from Cologne. This approach again is strongly influenced by Paolo Freire and demonstrates how his methods can be transferred into the European geographic-economic-cultural area. The main principles of Sayler's approach are concerned with "learning in dialogue," which can take place only in a relationship of equal status between teacher and student (Sayler, 1992, p. 80). She offers the following goals for intercultural learning: empathy; respect for the peculiarities of strangers; and development of strategies to deal with xenophobia and racism. Dialogue and cooperation are the key methods of delivery, involving people of different ethnic and cultural backgrounds. Regrettably, she limits intercultural education to school while neglecting the influence of mass media and of learning in preschool institutions and within the family, youth clubs, and adult education settings.

Women's Studies in Multicultural Education

From the very beginnings of *Ausländerpädagogik,* women were well represented in both professional and research personnel in the fields of multicultural education. And they raised issues concerning the obvious discrepancies that are provided for the role of women in rural—most frequently Muslim—societies and modern postindustrial European countries such as Germany. German women teachers, still supporting the fight for equal representation in their own society, felt the potential threat of the growing influence of male fundamentalist teachers in Qur'an schools (private Muslim schools in the Turkish community), of "autocratic fathers," and of "obedient mothers" of their pupils.

Although most of the work in women's studies has been done by White scientists of the majority group (e.g., Wolbert, 1984), it is a field where immigrant female researchers contributed their share from the very beginning (e.g., Akkent & Franger, 1987; Morokvasic, 1984; Özerturgut-Yurtdas, 1983). The main "target" group consisted of Turkish girls and women, not only because of their prominent representation among the "foreigners" in Germany but because they looked obviously different from the "majority" culture. In numerous publications Turkish women on the whole appeared as victimized, stigmatized personalities. Most of these projects were part of educational programs, welfare schemes, or health projects, but few reflected work in the classroom. With very few exceptions, all the work that examined the background components of gender, rural tradition, and culture was bound to a very static view of the "Oriental" woman. *Oriental* is to be understood, according to Said (1978), as a word into which Western scientific discussion has constructed findings and knowledge about the Middle Eastern countries and cultures in 200 years as results of biased research. Western scholars will still have to learn to find and use adequate methods to do justice to these cultures.

The German sociologist Helma Lutz, now based in the Netherlands, gave an overview and report on the research in this field (Lutz, 1986). In her critique, she sees a lack of interest in the position of immigrant or minority women. The main concern remains for the role of White Western European women. The relationship between race, culture, and gender is often neglected. The first signs of change appeared in the work of Anthius and Yuval-Davis (1983), Hebenstreit (1984), Mies (1984), and especially Schulz (1992). Lutz's more recent publication shows the strategies Turkish immigrant women of the second generation adopted to survive between the demands of two conflicting cultural norm systems (1991).

Teachers in West European immigration countries have been quite obsessed by the "veil problem." In France, where there have been violent clashes between Muslim parents and the police, it is forbidden to wear religious dress (e.g., the veil) in schools. This is not the case in Germany, but girls are quite strongly discouraged to do so by Turkish and German non-Muslim teachers and peers. Very often girls wear their head scarfs on the way to and from school but not inside the building (Akkent & Franger, 1987). Lutz pleads here (1991) for a change in thinking toward these issues and refers to female Arabian authors from the United States (e.g., Mernissi, 1975) who argue similarly.

Antiracist Education

Finally, it is necessary to refer in more detail to those who consider their work to be antiracist. As outlined earlier, there has been great restriction in academic discussion of issues of race and racism in Germany outside the study of national socialism and the fascist legacy. Repressed by the reeducation programs of the Allied Forces in Germany after 1945, most academics simply denied the existence of racism in postwar Germany. At most, there were still a few fanatics, "forever yesterday oriented" (*Ewiggestrigen*), whom academics believed would die with old age, who attacked tombstones in Jewish cemeteries and gathered occasionally in obscure cult places to celebrate and remember dead fascist war heroes. As racism was reserved for an attitude against Jews only, and as such criminalized by law, all insults and attacks against immigrants and minorities were summarized under the term *hostility against aliens* (*Ausländerfeindlichkeit*), even if they were aiming their hatred against German nationals such as Black Germans or nationalized immigrants. Shuffled this way in human consciences from "the interior office" to "foreign affairs," this behavior became a lesser offense—to be criticized but not persecuted.

The British scholar immigration expert Castles, now in Australia, published a comparative study of "racism" in Western Europe (1984; German edition, 1987) using the term *racism* in today's context. Mullard (1984) criticized the "liberal" terminology of multiculturalism in Great Britain for neglecting the issues of race, class, and gender. Together with the Dutch researcher Essed, his theories were later published in Germany, where they were major influences on the development of antiracist strategies in education (Essed & Mullard, 1991). Independently, the German scholars Kurt G. Fischer (political science), Hans J. Gamm (education), and Ernst Tugendhat (philosophy) influenced the work of Essinger, another founding member of the Berlin Institute for Intercultural Education. Essinger and Graf (1984) originally placed great emphasis on the contribution of intercultural work to "peace education," which Essinger claimed as a necessity for the survival of the human race in the atomic age. He later developed an outspoken interventionist, political, and antiracist focus based on the principle of "education as a contradiction to national thinking, in favour of a universal approach and education against racism, supporting a humanistic approach and an idea of a one-world civilisation" (Essinger, 1991, p. 17).

Another British influence in the field came from the work of Cole (1986), who criticized multiculturalists for not taking into account the different standards in living conditions between Black and White citizens in Britain. Troyna (1987) also challenged those researchers whom he believed were ignorant about the inequality of opportunity offered to Black pupils in the British educational system. They both blamed multiculturalists for individualizing the problems of racism and showing a paternalistic attitude toward the Black population. On the other hand, Cohen argued that this approach, which supports a program of "racism awareness training," does not offer any counsel or guidance for the White pupil who must overcome his or her "innate guilt" (Cohen, 1988, p. 83).

Following this argument, the German scholar Auernheimer (1990) sees the necessity for cooperation between the antiracist and the intercultural approaches in multicultural education. Generally, it is this cooperative approach that dominates today's discussion among scholars in Germany. Antiracism is perceived as a productive challenge to multiculturalism. This is reflected in the largest current intercultural project in Germany, Folgen der Arbeitsmigration für Bildung und Erziehung (FABER, 1989), situated in Hamburg University and directed by Ursula Neumann and Ingrid Gogolin. Here the London scholar Cohen is developing his approach to "cultural studies" and language acquisition.

Multicultural Education in Language Learning and Literature

The need for "special" education for immigrant children in schools was first articulated by teachers who were concerned by their inability to communicate in German. This need was equally felt by adults in the workplace. As a result, Ausländerpädagogik was born.

Since the 1960s the German linguistic profession has developed many different areas of research, including studies of first- and second-language acquisition (Pfaff, 1993), in psycho- and sociolinguistics, in preschool and adult education programs, of mother-tongue teachers, and in mono- and bilingual alphabetization.

Some 20 years later the science of literature discovered a new field of research: Ausländer- or Gastarbeiterliteratur, which focused on the work of migrants or immigrants writing either in their mother tongue or in German but being pub-lished exclusively in German and in Germany. Although only marginally established in mainstream school curricula for literature education, there is a vast and diverse body of literature written by Germans of a nondominant ethnic group, most of them originating from the different former guest-worker communities.

As an act of recognition of this work, the Robert Bosch Foundation and the Bavarian Academy of Fine Arts initiated a special award in 1985, the Adalbert von Chamisso Prize, which is granted every year to an author of non-German mother tongue who is writing in German or whose work is translated into German for its first publication (Friedrich, 1986). Among the award winners are the German Turkish author Aras Ören, the German Syrian Rafik Schami, and the German Italians Franco Biondi and Gino Chiellino. The female German Turkish novelists Aysel Özakin and Yüksel Pazarkaya have not won this prize yet, but they must be mentioned as representatives of this artistically productive group of the largest ethnic minority in Germany, perhaps together with the female German Turkish poet Zehra Cirak. Their names stand for dozens of stimulating writers who contribute in an outstanding manner to modern literature in Germany (Rösch, 1991).

The group of researchers in the field of language and literature include those working in the area of teacher training, those promoting the teaching of German as a foreign or second language, and those developing curriculum reform with projects or bi- or multilingual education in the classroom.

Another influence on multicultural studies came from the cross-cultural approach adopted by regional-studies experts within traditional foreign-language teaching for languages such as English and French. As they had earlier discovered the importance of implementing cultural studies in teaching foreign languages successfully, teachers in schools could rely on their experiences in this field when they attempted to make Ausländerpädagogik work. This regional-studies approach developed further in the work of Hans Nicklas and particularly Gabriele Steffen. Steffen shows that "language and culture are following different mutual dependent aspects of communication. That is why bilingual teaching can never be conceived of as monocultural or neutral in terms of culture" (Steffen, 1991, p. 231). As an example she discusses the change of the cultural and social context of the Turkish word ayle as it is translated into family: Does it really mean the same in the new culture? Is it possible to create this empathic type of language awareness to make it understood in the German (or English) language that, for example, family may mean to children of some cultures some 150 persons or even more?

As multicultural education became a discipline in its own right, many working in the field of language and literature (e.g., Luchtenberg, 1993) became interested in interdisciplinary approaches and contributed to research and projects in the field of education. Gabriele Pommerin, a language-acquisition specialist in primary schooling in Erlangen, coedited a widely acknowledged reader entitled Learning German Together: Intercultural Work in Language With Foreign and German Pupils (Hegele & Pommerin, 1983). In 1992 she chose for a similar publication aiming at the same readership the title Living and

Learning in the Multicultural Society (Pommerin-Götze, Tehle-Santoso, & Bozikake-Leisch, 1992). The importance of social learning as prerequisite to language acquisition remains at the heart of the work of many researchers in this field. Reich, Steinmüller, and Barkowski are all linguists who are determined educators.

Hans Reich inspired two major research projects: Aus- und Fortbildung für Lehrkräfte für Ausländerkinder (ALFA; Training of Teachers for Immigrant Children), focusing on the relations between immigration, education, and school politics (ALFA, 1983); and FABER, an even more ambitious follow-up project on the same topic that included additional European research results and involved the entire German federation (outlines published in Reich & Gogolin, 1990).

Ulrich Steinmüller did research with Turkish learners on German grammar acquisition relying on information they gained in the Turkish language, and on the cognitive development of bilingual children, implementing and evaluating data Skutnabb-Kangas had collected in Scandinavia (Steinmüller, 1981). He founded a permanent research center (Interkulturelle Forschungs- und Arbeitsstelle) at the Technische Universität Berlin and, as vice-president of the university, he created in 1989 the first chair for intercultural education in Germany, held by Helga Marburger in 1994. His center encourages studies in immigrant literature and comparative research with Eastern European countries as well as with Turkey and China, with a special emphasis on linguistic studies (Steinmüller, 1991), German studies, and school organization.

Hans Barkowski was initially involved in a German for Turkish Workers project in Heidelberg. In the 1980s, realizing the predominant influence of videotapes on the immigrant culture of the "guest-worker" community, he became responsible for a series produced by the German Federal TV Education Program (FWU/Munich), a sitcom situated among a Turkish guest-worker family that speaks Turkish but incorporates German in everyday life. A professor at the Berlin Institute for Intercultural Education since 1989, he is now cooperating in research with the Berlin-based projects on bilingual alphabetization in primary schools. In his recent article "Sit Down, Next to Me, My Camel" (Barkowski, 1992), he reflects on what he sees as the main obstacle to intercultural learning—the failure of the majority to empathize with people of different cultural traditions.

Finally, two Berlin linguists and educationalists, Monika Nehr (in Nehr, Birnkott-Rixius, Kubat, & Masuch, 1988) and Ulrike Harnisch (1991), developed significant school-based models on bilingual learning in the primary school. The projects were carried out independently at the request of teaching staff in the school but produced similar materials to be used in the bicultural classes of school beginners. Both projects are aimed at Turkish learners, who are taught to read the Turkish and German alphabets and at the same time given a bilingual thesaurus of first words for reading and writing. Both take place in equally mixed biethnic classrooms with two teachers, one Turkish, one German, teaching simultaneously. After overcoming many initial difficulties, material has been tested and evaluated and now exists for the first four grades in school. Financed by special project funds, more than 20 Berlin schools eventually became involved. The final report on the projects, covering four grades, was to be published in 1993, but the Berlin government only reluctantly guarantees the continuation of the program because of financial problems and political objections.

Putting Multicultural Education into Practice

The political reasons why there remains such a poor record of putting multicultural education into practice in Germany were discussed in the beginning of this chapter. Some (more "progressive") German states require an obligatory course for student teachers in order to pass their first exam, and this is described in the regulations as "work with foreign pupils in school." Some states offer special additional qualifications focusing basically on Turkish as a foreign language (TFL), which does not result in better pay or higher status for the qualified. Nevertheless, such teachers are in demand and are taught and evaluated very often by the most senior multicultural specialists.

Modellversuche. A popular method of funding studies in the humanities in Germany is the *Modellversuche* (experimental models). As a rule either the European Community or the federal government and the state(s) and sometimes the community (town/county) involved share the costs. The duration of these models is between 3 and 5 years. One or two academics are appointed directors of the project and are responsible for the design, conduct, and finances of the model. Individual scholars, research teams, and communities can apply for funding. Central research advisory boards or individuals give opinions on the applications. Final decisions are made anonymously inside the higher ranks of the civil service involved and returned to the applicant(s) without further explanation. The decisions therefore likely reflect the political opinion of the "bureaucracy." Due to this system of financing, a *Modellversuch* is normally not made part of everyday reality after its termination, even if the results are promising.

A famous example in this category became the so-called Krefelder Modell (Dickopp, 1982), named after a city in the Rhineland industrial region and running from 1975 to 1979. Three primary schools were at the center of the project, but all other primary education in the area was involved to a certain degree. The idea was to grant bicultural education for immigrant children and concentrate resources by creating two Turkish/German schools and one Greek/German school, according to the representation of minorities in the town. At the same time the other primary schools would be run as German-only schools. The schools involved provided intensive mother-tongue teaching and national culture studies. In the first grade only mathematics, sports, arts, and music were offered in the integrated classroom. In the fourth grade all subjects were taught in German for all children, except for 8 hours of mother-tongue teaching. A framework of supportive special care units was provided. Clearly a model in favor of assimilative integration, it is remarkable that mother-tongue teaching received such an emphasis. The results, according to the aims of the project, were very promising. The teachers and schools involved were willing to continue; other schools and communities were interested in following. However, nothing happened. The model was discontinued due to "lack of funding," which in German state politics is a phrase meaning "putting money into this matter will not help us win the next election." Because immigrants, even after 20 or more years of residential status in Germany, have no right to vote unless they can claim full citizenship, regional politicians do not have to care a lot about the well-being of this particular clientele.

Similar fortunes were in stock for other *Modellversuche* taking place in Berlin during the 1980s in the areas of kindergarten and primary and secondary education. These were organized and evaluated by the Freie Universität and Technische Universität of Berlin. Only one German/Turkish comprehensive school (Hector Petersen School) managed to continue a modified version of the model design into ordinary school routine because it was fortunate to have sympathetic people in political power at the time the model was terminated. As a result of the project this school came to see itself as an "antiracist-oriented school" (Pagel, 1993).

There have been a few other models similar to the Krefelder model, most prominently of which is the Mainzer Modell (Piroth, 1981), which involved the Italian and the Turkish minorities. This project individualized the time of transfer of pupils from the national to the integrated learning group according to their German-language ability. The models were most effective when they not only published the report of the project but developed classroom material for wide-ranging publication.

This is the reason why the two Berlin models directed by the Institute of Education have become well known and are followed by teachers and schools all over the nation. A four-volume handbook entitled *Where Are You From?* (Akpinar & Zimmer, 1984), on multicultural work in kindergarten, was a result of one project, and 11 booklets, reflecting all aspects and subjects of primary education, represent a major contribution to multicultural education in primary schools (Zimmer, 1988–90).

Finally, there is a major project conducted by the state of Northrhine-Westfalia that is basically community oriented but has at the same time a strict focus on multicultural education. Here the state organized centers (Regionale Arbeitsstelle für Ausländerarbeit [RAA], meaning regional centers for liaison work with foreigners) in the different regions to promote work and initiatives in favor of immigrant children (Raschert, 1987). These centers also support multicultural and antiracist approaches in schools and favor a kind of "district approach" following British or U.S. examples. In the 1990s new RAAs have been created in the former East German states, especially in (East) Berlin and Brandenburg, to deal with xenophobia, immigrants, and asylum seekers inside the communities (Schill, Preuß, & Dulabaum, 1993).

The French German Youth Foundation (DFAJ). This organization is constructed according to a special cross-cultural program that has been going on between France and Germany over several decades. It is debatable whether its achievements can be seen as an aspect of work in multicultural education, but the results do offer striking evidence that it is possible to overcome age-old prejudices through education, and so it has served as a model for intercultural programs in Germany.

At the time of the Napoleonic conquest of European nations, France became the natural adversary, the *Erbfeind* (enemy by heritage) of Germany. This discord lasted for the next 150 years and resulted in three wars and the occupation of provinces along the border by both sides.

After World War II, the two charismatic leaders de Gaulle and Adenauer saw that they needed to reduce these antagonisms in order to realize their dream of a united Western Europe. In 1961 they established Deutsch-Französisches Jugend Werle (DFJW) as a binational foundation with two directors, an equal amount of bilingual counselors from both nations, and offices in both capitals.

The organization has been in continuous operation since 1961 and has created numerous programs and projects, all focusing on exchange visits between the two countries. Not only do school classes and individual pupils learn about the everyday life of their counterparts, but civil servants, apprentices, local politicians, craftsmen, farmers, and people from numerous other trades and professions meet people in similar positions in the other country. Cities and villages in all provinces have been involved; many contacts have developed into business relationships as well as personal friendships. Participants do not have to speak the other language, but there is very little help given by professional interpreters. Instead, those leading the programs are trained in other ways of communication such as third languages, sign language, or pantomime. Sometimes an additional group of bilingual people become involved.

From the beginning there was permanent assessment through parallel research and careful monitoring. Foreign-language teachers, teacher trainers, regional-studies specialists, and finally scholars in the field of intercultural education became involved. After the collapse of the Iron Curtain in Europe, the two countries started to work with trinational groups (e.g., French-German-Romanian) to tackle the problems of racism, minorities, culture gap, language education, and religious fundamentalism in three countries, based on their long-term experiences of cross-cultural learning.

It is interesting that recent polls show that France and Germany regard each other as most favorable nations. Most of the resentments are gone, but the project described recently as a "difficult utopia" (Haumersen & Liebe, 1990) will carry on. Its success may be due to the regular visits of heads of states, or because many Germans learn French at the Gymnasium, but the example does show that it is possible to alter prejudices in long-term programs, even if there are setbacks in the process.

Deconstructionists in Multicultural Education

More recently, educationists with a strong affinity in their work to the neighboring disciplines of sociology or political science criticized the mainstream theories and practices of multicultural education as serving to distance and disempower minorities and immigrants. They claim that their multiculturalist colleagues do so by naming and emphasizing cultural differences between the indigenous majority of Germans and the various ethnic minorities of immigrants.

A review of the conceptual literature of multicultural education would not be complete without mentioning the work of some deconstructionist scholars, based in Bielefeld, Cologne, and Zurich, Switzerland, which was published from 1988 onwards. Their critique focuses on the social construction of minorities as the marginalized "cultural other," which they detect in mainstream multicultural research and the materials that have been developed in the aftermath. To overcome this "undesirable" trend, they attempt to deconstruct the artificial paradigm that they see as being created by some sociologists as an instrument to keep the majority in power.

Steiner-Khamsi (1992) demonstrates that the Anglo-American critical pedagogy of Henry Giroux and Peter McLaren, as developed in connection with the Birmingham Centre for Contemporary Cultural Studies, would be a useful model in defining the basic theory and the ethical concepts that she believes are still missing in Germany's intercultural education. The possible connection between ethnological and sociological studies already using this approach in Germany is made evident by Bukow and Llaryora (1993). They, together with Dittrich and Radtke (1990), ask why those groups of the population that are formed by migration processes are especially marked and stigmatized. The processes of ethnization and labeling as such are generally seen to be interdependent. Bukow and Llaryora and Steiner-Khamsi refer to the making of "ethnicity" for political purposes as having the "unifying" effect of alienating minorities from the "native" groups of a population and of promoting the rights of those who have been in a particular country first.

Ethnic differences are often used to stigmatize and marginalize minorities and to construct ethnic minorities as the "other." In contrast, the deconstructionist approach views schools as public democratic spheres in which the various communities have to struggle on equal grounds over the construction of meaning, which is reflected in the curriculum, in the educational setting, and in educational programs.

THE STATUS OF MULTICULTURAL EDUCATION IN TODAY'S UNIFIED GERMANY

Long before the collapse of the socialist world, the Black writer Sivanandan (1988), director of the London Institute of Race Relations, warned that "a new racism is emerging, . . . less visible, more virulent and, above all, European, directed against the migrants, refugees and asylum seekers, displaced from their own countries by the depredations of international capital" (p. 8). There are many more causes for recent emigration to Germany, all of which have led to the current increase of racism. This has all influenced a new willingness by state and federal governments to finance research into multicultural education.

Changes in Race Relations Since 1989

Race relations have become headline news since the Berlin Wall came down. German society as a whole is undergoing a fundamental change in its self-understanding as a consequence of the breakdown of communist countries and of unification in 1989. It is a sort of mass-identity crisis resulting from the fact

that there is no positive understanding of nation and nationality existing in Germany. Since the invention of the modern concept of nation, about 200 years ago, it has been abused by illiberal, antimodern, imperialistic, and finally megalomaniac and treacherous leaders. That is why it has been further repressed and tabooed completely since 1945, with different emphases in both German states. The essayist Enzensberger (1992) describes the special German way of xenophobia: The causes

lie in the precarious self-consciousness of the nation. It is a fact that Germans cannot tolerate each other—or even themselves. . . . This condition of self-loathing is evident not only in the hostility to foreigners, but also in the opposition to it. . . . The immigrant is defended in a tone of utter moralizing self-righteousness: "Foreigners, don't leave us alone with the Germans!", or: "Never again Germany!" Immigrants are idealized in a manner reminiscent of philo-Semitism. Self-hatred is projected on to others—most notably in the insidious assertion "I am a foreigner", which numerous German "celebrities" have adopted. (p. 40)

"Together we are detestable" is the summary of a report about a psychological study presented at a conference of the New Association for Psychology in Berlin in March 1993 by the Berlin-based scholar Eva Jaeggi. Her team analyzed the changes of intrafamiliar patterns of communication in families that had been divided into an eastern and western branch since the German separation and had to cope with normal accessibility after the wall came down (cited in Stein, 1993). They not only reported predictable difficulties but found out that both sides tended to project their own weaknesses onto their counterparts. When questioned about their differences, the family members, particularly those from the former East, strongly denied any estrangement but tended to project their hostility toward imaginary adversaries such as "foreigners" (Sturzbecher, 1990).

"Foreigners" are also one of the main concerns of young people in the former East German state of Brandenburg, surrounding Berlin. Fifty-four percent were worried about a possible "flooding of foreigners," following a representative survey in the state conducted by the regional Ministry of Education in autumn 1991 ("Vorurteile und Meinungslosigkeit," 1992).

These results are not surprising; there are few concepts existing for an understanding of the new German nation. Legal decisions have already been handed over to Brussels (seat of the EEC bureaucracy), but "United Europe" is still utopia and will remain so for many years to come. People are reluctant to face the facts that living in the country are millions of immigrants who will have offspring and that there will be more immigration into their territory, no matter how preventive the legislation might be. "There is the choice between 'apartheid' and an open society and in a multicultural society we must retain the optional character of cultural autonomy for the individual" (Brumlik & Leggewie, 1992, p. 433).

The Rise of Nationalism and Racism

The files of STASI, the former East German state security service, indicate that there have been neofascist activities observed since the end of the 1970s, according to reports in the daily newspapers in October 1992. This means there is a history of a neo-Nazi underground inside both parts of Germany.

However, it is too early to have a clear picture about the main causes of the horrifying surge in right-wing extremism that is dominating the recent news about Germany. Many surveys and scientific studies are in the making, but first results have been quite contradictory. This makes the possibility of a peaceful development into a multicultural society bleak and fuels the rising fears of those abroad that a Fourth Reich will emerge in Germany. For East Germany the old Nazi traditions lingered on under another name: Obedience, politeness, and order were the dominant virtues inside the family (Sturzbecher, 1990). These qualities were complemented by flag appeals and torchlight processions, compulsory membership in the state youth organization, and the belief that the army was a main pillar of values in the society. This has all been swept away by unification and replaced by a weak central government, the national problems of a divided economy, and unemployment approaching 50% in the East, with frozen wages and soaring rents. While the world recession cut jobs in the West and reduced social security, and taxes were raised to finance the *Aufschwung Ost* (Eastern stimulus), Germany had to absorb 3 million asylum seekers from 1989 to 1992, twice as many as the United States in the 1920s ("Hitler's Youths," 1992). As a result, in a representative survey (Tomic, 1993) in August 1992, 67% of Brandenburg's youths agreed that there are too many foreigners in Germany (actual rate in Brandenburg: 2%). Fifteen percent supported the opinion "Every foreigner is one too many!"

Changes in Legislation

In spite of more than 4,000 reported criminal acts caused by "hostility against foreigners" in Germany in 1992, the government still hesitates to tackle immigration laws. (More than half of these criminal acts include violence, and at least 21 people, Germans and *Ausländer*, have been killed between March 1992 and May 1993). Only after the second horrific arson attack against a house inhabited by a Turkish family, this time in Solingen, in which five Turkish women and girls lost their lives (May 30, 1993), politicians from all political parties stood up for the first time to demand a change of the constitution giving "guest workers" the right to German citizenship. It is significant that after Solingen, the most influential political magazine, *Der Spiegel*, changed its terminology from "foreigners" to "immigrants" and from "Turks in Germany" to "Turkish Germans" ("Die Deutschen Türken," 1993).

At last some changes seem to be possible. "Guest-worker" organizations, the Frankfurt City Directorate of Multicultural Affairs, and the Berlin ombudsperson for foreigners have been pressing for the acceptance of immigrants as German citizens to make dual citizenship possible. But as Turkish youths start "to fight back," demonstrate, smash windows, and threaten to take revenge for the burnings, conservative representatives are already calling for martial law and deportations.

One major change has already taken place. Germany has recently moved to help in the creation of a "fortress Europe" against a "growing tide of immigration" from countries stricken by poverty and war (more than 118,000 refugees arrived in the first 3 months of 1993). On May 26, 1993, after years of passionate negotiations, the German Parliament amended the constitution, the "basic law," to restrict refugees' access to and presence in Germany. The 521 to 132 vote to dispose the guaranteed right for all foreigners to seek asylum became law on July 1, 1993. Officials say the law would protect those threatened with political repression while keeping out economic immigrants. The leader of the Social Democratic opposition, who voted in favor of the bill, said, "unregulated immigration endangers the stability of democracy and only serves right-wing rabble-rousers" (Tomforde, 1993).

FUTURE PERSPECTIVES

There is no doubt that, given the facts of German society in 1994, immediate political action is needed. Educational programs can support developments in society only when there is a certain public consent on the direction a nation wants to go. Brumlik and Leggewie (1993) argue that "positive discrimination" of ethnic minorities apparently does not work. What is needed is active protection against discrimination, based on equal treatment and an equal legal position given to all inhabitants. The ombudspersons, responsible for immigrants, need more executive power. The traditional ways of state intervention (force, money, law) will have to be used to guarantee effective changes, as persuasion did not succeed (Leggewie, 1990). As the German economy will need continued immigration of about 300,000 people a year to keep the usual rates of economic growth (Informationsdienst des Bundestages, 1992, September 13) and secure old-age pensions for its citizens after the year 2020, it is high time to agree on annual immigration quotas and pass antidiscrimination laws.

As pupils in Germany have one of the longest compulsory schooling times in the Western world, one might question whether the existing schools are able to handle the problem of racism and discrimination adequately at all. A hiring system of teachers in which promotion is often the only way to get rid of incompetent personnel, and a streaming system in secondary schools, where general educational tasks are neglected in favor of subject teaching, show that the educational system is in desperate need of major reform itself.

There are promising proposals and well-researched alternatives, as shown above, but the crucial question is whether there will be strong public demand for school reform to open the gates for multicultural education in mainstream classrooms, especially in "White" schools. Major changes need to be implemented in all schools, in the general curriculum, and in the materials and textbooks used. Schools will have to open themselves to the requirements of the community and attempt to tackle today's problems within the school.

In February 1993 Berlin's ombudsperson for foreigners published a review that gives evidence that the majority in East and West Berlin object to xenophobia and support legal equality for non-Germans. But it is important to remember that there was no majority for Hitler's Nazi Party in the last free elections in Berlin in 1933.

There are new initiatives: The authorities in the city of Nuremberg developed "100 ideas for projects" in antiracist education focusing on social studies in pedagogical practice ("100 Projektideen," 1993), and there are new examples of learning second languages (e.g., those represented in the classroom as mother tongue) in elementary schools (Landesinstitut für Schule and Weiterbildung, 1992).

There still remains a major task for teachers and researchers in the field of multicultural education: "to institutionalize learn-

ing for all children, to enable them to develop their own culture—not just one adapted from a group, to communicate with other cultures, and to become self-determined in a growingly differentiated world" (Krüger-Potratz, 1993, p. 87). But until these initiatives become compulsory components of the curriculum for all schools, they will have little effect in preventing the growing tide of racism and nationalism in Germany.

References

(Note: All translations from German into English are by the author of this chapter, unless otherwise stated.)

100 Projektideen für die Pädagogische Praxis. (1993, March). *Erziehung und Wissenschaft*, pp. 23–26.

ALFA. Forschungsgruppe (Eds.) (1983). *Materialien zum Abschluß-bericht*. Landau: Erziehungswissenschaftliche Hochschule Rheinland Pfalz.

Aissen-Crewett, M. (1989/90). Musisch-ästhetische Erziehung in der multikulturellen Gesellschaft. *Die Grundschule*, nos. 10 (1989), 1 & 2 (1990).

Akkent, M., & Franger, G. (1987). *Das Kopftuch/BaSörtü. Ein Stückchen Stoff in Geschichte und Gegenwart*. Frankfurt am Main: Dagyeli.

Akpinar, Ü. (1976). *Sozialisationsbedingungen in der Türkei*. Materialien zum Projektbereich "Ausländische Arbeitnehmer." Bonn: AGG and Konrad Adenauer Stiftung.

Akpinar, Ü. (1980). Zur interkulturellen Erziehung. *Westermanns pädagogische Beiträge, 32*, 68–73.

Akpinar, Ü., & Zimmer, J., (Eds.). (1984). *Von wo kommst'n du? Interkulturelle Erziehung im Kindergarten* (4 Vols.). München: Kösel.

Anthius, F., & Yuval-Davis, N. (1983). Contextualizing feminism: Gender, ethnic and class division. *Feminist Review, 15*, 62–75.

Ardagh, J. (1991). *Germany and the Germans* (3rd ed.). London: Penguin Books.

Auernheimer, G. (Ed.). (1984). *Handwörterbuch Ausländerarbeit*. Weinheim/Basel: Beltz-Verlag.

Auernheimer, G. (1990). *Einführung in die interkulturelle Erziehung*. Darmstadt: Wissenschaftliche Buchgesellschaft.

Auernheimer, G. (1992). Ethnizität and Modernität. In A. Kalpaka & N. Räthzel (Eds.), *Rassismus und Migration in Europa* (pp. 118–132). Hamburg: Argument Verlag.

Bade, K. J. (1992). Asyl bei den Deutschen: Idee und Wirklichkeit. In K. J. Bade (Ed.), *Deutsche im Ausland, Fremde in Deutschland* (pp. 422–441). Munich: C. H. Beck.

Barkowski, H. (1982). *Kommunikative Grammatik und Deutschlernen mit ausländischen Arbeitern*. Kronberg im Taunus: Scriptor.

Barkowski, H. (1992). "Setz Dich zu mir, mein Kamel!" Interkulturelles Lernen und Lehren und der Erwerb des Deutschen als Zweitsprache. *Deutsch lernen, 2*, 144–166.

Batelaan, P. (1983). *The practice of intercultural education*. London: Commission for Racial Equality, Elliot House.

Blaschke, J. (1985). *Volk, Nation und interner Kolonialismus*. Berlin: Express Edition.

Boos-Nünning, U. (1983). Berufliche Orientierung und Berufswahlprozesse türkischer Jugendlicher: Darstellung und Analyse von zwei Fallbeispielen. In R. Hohberg (Ed.), *Sprachprobleme ausländischer Jugendlicher: Aufgaben der beruflichen Bildung* (pp. 147–172). Frankfurt am Main: Scriptor.

Boos-Nünning, U., Hohmann, M., & Reich, H. (1977). *Ausländische Kinder, Schule und Gesellschaft im Herkunftsland*. Düsseldorf: Publikation, ALFA, Verlag Schwann.

Borrelli, M. (1984). Interkulturelle Pädagogik: "Exotik"-Pädagogik? *Ausländerkinder, 18*, 5–50.

Borrelli, M. (1988). Gegen den affirmativen Charakter von Kultur und Bildung. In M. Borrelli & G. R. Hoff (Eds.), *Interkulturelle Pädagogik im internationalen Vergleich* (pp. 20–36). Baltmannsweiler: Pädagogischer Verlag Burgbücherei Schneider GmbH.

Brumlik, M., & Leggewie, C. (1992). Konturen der Einwanderungsgesellschaft. In K. J. Bade (Ed.), *Deutsche im Ausland, Fremde in Deutschland* (pp. 430–442). Munich: C. H. Beck.

Bukow, W. D., & Llaryora, R. (1993). *Mitbürger aus der Fremde: Soziogenese ethnischer Minoritäten* (2nd ed.). Opladen: Westdeutscher Verlag.

Castles, S. (1984). *Here for good: Western Europe's ethnic minorities*. London: Pinto Press.

Castles, S. (1987). *Migration und Rassismus in Westeuropa*. Berlin: Express Edition.

Cohen, P. (1988). The perversions of inheritance: Studies in the making of multi-racist Britain. In P. Cohen & H. Bains (Eds.), *Multi-racist Britain*. London: Macmillan.

Cole, M. (1986). Teaching and learning about racism: A critique of multicultural education in Britain. In S. Modgil, G. K. Verma, K. Mallick, & C. Modgil (Eds.), *Multicultural education: The interminable debate* (pp. 123–147). London: Falmer Press.

Cummins, J. (1984). Zweisprachigkeit und Schulerfolg. *Die Deutsche Schule, 3,* 187ff.

Dann, O. (1993). *Nation und Nationalismus in Deutschland 1770–1990*. Munich: C. H. Beck.

DECS/EGT [Directorate for Education, Culture, & Sport]. (1986). *The education and cultural development of migrants* (Project No. 7 final report). Strasbourg: Council of Europe.

Dickopp, K. H. (1982). *Erziehung ausländischer Kinder als pädagogische Herausforderung: Das Krefelder Modell*. Düsseldorf: Schwann.

Die Deutschen Türken: Weder Heimat noch Freunde. (1993, June 7). *Der Spiegel*, pp. 16–31.

Diehm, I., & Kodron, C. (1990). *Unterricht und Erziehung für eine multikulturelle Gesellschaft*. Frankfurt am Main: Deutsches Institut für Internationale Pädagogische Forschung.

Dittmar, N. (1979). Zum Nutzen von Ergebnissen der Untersuchung des ungesteuerten Zweitspracherwerbs ausländischer Arbeiter. In *Bildung und Ausbildung in der Romania (15 Romanistentag 1977, Gießen): Vol. 2. Sprachwissenschaft und Landeskunde* (pp. 371–396). München: Fink.

Dittrich, E. J., & Radtke, F.-O. (1990). Der Beitrag der Wissenschaften zur Konstruktion ethnischer Minderheiten. In E. J. Dittrich & F.-O. Radtke (Eds.), *Ethnizität, Wissenschaft und Minderheiten* (pp. 11–40). Opladen: Westdeutscher Verlag.

Ein einig Volk von Blutsbrüdern. (1993, March 15). *Der Spiegel*, pp. 50–71.

Enzensberger, H. M. (1992). The great migration. In B. Buford (Ed.), *"Krauts"* (pp. 15–51). Harmondsworth, England: Granta.

Essed, P. C., & Mullard, C. (1991). *Antirassistische Erziehung*. Felsberg: Migros Verlag.

Essinger, H. (1991). Interkulturelle Erziehung in multiethnischen Gesellschaften. In H. Marburger (Ed.), *Schule in der multikulturellen Gesellschaft* (pp. 3–18). Frankfurt: Verlag für Interkulturelle Kommunikation.

Essinger, H., & Graf, J. (1984). Interkulturelle Erziehung als Friedenserziehung. In H. Essinger & A. Uçar (Eds.), *Erziehung in der multikulturellen Gesellschaft* (pp. 15–34). Baltmannsweiler: Pädagogischer Verlag Burgbücherei Schneider.

Essinger, H., & Kula, O. B. (Eds.). (1987). *Pädagogik als interkultureller Prozeß*. Felsberg: Migro Verlag.

FABER (1989). *Forschungsschwerpunktprogramm—Folgen der Arbeitsmigration für Bildung und Erziehung—der Deutschen Forschungsgemeinschaft 1990–1995*. Unpublished manuscript.

Flechsig, K.-H. (1985). Die Sicherung didaktischer Vielfalt als Aufgabe einer interkulturellen Didaktik. *SSIP Bulletin, 55,* pp. 3–30.

Frey, H., Piroth, G., & Renner, E. (1982). *Ausländische Kinder im Unterricht: Erfahrungen, Materialien, Hilfen zu einer mehrkulturellen und integrativen Pädagogik*. Heinsberg: Dieck.

Friedrich, H. (Ed.). (1986). *Chamissos Enkel: Literatur von Ausländern in Deutschland*. München: Deutscher Taschenbuch Verlag.

Friesenhahn, G. J. (1988). *Zur Entwicklung interkultureller Pädagogik*. Berlin: Express Edition.

Fromeyer, M. (1993). Die drei Sackgassen der Interkulturellen Erziehung. In S. Kroon, D. Pagel, & T. Vallen (Eds.), *Multiethnische Gesellschaft und Schule in Berlin* (pp. 41–50). Münster: Waxmann.

Fthenakis, W. E., Sonner, A., Thrul, R., & Walbiner, W. (Eds.). (1985). *Bilingual-bikulturelle Entwicklung des Kindes*. Ismaning: Hueber.

Gondolf, U., Hegele, I., Pommerin, G., Röber-Siekmeyer, C., Schellong, I., & Steffen, G. (1983). *Gemeinsames Lernen mit ausländischen und deutschen Schülern*. Tübingen: DIFF, Projekt Ausländerkinder in der Schule.

Gotowos, A. (1991). "Ausländer bleibt Ausländer": Zum Verhältnis ausländerfreundlicher Positionen und anhaltender staatsbürgerlicher Diskriminierung von Immigranten. In H. Barkowski & G. R. Hoff (Eds.), *Berlin Interkulturell* (pp. 75–106). Berlin: Colloquium Verlag.

Griese, H. (Ed.). (1984). *"Der gläserne Fremde": Bilanz und Kritik der Gastarbeiterforschung und Ausländerpädagogik*. Opladen: Leske & Budrich.

Gundara, J. S. (1991). Western Europe: Multicultural or xenophobic? In H. Barkowski & G. R. Hoff (Eds.), *Berlin Interkulturell* (pp. 3–22). Berlin: Colloquium Verlag.

Haller, I. (1991). Multikulturell ist "in." *Europa, 9,* 72–73.

Harnisch, U. (1991). Zur Begriffsentwicklung in zwei Sprachen. In H. Barkowski & G. R. Hoff (Eds.), *Berlin Interkulturell* (pp. 109–120). Berlin: Colloquium Verlag.

Haumersen, P., & Liebe, F. (1990). *Eine schwierige Utopie*. Berlin: Verlag für Wissenschaft und Bildung.

Hebenstreit, S. (1984). Rückständig, isoliert, hilfsbedürftig: Das Bild der ausländischen Frau in der deutschen Literatur. *Informationsdienst des Forschungsinstituts Frau und Gesellschaft,* Hannover.

Heckmann, F. (1981). *Die Bundesrepublik: Ein Einwanderungsland? Zur Soziologie der Gastarbeiterbevölkerung als Einwandererminorität*. Stuttgart: Ernst Klett Verlag.

Hegele, I., & Pommerin, G. (1983). *Gemeinsam Deutsch lernen: Interkulturelle Spracharbeit mit ausländischen und deutschen Schulern*. Heidelberg: Quelle & Meyer.

Herrmann, H. (1992a). Ungelöste Probleme: Asylbewerber, Einwanderer, Flüchtlinge. *Informationen zur politischen Bildung, 237,* 32–40.

Herrmann, H. (1992b). Ursachen und Entwicklung der Ausländerbeschäftigung. *Informationen zur politischen Bildung, 237,* 4–7.

Hessler, M. (1993). *Zwischen Nationalstaat und multikultureller Gesellschaft: Einwanderung und Fremdenfeindlichkeit in der Bundesrepublik Deutschland*. Berlin: Hitit Verlag.

Hitler's Youths. (1992, December 5). *The Guardian Weekend,* pp. 6–10.

Hoff, G. R. (1991). Konzepte Interkultureller Erziehung in angelsächsischen Ländern. In H. Marburger (Ed.), *Schule in der multikulturellen Gesellschaft* (pp. 35–51). Frankfurt: Verlag für Interkulturelle Kommunikation.

Hoff, G. R. (1992). Culture in transition: A view from West Berlin. In K. A. Moodley (Ed.), *Beyond multicultural education: International perspectives* (pp. 67–77). Calgary: Detselig Enterprises.

Hohmann, M. (1976). *Unterricht mit ausländischen Kindern*. Düsseldorf: Schwann.

Hohmann, M. (1987). Interkulturelle Erziehung als Herausforderung für allgemeine Bildung? In D. Glowka & M. Krüger-Potratz (Eds., im Auftrag der Kommission für vergleichende Erziehungswissenschaft in der DGFE), *Vergleichende Erziehungswissenschaft, Informationen—Berichte–Studien* (Vol. 17, pp. 98–115). Berlin: DGFE.

IMAZ [Institut für Migrationsforschung, Ausländerpädagogik und Zweitsprachdidaktik]. (1993). *Verzeichnis der Publikationen*. Essen: Universität GH - Publikation.

Informationsdienst des Bundestages (1992, September 13). Pressemitteilung. *Der Tagesspiegel,* p. 14.

Klement, C. (1990). *Gemeinwesenorientierte Erziehung und Bildung im Sinne von Community Education als Antwort auf gesellschaftspolitische Herausforderungen der Gegenwart*. Frankfurt am Main: Lang.

Klemm, K. (1985). Interkulturelle Erziehung: Versuch einer Eingrenzung. *Die deutsche Schule, 3,* 176–187.

Kodron, C. (1984). Schule und Minderheiten in der europäischen Gemeinschaft: Heutiger Stand und Zukunftsperspektiven. *Zeitschrift für erziehungs- und sozialwissenschaftliche Forschung, 1,* 55ff.

Krüger-Potratz, M. (1983). Die problematische Verkürzung der Ausländerpädagogik als Subdisziplin der Erziehungswissenschaft. *Sozialarbeit und Ausländerpädagogik: Neue Praxis,* Sonderheft 7, 172ff.

Krüger-Potratz, M. (1987). Interkulturelle Erziehung: Eine Daueraufgabe der Ausbildung. *Infodienst zur Ausländerarbeit, 1,* 70ff.

Krüger-Potratz, M. (1993). Die (ehemalige) DDR auf dem Weg in eine multikulturelle Gesellschaft? In S. Kroon, D. Pagel, & T. Vallen (Eds.), *Multiethnische Gesellschaft und Schule in Berlin* (pp. 69–91). Münster: Waxmann.

Landesinstitut für Schule und Weiterbildung. (1992). *Begegnung mit Sprachen in der Grundschule*. Soest, NRW: Verlagskontor.

Leggewie, C. (1990). *MultiKulti: Spielregeln für die Vielvölkerrepublik*. Berlin: Rotbuch-Verlag.

Link, J. (1986). Asylanten: Ein Schimpfwort. In H. Kauffmann (Ed.), *Kein Asyl bei den Deutschen* (pp. 55–59). Reinbek: rororo aktuell.

Luchtenberg, S. (1993) "Ohne Fleiß kein Preis": Überlegungen zu Sprichwörtern und Redensarten im interkulturellen Deutschunterricht. *Lernen im Deutschland, 1,* 6–18.

Lutz, H. (1986). Migrantinnen aus der Türkei: Eine Kritik des gegenwärtigen Forschungsstandes. *Migration und Ethnizität, 0,* 9–44.

Lutz, H. (1991). Orientalische Weiblichkeit. In H. Barkowski & G. R. Hoff (Eds.), *Berlin Interkulturell* (pp. 245–260). Berlin: Colloquium Verlag.

Maas, U. (1984). Versuch einer kulturanalytischen Bestimmung ausländerpädagogischer Aufgaben. *Deutsch lernen, 1,* 3–24.

Marburger, H. (1991). Von der Ausländerpädagogik zur Interkulturellen Erziehung. In H. Marburger (Ed.), *Schule in der multikulturellen Gesellschaft* (pp. 19–34). Frankfurt: Verlag für Interkulturelle Kommunikation.

Mernissi, F. (1975). *Beyond the veil: Male-female dynamics in a modern Muslim society*. Cambridge, Mass.: Schenkmann; New York: Wiley.

Meyer-Ingwersen, J., Neumann, R., & Kummer, M. (1977). *Zur Sprachentwicklung türkischer Kinder in der Bundesrepublik* (2 Vols.). Königstein im Taŭnŭs Scriptor.

Michaelis, H. (1965). *Der zweite Weltkrieg.* Konstanz: Akademische Verlagsanstalt Athenaion.

Mies, M. (1984). Frauenforschung oder feministische Forschung. *Beiträge zur feministischen Theorie und Praxis, 11,* 40–60.

Molony, C., Zobl, H., & Stölting, W. (Eds.) (1978). *German in contact with other languages.* Kronberg im Taunus: Athenäum.

Morokvaśic, M. (1984). Birds of passage are also women. *International Migration Review, 18*(4), 886–907.

Mullard, C. (1984). *Antiracist education: The three "O's"* (Conference papers). Derby, England: National Association for Multi-Racial Education.

Nehr, M., Birnkott-Rixius, K., Kubat, L., & Masuch, S. (1988). *In zwei Sprachen lesen lernen: Geht denn das?* (Erfahrungsbericht). Weinheim: Beltz Verlag.

Nestvogel, R. (1983). Lernen von der dritten Welt: Traditionelle afrikanische Erziehungsmuster. *Zeitschrift für moderne Afrikaforschung, 1,* 27 ff.

Nieke, W. (1984). Multikulturelle Gesellschaft und interkulturelle Erziehung: Zur Theoriebildung in der Ausländerpädagogik. *Die Deutsche Schule, 1,* 462–473.

Otto, K. A. (1990). *Westwärts—Heimwärts?: Aussiedlerpolitik zwischen "Deutschtümelei" und "Verfassungsauftrag."* Bielefeld: AJZ.

Özerturgut-Yurtdas, H. (1983, July). *Muslim women in highly industrialized societies: The case of Turkish women in the Federal Republic of Germany.* Paper presented at the Seventh World Congress of Psychiatry, section on transcultural psychiatry, Vienna.

Pagel, D. (1993). Thesen für eine antirassistisch geprägte Schule. In S. Kroon, D. Pagel, & T. Vallen (Eds.), *Multiethnische Gesellschaft und Schule in Berlin* (pp. 113–134). Münster: Waxmann.

Pfaff, C. W. (1993). Turkish language development in Germany. In G. Extra & L. Verhoeven (Eds.), *Immigrant languages in Europe* (pp. 119–146). Clevedon: Multilingual Matters.

Piroth, G. (1981). Das Mainzer Modell: Schrittweise schulische Eingliederung von Kindern and Jugendlichen fremder Muttersprache. *Ausländerkinder, 8,* 50 ff.

Pommerin-Götze, G., Tehle-Santoso, B., & E. Bozikake-Leisch. (1992). *Es geht auch anders!–Leben und Lernen in der multikulturellen Gesellschaft.* Frankfurt, Dagyeli.

Raschert, J. (1987). Wie Schulen zu interkulturellen Handlungeinheiten werden. *Zeitschrift für Pädagogik, 6,* 841 ff.

Reich, H. H., & Gogolin, I. (1990). *Migrantenkinder in den Schulen Europas.* Münster: Waxmann.

Rösch, H. (1991). Migrationsliteratur und ihre Bedeutung für die interkulturelle Kommunikation. In H. Marburger (Ed.), *Schule in der multikulturellen Gesellschaft* (pp. 19–34). Frankfurt: Verlag für Interkulturelle Kommunikation.

Said, E. W. (1978). *Orientalism.* London: Penguin.

Sandfuchs, U. (Ed.). (1981). *Lehren und Lernen mit Ausländerkindern.* Bad Heilbrunn: Klinckhardt.

Sayler, W. M. (1991). Ausländerpädagogik—Integrative Pädagogik: Zum Problemhorizont einer wissenschaftlichen Teildisziplin. *Lernen in Deutschland, 1,* 16–36.

Sayler, W. M. (1992). Interkulturelle Pädagogik im Dialog. *Lernen in Deutschland, 1,* 80–82.

Schill, A., Preuβ, M., & Dulabaum, N. (1993). Für Toleranz: Gegen Rassismus! In S. Kroon, D. Pagel, & T. Vallen (Eds.), *Multiethnische Gesellschaft und Schule in Berlin* (pp. 153–160). Münster: Waxmann.

Schmidt, S. J. (1980). Was ist bei der Selektion landeskundlichen Wissens zu berücksichtigen? *Fremdsprache Deutsch, 1,* 289–299.

Schulz, M. (Ed.). (1992). *Fremde Frauen: Von der Gastarbeiterin zur Bürgerin.* Frankfurt am Main: Verlag für Interkulturelle Kommunikation.

Sivanandan, A. (1988, November 4). The new racism. *New Statesman and Society,* pp. 8–9.

Statistisches Bundesamt. (1992). *Statistisches Jahrbuch für die Bundesrepublik Deutschland.* Wiesbaden: Metzler Poeschel Verlag.

Statistisches Landesamt Berlin. (1992). *Statistisches Jahrbuch Berlin.* Berlin: Kulturbuch Verlag.

Steffen, G. (1991). Kulturvergleich und Landeskunde in einer sich internationalisierenden Welt. In H. Barkowski & G. R. Hoff (Eds.), *Berlin Interkulturell* (pp. 221–235). Berlin: Colloquium Verlag.

Stein, R. (1993, March 9). Gemeinsam sind wir unausstehlich. *Der Tagesspiegel,* p. 15.

Steiner-Khamsi, G. (1992). *Multikulturelle Bildungspolitik in der Postmoderne.* Opladen: Leske und Budrich.

Steinmüller, U. (1981). Begriffsbildung und Zweitspracherwerb. In H. Essinger, A. Hellmich, & G. R. Hoff (Eds.), *Ausländerkinder im Konflikt* (pp. 130–156). Königstein im Taunus: Athenäum.

Steinmüller, U. (1991). Spracherwerb und Zweisprachigkeit. In H. Marburger (Ed.), *Schule in der multikulturellen Gesellschaft* (pp. 114–131). Frankfurt: Verlag für Interkulturelle Kommunikation.

Sturzbecher, D. (1990). *Comparative survey on dominant goals in family education.* Unpublished manuscript, University of Potsdam, Institut für Familien- und Kindheitsforschung.

Thomas, A. (Ed.). (1988). *Interkulturelles Lernen im Schüleraustausch.* Saarbrücken: SSIP.

Thomas, H. (1987). Abschließender Sachbericht—Zusammenfassende Darstellung. In H. Thomas (Ed.), *Modellversuch "Integration ausländischer Schüler an Gesamtschulen," 1982–86* (Vol. 1, pp. 2–46). Berlin: Technische Universität (Fachbereich) FB 22.

Thum, B. (1986). Auf dem Wege zu einer interkulturellen Germanistik. *Jahrbuch Deutsch als Fremdsprache, 11,* 329–341.

Tomforde, A. (1993, May 27). Bohn defies protesters. *The Guardian,* p. 18.

Tomic, B. (1993, March 24). Weiterhin rechtsradikal. *Der Tagesspiegel,* p. 19.

Troyna, B. (1987). Beyond multiculturalism: Towards the enactment of antiracist education in policy, provision, and pedagogy. *Oxford Review of Education, 13*(3), 307 ff.

Vorurteile und Meinungslosigkeit in der Wende (1992, October 31). *Der Tagesspiegel,* p. 13.

Wolbert, B. (1984). *Migrationsbewältigung: Orientierungen und Strategien.* Biographisch-interpretative Fallstudien über die "Heirats-Migration" dreier Türkinnen. Göttingen: Herodot.

Zimmer, J. (1982). Situationsansatz und interkulturelle Erziehung. *Die Deutsche Schule, 5,* 378ff.

Zimmer, J. (1986). Federal Republic of Germany: Intercultural education as education for international understanding. In *International Education in Twelve Countries* (Publication No. 37). Jyväskylä: Publications of the Finnish National Commission for UNESCO.

Zimmer, J. (Ed.). (1988–90). *Interkulturelle Erziehung in der Grundschule* (11 Vols.). Weinheim: Beltz-Verlag.

NAME INDEX

N

NAACP Legal Defense and Educational Fund, 336
Nabokov, P., 331
NACCME (National Advisory and Co-ordinating Committee on Multicultural Education), 768, 770, 772
NAEC (National Aboriginal Education Committee), 764
NAEP (National Assessment for Educational Progress), 477
Nagel, J., 247, 253, 254, 255
Nagel, T., 527, 536
Nain, G. T., 192
Nakagawa, K., 132, 349, 355, 364, 421, 505, 506, 509
Nakajima, K., 436
Nakanishi, D. T., 670, 683, 685, 687, 689, 690, 691, 692, 693
Narot, R., 598
Narvaez, A. A., 305
Nasar, S., 699
Nash, G. B., 133, 134, 136, 274, 570
Nasstrom, R. R., 75–76
National Aboriginal Education Committee (NAEC), 764
National Accreditation of Teacher Education (NCATE), 479
National Advisory and Co-ordinating Committee on Multicultural Education (NACCME), 768, 770, 772
National Alliance of Black School Educators, 638
National Archives, 331
National Assessment for Educational Progress (NAEP), 477
National Association for the Advancement of Colored People (NAACP), 148
National Center for Education Statistics (NCES), 70, 333, 337, 372, 375, 376, 446, 466, 470, 473, 474, 664
National Clearinghouse for Bilingual Education, 451
National Coalition of Advocates for Students, 664
National Commission on Children, 375, 558
National Commission on Excellence in Education, 33, 403
National Commission on Secondary Education for Hispanics, 403, 404, 407, 604
National Committee for Commonwealth Immigrants (NCCI), 783–784
National Council for the Accreditation of Teacher Education (NCATE), 57, 58, 60, 750
National Council of La Raza (NCLR), 389, 390, 391, 402, 664
National Curriculum Council (NCC), 794, 795
National Curriculum Council (NCC), Multicultural Task Group, 795
National Education Association (NEA), 184, 336
National Education Crisis Committee, 283
National Governors' Association, 637
National Institute of Education, 603, 637
National Opinion Research Center (NORC), 638
   General Social Surveys, 322
National Puerto Rican Task Force, 392, 402
National Research Council (NRC), 334

National Science Board, 156
National Union of Teachers (NUT), 792
National Women's Studies Association (NWSA), 709
Natriello, G., 17, 152, 551, 555, 558
Nava, A., 151
Navarro, A., 214
Navarro, R. A., 401
NCATE (National Council for the Accreditation of Teacher Education), 57, 58, 60, 479, 750
NCC (National Curriculum Council), 794, 795
   Multicultural Task Group, 795
NCCI (National Committee for Commonwealth Immigrants), 783–784
NCES (National Center for Education Statistics), 70, 333, 337, 372, 375, 376, 446, 466, 470, 473, 474
NCLR (National Council of La Raza), 389, 390, 391, 402
NEA (National Education Association), 184, 336
Nederhof, A. J., 108
Nee, B., 685
Nee, V. C., 262, 685
Neely, M. A., 70
Neely, S., 335
Neff, D., 276
Negrón, A., 388, 393
Negrón de Montilla, A., 225
Nehr, M., 832
Neimever, G. J., 650
Neisser, U., 100
Nelle, J., 335
Nelson, A., 341
Nelson, C., 733, 734
Nelson, C. M., 555
Nelson, D., 511, 639, 640
Nelson, K., 429, 431
Nelson, L. D., 448
Nelson, P., 16, 340–341, 341
Nelson, R., 331
Nelson-Barber, S., 558, 559, 755
Nestvogel, R., 829
Network of Regional Desegregation Assistance Centers, 45, 46, 47, 48
Neuendorf, K. A., 177
Neufield, B., 560
Neumann, R., 826
Neumann, U., 829
Neusner, J., 275
New South Wales Department of Education, 768, 773, 775
"The New Whiz Kids," 688
New York City, Office of the Mayor, 398
New York City Board of Education, 510
New York Study Group on Outcome Equity, 467
Newhall, A., 718
Newman, F. M., 476
Newton, P. M., 68
Nichols, N. A., 73
Nicholson, L., 711
Nicolau, S., 503
Niedermeyer, F., 533, 539
Nieke, W., 826
Nieto, S., 3, 10, 28, 29, 30, 34, 35, 36, 38, 85, 281, 390, 394, 405, 406, 415, 492, 503, 517
Nieves, J., 237
Nieves, L., 606
Nieves-Squires, S., 715
Niggle, T., 150, 160, 679

Ninio, A., 432
Nishimoto, R., 261
Nixon, J., 816
Njeri, I., 687
Noble, G., 764, 766
Noble, J., 599
Nobles, W. W., 99, 270, 271, 356, 361
Noblit, G. W., 577, 610, 636, 638
Noddings, N., 576, 754
Noggle, B., 204
Noley, G., 335
Noordhoff, K., 150, 160, 754
Noorst, M., 769
NORC (National Opinion Research Center), 638
   General Social Surveys, 322
Norcross, J. C., 648, 652
Nordquist, J., 730
Noriega, C., 171, 177
Novak, M., 10, 32
NRC (National Research Council), 334
NUT (National Union of Teachers), 792
Nwachuku, U., 652, 654
Nwokah, O., 356
NWSA (National Women's Studies Association), 709
Nystrand, R. O., 69

O

Oakes, J., 5, 50, 51, 354, 375, 383, 470, 471, 472, 473, 474, 475, 531, 555, 559, 561, 562, 563, 564, 598, 637, 638, 664
Oanh, N. T., 416
Obenga, T., 281
Obiakor, F. E., 361
O'Brien, E. M., 666, 671, 672, 674, 685, 686, 687, 692
O'Brien, H., 296
O'Brien, M., 99–100
O'Brien, S., 248, 251, 252
Ochoa, A. S., 11, 30, 602
Ochs, E., 431, 432, 440
O'Conner, R. P., 129
O'Connor, J., 171
O'Connor, T., 35, 38
Odo, F., 262
O'Donnell, S. R., 734
Odum, H., 186
Oetting, E. R., 107
Office of Civil Rights, 402
Office of Multicultural Affairs, 767
Office of Research and Evaluation, 540
Office of Technology Assessment (OTA), 251
Ogbu, J. U., 5, 16, 89–90, 100, 129, 139, 195, 265, 284, 320, 324, 325, 337, 338, 340, 341, 358, 364, 372, 378, 382, 394, 421, 438, 439, 489, 507, 508, 510, 557, 558, 559, 560, 582, 583, 584, 585, 586, 587, 588, 590, 683, 756, 814
Ogi, A. Y., 674
Ogilvie, D. H., 10
Ogundipe-Leslie, M., 270, 271
Ogunyemi, C. O., 711
Oh, M. Y., 650, 654, 655
O'Hara, W. T., 635
Ohlin, L., 235, 236
Oickle, E., 360, 361, 631, 632
Oishi, S., 631, 633
Okada, F., 422
Okada, T., 551
Okakok, L., 341

Okamoto, D., 129, 133, 137
Okazaki, S., 100, 381, 422, 508
Okihiro, G., 698, 700
Okinaka, A., 674
O'Leary, M., 485
O'Leary, V. E., 68
Oliva, P. F., 26
Olivas, M. S., 666, 670, 671, 674, 675
Oliver, J., 669
Oliver, L., 148
Oliver, W., 364
Olmeda, E., 107
Olmos, E. J., 174
Olneck, M. R., 89, 90, 155, 310, 311, 312, 314, 316, 320, 322, 325, 755
Olsen, L., 376
Olsen, R. J., 471
Olson, D. R., 433, 436
Olson, J., 331
Olson, M., 250
Olson, T. A., 543
Olstad, R., 416
O'Malley, P. M., 108
Omatsu, G., 698
Omi, M., 86, 91
Omolade, B., 715
O'Neil, J., 363
O'Neill, K., 530, 537, 539
Ong, A., 714
Ong, P., 412, 698, 699
Ontario Ministry of Education, 804
Opitz, M., 191
Opler, M. K., 231, 233, 234
Oral History Task Force, 238
Oren, D. A., 691
Orfield, G., 355, 389, 403, 404, 406, 407, 466, 598, 602, 603, 637, 641, 664, 675
Orfield, G. F., 466
Organization of American Historians, 734
Oritz, F. I., 66
Orland, M. E., 555
Orlich, D. C., 538
Orlosky, D. E., 26, 30, 31
Ormseth, T., 473
Ornelas, C., 214
Ornstein, A. C., 26, 30
Orozco, C. E., 713
Orr, D. W., 280, 283
Orr, E. W., 359, 429, 440
Ortega, E., 713
Ortiz, A. A., 152, 160, 239
Ortiz, F. I., 69, 74, 75, 76
Ortiz, R. D., 698
Ortíz-Colón, R., 503
Ortner, S., 710
Orum, L. S., 389, 390, 403, 404
Osayande, K. I. M., 751
Osborne, B., 340
Osherow, N., 639
Ostriker, A. S., 713
OTA (Office of Technology Assessment), 251
Otani, J., 712
Otero, M., 207
Ottavi, T. M., 656
Otto, K. A., 823
Ouellet, F., 808, 809
Ouston, I., 17
Ovando, C. J., 17, 23, 29, 427, 434, 436, 437, 439, 441
Owen, D., 779
Owens, R. G., 489
Oyemade, U. J., 349
Özerturgut-Yurtdas, H., 830
Ozolins, U., 768

P
Pachon, H., 298
Packer, A. H., 647
Paddock, S. C., 76
Padfield, H., 116
Padget, M., 205
Padilla, A. M., 97, 103, 107, 381, 445, 457
Padilla, E., 227, 228, 233–234, 393, 395
Padilla, F. M., 117, 217, 237–238, 239
Padilla, G., 207
Padilla Seda, E., 227, 234
Page, C., 689
Page, R. N., 153, 354, 555, 562, 563, 564
Pagel, D., 833
Pai, Y., 32, 749
Painter, N. I., 571
Pajak, E. F., 531, 534, 535, 536, 537
Palanki, A., 518
Paley, V., 749
Palinscar, A. M., 132
Pallas, A. M., 17, 152, 551, 555, 558
Pallay, A., 532–533
Palmer, A. F., 191
Palmer, F., 813
Palmer, G., 341
Palmer, H., 801
Palmer, P. M., 711
Pang, V. O., 30, 412, 416, 417, 422, 685, 692
Pantoja, A., 119
Pantojas-Garcia, E., 237
Papajohn, J., 649
Pardes, I., 713
Pardo, W. E., 38
Paredes, J. A., 342
Paredes, R., 735
Paredes, R. A., 204
Parekh, B., 3, 28, 36, 793
Parents United in Education and the Development of Others (PUEDO), 504
Parham, T. A., 648, 650, 651, 652
Parish, R., 528
Parish, T. S., 14, 618
Park, B., 378, 636, 640
Park, C., 422
Park, R. E., 186, 260, 261
Parkay, F. W., 154
Parker, B. J., 612
Parmee, E., 337
Parsons, P. F., 136, 137
Parsons, T., 69
Parsons, T. W., Jr., 598, 607
Pascal, A., 470, 527, 528, 530, 534, 535
Pascal, R., 331
Pascall, D., 795
Passalacqua, J., 533
Passell, J. S., 247
Passeron, J., 549, 558, 559
Passow, A. H., 15, 583
Pasta, D. J., 446, 447, 452, 453, 454, 455, 456
Pasteur, A., 356
Pasteur, A. B., 490
Patai, D., 714
Patchen, M., 603, 608, 629, 635, 636, 637, 641–642
Patterson, J. N., 624
Patterson, O., 617, 743
Patterson, S., 781, 783
Pattie, J. O., 204
Pauldi, M. A., 68
Paulhus, D. L., 108
Paulsen, K., 485
Pauly, E., 527, 528, 530, 534, 535

Pavan, B. N., 75
Pave, M., 302
Pavel, D., 337
Payne, C. M., 364, 526, 535, 576
Payne, D. D., 492
Payton-Stewart, L., 12, 362, 363
Paz, O., 212, 213
Peal, E., 436, 446, 447, 448, 449
Pearce, D., 610
Pearce, J., 650, 717, 734
Pearl, A., 382, 599
Pearson, P. D., 357, 358, 537
Pease-Alvarez, L., 376, 377, 383
Pecheone, R. L., 536, 538
Pedersen, P. B., 647, 648, 650, 652, 654, 655
Pedhazur, E. J., 109, 110
Pedhazur-Schmelkin, L., 109, 110
Pedraza, P., 238
Pedro, J. D., 152, 160
Peeples, K., 268, 269
Peichert, J. R., 605
Pelavin, S. H., 473
Pelz, D. C., 66
Penfield, J., 440
Penn, W., 294
Penna, A. N., 26, 31
PEP & Research Services, 784
Pepinsky, H. B., 652
Pepper, F., 336, 342
Perez, A. L., 148, 160
Pérez de Jesús, M., 234
Pérez y Mena, A. I., 238
Perkins, L. M., 70, 571
Perkins, U. E., 364
Perlmann, J., 321, 511, 512
Perloff, H. S., 227, 228
Perlstein, D., 281
Perrone, L., 550, 552
Perry, J., 380
Perry, T., 515
Persell, C. H., 551, 552, 553, 554, 555, 558, 559
Peshkin, A., 71, 129, 136, 137, 140, 609–610
Pesquera, B. M., 713
Peston, M., 779, 780, 781, 783, 784
Peter, K., 803
Peters, M. F., 338, 506
Peters, T. J., 537
Peters, W., 19, 621
Petersen, W., 262
Peterson, C., 429
Peterson, K. D., 528
Peterson, M. D., 295
Peterson, P., 69
Peterson, R. C., 176
Petras, J., 237
Petrie, P., 742
Petroni, F. A., 586, 588
Petrullo, V., 227
Pettigrew, T. F., 15, 599, 608, 628, 637
Pettit, A. G., 171, 204, 213
Pfaff, C. W., 831
Phenix, P. H., 26, 32
Philion, W. L., 341
Philips, S. U., 16, 130, 140, 338–340, 428, 434, 577, 586, 588
Phillip, M., 156
Phillips, B. R., 471
Phillips, D. L., 71, 606, 607, 608
Phillips, U. B., 11, 12
Phillips, W., 739
Philp, K., 332, 335
Phinney, J. S., 12, 13, 107, 188

SUBJECT INDEX

A

AACTE (American Association of Colleges for Teacher Education), 11, 28, 35, 57, 572, 750
A Beka curriculum, 138
Ability, 485, 666
Aborigines, 763–764
Academic curriculum, 132–133
Academic Learning Time (ALT), 452
Academic tradition of teacher education, 749
Accelerated Schools, 540
Accreditation standards
  National Council for Accreditation of Teacher education, 44, 57–58, 62, 750–751
  state initiatives and, 49
Acculturation, 108, 210, 310–313
Achievement
  African American education and, 352–355
  of African Americans, 492, 505, 599–602
  Asian Pacific American education and, 417–419
  of Chinese Americans, 508
  cooperative learning and, 632
  desegregation and, 599–603, 610
  funding and, 469–470
  of Hispanics, 602–603
  improving, 540
  of Irish Americans, 512–513
  mathematics, 359–360, 599–602
  Mexican American education and, 375
  of Mexican Americans, 375, 487
  minorities and, 85, 476
  Puerto Rican education and, 404
  reading, 339, 577, 599–602
  scales, 105–106, 110
  socioeconomic status and, 664
  tests of, 105–106, 477–478
  tracking and, 638–639
  of Whites, 603
Acquiescence, social, 108–109
Additive approach to content integration, 12, 37
Administrative roles. *See* Leadership
Admissions quotas controversy, 683, 688–692
AERA (American Educational Research Association), 30, 100
Affirmative action, 67–68, 75, 673, 688–689

African American education
  achievement and, 352–355
  African American teachers and, 360–361
  Afrocentrism and, 355–356
  Black studies and, 355–356
  Brown v. Board of Education of Topeka decision and, 353, 354, 355
  cultural contexts and, 356–361
  desegregation and, 354–355
  DuBois (W.E.B.) and, 350, 351–352
  family involvement in, 504–508, 514–515
  future research on, 364–365
  historical perspective of, 349–352
  improvement in, 361–364
  language and, 357–359
  literacy and, 353, 357–359
  policy implications of, 364–365
  practice implications of, 364–365
  private schools and, 136, 361–362
  problems in schools and, 348–349
  Washington (Booker T.) and, 350, 351
  Woodson (Carter G.) and, 352
African Americans. *See also* Black studies
  in A Beka curriculum, 138
  achievement of, 492, 505, 599–602
  Asian immigrants and, 303
  assimilation of, 272–273
  Black English and, 17, 139, 357–359, 429, 440
  Black English Vernacular and, 139, 429, 440, 674
  Black studies movement and, 7
  children, 195
  civil rights movement and, 9
  cognition of, 492
  college completion rates of, 605
  college enrollment of, 664, 666
  college participation rates of, 439, 605, 664
  community of, rural, 115, 121–122, 125
  content integration and, 7
  cultural compatibility and, 130–131
  cultural knowledge/thought of, 271–273
  demography of, 504–505
  desegregation and, 7, 599–602, 606, 607
  family involvement in education and, 504–508, 514–515
  graduate/professional school enrollment for, 667, 668–669
  graduation rates of, 664
  identity of, 14

  immigrants and, 303
  individual racism and, 673
  inequality in U.S. education and, 466
  intergroup education and, 9–10
  IQ tests and, 353–354, 355
  leadership and, 70, 73–76
  learning styles of, 16, 490, 491
  linguistic and cultural expression of, critique of, 139–140
  mathematics and, 359–360, 599–602
  media and, 171, 174–175, 177–178
  parents, 504–508, 514–515
  persistence in college and, 666
  racial attitudes and, 620, 621
  reading and, 599–602
  self-determination of, 576–577
  self-esteem of, 106
  self-rejection paradigm and, 13–14
  slavery and, 12, 134
  socioeconomic status of, 504–505, 514
  teachers
    African American education and, 360–361
    American Association of Colleges for Teacher Education and, 572
    Black Artful Style and, 577–578
    Brown v. Board of Education of Topeka decision and, 361, 571, 572, 578
    communication patterns and, 577–578
    content-students' experiences link and, 576
    cultural patterns and, 577
    cultural solidarity and, 575–576
    culture-of-poverty perspective and, 139–140
    desegregation and, 572
    historical perspective of, 570–571
    narratives of, first-person, 572–573
    pedagogy of effective, 578
    policy research on, 571–572
    sociological/anthropological literature on, 574–578
    whole-child focus and, 576–577
  in U.S. history, 10, 11–12, 133–136, 363
  Western ideological hegemony and, 184–185, 189
  women, 190–192
  women's studies in higher education and, 74, 711–712
African American studies. *See* Black studies

866

resettlers and, 823
school system and, 824–825
"third world studies" and, 829
traditional, 828–829
women's studies and, 830
Gesellschaft, 114
Gestalt psychology, 178
GFL (German as a Foreign Language), 826
Ghost Dances, 253
Graduate school enrollment, 667–672
Graduation rates, 250, 663–664
Great Britain. *See* British multicultural
　　education
Grouping of students, 531–535, 638
Group Investigation, 630, 632
"The Growth of Democracy" lectures, 619
GSL (German as a Second Language)
　　students, 826
Guest workers, 823–824, 835

H
Haitian immigrants, 303
Haitian students, 132
Harter scale, 106
Hawaiians, 45, 48, 131, 422–423, 577
Hays Code, 172, 173
Head Start, 16, 349, 380, 503, 559
Health Professions Education Assistance
　　Act, 479
Heath Anthology of American Literature,
　　733, 735, 744
Hegemony, cultural. *See* Western
　　ideological hegemony
Hemos Trabajado Bien, 398–399
Hermeneutic curriculum theory, 26
Heterogeneity, 103, 312
Higher education. *See also* College
　Asian Pacific Americans in
　　admission quotas controversy and,
　　　683, 688–692
　　demography and, 684–686
　　faculty/administrative representation
　　　and, 686–688
　　increase in, research on, 683
　　limitations of research on, 683, 684,
　　　692–693
　core curricula in
　　cultural diversity requirement and,
　　　735–738
　　curriculum transformation and, 733
　　definition of, 729
　　disciplinary changes and, 733–735
　　general education and, 730–731
　　multiculturalism and, 729–730,
　　　741–744
　　new directions in, 744–745
　　patterns of, in last 25 years, 731–733
　　specialized education and, 730–731
　　textbook changes and, 733–735
　　types of, 729–730
　　"Western civilization" reconstruction
　　　and, 738–741
　curriculum in, 675–676
　equity in
　　college completion rates and, 605
　　college enrollment and, 664, 666
　　college participation rates and, 439,
　　　605, 664
　　drop-out rates and, 663–666
　　graduate/professional school
　　　enrollment and, 667–672
　　limitations of research on, 663
　　persistence in college and, 666
　ethnic studies in
　　backlash against, 703–704

conservativism and, 704
current status of, 697, 699
debates/issues within, 701–703
definition of, 699–701
establishment of, 699
fire insurance approach to, 696
future challenges for, 704–705
historical perspective of, 696–697
pluralism and, cultural, 705
professional associations representing,
　697
programs of, 697–699
financial aid programs for, 673, 675
future research on racial issues in, 679
graduate/professional school enrollment
　and, 667–672
pluralism in, integrated, 676–679
racism in, 672–676
women's studies in
　African American, 74, 711–712
　Asian Pacific American, 712–713
　Chicana, 713
　curriculum transformation and,
　　716–721
　definition of, 708–709
　development of, 709
　feminist theory and, 709–711
　gender and, 708
　as global phenomenon, 709
　impact of, 716, 720–721
　institutionalization of, 709
　Jewish, 713
　Latina, 713
　lesbian, 713–714
　Native American, 712
　new fields of study in, 711–714
　pedagogy and, 715–716
　programs, 736
　third world, 714
Higher Order Thinking Skills (HOTS)
　program, 540
Hispanic Policy Development Project, 390
Hispanics. *See also* Latinos
　achievement of, 602–603
　acquiescence and, social, 108
　college enrollment of, 664, 666
　college participation rates of, 664
　desegregation and, 598, 602–603, 606,
　　607
　graduate/professional school enrollment
　　of, 667, 670–671
　graduation rates of, 664
　inequality in U.S. education and, 466
　learning styles of, 490, 491
　persistence in college and, 666
　self-esteem of, 106
　social acquiescence and, 108
　term of, 389
Hmong, 303, 318, 319, 324
Hobart College, 731
Hobson v. Hansen, 466
Home-to-school mismatch, 381
Homogeneous grouping, 532
HOTS (Higher Order Thinking Skills)
　program, 540
Humanities Curriculum Project (United
　Kingdom), 786
Human relations, 51, 53
Human Relations approach, 147, 151
Human rights, property rights versus, 155
"Hypodermic needle effect" of media, 175

I
Identity
　of African Americans, 14

of clients, 653
cognition and, 14
of counselors, 653
cultural development of, 651–654
cultural diversity and, 585–586
ethnic, 492
levels of, 653
media and, 176
models of, 653–654
multicultural counseling and therapy
　and, 653–654
racial-ethnic, 136–140, 318–320
of Whites, 651–652
Idiographic approach to educational
　research, 98, 99
ILC (Intensive Language Centres), 773
ILEA (Inner London Education Authority),
　784, 789
Illinois Test of Psycholinguistic Abilities
　(ITPA), 489
IMBS (Integrative Multicultural Basic Skills)
　model, 39
Immigrant education
　acculturation and, 310–313
　American beliefs about, 310
　Americanization and, 311–312
　cross-group interactions and, 318
　cultural discontinuities and, 317–318
　cultural diversity and, 313–315
　culture of school and, 315
　differences among groups and,
　　educational, 321–322
　ethnic identity and, 318–320
　Eurocentrism and, 325
　federal initiatives and, 48
　gender and, 317
　intergroup relations and, 315–316, 318
　meaning of schooling and, 318
　occupational outcomes and, 322–323
　parents and, 317, 318, 320
　performance among groups and,
　　320–321, 323–325
　practices and, educational, 316–317
　schools and, 310, 315–320, 325
Immigrants
　African Americans and, 303
　aliens, 297, 304, 305
　Asian, 259, 260, 296–297, 302–303, 312
　Asian Pacific Americans as, 413–414
　asylum seekers, 304–305, 306–307, 824,
　　835
　Australian multicultural education and
　　assimilation of, 767–768
　　educational responses to, 767–770
　　performance of, 770–772
　　popular responses to, 765–767
　British multicultural education and
　　antiracism and, 791–794
　　assimilation of, 781–783
　　Black, 779, 781
　　dispersal policy and, 781, 782–783
　　integrationism and, 783–784
　　laissez-faire approach to, 780–781
　　pluralism and, 784–791, 793–794
　Catholic, 313–314
　Chinese, 259, 260, 296–297, 321, 765
　Chinese Americans as, 303
　circulatory migration and, 391–392
　community and, 115
　Cuban, 303
　cultural discontinuities and, 317–318
　European, 293–296, 298–299, 312,
　　325
　Filipino, 259, 260, 297
　German, 313

school, 32
social effects of, 279–280
social organization of, 277–279
transformative academic, 32–33
Knowledge construction
Black studies and, 268–270
conceptual system of society and,
184–185
content integration and, 5
as dimension of multicultural education,
412
feminist theory and, 12
future research on, 18
media and, 169–170, 176, 179–180
process, 4, 11–12
quantitative educational research and
social, 98–100
social contexts and, 268
teacher education and multicultural
education and, 752
Koreans, 585
Kpelle, 585–586
Krefelder Modell (Germany), 832

L

LAD (language acquisition device),
428–429
Laissez-faire approach to British
multicultural education, 780–781
Language. *See also* Bilingual education; ESL
(English as a Second Language)
students; LEP (Limited English
Proficient) students
acquisition, 428–429, 433, 446
African American education and,
357–359
Asian Pacific American education and,
415–416
Australian multicultural education and,
769, 773–775
barriers, 103–104
biculturalism and, 357
bilingual education and, 435–440
Black English, 17, 139, 357–359, 429, 440
Black English Vernacular, 139, 429, 440,
674
Chomsky (Noam) and, 428–429
classic theoretical approaches to,
428–430
communicative competence and,
429–430, 433, 434
community in successful outcomes of,
439–440
cultural difference theory and, 16–17
cultural discontinuities and, 317
cultural diversity and, 313, 584–585,
589–590
decontextualization and, 430, 436
diglossia and, 357
direct instruction and, 432
elaborated code in, 430
German, 313, 826, 831–832
German multicultural education and,
831–832
of home versus school, 130
intelligence and, 212
language acquisition device and,
428–429
language-parole distinction and, 429
learning and, 490
linguicism and, 394–395
literacy and, 357–359, 430, 433–435
match-mismatch formulation and,
433–434, 435, 437, 438

multicultural education and, 188–189,
435–440, 440–441
narrative discourse styles and, 434–435
Native American education and, 338–339,
341
Navajo Reservation study on, 437
1970s studies on, 429–430
oral-literate dichotomy of, 433–435
parental involvement in successful
outcomes of, 439
performance and, 429–430
in Puerto Rican education of future,
406–407
questions regarding, 428, 440
research literature on, 427–428
restricted code in, 430
scaffolding and, 431
social interaction theory and, 430–432,
434
socialization, 130, 432
sociocultural nature of, 430–435
stanza analysis and, 434
text and, 436
threshold hypothesis and, 438
utterance and, 436
Yiddish, 317
zone of proximal development and,
431
Language acquisition device (LAD),
428–429
Language-parole distinction, 429
Languages Other Than English (LOTE)
students, 769, 774–775
Lateral transmission of values hypothesis,
599
Latinas, 664, 713
Latino Commission, 405–406
Latinos, 131, 171, 177, 303, 389, 664. *See
also* specific groups
Latino studies, 698–699
"The Lau Remedies," 402
Lau v. Nichols decision, 402, 422, 449, 510,
518, 688
LBDQ (Leader Behavior Description
Questionnaire), 66
Leader Behavior Description Questionnaire
(LBDQ), 66
Leadership
African Americans and, 70, 73–76
approaches to research on, 66
career outcomes and, 74–75
current state of, 66
definitions of, 65–66
future research on, 76–77
gender and, 65, 69–76
minorities and, 67, 70, 71, 73–76
nature of, 65–66
prejudice and, 67–68
principals, 72, 76
race and, 65, 69–76
role theory and, 66–69
as school effectiveness correlate,
528–530, 543
social theory and, 66–69
superintendents, 69, 71, 72, 75
women and, 65, 69–76
Learning
acquisition of skills in, 527
active/enriched, 533–535
biological effects on, 490
childhood socialization and, 489
cognition and, 564
cultural diversity and, 586–588
ecological adaptation on, 489–490
family's influence on, 499

higher-order, 534, 535
language and, 490
opportunities for, 535
"overlapping spheres of influence"
model and, 499
school's influence on, 499
social class and, 556–561, 564
sociocultural tightness and, 489
Learning Style Inventory (LSI), 487
Learning styles
ability and, 485
affective, 484
of African Americans, 16, 490, 491
"apprenticeship" situations and, 431
cognitive, 484–485
cultural diversity and, 484, 494
culture and, 489–490, 492
definition of, 484
field dependence/independence and,
487–488, 489, 492
generalizations about, dangers of,
492–493
of Hispanics, 490, 491
impulsivity/reflectivity and, 488
instruction and, 493
instrumentation, 485–489, 494
locus of control and, 487, 488
of Mexican Americans, 16
of Native Americans, 16, 131–132,
338–340, 490–491, 577
physiological, 484
problems in research on, 491–493
promising aspects of research on,
494
teachers and, 492–494
strategies for, 491, 493
tests, 485
theory, 16
variables influencing, critical, 491–492
LEAs (local education authorities), 781,
788–789, 793
Legislation. *See* Federal initiatives; State
initiatives; specific names
LEP (Limited English Proficient) students.
See also Bilingual education
bilingual education and, 451–452
education of, 47–48
federal initiatives and, 47–48
programs for
growth of, 445
maintenance, 437, 446
studies of, 450–452
Significant Bilingual Instructional
Features study and, 451–452, 459
state initiatives and, 50, 51, 57
statistics on, 427
term of, 445, 447
Lesbian studies, 713–714
Leveling, 532
Liberalism, 82
Licensure, state, 58–59
Lieu de memoire, 193–194
Likert scale, 108
Limited English Proficient students. *See* LEP
(Limited English Proficient) students
Linguicism, 394–395
Literacy
African American education and, 353,
357–359
critical, 438
cultural, 438
Diaspora, 363
functional, 438
Gee's view of, 434
language and, 357–359, 430, 433–435

programs, 698, 699
sociological, 227
subthemes in, 223
The Puerto Rican Study, 397, 398, 405, 406
Punjabis, 584

Q

Quantitative educational research
Afrocentrism and, 99, 110
challenges in, 100–104, 110
Eurocentrism and, 98–99, 110
historical perspective of, 97
instrumentation, 104–110
knowledge construction and, social, 98–100
measurement, 104–110
nomothetic approach to, 98–99
Quebec (Canada), 806
Quintin Kynaston Comprehensive School (United Kingdom), 791

R

Race
belief structure of, 271, 278
career outcomes and, 74–75
critical theory and, 190
federal initiatives, 45–46
feminist theory and, 190–192
leadership and, 65, 69–76
media and, 170–172
research literature on, 146–147
social class and, 548
socialization and, 67
Race relations
in British Columbia (Canada), 806
Canadian multicultural education and, 806, 814–815
German multicultural education and, 834
intergroup education and, 8
Racial attitudes
African Americans and, 620, 621
cooperative learning and, 14, 15, 619
curricular intervention studies, 14, 18, 619–621
curriculum and, 619–621
intergroup education and, 619
Mexican Americans and, 620–621
modification studies, 14–15, 618–619, 619–622
Native Americans and, 620
nature of, 8, 12–14
perceptual differentiation studies, 14–15
practice implications of, 625
principle testing and, 621–622
reinforcement studies, 14, 621
research implications of, 624–626
teaching methods and, 621–622
Whites and, 621
Racial-ethnic identity, 136–140, 318–320
Racism
Asian Pacific American education and, 420
British multicultural education and, 779
in Chicano movement, 215
colonialism and, internal, 214
cultural, 673, 674–676
environmental, 673
German multicultural education and, 821–822, 827, 834–835
in higher education, 672–676
immigration policy and, 293, 302–303
individual, 673–674
institutional, 16, 672, 674–676
media and, 176–177, 178
myth of American republic and, 293–294

Puerto Rican education and, 394–395
socialization and, 67
in textbooks, 148–149
Radical curriculum theory, 33
Radicalism
capitalism and, 91–92
charges against multicultural education and, 89–90
feminist analysis of multicultural education and, 91
in future, 92
goal of, 89
implications of, for multicultural education, 91–92
oppression and, 91–92
patriarchy and, 91–92
position of, 82
proponents of, visible, 89
weaknesses of arguments and, 90–91
RAL (Reconstructing American Literature), 733, 734–735
Rampton report, 788, 790
RAT (Regular Auxiliary Teacher), 397
Reading
achievement, 339, 577, 599–602
African Americans and, 599–602
Degrees of Reading Power Test and, 534, 540
gender role attitudes and, 622–623
Heath Anthology of American Literature and, 733, 735, 744
Kamehameha Early Education Program (KEEP) and, 339, 577
Recitation script, 129–130, 137
Reconceptualist curriculum theory, 31
Reconstructing American Literature (RAL), 733, 734–735
Recontextualization, 430, 436
"Recruitment and Retention," 678
"Redbook," 729, 731
Reflectivity-impulsivity, 488
Reformist curriculum theory, 33
Refugee Education Assistance Act of 1980 (ESEA), 45, 48
Refugees, 823
Regular Auxiliary Teacher (RAT), 397
Reinforcement studies, 14
Religion
cultural diversity accommodations and, 313–314
immigration policy and, 294–296, 299
Native American education and, 335
of Native Americans, 254–256
private schools
creation of, 136
curriculum of, 138–140
documentation of, 136–137
social organization of church and, 137–138
Report of the Review of Post-Arrival Programs and Services for Migrants, 766, 769
Researcher's background, knowledge, and epistemological bias, 155–157
Research literature. *See also* Ethnic studies; specific types
American, 29–30
approaches to multicultural education and, 147
barriers to
confusion over multicultural education, 158
exceptionalism within academic discourse, 157–158
funding, 158

property rights versus human rights, 155
researcher's background, knowledge, and epistemological bias, 155–157
concerns/suggestions, 160–161
on content integration, 5
on curriculum, 148–149
on desegregation, 146, 355
frameworks in, paradigmatic, 159–160
future, 161
on gender, 146–147
historical perspective of, 145–146
ideologies emerging from, 158–159
international, 29
on language, 428–429
on Native American education, 336–342
paradigmatic frameworks of, 159–160
on practicing teachers, 152
on preservice programs, 149–152
on race, 146–147
since 1960s, 11
on social class, 146–147
on socioeconomic status, 146–147
on teacher-student relationships, 152–154
on textbooks, 148–149
Resegregation, 598, 636–637, 638
Resettlers, 823
Response patterns, 108–110
Response sets, 108
Reverse discrimination, 673, 689
Robinson v. Cahill, 468
Rockland (New York) Community College, 741–742
Rodriguez et al. v. Los Angeles Unified School District, 466, 477
Role conflict, 69, 75
Role models, 421–422
Role socialization, 67
Role stress, 69
Role theory, 66–69
Rough Rock Indian reservation school, 132, 341, 342

S

SABE (Spanish Assessment of Basic Education), 105
Samoan Americans, 419
Samples, identifying, describing, and selecting, 99–103
San Antonio Independent School District v. Rodriguez, 468
Sapir-Whorf hypothesis, 440
Saskatchewan (Canada), 805–806
SAT (Scholastic Aptitude Test), 417–418, 686
SAT (Substitute Auxiliary Teacher), 396, 397
Savage Inequalities (Kozol, Jonathan), 466–467
SBIF (Significant Bilingual Instructional Features) study, 451–452, 459
SBMI (Swassing-Barbe Modalities Index), 489
Scaffolding, 431
Scarman report, 790
SCCRI (Select Committee on Race Relations and Immigration), 785–789
Schemata theory, 178
Scholastic Aptitude Test (SAT), 417–418, 686
School-Based Instructional Leadership Program, 540
School boards, 71
School Development Program, 540